The Sporting News
COMPLETE HOCKEY BOOK
1995-96 EDITION

Editors / Complete Hockey Book
CRAIG CARTER
GEORGE PURO
KYLE VELTROP

Contributing Editor / Complete Hockey Book
LARRY WIGGE

D1416072

— PUBLISHING CO. —

Francis P. Pandolfi, Chairman; **Nicholas H. Niles,** President and Chief Executive Officer; **Francis X. Farrell,** Senior Vice President, Publisher; **John D. Rawlings,** Senior Vice President, Editorial Director; **John Kastberg,** Vice President, General Manager; **Kathy Kinkeade,** Vice President, Production; **Mike Nahrstedt,** Managing Editor; **Mike Huguenin,** Assistant Managing Editor; **Joe Hoppel,** Senior Editor; **Tom Dienhart and Dave Sloan,** Associate Editors; **Craig Carter,** Statistical Editor; **George Puro and Kyle Veltrop,** Assistant Editors; **Graham Boain, Mark Bonavita, Jay Davis, Robb McSorley and Josh Smith,** Editorial Assistants; **Fred Barnes,** Director of Graphics; **Angie Blackwell,** Art Director; **Albert Dickson,** Chief Photographer; **Gary Brinker,** Director, Information Systems; **Bob Parajon,** Prepress Director; **Patrick Kolieboi,** Network Manager; **Terry Shea,** Database Analyst; **Marilyn Kasal,** Production Manager; **Mike Bruner,** Graphics Network Manager; **Michael Behrens,** Macintosh Production Artist; **Vern Kasal,** Composing Room Supervisor.

A Times Mirror
Company

CONTENTS

ON THE COVER: Pittsburgh Penguins right winger Jaromir Jagr led the NHL with 70 points last season to win the Art Ross Trophy. He finished second in the league with 32 goals and tied for seventh with 38 assists. (Photo by Bruce Bennett/Bruce Bennett Studios)

Spine photo of Wayne Gretzky by Glenn Cratty/Allsport.

Editorial assistance provided by Igor Kuperman of the Winnipeg Jets.

ISBN: 0-89204-529-9 (perfect-bound)
     0-89204-530-2 (comb-bound)

10 9 8 7 6 5 4 3 2 1

1995-96 NHL SEASON

NHL directory

Team information

Schedule

NOTE: The Quebec Nordiques franchise of the NHL moved to the city of Denver following the 1994-95 season. At press time the team had not announced its new name, although "Rocky Mountain Avalanche" and "Colorado Avalanche" were reported to be the leading candidates. With the only certainty being that the team would play its home games in Denver, The Sporting News refers to the team as Denver throughout this book except in the NHL schedules, where the team is listed as "Colorado," as per the official schedules released by the league.

NHL DIRECTORY

LEAGUE OFFICES

OFFICERS

Commissioner
Gary B. Bettman
Senior V.P. and chief operating officer
Stephen J. Solomon
Senior V.P. and dir. of hockey operations
Brian P. Burke
Senior vice president and general counsel
Jeffrey Pash
Vice president and chief financial officer
John M. Houston
Vice president, public relations
Arthur Pincus
Vice president, corporate communications
Bernadette Mansur
Vice president, broadcasting
Glenn Adamo
Vice president, team service and television
Ellis T. "Skip" Prince
Vice president, special events
Frank A. Supovitz
Vice president, security
Dennis Cunningham

NHL ENTERPRISES

Senior V.P. and chief operating officer
Richard Dudley
Senior V.P. and general counsel
Richard Zahnd

Vice president, corporate Marketing
Edward G. Horne
Vice president, retail licensing
Fred Scalera

PUBLIC RELATIONS

Vice president, public relations
Arthur Pincus
Director, public relations
Gary Meagher
Mgr., public relations and news services
Andrew McGowan
Manager, media relations
Susan Aglietti
Manager, news services
Greg Inglis
Statistician
Benny Ercolani
Communications assistant
David Keon
News service assistant
Tamir Lipton
Administrative assistants
Karen Levine
Kay Merritts

NEW YORK OFFICE (NHL and NHLE)

Address
1251 Avenue of the Americas
47th Floor
New York, NY 10020

Phone
212-789-2000
FAX
212-789-2020

TORONTO OFFICE

Address
75 International Blvd.
Suite 300
Rexdale, Ont. M9W 6L9
Phone
416-798-0809
FAX
416-798-0852

MONTREAL OFFICE

Address
1800 McGill College Avenue
Suite 2600
Montreal, Que., Canada H3A 3J6
Phone
514-288-9220
FAX
514-284-0300

BOARD OF GOVERNORS

Anaheim
Michael D. Eisner
Boston
Jeremy M. Jacobs
Buffalo
Seymour H. Knox III
Calgary
Harley N. Hotchkiss
Chicago
William W. Wirtz
Colorado
Charles Lyons
Dallas
Norman N. Green

Detroit
Michael Ilitch
Edmonton
Peter Pocklington
Florida
William A. Torrey
Hartford
Peter Karmanos Jr.
Los Angeles
Joe Cohen
Montreal
Ronald L. Corey
New Jersey
Dr. John J. McMullen

New York Islanders
Robert Rosenthal
New York Rangers
Charles D. Dolan
Ottawa
Roderick M. Bryden
Philadelphia
Edward M. Snider
Pittsburgh
Howard L. Baldwin
St. Louis
Jack Quinn
San Jose
George Gund III

Tampa Bay
David E. LeFevre
Toronto
Steve A. Stavro
Vancouver
Arthur R. Griffiths
Washington
Richard M. Patrick
Winnipeg
Barry L. Shenkarow
Chairman, board of governors
Harley N. Hotchkiss

DIVISIONAL ALIGNMENT

EASTERN CONFERENCE

ATLANTIC DIVISION
Florida Panthers
New Jersey Devils
New York Islanders
New York Rangers
Philadelphia Flyers
Tampa Bay Lightning
Washington Capitals

NORTHEAST DIVISION
Boston Bruins
Buffalo Sabres
Hartford Whalers
Montreal Canadiens
Ottawa Senators
Pittsburgh Penguins

WESTERN CONFERENCE

CENTRAL DIVISION
Chicago Blackhawks
Dallas Stars
Detroit Red Wings
St. Louis Blues
Toronto Maple Leafs
Winnipeg Jets

PACIFIC DIVISION
Mighty Ducks of Anaheim
Calgary Flames
Denver
Edmonton Oilers
Los Angeles Kings
San Jose Sharks
Vancouver Canucks

MIGHTY DUCKS OF ANAHEIM
WESTERN CONFERENCE/PACIFIC DIVISION

1995-96 SCHEDULE

Home games shaded.
* — All-Star Game at FleetCenter, Boston.
D — Day game.

OCTOBER
SUN	MON	TUE	WED	THU	FRI	SAT
1	2	3	4	5	6	7
8	9 WIN	10	11 HAR	12	13 BUF	14 PIT
15	16	17	18 VAN	19	20 PHI	21
22 WIN	23 COL	24	25	26 DAL	27 STL	28
29 CAL	30	31				

NOVEMBER
SUN	MON	TUE	WED	THU	FRI	SAT
			1 STL	2	3 NYR	4
5 NJ	6	7 TOR	8 MON	9	10	11 D OTT
12	13	14	15 COL	16	17 NYI	18
19 FLA	20	21 CAL	22 EDM	23	24 D CHI	25
26	27	28	29 WAS	30		

DECEMBER
SUN	MON	TUE	WED	THU	FRI	SAT
					1 DET	2 TOR
3	4 NYR	5	6 TB	7 FLA	8	9
10 EDM	11	12	13 PIT	14	15 OTT	16
17 TOR	18	19 SJ	20 DET	21	22 VAN	23
24	25	26	27 LA	28	29 SJ	30
31 D LA						

JANUARY
SUN	MON	TUE	WED	THU	FRI	SAT
	1	2	3	4	5 CAL	6
7 EDM	8	9 PHI	10	11 BOS	12 CHI	13
14 WIN	15	16	17 CAL	18	19	20 *
21	22	23	24 VAN	25	26	27 D LA
28	29	30	31 COL			

FEBRUARY
SUN	MON	TUE	WED	THU	FRI	SAT
				1	2 HAR	3
4 CHI	5	6	7 TOR	8	9	10 D NYI
11 NJ	12	13	14 EDM	15 VAN	16	17 LA
18	19	20	21 BOS	22	23 CAL	24
25 D SJ	26 COL	27	28 MON	29		

MARCH
SUN	MON	TUE	WED	THU	FRI	SAT
					1	2
3 TB	4	5 DAL	6	7	8 BUF	9
10 LA	11	12	13 COL	14	15	16
17 STL	18	19 WAS	20	21	22 STL	23
24 D CHI	25 DET	26	27	28 DAL	29	30
31 D SJ						

APRIL
SUN	MON	TUE	WED	THU	FRI	SAT
	1	2	3 EDM	4	5 DET	6
7 D SJ	8 VAN	9	10 COL	11	12 DAL	13
14 WIN	15	16	17	18	19	20

1995-96 SEASON

CLUB DIRECTORY

Governor
Michael Eisner
President and alternate governor
Tony Tavares
Vice president and general manager
Jack Ferreira
Vice president of finance/administration
Andy Roundtree
Assistant general manager
Pierre Gauthier
Head coach
Ron Wilson
Assistant coaches
Tim Army
Al Sims
Vice president of hockey operations
Kevin Gilmore
Director of player personnel
David McNab
Pro scout
Paul Fenton

Regional scouts
Thommie Bergman
Alain Chainey
Al Godfrey
Richard Green
Trainer
Blynn DeNiro
Equipment manager
Mark O'Neill
Director of sales and marketing
Bill Holford
Director of public relations
Bill Robertson
Controller
Marty Greenspun
Manager of community relations
Jenny Price
Manager of premium ticketing services
Anne McNiff

DRAFT CHOICES

Rd. — Player	H/W	Overall	Pos.	Last team
1—Chad Kilger	6-3/204	4	C	Kingston (OHL)
2—Brian Wesenberg	6-3/173	29	RW	Guelph (OHL)
3—Mike Leclerc	6-1/205	55	LW	Brandon (WHL)
5—Igor Nikulin	6-1/180	107	RW	Cherepovets, CIS
6—Peter Leboutillier	6-2/195	133	RW	Red Deer (WHL)
7—Mike Laplante	6-1/176	159	D	Calgary (AJHL)
8—Igor Karpenko	5-8/158	185	G	Kiev, Ukraine

MISCELLANEOUS DATA

Home ice (capacity)
The Arrowhead Pond of Anaheim
(17,250)
Address
2695 E. Katella Avenue
P.O. Box 61077
Anaheim, CA 92803-6177
Business phone
714-704-2700

Rink dimensions
200 feet by 85 feet
Club colors
Purple, jade, silver and white
Radio affiliation
KEZY (95.9 FM)
TV affiliation
KCAL (Channel 9),
Prime Sports (Cable)

TRAINING CAMP ROSTER

No.	FORWARDS	Ht./Wt.	Place	BORN Date	NHL exp.	1994-95 clubs
21	Patrik Carnback (C/LW) .	6-0/187	Goteborg, Sweden	2-1-68	3	Vastra Frolunda (Sweden), Anaheim
19	Bob Corkum (C/RW).....	6-2/212	Salisbury, Mass.	12-18-67	5	Anaheim
16	Peter Douris (RW)........	6-1/195	Toronto	2-19-66	9	Anaheim
36	Todd Ewen (RW)	6-2/220	Saskatoon, Sask.	3-22-66	9	Anaheim
9	Paul Kariya (LW)	5-11/175	Vancouver	10-16-74	1	Anaheim
11	Valeri Karpov (RW/LW) ..	5-10/176	Chelyabinsk, U.S.S.R.	8-5-71	1	Traktor Chelyabinsk (CIS), Anaheim, San Diego (IHL)
17	Steven King (LW/RW)..	6-0/195	East Greenwich, R.I.	7-22-69	3	Anaheim
25	Todd Krygier (LW)	6-0/185	Northville, Mich.	10-12-65	6	Anaheim
42	Denny Lambert (LW) ...	5-11/200	Wawa, Ont.	1-7-70	1	San Diego (IHL), Anaheim
27	John Lilley (RW)	5-0/170	Wakefield, Mass.	8-3-72	2	San Diego (IHL), Anaheim
20	Steve Rucchin (C)	6-3/210	London, Ont.	7-4-71	1	San Diego (IHL), Anaheim
12	David Sacco (LW/RW).	6-0/180	Medford, Mass.	7-31-70	2	San Diego (IHL), Anaheim
14	Joe Sacco (RW/LW)	6-1/195	Medford, Mass.	2-4-69	5	Anaheim
23	Mike Sillinger (LW/C)..	5-10/190	Regina, Sask.	6-29-71	5	Wien (Austria), Detroit, Anaheim
33	Jim Thomson (RW)	6-1/220	Edmonton	12-30-65	7	
18	Garry Valk (LW/RW) ...	6-1/205	Edmonton	11-27-67	5	Anaheim
22	Shaun Van Allen (C)	6-1/200	Shaunavon, Sask.	8-29-67	4	Anaheim
	DEFENSEMEN					
5	Robert Dirk	6-4/210	Regina, Sask.	8-20-66	8	Anaheim
2	Bobby Dollas	6-2/212	Montreal	1-31-65	10	Anaheim
7	Milos Holan..................	5-11/191	Bilovec, Czechoslovakia	4-22-71	2	Hershey (AHL), Anaheim
15	David Karpa.................	6-1/202	Regina, Sask.	5-7-71	4	Cornwall (AHL), Quebec, Anaheim
24	Tom Kurvers	6-0/195	Minneapolis	9-14-62	11	Anaheim
29	Randy Ladouceur..........	6-2/220	Brockville, Ont.	6-30-60	13	Anaheim
23	Jason Marshall..............	6-2/195	Cranbrook, B.C.	2-22-71	2	San Diego (IHL), Anaheim
6	Don McSween	5-11/197	Detroit	6-9-64	4	Anaheim
10	Oleg Tverdovsky	6-0/183	Donetsk, U.S.S.R.	5-18-76	1	Brandon (WHL), Anaheim
48	Darren Van Impe	6-0/195	Saskatoon, Sask.	5-18-73	1	San Diego (IHL), Anaheim
3	Jason York....................	6-0/205	Nepean, Ont.	5-20-70	3	Adirondack (AHL), Detroit, Anaheim
	GOALTENDERS					
31	Guy Hebert....................	5-11/185	Troy, N.Y.	1-7-67	4	Anaheim
35	Mikhail Shtalenkov	6-2/180	Moscow, U.S.S.R.	10-20-65	2	Anaheim

1994-95 REVIEW

INDIVIDUAL STATISTICS

SCORING

	Games	G	A	Pts.	PIM	+/-	PPG	SHG	Shots	Shooting Pct.
Paul Kariya	47	18	21	39	4	-17	7	1	134	13.4
Shaun Van Allen	45	8	21	29	32	-4	1	1	68	11.8
Stephan Lebeau	38	8	16	24	12	6	1	0	70	11.4
Todd Krygier	35	11	11	22	10	1	1	0	90	12.2
Peter Douris	46	10	11	21	12	4	0	0	69	14.5
Patrik Carnback	41	6	15	21	32	-8	0	0	58	10.3
Bobby Dollas	45	7	13	20	12	-3	3	1	70	10.0
Bob Corkum	44	10	9	19	25	-7	0	0	100	10.0
Joe Sacco	41	10	8	18	23	-8	2	0	77	13.0
Steve Rucchin	43	6	11	17	23	7	0	0	59	10.2
Oleg Tverdovsky	36	3	9	12	14	-6	1	1	26	11.5
Valeri Karpov	30	4	7	11	6	-4	0	0	48	8.3
Milos Holan	25	2	8	10	14	4	1	0	93	2.2
Garry Valk	36	3	6	9	34	-4	0	0	53	5.7
Jason York*	15	0	8	8	12	4	0	0	22	0.0
Tom Kurvers	22	4	3	7	6	-13	1	0	44	9.1
Anatoli Semenov*	15	3	4	7	4	-10	2	0	33	9.1
Mike Sillinger*	15	2	5	7	6	1	0	0	28	7.1
Randy Ladouceur	44	2	4	6	36	2	0	0	42	4.8
Dave Karpa*	26	1	5	6	91	0	0	0	32	3.1
John Lilley	9	2	2	4	5	2	1	0	10	20.0
David Williams	21	2	2	4	26	-5	0	0	30	6.7
Denny Lambert	13	1	3	4	4	3	0	0	14	7.1
Robert Dirk	38	1	3	4	56	-3	0	0	15	6.7
Tim Sweeney	13	1	1	2	2	-3	0	0	11	9.1
David Sacco	8	0	2	2	0	-3	0	0	5	0.0
Darren Van Impe	1	0	1	1	4	0	0	0	0	0.0
Mark Ferner*	14	0	1	1	6	-4	0	0	15	0.0
Stu Grimson*	31	0	1	1	110	-7	0	0	14	0.0

	Games	G	A	Pts.	PIM	+/-	PPG	SHG	Shots	Shooting Pct.
Jason Marshall	1	0	0	0	0	-2	0	0	1	0.0
Don McSween	2	0	0	0	0	0	0	0	1	0.0
Mikhail Shtalenkov (goalie)	18	0	0	0	2	0	0	0	0	0.0
Todd Ewen	24	0	0	0	90	-2	0	0	14	0.0
Guy Hebert (goalie)	39	0	0	0	2	0	0	0	0	0.0

GOALTENDING

	Games	Min.	Goals	SO	Avg.	W	L	T	Shots	Sv. Pct.
Guy Hebert	39	2092	109	2	3.13	12	20	4	1132	.904
Mikhail Shtalenkov	18	810	49	0	3.63	4	7	1	448	.891

Empty-net goals (do not count against a goaltender's average): Hebert 4, Shtalenkov 2.
*Played with two or more NHL teams.

RESULTS

JANUARY
20—At Edmonton	L	1-2
21—At Winnipeg	W	4-3
23—Edmonton	W	*5-4
25—Dallas	L	1-4
27—Winnipeg	W	3-2
31—At St. Louis	L	2-7

FEBRUARY
1—At Dallas	L	2-9
3—Detroit	L	2-5
5—At Los Angeles	W	3-2
7—Chicago	L	0-3
9—At Calgary	L	1-5
12—At Edmonton	L	0-2
17—Vancouver	T	*2-2
18—At San Jose	W	6-3
23—At Toronto	L	1-3
24—At Winnipeg	L	2-4
26—Calgary	L	3-5

MARCH
1—Chicago	W	3-1
3—At Dallas	L	0-4
5—At Chicago	L	0-3
7—At St. Louis	L	3-6
9—Detroit	T	*4-4
11—At Vancouver	L	3-5
15—At Calgary	W	5-0
17—Toronto	T	*3-3
19—St. Louis	L	2-4
21—Los Angeles	T	*3-3
23—At San Jose	W	6-3
26—At Chicago	L	2-5
28—At Detroit	L	4-6
30—Winnipeg	W	3-1
31—At Vancouver	L	1-6

APRIL
2—San Jose	W	5-4
5—Edmonton	W	*4-3
7—Dallas	L	0-2
9—Los Angeles	W	5-1
11—At Vancouver	L	0-5
13—Calgary	W	4-2
15—Vancouver	L	1-3
17—San Jose	W	3-0
19—At Toronto	L	2-3
21—At Detroit	L	5-6
23—At Los Angeles	T	*2-2
24—Calgary	W	2-1
26—San Jose	L	2-5
30—At Los Angeles	L	1-2

MAY
1—St. Louis	L	3-5
3—Toronto	W	6-1

*Denotes overtime game.

BOSTON BRUINS
EASTERN CONFERENCE/NORTHEAST DIVISION

1995-96 SCHEDULE

Home games shaded.
* — All-Star Game at FleetCenter, Boston.
D — Day game.

OCTOBER

SUN	MON	TUE	WED	THU	FRI	SAT
1	2	3	4	5	6	7 NYI
8	9 D BUF	10	11 COL	12 SJ	13	14 DAL
15	16	17 STL	18	19	20	21 D DET
22	23	24	25	26 WAS	27	28 HAR
29	30	31 MON				

NOVEMBER

SUN	MON	TUE	WED	THU	FRI	SAT
			1	2 DET	3	4 MON
5	6	7 WAS	8	9 OTT	10	11 TOR
12	13	14 TB	15	16 NJ	17	18 STL
19	20	21 WIN	22	23	24 D LA	25 OTT
26	27	28	29	30 PIT		

DECEMBER

SUN	MON	TUE	WED	THU	FRI	SAT
					1	2 BUF
3 PHI	4	5 DAL	6	7	8 TB	9 FLA
10	11	12	13 NYR	14 FLA	15	16 CAL
17	18	19	20	21	22 BUF	23 TB
24	25	26 NYI	27	28	29	30
31 D WIN						

JANUARY

SUN	MON	TUE	WED	THU	FRI	SAT
	1	2 CHI	3 TOR	4	5	6 HAR
7	8 COL	9	10	11 NJ	12	13 D NJ
14	15 D VAN	16	17 NJ	18	19	20 *
21	22 PIT	23	24	25 D TB	26	27 D NYR
28 D MON	29	30	31 OTT			

FEBRUARY

SUN	MON	TUE	WED	THU	FRI	SAT
				1	2 FLA	3 D BUF
4	5	6 PIT	7 BUF	8	9	10 D PHI
11	12	13	14 HAR	15 CHI	16	17 VAN
18	19 D LA	20	21 ANA	22	23 EDM	24 CAL
25	26	27 EDM	28 NYR	29		

MARCH

SUN	MON	TUE	WED	THU	FRI	SAT
					1	2 D WAS
3	4	5 NYI	6	7 NYI	8	9 D PHI
10 FLA	11	12	13	14 PIT	15 WAS	16
17 SJ	18	19	20 NJ	21 OTT	22	23 D NYR
24	25	26	27 HAR	28 MON	29	30
31 D BUF						

APRIL

SUN	MON	TUE	WED	THU	FRI	SAT
	1 OTT	2	3 MON	4 MON	5	6
7 D PHI	8	9	10	11 HAR	12	13 D HAR
14 D PIT	15	16	17	18	19	20

1995-96 SEASON

CLUB DIRECTORY

Owner and governor
Jeremy M. Jacobs
Alternative governor
Louis Jacobs
Alternate governor, president and G.M.
Harry Sinden
Vice president
Tom Johnson
Assistant to the president
Nate Greenberg
Director of administration
Dale Hamilton
Coach
Steve Kasper
Assistant coaches
Cap Raeder
Tim Watters
Chief scouting coordinator
Gordie Clark

Scouting staff
Jim Morrison
Joe Lyons
Don Saatzer
Marcel Pelletier
Jean Ratelle
Harvey Keck
Sven-Ake Svensson
Controller
Bob Vogel
Trainer
Don DelNegro
Assistant trainer
Tim Trahant
Equipment manager
Ken Fleger
Director of media relations
Heidi Holland

DRAFT CHOICES

Rd.—Player	H/W	Overall	Pos.	Last team
1—Kyle McLaren	6-4/210	9	D	Tacoma (WHL)
1—Sean Brown	6-2/196	21	D	Belleville (OHL)
2—Paxton Schafer	5-9/152	47	G	Medicine Hat (WHL)
3—Bill McCauley	6-0/173	73	C	Detroit (OHL)
4—Cameron Mann	5-11/185	99	RW	Peterborough (OHL)
6—Yevgeny Shaldybin	6-1/198	151	D	Yaroslavl, CIS
7—Per Johan Axelsson	6-1/163	177	LW	Frolunda, Sweden
8—Sergei Zhukov		203		CIS
9—Jonathan Murphy	6-2/210	229	D	Peterborough (OHL)

MISCELLANEOUS DATA

Home ice (capacity)
FleetCenter (17,200)
Address
To be announced
Business phone
617-557-1351 (This is latest
number at deadline. Bruins will
likely have another number when
they move into FleetCenter.)

Rink dimensions
191 feet by 83 feet
Club colors
Gold, black and white
Radio affiliation
WBZ (1030 AM)
TV affiliation
WSBK (Channel 38)

No.	FORWARDS	Ht./Wt.	BORN Place	Date	NHL exp.	1994-95 clubs
	Clayton Beddoes (C)	5-10/180	Bentley, Alta.	11-10-70	0	Providence (AHL)
19	Mariusz Czerkawski (RW)	5-11/185	Radomski, Poland	4-13-72	2	Kiekko-Espoo (Finland), Boston
21	Ted Donato (C)	5-10/170	Dedham, Mass.	4-28-68	4	TuTo Turku (Finland), Boston
	Brett Harkins (LW/C)	6-1/170	North Ridgefield, O.	7-2-70	1	Providence (AHL), Boston
23	Steve Heinze (RW)	5-11/180	Lawrence, Mass.	1-30-70	4	Boston
42	Brent Hughes (LW)	5-11/180	New Westminster, B.C.	4-5-66	6	Boston
48	Fred Knipscheer (C)	5-11/185	Fort Wayne, Ind.	9-3-69	2	Providence (AHL), Boston
11	Guy Larose (C/LW)	5-10/175	Hull, Que.	7-31-67	6	Providence (AHL), Boston
27	Steve Leach (RW)	5-11/200	Cambridge, Mass.	1-16-66	10	Boston
	Shawn McEachern (C)	6-0/195	Waltham, Mass.	2-28-69	4	Kiekko-Espoo (Finland), Pittsburgh
	Sandy Moger (RW)	6-2/190	100 Mile House, B.C.	3-21-69	1	Providence (AHL), Boston
26	Mats Naslund (LW)	5-7/160	Timra, Sweden	10-31-59	9	Boston
8	Cam Neely (RW)	6-1/210	Comox, B.C.	6-6-65	12	Boston
12	Adam Oates (C)	5-11/190	Weston, Ont.	8-27-62	10	Boston
27	Marc Potvin (RW)	6-1/215	Ottawa	1-29-67	5	Boston, Providence (AHL)
17	Dave Reid (LW)	6-1/205	Toronto	5-15-64	12	Boston
	Kevin Stevens (LW)	6-3/217	Brockton, Mass.	4-15-65	8	Pittsburgh
	Cam Stewart (C)	5-10/188	Kitchener, Ont.	9-18-71	2	Boston, Providence (AHL)
22	Jozef Stumpel (LW)	6-1/190	Nitra, Czechoslovakia	6-20-72	4	Koln (Germany), Boston

	DEFENSEMEN					
	Bill Armstrong	6-5/220	Richmond Hill, Ont.	5-18-70	0	Providence (AHL)
77	Ray Bourque	5-11/210	Montreal	12-28-60	16	Boston
	Sean Brown	6-2/196	Oshawa, Ont.	11-5-76	0	Belleville (OHL), Phoenix (IHL)
29	John Gruden	6-0/180	Hastings, Minn.	4-6-70	2	Boston, Providence (AHL)
	Jamie Huscroft	6-2/200	Creston, B.C.	1-9-67	5	Boston
34	Al Iafrate	6-3/220	Dearborn, Mich.	3-21-66	10	
7	Alexei Kasatonov	6-1/215	Leningrad, U.S.S.R.	10-14-59	6	CSKA Moscow (CIS), Boston
	Milt Mastad	6-3/205	Regina, Sask.	3-5-75	0	Moose Jaw (WHL)
	Kyle McLaren	6-4/210	Coaldale, Alta.	6-18-77	0	Tacoma (WHL)
	Jon Rohloff	6-0/200	Mankato, Minn.	10-3-69	1	Boston, Providence (AHL)
34	David Shaw	6-2/204	St. Thomas, Ont.	5-25-64	13	Boston
32	Don Sweeney	5-11/170	St. Stephen, N.B.	8-17-66	7	Boston
	Mattias Timander	6-1/194	Solleftea, Sweden	4-16-74	0	MoDo Hockey Ornskoldvik (Sweden)
	Phil Von Stefenelli	6-1/183	Vancouver	4-10-69	0	Providence (AHL)

	GOALTENDERS					
	Scott Bailey	5-11/185	Calgary	5-2-72	0	Providence (AHL)
1	Craig Billington	5-10/170	London, Ont.	9-11-66	7	Ottawa, Boston
	Blaine Lacher	6-1/205	Medicine Hat, Alta.	9-5-70	1	Boston, Providence (AHL)
37	Vince Riendeau	5-10/185	St. Hyacinthe, Que.	4-20-66	8	Boston, Providence (AHL)
	Yevgeni Ryabchikov	5-11/167	Yaroslavl, U.S.S.R.	1-16-74	0	Metallurg Cherepovets (CIS), Providence (AHL)
	Paxton Schafer	5-9/152	Medicine Hat, Alta.	2-26-76	0	Medicine Hat (WHL)

1994-95 REVIEW

INDIVIDUAL STATISTICS

SCORING

	Games	G	A	Pts.	PIM	+/-	PPG	SHG	Shots	Shooting Pct.
Adam Oates	48	12	41	53	8	-11	4	1	109	11.0
Ray Bourque	46	12	31	43	20	3	9	0	†210	5.7
Cam Neely	42	27	14	41	72	7	†16	0	178	15.2
Bryan Smolinski	44	18	13	31	31	-3	6	0	121	14.9
Mariusz Czerkawski	47	12	14	26	31	4	1	0	126	9.5
Mats Naslund	34	8	14	22	4	-4	2	0	48	16.7
Don Sweeney	47	3	19	22	24	6	1	0	102	2.9
Ted Donato	47	10	10	20	10	3	1	0	71	14.1
Jozef Stumpel	44	5	13	18	8	4	1	0	46	10.9
Steve Heinze	36	7	9	16	23	0	0	1	70	10.0
Alexei Kasatonov	44	2	14	16	33	-2	0	1	50	4.0
Brent Hughes	44	6	6	12	139	6	0	0	75	8.0
Stephen Leach	35	5	6	11	68	-3	1	0	82	6.1
Jon Rohloff	34	3	8	11	39	1	0	0	51	5.9
Dave Reid	38	5	5	10	10	8	0	0	47	10.6
Sandy Moger	18	2	6	8	6	-1	2	0	32	6.3
Glen Murray	35	5	2	7	46	-11	0	0	64	7.8
David Shaw	44	3	4	7	36	-9	1	0	58	5.2
Jamie Huscroft	34	0	6	6	103	-3	0	0	30	0.0
John Gruden	38	0	6	6	22	3	0	0	30	0.0
Fred Knipscheer	16	3	1	4	2	1	0	0	20	15.0

	Games	G	A	Pts.	PIM	+/-	PPG	SHG	Shots	Shooting Pct.
Mikko Makela	11	1	2	3	0	0	1	0	10	10.0
Dan Lacroix*	23	1	0	1	38	-2	0	0	14	7.1
Brett Harkins	1	0	1	1	0	0	0	0	1	0.0
Marc Potvin	6	0	1	1	4	1	0	0	4	0.0
Blaine Lacher (goalie)	35	0	1	1	4	0	0	0	0	0.0
Grigori Panteleev	1	0	0	0	0	0	0	0	0	0.0
Jeff Serowik	1	0	0	0	0	1	0	0	0	0.0
Cameron Stewart	5	0	0	0	2	0	0	0	2	0.0
Craig Billington* (goalie)	8	0	0	0	2	0	0	0	0	0.0
Vincent Riendeau (goalie)	11	0	0	0	2	0	0	0	0	0.0

GOALTENDING

	Games	Min.	Goals	SO	Avg.	W	L	T	Shots	Sv. Pct.
Blaine Lacher	35	1965	79	4	2.41	19	11	2	805	.902
Vincent Riendeau	11	565	27	0	2.87	3	6	1	221	.878
Craig Billington*	8	373	19	0	3.06	5	1	0	140	.864

Empty-net goals (do not count against a goaltender's average): Riendeau 2.
*Played with two or more NHL teams.
†Led league.

RESULTS

JANUARY
22—Philadelphia	W	4-1
23—At N.Y. Rangers	W	2-1
26—New Jersey	W	*1-0
28—At Philadelphia	L	1-2
30—Florida	L	1-2

FEBRUARY
2—Ottawa	W	6-4
4—Hartford	W	5-4
7—Montreal	W	7-4
9—Quebec	L	3-4
11—Washington	T	*1-1
12—At Buffalo	W	2-1
14—At Pittsburgh	L	3-5
17—At Florida	W	5-4
18—At Tampa Bay	L	1-3
22—At Hartford	L	*2-3
23—At New Jersey	W	3-2
25—At Quebec	T	*1-1
27—At Ottawa	W	2-0

MARCH
2—New Jersey	W	7-2
4—Pittsburgh	L	*3-4
5—At Hartford	W	5-2
7—Washington	L	1-3
9—At Philadelphia	L	2-3
11—Florida	L	0-2
16—Montreal	W	6-0
18—N.Y. Islanders	W	4-3
19—At New Jersey	L	*3-4
22—At Quebec	L	2-6
24—At Tampa Bay	W	*4-3
28—Philadelphia	W	5-1
30—At N.Y. Islanders	W	3-2

APRIL
1—N.Y. Rangers	L	2-3
2—At Washington	L	1-2
6—Buffalo	T	*1-1
8—Tampa Bay	W	5-1
9—At Buffalo	W	6-5

12—Quebec	L	0-4
14—At N.Y. Rangers	L	3-5
15—At Montreal	W	3-2
19—Buffalo	W	4-1
20—At Ottawa	W	6-5
23—N.Y. Rangers	W	5-4
24—At N.Y. Islanders	L	3-5
26—Hartford	W	1-0
28—At Pittsburgh	L	1-4
30—Pittsburgh	W	5-2

MAY
1—Ottawa	W	5-4
3—At Montreal	W	4-2

*Denotes overtime game.

BUFFALO SABRES
EASTERN CONFERENCE/NORTHEAST DIVISION

1995-96 SCHEDULE

Home games shaded.
● — All-Star Game at FleetCenter, Boston.
D — Day game.

OCTOBER

SUN	MON	TUE	WED	THU	FRI	SAT
1	2	3	4	5	6	7 OTT
8	9 D BOS	10	11	12	13 ANA	14
15 NJ	16	17	18 EDM	19	20 NYR	21
22 STL	23	24 DAL	25	26	27 COL	28
29 CHI	30	31				

NOVEMBER

SUN	MON	TUE	WED	THU	FRI	SAT
			1 DET	2	3 PIT	4
5 WIN	6	7	8 SJ	9	10	11 FLA
12 TB	13	14	15 DAL	16	17	18 D NJ
19 OTT	20	21	22	23	24 NYI	25 PIT
26	27 STL	28	29 NYR	30		

DECEMBER

SUN	MON	TUE	WED	THU	FRI	SAT
					1 HAR	2 BOS
3	4	5	6	7 PHI	8 WAS	9
10 TB	11	12	13 COL	14	15 NYR	16
17	18	19	20 MON	21	22 BOS	23 OTT
24	25	26 PIT	27 OTT	28	29 CHI	30
31 NYI						

JANUARY

SUN	MON	TUE	WED	THU	FRI	SAT
	1	2	3	4	5 TOR	6 MON
7	8	9	10 WIN	11	12 CAL	13 EDM
14	15	16	17 PIT	18	19	20 ●
21	22	23	24 HAR	25	26 WAS	27 FLA
28	29	30 NYI	31 FLA			

FEBRUARY

SUN	MON	TUE	WED	THU	FRI	SAT
				1	2	3 D BOS
4 D	5	6	7 BOS	8 PHI	9	10 TOR
11	12	13	14 LA	15	16 NJ	17 HAR
18	19	20	21 PIT	22	23 PHI	24
25 FLA	26	27	28 OTT	29		

MARCH

SUN	MON	TUE	WED	THU	FRI	SAT
					1 NYR	2
3 D VAN	4	5	6 VAN	7	8 ANA	9
10 D SJ	11	12	13 LA	14	15 CAL	16 HAR
17	18 MON	19	20	21	22 MON	23 PIT
24	25	26	27 DET	28	29 PHI	30
31 D BOS						

APRIL

SUN	MON	TUE	WED	THU	FRI	SAT
	1 MON	2	3 WAS	4	5 TB	6 NYI
7	8	9	10 OTT	11	12	13 WAS
14 HAR	15	16	17	18	19	20

1995-96 SEASON

CLUB DIRECTORY

Chief executive officer and president
Douglas G. Moss
Chairman of the board
Seymour H. Knox III
Vice chairman of the board and counsel
Robert O. Swados
Vice chairman of the board
Robert E. Rich Jr.
Treasurer
Joseph T.J. Stewart
Assistant to the president
Seymour H. Knox IV
Senior vice president, administration
George Bergantz
V.P. of finance and chief financial officer
Dan DiPofi
V.P. of sales and marketing
Jeff Eisenberg
General manager
John Muckler
Head coach
Ted Nolan
Associate coach
Don Lever
Assistant coach
Terry Martin

Director of player evaluation
Larry Carriere
Director of player personnel
Don Luce
Scouting staff
Don Barrie
Jack Bowman
Boris Janicek
Paul Merritt
Mike Racicot
Gleb Tchistyakov
Director of communications
To be announced
Director of information
Bruce Wawrzyniak
Director of public relations
Jeff Holbrook
Head athletic trainer
Jim Pizzutelli
Trainer
Rip Simonick
Equipment supervisor
George Babcock

DRAFT CHOICES

Rd. — Player	H/W	Overall	Pos.	Last team
1 — Jay McKee	6-2/175	14	D	Niagara Falls (OHL)
1 — Martin Biron	6-1/154	16	G	Beauport (QMJHL)
2 — Mark Dutiaume	6-0/200	42	LW	Brandon (WHL)
3 — Mathieu Sunderland	6-4/192	68	RW	Drummondville (QMJHL)
4 — Matt Davidson	6-2/190	94	RW	Portland (WHL)
5 — Marian Menhart	6-3/220	111	D	Litinov Jrs., Czech Rep.
5 — Kevin Popp	6-1/198	119	D	Seattle (WHL)
5 — Daniel Bienvenue	6-0/196	123	LW	Val d'Or (QMJHL)
7 — Brian Scott	6-0/189	172	LW	Kitchener (OHL)
8 — Mike Zanutto	6-0/190	198	C	Oshawa (OHL)
9 — Rob Skrlac	6-4/230	224	LW	Kamloops (WHL)

MISCELLANEOUS DATA

Home ice (capacity)
Memorial Auditorium
(16,284, including standees)
Address
Memorial Auditorium
140 Main St.
Buffalo, NY 14202
Business phone
716-856-7300 or 800-333-7825

Rink dimensions
193 feet by 84 feet
Club colors
Blue, white and gold
Radio affiliation
To be announced
TV affiliation
Empire Sports Network

TRAINING CAMP ROSTER

No.	FORWARDS	Ht./Wt.	Place	BORN Date	NHL exp.	1994-95 clubs
28	Donald Audette (RW)	5-8/175	Laval, Que.	9-23-69	6	Buffalo
36	Matthew Barnaby (LW)	6-0/170	Ottawa	5-4-73	3	Rochester (AHL), Buffalo
	Curtis Brown (C)	6-0/182	Unity, Sask.	2-12-76	1	Moose Jaw (WHL), Buffalo
	Jason Dawe (LW/RW)..	5-10/195	North York, Ont.	5-29-73	2	Rochester (AHL), Buffalo
9	Viktor Gordiouk (RW) ...	5-10/176	Moscow, U.S.S.R.	4-11-70	2	Rochester (AHL), Buffalo
14	Dave Hannan (C)..........	5-10/180	Sudbury, Ont.	11-26-61	14	Buffalo
	Brian Holzinger (C)	5-11/180	Parma, O.	10-10-72	1	Bowling Green St. (CCHA), Buffalo
13	Yuri Khmylev (LW)	6-1/189	Moscow, U.S.S.R.	8-9-64	3	Buffalo
16	Pat LaFontaine (C)	5-10/180	St. Louis	2-22-65	12	Buffalo
27	Brad May (LW)	6-1/210	Toronto	11-29-71	4	Buffalo
33	Scott Pearson (LW)	6-1/205	Cornwall, Ont.	12-19-69	7	Edmonton, Buffalo
33	Mike Peca (RW/C)	5-11/175	Toronto	3-26-74	2	Syracuse (AHL), Vancouver
	Derek Plante (C)............	5-11/180	Cloquet, Minn.	1-17-71	2	Buffalo
	Wayne Primeau (C)......	6-3/193	Scarborough, Ont.	6-4-76	1	Owen Sound (OHL), Buffalo
32	Rob Ray (LW)	6-0/203	Stirling, Ont.	6-8-68	6	Buffalo
20	Bob Sweeney (C)	6-3/200	Boxborough, Mass.	1-25-64	9	Buffalo
21	Scott Thomas (RW)	6-2/195	Buffalo, N.Y.	1-18-70	2	Rochester (AHL)
	DEFENSEMEN					
	Mark Astley	5-11/185	Calgary	3-30-69	2	Rochester (AHL), Buffalo
8	Doug Bodger	6-2/213	Chemainus, B.C.	6-18-66	11	Buffalo
3	Garry Galley	6-0/204	Ottawa	4-16-63	11	Philadelphia, Buffalo
27	Doug Houda	6-2/190	Blairmore, Alta.	6-3-66	9	Buffalo
22	Charlie Huddy...............	6-0/210	Oshawa, Ont.	6-2-59	15	Los Angeles, Buffalo
3	Craig Muni	6-3/208	Toronto	7-19-62	13	Buffalo
42	Richard Smehlik	6-3/208	Ostrava, Czechoslovakia	1-23-70	3	HC Vitkovice (Czech.), Buffalo
	Mike Wilson	6-5/180	Brampton, Ont.	2-26-75	0	Sudbury (OHL)
2	Alexei Zhitnik	5-11/190	Kiev, U.S.S.R.	10-10-72	3	Los Angeles, Buffalo
	GOALTENDERS					
39	Dominik Hasek	5-11/168	Pardubice, Czechoslovakia	1-29-65	5	HC Pardubice (Czech.), Buffalo
35	Robb Stauber.................	5-11/180	Duluth, Minn.	11-25-67	4	Los Angeles, Buffalo
1	Andrei Trefilov	6-0/180	Moscow, U.S.S.R.	8-31-69	3	Saint John (AHL), Calgary

1994-95 REVIEW

INDIVIDUAL STATISTICS

SCORING

	Games	G	A	Pts.	PIM	+/-	PPG	SHG	Shots	Shooting Pct.
Alexander Mogilny	44	19	28	47	36	0	12	0	148	12.8
Donald Audette..........................	46	24	13	37	27	-3	13	0	124	19.4
Pat LaFontaine	22	12	15	27	4	2	6	1	54	22.2
Yuri Khmylev	48	8	17	25	14	8	2	1	71	11.3
Derek Plante	47	3	19	22	12	-4	2	0	94	3.2
Doug Bodger	44	3	17	20	47	-3	2	0	87	3.4
Wayne Presley...........................	46	14	5	19	41	5	0	5	90	15.6
Dale Hawerchuk	23	5	11	16	2	-2	2	0	56	8.9
Dave Hannan	42	4	12	16	32	3	0	2	36	11.1
Jason Dawe	42	7	4	11	19	-6	0	1	51	13.7
Craig Simpson	24	4	7	11	26	-5	1	0	20	20.0
Richard Smehlik	39	4	7	11	46	5	0	1	49	8.2
Garry Galley*	14	1	9	10	10	4	1	0	31	3.2
Bob Sweeney	45	5	4	9	18	-6	1	2	47	10.6
Alexei Zhitnik*	21	2	5	7	34	-3	1	0	33	6.1
Brad May	33	3	3	6	87	5	1	0	42	7.1
Charlie Huddy*	32	2	4	6	36	-1	1	0	40	5.0
Craig Muni	40	0	6	6	36	-4	0	0	32	0.0
Philippe Boucher*	9	1	4	5	0	6	0	0	15	6.7
Petr Svoboda*	26	0	5	5	60	-5	0	0	22	0.0
Mark Astley	14	2	1	3	12	-2	0	0	21	9.5
Scott Pearson*	14	2	1	3	20	-3	0	0	19	10.5
Ken Sutton*	12	1	2	3	30	-2	0	0	12	8.3
Doug Houda	28	1	2	3	68	1	0	0	21	4.8
Brian Holzinger	4	0	3	3	0	2	0	0	3	0.0
Rob Ray	47	0	3	3	173	-4	0	0	7	0.0
Curtis Brown.............................	1	1	1	2	2	2	0	0	4	25.0
Matthew Barnaby	23	1	1	2	116	-2	0	0	27	3.7
Viktor Gordiouk	10	0	2	2	0	-3	0	0	10	0.0
Wayne Primeau	1	1	0	1	0	-2	0	0	2	50.0
Peter Ambroziak	12	0	1	1	0	-1	0	0	3	0.0

	Games	G	A	Pts.	PIM	+/−	PPG	SHG	Shots	Shooting Pct.
Doug MacDonald	2	0	0	0	0	−1	0	0	0	0.0
Grant Fuhr* (goalie)	3	0	0	0	0	0	0	0	0	0.0
Denis Tsygurov*	4	0	0	0	4	−1	0	0	4	0.0
Dean Melanson	5	0	0	0	4	−1	0	0	1	0.0
Robb Stauber* (goalie)	6	0	0	0	0	0	0	0	0	0.0
Dominik Hasek (goalie)	41	0	0	0	2	0	0	0	0	0.0

GOALTENDING

	Games	Min.	Goals	SO	Avg.	W	L	T	Shots	Sv. Pct.
Dominik Hasek	41	2416	85	‡5	†2.11	19	14	7	1221	†.930
Robb Stauber*	6	317	20	0	3.79	2	3	0	150	.867
Grant Fuhr*	3	180	12	0	4.00	1	2	0	85	.859

Empty-net goals (do not count against a goaltender's average): Hasek 2.
*Played with two or more NHL teams.
†Led league.
‡Tied for league lead.

RESULTS

JANUARY

20—At N.Y. Rangers	W	2-1
22—At Tampa Bay	W	5-2
25—New Jersey	W	2-1
27—Quebec	L	3-7
28—At Ottawa	T	*2-2
31—At New Jersey	L	1-2

FEBRUARY

2—At Washington	W	1-0
4—At Philadelphia	L	2-4
5—Tampa Bay	W	2-1
7—Washington	W	2-1
11—At N.Y. Islanders	L	1-2
12—Boston	L	1-2
15—N.Y. Rangers	L	1-2
19—At Pittsburgh	T	*3-3
22—N.Y. Islanders	T	*3-3
25—At Hartford	W	3-1
26—N.Y. Rangers	L	2-4

MARCH

2—Pittsburgh	W	6-3
4—At Quebec	T	*1-1
5—Montreal	W	4-1
8—At Montreal	T	*2-2
11—At Pittsburgh	L	2-6
14—At Florida	W	*2-1
16—N.Y. Islanders	W	6-3
18—At Ottawa	L	*3-4
19—Tampa Bay	L	1-6
21—Pittsburgh	L	2-3
24—Florida	W	3-0
26—At Philadelphia	L	1-3
28—Quebec	W	5-3
30—Ottawa	W	7-0

APRIL

1—At N.Y. Islanders	W	5-1
4—Hartford	W	6-3
6—At Boston	T	*1-1
8—At Hartford	L	2-4
9—Boston	L	5-6
12—At N.Y. Rangers	L	1-3
14—At Quebec	L	2-5
16—Ottawa	W	2-1
18—Hartford	L	1-2
19—At Boston	L	1-4
23—Philadelphia	W	4-2
24—At Tampa Bay	W	3-1
26—Florida	W	5-0
28—At Washington	L	1-5
29—At Montreal	T	*3-3

MAY

1—Montreal	W	2-0
3—New Jersey	W	5-4

*Denotes overtime game.

CALGARY FLAMES
WESTERN CONFERENCE/PACIFIC DIVISION

Home games shaded.
* — All-Star Game at FleetCenter, Boston.
D — Day game.

OCTOBER

SUN	MON	TUE	WED	THU	FRI	SAT
1	2	3	4	5	6	7 TB
8 FLA	9	10 DAL	11	12	13	14
15 CHI	16	17 DET	18	19 OTT	20 TOR	21
22	23	24	25 COL	26	27 DET	28
29 ANA	30	31 LA				

NOVEMBER

SUN	MON	TUE	WED	THU	FRI	SAT
			1 COL	2	3	4 VAN
5	6 NYR	7	8 NJ	9 PHI	10	11 MON
12	13	14 EDM	15	16	17 COL	18 COL
19	20	21 ANA	22	23	24 EDM	25
26 CHI	27	28	29 SJ	30		

DECEMBER

SUN	MON	TUE	WED	THU	FRI	SAT
					1 EDM	2
3 WIN	4	5 STL	6	7	8	9 VAN
10	11 LA	12	13 DAL	14 STL	15	16 BOS
17	18	19 PIT	20 HAR	21	22 DET	23
24	25	26 VAN	27 TOR	28	29 PHI	30
31 NYR						

JANUARY

SUN	MON	TUE	WED	THU	FRI	SAT
	1	2 TB	3	4	5 FLA	6
7	8	9	10 HAR	11	12 FLA	13
14 COL	15	16 LA	17 ANA	18	19	20 *
21	22	23	24 NYI	25	26 DAL	27
28	29	30 EDM	31			

FEBRUARY

SUN	MON	TUE	WED	THU	FRI	SAT
				1 NJ	2	3 LA
4	5	6 OTT	7	8 WAS	9	10 WIN
11 EDM	12	13 WAS	14	15 NYI	16	17 MON
18	19	20 SJ	21	22	23 ANA	24 BOS
25	26	27	28	29 PIT		

MARCH

SUN	MON	TUE	WED	THU	FRI	SAT
					1	2
3 SJ	D 4	5	6	7 STL	8	9 TOR
10	11	12 STL	13	14 BUF	15	16
17 DET	D 18	19	20 CHI	21	22 SJ	23 VAN
24	25 TOR	26	27 CHI	28	29 LA	30
31 WIN						

APRIL

SUN	MON	TUE	WED	THU	FRI	SAT
	1	2	3 VAN	4	5	6 WIN
7	8 EDM	9 DAL	10	11	12 SJ	13 VAN
14	15	16	17	18	19	20

CLUB DIRECTORY

Chief exec. officer/governor
Harley N. Hotchkiss
Exec. V.P./alternate governor
Al Coates
Co-owners
Grant A. Bartlett
N. Murray Edwards
Harley N. Hotchkiss
Ronald V. Joyce
Alvin G. Libin
Allan P. Markin
J.R. McCaig
Byron J. Seaman
Daryl K. Seaman
General manager
Doug Risebrough
Vice president, business and finance
Clare Rhyasen
Director, hockey operations
Al MacNeil
Vice president, marketing
Lanny McDonald
Head Coach
Pierre Page
Assistant coaches
To be announced

Director of public relations
Rick Skaggs
Assistant public relations director
Mike Burke
Director of amateur scouting
Tom Thompson
Scouts
Ray Clearwater
Jiri Hrdina
Guy Lapointe
Ian McKenzie
Nick Polano
Larry Popein
Scouting staff
Glen Giovanacci
Paul MacIntosh
Anders Steen
Ernie Vargus
Controller
Michael Holditch
Trainer
Jim "Bearcat" Murray
Equipment manager
Bobby Stewart
Physiotherapist
James Gattinger

DRAFT CHOICES

Rd.—Player	H/W	Overall	Pos.	Last team
1—Denis Gauthier	6-1/195	20	D	Drummondville (QMJHL)
2—Pavel Smirnov	6-3/191	46	C	Molot Perm, CIS
3—Rocky Thompson	6-2/189	72	D	Medicine Hat (WHL)
4—Jan Labraaten	6-2/198	98	LW	Farjestad Jrs., Sweden
6—Clarke Wilm	5-11/201	150	C	Saskatoon (WHL)
7—Ryan Gillis	6-1/195	176	D	North Bay (OHL)
9—Steve Shirreffs		233		Hotchkiss H.S. (Conn.)

MISCELLANEOUS DATA

Home ice (capacity)
Olympic Saddledome (20,230)
Address
P.O. Box 1540
Station M
Calgary, Alta. T2P 3B9
Business phone
403-777-2177

Rink dimensions
200 feet by 85 feet
Club colors
Red, white and gold
Radio affiliation
66 CFR (660 AM)
TV affiliation
Calgary 7, CBC-TV, TSN

No.	FORWARDS	Ht./Wt.	Place (BORN)	Date	NHL exp.	1994-95 clubs
	Chris Dingman (LW)	6-4/225	Edmonton	7-6-76	0	Brandon (WHL)
14	Theo Fleury (C/RW)	5-6/160	Oxbow, Sask.	6-29-68	7	Tappara (Finland), Calgary
38	Todd Hlushko (LW)	5-11/185	Toronto	2-7-70	2	Saint John (AHL), Calgary
23	Sheldon Kennedy (RW)	5-11/180	Brandon, Man.	6-15-69	6	Calgary
11	Kelly Kisio (C)	5-10/185	Peace River, Alta.	9-18-59	13	Calgary
12	Paul Kruse (LW)	6-0/205	Merritt, B.C.	3-15-70	5	Calgary
	Jesper Mattsson (C)	6-0/173	Malmo, Sweden	5-13-75	0	Malmo (Sweden)
	Sandy McCarthy (RW)	6-3/225	Toronto	6-15-72	2	Calgary
	Marty Murray (C)	5-9/170	Deloraine, Man.	2-16-75	0	Brandon (WHL)
68	Barry Nieckar (LW)	6-3/200	Rama, Sask.	12-16-67	2	Saint John (AHL), Calgary
25	Joe Nieuwendyk (C)	6-1/195	Oshawa, Ont.	9-10-66	9	Calgary
92	Michael Nylander (C)	5-11/190	Stockholm, Sweden	10-3-72	3	JyP HT (Finland), Calgary
	Mike Peluso (C)	6-0/200	Denver, Colo.	9-2-74	0	Minnesota-Duluth (WCHA)
24	Jim Peplinski (C)	6-3/210	Renfrew, Ont.	10-24-60	11	Calgary
26	Robert Reichel (C)	5-10/185	Litvinov, Czechoslovakia	6-25-71	5	Frankfurt (Germany), Calgary
10	Gary Roberts (LW)	6-1/190	North York, Ont.	5-23-66	9	Calgary
13	German Titov (C)	6-0/190	Borovsk, U.S.S.R.	10-16-65	2	TPS Turku (Finland), Calgary
	Ed Ward (RW)	6-3/205	Edmonton	11-10-69	2	Cornwall (AHL), Saint John (AHL), Calgary
	DEFENSEMEN					
	Jamie Allison	6-1/190	Lindsay, Ont.	5-13-75	1	Detroit (OHL), Calgary
	Joel Bouchard	6-0/185	Montreal	1-23-74	1	Saint John (AHL), Calgary
21	Steve Chiasson	6-1/205	Barrie, Ont.	4-14-67	9	Calgary
4	Kevin Dahl	5-11/190	Regina, Sask.	12-30-68	3	Calgary
43	Len Esau	6-3/190	Meadow Lake, Sask.	3-16-68	4	Saint John (AHL), Edmonton, Calgary
6	Phil Housley	5-10/185	St. Paul, Minn.	3-9-64	13	Grasshoppers (Switzerland Div. II), Calgary
39	Dan Keczmer	6-1/190	Mt. Clemens, Mich.	5-25-68	5	Calgary
3	Frank Musil	6-3/215	Pardubice, Czechoslovakia	12-17-64	9	Sparta Prague (Czechoslovakia), Sachsen (Germany), Calgary
5	James Patrick	6-2/200	Winnipeg	6-14-63	12	Calgary
	Dmitri Ryabykin	6-1/183	Moscow, U.S.S.R.	3-24-76	0	Dynamo Moscow (CIS)
	Rocky Thompson	6-2/189	Calgary.	8-8-77	0	Medicine Hat (WHL)
18	Trent Yawney	6-3/195	Hudson Bay, Sask.	9-29-65	8	Calgary
33	Zarley Zalapski	6-1/215	Edmonton	4-22-68	8	Calgary
	GOALTENDERS					
	Trevor Kidd	6-2/190	St. Boniface, Man.	3-29-72	3	Calgary
	Jason Muzzatti	6-1/190	Toronto	2-3-70	2	Saint John (AHL), Calgary
	Dwayne Roloson	6-1/185	Simcoe, Ont.	10-12-69	0	Saint John (AHL)
31	Rick Tabaracci	5-11/180	Toronto	1-2-69	6	Washington, Chicago (IHL), Calgary

1994-95 REVIEW

INDIVIDUAL STATISTICS

SCORING

	Games	G	A	Pts.	PIM	+/-	PPG	SHG	Shots	Shooting Pct.
Theoren Fleury	47	29	29	58	112	6	9	2	173	16.8
Joe Nieuwendyk	46	21	29	50	33	11	3	0	122	17.2
Phil Housley	43	8	35	43	18	17	3	0	135	5.9
Robert Reichel	48	18	17	35	28	-2	5	0	160	11.3
Zarley Zalapski	48	4	24	28	46	9	1	0	76	5.3
Steve Chiasson	45	2	23	25	39	10	1	0	110	1.8
German Titov	40	12	12	24	16	6	3	2	88	13.6
Joel Otto	47	8	13	21	130	8	0	2	46	17.4
Wes Walz	39	6	12	18	11	7	4	0	73	8.2
Paul Kruse	45	11	5	16	141	13	0	0	52	21.2
Sheldon Kennedy	30	7	8	15	45	5	1	0	44	15.9
Ronnie Stern	39	9	4	13	163	4	1	0	69	13.0
Kevin Dahl	34	4	8	12	38	8	0	0	30	13.3
Kelly Kisio	12	7	4	11	6	2	5	1	26	26.9
Mike Sullivan	38	4	7	11	14	-2	0	0	31	12.9
James Patrick	43	0	10	10	14	-3	0	0	43	0.0
Sandy McCarthy	37	5	3	8	101	1	0	0	29	17.2
Dan Keczmer	28	2	3	5	10	7	0	0	33	6.1
Nikolai Borschevsky*	8	0	5	5	0	7	0	0	12	0.0
Frank Musil	35	0	5	5	61	6	0	0	18	0.0
Gary Roberts	8	2	2	4	43	1	2	0	20	10.0
Alan May*	7	1	2	3	13	2	0	0	5	20.0

	Games	G	A	Pts.	PIM	+/-	PPG	SHG	Shots	Shooting Pct.
Vesa Viitakoski	10	1	2	3	6	-1	1	0	6	16.7
Ed Ward	2	1	1	2	2	-2	0	0	1	100.0
Mark Greig	8	1	1	2	2	1	0	0	5	20.0
Cory Stillman	10	0	2	2	2	1	0	0	7	0.0
Trent Yawney	37	0	2	2	108	-4	0	0	20	0.0
Todd Hlushko	2	0	1	1	2	1	0	0	3	0.0
Rick Tabaracci* (goalie)	5	0	1	1	0	0	0	0	0	0.0
Michael Nylander	6	0	1	1	2	1	0	0	2	0.0
Jim Peplinski	6	0	1	1	11	-2	0	0	5	0.0
Trevor Kidd (goalie)	43	0	1	1	2	0	0	0	0	0.0
Jamie Allison	1	0	0	0	0	0	0	0	0	0.0
Leonard Esau*	1	0	0	0	0	-2	0	0	4	0.0
Steve Konroyd	1	0	0	0	0	0	0	0	0	0.0
Jason Muzzatti (goalie)	1	0	0	0	0	0	0	0	0	0.0
Joel Bouchard	2	0	0	0	0	0	0	0	0	0.0
Neil Eisenhut	3	0	0	0	0	0	0	0	2	0.0
Barry Nieckar	3	0	0	0	12	0	0	0	0	0.0
Scott Morrow	4	0	0	0	0	0	0	0	1	0.0
Andrei Trefilov (goalie)	6	0	0	0	0	0	0	0	0	0.0

GOALTENDING

	Games	Min.	Goals	SO	Avg.	W	L	T	Shots	Sv. Pct.
Jason Muzzatti	1	10	0	0	.00	0	0	0	8	1.000
Rick Tabaracci*	5	202	5	0	1.49	2	0	1	93	.946
Trevor Kidd	‡43	2463	107	3	2.61	22	14	6	1170	.909
Andrei Trefilov	6	236	16	0	4.07	0	3	0	130	.877

Empty-net goals (do not count against a goaltender's average): Kidd 4, Trefilov 3.
*Played with two or more NHL teams.
‡Tied for league lead.

RESULTS

JANUARY
20—At Winnipeg	T	*3-3
22—At Detroit	W	4-1
24—St. Louis	W	6-4
26—At Detroit	L	1-5
28—At Toronto	L	1-2

FEBRUARY
1—Detroit	W	2-1
3—Chicago	L	*3-4
4—Toronto	W	4-1
6—Winnipeg	L	4-5
9—Anaheim	W	5-1
11—At Dallas	W	6-0
13—At St. Louis	L	2-4
16—At Chicago	T	*2-2
18—Dallas	W	*3-2
20—Dallas	L	1-2
23—At Los Angeles	T	*3-3
24—At San Jose	W	3-0
26—At Anaheim	W	5-3
28—Edmonton	W	5-2

MARCH
2—Vancouver	T	*2-2
4—At Toronto	L	2-3
5—At Winnipeg	L	2-3
7—At Chicago	W	6-3
9—At St. Louis	L	1-5
12—At Dallas	T	*4-4
15—Anaheim	L	0-5
17—Winnipeg	W	8-4
19—San Jose	L	3-5
20—At Edmonton	L	2-5
22—St. Louis	W	4-3
24—Detroit	W	3-2
26—Vancouver	W	2-0
28—Los Angeles	L	3-5
31—At Edmonton	W	6-2

APRIL
4—Chicago	W	3-2
7—Los Angeles	W	7-4
8—Vancouver	L	2-4
10—San Jose	W	8-3

12—At Los Angeles	W	4-1
13—At Anaheim	L	2-4
15—At Edmonton	W	4-2
17—Los Angeles	W	5-2
20—At Vancouver	T	*2-2
24—At Anaheim	L	1-2
25—At San Jose	W	3-2
29—Toronto	T	*2-2
30—At Vancouver	L	4-6

MAY
3—Edmonton	W	5-3

*Denotes overtime game.

CHICAGO BLACKHAWKS
WESTERN CONFERENCE/CENTRAL DIVISION

1995-96 SCHEDULE

Home games shaded.
* — All-Star Game at FleetCenter, Boston.
D — Day game.

OCTOBER

SUN	MON	TUE	WED	THU	FRI	SAT
1	2	3	4	5	6	7 SJ
8	9	10 LA	11	12 PIT	13	14 HAR
15 CAL	16	17 FLA	18	19 TB	20	21 STL
22 PHI	23	24	25	26 TOR	27	28 MON
29 BUF	30	31				

NOVEMBER

SUN	MON	TUE	WED	THU	FRI	SAT
			1 DAL	2	3	4
5 COL	6	7	8	9 VAN	10	11 WAS
12 EDM	13	14 WIN	15	16 NYR	17	18
19 SJ	20	21	22 COL	23	24 D ANA	25
26 CAL	27	28 EDM	29 VAN	30		

DECEMBER

SUN	MON	TUE	WED	THU	FRI	SAT
					1	2 WIN
3	4	5	6 NYR	7 OTT	8	9
10 HAR	11	12	13 DET	14	15 MON	16
17 WIN	18	19	20 TOR	21 TOR	22	23 DAL
24	25	26 DAL	27	28 WIN	29 BUF	30
31 NJ						

JANUARY

SUN	MON	TUE	WED	THU	FRI	SAT
	1	2 BOS	3	4 STL	5	6 DET
7 DAL	8	9 NYI	10	11	12 ANA	13
14 LA	15	16	17 WAS	18	19	20 *
21	22 OTT	23	24 TOR	25 SJ	26	27 D DET
28	29	30	31 EDM			

FEBRUARY

SUN	MON	TUE	WED	THU	FRI	SAT
				1	2	3 D SJ
4 ANA	5	6 LA	7	8 STL	9	10 D PIT
11	12	13	14	15 BOS	16	17
18 D EDM	19	20	21	22 STL	23 WIN	24
25 PHI	26	27	28	29 COL		

MARCH

SUN	MON	TUE	WED	THU	FRI	SAT
					1 COL	2
3 DET	4	5 TB	6	7	8 LA	9
10	11 FLA	12	13	14 VAN	15	16
17 D NYI	18	19	20 CAL	21	22 NJ	23
24 D ANA	25	26	27 CAL	28	29 VAN	30
31 D DAL						

APRIL

SUN	MON	TUE	WED	THU	FRI	SAT
	1	2	3 TOR	4	5 DAL	6
7 D DET	8	9	10	11 TOR	12 DET	13
14 D STL	15	16	17	18	19	20

1995-96 SEASON

CLUB DIRECTORY

President
William W. Wirtz
Vice president
Arthur M. Wirtz Jr.
Vice president and asst. to the president
Thomas N. Ivan
Senior vice president/general manager
Bob Pulford
Assistant general manager
Bob Murray
Head coach
Craig Hartsburg
Assistant coaches
To be announced

Scouts
Jimmy Walker
Dave Lucas
Kerry Davison
Bruce Franklin
Michel Dumas
Jim Pappin
Steve Lyons
Public relations
Jim DeMaria
Trainers
Mike Gapski
Lou Varga
Troy Parchman

DRAFT CHOICES

Rd.—Player	H/W	Overall	Pos.	Last team
1—Dimitri Nabokov	6-2/209	19	C	Krylja Sovetov, CIS
2—Christian Laflamme	6-1/195	45	D	Beauport (QMJHL)
3—Kevin McKay	6-2/198	71	D	Moose Jaw (WHL)
4—Chris Van Dyk	6-2/185	82	D	Windsor (OHL)
4—Pavel Kriz	6-1/205	97	D	Tri-City (WHL)
6—Marc Magliarditi	5-11/170	146	G	Des Moines (Jr. A)
6—Marty Wilford	6-0/207	149	D	Oshawa (OHL)
7—Steve Tardif	5-11/178	175	C	Drummondville (QMJHL)
8—Casey Hankinson	6-1/187	201	LW	University of Minnesota
9—Mike Pittman	5-11/180	227	C	Guelph (OHL)

MISCELLANEOUS DATA

Home ice (capacity)
United Center (17,742)
Address
1901 W. Madison Street
Chicago, IL 60612
Business phone
312-455-7000
Rink dimensions
200 feet by 85 feet

Club colors
Red, black and white
Radio affiliation
WMVP (1000 AM)
TV affiliation
SportsChannel (road games)

FORWARDS

No.	FORWARDS	Ht./Wt.	Place	Date	NHL exp.	1994-95 clubs
33	Tony Amonte (RW)	6-0/186	Weymouth, Mass.	8-2-70	5	Fassa (Italy), Chicago
32	Murray Craven (C/LW)	6-2/185	Medicine Hat, Alta.	7-20-64	13	Chicago
12	Jim Cummins (LW)	6-2/205	Dearborn, Mich.	5-17-70	4	Tampa Bay, Chicago
	Eric Daze (LW)	6-4/202	Montreal	7-2-75	1	Beauport (QMJHL), Chicago
32	Steve Dubinsky (C)	6-0/190	Montreal	7-9-70	2	Indianapolis (IHL), Chicago
	Brent Grieve (LW)	6-1/205	Oshawa, Ont.	5-9-69	2	Chicago
29	Darin Kimble (RW)	6-2/205	Lucky Lake, Sask.	11-22-68	7	Chicago
	Sergei Klimovich (C)	6-2/189	Novosibirsk, U.S.S.R.	5-8-74	0	Dynamo Moscow (CIS), Indianapolis (IHL)
59	Sergei Krivokrasov (RW)	5-11/175	Angarsk, U.S.S.R.	4-15-74	3	Indianapolis (IHL), Chicago
	Eric Lecompte (LW)	6-4/190	Montreal	4-4-75	0	Hull (QMJHL), St. Jean (QMJHL), Sherbrooke (QMJHL), Indianapolis (IHL)
	Jean-Yves Leroux (LW)	6-2/193	Montreal	6-24-76	0	Beauport (QMJHL)
	Ethan Moreau (LW)	6-2/205	Orillia, Ont.	9-22-75	0	Niagara Falls (OHL), Sudbury (OHL)
17	Joe Murphy (RW)	6-1/190	London, Ont.	10-16-67	9	Chicago
	Dimitri Nabokov (C/LW)	6-2/209	Novosibirsk, U.S.S.R.	1-4-77	0	Soviet Wings (CIS)
19	Bernie Nicholls (C)	6-0/185	Haliburton, Ont.	6-24-61	14	Chicago
	Mike Pomichter (C)	6-1/200	New Haven, Conn.	9-10-73	0	Indianapolis (IHL)
24	Patrick Poulin (LW)	6-1/208	Vanier, Que.	4-23-73	4	Chicago
24	Bob Probert (LW)	6-3/215	Windsor, Ont.	6-5-65	9	Did not play
	Mike Prokopec (RW)	6-2/190	Toronto	5-17-74	0	Indianapolis (IHL)
27	Jeremy Roenick (C)	6-0/170	Boston	1-17-70	7	Koln (Germany), Chicago
9	Denis Savard (C)	5-10/175	Pointe Gatineau, Que.	2-4-61	15	Tampa Bay, Chicago
	Jeff Shantz (C)	6-0/185	Edmonton	10-10-73	2	Indianapolis (IHL), Chicago
12	Brent Sutter (C)	5-11/180	Viking, Alta.	6-10-62	15	Chicago

DEFENSEMEN

No.	DEFENSEMEN	Ht./Wt.	Place	Date	NHL exp.	1994-95 clubs
6	Keith Carney	6-2/205	Pawtucket, R.I.	2-3-70	4	Chicago
7	Chris Chelios	6-1/186	Chicago	1-25-62	12	Biel-Bienne (Switzerland), Chicago
	Ivan Droppa	6-2/209	Liptovsky Mikulas, Czech.	2-1-72	1	Indianapolis (IHL)
34	Roger Johansson	6-3/190	Ljungby, Sweden	4-17-67	4	Leksand (Sweden), Chicago
8	Cam Russell	6-4/206	Halifax, N.S.	1-12-69	6	Chicago
5	Steve Smith	6-4/215	Glasgow, Scotland	4-30-63	11	Chicago
6	Greg Smyth	6-3/212	Oakville, Ont.	4-23-66	9	Chicago, Indianapolis (IHL)
20	Gary Suter	6-0/190	Madison, Wis.	6-24-64	10	Chicago
	Tom Tilley	6-0/190	Trenton, Ont.	3-28-65	4	Atlanta (IHL), Indianapolis (IHL)
5	Eric Weinrich	6-0/210	Roanoke, Va.	12-19-66	7	Chicago

GOALTENDERS

No.	GOALTENDERS	Ht./Wt.	Place	Date	NHL exp.	1994-95 clubs
30	Ed Belfour	5-11/182	Carman, Man.	4-21-65	7	Chicago
30	Jeff Hackett	6-1/185	London, Ont.	6-1-68	6	Chicago
29	Jimmy Waite	6-1/180	Sherbrooke, Que.	4-15-69	7	Chicago, Indianapolis (IHL)

1994-95 REVIEW

| INDIVIDUAL STATISTICS |

SCORING

	Games	G	A	Pts.	PIM	+/-	PPG	SHG	Shots	Shooting Pct.
Bernie Nicholls	48	22	29	51	32	4	11	2	114	19.3
Joe Murphy	40	23	18	41	89	7	7	0	120	19.2
Chris Chelios	48	5	33	38	72	17	3	1	166	3.0
Gary Suter	48	10	27	37	42	14	5	0	144	6.9
Tony Amonte	48	15	20	35	41	7	6	1	105	14.3
Jeremy Roenick	33	10	24	34	14	5	5	0	93	10.8
Patrick Poulin	45	15	15	30	53	13	4	0	77	19.5
Sergei Krivokrasov	41	12	7	19	33	9	6	0	72	16.7
Jeff Shantz	45	6	12	18	33	11	0	2	58	10.3
Brent Sutter	47	7	8	15	51	6	1	0	65	10.8
Dirk Graham	40	4	9	13	42	2	1	1	68	5.9
Eric Weinrich	48	3	10	13	33	1	1	0	50	6.0
Steve Smith	48	1	12	13	128	6	0	0	43	2.3
Paul Ysebaert*	15	4	5	9	6	4	0	0	23	17.4
Denis Savard*	12	4	4	8	8	3	1	0	26	15.4
Murray Craven	16	4	3	7	2	2	1	0	29	13.8
Christian Ruuttu*	20	2	5	7	6	3	0	0	25	8.0
Brent Grieve	24	1	5	6	23	2	0	0	30	3.3
Jim Cummins*	27	3	1	4	117	-3	0	0	20	15.0
Cam Russell	33	1	3	4	88	4	0	0	18	5.6
Greg Smyth	22	0	3	3	33	2	0	0	10	0.0

	Games	G	A	Pts.	PIM	+/-	PPG	SHG	Shots	Shooting Pct.
Ed Belfour (goalie)	42	0	3	3	11	0	0	0	0	0.0
Eric Daze	4	1	1	2	2	2	0	0	1	100.0
Roger Johansson	11	1	0	1	6	1	0	0	10	10.0
Gerald Diduck*	13	1	0	1	48	3	0	0	17	5.9
Keith Carney	18	1	0	1	11	-1	0	0	14	7.1
Tony Horacek	19	0	1	1	25	-4	0	0	6	0.0
Jim Waite (goalie)	2	0	0	0	0	0	0	0	0	0.0
Daniel Gauthier	5	0	0	0	0	0	0	0	4	0.0
Jeff Hackett (goalie)	7	0	0	0	0	0	0	0	0	0.0
Darin Kimble	14	0	0	0	30	-5	0	0	2	0.0
Rich Sutter*	15	0	0	0	28	1	0	0	17	0.0
Steve Dubinsky	16	0	0	0	8	-5	0	0	16	0.0

GOALTENDING

	Games	Min.	Goals	SO	Avg.	W	L	T	Shots	Sv. Pct.
Ed Belfour	42	2450	93	‡5	2.28	22	15	3	990	.906
Jeff Hackett	7	328	13	0	2.38	1	3	2	150	.913
Jim Waite	2	119	5	0	2.52	1	1	0	51	.902

Empty-net goals (do not count against a goaltender's average): Belfour 4.
*Played with two or more NHL teams.
‡Tied for league lead.

RESULTS

JANUARY
20—At Detroit	L	1-4
23—At Winnipeg	L	3-5
25—Edmonton	W	5-1
27—Toronto	W	4-1
29—At Los Angeles	W	6-3
30—At San Jose	L	1-2

FEBRUARY
1—At Edmonton	W	7-0
3—At Calgary	W	*4-3
5—At Vancouver	W	9-4
7—At Anaheim	W	3-0
9—At St. Louis	W	5-0
13—At Toronto	L	2-4
16—Calgary	T	*2-2
19—Edmonton	W	4-1
20—San Jose	W	3-2
23—Detroit	L	2-4
26—At Dallas	W	2-1
28—At Los Angeles	W	8-4

MARCH
1—At Anaheim	L	1-3
3—At Edmonton	W	5-2
5—Anaheim	W	3-0
7—Calgary	L	3-6
9—Los Angeles	L	3-4
11—At Toronto	T	*2-2
13—At Dallas	L	2-4
16—Vancouver	W	9-2
19—At Winnipeg	W	3-2
21—At San Jose	W	7-3
23—At Vancouver	W	3-1
26—Anaheim	W	5-2
29—St. Louis	L	1-3
31—Toronto	T	*3-3

APRIL
2—Dallas	L	1-2
4—At Calgary	L	2-3
5—At Winnipeg	L	1-4
9—Detroit	L	1-4
12—San Jose	L	2-3
14—Detroit	L	1-3
16—At Dallas	L	0-2
17—Toronto	L	1-3
19—St. Louis	T	*2-2
21—Winnipeg	L	1-2
23—At St. Louis	T	*2-2
25—Vancouver	W	*4-3
27—Dallas	W	5-1
30—At Detroit	W	4-0

MAY
1—Winnipeg	W	3-2
3—Los Angeles	W	5-1

*Denotes overtime game.

DALLAS STARS
WESTERN CONFERENCE/CENTRAL DIVISION

Home games shaded.
* — All-Star Game at FleetCenter, Boston.
D — Day game.

OCTOBER

SUN	MON	TUE	WED	THU	FRI	SAT
1	2	3	4	5	6	7 WIN
8	9	10 CAL	11	12 STL	13	14 BOS
15	16	17 WAS	18	19 STL	20	21 TB
22	23	24 BUF	25	26 ANA	27	28 D SJ
29	30 COL	31				

NOVEMBER

SUN	MON	TUE	WED	THU	FRI	SAT
			1 CHI	2	3	4 D DET
5	6	7	8 LA	9 COL	10	11
12	13	14 PIT	15 BUF	16	17 SJ	18
19	20	21	22 VAN	23	24	25 NJ
26	27	28	29	30		

DECEMBER

SUN	MON	TUE	WED	THU	FRI	SAT
					1	2 LA
3 COL	4	5 BOS	6	7 DET	8	9 TOR
10	11 NYR	12	13 CAL	14	15 PIT	16
17 SJ	18	19	20	21 NYI	22	23 CHI
24	25	26 CHI	27	28 STL	29 DET	30
31						

JANUARY

SUN	MON	TUE	WED	THU	FRI	SAT
	1 D	2	3 DET	4	5 WIN	6
7 CHI	8	9	10 DET	11	12 FLA	13
14 NJ	15 PHI	16	17 EDM	18	19	20 *
21	22 VAN	23	24 EDM	25	26 CAL	27
28	29 WIN	30	31 NYR			

FEBRUARY

SUN	MON	TUE	WED	THU	FRI	SAT
				1	2 VAN	3
4 NYI	5	6 STL	7 MON	8	9	10 D STL
11 D HAR	12	13	14	15	16 EDM	17
18 FLA	19 TB	20	21	22 OTT	23	24 TOR
25 HAR	26	27	28 PHI	29		

MARCH

SUN	MON	TUE	WED	THU	FRI	SAT
					1	2 TOR
3	4	5 ANA	6 SJ	7	8	9
10	11 MON	12	13 OTT	14	15 TOR	16
17 D WAS	18	19	20 STL	21	22 VAN	23 LA
24	25	26 WIN	27	28 ANA	29	30
31 D CHI						

APRIL

SUN	MON	TUE	WED	THU	FRI	SAT
	1	2	3 WIN	4	5 CHI	6
7 D COL	8	9 CAL	10 EDM	11	12 ANA	13
14 D DET	15	16	17	18	19	20

CLUB DIRECTORY

Owner and governor
Norman N. Green
President and alternate governor
Jim Lites
Vice president/g.m. and head coach
Bob Gainey
V.P of marketing and promotion
Jeff Cogen
Vice president of finance
Rick McLaughlin
Vice president of marketing
Bill Strong
Assistant coaches
Doug Jarvis
Rick Wilson
Director of player personnel
Les Jackson
Director of amateur scouting
Craig Button

Assistant to the general manager
Doug Armstrong
Director of team services
Dan Stuchal
Director of public relations
Larry Kelly
Director of merchandising
Steve Schilts
Director of ticket sales
Brian Byrnes
Head trainer
Dave Surprenant
Assistant trainer
Dave Smith
Equipment manager
Lance Vogt

DRAFT CHOICES

Rd.—Player	H/W	Overall	Pos.	Last team
1—Jarome Iginla	6-1/193	11	C	Kamloops (WHL)
2—Patrick Cote	6-2/199	37	LW	Beauport (QMJHL)
3—Petr Buzek	6-0/183	63	D	Dukla Jihlava, Czech Rep.
3—Sergei Gusev	5-11/176	69	D	Mayak Samara, CIS
5—Wade Strand	6-3/185	115	D	Regina (WHL)
6—Dominic Marleau	6-1/194	141	D	Victoriaville (QMJHL)
7—Jeff Dewar	6-2/200	173	RW	Moose Jaw (WHL)
8—Anatoli Kovesnikov ..	5-11/187	193	LW	Kiev, Ukraine
8—Sergei Luchinkin.......	5-11/172	202	LW	Dimitrov, CIS
9—Stephen Lowe	5-11/164	219	C	Sault Ste. Marie (OHL)

MISCELLANEOUS DATA

Home ice (capacity)
Reunion Arena (16,924)
Address
211 Cowboys Parkway
Irving, TX 75063
Business phone
214-868-2890
Rink dimensions
200 feet by 85 feet

Club colors
Black, gold, green and white
Radio affiliation
WBAP (820 AM)
TV affiliation
Prime Sports (Cable), KDFW
(Channel 4), KDFI (Channel 27)

TRAINING CAMP ROSTER

No.	FORWARDS	Ht./Wt.	BORN Place	Date	NHL exp.	1994-95 clubs
8	Greg Adams (LW)	6-3/198	Nelson, B.C.	8-1-63	11	Vancouver, Dallas
28	Bob Bassen (C)	5-10/180	Calgary	5-6-65	10	Quebec
	Jason Botterill (LW)	6-3/205	Edmonton	5-19-76	0	Univ. of Michigan (CCHA)
	Zac Boyer (RW)	6-1/199	Inuvik, N.W.T.	10-25-71	1	Kalamazoo (IHL), Dallas
37	Paul Broten (RW)	5-11/190	Roseau, Minn.	10-27-65	6	Dallas
27	Shane Churla (RW)	6-1/200	Fernie, B.C.	6-24-65	9	Dallas
	Patrick Cote (LW)	6-2/199	Lasalle, Que.	1-24-75	0	Beauport (QMJHL)
11	Mike Donnelly (LW)	5-11/185	Livonia, Mich.	10-10-63	9	Los Angeles, Dallas
16	Dean Evason (C)	5-10/180	Flin Flon, Man.	8-22-64	12	Dallas
	Marty Flichel (RW)	5-11/175	Hodgeville, Sask.	3-6-76	0	Tacoma (WHL)
15	Dave Gagner (LW/C)	5-10/180	Chatham, Ont.	12-11-64	11	Courmaosta (Italy), Dallas
41	Brent Gilchrist (LW)	5-11/185	Moose Jaw, Sask.	4-3-67	7	Dallas
	Todd Harvey (RW/C)	6-0/195	Hamilton, Ont.	2-17-75	1	Detroit (OHL), Dallas
	Lee Jinman (C)	5-10/160	Scarborough, Ont.	1-10-76	0	North Bay (OHL)
	Mike Kennedy (LW)	6-1/170	Vancouver	4-3-72	1	Kalamazoo (IHL), Dallas
25	Dan Kesa (RW)	6-0/198	Vancouver	11-23-71	1	Syracuse (AHL)
29	Trent Klatt (RW)	6-1/205	Robbinsdale, Minn.	1-30-71	4	Dallas
	Jamie Langenbrunner (C)	5-11/185	Edmonton	4-21-75	1	Peterborough (OHL), Dallas, Kalamazoo (IHL)
	Mark Lawrence (RW)	6-4/215	Burlington, Ont.	1-27-72	1	Kalamazoo (IHL), Dallas
	Jere Lehtinen (RW)	6-0/185	Espoo, Finland	6-24-73	0	TPS Turku (Finland)
	Juha Lind (C)	5-11/160	Helsinki, Finland	1-2-74	0	Jokerit Helsinki (Finland)
	Grant Marshall (RW)	6-1/185	Toronto	6-9-73	1	Kalamazoo (IHL), Dallas
23	Corey Millen (C)	5-7/170	Cloquet, Minn.	4-29-64	6	New Jersey, Dallas
9	Mike Modano (RW/C)	6-3/190	Livonia, Mich.	6-7-70	7	Dallas
	Kyle Peterson (C)	6-3/195	Calgary	4-17-74	0	Michigan Tech (WCHA)
	Per Svartvadet (LW/C)	6-1/180	Ornskoldsvik, Sweden	5-17-75	0	MoDo Hockey Ornskoldvik (Sweden)
	Jarkko Varvio (LW)	5-9/172	Tampere, Finland	4-28-72	2	HPK Hameenlinna (Finland), Dallas, Kalamazoo (IHL)
	Jamie Wright (LW)	6-0/172	Kitchener, Ont.	5-13-76	0	Guelph (OHL)
25	Peter Zezel (C)	5-11/209	Toronto	4-22-65	11	Dallas, Kalamazoo (IHL)

No.	DEFENSEMEN	Ht./Wt.	Place	Date	NHL exp.	1994-95 clubs
	Craig Bonner	6-4/205	Edmonton	7-25-72	0	Kalamazoo (IHL)
14	Paul Cavallini	6-1/202	Toronto	10-13-65	9	Dallas
34	Gord Donnelly	6-1/202	Montreal	4-5-62	12	Dallas, Kalamazoo (IHL)
2	Derian Hatcher	6-5/225	Sterling Heights, Mich.	6-4-72	4	Dallas
4	Kevin Hatcher	6-4/225	Detroit	9-9-66	11	Dallas
	Jason Herter	6-1/190	Hafford, Sask.	10-2-70	0	Kalamazoo (IHL)
22	Mike Lalor	6-0/200	Fort Erie, Ont.	3-8-63	10	Dallas, Kalamazoo (IHL)
12	Grant Ledyard	6-2/195	Winnipeg	11-19-61	11	Dallas
3	Craig Ludwig	6-3/217	Rhinelander, Wis.	3-15-61	13	Dallas
4	Richard Matvichuk	6-2/190	Edmonton	2-5-73	3	Dallas, Kalamazoo (IHL)
	Yevgeny Petrochinin	5-9/165	Murmansk, U.S.S.R.	2-7-76	0	Spartak Moscow (CIS)
	Travis Richards	6-1/185	Crystal, Minn.	3-22-70	1	Kalamazoo (IHL), Dallas
5	Doug Zmolek	6-2/220	Rochester, Minn.	11-3-70	3	Dallas

No.	GOALTENDERS	Ht./Wt.	Place	Date	NHL exp.	1994-95 clubs
30	Manny Fernandez	6-0/185	Etobicoke, Ont.	8-27-74	1	Kalamazoo (IHL), Dallas
35	Andy Moog	5-8/170	Penticton, B.C.	2-18-60	15	Dallas
	Marty Turco	5-11/175	Sault Ste. Marie, Ont.	8-13-75	0	Univ. of Michigan (CCHA)
34	Darcy Wakaluk	5-11/180	Pincher Creek, Alta.	3-14-66	6	Dallas

1994-95 REVIEW

INDIVIDUAL STATISTICS

SCORING

	Games	G	A	Pts.	PIM	+/-	PPG	SHG	Shots	Shooting Pct.
Dave Gagner	48	14	28	42	42	2	7	0	138	10.1
Mike Modano	30	12	17	29	8	7	4	1	100	12.0
Kevin Hatcher	47	10	19	29	66	-4	3	0	138	7.2
Mike Donnelly*	35	11	14	25	29	3	3	0	94	11.7
Trent Klatt	47	12	10	22	26	-2	5	0	91	13.2
Todd Harvey	40	11	9	20	67	-3	2	0	64	17.2
Mike Kennedy	44	6	12	18	33	4	2	0	76	7.9
Grant Ledyard	38	5	13	18	20	6	4	0	79	6.3
Corey Millen*	28	3	15	18	28	4	1	0	44	6.8
Russ Courtnall*	32	7	10	17	13	-8	2	0	90	7.8
Paul Broten	47	7	9	16	36	-7	0	0	67	10.4
Derian Hatcher	43	5	11	16	105	3	2	0	74	6.8

	Games	G	A	Pts.	PIM	+/-	PPG	SHG	Shots	Shooting Pct.
Dean Evason	47	8	7	15	48	3	1	0	53	15.1
Brent Gilchrist	32	9	4	13	16	-3	1	3	70	12.9
Paul Cavallini	44	1	11	12	28	8	0	0	69	1.4
Peter Zezel	30	6	5	11	19	-6	0	0	47	12.8
Craig Ludwig	47	2	7	9	61	-6	0	0	55	3.6
Greg Adams*	12	3	3	6	4	-4	1	0	16	18.8
Doug Zmolek	42	0	5	5	67	-6	0	0	28	0.0
Shane Churla	27	1	3	4	186	0	0	0	22	4.5
Neal Broten*	17	0	4	4	4	-8	0	0	29	0.0
Jarkko Varvio	5	1	1	2	0	1	1	0	9	11.1
Alan May*	27	1	1	2	106	1	0	0	23	4.3
Richard Matvichuk	14	0	2	2	14	-7	0	0	21	0.0
Gord Donnelly	16	1	0	1	52	1	0	0	9	11.1
Grant Marshall	2	0	1	1	0	1	0	0	0	0.0
Andy Moog (goalie)	31	0	1	1	14	0	0	0	0	0.0
Zac Boyer	1	0	0	0	0	0	0	0	1	0.0
Manny Fernandez (goalie)	1	0	0	0	0	0	0	0	0	0.0
Jamie Langenbrunner	2	0	0	0	2	0	0	0	1	0.0
Mark Lawrence	2	0	0	0	0	0	0	0	3	0.0
Travis Richards	2	0	0	0	0	0	0	0	1	0.0
Iain Fraser*	4	0	0	0	0	-3	0	0	2	0.0
Mike Torchia (goalie)	6	0	0	0	0	0	0	0	0	0.0
Mike Lalor	12	0	0	0	9	0	0	0	6	0.0
Darcy Wakaluk (goalie)	15	0	0	0	4	0	0	0	0	0.0

GOALTENDING

	Games	Min.	Goals	SO	Avg.	W	L	T	Shots	Sv. Pct.
Andy Moog	31	1770	72	2	2.44	10	12	7	846	.915
Manny Fernandez	1	59	3	0	3.05	0	1	0	27	.889
Darcy Wakaluk	15	754	40	2	3.18	4	8	0	341	.883
Mike Torchia	6	327	18	0	3.30	3	2	1	172	.895

Empty-net goals (do not count against a goaltender's average): Moog 1, Wakaluk 1.
*Played with two or more NHL teams.

RESULTS

JANUARY

20—At Vancouver	T	*1-1
24—At Los Angeles	W	4-2
25—At Anaheim	W	4-1
28—At San Jose	L	2-3
30—Toronto	L	1-2

FEBRUARY

1—Anaheim	W	9-2
2—San Jose	L	1-2
4—At St. Louis	L	4-7
8—At Toronto	T	*3-3
11—Calgary	L	0-6
13—Winnipeg	L	4-7
15—Los Angeles	L	1-3
18—At Calgary	L	*2-3
20—At Calgary	W	2-1
22—At Edmonton	L	1-2
24—Vancouver	T	*3-3
26—Chicago	L	1-2
28—At Winnipeg	W	4-0

MARCH

1—At Edmonton	W	5-3
3—Anaheim	W	4-0
5—St. Louis	W	2-1
6—Los Angeles	W	8-2
8—At Toronto	L	2-3
10—At Winnipeg	L	3-4
12—Calgary	T	*4-4
13—Chicago	W	4-2
16—At Detroit	L	4-5
22—Edmonton	T	*4-4
23—Edmonton	W	2-1
27—St. Louis	L	2-3
30—At Detroit	L	2-3

APRIL

1—Detroit	L	2-3
2—At Chicago	W	2-1
4—At Vancouver	T	*2-2
6—At Los Angeles	L	2-3
7—At Anaheim	W	2-0
9—At St. Louis	W	3-2
11—Detroit	L	1-4
14—At Toronto	L	1-2
16—Chicago	W	2-0
17—Vancouver	T	*2-2
19—San Jose	T	*5-5
22—Toronto	W	6-4
23—Winnipeg	W	5-2
25—St. Louis	L	4-8
27—At Chicago	L	1-5
29—At Detroit	L	2-4

MAY

1—At San Jose	L	1-3

*Denotes overtime game.

DENVER
WESTERN CONFERENCE/PACIFIC DIVISION

1995-96 SCHEDULE

1995-96 SEASON

CLUB DIRECTORY

President and governor
To be announced
General manager
Pierre Lacroix
Assistant to the g.m./hockey operations
Sherry Bassin
Admin. asst. to the general manager
Francois Giguere
Head coach
Marc Crawford
Assistant coaches
Jacques Martin
Joel Quenneville
Director of public relations
To be announced
Director of team services
Jean Martineau

Psylotherapist
Pat Karns
Assistant physiotherapist
Matthew Sokolowski
Trainer
Rob McLean
Chief scout
Dave Draper
Scouts
Yvon Gendron
Jan Janda
Bengt Lundholm
Brian MacDonald
Don McKenney
Don Paarup
Orval Tessier

DRAFT CHOICES

Rd.—Player	H/W	Overall	Pos.	Last team
1—Marc Denis	6-0/188	25	G	Chicoutimi (QMJHL)
2—Nic Beaudoin	6-3/192	51	LW	Detroit (OHL)
3—John Tripp	6-2/209	77	RW	Oshawa (OHL)
4—Tomi Kallio	6-1/176	81	LW	Kiekko-67, Finland
5—Brent Johnson	6-1/175	129	G	Owen Sound (OHL)
6—John Cirjak	6-1/185	155	RW	Spokane (WHL)
7—Dan Smith	6-2/185	181	D	U. of British Columbia
8—Tomi Hirvonen	5-11/180	207	C	Ilves Jrs., Finland
9—Chris George	6-3/190	228	RW	Sarnia (OHL)

MISCELLANEOUS DATA

Home ice (capacity)
McNichols Arena (17,000)
Address
1635 Clay St.
Denver, CO 80204
Business phone
303-893-6700
Rink dimensions
200 feet by 85 feet

Club colors
To be announced
Radio affiliation
To be announced
TV affiliation
To be announced

TRAINING CAMP ROSTER

No.	FORWARDS	Ht./Wt.	Place	BORN Date	NHL exp.	1994-95 clubs
	Nic Beaudoin (LW)	6-3/192	Ottawa	12-25-76	0	Detroit (OHL)
	Paul Brousseau (RW)	6-1/203	Montreal	9-18-73	0	Cornwall (AHL)
17	Wendel Clark (LW)	5-10/194	Kelvington, Sask.	10-25-66	10	Quebec
	Rene Corbet (LW)	6-0/187	Victoriaville, Que.	6-25-73	2	Cornwall (AHL), Quebec
	Adam Deadmarsh (RW)	6-0/195	Trail, B.C.	5-10-75	1	Portland (WHL), Quebec
	Peter Forsberg (C)	5-11/190	Ornskoldsvik, Sweden	7-20-73	1	MoDo Hockey Ornskoldvik (Sweden), Quebec
61	Bill Huard (LW)	6-1/215	Alland, Ont.	6-24-67	3	Ottawa, Quebec
31	Valeri Kamensky (LW)	6-2/198	Voskresensk, U.S.S.R.	4-18-66	4	Ambri Piotta (Switzerland), Quebec
51	Andrei Kovalenko (RW)	5-10/200	Gorky, U.S.S.R.	7-7-70	3	Lada Togliatti (CIS), Quebec
47	Claude Lapointe (C)	5-9/181	Ville Emard, Que.	10-11-68	5	Quebec
	Josef Marha (C)	6-0/176	Havl. Brod, Czech.	6-2-76	0	Dukla Jihlava (Czech Rep.)
	Christian Matte (RW)	5-11/166	Hull, Que.	1-20-75	0	Granby (QMJHL), Cornwall (AHL)
11	Owen Nolan (RW)	6-1/201	Belfast, Northern Ireland	2-12-72	5	Quebec
9	Mike Ricci (C)	6-0/190	Scarborough, Ont.	10-27-71	5	Quebec
25	Martin Rucinsky (LW)	6-0/190	Most, Czechoslovakia	3-11-71	4	Chemopetrol Litvinov (Czech.), Quebec
19	Joe Sakic (C)	5-11/185	Burnaby, B.C.	7-7-69	7	Quebec
12	Chris Simon (LW)	6-3/219	Wawa, Ont.	1-30-72	3	Quebec
48	Scott Young (RW)	6-0/190	Clinton, Mass.	10-1-67	7	Frankfurt (Germany), Landshut (Germany), Quebec
	DEFENSEMEN					
	Wade Belak	6-4/213	North Battleford, Sask.	7-3-76	0	Saskatoon (WHL), Cornwall (AHL)
29	Steven Finn	6-0/191	Laval, Que.	8-20-66	10	Quebec
52	Adam Foote	6-1/202	Toronto	7-10-71	4	Quebec
5	Alexei Gusarov	6-3/185	Leningrad, U.S.S.R.	7-8-64	5	Quebec
	Jon Klemm	6-3/200	Cranbrook, B.C.	1-6-70	3	Cornwall (AHL), Quebec
4	Uwe Krupp	6-6/235	Cologne, West Germany	6-24-65	9	Landshut (Germany), Quebec
	Janne Laukkanen	6-0/180	Lahti, Finland	3-19-70	1	Cornwall (AHL), Quebec
2	Sylvain Lefebvre	6-2/205	Richmond, Que.	10-14-67	6	Quebec
7	Curtis Leschyshyn	6-1/205	Thompson, Man.	9-21-69	7	Quebec
	Aaron Miller	6-3/197	Buffalo, N.Y.	8-11-71	2	Cornwall (AHL), Quebec
	Anders Myrvold	6-1/178	Lorenskog, Norway	8-12-75	0	Laval (QMJHL), Cornwall (AHL)
28	John Slaney	6-0/195	St. John's, Nfld.	2-7-72	2	Washington, Portland (AHL)
6	Craig Wolanin	6-3/205	Grosse Point, Mich.	7-27-67	10	Quebec
	GOALTENDERS					
	Marc Denis	6-0/188	Montreal	8-1-77	0	Chicoutimi (QMJHL)
35	Stephane Fiset	6-1/195	Montreal	6-17-70	6	Quebec
	Jocelyn Thibault	5-11/170	Montreal	1-12-75	2	Sherbrooke (QMJHL), Quebec
	Tim Thomas	5-11/180	Flint, Mich.	4-15-74	0	Univ. of Vermont (ECAC)

1994-95 REVIEW

INDIVIDUAL STATISTICS

SCORING

	Games	G	A	Pts.	PIM	+/-	PPG	SHG	Shots	Shooting Pct.
Joe Sakic	47	19	43	62	30	7	3	2	157	12.1
Peter Forsberg	47	15	35	50	16	17	3	0	86	17.4
Owen Nolan	46	30	19	49	46	21	13	2	137	21.9
Scott Young	48	18	21	39	14	9	3	3	167	10.8
Mike Ricci	48	15	21	36	40	5	9	0	73	20.5
Wendel Clark	37	12	18	30	45	-1	5	0	95	12.6
Valeri Kamensky	40	10	20	30	22	3	5	1	70	14.3
Bob Bassen	47	12	15	27	33	14	0	1	66	18.2
Andrei Kovalenko	45	14	10	24	31	-4	1	0	63	22.2
Uwe Krupp	44	6	17	23	20	14	3	0	102	5.9
Adam Deadmarsh	48	9	8	17	56	16	0	0	48	18.8
Curtis Leschyshyn	44	2	13	15	20	29	0	0	43	4.7
Sylvain Lefebvre	48	2	11	13	17	13	0	0	81	2.5
Claude Lapointe	29	4	8	12	41	5	0	0	40	10.0
Chris Simon	29	3	9	12	106	14	0	0	33	9.1
Martin Rucinsky	20	3	6	9	14	5	0	0	32	9.4
Craig Wolanin	40	3	6	9	40	12	0	0	36	8.3
Adam Foote	35	0	7	7	52	17	0	0	24	0.0
Paul MacDermid	14	3	1	4	22	3	0	0	13	23.1
Bill Huard*	7	2	2	4	13	2	0	0	6	33.3
Dwayne Norris	13	1	2	3	2	1	0	0	7	14.3
Alexei Gusarov	14	1	2	3	6	-1	0	0	7	14.3

	Games	G	A	Pts.	PIM	+/-	PPG	SHG	Shots	Shooting Pct.
Rene Corbet	8	0	3	3	2	3	0	0	4	0.0
Aaron Miller	9	0	3	3	6	2	0	0	12	0.0
Janne Laukkanen	11	0	3	3	4	3	0	0	12	0.0
Stephane Fiset (goalie)	32	0	3	3	2	0	0	0	0	0.0
Steven Finn	40	0	3	3	64	1	0	0	28	0.0
Jon Klemm	4	1	0	1	2	3	0	0	5	20.0
Dave Karpa*	2	0	0	0	0	-1	0	0	1	0.0
Garth Snow (goalie)	2	0	0	0	0	0	0	0	0	0.0
Jocelyn Thibault (goalie)	18	0	0	0	0	0	0	0	0	0.0

GOALTENDING

	Games	Min.	Goals	SO	Avg.	W	L	T	Shots	Sv. Pct.
Jocelyn Thibault	18	898	35	1	2.34	12	2	2	423	.917
Stephane Fiset	32	1879	87	2	2.78	17	10	3	968	.910
Garth Snow	2	119	11	0	5.55	1	1	0	63	.825

Empty-net goals (do not count against a goaltender's average): Fiset 1.
*Played with two or more NHL teams.

RESULTS

JANUARY
21—At Philadelphia	W	3-1	
24—Washington	W	5-1	
27—At Buffalo	W	7-3	
28—N.Y. Rangers	W	2-0	
31—Philadelphia	W	5-2	

FEBRUARY
2—At New Jersey	L	4-5	
4—New Jersey	W	2-0	
5—Hartford	W	3-1	
8—At Hartford	W	3-2	
9—At Boston	W	4-3	
11—Ottawa	W	5-2	
14—At N.Y. Islanders	W	3-2	
16—At Philadelphia	W	4-2	
18—At Washington	L	2-4	
19—At Florida	W	4-1	
21—At Pittsburgh	L	4-5	
23—Philadelphia	T	*6-6	

25—Boston	T	*1-1	
27—Pittsburgh	L	5-7	

MARCH
1—Tampa Bay	W	8-2	
4—Buffalo	T	*1-1	
6—New Jersey	W	6-3	
7—At Pittsburgh	W	5-4	
9—At Hartford	L	1-2	
11—N.Y. Islanders	W	2-1	
16—Pittsburgh	W	3-2	
18—At Montreal	L	4-5	
20—Florida	W	*5-4	
22—Boston	W	6-2	
25—N.Y. Rangers	W	2-1	
26—At Ottawa	W	11-4	
28—At Buffalo	L	3-5	
30—At N.Y. Rangers	W	5-4	
31—At Washington	L	4-6	

APRIL
2—Ottawa	W	7-5	
5—At Montreal	L	5-6	
6—Montreal	W	3-2	
8—At Ottawa	T	*2-2	
12—At Boston	W	4-0	
14—Buffalo	W	5-2	
16—Washington	W	4-2	
18—At N.Y. Islanders	L	2-5	
20—At Tampa Bay	L	2-5	
22—At Florida	L	2-4	
26—Montreal	T	*1-1	
29—Tampa Bay	W	4-1	
30—At New Jersey	L	2-4	

MAY
3—Hartford	W	4-1	

*Denotes overtime game.

DETROIT RED WINGS
WESTERN CONFERENCE/CENTRAL DIVISION

1995-96 SCHEDULE

Home games shaded.
* — All-Star Game at FleetCenter, Boston.
D — Day game.

OCTOBER

SUN	MON	TUE	WED	THU	FRI	SAT
1	2	3	4	5	6 COL	7
8 EDM	9 VAN	10	11	12	13 EDM	14
15 WIN	16	17 CAL	18	19 NJ	20	21 D BOS
22	23	24 OTT	25	26	27 CAL	28
29	30 WIN	31				

NOVEMBER

SUN	MON	TUE	WED	THU	FRI	SAT
			1 BUF	2 BOS	3	4 D DAL
5	6	7 EDM	8	9	10	11 SJ
12	13	14 LA	15	16	17 EDM	18
19	20	21	22 SJ	23	24 D PHI	25 NYR
26	27	28 MON	29	30		

DECEMBER

SUN	MON	TUE	WED	THU	FRI	SAT
					1 ANA	2 MON
3	4	5 PHI	6	7 DAL	8 NYR	9
10	11	12 STL	13 CHI	14	15 NJ	16
17	18	19	20 ANA	21	22 CAL	23 VAN
24	25	26 STL	27	28	29 DAL	30
31 HAR						

JANUARY

SUN	MON	TUE	WED	THU	FRI	SAT
1	2	3 DAL	4	5 PIT	6
7	8 WIN	9	10 DAL	11	12 LA	13 WAS
14	15	16	17 COL	18	19	20 *
21	22	23	24 SJ	25 OTT	26	27 D CHI
28	29	30 TOR	31			

FEBRUARY

SUN	MON	TUE	WED	THU	FRI	SAT
				1	2	3 D PIT
4	5	6 FLA	7	8 FLA	9	10 D TB
11	12	13 LA	14	15 WAS	16 STL	17
18 D TOR	19 VAN	20	21	22 TOR	23	24 TB
25	26	27 NYI	28	29 NYI		

MARCH

SUN	MON	TUE	WED	THU	FRI	SAT
					1	2 D VAN
3 CHI	4	5	6 HAR	7	8 COL	9
10 WIN	11	12 WIN	13	14	15	16
17 D CAL	18	19 TOR	20 TOR	21	22 COL	23
24 STL	25 ANA	26	27 BUF	28	29	30
31 D STL						

APRIL

SUN	MON	TUE	WED	THU	FRI	SAT
	1	2 SJ	3 LA	4	5 ANA	6
7 D CHI	8	9	10 WIN	11	12 CHI	13
14 D DAL	15	16	17	18	19	20

1995-96 SEASON

CLUB DIRECTORY

Owner and president
Michael Ilitch
Owner and secretary/treasurer
Marian Ilitch
Senior vice president
Jim Devellano
Dir. of player personnel/head coach
Scott Bowman
Assistant general manager
Ken Holland
Assistant coaches
Dave Lewis
Barry Smith
Pro scouting director
Dan Belisle
Scouts
Billy Dea
Wayne Meier

Chris Coury
Ken Hoodikoff
Paul Crowley
Mark Leach
Hakan Andersson
Vladimir Havluj
Director of public relations
Bill Jamieson
Director of advertising sales
Jack Johnson
Director of marketing
Ted Speers
Athletic trainer
John Wharton
Equipment manager
Paul Boyer
Assistant equipment manager
Tim Abbott

DRAFT CHOICES

Rd.—Player	H/W	Overall	Pos.	Last team
1—Maxim Kuznetsov	6-5/198	26	D	Moscow Dynamo, CIS
2—Philippe Audet..........	6-1/175	52	LW	Granby (QMJHL)
3—Darryl Laplante	6-0/185	58	C	Moose Jaw (WHL)
4—Anatoly Ustyugov..	5-10/165	104	LW	Yaroslavl, CIS
5—Chad Wilchynski	6-3/179	125	D	Regina (WHL)
5—David Arsenault........	6-1/165	126	G	Drummondville (QMJHL)
6—Tyler Perry	6-0/175	156	C	Seattle (WHL)
7—Per Eklund................	5-11/196	182	LW	Djurgarden-Stockholm, Swe.
8—Andrei Samokvalov.	5-11/169	208	RW	UST-Kamenogorsk, CIS
9—David Engblom	6-1/183	234	C	Vallentuna, Sweden

MISCELLANEOUS DATA

Home ice (capacity)
Joe Louis Arena (19,275)
Address
600 Civic Center Drive
Detroit, MI 48226
Business phone
313-396-7544
Rink dimensions
200 feet by 85 feet

Club colors
Red and white
Radio affiliation
WJR (760 AM)
TV affiliation
WKBD, Pro-Am Sports

TRAINING CAMP ROSTER

No.	FORWARDS	Ht./Wt.	Place	BORN Date	NHL exp.	1994-1995 clubs
17	Doug Brown (RW)	5-10/185	Southborough, Mass.	6-12-64	9	Detroit
11	Shawn Burr (LW)	6-1/195	Sarnia, Ont.	7-1-66	11	Detroit
22	Dino Ciccarelli (RW)	5-10/175	Sarnia, Ont.	2-8-60	15	Detroit
	Sylvain Cloutier (C)	6-0/195	Mont-Laurier, Que.	2-13-74	0	Adirondack (AHL)
	Mathieu Dandenault (RW)	6-0/174	Magog, Que.	2-3-76	0	Sherbrooke (QMJHL)
33	Kris Draper (C)	5-11/185	Toronto	5-24-71	5	Detroit
12	Bob Errey (LW)	5-10/185	Montreal	9-21-64	12	San Jose, Detroit
91	Sergei Fedorov (C)	6-1/200	Minsk, U.S.S.R.	12-13-69	5	Detroit
	Joe Frederick (RW)	6-1/190	St. Hubert, Que.	8-6-69	0	Adirondack (AHL)
32	Stu Grimson (LW)	6-5/227	Kamloops, B.C.	5-20-65	7	Anaheim, Detroit
	Greg Johnson (C/RW)	5-10/174	Thunder Bay, Ont.	3-16-71	2	Detroit
	Michael Knuble (RW)	6-3/200	Toronto	7-4-72	0	University of Michigan (CCHA)
13	Slava Kozlov (LW)	5-10/180	Voskresensk, U.S.S.R.	5-3-72	4	CSKA Moscow (CIS), Detroit
18	Mike Krushelnyski (C)	6-2/200	Montreal	4-27-60	14	Detroit
20	Martin Lapointe (RW)	5-11/200	Lachine, Que.	9-12-73	4	Adirondack (AHL), Detroit
25	Darren McCarty (RW)	6-1/210	Burnaby, B.C.	4-1-72	2	Detroit
55	Keith Primeau (C)	6-4/220	Toronto	11-24-71	5	Detroit
26	Ray Sheppard (RW)	6-1/195	Pembroke, Ont.	5-27-66	8	Detroit
37	Tim Taylor (LW)	6-1/185	Stratford, Ont.	2-6-69	2	Detroit
19	Steve Yzerman (C)	5-11/185	Cranbrook, B.C.	5-9-65	12	Detroit
	DEFENSEMEN					
2	Terry Carkner	6-3/210	Smith Falls, Ont.	3-7-66	9	Detroit
77	Paul Coffey	6-1/190	Weston, Ont.	6-1-61	15	Detroit
	Anders Eriksson	6-3/218	Bollnas, Sweden	1-9-75	0	MoDo Hockey Ornskoldvik (Sweden)
	Mark Ferner	6-0/193	Regina, Sask.	9-5-65	6	San Diego (IHL), Anaheim, Adirondack (AHL), Detroit
44	Slava Fetisov	6-1/220	Moscow, U.S.S.R.	5-20-58	6	Spartak Moscow (CIS), New Jersey, Detroit
	Yan Golubovsky	6-3/185	Novosibirsk, U.S.S.R.	3-9-76	0	Adirondack (AHL)
4	Mark Howe	5-11/185	Detroit	5-28-55	16	Detroit
16	Vladimir Konstantinov	6-0/190	Murmansk, U.S.S.R.	3-19-67	4	Wedemark (Germany Div. II), Detroit
5	Nicklas Lidstrom	6-2/185	Vasteras, Sweden	4-28-70	4	Vasteras (Sweden), Detroit
15	Mike Ramsey	6-3/195	Minneapolis	12-3-60	16	Detroit
3	Bob Rouse	6-2/210	Surrey, B.C.	6-18-64	12	Detroit
	Aaron Ward	6-2/200	Windsor, Ont.	1-17-73	2	Adirondack (AHL), Detroit
	GOALTENDERS					
	Kevin Hodson	6-0/182	Winnipeg.	3-27-72	0	Adirondack (AHL)
	Norm Maracle	5-9/175	Belleville, Ont.	10-2-74	0	Adirondack (AHL)
30	Chris Osgood	5-10/160	Peace River, Alta.	11-26-72	2	Adirondack (AHL), Detroit
29	Mike Vernon	5-9/165	Calgary	2-24-63	12	Detroit

1994-95 REVIEW

INDIVIDUAL STATISTICS

SCORING

	Games	G	A	Pts.	PIM	+/-	PPG	SHG	Shots	Shooting Pct.
Paul Coffey	45	14	44	58	72	18	4	1	181	7.7
Sergei Fedorov	42	20	30	50	24	6	7	3	147	13.6
Dino Ciccarelli	42	16	27	43	39	12	6	0	106	15.1
Keith Primeau	45	15	27	42	99	17	1	0	96	15.6
Ray Sheppard	43	30	10	40	17	11	11	0	125	24.0
Steve Yzerman	47	12	26	38	40	6	4	0	134	9.0
Vyacheslav Kozlov	46	13	20	33	45	12	5	0	97	13.4
Nicklas Lidstrom	43	10	16	26	6	15	7	0	90	11.1
Doug Brown	45	9	12	21	16	14	1	1	69	13.0
Bob Errey*	30	6	11	17	31	9	0	0	53	11.3
Shawn Burr	42	6	8	14	60	13	0	0	65	9.2
Viacheslav Fetisov*	14	3	11	14	2	3	3	0	36	8.3
Vladimir Konstantinov	47	3	11	14	101	10	0	0	57	5.3
Darren McCarty	31	5	8	13	88	5	1	0	27	18.5
Martin Lapointe	39	4	6	10	73	1	0	0	46	8.7
Greg Johnson	22	3	5	8	14	1	2	0	32	9.4
Mike Sillinger*	13	2	6	8	2	3	0	0	11	18.2
Kris Draper	36	2	6	8	22	1	0	0	44	4.5
Bob Rouse	48	1	7	8	36	14	0	0	51	2.0
Mark Howe	18	1	5	6	10	-3	0	0	14	7.1
Mike Krushelnyski	20	2	3	5	6	3	0	0	20	10.0
Tim Taylor	22	0	4	4	16	3	0	0	21	0.0
Jason York*	10	1	2	3	2	0	0	0	6	16.7

	Games	G	A	Pts.	PIM	+/-	PPG	SHG	Shots	Shooting Pct.
Terry Carkner	20	1	2	3	21	7	0	0	9	11.1
Mike Ramsey	33	1	2	3	23	11	0	0	29	3.4
Aaron Ward	1	0	1	1	2	1	0	0	0	0.0
Bob Halkidis*	4	0	1	1	6	2	0	0	0	0.0
Andrew McKim	2	0	0	0	2	0	0	0	0	0.0
Mark Ferner*	3	0	0	0	0	0	0	0	1	0.0
Stu Grimson*	11	0	0	0	37	-4	0	0	4	0.0
Chris Osgood (goalie)	19	0	0	0	2	0	0	0	0	0.0
Mike Vernon (goalie)	30	0	0	0	8	0	0	0	0	0.0

GOALTENDING

	Games	Min.	Goals	SO	Avg.	W	L	T	Shots	Sv. Pct.
Chris Osgood	19	1087	41	1	2.26	14	5	0	496	.917
Mike Vernon	30	1807	76	1	2.52	19	6	4	710	.893

Empty-net goals (do not count against a goaltender's average): None.
*Played with two or more NHL teams.

RESULTS

JANUARY

20—Chicago	W	4-1
22—Calgary	L	1-4
24—Vancouver	W	6-3
26—Calgary	W	5-1
28—Edmonton	W	5-2
30—At Edmonton	W	4-2

FEBRUARY

1—At Calgary	L	1-2
3—At Anaheim	W	5-2
4—At Los Angeles	L	3-4
7—San Jose	W	6-0
10—Toronto	L	1-2
12—Los Angeles	T	*4-4
15—At Winnipeg	W	5-1
17—Edmonton	W	4-2
20—At Toronto	W	4-2
22—Toronto	W	4-1
23—At Chicago	W	4-2
25—St. Louis	L	2-3

MARCH

2—Winnipeg	W	6-1
5—At Edmonton	L	2-4
6—At Vancouver	W	5-2
9—At Anaheim	T	*4-4
12—At St. Louis	W	2-1
14—Los Angeles	W	5-2
16—Dallas	W	5-4
17—Vancouver	W	3-1
22—Winnipeg	W	6-3
24—At Calgary	L	2-3
25—At Vancouver	W	2-1
28—Anaheim	W	6-4
30—Dallas	W	3-2

APRIL

1—At Dallas	W	3-2
2—St. Louis	T	*3-3
5—At San Jose	W	5-3
7—At Toronto	W	4-2
9—At Chicago	W	4-1
11—At Dallas	W	4-1
13—San Jose	W	3-0
14—At Chicago	W	3-1
16—At St. Louis	L	5-6
19—Winnipeg	T	*5-5
21—Anaheim	W	6-5
23—At San Jose	W	5-1
25—At Los Angeles	L	1-5
27—At Winnipeg	L	3-4
29—Dallas	W	4-2
30—Chicago	L	0-4

MAY

3—At St. Louis	W	3-2

*Denotes overtime game.

EDMONTON OILERS
WESTERN CONFERENCE/PACIFIC DIVISION

Home games shaded.
* — All-Star Game at FleetCenter, Boston.
D — Day game.

OCTOBER

SUN	MON	TUE	WED	THU	FRI	SAT
1	2	3	4	5	6	7
8 DET	9	10 STL	11	12	13 DET	14
15 PHI	16	17 NJ	18 BUF	19	20	21 VAN
22 SJ	23	24	25	26	27 WIN	28
29	30	31 NJ				

NOVEMBER

SUN	MON	TUE	WED	THU	FRI	SAT
			1 VAN	2	3	4 TOR
5	6	7 DET	8	9 FLA	10 TB	11
12 CHI	13	14 CAL	15 MON	16	17 DET	18
19	20 COL	21	22 ANA	23	24 CAL	25
26 WIN	27	28 CHI	29	30		

DECEMBER

SUN	MON	TUE	WED	THU	FRI	SAT
					1 CAL	2 STL
3	4	5 VAN	6	7 COL	8	9 SJ
10 ANA	11	12	13 VAN	14	15 WIN	16
17	18 OTT	19	20 COL	21	22 WAS	23 TOR
24	25	26	27 PHI	28	29 LA	30 NYR
31						

JANUARY

SUN	MON	TUE	WED	THU	FRI	SAT
	1	2	3 TB	4	5 FLA	6
7 ANA	8	9 HAR	10	11	12	13 BUF
14	15	16 STL	17 DAL	18	19	20 *
21	22	23 DAL	24 NYI	25	26 NYI	27
28	29	30 CAL	31 CHI			

FEBRUARY

SUN	MON	TUE	WED	THU	FRI	SAT
				1	2	3
4	5	6	7 WAS	8	9 VAN	10
11 CAL	12	13	14 ANA	15	16 DAL	17
18 CHI	D 19 COL	20	21 LA	22	23 BOS	24
25 NYI	D 26	27 BOS	28 HAR	29		

MARCH

SUN	MON	TUE	WED	THU	FRI	SAT
					1 PIT	2
3 STL	D 4	5	6 LA	7	8 SJ	9
10	11	12	13 SJ	14	15	16 LA
17 COL	18	19 NYR	20	21 PIT	22	23 MON
24 OTT	25	26	27 LA	28	29 WIN	30 TOR
31						

APRIL

SUN	MON	TUE	WED	THU	FRI	SAT
	1 VAN	2	3 ANA	4 SJ	5	6
7	8 CAL	9	10 DAL	11	12	13 TOR
14	15	16	17	18	19	20

CLUB DIRECTORY

Owner/governor
Peter Pocklington

Alternate governor
Glen Sather

General counsels
Lorne Ruzicka

President/general manager
Glen Sather

Coach
Ron Low

Assistant coach
Kevin Primeau

Exec. V.P./assistant general manager
Bruce MacGregor

Vice president, finance
Werner Baum

Executive secretary
Betsy Freedman

Director of public relations
Bill Tuele

Coord. of publications & statistics
Steve Knowles

Director of player personnel
Kevin Prendergast

Scouting staff
Ed Chadwick
Lorne Davis
Barry Fraser
Harry Howell
Brad MacGregor
Peter Mahovlich
Kent Nilsson
Curly Reeves
Brad Smith

Athletic trainer
Barrie Stafford

Assistant trainer
Lyle Kulchisky

Athletic trainer/therapist
Ken Lowe

Massage therapist
Roland Kelly

Team physicians
Dr. David C. Reid
Dr. Boris Boyko

DRAFT CHOICES

Rd.—Player	H/W	Overall	Pos.	Last team
1—Steve Kelly	6-1/188	6	C	Prince Albert (WHL)
2—Georges Laraque	6-3/225	31	RW	St. Jean (QMJHL)
3—Lukas Zib	6-1/198	57	D	C Ceske-Budejovice, Czech
4—Mike Minard	6-3/205	83	G	Chilliwack (BCJHL)
5—Jan Snopek	6-3/212	109	D	Oshawa (OHL)
7—Martin Cerven	6-4/200	161	C	Trencin Jrs., Slovakia
8—Stephen Douglas	6-5/195	187	D	Niagara Falls (OHL)
9—Jiri Antonin	6-4/207	213	D	Pardubice Jrs., Czech Rep.

MISCELLANEOUS DATA

Home ice (capacity)
Edmonton Coliseum (17,111)

Address
Edmonton, Alta. T5B 4M9

Business phone
403-474-8561

Rink dimensions
200 feet by 85 feet

Club colors
Blue, orange and white

Radio affiliation
CFCW (790 AM)

TV affiliation
CFRN (Channel 3, Cable 2)

FORWARDS

No.	FORWARDS	Ht./Wt.	Place	BORN Date	NHL exp.	1994-95 clubs
7	Jason Arnott (C)	6-3/195	Collingworth, Ont.	10-11-74	2	Edmonton
	Jason Bonsignore (C) ...	6-4/208	Rochester, N.Y.	4-15-76	1	Niagara Falls (OHL), Edmonton, Sudbury (OHL)
	Dennis Bonvie (RW/D) .	5-11/210	Antigonish, N.S.	7-23-73	1	Cape Breton (AHL), Edmonton
16	Kelly Buchberger (RW)....	6-2/210	Langenburg, Sask.	12-12-66	9	Edmonton
8	Zdeno Ciger (LW)	6-1/190	Martin, Czechoslovakia	10-19-69	5	Dukla Trencin (Slovakia), Edmonton
29	Louie DeBrusk (LW)	6-2/215	Cambridge, Ont.	3-19-71	4	Edmonton
	Steve Kelly (C)	6-1/188	Vancouver	10-26-76	0	Prince Albert (WHL)
	Georges Laraque (RW) .	6-3/225	Montreal	12-7-76	0	St. Jean (QMJHL)
	Mats Lindgren (C)	6-1/190	Skellestea, Sweden	10-1-74	0	Farjestad Karlstad (Sweden)
18	Kirk Maltby (RW)	6-0/180	Guelph, Ont.	12-22-72	2	Edmonton
36	Todd Marchant (C/LW)	6-0/190	Buffalo, N.Y.	8-12-73	2	Cape Breton (AHL), Edmonton
37	Dean McAmmond (C)....	5-11/185	Grand Cache, Alta.	6-15-73	3	Edmonton
	David Oliver (RW)	5-11/185	Sechelt, B.C.	4-17-71	1	Cape Breton (AHL), Edmonton
	Kevin Paden (C/LW)......	6-3/175	Woodhaven, Mich.	2-12-75	0	Windsor (OHL)
	Miroslav Satan (C).......	6-1/176	Topolcany, Czechoslovakia	10-22-74	0	Detroit (IHL), San Diego (IHL), Cape Breton (AHL)
	Colin Schmidt (C)	5-11/185	Regina, Sask.	2-3-74	0	Colorado College (WCHA)
17	Scott Thornton (C)	6-2/200	London, Ont.	1-9-71	5	Edmonton
	Marko Tuomainen (RW) ..	6-2/190	Kuopio, Finland	4-25-72	1	Clarkson (ECAC), Edmonton
39	Doug Weight (C)...........	5-11/191	Warren, Mich.	1-21-71	5	Rosenheim (Germany), Edmonton
	Peter White (C)...........	5-11/200	Montreal	3-15-69	2	Cape Breton (AHL), Edmonton
19	Tyler Wright (C)	5-11/185	Canora, Sask.	4-6-73	3	Cape Breton (AHL), Edmonton

DEFENSEMEN

No.	DEFENSEMEN	Ht./Wt.	Place	Date	NHL exp.	1994-95 clubs
26	Dean Kennedy	6-2/212	Redvers, Sask.	1-18-63	12	Edmonton
21	Igor Kravchuk..............	6-1/200	Ufa, U.S.S.R.	9-13-66	4	Edmonton
27	Bryan Marchment	6-1/198	Scarborough, Ont.	5-1-69	7	Edmonton
27	Ryan McGill	6-2/205	Prince Albert, Sask.	2-28-69	4	Philadelphia, Edmonton
20	Boris Mironov	6-3/220	Moscow, U.S.S.R.	3-21-72	2	Cape Breton (AHL), Edmonton
22	Luke Richardson	6-4/210	Ottawa	3-26-69	8	Edmonton
24	Jiri Slegr	6-1/205	Litvinov, Czechoslovakia	5-30-71	3	Chemopetrol Litvinov (Czech.), Vancouver, Edmonton
	Jan Snopek	6-3/212	Prague, Czechoslovakia	6-22-76	0	Oshawa (OHL)
	Nick Stajduhar	6-2/1195	Kitchener, Ont.	12-6-74	0	Cape Breton (AHL)
41	Ken Sutton	6-0/198	Edmonton	5-11-69	5	Buffalo, Edmonton

GOALTENDERS

No.	GOALTENDERS	Ht./Wt.	Place	Date	NHL exp.	1994-95 clubs
31	Fred Brathwaite	5-7/170	Ottawa	11-24-72	2	Edmonton
	Joaquin Gage...............	6-0/200	Vancouver	10-19-73	1	Cape Breton (AHL), Edmonton
	Curtis Joseph	5-10/182	Keswick, Ont.	4-29-67	6	St. Louis
	Steve Passmore	5-9/165	Thunder Bay, Ont.	1-29-73	0	Cape Breton (AHL)
30	Bill Ranford.................	5-11/185	Brandon, Man.	12-14-66	10	Edmonton

	Games	G	A	Pts.	PIM	+/-	PPG	SHG	Shots	Shooting Pct.
Doug Weight	48	7	33	40	69	-17	1	0	104	6.7
Jason Arnott................	42	15	22	37	128	-14	7	0	156	9.6
Shayne Corson	48	12	24	36	86	-17	2	0	131	9.2
David Oliver	44	16	14	30	20	-11	10	0	79	20.3
Todd Marchant	45	13	14	27	32	-3	3	2	95	13.7
Kelly Buchberger	48	7	17	24	82	0	2	1	73	9.6
Scott Thornton	47	10	12	22	89	-4	0	1	69	14.5
Igor Kravchuk	36	7	11	18	29	-15	3	1	93	7.5
Mike Stapleton	46	6	11	17	21	-12	3	0	59	10.2
Roman Oksiuta*	26	11	2	13	8	-14	5	0	52	21.2
Luke Richardson	46	3	10	13	40	-6	1	1	51	5.9
Kirk Maltby	47	8	3	11	49	-11	0	2	73	11.0
Dean Kennedy...............	40	2	8	10	25	2	0	0	45	4.4
Fredrik Olausson	33	0	10	10	20	-4	0	0	52	0.0
Boris Mironov	29	1	7	8	40	-9	0	0	48	2.1
Peter White	9	2	4	6	0	1	2	0	13	15.4
Jiri Slegr*	12	1	5	6	14	-5	1	0	27	3.7
Bryan Marchment	40	1	5	6	184	-11	0	0	57	1.8
Leonard Esau*	14	0	6	6	15	-8	0	0	17	0.0
Scott Pearson*	28	1	4	5	54	-11	0	0	21	4.8
Ken Sutton*	12	3	1	4	12	-1	0	0	28	10.7
Zdeno Ciger	5	2	2	4	0	-1	1	0	10	20.0

	Games	G	A	Pts.	PIM	+/-	PPG	SHG	Shots	Shooting Pct.
Iain Fraser*	9	3	0	3	0	3	0	0	5	60.0
Louie Debrusk	34	2	0	2	93	-4	0	0	14	14.3
Gordon Mark	18	0	2	2	35	-9	0	0	21	0.0
Bill Ranford (goalie)	40	0	2	2	2	0	0	0	0	0.0
Jason Bonsignore	1	1	0	1	0	-1	0	0	3	33.3
Kent Nilsson	6	1	0	1	0	-5	1	0	2	50.0
Tyler Wright	6	1	0	1	14	1	0	0	6	16.7
Ralph Intranuovo	1	0	1	1	0	1	0	0	1	0.0
Joaquin Gage (goalie)	2	0	1	1	0	0	0	0	0	0.0
Micah Aivazoff	21	0	1	1	2	-2	0	0	6	0.0
Dennis Bonvie	2	0	0	0	0	0	0	0	0	0.0
Ryan Smyth	3	0	0	0	0	-1	0	0	2	0.0
Marko Tuomainen	4	0	0	0	0	0	0	0	5	0.0
Dean McAmmond	6	0	0	0	0	-1	0	0	3	0.0
Ryan McGill*	8	0	0	0	8	-4	0	0	6	0.0
Fred Brathwaite (goalie)	14	0	0	0	0	0	0	0	0	0.0

GOALTENDING

	Games	Min.	Goals	SO	Avg.	W	L	T	Shots	Sv. Pct.
Bill Ranford	40	2203	†133	2	3.62	15	20	3	1134	.883
Fred Brathwaite	14	601	40	0	3.99	2	5	1	292	.863
Joaquin Gage	2	99	7	0	4.24	0	2	0	40	.825

Empty-net goals (do not count against a goaltender's average): Ranford 2, Brathwaite 1.
*Played with two or more NHL teams.
†Led league.

RESULTS

JANUARY

20—Anaheim	W	2-1
22—At Los Angeles	W	4-3
23—At Anaheim	L	*4-5
25—At Chicago	L	1-5
28—At Detroit	L	2-5
30—Detroit	L	2-4

FEBRUARY

1—Chicago	L	0-7
3—Toronto	W	5-3
7—At Vancouver	T	*4-4
8—Winnipeg	T	*3-3
10—San Jose	W	5-1
12—Anaheim	W	2-0
15—At Toronto	W	4-1
17—At Detroit	L	2-4
19—At Chicago	L	1-4
20—At St. Louis	L	0-4
22—Dallas	W	2-1
25—Los Angeles	L	3-4
28—At Calgary	L	2-5

MARCH

1—Dallas	L	3-5
3—Chicago	L	2-5
5—Detroit	W	4-2
8—At San Jose	W	5-2
12—Vancouver	L	2-5
14—St. Louis	W	6-5
17—San Jose	W	5-3
20—Calgary	W	5-2
22—At Dallas	T	*4-4
23—At Dallas	L	1-2
26—At St. Louis	L	1-5
27—At Toronto	L	3-4
31—Calgary	L	2-6

APRIL

1—Vancouver	L	1-5
3—At Los Angeles	L	2-7
5—At Anaheim	L	*3-4
7—At San Jose	L	0-5
9—San Jose	L	2-5
13—At Vancouver	W	6-4

15—Calgary	L	2-4
17—At Winnipeg	W	6-5
19—Los Angeles	W	2-0
21—At Los Angeles	T	*3-3
22—At Vancouver	L	1-6
25—At Winnipeg	W	5-3
27—St. Louis	W	3-2
29—Winnipeg	L	1-5

MAY

1—Toronto	L	5-6
3—At Calgary	L	3-5

*Denotes overtime game.

FLORIDA PANTHERS

EASTERN CONFERENCE/ATLANTIC DIVISION

1995-96 SCHEDULE

Home games shaded.
* — All-Star Game at FleetCenter, Boston.
D — Day game.

OCTOBER

SUN	MON	TUE	WED	THU	FRI	SAT
1	2	3	4	5	6	7 D NJ
8 CAL	9	10	11 MON	12	13 OTT	14
15 NYI	16	17 CHI	18	19	20	21 HAR
22	23	24 TOR	25 MON	26	27	28 D OTT
29	30	31 NYI				

NOVEMBER

SUN	MON	TUE	WED	THU	FRI	SAT
			1	2 PHI	3 WAS	4
5 TB	6	7 PHI	8	9 EDM	10	11 BUF
12	13	14 TOR	15	16 VAN	17	18 LA
19 ANA	20	21 NJ	22	23	24	25
26 LA	27	28	29 PHI	30		

DECEMBER

SUN	MON	TUE	WED	THU	FRI	SAT
					1 PIT	2 HAR
3	4	5 WAS	6	7 ANA	8	9 BOS
10	11 NJ	12 NYI	13	14 BOS	15	16 TB
17	18	19	20	21 WIN	22	23 NJ
24	25	26	27	28 WAS	29	30 PIT
31						

JANUARY

SUN	MON	TUE	WED	THU	FRI	SAT
	1 NYI	2	3 VAN	4	5 EDM	6 CAL
7	8 SJ	9	10 COL	11	12 DAL	13
14	15	16 SJ	17	18	19	20 *
21	22 PHI	23 WAS	24	25 MON	26	27 BUF
28	29 PIT	30	31 BUF			

FEBRUARY

SUN	MON	TUE	WED	THU	FRI	SAT
				1 BOS	2	3 D TB
4	5	6 DET	7	8 DET	9	10
11 STL	12	13	14 PHI	15	16 COL	17
18 DAL	19	20	21 NJ	22	23	24 NYR
25 BUF	26	27	28	29 WAS		

MARCH

SUN	MON	TUE	WED	THU	FRI	SAT
					1	2 HAR
3	4	5 STL	6	7 WIN	8	9
10 BOS	11 CHI	12	13 NYR	14	15	16
17 NJ	18	19 OTT	20	21	22	23 TB
24	25	26	27 NYR	28 PIT	29	30 TB
31						

APRIL

SUN	MON	TUE	WED	THU	FRI	SAT
	1 HAR	2	3 OTT	4	5	6 MON
7	8 NYR	9	10 TB	11	12 NYI	13
14 D NYR	15	16	17	18	19	20

1995-96 SEASON

CLUB DIRECTORY

Owner
H. Wayne Huizenga
President
William A. Torrey
General manager
Bryan Murray
Vice president, business and marketing
Dean Jordan
Chief financial officer
Steve Dauria
Consultant
Gary Green
Director of player personnel
John Chapman
Assistant general manager
Chuck Fletcher
Head coach
Doug MacLean
Assistant coach
Lindy Ruff
Goaltending coach
Bill Smith

Dir. of player development & pro scout
Doug MacLean
Eastern scout
Ron Harris
European scout
Matti Vausanen
Director, public/media relations
Greg Bouris
Public/media relations associates
Kevin Dessart
Ron Colangelo
Director, promotions and special projects
Declan J. Bolger
Director, ticket and game day operations
Steve Dangerfield
Director, corporate sales and sponsorship
Kimberly Terranova
Director, merchandise
Ron Dennis
Athletic trainer
David Smith

DRAFT CHOICES

Rd.—Player	H/W	Overall	Pos.	Last team
1—Radek Dvorak	6-2/185	10	RW	Budejovice, Czech Rep.
2—Aaron MacDonald.....	6-1/186	36	G	Swift Current (WHL)
3—Mike O'Grady	6-3/200	62	D	Lethbridge (WHL)
4—Dave Duerden	6-2/182	80	LW	Peterborough (OHL)
4—Daniel Tjarnqvist	6-2/178	88	D	Rogle Angelholm, Sweden
5—Francois Cloutier	6-2/202	114	LW	Hull (QMJHL)
7—Peter Worrell............	6-6/225	166	LW	Hull (QMJHL)
8—Filip Kuba	6-4/202	192	D	Czech Republic
9—David Lemanowicz ...	6-2/190	218	G	Spokane (WHL)

MISCELLANEOUS DATA

Home ice (capacity)
Miami Arena (14,703)
Address
100 North East Third Avenue
10th Floor
Fort Lauderdale, FL 33301
Business phone
305-768-1900
Rink dimensions
200 feet by 85 feet

Club colors
Red, navy blue and yellow-gold
Radio affiliation
WQAM (560 AM),
WCMQ (1210 AM, Spanish)
TV affiliation
Sunshine Network,
WBFS-TV (Channel 33)

No.	FORWARDS	Ht./Wt.	Place BORN	Date	NHL exp.	1994-95 clubs
14	Stu Barnes (C)	5-11/174	Edmonton	12-25-70	4	Florida
26	Jesse Belanger (C)	6-0/186	St. Georges Beauce, Que.	6-15-69	4	Florida
	Chad Cabana (LW)	6-1/200	Bonnyville, Alta.	10-1-74	0	Tri-City (WHL)
	Radek Dvorak (LW)	6-2/187	Ceske Budejovice, Czech.	3-9-77	0	HC Ceske Budejovice (Czech Rep.)
21	Tom Fitzgerald (RW/C)	6-1/191	Melrose, Mass.	8-28-68	7	Florida
10	Johan Garpenlov (LW)	5-11/184	Stockholm, Sweden	3-21-68	5	San Jose, Florida
15	Todd Harkins (RW)	6-3/210	Cleveland	10-8-68	3	Chicago (IHL), Houston (IHL)
18	Mike Hough (LW)	6-1/197	Montreal	2-6-63	9	Florida
17	Jody Hull (RW)	6-2/195	Petrolia, Ont.	2-2-69	7	Florida
22	Bob Kudelski (RW)	6-1/206	Springfield, Mass.	3-3-64	8	Florida
	Jamie Linden (RW)	6-3/185	Medicine Hat, Alta.	7-19-72	1	Cincinnati (IHL), Florida
11	Bill Lindsay (LW)	5-11/190	Big Fork, Mont.	5-17-71	4	Florida
10	Dave Lowry (LW)	6-1/200	Sudbury, Ont.	1-14-65	10	Florida
27	Scott Mellanby (RW)	6-1/199	Montreal	6-11-66	10	Florida
44	Rob Niedermayer (C)	6-2/201	Cassiar, B.C.	12-28-74	2	Medicine Hat (WHL), Florida
	Jason Podollan (RW/C)	6-1/181	Vernon, B.C.	2-18-76	0	Spokane (WHL), Cincinnati (IHL)
20	Brian Skrudland (C)	6-0/196	Peace River, Alta.	7-31-63	10	Florida
37	Dave Tomlinson (C)	5-11/180	North Vancouver	5-8-68	4	Cincinnati (IHL), Florida
	Steve Washburn (C)	6-1/185	Ottawa	4-10-75	0	Ottawa (OHL), Cincinnati (IHL)
	DEFENSEMEN					
	Chris Armstrong	6-0/184	Regina, Sask.	6-26-75	0	Moose Jaw (WHL), Cincinnati (IHL)
4	Keith Brown	6-1/196	Corner Brook, Nfld.	5-6-60	16	Florida
52	Dallas Eakins	6-2/195	Dade City, Fla.	1-20-67	3	Cincinnati (IHL), Florida
	Ed Jovanovski	6-2/210	Windsor, Ont.	6-26-76	0	Windsor (OHL)
3	Paul Laus	6-1/216	Beamsville, Ont.	9-26-70	2	Florida
24	Randy Moller	6-2/210	Red Deer, Alta.	8-23-63	14	Florida
5	Gord Murphy	6-2/191	Willowdale, Ont.	2-23-67	7	Florida
	Alain Nasreddine	6-1/201	Montreal	7-10-75	0	Chicoutimi (QMJHL)
25	Geoff Smith	6-3/194	Edmonton	3-7-69	6	Florida
	Robert Svehla	6-1/190	Martin, Czechoslovakia	1-2-69	1	Malmo (Sweden), Florida
	Magnus Svensson	5-11/180	Tranas, Sweden	3-1-63	1	Davos HC (Switzerland), Florida
	Rhett Warrener	6-1/209	Shaunavon, Sask.	1-27-76	0	Saskatoon (WHL)
25	Jason Woolley	6-0/188	Toronto	7-27-69	4	Detroit (IHL), Florida
	GOALTENDERS					
30	Mark Fitzpatrick	6-2/198	Toronto	11-13-68	7	Florida
34	John Vanbiesbrouck	5-8/176	Detroit	9-4-63	13	Florida

1994-95 REVIEW

INDIVIDUAL STATISTICS

SCORING

	Games	G	A	Pts.	PIM	+/-	PPG	SHG	Shots	Shooting Pct.
Jesse Belanger	47	15	14	29	18	-5	6	0	89	16.9
Stu Barnes	41	10	19	29	8	7	1	0	93	10.8
Scott Mellanby	48	13	12	25	90	-16	4	0	130	10.0
Gord Murphy	46	6	16	22	24	-14	5	0	94	6.4
Dave Lowry	45	10	10	20	25	-3	2	0	70	14.3
Jody Hull	46	11	8	19	8	-1	0	0	63	17.5
Bill Lindsay	48	10	9	19	46	1	0	1	63	15.9
Tom Fitzgerald	48	3	13	16	31	-3	0	0	78	3.8
Brian Skrudland	47	5	9	14	88	0	1	0	44	11.4
Mike Hough	48	6	7	13	38	1	0	0	58	10.3
Jason Woolley	34	4	9	13	18	-1	1	0	76	5.3
Johan Garpenlov*	27	3	9	12	0	4	1	0	28	10.7
Rob Niedermayer	48	4	6	10	36	-13	1	0	58	6.9
Bob Kudelski	26	6	3	9	2	2	3	0	29	20.7
Brian Benning	24	1	7	8	18	-6	1	0	26	3.8
Magnus Svensson	19	2	5	7	10	5	1	0	41	4.9
Andrei Lomakin	31	1	6	7	6	-5	1	0	25	4.0
Paul Laus	37	0	7	7	138	12	0	0	18	0.0
Geoff Smith	47	2	4	6	22	-5	0	0	40	5.0
Gaetan Duchesne*	13	1	2	3	0	3	0	0	14	7.1
Randy Moller	17	0	3	3	16	-5	0	0	12	0.0
Robert Svehla	5	1	1	2	0	3	1	0	6	16.7
Brent Severyn*	9	1	1	2	37	-3	1	0	10	10.0
Dallas Eakins	17	0	1	1	35	2	0	0	3	0.0
Joe Cirella	20	0	1	1	21	-7	0	0	13	0.0
John Vanbiesbrouck (goalie)	37	0	1	1	6	0	0	0	0	0.0
Stephane Richer	1	0	0	0	2	0	0	0	0	0.0

	Games	G	A	Pts.	PIM	+/-	PPG	SHG	Shots	Shooting Pct.
Jeff Daniels	3	0	0	0	0	0	0	0	0	0.0
Jamie Linden	4	0	0	0	17	-1	0	0	0	0.0
Dave Tomlinson	5	0	0	0	0	-2	0	0	0	0.0
Keith Brown	13	0	0	0	2	1	0	0	10	0.0
Mark Fitzpatrick (goalie)	15	0	0	0	0	0	0	0	0	0.0

GOALTENDING

	Games	Min.	Goals	SO	Avg.	W	L	T	Shots	Sv. Pct.
John Vanbiesbrouck	37	2087	86	4	2.47	14	15	4	1000	.914
Mark Fitzpatrick	15	819	36	2	2.64	6	7	2	361	.900

Empty-net goals (do not count against a goaltender's average): Vanbiesbrouck 4, Fitzpatrick 1.
*Played with two or more NHL teams.

RESULTS

JANUARY

21—At N.Y. Islanders	L		1-2
23—Pittsburgh	L		5-6
25—At Tampa Bay	L		2-3
26—Tampa Bay	W		4-2
28—At Hartford	W		2-1
30—At Boston	W		2-1
31—N.Y. Islanders	L		1-5

FEBRUARY

2—Montreal	T	*	1-1
4—At Washington	L		2-3
7—At Pittsburgh	L		3-7
9—At Philadelphia	W		3-0
11—Hartford	W		4-3
12—New Jersey	L		2-4
15—Ottawa	W		2-0
17—Boston	L		4-5
19—Quebec	L		1-4
21—N.Y. Rangers	L		3-5
23—Montreal	L		2-5

25—At Ottawa	W		4-1
28—At N.Y. Rangers	T	*	0-0

MARCH

2—At Philadelphia	T	*	2-2
4—At New Jersey	L		1-6
8—Ottawa	W		3-2
11—At Boston	W		2-0
12—At Hartford	W		4-1
14—Buffalo	L	*	1-2
16—Washington	W		5-1
18—Philadelphia	L	*	3-4
20—At Quebec	L	*	4-5
22—At Montreal	W		3-2
24—At Buffalo	L		0-3
26—Pittsburgh	W		2-0
29—Hartford	T	*	4-4

APRIL

2—At Tampa Bay	W		4-1
5—N.Y. Rangers	L		0-5

8—At N.Y. Islanders	T	*	2-2
12—N.Y. Islanders	L		1-3
14—At Washington	L		0-3
16—Tampa Bay	W		4-1
18—Philadelphia	L		1-3
20—New Jersey	W		1-0
22—Quebec	W		4-2
24—At Ottawa	W		5-1
26—At Buffalo	L		0-5
28—At New Jersey	L		1-3
30—Washington	T	*	2-2

MAY

2—At N.Y. Rangers	W		4-3
3—At Pittsburgh	W		4-3

*Denotes overtime game.

HARTFORD WHALERS
EASTERN CONFERENCE/NORTHEAST DIVISION

1995-96 SCHEDULE

Home games shaded.
* — All-Star Game at FleetCenter, Boston.
D — Day game.

OCTOBER
SUN	MON	TUE	WED	THU	FRI	SAT
1	2	3	4	5	6	7 NYR
8	9	10	11 ANA	12	13	14 CHI
15	16 NYR	17	18	19	20 PIT	21 FLA
22	23	24	25 STL	26	27 MON	28 BOS
29	30	31				

NOVEMBER
SUN	MON	TUE	WED	THU	FRI	SAT
			1	2 OTT	3	4 OTT
5 PHI	6	7 SJ	8	9	10	11 NYR
12	13	14 NJ	15 OTT	16	17	18 D PHI
19	20 MON	21	22 MON	23	24 TOR	25 WAS
26	27	28	29 TB	30		

DECEMBER
SUN	MON	TUE	WED	THU	FRI	SAT
					1 BUF	2 FLA
3	4	5	6 NYI	7	8	9 PIT
10 CHI	11	12	13 TB	14	15 COL	16 NYI
17	18 MON	19	20 CAL	21	22 NYR	23 PHI
24	25	26	27	28 PIT	29	30 WAS
31 DET						

JANUARY
SUN	MON	TUE	WED	THU	FRI	SAT
	1	2	3 WAS	4	5 OTT	6 BOS
7	8	9 EDM	10 CAL	11	12 WIN	13
14	15	16 VAN	17 NYI	18	19	20 *
21	22	23	24 BUF	25 LA	26	27 NJ
28	29	30 SJ	31 LA			

FEBRUARY
SUN	MON	TUE	WED	THU	FRI	SAT
				1	2 ANA	3
4	5	6	7 VAN	8	9 COL	10
11 DAL	D 12	13	14 BOS	15	16	17 BUF
18	19	20	21 MON	22	23 PIT	24
25 DAL	26	27	28 EDM	29		

MARCH
SUN	MON	TUE	WED	THU	FRI	SAT
					1 WIN	2 FLA
3	4	5	6 DET	7	8 TOR	9 STL
10	11	12	13 PIT	14	15	16 BUF
17	18 TB	19	20 MON	21	22 OTT	23 WAS
24	25 PHI	26	27 BOS	28	29	30 D NYI
31						

APRIL
SUN	MON	TUE	WED	THU	FRI	SAT
	1 FLA	2	3 TB	4 NJ	5	6 D NJ
7	8 PIT	9	10	11 BOS	12	13 D BOS
14 BUF	15	16	17	18	19	20

1995-96 SEASON

CLUB DIRECTORY

Chief executive officer/governor
Peter Karmanos Jr.
General manager
Thomas Thewes
COO/president/general manager
Jim Rutherford
Vice president of hockey operations
Terry McDonnell
Head coach
Paul Holmgren
Assistant coaches
Paul Maurice
Ted Sator
Strength and conditioning coach
Jim M. McCrossin
Goaltending instructor
Steve Weeks
Sr. V.P. of marketing and communications
Russ Gregory
V.P. of finance and administration
Mike Amendola
V.P. of marketing and sales
Rick Francis
Director of communications/team services
John Forslund

Director of media relations
To be announced
Director of community relations director
Mary Lynn Gorman
Director of publications/statistics
Frank Polnaszek
Director of amateur hockey development
Mike Veisor
Director of player personnel
Sheldon Ferguson
Scouting staff
Tony MacDonald
Larry Johnston
Yves Sansfacon
Claude Larose
Kevin Maxwell
Willy Lindstrom
Willy Langer
Bruce Haralson
Ken Schinkel
Medical trainer
Bud Gouveia
Equipment manager
Skip Cunningham

DRAFT CHOICES

Rd.—Player	H/W	Overall	Pos.	Last team
1—J.-Sebastien Giguere ..	6-0/178	13	G	Halifax (QMJHL)
2—Sergei Fedotov.........	6-1/185	35	D	Dynamo, CIS
4—Ian MacNeil..............	6-2/177	85	C	Oshawa (OHL)
4—Sami Kapanen	5-10/169	87	LW	HIFK Helsinki, Finland
5—Hugh Hamilton	6-1/175	113	D	Spokane (WHL)
7—Byron Ritchie...........	5-10/180	165	C	Lethbridge (WHL)
8—Milan Kostolny	6-2/190	191	RW	Detroit (OHL)
9—Mike Rucinski	5-11/179	217	D	Detroit (OHL)

MISCELLANEOUS DATA

Home ice (capacity)
Hartford Civic Center (15,635)
Address
242 Trumbull Street
8th Floor
Hartford, CT 06103
Business phone
203-728-3366

Rink dimensions
200 feet by 85 feet
Club colors
Silver, blue, white and green
Radio affiliation
WTIC (1080 AM)
TV affiliation
SportsChannel New England

TRAINING CAMP ROSTER

No.	FORWARDS	Ht./Wt.	Place	Born Date	NHL exp.	1994-95 clubs
	Jeff Bes (C)	6-0/190	Tillsonburg, Ont.	7-31-73	0	Kalamazoo (IHL)
33	Jimmy Carson (C)	6-1/200	Southfield, Mich.	7-20-68	9	Hartford
21	Andrew Cassels (C)	6-0/192	Mississauga, Ont.	7-23-69	6	Hartford
27	Kelly Chase (RW)	5-11/195	Porcupine Plain, Sask.	10-25-67	6	Hartford
17	Scott Daniels (LW)	6-3/200	Prince Albert, Sask.	9-19-69	2	Springfield (AHL), Hartford
13	Ted Drury (C)	6-0/185	Boston	9-13-71	2	Hartford, Springfield (AHL)
	Mike Harding (RW)	6-4/221	Edsow, Alta.	2-24-71	0	Northern Michigan Univ. (WCHA)
22	Mark Janssens (C)	6-3/216	Surrey, B.C.	5-19-68	8	Hartford
	Dale Junkin (LW)	5-11/196	Oshawa, Ont.	5-23-73	0	
	Sami Kapanen (LW)	5-10/169	Vantaa, Finland	6-14-73	0	HIFK Helsinki (Finland)
18	Robert Kron (LW)	5-10/180	Brno, Czechoslovakia	2-27-67	5	Hartford
26	Jocelyn Lemieux (RW)	5-10/200	Mont-Laurier, Que.	11-18-67	9	Hartford
11	Andrei Nikolishin (C)	5-11/180	Vorkuta, U.S.S.R.	3-25-73	1	Dynamo Moscow (CIS), Hartford
	Jeff O'Neill (C)	6-0/176	Richmond Hill, Ont.	2-23-76	0	Guelph (OHL)
39	Robert Petrovicky (C)	5-11/172	Kosice, Czechoslovakia	10-26-73	3	Springfield (AHL), Hartford
28	Paul Ranheim (RW)	6-0/195	St. Louis	1-25-66	7	Hartford
8	Geoff Sanderson (LW)	6-0/185	Hay River, N.W.T.	2-1-72	5	HPK Hameenlinna (Finland), Hartford
	Brendan Shanahan	6-3/215	Mimico, Ont.	1-23-69	8	Dusseldorf (Germany), St. Louis
14	Kevin Smyth (LW)	6-2/217	Banff, Alta.	11-22-73	2	Springfield (AHL), Hartford
24	Jim Storm (LW)	6-2/200	Detroit	2-5-71	2	Springfield (AHL), Hartford
89	Darren Turcotte (C)	6-0/178	Boston	3-2-68	7	Hartford
	Bob Wren (LW)	5-10/175	Preston, Ont.	9-16-74	0	Springfield (AHL), Richmond (ECHL)
	DEFENSEMEN					
6	Adam Burt	6-0/190	Detroit	1-15-69	7	Hartford
	Gerald Diduck	6-2/207	Edmonton	4-6-65	11	Vancouver, Chicago
36	Glen Featherstone	6-4/215	Toronto	7-8-68	7	New York Rangers, Hartford
7	Brian Glynn	6-4/224	Iserlohn, West Germany	11-23-67	8	Hartford
5	Alexander Godynyuk	6-0/207	Kiev, U.S.S.R.	1-27-70	5	Hartford
4	Frantisek Kucera	6-2/205	Prague, Czechoslovakia	2-3-68	5	Sparta Prague (Czech.), Hartford
23	Marek Malik	6-5/190	Ostrava, Czechoslovakia	6-24-75	1	Springfield (AHL), Hartford
25	Jason McBain	6-2/178	Ilion, N.Y.	4-12-74	0	Springfield (AHL)
10	Brad McCrimmon	5-11/197	Dodsland, Sask.	3-29-59	16	Hartford
	Brian Mueller	5-11/225	Liverpool, N.Y.	6-2-72	0	Clarkson (ECAC)
45	John Stevens	6-1/195	Completon, N.B.	5-4-66	5	Springfield (AHL)
3	Michael Stewart	6-2/210	Calgary	3-30-72	0	Binghamton (AHL), Springfield (AHL)
20	Glen Wesley	6-1/195	Red Deer, Alta.	10-2-68	8	Hartford
	Steve Yule	6-0/210	Gleichen, Alta.	5-27-72	0	Springfield (AHL)
	GOALTENDERS					
1	Sean Burke	6-4/210	Windsor, Ont.	1-29-67	7	Hartford
	Jean Giguere	6-0/178	Montreal	5-16-77	0	Halifax (QMJHL)
30	Manny Legace	5-9/162	Toronto	2-4-73	0	Springfield (AHL)
35	Jeff Reese	5-9/175	Brantford, Ont.	3-24-66	8	Hartford

1994-95 REVIEW

INDIVIDUAL STATISTICS

SCORING

	Games	G	A	Pts.	PIM	+/-	PPG	SHG	Shots	Shooting Pct.
Andrew Cassels	46	7	30	37	18	-3	1	0	74	9.5
Darren Turcotte	47	17	18	35	22	1	3	1	121	14.0
Geoff Sanderson	46	18	14	32	24	-10	4	0	170	10.6
Steven Rice	40	11	10	21	61	2	4	0	57	19.3
Paul Ranheim	47	6	14	20	10	-3	0	0	73	8.2
Frantisek Kucera	48	3	17	20	30	3	0	0	73	4.1
Jimmy Carson	38	9	10	19	29	5	4	0	58	15.5
Robert Kron	37	10	8	18	10	-3	3	1	88	11.4
Andrei Nikolishin	39	8	10	18	10	7	1	1	57	14.0
Pat Verbeek*	29	7	11	18	53	0	3	0	75	9.3
Adam Burt	46	7	11	18	65	0	3	0	73	9.6
Glen Wesley	48	2	14	16	50	-6	1	0	125	1.6
Chris Pronger	43	5	9	14	54	-12	3	0	94	5.3
Jocelyn Lemieux	41	6	5	11	32	-7	0	0	78	7.7
Ted Drury	34	3	6	9	21	-3	0	0	31	9.7
Mark Janssens	46	2	5	7	93	-8	0	0	33	6.1
Brian Glynn	43	1	6	7	32	-2	0	0	35	2.9
Kevin Smyth	16	1	5	6	13	-3	0	0	20	5.0
Igor Chibirev	8	3	1	4	0	1	0	0	9	33.3
Kelly Chase	28	0	4	4	141	1	0	0	15	0.0
Jim Storm	6	0	3	3	0	2	0	0	3	0.0
Glen Featherstone*	13	1	1	2	32	-7	0	0	16	6.3
Scott Daniels	12	0	2	2	55	1	0	0	7	0.0

	Games	G	A	Pts.	PIM	+/-	PPG	SHG	Shots	Shooting Pct.
Marek Malik	1	0	1	1	0	1	0	0	0	0.0
Brad McCrimmon	33	0	1	1	42	7	0	0	13	0.0
Sean Burke (goalie)	42	0	1	1	8	0	0	0	0	0.0
Robert Petrovicky	2	0	0	0	0	0	0	0	1	0.0
Jeff Reese (goalie)	11	0	0	0	0	0	0	0	0	0.0
Jim Sandlak	13	0	0	0	0	-10	0	0	13	0.0
Alexander Godynyuk	14	0	0	0	8	1	0	0	16	0.0

GOALTENDING

	Games	Min.	Goals	SO	Avg.	W	L	T	Shots	Sv. Pct.
Sean Burke	42	2418	108	0	2.68	17	19	4	1233	.912
Jeff Reese	11	477	26	0	3.27	2	5	1	234	.889

Empty-net goals (do not count against a goaltender's average): Burke 6, Reese 1.
*Played with two or more NHL teams.

RESULTS

JANUARY

21—Washington	T	*1-1
22—New Jersey	T	*2-2
25—Ottawa	W	4-1
26—At Philadelphia	L	2-3
28—Florida	L	1-2

FEBRUARY

1—At Ottawa	W	2-1
4—At Boston	L	4-5
5—At Quebec	L	1-3
8—Quebec	L	2-3
10—At Tampa Bay	L	3-4
11—At Florida	L	3-4
13—At Montreal	T	*2-2
15—Montreal	W	4-1
16—At Pittsburgh	L	2-5
18—Pittsburgh	W	4-2
22—Boston	W	*3-2
24—At N.Y. Rangers	W	2-1
25—Buffalo	L	1-3
28—At Ottawa	W	6-3

MARCH

1—N.Y. Rangers	L	2-5
4—Tampa Bay	W	*3-2
5—Boston	L	2-5
7—At N.Y. Islanders	L	1-3
9—Quebec	W	2-1
12—Florida	L	1-4
14—N.Y. Islanders	W	6-4
16—At New Jersey	T	*2-2
20—Washington	L	0-5
22—Philadelphia	W	4-3
25—N.Y. Islanders	W	5-1
26—At Washington	W	*4-3
29—At Florida	T	*4-4
31—At Tampa Bay	L	0-2

APRIL

4—At Buffalo	L	3-6
5—At Pittsburgh	W	8-4
8—Buffalo	W	4-2
9—Tampa Bay	L	0-3
12—Ottawa	W	4-2
14—Montreal	W	*4-3
16—At New Jersey	L	2-3
18—At Buffalo	W	2-1
20—At N.Y. Rangers	L	2-3
21—At Washington	L	3-6
23—Pittsburgh	L	2-4
24—At Montreal	W	4-3
26—At Boston	L	0-1
28—Philadelphia	L	3-4

MAY

3—At Quebec	L	1-4

*Denotes overtime game.

LOS ANGELES KINGS
WESTERN CONFERENCE/PACIFIC DIVISION

1995-96 SCHEDULE

Home games shaded.
* — All-Star Game at FleetCenter, Boston.
D — Day game.

OCTOBER
SUN	MON	TUE	WED	THU	FRI	SAT
1	2	3	4	5	6	7 COL
8	9	10 CHI	11	12 VAN	13	14
15 VAN	16	17	18 PHI	19	20 WAS	21 PIT
22	23 MON	24	25	26 OTT	27	28 TOR
29	30	31 CAL				

NOVEMBER
SUN	MON	TUE	WED	THU	FRI	SAT
			1	2 NYR	3	4 NJ
5	6	7 STL	8 DAL	9	10	11 PIT
12	13 ANA	14 DET	15	16 NYI	17	18 FLA
19	20	21 PHI	22 NYI	23	24 D BOS	25
26 FLA	27 TB	28	29	30 WAS		

DECEMBER
SUN	MON	TUE	WED	THU	FRI	SAT
					1	2 DAL
3	4	5	6 WIN	7	8	9 STL
10	11 CAL	12	13 OTT	14	15	16 TOR
17	18	19	20 VAN	21	22 SJ	23 COL
24	25	26	27 ANA	28	29 EDM	30
31 D ANA						

JANUARY
SUN	MON	TUE	WED	THU	FRI	SAT
	1	2	3 WIN	4	5 SJ	6 SJ
7	8 DAL	9	10 TOR	11	12 DET	13
14 CHI	15	16 CAL	17	18	19	20 *
21	22 NYR	23 NJ	24	25 HAR	26	27 D ANA
28	29	30	31 HAR			

FEBRUARY
SUN	MON	TUE	WED	THU	FRI	SAT
				1 SJ	2	3 CAL
4	5	6 CHI	7	8 D SJ	9	10 D SJ
11	12	13 DET	14 BUF	15	16	17 ANA
18	19 D BOS	20	21 EDM	22	23 COL	24 STL
25	26 WIN	27	28 TB	29		

MARCH
SUN	MON	TUE	WED	THU	FRI	SAT
					1	2 MON
3	4	5	6 EDM	7	8 CHI	9
10 ANA	11	12	13 BUF	14	15	16 EDM
17	18 STL	19	20 COL	21	22	23 DAL
24	25 VAN	26	27 EDM	28	29 CAL	30
31						

APRIL
SUN	MON	TUE	WED	THU	FRI	SAT
	1	2	3 DET	4	5	6 VAN
7	8	9	10 SJ	11	12 WIN	13
14 D COL	15	16	17	18	19	20

1995-96 SEASON

CLUB DIRECTORY

Owners
Jeffrey Sudikoff
Joseph Cohen
Chairman of the board
Joseph Cohen
President
Rogie Vachon
General manager
Sam McMaster
Executive vice president
Lester Wintz
Coach
Larry Robinson
Assistant coach
John Perpich
Assistant to general manager
Dave Taylor
Administrative assistant to general manager
John Wolf

Director of amateur scouting
Al Murray
Director of pro scouting
Ace Bailey
Scouting staff
Serge Aubry
Gary Harker
Jan Lindegren
Vaclav Nedomansky
John Stanton
Vice president, finance
Michael Handelman, CPA
Director, media relations
Rick Minch
Trainers
Pete Demers
Peter Millar
Robert Zolg
Rick Garcia

DRAFT CHOICES

Rd.—Player	H/W	Overall	Pos.	Last team
1—Aki-Petteri Berg	6-3/196	3	D	TPS Jrs., Finland
2—Donald MacLean.......	6-2/174	33	C	Beauport (QMJHL)
2—Pavel Rosa	5-11/180	50	RW	Litinov Jrs., Czech Rep.
3—Vladimir Tsyplakov ..		59	W	Fort Wayne (IHL)
5—Jason Morgan	6-1/190	118	C	Kingston (OHL)
6—Igor Melyakov	5-10/176	137	LW	Yaroslavl, CIS
7—Beniot Larose............	6-5/195	157	D	Shawinigan (QMJHL)
7—Juha Vuorivirta.........	6-3/189	163	C	Tappara Tampere, Finland
9—Brian Stewart............	6-3/175	215	D	Sault Ste. Marie (OHL)

MISCELLANEOUS DATA

Home ice (capacity)
The Great Western Forum (16,005)
Address
3900 West Manchester Blvd.
Inglewood, CA 90305
Business phone
310-419-3160
Rink dimensions
200 feet by 85 feet

Club colors
Black, white and silver
Radio affiliation
XTRA (690 AM), KWIZ (1480 AM, Spanish)
TV affiliation
Prime Sports, KTLA (Channel 5), La Cadena Deportiva (Spanish)

TRAINING CAMP ROSTER

No.	FORWARDS	Ht./Wt.	Place	BORN Place	Date	NHL exp.	1994-95 clubs
	Kevin Brown (RW)	6-1/212	Birmingham, England		5-11-74	1	Phoenix (IHL), Los Angeles
18	Randy Burridge (LW)	5-9/185	Fort Erie, Ont.		1-7-66	10	Washington, Los Angeles
15	Pat Conacher (LW/C)	5-9/190	Edmonton		5-1-59	13	Los Angeles
	Troy Crowder (RW)	6-4/220	Sudbury, Ont.		5-3-68	5	Los Angeles
15	John Druce (RW)	6-2/195	Peterborough, Ont.		2-23-66	7	Los Angeles
21	Tony Granato (RW)	5-10/185	Downers Grove, Ill.		7-25-64	7	Los Angeles
99	Wayne Gretzky (C)	6-0/170	Brantford, Ont.		1-26-61	16	Los Angeles
	Matt Johnson (LW)	6-5/223	Pelham, Ont.		11-23-75	1	Peterborough (OHL), Los Angeles
8	Dimitri Khristich (LW)	6-2/200	Kiev, U.S.S.R.		7-23-69	5	Washington
17	Jari Kurri (C/RW)	6-1/195	Helsinki, Finland		5-18-60	14	Jokerit Helsinki (Finland), Los Angeles
41	Eric Lacroix (LW)	6-1/200	Montreal		7-15-71	2	St. John's (AHL), Phoenix (IHL), Los Angeles
13	Robert Lang (C)	6-2/180	Teplice, Czechoslovakia		12-19-70	3	Chemopetrol Litvinov (Czech.), Los Angeles
	Brian McReynolds (C)	6-1/192	Penetanguishene, Ont.		1-5-65	3	Phoenix (IHL), Atlanta (IHL)
	Yanic Perreault (C)	5-11/182	Sherbrooke, Que.		4-4-71	2	Phoenix (IHL), Los Angeles
	Keith Redmond (LW)	6-3/208	Richmond Hill, Ont.		10-25-72	1	Phoenix (IHL)
	Daniel Rydmark (C)	5-10/180	Vasteras, Sweden		2-23-70	0	Malmo (Sweden)
	Jeff Shevalier (LW/C)	5-11/180	Mississauga, Ont.		3-14-74	1	Phoenix (IHL), Los Angeles
14	Gary Shuchuk (RW/C)	5-10/185	Edmonton		2-17-67	4	Los Angeles, Phoenix (IHL)
	Dave Thomlinson (LW)	6-1/215	Edmonton		10-22-66	5	Phoenix (IHL), Los Angeles
22	Rick Tocchet (RW)	6-0/205	Scarborough, Ont.		4-9-64	11	Los Angeles
15	Kevin Todd (C)	5-10/180	Winnipeg		5-4-68	6	Los Angeles
	Vladimir Tsyplakov (LW)	6-2/194	Inta, U.S.S.R.		4-18-69	0	Fort Wayne (IHL)
	Vitali Yachmenev (RW)	5-9/180	Chelyabinsk, U.S.S.R.		1-8-75	0	North Bay (OHL), Phoenix (IHL)
	DEFENSEMEN						
	Ruslan Batyrshin	6-1/180	Moscow, U.S.S.R.		2-19-75	0	Dynamo Moscow (CIS)
	Aki-Petteri Berg	6-3/196	Turku, Finland		7-28-77	0	Kiekko-67 (Finland Div. II), TPS Jr. (Fin.), TPS Turku (Fin.)
4	Rob Blake	6-3/215	Simcoe, Ont.		12-10-69	6	Los Angeles
4	Philippe Boucher	6-2/188	St. Apollnaire, Que.		3-24-73	3	Rochester (AHL), Buffalo, Los Angeles
	Rob Cowie	6-0/195	Toronto		11-3-67	1	Phoenix (IHL), Los Angeles
	Justin Hocking	6-4/206	Stettler, Alta.		1-9-74	1	Phoenix (IHL), Syracuse (AHL), Portland (AHL), Knoxville (ECHL)
	Eric Lavigne	6-3/194	Victoriaville, Que.		11-14-72	1	Phoenix (IHL), Los Angeles, Detroit (IHL)
33	Marty McSorley (D/RW)	6-1/225	Hamilton, Ont.		5-18-63	12	Los Angeles
	Sean O'Donnell	6-3/225	Ottawa		9-13-71	1	Phoenix (IHL), Los Angeles
4	Michel Petit	6-1/185	St. Malo, Que.		2-12-64	13	Los Angeles
38	Chris Snell	5-10/200	Regina, Sask.		5-12-71	2	Minnesota-Duluth (WCHA), Phoenix (IHL), Los Angeles
25	Darryl Sydor	6-0/205	Edmonton		5-13-72	4	Los Angeles
	Denis Tsygurov	6-3/198	Chelyabinsk, U.S.S.R.		2-26-71	2	Lada Togliatti (CIS), Buffalo, Los Angeles
	Jan Vopat	6-0/198	Most, Czechoslovakia		3-22-73	0	Chemopetrol Litvinov (Czech Rep.)
	GOALTENDERS						
	Frederick Beaubien	6-1/204	Levis, Que.		4-1-75	0	St. Hyacinthe (QMJHL)
35	Byron Dafoe	5-11/195	Duncan, B.C.		2-25-71	3	Portland (AHL), Phoenix (IHL), Washington
32	Kelly Hrudey	5-10/189	Edmonton		1-13-61	12	Los Angeles
	Jamie Storr	6-2/192	Brampton, Ont.		12-28-75	1	Owen Sound (OHL), Los Angeles, Windsor (OHL)

1994-95 REVIEW

INDIVIDUAL STATISTICS

SCORING

	Games	G	A	Pts.	PIM	+/-	PPG	SHG	Shots	Shooting Pct.
Wayne Gretzky	48	11	37	48	6	-20	3	0	142	7.7
Rick Tocchet	36	18	17	35	70	-8	7	1	95	18.9
Dan Quinn	44	14	17	31	32	-3	2	0	78	17.9
Jari Kurri	38	10	19	29	24	-17	2	0	84	11.9
Tony Granato	33	13	11	24	68	9	2	0	106	12.3
Darryl Sydor	48	4	19	23	36	-2	3	0	96	4.2
Marty McSorley	41	3	18	21	83	-14	1	0	75	4.0
John Druce	43	15	5	20	20	-3	3	0	75	20.0

	Games	G	A	Pts.	PIM	+/-	PPG	SHG	Shots	Shooting Pct.
Randy Burridge*	38	4	15	19	8	-4	2	0	50	8.0
Michel Petit	40	5	12	17	84	4	2	0	70	7.1
Eric Lacroix	45	9	7	16	54	2	2	1	64	14.1
Pat Conacher	48	7	9	16	12	-9	0	1	64	10.9
Robert Lang	36	4	8	12	4	-7	0	0	38	10.5
Rob Blake	24	4	7	11	38	-16	4	0	76	5.3
Kevin Todd	33	3	8	11	12	-5	0	0	34	8.8
Gary Shuchuk	22	3	6	9	6	-2	0	0	16	18.8
Rob Cowie	32	2	7	9	20	-6	0	0	39	5.1
Chris Snell	32	2	7	9	22	-7	0	2	45	4.4
Alexei Zhitnik*	11	2	5	7	27	-3	2	0	33	6.1
Yanic Perreault	26	2	5	7	20	3	0	0	43	4.7
Kevin Brown	23	2	3	5	18	-7	0	0	25	8.0
Troy Crowder*	29	1	2	3	99	0	0	0	4	25.0
Mike Donnelly*	9	1	1	2	4	-7	0	0	22	4.5
Sean O'Donnell	15	0	2	2	49	-2	0	0	12	0.0
Jeff Shevalier	1	1	0	1	0	1	0	0	1	100.0
Philippe Boucher*	6	1	0	1	4	-3	0	0	15	6.7
Matt Johnson	14	1	0	1	102	0	0	0	4	25.0
Arto Blomsten*	4	0	1	1	0	2	0	0	1	0.0
Charlie Huddy*	9	0	1	1	6	-6	0	0	11	0.0
Pauli Jaks (goalie)	1	0	0	0	0	0	0	0	0	0.0
Eric Lavigne	1	0	0	0	0	-1	0	0	0	0.0
Robb Stauber* (goalie)	1	0	0	0	0	0	0	0	0	0.0
Dave Thomlinson	1	0	0	0	0	-1	0	0	0	0.0
Tim Watters	1	0	0	0	0	1	0	0	1	0.0
Rob Brown	2	0	0	0	0	-2	0	0	1	0.0
Jamie Storr (goalie)	5	0	0	0	0	0	0	0	0	0.0
Warren Rychel*	7	0	0	0	19	-5	0	0	7	0.0
Grant Fuhr* (goalie)	14	0	0	0	2	0	0	0	0	0.0
Denis Tsygurov*	21	0	0	0	11	-2	0	0	16	0.0
Kelly Hrudey (goalie)	35	0	0	0	0	0	0	0	0	0.0

GOALTENDING

	Games	Min.	Goals	SO	Avg.	W	L	T	Shots	Sv. Pct.
Pauli Jaks	1	40	2	0	3.00	0	0	0	25	.920
Kelly Hrudey	35	1894	99	0	3.14	14	13	5	1099	.910
Jamie Storr	5	263	17	0	3.88	1	3	1	152	.888
Grant Fuhr*	14	698	47	0	4.04	1	7	3	379	.876
Robb Stauber*	1	16	2	0	7.50	0	0	0	6	.667

Empty-net goals (do not count against a goaltender's average): Fuhr 3, Hrudey 3, Storr 1.
*Played with two or more NHL teams.

RESULTS

JANUARY

20—Toronto	T	*3-3
22—Edmonton	L	3-4
24—Dallas	L	2-4
26—At St. Louis	L	1-3
28—Winnipeg	W	4-2
29—Chicago	L	3-6

FEBRUARY

4—Detroit	W	4-3
5—Anaheim	L	2-3
7—At St. Louis	T	*5-5
11—At Toronto	W	5-2
12—At Detroit	T	*4-4
15—At Dallas	W	3-1
17—San Jose	L	0-2
18—Vancouver	L	2-6
20—At Vancouver	L	2-8
23—Calgary	T	*3-3
25—At Edmonton	W	4-3
28—Chicago	L	4-8

MARCH

4—Vancouver	L	4-5
6—At Dallas	L	2-8
9—At Chicago	W	4-3
11—At Winnipeg	W	4-2
13—At Toronto	W	4-1
14—At Detroit	L	2-5
16—St. Louis	T	*2-2
18—Toronto	L	3-5
20—St. Louis	W	5-3
21—At Anaheim	T	*3-3
25—San Jose	L	1-3
26—At San Jose	W	7-3
28—At Calgary	W	5-3
29—At Vancouver	L	2-5

APRIL

1—Winnipeg	T	*7-7
3—Edmonton	W	7-2
6—Dallas	W	3-2
7—At Calgary	L	4-7
9—At Anaheim	L	1-5
12—Calgary	L	1-4
16—At San Jose	L	0-2
17—At Calgary	L	2-5
19—At Edmonton	L	0-2
21—Edmonton	T	*3-3
23—Anaheim	T	*2-2
25—Detroit	W	5-1
28—At San Jose	L	0-4
30—Anaheim	W	2-1

MAY

2—At Winnipeg	W	2-1
3—At Chicago	L	1-5

*Denotes overtime game.

MONTREAL CANADIENS
EASTERN CONFERENCE/NORTHEAST DIVISION

1995-96 SCHEDULE

Home games shaded.
* — All-Star Game at FleetCenter, Boston.
D — Day game.

OCTOBER

SUN	MON	TUE	WED	THU	FRI	SAT
1	2	3	4	5	6	7 PHI
8	9	10	11 FLA	12 TB	13	14 NJ
15	16	17	18	19	20 NYI	21 TOR
22	23 LA	24	25 FLA	26	27 HAR	28 CHI
29	30	31 BOS				

NOVEMBER

SUN	MON	TUE	WED	THU	FRI	SAT
			1 WAS	2	3	4 BOS
5	6	7	8 ANA	9	10	11 CAL
12 VAN	13	14	15 EDM	16	17	18 OTT
19	20 HAR	21	22 HAR	23	24	25 COL
26	27	28 DET	29 STL	30		

DECEMBER

SUN	MON	TUE	WED	THU	FRI	SAT
					1	2 DET
3	4	5	6 NJ	7 PIT	8	9 NYR
10	11	12 WIN	13	14	15 CHI	16 PHI
17	18 HAR	19	20 BUF	21	22 PIT	23 PIT
24	25	26 WAS	27	28 TB	29	30 OTT
31						

JANUARY

SUN	MON	TUE	WED	THU	FRI	SAT
	1	2	3 NYR	4 NYI	5	6 BUF
7	8 TB	9	10 VAN	11	12 PIT	13 STL
14	15	16	17 OTT	18	19	20 *
21	22 TB	23	24	25 FLA	26	27 D WIN
28 D BOS	29	30	31 WAS			

FEBRUARY

SUN	MON	TUE	WED	THU	FRI	SAT
				1 PHI	2	3 TOR
4	5 COL	6	7 DAL	8	9	10 OTT
11	12 SJ	13	14	15 NYR	16	17 CAL
18	19	20	21 HAR	22	23 NJ	24 PIT
25	26 SJ	27	28 ANA	29		

MARCH

SUN	MON	TUE	WED	THU	FRI	SAT
					1	2 LA
3	4	5	6	7	8	9 OTT
10	11 DAL	12	13 NJ	14	15	16 NYR
17	18 BUF	19	20 HAR	21	22 BUF	23 EDM
24	25 NYI	26	27 WAS	28 BOS	29	30 OTT
31						

APRIL

SUN	MON	TUE	WED	THU	FRI	SAT
	1 BUF	2	3 BOS	4 BOS	5	6 FLA
7	8	9	10	11 PHI	12	13 NYI
14	15	16	17	18	19	20

1995-96 SEASON

CLUB DIRECTORY

Chairman of the board, pres. and governor
Ronald Corey
V.P. hockey and managing director
Serge Savard
V.P., communications and marketing services
Bernard Brisset
Vice president, Forum operations
Aldo Giampaolo
Vice president, finance and administration
Fred Steer
Dir. of recruitment and asst. to managing dir.
Andre Boudrias
Coach
Jacques Demers
Assistant coaches
Jacques Laperriere
Steve Shutt
Charles Thiffault
Goaltending instructor
Francois Allaire

Director of player development and scout
Claude Ruel
Chief scout
Doug Robinson
Director of communications
Donald Beauchamp
Director of team services
Michele Lapointe
Club physician
Dr. D.G. Kinnear
Athletic trainer
Gaetan Lefebvre
Equipment manager
Eddy Palchak
Assistants to the equipment manager
Pierre Gervais
Robert Boulanger
Pierre Ouellette

DRAFT CHOICES

Rd. — Player	H/W	Overall	Pos.	Last team
1 — Terry Ryan	6-1/207	8	LW	Tri-City (WHL)
3 — Miroslav Guren	6-2/205	60	D	ZPS Zlin Jrs., Czech Rep.
3 — Martin Hohenberger	6-0/195	74	C	Prince George (WHL)
4 — Jonathan Delisle	5-10/186	86	RW	Hull (QMJHL)
5 — Niklas Anger	6-1/185	112	RW	Djurgarden Jrs., Sweden
6 — Boyd Olson	6-1/170	138	C	Tri-City (WHL)
7 — Stephane Robidas	5-10/182	164	D	Shawinigan (QMJHL)
8 — Greg Hart	5-11/202	190	RW	Kamloops (WHL)
9 — Eric Houde	5-10/186	216	C	Halifax (QMJHL)

MISCELLANEOUS DATA

Home ice (capacity)
Montreal Forum (17,959)
Address
2313 St. Catherine Street West
Montreal, Que. H3H 1N2
Business phone
514-932-2582
Rink dimensions
200 feet by 85 feet

Club colors
Red, white and blue
Radio affiliation
CJAD (800 AM), CBF (690 AM)
TV affiliation
CBFT (Channel 2), CBC (Channel 6),
RDS-TV (Cable), CFJP-TV
(Cable 5 or UHH 35)

TRAINING CAMP ROSTER

No.	FORWARDS	Ht./Wt.	Place	BORN Date	NHL exp.	1994-95 clubs
	Sebastien Bordeleau (C)..	5-10/176	Vancouver	2-15-75	0	Hull (QMJHL)
35	Donald Brashear (LW)..	6-3/214	Bedford, Ind.	1-7-72	2	Montreal, Fredericton (AHL)
22	Benoit Brunet (LW)	5-11/193	Montreal	8-24-68	6	Montreal
18	Valeri Bure (RW/LW) ...	5-10/168	Moscow, U.S.S.R.	6-13-74	1	Fredericton (AHL), Montreal
	Jim Campbell (C)	6-1/175	Worcester, Mass.	2-3-73	0	Fredericton (AHL)
	Craig Conroy (C)	6-2/190	Potsdam, N.Y.	9-4-71	1	Fredericton (AHL), Montreal
25	Vincent Damphousse (LW)	6-1/199	Montreal	12-17-67	9	Ratingen (Germany), Montreal
	Robert Guillet (RW)	5-11/189	Montreal	2-22-72	0	Fredericton (AHL)
12	Mike Keane (RW)	5-10/180	Winnipeg	5-29-67	7	Montreal
	Saku Koivu (C)	5-9/163	Turku, Finland	11-23-74	0	TPS Turku (Finland)
	Chris Murray (RW)	6-2/214	Port Hardy, B.C.	10-25-74	1	Fredericton (AHL), Montreal
6	Oleg Petrov (RW)	5-9/166	Moscow, U.S.S.R.	4-18-71	3	Montreal, Fredericton (AHL)
8	Mark Recchi (RW)	5-10/185	Kamloops, B.C.	2-1-68	7	Philadelphia, Montreal
32	Mario Roberge (LW)	5-10/200	Quebec City	1-31-64	5	Fredericton (AHL)
31	Ed Ronan (RW)	6-0/197	Quincy, Mass.	3-21-68	4	Montreal
	Terry Ryan (LW)	6-1/207	St. John's, Nfld.	1-14-77	0	Tri-City (WHL)
49	Brian Savage (C)	6-1/196	Sudbury, Ont.	2-24-71	2	Montreal
20	Pierre Sevigny (LW)	6-0/189	Trois-Rivieres, Que.	9-8-71	2	Montreal
30	Turner Stevenson (RW)	6-3/224	Port Alberni, B.C.	5-18-72	3	Fredericton (AHL), Montreal
	Darcy Tucker (C)	5-10/163	Castor, Alta.	3-15-75	0	Kamloops (WHL)
77	Pierre Turgeon (C)	6-1/195	Rouyn, Que.	8-29-69	8	New York Islanders, Montreal
	DEFENSEMEN					
	Brent Bilodeau	6-4/215	Dallas	3-27-73	0	Fredericton (AHL)
43	Patrice Brisebois	6-2/192	Montreal	1-27-71	5	Montreal
	Brad Brown	6-3/218	Mississauga, Ont.	12-27-75	0	North Bay (OHL)
48	J.J. Daigneault	5-11/199	Montreal	10-12-65	10	Montreal
	Rory Fitzpatrick	6-1/190	Rochester, N.Y.	1-11-75	0	Sudbury (OHL), Fredericton (AHL)
36	Gerry Fleming	6-5/240	Montreal	10-16-67	2	Montreal, Fredericton (AHL)
44	Bryan Fogarty	6-2/206	Montreal	6-11-69	6	Montreal
	Marko Kiprusoff	6-0/194	Turku, Finland	6-6-72	0	TPS Turku (Finland)
38	Vladimir Malakhov	6-3/220	Sverdlovsk, U.S.S.R.	8-30-68	3	New York Islanders, Montreal
24	Lyle Odelein	5-10/206	Quill Lake, Sask.	7-21-68	6	Montreal
34	Peter Popovic	6-5/241	Koping, Sweden	2-10-68	2	Vasteras (Sweden), Montreal
29	Yves Racine	6-0/200	Matane, Que.	2-7-69	6	Montreal
	Craig Rivet	6-2/172	North Bay, Ont.	9-13-74	1	Fredericton (AHL), Montreal
	David Wilkie	6-2/202	Ellensburg, Wash.	5-30-74	1	Fredericton (AHL), Montreal
	GOALTENDERS					
	Martin Brochu	5-11/195	Anjou, Que.	3-10-73	0	Fredericton (AHL)
	Patrick Labrecque	6-0/187	Laval, Que.	3-6-71	0	Wheeling (ECHL), Fredericton (AHL)
33	Patrick Roy	6-0/192	Quebec City	10-5-65	11	Montreal
	Jose Theodore	5-10/176	Laval, Que.	9-13-76	0	Hull (QMJHL), Fredericton (AHL)
1	Ron Tugnutt	5-11/155	Scarborough, Ont.	10-22-67	8	Montreal

1994-95 REVIEW

INDIVIDUAL STATISTICS

SCORING

	Games	G	A	Pts.	PIM	+/-	PPG	SHG	Shots	Shooting Pct.
Mark Recchi*	39	14	29	43	16	-3	8	0	104	13.5
Vincent Damphousse	48	10	30	40	42	15	4	0	123	8.1
Benoit Brunet	45	7	18	25	16	7	1	1	80	8.8
Pierre Turgeon*	15	11	9	20	4	12	2	0	67	16.4
Mike Keane	48	10	10	20	15	5	1	0	75	13.3
Mathieu Schneider*	30	5	15	20	49	-3	2	0	82	6.1
Brian Savage	37	12	7	19	27	5	0	0	64	18.8
Kirk Muller*	33	8	11	19	33	-21	3	0	81	9.9
Brian Bellows	41	8	8	16	8	-7	1	0	110	7.3
Patrice Brisebois	35	4	8	12	26	-2	0	0	67	6.0
Yves Racine	47	4	7	11	42	-1	2	0	63	6.3
Lyle Odelein	48	3	7	10	152	-13	0	0	74	4.1
Paul Dipietro*	22	4	5	9	4	-3	0	0	41	9.8
J.J. Daigneault	45	3	5	8	40	2	0	0	36	8.3
Turner Stevenson	41	6	1	7	86	0	0	0	35	17.1
Bryan Fogarty	21	5	2	7	34	-3	3	0	41	12.2
Eric Desjardins*	9	0	6	6	2	2	0	0	14	0.0
Oleg Petrov	12	2	3	5	4	-7	0	0	26	7.7
John LeClair*	9	1	4	5	10	-1	1	0	18	5.6
Vladimir Malakhov*	14	1	4	5	14	-2	0	0	30	3.3
Ed Ronan	30	1	4	5	12	-7	0	0	14	7.1

	Games	G	A	Pts.	PIM	+/-	PPG	SHG	Shots	Shooting Pct.
Peter Popovic	33	0	5	5	8	-10	0	0	23	0.0
Valeri Bure	24	3	1	4	6	-1	0	0	39	7.7
Gilbert Dionne*	6	0	3	3	2	-3	0	0	4	0.0
Donald Brashear	20	1	1	2	63	-5	0	0	10	10.0
Craig Darby*	10	0	2	2	0	-5	0	0	4	0.0
Craig Conroy	6	1	0	1	0	-1	0	0	4	25.0
Mark Lamb*	39	1	0	1	18	-13	0	0	23	4.3
Craig Rivet	5	0	1	1	5	2	0	0	2	0.0
Yves Sarault	8	0	1	1	0	-1	0	0	9	0.0
Patrick Roy (goalie)	43	0	1	1	20	0	0	0	0	0.0
Craig Ferguson	1	0	0	0	0	0	0	0	3	0.0
David Wilkie	1	0	0	0	0	0	0	0	0	0.0
Chris Murray	3	0	0	0	4	0	0	0	0	0.0
Jim Montgomery*	5	0	0	0	2	-2	0	0	3	0.0
Gerry Fleming	6	0	0	0	17	-1	0	0	1	0.0
Ron Tugnutt (goalie)	7	0	0	0	0	0	0	0	0	0.0
Mario Roberge	9	0	0	0	34	-2	0	0	0	0.0
Pierre Sevigny	19	0	0	0	15	-5	0	0	6	0.0

GOALTENDING

	Games	Min.	Goals	SO	Avg.	W	L	T	Shots	Sv. Pct.
Patrick Roy	‡43	†2566	127	1	2.97	17	20	6	†1357	.906
Ron Tugnutt	7	346	18	0	3.12	1	3	1	172	.895

Empty-net goals (do not count against a goaltender's average): Roy 3.
*Played with two or more NHL teams.
†Led league.
‡Tied for league lead.

RESULTS

JANUARY

21—At N.Y. Rangers	L		2-5
25—Washington	W		2-0
28—New Jersey	W		5-1
29—Philadelphia	T	*	2-2
31—At Tampa Bay	L		1-4

FEBRUARY

2—At Florida	T	*	1-1
4—N.Y. Islanders	W		4-2
7—At Boston	L		4-7
8—At Ottawa	W		4-2
11—At Pittsburgh	L		1-3
13—Hartford	T	*	2-2
15—At Hartford	L		1-4
16—At N.Y. Rangers	T	*	2-2
18—N.Y. Rangers	L		5-2
20—N.Y. Islanders	W	*	3-2
23—At Florida	W		5-2
25—Philadelphia	L		0-7

27—At New Jersey	L		1-6
28—At N.Y. Islanders	L		1-2

MARCH

4—At Washington	L		1-5
5—At Buffalo	L		1-4
8—Buffalo	T	*	2-2
11—N.Y. Rangers	W		3-1
13—At Pittsburgh	L		2-4
15—Pittsburgh	W		8-5
16—At Boston	L		0-6
18—Quebec	W		5-4
20—At Philadelphia	L		4-8
22—Florida	L		2-3
25—Ottawa	W		3-1
27—At Tampa Bay	L	*	2-3

APRIL

1—At New Jersey	L		1-4
3—At Ottawa	W		5-4

5—Quebec	W		6-5
6—At Quebec	L		2-3
8—Pittsburgh	W		2-1
10—New Jersey	W		2-1
12—At Philadelphia	L		2-3
14—At Hartford	L	*	3-4
15—Boston	L		2-3
17—Washington	W		5-2
19—Ottawa	W		4-1
22—Tampa Bay	W		3-1
24—Hartford	L		3-4
26—At Quebec	T	*	1-1
29—Buffalo	T	*	3-3

MAY

1—At Buffalo	L		0-2
3—Boston	L		2-4

*Denotes overtime game.

NEW JERSEY DEVILS
EASTERN CONFERENCE/ATLANTIC DIVISION

1995-96 SCHEDULE

Home games shaded.
* — All-Star Game at FleetCenter, Boston.
D — Day game.

OCTOBER
SUN	MON	TUE	WED	THU	FRI	SAT
1	2	3	4	5	6	7 / FLA
8	9	10	11	12 WIN	13	14 MON
15 BUF	16	17 EDM	18	19 DET	20	21 OTT
22	23	24	25 VAN	26	27	28 PIT
29	30	31 EDM				

NOVEMBER
SUN	MON	TUE	WED	THU	FRI	SAT
			1	2 SJ	3	4 LA
5 ANA	6	7	8 CAL	9	10	11 D PHI
12 D PHI	13	14 HAR	15	16 BOS	17	18 D BUF
19	20	21 FLA	22 TB	23	24	25 DAL
26	27 NYR	28	29 COL	30		

DECEMBER
SUN	MON	TUE	WED	THU	FRI	SAT
					1 TB	2 NYI
3	4	5	6 MON	7 TOR	8	9 NYI
10	11 FLA	12	13	14	15 DET	16 BUF
17	18	19 PHI	20	21 TB	22	23 FLA
24	25	26	27 NYI	28	29 WIN	30
31 CHI						

JANUARY
SUN	MON	TUE	WED	THU	FRI	SAT
	1	2	3 COL	4	5	6 WAS
7	8 STL	9	10	11 SJ	12	13 D BOS
14 DAL	15	16	17 BOS	18	19	20 *
21	22	23 LA	24	25 WAS	26	27 HAR
28	29	30 VAN	31			

FEBRUARY
SUN	MON	TUE	WED	THU	FRI	SAT
				1 CAL	2	3 OTT
4	5	6	7 PIT	8	9	10 D NYR
11 ANA	12	13	14	15	16 BUF	17
18 D WAS	19 D PHI	20	21 FLA	22	23 MON	24 WAS
25	26	27	28	29		

MARCH
SUN	MON	TUE	WED	THU	FRI	SAT
					1 NYI	2 OTT
3	4 NYR	5	6 TOR	7	8	9 D PIT
10 PHI	11	12	13 MON	14	15 TB	16
17 FLA	18	19	20 BOS	21	22 CHI	23 NYI
24	25	26 TB	27	28 STL	29	30 D PIT
31						

APRIL
SUN	MON	TUE	WED	THU	FRI	SAT
	1	2 NYR	3	4 HAR	5	6 D HAR
7 D NYR	8	9	10 PHI	11 WAS	12	13 D OTT
14	15	16	17	18	19	20

1995-96 SEASON

CLUB DIRECTORY

Chairman
John J. McMullen
President and general manager
Louis A. Lamoriello
Executive vice president
Max McNab
Head coach
Jacques Lemaire
Assistant coaches
Dennis Gendron
Chris Nilan
Goaltending coach
Jacques Caron
Director, media relations
Mike Levine
Equipment manager
Dave Nichols
Medical trainer
Ted Schuch

Director of scouting
David Conte
Scouts
Claude Carrier
Marcel Pronovost
Milt Fisher
Ed Thomlinson
Dan Labraaten
Glen Dirk
Les Widdifield
Joe Mahoney
Ferny Flaman
Larry Perris
Lou Reycroft
Yvon Lemaire
John Cunniff
Bob Hoffmeyer
Jan Ludvig

DRAFT CHOICES

Rd. — Player	H/W	Overall	Pos.	Last team
1—Petr Sykora	5-11/183	18	C	Detroit (IHL)
2—Nathan Perrott	6-0/213	44	RW	Oshawa (OHL)
3—Sergei Vyshedkevich	6-0/185	70	D	Dynamo, CIS
3—David Gosselin	6-0/174	78	RW	Sherbrooke (QMJHL)
4—Alyn McCauley	5-11/185	79	C	Ottawa (OHL)
4—Henrik Rehnberg	6-2/194	96	D	Farjestad Jrs., Sweden
5—Chris Mason	5-11/180	122	G	Prince George (WHL)
6—Adam Young	6-4/222	148	D	Windsor (OHL)
7—Richard Rochefort	5-9/179	174	C	Sudbury (OHL)
8—Frederic Henry	5-10/152	200	G	Granby (QMJHL)
9—Colin O'Hara	6-1/190	226	D	Winnipeg (MJHL)

MISCELLANEOUS DATA

Home ice (capacity)
Byrne Meadowlands Arena (19,040)
Address
P.O. Box 504
East Rutherford, N.J. 07073
Business phone
201-935-6050
Rink dimensions
200 feet by 85 feet

Club colors
Red, black and white
Radio affiliation
WABC (770 AM), WEVD (1050 AM)
TV affiliation
SportsChannel

TRAINING CAMP ROSTER

No.	FORWARDS	Ht./Wt.	Place	Born Date	NHL exp.	1994-95 clubs
	Bill Armstrong (LW)	6-2/195	London, Ont.	6-25-66	1	Albany (AHL)
9	Neal Broten (C)	5-9/175	Roseau, Minn.	11-29-59	15	Dallas, New Jersey
	Steve Brule (C)	5-11/185	Montreal	1-15-75	0	St. Jean (QMJHL), Albany (AHL)
18	Sergei Brylin (C)...........	5-9/175	Moscow, U.S.S.R.	1-13-74	1	Albany (AHL), New Jersey
19	Bob Carpenter (LW)	6-0/200	Beverly, Mass.	7-13-63	14	New Jersey
17	Tom Chorske (RW)........	6-1/205	Minneapolis	9-18-66	6	Milan (Italy), New Jersey
20	Danton Cole (RW)	5-11/185	Pontiac, Mich.	1-10-67	6	Tampa Bay, New Jersey
12	Bill Guerin (RW/C)	6-2/200	Wilbraham, Mass.	11-9-70	4	New Jersey
16	Bobby Holik (RW)	6-3/200	Jihlava, Czechoslovakia	1-1-71	5	New Jersey
22	Claude Lemieux (RW)	6-1/215	Buckingham, Que.	7-16-65	12	New Jersey
15	John MacLean (RW)	6-0/200	Oshawa, Ont.	11-20-64	12	New Jersey
	Alyn McCauley (C)	5-10/185	Brockville, Ont.	5-29-77	0	Ottawa (OHL)
21	Randy McKay (RW)	6-1/205	Montreal	1-25-67	7	New Jersey
	Denis Pederson (C)	6-2/197	Prince Albert, Sask.	9-10-75	0	Prince Albert (WHL), Albany (AHL)
8	Mike Peluso (LW)	6-4/200	Hibbing, Minn.	11-8-65	6	New Jersey
44	Stephane Richer (RW) ..	6-2/215	Buckingham, Que.	6-7-66	11	New Jersey
14	Brian Rolston (C)	6-2/185	Flint, Mich.	2-21-73	1	Albany (AHL), New Jersey
	Vadim Sharifijanov (RW) ..	6-0/183	Ufa, U.S.S.R.	12-23-75	0	CSKA Moscow (CIS), Albany (AHL)
44	Reid Simpson (LW)	6-1/210	Flin Flon, Man.	5-21-69	3	Albany (AHL), New Jersey
	Petr Sykora (C)	5-11/180	Plzen, Czechoslovakia	11-19-76	0	Detroit (IHL)
25	Valeri Zelepukin (RW) ...	5-11/180	Voskresensk, U.S.S.R.	9-17-68	4	New Jersey

DEFENSEMEN

No.		Ht./Wt.	Place	Date	exp.	1994-95 clubs
6	Tommy Albelin	6-1/190	Stockholm, Sweden	5-21-64	8	New Jersey
22	Shawn Chambers	6-2/200	Royal Oak, Mich.	10-11-66	8	Tampa Bay, New Jersey
3	Ken Daneyko	6-0/210	Windsor, Ont.	4-17-64	12	New Jersey
	Kevin Dean	6-2/195	Madison, Wis.	4-1-69	1	Albany (AHL), New Jersey
23	Bruce Driver	6-0/185	Toronto	4-29-62	12	New Jersey
7	Chris McAlpine.............	6-0/190	Roseville, Minn.	12-1-71	1	Albany (AHL), New Jersey
27	Scott Niedermayer	6-0/200	Edmonton	8-31-73	4	New Jersey
	Rickard Persson	6-1/205	Ostersund, Sweden	8-24-69	0	Malmo (Sweden), Albany (AHL)
	Jason Smith.................	6-3/195	Calgary	11-2-73	2	Albany (AHL), New Jersey
4	Scott Stevens	6-2/210	Kitchener, Ont.	4-1-64	13	New Jersey

GOALTENDERS

No.		Ht./Wt.	Place	Date	exp.	1994-95 clubs
30	Martin Brodeur	6-1/205	Montreal	5-6-72	3	New Jersey
	Mike Dunham	6-3/185	Johnson City, N.Y.	6-1-72	0	Albany (AHL)
	Corey Schwab	6-0/180	Battleford, Sask.	11-4-70	0	Albany (AHL)
31	Chris Terreri	5-8/160	Warwick, R.I.	11-15-64	8	New Jersey

1994-95 REVIEW

INDIVIDUAL STATISTICS

SCORING

	Games	G	A	Pts.	PIM	+/-	PPG	SHG	Shots	Shooting Pct.
Stephane Richer	45	23	16	39	10	8	1	2	133	17.3
John MacLean	46	17	12	29	32	13	2	1	139	12.2
Neal Broten*	30	8	20	28	20	9	2	0	43	18.6
Bill Guerin	48	12	13	25	72	6	4	0	96	12.5
Scott Stevens..	48	2	20	22	56	4	1	0	111	1.8
Bobby Holik	48	10	10	20	18	9	0	0	84	11.9
Claude Lemieux	45	6	13	19	86	2	1	0	117	5.1
Scott Niedermayer	48	4	15	19	18	19	4	0	52	7.7
Tom Chorske...	42	10	8	18	16	-4	0	0	59	16.9
Brian Rolston	40	7	11	18	17	5	2	0	92	7.6
Bob Carpenter	41	5	11	16	19	-1	0	0	69	7.2
Bruce Driver	41	4	12	16	18	-1	1	0	62	6.5
Tommy Albelin	48	5	10	15	20	9	2	0	60	8.3
Sergei Brylin	26	6	8	14	8	12	0	0	41	14.6
Randy McKay	33	5	7	12	44	10	0	0	44	11.4
Mike Peluso..	46	2	9	11	167	5	0	0	27	7.4
Alexander Semak*	19	2	6	8	13	-4	0	0	32	6.3
Shawn Chambers*	21	2	5	7	6	2	1	0	23	8.7
Corey Millen*	17	2	3	5	8	2	0	0	30	6.7
Jim Dowd	10	1	4	5	0	-5	1	0	14	7.1
Valeri Zelepukin...	4	1	2	3	6	3	0	0	6	16.7
Danton Cole*	12	1	2	3	8	0	0	0	20	5.0
Ken Daneyko	25	1	2	3	54	4	0	0	27	3.7
Chris McAlpine	24	0	3	3	17	4	0	0	19	0.0
Martin Brodeur (goalie)	40	0	2	2	2	0	0	0	0	0.0
Viacheslav Fetisov*	4	0	1	1	0	-2	0	0	1	0.0

	Games	G	A	Pts.	PIM	+/-	PPG	SHG	Shots	Shooting Pct.
David Emma	6	0	1	1	0	-2	0	0	4	0.0
Kevin Dean	17	0	1	1	4	6	0	0	11	0.0
Jason Smith	2	0	0	0	0	-3	0	0	5	0.0
Ben Hankinson*	8	0	0	0	7	-6	0	0	8	0.0
Reid Simpson	9	0	0	0	27	-1	0	0	5	0.0
Jaroslav Modry	11	0	0	0	0	-1	0	0	10	0.0
Chris Terreri (goalie)	15	0	0	0	0	0	0	0	0	0.0

GOALTENDING

	Games	Min.	Goals	SO	Avg.	W	L	T	Shots	Sv. Pct.
Martin Brodeur	40	2184	89	3	2.45	19	11	6	908	.902
Chris Terreri	15	734	31	0	2.53	3	7	2	309	.900

Empty-net goals (do not count against a goaltender's average): Brodeur 1.
*Played with two or more NHL teams.

RESULTS

JANUARY

22—At Hartford	T	*2-2
25—At Buffalo	L	1-2
26—At Boston	L	*0-1
28—At Montreal	L	1-5
31—Buffalo	W	2-1

FEBRUARY

2—Quebec	W	5-4
4—At Quebec	L	0-2
5—Pittsburgh	T	*3-3
9—N.Y. Rangers	W	4-1
11—Philadelphia	L	1-3
12—At Florida	W	4-2
15—Washington	W	4-2
17—N.Y. Islanders	T	*2-2
18—At N.Y. Islanders	L	2-3
20—At Washington	W	2-0
23—Boston	L	2-3

25—Washington	T	*3-3
27—Montreal	W	6-1

MARCH

2—At Boston	L	2-7
4—Florida	W	6-1
6—At Quebec	L	3-6
8—At N.Y. Rangers	L	4-6
10—At Tampa Bay	W	3-2
12—At Philadelphia	L	3-4
14—Ottawa	W	4-2
16—Hartford	T	*2-2
18—Tampa Bay	L	1-2
19—Boston	W	*4-3
22—At N.Y. Rangers	W	5-2
24—At Pittsburgh	L	2-5
26—At N.Y. Islanders	T	*5-5
29—At Ottawa	W	4-2
30—At Philadelphia	W	4-3

APRIL

1—Montreal	W	4-1
4—Tampa Bay	T	*1-1
5—At Ottawa	W	2-0
9—N.Y. Rangers	W	2-0
10—At Montreal	L	1-2
12—At Washington	W	2-1
14—N.Y. Islanders	W	6-3
16—Hartford	W	3-2
18—At Tampa Bay	L	2-3
20—At Florida	L	0-1
22—Philadelphia	L	*3-4
26—Pittsburgh	T	*3-3
28—Florida	W	3-1
30—Quebec	W	4-2

MAY

3—At Buffalo	L	4-5

*Denotes overtime game.

NEW YORK ISLANDERS
EASTERN CONFERENCE/ATLANTIC DIVISION

1995-96 SCHEDULE

Home games shaded.
* — All-Star Game at FleetCenter, Boston.
D — Day game.

OCTOBER

SUN	MON	TUE	WED	THU	FRI	SAT
1	2	3	4	5	6	7 BOS
8	9	10 TOR	11	12	13	14 PHI
15 FLA	16	17 NYR	18	19	20 MON	21
22	23	24	25 PHI	26 PIT	27	28 PHI
29	30	31 FLA				

NOVEMBER

SUN	MON	TUE	WED	THU	FRI	SAT
			1	2	3 TB	4 WAS
5	6	7 VAN	8	9	10 NYR	11 STL
12	13	14 SJ	15	16	17 ANA	18
19	20	21	22 LA	23	24 BUF	25 TB
26	27	28 COL	29	30 OTT		

DECEMBER

SUN	MON	TUE	WED	THU	FRI	SAT
					1	2 NJ
3	4	5 PIT	6 HAR	7	8	9 D NJ
10 PHI	11	12 FLA	13	14 WAS	15	16 HAR
17	18	19 STL	20	21 DAL	22	23 WAS
24	25	26 BOS	27 NJ	28	29	30
31 BUF						

JANUARY

SUN	MON	TUE	WED	THU	FRI	SAT
	1 FLA	2	3	4 MON	5	6 OTT
7	8	9 CHI	10	11 TOR	12	13
14	15 D TB	16	17 HAR	18	19	20 *
21	22 COL	23	24 CAL	25	26 EDM	27 VAN
28	29	30 BUF	31			

FEBRUARY

SUN	MON	TUE	WED	THU	FRI	SAT
				1	2	3 WAS
4 DAL	5	6 NYR	7	8 NYR	9	10 D WAS
11	12 OTT	13	14	15 CAL	16	17 D SJ
18	19	20	21	22 NYR	23 TB	24
25 EDM	26	27 DET	28	29 DET		

MARCH

SUN	MON	TUE	WED	THU	FRI	SAT
					1 NJ	2
3 WIN	4 D	5 BOS	6	7 BOS	8	9 D NJ
10	11	12	13	14	15	16 D PIT
17 D CHI	18	19 PHI	20	21	22	23 NJ
24	25 MON	26 WAS	27	28	29	30 D HAR
31 NYR						

APRIL

SUN	MON	TUE	WED	THU	FRI	SAT
	1	2 PHI	3	4	5 OTT	6 BUF
7	8 TB	9	10 PIT	11	12 FLA	13 MON
14	15	16	17	18	19	20

1995-96 SEASON

CLUB DIRECTORY

Co-chairmen
Robert Rosenthal
Stephen Walsh
Chief operating officer
Ralph Palleschi
Executive vice president
Paul Greenwood
Senior vice president & CFO
Arthur J. McCarthy
Vice president of hockey operations
Al Arbour
Consultant
John H. Krumpe
General counsel
William M. Skehan
General manager
Don Maloney
Asst. g.m./dir. of player personnel
Darcy Regier
Coach
Mike Milbury
Assistant coaches
To be announced
Assistant to general manager
Gerry Ehman
Director of pro scouting
Ken Morrow
Scouts
Harry Boyd
Earl Ingarfield
Jim Madigan
Bert Marshall
Mario Saraceno
Vice president/communications
Pat Calabria

Director of media relations
Ginger Killian-Serby
Media relations assistant
Eric Mirlis
Dir. of publications/media relations assoc.
Chris Botta
Director of community relations
Maureen Brady
Director of game events
Tim Beach
Dir. of amateur hoc. dev. & alumni relations
Bob Nystrom
Director of marketing/ticket sales
Brian Edwards
Director of administration
Joseph Dreyer
Controller
Ralph Sellitti
Athletic trainer
Ed Tyburski
Equipment manager
John Doolan
Assistant trainer
Jerry Iannarelli
Team orthopedists
Jeffery Minkoff, M.D.
Barry Simonson, M.D.
Team internists
Gerald Cordani, M.D.
Larry Smith, M.D.
Physical therapist
Steve Wirth
Team dentists
Bruce Michnick, D.D.S.
Jan Sherman, D.D.S.

DRAFT CHOICES

Rd.—Player	H/W	Overall	Pos.	Last team
1—Wade Redden	6-1/193	2	D	Brandon (WHL)
2—Jan Hlavac	6-0/185	28	LW	Sparta Praha, Czech Rep.
2—D.J. Smith	6-1/210	41	D	Windsor (OHL)
5—Vladimir Orsagh	5-10/172	106	LW	Banska Bystrica, Slovakia
7—Andrew Taylor	6-2/193	158	LW	Detroit (OHL)
9—David MacDonald	5-9/181	210	G	Sudbury (OHL)
9—Mike Broda	6-1/189	211	LW	Moose Jaw (WHL)

MISCELLANEOUS DATA

Home ice (capacity)
Nassau Veterans Memorial Coliseum
(16,297)
Address
Uniondale, NY 11553
Business phone
516-794-4100
Rink dimensions
200 feet by 85 feet

Club colors
Blue, orange, Atlantic green
and silver
Radio affiliation
WRCN (94.3 FM and 103.9 FM),
WGSM (740 AM, day games)
TV affiliation
SportsChannel

No.	FORWARDS	Ht./Wt.	Place BORN	Date	NHL exp.	1994-95 clubs
46	Niclas Andersson (LW)	5-9/175	Kunglav, Sweden	5-20-71	1	Denver (IHL)
38	Derek Armstrong (C)	5-11/180	Ottawa	4-23-73	0	Denver (IHL)
	Todd Bertuzzi (LW)	6-3/227	Sudbury, Ont.	2-2-75	0	Guelph (OHL)
15	Brad Dalgarno (RW)	6-3/217	Vancouver	8-8-67	9	New York Islanders
	Craig Darby (C)	6-3/180	Oneida, N.Y.	9-26-72	1	Fredericton (AHL), Montreal, New York Islanders
	Jarrett Deuling (LW)	5-11/194	Vernon, B.C.	3-4-74	0	Worcester (AHL)
26	Patrick Flatley (RW)	6-2/201	Toronto	10-3-63	12	New York Islanders
39	Travis Green (C)	6-2/195	Creston, B.C.	12-20-70	3	New York Islanders
17	Yan Kaminsky (RW)	6-1/176	Penza, U.S.S.R.	7-28-71	2	Denver (IHL), New York Islanders
27	Derek King (LW)	6-1/206	Hamilton, Ont.	2-11-67	9	New York Islanders
	Brett Lindros (RW)	6-4/215	Toronto	12-2-75	1	Kingston (OHL), New York Islanders
	Chris Marinucci (LW)	6-0/175	Grand Rapids, Minn.	12-29-71	1	Denver (IHL), New York Islanders
18	Marty McInnis (C/LW)	6-0/183	Weymouth, Mass.	6-2-70	4	New York Islanders
	Kip Miller (C)	5-10/185	Lansing, Mich.	6-11-69	4	Denver (IHL), New York Islanders
11	Kirk Muller (LW)	6-0/205	Kingston, Ont.	2-8-66	11	Montreal, New York Islanders
68	Zigmund Palffy (RW)	5-10/169	Skalica, Czechoslovakia	5-5-72	2	Denver (IHL), New York Islanders
	Chris Taylor (C)	6-1/198	Stratford, Ont.	3-6-72	1	Denver (IHL), Roanoke (ECHL), New York Islanders
32	Steve Thomas (LW/RW)	5-11/184	Stockport, England	7-15-63	11	New York Islanders
12	Mick Vukota (RW)	6-2/215	Saskatoon, Sask.	9-14-66	8	New York Islanders

DEFENSEMEN

No.	DEFENSEMEN	Ht./Wt.	Place	Date	NHL exp.	1994-95 clubs
2	Bob Beers	6-2/200	Pittsburgh	5-20-67	6	New York Islanders
3	Dean Chynoweth	6-2/193	Saskatoon, Sask.	10-30-68	6	New York Islanders
11	Darius Kasparaitis	5-11/190	Elektrenai, U.S.S.R.	10-16-72	3	New York Islanders
7	Scott Lachance	6-2/198	Charlottesville, Va.	10-22-72	4	New York Islanders
2	Christopher Luongo	6-0/199	Detroit	3-17-67	4	Denver (IHL), New York Islanders
	Bryan McCabe	6-1/200	St. Catherines, Ont.	6-8-75	0	Spokane (WHL), Brandon (WHL)
47	Rich Pilon	6-0/205	Saskatoon, Sask.	4-30-68	7	New York Islanders, Chicago (IHL)
8	Mathieu Schneider	5-11/189	New York	6-12-69	7	Montreal, New York Islanders
24	Brent Severyn	6-2/210	Vegreville, Alta.	2-22-66	3	Florida, New York Islanders
	D.J. Smith	6-1/210	Windsor, Ont.	5-13-77	0	Windsor (OHL)
37	Dennis Vaske	6-2/210	Rockford, Ill.	10-11-67	5	New York Islanders

GOALTENDERS

No.	GOALTENDERS	Ht./Wt.	Place	Date	NHL exp.	1994-95 clubs
	Eric Fichaud	5-11/160	Montreal	11-4-75	0	Chicoutimi (QMJHL)
	Milan Hnilicka	6-0/180	Kladno, Czechoslovakia	6-24-73	0	Denver (IHL)
29	Jamie McLennan	6-0/189	Edmonton	6-30-71	2	New York Islanders, Denver (IHL)
	Tommy Salo	5-11/161	Surahammar, Sweden	2-1-71	1	Denver (IHL), New York Islanders
30	Tommy Soderstrom	5-9/156	Stockholm, Sweden	7-17-69	3	New York Islanders

1994-95 REVIEW

INDIVIDUAL STATISTICS

SCORING

	Games	G	A	Pts.	PIM	+/-	PPG	SHG	Shots	Shooting Pct.
Ray Ferraro	47	22	21	43	30	1	2	0	94	23.4
Pierre Turgeon*	34	13	14	27	10	-12	3	2	93	14.0
Patrick Flatley	45	7	20	27	12	9	1	0	81	8.6
Steve Thomas	47	11	15	26	60	-14	3	0	133	8.3
Derek King	43	10	16	26	41	-5	7	0	118	8.5
Zigmund Palffy	33	10	7	17	6	3	1	0	75	13.3
Marty McInnis	41	9	7	16	8	-1	0	0	68	13.2
Vladimir Malakhov*	26	3	13	16	32	-1	1	0	61	4.9
Scott Lachance	26	6	7	13	26	2	3	0	56	10.7
Travis Green	42	5	7	12	25	-10	0	0	59	8.5
Dennis Vaske	41	1	11	12	53	3	0	0	48	2.1
Benoit Hogue*	33	6	4	10	34	0	1	0	50	12.0
Troy Loney*	26	5	4	9	23	0	2	0	45	11.1
Mathieu Schneider*	13	3	6	9	30	-5	1	0	36	8.3
Bob Beers	22	2	7	9	6	-8	1	0	38	5.3
Kirk Muller*	12	3	5	8	14	3	1	1	16	18.8
Brad Dalgarno	22	3	2	5	14	-8	1	1	18	16.7
Chris Marinucci	12	1	4	5	2	-1	0	0	11	9.1
Ron Sutter	27	1	4	5	21	-8	0	0	29	3.4
Brent Severyn*	19	1	3	4	34	1	0	0	22	4.5
Brett Lindros	33	1	3	4	100	-8	0	0	35	2.9
Chris Luongo	47	1	3	4	36	-2	0	0	44	2.3
Paul Stanton	18	0	4	4	9	-6	0	0	28	0.0
Chris Taylor	10	0	3	3	2	1	0	0	13	0.0

	Games	G	A	Pts.	PIM	+/-	PPG	SHG	Shots	Shooting Pct.
Yan Kaminsky	2	1	1	2	0	2	0	0	4	25.0
Richard Pilon	20	1	1	2	40	-3	0	0	11	9.1
Dean Chynoweth	32	0	2	2	77	9	0	0	22	0.0
Mick Vukota	40	0	2	2	109	1	0	0	11	0.0
Tommy Salo (goalie)	6	0	1	1	0	0	0	0	0	0.0
Kip Miller	8	0	1	1	0	1	0	0	11	0.0
Darius Kasparaitis	13	0	1	1	22	-11	0	0	8	0.0
Jason Widmer	1	0	0	0	0	-1	0	0	0	0.0
Milan Tichy	2	0	0	0	2	-1	0	0	1	0.0
Andrei Vasiliev	2	0	0	0	2	0	0	0	2	0.0
Craig Darby*	3	0	0	0	0	-1	0	0	1	0.0
Gord Dineen	9	0	0	0	2	-5	0	0	4	0.0
Dave Chyzowski	13	0	0	0	11	-2	0	0	11	0.0
Jamie McLennan (goalie)	21	0	0	0	2	0	0	0	0	0.0
Tommy Soderstrom (goalie)	26	0	0	0	2	0	0	0	0	0.0

GOALTENDING

	Games	Min.	Goals	SO	Avg.	W	L	T	Shots	Sv. Pct.
Tommy Salo	6	358	18	0	3.02	1	5	0	189	.905
Tommy Soderstrom	26	1350	70	1	3.11	8	12	3	717	.902
Jamie McLennan	21	1185	67	0	3.39	6	11	2	539	.876

Empty-net goals (do not count against a goaltender's average): Soderstrom 2, McLennan 1.
*Played with two or more NHL teams.

RESULTS

JANUARY
21—Florida	W	2-1	
22—Ottawa	T	*3-3	
24—Philadelphia	W	4-3	
27—At Washington	L	2-5	
28—Tampa Bay	L	1-4	
31—At Florida	W	5-1	

FEBRUARY
2—At Philadelphia	W	*5-4	
4—At Montreal	L	2-4	
7—At Tampa Bay	L	2-5	
9—Pittsburgh	L	2-5	
11—Buffalo	W	2-1	
14—Quebec	L	2-3	
17—At New Jersey	T	*2-2	
18—New Jersey	W	3-2	
20—At Montreal	L	*2-3	
22—At Buffalo	T	*3-3	
23—Tampa Bay	L	1-4	
25—Pittsburgh	W	3-1	
28—Montreal	W	2-1	

MARCH
2—Washington	L	3-4	
5—At Ottawa	L	1-3	
7—Hartford	W	3-1	
9—At Pittsburgh	L	2-4	
11—At Quebec	L	1-2	
14—At Hartford	L	4-6	
16—At Buffalo	L	3-6	
18—At Boston	L	3-4	
23—N.Y. Rangers	W	1-0	
25—At Hartford	L	1-5	
26—New Jersey	T	*5-5	
28—At Pittsburgh	L	3-6	
30—Boston	L	2-3	

APRIL
1—Buffalo	L	1-5	
4—Washington	L	4-5	
7—At N.Y. Rangers	W	4-3	
8—Florida	T	*2-2	
11—At Tampa Bay	L	2-5	
12—At Florida	W	3-1	

14—At New Jersey	L	3-6	
16—N.Y. Rangers	L	2-3	
18—Quebec	W	5-2	
20—At Philadelphia	L	1-2	
22—Ottawa	L	2-3	
24—Boston	W	5-3	
26—At Washington	L	5-6	
28—At N.Y. Rangers	W	4-2	
29—At Ottawa	L	3-4	

MAY
2—Philadelphia	L	0-2	

*Denotes overtime game.

NEW YORK RANGERS
EASTERN CONFERENCE/ATLANTIC DIVISION

1995-96 SCHEDULE

Home games shaded.
* — All-Star Game at FleetCenter, Boston.
D — Day game.

OCTOBER

SUN	MON	TUE	WED	THU	FRI	SAT
1	2	3	4	5	6	7 HAR
8	9	10	11 WIN	12	13	14 TOR
15	16 HAR	17 NYI	18	19	20 BUF	21
22 OTT	23	24 VAN	25	26 TB	27	28
29 TOR	30	31 SJ				

NOVEMBER

SUN	MON	TUE	WED	THU	FRI	SAT
			1	2 LA	3 ANA	4
5	6 CAL	7	8 TB	9	10 NYI	11 HAR
12	13	14 STL	15	16 CHI	17 WIN	18
19	20	21 PIT	22 PIT	23	24	25 DET
26	27 NJ	28	29 BUF	30		

DECEMBER

SUN	MON	TUE	WED	THU	FRI	SAT
					1 COL	2 OTT
3	4 ANA	5	6 CHI	7	8 DET	9 MON
10	11 DAL	12	13 BOS	14	15 BUF	16 WAS
17	18 WAS	19	20	21 PHI	22 HAR	23
24	25	26 OTT	27	28 VAN	29	30 EDM
31 CAL						

JANUARY

SUN	MON	TUE	WED	THU	FRI	SAT
	1	2	3 MON	4	5 WAS	6
7	8 WAS	9	10 SJ	11	12	13 D PHI
14 STL	15	16	17	18	19	20 *
21	22 LA	23	24 PHI	25	26	27 D BOS
28	29	30	31 DAL			

FEBRUARY

SUN	MON	TUE	WED	THU	FRI	SAT
				1	2	3 D COL
4	5	6 NYI	7	8 NYI	9	10 D NJ
11 D TB	12	13	14	15 MON	16	17 OTT
18 PIT	19	20	21	22 NYI	23	24 FLA
25	26	27	28 BOS	29		

MARCH

SUN	MON	TUE	WED	THU	FRI	SAT
				1 BUF		2
3	4 NJ	5	6	7 TB	8	9 D WAS
10	11	12	13 FLA	14	15	16 MON
17	18	19 EDM	20	21	22	23 D BOS
24 PIT	25	26	27 FLA	28	29	30
31 D NYI						

APRIL

SUN	MON	TUE	WED	THU	FRI	SAT
	1	2 NJ	3	4 PHI	5 PHI	6
7 D NJ	8 FLA	9	10 WAS	11	12 TB	13
14 D FLA	15	16	17	18	19	20

1995-96 SEASON

CLUB DIRECTORY

President and general manager
Neil Smith
Governor
Chuck Dolan
Alternate NHL governors
Rand Araskog
Ken Munoz
Neil Smith
Vice president, general counsel
Ken Munoz
Vice president of marketing
Kevin Kennedy
Director of communications
To be announced
Director of administration
John Gentile
Assistant G.M., player development
Larry Pleau
Coach
Colin Campbell
Assistant coaches
Mike Murphy
Dick Todd

Scouting staff
Darwin Bennett
Tony Feltrin
Herb Hammond
Martin Madden
Christer Rockstrom
Scouting manager
Bill Short
Director of team operations
Matthew Loughran
Asst. director of communications
John Rosasco
Public relations assistant
Rob Koch
Team physician and orthopedic surgeon
Barton Nisonson, M.D.
Medical trainer
Jim Ramsay
Equipment trainer
Joe Murphy

DRAFT CHOICES

Rd.—Player	H/W	Overall	Pos.	Last team
2—Christian Dube	5-11/170	39	C	Sherbrooke (QMJHL)
3—Mike Martin	6-2/204	65	D	Windsor (OHL)
4—Marc Savard	5-10/174	91	C	Oshawa (OHL)
5—Alexei Vasiljev	6-1/189	110	D	Yaroslavl, CIS
5—Dale Purinton	6-1/201	117	D	Tacoma (WHL)
6—Peter Slamiar	5-11/174	143	RW	Zvolen Jrs., Slovakia
7—Jeff Heil		169	G	Wisconsin-River Falls
8—Ilja Gorchov	6-0/172	195	D	Yaroslavl, CIS
9—Bob Maudie	5-11/180	221	C	Kamloops (WHL)

MISCELLANEOUS DATA

Home ice (capacity)
Madison Square Garden (18,200)
Address
4 Pennsylvania Plaza
New York, NY 10001
Business phone
212-465-6000
Rink dimensions
200 feet by 85 feet

Club colors
Blue, red and white
Radio affiliation
WFAN (660 AM)
TV affiliation
MSG Network

No.	FORWARDS	Ht./Wt.	Place	Born Date	NHL exp.	1994-95 clubs
	Chris Ferraro (RW)	5-10/175	Port Jefferson, N.Y.	1-24-73	0	Atlanta (IHL), Binghamton (AHL)
	Peter Ferraro (C)	5-10/175	Port Jefferson, N.Y.	1-24-73	0	Atlanta (IHL), Binghamton (AHL)
	Ray Ferraro (C)	5-10/186	Trail, B.C.	8-23-64	11	New York Islanders
9	Adam Graves (LW)	6-0/207	Toronto	4-12-68	8	New York Rangers
26	Joey Kocur (RW)	6-0/201	Calgary	12-21-64	11	New York Rangers
27	Alexei Kovalev (RW)	6-0/200	Moscow, U.S.S.R.	2-24-73	3	Lada Togliatti (CIS), New York Rangers
19	Nick Kypreos (LW)	6-0/195	Toronto	6-4-66	6	New York Rangers
25	Nathan LaFayette (C)	6-1/195	New Westminster, B.C.	2-17-73	2	Syracuse (AHL), Vancouver, New York Rangers
	Darren Langdon (LW)	6-1/200	Deer Lake, Nfld.	1-8-71	1	Binghamton (AHL), New York Rangers
28	Steve Larmer (RW)	5-11/185	Peterborough, Ont.	6-16-61	15	New York Rangers
32	Stephane Matteau (LW)	6-3/210	Rouyn, Que.	9-2-69	5	New York Rangers
11	Mark Messier (C)	6-1/210	Edmonton	1-18-61	16	New York Rangers
10	Petr Nedved (C)	6-3/195	Liberec, Czechoslovakia	12-9-71	5	New York Rangers
13	Sergei Nemchinov (C)	6-0/210	Moscow, U.S.S.R.	1-14-64	4	New York Rangers
	Jeff Nielsen (RW)	6-0/170	Grand Rapids, Minn.	9-20-71	0	Binghamton (AHL)
	Wayne Presley (RW)	5-11/180	Dearborn, Mich.	3-23-65	11	Buffalo
	Dimitri Starostenko (RW)	6-0/185	Minsk, U.S.S.R.	3-18-73	0	Binghamton (AHL)
	Niklas Sundstrom (LW)	5-11/183	Ornskoldsvik, Sweden	6-6-75	0	MoDo Hockey Ornskoldvik (Sweden)
16	Pat Verbeek (RW)	5-9/190	Sarnia, Ont.	5-24-64	13	Hartford, New York Rangers
	Rudolf Vercik (LW)	6-1/189	Bratislava, Czech.	3-19-76	0	Slovan Bratislava (Slovakia)
	DEFENSEMEN					
23	Jeff Beukeboom	6-5/225	Ajax, Ont.	3-28-65	10	New York Rangers
	Eric Cairns	6-6/217	Oakville, Ont.	6-27-74	0	Binghamton (AHL), Birmingham (ECHL)
	Maxim Galanov	6-1/167	Krasnoyarsk, U.S.S.R.	3-13-74	0	Lada Togliatti (CIS)
25	Alexander Karpovtsev	6-1/210	Moscow, U.S.S.R.	4-7-70	2	Dynamo Moscow (CIS), New York Rangers
2	Brian Leetch	5-11/195	Corpus Christi, Tex.	3-3-68	8	New York Rangers
	Doug Lidster	6-1/201	Kamloops, B.C.	10-18-60	12	St. Louis
4	Kevin Lowe	6-2/195	Lachute, Que.	4-15-59	16	New York Rangers
	Mike Martin	6-2/204	Stratford, Ont.	10-27-76	0	Windsor (OHL)
5	Mattias Norstrom	6-1/205	Stockholm, Sweden	1-2-72	2	Binghamton (AHL), New York Rangers
3	Barry Richter	6-2/203	Madison, Wis.	9-11-70	0	Binghamton (AHL)
21	Sergei Zubov	6-1/200	Moscow, U.S.S.R.	7-22-70	3	New York Rangers
	GOALTENDERS					
	Dan Cloutier	6-1/182	Mont-Laurier, Que.	4-22-76	0	Sault Ste. Marie (OHL)
30	Glenn Healy	5-10/183	Pickering, Ont.	8-23-62	9	New York Rangers
	Jamie Ram	5-11/175	Scarborough, Ont.	1-18-71	0	Binghamton (AHL)
35	Mike Richter	5-11/182	Philadelphia	9-22-66	7	New York Rangers

1994-95 REVIEW

INDIVIDUAL STATISTICS

SCORING

	Games	G	A	Pts.	PIM	+/-	PPG	SHG	Shots	Shooting Pct.
Mark Messier	46	14	39	53	40	8	3	3	126	11.1
Brian Leetch	48	9	32	41	18	0	3	0	182	4.9
Sergei Zubov	38	10	26	36	18	-2	6	0	116	8.6
Adam Graves	47	17	14	31	51	9	9	0	185	9.2
Steve Larmer	47	14	15	29	16	8	3	1	116	12.1
Alexei Kovalev	48	13	15	28	30	-6	1	1	103	12.6
Brian Noonan	45	14	13	27	26	-3	7	0	95	14.7
Petr Nedved	46	11	12	23	26	-1	1	0	123	8.9
Pat Verbeek*	19	10	5	15	18	-2	4	0	56	17.9
Sergei Nemchinov	47	7	6	13	16	-6	0	0	67	10.4
Alexander Karpovtsev	47	4	8	12	30	-4	1	0	82	4.9
Jay Wells	43	2	7	9	36	0	0	0	38	5.3
Stephane Matteau	41	3	5	8	25	-8	0	0	37	8.1
Kevin Lowe	44	1	7	8	58	-2	1	0	35	2.9
Mark Osborne	37	1	3	4	19	-2	0	0	32	3.1
Nick Kypreos	40	1	3	4	93	0	0	0	16	6.3
Jeff Beukeboom	44	1	3	4	70	3	0	0	29	3.4
Ed Olczyk*	20	2	1	3	4	-2	1	0	29	6.9
Joey Kocur	48	1	2	3	71	-4	0	0	25	4.0
Mattias Norstrom	9	0	3	3	2	2	0	0	4	0.0
Darren Langdon	18	1	1	2	62	0	0	0	6	16.7

	Games	G	A	Pts.	PIM	+/-	PPG	SHG	Shots	Shooting Pct.
Joby Messier	10	0	2	2	18	2	0	0	4	0.0
Glenn Healy (goalie)	17	0	2	2	2	0	0	0	0	0.0
Jean-Yves Roy	3	1	0	1	2	-1	0	0	8	12.5
Shawn McCosh	5	1	0	1	2	1	0	0	2	50.0
Glen Featherstone*	6	1	0	1	18	0	0	0	6	16.7
Mike Hartman	1	0	0	0	4	0	0	0	0	0.0
Dan Lacroix*	1	0	0	0	0	0	0	0	0	0.0
Troy Loney*	4	0	0	0	0	-2	0	0	2	0.0
Nathan Lafayette*	12	0	0	0	0	1	0	0	5	0.0
Mike Richter (goalie)	35	0	0	0	2	0	0	0	0	0.0

GOALTENDING

	Games	Min.	Goals	SO	Avg.	W	L	T	Shots	Sv. Pct.
Glenn Healy	17	888	35	1	2.36	8	6	1	377	.907
Mike Richter	35	1993	97	2	2.92	14	17	2	884	.890

Empty-net goals (do not count against a goaltender's average): Richter 2.
*Played with two or more NHL teams.

RESULTS

JANUARY
20—Buffalo	L	1-2
21—Montreal	W	5-2
23—Boston	L	1-2
25—Pittsburgh	L	2-3
28—At Quebec	L	0-2
30—Ottawa	W	6-2

FEBRUARY
1—At Pittsburgh	L	3-4
2—Tampa Bay	T	*3-3
4—At Ottawa	W	2-1
8—Washington	W	5-4
9—At New Jersey	L	1-4
11—At Tampa Bay	W	3-2
15—At Buffalo	W	2-1
16—Montreal	T	*2-2
18—At Montreal	L	2-5
20—At Tampa Bay	W	3-1
21—At Florida	W	5-3
24—Hartford	L	1-2

26—At Buffalo	W	4-2
28—Florida	T	*0-0

MARCH
1—At Hartford	W	5-2
3—Philadelphia	W	5-3
5—At Washington	L	2-4
6—Ottawa	W	4-3
8—New Jersey	W	6-4
11—At Montreal	L	1-3
15—Philadelphia	L	3-4
18—At Washington	L	1-4
22—New Jersey	L	2-5
23—At N.Y. Islanders	L	0-1
25—At Quebec	L	1-2
30—Quebec	L	4-5

APRIL
1—At Boston	W	3-2
2—At Philadelphia	L	2-4
5—At Florida	W	5-0

7—N.Y. Islanders	L	3-4
9—At New Jersey	L	0-2
12—Buffalo	W	3-1
14—Boston	W	5-3
16—At N.Y. Islanders	W	3-2
18—At Pittsburgh	L	5-6
20—Hartford	W	3-2
23—At Boston	L	4-5
24—Washington	W	5-4
26—Tampa Bay	W	6-4
28—N.Y. Islanders	L	2-4
30—At Philadelphia	W	2-0

MAY
2—Florida	L	3-4

*Denotes overtime game.

OTTAWA SENATORS
EASTERN CONFERENCE/NORTHEAST DIVISION

1995-96 SCHEDULE

Home games shaded.
* — All-Star Game at FleetCenter, Boston.
D — Day game.

OCTOBER

SUN	MON	TUE	WED	THU	FRI	SAT
1	2	3	4	5	6	7 BUF
8	9	10	11	12	13 FLA	14
15 TB	16	17	18	19 CAL	20	21 NJ
22 NYR	23	24 DET	25	26 LA	27	28 D FLA
29 PHI	30	31				

NOVEMBER

SUN	MON	TUE	WED	THU	FRI	SAT
			1	2 HAR	3	4 HAR
5	6	7	8 PIT	9 BOS	10	11 D ANA
12	13	14	15 HAR	16 PHI	17	18 MON
19 BUF	20	21	22 WIN	23	24	25 BOS
26	27	28 PIT	29	30 NYI		

DECEMBER

SUN	MON	TUE	WED	THU	FRI	SAT
					1	2 NYR
3	4	5 TOR	6	7 CHI	8	9 COL
10	11	12 SJ	13 LA	14	15 ANA	16
17 D VAN	18 EDM	19	20	21	22	23 BUF
24	25	26 NYR	27 BUF	28	29	30 MON
31 TB						

JANUARY

SUN	MON	TUE	WED	THU	FRI	SAT
	1	2	3 PIT	4	5 HAR	6 NYI
7	8	9	10 WAS	11	12	13 TB
14	15	16	17 MON	18	19	20 *
21	22 CHI	23	24 PIT	25 DET	26	27 TOR
28	29 STL	30	31 BOS			

FEBRUARY

SUN	MON	TUE	WED	THU	FRI	SAT
				1 WAS	2	3 NJ
4	5	6 CAL	7	8 WIN	9	10 MON
11	12 NYI	13	14	15 SJ	16	17 NYR
18	19	20 STL	21	22 DAL	23	24
25 COL	26	27	28 BUF	29		

MARCH

SUN	MON	TUE	WED	THU	FRI	SAT
					1 PHI	2 NJ
3	4	5	6	7 PIT	8	9 MON
10	11	12	13 DAL	14	15 VAN	16
17 D TB	18	19 FLA	20	21 BOS	22 HAR	23
24 EDM	25	26	27 PHI	28	29 WAS	30 MON
31						

APRIL

SUN	MON	TUE	WED	THU	FRI	SAT
	1 BOS	2	3 FLA	4	5 NYI	6 WAS
7	8	9	10 BUF	11 PIT	12	13 D NJ
14	15	16	17	18	19	20

1995-96 SEASON

CLUB DIRECTORY

Chairman, governor, and CEO
Rod Bryden
President, G.M., and alt. governor
Randy J. Sexton
Senior V.P., commercial operations and CFO
Bernie Ashe
Assistant general manager
Ray Shero
Head coach
Rick Bowness
Assistant coaches
Alain Vigneault
Chico Resch
Director of player personnel
John Ferguson
Athletic trainer
Conrad Lackten

Assistant trainer
John Gervais
Head equipment trainer
Ed Georgica
Executive secretary to the president
Allison Vaughan
Vice president of marketing
Jim Steel
Vice president of sales
Mark Bonneau
Director of media relations
Laurent Benoit
Media relations assistant
Dominick Saillant

DRAFT CHOICES

Rd. — Player	H/W	Overall	Pos.	Last team
1 — Bryan Berard	6-1/190	1	D	Detroit (OHL)
2 — Marc Moro	6-0/209	27	D	Kingston (OHL)
3 — Brad Larsen	5-11/198	53	LW	Swift Current (WHL)
4 — Kevin Bolibruck	6-1/197	89	D	Peterborough (OHL)
4 — Kevin Boyd	6-2/201	103	LW	London (OHL)
6 — David Hruska	6-0/189	131	RW	Sokolov, Czech Republic
8 — Kaj Linna	6-2/210	183	D	Boston University
8 — Ray Schultz	6-1/200	184	D	Tri-City (WHL)
9 — Erik Kasminski		231		Cleveland (Jr. A)

MISCELLANEOUS DATA

Home ice (capacity)
Ottawa Civic Centre (10,575)
Note: The Senators will play in the
Palladium (18,500), beginning in
January, 1996.
Address
301 Moodie Drive
Nepean, Ont. K2H 9C4
Business phone
613-721-0115

Rink dimensions
200 feet by 85 feet
Club colors
Black, red and gold
Radio affiliation
CFRA (580 AM, English)
CJRC (1150 AM, French)
TV affiliation
CHRO (English)

TRAINING CAMP ROSTER

No.	FORWARDS	Ht./Wt.	Place	BORN Date	NHL exp.	1994-95 clubs
15	Dave Archibald (C/LW)	6-1/211	Chilliwack, B.C.	4-14-69	6	Ottawa
10	Claude Boivin (LW)	6-2/200	St. Foy, Que.	3-1-70	4	Prince Edward Island (AHL), Ottawa
76	Radek Bonk (C)	6-3/216	Kronov, Czechoslovakia	1-9-76	1	Las Vegas (IHL), Ottawa, Prince Edward Island (AHL)
29	Phil Bourque (LW)	6-1/196	Chelmsford, Mass.	6-8-62	11	Ottawa
7	Randy Cunneyworth (LW)	6-0/193	Etobicoke, Ont.	5-10-61	12	Ottawa
91	Alexandre Daigle (C)	6-0/184	Montreal	2-7-75	2	Victoriaville (QMJHL), Ottawa
78	Pavol Demitra (LW)	6-0/184	Dubnica, Czechoslovakia	11-29-74	2	Prince Edward Island (AHL), Ottawa
25	Pat Elynuik (RW)	6-1/192	Foam Lake, Sask.	10-30-67	8	Ottawa
	Bruce Gardiner (C)	6-1/185	Barrie, Ont.	2-11-71	0	Prince Edward Island (AHL)
10	Rob Gaudreau (RW)	5-11/185	Cranston, R.I.	1-20-70	3	Ottawa
	Daniel Guerard (RW)	6-4/215	La Salle, Que.	4-9-74	1	Prince Edward Island (AHL), Ottawa
74	Steve Larouche (C)	6-0/184	Rouyn, Que.	4-14-71	1	Prince Edward Island (AHL), Ottawa
26	Scott Levins (C/RW)	6-4/216	Portland, Ore.	1-30-70	3	Ottawa, Prince Edward Island (AHL)
18	Troy Mallette (LW)	6-2/214	Sudbury, Ont.	2-25-70	6	Ottawa, Prince Edward Island (AHL)
17	David McLlwain (C/RW)	6-0/185	Seaforth, Ont.	1-9-67	8	Ottawa
	Chad Penney (LW)	6-0/195	Labrador City, Nfld.	9-18-73	1	Prince Edward Island (AHL)
44	Michel Picard (LW)	5-11/190	Beauport, Que.	11-7-69	4	Prince Edward Island (AHL), Ottawa
	Dan Quinn (C/RW)	5-11/182	Ottawa	6-1-65	12	Zug (Switzerland), Los Angeles
	Claude Savoie (RW)	5-11/200	Montreal	3-12-73	0	Prince Edward Island (AHL)
82	Martin Straka (C)	5-10/180	Plzen, Czechoslovakia	9-3-72	3	Pittsburgh, Ottawa
	Antti Tormannen (RW)	6-1/190	Espoo, Finland	9-19-70	0	Jokerit (Finland)
61	Sylvain Turgeon (LW)	6-0/195	Noranda, Que.	1-17-65	12	Ottawa
19	Alexei Yashin (C)	6-3/216	Sverdlovsk, U.S.S.R.	11-5-73	2	Las Vegas (IHL), Ottawa
	DEFENSEMEN					
	Bryan Berard	6-1/195	Woonsocket, R.I.	3-5-77	0	Detroit (OHL)
	Radim Bicanek	6-1/195	Uherske Hradiste, Czech.	1-18-75	1	Belleville (OHL), Ottawa, Prince Edward Island (AHL)
6	Chris Dahlquist	6-1/196	Fridley, Minn.	12-14-62	10	Ottawa
	Steve Duchesne	5-11/195	Sept-Iles, Que.	6-30-65	9	St. Louis
3	Sean Hill	6-0/196	Duluth, Minn.	2-14-70	5	Ottawa
5	Kerry Huffman	6-2/214	Peterborough, Ont.	1-3-68	9	Ottawa
41	Dan Laperriere	6-1/180	Laval, Que.	3-28-69	3	Peoria (IHL), St. Louis, Ottawa
	Jaroslav Modry	6-2/195	Ceske-Budejovice, Czech.	2-27-71	2	HC Ceske Budejovice (Czech.), New Jersey, Albany (AHL)
94	Stan Neckar	6-0/196	Ceske-Budejovice, Czech.	12-22-75	1	Detroit (IHL), Ottawa
2	Jim Paek	6-1/200	Seoul, South Korea	4-7-67	5	Ottawa
	Lance Pitlick	6-0/190	Fridley, Minn.	11-5-67	1	Prince Edward Island (AHL), Ottawa
	Patrick Traverse	6-3/200	Montreal	3-14-74	0	Prince Edward Island (AHL)
21	Dennis Vial	6-1/222	Sault Ste. Marie, Ont.	4-10-69	5	Ottawa
	GOALTENDERS					
30	Mike Bales	6-1/180	Saskatoon, Sask.	8-6-71	2	Prince Edward Island (AHL), Ottawa
31	Don Beaupre	5-10/172	Kitchener, Ont.	9-19-61	15	Ottawa
	Jean-Francois Labbe	5-9/170	Sherbrooke, Quebec	6-15-72	0	Prince Edward Island (AHL)
30	Darrin Madeley	5-11/168	Holland Landing, Ont.	2-25-68	3	Ottawa, Prince Edward Island (AHL), Detroit (IHL)

1994-95 REVIEW

INDIVIDUAL STATISTICS

SCORING

	Games	G	A	Pts.	PIM	+/-	PPG	SHG	Shots	Shooting Pct.
Alexei Yashin	47	21	23	44	20	-20	11	0	154	13.6
Alexandre Daigle	47	16	21	37	14	-22	4	1	105	15.2
Sylvain Turgeon	33	11	8	19	29	-1	2	0	83	13.3
Steve Larouche	18	8	7	15	6	-5	2	0	38	21.1
Sean Hill	45	1	14	15	30	-11	0	0	107	0.9
Rob Gaudreau	36	5	9	14	8	-16	0	0	65	7.7
Troy Murray*	33	4	10	14	16	-1	0	0	38	10.5
Michel Picard	24	5	8	13	14	-1	1	0	33	15.2
Scott Levins	24	5	6	11	51	4	0	0	34	14.7
Dave McLlwain	43	5	6	11	22	-26	1	0	48	10.4
Norm Maciver*	28	4	7	11	10	-9	2	0	30	13.3
Radek Bonk	42	3	8	11	28	-5	1	0	40	7.5
Randy Cunneyworth	48	5	5	10	68	-19	2	0	71	7.0
Pat Elynuik	41	3	7	10	51	-11	0	0	58	5.2
Troy Mallette	23	3	5	8	35	6	0	0	21	14.3
Chris Dahlquist	46	1	7	8	36	-30	1	0	45	2.2
Pavol Demitra	16	4	3	7	0	-4	1	0	21	19.0
Phil Bourque	38	4	3	7	20	-17	0	0	34	11.8

	Games	G	A	Pts.	PIM	+/-	PPG	SHG	Shots	Shooting Pct.
Kerry Huffman	37	2	4	6	46	-17	2	0	68	2.9
David Archibald	14	2	2	4	19	-7	0	0	27	7.4
Stanislav Neckar	48	1	3	4	37	-20	0	0	34	2.9
Dennis Vial	27	0	4	4	65	0	0	0	9	0.0
Evgeny Davydov	3	1	2	3	0	2	0	0	2	50.0
Martin Straka*	6	1	1	2	0	-1	0	0	13	7.7
Daniel Laperriere*	13	1	1	2	0	-4	1	0	18	5.6
Bill Huard*	26	1	1	2	64	-2	0	0	15	6.7
Jim Paek	29	0	2	2	28	-5	0	0	16	0.0
Claude Boivin	3	0	1	1	6	-1	0	0	0	0.0
Lance Pitlick	15	0	1	1	6	-5	0	0	11	0.0
Mike Bales (goalie)	1	0	0	0	0	0	0	0	0	0.0
Daniel Guerard	2	0	0	0	0	0	0	0	0	0.0
Brad Shaw	2	0	0	0	0	3	0	0	3	0.0
Darrin Madeley (goalie)	5	0	0	0	0	0	0	0	0	0.0
Radim Bicanek	6	0	0	0	0	3	0	0	6	0.0
Craig Billington* (goalie)	9	0	0	0	2	0	0	0	0	0.0
Don Beaupre (goalie)	38	0	0	0	10	0	0	0	0	0.0

GOALTENDING

	Games	Min.	Goals	SO	Avg.	W	L	T	Shots	Sv. Pct.
Mike Bales	1	3	0	0	.00	0	0	0	1	1.000
Don Beaupre	38	2161	121	1	3.36	8	†25	3	1167	.896
Darrin Madeley	5	255	15	0	3.53	1	3	0	147	.898
Craig Billington*	9	472	32	0	4.07	0	6	2	240	.867

Empty-net goals (do not count against a goaltender's average): Beaupre 3, Billington 2, Madeley 1.
*Played with two or more NHL teams.
†Led league.

RESULTS

JANUARY
22—At N.Y. Islanders	T	*3-3
25—At Hartford	L	1-4
27—At Pittsburgh	L	4-5
28—Buffalo	T	*2-2
30—At N.Y. Rangers	L	2-6

FEBRUARY
1—Hartford	L	1-2
2—At Boston	L	4-6
4—N.Y. Rangers	L	1-2
6—Philadelphia	W	3-0
8—Montreal	L	2-4
11—At Quebec	L	2-5
15—At Florida	L	0-2
17—At Tampa Bay	W	2-1
23—Washington	T	*5-5
25—Florida	L	1-4
27—Boston	L	0-2
28—Hartford	L	3-6

MARCH
2—Tampa Bay	L	*2-3
5—N.Y. Islanders	W	3-1
6—At N.Y. Rangers	L	3-4
8—At Florida	L	2-3
10—At Washington	T	*2-2
14—At New Jersey	L	2-4
16—Philadelphia	L	1-3
18—Buffalo	W	*4-3
19—Pittsburgh	L	3-4
21—At Washington	L	0-1
25—At Montreal	L	1-3
26—Quebec	L	4-11
29—New Jersey	L	2-4
30—At Buffalo	L	0-7

APRIL
2—At Quebec	L	5-7
3—Montreal	L	4-5
5—New Jersey	L	0-2

8—Quebec	T	*2-2
10—Pittsburgh	L	3-4
12—At Hartford	L	2-4
15—At Pittsburgh	L	2-5
16—At Buffalo	L	1-2
19—At Montreal	L	1-4
20—Boston	L	5-6
22—At N.Y. Islanders	W	3-2
24—Florida	L	1-5
26—At Philadelphia	W	5-2
27—Tampa Bay	W	6-1
29—N.Y. Islanders	W	4-3

MAY
| 1—At Boston | L | 4-5 |
| 3—At Tampa Bay | W | 4-3 |

*Denotes overtime game.

PHILADELPHIA FLYERS
EASTERN CONFERENCE/ATLANTIC DIVISION

Home games shaded.
* — All-Star Game at FleetCenter, Boston.
D — Day game.

OCTOBER

SUN	MON	TUE	WED	THU	FRI	SAT
1	2	3	4	5	6	7 MON
8	9	10	11 WAS	12	13	14 NYI
15 EDM	16	17	18 LA	19	20 ANA	21
22 CHI	23	24	25 NYI	26	27	28 NYI
29 OTT	30	31 TB				

NOVEMBER

SUN	MON	TUE	WED	THU	FRI	SAT
			1	2 FLA	3	4 PIT
5 HAR	6	7 FLA	8	9 CAL	10	11 D NJ
12 D NJ	13	14 WAS	15	16 OTT	17	18 D HAR
19 VAN	20	21 LA	22	23	24 D DET	25
26	27	28	29 FLA	30 TOR		

DECEMBER

SUN	MON	TUE	WED	THU	FRI	SAT
					1	2
3 BOS	4	5 DET	6	7 BUF	8	9
10 NYI	11	12	13	14 TB	15	16 MON
17 PIT	18	19 NJ	20	21 NYR	22	23 HAR
24	25	26	27 EDM	28	29 CAL	30
31 D VAN						

JANUARY

SUN	MON	TUE	WED	THU	FRI	SAT
	1	2	3 SJ	4 COL	5	6
7	8	9 ANA	10	11 STL	12	13 D NYR
14	15 DAL	16	17	18	19	20 *
21	22 FLA	23	24 NYR	25	26	27 D PIT
28 D WAS	29	30	31			

FEBRUARY

SUN	MON	TUE	WED	THU	FRI	SAT
				1 MON	2	3 D STL
4	5	6	7	8 BUF	9	10 D BOS
11 COL	12	13	14 FLA	15	16	17 TB
18	19 D WAS	20	21	22 WAS	23 BUF	24
25 CHI	26	27	28 DAL	29		

MARCH

SUN	MON	TUE	WED	THU	FRI	SAT
					1 OTT	2
3 D WAS	4	5	6	7	8	9 D BOS
10 NJ	11	12	13 TB	14	15	16 WIN
17 SJ	18	19 NYI	20	21	22 WIN	23 TOR
24	25 HAR	26	27 OTT	28	29 BUF	30
31 D PIT						

APRIL

SUN	MON	TUE	WED	THU	FRI	SAT
	1	2 NYI	3	4 NYR	5 NYR	6
7 D BOS	8	9	10 NJ	11 MON	12	13
14 D TB	15	16	17	18	19	20

CLUB DIRECTORY

Chairman of the exec. committee/owner
Edward M. Snider
President and general manager
Bob Clarke
Chairman of the board emeritus
Joseph C. Scott
Executive vice president
Keith Allen
Chief operating officer
Ron Ryan
Assistant general manager
John Blackwell
Vice president, finance
Dan Clemmens
Coach
Terry Murray
Assistant coaches
Keith Acton
Tom Webster
Goaltending coach
Rejean Lemelin
Director of pro scouting
Bill Barber
Chief scout
Jerry Melnyk

Scouts
Inge Hammarstrom
Vaclav Slansky
Simon Nolet
Dennis Patterson
Bill Dineen
Evgeny Zimin
Vice president, public relations
Mark Piazza
Ticket manager
Ceil Baker
Vice president, sales
Jack Betson
Director of team services
Joe Kadlec
Medical trainer
John Worley
Head trainer
Dave Settlemyre
Trainers
Jim Evers
Harry Bricker
Derek Settlemyre
Orthopedic surgeon
Arthur Bartolozzi

DRAFT CHOICES

Rd. — Player	H/W	Overall	Pos.	Last team
1 — Brian Boucher	6-1/180	22	G	Tri-City (WHL)
2 — Shane Kenny	6-2/242	48	D	Owen Sound (OHL)
4 — Radovan Somik	6-2/194	100	RW	ZTS Martin, Slovakia
6 — Dmitri Tertyshny	6-1/176	132	D	Chelybinsk, CIS
6 — Jamie Sokolsky	6-2/201	135	D	Belleville (OHL)
6 — Martin Spahnel	6-2/187	152	LW	Zlin Jrs., Czech Rep.
7 — Martin Streit	6-2/191	178	RW	HC Olomouc, Czech Rep.
8 — Ruslan Shafikov	5-10/176	204	C	Salavat Yulayev, CIS
9 — Jeff Lank	6-3/200	230	D	Prince Albert (WHL)

MISCELLANEOUS DATA

Home ice (capacity)
The Spectrum (17,380)
Address
CoreStates Spectrum
3601 S. Broad Street
Philadelphia, PA 19148
Business phone
215-465-4500
Rink dimensions
200 feet by 85 feet

Club colors
Orange, white and black
Radio affiliation
WIP-AM (610 AM)
TV affiliation
WPHL-TV (Channel 17), Prism
(Cable), Sports Channel
Philadelphia (Cable)

FORWARDS

No.	FORWARDS	Ht./Wt.	Place	Date	NHL exp.	1994-95 clubs
				BORN		
36	Shawn Anderson (D/LW)	6-1/200	Montreal	2-7-68	8	Hershey (AHL), Philadelphia
18	Shawn Antoski (LW/RW)	6-4/235	Brantford, Ont.	5-25-70	5	Vancouver, Philadelphia
17	Rod Brind'Amour (C/LW) .	6-1/200	Ottawa	8-9-70	7	Philadelphia
21	Dave Brown (RW)	6-5/222	Saskatoon, Sask.	10-12-62	13	Philadelphia
23	Phil Crowe (LW)	6-2/220	Red Deer, Alta.	4-14-70	1	Hershey (AHL)
20	Rob DiMaio (C)	5-10/190	Calgary	2-19-68	7	Philadelphia
11	Kevin Dineen (RW)	5-11/190	Quebec City	10-28-63	11	Houston (IHL), Philadelphia
45	Gilbert Dionne (LW)	6-0/205	Drummondville, Que.	9-19-70	5	Montreal, Philadelphia
	Yanick Dupre (LW)	6-0/192	Montreal	11-20-72	2	Hershey (AHL), Philadelphia
36	Andre Faust (C)	6-1/190	Joliette, Que.	10-7-69	2	Hershey (AHL)
18	Brent Fedyk (LW)	6-0/196	Yorkton, Sask.	3-8-67	8	Philadelphia
	Patrik Juhlin (LW)	6-0/187	Huddinge, Sweden	4-24-70	1	Vasteras (Sweden), Philadelphia
17	John LeClair (C)	6-2/220	St. Albans, Vt.	7-5-69	5	Montreal, Philadelphia
88	Eric Lindros (C)	6-4/229	London, Ont.	2-28-73	3	Philadelphia
14	Craig MacTavish (C)	6-1/195	London, Ont.	8-15-58	16	Philadelphia
	Jim Montgomery (C)	5-9/180	Montreal	6-30-69	2	Montreal, Philadelphia, Hershey (AHL)
	Joel Otto (C)	6-4/220	Elk River, Minn.	10-29-61	11	Calgary
26	Shjon Podein (LW)	6-2/200	Rochester, Minn.	3-5-68	3	Philadelphia
19	Mikael Renberg (LW)	6-2/218	Pitea, Sweden	5-5-72	2	Lulea (Sweden), Philadelphia
20	Anatoli Semenov (C/LW)	6-2/190	Moscow, U.S.S.R.	3-5-62	6	Anaheim, Philadelphia
	Ryan Sittler (LW/C)	6-2/185	London, Ont.	1-28-74	0	Hershey (AHL), Johnstown (ECHL)
40	Chris Winnes (RW)	6-0/170	Ridgefield, Conn.	2-12-68	4	Hershey (AHL)

DEFENSEMEN

No.	DEFENSEMEN	Ht./Wt.	Place	Date	NHL exp.	1994-95 clubs
28	Jason Bowen	6-4/208	Courtenay, B.C.	11-11-73	3	Hershey (AHL), Philadelphia
	Aris Brimanis	6-3/195	Cleveland	3-14-72	1	Hershey (AHL)
28	Eric Desjardins	6-1/200	Rouyn, Que.	6-14-69	7	Montreal, Philadelphia
45	Karl Dykhuis	6-3/195	Sept-Iles, Que.	7-8-72	3	Indianapolis (IHL), Hershey (AHL)
14	Kevin Haller	6-2/183	Trochu, Alta.	12-5-70	6	Philadelphia
	Dan Kordic	6-5/220	Edmonton	4-18-71	2	Hershey (AHL)
23	Stewart Malgunas	6-0/200	Prince George, B.C.	4-21-70	2	Hershey (AHL), Philadelphia
	Kjell Samuelsson	6-6/233	Tyngsryd, Sweden	10-18-58	10	Pittsburgh
7	Petr Svoboda	6-1/175	Most, Czechoslovakia	2-14-66	11	Chemopetrol Litvinov (Czech Rep.), Buffalo, Philadelphia
	Chris Therien	6-4/230	Ottawa	12-14-71	1	Hershey (AHL), Philadelphia
2	Dimitri Yushkevich	5-11/208	Yaroslavl, U.S.S.R.	11-19-71	3	Torpedo Yaroslavl (CIS), Philadelphia

GOALTENDERS

No.	GOALTENDERS	Ht./Wt.	Place	Date	NHL exp.	1994-95 clubs
72	Ron Hextall	6-3/192	Winnipeg	5-3-64	9	Philadelphia
	Les Kuntar	6-2/195	Buffalo, N.Y.	7-28-69	1	Worcester (AHL), Hershey (AHL)
33	Dominic Roussel	6-1/190	Hull, Que.	2-22-70	4	Philadelphia, Hershey (AHL)
	Garth Snow	6-3/200	Wrentham, Mass.	7-28-69	2	Cornwall (AHL), Quebec

1994-95 REVIEW

INDIVIDUAL STATISTICS

SCORING

	Games	G	A	Pts.	PIM	+/-	PPG	SHG	Shots	Shooting Pct.
Eric Lindros	46	29	41	‡70	60	27	7	0	144	20.1
Mikael Renberg	47	26	31	57	20	20	8	0	143	18.2
John LeClair*	37	25	24	49	20	21	5	0	113	22.1
Rod Brind'Amour	48	12	27	39	33	-4	4	1	86	14.0
Eric Desjardins*	34	5	18	23	12	10	1	0	79	6.3
Garry Galley*	33	2	20	22	20	0	1	0	66	3.0
Dimitri Yushkevich	40	5	9	14	47	-4	3	1	80	6.3
Kevin Dineen	40	8	5	13	39	-1	4	0	55	14.5
Chris Therien	48	3	10	13	38	8	1	0	53	5.7
Brent Fedyk	30	8	4	12	14	-2	3	0	41	19.5
Craig MacTavish	45	3	9	12	23	2	0	0	38	7.9
Josef Beranek*	14	5	5	10	2	3	1	0	39	12.8
Shjon Podein	44	3	7	10	33	-2	0	0	48	6.3
Kevin Haller	36	2	8	10	48	16	0	0	26	7.7
Karl Dykhuis	33	2	6	8	37	7	1	0	46	4.3
Patrik Juhlin	42	4	3	7	6	-13	0	0	44	9.1
Gilbert Dionne*	20	0	6	6	2	-1	0	0	29	0.0
Mark Recchi*	10	2	3	5	12	-6	1	0	17	11.8
Rob DiMaio	36	3	1	4	53	8	0	0	34	8.8
Anatoli Semenov*	26	1	2	3	6	-2	0	0	36	2.8
Dave Brown	28	1	2	3	53	-1	0	0	8	12.5
Petr Svoboda*	11	0	3	3	10	0	0	0	17	0.0
Jim Montgomery*	8	1	1	2	6	-2	0	0	10	10.0

	Games	G	A	Pts.	PIM	+/-	PPG	SHG	Shots	Shooting Pct.
Mark Lamb*	8	0	2	2	2	1	0	0	7	0.0
Rob Zettler	32	0	1	1	34	-3	0	0	17	0.0
Shawn Anderson	1	0	0	0	0	0	0	0	0	0.0
Jason Bowen	4	0	0	0	0	-2	0	0	2	0.0
Stewart Malgunas	4	0	0	0	4	-1	0	0	1	0.0
Ryan McGill*	12	0	0	0	13	0	0	0	2	0.0
Dominic Roussel (goalie)	19	0	0	0	6	0	0	0	0	0.0
Yanick Dupre	22	0	0	0	8	-7	0	0	21	0.0
Shawn Antoski*	25	0	0	0	61	0	0	0	12	0.0
Ron Hextall (goalie)	31	0	0	0	13	0	0	0	0	0.0

GOALTENDING

	Games	Min.	Goals	SO	Avg.	W	L	T	Shots	Sv. Pct.
Dominic Roussel	19	1075	42	1	2.34	11	7	0	486	.914
Ron Hextall	31	1824	88	1	2.89	17	9	4	801	.890

Empty-net goals (do not count against a goaltender's average): Hextall 1, Roussel 1.
*Played with two or more NHL teams.
‡Tied for league lead.

RESULTS

JANUARY

21—Quebec	L	1-3
22—At Boston	L	1-4
24—At N.Y. Islanders	L	3-4
26—Hartford	W	3-2
28—Boston	W	2-1
29—At Montreal	T	*2-2
31—At Quebec	L	2-5

FEBRUARY

2—N.Y. Islanders	L	*4-5
4—Buffalo	W	4-2
6—At Ottawa	L	0-3
9—Florida	L	0-3
11—At New Jersey	W	3-1
13—Washington	W	5-3
14—At Tampa Bay	W	5-2
16—Quebec	L	2-4
23—At Quebec	T	*6-6
25—At Montreal	W	7-0
28—Washington	W	4-2

MARCH

2—Florida	T	*2-2
3—At N.Y. Rangers	L	3-5
5—Pittsburgh	W	6-2
7—At Tampa Bay	W	4-3
9—Boston	W	3-2
12—New Jersey	W	4-3
15—At N.Y. Rangers	W	4-3
16—At Ottawa	W	3-1
18—At Florida	W	*4-3
20—Montreal	W	8-4
22—At Hartford	L	3-4
25—At Washington	T	*2-2
26—Buffalo	W	3-1
28—At Boston	L	1-5
30—New Jersey	L	3-4

APRIL

1—At Pittsburgh	L	2-3
2—N.Y. Rangers	W	4-2
6—Tampa Bay	W	5-4
8—At Washington	W	3-1
12—Montreal	W	3-2
14—Tampa Bay	W	3-2
16—Pittsburgh	W	*4-3
18—At Florida	W	3-1
20—N.Y. Islanders	W	2-1
22—At New Jersey	W	*4-3
23—At Buffalo	L	2-4
26—Ottawa	L	2-5
28—At Hartford	W	4-3
30—N.Y. Rangers	L	0-2

MAY

2—At N.Y. Islanders	W	2-0

*Denotes overtime game.

PITTSBURGH PENGUINS
EASTERN CONFERENCE/NORTHEAST DIVISION

1995-96 SCHEDULE

Home games shaded.
* — All-Star Game at FleetCenter, Boston.
D — Day game.

OCTOBER

SUN	MON	TUE	WED	THU	FRI	SAT
1	2	3	4	5	6	7 TOR
8	9 COL	10	11	12 CHI	13	14 ANA
15	16	17	18	19	20 HAR	21 LA
22	23	24	25	26 NYI	27	28 NJ
29	30	31				

NOVEMBER

SUN	MON	TUE	WED	THU	FRI	SAT
			1 TB	2	3 BUF	4 PHI
5	6	7	8 OTT	9	10 SJ	11 LA
12	13	14 DAL	15	16	17 WAS	18 WAS
19	20	21 NYR	22 NYR	23	24	25 BUF
26	27	28 OTT	29	30 BOS		

DECEMBER

SUN	MON	TUE	WED	THU	FRI	SAT
					1 FLA	2
3 TB	4	5 NYI	6	7 MON	8	9 HAR
10	11	12	13 ANA	14	15 DAL	16
17 PHI	18	19 CAL	20	21	22 MON	23 MON
24	25	26 BUF	27	28 HAR	29	30 FLA
31						

JANUARY

SUN	MON	TUE	WED	THU	FRI	SAT
	1 D WAS	2	3 OTT	4	5 DET	6 STL
7	8 VAN	9	10	11	12 MON	13 SJ
14	15	16 COL	17 BUF	18	19	20 *
21	22 BOS	23	24 OTT	25	26	27 PHI
28	29 FLA	30	31 TB			

FEBRUARY

SUN	MON	TUE	WED	THU	FRI	SAT
				1	2	3 DET D
4	5	6 BOS	7 NJ	8	9	10 CHI D
11	12 TOR	13	14	15	16 WIN	17
18 NYR	19	20	21 BUF	22	23 HAR	24 MON
25	26	27 VAN	28	29 CAL		

MARCH

SUN	MON	TUE	WED	THU	FRI	SAT
				1 EDM	2	
3	4	5 WIN	6	7 OTT	8	9 NJ D
10	11	12	13 HAR	14 BOS	15	16 NYI D
17	18	19	20	21 EDM	22	23 BUF
24 NYR	25	26 STL	27	28 FLA	29	30 NJ D
31 D PHI						

APRIL

SUN	MON	TUE	WED	THU	FRI	SAT
	1	2	3	4 WAS	5	6 TB
7	8 HAR	9	10 NYI	11 OTT	12	13
14 D BOS	15	16	17	18	19	20

1995-96 SEASON

CLUB DIRECTORY

Owners
Howard Baldwin
Morris Belzberg
Thomas Ruta
Chairman of the board and governor
Howard Baldwin
President and chief executive officer
Pittsburgh Sports Associates
Steve Ryan
President
Jack Kelley
Executive V.P. and general manager
Craig Patrick
Head coach
Ed Johnston
Assistant coaches
Rick Kehoe
Bryan Trottier
Scouts
Greg Malone
Gilles Meloche
Mark Kelley
Les Binkley
Charlie Hodge
Ralph Cox
Senior executive vice president
Bill Barnes

Executive V.P. and chief financial officer
Donn Patton
V.P. public and community relations
Phil Langan
Assistant to the president
Howard Baldwin Jr.
Controller
Kevin Hart
Director of public relations
Cindy Himes
Director of media relations
Harry Sanders
Assistant director of media relations
Steve Bovino
Director of ticket sales
Jeff Mercer
Trainer
Charles Thayer
Strength and conditioning coach
John Welday
Equipment manager
Steve Latin
Team physician
Dr. Charles Burke

DRAFT CHOICES

Rd.—Player	H/W	Overall	Pos.	Last team
1—Alexei Morozov	6-1/174	24	LW	Krylja Sovetov, CIS
3—J.-Sebastien Aubin	5-11/179	76	G	Sherbrooke (QMJHL)
4—Oleg Belov	6-1/180	102	C	CSKA Moskow, CIS
5—Jan Hrdina	5-11/180	128	C	Seattle (WHL)
6—Alexei Kolkunov	6-0/185	154	C	Krylja Sovetov, CIS
7—Derrick Pyke	6-1/161	180	RW	Halifax (QMJHL)
8—Sergei Voronov	6-2/200	206	D	Dynamo, CIS
9—Frank Ivankovic	6-4/194	232	G	Oshawa (OHL)

MISCELLANEOUS DATA

Home ice (capacity)
Civic Arena (17,181)
Address
Gate No. 9
Pittsburgh, PA 15219
Business phone
412-642-1300
Rink dimensions
200 feet by 85 feet

Club colors
Black, gold and white
Radio affiliation
WTAE (1250 AM)
TV affiliation
Prime Sports

TRAINING CAMP ROSTER

No.	FORWARDS	Ht./Wt.	Place	BORN Date	NHL exp.	1994-95 clubs
	Serge Aubin (C)	6-0/180	Val d'Or, Que.	2-15-75	0	Granby (QMJHL)
	Joe Dziedzic (LW)	6-3/220	Minneapolis	12-18-71	0	Cleveland (IHL)
34	Rusty Fitzgerald (C)	6-1/195	Minneapolis	10-4-72	1	Minnesota-Duluth (WCHA), Pittsburgh, Cleveland (IHL)
10	Ron Francis (C)	6-2/200	Sault Ste. Marie, Ont.	3-1-63	14	Pittsburgh
16	Mike Hudson (C)	6-1/205	Guelph, Ont.	2-6-67	7	Pittsburgh
68	Jaromir Jagr (RW)	6-2/208	Kladno, Czechoslovakia	2-15-72	5	HC Kladno (Czech.), HC Bolzano (EURO), HC Bolzano (Italy), Schalker Haie (Germany Div. II), Pittsburgh
66	Mario Lemieux (C)	6-4/220	Montreal	10-5-65	11	Did not play
33	Jim McKenzie (LW)	6-3/205	Gull Lake, Sask.	11-3-69	6	Pittsburgh
	Alexei Morozov (RW)	6-1/178	Moscow, U.S.S.R.	2-16-77	0	Soviet Wings (CIS)
	Glen Murray (RW)	6-2/200	Halifax, N.S.	11-1-72	4	Boston
29	Markus Naslund (LW)	5-11/185	Harnosand, Sweden	7-30-73	2	Pittsburgh, Cleveland (IHL)
26	Richard Park (C)	6-0/187	Seoul, South Korea	5-27-76	1	Belleville (OHL), Pittsburgh
44	Ed Patterson (RW)	6-2/210	Delta, B.C.	11-14-72	1	Cleveland (IHL)
	Domenic Pittis (C)	5-11/180	Calgary	10-1-74	0	Cleveland (IHL)
20	Luc Robitaille (LW)	6-1/195	Montreal	2-17-66	9	Pittsburgh
	Dave Roche (LW)	6-4/224	Lindsay, Ont.	6-13-75	0	Windsor (OHL)
17	Tomas Sandstrom (RW)	6-2/200	Jakobstad, Finland	9-4-64	11	Malmo (Sweden), Pittsburgh
	Bryan Smolinski (C)	6-0/185	Toledo, O.	12-27-71	3	Boston
	Chris Wells (C)	6-6/215	Calgary	11-12-75	0	Seattle (WHL), Cleveland (IHL)
	DEFENSEMEN					
	Greg Andrusak	6-1/185	Cranbrook, B.C.	11-14-69	2	Cleveland (IHL), Detroit (IHL), Pittsburgh
44	Drake Berehowsky	6-2/211	Toronto	1-3-72	5	Toronto, Pittsburgh
	Sven Butenschon	6-5/201	Itzehoe, West Germany	3-22-76	0	Brandon (WHL)
23	Chris Joseph	6-2/210	Burnaby, B.C.	9-10-69	8	Pittsburgh
18	Francois Leroux	6-6/234	St. Adele, Que.	4-18-70	1	Prince Edward Island (AHL), Pittsburgh
22	Norm Maciver	5-11/185	Thunder Bay, Ont.	9-8-64	9	Ottawa, Pittsburgh
6	Wayne McBean	6-2/185	Calgary	2-21-69	7	Did not play
15	Dmitri Mironov	6-2/214	Moscow, U.S.S.R.	12-25-65	4	Toronto
37	Ian Moran	5-11/175	Cleveland	8-24-72	1	Cleveland (IHL), Pittsburgh
5	Ulf Samuelsson	6-1/195	Fagersta, Sweden	3-26-64	11	Leksand (Sweden), Pittsburgh
2	Chris Tamer	6-2/185	Dearborn, Mich.	11-17-70	2	Cleveland (IHL), Pittsburgh
	GOALTENDERS					
35	Jean-Sebastien Aubin	5-11/179	Montreal	7-19-77	0	Sherbrooke (QMJHL)
	Tom Barrasso	6-3/211	Boston	3-31-65	12	Pittsburgh
	Phillippe DeRouville	6-1/185	Arthabaska, Que.	8-7-74	0	Verdun (QMJHL), Cleveland (IHL)
	Patrick Lalime	6-2/170	St. Bonaventure, Que.	7-7-74	0	Hampton Roads (ECHL), Cleveland (IHL)
31	Ken Wregget	6-1/195	Brandon, Man.	3-25-64	12	Pittsburgh

1994-95 REVIEW

INDIVIDUAL STATISTICS

SCORING

	Games	G	A	Pts.	PIM	+/-	PPG	SHG	Shots	Shooting Pct.
Jaromir Jagr	48	32	38	‡70	37	23	8	3	192	16.7
Ron Francis	44	11	†48	59	18	†30	3	0	94	11.7
Tomas Sandstrom	47	21	23	44	42	1	4	1	116	18.1
Luc Robitaille	46	23	19	42	37	10	5	0	109	21.1
Larry Murphy	48	13	25	38	18	12	4	0	124	10.5
Joe Mullen	45	16	21	37	6	15	5	2	78	20.5
John Cullen	46	13	24	37	66	-4	2	0	88	14.8
Kevin Stevens	27	15	12	27	51	0	6	0	80	18.8
Shawn McEachern	44	13	13	26	22	4	1	2	97	13.4
Martin Straka*	31	4	12	16	16	0	0	0	36	11.1
Ulf Samuelsson	44	1	15	16	113	11	0	0	47	2.1
Chris Joseph	33	5	10	15	46	3	3	0	73	6.8
Len Barrie	48	3	11	14	66	-4	0	0	37	8.1
Mike Hudson	40	2	9	11	34	-1	0	0	33	6.1
Norm Maciver*	13	0	9	9	6	7	0	0	20	0.0
Kjell Samuelsson	41	1	6	7	54	8	0	0	37	2.7
Greg Hawgood	21	1	4	5	25	2	1	0	17	5.9
Markus Naslund	14	2	2	4	2	0	0	0	13	15.4
Greg Andrusak	7	0	4	4	6	-1	0	0	7	0.0

	Games	G	A	Pts.	PIM	+/-	PPG	SHG	Shots	Shooting Pct.
Grant Jennings*	25	0	4	4	36	2	0	0	16	0.0
Jim McKenzie	39	2	1	3	63	-7	0	0	16	12.5
Chris Tamer	36	2	0	2	82	0	0	0	26	7.7
Troy Murray*	13	0	2	2	23	-1	0	0	7	0.0
Francois Leroux	40	0	2	2	114	7	0	0	19	0.0
Rusty Fitzgerald	4	1	0	1	0	2	0	0	5	20.0
Richard Park	1	0	1	1	2	1	0	0	4	0.0
Peter Taglianetti	13	0	1	1	12	1	0	0	5	0.0
Jeff Christian	1	0	0	0	0	0	0	0	2	0.0
Philippe DeRouville (goalie)	1	0	0	0	0	0	0	0	0	0.0
Tom Barrasso (goalie)	2	0	0	0	0	0	0	0	0	0.0
Drake Berehowsky*	4	0	0	0	13	1	0	0	2	0.0
Wendell Young (goalie)	10	0	0	0	2	0	0	0	0	0.0
Ken Wregget (goalie)	38	0	0	0	14	0	0	0	0	0.0

GOALTENDING

	Games	Min.	Goals	SO	Avg.	W	L	T	Shots	Sv. Pct.
Philippe DeRouville	1	60	3	0	3.00	1	0	0	27	.889
Ken Wregget	38	2208	118	0	3.21	†25	9	2	1219	.903
Wendell Young	10	497	27	0	3.26	3	6	0	255	.894
Tom Barrasso	2	125	8	0	3.84	0	1	1	75	.893

Empty-net goals (do not count against a goaltender's average): Wregget 1, Young 1.
*Played with two or more NHL teams.
†Led league.
‡Tied for league lead.

RESULTS

JANUARY
20—At Tampa Bay	W	5-3
23—At Florida	W	6-5
25—At N.Y. Rangers	W	3-2
27—Ottawa	W	5-4
29—At Washington	W	4-1

FEBRUARY
1—N.Y. Rangers	W	4-3
4—Tampa Bay	W	6-3
5—At New Jersey	T	*3-3
7—Florida	W	7-3
9—At N.Y. Islanders	W	5-2
11—Montreal	W	3-1
14—Boston	W	5-3
16—Hartford	W	5-2
18—At Hartford	L	2-4
19—Buffalo	T	*3-3
21—Quebec	W	5-4

24—Tampa Bay	L	2-4
25—At N.Y. Islanders	L	1-3
27—At Quebec	W	7-5

MARCH
2—At Buffalo	L	3-6
4—At Boston	W	*4-3
5—At Philadelphia	L	2-6
7—Quebec	L	4-5
9—N.Y. Islanders	W	4-2
11—Buffalo	W	6-2
13—Montreal	W	4-2
15—At Montreal	L	5-8
16—At Quebec	L	2-3
19—At Ottawa	W	4-3
21—At Buffalo	W	3-2
24—New Jersey	W	5-2
26—At Florida	L	0-2
28—N.Y. Islanders	W	6-3

APRIL
1—Philadelphia	W	3-2
5—Hartford	L	4-8
8—At Montreal	L	1-2
10—At Ottawa	W	4-3
11—Washington	W	3-1
15—Ottawa	W	5-2
16—At Philadelphia	L	*3-4
18—N.Y. Rangers	W	6-5
22—Washington	L	1-2
23—At Hartford	W	4-2
26—At New Jersey	T	*3-3
28—Boston	W	4-1
30—At Boston	L	2-5

MAY
2—At Washington	L	2-7
3—Florida	L	3-4

*Denotes overtime game.

ST. LOUIS BLUES
WESTERN CONFERENCE/CENTRAL DIVISION

1995-96 SCHEDULE

Home games shaded.
* — All-Star Game at FleetCenter, Boston.
D — Day game.

OCTOBER

SUN	MON	TUE	WED	THU	FRI	SAT
1	2	3	4	5	6	7 WAS
8	9	10 EDM	11	12 DAL	13	14 COL
15	16	17 BOS	18	19 DAL	20	21 CHI
22 BUF	23	24	25 HAR	26	27 ANA	28
29 WAS	30	31				

NOVEMBER

SUN	MON	TUE	WED	THU	FRI	SAT
			1 ANA	2	3	4 SJ
5	6	7 LA	8	9	10 WIN	11 NYI
12	13	14 NYR	15	16 SJ	17	18 BOS
19	20	21 TOR	22	23 VAN	24	25 TOR
26	27 BUF	28	29 MON	30 WIN		

DECEMBER

SUN	MON	TUE	WED	THU	FRI	SAT
					1	2 EDM
3	4	5 CAL	6	7	8 VAN	9 LA
10	11	12 DET	13	14 CAL	15	16 SJ
17	18	19 NYI	20	21	22 COL	23 WIN
24	25	26 DET	27	28 DAL	29	30 TOR
31						

JANUARY

SUN	MON	TUE	WED	THU	FRI	SAT
	1	2	3	4 CHI	5	6 PIT
7	8	9 NJ	10	11 PHI	12	13 MON
14 NYR	15	16 EDM	17	18	19	20 *
21	22	23	24 WIN	25	26	27 TB
28	29 OTT	30	31 TOR			

FEBRUARY

SUN	MON	TUE	WED	THU	FRI	SAT
				1 VAN	2	3 D PHI
4	5	6 DAL	7	8 CHI	9	10 D DAL
11 FLA	12	13 TB	14	15	16 DET	17
18 WIN	19	20 OTT	21	22 CHI	23	24 LA
25	26	27	28	29 VAN		

MARCH

SUN	MON	TUE	WED	THU	FRI	SAT
					1	2
3 EDM	4	5 FLA	6	7 CAL	8	9 HAR
10	11	12 CAL	13	14	15 SJ	16
17 ANA	18 LA	19	20 DAL	21	22 ANA	23
24 DET	25	26 PIT	27	28 NJ	29	30
31 D DET						

APRIL

SUN	MON	TUE	WED	THU	FRI	SAT
	1	2	3 COL	4 TOR	5	6 TOR
7	8 WIN	9	10	11 COL	12	13
14 D CHI	15	16	17	18	19	20

1995-96 SEASON

CLUB DIRECTORY

Board of directors
Jud Perkins
Al Kerth
Jack Quinn
Ed Trusheim
Andy Craig
Horace Wilkins
Chairman of the board & president
Jack J. Quinn
Executive vice president
Ronald Caron
General manager/head coach
Mike Keenan
Associate coach
Bob Berry
Vice president/director of sales
Bruce Affleck
V.P./dir. of player personnel and scouting/ assistant general manager
Ted Hampson
V.P./director of player development
Bob Plager
Dir. of professional playing personnel
Jim Papin

V.P./dir. of broadcast sales
Matt Hyland
V.P./dir. of finance and administration
Jerry Jasiek
Asst. dir. of marketing and P.R.
Adam Fell
Assistant director of scouting
Jack Evans
Western Canada/U.S. scout
Pat Ginnell
New England scout
Matt Keator
Assistant director of public relations
Mike Eiskant
Director of team services
Mike Caruso
Training staff
Ray Barile
Jeff Cope
Mark Roof
Terry Roof

DRAFT CHOICES

Rd.—Player	H/W	Overall	Pos.	Last team
2—Jochen Hecht	6-1/180	49	C	Mannheim, Germany
3—Scott Roche	6-4/220	75	G	North Bay (OHL)
4—Michal Handzus	6-3/191	101	C	Banska Bystrica, Slovakia
5—Jeff Ambrosio	6-0/190	127	LW	Belleville (OHL)
6—Denis Hamel	6-2/188	153	LW	Chicoutimi (QMJHL)
7—J.-Luc Grand-Pierre	6-2/197	179	D	Val d'Or (QMJHL)
8—Derek Bekar	6-2/180	205	C	Powell River (BCJHL)
9—Libor Zabransky	5-10/191	209	W	CSKE Budjovice, Czech Rep.

MISCELLANEOUS DATA

Home ice (capacity)
Kiel Center (18,500)
Address
1401 Clark
St. Louis, MO 63103
Business phone
314-622-2500
Rink dimensions
200 feet by 85 feet

Club colors
Blue, gold, red and white
Radio affiliation
KMOX (1120 AM)
TV affiliation
KPLR (Channel 11)

No.	FORWARDS	Ht./Wt.	Place	BORN Date	NHL exp.	1994-95 clubs
21	Guy Carbonneau (C)	5-11/185	Sept-Iles, Que.	3-18-60	14	St. Louis
27	Denis Chasse (RW)	6-2/200	Montreal	2-7-70	2	St. Louis
	Shayne Corson (LW/C)	6-1/200	Barrie, Ont.	8-13-66	10	Edmonton
14	Geoff Courtnall (LW)	6-1/195	Victoria, B.C.	8-18-62	12	Vancouver
20	Adam Creighton (C)	6-5/220	Burlington, Ont.	6-2-65	12	St. Louis
7	Greg Gilbert (LW)	6-1/191	Mississauga, Ont.	1-22-67	14	St. Louis
10	Dale Hawerchuk (C)	5-11/190	Toronto	4-4-63	14	Buffalo
16	Brett Hull (RW)	5-10/200	Belleville, Ont.	8-9-64	10	St. Louis
	Craig Johnson (LW)	6-2/185	St. Paul, Minn.	3-18-72	1	Peoria (IHL), St. Louis
22	Ian Laperriere (C)	6-1/195	Montreal	1-19-74	2	Peoria (IHL), St. Louis
17	Basil McRae (LW)	6-2/210	Beaverton, Ont.	1-5-61	14	St. Louis, Peoria (IHL)
16	Brian Noonan (RW)	6-1/200	Boston	5-29-65	8	New York Rangers
15	Dave Roberts (C/LW)	6-0/185	Alameda, Calif.	5-28-70	2	Peoria (IHL), St. Louis
	Kevin Sawyer (LW)	6-2/205	Christina Lake, B.C.	2-18-74	0	Spokane (WHL), Peoria (IHL)
26	Peter Stastny (C)	6-1/200	Bratislava, Czech.	9-18-56	15	St. Louis
25	Patrice Tardif (RW/C)	6-2/202	Thetford Mines, Que.	10-30-70	1	Peoria (IHL), St. Louis
10	Esa Tikkanen (LW)	6-1/200	Helsinki, Finland	1-25-68	11	HIFK Helsinki (Finland), St. Louis
18	Tony Twist (LW)	6-1/220	Sherwood Park, Alta.	5-9-68	6	St. Louis
	Alex Vasilevskii (RW)	5-11/190	Kiev, U.S.S.R.	1-8-75	0	Prince George (WHL), Brandon (WHL)
	Roman Vopat (C)	6-3/216	Litvinov, Czechoslovakia	4-21-76	0	Moose Jaw (WHL), Peoria (IHL)
	DEFENSEMEN					
34	Murray Baron	6-3/215	Prince George, B.C.	6-1-67	6	St. Louis
32	Donald Dufresne	6-1/206	Quebec City	4-10-67	7	St. Louis
	Martin Hamrlik	5-11/176	Zlin, Czechoslovakia	5-6-73	0	Peoria (IHL)
2	Al MacInnis	6-2/196	Inverness, N.S.	7-11-63	14	St. Louis
5	Jeff Norton	6-2/200	Cambridge, Mass.	11-25-65	8	San Jose, St. Louis
	Chris Pronger	6-5/190	Dryden, Ont.	10-10-74	2	Hartford
	Jamie Rivers	6-0/180	Ottawa	3-16-75	0	Sudbury (OHL)
	Steve Staios	6-0/183	Hamilton, Ont.	7-28-73	0	Peoria (IHL)
	Jay Wells	6-1/210	Paris, Ont.	5-18-59	16	New York Rangers
4	Rick Zombo	6-1/202	Des Plaines, Ill.	5-8-63	11	St. Louis
	GOALTENDERS					
	Mike Buzak	6-3/190	Edson, Alta.	2-10-73	0	Michigan State (CCHA)
30	Jon Casey	5-10/155	Grand Rapids, Minn.	8-29-62	10	St. Louis
	Grant Fuhr	5-9/190	Spruce Grove, Alta.	9-28-62	14	Buffalo, Los Angeles

1994-95 REVIEW

INDIVIDUAL STATISTICS

SCORING

	Games	G	A	Pts.	PIM	+/-	PPG	SHG	Shots	Shooting Pct.
Brett Hull	48	29	21	50	10	13	9	3	200	14.5
Brendan Shanahan	45	20	21	41	136	7	6	2	153	13.1
Steve Duchesne	47	12	26	38	36	29	1	0	116	10.3
Esa Tikkanen	43	12	23	35	22	13	5	2	107	11.2
Adam Creighton	48	14	20	34	74	17	3	0	81	17.3
Al MacInnis	32	8	20	28	43	19	2	0	110	7.3
Ian Laperriere	37	13	14	27	85	12	1	0	53	†24.5
Glenn Anderson	36	12	14	26	37	9	0	0	54	22.2
Greg Gilbert	46	11	14	25	11	22	0	0	57	19.3
Jeff Norton*	28	2	18	20	33	21	0	0	27	7.4
Bill Houlder	41	5	13	18	20	16	1	0	59	8.5
Denis Chasse	47	7	9	16	133	12	1	0	48	14.6
Guy Carbonneau	42	5	11	16	16	11	1	0	33	15.2
Patrice Tardif	27	3	10	13	29	4	1	0	46	6.5
David Roberts	19	6	5	11	10	2	3	0	41	14.6
Vitali Karamnov	26	3	7	10	14	7	0	0	22	13.6
Doug Lidster	37	2	7	9	12	9	1	0	37	5.4
Craig Janney*	8	2	5	7	0	3	1	0	9	22.2
Kevin Miller*	15	2	5	7	0	4	0	0	19	10.5
Craig Johnson	15	3	3	6	6	4	0	0	19	15.8
Todd Elik*	13	2	4	6	4	5	0	0	26	7.7
Rick Zombo	23	1	4	5	24	7	0	0	18	5.6
Basil McRae	21	0	5	5	72	4	0	0	14	0.0
Murray Baron	39	0	5	5	93	9	0	0	28	0.0

	Games	G	A	Pts.	PIM	+/-	PPG	SHG	Shots	Shooting Pct.
Tony Twist	28	3	0	3	89	0	0	0	8	37.5
Donald Dufresne	22	0	3	3	10	2	0	0	11	0.0
Peter Stastny	6	1	1	2	0	1	0	0	9	11.1
Geoff Sarjeant (goalie)	4	0	1	1	2	0	0	0	0	0.0
Curtis Joseph (goalie)	36	0	1	1	0	0	0	0	0	0.0
Philippe Bozon	1	0	0	0	0	0	0	0	0	0.0
Vitali Prokhorov	2	0	0	0	0	1	0	0	0	0.0
Denny Felsner	3	0	0	0	2	-1	0	0	2	0.0
Daniel Laperriere*	4	0	0	0	15	1	0	0	0	0.0
Terry Hollinger	5	0	0	0	2	-1	0	0	1	0.0
Jeff Batters	10	0	0	0	21	-5	0	0	3	0.0
Jon Casey (goalie)	19	0	0	0	0	0	0	0	0	0.0

GOALTENDING

	Games	Min.	Goals	SO	Avg.	W	L	T	Shots	Sv. Pct.
Jon Casey	19	872	40	0	2.75	7	5	4	400	.900
Curtis Joseph	36	1914	89	1	2.79	20	10	1	904	.902
Geoff Sarjeant	4	120	6	0	3.00	1	0	0	52	.885

Empty-net goals (do not count against a goaltender's average): None.
*Played with two or more NHL teams.
†Led league.

RESULTS

JANUARY

20—At San Jose	W	5-2
21—At Vancouver	W	7-1
24—At Calgary	L	4-6
26—Los Angeles	W	3-1
28—Vancouver	L	1-3
31—Anaheim	W	7-2

FEBRUARY

2—At Winnipeg	W	*5-4
4—Dallas	W	7-4
7—Los Angeles	T	*5-5
9—Chicago	L	0-5
11—Winnipeg	L	2-3
13—Calgary	W	4-2
17—At Winnipeg	W	4-3
18—At Toronto	L	1-3
20—Edmonton	W	4-0
22—San Jose	W	4-3
25—At Detroit	W	3-2
27—Toronto	W	3-2

MARCH

5—At Dallas	L	1-2
7—Anaheim	W	6-3
9—Calgary	W	5-1
12—Detroit	L	1-2
14—At Edmonton	L	5-6
16—At Los Angeles	T	*2-2
19—At Anaheim	W	4-2
20—At Los Angeles	L	3-5
22—At Calgary	L	3-4
26—Edmonton	W	5-1
27—At Dallas	W	3-2
29—At Chicago	W	3-1
31—San Jose	W	4-1

APRIL

2—At Detroit	T	*3-3
3—Toronto	W	5-2
5—At Toronto	W	6-4
9—Dallas	L	2-3
11—Winnipeg	W	7-5

13—At Winnipeg	L	2-5
16—Detroit	W	6-5
18—Vancouver	W	4-1
19—At Chicago	T	*2-2
21—Toronto	W	3-1
23—Chicago	T	*2-2
25—At Dallas	W	8-4
27—At Edmonton	L	2-3
28—At Vancouver	L	1-3
30—At San Jose	W	4-3

MAY

1—At Anaheim	W	5-3
3—Detroit	L	2-3

*Denotes overtime game.

SAN JOSE SHARKS
WESTERN CONFERENCE/PACIFIC DIVISION

1995-96 SCHEDULE

Home games shaded.
* — All-Star Game at FleetCenter, Boston.
D — Day game.

OCTOBER

SUN	MON	TUE	WED	THU	FRI	SAT
1	2	3	4	5	6	7 CHI
8	9	10	11	12 BOS	13	14 VAN
15	16	17	18	19 WIN	20	21
22 EDM	23	24	25 WIN	26	27	28 D DAL
29	30 VAN	31 NYR				

NOVEMBER

SUN	MON	TUE	WED	THU	FRI	SAT
			1	2 NJ	3	4 STL
5	6	7 HAR	8 BUF	9	10 PIT	11 DET
12	13	14 NYI	15	16 STL	17 DAL	18
19 CHI	20	21 WAS	22 DET	23	24	25 VAN
26	27	28	29 CAL	30		

DECEMBER

SUN	MON	TUE	WED	THU	FRI	SAT
					1 VAN	2 WAS
3	4	5 COL	6	7 WIN	8	9 EDM
10	11	12 OTT	13	14 TOR	15	16 STL
17 DAL	18	19 ANA	20	21	22 LA	23
24	25	26 COL	27	28	29 ANA	30
31						

JANUARY

SUN	MON	TUE	WED	THU	FRI	SAT
	1	2	3 PHI	4	5 LA	6 LA
7	8 FLA	9	10 NYR	11 NJ	12	13 PIT
14	15	16 FLA	17 TB	18	19	20 *
21	22	23	24 DET	25 CHI	26	27 D COL
28	29	30 HAR	31			

FEBRUARY

SUN	MON	TUE	WED	THU	FRI	SAT
				1 LA	2	3 D CHI
4	5 TOR	6	7	8	9	10 D LA
11	12 MON	13	14 TOR	15 OTT	16	17 D NYI
18	19	20 CAL	21	22	23 VAN	24
25 D ANA	26 MON	27	28	29		

MARCH

SUN	MON	TUE	WED	THU	FRI	SAT
					1 TB	2
3 D CAL	4	5 COL	6 DAL	7	8 EDM	9
10 D BUF	11	12	13 EDM	14	15 STL	16
17 PHI	18 BOS	19	20 WIN	21	22 CAL	23
24	25	26	27	28 COL	29	30
31 D ANA						

APRIL

SUN	MON	TUE	WED	THU	FRI	SAT
	1	2 DET	3	4 EDM	5	6 D COL
7 D ANA	8	9	10 LA	11	12 CAL	13
14	15	16	17	18	19	20

1995-96 SEASON

CLUB DIRECTORY

Majority owner & chairman
George Gund III
Co-owner
Gordon Gund
President & chief executive officer
Arthur L. Savage
Exec. V.P. & chief operating officer
Greg Jamison
Exec. V.P., development
Matt Levine
Exec. V.P., building operations
Frank Jirik
Exec. V.P., dir. of hockey operations
Dean Lombardi
Exec. V.P., dir. of player personnel
Chuck Grillo
Vice chairman
Tom McEnery
Vice president, chief financial officer
Gregg Olson
Head coach
Kevin Constantine
Asst. coach & asst. to dir. of hoc. operations
Wayne Thomas
Assistant coaches
Drew Remenda
Vasily Tikhonov
Strength & conditioning coach
Steve Millard

Asst. director of player personnel
Joe Will
Director of hockey administration
Brenda Will
Asst. director of media relations
Paul Turner
Media relations assistant
Roger Ross
Scouting staff
Tim Burke
Rob Grillo
Pat Funk
Konstantin Krylov
Karel Masopust
Jack Morganstern
Dan Summers
Bob Friedlander
Head trainer
Tom Woodcock
Equipment manager
Bob Crocker Jr.
Asst. equip. manager/massage therapist
Sergei Tchekmarev
Team physician
Dr. Arthur Ting
Director of ticket operations
Daniel DeBoer

DRAFT CHOICES

Rd.—Player	H/W	Overall	Pos.	Last team
1—Teemu Riihijarvi	6-6/202	12	LW	Espoo Jrs., Finland
2—Peter Roed	5-10/210	38	C	White Bear Lake H.S. (Min.)
3—Marko Makinen	6-4/198	64	RW	TPS Jrs., Finland
4—Vesa Toskala	5-9/172	90	G	Ilves Jrs., Finland
5—Miikka Kiprusoff	6-0/176	116	G	TPS Jrs., Finland
5—Michal Bros	6-1/174	130	C	HC Olomouc, Czech Rep.
6—Timo Hakanen	6-2/189	140	C	Assat Jrs., Finland
6—Jaroslav Kudrna	5-11/176	142	LW	Penticton (BCJHL)
7—Brad Mehalko	5-11/182	167	RW	Lethbridge (WHL)
7—Robert Jindrich	5-11/167	168	D	Plzen, Czech Republic
8—Ryan Kraft	5-9/181	194	C	University of Minnesota
9—Miiko Markkanen	5-9/165	220	RW	TPS Jrs., Finland

MISCELLANEOUS DATA

Home ice (capacity)
San Jose Arena (17,190)
Address
525 West Santa Clara Street
San Jose, CA 95113
Business phone
408-287-7070
Rink dimensions
200 feet by 85 feet

Club colors
Pacific teal, gray, black and white
Radio affiliation
KFRC (610 AM & 99.7 FM),
KLOK (1170 AM, Spanish)
TV affiliation
KICU (Channel 36), SportsChannel

TRAINING CAMP ROSTER

No.	FORWARDS	Ht./Wt.	Place (BORN)	Date	NHL exp.	1994-95 clubs
13	Jamie Baker (C)	6-0/190	Nepean, Ont.	8-31-66	6	San Jose
	Michal Bros (C)	6-1/175	Olomouc, Czechoslovakia	1-25-76	0	HC Olomouc (Czech Rep.)
	Jan Caloun (RW)	5-10/175	Usti-nad-Labem, Czech.	12-20-72	0	Kansas City (IHL)
	Alexander Cherbayev	6-1/190	Voskresensk, U.S.S.R.	8-13-73	0	Kansas City (IHL)
22	Ulf Dahlen (RW)	6-3/200	Ostersund, Sweden	1-12-67	8	San Jose
	Shean Donovan (RW)	6-1/172	Timmins, Ont.	1-22-75	1	Ottawa (OHL), San Jose, Kansas City (IHL)
17	Pat Falloon (RW)	5-11/190	Foxwarren, Man.	9-22-72	4	San Jose
39	Jeff Friesen (C/LW)	6-1/190	Meadow Lake, Sask.	8-5-76	1	Regina (WHL), San Jose
	Dean Grillo (RW)	6-2/210	Bemidji, Minn.	12-8-72	0	Kansas City (IHL)
15	Craig Janney (C)	6-1/190	Hartford, Conn.	9-26-67	8	St. Louis, San Jose
	Alexander Korolyuk (RW)	5-9/165	Moscow, U.S.S.R.	1-15-76	0	Soviet Wings (CIS)
	Viktor Kozlov (RW)	6-5/209	Togliatti, U.S.S.R.	2-14-75	1	Dynamo Moscow (CIS), San Jose, Kansas City (IHL)
7	Igor Larionov (C)	5-9/170	Voskresensk, U.S.S.R.	12-3-60	5	San Jose
	Lee Leslie (LW)	6-4/190	Prince George, B.C.	8-15-72	0	Kansas City (IHL), Canadian National Team (Int'l)
24	Sergei Makarov (RW)	5-11/195	Chelyabinsk, U.S.S.R.	6-19-58	6	San Jose
8	Kevin Miller (LW)	5-11/190	Lansing, Mich.	8-9-65	7	St. Louis, San Jose
23	Andrei Nazarov (LW)	6-6/230	Chelyabinsk, U.S.S.R.	3-21-72	2	Kansas City (IHL), San Jose
	Fredrick Nilsson (C)	6-1/200	Vasteras, Sweden	4-16-71	0	Kansas City (IHL)
36	Jeff Odgers (RW)	6-0/195	Spy Hill, Sask.	5-31-69	4	San Jose
	Ville Peltonen (LW/RW)	5-10/172	Vantaa, Finland	5-24-73	0	HIFK Helsinki (Finland)
18	Chris Tancill (LW)	5-10/185	Livonia, Mich.	2-7-68	5	San Jose, Kansas City (IHL)
	Vaclav Varada (LW)	6-0/198	Valasske Mezirici, Czech.	4-26-76	0	Tacoma (WHL)
	Petri Varis (LW)	6-1/200	Varkaus, Finland	5-13-69	0	Jokerit Helsinki (Finland)
14	Ray Whitney (C)	5-10/170	Edmonton	5-8-72	4	San Jose
45	Dody Wood (C/LW)	5-11/180	Chetwynd, B.C.	5-8-72	2	Kansas City (IHL), San Jose
	Alexei Yegorov (C)	5-9/174	Leningrad, U.S.S.R.	5-21-75	0	SKA St. Petersburg (CIS), Fort Worth (CHL)

DEFENSEMEN

No.	DEFENSEMEN	Ht./Wt.	Place (BORN)	Date	NHL exp.	1994-95 clubs
44	Shawn Cronin	6-2/225	Flushing, Mich.	8-20-63	7	San Jose
	Vlastimil Kroupa	6-2/176	Most, Czechoslovakia	4-27-75	2	Kansas City (IHL), San Jose
2	Jim Kyte	6-5/220	Ottawa	3-21-64	12	Las Vegas (IHL), San Jose
4	Jay More	6-2/210	Souris, Man.	1-12-69	6	San Jose
	Angel Nikolov	6-1/176	Most, Czechoslovakia	11-18-75	0	Chemopetrol Litvinov (Czech Rep.)
6	Sandis Ozolinsh	6-3/205	Riga, U.S.S.R.	8-3-72	3	San Jose
41	Tom Pederson	5-9/180	Bloomington, Minn.	1-14-70	3	San Jose
	Marcus Ragnarsson	6-1/200	Ostervala, Sweden	8-13-71	0	Djurgarden Stockholm (Sweden)
40	Mike Rathje	6-6/220	Manville, Alta.	5-11-74	2	Kansas City (IHL), San Jose
38	Michal Sykora	6-5/225	Pardubice, Czech.	7-5-73	2	Kansas City (IHL), San Jose

GOALTENDERS

No.	GOALTENDERS	Ht./Wt.	Place (BORN)	Date	NHL exp.	1994-95 clubs
31	Wade Flaherty	6-0/190	Terreace, B.C.	1-11-68	3	San Jose
32	Arturs Irbe	5-8/190	Riga, U.S.S.R.	2-2-67	4	San Jose

1994-95 REVIEW

INDIVIDUAL STATISTICS

SCORING

	Games	G	A	Pts.	PIM	+/-	PPG	SHG	Shots	Shooting Pct.
Ulf Dahlen	46	11	23	34	11	-2	4	1	85	12.9
Jeff Friesen	48	15	10	25	14	-8	5	1	86	17.4
Ray Whitney	39	13	12	25	14	-7	4	0	67	19.4
Sandis Ozolinsh	48	9	16	25	30	-6	3	1	83	10.8
Sergei Makarov	43	10	14	24	40	-4	1	0	56	17.9
Igor Larionov	33	4	20	24	14	-3	0	0	69	5.8
Craig Janney*	27	5	15	20	10	-4	2	0	31	16.1
Pat Falloon	46	12	7	19	25	-4	0	0	91	13.2
Todd Elik*	22	7	10	17	18	3	4	0	50	14.0
Tom Pederson	47	5	11	16	31	-14	0	0	59	8.5
Chris Tancill	26	3	11	14	10	1	0	1	39	7.7
Kevin Miller*	21	6	7	13	13	0	1	1	41	14.6
Jamie Baker	43	7	4	11	22	-7	0	1	60	11.7
Jeff Norton*	20	1	9	10	39	1	0	0	21	4.8
Gaetan Duchesne*	33	2	7	9	16	-6	0	0	48	4.2
Mike Rathje	42	2	7	9	29	-1	0	0	38	5.3
Andrei Nazarov	26	3	5	8	94	-1	0	0	19	15.8
Jeff Odgers	48	4	3	7	117	-8	0	0	47	8.5
Jim Kyte	18	2	5	7	33	-7	0	0	14	14.3

	Games	G	A	Pts.	PIM	+/-	PPG	SHG	Shots	Shooting Pct.
Jay More	45	0	6	6	71	7	0	0	25	0.0
Ilya Byakin	13	0	5	5	14	-9	0	0	19	0.0
Bob Errey*	13	2	2	4	27	4	0	0	19	10.5
Michal Sykora	16	0	4	4	10	6	0	0	6	0.0
Slava Butsayev	6	2	0	2	0	-2	0	0	6	33.3
Viktor Kozlov	16	2	0	2	2	-5	0	0	23	8.7
Dody Wood	9	1	1	2	29	0	0	0	5	20.0
Johan Garpenlov*	13	1	1	2	2	-3	0	0	16	6.3
Vlastimil Kroupa	14	0	2	2	16	-7	0	0	4	0.0
Shawn Cronin	29	0	2	2	61	0	0	0	12	0.0
Wade Flaherty (goalie)	18	0	1	1	0	0	0	0	0	0.0
Shean Donovan	14	0	0	0	6	-6	0	0	13	0.0
Arturs Irbe (goalie)	38	0	0	0	4	0	0	0	0	0.0

GOALTENDING

	Games	Min.	Goals	SO	Avg.	W	L	T	Shots	Sv. Pct.
Wade Flaherty	18	852	44	1	3.10	5	6	1	455	.903
Arturs Irbe	38	2043	111	4	3.26	14	19	3	1056	.895

Empty-net goals (do not count against a goaltender's average): Irbe 4, Flaherty 2.
*Played with two or more NHL teams.

RESULTS

JANUARY

20—St. Louis	L	2-5
21—Toronto	W	3-2
25—Winnipeg	W	4-0
28—Dallas	W	3-2
30—Chicago	W	2-1

FEBRUARY

2—At Dallas	W	2-1
4—At Winnipeg	T	*3-3
6—At Toronto	L	3-7
7—At Detroit	L	0-6
10—At Edmonton	L	1-5
11—At Vancouver	T	*1-1
15—Vancouver	W	3-1
17—At Los Angeles	W	2-0
18—Anaheim	L	3-6
20—At Chicago	L	2-3
22—At St. Louis	L	3-4
24—Calgary	L	0-3

26—Vancouver	L	1-5
28—At Vancouver	W	4-3

MARCH

2—At Toronto	W	4-3
4—At Winnipeg	L	2-4
8—Edmonton	L	2-5
15—Toronto	L	1-2
17—At Edmonton	L	3-5
19—At Calgary	W	5-3
21—Chicago	L	3-7
23—Anaheim	L	3-6
25—At Los Angeles	W	3-1
26—Los Angeles	L	3-7
28—Winnipeg	W	*6-5
31—At St. Louis	L	1-4

APRIL

2—At Anaheim	L	4-5
5—Detroit	L	3-5
7—Edmonton	W	5-0

9—At Edmonton	W	5-2
10—At Calgary	L	3-8
12—At Chicago	W	3-2
13—At Detroit	L	0-3
16—Los Angeles	W	2-0
17—At Anaheim	L	0-3
19—At Dallas	T	*5-5
23—Detroit	L	1-5
25—Calgary	L	2-3
26—At Anaheim	W	5-2
28—Los Angeles	W	4-0
30—St. Louis	L	3-4

MAY

1—Dallas	W	3-1
3—Vancouver	T	*3-3

*Denotes overtime game.

TAMPA BAY LIGHTNING
EASTERN CONFERENCE/ATLANTIC DIVISION

Home games shaded.
* — All-Star Game at FleetCenter, Boston.
D — Day game.

OCTOBER

SUN	MON	TUE	WED	THU	FRI	SAT
1	2	3	4	5	6	7 CAL
8	9	10	11	12 MON	13	14 WAS
15 OTT	16	17 WIN	18	19 CHI	20	21 DAL
22	23	24	25	26 NYR	27	28 WAS
29	30	31 PHI				

NOVEMBER

SUN	MON	TUE	WED	THU	FRI	SAT
			1 PIT	2	3 NYI	4
5 FLA	6	7	8 NYR	9	10 EDM	11
12 BUF	13	14 BOS	15	16 TOR	17	18 VAN
19	20	21	22 NJ	23	24 WAS	25 NYI
26	27 LA	28	29 HAR	30		

DECEMBER

SUN	MON	TUE	WED	THU	FRI	SAT
					1 NJ	2
3 PIT	4	5	6 ANA	7	8 BOS	9
10 BUF	11	12	13 HAR	14 PHI	15	16 FLA
17	18	19 WIN	20	21 NJ	22	23 BOS
24	25	26	27	28 MON	29	30
31 OTT						

JANUARY

SUN	MON	TUE	WED	THU	FRI	SAT
	1	2 CAL	3 EDM	4	5	6 VAN
7	8 MON	9	10	11	12	13 OTT
14	15 D NYI	16	17 SJ	18	19	20 *
21	22 MON	23	24	25 BOS	26	27 D STL
28	29	30	31 PIT			

FEBRUARY

SUN	MON	TUE	WED	THU	FRI	SAT
				1	2	3 D FLA
4 BUF	5 D	6	7 COL	8	9	10 D DET
11 NYR	12	13 STL	14	15 COL	16	17 PHI
18	19 DAL	20	21 TOR	22	23 NYI	24 DET
25	26	27	28 LA	29		

MARCH

SUN	MON	TUE	WED	THU	FRI	SAT
					1 SJ	2
3 ANA	4	5 CHI	6	7 NYR	8	9
10 D WAS	11	12	13 PHI	14	15 NJ	16
17 OTT	18 D HAR	19	20	21 WAS	22	23 FLA
24	25	26 NJ	27	28	29	30 FLA
31 WAS						

APRIL

SUN	MON	TUE	WED	THU	FRI	SAT
	1	2	3 HAR	4	5 BUF	6 PIT
7	8 NYI	9	10 FLA	11	12 NYR	13
14 D PHI	15	16	17	18	19	20

CLUB DIRECTORY

Pres., Lightning Partners, Ltd.
Steve Oto
Governor
David LeFevre
Pres., general manager and alt. gov.
Phil Esposito
Executive V.P., treasurer and alt. gov.
Mel Lowell
Executive V.P., alternate governor
Chris Phillips
Counsel
Henry Paul
Director of hockey operations
Tony Esposito
Head coach
Terry Crisp
Assistant coaches
Wayne Cashman
Danny Gare
Chief financial officer
Frank Sato
Accounting manager
Vincent Ascanio
Vice president, communications
Gerry Helper

Media relations manager
Barry Hanrahan
Director of team services
Carrie Esposito
Director of sales
Paul D'Aiuto
Director of merchandising
Kevin Murphy
Director of ticket operations
Jeff Morander
Head scout
Don Murdoch
Scouting staff
Angelo Bumbacco
Jacques Campeau
Jake Goertzen
Doug Macauley
Richard Rose
Luke Williams
Head trainer
Larry Ness
Assistant trainer
Bill Cronin
Equipment manager
Jocko Cayer

DRAFT CHOICES

Rd. — Player	H/W	Overall	Pos.	Last team
1—Daymond Langkow...	5-10/170	5	C	Tri-City (WHL)
2—Mike McBain	6-1/191	30	D	Red Deer (WHL)
3—Shane Willis	6-0/170	56	RW	Prince Albert (WHL)
5—Konst. Golokhvastov...	6-1/185	108	RW	Dynamo, Ukraine
6—Eduard Pershin	6-0/191	134	C	Dynamo, CIS
7—Cory Murphy.............	6-2/202	160	D	Sault Ste. Marie (OHL)
8—Joseph Cardarelli	5-11/205	186	LW	Spokane (WHL)
9—Zac Bierk	6-4/186	212	G	Peterborough (OHL)

MISCELLANEOUS DATA

Home ice (capacity)
Florida Suncoast Dome (26,000)
Address
501 East Kennedy Blvd.
Tampa, Fla. 33602
Business phone
813-229-2658
Rink dimensions
200 feet by 85 feet

Club colors
Black, blue, silver and white
Radio affiliation
WFNS (910 AM), WSUN (620 AM)
TV affiliation
Sunshine Network (Cable),
WTOG (Channel 44)

No.	FORWARDS	Ht./Wt.	Place	BORN Date	NHL exp.	1994-95 clubs
34	Mikael Andersson (RW)	5-11/185	Malmo, Sweden	5-10-66	10	Vastra Frolunda (Sweden), Tampa Bay
23	Brian Bellows (LW)	5-11/209	St. Catharines, Ont.	9-1-64	13	Montreal
19	Brian Bradley (C)	5-10/177	Kitchener, Ont.	1-21-65	10	Tampa Bay
	Colin Cloutier (C)	6-3/224	Winnipeg	1-27-76	0	Brandon (WHL)
	Allan Egeland (C)	6-0/184	Lethbridge, Alta.	1-31-73	0	Atlanta (IHL)
	Aaron Gavey (C)	6-1/169	Sudbury, Ont.	2-22-74	0	Atlanta (IHL)
77	Chris Gratton (C)	6-3/202	Brantford, Ont.	7-5-75	2	Tampa Bay
	Brent Gretzky (C)	5-10/160	Brantford, Ont.	2-20-72	2	Atlanta (IHL), Tampa Bay
14	Ben Hankinson (RW)	6-2/215	Edina, Minn.	1-5-69	3	New Jersey, Albany (AHL), Tampa Bay
	Marian Kacir (RW)	6-1/183	Hodonin, Czechoslovakia	9-29-74	0	Chicago (IHL), Charlotte (ECHL), Nashville (ECHL)
85	Petr Klima (LW/RW)	6-0/190	Chaomutov, Czech.	12-23-64	10	Wolfsburg (Germany Div. II), ZPS Zlin (Czech.), Tampa Bay
	Brantt Myhres (LW)	6-3/195	Edmonton	3-18-74	1	Tampa Bay
	Eduard Pershin (RW)	6-0/191	Nizhnekamsk, U.S.S.R.	9-1-77	0	Dynamo Moscow (CIS)
	Brent Peterson (LW)	6-3/195	Calgary	7-20-72	0	Michigan Tech (WCHA)
8	Jason Ruff (LW)	6-2/192	Kelowna, B.C.	1-27-70	2	Atlanta (IHL)
	Alexander Selivanov (RW)	6-0/180	Moscow, U.S.S.R.	3-23-71	1	Atlanta (IHL), Chicago (IHL), Tampa Bay
20	Alexander Semak (C)	5-10/185	Ufa, U.S.S.R.	2-11-66	4	Salavat Yulayev Ufa (CIS), New Jersey, Tampa Bay
	Jeff Toms (LW)	6-3/180	Swift Current, Sask.	6-4-74	0	Atlanta (IHL)
14	John Tucker (RW)	6-0/200	Windsor, Ont.	9-29-64	11	Tampa Bay
	Jason Wiemer (LW)	6-1/215	Kimberley, B.C.	4-14-76	1	Portland (WHL), Tampa Bay
21	Paul Ysebaert (LW)	6-1/190	Sarnia, Ont.	5-15-66	7	Chicago, Tampa Bay
7	Rob Zamuner (LW/C)	6-2/202	Oakville, Ont.	9-17-69	4	Tampa Bay
	DEFENSEMEN					
	Drew Bannister	6-1/193	Belleville, Ont.	9-4-74	0	Atlanta (IHL)
25	Marc Bergevin	6-1/197	Montreal	8-11-65	11	Tampa Bay
3	Eric Charron	6-3/192	Verdun, Que.	1-14-70	3	Tampa Bay
39	Enrico Ciccone	6-4/200	Montreal	4-10-70	4	Tampa Bay
4	Cory Cross	6-5/212	Prince Albert, Sask.	1-3-71	2	Atlanta (IHL), Tampa Bay
	Eric DuBois	6-0/195	Moncton, N.B.	5-10-70	0	Atlanta (IHL)
	Bob Halkidis	5-11/205	Toronto	3-5-66	10	Detroit, Tampa Bay
44	Roman Hamrlik	6-2/189	Gottwaldov, Czech.	4-12-74	3	ZPS Zlin (Czech.), Tampa Bay
	Bill Houlder	6-3/218	Thunder Bay, Ont.	3-11-67	8	St. Louis
40	Chris LiPuma	6-0/183	Chicago	3-23-71	3	Atlanta (IHL), Tampa Bay, Nashville (ECHL)
6	Adrien Plavsic	6-1/200	Montreal	1-13-70	6	Vancouver, Tampa Bay
20	Rudy Poeschek	6-2/210	Terrace, B.C.	9-29-66	7	Tampa Bay
	Mathieu Raby	6-2/204	Hull, Que.	1-19-75	0	Victoriaville (QMJHL), Sherbrooke (QMJHL)
	GOALTENDERS					
30	Jean-Claude Bergeron	5-9/181	Hauterive, Que.	10-14-68	4	Tampa Bay, Atlanta (IHL)
	Tyler Moss	6-0/168	Ottawa	6-29-75	0	Kingston (OHL)
93	Daren Puppa	6-3/205	Kirkland Lake, Ont.	3-23-65	10	Tampa Bay
	Derek Wilkinson	6-0/160	Windsor, Ont.	7-29-74	0	Atlanta (IHL)

1994-95 REVIEW

INDIVIDUAL STATISTICS

SCORING

	Games	G	A	Pts.	PIM	+/-	PPG	SHG	Shots	Shooting Pct.
Brian Bradley	46	13	27	40	42	-6	3	0	111	11.7
Chris Gratton	46	7	20	27	89	-2	2	0	91	7.7
Petr Klima	47	13	13	26	26	-13	4	0	75	17.3
John Tucker	46	12	13	25	14	-10	2	0	81	14.8
Roman Hamrlik	48	12	11	23	86	-18	7	1	134	9.0
Paul Ysebaert*	29	8	11	19	12	-1	0	0	70	11.4
Denis Savard*	31	6	11	17	10	-6	1	0	56	10.7
Alexander Selivanov	43	10	6	16	14	-2	4	0	94	10.6
Rob Zamuner	43	9	6	15	24	-3	0	3	74	12.2
Shawn Chambers*	24	2	12	14	6	0	1	0	44	4.5
Marc Bureau	48	2	12	14	30	-8	0	1	72	2.8
Mikael Andersson	36	4	7	11	4	-3	0	0	36	11.1
Alexander Semak*	22	5	5	10	12	-3	0	0	39	12.8
Danton Cole*	26	3	3	6	6	-1	1	0	56	5.4
Enrico Ciccone	41	2	4	6	†225	3	0	0	43	4.7
Marc Bergevin	44	2	4	6	51	-6	0	1	32	6.3
Cory Cross	43	1	5	6	41	-6	0	0	35	2.9

	Games	G	A	Pts.	PIM	+/-	PPG	SHG	Shots	Shooting Pct.
Jason Wiemer	36	1	4	5	44	-2	0	0	10	10.0
Eric Charron	45	1	4	5	26	1	0	0	33	3.0
Bob Halkidis*	27	1	3	4	40	-12	0	0	25	4.0
Adrien Plavsic*	15	2	1	3	4	5	0	0	24	8.3
Brantt Myhres	15	2	0	2	81	-2	0	0	4	50.0
Rudy Poeschek	25	1	1	2	92	0	0	0	14	7.1
Ben Hankinson*	18	0	2	2	6	1	0	0	18	0.0
Jim Cummins*	10	1	0	1	41	-3	0	0	3	33.3
Brent Gretzky	3	0	1	1	0	-2	0	0	1	0.0
Daren Puppa (goalie)	36	0	1	1	2	0	0	0	0	0.0
Gerard Gallant	1	0	0	0	0	0	0	0	1	0.0
Chris Lipuma	1	0	0	0	0	2	0	0	1	0.0
Rich Sutter*	4	0	0	0	0	0	0	0	3	0.0
J.C. Bergeron (goalie)	17	0	0	0	2	0	0	0	0	0.0

GOALTENDING

	Games	Min.	Goals	SO	Avg.	W	L	T	Shots	Sv. Pct.
Daren Puppa	36	2013	90	1	2.68	14	19	2	946	.905
J.C. Bergeron	17	883	49	1	3.33	3	9	1	374	.869

Empty-net goals (do not count against a goaltender's average): Puppa 4, Bergeron 1.
*Played with two or more NHL teams.
†Led league.

RESULTS

JANUARY
20—Pittsburgh ..... L 3-5
22—Buffalo ..... L 2-5
25—Florida ..... W 3-2
26—At Florida ..... L 2-4
28—At N.Y. Islanders ..... W 4-1
31—Montreal ..... W 4-1

FEBRUARY
2—At N.Y. Rangers ..... T *3-3
4—At Pittsburgh ..... L 3-6
5—At Buffalo ..... L 1-2
7—N.Y. Islanders ..... W 5-2
10—Hartford ..... W 4-3
11—N.Y. Rangers ..... L 2-3
14—Philadelphia ..... L 2-5
17—Ottawa ..... L 1-2
18—Boston ..... W 3-1
20—N.Y. Rangers ..... L 1-3
23—At N.Y. Islanders ..... W 4-1
24—At Pittsburgh ..... W 4-2
26—At Washington ..... T *1-1

MARCH
1—At Quebec ..... L 2-8
2—At Ottawa ..... W *3-2
4—At Hartford ..... L *2-3
7—Philadelphia ..... L 3-4
10—New Jersey ..... L 2-3
12—At Washington ..... L 1-3
13—Washington ..... L 0-3
18—At New Jersey ..... W 2-1
19—At Buffalo ..... W 6-1
24—Boston ..... L *3-4
27—Montreal ..... W *3-2
29—Washington ..... L 2-4
31—Hartford ..... W 2-0

APRIL
2—Florida ..... L 1-4
4—At New Jersey ..... T *1-1
6—At Philadelphia ..... L 4-5
8—At Boston ..... L 1-5
9—At Hartford ..... W 3-0
11—N.Y. Islanders ..... W 5-2
14—At Philadelphia ..... L 2-3
16—At Florida ..... L 1-4
18—New Jersey ..... W 3-2
20—Quebec ..... W 5-2
22—At Montreal ..... L 1-3
24—Buffalo ..... L 1-3
26—At N.Y. Rangers ..... L 4-6
27—At Ottawa ..... L 1-6
29—At Quebec ..... L 1-4

MAY
3—Ottawa ..... L 3-4
*Denotes overtime game.

— 70 —

TORONTO MAPLE LEAFS
WESTERN CONFERENCE/CENTRAL DIVISION

1995-96 SCHEDULE

Home games shaded.
* — All-Star Game at FleetCenter, Boston.
D — Day game.

OCTOBER

SUN	MON	TUE	WED	THU	FRI	SAT
1	2	3	4	5	6	7 PIT
8	9	10 NYI	11	12	13	14 NYR
15	16	17 SJ	18	19	20 CAL	21 MON
22	23	24 FLA	25	26 CHI	27	28 LA
29 NYR	30	31				

NOVEMBER

SUN	MON	TUE	WED	THU	FRI	SAT
			1 WIN	2	3 VAN	4 EDM
5	6	7 ANA	8	9	10 WAS	11 BOS
12	13	14 FLA	15	16 TB	17	18 WIN
19	20	21 STL	22	23	24 HAR	25 STL
26	27	28 WIN	29	30 PHI		

DECEMBER

SUN	MON	TUE	WED	THU	FRI	SAT
					1	2 ANA
3	4	5 OTT	6	7 NJ	8	9 DAL
10	11 COL	12	13	14 LA	15	16 LA
17 ANA	18	19	20 CHI	21 CHI	22	23 EDM
24	25	26	27 CAL	28	29 COL	30 STL
31						

JANUARY

SUN	MON	TUE	WED	THU	FRI	SAT
	1 DAL	D 2	3 BOS	4	5 BUF	6 COL
7	8	9	10 LA	11 NYI	12	13 VAN
14	15	16	17 WIN	18	19	20 *
21	22	23	24 CHI	25	26	27 OTT
28	29	30 DET	31 STL			

FEBRUARY

SUN	MON	TUE	WED	THU	FRI	SAT
				1	2	3 MON
4	5 SJ	6	7 ANA	8 LA	9	10 BUF
11	12 PIT	13	14 SJ	15	16 WAS	17
18 D DET	19	20	21 TB	22 DET	23	24 DAL
25	26	27	28 WIN	29		

MARCH

SUN	MON	TUE	WED	THU	FRI	SAT
					1	2 DAL
3 COL	4	5	6 NJ	7	8 HAR	9 CAL
10	11	12	13 WIN	14	15 DAL	16
17 D VAN	18	19 DET	20 DET	21	22	23 PHI
24	25 CAL	26	27 VAN	28	29	30 EDM
31						

APRIL

SUN	MON	TUE	WED	THU	FRI	SAT
	1	2	3 CHI	4 STL	5	6 STL
7	8	9	10	11 CHI	12	13 EDM
14	15	16	17	18	19	20

1995-96 SEASON

CLUB DIRECTORY

Chairman of the board and CEO
Steve A. Stavro
President, COO and general manager
Cliff Fletcher
Secretary-treasurer
J. Donald Crump
Alternate governors
Cliff Fletcher
Brian P. Bellmore
Assistant general manager
Bill Watters
Special consultant to the president
Darryl Sittler
Dir. of scouting and player personnel
Nick Beverley
Dir. of bus. operations and communications
Bob Stellick
Controller
Ian Clarke
Head coach
Pat Burns
Assistant coaches
Mike Kitchen
Rick Wamsley
Director of professional development
Floyd Smith
Director of marketing
Bill Cluff
Media relations coordinator
Pat Park

Box office manager
Donna Henderson
Scouts
George Armstrong
John Choyce
Anders Hedberg
Peter Johnson
Garth Malarchuk
Dan Marr
Dick Bouchard
Jack Gardiner
Bob Johnson
Ernie Gare
Doug Woods
Head athletic therapist
Chris Broadhurst
Athletic therapist
Brent Smith
Trainer
Brian Papineau
Team doctors
Dr. Michael Clarfield
Dr. Darrell Olgilvie-Harris
Dr. Leith Douglas
Dr. Michael Easterbrook
Dr. Simon McGrail
Dr. Ernie Lewis

DRAFT CHOICES

Rd.—Player	H/W	Overall	Pos.	Last team
1—Jeff Ware	6-4/214	15	D	Oshawa (OHL)
3—Ryan Pepperall	6-1/175	54	RW	Kitchener (OHL)
6—Doug Bonner	5-9/170	139	G	Seattle (WHL)
6—Yannick Tremblay	6-2/175	145	D	Beauport (QMJHL)
7—Marek Melenovsky	5-9/176	171	C	Czech Republic
8—Mark Murphy	5-11/195	197	LW	Stratford, Ont. (Jr. B)
9—Danlil Markov	5-11/176	223	D	Spartak, CIS

MISCELLANEOUS DATA

Home ice (capacity)
Maple Leaf Gardens
(15,746, including standees)
Address
60 Carlton Street
Toronto, Ont. M5B 1L1
Business phone
416-977-1641
Rink dimensions
200 feet by 85 feet

Club colors
Blue and white
Radio affiliation
Telemedia Radio Network
(The Fan 590)
TV affiliation
CBC, Global TV

No.	FORWARDS	Ht./Wt.	Place (BORN)	Date	NHL exp.	1994-95 clubs
14	Dave Andreychuk (LW)	6-3/220	Hamilton, Ont.	9-29-63	13	Toronto
	Ken Belanger (LW)	6-4/225	Sault Ste. Marie, Ont.	5-14-74	1	St. John's (AHL), Toronto
10	Bill Berg (LW)	6-1/205	St. Catharines, Ont.	10-21-67	6	Toronto
20	Mike Craig (RW)	6-1/180	London, Ont.	6-6-71	5	Toronto
15	Paul Dipietro (C)	5-8/179	Sault Ste. Marie, Ont.	9-8-70	4	Montreal, Toronto
20	Tie Domi (RW)	5-10/200	Windsor, Ont.	11-1-69	6	Winnipeg, Toronto
22	Mike Gartner (RW)	6-0/187	Ottawa	10-29-59	16	Toronto
93	Doug Gilmour (C)	5-11/172	Kingston, Ont.	6-25-63	12	Rapperswil (Switzerland Div. II), Toronto
	Sean Haggerty (LW)	6-1/186	Greenwich, Conn.	2-11-76	0	Detroit (OHL)
	Darby Hendrickson (C)	6-0/185	Richfield, Minn.	8-28-72	2	St. John's (AHL), Toronto
33	Benoit Hogue (LW)	5-10/194	Repentigny, Que.	10-28-66	8	New York Islanders, Toronto
18	Kent Manderville (LW)	6-3/207	Edmonton	4-12-71	4	Toronto
27	Sergio Momesso (LW)	6-3/215	Montreal	9-4-65	11	Milan (Italy), Vancouver
	Zdenek Nedved (RW)	6-0/180	Lany, Czechoslovakia	3-3-75	1	Sudbury (OHL), Toronto
10	Warren Rychel (LW)	6-0/202	Tecumseh, Ont.	5-12-67	5	Los Angeles, Toronto
13	Mats Sundin (RW)	6-4/215	Sollentuna, Sweden	2-13-71	5	Djurgarden Stockholm (Sweden), Toronto
	Todd Warriner (LW/C)	6-1/188	Chatham, Ont.	1-3-74	1	St. John's (AHL), Toronto
19	Randy Wood (LW)	6-0/195	Princeton, N.J.	10-12-63	9	Toronto

DEFENSEMEN

No.	DEFENSEMEN	Ht./Wt.	Place	Date	NHL exp.	1994-95 clubs
22	Ken Baumgartner (D/LW)	6-1/205	Flin Flon, Man.	3-11-66	8	Toronto
5	Garth Butcher	6-0/204	Regina, Sask.	1-8-63	14	Toronto
4	Dave Ellett	6-2/205	Cleveland	3-30-64	11	Toronto
23	Todd Gill	6-0/180	Brockville, Ont.	11-9-65	11	Toronto
	David Harlock	6-2/205	Toronto	3-16-71	2	St. John's (AHL), Toronto
	Kenny Jonsson	6-3/195	Angelholm, Sweden	10-5-74	1	Rogle (Sweden), St. John's (AHL), Toronto
34	Jamie Macoun	6-2/200	Newmarket, Ont.	8-17-61	13	Toronto
	Matt Martin	6-3/205	Hamden, Conn.	4-30-71	2	St. John's (AHL), Toronto
55	Larry Murphy	6-2/210	Scarborough, Ont.	3-8-61	15	Pittsburgh

GOALTENDERS

No.	GOALTENDERS	Ht./Wt.	Place	Date	NHL exp.	1994-95 clubs
	Doug Bonner	5-9/170	Tacoma, MA.	10-15-76	0	Seattle (WHL)
	Marcel Cousineau	5-10/175	Delson, Que.	4-30-73	0	St. John's (AHL)
35	Pat Jablonski	6-0/180	Toledo, O.	6-20-67	5	Chicago (IHL), Houston (IHL)
29	Felix Potvin	6-0/190	Anjou, Que.	6-23-71	4	Toronto
	Damian Rhodes	6-0/190	St. Paul, Minn.	5-28-69	3	Toronto

1994-95 REVIEW

INDIVIDUAL STATISTICS

SCORING

	Games	G	A	Pts.	PIM	+/-	PPG	SHG	Shots	Shooting Pct.
Mats Sundin	47	23	24	47	14	-5	9	0	173	13.3
Dave Andreychuk	48	22	16	38	34	-7	8	0	168	13.1
Mike Ridley	48	10	27	37	14	1	2	2	88	11.4
Doug Gilmour	44	10	23	33	26	-5	3	0	73	13.7
Todd Gill	47	7	25	32	64	-8	3	1	82	8.5
Randy Wood	48	13	11	24	34	7	1	1	125	10.4
Mike Gartner	38	12	8	20	6	0	2	1	91	13.2
Dmitri Mironov	33	5	12	17	28	6	2	0	68	7.4
Benoit Hogue	45	9	7	16	34	0	2	0	66	13.6
Dave Ellett	33	5	10	15	26	-6	3	0	84	6.0
Mike Eastwood*	36	5	5	10	32	-12	0	0	38	13.2
Mike Craig	37	5	5	10	12	-21	1	0	61	8.2
Jamie Macoun	46	2	8	10	75	-6	1	0	84	2.4
Kenny Jonsson	39	2	7	9	16	-8	0	0	50	4.0
Garth Butcher	45	1	7	8	59	-5	0	0	24	4.2
Warren Rychel*	26	1	6	7	101	1	0	0	34	2.9
Bill Berg	32	5	1	6	26	-11	0	0	57	8.8
Benoit Hogue*	12	3	3	6	0	0	1	0	16	18.8
Terry Yake	19	3	2	5	2	1	1	0	26	11.5
Nikolai Borschevsky*	19	0	5	5	0	3	0	0	28	0.0
Rich Sutter*	18	0	3	3	10	-7	0	0	19	0.0
Dixon Ward	22	0	3	3	31	-4	0	0	15	0.0
Paul Dipietro*	12	1	1	2	6	-6	0	0	19	5.3
Grant Jennings*	10	0	2	2	7	-6	0	0	9	0.0
Drake Berehowsky*	25	0	2	2	15	-10	0	0	12	0.0
Darby Hendrickson	8	0	1	1	4	0	0	0	4	0.0

	Games	G	A	Pts.	PIM	+/-	PPG	SHG	Shots	Shooting Pct.
Tie Domi*	9	0	1	1	31	1	0	0	12	0.0
Kent Manderville	36	0	1	1	22	-2	0	0	43	0.0
David Harlock	1	0	0	0	0	-1	0	0	0	0.0
Zdenek Nedved	1	0	0	0	2	0	0	0	0	0.0
Ken Baumgartner	2	0	0	0	5	0	0	0	1	0.0
Ken Belanger	3	0	0	0	9	0	0	0	1	0.0
Todd Warriner	5	0	0	0	0	-3	0	0	1	0.0
Damian Rhodes (goalie)	13	0	0	0	4	0	0	0	0	0.0
Matt Martin	15	0	0	0	13	2	0	0	14	0.0
Felix Potvin (goalie)	36	0	0	0	4	0	0	0	0	0.0

GOALTENDING

	Games	Min.	Goals	SO	Avg.	W	L	T	Shots	Sv. Pct.
Damian Rhodes	13	760	34	0	2.68	6	6	1	404	.916
Felix Potvin	36	2144	104	0	2.91	15	13	7	1120	.907

Empty-net goals (do not count against a goaltender's average): Potvin 6, Rhodes 2.
*Played with two or more NHL teams.

RESULTS

JANUARY

20—At Los Angeles	T	*3-3	
21—At San Jose	L	2-3	
25—Vancouver	W	6-2	
27—At Chicago	L	1-4	
28—Calgary	W	2-1	
30—At Dallas	W	2-1	

FEBRUARY

1—At Vancouver	T	*4-4	
3—At Edmonton	L	3-5	
4—At Calgary	L	1-4	
6—San Jose	W	7-3	
8—Dallas	T	*3-3	
10—At Detroit	W	2-1	
11—Los Angeles	L	2-5	
13—Chicago	W	4-2	
15—Edmonton	L	1-4	
18—St. Louis	W	3-1	
20—Detroit	L	2-4	
22—At Detroit	L	1-4	
23—Anaheim	W	3-1	

25—Winnipeg	W	5-2	
27—At St. Louis	L	2-3	

MARCH

2—San Jose	L	3-4	
4—Calgary	W	3-2	
8—Dallas	W	3-2	
11—Chicago	T	*2-2	
13—Los Angeles	L	1-4	
15—At San Jose	W	2-1	
17—At Anaheim	T	*3-3	
18—At Los Angeles	W	5-3	
21—At Vancouver	L	1-3	
24—Winnipeg	W	3-2	
25—At Winnipeg	T	*3-3	
27—Edmonton	W	4-3	
31—At Chicago	T	*3-3	

APRIL

3—At St. Louis	L	2-5	
5—St. Louis	L	4-6	
7—Detroit	L	2-4	

8—Winnipeg	W	4-3	
14—Dallas	W	2-1	
15—At Winnipeg	L	1-5	
17—At Chicago	W	3-1	
19—Anaheim	W	3-2	
21—At St. Louis	L	1-3	
22—At Dallas	L	4-6	
26—Vancouver	W	5-2	
29—At Calgary	T	*2-2	

MAY

1—At Edmonton	W	6-5	
3—At Anaheim	L	1-6	

*Denotes overtime game.

VANCOUVER CANUCKS
WESTERN CONFERENCE/PACIFIC DIVISION

1995-96 SCHEDULE

Home games shaded.
* — All-Star Game at FleetCenter, Boston.
D — Day game.

OCTOBER
SUN	MON	TUE	WED	THU	FRI	SAT
1	2	3	4	5	6	7
8	9 DET	10	11	12 LA	13	14 SJ
15 LA	16	17	18 ANA	19	20	21 EDM
22	23	24 NYR	25 NJ	26	27	28 WIN
29	30 SJ	31				

NOVEMBER
SUN	MON	TUE	WED	THU	FRI	SAT
			1 EDM	2	3 TOR	4 CAL
5	6	7 NYI	8	9 CHI	10	11 COL
12 MON	13	14	15	16 FLA	17	18 TB
19 PHI	20	21	22 DAL	23 STL	24	25 SJ
26	27	28	29 CHI	30		

DECEMBER
SUN	MON	TUE	WED	THU	FRI	SAT
					1 SJ	2
3	4	5 EDM	6	7	8 STL	9 CAL
10	11	12	13 EDM	14	15	16
17 D OTT	18 COL	19	20 LA	21	22 ANA	23 DET
24	25	26 CAL	27	28 NYR	29	30
31 D PHI						

JANUARY
SUN	MON	TUE	WED	THU	FRI	SAT
	1	2	3 FLA	4	5	6 TB
7	8 PIT	9	10 MON	11	12	13 TOR
14	15 D BOS	16 HAR	17	18	19	20 *
21	22 DAL	23	24 ANA	25 COL	26	27 NYI
28	29	30 NJ	31			

FEBRUARY
SUN	MON	TUE	WED	THU	FRI	SAT
				1 STL	2 DAL	3
4 D WIN	5	6	7 HAR	8	9 EDM	10 WAS
11	12	13 WIN	14	15 ANA	16	17 BOS
18	19 DET	20	21 WIN	22	23 SJ	24
25	26	27 PIT	28	29 STL		

MARCH
SUN	MON	TUE	WED	THU	FRI	SAT
					1	2 D DET
3 D BUF	4	5	6 D BUF	7	8	8 D COL
10	11	12 WAS	13	14 CHI	15 OTT	16
17 D TOR	18	19 COL	20	21	22 DAL	23 CAL
24	25 LA	26	27 TOR	28	29 CHI	30
31						

APRIL
SUN	MON	TUE	WED	THU	FRI	SAT
	1 EDM	2	3 CAL	4	5	6 LA
7	8 ANA	9	10	11	12	13 CAL
14	15	16	17	18	19	20

1995-96 SEASON

CLUB DIRECTORY

Chairman, CEO, governor
Arthur R. Griffiths
Vice chairman and alternate governor
John E. McCaw Jr.
President and chief operating officer
John H. Chapple
Deputy chairman and alternate governor
Michael J. Korenberg
Executive vice president
Stanley B. McCammon
Executive vice president, business
Tod Leiweke
Vice president, consumer sales
John Rizzardini
President, g.m., alternate governor
Pat Quinn
Vice president, finance and administration
Carlos Mascarenhas
Vice president, assistant to president
Steve Tambellini
Vice president, hockey operations
George McPhee
Director of corporate sales and promotions
Ric Thomsen
Director, customer sales and service
John Rocha
Director, player development/scouting
Mike Penny
Manager, hockey information
Devin Smith
Public relations assistant
Veronica Bateman
Game presentation
Jane Bremner
Head coach
Rick Ley

Assistant coaches
Glen Hanlon
Stan Smyl
Strength and conditioning coach
Peter Twist
Director of pro scouting
Murray Oliver
Scouting information coordinator
Frank Provenzano
Scouts
Ron Delorme
Jack McCartan
Noel Price
Ken Slater
Jack Birch
Ross Mahoney
Mike Backman
Sergei Chibisov
Jim Eagle
Thomas Gradin
Ed McColgan
Ray Miron
Al McDonald
Medical trainer
Larry Ashley
Message therapist
Dave Schima
Equipment trainers
Pat O'Neill
Darren Granger
Team doctors
Dr. Ross Davidson
Dr. Doug Clement
Team dentist
Dr. David Lawson

DRAFT CHOICES

Rd.—Player	H/W	Overall	Pos.	Last team
2—Chris McAllister	6-6/236	40	D	Saskatoon (WHL)
3—Larry Courville	6-2/184	61	LW	Oshawa (OHL)
3—Peter Schaefer	5-11/178	66	LW	Brandon (WHL)
4—Lloyd Shaw	6-3/215	92	D	Seattle (WHL)
5—Todd Norman	5-10/186	120	LW	Guelph (OHL)
6—Brent Sopel	6-1/185	144	D	Swift Current (WHL)
7—Stewart Bodtker	6-1/175	170	C	Colorado College
8—Tyler Willis	5-8/160	196	RW	Swift Current (WHL)
9—Jason Cugnet	6-1/170	222	G	Kelowna (BCJHL)

MISCELLANEOUS DATA

Home ice (capacity)
General Motors Place (19,056)
Address
800 Griffiths Way
Vancouver, B.C.
Business phone
604-899-4600
Rink dimensions
200 feet by 85 feet

Club colors
White, black, red and gold
Radio affiliation
CKNW (980 AM)
TV affiliation
BCTV (Channel 8)

No.	FORWARDS	Ht./Wt.	Place	Born Date	NHL exp.	1994-95 clubs
42	Josef Beranek (C)	6-2/189	Litvinov, Czechoslovakia	10-25-69	4	Dadak Vsetin (Czech Rep.), Philadelphia, Vancouver
	Lonny Bohonos (RW)	5-11/190	Winnipeg	5-20-73	0	Syracuse (AHL)
10	Pavel Bure (RW/LW)	5-10/187	Moscow, U.S.S.R.	3-31-71	4	Landshut (Germany), Spartak Moscow (CIS), Vancouver
9	Russ Courtnall (RW)	5-11/190	Victoria, B.C.	6-3-65	12	Dallas, Vancouver
23	Martin Gelinas (LW)	5-11/195	Shawinigan, Que.	6-5-70	7	Vancouver
	Rick Girard (C)	5-11/180	Edmonton	5-1-74	0	Syracuse (AHL)
19	Tim Hunter (LW/RW)	6-2/202	Calgary	9-10-60	14	Vancouver
36	Dane Jackson (RW)	6-1/200	Winnipeg	5-17-70	2	Syracuse (AHL), Vancouver
16	Trevor Linden (RW)	6-4/210	Medicine Hat, Alta.	4-11-70	7	Vancouver
	Brian Loney (RW)	6-2/195	Winnipeg	8-9-72	0	Syracuse (AHL)
15	John McIntyre (C/LW)	6-1/180	Ravenswood, Ont.	4-29-69	6	Vancouver
89	Alexander Mogilny (RW)	5-11/187	Khabarovsk, U.S.S.R.	2-18-69	6	Spartak Moscow (CIS), Buffalo
29	Gino Odjick (LW)	6-3/210	Maniwaki, Que.	9-7-70	5	Vancouver
28	Roman Oksiuta (RW)	6-3/229	Murmansk, U.S.S.R.	8-21-70	2	Cape Breton (AHL), Edmonton, Vancouver
17	Mike Ridley (C)	6-0/195	Winnipeg	7-8-63	10	Toronto
7	Cliff Ronning (C)	5-8/180	Vancouver	10-1-65	9	Vancouver
	Rod Stevens (C)	5-10/175	Fort St. John, B.C.	4-5-74	0	Syracuse (AHL)
25	Alex Stojanov (LW)	6-4/230	Windsor, Ont.	4-25-73	1	Syracuse (AHL), Vancouver
24	Scott Walker (RW)	5-9/185	Montreal	7-19-73	1	Syracuse (AHL), Vancouver
	DEFENSEMEN					
6	Adrian Aucoin	6-1/194	London, Ont.	7-3-73	1	Syracuse (AHL), Vancouver
44	Dave Babych	6-2/215	Edmonton	5-23-61	15	Vancouver
22	Jeff Brown	6-1/204	Ottawa	4-30-66	10	Vancouver
34	Jassen Cullimore	6-5/220	Simcoe, Ont.	12-4-72	1	Syracuse (AHL), Vancouver
3	Bret Hedican	6-2/195	St. Paul, Minn.	8-10-70	4	Vancouver
21	Jyrki Lumme	6-1/207	Tampere, Finland	7-16-66	7	Ilves Tampere (Finland), Vancouver
5	Dana Murzyn	6-2/210	Regina, Sask.	12-9-66	10	Vancouver
2	John Namestnikov	5-11/190	Novgorod, U.S.S.R.	10-9-71	2	Syracuse (AHL), Vancouver
	Leif Rohlin	6-1/198	Vasteras, Sweden	2-26-68	0	Vasteras (Sweden)
4	Mark Wotton	6-0/190	Foxwarren, Man.	11-16-73	1	Syracuse (AHL), Vancouver
	GOALTENDERS					
	Mike Fountain	6-1/176	Gravenhurst, Ont.	1-26-72	0	Syracuse (AHL)
31	Corey Hirsch	5-10/160	Medicine Hat, Alta.	7-1-72	1	Binghamton (AHL)
1	Kirk McLean	6-0/180	Willowdale, Ont.	6-26-66	10	Vancouver
	Sonny Mignacca	5-8/175	Winnipeg	1-4-74	0	Syracuse (AHL)
35	Kay Whitmore	5-11/180	Sudbury, Ont.	4-10-67	7	Vancouver

1994-95 REVIEW

INDIVIDUAL STATISTICS

SCORING

	Games	G	A	Pts.	PIM	+/-	PPG	SHG	Shots	Shooting Pct.
Pavel Bure	44	20	23	43	47	-8	6	2	198	10.1
Trevor Linden	48	18	22	40	40	-5	9	0	129	14.0
Geoff Courtnall	45	16	18	34	81	2	7	0	144	11.1
Jeff Brown	33	8	23	31	16	-2	3	0	111	7.2
Sergio Momesso	48	10	15	25	65	-2	6	0	82	12.2
Cliff Ronning	41	6	19	25	27	-4	3	0	93	6.5
Martin Gelinas	46	13	10	23	36	8	1	0	75	17.3
Josef Beranek*	37	8	13	21	28	-10	2	0	95	8.4
Russ Courtnall*	13	4	14	18	4	10	0	2	42	9.5
Jyrki Lumme	36	5	12	17	26	4	3	0	78	6.4
Greg Adams*	31	5	10	15	12	1	2	2	56	8.9
Dave Babych	40	3	11	14	18	-13	1	0	58	5.2
Bret Hedican	45	2	11	13	34	-3	0	0	56	3.6
Mike Peca	33	6	6	12	30	-6	2	0	46	13.0
Christian Ruuttu*	25	5	6	11	23	11	0	0	19	26.3
Gino Odjick	23	4	5	9	109	-3	0	0	35	11.4
Nathan Lafayette*	27	4	4	8	2	2	0	1	30	13.3
Dana Murzyn	40	0	8	8	129	14	0	0	29	0.0
Roman Oksiuta*	12	5	2	7	2	2	1	0	15	33.3
Jiri Slegr*	19	1	5	6	32	0	0	0	42	2.4
Tim Hunter	34	3	2	5	120	1	0	0	17	17.6
Gerald Diduck*	22	1	3	4	15	-8	1	0	25	4.0
John McIntyre	28	0	4	4	37	-3	0	0	6	0.0
Jassen Cullimore	34	1	2	3	39	-2	0	0	30	3.3

	Games	G	A	Pts.	PIM	+/-	PPG	SHG	Shots	Shooting Pct.
Yevgeny Namestnikov	16	0	3	3	4	2	0	0	18	0.0
Gary Leeman	10	2	0	2	0	-3	0	0	14	14.3
Adrian Aucoin	1	1	0	1	0	1	0	0	2	50.0
Jose Charbonneau	3	1	0	1	0	0	0	0	2	50.0
Dane Jackson	3	1	0	1	4	0	0	0	6	16.7
Adrien Plavsic*	3	0	1	1	4	3	0	0	11	0.0
Scott Walker	11	0	1	1	33	0	0	0	8	0.0
Kay Whitmore (goalie)	11	0	1	1	7	0	0	0	0	0.0
Kirk McLean (goalie)	40	0	1	1	4	0	0	0	0	0.0
Mark Wotton	1	0	0	0	0	1	0	0	2	0.0
Alek Stojanov	4	0	0	0	13	-2	0	0	1	0.0
Shawn Antoski*	7	0	0	0	46	-4	0	0	4	0.0

GOALTENDING

	Games	Min.	Goals	SO	Avg.	W	L	T	Shots	Sv. Pct.
Kirk McLean	40	2374	109	1	2.75	18	12	†10	1140	.904
Kay Whitmore	11	558	37	0	3.98	0	6	2	279	.867

Empty-net goals (do not count against a goaltender's average): McLean 1, Whitmore 1.
*Played with two or more NHL teams.
†Led league.

RESULTS

JANUARY

20—Dallas	T	*1-1
21—St. Louis	L	1-7
24—At Detroit	L	3-6
25—At Toronto	L	2-6
28—At St. Louis	W	3-1

FEBRUARY

1—Toronto	T	*4-4
5—Chicago	L	4-9
7—Edmonton	T	*4-4
9—Winnipeg	W	5-1
11—San Jose	T	*1-1
15—At San Jose	L	1-3
17—At Anaheim	T	*2-2
18—At Los Angeles	W	6-2
20—Los Angeles	W	8-2
22—Winnipeg	L	1-4
24—At Dallas	T	*3-3
26—At San Jose	W	5-1
28—San Jose	L	3-4

MARCH

2—At Calgary	T	*2-2
4—At Los Angeles	W	5-4
6—Detroit	L	2-5
11—Anaheim	W	5-3
12—At Edmonton	W	5-2
14—At Winnipeg	T	*3-3
16—At Chicago	L	2-9
17—At Detroit	L	1-3
21—Toronto	W	3-1
23—Chicago	L	1-3
25—Detroit	L	1-2
26—At Calgary	L	0-2
29—Los Angeles	W	5-2
31—Anaheim	W	6-1

APRIL

1—At Edmonton	W	5-1
4—Dallas	T	*2-2
7—At Winnipeg	L	4-7

8—At Calgary	W	4-2
11—Anaheim	W	5-0
13—Edmonton	L	4-6
15—At Anaheim	W	3-1
17—At Dallas	T	*2-2
18—At St. Louis	L	1-4
20—Calgary	T	*2-2
22—Edmonton	W	6-1
25—At Chicago	L	*3-4
26—At Toronto	L	2-5
28—St. Louis	W	3-1
30—Calgary	W	6-4

MAY

3—At San Jose	T	*3-3

*Denotes overtime game.

WASHINGTON CAPITALS
EASTERN CONFERENCE/ATLANTIC DIVISION

1995-96 SCHEDULE

Home games shaded.
* — All-Star Game at FleetCenter, Boston.
D — Day game.

OCTOBER
SUN	MON	TUE	WED	THU	FRI	SAT
1	2	3	4	5	6	7 STL
8	9	10	11 PHI	12	13 COL	14 TB
15	16	17 DAL	18 COL	19	20 LA	21
22	23	24	25	26 BOS	27	28 TB
29 STL	30	31				

NOVEMBER
SUN	MON	TUE	WED	THU	FRI	SAT
			1 MON	2	3 FLA	4 NYI
5	6	7 BOS	8	9	10 TOR	11 CHI
12	13	14 PHI	15	16	17 PIT	18 PIT
19	20	21 SJ	22	23	24 TB	25 HAR
26	27	28	29 ANA	30 LA		

DECEMBER
SUN	MON	TUE	WED	THU	FRI	SAT
					1	2 SJ
3	4	5 FLA	6	7	8 BUF	9
10 WIN	11	12	13	14 NYI	15	16 NYR
17	18 NYR	19	20	21	22 EDM	23 NYI
24	25	26 MON	27	28 FLA	29	30 HAR
31						

JANUARY
SUN	MON	TUE	WED	THU	FRI	SAT
	1 D PIT	2	3 HAR	4	5 NYR	6 NJ
7	8 NYR	9	10	11 OTT	12	13 DET
14	15	16 WIN	17 CHI	18	19	20 *
21	22	23 FLA	24	25 NJ	26 BUF	27
28 D PHI	29	30	31 MON			

FEBRUARY
SUN	MON	TUE	WED	THU	FRI	SAT
				1 OTT	2	3 NYI
4	5	6	7 EDM	8	9	10 VAN
11	12	13 CAL	14	15 DET	16 TOR	17
18 D NJ	19	20	21	22 PHI	23	24 NJ
25	26	27	28	29 FLA		

MARCH
SUN	MON	TUE	WED	THU	FRI	SAT
					1	2 D BOS
3 D PHI	4	5	6	7	8	9 D NYR
10 D TB	11	12 VAN	13	14	15 BOS	16
17 D DAL	18 D	19 ANA	20	21 TB	22	23 HAR
24	25	26 NYI	27 MON	28	29 OTT	30
31 TB						

APRIL
SUN	MON	TUE	WED	THU	FRI	SAT
	1	2	3 BUF	4 PIT	5	6 OTT
7	8	9	10 NYR	11 NJ	12	13 BUF
14	15	16	17	18	19	20

1995-96 SEASON

CLUB DIRECTORY

Chairman and governor
Abe Pollin
President and alternate governor
Richard M. Patrick
Vice president and general manager
David Poile
Legal counselors and alternate governors
David M. Osnos
Peter O'Malley
Vice president/finance
Edmund Stelzer
Vice president/communications
Ed Quinlan
Communications manager
Dan Kaufman
Vice president/marketing
Lew Strudler
Assistant director of marketing
Debi Angus
Director of community relations
Yvon Labre
Admin. assistant to communications
Julie Hensley
Admin. assistant to the general manager
Pat Young

Coach
Jim Schoenfeld
Assistant coaches
Tod Button
Keith Allain
Strength and conditioning coach
Frank Costello
Dir. of player personnel and recruitment
Jack Button
Scouts
Craig Channell
Gilles Cote
Fred Devereaux
Bud Quinn
Hugh Rogers
Bob Schmidt
Shawn Simpson
Dan Sylvester
Niklas Wikegard
Darrell Young
Alexei Yudin
Trainer
Stan Wong
Assistant trainer/head equipment manager
Doug Shearer

DRAFT CHOICES

Rd. — Player	H/W	Overall	Pos.	Last team
1 — Brad Church	6-1/210	17	LW	Prince Albert (WHL)
1 — Miikka Elomo	6-0/183	23	C	Kiekko-67, Finland
2 — Dwayne Hay	6-1/183	43	LW	Guelph (OHL)
4 — Sebastien Charpentier	5-9/161	93	G	Laval (QMJHL)
4 — Joel Theriault	6-3/201	95	D	Beauport (QMJHL)
5 — Benoit Gratton	5-10/163	105	C	Laval (QMJHL)
5 — Joel Cort	6-3/227	124	D	Guelph (OHL)
6 — Frederic Jobin	6-0/210	147	D	Laval (QMJHL)
8 — Vasili Turkovsky	6-0/194	199	D	CSKA Moskow, CIS
9 — Scott Swanson	6-2/186	225	D	Omaha (Jr. A)

MISCELLANEOUS DATA

Home ice (capacity)
USAir Arena (18,130)
Address
Landover, MD 20785
Business phone
301-386-7000
Rink dimensions
200 feet by 85 feet

Club colors
Bronze and blue
Radio affiliation
To be announced
TV affiliation
HTS, WFTY (Channel 50)

TRAINING CAMP ROSTER

No.	FORWARDS	Ht./Wt.	Place	BORN Date	NHL exp.	1994-95 clubs
41	Jason Allison (C)	6-3/205	Toronto	5-29-75	2	London (OHL), Washington, Portland (AHL)
27	Craig Berube (LW)	6-1/205	Calihoo, Alta.	12-17-65	9	Washington
12	Peter Bondra (RW)	6-1/200	Luck, U.S.S.R.	2-7-68	5	HC Kosice (Slovakia), Washington
36	Mike Eagles (C)	5-10/190	Sussex, N.B.	3-7-63	11	Winnipeg, Washington
34	Martin Gendron (RW)	5-9/190	Valleyfield, Que.	2-15-74	1	Portland (AHL), Washington
32	Dale Hunter (C)	5-10/200	Petrolia, Ont.	7-31-60	15	Washington
26	Keith Jones (RW)	6-0/200	Brantford, Ont.	11-8-68	3	Washington
90	Joe Juneau (C)	6-0/195	Pont-Rouge, Que.	1-5-68	4	Washington
23	Kevin Kaminski (C)	5-10/190	Churchbridge, Sask.	3-13-69	5	Portland (AHL), Washington
	Alexander Kharlamov (LW)	5-10/180	Moscow, U.S.S.R.	9-23-75	0	CSKA Moscow (CIS)
22	Steve Konowalchuk (C)	6-1/195	Salt Lake City	11-11-72	4	Washington
10	Kelly Miller (LW)	5-11/195	Lansing, Mich.	3-3-63	11	Washington
15	Jeff Nelson (C)	6-0/190	Prince Albert, Sask.	12-18-72	1	Portland (AHL), Washington
33	Greg Pankewicz (RW)	6-0/189	Valley, Alta.	10-6-70	1	Prince Edward Island (AHL)
14	Pat Peake (RW)	6-1/195	Detroit	5-28-73	2	Washington, Portland (AHL)
25	Rob Pearson (RW)	6-3/200	Oshawa, Ont.	8-3-71	4	Washington
20	Michal Pivonka (C)	6-2/195	Kladno, Czechoslovakia	1-28-66	9	Klagenfurt (Austria), Washington
	Joel Poirier (LW)	6-0/190	Richmond Hill, Ont.	1-15-75	0	Windsor (OHL)
39	Stefan Ustorf (C)	6-0/185	Kaufbeuren, W. Germany	1-3-74	0	Portland (AHL)

DEFENSEMEN

No.	DEFENSEMEN	Ht./Wt.	Place	BORN Date	NHL exp.	1994-95 clubs
	Nolan Baumgartner	6-1/200	Calgary	3-23-76	0	Kamloops (WHL)
	Patrick Boileau	6-0/190	Montreal	2-22-75	0	Laval (QMJHL)
3	Sylvain Cote	6-0/190	Quebec City	1-19-66	11	Washington
	Brian Curran	6-4/230	Toronto	11-5-63	10	Portland (AHL)
17	Sergei Gonchar	6-2/212	Chelyabinsk, U.S.S.R.	4-13-74	1	Portland (AHL), Washington
6	Calle Johansson	5-11/200	Goteborg, Sweden	2-14-67	8	Kloten (Switzerland), Washington
4	Jim Johnson	6-1/190	New Hope, Minn.	8-9-62	10	Washington
2	Ken Klee	6-1/205	Indianapolis	4-24-71	1	Portland (AHL), Washington
38	Steve Poapst	6-0/180	Cornwall, Ont.	1-3-69	0	Portland (AHL)
29	Joe Reekie	6-3/220	Victoria, B.C.	2-22-65	10	Washington
	Sergei Tertyshny	6-0/187	Chelyabinsk, U.S.S.R.	6-3-70	0	Portland (AHL)
24	Mark Tinordi	6-4/213	Red Deer, Alta.	5-9-66	8	Washington
5	Igor Ulanov	6-2/202	Kraskokamsk, U.S.S.R.	10-1-69	4	Winnipeg, Washington
19	Brendan Witt	6-1/205	Humboldt, Sask.	2-20-75	0	Did not play

GOALTENDERS

No.	GOALTENDERS	Ht./Wt.	Place	BORN Date	NHL exp.	1994-95 clubs
30	Jim Carey	6-2/205	Dorchester, Mass.	5-31-74	1	Portland (AHL), Washington
37	Olaf Kolzig	6-3/225	Johannesburg, S. Africa	4-6-70	4	Washington, Portland (AHL)

1994-95 REVIEW

INDIVIDUAL STATISTICS

SCORING

	Games	G	A	Pts.	PIM	+/-	PPG	SHG	Shots	Shooting Pct.
Peter Bondra	47	†34	9	43	24	9	12	†6	177	19.2
Joe Juneau	44	5	38	43	8	-1	3	0	70	7.1
Michal Pivonka	46	10	23	33	50	3	4	2	80	12.5
Calle Johansson	46	5	26	31	35	-6	4	0	112	4.5
Dimitri Khristich	48	12	14	26	41	0	8	0	92	13.0
Steve Konowalchuk	46	11	14	25	44	7	3	3	88	12.5
Kelly Miller	48	10	13	23	6	5	2	0	70	14.3
Dale Hunter	45	8	15	23	101	-4	3	0	73	11.0
Keith Jones	40	14	6	20	65	-2	1	0	85	16.5
Sylvain Cote	47	5	14	19	53	2	1	0	124	4.0
Jim Johnson	47	0	13	13	43	6	0	0	46	0.0
Mark Tinordi	42	3	9	12	71	-5	2	0	71	4.2
Dave Poulin	29	4	5	9	10	2	0	2	30	13.3
Sergei Gonchar	31	2	5	7	22	4	0	0	38	5.3
Joe Reekie	48	1	6	7	97	10	0	0	52	1.9
Craig Berube	43	2	4	6	173	-5	0	0	22	9.1
Rob Pearson	32	0	6	6	96	-6	0	0	34	0.0
Ken Klee	23	3	1	4	41	2	0	0	18	16.7
Mike Eagles*	13	1	3	4	8	2	0	0	15	6.7
Pat Peake	18	0	4	4	12	-6	0	0	30	0.0
Martin Gendron	8	2	1	3	2	3	0	0	11	18.2
Jason Allison	12	2	1	3	6	-3	2	0	9	22.2
John Slaney	16	0	3	3	6	-3	0	0	21	0.0
Kevin Kaminski	27	1	1	2	102	-6	0	0	12	8.3
Jeff Nelson	10	1	0	1	2	-2	0	0	4	25.0

	Games	G	A	Pts.	PIM	+/-	PPG	SHG	Shots	Shooting Pct.
Igor Ulanov*	3	0	1	1	2	3	0	0	0	0.0
Rick Tabaracci* (goalie)	8	0	1	1	2	0	0	0	0	0.0
Randy Burridge*	2	0	0	0	2	0	0	0	2	0.0
Byron Dafoe (goalie)	4	0	0	0	0	0	0	0	0	0.0
Olaf Kolzig (goalie)	14	0	0	0	4	0	0	0	0	0.0
Jim Carey (goalie)	28	0	0	0	0	0	0	0	0	0.0

GOALTENDING

	Games	Min.	Goals	SO	Avg.	W	L	T	Shots	Sv. Pct.
Jim Carey	28	1604	57	4	2.13	18	6	3	654	.913
Rick Tabaracci*	8	394	16	0	2.44	1	3	2	147	.891
Olaf Kolzig	14	724	30	0	2.49	2	8	2	305	.902
Byron Dafoe	4	187	11	0	3.53	1	1	1	80	.863

Empty-net goals (do not count against a goaltender's average): Kolzig 4, Carey 2.
*Played with two or more NHL teams.
†Led league.

RESULTS

JANUARY

21—At Hartford	T	*1-1
24—At Quebec	L	1-5
25—At Montreal	L	0-2
27—N.Y. Islanders	W	5-2
29—Pittsburgh	L	1-4

FEBRUARY

2—Buffalo	L	0-1
4—Florida	W	3-2
7—At Buffalo	L	1-2
8—At N.Y. Rangers	L	4-5
11—At Philadelphia	T	*1-1
13—At Philadelphia	L	3-5
15—At New Jersey	L	2-4
18—Quebec	W	4-2
20—New Jersey	L	0-2
23—At Ottawa	T	*5-5
25—At New Jersey	T	*3-3
26—Tampa Bay	T	*1-1
28—At Philadelphia	L	2-4

MARCH

2—At N.Y. Islanders	W	4-3
4—Montreal	W	5-1
5—N.Y. Rangers	W	4-2
7—At Boston	W	3-1
10—Ottawa	T	*2-2
12—Tampa Bay	W	3-1
13—At Tampa Bay	W	3-0
16—At Florida	L	1-5
18—N.Y. Rangers	W	4-1
20—At Hartford	W	5-0
21—Ottawa	W	1-0
25—Philadelphia	T	*2-2
26—Hartford	L	*3-4
29—At Tampa Bay	W	4-2
31—Quebec	W	6-4

APRIL

2—Boston	W	2-1
4—At N.Y. Islanders	W	5-4
8—Philadelphia	L	1-3
11—At Pittsburgh	L	1-3
12—New Jersey	L	1-2
14—Florida	W	3-0
16—At Quebec	L	2-4
17—At Montreal	L	2-5
21—Hartford	W	6-3
22—At Pittsburgh	W	2-1
24—At N.Y. Rangers	L	4-5
26—N.Y. Islanders	W	6-5
28—Buffalo	W	5-1
30—At Florida	T	*2-2

MAY

2—Pittsburgh	W	7-2

*Denotes overtime game.

WINNIPEG JETS
WESTERN CONFERENCE/CENTRAL DIVISION

Home games shaded.
* — All-Star Game at FleetCenter, Boston.
D — Day game.

OCTOBER
SUN	MON	TUE	WED	THU	FRI	SAT
1	2	3	4	5	6	7 DAL
8	9 ANA	10	11 NYR	12 NJ	13	14
15 DET	16	17 TB	18	19 SJ	20	21
22 ANA	23	24	25 SJ	26	27 EDM	28 VAN
29	30 DET	31				

NOVEMBER
SUN	MON	TUE	WED	THU	FRI	SAT
			1 TOR	2	3 COL	4
5 BUF	6	7	8	9	10 STL	11
12	13	14 CHI	15	16	17 NYR	18 TOR
19	20	21 BOS	22 OTT	23	24	25
26 EDM	27	28 TOR	29	30 STL		

DECEMBER
SUN	MON	TUE	WED	THU	FRI	SAT
					1	2 CHI
3 CAL	4	5	6 LA	7 SJ	8	9
10 WAS	11	12 MON	13	14	15 EDM	16
17 CHI	18	19 TB	20	21 FLA	22	23 STL
24	25	26	27	28 CHI	29 NJ	30
31 D BOS						

JANUARY
SUN	MON	TUE	WED	THU	FRI	SAT
	1	2	3 LA	4	5 DAL	6
7	8 DET	9	10 BUF	11	12 HAR	13
14 ANA	15	16 WAS	17 TOR	18	19	20 *
21	22	23 STL	25	26	27 D MON	
28	29 DAL	30	31			

FEBRUARY
SUN	MON	TUE	WED	THU	FRI	SAT
				1 COL	2	3
4 D VAN	5	6	7	8 OTT	9	10 CAL
11	12	13 VAN	14	15	16 PIT	17
18 STL	19	20	21 VAN	22	23 CHI	24
25	26 LA	27	28 TOR	29		

MARCH
SUN	MON	TUE	WED	THU	FRI	SAT
				1 HAR	2	
3 D NYI	4	5 PIT	6	7 FLA	8	9 D NYI
10 DET	11	12 DET	13 TOR	14	15	16 PHI
17	18	19	20 SJ	21	22 PHI	23
24 D COL	25	26 DAL	27 COL	28	29 EDM	30
31 CAL						

APRIL
SUN	MON	TUE	WED	THU	FRI	SAT
	1	2	3 DAL	4	5	6 CAL
7	8 STL	9	10 DET	11	12 LA	13
14 ANA	15	16	17	18	19	20

1995-96 SEASON

CLUB DIRECTORY

President and governor
Barry L. Shenkarow
Alternate governor
Bill Davis
General manager
John Paddock
Asst. G.M./V.P of communications
Mike O'Hearn
Head coach
Terry Simpson
Assistant coaches
Randy Carlyle
Zinetula Bilvaletdinov
Goaltending coach
Pete Peeters
Coordinator of coaching services
Glenn Williamson
V.P. of finance and administration
Don Binda
Director, hockey information
Igor Kuperman
Media/public relations
Richard Nairn
Communications assistant
Jeffrey Hecht

Director of scouting
Bill Lesuk
Assistant director of scouting
Joe Yannetti
Scouts
Tom Savage
Connie Broden
Sean Coady
Charlie Burroughs
Boris Yemeljanov
Larry Hornung
Vaughn Karpan
Special events director
Lori Summers
Athletic trainers
Gord Hart
Phil Walker
Equipment managers
Craig Heisinger
Stan Wilson
Team physician
Dr. Brian Lukie

DRAFT CHOICES

Rd.—Player	H/W	Overall	Pos.	Last team
1—Shane Doan	6-1/215	7	RW	Kamloops (WHL)
2—Marc Chouinard	6-4/187	32	C	Beauport (QMJHL)
2—Jason Doig	6-3/216	34	D	Laval (QMJHL)
3—Brad Isbister	6-2/198	67	RW	Portland (WHL)
4—Justin Kurtz	5-11/188	84	D	Brandon (WHL)
5—Brian Elder	6-0/175	121	G	Brandon (WHL)
6—Sylvain Daigle	5-7/182	136	G	Shawinigan (QMJHL)
7—Paul Traynor	6-1/170	162	D	Kitchener (OHL)
8—Jaroslav Obsut	6-1/185	188	D	North Battleford (SJHL)
8—Frederik Loven	6-2/183	189	C	Djurgarden-Stockholm, Swe.
9—Rob Deciantis	5-11/175	214	C	Kitchener (OHL)

MISCELLANEOUS DATA

Home ice (capacity)
Winnipeg Arena (15,393)
Address
15-1430 Maroons Road
Winnipeg, Man. R3G 0L5
Business phone
204-982-5387
Rink dimensions
200 feet by 85 feet

Club colors
Blue, red and white
Radio affiliation
CJOB (680 AM)
TV affiliation
CKND (Channel 9—Cable 12)

No.	FORWARDS	Ht./Wt.	Place	Born Date	NHL exp.	1994-95 clubs
61	Dorian Anneck (C)	6-1/183	Winnipeg, Man.	4-24-76	0	Prince George (WHL), Tri-City (WHL)
38	Luciano Borsato (C)	5-11/190	Richmond Hill, Ont.	1-7-66	5	Winnipeg, Springfield (AHL)
	Shane Doan (RW)	6-1/215	Eston, Sask.	10-10-76	0	Kamloops (WHL)
18	Dallas Drake (C)	6-0/180	Trail, B.C.	2-4-69	3	Winnipeg
32	Michael Eastwood (C/RW)	6-3/205	Cornwall, Ont.	7-1-67	4	Toronto, Winnipeg
19	Nelson Emerson (C)	5-11/175	Hamilton, Ont.	8-17-67	5	Winnipeg
15	Randy Gilhen (C)	6-0/190	Zweibrucken, W. Germany	6-13-63	10	Winnipeg
75	Michal Grosek (LW)	6-2/200	Gottwaldov, Czech.	6-1-75	2	Springfield (AHL), Winnipeg
43	Ravil Gusmanov	6-2/185	Nab. Chelny, U.S.S.R.	7-22-72	0	Springfield (AHL)
47	Tavis Hansen (C/RW)	6-1/180	Prince Albert, Sask.	6-17-75	1	Tacoma (WHL)
17	Kris King (LW)	5-11/208	Bracebridge, Ont.	2-18-66	8	Winnipeg
23	Igor Korolev (RW/C)	6-1/187	Moscow, U.S.S.R.	9-6-70	3	Dynamo Moscow (CIS), Winnipeg
28	Craig Martin (RW)	6-2/215	Amherst, N.S.	1-21-71	1	Winnipeg, Springfield (AHL)
48	Craig Mills (RW)	5-11/174	Toronto	8-27-76	0	Belleville (OHL)
12	Rob Murray (C)	6-1/180	Toronto	4-4-67	6	Springfield (AHL), Winnipeg
12	Ed Olczyk (C)	6-1/205	Chicago	8-16-66	11	New York Rangers, Winnipeg
8	Teemu Selanne (RW)	6-0/200	Helsinki, Finland	7-3-70	3	Jokerit Helsinki (Finland), Winnipeg
34	Darrin Shannon (LW)	6-2/210	Barrie, Ont.	12-8-69	7	Winnipeg
7	Keith Tkachuk (LW)	6-2/210	Melrose, Mass.	3-28-72	4	Winnipeg
	Juha Ylonen (C)	6-0/180	Helsinki, Finland	2-13-72	0	Jokerit Helsinki (Finland)
10	Alexei Zhamnov (C)	6-1/195	Moscow, U.S.S.R.	10-1-70	3	Winnipeg
	DEFENSEMEN					
34	Greg Brown	6-0/185	Hartford, Conn.	3-7-68	4	Cleveland (IHL), Winnipeg
46	Steve Cheredaryk	6-2/197	Calgary	11-20-75	0	Medicine Hat (WHL), Springfield (AHL)
3	Dave Manson	6-2/202	Prince Albert, Sask.	1-27-67	9	Winnipeg
42	Oleg Mikulchik	6-2/200	Minsk, U.S.S.R.	6-27-64	2	Springfield (AHL), Winnipeg
44	Mike Muller	6-2/205	Minneapolis	9-18-71	0	Springfield (AHL)
27	Teppo Numminen	6-1/190	Tampere, Finland	7-3-68	7	TuTo Turku (Finland), Winnipeg
	Deron Quint	6-1/182	Dover, N.H.	3-12-76	0	Seattle (WHL)
24	Darryl Shannon	6-2/200	Barrie, Ont.	6-21-68	7	Winnipeg
39	Mark Visheau	6-4/200	Burlington, Ont.	6-27-73	1	Springfield (AHL)
2	Neil Wilkinson	6-3/190	Selkirk, Man.	8-15-67	6	Winnipeg
	GOALTENDERS					
29	Tim Cheveldae	5-10/195	Melville, Sask.	2-15-68	7	Winnipeg
	Sylvain Daigle	5-8/185	St. Hyacinthe, Que.	10-20-76	0	Shawinigan (QMJHL)
	Parris Duffus	6-2/192	Denver	1-27-70	0	Peoria (IHL)
	Brian Elder	6-0/175	Oak Lake, Man.	6-8-76	0	Brandon (WHL)
35	Nikolai Khabibulin	6-1/176	Sverdlovsk, U.S.S.R.	1-13-73	1	Springfield (AHL), Winnipeg
31	Scott Langkow	5-11/190	Edmonton	4-21-75	0	Portland (WHL)

1994-95 REVIEW

INDIVIDUAL STATISTICS

SCORING

	Games	G	A	Pts.	PIM	+/-	PPG	SHG	Shots	Shooting Pct.
Alexei Zhamnov	48	30	35	65	20	5	9	0	155	19.4
Keith Tkachuk	48	22	29	51	152	-4	7	2	129	17.1
Teemu Selanne	45	22	26	48	2	1	8	2	167	13.2
Nelson Emerson	48	14	23	37	26	-12	4	1	122	11.5
Igor Korolev	45	8	22	30	10	1	1	0	85	9.4
Dallas Drake	43	8	18	26	30	-6	0	0	66	12.1
Stephane Quintal	43	6	17	23	78	0	3	0	107	5.6
Teppo Numminen	42	5	16	21	16	12	2	0	86	5.8
Dave Manson	44	3	15	18	139	-20	2	0	104	2.9
Thomas Steen	31	5	10	15	14	-13	2	0	32	15.6
Darryl Shannon	40	5	9	14	48	1	0	1	42	11.9
Randy Gilhen	44	5	6	11	52	-17	0	1	47	10.6
Ed Olczyk*	13	2	8	10	8	1	1	0	27	7.4
Mike Eastwood*	13	3	6	9	4	3	0	0	17	17.6
Darrin Shannon	19	5	3	8	14	-6	3	0	26	19.2
Tie Domi*	31	4	4	8	128	-6	0	0	34	11.8
Kris King	48	4	2	6	85	0	0	0	58	6.9
Neil Wilkinson	40	1	4	5	75	-26	0	0	25	4.0
Michal Grosek	24	2	2	4	21	-3	0	0	27	7.4
Igor Ulanov*	19	1	3	4	27	-2	0	0	13	7.7
Mike Eagles*	27	2	1	3	40	-13	0	0	13	15.4
Greg Brown*	9	0	3	3	17	1	0	0	12	0.0
Rob Murray	10	0	2	2	2	1	0	0	5	0.0
Oleg Mikulchik	25	0	2	2	12	10	0	0	5	0.0

	Games	G	A	Pts.	PIM	+/-	PPG	SHG	Shots	Shooting Pct.
Craig Martin	20	0	1	1	19	-4	0	0	3	0.0
Nikolai Khabibulin (goalie)	26	0	1	1	4	0	0	0	0	0.0
Tim Cheveldae (goalie)	30	0	1	1	2	0	0	0	0	0.0
Arto Blomsten*	1	0	0	0	2	0	0	0	0	0.0
Tavis Hansen	1	0	0	0	0	0	0	0	0	0.0
John LeBlanc	2	0	0	0	0	0	0	0	0	0.0
Luciano Borsato	4	0	0	0	0	-1	0	0	2	0.0
Russ Romaniuk	6	0	0	0	0	-3	0	0	3	0.0
Brent Thompson	29	0	0	0	78	-17	0	0	16	0.0

GOALTENDING

	Games	Min.	Goals	SO	Avg.	W	L	T	Shots	Sv. Pct.
Nikolai Khabibulin	26	1339	76	0	3.41	8	9	4	723	.895
Tim Cheveldae	30	1571	97	0	3.70	8	16	3	818	.881

Empty-net goals (do not count against a goaltender's average): Cheveldae 3, Khabibulin 1.
*Played with two or more NHL teams.

RESULTS

JANUARY

20—Calgary	T	*3-3
21—Anaheim	L	3-4
23—Chicago	W	5-3
25—At San Jose	L	0-4
27—At Anaheim	L	2-3
28—At Los Angeles	L	2-4

FEBRUARY

2—St. Louis	L	*4-5
4—San Jose	T	*3-3
6—At Calgary	W	5-4
8—At Edmonton	T	*3-3
9—At Vancouver	L	1-5
11—At St. Louis	W	3-2
13—At Dallas	W	7-4
15—Detroit	L	1-5
17—St. Louis	L	3-4
22—At Vancouver	W	4-1
24—Anaheim	W	4-2
25—At Toronto	L	2-5
28—Dallas	L	0-4

MARCH

2—At Detroit	L	1-6
4—San Jose	W	4-2
5—Calgary	W	3-2
10—Dallas	W	4-3
11—Los Angeles	L	2-4
14—Vancouver	T	*3-3
17—At Calgary	L	4-8
19—Chicago	L	2-3
22—At Detroit	L	3-6
24—At Toronto	L	2-3
25—Toronto	T	*3-3
28—At San Jose	L	*5-6
30—At Anaheim	L	1-3

APRIL

1—At Los Angeles	T	*7-7
5—Chicago	W	4-1
7—Vancouver	W	7-4
8—At Toronto	L	3-4
11—At St. Louis	L	5-7
13—St. Louis	W	5-2
15—Toronto	W	5-1
17—Edmonton	L	5-6
19—At Detroit	T	*5-5
21—At Chicago	W	2-1
23—At Dallas	L	2-5
25—Edmonton	L	3-5
27—Detroit	W	4-3
29—At Edmonton	W	5-1

MAY

1—At Chicago	L	2-3
2—Los Angeles	L	1-2

*Denotes overtime game.

SCHEDULE

*Denotes afternoon game.

FRIDAY, OCTOBER 6
Detroit at Colorado

SATURDAY, OCTOBER 7
N.Y. Islanders at Boston
N.Y. Rangers at Hartford
Toronto at Pittsburgh
Buffalo at Ottawa
Philadelphia at Montreal
Florida at New Jersey*
St. Louis at Washington
Calgary at Tampa Bay
Dallas at Winnipeg
Chicago at San Jose
Colorado at Los Angeles

SUNDAY, OCTOBER 8
Calgary at Florida
Detroit at Edmonton

MONDAY, OCTOBER 9
Buffalo at Boston*
Anaheim at Winnipeg
Pittsburgh at Colorado
Detroit at Vancouver

TUESDAY, OCTOBER 10
N.Y. Islanders at Toronto
Edmonton at St. Louis
Calgary at Dallas
Chicago at Los Angeles

WEDNESDAY, OCTOBER 11
Anaheim at Hartford
Winnipeg at N.Y. Rangers
Washington at Philadelphia
Montreal at Florida
Boston at Colorado

THURSDAY, OCTOBER 12
Winnipeg at New Jersey
Montreal at Tampa Bay
Pittsburgh at Chicago
St. Louis at Dallas
Boston at San Jose
Vancouver at Los Angeles

FRIDAY, OCTOBER 13
Anaheim at Buffalo
Colorado at Washington
Ottawa at Florida
Edmonton at Detroit

SATURDAY, OCTOBER 14
Chicago at Hartford
Anaheim at Pittsburgh
New Jersey at Montreal
Philadelphia at N.Y. Islanders
Tampa Bay at Washington
N.Y. Rangers at Toronto
Colorado at St. Louis
Boston at Dallas
Vancouver at San Jose

SUNDAY, OCTOBER 15
New Jersey at Buffalo
Edmonton at Philadelphia
Ottawa at Tampa Bay
N.Y. Islanders at Florida

Calgary at Chicago
Detroit at Winnipeg
Los Angeles at Vancouver

MONDAY, OCTOBER 16
Hartford at N.Y. Rangers

TUESDAY, OCTOBER 17
N.Y. Rangers at N.Y. Islanders
Edmonton at New Jersey
Chicago at Florida
San Jose at Toronto
Calgary at Detroit
Boston at St. Louis
Washington at Dallas
Tampa Bay at Winnipeg

WEDNESDAY, OCTOBER 18
Edmonton at Buffalo
Washington at Colorado
Philadelphia at Los Angeles
Vancouver at Anaheim

THURSDAY, OCTOBER 19
Calgary at Ottawa
Detroit at New Jersey
Tampa Bay at Chicago
Dallas at St. Louis
San Jose at Winnipeg

FRIDAY, OCTOBER 20
Pittsburgh at Hartford
N.Y. Rangers at Buffalo
Montreal at N.Y. Islanders
Los Angeles at Washington
Calgary at Toronto
Philadelphia at Anaheim

SATURDAY, OCTOBER 21
Los Angeles at Pittsburgh
Toronto at Montreal
Ottawa at New Jersey
Hartford at Florida
Boston at Detroit*
Chicago at St. Louis
Tampa Bay at Dallas
Vancouver at Edmonton

SUNDAY, OCTOBER 22
St. Louis at Buffalo
Ottawa at N.Y. Rangers
Philadelphia at Chicago
San Jose at Edmonton
Winnipeg at Anaheim

MONDAY, OCTOBER 23
Los Angeles at Montreal
Anaheim at Colorado

TUESDAY, OCTOBER 24
Vancouver at N.Y. Rangers
Florida at Toronto
Ottawa at Detroit
Buffalo at Dallas

WEDNESDAY, OCTOBER 25
St. Louis at Hartford
Florida at Montreal
Vancouver at New Jersey
N.Y. Islanders at Philadelphia
Colorado at Calgary
Winnipeg at San Jose

THURSDAY, OCTOBER 26
Washington at Boston
Los Angeles at Ottawa
Pittsburgh at N.Y. Islanders
N.Y. Rangers at Tampa Bay
Toronto at Chicago
Anaheim at Dallas

FRIDAY, OCTOBER 27
Montreal at Hartford
Anaheim at St. Louis
Buffalo at Colorado
Detroit at Calgary
Winnipeg at Edmonton

SATURDAY, OCTOBER 28
Hartford at Boston
Florida at Ottawa*
Chicago at Montreal
Philadelphia at N.Y. Islanders
Pittsburgh at New Jersey
Washington at Tampa Bay
Los Angeles at Toronto
Winnipeg at Vancouver
Dallas at San Jose*

SUNDAY, OCTOBER 29
Toronto at N.Y. Rangers
Ottawa at Philadelphia
Buffalo at Chicago
Washington at St. Louis
Calgary at Anaheim

MONDAY, OCTOBER 30
Colorado at Dallas
Detroit at Winnipeg
San Jose at Vancouver

TUESDAY, OCTOBER 31
Montreal at Boston
Tampa Bay at Philadelphia
N.Y. Islanders at Florida
New Jersey at Edmonton
N.Y. Rangers at San Jose
Calgary at Los Angeles

WEDNESDAY, NOVEMBER 1
Tampa Bay at Pittsburgh
Detroit at Buffalo
Montreal at Washington
Chicago at Dallas
Toronto at Winnipeg
Calgary at Colorado
Edmonton at Vancouver
St. Louis at Anaheim

THURSDAY, NOVEMBER 2
Detroit at Boston
Ottawa at Hartford
Florida at Philadelphia
New Jersey at San Jose
N.Y. Rangers at Los Angeles

FRIDAY, NOVEMBER 3
Pittsburgh at Buffalo
Florida at Washington
N.Y. Islanders at Tampa Bay
Colorado at Winnipeg
Toronto at Vancouver
N.Y. Rangers at Anaheim

— 83 —

SATURDAY, NOVEMBER 4
Philadelphia at Pittsburgh
Hartford at Ottawa
Boston at Montreal
Washington at N.Y. Islanders
Dallas at Detroit*
Vancouver at Calgary
Toronto at Edmonton
St. Louis at San Jose
New Jersey at Los Angeles

SUNDAY, NOVEMBER 5
Winnipeg at Buffalo
Hartford at Philadelphia
Tampa Bay at Florida
Colorado at Chicago
New Jersey at Anaheim

MONDAY, NOVEMBER 6
Calgary at N.Y. Rangers

TUESDAY, NOVEMBER 7
San Jose at Hartford
Vancouver at N.Y. Islanders
Boston at Washington
Philadelphia at Florida
Anaheim at Toronto
Edmonton at Detroit
Los Angeles at St. Louis

WEDNESDAY, NOVEMBER 8
San Jose at Buffalo
Pittsburgh at Ottawa
Anaheim at Montreal
Tampa Bay at N.Y. Rangers
Calgary at New Jersey
Los Angeles at Dallas

THURSDAY, NOVEMBER 9
Ottawa at Boston
Calgary at Philadelphia
Edmonton at Florida
Vancouver at Chicago
Dallas at Colorado

FRIDAY, NOVEMBER 10
N.Y. Islanders at N.Y. Rangers
Edmonton at Tampa Bay
Washington at Toronto
Winnipeg at St. Louis
Pittsburgh at San Jose

SATURDAY, NOVEMBER 11
Toronto at Boston
N.Y. Rangers at Hartford
Anaheim at Ottawa*
St. Louis at N.Y. Islanders
Philadelphia at New Jersey*
Chicago at Washington
Buffalo at Florida
Montreal at Calgary
Colorado at Vancouver
Detroit at San Jose
Pittsburgh at Los Angeles

SUNDAY, NOVEMBER 12
New Jersey at Philadelphia*
Buffalo at Tampa Bay
Edmonton at Chicago
Montreal at Vancouver

MONDAY, NOVEMBER 13
Los Angeles at Anaheim

TUESDAY, NOVEMBER 14
Dallas at Pittsburgh
Hartford at New Jersey
Philadelphia at Washington

Boston at Tampa Bay
Toronto at Florida
N.Y. Rangers at St. Louis
Chicago at Winnipeg
Edmonton at Calgary
N.Y. Islanders at San Jose
Detroit at Los Angeles

WEDNESDAY, NOVEMBER 15
Ottawa at Hartford
Dallas at Buffalo
Montreal at Edmonton
Colorado at Anaheim

THURSDAY, NOVEMBER 16
New Jersey at Boston
Ottawa at Philadelphia
Toronto at Tampa Bay
Vancouver at Florida
N.Y. Rangers at Chicago
San Jose at St. Louis
N.Y. Islanders at Los Angeles

FRIDAY, NOVEMBER 17
Pittsburgh at Washington
San Jose at Dallas
N.Y. Rangers at Winnipeg
Colorado at Calgary
Detroit at Edmonton
N.Y. Islanders at Anaheim

SATURDAY, NOVEMBER 18
St. Louis at Boston
Philadelphia at Hartford*
Washington at Pittsburgh
Ottawa at Montreal
Buffalo at New Jersey*
Vancouver at Tampa Bay
Winnipeg at Toronto
Calgary at Colorado
Florida at Los Angeles

SUNDAY, NOVEMBER 19
Ottawa at Buffalo
Vancouver at Philadelphia
San Jose at Chicago
Florida at Anaheim

MONDAY, NOVEMBER 20
Hartford at Montreal
Colorado at Edmonton

TUESDAY, NOVEMBER 21
Winnipeg at Boston
Pittsburgh at N.Y. Rangers
Los Angeles at Philadelphia
San Jose at Washington
New Jersey at Florida
St. Louis at Toronto
Anaheim at Calgary

WEDNESDAY, NOVEMBER 22
Montreal at Hartford
N.Y. Rangers at Pittsburgh
Winnipeg at Ottawa
Los Angeles at N.Y. Islanders
New Jersey at Tampa Bay
San Jose at Detroit
Vancouver at Dallas
Chicago at Colorado
Anaheim at Edmonton

THURSDAY, NOVEMBER 23
Vancouver at St. Louis

FRIDAY, NOVEMBER 24
Los Angeles at Boston*
N.Y. Islanders at Buffalo

Detroit at Philadelphia*
Tampa Bay at Washington
Hartford at Toronto
Edmonton at Calgary
Chicago at Anaheim*

SATURDAY, NOVEMBER 25
Washington at Hartford
Buffalo at Pittsburgh
Boston at Ottawa
Colorado at Montreal
Tampa Bay at N.Y. Islanders
N.Y. Rangers at Detroit
Toronto at St. Louis
New Jersey at Dallas
Vancouver at San Jose

SUNDAY, NOVEMBER 26
Los Angeles at Florida
Edmonton at Winnipeg
Chicago at Calgary

MONDAY, NOVEMBER 27
New Jersey at N.Y. Rangers
Los Angeles at Tampa Bay
Buffalo at St. Louis

TUESDAY, NOVEMBER 28
Ottawa at Pittsburgh
Colorado at N.Y. Islanders
Montreal at Detroit
Toronto at Winnipeg
Chicago at Edmonton

WEDNESDAY, NOVEMBER 29
Buffalo at N.Y. Rangers
Colorado at New Jersey
Hartford at Tampa Bay
Philadelphia at Florida
Montreal at St. Louis
Chicago at Vancouver
Calgary at San Jose
Washington at Anaheim

THURSDAY, NOVEMBER 30
Pittsburgh at Boston
N.Y. Islanders at Ottawa
Toronto at Philadelphia
St. Louis at Winnipeg
Washington at Los Angeles

FRIDAY, DECEMBER 1
Florida at Pittsburgh
Hartford at Buffalo
Colorado at N.Y. Rangers
Tampa Bay at New Jersey
Anaheim at Detroit
Calgary at Edmonton
San Jose at Vancouver

SATURDAY, DECEMBER 2
Buffalo at Boston
Florida at Hartford
N.Y. Rangers at Ottawa
Detroit at Montreal
New Jersey at N.Y. Islanders
Anaheim at Toronto
Chicago at Winnipeg
St. Louis at Edmonton
Washington at San Jose
Dallas at Los Angeles

SUNDAY, DECEMBER 3
Boston at Philadelphia
Pittsburgh at Tampa Bay
Calgary at Winnipeg
Dallas at Colorado

MONDAY, DECEMBER 4
Anaheim at N.Y. Rangers

TUESDAY, DECEMBER 5
Dallas at Boston
Pittsburgh at N.Y. Islanders
Florida at Washington
Ottawa at Toronto
Philadelphia at Detroit
San Jose at Colorado
St. Louis at Calgary
Edmonton at Vancouver

WEDNESDAY, DECEMBER 6
N.Y. Islanders at Hartford
New Jersey at Montreal
Chicago at N.Y. Rangers
Anaheim at Tampa Bay
Winnipeg at Los Angeles

THURSDAY, DECEMBER 7
Montreal at Pittsburgh
Toronto at New Jersey
Buffalo at Philadelphia
Anaheim at Florida
Dallas at Detroit
Ottawa at Chicago
Edmonton at Colorado
Winnipeg at San Jose

FRIDAY, DECEMBER 8
Washington at Buffalo
Detroit at N.Y. Rangers
Boston at Tampa Bay
St. Louis at Vancouver

SATURDAY, DECEMBER 9
Hartford at Pittsburgh
Colorado at Ottawa
N.Y. Rangers at Montreal
N.Y. Islanders at New Jersey*
Boston at Florida
Dallas at Toronto
Vancouver at Calgary
Edmonton at San Jose
St. Louis at Los Angeles

SUNDAY, DECEMBER 10
Tampa Bay at Buffalo
N.Y. Islanders at Philadelphia
Hartford at Chicago
Washington at Winnipeg
Edmonton at Anaheim

MONDAY, DECEMBER 11
Dallas at N.Y. Rangers
Florida at New Jersey
Colorado at Toronto
Los Angeles at Calgary

TUESDAY, DECEMBER 12
Florida at N.Y. Islanders
Detroit at St. Louis
Montreal at Winnipeg
Ottawa at San Jose

WEDNESDAY, DECEMBER 13
Tampa Bay at Hartford
Colorado at Buffalo
Boston at N.Y. Rangers
Chicago at Detroit
Calgary at Dallas
Vancouver at Edmonton
Ottawa at Los Angeles
Pittsburgh at Anaheim

THURSDAY, DECEMBER 14
Florida at Boston

Tampa Bay at Philadelphia
N.Y. Islanders at Washington
Calgary at St. Louis
Toronto at San Jose

FRIDAY, DECEMBER 15
Colorado at Hartford
N.Y. Rangers at Buffalo
New Jersey at Detroit
Montreal at Chicago
Pittsburgh at Dallas
Edmonton at Winnipeg
Ottawa at Anaheim

SATURDAY, DECEMBER 16
Calgary at Boston
Philadelphia at Montreal
Hartford at N.Y. Islanders
Buffalo at New Jersey
N.Y. Rangers at Washington
Florida at Tampa Bay
San Jose at St. Louis
Toronto at Los Angeles

SUNDAY, DECEMBER 17
Pittsburgh at Philadelphia
Winnipeg at Chicago
San Jose at Dallas
Ottawa at Vancouver*
Toronto at Anaheim

MONDAY, DECEMBER 18
Hartford at Montreal
Washington at N.Y. Rangers
Vancouver at Colorado
Ottawa at Edmonton

TUESDAY, DECEMBER 19
Calgary at Pittsburgh
Philadelphia at New Jersey
Winnipeg at Tampa Bay
N.Y. Islanders at St. Louis
San Jose at Anaheim

WEDNESDAY, DECEMBER 20
Calgary at Hartford
Montreal at Buffalo
Chicago at Toronto
Colorado at Edmonton
Vancouver at Los Angeles
Detroit at Anaheim

THURSDAY, DECEMBER 21
N.Y. Rangers at Philadelphia
New Jersey at Tampa Bay
Winnipeg at Florida
Toronto at Chicago
N.Y. Islanders at Dallas

FRIDAY, DECEMBER 22
Montreal at Pittsburgh
Boston at Buffalo
Hartford at N.Y. Rangers
Edmonton at Washington
St. Louis at Colorado
Detroit at Calgary
Los Angeles at San Jose
Vancouver at Anaheim

SATURDAY, DECEMBER 23
Tampa Bay at Boston
Philadelphia at Hartford
Buffalo at Ottawa
Pittsburgh at Montreal
Washington at N.Y. Islanders
New Jersey at Florida
Edmonton at Toronto
Chicago at Dallas

St. Louis at Winnipeg
Detroit at Vancouver
Colorado at Los Angeles

TUESDAY, DECEMBER 26
Buffalo at Pittsburgh
Boston at N.Y. Islanders
Ottawa at N.Y. Rangers
Montreal at Washington
St. Louis at Detroit
Dallas at Chicago
Calgary at Vancouver
Colorado at San Jose

WEDNESDAY, DECEMBER 27
Ottawa at Buffalo
N.Y. Islanders at New Jersey
Toronto at Calgary
Philadelphia at Edmonton
Anaheim at Los Angeles

THURSDAY, DECEMBER 28
Hartford at Pittsburgh
Montreal at Tampa Bay
Washington at Florida
Winnipeg at Chicago
Dallas at St. Louis
N.Y. Rangers at Vancouver

FRIDAY, DECEMBER 29
Chicago at Buffalo
Detroit at Dallas
New Jersey at Winnipeg
Toronto at Colorado
Philadelphia at Calgary
Los Angeles at Edmonton
San Jose at Anaheim

SATURDAY, DECEMBER 30
Florida at Pittsburgh
Montreal at Ottawa
Hartford at Washington
Toronto at St. Louis
N.Y. Rangers at Edmonton

SUNDAY, DECEMBER 31
N.Y. Islanders at Buffalo
Tampa Bay at Ottawa
Hartford at Detroit
New Jersey at Chicago
Boston at Winnipeg*
N.Y. Rangers at Calgary
Philadelphia at Vancouver*
Los Angeles at Anaheim*

MONDAY, JANUARY 1
Pittsburgh at Washington*
N.Y. Islanders at Florida
Toronto at Dallas*

TUESDAY, JANUARY 2
Chicago at Boston
Tampa Bay at Calgary

WEDNESDAY, JANUARY 3
Washington at Hartford
Ottawa at Pittsburgh
Montreal at N.Y. Rangers
Boston at Toronto
Dallas at Detroit
New Jersey at Colorado
Tampa Bay at Edmonton
Florida at Vancouver
Philadelphia at San Jose
Winnipeg at Los Angeles

THURSDAY, JANUARY 4
Montreal at N.Y. Islanders

St. Louis at Chicago
Philadelphia at Colorado

FRIDAY, JANUARY 5

Ottawa at Hartford
Detroit at Pittsburgh
Toronto at Buffalo
N.Y. Rangers at Washington
Winnipeg at Dallas
Anaheim at Calgary
Florida at Edmonton
Los Angeles at San Jose

SATURDAY, JANUARY 6

Hartford at Boston
Buffalo at Montreal
Ottawa at N.Y. Islanders
Washington at New Jersey
Colorado at Toronto
Chicago at Detroit
Pittsburgh at St. Louis
Florida at Calgary
Tampa Bay at Vancouver
San Jose at Los Angeles

SUNDAY, JANUARY 7

Dallas at Chicago
Anaheim at Edmonton

MONDAY, JANUARY 8

Colorado at Boston
Vancouver at Pittsburgh
Tampa Bay at Montreal
Washington at N.Y. Rangers
Winnipeg at Detroit
Los Angeles at Dallas
Florida at San Jose

TUESDAY, JANUARY 9

Chicago at N.Y. Islanders
St. Louis at New Jersey
Anaheim at Philadelphia
Hartford at Edmonton

WEDNESDAY, JANUARY 10

Vancouver at Montreal
San Jose at N.Y. Rangers
Los Angeles at Toronto
Detroit at Dallas
Buffalo at Winnipeg
Florida at Colorado
Hartford at Calgary

THURSDAY, JANUARY 11

Anaheim at Boston
Toronto at N.Y. Islanders
San Jose at New Jersey
St. Louis at Philadelphia
Ottawa at Washington

FRIDAY, JANUARY 12

Montreal at Pittsburgh
Los Angeles at Detroit
Anaheim at Chicago
Florida at Dallas
Hartford at Winnipeg
Buffalo at Calgary

SATURDAY, JANUARY 13

New Jersey at Boston*
San Jose at Pittsburgh
St. Louis at Montreal
N.Y. Rangers at Philadelphia*
Detroit at Washington
Ottawa at Tampa Bay
Vancouver at Toronto
Buffalo at Edmonton

SUNDAY, JANUARY 14

St. Louis at N.Y. Rangers
Dallas at New Jersey
Los Angeles at Chicago
Anaheim at Winnipeg
Calgary at Colorado

MONDAY, JANUARY 15

Vancouver at Boston*
Tampa Bay at N.Y. Islanders*
Dallas at Philadelphia

TUESDAY, JANUARY 16

Vancouver at Hartford
Colorado at Pittsburgh
Winnipeg at Washington
San Jose at Florida
Edmonton at St. Louis
Calgary at Los Angeles

WEDNESDAY, JANUARY 17

Pittsburgh at Buffalo
Montreal at Ottawa
Hartford at N.Y. Islanders
Boston at New Jersey
San Jose at Tampa Bay
Winnipeg at Toronto
Colorado at Detroit
Washington at Chicago
Edmonton at Dallas
Calgary at Anaheim

SATURDAY, JANUARY 20

All-Star Game at Boston*

MONDAY, JANUARY 22

Boston at Pittsburgh
Chicago at Ottawa
Tampa Bay at Montreal
Los Angeles at N.Y. Rangers
Florida at Philadelphia
N.Y. Islanders at Colorado
Dallas at Vancouver

TUESDAY, JANUARY 23

Los Angeles at New Jersey
Florida at Washington

WEDNESDAY, JANUARY 24

Hartford at Buffalo
Pittsburgh at Ottawa
Philadelphia at N.Y. Rangers
Chicago at Toronto
San Jose at Detroit
St. Louis at Winnipeg
N.Y. Islanders at Calgary
Dallas at Edmonton
Anaheim at Vancouver

THURSDAY, JANUARY 25

Tampa Bay at Boston
Los Angeles at Hartford
Detroit at Ottawa
Washington at New Jersey
Montreal at Florida
San Jose at Chicago
Vancouver at Colorado

FRIDAY, JANUARY 26

Buffalo at Washington
Dallas at Calgary
N.Y. Islanders at Edmonton

SATURDAY, JANUARY 27

N.Y. Rangers at Boston*
New Jersey at Hartford
Philadelphia at Pittsburgh*
Toronto at Ottawa

Winnipeg at Montreal*
Buffalo at Florida
Detroit at Chicago*
Tampa Bay at St. Louis*
N.Y. Islanders at Vancouver
Colorado at San Jose*
Anaheim at Los Angeles*

SUNDAY, JANUARY 28

Boston at Montreal*
Philadelphia at Washington*

MONDAY, JANUARY 29

St. Louis at Ottawa
Pittsburgh at Florida
Winnipeg at Dallas

TUESDAY, JANUARY 30

Buffalo at N.Y. Islanders
Toronto at Detroit
Edmonton at Calgary
New Jersey at Vancouver
Hartford at San Jose

WEDNESDAY, JANUARY 31

Florida at Buffalo
Boston at Ottawa
Washington at Montreal
Pittsburgh at Tampa Bay
St. Louis at Toronto
N.Y. Rangers at Dallas
Chicago at Edmonton
Hartford at Los Angeles
Colorado at Anaheim

THURSDAY, FEBRUARY 1

Florida at Boston
Washington at Ottawa
Montreal at Philadelphia
Vancouver at St. Louis
Winnipeg at Colorado
New Jersey at Calgary
Los Angeles at San Jose

FRIDAY, FEBRUARY 2

Vancouver at Dallas
Hartford at Anaheim

SATURDAY, FEBRUARY 3

Buffalo at Boston*
New Jersey at Ottawa
N.Y. Islanders at Washington
Florida at Tampa Bay*
Montreal at Toronto
Pittsburgh at Detroit*
Philadelphia at St. Louis*
N.Y. Rangers at Colorado*
Los Angeles at Calgary
Chicago at San Jose*

SUNDAY, FEBRUARY 4

Tampa Bay at Buffalo*
Dallas at N.Y. Islanders
Vancouver at Winnipeg*
Chicago at Anaheim

MONDAY, FEBRUARY 5

Montreal at Colorado
Toronto at San Jose

TUESDAY, FEBRUARY 6

Boston at Pittsburgh
N.Y. Rangers at N.Y. Islanders
Florida at Detroit
Dallas at St. Louis
Ottawa at Calgary
Chicago at Los Angeles

WEDNESDAY, FEBRUARY 7
Boston at Buffalo
Pittsburgh at New Jersey
Montreal at Dallas
Tampa Bay at Colorado
Washington at Edmonton
Hartford at Vancouver
Toronto at Anaheim

THURSDAY, FEBRUARY 8
N.Y. Islanders at N.Y. Rangers
Buffalo at Philadelphia
Detroit at Florida
Chicago at St. Louis
Ottawa at Winnipeg
Washington at Calgary
Toronto at Los Angeles

FRIDAY, FEBRUARY 9
Hartford at Colorado
Vancouver at Edmonton

SATURDAY, FEBRUARY 10
Philadelphia at Boston*
Chicago at Pittsburgh*
Ottawa at Montreal
Anaheim at N.Y. Islanders*
N.Y. Rangers at New Jersey*
Detroit at Tampa Bay*
Buffalo at Toronto
St. Louis at Dallas*
Winnipeg at Calgary
Washington at Vancouver
San Jose at Los Angeles*

SUNDAY, FEBRUARY 11
Anaheim at New Jersey
Colorado at Philadelphia
N.Y. Rangers at Tampa Bay*
St. Louis at Florida
Hartford at Dallas*
Calgary at Edmonton

MONDAY, FEBRUARY 12
San Jose at Montreal
Ottawa at N.Y. Islanders
Pittsburgh at Toronto

TUESDAY, FEBRUARY 13
Calgary at Washington
St. Louis at Tampa Bay
Los Angeles at Detroit
Winnipeg at Vancouver

WEDNESDAY, FEBRUARY 14
Boston at Hartford
Los Angeles at Buffalo
Philadelphia at Florida
San Jose at Toronto
Anaheim at Edmonton

THURSDAY, FEBRUARY 15
San Jose at Ottawa
Calgary at N.Y. Islanders
Montreal at N.Y. Rangers
Colorado at Tampa Bay
Washington at Detroit
Boston at Chicago
Anaheim at Vancouver

FRIDAY, FEBRUARY 16
New Jersey at Buffalo
Toronto at Washington
Colorado at Florida
Detroit at St. Louis
Edmonton at Dallas
Pittsburgh at Winnipeg

SATURDAY, FEBRUARY 17
Buffalo at Hartford
N.Y. Rangers at Ottawa
Calgary at Montreal
San Jose at N.Y. Islanders*
Philadelphia at Tampa Bay
Boston at Vancouver
Anaheim at Los Angeles

SUNDAY, FEBRUARY 18
N.Y. Rangers at Pittsburgh
Washington at New Jersey*
Dallas at Florida
Detroit at Toronto*
Edmonton at Chicago*
Winnipeg at St. Louis

MONDAY, FEBRUARY 19
New Jersey at Philadelphia*
Dallas at Tampa Bay
Vancouver at Detroit
Edmonton at Colorado
Boston at Los Angeles*

TUESDAY, FEBRUARY 20
Ottawa at St. Louis
San Jose at Calgary

WEDNESDAY, FEBRUARY 21
Montreal at Hartford
Pittsburgh at Buffalo
Florida at New Jersey
Tampa Bay at Toronto
Vancouver at Winnipeg
Los Angeles at Edmonton
Boston at Anaheim

THURSDAY, FEBRUARY 22
N.Y. Islanders at N.Y. Rangers
Washington at Philadelphia
Toronto at Detroit
St. Louis at Chicago
Ottawa at Dallas

FRIDAY, FEBRUARY 23
Hartford at Pittsburgh
Philadelphia at Buffalo
Tampa Bay at N.Y. Islanders
Montreal at New Jersey
Chicago at Winnipeg
Los Angeles at Colorado
Anaheim at Calgary
Boston at Edmonton
San Jose at Vancouver

SATURDAY, FEBRUARY 24
Pittsburgh at Montreal
New Jersey at Washington
N.Y. Rangers at Florida
Dallas at Toronto
Tampa Bay at Detroit
Los Angeles at St. Louis
Boston at Calgary

SUNDAY, FEBRUARY 25
Dallas at Hartford
Florida at Buffalo
Edmonton at N.Y. Islanders*
Chicago at Philadelphia
Ottawa at Colorado
San Jose at Anaheim*

MONDAY, FEBRUARY 26
Los Angeles at Winnipeg
Anaheim at Colorado
Montreal at San Jose

TUESDAY, FEBRUARY 27
Edmonton at Boston
Detroit at N.Y. Islanders
Pittsburgh at Vancouver

WEDNESDAY, FEBRUARY 28
Edmonton at Hartford
Buffalo at Ottawa
Boston at N.Y. Rangers
Philadelphia at Dallas
Toronto at Winnipeg
Tampa Bay at Los Angeles
Montreal at Anaheim

THURSDAY, FEBRUARY 29
Washington at Florida
N.Y. Islanders at Detroit
Colorado at Chicago
Pittsburgh at Calgary
St. Louis at Vancouver

FRIDAY, MARCH 1
Winnipeg at Hartford
Philadelphia at Ottawa
Buffalo at N.Y. Rangers
N.Y. Islanders at New Jersey
Chicago at Colorado
Pittsburgh at Edmonton
Tampa Bay at San Jose

SATURDAY, MARCH 2
Washington at Boston*
Florida at Hartford
New Jersey at Ottawa
Vancouver at Detroit*
Toronto at Dallas
Montreal at Los Angeles

SUNDAY, MARCH 3
Vancouver at Buffalo*
Winnipeg at N.Y. Islanders*
Philadelphia at Washington*
Detroit at Chicago
Toronto at Colorado
St. Louis at Edmonton*
Calgary at San Jose*
Tampa Bay at Anaheim

MONDAY, MARCH 4
New Jersey at N.Y. Rangers

TUESDAY, MARCH 5
Winnipeg at Pittsburgh
Boston at N.Y. Islanders
Chicago at Tampa Bay
Florida at St. Louis
San Jose at Colorado
Dallas at Anaheim

WEDNESDAY, MARCH 6
Detroit at Hartford
New Jersey at Toronto
Buffalo at Vancouver
Dallas at San Jose
Edmonton at Los Angeles

THURSDAY, MARCH 7
N.Y. Islanders at Boston
Ottawa at Pittsburgh
N.Y. Rangers at Tampa Bay
Calgary at St. Louis
Florida at Winnipeg

FRIDAY, MARCH 8
Toronto at Hartford
Los Angeles at Chicago
Detroit at Colorado

San Jose at Edmonton
Buffalo at Anaheim

SATURDAY, MARCH 9
Philadelphia at Boston*
New Jersey at Pittsburgh*
Ottawa at Montreal
N.Y. Rangers at Washington*
Calgary at Toronto
Hartford at St. Louis
N.Y. Islanders at Winnipeg*
Colorado at Vancouver

SUNDAY, MARCH 10
New Jersey at Philadelphia
Washington at Tampa Bay*
Boston at Florida
Detroit at Winnipeg
Buffalo at San Jose*
Los Angeles at Anaheim

MONDAY, MARCH 11
Dallas at Montreal
Florida at Chicago

TUESDAY, MARCH 12
Vancouver at Washington
Winnipeg at Detroit
St. Louis at Calgary

WEDNESDAY, MARCH 13
Pittsburgh at Hartford
Dallas at Ottawa
Florida at N.Y. Rangers
Montreal at New Jersey
Tampa Bay at Philadelphia
Winnipeg at Toronto
Edmonton at San Jose
Buffalo at Los Angeles
Colorado at Anaheim

THURSDAY, MARCH 14
Pittsburgh at Boston
Vancouver at Chicago

FRIDAY, MARCH 15
Calgary at Buffalo
Vancouver at Ottawa
Tampa Bay at New Jersey
Boston at Washington
Dallas at Toronto
St. Louis at San Jose

SATURDAY, MARCH 16
Buffalo at Hartford
N.Y. Islanders at Pittsburgh*
N.Y. Rangers at Montreal
Winnipeg at Philadelphia
Edmonton at Los Angeles

SUNDAY, MARCH 17
Tampa Bay at Ottawa*
San Jose at Philadelphia
Dallas at Washington*
New Jersey at Florida
Vancouver at Toronto*
Calgary at Detroit*
N.Y. Islanders at Chicago*
Edmonton at Colorado
St. Louis at Anaheim

MONDAY, MARCH 18
San Jose at Boston
Tampa Bay at Hartford
Buffalo at Montreal
St. Louis at Los Angeles

TUESDAY, MARCH 19
Edmonton at N.Y. Rangers

N.Y. Islanders at Philadelphia
Anaheim at Washington
Ottawa at Florida
Toronto at Detroit
Colorado at Vancouver

WEDNESDAY, MARCH 20
Hartford at Montreal
Boston at New Jersey
Detroit at Toronto
Calgary at Chicago
St. Louis at Dallas
San Jose at Winnipeg
Colorado at Los Angeles

THURSDAY, MARCH 21
Ottawa at Boston
Edmonton at Pittsburgh
Washington at Tampa Bay

FRIDAY, MARCH 22
Montreal at Buffalo
Hartford at Ottawa
Chicago at New Jersey
Colorado at Detroit
Anaheim at St. Louis
Philadelphia at Winnipeg
San Jose at Calgary
Dallas at Vancouver

SATURDAY, MARCH 23
N.Y. Rangers at Boston*
Buffalo at Pittsburgh
Edmonton at Montreal
New Jersey at N.Y. Islanders
Hartford at Washington
Florida at Tampa Bay
Philadelphia at Toronto
Calgary at Vancouver
Dallas at Los Angeles

SUNDAY, MARCH 24
Edmonton at Ottawa
Pittsburgh at N.Y. Rangers
Anaheim at Chicago*
Detroit at St. Louis
Colorado at Winnipeg*

MONDAY, MARCH 25
N.Y. Islanders at Montreal
Hartford at Philadelphia
Anaheim at Detroit
Toronto at Calgary
Los Angeles at Vancouver

TUESDAY, MARCH 26
St. Louis at Pittsburgh
Washington at N.Y. Islanders
New Jersey at Tampa Bay
Winnipeg at Dallas

WEDNESDAY, MARCH 27
Boston at Hartford
Philadelphia at Ottawa
Washington at Montreal
Florida at N.Y. Rangers
Buffalo at Detroit
Winnipeg at Colorado
Chicago at Calgary
Los Angeles at Edmonton
Toronto at Vancouver

THURSDAY, MARCH 28
Montreal at Boston
Pittsburgh at Florida
New Jersey at St. Louis
Anaheim at Dallas
Colorado at San Jose

FRIDAY, MARCH 29
Philadelphia at Buffalo
Ottawa at Washington
Los Angeles at Calgary
Winnipeg at Edmonton
Chicago at Vancouver

SATURDAY, MARCH 30
N.Y. Islanders at Hartford*
New Jersey at Pittsburgh*
Montreal at Ottawa
Tampa Bay at Florida
Toronto at Edmonton

SUNDAY, MARCH 31
Boston at Buffalo*
N.Y. Rangers at N.Y. Islanders*
Pittsburgh at Philadelphia*
Tampa Bay at Washington
St. Louis at Detroit*
Dallas at Chicago*
Winnipeg at Calgary
Anaheim at San Jose*

MONDAY, APRIL 1
Boston at Ottawa
Buffalo at Montreal
Hartford at Florida
Edmonton at Vancouver

TUESDAY, APRIL 2
Philadelphia at N.Y. Islanders
New Jersey at N.Y. Rangers
Detroit at San Jose

WEDNESDAY, APRIL 3
Washington at Buffalo
Florida at Ottawa
Boston at Montreal
Hartford at Tampa Bay
Chicago at Toronto
Dallas at Winnipeg
St. Louis at Colorado
Vancouver at Calgary
Detroit at Los Angeles
Edmonton at Anaheim

THURSDAY, APRIL 4
Montreal at Boston
Washington at Pittsburgh
Hartford at New Jersey
N.Y. Rangers at Philadelphia
Toronto at St. Louis
Edmonton at San Jose

FRIDAY, APRIL 5
N.Y. Islanders at Ottawa
Philadelphia at N.Y. Rangers
Buffalo at Tampa Bay
Chicago at Dallas
Detroit at Anaheim

SATURDAY, APRIL 6
New Jersey at Hartford*
Tampa Bay at Pittsburgh
Washington at Ottawa
Florida at Montreal
Buffalo at N.Y. Islanders
St. Louis at Toronto
Calgary at Winnipeg
San Jose at Colorado*
Vancouver at Los Angeles

SUNDAY, APRIL 7
N.Y. Rangers at New Jersey*
Boston at Philadelphia*
Detroit at Chicago*

— 88 —

Colorado at Dallas*
Anaheim at San Jose*

MONDAY, APRIL 8
Pittsburgh at Hartford
Florida at N.Y. Rangers
N.Y. Islanders at Tampa Bay
Winnipeg at St. Louis
Calgary at Edmonton
Vancouver at Anaheim

TUESDAY, APRIL 9
Dallas at Calgary

WEDNESDAY, APRIL 10
N.Y. Islanders at Pittsburgh
Ottawa at Buffalo
Washington at N.Y. Rangers
Philadelphia at New Jersey
Tampa Bay at Florida

Winnipeg at Detroit
Anaheim at Colorado
Dallas at Edmonton
San Jose at Los Angeles

THURSDAY, APRIL 11
Hartford at Boston
Pittsburgh at Ottawa
Montreal at Philadelphia
New Jersey at Washington
Toronto at Chicago
Colorado at St. Louis

FRIDAY, APRIL 12
Florida at N.Y. Islanders
Tampa Bay at N.Y. Rangers
Chicago at Detroit
Los Angeles at Winnipeg
Calgary at San Jose
Dallas at Anaheim

SATURDAY, APRIL 13
Boston at Hartford*
N.Y. Islanders at Montreal
Ottawa at New Jersey*
Buffalo at Washington
Edmonton at Toronto
Calgary at Vancouver

SUNDAY, APRIL 14
Pittsburgh at Boston*
Hartford at Buffalo
Philadelphia at Tampa Bay*
N.Y. Rangers at Florida*
St. Louis at Chicago*
Detroit at Dallas*
Los Angeles at Colorado*
Winnipeg at Anaheim

1994-95 NHL REVIEW

Regular season

Stanley Cup playoffs

Awards

Player drafts

REGULAR SEASON

EASTERN CONFERENCE

NORTHEAST DIVISION

	G	W	L	T	Pts.	GF	GA	Home	Away	Div. Rec.
Quebec Nordiques	48	30	13	5	65	185	134	19- 1- 4	11-12- 1	14- 6- 4
Pittsburgh Penguins	48	29	16	3	61	181	158	18- 5- 1	11-11- 2	15- 8- 1
Boston Bruins	48	27	18	3	57	150	127	15- 7- 2	12-11- 1	15- 7- 2
Buffalo Sabres	48	22	19	7	51	130	119	15- 8- 1	7-11- 6	8-10- 6
Hartford Whalers	48	19	24	5	43	127	141	12-10- 2	7-14- 3	13-10- 1
Montreal Canadiens	48	18	23	7	43	125	148	15- 5- 4	3-18- 3	8-12- 4
Ottawa Senators	48	9	34	5	23	117	174	5-16- 3	4-18- 2	1-21- 2

ATLANTIC DIVISION

	G	W	L	T	Pts.	GF	GA	Home	Away	Div. Rec.
Philadelphia Flyers	48	28	16	4	60	150	132	16- 7- 1	12- 9- 3	16- 6- 2
New Jersey Devils	48	22	18	8	52	136	121	14- 4- 6	8-14- 2	12- 8- 4
Washington Capitals	48	22	18	8	52	136	120	15- 6- 3	7-12- 5	11- 9- 4
New York Rangers	48	22	23	3	47	139	134	11-10- 3	11-13- 0	11-11- 2
Florida Panthers	48	20	22	6	46	115	127	9-12- 3	11-10- 3	7-13- 4
Tampa Bay Lightning	48	17	28	3	37	120	144	10-14- 0	7-14- 3	7-14- 3
New York Islanders	48	15	28	5	35	126	158	10-11- 3	5-17- 2	9-12- 3

WESTERN CONFERENCE

CENTRAL DIVISION

	G	W	L	T	Pts.	GF	GA	Home	Away	Div. Rec.
Detroit Red Wings	48	33	11	4	70	180	117	17- 4- 3	16- 7- 1	17- 5- 2
St. Louis Blues	48	28	15	5	61	178	135	16- 6- 2	12- 9- 3	13- 8- 3
Chicago Blackhawks	48	24	19	5	53	156	115	11-10- 3	13- 9- 2	7-13- 4
Toronto Maple Leafs	48	21	19	8	50	135	146	15- 7- 2	6-12- 6	10-10- 4
Dallas Stars	48	17	23	8	42	136	135	9-10- 5	8-13- 3	8-15- 1
Winnipeg Jets	48	16	25	7	39	157	177	10-10- 4	6-15- 3	9-13- 2

PACIFIC DIVISION

	G	W	L	T	Pts.	GF	GA	Home	Away	Div. Rec.
Calgary Flames	48	24	17	7	55	163	135	15- 7- 2	9-10- 5	13- 8- 3
Vancouver Canucks	48	18	18	12	48	153	148	10- 8- 6	8-10- 6	14- 4- 6
San Jose Sharks	48	19	25	4	42	129	161	10-13- 1	9-12- 3	10-12- 2
Los Angeles Kings	48	16	23	9	41	142	174	7-11- 6	9-12- 3	5-15- 4
Edmonton Oilers	48	17	27	4	38	136	183	11-12- 1	6-15- 3	9-13- 2
Mighty Ducks of Anaheim	48	16	27	5	37	125	164	11- 9- 4	5-18- 1	11-10- 3

INDIVIDUAL LEADERS

SCORING

TOP SCORERS

	Games	G	A	Pts.	PIM	+/-	PPG	SHG	Shots	Shooting Pct.
Jaromir Jagr, Pittsburgh	48	32	38	†70	37	23	8	3	192	16.7
Eric Lindros, Philadelphia	46	29	41	†70	60	27	7	0	144	20.1
Alexei Zhamnov, Winnipeg	48	30	35	65	20	5	9	0	155	19.4
Joe Sakic, Quebec	47	19	43	62	30	7	3	2	157	12.1
Ron Francis, Pittsburgh	44	11	*48	59	18	*30	3	0	94	11.7
Theoren Fleury, Calgary	47	29	29	58	112	6	9	2	173	16.8
Paul Coffey, Detroit	45	14	44	58	72	18	4	1	181	7.7
Mikael Renberg, Philadelphia	47	26	31	57	20	20	8	0	143	18.2
John LeClair, Mon.-Phi.	46	26	28	54	30	20	6	0	131	19.8
Mark Messier, N.Y. Rangers	46	14	39	53	40	8	3	3	126	11.1
Adam Oates, Boston	48	12	41	53	8	-11	4	1	109	11.0
Bernie Nicholls, Chicago	48	22	29	51	32	4	11	2	114	19.3
Keith Tkachuk, Winnipeg	48	22	29	51	152	-4	7	2	129	17.1
Brett Hull, St. Louis	48	29	21	50	10	13	9	3	200	14.5
Joe Nieuwendyk, Calgary	46	21	29	50	33	11	3	0	122	17.2
Sergei Fedorov, Detroit	42	20	30	50	24	6	7	3	147	13.6
Peter Forsberg, Quebec	47	15	35	50	16	17	3	0	86	17.4
Owen Nolan, Quebec	46	30	19	49	46	21	13	2	137	21.9
Teemu Selanne, Winnipeg	45	22	26	48	2	1	8	2	167	13.2

	Games	G	A	Pts.	PIM	+/-	PPG	SHG	Shots	Shooting Pct.
Mark Recchi, Phi.-Mon.	49	16	32	48	28	-9	9	0	121	13.2
Wayne Gretzky, Los Angeles	48	11	37	48	6	-20	3	0	142	7.7

The scoring leader is awarded the Art Ross Memorial Trophy.
*Led league.
†Tied for league lead.

Games

Josef Beranek, Phi./Van.	51
Mike Eastwood, Tor./Win.	49
Mark Recchi, Phi./Mon.	49
Pierre Turgeon, NYI/Mon.	49
Many tied with	48

Points

Jaromir Jagr, Pittsburgh	70
Eric Lindros, Philadelphia	70
Alexei Zhamnov, Winnipeg	65
Joe Sakic, Quebec	62
Ron Francis, Pittsburgh	59
Theoren Fleury, Calgary	58
Paul Coffey, Detroit	58
Mikael Renberg, Philadelphia	57
John LeClair, Mon./Phi.	54
Mark Messier, N.Y. Rangers	53
Adam Oates, Boston	53

Points by a defenseman

Paul Coffey, Detroit	58
Ray Bourque, Boston	43
Phil Housley, Calgary	43
Brian Leetch, N.Y. Rangers	41
Chris Chelios, Chicago	38
Steve Duchesne, St. Louis	38
Larry Murphy, Pittsburgh	38

Goals

Peter Bondra, Washington	34
Jaromir Jagr, Pittsburgh	32
Owen Nolan, Quebec	30
Ray Sheppard, Detroit	30
Alexei Zhamnov, Winnipeg	30
Theoren Fleury, Calgary	29
Brett Hull, St. Louis	29
Eric Lindros, Philadelphia	29
Cam Neely, Boston	27
John LeClair, Mon./Phi.	26
Mikael Renberg, Philadelphia	26

Assists

Ron Francis, Pittsburgh	48
Paul Coffey, Detroit	44
Joe Sakic, Quebec	43
Eric Lindros, Philadelphia	41
Adam Oates, Boston	41
Mark Messier, N.Y. Rangers	39
Joe Juneau, Washington	38
Jaromir Jagr, Pittsburgh	38
Wayne Gretzky, Los Angeles	37
Phil Housley, Calgary	35
Peter Forsberg, Quebec	35
Alexei Zhamnov, Winnipeg	35

Power-play goals

Cam Neely, Boston	16
Donald Audette, Buffalo	13

Owen Nolan, Quebec	13
Peter Bondra, Washington	12
Alexander Mogilny, Buffalo	12

Shorthanded goals

Peter Bondra, Washington	6
Wayne Presley, Buffalo	5
Sergei Fedorov, Detroit	3
Brent Gilchrist, Dallas	3
Brett Hull, St. Louis	3
Jaromir Jagr, Pittsburgh	3
Steve Konowalchuk, Washington	3
Mark Messier, N.Y. Rangers	3
Scott Young, Quebec	3
Rob Zamuner, Tampa Bay	3

Game-winning goals

Owen Nolan, Quebec	8
Donald Audette, Buffalo	7
Jaromir Jagr, Pittsburgh	7
John LeClair, Mon./Phi.	7
Brett Hull, St. Louis	6
Brendan Shanahan, St. Louis	6

Game-tying goals

Trevor Linden, Vancouver	3
Dan Quinn, Los Angeles	3
Dave Andreychuk, Toronto	2
Bob Carpenter, New Jersey	2
Todd Elik, S.J./St.L.	2
Ray Ferraro, N.Y. Islanders	2
Dimitri Khristich, Washington	2
Tom Pederson, San Jose	2

Shots

Ray Bourque, Boston	210
Brett Hull, St. Louis	200
Pavel Bure, Vancouver	198
Jaromir Jagr, Pittsburgh	192
Adam Graves, N.Y. Rangers	185

Shooting percentage (48 shots minimum)

Ian Laperriere, St. Louis	24.5
Ray Sheppard, Detroit	24.0
Roman Oksiuta, Edm./Van.	23.9
Ray Ferraro, N.Y. Islanders	23.4
Andrei Kovalenko, Quebec	22.2

Plus/minus

Ron Francis, Pittsburgh	30
Steve Duchesne, St. Louis	29
Curtis Leschyshyn, Quebec	29
Eric Lindros, Philadelphia	27
Jaromir Jagr, Pittsburgh	23

Penalty minutes

Enrico Ciccone, Tampa Bay	225
Shane Churla, Dallas	186
Bryan Marchment, Edmonton	184
Craig Berube, Washington	173
Rob Ray, Buffalo	173
Mike Peluso, New Jersey	167
Ronnie Stern, Calgary	163
Tie Domi, Win./Tor.	159
Jim Cummins, T.B./Chi.	158
Keith Tkachuk, Winnipeg	152
Lyle Odelein, Montreal	152

Consecutive-game point streaks

Eric Lindros, Philadelphia	14
Pierre Turgeon, NYI/Mon.	14
Paul Coffey, Detroit	13
Ron Francis, Pittsburgh	13
Mikael Renberg, Philadelphia	13

Consecutive-game goal streaks

Peter Bondra, Washington	7
Ray Sheppard, Detroit	7
Kelly Kisio, Calgary	6
Eric Lindros, Philadelphia	6
Joe Murphy, Chicago	6

Consecutive-game assist streaks

Phil Housley, Calgary	8
Eric Lindros, Philadelphia	8
Mark Messier, N.Y. Rangers	8
Many tied with	7

Most games scoring three or more goals

Eric Lindros, Philadelphia	3
Bernie Nicholls, Chicago	3
Owen Nolan, Quebec	3
Brett Hull, St. Louis	2
John LeClair, Philadelphia	2
Cam Neely, Boston	2
Alexei Zhamnov, Winnipeg	2

Points by a rookie

Peter Forsberg, Quebec	50
Paul Kariya, Anaheim	39
David Oliver, Edmonton	30
Ian Laperriere, St. Louis	27
Todd Marchant, Edmonton	27

Goals by a rookie

Paul Kariya, Anaheim	18
Roman Oksiuta, Edm./Van.	16
David Oliver, Edmonton	16
Peter Forsberg, Quebec	15
Jeff Friesen, San Jose	15

Assists by a rookie

Peter Forsberg, Quebec	35
Paul Kariya, Anaheim	21
Mariusz Czerkawski, Boston	14
Ian Laperriere, St. Louis	14
Todd Marchant, Edmonton	14
David Oliver, Edmonton	14

GOALTENDING

Games

Trevor Kidd, Calgary	43
Patrick Roy, Montreal	43
Ed Belfour, Chicago	42
Sean Burke, Hartford	42
Dominik Hasek, Buffalo	41

Minutes

Patrick Roy, Montreal	2566
Trevor Kidd, Calgary	2463
Ed Belfour, Chicago	2450
Sean Burke, Hartford	2418
Dominik Hasek, Buffalo	2416

Goals allowed

Bill Ranford, Edmonton	133
Patrick Roy, Montreal	127
Don Beaupre, Ottawa	121
Ken Wregget, Pittsburgh	118
Arturs Irbe, San Jose	111

Shutouts

Ed Belfour, Chicago 5
Dominik Hasek, Buffalo 5
Jim Carey, Washington 4
Arturs Irbe, San Jose 4
Blaine Lacher, Boston 4
John Vanbiesbrouck, Florida 4

Lowest goals-against average
(13 games played minimum)

Dominik Hasek, Buffalo 2.111
Rick Tabaracci, Was./Cal. 2.114
Jim Carey, Washington 2.13
Chris Osgood, Detroit 2.26
Ed Belfour, Chicago 2.28

Highest goals-against average
(13 games played minimum)

Grant Fuhr, Buf.-L.A. 4.03
Fred Brathwaite, Edmonton 3.99
Tim Cheveldae, Winnipeg 3.70
Mikhail Shtalenkov, Anaheim 3.63
Craig Billington, Ott.-Bos. 3.621
Bill Ranford, Edmonton 3.622

Games won

Ken Wregget, Pittsburgh 25
Ed Belfour, Chicago 22
Trevor Kidd, Calgary 22
Curtis Joseph, St. Louis 20

Martin Brodeur, New Jersey 19
Dominik Hasek, Buffalo 19
Blaine Lacher, Boston 19
Mike Vernon, Detroit 19

Best winning percentage
(13 games played minimum)

Jocelyn Thibault, Que. (12-2-2) .. .813
Chris Osgood, Det. (14-5-0) .... .737
Mike Vernon, Det. (19-6-4) .... .724
Ken Wregget, Pit. (25-9-2) .... .722
Jim Carey, Was. (18-6-3) .... .722

Worst winning percentage
(13 games played minimum)

Grant Fuhr, Buf.-L.A. (2-9-3) .... .250
Olaf Kolzig, Was. (2-8-2) .... .250
Don Beaupre, Ott. (8-25-3) .... .264
J.C. Bergeron, T.B. (3-9-1) .... .269
Fred Brathwaite, Edm. (2-5-1) .... .313

Games lost

Don Beaupre, Ottawa 25
Guy Hebert, Anaheim 20
Bill Ranford, Edmonton 20
Patrick Roy, Montreal 20
Sean Burke, Hartford 19
Arturs Irbe, San Jose 19
Daren Puppa, Tampa Bay 19

Shots against

Patrick Roy, Montreal 1357
Sean Burke, Hartford 1233
Dominik Hasek, Buffalo 1221
Ken Wregget, Pittsburgh 1219
Trevor Kidd, Calgary 1170

Saves

Patrick Roy, Montreal 1230
Dominik Hasek, Buffalo 1136
Sean Burke, Hartford 1125
Ken Wregget, Pittsburgh 1101
Trevor Kidd, Calgary 1063

Highest save percentage
(13 games played minimum)

Dominik Hasek, Buffalo .... .930
Chris Osgood, Detroit .... .91734
Jocelyn Thibault, Quebec .... .91725
Damian Rhodes, Toronto .... .916
Andy Moog, Dallas .... .915

Lowest save percentage
(13 games played minimum)

Fred Brathwaite, Edmonton .... .863
Craig Billington, Ott.-Bos. .... .866
J.C. Bergeron, Tampa Bay .... .869
Grant Fuhr, Buf.-L.A. .... .873
Jamie McLennan, N.Y. Islanders ... .876

STATISTICS OF PLAYERS WITH TWO OR MORE TEAMS

SCORING

	Games	G	A	Pts.	PIM	+/-	PPG	SHG	Shots	Shooting Pct.
Greg Adams, Vancouver	31	5	10	15	12	1	2	2	56	8.9
Greg Adams, Dallas	12	3	3	6	4	-4	1	0	16	18.8
Totals	43	8	13	21	16	-3	3	2	72	11.1
Shawn Antoski, Vancouver	7	0	0	0	46	-4	0	0	4	0.0
Shawn Antoski, Philadelphia	25	0	0	0	61	0	0	0	12	0.0
Totals	32	0	0	0	107	-4	0	0	16	0.0
Josef Beranek, Philadelphia	14	5	5	10	2	3	1	0	39	12.8
Josef Beranek, Vancouver	37	8	13	21	28	-10	2	0	95	8.4
Totals	†51	13	18	31	30	-7	3	0	134	9.7
Drake Berehowsky, Toronto	25	0	2	2	15	-10	0	0	12	0.0
Drake Berehowsky, Pittsburgh	4	0	0	0	13	1	0	0	2	0.0
Totals	29	0	2	2	28	-9	0	0	14	0.0
Craig Billington, Ottawa (goalie)	9	0	0	0	2	0	0	0	0	0.0
Craig Billington, Boston (goalie)	8	0	0	0	2	0	0	0	0	0.0
Totals	17	0	0	0	4	0	0	0	0	0.0
Arto Blomsten, Winnipeg	1	0	0	0	2	0	0	0	0	0.0
Arto Blomsten, Los Angeles	4	0	1	1	0	2	0	0	1	0.0
Totals	5	0	1	1	2	2	0	0	1	0.0
Nikolai Borschevsky, Toronto	19	0	5	5	0	3	0	0	28	0.0
Nikolai Borschevsky, Calgary	8	0	5	5	0	7	0	0	12	0.0
Totals	27	0	10	10	0	10	0	0	40	0.0
Philippe Boucher, Buffalo	9	1	4	5	0	6	0	0	15	6.7
Philippe Boucher, Los Angeles	6	1	0	1	4	-3	0	0	15	6.7
Totals	15	2	4	6	4	3	0	0	30	6.7
Neal Broten, Dallas	17	0	4	4	4	-8	0	0	29	0.0
Neal Broten, New Jersey	30	8	20	28	20	9	2	0	43	18.6
Totals	47	8	24	32	24	1	2	0	72	11.1
Randy Burridge, Washington	2	0	0	0	2	0	0	0	2	0.0
Randy Burridge, Los Angeles	38	4	15	19	8	-4	2	0	50	8.0
Totals	40	4	15	19	10	-4	2	0	52	7.7
Shawn Chambers, Tampa Bay	24	2	12	14	6	0	1	0	44	4.5
Shawn Chambers, New Jersey	21	2	5	7	6	2	1	0	23	8.7
Totals	45	4	17	21	12	2	2	0	67	6.0
Danton Cole, Tampa Bay	26	3	3	6	6	-1	1	0	56	5.4
Danton Cole, New Jersey	12	1	2	3	8	0	0	0	20	5.0
Totals	38	4	5	9	14	-1	1	0	76	5.3
Russ Courtnall, Dallas	32	7	10	17	13	-8	2	0	90	7.8
Russ Courtnall, Vancouver	13	4	14	18	4	10	0	2	42	9.5
Totals	45	11	24	35	17	2	2	2	132	8.3

	Games	G	A	Pts.	PIM	+/-	PPG	SHG	Shots	Shooting Pct.
Jim Cummins, Tampa Bay	10	1	0	1	41	-3	0	0	3	33.3
Jim Cummins, Chicago	27	3	1	4	117	-3	0	0	20	15.0
Totals	37	4	1	5	158	-6	0	0	23	17.4
Craig Darby, Montreal	10	0	2	2	0	-5	0	0	4	0.0
Craig Darby, N.Y. Islanders	3	0	0	0	0	-1	0	0	1	0.0
Totals	13	0	2	2	0	-6	0	0	5	0.0
Eric Desjardins, Montreal	9	0	6	6	2	2	0	0	14	0.0
Eric Desjardins, Philadelphia	34	5	18	23	12	10	1	0	79	6.3
Totals	43	5	24	29	14	12	1	0	93	5.4
Paul Dipietro, Montreal	22	4	5	9	4	-3	0	0	41	9.8
Paul Dipietro, Toronto	12	1	1	2	6	-6	0	0	19	5.3
Totals	34	5	6	11	10	-9	0	0	60	8.3
Gerald Diduck, Vancouver	22	1	3	4	15	-8	1	0	25	4.0
Gerald Diduck, Chicago	13	1	0	1	48	3	0	0	17	5.9
Totals	35	2	3	5	63	-5	1	0	42	4.8
Gilbert Dionne, Montreal	6	0	3	3	2	-3	0	0	4	0.0
Gilbert Dionne, Philadelphia	20	0	6	6	2	-1	0	0	29	0.0
Totals	26	0	9	9	4	-4	0	0	33	0.0
Tie Domi, Winnipeg	31	4	4	8	128	-6	0	0	34	11.8
Tie Domi, Toronto	9	0	1	1	31	1	0	0	12	0.0
Totals	40	4	5	9	159	-5	0	0	46	8.7
Mike Donnelly, Los Angeles	9	1	1	2	4	-7	0	0	22	4.5
Mike Donnelly, Dallas	35	11	14	25	29	3	3	0	94	11.7
Totals	44	12	15	27	33	-4	3	0	116	10.3
Gaetan Duchesne, San Jose	33	2	7	9	16	-6	0	0	48	4.2
Gaetan Duchesne, Florida	13	1	2	3	0	3	0	0	14	7.1
Totals	46	3	9	12	16	-3	0	0	62	4.8
Mike Eagles, Winnipeg	27	2	1	3	40	-13	0	0	13	15.4
Mike Eagles, Washington	13	1	3	4	8	2	0	0	15	6.7
Totals	40	3	4	7	48	-11	0	0	28	10.7
Mike Eastwood, Toronto	36	5	5	10	32	-12	0	0	38	13.2
Mike Eastwood, Winnipeg	13	3	6	9	4	3	0	0	17	17.6
Totals	49	8	11	19	36	-9	0	0	55	14.5
Todd Elik, San Jose	22	7	10	17	18	3	4	0	50	14.0
Todd Elik, St. Louis	13	2	4	6	4	5	0	0	26	7.7
Totals	35	9	14	23	22	8	4	0	76	11.8
Bob Errey, San Jose	13	2	2	4	27	4	0	0	19	10.5
Bob Errey, Detroit	30	6	11	17	31	9	0	0	53	11.3
Totals	43	8	13	21	58	13	0	0	72	11.1
Leonard Esau, Edmonton	14	0	6	6	15	-8	0	0	17	0.0
Leonard Esau, Calgary	1	0	0	0	0	-2	0	0	4	0.0
Totals	15	0	6	6	15	-10	0	0	21	0.0
Glen Featherstone, N.Y. Rangers	6	1	0	1	18	0	0	0	6	16.7
Glen Featherstone, Hartford	13	1	1	2	32	-7	0	0	16	6.3
Totals	19	2	1	3	50	-7	0	0	22	9.1
Mark Ferner, Anaheim	14	0	1	1	6	-4	0	0	15	0.0
Mark Ferner, Detroit	3	0	0	0	0	0	0	0	1	0.0
Totals	17	0	1	1	6	-4	0	0	16	0.0
Viacheslav Fetisov, New Jersey	4	0	1	1	0	-2	0	0	1	0.0
Viacheslav Fetisov, Detroit	14	3	11	14	2	3	3	0	36	8.3
Totals	18	3	12	15	2	1	3	0	37	8.1
Iain Fraser, Dallas	4	0	0	0	0	-3	0	0	2	0.0
Iain Fraser, Edmonton	9	3	0	3	0	3	0	0	5	60.0
Totals	13	3	0	3	0	0	0	0	7	42.9
Grant Fuhr, Buffalo (goalie)	3	0	0	0	0	0	0	0	0	0.0
Grant Fuhr, Los Angeles (goalie)	14	0	0	0	2	0	0	0	0	0.0
Totals	17	0	0	0	2	0	0	0	0	0.0
Garry Galley, Philadelphia	33	2	20	22	20	0	1	0	66	3.0
Garry Galley, Buffalo	14	1	9	10	10	4	1	0	31	3.2
Totals	47	3	29	32	30	4	2	0	97	3.1
Johan Garpenlov, San Jose	13	1	1	2	2	-3	0	0	16	6.3
Johan Garpenlov, Florida	27	3	9	12	0	4	0	0	28	10.7
Totals	40	4	10	14	2	1	0	0	44	9.1
Stu Grimson, Anaheim	31	0	1	1	110	-7	0	0	14	0.0
Stu Grimson, Detroit	11	0	0	0	37	-4	0	0	4	0.0
Totals	42	0	1	1	147	-11	0	0	18	0.0
Bob Halkidis, Detroit	4	0	1	1	6	2	0	0	0	0.0
Bob Halkidis, Tampa Bay	27	1	3	4	40	-12	0	0	25	4.0
Totals	31	1	4	5	46	-10	0	0	25	4.0
Ben Hankinson, New Jersey	8	0	0	0	7	-6	0	0	8	0.0
Ben Hankinson, Tampa Bay	18	0	2	2	6	1	0	0	18	0.0
Totals	26	0	2	2	13	-5	0	0	26	0.0
Benoit Hogue, N.Y. Islanders	33	6	4	10	34	0	1	0	50	12.0
Benoit Hogue, Toronto	12	3	3	6	0	0	1	0	16	18.8
Totals	45	9	7	16	34	0	2	0	66	13.6

	Games	G	A	Pts.	PIM	+/-	PPG	SHG	Shots	Shooting Pct.
Bill Huard, Ottawa	26	1	1	2	64	-2	0	0	15	6.7
Bill Huard, Quebec	7	2	2	4	13	2	0	0	6	33.3
Totals	33	3	3	6	77	0	0	0	21	14.3
Charlie Huddy, Los Angeles	9	0	1	1	6	-6	0	0	11	0.0
Charlie Huddy, Buffalo	32	2	4	6	36	-1	1	0	40	5.0
Totals	41	2	5	7	42	-7	1	0	51	3.9
Craig Janney, St. Louis	8	2	5	7	0	3	1	0	9	22.2
Craig Janney, San Jose	27	5	15	20	10	-4	2	0	31	16.1
Totals	35	7	20	27	10	-1	3	0	40	17.5
Grant Jennings, Pittsburgh	25	0	4	4	36	2	0	0	16	0.0
Grant Jennings, Toronto	10	0	2	2	7	-6	0	0	9	0.0
Totals	35	0	6	6	43	-4	0	0	25	0.0
Dave Karpa, Quebec	2	0	0	0	0	-1	0	0	1	0.0
Dave Karpa, Anaheim	26	1	5	6	91	0	0	0	32	3.1
Totals	28	1	5	6	91	-1	0	0	33	3.0
Dan Lacroix, Boston	23	1	0	1	38	-2	0	0	14	7.1
Dan Lacroix, N.Y. Rangers	1	0	0	0	0	0	0	0	0	0.0
Totals	24	1	0	1	38	-2	0	0	14	7.1
Nathan Lafayette, Vancouver	27	4	4	8	2	2	0	1	30	13.3
Nathan Lafayette, N.Y. Rangers	12	0	0	0	0	1	0	0	5	0.0
Totals	39	4	4	8	2	3	0	1	35	11.4
Mark Lamb, Philadelphia	8	0	2	2	2	1	0	0	7	0.0
Mark Lamb, Montreal	39	1	0	1	18	-13	0	0	23	4.3
Totals	47	1	2	3	20	-12	0	0	30	3.3
Daniel Laperriere, St. Louis	4	0	0	0	15	1	0	0	0	0.0
Daniel Laperriere, Ottawa	13	1	1	2	0	-4	1	0	18	5.6
Totals	17	1	1	2	15	-3	1	0	18	5.6
John LeClair, Montreal	9	1	4	5	10	-1	1	0	18	5.6
John LeClair, Philadelphia	37	25	24	49	20	21	5	0	113	22.1
Totals	46	26	28	54	30	20	6	0	131	19.8
Troy Loney, N.Y. Islanders	26	5	4	9	23	0	2	0	45	11.1
Troy Loney, N.Y. Rangers	4	0	0	0	0	-2	0	0	2	0.0
Totals	30	5	4	9	23	-2	2	0	47	10.6
Norm Maciver, Ottawa	28	4	7	11	10	-9	2	0	30	13.3
Norm Maciver, Pittsburgh	13	0	9	9	6	7	0	0	20	0.0
Totals	41	4	16	20	16	-2	2	0	50	8.0
Vladimir Malakhov, N.Y. Islanders	26	3	13	16	32	-1	1	0	61	4.9
Vladimir Malakhov, Montreal	14	1	4	5	14	-2	0	0	30	3.3
Totals	40	4	17	21	46	-3	1	0	91	4.4
Alan May, Dallas	27	1	1	2	106	1	0	0	23	4.3
Alan May, Calgary	7	1	2	3	13	2	0	0	5	20.0
Totals	34	2	3	5	119	3	0	0	28	7.1
Ryan McGill, Philadelphia	12	0	0	0	13	0	0	0	2	0.0
Ryan McGill, Edmonton	8	0	0	0	8	-4	0	0	6	0.0
Totals	20	0	0	0	21	-4	0	0	8	0.0
Corey Millen, New Jersey	17	2	3	5	8	2	0	0	30	6.7
Corey Millen, Dallas	28	3	15	18	28	4	1	0	44	6.8
Totals	45	5	18	23	36	6	1	0	74	6.8
Kevin Miller, St. Louis	15	2	5	7	0	4	0	0	19	10.5
Kevin Miller, San Jose	21	6	7	13	13	0	1	1	41	14.6
Totals	36	8	12	20	13	4	1	1	60	13.3
Jim Montgomery, Montreal	5	0	0	0	2	-2	0	0	3	0.0
Jim Montgomery, Philadelphia	8	1	1	2	6	-2	0	0	10	10.0
Totals	13	1	1	2	8	-4	0	0	13	7.7
Kirk Muller, Montreal	33	8	11	19	33	-21	3	0	81	9.9
Kirk Muller, N.Y. Islanders	12	3	5	8	14	3	1	1	16	18.8
Totals	45	11	16	27	47	-18	4	1	97	11.3
Troy Murray, Ottawa	33	4	10	14	16	-1	0	0	38	10.5
Troy Murray, Pittsburgh	13	0	2	2	23	-1	0	0	7	0.0
Totals	46	4	12	16	39	-2	0	0	45	8.9
Jeff Norton, San Jose	20	1	9	10	39	1	0	0	21	4.8
Jeff Norton, St. Louis	28	2	18	20	33	21	0	0	27	7.4
Totals	48	3	27	30	72	22	0	0	48	6.3
Roman Oksiuta, Edmonton	26	11	2	13	8	-14	5	0	52	21.2
Roman Oksiuta, Vancouver	12	5	2	7	2	2	1	0	15	33.3
Totals	38	16	4	20	10	-12	6	0	67	23.9
Ed Olczyk, N.Y. Rangers	20	2	1	3	4	-2	1	0	29	6.9
Ed Olczyk, Winnipeg	13	2	8	10	8	1	1	0	27	7.4
Totals	33	4	9	13	12	-1	2	0	56	7.1
Scott Pearson, Edmonton	28	1	4	5	54	-11	0	0	21	4.8
Scott Pearson, Buffalo	14	2	1	3	20	-3	0	0	19	10.5
Totals	42	3	5	8	74	-14	0	0	40	7.5
Adrien Plavsic, Vancouver	3	0	1	1	4	3	0	0	11	0.0
Adrien Plavsic, Tampa Bay	15	2	1	3	4	5	0	0	24	8.3
Totals	18	2	2	4	8	8	0	0	35	5.7

	Games	G	A	Pts.	PIM	+/-	PPG	SHG	Shots	Shooting Pct.
Mark Recchi, Philadelphia	10	2	3	5	12	-6	1	0	17	11.8
Mark Recchi, Montreal	39	14	29	43	16	-3	8	0	104	13.5
Totals	49	16	32	48	28	-9	9	0	121	13.2
Christian Ruuttu, Chicago	20	2	5	7	6	3	0	0	25	8.0
Christian Ruuttu, Vancouver	25	5	6	11	23	11	0	0	19	26.3
Totals	45	7	11	18	29	14	0	0	44	15.9
Warren Rychel, Los Angeles	7	0	0	0	19	-5	0	0	7	0.0
Warren Rychel, Toronto	26	1	6	7	101	1	0	0	34	2.9
Totals	33	1	6	7	120	-4	0	0	41	2.4
Denis Savard, Tampa Bay	31	6	11	17	10	-6	1	0	56	10.7
Denis Savard, Chicago	12	4	4	8	8	3	1	0	26	15.4
Totals	43	10	15	25	18	-3	2	0	82	12.2
Mathieu Schneider, Montreal	30	5	15	20	49	-3	2	0	82	6.1
Mathieu Schneider, N.Y. Islanders	13	3	6	9	30	-5	1	0	36	8.3
Totals	43	8	21	29	79	-8	3	0	118	6.8
Alexander Semak, New Jersey	19	2	6	8	13	-4	0	0	32	6.3
Alexander Semak, Tampa Bay	22	5	5	10	12	-3	0	0	39	12.8
Totals	41	7	11	18	25	-7	0	0	71	9.9
Anatoli Semenov, Anaheim	15	3	4	7	4	-10	2	0	33	9.1
Anatoli Semenov, Philadelphia	26	1	2	3	6	-2	0	0	36	2.8
Totals	41	4	6	10	10	-12	2	0	69	5.8
Brent Severyn, Florida	9	1	1	2	37	-3	1	0	10	10.0
Brent Severyn, N.Y. Islanders	19	1	3	4	34	1	0	0	22	4.5
Totals	28	2	4	6	71	-2	1	0	32	6.3
Mike Sillinger, Detroit	13	2	6	8	2	3	0	0	11	18.2
Mike Sillinger, Anaheim	15	2	5	7	6	1	2	0	28	7.1
Totals	28	4	11	15	8	4	2	0	39	10.3
Jiri Slegr, Vancouver	19	1	5	6	32	0	0	0	42	2.4
Jiri Slegr, Edmonton	12	1	5	6	14	-5	1	0	27	3.7
Totals	31	2	10	12	46	-5	1	0	69	2.9
Robb Stauber, Los Angeles (goalie)	1	0	0	0	0	0	0	0	0	0.0
Robb Stauber, Buffalo (goalie)	6	0	0	0	0	0	0	0	0	0.0
Totals	7	0	0	0	0	0	0	0	0	0.0
Martin Straka, Pittsburgh	31	4	12	16	16	0	0	0	36	11.1
Martin Straka, Ottawa	6	1	1	2	0	-1	0	0	13	7.7
Totals	37	5	13	18	16	-1	0	0	49	10.2
Rich Sutter, Chicago	15	0	0	0	28	1	0	0	17	0.0
Rich Sutter, Tampa Bay	4	0	0	0	0	0	0	0	3	0.0
Rich Sutter, Toronto	18	0	3	3	10	-7	0	0	19	0.0
Totals	37	0	3	3	38	-6	0	0	39	0.0
Ken Sutton, Buffalo	12	1	2	3	30	-2	0	0	12	8.3
Ken Sutton, Edmonton	12	3	1	4	12	-1	0	0	28	10.7
Totals	24	4	3	7	42	-3	0	0	40	10.0
Petr Svoboda, Buffalo	26	0	5	5	60	-5	0	0	22	0.0
Petr Svoboda, Philadelphia	11	0	3	3	10	0	0	0	17	0.0
Totals	37	0	8	8	70	-5	0	0	39	0.0
Rick Tabaracci, Washington (goalie)	8	0	1	1	2	0	0	0	0	0.0
Rick Tabaracci, Calgary (goalie)	5	0	1	1	0	0	0	0	0	0.0
Totals	13	0	2	2	2	0	0	0	0	0.0
Denis Tsygurov, Buffalo	4	0	0	0	4	-1	0	0	4	0.0
Denis Tsygurov, Los Angeles	21	0	0	0	11	-2	0	0	16	0.0
Totals	25	0	0	0	15	-3	0	0	20	0.0
Pierre Turgeon, N.Y. Islanders	34	13	14	27	10	-12	3	2	93	14.0
Pierre Turgeon, Montreal	15	11	9	20	4	12	2	0	67	16.4
Totals	49	24	23	47	14	0	5	2	160	15.0
Igor Ulanov, Winnipeg	19	1	3	4	27	-2	0	0	13	7.7
Igor Ulanov, Washington	3	0	1	1	2	3	0	0	0	0.0
Totals	22	1	4	5	29	1	0	0	13	7.7
Pat Verbeek, Hartford	29	7	11	18	53	0	3	0	75	9.3
Pat Verbeek, N.Y. Rangers	19	10	5	15	18	-2	4	0	56	17.9
Totals	48	17	16	33	71	-2	7	0	131	13.0
Jason York, Detroit	10	1	2	3	2	0	0	0	6	16.7
Jason York, Anaheim	15	0	8	8	12	4	0	0	22	0.0
Totals	25	1	10	11	14	4	0	0	28	3.6
Paul Ysebaert, Chicago	15	4	5	9	6	4	0	0	23	17.4
Paul Ysebaert, Tampa Bay	29	8	11	19	12	-1	0	0	70	11.4
Totals	44	12	16	28	18	3	0	0	93	12.9
Alexei Zhitnik, Los Angeles	11	2	5	7	27	-3	2	0	33	6.1
Alexei Zhitnik, Buffalo	21	2	5	7	34	-3	1	0	33	6.1
Totals	32	4	10	14	61	-6	3	0	66	6.1

GOALTENDING

	Games	Min.	Goals	SO	Avg.	W	L	T	Shots	Sv. Pct.
Craig Billington, Ottawa	9	472	32	0	4.07	0	6	2	240	.867
Craig Billington, Boston	8	373	19	0	3.06	5	1	0	140	.864
Totals	17	845	51	0	3.62	5	7	2	380	.866
Grant Fuhr, Buffalo	3	180	12	0	4.00	1	2	0	85	.859
Grant Fuhr, Los Angeles	14	698	47	0	4.04	1	7	3	379	.876
Totals	17	878	59	0	4.03	2	9	3	464	.873
Robb Stauber, Los Angeles	1	16	2	0	7.50	0	0	0	6	.667
Robb Stauber, Buffalo	6	317	20	0	3.79	2	3	0	150	.867
Totals	7	333	22	0	3.96	2	3	0	156	.859
Rick Tabaracci, Washington	8	394	16	0	2.44	1	3	2	147	.891
Rick Tabaracci, Calgary	5	202	5	0	1.49	2	0	1	93	.946
Totals	13	596	21	0	2.11	3	3	3	240	.913

†Led league.

MISCELLANEOUS

HAT TRICKS

(Players scoring three or more goals in a game)

Date	Player, Team	Opp.	Goals	Date	Player, Team	Opp.	Goals
1-22-95	Cam Neely, Boston	Phi.	3	3-18-95	Eric Lindros, Philadelphia	Fla.	3
1-24-95	Ray Sheppard, Detroit	Van.	3	3-20-95	Jason Arnott, Edmonton	Cal.	3
1-30-95	Adam Graves, N.Y. Rangers	Ott.	3	3-20-95	Eric Lindros, Philadelphia	Mon.	3
2- 2-95	Josef Beranek, Philadelphia	NYI	3	3-21-95	Bernie Nicholls, Chicago	S.J.	3
2- 4-95	Brett Hull, St. Louis	Dal.	3	3-22-95	David Oliver, Edmonton	Dal.	3
2- 4-95	German Titov, Calgary	Tor.	3	3-26-95	Alexandre Daigle, Ottawa	Que.	3
2- 4-95	Rick Tocchet, Los Angeles	Det.	3	3-26-95	Scott Young, Quebec	Ott.	3
2- 5-95	Bernie Nicholls, Chicago	Van.	4	3-28-95	Nelson Emerson, Winnipeg	S.J.	3
2- 9-95	Wendel Clark, Quebec	Bos.	3	3-29-95	Steven Rice, Hartford	Fla.	3
2-11-95	Alexei Zhamnov, Winnipeg	St.L.	3	3-30-95	Owen Nolan, Quebec	NYR	3
2-12-95	Sergei Fedorov, Detroit	L.A.	4	3-30-95	Donald Audette, Buffalo	Ott.	3
2-14-95	John LeClair, Philadelphia	T.B.	3	4- 1-95	Alexei Zhamnov, Winnipeg	L.A.	5
2-14-95	Jaromir Jagr, Pittsburgh	Bos.	3	4- 2-95	Owen Nolan, Quebec	Ott.	3
2-15-95	Geoff Sanderson, Hartford	Mon.	3	4- 3-95	Steve Larouche, Ottawa	Mon.	3
2-16-95	Luc Robitaille, Pittsburgh	Har.	4	4- 3-95	Tony Granato, Los Angeles	Edm.	3
2-23-95	Alexei Yashin, Ottawa	Was.	3	4- 5-95	Igor Chibirev, Hartford	Pit.	3
2-23-95	Eric Lindros, Philadelphia	Que.	3	4-10-95	Joe Nieuwendyk, Calgary	S.J.	3
2-25-95	John LeClair, Philadelphia	Mon.	3	4-11-95	Pavel Bure, Vancouver	Ana.	3
2-28-95	Bernie Nicholls, Chicago	L.A.	4	4-16-95	Brett Hull, St. Louis	Det.	4
3- 1-95	Brian Noonan, N.Y. Rangers	Har.	3	4-17-95	Pierre Turgeon, Montreal	Was.	3
3- 1-95	Uwe Krupp, Quebec	T.B.	3	4-21-95	Peter Bondra, Washington	Har.	3
3- 2-95	Bryan Smolinski, Boston	N.J.	3	4-22-95	Russ Courtnall, Vancouver	Edm.	3
3- 6-95	Owen Nolan, Quebec	N.J.	3	4-22-95	Todd Harvey, Dallas	Tor.	3
3-12-95	Ronnie Stern, Calgary	Dal.	3	4-23-95	Cam Neely, Boston	NYR	3

OVERTIME GOALS

Date	Player, Team	Opponent	Time	Final score
1-23-95	Peter Douris, Anaheim	Edmonton	4:20	Anaheim 5, Edmonton 4
1-26-95	Adam Oates, Boston	New Jersey	3:43	Boston 1, New Jersey 0
2- 2-95	Ray Ferraro, N.Y. Islanders	Philadelphia	1:43	N.Y. Islanders 5, Philadelphia 4
2- 2-95	Brett Hull, St. Louis	Winnipeg	3:32	St. Louis 5, Winnipeg 4
2- 3-95	Tony Amonte, Chicago	Calgary	2:25	Chicago 4, Calgary 3
2-18-95	Theoren Fleury, Calgary	Dallas	4:34	Calgary 3, Dallas 2
2-20-95	Donald Brashear, Montreal	N.Y. Islanders	1:54	Montreal 3, N.Y. Islanders 2
2-22-95	Darren Turcotte, Hartford	Boston	2:59	Hartford 3, Boston 2
3- 2-95	Brian Bradley, Tampa Bay	Ottawa	3:55	Tampa Bay 3, Ottawa 2
3- 4-95	Robert Kron, Hartford	Tampa Bay	1:11	Hartford 3, Tampa Bay 2
3- 4-95	Larry Murphy, Pittsburgh	Boston	4:36	Pittsburgh 4, Boston 3
3-14-95	Yuri Khmylev, Buffalo	Florida	0:54	Buffalo 2, Florida 1
3-18-95	Troy Murray, Ottawa	Buffalo	3:42	Ottawa 4, Buffalo 3
3-18-95	Eric Lindros, Philadelphia	Florida	2:13	Philadelphia 4, Florida 3
3-19-95	Stephane Richer, New Jersey	Boston	1:36	New Jersey 4, Boston 3
3-20-95	Owen Nolan, Quebec	Florida	2:33	Quebec 5, Florida 4
3-24-95	Fred Knipscheer, Boston	Tampa Bay	3:32	Boston 4, Tampa Bay 3
3-26-95	Geoff Sanderson, Hartford	Washington	2:16	Hartford 4, Washington 3
3-27-95	Petr Klima, Tampa Bay	Montreal	2:23	Tampa Bay 3, Montreal 2
3-28-95	Jeff Friesen, San Jose	Winnipeg	4:27	San Jose 6, Winnipeg 5
4- 5-95	Stephan Lebeau, Anaheim	Edmonton	4:09	Anaheim 4, Edmonton 3
4-14-95	Darren Turcotte, Hartford	Montreal	2:04	Hartford 4, Montreal 3
4-16-95	Rod Brind'Amour, Philadelphia	Pittsburgh	1:30	Philadelphia 4, Pittsburgh 3

Date	Player, Team	Opponent	Time	Final score
4-22-95	—John LeClair, Philadelphia	New Jersey	0:54	Philadelphia 4, New Jersey 3
4-25-95	—Murray Craven, Chicago	Vancouver	2:00	Chicago 4, Vancouver 3
4-27-95	—Zdeno Ciger, Edmonton	St. Louis	3:19	Edmonton 3, St. Louis 2

PENALTY-SHOT INFORMATION

Date	Shooter	Goaltender	Scored	Final score
1-21-95	Michal Pivonka, Washington	Sean Burke, Hartford	No	Washington 1, Hartford 1
1-24-95	Benoit Hogue, N.Y. Islanders	Ron Hextall, Philadelphia	Yes	N.Y. Islanders 4, Philadelphia 3
2- 6-95	Mark Recchi, Philadelphia	Don Beaupre, Ottawa	No	Ottawa 3, Philadelphia 0
2- 6-95	Teemu Selanne, Winnipeg	Trevor Kidd, Calgary	No	Winnipeg 5, Calgary 4
2-12-95	Sergei Fedorov, Detroit	Kelly Hrudey, Los Angeles	No	Los Angeles 4, Detroit 4
3- 5-95	Steve Konowalchuk, Washington	Mike Richter, N.Y. Rangers	No	Washington 4, N.Y. Rangers 2
3- 7-95	Jeremy Roenick, Chicago	Andrei Trefilov, Calgary	No	Calgary 6, Chicago 3
3- 8-95	Mark Recchi, Montreal	Dominik Hasek, Buffalo	No	Buffalo 2, Montreal 2
3- 9-95	Dirk Graham, Chicago	Kelly Hrudey, Los Angeles	No	Los Angeles 4, Chicago 3
3-15-95	Mats Sundin, Toronto	Arturs Irbe, San Jose	Yes	Toronto 2, San Jose 1
3-16-95	Martin Straka, Pittsburgh	Jocelyn Thibault, Quebec	No	Quebec 3, Pittsburgh 2
3-21-95	Geoff Courtnall, Vancouver	Damian Rhodes, Toronto	No	Vancouver 3, Toronto 1
3-21-95	Dan Quinn, Los Angeles	Mikhail Shtalenkov, Anaheim	Yes	Los Angeles 3, Anaheim 3
3-22-95	Bob Errey, Detroit	Nikolai Khabibulin, Winnipeg	No	Detroit 6, Winnipeg 3
3-26-95	Brett Hull, St. Louis	Bill Ranford, Edmonton	No	St. Louis 5, Edmonton 1
4- 1-95	Dave Gagner, Dallas	Chris Osgood, Detroit	No	Detroit 3, Dallas 2
4- 8-95	Dave Andreychuk, Toronto	Tim Cheveldae, Winnipeg	No	Toronto 4, Winnipeg 3

TEAM STREAKS

Most consecutive games won

Philadelphia, Apr. 2-22 9
Philadelphia, Mar. 5-20 8
Pittsburgh, Jan. 20-Feb. 4 7
Quebec, Feb. 4-16 7
Detroit, Apr. 5-14 6

Most consecutive home games won

Quebec, Mar. 6-Apr. 16 10
Pittsburgh, Jan. 27-Feb. 16 7
Detroit, Mar. 2-30 7

Most consecutive road games won

Detroit, Mar. 25-Apr. 14 7
Chicago, Feb. 1-9 5

Most consecutive games undefeated

Pittsburgh, Jan. 20-Feb. 16 13
Detroit, Mar. 25-Apr. 14 11
Philadelphia, Apr. 2-22 9
Philadelphia, Mar. 5-20 8

Most consecutive home games undefeated

Quebec, Mar. 1-May 3 15
Detroit, Mar. 2-Apr. 29 12
Pittsburgh, Jan. 27-Feb. 21 9
Quebec, Jan. 24-Feb. 25 8
Washington, Feb. 26-Mar. 25 8

Most consecutive road games undefeated

Vancouver, Feb. 17-Mar. 14 8
Detroit, Mar. 25-Apr. 14 7
Pittsburgh, Jan. 20-Feb. 9 6
Chicago, Feb. 1-9 5

TEAM OVERTIME GAMES

Team	OVERALL					HOME					AWAY				
	G	W	L	T	Pct.	G	W	L	T	Pct.	G	W	L	T	Pct.
Hartford	9	4	0	5	.722	5	3	0	2	.800	4	1	0	3	.625
Anaheim	7	2	0	5	.643	6	2	0	4	.667	1	0	0	1	.500
Chicago	7	2	0	5	.643	4	1	0	3	.625	3	1	0	2	.667
Philadelphia	8	3	1	4	.625	3	1	1	1	.500	5	2	0	3	.700
San Jose	5	1	0	4	.600	2	1	0	1	.750	3	0	0	3	.500
Quebec	6	1	0	5	.583	5	1	0	4	.600	1	0	0	1	.500
Calgary	9	1	1	7	.500	4	1	1	2	.500	5	0	0	5	.500
Buffalo	9	1	1	7	.500	1	0	0	1	.500	8	1	1	6	.500
Los Angeles	9	0	0	9	.500	6	0	0	6	.500	3	0	0	3	.500
Toronto	8	0	0	8	.500	2	0	0	2	.500	6	0	0	6	.500
Tampa Bay	7	2	2	3	.500	2	1	1	0	.500	5	1	1	3	.500
Ottawa	7	1	1	5	.500	5	1	1	3	.500	2	0	0	2	.500
N.Y. Islanders	7	1	1	5	.500	3	0	0	3	.500	4	1	1	2	.500
St. Louis	7	1	1	5	.500	2	0	0	2	.500	5	1	1	3	.500
Pittsburgh	5	1	1	3	.500	1	0	0	1	.500	4	1	1	2	.500
Detroit	4	0	0	4	.500	3	0	0	3	.500	1	0	0	1	.500
N.Y. Rangers	3	0	0	3	.500	3	0	0	3	.500	0	0	0	0	.000
Vancouver	13	0	1	12	.462	6	0	0	6	.500	7	0	1	6	.429
New Jersey	11	1	2	8	.455	8	1	1	6	.500	3	0	1	2	.333
Montreal	10	1	2	7	.450	5	1	0	4	.600	5	0	2	3	.300
Dallas	9	0	1	8	.444	5	0	0	5	.500	4	0	1	3	.375
Washington	9	0	1	8	.444	4	0	1	3	.375	5	0	0	5	.500
Boston	8	2	3	3	.438	4	1	1	2	.500	4	1	2	1	.375
Edmonton	7	1	2	4	.429	2	1	0	1	.750	5	0	2	3	.300
Winnipeg	9	0	2	7	.389	5	0	1	4	.400	4	0	1	3	.375
Florida	9	0	3	6	.333	5	0	2	3	.300	4	0	1	3	.375
Totals	101	26	26	75	.500	101	16	10	75	.530	101	10	16	75	.470

RESULTS

CONFERENCE QUARTERFINALS

EASTERN CONFERENCE

	W	L	Pts.	GF	GA
N.Y. Rangers	4	2	8	25	19
Quebec Nordiques	2	4	4	19	25

(N.Y. Rangers won Eastern Conference quarterfinals, 4-2)

Sat.	May 6—N.Y. Rangers 4, at Quebec 5	
Mon.	May 8—N.Y. Rangers 8, at Quebec 3	
Wed.	May 10—Quebec 3, at N.Y. Rangers 4	
Fri.	May 12—Quebec 2, at N.Y. Rangers 3 (a)	
Sun.	May 14—N.Y. Rangers 2, at Quebec 4	
Tue.	May 16—Quebec 2, at N.Y. Rangers 4	

(a)—Steve Larmer scored at 8:09 (OT) for N.Y. Rangers.

	W	L	Pts.	GF	GA
Pittsburgh Penguins	4	3	8	29	26
Washington Capitals	3	4	6	26	29

(Pittsburgh won Eastern Conference quarterfinals, 4-3)

Sat.	May 6—Washington 5, at Pittsburgh 4
Mon.	May 8—Washington 3, at Pittsburgh 5
Wed.	May 10—Pittsburgh 2, at Washington 6
Fri.	May 12—Pittsburgh 2, at Washington 6
Sun.	May 14—Washington 5, at Pittsburgh 6 (b)
Tue.	May 16—Pittsburgh 7, at Washington 1
Thur.	May 18—Washington 0, at Pittsburgh 3

(b)—Luc Robitaille scored at 4:30 (OT) for Pittsburgh.

	W	L	Pts.	GF	GA
Philadelphia Flyers	4	1	8	20	11
Buffalo Sabres	1	4	2	11	20

(Philadelphia won Eastern Conference quarterfinals, 4-1)

Sun.	May 7—Buffalo 3, at Philadelphia 4 (c)
Mon.	May 8—Buffalo 1, at Philadelphia 3
Wed.	May 10—Philadelphia 1, at Buffalo 3
Fri.	May 12—Philadelphia 4, at Buffalo 2
Sun.	May 14—Buffalo 4, at Philadelphia 6

(c)—Karl Dykhuis scored at 10:06 (OT) for Philadelphia.

	W	L	Pts.	GF	GA
New Jersey Devils	4	1	8	14	5
Boston Bruins	1	4	2	5	14

(New Jersey won Eastern Conference quarterfinals, 4-1)

Sun.	May 7—New Jersey 5, at Boston 0
Mon.	May 8—New Jersey 3, at Boston 0
Wed.	May 10—Boston 3, at New Jersey 2
Fri.	May 12—Boston 0, at New Jersey 1 (d)
Sun.	May 14—New Jersey 3, at Boston 2

(d)—Randy McKay scored at 8:51 (OT) for New Jersey.

WESTERN CONFERENCE

	W	L	Pts.	GF	GA
Detroit Red Wings	4	1	8	17	10
Dallas Stars	1	4	2	10	17

(Detroit won Western Conference quarterfinals, 4-1)

Sun.	May 7—Dallas 3, at Detroit 4
Tue.	May 9—Dallas 1, at Detroit 4
Thur.	May 11—Detroit 1, at Dallas 1
Sun.	May 14—Detroit 1, at Dallas 4
Mon.	May 15—Dallas 1, at Detroit 3

	W	L	Pts.	GF	GA
Vancouver Canucks	4	3	8	27	27
St. Louis Blues	3	4	6	27	27

(Vancouver won Western Conference quarterfinals, 4-3)

Sun.	May 7—Vancouver 1, at St. Louis 2
Tue.	May 9—Vancouver 5, at St. Louis 3
Thur.	May 11—St. Louis 1, at Vancouver 6
Sat.	May 13—St. Louis 5, at Vancouver 2
Mon.	May 15—Vancouver 6, at St. Louis 5 (e)
Wed.	May 17—St. Louis 8, at Vancouver 2
Fri.	May 19—Vancouver 5, at St. Louis 3

(e)—Cliff Ronning scored at 1:48 (OT) for Vancouver.

	W	L	Pts.	GF	GA
Chicago Blackhawks	4	3	8	22	20
Toronto Maple Leafs	3	4	6	20	22

(Chicago won Western Conference quarterfinals, 4-3)

Sun.	May 7—Toronto 5, at Chicago 3
Tue.	May 9—Toronto 3, at Chicago 0
Thur.	May 11—Chicago 3, at Toronto 2
Sat.	May 13—Chicago 3, at Toronto 1
Mon.	May 15—Toronto 2, at Chicago 4
Wed.	May 17—Chicago 4, at Toronto 5 (f)
Fri.	May 19—Toronto 2, at Chicago 5

(f)—Randy Wood scored at 10:00 (OT) for Toronto.

	W	L	Pts.	GF	GA
San Jose Sharks	4	3	8	26	35
Calgary Flames	3	4	6	35	26

(San Jose won Western Conference quarterfinals, 4-3)

Sun.	May 7—San Jose 5, at Calgary 4
Tue.	May 9—San Jose 5, at Calgary 4 (g)
Thur.	May 11—Calgary 9, at San Jose 2
Sat.	May 13—Calgary 6, at San Jose 4
Mon.	May 15—San Jose 0, at Calgary 5
Wed.	May 17—Calgary 3, at San Jose 5
Fri.	May 19—San Jose 5, at Calgary 4 (h)

(g)—Ulf Dahlen scored at 12:21 (OT) for San Jose.
(h)—Ray Whitney scored at 1:54 (2 OT) for San Jose.

CONFERENCE SEMIFINALS

EASTERN CONFERENCE

	W	L	Pts.	GF	GA
New Jersey Devils	4	1	8	17	8
Pittsburgh Penguins	1	4	2	8	17

(New Jersey won Eastern Conference semifinals, 4-1)

Sat.	May 20—New Jersey 2, at Pittsburgh 3
Mon.	May 22—New Jersey 4, at Pittsburgh 2
Wed.	May 24—Pittsburgh 1, at New Jersey 5
Fri.	May 26—Pittsburgh 1, at New Jersey 2 (i)
Sun.	May 28—New Jersey 4, at Pittsburgh 1

(i)—Neal Broten scored at 18:36 (OT) for New Jersey.

	W	L	Pts.	GF	GA
Philadelphia Flyers	4	0	8	18	10
N.Y. Rangers	0	4	0	10	18

(Philadelphia won Eastern Conference semifinals, 4-0)

Sun.	May 21—N.Y. Rangers 4, at Philadelphia 5 (j)
Mon.	May 22—N.Y. Rangers 3, at Philadelphia 4 (k)
Wed.	May 24—Philadelphia 5, at N.Y. Rangers 2
Fri.	May 26—Philadelphia 4, at N.Y. Rangers 1

(j)—Eric Desjardins scored at 7:03 (OT) for Philadelphia.
(k)—Kevin Haller scored at 0:25 (OT) for Philadelphia.

WESTERN CONFERENCE

	W	L	Pts.	GF	GA
Detroit Red Wings	4	0	8	24	6
San Jose Sharks	0	4	0	6	24

(Detroit won Western Conference semifinals, 4-0)

Sun.　May 21—San Jose 0, at Detroit 6
Tue.　May 23—San Jose 2, at Detroit 6
Thur.　May 25—Detroit 6, at San Jose 2
Sat.　May 27—Detroit 6, at San Jose 2

	W	L	Pts.	GF	GA
Chicago Blackhawks	4	0	8	11	6
Vancouver Canucks	0	4	0	6	11

(Chicago won Western Conference semifinals, 4-0)

Sun.　May 21—Vancouver 1, at Chicago 2 (l)
Tue.　May 23—Vancouver 0, at Chicago 2
Thur.　May 25—Chicago 3, at Vancouver 2 (m)
Sat.　May 27—Chicago 4, at Vancouver 3 (n)
(l)—Joe Murphy scored at 9:04 (OT) for Chicago.
(m)—Chris Chelios scored at 6:22 (OT) for Chicago.
(n)—Chris Chelios scored at 5:35 (OT) for Chicago.

CONFERENCE FINALS

EASTERN CONFERENCE

	W	L	Pts.	GF	GA
New Jersey Devils	4	2	8	20	14
Philadelphia Flyers	2	4	4	14	20

(New Jersey won Eastern Conference finals, 4-2)

Sat.　June 3—New Jersey 4, at Philadelphia 1
Mon.　June 5—New Jersey 5, at Philadelphia 2
Wed.　June 7—Philadelphia 3, at New Jersey 2 (o)
Sat.　June 10—Philadelphia 4, at New Jersey 2
Sun.　June 11—New Jersey 3, at Philadelphia 2
Tue.　June 13—Philadelphia 2, at New Jersey 4
(o)—Eric Lindros scored at 4:19 (OT) for Philadelphia.

WESTERN CONFERENCE

	W	L	Pts.	GF	GA
Detroit Red Wings	4	1	8	13	12
Chicago Blackhawks	1	4	2	12	13

(Detroit won Western Conference finals, 4-1)

Thur.　June 1—Chicago 1, at Detroit 2 (p)
Sun.　June 4—Chicago 2, at Detroit 3
Tue.　June 6—Detroit 4, at Chicago 3 (q)
Thur.　June 8—Detroit 2, at Chicago 5
Sun.　June 11—Chicago 1, at Detroit 2 (r)
(p)—Nicklas Lidstrom scored at 1:01 (OT) for Detroit.
(q)—Vladimir Konstantinov scored at 9:25 (2 OT) for Detroit.
(r)—Vyacheslav Kozlov scored at 2:25 (2 OT) for Detroit.

STANLEY CUP FINALS

	W	L	Pts.	GF	GA
New Jersey Devils	4	0	8	16	7
Detroit Red Wings	0	4	0	7	16

(New Jersey won Stanley Cup championship, 4-0)

Sat.　June 17—New Jersey 2, at Detroit 1
Tue.　June 20—New Jersey 4, at Detroit 2
Thur.　June 22—Detroit 2, at New Jersey 5
Sat.　June 24—Detroit 2, at New Jersey 5

GAME SUMMARIES, STANLEY CUP FINALS

GAME 1

AT DETROIT, JUNE 17

New Jersey 2, Detroit 1

New Jersey	0	1	1—2
Detroit	0	1	0—1

FIRST PERIOD—None. Penalties—Guerin, New Jersey (holding), 6:47; Konstantinov, Detroit (holding stick), 11:05.
SECOND PERIOD—1. New Jersey, Richer 5 (Albelin, Broten), 9:41 (pp). 2. Detroit, Ciccarelli 9 (Lidstrom, Coffey), 13:08 (pp). Penalties—Draper, Detroit (roughing), 9:35; Holik, New Jersey (high-sticking), 11:37; Lemieux, New Jersey (hooking), 13:41; Daneyko, New Jersey (roughing), 15:44; Ciccarelli, Detroit (roughing), 15:44.
THIRD PERIOD—3. New Jersey, Lemieux 12 (MacLean, Chorske), 3:17. Penalty—Brown, Detroit (tripping), 4:48.
Shots on goal—New Jersey 9-10-9-28; Detroit 7-5-5-17. Power-play opportunities—New Jersey 1 of 3; Detroit 1 of 3. Goalies—New Jersey, Brodeur 13-4 (17 shots-16 saves); Detroit, Vernon, 12-3 (28-26). A—19,875. Referee—Bill McCreary. Linesmen—Brian Murphy, Kevin Collins.

GAME 2

AT DETROIT, JUNE 20

New Jersey 4, Detroit 2

New Jersey	0	1	3—4
Detroit	0	1	1—2

FIRST PERIOD—None. Penalties—Stevens, New Jersey (roughing), 0:37; Ciccarelli, Detroit (slashing), 5:57; McCarty, Detroit (roughing), 8:49; Broten, New Jersey (high-sticking), 9:27.
SECOND PERIOD—1. Detroit, Kozlov 9 (Ciccarelli, Fedorov), 7:17 (pp). 2. New Jersey, MacLean 5 (Niedermayer, Broten), 9:40. Penalties—Brodeur, New Jersey, served by Rolston (delay of game), 6:56; Guerin, New Jersey (slash-

ing), 8:58; McCarty, Detroit (slashing), 8:58; Errey, Detroit (charging), 16:01; Dowd, New Jersey (interference), 18:30.
THIRD PERIOD—3. Detroit, Fedorov 5 (Brown, Fetisov), 1:36. 4. New Jersey, Niedermayer 4 (Dowd), 9:47. 5. New Jersey, Dowd 2 (Chambers, Albelin), 18:36. 6. New Jersey, Richer 6 (Niedermayer), 19:39 (en). Penalty—Holik, New Jersey (boarding), 4:58.
Shots on goal—New Jersey 3-9-11—23; Detroit 7-6-5—18. Power-play opportunities—New Jersey 0 of 3; Detroit 1 of 5. Goalies—New Jersey, Brodeur, 14-4 (18 shots-16 saves); Detroit, Vernon, 12-4 (22-19). A—19,875. Referee—Terry Gregson. Linesmen—Ray Scapinello, Wayne Bonney.

GAME 3

AT NEW JERSEY, JUNE 22

New Jersey 5, Detroit 2

Detroit	0	0	2—2
New Jersey	2	2	1—5

FIRST PERIOD—1. New Jersey, Driver 1 (Broten, MacLean), 10:30 (pp). 2. New Jersey, Lemieux 13 (Carpenter, Stevens), 16:52. Penalties—Primeau, Detroit (slashing), 1:09; Lemieux, New Jersey (roughing), 1:09; Konstantinov, Detroit (holding stick), 8:56; Holik, New Jersey (tripping), 10:58; Lapointe, Detroit (unsportsmanlike conduct), 16:38; Guerin, New Jersey (unsportsmanlike conduct), 16:38.
SECOND PERIOD—3. New Jersey, Broten 5 (Stevens, MacLean), 6:59. 4. New Jersey, McKay 8 (Holik, Driver), 8:20. Penalties—Broten, New Jersey (holding stick), 11:01; Primeau, Detroit (tripping), 16:03; Carpenter, New Jersey (cross-checking), 19:47.
THIRD PERIOD—5. New Jersey, Holik 4 (Guerin, Richer), 8:14 (pp). 6. Detroit, Fedorov 6 (Fetisov, Brown), 16:57 (pp). 7. Detroit, Yzerman 4 (Sheppard, Lidstrom), 18:27 (pp). Penalties—Albelin, New Jersey (high-sticking), 2:30; Konstantinov, Detroit (high-sticking), 4:25; Draper, Detroit

(high-sticking), 5:17; Primeau, Detroit (cross-checking), 6:31; Holik, New Jersey (interference), 8:44; Richer, New Jersey (hooking), 12:28; Taylor, Detroit (roughing), 15:37; Lapointe, Detroit, double minor (roughing), 15:37; Ciccarelli, Detroit (roughing), 15:37; Guerin, New Jersey, double minor (boarding, roughing), 15:37; Brylin, New Jersey, double minor (high-sticking, roughing), 15:37; Zelepukin, New Jersey, double minor (roughing), 15:37.

Shots on goal—Detroit 7-5-12—24; New Jersey 15-8-8—31. Power-play opportunities—Detroit 2 of 8; New Jersey 2 of 5. Goalies—Detroit, Vernon, 12-5 (20 shots-16 saves), Osgood (8:20 second, 11-10); New Jersey, Brodeur, 15-4 (24-22). A—16,150. Referee—Kerry Fraser. Linesmen—Kevin Collins, Brian Murphy.

```
┌──────────────────┐
│      GAME 4      │
└──────────────────┘
```

AT NEW JERSEY, JUNE 24

New Jersey 5, Detroit 2

Detroit	2	0	0	—2
New Jersey	2	1	2	—5

FIRST PERIOD—1. New Jersey, Broten 6 (Richer, Chorske), 1:08. 2. Detroit, Fedorov 7 (Lapointe, Fetisov), 2:03. 3. Detroit, Coffey 6 (Brown, Fedorov), 13:01 (sh). 4. New Jersey, Chambers 3 (Driver, MacLean), 17:45. Penalties—Errey, Detroit (hooking), 11:03; Daneyko, New Jersey (roughing), 13:36; Primeau, Detroit (goalie interference), 15:36.

SECOND PERIOD—5. New Jersey, Broten 7 (Niedermayer, Guerin), 7:56. Penalties—Daneyko, New Jersey (slashing), 0:30; Lapointe, Detroit (roughing), 10:09; Stevens, New Jersey (roughing), 10:09; Guerin, New Jersey (interference), 12:40; Konstantinov, Detroit (hooking), 19:12.

THIRD PERIOD—6. New Jersey, Brylin 1 (Rolston, Guerin), 7:46. 7. New Jersey, Chambers 4 (Brylin, Guerin), 12:32. Penalty—Grimson, Detroit (roughing), 10:24.

Shots on goal—Detroit 8-7-1—16; New Jersey 8-8-10—26. Power-play opportunities—Detroit 0 of 3; New Jersey 0 of 4. Goalies—Detroit, Vernon 12-6 (26 shots-21 saves); New Jersey, Brodeur 16-4 (16-14). A—19,040. Referee—Bill McCreary. Linesmen—Wayne Bonney, Ray Scapinello.

INDIVIDUAL LEADERS

Goals: Claude Lemieux, New Jersey (13)
Assists: Sergei Fedorov, Detroit (17)
Points: Sergei Fedorov, Detroit (24)
Penalty minutes: Glenn Anderson, St. Louis (49)
Goaltending average: Martin Brodeur, New Jersey (1.67)
Shutouts: Martin Brodeur, New Jersey (3)

TOP SCORERS

	Games	G	A	Pts.	PIM
Sergei Fedorov, Detroit	17	7	17	24	6
Stephane Richer, New Jersey	19	6	15	21	2
Neal Broten, New Jersey	20	7	12	19	6
Ron Francis, Pittsburgh	12	6	13	19	4
Denis Savard, Chicago	16	7	11	18	10
Paul Coffey, Detroit	18	6	12	18	10
John MacLean, New Jersey	20	5	13	18	14
Claude Lemieux, New Jersey	20	13	3	16	20
Vyacheslav Kozlov, Detroit	18	9	7	16	10
Nicklas Lidstrom, Detroit	18	4	12	16	8

INDIVIDUAL STATISTICS

BOSTON BRUINS

(Lost Eastern Conference quarterfinals to New Jersey, 4-1)

SCORING

	Games	G	A	Pts.	PIM
Ray Bourque	5	0	3	3	0
Cam Neely	5	2	0	2	2
Mariusz Czerkawski	5	1	0	1	0
Mats Naslund	5	1	0	1	0
Adam Oates	5	1	0	1	2
David Shaw	5	0	1	1	4
Bryan Smolinski	5	0	1	1	4
Craig Billington (goalie)	1	0	0	0	0
Glen Murray	2	0	0	0	2
Fred Knipscheer	4	0	0	0	0
Guy Larose	4	0	0	0	0
Ted Donato	5	0	0	0	4
Steve Heinze	5	0	0	0	0
Brent Hughes	5	0	0	0	4
Jamie Huscroft	5	0	0	0	11
Alexei Kasatonov	5	0	0	0	2
Blaine Lacher (goalie)	5	0	0	0	0
Dave Reid	5	0	0	0	0
Jon Rohloff	5	0	0	0	6
Jozef Stumpel	5	0	0	0	0
Don Sweeney	5	0	0	0	4

GOALTENDERS

	Games	Min.	W	L	T	Goals	SO	Avg.
Craig Billington	1	25	0	0	0	1	0	2.40
Blaine Lacher	5	283	1	4	0	12	0	2.54

BUFFALO SABRES

(Lost Eastern Conference quarterfinals to Philadelphia, 4-1)

SCORING

	Games	G	A	Pts.	PIM
Alexander Mogilny	5	3	2	5	2
Wayne Presley	5	3	1	4	8
Pat LaFontaine	5	2	2	4	2
Doug Bodger	5	0	4	4	0
Brian Holzinger	4	2	1	3	2
Jason Dawe	5	2	1	3	6
Garry Galley	5	0	3	3	4
Donald Audette	5	1	1	2	4
Dave Hannan	5	0	2	2	2
Yuri Khmylev	5	0	1	1	8
Craig Muni	5	0	1	1	2
Alexei Zhitnik	5	0	1	1	14
Mark Astley	2	0	0	0	0
Dale Hawerchuk	2	0	0	0	0
Charlie Huddy	3	0	0	0	0
Brad May	4	0	0	0	2
Dominik Hasek (goalie)	5	0	0	0	0
Scott Pearson	5	0	0	0	4
Rob Ray	5	0	0	0	14
Richard Smehlik	5	0	0	0	2
Bob Sweeney	5	0	0	0	4

GOALTENDERS

	Games	Min.	W	L	T	Goals	SO	Avg.
Dominik Hasek	5	309	1	4	0	18	0	3.50

CALGARY FLAMES

(Lost Western Conference quarterfinals to San Jose, 4-3)

SCORING

	Games	G	A	Pts.	PIM
Theoren Fleury	7	7	7	14	2
Phil Housley	7	0	9	9	0

	Games	G	A	Pts.	PIM
German Titov	7	5	3	8	10
Mike Sullivan	7	3	5	8	2
Joe Nieuwendyk	5	4	3	7	0
Paul Kruse	7	4	2	6	10
Robert Reichel	7	2	4	6	4
Michael Nylander	6	0	6	6	2
Kelly Kisio	7	3	2	5	19
Sheldon Kennedy	7	3	1	4	16
Ronnie Stern	7	3	1	4	8
Zarley Zalapski	7	0	4	4	4
Steve Chiasson	7	1	2	3	9
Joel Otto	7	0	3	3	2
Frank Musil	5	0	1	1	0
James Patrick	5	0	1	1	0
Sandy Mccarthy	6	0	1	1	17
Dan Keczmer	7	0	1	1	2
Todd Hlushko	1	0	0	0	2
Rick Tabaracci (goalie)	1	0	0	0	0
Wes Walz	1	0	0	0	0
Trent Yawney	2	0	0	0	2
Kevin Dahl	3	0	0	0	0
Trevor Kidd (goalie)	7	0	0	0	0

GOALTENDERS

	Games	Min.	W	L	T	Goals	SO	Avg.
Rick Tabaracci	1	19	0	0	0	0	0	0.00
Trevor Kidd	7	434	3	4	0	26	1	3.59

CHICAGO BLACKHAWKS

(Lost Western Conference finals to Detroit, 4-1)

SCORING

	Games	G	A	Pts.	PIM
Denis Savard	16	7	11	18	10
Joe Murphy	16	9	3	12	29
Bernie Nicholls	16	1	11	12	8
Chris Chelios	16	4	7	11	12
Murray Craven	16	5	5	10	4
Gary Suter	12	2	5	7	10
Tony Amonte	16	3	3	6	10
Eric Weinrich	16	1	5	6	4
Patrick Poulin	16	4	1	5	8
Dirk Graham	16	2	3	5	8
Jeff Shantz	16	3	1	4	2
Gerald Diduck	16	1	3	4	22
Jeremy Roenick	8	1	2	3	16
Brent Sutter	16	1	2	3	4
Cam Russell	16	0	3	3	8
Jim Cummins	14	1	1	2	4
Keith Carney	4	0	1	1	0
Eric Daze	16	0	1	1	4
Steve Smith	16	0	1	1	26
Jeff Hackett (goalie)	2	0	0	0	0
Sergei Krivokrasov	10	0	0	0	8
Ed Belfour (goalie)	16	0	0	0	6

GOALTENDERS

	Games	Min.	W	L	T	Goals	SO	Avg.
Ed Belfour	16	1014	9	7	0	37	1	2.19
Jeff Hackett	2	26	0	0	0	1	0	2.31

DALLAS STARS

(Lost Western Conference quarterfinals to Detroit, 4-1)

SCORING

	Games	G	A	Pts.	PIM
Kevin Hatcher	5	2	1	3	2
Paul Broten	5	1	2	3	2
Dean Evason	5	1	2	3	12
Greg Adams	5	2	0	2	0
Dave Gagner	5	1	1	2	4
Paul Cavallini	5	0	2	2	6
Richard Matvichuk	5	0	2	2	4
Peter Zezel	3	1	0	1	0
Trent Klatt	5	1	0	1	0
Corey Millen	5	1	0	1	2

	Games	G	A	Pts.	PIM
Craig Ludwig	4	0	1	1	2
Mike Donnelly	5	0	1	1	6
Brent Gilchrist	5	0	1	1	2
Darcy Wakaluk (goalie)	1	0	0	0	0
Zac Boyer	2	0	0	0	0
Mike Lalor	3	0	0	0	2
Grant Ledyard	3	0	0	0	2
Shane Churla	5	0	0	0	20
Todd Harvey	5	0	0	0	8
Mike Kennedy	5	0	0	0	9
Andy Moog (goalie)	5	0	0	0	2
Doug Zmolek	5	0	0	0	10

GOALTENDERS

	Games	Min.	W	L	T	Goals	SO	Avg.
Darcy Wakaluk	1	20	0	0	0	1	0	3.00
Andy Moog	5	277	1	4	0	16	0	3.47

DETROIT RED WINGS

(Lost Stanley Cup finals to New Jersey, 4-0)

SCORING

	Games	G	A	Pts.	PIM
Sergei Fedorov	17	7	17	24	6
Paul Coffey	18	6	12	18	10
Vyacheslav Kozlov	18	9	7	16	10
Nicklas Lidstrom	18	4	12	16	8
Steve Yzerman	15	4	8	12	0
Doug Brown	18	4	8	12	2
Dino Ciccarelli	16	9	2	11	22
Keith Primeau	17	4	5	9	45
Viacheslav Fetisov	18	0	8	8	14
Ray Sheppard	17	4	3	7	5
Bob Errey	18	1	5	6	30
Kris Draper	18	4	1	5	12
Darren McCarty	18	3	2	5	14
Bob Rouse	18	0	3	3	8
Vladimir Konstantinov	18	1	1	2	22
Shawn Burr	16	0	2	2	6
Stu Grimson	11	1	0	1	26
Martin Lapointe	2	0	1	1	8
Tim Taylor	6	0	1	1	12
Mike Ramsey	15	0	1	1	4
Greg Johnson	1	0	0	0	0
Chris Osgood (goalie)	2	0	0	0	0
Mark Howe	3	0	0	0	0
Mike Krushelnyski	8	0	0	0	0
Mike Vernon (goalie)	18	0	0	0	0

GOALTENDERS

	Games	Min.	W	L	T	Goals	SO	Avg.
Chris Osgood	2	68	0	0	0	2	0	1.76
Mike Vernon	18	1063	12	6	0	41	1	2.31

NEW JERSEY DEVILS

(Winner of 1995 Stanley Cup)

SCORING

	Games	G	A	Pts.	PIM
Stephane Richer	19	6	15	21	2
Neal Broten	20	7	12	19	6
John MacLean	20	5	13	18	14
Claude Lemieux	20	13	3	16	20
Randy McKay	19	8	4	12	11
Scott Niedermayer	20	4	7	11	10
Bill Guerin	20	3	8	11	30
Shawn Chambers	20	4	5	9	2
Bobby Holik	20	4	4	8	22
Tommy Albelin	20	1	7	8	2
Scott Stevens	20	1	7	8	24
Bruce Driver	17	1	6	7	8
Tom Chorske	17	1	5	6	4
Bob Carpenter	17	1	4	5	6
Brian Rolston	6	2	1	3	4
Jim Dowd	11	2	1	3	8
Sergei Brylin	12	1	2	3	4

	Games	G	A	Pts.	PIM
Valeri Zelepukin	18	1	2	3	12
Mike Peluso	20	1	2	3	8
Kevin Dean	3	0	2	2	0
Ken Daneyko	20	1	0	1	22
Martin Brodeur (goalie)	20	0	1	1	6
Danton Cole	1	0	0	0	0
Chris Terreri (goalie)	1	0	0	0	0

GOALTENDERS

	Games	Min.	W	L	T	Goals	SO	Avg.
Chris Terreri	1	8	0	0	0	0	0	0.00
Martin Brodeur	20	1222	16	4	0	34	3	1.67

NEW YORK RANGERS

(Lost Eastern Conference semifinals to Philadelphia, 4-0)

SCORING

	Games	G	A	Pts.	PIM
Brian Leetch	10	6	8	14	8
Mark Messier	10	3	10	13	8
Alexei Kovalev	10	4	7	11	10
Sergei Zubov	10	3	8	11	2
Pat Verbeek	10	4	6	10	20
Sergei Nemchinov	10	4	5	9	2
Adam Graves	10	4	4	8	8
Petr Nedved	10	3	2	5	6
Steve Larmer	10	2	2	4	6
Nick Kypreos	10	0	2	2	6
Mark Osborne	7	1	0	1	2
Alexander Karpovtsev	8	1	0	1	0
Stephane Matteau	9	0	1	1	10
Kevin Lowe	10	0	1	1	12
Troy Loney	1	0	0	0	0
Mattias Norstrom	3	0	0	0	0
Glenn Healy (goalie)	5	0	0	0	0
Brian Noonan	5	0	0	0	8
Mike Richter (goalie)	7	0	0	0	0
Nathan Lafayette	8	0	0	0	2
Jeff Beukeboom	9	0	0	0	10
Joey Kocur	10	0	0	0	8
Jay Wells	10	0	0	0	8

GOALTENDERS

	Games	Min.	W	L	T	Goals	SO	Avg.
Glenn Healy	5	230	2	1	0	13	0	3.39
Mike Richter	7	384	2	5	0	23	0	3.59

PHILADELPHIA FLYERS

(Lost Eastern Conference finals to New Jersey, 4-2)

SCORING

	Games	G	A	Pts.	PIM
Rod Brind'Amour	15	6	9	15	8
Eric Lindros	12	4	11	15	18
Mikael Renberg	15	6	7	13	6
John LeClair	15	5	7	12	4
Kevin Dineen	15	6	4	10	18
Eric Desjardins	15	4	4	8	8
Karl Dykhuis	15	4	4	8	14
Kevin Haller	15	4	4	8	10
Rob DiMaio	15	2	4	6	4
Anatoli Semenov	15	2	4	6	0
Dimitri Yushkevich	15	1	5	6	12
Craig MacTavish	15	1	4	5	20
Brent Fedyk	9	2	2	4	8
Shjon Podein	15	1	3	4	10
Petr Svoboda	14	0	4	4	8
Jim Montgomery	7	1	0	1	2
Patrik Juhlin	13	1	0	1	2
Shawn Antoski	13	0	1	1	10
Ron Hextall (goalie)	15	0	1	1	4
Dominic Roussel (goalie)	1	0	0	0	0
Rob Zettler	1	0	0	0	2
Dave Brown	3	0	0	0	0
Gilbert Dionne	3	0	0	0	4
Chris Therien	15	0	0	0	10

GOALTENDERS

	Games	Min.	W	L	T	Goals	SO	Avg.
Dominic Roussel	1	23	0	0	0	0	0	0.00
Ron Hextall	15	897	10	5	0	42	0	2.81

PITTSBURGH PENGUINS

(Lost Eastern Conference semifinals to New Jersey, 4-1)

SCORING

	Games	G	A	Pts.	PIM
Ron Francis	12	6	13	19	4
Jaromir Jagr	12	10	5	15	6
Larry Murphy	12	2	13	15	0
Luc Robitaille	12	7	4	11	26
Kevin Stevens	12	4	7	11	21
Tomas Sandstrom	12	3	3	6	16
Norm Maclver	12	1	4	5	8
Troy Murray	12	2	1	3	12
Joe Mullen	12	0	3	3	4
Chris Joseph	10	1	1	2	12
Ulf Samuelsson	7	0	2	2	8
John Cullen	9	0	2	2	8
Shawn McEachern	11	0	2	2	8
Francois Leroux	12	0	2	2	14
Len Barrie	4	1	0	1	8
Kjell Samuelsson	11	0	1	1	32
Drake Berehowsky	1	0	0	0	0
Tom Barrasso (goalie)	2	0	0	0	2
Richard Park	3	0	0	0	2
Peter Taglianetti	4	0	0	0	2
Chris Tamer	4	0	0	0	18
Rusty Fitzgerald	5	0	0	0	4
Jim McKenzie	5	0	0	0	4
Ian Moran	8	0	0	0	0
Mike Hudson	11	0	0	0	6
Ken Wregget (goalie)	11	0	0	0	7

GOALTENDERS

	Games	Min.	W	L	T	Goals	SO	Avg.
Ken Wregget	11	661	5	6	0	33	1	3.00
Tom Barrasso	2	80	0	1	0	8	0	6.00

QUEBEC NORDIQUES

(Lost Eastern Conference quarterfinals to N.Y. Rangers, 4-2)

SCORING

	Games	G	A	Pts.	PIM
Scott Young	6	3	3	6	2
Bob Bassen	5	2	4	6	4
Peter Forsberg	6	2	4	6	4
Joe Sakic	6	4	1	5	0
Owen Nolan	6	2	3	5	6
Mike Ricci	6	1	3	4	8
Wendel Clark	6	1	2	3	6
Chris Simon	6	1	1	2	19
Craig Wolanin	6	1	1	2	4
Uwe Krupp	5	0	2	2	2
Sylvain Lefebvre	6	0	2	2	2
Valeri Kamensky	2	1	0	1	0
Janne Laukkanen	6	1	0	1	2
Rene Corbet	2	0	1	1	0
Curtis Leschyshyn	3	0	1	1	4
Steven Finn	4	0	1	1	2
Adam Deadmarsh	6	0	1	1	0
Adam Foote	6	0	1	1	14
Andrei Kovalenko	6	0	1	1	2
Bill Huard	1	0	0	0	0
Garth Snow (goalie)	1	0	0	0	0
Paul MacDermid	3	0	0	0	2
Jocelyn Thibault (goalie)	3	0	0	0	0
Stephane Fiset (goalie)	4	0	0	0	0
Claude Lapointe	5	0	0	0	8

GOALTENDERS

	Games	Min.	W	L	T	Goals	SO	Avg.
Jocelyn Thibault	3	148	1	2	0	8	0	3.24
Stephane Fiset	4	209	1	2	0	16	0	4.59
Garth Snow	1	9	0	0	0	1	0	6.67

ST. LOUIS BLUES

(Lost Western Conference quarterfinals to Vancouver, 4-3)

SCORING

	Games	G	A	Pts.	PIM
Brendan Shanahan	5	4	5	9	14
Brett Hull	7	6	2	8	0
Denis Chasse	7	1	7	8	23
Todd Elik	7	4	3	7	2
Al MacInnis	7	1	5	6	10
Esa Tikkanen	7	2	2	4	20
Steve Duchesne	7	0	4	4	2
Ian Laperriere	7	0	4	4	21
Basil McRae	7	2	1	3	4
Guy Carbonneau	7	1	2	3	6
Greg Gilbert	7	0	3	3	6
Adam Creighton	7	2	0	2	16
Bill Houlder	4	1	1	2	0
Glenn Anderson	6	1	1	2	49
Murray Baron	7	1	1	2	2
Jeff Norton	7	1	1	2	11
Curtis Joseph (goalie)	7	0	1	1	0
Craig Johnson	1	0	0	0	2
Tony Twist	1	0	0	0	6
Jon Casey (goalie)	2	0	0	0	0
Vitali Karamnov	2	0	0	0	2
Donald Dufresne	3	0	0	0	4
Rick Zombo	3	0	0	0	2
Doug Lidster	4	0	0	0	2
David Roberts	6	0	0	0	4

GOALTENDERS

	Games	Min.	W	L	T	Goals	SO	Avg.
Curtis Joseph	7	392	3	3	0	24	0	3.67
Jon Casey	2	30	0	1	0	2	0	4.00

SAN JOSE SHARKS

(Lost Western Conference semifinals to Detroit, 4-0)

SCORING

	Games	G	A	Pts.	PIM
Ulf Dahlen	11	5	4	9	0
Igor Larionov	11	1	8	9	2
Ray Whitney	11	4	4	8	2
Mike Rathje	11	5	2	7	4
Craig Janney	11	3	4	7	4
Sergei Makarov	11	3	3	6	4
Jeff Friesen	11	1	5	6	4
Sandis Ozolinsh	11	3	2	5	6
Tom Pederson	10	0	5	5	8
Pat Falloon	11	3	1	4	0
Jamie Baker	11	2	2	4	12
Jay More	11	0	4	4	6
Jeff Odgers	11	1	1	2	23
Chris Tancill	11	1	1	2	8
Jim Kyte	11	0	2	2	14
Shean Donovan	7	0	1	1	6
Arturs Irbe (goalie)	6	0	0	0	10
Vlastimil Kroupa	6	0	0	0	4
Kevin Miller	6	0	0	0	2
Andrei Nazarov	6	0	0	0	9
Wade Flaherty (goalie)	7	0	0	0	0
Shawn Cronin	9	0	0	0	5

GOALTENDERS

	Games	Min.	W	L	T	Goals	SO	Avg.
Wade Flaherty	7	377	2	3	0	31	0	4.93
Arturs Irbe	6	316	2	4	0	27	0	5.13

TORONTO MAPLE LEAFS

(Lost Western Conference quarterfinals to Chicago, 4-3)

SCORING

	Games	G	A	Pts.	PIM
Mats Sundin	7	5	4	9	4
Doug Gilmour	7	0	6	6	6
Dave Andreychuk	7	3	2	5	25
Mike Ridley	7	3	1	4	2
Mike Gartner	5	2	2	4	2
Dmitri Mironov	6	2	1	3	2
Jamie Macoun	7	1	2	3	8
Todd Gill	7	0	3	3	6
Randy Wood	7	2	0	2	6
Paul Dipietro	7	1	1	2	0
Dave Ellett	7	0	2	2	0
Tie Domi	7	1	0	1	0
Mike Craig	2	0	1	1	0
Bill Berg	7	0	1	1	4
Warren Rychel	3	0	0	0	0
Grant Jennings	4	0	0	0	0
Kenny Jonsson	4	0	0	0	0
Rich Sutter	4	0	0	0	2
Garth Butcher	7	0	0	0	8
Benoit Hogue	7	0	0	0	6
Kent Manderville	7	0	0	0	6
Felix Potvin (goalie)	7	0	0	0	0

GOALTENDERS

	Games	Min.	W	L	T	Goals	SO	Avg.
Felix Potvin	7	424	3	4	0	20	1	2.83

VANCOUVER CANUCKS

(Lost Western Conference semifinals to Chicago, 4-0)

SCORING

	Games	G	A	Pts.	PIM
Pavel Bure	11	7	6	13	10
Russ Courtnall	11	4 ·	8	12	21
Cliff Ronning	11	3	5	8	2
Trevor Linden	11	2	6	8	12
Jyrki Lumme	11	2	6	8	8
Geoff Courtnall	11	4	2	6	34
Roman Oksiuta	10	2	3	5	0
Sergio Momesso	11	3	1	4	16
Dave Babych	11	2	2	4	14
Jeff Brown	5	1	3	4	2
Christian Ruuttu	9	1	1	2	0
Josef Beranek	11	1	1	2	12
Bret Hedican	11	0	2	2	6
Adrian Aucoin	4	1	0	1	0
Martin Gelinas	3	0	1	1	0
Mike Peca	5	0	1	1	8
Dana Murzyn	8	0	1	1	22
Kirk McLean (goalie)	11	0	1	1	0
Yevgeny Namestnikov	1	0	0	0	2
Kay Whitmore (goalie)	1	0	0	0	0
Gino Odjick	5	0	0	0	47
Alek Stojanov	5	0	0	0	2
Mark Wotton	5	0	0	0	4
Dane Jackson	6	0	0	0	10
Jassen Cullimore	11	0	0	0	12
Tim Hunter	11	0	0	0	22

GOALTENDERS

	Games	Min.	W	L	T	Goals	SO	Avg.
Kirk McLean	11	660	4	7	0	36	0	3.27
Kay Whitmore	1	20	0	0	0	2	0	6.00

WASHINGTON CAPITALS

(Lost Eastern Conference quarterfinals to Pittsburgh, 4-3)

SCORING

	Games	G	A	Pts.	PIM
Peter Bondra	7	5	3	8	10
Dale Hunter	7	4	4	8	24
Keith Jones	7	4	4	8	22
Joe Juneau	7	2	6	8	2
Steve Konowalchuk	7	2	5	7	12
Dimitri Khristich	7	1	4	5	0
Michal Pivonka	7	1	4	5	21
Calle Johansson	7	3	1	4	0
Sergei Gonchar	7	2	2	4	2
Sylvain Cote	7	1	3	4	2

	Games	G	A	Pts.	PIM
Kelly Miller	7	0	3	3	4
Mike Eagles	7	0	2	2	4
Jim Johnson	7	0	2	2	8
Rob Pearson	3	1	0	1	17
Byron Dafoe (goalie)	1	0	0	0	0
Mark Tinordi	1	0	0	0	2
Olaf Kolzig (goalie)	2	0	0	0	0
Dave Poulin	2	0	0	0	0
Igor Ulanov	2	0	0	0	4
Kevin Kaminski	5	0	0	0	36

	Games	G	A	Pts.	PIM
Craig Berube	7	0	0	0	29
Jim Carey (goalie)	7	0	0	0	4
Ken Klee	7	0	0	0	4
Joe Reekie	7	0	0	0	2

GOALTENDERS

	Games	Min.	W	L	T	Goals	SO	Avg.
Olaf Kolzig	2	44	1	0	0	1	0	1.36
Byron Dafoe	1	20	0	0	0	1	0	3.00
Jim Carey	7	358	2	4	0	25	0	4.19

MISCELLANEOUS

HAT TRICKS

(Players scoring three or more goals in a game)

Date	Player, Team	Opp.	Goals	Date	Player, Team	Opp.	Goals
5-11-95	Mike Sullivan, Calgary	S.J.	3	5-21-95	John LeClair, Philadelphia	NYR	3
5-11-95	Dino Ciccarelli, Detroit	Dal.	3	5-22-95	Joe Sakic, Quebec	NYR	3
5-13-95	Brendan Shanahan, St. Louis	Van.	3	5-22-95	Brian Leetch, N.Y. Rangers	Phi.	3
5-13-95	Theoren Fleury, Calgary	S.J.	4				

OVERTIME GOALS

Date	Player, Team	Opponent	Time	Final score
5- 7-95	Karl Dykhuis, Philadelphia	Buffalo	10:06	Philadelphia 4, Buffalo 3
5- 9-95	Ulf Dahlen, San Jose	Calgary	12:21	San Jose 5, Calgary 4
5-12-95	Randy McKay, New Jersey	Boston	8:51	New Jersey 1, Boston 0
5-12-95	Steve Larmer, N.Y. Rangers	Quebec	8:09	N.Y. Rangers 3, Quebec 2
5-14-95	Luc Robitaille, Pittsburgh	Washington	4:30	Pittsburgh 6, Washington 5
5-15-95	Cliff Ronning, Vancouver	St. Louis	1:48	Vancouver 6, St. Louis 5
5-17-95	Randy Wood, Toronto	Chicago	10:00	Toronto 5, Chicago 4
5-19-95	Ray Whitney, San Jose	Calgary	*1:54	San Jose 5, Calgary 4
5-21-95	Eric Desjardins, Philadelphia	N.Y. Rangers	7:03	Philadelphia 5, N.Y. Rangers 4
5-21-95	Joe Murphy, Chicago	Vancouver	9:04	Chicago 2, Vancouver 1
5-22-95	Kevin Haller, Philadelphia	N.Y. Rangers	0:25	Philadelphia 4, N.Y. Rangers 3
5-25-95	Chris Chelios, Chicago	Vancouver	6:22	Chicago 3, Vancouver 2
5-26-95	Neal Broten, New Jersey	Pittsburgh	18:36	New Jersey 2, Pittsburgh 1
5-27-95	Chris Chelios, Chicago	Vancouver	5:35	Chicago 4, Vancouver 3
6- 1-95	Niklas Lidstrom, Detroit	Chicago	1:01	Detroit 2, Chicago 1
6- 6-95	Vladimir Konstantinov, Detroit	Chicago	*9:25	Detroit 4, Chicago 3
6- 7-95	Eric Lindros, Philadelphia	New Jersey	4:19	Philadelphia 3, New Jersey 2
6-11-95	Vyacheslav Kozlov, Detroit	Chicago	*2:25	Detroit 2, Chicago 1

*Goal scored in second overtime.

PENALTY - SHOT INFORMATION

Date	Shooter	Goaltender	Scored	Final score
5- 9-95	Patrick Poulin, Chicago	Felix Potvin, Toronto	No	Toronto 3, Chicago 0
5-10-95	Michal Pivonka, Washington	Tom Barrasso, Pittsburgh	No	Washington 6, Pittsburgh 2

AWARDS

ALL-STAR TEAM

Dominik Hasek, Buffalo..Goaltender
Ray Bourque, Boston...Defense
Paul Coffey, Detroit...Defense

John LeClair, Montreal-Philadelphia.......................Left wing
Eric Lindros, Philadelphia...Center
Jaromir Jagr, Pittsburgh...Right wing

Note: THE SPORTING NEWS All-Star Team is selected by the NHL players.

AWARD WINNERS

Player of the Year: Eric Lindros, Philadelphia
Rookie of the Year: Peter Forsberg, Quebec

Coach of the Year: Marc Crawford, Quebec
Executive of the Year: Bobby Clarke, Philadelphia

Note: THE SPORTING NEWS player and rookie awards are selected by the NHL players, the coaches award by the NHL coaches and the executive award by NHL executives.

NATIONAL HOCKEY LEAGUE

ALL-STAR TEAMS

First team	Position	Second team
Dominik Hasek, Buffalo	Goaltender	Ed Belfour, Chicago
Chris Chelios, Chicago	Defense	Ray Bourque, Boston
Paul Coffey, Detroit	Defense	Larry Murphy, Pittsburgh
John LeClair, Montreal-Philadelphia	Left wing	Keith Tkachuk, Winnipeg
Eric Lindros, Philadelphia	Center	Alexei Zhamnov, Winnipeg
Jaromir Jagr, Pittsburgh	Right wing	Theoren Fleury, Calgary

AWARD WINNERS

Art Ross Trophy: Jaromir Jagr, Pittsburgh
Hart Memorial Trophy: Eric Lindros, Philadelphia
James Norris Memorial Trophy: Paul Coffey, Detroit
Vezina Trophy: Dominik Hasek, Buffalo
Bill Jennings Trophy: Ed Belfour, Chicago
Calder Memorial Trophy: Peter Forsberg, Quebec

Lady Byng Memorial Trophy: Ron Francis, Pittsburgh
Conn Smythe Trophy: Claude Lemieux, New Jersey
Bill Masterton Memorial Trophy: Pat LaFontaine, Buffalo
Frank J. Selke Trophy: Ron Francis, Pittsburgh
Jack Adams Award: Marc Crawford, Quebec
King Clancy Trophy: Joe Nieuwendyk, Calgary

PLAYER DRAFTS

ENTRY DRAFT—JULY 8, 1995

FIRST ROUND

No.—Selecting club	Player	Pos.	Previous team (league)
1—Ottawa	Bryan Berard	D	Detroit (OHL)
2—N.Y. Islanders	Wade Redden	D	Brandon (WHL)
3—Los Angeles	Aki-Petteri Berg	D	TPS Jrs., Finland
4—Anaheim	Chad Kilger	C	Kingston (OHL)
5—Tampa Bay	Daymond Langkow	C	Tri-City (WHL)
6—Edmonton	Steve Kelly	C	Prince Albert (WHL)
7—Winnipeg	Shane Doan	RW	Kamloops (WHL)
8—Montreal	Terry Ryan	LW	Tri-City (WHL)
9—Boston (from Hartford)	Kyle McLaren	D	Tacoma (WHL)
10—Florida	Radek Dvorak	RW	Budejovice, Czech Republic
11—Dallas	Jarome Iginla	C	Kamloops (WHL)
12—San Jose	Teemu Riihijarvi	LW	Espoo Jrs., Finland
13—Hartford (from N.Y. Rangers)	Jean-Sebastien Giguere	G	Halifax (QMJHL)
14—Buffalo (from Vancouver)	Jay McKee	D	Niagara Falls (OHL)
15—Toronto	Jeff Ware	D	Oshawa (OHL)
16—Buffalo	Martin Biron	G	Beauport (QMJHL)
17—Washington	Brad Church	LW	Prince Albert (WHL)
18—New Jersey	Petr Sykora	C	Detroit (IHL)
19—Chicago	Dimitri Nabokov	C	Krylja Sovetov, CIS
20—Calgary	Denis Gauthier	D	Drummondville (QMJHL)
21—Boston	Sean Brown	D	Belleville (OHL)
22—Philadelphia	Brian Boucher	G	Tri-City (WHL)
23—Washington (from St. Louis)	Miikka Elomo	C	Kiekko-67, Finland
24—Pittsburgh	Alexei Morozov	LW	Krylja Sovetov, CIS
25—Denver	Marc Denis	G	Chicoutimi (QMJHL)
26—Detroit	Maxim Kuznetsov	D	Moscow Dynamo, CIS

SECOND ROUND

No.—Selecting club	Player	Pos.	Previous team (league)
27—Ottawa	Marc Moro	D	Kingston (OHL)
28—N.Y. Islanders	Jan Hlavac	LW	Sparta Praha, Czech Republic
29—Anaheim	Brian Wesenberg	RW	Guelph (OHL)
30—Tampa Bay	Mike McBain	D	Red Deer (WHL)
31—Edmonton	Georges Laraque	RW	St. Jean (QMJHL)
32—Winnipeg	Marc Chouinard	C	Beauport (QMJHL)
33—Los Angeles	Donald MacLean	C	Beauport (QMJHL)
34—Winnipeg (from Montreal)	Jason Doig	D	Laval (QMJHL)
35—Hartford	Sergei Fedotov	D	Dynamo, CIS
36—Florida	Aaron MacDonald	G	Swift Current (WHL)
37—Dallas	Patrick Cote	LW	Beauport (QMJHL)
38—San Jose	Peter Roed	C	White Bear Lake H.S. (Min.)
39—N.Y. Rangers	Christian Dube	C	Sherbrooke (QMJHL)
40—Vancouver	Chris McAllister	D	Saskatoon (WHL)
41—N.Y. Islanders (from Toronto)	D.J. Smith	D	Windsor (OHL)
42—Buffalo	Mark Dutiaume	LW	Brandon (WHL)
43—Washington	Dwayne Hay	LW	Guelph (OHL)
44—New Jersey	Nathan Perrott	RW	Oshawa (OHL)
45—Chicago	Christian Laflamme	D	Beauport (QMJHL)
46—Calgary	Pavel Smirnov	C	Molot Perm, CIS
47—Boston	Paxton Schafer	G	Medicine Hat (WHL)
48—Philadelphia	Shane Kenny	D	Owen Sound (OHL)
49—St. Louis	Jochen Hecht	C	Mannheim, Germany
50—Los Angeles (from Pittsburgh)	Pavel Rosa	RW	Litinov Jrs., Czech Republic
51—Denver	Nic Beaudoin	LW	Detroit (OHL)
52—Detroit	Philippe Audet	LW	Granby (QMJHL)

THIRD ROUND

No.—Selecting club	Player	Pos.	Previous team (league)
53—Ottawa	Brad Larsen	LW	Swift Current (WHL)
54—Toronto (from N.Y. Islanders)	Ryan Pepperall	RW	Kitchener (OHL)
55—Anaheim	Mike Leclerc	LW	Brandon (WHL)
56—Tampa Bay	Shane Willis	RW	Prince Albert (WHL)
57—Edmonton	Lukas Zib	D	C Ceske-Budejovice, Czech Rep.
58—Detroit (from Winnipeg)	Darryl Laplante	C	Moose Jaw (WHL)
59—Los Angeles	Vladimir Tsyplakov	W	Fort Wayne (IHL)

No.—Selecting club	Player	Pos.	Previous team (league)
60—Montreal	Miroslav Guren	D	ZPS Zlin Jrs., Czech Republic
61—Vancouver (from Hartford through Chicago)	Larry Courville	LW	Oshawa (OHL)
62—Florida	Mike O'Grady	D	Lethbridge (WHL)
63—Dallas	Petr Buzek	D	Dukla Jihlava, Czech Republic
64—San Jose	Marko Makinen	RW	TPS Jrs., Finland
65—N.Y. Rangers	Mike Martin	D	Windsor (OHL)
66—Vancouver	Peter Schaefer	LW	Brandon (WHL)
67—Winnipeg (from Toronto)	Brad Isbister	RW	Portland (WHL)
68—Buffalo	Mathieu Sunderland	RW	Drummondville (QMJHL)
69—Dallas (from Washington through Winnipeg)	Sergei Gusev	D	Mayak Samara, CIS
70—New Jersey	Sergei Vyshedkevich	D	Dynamo, CIS
71—Chicago	Kevin McKay	D	Moose Jaw (WHL)
72—Calgary	Rocky Thompson	D	Medicine Hat (WHL)
73—Boston	Bill McCauley	C	Detroit (OHL)
74—Montreal (from Philadelphia)	Martin Hohenberger	C	Prince George (WHL)
75—St. Louis	Scott Roche	G	North Bay (OHL)
76—Pittsburgh	Jean-Sebastien Aubin	G	Sherbrooke (QMJHL)
77—Denver	John Tripp	RW	Oshawa (OHL)
78—New Jersey (from Detroit)	David Gosselin	RW	Sherbrooke (QMJHL)

FOURTH ROUND

No.—Selecting club	Player	Pos.	Previous team (league)
79—New Jersey (from Ottawa)	Alyn McCauley	C	Ottawa (OHL)
80—Florida (from N.Y. Islanders)	Dave Duerden	LW	Peterborough (OHL)
81—Denver (from Anaheim)	Tomi Kallio	LW	Kiekko-67, Finland
82—Chicago (from Tampa Bay through Anaheim)	Chris Van Dyk	D	Windsor (OHL)
83—Edmonton	Mike Minard	G	Chilliwack (BCJHL)
84—Winnipeg	Justin Kurtz	D	Brandon (WHL)
85—Hartford (from Los Angeles)	Ian MacNeil	C	Oshawa (OHL)
86—Montreal	Jonathan Delisle	RW	Hull (QMJHL)
87—Hartford	Sami Kapanen	LW	HIFK Helsinki, Finland
88—Florida	Daniel Tjarnqvist	D	Rogle Angelholm, Sweden
89—Ottawa (from Dallas through Florida)	Kevin Bolibruck	D	Peterborough (OHL)
90—San Jose	Vesa Toskala	G	Ilves Jrs., Finland
91—N.Y. Rangers	Marc Savard	C	Oshawa (OHL)
92—Vancouver	Lloyd Shaw	D	Seattle (WHL)
93—Washington (from Toronto)	Sebastien Charpentier	G	Laval (QMJHL)
94—Buffalo	Matt Davidson	RW	Portland (WHL)
95—Washington	Joel Theriault	D	Beauport (QMJHL)
96—New Jersey	Henrik Rehnberg	D	Farjestad Jrs., Sweden
97—Chicago	Pavel Kriz	D	Tri-City (WHL)
98—Calgary	Jan Labraaten	LW	Farjestad Jrs., Sweden
99—Boston	Cameron Mann	RW	Peterborough (OHL)
100—Philadelphia	Radovan Somik	RW	ZTS Martin, Slovakia
101—St. Louis	Michal Handzus	C	Banska Bystrica, Slovakia
102—Pittsburgh	Oleg Belov	C	CSKA Moskow, CIS
103—Ottawa (from Denver)	Kevin Boyd	LW	London (OHL)
104—Detroit	Anatoly Ustyugov	LW	Yaroslavl, CIS

FIFTH ROUND

No.—Selecting club	Player	Pos.	Previous team (league)
105—Washington (from Ottawa)	Benoit Gratton	C	Laval (QMJHL)
106—N.Y. Islanders	Vladimir Orsagh	LW	Banska Bystrica, Slovakia
107—Anaheim	Igor Nikulin	RW	Cherepovets, CIS
108—Tampa Bay	Konstantin Golokhvastov	RW	Dynamo, Ukraine
109—Edmonton	Jan Snopek	D	Oshawa (OHL)
110—N.Y. Rangers (from Winnipeg)	Alexei Vasiljev	D	Yaroslavl, CIS
111—Buffalo (from Los Angeles)	Marian Menhart	D	Litinov Jrs., Czech Republic
112—Montreal	Niklas Anger	RW	Djurgarden Jrs., Sweden
113—Hartford	Hugh Hamilton	D	Spokane (WHL)
114—Florida	Francois Cloutier	LW	Hull (QMJHL)
115—Dallas	Wade Strand	D	Regina (WHL)
116—San Jose	Miikka Kiprusoff	G	TPS Jrs., Finland
117—N.Y. Rangers	Dale Purinton	D	Tacoma (WHL)
118—Los Angeles (from Van. through Dal.)	Jason Morgan	C	Kingston (OHL)
119—Buffalo (from Toronto)	Kevin Popp	D	Seattle (WHL)
120—Vancouver (from Buffalo)	Todd Norman	LW	Guelph (OHL)
121—Winnipeg (from Washington)	Brian Elder	G	Brandon (WHL)
122—New Jersey	Chris Mason	G	Prince George (WHL)
123—Buffalo (from Chicago)	Daniel Bienvenue	LW	Val d'Or (QMJHL)
124—Washington (from Calgary)	Joel Cort	D	Guelph (OHL)
125—Detroit (from Boston)	Chad Wilchynski	D	Regina (WHL)
126—Detroit (from Philadelphia)	David Arsenault	G	Drummondville (QMJHL)

No.—Selecting club	Player	Pos.	Previous team (league)
127—St. Louis	Jeff Ambrosio	LW	Belleville (OHL)
128—Pittsburgh	Jan Hrdina	C	Seattle (WHL)
129—Denver	Brent Johnson	G	Owen Sound (OHL)
130—San Jose (from Detroit)	Michal Bros	C	HC Olomouc, Czech Republic

SIXTH ROUND

No.—Selecting club	Player	Pos.	Previous team (league)
131—Ottawa	David Hruska	RW	Sokolov, Czech Republic
132—Philadelphia (from N.Y. Islanders)	Dmitri Tertyshny	D	Chelybinsk, CIS
133—Anaheim	Peter Leboutillier	RW	Red Deer (WHL)
134—Tampa Bay	Eduard Pershin	C	Dynamo, CIS
135—Philadelphia (from Edmonton)	Jamie Sokolsky	D	Belleville (OHL)
136—Winnipeg	Sylvain Daigle	G	Shawinigan (QMJHL)
137—Los Angeles	Igor Melyakov	LW	Yaroslavl, CIS
138—Montreal	Boyd Olson	C	Tri-City (WHL)
139—Toronto (from Hartford)	Doug Bonner	G	Seattle (WHL)
140—San Jose (from Florida)	Timo Hakanen	C	Assat Jrs., Finland
141—Dallas	Dominic Marleau	D	Victoriaville (QMJHL)
142—San Jose	Jaroslav Kudrna	LW	Penticton (BCJHL)
143—N.Y. Rangers	Peter Slamiar	RW	Zvolen Jrs., Slovakia
144—Vancouver	Brent Sopel	D	Swift Current (WHL)
145—Toronto	Yannick Tremblay	D	Beauport (QMJHL)
146—Chicago (from Buffalo)	Marc Magliarditi	G	Des Moines (Jr. A)
147—Washington	Frederic Jobin	D	Laval (QMJHL)
148—New Jersey	Adam Young	D	Windsor (OHL)
149—Chicago	Marty Wilford	D	Oshawa (OHL)
150—Calgary	Clarke Wilm	C	Saskatoon (WHL)
151—Boston	Yevgeny Shaldybin	D	Yaroslavl, CIS
152—Philadelphia	Martin Spahnel	LW	Zlin Jrs., Czech Republic
153—St. Louis (from St. Louis through Anaheim)	Denis Hamel	LW	Chicoutimi (QMJHL)
154—Pittsburgh	Alexei Kolkunov	C	Krylja Sovetov, CIS
155—Denver	John Cirjak	RW	Spokane (WHL)
156—Detroit	Tyler Perry	C	Seattle (WHL)

SEVENTH ROUND

No.—Selecting club	Player	Pos.	Previous team (league)
157—Los Angeles (from Ottawa)	Beniot Larose	D	Shawinigan (QMJHL)
158—N.Y. Islanders	Andrew Taylor	LW	Detroit (OHL)
159—Anaheim	Mike Laplante	D	Calgary (AJHL)
160—Tampa Bay	Cory Murphy	D	Sault Ste. Marie (OHL)
161—Edmonton	Martin Cerven	C	Trencin Jrs., Slovakia
162—Winnipeg	Paul Traynor	D	Kitchener (OHL)
163—Los Angeles	Juha Vuorivirta	C	Tappara Tampere, Finland
164—Montreal	Stephane Robidas	D	Shawinigan (QMJHL)
165—Hartford	Byron Ritchie	C	Lethbridge (WHL)
166—Florida	Peter Worrell	LW	Hull (QMJHL)
167—San Jose (from Dallas)	Brad Mehalko	RW	Lethbridge (WHL)
168—San Jose	Robert Jindrich	D	Plzen, Czech Republic.
169—N.Y. Rangers	Jeff Heil	G	Wisconsin-River Falls
170—Vancouver	Stewart Bodtker	C	Colorado College
171—Toronto	Marek Melenovsky	C	Czech Republic
172—Buffalo	Brian Scott	LW	Kitchener (OHL)
173—Dallas (from Washington)	Jeff Dewar	RW	Moose Jaw (WHL)
174—New Jersey	Richard Rochefort	C	Sudbury (OHL)
175—Chicago	Steve Tardif	C	Drummondville (QMJHL)
176—Calgary	Ryan Gillis	D	North Bay (OHL)
177—Boston	Per Johan Axelsson	LW	Frolunda, Sweden
178—Philadelphia	Martin Streit	RW	HC Olomouc, Czech Republic
179—St. Louis	Jean-Luc Grand-Pierre	D	Val d'Or (QMJHL)
180—Pittsburgh	Derrick Pyke	RW	Halifax (QMJHL)
181—Denver	Dan Smith	D	U. of British Columbia
182—Detroit	Per Eklund	LW	Djurgarden-Stockholm, Sweden

EIGHTH ROUND

No.—Selecting club	Player	Pos.	Previous team (league)
183—Ottawa	Kaj Linna	D	Boston University
184—Ottawa (from N.Y. Islanders through Boston)	Ray Schultz	D	Tri-City (WHL)
185—Anaheim	Igor Karpenko	G	Kiev, Ukraine
186—Tampa Bay	Joseph Cardarelli	LW	Spokane (WHL)
187—Edmonton	Stephen Douglas	D	Niagara Falls (OHL)
188—Winnipeg	Jaroslav Obsut	D	North Battleford (SJHL)
189—Winnipeg (from Los Angeles)	Frederik Loven	C	Djurgarden-Stockholm, Sweden

No.—Selecting club	Player	Pos.	Previous team (league)
190—Montreal	Greg Hart	RW	Kamloops (WHL)
191—Hartford	Milan Kostolny	RW	Detroit (OHL)
192—Florida	Filip Kuba	D	Czech Republic
193—Dallas	Anatoli Kovesnikov	LW	Kiev, Ukraine
194—San Jose	Ryan Kraft	C	Univ. of Minnesota
195—N.Y. Rangers	Ilja Gorchov	D	Yaroslavl, CIS
196—Vancouver	Tyler Willis	RW	Swift Current (WHL)
197—Toronto	Mark Murphy	LW	Stratford, Ont. (Jr. B)
198—Buffalo	Mike Zanutto	C	Oshawa (OHL)
199—Washington	Vasili Turkovsky	D	CSKA Moskow, CIS
200—New Jersey	Frederic Henry	G	Granby (QMJHL)
201—Chicago	Casey Hankinson	LW	Univ. of Minnesota
202—Dallas (from Calgary)	Sergei Luchinkin	LW	Dimitrov, CIS
203—Boston	Sergei Zhukov		CIS
204—Philadelphia	Ruslan Shafikov	C	Salavat Yulayev, CIS
205—St. Louis	Derek Bekar	C	Powell River (BCJHL)
206—Pittsburgh	Sergei Voronov	D	Dynamo, CIS
207—Denver	Tomi Hirvonen	C	Ilves Jrs., Finland
208—Detroit	Andrei Samokvalov	RW	UST-Kamenogorsk, CIS

NINTH ROUND

No.—Selecting club	Player	Pos.	Previous team (league)
209—St. Louis (from Ottawa)	Libor Zabransky	W	CSKE Budjovice, Czech Republic
210—N.Y. Islanders	David MacDonald	G	Sudbury (OHL)
211—N.Y. Islanders (from Anaheim)	Mike Broda	LW	Moose Jaw (WHL)
212—Tampa Bay	Zac Bierk	G	Peterborough (OHL)
213—Edmonton	Jiri Antonin	D	Pardubice Jrs., Czech Republic
214—Winnipeg	Rob Deciantis	C	Kitchener (OHL)
215—Los Angeles	Brian Stewart	D	Sault Ste. Marie (OHL)
216—Montreal	Eric Houde	C	Halifax (QMJHL)
217—Hartford	Mike Rucinski	D	Detroit (OHL)
218—Florida	David Lemanowicz	G	Spokane (WHL)
219—Dallas	Stephen Lowe	C	Sault Ste. Marie (OHL)
220—San Jose	Miiko Markkanen	RW	TPS Jrs., Finland
221—N.Y. Rangers	Bob Maudie	C	Kamloops (WHL)
222—Vancouver	Jason Cugnet	G	Kelowna (BCJHL)
223—Toronto	Danlil Markov	D	Spartak, CIS
224—Buffalo	Rob Skrlac	LW	Kamloops (WHL)
225—Washington	Scott Swanson	D	Omaha (Jr. A)
226—New Jersey	Colin O'Hara	D	Winnipeg (MJHL)
227—Chicago	Mike Pittman	C	Guelph (OHL)
228—Denver (from Calgary)	Chris George	RW	Sarnia (OHL)
229—Boston	Jonathan Murphy	D	Peterborough (OHL)
230—Philadelphia	Jeff Lank	D	Prince Albert (WHL)
231—Ottawa (from St. Louis)	Erik Kasminski		Cleveland (Jr. A)
232—Pittsburgh	Frank Ivankovic	G	Oshawa (OHL)
233—Calgary (from Denver)	Steve Shirreffs		Hotchkiss H.S. (Conn.)
234—Detroit	David Engblom	C	Vallentuna, Sweden

NHL HISTORY

Stanley Cup champions

All-Star Games

Records

Award winners

The Sporting News awards

Hall of Fame

Milestones

Team histories

STANLEY CUP CHAMPIONS

The Stanley Cup was donated in 1893 to be awarded to signify supremacy in Canadian amateur hockey. Eventually, other teams, including professional clubs and clubs outside of Canada, began vying for the trophy. Since 1926 only NHL clubs have competed for the Stanley Cup.

Season	Club	Coach
1892-93	Montreal Am. Ath. Assn.*	
1893-94	Montreal Am. Ath. Assn.*	
1894-95	Montreal Victorias*	Mike Grant†
1895-96	(Feb. '96) Winnipeg Victorias*	J. Armitage
1895-96	(Dec. '96) Montreal Victorias*	Mike Grant†
1896-97	Montreal Victorias*	Mike Grant†
1897-98	Montreal Victorias*	F. Richardson
1898-99	Montreal Shamrocks*	H.J. Trihey†
1899-1900	Montreal Shamrocks*	H.J. Trihey†
1900-01	Winnipeg Victorias*	D.H. Bain
1901-02	Montreal Am. Ath. Assn.*	C. McKerrow
1902-03	Ottawa Silver Seven*	A.T. Smith
1903-04	Ottawa Silver Seven*	A.T. Smith
1904-05	Ottawa Silver Seven*	A.T. Smith
1905-06	Montreal Wanderers*	Cecil Blachford†
1906-07	(Jan. '07) Kenora Thistles*	Tommy Phillips†
1906-07	(Mar. '07) Montreal Wanderers*	Cecil Blachford
1907-08	Montreal Wanderers*	Cecil Blachford
1908-09	Ottawa Senators*	Bruce Stuart†
1909-10	Montreal Wanderers*	Pud Glass†
1910-11	Ottawa Senators*	Bruce Stuart†
1911-12	Quebec Bulldogs*	C. Nolan
1912-13	Quebec Bulldogs*	Joe Malone†
1913-14	Toronto Blueshirts*	Scotty Davidson†
1914-15	Vancouver Millionaires*	Frank Patrick
1915-16	Montreal Canadiens*	George Kennedy
1916-17	Seattle Metropolitans*	Pete Muldoon
1917-18	Toronto Arenas	Dick Carroll
1919-20	Ottawa Senators	Pete Green
1920-21	Ottawa Senators	Pete Green
1921-22	Toronto St. Pats	Eddie Powers
1922-23	Ottawa Senators	Pete Green
1923-24	Montreal Canadiens	Leo Dandurand
1924-25	Victoria Cougars*	Lester Patrick
1925-26	Montreal Maroons	Eddie Gerard
1926-27	Ottawa Senators	Dave Gill
1927-28	New York Rangers	Lester Patrick
1928-29	Boston Bruins	Cy Denneny
1929-30	Montreal Canadiens	Cecil Hart
1930-31	Montreal Canadiens	Cecil Hart
1931-32	Toronto Maple Leafs	Dick Irvin
1932-33	New York Rangers	Lester Patrick
1933-34	Chicago Black Hawks	Tommy Gorman
1934-35	Montreal Maroons	Tommy Gorman
1935-36	Detroit Red Wings	Jack Adams
1936-37	Detroit Red Wings	Jack Adams
1937-38	Chicago Black Hawks	Bill Stewart
1938-39	Boston Bruins	Art Ross
1939-40	New York Rangers	Frank Boucher
1940-41	Boston Bruins	Cooney Weiland
1941-42	Toronto Maple Leafs	Hap Day
1942-43	Detroit Red Wings	Jack Adams
1943-44	Montreal Canadiens	Dick Irvin
1944-45	Toronto Maple Leafs	Hap Day
1945-46	Montreal Canadiens	Dick Irvin
1946-47	Toronto Maple Leafs	Hap Day
1947-48	Toronto Maple Leafs	Hap Day
1948-49	Toronto Maple Leafs	Hap Day
1949-50	Detroit Red Wings	Tommy Ivan
1950-51	Toronto Maple Leafs	Joe Primeau
1951-52	Detroit Red Wings	Tommy Ivan
1952-53	Montreal Canadiens	Dick Irvin
1953-54	Detroit Red Wings	Tommy Ivan
1954-55	Detroit Red Wings	Jimmy Skinner
1955-56	Montreal Canadiens	Toe Blake
1956-57	Montreal Canadiens	Toe Blake
1957-58	Montreal Canadiens	Toe Blake
1958-59	Montreal Canadiens	Toe Blake
1959-60	Montreal Canadiens	Toe Blake
1960-61	Chicago Black Hawks	Rudy Pilous
1961-62	Toronto Maple Leafs	Punch Imlach
1962-63	Toronto Maple Leafs	Punch Imlach
1963-64	Toronto Maple Leafs	Punch Imlach
1964-65	Montreal Canadiens	Toe Blake
1965-66	Montreal Canadiens	Toe Blake
1966-67	Toronto Maple Leafs	Punch Imlach
1967-68	Montreal Canadiens	Toe Blake
1968-69	Montreal Canadiens	Claude Ruel
1969-70	Boston Bruins	Harry Sinden
1970-71	Montreal Canadiens	Al MacNeil
1971-72	Boston Bruins	Tom Johnson
1972-73	Montreal Canadiens	Scotty Bowman
1973-74	Philadelphia Flyers	Fred Shero
1974-75	Philadelphia Flyers	Fred Shero
1975-76	Montreal Canadiens	Scotty Bowman
1976-77	Montreal Canadiens	Scotty Bowman
1977-78	Montreal Canadiens	Scotty Bowman
1978-79	Montreal Canadiens	Scotty Bowman
1979-80	New York Islanders	Al Arbour
1980-81	New York Islanders	Al Arbour
1981-82	New York Islanders	Al Arbour
1982-83	New York Islanders	Al Arbour
1983-84	Edmonton Oilers	Glen Sather
1984-85	Edmonton Oilers	Glen Sather
1985-86	Montreal Canadiens	Jean Perron
1986-87	Edmonton Oilers	Glen Sather
1987-88	Edmonton Oilers	Glen Sather
1988-89	Calgary Flames	Terry Crisp
1989-90	Edmonton Oilers	John Muckler
1990-91	Pittsburgh Penguins	Bob Johnson
1991-92	Pittsburgh Penguins	Scotty Bowman
1992-93	Montreal Canadiens	Jacques Demers
1993-94	New York Rangers	Mike Keenan
1994-95	New Jersey Devils	Jacques Lemaire

NOTE: 1918-19 series between Montreal and Seattle cancelled after five games because of influenza epidemic.
*Stanley Cups won by non-NHL clubs.
†Team captain.

STANLEY CUP (

ALL-STAR GAMES

Date	Site	Winning team, score	Losing team, score	Att.
2-14-34†	Maple Leaf Gardens, Toronto	Toronto Maple Leafs, 7	NHL All-Stars, 3	*14,000
11-3-37‡	Montreal Forum	NHL All-Stars, 6	Montreal All-Stars§, 5	8,683
10-29-39*	Montreal Forum	NHL All-Stars, 5	Montreal Canadiens, 2	*6,000
10-13-47	Maple Leaf Gardens, Toronto	NHL All-Stars, 4	Toronto Maple Leafs, 3	14,169
11-3-48	Chicago Stadium	NHL All-Stars, 3	Toronto Maple Leafs, 1	12,794
10-10-49	Maple Leaf Gardens, Toronto	NHL All-Stars, 3	Toronto Maple Leafs, 1	13,541
10-8-50	Olympia Stadium, Detroit	Detroit Red Wings, 7	NHL All-Stars, 1	9,166
10-9-51	Maple Leaf Gardens, Toronto	First Team•, 2	Second Team•, 2	11,469
10-5-52	Olympia Stadium, Detroit	First Team•, 1	Second Team•, 1	10,680
10-3-53	Montreal Forum	NHL All-Stars, 3	Montreal Canadiens, 1	14,153
10-2-54	Olympia Stadium, Detroit	NHL All-Stars, 2	Detroit Red Wings, 2	10,689
10-2-55	Olympia Stadium, Detroit	Detroit Red Wings, 3	NHL All-Stars, 1	10,111
10-9-56	Montreal Forum	NHL All-Stars, 1	Montreal Canadiens, 1	13,095
10-5-57	Montreal Forum	NHL All-Stars, 5	Montreal Canadiens, 3	13,095
10-4-58	Montreal Forum	Montreal Canadiens, 6	NHL All-Stars, 3	13,989
10-3-59	Montreal Forum	Montreal Canadiens, 6	NHL All-Stars, 1	13,818
10-1-60	Montreal Forum	NHL All-Stars, 2	Montreal Canadiens, 1	13,949
10-7-61	Chicago Stadium	NHL All-Stars, 3	Chicago Blackhawks, 1	14,534
10-6-62	Maple Leaf Gardens, Toronto	Toronto Maple Leafs, 4	NHL All-Stars, 1	14,236
10-5-63	Maple Leaf Gardens, Toronto	NHL All-Stars, 3	Toronto Maple Leafs, 3	14,034
10-10-64	Maple Leaf Gardens, Toronto	NHL All-Stars, 3	Toronto Maple Leafs, 2	14,232
10-20-65	Montreal Forum	NHL All-Stars, 5	Montreal Canadiens, 2	14,284
1-18-67	Montreal Forum	Montreal Canadiens, 3	NHL All-Stars, 0	14,284
1-16-68	Maple Leaf Gardens, Toronto	Toronto Maple Leafs, 4	NHL All-Stars, 3	15,753
1-21-69	Montreal Forum	West Division, 3	East Division, 3	16,260
1-20-70	St. Louis Arena	East Division, 4	West Division, 1	16,587
1-19-71	Boston Garden	West Division, 2	East Division, 1	14,790
1-25-72	Met Sports Center, Bloomington, Minn.	East Division, 3	West Division, 2	15,423
1-30-73	Madison Square Garden, New York	East Division, 5	West Division, 4	16,986
1-29-74	Chicago Stadium	West Division, 6	East Division, 4	16,426
1-21-75	Montreal Forum	Wales Conference, 7	Campbell Conference, 1	16,080
1-20-76	The Spectrum, Philadelphia	Wales Conference, 7	Campbell Conference, 5	16,436
1-25-77	Pacific Coliseum, Vancouver	Wales Conference, 4	Campbell Conference, 3	15,607
1-24-78	Buffalo Memorial Auditorium	Wales Conference, 3	Campbell Conference, 2 (OT)	16,433
1979 All-Star Game replaced by Challenge Cup series between Team NHL and Soviet Union				
2-5-80	Joe Louis Arena, Detroit	Wales Conference, 6	Campbell Conference, 3	21,002
2-10-81	The Forum, Los Angeles	Campbell Conference, 4	Wales Conference, 1	15,761
2-9-82	Capital Centre, Landover, Md.	Wales Conference, 4	Campbell Conference, 2	18,130
2-8-83	Nassau Coliseum, Long Island, N.Y.	Campbell Conference, 9	Wales Conference, 3	15,230
1-31-84	Meadowlands Arena, East Rutherford, N.J.	Wales Conference, 7	Campbell Conference, 6	18,939
2-12-85	Olympic Saddledome, Calgary	Wales Conference, 6	Campbell Conference, 4	16,683
2-4-86	Hartford Civic Center	Wales Conference, 4	Campbell Conference, 3 (OT)	15,126
1987 All-Star Game replaced by Rendez-Vous '87 between Team NHL and Soviet Union				
2-9-88	St. Louis Arena	Wales Conference, 6	Campbell Conference, 5 (OT)	17,878
2-7-89	Northlands Coliseum, Edmonton	Campbell Conference, 9	Wales Conference, 5	17,503
1-21-90	Pittsburgh Civic Arena	Wales Conference, 12	Campbell Conference, 7	17,503
1-19-91	Chicago Stadium	Campbell Conference, 11	Wales Conference, 5	18,472
1-18-92	The Spectrum, Philadelphia	Campbell Conference, 10	Wales Conference, 6	17,380
2-6-93	Montreal Forum	Wales Conference, 16	Campbell Conference, 6	17,137
1-22-94	Madison Square Garden, New York	Eastern Conference, 9	Western Conference, 8	18,200
1995 All-Star Game canceled because of NHL lockout				

*Estimated figure.
†Benefit game for Toronto Maple Leafs left wing Ace Bailey, who suffered a career-ending skull injury earlier in the season.
‡Benefit game for the family of Montreal Canadiens center Howie Morenz, who died of a heart attack earlier in the year.
§Montreal All-Star roster made up of players from Montreal Canadiens and Maroons.
*Benefit game for the family of Montreal Canadiens defenseman Babe Siebert, who drowned earlier in the year.
•First Team roster supplemented by players from the four American clubs and Second Team roster supplemented by players from the two Canadian clubs.

Date	Player, All-Star Game team (regular-season team)	Date	Player, All-Star Game team (regular-season team)
10-6-62	Eddie Shack, Toronto Maple Leafs	1-20-70	Bobby Hull, East Div. (Chicago Blackhawks)
10-5-63	Frank Mahovlich, Toronto Maple Leafs	1-19-71	Bobby Hull, West Div. (Chicago Blackhawks)
10-10-64	Jean Beliveau, All-Stars (Montreal Canadiens)	1-25-72	Bobby Orr, East Division (Boston Bruins)
10-20-65	Gordie Howe, All-Stars (Detroit Red Wings)	1-30-73	Greg Polis, West Division (Pittsburgh Penguins)
1-18-67	Henri Richard, Montreal Canadiens	1-29-74	Garry Unger, West Division (St. Louis Blues)
1-16-68	Bruce Gamble, Toronto Maple Leafs	1-21-75	Syl Apps Jr., Wales Conf. (Pittsburgh Penguins)
1-21-69	Frank Mahovlich, East Div. (Detroit Red Wings)	1-20-76	Peter Mahovlich, Wales Conf. (Mon. Canadiens)

Date	Player, All-Star Game team (regular-season team)	Date	Player, All-Star Game team (regular-season team)
1-25-77	Rick Martin, Wales Conference (Buffalo Sabres)	2-4-86	Grant Fuhr, Campbell Conf. (Edmonton Oilers)
1-24-78	Billy Smith, Campbell Conf. (New York Islanders)	2-9-88	Mario Lemieux, Wales Conf. (Pittsburgh Penguins)
2-5-80	Reggie Leach, Campbell Conf. (Phila. Flyers)	2-7-89	Wayne Gretzky, Campbell Conf. (L.A. Kings)
2-10-81	Mike Liut, Campbell Conf. (St. Louis Blues)	1-21-90	Mario Lemieux, Wales Conf. (Pittsburgh Penguins)
2-9-82	Mike Bossy, Wales Conf. (New York Islanders)	1-19-91	Vincent Damphousse, Camp. Conf. (T. Maple Leafs)
2-8-83	Wayne Gretzky, Campbell Conf. (Edmonton Oilers)	1-18-92	Brett Hull, Campbell Conf. (St. Louis Blues)
1-31-84	Don Maloney, Wales Conf. (New York Rangers)	2-6-93	Mike Gartner, Wales Conf. (New York Rangers)
2-12-85	Mario Lemieux, Wales Conf. (Pittsburgh Penguins)	1-22-94	Mike Richter, Eastern Conf. (New York Rangers)

RECORDS

INDIVIDUAL — CAREER

Most seasons

- NHL: 26—Gordie Howe, Detroit Red Wings and Hartford Whalers, 1946-47 through 1970-71 and 1979-80.
- CHL: 9—Richie Hansen, Fort Worth Texans, Salt Lake Golden Eagles, Wichita Wind, 1975-76 through 1983-84.
- AHL: 20—Fred Glover, Indianapolis Caps, St. Louis Flyers, Cleveland Barons.
  Willie Marshall, Pittsburgh Hornets, Rochester Americans, Hershey Bears, Providence Reds, Baltimore Clippers.
- IHL: 18—Glenn Ramsay, Cincinnati Mohawks, Fort Wayne Komets, Troy Bruins, Toledo Blades, St. Paul Saints, Omaha Knights, Des Moines Oak Leafs, Toledo Hornets, Port Huron Flags, 1956-57 through 1973-74.

Most games played

- NHL: 1,767—Gordie Howe, Detroit Red Wings and Hartford Whalers (26 seasons).
- AHL: 1,205—Willie Marshall, Pittsburgh Hornets, Rochester Americans, Hershey Bears, Providence Reds, Baltimore Clippers (20 seasons).
- IHL: 1,053—Glenn Ramsay, Cincinnati Mohawks, Fort Wayne Komets, Troy Bruins, Toledo Blades, St. Paul Saints, Omaha Knights, Des Moines Oak Leafs, Toledo Hornets, Port Huron Flags (18 seasons).
- CHL: 575—Richie Hansen, Fort Worth Texans, Salt Lake Golden Eagles, Wichita Wind (9 seasons).
- WHA: 551—Andre Lacroix, Philadelphia Blazers, New York Golden Blades, Jersey Knights, San Diego Mariners, Houston Aeros and New England Whalers (7 seasons).

Most goals

- NHL: 814—Wayne Gretzky, Edmonton Oilers, Los Angeles Kings (16 seasons).
- IHL: 526—Joe Kastelic, Fort Wayne Komets, Troy Burins, Louisville Rebels, Muskegon Zephyrs, Muskegon Mohawks (15 seasons).
- AHL: 523—Willie Marshall, Pittsburgh Hornets, Rochester Americans, Hershey Bears, Providence Reds, Baltimore Clippers (20 seasons).
- WHA: 316—Marc Tardif, Quebec Nordiques (6 seasons).
- CHL: 204—Richie Hansen, Fort Worth Texans, Salt Lake Golden Eagles, Wichita Wind (9 seasons).

Most assists

- NHL: 1,692—Wayne Gretzky, Edmonton Oilers, Los Angeles Kings (16 seasons).
- AHL: 852—Willie Marshall, Pittsburgh Hornets, Hershey Bears, Rochester Americans, Providence Reds, Baltimore Clippers (20 seasons).
- IHL: 826—Len Thornson, Huntington Hornets, Indianapolis Chiefs, Fort Wayne Komets (13 seasons).
- WHA: 547—Andre Lacroix, Philadelphia Blazers, Jersey Knights, San Diego Mariners, Houston Aeros, New England Whalers (7 seasons).
- CHL: 374—Richie Hansen, Fort Worth Texans, Salt Lake Golden Eagles, Wichita Wind (9 seasons).

Most points

- NHL: 2,506—Wayne Gretzky, Edmonton Oilers, Los Angeles Kings (16 seasons).
- AHL: 1,375—Willie Marshall, Pittsburgh Hornets, Hershey Bears, Rochester Americans, Providence Reds, Baltimore Clippers (20 seasons).
- IHL: 1,252—Len Thornson, Huntington Hornets, Indianapolis Chiefs, Fort Wayne Komets (13 seasons).
- WHA: 798—Andre Lacroix, Philadelphia Blazers, Jersey Knights, San Diego Mariners, Houston Aeros, New England Whalers (7 seasons).
- CHL: 578—Richie Hansen, Fort Worth Texans, Salt Lake Golden Eagles, Wichita Wind (9 seasons).

Most penalty minutes

- NHL: 3,966—Dave "Tiger" Williams, Toronto Maple Leafs, Vancouver Canucks, Detroit Red Wings, Los Angeles Kings, Hartford Whalers (13 seasons).
- AHL: 2,402—Fred Glover, Indianapolis Caps, St. Louis Flyers, Cleveland Barons (20 seasons).
- IHL: 2,175—Gord Malinoski, Dayton Gems, Saginaw Gears (9 seasons).
- WHA: 962—Paul Baxter, Cleveland Crusaders, Quebec Nordiques (5 seasons).
- CHL: 899—Brad Gassoff, Tulsa Oilers, Dallas Black Hawks (5 seasons).

Most shutouts

- NHL: 103—Terry Sawchuk, Detroit Red Wings, Boston Bruins, Los Angeles Kings, New York Rangers, Toronto Maple Leafs (20 seasons).
- AHL: 45—Johnny Bower, Cleveland Barons, Providence Reds (11 seasons).
- IHL: 45—Glenn Ramsay, Cincinnati Mohawks, Fort Wayne Komets, Troy Bruins, Toledo Blades, St. Paul Saints, Omaha Knights, Des Moines Oak Leafs, Toledo Hornets, Port Huron Flags (18 seasons).
- WHA: 16—Ernie Wakely, Winnipeg Jets, San Diego Mariners, Houston Aeros (6 seasons).
- CHL: 12—Michel Dumas, Dallas Black Hawks (4 seasons).
  Mike Veisor, Dallas Black Hawks (5 seasons).

INDIVIDUAL — SEASON

Most goals

- NHL: 92—Wayne Gretzky, Edmonton Oilers, 1981-82 season.
- WHA: 77—Bobby Hull, Winnipeg Jets, 1974-75 season.

CHL: 77—Alain Caron, St. Louis Braves, 1963-64 season.
IHL: 75—Dan Lecours, Milwaukee Admirals, 1982-83 season.
AHL: 70—Stephan Lebeau, Sherbrooke Canadiens, 1988-89 season.

Most goals by a defenseman

NHL: 48—Paul Coffey, Edmonton Oilers, 1985-86 season.
IHL: 34—Roly McLenahan, Cincinnati Mohawks, 1955-56 season.
CHL: 29—Dan Poulin, Nashville South Stars, 1981-82 season.
AHL: 28—Greg Tebbutt, Baltimore Skipjacks, 1982-83 season.
WHA: 24—Kevin Morrison, Jersey Knights, 1973-74 season.

Most assists

NHL: 163—Wayne Gretzky, Edmonton Oilers, 1985-86 season.
IHL: 109—John Cullen, Flint Spirits, 1987-88 season.
WHA: 106—Andre Lacroix, San Diego Mariners, 1974-75 season.
AHL: 89—George "Red" Sullivan, Hershey Bears, 1953-54 season.
CHL: 81—Richie Hansen, Salt Lake Golden Eagles, 1981-82 season.

Most assists by a defenseman

NHL: 102—Bobby Orr, Boston Bruins, 1970-71 season.
IHL: 86—Gerry Glaude, Muskegon Zephyrs, 1962-63 season.
WHA: 77—J. C. Tremblay, Quebec Nordiques, 1975-76 season.
AHL: 62—Craig Levie, Nova Scotia Voyageurs, 1980-81 season.
        Shawn Evans, Nova Scotia Oilers, 1987-88 season.
CHL: 61—Barclay Plager, Omaha Knights, 1963-64 season.

Most points

NHL: 215—Wayne Gretzky, Edmonton Oilers, 1985-86 season.
IHL: 157—John Cullen, Flint Spirits, 1987-88 season.
WHA: 154—Marc Tardif, Quebec Nordiques, 1977-78 season.
AHL: 138—Don Biggs, Binghamton Rangers, 1992-93 season.
CHL: 125—Alain Caron, St. Louis Braves, 1963-64 season.

Most points by a defenseman

NHL: 139—Bobby Orr, Boston Bruins, 1970-71 season.
IHL: 101—Gerry Glaude, Muskegon Zephyrs, 1962-63 season.
WHA: 89—J. C. Tremblay, Quebec Nordiques, 1972-73 and 1975-76 seasons.
CHL: 85—Dan Poulin, Nashville South Stars, 1981-82 season.
AHL: 84—Greg Tebbutt, Baltimore Skipjacks, 1982-83 season.

Most penalty minutes

IHL: 648—Kevin Evans, Kalamazoo, 1986-87 season.
NHL: 472—Dave Schultz, Philadelphia Flyers, 1974-75 season.
AHL: 446—Robert Ray, Rochester Americans, 1988-89 season.
CHL: 411—Randy Holt, Dallas Black Hawks, 1974-75 season.
WHA: 365—Curt Brackenbury, Minnesota Fighting Saints and Quebec Nordiques, 1975-76 season.

Most shutouts

NHL: 22—George Hainsworth, Montreal Canadiens, 1928-29 season.
NHL: 15—(modern era) Tony Esposito, Chicago Black Hawks, 1969-70 season.
IHL: 10—Charlie Hodge, Cincinnati Mohawks, 1953-54 season.
        Joe Daley, Winnipeg Jets, 1975-76 season.
CHL: 9—Marcel Pelletier, St. Paul Rangers, 1963-64 season.
AHL: 9—Gordie Bell, Buffalo Bisons, 1942-43 season.
WHA: 5—Gerry Cheevers, Cleveland Crusaders, 1972-73 season.

Lowest goals against average

NHL: 0.98—George Hainsworth, Montreal Canadiens, 1928-29 season.
AHL: 1.79—Frank Brimsek, Providence Reds, 1937-38 season.
IHL: 1.88—Glenn Ramsay, Cincinnati Mohawks, 1956-57 season.
CHL: 2.16—Russ Gillow, Oklahoma City Blazers, 1967-68 season.
WHA: 2.57—Don McLeod, Houston Aeros, 1973-74 season.

INDIVIDUAL—GAME

Most goals

NHL: 7—Joe Malone, Quebec Bulldogs vs. Toronto St. Pats, January 31, 1920.
NHL: 6—(modern era) Syd Howe, Detroit Red Wings vs. N.Y. Rangers, Feb. 3, 1944.
        Gordon "Red" Berenson, St. Louis Blues vs. Philadelphia, Nov. 7, 1968.
        Darryl Sittler, Toronto Maple Leafs vs. Boston, Feb. 7, 1976.
CHL: 6—Jim Mayer, Dallas Black Hawks, February 23, 1979.
AHL: 6—Bob Heron, Pittsburgh Hornets, 1941-42.
        Harry Pidhirny, Springfield Indians, 1953-54.
        Camille Henry, Providence Reds, 1955-56.
        Patrick Lebeau, Fredericton Canadiens, Feb. 1, 1991.

IHL: 6—Pierre Brillant, Indianapolis Chiefs, Feb. 18, 1959.
　　　　Bryan McLay, Muskegon Zephyrs, Mar. 8, 1961.
　　　　Elliott Chorley, St. Paul Saints, Jan. 17, 1962.
　　　　Joe Kastelic, Muskegon Zephyrs, Mar. 1, 1962.
　　　　Tom St. James, Flint Generals, Mar. 15, 1985.
WHA: 5—Ron Ward, New York Raiders vs. Ottawa, January 4, 1973.
　　　　Ron Climie, Edmonton Oilers vs. N.Y. Golden Blades, November 6, 1973.
　　　　Andre Hinse, Houston Aeros vs. Edmonton, Jan. 16, 1975.
　　　　Vaclav Nedomansky, Toronto Toros vs. Denver Spurs, Nov. 13, 1975.
　　　　Wayne Connelly, Minnesota Fighting Saints vs. Cincinnati Stingers, Nov. 27, 1975.
　　　　Ron Ward, Cleveland Crusaders vs. Toronto Toros, Nov. 30, 1975.
　　　　Real Cloutier, Quebec Nordiques fs. Phoenix Roadrunners, Oct. 26, 1976.

Most assists

AHL: 9—Art Stratton, Buffalo Bisons vs. Pittsburgh, Mar. 17, 1963.
IHL: 9—Jean-Paul Denis, St. Paul Saints, Jan. 17, 1962.
NHL: 7—Billy Taylor, Detroit Red Wings vs. Chicago, Mar. 16, 1947.
　　　　Wayne Gretzky, Edmonton Oilers vs. Washington, Feb. 15, 1980.
WHA: 7—Jim Harrison, Alberta Oilers vs. New York, January 30, 1973.
　　　　Jim Harrison, Cleveland Crusaders vs. Toronto, Nov. 30, 1975.
CHL: 6—Art Stratton, St. Louis Braves, 1966-67.
　　　　Ron Ward, Tulsa Oilers, 1967-68.
　　　　Bill Hogaboam, Omaha Knights, January 15, 1972.
　　　　Jim Wiley, Tulsa Oilers, 1974-75.

Most points

IHL: 11—Elliott Chorley, St. Paul Saints, Jan. 17, 1962.
　　　　Jean-Paul Denis, St. Paul Saints, Jan. 17, 1962.
NHL: 10—Darryl Sittler, Toronto Maple Leafs vs. Boston, Feb. 7, 1976.
WHA: 10—Jim Harrison, Alberta Oilers vs. New York, January 30, 1973.
AHL: 9—Art Stratton, Buffalo Bisons vs Pittsburgh, Mar. 17, 1963.
CHL: 8—Steve Vickers, Omaha Knights vs. Kansas City, Jan. 15, 1972.

Most penalty minutes

NHL: 67—Randy Holt, Los Angeles Kings vs. Philadelphia, March 11, 1979.
IHL: 63—Willie Trognitz, Dayton Gems, Oct. 29, 1977.
AHL: 54—Wally Weir, Rochester Americans vs. New Brunswick, Jan. 16, 1981.
CHL: 49—Gary Rissling, Birmingham Bulls vs. Salt Lake, Dec. 5, 1980.
WHA: 46—Dave Hanson, Birmingham Bulls vs. Indianapolis, Feb. 5, 1978.

STANLEY CUP PLAYOFFS

INDIVIDUAL—CAREER

Most years in playoffs: 20—Gordie Howe, Detroit, Hartford.
　　　　　　　　　　　　Larry Robinson, Montreal, Los Angeles.
Most consecutive years in playoffs: 20—Larry Robinson, Montreal, Los Angeles.
Most games: 227—Larry Robinson, Montreal, Los Angeles.
Most games by goaltender: 131—Billy Smith, N.Y. Islanders.
Most goals: 110—Wayne Gretzky, Edmonton, Los Angeles.
Most assists: 236—Wayne Gretzky, Edmonton, Los Angeles.
Most points: 346—Wayne Gretzky, Edmonton, Los Angeles.
Most penalty minutes: 605—Dale Hunter, Quebec, Washington.
Most shutouts: 14—Jacques Plante, Montreal, St. Louis.

INDIVIDUAL—SEASON

Most goals: 19—Reggie Leach, Philadelphia (1975-76).
　　　　　　　Jari Kurri, Edmonton (1984-85).
Most goals by a defenseman: 12—Paul Coffey, Edmonton (1984-85).
Most assists: 31—Wayne Gretzky, Edmonton (1987-88).
Most assists by a defenseman: 25—Paul Coffey, Edmonton (1984-85).
Most points: 47—Wayne Gretzky, Edmonton (1984-85).
Most points by a defenseman: 37—Paul Coffey, Edmonton (1984-85).
Most penalty minutes: 141—Chris Nilan, Montreal (1985-86).
Most shutouts: 4—Clint Benedict, Montreal Maroons (1927-28).
　　　　　　　Dave Kerr, N.Y. Rangers (1936-37).
　　　　　　　Frank McCool, Toronto (1944-45).
　　　　　　　Terry Sawchuk, Detroit (1951-52).
　　　　　　　Bernie Parent, Philadelphia (1974-75).
　　　　　　　Ken Dryden, Montreal (1976-77).
Most consecutive shutouts: 3—Frank McCool, Toronto (1944-45).

INDIVIDUAL — GAME

Most goals: 5—Maurice Richard, Montreal vs. Toronto, March 23, 1944.
　　　　　　 Darryl Sittler, Toronto vs. Philadelphia, April 22, 1976.
　　　　　　 Reggie Leach, Philadelphia vs. Boston, May 6, 1976.
　　　　　　 Mario Lemieux, Pittsburgh vs. Philadelphia, April 25, 1989.
Most assists: 6—Mikko Leinonen, N.Y. Rangers vs. Philadelphia, April 8, 1982.
　　　　　　 Wayne Gretzky, Edmonton vs. Los Angeles, April 9, 1987.
Most points: 8—Patrik Sundstrom, New Jersey vs. Washington, April 22, 1988.
　　　　　　 Mario Lemieux, Pittsburgh vs. Philadelphia, April 25, 1989.

CLUB

Most Stanley Cup championships: 24—Montreal Canadiens.
Most consecutive Stanley Cup championships: 5—Montreal Canadiens.
Most final series apperances: 32—Montreal Canadiens.
Most years in playoffs: 69—Montreal Canadiens.
Most consecutive playoff appearances: 28—Boston Bruins.
Most consecutive playoff game victories: 12—Edmonton Oilers.
Most goals, one team, one game: 13—Edmonton vs. Los Angeles, April 9, 1987.
Most goals, one team, one period: 7—Montreal Canadiens vs. Toronto, March 30, 1944, 3rd period.

AWARD WINNERS

ART ROSS TROPHY

(Leading scorer)

Season	Player, Team	Pts.
1917-18	Joe Malone, Montreal	44
1918-19	Newsy Lalonde, Montreal	32
1919-20	Joe Malone, Quebec Bulldogs	45
1920-21	Newsy Lalonde, Montreal	41
1921-22	Punch Broadbelt, Ottawa	46
1922-23	Babe Dye, Toronto	37
1923-24	Cy Denneny, Ottawa	23
1924-25	Babe Dye, Toronto	44
1925-26	Nels Stewart, Montreal Maroons	42
1926-27	Bill Cook, N.Y. Rangers	37
1927-28	Howie Morenz, Montreal	51
1928-29	Ace Bailey, Toronto	32
1929-30	Cooney Weiland, Boston	73
1930-31	Howie Morenz, Montreal	51
1931-32	Harvey Jackson, Toronto	53
1932-33	Bill Cook, N.Y. Rangers	50
1933-34	Charlie Conacher, Toronto	52
1934-35	Charlie Conacher, Toronto	57
1935-36	Dave Schriner, N.Y. Americans	45
1936-37	Dave Schriner, N.Y. Americans	46
1937-38	Gordie Drillion, Toronto	52
1938-39	Toe Blake, Montreal	47
1939-40	Milt Schmidt, Boston	52
1940-41	Bill Cowley, Boston	62
1941-42	Bryan Hextall, N.Y. Rangers	56
1942-43	Doug Bentley, Chicago	73
1943-44	Herbie Cain, Boston	82
1944-45	Elmer Lach, Montreal	80
1945-46	Max Bentley, Chicago	61
1946-47	Max Bentley, Chicago	72
1947-48	Elmer Lach, Montreal	61
1948-49	Roy Conacher, Chicago	68
1949-50	Ted Lindsay, Detroit	78
1950-51	Gordie Howe, Detroit	86
1951-52	Gordie Howe, Detroit	86
1952-53	Gordie Howe, Detroit	95
1953-54	Gordie Howe, Detroit	81
1954-55	Bernie Geoffrion, Montreal	75
1955-56	Jean Beliveau, Montreal	88
1956-57	Gordie Howe, Detroit	89
1957-58	Dickie Moore, Montreal	84
1958-59	Dickie Moore, Montreal	96
1959-60	Bobby Hull, Chicago	81
1960-61	Bernie Geoffrion, Montreal	95
1961-62	Bobby Hull, Chicago	84
1962-63	Gordie Howe, Detroit	86
1963-64	Stan Mikita, Chicago	89
1964-65	Stan Mikita, Chicago	87
1965-66	Bobby Hull, Chicago	97
1966-67	Stan Mikita, Chicago	97
1967-68	Stan Mikita, Chicago	87
1968-69	Phil Esposito, Boston	126
1969-70	Bobby Orr, Boston	120
1970-71	Phil Esposito, Boston	152
1971-72	Phil Esposito, Boston	133
1972-73	Phil Esposito, Boston	130
1973-74	Phil Esposito, Boston	145
1974-75	Bobby Orr, Boston	135
1975-76	Guy Lafleur, Montreal	125
1976-77	Guy Lafleur, Montreal	136
1977-78	Guy Lafleur, Montreal	132
1978-79	Bryan Trottier, N.Y. Islanders	134
1979-80	Marcel Dionne, Los Angeles	137
1980-81	Wayne Gretzky, Edmonton	164
1981-82	Wayne Gretzky, Edmonton	212
1982-83	Wayne Gretzky, Edmonton	196
1983-84	Wayne Gretzky, Edmonton	205
1984-85	Wayne Gretzky, Edmonton	208
1985-86	Wayne Gretzky, Edmonton	215
1986-87	Wayne Gretzky, Edmonton	183
1987-88	Mario Lemieux, Pittsburgh	168
1988-89	Mario Lemieux, Pittsburgh	199
1989-90	Wayne Gretzky, Los Angeles	142
1990-91	Wayne Gretzky, Los Angeles	163
1991-92	Mario Lemieux, Pittsburgh	131
1992-93	Mario Lemieux, Pittsburgh	160
1993-94	Wayne Gretzky, Los Angeles	130
1994-95	Jaromir Jagr, Pittsburgh	70

The award was originally known as the Leading Scorer Trophy. The present trophy, first given in 1947, was presented to the NHL by Art Ross, former manager-coach of the Boston Bruins. In event of a tie, the player with the most goals receives the award.

HART MEMORIAL TROPHY

(Most Valuable Player)

Season	Player, Team
1923-24	Frank Nighbor, Ottawa
1924-25	Billy Burch, Hamilton
1925-26	Nels Stewart, Montreal Maroons
1926-27	Herb Gardiner, Montreal
1927-28	Howie Morenz, Montreal
1928-29	Roy Worters, N.Y. Americans
1929-30	Nels Stewart, Montreal Maroons
1930-31	Howie Morenz, Montreal
1931-32	Howie Morenz, Montreal
1932-33	Eddie Shore, Boston
1933-34	Aurel Joliat, Montreal
1934-35	Eddie Shore, Boston
1935-36	Eddie Shore, Boston
1936-37	Babe Siebert, Montreal
1937-38	Eddie Shore, Boston
1938-39	Toe Blake, Montreal
1939-40	Ebbie Goodfellow, Detroit
1940-41	Bill Cowley, Boston
1941-42	Tom Anderson, N.Y. Americans
1942-43	Bill Cowley, Boston
1943-44	Babe Pratt, Toronto
1944-45	Elmer Lach, Montreal
1945-46	Max Bentley, Chicago
1946-47	Maurice Richard, Montreal
1947-48	Buddy O'Connor, N.Y. Rangers
1948-49	Sid Abel, Detroit
1949-50	Chuck Rayner, N.Y. Rangers
1950-51	Milt Schmidt, Boston
1951-52	Gordie Howe, Detroit
1952-53	Gordie Howe, Detroit
1953-54	Al Rollins, Chicago
1954-55	Ted Kennedy, Toronto
1955-56	Jean Beliveau, Montreal
1956-57	Gordie Howe, Detroit
1957-58	Gordie Howe, Detroit
1958-59	Andy Bathgate, N.Y. Rangers
1959-60	Gordie Howe, Detroit
1960-61	Bernie Geoffrion, Montreal
1961-62	Jacques Plante, Montreal
1962-63	Gordie Howe, Detroit
1963-64	Jean Beliveau, Montreal
1964-65	Bobby Hull, Chicago
1965-66	Bobby Hull, Chicago
1966-67	Stan Mikita, Chicago
1967-68	Stan Mikita, Chicago
1968-69	Phil Esposito, Boston
1969-70	Bobby Orr, Boston
1970-71	Bobby Orr, Boston
1971-72	Bobby Orr, Boston
1972-73	Bobby Clarke, Philadelphia
1973-74	Phil Esposito, Boston
1974-75	Bobby Clarke, Philadelphia
1975-76	Bobby Clarke, Philadelphia
1976-77	Guy Lafleur, Montreal
1977-78	Guy Lafleur, Montreal
1978-79	Bryan Trottier, N.Y. Islanders
1979-80	Wayne Gretzky, Edmonton
1980-81	Wayne Gretzky, Edmonton
1981-82	Wayne Gretzky, Edmonton
1982-83	Wayne Gretzky, Edmonton
1983-84	Wayne Gretzky, Edmonton
1984-85	Wayne Gretzky, Edmonton

Season	Player, Team
1985-86	Wayne Gretzky, Edmonton
1986-87	Wayne Gretzky, Edmonton
1987-88	Mario Lemieux, Pittsburgh
1988-89	Wayne Gretzky, Los Angeles
1989-90	Mark Messier, Edmonton
1990-91	Brett Hull, St. Louis
1991-92	Mark Messier, N.Y. Rangers
1992-93	Mario Lemieux, Pittsburgh
1993-94	Sergei Fedorov, Detroit
1994-95	Eric Lindros, Philadelphia

JAMES NORRIS MEMORIAL TROPHY

(Outstanding defenseman)

Season	Player, Team
1953-54	Red Kelly, Detroit
1954-55	Doug Harvey, Montreal
1955-56	Doug Harvey, Montreal
1956-57	Doug Harvey, Montreal
1957-58	Doug Harvey, Montreal
1958-59	Tom Johnson, Montreal
1959-60	Doug Harvey, Montreal
1960-61	Doug Harvey, Montreal
1961-62	Doug Harvey, N.Y. Rangers
1962-63	Pierre Pilote, Chicago
1963-64	Pierre Pilote, Chicago
1964-65	Pierre Pilote, Chicago
1965-66	Jacques Laperriere, Montreal
1966-67	Harry Howell, N.Y. Rangers
1967-68	Bobby Orr, Boston
1968-69	Bobby Orr, Boston
1969-70	Bobby Orr, Boston
1970-71	Bobby Orr, Boston
1971-72	Bobby Orr, Boston
1972-73	Bobby Orr, Boston
1973-74	Bobby Orr, Boston
1974-75	Bobby Orr, Boston
1975-76	Denis Potvin, N.Y. Islanders
1976-77	Larry Robinson, Montreal
1977-78	Denis Potvin, N.Y. Islanders
1978-79	Denis Potvin, N.Y. Islanders
1979-80	Larry Robinson, Montreal
1980-81	Randy Carlyle, Pittsburgh
1981-82	Doug Wilson, Chicago
1982-83	Rod Langway, Washington
1983-84	Rod Langway, Washington
1984-85	Paul Coffey, Edmonton
1985-86	Paul Coffey, Edmonton
1986-87	Ray Bourque, Boston
1987-88	Ray Bourque, Boston
1988-89	Chris Chelios, Montreal
1989-90	Ray Bourque, Boston
1990-91	Ray Bourque, Boston
1991-92	Brian Leetch, N.Y. Rangers
1992-93	Chris Chelios, Chicago
1993-94	Ray Bourque, Boston
1994-95	Paul Coffey, Detroit

VEZINA TROPHY

(Outstanding goaltender)

Season	Player, Team	GAA
1926-27	George Hainsworth, Montreal	1.52
1927-28	George Hainsworth, Montreal	1.09
1928-29	George Hainsworth, Montreal	0.98
1929-30	Tiny Thompson, Boston	2.23
1930-31	Roy Worters, N.Y. Americans	1.68
1931-32	Charlie Gardiner, Chicago	2.10
1932-33	Tiny Thompson, Boston	1.83
1933-34	Charlie Gardiner, Chicago	1.73
1934-35	Lorne Chabot, Chicago	1.83
1935-36	Tiny Thompson, Boston	1.71
1936-37	Normie Smith, Detroit	2.13
1937-38	Tiny Thompson, Boston	1.85
1938-39	Frank Brimsek, Boston	1.60
1939-40	Dave Kerr, N.Y. Rangers	1.60
1940-41	Turk Broda, Toronto	2.60
1941-42	Frank Brimsek, Boston	2.38
1942-43	Johnny Mowers, Detroit	2.48
1943-44	Bill Durnan, Montreal	2.18

Season	Player, Team	GAA
1944-45	Bill Durnan, Montreal	2.42
1945-46	Bill Durnan, Montreal	2.60
1946-47	Bill Durnan, Montreal	2.30
1947-48	Turk Broda, Toronto	2.38
1948-49	Bill Durnan, Montreal	2.10
1949-50	Bill Durnan, Montreal	2.20
1950-51	Al Rollins, Toronto	1.75
1951-52	Terry Sawchuk, Detroit	1.98
1952-53	Terry Sawchuk, Detroit	1.94
1953-54	Harry Lumley, Toronto	1.85
1954-55	Terry Sawchuk, Detroit	1.94
1955-56	Jacques Plante, Montreal	1.86
1956-57	Jacques Plante, Montreal	2.02
1957-58	Jacques Plante, Montreal	2.09
1958-59	Jacques Plante, Montreal	2.15
1959-60	Jacques Plante, Montreal	2.54
1960-61	Johnny Bower, Toronto	2.50
1961-62	Jacques Plante, Montreal	2.37
1962-63	Glenn Hall, Chicago	2.51
1963-64	Charlie Hodge, Montreal	2.26
1964-65	Terry Sawchuk, Toronto	2.56
	Johnny Bower, Toronto	2.38
1965-66	Lorne Worsley, Montreal	2.36
	Charlie Hodge, Montreal	2.58
1966-67	Glenn Hall, Chicago	2.38
	Denis DeJordy, Chicago	2.46
1967-68	Lorne Worsley, Montreal	1.98
	Rogatien Vachon, Montreal	2.48
1968-69	Glenn Hall, St. Louis	2.17
	Jacques Plante, St. Louis	1.96
1969-70	Tony Esposito, Chicago	2.17
1970-71	Ed Giacomin, N.Y. Rangers	2.15
	Gilles Villemure, N.Y. Rangers	2.29
1971-72	Tony Esposito, Chicago	1.76
	Gary Smith, Chicago	2.41
1972-73	Ken Dryden, Montreal	2.26
1973-74	Bernie Parent, Philadelphia	1.89
	Tony Esposito, Chicago	2.04
1974-75	Bernie Parent, Philadelphia	2.03
1975-76	Ken Dryden, Montreal	2.03
1976-77	Ken Dryden, Montreal	2.14
	Michel Larocque, Montreal	2.09
1977-78	Ken Dryden, Montreal	2.05
	Michel Larocque, Montreal	2.67
1978-79	Ken Dryden, Montreal	2.30
	Michel Larocque, Montreal	2.84
1979-80	Bob Sauve, Buffalo	2.36
	Don Edwards, Buffalo	2.57
1980-81	Richard Sevigny, Montreal	2.40
	Michel Larocque, Montreal	3.03
	Denis Herron, Montreal	3.50
1981-82	Billy Smith, N.Y. Islanders	2.97
1982-83	Pete Peeters, Boston	2.36
1983-84	Tom Barrasso, Buffalo	2.84
1984-85	Pelle Lindbergh, Philadelphia	3.02
1985-86	John Vanbiesbrouck, N.Y. Rangers	3.32
1986-87	Ron Hextall, Philadelphia	3.00
1987-88	Grant Fuhr, Edmonton	3.43
1988-89	Patrick Roy, Montreal	2.47
1989-90	Patrick Roy, Montreal	2.53
1990-91	Ed Belfour, Chicago	2.47
1991-92	Patrick Roy, Montreal	2.36
1992-93	Ed Belfour, Chicago	2.59
1993-94	Dominik Hasek, Buffalo	1.95
1994-95	Dominik Hasek, Buffalo	2.11

The award was formerly presented to the goaltender(s) having played a minimum of 25 games for the team with the fewest goals scored against. Beginning with the 1981-82 season, it was awarded to the outstanding goaltender.

BILL JENNINGS TROPHY

(Leading goaltender)

Season	Player, Team	GAA
1981-82	Denis Herron, Montreal	2.64
	Rick Wamsley, Montreal	2.75
1982-83	Roland Melanson, N.Y. Islanders	2.66
	Billy Smith, N.Y. Islanders	2.87
1983-84	Pat Riggin, Washington	2.66
	Al Jensen, Washington	2.91

Season	Player, Team	GAA
1984-85	Tom Barrasso, Buffalo	2.66
	Bob Sauve, Buffalo	3.22
1985-86	Bob Froese, Philadelphia	2.55
	Darren Jensen, Philadelphia	3.68
1986-87	Brian Hayward, Montreal	2.81
	Patrick Roy, Montreal	2.93
1987-88	Brian Hayward, Montreal	2.86
	Patrick Roy, Montreal	2.90
1988-89	Patrick Roy, Montreal	2.47
	Brian Hayward, Montreal	2.90
1989-90	Rejean Lemelin, Boston	2.81
	Andy Moog, Boston	2.89
1990-91	Ed Belfour, Chicago	2.47
1991-92	Patrick Roy, Montreal	2.36
1992-93	Ed Belfour, Chicago	2.59
1993-94	Dominik Hasek, Buffalo	1.95
	Grant Fuhr, Buffalo	3.68
1994-95	Ed Belfour, Chicago	2.28

The award is presented to the goaltender(s) having played a minimum of 25 games for the team with the fewest goals scored against.

CALDER MEMORIAL TROPHY

(Rookie of the year)

Season	Player, Team
1932-33	Carl Voss, Detroit
1933-34	Russ Blinco, Montreal Maroons
1934-35	Dave Schriner, N.Y. Americans
1935-36	Mike Karakas, Chicago
1936-37	Syl Apps, Toronto
1937-38	Cully Dahlstrom, Chicago
1938-39	Frank Brimsek, Boston
1939-40	Kilby Macdonald, N.Y. Rangers
1940-41	John Quilty, Montreal
1941-42	Grant Warwick, N.Y. Rangers
1942-43	Gaye Stewart, Toronto
1943-44	Gus Bodnar, Toronto
1944-45	Frank McCool, Toronto
1945-46	Edgar Laprade, N.Y. Rangers
1946-47	Howie Meeker, Toronto
1947-48	Jim McFadden, Detroit
1948-49	Pentti Lund, N.Y. Rangers
1949-50	Jack Gelineau, Boston
1950-51	Terry Sawchuk, Detroit
1951-52	Bernie Geoffrion, Montreal
1952-53	Lorne Worsley, N.Y. Rangers
1953-54	Camille Henry, N.Y. Rangers
1954-55	Ed Litzenberger, Chicago
1955-56	Glenn Hall, Detroit
1956-57	Larry Regan, Boston
1957-58	Frank Mahovlich, Toronto
1958-59	Ralph Backstrom, Montreal
1959-60	Bill Hay, Chicago
1960-61	Dave Keon, Toronto
1961-62	Bobby Rousseau, Montreal
1962-63	Kent Douglas, Toronto
1963-64	Jacques Laperriere, Montreal
1964-65	Roger Crozier, Detroit
1965-66	Brit Selby, Toronto
1966-67	Bobby Orr, Boston
1967-68	Derek Sanderson, Boston
1968-69	Danny Grant, Minnesota
1969-70	Tony Esposito, Chicago
1970-71	Gilbert Perreault, Buffalo
1971-72	Ken Dryden, Montreal
1972-73	Steve Vickers, N.Y. Rangers
1973-74	Denis Potvin, N.Y. Islanders
1974-75	Eric Vail, Atlanta
1975-76	Bryan Trottier, N.Y. Islanders
1976-77	Willi Plett, Atlanta
1977-78	Mike Bossy, N.Y. Islanders
1978-79	Bobby Smith, Minnesota
1979-80	Ray Bourque, Boston
1980-81	Peter Stastny, Quebec
1981-82	Dale Hawerchuk, Winnipeg
1982-83	Steve Larmer, Chicago
1983-84	Tom Barrasso, Buffalo
1984-85	Mario Lemieux, Pittsburgh
1985-86	Gary Suter, Calgary

Season	Player, Team
1986-87	Luc Robitaille, Los Angeles
1987-88	Joe Nieuwendyk, Calgary
1988-89	Brian Leetch, N.Y. Rangers
1989-90	Sergei Makarov, Calgary
1990-91	Ed Belfour, Chicago
1991-92	Pavel Bure, Vancouver
1992-93	Teemu Selanne, Winnipeg
1993-94	Martin Brodeur, New Jersey
1994-95	Peter Forsberg, Quebec

The award was originally known as the Leading Rookie Award. It was renamed the Calder Trophy in 1936-37 and became the Calder Memorial Trophy in 1942-43, following the death of NHL President Frank Calder.

LADY BYNG MEMORIAL TROPHY

(Most gentlemanly player)

Season	Player, Team
1924-25	Frank Nighbor, Ottawa
1925-26	Frank Nighbor, Ottawa
1926-27	Billy Burch, N.Y. Americans
1927-28	Frank Boucher, N.Y. Rangers
1928-29	Frank Boucher, N.Y. Rangers
1929-30	Frank Boucher, N.Y. Rangers
1930-31	Frank Boucher, N.Y. Rangers
1931-32	Joe Primeau, Toronto
1932-33	Frank Boucher, N.Y. Rangers
1933-34	Frank Boucher, N.Y. Rangers
1934-35	Frank Boucher, N.Y. Rangers
1935-36	Doc Romnes, Chicago
1936-37	Marty Barry, Detroit
1937-38	Gordie Drillon, Toronto
1938-39	Clint Smith, N.Y. Rangers
1939-40	Bobby Bauer, Boston
1940-41	Bobby Bauer, Boston
1941-42	Syl Apps, Toronto
1942-43	Max Bentley, Chicago
1943-44	Clint Smith, Chicago
1944-45	Bill Mosienko, Chicago
1945-46	Toe Blake, Montreal
1946-47	Bobby Bauer, Boston
1947-48	Buddy O'Connor, N.Y. Rangers
1948-49	Bill Quackenbush, Detroit
1949-50	Edgar Laprade, N.Y. Rangers
1950-51	Red Kelly, Detroit
1951-52	Sid Smith, Toronto
1952-53	Red Kelly, Detroit
1953-54	Red Kelly, Detroit
1954-55	Sid Smith, Toronto
1955-56	Earl Reibel, Detroit
1956-57	Andy Hebenton, N.Y. Rangers
1957-58	Camille Henry, N.Y. Rangers
1958-59	Alex Delvecchio, Detroit
1959-60	Don McKenney, Boston
1960-61	Red Kelly, Toronto
1961-62	Dave Keon, Toronto
1962-63	Dave Keon, Toronto
1963-64	Ken Wharram, Chicago
1964-65	Bobby Hull, Chicago
1965-66	Alex Delvecchio, Detroit
1966-67	Stan Mikita, Chicago
1967-68	Stan Mikita, Chicago
1968-69	Alex Delvecchio, Detroit
1969-70	Phil Goyette, St. Louis
1970-71	John Bucyk, Boston
1971-72	Jean Ratelle, N.Y. Rangers
1972-73	Gilbert Perreault, Buffalo
1973-74	John Bucyk, Boston
1974-75	Marcel Dionne, Detroit
1975-76	Jean Ratelle, N.Y. R.-Boston
1976-77	Marcel Dionne, Los Angeles
1977-78	Butch Goring, Los Angeles
1978-79	Bob MacMillan, Atlanta
1979-80	Wayne Gretzky, Edmonton
1980-81	Butch Goring, N.Y. Islanders
1981-82	Rick Middleton, Boston
1982-83	Mike Bossy, N.Y. Islanders
1983-84	Mike Bossy, N.Y. Islanders
1984-85	Jari Kurri, Edmonton
1985-86	Mike Bossy, N.Y. Islanders
1986-87	Joe Mullen, Calgary

Season	Player, Team
1987-88	Mats Naslund, Montreal
1988-89	Joe Mullen, Calgary
1989-90	Brett Hull, St. Louis
1990-91	Wayne Gretzky, Los Angeles
1991-92	Wayne Gretzky, Los Angeles
1992-93	Pierre Turgeon, N.Y. Islanders
1993-94	Wayne Gretzky, Los Angeles
1994-95	Ron Francis, Pittsburgh

The award was originally known as the Lady Byng Trophy. After winning the award seven times, Frank Boucher received permanent possession and a new trophy was donated to the NHL in 1936. After Lady Byng's death in 1949, the NHL changed the name to Lady Byng Memorial Trophy.

CONN SMYTHE TROPHY

(Playoff MVP)

Season	Player, Team
1964-65	Jean Beliveau, Montreal
1965-66	Roger Crozier, Detroit
1966-67	Dave Keon, Toronto
1967-68	Glenn Hall, St. Louis
1968-69	Serge Savard, Montreal
1969-70	Bobby Orr, Boston
1970-71	Ken Dryden, Montreal
1971-72	Bobby Orr, Boston
1972-73	Yvan Cournoyer, Montreal
1973-74	Bernie Parent, Philadelphia
1974-75	Bernie Parent, Philadelphia
1975-76	Reggie Leach, Philadelphia
1976-77	Guy Lafleur, Montreal
1977-78	Larry Robinson, Montreal
1978-79	Bob Gainey, Montreal
1979-80	Bryan Trottier, N.Y. Islanders
1980-81	Butch Goring, N.Y. Islanders
1981-82	Mike Bossy, N.Y. Islanders
1982-83	Billy Smith, N.Y. Islanders
1983-84	Mark Messier, Edmonton
1984-85	Wayne Gretzky, Edmonton
1985-86	Patrick Roy, Montreal
1986-87	Ron Hextall, Philadelphia
1987-88	Wayne Gretzky, Edmonton
1988-89	Al MacInnis, Calgary
1989-90	Bill Ranford, Edmonton
1990-91	Mario Lemieux, Pittsburgh
1991-92	Mario Lemieux, Pittsburgh
1992-93	Patrick Roy, Montreal
1993-94	Brian Leetch, N.Y. Rangers
1994-95	Claude Lemieux, New Jersey

BILL MASTERTON MEMORIAL TROPHY

(Sportsmanship—dedication to hockey)

Season	Player, Team
1967-68	Claude Provost, Montreal
1968-69	Ted Hampson, Oakland
1969-70	Pit Martin, Chicago
1970-71	Jean Ratelle, N.Y. Rangers
1971-72	Bobby Clarke, Philadelphia
1972-73	Lowell MacDonald, Pittsburgh
1973-74	Henri Richard, Montreal
1974-75	Don Luce, Buffalo
1975-76	Rod Gilbert, N.Y. Rangers
1976-77	Ed Westfall, N.Y. Islanders
1977-78	Butch Goring, Los Angeles
1978-79	Serge Savard, Montreal
1979-80	Al MacAdam, Minnesota
1980-81	Blake Dunlop, St. Louis
1981-82	Glenn Resch, Colorado
1982-83	Lanny McDonald, Calgary
1983-84	Brad Park, Detroit
1984-85	Anders Hedberg, N.Y. Rangers
1985-86	Charlie Simmer, Boston
1986-87	Doug Jarvis, Hartford

Season	Player, Team
1987-88	Bob Bourne, Los Angeles
1988-89	Tim Kerr, Philadelphia
1989-90	Gord Kluzak, Boston
1990-91	Dave Taylor, Los Angeles
1991-92	Mark Fitzpatrick, N.Y. Islanders
1992-93	Mario Lemieux, Pittsburgh
1993-94	Cam Neely, Boston
1994-95	Pat LaFontaine, Buffalo

Presented by the Professional Hockey Writers' Association to the player who best exemplifies the qualities of perseverance, sportsmanship and dedication to hockey.

FRANK J. SELKE TROPHY

(Best defensive forward)

Season	Player, Team
1977-78	Bob Gainey, Montreal
1978-79	Bob Gainey, Montreal
1979-80	Bob Gainey, Montreal
1980-81	Bob Gainey, Montreal
1981-82	Steve Kasper, Boston
1982-83	Bobby Clarke, Philadelphia
1983-84	Doug Jarvis, Washington
1984-85	Craig Ramsay, Buffalo
1985-86	Troy Murray, Chicago
1986-87	Dave Poulin, Philadelphia
1987-88	Guy Carbonneau, Montreal
1988-89	Guy Carbonneau, Montreal
1989-90	Rick Meagher, St. Louis
1990-91	Dirk Graham, Chicago
1991-92	Guy Carbonneau, Montreal
1992-93	Doug Gilmour, Toronto
1993-94	Sergei Fedorov, Detroit
1994-95	Ron Francis, Pittsburgh

JACK ADAMS AWARD

(Coach of the year)

Season	Coach, Team
1973-74	Fred Shero, Philadelphia
1974-75	Bob Pulford, Los Angeles
1975-76	Don Cherry, Boston
1976-77	Scotty Bowman, Montreal
1977-78	Bobby Kromm, Detroit
1978-79	Al Arbour, N.Y. Islanders
1979-80	Pat Quinn, Philadelphia
1980-81	Red Berenson, St. Louis
1981-82	Tom Watt, Winnipeg
1982-83	Orval Tessier, Chicago
1983-84	Bryan Murray, Washington
1984-85	Mike Keenan, Philadelphia
1985-86	Glen Sather, Edmonton
1986-87	Jacques Demers, Detroit
1987-88	Jacques Demers, Detroit
1988-89	Pat Burns, Montreal
1989-90	Bob Murdoch, Winnipeg
1990-91	Brian Sutter, St. Louis
1991-92	Pat Quinn, Vancouver
1992-93	Pat Burns, Toronto
1993-94	Jacques Lemaire, New Jersey
1994-95	Marc Crawford, Quebec

KING CLANCY TROPHY

(Humanitarian contributions)

Season	Player, Team
1987-88	Lanny McDonald, Calgary
1988-89	Bryan Trottier, N.Y. Islanders
1989-90	Kevin Lowe, Edmonton
1990-91	Dave Taylor, Los Angeles
1991-92	Ray Bourque, Boston
1992-93	Dave Poulin, Boston
1993-94	Adam Graves, N.Y. Rangers
1994-95	Joe Nieuwendyk, Calgary

NHL EXECUTIVE OF THE YEAR

1972-73—Sam Pollock, Montreal
1973-74—Keith Allen, Philadelphia
1974-75—Bill Torrey, N.Y. Islanders
1975-76—Sam Pollock, Montreal
1976-77—Harry Sinden, Boston
1977-78—Ted Lindsay, Detroit
1978-79—Bill Torrey, N.Y. Islanders
1979-80—Scotty Bowman, Buffalo
1980-81—Emile Francis, St. Louis
1981-82—John Ferguson, Winnipeg
1982-83—David Poile, Washington
1983-84—David Poile, Washington

1984-85—John Ferguson, Winnipeg
1985-86—Emile Francis, Hartford
1986-87—John Ferguson, Winnipeg
1987-88—Cliff Fletcher, Calgary
1988-89—Bruce McNall, Los Angeles
1989-90—Harry Sinden, Boston
1990-91—Craig Patrick, Pittsburgh
1991-92—Neil Smith, N.Y. Rangers
1992-93—Cliff Fletcher, Toronto
1993-94—Bobby Clarke, Florida
1994-95—Bobby Clarke, Philadelphia

NHL COACH OF THE YEAR

1944-45—Dick Irvin, Montreal
1945-46—Johnny Gottselig, Chicago
1979-80—Pat Quinn, Philadelphia
1980-81—Red Berenson, St. Louis
1981-82—Herb Brooks, N.Y. Rangers
1982-83—Gerry Cheevers, Boston
1983-84—Bryan Murray, Washington
1984-85—Mike Keenan, Philadelphia
1985-86—Jacques Demers, St. Louis

1986-87—Jacques Demers, Detroit
1987-88—Terry Crisp, Calgary
1988-89—Pat Burns, Montreal
1989-90—Mike Milbury, Boston
1990-91—Tom Webster, Los Angeles
1991-92—Pat Quinn, Vancouver
1992-93—Pat Burns, Toronto
1993-94—Jacques Lemaire, New Jersey
1994-95—Marc Crawford, Quebec

NOTE: The Coach of the Year Award was not given from 1946-47 through 1978-79 seasons.

ROOKIE OF THE YEAR

1967-68—E. Div.: Derek Sanderson, Boston
        W. Div.: Bill Flett, Los Angeles
1968-69—E. Div.: Brad Park, N.Y. Rangers
        W. Div.: Norm Ferguson, Oakland
1969-70—E. Div.: Tony Esposito, Chicago
        W. Div.: Bobby Clarke, Philadelphia
1970-71—E. Div.: Gil Perreault, Buffalo
        W. Div.: Jude Drouin, Minnesota
1971-72—E. Div.: Richard Martin, Buffalo
        W. Div.: Gilles Meloche, California
1972-73—E. Div.: Steve Vickers, N.Y. Rangers
        W. Div.: Bill Barber, Philadelphia
1973-74—E. Div.: Denis Potvin, N.Y. Islanders
        W. Div.: Tom Lysiak, Atlanta
1974-75—Camp. Conf.: Eric Vail, Atlanta
        Wales Conf.: Pierre Larouche, Pittsburgh
1975-76—Bryan Trottier, N.Y. Islanders
1976-77—Willi Plett, Atlanta

1977-78—Mike Bossy, N.Y. Islanders
1978-79—Bobby Smith, Minnesota
1979-80—Ray Bourque, Boston
1980-81—Peter Stastny, Quebec
1981-82—Dale Hawerchuk, Winnipeg
1982-83—Steve Larmer, Chicago
1983-84—Steve Yzerman, Detroit
1984-85—Mario Lemieux, Pittsburgh
1985-86—Wendel Clark, Toronto
1986-87—Ron Hextall, Philadelphia
1987-88—Joe Nieuwendyk, Calgary
1988-89—Brian Leetch, N.Y. Rangers
1989-90—Jeremy Roenick, Chicago
1990-91—Ed Belfour, Chicago
1991-92—Tony Amonte, N.Y. Rangers
1992-93—Teemu Selanne, Winnipeg
1993-94—Jason Arnott, Edmonton
1994-95—Peter Forsberg, Quebec

PLAYER OF THE YEAR

1967-68—E. Div.: Stan Mikita, Chicago
        W. Div.: Red Berenson, St. Louis
1968-69—E. Div.: Phil Esposito, Boston
        W. Div.: Red Berenson, St. Louis
1969-70—E. Div.: Bobby Orr, Boston
        W. Div.: Red Berenson, St. Louis
1970-71—E. Div.: Phil Esposito, Boston
        W. Div.: Bobby Hull, Chicago
1971-72—E. Div.: Jean Ratelle, N.Y. Rangers
        W. Div.: Bobby Hull, Chicago
1972-73—E. Div.: Phil Esposito, Boston
        W. Div.: Bobby Clarke, Philadelphia
1973-74—E. Div.: Phil Esposito, Boston
        W. Div.: Bernie Parent, Philadelphia
1974-75—Camp. Conf.: Bobby Clarke, Philadelphia
        Wales Conf.: Guy Lafleur, Montreal
1975-76—Bobby Clarke, Philadelphia
1976-77—Guy Lafleur, Montreal

1977-78—Guy Lafleur, Montreal
1978-79—Bryan Trottier, N.Y. Islanders
1979-80—Marcel Dionne, Los Angeles
1980-81—Wayne Gretzky, Edmonton
1981-82—Wayne Gretzky, Edmonton
1982-83—Wayne Gretzky, Edmonton
1983-84—Wayne Gretzky, Edmonton
1984-85—Wayne Gretzky, Edmonton
1985-86—Wayne Gretzky, Edmonton
1986-87—Wayne Gretzky, Edmonton
1987-88—Mario Lemieux, Pittsburgh
1988-89—Mario Lemieux, Pittsburgh
1989-90—Mark Messier, Edmonton
1990-91—Brett Hull, St. Louis
1991-92—Mark Messier, N.Y. Rangers
1992-93—Mario Lemieux, Pittsburgh
1993-94—Sergei Fedorov, Detroit
1994-95—Eric Lindros, Philadelphia

HALL OF FAME

NOTE: Leagues other than the NHL with which Hall of Fame members are associated are denoted in parentheses. Abbreviations: **AAHA:** Alberta Amateur Hockey Association. **AHA:** Amateur Hockey Association of Canada. **CAHL:** Canadian Amateur Hockey League. **EAA:** Eaton Athletic Association. **ECAHA:** Eastern Canada Amateur Hockey Association. **ECHA:** Eastern Canada Hockey Association. **FAHL:** Federal Amateur Hockey League. **IHL:** International Professional Hockey League. **MHL:** Manitoba Hockey League. **MNSHL:** Manitoba and Northwestern Senior Hockey League. **MPHL:** Maritime Pro Hockey League. **MSHL:** Manitoba Senior Hockey League. **NHA:** National Hockey Association. **NOHA:** Northern Ontario Hockey Association. **OHA:** Ontario Hockey Association. **OPHL:** Ontario Professional Hockey League. **PCHA:** Pacific Coast Hockey Association. **WCHL:** Western Canada Hockey League. **WHA:** World Hockey Association. **WHL:** Western Hockey League. **WinHL:** Winnipeg Hockey League. **WOHA:** Western Ontario Hockey Association.

PLAYERS

Player	Elec. year/ how elected*	Pos.†	First season	Last season	Stanley Cup wins‡	Teams as player
Abel, Sid	1969/P	C	1938-39	1953-54	3	Detroit Red Wings, Chicago Blackhawks
Adams, Jack	1959/P	C	1917-18	1926-27	2	Toronto Arenas, Vancouver Millionaires (PCHA), Toronto St. Pats, Ottawa Senators
Apps, Syl	1961/P	C	1936-37	1947-48	3	Toronto Maple Leafs
Armstrong, George	1975/P	RW	1949-50	1970-71	4	Toronto Maple Leafs
Bailey, Ace	1975/P	RW	1926-27	1933-34	1	Toronto Maple Leafs
Bain, Dan	1945/P	C	1895-96	1901-02	3	Winnipeg Victorias (MHL)
Baker, Hobey	1945/P	Ro.	1910	1915	0	Princeton University, St. Nicholas
Barber, Bill	1990/P	LW	1972-73	1983-84	2	Philadelphia Flyers
Barry, Marty	1965/P	C	1927-28	1939-40	2	New York Americans, Boston Bruins, Detroit Red Wings, Montreal Canadiens
Bathgate, Andy	1978/P	RW	1952-53	1974-75	1	New York Rangers, Toronto Maple Leafs, Detroit Red Wings, Pittsburgh Penguins, Vancouver Blazers (WHA)
Beliveau, Jean	1972/P	C	1950-51	1970-71	10	Montreal Canadiens
Benedict, Clint	1965/P	C	1917-18	1929-30	4	Ottawa Senators, Montreal Maroons
Bentley, Doug	1964/P	LW	1939-40	1953-54	0	Chicago Blackhawks, New York Rangers
Bentley, Max	1966/P	C	1940-41	1953-54	3	Toronto Maple Leafs, New York Rangers
Blake, Toe	1966/P	LW	1932-33	1947-48	3	Montreal Maroons, Montreal Canadiens
Boivin, Leo	1986/P	D	1951-52	1969-70	0	Toronto Maple Leafs, Boston Bruins, Detroit Red Wings, Pittsburgh Penguins, Minnesota North Stars
Boon, Dickie	1952/P	D	1897	1905	2	Montreal Monarchs, Montreal AAA (CAHL), Montreal Wanderers (FAHL)
Bossy, Mike	1991/P	RW	1977-78	1986-87	4	New York Islanders
Bouchard, Butch	1966/P	D	1941-42	1955-56	4	Montreal Canadiens
Boucher, Frank	1958/P	C	1921-22	1943-44	2	Ottawa Senators, Vancouver Maroons, New York Rangers
Boucher, George	1960/P	F/D	1915-16	1931-32	4	Ottawa Senators, Montreal Maroons, Chicago Blackhawks
Bower, Johnny	1976/P	G	1953-54	1969-70	0	New York Rangers, Toronto Maple Leafs
Bowie, Russell	1945/P	C	1898-99	1907-08	1	Montreal Victorias
Brimsek, Frank	1966/P	G	1938-39	1951-52	0	Boston Bruins, Chicago Blackhawks
Broadbent, Punch	1962/P	RW	1912-13	1928-29	4	Ottawa Senators, Montreal Maroons, New York Americans
Broda, Turk	1967/P	G	1936-37	1928-29	0	Toronto Maple Leafs
Bucyk, John	1981/P	LW	1955-56	1977-78	2	Detroit Red Wings, Boston Bruins
Burch, Billy	1974/P	C	1922-23	1932-33	0	Hamilton Tigers, New York Americans, Chicago Blackhawks
Cameron, Harry	1962/P	D	1912-13	1925-26	3	Toronto Blueshirts, Toronto Arenas, Montreal Wanderers, Ottawa Senators, Toronto St. Pats, Montreal Canadiens, Saskatoon (WCHL)
Cheevers, Gary	1985/P	G	1961-62	1979-80	2	Toronto Maple Leafs, Boston Bruins, Cleveland Crusaders (WHA)
Clancy, King	1958/P	D	1921-22	1936-37	3	Ottawa Senators, Toronto Maple Leafs
Clapper, Dit	1947/P	RW	1927-28	1946-47	3	Boston Bruins
Clarke, Bobby	1987/P	C	1969-70	1983-84	2	Philadelphia Flyers
Cleghorn, Sprague	1958/P	D	1909-10	1927-28	3	New York Crescents, Renfrew Creamery Kings (NHA), Montreal Wanderers, Ottawa Senators, Toronto St. Pats, Montreal Canadiens, Boston Bruins
Colville, Neil	1967/P	C/D	1935-36	1948-49	1	New York Rangers
Conacher, Charlie	1961/P	RW	1929-30	1940-41	1	Toronto Maple Leafs, Detroit Red Wings, New York Americans
Conacher, Lionel	1994/V	D	1925-26	1936-37	2	Pittsburgh Pirates, New York Americans, Montreal Maroons, Chicago Blackhawks
Connell, Alex	1958/P	G	1924-25	1936-37	2	Ottawa Senators, Detroit Red Wings, New York Americans, Montreal Maroons

Player	Elec. year/ how elected*	Pos.†	First season	Last season	Stanley Cup wins‡	Teams as player
Cook, Bill	1952/P	RW	1921-22	1936-37	2	Saskatoon, New York Rangers
Coulter, Art	1974/P	D	1931-32	1941-42	2	Chicago Blackhawks, New York Rangers
Cournoyer, Yvan	1982/P	RW	1963-64	1978-79	10	Montreal Canadiens
Cowley, Bill	1968/P	C	1934-35	1946-47	2	St. Louis Eagles, Boston Bruins
Crawford, Rusty	1962/P	LW	1912-13	1925-26	1	Quebec Bulldogs, Ottawa Senators, Toronto Arenas, Saskatoon (WCHL), Calgary (WCHL), Vancouver (WHL)
Darragh, Jack	1962/P	RW	1910-11	1923-24	4	Ottawa Senators
Davidson, Scotty	1950/P	RW	1912-13	1913-14	0	Toronto (NHA)
Day, Hap	1961/P	LW	1924-25	1937-38	1	Toronto St. Pats, Toronto Maple Leafs, New York Americans
Delvecchio, Alex	1977/P	C	1950-51	1973-74	3	Detroit Red Wings
Denneny, Cy	1959/P	LW	1914-15	1928-29	5	Toronto Shamrocks (NHA), Toronto Arenas (NHA), Ottawa Senators, Boston Bruins
Dionne, Marcel	1992/P	C	1971-72	1988-89	0	Detroit Red Wings, Los Angeles Kings, New York Rangers
Drillon, Gord	1975/P	LW	1936-37	1942-43	1	Toronto Maple Leafs, Montreal Canadiens
Drinkwater, Graham	1950/P	F/D	1892-93	1898-99	5	Montreal Victorias
Dryden, Ken	1983/P	G	1970-71	1978-79	6	Montreal Canadiens
Dumart, Woody	1992/V	LW	1935-36	1953-54	2	Boston Bruins
Dunderdale, Tommy	1974/P	C	1906-07	1923-24	0	Winnipeg Maple Leafs (MHL), Montreal Shamrocks (NHA), Quebec Bulldogs (NHA), Victoria (PCHA), Portland (PCHA), Saskatoon (WCHL), Edmonton (WCHL)
Durnam, Bill	1964/P	G	1943-44	1949-50	2	Montreal Canadiens
Dutton, Red	1958/P	D	1921-22	1935-36	0	Calgary Tigers (WCHL), Montreal Maroons, New York Americans
Dye, Babe	1970/P	RW	1919-20	1930-31	1	Toronto St. Pats, Hamilton Tigers, Chicago Blackhawks, New York Americans, Toronto Maple Leafs
Esposito, Phil	1984/P	C	1963-64	1980-81	2	Chicago Blackhawks, Boston Bruins, New York Rangers
Esposito, Tony	1988/P	G	1968-69	1983-84	1	Montreal Canadiens, Chicago Blackhawks
Farrell, Arthur	1965/P	F	1896-97	1900-01	2	Montreal Shamrocks (AHA/CAHL)
Flaman, Fern	1990/V	D	1944-45	1960-61	1	Boston Bruins, Toronto Maple Leafs
Foyston, Frank	1958/P	C	1912-13	1927-28	3	Toronto Blueshirts (NHA), Seattle Metropolitans (PCHA), Victoria Cougars (WCHL/WHL), Detroit Cougars
Fredrickson, Frank	1958/P	C	1920-21	1930-31	1	Victoria Aristocrats (PCHA), Victoria Cougars (PCHA/WCHL/WHL), Detroit Cougars, Boston Bruins, Pittsburgh Pirates, Detroit Falcons
Gadsby, Bill	1970/P	D	1946-47	1965-66	0	Chicago Blackhawks, New York Rangers, Detroit Red Wings
Gainey, Bob	1992/P	LW	1973-74	1988-89	5	Montreal Canadiens
Gardiner, Chuck	1945/P	G	1927-28	1933-34	1	Chicago Blackhawks
Gardiner, Herb	1958/P	D	1921-22	1928-29	0	Calgary Tigers (WCHL), Montreal Canadiens, Chicago Blackhawks
Gardner, Jimmy	1962/P	LW	1900-01	1914-15	3	Montreal Hockey Club (CAHL), Montreal Wanderers (FAHL/ECHA/NHA), Calumet (IHL), Pittsburgh (IHL), Montreal Shamrocks (ECAHA), New Westminster Royals (PCHA), Montreal Canadiens (NHA)
Geoffrion, Boom Boom	1972/P	RW	1950-51	1967-68	6	Montreal Canadiens, New York Rangers
Gerard, Eddie	1945/P	F/D	1913-14	1922-23	4	Ottawa Senators (NHA/NHL), Toronto St. Pats
Giacomin, Eddie	1987/P	G	1965-66	1977-78	0	New York Rangers, Detroit Red Wings
Gilbert, Rod	1982/P	RW	1960-61	1977-78	0	New York Rangers
Gilmour, Billy	1962/P	RW	1902-03	1915-16	5	Ottawa Silver Seven (CAHL/FAHL/ECAHA), Montreal Victorias (ECAHA), Ottawa Senators (ECHA/NHA)
Goheen, Moose	1952/P	D	1914	1918	0	St. Paul Athletic Club, 1920 U.S. Olympic Team
Goodfellow, Ebbie	1963/P	C	1929-30	1942-43	3	Detroit Cougars, Detroit Falcons, Detroit Red Wings
Grant, Mike	1950/P	D	1893-94	1901-02	5	Montreal Victorias (AHA/CAHL), Montreal Shamrocks (CAHL)
Green, Shorty	1962/P	RW	1923-24	1926-27	0	Hamilton Tigers, New York Americans
Griffis, Si	1950/P	Ro./D	1902-03	1918-19	2	Rat Portage Thistles (MNSHL), Kenora Thistles (MSHL), Vancouver Millionaires (PCHA)
Hainsworth, George	1961/P	G	1923-24	1936-37	2	Saskatoon Crescents (WCHL/WHL), Montreal Canadiens
Hall, Glenn	1975/P	G	1952-53	1970-71	1	Detriot Red Wings, Chicago Blackhawks, St. Louis Blues
Hall, Joe	1961/P	F/D	1903-04	1918-19	2	Winnipeg (MSHL), Quebec Bulldogs (ECAHA/NHA), Brandon (MHL), Montreal (ECAHA), Montreal Shamrocks (ECAHA/NHA), Montreal Wanderers (ECHA), Montreal Canadiens
Harvey, Doug	1973/P	D	1947-48	1968-69	6	Montreal Canadiens, New York Rangers, Detroit Red Wings, St. Louis Blues

Player	Elec. year/ how elected*	Pos.†	First season	Last season	Stanley Cup wins‡	Teams as player
Hay, George	1958/P	LW	1921-22	1933-34	0	Regina Capitals (WCHL), Portland Rosebuds (WHL), Chicago Blackhawks, Detroit Cougars, Detroit Falcons, Detroit Red Wings
Hern, Riley	1962/P	G	1906-07	1910-11	3	Montreal Wanderers (ECAHA/ECHA/NHA)
Hextall, Bryan	1969/P	RW	1936-37	1947-48	1	New York Rangers
Holmes, Hap	1972/P	G	1912-13	1927-28	0	Toronto Blueshirts (NHA), Seattle Metropolitans (PCHA), Toronto Arenas, Victoria Cougars, Detroit Cougars
Hooper, Tom	1962/P	F	1904-05	1907-08	2	Rat Portage Thistles (MNSHL), Kenora Thistles (MSHL), Montreal Wanderers (ECAHA), Montreal (ECAHA)
Horner, Red	1965/P	D	1928-29	1939-40	1	Toronto Maple Leafs
Horton, Tim	1977/P	D	1949-50	1973-74	4	Toronto Maple Leafs, New York Rangers, Pittsburgh Penguins, Buffalo Sabres
Howe, Gordie	1972/P	RW	1946-47	1979-80	4	Detroit Red Wings, Houston Aeros (WHA), New England Whalers (WHA), Hartford Whalers
Howe, Syd	1965/P	F/D	1929-30	1945-46	3	Ottawa Senators, Philadelphia Quakers, Toronto Maple Leafs, St. Louis Eagles, Detroit Red Wings
Howell, Harry	1979/P	D	1952-53	1975-76	0	New York Rangers, Oakland Seals, California Golden Seals, New York Golden Blades/ Jersey Knights (WHA), San Diego Mariners (WHA), Calgary Cowboys (WHA)
Hull, Bobby	1983/P	LW	1957-58	1979-80	1	Chicago Blackhawks, Winnipeg Jets (WHA/NHL), Hartford Whalers
Hutton, Bouse	1962/P	G	1898-99	1903-04	1	Ottawa Silver Seven (CAHL)
Hyland, Harry	1962/P	RW	1908-09	1917-18	1	Montreal Shamrocks (ECHA), Montreal Wanderers (NHA), New Westminster Royals (PCHA), Ottawa Senators
Irvin, Dick	1958/P	C	1916-17	1928-29	0	Portland Rosebuds (PCHA), Regina Capitals (WCHL), Chicago Blackhawks
Jackson, Busher	1971/P	LW	1929-30	1943-44	1	Toronto Maple Leafs, New York Americans, Boston Bruins
Johnson, Ching	1958/P	D	1926-27	1937-38	2	New York Rangers, New York Americans
Johnson, Moose	1952/P	LW/D	1903-04	1921-22	4	Montreal AAA (CAHL), Montreal Wanderers (ECAHA/ECHA/NHA), New Westminster Royals (PCHA), Portland Rosebuds (PCHA), Victoria Aristocrats (PCHA)
Johnson, Tom	1970/P	D	1947-48	1964-65	6	Montreal Canadiens, Boston Bruins
Joliat, Aurel	1947/P	LW	1922-23	1937-38	3	Montreal Canadiens
Keats, Duke	1958/P	C	1915-16	1928-29	0	Toronto Arenas (NHA), Edmonton Eskimos (WCHL/WHL), Detroit Cougars, Chicago Blackhawks
Kelly, Red	1969/P	C	1947-48	1966-67	8	Detroit Red Wings, Toronto Maple Leafs
Kennedy, Ted	1966/P	C	1942-43	1956-57	5	Toronto Maple Leafs
Keon, Dave	1986/P	C	1960-61	1981-82	4	Toronto Maple Leafs, Minnesota Fighting Saints (WHA), Indianapolis Racers (WHA), New England Whalers (WHA), Hartford Whalers
Lach, Elmer	1966/P	C	1940-41	1953-54	3	Montreal Canadiens
Lafleur, Guy	1988/P	RW	1971-72	1990-91	5	Montreal Canadiens, New York Rangers, Quebec Nordiques
Lalonde, Newsy	1950/P	C/Ro.	1904-05	1926-27	1	Cornwall (FAHL), Portage La Prairie (MHL), Toronto (OPHL), Montreal Canadiens (NHA/NHL), Renfrew Creamery Kings (NHA), Vancouver Millionaires (PCHA), Saskatoon Sheiks (WCHL), Saskatoon Crescents (WCHL/WHL), New York Americans
Laperriere, Jacques	1987/P	D	1962-63	1973-74	6	Montreal Canadiens
Lapointe, Guy	1993/P	D	1968-69	1983-84	6	Montreal Canadiens, St. Louis Blues, Boston Bruins
Laprade, Edgar	1993/V	C	1945-46	1954-55	0	New York Rangers
Laviolette, Jack	1962/P	D/LW	1903-04	1917-18	1	Montreal Nationals (FAHL), Montreal Shamrocks (ECAHA/ECHA), Montreal Canadiens (NHA/NHL)
Lehman, Hughie	1958/P	G	1908-09	1927-28	1	Berlin Dutchmen (OPHL), Galt (OPHL), New Westminster Royals (PCHA), Vancouver Millionaires, Vancouver Maroons, Chicago Blackhawks
Lemaire, Jacques	1984/P	C	1967-68	1978-79	8	Montreal Canadiens
LeSueur, Percy	1961/P	G	1905-06	1915-16	3	Smith Falls (FAHL), Ottawa Senators (ECAHA/ECHA/NHA), Toronto Shamrocks (NHA), Toronto Blueshirts (NHA)
Lewis, Herbie	1989/V	LW	1928-29	1938-39	2	Detroit Cougars, Detroit Falcons, Detroit Red Wings
Lindsay, Ted	1966/P	LW	1944-45	1964-65	4	Detroit Red Wings, Chicago Blackhawks
Lumley, Harry	1980/P	G	1943-44	1959-60	1	Detroit Red Wings, New York Rangers, Chicago Blackhawks, Toronto Maple Leafs, Boston Bruins
MacKay, Mickey	1952/P	C/Ro.	1914-15	1929-30	1	Vancouver Millionaires (PCHA), Vancouver Maroons (PCHA/WCHL/WHL),

Player	Elec. year/ how elected*	Pos.†	First season	Last season	Stanley Cup wins‡	Teams as player
						Chicago Blackhawks, Pittsburgh Pirates, Boston Bruins
Mahovlich, Frank	1981/P	LW	1956-57	1977-78	6	Toronto Maple Leafs, Detroit Red Wings, Montreal Canadiens, Toronto Toros (WHA), Birmingham Bulls (WHA)
Malone, Joe	1950/P	C/LW	1908-09	1923-24	3	Quebec (ECHA), Waterloo (OPHL), Quebec Bulldogs (NHA/NHL), Montreal Canadiens, Hamilton Tigers
Mantha, Sylvio	1960/P	D	1923-24	1936-37	3	Montreal Canadiens, Boston Bruins
Marshall, Jack	1965/P	C/D	1900-01	1916-17	6	Winnipeg Victorias, Montreal AAA (CAHL), Montreal Wanderers (FAHL/ECAHA/NHA), Montreal Montagnards (FAHL), Montreal Shamrocks (ECAHA/ECHA), Toronto Blueshirts (NHA)
Maxwell, Fred	1962/P	Ro.	1914	1925	0	Winnipeg Monarchs (MSHL), Winnipeg Falcons (MSHL)
McDonald, Lanny	1992/P	RW	1973-74	1988-89	1	Toronto Maple Leafs, Colorado Rockies, Calgary Flames
McGee, Frank	1945/P	C/Ro.	1902-03	1905-06	4	Ottawa Silver Seven
McGimsie, Billy	1962/P	F	1902-03	1906-07	1	Rat Portage Thistles (MNSHL/MSHL), Kenora Thistles (MSHL)
McNamara, George	1958/P	D	1907-08	1916-17	1	Montreal Shamrocks (ECAHA/ECHA), Waterloo (OPHL), Toronto Tecumsehs (NHA), Toronto Ontarios (NHA), Toronto Blueshirts (NHA), Toronto Shamrocks (NHA), 228th Battalion (NHA)
Mikita, Stan	1983/P	C	1958-59	1979-80	1	Chicago Blackhawks
Moore, Dickie	1974/P	RW	1951-52	1967-68	6	Montreal Canadiens, Toronto Maple Leafs, St. Louis Blues
Moran, Paddy	1958/P	G	1901-02	1916-17	2	Quebec Bulldogs (CAHL/ECAHA/ECHA/NHA), Haileybury (NHA)
Morenz, Howie	1945/P	C	1923-24	1936-37	3	Montreal Canadiens, Chicago Blackhawks, New York Rangers
Mosienko, Bill	1965/P	RW	1941-42	1954-55	0	Chicago Blackhawks
Nighbor, Frank	1947/P	LW/C	1912-13	1929-30	5	Toronto Blueshirts (NHA), Vancouver Millionaires, (PCHA), Ottawa Senators, Toronto Maple Leafs
Noble, Reg	1962/P	LW/C/D	1916-17	1932-33	3	Toronto Blueshirts (NHA), Montreal Canadiens (NHA), Toronto Arenas, Toronto St. Pats, Montreal Maroons, Detroit Cougars, Detroit Falcons, Detroit Red Wings
O'Connor, Buddy	1988/V	C	1941-42	1950-51	2	Montreal Canadiens, New York Rangers
Oliver, Harry	1967/P	F	1921-22	1936-37	1	Calgary Tigers (WCHL/WHL), Boston Bruins, New York Americans
Olmstead, Bert	1985/P	LW	1948-49	1961-62	5	Chicago Blackhawks, Montreal Canadiens, Toronto Maple Leafs
Orr, Bobby	1979/P	D	1966-67	1978-79	2	Boston Bruins, Chicago Blackhawks
Parent, Bernie	1984/P	G	1965-66	1978-79	2	Boston Bruins, Philadelphia Flyers, Toronto Maple Leafs, Philadelphia Blazers (WHA)
Park, Brad	1988/P	D	1968-69	1984-85	0	New York Rangers, Boston Bruins, Detroit Red Wings
Patrick, Lester	1947/P	D/Ro./G	1903-04	1926-27	3	Brandon, Westmount (CAHL), Montreal Wanderers (ECAHA), Edmonton Eskimos (AAHA), Renfrew Millionaires (NHA), Victoria Aristocrats (PCHA), Spokane Canaries (PCHA), Seattle Metropolitans(PCHA), Victoria Cougars (WHA), New York Rangers
Patrick, Lynn	1980/P	LW	1934-35	1945-46	1	New York Rangers
Perreault, Gilbert	1990/P	C	1970-71	1986-87	0	Buffalo Sabres
Phillips, Tommy	1945/P	LW	1902-03	1911-12	1	Montreal AAA (CAHL), Toronto Marlboros (OHA), Rat Portage Thistles, Kenora Thistles (MHL), Ottawa Senators (ECAHA), Edmonton Eskimos (AAHA), Vancouver Millionaires (PCHA)
Pilote, Pierre	1975/P	D	1955-56	168-69	1	Chicago Blackhawks, Toronto Maple Leafs
Pitre, Didier	1962/P	D/Ro./RW	1903-04	1922-23	0	Montreal Nationals (FAHL/CAHL), Montreal Shamrocks (ECAHA), Edmonton Eskimos (AAHA), Montreal Canadiens (NHA/NHL), Vancouver Millionaires (PCHA)
Plante, Jacques	1978/P	G	1952-53	1974-75	6	Montreal Canadiens, New York Rangers, St. Louis Blues, Toronto Maple Leafs, Boston Bruins, Edmonton Oilers
Potvin, Denis	1991/P	D	1973-74	1987-88	4	New York Islanders
Pratt, Babe	1966/P	D	1935-36	1946-47	2	New York Rangers, Toronto Maple Leafs, Boston Bruins
Primeau, Joe	1963/P	C	1927-28	1935-36	1	Toronto Maple Leafs
Pronovost, Marcel	1978/P	D	1950-51	1966-67	5	Detroit Red Wings, Toronto Maple Leafs
Pulford, Bob	1991/P	LW	1956-57	1971-72	4	Toronto Maple Leafs, Los Angeles Kings
Pulford, Harvey	1945/P	D	1893-94	1907-08	4	Ottawa Silver Seven/Senators (AHA/CAHL/FAHL/ECAHA)

Player	Elec. year/ how elected*	Pos.†	First season	Last season	Stanley Cup wins‡	Teams as player
Quackenbush, Bill	1976/P	D	1942-43	1955-56	0	Detroit Red Wings, Boston Bruins
Rankin, Frank	1961/P	Ro.	1906	1914	0	Stratford (OHA), Eatons (EAA), Toronto St. Michaels (OHA)
Ratelle, Jean	1985/P	C	1960-61	1980-81	0	New York Rangers, Boston Bruins
Rayner, Chuck	1973/P	G	1940-41	1952-53	0	New York Americans, New York Rangers
Reardon, Ken	1966/P	D	1940-41	1949-50	1	Montreal Canadiens
Richard, Henri	1979/P	C	1955-56	1974-75	11	Montreal Canadiens
Richard, Rocket	1961/P	RW	1942-43	1959-60	8	Montreal Canadiens
Richardson, George	1950/P		1906	1912	0	14th Regiment, Queen's University
Roberts, Gordon	1971/P	LW	1909-10	1919-20	0	Ottawa Senators (NHA), Montreal Wanderers (NHA), Vancouver Millionaires (PCHA), Seattle Metropolitans (PCHA)
Ross, Art	1945/P	D	1904-05	1917-18	2	Westmount (CAHL), Brandon (MHL), Kenora Thistles (MHL), Montreal Wanderers (ECAHA/ECHA/NHA/NHL), Haileybury (NHA), Ottawa Senators (NHA)
Russell, Blair	1965/P	RW/C	1899-00	1907-08	0	Montreal Victorias (CAHL/ECAHA)
Russell, Ernie	1965/P	Ro./C	1904-05	1913-14	4	Montreal Winged Wheelers (CAHL), Montreal Wanderers (ECAHA/NHA)
Ruttan, Jack	1962/P		1905	1913	0	Armstrong's Point, Rustler, St. John's College, Manitoba Varsity (WSHL), Winnipeg (WinHL)
Savard, Serge	1986/P	D	1966-67	1982-83	7	Montreal Canadiens, Winnipeg Jets
Sawchuk, Terry	1971/P	G	1949-50	1969-70	4	Detroit Red Wings, Boston Bruins, Toronto Maple Leafs, Los Angeles Kings, New York Rangers
Scanlan, Fred	1965/P	F	1897-98	1902-03	3	Montreal Shamrocks (AHA/CAHL), Winnipeg Victorias (MSHL)
Schmidt, Milt	1961/P	C	1936-37	1954-55	2	Boston Bruins
Schriner, Sweeney	1962/P	LW	1934-35	1945-46	2	New York Americans, Toronto Maple Leafs
Seibert, Earl	1963/P	D	1931-32	1945-46	2	New York Rangers, Chicago Blackhawks, Detroit Red Wings
Seibert, Oliver	1961/P	D	1900	1906	0	Berlin Rangers (WOHA), Houghton (IHL), Guelph (OPHL), London (OPHL)
Shore, Eddie	1947/P	D	1924-25	1939-40	2	Regina Capitals (WCHL), Edmonton Eskimos (WHL), Boston Bruins, New York Americans
Shutt, Steve	1993/P	LW	1972-73	1984-85	5	Montreal Canadiens, Los Angeles Kings
Siebert, Babe	1964/P	LW/D	1925-26	1938-39	2	Montreal Maroons, New York Rangers, Boston Bruins, Montreal Canadiens
Simpson, Joe	1962/P	D	1921-22	1930-31	0	Edmonton Eskimos (WCHL), New York Americans
Sittler, Darryl	1989/P	C	1970-71	1984-85	0	Toronto Maple Leafs, Philadelphia Flyers, Detroit Red Wings
Smith, Alf	1962/P	RW	1894-95	1907-08	4	Ottawa Silver Seven/Senators (AHA/CAHL/FAHL/ECAHA), Kenora Thistles (MHL)
Smith, Billy	1993/P	G	1971-72	1988-89	4	Los Angeles Kings, New York Islanders
Smith, Clint	1991/V	C	1936-37	1946-47	1	New York Rangers, Chicago Blackhawks
Smith, Hooley	1972/P	RW	1924-25	1940-41	2	1924 Canadian Olympic Team, Ottawa Senators, Montreal Maroons, Boston Bruins, New York Americans
Smith, Tommy	1973/P	LW/C	1905-06	1919-20	1	Ottawa Vics (FAHL), Ottawa Senators (ECAHA), Brantford (OPHL), Moncton (MPHL), Quebec Bulldogs (NHA/NHL), Toronto Ontarios (NHA), Montreal Canadiens (NHA)
Stanley, Allan	1981/P	D	1948-49	1968-69	4	New York Rangers, Chicago Blackhawks, Boston Bruins, Toronto Maple Leafs, Philadelphia Flyers
Stanley, Barney	1962/P	RW/D	1914-15	1925-26	1	Vancouver Millionaires (PCHA), Calgary Tigers (WCHL), Regina Capitals (WCHL), Edmonton Eskimos (WCHL/WHL)
Stewart, Black Jack	1964/P	D	1938-39	1951-52	2	Detroit Red Wings, Chicago Blackhawks
Stewart, Nels	1962/P	C	1925-26	1939-40	1	Montreal Maroons, Boston Bruins, New York Americans, Boston Bruins
Stuart, Bruce	1961/P	F	1989-99	1910-11	3	Ottawa Senators (CAHL/ECHA/NHA), Quebec Bulldogs (CAHL), Pittsburgh (IHL), Houghton (IHL), Portage Lake (IHL), Montreal Wanderers (ECAHA)
Stuart, Hod	1945/P	D	1898-99	1906-07	1	Ottawa Senators, Quebec Bulldogs, Calumet (IHL), Pittsburgh (IHL), Montreal Wanderers
Taylor, Cyclone	1947/P	D/Ro./C	1907-08	1922-23	2	Ottawa Senators (ECAHA/ECHA), Renfrew Creamery Kings (NHA), Vancouver Maroons (PCHA)
Thompson, Tiny	1959/P	G	1928-29	1939-40	1	Boston Bruins, Detroit Red Wings
Tretiak, Vladislav	1989/P	G	1969	1984	0	Central Red Army
Trihey, Harry	1950/P	C	1896-97	1900-01	2	Montreal Shamrocks (AHA/CAHL)
Ullman, Norm	1982/P	C	1955-56	1976-77	0	Detroit Red Wings, Toronto Maple Leafs, Edmonton Oilers (WHA)
Vezina, Georges	1945/P	G	1910-11	1925-26	2	Montreal Canadiens (NHA/NHL)
Walker, Jack	1960/P	LW/Ro.	1910-11	1927-28	3	Port Arthur, Toronto Blueshirts (NHA),

Player	Elec. year/ how elected*	Pos.†	First season	Last season	Stanley Cup wins‡	Teams as player
Walsh, Marty	1962/P	C	1905-06	1911-12	2	Seattle Metropolitans (PCHA), Victoria Cougars (WCHL/WHL), Detroit Cougars Queens University (OHA), Ottawa Senators (ECAHA/ECHA/NHA)
Watson, Harry E.	1962/P	C	1915	1931	0	St. Andrews (OHA), Aura Lee Juniors (OHA), Toronto Dentals (OHA), Toronto Granites (OHA), 1924 Canadian Olympic Team, Toronto National Sea Fleas (OHA)
Watson, Harry P.	1994/V	LW	1941-42	1956-57	5	Brooklyn Americans, Detroit Red Wings, Toronto Maple Leafs, Chicago Blackhawks
Weiland, Cooney	1971/P	C	1928-29	1938-39	0	Boston Bruins, Ottawa Senators, Detroit Red Wings
Westwick, Harry	1962/P	Ro.	1894-95	1907-08	4	Ottawa Senators/Silver Seven (AHA/CAHL/FAHL/ECAHA/), Kenora Thistles
Whitcroft, Frederick	1962/P	Ro.	1906-07	1909-10	0	Kenora Thistles (MSHL), Edmonton Eskimos (AAHA), Renfrew Millionaires (NHA)
Wilson, Gord	1962/P	D	1918	1933	0	Port Arthur War Veterans (OHA), Iroquois Falls (NOHA), Port Arthur Bearcats (OHA)
Worsley, Gump	1980/P	G	1952-53	1973-74	4	New York Rangers, Montreal Canadiens, Minnesota North Stars
Worters, Roy	1969/P	G	1925-26	1936-37	0	Pittsburgh Pirates, New York Americans, Montreal Canadiens

*Denotes whether enshrinee was elected by regular election (P) or veterans committee (V).
†Primary positions played during career: C—center; D—defense; G—goaltender; LW—left wing; Ro.—rover; RW—right wing.
‡Stanley Cup wins column refers to wins as a player in the players section and as a coach in the coaches section.

BUILDERS

Builder	Election year	Stanley Cup wins‡	Designation for induction
Adams, Charles F.	1960		Founder, Boston Bruins (1924)
Adams, Weston W.	1972		President and chairman, Boston Bruins (1936-69)
Aheam, Frank	1962		Owner, Ottawa Senators (1924-34)
Ahearne, Bunny	1977		President, International Hockey Federation (1957-75)
Allan, Sir Montagu	1945		Donator of Allan Cup, awarded anually to senior amateur champion of Canada (1908)
Allen, Keith	1992	0	Coach, Philadelphia Flyers (1967-68 and 1968-69); general manager and executive, Philadelphia Flyers (1966-present)
Ballard, Harold	1977		Owner and chief executive, Toronto Maple Leafs (1961-90)
Bauer, Father David	1989		Developer and coach of first Canadian National Hockey Team
Bickell, J.P.	1978		First president and chairman of the board, Toronto Maple Leafs (1927-51)
Bowman, Scott	1991	6	Coach, St. Louis Blues, Montreal Canadiens, Buffalo Sabres, Pittsburgh Penguins, Detroit Red Wings (1967-68 through 1979-80, 1981-82 through 1986-87 and 1991-92 through present); general manager, St. Louis Blues, Buffalo Sabres (1969-70, 1970-71 and 1979-80 through 1986-87)
Brown, George V.	1961		U.S. hockey pioneer; organizer, Boston Athletic Association hockey team (1910); general manager, Boston Arena and Boston Garden (1934-37)
Brown, Walter A.	1962		Co-owner and president, Boston Bruins (1951-64); general manager, Boston Gardens
Buckland, Frank	1975		Amateur hockey coach and manager; president and treasurer, Ontario Hockey Association
Butterfield, Jack	1980		President, American Hockey League
Calder, Frank	1947		First president, National Hockey League (1917-43)
Campbell, Angus	1964		First president, Northern Ontario Hockey Association (1919); executive, Ontario Hockey Association
Campbell, Clarence	1966		referee (1929-40); president, National Hockey League (1946-77)
Cattarinich, Joseph	1977		General manager, Montreal Canadiens (1909-10); co-owner, Montreal Canadiens (1921-35)
Dandurand, Leo	1963	1	Co-owner, Montreal Canadiens (1921-35); coach, Montreal Canadiens (1920-21 through 1924-25 and 1934-35); general manager, Montreal Canadiens (1920-21 through 1934-35)
Dilio, Frank	1964		Secretary and president, Junior Amateur Hockey Association; registrar and secretary, Quebec Amateur Hockey League (1943-62)
Dudley, George	1958		President, Canadian Amateur Hockey Association (1940-42); treasurer, Ontario Hockey Association; president, International Ice Hockey Federation
Dunn, Jimmy	1968		President, Manitoba Amateur Hockey Association (1945-51); president, Canadian Amateur Hockey Association
Eagleson, Alan	1989		Executive director, National Hockey League Players' Association
Francis, Emile	1982	0	General manager, New York Rangers, St. Louis Blues, Hartford Whalers (1964-65 through 1988-89); coach, New York Rangers, St. Louis Blues (1965-66 through 1974-75, 1976-77, 1981-82 and 1982-83); president, Hartford Whalers (1983-1993)
Gibson, Jack	1976		Organizer, International League (1903-07), world's first professional hockey league

Builder	Election year	Stanley Cup wins‡	Designation for induction
Gorman, Tommy	1963	2	Co-founder, National Hockey League (1917); coach, Ottawa Senators, New York Americans, Chicago Blackhawks, Montreal Maroons (1917-1938); general manager, Montreal Canadiens (1941-42 through 1945-46)
Griffiths, Frank	1993		Chairman, Vancouver Canucks (1974 through 1994)
Hanley, Bill	1986		Secretary-manager, Ontario Hockey Association
Hay, Charles	1974		Coordinator, 1972 series between Canada and Soviet Union; president, Hockey Canada
Hendy, Jim	1968		President, United States Hockey League; general manager, Cleveland Barons (AHL); publisher, Hockey Guide (1933-51)
Hewitt, Foster	1965		Hockey broadcaster
Hewitt, William	1947		Sports editor, Toronto Star; secretary, Ontario Hockey Association (1903-61); registrar and treasurer, Canadian Amateur Hockey Association
Hume, Fred	1962		Co-developer, Western Hockey League, New Westminster Royals
Imlach, Punch	1984	4	Coach, Toronto Maple Leafs, Buffalo Sabres (1958-59 through 1968-69, 1970-71, 1971-72 and 1979-80); general manager, Toronto Maple Leafs, Buffalo Sabres (1958-59 through 1968-69, 1970-71 through 1977-78 and 1979-80 through 1981-82)
Ivan, Tommy	1974	3	Coach, Detroit Red Wings, Chicago Blackhawks (1947-48 through 1953-54, 1956-57 and 1957-58); general manager, Chicago Blackhawks (1954-55 through 1976-77)
Jennings, Bill	1975		President, New York Rangers
Johnson, Bob	1992	1	Coach, Calgary Flames, Pittsburgh Penguins (1982-83 through 1986-87, 1990-91 and 1991-92)
Juckes, Gordon	1979		President, Saskatchewan Amateur Hockey Association; director, Canadian Amateur Hockey Association (1960-78)
Kilpatrick, General J.R.	1960		President, New York Rangers, Madison Square Garden; director, NHL Players' Pension Society; NHL Governor
Knox III, Seymour	1993		Chairman and president, Buffalo Sabres (1970-71 through present)
Leader, Al	1969		President, Western Hockey League (1944-69)
LeBel, Bob	1970		Founder and president, Interprovincial Senior League (1944-47); president, Quebec Amateur Hockey League, Canadian Amateur Hockey Association, International Ice Hockey Federation (1955-63)
Lockhart, Tommy	1965		Organizer and president, Eastern Amateur Hockey League, Amateur Hockey Association of the United States; business manager, New York Rangers
Loicq, Paul	1961		President and referee, International Ice Hockey Federation (1922-47)
Mariucci, John	1985		Minnesota hockey pioneer; coach, 1956 U.S. Olympic Team
Mathers, Frank	1992		Coach, president and general manager, Hershey Bears (AHL)
McLaughlin, Major Frederic	1963		Owner and first president, Chicago Blackhawks; general manager, Chicago Blackhawks (1926-27 through 1941-42)
Milford, Jake	1984		Coach, New York Rangers organization; general manager, Los Angeles Kings, Vancouver Canucks (1973-74 through 1981-82)
Molson, Senator Hartland De Montarville	1973		President and chairman, Montreal Canadiens (1957-68)
Nelson, Francis	1947		Sports editor, Toronto Globe; vice president, Ontario Hockey Association (1903-05); Governor, Amateur Athletic Union of Canada
Norris, Bruce	1969		Owner, Detroit Red Wings, Olympic Stadium (1955-82)
Norris, James	1958		Co-owner, Detroit Red Wings (1933-43)
Norris, James D.	1962		Co-owner, Detroit Red Wings (1933-43), Chicago Blackhawks (1946-66)
Northey, William	1947		President, Montreal Amateur Athletic Association; managing director, Montreal Forum; first trustee, Allan Cup (1908)
O'Brien, J. Ambrose	1962		Organizer, National Hockey Association (1909); co-founder, Montreal Canadiens
O'Neil, Brian	1994		Director of administration, NHL (1966); executive director, NHL (1971); executive vice-president, NHL (1977)
Page, Fred	1993		President, Canadian Amateur Hockey Association (1966-68); chairman of the board, British Columbia Junior Hockey League (1983 through present)
Patrick, Frank	1958		Co-organizer and president, Pacific Coast Hockey Association (1911); owner, manager, player/coach, Vancouver Millionaires (PCHA), managing director, National Hockey League; coach, Boston Bruins (1934-35 and 1935-36); manager, Montreal Canadiens
Pickard, Allan	1958		President, Saskatchewan Amateur Hockey Association, Saskatchewan Senior League, Western Canada Senior League; governor, Saskatchewan Junior League, Western Canada Junior League; president, Canadian Amateur Hockey Association (1947-50)
Pilous, Rudy	1985	1	Coach, Chicago Blackhawks, Winnipeg Jets (1957-58 through 1962-63 and 1974-75); manager, Winnipeg Jets (WHA); scout, Detroit Red Wings, Los Angeles Kings
Poile, Bud	1990		General manager, Philadelphia Flyers, Vancouver Canucks (1967-68 through 1972-73); vice president, World Hockey Association; commissioner, Central Hockey League, International Hockey League
Pollock, Sam	1978		Director of personnel, Montreal Canadiens (1950-64); general manager, Montreal Canadiens (1964-65 through 1977-78)
Raymond, Sen. Donat	1958		President, Canadian Arena Company (Montreal Maroons, Montreal Canadiens) (1924-25 through 1955); chairman, Canadian Arena Company (1955-63)
Robertson, John Ross	1947		President, Ontario Hockey Association (1901-05)

Builder	Election year	Stanley Cup wins‡	Designation for induction
Robinson, Claude	1947		First secretary, Canadian Amateur Hockey Association (1914); manager, 1932 Canadian Olympic Team
Ross, Philip	1976		Trustee, Stanley Cup (1893-1949)
Selke, Frank	1960		Assistant general manager, Toronto Maple Leafs; general manager, Montreal Canadiens (1946-47 through 1963-64)
Sinden, Harry	1983	1	Coach, Boston Bruins (1966-67 through 1969-70, 1979-80 and 1984-85); coach, 1972 Team Canada; general manager, Boston Bruins (1972-73 through present)
Smith, Frank	1962		Co-founder and secretary, Beaches Hockey League (later Metropolitan Toronto Hockey League (1911-62)
Smyth, Conn	1958	0	President, Toronto Maple Leafs, Maple Leaf Gardens, general manager, Toronto Maple Leafs (1927-28 through 1956-57); coach, Toronto Maple Leafs (1926-27 through 1930-31)
Snider, Ed	1988		Owner, Philadelphia Flyers (1967-68 through present)
Stanley of Preston, Lord	1945		Donator, Stanley Cup (1893)
Sutherland, Capt. James	1947		President, Ontario Hockey Association (1915-17); president, Canadian Amateur Hockey Association (1919-21)
Tarasov, Anatoli	1974		Coach, Soviet National Team
Turner, Lloyd	1958		Co-organizer, Western Canadian Hockey League (1918); organizer, Calgary Tigers
Tutt, Thayer	1978		President, International Ice Hockey Federation (1966-69), Amateur Hockey Association of the United States
Voss, Carl	1974		President, U.S. Hockey League; first NHL referee-in-chief
Waghorne, Fred	1961		Pioneer and hockey official, Toronto Hockey League
Wirtz, Arthur	1971		Co-owner, Detroit Red Wings, Olympia Stadium, Chicago Stadium, St. Louis Arena, Madison Square Garden, Chicago Blackhawks
Wirtz, Bill	1976		President, Chicago Blackhawks (1966 through present); chairman, NHL Board of Governors
Ziegler, John	1987		President, National Hockey League (1977-92)

REFEREES/LINESMEN

Referee/linesman	Election year	First season	Last season	Position
Armstrong, Neil	1991	1957	1977	Linesman and referee
Ashley, John	1981	1959	1972	Referee
Chadwick, Bill	1964	1940	1955	Linesman and referee
D'Amico, John	1993	1964-65	1987-88	Linesman
Elliott, Chaucer	1961	1903	1913	Referee (OHA)
Hayes, George	1988	1946-47	1964-65	Linesman
Hewitson, Bobby	1963	1924	1934	Referee
Ion, Mickey	1961	1913	1943	Referee (PCHL/NHL)
Pavelich, Marty	1987	1956-57	1978-79	Linesman
Rodden, Mike	1962			Referee
Smeaton, Cooper	1961			Referee (NHA/NHL); referee-in-chief (NHL) (1931-37); trustee, Stanley Cup (1946-78)
Storey, Red	1967	1951	1959	Referee
Udvari, Frank	1973	1951-52	1965-66	Referee; supervisor of NHL officials

‡Stanley Cup wins column refers to wins as a player in the players section and as a coach in the coaches section.

MILESTONES

(Players active in the NHL in the 1994-95 season are in boldface.)

CAREER

☐ FORWARDS AND DEFENSEMEN ☐

20 SEASONS

Rk.	Player (Pos.)	No.
1.	Gordie Howe (RW)	26
2.	Alex Delvecchio (C)	24
	Tim Horton (D)	24
4.	John Bucyk (LW)	23
5.	Stan Mikita (D)	22
	Doug Mohns (D)	22
	Dean Prentice (LW)	22
8.	George Armstrong (RW)	21
	Harry Howell (D)	21
	Eric Nesterenko (RW)	21
	Marcel Pronovost (D)	21
	Jean Ratelle (D)	21
	Allan Stanley (D)	21
	Ron Stewart (RW)	21
15.	Jean Beliveau (C)	20
	Bill Gadsby (D)	20
	Red Kelly (C)	20
	Henri Richard (C)	20
	Larry Robinson (D)	20
	Norm Ullman (C)	20

Total number of players: (20)

1,200 GAMES

Rk.	Player (Pos.)	No.
1.	Gordie Howe (RW)	1,767
2.	Alex Delvecchio (C)	1,549
3.	John Bucyk (LW)	1,540
4.	Tim Horton (D)	1,446
5.	Harry Howell (D)	1,411
6.	Norm Ullman (C)	1,410
7.	Stan Mikita (C)	1,394
8.	Doug Mohns (D)	1,390
9.	Larry Robinson (D)	1,384
10.	Dean Prentice (LW)	1,378
11.	Ron Stewart (RW)	1,353
12.	Marcel Dionne (C)	1,348
13.	Red Kelly (C)	1,316
14.	Dave Keon (C)	1,296
15.	Phil Esposito (C)	1,282
16.	Jean Ratelle (C)	1,281
17.	Bryan Trottier (C)	1,279
18.	Henri Richard (C)	1,256
19.	Bill Gadsby (D)	1,248
20.	Allan Stanley (D)	1,244
21.	Eddie Westfall (RW)	1,227
22.	Eric Nesterenko (RW)	1,219
23.	Marcel Pronovost (D)	1,206

Total number of players: (23)

500 GOALS

Rk.	Player (Pos.)	No.
1.	**Wayne Gretzky (C)**	**814**
2.	Gordie Howe (RW)	801
3.	Marcel Dionne (C)	731
4.	Phil Esposito (C)	717
5.	**Mike Gartner (RW)**	**629**
6.	Bobby Hull (LW)	610
7.	Mike Bossy (RW)	573
8.	**Jari Kurri (RW)**	**565**
9.	Guy Lafleur (RW)	560

Rk.	Player (Pos.)	No.
10.	John Bucyk (LW)	556
11.	Michel Goulet (LW)	548
12.	Maurice Richard (RW)	544
13.	Stan Mikita (C)	541
14.	Frank Mahovlich (LW)	533
15.	**Dino Ciccarelli (RW)**	**529**
16.	Bryan Trottier (C)	524
17.	Gilbert Perreault (C)	512
18.	Jean Beliveau (C)	507
19.	Lanny McDonald (RW)	500

Total number of players: (19)

700 ASSISTS

Rk.	Player (Pos.)	No.
1.	**Wayne Gretzky (C)**	**1,692**
2.	Gordie Howe (RW)	1,049
3.	Marcel Dionne (C)	1,040
4.	**Paul Coffey (D)**	**978**
5.	Stan Mikita (C)	926
6.	**Ray Bourque (D)**	**908**
7.	Bryan Trottier (C)	901
8.	**Mark Messier (C)**	**877**
9.	Phil Esposito (C)	873
10.	Bobby Clarke (C)	852
11.	Alex Delvecchio (C)	825
	Dale Hawerchuk (C)	**825**
13.	Gilbert Perreault (C)	814
14.	John Bucyk (LW)	813
15.	**Denis Savard (C)**	**812**
16.	Guy Lafleur (RW)	793
17.	**Ron Francis (C)**	**789**
	Peter Stastny (C)	**789**
19.	Jean Ratelle (C)	776
20.	Bernie Federko (C)	761
21.	Larry Robinson (D)	750
22.	Denis Potvin (D)	742
23.	Norm Ullman (C)	739
24.	**Jari Kurri (RW)**	**731**
25.	**Mario Lemieux (C)** *	**717**
26.	Jean Beliveau (C)	712
	Larry Murphy (D)	712

Total number of players: (27)

*On medical leave of absence entire 1994-95 season.

1,000 POINTS

Rk.	Player (Pos.)	No.
1.	**Wayne Gretzky (C)**	**2,506**
2.	Gordie Howe (RW)	1,850
3.	Marcel Dionne (C)	1,771
4.	Phil Esposito (C)	1,590
5.	Stan Mikita (C)	1,467
6.	Bryan Trottier (C)	1,425
7.	John Bucyk (LW)	1,369
8.	**Mark Messier (C)**	**1,369**
9.	Guy Lafleur (RW)	1,353
10.	**Paul Coffey (D)**	**1,336**
11.	Gilbert Perreault (C)	1,326
12.	**Dale Hawerchuk (C)**	**1,314**
13.	**Jari Kurri (RW)**	**1,296**
14.	Alex Delvecchio (C)	1,281
15.	Jean Ratelle (C)	1,267
16.	**Denis Savard (C)**	**1,263**
17.	**Peter Stastny (C)**	**1,239**
18.	**Ray Bourque (D)**	**1,231**
19.	Norm Ullman (C)	1,229
20.	Jean Beliveau (C)	1,219

Rk.	Player (Pos.)	No.
21.	**Mario Lemieux (C)** *	**1,211**
22.	Bobby Clarke (C)	1,210
23.	**Mike Gartner (RW)**	**1,191**
24.	Bobby Hull (LW)	1,170
25.	**Steve Yzerman (C)**	**1,160**
26.	Michel Goulet (LW)	1,152
27.	**Ron Francis (C)**	**1,138**
28.	Bernie Federko (C)	1,130
29.	Mike Bossy (RW)	1,126
30.	Darryl Sittler (C)	1,121
31.	Frank Mahovlich (LW)	1,103
32.	**Glenn Anderson (LW)**	**1,085**
33.	**Bernie Nichols (C)**	**1,074**
34.	Dave Taylor (RW)	1,069
35.	**Dino Ciccarelli (RW)**	**1,057**
36.	Denis Potvin (D)	1,052
37.	Henri Richard (C)	1,046
38.	Bobby Smith (C)	1,036
39.	**Joey Mullen (RW)**	**1,026**
40.	Rod Gilbert (RW)	1,021
41.	**Steve Larmer (RW)**	**1,012**
42.	Lanny McDonald (RW)	1,006
43.	Brian Propp (LW)	1,004

Total number of players: (43)

*On medical leave of absence entire 1994-95 season.

1,800 PENALTY MINUTES

Rk.	Player (Pos.)	No.
1.	Dave Williams (LW)	3,966
2.	**Dale Hunter (C)**	**3,106**
3.	Chris Nilan (RW)	3,043
4.	**Tim Hunter (RW)**	**2,889**
5.	**Marty McSorley (D)**	**2,723**
6.	Willie Plett (RW)	2,572
7.	**Basil McRae (LW)**	**2,405**
8.	**Garth Butcher (D)**	**2,302**
9.	Dave Schultz (LW)	2,294
10.	**Jay Wells (D)**	**2,279**
11.	Laurie Boschman (C)	2,265
12.	Rob Ramage (D)	2,226
13.	Bryan Watson (D)	2,212
14.	**Joey Kocur (RW)**	**2,202**
15.	**Scott Stevens (D)**	**2,190**
16.	**Rick Tocchet (RW)**	**2,190**
17.	**Pat Verbeek (LW/RW)**	**2,105**
18.	Terry O'Reilly (RW)	2,095
19.	Al Secord (LW)	2,093
20.	**Bob Probert (LW)** *	**2,090**
21.	**Gord Donnelly (RW)**	**2,069**
22.	Mike Foligno (RW)	2,049
23.	Phil Russell (D)	2038
24.	Harold Snepsts (D)	2,009
25.	Andre Dupont (D)	1,986
26.	**Shane Churla (RW)**	**1,964**
27.	**Dave Manson (D)**	**1,935**
28.	**Ken Daneyko (D)**	**1,933**
29.	**Ulf Samuelsson (D)**	**1,914**
30.	**Steve Smith (D)**	**1,900**
31.	**Craig Berube (LW)**	**1,899**
32.	Garry Howatt (LW)	1,836
33.	Carol Vadnais (D)	1,813
34.	Larry Playfair (D)	1,812
35.	Ted Lindsay (LW)	1,808
36.	Jim Korn (D)	1,801

Total number of players: (36)

*Suspended entire 1994-95 season.

15 SEASONS

Rk.	Goaltender	No.
1.	Terry Sawchuk	21
	Gump Worsley	21
3.	Glenn Hall	18
	Gilles Meloche	18
	Jacques Plante	18
	Billy Smith	18
7.	Tony Esposito	16
	Eddie Johnston	16
	Harry Lumley	16
	Rogie Vachon	16
11.	Don Beaupre	15
	Johnny Bower	15
	Reggie Lemelin	15
	Cesare Maniago	15
	Andy Moog	15

Total number of goaltenders: (15)

600 GAMES

Rk.	Goaltender	No.
1.	Terry Sawchuk	971
2.	Glenn Hall	906
3.	Tony Esposito	886
4.	Gump Worsley	862
5.	Jacques Plante	837
6.	Harry Lumley	804
7.	Rogie Vachon	795
8.	Gilles Meloche	788
9.	Billy Smith	680
10.	Mike Liut	663
11.	Dan Bouchard	655
12.	Turk Broda	629
13.	Don Beaupre	623
14.	Ed Giacomin	610
15.	Bernie Parent	608
16.	Greg Millen	604

Total number of goaltenders: (16)

25,000 MINUTES

Rk.	Goaltender	No.
1.	Terry Sawchuk	57,205
2.	Glenn Hall	53,484
3.	Tony Esposito	52,585
4.	Gump Worsley	50,232
5.	Jacques Plante	49,553
6.	Harry Lumley	48,107
7.	Rogie Vachon	46,298
8.	Gilles Meloche	45,401
9.	Billy Smith	38,431
10.	Turk Broda	38,173
11.	Mike Liut	38,155
12.	Dan Bouchard	37,919
13.	Ed Giacomin	35,693
14.	Greg Millen	35,377
15.	Bernie Parent	35,136
16.	Eddie Johnston	34,209
17.	Tiny Thompson	34,174
18.	Grant Fuhr	33,647
19.	Cesare Maniago	32,570
20.	Glenn Resch	32,279
21.	Johnny Bower	32,077
22.	Kelly Hrudey	32,016
23.	Frank Brimsek	31,210
24.	John Vanbiesbrouck	30,907
25.	Patrick Roy	30,658
26.	John Roach	30,423
27.	Roy Worters	30,175
28.	Gary Smith	29,619
29.	George Hainsworth	29,415

Rk.	Goaltender	No.
30.	Roger Crozier	28,567
31.	Mike Vernon	28,385
32.	Reggie Lemelin	28,006
33.	Pete Peeters	27,699
34.	Dave Kerr	26,519
35.	Don Edwards	26,181
36.	Glen Hanlon	26,037
37.	Alex Connell	26,030
38.	Jim Rutherford	25,895
39.	Al Rollins	25,717
40.	Denis Herron	25,608
41.	Chuck Rayner	25,491
42.	Lorne Chabot	25,309
43.	Phil Myre	25,220

Total number of goaltenders: (43)

2.50 OR UNDER GOALS - AGAINST AVG.

(Goaltenders with 10,000 or more minutes)

Rk.	Goaltender	Min.	GAA
1.	Alex Connell	26,030	1.91
	George Hainsworth	29,415	1.91
3.	Chuck Gardiner	19,687	2.02
4.	Lorne Chabot	25,309	2.04
5.	Tiny Thompson	34,174	2.08
6.	Dave Kerr	26,519	2.17
7.	Ken Dryden	23,352	2.24
8.	Roy Worters	30,175	2.27
9.	Clint Benedict	22,321	2.32
10.	Norman Smith	12,297	2.32
11.	Bill Durnan	22,945	2.36
	Gerry McNeil	16,535	2.36
13.	Jacques Plante	49,553	2.38
14.	John Roach	30,423	2.46

Total number of goaltenders: (14)

200 GAMES WON

Rk.	Goaltender	No.
1.	Terry Sawchuk	435
2.	Jacques Plante	434
3.	Tony Esposito	423
4.	Glenn Hall	407
5.	Rogie Vachon	355
6.	Gump Worsley	335
7.	Harry Lumley	332
8.	Andy Moog	313
9.	Billy Smith	305
10.	Turk Broda	302
11.	Mike Liut	293
12.	Grant Fuhr	290
13.	Ed Giacomin	289
14.	Dan Bouchard	286
15.	Tiny Thompson	284
16.	Patrick Roy	277
17.	Gilles Meloche	270
	Bernie Parent	270
19.	Mike Vernon	267
20.	Tom Barrasso	266
21.	Don Beaupre	262
22.	Ken Dryden	258
23.	Frank Brimsek	252
24.	Johnny Bower	251
25.	George Hainsworth	247
26.	Pete Peeters	246
27.	Kelly Hrudey	244
28.	Eddie Johnston	236
	Reggie Lemelin	236
30.	John Vanbiesbrouck	235
31.	Glen Resch	231
32.	Gerry Cheevers	230
33.	John Roach	218
34.	Greg Millen	215
35.	Bill Durnan	208
	Don Edwards	208

Rk.	Goaltender	No.
37.	Lorne Chabot	206
	Roger Crozier	206
39.	Rick Wamsley	204
40.	Ron Hextall	203
	Dave Kerr	203

Total number of goaltenders: (41)

150 GAMES LOST

Rk.	Goaltender	No.
1.	Gump Worsley	353
2.	Gilles Meloche	351
3.	Terry Sawchuk	337
4.	Glenn Hall	327
5.	Harry Lumley	324
6.	Tony Esposito	307
7.	Rogie Vachon	291
8.	Greg Millen	284
9.	Mike Liut	271
10.	Cesare Maniago	261
11.	Eddie Johnston	256
12.	Don Beaupre	246
	Jacques Plante	246
14.	Gary Smith	237
15.	Billy Smith	233
	Roy Worters	233
17.	Dan Bouchard	232
18.	Jim Rutherford	227
19.	Turk Broda	224
	Glenn Resch	224
21.	John Vanbiesbrouck	217
22.	Kelly Hrudey	210
23.	Chuck Rayner	209
24.	Ed Giacomin	206
25.	Al Rollins	205
26.	John Roach	204
27.	Denis Herron	203
	Ron Low	203
29.	Glen Hanlon	202
30.	Phil Myre	198
31.	Tom Barrasso	197
	Roger Crozier	197
	Bernie Parent	197
34.	Johnny Bower	196
35.	Grant Fuhr	195
36.	Tiny Thompson	194
37.	Bill Ranford	190
	Ken Wregget	190
39.	Frank Brimsek	182
40.	Jim Henry	178
41.	Richard Brodeur	176
42.	Kirk McLean	174
43.	Mike Karakas	169
44.	Bill Beveridge	166
	Patrick Roy	166
46.	Reggie Lemelin	162
47.	Ron Hextall	161
	Mike Vernon	161
49.	Andy Moog	160
50.	Brian Haywood	156
51.	Alex Connell	155
	Don Edwards	155
	Pete Peeters	155
54.	Gerry Desjardins	153
	Doug Favell	153
56.	Chuck Gardiner	152
57.	Dunc Wilson	150

Total number of goaltenders: (57)

75 GAMES TIED

Rk.	Goaltender	No.
1.	Terry Sawchuk	188
2.	Glenn Hall	165

Rk.	Goaltender	No.
3.	Tony Esposito	151
4.	Gump Worsley	150
5.	Harry Lumley	143
6.	Jacques Plante	137
7.	Gilles Meloche	131
8.	Bernie Parent	121
9.	Rogie Vachon	115
10.	Dan Bouchard	113
11.	Billy Smith	105
12.	Turk Broda	101
13.	Ed Giacomin	97
14.	Cesare Maniago	96
15.	Johnny Bower	90
16.	Greg Millen	89
17.	Eddie Johnston	87
18.	Al Rollins	84
19.	Glenn Resch	82
20.	Frank Brimsek	80
21.	Don Edwards	77
	Chuck Rayner	77
23.	Denis Herron	76
	Phil Myre	76
25.	Don Beaupre	75
	Dave Kerr	75
	Tiny Thompson	75

Total number of goaltenders: (27)

25 SHUTOUTS

Rk.	Goaltender	No.
1.	Terry Sawchuk	103
2.	George Hainsworth	94
3.	Glenn Hall	84
4.	Jacques Plante	82
5.	Tiny Thompson	81
	Alex Connell	81
7.	Tony Esposito	76
8.	Lorne Chabot	73
9.	Harry Lumley	71
10.	Roy Worters	66
11.	Turk Broda	62
12.	John Roach	58
13.	Clint Benedict	57
14.	Bernie Parent	55
15.	Ed Giacomin	54
16.	Dave Kerr	51
	Rogie Vachon	51
18.	Ken Dryden	46
19.	Gump Worsley	43
20.	Charlie Gardiner	42
21.	Frank Brimsek	40
22.	Johnny Bower	37
23.	Bill Durnan	34
24.	Eddie Johnston	32
25.	Roger Crozier	30
	Cesare Maniago	30
27.	Ed Belfour	28
	Jim Henry	28
	Mike Karakas	28
	Gerry McNeil	28
	Al Rollins	28
	Patrick Roy	28
33.	Dan Bouchard	27
34.	Gerry Cheevers	26
	Glenn Resch	26
	Gary Smith	26
37.	Mike Liut	25
	Chuck Rayner	25

Total number of goaltenders: (38)

COACHES

500 GAMES

Rk.	Coach	No.
1.	Al Arbour	1,606
2.	Scott Bowman	1,572
3.	Dick Irvin	1,437
4.	Billy Reay	1,102
5.	Jack Adams	982
6.	Sid Abel	963
7.	Bryan Murray	916
8.	Toe Blake	914
9.	Punch Imlach	879
10.	Bob Berry	860
11.	Jacques Demers	856
12.	Glen Sather	842
13.	Roger Neilson	839
14.	Michel Bergeron	792
15.	Emile Francis	778
16.	Mike Keenan	772
17.	Bob Pulford	771
18.	Milt Schmidt	769
19.	Red Kelly	742
20.	Pat Quinn	738
21.	Fred Shero	734
22.	Art Ross	728
23.	Jack Evans	614
24.	Tommy Ivan	610
25.	Lester Patrick	604
26.	Hap Day	546
27.	Pat Burns	536
	Brian Sutter	536
29.	Frank Boucher	525
30.	Johnny Wilson	517
31.	Bob McCammon	511

Total number of coaches: (31)

250 GAMES WON

Rk.	Coach	No.
1.	Scott Bowman	913
2.	Al Arbour	781
3.	Dick Irvin	690
4.	Billy Reay	542
5.	Toe Blake	500
6.	Bryan Murray	467
7	Glen Sather	464
8.	Jack Adams	423
	Mike Keenan	423
10.	Punch Imlach	395
11.	Emile Francis	393
12.	Fred Shero	390
13.	Bob Berry	384
14.	Sid Abel	382
15.	Roger Neilson	381
16.	Jacques Demers	375
17.	Art Ross	361
18.	Pat Quinn	354
19.	Michel Bergeron	338
20.	Bob Pulford	336
21.	Tommy Ivan	302
22.	Pat Burns	282
23.	Lester Patrick	281
24.	Red Kelly	278
25.	Brian Sutter	273
26.	Hap Day	259
27.	Don Cherry	250
	Milt Schmidt	250

Total number of coaches: (28)

250 GAMES LOST

Rk.	Coach	No.
1.	Al Arbour	577
2.	Dick Irvin	521
3.	Sid Abel	426
4.	Scott Bowman	421
5.	Jack Adams	397
6.	Milt Schmidt	393
7.	Billy Reay	385
8.	Jacques Demers	368
9.	Bob Berry	355
10.	Michel Bergeron	350
11.	Bryan Murray	337
12.	Punch Imlach	336
13.	Red Kelly	330
14.	Roger Neilson	326
15.	Bob Pulford	305
16.	Jack Evans	303
17.	Pat Quinn	282
18.	Art Ross	277
19.	Emile Francis	273
20.	Glen Sather	268
21.	Mike Keenan	267
22.	Frank Boucher	263
	Tom Mcvie	263
24.	Toe Blake	255
25.	Tom Watt	252

Total number of coaches: (25)

100 GAMES TIED

Rk.	Coach	No.
1.	Al Arbour	248
2.	Scott Bowman	238
3.	Dick Irvin	226
4.	Billy Reay	175
5.	Jack Adams	162
6.	Toe Blake	159
7.	Sid Abel	155
8.	Punch Imlach	148
9.	Red Kelly	134
10.	Roger Neilson	132
11.	Bob Pulford	130
12.	Milt Schmidt	126
13.	Bob Berry	121
14.	Fred Shero	119
15.	Jacques Demers	113
16.	Emile Francis	112
	Tommy Ivan	112
	Bryan Murray	112
19.	Glen Sather	110
20.	Lester Patrick	107
21.	Michel Bergeron	104
22.	Pat Quinn	102

Total number of coaches: (22)

.525 WINNING PERCENTAGE

(Coaches with 300 or more games)

Rk.	Coach	Games	Pct.
1.	Scott Bowmann	1,572	.656
2.	Claude Ruel	305	.648
3.	Toe Blake	914	.634
4.	Floyd Smith	309	.626
5.	Glen Sather	842	.616
6.	Fred Shero	734	.612
7.	Gerry Cheevers	376	.604
8.	Don Cherry	480	.601
	Mike Keenan	772	.601
10.	Pat Burns	536	.594
11.	Tommy Ivan	610	.587
12.	Emile Francis	778	.577
13.	Bryan Murray	916	.571
	Billy Reay	1,102	.571
15.	Al Arbour	1,606	.564
16.	Dick Irvin	1,437	.559
17.	Art Ross	728	.558
18.	Lester Patrick	604	.554
19.	Terry Murray	373	.553
20.	Brian Sutter	536	.552
21.	Hap Day	546	.549
	Pat Quinn	738	.549

Rk.	Coach	Games	Pct.
23.	Fred Creighton	421	.548
	Bob Johnson	480	.548
25.	Harry Sinden	330	.545
26.	Punch Imlach	879	.534
27.	Terry Crisp	456	.529

Total number of coaches: (27)

STANLEY CUP CHAMPIONSHIPS

(Includes Stanley Cup championships
as NHL coach only)

Rk.	Coach	No.
1.	Toe Blake	8
2.	Scott Bowman	6
3.	Hap Day	5
4.	Al Arbour	4
	Dick Irvin	4
	Punch Imlach	4
	Glen Sather	4
8.	Jack Adams	3
	Pete Green	3
	Tommy Ivan	3
11.	Tommy Gorman	2
	Cecil Hart	2
	Lester Patrick	2
	Fred Shero	2

Total number of coaches: (14)

SEASON

☐ FORWARDS AND DEFENSEMEN ☐

60 GOALS

Season—Player (Pos.)	No.
1981-82—Wayne Gretzky (C)	92
1983-84—Wayne Gretzky (C)	87
1990-91—Brett Hull (RW)	86
1988-89—Mario Lemieux (C)*	85
1971-72—Phil Esposito (C)	76
1992-93—Alexander Mogilny (RW)	76
1992-93—Teemu Selanne (RW)	76
1984-85—Wayne Gretzky (C)	73
1989-90—Brett Hull (RW)	72
1982-83—Wayne Gretzky (C)	71
1984-85—Jari Kurri (RW)	71
1991-92—Brett Hull (RW)	70
1987-88—Mario Lemieux (C)*	70
1988-89—Bernie Nicholls (C)	70
1978-79—Mike Bossy (RW)	69
1992-93—Mario Lemieux (C)*	69
1980-81—Mike Bossy (RW)	68
1973-74—Phil Esposito (C)	68
1985-86—Jari Kurri (RW)	68
1972-73—Phil Esposito (C)	66
1982-83—Lanny McDonald (RW)	66
1988-89—Steve Yzerman (C)	65
1981-82—Mike Bossy (RW)	64
1992-93—Luc Robitaille (LW)	63
1986-87—Wayne Gretzky (C)	62
1989-90—Steve Yzerman (C)	62
1985-86—Mike Bossy (RW)	61
1974-75—Phil Esposito (C)	61
1975-76—Reggie Leach (RW)	61
1982-83—Mike Bossy (RW)	60
1992-93—Pavel Bure (RW)	60
1993-94—Pavel Bure (RW)	60
1977-78—Guy Lafleur (RW)	60
1981-82—Dennis Maruk (C)	60
1976-77—Steve Shutt (LW)	60

Total number of occurrences: (35)

*On medical leave of absence entire
1994-95 season.

50-GOAL SEASONS

Rk.	Player (Pos.)	No.	Cons.
1.	Mike Bossy (RW)	9	9
	Wayne Gretzky (C)	9	8
3.	Guy Lafleur (RW)	6	6
	Marcel Dionne (C)	6	5
5.	Phil Esposito (C)	5	5
	Brett Hull (RW)	5	5
	Steve Yzerman (C)	5	4
	Bobby Hull (LW)	5	2
9.	Michel Goulet (LW)	4	4
	Tim Kerr (C)	4	4
	Jari Kurri (C)	4	4
12.	Rick Vaive (RW)	3	3
	Mario Lemieux (C)*	3	2
	Cam Neely (RW)	3	2
	Luc Robitaille (LW)	3	1
16.	Dave Andreychuk (C)	2	2
	Pavel Bure (RW)	2	2
	Rick Martin (LW)	2	2
	Dennis Maruk (C)	2	2
	Joe Nieuwendyk (C)	2	2
	Mickey Redmond (RW)	2	2
	Jeremy Roenick (C)	2	2
	Brendan Shanahan (RW)	2	2
	Charlie Simmer (LW)	2	2
	Kevin Stevens (LW)	2	2
	Glenn Anderson (LW)	2	1
	Dino Ciccarelli (RW)	2	1
	Danny Gare (RW)	2	1
	Pat Lafontaine (C)	2	1
	Pierre Larouche (C)	2	1
	Reggie Leach (RW)	2	1
	Stephane Richer (RW)	2	1
	Blaine Stoughton (RW)	2	1
34.	Wayne Babych (RW)	1	1
	Bill Barber (LW)	1	1
	Brian Bellows (RW)	1	1
	John Bucyk (LW)	1	1
	Mike Bullard (C)	1	1
	Bob Carpenter (C/LW)	1	1
	Jimmy Carson (C)	1	1
	Guy Chouinard (C)	1	1
	Sergei Fedorov (C)	1	1
	Theoren Fleury (C)	1	1
	Mike Gartner (RW)	1	1
	Bernie Geoffrion (RW)	1	1
	Danny Grant (LW)	1	1
	Adam Graves (C)	1	1
	Vic Hadfield (LW)	1	1
	Dale Hawerchuk (C)	1	1
	Ken Hodge (RW)	1	1
	Rick Kehoe (RW)	1	1
	Gary Leeman (RW)	1	1
	Hakan Loob (RW)	1	1
	Rick MacLeish (C)	1	1
	Lanny McDonald (RW)	1	1
	Mark Messier (C)	1	1
	Rick Middleton (RW)	1	1
	Mike Modano (C)	1	1
	Alexander Mogilny (LW)	1	1
	Joe Mullen (RW)	1	1
	Bernie Nicholls (C)	1	1
	John Ogrodnick (LW)	1	1
	Jean Pronovost (RW)	1	1
	Mark Recchi (RW)	1	1
	Jacques Richard (LW)	1	1
	Maurice Richard (RW)	1	1
	Gary Roberts (LW)	1	1
	Al Secord (LW)	1	1
	Teemu Selanne (RW)	1	1
	Ray Sheppard (RW)	1	1
	Steve Shutt (LW)	1	1
	Craig Simpson (LW)	1	1
	Bryan Trottier (C)	1	1
	Pierre Turgeon (C)	1	1

Total number of players: (74)

40 GOALS BY ROOKIES

Season—Player (Pos.)	No.
1992-93—Teemu Selanne (RW)	76
1977-78—Mike Bossy (RW)	53
1987-88—Joe Nieuwendyk (C)	51
1981-82—Dale Hawerchuk (C)	45
1986-87—Luc Robitaille (LW)	45
1971-72—Rick Martin (LW)	44
1981-82—Barry Pederson (C)	44
1982-83—Steve Larmer (RW)	43
1984-85—Mario Lemieux (C)*	43
1992-93—Eric Lindros (C)	41
1980-81—Darryl Sutter (LW)	40
1983-84—Sylvain Turgeon (LW)	40
1984-85—Warren Young (C)	40

Total number of players: (13)

*On medical leave of absence entire
1994-95 season.

125 POINTS

Season—Player (Pos.)	No.
1985-86—Wayne Gretzky (C)	215
1981-82—Wayne Gretzky (C)	212
1984-85—Wayne Gretzky (C)	208
1983-84—Wayne Gretzky (C)	205
1988-89—Mario Lemieux (C)*	199
1982-83—Wayne Gretzky (C)	196
1986-87—Wayne Gretzky (C)	183
1988-89—Wayne Gretzky (C)	168
1987-88—Mario Lemieux (C)*	168
1980-81—Wayne Gretzky (C)	164
1990-91—Wayne Gretzky (C)	163
1992-93—Mario Lemieux (C)*	160
1988-89—Steve Yzerman (C)	155
1970-71—Phil Esposito (C)	152
1988-89—Bernie Nichols (C)	150
1987-88—Wayne Gretzky (C)	149
1992-93—Pat Lafontaine (C)	148
1981-82—Mike Bossy (RW)	147
1973-74—Phil Esposito (C)	145
1989-90—Wayne Gretzky (C)	142
1992-93—Adam Oates (C)	142
1985-86—Mario Lemieux (C)*	141
1970-71—Bobby Orr (D)	139
1981-82—Peter Stastny (C)	139
1985-86—Paul Coffey (D)	138
1979-80—Wayne Gretzky (C)	137
1992-93—Steve Yzerman (C)	137
1976-77—Guy Lafleur (RW)	136
1981-82—Dennis Maruk (C)	136
1980-81—Marcel Dionne (C)	135
1984-85—Jari Kurri (RW)	135
1974-75—Bobby Orr (D)	135
1978-79—Brian Trottier (C)	134
1971-72—Phil Esposito (C)	133
1977-78—Guy Lafleur (RW)	132
1992-93—Pierre Turgeon (C)	132
1992-93—Teemu Selanne (RW)	132
1990-91—Brett Hull (RW)	131
1991-92—Mario Lemieux (C)*	131
1985-86—Jari Kurri (RW)	131
1980-81—Kent Nilsson (C)	131
1987-88—Dennis Savard (C)	131
1972-73—Phil Esposito (C)	130
1978-79—Marcel Dionne (C)	130
1984-85—Dale Hawerchuck (C)	130
1993-94—Wayne Gretzky (C)	130
1989-90—Mark Messier (C)	129
1978-79—Guy Lafleur (RW)	129
1981-82—Bryan Trottier (C)	129
1974-75—Phil Esposito (C)	127
1992-93—Doug Gilmour (C)	127
1992-93—Alexander Mogilny (LW)	127
1989-90—Steve Yzerman (C)	127

Season—Player (Pos.)	No.
1968-69—Phil Esposito (C)	126
1978-79—Mike Bossy (RW)	126
1983-84—Paul Coffey (D)	**126**
1984-85—Marcel Dionne (C)	126
1975-76—Guy Lafleur (RW)	125
1979-80—Guy Lafleur (RW)	125

Total number of occurrences: (60)

*On medical leave of absence entire 1994-95 season.

100-POINT SEASONS

Rk.	Player (Pos.)	No.	Cons.
1.	**Wayne Gretzky (C)**	**14**	**13**
2.	**Mario Lemieux (RW) ***	**8**	**6**
3.	Marcel Dionne (C)	8	5
4.	Mike Bossy (LW)	7	6
	Peter Stastny (C)	7	6
	Guy Lafleur (RW)	6	6
7.	Bobby Orr (D)	6	6
	Steve Yzerman (C)	6	6
	Dale Hawerchuk (C)	6	5
	Jari Kurri (RW)	6	5
	Brian Trottier (C)	6	5
	Mark Messier (C)	6	2
13.	Dennis Savard (C)	5	2
14.	Brett Hull (RW)	4	4
	Paul Coffey (D)	4	3
	Bernie Federko (C)	4	3
	Michel Goulet (LW)	4	2
	Adam Oates (C)	4	2
	Luc Robitaille (LW)	4	2
20.	Mike Rogers (C)	3	3
	Glenn Anderson (RW)	3	2
	Bobby Clarke (C)	3	2
	Doug Gilmour (C)	3	2
	Bernie Nicholls (C)	3	2
	Mark Recchi (RW)	3	2
	Joe Sakic (C)	3	2
	Pavel Bure (RW)	2	2
	Jimmy Carson (C)	2	2
29.	Pete Mahovlich (C)	2	2
	Barry Pederson (C)	2	2
	Jeremy Roenick (C)	2	2
	Charlie Simmer (LW)	2	2
	Kevin Stevens (LW)	2	2
	Dave Taylor (C)	2	2
	Dino Ciccarelli (RW)	2	0
	Theoren Fleury (C)	2	0
	Ron Francis (C)	2	0
	Pat Lafontaine (C)	2	0
	Rick Middleton (RW)	2	0
	Kent Nilsson (C)	2	0
	Gilbert Perreault (C)	2	0
	Jean Ratelle (LW)	2	0
	Darryl Sittler (C)	2	0
	Pierre Turgeon (C)	2	0

Total number of players: (44)

*On medical leave of absence entire 1994-95 season.

75 POINTS BY ROOKIES

Season—Player (Pos.)	No.
1992-93—Teemu Selanne (RW)	**132**
1980-81—Peter Stastny (C)	**109**
1981-82—Dale Hawerchuk (C)	**103**
1992-93—Joe Juneau (C)	102
1984-85—Mario Lemieux (C) *	**100**
1981-82—Neal Broten (C)	98
1975-76—Brian Trottier (C)	95
1987-88—Joe Nieuwendyk (C)	**92**
1981-82—Barry Pederson (C)	92
1977-78—Mike Bossy (RW)	91
1982-83—Steve Larmer (RW)	**90**
1981-82—Marian Stastny (RW) ..	89
1983-84—Steve Yzerman (C)	**87**
1989-90—Sergei Makarov (RW)	**86**
1980-81—Anton Stastny (LW)	85
1986-87—Luc Robitaille (LW)	**84**
1993-94—Mikael Renberg (LW)	**82**
1986-87—Jimmy Carson (C)	**79**
1990-91—Sergei Fedorov (C)	**79**
1993-94—Alexei Yashin (C)	**79**
1971-72—Marcel Dionne (C)	77
1980-81—Larry Murphy (D)	**76**
1981-82—Mark Pavelich (C)	76
1983-84—Dave Poulin (C)	**76**
1992-93—Eric Lindros (C)	75
1980-81—Jari Kurri (RW)	**75**
1989-90—Mike Modano (C)	**75**
1979-80—Brian Propp (LW)	75
1980-81—Dennis Savard (C)	**75**

Total number of players: (29)

250 PENALTY MINUTES

Season—Player (Pos.)	No.
1974-75—Dave Schultz (LW)	472
1981-82—Paul Baxter (D)	409
1991-92—Mike Peluso (LW)	**408**
1977-78—Dave Schultz (LW)	405
1992-93—Marty McSorley (D)	**399**
1987-88—Bob Probert (LW) *	**398**
1985-86—Joey Kocur (RW)	**377**
1988-89—Tim Hunter (RW)	**375**
1975-76—Steve Durbano (D)	370
1986-87—Tim Hunter (RW)	**361**
1984-85—Chris Nilan (RW)	358
1989-90—Basil McRae (LW)	**351**
1990-91—Rob Ray (LW)	**350**
1973-74—Dave Schultz (RW)	348
1993-94—Tie Domi (RW)	**347**
1980-81—Dave Williams (LW)	343

*On medical leave of absence entire 1994-95 season.

Season—Player (Pos.)	No.
1983-84—Chris Nilan (RW)	338
1976-77—Dave Williams (LW)	338
1978-79—Dave Williams (LW)	298
1970-71—Keith Magnuson (D)	291
1979-80—Jimmy Mann (RW)	287
1982-83—Randy Holt (D)	275
1962-63—Howie Young (D)	273
1972-73—Dave Schultz (LW)	259

Total number of occurrences: (24)

*Suspended entire 1994-95 season.

GOALTENDERS

10 SHUTOUTS

Season—Goaltender	No.
1928-29—George Hainsworth	22
1925-26—Alex Connell	15
1927-28—Alex Connell	15
1969-70—Tony Esposito	15
1927-28—Hal Winkler	15
1926-27—George Hainsworth	14
1926-27—Clint Benedict	13
1926-27—Alex Connell	13
1927-28—George Hainsworth	13
1953-54—Harry Lumley	13
1928-29—John Roach	13
1928-29—Roy Worters	13
1928-29—Lorne Chabot	12
1930-31—Chuck Gardiner	12
1955-56—Glenn Hall	12
1973-74—Bernie Parent	12
1974-75—Bernie Parent	12
1951-52—Terry Sawchuk	12
1953-54—Terry Sawchuk	12
1954-55—Terry Sawchuk	12
1928-29—Tiny Thompson	12
1928-29—Clint Benedict	11
1927-28—Lorne Chabot	11
1927-28—Harry Holmes	11
1928-29—Joe Miller	11
1950-51—Terry Sawchuk	11
1932-33—Tiny Thompson	11
1938-39—Frank Brimsek	10
1926-27—Lorne Chabot	10
1928-29—Clarence Dolson	10
1976-77—Ken Dryden	10
1948-49—Bill Durnan	10
1973-74—Tony Esposito	10
1933-34—Chuck Gardiner	10
1952-53—Harry Lumley	10
1952-53—Gerry McNeil	10
1932-33—John Roach	10
1935-36—Tiny Thompson	10
1927-28—Roy Worters	10

Total number of occurrences: (39)

GAME

FORWARDS AND DEFENSEMEN

FIVE GOALS

Date	Player	Club	Opponents	Goals
December 19, 1917	Joe Malone	Montreal	at Ottawa	5
December 19, 1917	Harry Hyland	Montreal Wanderers	vs. Toronto	5
January 12, 1918	Joe Malone	Montreal	vs. Ottawa	5
February 2, 1918	Joe Malone	Montreal	vs. Toronto	5
January 10, 1920	Newsy Lalonde	Montreal	vs Toronto	6
January 31, 1920	Joe Malone	Quebec Bulldogs	vs. Toronto	7
March 6, 1920	Mickey Roach	Toronto St. Pats	vs. Quebec	5
March 10, 1920	Joe Malone	Quebec Bulldogs	vs. Ottawa	6

Date	Player	Club	Opponents	Goals
January 26, 1921	Corb Denneny	Toronto St. Pats	vs. Hamilton	6
February 16, 1921	Newsy Lalonde	Montreal	vs. Hamilton	5
March 7, 1921	Cy Denneny	Ottawa Senators	vs. Hamilton	6
December 16, 1922	Babe Dye	Toronto St. Pats	vs. Montreal	5
December 5, 1924	Redvers Green	Hamilton Tigers	at Toronto	5
December 22, 1924	Babe Dye	Toronto St. Pats	at Boston	5
January 7, 1925	Harry Broadbent	Montreal Maroons	at Hamilton	5
December 14, 1929	Pit Lepine	Montreal	vs. Ottawa	5
March 18, 1930	Howie Morenz	Montreal	vs. New York Americans	5
January 19, 1932	Charlie Conacher	Toronto	vs. New York Americans	5
February 6, 1943	Ray Getliffe	Montreal	vs. Boston	5
December 28, 1944	Maurice Richard	Montreal	vs. Detroit	5
February 3, 1944	Syd Howe	Detroit	vs. New York Rangers	6
January 8, 1947	Howie Meeker	Toronto	vs. Chicago	5
February 19, 1955	Bernie Geoffrion	Montreal	vs. New York Rangers	5
February 1, 1964	Bobby Rousseau	Montreal	vs. Detroit	5
November 7, 1968	Red Berenson	St. Louis	at Philadelphia	6
February 15, 1975	Yvan Cournoyer	Montreal	vs. Chicago	5
October 12, 1976	Don Murdoch	New York Rangers	at Minnesota	5
November 7, 1976	Darryl Sittler	Toronto	vs. Boston	6
February 2, 1977	Ian Turnbull	Toronto	vs. Detroit	5
December 23, 1978	Bryan Trottier	New York Islanders	vs. New York Rangers	5
January 15, 1979	Tim Young	Minnesota	at New York Rangers	5
January 6, 1981	John Tonelli	New York Islanders	vs. Toronto	5
February 18, 1981	**Wayne Gretzky**	**Edmonton**	**vs. St. Louis**	**5**
December 30, 1981	**Wayne Gretzky**	**Edmonton**	**vs. Philadelphia**	**5**
February 3, 1982	Grant Mulvey	Chicago	vs. St. Louis	5
February 13, 1982	Bryan Trottier	New York Islanders	vs. Philadelphia	5
March 2, 1982	Willie Lindstrom	Winnipeg	at Philadelphia	5
February 23, 1983	Mark Pavelich	New York Rangers	vs. Hartford	5
November 19, 1983	**Jari Kurri**	**Edmonton**	**vs. New Jersey**	**5**
January 8, 1984	Bengt Gustafsson	Washington	at Philadelphia	5
February 3, 1984	Pat Hughes	Edmonton	vs. Calgary	5
December 15, 1984	**Wayne Gretzky**	**Edmonton**	**at St. Louis**	**5**
February 6, 1986	**Dave Andreychuk**	**Buffalo**	**at Boston**	**5**
December 6, 1987	**Wayne Gretzky**	**Edmonton**	**vs. Minnesota**	**5**
December 31, 1988	**Mario Lemieux** *	**Pittsburgh**	**vs. New Jersey**	**5**
January 11, 1989	**Joe Nieuwendyk**	**Calgary**	**vs. Winnipeg**	**5**
March 5, 1992	Mats Sundin	Quebec	at Hartford	5
April 9, 1993	Mario Lemieux *	Pittsburgh	at New York Rangers	5
February 5, 1994	**Peter Bondra**	**Washington**	**vs. Tampa Bay**	**5**
February 17, 1994	**Mike Ricci**	**Quebec**	**vs. San Jose**	**5**
April 1, 1995	Alexei Zhamnov	Winnipeg	at Los Angeles	5

Total number of occurrences: (51)
  *On medical leave of absence entire 1994-95 season.

TEAM HISTORIES

MIGHTY DUCKS OF ANAHEIM

YEAR-BY-YEAR RECORDS

	REGULAR SEASON					PLAYOFFS			
Season	W	L	T	Pts.	Finish	W	L	Highest round	Coach
1993-94	33	46	5	71	4th/Pacific	—	—		Ron Wilson
1994-95	16	27	5	37	6th/Pacific	—	—		Ron Wilson

FIRST-ROUND ENTRY DRAFT CHOICES

Year Player, Overall, Last Amateur Team (League)	Year Player, Overall, Last Amateur Team (League)
1993—Paul Kariya, 4, University of Maine	1995—Chad Kilger, 4, Kingston (OHL)
1994—Oleg Tverdovsky, 2, Krylja Sovetov, CIS	

FRANCHISE LEADERS

Players in boldface played
for club in '94-95

FORWARDS/DEFENSEMEN

Games

Randy Ladouceur	125
Joe Sacco	125
Shaun Van Allen	125
Bobby Dollas	122
Bob Corkum	120
Peter Douris	120
Patrik Carnback	114
Garry Valk	114
Stu Grimson	108
Todd Ewen	100

Goals

Bob Corkum	33
Joe Sacco	29
Peter Douris	22
Garry Valk	21
Terry Yake	21
Patrik Carnback	18
Paul Kariya	18
Tim Sweeney	17
Bobby Dollas	16
Shaun Van Allen	16

Assists

Shaun Van Allen	46
Bob Corkum	37
Peter Douris	33
Garry Valk	33
Terry Yake	31
Tim Sweeney	28
Patrik Carnback	26
Joe Sacco	26
Bill Houlder	25
Bobby Dollas	24

Points

Bob Corkum	70
Shaun Van Allen	62
Peter Douris	55
Joe Sacco	55
Garry Valk	54
Terry Yake	52
Tim Sweeney	45
Patrik Carnback	44
Bobby Dollas	40
Bill Houlder	39
Paul Kariya	39

Penalty minutes

Todd Ewen	362
Stu Grimson	309
Garry Valk	134

Penalty minutes (Franchise Leaders right column)

Randy Ladouceur	110
Shaun Van Allen	96
David Karpa	91
Troy Loney	88
Patrik Carnback	86
Joe Sacco	84
Sean Hill	78

GOALTENDERS

Games

Guy Hebert	91
Mikhail Shtalenkov	28
Ron Tugnutt	28

Shutouts

Guy Hebert	4
Ron Tugnutt	1

Goals-against average
(1200 minutes minimum)

Guy Hebert	2.95
Ron Tugnutt	3.00
Mikhail Shtalenkov	3.24

Wins

Guy Hebert	32
Ron Tugnutt	10
Mikhail Shtalenkov	7

BOSTON BRUINS

YEAR-BY-YEAR RECORDS

	REGULAR SEASON					PLAYOFFS			
Season	W	L	T	Pts.	Finish	W	L	Highest round	Coach
1924-25	6	24	0	12	6th	—	—		Art Ross
1925-26	17	15	4	38	4th	—	—		Art Ross
1926-27	21	20	3	45	2nd/American	*2	2	Stanley Cup finals	Art Ross
1927-28	20	13	11	51	1st/American	*0	1	Semifinals	Art Ross
1928-29	26	13	5	57	1st/American	5	0	Stanley Cup champ	Cy Denneny
1929-30	38	5	1	77	1st/American	3	3	Stanley Cup finals	Art Ross
1930-31	28	10	6	62	1st/American	2	3	Semifinals	Art Ross
1931-32	15	21	12	42	4th/American	—	—		Art Ross
1932-33	25	15	8	58	1st/American	2	3	Semifinals	Art Ross
1933-34	18	25	5	41	4th/American	—	—		Art Ross
1934-35	26	16	6	58	1st/American	1	3	Semifinals	Frank Patrick
1935-36	22	20	6	50	2nd/American	1	1	Quarterfinals	Frank Patrick
1936-37	23	18	7	53	2nd/American	1	2	Quarterfinals	Art Ross
1937-38	30	11	7	67	1st/American	0	3	Semifinals	Art Ross
1938-39	36	10	2	74	1st	8	4	Stanley Cup champ	Art Ross
1939-40	31	12	5	67	1st	2	4	Semifinals	Ralph (Cooney) Weiland
1940-41	27	8	13	67	1st	8	3	Stanley Cup champ	Ralph (Cooney) Weiland

		REGULAR SEASON					PLAYOFFS		
Season	W	L	T	Pts.	Finish	W	L	Highest round	Coach
1941-42	25	17	6	56	3rd	2	3	Semifinals	Art Ross
1942-43	24	17	9	57	2nd	4	5	Stanley Cup finals	Art Ross
1943-44	19	26	5	43	5th	—	—		Art Ross
1944-45	16	30	4	36	4th	3	4	League semifinals	Art Ross
1945-46	24	18	8	56	2nd	5	5	Stanley Cup finals	Dit Clapper
1946-47	26	23	11	63	3rd	1	4	League semifinals	Dit Clapper
1947-48	23	24	13	59	3rd	1	4	League semifinals	Dit Clapper
1948-49	29	23	8	66	2nd	1	4	League semifinals	Dit Clapper
1949-50	22	32	16	60	5th	—	—		George Boucher
1950-51	22	30	18	62	4th	+1	4	League semifinals	Lynn Patrick
1951-52	25	29	16	66	4th	3	4	League semifinals	Lynn Patrick
1952-53	28	29	13	69	3rd	5	6	League semifinals	Lynn Patrick
1953-54	32	28	10	74	4th	0	4	League semifinals	Lynn Patrick
1954-55	23	26	21	67	4th	1	4	League semifinals	Lynn Patrick, Milt Schmidt
1955-56	23	34	13	59	5th	—	—		Milt Schmidt
1956-57	34	24	12	80	3rd	5	5	Stanley Cup finals	Milt Schmidt
1957-58	27	28	15	69	4th	6	6	Stanley Cup finals	Milt Schmidt
1958-59	32	29	9	73	2nd	3	4	League semifinals	Milt Schmidt
1959-60	28	34	8	64	5th	—	—		Milt Schmidt
1960-61	15	42	13	43	6th	—	—		Milt Schmidt
1961-62	15	47	8	38	6th	—	—		Phil Watson
1962-63	14	39	17	45	6th	—	—		Phil Watson, Milt Schmidt
1963-64	18	40	12	48	6th	—	—		Milt Schmidt
1964-65	21	43	6	48	6th	—	—		Milt Schmidt
1965-66	21	43	6	48	5th	—	—		Milt Schmidt
1966-67	17	43	10	44	6th	—	—		Harry Sinden
1967-68	37	27	10	84	3rd/East	0	4	Division semifinals	Harry Sinden
1968-69	42	18	16	100	2nd/East	6	4	Division finals	Harry Sinden
1969-70	40	17	19	99	2nd/East	12	2	Stanley Cup champ	Harry Sinden
1970-71	57	14	7	121	1st/East	3	4	Division semifinals	Tom Johnson
1971-72	54	13	11	119	1st/East	12	3	Stanley Cup champ	Tom Johnson
1972-73	51	22	5	107	2nd/East	1	4	Division semifinals	Tom Johnson, Bep Guidolin
1973-74	52	17	9	113	1st/East	10	6	Stanley Cup finals	Bep Guidolin
1974-75	40	26	14	94	2nd/Adams	1	2	Preliminaries	Don Cherry
1975-76	48	15	17	113	1st/Adams	5	7	Semifinals	Don Cherry
1976-77	49	23	8	106	1st/Adams	8	6	Stanley Cup finals	Don Cherry
1977-78	51	18	11	113	1st/Adams	10	5	Stanley Cup finals	Don Cherry
1978-79	43	23	14	100	1st/Adams	7	4	Semifinals	Don Cherry
1979-80	46	21	13	105	2nd/Adams	4	6	Quarterfinals	Fred Creighton, Harry Sinden
1980-81	37	30	13	87	2nd/Adams	0	3	Preliminaries	Gerry Cheevers
1981-82	43	27	10	96	2nd/Adams	6	5	Division finals	Gerry Cheevers
1982-83	50	20	10	110	1st/Adams	9	8	Conference finals	Gerry Cheevers
1983-84	49	25	6	104	1st/Adams	0	3	Division semifinals	Gerry Cheevers
1984-85	36	34	10	82	4th/Adams	2	3	Division semifinals	Gerry Cheevers, Harry Sinden
1985-86	37	31	12	86	3rd/Adams	0	3	Division semifinals	Butch Goring
1986-87	39	34	7	85	3rd/Adams	0	4	Division semifinals	Butch Goring, Terry O'Reilly
1987-88	44	30	6	94	2nd/Adams	12	6	Stanley Cup finals	Terry O'Reilly
1988-89	37	29	14	88	2nd/Adams	5	5	Division finals	Terry O'Reilly
1989-90	46	25	9	101	1st/Adams	13	8	Stanley Cup finals	Mike Milbury
1990-91	44	24	12	100	1st/Adams	10	9	Conference finals	Mike Milbury
1991-92	36	32	12	84	2nd/Adams	8	7	Conference finals	Rick Bowness
1992-93	51	26	7	109	1st/Adams	0	4	Division semifinals	Brian Sutter
1993-94	42	29	13	97	2nd/Northeast	6	7	Conference semifinals	Brian Sutter
1994-95	27	18	3	57	3rd/Northeast	1	4	Conference quarterfinals	Brian Sutter

*Won-lost record does not indicate tie(s) resulting from two-game, total-goals series that year (two-game, total-goals series were played from 1917-18 through 1935-36).
+Tied after one overtime (curfew law).

FIRST-ROUND ENTRY DRAFT CHOICES

Year Player, Overall, Last Amateur Team (League)

1969 — Don Tannahill, 3, Niagara Falls (OHL)
  Frank Spring, 4, Edmonton (WCHL)
  Ivan Boldirev, 11, Oshawa (OHL)
1970 — Reggie Leach, 3, Flin Flon (WCHL)
  Rick MacLeish, 4, Peterborough (OHL)
  Ron Plumb, 9, Peterborough (OHL)
  Bob Stewart, 13, Oshawa (OHL)
1971 — Ron Jones, 6, Edmonton (WCHL)
  Terry O'Reilly, 14, Oshawa (OHL)
1972 — Mike Bloom, 16, St. Catharines (OHL)
1973 — Andre Savard, 6, Quebec (QMJHL)
1974 — Don Laraway, 18, Swift Current (WCHL)
1975 — Doug Halward, 14, Peterborough (OHL)

Year Player, Overall, Last Amateur Team (League)

1976 — Clayton Pachal, 16, New Westminster (WCHL)
1977 — Dwight Foster, 16, Kitchener (OHL)
1978 — Al Secord, 16, Hamilton (OHL)
1979 — Ray Bourque, 8, Verdun (QMJHL)
  Brad McCrimmon, 15, Brandon (WHL)
1980 — Barry Pederson, 18, Victoria (WHL)
1981 — Norm Leveille, 14, Chicoutimi (QMJHL)
1982 — *Gord Kluzak, 1, Billings (WHL)
1983 — Nevin Markwart, 21, Regina (WHL)
1984 — Dave Pasin, 19, Prince Albert (WHL)
1985 — No first round selection
1986 — Craig Janney, 13, Boston College
1987 — Glen Wesley, 3, Portland (WHL)

Year   Player, Overall, Last Amateur Team (League)
        Stephane Quintal, 14, Granby (QMJHL)
1988—Robert Cimetta, 18, Toronto (OHL)
1989—Shayne Stevenson, 17, Kitchener (OHL)
1990—Bryan Smolinski, 21, Michigan State University
1991—Glen Murray, 18, Sudbury (OHL)
1992—Dmitri Kvartalnov, 16, San Diego (IHL)

Year   Player, Overall, Last Amateur Team (League)
1993—Kevyn Adams, 25, Miami of Ohio
1994—Evgeni Riabchikov, 21, Molot-Perm (Russia)
1995—Kyle McLaren, 9, Tacoma (WHL)
        Sean Brown, 21, Belleville (OHL)
*Designates first player chosen in draft.

FRANCHISE LEADERS

Players in boldface played
for club in '94-95

FORWARDS/DEFENSEMEN

Games

John Bucyk	1436
Ray Bourque	**1146**
Wayne Cashman	1027
Terry O'Reilly	891
Rick Middleton	881
Don Marcotte	868
Dallas Smith	861
Dit Clapper	833
Milt Schmidt	776
Woody Dumart	771

Goals

John Bucyk	545
Phil Esposito	459
Rick Middleton	402
Ray Bourque	**323**
Cam Neely	**218**
Ken Hodge	289
Wayne Cashman	277
Bobby Orr	264
Peter McNab	263
Don Marcotte	230

Assists

Ray Bourque	**908**
John Bucyk	794

Bobby Orr	624
Phil Esposito	553
Wayne Cashman	516
Rick Middleton	496
Terry O'Reilly	402
Ken Hodge	385
Bill Cowley	346
Milt Schmidt	346

Points

John Bucyk	1339
Ray Bourque	**1231**
Phil Esposito	1012
Rick Middleton	898
Bobby Orr	888
Wayne Cashman	793
Ken Hodge	674
Terry O'Reilly	606
Peter McNab	587
Milt Schmidt	575

Penalty minutes

Terry O'Reilly	2095
Mike Milbury	1552
Keith Crowder	1261
Wayne Cashman	1041
Eddie Shore	1038
Ted Green	1029

GOALTENDERS

Games

Cecil Thompson	468
Frankie Brimsek	444

Eddie Johnston	443
Gerry Cheevers	416
Gilles Gilbert	277
Jim Henry	236

Shutouts

Cecil Thompson	74
Frankie Brimsek	35
Eddie Johnston	27
Gerry Cheevers	26
Jim Henry	24
Hal Winkler	19
Gilles Gilbert	16
Don Simmons	15

Goals-against average
(2400 minutes minimum)

Hal Winkler	1.56
Cecil Thompson	1.99
Charles Stewart	2.46
John Henderson	2.52
Terry Sawchuk	2.57
Frankie Brimsek	2.58
Jim Henry	2.58

Wins

Cecil Thompson	252
Frankie Brimsek	230
Gerry Cheevers	229
Eddie Johnston	182
Gilles Gilbert	155

BUFFALO SABRES

YEAR-BY-YEAR RECORDS

	REGULAR SEASON					PLAYOFFS			
Season	W	L	T	Pts.	Finish	W	L	Highest round	Coach
1970-71	24	39	15	63	5th/East	—	—		Punch Imlach
1971-72	16	43	19	51	6th/East	—	—		Punch Imlach, Joe Crozier
1972-73	37	27	14	88	4th/East	2	4	Division semifinals	Joe Crozier
1973-74	32	34	12	76	5th/East	—	—		Joe Crozier
1974-75	49	16	15	113	1st/Adams	10	4	Stanley Cup finals	Floyd Smith
1975-76	46	21	13	105	2nd/Adams	4	5	Quarterfinals	Floyd Smith
1976-77	48	24	8	104	2nd/Adams	2	4	Quarterfinals	Floyd Smith
1977-78	44	19	17	105	2nd/Adams	3	5	Quarterfinals	Marcel Pronovost
1978-79	36	28	16	88	2nd/Adams	1	2	Preliminaries	Marcel Pronovost, Bill Inglis
1979-80	47	17	16	110	1st/Adams	9	5	Semifinals	Scotty Bowman
1980-81	39	20	21	99	1st/Adams	4	4	Quarterfinals	Roger Neilson
1981-82	39	26	15	93	3rd/Adams	1	3	Division semifinals	Jim Roberts, Scotty Bowman
1982-83	38	29	13	89	3rd/Adams	6	4	Division finals	Scotty Bowman
1983-84	48	25	7	103	2nd/Adams	0	3	Division semifinals	Scotty Bowman
1984-85	38	28	14	90	3rd/Adams	2	3	Divison semifinals	Scotty Bowman
1985-86	37	37	6	80	5th/Adams	—	—		Jim Schoenfeld, Scotty Bowman
1986-87	28	44	8	64	5th/Adams	—	—		Scotty Bowman, Craig Ramsay
									Ted Sator
1987-88	37	32	11	85	3rd/Adams	2	4	Division semifinals	Ted Sator
1988-89	38	35	7	83	3rd/Adams	1	4	Division semifinals	Ted Sator
1989-90	45	27	8	98	2nd/Adams	2	4	Division semifinals	Rick Dudley
1990-91	31	30	19	81	3rd/Adams	2	4	Division semifinals	Rick Dudley
1991-92	31	37	12	74	3rd/Adams	3	4	Division semifinals	Rick Dudley, John Muckler
1992-93	38	36	10	86	4th/Adams	4	4	Division finals	John Muckler
1993-94	43	32	9	95	4th/Northeast	3	4	Conference quarterfinals	John Muckler
1994-95	22	19	7	51	4th/Northeast	1	4	Conference quarterfinals	John Muckler

FIRST-ROUND ENTRY DRAFT CHOICES

Year	Player, Overall, Last Amateur Team (League)
1970—	*Gilbert Perreault, 1, Montreal (OHL)
1971—	Rick Martin, 5, Montreal (OHL)
1972—	Jim Schoenfeld, 5, Niagara Falls (OHL)
1973—	Morris Titanic, 12, Sudbury (OHL)
1974—	Lee Fogolin, 11, Oshawa (OHL)
1975—	Robert Sauve, 17, Laval (QMJHL)
1976—	No first round selection
1977—	Ric Seiling, 14, St. Catharines (OHL)
1978—	Larry Playfair, 13, Portland (WHL)
1979—	Mike Ramsey, 11, University of Minnesota
1980—	Steve Patrick, 20, Brandon (WHL)
1981—	Jiri Dudacek, 17, Kladno (Czechoslovakia)
1982—	Phil Housley, 6, South St. Paul H.S. (Minn.)
	Paul Cyr, 9, Victoria (WHL)
	Dave Andreychuk, 16, Oshawa (OHL)
1983—	Tom Barrasso, 5, Acton Boxboro H.S. (Mass.)
	Norm Lacombe, 10, Univ. of New Hampshire
	Adam Creighton, 11, Ottawa (OHL)

Year	Player, Overall, Last Amateur Team (League)
1984—	Bo Andersson, 18, Vastra Frolunda (Sweden)
1985—	Carl Johansson, 14, Vastra Frolunda (Sweden)
1986—	Shawn Anderson, 5, Team Canada
1987—	*Pierre Turgeon, 1, Granby (QMJHL)
1988—	Joel Savage, 13, Victoria (WHL)
1989—	Kevin Haller, 14, Regina (WHL)
1990—	Brad May, 14, Niagara Falls (OHL)
1991—	Philippe Boucher, 13, Granby (QMJHL)
1992—	David Cooper, 11, Medicine Hat (WHL)
1993—	No first round selection
1994—	Wayne Primeau, 17, Owen Sound (OHL)
1995—	Jay McKee, 14, Niagara Falls (OHL)
	Martin Biron, 16, Beauport (QMJHL)

*Designates first player chosen in draft.

FRANCHISE LEADERS

Players in boldface played
for club in '94-95

FORWARDS/DEFENSEMEN

Games

Gilbert Perreault	1191
Craig Ramsay	1070
Mike Ramsey	911
Bill Hajt	854
Don Luce	766
Dave Andreychuk	763
Rick Martin	681
Ric Seiling	664
Mike Foligno	662
Lindy Ruff	608
Phil Housley	608

Goals

Gilbert Perreault	512
Rick Martin	382
Dave Andreychuk	348
Danny Gare	267
Craig Ramsay	252
Mike Foligno	247
Rene Robert	222
Don Luce	216
Alexander Mogilny	**211**
Phil Housley	178

Assists

Gilbert Perreault	814
Dave Andreychuk	423
Craig Ramsay	420
Phil Housley	380
Rene Robert	330

Rick Martin	313
Don Luce	310
Dale Hawerchuk	**275**
Mike Foligno	264
Mike Ramsey	256

Points

Gilbert Perreault	1326
Dave Andreychuk	710
Rick Martin	771
Criag Ramsay	672
Phil Housley	558
Rene Robert	552
Don Luce	526
Mike Foligno	511
Danny Gare	500
Alexander Mogilny	**444**

Penalty minutes

Rob Ray	**1459**
Mike Foligno	1450
Larry Playfair	1390
Lindy Ruff	1126
Jim Schoenfeld	1025
Mike Ramsey	924
Mike Hartman	890
Jerry Korab	870
Brad May	**809**
Danny Gare	686

GOALTENDERS

Games

Don Edwards	307
Tom Barrasso	266
Bob Sauve	246

Daren Puppa	215
Roger Crozier	202
Jacques Cloutier	144
Dominik Hasek	**127**
Dave Dryden	120
Gerry Desjardins	116
Clint Malarchuk	102

Shutouts

Don Edwards	14
Tom Barrasso	13
Dominik Hasek	**12**
Roger Crozier	10
Bob Sauve	7

Goals-against average
(2400 minutes minimum)

Dominik Hasek	**2.24**
Gerry Desjardins	2.81
Don Edwards	2.90
Dave Dryden	3.06
Bob Sauve	3.20
Roger Crozier	3.23
Tom Barrasso	3.28
Clint Malarchuk	3.40
Daren Puppa	3.41
Grant Fuhr	**3.60**

Wins

Don Edwards	156
Tom Barrasso	124
Bob Sauve	119
Daren Puppa	96
Roger Crozier	74
Gerry Desjardins	66

CALGARY FLAMES

YEAR-BY-YEAR RECORDS

Season	W	L	T	Pts.	Finish	W	L	Highest round	Coach
1972-73*	25	38	15	65	7th/West	—	—		Bernie Geoffrion
1973-74*	30	34	14	74	4th/West	0	4	Division semifinals	Bernie Geoffrion
1974-75*	34	31	15	83	4th/Patrick	—	—		Bernie Geoffrion, Fred Creighton
1975-76*	35	33	12	82	3rd/Patrick	0	2	Preliminaries	Fred Creighton
1976-77*	34	34	12	80	3rd/Patrick	1	2	Preliminaries	Fred Creighton
1977-78*	34	27	19	87	3rd/Patrick	0	2	Preliminaries	Fred Creighton
1978-79*	41	31	8	90	4th/Patrick	0	2	Preliminaries	Fred Creighton
1979-80*	35	32	13	83	4th/Patrick	1	3	Preliminaries	Al MacNeil
1980-81	39	27	14	92	3rd/Patrick	9	7	Semifinals	Al MacNeil

Season	W	L	T	Pts.	Finish	W	L	Highest round	Coach
1981-82	29	34	17	75	3rd/Smythe	0	3	Division semifinals	Al MacNeil
1982-83	32	34	14	78	2nd/Smythe	4	5	Division finals	Bob Johnson
1983-84	34	32	14	82	2nd/Smythe	6	5	Division finals	Bob Johnson
1984-85	41	27	12	94	3rd/Smythe	1	3	Division semifinals	Bob Johnson
1985-86	40	31	9	89	2nd/Smythe	12	10	Stanley Cup finals	Bob Johnson
1986-87	46	31	3	95	2nd/Smythe	2	4	Division semifinals	Bob Johnson
1987-88	48	23	9	105	1st/Smythe	4	5	Division finals	Terry Crisp
1988-89	54	17	9	117	1st/Smythe	16	6	Stanley Cup champ	Terry Crisp
1989-90	42	23	15	99	1st/Smythe	2	4	Division semifinals	Terry Crisp
1990-91	46	26	8	100	2nd/Smythe	3	4	Division semifinals	Doug Risebrough
1991-92	31	37	12	74	5th/Smythe	—	—		Doug Risebrough, Guy Charron
1992-93	43	30	11	97	2nd/Smythe	2	4	Division semifinals	Dave King
1993-94	42	29	13	97	1st/Pacific	3	4	Conference quarterfinals	Dave King
1994-95	24	17	7	55	1st/Pacific	3	4	Conference quarterfinals	Dave King

*Atlanta Flames.

FIRST-ROUND ENTRY DRAFT CHOICES

Year   Player, Overall, Last Amateur Team (League)

1972—Jacques Richard, 2, Quebec (QMJHL)
1973—Tom Lysiak, 2, Medicine Hat (WCHL)
       Vic Mercredi, 16, New Westminster (WCHL)
1974—No first round selection
1975—Richard Mulhern, 8, Sherbrooke (QMJHL)
1976—Dave Shand, 8, Peterborough (OHL)
       Harold Phillipoff, 10, New Westminster (WCHL)
1977—No first round selection
1978—Brad Marsh, 11, London (OHL)
1979—Paul Reinhart, 12, Kitchener (OHL)
1980—Denis Cyr, 13, Montreal (OHL)
1981—Al MacInnis, 15, Kitchener (OHL)
1982—No first round selection

1983—Dan Quinn, 13, Belleville (OHL)
1984—Gary Roberts, 12, Ottawa (OHL)
1985—Chris Biotti, 17, Belmont Hill H.S. (Mass.)
1986—George Pelawa, 16, Bemidji H.S. (Minn.)
1987—Bryan Deasley, 19, University of Michigan
1988—Jason Muzzatti, 21, Michigan State University
1989—No first round selection
1990—Trevor Kidd, 11, Brandon (WHL)
1991—Niklas Sundblad, 19, AIK (Sweden)
1992—Cory Stillman, 6, Windsor (OHL)
1993—Jesper Mattsson, 18, Malmo (Sweden)
1994—Chris Dingman, 19, Brandon (WHL)
1995—Denis Gauthier, 20, Drummondville (QMJHL)

FRANCHISE LEADERS

Players in boldface played
for club in '94-95

FORWARDS/DEFENSEMEN

Games

Al MacInnis	803
Joel Otto	**730**
Jim Peplinski	705
Gary Suter	617
Jamie Macoun	586
Joe Nieuwendyk	**577**
Gary Roberts	**550**
Tim Hunter	545
Eric Vail	539
Paul Reinhart	517

Goals

Joe Nieuwendyk	**314**
Gary Roberts	**235**
Theoren Fleury	**232**
Kent Nilsson	229
Lanny McDonald	215
Al MacInnis	213
Eric Vail	206
Guy Chouinard	193
Hakan Loob	193
Joe Mullen	190

Assists

Al MacInnis	609
Gary Suter	437
Guy Chouinard	336
Paul Reinhart	335
Kent Nilsson	333
Joe Nieuwendyk	**302**

Theoren Fleury	**288**
Tom Lysiak	276
Jim Peplinski	262
Joel Otto	**261**

Points

Al MacInnis	822
Joe Nieuwendyk	**616**
Gary Suter	565
Kent Nilsson	562
Guy Chouinard	529
Theoren Fleury	**520**
Gary Roberts	**463**
Eric Vail	452
Paul Reinhart	444
Tom Lysiak	431

Penalty minutes

Tim Hunter	2405
Gary Roberts	**1658**
Joel Otto	**1642**
Jim Peplinski	1456
Willi Plett	1267
Ronnie Stern	**1020**
Al MacInnis	960
Gary Suter	874
Theoren Fleury	**858**
Jamie Macoun	666

GOALTENDERS

Games

Mike Vernon	467
Dan Bouchard	398

Reggie Lemelin	324
Phil Myre	211
Pat Riggin	119
Don Edwards	114
Rick Wamsley	111

Shutouts

Dan Bouchard	20
Phil Myre	11
Mike Vernon	9
Reggie Lemelin	6
Pat Riggin	4
Rick Wamsley	4

Goals-against average
(2400 minutes minimum)

Trevor Kidd	**2.86**
Dan Bouchard	3.03
Phil Myre	3.21
Rick Wamsley	3.21
Mike Vernon	3.28
Reggie Lemelin	3.67
Pat Riggin	3.88
Don Edwards	4.06

Wins

Mike Vernon	248
Dan Bouchard	170
Reggie Lemelin	144
Phil Myre	76
Rick Wamsley	53
Pat Riggin	50
Don Edwards	40

YEAR-BY-YEAR RECORDS

Season	W	L	T	Pts.	Finish	W	L	Highest round	Coach
					REGULAR SEASON			PLAYOFFS	
1926-27	19	22	3	41	3rd/American	*0	1	Quarterfinals	Pete Muldoon
1927-28	7	34	3	17	5th/American	—	—		Barney Stanley, Hugh Lehman
1928-29	7	29	8	22	5th/American	—	—		Herb Gardiner
1929-30	21	18	5	47	2nd/American	*0	1	Quarterfinals	Tom Schaughnessy, Bill Tobin
1930-31	24	17	3	51	2nd/American	*5	3	Stanley Cup finals	Dick Irvin
1931-32	18	19	11	47	2nd/American	1	1	Quarterfinals	Dick Irvin, Bill Tobin
1932-33	16	20	12	44	4th/American	—	—		Godfrey Matheson, Emil Iverson
1933-34	20	17	11	51	2nd/American	6	2	Stanley Cup champ	Tom Gorman
1934-35	26	17	5	57	2nd/American	*0	1	Quarterfinals	Clem Loughlin
1935-36	21	19	8	50	3rd/American	1	1	Quarterfinals	Clem Loughlin
1936-37	14	27	7	35	4th/American	—	—		Clem Loughlin
1937-38	14	25	9	37	3rd/American	7	3	Stanley Cup champ	Bill Stewart
1938-39	12	28	8	32	7th	—	—		Bill Stewart, Paul Thompson
1939-40	23	19	6	52	4th	0	2	Quarterfinals	Paul Thompson
1940-41	16	25	7	39	5th	2	3	Semifinals	Paul Thompson
1941-42	22	23	3	47	4th	1	2	Quarterfinals	Paul Thompson
1942-43	17	18	15	49	5th	—	—		Paul Thompson
1943-44	22	23	5	49	4th	4	5	Stanley Cup finals	Paul Thompson
1944-45	13	30	7	33	5th	—	—		Paul Thompson, John Gottselig
1945-46	23	20	7	53	3rd	0	4	League semifinals	John Gottselig
1946-47	19	37	4	42	6th	—	—		John Gottselig
1947-48	20	34	6	46	6th	—	—		John Gottselig, Charlie Conacher
1948-49	21	31	8	50	5th	—	—		Charlie Conacher
1949-50	22	38	10	54	6th	—	—		Charlie Conacher
1950-51	13	47	10	36	6th	—	—		Ebbie Goodfellow
1951-52	17	44	9	43	6th	—	—		Ebbie Goodfellow
1952-53	27	28	15	69	4th	3	4	League semifinals	Sid Abel
1953-54	12	51	7	31	6th	—	—		Sid Abel
1954-55	13	40	17	43	6th	—	—		Frank Eddolls
1955-56	19	39	12	50	6th	—	—		Dick Irvin
1956-57	16	39	15	47	6th	—	—		Tommy Ivan
1957-58	24	39	7	55	5th	—	—		Tommy Ivan, Rudy Pilous
1958-59	28	29	13	69	3rd	2	4	League semifinals	Rudy Pilous
1959-60	28	29	13	69	3rd	0	4	League semifinals	Rudy Pilous
1960-61	29	24	17	75	3rd	8	4	Stanley Cup champ	Rudy Pilous
1961-62	31	26	13	75	3rd	6	6	Stanley Cup finals	Rudy Pilous
1962-63	32	21	17	81	2nd	2	4	League semifinals	Rudy Pilous
1963-64	36	22	12	84	2nd	3	4	League semifinals	Billy Reay
1964-65	34	28	8	76	3rd	7	7	Stanley Cup finals	Billy Reay
1965-66	37	25	8	82	2nd	2	4	League semifinals	Billy Reay
1966-67	41	17	12	94	1st	2	4	League semifinals	Billy Reay
1967-68	32	26	16	80	4th/East	5	6	Division finals	Billy Reay
1968-69	34	33	9	77	6th/East	—	—		Billy Reay
1969-70	45	22	9	99	1st/East	4	4	Division finals	Billy Reay
1970-71	49	20	9	107	1st/West	11	7	Stanley Cup finals	Billy Reay
1971-72	46	17	15	107	1st/West	4	4	Division finals	Billy Reay
1972-73	42	27	9	93	1st/West	10	6	Stanley Cup finals	Billy Reay
1973-74	41	14	23	105	2nd/West	6	5	Division finals	Billy Reay
1974-75	37	35	8	82	3rd/Smythe	3	5	Quarterfinals	Billy Reay
1975-76	32	30	18	82	1st/Smythe	0	4	Quarterfinals	Billy Reay
1976-77	26	43	11	63	3rd/Smythe	0	2	Preliminaries	Billy Reay, Bill White
1977-78	32	29	19	83	1st/Smythe	0	4	Quarterfinals	Bob Pulford
1978-79	29	36	15	73	1st/Smythe	0	4	Quarterfinals	Bob Pulford
1979-80	34	27	19	87	1st/Smythe	3	4	Quarterfinals	Eddie Johnston
1980-81	31	33	16	78	2nd/Smythe	0	3	Preliminaries	Keith Magnuson
1981-82	30	38	12	72	4th/Norris	8	7	Conference finals	Keith Magnuson, Bob Pulford
1982-83	47	23	10	104	1st/Norris	7	6	Conference finals	Orval Tessier
1983-84	30	42	8	68	4th/Norris	2	3	Division semifinals	Orval Tessier
1984-85	38	35	7	83	2nd/Norris	9	6	Conference finals	Orval Tessier, Bob Pulford
1985-86	39	33	8	86	1st/Norris	0	3	Division semifinals	Bob Pulford
1986-87	29	37	14	72	3rd/Norris	0	4	Division semifinals	Bob Pulford
1987-88	30	41	9	69	3rd/Norris	1	4	Division semifinals	Bob Murdoch
1988-89	27	41	12	66	4th/Norris	9	7	Conference finals	Mike Keenan
1989-90	41	33	6	88	1st/Norris	10	10	Conference finals	Mike Keenan
1990-91	49	23	8	106	1st/Norris	2	4	Division semifinals	Mike Keenan
1991-92	36	29	15	87	2nd/Norris	12	6	Stanley Cup finals	Mike Keenan
1992-93	47	25	12	106	1st/Norris	0	4	Division semifinals	Darryl Sutter
1993-94	39	36	9	87	5th/Central	2	4	Conference quarterfinals	Darryl Sutter
1994-95	24	19	5	53	3rd/Central	9	7	Conference finals	Darryl Sutter

*Won-lost record does not indicate tie(s) resulting from two-game, total-goals series that year (two-game, total-goals series were played from 1917-18 through 1935-36).

FIRST - ROUND ENTRY DRAFT CHOICES

Year   Player, Overall, Last Amateur Team (League)
1969—J.P. Bordeleau, 13, Montreal (OHL)
1970—Dan Maloney, 14, London (OHL)
1971—Dan Spring, 12, Edmonton (WCHL)
1972—Phil Russell, 13, Edmonton (WCHL)
1973—Darcy Rota, 13, Edmonton (WCHL)
1974—Grant Mulvey, 16, Calgary (WCHL)
1975—Greg Vaydik, 7, Medicine Hat (WCHL)
1976—Real Cloutier, 9, Quebec (WHA)
1977—Doug Wilson, 6, Ottawa (OHL)
1978—Tim Higgins, 10, Ottawa (OHL)
1979—Keith Brown, 7, Portland (WHL)
1980—Denis Savard, 3, Montreal (QMJHL)
　　　Jerome Dupont, 15, Toronto (OHL)
1981—Tony Tanti, 12, Oshawa (OHL)

Year   Player, Overall, Last Amateur Team (League)
1982—Ken Yaremchuk, 7, Portland (WHL)
1983—Bruce Cassidy, 18, Ottawa (OHL)
1984—Ed Olczyk, 3, U.S. Olympic Team
1985—Dave Manson, 11, Prince Albert (WHL)
1986—Everett Sanipass, 14, Verdun (QMJHL)
1987—Jimmy Waite, 8, Chicoutimi (QMJHL)
1988—Jeremy Roenick, 8, Thayer Academy (Mass.)
1989—Adam Bennett, 6, Sudbury (OHL)
1990—Karl Dykhuis, 16, Hull (QMJHL)
1991—Dean McAmmond, 22, Prince Albert (WHL)
1992—Sergei Krivokrasov, 12, Central Red Army, CIS
1993—Eric Lecompte, 24, Hull (QMJHL)
1994—Ethan Moreau, 14, Niagara Falls (OHL)
1995—Dimitri Nabokov, 19, Krylja Sovetov, CIS

FRANCHISE LEADERS

Players in boldface played
for club in '94-95

FORWARDS/DEFENSEMEN

Games
Stan Mikita 1394
Bobby Hull................................. 1036
Eric Nesterenko 1013
Bob Murray 1008
Doug Wilson 938
Dennis Hull................................. 904
Steve Larmer 891
Chico Maki.................................. 841
Pierre Pilote 821
Cliff Koroll 814
Keith Brown 812
Ken Wharram............................. 766
Harold March............................. 758
Denis Savard 748
Pit Martin 740

Goals
Bobby Hull.................................. 604
Stan Mikita 541
Steve Larmer 406
Denis Savard 355
Dennis Hull................................. 298
Bill Mosienko 258

Ken Wharram 252
Pit Martin 243
Jeremy Roenick........................ **235**
Doug Wilson 225
Doug Bentley 217
Jim Pappin 216
Al Secord................................... 213
Cliff Koroll 208
Eric Nesterenko 207

Assists
Stan Mikita 926
Denis Savard 666
Doug Wilson 554
Bobby Hull.................................. 549
Steve Larmer 517
Pierre Pilote 400
Pit Martin 384
Bob Murray 382
Dennis Hull................................. 342
Doug Bentley 314
Jeremy Roenick........................ **294**
Chico Maki.................................. 292
Troy Murray 291
Eric Nesterenko 288
Pat Stapleton 286

Points
Stan Mikita 1467
Bobby Hull................................ 1153

Denis Savard 1021
Steve Larmer 923
Doug Wilson 779
Dennis Hull................................. 640
Pit Martin 627
Bill Mosienko 540
Ken Wharram 533
Doug Bentley 531
Jeremy Roenick........................ **529**
Bob Murray 514
Eric Nesterenko 495
Troy Murray 488
Pierre Pilote 477

GOALTENDERS
Shutouts
Tony Esposito.............................. 74
Glenn Hall................................... 51
Chuck Gardiner............................ 42
Ed Belfour................................. **28**
Mike Karakas.............................. 28
Al Rollins................................... 17
Denis DeJordy 13
Murray Bannerman 8
Lorne Chabot 8
Paul Goodman 6
Hugh Lehman 6

CLEVELAND BARONS (DEFUNCT)

YEAR - BY - YEAR RECORDS

Season	W	L	T	Pts.	Finish	W	L	Highest round	Coach
			REGULAR SEASON					PLAYOFFS	
1967-68†	15	42	17	42	6th/West	—	—		Bert Olmstead, Gordie Fashoway
1968-69†	29	36	11	69	2nd/West	3	4	Division semifinals	Fred Glover
1969-70†	22	40	14	58	4th/West	0	4	Division semifinals	Fred Glover
1970-71‡	20	53	5	45	7th/West	—	—		Fred Glover
1971-72‡	21	39	18	60	6th/West	—	—		Fred Glover, Vic Stasiuk
1972-73‡	16	46	16	48	8th/West	—	—		Garry Young, Fred Glover
1973-74‡	13	55	10	36	8th/West	—	—		Fred Glover, Marsh Johnston
1974-75‡	19	48	13	51	4th/Adams	—	—		Marsh Johnston
1975-76‡	27	42	11	65	4th/Adams	—	—		Jack Evans
1976-77	25	42	13	63	4th/Adams	—	—		Jack Evans
1977-78*	22	45	13	57	4th/Adams	—	—		Jack Evans

*Team disbanded after 1977-78 season. Owners bought Minnesota franchise and a number of Cleveland players were awarded to North Stars; remaining Cleveland players were dispersed to other clubs in draft.
†Oakland Seals.
†California Golden Seals.

Year	Player, Overall, Last Amateur Team (League)
1969	Tony Featherstone, 7, Peterborough (OHA)
1970	Chris Oddleifson, 10 Winnipeg (WCHL)
1971	No first-round selection
1972	No first-round selection
1973	No first-round selection
1974	Rick Hampton, 3, St. Catharines (OHA)
	Ron Chipperfield, 17, Brandon (WCHL)
1975	Ralph Klassen, 3, Saskatoon (WCHL)
1976	Bjorn Johansson, 5, Orebro IK (Sweden)
1977	Mike Crombeen, 5, Kingston (OHA)

DALLAS STARS

YEAR-BY-YEAR RECORDS

	REGULAR SEASON					PLAYOFFS			
Season	W	L	T	Pts.	Finish	W	L	Highest round	Coach
1967-68*	27	32	15	69	4th/West	7	7	Division finals	Wren Blair
1968-69*	18	43	15	51	6th/West	—	—		Wren Blair, John Muckler
1969-70*	19	35	22	60	3rd/West	2	4	Division semifinals	Wren Blair, Charlie Burns
1970-71*	28	34	16	72	4th/West	6	6	Division finals	Jack Gordon
1971-72*	37	29	12	86	2nd/West	3	4	Division semifinals	Jack Gordon
1972-73*	37	30	11	85	3rd/West	2	4	Division semifinals	Jack Gordon
1973-74*	23	38	17	63	7th/West	—	—		Jack Gordon, Parker MacDonald
1974-75*	23	50	7	53	4th/Smythe	—	—		Jack Gordon, Charlie Burns
1975-76*	20	53	7	47	5th/Smythe	—	—		Ted Harris
1976-77*	23	39	18	64	2nd/Smythe	0	2	Preliminaries	Ted Harris
1977-78*	18	53	9	45	5th/Smythe	—	—		Ted Harris, Andre Beaulieu, Lou Nanne
1978-79*	28	40	12	68	4th/Adams	—	—		Harry Howell, Glen Sonmor
1979-80*	36	28	16	88	3rd/Adams	8	7	Semifinals	Glen Sonmor
1980-81*	35	28	17	87	3rd/Adams	12	7	Stanley Cup finals	Glen Sonmor
1981-82*	37	23	20	94	1st/Norris	1	3	Division semifinals	Glen Sonmor, Murray Oliver
1982-83*	40	24	16	96	2nd/Norris	4	5	Division finals	Glen Sonmor, Murray Oliver
1983-84*	39	31	10	88	1st/Norris	7	9	Conference finals	Bill Maloney
1984-85*	25	43	12	62	4th/Norris	5	4	Division finals	Bill Maloney, Glen Sonmor
1985-86*	38	33	9	85	2nd/Norris	2	3	Division semifinals	Lorne Henning
1986-87*	30	40	10	70	5th/Norris	—	—		Lorne Henning, Glen Sonmor
1987-88*	19	48	13	51	5th/Norris	—	—		Herb Brooks
1988-89*	27	37	16	70	3rd/Norris	1	4	Division semifinals	Pierre Page
1989-90*	36	40	4	76	4th/Norris	3	4	Division semifinals	Pierre Page
1990-91*	27	39	14	68	4th/Norris	14	9	Stanley Cup finals	Bob Gainey
1991-92*	32	42	6	70	4th/Norris	3	4	Division semifinals	Bob Gainey
1992-93*	36	38	10	82	5th/Norris	—	—		Bob Gainey
1993-94	42	29	13	97	3rd/Central	5	4	Conference semifinals	Bob Gainey
1994-95	17	23	8	42	5th/Central	1	4	Conference quarterfinals	Bob Gainey

*Minnesota North Stars.

FIRST-ROUND ENTRY DRAFT CHOICES

Year	Player, Overall, Last Amateur Team (League)
1969	Dick Redmond, 5, St. Catharines (OHL)
	Dennis O'Brien, 14, St. Catharines (OHL)
1970	No first-round selection
1971	No first-round selection
1972	Jerry Byers, 12, Kitchener (OHL)
1973	No first-round selection
1974	Doug Hicks, 6, Flin Flon (WCHL)
1975	Brian Maxwell, 4, Medicine Hat (WCHL)
1976	Glen Sharpley, 3, Hull (QMJHL)
1977	Brad Maxwell, 7, New Westminster (WCHL)
1978	*Bobby Smith, 1, Ottawa (OHL)
1979	Craig Hartsburg, 6, Birmingham (WHA)
	Tom McCarthy, 10, Oshawa (OHL)
1980	Brad Palmer, 16, Victoria (WHL)
1981	Ron Meighan, 13, Niagara Falls (OHL)
1982	Brian Bellows, 2, Kitchener (OHL)
1983	*Brian Lawton, 1, Mount St. Charles H.S. (R.I.)
1984	David Quinn, 13, Kent H.S. (Ct.)
1985	No first-round selection
1986	Warren Babe, 12, Lethbridge (WHL)
1987	Dave Archibald, 6, Portland (WHL)
1988	*Mike Modano, 1, Prince Albert (WHL)
1989	Doug Zmolek, 7, John Marshall H.S. (Minn.)
1990	Derian Hatcher, 8, North Bay (OHL)
1991	Richard Matvichuk, 8, Saskatoon (WHL)
1992	No first-round selection
1993	Todd Harvey, 9, Detroit (OHL)
1994	Jason Botterill, 20, Michigan (CCHA)
1995	Jarome Iginla, 11, Kamloops (WHL)

*Designates first player chosen in draft.

FRANCHISE LEADERS

Players in boldface played
for club in '94-95

FORWARDS/DEFENSEMEN

Games

Neal Broten	972
Curt Giles	760

Brian Bellows	753
Fred Barrett	730
Bill Goldsworthy	670
Lou Nanne	635
Tom Reid	615
Steve Payne	613
Dino Ciccarelli	602
J.P. Parise	588

Goals

Brian Bellows	342
Dino Ciccarelli	332
Bill Goldsworthy	267
Neal Broten	266
Dave Gagner	233
Steve Payne	228
Bobby Smith	185

Mike Modano	....	185
Tim Young	....	178
Danny Grant	....	176

Assists

Neal Broten	582
Brian Bellows	380
Bobby Smith	369
Dino Ciccarelli	319
Tim Young	316
Craig Hartsburg	315
Dave Gagner	274
Mike Modano	246
J.P. Parise	242
Bill Goldsworthy	239

Points

Neal Broten	852
Brian Bellows	722
Dino Ciccarelli	651
Bobby Smith	554
Dave Gagner	507
Bill Goldsworthy	506
Tim Young	494
Steve Payne	466

Mike Modano	423
Craig Hartsburg	413

Penalty minutes

Shane Churla	1715
Basil McRae	1567
Willi Plett	1137
Brad Maxwell	1031
Mark Tinordi	1015
Dennis O'Brien	836
Gordie Roberts	832
Craig Hartsburg	818
Bob Rouse	735

GOALTENDERS

Games

Cesare Maniago	420
Gilles Meloche	328
Jon Casey	325
Don Beaupre	316
Pete LoPresti	173
Kari Takko	131
Darcy Wakaluk	116

Shutouts

Cesare Maniago	29
Jon Casey	12
Gilles Meloche	9
Darcy Wakaluk	7
Pete LoPresti	5

Goals-against average
(2400 minutes minimum)

Gump Worsley	2.62
Cesare Maniago	3.17
Darcy Wakaluk	3.20
Andy Moog	3.27
Jon Casey	3.28
Gilles Gilbert	3.39
Gary Edwards	3.44
Gilles Meloche	3.51
Don Beaupre	3.74
Kari Takko	3.87

Wins

Cesare Maniago	143
Gilles Meloche	141
Jon Casey	128
Don Beaupre	126
Darcy Wakaluk	45

DETROIT RED WINGS

YEAR-BY-YEAR RECORDS

		REGULAR SEASON					PLAYOFFS			
Season	W	L	T	Pts.	Finish	W	L	Highest round	Coach
1926-27†	12	28	4	28	5th/American	—	—		Art Duncan, Duke Keats
1927-28†	19	19	6	44	4th/American	—	—		Jack Adams
1928-29†	19	16	9	47	3rd/American	0	2	Quarterfinals	Jack Adams
1929-30†	14	24	6	34	4th/American	—	—		Jack Adams
1930-31‡	16	21	7	39	4th/American	—	—		Jack Adams
1931-32‡	18	20	10	46	3rd/American	*0	1	Quarterfinals	Jack Adams
1932-33	25	15	8	58	2nd/American	2	2	Semifinals	Jack Adams
1933-34	24	14	10	58	1st/American	4	5	Stanley Cup finals	Jack Adams
1934-35	19	22	7	45	4th/American	—	—		Jack Adams
1935-36	24	16	8	56	1st/American	6	1	Stanley Cup champ	Jack Adams
1936-37	25	14	9	59	1st/American	6	4	Stanley Cup champ	Jack Adams
1937-38	12	25	11	35	4th/American	—	—		Jack Adams
1938-39	18	24	6	42	5th	3	3	Semifinals	Jack Adams
1939-40	16	26	6	38	5th	2	3	Semifinals	Jack Adams
1940-41	21	16	11	53	3rd	4	5	Stanley Cup finals	Jack Adams
1941-42	19	25	4	42	5th	7	5	Stanley Cup finals	Jack Adams
1942-43	25	14	11	61	1st	8	2	Stanley Cup champ	Jack Adams
1943-44	26	18	6	58	2nd	1	4	League semifinals	Jack Adams
1944-45	31	14	5	67	2nd	7	7	Stanley Cup finals	Jack Adams
1945-46	20	20	10	50	4th	1	4	League semifinals	Jack Adams
1946-47	22	27	11	55	4th	1	4	League semifinals	Jack Adams
1947-48	30	18	12	72	2nd	4	6	Stanley Cup finals	Tommy Ivan
1948-49	34	19	7	75	1st	4	7	Stanley Cup finals	Tommy Ivan
1949-50	37	19	14	88	1st	8	6	Stanley Cup champ	Tommy Ivan
1950-51	44	13	13	101	1st	2	4	League semifinals	Tommy Ivan
1951-52	44	14	12	100	1st	8	0	Stanley Cup champ	Tommy Ivan
1952-53	36	16	18	90	1st	2	4	League semifinals	Tommy Ivan
1953-54	37	19	14	88	1st	8	4	Stanley Cup champ	Tommy Ivan
1954-55	42	17	11	95	1st	8	3	Stanley Cup champ	Jimmy Skinner
1955-56	30	24	16	76	2nd	5	5	Stanley Cup finals	Jimmy Skinner
1956-57	38	20	12	88	1st	1	4	League semifinals	Jimmy Skinner
1957-58	29	29	12	70	3rd	0	4	League semifinals	Jimmy Skinner, Sid Abel
1958-59	25	37	8	58	6th	—	—		Sid Abel
1959-60	26	29	15	67	4th	2	4	League semifinals	Sid Abel
1960-61	25	29	16	66	4th	6	5	Stanley Cup finals	Sid Abel
1961-62	23	33	14	60	5th	—	—		Sid Abel
1962-63	32	25	13	77	4th	5	6	Stanley Cup finals	Sid Abel
1963-64	30	29	11	71	4th	7	7	Stanley Cup finals	Sid Abel
1964-65	40	23	7	87	1st	3	4	League semifinals	Sid Abel
1965-66	31	27	12	74	4th	6	6	Stanley Cup finals	Sid Abel
1966-67	27	39	4	58	5th	—	—		Sid Abel
1967-68	27	35	12	66	6th/East	—	—		Sid Abel
1968-69	33	31	12	78	5th/East	—	—		Bill Gadsby
1969-70	40	21	15	95	3rd/East	0	4	Division semifinals	Bill Gadsby, Sid Abel

Season	W	L	T	Pts.	Finish	W	L	Highest round	Coach
1970-71	22	45	11	55	7th/East	—	—		Ned Harkness, Doug Barkley
1971-72	33	35	10	76	5th/East	—	—		Doug Barkley, Johnny Wilson
1972-73	37	29	12	86	5th/East	—	—		Johnny Wilson
1973-74	29	39	10	68	6th/East	—	—		Ted Garvin, Alex Delvecchio
1974-75	23	45	12	58	4th/Norris	—	—		Alex Delvecchio
1975-76	26	44	10	62	4th/Norris	—	—		Ted Garvin, Alex Delvecchio
1976-77	16	55	9	41	5th/Norris	—	—		Alex Delvecchio, Larry Wilson
1977-78	32	34	14	78	2nd/Norris	3	4	Quarterfinals	Bobby Kromm
1978-79	23	41	16	62	5th/Norris	—	—		Bobby Kromm
1979-80	26	43	11	63	5th/Norris	—	—		Bobby Kromm, Ted Lindsay
1980-81	19	43	18	56	5th/Norris	—	—		Ted Lindsay, Wayne Maxner
1981-82	21	47	12	54	6th/Norris	—	—		Wayne Maxner, Billy Dea
1982-83	21	44	15	57	5th/Norris	—	—		Nick Polano
1983-84	31	42	7	69	3rd/Norris	1	3	Division semifinals	Nick Polano
1984-85	27	41	12	66	3rd/Norris	0	3	Division semifinals	Nick Polano
1985-86	17	57	6	40	5th/Norris	—	—		Harry Neale, Brad Park, Dan Belisle
1986-87	34	36	10	78	2nd/Norris	9	7	Conference finals	Jacques Demers
1987-88	41	28	11	93	1st/Norris	9	7	Conference finals	Jacques Demers
1988-89	34	34	12	80	1st/Norris	2	4	Division semifinals	Jacques Demers
1989-90	28	38	14	70	5th/Norris	—	—		Jacques Demers
1990-91	34	38	8	76	3rd/Norris	3	4	Division semifinals	Bryan Murray
1991-92	43	25	12	98	1st/Norris	4	7	Division finals	Bryan Murray
1992-93	47	28	9	103	2nd/Norris	3	4	Division semifinals	Bryan Murray
1993-94	46	30	8	100	1st/Central	3	4	Conference quarterfinals	Scotty Bowman
1994-95	33	11	4	70	1st/Central	12	6	Stanley Cup finals	Scotty Bowman

*Won-lost record does not indicate tie(s) resulting from two-game, total goals series that year (two-game, total-goals series were played from 1917-18 through 1935-36).
†Detroit Cougars.
‡Detroit Falcons.

FIRST-ROUND ENTRY DRAFT CHOICES

Year	Player, Overall, Last Amateur Team (League)
1969	Jim Rutherford, 10, Hamilton (OHL)
1970	Serge Lajeunesse, 12, Montreal (OHL)
1971	Marcel Dionne, 2, St. Catharines (OHL)
1972	No first-round selection
1973	Terry Richardson, 11, New Westminster (WCHL)
1974	Bill Lochead, 9, Oshawa (OHL)
1975	Rick Lapointe, 5, Victoria (WCHL)
1976	Fred Williams, 4, Saskatoon (WCHL)
1977	*Dale McCourt, 1, St. Catharines (OHL)
1978	Willie Huber, 9, Hamilton (OHL)
	Brent Peterson, 12, Portland (WCHL)
1979	Mike Foligno, 3, Sudbury (OHL)
1980	Mike Blaisdell, 11, Regina (WHL)
1981	No first-round selection
1982	Murray Craven, 17, Medicine Hat (WHL)
1983	Steve Yzerman, 4, Peterborough (OHL)
1984	Shawn Burr, 7, Kitchener (OHL)
1985	Brent Fedyk, 8, Regina (WHL)
1986	*Joe Murphy, 1, Michigan State University
1987	Yves Racine, 11, Longueuil (QMJHL)
1988	Kory Kocur, 17, Saskatoon (WHL)
1989	Mike Sillinger, 11, Regina (WHL)
1990	Keith Primeau, 3, Niagara Falls (OHL)
1991	Martin Lapointe, 10, Laval (QMJHL)
1992	Curtis Bowen, 22, Ottawa (OHL)
1993	Anders Eriksson, 22, MoDo (Sweden)
1994	Yan Golvbovsky, 23, Dynamo Moscow, CIS
1995	Maxim Kuznetsov, 26, Dynamo Moscow, CIS

*Designates first player chosen in draft.

FRANCHISE LEADERS

Players in boldface played for club in '94-95

FORWARDS/DEFENSEMEN

Games

Gordie Howe	1687
Alex Delvecchio	1549
Marcel Pronovost	983
Norm Ullman	875
Ted Lindsay	862
Steve Yzerman	862
Nick Libett	861
Red Kelly	846
Syd Howe	793
Reed Larson	708

Goals

Gordie Howe	786
Steve Yzerman	481
Alex Delvecchio	456
Ted Lindsay	335
Norm Ullman	324

John Ogrodnick	259
Nick Libett	217
Gerard Gallant	207
Syd Howe	202
Reed Larson	188

Assists

Gordie Howe	1023
Alex Delvecchio	825
Steve Yzerman	679
Norm Ullman	434
Ted Lindsay	393
Reed Larson	382
Red Kelly	297
Sid Abel	279
John Ogrodnick	275
Gerard Gallant	260

Points

Gordie Howe	1809
Alex Delvecchio	1281
Steve Yzerman	1160

Norm Ullman	758
Ted Lindsay	728
Reed Larson	570
John Ogrodnick	534
Gerard Gallant	467
Nick Libett	467
Sid Abel	463

GOALTENDERS

Games

Terry Sawchuk	734
Harry Lumley	324
Jim Rutherford	314
Roger Crozier	310
Greg Stefan	299
Tim Cheveldae	264
Roy Edwards	221
Glen Hanlon	186
Norm Smith	178
John Mowers	152

Shutouts

Terry Sawchuk	85
Harry Lumley	26
Roger Crozier	20
Clarence Dolson	17
Glenn Hall	17
Harry Holmes	17
Norm Smith	17

Goals - against average
(2400 minutes minimum)

Clarence Dolson	2.06

Harry Holmes	2.11
Glenn Hall	2.14
Alex Connell	2.25
John Ross Roach	2.26
Norm Smith	2.34
Terry Sawchuk	2.46
John Mowers	2.63
Cecil Thompson	2.65
Harry Lumley	2.73

Wins

Terry Sawchuk	352

Harry Lumley	163
Roger Crozier	130
Tim Cheveldae	128
Greg Stefan	115
Jim Rutherford	97
Roy Edwards	95
Norm Smith	76

EDMONTON OILERS

YEAR-BY-YEAR RECORDS

Season	W	L	T	Pts.	Finish	W	L	Highest round	Coach
1972-73*	38	37	3	79	5th	—	—		Ray Kinasewich
1973-74†	38	37	3	79	3rd	1	4	League quarterfinals	Brian Shaw
1974-75†	36	38	4	76	5th	—	—		Brian Shaw, Bill Hunter
1975-76†	27	49	5	59	4th	0	4	League quarterfinals	Clare Drake, Bill Hunter
1976-77†	34	43	4	72	4th	1	4	League quarterfinals	Bep Guidolin, Glen Sather
1977-78†	38	39	3	79	5th	1	4	League quarterfinals	Glen Sather
1978-79†	48	30	2	98	1st	6	7	Avco World Cup finals	Glen Sather
1979-80	28	39	13	69	4th/Smythe	0	3	Preliminaries	Glen Sather
1980-81	29	35	16	74	4th/Smythe	5	4	Quarterfinals	Glen Sather
1981-82	48	17	15	111	1st/Smythe	2	3	Division semifinals	Glen Sather
1982-83	47	21	12	106	1st/Smythe	11	5	Stanley Cup finals	Glen Sather
1983-84	57	18	5	119	1st/Smythe	15	4	Stanley Cup champ	Glen Sather
1984-85	49	20	11	109	1st/Smythe	15	3	Stanley Cup champ	Glen Sather
1985-86	56	17	7	119	1st/Smythe	6	4	Division finals	Glen Sather
1986-87	50	24	6	106	1st/Smythe	16	5	Stanley Cup champ	Glen Sather
1987-88	44	25	11	99	2nd/Smythe	16	2	Stanley Cup champ	Glen Sather
1988-89	38	34	8	84	3rd/Smythe	3	4	Division semifinals	Glen Sather
1989-90	38	28	14	90	2nd/Smythe	16	6	Stanley Cup champ	John Muckler
1990-91	37	37	6	80	3rd/Smythe	9	9	Conference finals	John Muckler
1991-92	36	34	10	82	3rd/Smythe	8	8	Conference finals	Ted Green
1992-93	26	50	8	60	5th/Smythe	—	—		Ted Green
1993-94	25	45	14	64	6th/Pacific	—	—		Ted Green, Glen Sather
1994-95	17	27	4	38	5th/Pacific	—	—		George Burnett, Ron Low

*Alberta Oilers, members of World Hockey Association.
†Members of World Hockey Association.

FIRST-ROUND ENTRY DRAFT CHOICES

Year   Player, Overall, Last Amateur Team (League)
1979—Kevin Lowe, 21, Quebec (QMJHL)
1980—Paul Coffey, 6, Kitchener (OHL)
1981—Grant Fuhr, 8, Victoria (WHL)
1982—Jim Playfair, 20, Portland (WHL)
1983—Jeff Beukeboom, 19, Sault Ste. Marie (OHL)
1984—Selmar Odelein, 21, Regina (WHL)
1985—Scott Metcalfe, 20, Kingston (OHL)
1986—Kim Issel, 21, Prince Albert (WHL)
1987—Peter Soberlak, 21, Swift Current (WHL)
1988—Francois Leroux, 19, St. Jean (QMJHL)
1989—Jason Soules, 15, Niagara Falls (OHL)
1990—Scott Allison, 17, Prince Albert (WHL)

Year   Player, Overall, Last Amateur Team (League)
1991—Tyler Wright, 12, Swift Current (WHL)
        Martin Rucinsky, 20, Litvinov (Czech.)
1992—Joe Hulbig, 13, St. Sebastian H.S. (Mass.)
1993—Jason Arnott, 7, Oshawa (OHL)
        Nick Stajduhar, 16, London (OHL)
1994—Jason Bonsignore, 4, Niagara Falls (OHL)
        Ryan Smyth, 6, Moose Jaw (WHL)
1995—Steve Kelly, 6, Prince Albert (WHL)

NOTE: Edmonton chose Dave Dryden, Bengt Gustafsson and Ed Mio as priority selections before the 1979 expansion draft.

FRANCHISE LEADERS

Players in boldface played
for club in '94-95

FORWARDS/DEFENSEMEN

Games

Kevin Lowe	966
Mark Messier	851
Glenn Anderson	828
Jari Kurri	754
Craig MacTavish	701
Wayne Gretzky	696

Charlie Huddy	694
Dave Hunter	653
Lee Fogolin	586
Paul Coffey	532

Goals

Wayne Gretzky	583
Jari Kurri	474
Glenn Anderson	413
Mark Messier	392
Paul Coffey	209
Craig Simpson	185

Esa Tikkanen	178
Craig MacTavish	155
Dave Hunter	119
Petr Klima	118

Assists

Wayne Gretzky	1086
Mark Messier	642
Jari Kurri	569
Glenn Anderson	483
Paul Coffey	460
Kevin Lowe	295

Charlie Huddy	287
Esa Tikkanen	258
Craig Simpson	180
Craig MacTavish	176

Points

Wayne Gretzky	1669
Jari Kurri	1043
Mark Messier	1034
Glenn Anderson	896
Paul Coffey	669
Esa Tikkanen	436
Charlie Huddy	368
Kevin Lowe	368
Craig Simpson	365
Craig MacTavish	331

Penalty minutes

Kevin McClelland	1298
Kelly Buchberger	1214
Kevin Lowe	1164

Mark Messier	1122
Steve Smith	1080
Dave Semenko	976
Lee Fogolin	886
Dave Hunter	776
Glenn Anderson	771
Esa Tikkanen	759

GOALTENDERS
Games

Grant Fuhr	423
Bill Ranford	396
Andy Moog	235
Eddie Mio	77
Ron Low	67
Fred Brathwaite	33
Ron Tugnutt	29
Jim Corsi	26
Gary Edwards	15
Dave Dryden	14

Shutouts

Grant Fuhr	9
Bill Ranford	7
Andy Moog	4
Eddie Mio	1

Goals-against average
(2400 minutes minimum)

Bill Ranford	3.48
Andy Moog	3.61
Grant Fuhr	3.69
Eddie Mio	4.02
Ron Low	4.03

Wins

Grant Fuhr	226
Bill Ranford	150
Andy Moog	143
Ron Low	30
Eddie Mio	25
Ron Tugnutt	10
Jim Corsi	8

FLORIDA PANTHERS

YEAR-BY-YEAR RECORDS

	REGULAR SEASON					PLAYOFFS			
Season	W	L	T	Pts.	Finish	W	L	Highest round	Coach
1993-94	33	34	17	83	5th/Atlantic	—	—		Roger Neilson
1994-95	20	22	6	46	5th/Atlantic	—	—		Roger Neilson

FIRST-ROUND ENTRY DRAFT CHOICES

Year Player, Overall, Last Amateur Team (League)
1993—Rob Niedermayer, 5, Medicine Hat (WHL)
1994—*Ed Jovanovski, 1, Windsor (OHL)

Year Player, Overall, Last Amateur Team (League)
1995—Radek Dvorak, 10, Budejovice, Czech Republic
*Designates first player chosen in draft.

FRANCHISE LEADERS

Players in boldface played
for club in '94-95

FORWARDS/DEFENSEMEN
Games

Bill Lindsay	132
Tom Fitzgerald	131
Gord Murphy	130
Scott Mellanby	127
Mike Hough	126
Brian Skrudland	126
Dave Lowry	125
Jody Hull	115
Rob Niedermayer	113
Andrei Lomakin	107

Goals

Scott Mellanby	43
Jesse Belanger	32
Stu Barnes	28
Dave Lowry	25
Jody Hull	24
Tom Fitzgerald	21
Bob Kudelski	20
Andrei Lomakin	20
Gord Murphy	20
Brian Skrudland	20

Assists

Jesse Belanger	47
Gord Murphy	45
Scott Mellanby	42
Stu Barnes	39
Andrei Lomakin	35
Brian Skrudland	34
Dave Lowry	32
Brian Benning	31
Mike Hough	30
Tom Fitzgerald	27

Points

Scott Mellanby	85
Jesse Belanger	79
Stu Barnes	67
Gord Murphy	65
Dave Lowry	57
Andrei Lomakin	54
Brian Skrudland	54
Tom Fitzgerald	48
Mike Hough	42
Jody Hull	42

Penalty minutes

Paul Laus	242
Scott Mellanby	237

Brian Skrudland	224
Brent Severyn	193
Bill Lindsay	139
Brian Benning	125
Joe Cirella	120
Gord Murphy	95
Dave Lowry	89
Scott Levins	69

GOALTENDERS
Games

John Vanbiesbrouck	94
Mark Fitzpatrick	43
Pokey Reddick	2

Shutouts

John Vanbiesbrouck	5
Mark Fitzpatrick	3

Goals-against average
(1200 minutes minimum)

John Vanbiesbrouck	2.51
Mark Fitzpatrick	2.70

Wins

John Vanbiesbrouck	35
Mark Fitzpatrick	18

HARTFORD WHALERS

YEAR-BY-YEAR RECORDS

	REGULAR SEASON					PLAYOFFS			
Season	W	L	T	Pts.	Finish	W	L	Highest round	Coach
1972-73*	46	30	2	94	1st	12	3	Avco World Cup champ	Jack Kelley
1973-74*	43	31	4	90	1st	3	4	League quarterfinals	Ron Ryan

		REGULAR SEASON						PLAYOFFS	
Season	W	L	T	Pts.	Finish	W	L	Highest round	Coach
1974-75*	43	30	5	91	1st	2	4	League quarterfinals	Ron Ryan, Jack Kelley
1975-76*	33	40	7	73	3rd	6	4	League semifinals	Jack Kelley, Don Blackburn, Harry Neale
1976-77*	35	40	6	76	4th	1	4	League quarterfinals	Harry Neale
1977-78*	44	31	5	93	2nd	8	6	Avco World Cup finals	Harry Neale
1978-79*	37	34	9	83	4th	5	5	League semifinals	Bill Dineen, Don Blackburn
1979-80	27	34	19	73	4th/Norris	0	3	Preliminaries	Don Blackburn
1980-81	21	41	18	60	4th/Norris	—	—		Don Blackburn, Larry Pleau
1981-82	21	41	18	60	5th/Adams	—	—		Larry Pleau
1982-83	19	54	7	45	5th/Adams	—	—		Larry Kish, Larry Pleau, John Cunniff
1983-84	28	42	10	66	5th/Adams	—	—		Jack Evans
1984-85	30	41	9	69	5th/Adams	—	—		Jack Evans
1985-86	40	36	4	84	4th/Adams	6	4	Division finals	Jack Evans
1986-87	43	30	7	93	1st/Adams	2	4	Division semifinals	Jack Evans
1987-88	35	38	7	77	4th/Adams	2	4	Division semifinals	Jack Evans, Larry Pleau
1988-89	37	38	5	79	4th/Adams	0	4	Division semifinals	Larry Pleau
1989-90	38	33	9	85	4th/Adams	3	4	Division semifinals	Rick Ley
1990-91	31	38	11	73	4th/Adams	2	4	Division semifinals	Rick Ley
1991-92	26	41	13	65	4th/Adams	3	4	Division semifinals	Jim Roberts
1992-93	26	52	6	58	5th/Adams	—	—		Paul Holmgren
1993-94	27	48	9	63	6th/Northeast	—	—		Paul Holmgren, Pierre McGuire
1994-95	19	24	5	43	5th/Northeast	—	—		Paul Holmgren

*New England Whalers, members of World Hockey Association.

FIRST-ROUND ENTRY DRAFT CHOICES

Year   Player, Overall, Last Amateur Team (League)

1979—Ray Allison, 18, Brandon (WHL)
1980—Fred Arthur, 8, Cornwall (QMJHL)
1981—Ron Francis, 4, Sault Ste. Marie (OHL)
1982—Paul Lawless, 14, Windsor (OHL)
1983—Sylvain Turgeon, 2, Hull (QMJHL)
　　　David A. Jensen, 20, Lawrence Academy (Mass.)
1984—Sylvain Cote, 11, Quebec (QMJHL)
1985—Dana Murzyn, 5, Calgary (WHL)
1986—Scott Young, 11, Boston University
1987—Jody Hull, 18, Peterborough (OHL)
1988—Chris Govedaris, 11, Toronto (OHL)

1989—Robert Holik, 10, Jihlava (Czechoslovakia)
1990—Mark Greig, 15, Lethbridge (WHL)
1991—Patrick Poulin, 9, St. Hyacinthe (QMJHL)
1992—Robert Petrovicky, 9, Dukla Trencin (Czech.)
1993—Chris Pronger, 2, Peterborough (OHL)
1994—Jeff O'Neill, 5, Guelph (OHL)
1995—Jean-Sebastien Giguere, 13, Halifax (QMJHL)

NOTE: Hartford chose Jordy Douglas, John Garrett and Mark Howe as priority selections before the 1979 expansion draft.

FRANCHISE LEADERS

Players in boldface played for club in '94-95

FORWARDS/DEFENSEMEN

Games

Ron Francis	714
Kevin Dineen	489
Dave Tippett	483
Ulf Samuelsson	463
Joel Quenneville	457
Randy Ladouceur	452
Ray Ferraro	442
Dean Evason	434
Pat Verbeek	**433**
Sylvain Cote	382
Paul MacDermid	373

Goals

Ron Francis	264
Blaine Stoughton	219
Kevin Dineen	214
Pat Verbeek	**192**
Sylvain Turgeon	178
Ray Ferraro	157
Geoff Sanderson	**119**
Ray Neufeld	106
Dean Evason	87
Mark Johnson	85
Mike Rogers	85

Assists

Ron Francis	557
Kevin Dineen	262
Pat Verbeek	**211**
Dave Babych	196
Ray Ferraro	194
Andrew Cassels	**166**
Blaine Stoughton	158
Sylvain Turgeon	150
Dean Evason	148
Mark Howe	147

Points

Ron Francis	821
Kevin Dineen	446
Pat Verbeek	**403**
Blaine Stoughton	377
Ray Ferraro	351
Sylvain Turgeon	328
Dave Babych	240
Dean Evason	235
Ray Neufeld	226
Andrew Cassels	**221**
Geoff Sanderson	**220**

Penalty minutes

Torrie Robertson	1368
Pat Verbeek	**1144**
Ulf Samuelsson	1108
Kevin Dineen	1029
Randy Ladouceur	717
Paul MacDermid	706
Dean Evason	617
Ron Francis	540
Adam Burt	**523**
Ed Kastelic	485

GOALTENDERS

Games

Mike Liut	252
Greg Millen	219
Peter Sidorkiewicz	178
Sean Burke	**139**
John Garrett	122
Steve Weeks	94
Kay Whitmore	75
Mike Veisor	69

Shutouts

Mike Liut	13
Peter Sidorkiewicz	8
Greg Millen	4
Steve Weeks	4
Sean Burke	**2**

Goals-against average
(2400 minutes minimum)

Sean Burke	**3.29**
Peter Sidorkiewicz	3.33
Mike Liut	3.36
Kay Whitmore	3.61
Steve Weeks	3.68
Greg Millen	4.25
John Garrett	4.28
Mike Veisor	4.87

Wins

Mike Liut	115
Peter Sidorkiewicz	71
Greg Millen	62
Sean Burke	**50**
Steve Weeks	42
John Garrett	36

YEAR-BY-YEAR RECORDS

	REGULAR SEASON					PLAYOFFS			
Season	W	L	T	Pts.	Finish	W	L	Highest round	Coach
1967-68	31	33	10	72	2nd/West	3	4	Division semifinals	Red Kelly
1968-69	24	42	10	58	4th/West	4	7	Division finals	Red Kelly
1969-70	14	52	10	38	6th/West	—	—		Hal Laycoe, Johnny Wilson
1970-71	25	40	13	63	5th/West	—	—		Larry Regan
1971-72	20	49	9	49	7th/West	—	—		Larry Regan, Fred Glover
1972-73	31	36	11	73	6th/West	—	—		Bob Pulford
1973-74	33	33	12	78	3rd/West	1	4	Division semifinals	Bob Pulford
1974-75	42	17	21	105	2nd/Norris	1	2	Preliminaries	Bob Pulford
1975-76	38	33	9	85	2nd/Norris	5	4	Quarterfinals	Bob Pulford
1976-77	34	31	15	83	2nd/Norris	4	5	Quarterfinals	Bob Pulford
1977-78	31	34	15	77	3rd/Norris	0	2	Preliminaries	Ron Stewart
1978-79	34	34	12	80	3rd/Norris	0	2	Preliminaries	Bob Berry
1979-80	30	36	14	74	2nd/Norris	1	3	Preliminaries	Bob Berry
1980-81	43	24	13	99	2nd/Norris	1	3	Preliminaries	Bob Berry
1981-82	24	41	15	63	4th/Smythe	4	6	Division finals	Parker MacDonald, Don Perry
1982-83	27	41	12	66	5th/Smythe	—	—		Don Perry
1983-84	23	44	13	59	5th/Smythe	—	—		Don Perry, Rogie Vachon, Roger Neilson
1984-85	34	32	14	82	4th/Smythe	0	3	Division semifinals	Pat Quinn
1985-86	23	49	8	54	5th/Smythe	—	—		Pat Quinn
1986-87	31	41	8	70	4th/Smythe	1	4	Division semifinals	Pat Quinn, Mike Murphy
1987-88	30	42	8	68	4th/Smythe	1	4	Division semifinals	Mike Murphy, Rogie Vachon, Robbie Ftorek
1988-89	42	31	7	91	2nd/Norris	4	7	Division finals	Robbie Ftorek
1989-90	34	39	7	75	4th/Smythe	4	6	Division finals	Tom Webster
1990-91	46	24	10	102	1st/Smythe	6	6	Division finals	Tom Webster
1991-92	35	31	14	84	2nd/Smythe	2	4	Division semifinals	Tom Webster
1992-93	39	35	10	88	3rd/Smythe	13	11	Stanley Cup finals	Barry Melrose
1993-94	27	45	12	66	5th/Pacific	—	—		Barry Melrose
1994-95	16	23	9	41	4th/Pacific	—	—		Barry Melrose, Rogie Vachon

FIRST-ROUND ENTRY DRAFT CHOICES

Year Player, Overall, Last Amateur Team (League)
1969—No first-round selection
1970—No first-round selection
1971—No first-round selection
1972—No first-round selection
1973—No first-round selection
1974—No first-round selection
1975—Tim Young, 16, Ottawa (OHL)
1976—No first-round selection
1977—No first-round selection
1978—No first-round selection
1979—Jay Wells, 16, Kingston (OHL)
1980—Larry Murphy, 4, Peterborough (OHL)
        Jim Fox, 10, Ottawa (OHL)
1981—Doug Smith, 2, Ottawa (OHL)
1982—No first-round selection

Year Player, Overall, Last Amateur Team (League)
1983—No first-round selection
1984—Craig Redmond, 6, Canadian Olympic Team
1985—Craig Duncanson, 9, Sudbury (OHL)
        Dan Gratton, 10, Oshawa (OHL)
1986—Jimmy Carson, 2, Verdun (QMJHL)
1987—Wayne McBean, 4, Medicine Hat (WHL)
1988—Martin Gelinas, 7, Hull (QMJHL)
1989—No first-round selection
1990—Darryl Sydor, 7, Kamloops (WHL)
1991—No first-round selection
1992—No first-round selection
1993—No first-round selection
1994—Jamie Storr, 7, Owen Sound (OHL)
1995—Aki-Petteri Berg, 3, TPS Jrs., Finland

FRANCHISE LEADERS

Players in boldface played
for club in '94-95

FORWARDS/DEFENSEMEN

Games

Dave Taylor	1111
Marcel Dionne	921
Butch Goring	736
Mike Murphy	673
Luc Robitaille	640
Mark Hardy	616
Jay Wells	604
Bernie Nicholls	602
Jim Fox	578
Bob Berry	539

Goals

Marcel Dionne	550
Dave Taylor	431

Luc Robitaille	392
Bernie Nicholls	327
Butch Goring	275
Wayne Gretzky	**231**
Charlie Simmer	222
Mike Murphy	194
Jim Fox	186
Bob Berry	159

Assists

Marcel Dionne	757
Dave Taylor	638
Wayne Gretzky	**606**
Bernie Nicholls	431
Luc Robitaille	411
Butch Goring	384
Jim Fox	292
Mike Murphy	262
Mark Hardy	250

Charlie Simmer	244

Points

Marcel Dionne	1307
Dave Taylor	1069
Wayne Gretzky	**837**
Luc Robitaille	803
Bernie Nicholls	758
Butch Goring	659
Jim Fox	478
Charlie Simmer	466
Mike Murphy	456
Bob Berry	350

Penalty minutes

Marty McSorley	**1698**
Dave Taylor	1589
Jay Wells	1446
Jay Miller	865
Mark Hardy	858

GOALTENDERS

Games

Rogie Vachon	389
Kelly Hrudey	**324**
Mario Lessard	240
Gary Edwards	155
Roland Melanson	119
Gerry Desjardins	103
Bob Janecyk	102
Dennis DeJordy	86

Shutouts

Rogie Vachon	32

Kelly Hrudey	10
Mario Lessard	9
Gerry Desjardins	7
Gary Edwards	7

Goals-against average
(2400 minutes minimum)

Rogie Vachon	2.86
Wayne Rutledge	3.34
Gary Edwards	3.39
Kelly Hrudey	**3.50**
Gerry Desjardins	3.52
Daniel Berthiaume	3.54

Dennis DeJordy	3.73
Mario Lessard	3.74
Robb Stauber	**3.81**

Wins

Rogie Vachon	171
Kelly Hrudey	**138**
Mario Lessard	92
Gary Edwards	54
Bob Janecyk	41
Roland Melanson	40
Glenn Healy	37

MONTREAL CANADIENS

YEAR-BY-YEAR RECORDS

	REGULAR SEASON					PLAYOFFS			
Season	W	L	T	Pts.	Finish	W	L	Highest round	Coach
1917-18	13	9	0	26	1st/3rd	1	1	Semifinals	George Kennedy
1918-19	10	8	0	20	1st/2nd	†*6	3	Stanley Cup finals	George Kennedy
1919-20	13	11	0	26	2nd/3rd	—	—		George Kennedy
1920-21	13	11	0	26	3rd/2nd	—	—		George Kennedy
1921-22	12	11	1	25	3rd	—	—		Leo Dandurand
1922-23	13	9	2	28	2nd	1	1	Quarterfinals	Leo Dandurand
1923-24	13	11	0	26	2nd	6	0	Stanley Cup champ	Leo Dandurand
1924-25	17	11	2	36	3rd	3	3	Stanley Cup finals	Leo Dandurand
1925-26	11	24	1	23	7th	—	—		Cecil Hart
1926-27	28	14	2	58	2nd/Canadian	*1	1	Semifinals	Cecil Hart
1927-28	26	11	7	59	1st/Canadian	*0	1	Semifinals	Cecil Hart
1928-29	22	7	15	59	1st/Canadian	0	3	Semifinals	Cecil Hart
1929-30	21	14	9	51	2nd/Canadian	*5	0	Stanley Cup champ	Cecil Hart
1930-31	26	10	8	60	1st/Canadian	6	4	Stanley Cup champ	Cecil Hart
1931-32	25	16	7	57	1st/Canadian	1	3	Semifinals	Cecil Hart
1932-33	18	25	5	41	3rd/Canadian	*0	1	Quarterfinals	Newsy Lalonde
1933-34	22	20	6	50	2nd/Canadian	*0	1	Quarterfinals	Newsy Lalonde
1934-35	19	23	6	44	3rd/Canadian	*0	1	Quarterfinals	Newsy Lalonde, Leo Dandurand
1935-36	11	26	11	33	4th/Canadian	—	—		Sylvio Mantha
1936-37	24	18	6	54	1st/Canadian	2	3	Semifinals	Cecil Hart
1937-38	18	17	13	49	3rd/Canadian	1	2	Quarterfinals	Cecil Hart
1938-39	15	24	9	39	6th	1	2	Quarterfinals	Cecil Hart, Jules Dugal
1939-40	10	33	5	25	7th	—	—		Pit Lepine
1940-41	16	26	6	38	6th	1	2	Quarterfinals	Dick Irvin
1941-42	18	27	3	39	6th	1	2	Quarterfinals	Dick Irvin
1942-43	19	19	12	50	4th	1	4	League semifinals	Dick Irvin
1943-44	38	5	7	83	1st	8	1	Stanley Cup champ	Dick Irvin
1944-45	38	8	4	80	1st	2	4	League semifinals	Dick Irvin
1945-46	28	17	5	61	1st	8	1	Stanley Cup champ	Dick Irvin
1946-47	34	16	10	78	1st	6	5	Stanley Cup finals	Dick Irvin
1947-48	20	29	11	51	5th	—	—		Dick Irvin
1948-49	28	23	9	65	3rd	3	4	League semifinals	Dick Irvin
1949-50	29	22	19	77	2nd	1	4	League semifinals	Dick Irvin
1950-51	25	30	15	65	3rd	5	6	Stanley Cup finals	Dick Irvin
1951-52	34	26	10	78	2nd	4	7	Stanley Cup finals	Dick Irvin
1952-53	28	23	19	75	2nd	8	4	Stanley Cup champ	Dick Irvin
1953-54	35	24	11	81	2nd	7	4	Stanley Cup finals	Dick Irvin
1954-55	41	18	11	93	2nd	7	5	Stanley Cup finals	Dick Irvin
1955-56	45	15	10	100	1st	8	2	Stanley Cup champ	Toe Blake
1956-57	35	23	12	82	2nd	8	2	Stanley Cup champ	Toe Blake
1957-58	43	17	10	96	1st	8	2	Stanley Cup champ	Toe Blake
1958-59	39	18	13	91	1st	8	3	Stanley Cup champ	Toe Blake
1959-60	40	18	12	92	1st	8	0	Stanley Cup champ	Toe Blake
1960-61	41	19	10	92	1st	2	4	League semifinals	Toe Blake
1961-62	42	14	14	98	1st	2	4	League semifinals	Toe Blake
1962-63	28	19	23	79	3rd	1	4	League semifinals	Toe Blake
1963-64	36	21	13	85	1st	3	4	League semifinals	Toe Blake
1964-65	36	23	11	83	2nd	8	5	Stanley Cup champ	Toe Blake
1965-66	41	21	8	90	1st	8	2	Stanley Cup champ	Toe Blake
1966-67	32	25	13	77	2nd	6	4	Stanley Cup finals	Toe Blake
1967-68	42	22	10	54	1st/East	12	1	Stanley Cup champ	Claude Ruel
1968-69	46	19	11	103	1st/East	12	2	Stanley Cup champ	Claude Ruel
1969-70	38	22	16	92	5th/East	—	—		Claude Ruel
1970-71	42	23	13	97	3rd/East	12	8	Stanley Cup champ	Claude Ruel, Al MacNeil
1971-72	46	16	16	108	3rd/East	2	4	Division semifinals	Scotty Bowman
1972-73	52	10	16	120	1st/East	12	5	Stanley Cup champ	Scotty Bowman

— 154 —

		REGULAR SEASON				PLAYOFFS			
Season	W	L	T	Pts.	Finish	W	L	Highest round	Coach
1973-74	45	42	9	99	2nd/East	2	4	Division semifinals	Scotty Bowman
1974-75	47	14	19	113	1st/Norris	6	5	Semifinals	Scotty Bowman
1975-76	58	11	11	127	1st/Norris	12	1	Stanley Cup champ	Scotty Bowman
1976-77	60	8	12	132	1st/Norris	12	2	Stanley Cup champ	Scotty Bowman
1977-78	59	10	11	129	1st/Norris	12	3	Stanley Cup champ	Scotty Bowman
1978-79	52	17	11	115	1st/Norris	12	4	Stanley Cup champ	Scotty Bowman
1979-80	47	20	13	107	1st/Norris	6	4	Quarterfinals	Bernie Geoffrion, Claude Ruel
1980-81	45	22	13	103	1st/Norris	0	3	Preliminaries	Claude Ruel
1981-82	46	17	17	109	1st/Adams	2	3	Division semifinals	Bob Berry
1982-83	42	24	14	98	2nd/Adams	0	3	Division semifinals	Bob Berry
1983-84	35	40	5	75	4th/Adams	9	6	Conference finals	Bob Berry, Jacques Lemaire
1984-85	41	27	12	94	1st/Adams	6	6	Division finals	Jacques Lemaire
1985-86	40	33	7	87	2nd/Adams	15	5	Stanley Cup champ	Jean Perron
1986-87	41	29	10	92	2nd/Adams	10	7	Conference finals	Jean Perron
1987-88	45	22	13	103	1st/Adams	5	6	Division finals	Jean Perron
1988-89	53	18	9	115	1st/Adams	14	7	Stanley Cup finals	Pat Burns
1989-90	41	28	11	93	3rd/Adams	5	6	Division finals	Pat Burns
1990-91	39	30	11	89	2nd/Adams	7	6	Division finals	Pat Burns
1991-92	41	28	11	93	1st/Adams	4	7	Division finals	Pat Burns
1992-93	48	30	6	102	3rd/Adams	16	4	Stanley Cup champ	Jacques Demers
1993-94	41	29	14	96	3rd/Northeast	3	4	Conference quarterfinals	Jacques Demers
1994-95	18	23	7	43	6th/Northeast	—	—		Jacques Demers

*Won-lost record does not indicate tie(s) resulting from two-game, total-goals series that year (two-game, total-goals series were played from 1917-18 through 1935-36).
† 1918-19 series abandoned with no Cup holder due to influenza epidemic.

FIRST-ROUND ENTRY DRAFT CHOICES

Year Player, Overall, Last Amateur Team (League)
1969—*Rejean Houle, 1, Montreal (OHL)
  Marc Tardif, 2, Montreal (OHL)
1970—Ray Martiniuk, 5, Flin Flon (WCHL)
  Chuck Lefley, 6, Canadian Nationals
1971—*Guy Lafleur, 1, Quebec (QMJHL)
  Chuck Arnason, 7, Flin Flon (WCHL)
  Murray Wilson, 11, Ottawa (OHL)
1972—Steve Shutt, 4, Toronto (OHL)
  Michel Larocque, 6, Ottawa (OHL)
  Dave Gardner, 8, Toronto (OHL)
  John Van Boxmeer, 14, Guelph (SOJHL)
1973—Bob Gainey, 8, Peterborough (OHL)
1974—Cam Connor, 5, Flin Flon (WCHL)
  Doug Risebrough, 7, Kitchener (OHL)
  Rick Chartraw, 10, Kitchener (OHL)
  Mario Tremblay, 12, Montreal (OHL)
  Gord McTavish, 15, Sudbury (OHL)
1975—Robin Sadler, 9, Edmonton (WCHL)
  Pierre Mondou, 15, Montreal (QMJHL)
1976—Peter Lee, 12, Ottawa (OHL)
  Rod Schutt, 13, Sudbury (OHL)
  Bruce Baker, 18, Ottawa (OHL)
1977—Mark Napier, 10, Birmingham (WHA)
  Normand Dupont, 18, Montreal (QMJHL)
1978—Danny Geoffrion, 8, Cornwall (QMJHL)
  Dave Hunter, 17, Sudbury (OHL)

Year Player, Overall, Last Amateur Team (League)
1979—No first-round selection
1980—*Doug Wickenheiser, 1, Regina (WHL)
1981—Mark Hunter, 7, Brantford (OHL)
  Gilbert Delorme, 18, Chicoutimi (QMJHL)
  Jan Ingman, 19, Farjestads (Sweden)
1982—Alain Heroux, 19, Chicoutimi (QMJHL)
1983—Alfie Turcotte, 17, Portland (WHL)
1984—Petr Svoboda, 5, Czechoslovakia
  Shayne Corson, 8, Brantford (OHL)
1985—Jose Charbonneau, 12, Drummondville (QMJHL)
  Tom Chorske, 16, Minneapolis SW H.S. (Minn.)
1986—Mark Pederson, 15, Medicine Hat (WHL)
1987—Andrew Cassels, 17, Ottawa (OHL)
1988—Eric Charron, 20, Trois-Rivieres (QMJHL)
1989—Lindsay Vallis, 13, Seattle (WHL)
1990—Turner Stevenson, 12, Seattle (WHL)
1991—Brent Bilodeau, 17, Seattle (WHL)
1992—David Wilkie, 20, Kamloops (WHL)
1993—Saku Koivu, 21, TPS Turku (Finland)
1994—Brad Brown, 18, North Bay (OHL)
1995—Terry Ryan, 8, Tri-City (WHL)

*Designates first player chosen in draft.

FRANCHISE LEADERS

Players in boldface played
for club in '94-95

FORWARDS/DEFENSEMEN
Games
Henri Richard 1256
Larry Robinson 1202
Bob Gainey 1160
Jean Beliveau 1125
Claude Provost 1005
Maurice Richard 978
Yvan Cournoyer 968
Guy Lafleur 961
Serge Savard 917
Guy Carbonneau 912

Goals
Maurice Richard 544
Guy Lafleur 518
Jean Beliveau 507
Yvan Cournoyer 428
Steve Shutt 408
Bernie Geoffrion 371
Jacques Lemaire 366
Henri Richard 358
Aurele Joliat 270
Mario Tremblay 258

Assists
Guy Lafleur 728
Jean Beliveau 712
Henri Richard 688

Larry Robinson 686
Jacques Lemaire 469
Yvan Cournoyer 435
Maurice Richard 421
Elmer Lach 408
Guy Lapointe 406
Bernie Geoffrion 388

Points
Guy Lafleur 1246
Jean Beliveau 1219
Henri Richard 1046
Maurice Richard 965
Larry Robinson 883
Yvan Cournoyer 863
Jacques Lemaire 835

Steve Shutt 776	Henri Richard................................ 928	Charlie Hodge 236
Bernie Geoffrion 759	Tom Johnson 897	Michel Larocque........................... 231
Elmer Lach...................................... 623		

GOALTENDERS

Shutouts

Penalty minutes	Games	
		George Hainsworth........................... 74
Chris Nilan 2248	Jacques Plante 556	Jacques Plante.............................. 58
Maurice Richard......................... 1285	**Patrick Roy** **529**	Ken Dryden................................. 46
John Ferguson.............................. 1214	Ken Dryden 397	Bill Durnan................................. 34
Lyle Odelein **1137**	Bill Durnan 383	Gerry McNeil.............................. 28
Mario Tremblay 1043	Georges Vezina 328	**Patrick Roy** **28**
Doug Harvey 1042	George Hainsworth........................ 321	Wilf Cude...................................... 22
Jean Beliveau 1029	Gerry McNeil................................ 276	Charlie Hodge 21
Doug Risebrough 959	Wilf Cude...................................... 249	Michel Larocque 17
		Gump Worsley 16

MONTREAL MAROONS (DEFUNCT)

YEAR - BY - YEAR RECORDS

	REGULAR SEASON					PLAYOFFS			
Season	W	L	T	Pts.	Finish	W	L	Highest round	Coach
1924-25	9	19	2	20	5th	—	—		Eddie Gerard
1925-26	20	11	5	45	2nd	3	1	Stanley Cup champ	Eddie Gerard
1926-27	20	20	4	44	3rd/Canadian	*0	1	Quarterfinals	Eddie Gerard
1927-28	24	14	6	54	2nd/Canadian	*5	3	Stanley Cup finals	Eddie Gerard
1928-29	15	20	9	39	5th/Canadian	—			Eddie Gerard
1929-30	23	16	5	51	1st/Canadian	1	3	Semifinals	Dunc Munro
1930-31	20	18	6	46	3rd/Canadian	*0	2	Quarterfinals	Dunc Munro, George Boucher
1931-32	19	22	7	45	3rd/Canadian	*1	1	Semifinals	Sprague Cleghorn
1932-33	22	20	6	50	2nd/Canadian	0	2	Quarterfinals	Eddie Gerard
1933-34	19	18	11	49	3rd/Canadian	*1	2	Semifinals	Eddie Gerard
1934-35	24	19	5	53	2nd/Canadian	*5	0	Stanley Cup champ	Tommy Gorman
1935-36	22	16	10	54	1st/Canadian	0	1	Semifinals	Tommy Gorman
1936-37	22	17	9	53	2nd/Canadian	2	3	Semifinals	Tommy Gorman
1937-38	12	30	6	30	4th/Canadian	—			King Clancy, Tommy Gorman

*Won-lost record does not indicate tie(s) resulting from two-game, total goals series that year (two-game, total-goals series were played from 1917-18 through 1935-36).

MONTREAL WANDERERS (DEFUNCT)

YEAR - BY - YEAR RECORDS

	REGULAR SEASON					PLAYOFFS			
Season	W	L	T	Pts.	Finish	W	L	Highest round	Coach
1917-18*	1	5	0	2	4th	—	—		Art Ross

*Franchise disbanded after Montreal Arena burned down. Montreal Canadiens and Toronto each counted one win for defaulted games with Wanderers.

NEW JERSEY DEVILS

YEAR - BY - YEAR RECORDS

	REGULAR SEASON					PLAYOFFS			
Season	W	L	T	Pts.	Finish	W	L	Highest round	Coach
1974-75*	15	54	11	41	5th/Smythe	—	—		Bep Guidolin
1975-76*	12	56	12	36	5th/Smythe	—	—		Bep Guidolin, Sid Abel, Eddie Bush
1976-77†	20	46	14	54	5th/Smythe	—	—		John Wilson
1977-78†	19	40	21	59	2nd/Smythe	0	2	Preliminaries	Pat Kelly
1978-79†	15	53	12	42	4th/Smythe	—	—		Pat Kelly, Bep Guidolin
1979-80†	19	48	13	51	6th/Smythe	—	—		Don Cherry
1980-81†	22	45	13	57	5th/Smythe	—	—		Billy MacMillan
1981-82†	18	49	13	49	5th/Smythe	—	—		Bert Marshall, Marshall Johnston
1982-83	17	49	14	48	5th/Patrick	—	—		Billy MacMillan
1983-84	17	56	7	41	5th/Patrick	—	—		Billy MacMillan, Tom McVie
1984-85	22	48	10	54	5th/Patrick	—	—		Doug Carpenter
1985-86	28	49	3	59	5th/Patrick	—	—		Doug Carpenter
1986-87	29	45	6	64	6th/Patrick	—	—		Doug Carpenter
1987-88	38	36	6	82	4th/Patrick	11	9	Conference finals	Doug Carpenter, Jim Schoenfeld
1988-89	27	41	12	66	5th/Patrick	—	—		Jim Schoenfeld
1989-90	37	34	9	83	2nd/Patrick	2	4	Division semifinals	Jim Schoenfeld, John Cunniff
1990-91	32	33	15	79	4th/Patrick	3	4	Division semifinals	John Cunniff, Tom McVie
1991-92	38	31	11	87	4th/Patrick	3	4	Division semifinals	Tom McVie
1992-93	40	37	7	87	4th/Patrick	1	4	Division semifinals	Herb Brooks

Season	W	L	T	Pts.	REGULAR SEASON Finish	W	L	PLAYOFFS Highest round	Coach
1993-94	47	25	12	106	2nd/Atlantic	11	9	Conference finals	Jacques Lemaire
1994-95	22	18	8	52	2nd/Atlantic	16	4	Stanley Cup champ	Jacques Lemaire

*Kansas City Scouts.
†Colorado Rockies.

FIRST-ROUND ENTRY DRAFT CHOICES

Year	Player, Overall, Last Amateur Team (League)
1974	Wilf Paiement, 2, St. Catharines (OHL)
1975	Barry Dean, 2, Medicine Hat (WCHL)
1976	Paul Gardner, 11, Oshawa (OHL)
1977	Barry Beck, 2, New Westminster (WCHL)
1978	Mike Gillis, 5, Kingston (OHL)
1979	*Rob Ramage, 1, Birmingham (WHA)
1980	Paul Gagne, 19, Windsor (OHL)
1981	Joe Cirella, 5, Oshawa (OHL)
1982	Rocky Trottier, 8, Billings (WHL)
	Ken Daneyko, 18, Seattle (WHL)
1983	John MacLean, 6, Oshawa (OHL)
1984	Kirk Muller, 2, Guelph (OHL)
1985	Craig Wolanin, 3, Kitchener (OHL)
1986	Neil Brady, 3, Medicine Hat (WHL)

Year	Player, Overall, Last Amateur Team (League)
1987	Brendan Shanahan, 2, London (OHL)
1988	Corey Foster, 12, Peterborough (OHL)
1989	Bill Guerin, 5, Springfield (Mass.) Jr.
	Jason Miller, 18, Medicine Hat (WHL)
1990	Martin Brodeur, 20, St. Hyacinthe (QMJHL)
1991	Scott Niedermayer, 3, Kamloops (WHL)
	Brian Rolston, 11, Detroit Compuware Jr.
1992	Jason Smith, 18, Regina (WHL)
1993	Denis Pederson, 13, Prince Albert (WHL)
1994	Vadim Sharifjanov, 25, Salavat (Russia)
1995	Petr Sykora, 18, Detroit (IHL)

*Designates first player chosen in draft.

FRANCHISE LEADERS

Players in boldface played
for club in '94-95

FORWARDS/DEFENSEMEN

Games

John MacLean	752
Ken Daneyko	716
Bruce Driver	702
Aaron Broten	641
Kirk Muller	556
Joe Cirella	503
Mike Kitchen	474
Pat Verbeek	463
Wilf Paiement	392
Gary Croteau	390

Goals

John MacLean	295
Kirk Muller	185
Pat Verbeek	170
Aaron Broten	162
Wilf Paiement	153
Stephane Richer	126
Claude Lemieux	125
Paul Gagne	106
Brendan Shanahan	96
Gary Croteau	92

Assists

Kirk Muller	335
Bruce Driver	316
Aaron Broten	307
John MacLean	293
Wilf Paiement	183
Scott Stevens	167
Patrik Sundstrom	160
Joe Cirella	159
Pat Verbeek	151
Mel Bridgman	148

Points

John MacLean	588
Kirk Muller	520
Aaron Broten	469
Bruce Driver	399
Wilf Paiement	336
Pat Verbeek	321
Claude Lemieux	259
Stephane Richer	248
Patrik Sundstrom	246
Mark Johnson	229

Penalty minutes

Ken Daneyko	1936
John MacLean	1014
Pat Verbeek	943

Joe Cirella	938
Randy McKay	740
David Maley	683
Kirk Muller	572
Wilf Paiement	558
Perry Anderson	553
Claude Lemieux	539

GOALTENDERS

Games

Chico Resch	267
Chris Terreri	264
Sean Burke	162

Shutouts

Martin Brodeur	6
Chris Terreri	6
Craig Billington	4
Sean Burke	4

Goals-against average
(2400 minutes minimum)

Martin Brodeur	2.45
Chris Terreri	3.10
Sean Burke	3.66

Wins

Chris Terreri	103
Chico Resch	67
Sean Burke	62

NEW YORK AMERICANS (DEFUNCT)

YEAR-BY-YEAR RECORDS

Season	W	L	T	Pts.	REGULAR SEASON Finish	W	L	PLAYOFFS Highest round	Coach
1919-20‡	4	20	0	8	4th	—	—		Mike Quinn
1920-21§	6	18	0	12	4th	—	—		Percy Thompson
1921-22§	7	17	0	14	4th	—	—		Percy Thompson
1922-23§	6	18	0	12	4th	—	—		Art Ross
1923-24§	9	15	0	18	4th	—	—		Percy Lesueur
1924-25§	19	10	1	39	1st	† —	—		Jimmy Gardner
1925-26	12	20	4	28	5th	—	—		Tommy Gorman
1926-27	17	25	2	36	4th/Canadian	—	—		Newsy Lalonde
1927-28	11	27	6	28	5th/Canadian	—	—		Wilf Green
1928-29	19	13	12	50	2nd/Canadian	*0	1	Semifinals	Tommy Gorman
1929-30	14	25	5	33	5th/Canadian	—	—		Lionel Conacher
1930-31	18	16	10	46	4th/Canadian	—	—		Eddie Gerard

			REGULAR SEASON			PLAYOFFS		
Season	W	L	T	Pts.	Finish	W	L	Highest round	Coach
1931-32	16	24	8	40	4th/Canadian	—	—		Eddie Gerard
1932-33	15	22	11	41	4th/Canadian	—	—		Joe Simpson
1933-34	15	23	10	40	4th/Canadian	—	—		Joe Simpson
1934-35	12	27	9	33	4th/Canadian	—	—		Joe Simpson
1935-36	16	25	7	39	3rd/Canadian	2	3	Semifinals	Red Dutton
1936-37	15	29	4	34	4th/Canadian	—	—		Red Dutton
1937-38	19	18	11	49	2nd/Canadian	3	3	Semifinals	Red Dutton
1938-39	17	21	10	44	4th	0	2	Quarterfinals	Red Dutton
1939-40	15	29	4	34	6th	1	2	Quarterfinals	Red Dutton
1940-41	8	29	11	27	7th	—	—		Red Dutton
1941-42*	16	29	3	35	7th	—	—		Red Dutton

*Won-lost record does not indicate tie(s) resulting from two-game, total goals series that year (two-game, total-goals series were played from 1917-18 through 1935-36).
†Refused to participate in playoffs—held out for more compensation.
‡Quebec Bulldogs.
§Hamilton Tigers.
*Brooklyn Americans.

NEW YORK ISLANDERS

YEAR-BY-YEAR RECORDS

			REGULAR SEASON			PLAYOFFS		
Season	W	L	T	Pts.	Finish	W	L	Highest round	Coach
1972-73	12	60	6	30	8th/East	—	—		Phil Goyette, Earl Ingarfield
1973-74	19	41	18	56	8th/East	—	—		Al Arbour
1974-75	33	25	22	88	3rd/Patrick	9	8	Semifinals	Al Arbour
1975-76	42	21	17	101	2nd/Patrick	7	6	Semifinals	Al Arbour
1976-77	47	21	12	106	2nd/Patrick	8	4	Semifinals	Al Arbour
1977-78	48	17	15	111	1st/Patrick	3	4	Quarterfinals	Al Arbour
1978-79	51	15	14	116	1st/Patrick	6	4	Semifinals	Al Arbour
1979-80	39	28	13	91	2nd/Patrick	15	6	Stanley Cup champ	Al Arbour
1980-81	48	18	14	110	1st/Patrick	15	3	Stanley Cup champ	Al Arbour
1981-82	54	16	10	118	1st/Patrick	15	4	Stanley Cup champ	Al Arbour
1982-83	42	26	12	96	2nd/Patrick	15	5	Stanley Cup champ	Al Arbour
1983-84	50	26	4	104	1st/Patrick	12	9	Stanley Cup finals	Al Arbour
1984-85	40	34	6	86	3rd/Patrick	4	6	Division finals	Al Arbour
1985-86	39	29	12	90	3rd/Patrick	0	3	Division semifinals	Al Arbour
1986-87	35	33	12	82	3rd/Patrick	7	7	Division finals	Terry Simpson
1987-88	39	31	10	88	1st/Patrick	2	4	Division semifinals	Terry Simpson
1988-89	28	47	5	61	6th/Patrick	—	—		Terry Simpson, Al Arbour
1989-90	31	38	11	73	4th/Patrick	1	4	Division semifinals	Al Arbour
1990-91	25	45	10	60	6th/Patrick	—	—		Al Arbour
1991-92	34	35	11	79	5th/Patrick	—	—		Al Arbour
1992-93	40	37	7	87	3rd/Patrick	9	9	Conference finals	Al Arbour
1993-94	36	36	12	84	4th/Atlantic	0	4	Conference quarterfinals	Al Arbour, Lorne Henning
1994-95	15	28	5	35	7th/Atlantic	—	—		Lorne Henning

FIRST-ROUND ENTRY DRAFT CHOICES

Year Player, Overall, Last Amateur Team (League)
1972—*Billy Harris, 1, Toronto (OHL)
1973—*Denis Potvin, 1, Ottawa (OHL)
1974—Clark Gillies, 4, Regina (WCHL)
1975—Pat Price, 11, Vancouver (WHA)
1976—Alex McKendry, 14, Sudbury (OHL)
1977—Mike Bossy, 15, Laval (QMJHL)
1978—Steve Tambellini, 15, Lethbridge (WCHL)
1979—Duane Sutter, 17, Lethbridge (WHL)
1980—Brent Sutter, 17, Red Deer (AJHL)
1981—Paul Boutilier, 21, Sherbrooke (QMJHL)
1982—Pat Flatley, 21, University of Wisconsin
1983—Pat LaFontaine, 3, Verdun (QMJHL)
          Gerald Diduck, 16, Lethbridge (WHL)
1984—Duncan MacPherson, 20, Saskatoon (WHL)

Year Player, Overall, Last Amateur Team (League)
1985—Brad Dalgarno, 6, Hamilton (OHL)
          Derek King, 13, Sault Ste. Marie (OHL)
1986—Tom Fitzgerald, 17, Austin Prep (Mass.)
1987—Dean Chynoweth, 13, Medicine Hat (WHL)
1988—Kevin Cheveldayoff, 16, Brandon (WHL)
1989—Dave Chyzowski, 2, Kamloops (WHL)
1990—Scott Scissons, 6, Saskatoon (WHL)
1991—Scott Lachance, 4, Boston University
1992—Darius Kasparaitis, 5, Dynamo Moscow (CIS)
1993—Todd Bertuzzi, 23, Guelph (OHL)
1994—Brett Lindros, 9, Kingston (OHL)
1995—Wade Redden, 2, Brandon (WHL)

*Designates first player chosen in draft.

Players in boldface played
for club in '94-95

FORWARDS/DEFENSEMEN

Games
Bryan Trottier	1123
Denis Potvin	1080
Bob Nystrom	900
Clark Gillies	872
Bob Bourne	814
Mike Bossy	752
Brent Sutter	694
Billy Smith	675
Billy Harris	623
Stefan Persson	622

Goals
Mike Bossy	573
Bryan Trottier	500
Denis Potvin	310
Clark Gillies	304
Pat LaFontaine	287
Brent Sutter	287
Bob Bourne	238
Bob Nystrom	235
John Tonelli	206
Billy Harris	184

Assists
Bryan Trottier	853
Denis Potvin	742

Mike Bossy	553
Clark Gillies	359
John Tonelli	338
Brent Sutter	323
Stefan Persson	317
Bob Bourne	304
Pat LaFontaine	279
Bob Nystrom	278

Points
Bryan Trottier	1353
Mike Bossy	1126
Denis Potvin	1052
Clark Gillies	663
Brent Sutter	610
Pat LaFontaine	566
John Tonelli	544
Bob Bourne	542
Bob Nystrom	513
Billy Harris	443

Penalty minutes
Mick Vukota	**1702**
Garry Howatt	1466
Denis Potvin	1354
Bob Nystrom	1248
Clark Gillies	891
Duane Sutter	891
Rich Pilon	**861**
Bryan Trottier	798
Gerry Hart	783
Brent Sutter	761

GOALTENDERS

Games
Billy Smith	675
Chico Resch	282
Kelly Hrudey	241
Glenn Healy	176
Roland Melanson	136
Mark Fitzpatrick	129
Gerry Desjardins	80

Shutouts
Chico Resch	25
Billy Smith	22
Kelly Hrudey	6

Goals-against average
(2400 minutes minimum)
Chico Resch	2.56
Ron Hextall	3.08
Jamie McLennan	**3.11**
Roland Melanson	3.14
Billy Smith	3.16
Mark Fitzpatrick	3.41
Glenn Healy	3.45
Kelly Hrudey	3.46

Wins
Billy Smith	304
Chico Resch	157
Kelly Hrudey	106
Roland Melanson	77
Glenn Healy	66
Mark Fitzpatrick	51
Ron Hextall	27
Gerry Desjardins	14
Jamie McLennan	**14**

NEW YORK RANGERS

YEAR-BY-YEAR RECORDS

Season	W	L	T	Pts.	Finish	W	L	Highest round	Coach
1926-27	25	13	6	56	1st/American	*0	1	Semifinals	Lester Patrick
1927-28	19	16	9	47	2nd/American	*5	3	Stanley Cup champ	Lester Patrick
1928-29	21	13	10	52	2nd/American	*3	2	Stanley Cup finals	Lester Patrick
1929-30	17	17	10	44	3rd/American	*1	2	Semifinals	Lester Patrick
1930-31	19	16	9	47	3rd/American	2	2	Semifinals	Lester Patrick
1931-32	23	17	8	54	1st/American	3	4	Stanley Cup finals	Lester Patrick
1932-33	23	17	8	54	3rd/American	*6	1	Stanley Cup champ	Lester Patrick
1933-34	21	19	8	50	3rd/American	*0	1	Quarterfinals	Lester Patrick
1934-35	22	20	6	50	3rd/American	*1	1	Semifinals	Lester Patrick
1935-36	19	17	12	50	4th/American	—	—		Lester Patrick
1936-37	19	20	9	47	3rd/American	6	3	Stanley Cup finals	Lester Patrick
1937-38	27	15	6	60	2nd/American	1	2	Quarterfinals	Lester Patrick
1938-39	26	16	6	58	2nd	3	4	Semifinals	Lester Patrick
1939-40	27	11	10	64	2nd	8	4	Stanley Cup champ	Frank Boucher
1940-41	21	19	8	50	4th	1	2	Quarterfinals	Frank Boucher
1941-42	29	17	2	60	1st	2	4	Semifinals	Frank Boucher
1942-43	11	31	8	30	6th	—	—		Frank Boucher
1943-44	6	39	5	17	6th	—	—		Frank Boucher
1944-45	11	29	10	32	6th	—	—		Frank Boucher
1945-46	13	28	9	35	6th	—	—		Frank Boucher
1946-47	22	32	6	50	5th	—	—		Frank Boucher
1947-48	21	26	13	55	4th	2	4	League semifinals	Frank Boucher
1948-49	18	31	11	47	6th	—	—		Frank Boucher, Lynn Patrick
1949-50	28	31	11	67	4th	7	5	Stanley Cup finals	Lynn Patrick
1950-51	20	29	21	61	5th	—	—		Neil Colville
1951-52	23	34	13	59	5th	—	—		Neil Colville, Bill Cook
1952-53	17	37	16	50	6th	—	—		Bill Cook
1953-54	29	31	10	68	5th	—	—		Frank Boucher, Muzz Patrick
1954-55	17	35	18	52	5th	—	—		Muzz Patrick
1955-56	32	28	10	74	3rd	1	4	League semifinals	Phil Watson
1956-57	26	30	14	66	4th	1	4	League semifinals	Phil Watson
1957-58	32	25	13	77	2nd	2	4	League semifinals	Phil Watson

| | REGULAR SEASON | | | | | PLAYOFFS | | | |
Season	W	L	T	Pts.	Finish	W	L	Highest round	Coach
1958-59	26	32	12	64	5th	—	—		Phil Watson
1959-60	17	38	15	49	6th	—	—		Phil Watson, Alf Pike
1960-61	22	38	10	54	5th	—	—		Alf Pike
1961-62	26	32	12	64	4th	2	4	League semifinals	Doug Harvey
1962-63	22	36	12	56	5th	—	—		Muzz Patrick, Red Sullivan
1963-64	22	38	10	54	5th	—	—		Red Sullivan
1964-65	20	38	12	52	5th	—	—		Red Sullivan
1965-66	18	41	11	47	6th	—	—		Red Sullivan, Emile Francis
1966-67	30	28	12	72	4th	0	4	League semifinals	Emile Francis
1967-68	39	23	12	90	2nd/East	2	4	Division semifinals	Emile Francis
1968-69	41	26	9	91	3rd/East	0	4	Division semifinals	Bernie Geoffrion, Emile Francis
1969-70	38	22	16	92	4th/East	2	4	Division semifinals	Emile Francis
1970-71	49	18	11	109	2nd/East	7	6	Division finals	Emile Francis
1971-72	48	17	13	109	2nd/East	10	6	Stanley Cup finals	Emile Francis
1972-73	47	23	8	102	3rd/East	5	5	Division finals	Emile Francis
1973-74	40	24	14	94	3rd/East	7	6	Division finals	Larry Popein, Emile Francis
1974-75	37	29	14	88	2nd/Patrick	1	2	Preliminaries	Emile Francis
1975-76	29	42	9	67	4th/Patrick	—	—		Ron Stewart, John Ferguson
1976-77	29	37	14	72	4th/Patrick	—	—		John Ferguson
1977-78	30	37	13	73	4th/Patrick	1	2	Preliminaries	Jean-Guy Talbot
1978-79	40	29	11	91	3rd/Patrick	11	7	Stanley Cup finals	Fred Shero
1979-80	38	32	10	86	3rd/Patrick	4	5	Quarterfinals	Fred Shero
1980-81	30	36	14	74	4th/Patrick	7	7	Semifinals	Fred Shero, Craig Patrick
1981-82	39	27	14	92	2nd/Patrick	5	5	Division finals	Herb Brooks
1982-83	35	35	10	80	4th/Patrick	5	4	Division finals	Herb Brooks
1983-84	42	29	9	93	4th/Patrick	2	3	Division semifinals	Herb Brooks
1984-85	26	44	10	62	4th/Patrick	0	3	Division semifinals	Herb Brooks, Craig Patrick
1985-86	36	38	8	78	4th/Patrick	8	8	Conference finals	Ted Sator
1986-87	34	38	8	76	4th/Patrick	2	4	Division semifinals	Ted Sator, Tom Webster, Phil Esposito
1987-88	36	34	10	82	4th/Patrick	—	—		Michel Bergeron
1988-89	37	35	8	82	3rd/Patrick	0	4	Division semifinals	Michel Bergeron, Phil Esposito
1989-90	36	31	13	85	1st/Patrick	5	5	Division finals	Roger Neilson
1990-91	36	31	13	85	2nd/Patrick	2	4	Division semifinals	Roger Neilson
1991-92	50	25	5	105	1st/Patrick	6	7	Division finals	Roger Neilson
1992-93	34	39	11	79	6th/Patrick	—	—		Roger Neilson, Ron Smith
1993-94	52	24	8	112	1st/Atlantic	16	7	Stanley Cup champ	Mike Keenan
1994-95	22	23	3	47	4th/Atlantic	4	6	Conference semifinals	Colin Campbell

*Won-lost record does not indicate tie(s) resulting from two-game, total goals series that year (two-game, total-goals series were played from 1917-18 through 1935-36).

FIRST-ROUND ENTRY DRAFT CHOICES

Year Player, Overall, Last Amateur Team (League)
1969—Andre Dupont, 8, Montreal (OHL)
    Pierre Jarry, 12, Ottawa (OHL)
1970—Normand Gratton, 11, Montreal (OHL)
1971—Steve Vickers, 10, Toronto (OHL)
    Steve Durbano, 13, Toronto (OHL)
1972—Albert Blanchard, 10, Kitchener (OHL)
    Bobby MacMillan, 15, St. Catharines (OHL)
1973—Rick Middleton, 14, Oshawa (OHL)
1974—Dave Maloney, 14, Kitchener (OHL)
1975—Wayne Dillon, 12, Toronto (WHA)
1976—Don Murdoch, 6, Medicine Hat (WCHL)
1977—Lucien DeBlois, 8, Sorel (QMJHL)
    Ron Duguay, 13, Sudbury (OHL)
1978—No first-round selection
1979—Doug Sulliman, 13, Kitchener (OHL)
1980—Jim Malone, 14, Toronto (OHL)

Year Player, Overall, Last Amateur Team (League)
1981—James Patrick, 9, Prince Albert (AJHL)
1982—Chris Kontos, 15, Toronto (OHL)
1983—Dave Gagner, 12, Brantford (OHL)
1984—Terry Carkner, 14, Peterborough (OHL)
1985—Ulf Dahlen, 7, Ostersund (Sweden)
1986—Brian Leetch, 9, Avon Old Farms Prep (Ct.)
1987—Jayson More, 10, New Westminster (WCHL)
1988—No first-round selection
1989—Steven Rice, 20, Kitchener (OHL)
1990—Michael Stewart, 13, Michigan State University
1991—Alexei Kovalev, 15, Dynamo Moscow (USSR)
1992—Peter Ferraro, 24, Waterloo (USHL)
1993—Niklas Sundstrom, 8, Ornskoldsvik (Sweden)
1994—Dan Cloutier, 26, Sault Ste. Marie (OHL)
1995—No first-round selection

FRANCHISE LEADERS

Players in boldface played
for club in '94-95

FORWARDS/DEFENSEMEN

Games					
Harry Howell	1160				
Rod Gilbert	1065				
Ron Greschner	982				
Walt Tkaczuk	945				
Jean Ratelle	862				
Vic Hadfield	838				

	Games		Goals		Assists
Jim Neilson	810	Rod Gilbert	406	Rod Gilbert	615
Andy Bathgate	719	Jean Ratelle	336	Jean Ratelle	481
Steve Vickers	698	Andy Bathgate	272	Andy Bathgate	457
Dean Prentice	666	Vic Hadfield	262	Walt Tkaczuk	451
Bill Cook	228	Camille Henry	256	Ron Greschner	431
Walt Tkaczuk	227	Steve Vickers	246	**Brian Leetch**	**375**
Don Maloney	195				
Bryan Hextall	187				

James Patrick	363
Steve Vickers	340
Vic Hadfield	310
Don Maloney	307
Brad Park	283

Points

Rod Gilbert	1021
Jean Ratelle	817
Andy Bathgate	729
Walt Tkaczuk	678
Ron Greschner	610
Steve Vickers	586
Vic Hadfield	572
Don Maloney	502
Brian Leetch	**487**
Camille Henry	478

Penalty minutes

| Ron Greschner | 1226 |
| Harry Howell | 1147 |

Don Maloney	1113
Vic Hadfield	1036
Nick Fotiu	970

GOALTENDERS

Games

Gump Worsley	583
Ed Giacomin	539
John Vanbiesbrouck	449
Chuck Rayner	377
Dave Kerr	324
Mike Richter	**250**
John Davidson	222
Gilles Villemure	184

Shutouts

Ed Giacomin	49
Dave Kerr	40
John Ross Roach	30
Chuck Rayner	24
Gump Worsley	24

| Lorne Chabot | 21 |

Goals - against average
(2400 minutes minimum)

Lorne Chabot	1.61
Dave Kerr	2.07
John Ross Roach	2.16
Andy Aitkenhead	2.42
Johnny Bower	2.62
Gilles Villemure	2.62
Ed Giacomin	2.73

Wins

Ed Giacomin	266
Gump Worsley	204
John Vanbiesbrouck	200
Dave Kerr	157
Mike Richter	**125**
Chuck Rayner	123
Gilles Villemure	96
John Davidson	93

OTTAWA SENATORS (FIRST CLUB—DEFUNCT)

YEAR-BY-YEAR RECORDS

	REGULAR SEASON					PLAYOFFS			
Season	W	L	T	Pts.	Finish	W	L	Highest round	Coach
1917-18	9	13	0	18	3rd	—	—		Eddie Gerard
1918-19	12	6	0	24	1st	1	4	Semifinals	Alf Smith
1919-20	19	5	0	38	1st	3	2	Stanley Cup champ	Pete Green
1920-21	14	10	0	28	2nd	*4	2	Stanley Cup champ	Pete Green
1921-22	14	8	2	30	1st	*0	1	Semifinals	Pete Green
1922-23	14	9	1	29	1st	6	2	Stanley Cup champ	Pete Green
1923-24	16	8	0	32	1st	0	2	Semifinals	Pete Green
1924-25	17	12	1	35	4th	—	—		Pete Green
1925-26	24	8	4	52	1st	*0	1	Semifinals	Pete Green
1926-27	30	10	4	64	1st/Canadian	*3	0	Stanley Cup champ	Dave Gill
1927-28	20	14	10	50	3rd/Canadian	0	2	Quarterfinals	Dave Gill
1928-29	14	17	13	41	4th/Canadian	—	—		Dave Gill
1929-30	21	15	8	50	3rd/Canadian	*0	1	Semifinals	Newsy Lalonde
1930-31	10	30	4	24	5th/Canadian	—	—		Newsy Lalonde
1931-32					Club suspended operations for one season.				
1932-33	11	27	10	32	5th/Canadian	—	—		Cy Denneny
1933-34	13	29	6	32	5th/Canadian	—	—		George Boucher
1934-35†	11	31	6	28	5th/Canadian	—	—		Eddie Gerard, George Boucher

*Won-lost record does not indicate tie(s) resulting from two-game, total goals series that year (two-game, total-goals series were played from 1917-18 through 1935-36).
†St. Louis Eagles.

OTTAWA SENATORS (SECOND CLUB)

YEAR-BY-YEAR RECORDS

	REGULAR SEASON					PLAYOFFS			
Season	W	L	T	Pts.	Finish	W	L	Highest round	Coach
1992-93	10	70	4	24	6th/Adams	—	—		Rick Bowness
1993-94	14	61	9	37	7th/Northeast	—	—		Rick Bowness
1994-95	9	34	5	23	7th/Northeast	—	—		Rick Bowness

FIRST-ROUND ENTRY DRAFT CHOICES

Year   Player, Overall, Last Amateur Team (League)
1992—Alexei Yashin, 2, Dynamo Moscow (CIS)
1993—*Alexandre Daigle, 1, Victoriaville (QMJHL)
1994—Radek Bonk, 3, Las Vegas (IHL)

Year   Player, Overall, Last Amateur Team (League)
1995—*Bryan Berard, 1, Detroit (OHL)
*Designates first player chosen in draft.

Players in boldface played
for club in '94-95

FORWARDS/DEFENSEMEN

Games

Norm Maciver	161
Sylvain Turgeon	152
Brad Shaw	149
Darren Rumble	139
Mark Lamb	137
Alexandre Daigle	131
Alexei Yashin	130
Darcy Loewen	123
Andrew McBain	114
Gord Dineen	109
Dave McLlwain	109

Goals

Alexei Yashin	51
Bob Kudelski	47
Sylvain Turgeon	47
Alexandre Daigle	36
Norm Maciver	24
Dave McLlwain	22
David Archibald	21
Jamie Baker	19
Mark Lamb	18
Andrew McBain	18

Assists

Norm Maciver	73
Alexei Yashin	72
Brad Shaw	53
Alexandre Daigle	52
Sylvain Turgeon	41
Mark Lamb	37
Dave McLlwain	32
Jamie Baker	29
Bob Kudelski	29
Gord Dineen	25

Points

Alexei Yashin	123
Norm Maciver	97
Alexandre Daigle	88
Sylvain Turgeon	88
Bob Kudelski	76
Brad Shaw	64
Mark Lamb	55
Jamie Baker	48
Dave McLlwain	43
Andrew McBain	42

Penalty minutes

Mike Peluso	318
Dennis Vial	279
Bill Huard	226
Troy Mallette	201
Darcy Loewen	197

Sylvain Turgeon	185
Darren Rumble	177
Scott Levins	144
Mark Lamb	120
Norm Maciver	120

GOALTENDERS

Games

Craig Billington	72
Peter Sidorkiewicz	64
Darrin Madeley	39
Don Beaupre	38
Daniel Berthiaume	26

Shutouts

Don Beaupre	1

Goals-against average
(1200 minutes minimum)

Don Beaupre	3.36
Darrin Madeley	4.36
Daniel Berthiaume	4.39
Peter Sidorkiewicz	4.43
Craig Billington	4.53

Wins

Craig Billington	11
Don Beaupre	8
Peter Sidorkiewicz	8
Darrin Madeley	4
Daniel Berthiaume	2'

PHILADELPHIA FLYERS

YEAR-BY-YEAR RECORDS

	REGULAR SEASON					PLAYOFFS			
Season	W	L	T	Pts.	Finish	W	L	Highest round	Coach
1967-68	31	32	11	73	1st/West	3	4	Division semifinals	Keith Allen
1968-69	20	35	21	61	3rd/West	0	4	Division semifinals	Keith Allen
1969-70	17	35	24	58	5th/West	—	—		Vic Stasiuk
1970-71	28	33	17	73	3rd/West	0	4	Division semifinals	Vic Stasiuk
1971-72	26	38	14	66	5th/West	—	—		Fred Shero
1972-73	37	30	11	85	2nd/West	5	6	Division finals	Fred Shero
1973-74	50	16	12	112	1st/West	12	5	Stanley Cup champ	Fred Shero
1974-75	51	18	11	113	1st/Patrick	12	5	Stanley Cup champ	Fred Shero
1975-76	51	13	16	118	1st/Patrick	8	8	Stanley Cup finals	Fred Shero
1976-77	48	16	16	112	1st/Patrick	4	6	Semifinals	Fred Shero
1977-78	45	20	15	105	2nd/Patrick	7	5	Semifinals	Fred Shero
1978-79	40	25	15	95	2nd/Patrick	3	5	Quarterfinals	Bob McCammon, Pat Quinn
1979-80	48	12	20	116	1st/Patrick	13	6	Stanley Cup finals	Pat Quinn
1980-81	41	24	15	97	2nd/Patrick	6	6	Quarterfinals	Pat Quinn
1981-82	38	31	11	87	3rd/Patrick	1	3	Division semifinals	Pat Quinn, Bob McCammon
1982-83	49	23	8	106	1st/Patrick	0	3	Division semifinals	Bob McCammon
1983-84	44	26	10	98	3rd/Patrick	0	3	Division semifinals	Bob McCammon
1984-85	53	20	7	113	1st/Patrick	12	7	Stanley Cup finals	Mike Keenan
1985-86	53	23	4	110	1st/Patrick	2	3	Division semifinals	Mike Keenan
1986-87	46	26	8	100	1st/Patrick	15	11	Stanley Cup finals	Mike Keenan
1987-88	38	33	9	85	2nd/Patrick	3	4	Division semifinals	Mike Keenan
1988-89	36	36	8	80	4th/Patrick	10	9	Conference finals	Paul Holmgren
1989-90	30	39	11	71	6th/Patrick	—	—		Paul Holmgren
1990-91	33	37	10	76	5th/Patrick	—	—		Paul Holmgren
1991-92	32	37	11	75	6th/Patrick	—	—		Paul Holmgren, Bill Dineen
1992-93	36	37	11	83	6th/Patrick	—	—		Bill Dineen
1993-94	35	39	10	80	6th/Atlantic	—	—		Terry Simpson
1994-95	28	16	4	60	1st/Atlantic	10	5	Conference finals	Terry Murray

FIRST-ROUND ENTRY DRAFT CHOICES

Year   Player, Overall, Last Amateur Team (League)
1969—Bob Currier, 6, Cornwall (QMJHL)
1970—No first-round selection
1971—Larry Wright, 8, Regina (WCHL)
   Pierre Plante, 9, Drummondville (QMJHL)

Year   Player, Overall, Last Amateur Team (League)
1972—Bill Barber, 7, Kitchener (OHL)
1973—No first-round selection
1974—No first-round selection
1975—*Mel Bridgeman, 1, Victoria (WCHL)

Year	Player, Overall, Last Amateur Team (League)
1976	Mark Suzor, 17, Kingston (OHL)
1977	Kevin McCarthy, 17, Winnipeg (WCHL)
1978	Behn Wilson, 6, Kingston (OHL)
	Ken Linseman, 7, Birmingham (WHA)
	Dan Lucas, 14, Sault Ste. Marie (OHL)
1979	Brian Propp, 14, Brandon (WHL)
1980	Mike Stothers, 21, Kingston (OHL)
1981	Steve Smith, 16, Sault Ste. Marie (OHL)
1982	Ron Sutter, 4, Lethbridge (WHL)
1983	No first-round selection
1984	No first-round selection
1985	Glen Seabrooke, 21, Peterborough (OHL)

Year	Player, Overall, Last Amateur Team (League)
1986	Kerry Huffman, 20, Guelph (OHL)
1987	Darren Rumble, 20, Kitchener (OHL)
1988	Claude Boivin, 14, Drummondville (QMJHL)
1989	No first-round selection
1990	Mike Ricci, 4, Peterborough (OHL)
1991	Peter Forsberg, 6, Modo (Sweden)
1992	Ryan Sittler, 7, Nichols H.S. (N.Y.)
	Jason Bowen, 15, Tri-City (WHL)
1993	No first-round selection
1994	No first-round selection
1995	Brian Boucher, 22, Tri-City (WHL)

*Designates first player chosen in draft.

FRANCHISE LEADERS

Players in boldface played
for club in '94-95

FORWARDS/DEFENSEMEN
Games
Bobby Clarke	1144
Bill Barber	903
Brian Propp	790
Joe Watson	746
Bob Kelly	741
Rick MacLeish	741
Gary Dornhoefer	725
Ed Van Impe	617
Jim Watson	613
Reggie Leach	606

Goals
Bill Barber	420
Brian Propp	369
Tim Kerr	363
Bobby Clarke	358
Rick MacLeish	328
Reggie Leach	306
Rick Tocchet	215
Gary Dornhoefer	202
Ilkka Sinisalo	199
Dave Poulin	161

Assists
Bobby Clarke	852
Brian Propp	480

Bill Barber	463
Rick MacLeish	369
Mark Howe	342
Pelle Eklund	334
Gary Dornhoefer	316
Tim Kerr	287
Murray Craven	272
Rick Tocchet	247

Points
Bobby Clarke	1210
Bill Barber	883
Brian Propp	849
Rick MacLeish	697
Tim Kerr	650
Gary Dornhoefer	518
Reggie Leach	514
Mark Howe	480
Rick Tocchet	462
Pelle Eklund	452

Penalty minutes
Rick Tocchet	1683
Paul Holmgren	1600
Andre Dupont	1505
Bobby Clarke	1453
Dave Schultz	1386
Dave Brown	1382
Bob Kelly	1285
Gary Dornhoefer	1256
Glen Cochrane	1110

GOALTENDERS
Games
Bernie Parent	486
Ron Hextall	312
Doug Favell	215
Pete Peeters	179
Wayne Stephenson	165
Pelle Lindbergh	157
Bob Froese	144

Shutouts
Bernie Parent	50
Doug Favell	16
Bob Froese	12
Wayne Stephenson	10

Goals-against average
(2400 minutes minimum)
Bernie Parent	2.42
Bob Froese	2.74
Wayne Stephenson	2.77
Doug Favell	2.78
Pete Peeters	3.19
Rick St. Croix	3.23
Ron Hextall	3.24
Pelle Lindbergh	3.30

Wins
Bernie Parent	232
Ron Hextall	147
Wayne Stephenson	93
Bob Froese	92
Pelle Lindbergh	87

PITTSBURGH PENGUINS

YEAR-BY-YEAR RECORDS

Season	W	L	T	Pts.	Finish	W	L	Highest round	Coach
1967-68	27	34	13	67	5th/West	—	—		Red Sullivan
1968-69	20	45	11	51	5th/West	—	—		Red Sullivan
1969-70	26	38	12	64	2nd/West	6	4	Division finals	Red Kelly
1970-71	21	37	20	62	6th/West	—	—		Red Kelly
1971-72	26	38	14	66	4th/West	0	4	Division semifinals	Red Kelly
1972-73	32	37	9	73	5th/West	—	—		Red Kelly, Ken Schinkel
1973-74	28	41	9	65	5th/West	—	—		Ken Schinkel, Marc Boileau
1974-75	37	28	15	89	3rd/Norris	5	4	Quarterfinals	Marc Boileau
1975-76	35	33	12	82	3rd/Norris	1	2	Preliminaries	Marc Boileau, Ken Schinkel
1976-77	34	33	13	81	3rd/Norris	1	2	Preliminaries	Ken Schinkel
1977-78	25	37	18	68	4th/Norris	—	—		Johnny Wilson
1978-79	36	31	13	85	2nd/Norris	2	5	Quarterfinals	Johnny Wilson
1979-80	30	37	13	73	3rd/Norris	2	3	Preliminaries	Johnny Wilson
1980-81	30	37	13	73	3rd/Norris	2	3	Preliminaries	Eddie Johnston
1981-82	31	36	13	75	4th/Patrick	2	3	Division semifinals	Eddie Johnston
1982-83	18	53	9	45	6th/Patrick	—	—		Eddie Johnston
1983-84	16	58	6	38	6th/Patrick	—	—		Lou Angotti
1984-85	24	51	5	53	5th/Patrick	—	—		Bob Berry
1985-86	34	38	8	76	5th/Patrick	—	—		Bob Berry
1986-87	30	38	12	72	5th/Patrick	—	—		Bob Berry

Season	REGULAR SEASON W	L	T	Pts.	Finish	PLAYOFFS W	L	Highest round	Coach
1987-88	36	35	9	81	6th/Patrick	—	—		Pierre Creamer
1988-89	40	33	7	87	2nd/Patrick	7	4	Division finals	Gene Ubriaco
1989-90	32	40	8	72	5th/Patrick	—	—		Gene Ubriaco, Craig Patrick
1990-91	41	33	6	88	1st/Patrick	16	8	Stanley Cup champ	Bob Johnson
1991-92	39	32	9	87	3rd/Patrick	16	5	Stanley Cup champ	Scotty Bowman
1992-93	56	21	7	119	1st/Patrick	7	5	Division finals	Scotty Bowman
1993-94	44	27	13	101	1st/Northeast	2	4	Conference quarterfinals	Eddie Johnston
1994-95	29	16	3	61	2nd/Northeast	5	7	Conference semifinals	Eddie Johnston

FIRST-ROUND ENTRY DRAFT CHOICES

Year	Player, Overall, Last Amateur Team (League)
1969	No first-round selection
1970	Greg Polis, 7, Estevan (WCHL)
1971	No first-round selection
1972	No first-round selection
1973	Blaine Stoughton, 7, Flin Flon (WCHL)
1974	Pierre Larouche, 8, Sorel (QMJHL)
1975	Gord Laxton, 13, New Westminster (WCHL)
1976	Blair Chapman, 2, Saskatoon (WCHL)
1977	No first-round selection
1978	No first-round selection
1979	No first-round selection
1980	Mike Bullard, 9, Brantford (OHL)
1981	No first-round selection
1982	Rich Sutter, 10, Lethbridge (WHL)
1983	Bob Errey, 15, Peterborough (OHL)

Year	Player, Overall, Last Amateur Team (League)
1984	*Mario Lemieux, 1, Laval (QMJHL)
	Doug Bodger, 9, Kamloops (WHL)
	Roger Belanger, 16, Kingston (OHL)
1985	Craig Simpson, 2, Michigan State University
1986	Zarley Zalapski, 4, Team Canada
1987	Chris Joseph, 5, Seattle (WHL)
1988	Darrin Shannon, 4, Windsor (OHL)
1989	Jamie Heward, 16, Regina (WHL)
1990	Jaromir Jagr, 5, Poldi Kladno (Czech.)
1991	Markus Naslund, 16, MoDo (Sweden)
1992	Martin Straka, 19, Skoda Plzen (Czech.)
1993	Stefan Bergqvist, 26, Leksand (Sweden)
1994	Chris Wells, 24, Seattle (WHL)
1995	Alexei Morozov, 24, Krylja Sovetov, CIS

*Designates first player chosen in draft.

FRANCHISE LEADERS

Players in boldface played for club in '94-95, except for Mario Lemieux, who was on medical leave of absence

FORWARDS/DEFENSEMEN

Games
Jean Pronovost	753
Rick Kehoe	722
Ron Stackhouse	621
Ron Schock	619
Mario Lemieux	599
Dave Burrows	573
Bob Errey	518
Troy Loney	532
Syl Apps	495
Greg Malone	495

Goals
Mario Lemieux	494
Jean Pronovost	316
Rick Kehoe	312
Kevin Stevens	251
Mike Bullard	186
Jaromir Jagr	157
Syl Apps	151
Joe Mullen	146
Greg Malone	143
Lowell MacDonald	140

Assists
Mario Lemieux	717
Syl Apps	349
Paul Coffey	332
Rick Kehoe	324
Jean Pronovost	287

Ron Schock	280
Ron Stackhouse	277
Kevin Stevens	276
Randy Carlyle	257
Jaromir Jagr	235

Points
Mario Lemieux	1211
Rick Kehoe	636
Jean Pronovost	603
Kevin Stevens	527
Syl Apps	500
Paul Coffey	440
Ron Schock	404
Jaromir Jagr	389
Greg Malone	364
Mike Bullard	361

Penalty minutes
Troy Loney	980
Kevin Stevens	968
Rod Buskas	959
Bryan Watson	871
Paul Baxter	851
Gary Rissling	832
Jay Caufield	714
Russ Anderson	684
Jim Johnson	658
Bob Errey	651

GOALTENDERS

Games
Denis Herron	290
Tom Barrasso	282

Les Binkley	196
Michel Dion	151
Greg Millen	135
Roberto Romano	123
Jim Rutherford	115
Ken Wregget	114
Gilles Meloche	104
Wendell Young	101

Shutouts
Les Binkley	11
Tom Barrasso	8
Denis Herron	6
Dunc Wilson	5

Goals-against average
(2400 minutes minimum)
Al Smith	3.07
Les Binkley	3.12
Jim Rutherford	3.14
Gary Inness	3.34
Ken Wregget	3.38
Dunc Wilson	3.53
Tom Barrasso	3.57
Michel Plasse	3.59
Gilles Meloche	3.65
Andy Brown	3.78

Wins
Tom Barrasso	142
Denis Herron	88
Ken Wregget	64
Les Binkley	58
Greg Millen	57
Roberto Romano	45
Jim Rutherford	44

PITTSBURGH PIRATES (DEFUNCT)

YEAR-BY-YEAR RECORDS

Season	REGULAR SEASON W	L	T	Pts.	Finish	PLAYOFFS W	L	Highest round	Coach
1925-26	19	16	1	39	3rd	—	—		Odie Cleghorn
1926-27	15	26	3	33	4th/American	—	—		Odie Cleghorn

Season	W	L	T	Pts.	Finish	W	L	Highest round	Coach
			REGULAR SEASON				PLAYOFFS		
1927-28	19	17	8	46	3rd/American	1	1	Quarterfinals	Odie Cleghorn
1928-29	9	27	8	26	4th/American	—	—		Odie Cleghorn
1929-30	5	36	3	13	5th/American	—	—		Frank Frederickson
1930-31*	4	36	4	12	5th/American	—	—		Cooper Smeaton

*Philadelphia Quakers.

QUEBEC NORDIQUES

YEAR-BY-YEAR RECORDS

Season	W	L	T	Pts.	Finish	W	L	Highest round	Coach
			REGULAR SEASON				PLAYOFFS		
1972-73*	33	40	5	71	5th	—	—		Maurice Richard, Maurice Filion
1973-74*	38	36	4	80	5th	—	—		Jacques Plante
1974-75*	46	32	0	92	1st	8	7	Avco World Cup finals	Jean-Guy Gendron
1975-76*	50	27	4	104	2nd	1	4	League quarterfinals	Jean-Guy Gendron
1976-77*	47	31	3	97	1st	12	5	Avco World Cup champ	Marc Boileau
1977-78*	40	37	3	83	4th	5	6	League semifinals	Marc Boileau
1978-79*	41	34	5	87	2nd	0	4	League semifinals	Jacques Demers
1979-80	25	44	11	61	5th/Adams	—	—		Jacques Demers
1980-81	30	32	18	78	4th/Adams	2	3	Preliminaries	Maurice Filion, Michel Bergeron
1981-82	33	31	16	82	4th/Adams	7	9	Conference finals	Michel Bergeron
1982-83	34	34	12	80	4th/Adams	1	3	Division semifinals	Michel Bergeron
1983-84	42	28	10	94	3rd/Adams	5	4	Division finals	Michel Bergeron
1984-85	41	30	9	91	2nd/Adams	9	9	Conference finals	Michel Bergeron
1985-86	43	31	6	92	1st/Adams	0	3	Division semifinals	Michel Bergeron
1986-87	31	39	10	72	4th/Adams	7	6	Division finals	Michel Bergeron
1987-88	32	43	5	69	5th/Adams	—	—		Andre Savard, Ron Lapointe
1988-89	27	46	7	61	5th/Adams	—	—		Ron Lapointe, Jean Perron
1989-90	12	61	7	31	5th/Adams	—	—		Michel Bergeron
1990-91	16	50	14	46	5th/Adams	—	—		Dave Chambers
1991-92	20	48	12	52	5th/Adams	—	—		Dave Chambers, Pierre Page
1992-93	47	27	10	104	2nd/Adams	2	4	Division semifinals	Pierre Page
1993-94	34	42	8	76	5th/Northeast	—	—		Pierre Page
1994-95	30	13	5	65	1st/Northeast	2	4	Conference quarterfinals	Marc Crawford

*Members of World Hockey Association.

FIRST-ROUND ENTRY DRAFT CHOICES

Year	Player, Overall, Last Amateur Team (League)
1979	Michel Goulet, 20, Birmingham (WHA)
1980	No first-round selection
1981	Randy Moller, 11, Lethbridge (WHL)
1982	David Shaw, 13, Kitchener (OHL)
1983	No first-round selection
1984	Trevor Steinburg, 15, Guelph (OHL)
1985	Dave Latta, 15, Kitchener (OHL)
1986	Ken McRae, 18, Sudbury (OHL)
1987	Bryan Fogarty, 9, Kingston (OHL)
	Joe Sakic, 15, Swift Current (WHL)
1988	Curtis Leschyshyn, 3, Saskatoon (WHL)
	Daniel Dore, 5, Drummondville (QMJHL)
1989	*Mats Sundin, 1, Nacka (Sweden)

Year	Player, Overall, Last Amateur Team (League)
1990	*Owen Nolan, 1, Cornwall (OHL)
1991	*Eric Lindros, 1, Oshawa (OHL)
1992	Todd Warriner, 4, Windsor (OHL)
1993	Jocelyn Thibault, 10, Sherbrooke (QMJHL)
	Adam Deadmarsh, 14, Portland (WHL)
1994	Wade Belak, 12, Saskatoon (WHL)
	Jeffrey Kealty, 22, Catholic Memorial H.S.
1995	Marc Denis, 25, Chicoutimi (QMJHL)

*Designates first player chosen in draft.
NOTE: Quebec chose Paul Baxter, Richard Brodeur and Garry Lariviere as priority selections before the 1979 expansion draft.

FRANCHISE LEADERS

Players in boldface played
for club in '94-95

FORWARDS/DEFENSEMEN

Games

Michel Goulet	813
Peter Stastny	737
Alain Cote	696
Anton Stastny	650
Steven Finn	**606**
Paul Gillis	576
Dale Hunter	523
Joe Sakic	**509**
Randy Moller	508
Normand Rochefort	480

Goals

Michel Goulet	456
Peter Stastny	380
Anton Stastny	252
Joe Sakic	**235**
Dale Hunter	140
Mats Sundin	135
Real Cloutier	122
Marc Tardif	116
Owen Nolan	**113**
Alain Cote	103

Assists

Peter Stastny	668
Michel Goulet	489
Joe Sakic	**391**

Anton Stastny	384
Dale Hunter	318
Mats Sundin	199
Alain Cote	190
Real Cloutier	162
Mario Marois	162
Paul Gillis	146

Points

Peter Stastny	1048
Michel Goulet	945
Anton Stastny	636
Joe Sakic	**626**
Dale Hunter	458
Mats Sundin	334
Alain Cote	293

Real Cloutier	284
Marc Tardif	244
Marian Stastny	241

Penalty minutes

Dale Hunter	1545
Steven Finn	**1511**
Paul Gillis	1351
Randy Moller	1002
Mario Marois	778
Peter Stastny	687
Gord Donnelly	668
Wilf Paiement	619
Michel Goulet	613
Wally Weir	535

GOALTENDERS
Games

Dan Bouchard	225
Mario Gosselin	192
Stephane Fiset	**152**
Ron Tugnutt	150
Clint Malarchuk	140
Michel Dion	62

Shutouts

Mario Gosselin	6
Dan Bouchard	5
Stephane Fiset	**5**
Clint Malarchuk	5

Goals - against average
(2400 minutes minimum)

Jocelyn Thibault	**2.95**

Ron Hextall	3.42
Dan Bouchard	3.59
Stephane Fiset	**3.61**
Clint Malarchuk	3.63
Mario Gosselin	3.67
Jacques Cloutier	3.91
Michel Dion	4.02
Ron Tugnutt	4.07

Wins

Dan Bouchard	107
Mario Gosselin	79
Stephane Fiset	**62**
Clint Malarchuk	62
Ron Tugnutt	35
Ron Hextall	29

ST. LOUIS BLUES
YEAR - BY - YEAR RECORDS

	REGULAR SEASON					PLAYOFFS			
Season	W	L	T	Pts.	Finish	W	L	Highest round	Coach
1967-68	27	31	16	70	3rd/West	8	10	Stanley Cup finals	Lynn Patrick, Scotty Bowman
1968-69	37	25	14	88	1st/West	8	4	Stanley Cup finals	Scotty Bowman
1969-70	37	27	12	86	1st/West	8	8	Stanley Cup finals	Scotty Bowman
1970-71	34	25	19	87	2nd/West	2	4	Division semifinals	Al Arbour, Scotty Bowman
1971-72	28	39	11	67	3rd/West	4	7	Division finals	Sid Abel, Bill McCreary, Al Arbour
1972-73	32	34	12	76	4th/West	1	4	Division semifinals	Al Arbour, Jean-Guy Talbot
1973-74	26	40	12	64	6th/West	—	—		Jean-Guy Talbot, Lou Angotti
1974-75	35	31	14	84	2nd/Smythe	0	2	Preliminaries	Lou Angotti, Lynn Patrick, Garry Young
1975-76	29	37	14	72	3rd/Smythe	1	2	Preliminaries	Garry Young, Lynn Patrick, Leo Boivin
1976-77	32	39	9	73	1st/Smythe	0	4	Quarterfinals	Emile Francis
1977-78	20	47	13	53	4th/Smythe	—	—		Leo Boivin, Barclay Plager
1978-79	18	50	12	48	3rd/Smythe	—	—		Barclay Plager
1979-80	34	34	12	80	2nd/Smythe	0	3	Preliminaries	Barclay Plager, Red Berenson
1980-81	45	18	17	107	1st/Smythe	5	6	Quarterfinals	Red Berenson
1981-82	32	40	8	72	3rd/Norris	5	5	Division finals	Red Berenson, Emile Francis
1982-83	25	40	15	65	4th/Norris	1	3	Division semifinals	Emile Francis, Barclay Plager
1983-84	32	41	7	71	2nd/Norris	6	5	Division finals	Jacques Demers
1984-85	37	31	12	86	3rd/Norris	0	3	Division semifinals	Jacques Demers
1985-86	37	34	9	83	3rd/Norris	10	9	Conference finals	Jacques Demers
1986-87	32	33	15	79	1st/Norris	2	4	Division semifinals	Jacques Martin
1987-88	34	38	8	76	2nd/Norris	5	5	Division finals	Jacques Martin
1988-89	33	35	12	78	2nd/Norris	5	5	Division finals	Brian Sutter
1989-90	37	34	9	83	2nd/Norris	7	5	Division finals	Brian Sutter
1990-91	47	22	11	105	2nd/Norris	6	7	Division finals	Brian Sutter
1991-92	36	33	11	83	3rd/Norris	2	4	Division semifinals	Brian Sutter
1992-93	37	36	11	85	4th/Norris	7	4	Division finals	Bob Plager, Bob Berry
1993-94	40	33	11	91	4th/Central	0	4	Conference quarterfinals	Bob Berry
1994-95	28	15	5	61	2nd/Central	3	4	Conference quarterfinals	Mike Keenan

FIRST - ROUND ENTRY DRAFT CHOICES

Year   Player, Overall, Last Amateur Team (League)
1969—No first-round selection
1970—No first-round selection
1971—Gene Carr, 4, Flin Flon (WCHL)
1972—Wayne Merrick, 9, Ottawa (OHL)
1973—John Davidson, 5, Calgary (WCHL)
1974—No first-round selection
1975—No first-round selection
1976—Bernie Federko, 7, Saskatoon (WCHL)
1977—Scott Campbell, 9, London (OHL)
1978—Wayne Babych, 3, Portland (WCHL)
1979—Perry Turnbull, 2, Portland (WHL)
1980—Rik Wilson, 12, Kingston (OHL)
1981—Marty Ruff, 20, Lethbridge (WHL)
1982—No first-round selection

Year   Player, Overall, Last Amateur Team (League)
1983—No first-round selection
1984—No first-round selection
1985—No first-round selection
1986—Jocelyn Lemieux, 10, Laval (QMJHL)
1987—Keith Osborne, 12, North Bay (OHL)
1988—Rod Brind'Amour, 9, Notre Dame Academy (Sask.)
1989—Jason Marshall, 9, Vernon (B.C.) Tier II
1990—No first-round selection
1991—No first-round selection
1992—No first-round selection
1993—No first-round selection
1994—No first-round selection
1995—No first-round selection

FRANCHISE LEADERS

Players in boldface played
for club in '94-95

FORWARDS/DEFENSEMEN
Games
Bernie Federko 927
Brian Sutter 779
Garry Unger 662
Bob Plager 615
Barclay Plager 614
Larry Patey 603
Brett Hull 531
Red Berenson 519
Gary Sabourin 463
Jack Brownschidle 455

Goals
Brett Hull 415
Bernie Federko 352
Brian Sutter 303
Garry Unger 292
Red Berenson 172
Jorgen Pettersson 161
Wayne Babych 155
Joe Mullen 151
Doug Gilmour 149
Perry Turnbull 139

Assists
Bernie Federko 721
Brian Sutter 334
Brett Hull 284
Garry Unger 283
Red Berenson 240
Rob Ramage 229

Adam Oates 228
Doug Gilmour 205
Blake Dunlop 201
Wayne Babych 190

Points
Bernie Federko 1073
Brett Hull 699
Brian Sutter 636
Garry Unger 575
Red Berenson 412
Doug Gilmour 354
Wayne Babych 345
Joe Mullen 335
Jorgen Pettersson 332
Rob Ramage 296

Penalty minutes
Brian Sutter 1786
Barclay Plager 1115
Kelly Chase 1005
Rob Ramage 998
Bob Gassoff 866
Perry Turnbull 829
Bob Plager 760
Garry Unger 744
Brendan Shanahan 692
Herb Raglan 571

GOALTENDERS
Games
Mike Liut 347
Curtis Joseph 280
Greg Millen 209
Rick Wamsley 154

Glenn Hall 140
Ed Staniowski 137
Vincent Riendeau 122
Ernie Wakely 111
Eddie Johnston 108
Wayne Stephenson 87

Shutouts
Glenn Hall 16
Mike Liut 10
Jacques Plante 10
Ernie Wakely 8
Greg Millen 7

Goals-against average
(2400 minutes minimum)
Jacques Plante 2.07
Glenn Hall 2.43
Ernie Wakely 2.77
Jacques Caron 3.02
Curtis Joseph 3.04
Wayne Stephenson 3.12
Vincent Riendeau 3.34
Eddie Johnston 3.36
John Davidson 3.37
Rick Wamsley 3.41
Greg Millen 3.43

Wins
Mike Liut 151
Curtis Joseph 137
Greg Millen 85
Rick Wamsley 75
Glenn Hall 58
Vincent Riendeau 58

SAN JOSE SHARKS

YEAR-BY-YEAR RECORDS

Season	W	L	T	Pts.	Finish	W	L	Highest round	Coach
1991-92	17	58	5	39	6th/Smythe	—	—		George Kingston
1992-93	11	71	2	24	6th/Smythe	—	—		George Kingston
1993-94	33	35	16	82	3rd/Pacific	7	7	Conference semifinals	Kevin Constantine
1994-95	19	25	4	42	3rd/Pacific	4	7	Conference semifinals	Kevin Constantine

FIRST-ROUND ENTRY DRAFT CHOICES

Year   Player, Overall, Last Amateur Team (League)
1991—Pat Falloon, 2, Spokane (WHL)
1992—Mike Rathje, 3, Medicine Hat (WHL)
    Andrei Nazarov, 10, Dynamo Moscow, CIS

Year   Player, Overall, Last Amateur Team (League)
1993—Viktor Kozlov, 6, Moscow, CIS
1994—Jeff Friesen, 11, Regina (WHL)
1995—Teemu Riihijarvi, 12, Espoo Jrs., Finland

FRANCHISE LEADERS

Players in boldface played
for club in '94-95

FORWARDS/DEFENSEMEN
Games
Jeff Odgers 256
Pat Falloon 249
Jay More 213
Rob Zettler 196
Johan Garpenlov 184
Mike Sullivan 171
Sandis Ozolinsh 166
Tom Pederson 165
Dean Evason 158
Doug Zmolek 152

Goals
Pat Falloon 73
Johan Garpenlov 46
Sandis Ozolinsh 42
Sergei Makarov 40
Rob Gaudreau 38
Kelly Kisio 37
Jeff Odgers 36
Todd Elik 32
Ray Whitney 31
David Bruce 24

Assists
Pat Falloon 86
Johan Garpenlov 86
Kelly Kisio 78

Sandis Ozolinsh 70
Igor Larionov 58
Sergei Makarov 52
Todd Elik 51
Ray Whitney 47
Tom Pederson 43
Rob Gaudreau 40

Points
Pat Falloon 159
Johan Garpenlov 132
Kelly Kisio 115
Sandis Ozolinsh 112
Sergei Makarov 92
Todd Elik 83
Igor Larionov 80

— 167 —

Rob Gaudreau	78
Ray Whitney	78
Jeff Odgers	66

Penalty minutes

Jeff Odgers	809
Jay More	398
Doug Zmolek	351
Link Gaetz	326
Rob Zettler	314
Dean Evason	231
Neil Wilkinson	203
Dave Maley	156
Bob Errey	153

Kelly Kisio	144

GOALTENDERS
Games

Arturs Irbe	161
Jeff Hackett	78
Jarmo Myllys	27
Brian Hayward	25
Wade Flaherty	22
Jimmy Waite	15

Shutouts

Arturs Irbe	8
Wade Flaherty	1

Goals-against average
(1200 minutes minimum)

Arturs Irbe	3.34
Jeff Hackett	4.51
Jarmo Myllys	5.02
Brian Hayward	5.39

Wins

Arturs Irbe	53
Jeff Hackett	13
Wade Flaherty	5
Brian Hayward	3
Jarmo Myllys	3
Jimmy Waite	3

TAMPA BAY LIGHTNING

YEAR-BY-YEAR RECORDS

		REGULAR SEASON					PLAYOFFS			
Season	W	L	T	Pts.	Finish	W	L	Highest round	Coach
1992-93	23	54	7	53	6th/Norris	—	—		Terry Crisp
1993-94	30	43	11	71	7th/Atlantic	—	—		Terry Crisp
1994-95	17	28	3	37	6th/Atlantic	—	—		Terry Crisp

FIRST-ROUND ENTRY DRAFT CHOICES

Year   Player, Overall, Last Amateur Team (League)
1992—*Roman Hamrlik, 1, Zlin (Czech.)
1993—Chris Gratton, 3, Kingston (OHL)
1994—Jason Weimer, 8, Portland (WHL)

Year   Player, Overall, Last Amateur Team (League)
1995—Daymond Langkow, 5, Tri-City (WHL)
*Designates first player chosen in draft.

FRANCHISE LEADERS

Players in boldface played
for club in '94-95

FORWARDS/DEFENSEMEN
Games

Marc Bergevin	205
Brian Bradley	204
John Tucker	190
Mikael Andersson	189
Rob Zamuner	188
Marc Bureau	186
Roman Hamrlik	179
Danton Cole	174
Shawn Chambers	145
Adam Creighton	136

Goals

Brian Bradley	79
John Tucker	46
Petr Klima	41
Danton Cole	35
Mikael Andersson	33
Rob Zamuner	30
Adam Creighton	29
Chris Kontos	27
Denis Savard	24
Shawn Chambers	23

Assists

Brian Bradley	111

John Tucker	75
Shawn Chambers	64
Chris Gratton	49
Roman Hamrlik	44
Danton Cole	41
Marc Bureau	40
Rob Zamuner	40
Petr Klima	40
Denis Savard	39

Points

Brian Bradley	190
John Tucker	121
Shawn Chambers	87
Petr Klima	85
Danton Cole	76
Rob Zamuner	70
Chris Gratton	69
Roman Hamrlik	65
Mikael Andersson	63
Denis Savard	63

Penalty minutes

Roman Hamrlik	292
Enrico Ciccone	277
Chris Gratton	212
Rudy Poeschek	210
Marc Bergevin	204
Brian Bradley	190
Marc Bureau	171

Mike Hartman	154
Peter Taglianetti	150
Adam Creighton	147

GOALTENDERS
Games

Darren Puppa	99
Pat Jablonski	58
J.C. Bergeron	41
Wendell Young	40
Dave Littman	1

Shutouts

Darren Puppa	5
J.C. Bergeron	1
Pat Jablonski	1
Wendell Young	1

Goals-against average
(1200 minutes minimum)

Darren Puppa	2.70
Wendell Young	3.39
J.C. Bergeron	3.50
Pat Jablonski	3.95

Wins

Darren Puppa	36
Pat Jablonski	13
J.C. Bergeron	12
Wendell Young	9

TORONTO MAPLE LEAFS

YEAR-BY-YEAR RECORDS

		REGULAR SEASON					PLAYOFFS			
Season	W	L	T	Pts.	Finish	W	L	Highest round	Coach
1917-18‡	13	9	0	26	2nd	4	3	Stanley Cup champ	Dick Carroll
1918-19‡	5	13	0	10	3rd	—	—		Dick Carroll
1919-20§	12	12	0	24	3rd	—	—		Frank Heffernan, Harry Sproule

Season	W	L	T	Pts.	Finish	W	L	Highest round	Coach
1920-21§	15	9	0	30	1st	0	2	Semifinals	Dick Carroll
1921-22§	13	10	1	27	2nd	*4	2	Stanley Cup champ	Eddie Powers
1922-23§	13	10	1	27	3rd	—	—		Charlie Querrie, Jack Adams
1923-24§	10	14	0	20	3rd	—	—		Eddie Powers
1924-25§	19	11	0	38	2nd	0	2	Semifinals	Eddie Powers
1925-26§	12	21	3	27	6th	—	—		Eddie Powers
1926-27§	15	24	5	35	5th/Canadian	—	—		Conn Smythe
1927-28	18	18	8	44	4th/Canadian	—	—		Alex Roveril, Conn Smythe
1928-29	21	18	5	47	3rd/Canadian	2	2	Semifinals	Alex Roveril, Conn Smythe
1929-30	17	21	6	40	4th/Canadian	—	—		Alex Roveril, Conn Smythe
1930-31	22	13	9	53	2nd/Canadian	*0	1	Quarterfinals	Conn Smythe, Art Duncan
1931-32	23	18	7	53	2nd/Canadian	5	2	Stanley Cup champ	Art Duncan, Dick Irvin
1932-33	24	18	6	54	1st/Canadian	4	5	Stanley Cup finals	Dick Irvin
1933-34	26	13	9	61	1st/Canadian	2	3	Semifinals	Dick Irvin
1934-35	30	14	4	64	1st/Canadian	3	4	Stanley Cup finals	Dick Irvin
1935-36	23	19	6	52	2nd/Canadian	4	5	Stanley Cup finals	Dick Irvin
1936-37	22	21	5	49	3rd/Canadian	0	2	Quarterfinals	Dick Irvin
1937-38	24	15	9	57	1st/Canadian			Stanley Cup finals	Dick Irvin
1938-39	19	20	9	47	3rd	5	5	Stanley Cup finals	Dick Irvin
1939-40	25	17	6	56	3rd	6	4	Stanley Cup finals	Dick Irvin
1940-41	28	14	6	62	2nd	3	4	Semifinals	Hap Day
1941-42	27	18	3	57	2nd	8	5	Stanley Cup champ	Hap Day
1942-43	22	19	9	53	3rd	2	4	League semifinals	Hap Day
1943-44	23	23	4	50	3rd	1	4	League semifinals	Hap Day
1944-45	24	22	4	52	3rd	8	5	Stanley Cup champ	Hap Day
1945-46	19	24	7	45	5th	—	—		Hap Day
1946-47	31	19	10	72	2nd	8	3	Stanley Cup champ	Hap Day
1947-48	32	15	13	77	1st	8	1	Stanley Cup champ	Hap Day
1948-49	22	25	13	57	4th	8	1	Stanley Cup champ	Hap Day
1949-50	31	27	12	74	3rd	3	4	League semifinals	Hap Day
1950-51	41	16	13	95	2nd	†8	2	Stanley Cup champ	Joe Primeau
1951-52	29	25	16	74	3rd	0	4	League semifinals	Joe Primeau
1952-53	27	30	13	67	5th	—	—		Joe Primeau
1953-54	32	24	14	78	3rd	1	4	League semifinals	King Clancy
1954-55	24	24	22	70	3rd	0	4	League semifinals	King Clancy
1955-56	24	33	13	61	4th	1	4	League semifinals	King Clancy
1956-57	21	34	15	57	5th	—	—		Howie Meeker
1957-58	21	38	11	53	6th	—	—		Billy Reay
1958-59	27	32	11	65	4th	5	7	Stanley Cup finals	Billy Reay, Punch Imlach
1959-60	35	26	9	79	2nd	4	6	Stanley Cup finals	Punch Imlach
1960-61	39	19	12	90	2nd	1	4	League semifinals	Punch Imlach
1961-62	37	22	11	85	2nd	8	4	Stanely Cup champ	Punch Imlach
1962-63	35	23	12	82	1st	8	2	Stanely Cup champ	Punch Imlach
1963-64	33	25	12	78	3rd	8	6	Stanely Cup champ	Punch Imlach
1964-65	30	26	14	74	4th	2	4	League semifinals	Punch Imlach
1965-66	34	25	11	79	3rd	0	4	League semifinals	Punch Imlach
1966-67	32	27	11	75	3rd	8	4	Stanley Cup champ	Punch Imlach
1967-68	33	31	10	76	5th/East	—	—		Punch Imlach
1968-69	35	26	15	85	4th/East	0	4	Division semifinals	Punch Imlach
1969-70	29	34	13	71	6th/East	—	—		John McLellan
1970-71	37	33	8	82	4th/East	2	4	Division semifinals	John McLellan
1971-72	33	31	14	80	4th/East	1	4	Division semifinals	John McLellan
1972-73	27	41	10	64	6th/East	—	—		John McLellan
1973-74	35	27	16	86	4th/East	0	4	Division semifinals	Red Kelly
1974-75	31	33	16	78	3rd/Adams	2	5	Quarterfinals	Red Kelly
1975-76	34	31	15	83	3rd/Adams	5	5	Quarterfinals	Red Kelly
1976-77	33	32	15	81	3rd/Adams	4	5	Quarterfinals	Red Kelly
1977-78	41	29	10	92	3rd/Adams	4	2	Quarterfinals	Roger Neilson
1978-79	34	33	13	81	3rd/Adams	4	7	Quarterfinals	Roger Neilson
1979-80	35	40	5	75	4th/Adams	0	3	Preliminaries	Floyd Smith
1980-81	28	37	15	71	5th/Adams	0	3	Preliminaries	Punch Imlach, Joe Crozier
1981-82	20	44	16	56	5th/Norris	—	—		Mike Nykoluk
1982-83	28	40	12	68	3rd/Norris	1	3	Division semifinals	Mike Nykoluk
1983-84	26	45	9	61	5th/Norris	—	—		Mike Nykoluk
1984-85	20	52	8	48	5th/Norris	—	—		Dan Maloney
1985-86	25	48	7	57	4th/Norris	6	4	Division finals	Dan Maloney
1986-87	32	42	6	70	4th/Norris	7	6	Division finals	John Brophy
1987-88	21	49	10	52	4th/Norris	2	4	Division semifinals	John Brophy
1988-89	28	46	6	62	5th/Norris	—	—		John Brophy, George Armstrong
1989-90	38	38	4	80	3rd/Norris	1	4	Division semifinals	Doug Carpenter
1990-91	23	46	11	57	5th/Norris	—	—		Doug Carpenter, Tom Watt
1991-92	30	43	7	67	5th/Norris	—	—		Tom Watt
1992-93	44	29	11	99	3rd/Norris	11	10	Conference finals	Pat Burns
1993-94	43	29	12	98	2nd/Central	9	9	Conference finals	Pat Burns
1994-95	21	19	8	50	4th/Central	3	4	Conference quarterfinals	Pat Burns

*Won-lost record does not indicate tie(s) resulting from two-game, total-goals series that year (two-game, total-goals series were played from 1917-18 through 1935-36).
†Tied after one overtime (curfew law).
‡Toronto Arenas.
§Toronto St. Patricks (until April 14, 1927).

FIRST-ROUND ENTRY DRAFT CHOICES

Year	Player, Overall, Last Amateur Team (League)
1969	Ernie Moser, 9, Esteven (WCHL)
1970	Darryl Sittler, 8, London (OHL)
1971	No first-round selection
1972	George Ferguson, 11, Toronto (OHL)
1973	Lanny McDonald, 4, Medicine Hat (WCHL)
	Bob Neely, 10, Peterborough (OHL)
	Ian Turnbull, 15, Ottawa (OHL)
1974	Jack Valiquette, 13, Sault Ste. Marie (OHL)
1975	Don Ashby, 6, Calgary (WCHL)
1976	No first-round selection
1977	John Anderson, 11, Toronto (OHA)
	Trevor Johansen, 12, Toronto (OHA)
1978	No first-round selection
1979	Laurie Boschman, 9, Brandon (WHL)
1980	No first-round selection
1981	Jim Benning, 6, Portland (WHL)
1982	Gary Nylund, 3, Portland (WHL)
1983	Russ Courtnall, 7, Victoria (WHL)

Year	Player, Overall, Last Amateur Team (League)
1984	Al Iafrate, 4, U.S. Olympics/Belleville (OHL)
1985	*Wendel Clark, 1, Saskatoon (WHL)
1986	Vincent Damphousse, 6, Laval (QMJHL)
1987	Luke Richardson, 7, Peterborough (OHL)
1988	Scott Pearson, 6, Kingston (OHL)
1989	Scott Thornton, 3, Belleville (OHL)
	Rob Pearson, 12, Belleville (OHL)
	Steve Bancroft, 21, Belleville (OHL)
1990	Drake Berehowsky, 10, Kingston (OHL)
1991	No first-round selection
1992	Brandon Convery, 8, Sudbury (OHL)
	Grant Marshall, 23, Ottawa (OHL)
1993	Kenny Jonsson, 12, Rogle (Sweden)
	Landon Wilson, 19, Dubuque (USHL)
1994	Eric Fichaud, 16, Chicoutimi (QMJHL)
1995	Jeff Ware, 15, Oshawa (OHL)

*Designates first player chosen in draft.

FRANCHISE LEADERS

Players in boldface played for club in '94-95

FORWARDS/DEFENSEMEN

Games
George Armstrong	1187
Tim Horton	1185
Borje Salming	1099
Dave Keon	1062
Ron Ellis	1034
Bob Pulford	947
Darryl Sittler	844
Ron Stewart	838
Bob Baun	739
Frank Mahovlich	720

Goals
Darryl Sittler	389
Dave Keon	365
Ron Ellis	332
Rick Vaive	299
George Armstrong	296
Frank Mahovlich	296
Bob Pulford	251
Ted Kennedy	231
Lanny McDonald	219
Syl Apps	201

Assists
Borje Salming	620
Darryl Sittler	527
Dave Keon	493
George Armstrong	417
Tim Horton	349
Ted Kennedy	329

Bob Pulford	312
Ron Ellis	308
Norm Ullman	305
Ian Turnbull	302

Points
Darryl Sittler	916
Dave Keon	858
Borje Salming	768
George Armstrong	713
Ron Ellis	640
Frank Mahovlich	597
Bob Pulford	563
Ted Kennedy	560
Rick Vaive	537
Norm Ullman	471

Penalty minutes
Dave Williams	1670
Tim Horton	1389
Wendel Clark	1343
Borje Salming	1292
Red Horner	1264
Bob Baun	1155
Bob McGill	988
Rick Vaive	940
Carl Brewer	917
Jim Thomson	830

GOALTENDERS

Games
Turk Broda	629
Johnny Bower	472

Mike Palmateer	296
Harry Lumley	267
Lorne Chabot	214
Bruce Gamble	210
Ken Wregget	200

Shutouts
Turk Broda	62
Harry Lumley	34
Lorne Chabot	33
Johnny Bower	32
George Hainsworth	19

Goals-against average
(2400 minutes minimum)
John Ross Roach	2.00
Al Rollins	2.05
Lorne Chabot	2.20
Harry Lumley	2.21
George Hainsworth	2.26
Jacques Plante	2.46
Johnny Bower	2.51
Turk Broda	2.53
Bernie Parent	2.59
Don Simmons	2.71
Felix Potvin	**2.76**

Wins
Turk Broda	302
Johnny Bower	220
Mike Palmateer	129
Lorne Chabot	108
Harry Lumley	104

VANCOUVER CANUCKS

YEAR-BY-YEAR RECORDS

	REGULAR SEASON					PLAYOFFS			
Season	W	L	T	Pts.	Finish	W	L	Highest round	Coach
1970-71	24	46	8	56	6th/East	—	—		Hal Laycoe
1971-72	20	50	8	48	7th/East	—	—		Hal Laycoe

Season	W	L	T	Pts.	Finish	W	L	Highest round	Coach
1972-73	22	47	9	53	7th/East	—	—		Vic Stasiuk
1973-74	24	43	11	59	7th/East	—	—		Bill McCreary, Phil Maloney
1974-75	38	32	10	86	1st/Smythe	1	4	Quarterfinals	Phil Maloney
1975-76	33	32	15	81	2nd/Smythe	0	2	Preliminaries	Phil Maloney
1976-77	25	42	13	63	4th/Smythe	—	—		Phil Maloney, Orland Kurtenbach
1977-78	20	43	17	57	3rd/Smythe	—	—		Orland Kurtenbach
1978-79	25	42	13	63	2nd/Smythe	1	2	Preliminaries	Harry Neale
1979-80	27	37	16	70	3rd/Smythe	1	3	Preliminaries	Harry Neale
1980-81	28	32	20	76	3rd/Smythe	0	3	Preliminaries	Harry Neale
1981-82	30	33	17	77	2nd/Smythe	11	6	Stanley Cup finals	Harry Neale, Roger Neilson
1982-83	30	35	15	75	3rd/Smythe	1	3	Division semifinals	Roger Neilson
1983-84	32	39	9	73	3rd/Smythe	1	3	Division semifinals	Roger Neilson, Harry Neale
1984-85	25	46	9	59	5th/Smythe	—	—		Bill Laforge, Harry Neale
1985-86	23	44	13	59	4th/Smythe	0	3	Division semifinals	Tom Watt
1986-87	29	43	8	66	5th/Smythe	—	—		Tom Watt
1987-88	25	46	9	59	5th/Smythe	—	—		Bob McCammon
1988-89	33	39	8	74	4th/Smythe	3	4	Division semifinals	Bob McCammon
1989-90	25	41	14	64	5th/Smythe	—	—		Bob McCammon
1990-91	28	43	9	65	4th/Smythe	2	4	Division semifinals	Bob McCammon, Pat Quinn
1991-92	42	26	12	96	1st/Smythe	6	7	Division finals	Pat Quinn
1992-93	46	29	9	101	1st/Smythe	6	6	Division finals	Pat Quinn
1993-94	41	40	3	85	2nd/Pacific	15	9	Stanley Cup finals	Pat Quinn
1994-95	18	18	12	48	2nd/Pacific	4	7	Conference semifinals	Rick Ley

Column headers: REGULAR SEASON (W, L, T, Pts., Finish); PLAYOFFS (W, L, Highest round); Coach

FIRST-ROUND ENTRY DRAFT CHOICES

Year — Player, Overall, Last Amateur Team (League)

1970—Dale Tallon, 2, Toronto (OHL)
1971—Jocelyn Guevremont, 3, Montreal (OHL)
1972—Don Lever, 3, Niagara Falls (OHL)
1973—Dennis Ververgaert, 3, London (OHL)
       Bob Dailey, 9, Toronto (OHL)
1974—No first-round selection
1975—Rick Blight, 10, Brandon (WCHL)
1976—No first-round selection
1977—Jere Gillis, 4, Sherbrooke (QMJHL)
1978—Bill Derlago, 4, Brandon (WCHL)
1979—Rick Vaive, 5, Birmingham (WHA)
1980—Rick Lanz, 7, Oshawa (OHL)
1981—Garth Butcher, 10, Regina (WHL)
1982—Michel Petit, 11, Sherbrooke (QMJHL)

1983—Cam Neely, 9, Portland (WHL)
1984—J.J. Daigneault, 10, Can. Ol./Longueuil (QMJHL)
1985—Jim Sandlak, 4, London (OHL)
1986—Dan Woodley, 7, Portland (WHL)
1987—No first-round selection
1988—Trevor Linden, 2, Medicine Hat (WHL)
1989—Jason Herter, 8, University of North Dakota
1990—Petr Nedved, 2, Seattle (WHL)
       Shawn Antoski, 18, North Bay (OHL)
1991—Alex Stojanov, 7, Hamilton (OHL)
1992—Libor Polasek, 21, TJ Vikovice (Czech.)
1993—Mike Wilson, 20, Sudbury (OHL)
1994—Mattias Ohlund, 13, Pitea Div. I (Sweden)
1995—No first-round selection

FRANCHISE LEADERS

Players in boldface played for club in '94-95

FORWARDS/DEFENSEMEN

Games

Stan Smyl	896
Harold Snepsts	781
Dennis Kearns	677
Doug Lidster	666
Thomas Gradin	613
Garth Butcher	610
Don Lever	593
Tony Tanti	531
Trevor Linden	**529**
Greg Adams	**489**

Goals

Stan Smyl	262
Tony Tanti	250
Trevor Linden	**198**
Thomas Gradin	197
Don Lever	186
Greg Adams	**179**
Pavel Bure	**174**
Petri Skriko	171
Dennis Ververgaert	139
Patrik Sundstrom	133

Assists

Stan Smyl	411
Thomas Gradin	353
Dennis Kearns	290

Andre Boudrias	267
Doug Lidster	244
Trevor Linden	**230**
Don Lever	221
Tony Tanti	220
Patrik Sundstrom	209
Petri Skriko	207

Points

Stan Smyl	673
Thomas Gradin	550
Tony Tanti	470
Trevor Linden	**428**
Don Lever	407
Andre Boudrias	388
Petri Skriko	373
Greg Adams	**369**
Patrik Sundstrom	342
Dennis Kearns	321

Penalty minutes

Garth Butcher	1668
Stan Smyl	1556
Harold Snepsts	1446
Gino Odjick	**1394**
Tiger Williams	1314
Jim Sandlak	783
Sergio Momesso	**655**
Curt Fraser	651
Dana Murzyn	**587**
Gerald Diduck	**548**

GOALTENDERS

Games

Kirk McLean	398
Richard Brodeur	377
Gary Smith	208
Dunc Wilson	148
Glen Hanlon	137

Shutouts

Kirk McLean	**17**
Gary Smith	11
Richard Brodeur	6
Glen Hanlon	5
Gary Bromley	3

Goals-against average (2400 minutes minimum)

Kirk McLean	**3.23**
Gary Smith	3.33
Kay Whitmore	**3.41**
Steve Weeks	3.44
Glen Hanlon	3.56

Wins

Kirk McLean	**169**
Richard Brodeur	126
Gary Smith	72
Glen Hanlon	43
Kay Whitmore	**36**

YEAR-BY-YEAR RECORDS

Season	W	L	T	Pts.	Finish	W	L	Highest round	Coach
				REGULAR SEASON				PLAYOFFS	
1974-75	8	67	5	21	5th/Norris	—	—		Jim Anderson, Red Sullivan
									Milt Schmidt
1975-76	11	59	10	32	5th/Norris	—	—		Milt Schmidt, Tom McVie
1976-77	24	42	14	62	4th/Norris	—	—		Tom McVie
1977-78	17	49	14	48	5th/Norris	—	—		Tom McVie
1978-79	24	41	15	63	4th/Norris	—	—		Dan Belisle
1979-80	27	40	13	67	5th/Patrick	—	—		Dan Belisle, Gary Green
1980-81	26	36	18	70	5th/Patrick	—	—		Gary Green
1981-82	26	41	13	65	5th/Patrick	—	—		Gary Green, Roger Crozier
									Bryan Murray
1982-83	39	25	16	94	3rd/Patrick	1	3	Division semifinals	Bryan Murray
1983-84	48	27	5	101	2nd/Patrick	4	4	Division finals	Bryan Murray
1984-85	46	25	9	101	2nd/Patrick	2	3	Division semifinals	Bryan Murray
1985-86	50	23	7	107	2nd/Patrick	5	4	Division finals	Bryan Murray
1986-87	38	32	10	86	2nd/Patrick	3	4	Division semifinals	Bryan Murray
1987-88	38	33	9	85	2nd/Patrick	7	7	Division finals	Bryan Murray
1988-89	41	29	10	92	1st/Patrick	2	4	Division semifinals	Bryan Murray
1989-90	36	38	6	78	3rd/Patrick	8	7	Conference finals	Bryan Murray, Terry Murray
1990-91	37	36	7	81	3rd/Patrick	5	6	Division finals	Terry Murray
1991-92	45	27	8	98	2nd/Patrick	3	4	Division semifinals	Terry Murray
1992-93	43	34	7	93	2nd/Patrick	2	4	Division semifinals	Terry Murray
1993-94	39	35	10	88	3rd/Atlantic	5	6	Conference semifinals	Terry Murray, Jim Schoenfeld
1994-95	22	18	8	52	3rd/Atlantic	4	3	Conference quarterfinals	Jim Schoenfeld

FIRST-ROUND ENTRY DRAFT CHOICES

Year — Player, Overall, Last Amateur Team (League)

1974—*Greg Joly, 1, Regina (WCHL)
1975—Alex Forsyth, 18, Kingston (OHA)
1976—*Rick Green, 1, London (OHL)
     Greg Carroll, 15, Medicine Hat (WCHL)
1977—Robert Picard, 3, Montreal (QMJHL)
1978—Ryan Walter, 2, Seattle (WCHL)
     Tim Coulis, 18, Hamilton (OHL)
1979—Mike Gartner, 4, Cincinnati (WHA)
1980—Darren Veitch, 5, Regina (WHL)
1981—Bobby Carpenter, 3, St. John's H.S. (Mass.)
1982—Scott Stevens, 5, Kitchener (OHL)
1983—No first-round selection
1984—Kevin Hatcher, 17, North Bay (OHL)
1985—Yvon Corriveau, 19, Toronto (OHL)
1986—Jeff Greenlaw, 19, Team Canada

1987—No first-round selection
1988—Reggie Savage, 15, Victoriaville (QMJHL)
1989—Olaf Kolzig, 19, Tri-City (WHL)
1990—John Slaney, 9, Cornwall (OHL)
1991—Pat Peake, 14, Detroit (OHL)
     Trevor Halverson, 21, North Bay (OHL)
1992—Sergei Gonchar, 14, Dynamo Moscow, CIS
1993—Brendan Witt, 11, Seattle (WHL)
     Jason Allison, 17, London (OHL)
1994—Nolan Baumgartner, 10, Kamloops (WHL)
     Alexander Kharlamov, 15, CSKA Moscow, CIS
1995—Brad Church, 17, Prince Albert (WHL)
     Miikka Elomo, 23, Kiekko-67, Finland

*Designates first player chosen in draft.

FRANCHISE LEADERS

Players in boldface played
for club in '94-95

FORWARDS/DEFENSEMEN

Games

Mike Gartner	758
Rod Langway	726
Kevin Hatcher	685
Kelly Miller	**651**
Bengt Gustafsson	629
Michal Pivonka	**629**
Scott Stevens	601
Bobby Gould	600
Mike Ridley	588
Dale Hunter	**576**

Goals

Mike Gartner	397
Mike Ridley	218
Bengt Gustafsson	196
Dave Christian	193
Bob Carpenter	188
Dennis Maruk	182

Michal Pivonka	**150**
Kevin Hatcher	149
Dale Hunter	**146**
Kelly Miller	**136**

Assists

Mike Gartner	392
Bengt Gustafsson	359
Scott Stevens	331
Mike Ridley	329
Michal Pivonka	**325**
Dale Hunter	**296**
Kevin Hatcher	277
Larry Murphy	259
Dennis Maruk	249
Dave Christian	224

Points

Mike Gartner	789
Bengt Gustafsson	555
Mike Ridley	547
Michal Pivonka	**475**
Dale Hunter	**442**

Dennis Maruk	431
Scott Stevens	429
Kevin Hatcher	**426**
Dave Christian	417
Bobby Carpenter	395

Penalty minutes

Scott Stevens	1630
Dale Hunter	**1561**
Alan May	1189
Kevin Hatcher	**998**
Mike Gartner	770
Yvon Labre	756
Greg Adams	694
Al Iafrate	616
Gord Lane	614
Lou Franceschetti	562

GOALTENDERS

Games

Don Beaupre	269
Al Jensen	173
Ron Low	145

Pat Riggin	143
Pete Peeters	139
Bernie Wolfe	120
Clint Malarchuk	96

Goals-against average
(2400 minutes minimum)

| Pat Riggin | 3.02 |

Pete Peeters	3.06
Don Beaupre	3.05
Bob Mason	3.16
Al Jensen	3.26

Wins

Don Beaupre	128
Al Jensen	94
Pete Peeters	70

| Pat Riggin | 67 |
| Clint Malarchuk | 40 |

Shutouts

Don Beaupre	12
Al Jensen	8
Pete Peeters	7
Pat Riggin	6
Clint Malarchuk	5

WINNIPEG JETS

YEAR-BY-YEAR RECORDS

	REGULAR SEASON					PLAYOFFS			
Season	W	L	T	Pts.	Finish	W	L	Highest round	Coach
1972-73*	43	31	4	90	1st	9	5	Avco World Cup finals	Nick Mickoski, Bobby Hull
1973-74*	34	39	5	73	4th	0	4	League quarterfinals	Nick Mickoski, Bobby Hull
1974-75*	38	35	5	81	3rd	—	—		Rudy Pilous
1975-76*	52	27	2	106	1st	12	1	Avco World Cup champ	Bobby Kromm
1976-77*	46	32	2	94	2nd	11	9	Avco World Cup finals	Bobby Kromm
1977-78*	50	28	2	102	1st	8	1	Avco World Cup champ	Larry Hillman
1978-79*	39	35	6	84	3rd	8	2	Avco World Cup champ	Larry Hillman, Tom McVie
1979-80	20	49	11	51	5th/Smythe	—	—		Tom McVie
1980-81	9	57	14	32	6th/Smythe	—	—		Tom McVie, Bill Sutherland, Mike Smith
1981-82	33	33	14	80	2nd/Norris	1	3	Division semifinals	Tom Watt
1982-83	33	39	8	74	4th/Smythe	0	3	Division semifinals	Tom Watt
1983-84	31	38	11	73	3rd/Smythe	0	3	Division semifinals	Tom Watt, Barry Long
1984-85	43	27	10	96	2nd/Smythe	3	5	Division finals	Barry Long
1985-86	26	47	7	59	3rd/Smythe	0	3	Division semifinals	Barry Long, John Ferguson
1986-87	40	32	8	88	3rd/Smythe	4	6	Division finals	Dan Maloney
1987-88	33	36	11	77	3rd/Smythe	1	4	Division semifinals	Dan Maloney
1988-89	26	42	12	64	5th/Smythe	—	—		Dan Maloney, Rick Bowness
1989-90	37	32	11	85	3rd/Smythe	3	4	Division semifinals	Bob Murdoch
1990-91	26	43	11	63	5th/Smythe	—	—		Bob Murdoch
1991-92	33	32	15	81	4th/Smythe	3	4	Division semifinals	John Paddock
1992-93	40	37	7	87	4th/Smythe	2	4	Division semifinals	John Paddock
1993-94	24	51	9	57	6th/Central	—	—		John Paddock
1994-95	16	25	7	39	6th/Central	—	—		John Paddock, Terry Simpson

*Members of World Hockey Association.

FIRST-ROUND ENTRY DRAFT CHOICES

Year   Player, Overall, Last Amateur Team (League)
1979—Jimmy Mann, 19, Sherbrooke (QMJHL)
1980—David Babych, 2, Portland (WHL)
1981—*Dale Hawerchuk, 1, Cornwall (QMJHL)
1982—Jim Kyte, 12, Cornwall (OHL)
1983—Andrew McBain, 8, North Bay (OHL)
        Bobby Dollas, 14, Laval (QMJHL)
1984—No first-round selection
1985—Ryan Stewart, 18, Kamloops (WHL)
1986—Pat Elynuik, 8, Prince Albert (WHL)
1987—Bryan Marchment, 16, Belleville (OHL)
1988—Teemu Selanne, 10, Jokerit (Finland)
1989—Stu Barnes, 4, Tri-City (WHL)

Year   Player, Overall, Last Amateur Team (League)
1990—Keith Tkachuk, 19, Malden Cath. H.S. (Mass.)
1991—Aaron Ward, 5, University of Michigan
1992—Sergei Bautin, 17, Dynamo Moscow (CIS)
1998—Mats Lindgren, 15, Skelleftea (Sweden)
1994—No first-round selection
1995—Shane Doan, 7, Kamloops (WHL)

*Designates first player chosen in draft.
  NOTE: Winnipeg chose Scott Campbell, Morris Lukowich and Markus Mattsson as priority selections before the 1979 expansion draft.

FRANCHISE LEADERS

Players in boldface played
for club in '94-95

FORWARDS/DEFENSEMEN
Games

Thomas Steen	950
Dale Hawerchuk	713
Doug Smail	691
Randy Carlyle	564
Ron Wilson	536

Goals

Dale Hawerchuk	379
Thomas Steen	264
Paul MacLean	248
Doug Smail	189
Morris Lukowich	168

Assists

Thomas Steen	553
Dale Hawerchuk	550
Paul MacLean	270
Fredrik Olausson	249
Dave Babych	248

Points

Dale Hawerchuk	929
Thomas Steen	817
Paul MacLean	518
Doug Smail	397
Laurie Boschman	379

Penalty minutes

Laurie Boschman	1338
Jim Kyte	772
Tim Watters	760
Thomas Steen	753

| Randy Carlyle | 736 |

GOALTENDERS
Shutouts

Bob Essensa	14
Daniel Berthiaume	4
Markus Mattsson	3
Stephane Beauregard	2
Dan Bouchard	2
Doug Soetaert	2
Ed Staniowski	2

Wins

Bob Essensa	116
Brian Hayward	63
Daniel Berthiaume	50
Pokey Reddick	41

MINOR LEAGUES

American Hockey League

International Hockey League

East Coast Hockey League

Central Hockey League

Colonial Hockey League

AMERICAN HOCKEY LEAGUE

LEAGUE OFFICE

Chairman of the board
  Jack Butterfield
President and treasurer
  David Andrews
Vice president and general counsel
  Macgregor Kilpatrick
Sr. V.P., hockey operations
  Gordon C. Anziano

Asst. dir. of com. and media relations
  Maria D'Agostino
Executive assistant
  Steve Luce

Address
  425 Union Street
  West Springfield, MA 01089
Phone
  413-781-2030
FAX
  413-733-4767

TEAMS

ADIRONDACK RED WINGS

General manager
  Ken Holland
Head coach
  Newell Brown
Home ice
  Glens Falls Civic Center
Address
  1 Civic Center Plaza
  Glens Falls, NY 12801
Seating capacity
  4,806
Phone
  518-798-0366
FAX
  518-798-0816

ALBANY RIVER RATS

President
  Doug Burch
Head coach
  Robbie Ftorek
Home ice
  Knickerbocker Arena
Address
  51 South Pearl St.
  Albany, NY 12207
Seating capacity
  6,500
Phone
  518-487-2244
FAX
  518-487-2248

BALTIMORE BANDITS

General manager
  Pierre Gauthier
Head coach
  Walt Kyle
Home ice
  Baltimore Arena
Address
  201 West Baltimore St.
  Baltimore, MD 21201
Seating capacity
  12,142
Phone
  908-364-6588
FAX
  To be announced

BINGHAMTON RANGERS

Managing partner
  Tom Mitchell
Head coach
  George Burnett
Home ice
  Broome County Veterans
  Memorial Arena
Address
  One Stuart Street
  Binghamton, NY 13901
Seating capacity
  4,643
Phone
  607-723-8937
FAX
  607-724-6892

CAPE BRETON OILERS

General manager
  Scott Howson
Head coach
  Lorne Mulligan
Home ice
  Centre 200
Address
  P.O. Box 1510
  Sydney, Nova Scotia B1T 6R7
Seating capacity
  4,763
Phone
  902-562-0780
FAX
  902-562-1806

CAROLINA MONARCHS

President
  Bill Black
Head coach
  To be announced
Home ice
  Greensboro Colliseum
Address
  P.O. Box 5447
  Greensboro, NC 27435
Seating capacity
  21,500
Phone
  910-852-6170
FAX
  910-852-6259

CORNWALL ACES

General manager
  Pierre Lacroix
Head coach
  Robert Hartley
Home ice
  Cornwall Civic Complex
Address
  100 Water Street
  Cornwall, Ont. K6H 6G4
Seating capacity
  3,991
Phone
  613-937-4132
FAX
  613-933-9632

FREDERICTON CANADIENS

Director of operations
  Wayne Gamble
Head coach
  Paulin Bordeleau
Home ice
  Aitken University Centre
Address
  P.O. Box HABS
  Fredericton, N.B. E3B 4Y2
Seating capacity
  3,712
Phone
  506-459-4227
FAX
  506-457-4250

HERSHEY BEARS

General manager
  Jay Feaster
Head coach
  Jay Leach
Home ice
  Hersheypark Arena
Address
  P.O. Box 866
  Hershey, PA 17033
Seating capacity
  7,256
Phone
  717-534-3380
FAX
  717-534-3383

PORTLAND PIRATES

President
Godfrey Wood
Head coach
Barry Trotz
Home ice
Cumberland County Civic Center
Address
85 Free St.
Portland, ME 04101
Seating capacity
6,736
Phone
207-828-4665
FAX
207-773-3278

ROCHESTER AMERICANS

President
Steve Donner
Head coach
John Tortorella
Home ice
War Memorial Auditorium
Address
100 Exchange Street
Rochester, NY 14614
Seating capacity
6,973
Phone
716-454-5335
FAX
716-454-3954

SPRINGFIELD FALCONS

General Manager
Bruce Landon
Head coach
Kevin McCarthy
Home ice
Springfield Civic Center
Address
P.O. Box 3190
Springfield, MA 01110
Seating capacity
7,452
Phone
413-739-3344
FAX
413-739-3389

PRINCE EDWARD ISLAND SENATORS

Director of operations
Gary Thompson
Head coach
Dave Allison
Home ice
Charlottetown Civic Centre
Address
P.O. Box 22093
Charlottetown, PEI C1A 9J2
Seating capacity
3,340
Phone
902-566-5450
FAX
902-566-5170

SAINT JOHN FLAMES

Director of operations
Alan Millar
Head coach
Bob Francis
Home ice
Harbour Station
Address
P.O. Box 4040, Station B
Saint John, NB E2M 5E6
Seating capacity
6,114
Phone
506-635-2637
FAX
506-633-4625

SYRACUSE CRUNCH

General manager
David Gregory
Head coach
Jack McIlhargey
Home ice
Onondaga County War Memorial
Address
800 S. State St.
Syracuse, NY 13202
Seating capacity
6,230
Phone
315-473-4444
FAX
315-473-4449

PROVIDENCE BRUINS

Chief executive officer
Ed Anderson
Head coach
To be announced
Home ice
Providence Civic Center
Address
1 LaSalle Square
Providence, RI 02903
Seating capacity
11,909
Phone
401-273-5000
FAX
401-273-5004

ST. JOHN'S MAPLE LEAFS

General manager
Glenn Stanford
Head coach
Tom Watt
Home ice
St. John's Memorial Stadium
Address
6 Logy Bay Road
St. John's, Newfoundland A1A 1J3
Seating capacity
3,910
Phone
709-726-1010
FAX
709-726-1511

WORCESTER ICECATS

General manager and head coach
Jim Roberts
Home ice
Worcester Centrum
Address
303 Main St.
Worcester, MA 01608
Seating capacity
12,316
Phone
508-798-5400
FAX
508-799-5267

1994-95 REGULAR SEASON

FINAL STANDINGS

ATLANTIC DIVISION

Team	G	W	L	T	Pts.	GF	GA
Prince Edward Island	80	41	31	8	90	305	271
St. John's	80	33	37	10	76	263	263
Fredericton	80	35	40	5	75	274	288
Saint John	80	27	40	13	67	250	286
Cape Breton	80	27	44	9	63	298	342

NORTHERN DIVISION

Team	G	W	L	T	Pts.	GF	GA
Albany	80	46	17	17	109	293	219
Portland	80	46	22	12	104	333	233
Providence	80	39	30	11	89	300	268
Adirondack	80	32	38	10	74	271	294
Springfield	80	31	37	12	74	269	289
Worcester	80	24	45	11	59	234	300

SOUTHERN DIVISION

Team	G	W	L	T	Pts.	GF	GA
Binghamton	80	43	30	7	93	302	261
Cornwall	80	38	33	9	85	236	248
Hershey	80	34	36	10	78	275	300
Rochester	80	35	38	7	77	300	304
Syracuse	80	29	42	9	67	288	325

Goals: Steve Larouche, Prince Edward Island (53)
Assists: Brett Harkins, Providence (69)
Peter White, Cape Breton (69)
Points: Peter White, Cape Breton (105)
Penalty minutes: Barry Nieckar, Saint John (491)
Goaltending average: Corey Schwab, Albany (2.59)
Shutouts: Jim Carey, Portland (6)

	Games	G	A	Pts.
Todd Simon, Rochester	69	25	65	90
Michel Picard, Prince Edward	57	32	57	89
Mitch Lamoureux, Hershey	76	39	46	85
Jeff Nelson, Portland	64	33	50	83
Shawn McCosh, Binghamton	67	23	60	83
Robert Petrovicky, Springfield	74	30	52	82
Mark Greig, Saint John	67	31	50	81
Steve Sullivan, Albany	75	31	50	81
Cory Stillman, Saint John	63	28	53	81
Andrew Brunette, Portland	79	30	50	80
Bill Armstrong, Albany	76	32	47	79
Alexei Kudashov, St. John's	75	25	54	79
Dan Kesa, Syracuse	70	34	44	78
Jean-Yves Roy, Binghamton	67	41	36	77
Chris Jensen, Portland	67	35	42	77

TOP SCORERS

	Games	G	A	Pts.
Peter White, Cape Breton	65	36	69	105
Steve Larouche, Prince Edward	70	53	48	101
Andrew McKim, Adirondack	77	39	55	94
Ralph Intranuovo, Cape Breton	70	46	47	93
Brett Harkins, Providence	80	23	69	92

ADIRONDACK RED WINGS

SCORING

	Games	G	A	Pts.	PIM
Andrew McKim	77	39	55	94	22
Jason Miller	77	32	33	65	39
Mike Casselman	60	17	43	60	42
Joe Frederick	71	27	28	55	124
Martin Lapointe	39	29	16	45	80
Kurt Miller	78	22	18	40	45
Jason MacDonald	68	14	21	35	238
Aaron Ward	76	11	24	35	87
Sylvain Cloutier	71	7	26	33	144
Chris Govedaris	24	19	11	30	34
Scott Hollis	48	12	15	27	118
Jeff Bloemberg	44	5	19	24	10
Troy Neumeier	60	4	17	21	26
Curtis Bowen	64	6	11	17	71
Tod Hartje	31	6	10	16	33
Jason Gladney	44	3	13	16	65
Lev Berdichevsky	38	4	9	13	28
Jamie Pushor	58	2	11	13	129
Gord Kruppke	48	2	9	11	157
Sergei Bautin	32	0	10	10	57
Yan Golubovsky	57	4	2	6	39
Dmitri Motkov	31	1	5	6	49
Darren Banks	20	3	2	5	65
Jason York	5	1	3	4	4
Brandon Smith	14	1	2	3	7
Mark Green	4	0	3	3	2
Norm Maracle (goalie)	39	0	2	2	4
Lorne Knauft	2	0	1	1	6
Murray Eaves	4	0	1	1	0
Darren Perkins	4	0	1	1	0
Cam Brown	10	0	1	1	30
Kevin Hodson (goalie)	51	0	1	1	2
Todd Walker	1	0	0	0	0
Mike Latendresse	2	0	0	0	0
Chris Osgood (goalie)	2	0	0	0	2
Tim Spitzig	2	0	0	0	0
Mark Ferner	3	0	0	0	2
Clark Polglase	3	0	0	0	7
Stacy Roest	3	0	0	0	0
Derek Grant	4	0	0	0	15

GOALTENDING

	Games	Min.	W	L	T	Goals	SO	Avg.
Chris Osgood	2	120	1	1	0	6	0	3.00
Kevin Hodson	51	2731	19	22	8	161	1	3.54
Norm Maracle	39	1997	12	15	2	119	0	3.57

ALBANY RIVER RATS

SCORING

	Games	G	A	Pts.	PIM
Steve Sullivan	75	31	50	81	124
Bill H. Armstrong	76	32	47	79	115
Rob Conn	68	35	32	67	76
Scott Pellerin	74	23	33	56	95
Sergei Brylin	63	19	35	54	78
Matt Ruchty	78	26	23	49	348
Curt Regnier	73	20	26	46	34
Pascal Rheaume	78	19	25	44	46
Reid Simpson	70	18	25	43	268
Bryan Helmer	77	7	36	43	101
Kevin Dean	68	5	37	42	66
Mike Vukonich	61	16	14	30	16
Brad Bombardir	77	5	22	27	22
Chris McAlpine	48	4	18	22	49
Brian Rolston	18	9	11	20	10
Cale Hulse	77	5	13	18	215
Geordie Kinnear	68	5	11	16	136
Jaroslav Modry	18	5	6	11	14
Bobby House	26	4	7	11	12
Chad Quenneville	8	1	5	6	0
Steve Brule	3	1	4	5	0
Vadim Sharifijanov	1	1	1	2	0
Krzysztof Oliwa	20	1	1	2	77
Jason Smith	7	0	2	2	15
Sheldon Souray	7	0	2	2	8
Ben Hankinson	1	1	0	1	6
Todd Reirden	2	0	1	1	2
Dean Malkoc	9	0	1	1	52
Corey Schwab (goalie)	45	0	1	1	46
David Emma	1	0	0	0	0
Chad Erickson (goalie)	1	0	0	0	0
Brett Duncan	3	0	0	0	0
Todd Person	3	0	0	0	0
Mike Dunham (goalie)	35	0	0	0	2

GOALTENDING

	Games	Min.	W	L	T	Goals	SO	Avg.
Chad Erickson	1	60	1	0	0	2	0	2.00
Corey Schwab	45	2711	25	10	9	117	3	2.59
Mike Dunham	35	2120	20	7	8	99	1	2.80

BINGHAMTON RANGERS

SCORING

	Games	G	A	Pts.	PIM
Shawn McCosh	67	23	60	83	73
Jean-Yves Roy	67	41	36	77	28
Craig Duncanson	62	21	43	64	105
Dave Smith	77	20	40	60	225
Barry Richter	73	15	41	56	54
Ken Gernander	80	28	25	53	24
Darcy Werenka	73	17	29	46	12
Dmitri Starostenko	69	19	22	41	40
Jeff Nielsen	76	24	13	37	139
Andrei Kudinov	65	14	22	36	45
Jim Hiller	49	15	13	28	44

	Games	G	A	Pts.	PIM
Michael Stewart	68	6	21	27	83
Mike McLaughlin	60	10	16	26	27
Peter Fiorentino	66	9	16	25	183
Darren Langdon	55	6	14	20	296
Mattias Norstrom	63	9	10	19	91
Scott Malone	48	3	14	17	85
Brad Rubachuk	30	6	8	14	54
Rob Kenny	17	2	9	11	32
Joby Messier	25	2	9	11	36
Chris Ferraro	13	6	4	10	38
Peter Ferraro	12	2	6	8	67
Shawn Reid	18	3	4	7	8
Eric Cairns	27	0	3	3	134
Sylvain Blouin	10	1	0	1	46
Andy Silverman	5	0	1	1	2
Jamie Ram (goalie)	26	0	1	1	4
Corey Hirsch (goalie)	57	0	1	1	10
Oavel Komarov	2	0	0	0	2
Jan Benda	4	0	0	0	0

GOALTENDING

	Games	Min.	W	L	T	Goals	SO	Avg.
Corey Hirsch	57	3371	31	20	5	175	0	3.11
Jamie Ram	26	1472	12	10	2	81	1	3.30

CAPE BRETON OILERS

SCORING

	Games	G	A	Pts.	PIM
Peter White	65	36	69	105	30
Ralph Intranuovo	70	46	47	93	62
David Vyborny	76	23	38	61	30
Jozef Cierny	73	28	24	52	58
Todd Marchant	38	22	25	47	25
Miroslav Satan	25	24	16	40	15
Nick Stajduhar	54	12	26	38	55
Brad Zavisha	62	13	20	33	55
Tyler Wright	70	16	15	31	184
David Oliver	32	11	18	29	8
Greg DeVries	77	5	19	24	68
Vladimir Vujtek	30	10	11	21	30
Martin Bakula	57	2	19	21	38
Scott Allison	58	6	14	20	104
Dennis Bonvie	74	5	15	20	422
John Van Kessel	38	8	9	17	148
Roman Oksiuta	25	9	7	16	20
Darcy Martini	31	2	13	15	75
Ian Herbers	36	1	11	12	104
Claude Jutras	25	6	5	11	95
Scott Ferguson	58	4	6	10	103
Ladislav Benysek	58	2	7	9	54
Boris Mironov	4	2	5	7	23
Duane Dennis	28	2	4	6	16
Joe Mittelsteadt	37	2	3	5	74
Stephen Tepper	26	1	4	5	16
Steve Passmore (goalie)	25	0	4	4	14
Adam Bennett	10	0	3	3	6
Joaquin Gage (goalie)	54	0	2	2	16
Gairin Smith	6	0	1	1	16
Brent Pope	9	0	1	1	25
Marc Laforge	18	0	1	1	80
Chad Dameworth	1	0	0	0	0
Dominic Fafard	1	0	0	0	0
Andrew Verner (goalie)	1	0	0	0	0
Pat Barton	2	0	0	0	0
Greg Louder (goalie)	3	0	0	0	0
Geoff Finch (goalie)	4	0	0	0	2

GOALTENDING

	Games	Min.	W	L	T	Goals	SO	Avg.
Steve Passmore	25	1455	8	13	3	93	0	3.83
Greg Louder	3	58	0	0	1	4	0	4.08
Joaquin Gage	54	3010	17	28	5	207	0	4.13
Geoff Finch	4	238	2	2	0	17	0	4.28
Andrew Verner	1	60	0	1	0	8	0	8.00

CORNWALL ACES

SCORING

	Games	G	A	Pts.	PIM
Dwayne Norris	60	30	43	73	61
Mike Hurlbut	74	11	49	60	69
Rene Corbet	65	33	24	57	79
Ryan Hughes	72	15	24	39	48
Paul Brousseau	57	19	17	36	29
Paxton Schulte	74	14	22	36	217
Eric Veilleux	70	13	23	36	93
Janne Laukkanen	55	8	26	34	41
Stephane Yelle	40	18	15	33	22
Ed Ward	56	10	14	24	118
Blair Scott	56	8	16	24	108
Aaron Miller	76	4	18	22	69
Reggie Savage	34	13	7	20	56
Jon Klemm	65	6	13	19	84
Doug Friedman	55	6	9	15	56
Cory Banika	56	3	11	14	225
Mike McKee	36	2	11	13	24
Karson Kaebel	25	3	7	10	17
Landon Wilson	8	4	4	8	25
Jeff Parrott	65	2	5	7	99
Craig Charron	6	5	0	5	0
Francois Leroux	18	5	0	5	23
Rick Kowalsky	9	2	1	3	38
Francois Groleau	8	1	2	3	7
Norman Desjardins	15	0	3	3	35
Serge Roberge	73	0	3	3	342
David Karpa	6	0	2	2	19
Brent Brekke	29	1	0	1	24
Stephane Charbonneau	1	0	1	1	0
Mark Matier	3	0	1	1	4
Garth Snow (goalie)	62	0	1	1	73
Steve Gibson	2	0	0	0	0
Chris Phelps	3	0	0	0	0
Mike Taylor	3	0	0	0	2
Pascal Trepanier	4	0	0	0	9
Paul Krake (goalie)	7	0	0	0	0
Rich Shulmistra (goalie)	20	0	0	0	2

GOALTENDING

	Games	Min.	W	L	T	Goals	SO	Avg.
Garth Snow	62	3558	32	20	7	162	3	2.73
Rich Shulmistra	20	937	4	9	2	58	0	3.71
Paul Krake	7	359	2	4	0	24	0	4.01

FREDERICTON CANADIENS

SCORING

	Games	G	A	Pts.	PIM
Craig Darby	64	21	47	68	82
Craig Ferguson	80	27	35	62	62
David Wilkie	70	10	43	53	34
Jim Campbell	77	27	24	51	103
Valeri Bure	45	23	25	48	32
Scott Fraser	65	23	25	48	36
Yves Sarault	69	24	21	45	96
Craig Conroy	55	26	18	44	29
Craig Rivet	78	5	27	32	126
Robert Guillet	48	14	15	29	23
Turner Stevenson	37	12	12	24	109
Mario Roberge	28	8	12	20	91
Derek Maguire	52	6	14	20	19
Donald Brashear	29	10	9	19	182
Oleg Petrov	17	7	11	18	12
Chris Murray	55	6	12	18	234
Martin Sychra	39	4	10	14	4
Brent Bilodeau	50	4	8	12	146
Christian Proulx	75	1	9	10	184
Gaston Gingras	19	3	6	9	4
Gerry Fleming	16	3	3	6	60
Xavier Majic	21	2	3	5	4
Brady Kramer	6	3	0	3	7
Louis Bernard	31	2	1	3	34
Tim Tisdale	12	1	2	3	0

	Games	G	A	Pts.	PIM
Brad Layzell	24	1	2	3	8
Patrick Labrecque (goalie)	35	0	3	3	20
Christian Lariviere	32	1	1	2	36
Kevin O'Sullivan	22	0	2	2	20
Dion Darling	51	0	2	2	153
Marc Lamothe (goalie)	9	0	1	1	0
Martin Brochu (goalie)	44	0	1	1	6
Alexandre Duchesne	1	0	0	0	2

GOALTENDING

	Games	Min.	W	L	T	Goals	SO	Avg.
Patrick Labrecque	35	1913	15	17	1	104	1	3.26
Martin Brochu	44	2475	18	18	4	145	0	3.51
Marc Lamothe	9	428	2	5	0	32	0	4.48

HERSHEY BEARS

SCORING

	Games	G	A	Pts.	PIM
Mitch Lamoureux	76	39	46	85	112
Chris Winnes	78	26	40	66	39
Mike McHugh	68	24	26	50	102
Milos Holan	55	22	27	49	75
Vaclav Prospal	69	13	32	45	36
Bruce Coles	51	16	25	41	73
Andre Faust	55	12	28	40	72
Bob Wilkie	50	9	30	39	46
Yanick Dupre	41	15	19	34	35
Clayton Norris	76	12	21	33	287
Shawn Anderson	31	9	21	30	18
Paul Jerrard	66	17	11	28	118
Aris Brimanis	76	8	17	25	68
Phil Crowe	46	11	6	17	132
Chris Therien	34	3	13	16	27
Jim Montgomery	16	8	6	14	14
Keith Acton	12	5	7	12	58
Jeff Finley	36	2	9	11	33
Tracy Egeland	37	5	5	10	83
Jason Bowen	55	5	5	10	116
Ryan Sittler	42	2	7	9	48
Stewart Malgunas	32	3	5	8	28
Vladislav Boulin	52	1	7	8	30
Rick Bennett	30	3	4	7	40
Brad Zavisha	9	3	0	3	12
Terran Sandwith	11	1	1	2	32
Dan Kordic	37	0	2	2	121
Denis Metlyuk	7	1	0	1	8
Rod Hinks	3	0	1	1	0
Rob Leask	15	0	1	1	6
Mike Greenlay (goalie)	16	0	1	1	4
Neil Little (goalie)	19	0	1	1	2
Les Kuntar (goalie)	32	0	1	1	21
Karl Dykhuis	1	0	0	0	0
Dominic Roussel (goalie)	1	0	0	0	0
Chris Herperger	4	0	0	0	0
Aaron Israel (goalie)	7	0	0	0	0
Jan Lipiansky	7	0	0	0	2
Scott LaGrand (goalie)	21	0	0	0	0

GOALTENDING

	Games	Min.	W	L	T	Goals	SO	Avg.
Les Kuntar	32	1802	15	13	2	89	0	2.96
Scott LaGrand	21	1104	7	9	3	71	1	3.86
Neil Little	19	919	5	7	3	60	0	3.91
Aaron Israel	7	245	2	1	0	16	0	3.92
Mike Greenlay	16	704	5	5	2	46	0	3.92
Dominic Roussel	1	59	0	1	0	5	0	5.07

PORTLAND PIRATES

SCORING

	Games	G	A	Pts.	PIM
Jeff Nelson	64	33	50	83	57
Andrew Brunette	79	30	50	80	53
Chris Jensen	67	35	42	77	89

	Games	G	A	Pts.	PIM
Martin Gendron	72	36	32	68	54
Norm Batherson	77	27	34	61	64
Jason Christie	71	20	40	60	130
Stefan Ustorf	63	21	38	59	51
Mike Boback	32	14	36	50	20
Todd Nelson	75	10	35	45	76
Sergei Gonchar	61	10	32	42	67
Kevin Kaminski	34	15	20	35	292
Steve Poapst	71	8	22	30	60
Kent Hulst	29	10	17	27	80
Darren McAusland	46	12	9	21	33
Kerry Clark	57	9	12	21	282
Chris Longo	57	8	13	21	33
Sergei Tertyshny	55	0	17	17	12
John Slaney	8	3	10	13	4
Ken Klee	49	5	7	12	89
Brian Curran	59	2	10	12	328
Jim Mathieson	35	5	5	10	119
Jason Allison	8	5	4	9	2
Darcy Martini	22	3	6	9	28
Stephane Charbonneau	7	3	5	8	0
Scott Humeniuk	8	3	1	4	30
Steve Gibson	12	3	1	4	2
Pat Peake	5	1	3	4	2
Darren Banks	12	1	2	3	38
John Byce	6	1	1	2	2
Alexander Alexeev	2	0	2	2	4
Jim Carey (goalie)	55	0	2	2	10
John Varga	2	0	1	1	0
Matt Mallgrave	3	0	1	1	0
Trevor Halverson	5	0	1	1	9
Brian Goudie	9	0	1	1	35
Justin Hocking	9	0	1	1	34
Mike Parson (goalie)	1	0	0	0	0
Olaf Kolzig (goalie)	2	0	0	0	0
Scott Matusovich	4	0	0	0	6
Byron Dafoe (goalie)	6	0	0	0	6
Andre Racicot (goalie)	19	0	0	0	0

GOALTENDING

	Games	Min.	W	L	T	Goals	SO	Avg.
Olaf Kolzig	2	125	1	0	1	3	0	1.44
Jim Carey	55	3281	30	14	11	151	6	2.76
Byron Dafoe	6	330	5	0	0	16	0	2.91
Andre Racicot	19	1080	10	7	0	53	1	2.94
Mike Parson	1	29	0	1	0	4	0	8.01

PRINCE EDWARD ISLAND SENATORS

SCORING

	Games	G	A	Pts.	PIM
Steve Larouche	70	53	48	101	54
Michel Picard	57	32	57	89	58
Pavol Demitra	61	26	48	74	23
Greg Pankewicz	75	37	30	67	161
Darren Rumble	70	7	46	53	77
Corey Foster	78	13	34	47	61
Daniel Guerard	68	20	22	42	95
Bruce Gardiner	72	17	20	37	132
Chad Penney	66	16	16	32	19
Trent McCleary	51	9	20	29	60
Lance Pitlick	61	8	19	27	55
Jason Zent	55	15	11	26	46
Dimitri Filimonov	32	6	19	25	14
Claude Savoie	59	9	14	23	67
Claude Boivin	22	10	9	19	89
Patrick Traverse	70	5	13	18	19
Francois Leroux	45	4	14	18	137
Darcy Simon	65	4	10	14	220
Guy Gadowsky	38	4	5	9	12
Greg Spenrath	58	3	5	8	216
Troy Mallette	5	1	5	6	19
Barry McKinlay	8	1	5	6	0
Andy Schneider	10	1	5	6	25
Scott Levins	6	0	4	4	14
Steve Parson	8	2	1	3	0
Darren W. Perkins	26	0	3	3	56

	Games	G	A	Pts.	PIM
Mike Bales (goalie)	45	0	3	3	4
Jean-Francois Labbe (goalie)	32	0	2	2	6
Jason Firth	4	1	0	1	2
Chris Rowland	8	1	0	1	5
Dan Brown	1	0	1	1	0
Bruce Ramsay	2	0	1	1	10
Cosmo DuPaul	3	0	1	1	2
Radek Hamr	7	0	1	1	2
Chris Hynnes	14	0	1	1	4
Jean Blouin	1	0	0	0	0
Lance Leslie (goalie)	1	0	0	0	0
Patrick Charbonneau (goalie)	2	0	0	0	0
Mel Angelstad	3	0	0	0	16
Darrin Madeley (goalie)	3	0	0	0	0

GOALTENDING

	Games	Min.	W	L	T	Goals	SO	Avg.
Lance Leslie	1	65	0	0	1	2	0	1.85
Patrick Charbonneau	2	120	2	0	0	4	0	2.00
Darrin Madeley	3	185	1	1	1	8	0	2.59
J.-F. Labbe	32	1817	13	14	3	94	2	3.10
Mike Bales	45	2649	25	16	3	160	2	3.62

PROVIDENCE BRUINS

SCORING

	Games	G	A	Pts.	PIM
Brett Harkins	80	23	69	92	32
Fred Knipscheer	71	29	34	63	81
Jeff Serowik	78	28	34	62	102
Sandy Moger	63	32	29	61	105
Guy Larose	68	25	33	58	93
Sergei Zholtok	78	23	35	58	42
Tim Tookey	50	14	30	44	28
Grigori Panteleev	70	20	23	43	36
Clayton Beddoes	65	16	20	36	39
Peter Laviolette	65	7	23	30	84
Daniel Lacroix	40	15	11	26	266
Cam Stewart	31	13	11	24	38
Phil Von Stefenelli	75	6	13	19	93
Mike Bodnarchuk	40	4	15	19	22
Denis Chervyakov	65	1	18	19	130
Jon Pratt	44	12	6	18	31
Marc Potvin	21	4	14	18	84
Alex Nikolic	57	6	8	14	229
Jeff Wells	51	3	11	14	23
Bill C. Armstrong	75	3	10	13	244
Darren Stolk	23	3	6	9	13
Paul Stanton	8	4	4	8	4
Andrei Sapozhnikov	19	1	5	6	23
Tim Sweeney	2	2	2	4	0
Scott Bailey (goalie)	52	0	4	4	6
Dave Reid	7	3	0	3	0
Jon Rohloff	4	2	1	3	6
Kurt Seher	15	0	3	3	4
Davis Payne	2	1	0	1	0
John Gruden	1	0	1	1	0
Evgeny Ryabchikov (goalie)	14	0	1	1	12
Derek Eberle	1	0	0	0	0
Claude Fillion	1	0	0	0	0
Alexander Kerch	1	0	0	0	15
Blaine Lacher (goalie)	1	0	0	0	0
Daniel Berthiaume (goalie)	2	0	0	0	0
Rob Tallas (goalie)	2	0	0	0	0
Howie Rosenblatt	3	0	0	0	7
Steve Norton	6	0	0	0	2
Chad Erickson (goalie)	7	0	0	0	0
John Blue (goalie)	10	0	0	0	0

GOALTENDING

	Games	Min.	W	L	T	Goals	SO	Avg.
Rob Tallas	2	82	1	0	0	4	1	2.90
Scott Bailey	52	2936	25	16	9	147	2	3.00
Blaine Lacher	1	59	0	1	0	3	0	3.03
John Blue	10	577	6	3	0	30	0	3.11
Daniel Berthiaume	2	126	0	1	1	7	0	3.32

	Games	Min.	W	L	T	Goals	SO	Avg.
Evgeny Ryabchikov	14	721	6	3	1	42	0	3.49
Chad Erickson	7	351	1	6	0	33	0	5.63

ROCHESTER AMERICANS

SCORING

	Games	G	A	Pts.	PIM
Todd Simon	69	25	65	90	78
Viktor Gordiouk	63	31	30	61	36
Scott Metcalfe	63	19	36	55	216
Matthew Barnaby	56	21	29	50	274
Jason Dawe	44	27	19	46	24
Scott Thomas	55	21	25	46	115
Doug MacDonald	58	21	25	46	73
Mikhail Volkov	56	17	27	44	52
Philippe Boucher	43	14	27	41	26
Jim Wiemer	45	9	29	38	74
Jason Young	51	18	17	35	80
Mark Astley	46	5	24	29	49
Sergei Petrenko	43	12	16	28	16
Scott Nichol	71	11	16	27	136
Peter Ambroziak	46	14	11	25	35
Tom Nemeth	56	4	17	21	32
Mark Krys	70	3	16	19	113
Todd Copeland	77	4	12	16	152
Paul Rushforth	25	8	6	14	10
Dean Melanson	43	4	7	11	84
Jody Gage	23	4	5	9	20
Eric Germain	18	1	7	8	13
Mike Bavis	27	3	4	7	100
David Cooper	21	2	4	6	48
Mike Barrie	16	1	3	4	40
Scott Boston	16	1	1	2	6
Lorne Knauft	5	0	2	2	8
Steve Shields (goalie)	13	0	2	2	0
Kevin McClelland	22	0	2	2	93
Don Martin	1	0	1	1	2
Chris Foy	5	0	1	1	2
Jacques Mailhot	15	0	1	1	52
Markus Ketterer (goalie)	47	0	1	1	0
Bruce Shoebottom	1	0	0	0	0
Cal Benazic	2	0	0	0	0
Doug Evans	2	0	0	0	0
Shayne Wright	2	0	0	0	0
Scott Campbell	3	0	0	0	15
Brian McCarthy	4	0	0	0	5
Sergei Klimentiev	7	0	0	0	8
Eric Raymond (goalie)	29	0	0	0	6

GOALTENDING

	Games	Min.	W	L	T	Goals	SO	Avg.
Eric Raymond	29	1592	13	10	4	92	0	3.47
Markus Ketterer	47	2563	19	20	3	154	1	3.60
Steve Shields	13	673	3	8	0	53	0	4.72

SAINT JOHN SAINTS

SCORING

	Games	G	A	Pts.	PIM
Mark Greig	67	31	50	81	82
Cory Stillman	63	28	53	81	70
Neil Eisenhut	75	16	39	55	30
Vesa Viitakoski	56	17	26	43	8
Len Esau	54	13	27	40	73
Francois Groleau	65	6	34	40	28
Scott Morrow	64	18	21	39	105
Ryan Duthie	72	18	21	39	70
Mike Murray	65	8	27	35	53
Todd Hlushko	46	22	10	32	36
Bobby Marshall	77	7	24	31	62
Joel Bouchard	77	6	25	31	63
Dale Kushner	38	13	10	23	97
Barry Nieckar	65	8	7	15	491
Niklas Sundblad	72	9	5	14	151
Todd Simpson	80	3	10	13	321
Ed Ward	11	4	5	9	20

	Games	G	A	Pts.	PIM
Sami Helenius	69	2	5	7	217
David St. Pierre	17	4	2	6	0
Jeff Perry	28	4	2	6	128
Dennis Purdie	12	4	1	5	11
Nicolas Perreault	36	3	2	5	46
Krzysztof Oliwa	14	1	4	5	79
Chris Gotziaman	12	2	2	4	4
Dwayne Roloson (goalie)	46	0	4	4	19
Travis Thiessen	9	1	2	3	12
Jeff Sebastian	11	1	1	2	0
John Porco	3	1	0	1	2
David Struch	7	0	1	1	4
Jason Muzzatti (goalie)	31	0	1	1	37
Patrick Bisillon	1	0	0	0	0
Dave Cameron	1	0	0	0	0
Brian Caruso	1	0	0	0	2
Ladislav Kohn	1	0	0	0	0
Rob Moffat	1	0	0	0	0
Andrei Trefilov (goalie)	7	0	0	0	2

GOALTENDING

	Games	Min.	W	L	T	Goals	SO	Avg.
Andrei Trefilov	7	383	1	5	1	20	0	3.13
Dwayne Roloson	46	2734	16	21	8	156	1	3.42
Jason Muzzatti	31	1741	10	14	4	101	2	3.48

ST. JOHN'S MAPLE LEAFS

SCORING

	Games	G	A	Pts.	PIM
Alexei Kudashov	75	25	54	79	17
Brandon Convery	76	34	37	71	43
Patrik Augusta	71	37	32	69	98
Rich Chernomaz	77	24	45	69	235
Kelly Fairchild	53	27	23	50	51
Steffon Walby	70	23	23	46	30
Janne Gronvall	76	8	29	37	75
Nathan Dempsey	74	7	30	37	91
Darby Hendrickson	59	16	20	36	48
Mark Kolesar	65	12	18	30	62
Guy Leveque	37	8	14	22	31
Todd Warriner	46	8	10	18	22
Matt Martin	49	2	16	18	54
Mike Speer	27	5	12	17	30
Ryan VandenBussche	53	2	13	15	239
Guy Lehoux	77	4	9	13	255
Ken Belanger	47	5	5	10	246
Kenny Jonsson	10	2	5	7	2
Dixon Ward	6	3	3	6	19
David Harlock	58	0	6	6	44
Frank Bialowas	51	2	3	5	277
Robb McIntyre	19	4	0	4	4
Bruce Racine (goalie)	27	0	3	3	6
Mike Ware	1	2	0	2	0
Steve Bancroft	4	2	0	2	2
Paul Holden	6	1	1	2	4
Paul Vincent	2	0	2	2	0
Marcel Cousineau (goalie)	58	0	2	2	20
Gord Kruppke	3	0	1	1	6
Mike Taylor	4	0	1	1	0
Terry Chitaroni	5	0	1	1	14
Marc Hussey	11	0	1	1	20
Trent Cull	43	0	1	1	53
Marc Aussey	1	0	0	0	0
Eric Lacroix	1	0	0	0	2
Andy Sullivan	1	0	0	0	0
Wayne Clark	3	0	0	0	0
Beat Equilino	3	0	0	0	0
Jason Cipolla	4	0	0	0	0
Jason Denomme	4	0	0	0	0

GOALTENDING

	Games	Min.	W	L	T	Goals	SO	Avg.
Marcel Cousineau	58	3342	22	27	6	171	4	3.07
Bruce Racine	27	1492	11	10	4	85	1	3.42

SPRINGFIELD INDIANS

SCORING

	Games	G	A	Pts.	PIM
Robert Petrovicky	74	30	52	82	121
John LeBlanc	65	39	34	73	32
Rob Murray	78	16	38	54	373
Brad Jones	61	23	22	45	47
Jason McBain	77	16	28	44	92
Marek Malik	58	11	30	41	91
Kevin Smyth	57	17	22	39	72
Ravil Gusmanov	72	18	15	33	14
Michal Grosek	45	10	22	32	98
Bob Wren	61	16	15	31	118
Dale Junkin	63	11	13	24	30
Jim Storm	33	11	11	22	29
Oleg Mikulchik	50	5	16	21	59
Luciano Borsato	22	9	11	20	14
John Stevens	79	5	15	20	122
Arto Blomsten	27	3	16	19	20
Scott Daniels	48	9	5	14	277
Russ Romaniuk	17	5	7	12	29
Steve Yule	61	1	10	11	143
Rick Bennett	34	3	5	8	74
Mike Muller	64	2	5	7	61
Len Hachborn	5	2	4	6	2
Shayne McCosh	18	2	3	5	4
Jeff Hoad	11	2	2	4	33
Mark Visheau	35	0	4	4	94
Jarrett Reid	8	1	2	3	0
Tim Roberts	5	0	3	3	0
Michael Stewart	7	0	3	3	21
Mark Deazeley	26	2	0	2	141
Nikolai Khabibulin (goalie)	23	0	2	2	2
Stephane Beauregard (goalie)	24	0	2	2	4
Ted Drury	2	0	1	1	0
Steve Cheredaryk	3	0	1	1	0
Ian Hebert	4	0	1	1	2
Craig Martin	6	0	1	1	21
Chad Erickson (goalie)	1	0	0	0	0
Doug Smith	1	0	0	0	14
Brad Mullahy (goalie)	2	0	0	0	0
Brad Smyth	3	0	0	0	7
Manny Legace (goalie)	39	0	0	0	18

GOALTENDING

	Games	Min.	W	L	T	Goals	SO	Avg.
Brad Mullahy	2	38	0	0	0	0	0	0.00
S. Beauregard	24	1381	10	11	3	73	2	3.17
Manny Legace	39	2169	12	17	6	128	2	3.54
Nikolai Khabibulin	23	1240	9	9	3	80	0	3.87
Chad Erickson	1	23	0	0	0	3	0	7.78

SYRACUSE CRUNCH

SCORING

	Games	G	A	Pts.	PIM
Dan Kesa	70	34	44	78	81
Lonny Bohonos	67	30	45	75	71
Dane Jackson	78	30	28	58	162
Scott Walker	74	14	38	52	334
Rod Stevens	78	21	21	42	63
Mark Wotton	75	12	29	41	50
Brian Loney	67	23	17	40	98
Mike Peca	35	10	24	34	75
John Namestnikov	59	11	22	33	59
Adrian Aucoin	71	13	18	31	52
Alex Stojanov	73	18	12	30	270
Yuri Kuznetsov	54	10	17	27	37
Rick Girard	26	10	13	23	22
Yannick Dube	39	10	11	21	8
Daryl Filipek	71	6	13	19	46
Nathan Lafayette	27	9	9	18	10
Jason Firth	20	4	13	17	4
Libor Polasek	45	2	8	10	16
Brent Tully	63	6	3	9	106
Jassen Cullimore	33	2	7	9	66

	Games	G	A	Pts.	PIM
John Badduke	44	6	0	6	334
Marc Laforge	39	1	5	6	202
Mikhail Kravets	7	2	2	4	8
Cam Danyluk	12	1	3	4	19
Mike Fountain (goalie)	61	0	4	4	18
Trevor Sim	3	2	0	2	0
Artur Oktyabrev	7	1	1	2	2
Mark Cornforth	2	0	1	1	2
Jacque Rodrigue	2	0	1	1	0
Norm Dezainde	6	0	1	1	17
Larry Empey	1	0	0	0	0
Danny Beauregard	2	0	0	0	15
Louis Dumont	2	0	0	0	0
Shawn Hannah	2	0	0	0	2
Sergei Tkachenko (goalie)	2	0	0	0	2
Travis Tucker	2	0	0	0	2
Rob Trumbley	3	0	0	0	12
Michael Whitton	4	0	0	0	5
Justin Hocking	7	0	0	0	24
Sonny Mignacca (goalie)	19	0	0	0	2

GOALTENDING

	Games	Min.	W	L	T	Goals	SO	Avg.
Mike Fountain	61	3618	25	29	7	225	2	3.73
Sergei Tkachenko	2	118	0	2	0	9	0	4.57
Sonny Mignacca	19	1097	4	11	2	85	0	4.65

WORCESTER ICECATS

SCORING

	Games	G	A	Pts.	PIM
Denis Chalifoux	65	21	32	53	32
Shawn Heaphy	70	23	28	51	50
Blair Atcheynum	55	17	29	46	26
Cal McGowan	64	22	21	43	28
Mark Ouimet	61	13	29	42	24
Ross Wilson	70	17	24	41	82
Terry Virtue	73	14	25	39	186
Dave Baseggio	72	10	28	38	38
Jason Widmer	73	8	26	34	136
Roy Mitchell	80	5	25	30	97
Jim Nesich	77	7	21	28	128
John Carter	64	18	9	27	96
Sean Whyte	59	13	8	21	76
David Haas	28	11	10	21	88
Jarrett Deuling	63	11	8	19	37
Martin Mercier	39	8	10	18	31
Shaun Kane	77	1	14	15	52
Walt Poddubny	34	7	6	13	62
Jim Bermingham	10	3	4	7	4
Lindsay Vallis	14	0	7	7	28
Yves Heroux	7	3	1	4	2
Jason Weinrich	31	0	3	3	21
Rob Melanson	59	0	3	3	210
Maxim Bets	9	1	1	2	6
Brian Straub	7	0	2	2	39
Wayne Cowley (goalie)	45	0	2	2	4
Mark Woolf	7	1	0	1	0
Chris Valicevic	3	0	1	1	2
Lance Brady	4	0	1	1	0
Chris Bright	1	0	0	0	4
Tom Cole (goalie)	1	0	0	0	0
Francis Ouellette	1	0	0	0	0
B.J. MacPherson	2	0	0	0	8
Marquis Mathieu	2	0	0	0	0
Chris Gordon (goalie)	17	0	0	0	0
Les Kuntar (goalie)	24	0	0	0	0

GOALTENDING

	Games	Min.	W	L	T	Goals	SO	Avg.
Wayne Cowley	45	2597	11	25	6	153	1	3.53
Les Kuntar	24	1241	6	10	5	77	2	3.72
Chris Gordon	17	993	7	10	0	67	0	4.05
Tom Cole	1	28	0	0	0	2	0	4.23

PLAYERS WITH TWO OR MORE TEAMS

SCORING

	Games	G	A	Pts.	PIM
Darren Banks, Adirondack	20	3	2	5	65
Darren Banks, Portland	12	1	2	3	38
Totals	32	4	4	8	103
Rick Bennett, Springfield	34	3	5	8	74
Rick Bennett, Hershey	30	3	4	7	40
Totals	64	6	9	15	114
Stephane Charbonneau, Corn.	1	0	1	1	0
Stephane Charbonneau, Port.	7	3	5	8	0
Totals	8	3	6	9	0
Chad Erickson, Albany (g)	1	0	0	0	0
Chad Erickson, Providence (g)	7	0	0	0	0
Chad Erickson, Springfield (g)	1	0	0	0	0
Totals	9	0	0	0	0
Jason Firth, Prince Edward Is.	4	1	0	1	2
Jason Firth, Syracuse	20	4	13	17	4
Totals	24	5	13	18	6
Steve Gibson, Portland	12	3	1	4	2
Steve Gibson, Cornwall	2	0	0	0	0
Totals	14	3	1	4	2
Francois Groleau, Saint John	65	6	34	40	28
Francois Groleau, Cornwall	8	1	2	3	7
Totals	73	7	36	43	35
Justin Hocking, Syracuse	7	0	0	0	24
Justin Hocking, Portland	9	0	1	1	34
Totals	16	0	1	1	58
Lorne Knauft, Adirondack	2	0	1	1	6
Lorne Knauft, Rochester	5	0	2	2	8
Totals	7	0	3	3	14
Gord Kruppke, Adirondack	48	2	9	11	157
Gord Kruppke, St. John's	3	0	1	1	6
Totals	51	2	10	12	163
Les Kuntar, Worcester (g)	24	0	0	0	0
Les Kuntar, Hershey (g)	32	0	1	1	21
Totals	56	0	1	1	21
Marc Laforge, Cape Breton	18	0	1	1	80
Marc Laforge, Syracuse	39	1	5	6	202
Totals	57	1	6	7	282
Darcy Martini, Cape Breton	31	2	13	15	75
Darcy Martini, Portland	22	3	6	9	28
Totals	53	5	19	24	103
Krzysztof Oliwa, Albany	20	1	1	2	77
Krzysztof Oliwa, Saint John	14	1	4	5	79
Totals	34	2	5	7	156
Michael Stewart, Binghamton	68	6	21	27	83
Michael Stewart, Springfield	7	0	3	3	21
Totals	75	6	24	30	104
Mike Taylor, St. John's	4	0	1	1	0
Mike Taylor, Cornwall	3	0	0	0	2
Totals	7	0	1	1	2
Ed Ward, Cornwall	56	10	14	24	118
Ed Ward, Saint John	11	4	5	9	20
Totals	67	14	19	33	138
Brad Zavisha, Cape Breton	62	13	20	33	55
Brad Zavisha, Hershey	9	3	0	3	12
Totals	71	16	20	36	67

GOALTENDING

	Games	Min.	W	L	T	Goals	SO	Avg.
C. Erickson, Albany.	1	60	1	0	0	2	0	2.00
C. Erickson, Prov..	7	351	1	6	0	33	0	5.63
C. Erickson, Spring..	1	23	0	0	0	3	0	7.78
Totals	9	434	2	6	0	38	0	5.24
L. Kuntar, Worcester	24	1241	6	10	5	77	2	3.72
L. Kuntar, Hershey.	32	1802	15	13	2	89	0	2.96
Totals	56	3044	21	23	7	166	2	3.27

RESULTS

DIVISION SEMIFINALS

Series "A"

	W	L	Pts.	GF	GA
Prince Edward Island	4	1	8	15	9
Saint John	1	4	2	9	15

(Prince Edward Island won series, 4-1)

Series "B"

	W	L	Pts.	GF	GA
Fredericton	4	1	8	15	10
St. John's	1	4	2	10	15

(Fredericton won series, 4-1)

Series "C"

	W	L	Pts.	GF	GA
Albany	4	0	8	15	7
Adirondack	0	4	0	7	15

(Albany won series, 4-0)

Series "D"

	W	L	Pts.	GF	GA
Providence	4	3	8	30	30
Portland	3	4	6	30	30

(Providence won series, 4-3)

Series "E"

	W	L	Pts.	GF	GA
Binghamton	4	1	8	21	10
Rochester	1	4	2	10	21

(Binghamton won series, 4-1)

Series "F"

	W	L	Pts.	GF	GA
Cornwall	4	2	8	18	19
Hershey	2	4	4	19	18

(Cornwall won series, 4-2)

DIVISION FINALS

Series "G"

	W	L	Pts.	GF	GA
Fredericton	4	2	8	29	18
Prince Edward Island	2	4	4	18	29

(Fredericton won series, 4-2)

Series "H"

	W	L	Pts.	GF	GA
Albany	4	2	8	24	26
Providence	2	4	4	26	24

(Albany won series, 4-2)

Series "J"

	W	L	Pts.	GF	GA
Cornwall	4	2	8	21	13
Binghamton	2	4	6	13	21

(Cornwall won series, 4-2)

LEAGUE SEMIFINALS

Series "K"

	W	L	Pts.	GF	GA
Fredericton	2	0	4	5	2
Cornwall	0	2	0	2	5

(Fredericton won series, 2-0)

FINALS—FOR THE CALDER CUP

Series "L"

	W	L	Pts.	GF	GA
Albany	4	0	8	15	7
Fredericton	0	4	0	7	15

(Albany won series, 4-0)

INDIVIDUAL LEADERS

Goals: Robert Guillet, Fredericton (10)
Assists: Tim Sweeney, Providence (17)
Points: Tim Sweeney, Providence (25)
Penalty minutes: Darren Langdon, Binghamton (84)
Goaltending average: Garth Snow (2.09)
Shutouts: Scott Bailey, Providence (2)
Mike Bales, Prince Edward Island (2)
Garth Snow, Cornwall (2)

TOP SCORERS

	Games	G	A	Pts.
Tim Sweeney, Providence	13	8	17	25
Brett Harkins, Providence	13	8	14	22
Grigori Panteleev, Providence	13	8	11	19
Robert Guillet, Fredericton	17	10	6	16
Dwayne Norris, Cornwall	12	7	8	15
Matt Ruchty, Albany	12	5	10	15
Steve Brule, Albany	14	9	5	14
Stephane Yelle, Cornwall	13	7	7	14
Gaston Gingras, Fredericton	17	2	12	14
Sergei Zholtok, Providence	13	8	5	13

INDIVIDUAL STATISTICS

ADIRONDACK RED WINGS

(Lost division semifinals to Albany, 4-0)

SCORING

	Games	G	A	Pts.	PIM
Andrew McKim	4	3	3	6	0
Chris Govedaris	4	2	1	3	10
Kurt Miller	4	1	1	2	2
Curtis Bowen	4	0	2	2	4
Jason Miller	4	1	0	1	0
Jamie Pushor	4	0	1	1	0
Aaron Ward	4	0	1	1	0
Sergei Bautin	1	0	0	0	4

	Games	G	A	Pts.	PIM
Mark Ferner	1	0	0	0	0
Mike Knuble	3	0	0	0	0
Brandon Smith	3	0	0	0	2
Jeff Bloemberg	4	0	0	0	0
Cam Brown	4	0	0	0	24
Mike Casselman	4	0	0	0	2
Joe Frederick	4	0	0	0	10
Tod Hartje	4	0	0	0	4
Kevin Hodson (goalie)	4	0	0	0	0
Jason MacDonald	4	0	0	0	2
Troy Neumeier	4	0	0	0	2

GOALTENDING

	Games	Min.	W	L	T	Goals	SO	Avg.
Kevin Hodson	4	238	0	4	0	14	0	3.53

ALBANY RIVER RATS

(Winner of 1995 Calder Cup playoffs)

SCORING

	Games	G	A	Pts.	PIM
Matt Ruchty	12	5	10	15	43
Steve Brule	14	9	5	14	4
Bill H. Armstrong	13	6	5	11	20
Steve Sullivan	14	4	7	11	10
Scott Pellerin	14	6	4	10	8
Rob Conn	14	4	6	10	16
Pascal Rheaume	14	3	6	9	19
Reid Simpson	14	1	8	9	13
Rickard Persson	9	3	5	8	7
Vadim Sharifijanov	9	3	3	6	10
Jaroslav Modry	14	3	3	6	4
Jason Smith	11	2	2	4	19
Kevin Dean	8	0	4	4	4
Brad Bombardir	14	0	3	3	6
Curt Regnier	6	1	1	2	2
Bobby House	8	1	1	2	0
Geordie Kinnear	9	1	1	2	7
Cale Hulse	12	1	1	2	17
Corey Schwab (goalie)	7	0	2	2	0
Bryan Helmer	7	1	0	1	0
Denis Pederson	3	0	0	0	2
Mike Vukonich	4	0	0	0	0
Mike Dunham (goalie)	7	0	0	0	6

GOALTENDING

	Games	Min.	W	L	T	Goals	SO	Avg.
Corey Schwab	7	425	6	1	0	19	0	2.68
Mike Dunham	7	420	6	1	0	20	1	2.86

BINGHAMTON RANGERS

(Lost division finals to Cornwall, 4-2)

SCORING

	Games	G	A	Pts.	PIM
Shawn McCosh	8	3	9	12	6
Jean-Yves Roy	11	4	6	10	12
Barry Richter	11	4	5	9	12
Craig Duncanson	11	4	4	8	16
Peter Ferraro	11	4	3	7	51
Darcy Werenka	11	4	3	7	2
Dave Smith	8	2	4	6	38
Brad Rubachuk	8	2	3	5	33
Chris Ferraro	10	2	3	5	16
Ken Gernander	11	2	2	4	6
Darren Langdon	11	1	3	4	84
Mike McLaughlin	8	0	3	3	0
Shawn Reid	9	0	3	3	6
Dmitri Starostenko	5	1	1	2	0
Eric Cairns	9	1	1	2	28
Scott Malone	11	0	2	2	12
Jamie Ram (goalie)	11	0	2	2	2
Peter Fiorentino	2	0	1	1	11
Jon Hillebrandt (goalie)	1	0	0	0	0
Joby Messier	1	0	0	0	0
Sylvain Blouin	2	0	0	0	24
Andrei Kudinov	3	0	0	0	0
Jeff Nielsen	7	0	0	0	22
Lee Sorochan	8	0	0	0	11

GOALTENDING

	Games	Min.	W	L	T	Goals	SO	Avg.
Jamie Ram	11	664	6	5	0	29	1	2.62
Jon Hillebrandt	1	6	0	0	U	1	0	10.20

CORNWALL ACES

(Lost league semifinals to Fredericton, 2-0)

SCORING

	Games	G	A	Pts.	PIM
Dwayne Norris	12	7	8	15	4
Stephane Yelle	13	7	7	14	8
Reggie Savage	14	5	6	11	40
Rene Corbet	12	2	8	10	27
Francois Groleau	14	2	7	9	16
Pascal Trepanier	14	2	7	9	32
Blair Scott	14	3	5	8	12
Landon Wilson	13	3	4	7	68
Ryan Hughes	14	0	7	7	10
Paxton Schulte	14	3	3	6	29
Paul Brousseau	7	2	1	3	10
Wade Belak	11	1	2	3	40
Eric Veilleux	13	1	1	2	20
Chris Phelps	1	1	0	1	0
Mike Hurlbut	3	1	0	1	15
Cory Banika	7	1	0	1	47
Christian Matte	3	0	1	1	2
Anders Myrvold	3	0	1	1	2
Jeff Parrott	14	0	1	1	12
Brent Brekke	1	0	0	0	4
Craig Charron	2	0	0	0	0
Doug Friedman	3	0	0	0	0
Darren Wetherill	3	0	0	0	12
Jason Downey	7	0	0	0	28
Rich Shulmistra (goalie)	8	0	0	0	4
Garth Snow (goalie)	8	0	0	0	29
Serge Roberge	11	0	0	0	29

GOALTENDING

	Games	Min.	W	L	T	Goals	SO	Avg.
Garth Snow	8	402	4	3	0	14	2	2.09
Rich Shulmistra	8	447	4	3	0	22	0	2.95

FREDERICTON CANADIENS

(Lost league finals to Albany, 4-0)

SCORING

	Games	G	A	Pts.	PIM
Robert Guillet	17	10	6	16	28
Gaston Gingras	17	2	12	14	8
Donald Brashear	17	7	5	12	77
Xavier Majic	17	3	9	12	0
Oleg Petrov	17	5	6	11	10
Craig Conroy	11	7	3	10	6
Craig Ferguson	17	6	2	8	6
Scott Fraser	16	3	5	8	14
Jim Campbell	12	0	7	7	8
Brent Bilodeau	12	3	3	6	28
Brady Kramer	12	3	2	5	2
Christian Lariviere	15	0	5	5	18
Craig Rivet	12	0	4	4	17
Derek Maguire	17	0	4	4	4
Yves Sarault	13	2	1	3	33
Rory Fitzpatrick	10	1	2	3	5
Gerry Fleming	10	2	0	2	67
Mario Roberge	6	1	1	2	6
Chris Murray	12	1	1	2	50
Christian Proulx	9	0	1	1	8
Patrick Labrecque (goalie)	16	0	1	1	2
Louis Bernard	1	0	0	0	0
Sebastian Bordeau	1	0	0	0	0
Jose Theodore (goalie)	1	0	0	0	0
David Wilkie	1	0	0	0	0

GOALTENDING

	Games	Min.	W	L	T	Goals	SO	Avg.
Patrick Labrecque	16	968	10	6	0	40	1	2.48
Jose Theodore	1	60	0	1	0	3	0	3.00

HERSHEY BEARS

(Lost division semifinals to Cornwall, 4-2)

SCORING

	Games	G	A	Pts.	PIM
Bruce Coles	6	1	5	6	14
Andre Faust	6	1	5	6	12
Mike McHugh	6	3	2	5	6
Jim Montgomery	6	3	2	5	25
Shawn Anderson	6	2	3	5	19
Chris Winnes	6	2	2	4	17
Rick Bennett	3	2	1	3	14
Stewart Malgunas	6	2	1	3	31
Aris Brimanis	6	1	1	2	14
Mitch Lamoureux	6	0	2	2	8
Tracy Egeland	2	1	0	1	15
Vaclav Prospal	2	1	0	1	4
Phil Crowe	6	0	1	1	19
Jeff Finley	6	0	1	1	8
Paul Jerrard	6	0	1	1	19
Dan Kordic	6	0	1	1	21
Rod Hinks	1	0	0	0	2
Aaron Israel (goalie)	1	0	0	0	0
Les Kuntar (goalie)	2	0	0	0	0
Clayton Norris	4	0	0	0	8
Mike Greenlay (goalie)	5	0	0	0	19
Jason Bowen	6	0	0	0	46

GOALTENDING

	Games	Min.	W	L	T	Goals	SO	Avg.
Mike Greenlay	5	270	2	3	0	12	0	2.66
Aaron Israel	1	21	0	0	0	1	0	2.81
Les Kuntar	2	70	0	1	0	5	0	4.28

PORTLAND PIRATES

(Lost division semifinals to Providence, 4-3)

SCORING

	Games	G	A	Pts.	PIM
Jason Allison	7	3	8	11	2
Chris Jensen	7	4	3	7	0
Norm Batherson	7	3	4	7	4
Stefan Ustorf	7	1	6	7	7
Martin Gendron	4	5	1	6	2
Andrew Brunette	7	3	3	6	10
Scott Humeniuk	7	3	3	6	2
Mike Boback	5	1	4	5	2
Jeff Nelson	7	1	4	5	8
Kent Hulst	7	3	1	4	2
John Slaney	7	1	3	4	4
Todd Nelson	7	0	4	4	6
Pat Peake	4	0	3	3	6
Darren McAusland	2	2	2	2	2
Jason Christie	3	1	0	1	0
Jim Mathieson	7	1	0	1	4
Steve Poapst	7	0	1	1	16
Kerry Clark	1	0	0	0	0
Chris Longo	2	0	0	0	0
Brian Curran	7	0	0	0	24
Byron Dafoe (goalie)	7	0	0	0	0

GOALTENDING

	Games	Min.	W	L	T	Goals	SO	Avg.
Byron Dafoe	7	417	3	4	0	29	0	4.18

PRINCE EDWARD ISLAND SENATORS

(Lost division finals to Fredericton, 4-2)

SCORING

	Games	G	A	Pts.	PIM
Andy Schneider	11	5	5	10	11
Michel Picard	8	4	4	8	6
Jason Zent	9	6	1	7	6
Corey Foster	11	2	5	7	12
Pavol Demitra	5	0	7	7	0
Darren Rumble	11	0	6	6	4

	Games	G	A	Pts.	PIM
Bruce Gardiner	7	4	1	5	4
Trent McCleary	9	2	3	5	26
Lance Pitlick	11	1	4	5	10
Darcy Simon	11	1	4	5	38
Chad Penney	11	2	2	4	2
Claude Boivin	9	1	2	3	32
Claude Savoie	4	2	0	2	7
Greg Pankewicz	6	1	1	2	24
Guy Gadowsky	10	1	1	2	4
Patrick Traverse	7	0	2	2	0
Greg Spenrath	9	0	2	2	28
Steve Larouche	2	1	0	1	0
Radim Bicanek	3	0	1	1	0
Daniel Guerard	8	0	1	1	16
Dimitri Filimonov	9	0	1	1	2
Radek Bonk	1	0	0	0	0
Cosmo DuPaul	1	0	0	0	0
Bruce Ramsay	1	0	0	0	2
Darren W. Perkins	2	0	0	0	21
Patrick Charbonneau (goalie)	3	0	0	0	0
Mike Bales (goalie)	9	0	0	0	2

GOALTENDING

	Games	Min.	W	L	T	Goals	SO	Avg.
Mike Bales	9	530	6	3	0	24	2	2.72
Patrick Charbonneau	3	137	0	2	0	12	0	5.24

PROVIDENCE BRUINS

(Lost division finals to Albany, 4-2)

SCORING

	Games	G	A	Pts.	PIM
Tim Sweeney	13	8	17	25	6
Brett Harkins	13	8	14	22	4
Grigori Panteleev	13	8	11	19	6
Sergei Zholtok	13	8	5	13	6
Guy Larose	12	4	6	10	22
Jeff Serowik	13	4	6	10	10
Peter Laviolette	13	2	8	10	17
Cam Stewart	9	2	5	7	0
Mikko Makela	7	2	4	6	2
Marc Potvin	12	2	4	6	25
Phil Von Stefenelli	13	2	4	6	6
Clayton Beddoes	13	3	1	4	18
Jeff Wells	9	2	1	3	0
Jon Pratt	9	1	1	2	8
Alexander Kerch	4	0	2	2	0
Scott Bailey (goalie)	9	0	2	2	8
Denis Chervyakov	10	0	2	2	14
Bill C. Armstrong	13	0	2	2	8
Tim Tookey	1	0	1	1	2
Darren Stolk	4	0	1	1	4
Mike Bodnarchuk	1	0	0	0	0
Vincent Riendeau (goalie)	1	0	0	0	0
Howie Rosenblatt	1	0	0	0	0
John Blue (goalie)	4	0	0	0	0
Alex Nikolic	6	0	0	0	18
Kurt Seher	6	0	0	0	2

GOALTENDING

	Games	Min.	W	L	T	Goals	SO	Avg.
Vincent Riendeau	1	60	1	0	0	3	0	3.00
Scott Bailey	9	505	4	4	0	31	2	3.69
John Blue	4	220	1	3	0	19	0	5.19

ROCHESTER AMERICANS

(Lost division semifinals to Binghamton, 4-1)

SCORING

	Games	G	A	Pts.	PIM
Scott Thomas	5	4	0	4	4
Tom Nemeth	4	2	1	3	4
Scott Nichol	5	0	3	3	14
Scott Metcalfe	5	1	1	2	4
Mark Astley	3	0	2	2	2
Viktor Gordiouk	3	0	2	2	0

	Games	G	A	Pts.	PIM
Eric Germain	5	0	2	2	18
Todd Simon	5	0	2	2	21
Jim Wiemer	5	0	2	2	6
Mikhail Volkov	4	1	0	1	2
Jason Young	4	1	0	1	16
Todd Copeland	5	1	0	1	14
Shayne Wright	4	0	1	1	0
Mike Bavis	5	0	1	1	9
Doug MacDonald	5	0	1	1	0
Sergei Klimentiev	1	0	0	0	0
Steve Shields (goalie)	1	0	0	0	0
Jody Gage	2	0	0	0	0
Paul Rushforth	2	0	0	0	0
Mark Krys	3	0	0	0	0
Peter Ambroziak	4	0	0	0	6
Eric Raymond (goalie)	5	0	0	0	0

GOALTENDING

	Games	Min.	W	L	T	Goals	SO	Avg.
Eric Raymond	5	286	1	4	0	18	0	3.77
Steve Shields	1	20	0	0	0	3	0	9.00

SAINT JOHN FLAMES

(Lost division semifinals to Prince Edward Island, 4-1)

SCORING

	Games	G	A	Pts.	PIM
Todd Hlushko	4	2	2	4	22
Dale Kushner	5	0	3	3	14
David St. Pierre	3	2	0	2	0
Scott Morrow	5	2	0	2	4
Neil Eisenhut	5	1	1	2	6
Len Esau	5	0	2	2	0
Dwayne Roloson (goalie)	5	0	2	2	2
Cory Stillman	5	0	2	2	2
Joel Bouchard	5	1	0	1	4
Ed Ward	5	1	0	1	10
Mark Greig	2	0	1	1	0
Vesa Viitakoski	4	0	1	1	2
Jeff Sebastian	5	0	1	1	0
Travis Thiessen	5	0	1	1	0

	Games	G	A	Pts.	PIM
Ryan Duthie	2	0	0	0	0
Niklas Sundblad	2	0	0	0	6
Mike Murray	4	0	0	0	6
Barry Nieckar	4	0	0	0	22
Bobby Marshall	5	0	0	0	4
Todd Simpson	5	0	0	0	4

GOALTENDING

	Games	Min.	W	L	T	Goals	SO	Avg.
Dwayne Roloson	5	299	1	4	0	13	0	2.61

ST. JOHN'S MAPLE LEAFS

(Lost division semifinals to Fredericton, 4-1)

SCORING

	Games	G	A	Pts.	PIM
Alexei Kudashov	5	1	4	5	2
Brandon Convery	5	2	2	4	4
Steve Bancroft	5	0	3	3	8
Patrik Augusta	4	2	0	2	7
Rich Chernomaz	5	1	1	2	8
Steffon Walby	5	1	1	2	4
Kelly Fairchild	4	0	2	2	4
Todd Warriner	4	1	0	1	2
Nathan Dempsey	5	1	0	1	11
Mark Kolesar	5	1	0	1	2
Bruce Racine (goalie)	2	0	0	0	0
Marcel Cousineau (goalie)	3	0	0	0	0
Guy Leveque	3	0	0	0	0
Ryan VandenBussche	3	0	0	0	17
Ken Belanger	4	0	0	0	30
Frank Bialowas	4	0	0	0	12
Paul Holden	4	0	0	0	0
Janne Gronvall	5	0	0	0	0
David Harlock	5	0	0	0	0
Guy Lehoux	5	0	0	0	2

GOALTENDING

	Games	Min.	W	L	T	Goals	SO	Avg.
Bruce Racine	2	119	1	1	0	3	0	1.51
Marcel Cousineau	3	180	0	3	0	9	0	3.01

1994-95 AWARD WINNERS

ALL-STAR TEAMS

First team	Pos.	Second team
Jim Carey, Portland	G	Corey Schwab, Albany
Jeff Serowik, Providence	D	Darren Rumble, P.E.I.
Kevin Dean, Albany	D	Mike Hurlbut, Cornwall
Steve Larouche, P.E.I.	C	Peter White, Cape Breton
Michel Picard, P.E.I.	LW	Andrew Brunette, Portland
Dwayne Norris, Cornwall	RW	Ralph Intranuovo, C.B.

TROPHY WINNERS

John B. Sollenberger Trophy: Peter White, Cape Breton
Les Cunningham Plaque: Steve Larouche, Prince Edward Island
Harry (Hap) Holmes Memorial Trophy: Mike Dunham, Albany
   Corey Schwab, Albany
Dudley (Red) Garrett Memorial Trophy: Jim Carey, Portland
Eddie Shore Plaque: Jeff Serowik, Providence
Fred Hunt Memorial Award: Steve Larouche, Prince Edward Island
Louis A.R. Pieri Memorial Award: Robbie Ftorek, Albany
Baz Bastien Trophy: Jim Carey, Portland
Jack Butterfield Trophy: Mike Dunham, Albany
   Corey Schwab, Albany

ALL-TIME AWARD WINNERS

JOHN B. SOLLENBERGER TROPHY

(Leading scorer)

Season	Player, Team
1936-37	Jack Markle, Syracuse
1937-38	Jack Markle, Syracuse
1938-39	Don Deacon, Pittsburgh
1939-40	Norm Locking, Syracuse
1940-41	Les Cunningham, Cleveland
1941-42	Pete Kelly, Springfield
1942-43	Wally Kilrea, Hershy
1943-44	Tommy Burlington, Cleveland
1944-45	Bob Gracie, Pittsburgh
	Bob Walton, Pittsburgh

Season	Player, Team
1945-46	Les Douglas, Indianapolis
1946-47	Phil Hergesheimer, Philadelphia
1947-48	Carl Liscombe, Providence
1948-49	Sid Smith, Pittsburgh
1949-50	Les Douglas, Cleveland
1950-51	Ab DeMarco, Buffalo
1951-52	Ray Powell, Providence
1952-53	Eddie Olson, Cleveland
1953-54	George Sullivan, Hershey
1954-55	Eddie Olson, Cleveland
1955-56	Zellio Toppazzini, Providence
1956-57	Fred Glover, Cleveland
1957-58	Willie Marshall, Hershey

Season	Player, Team
1958-59	Bill Hicke, Rochester
1959-60	Fred Glover, Cleveland
1960-61	Bill Sweeney, Springfield
1961-62	Bill Sweeney, Springfield
1962-63	Bill Sweeney, Springfield
1963-64	Gerry Ehman, Rochester
1964-65	Art Stratton, Buffalo
1965-66	Dick Gamble, Rochester
1966-67	Gordon Labossiere, Quebec
1967-68	Simon Nolet, Quebec
1968-69	Jeannot Gilbert, Hershey
1969-70	Jude Drouin, Montreal
1970-71	Fred Speck, Baltimore
1971-72	Don Blackburn, Providence
1972-73	Yvon Lambert, Nova Scotia
1973-74	Steve West, New Haven
1974-75	Doug Gibson, Rochester
1975-76	Jean-Guy Gratton, Hershey
1976-77	Andre Peloffy, Springfield
1977-78	Gord Brooks, Philadelphia
	Rick Adduono, Rochester
1978-79	Bernie Johnston, Maine
1979-80	Norm Dube, Nova Scotia
1980-81	Mark Lofthouse, Hershey
1981-82	Mike Kasczyki, New Brunswick
1982-83	Ross Yates, Binghamton
1983-84	Claude Larose, Sherbrooke
1984-85	Paul Gardner, Binghamton
1985-86	Paul Gardner, Rochester
1986-87	Tim Tookey, Hershey
1987-88	Bruce Boudreau, Springfield
1988-89	Stephan Lebeau, Sherbrooke
1989-90	Paul Ysebaert, Utica
1990-91	Kevin Todd, Utica
1991-92	Shaun Van Allen, Cape Breton
1992-93	Don Biggs, Binghamton
1993-94	Tim Taylor, Adirondack
1994-95	Peter White, Cape Breton

LES CUNNINGHAM PLAQUE

(Most Valuable Player)

Season	Player, Team
1947-48	Carl Liscombe, Providence
1948-49	Carl Liscombe, Providence
1949-50	Les Douglas, Cleveland
1950-51	Ab DeMarco, Buffalo
1951-52	Ray Powell, Providence
1952-53	Eddie Olson, Cleveland
1953-54	George "Red" Sullivan, Hershey
1954-55	Ross Lowe, Springfield
1955-56	Johnny Bower, Providence
1956-57	Johnny Bower, Providence
1957-58	Johnny Bower, Cleveland
1958-59	Bill Hicke, Rochester
	Rudy Migay, Rochester
1959-60	Fred Glover, Cleveland
1960-61	Phil Maloney, Buffalo
1961-62	Fred Glover, Cleveland
1962-63	Denis DeJordy, Buffalo
1963-64	Fred Glover, Cleveland
1964-65	Art Stratton, Buffalo
1965-66	Dick Gamble, Rochester
1966-67	Mike Nykoluk, Hershey
1967-68	Dave Creighton, Providence
1968-69	Gilles Villemure, Buffalo
1969-70	Gilles Villemure, Buffalo
1970-71	Fred Speck, Baltimore
1971-72	Garry Peters, Boston
1972-73	Billy Inglis, Cincinnati
1973-74	Art Stratton, Rochester
1974-75	Doug Gibson, Rochester
1975-76	Ron Andruff, Nova Scotia
1976-77	Doug Gibson, Rochester
1977-78	Blake Dunlop, Maine
1978-79	Rocky Saganiuk, New Brunswick

Season	Player, Team
1979-80	Norm Dube, Nova Scotia
1980-81	Pelle Lindbergh, Maine
1981-82	Mike Kasczyki, New Brunswick
1982-83	Ross Yates, Binghamton
1983-84	Mal Davis, Rochester
	Garry Lariviere, St. Catharines
1984-85	Paul Gardner, Binghamton
1985-86	Paul Gardner, Rochester
1986-87	Tim Tookey, Hershey
1987-88	Jody Gage, Rochester
1988-89	Stephan Lebeau, Sherbrooke
1989-90	Paul Ysebaert, Utica
1990-91	Kevin Todd, Utica
1991-92	John Anderson, Hew Haven
1992-93	Don Biggs, Binghamton
1993-94	Rich Chernomaz, St. John's
1994-95	Steve Larouche, Prince Edward Island

HARRY (HAP) HOLMES MEMORIAL TROPHY

(Outstanding goaltender)

Season	Player, Team
1936-37	Bert Gardiner, Philadelphia
1937-38	Frank Brimsek, Providence
1938-39	Alfie Moore, Hershey
1939-40	Moe Roberts, Cleveland
1940-41	Chuck Rayner, Springfield
1941-42	Bill Beveridge, Cleveland
1942-43	Gordie Bell, Buffalo
1943-44	Nick Damore, Hershey
1944-45	Yves Nadon, Buffalo
1945-46	Connie Dion, St. Louis-Buffalo
1946-47	Baz Bastien, Pittsburgh
1947-48	Baz Bastien, Pittsburgh
1948-49	Baz Bastien, Pittsburgh
1949-50	Gil Mayer, Pittsburgh
1950-51	Gil Mayer, Pittsburgh
1951-52	Johnny Bower, Cleveland
1952-53	Gil Mayer, Pittsburgh
1953-54	Jacques Plante, Buffalo
1954-55	Gil Mayer, Pittsburgh
1955-56	Gil Mayer, Pittsburgh
1956-57	Johnny Bower, Providence
1957-58	Johnny Bower, Cleveland
1958-59	Bob Perreault, Hershey
1959-60	Ed Chadwick, Rochester
1960-61	Marcel Paille, Springfield
1961-62	Marcel Paille, Springfield
1962-63	Denis DeJordy, Buffalo
1963-64	Roger Crozier, Pittsburgh
1964-65	Gerry Cheevers, Rochester
1965-66	Les Binkley, Cleveland
1966-67	Andre Gill, Hershey
1967-68	Bob Perreault, Rochester
1968-69	Gilles Villemure, Buffalo
1969-70	Gilles Villemure, Buffalo
1970-71	Gary Kurt, Cleveland
1971-72	Dan Bouchard, Boston
	Ross Brooks, Boston
1972-73	Michel Larocque, Nova Scotia
1973-74	Jim Shaw, Nova Scotia
	Dave Elenbaas, Nova Scotia
1974-75	Ed Walsh, Nova Scotia
	Dave Elenbaas, Nova Scotia
1975-76	Dave Elenbaas, Nova Scotia
	Ed Walsh, Nova Scotia
1976-77	Ed Walsh, Nova Scotia
	Dave Elenbaas, Nova Scotia
1977-78	Bob Holland, Nova Scotia
	Maurice Barrette, Nova Scotia
1978-79	Pete Peeters, Maine
	Robbie Moore, Maine
1979-80	Rick St. Croix, Maine
	Robbie Moore, Maine
1980-81	Pelle Lindbergh, Maine
	Robbie Moore, Maine

Season	Player, Team
1981-82	Bob Janecyk, New Brunswick
	Warren Skorodenski, New Brunswick
1982-83	Brian Ford, Fredericton
	Clint Malarchuk, Fredericton
1983-84	Brian Ford, Fredericton
1984-85	Jon Casey, Baltimore
1985-86	Sam St. Laurent, Maine
	Karl Friesen, Maine
1986-87	Vincent Riendeau, Sherbrooke
1987-88	Vincent Riendeau, Sherbrooke
	Jocelyn Perreault, Sherbrooke
1988-89	Randy Exelby, Sherbrooke
	Francois Gravel, Sherbrooke
1989-90	Jean Claude Bergeron, Sherbrooke
	Andre Racicot, Sherbrooke
1990-91	David Littman, Rochester
	Darcy Wakaluk, Rochester
1991-92	David Littman, Rochester
1992-93	Corey Hirsch, Binghamton
	Boris Rousson, Binghamton
1993-94	Byron Dafoe, Portland
	Olaf Kolzig, Portland
1994-95	Mike Dunham, Albany
	Corey Schwab, Albany

Beginning with the 1983-84 season, the award goes to the top goaltending team with each goaltender having played a minimum of 25 games for the team with the fewest goals against.

DUDLEY (RED) GARRETT MEMORIAL TROPHY

(Top rookie)

Season	Player, Team
1947-48	Bob Solinger, Cleveland
1948-49	Terry Sawchuk, Indianapolis
1949-50	Paul Meger, Buffalo
1950-51	Wally Hergesheimer, Cleveland
1951-52	Earl "Dutch" Reibel, Indianapolis
1952-53	Guyle Fielder, St. Louis
1953-54	Don Marshall, Buffalo
1954-55	Jimmy Anderson, Springfield
1955-56	Bruce Cline, Providence
1956-57	Boris "Bo" Elik, Cleveland
1957-58	Bill Sweeney, Providence
1958-59	Bill Hicke, Rochester
1959-60	Stan Baluik, Providence
1960-61	Ronald "Chico" Maki, Buffalo
1961-62	Les Binkley, Cleveland
1962-63	Doug Robinson, Buffalo
1963-64	Roger Crozier, Pittsburgh
1964-65	Ray Cullen, Buffalo
1965-66	Mike Walton, Rochester
1966-67	Bob Rivard, Quebec
1967-68	Gerry Desjardins, Cleveland
1968-69	Ron Ward, Rochester
1969-70	Jude Drouin, Montreal
1970-71	Fred Speck, Baltimore
1971-72	Terry Caffery, Cleveland
1972-73	Ron Anderson, Boston
1973-74	Rick Middleton, Providence
1974-75	Jerry Holland, Providence
1975-76	Greg Holst, Providence
	Pierre Mondou, Nova Scotia
1976-77	Rod Schutt, Nova Scotia
1977-78	Norm Dupont, Nova Scotia
1978-79	Mike Meeker, Binghamton
1979-80	Darryl Sutter, New Brunswick
1980-81	Pelle Lindbergh, Maine
1981-82	Bob Sullivan, Binghamton
1982-83	Mitch Lamoureux, Baltimore
1983-84	Claude Verret, Rochester
1984-85	Steve Thomas, St. Catharines
1985-86	Ron Hextall, Hershey
1986-87	Brett Hull, Moncton
1987-88	Mike Richard, Binghamton

Season	Player, Team
1988-89	Stephan Lebeau, Sherbrooke
1989-90	Donald Audette, Rochester
1990-91	Patrick Lebeau, Fredericton
1991-92	Felix Potvin, St. John's
1992-93	Corey Hirsch, Binghamton
1993-94	Rene Corbet, Cornwall
1994-95	Jim Carey, Portland

EDDIE SHORE PLAQUE

(Outstanding defenseman)

Season	Player, Team
1958-59	Steve Kraftcheck, Rochester
1959-60	Larry Hillman, Providence
1960-61	Bob McCord, Springfield
1961-62	Kent Douglas, Springfield
1962-63	Marc Reaume, Hershey
1963-64	Ted Harris, Cleveland
1964-65	Al Arbour, Rochester
1965-66	Jim Morrison, Quebec
1966-67	Bob McCord, Pittsburgh
1967-68	Bill Needham, Cleveland
1968-69	Bob Blackburn, Buffalo
1969-70	Noel Price, Springfield
1970-71	Marshall Johnston, Cleveland
1971-72	Noel Price, Nova Scotia
1972-73	Ray McKay, Cincinnati
1973-74	Gordon Smith, Springfield
1974-75	Joe Zanussi, Providence
1975-76	Noel Price, Nova Scotia
1976-77	Brian Engblom, Nova Scotia
1977-78	Terry Murray, Maine
1978-79	Terry Murray, Maine
1979-80	Rick Vasko, Adirondack
1980-81	Craig Levie, Nova Scotia
1981-82	Dave Farrish, New Brunswick
1982-83	Greg Tebbutt, Baltimore
1983-84	Garry Lariviere, St. Catharines
1984-85	Richie Dunn, Binghamton
1985-86	Jim Wiemer, New Haven
1986-87	Brad Shaw, Binghamton
1987-88	Dave Fenyves, Hershey
1988-89	Dave Fenyves, Hershey
1989-90	Eric Weinrich, Utica
1990-91	Norm Maciver, Cape Breton
1991-92	Greg Hawgood, Cape Breton
1992-93	Bobby Dollas, Adirondack
1993-94	Chris Snell, St. John's
1994-95	Jeff Serowik, Providence

FRED HUNT MEMORIAL AWARD

(Sportsmanship, determination and dedication)

Season	Player, Team
1977-78	Blake Dunlop, Maine
1978-79	Bernie Johnston, Maine
1979-80	Norm Dube, Nova Scotia
1980-81	Tony Cassolato, Hershey
1981-82	Mike Kasczyki, New Brunswick
1982-83	Ross Yates, Binghamton
1983-84	Claude Larose, Sherbrooke
1984-85	Paul Gardner, Binghamton
1985-86	Steve Tsujiura, Maine
1986-87	Glenn Merkosky, Adirondack
1987-88	Bruce Boudreau, Springfield
1988-89	Murray Eaves, Adirondack
1989-90	Murray Eaves, Adirondack
1990-91	Glenn Merkosky, Adirondack
1991-92	John Anderson, New Haven
1992-93	Tim Tookey, Hershey
1993-94	Jim Nesich, Cape Breton
1994-95	Steve Larouche, Prince Edward Island

LOUIS A.R. PIERI MEMORIAL AWARD
(Top coach)

Season	Coach, Team
1967-68	Vic Stasiuk, Quebec
1968-69	Frank Mathers, Hershey
1969-70	Fred Shero, Buffalo
1970-71	Terry Reardon, Baltimore
1971-72	Al MacNeil, Nova Scotia
1972-73	Floyd Smith, Cincinnati
1973-74	Don Cherry, Rochester
1974-75	John Muckler, Providence
1975-76	Chuck Hamilton, Hershey
1976-77	Al MacNeil, Nova Scotia
1977-78	Bob McCammon, Maine
1978-79	Parker MacDonald, New Haven
1979-80	Doug Gibson, Hershey
1980-81	Bob McCammon, Maine
1981-82	Orval Tessier, New Brunswick
1982-83	Jacques Demers, Fredericton
1983-84	Gene Ubriaco, Baltimore
1984-85	Bill Dineen, Adirondack
1985-86	Bill Dineen, Adirondack
1986-87	Larry Pleau, Binghamton
1987-88	John Paddock, Hershey
	Mike Milbury, Maine
1988-89	Tom McVie, Utica
1989-90	Jimmy Roberts, Springfield
1990-91	Don Lever, Rochester
1991-92	Doug Carpenter, New Haven
1992-93	Marc Crawford, St. John's
1993-94	Barry Trotz, Portland
1994-95	Robbie Ftorek, Albany

BAZ BASTIEN TROPHY
(Coaches pick as top goaltender)

Season	Player, Team
1983-84	Brian Ford, Fredericton
1984-85	Jon Casey, Baltimore
1985-86	Sam St. Laurent, Maine
1986-87	Mark Laforest, Adirondack
1987-88	Wendell Young, Hershey
1988-89	Randy Exelby, Sherbrooke
1989-90	Jean Claude Bergeron, Sherbrooke
1990-91	Mark Laforest, Binghamton
1991-92	Felix Potvin, St. John's
1992-93	Corey Hirsch, Binghamton
1993-94	Frederic Chabot, Hershey
1994-95	Jim Carey, Portland

JACK BUTTERFIELD TROPHY
(Calder Cup playoff MVP)

Season	Player, Team
1983-84	Bud Stefanski, Maine
1984-85	Brian Skrudland, Sherbrooke
1985-86	Tim Tookey, Hershey
1986-87	Dave Fenyves, Rochester
1987-88	Wendell Young, Hershey
1988-89	Sam St. Laurent, Adirondack
1989-90	Jeff Hackett, Springfield
1990-91	Kay Whitmore, Springfield
1991-92	Allan Bester, Adirondack
1992-93	Bill McDougall, Cape Breton
1993-94	Olaf Kolzig, Portland
1994-95	Mike Dunham, Albany
	Corey Schwab, Albany

ALL-TIME LEAGUE CHAMPIONS

	REGULAR-SEASON CHAMPION		PLAYOFF CHAMPION	
Season	**Team**	**Coach**	**Team**	**Coach**
1936-37	E—Philadelphia	Herb Gardiner	Syracuse	Eddie Powers
	W—Syracuse	Eddie Powers		
1937-38	E—Providence	Bun Cook	Providence	Bun Cook
	W—Cleveland	Bill Cook		
1938-39	E—Philadelphia	Herb Gardiner	Cleveland	Bill Cook
	W—Hershey	Herb Mitchell		
1939-40	E—Providence	Bun Cook	Providence	Bun Cook
	W—Indianapolis	Herb Lewis		
1940-41	E—Providence	Bun Cook	Cleveland	Bill Cook
	W—Cleveland	Bill Cook		
1941-42	E—Springfield	Johnny Mitchell	Indianapolis	Herb Lewis
	W—Indianapolis	Herb Lewis		
1942-43	—Hershey	Cooney Weiland	Buffalo	Art Chapman
1943-44	E—Hershey	Cooney Weiland	Buffalo	Art Chapman
	W—Cleveland	Bun Cook		
1944-45	E—Buffalo	Art Chapman	Cleveland	Bun Cook
	W—Cleveland	Bun Cook		
1945-46	E—Buffalo	Frank Beisler	Buffalo	Frank Beisler
	W—Indianapolis	Earl Seibert		
1946-47	E—Hershey	Don Penniston	Hershey	Don Penniston
	W—Cleveland	Bun Cook		
1947-48	E—Providence	Terry Reardon	Cleveland	Bun Cook
	W—Cleveland	Bun Cook		
1948-49	E—Providence	Terry Reardon	Providence	Terry Reardon
	W—St. Louis	Ebbie Goodfellow		
1949-50	E—Buffalo	Roy Goldsworthy	Indianapolis	Ott Heller
	W—Cleveland	Bun Cook		
1950-51	E—Buffalo	Roy Goldsworthy	Cleveland	Bun Cook
	W—Cleveland	Bun Cook		
1951-52	E—Hershey	John Crawford	Pittsburgh	King Clancy
	W—Pittsburgh	King Clancy		
1952-53	—Cleveland	Bun Cook	Cleveland	Bun Cook
1953-54	—Buffalo	Frank Eddolls	Cleveland	Bun Cook
1954-55	—Pittsburgh	Howie Meeker	Pittsburgh	Howie Meeker
1955-56	—Providence	John Crawford	Providence	John Crawford
1956-57	—Providence	John Crawford	Cleveland	Jack Gordon
1957-58	—Hershey	Frank Mathers	Hershey	Frank Mathers
1958-59	—Buffalo	Bobby Kirk	Hershey	Frank Mathers

— 190 —

	REGULAR-SEASON CHAMPION		PLAYOFF CHAMPION	
Season	Team	Coach	Team	Coach
1959-60	—Springfield	Pat Egan	Springfield	Pat Egan
1960-61	—Springfield	Pat Egan	Springfield	Pat Egan
1961-62	E—Springfield	Pat Egan	Springfield	Pat Egan
	W—Cleveland	Jack Gordon		
1962-63	E—Providence	Fern Flaman	Buffalo	Billy Reay
	W—Buffalo	Billy Reay		
1963-64	E—Quebec	Floyd Curry	Cleveland	Fred Glover
	W—Pittsburgh	Vic Stasiuk		
1964-65	E—Quebec	Bernie Geoffrion	Rochester	Joe Crozier
	W—Rochester	Joe Crozier		
1965-66	E—Quebec	Bernie Geoffrion	Rochester	Joe Crozier
	W—Rochester	Joe Crozier		
1966-67	E—Hershey	Frank Mathers	Pittsburgh	Baz Bastien
	W—Pittsburgh	Baz Bastien		
1967-68	E—Hershey	Frank Mathers	Rochester	Joe Crozier
	W—Rochester	Joe Crozier		
1968-69	E—Hershey	Frank Mathers	Hershey	Frank Mathers
	W—Buffalo	Fred Shero		
1969-70	E—Montreal	Al MacNeil	Buffalo	Fred Shero
	W—Buffalo	Fred Shero		
1970-71	E—Providence	Larry Wilson	Springfield	John Wilson
	W—Baltimore	Terry Reardon		
1971-72	E—Boston	Armond Guidolin	Nova Scotia	Al MacNeil
	W—Baltimore	Terry Reardon		
1972-73	E—Nova Scotia	Al MacNeil	Cincinnati	Floyd Smith
	W—Cincinnati	Floyd Smith		
1973-74	N—Rochester	Don Cherry	Hershey	Chuck Hamilton
	S—Baltimore	Terry Reardon		
1974-75	N—Providence	John Muckler	Springfield	Ron Stewart
	S—Virginia	Doug Barkley		
1975-76	N—Nova Scotia	Al MacNeil	Nova Scotia	Al MacNeil
	S—Hershey	Chuck Hamilton		
1976-77	—Nova Scotia	Al MacNeil	Nova Scotia	Al MacNeil
1977-78	N—Maine	Bob McCammon	Maine	Bob McCammon
	S—Rochester	Duane Rupp		
1978-79	N—Maine	Bob McCammon	Maine	Bob McCammon
	S—New Haven	Parker MacDonald		
1979-80	N—New Brunswick	Joe Crozier-Lou Angotti	Hershey	Doug Gibson
	S—New Haven	Parker MacDonald		
1980-81	N—Maine	Bob McCammon	Adirondack	Tom Webster-J.P. LeBlanc
	S—Hershey	Bryan Murray		
1981-82	N—New Brunswick	Orval Tessier	New Brunswick	Orval Tessier
	S—Binghamton	Larry Kish		
1982-83	N—Fredericton	Jacques Demers	Rochester	Mike Keenan
	S—Rochester	Mike Keenan		
1983-84	N—Fredericton	Earl Jessiman	Maine	John Paddock
	S—Baltimore	Gene Ubriaco		
1984-85	N—Maine	Tom McVie-John Paddock	Sherbrooke	Pierre Creamer
	S—Binghamton	Larry Pleau		
1985-86	N—Adirondack	Bill Dineen	Adirondack	Bill Dineen
	S—Hershey	John Paddock		
1986-87	N—Sherbrooke	Pierre Creamer	Rochester	John Van Boxmeer
	S—Rochester	John Van Boxmeer*		
1987-88	N—Maine	Mike Milbury	Hershey	John Paddock
	S—Hershey	John Paddock		
1988-89	N—Sherbrooke	Jean Hamel	Adirondack	Bill Dineen
	S—Adirondack	Bill Dineen		
1989-90	N—Sherbrooke	Jean Hamel	Springfield	Jimmy Roberts
	S—Rochester	John Van Boxmeer		
1990-91	N—Springfield	Jimmy Roberts	Springfield	Jimmy Roberts
	S—Rochester	Don Lever		
1991-92	N—Springfield	Jay Leach	Adirondack	Barry Melrose
	S—Binghamton	Ron Smith		
	A—Fredericton	Paulin Bordeleau		
1992-93	N—Providence	Mike O'Connell	Cape Breton	George Burnett
	S—Binghamton	Ron Smith-Colin Campbell		
	A—St. John's	Marc Crawford		
1993-94	N—Adirondack	Newell Brown	Portland	Barry Trotz
	S—Hershey	Jay Leach		
	A—St. John's	Marc Crawford		
1994-95	N—Albany	Robbie Ftorek	Albany	Robbie Ftorek
	S—Binghamton	Al Hill		
	A—Prince Edward Island	Dave Allison		

*Rochester awarded division championship based on season-series record.

INTERNATIONAL HOCKEY LEAGUE

LEAGUE OFFICE

Commissioner
Robert P. Ufer
Chairman of the board of governors
Larry Gordon
Senior V.P. of hockey operations
N. Thomas Berry Jr.
Senior V.P. of business operations
W. David Andrews
Director of operations
Michael A. Meyers
Consultants
N.R. (Bud) Poile
Jack Riley
Vice president of marketing
Greg Elliott

Director of corporate marketing
Matt Strelo
Vice president of communications
Tim Bryant
Asst. director of communications
Scott Woods
Controller
Don Smolenski
Business office address
1577 N. Woodward Ave., Suite 212
Bloomfield Hills, MI 48304
Phone
810-258-0580
FAX
810-258-0940

Hockey operations address
3850 Priority Way, Suite 100
Indianapolis, IN 46240
Phone
317-573-3888
FAX
317-573-3880

TEAMS

ATLANTA KNIGHTS

General manager
Joe Bucchino
Coach
John Paris Jr.
Home ice
The Omni
Address
100 Techwood Drive
Atlanta, GA 30303
Seating capacity
14,865
Phone
404-525-5800
FAX
404-525-0044

CHICAGO WOLVES

General manager
Grant Mulvey
Head coach
Gene Ubriaco
Home ice
Rosemont Horizon
Address
10550 Lunt Avenue
Rosemont, IL 60018
Seating capacity
16,535
Phone
708-390-0404
FAX
708-390-9792

CINCINNATI CYCLONES

General manager
Doug Kirchhofer
Head coach
Don Jackson
Home ice
Cincinnati Gardens
Address
2250 Seymour Avenue
Cincinnati, OH 45212

Seating capacity
10,326
Phone
513-531-7825
FAX
513-531-0209

CLEVELAND LUMBERJACKS

General manager
Larry Gordon
Coach
Rick Paterson
Home ice
Gund Arena
Address
One Center Ice
200 Huron Road
Cleveland, OH 44115
Seating capacity
19,941
Phone
216-420-0000
FAX
216-420-2500

DENVER GRIZZLIES

General manager
Bernie Mullin
Head coach
Butch Goring
Home ice
McNichols Arena
Address
1635 Clay Street
Denver, CO 80204
Seating capacity
16,215
Phone
303-592-7825
FAX
303-592-7171

DETROIT VIPERS

General manager and head coach
Rick Dudley

Home ice
The Palace of Auburn Hills
Address
2 Championship Drive
Auburn Hills, MI 48326
Seating capacity
20,182
Phone
810-377-8613
FAX
810-377-2695

FORT WAYNE KOMETS

General manager
David Franke
Head coach
Dave Farrish
Home ice
Allen County War Memorial Coliseum
Address
1010 Memorial Way, Suite 100
Fort Wayne, IN 46805
Seating capacity
8,003
Phone
219-483-0011
FAX
219-483-3899

HOUSTON AEROS

General manager
Steve Patterson
Head coach
Terry Ruskowski
Home ice
The Summit
Address
P.O. Box 271469
Houston, TX 77277-1469
Seating capacity
15,552
Phone
713-621-2842
FAX
713-627-0399

INDIANAPOLIS ICE

General manager
Ray Compton
Coach
Duane Sutter
Home ice
Market Square Arena
Address
222 E. Ohio St., Suite 810
Indianapolis, IN 46204
Seating capacity
15,993
Phone
317-266-1234
FAX
317-266-1233

KANSAS CITY BLADES

Vice president and general manager
Doug Soetaert
Head coach
Jim Wiley
Home ice
Kemper Arena
Address
1800 Genesee
Kansas City, MO 64102
Seating capacity
15,771
Phone
816-842-5233
FAX
816-842-5610

LAS VEGAS THUNDER

General manager and head coach
Bob Strumm
Home ice
Thomas & Mack Center
Address
P.O. Box 70065
Las Vegas, NV 89170-0065
Seating capacity
12,604
Phone
702-798-7825
FAX
702-798-9464

LOS ANGELES ICE DOGS

General manager and head coach
John Van Boxmeer
Home ice
Los Angeles Sports Arena
Address
3939 South Figueroa Street
Los Angeles, CA 90037-1292
Seating capacity
14,700

Phone
213-749-7825
FAX
213-747-8083

MICHIGAN K-WINGS

General manager
Bill Inglis
Coach
Ken Hitchcock
Home ice
Wings Stadium
Address
3620 Van Rick Drive
Kalamazoo, MI 49002
Seating capacity
5,113
Phone
616-349-9772
FAX
616-345-6584

MILWAUKEE ADMIRALS

General manager and head coach
Phil Wittliff
Home ice
The Bradley Center
Address
1001 North Fourth Street
Milwaukee, WI 53203
Seating capacity
17,845
Phone
414-227-0550
FAX
414-227-0568

MINNESOTA MOOSE

Business operations/marketing
Ron Minegar
Head coach
Frank Serratore
Home ice
St. Paul Civic Center
Address
28 W. Sixth Street
St. Paul, MN 55102
Seating capacity
15,594
Phone
612-292-3333
FAX
612-221-0292

ORLANDO SOLAR BEARS

General manager
Don Waddell
Head coach
To be announced

Home ice
Orlando Arena
Address
P.O. Box 95
Orlando, FL 32802-0095
Seating capacity
15,732
Phone
407-428-6600
FAX
407-841-6363

PEORIA RIVERMEN

General manager
Denis Cyr
Coach
Paul MacLean
Home ice
Peoria Civic Center
Address
201 S.W. Jefferson
Peoria, IL 61602
Seating capacity
9,470
Phone
309-676-1040
FAX
309-676-2488

PHOENIX ROADRUNNERS

General manager
Adam Keller
Head coach
Rob Laird
Home ice
Arizona Veterans Memorial Coliseum
Address
1826 West McDowell Road
Phoenix, AZ 85007
Seating capacity
13,747
Phone
602-340-0001
FAX
602-340-0041

SAN FRANCISCO SPIDERS

General manager and head coach
Jean Perron
Home ice
Cow Palace
Address
5 Thomas Mellon Circle, Suite 156
San Francisco, CA 94134
Seating capacity
10,800
Phone
415-656-3000
FAX
415-656-3099

1994-95 REGULAR SEASON

FINAL STANDINGS

EASTERN CONFERENCE

NORTHERN DIVISION

Team	G	W	L		Pts.	GF	GA
Detroit	81	48	27	(6)	102	311	273
Kalamazoo	81	43	24	(14)	100	288	249
Chicago	81	34	33	(14)	82	261	306
Cleveland	81	34	37	(10)	78	306	339

MIDWEST DIVISION

Team	G	W	L		Pts.	GF	GA
Peoria	81	51	19	(11)	113	311	245
Cincinnati	81	49	22	(10)	108	305	272
Fort Wayne	81	34	39	(8)	76	296	324
Indianapolis	81	32	41	(8)	72	273	330

( )—Indicates overtime losses and are worth one point.

WESTERN CONFERENCE

CENTRAL DIVISION

Team	G	W	L		Pts.	GF	GA
Milwaukee	81	44	27	(10)	98	317	298
Houston	81	38	35	(8)	84	272	283
Atlanta	81	39	37	(5)	83	279	296
Minnesota	81	34	35	(12)	80	271	336
Kansas City	81	35	40	(6)	76	277	300

SOUTHWEST DIVISION

Team	G	W	L		Pts.	GF	GA
Denver	81	57	18	(6)	120	339	235
Las Vegas	81	46	30	(5)	97	328	278
Phoenix	81	41	26	(14)	96	325	310
San Diego	81	37	36	(8)	82	268	301

INDIVIDUAL LEADERS

Goals: Steve Maltais, Chicago (57)
Assists: Stephane Morin, Minnesota (81)
Points: Stephane Morin, Minnesota (114)
Penalty minutes: Kevin MacDonald, Chicago (390)
Goaltending average: Tommy Salo, Denver (2.60)
Shutouts: Parris Duffus, Peoria (3)
    Rick Knickle, Detroit (3)
    Pokey Reddick, Las Vegas (3)
    Tommy Salo, Denver (3)
    Mike Torchia, Kalamazoo (3)

	Games	G	A	Pts.
Yanic Perreault, Phoenix	68	51	48	99
Hubie McDonough, San Diego	80	43	55	98
Steve Maltais, Chicago	79	57	40	97
Paul Lawless, Cincinnati	64	44	52	96
Patrice Lefebvre, Las Vegas	75	32	62	94
Craig Fisher, Indianapolis	77	53	40	93
Tony Hrkac, Milwaukee	71	24	67	91
Stan Drulia, Atlanta	66	41	49	90
Gino Cavallini, Milwaukee	80	53	35	88
Lonnie Loach, Detroit	77	35	53	88
Daniel Shank, Detroit	73	48	38	86
Chris Taylor, Denver	78	38	48	86
Ken Quinney, Las Vegas	78	40	42	82
Michel Mongeau, Peoria	74	30	52	82
Peter Ciavaglia, Detroit	73	22	59	81
Mark Freer, Houston	80	38	42	80
Dave Christian, Minnesota	81	38	42	80

TOP SCORERS

	Games	G	A	Pts.
Stephane Morin, Minnesota	81	33	81	114
Dave Tomlinson, Cincinnati	78	38	72	110
Rob Brown, Phoenix	69	34	73	107
Kip Miller, Denver	71	46	60	106

INDIVIDUAL STATISTICS

ATLANTA KNIGHTS

SCORING

	Games	G	A	Pts.	PIM
Stan Drulia	66	41	49	90	60
Jason Ruff	64	42	34	76	161
Yves Heroux	66	31	24	55	56
Brent Gretzky	67	19	32	51	42
Peter Ferraro	61	15	24	39	118
Aaron Gavey	66	18	17	35	85
Eric Dubois	56	3	25	28	56
Chris Ferraro	54	13	14	27	72
Allan Egeland	60	8	16	24	112
Derek Mayer	55	7	17	24	77
Christian Campeau	76	10	13	23	96
Colin Miller	36	5	14	19	29
Brad Shaw	26	1	18	19	17
Chris LiPuma	41	5	12	17	191
Jeff Toms	40	7	8	15	10
Jim Hiller	17	5	10	15	28
Cory Cross	41	5	10	15	67
Brian McReynolds	11	5	7	12	14
Drew Bannister	72	5	7	12	74
Brantt Mhyres	40	5	5	10	213
Aigar Cipruss	11	3	7	10	2
Devin Edgerton	18	2	8	10	8
Chris Nelson	49	0	9	9	46
Tom Tilley	10	2	6	8	14
Aaron Boh	20	2	6	8	15
Trevor Jobe	10	4	3	7	2
Brian Straub	22	3	4	7	39
Gerard Gallant	16	3	3	6	31
Colin Ward	5	2	3	5	2
Rich Sutter	4	0	5	5	0
Allen Pedersen	71	0	5	5	61
Derek Eberle	13	2	1	3	4
Alexander Selivanov	4	0	3	3	2
Jeff Buchanan	4	0	1	1	9
Derek Wilkinson (goalie)	46	0	1	1	6
Pat Cavanagh	1	0	0	0	0
Matt DelGuidice (goalie)	1	0	0	0	0
Jeff Hill	1	0	0	0	0
Terry Virtue	1	0	0	0	2

	Games	G	A	Pts.	PIM
Tod Hartje	2	0	0	0	0
Marc Tardif	5	0	0	0	2
Brock Woods	5	0	0	0	21
J.C. Bergeron (goalie)	6	0	0	0	0
Mike Greenlay (goalie)	20	0	0	0	6
Scott LaGrand (goalie)	21	0	0	0	2

GOALTENDING

	Games	Min.	W	L	OTL	Goals	SO	Avg.
Derek Wilkinson	46	2415	22	17	2	121	1	3.01
Scott LaGrand	21	994	7	7	3	67	0	4.04
Mike Greenlay	20	1059	7	10	0	72	0	4.08
J.C. Bergeron	6	324	3	3	0	24	0	4.44
Matt DelGuidice	1	53	0	0	0	5	0	5.70

CHICAGO WOLVES

SCORING

	Games	G	A	Pts.	PIM
Steve Maltais	79	57	40	97	145
Brian Wiseman	75	17	55	72	52
Lee Davidson	76	28	37	65	36
Bob Nardella	74	9	40	49	36
Todd Harkins	52	18	25	43	136
Shawn Rivers	68	8	29	37	69
Clayton Young	68	19	16	35	194
Al Secord	59	13	20	33	195
Tim Bergland	81	12	21	33	70
Ted Crowley	53	8	23	31	68
Ed Courtenay	47	14	16	30	20
Tim Breslin	71	7	21	28	62
Gordie Roberts	68	6	22	28	80
Evgeny Davydov	18	10	12	22	26
Todd Gillingham	54	8	11	19	208
Jack Duffy	69	3	11	14	98
Kevin MacDonald	75	1	12	13	390
Marian Kacir	29	4	6	10	6
Clayton Young	21	2	7	9	54
Jeff Rohlicek	18	4	4	8	13
Frank Evans	26	3	4	7	49
Mick Kempffer	35	2	5	7	26
Alexander Selivanov	14	4	1	5	8

	Games	G	A	Pts.	PIM
Brian Pellerin	24	4	1	5	80
Greg Walters	18	1	4	5	110
Steve Konroyd	16	2	2	4	4
Steve Gosselin	19	2	2	4	43
Justin Duberman	13	1	3	4	39
Joe Crowley	17	2	1	3	32
Ian Kidd	22	2	0	2	20
Sylvain Blouin	1	0	0	0	2
Richard Pion	2	0	0	0	0
Jason Rushton	2	0	0	0	10
Rick Tabaracci (goalie)	2	0	0	0	2
Pat Jablonski (goalie)	4	0	0	0	2
Grant Sjerven (goalie)	7	0	0	0	0
Wendell Young (goalie)	37	0	0	0	4
Ray LeBlanc (goalie)	44	0	0	0	2

GOALTENDING

	Games	Min.	W	L	OTL	Goals	SO	Avg.
Ray LeBlanc	44	2375	19	14	6	129	1	3.26
Wendell Young	37	1882	14	11	7	112	0	3.57
Grant Sjerven	7	252	0	3	1	18	0	4.29
Rick Tabaracci	2	120	1	1	0	9	0	4.51
Pat Jablonski	4	217	0	4	0	17	0	4.71

CINCINNATI CYCLONES

SCORING

	Games	G	A	Pts.	PIM
Dave Tomlinson	78	38	72	110	79
Paul Lawless	64	44	52	96	119
Mike Stevens	80	34	43	77	274
Don Biggs	77	27	49	76	152
Stephane J.G. Richer	80	16	53	69	67
Doug Barrault	74	20	40	60	57
Chris Cichocki	75	22	30	52	50
Sergei Kharin	56	14	29	43	24
Jason Cirone	74	22	15	37	170
Marc Laniel	70	5	29	34	34
Jeff Greenlaw	67	10	21	31	117
Sean McCann	76	10	12	22	58
Yuri Krivokhija	57	9	9	18	67
Dallas Eakins	59	6	12	18	69
Bob Boughner	81	2	14	16	192
Brad Smyth	26	2	11	13	34
Jamie Linden	51	3	6	9	173
Marc LaBelle	54	3	4	7	173
Steve Washburn	6	3	1	4	0
Chris Bergeron	14	1	3	4	2
Trevor Doyle	52	0	3	3	139
Ian Kidd	13	1	1	2	10
Jamie Leach	11	0	2	2	9
Danny Lorenz (goalie)	41	0	2	2	12
Frederic Chabot (goalie)	48	0	1	1	12

GOALTENDING

	Games	Min.	W	L	OTL	Goals	SO	Avg.
Frederic Chabot	48	2622	25	12	7	128	1	2.93
Danny Lorenz	41	2223	24	10	3	126	0	3.40

CLEVELAND LUMBERJACKS

SCORING

	Games	G	A	Pts.	PIM
Dale DeGray	64	19	49	68	134
Eric Murano	77	32	33	65	42
Jock Callander	61	24	36	60	90
Brad Lauer	51	32	27	59	48
Victor Gervais	52	20	32	52	55
Domenic Pittis	62	18	32	50	66
Len Barrie	28	13	30	43	137
Ladislav Karabin	47	15	25	40	26
Ian Moran	64	7	31	38	94
Jeff Christian	56	13	24	37	126
Dave Michayluk	60	19	17	36	22
Joe Dziedzic	68	15	15	30	74

	Games	G	A	Pts.	PIM
Ed Patterson	58	13	17	30	93
Perry Ganchar	60	11	17	28	56
Michal Straka	30	3	18	21	0
Greg Brown	28	5	14	19	22
Brian Farrell	46	7	11	18	28
Paul Dyck	79	5	12	17	59
Jamie Black	20	5	10	15	14
Chris Tamer	48	4	10	14	204
Corey Beaulieu	65	2	11	13	180
Larry DePalma	25	6	6	12	113
Mike Dagenais	38	3	5	8	84
Greg Andrusak	8	0	8	8	14
Markus Naslund	7	3	4	7	6
Rick Hayward	56	1	3	4	269
Todd Hawkins	4	2	0	2	29
Darren Wetherill	12	0	2	2	8
Rusty Fitzgerald	2	0	1	1	0
Shane Henry	2	0	1	1	2
Peter Taglianetti	3	0	1	1	7
Chris Wells	3	0	1	1	2
Philippe DeRouville (goalie)	41	0	1	1	4
Ryan Savoia	1	0	0	0	0
Patrick Neaton	2	0	0	0	4
Craig Woodcroft	2	0	0	0	0
Lance Brady	3	0	0	0	5
Patrick LaLime (goalie)	23	0	0	0	6
Olie Sundstrom (goalie)	23	0	0	0	12

GOALTENDING

	Games	Min.	W	L	OTL	Goals	SO	Avg.
Philippe DeRouville	41	2370	24	10	5	131	1	3.32
Patrick LaLime	23	1230	7	10	4	91	0	4.44
Olie Sundstrom	23	1235	3	17	1	104	0	5.05

DENVER GRIZZLIES

SCORING

	Games	G	A	Pts.	PIM
Kip Miller	71	46	60	106	54
Chris Taylor	78	38	48	86	47
Chris Marinucci	74	29	40	69	42
Jeff Madill	73	35	30	65	207
Andrei Vasiliev	74	28	37	65	48
Niklas Andersson	66	22	39	61	28
Milan Tichy	71	18	36	54	90
Andy Brickley	58	15	35	50	16
Doug Crossman	77	6	43	49	31
Zigmund Palffy	33	20	23	43	40
Yan Kaminsky	38	17	16	33	14
Gord Dineen	68	5	27	32	75
Derek Armstrong	59	13	18	31	65
Steve Junker	72	13	16	29	37
Jeff Sirkka	58	4	18	22	86
Normand Rochefort	77	4	13	17	46
Chris Luongo	41	1	14	15	26
Victor Ignatjev	23	2	11	13	4
Mike MacWilliam	30	5	6	11	218
Jason Simon	61	3	6	9	300
Paul Stanton	11	2	6	8	15
Rod Miller	47	2	5	7	65
Scott Scissons	7	2	3	5	6
Terry Yake	2	0	3	3	3
Brent Sapergia	2	1	1	2	2
Egor Bashkatov	2	0	2	2	0
Jim Paradise	2	1	0	1	0
Kevan Guy	3	0	1	1	0
Tommy Salo (goalie)	65	0	1	1	12
Iain Fraser	1	0	0	0	0
Ron Handy	1	0	0	0	0
Martin Laitre	1	0	0	0	18
Paul Polillo	1	0	0	0	0
Eric Ricard	1	0	0	0	0
Darren Schwartz	1	0	0	0	0
Dan Plante	2	0	0	0	4
Jamie McLennan (goalie)	4	0	0	0	2
Milan Hnilicka (goalie)	15	0	0	0	2

	Games	Min.	W	L	OTL	Goals	SO	Avg.
Tommy Salo	65	3810	45	14	4	165	3	2.60
Jamie McLennan	4	240	3	0	1	12	0	3.00
Milan Hnilicka	15	798	9	4	1	47	1	3.53

DETROIT VIPERS

SCORING

	Games	G	A	Pts.	PIM
Peter Ciavaglia	73	22	59	81	83
Lonnie Loach	64	32	43	75	45
Daniel Shank	54	44	27	71	142
Al Conroy	71	18	40	58	151
Jay Mazur	64	23	27	50	64
Sandy Smith	60	19	21	40	86
Gord Hynes	62	4	35	39	32
Mark Major	78	17	19	36	229
Jason Woolley	48	8	28	36	38
Greg Andrusak	37	5	26	31	50
Petr Sykora	29	12	17	29	16
Mark Hardy	41	6	21	27	35
Joe Day	32	16	10	26	126
Brad Tiley	56	7	19	26	32
Darryl Williams	66	10	12	22	268
Steve Strunk	57	6	16	22	48
Jeff Daniels	25	8	12	20	6
Ron Wilson	12	6	9	15	10
Ken McRae	24	4	9	13	38
John Craighead	44	5	7	12	285
Bobby Jay	57	3	8	11	51
Jeff Buchanan	50	4	6	10	125
Dixon Ward	7	3	6	9	7
Igor Malykhin	13	1	8	9	8
Dale DeGray	14	1	8	9	18
Oleg Shargorodsky	10	3	4	7	10
Ian Herbers	37	1	5	6	46
Stanislav Neckar	15	2	2	4	15
Steve Bancroft	6	1	3	4	0
Miroslav Satan	8	1	3	4	4
Sverre Sears	15	0	3	3	15
Dennis Smith	8	2	0	2	12
Rick Knickle (goalie)	49	0	2	2	17
Clark Polglase	5	1	0	1	7
Mike Hartman	6	1	0	1	52
David Haas	1	0	1	1	0
Krzysztof Oliwa	4	0	1	1	24
Kevin Malgunas	17	0	1	1	52
Dave Baseggio	1	0	0	0	0
Scott Feasby	1	0	0	0	2
Eric Lavigne	1	0	0	0	2
Maxim Michailovsky (goalie)	1	0	0	0	0
Egor Bashkatov	2	0	0	0	2
Garry Gulash	3	0	0	0	0
Jeff Winstanley	3	0	0	0	0
Steve Beadle	4	0	0	0	2
Mark Osiecki	4	0	0	0	4
Mikhail Kravets	7	0	0	0	4
Darrin Madeley (goalie)	9	0	0	0	0
David Goverde (goalie)	15	0	0	0	16
Norm Foster (goalie)	18	0	0	0	0

GOALTENDING

	Games	Min.	W	L	OTL	Goals	SO	Avg.
Maxim Michailovsky	1	6	0	0	0	0	0	0.00
Darrin Madeley	9	498	7	2	0	20	1	2.41
Rick Knickle	49	2726	24	15	5	134	3	2.95
David Goverde	15	814	8	5	0	49	0	3.61
Norm Foster	18	798	9	5	1	59	0	4.44

FORT WAYNE KOMETS

SCORING

	Games	G	A	Pts.	PIM
Vladimir Tsyplakov	79	38	40	78	39
Paul Willett	80	26	47	73	74

	Games	G	A	Pts.	PIM
John Purves	60	30	33	63	16
Igor Chibirev	56	34	28	62	10
Kelly Hurd	59	16	33	49	36
Ian Boyce	76	26	22	48	20
Rob Doyle	72	18	21	39	61
Darin Smith	53	16	23	39	77
Kevin Miehm	30	10	25	35	18
Guy Dupuis	77	9	26	35	125
Dan Ratushny	72	3	25	28	46
Colin Chin	22	10	15	25	10
Steve Bancroft	50	7	17	24	100
Jeff Rohlicek	22	9	14	23	8
Grant Richison	72	3	16	19	62
Radek Hamr	58	3	13	16	14
Greg Walters	44	4	9	13	142
Shawn Reid	42	4	8	12	28
Shawn Evans	11	2	8	10	6
Brad Tiley	14	1	6	7	2
Scott Burfoot	10	4	2	6	6
Jason Renard	27	4	2	6	129
Igor Malykhin	25	3	3	6	21
Carey Lucyk	59	1	5	6	30
Oleg Yashin	4	2	3	5	0
Max Middendorf	15	1	4	5	34
Peter Ing (goalie)	36	0	4	4	4
Brad Rubachuk	11	0	3	3	16
Jeff Whittle	2	2	0	2	0
Brad Jones	4	1	1	2	6
Mike Speer	7	1	1	2	18
Dan Gravelle	3	0	2	2	0
Peter Sidorkiewicz (goalie)	16	0	2	2	0
Mike O'Neill (goalie)	28	0	2	2	0
Steve Fletcher	43	0	2	2	204
Craig Charron	2	1	0	1	4
Andy Bezeau	3	0	1	1	26
Chris Rowland	5	0	1	1	14
Kirk Tomlinson	13	0	1	1	82
Rob Donovan	1	0	0	0	2
Jamey Hicks	1	0	0	0	2
Bob Mason (goalie)	1	0	0	0	0
Stephane Charbonneau	4	0	0	0	8
Sean Gauthier (goalie)	5	0	0	0	0
Kyle Reeves	7	0	0	0	17

GOALTENDING

	Games	Min.	W	L	OTL	Goals	SO	Avg.
Peter Ing	36	2018	15	18	2	119	2	3.54
Peter Sidorkiewicz	16	942	8	6	1	58	1	3.70
Mike O'Neill	28	1603	11	12	4	109	0	4.08
Sean Gauthier	5	218	0	2	1	15	0	4.13
Bob Mason	1	60	0	1	0	5	0	5.00

HOUSTON AEROS

SCORING

	Games	G	A	Pts.	PIM
Mark Freer	80	38	42	80	54
Scott Arniel	72	37	40	77	102
Dave Tippett	75	18	48	66	56
Mario Chitaroni	79	24	32	56	157
Michael Maurice	71	20	26	46	64
Len Hachborn	53	12	30	42	10
Graeme Townshend	71	19	21	40	204
Oleg Shargorodsky	62	7	26	33	52
Clayton Young	47	17	9	26	140
Carl Valimont	69	5	18	23	66
Todd Harkins	25	9	10	19	77
Vadim Slivchenko	29	8	9	17	30
Mike Yeo	63	5	12	17	100
Steve Jaques	75	2	14	16	233
Rob Robinson	70	3	12	15	54
Ted Crowley	23	4	9	13	35
Kevin Grant	57	4	9	13	182
Murray Eaves	31	3	9	12	18
Curtis Hunt	44	0	12	12	103
Kevin Dineen	17	6	4	10	42

	Games	G	A	Pts.	PIM
Steve Gosselin	28	5	5	10	36
Brian Pellerin	46	3	7	10	176
Al Conroy	9	3	4	7	17
Brian McKee	10	3	4	7	18
Kevin Malgunas	20	2	5	7	58
Scott McCrory	3	1	4	5	0
Chris Foy	14	0	4	4	12
Sean O'Brien	13	2	1	3	23
Gerry St. Cyr	15	0	2	2	76
Rob Dopson (goalie)	41	0	2	2	2
Trevor Buchanan	9	1	0	1	18
Darryl Olsen	4	0	1	1	12
Steve Martinson	6	0	1	1	30
Brock Woods	1	0	1	1	0
Marc Laniel	2	0	0	0	0
Carl LeBlanc	2	0	0	0	5
Pat Jablonski (goalie)	3	0	0	0	0
Alan Perry (goalie)	3	0	0	0	0
Troy Gamble (goalie)	43	0	0	0	25

GOALTENDING

	Games	Min.	W	L	OTL	Goals	SO	Avg.
Pat Jablonski	3	179	1	1	1	9	0	3.01
Troy Gamble	43	2422	18	17	5	132	1	3.27
Rob Dopson	41	2103	17	16	2	119	0	3.40
Alan Perry	3	130	2	1	0	9	0	4.16

INDIANAPOLIS ICE

SCORING

	Games	G	A	Pts.	PIM
Craig Fisher	77	53	40	93	65
Daniel Gauthier	66	22	50	72	53
Hugo Belanger	66	20	25	45	8
Sergei Klimovich	71	14	30	44	20
Bogdan Savenko	62	18	17	35	49
Mike Prokopec	70	21	12	33	80
Ivan Droppa	67	5	28	33	91
Steve Dubinsky	62	16	11	27	29
Sergei Krivokrasov	29	12	15	27	41
Bob Wilkie	29	5	22	27	30
Tony Horacek	51	7	19	26	201
Jeff Shantz	32	9	15	24	20
Karl Dykhuis	52	2	21	23	63
Mike Pomichter	76	13	9	22	47
Andy MacIntyre	51	9	8	17	17
Tom Tilley	25	2	13	15	19
Bruce Cassidy	29	2	13	15	16
Jeff Ricciardi	60	2	11	13	187
Jeff Buchanan	25	3	9	12	63
Colin Miller	13	5	6	11	10
Kevin St. Jacques	12	4	5	9	10
Bob Kellogg	51	3	6	9	30
Matt Oates	59	3	6	9	18
Rob Conn	10	4	4	8	11
Bobby House	26	2	3	5	26
Travis Thiessen	41	2	3	5	36
Dean Malkoc	62	1	3	4	193
Eric LeCompte	3	2	0	2	2
Christian Soucy (goalie)	42	0	2	2	2
Gerry Skrypec	14	1	0	1	27
Jim Waite (goalie)	4	0	1	1	0
Chris Rogles (goalie)	43	0	1	1	8
Greg Smyth	2	0	0	0	0
Joe Bonvie (goalie)	3	0	0	0	0

GOALTENDING

	Games	Min.	W	L	OTL	Goals	SO	Avg.
Jim Waite	4	240	2	1	1	13	0	3.25
Chris Rogles	43	2269	14	22	2	140	0	3.70
Christian Soucy	42	2217	15	17	5	148	0	4.01
Joe Bonvie	3	118	1	1	0	13	0	6.60

KALAMAZOO WINGS

SCORING

	Games	G	A	Pts.	PIM
Mark Pederson	75	31	32	63	47
Dave Barr	66	18	41	59	77
Neil Brady	70	13	45	58	140
Derrick Smith	68	30	21	51	103
Mark Lawrence	77	21	29	50	92
Mike Kennedy	42	20	28	48	29
Grant Marshall	61	17	29	46	96
Shane Peacock	71	13	23	36	42
Robin Bawa	71	22	12	34	184
Jeff McLean	41	16	18	34	22
Jason Herter	60	12	20	32	70
Jeff Bes	52	8	17	25	47
Collin Bauer	70	6	19	25	51
Pat Murray	33	11	10	21	16
Travis Richards	63	4	16	20	53
Mike Needham	37	9	9	18	31
Zac Boyer	22	9	7	16	22
Brad Berry	65	4	11	15	146
Scott McCrory	22	3	12	15	12
Dean Fedorchuk	28	4	9	13	8
Herb Raglan	31	4	4	8	94
Gil Delorme	28	1	5	6	26
Richard Matvichuk	17	0	6	6	16
Gord Donnelly	7	2	2	4	18
Dave Chyzowski	4	0	4	4	8
Dennis Smith	31	2	1	3	41
Pascal Trepanier	14	1	2	3	47
John Brill	11	0	3	3	4
Craig Bonner	23	0	3	3	42
Scott Feasby	2	0	1	1	0
Mike Lalor	5	0	1	1	11
Mike Torchia (goalie)	41	0	1	1	10
Alain Harvey	1	0	0	0	0
Cal McGowan	1	0	0	0	0
Craig Charron	2	0	0	0	0
Peter Zezel	2	0	0	0	0
Jason Downey	3	0	0	0	2
Dave Marcinyshyn	3	0	0	0	6
Steve Lingren	4	0	0	0	0
Darryl Gilmour (goalie)	5	0	0	0	0
Scott Loucks	5	0	0	0	2
Jarkko Varvio	7	0	0	0	2
Manny Fernandez (goalie)	46	0	0	0	4

GOALTENDING

	Games	Min.	W	L	OTL	Goals	SO	Avg.
Darryl Gilmour	5	233	3	0	0	8	0	2.06
Manny Fernandez	46	2470	21	10	9	115	2	2.79
Mike Torchia	41	2140	19	14	5	106	3	2.97

KANSAS CITY BLADES

SCORING

	Games	G	A	Pts.	PIM
Jan Caloun	76	34	39	73	50
Gary Emmons	81	22	38	60	42
Chris Tancill	64	31	28	59	40
David Bruce	63	33	25	58	80
J.F. Quintin	63	23	35	58	130
Alex Cherbayev	62	17	28	45	56
Ken Hodge	62	15	25	40	18
Claudio Scremin	61	8	30	38	29
Dean Grillo	72	15	21	36	24
Kevin Wortman	80	6	28	34	22
Duane Joyce	71	9	21	30	31
Andrei Buschan	66	3	27	30	78
Pat Ferschweiler	49	11	18	29	28
Ken Hammond	76	3	24	27	151
Andrei Nazarov	43	15	10	25	55
Dody Wood	44	5	13	18	255
Vlastimil Kroupa	51	4	8	12	49
Michal Sykora	36	1	10	11	30
Kevin Evans	26	3	6	9	192

	Games	G	A	Pts.	PIM
Todd Holt	28	4	4	8	12
Viacheslav Butsayev	13	4	3	7	12
Lee Leslie	10	2	5	7	4
Stewart Gavin	18	2	2	4	32
Fredrick Nilsson	13	3	0	3	2
Terran Sandwith	25	0	3	3	73
Andrei Kozlov	4	1	1	2	0
Ilya Byakin	1	0	2	2	0
Shean Donovan	5	0	2	2	7
Mike Rathje	6	0	1	1	7
Ron Pascucci	10	0	1	1	8
Larry Dyck (goalie)	21	0	1	1	0
Trevor Robins (goalie)	39	0	1	1	6
Martin Masa	3	0	0	0	0
Dan Ryder (goalie)	3	0	0	0	2
Andrew Kemper	5	0	0	0	2
Corwin Saurdiff (goalie)	6	0	0	0	0
Pat McGarry (goalie)	7	0	0	0	0
Jim Hrivnak (goalie)	10	0	0	0	0

GOALTENDING

	Games	Min.	W	L	OTL	Goals	SO	Avg.
Larry Dyck	21	1258	13	6	2	52	1	2.48
Pat McGarry	7	371	2	2	1	20	0	3.23
Jim Hrivnak	10	551	3	5	2	35	0	3.81
Trevor Robins	39	2230	15	20	1	144	1	3.87
Dan Ryder	3	140	1	2	0	11	0	4.71
Corwin Saurdiff	6	299	1	5	0	27	0	5.42

LAS VEGAS THUNDER

SCORING

	Games	G	A	Pts.	PIM
Patrice Lefebvre	75	32	62	94	74
Ken Quinney	78	40	42	82	40
Jarrod Skalde	74	34	41	75	103
James Black	78	29	44	73	54
Alex Hicks	78	24	42	66	212
Todd Richards	80	12	49	61	130
Jean-Marc Richard	81	16	41	57	76
Jeff Sharples	72	20	33	53	63
Andrew McBain	62	15	27	42	111
Marc Rodgers	58	17	19	36	131
Marc Habscheid	43	11	25	36	38
Alexei Yashin	24	15	20	35	32
Darcy Loewen	64	9	21	30	183
Bob Joyce	60	15	12	27	52
Jose Charbonneau	27	8	12	20	102
Radek Bonk	33	7	13	20	62
Jim Kyte	76	3	17	20	195
Jeff Reid	45	5	13	18	14
Rod Buskas	27	2	3	5	53
Frank Evans	41	2	3	5	111
Kerry Toporowski	37	1	4	5	300
Rhett Trombley	30	4	0	4	141
Alain Deeks	13	1	2	3	27
Mike Johnson	2	1	0	1	0
Rick Judson	2	0	1	1	0
Colin Miller	7	0	1	1	2
Doug Searle	7	0	1	1	18
Dave Neilson	13	0	1	1	51
Pokey Reddick (goalie)	40	0	1	1	2
Vladimir Vujtek	1	0	0	0	0
Darren Banks	2	0	0	0	19
Chris McSorley	2	0	0	0	20
Manon Rheaume (goalie)	2	0	0	0	0
Norm Foster (goalie)	14	0	0	0	0
Clint Malarchuk (goalie)	38	0	0	0	31

GOALTENDING

	Games	Min.	W	L	OTL	Goals	SO	Avg.
Pokey Reddick	40	2075	23	13	1	104	3	3.01
Norm Foster	14	677	8	3	1	35	0	3.10
Manon Rheaume	2	53	0	1	0	3	0	3.41
Clint Malarchuk	38	2039	15	13	3	127	0	3.74

MILWAUKEE ADMIRALS

SCORING

	Games	G	A	Pts.	PIM
Tony Hrkac	71	24	67	91	26
Gino Cavallini	80	53	35	88	54
Sylvain Couturier	77	31	41	72	77
Mike Tomlak	63	27	41	68	54
Brian Dobbin	76	21	40	61	62
Chris Govedaris	54	34	25	59	71
Brad Werenka	80	8	45	53	161
Pat MacLeod	69	11	36	47	16
Shawn Evans	58	6	34	40	20
Mike McNeill	80	23	15	38	30
Dave Mackey	74	19	18	37	261
Fabian Joseph	78	7	27	34	32
Kent Paynter	73	3	22	25	104
John Byce	30	9	11	20	10
Trevor Sim	37	9	10	19	26
Ken Sabourin	75	3	16	19	297
Dave Marcinyshyn	63	2	14	16	176
Martin Simard	57	7	5	12	100
Matt Block	28	4	5	9	63
Randy Velischek	35	3	3	6	24
Steve Tuttle	21	3	1	4	8
Mark Laforest (goalie)	42	0	3	3	8
Robin Bawa	4	1	1	2	19
Kevin Grant	3	0	1	1	6
Bob Mason (goalie)	13	0	1	1	2
Jim Hrivnak (goalie)	28	0	1	1	0
Don Martin	1	0	0	0	0
Trevor Robins (goalie)	1	0	0	0	0
John Varga	1	0	0	0	0
Wayne Cowley (goalie)	2	0	0	0	0
Dave MacIsaac	2	0	0	0	5

GOALTENDING

	Games	Min.	W	L	OTL	Goals	SO	Avg.
Trevor Robins	1	60	1	0	0	1	0	1.00
Wayne Cowley	2	79	0	1	0	4	0	3.04
Mark Laforest	42	2326	19	13	7	123	2	3.17
Jim Hrivnak	28	1634	17	10	1	106	0	3.89
Bob Mason	13	745	7	4	1	50	0	4.03

MINNESOTA MOOSE

SCORING

	Games	G	A	Pts.	PIM
Stephane Morin	81	33	81	114	53
Dave Christian	81	38	42	80	16
Dan Currie	54	18	35	53	34
John Young	70	17	32	49	24
Dave Snuggerud	72	25	23	48	57
Sean Williams	81	20	26	46	34
Yvon Corriveau	62	18	24	42	26
Larry Olimb	75	13	14	27	34
Scott Humeniuk	47	10	15	25	55
Dean Kolstad	73	6	18	24	71
Mikhail Kravets	37	7	15	22	21
Kris Miller	71	4	16	20	61
Todd Hawkins	47	10	8	18	95
Dave Hakstol	76	3	14	17	128
Scott Scissons	23	7	9	16	6
Daniel Shank	19	4	11	15	30
Brad Miller	55	1	13	14	181
Stewart Gavin	22	4	7	11	21
Blair Atcheynum	17	4	6	10	7
Chris Hynnes	25	3	4	7	22
John Brill	29	3	4	7	16
Kimbi Daniels	10	1	4	5	2
Dave Morissette	50	1	4	5	174
Darcy Martini	10	3	1	4	10
Reed Larson	9	2	2	4	11
Scott Bell	3	2	1	3	2
Mark Osiecki	35	1	2	3	18
Tod Hartje	6	1	1	2	6
Shannon Finn	3	0	2	2	6

	Games	G	A	Pts.	PIM
Mike Smith	13	0	2	2	0
Derek Linnell	3	1	0	1	2
Lou Franceschetti	4	1	0	1	12
Lyndon Byers	7	1	0	1	16
Ross Wilson	2	0	1	1	0
Phil Huber	3	0	1	1	0
Doug Torrel	4	0	1	1	0
Dave Gagnon (goalie)	16	0	1	1	6
Tom Draper (goalie)	59	0	1	1	20
Pat Ferschweiler	1	0	0	0	0
Kevin McKinnon	1	0	0	0	0
Brandon Smith	1	0	0	0	0
Nick Wohlers	1	0	0	0	2
David Craievich	2	0	0	0	0
Chris Imes	2	0	0	0	4
Duane Derksen (goalie)	7	0	0	0	4
Frank Pietrangelo (goalie)	15	0	0	0	6

GOALTENDING

	Games	Min.	W	L	OTL	Goals	SO	Avg.
Tom Draper	59	3063	25	20	6	187	1	3.66
Frank Pietrangelo	15	757	3	8	1	52	0	4.12
Dave Gagnon	16	767	5	4	2	55	0	4.30
Duane Derksen	7	251	1	3	3	21	0	5.02

PEORIA RIVERMEN

SCORING

	Games	G	A	Pts.	PIM
Michel Mongeau	74	30	52	82	72
Greg Paslawski	69	26	43	69	15
David Roberts	65	30	38	68	65
Daniel Laperriere	65	19	33	52	42
Doug Evans	74	13	39	52	103
Darren Veitch	75	8	42	50	42
Ian Laperriere	51	16	32	48	111
Patrice Tardif	53	27	18	45	83
Ron Hoover	76	22	20	42	70
Dave MacIntyre	71	10	31	41	52
Terry Hollinger	69	7	25	32	137
Steve Tuttle	38	14	13	27	14
Denny Felsner	25	10	12	22	14
Kirk Tomlinson	41	11	9	20	171
Martin Hamrlik	77	5	13	18	120
Glenn Mulvenna	48	7	9	16	20
Steve Staios	60	3	13	16	64
Vitaly Karamnov	15	6	9	15	7
Kevin Evans	29	5	9	14	121
Jeff Batters	42	0	11	11	128
Butch Kaebel	43	7	2	9	61
Vitali Prokhorov	20	6	3	9	6
Craig Johnson	16	2	6	8	25
Kevin Miehm	5	1	5	6	2
Ed Courtenay	9	5	0	5	4
Rene Chapdelaine	45	3	2	5	62
Eric Fenton	8	1	1	2	20
Steve Potvin	2	1	0	1	0
Chris MacDonald	4	1	0	1	4
Keith Morris	2	0	1	1	0
Jeff Petruic	3	0	1	1	0
Pat Cavanagh	11	0	1	1	49
Geoff Sarjeant (goalie)	55	0	1	1	20
Mike Dagenais	2	0	0	0	2
Jeff Gabriel	2	0	0	0	2
Basil McRae	2	0	0	0	12
Paul Taylor (goalie)	2	0	0	0	0
Jason Downey	4	0	0	0	14
Parris Duffus (goalie)	29	0	0	0	6

GOALTENDING

	Games	Min.	W	L	OTL	Goals	SO	Avg.
Paul Taylor	2	120	2	0	0	5	0	2.50
Parris Duffus	29	1581	17	7	3	71	3	2.69
Geoff Sarjeant	55	3147	32	12	8	158	0	3.01

PHOENIX ROADRUNNERS

SCORING

	Games	G	A	Pts.	PIM
Rob Brown	69	34	73	107	135
Yanic Perreault	68	51	48	99	52
Jeff Shevalier	68	31	39	70	44
Dave Thomlinson	77	30	40	70	87
Chris Snell	57	15	49	64	122
Kevin Brown	48	19	31	50	64
Rob Cowie	51	14	33	47	71
Dan Bylsma	81	19	23	42	41
Nicholas Vachon	64	13	26	39	137
Devin Edgerton	42	15	20	35	16
Brian McReynolds	55	5	27	32	60
Vaclav Nedomansky	41	15	11	26	77
Brian Chapman	60	2	23	25	181
Jim Vesey	41	10	10	20	62
Sean O'Donnell	61	2	18	20	132
Brian Straub	35	3	13	16	46
Gary Shuchuk	13	8	7	15	12
Eric Lavigne	69	4	10	14	233
Barry Potomski	42	5	6	11	171
Brian McKee	17	4	6	10	26
Steve Wilson	54	3	6	9	61
Tim Watters	36	1	8	9	58
Eric Lacroix	25	7	1	8	31
Dan Currie	16	2	6	8	8
Randy Pearce	14	2	3	5	30
Arto Blomsten	2	1	2	3	0
Keith Redmond	20	0	3	3	81
Ken McRae	2	2	0	2	0
Justin Hocking	20	1	1	2	50
Brett Seguin	2	0	2	2	0
Byron Dafoe (goalie)	49	0	2	2	12
Sean Brown	3	0	1	1	0
Mike Gaul	4	0	1	1	2
Mike O'Neill (goalie)	21	0	1	1	4
Doug Smith	1	0	0	0	0
Mark Straub	1	0	0	0	0
David Goverde (goalie)	2	0	0	0	0
Guy Leveque	2	0	0	0	15
Rob Murphy	2	0	0	0	10
Andre Racicot (goalie)	3	0	0	0	0
Wayne Doucet	4	0	0	0	2
Andy Bezeau	6	0	0	0	23
Scott Feasby	6	0	0	0	4
Pauli Jaks (goalie)	15	0	0	0	0

GOALTENDING

	Games	Min.	W	L	OTL	Goals	SO	Avg.
Mike O'Neill	21	1257	13	4	4	64	1	3.06
Andre Racicot	3	132	1	0	0	8	0	3.62
Byron Dafoe	49	2744	25	16	6	169	2	3.70
David Goverde	2	76	0	2	0	5	0	3.95
Pauli Jaks	15	636	2	4	4	44	0	4.15

SAN DIEGO GULLS

SCORING

	Games	G	A	Pts.	PIM
Hubie McDonough	80	43	55	98	10
Mark Beaufait	68	24	39	63	22
Denny Lambert	75	25	35	60	222
Brian Sullivan	74	24	23	47	97
Clark Donatelli	70	22	25	47	48
David Sacco	45	11	25	36	57
Patrick Neaton	71	8	27	35	86
Ron Wilson	58	8	25	33	60
Steve Rucchin	41	11	15	26	14
Jason Marshall	80	7	18	25	218
Dan Lambert	70	6	19	25	95
John Lilley	45	9	15	24	71
Darren Van Impe	76	6	17	23	74
Larry DePalma	38	14	8	22	86
Anatoli Fedotov	53	5	12	17	16
Craig Reichert	49	4	12	16	28

	Games	G	A	Pts.	PIM
Mark Ferner	46	3	12	15	51
Lonnie Loach	13	3	10	13	21
Barry Dreger	60	5	6	11	217
Maxim Bets	36	2	6	8	31
Dean Ewen	36	4	3	7	187
Valeri Karpov	5	3	3	6	0
John Byce	5	2	3	5	2
Myles O'Connor	16	1	4	5	50
John Porco	6	2	1	3	4
Evgeny Davydov	11	2	1	3	14
Todd Gillingham	16	1	1	2	60
Dennis Holland	1	0	2	2	2
Miroslav Satan	6	0	2	2	6
David Williams	2	0	1	1	0
Mike Maneluk	10	0	1	1	4
Jon Hillebrandt (goalie)	1	0	0	0	0
Scott McKay	1	0	0	0	2
Scott Chartier	8	0	0	0	0
Mark DeSantis	8	0	0	0	23
Bill Horn (goalie)	8	0	0	0	0
Sean Pronger	8	0	0	0	2
John Tanner (goalie)	8	0	0	0	6
Bob Essensa (goalie)	16	0	0	0	0
Allan Bester (goalie)	58	0	0	0	36

GOALTENDING

	Games	Min.	W	L	OTL	Goals	SO	Avg.
Bill Horn	8	289	2	1	1	15	0	3.12
Allan Bester	58	3251	28	23	5	183	1	3.38
Bob Essensa	16	919	6	8	1	52	0	3.39
John Tanner	8	345	1	3	1	28	0	4.87
Jon Hillebrandt	1	40	0	1	0	6	0	9.00

PLAYERS WITH TWO OR MORE TEAMS

SCORING

	Games	G	A	Pts.	PIM
Greg Andrusak, Cleveland	8	0	8	8	14
Greg Andrusak, Detroit	37	5	26	31	50
Totals	45	5	34	39	64
Steve Bancroft, Ft. Wayne	50	7	17	24	100
Steve Bancroft, Detroit	6	1	3	4	0
Totals	56	8	20	28	100
Egor Bashkatov, Detroit	2	0	0	0	2
Egor Bashkatov, Denver	2	0	2	2	0
Totals	4	0	2	2	2
Robin Bawa, Kalamazoo	71	22	12	34	184
Robin Bawa, Milwaukee	4	1	1	2	19
Totals	75	23	13	36	203
Andy Bezeau, Phoenix	6	0	0	0	23
Andy Bezeau, Ft. Wayne	3	0	1	1	26
Totals	9	0	1	1	49
John Brill, Kalamazoo	11	0	3	3	4
John Brill, Minnesota	29	3	4	7	16
Totals	40	3	7	10	20
Jeff Buchanan, Atlanta	4	0	1	1	9
Jeff Buchanan, Detroit	50	4	6	10	125
Jeff Buchanan, Indianapolis	25	3	9	12	63
Totals	79	7	16	23	197
John Byce, San Diego	5	2	3	5	2
John Byce, Milwaukee	30	9	11	20	10
Totals	35	11	14	25	12
Pat Cavanagh, Peoria	11	0	1	1	49
Pat Cavanagh, Atlanta	1	0	0	0	0
Totals	12	0	1	1	49
Craig Charron, Kalamazoo	2	0	0	0	0
Craig Charron, Ft. Wayne	2	1	0	1	4
Totals	4	1	0	1	4
Al Conroy, Detroit	71	18	40	58	151
Al Conroy, Houston	9	3	4	7	17
Totals	80	21	44	65	168
Ed Courtenay, Chicago	47	14	16	30	20
Ed Courtenay, Peoria	9	5	0	5	4
Totals	56	19	16	35	24
Ted Crowley, Chicago	53	8	23	31	68
Ted Crowley, Houston	23	4	9	13	35
Totals	76	12	32	44	103

	Games	G	A	Pts.	PIM
Dan Currie, Phoenix	16	2	6	8	8
Dan Currie, Minnesota	54	18	35	53	34
Totals	70	20	41	61	42
Mike Dagenais, Cleveland	38	3	5	8	84
Mike Dagenais, Peoria	2	0	0	0	2
Totals	40	3	5	8	86
Evgeny Davydov, San Diego	11	2	1	3	14
Evgeny Davydov, Chicago	18	10	12	22	26
Totals	29	12	13	25	40
Dale DeGray, Detroit	14	1	8	9	18
Dale DeGray, Cleveland	64	19	49	68	134
Totals	78	20	57	77	152
Larry DePalma, Cleveland	25	6	6	12	113
Larry DePalma, San Diego	38	14	8	22	86
Totals	63	20	14	34	199
Jason Downey, Peoria	4	0	0	0	14
Jason Downey, Kalamazoo	3	0	0	0	2
Totals	7	0	0	0	16
Devin Edgerton, Atlanta	18	2	8	10	8
Devin Edgerton, Phoenix	42	15	20	35	16
Totals	60	17	28	45	24
Frank Evans, Las Vegas	41	2	3	5	111
Frank Evans, Chicago	26	3	4	7	49
Totals	67	5	7	12	160
Kevin Evans, Peoria	29	5	9	14	121
Kevin Evans, Kansas City	26	3	6	9	192
Totals	55	8	15	23	313
Shawn Evans, Milwaukee	58	6	34	40	20
Shawn Evans, Ft. Wayne	11	2	8	10	6
Totals	69	8	42	50	26
Scott Feasby, Phoenix	6	0	0	0	4
Scott Feasby, Kalamazoo	2	0	1	1	0
Scott Feasby, Detroit	1	0	0	0	2
Totals	9	0	1	1	6
Pat Ferschweiler, Minnesota	1	0	0	0	0
Pat Ferschweiler, Kansas City	49	11	18	29	28
Totals	50	11	18	29	28
Norm Foster, Detroit (g)	18	0	0	0	0
Norm Foster, Las Vegas (g)	14	0	0	0	0
Totals	32	0	0	0	0
Stewart Gavin, Kansas City	18	2	2	4	32
Stewart Gavin, Minnesota	22	4	7	11	21
Totals	40	6	9	15	53
Todd Gillingham, Chicago	54	8	11	19	208
Todd Gillingham, San Diego	16	1	1	2	60
Totals	70	9	12	21	268
Steve Gosselin, Houston	28	5	5	10	36
Steve Gosselin, Chicago	19	2	2	4	43
Totals	47	7	7	14	79
David Goverde, Phoenix (g)	2	0	0	0	0
David Goverde, Detroit (g)	15	0	0	0	16
Totals	17	0	0	0	16
Kevin Grant, Milwaukee	3	0	1	1	6
Kevin Grant, Houston	57	4	9	13	182
Totals	60	4	10	14	188
Todd Harkins, Chicago	52	18	25	43	136
Todd Harkins, Houston	25	9	10	19	77
Totals	77	27	35	62	213
Tod Hartje, Minnesota	6	1	1	2	6
Tod Hartje, Atlanta	2	0	0	0	0
Totals	8	1	1	2	6
Todd Hawkins, Cleveland	4	2	0	2	29
Todd Hawkins, Minnesota	47	10	8	18	95
Totals	51	12	8	20	124
Jim Hrivnak, Milwaukee (g)	28	0	0	1	0
Jim Hrivnak, Kansas City (g)	10	0	0	0	0
Totals	38	0	0	1	0
Pat Jablonski, Chicago (g)	4	0	0	0	2
Pat Jablonski, Houston (g)	3	0	0	0	0
Totals	7	0	0	0	2
Ian Kidd, Chicago	22	2	0	2	20
Ian Kidd, Cincinnati	13	1	1	2	10
Totals	35	3	1	4	30
Mikhail Kravets, Detroit	7	0	0	0	4
Mikhail Kravets, Minnesota	37	7	15	22	21
Totals	44	7	15	22	25

	Games	G	A	Pts.	PIM
Marc Laniel, Houston	2	0	0	0	0
Marc Laniel, Cincinnati	70	5	29	34	34
Totals	72	5	29	34	34
Eric Lavigne, Phoenix	69	4	10	14	233
Eric Lavigne, Detroit	1	0	0	0	2
Totals	70	4	10	14	235
Lonnie Loach, San Diego	13	3	10	13	21
Lonnie Loach, Detroit	64	32	43	75	45
Totals	77	35	53	88	66
Kevin Malgunas, Detroit	17	0	1	1	52
Kevin Malgunas, Houston	20	2	5	7	58
Totals	37	2	6	8	110
Igor Malykhin, Ft. Wayne	25	3	3	6	21
Igor Malykhin, Detroit	13	1	8	9	8
Totals	38	4	11	15	29
Dave Marcinyshyn, Milwaukee ..	63	2	14	16	176
Dave Marcinyshyn, Kalamazoo..	3	0	0	0	6
Totals	66	2	14	16	182
Bob Mason, Ft. Wayne (g)	1	0	0	0	0
Bob Mason, Milwaukee (g)	13	0	1	1	2
Totals	14	0	1	1	2
Scott McCrory, Kalamazoo	22	3	12	15	12
Scott McCrory, Houston	3	1	4	5	0
Totals	25	4	16	20	12
Brian McKee, Houston	10	3	4	7	18
Brian McKee, Phoenix	17	4	6	10	26
Totals	27	7	10	17	44
Ken McRae, Detroit	24	4	9	13	38
Ken McRae, Phoenix	2	2	0	2	0
Totals	26	6	9	15	38
Brian McReynolds, Phoenix	55	5	27	32	60
Brian McReynolds, Atlanta	11	5	7	12	14
Totals	66	10	34	44	74
Kevin Miehm, Peoria	5	1	5	6	2
Kevin Miehm, Ft. Wayne	30	10	25	35	18
Totals	35	11	30	41	20
Colin Miller, Las Vegas	7	0	1	1	2
Colin Miller, Atlanta	36	5	14	19	29
Colin Miller, Indianapolis	13	5	6	11	10
Totals	56	10	21	31	41
Patrick Neaton, Cleveland	2	0	0	0	4
Patrick Neaton, San Diego	71	8	27	35	86
Totals	73	8	27	35	90
Mark Osiecki, Detroit	4	0	0	0	4
Mark Osiecki, Minnesota	35	1	2	3	18
Totals	39	1	2	3	22
Mike O'Neill, Ft. Wayne (g)	28	0	2	2	0
Mike O'Neill, Phoenix (g)	21	0	1	1	4
Totals	49	0	3	3	4
Brian Pellerin, Houston	46	3	7	10	176
Brian Pellerin, Chicago	24	4	1	5	80
Totals	70	7	8	15	256
Trevor Robins, Kansas City (g) .	39	0	1	1	6
Trevor Robins, Milwaukee (g) ...	1	0	0	0	0
Totals	40	0	1	1	6
Jeff Rohlicek, Chicago	18	4	4	8	13
Jeff Rohlicek, Ft. Wayne	22	9	14	23	8
Totals	40	13	18	31	21
Miroslav Satan, Detroit	8	1	3	4	4
Miroslav Satan, San Diego	6	0	2	2	6
Totals	14	1	5	6	10
Scott Scissons, Denver	7	2	3	5	6
Scott Scissons, Minnesota	23	7	9	16	6
Totals	30	9	12	21	12

	Games	G	A	Pts.	PIM
Alexander Selivanov, Atlanta	4	0	3	3	2
Alexander Selivanov, Chicago	14	4	1	5	8
Totals	18	4	4	8	10
Daniel Shank, Minnesota	19	4	11	15	30
Daniel Shank, Detroit	54	44	27	71	142
Totals	73	48	38	86	172
Oleg Shargorodsky, Houston	62	7	26	33	52
Oleg Shargorodsky, Detroit	10	3	4	7	10
Totals	72	10	30	40	62
Dennis Smith, Detroit	8	2	0	2	12
Dennis Smith, Kalamazoo	31	2	1	3	41
Totals	39	4	1	5	53
Brian Straub, Atlanta	22	3	4	7	39
Brian Straub, Phoenix	35	3	13	16	46
Totals	57	6	17	23	85
Brad Tiley, Detroit	56	7	19	26	32
Brad Tiley, Ft. Wayne	14	1	6	7	2
Totals	70	8	25	33	34
Tom Tilley, Atlanta	10	2	6	8	14
Tom Tilley, Indianapolis	25	2	13	15	19
Totals	35	4	19	23	33
Kirk Tomlinson, Ft. Wayne	13	0	1	1	82
Kirk Tomlinson, Peoria	41	11	9	20	171
Totals	54	11	10	21	253
Steve Tuttle, Peoria	38	14	13	27	14
Steve Tuttle, Milwaukee	21	3	1	4	8
Totals	59	17	14	31	22
Greg Walters, Ft. Wayne	44	4	9	13	142
Greg Walters, Chicago	18	1	4	5	110
Totals	62	5	13	18	252
Ron Wilson, Detroit	12	6	9	15	10
Ron Wilson, San Diego	58	8	25	33	60
Totals	70	14	34	48	70
Brock Woods, Houston	1	0	0	0	0
Brock Woods, Atlanta	5	0	0	0	21
Totals	6	0	0	0	21
Clayton Young, Houston	47	17	9	26	140
Clayton Young, Chicago	21	2	7	9	54
Totals	68	19	16	35	194

GOALTENDING

	Games	Min.	W	L	OTL	Goals	SO	Avg.
Norm Foster, Det.	18	798	9	5	1	59	0	4.44
Norm Foster, L.V.	14	677	8	3	1	35	0	3.10
Totals	32	1475	17	8	2	94	0	3.82
David Goverde, Pho.	2	76	0	2	0	5	0	3.95
David Goverde, Det..	15	814	8	5	0	49	0	3.61
Totals	17	890	8	7	0	54	0	3.64
Jim Hrivnak, Mil.	28	1634	17	10	1	106	0	3.89
Jim Hrivnak, K.C.	10	551	3	5	2	35	0	3.81
Totals	38	2185	20	15	3	141	0	3.87
Pat Jablonski, Chi. .	4	217	0	4	0	17	0	4.71
Pat Jablonski, Hou. .	3	179	1	1	1	9	0	3.01
Totals	7	396	1	5	1	26	0	3.94
Bob Mason, Ft.W.	1	60	0	1	0	5	0	5.00
Bob Mason, Mil.	13	745	7	4	1	50	0	4.03
Totals	14	805	7	5	1	55	0	4.10
Mike O'Neill, Ft.W.	28	1603	11	12	4	109	0	4.08
Mike O'Neill, Pho.	21	1257	13	4	4	64	1	3.06
Totals	49	2860	24	16	8	173	1	3.63
Trevor Robins, K.C.	39	2230	15	20	1	144	1	3.87
Trevor Robins, Mil. ..	1	60	1	0	0	1	0	1.00
Totals	40	2290	16	20	1	145	1	3.80

1995 TURNER CUP PLAYOFFS

RESULTS

QUARTERFINALS

EASTERN CONFERENCE

Series "A"

	W	L	Pts.	GF	GA
Peoria	3	1	6	18	17
Ft. Wayne	1	3	2	17	18

(Peoria won series, 3-1)

Series "B"

	W	L	Pts.	GF	GA
Kansas City	3	2	6	14	11
Detroit	2	3	4	11	14

(Kansas City won series, 3-2)

Series "C"

	W	L	Pts.	GF	GA
Cincinnati	3	1	6	18	15
Cleveland	1	3	2	15	18

(Cincinnati won series, 3-1)

Series "D"

	W	L	Pts.	GF	GA
Kalamazoo	3	0	6	16	9
Chicago	0	3	0	9	16

(Kalamazoo City won series, 3-0)

WESTERN CONFERENCE

Series "E"

	W	L	Pts.	GF	GA
Denver	3	0	6	19	4
Minnesota	0	3	0	4	19

(Denver won series, 3-0)

Series "F"

	W	L	Pts.	GF	GA
Milwaukee	3	2	6	16	11
San Diego	2	3	4	11	16

(Milwaukee won series, 3-2)

Series "G"

	W	L	Pts.	GF	GA
Las Vegas	3	2	6	19	19
Atlanta	2	3	4	19	19

(Las Vegas won series, 3-2)

Series "H"

	W	L	Pts.	GF	GA
Phoenix	3	1	6	22	12
Houston	1	3	2	12	22

(Phoenix won series, 3-1)

SEMIFINALS

EASTERN CONFERENCE

Series "I"

	W	L	Pts.	GF	GA
Kansas City	4	1	8	20	13
Peoria	1	4	2	13	20

(Kansas City won series, 4-1)

Series "J"

	W	L	Pts.	GF	GA
Kalamazoo	4	2	8	19	15
Cincinnati	2	4	4	15	19

(Kalamazoo won series, 4-2)

WESTERN CONFERENCE

Series "K"

	W	L	Pts.	GF	GA
Denver	4	1	8	21	16
Phoenix	1	4	2	16	21

(Denver won series, 4-1)

Series "L"

	W	L	Pts.	GF	GA
Milwaukee	4	1	8	16	8
Las Vegas	1	4	2	8	16

(Milwaukee won series, 4-1)

FINALS

EASTERN CONFERENCE

Series "M"

	W	L	Pts.	GF	GA
Kansas City	4	3	8	29	23
Kalamazoo	3	4	6	23	29

(Kansas City won series, 4-3)

WESTERN CONFERENCE

Series "N"

	W	L	Pts.	GF	GA
Denver	4	1	8	27	14
Milwaukee	1	4	2	14	27

(Denver won series, 4-1)

TURNER CUP FINALS

Series "O"

	W	L	Pts.	GF	GA
Denver	4	0	8	16	10
Kansas City	0	4	0	10	16

(Denver won series, 4-0)

INDIVIDUAL LEADERS

Goals: Kip Miller, Denver (15)
Assists: Andy Brickley, Denver (25)
Points: Andy Brickley, Denver (30)
Penalty minutes: Kevin Evans, Kansas City (111)
Goaltending average: Jamie McLennan, Denver (2.15)
Shutouts: Mark Laforest, Milwaukee (2)

TOP SCORERS

	Games	G	A	Pts.
Andy Brickley, Denver	16	5	25	30
Kip Miller, Denver	17	15	14	29
Gary Emmons, Kansas City	21	9	19	28
Jan Caloun, Kansas City	21	13	10	23
Niklas Andersson, Denver	15	8	13	21
Claudio Scremin, Kansas City	20	8	12	20
Neil Brady, Kalamazoo	15	5	14	19
Paul Lawless, Cincinnati	10	9	9	18
Dody Wood, Kansas City	21	7	10	17
Rob Brown, Phoenix	9	4	12	16

INDIVIDUAL STATISTICS

ATLANTA KNIGHTS

(Lost quarterfinals to Las Vegas, 3-2)

SCORING

	Games	G	A	Pts.	PIM
Brian McReynolds	5	4	5	9	4
Brad Shaw	5	3	4	7	9
Stan Drulia	5	1	5	6	2
Brent Gretzky	5	4	1	5	4
Yves Heroux	5	2	3	5	6
Jason Ruff	3	3	1	4	10
Eric Dubois	5	0	3	3	24
Jim Hiller	5	0	3	3	8
Derek Mayer	5	1	1	2	10
Drew Bannister	5	0	2	2	22
Christian Campeau	5	1	0	1	11
Allan Egeland	5	0	1	1	16
Aaron Gavey	5	0	1	1	9
Derek Eberle	2	0	0	0	0
Colin Ward	2	0	0	0	0
Scott LaGrand (goalie)	3	0	0	0	0
Brock Woods	3	0	0	0	12
Jeff Toms	4	0	0	0	4
Derek Wilkinson (goalie)	4	0	0	0	0
Allen Pedersen	5	0	0	0	2

GOALTENDING

	Games	Min.	W	L	OTL	Goals	SO	Avg.
Derek Wilkinson	4	197	2	1	0	8	0	2.43
Scott LaGrand	3	102	0	2	0	10	0	5.91

CHICAGO WOLVES

(Lost quarterfinals to Kalamazoo, 3-0)

SCORING

	Games	G	A	Pts.	PIM
Tim Bergland	3	1	2	3	4
Bob Nardella	3	1	2	3	0
Jack Duffy	3	0	3	3	4
Lee Davidson	3	2	0	2	2
Tim Breslin	3	1	1	2	0
Steve Maltais	3	1	1	2	2
Al Secord	3	1	1	2	19
Brian Wiseman	3	1	1	2	4
Brian Pellerin	3	0	2	2	13
Evgeny Davydov	3	1	0	1	0
Clayton Young	1	0	1	1	0
Steve Konroyd	3	0	1	1	2
Shawn Rivers	3	0	1	1	0
Steve Gosselin	1	0	0	0	2
Frank Evans	2	0	0	0	2
Greg Walters	2	0	0	0	0
Ray LeBlanc (goalie)	3	0	0	0	2
Kevin MacDonald	3	0	0	0	17
Gordie Roberts	3	0	0	0	4

GOALTENDING

	Games	Min.	W	L	OTL	Goals	SO	Avg.
Ray LeBlanc	3	178	0	3	0	14	0	4.73

CINCINNATI CYCLONES

(Lost semifinals to Kalamazoo, 4-2)

SCORING

	Games	G	A	Pts.	PIM
Paul Lawless	10	9	9	18	8
Dave Tomlinson	10	7	3	10	8
Don Biggs	10	1	9	10	29
Mike Stevens	10	6	3	9	16
Stephane J.G. Richer	10	2	7	9	18
Doug Barrault	10	2	6	8	20
Ian Kidd	8	1	3	4	6
Chris Armstrong	9	1	3	4	10
Steve Washburn	9	1	3	4	4

	Games	G	A	Pts.	PIM
Chris Cichocki	8	0	3	3	6
Jeff Greenlaw	10	2	0	2	22
Jason Cirone	9	1	1	2	14
Sean McCann	10	0	2	2	8
Frederic Chabot (goalie)	5	0	1	1	2
Sergei Kharin	1	0	0	0	0
Brad Smyth	1	0	0	0	2
Chris Bergeron	2	0	0	0	0
Jason Podollan	3	0	0	0	2
Yuri Krivokhija	5	0	0	0	2
Danny Lorenz (goalie)	5	0	0	0	0
Trevor Doyle	6	0	0	0	13
Marc LaBelle	8	0	0	0	7
Bob Boughner	10	0	0	0	18

GOALTENDING

	Games	Min.	W	L	OTL	Goals	SO	Avg.
Frederic Chabot	5	326	3	0	2	16	0	2.94
Danny Lorenz	5	308	2	2	1	16	0	3.12

CLEVELAND LUMBERJACKS

(Lost quarterfinals to Cincinnati, 3-1)

SCORING

	Games	G	A	Pts.	PIM
Brad Lauer	4	4	2	6	6
Jock Callander	4	2	2	4	6
Paul Dyck	4	1	3	4	4
Victor Gervais	4	1	3	4	4
Markus Naslund	4	1	3	4	8
Dale DeGray	4	0	4	4	10
Rusty Fitzgerald	3	3	0	3	6
Ed Patterson	4	1	2	3	6
Eric Murano	3	0	2	2	0
Domenic Pittis	3	0	2	2	2
Greg Hawgood	3	1	0	1	4
Joe Dziedzic	4	1	0	1	10
Corey Beaulieu	1	0	1	1	0
Jeff Christian	2	0	1	1	8
Ian Moran	4	0	1	1	2
Dave Michayluk	1	0	0	0	0
Rick Hayward	3	0	0	0	13
Philippe DeRouville (goalie)	4	0	0	0	0
Ladislav Karabin	4	0	0	0	2
Peter Taglianetti	4	0	0	0	19

GOALTENDING

	Games	Min.	W	L	OTL	Goals	SO	Avg.
Philippe DeRouville	4	264	1	1	2	18	0	4.09

DENVER GRIZZLIES

(Winner of 1995 Turner Cup playoffs)

SCORING

	Games	G	A	Pts.	PIM
Andy Brickley	16	5	25	30	2
Kip Miller	17	15	14	29	8
Niklas Andersson	15	8	13	21	10
Terry Yake	17	4	11	15	16
Jeff Madill	17	8	6	14	53
Andrei Vasiliev	13	9	4	13	22
Chris Taylor	14	7	6	13	10
Milan Tichy	17	4	9	13	12
Yan Kaminsky	15	6	6	12	0
Victor Ignatjev	17	3	8	11	8
Doug Crossman	17	3	6	9	7
Steve Junker	11	3	4	7	4
Chris Marinucci	14	3	4	7	12
Gord Dineen	17	1	6	7	8
Normand Rochefort	17	1	4	5	12
Mike MacWilliam	12	2	2	4	56
Rod Miller	12	1	3	4	11
Derek Armstrong	6	0	2	2	0

	Games	G	A	Pts.	PIM
Jeff Sirkka	5	0	1	1	19
Jamie McLennan (goalie)	11	0	1	1	29
Jason Simon	1	0	0	0	12
Tommy Salo (goalie)	8	0	0	0	2

GOALTENDING

	Games	Min.	W	L	OTL	Goals	SO	Avg.
Jamie McLennan	11	641	8	2	0	23	1	2.15
Tommy Salo	8	390	7	0	0	20	0	3.07

DETROIT VIPERS

(Lost quarterfinals to Kansas City, 3-2)

SCORING

	Games	G	A	Pts.	PIM
Daniel Shank	5	2	2	4	6
Dixon Ward	5	3	0	3	7
Lonnie Loach	3	2	1	3	2
Peter Ciavaglia	5	1	1	2	6
Mark Hardy	5	1	1	2	7
Ian Herbers	5	1	1	2	6
Joe Day	5	0	2	2	21
Oleg Shargorodsky	5	0	2	2	11
Jeff Daniels	5	1	0	1	0
Len Hachborn	1	0	1	1	0
Jay Mazur	1	0	1	1	2
Igor Malykhin	2	0	1	1	0
John Craighead	3	0	1	1	4
Mark Major	5	0	1	1	23
David Goverde	1	0	0	0	0
Mike Hartman	1	0	0	0	0
Sandy Smith	2	0	0	0	0
Sverre Sears	3	0	0	0	2
Darryl Williams	4	0	0	0	14
Daniel Berthiaume (goalie)	5	0	0	0	0
Bobby Jay	5	0	0	0	10
Eric Lavigne	5	0	0	0	26
Steve Strunk	5	0	0	0	0

GOALTENDING

	Games	Min.	W	L	OTL	Goals	SO	Avg.
Daniel Berthiaume	5	332	2	2	1	14	0	2.53

FORT WAYNE KOMETS

(Lost quarterfinals to Peoria, 3-1)

SCORING

	Games	G	A	Pts.	PIM
Vladimir Tsyplakov	4	2	4	6	2
John Purves	4	4	1	5	6
Kevin Miehm	4	1	4	5	0
Shawn Evans	4	1	3	4	2
Kelly Hurd	4	3	0	3	4
Ian Boyce	4	2	1	3	4
Brad Tiley	3	1	2	3	0
Jeff Rohlicek	4	1	2	3	4
Grant Richison	4	0	3	3	2
Darin Smith	4	1	1	2	8
Rob Doyle	4	1	0	1	6
Paul Willett	1	0	1	1	0
Jason Renard	3	0	1	1	16
Dan Ratushny	4	0	1	1	8
Steve Fletcher	1	0	0	0	0
Radek Hamr	1	0	0	0	0
Peter Ing (goalie)	2	0	0	0	0
Colin Chin	3	0	0	0	2
Peter Sidorkiewicz (goalie)	3	0	0	0	0
Guy Dupuis	4	0	0	0	6
Carey Lucyk	4	0	0	0	10

GOALTENDING

	Games	Min.	W	L	OTL	Goals	SO	Avg.
Peter Ing	2	94	0	1	0	5	0	3.19
Peter Sidorkiewicz	3	144	1	2	0	12	0	5.00

HOUSTON AEROS

(Lost quarterfinals to Phoenix, 3-1)

SCORING

	Games	G	A	Pts.	PIM
Scott McCrory	4	2	2	4	2
Mario Chitaroni	4	1	3	4	4
Al Conroy	4	1	2	3	8
Michael Maurice	4	1	2	3	6
Dave Tippett	4	1	2	3	4
Kevin Grant	4	1	1	2	19
Todd Harkins	4	1	1	2	28
Steve Jaques	4	1	1	2	11
Marc Laniel	4	0	2	2	6
Graeme Townshend	4	0	2	2	22
Kevin Malgunas	2	1	0	1	12
Vadim Slivchenko	2	1	0	1	0
Scott Arniel	4	1	0	1	10
Ted Crowley	3	0	1	1	0
Mark Freer	4	0	1	1	4
Rob Robinson	4	0	1	1	4
Rob Dopson (goalie)	1	0	0	0	0
Carl Valimont	2	0	0	0	0
Curtis Hunt	3	0	0	0	12
Troy Gamble (goalie)	4	0	0	0	0

GOALTENDING

	Games	Min.	W	L	OTL	Goals	SO	Avg.
Troy Gamble	4	203	1	2	1	16	0	4.72
Rob Dopson	1	40	0	0	0	6	0	9.00

KALAMAZOO WINGS

(Lost conference finals to Kansas City, 4-3)

SCORING

	Games	G	A	Pts.	PIM
Neil Brady	15	5	14	19	22
Dave Chyzowski	16	9	5	14	27
Grant Marshall	16	9	3	12	27
Mark Pederson	16	8	4	12	2
Zac Boyer	15	3	9	12	8
Derrick Smith	16	3	8	11	8
Mike Needham	14	5	5	10	11
Mark Lawrence	16	3	7	10	28
Jason Herter	16	2	8	10	10
Collin Bauer	16	1	9	10	8
Shane Peacock	12	3	5	8	8
Travis Richards	15	1	5	6	12
Jeff McLean	4	1	4	5	0
Dave Barr	16	1	4	5	8
Jamie Langenbrunner	11	1	3	4	2
Pat Murray	6	3	0	3	2
Dennis Smith	13	0	2	2	33
Dave Marcinyshyn	16	0	1	1	16
Brad Berry	1	0	0	0	0
Herb Raglan	6	0	0	0	15
Mike Torchia (goalie)	6	0	0	0	0
Manny Fernandez (goalie)	14	0	0	0	0

GOALTENDING

	Games	Min.	W	L	OTL	Goals	SO	Avg.
Manny Fernandez	14	754	10	1	1	34	1	2.71
Mike Torchia	6	257	0	4	0	17	0	3.97

KANSAS CITY BLADES

(Lost Turner Cup finals to Denver, 4-0)

SCORING

	Games	G	A	Pts.	PIM
Gary Emmons	21	9	19	28	24
Jan Caloun	21	13	10	23	18
Claudio Scremin	20	8	12	20	14
Dody Wood	21	7	10	17	87
Ilya Byakin	16	4	10	14	43
J.F. Quintin	19	2	9	11	57
Ken Hodge	17	4	6	10	4

	Games	G	A	Pts.	PIM
Viktor Kozlov	13	4	5	9	12
Shean Donovan	14	5	3	8	23
Dean Grillo	18	3	5	8	18
Duane Joyce	21	2	5	7	4
Vlastimil Kroupa	12	2	4	6	22
Kevin Evans	19	2	4	6	111
Pat Ferschweiler	20	2	4	6	22
Fredrick Nilsson	12	3	2	5	4
Ken Hammond	21	1	4	5	45
Ron Pascucci	10	1	1	2	4
Kevin Wortman	21	1	1	2	4
Alex Cherbayev	11	0	2	2	10
Andrei Buschan	5	0	1	1	7
Viacheslav Butsayev	3	0	0	0	2
Jim Hrivnak (goalie)	3	0	0	0	0
Larry Dyck (goalie)	19	0	0	0	0

GOALTENDING

	Games	Min.	W	L	OTL	Goals	SO	Avg.
Larry Dyck	19	1291	11	4	4	56	1	2.60
Jim Hrivnak	2	118	0	2	0	7	0	3.55

LAS VEGAS THUNDER

(Lost semifinals to Milwaukee, 4-1)

SCORING

	Games	G	A	Pts.	PIM
Jeff Sharples	10	4	4	8	18
Marc Rodgers	10	2	6	8	25
Bob Joyce	10	4	3	7	26
James Black	10	1	6	7	4
Alex Hicks	9	2	4	6	47
Jarrod Skalde	9	2	4	6	8
Ken Quinney	10	3	2	5	9
Patrice Lefebvre	10	2	3	5	2
Todd Richards	9	1	2	3	6
Andrew McBain	8	0	3	3	33
Jean-Marc Richard	10	0	3	3	4
Mike Johnson	8	2	0	2	35
Alain Deeks	5	1	1	2	6
Darcy Loewen	7	1	1	2	16
Jose Charbonneau	9	1	1	2	71
Rod Buskas	10	1	0	1	19
Kerry Toporowski	5	0	1	1	69
Jeff Reid	7	0	1	1	4
Bill Bowler	1	0	0	0	0
Clint Malarchuk (goalie)	2	0	0	0	0
Rhett Trombley	3	0	0	0	10
Pokey Reddick (goalie)	10	0	0	0	0

GOALTENDING

	Games	Min.	W	L	OTL	Goals	SO	Avg.
Pokey Reddick	10	592	4	4	2	31	0	3.14
Clint Malarchuk	2	32	0	0	0	2	0	3.70

MILWAUKEE ADMIRALS

(Lost conference finals to Denver, 4-1)

SCORING

	Games	G	A	Pts.	PIM
Tony Hrkac	15	4	9	13	16
Brad Werenka	15	3	10	13	36
Dave Mackey	15	6	4	10	34
Gino Cavallini	15	7	2	9	10
John Byce	15	4	5	9	4
Mike Tomlak	15	4	5	9	8
Pat MacLeod	15	3	6	9	8
Fabian Joseph	14	3	4	7	6
Robin Bawa	15	1	5	6	48
Kent Paynter	5	2	3	5	8
Sylvain Couturier	15	1	4	5	10
Randy Velischek	12	2	2	4	6
Mike McNeill	15	2	2	4	14
Brian Dobbin	9	0	4	4	2
Matt Block	14	2	1	3	13
Trevor Sim	7	1	2	3	4

	Games	G	A	Pts.	PIM
Ken Sabourin	15	1	1	2	69
Dave MacIsaac	9	0	2	2	2
Trevor Robins (goalie)	1	0	0	0	0
Martin Simard	5	0	0	0	2
Mark Laforest (goalie)	15	0	0	0	8

GOALTENDING

	Games	Min.	W	L	OTL	Goals	SO	Avg.
Mark Laforest	15	938	8	5	2	40	2	2.56
Trevor Robins	1	20	0	0	0	3	0	9.00

MINNESOTA MOOSE

(Lost quarterfinals to Denver, 3-0)

SCORING

	Games	G	A	Pts.	PIM
Yvon Corriveau	3	1	1	2	0
John Young	3	1	1	2	0
Kris Miller	3	1	0	1	0
Sean Williams	3	1	0	1	0
Stephane Morin	2	0	1	1	0
Scott Bell	3	0	1	1	15
Dave Christian	3	0	1	1	0
Todd Hawkins	3	0	1	1	12
Dave Snuggerud	3	0	1	1	2
Dave Gagnon (goalie)	1	0	0	0	0
Dean Kolstad	1	0	0	0	2
Darcy Martini	1	0	0	0	2
Larry Olimb	1	0	0	0	2
John Brill	2	0	0	0	0
Tom Draper (goalie)	2	0	0	0	10
Mark Osiecki	2	0	0	0	2
Dan Currie	3	0	0	0	2
Lou Franceschetti	3	0	0	0	0
Dave Hakstol	3	0	0	0	6
Chris Imes	3	0	0	0	0
Brad Miller	3	0	0	0	12

GOALTENDING

	Games	Min.	W	L	OTL	Goals	SO	Avg.
Tom Draper	2	118	0	2	0	10	0	5.07
Dave Gagnon	1	60	0	1	0	9	0	9.00

PEORIA RIVERMEN

(Lost semifinals to Kansas City, 4-1)

SCORING

	Games	G	A	Pts.	PIM
Vitali Prokhorov	9	4	7	11	6
Doug Evans	9	2	9	11	10
Greg Paslawski	9	9	1	10	4
Ed Courtenay	9	5	3	8	2
Terry Hollinger	4	2	4	6	8
Denny Felsner	8	2	3	5	0
Dave MacIntyre	8	2	3	5	0
Craig Johnson	9	0	4	4	10
Glenn Mulvenna	7	3	0	3	2
Ron Hoover	9	2	1	3	12
Roman Vopat	6	0	2	2	2
Mike Dagenais	7	0	2	2	20
Rene Chapdelaine	9	0	2	2	12
Darren Veitch	9	0	2	2	8
Jeff Batters	5	0	1	1	18
Kirk Tomlinson	9	0	1	1	17
Eric Fenton	2	0	0	0	8
Steve Potvin	2	0	0	0	0
Kevin Sawyer	2	0	0	0	12
Martin Hamrlik	3	0	0	0	2
Butch Kaebel	3	0	0	0	2
Geoff Sarjeant (goalie)	4	0	0	0	2
Steve Staios	6	0	0	0	10
Parris Duffus (goalie)	7	0	0	0	0

GOALTENDING

	Games	Min.	W	L	OTL	Goals	SO	Avg.
Parris Duffus	7	410	4	1	1	17	0	2.49
Geoff Sarjeant	4	207	0	2	1	20	0	5.81

PHOENIX ROADRUNNERS

(Lost semifinals to Denver, 4-1)

SCORING

	Games	G	A	Pts.	PIM
Rob Brown	9	4	12	16	0
Ken McRae	9	3	8	11	21
Jeff Shevalier	9	5	4	9	0
Arto Blomsten	8	3	6	9	6
Devin Edgerton	9	6	2	8	2
Dave Thomlinson	9	5	3	8	8
Dan Bylsma	9	4	4	8	4
Brian Chapman	9	1	5	6	31
Brian Straub	9	0	6	6	10
Steve Wilson	9	0	6	6	0
Randy Pearce	9	3	1	4	8
Vaclav Nedomansky	6	0	4	4	23
Keith Redmond	6	2	1	3	29
Nicholas Vachon	9	1	2	3	24
Vitali Yachmenev	4	1	0	1	0
Rob Murphy	2	0	1	1	0
Tim Watters	7	0	1	1	10
Sean O'Donnell	9	0	1	1	21
Justin Hocking	1	0	0	0	0
Brian McKee	1	0	0	0	0
Andre Racicot (goalie)	2	0	0	0	0
Mike O'Neill (goalie)	9	0	0	0	0

GOALTENDING

	Games	Min.	W	L	OTL	Goals	SO	Avg.
Andre Racicot	2	21	0	0	0	0	0	0.00
Mike O'Neill	9	536	4	4	1	33	0	3.70

SAN DIEGO GULLS

(Lost quarterfinals to Milwaukee, 3-2)

SCORING

	Games	G	A	Pts.	PIM
Todd Gillingham	5	2	3	5	10
Dan Lambert	5	0	5	5	10
David Sacco	4	3	1	4	0
Mark Beaufait	5	2	2	4	2
Ron Wilson	5	2	0	2	8
Dennis Holland	4	1	0	1	2
David Williams	5	1	0	1	0
Allan Bester (goalie)	4	0	1	1	0
Clark Donatelli	5	0	1	1	6
Jason Marshall	5	0	1	1	8
Hubie McDonough	5	0	1	1	4
Patrick Neaton	5	0	1	1	0
Myles O'Connor	5	0	1	1	0
Brian Sullivan	5	0	1	1	7
Bob Essensa (goalie)	1	0	0	0	0
Larry DePalma	2	0	0	0	20
John Lilley	2	0	0	0	2
Dean Ewen	4	0	0	0	10
Jamie Leach	4	0	0	0	0
Darren Van Impe	5	0	0	0	0

GOALTENDING

	Games	Min.	W	L	OTL	Goals	SO	Avg.
Allan Bester	4	272	2	2	0	13	0	2.86
Bob Essensa	1	59	0	1	0	3	0	3.05

1994-95 AWARD WINNERS

ALL-STAR TEAMS

First team	Pos.	Second team
Tommy Salo, Denver	G	Manny Fernandez, Kal.
Todd Richards, Las Vegas	D	Dale DeGray, Cleveland
Chris Snell, Phoenix	D	Stephane Richer, Cin.
Steve Maltais, Chicago	LW	Gino Cavallini, Milwaukee
Stephane Morin, Minnesota	C	Hubie McDonough, S.D.
Stan Drulia, Atlanta	RW	Rob Brown, Phoenix

TROPHY WINNERS

James Gatschene Memorial Trophy: Tommy Salo, Denver
Leo P. Lamoureux Memorial Trophy: Stephane Morin, Minnesota
James Norris Memorial Trophy: Tommy Salo, Denver
Governors Trophy: Todd Richards, Las Vegas
Garry F. Longman Memorial Trophy: Tommy Salo, Denver
Ken McKenzie Trophy: Chris Marinucci, Denver
Commissioner's Trophy: Butch Goring, Denver
N.R. (Bud) Poile Trophy: Kip Miller, Denver
Fred A. Huber Trophy: Denver Grizzlies
Joseph Turner Memorial Cup Winner: Denver Grizzlies

ALL-TIME AWARD WINNERS

JAMES GATSCHENE MEMORIAL TROPHY

(Most Valuable Player)

Season	Player, Team
1946-47	Herb Jones, Detroit Auto Club
1947-48	Lyle Dowell, Det. Bright's Goodyears
1948-49	Bob McFadden, Det. Jerry Lynch
1949-50	Dick Kowcinak, Sarnia
1950-51	John McGrath, Toledo
1951-52	Ernie Dick, Chatham
1952-53	Donnie Marshall, Cincinnati
1953-54	No award given
1954-55	Phil Goyette, Cincinnati
1955-56	George Hayes, Grand Rapids
1956-57	Pierre Brillant, Indianapolis
1957-58	Pierre Brillant, Indianapolis
1958-59	Len Thornson, Fort Wayne
1959-60	Billy Reichart, Minneapolis
1960-61	Len Thornson, Fort Wayne
1961-62	Len Thornson, Fort Wayne
1962-63	Len Thornson, Fort Wayne
	Eddie Lang, Fort Wayne
1963-64	Len Thornson, Fort Wayne
1964-65	Chick Chalmers, Toledo
1965-66	Gary Schall, Muskegon

Season	Player, Team
1966-67	Len Thornson, Fort Wayne
1967-68	Len Thornson, Fort Wayne
	Don Westbrooke, Dayton
1968-69	Don Westbrooke, Dayton
1969-70	Cliff Pennington, Des Moines
1970-71	Lyle Carter, Muskegon
1971-72	Len Fontaine, Port Huron
1972-73	Gary Ford, Muskegon
1973-74	Pete Mara, Des Moines
1974-75	Gary Ford, Muskegon
1975-76	Len Fontaine, Port Huron
1976-77	Tom Mellor, Toledo
1977-78	Dan Bonar, Fort Wayne
1978-79	Terry McDougall, Fort Wayne
1979-80	Al Dumba, Fort Wayne
1980-81	Marcel Comeau, Saginaw
1981-82	Brent Jarrett, Kalamazoo
1982-83	Claude Noel, Toledo
1983-84	Darren Jensen, Fort Wayne
1984-85	Scott Gruhl, Muskegon
1985-86	Darrell May, Peoria
1986-87	Jeff Pyle, Saginaw
	Jock Callander, Muskegon
1987-88	John Cullen, Flint

Season	Player, Team
1988-89	Dave Michayluk, Muskegon
1989-90	Michel Mongeau, Peoria
1990-91	David Bruce, Peoria
1991-92	Dmitri Kvartalnov, San Diego
1992-93	Tony Hrkac, Indianapolis
1993-94	Rob Brown, Kalamazoo
1994-95	Tommy Salo, Denver

LEO P. LAMOUREUX MEMORIAL TROPHY

(Leading scorer)

Season	Player, Team
1946-47	Harry Marchand, Windsor
1947-48	Dick Kowcinak, Det. Auto Club
1948-49	Leo Richard, Toledo
1949-50	Dick Kowcinak, Sarnia
1950-51	Herve Parent, Grand Rapids
1951-52	George Parker, Grand Rapids
1952-53	Alex Irving, Milwaukee
1953-54	Don Hall, Johnstown
1954-55	Phil Goyette, Cincinnati
1955-56	Max Mekilok, Cincinnati
1956-57	Pierre Brillant, Indianapolis
1957-58	Warren Hynes, Cincinnati
1958-59	George Ranieri, Louisville
1959-60	Chick Chalmers, Louisville
1960-61	Ken Yackel, Minneapolis
1961-62	Len Thornson, Fort Wayne
1962-63	Moe Bartoli, Minneapolis
1963-64	Len Thornson, Fort Wayne
1964-65	Lloyd Maxfield, Port Huron
1965-66	Bob Rivard, Fort Wayne
1966-67	Len Thornson, Fort Wayne
1967-68	Gary Ford, Muskegon
1968-69	Don Westbrooke, Dayton
1969-70	Don Westbrooke, Dayton
1970-71	Darrel Knibbs, Muskegon
1971-72	Gary Ford, Muskegon
1972-73	Gary Ford, Muskegon
1973-74	Pete Mara, Des Moines
1974-75	Rick Bragnalo, Dayton
1975-76	Len Fontaine, Port Huron
1976-77	Jim Koleff, Flint
1977-78	Jim Johnston, Flint
1978-79	Terry McDougall, Fort Wayne
1979-80	Al Dumba, Fort Wayne
1980-81	Marcel Comeau, Saginaw
1981-82	Brent Jarrett, Kalamazoo
1982-83	Dale Yakiwchuk, Milwaukee
1983-84	Wally Schreiber, Fort Wayne
1984-85	Scott MacLeod, Salt Lake
1985-86	Scott MacLeod, Salt Lake
1986-87	Jock Callander, Muskegon
	Jeff Pyle, Saginaw
1987-88	John Cullen, Flint
1988-89	Dave Michayluk, Muskegon
1989-90	Michel Mongeau, Peoria
1990-91	Lonnie Loach, Fort Wayne
1991-92	Dmitri Kvartalnov, San Diego
1992-93	Tony Hrkac, Indianapolis
1993-94	Rob Brown, Kalamazoo
1994-95	Stephane Morin, Minnesota

The award was originally known as the George H. Wilkinson Trophy from 1946-47 through 1959-60.

JAMES NORRIS MEMORIAL TROPHY

(Outstanding goaltenders)

Season	Player, Team
1955-56	Bill Tibbs, Troy
1956-57	Glenn Ramsey, Cincinnati
1957-58	Glenn Ramsey, Cincinnati
1958-59	Don Rigazio, Louisville
1959-60	Rene Zanier, Fort Wayne
1960-61	Ray Mikulan, Minneapolis
1961-62	Glenn Ramsey, Omaha
1962-63	Glenn Ramsey, Omaha
1963-64	Glenn Ramsey, Toledo
1964-65	Chuck Adamson, Fort Wayne
1965-66	Bob Sneddon, Port Huron
1966-67	Glenn Ramsey, Toledo
1967-68	Tim Tabor, Muskegon
	Bob Perani, Muskegon
1968-69	Pat Rupp, Dayton
	John Adams, Dayton
1969-70	Gaye Cooley, Des Moines
	Bob Perreault, Des Moines
1970-71	Lyle Carter, Muskegon
1971-72	Glenn Resch, Muskegon
1972-73	Robbie Irons, Fort Wayne
	Don Atchison, Fort Wayne
1973-74	Bill Hughes, Muskegon
1974-75	Bob Volpe, Flint
	Merlin Jenner, Flint
1975-76	Don Cutts, Muskegon
1976-77	Terry Richardson, Kalamazoo
1977-78	Lorne Molleken, Saginaw
	Pierre Chagnon, Saginaw
1978-79	Gord Laxton, Grand Rapids
1979-80	Larry Lozinski, Kalamazoo
1980-81	Claude Legris, Kalamazoo
	Georges Gagnon, Kalamazoo
1981-82	Lorne Molleken, Toledo
	Dave Tardich, Toledo
1982-83	Lorne Molleken, Toledo
1983-84	Darren Jensen, Fort Wayne
1984-85	Rick Heinz, Peoria
1985-86	Rick St. Croix, Fort Wayne
	Pokey Reddick, Fort Wayne
1986-87	Alain Raymond, Fort Wayne
	Michel Dufour, Fort Wayne
1987-88	Steve Guenette, Muskegon
1988-89	Rick Knickle, Fort Wayne
1989-90	Jimmy Waite, Indianapolis
1990-91	Guy Hebert, Peoria
	Pat Jablonski, Peoria
1991-92	Arturs Irbe, Kansas City
	Wade Flaherty, Kansas City
1992-93	Rick Knickle, San Diego
	Clint Malarchuk, San Diego
1993-94	J.C. Bergeron, Atlanta
	Mike Greenlay, Atlanta
1994-95	Tommy Salo, Denver

GOVERNORS TROPHY

(Outstanding defenseman)

Season	Player, Team
1964-65	Lionel Repka, Fort Wayne
1965-66	Bob Lemieux, Muskegon
1966-67	Larry Mavety, Port Huron
1967-68	Carl Brewer, Muskegon
1968-69	Al Breaule, Dayton
	Moe Benoit, Dayton
1969-70	John Gravel, Toledo
1970-71	Bob LaPage, Des Moines
1971-72	Rick Pagnutti, Fort Wayne
1972-73	Bob McCammon, Port Huron
1973-74	Dave Simpson, Dayton
1974-75	Murry Flegel, Muskegon
1975-76	Murry Flegel, Muskegon
1976-77	Tom Mellor, Toledo
1977-78	Michel LaChance, Milwaukee
1978-79	Guido Tenesi, Grand Rapids
1979-80	John Gibson, Saginaw
1980-81	Larry Goodenough, Saginaw
1981-82	Don Waddell, Saginaw
1982-83	Jim Burton, Fort Wayne
	Kevin Willison, Milwaukee
1983-84	Kevin Willison, Milwaukee
1984-85	Lee Norwood, Peoria
1985-86	Jim Burton, Fort Wayne

Season	Player, Team
1986-87	Jim Burton, Fort Wayne
1987-88	Phil Bourque, Muskegon
1988-89	Randy Boyd, Milwaukee
1989-90	Brian Glynn, Salt Lake
1990-91	Brian McKee, Fort Wayne
1991-92	Jean-Marc Richard, Fort Wayne
1992-93	Bill Houlder, San Diego
1993-94	Darren Veitch, Peoria
1994-95	Todd Richards, Las Vegas

GARRY F. LONGMAN MEMORIAL TROPHY
(Outstanding rookie)

Season	Player, Team
1961-62	Dave Richardson, Fort Wayne
1962-63	John Gravel, Omaha
1963-64	Don Westbrooke, Toledo
1964-65	Bob Thomas, Toledo
1965-66	Frank Golembrowsky, Port Huron
1966-67	Kerry Bond, Columbus
1967-68	Gary Ford, Muskegon
1968-69	Doug Volmar, Columbus
1969-70	Wayne Zuk, Toledo
1970-71	Corky Agar, Flint
	Herb Howdle, Dayton
1971-72	Glenn Resch, Muskegon
1972-73	Danny Gloor, Des Moines
1973-74	Frank DeMarco, Des Moines
1974-75	Rick Bragnalo, Dayton
1975-76	Sid Veysey, Fort Wayne
1976-77	Ron Zanussi, Fort Wayne
	Garth MacGuigan, Muskegon
1977-78	Dan Bonar, Fort Wayne
1978-79	Wes Jarvis, Port Huron
1979-80	Doug Robb, Milwaukee
1980-81	Scott Vanderburgh, Kalamazoo
1981-82	Scott Howson, Toledo
1982-83	Tony Fiore, Flint
1983-84	Darren Jensen, Fort Wayne
1984-85	Gilles Thibaudeau, Flint
1965-66	Guy Benoit, Muskegon
1986-87	Michel Mongeau, Saginaw
1987-88	Ed Belfour, Saginaw
	John Cullen, Flint
1988-89	Paul Ranheim, Salt Lake
1989-90	Rob Murphy, Milwaukee
1990-91	Nelson Emerson, Peoria
1991-92	Dmitri Kvartalnov, Kansas City
1992-93	Mikhail Shtalenkov, Milwaukee
1993-94	Radek Bonk, Las Vegas
1994-95	Tommy Salo, Denver

KEN McKENZIE TROPHY
(Outstanding American-born rookie)

Season	Player, Team
1977-78	Mike Eruzione, Toledo
1978-79	Jon Fontas, Saginaw

Season	Player, Team
1979-80	Bob Janecyk, Fort Wayne
1980-81	Mike Labianca, Toledo
	Steve Janaszak, Fort Wayne
1981-82	Steve Salvucci, Saginaw
1982-83	Paul Fenton, Peoria
1983-84	Mike Krensing, Muskegon
1984-85	Bill Schafhauser, Kalamazoo
1985-86	Brian Noonan, Saginaw
1986-87	Ray LeBlanc, Flint
1987-88	Dan Woodley, Flint
1988-89	Paul Ranheim, Salt Lake
1989-90	Tim Sweeney, Salt Lake
1990-91	C.J. Young, Salt Lake
1991-92	Kevin Wortman, Salt Lake
1992-93	Mark Beaufait, Kansas City
1993-94	Chris Rogles, Indianapolis
1994-95	Chris Marinucci, Denver

COMMISSIONER'S TROPHY
(Coach of the year)

Season	Coach, Team
1984-85	Rick Ley, Muskegon
	Pat Kelly, Peoria
1985-86	Rob Laird, Fort Wayne
1986-87	Wayne Thomas, Salt Lake
1987-88	Rick Dudley, Flint
1988-89	B. J. MacDonald, Muskegon
	Phil Russell, Muskegon
1989-90	Darryl Sutter, Indianapolis
1990-91	Bob Plager, Peoria
1991-92	Kevin Constantine, Kansas City
1992-93	Al Sims, Fort Wayne
1993-94	Bruce Boudreau, Fort Wayne
1994-95	Butch Goring, Denver

N.R. (BUD) POILE TROPHY
(Playoff MVP)

Season	Player, Team
1984-85	Denis Cyr, Peoria
1985-86	Jock Callander, Muskegon
1986-87	Rick Heinz, Salt Lake
1987-88	Peter Lappin, Salt Lake
1988-89	Dave Michayluk, Muskegon
1989-90	Mike McNeill, Indianapolis
1990-91	Michel Mongeau, Peoria
1991-92	Ron Handy, Kansas City
1992-93	Pokey Reddick, Fort Wayne
1993-94	Stan Drulia, Atlanta
1994-95	Kip Miller, Denver

The award was originally known as the Turner Cup Playoff MVP from 1984-85 through 1988-89.

ALL-TIME LEAGUE CHAMPIONS

REGULAR-SEASON CHAMPION

PLAYOFF CHAMPION

Season	Team	Coach	Team	Coach
1945-46	No trophy awarded		Detroit Auto Club	Jack Ward
1946-47	Windsor Staffords	Jack Ward	Windsor Spitfires	Ebbie Goodfellow
1947-48	Windsor Hettche Spitfires	Dent-Goodfellow	Toledo Mercurys	Andy Mulligan
1948-49	Toledo Mercurys	Andy Mulligan	Windsor Hettche Spitfires	Jimmy Skinner
1949-50	Sarnia Sailors	Dick Kowcinak	Catham Maroons	Bob Stoddart
1950-51	Grand Rapids Rockets	Lou Trudell	Toledo Mercurys	Alex Wood
1951-52	Grand Rapids Rockets	Lou Trudell	Toledo Mercurys	Alex Wood
1952-53	Cincinnati Mohawks	Buddy O'Conner	Cincinnati Mohawks	Buddy O'Conner
1953-54	Cincinnati Mohawks	Roly McLenahan	Cincinnati Mohawks	Roly McLenahan
1954-55	Cincinnati Mohawks	Roly McLenahan	Cincinnati Mohawks	Roly McLenahan
1955-56	Cincinnati Mohawks	Roly McLenahan	Cincinnati Mohawks	Roly McLenahan
1956-57	Cincinnati Mohawks	Roly McLenahan	Cincinnati Mohawks	Roly McLenahan
1957-58	Cincinnati Mohawks	Bill Gould	Indiana. Chiefs	Leo Lamoureux
1958-59	Louisville Rebels	Leo Gasparini	Louisville Rebels	Leo Gasparini
1959-60	Fort Wayne Komets	Ken Ullyot	St. Paul Saints	Fred Shero
1960-61	Minneapolis Millers	Ken Yachel	St. Paul Saints	Fred Shero
1961-62	Muskegon Zephrys	Moose Lallo	Muskegon Zephrys	Moose Lallo
1962-63	Fort Wayne Komets	Ken Ullyot	Fort Wayne Komets	Ken Ullyot
1963-64	Toledo Blades	Moe Benoit	Toledo Blades	Moe Benoit
1964-65	Port Huron Flags	Lloyd Maxfield	Fort Wayne Komets	Eddie Long
1965-66	Muskegon Mohawks	Moose Lallo	Port Huron Flags	Lloyd Maxfield
1966-67	Dayton Gems	Warren Back	Toledo Blades	Terry Slater
1967-68	Muskegon Mohawks	Moose Lallo	Muskegon Mohawks	Moose Lallo
1968-69	Dayton Gems	Larry Wilson	Dayton Gems	Larry Wilson
1969-70	Muskegon Mohawks	Moose Lallo	Dayton Gems	Larry Wilson
1970-71	Muskegon Mohawks	Moose Lallo	Port Huron Flags	Ted Garvin
1971-72	Muskegon Mohawks	Moose Lallo	Port Huron Flags	Ted Garvin
1972-73	Fort Wayne Komets	Marc Boileau	Fort Wayne Komets	Marc Boileau
1973-74	Des Moines Capitals	Dan Belisle	Des Moines Capitals	Dan Belisle
1974-75	Muskegon Mohawks	Moose Lallo	Toledo Goaldiggers	Ted Garvin
1975-76	Dayton Gems	Ivan Prediger	Dayton Gems	Ivan Prediger
1976-77	Saginaw Gears	Don Perry	Saginaw Gears	Don Perry
1977-78	Fort Wayne Komets	Gregg Pilling	Toledo Goaldiggers	Ted Garvin
1978-79	Grand Rapids Owls	Moe Bartoli	Kalamazoo Wings	Bill Purcell
1979-80	Kalamazoo Wings	Doug McKay	Kalamazoo Wings	Doug McKay
1980-81	Kalamazoo Wings	Doug McKay	Saginaw Gears	Don Perry
1981-82	Toledo Goaldiggers	Bill Inglis	Toledo Goaldiggers	Bill Inglis
1982-83	Toledo Goaldiggers	Bill Inglis	Toledo Goaldiggers	Bill Inglis
1983-84	Fort Wayne Komets	Ron Ullyot	Flint Generals	Dennis Desrosiers
1984-85	Peoria Rivermen	Pat Kelly	Peoria Rivermen	Pat Kelly
1985-86	Fort Wayne Komets	Rob Laird	Muskegon Lumberjacks	Rick Ley
1986-87	Fort Wayne Komets	Rob Laird	Salt Lake Golden Eagles	Wayne Thomas
1987-88	Muskegon Lumberjacks	Rick Ley	Salt Lake Golden Eagles	Paul Baxter
1988-89	Muskegon Lumberjacks	B.J. MacDonald	Muskegon Lumberjacks	B.J. MacDonald
1989-90	Muskegon Lumberjacks	B.J. MacDonald	Indianapolis Ice	Darryl Sutter
1990-91	Peoria Rivermen	Bob Plager	Peoria Rivermen	Bob Plager
1991-92	Kansas City Blades	Kevin Constantine	Kansas City Blades	Kevin Constantine
1992-93	San Diego Gulls	Rick Dudley	Fort Wayne Komets	Al Sims
1993-94	Las Vegas Thunder	Butch Goring	Atlanta Knights	Gene Ubriaco
1994-95	Denver Grizzlies	Butch Goring	Denver Grizzlies	Butch Goring

The IHL regular-season champion is awarded the Fred A. Huber Trophy and the playoff champion is awarded the Joseph Turner Memorial Cup.

The regular-season championship award was originally called the J.P. McGuire Trophy from 1946-47 through 1953-54.

EAST COAST HOCKEY LEAGUE

LEAGUE OFFICE

President/chief executive officer
Richard Adams
Commissioner
Patrick Kelly
Director of operations
Doug Price

Address
DD 518
Mart Office Building
800 Briar Creek Road
Charlotte, NC 28205

Phone
704-358-3658
FAX
704-358-3560

TEAMS

BIRMINGHAM BULLS

General manager
Art Clarkson
Head coach
Phil Roberto
Home ice
Birmingham-Jefferson Civic Center
Address
P.O. Box 1506
Birmingham, AL 35201
Seating capacity
16,850
Phone
205-458-8833
FAX
205-458-8489

CHARLOTTE CHECKERS

General manager
Carl Scheer
Head coach
John Marks
Home ice
Independence Arena
Address
2700 E. Independence Blvd.
Charlotte, NC 28205
Seating capacity
9,559
Phone
704-342-4423
FAX
704-377-4595

COLUMBUS CHILL

General manager
David Paitson
Head coach
Moe Mantha
Home ice
Ohio Fair Ground Coliseum
Address
7001 Dublin Park Drive
Dublin, OH 43017
Seating capacity
5,700
Phone
614-791-9999
FAX
614-791-9302

DAYTON BOMBERS

General manager
Arnold Johnson
Head coach
Jim Playfair
Home ice
Hara Arena
Address
P.O. Box 5952
Dayton, OH 45405-5952
Seating capacity
5,543
Phone
513-277-3765
FAX
513-278-3007

ERIE PANTHERS

General manager and head coach
Ron Hansis
Home ice
Erie Civic Center
Address
P.O. Box 6116
Erie, PA 16512
Seating capacity
5,374
Phone
814-455-3936
FAX
814-456-8287

HAMPTON ROADS ADMIRALS

General manager and head coach
John Brophy
Home ice
Scope Plaza
Address
P.O. Box 299
Norfolk, VA 23501
Seating capacity
8,994
Phone
804-640-1212
FAX
804-640-8447

HUNTINGTON BLIZZARD

General manager
Bob Henry
Head coach
To be announced
Home ice
Huntington Civic Center
Address
763 Third Avenue
Huntington, WV 25701
Seating capacity
5,376
Phone
304-697-7825
FAX
304-697-7832

JACKSONVILLE LIZARD KINGS

General manager
Larry Lane
Head coach
To be announced
Home ice
Jacksonville Veterans Memorial Coliseum
Address
5569-7 Bowden Road
Jacksonville, FL 32216
Seating capacity
8,000
Phone
904-448-8800
FAX
904-733-4413

JOHNSTOWN CHIEFS

General manager
Les Crooks
Head coach
To be announced
Home ice
War Memorial Arena
Address
326 Napoleon Street
Johnstown, PA 15901
Seating capacity
4,050
Phone
814-539-1799
FAX
814-536-1316

KNOXVILLE CHEROKEES

General manager
Ken Carringer
Head coach
Barry Smith
Home ice
Civic Coliseum

Address
500 East Church St.
Knoxville, TN 37915
Seating capacity
4,884
Phone
615-546-7825
FAX
615-546-5521

LOUISIANA ICEGATORS

General manager
Dave Berryman
Head coach
Doug Shedden
Home ice
Cajundome
Address
444 Cajundome Blvd.
Lafayette, LA 70506
Seating capacity
11,000
Phone
318-234-4423
FAX
318-232-1254

LOUISVILLE RIVERFROGS

General manager
Dale Owens
Head coach
Warren Young
Home ice
Broadbent Arena
Address
P.O. Box 36407
Louisville, KY 40233
Seating capacity
6,618
Phone
502-367-9121
FAX
502-368-5120

MOBILE MYSTICKS

General manager
Steve Chapman
Head coach
Eddie Johnstone
Home ice
Mobile Civic Center
Address
P.O. Box 263
Mobile, AL 36601-0263
Seating capacity
8,600
Phone
334-434-7932
FAX
334-434-7931

NASHVILLE KNIGHTS

General manager
Greg Lutz
Head coach
Mark Kumpel

Home ice
Municipal Coliseum
Address
417 4th Avenue North
Nashville, TN 37201
Seating capacity
7,985
Phone
615-255-7825
FAX
615-255-0024

RALEIGH ICECAPS

General manager
Pete Bock
Head coach
Kurt Kleinendorst
Home ice
Dorton Arena
Address
P.O. Box 33219
Raleigh, NC 27636
Seating capacity
5,700
Phone
919-755-1427
FAX
919-755-0899

RICHMOND RENEGADES

General manager
Craig Laughlin
Head coach
Roy Sommer
Home ice
Richmond Coliseum
Address
601 East Leigh Street
Richmond, VA 23219
Seating capacity
10,324
Phone
804-643-7825
FAX
804-649-0651

ROANOKE EXPRESS

General manager
Pierre Paiement
Head coach
Frank Anzalone
Home ice
Roanoke Civic Center
Address
4502 Starkey Road S.W., Ste. 211
Roanoke, VA 24014
Seating capacity
8,372
Phone
703-989-4625
FAX
703-989-8681

SOUTH CAROLINA STRINGRAYS

General manager
Frank Milne

Head coach
Rick Vaive
Home ice
North Charleston Coliseum
Address
3107 Firestone Road
N. Charleston, SC 29418
Seating capacity
11,000
Phone
803-744-2248
FAX
803-744-2898

TALLAHASSEE TIGER SHARKS

General manager
Tim Mouser
Head coach
Terry Christensen
Home ice
Tallahassee Leon County Civic Center
Address
505 West Pensacola Street
Tallahassee, FL 32302
Seating capacity
11,032
Phone
904-224-7700
FAX
904-224-6300

TOLEDO STORM

General manager
Barry Soskin
Head coach
Greg Puhalski
Home ice
Toledo Sports Arena
Address
One Main Street
Toledo, OH 43605
Seating capacity
5,160
Phone
419-691-0200
FAX
419-698-8998

WHEELING THUNDERBIRDS

General manager
Larry Kish
Head coach
Doug Sauter
Home ice
Wheeling Civic Center
Address
P.O. Box 6563
Wheeling, WV 26003-0815
Seating capacity
5,608
Phone
304-234-4625
FAX
304-233-4846

FINAL STANDINGS

EAST DIVISION

Team	G	W	L		Pts.	GF	GA
Richmond	68	41	20	(7)	89	271	232
Roanoke	68	39	19	(10)	88	255	223
Charlotte	68	37	22	(9)	83	274	261
Hampton Roads	68	37	23	(8)	82	255	239
Greensboro	68	31	28	(9)	71	277	293
Raleigh	68	23	39	(6)	52	239	295

NORTH DIVISION

Team	G	W	L		Pts.	GF	GA
Wheeling	68	46	17	(5)	97	313	243
Dayton	68	42	17	(9)	93	307	224
Toledo	68	41	22	(5)	87	287	230
Columbus	68	31	32	(5)	67	282	315
Johnstown	68	31	32	(5)	67	256	297
Erie	68	18	46	(4)	40	256	356

WEST DIVISION

Team	G	W	L		Pts.	GF	GA
South Carolina	68	42	19	(7)	91	255	215
Tallahassee	68	36	25	(7)	79	268	227
Nashville	68	32	30	(6)	70	263	279
Knoxville	68	30	30	(8)	68	241	267
Huntington	68	28	37	(3)	59	224	275
Birmingham	68	26	38	(4)	56	273	325

( )—Indicates overtime losses and are worth one point.

INDIVIDUAL LEADERS

Goals: Stephane Charbonneau, Erie (50)
Assists: Scott Burfoot, Erie (68)
Points: Scott Burfoot, Erie (97)
Penalty minutes: Jason Clarke, Roanoke (467)
Goaltending average: Chris Gordon, Huntington (2.55)
Shutouts: Paul Taylor, Dayton (3)
  Nick Vitucci, Toledo (3)

	Games	G	A	Pts.
Kevin McKinnon, Erie	67	37	48	85
Darren Schwartz, Tallahassee	66	47	35	82
Craig Charron, Dayton	48	35	47	82
Chris Bergeron, Birmingham	53	27	55	82
Jamie Steer, Dayton	62	33	48	81
John Porco, Hampton Roads	54	36	44	80
Kevin Riehl, Raleigh	64	33	46	79
Rod Taylor, Hampton Roads	68	38	40	78
Glenn Stewart, Greensboro	57	33	45	78
Derek DeCosty, Wheeling	62	41	35	76
Don Parsons, Tallahassee	66	41	35	76
Vadim Slivchenko, Wheeling	49	37	39	76
Rod Hinks, Johnstown	66	30	46	76
Oleg Yashin, Charlotte	65	30	46	76
Ilya Dubkov, Roanoke	68	28	47	75

TOP SCORERS

	Games	G	A	Pts.
Scott Burfoot, Erie	56	29	68	97
Stephane Charbonneau, Erie	64	50	41	91
Matt Robbins, Charlotte	68	28	61	89
Darryl Noren, Charlotte	62	46	41	87
Derek Clancey, Columbus	63	21	66	87

INDIVIDUAL STATISTICS

BIRMINGHAM BULLS

SCORING

	Games	G	A	Pts.	PIM
Chris Bergeron	53	27	55	82	128
Brad Smyth	36	33	35	68	52
David Craievich	59	20	46	66	140
Olaf Kjenstad	62	29	30	59	107
Ian Hebert	67	26	33	59	55
Rob Donovan	60	15	41	56	117
John Joyce	55	15	35	50	80
Craig Lutes	66	23	26	49	139
Jerome Bechard	67	22	26	48	427
Jim Larkin	47	13	20	33	33
Peter Marek	23	8	16	24	26
Jon Duval	60	4	16	20	208
Todd Harris	37	3	17	20	50
Colin Gregor	19	8	9	17	12
Jason Dexter	19	5	10	15	0
Norm Bazin	18	6	8	14	77
Brendan Creagh	30	3	8	11	42
Brad Pascall	38	2	9	11	53
Chris Tschupp	27	5	3	8	23
Ty Eigner	44	0	7	7	20
Scott Malone	8	1	4	5	36
Eric Cairns	11	1	3	4	49
Craig Johnson	37	3	0	3	150
Greg Bailey	18	0	2	2	149
Sandy Galuppo (goalie)	23	0	2	2	21
Mark Michaud (goalie)	44	0	2	2	10
Joel Eagan	12	1	0	1	18
Billy Tibbetts	2	0	1	1	18
Igor Bonderev	3	0	1	1	0
Doug Famigletti	1	0	0	0	0
Tom O'Connor	1	0	0	0	0
Sergei Tkachenko (goalie)	6	0	0	0	0
Dave Boyd	12	0	0	0	57

GOALTENDING

	Games	Min.	W	L	OTL	Goals	SO	Avg.
Sergei Tkachenko	6	359	2	4	0	25	0	4.17
Sandy Galuppo	23	1217	10	10	0	92	1	4.53
Mark Michaud	44	2529	14	24	4	200	1	4.75

CHARLOTTE CHECKERS

SCORING

	Games	G	A	Pts.	PIM
Matt Robbins	68	28	61	89	20
Sergei Berdnikov	62	37	37	74	36
Shawn Wheeler	68	34	39	73	226
Darryl Noren	45	39	25	64	63
Andrei Bashkirov	61	19	27	46	20
Joe Hawley	33	19	22	41	57
Eric Fenton	58	11	26	37	269
Daniel Murphy	68	4	33	37	57
Ken Thibodeau	28	10	17	27	30
Oleg Yashin	20	6	20	26	30

	Games	G	A	Pts.	PIM
Kurt Seher	49	8	13	21	51
Roman Gorev	20	10	7	17	2
Scott Meehan	68	1	16	17	142
Travis Tucker	62	5	11	16	250
Daniel Ruoho	28	8	6	14	41
Andy Silverman	64	3	11	14	57
Sylvain Blouin	50	5	7	12	280
Joe Crowley	24	7	3	10	70
Ted Dent	17	3	7	10	40
Jay Ness	20	7	2	9	10
Mick Kempffer	12	1	6	7	16
Marian Kacir	5	2	3	5	2
Steve Norton	15	2	3	5	16
Steve Foster	21	1	4	5	21
Scott MacNair	8	0	4	4	4
Scott Lindsay	9	2	0	2	13
Howie Rosenblatt	5	1	1	2	38
Reginald Brezeault	8	1	0	1	48
Jon Hillebrandt (goalie)	32	0	1	1	6
Rob Tallas (goalie)	36	0	1	1	14
Scott Vettraino (goalie)	1	0	0	0	0
Matt DelGuidice (goalie)	5	0	0	0	0
Jeff Marshall	5	0	0	0	4
Alexei Deev	6	0	0	0	0

GOALTENDING

	Games	Min.	W	L	OTL	Goals	SO	Avg.
Scott Vettraino	1	31	0	0	0	1	0	1.94
Matt DelGuidice	5	303	2	2	1	15	0	2.97
Rob Tallas	36	2011	21	9	3	114	0	3.40
Jon Hillebrandt	32	1790	14	11	5	121	0	4.05

COLUMBUS CHILL

SCORING

	Games	G	A	Pts.	PIM
Derek Clancey	63	21	66	87	20
Keith Morris	62	32	41	73	32
Robin Bouchard	46	30	33	63	188
Mike Ross	67	24	37	61	44
Chris Gotziaman	56	35	19	54	57
Kevin St. Jacques	46	14	38	52	88
Roman Gorev	40	21	21	42	6
Lance Brady	66	6	25	31	151
Aaron Boh	58	5	25	30	186
Brad Treliving	58	7	16	23	107
Rob Schriner	42	14	8	22	29
Craig Woodcroft	16	7	14	21	22
Bobby House	9	11	6	17	2
Craig Binns	48	7	10	17	110
Jesse Cooper	56	2	14	16	38
Andy MacIntyre	22	7	8	15	5
Greg Murray	19	8	5	13	4
Pat Meehan	15	6	4	10	14
Mark Kuntz	25	6	4	10	91
Matt Oates	11	4	5	9	11
Jason Smart	15	2	6	8	46
Gerry Skrypec	48	1	7	8	84
Rick Rougeau	8	3	3	6	2
Darwin McClelland	14	2	4	6	17
Wyatt Buckland	11	3	1	4	51
Brett Abel (goalie)	49	0	4	4	6
Bill Lang	10	2	1	3	7
Kelvin Solari	11	1	1	2	25
Kevin Quinn	15	1	1	2	66
Clayton Gainer	7	0	2	2	16
Glen Lang	3	0	1	1	0
Dave Pensa	6	0	1	1	14
Shawn Yakimishyn	6	0	1	1	24
Matt Yingst	10	0	1	1	4
Tom Newman (goalie)	17	0	1	1	6
Ron Bertrand (goalie)	1	0	0	0	0
Andrew Dickson	1	0	0	0	0
Brad Kirkwood (goalie)	1	0	0	0	0
Jerome Butler (goalie)	3	0	0	0	0

	Games	G	A	Pts.	PIM
Brad Cook	3	0	0	0	0
Joe Bonvie (goalie)	10	0	0	0	0

GOALTENDING

	Games	Min.	W	L	OTL	Goals	SO	Avg.
Brett Abel	49	2649	21	18	4	180	1	4.08
Ron Bertrand	1	65	1	0	0	5	0	4.62
Tom Newman	17	759	7	6	0	59	0	4.67
Jerome Butler	3	141	0	3	0	12	0	5.12
Joe Bonvie	10	495	2	5	1	44	0	5.34
Brad Kirkwood	1	19	0	0	0	4	0	12.69

DAYTON BOMBERS

SCORING

	Games	G	A	Pts.	PIM
Craig Charron	48	35	47	82	82
Jamie Steer	62	33	48	81	54
Kevin Brown	66	29	42	71	34
Brandon Smith	60	16	49	65	57
Rob Hartnell	62	21	26	47	211
Karson Kaebel	33	14	33	47	68
Pascal Trepanier	36	16	28	44	113
Jim Lessard	66	14	30	44	199
John Brill	35	14	27	41	59
Tony Gruba	44	18	20	38	55
Steve Lingren	64	11	23	34	128
Sean Gagnon	68	9	23	32	339
Jason Downey	62	7	23	30	282
Nicolas Turmel	41	10	18	28	52
Mike Doers	64	12	15	27	31
Scott Loucks	35	10	15	25	46
Steve Wilson	16	12	9	21	30
Dean Fedorchuk	15	8	11	19	12
Greg Hagen	17	7	6	13	6
Pat Cavanagh	27	7	5	12	167
Mike Vandenberghe	24	1	9	10	75
Brent Brekke	24	1	7	8	31
Brett Strot	4	1	3	4	0
Pat Meehan	10	1	1	2	0
Paul Taylor (goalie)	32	0	2	2	55
Mike Dennis	3	0	1	1	15
John Bradley	4	0	1	1	0
Mike Black	3	0	0	0	0
Jeff Stolp (goalie)	40	0	0	0	8

GOALTENDING

	Games	Min.	W	L	OTL	Goals	SO	Avg.
Jeff Stolp	40	2181	22	5	6	112	1	3.08
Paul Taylor	32	1685	18	11	2	97	3	3.45

ERIE PANTHERS

SCORING

	Games	G	A	Pts.	PIM
Scott Burfoot	56	29	68	97	66
Stephane Charbonneau	64	50	41	91	129
Kevin McKinnon	67	37	48	85	28
Eric Bellerose	44	12	31	43	69
Cam Brown	60	14	28	42	341
Jason Smith	56	7	34	41	38
Vyacheslav Polikarkin	34	12	22	34	26
Jeff Hoad	35	13	17	30	112
Carl Fleury	43	13	15	28	79
Brad Harrison	34	14	7	21	129
Ian DeCorby	40	5	15	20	30
Casey Hungle	45	9	8	17	49
Todd Dvorak	46	7	9	16	44
Sergei Stas	35	1	15	16	108
Justin Peca	23	7	6	13	18
Todd Harris	27	6	7	13	49
Herve LaPointe	58	1	12	13	253
Chris Morque	26	3	8	11	83
Gerry St. Cyr	11	4	6	10	33

	Games	G	A	Pts.	PIM
Sverre Sears	21	0	8	8	83
Pete Mehalic	11	3	4	7	13
Chris Tschupp	16	3	3	6	25
Vassili Demin	32	0	5	5	20
Francis Ouellette (goalie)	45	0	4	4	36
Rouslan Toujikov	5	2	1	3	8
Brian Caruso	12	1	2	3	36
Henrich Hluchan	2	1	1	2	4
Jason Winch	5	0	2	2	2
Rick Rougeau	6	0	2	2	2
Ilia Borisychev	3	1	0	1	0
Jamie Bailey	9	1	0	1	13
Trevor Hunt	2	0	1	1	0
Justin Proud	2	0	1	1	15
Andrei Kozlov	8	0	1	1	52
Larry Empey	23	0	1	1	52
Jason Eckel	1	0	0	0	2
John Johnson	1	0	0	0	0
Wade Gibson	2	0	0	0	0
Vern Guetens (goalie)	4	0	0	0	0
Jason Richard	6	0	0	0	0
Brad Cook	7	0	0	0	2
Paul Krake (goalie)	10	0	0	0	2
Todd Chin (goalie)	13	0	0	0	0
Brian McCarthy	16	0	0	0	7

GOALTENDING

	Games	Min.	W	L	OTL	Goals	SO	Avg.
Francis Ouellette	45	2559	15	28	1	202	1	4.74
Vern Guetens	4	245	1	2	1	20	0	4.90
Todd Chin	13	711	1	8	1	65	0	5.48
Paul Krake	10	597	1	8	1	61	0	6.13

GREENSBORO MONARCHS

SCORING

	Games	G	A	Pts.	PIM
Glenn Stewart	57	33	45	78	51
Davis Payne	62	25	36	61	195
Jeff Gabriel	66	24	27	51	92
Phil Berger	40	23	27	50	114
Hugo Proulx	40	18	28	46	116
Artur Kupacs	63	14	30	44	89
Mark DeSantis	57	10	34	44	196
Howie Rosenblatt	41	12	24	36	245
Chris Valicevic	37	5	28	33	39
Francois Leroux	36	16	16	32	79
Jeremy Stevenson	43	14	13	27	231
Vyacheslav Polikarkin	23	7	20	27	6
Doug Evans	59	10	15	25	151
Darryl Noren	17	7	16	23	43
Scott Chartier	30	6	14	20	82
Colin Foley	28	12	6	18	58
Dean Zayonce	60	2	14	16	245
Brandon Coates	22	8	6	14	14
Scott McKay	17	7	7	14	54
B.J. MacPherson	15	4	7	11	34
Brendan Creagh	21	4	7	11	39
Ron Pasco	18	3	8	11	32
Chad Seibel	17	1	9	10	46
Dwayne Gylywoychuk	27	1	9	10	42
Trevor Senn	15	3	5	8	141
Sergei Stas	21	1	7	8	102
Eric Bellerose	13	4	3	7	32
Dean Hulett	4	1	3	4	15
Tavis MacMillan	8	2	1	3	20
Sean Pronger	2	0	2	2	0
Petr Skudra (goalie)	33	0	2	2	14
John Tanner (goalie)	6	0	1	1	2
Tom Newman (goalie)	10	0	1	1	0
Herve LaPointe	1	0	0	0	2
Paul Spagnoletti (goalie)	1	0	0	0	0
Rival Fullum	2	0	0	0	0
Brian Caruso	7	0	0	0	13
Sverre Sears	9	0	0	0	14
Rob Laurie (goalie)	10	0	0	0	0
Bill Horn (goalie)	20	0	0	0	2

GOALTENDING

	Games	Min.	W	L	OTL	Goals	SO	Avg.
Bill Horn	20	1135	13	5	1	58	0	3.07
Petr Skudra	33	1613	13	9	5	113	0	4.20
Tom Newman	10	500	1	6	1	36	0	4.32
Rob Laurie	10	514	4	4	1	39	0	4.55
John Tanner	6	342	0	4	1	27	0	4.73
Paul Spagnoletti	1	20	0	0	0	3	0	9.00

HAMPTON ROADS ADMIRALS

SCORING

	Games	G	A	Pts.	PIM
John Porco	54	36	44	80	97
Rod Taylor	68	38	40	78	118
Rob MacInnis	54	11	44	55	247
Rick Kowalsky	49	29	24	53	114
Chris Phelps	67	13	39	52	161
Jim Brown	49	24	21	45	50
Ron Pascucci	52	8	37	45	108
Brendan Curley	60	7	35	42	50
Trevor Halverson	42	14	26	40	194
Matt Mallgrave	48	18	17	35	81
Tom Menicci	50	11	12	23	47
Kelly Sorensen	60	10	13	23	214
Brian Goudie	51	5	16	21	278
Mikhail Nemirovsky	29	6	14	20	33
Jason MacIntyre	61	6	11	17	227
Ron Majic	51	7	8	15	241
Dennis McEwen	25	6	8	14	32
Tony MacAuley	57	1	6	7	90
George Zajankala	6	1	5	6	2
Colin Gregor	21	3	2	5	48
Corwin Saurdiff (goalie)	22	1	4	5	27
Bill Lang	11	0	4	4	19
Shamus Gregga (goalie)	18	0	2	2	2
Patrick LaLime (goalie)	26	0	1	1	0
Bob Jones (goalie)	1	0	0	0	0
Martin Laitre	5	0	0	0	4
Todd Hunter (goalie)	10	0	0	0	14

GOALTENDING

	Games	Min.	W	L	OTL	Goals	SO	Avg.
Corwin Saurdiff	22	1261	13	6	2	66	1	3.14
Patrick Lalime	26	1471	15	7	3	82	2	3.35
Todd Hunter	10	498	3	5	1	29	0	3.49
Shamus Gregga	18	853	6	5	2	52	0	3.66
Bob Jones	1	31	0	0	0	2	0	3.86

HUNTINGTON BLIZZARD

SCORING

	Games	G	A	Pts.	PIM
Mark Woolf	59	38	36	74	96
Jim Bermingham	43	29	36	65	96
Mike Stone	68	27	30	57	18
Jared Bednar	64	9	36	45	211
Gordie Frantti	34	19	23	42	102
Todd Brost	68	14	26	40	108
Mark Franks	55	21	16	37	34
Trent Eigner	59	8	25	33	164
Dan Fournel	55	11	20	31	176
Kelly Harper	60	12	14	26	100
Jim Larkin	24	6	16	22	18
Derek Schooley	66	3	15	18	151
Mitch Kean	30	6	8	14	10
Jim Solly	31	10	3	13	19
Jason Weinrich	21	1	9	10	42
Steve Barnes	29	1	9	10	36
Chris Morque	36	1	9	10	126
Ray Edwards	32	3	5	8	129
Ian DeCorby	32	0	8	8	26
Cory Bricknell	34	0	8	8	136
Ed Henrich	34	3	3	6	24
Joe Crowley	7	1	2	3	4

	Games	G	A	Pts.	PIM
Ty Eigner	9	0	3	3	7
Craig Mittleholt	10	1	1	2	2
Andrew Dickson	2	0	1	1	2
Ken Thibodeau	3	0	1	1	0
Jeff Pawluk	7	0	1	1	26
Adam Hooper	1	0	0	0	4
Derek MacNair	1	0	0	0	0
Derek McNair	1	0	0	0	2
Jim Mill (goalie)	1	0	0	0	0
Brian Sutton	2	0	0	0	2
Frank Cirone	3	0	0	0	2
Wyatt Buckland	6	0	0	0	12
Jason Currie (goalie)	6	0	0	0	0
Alan Brown	12	0	0	0	8
Todd Chin (goalie)	12	0	0	0	0
Chris Gordon (goalie)	30	0	0	0	2
Jeff Levy (goalie)	36	0	0	0	12

GOALTENDING

	Games	Min.	W	L	OTL	Goals	SO	Avg.
Chris Gordon	30	1484	17	6	2	63	2	2.55
Jeff Levy	36	1845	6	22	1	138	0	4.49
Todd Chin	12	515	5	5	0	39	0	4.54
Jim Mill	1	46	0	1	0	4	0	5.25
Jason Currie	6	209	0	3	0	23	0	6.60

JOHNSTOWN CHIEFS

SCORING

	Games	G	A	Pts.	PIM
Rod Hinks	66	30	46	76	90
Jason Brousseau	57	35	26	61	74
Matt Hoffman	55	25	36	61	113
Rob Leask	60	16	45	61	110
Dennis Purdie	36	27	33	60	125
Jason Jennings	67	23	31	54	57
Bruce Coles	29	20	25	45	56
Ted Dent	46	9	24	33	125
Perry Florio	62	3	28	31	94
Justin Duberman	24	13	14	27	30
Mike Dennis	59	5	18	23	86
Brandon Christian	39	7	12	19	226
Jay Ness	38	6	11	17	12
Ben Wyzansky	64	4	12	16	66
Steve Norton	31	4	10	14	12
Martin D'Orsonnens	39	5	7	12	79
Paul MacLean	40	5	7	12	26
Anton Federov	13	5	6	11	2
Dan Sawyer	58	2	9	11	111
Matt Yingst	41	5	5	10	27
Brian McCarthy	12	4	4	8	2
Steve Foster	21	1	6	7	14
Peter Romeo	11	0	4	4	16
Aaron Israel (goalie)	30	0	4	4	16
Gord Christian	4	1	2	3	29
Ryan Sittler	1	1	1	2	0
Jeff Connelly	4	0	2	2	0
Rob Laurie (goalie)	26	0	2	2	2
Kevin Quinn	7	0	1	1	36
Philippe Boudreault	2	0	0	0	2
Joel Eagan	3	0	0	0	2
Jason Richard	4	0	0	0	4
Neil Little (goalie)	16	0	0	0	2

GOALTENDING

	Games	Min.	W	L	OTL	Goals	SO	Avg.
Neil Little	16	897	7	6	1	55	0	3.68
Aaron Israel	30	1775	17	10	2	119	1	4.02
Rob Laurie	26	1456	7	16	2	113	0	4.66

KNOXVILLE CHEROKEES

SCORING

	Games	G	A	Pts.	PIM
Mike Gaul	68	13	41	54	51
Carl LeBlanc	62	6	47	53	192

	Games	G	A	Pts.	PIM
Steve Flomenhoft	49	17	34	51	42
Mike Murray	53	24	23	47	56
George Zajankala	49	18	24	42	131
Sean Pronger	34	18	23	41	55
Sean Brown	62	14	21	35	243
Jon Jenkins	65	16	17	33	29
Chris Tucker	30	11	19	30	8
Alain Deeks	58	15	13	28	150
David Neilson	33	11	14	25	129
Jack Callahan	51	13	11	24	11
Vaclav Nedomansky	26	14	9	23	107
Chris Fess	48	7	11	18	77
Doug Searle	56	7	11	18	205
Pat Murray	11	7	9	16	4
Mike Burman	38	4	11	15	76
Robb McIntyre	30	9	5	14	23
Jim Brown	15	7	5	12	42
Mike Vandenberghe	30	3	9	12	99
Rob Dumas	22	3	8	11	47
Hayden O'Rear	53	0	11	11	44
Mike Krygier	23	3	3	6	9
Justin Hocking	20	0	6	6	70
Colin Miller	5	1	2	3	0
Stephane Menard (goalie)	27	0	1	1	0
Cory Cadden (goalie)	47	0	0	0	26

GOALTENDING

	Games	Min.	W	L	OTL	Goals	SO	Avg.
Cory Cadden	46	2688	19	20	5	154	0	3.44
Stephane Menard	27	1450	11	10	3	106	0	4.39

NASHVILLE KNIGHTS

SCORING

	Games	G	A	Pts.	PIM
Colin Ward	64	41	29	70	108
Aigar Cipruss	53	26	43	69	24
Derek Eberle	57	25	32	57	96
Greg Burke	67	18	29	47	186
Doug Lawrence	33	7	37	44	129
Marc Tardif	54	16	26	42	263
Tod Hartje	25	13	26	39	74
Alexander Chunchukov	29	11	25	36	32
Tim Sullivan	55	16	15	31	133
Trevor Jobe	18	16	13	29	40
Dan Carney	58	7	17	24	36
Tom MacDonald	55	9	12	21	137
Troy Stevens	25	5	16	21	23
Gordie Frantti	23	11	9	20	100
Brandon Coates	24	12	3	15	46
Chris Nelson	21	3	11	14	46
Stephan Phillips	34	6	7	13	24
Chad Seibel	35	3	10	13	79
Jeff Hill	58	4	8	12	81
Jason Courtemanche	45	1	8	9	223
Martin Smith	19	3	5	8	11
Dmitri Alekhin	22	2	6	8	10
Marian Kacir	9	1	7	8	2
Gary Lebsack	50	1	6	7	298
Derby Bognar	34	1	5	6	13
Brandy Semchuk	9	3	2	5	2
Pat Cavanagh	8	2	2	4	50
Martin Lepage	10	0	2	2	2
Mike DeCarle	3	0	1	1	2
Matt DelGuidice (goalie)	18	0	1	1	18
Craig Brown (goalie)	52	0	1	1	28
Chris LiPuma	1	0	0	0	0
Paul Spagnoletti (goalie)	5	0	0	0	0

GOALTENDING

	Games	Min.	W	L	OTL	Goals	SO	Avg.
Craig Brown	52	2848	24	20	3	165	2	3.48
Matt DelGuidice	18	1009	7	8	2	81	0	4.82
Paul Spagnoletti	5	257	1	2	1	23	0	5.37

RALEIGH ICECAPS

SCORING

	Games	G	A	Pts.	PIM
Kevin Riehl	64	33	46	79	79
Lyle Wildgoose	65	29	44	73	37
Lenny Periera	66	19	21	40	53
Trevor Jobe	23	18	22	40	42
Derek Linnell	68	16	17	33	46
Marquis Mathieu	33	15	17	32	181
Scott MacNair	50	15	14	29	28
Justin Tomberlin	53	11	18	29	17
Chic Pojar	60	9	17	26	38
Alexander Chunchukov	32	7	18	25	30
Spencer Meany	61	7	18	25	160
Wade Bartley	41	6	17	23	47
Jamie Erb	26	12	9	21	38
Eric Long	53	4	15	19	55
John Blessman	31	4	14	18	109
Jim Duhart	20	8	8	16	112
Jim Powers	13	7	8	15	17
Todd Reirden	26	2	13	15	33
Doug Sinclair	30	2	12	14	103
Rodrigo Lavinsh	25	2	7	9	30
Brett Duncan	63	4	4	8	216
Anton Federov	21	2	6	8	6
Gord Christian	8	2	4	6	23
Kyle Kirkpatrick	8	1	3	4	2
Trent Eigner	7	1	2	3	10
Brad Mullahy (goalie)	39	0	3	3	28
Jim Gibson	13	2	0	2	6
Krysztof Oliwa	5	0	2	2	32
Frank Cirone	12	1	0	1	2
Mike Guilbert	4	0	1	1	6
Chris Scourletis	4	0	1	1	2
Eddie Sabo	5	0	1	1	2
Todd Hunter (goalie)	21	0	1	1	16
Cooper Naylor	1	0	0	0	0
Todd Person	1	0	0	0	0
Randy Murphy	2	0	0	0	0
Andy Borggard	4	0	0	0	0
Scott Lindsay	7	0	0	0	4
Chad Erickson (goalie)	11	0	0	0	24

GOALTENDING

	Games	Min.	W	L	OTL	Goals	SO	Avg.
Todd Hunter	21	1273	9	9	3	82	0	3.87
Brad Mullahy	39	2264	13	22	2	154	0	4.08
Chad Erickson	11	587	1	8	1	45	0	4.60

RICHMOND RENEGADES

SCORING

	Games	G	A	Pts.	PIM
Scott Gruhl	49	31	40	71	288
Shane Henry	57	22	47	69	34
Andrew Shier	64	28	37	65	126
Blaine Moore	60	30	33	63	181
Jan Benda	62	21	39	60	187
Kurt Mallett	68	24	27	51	24
Jay Murphy	37	24	15	39	78
Steve Bogoyevac	46	13	20	33	80
Shawn Snesar	63	8	23	31	259
Mike Taylor	42	7	21	28	90
Garrett MacDonald	58	10	17	27	229
Lou Body	49	8	16	24	76
Sean O'Brien	52	5	18	23	147
Daniel Chaput	39	8	13	21	122
Mike Burman	24	7	14	21	49
Cooper Naylor	34	3	18	21	32
Chris Tucker	31	7	11	18	41
Darrin Wetherill	56	6	12	18	114
Don Lester	26	1	16	17	32
Chris Foy	16	3	5	8	12

	Games	G	A	Pts.	PIM
Chad Seibel	12	1	3	4	55
Eric Germain	10	0	2	2	55
Duane Derksen (goalie)	27	0	2	2	44
Jarrett Reid	1	1	0	1	0
Derby Bognar	2	1	0	1	0
Mike Vandenberghe	6	1	0	1	32
Trevor Senn	9	1	0	1	98
Bob Wren	2	0	1	1	0
Jason Currie (goalie)	13	0	1	1	4
Grant Sjerven (goalie)	26	0	1	1	6
Vern Guetens (goalie)	2	0	0	0	0
Oleg Santuryan	2	0	0	0	0
Todd Dougherty	3	0	0	0	15
Rod Langway	6	0	0	0	2
Nate Smith	7	0	0	0	2
David Littman (goalie)	8	0	0	0	0

GOALTENDING

	Games	Min.	W	L	OTL	Goals	SO	Avg.
Dave Littman	8	346	4	2	0	13	1	2.25
Grant Sjerven	26	1438	17	6	2	72	1	3.01
Dwayne Derksen	27	1558	15	8	2	83	0	3.20
Jason Currie	13	687	5	3	2	42	0	3.67
Vern Guetens	2	118	0	2	0	10	0	5.09

ROANOKE EXPRESS

SCORING

	Games	G	A	Pts.	PIM
Ilya Dubkov	68	28	47	75	78
Jeff Jestadt	62	26	44	70	39
Dave Stewart	68	14	46	60	200
Derek Laxdal	66	32	24	56	144
Craig Herr	48	24	29	53	54
Oleg Yashin	45	24	26	50	41
Michael Smith	57	6	40	46	59
Tony Szabo	36	22	22	44	32
Pat Ferschweiler	22	8	22	30	44
Jason Clarke	63	11	18	29	467
Jon Larson	67	11	17	28	132
Rouslan Toujikov	39	16	11	27	90
Marty Schriner	55	12	15	27	95
Mark Luger	67	3	24	27	60
Chris Potter	68	1	18	19	77
Darwin McClelland	27	7	7	14	14
Mike Krygier	17	2	9	11	5
Stephane Desjardins	58	2	5	7	64
Joe Hawley	20	4	2	6	15
Carl Fleury	16	1	1	2	35
Todd Holt	2	0	2	2	0
Robin Bouchard	10	1	0	1	25
Andrew Dickson	3	0	1	1	2
Brian Sutton	3	0	1	1	2
Reginald Brezeault	8	0	1	1	20
Dan Ryder (goalie)	21	0	1	1	6
Dave Gagnon (goalie)	29	0	1	1	12
Chris Taylor	1	0	0	0	2
Rocco Trentadue (goalie)	1	0	0	0	0
Stephan Phillips	2	0	0	0	2
Paul Belleza	3	0	0	0	21
John Bradley (goalie)	3	0	0	0	0
Nick Wohlers	3	0	0	0	5
Andrei Kozlov	4	0	0	0	6
Ryan Schmidt	4	0	0	0	0
Daniel Berthiaume (goalie)	21	0	0	0	18

GOALTENDING

	Games	Min.	W	L	OTL	Goals	SO	Avg.
Rocco Trentadue	1	16	0	0	0	0	0	0.00
Daniel Berthiaume	21	1196	15	4	2	47	0	2.36
Dave Gagnon	29	1738	17	7	5	82	1	2.83
John Bradley	3	171	0	2	1	10	0	3.52
Dan Ryder	21	1008	7	6	2	66	1	3.93

SOUTH CAROLINA STINGRAYS

SCORING

	Games	G	A	Pts.	PIM
Gary Socha	68	33	37	70	80
Brett Marietti	67	23	33	56	103
Cam Danyluk	50	26	27	53	188
Scott Boston	48	18	33	51	137
Craig Lyons	46	19	29	48	58
Sylvain Fleury	50	15	32	47	10
James O'Brien	63	7	39	46	38
Derek Booth	66	6	30	36	158
Yvon Corbin	35	15	20	35	10
Mark Bavis	43	16	16	32	85
David Cooper	39	9	19	28	90
Marty Dallman	22	11	16	27	22
Mike Barrie	39	8	14	22	122
Mike Bavis	39	8	14	22	108
Chris Foy	23	4	14	18	27
Paul Rushforth	41	6	8	14	130
Daniel Ruoho	22	7	6	13	25
Dean Hulett	15	8	3	11	34
Rob Sumner	35	1	9	10	114
Brian McCarthy	21	3	5	8	25
Vasili Demin	31	2	6	8	59
Jim Sprott	21	1	6	7	100
Tom Nemeth	5	3	3	6	2
Chris Bright	3	2	2	4	2
Gord Christian	15	1	3	4	17
Brad Pascall	28	0	4	4	76
Trevor Senn	15	2	1	3	139
Dan Wiebe	3	1	1	2	6
Kyle Reeves	2	0	1	1	4
Dominic Fafard	7	0	1	1	4
Hugo Proulx	10	0	1	1	12
Steve Shields (goalie)	21	0	1	1	10
Libor Polasek	7	0	0	0	6
Andy Grenier	8	0	0	0	12
Norm Dezainde	9	0	0	0	6
Sergei Tkachenko (goalie)	16	0	0	0	12
Jason Fitzsimmons (goalie)	37	0	0	0	16

GOALTENDING

	Games	Min.	W	L	OTL	Goals	SO	Avg.
Steve Shields	21	1158	11	5	2	52	2	2.69
Jason Fitzsimmons	37	2125	24	7	4	105	1	2.97
Sergei Tkachenko	16	868	7	7	1	47	0	3.25

TALLAHASSEE TIGER SHARKS

SCORING

	Games	G	A	Pts.	PIM
Darren Schwartz	66	47	35	82	150
Don Parsons	66	41	35	76	82
Greg Geldart	65	26	47	73	24
Tom Neziol	56	35	27	62	54
Ron Pasco	36	11	30	41	63
Rob Dumas	35	8	27	35	68
Matt Osiecki	68	6	27	33	28
Jim Paradise	66	14	16	30	59
Todd Reirden	43	5	25	30	61
Greg Hagen	39	14	14	28	8
Dean Hulett	42	10	18	28	160
Jon Engfer	42	12	14	26	22
Jarrett Reid	28	5	16	21	39
Robert Haddock	43	5	14	19	55
John Uniac	47	3	16	19	40
Wade Bartley	23	0	16	16	31
Tony Prpic	20	5	8	13	71
Rodrigo Lavinsh	44	3	9	12	36
Mikhail Zdanovsky	42	4	7	11	29
Wade Gibson	41	3	7	10	129
Craig Herr	14	1	8	9	10
Brett Strot	7	2	6	8	4
Cory Paterson	14	2	6	8	20
Kevan Guy	6	0	5	5	0

	Games	G	A	Pts.	PIM
Alexei Lojkin	1	3	1	4	0
Rob Madia	6	1	3	4	0
Chris George	8	1	1	2	4
Mikhail Nemirovsky	6	0	2	2	0
Louis Dumont	5	1	0	1	4
Chris O'Rourke	15	0	1	1	79
Mark Richards (goalie)	59	0	1	1	8
Phil Esposito	1	0	0	0	2
Yannick Gosselin (goalie)	1	0	0	0	0
Manon Rheaume (goalie)	1	0	0	0	0
Shawn Yakimishyn	1	0	0	0	0
Mark Chowaniec	2	0	0	0	2
Jim Mill (goalie)	15	0	0	0	2

GOALTENDING

	Games	Min.	W	L	OTL	Goals	SO	Avg.
Mark Richards	59	3369	31	16	7	163	0	2.90
Jim Mill	15	689	6	6	0	47	0	4.09
Yannick Gosselin	1	28	0	1	0	3	0	6.47
Manon Rheaume	1	20	0	1	0	4	0	12.00

TOLEDO STORM

SCORING

	Games	G	A	Pts.	PIM
Rick Corriveau	60	26	48	74	168
Rick Judson	54	27	41	68	29
Jay Neal	64	28	34	62	81
Mike Latendresse	43	36	20	56	23
John Hendry	56	25	30	55	141
Iain Duncan	37	9	34	43	133
Jim Maher	52	18	19	37	63
Darren Perkins	59	7	29	36	138
Dave Bankoske	48	13	15	28	19
Shawn Penn	63	14	13	27	208
Lev Berdichevsky	13	4	11	15	31
Mark Deazeley	14	5	1	6	136
Sam Raffoul	19	2	4	6	71
Steve Dykstra	10	1	5	6	19
Troy Neumeier	10	0	5	5	18
Tony Burns	10	0	3	3	4
Jason Gladney	3	1	1	2	10
Mike Mickelson	3	1	1	2	2
Page Klostereich	5	0	2	2	8
Rhett Trombley	13	0	2	2	80
Rob Radobenko	16	0	2	2	30
Tom Warden	13	1	0	1	113
Dave Gregory	9	0	1	1	9
Nick Vitucci (goalie)	56	0	1	1	16
Benoit Larose	1	0	0	0	0
Chris Tarsha	1	0	0	0	0
Greg Trewin	1	0	0	0	0
Bruce MacDonald	2	0	0	0	0
Ken Matlock	2	0	0	0	2
Jamie Patenall	9	0	0	0	2
Alain Harvey (goalie)	15	0	0	0	2

GOALTENDING

	Games	Min.	W	L	OTL	Goals	SO	Avg.
Nick Vitucci	56	3273	35	16	3	176	3	3.23
Alain Harvey	15	822	6	6	2	49	1	3.58

WHEELING THUNDERBIRDS

SCORING

	Games	G	A	Pts.	PIM
Derek DeCosty	62	41	35	76	83
Vadim Slivchenko	49	37	39	76	75
Tim Roberts	61	16	58	74	62
Steve Gibson	50	37	29	66	61
Louis Dumont	62	25	33	58	81
Xavier Majic	49	20	31	51	41
Tim Tisdale	33	19	31	50	54
Brock Woods	65	13	31	44	219

	Games	G	A	Pts.	PIM
Scott Matusovich	66	13	31	44	97
Dennis Holland	22	15	22	37	43
Tony Prpic	30	11	16	27	64
Brent Pope	57	7	17	24	235
Duane Dennis	17	10	12	22	25
Peter Marek	25	3	17	20	37
Kevin O'Sullivan	28	3	17	20	37
Gairin Smith	48	8	11	19	195
Lorne Toews	54	8	11	19	71
Brad Layzell	31	2	16	18	29
Claude Jutras	19	7	7	14	172
Pat Barton	27	3	7	10	49
Dominic Fafard	39	2	8	10	44
Christian Lariviere	17	0	8	8	40
Darren McAusland	11	6	1	7	8
Scott Fraser	8	4	2	6	8
Scott Ferguson	5	1	5	6	16
Louis Bernard	20	1	5	6	26
Alex Duchesne	9	1	4	5	15
Cory Paterson	12	0	4	4	35
Geoff Finch (goalie)	37	0	1	1	2
Mike Bajurny	1	0	0	0	0
John Bradley (goalie)	2	0	0	0	0
Jeff Connelly	2	0	0	0	0
Mike Parson (goalie)	2	0	0	0	0
Stephen Rohr	2	0	0	0	0
Dion Darling	4	0	0	0	24
Patrick Labrecque (goalie)	5	0	0	0	0
Greg Louder (goalie)	5	0	0	0	0
Daniel Berthiaume (goalie)	10	0	0	0	0
Marc Lamothe (goalie)	13	0	0	0	0

GOALTENDING

	Games	Min.	W	L	OTL	Goals	SO	Avg.
John Bradley	2	69	0	1	0	3	0	2.62
Geoff Finch	37	2071	26	8	3	104	2	3.01
Marc Lamothe	13	737	9	2	1	38	0	3.10
Mike Parson	2	113	1	1	0	7	0	3.73
Daniel Berthiaume	10	600	6	1	1	41	0	4.10
Greg Louder	5	260	2	1	0	19	0	4.39
Patrick Labrecque	5	281	2	3	0	22	0	4.69

PLAYERS WITH TWO OR MORE TEAMS

SCORING

	Games	G	A	Pts.	PIM
Steve Barnes, Huntington	29	1	9	10	36
Steve Barnes, Toledo	31	3	10	13	18
Totals	60	4	19	23	54
Wade Bartley, Tallahassee	23	0	16	16	31
Wade Bartley, Raleigh	41	6	17	23	47
Totals	64	6	33	39	78
Eric Bellerose, Greensboro	13	4	3	7	32
Eric Bellerose, Erie	44	12	31	43	69
Totals	57	16	34	50	101
Daniel Berthiaume, Whe. (g)	10	0	0	0	0
Daniel Berthiaume, Roa. (g)	21	0	0	0	18
Totals	31	0	0	0	18
John Blessman, Raleigh	31	4	14	18	109
John Blessman, Toledo	16	1	2	3	33
Totals	47	5	16	21	142
Derby Bognar, Richmond	2	1	0	1	0
Derby Bognar, Nashville	34	1	5	6	13
Totals	36	2	5	7	13
Robin Bouchard, Roanoke	10	1	0	1	25
Robin Bouchard, Columbus	46	30	33	63	188
Totals	56	31	33	64	213
John Bradley, Roanoke (g)	3	0	0	0	0
John Bradley, Dayton (g)	4	0	1	1	0
John Bradley, Wheeling (g)	2	0	0	0	0
Totals	9	0	1	1	0
Reginald Brezeault, Roanoke	8	0	1	1	20
Reginald Brezeault, Charlotte	8	1	0	1	48
Totals	16	1	1	2	68

	Games	G	A	Pts.	PIM
Jim Brown, Hampton Roads	49	24	21	45	50
Jim Brown, Knoxville	15	7	5	12	42
Totals	64	31	26	57	92
Wyatt Buckland, Toledo	30	9	9	18	62
Wyatt Buckland, Huntington	6	0	0	0	12
Wyatt Buckland, Columbus	11	3	1	4	51
Totals	47	12	10	22	125
Mike Burman, Knoxville	38	4	11	15	76
Mike Burman, Richmond	24	7	14	21	49
Totals	62	11	25	36	125
Brian Caruso, Greensboro	7	0	0	0	13
Brian Caruso, Erie	12	1	2	3	36
Totals	19	1	2	3	49
Pat Cavanagh, Dayton	27	7	5	12	167
Pat Cavanagh, Nashville	8	2	2	4	50
Totals	35	9	7	16	217
Todd Chin, Erie (g)	13	0	0	0	0
Todd Chin, Huntington (g)	12	0	0	0	0
Totals	25	0	0	0	0
Gord Christian, Johnstown	4	1	2	3	29
Gord Christian, South Carolina	15	1	3	4	17
Gord Christian, Raleigh	8	2	4	6	23
Totals	27	4	9	13	69
Alexander Chunchukov, Ral.	32	7	18	25	30
Alexander Chunchukov, Nash.	29	11	25	36	32
Totals	61	18	43	61	62
Frank Cirone, Huntington	3	0	0	0	2
Frank Cirone, Raleigh	12	1	0	1	2
Totals	15	1	0	1	4
Brandon Coates, Nashville	24	12	3	15	46
Brandon Coates, Greensboro	22	8	6	14	14
Totals	46	20	9	29	60
Jeff Connelly, Wheeling	2	0	0	0	0
Jeff Connelly, Johnstown	4	0	2	2	0
Totals	6	0	2	2	0
Brad Cook, Columbus	3	0	0	0	0
Brad Cook, Erie	7	0	0	0	2
Totals	10	0	0	0	2
Brendan Creagh, Greensboro	21	4	7	11	39
Brendan Creagh, Birmingham	30	3	8	11	42
Totals	51	7	15	22	81
Joe Crowley, Charlotte	24	7	3	10	70
Joe Crowley, Huntington	7	1	2	3	4
Totals	31	8	5	13	74
Jason Currie, Richmond (g)	13	0	1	1	4
Jason Currie, Huntington (g)	6	0	0	0	0
Totals	19	0	1	1	4
Ian DeCorby, Erie	40	5	15	20	30
Ian DeCorby, Huntington	32	0	8	8	26
Totals	72	5	23	28	56
Matt DelGuidice, Charlotte (g)	5	0	0	0	0
Matt DelGuidice, Nashville (g)	18	0	1	1	18
Totals	23	0	1	1	18
Mike Dennis, Dayton	3	0	1	1	15
Mike Dennis, Johnstown	59	5	18	23	86
Totals	62	5	19	24	101
Ted Dent, Johnstown	46	9	24	33	125
Ted Dent, Charlotte	17	3	7	10	40
Totals	63	12	31	43	165
Norm Dezainde, South Carolina	9	0	0	0	6
Norm Dezainde, Toledo	20	6	15	21	47
Totals	29	6	15	21	53
Andrew Dickson, Huntington	2	0	1	1	2
Andrew Dickson, Roanoke	3	0	1	1	2
Andrew Dickson, Columbus	1	0	0	0	0
Totals	6	0	2	2	4
Rob Dumas, Knoxville	22	3	8	11	47
Rob Dumas, Tallahassee	35	8	27	35	68
Totals	57	11	35	46	115
Louis Dumont, Tallahassee	5	1	0	1	4
Louis Dumont, Wheeling	62	25	33	58	81
Totals	67	26	33	59	85
Joel Eagan, Birmingham	12	1	0	1	18
Joel Eagan, Johnstown	3	0	0	0	2
Totals	15	1	0	1	20

	Games	G	A	Pts.	PIM
Trent Eigner, Raleigh	7	1	2	3	10
Trent Eigner, Huntington	59	8	25	33	164
Totals	66	9	27	36	174
Ty Eigner, Huntington	9	0	3	3	7
Ty Eigner, Birmingham	44	0	7	7	20
Totals	53	0	10	10	27
Dominic Fafard, Wheeling	39	2	8	10	44
Dominic Fafard, South Carolina	7	0	1	1	4
Totals	46	2	9	11	48
Anton Federov, Raleigh	21	2	6	8	6
Anton Federov, Johnstown	13	5	6	11	2
Totals	34	7	12	19	8
Carl Fleury, Roanoke	16	1	1	2	35
Carl Fleury, Erie	43	13	15	28	79
Totals	59	14	16	30	114
Steve Foster, Charlotte	21	1	4	5	21
Steve Foster, Johnstown	21	1	6	7	14
Totals	42	2	10	12	35
Chris Foy, Richmond	16	3	5	8	12
Chris Foy, South Carolina	23	4	14	18	27
Totals	39	7	19	26	39
Gordie Frantti, Huntington	34	19	23	42	102
Gordie Frantti, Nashville	23	11	9	20	100
Totals	57	30	32	62	202
Rival Fullum, Toledo	14	7	8	15	20
Rival Fullum, Greensboro	2	0	0	0	0
Totals	16	7	8	15	20
Wade Gibson, Tallahassee	41	3	7	10	129
Wade Gibson, Erie	2	0	0	0	0
Totals	43	3	7	10	129
Roman Gorev, Charlotte	20	10	7	17	2
Roman Gorev, Columbus	40	21	21	42	6
Totals	60	31	28	59	8
Colin Gregor, Hampton Roads	21	3	2	5	48
Colin Gregor, Birmingham	19	8	9	17	12
Totals	40	11	11	22	60
Vern Guetens, Erie (g)	4	0	0	0	0
Vern Guetens, Richmond (g)	2	0	0	0	0
Totals	6	0	0	0	0
Greg Hagen, Tallahassee	39	14	14	28	8
Greg Hagen, Dayton	17	7	6	13	6
Totals	56	21	20	41	14
Todd Harris, Birmingham	37	3	17	20	50
Todd Harris, Erie	27	6	7	13	49
Totals	64	9	24	33	99
Joe Hawley, Charlotte	33	19	22	41	57
Joe Hawley, Roanoke	20	4	2	6	15
Totals	53	23	24	47	72
Ed Henrich, Toledo	32	0	9	9	12
Ed Henrich, Huntington	34	3	3	6	24
Totals	66	3	12	15	36
Craig Herr, Tallahassee	14	1	8	9	10
Craig Herr, Roanoke	48	24	29	53	54
Totals	62	25	37	62	64
Jeff Hoad, Toledo	15	1	5	6	35
Jeff Hoad, Erie	35	13	17	30	112
Totals	50	14	22	36	147
Dean Hulett, Greensboro	4	1	3	4	15
Dean Hulett, Tallahassee	42	10	18	28	160
Dean Hulett, South Carolina	15	8	3	11	34
Totals	61	19	24	43	209
Todd Hunter, Raleigh (g)	21	0	1	1	16
Todd Hunter, H.R. (g)	10	0	0	0	14
Totals	31	0	1	1	30
Trevor Jobe, Nashville	18	16	13	29	40
Trevor Jobe, Raleigh	23	18	22	40	42
Totals	41	34	35	69	82
Marian Kacir, Charlotte	5	2	3	5	2
Marian Kacir, Nashville	9	1	7	8	2
Totals	14	3	10	13	4
Andrei Kozlov, Erie	8	0	1	1	52
Andrei Kozlov, Roanoke	4	0	0	0	6
Totals	12	0	1	1	58
Mike Krygier, Knoxville	23	3	3	6	9
Mike Krygier, Roanoke	17	2	9	11	5
Totals	40	5	12	17	14
Bill Lang, Hampton Roads	11	0	4	4	19
Bill Lang, Columbus	10	2	1	3	7
Totals	21	2	5	7	26
Herve LaPointe, Greensboro	1	0	0	0	2
Herve LaPointe, Erie	58	1	12	13	253
Totals	59	1	12	13	255
Jim Larkin, Birmingham	47	13	20	33	33
Jim Larkin, Huntington	24	6	16	22	18
Totals	71	19	36	55	51
Rob Laurie, Johnstown (g)	26	0	2	2	2
Rob Laurie, Greensboro (g)	10	0	0	0	0
Totals	36	0	2	2	2
Rodrigo Lavinsh, Raleigh	25	2	7	9	30
Rodrigo Lavinsh, Tallahassee	44	3	9	12	36
Totals	69	5	16	21	66
Scott Lindsay, Charlotte	9	2	0	2	13
Scott Lindsay, Raleigh	7	0	0	0	4
Totals	16	2	0	2	17
Scott MacNair, Charlotte	8	0	4	4	4
Scott MacNair, Raleigh	50	15	14	29	28
Totals	58	15	18	33	32
B.J. MacPherson, Greensboro	15	4	7	11	34
B.J. MacPherson, Toledo	54	16	30	46	117
Totals	69	20	37	57	151
Peter Marek, Wheeling	25	3	17	20	37
Peter Marek, Birmingham	23	8	16	24	26
Totals	48	11	33	44	63
Marquis Mathieu, Toledo	33	13	22	35	168
Marquis Mathieu, Raleigh	33	15	17	32	181
Totals	66	28	39	67	349
Brian McCarthy, South Carolina	21	3	5	8	25
Brian McCarthy, Erie	16	0	0	0	7
Brian McCarthy, Johnstown	12	4	4	8	2
Totals	49	7	9	16	34
Darwin McClelland, Columbus	14	2	4	6	17
Darwin McClelland, Roanoke	27	7	7	14	14
Totals	41	9	11	20	31
Pat Meehan, Dayton	10	1	1	2	0
Pat Meehan, Columbus	15	6	4	10	14
Totals	25	7	5	12	14
Jim Mill, Huntington (g)	1	0	0	0	0
Jim Mill, Tallahassee (g)	15	0	0	0	2
Totals	16	0	0	0	2
Chris Morque, Huntington	36	1	9	10	126
Chris Morque, Erie	26	3	8	11	83
Totals	62	4	17	21	209
Cooper Naylor, Raleigh	1	0	0	0	0
Cooper Naylor, Richmond	34	3	18	21	32
Totals	35	3	18	21	32
Mikhail Nemirovsky, Tal.	6	0	2	2	0
Mikhail Nemirovsky, H.R.	29	6	14	20	33
Totals	35	6	16	22	33
Jay Ness, Charlotte	20	7	2	9	10
Jay Ness, Johnstown	38	6	11	17	12
Totals	58	13	13	26	22
Tom Newman, Greensboro (g)	10	0	1	1	0
Tom Newman, Columbus (g)	17	0	1	1	6
Totals	27	0	2	2	6
Darryl Noren, Greensboro	17	7	16	23	43
Darryl Noren, Charlotte	45	39	25	64	63
Totals	62	46	41	87	106
Steve Norton, Charlotte	15	2	3	5	16
Steve Norton, Johnstown	31	4	10	14	12
Totals	46	6	13	19	28
Brad Pascall, South Carolina	28	0	4	4	76
Brad Pascall, Birmingham	38	2	9	11	53
Totals	66	2	13	15	129
Ron Pasco, Greensboro	18	3	8	11	32
Ron Pasco, Tallahassee	36	11	30	41	63
Totals	54	14	38	52	95
Cory Paterson, Wheeling	12	0	4	4	35
Cory Paterson, Tallahassee	14	2	6	8	20
Totals	26	2	10	12	55
Stephan Phillips, Roanoke	2	0	0	0	2
Stephan Phillips, Nashville	34	6	7	13	24
Totals	36	6	7	13	26

	Games	G	A	Pts.	PIM
Vyacheslav Polikarkin, Erie	34	12	22	34	26
Vyacheslav Polikarkin, Gre.	23	7	20	27	6
Totals	57	19	42	61	32
Sean Pronger, Knoxville	34	18	23	41	55
Sean Pronger, Greensboro	2	0	2	2	0
Totals	36	18	25	43	55
Hugo Proulx, South Carolina	10	0	1	1	12
Hugo Proulx, Greensboro	40	18	28	46	116
Totals	50	18	29	47	128
Tony Prpic, Tallahassee	20	5	8	13	71
Tony Prpic, Wheeling	30	11	16	27	64
Totals	50	16	24	40	135
Kevin Quinn, Johnstown	7	0	1	1	36
Kevin Quinn, Columbus	15	1	1	2	66
Totals	22	1	2	3	102
Jarrett Reid, Richmond	1	1	0	1	0
Jarrett Reid, Tallahassee	28	5	16	21	39
Totals	29	6	16	22	39
Todd Reirden, Raleigh	26	2	13	15	33
Todd Reirden, Tallahassee	43	5	25	30	61
Totals	69	7	38	45	94
Jason Richard, Johnstown	4	0	0	0	4
Jason Richard, Erie	6	0	0	0	0
Totals	10	0	0	0	4
Stephen Rohr, Wheeling	2	0	0	0	0
Stephen Rohr, Toledo	4	0	0	0	2
Totals	6	0	0	0	2
Howie Rosenblatt, Charlotte	5	1	1	2	38
Howie Rosenblatt, Greensboro	41	12	24	36	245
Totals	46	13	25	38	283
Rick Rougeau, Columbus	8	3	3	6	2
Rick Rougeau, Erie	6	0	2	2	2
Totals	14	3	5	8	4
Daniel Ruoho, South Carolina	22	7	6	13	25
Daniel Ruoho, Charlotte	28	8	6	14	41
Totals	50	15	12	27	66
Ryan Schmidt, Roanoke	4	0	0	0	0
Ryan Schmidt, Toledo	10	0	2	2	15
Totals	14	0	2	2	15
Sverre Sears, Greensboro	9	0	0	0	14
Sverre Sears, Erie	21	0	8	8	83
Totals	30	0	8	8	97
Chad Seibel, Richmond	12	1	3	4	55
Chad Seibel, Greensboro	17	1	9	10	46
Chad Seibel, Nashville	35	3	10	13	79
Totals	64	5	22	27	180
Trevor Senn, Greensboro	15	3	5	8	141
Trevor Senn, South Carolina	15	2	1	3	139
Trevor Senn, Richmond	9	1	0	1	98
Totals	39	6	6	12	378
Paul Spagnoletti, Nashville (g)	5	0	0	0	0
Paul Spagnoletti, Gre. (g)	1	0	0	0	0
Totals	6	0	0	0	0
Sergei Stas, Erie	35	1	15	16	108
Sergei Stas, Greensboro	21	1	7	8	102
Totals	56	2	22	24	210
Brett Strot, Tallahassee	7	2	6	8	4
Brett Strot, Dayton	4	1	3	4	0
Totals	11	3	9	12	4
Gerry St. Cyr, Erie	11	4	6	10	33
Gerry St. Cyr, Toledo	28	13	33	46	188
Totals	39	17	39	56	221
Brian Sutton, Huntington	2	0	0	0	2
Brian Sutton, Roanoke	3	0	1	1	2
Totals	5	0	1	1	4
Ken Thibodeau, Charlotte	28	10	17	27	30
Ken Thibodeau, Huntington	3	0	1	1	0
Totals	31	10	18	28	30

	Games	G	A	Pts.	PIM
Sergei Tkachenko, S.C. (g)	16	0	0	0	12
Sergei Tkachenko, Bir. (g)	6	0	0	0	0
Totals	22	0	0	0	12
Rouslan Toujikov, Roanoke	39	16	11	27	90
Rouslan Toujikov, Erie	5	2	1	3	8
Totals	44	18	12	30	98
Chris Tschupp, Erie	16	3	3	6	25
Chris Tschupp, Birmingham	27	5	3	8	23
Totals	43	8	6	14	48
Chris Tucker, Richmond	31	7	11	18	41
Chris Tucker, Knoxville	30	11	19	30	8
Totals	61	18	30	48	49
Mike Vandenberghe, Dayton	24	1	9	10	75
Mike Vandenberghe, Richmond	6	1	0	1	32
Mike Vandenberghe, Knox.	30	3	9	12	99
Totals	60	5	18	23	206
Shawn Yakimishyn, Columbus	6	0	1	1	24
Shawn Yakimishyn, Tal.	1	0	0	0	0
Totals	7	0	1	1	24
Oleg Yashin, Roanoke	45	24	26	50	41
Oleg Yashin, Charlotte	20	6	20	26	30
Totals	65	30	46	76	71
Matt Yingst, Johnstown	41	5	5	10	27
Matt Yingst, Columbus	10	0	1	1	4
Totals	51	5	6	11	31
George Zajankala, Knoxville	49	18	24	42	131
George Zajankala, H.R.	6	1	5	6	2
Totals	55	19	29	48	133

GOALTENDING

	Games	Min.	W	L	OTL	Goals	SO	Avg.
D. Berthiaume, Whe.	10	600	6	1	1	41	0	4.10
D. Berthiaume, Roa..	21	1196	15	4	2	47	0	2.36
Totals	31	1796	21	5	3	88	0	2.94
John Bradley, Roa..	3	171	0	2	1	10	0	3.52
John Bradley, Whe.	2	69	0	1	0	3	0	2.62
Totals	9	481	2	4	2	24	1	2.99
Todd Chin, Erie	13	711	1	8	1	65	0	5.48
Todd Chin, Hunt.	12	515	5	5	0	39	0	4.54
Totals	25	1226	6	13	1	104	0	5.09
Jason Currie, Rich..	13	687	5	2	3	42	0	3.67
Jason Currie, Hunt.	6	209	0	3	0	23	0	6.60
Totals	19	896	5	5	3	65	0	4.35
M. DelGuidice, Char.	5	303	2	2	1	15	0	2.97
M. DelGuidice, Nash.	18	1009	7	8	2	81	0	4.82
Totals	23	1312	9	10	3	96	0	4.39
Vern Guetens, Erie..	4	245	1	2	1	20	0	4.90
Vern Guetens, Rich.	2	118	0	2	0	10	0	5.09
Totals	6	363	1	4	1	30	0	4.99
Todd Hunter, Ral.	21	1273	9	9	3	82	0	3.87
Todd Hunter, H.R.	10	498	3	5	1	29	0	3.49
Totals	31	1771	12	14	4	111	0	3.76
Rob Laurie, John.	26	1456	7	16	2	113	0	4.66
Rob Laurie, Gre.	10	514	4	4	1	39	0	4.55
Totals	36	1970	11	20	3	152	0	4.63
Jim Mill, Hunt.	1	46	0	1	0	4	0	5.25
Jim Mill, Tal.	15	689	6	6	0	47	0	4.09
Totals	16	735	6	7	0	51	0	4.16
Tom Newman, Gre..	10	500	1	6	1	36	0	4.32
Tom Newman, Col..	17	759	7	6	0	59	0	4.67
Totals	27	1259	8	12	1	95	0	4.53
P. Spagnoletti, Nash.	5	257	1	2	1	23	0	5.37
P. Spagnoletti, Gre...	1	20	0	0	0	3	0	9.00
Totals	6	277	1	2	1	26	0	5.64
S. Tkachenko, S.C..	16	868	7	7	1	47	0	3.25
S. Tkachenko, Bir...	6	359	2	4	0	25	0	4.17
Totals	22	1228	9	11	1	72	0	3.52

RESULTS

PRELIMINARY ROUND

Series "A"

	W	L	Pts.	GF	GA
Birmingham	3	0	6	20	9
Wheeling	0	3	0	9	20

(Birmingham won series, 3-0)

Series "B"

	W	L	Pts.	GF	GA
Dayton	3	1	6	15	12
Huntington	1	3	2	12	15

(Dayton won series, 3-1)

Series "C"

	W	L	Pts.	GF	GA
South Carolina	3	2	6	25	20
Johnstown	2	3	4	20	25

(South Carolina won series, 3-2)

Series "D"

	W	L	Pts.	GF	GA
Richmond	3	0	6	25	13
Columbus	0	3	0	13	25

(Richmond won series, 3-0)

Series "E"

	W	L	Pts.	GF	GA
Roanoke	3	1	6	16	12
Knoxville	1	3	2	12	16

(Roanoke won series, 3-1)

Series "F"

	W	L	Pts.	GF	GA
Nashville	3	1	6	12	10
Toledo	1	3	2	10	12

(Nashville won series, 3-1)

Series "G"

	W	L	Pts.	GF	GA
Greensboro	3	0	6	12	9
Charlotte	0	3	0	9	12

(Greensboro won series, 3-0)

Series "H"

	W	L	Pts.	GF	GA
Tallahassee	3	1	6	12	10
Hampton Roads	1	3	2	10	12

(Tallahassee won series, 3-1)

QUARTERFINALS

Series "I"

	W	L	Pts.	GF	GA
Richmond	3	1	6	14	7
Roanoke	1	3	2	7	14

(Richmond won series, 3-1)

Series "J"

	W	L	Pts.	GF	GA
Tallahassee	3	1	6	17	15
Birmingham	1	3	2	15	17

(Tallahassee won series, 3-1)

Series "K"

	W	L	Pts.	GF	GA
Greensboro	3	2	6	19	26
Dayton	2	3	4	26	19

(Greensboro won series, 3-2)

Series "L"

	W	L	Pts.	GF	GA
Nashville	3	1	6	18	11
South Carolina	1	3	2	11	18

(Nashville won series, 3-1)

SEMIFINALS

Series "M"

	W	L	Pts.	GF	GA
Richmond	3	2	6	19	15
Tallahassee	2	3	4	15	19

(Richmond won series, 3-2)

Series "N"

	W	L	Pts.	GF	GA
Greensboro	3	2	6	23	25
Nashville	2	3	4	25	23

(Greensboro won series, 3-2)

RILEY CUP FINALS

Series "O"

	W	L	Pts.	GF	GA
Richmond	4	1	8	18	10
Greensboro	1	4	2	10	18

(Richmond won series, 4-1)

INDIVIDUAL LEADERS

Goals: Blaine Moore, Richmond (17)
Assists: Andrew Shier, Richmond (19)
Points: Blaine Moore, Richmond (34)
Penalty minutes: Trevor Senn, Richmond (138)
Goaltending average: Dave Littman, Richmond (2.33)
Shutouts: Dave Littman, Richmond (3)

TOP SCORERS

	Games	G	A	Pts.
Blaine Moore, Richmond	17	17	17	34
Andrew Shier, Richmond	17	8	19	27
Phil Berger, Greensboro	17	6	17	23

	Games	G	A	Pts.
Craig Charron, Dayton	9	9	13	22
Aigar Cipruss, Nashville	13	5	16	21
Hugo Proulx, Greensboro	18	6	14	20
Gordie Frantti, Nashville	13	8	11	19
Greg Geldart, Tallahassee	13	5	14	19
Scott Gruhl, Richmond	17	9	9	18
Francois Leroux, Greensboro	17	8	9	17
Davis Payne, Greensboro	17	7	10	17
Jeremy Stevenson, Greensboro	17	6	11	17
Mike Burman, Richmond	17	4	13	17
Mike Taylor, Richmond	17	3	14	17
Jason Downey, Dayton	9	2	15	17

INDIVIDUAL STATISTICS

BIRMINGHAM BULLS

(Lost quarterfinals to Tallahassee, 3-1)

SCORING

	Games	G	A	Pts.	PIM
Chris Bergeron	7	4	8	12	2
Ian Hebert	7	0	11	11	2
Craig Lutes	7	6	3	9	6
David Craievich	7	4	4	8	10
Peter Marek	7	3	5	8	2
John Joyce	7	1	7	8	14
Brad Smyth	3	5	2	7	0
Jason Dexter	7	3	4	7	2
Colin Gregor	7	2	5	7	8
Olaf Kjenstad	7	4	2	6	8
Rob Donovan	5	1	3	4	12
Jerome Bechard	7	1	3	4	14
Brendan Creagh	7	1	1	2	12
Jon Duval	4	0	2	2	6
Brad Pascall	7	0	2	2	12
Mark Michaud (goalie)	2	0	0	0	0
Ty Eigner	3	0	0	0	0
Sandy Galuppo (goalie)	5	0	0	0	0

GOALTENDING

	Games	Min.	W	L	OTL	Goals	SO	Avg.
Sandy Galuppo	5	306	3	2	0	18	0	3.53
Mark Michaud	2	120	1	1	0	8	0	4.00

CHARLOTTE CHECKERS

(Lost in first round to Greensboro, 3-0)

SCORING

	Games	G	A	Pts.	PIM
Matt Robbins	3	1	6	7	0
Darryl Noren	3	5	1	6	2
Daniel Murphy	3	0	4	4	6
Oleg Yashin	3	0	3	3	2
Sergei Berdnikov	3	0	2	2	0
Kurt Seher	1	1	0	1	0
Travis Tucker	3	1	0	1	6
Shawn Wheeler	3	1	0	1	8
Daniel Ruoho	3	0	1	1	2
Eric Fenton	2	0	0	0	4
Andy Silverman	3	0	0	0	2
Andrei Bashkirov	3	0	0	0	0
Scott Meehan	3	0	0	0	6
Reginald Brezeault	3	0	0	0	4
Ted Dent	3	0	0	0	14
Sylvain Blouin	3	0	0	0	6
Jon Hillebrandt (goalie)	3	0	0	0	4

GOALTENDING

	Games	Min.	W	L	OTL	Goals	SO	Avg.
Jon Hillebrandt	3	179	0	2	1	12	0	4.01

COLUMBUS CHILL

(Lost in first round to Richmond, 3-0)

SCORING

	Games	G	A	Pts.	PIM
Chris Gotziaman	3	4	1	5	15
Derek Clancey	3	3	2	5	6
Lance Brady	3	0	5	5	15
Craig Woodcroft	3	3	1	4	12
Keith Morris	3	1	2	3	2
Robin Bouchard	3	0	3	3	38
Roman Gorev	3	1	1	2	0
Mike Ross	3	1	0	1	5
Jesse Cooper	3	0	1	1	2
Craig Binns	3	0	1	1	4
Brett Abel (goalie)	1	0	0	0	0

	Games	G	A	Pts.	PIM
Pat Meehan	1	0	0	0	15
Tom Newmen (goalie)	2	0	0	0	0
Gerry Skrypec	2	0	0	0	36
Wyatt Buckland	3	0	0	0	2
Brad Treliving	3	0	0	0	14

GOALTENDING

	Games	Min.	W	L	OTL	Goals	SO	Avg.
Brett Abel	1	95	0	0	1	9	0	5.68
Tom Newman	2	120	0	2	0	16	0	8.00

DAYTON BOMBERS

(Lost quarterfinals to Greensboro, 3-2)

SCORING

	Games	G	A	Pts.	PIM
Craig Charron	9	9	13	22	10
Jason Downey	9	2	15	17	57
Greg Hagen	9	6	4	10	4
Steve Lingren	9	2	8	10	16
Kevin Brown	8	5	4	9	2
Jamie Steer	9	4	5	9	16
Dean Fedorchuk	9	5	2	7	6
Pascal Trepanier	9	2	4	6	20
Brandon Smith	4	2	3	5	0
Karson Kaebel	9	0	4	4	28
John Brill	1	2	1	3	0
Jim Lessard	8	1	2	3	9
Sean Gagnon	8	0	3	3	69
Rob Hartnell	7	1	1	2	15
Tony Gruba	9	0	2	2	8
Wade Klippenstein	2	0	1	1	0
Jeff Stolp (goalie)	8	0	1	1	0
Nicolas Turmel	9	0	1	1	2
Paul Taylor (goalie)	2	0	0	0	0

GOALTENDING

	Games	Min.	W	L	OTL	Goals	SO	Avg.
Paul Taylor	2	108	0	0	1	3	0	1.67
Jeff Stolp	8	438	5	3	0	28	1	3.84

GREENSBORO MONARCHS

(Lost finals to Richmond, 4-1)

SCORING

	Games	G	A	Pts.	PIM
Phil Berger	17	6	17	23	46
Hugo Proulx	18	6	14	20	58
Francois Leroux	17	8	9	17	78
Davis Payne	17	7	10	17	38
Jeremy Stevenson	17	6	11	17	64
Artur Kupacs	18	5	10	15	24
Jeff Gabriel	18	7	5	12	10
Sergei Stas	18	2	7	9	38
Vyacheslav Polikarkin	13	6	1	7	12
Glenn Stewart	6	2	5	7	27
Chris Valicevic	18	1	6	7	33
Howie Rosenblatt	14	5	1	6	76
Scott Chartier	18	2	3	5	41
Mark DeSantis	15	0	4	4	71
Doug Evans	18	1	2	3	34
Dean Zayonce	17	0	2	2	54
Mario DuMoulin	3	0	0	0	4
Peter Skudra (goalie)	7	0	0	0	2
Bill Horn (goalie)	13	0	0	0	8

GOALTENDING

	Games	Min.	W	L	OTL	Goals	SO	Avg.
Bill Horn	13	755	8	4	1	48	1	3.82
Peter Skudra	6	342	2	1	1	28	0	4.92

HAMPTON ROADS ADMIRALS

(Lost in first round to Tallahassee, 3-1)

SCORING

	Games	G	A	Pts.	PIM
John Porco	3	4	1	5	0
Brian Goudie	4	0	5	5	45
Rick Kowalsky	4	0	4	4	4
Rod Taylor	4	2	1	3	6
Rob MacInnis	4	0	3	3	12
Mikhail Nemirovsky	4	2	0	2	4
Trevor Halverson	4	1	1	2	2
Tom Menicci	4	1	0	1	0
Ron Majic	3	0	1	1	20
Matt Mallgrave	3	0	1	1	6
Corwin Saurdiff (goalie)	4	0	1	1	0
Chris Phelps	4	0	0	0	10
Brendan Curley	4	0	0	0	0
Tony MacAuley	4	0	0	0	0
Kelly Sorensen	4	0	0	0	6
Jason MacIntyre	4	0	0	0	16

GOALTENDING

	Games	Min.	W	L	OTL	Goals	SO	Avg.
Corwin Saurdiff	4	241	1	2	1	12	0	2.99

HUNTINGTON BLIZZARD

(Lost in first round to Dayton, 3-1)

SCORING

	Games	G	A	Pts.	PIM
Mark Franks	4	3	2	5	2
Jim Bermingham	4	3	1	4	4
Todd Brost	4	1	3	4	2
Jim Larkin	4	1	3	4	6
Kelly Harper	4	2	1	3	2
Mike Stone	4	1	2	3	0
Dan Fournel	3	1	1	2	16
Jared Bednar	2	0	2	2	4
Ian DeCorby	4	0	2	2	2
Mark Woolf	4	0	2	2	8
Ed Henrich	4	0	1	1	2
Ray Edwards	4	0	1	1	6
Trent Eigner	4	0	1	1	12
Derek Schooley	4	0	0	0	13
Jeff Levy (goalie)	4	0	0	0	0

GOALTENDING

	Games	Min.	W	L	OTL	Goals	SO	Avg.
Jeff Levy	4	236	1	3	0	15	0	3.81

JOHNSTOWN CHIEFS

(Lost in first round to South Carolina, 3-2)

SCORING

	Games	G	A	Pts.	PIM
Dennis Purdie	5	5	3	8	12
Justin Duberman	5	0	7	7	20
Matt Hoffman	5	2	4	6	10
Martin D'Orsonnens	5	1	5	6	4
Perry Florio	4	0	6	6	12
Brian McCarthy	5	4	1	5	2
Rod Hinks	5	4	1	5	4
Jay Ness	5	2	2	4	6
Jason Brousseau	5	1	2	3	6
Jason Jennings	5	0	3	3	2
Anton Federov	5	1	1	2	0
Steve Foster	5	0	1	1	2
Mike Dennis	5	0	1	1	28
Rob Leask	1	0	0	0	0
Aaron Israel (goalie)	3	0	0	0	0
Neil Little (goalie)	3	0	0	0	4
Dan Sawyer	5	0	0	0	2

GOALTENDING

	Games	Min.	W	L	OTL	Goals	SO	Avg.
Neil Little	3	145	0	2	0	11	0	4.55
Aaron Israel	3	157	2	1	0	14	0	5.35

KNOXVILLE CHEROKEES

(Lost in first round to Roanoke, 3-1)

SCORING

	Games	G	A	Pts.	PIM
Jim Brown	4	3	2	5	8
David Neilson	4	2	3	5	4
Chris Tucker	4	1	3	4	0
Mike Gaul	4	2	1	3	2
Robb McIntyre	4	2	1	3	14
Mike Murray	4	0	3	3	2
Jon Jenkins	4	1	1	2	0
Carl LeBlanc	4	0	2	2	19
Mike Vandenberghe	4	1	0	1	4
Hayden O'Rear	4	0	1	1	6
Alain Deeks	1	0	0	0	0
Scott Rogers	3	0	0	0	4
Doug Searle	4	0	0	0	15
Chris Fess	4	0	0	0	4
Justin Hocking	4	0	0	0	26
Cory Cadden (goalie)	4	0	0	0	4

GOALTENDING

	Games	Min.	W	L	OTL	Goals	SO	Avg.
Cory Cadden	4	247	1	1	2	16	0	3.89

NASHVILLE KNIGHTS

(Lost semifinals to Greensboro, 3-2)

SCORING

	Games	G	A	Pts.	PIM
Aigar Cipruss	13	5	16	21	6
Gordie Frantti	13	8	11	19	18
Colin Ward	12	11	4	15	10
Derek Eberle	12	5	10	15	20
Alexander Chunchukov	11	4	11	15	4
Chad Seibel	13	4	5	9	22
Tom MacDonald	13	2	7	9	55
Greg Burke	13	3	4	7	50
Tim Sullivan	11	2	5	7	32
Jeff Hill	13	1	6	7	14
Troy Stevens	12	4	1	5	8
Pat Cavanagh	12	2	3	5	94
Dan Carney	13	2	3	5	8
Marian Kacir	4	1	2	3	6
Gary Lebsack	13	0	2	2	68
Marc Tardif	8	1	0	1	30
Matt DelGuidice (goalie)	2	0	1	1	0
Craig Brown (goalie)	13	0	1	1	20
Bob Gohde	2	0	0	0	0

GOALTENDING

	Games	Min.	W	L	OTL	Goals	SO	Avg.
Craig Brown	13	731	8	2	2	37	0	3.04
Matt DelGuidice	2	74	0	1	0	6	0	4.84

RICHMOND RENEGADES

(Winner of Riley Cup playoffs)

SCORING

	Games	G	A	Pts.	PIM
Blaine Moore	17	17	17	34	34
Andrew Shier	17	8	19	27	33
Scott Gruhl	17	9	9	18	68
Mike Burman	17	4	13	17	14
Mike Taylor	17	3	14	17	23
Kurt Mallett	17	6	10	16	4
Shane Henry	17	3	12	15	6
Jan Benda	17	8	5	13	50
Trevor Senn	16	5	8	13	138
Garrett MacDonald	17	4	3	7	62
Sean O'Brien	17	2	5	7	77
Lou Body	17	2	4	6	26
Jay Murphy	6	2	3	5	9
Darrin Wetherill	17	1	2	3	41
Rod Langway	9	1	1	2	4

	Games	G	A	Pts.	PIM
Shawn Snesar	14	1	1	2	39
David Littman (goalie)	17	0	1	1	4
Duane Derksen (goalie)	4	0	0	0	0

GOALTENDING

	Games	Min.	W	L	OTL	Goals	SO	Avg.
Dave Littman	17	953	12	4	0	37	3	2.33
Dwayne Derksen	4	99	1	0	0	6	0	3.62

ROANOKE EXPRESS

(Lost quarterfinals to Richmond, 3-1)

SCORING

	Games	G	A	Pts.	PIM
Ilya Dubkov	8	5	3	8	4
Michael Smith	8	4	2	6	8
Derek Laxdal	8	2	4	6	25
Tony Szabo	8	1	5	6	8
Jeff Jestadt	8	4	1	5	6
Joe Hawley	8	2	3	5	40
Jason Clarke	8	1	4	5	64
Dave Stewart	8	2	1	3	20
Darwin McClelland	8	1	2	3	18
Mike Krygier	8	1	2	3	0
Craig Herr	8	0	2	2	14
Jon Larson	8	0	1	1	19
Mark Luger	8	0	1	1	8
Daniel Berthiaume (goalie)	8	0	1	1	0
Dan Ryder (goalie)	1	0	0	0	0
Stephane Desjardins	7	0	0	0	9
Chris Potter	8	0	0	0	12

GOALTENDING

	Games	Min.	W	L	OTL	Goals	SO	Avg.
Daniel Berthiaume	8	464	4	4	0	23	1	2.97
Dan Ryder	1	20	0	0	0	1	0	3.00

SOUTH CAROLINA STINGRAYS

(Lost quarterfinals to Nashville, 3-1)

SCORING

	Games	G	A	Pts.	PIM
Marty Dallman	6	5	9	14	4
Dean Hulett	9	3	8	11	30
David Cooper	9	3	8	11	24
Scott Boston	9	2	8	10	33
Cam Danyluk	9	5	4	9	76
Gary Socha	9	3	5	8	4
Derek Booth	9	3	4	7	28
James O'Brien	9	3	3	6	6
Mark Bavis	9	2	3	5	28
Yvon Corbin	7	1	4	5	0
Derek Grant	3	1	2	3	4
Brett Marietti	9	2	0	2	16
Mike Bavis	4	1	1	2	8
Vasili Demin	9	1	1	2	2
Chris Foy	9	0	2	2	10
Dominic Fafard	8	1	0	1	6
Steve McClaren	2	0	0	0	19
Steve Shields (goalie)	3	0	0	0	2
Jason Fitzsimmons (goalie)	7	0	0	0	12

GOALTENDING

	Games	Min.	W	L	OTL	Goals	SO	Avg.
Jason Fitzsimmons	7	418	4	2	1	25	0	3.59
Steve Shields	3	144	0	2	0	11	0	4.58

TALLAHASSEE TIGER SHARKS

(Lost semifinals to Richmond, 3-2)

SCORING

	Games	G	A	Pts.	PIM
Greg Geldart	13	5	14	19	6
Don Parsons	13	5	10	15	12

	Games	G	A	Pts.	PIM
Ron Pasco	13	8	6	14	22
Darren Schwartz	13	5	9	14	18
Tom Neziol	13	3	7	10	18
Rob Dumas	13	4	3	7	40
Todd Reirden	13	2	5	7	10
Robert Haddock	13	1	6	7	24
Jon Engfer	13	3	3	6	30
Cory Paterson	13	3	3	6	30
Chris George	13	1	4	5	0
John Uniac	13	2	2	4	6
Mikhail Zdanovsky	13	2	1	3	10
Rodrigo Lavinsh	11	0	3	3	8
Jim Mill (goalie)	2	0	0	0	0
Mark Richards (goalie)	13	0	0	0	4
Matt Osiecki	13	0	0	0	8

GOALTENDING

	Games	Min.	W	L	OTL	Goals	SO	Avg.
Mark Richards	13	760	8	4	1	40	1	3.16
Jim Mill	2	28	0	0	0	2	0	4.32

TOLEDO STORM

(Lost in first round to Nashville, 3-1)

SCORING

	Games	G	A	Pts.	PIM
Rick Judson	4	2	4	6	0
B.J. MacPherson	3	1	3	4	18
Mike Latendresse	4	1	3	4	2
Gerry St. Cyr	4	2	1	3	33
Iain Duncan	4	1	2	3	10
Darren Perkins	4	1	2	3	4
Jim Maher	4	1	1	2	6
Jason Gladney	4	1	1	2	4
Brad Haelzle	3	0	1	1	4
Jay Neal	4	0	1	1	4
Rick Corriveau	2	0	1	1	0
Steve Barnes	4	0	0	0	0
Paul O'Hagen	4	0	0	0	2
John Hendry	4	0	0	0	4
Shawn Penn	4	0	0	0	4
Nick Vitucci (goalie)	4	0	0	0	0

GOALTENDING

	Games	Min.	W	L	OTL	Goals	SO	Avg.
Nick Vitucci	4	239	1	3	0	12	0	3.01

WHEELING THUNDERBIRDS

(Lost in first round to Birmingham, 3-0)

SCORING

	Games	G	A	Pts.	PIM
Scott Matusovich	3	2	1	3	0
Claude Jutras	3	2	1	3	20
Tim Tisdale	3	1	2	3	2
Steve Gibson	3	0	3	3	6
Tim Roberts	3	1	1	2	6
Tony Prpic	3	1	1	2	2
Louis Dumont	3	1	1	2	4
Brent Pope	3	1	1	2	2
Brad Layzell	3	0	1	1	4
Lorne Toews	3	0	1	1	2
Brock Woods	3	0	1	1	20
Dennis Holland	2	0	0	0	0
Kevin O'Sullivan	3	0	0	0	2
Derek DeCosty	3	0	0	0	2
Geoff Finch (goalie)	3	0	0	0	0
Duane Dennis	3	0	0	0	8

GOALTENDING

	Games	Min.	W	L	OTL	Goals	SO	Avg.
Geoff Finch	3	180	0	3	0	20	0	6.69

ALL-STAR TEAMS

First team	Pos.	Second team
Chris Gordon, Huntington	G	Dave Gagnon, Roanoke
Brandon Smith, Dayton	D	Scott Boston, S.C.
Rick Corriveau, Toledo	D	Tim Roberts, Wheeling
Darren Schwartz, Tall.	LW	Rod Taylor, H.R.
John Porco, H.R.	C	Scott Burfoot, Erie
Vadim Slivchenko, Wheel.	RW	Stephane Charbonneau, Erie

Coach of the Year: Jim Playfair, Dayton

TROPHY WINNERS

Most Valuable Player: Vadim Slivchenko, Wheeling
Scoring leader: Scott Burfoot, Erie
Outstanding defenseman: Brandon Smith, Dayton
Outstanding goaltender: Chris Gordon, Huntington
Rookie of the Year: Kevin McKinnon, Erie
Playoff MVP: Blaine Moore, Richmond
Coach of the Year: Jim Playfair, Dayton

ALL-TIME AWARD WINNERS

MOST VALUABLE PLAYER

Season	Player, Team
1988-89	Daryl Harpe, Erie
1989-90	Bill McDougall, Erie
1990-91	Stan Drulia, Knoxville
1991-92	Phil Berger, Greensboro
1992-93	Trevor Jobe, Nashville
1993-94	Joe Flanagan, Birmingham
1994-95	Vadim Slivchenko, Wheeling

TOP SCORER

Season	Player, Team
1988-89	Daryl Harpe, Erie
1989-90	Bill McDougall, Erie
1990-91	Stan Drulia, Knoxville
1991-92	Phil Berger, Greensboro
1992-93	Trevor Jobe, Nashville
1993-94	Phil Berger, Greensboro
1994-95	Scott Burfoot, Erie

ROOKIE OF THE YEAR

Season	Player, Team
1988-89	Tom Sasso, Johnstown
1989-90	Bill McDougall, Erie
1990-91	Dan Gauthier, Knoxville
1991-92	Darren Colbourne, Dayton
1992-93	Joe Flanagan, Birmingham
1993-94	Dan Gravelle, Greensboro
1994-95	Kevin McKinnon, Erie

TOP GOALTENDER

Season	Player, Team
1988-89	Scott Gordon, Johnstown
1989-90	Alain Raymond, Hampton Roads
1990-91	Dean Anderson, Knoxville
1991-92	Frederic Chabot, Winston-Salem
1992-93	Nick Vitucci, Hampton Roads
1993-94	Cory Cadden, Knoxville
1994-95	Chris Gordon, Huntington

PLAYOFF MVP

Season	Player, Team
1988-89	Nick Vitucci, Carolina
1989-90	Wade Flaherty, Greensboro
1990-91	Dave Gagnon, Hampton Roads
	Dave Flanagan, Hampton Roads
1991-92	Mark Bernard, Hampton Roads
1992-93	Rick Judson, Toledo
1993-94	Dave Gagnon, Toledo
1994-95	Blaine Moore, Richmond

COACH OF THE YEAR

Season	Coach, Team
1988-89	Ron Hansis, Erie
1989-90	Dave Allison, Virginia
1990-91	Don Jackson, Knoxville
1991-92	Doug Sauter, Winston-Salem
1992-93	Kurt Kleinendorst, Raleigh
1993-94	Barry Smith, Knoxville
1994-95	Jim Playfair, Dayton

TOP DEFENSEMAN

Season	Player, Team
1988-89	Kelly Szautner, Erie
1989-90	Bill Whitfield, Virginia
1990-91	Brett McDonald, Nashville
1991-92	Scott White, Greensboro
1992-93	Derek Booth, Toledo
1993-94	Tom Nemeth, Dayton
1994-95	Brandon Smith, Dayton

ALL-TIME LEAGUE CHAMPIONS

REGULAR-SEASON CHAMPION

Season	Team	Coach
1988-89	Erie Panthers	Ron Hansis
1989-90	Winston-Salem Thunderbirds	C. McSorley, J. Fraser
1990-91	Knoxville Cherokees	Don Jackson
1991-92	Toledo Storm	Chris McSorley
1992-93	Wheeling Thunderbirds	Doug Sauter
1993-94	Knoxville Cherokees	Barry Smith
1994-95	Wheeling Thunderbirds	Doug Sauter

PLAYOFF CHAMPION

Team	Coach
Carolina Thunderbirds	Brendon Watson
Greensboro Monarchs	Jeff Brubaker
Hampton Roads Admirals	John Brophy
Hampton Roads Admirals	John Brophy
Toledo Storm	Chris McSorley
Toledo Storm	Chris McSorley
Richmond Renegades	Roy Sommer

The ECHL playoff champion is awarded the Bob Payne Trophy.

CENTRAL HOCKEY LEAGUE

TEAMS

FORT WORTH FIRE

General manager
Tom Weisenbach
Head coach
Steve Harrison
Home ice
Fort Worth/Tarrant County
Convention Center
Address
910 Houston Street, Suite 400
Fort Worth, TX 76102
Seating capacity
11,314
Phone
817-336-1992
FAX
817-336-1997

OKLAHOMA CITY BLAZERS

General manager
Brad Lund
Head coach
To be announced
Home ice
Myriad Convention Center
Address
119 N. Robinson, Suite 230
Oklahoma City, OK 73102-9201
Seating capacity
13,479
Phone
405-235-7825
FAX
405-272-9875

TULSA OILERS

General manager
Jeff D. Lund
Head coach
Garry Unger
Home ice
Tulsa Convention Center
Address
4528 S. Sheridan Road, Suite 212
Tulsa, OK 74145
Seating Capacity
7,109
Phone
918-663-5888
FAX
918-663-5977

MEMPHIS RIVERKINGS

General manager
Jim Riggs
Head coach
Herb Boxer
Home ice
Mid-South Coliseum
Address
The Fairgrounds
Memphis, TN 38104
Seating capacity
9,551
Phone
901-278-9009
FAX
901-274-3209

SAN ANTONIO IGUANAS

General manager
Jim Goodman
Head coach
John Torchetti
Home ice
Freeman Coliseum
Address
110 Broadway, Suite 25
San Antonio, TX 78205
Seating Capacity
9,600
Phone
210-227-4449
FAX
210-227-4484

WICHITA THUNDER

General manager
Bill Shuck
Head coach
To be announced
Home ice
Kansas Coliseum
Address
4328 E. Kellogg
Wichita, KS 67218
Seating Capacity
9,826
Phone
316-264-4625
FAX
316-264-3037

1994-95 REGULAR SEASON

FINAL STANDINGS

Team	G	W	L		Pts.	GF	GA
Wichita	66	44	18	(4)	92	320	268
San Antonio	66	37	22	(7)	81	336	281
Tulsa	66	36	24	(6)	78	307	281
Oklahoma City	66	34	23	(9)	77	274	267

Team	G	W	L		Pts.	GF	GA
Fort Worth	66	32	26	(8)	72	314	288
Memphis	66	24	35	(7)	55	259	327
Dallas	66	24	36	(6)	54	266	364

( )—Indicates overtime losses and are worth one point.

INDIVIDUAL LEADERS

Goals: Joe Burton, Oklahoma City (59)
Assists: Brian Shantz, San Antonio (80)
Points: Brian Shantz, San Antonio (119)
Penalty minutes: Rob McCaig, Dallas (380)
Goaltending average: Alan Perry, Oklahoma City (3.54)
Shutouts: Mark Bernard, San Antonio (3)

TOP SCORERS

	Games	G	A	Pts.
Brian Shantz, San Antonio	66	39	80	119
George Dupont, Oklahoma City	65	27	78	105
Bob Berg, Wichita	66	55	46	101

	Games	G	A	Pts.
Paul Jackson, San Antonio	53	51	49	100
Jim McGeough, Dallas	66	50	50	100
Joe Burton, Oklahoma City	66	59	38	97
Bobby Wallwork, Memphis	64	42	50	92
Dave Doucette, Wichita	64	20	70	90
Wayne Anchikoski, Dallas	53	32	50	82
Michael St. Jacques, Oklahoma City	64	48	33	81
John DePourcq, Wichita	59	28	53	81
Dominic Maltais, Fort Worth	66	40	38	78

	Games	G	A	Pts.
Troy Frederick, Fort Worth	66	38	37	75
Mark Karpen, Wichita	49	32	40	72
Sheldon Gorski, San Antonio	57	45	26	71
Ron Handy, Wichita	46	24	45	69
Stu Kulak, San Antonio	65	30	38	68
Taylor Hall, Tulsa	58	29	39	68
Martin Masa, Fort Worth	61	31	35	66
Dale Henry, San Antonio	55	28	36	64
Sylvain Naud, Tulsa	65	28	36	64

INDIVIDUAL STATISTICS

DALLAS FREEZE

SCORING

	Games	G	A	Pts.	PIM
Jim McGeough	66	50	50	100	38
Wayne Anchikoski	53	32	50	82	36
Frank LaScala	41	23	37	60	76
Troy Binnie	58	28	29	57	92
Jamie Adams	65	17	30	47	24
Rob Madia	60	27	19	46	35
Doug Roberts	60	21	25	46	46
Ross Harris	40	14	21	35	15
Jeff Beaudin	65	12	23	35	228
Jim Peters	40	7	28	35	56
Rob McCaig	65	5	23	28	380
Jason Taylor	26	6	12	18	118
Ray Desouza	35	4	13	17	97
Dan Williams	29	2	13	15	100
Don Burke	19	1	12	13	25
Derek Crawford	27	6	4	10	111
Greg MacEachern	35	3	7	10	44
Igor Bonderev	9	1	9	10	12
Andy Stewart	23	0	6	6	79
Ivan Roulette	9	1	3	4	0
Ryan Leschasin	16	3	0	3	9
Joe Mittelsteadt	8	1	1	2	29
Jon Gustafson (goalie)	52	0	2	2	34
Rick Kelly	4	1	0	1	12
Andy Borggard	6	1	0	1	6
Jason Christiansen	2	0	1	1	2
Kurt Walsten	2	0	1	1	2
Jason Heiland	20	0	1	1	25
Darren Naylor	2	0	0	0	4
Mike Sanderson	3	0	0	0	2
Stephen Sangermano	3	0	0	0	0
Joey McTamney	4	0	0	0	0
Rocco Trentadue (goalie)	7	0	0	0	2
James Jensen (goalie)	18	0	0	0	14

GOALTENDING

	Games	Min.	W	L	OTL	Goals	SO	Avg.
Rocco Trentadue	7	335	2	3	0	26	0	4.66
Jon Gustafson	52	2877	22	22	4	232	2	4.84
James Jensen	18	730	0	11	2	95	0	7.81

FORT WORTH FIRE

SCORING

	Games	G	A	Pts.	PIM
Dominic Maltais	66	40	38	78	204
Troy Frederick	66	38	37	75	99
Martin Masa	61	31	35	66	104
Sean Rowe	56	22	40	62	19
Bruce Bell	48	12	50	62	77
Alex Kholomeyev	63	31	29	60	91
Eric Ricard	60	11	45	56	141
Jeff Massey	57	23	29	52	41
Stephen Tepper	35	26	22	48	63
Scott Allen	64	18	25	43	57
Chad Johnson	42	18	23	41	21
Francois Bourdeau	60	7	21	28	119
Igor Bonderev	41	5	19	24	32
Dwight Mullins	45	10	11	21	197

	Games	G	A	Pts.	PIM
Mike McCormick	36	9	10	19	40
Mark Hilton	15	7	10	17	18
Alexei Yegorov	18	4	10	14	15
Andy Stewart	35	2	10	12	73
Steve Dykstra	10	0	2	2	12
Bryan Schoen (goalie)	32	0	1	1	53
Pat McGarry (goalie)	46	0	1	1	14
Jason Heiland	12	0	0	0	25
Darren Srochenski	14	0	0	0	47

GOALTENDING

	Games	Min.	W	L	OTL	Goals	SO	Avg.
Pat McGarry	46	2444	21	16	6	166	1	4.08
Bryan Schoen	32	1503	11	10	2	111	0	4.43

MEMPHIS RIVERKINGS

SCORING

	Games	G	A	Pts.	PIM
Bobby Wallwork	64	42	50	92	66
Brent Fleetwood	66	28	32	60	94
Mark McGinn	66	31	25	56	32
Steve Magnusson	65	17	39	56	119
Jamie Cooke	35	23	22	45	11
Brian Cook	50	13	29	42	50
Layne LeBel	45	13	27	40	12
Francois Gagnon	65	21	17	38	52
Andy Ross	47	18	17	35	55
Mike C. Jackson	52	13	22	35	67
Dan Brown	62	10	24	34	112
Jamie Hearn	57	6	28	34	154
Kyle Haviland	61	7	19	26	215
Nicolas Brousseau	24	5	7	12	40
Dennis Beauchamp	52	2	10	12	45
Doug Stromback	6	5	4	9	6
Scott Kelsey	31	1	5	6	40
Dominic Grand-Maison	20	2	2	4	82
Bill Davidson	11	1	1	2	17
Darren Miciak	31	1	1	2	245
Aaron Ellis (goalie)	11	0	1	1	2
Scott Brower (goalie)	48	0	1	1	2
Lance Carlson (goalie)	1	0	0	0	0
Sean Goldsworthy	2	0	0	0	2
Peter Skudra (goalie)	2	0	0	0	0
Mike Gregorio (goalie)	5	0	0	0	0
Paul Krake (goalie)	5	0	0	0	0

GOALTENDING

	Games	Min.	W	L	OTL	Goals	SO	Avg.
Paul Krake	5	260	4	1	0	19	0	4.38
Scott Brower	47	2695	15	22	6	208	0	4.63
Mike Gregorio	5	259	1	4	0	21	0	4.87
Aaron Ellis	11	629	4	6	1	56	1	5.34
Peter Skudra	2	80	0	1	0	8	0	6.00
Lance Carlson	1	29	0	1	0	5	0	10.25

OKLAHOMA CITY BLAZERS

SCORING

	Games	G	A	Pts.	PIM
George Dupont	65	27	78	105	250
Joe Burton	66	59	38	97	20

	Games	G	A	Pts.	PIM
Michael St. Jacques	64	48	33	81	52
Trent Pankewicz	54	16	32	48	129
Viktor Ignatjev	47	11	35	46	66
Tom Gomes	57	20	22	42	52
Steve Simoni	57	23	18	41	80
Eric Plante	51	17	23	40	34
Tom Thornbury	43	11	29	40	43
Derry Menard	60	11	20	31	78
Chris Laganas	59	9	13	22	177
Tom Frye	40	7	9	16	143
Sean Gorman	62	1	14	15	81
Dave Slifka	62	1	12	13	82
Kevin Meisner	10	2	8	10	11
Jason Disiewich	12	3	6	9	11
Ron Aubrey	16	4	3	7	155
Ken Venis	15	1	4	5	18
Michel Couvrette	10	1	3	4	4
Chris McMurtry	39	1	3	4	43
Craig Geekie	7	0	3	3	2
Joakim Wassberger	4	1	1	2	2
Angelo Karitrotis (goalie)	3	0	0	0	0
Sergei Naumov (goalie)	28	0	0	0	20
Alan Perry (goalie)	44	0	0	0	60

GOALTENDING

	Games	Min.	W	L	OTL	Goals	SO	Avg.
Alan Perry	44	2392	21	13	6	141	2	3.54
Sergei Naumov	28	1467	13	9	3	105	0	4.29
Angelo Karitrotis	3	91	0	1	0	9	0	5.91

SAN ANTONIO IGUANAS

SCORING

	Games	G	A	Pts.	PIM
Brian Shantz	66	39	80	119	125
Paul Jackson	53	51	49	100	251
Sheldon Gorski	57	45	26	71	96
Stu Kulak	65	30	38	68	97
Dale Henry	55	28	36	64	120
Trevor Buchanan	48	30	27	57	268
Dave Shute	53	22	31	53	68
Ken Plaquin	66	7	46	53	74
Fred Goltz	61	25	19	44	150
Brandy Semchuk	29	17	16	33	34
Dean Shmyr	60	3	29	32	225
Ken Venis	49	7	19	26	131
Jeff Winstanley	25	3	14	17	24
Sean Goldsworthy	23	11	6	17	32
Mark Yannetti	48	2	11	13	47
John Blessman	16	2	10	12	13
Scott Kelsey	32	4	7	11	84
John Klaers	13	2	4	6	6
Ron Aubrey	24	3	2	5	163
Stephen Cormat	18	2	3	5	80
Ross Harris	13	2	2	4	16
Bill Peters	1	1	2	3	2
Link Gaetz	13	0	3	3	156
Mark Bernard (goalie)	29	0	2	2	18
Malcom Cameron	4	0	1	1	0
Mike Williams (goalie)	38	0	1	1	35
Chuck Texeira	4	0	0	0	12
Adam Thompson (goalie)	9	0	0	0	0

GOALTENDING

	Games	Min.	W	L	OTL	Goals	SO	Avg.
Mark Bernard	29	1500	16	8	3	93	3	3.72
Mike Williams	38	2000	15	12	4	139	0	4.17
Adam Thompson	9	452	6	2	0	35	0	4.65

TULSA OILERS

SCORING

	Games	G	A	Pts.	PIM
Taylor Hall	58	29	39	68	33
Sylvain Naud	65	28	36	64	112

	Games	G	A	Pts.	PIM
David Moore	66	20	41	61	127
Shaun Clouston	65	25	32	57	95
Luc Beausoleil	41	27	26	53	26
Sasha Lakovic	40	20	24	44	214
Michel Couvrette	40	22	19	41	27
Chuck Loreto	49	18	22	40	16
Colin Baustad	66	12	26	38	27
Mike Sanderson	25	18	14	32	10
Dan O'Rourke	57	12	19	31	180
Jody Praznik	60	8	23	31	40
Mike Berger	46	10	20	30	64
Ryan Harrison	33	13	14	27	39
Doug Lawrence	19	8	15	23	87
Bill Campbell	31	4	18	22	14
Doug Stromback	27	9	10	19	19
Mike Shea	28	4	13	17	45
Chris Robertson	17	6	10	16	24
Craig Coxe	12	7	7	14	28
Andy Ross	17	4	6	10	12
Andy Borggard	4	2	1	3	0
Glen Lang	2	1	1	2	2
Mark Cavallin (goalie)	26	0	2	2	4
Tony Martino (goalie)	42	0	2	2	92
Don Burke	1	0	0	0	6

GOALTENDING

	Games	Min.	W	L	OTL	Goals	SO	Avg.
Tony Martino	42	2482	25	14	3	168	0	4.06
Mark Cavallin	26	1463	11	10	3	100	0	4.10

WICHITA THUNDER

SCORING

	Games	G	A	Pts.	PIM
Bob Berg	66	55	46	101	122
Dave Doucette	64	20	70	90	81
John DePourcq	59	28	53	81	10
Mark Karpen	49	32	40	72	45
Ron Handy	46	24	45	69	72
Brent Sapergia	32	32	26	58	297
John Vary	63	12	38	50	163
Jack Williams	53	16	20	36	58
Jim Latos	55	13	23	36	167
Rob Weingartner	49	20	11	31	274
Conrade Thomas	50	14	17	31	114
Greg Neish	59	12	19	31	337
Tom Roulston	23	11	19	30	8
Brian Wells	25	15	9	24	251
Mark Hilton	50	7	17	24	94
Mike McCormick	16	7	3	10	29
Jim Peters	11	0	5	5	18
Darcy Kaminski	24	1	3	4	38
Darren Srochenski	14	0	2	2	40
Craig Johnson	14	1	0	1	99
Jason Hines	5	0	1	1	2
Greg Smith (goalie)	29	0	1	1	33
George Maneluk (goalie)	44	0	1	1	50
Benoit Larose	1	0	0	0	0
Mike Heaney	4	0	0	0	0
Jason McQuat	7	0	0	0	45

GOALTENDING

	Games	Min.	W	L	OTL	Goals	SO	Avg.
George Maneluk	44	2439	27	10	2	153	2	3.76
Greg Smith	29	1513	17	8	2	103	1	4.08

PLAYERS WITH TWO OR MORE TEAMS

SCORING

	Games	G	A	Pts.	PIM
Ron Aubrey, Oklahoma City	16	4	3	7	155
Ron Aubrey, San Antonio	24	3	2	5	163
Totals	40	7	5	12	318
Igor Bonderev, Dallas	9	1	9	10	12
Igor Bonderev, Fort Worth	41	5	19	24	32
Totals	50	6	28	34	44

	Games	G	A	Pts.	PIM
Andy Borggard, Tulsa	4	2	1	3	0
Andy Borggard, Dallas	6	1	0	1	6
Totals	10	3	1	4	6
Don Burke, Tulsa	1	0	0	0	6
Don Burke, Dallas	19	1	12	13	25
Totals	27	1	15	16	39
Michel Couvrette, Tulsa	40	22	19	41	27
Michel Couvrette, Memphis	3	0	1	1	0
Michel Couvrette, O.C.	10	1	3	4	4
Totals	53	23	23	46	31
Sean Goldsworthy, San Antonio	23	11	6	17	32
Sean Goldsworthy, Memphis	2	0	0	0	2
Totals	25	11	6	17	34
Ross Harris, San Antonio	13	2	2	4	16
Ross Harris, Dallas	40	14	21	35	15
Totals	53	16	23	39	31
Jason Heiland, Dallas	20	0	1	1	25
Jason Heiland, Fort Worth	12	0	0	0	25
Totals	32	0	1	1	50
Mark Hilton, Wichita	50	7	17	24	94
Mark Hilton, Fort Worth	15	7	10	17	18
Totals	65	14	27	41	112
Scott Kelsey, San Antonio	32	4	7	11	84
Scott Kelsey, Memphis	31	1	5	6	40
Totals	63	5	12	17	124

	Games	G	A	Pts.	PIM
Mike McCormick, Fort Worth	36	9	10	19	40
Mike McCormick, Wichita	16	7	3	10	29
Totals	52	16	13	29	69
Jim Peters, Wichita	11	0	5	5	18
Jim Peters, Dallas	40	7	28	35	56
Totals	51	7	33	40	74
Andy Ross, Tulsa	17	4	6	10	12
Andy Ross, Memphis	47	18	17	35	55
Totals	64	22	23	45	67
Mike Sanderson, Dallas	3	0	0	0	2
Mike Sanderson, Tulsa	25	18	14	32	10
Totals	28	18	14	32	12
Darren Srochenski, Fort Worth	14	0	0	0	47
Darren Srochenski, Wichita	14	0	2	2	40
Totals	28	0	2	2	87
Andy Stewart, Fort Worth	35	2	10	12	73
Andy Stewart, Dallas	23	0	6	6	79
Totals	58	2	16	18	152
Doug Stromback, Tulsa	27	9	10	19	19
Doug Stromback, Memphis	6	5	4	9	6
Totals	33	14	14	28	25
Ken Venis, San Antonio	49	7	19	26	131
Ken Venis, Oklahoma City	15	1	4	5	18
Totals	64	8	23	31	149

1995 PLAYOFFS

RESULTS

SEMIFINALS

Series "A"

	W	L	Pts.	GF	GA
Wichita	4	1	8	36	18
Oklahoma City	1	4	2	18	36

(Wichita won series, 4-1)

Series "B"

	W	L	Pts.	GF	GA
San Antonio	4	3	8	35	25
Tulsa	3	4	6	25	35

(San Antonio won series, 4-3)

FINALS

Series "C"

	W	L	Pts.	GF	GA
Wichita	4	2	8	29	27
San Antonio	2	4	4	27	29

(Wichita won series, 4-2)

INDIVIDUAL LEADERS

Goals: Sheldon Gorski, San Antonio (15)
Ron Handy, Wichita (15)
Assists: Bob Berg, Wichita (17)
John Blessman, San Antonio (17)
Points: Ron Handy, Wichita (31)
Penalty minutes: Brent Sapergia, Wichita (117)
Goaltending average: Greg Smith, Wichita (2.30)
Shutouts: None

TOP SCORERS

	Games	G	A	Pts.
Ron Handy, Wichita	11	15	16	31
Sheldon Gorski, San Antonio	13	15	12	27
Brian Shantz, San Antonio	13	10	17	27
Tom Roulston, Wichita	11	13	11	24
Bob Berg, Wichita	11	6	17	23
John Blessman, San Antonio	13	4	17	21
Dave Shute, San Antonio	13	11	5	16
Brent Sapergia, Wichita	9	8	8	16
Dale Henry, San Antonio	13	6	8	14
Dave Doucette, Wichita	11	2	12	14

INDIVIDUAL STATISTICS

OKLAHOMA CITY BLAZERS

(Lost semifinals to Wichita, 4-1)

SCORING

	Games	G	A	Pts.	PIM
Joe Burton	5	3	4	7	4
George Dupont	5	2	4	6	31
Michael St. Jacques	5	2	4	6	0
Kevin Meisner	5	1	5	6	16
Tom Gomes	5	4	0	4	0
Michel Couvrette	5	3	1	4	14
Tom Frye	5	1	1	2	4

	Games	G	A	Pts.	PIM
Sean Gorman	5	1	1	2	8
Chris Laganas	5	1	1	2	14
Eric Plante	3	0	2	2	0
Steve Simoni	5	0	2	2	2
Ken Venis	5	0	2	2	2
Dave Slifka	5	0	1	1	12
Angelo Karitrotis (goalie)	1	0	0	0	0
Sergei Naumov (goalie)	1	0	0	0	0
Alan Perry (goalie)	4	0	0	0	2
Chris McMurtry	5	0	0	0	6

GOALTENDERS

	Games	Min.	W	L	OTL	Goals	SO	Avg.
Alan Perry	4	228	1	3	0	26	0	6.83
Sergei Naumov	1	60	0	1	0	8	0	8.00
Angelo Karitrotis	1	12	0	0	0	2	0	10.42

SAN ANTONIO IGUANAS

(Lost finals to Wichita, 4-3)

SCORING

	Games	G	A	Pts.	PIM
Sheldon Gorski	13	15	12	27	12
Brian Shantz	13	10	17	27	27
John Blessman	13	4	17	21	12
Dave Shute	13	11	5	16	12
Dale Henry	13	6	8	14	25
Paul Jackson	11	7	6	13	52
Jeff Winstanley	13	2	9	11	31
Ken Plaquin	13	1	6	7	20
Stu Kulak	13	3	3	6	36
Brandy Semchuk	13	1	5	6	33
Fred Goltz	13	2	1	3	45
Mark Yannetti	13	0	2	2	14
Mark Bernard (goalie)	13	0	2	2	18
Trevor Buchanan	2	0	1	1	19
Ron Aubrey	6	0	1	1	43
Dean Shmyr	12	0	1	1	30
Mike Williams (goalie)	4	0	0	0	0
Stephan Corfmat	8	0	0	0	2

GOALTENDERS

	Games	Min.	W	L	OTL	Goals	SO	Avg.
Mike Williams	4	144	1	1	0	7	0	2.91
Mark Bernard	13	636	5	4	2	47	0	4.43

TULSA OILERS

(Lost semifinals to San Antonio, 4-3)

SCORING

	Games	G	A	Pts.	PIM
Chris Robertson	7	5	4	9	6
David Moore	5	4	3	7	24
Luc Beausoleil	7	3	2	5	2
Mike Berger	6	2	3	5	54
Mike Sanderson	7	2	3	5	2

	Games	G	A	Pts.	PIM
Taylor Hall	7	2	3	5	17
Sasha Lakovic	5	1	3	4	88
Sylvain Naud	7	0	4	4	17
Shaun Clouston	7	3	0	3	12
Colin Baustad	7	1	2	3	2
Doug Lawrence	7	0	3	3	33
Jody Praznik	4	1	1	2	2
Glen Lang	2	1	0	1	0
Craig Coxe	7	0	1	1	30
Dan O'Rourke	7	0	1	1	53
Bill Campbell	4	0	0	0	2
Tony Martino (goalie)	7	0	0	0	29

GOALTENDERS

	Games	Min.	W	L	OTL	Goals	SO	Avg.
Tony Martino	7	421	3	4	0	31	0	4.41

WICHITA THUNDER

(Winner of 1995 CHL playoffs)

SCORING

	Games	G	A	Pts.	PIM
Ron Handy	11	15	16	31	4
Tom Roulston	11	13	11	24	10
Bob Berg	11	6	17	23	21
Brent Sapergia	9	8	8	16	117
Dave Doucette	11	2	12	14	6
Rob Weingartner	11	4	6	10	30
John Vary	11	3	5	8	16
Mike McCormick	11	3	5	8	9
John DePourcq	6	2	6	8	2
Conrade Thomas	11	2	6	8	16
Craig Johnson	7	2	5	7	14
Jim Latos	11	2	5	7	44
Jack Williams	11	2	3	5	20
Mike Heaney	9	0	4	4	12
Greg Neish	10	1	2	3	59
Darren Srochenski	3	0	0	0	26
Greg Smith (goalie)	5	0	0	0	0
George Maneluk (goalie)	9	0	0	0	2

GOALTENDERS

	Games	Min.	W	L	OTL	Goals	SO	Avg.
Greg Smith	5	183	2	0	0	7	0	2.30
George Maneluk	9	477	6	3	0	37	0	4.65

1994-95 AWARD WINNERS

ALL-STAR TEAMS

First team	Pos.	Second team
Alan Perry, Oklahoma City	G	George Maneluk, Wichita
Dave Doucette, Wichita	D	Bruce Bell, Fort Worth
Eric Ricard, Fort Worth	D	Viktor Ignatjev, Okla. City
Paul Jackson, San Antonio	C	George Dupont, Okla. City
Bob Berg, Wichita	LW	Jim McGeough, Dallas
Joe Burton, Oklahoma City	RW	Bobby Wallwork, Memphis

TROPHY WINNERS

Most Valuable Player: Paul Jackson, San Antonio
Ken McKenzie Trophy: Brian Shantz, San Antonio
John Voss Trophy: Alan Perry, Oklahoma City
Defenseman of the Year: Eric Ricard, Fort Worth
Rookie of the Year: Michel St. Jacques, Oklahoma City
President's Trophy: Ron Handy, Wichita
Commissioner's Trophy: John Torchetti, San Antonio

ALL-TIME AWARD WINNERS

MOST VALUABLE PLAYER

Season	Player, Team
1992-93	Sylvain Fleury, Oklahoma City
1993-94	Robert Desjardins, Wichita
1994-95	Paul Jackson, San Antonio

KEN McKENZIE TROPHY

(Leading Scorer)

Season	Player, Team
1992-93	Sylvain Fleury, Oklahoma City
1993-94	Paul Jackson, Wichita
1994-95	Brian Shantz, San Antonio

JOHN VOSS TROPHY

(Outstanding goaltender)

Season	Player, Team
1992-93	Tony Martino, Tulsa
1993-94	Alan Perry, Oklahoma City
1994-95	Alan Perry, Oklahoma City

DEFENSEMAN OF THE YEAR

Season	Player, Team
1992-93	Dave Doucette, Dallas
1993-94	Guy Girouard, Oklahoma City
1994-95	Eric Ricard, Fort Worth

ROOKIE OF THE YEAR

Season   Player, Team
1992-93 — Robert Desjardins, Wichita
1993-94 — Chad Seibel, Memphis
1994-95 — Michel St. Jacques, Oklahoma City

PRESIDENT'S TROPHY

(Playoff MVP)

Season   Player, Team
1992-93 — Tony Fiore, Tulsa

Season   Player, Team
1993-94 — Ron Handy, Wichita
1994-95 — Ron Handy, Wichita

COMMISSIONER'S TROPHY

(Coach of the year)

Season   Coach, Team
1992-93 — Garry Unger, Tulsa
1993-94 — Doug Shedden, Wichita
1994-95 — John Torchetti, San Antonio

ALL-TIME LEAGUE CHAMPIONS

REGULAR-SEASON CHAMPION

Season	Team	Coach
1992-93	Oklahoma City Blazers	Michael McEwen
1993-94	Wichita Thunder	Doug Shedden
1994-95	Wichita Thunder	Doug Shedden

PLAYOFF CHAMPION

Team	Coach
Tulsa Oilers	Garry Unger
Wichita Thunder	Doug Shedden
Wichita Thunder	Doug Shedden

COLONIAL HOCKEY LEAGUE

LEAGUE OFFICE

Commissioner
Mike Forbes
Director of information
Doug Kennedy
Director of officiating
Bob Myers

Address
34400 Utica Road
Fraser, MI 48026

Phone
810-296-5510/5514
FAX
810-296-5515

TEAMS

BRANTFORD SMOKE

General manager
To be announced
Head coach
To be announced
Home ice
Brantford Civic Centre
Address
69-79 Market Street, South
Brantford, Ontario N3T 5R7
Seating Capacity
3,300
Phone
519-751-9467
FAX
519-751-2366

DETROIT FALCONS

General manager and head coach
Larry Floyd
Home ice
Fraser Ice Arena (Falcon Dome)
Address
34400 Utica Road
Fraser, MI 48026
Seating capacity
2,800
Phone
810-294-2488
FAX
810-294-2358

FLINT GENERALS

General manager and head coach
Robbie Nichols
Home ice
IMA Sports Arena
Address
3501 Lapeer Road
Flint, MI 48503
Seating capacity
4,021
Phone
810-742-9422
FAX
810-742-5892

MADISON MONSTERS

General manager and head coach
Mark Johnson

Home ice
Dane County Exposition Center
Address
1881 Expo Mall East
Madison, WI 53713
Seating capacity
8,500
Phone
608-251-2884
FAX
608-251-2923

MUSKEGON FURY

General manager
Tony Lisman
Head coach
Steve Ludzik
Home ice
L.C. Walker Arena
Address
470 W. Western Avenue
Muskegon, MI 49440
Seating capacity
5,400
Phone
616-726-5058
FAX
616-728-0428

QUAD CITY MALLARDS

General manager
Dan Kable
Head coach
Brad Buetow
Home ice
The MARK of the Quad Cities
Address
P.O. Box 1003
Moline, IL 61266
Seating capacity
9,521
Phone
309-764-7825
FAX
309-764-7858

SAGINAW WHEELS

General manager/head coach
Tom Barrett
Home ice
Wendler Arena

Address
126 N. Franklin, Suite 502
Saginaw, MI 48607
Seating capacity
4,727
Phone
517-752-4200
FAX
517-752-1960

THUNDER BAY SENATORS

President and general manager
Gary Cook
Head coach
Bill MacDonald
Home ice
Fort William Gardens
Address
901 Myles Street E.
Thunder Bay, ONT P7C 1J9
Seating capacity
3,430
Phone
807-623-7121
FAX
807-622-3306

UTICA BLIZZARD

President and general manager
Jeff Croop
Head coach
Ric Seiling
Home ice
Utica Memorial Auditorium
Address
400 Oriskany St. West
Utica, NY 13502
Seating capacity
3,090
Phone
315-793-1111
FAX
315-793-1191

> NOTE: The London team had suspended operations as of deadline. The club may be sold and moved to another city.

FINAL STANDINGS

EAST DIVISION

Team	G	W	L		Pts.	GF	GA
Thunder Bay	74	48	22	(4)	100	341	279
London	74	34	38	(2)	70	341	380
Utica	74	31	38	(5)	67	299	349
Brantford	74	26	36	(12)	64	299	357

( )—Indicates overtime losses and are worth one point.

WEST DIVISION

Team	G	W	L		Pts.	GF	GA
Detroit	74	45	27	(2)	92	329	273
Muskegon	74	42	27	(5)	89	333	286
Saginaw	74	36	31	(7)	79	306	321
Flint	74	34	34	(6)	74	350	353

INDIVIDUAL LEADERS

Goals: Mark Green, Utica (71)
Assists: Paul Polillo, Brantford (99)
Points: Paul Polillo, Brantford (146)
Penalty minutes: Andy Bezeau, Brant.-Musk. (542)
Goaltending average: Maxim Michilosky, Detroit (3.02)
Shutouts: Lance Leslie, Thunder Bay (2)

	Games	G	A	Pts.
Jean Blouin, Thunder Bay	66	70	39	109
Jamie Hicks, Saginaw	71	42	60	102
Terry Menard, Thunder Bay	71	39	60	99
Kent Hawley, London	61	35	59	94
Jason Firth, Thunder Bay	59	29	65	94
Egor Bashkatov, Detroit	69	49	43	92
Wayne Thompson, London	50	43	45	88
Justin Morrison, Muskegon	74	32	54	86
Stanislav Tkach, Detroit	74	39	45	84
Wayne Muir, Brantford	71	38	46	84
Shane MacEachern, Brantford	71	30	52	82
Barry McKinlay, Thunder Bay	65	26	54	80
John Vecciarelli, Saginaw	40	33	46	79
Ted Miskolczi, Brantford	74	37	40	77
Bob McKillop, Detroit	63	32	45	77

TOP SCORERS

	Games	G	A	Pts.
Paul Polillo, Brantford	74	47	99	146
Mark Green, Utica	71	71	56	127
Brett Seguin, Muskegon	74	55	67	122
Kevin Kerr, Flint	62	63	56	119
Brian Sakic, Flint	62	28	85	113
Marc Saumier, Muskegon	69	33	77	110

INDIVIDUAL STATISTICS

BRANTFORD SMOKE

SCORING

	Games	G	A	Pts.	PIM
Paul Polillo	74	47	99	146	48
Wayne Muir	71	38	46	84	222
Shane MacEachern	71	30	52	82	58
Ted Miskolczi	74	37	40	77	34
Derek Gauthier	60	16	26	42	101
Lorne Knauft	29	12	19	31	80
Mike Speer	28	8	21	29	29
Rob Arabski	44	13	14	27	30
Paul Mitton	68	14	12	26	137
Terry Chitaroni	14	9	14	23	27
Brad Barton	65	5	15	20	122
Andy Bezeau	17	8	10	18	185
Glenn Clark	21	7	11	18	8
Sebastien Fortier	25	5	10	15	21
Pete Liptrott	64	3	12	15	90
Rob Peters	26	4	9	13	22
John East	29	1	9	10	59
Wayne MacPhee	46	0	10	10	26
Martin Laitre	28	2	5	7	161
Bruno Villeneuve	10	3	2	5	0
Pat Curcio	10	1	3	4	4
Jason Taylor	13	1	3	4	36
Marc Delorme (goalie)	25	0	4	4	22
Brian Blad	51	1	2	3	62
Trevor Smith	10	0	2	2	12
Luc Carbonneau	2	0	0	0	27
Wayne Marion (goalie)	13	0	0	0	0
Bob DeLorimiere (goalie)	14	0	0	0	0
Mike Risdale (goalie)	14	0	0	0	2
Jamie Organ (goalie)	18	0	0	0	4

GOALTENDING

	Games	Min.	W	L	OTL	Goals	SO	Avg.
Marc Delorme	25	1339	12	8	2	86	1	3.85
Wayne Marion	13	682	4	7	1	51	0	4.48
Bob DeLorimiere	14	702	2	6	3	54	0	4.61
Mike Risdale	14	693	2	6	3	62	0	5.37
Jamie Organ	18	901	3	9	3	84	0	5.59

DETROIT FALCONS

SCORING

	Games	G	A	Pts.	PIM
Egor Bashkatov	69	49	43	92	10
Stanislav Tkach	74	39	45	84	72
Bob McKillop	63	32	45	77	37
Savo Mitrovic	68	23	45	68	38
Jamie Allan	65	24	41	65	239
Chris MacKenzie	50	20	38	58	24
Dan Gravelle	51	23	33	56	54
Mike Jorgensen	74	15	33	48	19
Steve Beadle	73	5	40	45	61
Rick Lacroix	74	11	32	43	56
Garry Gulash	53	10	29	39	239
Kevin Malgunas	39	13	21	34	127
Clark Polglase	34	11	13	24	116
Darren Banks	22	9	10	19	51
Jamie Dabonovich	43	7	11	18	18
Darryl Brunoro	50	12	5	17	115
John Blum	71	1	14	15	98
Alan Schuler	13	2	10	12	12
Ryan Schmidt	19	2	3	5	50
Andrei Kozlov	21	1	4	5	105
Joel Gardner	2	1	2	3	0
Pat Fisher	23	0	3	3	6
Dave Wright	9	0	2	2	2
Sergei Zvyagin (goalie)	32	0	2	2	4
Dan Gardner	2	1	0	1	0
Robbie Nichols	1	0	1	1	0
Wayne Menard	11	0	1	1	24
David Goverde (goalie)	4	0	0	0	0
John Vivian	8	0	0	0	15
Mike Risdale (goalie)	12	0	0	0	0
Maxim Michailovsky (goalie)	29	0	0	0	4

GOALTENDING

	Games	Min.	W	L	OTL	Goals	SO	Avg.
David Goverde	4	240	4	0	0	10	0	2.50
M. Michialovsky	29	1666	20	7	0	84	1	3.02

	Games	Min.	W	L	OTL	Goals	SO	Avg.
Mike Risdale	12	661	7	4	0	43	0	3.90
Sergei Zvyagin	32	1705	12	15	2	124	0	4.36

FLINT GENERALS

SCORING

	Games	G	A	Pts.	PIM
Kevin Kerr	62	63	56	119	284
Brian Sakic	62	28	85	113	22
Jeff Whittle	58	31	44	75	133
Todd Humphrey	61	35	35	70	357
Kyle Reeves	36	38	16	54	133
Fredrik Jax	56	16	34	50	41
Stephan Brochu	60	12	37	49	39
Brett Strot	32	16	28	44	28
Keith Whitmore	45	6	29	35	50
Doug Jones	37	8	23	31	21
Kevin Barrett	71	16	14	30	254
Ken Blum	54	6	23	29	164
Ray Gallagher	33	6	21	27	25
Ken Spangler	55	6	20	26	135
Trevor Smith	28	6	18	24	38
Ken Murchison	31	9	13	22	30
Glen Mears	57	3	10	13	66
Blake Martin	24	5	7	12	8
Bobby Clouston	33	3	9	12	29
Chris O'Rourke	34	3	9	12	134
Mark Turner	10	1	11	12	16
Travis Thiessen	5	0	1	1	2
Rob Rabadenko	7	0	1	1	17
Mark Vichorek	7	0	1	1	10
Ryan Douglas (goalie)	19	0	1	1	0
Dave Boyd	3	0	0	0	4
Jamie Organ (goalie)	7	0	0	0	2
Joe Bonvie (goalie)	8	0	0	0	0
Vern Guetens (goalie)	22	0	0	0	0

GOALTENDING

	Games	Min.	W	L	OTL	Goals	SO	Avg.
Joe Bonvie	8	389	4	2	0	24	0	3.69
Jamie Organ	7	345	3	3	0	23	0	3.99
Vern Guetens	22	1224	8	10	2	89	0	4.36
Ryan Douglas	19	937	7	8	1	83	0	5.31

LONDON WILDCATS

SCORING

	Games	G	A	Pts.	PIM
Kent Hawley	61	35	59	94	54
Wayne Thompson	50	43	45	88	18
Trevor Dam	72	20	46	66	39
Alex Kuzminski	68	24	40	64	14
Wayne Doucet	68	25	36	61	100
Paul Holden	58	17	42	59	38
Tim Bean	54	35	21	56	72
Lou Franceschetti	37	14	41	55	64
Jason Glover	45	13	32	45	48
Donny Jones	37	19	17	36	59
Bernie Johns	46	10	22	32	10
Todd Coopman	69	10	21	31	68
Steve Pepin	30	15	13	28	28
Shane Johnson	43	9	8	17	14
John Batten	9	7	10	17	46
John East	37	4	12	16	34
Marcel Richard	22	7	8	15	2
Mark Matier	37	3	12	15	107
Rob Arabski	19	3	5	8	8
Andrew Plumb	45	1	6	7	20
John Laan	20	2	2	4	28
Jason Taylor	18	1	3	4	165
Shannon Bolton	10	0	4	4	25
Mike Lenarduzzi (goalie)	43	0	4	4	10
C.J. DeNomme (goalie)	28	0	1	1	4
Shawn Wright	1	0	0	0	0
Mark DaSilva (goalie)	2	0	0	0	0
Gary Miller	4	0	0	0	0
Alex Weinrich	8	0	0	0	0

GOALTENDING

	Games	Min.	W	L	OTL	Goals	SO	Avg.
C.J. DeNomme	28	1448	11	12	2	112	0	4.64
Mike Lenarduzzi	43	2198	19	16	0	172	0	4.69
Mark DaSilva	2	40	0	0	0	8	0	11.78

MUSKEGON FURY

SCORING

	Games	G	A	Pts.	PIM
Brett Seguin	74	55	67	122	74
Marc Saumier	69	33	77	110	219
Justin Morrison	74	32	54	86	224
Todd Charlesworth	62	21	49	70	60
Paul Kelly	65	29	40	69	64
Dan Woodley	43	25	26	51	87
Norm Krumpschmid	59	22	27	49	27
Steve Walker	72	20	26	46	42
Jamie Black	56	18	28	46	35
Wes McCauley	63	9	31	40	70
Scott Campbell	51	7	28	35	79
Grant Block	48	10	22	32	27
Andy Bezeau	46	14	17	31	357
Mark Turner	20	7	13	20	48
Scott Feasby	63	4	15	19	75
Brett MacDonald	11	3	8	11	14
Mark Vilneff	71	1	10	11	60
Lorne Knauft	16	2	7	9	48
Gary Coupal	18	4	4	8	100
Cory Johnson	7	1	2	3	2
Darryl Gilmour (goalie)	44	0	3	3	12
Steve Herniman	16	0	2	2	28
Rich Parent (goalie)	35	0	2	2	8
Jodi Murphy	39	1	0	1	178
Steve Wachter (goalie)	1	0	0	0	0

GOALTENDING

	Games	Min.	W	L	OTL	Goals	SO	Avg.
Steve Wachter	1	15	0	0	0	0	0	0.00
Rich Parent	35	1867	17	11	3	112	1	3.60
Darryl Gilmour	44	2567	25	16	2	166	1	3.88

SAGINAW WHEELS

SCORING

	Games	G	A	Pts.	PIM
Jamey Hicks	71	42	60	102	113
John Vecciarelli	40	33	46	79	155
Jim Ritchie	60	30	43	73	90
Jason Stos	72	15	50	65	78
Brett MacDonald	62	17	42	59	42
Niklas Barklund	61	21	24	45	196
Cory Johnson	57	13	29	42	22
Bob Jones	66	11	28	39	88
Richard Borgo	46	22	16	38	182
Scott Smith	72	21	13	34	16
Troy Stephens	37	15	18	33	24
Pat Curcio	30	12	15	27	20
Geoff Simpson	64	9	14	23	41
Dan Woodley	11	11	4	15	18
Lee Giffin	13	5	7	12	13
Mark Donahue	33	3	8	11	16
Shawn Yakimishyn	18	4	6	10	52
John Roderick	51	0	9	9	83
Luc Carbonneau	11	1	4	5	38
Chad Holloway	60	1	2	3	97
Mike Gruttadauria	41	0	3	3	110
Devin Derksen	35	0	2	2	29
Kevin Butt (goalie)	45	0	1	1	19
Ken MacLeod	2	0	0	0	5
Shannon Bolton	5	0	0	0	2
Jodi Murphy	5	0	0	0	29
Alain Roy (goalie)	21	0	0	0	10

GOALTENDING

	Games	Min.	W	L	OTL	Goals	SO	Avg.
Kevin Butt	45	2412	21	15	4	159	1	3.95
Alain Roy	21	1154	9	7	2	76	0	3.95

THUNDER BAY SENATORS

SCORING

	Games	G	A	Pts.	PIM
Jean Blouin	66	70	39	109	60
Terry Menard	71	39	60	99	152
Barry McKinlay	65	26	54	80	100
Chris Rowland	64	30	44	74	255
Todd Howarth	67	27	47	74	168
Mike McCourt	65	13	37	50	33
Steve Parson	62	16	29	45	36
Bruce Ramsay	62	14	29	43	462
Llew NcWana	74	4	36	40	81
Don Osborne	50	4	21	25	20
Alain Cote	74	13	11	24	20
Jake Grimes	15	10	12	22	4
Chris Hynnes	16	6	9	15	10
Darren Perkins	33	2	12	14	61
Mel Angelstad	46	0	8	8	317
Vern Ray	20	1	6	7	20
Jamie Hayden	32	1	5	6	21
Neal Purdon	20	2	2	4	4
Mike O'Leary	13	1	2	3	13
Pat Szturm (goalie)	35	0	3	3	0
Lance Leslie (goalie)	42	0	1	1	4

GOALTENDING

	Games	Min.	W	L	OTL	Goals	SO	Avg.
Lance Leslie	42	2420	29	10	3	130	2	3.22
Pat Szturm	35	1940	17	12	1	137	1	4.24

UTICA BLIZZARD

SCORING

	Games	G	A	Pts.	PIM
Mark Green	71	71	56	127	76
Tim Fingerhut	56	28	30	58	79
Shayne Stevenson	43	17	40	57	37
Don Martin	57	19	30	49	234
Bruno Villeneuve	49	22	25	47	30
Tim Harris	60	15	28	43	92
Mike Steckler	52	13	28	41	52
Mike Tomlinson	52	16	20	36	128
Gary Miller	63	5	25	30	128
Jacques Mailhot	59	11	17	28	302
Bill Wagner	55	5	18	23	44
Trevor Smith	32	7	13	20	26
Sebastien Fortier	33	5	14	19	86
Kyle Reeves	13	12	5	17	28
Ray Gallagher	39	4	13	17	30
Mark Turner	18	6	10	16	28
Richie Walcott	61	6	9	15	285
Rob Peters	43	3	12	15	77
Bill Gall	20	3	11	14	14
Bobby Clouston	27	5	5	10	22
Jamie Hayden	25	1	6	7	12
Todd Dougherty	21	0	7	7	92
Larry Empey	27	0	5	5	29
Stefan Boudrias	17	2	0	2	61
Ted Fauss	5	1	1	2	8
Mikhail Zakharov	4	0	2	2	4
Ryan Schmidt	11	1	0	1	6
Andrew Plumb	8	0	1	1	9
Ron Bertrand (goalie)	11	0	1	1	2
Wayne Marion (goalie)	27	0	1	1	0
Tom Cole (goalie)	36	0	1	1	6
John Batten	1	0	0	0	2
Ric Seiling	1	0	0	0	0
Mike Speer	1	0	0	0	0
Bob Woods	1	0	0	0	0
Brian Beigel	2	0	0	0	2
Bob Delormiere (goalie)	3	0	0	0	0

GOALTENDING

	Games	Min.	W	L	OTL	Goals	SO	Avg.
Wayne Marion	27	1565	12	8	3	110	1	4.22
Tom Cole	36	1992	13	20	2	144	0	4.34

	Games	Min.	W	L	OTL	Goals	SO	Avg.
Ron Bertrand	11	636	5	5	0	48	0	4.53
Bob Delormiere	3	123	0	2	0	21	0	10.17

PLAYERS WITH TWO OR MORE TEAMS

SCORING

	Games	G	A	Pts.	PIM
Rob Arabski, London	19	3	5	8	8
Rob Arabski, Brantford	44	13	14	27	30
Totals	63	16	19	35	38
John Batten, Utica	1	0	0	0	2
John Batten, London	9	7	10	17	46
Totals	10	7	10	17	48
Andy Bezeau, Brantford	17	8	10	18	185
Andy Bezeau, Muskegon	46	14	17	31	357
Totals	63	22	27	49	542
Shannon Bolton, London	10	0	4	4	25
Shannon Bolton, Saginaw	5	0	0	0	2
Totals	15	0	4	4	27
Luc Carbonneau, Brantford	2	0	0	0	27
Luc Carbonneau, Saginaw	11	1	4	5	38
Totals	13	1	4	5	65
Bobby Clouston, Utica	27	5	5	10	22
Bobby Clouston, Flint	33	3	9	12	29
Totals	60	8	14	22	51
Pat Curcio, Saginaw	30	12	15	27	20
Pat Curcio, Brantford	10	1	3	4	4
Totals	40	13	18	31	24
John East, Brantford	29	1	9	10	59
John East, London	37	4	12	16	34
Totals	66	5	21	26	93
Sebastien Fortier, Utica	33	5	14	19	86
Sebastien Fortier, Brantford	25	5	10	15	21
Totals	58	10	24	34	107
Ray Gallagher, Flint	33	6	21	27	25
Ray Gallagher, Utica	39	4	13	17	30
Totals	72	10	34	44	55
Jamie Hayden, Thunder Bay	32	1	5	6	21
Jamie Hayden, Utica	25	1	6	7	12
Totals	57	2	11	13	33
Cory Johnson, Saginaw	57	13	29	42	22
Cory Johnson, Muskegon	7	1	2	3	2
Totals	64	14	31	45	24
Lorne Knauft, Muskegon	16	2	7	9	48
Lorne Knauft, Brantford	29	12	19	31	80
Totals	45	14	26	40	128
Brett MacDonald, Saginaw	62	17	42	59	42
Brett MacDonald, Muskegon	11	3	8	11	14
Totals	73	20	50	70	56
Wayne Marion, Utica (g)	27	0	1	1	0
Wayne Marion, Brantford (g)	13	0	0	0	0
Totals	40	0	1	1	0
Gary Miller, London	4	0	0	0	0
Gary Miller, Utica	63	5	25	30	128
Totals	67	5	25	30	128
Jodi Murphy, Muskegon	39	1	0	1	178
Jodi Murphy, Saginaw	5	0	0	0	29
Totals	44	1	0	1	207
Jamie Organ, Brantford (g)	18	0	0	0	4
Jamie Organ, Flint (g)	7	0	0	0	2
Totals	25	0	0	0	6
Rob Peters, Utica	43	3	12	15	77
Rob Peters, Brantford	26	4	9	13	22
Totals	69	7	21	28	99
Andrew Plumb, Utica	8	0	1	1	9
Andrew Plumb, London	45	1	6	7	20
Totals	53	1	7	8	29
Kyle Reeves, Flint	36	38	16	54	133
Kyle Reeves, Utica	13	12	5	17	28
Totals	49	50	21	71	161
Mike Risdale, Brantford (g)	14	0	0	0	2
Mike Risdale, Detroit (g)	12	0	0	0	0
Totals	26	0	0	0	2
Ryan Schmidt, Utica	11	1	0	1	6
Ryan Schmidt, Detroit	19	2	3	5	50
Totals	30	3	3	6	56

	Games	G	A	Pts.	PIM
Trevor Smith, Utica	32	7	13	20	26
Trevor Smith, Flint	28	6	18	24	38
Trevor Smith, Brantford	10	0	2	2	12
Totals	70	13	33	46	76
Mike Speer, Brantford	28	8	21	29	29
Mike Speer, Utica	1	0	0	0	0
Totals	29	8	21	29	29
Jason Taylor, Brantford	13	1	3	4	36
Jason Taylor, London	18	1	3	4	165
Totals	31	2	6	8	201
Mark Turner, Muskegon	20	7	13	20	48
Mark Turner, Utica	18	6	10	16	28
Mark Turner, Flint	10	1	11	12	16
Totals	48	14	34	48	92
Bruno Villeneuve, Brantford	10	3	2	5	0
Bruno Villeneuve, Utica	49	22	25	47	30
Totals	59	25	27	52	30

	Games	G	A	Pts.	PIM
Dan Woodley, Muskegon	43	25	26	51	87
Dan Woodley, Saginaw	11	11	4	15	18
Totals	54	36	30	66	105

GOALTENDING

	Games	Min.	W	L	OTL	Goals	SO	Avg.
W. Marion, Utica	27	1565	12	8	3	110	1	4.22
W. Marion, Brandon	13	682	4	7	1	51	0	4.48
Totals	40	2247	16	15	4	161	1	4.30
J. Organ, Brandon	18	901	3	9	3	84	0	5.59
J. Organ, Flint	7	345	3	3	0	23	0	3.99
Totals	25	1246	6	12	3	107	0	5.15
M. Risdale, Brandon	14	693	2	6	3	62	0	5.37
M. Risdale, Detroit	12	661	7	4	0	43	0	3.90
Totals	26	1354	9	10	3	105	0	4.65

1995 COLONIAL CUP PLAYOFFS

RESULTS

PRELIMINARY ROUND

Series "A"

	W	L	Pts.	GF	GA
Detroit	4	2	8	16	15
Utica	2	4	4	15	16

(Detroit won series, 4-2)

Series "B"

	W	L	Pts.	GF	GA
Muskegon	4	1	8	24	22
London	1	4	2	22	24

(Muskegon won series, 4-1)

Series "C"

	W	L	Pts.	GF	GA
Saginaw	4	2	8	27	23
Flint	2	4	4	23	27

(Saginaw won series, 4-2)

SEMIFINALS

Series "D"

	W	L	Pts.	GF	GA
Thunder Bay	4	1	8	36	21
Saginaw	1	4	2	21	36

(Thunder Bay won series, 4-1)

Series "E"

	W	L	Pts.	GF	GA
Muskegon	4	2	8	31	21
Detroit	2	4	4	21	31

(Muskegon won series, 4-2)

FINALS

Series "F"

	W	L	Pts.	GF	GA
Thunder Bay	4	2	8	25	17
Muskegon	2	4	4	17	25

(Thunder Bay won series, 4-2)

INDIVIDUAL LEADERS

Goals: Jean Blouin, Thunder Bay (16)
Assists: Jason Firth, Thunder Bay (22)
Points: Brett Seguin, Muskegon (33)
Penalty minutes: Gary Coupal, Muskegon (95)
Goaltending average: Tom Cole, Utica (2.66)
Shutouts: Tom Cole, Utica (1)
Lance Leslie, Thunder Bay (1)
Rich Parent, Muskegon (1)

TOP SCORERS

	Games	G	A	Pts.
Brett Seguin, Muskegon	17	13	20	33
Jason Firth, Thunder Bay	11	6	22	28
Jean Blouin, Thunder Bay	11	16	11	27
John Vecchiarelli, Saginaw	11	8	13	21
Justin Morrison, Muskegon	15	4	15	19
Barry McKinlay, Thunder Bay	11	4	13	17
Richard Borgo, Saginaw	11	9	7	16
Andy Bezeau, Muskegon	17	9	7	16
Jamey Hicks, Saginaw	11	8	8	16
Todd Howarth, Thunder Bay	11	8	8	16
Steve Walker, Muskegon	17	7	9	16

INDIVIDUAL STATISTICS

DETROIT FALCONS

(Lost semifinals to Muskegon, 4-2)

SCORING

	Games	G	A	Pts.	PIM
Dan Gravelle	12	6	9	15	16
Savo Mitrovic	12	5	5	10	21
Rick Lacroix	12	2	7	9	14
Bob McKillop	9	6	2	8	4
Darren Banks	12	3	5	8	59

	Games	G	A	Pts.	PIM
Egor Bashkatov	12	2	6	8	2
Steve Beadle	12	1	7	8	4
Clark Polglase	12	1	6	7	4
Chris MacKenzie	7	2	4	6	6
Mike Jorgensen	12	2	3	5	19
Garry Gulash	7	1	3	4	56
Joel Gardner	12	3	0	3	8
Jamie Allan	7	2	0	2	20
Alan Schuler	6	1	1	2	6

	Games	G	A	Pts.	PIM
Stanislav Tkach	12	0	2	2	6
John Blum	12	0	2	2	20
Jamie Dabonovich	5	0	0	0	2
Mike Risdale (goalie)	6	0	0	0	0
Sergei Zvyagin (goalie)	8	0	0	0	2

GOALTENDING

	Games	Min.	W	L	OTL	Goals	SO	Avg.
Sergei Zvyagin	8	407	4	3	0	22	0	3.24
Mike Risdale	6	317	2	3	0	24	0	4.53

FLINT GENERALS

(Lost preliminary round to Saginaw, 4-2)

SCORING

	Games	G	A	Pts.	PIM
Stephan Brochu	6	0	9	9	8
Kevin Kerr	4	6	1	7	2
Brett Strot	6	4	3	7	6
Fredrik Jax	6	2	5	7	2
Brian Sakic	6	1	5	6	0
Todd Humphrey	6	1	5	6	40
Keith Whitmore	6	2	2	4	8
Mark Turner	6	2	2	4	33
Jeff Whittle	6	2	2	4	15
Doug Jones	6	2	0	2	6
Mark Vichorek	6	0	2	2	4
Ken Blum	5	1	0	1	10
Chris O'Rourke	6	0	1	1	25
Ken Spangler	6	0	1	1	20
Ken Murchison	6	0	1	1	21
Vern Guetens (goalie)	3	0	0	0	2
Glen Mears	3	0	0	0	2
Joe Bonvie (goalie)	4	0	0	0	2
Kevin Barrett	6	0	0	0	27

GOALTENDING

	Games	Min.	W	L	OTL	Goals	SO	Avg.
Joe Bonvie	4	218	1	2	1	13	0	3.57
Vern Guetens	3	141	1	1	0	13	0	5.52

LONDON WILDCATS

(Lost preliminary round to Chatham, 4-1)

SCORING

	Games	G	A	Pts.	PIM
Paul Holden	5	1	8	9	4
Wayne Doucet	5	4	3	7	18
Marcel Richard	5	4	3	7	0
Steve Pepin	5	4	2	6	14
Wayne Thompson	3	3	3	6	0
Alex Kuzminski	5	2	3	5	2
John Batten	5	1	4	5	26
Lou Franceschetti	5	0	5	5	16
Bernie Johns	5	1	1	2	2
Trevor Dam	5	1	1	2	0
Tim Bean	4	1	0	1	4
Andrew Plumb	5	0	1	1	8
John East	5	0	1	1	4
Todd Coopman	1	0	0	0	0
C.J. DeNomme (goalie)	1	0	0	0	0
Jason Glover	3	0	0	0	10
Mark Matier	5	0	0	0	10
Mike Lenarduzzi (goalie)	5	0	0	0	0

GOALTENDING

	Games	Min.	W	L	OTL	Goals	SO	Avg.
Mike Lenarduzzi	5	274	1	2	1	20	0	4.37
C.J. DeNomme	1	27	0	1	0	3	0	6.44

MUSKEGON FURY

(Lost finals to Thunder Bay, 4-2)

SCORING

	Games	G	A	Pts.	PIM
Brett Seguin	17	13	20	33	10
Justin Morrison	15	4	15	19	32

	Games	G	A	Pts.	PIM
Andy Bezeau	17	9	7	16	88
Steve Walker	17	7	9	16	6
Grant Block	17	8	7	15	12
Jamie Black	12	3	12	15	6
Todd Charlesworth	17	1	14	15	12
Wes McCauley	13	7	7	14	4
Marc Saumier	17	5	6	11	71
Scott Campbell	16	2	8	10	58
Norm Krumpschmid	17	4	4	8	8
Paul Kelly	17	2	6	8	6
Brett MacDonald	16	2	5	7	12
Cory Johnson	17	4	1	5	19
Mark Vilneff	14	1	3	4	6
Scott Feasby	17	0	4	4	40
Rich Parent (goalie)	13	0	1	1	4
Brad Guzda (goalie)	1	0	0	0	0
Darryl Gilmour (goalie)	5	0	0	0	0
Gary Coupal	12	0	0	0	95

GOALTENDING

	Games	Min.	W	L	OTL	Goals	SO	Avg.
Darryl Gilmour	5	263	3	2	0	15	0	3.42
Rich Parent	13	725	7	3	1	47	1	3.89
Brad Guzda	1	46	0	1	0	5	0	6.51

SAGINAW WHEELS

(Lost semifinals to Thunder Bay, 4-1)

SCORING

	Games	G	A	Pts.	PIM
John Vecciarelli	11	8	13	21	22
Richard Borgo	11	9	7	16	10
Jamey Hicks	11	8	8	16	16
Lee Giffin	10	2	13	15	24
Troy Stephens	11	4	8	12	12
Shawn Yakimishyn	11	5	3	8	55
Jim Ritchie	11	3	4	7	27
Jason Stos	11	1	6	7	14
Mark Donahue	9	3	3	6	15
Bob Jones	4	1	4	5	8
Geoff Simpson	4	2	2	4	0
Dan Woodley	2	1	1	2	24
Niklas Barklund	11	1	0	1	16
Scott Smith	9	0	1	1	6
Dennis Maxwell	10	0	1	1	36
John Roderick	10	0	1	1	30
Kevin Butt (goalie)	10	0	1	1	12
Scott Humphrey (goalie)	1	0	0	0	0
Alain Roy (goalie)	3	0	0	0	2
Jodi Murphy	9	0	0	0	15
Chad Holloway	11	0	0	0	43

GOALTENDING

	Games	Min.	W	L	OTL	Goals	SO	Avg.
Kevin Butt	10	542	5	3	0	39	0	4.31
Scott Humphrey	1	6	0	0	0	1	0	8.85
Alain Roy	3	110	0	3	0	18	0	9.82

THUNDER BAY SENATORS

(Winner of 1995 Colonial Hockey League playoffs)

SCORING

	Games	G	A	Pts.	PIM
Jason Firth	11	6	22	28	8
Jean Blouin	11	16	11	27	38
Barry McKinlay	11	4	13	17	4
Todd Howarth	11	8	8	16	45
Chris Rowland	11	7	7	14	34
Terry Menard	11	6	7	13	16
Brian Downey	11	5	7	12	2
Llew NcWana	10	3	6	9	17
Mike McCourt	11	3	5	8	6
Chris Hynnes	8	1	4	5	10
Don Osborne	11	1	4	5	6
Alain Cote	11	1	4	5	4
Mel Angelstad	7	0	3	3	62

	Games	G	A	Pts.	PIM
Bruce Ramsay	11	0	3	3	83
Lance Leslie (goalie)	10	0	1	1	0
Pat Szturm (goalie)	2	0	0	0	0
Darren Perkins	4	0	0	0	4
Vern Ray	11	0	0	0	14

GOALTENDING

	Games	Min.	W	L	OTL	Goals	SO	Avg.
Pat Szturm	2	80	1	0	0	2	0	1.50
Lance Leslie	10	587	7	2	1	35	1	3.58

UTICA BLIZZARD

(Lost preliminary round to Detroit, 4-2)

SCORING

	Games	G	A	Pts.	PIM
Mark Green	6	5	2	7	8
Tim Fingerhut	6	1	4	5	4

	Games	G	A	Pts.	PIM
Tim Harris	6	2	2	4	16
Kyle Reeves	6	2	2	4	12
Don Martin	6	1	3	4	44
Shayne Stevenson	6	0	3	3	14
Mike Steckler	6	2	0	2	4
Bruno Villeneuve	6	2	0	2	2
Mike Tomlinson	6	0	2	2	16
Bill Gall	6	0	2	2	8
Ray Gallagher	4	0	1	1	10
Gary Miller	6	0	1	1	32
Larry Empey	6	0	1	1	6
Jamie Hayden	6	0	1	1	6
Bill Wagner	6	0	1	1	14
Richie Walcott	6	0	0	0	16
Tom Cole (goalie)	6	0	0	0	0

GOALTENDING

	Games	Min.	W	L	OTL	Goals	SO	Avg.
Tom Cole	6	361	2	3	1	16	1	2.66

1994-95 AWARD WINNERS

ALL-STAR TEAMS

First team	Pos.	Second team
Lance Leslie, Thunder Bay	G	Maxim Mikhailovsky, Det.
Todd Charlesworth, Musk.	D	Paul Holden, London
Barry McKinlay, T.B.	D	Jason Stos, Saginaw
Jim Ritchie, Saginaw	LW	Egor Bashkatov, Detroit
Paul Polillo, Brantford	C	Brett Seguin, Muskegon
John Blouin, Thunder Bay	RW	Kevin Kerr, Flint

Coach of the Year: Steve Ludzik, Muskegon

TROPHY WINNERS

Most Valuable Player: Mark Green, Utica
Paul Polillo, Brantford
Scoring leader: Paul Polillo, Brantford
Outstanding defenseman: Barry McKinlay, Thunder Bay
Outstanding defensive forward: Terry Menard, Thunder Bay
Rookie of the Year: Lance Leslie, Thunder Bay
Most sportsmanlike player of the year: Paul Polillo, Brantford
Playoff MVP: Lance Leslie, Thunder Bay
Coach of the Year: Steve Ludzik, Muskegon

ALL-TIME AWARD WINNERS

MOST VALUABLE PLAYER

Season	Player, Team
1991-92	Terry McCutcheon, Brantford
1992-93	Jason Firth, Thunder Bay
1993-94	Kevin Kerr, Flint
1994-95	Mark Green, Utica
	Paul Polillo, Brantford

SCORING LEADER

Season	Player, Team
1991-92	Tom Sasso, Flint
1992-93	Len Soccio, St. Thomas
1993-94	Paul Polillo, Brantford
1994-95	Paul Polillo, Brantford

ROOKIE OF THE YEAR

Season	Player, Team
1991-92	Kevin Butt, St. Thomas
1992-93	Jason Firth, Thunder Bay
1993-94	Jean-Francois Labbe, Thunder Bay
1994-95	Lance Leslie, Thunder Bay

DEFENSEMAN OF THE YEAR

Season	Player, Team
1991-92	Tom Searle, Brantford
1992-93	Tom Searle, Brantford
1993-94	Barry McKinlay, Thunder Bay
1994-95	Barry McKinlay, Thunder Bay

BEST DEFENSIVE FORWARD

Season	Player, Team
1991-92	Tim Bean, St. Thomas
1992-93	Todd Howarth, Thunder Bay
1993-94	Jamie Hicks, Brantford
1994-95	Terry Menard, Thunder Bay

MOST SPORTSMANLIKE PLAYER

Season	Player, Team
1991-92	Tom Sasso, Flint
1992-93	Paul Polillo, Brantford
1993-94	Paul Polillo, Brantford
1994-95	Paul Polillo, Brantford

PLAYOFF MVP

Season	Player, Team
1991-92	Gary Callaghan, Thunder Bay
1992-93	Roland Melanson, Brantford
1993-94	Jean-Francois Labbe, Thunder Bay
1994-95	Lance Leslie, Thunder Bay

COACH OF THE YEAR

Season	Coach, Team
1991-92	Peter Horachek, St. Thomas
1992-93	Bill McDonald, Thunder Bay
1993-94	Tom Barrett, Chatham
1994-95	Steve Ludzik, Muskegon

ALL-TIME LEAGUE CHAMPIONS

	REGULAR-SEASON CHAMPION		PLAYOFF CHAMPION	
Season	Team	Coach	Team	Coach
1991-92	Michigan Falcons	Terry Christensen	Thunder Bay Thunder Hawks	Bill MacDonald
1992-93	Brantford Smoke	Ken Mann & Ken Gratton	Brantford Smoke	Ken Gratton
1993-94	Thunder Bay Senators	Bill MacDonald	Thunder Bay Senators	Bill MacDonald
1994-95	Thunder Bay Senators	Bill MacDonald	Thunder Bay Senators	Bill MacDonald

MAJOR JUNIOR LEAGUES

Canadian Hockey League

Ontario Hockey League

Quebec Major Junior Hockey League

Western Hockey League

CANADIAN HOCKEY LEAGUE

The Canadian Hockey League is an alliance of the three Major Junior leagues—Ontario Hockey League, Quebec Major Junior Hockey League and Western Hockey League. After the regular season, the three leagues compete in a round-robin tournament to decide the Memorial Cup championship. Originally awarded to the national Junior champion, the Memorial Cup later signified Junior A supremacy (after Junior hockey in Canada was divided into "A" and "B" classes). Beginning in 1971, when Junior A hockey was split into Major Junior and Tier II Junior A, the Memorial Cup was awarded to the Major Junior champion.

LEAGUE OFFICE

Address
305 Milner Ave.
Scarborough, Ont. M1B 3V4
Phone
416-298-3523
FAX
416-298-3187
President
Ed Chynoweth

Vice presidents
David E. Branch
Gilles Courteau
Director of information
Jim Price
Directors
Rick Gay
Marcel Robert
Rick Brodsky

Director of officiating
Richard Doerksen
Member leagues
Ontario Hockey League
Quebec Major Junior Hockey League
Western Hockey League

1995 MEMORIAL CUP

FINAL STANDINGS

Team (League)	W	L	Pts.	GF	GA
Kamloops (WHL)	4	0	8	23	11
Detroit (OHL)	3	2	6	17	19
Brandon (WHL)	1	3	2	17	14
Hull (QMJHL)	0	3	0	5	18

RESULTS

SATURDAY, MAY 13
Brandon 9, Hull 2

SUNDAY, MAY 14
Detroit 4, Brandon 3
Kamloops 4, Hull 1

TUESDAY, MAY 16
Kamloops 5, Detroit 4

WEDNESDAY, MAY 17
Detroit 5, Hull 2

THURSDAY, MAY 18
Kamloops 6, Brandon 4

SATURDAY, MAY 20
Detroit 2, Brandon 1

SUNDAY, MAY 21
Kamloops 8, Detroit 2

TOP TOURNAMENT SCORERS

	Games	G	A	Pts.
Shane Doan, Kamloops	4	4	5	*9
Sean Haggerty, Detroit	5	*5	2	7
Bryan McCabe, Brandon	4	3	4	7
Ryan Huska, Kamloops	4	2	5	7
Jarome Iginla, Kamloops	4	4	2	6
Tyson Nash, Kamloops	4	2	4	6
Darcy Tucker, Kamloops	4	2	4	6
Bill McCauley, Detroit	5	2	4	6
Nolan Baumgartner, Kamloops	4	0	*6	6
Bob Maudie, Kamloops	4	2	2	4

*Indicates tournament leader.

1994-95 AWARD WINNERS

ALL-STAR TEAMS

First team	Pos.	Second team
Martin Biron, Beauport	G	Paxton Schafer, M.H.
Nolan Baumgartner, Kam.	D	Wade Redden, Brandon
Bryan Berard, Detroit	D	Ed Jovanovski, Windsor
Ryan Smyth, Moose Jaw	LW	Curtis Brown, Moose Jaw
Daymond Langkow, T.C.	C	Jeff O'Neill, Guelph
David Ling, Kingston	RW	Darren Ritchie, Brandon

Coach of the Year: Craig Hartsburg, Guelph

TROPHY WINNERS

Player of the year: David Ling, Kingston
Plus/minus award: Darren Ritchie, Brandon
Rookie of the year: Bryan Berard, Detroit
Defenseman of the year: Nolan Baumgartner, Kamloops
Goaltender of the year: Martin Biron, Beauport
Scholastic player of the year: Perry Johnson, Regina
Coach of the year: Craig Hartsburg, Guelph
Executive of the year: Kelly McCrimmon, Brandon
Most sportsmanlike player of the year: Eric Daze, Beauport
Top draft prospect award: Bryan Berard, Detroit
Humanitarian award: David-Alexandre Beauregard, St. Hyacinthe

ALL-TIME MEMORIAL CUP WINNERS

Season	Team	Season	Team	Season	Team
1918-19	Univ. of Toronto Schools	1944-45	Toronto St. Michael's	1970-71	Quebec Remparts
1919-20	Toronto Canoe Club	1945-46	Winnipeg Monarchs	1971-72	Cornwall Royals
1920-21	Winnipeg Falcons	1946-47	Toronto St. Michael's	1972-73	Toronto Marlboros
1921-22	Fort William War Veterans	1947-48	Port Arthur W. End Bruins	1973-74	Regina Pats
1922-23	Univ. of Manitoba-Winnipeg	1948-49	Montreal Royals	1974-75	Toronto Marlboros
1923-24	Owen Sound Greys	1949-50	Montreal Jr. Canadiens	1975-76	Hamilton Fincups
1924-25	Regina Pats	1950-51	Barrie Flyers	1976-77	New Westminster Bruins
1925-26	Calgary Canadians	1951-52	Guelph Biltmores	1977-78	New Westminster Bruins
1926-27	Owen Sound Greys	1952-53	Barrie Flyers	1978-79	Peterborough Petes
1927-28	Regina Monarchs	1953-54	St. Catharines Tee Pees	1979-80	Cornwall Royals
1928-29	Toronto Marlboros	1954-55	Toronto Marlboros	1980-81	Cornwall Royals
1929-30	Regina Pats	1955-56	Toronto Marlboros	1981-82	Kitchener Rangers
1930-31	Winnipeg Elmwoods	1956-57	Flin Flon Bombers	1982-83	Portland Winter Hawks
1931-32	Sudbury Wolves	1957-58	Ottawa-Hull Jr. Canadiens	1983-84	Ottawa 67's
1932-33	Newmarket	1958-59	Winnipeg Braves	1984-85	Prince Albert Raiders
1933-34	Toronto St. Michael's	1959-60	St. Catharines Tee Pees	1985-86	Guelph Platers
1934-35	Winnipeg Monarchs	1960-61	Tor. St. Michael's Majors	1986-87	Medicine Hat Tigers
1935-36	West Toronto Redmen	1961-62	Hamilton Red Wings	1987-88	Medicine Hat Tigers
1936-37	Winnipeg Monarchs	1962-63	Edmonton Oil Kings	1988-89	Swift Current Broncos
1937-38	St. Boniface Seals	1963-64	Toronto Marlboros	1989-90	Oshawa Generals
1938-39	Oshawa Generals	1964-65	Niagara Falls Flyers	1990-91	Spokane Chiefs
1939-40	Oshawa Generals	1965-66	Edmonton Oil Kings	1991-92	Kamloops Blazers
1940-41	Winnipeg Rangers	1966-67	Toronto Marlboros	1992-93	Sault Ste. Marie Greyhounds
1941-42	Portage la Prairie	1967-68	Niagara Falls Flyers	1993-94	Kamloops Blazers
1942-43	Winnipeg Rangers	1968-69	Montreal Jr. Canadiens	1994-95	Kamloops Blazers
1943-44	Oshawa Generals	1969-70	Montreal Jr. Canadiens		

ALL-TIME AWARD WINNERS

PLAYER OF THE YEAR AWARD

Season	Player, Team
1974-75	Ed Staniowski, Regina
1975-76	Peter Lee, Ottawa
1976-77	Dale McCourt, Ste. Catharines
1977-78	Bobby Smith, Ottawa
1978-79	Pierre LaCroix, Trois-Rivieres
1979-80	Doug Wickenheiser, Regina
1980-81	Dale Hawerchuk, Cornwall
1981-82	Dave Simpson, London
1982-83	Pat LaFontaine, Verdun
1983-84	Mario Lemieux, Laval
1984-85	Dan Hodgson, Prince Albert
1985-86	Luc Robitaille, Hull
1986-87	Rob Brown, Kamloops
1987-88	Joe Sakic, Swift Current
1988-89	Bryan Fogarty, Niagara Falls
1989-90	Mike Ricci, Peterborough
1990-91	Eric Lindros, Oshawa
1991-92	Charles Poulin, St. Hyacinthe
1992-93	Pat Peake, Detroit
1993-94	Jason Allison, London
1994-95	David Ling, Kingston

Season	Player, Team
1989-90	Petr Nedved, Seattle
1990-91	Philippe Boucher, Granby
1991-92	Alexandre Daigle, Victoriaville
1992-93	Jeff Freisen, Regina
1993-94	Vitali Yachmenev, North Bay
1994-95	Bryan Berard, Detroit

DEFENSEMAN OF THE YEAR AWARD

Season	Player, Team
1987-88	Greg Hawgood, Kamloops
1988-89	Bryan Fogarty, Niagara Falls
1989-90	John Slaney, Cornwall
1990-91	Patrice Brisebois, Drummondville
1991-92	Drake Berehowsky, North Bay
1992-93	Chris Pronger, Peterborough
1993-94	Steve Gosselin, Chicoutimi
1994-95	Nolan Baumgartner, Kamloops

PLUS/MINUS AWARD

Season	Player, Team
1986-87	Rob Brown, Kamloops
1987-88	Marc Saumier, Hull
1988-89	Bryan Fogarty, Niagara Falls
1989-90	Len Barrie, Kamloops
1990-91	Eric Lindros, Oshawa
1991-92	Dean McAmmond, Prince Albert
1992-93	Chris Pronger, Peterborough
1993-94	Mark Wotton, Saskatoon
1994-95	Darren Ritchie, Brandon

GOALTENDER OF THE YEAR AWARD

Season	Player, Team
1987-88	Stephane Beauregard, St. Jean
1988-89	Stephane Fiset, Victoriaville
1989-90	Trevor Kidd, Brandon
1990-91	Felix Potvin, Chicoutimi
1991-92	Corey Hirsch, Kamloops
1992-93	Jocelyn Thibault, Sherbrooke
1993-94	Norm Maracle, Saskatoon
1994-95	Martin Biron, Beauport

ROOKIE OF THE YEAR AWARD

Season	Player, Team
1987-88	Martin Gelinas, Hull
1988-89	Yanic Perreault, Trois-Rivieres

SCHOLASTIC PLAYER OF THE YEAR AWARD

Season	Player, Team
1987-88	Darrin Shannon, Windsor
1988-89	Jeff Nelson, Prince Albert
1989-90	Jeff Nelson, Prince Albert
1990-91	Scott Niedermayer, Kamloops
1991-92	Nathan LaFayette, Cornwall
1992-93	David Trofimenkoff, Lethbridge
1993-94	Patrick Boileau, Laval
1994-95	Perry Johnson, Regina

COACH OF THE YEAR AWARD

Season	Coach, Team
1987-88	Alain Vigneault, Hull
1988-89	Joe McDonnell, Kitchener
1989-90	Ken Hitchcock, Kamloops
1990-91	Joe Canale, Chicoutimi
1991-92	Bryan Maxwell, Spokane
1992-93	Marcel Comeau, Tacoma
1993-94	Bert Templeton, North Bay
1994-95	Craig Hartsburg, Guelph

EXECUTIVE OF THE YEAR AWARD

Season	Executive, Team or League
1988-89	John Horman, QMJHL
1989-90	Russ Farwell, Seattle
1990-91	Sherwood Bassin, Sault Ste. Marie
1991-92	Bert Templeton, North Bay
1992-93	Jim Rutherford, Detroit
1993-94	Bob Brown, Kamloops
1994-95	Kelly McCrimmon, Brandon

MOST SPORTSMANLIKE PLAYER OF THE YEAR AWARD

Season	Player, Team
1989-90	Andrew McKim, Hull
1990-91	Pat Falloon, Spokane
1991-92	Martin Gendron, St. Hyacinthe
1992-93	Rick Girard, Swift Current
1993-94	Yanick Dube, Laval
1994-95	Eric Daze, Beauport

TOP DRAFT PROSPECT AWARD

Season	Player, Team
1990-91	Eric Lindros, Oshawa
1991-92	Todd Warriner, Windsor
1992-93	Alexandre Daigle, Victoriaville
1993-94	Jeff O'Neill, Guelph
1994-95	Bryan Berard, Detroit

HUMANITARIAN AWARD

Season	Player, Team
1992-93	Keli Corpse, Kingston
1993-94	Stephane Roy, Val-d'Or
1994-95	David-Alexandre Beauregard, St. Hyacinthe

ONTARIO HOCKEY LEAGUE

LEAGUE OFFICE

Commissioner
David E. Branch
Chairman of the board
Rick Gay
Director of administration
Herb Morell
Dir. of hockey operations/referee in chief
Ted Baker

Director of central scouting
Jack Ferguson
Address
305 Milner Avenue
Suite 208
Scarborough, Ontario M1B 3V4

Phone
416-299-8700
FAX
416-299-8787

1994-95 REGULAR SEASON

FINAL STANDINGS

EAST DIVISION

Team	G	W	L	T	Pts.	GF	GA
Kingston	66	40	19	7	87	284	224
Oshawa	66	40	21	5	85	300	242
North Bay	66	35	27	4	74	272	247
Belleville	66	32	31	3	67	295	287
Peterborough	66	26	34	6	58	255	286
Ottawa	66	22	38	6	50	232	276

CENTRAL DIVISION

Team	G	W	L	T	Pts.	GF	GA
Guelph	66	47	14	5	99	330	200
Sudbury	66	43	17	6	92	314	208
Owen Sound	66	22	38	6	50	239	299
Niagara Falls	66	18	40	8	44	231	298
Kitchener	66	18	42	6	42	216	296

WEST DIVISION

Team	G	W	L	T	Pts.	GF	GA
Detroit	66	44	18	4	92	306	223
Windsor	66	41	22	3	85	303	232
Sarnia	66	24	37	5	53	250	292
London	66	18	44	4	40	210	309
Sault Ste. Marie	66	17	45	4	38	228	346

INDIVIDUAL LEADERS

Goals: David Ling, Kingston (61)
Assists: Bill Bowler, Windsor (102)
Points: Marc Savard, Oshawa (139)
Penalty minutes: Adam Young, Windsor (262)
Goaltending average: Mark McArthur, Guelph (2.81)
Shutouts: Travis Scott, Windsor (3)

	Games	G	A	Pts.
Dave Roche, Windsor	66	55	59	114
Steve Washburn, Ottawa	63	43	63	106
Vitali Yachmenev, North Bay	59	53	52	105
Lee Jinman, North Bay	63	39	65	104
Bill McCauley, Detroit	66	41	61	102
Zdenek Nedved, Sudbury	59	47	51	98
Jamie Langenbrunner, Pet.	62	42	56	98
Ethan Moreau, Sudbury	62	38	58	96
Wayne Primeau, Owen Sound	66	34	62	96
Chad Kilger, Kingston	65	42	53	95
David Gilmore, London	61	34	56	90
Barrie Moore, Sudbury	60	47	42	89
Sean Haggerty, Detroit	61	40	49	89
Steve Potvin, Niagara Falls	60	32	57	89

TOP SCORERS

	Games	G	A	Pts.
Marc Savard, Oshawa	66	43	96	139
David Ling, Kingston	62	61	74	135
Bill Bowler, Windsor	61	33	102	135
Jeff O'Neill, Guelph	57	43	81	124
Darryl Lafrance, Oshawa	57	55	67	122
Todd Bertuzzi, Guelph	62	54	65	119

INDIVIDUAL STATISTICS

BELLEVILLE BULLS

SCORING

	Games	G	A	Pts.	PIM
Brian Secord	57	29	53	82	76
Daniel Cleary	62	26	55	81	62
Craig Mills	62	39	41	80	104
Richard Park	45	28	51	79	35
Joe Coombs	66	36	42	78	53
Paul Andrea	60	46	23	69	29
Dan Preston	62	10	44	54	65
Marc Dupuis	66	5	40	45	24
Radim Bicanek	49	13	26	39	61
Corey Isen	37	7	27	34	78

	Games	G	A	Pts.	PIM
Steve Carter	56	6	19	25	88
Jamie Sokolsky	63	4	18	22	28
Jeff Ambrosio	47	10	10	20	10
Doug Doull	29	7	12	19	71
Sean Brown	58	2	16	18	200
Andrew Clark	17	7	6	13	22
Steve Tracze	26	5	7	12	10
Rob Boyko	29	4	4	8	12
Larry Paleczny	66	4	4	8	10
Paul Dillon	37	1	6	7	24
Scott DeWolfe	39	2	4	6	29
Todd St. Louis	53	2	2	4	139
Ryan Appel	17	1	1	2	37

	Games	G	A	Pts.	PIM
Adam Robbins	31	1	1	2	15
Kory Cooper (goalie)	35	0	2	2	0
Mark Gowan (goalie)	39	0	2	2	2
Ryan Connolly	1	0	0	0	0
Dan Reja	2	0	0	0	0
Bill Laird	3	0	0	0	0
Kevin Barszcz	5	0	0	0	4
Aaron Ellis (goalie)	7	0	0	0	9

GOALTENDING

	Games	Min.	W	L	T	Goals	SO	Avg.
Kory Cooper	35	1731	15	12	1	115	1	3.99
Mark Gowan	39	1896	16	16	1	134	0	4.24
Aaron Ellis	7	372	1	3	1	35	0	5.65

DETROIT JR. RED WINGS

SCORING

	Games	G	A	Pts.	PIM
Bill McCauley	66	41	61	102	43
Sean Haggerty	61	40	49	89	37
Matt Ball	64	35	44	79	84
Bryan Berard	58	20	55	75	97
Tom Buckley	64	30	36	66	49
Jeff Mitchell	61	30	30	60	121
Dan Pawlaczyk	58	24	28	52	30
Duane Harmer	64	10	33	43	104
Milan Kostolny	51	13	25	38	40
Scott Blair	66	12	24	36	85
Mike Rucinski	64	9	18	27	61
Shayne McCosh	26	4	21	25	32
Mike Morrone	47	4	21	25	129
Todd Harvey	11	8	14	22	12
Eric Manlow	16	4	16	20	11
Jamie Allison	50	1	14	15	119
Gerry Lanigan	39	6	6	12	9
Quade Lightbody	64	1	10	11	128
Dylan Seca	42	4	6	10	56
Murray Sheehan	42	2	5	7	33
Jeremy Meehan	35	4	2	6	26
Jason Saal (goalie)	51	0	6	6	16
Ryan MacDonald	51	1	4	5	75
Andrew Taylor	18	2	2	4	11
Nic Beaudoin	11	1	3	4	16
Robin LaCour	32	0	3	3	24
Brad Cook	1	0	0	0	0
Chris Wilcox (goalie)	1	0	0	0	0
Don Ashley	2	0	0	0	0
Craig Pederson	2	0	0	0	0
Aaron Ellis (goalie)	4	0	0	0	0
Scott Smith	7	0	0	0	0
Darryl Foster (goalie)	18	0	0	0	6

GOALTENDING

	Games	Min.	W	L	T	Goals	SO	Avg.
Jason Saal	51	2887	32	13	3	153	1	3.18
Darryl Foster	18	888	10	4	1	50	0	3.38
Aaron Ellis	4	154	2	0	0	10	0	3.90
Chris Wilcox	1	60	0	1	0	6	0	6.00

GUELPH STORM

SCORING

	Games	G	A	Pts.	PIM
Jeff O'Neill	57	43	81	124	56
Todd Bertuzzi	62	54	65	119	58
Jamie Wright	65	43	39	82	36
Todd Norman	64	30	43	73	40
Dwayne Hay	65	26	28	54	37
Jeff Williams	52	15	32	47	21
Brian Wesenberg	66	17	27	44	81
Mike Rusk	64	9	31	40	51
Jason Jackman	60	14	21	35	16
Ryan Risidore	65	2	30	32	102
Rumun Ndur	63	10	21	31	187
Neil Fewster	28	3	25	28	30

	Games	G	A	Pts.	PIM
Regan Stocco	60	5	22	27	70
Mike Pittman	64	10	15	25	27
Andrew Clark	22	10	13	23	32
Pat Barton	24	9	14	23	34
Stephane Soulliere	22	10	8	18	48
Jeff Cowan	51	10	7	17	14
David Lylyk	36	5	5	10	25
Chris Hajt	57	1	7	8	35
Andrew Long	36	1	6	7	9
Bryan McKinney	39	1	6	7	42
Eric Landry	13	1	4	5	20
Joel Cort	29	1	3	4	20
Andy Adams (goalie)	22	0	1	1	7
Brett Thompson (goalie)	1	0	0	0	0
Derek Conn	2	0	0	0	0
Ryan O'Neill	2	0	0	0	0
Victor Reuta	4	0	0	0	2
Tom Johnson	14	0	0	0	0
Mark McArthur (goalie)	48	0	0	0	16

GOALTENDING

	Games	Min.	W	L	T	Goals	SO	Avg.
Brett Thompson	1	6	0	0	0	0	0	0.00
Mark McArthur	48	2776	34	8	4	130	1	2.81
Andy Adams	22	1207	13	6	1	68	1	3.38

KINGSTON FRONTENACS

SCORING

	Games	G	A	Pts.	PIM
David Ling	62	61	74	135	136
Chad Kilger	65	42	53	95	95
Mike Ware	64	25	41	66	98
Gord Walsh	61	27	37	64	43
Keli Corpse	25	12	41	53	6
Brett Lindros	26	24	23	47	63
Duncan Fader	59	21	23	44	93
Jeff DaCosta	58	6	36	42	43
Jason Disher	57	4	32	36	110
Brian Scott	38	5	24	29	15
Cail MacLean	65	11	17	28	17
Wes Swinson	20	7	20	27	16
Alexander Zhurik	54	3	21	24	51
Jason Sands	59	5	16	21	30
Marc Moro	64	4	12	16	255
Rob Mailloux	53	5	9	14	23
Ken Boone	46	4	9	13	73
Bill Maranduik	60	4	7	11	56
Colin Chaulk	51	2	9	11	42
Rob Schweyer	19	3	6	9	10
Chris Allen	43	3	5	8	15
Greg Kraemer	33	3	4	7	27
Bob Thornton	26	2	3	5	12
Jason Morgan	20	0	3	3	14
Tyler Moss (goalie)	57	0	3	3	12
Dave Bourque	42	1	1	2	37
Dan Beck	4	0	1	1	2
Eric Rylands	9	0	0	0	25
Tim Keyes (goalie)	16	0	0	0	0

GOALTENDING

	Games	Min.	W	L	T	Goals	SO	Avg.
Tyler Moss	57	3249	33	17	5	164	1	3.03
Tim Keyes	16	750	7	2	2	56	0	4.48

KITCHENER RANGERS

SCORING

	Games	G	A	Pts.	PIM
Trevor Gallant	43	23	36	59	17
Eric Manlow	44	25	29	54	26
Wes Swinson	42	12	38	50	71
Rob DeCiantis	63	19	24	43	26
Ryan Pepperall	62	17	16	33	86
Greg McLean	63	9	24	33	158

	Games	G	A	Pts.	PIM
Tim Spitzig	41	15	17	32	62
Chris Pittman	61	15	14	29	38
Bill McGuigan	37	7	20	27	112
Chris Brassard	24	6	14	20	12
Jason Hughes	60	2	18	20	176
Jim Ensom	21	10	8	18	9
Ryan Pawluk	19	8	10	18	10
Travis Riggin	60	7	11	18	26
Jason Morgan	35	3	15	18	25
Dan Godbout	56	3	11	14	85
Sergei Olympiev	25	4	9	13	27
Brian Scott	20	6	6	12	10
Lucas Miller	50	6	5	11	18
Paul Traynor	50	3	8	11	25
Keith Welsh	40	4	6	10	12
Rick Emmett	16	0	10	10	4
Andrew Taylor	42	4	5	9	65
Jason Byrnes	50	3	5	8	44
Rob Maric	58	1	6	7	10
Jason Gladney	2	1	5	6	6
Matt O'Dette	10	1	2	3	29
Luch Nasato	18	1	2	3	62
Robin LaCour	21	0	3	3	20
Paul Doyle	4	0	1	1	5
Dylan Seca	13	0	1	1	21
Garrett Burnett	22	0	1	1	74
James Boyd	1	0	0	0	0
Brian Jones	1	0	0	0	0
Chad Turner	2	0	0	0	4
Peter Brearley	3	0	0	0	5
Darryl Whyte (goalie)	25	0	0	0	0
David Belitski (goalie)	54	0	0	0	11

GOALTENDING

	Games	Min.	W	L	T	Goals	SO	Avg.
David Belitski	54	2888	12	34	4	210	1	4.36
Darryl Whyte	25	1111	6	8	2	82	0	4.43

LONDON KNIGHTS

SCORING

	Games	G	A	Pts.	PIM
David Gilmore	61	34	56	90	73
Chris Zanutto	66	7	39	46	99
Peter Brearley	59	24	21	45	52
Don Margettie	65	19	23	42	116
Ryan Burgoyne	64	17	24	41	69
Jason Allison	15	15	21	36	43
Rob Frid	51	16	16	32	216
Brian Stacey	36	8	18	26	47
Justin Steinbach	64	12	12	24	34
Kevin Slota	56	6	16	22	90
Stefan Bergkvist	64	3	17	20	93
Corey Isen	21	8	11	19	55
Dan Reja	18	6	13	19	31
Jason Doyle	45	4	10	14	7
Jason Brooks	28	6	7	13	42
Ben Walker	60	5	7	12	25
Troy Brownell	64	5	7	12	11
Roy Gray	60	1	10	11	190
Kevin Boyd	65	5	5	10	125
Jason Payne	20	4	1	5	45
Joel Dezainde	53	0	4	4	60
Ian Keiller	31	3	0	3	150
Andrew Power	9	1	2	3	4
Larry McMorran	5	1	1	2	0
Bob Graham	24	0	2	2	13
Ryan Appel	9	0	1	1	23
Chris Brassard	2	0	0	0	0
Cam Law	2	0	0	0	0
Joel Mercer	2	0	0	0	0
Matt St. Amand	2	0	0	0	12
Brandon Stubbington	19	0	0	0	21
Kevin Roach	22	0	0	0	34
Eoin McInerney (goalie)	28	0	0	0	12
Jordan Willis (goalie)	53	0	0	0	27

GOALTENDING

	Games	Min.	W	L	T	Goals	SO	Avg.
Jordan Willis	53	2824	16	29	3	202	0	4.29
Eoin McInerney	28	1171	2	15	1	101	0	5.18

NIAGARA FALLS THUNDER

SCORING

	Games	G	A	Pts.	PIM
Steve Potvin	60	32	57	89	95
Andrew Williamson	61	31	43	74	25
Jeff Johnstone	66	36	35	71	30
Ethan Moreau	39	25	41	66	69
Steve Nimigon	48	22	25	47	82
Jason Bonsignore	26	12	21	33	51
Victor Reuta	53	15	17	32	57
Jason Reesor	65	7	24	31	54
Matthew Mayo	51	10	18	28	19
Neil Fewster	37	6	19	25	48
Geoff Peters	57	11	9	20	37
Jay McKee	26	3	13	16	60
Corey Bricknell	38	2	14	16	124
Jeff Paul	57	3	10	13	64
Mike Perna	63	2	11	13	186
Yianni Ioannou	65	2	10	12	114
Mike VanVolsen	59	1	11	12	31
Chester Gallant	26	3	5	8	70
Rich Vrataric	61	1	5	6	48
Anatoli Filatov	12	2	3	5	6
Mark Cadotte	56	2	3	5	60
Chris Haskett	51	2	1	3	27
Derek Sylvester	10	1	2	3	12
Trent Walford	8	0	3	3	5
Ron Paleczny	31	0	2	2	14
Stephen Douglas	32	0	2	2	15
Lucas Miller	4	0	1	1	0
Jeff Salajko (goalie)	45	0	1	1	12
Simon Alary	1	0	0	0	0
Dustin McArthur	1	0	0	0	0
Chris Stevenson	2	0	0	0	0
Ryan Middleton	3	0	0	0	2
Pat Paone	3	0	0	0	2
Steve Guiney	4	0	0	0	0
Matt Kiereck	4	0	0	0	7
Darryl Foster (goalie)	11	0	0	0	0
Ryan Penney (goalie)	19	0	0	0	17

GOALTENDING

	Games	Min.	W	L	T	Goals	SO	Avg.
Jeff Salajko	45	2528	13	24	7	170	1	4.03
Ryan Penney	19	920	3	9	0	74	0	4.83
Darryl Foster	11	564	2	7	1	47	0	5.00

NORTH BAY CENTENNIALS

SCORING

	Games	G	A	Pts.	PIM
Vitali Yachmenev	59	53	52	105	8
Lee Jinman	63	39	65	104	41
Stefan Rivard	60	24	38	62	140
Alex Matvichuk	66	26	28	54	30
Scott Cherrey	62	16	32	48	78
Brad Brown	64	8	38	46	172
Jim Ensom	44	13	30	43	49
Dustin Virag	66	22	19	41	62
Jason Campeau	41	16	19	35	37
Ryan Gillis	65	4	31	35	58
Corey Neilson	64	6	27	33	86
John Guirestante	45	12	14	26	56
Damien Bloye	58	8	18	26	46
Andy Delmore	40	2	14	16	21
Trevor Gallant	16	3	12	15	15
Gary Roach	23	2	12	14	21
Steve McLaren	27	3	10	13	119
Derek Lahnalampi	56	3	6	9	66
Stephen Carpenter	51	5	3	8	9
Kris Cantu	50	4	2	6	45

	Games	G	A	Pts.	PIM
Scott Roche (goalie)	47	0	5	5	2
Brian Whitley	45	1	3	4	14
Mike Zanutto	13	1	1	2	2
Kam White	20	1	1	2	84
Denis Gaudet	9	0	1	1	6
Fred Corkum (goalie)	1	0	0	0	0
Michel Laplante	2	0	0	0	0
Rob Lave	2	0	0	0	4
Lloyd Lafrance (goalie)	8	0	0	0	0
Joel Gagnon (goalie)	21	0	0	0	4
Justin Robinson	21	0	0	0	12
Kody Grigg	45	0	0	0	89

GOALTENDING

	Games	Min.	W	L	T	Goals	SO	Avg.
Fred Corkum	1	31	0	0	0	0	0	0.00
Lloyd Lafrance	8	337	3	1	1	17	0	3.03
Joel Gagnon	21	1021	8	9	1	59	0	3.47
Scott Roche	47	2599	24	17	2	167	2	3.86

OSHAWA GENERALS

SCORING

	Games	G	A	Pts.	PIM
Marc Savard	66	43	96	139	78
Darryl Lafrance	57	55	67	122	10
Ryan Lindsay	61	31	46	77	63
Larry Courville	28	25	30	55	72
Nathan Perrott	63	18	28	46	233
Jan Snepek	64	14	30	44	97
David Froh	56	8	32	40	28
Rob McQuat	58	5	26	31	159
Mike Zanutto	42	13	17	30	2
Stephane Soulliere	18	9	21	30	27
Ian MacNeil	60	7	21	28	57
Jason Sweitzer	65	17	10	27	75
Ryan Tocher	36	6	14	20	60
John Tripp	58	6	11	17	53
Kurt Walsh	42	6	10	16	31
B.J. Johnston	21	5	11	16	10
Darrell Woodley	53	5	11	16	56
Jeff Ware	55	2	11	13	86
Eric Boulton	27	7	5	12	125
Darryl Moxam	27	4	7	11	4
Damon Hardy	20	5	3	8	21
Marty Wilford	63	1	6	7	95
Denis Gaudet	43	3	2	5	23
Robert Dubois	10	1	4	5	2
Brandon Gray	14	2	1	3	4
Billy Wallace	25	2	0	2	8
Frank Ivankovic (goalie)	19	0	2	2	6
Todd Newton	2	0	1	1	4
Chris Hall	3	0	1	1	0
Jeff Andrews	4	0	1	1	0
Ken Shepard (goalie)	42	0	1	1	25
Ryan Martin	1	0	0	0	0
Andrew Power	2	0	0	0	0
Shane Roney	3	0	0	0	0
Brad Domonsky	11	0	0	0	6
Joel Gagnon (goalie)	15	0	0	0	0
Kevin Vaughan	19	0	0	0	14

GOALTENDING

	Games	Min.	W	L	T	Goals	SO	Avg.
Ken Shepard	42	2404	24	11	3	128	2	3.19
Joel Gagnon	15	789	6	7	2	50	1	3.80
Frank Ivankovic	19	805	10	3	0	61	0	4.55

OTTAWA 67's

SCORING

	Games	G	A	Pts.	PIM
Steve Washburn	63	43	63	106	72
Derek Grant	42	22	40	62	14
Dave Nemirovsky	59	27	29	56	25
Alyn McCauley	65	16	38	54	20

	Games	G	A	Pts.	PIM
Mark Edmundson	65	18	25	43	50
Shean Donovan	29	22	19	41	41
Rich Bronilla	66	4	25	29	47
Mike Lavell	64	12	12	24	24
Daryl Rivers	55	4	20	24	57
Steve Zoryk	45	6	16	22	17
Jure Kovacevic	27	8	13	21	29
Akil Adams	25	6	15	21	22
David Bell	66	4	17	21	130
Troy Stonier	56	7	13	20	2
Rob Boyko	20	7	11	18	15
Joel Trottier	53	7	10	17	13
Fredrik Oduya	61	2	13	15	175
James Boyd	55	6	7	13	94
Sean Blanchard	59	2	5	7	24
Steve Jones	61	0	5	5	10
John Argiropoulos	14	4	0	4	4
Cory Murphy	20	2	2	4	33
Kevin Weekes (goalie)	41	0	4	4	4
Chris Brassard	17	1	2	3	8
Craig Whynot	62	1	2	3	27
Daryl Lavoie	3	1	1	2	4
Junior Lapointe (goalie)	1	0	1	1	0
Jeff Salajko (goalie)	11	0	1	1	2
Craig Hillier (goalie)	24	0	0	0	2

GOALTENDING

	Games	Min.	W	L	T	Goals	SO	Avg.
Craig Hillier	24	1078	6	7	2	69	1	3.84
Kevin Weekes	41	2266	13	23	4	154	1	4.08
Jeff Salajko	11	595	3	7	0	44	1	4.44
Junior Lapointe	1	60	0	1	0	6	0	6.00

OWEN SOUND PLATERS

SCORING

	Games	G	A	Pts.	PIM
Wayne Primeau	66	34	62	96	84
Jeff Kostuch	64	34	41	75	26
Shayne Wright	63	12	50	62	114
Peter MacKellar	50	18	29	47	21
Willie Skilliter	66	19	25	44	18
Jason Campbell	62	14	29	43	25
Jeremy Rebek	51	7	26	33	46
Shane Kenny	65	13	19	32	134
John Argiropoulos	54	12	17	29	35
Ryan Mougenel	66	11	18	29	72
Rob Fitzgerald	61	8	19	27	45
Rob Schweyer	30	13	10	23	38
Scott Seiling	58	8	9	17	22
Kevin Young	48	9	7	16	12
Brian Medeiros	27	7	8	15	43
Mike Loach	18	5	10	15	50
Scott Smith	53	3	9	12	33
Murray Hogg	53	3	4	7	69
Greg Kraemer	20	2	5	7	27
Matt Osborne	53	1	5	6	11
Chris Wismer	61	0	6	6	76
Peter Westerkamp	7	2	2	4	0
Joe Harris	16	1	2	3	30
David Zunic	23	0	3	3	6
Mike Morrone	8	1	1	2	14
Kirk Furey	34	1	1	2	14
Derek Lahnalampi	1	1	0	1	2
Jamie Storr (goalie)	17	0	0	0	2
Brent Johnson (goalie)	18	0	0	0	8
Shawn Silver (goalie)	38	0	0	0	4

GOALTENDING

	Games	Min.	W	L	T	Goals	SO	Avg.
Jamie Storr	17	977	5	9	2	64	0	3.93
Shawn Silver	38	2125	14	20	3	152	0	4.29
Brent Johnson	18	904	3	9	1	75	0	4.98

PETERBOROUGH PETES

SCORING

	Games	G	A	Pts.	PIM
Jamie Langenbrunner	62	42	57	99	84
Steve Hogg	66	41	40	81	40
Mike Williams	55	33	44	77	55
Rob Giffin	66	21	48	69	60
Dave Duerden	66	20	33	53	21
Briane Thompson	62	7	45	52	116
Cameron Mann	64	18	25	43	40
Todd Walker	37	14	20	34	16
Adrian Murray	64	4	22	26	115
Ryan Pawluk	42	7	18	25	8
Stephen Webb	42	8	16	24	109
Jason MacMillan	63	11	10	21	4
Rick Emmett	18	3	16	19	6
Kevin Bolibruck	66	2	16	18	88
Matt Lahey	63	6	6	12	87
Mike Martone	62	3	9	12	99
Dan DelMonte	8	5	5	10	7
Dan West	51	3	7	10	34
Pat Paone	12	4	4	8	15
Jonathan Murphy	50	1	4	5	46
Cory Peterson	66	1	4	5	97
Matt Johnson	14	1	2	3	43
Bill McGuigan	13	0	3	3	25
Zac Bierk (goalie)	35	0	3	3	10
Mike Sergeant	39	0	2	2	0
Chad Lang (goalie)	43	0	2	2	25
Mark Teskey	17	0	1	1	21
Andy Cadieux	1	0	0	0	0
Marty Davis	1	0	0	0	0
Darrin Gostlin	1	0	0	0	0
Scott Stephens	1	0	0	0	0
John Shamoon	11	0	0	0	33

GOALTENDING

	Games	Min.	W	L	T	Goals	SO	Avg.
Zac Bierk	35	1798	12	15	5	118	0	3.94
Chad Lang	43	2214	14	19	1	163	0	4.42

SARNIA STING

SCORING

	Games	G	A	Pts.	PIM
Aaron Brand	66	33	42	75	58
Dan DelMonte	55	13	56	69	72
Matt Hogan	64	21	33	54	70
B.J. Johnston	44	23	29	52	35
Brendan Yarema	58	24	25	49	103
Dennis Maxwell	55	16	30	46	227
Rob Massa	42	24	20	44	68
Trevor Letowski	66	22	19	41	33
Alan Letang	62	5	36	41	35
Paul McInnes	60	8	14	22	64
Jon Sim	25	9	12	21	19
Stephane Soulliere	22	10	9	19	38
Larry Courville	16	9	9	18	58
Andy Delmore	27	5	13	18	27
Jeff Brown	58	2	14	16	52
Darren Mortier	42	10	5	15	6
Damon Hardy	33	3	8	11	35
Rob Guinn	54	1	10	11	93
Eric Boulton	24	3	7	10	134
Wes Mason	38	1	8	9	50
Sasha Cucuz	27	3	3	6	16
Jeremy Miculinic	40	2	4	6	12
Ryan Tocher	12	1	5	6	17
Dustin McArthur	13	1	3	4	30
Chris George	41	1	3	4	102
Kurt Walsh	17	0	4	4	18
Kam White	31	0	4	4	77
Tom Brown	53	0	3	3	17
Ken Carroll (goalie)	37	0	2	2	8
Paul Andrea	1	0	1	1	0
Joe Doyle	33	0	1	1	94

	Games	G	A	Pts.	PIM
Scott Hay (goalie)	41	0	1	1	17
Troy Keating	1	0	0	0	0
Corey Prang	1	0	0	0	5
Joe McLean	3	0	0	0	9
Shawn Harris	4	0	0	0	7

GOALTENDING

	Games	Min.	W	L	T	Goals	SO	Avg.
Scott Hay	41	2188	16	19	3	155	0	4.25
Ken Carroll	37	1812	8	18	2	129	0	4.27

SAULT STE. MARIE GREYHOUNDS

SCORING

	Games	G	A	Pts.	PIM
Joe VanVolsen	57	42	40	82	101
Brad Baber	62	25	48	73	93
Chad Grills	53	19	46	65	97
Richard Uniacke	66	31	32	63	6
Steven Lowe	61	15	29	44	44
Gary Roach	42	5	27	32	41
Andre Payette	50	15	15	30	177
Jeff Gies	66	8	18	26	79
Jamie Wentzell	62	9	14	23	86
Blaine Fitzpatrick	39	10	8	18	88
Andrew Clark	18	9	9	18	27
Eric Landry	44	7	8	15	88
Craig Nelson	44	4	11	15	37
Matt O'Dette	42	3	12	15	94
Steve Spina	43	2	13	15	47
Peter MacKellar	17	4	10	14	11
Eric Rylands	51	3	11	14	154
Ben Schust	40	6	7	13	4
Kevin Murnaghan	59	0	11	11	88
Brian Stewart	44	3	7	10	6
Tim Swartz	46	1	7	8	72
Trevor Tokarczyk	43	1	5	6	18
Kevin Mylander	18	2	2	4	11
Andrew Morrison	27	1	3	4	33
Cory Murphy	11	0	4	4	18
Scott King	7	1	2	3	0
Steve Zoryk	11	1	2	3	0
Corey Moylan	15	0	3	3	27
Allan Carr	5	0	2	2	0
Joe Seroski	10	0	2	2	0
Stephane Lefebvre	4	1	0	1	0
Derrick MacCormick	6	0	1	1	2
Robert Dubois	7	0	1	1	11
Garrett Burnett	14	0	1	1	78
Dan Cloutier (goalie)	45	0	1	1	25
Lee Cole	2	0	0	0	7
Ivan Papineau (goalie)	3	0	0	0	0
Bryan Bertoncello (goalie)	7	0	0	0	0
Andrea Carpano (goalie)	23	0	0	0	6

GOALTENDING

	Games	Min.	W	L	T	Goals	SO	Avg.
Dan Cloutier	45	2517	15	25	2	184	1	4.39
Bryan Bertoncello	7	279	0	3	1	28	0	6.02
Andrea Carpano	23	1132	2	16	1	116	0	6.15
Ivan Papineau	3	63	0	1	0	8	0	7.62

SUDBURY WOLVES

SCORING

	Games	G	A	Pts.	PIM
Zdenek Nedved	59	47	51	98	36
Barrie Moore	60	47	42	89	67
Richard Rochefort	57	21	44	65	26
Jamie Rivers	46	9	56	65	30
Ryan Shanahan	65	21	34	55	153
Sean Venedam	65	25	28	53	42
Andrew Dale	65	21	30	51	99
Rory Fitzpatrick	56	12	36	48	72
Mike Wilson	64	13	34	47	46
Luc Gagne	66	19	25	44	29

	Games	G	A	Pts.	PIM
Neal Martin	62	4	32	36	61
Ethan Moreau	23	13	17	30	22
Jason Bonsignore	23	15	14	29	45
Ron Newhook	61	9	16	25	12
Shawn Frappier	45	6	19	25	61
Rick Bodkin	48	11	7	18	44
Jay McKee	39	6	6	12	91
Kiley Hill	27	4	7	11	50
Chester Gallant	37	3	5	8	63
Brian Stacey	21	0	8	8	15
Matt Mullin (goalie)	45	0	7	7	21
Liam MacEachern	54	3	3	6	34
Gary Coupal	17	1	5	6	61
Kris Secemski	22	2	2	4	10
Simon Sherry	50	1	3	4	130
Gregg Lalonde	29	1	0	1	4
Aaron Starnyski	17	0	1	1	24
Steve Valiquette (goalie)	4	0	0	0	0
David MacDonald (goalie)	26	0	0	0	4

GOALTENDING

	Games	Min.	W	L	T	Goals	SO	Avg.
Steve Valiquette	4	138	2	0	0	6	0	2.61
Matt Mullin	45	2525	27	10	4	128	2	3.04
David MacDonald	26	1327	14	7	2	68	1	3.07

WINDSOR SPITFIRES
SCORING

	Games	G	A	Pts.	PIM
Bill Bowler	61	33	102	135	63
Dave Roche	66	55	59	114	180
Tim Findlay	63	34	42	76	12
Ed Jovanovski	50	23	42	65	198
Vladimir Krechine	60	23	41	64	37
Joel Poirier	64	24	39	63	50
Rob Shearer	59	28	28	56	48
Kevin Paden	57	15	24	39	50
Mike Martin	53	9	28	37	79
Chris Van Dyk	51	4	23	27	55
Mike Loach	39	16	7	23	66
Akil Adams	20	4	14	18	20
Denis Smith	61	4	13	17	201
Glenn Crawford	61	5	11	16	17
Dave Geris	65	5	11	16	135
Cory Evans	30	3	12	15	107
Rick Emmett	20	2	13	15	21
Adam Young	63	4	10	14	260
David Pluck	54	1	11	12	45
Wes Ward	56	3	4	7	32
Caleb Ward	49	4	1	5	24
John Cooper	22	1	3	4	0
Luke Clowes	21	1	2	3	26
David Green	25	2	0	2	2
Travis Scott (goalie)	48	0	2	2	23
Paul Beazley (goalie)	18	0	1	1	8
Phil James	1	0	0	0	0
Jamie Foster	2	0	0	0	0
Paul Watson	2	0	0	0	0
Dan West	2	0	0	0	7
Derek Wells	3	0	0	0	0
Jamie Storr (goalie)	4	0	0	0	4
Ryan Gelinas (goalie)	6	0	0	0	0

GOALTENDING

	Games	Min.	W	L	T	Goals	SO	Avg.
Jamie Storr	4	241	3	1	0	8	1	1.99
Travis Scott	47	2644	26	14	3	147	3	3.34
Ryan Gelinas	6	340	3	3	0	22	0	3.88
Paul Beazley	18	768	9	4	0	51	0	3.98

PLAYERS WITH TWO OR MORE TEAMS
SCORING

	Games	G	A	Pts.	PIM
Akil Adams, Windsor	20	4	14	18	20
Akil Adams, Ottawa	25	6	15	21	22
Totals	45	10	29	39	42
Paul Andrea, Sarnia	1	0	1	1	0
Paul Andrea, Belleville	60	46	23	69	29
Totals	61	46	24	70	29
Ryan Appel, London	9	0	1	1	23
Ryan Appel, Belleville	17	1	1	2	37
Totals	26	1	2	3	60
John Argiropoulos, Ottawa	14	4	0	4	4
John Argiropoulos, Owen Sound	54	12	17	29	35
Totals	68	16	17	33	39
Jason Bonsignore, N.F.	26	12	21	33	51
Jason Bonsignore, Sudbury	23	15	14	29	45
Totals	49	27	35	62	96
Eric Boulton, Oshawa	27	7	5	12	125
Eric Boulton, Sarnia	24	3	7	10	134
Totals	51	10	12	22	259
James Boyd, Kitchener	1	0	0	0	0
James Boyd, Ottawa	55	6	7	13	94
Totals	56	6	7	13	94
Rob Boyko, Belleville	29	4	4	8	12
Rob Boyko, Ottawa	20	7	11	18	15
Totals	49	11	15	26	27
Chris Brassard, London	2	0	0	0	0
Chris Brassard, Ottawa	17	1	2	3	8
Chris Brassard, Kitchener	24	6	14	20	12
Totals	43	7	16	23	20
Peter Brearley, Kitchener	3	0	0	0	5
Peter Brearley, London	59	24	21	45	52
Totals	62	24	21	45	57
Garrett Burnett, Sault Ste. Marie	14	0	1	1	78
Garrett Burnett, Kitchener	22	0	1	1	74
Totals	36	0	2	2	152
Andrew Clark, Sault Ste. Marie	18	9	9	18	27
Andrew Clark, Guelph	22	10	13	23	32
Andrew Clark, Belleville	17	7	6	13	22
Totals	57	26	28	54	81
Larry Courville, Sarnia	16	9	9	18	58
Larry Courville, Oshawa	28	25	30	55	72
Totals	44	34	39	73	130
Dan DelMonte, Peterborough	8	5	5	10	7
Dan DelMonte, Sarnia	55	13	56	69	72
Totals	63	18	61	79	79
Andy Delmore, North Bay	40	2	14	16	21
Andy Delmore, Sarnia	27	5	13	18	27
Totals	67	7	27	34	48
Robert Dubois, Oshawa	10	1	4	5	2
Robert Dubois, Sault Ste. Marie	7	0	1	1	11
Totals	17	1	5	6	13
Aaron Ellis, Detroit (g)	4	0	0	0	0
Aaron Ellis, Belleville (g)	7	0	0	0	9
Totals	11	0	0	0	9
Rick Emmett, Peterborough	18	3	16	19	6
Rick Emmett, Windsor	20	2	13	15	21
Rick Emmett, Kitchener	16	0	10	10	4
Totals	54	5	39	44	31
Jim Ensom, North Bay	44	13	30	43	49
Jim Ensom, Kitchener	21	10	8	18	9
Totals	65	23	38	61	58
Neil Fewster, Niagara Falls	37	6	19	25	48
Neil Fewster, Guelph	28	3	25	28	30
Totals	65	9	44	53	78
Darryl Foster, Niagara Falls (g)	11	0	0	0	0
Darryl Foster, Detroit (g)	18	0	0	0	6
Totals	29	0	0	0	6
Joel Gagnon, Oshawa (g)	15	0	0	0	0
Joel Gagnon, North Bay (g)	21	0	0	0	4
Totals	36	0	0	0	4
Chester Gallant, Sudbury	37	3	5	8	63
Chester Gallant, Niagara Falls	26	3	5	8	70
Totals	63	6	10	16	133
Trevor Gallant, Kitchener	43	23	36	59	17
Trevor Gallant, North Bay	16	3	12	15	15
Totals	59	26	48	74	32
Denis Gaudet, North Bay	9	0	1	1	6
Denis Gaudet, Oshawa	43	3	2	5	23
Totals	52	3	3	6	29

	Games	G	A	Pts.	PIM
Damon Hardy, Oshawa	20	5	3	8	21
Damon Hardy, Sarnia	33	3	8	11	35
Totals	53	8	11	19	56
Corey Isen, Belleville	37	7	27	34	78
Corey Isen, London	21	8	11	19	55
Totals	58	15	38	53	133
B.J. Johnston, Oshawa	21	5	11	16	10
B.J. Johnston, Sarnia	44	23	29	52	35
Totals	65	28	40	68	45
Greg Kraemer, Kingston	33	3	4	7	27
Greg Kraemer, Owen Sound	20	2	5	7	27
Totals	53	5	9	14	54
Robin LaCour, Detroit	32	0	3	3	24
Robin LaCour, Kitchener	21	0	3	3	20
Totals	53	0	6	6	44
Derek Lahnalampi, Owen Sound.	1	1	0	1	2
Derek Lahnalampi, North Bay	56	3	6	9	66
Totals	57	4	6	10	68
Eric Landry, Guelph	13	1	4	5	20
Eric Landry, Sault Ste. Marie	44	7	8	15	88
Totals	57	8	12	20	108
Mike Loach, Windsor	39	16	7	23	66
Mike Loach, Owen Sound	18	5	10	15	50
Totals	57	21	17	38	116
Peter MacKellar, S. Ste. Marie	17	4	10	14	11
Peter MacKellar, Owen Sound	50	18	29	47	21
Totals	67	22	39	61	32
Eric Manlow, Kitchener	44	25	29	54	26
Eric Manlow, Detroit	16	4	16	20	11
Totals	60	29	45	74	37
Dustin McArthur, Sarnia	13	1	3	4	30
Dustin McArthur, Niagara Falls.	1	0	0	0	0
Totals	14	1	3	4	30
Bill McGuigan, Peterborough	13	0	3	3	25
Bill McGuigan, Kitchener	37	7	20	27	112
Totals	50	7	23	30	137
Jay McKee, Sudbury	39	6	6	12	91
Jay McKee, Niagara Falls	26	3	13	16	60
Totals	65	9	19	28	151
Lucas Miller, Niagara Falls	4	0	1	1	0
Lucas Miller, Kitchener	50	6	5	11	18
Totals	54	6	6	12	18
Ethan Moreau, Niagara Falls	39	25	41	66	69
Ethan Moreau, Sudbury	23	13	17	30	22
Totals	62	38	58	96	91
Jason Morgan, Kitchener	35	3	15	18	25
Jason Morgan, Kingston	20	0	3	3	14
Totals	55	3	18	21	39
Mike Morrone, Owen Sound	8	1	1	2	14
Mike Morrone, Detroit	47	4	21	25	129
Totals	55	5	22	27	143
Cory Murphy, Ottawa	20	2	2	4	33
Cory Murphy, Sault Ste. Marie	11	0	4	4	18
Totals	31	2	6	8	51
Matt O'Dette, Kitchener	10	1	2	3	29
Matt O'Dette, Sault Ste. Marie	42	3	12	15	94
Totals	52	4	14	18	123
Pat Paone, Peterborough	12	4	4	8	15
Pat Paone, Niagara Falls	3	0	0	0	2
Totals	15	4	4	8	17
Ryan Pawluk, Kitchener	19	8	10	18	10
Ryan Pawluk, Peterborough	42	7	18	25	8
Totals	61	15	28	43	18
Andrew Power, Oshawa	2	0	0	0	0
Andrew Power, London	9	1	2	3	4
Totals	11	1	2	3	4
Dan Reja, London	18	6	13	19	31
Dan Reja, Belleville	2	0	0	0	0
Totals	20	6	13	19	31
Victor Reuta, Guelph	4	0	0	0	2
Victor Reuta, Niagara Falls	53	15	17	32	57
Totals	57	15	17	32	59
Gary Roach, Sault Ste. Marie	42	5	27	32	41
Gary Roach, North Bay	23	2	12	14	21
Totals	65	7	39	46	62

	Games	G	A	Pts.	PIM
Eric Rylands, Kingston	9	0	0	0	25
Eric Rylands, Sault Ste. Marie	51	3	11	14	154
Totals	60	3	11	14	179
Jeff Salajko, Ottawa (g)	11	0	1	1	2
Jeff Salajko, Niagara Falls (g)	45	0	1	1	12
Totals	56	0	2	2	14
Rob Schweyer, Owen Sound	30	13	10	23	38
Rob Schweyer, Kingston	19	3	6	9	10
Totals	49	16	16	32	48
Brian Scott, Kingston	38	5	24	29	15
Brian Scott, Kitchener	20	6	6	12	10
Totals	58	11	30	41	25
Dylan Seca, Detroit	42	4	6	10	56
Dylan Seca, Kitchener	13	0	1	1	21
Totals	55	4	7	11	77
Scott Smith, Detroit	7	0	0	0	0
Scott Smith, Owen Sound	53	3	9	12	33
Totals	60	3	9	12	33
Stephane Soulliere, Oshawa	18	9	21	30	27
Stephane Soulliere, Sarnia	22	10	9	19	38
Stephane Soulliere, Guelph	22	10	8	18	48
Totals	62	29	38	67	113
Brian Stacey, London	36	8	18	26	47
Brian Stacey, Sudbury	21	0	8	8	15
Totals	57	8	26	34	62
Jamie Storr, Owen Sound (g)	17	0	0	0	2
Jamie Storr, Windsor (g)	4	0	0	0	4
Totals	21	0	0	0	4
Wes Swinson, Kitchener	42	12	38	50	71
Wes Swinson, Kingston	20	7	20	27	16
Totals	62	19	58	77	87
Andrew Taylor, Kitchener	42	4	5	9	65
Andrew Taylor, Detroit	18	2	2	4	11
Totals	60	6	7	13	76
Ryan Tocher, Sarnia	12	1	5	6	17
Ryan Tocher, Oshawa	36	6	14	20	60
Totals	48	7	19	26	77
Kurt Walsh, Sarnia	17	0	4	4	18
Kurt Walsh, Oshawa	42	6	10	16	31
Totals	59	6	14	20	49
Dan West, Windsor	2	0	0	0	7
Dan West, Peterborough	51	3	7	10	34
Totals	53	3	7	10	41
Kam White, Sarnia	31	0	4	4	77
Kam White, North Bay	20	1	1	2	84
Totals	51	1	5	6	161
Mike Zanutto, North Bay	13	1	1	2	2
Mike Zanutto, Oshawa	42	13	17	30	2
Totals	55	14	18	32	4
Steve Zoryk, Sault Ste. Marie	11	1	2	3	0
Steve Zoryk, Ottawa	45	6	16	22	17
Totals	56	7	18	25	17

GOALTENDING

	Games	Min.	W	L	T	Goals	SO	Avg.
Aaron Ellis, Det.	4	154	2	0	0	10	0	3.90
Aaron Ellis, Bel.	7	372	1	3	1	35	0	5.65
Totals	11	526	3	3	1	45	0	5.13
Darryl Foster, N.F.	11	564	2	7	1	47	0	5.00
Darryl Foster, Det.	18	888	10	4	1	50	0	3.38
Totals	29	1452	12	11	2	97	0	4.01
Joel Gagnon, Osh.	15	789	6	7	2	50	1	3.80
Joel Gagnon, N.B.	21	1021	8	9	1	59	0	3.47
Totals	36	1810	14	16	3	109	1	3.61
Jeff Salajko, Ott.	11	595	3	7	0	44	1	4.44
Jeff Salajko, N.F.	45	2528	13	24	7	170	1	4.03
Totals	56	3123	16	31	7	214	2	4.11
Jamie Storr, O.S.	17	977	5	9	2	64	0	3.93
Jamie Storr, Wind.	4	241	3	1	0	8	1	1.99
Totals	21	1218	8	10	2	72	1	3.55

RESULTS

FIRST ROUND

	W	L	Pts.	GF	GA
Peterborough	4	3	8	33	31
Oshawa	3	4	6	31	33

(Peterborough won series, 4-3)

	W	L	Pts.	GF	GA
Belleville	4	2	8	32	27
North Bay	2	4	4	27	32

(Belleville won series, 4-2)

	W	L	Pts.	GF	GA
Sudbury	4	1	8	32	12
Kitchener	1	4	2	12	32

(Sudbury won series, 4-1)

	W	L	Pts.	GF	GA
Owen Sound	4	2	8	22	17
Niagara Falls	2	4	4	17	22

(Owen Sound won series, 4-2)

	W	L	Pts.	GF	GA
Detroit	4	0	8	23	6
London	0	4	0	6	23

(Detroit won series, 4-0)

	W	L	Pts.	GF	GA
Windsor	4	0	8	22	10
London	0	4	0	10	22

(Windsor won series, 4-0)

SECOND ROUND

	W	L	Pts.	GF	GA
Guelph	4	0	8	20	9
Owen Sound	0	4	0	9	20

(Guelph won series, 4-0)

	W	L	Pts.	GF	GA
Detroit	4	0	8	19	8
Peterborough	0	4	0	8	19

(Detroit won series, 4-0)

	W	L	Pts.	GF	GA
Belleville	4	2	8	32	24
Kingston	2	4	4	24	32

(Belleville won series, 4-2)

	W	L	Pts.	GF	GA
Sudbury	4	2	8	30	20
Windsor	2	4	4	20	30

(Sudbury won series, 4-2)

THIRD ROUND

	W	L	Pts.	GF	GA
Detroit	4	3	8	30	23
Sudbury	3	4	6	23	30

(Detroit won series, 4-3)

	W	L	Pts.	GF	GA
Guelph	4	0	8	20	10
Belleville	0	4	0	10	20

(Guelph won series, 4-0)

J. ROSS ROBERTSON CUP FINALS

	W	L	Pts.	GF	GA
Detroit	4	2	8	28	24
Guelph	2	4	4	24	28

(Detroit won series, 4-2)

INDIVIDUAL LEADERS

Goals: Todd Bertuzzi, Guelph (15)
Assists: Bill McCauley, Detroit (27)
Points: Bill McCauley, Detroit (39)
Penalty minutes: Sean Brown, Belleville (67)
Goaltending average: Jason Saal, Detroit (2.88)
Shutouts: Jason Saal, Detroit (3)

TOP SCORERS

	Games	G	A	Pts.
Bill McCauley, Detroit	21	12	27	39
Sean Haggerty, Detroit	21	13	24	37
Todd Bertuzzi, Guelph	14	15	18	33
Jamie Rivers, Sudbury	18	7	26	33
Barrie Moore, Sudbury	18	15	14	29
Zdenek Nedved, Sudbury	18	12	16	28
Matt Ball, Detroit	21	9	19	28
Richard Park, Belleville	16	9	18	27
Jeff O'Neill, Guelph	14	8	18	26
Joe Coombs, Belleville	16	11	14	25

INDIVIDUAL STATISTICS

BELLEVILLE BULLS

(Lost in third round to Guelph, 4-0)

SCORING

	Games	G	A	Pts.	PIM
Richard Park	16	9	18	27	12
Joe Coombs	16	11	14	25	10
Paul Andrea	16	10	8	18	6
Daniel Cleary	16	7	10	17	23
Craig Mills	13	7	9	16	8
Dan Preston	16	4	11	15	10
Doug Doull	16	2	13	15	39

	Games	G	A	Pts.	PIM
Radim Bicanek	16	6	5	11	30
Andrew Clark	16	4	5	9	8
Jamie Sokolsky	16	3	6	9	14
Jeff Ambrosio	16	1	7	8	8
Marc Dupuis	16	1	7	8	4
Brian Secord	10	2	5	7	4
Steve Tracze	13	2	5	7	0
Sean Brown	16	4	2	6	67
Steve Carter	14	1	0	1	26
Ryan Appel	9	0	1	1	0
Larry Paleczny	14	0	1	1	4
Scott DeWolfe	4	0	0	0	0

	Games	G	A	Pts.	PIM
Adam Robbins	6	0	0	0	5
Todd St. Louis	13	0	0	0	30
Mark Gowan (goalie)	16	0	0	0	4

GOALTENDING

	Games	Min.	W	L	T	Goals	SO	Avg.
Mark Gowan	16	985	8	8	0	68	0	4.14

DETROIT JR. RED WINGS

(Winner of 1995 J. Ross Robertson Cup playoffs)

SCORING

	Games	G	A	Pts.	PIM
Bill McCauley	21	12	27	39	12
Sean Haggerty	21	13	24	37	18
Matt Ball	21	9	19	28	22
Bryan Berard	21	4	20	24	38
Shayne McCosh	20	7	16	23	12
Eric Manlow	21	11	10	21	18
Jeff Mitchell	21	9	12	21	48
Tom Buckley	21	10	9	19	8
Duane Harmer	21	4	9	13	12
Dan Pawlaczyk	21	4	9	13	15
Nic Beaudoin	21	5	7	12	16
Jamie Allison	18	2	7	9	35
Milan Kostolny	19	4	4	8	13
Mike Rucinski	21	3	3	6	8
Mike Morrone	21	1	1	2	11
Scott Blair	15	1	0	1	0
Quade Lightbody	20	1	0	1	26
Gerry Lanigan	19	0	1	1	0
Murray Sheehan	1	0	0	0	0
Darryl Foster (goalie)	4	0	0	0	0
Ryan MacDonald	5	0	0	0	0
Andrew Taylor	9	0	0	0	7
Jason Saal (goalie)	18	0	0	0	0

GOALTENDING

	Games	Min.	W	L	T	Goals	SO	Avg.
Darryl Foster	4	230	3	1	0	8	0	2.09
Jason Saal	18	1083	13	4	0	52	3	2.88

GUELPH STORM

(Lost J. Ross Robertson Cup finals to Detroit, 4-2)

SCORING

	Games	G	A	Pts.	PIM
Todd Bertuzzi	14	15	18	33	41
Jeff O'Neill	14	8	18	26	34
Jason Jackman	14	7	8	15	14
Jamie Wright	14	6	8	14	6
Dwayne Hay	14	5	7	12	6
Neil Fewster	14	3	9	12	14
Jeff Williams	14	5	5	10	0
Pat Barton	14	0	9	9	17
Todd Norman	13	3	2	5	4
Stephane Soulliere	14	3	2	5	21
Regan Stocco	14	3	2	5	6
Brian Wesenberg	14	2	3	5	18
Mike Rusk	14	1	4	5	8
Ryan Risidore	14	2	2	4	19
Rumun Ndur	14	0	4	4	28
Jeff Cowan	14	1	1	2	0
Chris Hajt	14	0	2	2	9
Mike Pittman	14	0	1	1	2
Andy Adams (goalie)	1	0	0	0	0
Dave Lylyk	1	0	0	0	0
Mark McArthur (goalie)	13	0	0	0	0

GOALTENDING

	Games	Min.	W	L	T	Goals	SO	Avg.
Andy Adams	1	60	1	0	0	2	0	2.00
Mark McArthur	13	797	9	4	0	44	0	3.31

KINGSTON FRONTENACS

(Lost in second round to Belleville, 4-2)

SCORING

	Games	G	A	Pts.	PIM
David Ling	6	7	8	15	12
Keli Corpse	6	4	9	13	10
Wes Swinson	6	2	7	9	6
Chad Kilger	6	5	2	7	10
Mike Ware	6	3	4	7	9
Duncan Fader	6	1	1	2	4
Jason Disher	6	0	2	2	23
Jason Morgan	6	0	2	2	0
Jason Sands	6	1	0	1	4
Gord Walsh	6	1	0	1	6
Ken Boone	4	0	1	1	16
Colin Chaulk	5	0	1	1	7
Bill Maranduik	6	0	1	1	6
Tyler Moss (goalie)	6	0	1	1	0
Dave Bourque	1	0	0	0	0
Tim Keyes (goalie)	1	0	0	0	0
Chris Allen	2	0	0	0	0
Jeff DaCosta	4	0	0	0	2
Rob Mailloux	4	0	0	0	0
Rob Schweyer	4	0	0	0	2
Cail MacLean	6	0	0	0	0
Marc Moro	6	0	0	0	23
Alexander Zhurik	6	0	0	0	0

GOALTENDING

	Games	Min.	W	L	T	Goals	SO	Avg.
Tyler Moss	6	333	2	4	0	27	0	4.86
Tim Keyes	1	27	0	0	0	5	0	11.11

KITCHENER RANGERS

(Lost in first round to Sudbury, 4-1)

SCORING

	Games	G	A	Pts.	PIM
Rob DeCiantis	5	4	3	7	2
Ryan Pepperall	5	2	2	4	8
Brian Scott	5	3	0	3	4
Tim Spitzig	5	2	1	3	8
Jim Ensom	3	1	1	2	6
Greg McLean	5	0	2	2	13
Garrett Burnett	3	0	1	1	23
Dan Godbout	5	0	1	1	0
Jason Hughes	5	0	1	1	12
Rob Maric	5	0	1	1	4
Bill McGuigan	5	0	1	1	17
Lucas Miller	5	0	1	1	4
Chris Pittman	5	0	1	1	2
Travis Riggin	5	0	1	1	0
Darryl Whyte (goalie)	2	0	0	0	0
Dylan Seca	4	0	0	0	4
David Belitski (goalie)	5	0	0	0	0
Jason Byrnes	5	0	0	0	0
Robin LaCour	5	0	0	0	14
Paul Traynor	5	0	0	0	4
Keith Welsh	5	0	0	0	0

GOALTENDING

	Games	Min.	W	L	T	Goals	SO	Avg.
David Belitski	5	268	1	4	0	27	0	6.04
Darryl Whyte	2	43	0	0	0	5	0	6.98

LONDON KNIGHTS

(Lost in first round to Detroit, 4-0)

SCORING

	Games	G	A	Pts.	PIM
David Gilmore	4	2	1	3	8
Joel Dezainde	4	0	3	3	0
Jason Doyle	4	1	1	2	0
Corey Isen	4	0	2	2	6

	Games	G	A	Pts.	PIM
Ryan Burgoyne	4	1	0	1	0
Kevin Slota	4	1	0	1	4
Chris Zanutto	4	1	0	1	8
Peter Brearley	4	0	1	1	2
Jason Brooks	4	0	1	1	5
Bob Graham	4	0	1	1	0
Justin Steinbach	4	0	1	1	0
Ian Keiller	2	0	0	0	6
Eoin McInerney (goalie)	2	0	0	0	0
Ben Walker	2	0	0	0	0
Jordan Willis (goalie)	3	0	0	0	2
Stefan Bergkvist	4	0	0	0	5
Kevin Boyd	4	0	0	0	0
Troy Brownell	4	0	0	0	0
Rob Frid	4	0	0	0	6
Roy Gray	4	0	0	0	8
Don Margettie	4	0	0	0	8

GOALTENDING

	Games	Min.	W	L	T	Goals	SO	Avg.
Jordan Willis	3	165	0	3	0	15	0	5.45
Eoin McInerney	2	75	0	1	0	8	0	6.40

NIAGARA FALLS THUNDER

(Lost in first round to Owen Sound, 4-2)

SCORING

	Games	G	A	Pts.	PIM
Jeff Johnstone	6	7	1	8	2
Steve Potvin	6	1	5	6	10
Jay McKee	6	2	3	5	10
Mike Perna	6	1	4	5	12
Andrew Williamson	6	1	3	4	2
Steve Nimigon	6	0	3	3	2
Geoff Peters	6	2	0	2	4
Jeff Paul	6	0	2	2	0
Victor Reuta	6	0	2	2	0
Chester Gallant	6	1	0	1	19
Jason Reesor	6	1	0	1	6
Rich Vrataric	6	1	0	1	9
Chris Stevenson	2	0	1	1	0
Mark Cadotte	6	0	1	1	14
Chris Haskett	6	0	1	1	4
Mike VanVolsen	6	0	1	1	8
Ron Paleczny	2	0	0	0	0
Stephen Douglas	6	0	0	0	4
Yianni Ioannou	6	0	0	0	10
Jeff Salajko (goalie)	6	0	0	0	4

GOALTENDING

	Games	Min.	W	L	T	Goals	SO	Avg.
Jeff Salajko	6	371	2	4	0	22	0	3.56

NORTH BAY CENTENNIALS

(Lost in first round to Belleville, 4-2)

SCORING

	Games	G	A	Pts.	PIM
Lee Jinman	6	5	5	10	4
Trevor Gallant	6	3	6	9	6
Vitali Yachmenev	6	1	8	9	2
Damien Bloye	6	4	2	6	0
Corey Neilson	6	3	3	6	9
Stefan Rivard	6	3	2	5	12
Brad Brown	6	1	4	5	8
Alex Matvichuk	6	1	4	5	4
Scott Cherrey	6	1	3	4	4
Steve McLaren	6	2	1	3	23
Dustin Virag	6	1	2	3	6
John Guirestante	3	0	3	3	2
Ryan Gillis	6	0	3	3	6
Gary Roach	3	1	1	2	2
Jason Campeau	5	1	1	2	8
Kody Grigg	6	0	1	1	4

	Games	G	A	Pts.	PIM
Kam White	6	0	1	1	10
Joel Gagnon (goalie)	2	0	0	0	0
Brian Whitley	3	0	0	0	0
Kris Cantu	4	0	0	0	4
Stephen Carpenter	5	0	0	0	0
Scott Roche (goalie)	6	0	0	0	0

GOALTENDING

	Games	Min.	W	L	T	Goals	SO	Avg.
Joel Gagnon	2	35	0	0	0	2	0	3.43
Scott Roche	6	348	2	4	0	30	0	5.17

OSHAWA GENERALS

(Lost in first round to Peterborough, 4-3)

SCORING

	Games	G	A	Pts.	PIM
Larry Courville	7	4	10	14	10
Darryl Lafrance	7	6	7	13	2
Marc Savard	7	5	6	11	8
Ryan Tocher	7	1	7	8	2
Ryan Lindsay	7	4	3	7	4
Mike Zanutto	7	4	1	5	0
David Froh	7	1	4	5	6
Darrell Woodley	7	0	4	4	11
Kurt Walsh	7	2	0	2	8
Nathan Perrott	2	1	1	2	9
Jeff Andrews	6	1	1	2	4
Jeff Ware	7	1	1	2	6
Marty Wilford	7	1	1	2	4
Jason Sweitzer	6	0	2	2	2
Ian MacNeil	7	2	0	2	0
Billy Wallace	4	0	1	1	0
Jan Snopek	7	0	1	1	4
John Tripp	7	0	1	1	4
Denis Gaudet	3	0	0	0	0
Frank Ivankovic (goalie)	3	0	0	0	2
Ken Shepard (goalie)	5	0	0	0	4
Rob McQuat	7	0	0	0	22

GOALTENDING

	Games	Min.	W	L	T	Goals	SO	Avg.
Frank Ivankovic	3	121	2	0	0	5	0	2.48
Ken Shepard	5	299	1	4	0	26	0	5.22

OWEN SOUND PLATERS

(Lost in second round to Guelph, 4-0)

SCORING

	Games	G	A	Pts.	PIM
Jason Campbell	10	7	6	13	4
Wayne Primeau	10	4	9	13	15
Jeff Kostuch	10	4	6	10	8
Shayne Wright	10	1	9	10	34
Peter MacKellar	10	4	3	7	2
Willie Skilliter	10	2	5	7	2
Ryan Mougenel	10	3	2	5	6
Mike Loach	10	1	3	4	14
Jeremy Rebek	10	1	3	4	8
John Argiropoulos	10	2	1	3	10
Rob Fitzgerald	10	2	1	3	13
Chris Wismer	10	0	3	3	8
Kevin Young	7	0	2	2	4
Scott Seiling	8	0	2	2	11
Shane Kenny	9	0	2	2	8
Greg Kraemer	9	0	2	2	15
Shawn Silver (goalie)	10	0	1	1	4
Scott Smith	7	0	0	0	0
Murray Hogg	10	0	0	0	26
Matt Osborne	10	0	0	0	4

GOALTENDING

	Games	Min.	W	L	T	Goals	SO	Avg.
Shawn Silver	10	611	4	6	0	36	0	3.54

PETERBOROUGH PETES

(Lost in second round to Detroit, 4-0)

SCORING

	Games	G	A	Pts.	PIM
Jamie Langenbrunner	11	8	14	22	12
Briane Thompson	11	1	13	14	18
Steve Hogg	11	4	9	13	2
Cameron Mann	11	3	8	11	4
Todd Walker	11	3	7	10	10
Rob Giffin	11	6	3	9	4
Dave Duerden	11	6	2	8	6
Steve Webb	11	3	3	6	22
Jason MacMillan	11	2	2	4	6
Kevin Bolibruck	11	1	1	2	14
Matt Lahey	11	1	1	2	18
Adrian Murray	11	1	1	2	18
Ryan Pawluk	11	1	1	2	4
Mike Martone	10	0	2	2	4
Jonathan Murphy	11	1	0	1	2
Mike Williams	5	0	1	1	0
Cory Peterson	11	0	1	1	6
Mark Teskey	1	0	0	0	0
Zac Bierk (goalie)	6	0	0	0	2
Chad Lang (goalie)	6	0	0	0	11
Mike Sergeant	6	0	0	0	0
Dan West	11	0	0	0	0

GOALTENDING

	Games	Min.	W	L	T	Goals	SO	Avg.
Chad Lang	6	376	2	4	0	25	0	3.99
Zac Bierk	6	301	2	3	0	24	0	4.78

SARNIA STING

(Lost in first round to Windsor, 4-0)

SCORING

	Games	G	A	Pts.	PIM
Jon Sim	4	3	2	5	2
B.J. Johnston	4	2	3	5	6
Alan Letang	4	2	2	4	6
Damon Hardy	4	0	3	3	4
Dan DelMonte	4	2	0	2	17
Brendan Yarema	4	1	1	2	13
Aaron Brand	3	0	2	2	4
Jeff Brown	4	0	2	2	2
Eric Boulton	4	0	1	1	10
Matt Hogan	4	0	1	1	15
Trevor Letowski	4	0	1	1	9
Rob Massa	4	0	1	1	2
Jeremy Miculinic	1	0	0	0	2
Joe Doyle	2	0	0	0	2
Wes Mason	2	0	0	0	9
Darren Mortier	2	0	0	0	0
Ken Carroll (goalie)	3	0	0	0	2
Andy Delmore	3	0	0	0	2
Scott Hay (goalie)	3	0	0	0	0
Dennis Maxwell	3	0	0	0	18
Chris George	4	0	0	0	12
Rob Guinn	4	0	0	0	9
Paul McInnes	4	0	0	0	2

GOALTENDING

	Games	Min.	W	L	T	Goals	SO	Avg.
Ken Carroll	3	114	0	2	0	9	0	4.74
Scott Hay	3	139	0	2	0	13	0	5.61

SUDBURY WOLVES

(Lost in third round to Detroit, 4-3)

SCORING

	Games	G	A	Pts.	PIM
Jamie Rivers	18	7	26	33	22
Barrie Moore	18	15	14	29	24
Zdenek Nedved	18	12	16	28	16
Jason Bonsignore	17	13	10	23	12
Ethan Moreau	18	6	12	18	26
Rory Fitzpatrick	18	3	15	18	21
Andrew Dale	18	2	9	11	37
Ryan Shanahan	18	5	5	10	21
Richard Rochefort	13	3	7	10	6
Luc Gagne	16	5	4	9	11
Mike Wilson	18	1	8	9	10
Ron Newhook	16	4	4	8	4
Rick Bodkin	18	3	3	6	4
Sean Venedam	15	2	4	6	12
Neal Martin	18	0	6	6	6
Simon Sherry	18	2	1	3	53
Brian Stacey	18	2	1	3	26
Matt Mullin (goalie)	18	0	1	1	4
Shawn Frappier	19	0	1	1	23
Krystof Secemski	2	0	0	0	0
David MacDonald (goalie)	4	0	0	0	0
Liam MacEachern	10	0	0	0	6

GOALTENDING

	Games	Min.	W	L	T	Goals	SO	Avg.
Matt Mullin	18	996	10	7	0	53	0	3.19
David MacDonald	4	117	1	0	0	9	0	4.62

WINDSOR SPITFIRES

(Lost in second round to Sudbury, 4-2)

SCORING

	Games	G	A	Pts.	PIM
Bill Bowler	10	7	15	22	13
Dave Roche	10	9	6	15	16
Tim Findlay	10	5	7	12	4
Joel Poirier	10	4	5	9	10
Ed Jovanovski	9	2	7	9	39
Rob Shearer	10	4	4	8	10
Glenn Crawford	10	2	5	7	8
Dave Geris	10	1	6	7	21
Rick Emmett	10	2	4	6	4
Vladimir Krechine	10	1	3	4	8
Mike Martin	10	1	3	4	21
Denis Smith	10	1	3	4	41
Adam Young	10	2	1	3	36
Chris Van Dyk	10	0	2	2	4
David Pluck	10	1	0	1	23
Caleb Ward	2	0	1	1	5
David Green	10	0	1	1	7
Travis Scott (goalie)	3	0	0	0	0
Wes Ward	3	0	0	0	4
Cory Evans	6	0	0	0	26
John Cooper	10	0	0	0	4
Jamie Storr (goalie)	10	0	0	0	2

GOALTENDING

	Games	Min.	W	L	T	Goals	SO	Avg.
Travis Scott	3	94	0	1	0	6	1	3.83
Jamie Storr	10	520	6	3	0	34	1	3.92

1994-95 AWARD WINNERS

ALL-STAR TEAMS

First team	Pos.	Second team
Tyler Moss, Kingston	G	Mark McArthur, Guelph
Ed Jovanovski, Windsor	D	Wes Swinson, Kingston
Bryan Berard, Detroit	D	Jamie Rivers, Sudbury

First team	Pos.	Second team
Dave Roche, Windsor	LW	Larry Courville, Oshawa
Jeff O'Neill, Guelph	C	Marc Savard, Oshawa
David Ling, Kingston	RW	Todd Bertuzzi, Guelph

Coach of the Year: Craig Hartsburg, Guelph

TROPHY WINNERS

Red Tilson Trophy: David Ling, Kingston
Eddie Powers Memorial Trophy: Marc Savard, Oshawa
Dave Pinkney Trophy: Andy Adams, Guelph
　　　　　　　　　　　Mark McArthur, Guelph
Max Kaminsky Trophy: Bryan Berard, Detroit

William Hanley Trophy: Vitali Yachmenev, North Bay
Emms Family Award: Bryan Berard, Detroit
Matt Leyden Trophy: Craig Hartsburg, Guelph
Jim Mahon Memorial Trophy: David Ling, Kingston
F.W. Dinty Moore Trophy: David MacDonald, Sudbury
Leo Lalonde Memorial Trophy: Bill Bowler, Windsor
Hamilton Spectator Trophy: Guelph Storm
J. Ross Robertson Cup: Detroit Jr. Red Wings

ALL - TIME AWARD WINNERS

RED TILSON TROPHY

(Outstanding player)

Season	Player, Team
1944-45	Doug McMurdy, St. Catharines
1945-46	Tod Sloan, St. Michael's
1946-47	Ed Sanford, St. Michael's
1947-48	George Armstrong, Stratford
1948-49	Gil Mayer, Barrie
1949-50	George Armstrong, Marlboros
1950-51	Glenn Hall, Windsor
1951-52	Bill Harrington, Kitchener
1952-53	Bob Attersley, Oshawa
1953-54	Brian Cullen, St. Catharines
1954-55	Hank Ciesla, St. Catharines
1955-56	Ron Howell, Guelph
1956-57	Frank Mahovlich, St. Michael's
1957-58	Murray Oliver, Hamilton
1958-59	Stan Mikita, St. Catharines
1959-60	Wayne Connelly, Peterborough
1960-61	Rod Gilbert, Guelph
1961-62	Pit Martin, Hamilton
1962-63	Wayne Maxner, Niagara Falls
1963-64	Yvan Cournoyer, Montreal
1964-65	Andre Lacroix, Peterborough
1965-66	Andre Lacroix, Peterborough
1966-67	Mickey Redmond, Peterborough
1967-68	Walt Tkaczuk, Kitchener
1968-69	Rejean Houle, Montreal
1969-70	Gilbert Perreault, Montreal
1970-71	Dave Gardner, Marlboros
1971-72	Don Lever, Niagara Falls
1972-73	Rick Middleton, Oshawa
1973-74	Jack Valiquette, Sault Ste. Marie
1974-75	Dennis Maruk, London
1975-76	Peter Lee, Ottawa
1976-77	Dale McCourt, St. Catharines
1977-78	Bobby Smith, Ottawa
1978-79	Mike Foligno, Sudbury
1979-80	Jim Fox, Ottawa
1980-81	Ernie Godden, Windsor
1981-82	Dave Simpson, London
1982-83	Doug Gilmour, Cornwall
1983-84	John Tucker, Kitchener
1984-85	Wayne Groulx, Sault Ste. Marie
1985-86	Ray Sheppard, Cornwall
1986-87	Scott McCrory, Oshawa
1987-88	Andrew Cassels, Ottawa
1988-89	Bryan Fogarty, Niagara Falls
1989-90	Mike Ricci, Peterborough
1990-91	Eric Lindros, Oshawa
1991-92	Todd Simon, Niagara Falls
1992-93	Pat Peake, Detroit
1993-94	Jason Allison, London
1994-95	David Ling, Kingston

EDDIE POWERS MEMORIAL TROPHY

(Scoring champion)

Season	Player, Team
1933-34	J. Groboski, Oshawa
1934-35	J. Good, Toronto Lions
1935-36	John O'Flaherty, West Toronto
1936-37	Billy Taylor, Oshawa
1937-38	Hank Goldup, Tor. Marlboros
1938-39	Billy Taylor, Oshawa
1939-40	Jud McAtee, Oshawa
1940-41	Gaye Stewart, Tor. Marlboros

Season	Player, Team
1941-42	Bob Wiest, Brantford
1942-43	Norman "Red" Tilson, Oshawa
1943-44	Ken Smith, Oshawa
1944-45	Leo Gravelle, St. Michael's
1945-46	Tod Sloan, St. Michael's
1946-47	Fleming Mackell, St. Michael's
1947-48	George Armstrong, Stratford
1948-49	Bert Giesebrecht, Windsor
1949-50	Earl Reibel, Windsor
1950-51	Lou Jankowski, Oshawa
1951-52	Ken Laufman, Guelph
1952-53	Jim McBurney, Galt
1953-54	Brian Cullen, St. Catharines
1954-55	Hank Ciesla, St. Catharines
1955-56	Stan Baliuk, Kitchener
1956-57	Bill Sweeney, Guelph
1957-58	John McKenzie, St. Catharines
1958-59	Stan Mikita, St. Catharines
1959-60	Chico Maki, St. Catharines
1960-61	Rod Gilbert, Guelph
1961-62	Andre Boudrias, Montreal
1962-63	Wayne Maxner, Niagara Falls
1963-64	Andre Boudrias, Montreal
1964-65	Ken Hodge, St. Catharines
1965-66	Andre Lacroix, Peterborough
1966-67	Derek Sanderson, Niagara Falls
1967-68	Tom Webster, Niagara Falls
1968-69	Rejean Houle, Montreal
1969-70	Marcel Dionne, St. Catharines
1970-71	Marcel Dionne, St. Catharines
1971-72	Bill Harris, Toronto
1972-73	Blake Dunlop, Ottawa
1973-74	Jack Valiquette, Sault Ste. Marie
	Rick Adduono, St. Catharines
1974-75	Bruce Boudreau, Toronto
1975-76	Mike Kaszycki, Sault Ste. Marie
1976-77	Dwight Foster, Kitchener
1977-78	Bobby Smith, Ottawa
1978-79	Mike Foligno, Sudbury
1979-80	Jim Fox, Ottawa
1980-81	John Goodwin, Sault Ste. Marie
1981-82	Dave Simpson, London
1982-83	Doug Gilmour, Cornwall
1983-84	Tim Salmon, Kingston
1984-85	Dave MacLean, Belleville
1985-86	Ray Sheppard, Cornwall
1986-87	Scott McCrory, Oshawa
1987-88	Andrew Cassels, Ottawa
1988-89	Bryan Fogarty, Niagara Falls
1989-90	Keith Primeau, Niagara Falls
1990-91	Eric Lindros, Oshawa
1991-92	Todd Simon, Niagara Falls
1992-93	Andrew Brunette, Owen Sound
1993-94	Jason Allison, London
1994-95	Marc Savard, Oshawa

DAVE PINKNEY TROPHY

(Top team goaltending)

Season	Player, Team
1948-49	Gil Mayer, Barrie
1949-50	Don Lockhart, Marlboros
1950-51	Don Lockhart, Marlboros
	Lorne Howes, Barrie
1951-52	Don Head, Marlboros
1952-53	John Henderson, Marlboros
1953-54	Dennis Riggin, Hamilton

Season	Player, Team
1954-55	John Albani, Marlboros
1955-56	Jim Crockett, Marlboros
1956-57	Len Broderick, Marlboros
1957-58	Len Broderick, Marlboros
1958-59	Jacques Caron, Peterborough
1959-60	Gerry Cheevers, St. Michael's
1960-61	Bud Blom, Hamilton
1961-62	George Holmes, Montreal
1962-63	Chuck Goddard, Peterborough
1963-64	Bernie Parent, Niagara Falls
1964-65	Bernie Parent, Niagara Falls
1965-66	Ted Quimet, Montreal
1966-67	Peter MacDuffe, St. Catharines
1967-68	Bruce Mullet, Montreal
1968-69	Wayne Wood, Montreal
1969-70	John Garrett, Peterborough
1970-71	John Garrett, Peterborough
1971-72	Michel Larocque, Ottawa
1972-73	Mike Palmateer, Toronto
1973-74	Don Edwards, Kitchener
1974-75	Greg Millen, Peterborough
1975-76	Jim Bedard, Sudbury
1976-77	Pat Riggin, London
1977-78	Al Jensen, Hamilton
1978-79	Nick Ricci, Niagara Falls
1979-80	Rick LaFerriere, Peterborough
1980-81	Jim Ralph, Ottawa
1981-82	Marc D'Amour, Sault Ste. Marie
1982-83	Peter Sidorkiewicz, Oshawa
	Jeff Hogg, Oshawa
1983-84	Darren Pang, Ottawa
	Greg Coram, Ottawa
1984-85	Scott Mosey, Sault Ste. Marie
	Marty Abrams, Sault Ste. Marie
1985-86	Kay Whitmore, Peterborough
	Ron Tugnutt, Peterborough
1986-87	Sean Evoy, Oshawa
	Jeff Hackett, Oshawa
1987-88	Todd Bojcun, Peterborough
	John Tanner, Peterborough
1988-89	Todd Bojcun, Peterborough
	John Tanner, Peterborough
1989-90	Jeff Wilson, Peterborough
	Sean Gauthier, Kingston
1990-91	Kevin Hodson, Sault Ste. Marie
	Mike Lenarduzzi, Sault Ste. Marie
1991-92	Kevin Hodson, Sault Ste. Marie
1992-93	Chad Lang, Peterborough
	Ryan Douglas, Peterborough
1993-94	Sandy Allan, North Bay
	Scott Roche, North Bay
1994-95	Andy Adams, Guelph
	Mark McArthur, Guelph

MAX KAMINSKY TROPHY

(Outstanding defenseman)

Season	Player, Team
1969-70	Ron Plumb, Peterborough
1970-71	Jocelyn Guevremont, Montreal
1971-72	Denis Potvin, Ottawa
1972-73	Denis Potvin, Ottawa
1973-74	Jim Turkiewicz, Peterborough
1974-75	Mike O'Connell, Kingston
1975-76	Rick Green, London
1976-77	Craig Hartsburg, S. Ste. Marie
1977-78	Brad Marsh, London
	Rob Ramage, London
1978-79	Greg Theberge, Peterborough
1979-80	Larry Murphy, Peterborough
1980-81	Steve Smith, Sault Ste. Marie
1981-82	Ron Meighan, Niagara Falls
1982-83	Allan MacInnis, Kitchener
1983-84	Brad Shaw, Ottawa
1984-85	Bob Halkidis, London
1985-86	Terry Carkner, Peterborough
	Jeff Brown, Sudbury
1986-87	Kerry Huffman, Guelph
1987-88	Darryl Shannon, Windsor
1988-89	Bryan Fogarty, Niagara Falls
1989-90	John Slaney, Cornwall

Season	Player, Team
1990-91	Chris Snell, Ottawa
1991-92	Drake Berehowsky, North Bay
1992-93	Chris Pronger, Peterborough
1993-94	Jamie Rivers, Sudbury
1994-95	Bryan Berard, Detroit

WILLIAM HANLEY TROPHY

(Most gentlemanly)

Season	Player, Team
1960-61	Bruce Draper, St. Michael's
1961-62	Lowell MacDonald, Hamilton
1962-63	Paul Henderson, Hamilton
1963-64	Fred Stanfield, St. Catharines
1964-65	Jimmy Peters, Hamilton
1965-66	Andre Lacroix, Peterborough
1966-67	Mickey Redmond, Peterborough
1967-68	Tom Webster, Niagara Falls
1968-69	Rejean Houle, Montreal
1969-74	No award presented
1974-75	Doug Jarvis, Peterborough
1975-76	Dale McCourt, Hamilton
1976-77	Dale McCourt, St. Catharines
1977-78	Waynbe Gretzky, S.S. Marie
1978-79	Sean Simpson, Ottawa
1979-80	Sean Simpson, Ottawa
1980-81	John Goodwin, Sault Ste. Marie
1981-82	Dave Simpson, London
1982-83	Kirk Muller, Guelph
1983-84	Kevin Conway, Kingston
1984-85	Scott Tottle, Peterborough
1985-86	Jason Lafreniere, Belleville
1986-87	Scott McCrory, Oshawa
	Keith Gretzky, Hamilton
1987-88	Andrew Cassels, Ottawa
1988-89	Kevin Miehm, Oshawa
1989-90	Mike Ricci, Peterborough
1990-91	Dale Craigwell, Oshawa
1991-92	John Spoltore, North Bay
1992-93	Pat Peake, Detroit
1993-94	Jason Allison, London
1994-95	Vitali Yachmenev, North Bay

EMMS FAMILY AWARD

(Rookie of the year)

Season	Player, Team
1972-73	Dennis Maruk, London
1973-74	Jack Valiquette, Sault Ste. Marie
1974-75	Danny Shearer, Hamilton
1975-76	John Travella, Sault Ste. Marie
1976-77	Yvan Joly, Ottawa
1977-78	Wayne Gretzky, S.S. Marie
1978-79	John Goodwin, Sault Ste. Marie
1979-80	Bruce Dowie, Toronto
1980-81	Tony Tanti, Oshawa
1981-82	Pat Verbeek, Sudbury
1982-83	Bruce Cassidy, Ottawa
1983-84	Shawn Burr, Kitchener
1984-85	Derek King, Sault Ste. Marie
1985-86	Lonnie Loach, Guelph
1986-87	Andrew Cassels, Ottawa
1987-88	Rick Corriveau, London
1988-89	Owen Nolan, Cornwall
1989-90	Chris Longo, Peterborough
1990-91	Cory Stillman, Windsor
1991-92	Chris Gratton, Kingston
1992-93	Jeff O'Neill, Guelph
1993-94	Vitali Yachmenev, North Bay
1994-95	Bryan Berard, Detroit

MATT LEYDEN TROPHY

(Coach of the year)

Season	Coach, Team
1971-72	Gus Bodnar, Oshawa
1972-73	George Armstrong, Toronto
1973-74	Jack Bownass, Kingston
1974-75	Bert Templeton, Hamilton
1975-76	Jerry Toppazzini, Sudbury

Season	Coach, Team
1976-77	Bill Long, London
1977-78	Bill White, Oshawa
1978-79	Gary Green, Peterborough
1979-80	Dave Chambers, Toronto
1980-81	Brian Kilrea, Ottawa
1981-82	Brian Kilrea, Ottawa
1982-83	Terry Crisp, Sault Ste. Marie
1983-84	Tom Barrett, Kitchener
1984-85	Terry Crisp, Sault Ste. Marie
1985-86	Jacques Martin, Guelph
1986-87	Paul Theriault, Oshawa
1987-88	Dick Todd, Peterborough
1988-89	Joe McDonnell, Kitchener
1989-90	Larry Mavety, Kingston
1990-91	George Burnett, Niagara Falls
1991-92	George Burnett, Niagara Falls
1992-93	Gary Agnew, London
1993-94	Bert Templeton, North Bay
1994-95	Craig Hartsburg, Guelph

JIM MAHON MEMORIAL TROPHY

(Top scoring right wing)

Season	Player, Team
1971-72	Bill Harris, Toronto
1972-73	Dennis Ververgaert, London
1973-74	Dave Gorman, St. Catharines
1974-75	Mark Napier, Toronto
1975-76	Peter Lee, Ottawa
1976-77	John Anderson, Toronto
1977-78	Dino Ciccarelli, London
1978-79	Mike Foligno, Sudbury
1979-80	Jim Fox, Ottawa
1980-81	Tony Tanti, Oshawa
1981-82	Tony Tanti, Oshawa
1982-83	Ian MacInnis, Cornwall
1983-84	Wayne Presley, Kitchener
1984-85	Dave MacLean, Belleville
1985-86	Ray Sheppard, Cornwall
1986-87	Ron Goodall, Kitchener
1987-88	Sean Williams, Oshawa
1988-89	Stan Drulia, Niagara Falls
1989-90	Owen Nolan, Cornwall
1990-91	Rob Pearson, Oshawa
1991-92	Darren McCarty, Belleville

Season	Player, Team
1992-93	Kevin J. Brown, Detroit
1993-94	Kevin J. Brown, Detroit
1994-95	David Ling, Kingston

F.W. DINTY MOORE TROPHY

(Lowest average by a rookie goalie)

Season	Player, Team
1975-76	Mark Locken, Hamilton
1976-77	Barry Heard, London
1977-78	Ken Ellacott, Peterborough
1978-79	Nick Ricci, Niagara Falls
1979-80	Mike Vezina, Ottawa
1980-81	John Vanbiesbrouck, Sault Ste. Marie
1981-82	Shawn Kilroy, Peterborough
1982-83	Dan Burrows, Belleville
1983-84	Jerry Iuliano, Sault Ste. Marie
1984-85	Ron Tugnutt, Peterborough
1985-86	Paul Henriques, Belleville
1986-87	Jeff Hackett, Oshawa
1987-88	Todd Bojcun, Peterborough
1988-89	Jeff Wilson, Kingston
1989-90	Sean Basilio, London
1990-91	Kevin Hodson, Sault Ste. Marie
1991-92	Sandy Allan, North Bay
1992-93	Ken Shepard, Oshawa
1993-94	Scott Roche, North Bay
1994-95	David MacDonald, Sudbury

LEO LALONDE MEMORIAL TROPHY

(Overage player of the year)

Season	Player, Team
1983-84	Don McLaren, Ottawa
1984-85	Dunc MacIntyre, Belleville
1985-86	Steve Guenette, Guelph
1986-87	Mike Richard, Toronto
1987-88	Len Soccio, North Bay
1988-89	Stan Drulia, Niagara Falls
1989-90	Iain Fraser, Oshawa
1990-91	Joey St. Aubin, Kitchener
1991-92	John Spoltore, North Bay
1992-93	Scott Hollis, Oshawa
1993-94	B.J. MacPherson, North Bay
1994-95	Bill Bowler, Windsor

ALL-TIME LEAGUE CHAMPIONS

REGULAR-SEASON CHAMPION

PLAYOFF CHAMPION

Season	Team	Team
1933-34	No trophy awarded	St. Michael's College
1934-35	No trophy awarded	Kitchener
1935-36	No trophy awarded	West Toronto Redmen
1936-37	No trophy awarded	St. Michael's College
1937-38	No trophy awarded	Oshawa Generals
1938-39	No trophy awarded	Oshawa Generals
1939-40	No trophy awarded	Oshawa Generals
1940-41	No trophy awarded	Oshawa Generals
1941-42	No trophy awarded	Oshawa Generals
1942-43	No trophy awarded	Oshawa Generals
1943-44	No trophy awarded	Oshawa Generals
1944-45	No trophy awarded	St. Michael's College
1945-46	No trophy awarded	St. Michael's College
1946-47	No trophy awarded	St. Michael's College
1947-48	No trophy awarded	Barrie Flyers
1948-49	No trophy awarded	Barrie Flyers
1949-50	No trophy awarded	Guelph Biltmores
1950-51	No trophy awarded	Barrie Flyers
1951-52	No trophy awarded	Guelph Biltmores
1952-53	No trophy awarded	Barrie Flyers
1953-54	No trophy awarded	St. Catharines Tee Pees
1954-55	No trophy awarded	Toronto Marlboros
1955-56	No trophy awarded	Toronto Marlboros
1956-57	No trophy awarded	Guelph Biltmores
1957-58	St. Catharines Tee Pees	Toronto Marlboros
1958-59	St. Catharines Tee Pees	Peterborough TPTs

REGULAR-SEASON CHAMPION	PLAYOFF CHAMPION
Season Team	**Team**
1959-60—Toronto Marlboros	St. Catharines Tee Pees
1960-61—Guelph Royals	St. Michael's College
1961-62—Montreal Jr. Canadiens	Hamilton Red Wings
1962-63—Niagara Falls Flyers	Niagara Falls Flyers
1963-64—Toronto Marlboros	Toronto Marlboros
1964-65—Niagara Falls Flyers	Niagara Falls Flyers
1965-66—Peterborough Petes	Oshawa Generals
1966-67—Kitchener Rangers	Toronto Marlboros
1967-68—Kitchener Rangers	Niagara Falls Flyers
1968-69—Montreal Jr. Canadiens	Montreal Jr. Canadiens
1969-70—Montreal Jr. Canadiens	Montreal Jr. Canadiens
1970-71—Peterborough Petes	St. Catharines Black Hawks
1971-72—Toronto Marlboros	Peterborough Petes
1972-73—Toronto Marlboros	Toronto Marlboros
1973-74—Kitchener Rangers	St. Catharines Black Hawks
1974-75—Toronto Marlboros	Toronto Marlboros
1975-76—Sudbury Wolves	Hamilton Steelhawks
1976-77—St. Catharines Fincups	Ottawa 67's
1977-78—Ottawa 67's	Peterborough Petes
1978-79—Peterborough Petes	Peterborough Petes
1979-80—Peterborough Petes	Peterborough Petes
1980-81—Sault St. Marie Greyhounds	Kitchener Rangers
1981-82—Ottawa 67's	Kitchener Rangers
1982-83—Sault Ste. Marie Greyhounds	Oshawa Generals
1983-84—Kitchener Rangers	Ottawa 67's
1984-85—Sault Ste. Marie Greyhounds	Sault Ste. Marie Greyhounds
1985-86—Peterborough Petes	Guelph Platers
1986-87—Oshawa Generals	Oshawa Generals
1987-88—Windsor Compuware Spitfires	Windsor Compuware Spitfires
1988-89—Kitchener Rangers	Peterborough Petes
1989-90—Oshawa Generals	Oshawa Generals
1990-91—Oshawa Generals	Sault Ste. Marie Greyhounds
1991-92—Peterborough Petes	Sault Ste. Marie Greyhounds
1992-93—Peterborough Petes	Peterborough Petes
1993-94—North Bay Centennials	North Bay Centennials
1994-95—Guelph Storm	Detroit Jr. Red Wings

The OHL regular-season champion is awarded the Hamilton Spectator Trophy and the playoff champion is awarded the J. Ross Robertson Cup.

QUEBEC MAJOR JUNIOR HOCKEY LEAGUE

LEAGUE OFFICE

President
  Gilles Courteau
Vice president
  Maurice Filion
Statistician
  Denis Demers
Communications assistant
  Manon Gagnon-Leroux

Administrative assistant
  Claire Lussier
Address
  255 Roland-Therien Blvd.
  Suite 101
  Longueuil, Quebec

Phone
  514-442-3590
FAX
  514-442-3593

1994-95 REGULAR SEASON

FINAL STANDINGS

ROBERT LE BEL DIVISION

Team	G	W	L	T	Pts.	GF	GA
Laval	72	48	22	2	98	302	232
Hull	72	42	28	2	86	340	274
St. Jean	72	39	27	6	84	282	277
Granby	72	31	36	5	67	314	294
St. Hyacinthe	72	26	42	4	56	241	310
Val-d'Or	72	21	49	2	44	232	341

FRANK DILIO DIVISION

Team	G	W	L	T	Pts.	GF	GA
Beauport	72	39	24	9	87	291	202
Shawinigan	72	40	28	4	84	325	270
Chicoutimi	72	38	29	5	81	290	259
Sherbrooke	72	37	30	5	79	297	261
Drummondville	72	31	38	3	65	272	302
Halifax	72	24	42	6	54	257	317
Victoriaville	72	24	45	3	51	266	371

INDIVIDUAL LEADERS

Goals: Alain Savage, Shawinigan (55)
Assists: Patrick Carignan, Shawinigan (100)
Points: Patrick Carignan, Shawinigan (137)
Penalty minutes: Danny Dupont, Granby (446)
Goaltending average: Martin Biron, Beauport (2.48)
Shutouts: Jose Theodore, Hull (5)

	Games	G	A	Pts.
Serge Aubin, Granby	60	37	73	110
Steve Brule, St. Jean	69	44	64	108
Mathieu Dandenault, Sherbrooke	67	37	70	107
Alexei Lojkin, Chicoutimi	57	43	58	101
Christian Dube, Sherbrooke	71	36	65	101
Martin Menard, Hull	64	44	56	100
Stephane St. Amour, Drummondville	57	41	49	100
Eric Daze, Beauport	57	54	45	99
Brant Blackned, Halifax	72	45	52	97
Eric Lecompte, Sherbrooke	64	42	48	90
Samuel Groleau, Chicoutimi	61	40	49	89
Patrick Deraspe, Drummondville	52	32	56	88
Benoit Gratton, Laval	71	30	58	88
Michael McKay, Hull	64	28	60	88

TOP SCORERS

	Games	G	A	Pts.
Patrick Carignan, Shawinigan	71	37	100	137
Sebastien Bordeleau, Hull	68	52	76	128
Daniel Briere, Drummondville	72	51	72	123
Christian Matte, Granby	66	50	66	116
Alain Savage, Shawinigan	71	55	57	112
Frederic Chartier, Laval	72	51	59	110

INDIVIDUAL STATISTICS

BEAUPORT HARFANGS

SCORING

	Games	G	A	Pts.	PIM
Eric Daze	57	54	45	99	20
Marc Chouinard	68	24	40	64	32
Eric Montreuil	70	21	39	60	186
Jean-Yves Leroux	59	19	33	52	125
Christian Laflamme	67	6	41	47	82
Ian McIntyre	56	10	33	43	149
Donald MacLean	64	15	27	42	37
Yannick Tremblay	70	10	32	42	22
Patrick Cote	56	20	20	40	314
Eric Belanger	71	12	28	40	24
Patrick Deraspe	24	16	22	38	45
Martin Ethier	68	4	26	30	125
Dimitri Goubar	60	10	15	25	4
Derrick Walser	48	4	18	22	34
Hugo Belanger	28	10	11	21	20
Jimmy Provencher	34	10	10	20	15
Eric Moreau	32	9	11	20	27

	Games	G	A	Pts.	PIM
Vincent Tremblay	33	9	10	19	52
Stephane Madore	46	5	12	17	115
Louis Bedard	33	3	9	12	162
Claude St. Cyr	28	6	3	9	7
Joel Theriault	51	2	5	7	293
Nick Spaccucci	29	4	0	4	51
Jean-Francois Tremblay	11	1	3	4	21
Rejean Dufour	34	1	3	4	17
Vitali Kozel	9	0	4	4	8
Emmanuel Labranche	26	0	4	4	90
Mario Cormier	13	2	1	3	12
Sebastien Berube	6	1	2	3	12
Patrice Paquin	1	1	1	2	2
Hugo Deschenes	4	1	1	2	2
Brad Hartlin	24	1	1	2	6
Jonathan Nantel	3	0	1	1	0
Michel Dodier	2	0	0	0	0
Bobby Rochon (goalie)	30	—	—	—	4
Martin Biron (goalie)	56	—	—	—	6

GOALTENDING

	Games	Min.	W	L	T	Goals	SO	Avg.
Martin Biron	56	3193	29	16	9	132	3	2.48
Bobby Rochon	30	1327	4	14	2	95	0	4.30

CHICOUTIMI SAGUENEENS

SCORING

	Games	G	A	Pts.	PIM
Alexei Lojkin	57	43	58	101	26
Samuel Groleau	61	40	49	89	47
Allan Sirois	68	23	41	64	184
Yannick Jean	71	7	46	53	155
Patrick Lacombe	72	5	47	52	197
Christian Caron	45	14	31	45	150
Jerome Boivin	66	14	30	44	55
Simon Harvey	61	16	25	41	44
Dominic Savard	53	20	19	39	14
Alain Nasreddine	67	8	31	39	342
Marc Bouchard	58	16	20	36	20
Steve Dulac	61	14	16	30	67
Denis Hamel	66	15	12	27	155
Andre Roy	20	15	8	23	90
Yan Laterreur	31	8	8	16	18
Hugo Veilleux	31	6	10	16	27
Valery Ermelov	31	5	8	13	6
Sebastien Bety	24	4	9	13	109
Jaysen Barbeau	65	2	11	13	46
Michel Lebouthillier	67	2	9	11	10
Christian Labonte	13	4	6	10	10
Yann Vaillancourt	32	3	7	10	47
Marco Cimon	57	2	4	6	70
Daniel Laflamme	12	1	4	5	12
Vincent Gignac	56	1	3	4	118
Carl Latulippe	6	1	2	3	7
Pascal Gagnon	3	0	2	2	15
Frederic Servant	4	1	0	1	0
Stefano Paduano	3	0	1	1	0
Marc-Etienne Hubert	2	0	0	0	0
Marc Drainville	10	0	0	0	11
Yohan Dufour (goalie)	1	—	—	—	0
Marc Denis (goalie)	32	—	—	—	6
Eric Fichaud (goalie)	46	—	—	—	14

GOALTENDING

	Games	Min.	W	L	T	Goals	SO	Avg.
Eric Fichaud	46	2637	21	19	4	151	4	3.44
Marc Denis	32	1688	17	9	1	98	0	3.48
Yohan Dufour	1	59	0	1	0	5	0	5.08

DRUMMONDVILLE VOLTIGEURS

SCORING

	Games	G	A	Pts.	PIM
Daniel Briere	72	51	72	123	54
Stephane St. Amour	57	41	59	100	87
Patrick Deraspe	28	16	34	50	21
Mathieu Sunderland	66	21	24	45	185
Steve Tardif	64	10	33	43	313
Denis Gauthier	64	9	31	40	190
Andre Roy	34	18	13	31	233
Francois Sasseville	62	18	11	29	80
David Thibeault	61	10	19	29	101
Martin Woods	22	8	15	23	82
Christian Drolet	64	7	16	23	40
Paolo DeRubertis	63	8	14	22	357
Martin Pouliot	62	7	15	22	98
Martin Latulippe	45	2	19	21	85
David Lessard	25	11	6	17	63
Sebastien Lefrancois	51	6	10	16	50
Bruno Gladu	22	4	12	16	19
Patrice Charbonneau	72	6	7	13	77
Carl Latulippe	36	4	8	12	36
Marc-Olivier Roy	59	0	10	10	52
Alexandre Duchesne	9	3	6	9	17
Sebastien Bety	22	1	7	8	77
Hugo Tremblay	35	1	7	8	29

	Games	G	A	Pts.	PIM
Yan St. Pierre	12	4	3	7	10
Christian Marcoux	24	1	5	6	35
Alexandre Laporte	23	0	6	6	28
Patrick Cassin	13	3	2	5	2
Mario Cormier	8	0	3	3	10
Emmanuel Labranche	32	1	1	2	95
Sylvain Brisson	16	1	0	1	28
Norbert Roy	3	0	1	1	0
Nicolas Savage	12	0	1	1	69
Iannique Renaud	24	0	1	1	126
Denys McDonald	1	0	0	0	0
Patrick Tremblay	1	0	0	0	0
Luc St. Germain	4	0	0	0	2
Martin Element	5	0	0	0	2
Benoit Cloutier	9	0	0	0	29
Herbie Bonvie	10	0	0	0	7
Denys McDonald (goalie)	1	—	—	—	0
Yannick Gagnon (goalie)	18	—	—	—	0
Kaven St. Pierre (goalie)	24	—	—	—	17
David Arsenault (goalie)	31	—	—	—	19
Steve Vezina (goalie)	42	—	—	—	2

GOALTENDING

	Games	Min.	W	L	T	Goals	SO	Avg.
Denys McDonald	1	1	0	0	0	0	0	0.00
Steve Vezina	42	2115	21	14	0	131	2	3.72
Yannick Gagnon	18	935	8	8	0	67	2	4.30
Kaven St. Pierre	24	1208	7	12	0	87	0	4.32
David Arsenault	31	1332	5	15	0	115	0	5.18

GRANBY BISONS

SCORING

	Games	G	A	Pts.	PIM
Christian Matte	66	50	66	116	86
Serge Aubin	60	37	73	110	55
Frederic Bouchard	70	17	49	66	190
Louis-Philippe Sevigny	72	17	39	56	165
Xavier Delisle	72	18	36	54	48
Dave Boudreault	42	24	27	51	143
Martin Chouinard	53	16	28	44	53
Hugues Gervais	71	17	25	42	341
Eric Bertrand	56	14	26	40	268
Maxime Blouin	45	15	23	38	46
Philippe Audet	62	19	17	36	93
Dave Douville	55	13	15	28	46
Martin Woods	19	6	16	22	116
Jean-Martin Morin	24	7	11	18	14
Martin Corbeil	68	8	8	16	132
Samy Nasreddine	65	4	12	16	82
David Brosseau	26	9	6	15	37
Martin Lepage	33	2	12	14	94
David Haynes	20	6	5	11	65
Martin Belanger	43	0	11	11	32
Kevin Bourque	44	4	4	8	25
Dave Savard	37	2	6	8	76
Martin Latulippe	16	1	4	5	28
Danny Dupont	16	2	2	4	130
Dave Belliveau	17	2	2	4	17
Yan Coulombe	51	1	3	4	67
Martin Brosseau	31	0	4	4	48
Marc Benoit	21	1	2	3	16
Christian Lefebvre	24	1	1	2	11
Michel Massie	8	1	0	1	2
Jean-Philippe Soucy	7	0	1	1	0
Frederic Henry (goalie)	15	—	—	—	0
Frederic Deschene (goalie)	45	—	—	—	2

GOALTENDING

	Games	Min.	W	L	T	Goals	SO	Avg.
Frederic Henry	15	866	8	5	0	47	0	3.26
Frederic Deschene	45	2375	16	23	1	160	0	4.04

HALIFAX MOOSEHEADS

SCORING

	Games	G	A	Pts.	PIM
Brant Blackned	72	45	52	97	76
Stephane Larocque	72	28	48	76	342
Mario Dumoulin	72	23	51	74	240
Chris Peyton	71	12	50	62	92
Etienne Drapeau	63	26	35	61	121
Derrick Pyke	71	20	22	42	99
Rocco Anoia	68	16	20	36	179
Eric Houde	28	13	23	36	8
Chris Angione	67	10	26	36	56
David Carson	45	16	16	32	12
Nicolas Maheux	46	12	15	27	31
Jody Shelley	72	10	12	22	194
Daniel Villeneuve	66	4	8	12	269
Steve Mongrain	55	6	4	10	122
Chris Cahoon	41	4	6	10	64
Claude Fillion	28	1	9	10	133
Jamie Brown	59	1	9	10	87
Dereck Michaud	14	2	6	8	18
Danny Dupont	27	1	5	6	239
Simon Godbout	31	0	5	5	51
Chris Halverson	49	1	3	4	239
Iannique Renaud	19	2	1	3	166
Elias Abrahamsson	25	0	3	3	41
Mark McNulty	35	0	3	3	126
Daniel Payette	28	1	1	2	53
Mark Johnson	22	0	2	2	63
Steeve Finn	8	1	0	1	7
Sebastien Berube	23	1	0	1	73
Yannick Gaucher	4	0	1	1	9
Ian Fontaine	2	0	0	0	0
Patrick Desjardins	10	0	0	0	8
Harlin Hayes (goalie)	7	—	—	—	0
Jean-Sebastien Giguere (g)	47	—	—	—	32

GOALTENDING

	Games	Min.	W	L	T	Goals	SO	Avg.
J.S. Giguere	47	2755	14	27	5	181	2	3.94
Harlin Hayes	7	275	1	3	0	24	0	5.24

HULL OLYMPIQUES

SCORING

	Games	G	A	Pts.	PIM
Sebastien Bordeleau	68	52	76	128	142
Martin Menard	64	44	56	100	48
Michael McKay	64	28	60	88	110
Jean-Guy Trudel	54	29	42	71	76
Jamie Bird	66	11	51	62	130
Jonathan Delisle	60	21	38	59	218
Harold Hersh	65	28	30	58	116
Carl Charland	67	22	21	43	159
Carl Beaudoin	69	4	33	37	150
Roddie MacKenzie	60	14	21	35	190
Jan Nemecek	49	10	16	26	48
Louis-Philippe Charbonneau	34	14	9	23	318
Francois Cloutier	58	15	5	20	70
Eric Lecompte	12	11	9	20	58
Alex Rodrigue	26	12	6	18	27
Richard Safarik	47	5	12	17	34
Eric Cloutier	25	3	11	14	181
Shane Doiron	16	5	8	13	65
Brandon Gray	12	3	8	11	11
Jason Groleau	43	2	9	11	175
Gordie Dwyer	57	3	7	10	204
Peter Worrell	56	1	8	9	243
Michael Coveny	66	0	7	7	236
Steve Gervais	35	1	4	5	73
Simon Provencher	15	1	3	4	59
Chris Hall	21	0	4	4	76
Sean Farmer	45	0	3	3	95
Pierre-Francois Lalonde	1	2	0	2	0
Colin White	5	0	1	1	4
Peter James Akiwenzie	11	0	1	1	18

	Games	G	A	Pts.	PIM
Kevin Felix	2	0	0	0	14
Patrick Lamey	2	0	0	0	12
Stephane Poulin	4	0	0	0	0
Carl Prud'homme	7	0	0	0	2
Eric Patry (goalie)	1	—	—	—	0
Gabriel Snauweart (goalie)	2	—	—	—	0
Matthew Carmichael (goalie)	9	—	—	—	6
Neil Savary (goalie)	30	—	—	—	18
Jose Theodore (goalie)	58	—	—	—	20

GOALTENDING

	Games	Min.	W	L	T	Goals	SO	Avg.
Gabriel Snauweart	2	54	0	0	0	3	0	3.33
Jose Theodore	58	3348	32	22	2	193	5	3.46
Neil Savary	30	1525	14	12	1	118	0	4.64
Matthew Carmichael	9	217	1	2	0	18	0	4.98
Eric Patry	1	20	0	0	0	3	0	9.00

LAVAL TITANS

SCORING

	Games	G	A	Pts.	PIM
Frederic Chartier	72	51	59	110	159
Benoit Gratton	71	30	58	88	199
Anders Myrvold	64	14	50	64	173
Jason Boudrias	52	24	37	61	43
Jason Doig	55	13	42	55	259
Dominic Perna	70	26	27	53	30
Jeff Loder	66	22	27	49	67
Daniel Goneau	56	16	31	47	78
Patrick Boileau	38	8	25	33	46
Francis Bouillon	72	8	25	33	115
Dave Boudreault	22	19	13	32	77
Jeff Mercer	49	14	9	23	318
Jean-Francois Brunelle	43	9	14	23	39
Jason Bermingham	58	10	12	22	22
Jean-Francois Robert	39	7	15	22	93
Marc Lirette	42	8	12	20	4
Francois Pilon	71	6	10	16	116
David Haynes	40	5	9	14	219
Frederic Jobin	70	0	13	13	285
Francois Veilleux	53	4	8	12	372
Eddy Gervais	17	3	5	8	16
Maxime Blouin	23	3	5	8	4
Eric Cloutier	23	3	3	6	133
Jeffrey Lagueux	6	0	2	2	0
Richard Goudie	23	0	2	2	6
Luc Boily	31	1	0	1	5
Yanick Dube	1	0	1	1	0
Danny Dupont	7	0	1	1	77
Colin White	7	0	1	1	32
Jon Sim	9	0	1	1	6
Marc-Andre Tousignant	13	0	1	1	98
Steve Parson	27	0	1	1	176
David Desjardins	1	0	0	0	0
Ian Monfils	1	0	0	0	0
Philippe Trudeau	2	0	0	0	2
Martin Villeneuve (goalie)	40	—	—	—	8
Sebastien Charpentier (goalie)	41	—	—	—	17

GOALTENDING

	Games	Min.	W	L	T	Goals	SO	Avg.
S. Charpentier	41	2152	25	12	1	99	2	2.76
Martin Villeneuve	40	2142	23	9	1	125	0	3.50

ST. HYACINTHE LASERS

SCORING

	Games	G	A	Pts.	PIM
Steve Brule	69	44	64	108	42
Eric Landry	68	38	36	74	249
Francois Methot	60	14	38	52	22
Jean-Francois Tremblay	71	19	26	45	270
David Desnoyers	67	12	32	44	226
Marc Sigouin	72	12	32	44	143

	Games	G	A	Pts.	PIM
Yannick Hubert	68	19	23	42	55
David-Alexandre Beauregard	37	24	16	40	22
Jimmy Drolet	68	9	27	36	126
Remy Boudreau	72	13	19	32	27
David Bernier	66	15	16	31	40
Hugo Bertrand	61	4	21	25	274
Gabriel Cote	53	8	16	24	116
Eric Gauvin	26	7	13	20	37
Nathan Morin	28	7	9	16	213
Yann Vaillancourt	30	10	5	15	15
Christian Gosselin	60	5	10	15	202
Yan St. Pierre	30	9	4	13	22
Maxime Leclair	53	4	9	13	19
Luc Dostaler	40	3	9	12	39
Hugo Veilleux	38	3	7	10	62
Alexandre Laporte	38	3	6	9	70
Martin Lacaille	63	1	5	6	83
Jonathan Levesque	40	1	4	5	42
Steeven Dussault	38	1	2	3	16
Pascal Ouellet	1	0	1	1	0
Frederic Delage	1	0	0	0	0
Brad Hartlin	1	0	0	0	0
Jean-Francois Lachance	1	0	0	0	2
Maxime Lessard	1	0	0	0	0
Hugo Tremblay	1	0	0	0	0
Yanick Plante	2	0	0	0	9
Jonathan Girard	6	0	0	0	0
Nicolas Savage	34	0	0	0	117
Stephane Routhier (goalie)	44	—	—	—	2
Frederick Beaubien (goalie)	51	—	—	—	14

GOALTENDING

	Games	Min.	W	L	T	Goals	SO	Avg.
Stephane Routhier	44	2378	15	20	3	149	0	3.76
Frederick Beaubien	51	2697	19	24	4	178	1	3.96

ST. JEAN LYNX

SCORING

	Games	G	A	Pts.	PIM
Stephane Roy	68	19	52	71	113
Patrice Paquin	53	22	32	54	147
Rony Valenti	68	23	26	49	229
Hugo Turcotte	32	17	28	45	0
Jan Melichercik	71	15	27	42	16
Georges Laraque	62	19	22	41	259
Jimmy Provencher	37	14	21	35	51
Eric Gauvin	33	11	19	30	16
Frederic Barbeau	68	7	23	30	104
Patrick Charbonneau	71	10	19	29	86
Yanick Turcotte	65	13	14	27	51
Jean-Francois Boutin	32	10	17	27	20
Shane Doiron	54	9	17	26	140
Sebastien Lessard	44	8	17	25	12
Eric Houde	40	10	13	23	23
Eric Normandin	64	6	16	22	37
Eric Moreau	32	6	15	21	30
Eric Lecompte	18	9	10	19	54
Alex Richard	39	3	10	13	17
Jean Theroux	29	5	5	10	17
Simon Provencher	41	3	6	9	90
Joel Theriault	18	2	7	9	94
Francois Archambault	18	4	4	8	60
Daniel Payette	33	2	5	7	46
Eric Drouin	57	1	6	7	29
Claude Fillion	23	0	6	6	87
Martin Poitras	18	1	3	4	12
Bruno Gladu	9	3	0	3	0
Francois Levesque	41	2	1	3	10
Jason Groleau	16	1	1	2	31
Martin Rozon	2	1	0	1	0
Steeven Dussault	20	0	1	1	10
Casey Wolak	1	0	0	0	0
Nathan Morin	2	0	0	0	11
Pierre Gauthier	3	0	0	0	2
Patrick Gladu	10	0	0	0	26

	Games	G	A	Pts.	PIM
Martin Rodrigue (goalie)	18	—	—	—	0
Carl Benoit (goalie)	29	—	—	—	6
Frederic Cassivi (goalie)	43	—	—	—	38

GOALTENDING

	Games	Min.	W	L	T	Goals	SO	Avg.
Carl Benoit	29	1509	11	8	5	85	1	3.38
Martin Rodrigue	18	962	10	5	0	61	2	3.80
Frederic Cassivi	43	2383	21	18	1	160	1	4.03

SHAWINIGAN CATARACTES

SCORING

	Games	G	A	Pts.	PIM
Patrick Carignan	71	37	100	137	43
Alain Savage	71	55	57	112	112
Yanick Evola	72	29	58	87	260
Carl Paradis	66	33	45	78	78
Jean-Francois Laroche	67	30	43	73	70
Stephane Robidas	71	13	56	69	44
Martin Lamarche	58	20	29	49	353
David Brosseau	39	28	20	48	65
Pavel Agarkov	55	19	26	45	34
David Grenier	67	16	24	40	190
Dereck Gosselin	72	9	24	33	115
Guy Loranger	61	9	17	26	93
Jean-Francois Bessette	65	3	17	20	178
Alexandre Jacques	71	9	8	17	18
Sergei Polichouk	63	1	15	16	151
David Bahl	60	3	12	15	63
Evan Levi	42	2	5	7	4
Sylvain Rodier	38	4	2	6	24
Mathieu Descoteaux	50	3	2	5	28
Dave Savard	23	2	1	3	53
Patrick Lafleur	20	0	2	2	41
Carl Benoit	63	0	2	2	44
Patrick Gladu	13	0	1	1	75
Eric Doucet	1	0	0	0	0
Benjamin Carpentier	2	0	0	0	0
Clark Udle	2	0	0	0	0
Steven Morneau	11	0	0	0	5
Steve Plouffe (goalie)	32	—	—	—	6
Sylvain Daigle (goalie)	48	—	—	—	2

GOALTENDING

	Games	Min.	W	L	T	Goals	SO	Avg.
Sylvain Daigle	48	2831	27	17	3	159	3	3.37
Steve Plouffe	32	1702	12	11	5	113	0	3.98

SHERBROOKE FAUCONS

SCORING

	Games	G	A	Pts.	PIM
Mathieu Dandenault	67	37	70	107	76
Christian Dube	71	36	65	101	43
Stephane Julien	66	22	59	81	103
Etienne Beaudry	56	37	28	65	20
Eric Lecompte	34	22	29	51	111
Radoslav Suchy	69	12	32	44	30
Charles Paquette	53	15	26	41	186
Pascal Bernier	57	11	25	36	67
Gaetan Royer	65	11	25	36	194
Hugo Turcotte	33	21	12	33	23
Vitali Kozel	31	10	21	31	8
Jean-Francois Boutin	36	12	17	29	42
Francois Rivard	49	7	10	17	46
Eric Jenkins	72	3	14	17	106
David Gosselin	58	8	8	16	36
Samuel Lacroix	60	8	8	16	35
Steven Low	42	3	13	16	130
Bruce Richardson	32	1	13	14	25
Jean-Francois Robert	28	5	4	9	27
Patrick Pelchat	37	5	3	8	43
Alex Richard	36	4	4	8	38
Louis-Simon Arguin	15	1	6	7	4

	Games	G	A	Pts.	PIM
Richard Lacasse	34	1	6	7	37
Yannick Tremblay	10	2	2	4	15
Mathieu Raby	25	2	2	4	106
Jean-Sebastien Gingras	32	1	3	4	48
Dave Bolduc	22	0	4	4	30
Patrick Gladu	7	1	0	1	39
Yannick Auger	7	0	1	1	0
Rick Horch	10	0	1	1	2
Kevin Vaughan	27	0	1	1	38
Sebastien Robitaille	1	0	0	0	0
Benoit Larose	28	0	0	0	32
Claude Fernet (goalie)	1	—	—	—	0
Jocelyn Thibault (goalie)	13	—	—	—	2
Jean-Sebastien Aubin (goalie)	27	—	—	—	4
Luc Belanger (goalie)	43	—	—	—	6

GOALTENDING

	Games	Min.	W	L	T	Goals	SO	Avg.
Jocelyn Thibault	13	776	6	6	1	38	1	2.94
Claude Fernet	1	59	0	1	0	3	0	3.05
J.S. Aubin	27	1287	13	10	1	73	1	3.40
Luc Belanger	43	2240	18	13	3	144	1	3.86

VAL-D'OR FOREURS

SCORING

	Games	G	A	Pts.	PIM
Cosmo DuPaul	71	29	44	73	60
Mathieu Carpentier	63	14	28	42	119
Daniel Bienvenue	67	27	14	41	40
Daniel Germain	55	10	30	40	140
Francois Archambault	40	14	23	37	54
Hugo Belanger	31	12	19	31	8
Yannick Gaucher	43	11	20	31	40
Dominic Chiasson	65	17	13	30	46
Pascal Chiasson	66	4	24	28	242
Louis Bedard	38	11	16	27	184
Mathieu Letourneau	67	6	21	27	154
Jean-Luc Grand-Pierre	59	10	13	23	126
Christian Fortin	56	15	6	21	24
Jason Dumont	30	7	14	21	25
Christian Neveu	63	8	12	20	42
Jean-Pierre Dumont	48	5	14	19	24
Claude St. Cyr	28	8	10	18	31
Christian Bigras	39	11	5	16	57
Marquis Gregoire	70	4	10	14	74
Eric Sylvestre	52	3	10	13	43
Yan Laterreur	13	4	1	5	10
Nicolas Morency	18	1	4	5	4
Daniel Archambault	54	3	1	4	165
Christian Labonte	14	2	2	4	52
Brandon Gray	18	1	3	4	39
Martin Belair	17	0	4	4	19
Frederic Servant	17	1	2	3	31
Craig Copeland	3	0	2	2	0
Francois Fortin	4	1	0	1	2
Domenico Scali	6	1	0	1	10
Kevin Papatie	14	1	0	1	61
Ryan Coughlan	17	1	0	1	7
Christian Deschenes	7	0	1	1	2
Marc Drainville	26	0	1	1	39
Dagan Kay	1	0	0	0	19
Alexandre Lauzon	1	0	0	0	0
Tommy Melancon	1	0	0	0	0
Pierre Frechette	2	0	0	0	5
Roberto Baldris	5	0	0	0	2
Guy Legault	5	0	0	0	0
Michel Lincourt (goalie)	1	—	—	—	0
Francis St. Onge (goalie)	3	—	—	—	0
Francis Larivee (goalie)	38	—	—	—	36
Hugo Hamelin (goalie)	46	—	—	—	53

GOALTENDING

	Games	Min.	W	L	T	Goals	SO	Avg.
Francis Larivee	38	1795	9	21	1	132	0	4.41
Hugo Hamelin	46	2455	12	25	1	192	0	4.69

	Games	Min.	W	L	T	Goals	SO	Avg.
Michel Lincourt	1	60	0	0	0	8	0	8.00
Francis St. Onge	3	70	0	1	0	13	0	11.14

VICTORIAVILLE TIGRES

SCORING

	Games	G	A	Pts.	PIM
Jean-Martin Morin	41	29	28	57	32
Sebastien Vallee	72	23	32	55	52
Maxime Roux	67	18	37	55	119
Philippe-Joseph Stock	70	9	46	55	386
Daniel Corso	65	27	26	53	6
Philippe Gelineau	64	21	32	53	66
David Lessard	42	15	24	39	116
Alexandre Daigle	18	14	20	34	16
Philippe Vezina	63	13	13	26	41
Sebastien Demers	70	12	12	24	45
Dany Larochelle	67	5	17	22	69
Remi Royer	57	3	17	20	144
Steven Low	28	8	9	17	112
Mathieu Raby	38	5	11	16	238
Eric Naud	62	4	12	16	139
Dominic Marleau	63	3	13	16	78
Dean Stock	56	8	7	15	119
Alexandre Duchesne	19	5	10	15	30
Alexandre Couture	24	4	7	11	4
Louis-Philippe Charbonneau	13	4	4	8	86
Patrick Pelchat	29	4	1	5	26
Pierre Morin	57	1	4	5	199
Marc-Andre Gaudet	59	1	3	4	71
Benoit Larose	23	0	3	3	99
Bryan Faucher	7	1	1	2	5
Patrick Berube	2	0	1	1	2
Marc Diamond	1	0	0	0	0
Francois Page	3	0	0	0	5
Karl Castonguay	5	0	0	0	0
Mario Dumais	8	0	0	0	0
Sebastien Decaens	17	0	0	0	4
Benoit Thibert (goalie)	1	—	—	—	0
David Dubuc (goalie)	24	—	—	—	0
Patrick Charbonneau (goalie)	47	—	—	—	68

GOALTENDING

	Games	Min.	W	L	T	Goals	SO	Avg.
Benoit Thibert	1	49	0	1	0	4	0	4.90
P. Charbonneau	47	2339	15	27	1	201	0	5.16
David Dubuc	24	798	5	5	0	73	0	5.49

PLAYERS WITH TWO OR MORE TEAMS

SCORING

	Games	G	A	Pts.	PIM
Francois Archambault, St. Jean	18	4	4	8	60
Francois Archambault, Val-D'Or	40	14	23	37	54
Totals	58	18	27	45	114
Louis Bedard, Val-D'Or	38	11	16	27	184
Louis Bedard, Beauport	33	3	9	12	162
Totals	71	14	25	39	346
Hugo Belanger, Beauport	28	10	11	21	20
Hugo Belanger, Val-D'Or	31	12	19	31	8
Totals	59	22	30	52	28
Sebastien Berube, Beauport	6	1	2	3	12
Sebastien Berube, Halifax	23	1	0	1	73
Totals	29	2	2	4	85
Sebastien Bety, Drummondville	22	1	7	8	77
Sebastien Bety, Chicoutimi	24	4	9	13	109
Totals	46	5	16	21	186
Maxime Blouin, Granby	45	15	23	38	46
Maxime Blouin, Laval	23	3	5	8	4
Totals	68	18	28	46	50
Dave Boudreault, Granby	42	24	27	51	143
Dave Boudreault, Laval	22	19	13	32	77
Totals	64	43	40	83	220
Jean-Francois Boutin, Sher.	36	12	17	29	42
Jean-Francois Boutin, St. Jean	32	10	17	27	20
Totals	68	22	34	56	62

	Games	G	A	Pts.	PIM
David Brosseau, Shawinigan	39	28	20	48	65
David Brosseau, Granby	26	9	6	15	37
Totals	65	37	26	63	102
Louis-Philippe Charbonneau, Vic.	13	4	4	8	86
Louis-Philippe Charbonneau, Hull	34	14	9	23	318
Totals	47	18	13	31	404
Eric Cloutier, Hull	25	3	11	14	181
Eric Cloutier, Laval	23	3	3	6	133
Totals	48	6	14	20	314
Mario Cormier, Beauport	13	2	1	3	12
Mario Cormier, Drummondville	8	0	3	3	10
Totals	21	2	4	6	22
Patrick Deraspe, Beauport	24	16	22	38	45
Patrick Deraspe, Drummondville	28	16	34	50	21
Totals	52	32	56	88	66
Shane Doiron, Hull	16	5	8	13	65
Shane Doiron, St. Jean	54	9	17	26	140
Totals	70	14	25	39	205
Marc Drainville, Chicoutimi	10	0	0	0	11
Marc Drainville, Val-D'Or	26	0	1	1	39
Totals	36	0	1	1	43
Alexandre Duchesne, Drum.	9	3	6	9	17
Alexandre Duchesne, Vic.	19	5	10	15	30
Totals	28	8	16	24	47
Danny Dupont, Halifax	27	1	5	6	239
Danny Dupont, Laval	7	0	1	1	77
Danny Dupont, Granby	16	2	2	4	130
Totals	50	3	8	11	446
Steeven Dussault, St. Jean	20	0	1	1	10
Steeven Dussault, St. Hy.	38	1	2	3	16
Totals	58	1	3	4	26
Claude Fillion, Halifax	28	1	9	10	133
Claude Fillion, St. Jean	23	0	6	6	87
Totals	51	1	15	16	220
Yannick Gaucher, Halifax	4	0	1	1	9
Yannick Gaucher, Val-D'Or	43	11	20	31	40
Totals	47	11	21	32	49
Eric Gauvin, St. Hyacinthe	26	7	13	20	37
Eric Gauvin, St. Jean	33	11	19	30	16
Totals	59	18	32	50	53
Bruno Gladu, Drummondville	22	4	12	16	19
Bruno Gladu, St. Jean	9	3	0	3	0
Totals	31	7	12	19	19
Patrick Gladu, Shawinigan	13	0	1	1	75
Patrick Gladu, Sherbrooke	7	1	0	1	39
Patrick Gladu, St. Jean	10	0	0	0	26
Totals	30	1	1	2	140
Brandon Gray, Hull	12	3	8	11	11
Brandon Gray, Val-D'Or	18	1	3	4	39
Totals	30	4	11	15	50
Jason Groleau, St. Jean	16	1	1	2	31
Jason Groleau, Hull	43	2	9	11	175
Totals	59	3	10	13	206
Brad Hartlin, St. Hyacinthe	1	0	0	0	0
Brad Hartlin, Beauport	24	1	1	2	6
Totals	25	1	1	2	6
David Haynes, Laval	40	5	9	14	219
David Haynes, Granby	20	6	5	11	65
Totals	60	11	14	25	284
Eric Houde, St. Jean	40	10	13	23	23
Eric Houde, Halifax	28	13	23	36	8
Totals	68	23	36	59	31
Vitali Kozel, Beauport	9	0	4	4	8
Vitali Kozel, Sherbrooke	31	10	21	31	8
Totals	40	10	25	35	16
Christian Labonte, Val-D'Or	14	2	2	4	52
Christian Labonte, Chicoutimi	13	4	6	10	10
Totals	27	6	8	14	62
Emmanuel Labranche, Drum.	32	1	1	2	95
Emmanuel Labranche, Beauport	26	0	4	4	90
Totals	58	1	5	6	185
Alexandre Laporte, St. Hy.	38	3	6	9	70
Alexandre Laporte, Drum.	23	0	6	6	28
Totals	61	3	12	15	98
Benoit Larose, Victoriaville	23	0	3	3	99
Benoit Larose, Sherbrooke	28	0	0	0	32

	Games	G	A	Pts.	PIM
Totals	51	0	3	3	131
Yan Laterreur, Val-D'Or	13	4	1	5	10
Yan Laterreur, Chicoutimi	31	8	8	16	18
Totals	44	12	9	21	28
Carl Latulippe, Chicoutimi	6	1	2	3	7
Carl Latulippe, Drummondville	36	4	8	12	36
Totals	42	5	10	15	43
Martin Latulippe, Drum.	45	2	19	21	85
Martin Latulippe, Granby	16	1	4	5	28
Totals	61	3	23	26	113
Eric Lecompte, Hull	12	11	9	20	58
Eric Lecompte, St. Jean	18	9	10	19	54
Eric Lecompte, Sherbrooke	34	22	29	51	111
Totals	64	42	48	90	223
David Lessard, Victoriaville	42	15	24	39	116
David Lessard, Drummondville	25	11	6	17	63
Totals	67	26	30	56	179
Steven Low, Sherbrooke	42	3	13	16	130
Steven Low, Victoriaville	28	8	9	17	112
Totals	70	11	22	33	242
Eric Moreau, Beauport	32	9	11	20	27
Eric Moreau, St. Jean	32	6	15	21	30
Totals	64	15	26	41	57
Jean-Martin Morin, Victoriaville	41	29	28	57	32
Jean-Martin Morin, Granby	24	7	11	18	14
Totals	65	36	39	75	46
Nathan Morin, St. Jean	2	0	0	0	11
Nathan Morin, St. Hyacinthe	28	7	9	16	213
Totals	30	7	9	16	224
Patrice Paquin, Beauport	1	1	1	2	2
Patrice Paquin, St. Jean	53	22	32	54	147
Totals	54	23	33	56	149
Daniel Payette, St. Jean	33	2	5	7	46
Daniel Payette, Halifax	28	1	1	2	53
Totals	61	3	6	9	99
Patrick Pelchat, Sherbrooke	37	5	3	8	43
Patrick Pelchat, Victoriaville	29	4	1	5	26
Totals	66	9	4	13	69
Jimmy Provencher, St. Jean	37	14	21	35	51
Jimmy Provencher, Beauport	34	10	10	20	15
Totals	71	24	31	55	66
Simon Provencher, Hull	15	1	3	4	59
Simon Provencher, St. Jean	41	3	6	9	90
Totals	56	4	9	13	149
Mathieu Raby, Victoriaville	38	5	11	16	238
Mathieu Raby, Sherbrooke	25	2	2	4	106
Totals	63	7	13	20	344
Iannique Renaud, Halifax	19	2	1	3	166
Iannique Renaud, Drum.	24	0	1	1	126
Totals	43	2	2	4	292
Alex Richard, St. Jean	39	3	10	13	17
Alex Richard, Sherbrooke	36	4	4	8	38
Totals	75	7	14	21	55
Jean-Francois Robert, Laval	39	7	15	22	93
Jean-Francois Robert, Sher.	28	5	4	9	27
Totals	67	12	19	31	120
Andre Roy, Chicoutimi	20	15	8	23	90
Andre Roy, Drummondville	34	18	13	31	233
Totals	54	33	21	54	323
Nicolas Savage, Drummondville	12	0	1	1	69
Nicolas Savage, St. Hyacinthe	34	0	0	0	117
Totals	46	0	1	1	186
Dave Savard, Granby	37	2	6	8	76
Dave Savard, Shawinigan	23	2	1	3	53
Totals	60	4	7	11	129
Frederic Servant, Chicoutimi	4	1	0	1	0
Frederic Servant, Val-D'Or	17	1	2	3	31
Totals	21	2	2	4	31
Claude St. Cyr, Beauport	28	6	3	9	7
Claude St. Cyr, Val-D'Or	28	8	10	18	31
Totals	56	14	13	27	38
Yan St. Pierre, Drummondville	12	4	3	7	10
Yan St. Pierre, St. Hyacinthe	30	9	4	13	22
Totals	42	13	7	20	32
Joel Theriault, St. Jean	18	2	7	9	94
Joel Theriault, Beauport	51	2	5	7	293

	Games	G	A	Pts.	PIM
Totals	69	4	12	16	387
Hugo Tremblay, Drummondville	35	1	7	8	29
Hugo Tremblay, St. Hyacinthe	1	0	0	0	0
Totals	36	1	7	8	29
Hugo Turcotte, Sherbrooke	33	21	12	33	23
Hugo Turcotte, St. Jean	32	17	28	45	0
Totals	65	38	40	78	23
Yann Vaillancourt, Chicoutimi	32	3	7	10	47
Yann Vaillancourt, St. Hy.	30	10	5	15	15
Totals	62	13	12	25	62

	Games	G	A	Pts.	PIM
Hugo Veilleux, St. Hyacinthe	38	3	7	10	62
Hugo Veilleux, Chicoutimi	31	6	10	16	27
Totals	69	9	17	26	89
Colin White, Laval	7	0	1	1	32
Colin White, Hull	5	0	1	1	4
Totals	12	0	2	2	36
Martin Woods, Granby	19	6	16	22	116
Martin Woods, Drummondville	22	8	15	23	82
Totals	41	14	31	45	198

1995 PRESIDENT CUP PLAYOFFS

RESULTS

QUARTERFINALS

NOTE: QMJHL playoff teams played round-robin tournaments in the early rounds to determine semifinalist teams.

	W	L	Pts.	GF	GA
Hull	4	1	8	17	11
Beauport	1	4	2	11	17

(Hull won series, 4-1)

SEMIFINALS

	W	L	Pts.	GF	GA
Laval	4	1	8	22	17
Shawinigan	1	4	2	17	22

(Laval won series, 4-1)

FINALS

	W	L	Pts.	GF	GA
Hull	4	1	8	19	16
Laval	1	4	2	16	19

(Hull won series, 4-1)

INDIVIDUAL LEADERS

Goals: Sebastien Bordeleau, Hull (13)
Assists: Benoit Gratton, Laval (21)
Points: Sebastien Bordeleau, Hull (32)
Penalty minutes: Joel Theriault, Beauport (162)
Goaltending average: Jean-Sebastien Giguere, Halifax (2.45)
Shutouts: Martin Biron, Beauport (4)

TOP SCORERS

	Games	G	A	Pts.
Sebastien Bordeleau, Hull	18	13	19	32
Benoit Gratton, Laval	20	8	21	29
Patrick Carignan, Shawinigan	15	8	20	28
Jason Boudrias, Laval	20	10	17	27
Dave Boudreault, Laval	20	9	14	23
Yanick Evola, Shawinigan	15	9	14	23
Serge Aubin, Granby	11	8	15	23
Eric Daze, Beauport	16	9	12	21
Alain Savage, Shawinigan	15	6	14	20
Patrick Boileau, Laval	20	4	16	20

INDIVIDUAL STATISTICS

BEAUPORT HARFANGS

(Lost semifinals to Hull, 4-1)

SCORING

	Games	G	A	Pts.	PIM
Eric Daze	16	9	12	21	23
Patrick Cote	17	8	8	16	115
Eric Montreuil	18	5	10	15	72
Yannick Tremblay	17	6	8	14	6
Eric Belanger	18	5	9	14	25
Jean-Yves Leroux	17	4	6	10	39
Joel Theriault	18	3	6	9	162
Donald MacLean	17	4	4	8	6
Jimmy Provencher	17	5	2	7	21
Derrick Walser	12	2	5	7	2
Marc Chouinard	18	1	6	7	4
Vincent Tremblay	16	2	3	5	18
Christian Laflamme	8	1	4	5	6
Ian McIntyre	18	1	4	5	49
Martin Ethier	18	0	5	5	53
Louis Bedard	15	1	1	2	86
Emmanuel Labranche	16	0	2	2	46
Stephane Madore	17	0	2	2	48
Brad Hartlin	5	1	0	1	0
Dimitri Goubar	11	1	0	1	2
Rejean Dufour	3	0	1	1	4
Jean-Francois Tremblay	5	0	0	0	21
Nick Spaccucci	7	0	0	0	13
Bobby Rochon (goalie)	4	—	—	—	—
Martin Biron (goalie)	16	—	—	—	—

GOALTENDING

	Games	Min.	W	L	T	Goals	SO	Avg.
Martin Biron	16	900	8	7	0	37	4	2.47
Bobby Rochon	4	172	2	1	0	11	0	3.84

CHICOUTIMI SAGUENEENS

SCORING

	Games	G	A	Pts.	PIM
Jerome Boivin	13	4	8	12	8
Alexei Lojkin	11	6	5	11	2
Samuel Groleau	13	6	5	11	13
Steve Dulac	13	4	7	11	4
Allan Sirois	13	2	8	10	10
Yannick Jean	13	2	7	9	25
Christian Caron	13	5	3	8	34
Alain Nasreddine	13	3	5	8	40
Patrick Lacombe	12	0	8	8	28
Sebastien Bety	13	1	5	6	46
Hugo Veilleux	13	2	3	5	16
Dominic Savard	12	3	1	4	4
Denis Hamel	13	2	0	2	29
Simon Harvey	13	1	1	2	10
Yan Laterreur	13	1	0	1	6
Vincent Gignac	3	0	0	0	15
Michel Lebouthillier	3	0	0	0	0
Jaysen Barbeau	12	0	0	0	8
Marco Cimon	12	0	0	0	2
Marc Bouchard	13	0	0	0	2

	Games	G	A	Pts.	PIM
Marc Denis (goalie)	6	—	—	—	—
Eric Fichaud (goalie)	7	—	—	—	—

GOALTENDING

	Games	Min.	W	L	T	Goals	SO	Avg.
Eric Fichaud	7	428	2	5	0	20	0	2.80
Marc Denis	6	372	4	2	0	19	1	3.06

DRUMMONDVILLE VOLTIGEURS

SCORING

	Games	G	A	Pts.	PIM
Mathieu Sunderland	3	2	4	6	12
Daniel Briere	4	2	3	5	2
Stephane St. Amour	4	2	3	5	8
Denis Gauthier	4	0	5	5	12
Martin Woods	4	2	2	4	11
Steve Tardif	4	1	2	3	9
Andre Roy	4	2	0	2	34
David Lessard	4	0	2	2	6
Carl Latulippe	3	1	0	1	6
Francois Sasseville	4	1	0	1	4
Martin Pouliot	1	0	1	1	0
Patrick Deraspe	3	0	1	1	6
Alexandre Laporte	4	0	1	1	0
Iannique Renaud	2	0	0	0	2
Patrice Charbonneau	4	0	0	0	15
Mario Cormier	4	0	0	0	2
Paolo DeRubertis	4	0	0	0	6
Christian Drolet	4	0	0	0	0
Marc-Olivier Roy	4	0	0	0	6
David Thibeault	4	0	0	0	0
David Arsenault (goalie)	2	—	—	—	—
Steve Vezina (goalie)	2	—	—	—	—

GOALTENDING

	Games	Min.	W	L	T	Goals	SO	Avg.
David Arsenault	2	122	0	2	0	8	0	3.93
Steve Vezina	2	119	0	2	0	15	0	7.56

GRANBY BISONS

SCORING

	Games	G	A	Pts.	PIM
Serge Aubin	11	8	15	23	4
Christian Matte	13	11	7	18	12
Eric Bertrand	13	3	8	11	50
Frederic Bouchard	13	3	6	9	20
Xavier Delisle	13	2	6	8	4
Martin Chouinard	13	3	4	7	14
Philippe Audet	13	2	5	7	10
Louis-Philippe Sevigny	13	1	6	7	21
Martin Lepage	13	2	4	6	46
Dave Belliveau	12	3	2	5	8
David Brosseau	13	2	2	4	4
Hugues Gervais	13	1	3	4	27
Martin Latulippe	11	1	1	2	76
Jean-Martin Morin	9	0	2	2	4
David Haynes	13	1	0	1	24
Marc Benoit	5	0	1	1	12
Samy Nasreddine	9	0	1	1	10
Martin Belanger	12	0	1	1	6
Yan Coulombe	3	0	0	0	2
Martin Corbeil	4	0	0	0	8
Christian Lefebvre	4	0	0	0	0
Danny Dupont	11	0	0	0	41
Frederic Henry (goalie)	6	—	—	—	—
Frederic Deschene (goalie)	11	—	—	—	—

GOALTENDING

	Games	Min.	W	L	T	Goals	SO	Avg.
Frederic Deschene	11	553	3	7	0	35	1	3.80
Frederic Henry	6	232	1	2	0	21	0	5.43

HALIFAX MOOSEHEADS

SCORING

	Games	G	A	Pts.	PIM
Chris Peyton	7	1	5	6	14
Stephane Larocque	7	1	4	5	22
Mario Dumoulin	7	0	5	5	27
Rocco Anoia	7	4	0	4	13
Brant Blackned	7	2	2	4	10
Etienne Drapeau	7	2	2	4	20
Eric Houde	3	2	1	3	4
Nicolas Maheux	6	0	3	3	2
Steve Mongrain	5	2	0	2	13
David Carson	5	1	0	1	0
Chris Angione	8	1	0	1	0
Jamie Brown	7	0	1	1	6
Daniel Payette	7	0	1	1	36
Derrick Pyke	7	0	1	1	4
Jody Shelley	7	0	1	1	12
Chris Cahoon	4	0	0	0	2
Mark Johnson	5	0	0	0	0
Daniel Villeneuve	6	0	0	0	24
Sebastien Berube	7	0	0	0	32
Chris Halverson	7	0	0	0	10
Jean-Sebastien Giguere (goalie)	7	—	—	—	—

GOALTENDING

	Games	Min.	W	L	T	Goals	SO	Avg.
J.S. Giguere	7	417	3	4	0	17	1	2.45

HULL OLYMPIQUES

(Winner of 1995 President Cup playoffs)

SCORING

	Games	G	A	Pts.	PIM
Sebastien Bordeleau	18	13	19	32	25
Jonathan Delisle	19	11	8	19	43
Martin Menard	21	7	11	18	19
Jean-Guy Trudel	19	4	13	17	25
Louis-Philippe Charbonneau	18	10	5	15	109
Carl Beaudoin	21	6	9	15	46
Michael McKay	21	7	7	14	37
Harold Hersh	21	5	9	14	14
Jan Nemecek	21	5	9	14	10
Jamie Bird	19	2	8	10	31
Carl Charland	16	4	3	7	74
Jason Groleau	21	0	7	7	37
Francois Cloutier	17	2	4	6	36
Gordie Dwyer	17	1	3	4	54
Roddie MacKenzie	18	0	3	3	42
Chris Hall	2	2	0	2	0
Alex Rodrigue	8	1	1	2	2
Richard Safarik	7	1	0	1	10
Michael Coveny	19	0	1	1	32
Peter Worrell	21	0	1	1	91
Sean Farmer	10	0	0	0	0
Carl Prud'homme	11	0	0	0	22
Colin White	12	0	0	0	23
Neil Savary (goalie)	1	—	—	—	—
Jose Theodore (goalie)	21	—	—	—	2

GOALTENDING

	Games	Min.	W	L	T	Goals	SO	Avg.
Jose Theodore	21	1263	15	6	0	59	1	2.80
Neil Savary	1	20	0	0	0	1	0	3.00

LAVAL TITANS

(Lost finals to Hull, 4-1)

SCORING

	Games	G	A	Pts.	PIM
Benoit Gratton	20	8	21	29	42
Jason Boudrias	20	10	17	27	2
Dave Boudreault	20	9	14	23	52
Patrick Boileau	20	4	16	20	24
Frederic Chartier	20	10	9	19	28

MAJOR JUNIOR LEAGUES

	Games	G	A	Pts.	PIM
Maxime Blouin	19	9	8	17	24
Jason Doig	20	4	13	17	39
Jeff Loder	19	9	6	15	12
Daniel Goneau	20	5	10	15	33
Yanick Dube	16	11	3	14	12
Anders Myrvold	20	4	10	14	68
Francis Bouillon	20	3	11	14	21
Jeff Mercer	18	7	6	13	125
Eric Cloutier	20	0	8	8	94
Dominic Perna	20	1	5	6	2
Francois Pilon	20	2	3	5	25
Jason Bermingham	9	1	1	2	6
Frederic Jobin	20	1	1	2	106
Francois Veilleux	2	0	1	1	5
Richard Goudie	1	0	0	0	0
Jean-Francois Brunelle	2	0	0	0	2
Steve Parson	14	0	0	0	52
Martin Villeneuve (goalie)	7	—	—	—	0
Sebastien Charpentier (goalie)	16	—	—	—	0

GOALTENDING

	Games	Min.	W	L	T	Goals	SO	Avg.
S. Charpentier	16	886	9	4	0	45	0	3.05
Martin Villeneuve	7	339	5	2	0	20	0	3.54

ST. HYACINTHE LASERS

SCORING

	Games	G	A	Pts.	PIM
Yann Vaillancourt	5	2	2	4	8
David-Alexandre Beauregard	5	1	3	4	0
Eric Landry	5	2	1	3	10
Nathan Morin	5	2	1	3	8
Jimmy Drolet	5	0	2	2	12
Gabriel Cote	3	1	0	1	2
David Desnoyers	5	1	0	1	19
Yannick Hubert	5	1	0	1	4
David Bernier	1	0	1	1	0
Hugo Bertrand	5	0	1	1	30
Remy Boudreau	5	0	1	1	7
Maxime Leclair	5	0	1	1	4
Francois Methot	5	0	1	1	0
Jonathan Levesque	1	0	0	0	0
Yan St. Pierre	4	0	0	0	6
Jean-Francois Tremblay	4	0	0	0	6
Steeven Dussault	5	0	0	0	0
Christian Gosselin	5	0	0	0	11
Martin Lacaille	5	0	0	0	8
Marc Sigouin	5	0	0	0	12
Frederick Beaubien (goalie)	3	—	—	—	—
Stephane Routhier (goalie)	3	—	—	—	—

GOALTENDING

	Games	Min.	W	L	T	Goals	SO	Avg.
Frederick Beaubien	3	176	1	2	0	9	0	3.07
Stephane Routhier	3	125	0	2	0	10	0	4.80

ST. JEAN LYNX

SCORING

	Games	G	A	Pts.	PIM
Hugo Turcotte	7	1	8	9	4
Jan Melichercik	7	4	3	7	4
Steve Brule	7	3	4	7	8
Rony Valenti	7	3	1	4	13
Patrice Paquin	5	2	2	4	6
Eric Gauvin	7	1	3	4	4
Shane Doiron	7	0	4	4	10
Jean-Francois Boutin	7	2	1	3	0
Eric Moreau	7	2	1	3	12
Georges Laraque	7	1	1	2	42
Jean Theroux	7	1	1	2	12
Sebastien Lessard	7	0	2	2	2
Patrick Charbonneau	7	1	0	1	6
Claude Fillion	7	1	0	1	31

	Games	G	A	Pts.	PIM
Yanick Turcotte	7	1	0	1	0
Frederic Barbeau	7	0	1	1	6
Eric Drouin	1	0	0	0	0
Bruno Gladu	1	0	0	0	0
Eric Normandin	3	0	0	0	0
Casey Wolak	5	0	0	0	4
Simon Provencher	6	0	0	0	2
Carl Benoit (goalie)	3	—	—	—	—
Frederic Cassivi (goalie)	5	—	—	—	—

GOALTENDING

	Games	Min.	W	L	T	Goals	SO	Avg.
Frederic Cassivi	5	258	2	2	0	18	0	4.19
Carl Benoit	3	170	1	1	0	13	0	4.59

SHAWINIGAN CATARACTES

(Lost semifinals to Laval, 4-1)

SCORING

	Games	G	A	Pts.	PIM
Patrick Carignan	15	8	20	28	6
Yanick Evola	15	9	14	23	78
Alain Savage	15	6	14	20	20
Stephane Robidas	15	7	12	19	4
Jean-Francois Laroche	12	7	8	15	21
Alexandre Jacques	14	8	5	13	8
Carl Paradis	15	5	8	13	29
Martin Lamarche	14	3	10	13	65
Pavel Agarkov	14	7	5	12	10
Dereck Gosselin	15	2	6	8	20
Guy Loranger	15	2	4	6	39
Sergei Polichouk	10	1	4	5	24
Jean-Francois Bessette	15	0	4	4	35
David Grenier	15	1	2	3	40
Dave Savard	15	0	3	3	14
Sylvain Rodier	15	2	0	2	14
Mathieu Descoteaux	15	1	1	2	19
David Bahl	15	0	1	1	18
Benjamin Carpentier	2	0	0	0	2
Steven Morneau	2	0	0	0	0
Carl Benoit	7	0	0	0	2
Steve Plouffe (goalie)	2	—	—	—	0
Sylvain Daigle (goalie)	14	—	—	—	4

GOALTENDING

	Games	Min.	W	L	T	Goals	SO	Avg.
Sylvain Daigle	14	824	7	6	0	57	0	4.15
Steve Plouffe	2	78	1	1	0	6	0	4.62

SHERBROOKE FAUCONS

SCORING

	Games	G	A	Pts.	PIM
Etienne Beaudry	7	6	3	9	6
Stephane Julien	7	4	5	9	6
Mathieu Dandenault	7	1	7	8	10
Christian Dube	7	1	7	8	8
Eric Lecompte	4	2	2	4	4
Jean-Francois Robert	7	1	2	3	6
Radoslav Suchy	7	0	3	3	2
Vitali Kozel	5	2	0	2	4
Yannick Tremblay	7	2	0	2	6
Charles Paquette	5	1	1	2	18
Gaetan Royer	7	0	2	2	6
Samuel Lacroix	7	1	0	1	6
Bruce Richardson	4	0	1	1	0
Mathieu Raby	7	0	1	1	24
Alex Richard	7	0	1	1	4
Benoit Larose	3	0	0	0	0
Yannick Auger	5	0	0	0	0
David Gosselin	7	0	0	0	2
Eric Jenkins	7	0	0	0	2
Kevin Vaughan	7	0	0	0	10
Jean-Sebastien Aubin (goalie)	3	—	—	—	0
Luc Belanger (goalie)	4	—	—	—	17

	Games	Min.	W	L	T	Goals	SO	Avg.
Luc Belanger	4	240	2	2	0	12	0	3.00
J.S. Aubin	3	185	1	2	0	11	0	3.57

VICTORIAVILLE TIGRES

SCORING

	Games	G	A	Pts.	PIM
Cosmo DuPaul	4	3	4	7	6
Daniel Corso	4	2	5	7	2
Philippe Gelineau	4	1	3	4	2
Dany Larochelle	4	2	1	3	0
Alexandre Couture	4	1	2	3	2
Alexandre Duchesne	4	2	0	2	14
Sebastien Demers	4	0	2	2	2
Sebastien Vallee	4	1	0	1	0
Philippe Vezina	4	1	0	1	2

	Games	G	A	Pts.	PIM
Pierre Morin	1	0	1	1	5
Maxime Roux	4	0	1	1	11
Remi Royer	4	0	1	1	7
Dominic Marleau	3	0	0	0	11
Eric Naud	3	0	0	0	2
Marc-Andre Gaudet	4	0	0	0	8
Steven Low	4	0	0	0	33
Patrick Pelchat	4	0	0	0	10
Dean Stock	4	0	0	0	13
Philippe-Joseph Stock	4	0	0	0	60
David Dubuc (goalie)	3	—	—	—	0
Patrick Charbonneau (goalie)	4	—	—	—	0

GOALTENDING

	Games	Min.	W	L	T	Goals	SO	Avg.
David Dubuc	3	97	0	1	0	12	0	7.42
Patrick Charbonneau	4	142	0	3	0	20	0	8.45

1994-95 AWARD WINNERS

ALL-STAR TEAMS

First team	Pos.	Second team
Eric Fichaud, Chi.	G	Jose Theodore, Hull
Stephane Julien, Sherbrooke	D	Christian Laflamme, Beau.
Charles Paquette, Sher.	D	Alain Nasreddine, Chi.
Patrick Carignan, Shaw.	LW	Brant Blackned, Halifax
Sebastien Bordeleau, Hull	C	Steve Brule, St. Jean
Eric Daze, Beauport	RW	Frederic Chartier, Laval

Coach of the Year: Michel Therrien, Laval

TROPHY WINNERS

Frank Selke Trophy: Eric Daze, Beauport
Michel Bergeron Trophy: Daniel Briere, Drummondville
Raymond Lagace Trophy: Martin Biron, Beauport
Jean Beliveau Trophy: Patrick Carignan, Shawinigan
Michel Briere Trophy: Frederic Chartier, Laval
Marcel Robert Trophy: Daniel Briere, Drummondville
Mike Bossy Trophy: Martin Biron, Beauport
Emile "Butch" Bouchard Trophy: Stephane Julien, Sherbrooke
Jacques Plante Trophy: Martin Biron, Beauport
Guy Lafleur Trophy: Jose Theodore, Hull
Robert LeBel Trophy: Beauport Harfangs
John Rougeau Trophy: Laval Titans
President Cup: Hull Olympiques

ALL-TIME AWARD WINNERS

FRANK SELKE TROPHY

(Most gentlemanly player)

Season	Player, Team
1970-71	Norm Dube, Sherbrooke
1971-72	Gerry Teeple, Cornwall
1972-73	Claude Larose, Drummondville
1973-74	Gary MacGregor, Cornwall
1974-75	Jean-Luc Phaneuf, Montreal
1975-76	Norm Dupont, Montreal
1976-77	Mike Bossy, Laval
1977-78	Kevin Reeves, Montreal
1978-79	Ray Bourque, Verdun
	Jean-Francois Sauve, Trois-Rivieres
1979-80	Jean-Francois Sauve, Trois-Rivieres
1980-81	Claude Verret, Trois-Rivieres
1981-82	Claude Verret, Trois-Rivieres
1982-83	Pat LaFontaine, Verdun
1983-84	Jerome Carrier, Verdun
1984-85	Patrick Emond, Chicoutimi
1985-86	Jimmy Carson, Verdun
1986-87	Luc Beausoleil, Laval
1987-88	Stephan Lebeau, Shawinigan
1988-89	Steve Cadieux, Shawinigan
1989-90	Andrew McKim, Hull
1990-91	Yanic Perreault, Trois-Rivieres
1991-92	Martin Gendron, St. Hyacinthe
1992-93	Martin Gendron, St. Hyacinthe
1993-94	Yanick Dube, Laval
1994-95	Eric Daze, Beauport

MICHEL BERGERON TROPHY

(Top rookie forward)

Season	Player, Team
1969-70	Serge Martel, Verdun

Season	Player, Team
1970-71	Bob Murphy, Cornwall
1971-72	Bob Murray, Cornwall
1972-73	Pierre Larouche, Sorel
1973-74	Mike Bossy, Laval
1974-75	Dennis Pomerleau, Hull
1975-76	Jean-Marc Bonamie, Shawinigan
1976-77	Rick Vaive, Sherbrooke
1977-78	Norm Rochefort, Trois-Rivieres
	Denis Savard, Montreal
1978-79	Alan Grenier, Laval
1979-80	Dale Hawerchuk, Cornwall
1980-81	Claude Verret, Trois-Rivieres
1981-82	Sylvain Turgeon, Hull
1982-83	Pat LaFontaine, Verdun
1983-84	Stephane Richer, Granby
1984-85	Jimmy Carson, Verdun
1985-86	Pierre Turgeon, Granby
1986-87	Rob Murphy, Laval
1987-88	Martin Gelinas, Hull
1988-89	Yanic Perreault, Trois-Rivieres
1989-90	Martin Lapointe, Laval
1990-91	Rene Corbet, Drummondville
1991-92	Alexandre Daigle, Victoriaville
1992-93	Steve Brule, St. Jean
1993-94	Christian Dube, Sherbrooke
1994-95	Daniel Briere, Drummondville

Prior to 1980-81 season, award was given to QMJHL rookie of the year.

RAYMOND LAGACE TROPHY

(Top rookie defenseman or goaltender)

Season	Player, Team
1980-81	Billy Campbell, Montreal
1981-82	Michel Petit, Sherbrooke

Season	Player, Team
1982-83	Bobby Dollas, Laval
1983-84	James Gasseau, Drummondville
1984-85	Robert Desjardins, Shawinigan
1985-86	Stephane Guerard, Shawinigan
1986-87	Jimmy Waite, Chicoutimi
1987-88	Stephane Beauregard, St. Jean
1988-89	Karl Dykhuis, Hull
1989-90	Francois Groleau, Shawinigan
1990-91	Philippe Boucher, Granby
1991-92	Philippe DeRouville, Longueuil
1992-93	Stephane Routhier, Drummondville
1993-94	Jimmy Drolet, St. Hyacinthe
1994-95	Martin Biron, Beauport

JEAN BELIVEAU TROPHY
(Scoring leader)

Season	Player, Team
1969-70	Luc Simard, Trois-Rivieres
1970-71	Guy Lafleur, Quebec
1971-72	Jacques Richard, Quebec
1972-73	Andre Savard, Quebec
1973-74	Pierre Larouche, Sorel
1974-75	Norm Dupont, Montreal
1975-76	Richard Dalpe, Trois-Rivieres
	Sylvain Locas, Chicoutimi
1976-77	Jean Savard, Quebec
1977-78	Ron Carter, Sherbrooke
1978-79	Jean-Francois Sauve, Trois-Rivieres
1979-80	Jean-Francois Sauve, Trois-Rivieres
1980-81	Dale Hawerchuk, Cornwall
1981-82	Claude Verret, Trois-Rivieres
1982-83	Pat LaFontaine, Verdun
1983-84	Mario Lemieux, Laval
1984-85	Guy Rouleau, Longueuil
1985-86	Guy Rouleau, Hull
1986-87	Marc Fortier, Chicoutimi
1987-88	Patrice Lefebvre, Shawinigan
1988-89	Stephane Morin, Chicoutimi
1989-90	Patrick Lebeau, Victoriaville
1990-91	Yanic Perreault, Trois-Rivieres
1991-92	Patrick Poulin, St. Hyacinthe
1992-93	Rene Corbet, Drummondville
1993-94	Yanick Dube, Laval
1994-95	Patrick Carignan, Shawinigan

MICHEL BRIERE TROPHY
(Most Valuable Player)

Season	Player, Team
1972-73	Andre Savard, Quebec
1973-74	Gary MacGregor, Cornwall
1974-75	Mario Viens, Cornwall
1975-76	Peter Marsh, Sherbrooke
1976-77	Lucien DeBlois, Sorel
1977-78	Kevin Reeves, Montreal
1978-79	Pierre Lacroix, Trois-Rivieres
1979-80	Denis Savard, Montreal
1980-81	Dale Hawerchuk, Cornwall
1981-82	John Chabot, Sherbrooke
1982-83	Pat LaFontaine, Verdun
1983-84	Mario Lemieux, Laval
1984-85	Daniel Berthiaune, Chicoutimi
1985-86	Guy Rouleau, Hull
1986-87	Robert Desjardins, Longueuil
1987-88	Marc Saumier, Hull
1988-89	Stephane Morin, Chicoutimi
1989-90	Andrew McKim, Hull
1990-91	Yanic Perreault, Trois-Rivieres
1991-92	Charles Poulin, St. Hyacinthe
1992-93	Jocelyn Thibault, Sherbrooke
1993-94	Emmanuel Fernandez, Laval
1994-95	Frederic Chartier, Laval

MARCEL ROBERT TROPHY
(Top scholastic/athletic performer)

Season	Player, Team
1981-82	Jacques Sylvestre, Granby
1982-83	Claude Gosselin, Quebec
1983-84	Gilbert Paiement, Chicoutimi
1984-85	Claude Gosselin, Longueuil
1985-86	Bernard Morin, Laval
1986-87	Patrice Tremblay, Chicoutimi
1987-88	Stephane Beauregard, St. Jean
1988-89	Daniel Lacroix, Granby
1989-90	Yanic Perreault, Trois-Rivieres
1990-91	Benoit Larose, Laval
1991-92	Simon Toupin, Beauport
1992-93	Jocelyn Thibault, Sherbrooke
1993-94	Patrick Boileau, Laval
1994-95	Daniel Briere, Drummondville

MIKE BOSSY TROPHY
(Top pro prospect)

Season	Player, Team
1980-81	Dale Hawerchuk, Cornwall
1981-82	Michel Petit, Sherbrooke
1982-83	Pat LaFontaine, Verdun
	Sylvain Turgeon, Hull
1983-84	Mario Lemieux, Laval
1984-85	Jose Charbonneau, Drummondville
1985-86	Jimmy Carson, Verdun
1986-87	Pierre Turgeon, Granby
1987-88	Daniel Dore, Drummondville
1988-89	Patrice Brisebois, Laval
1989-90	Karl Dykhuis, Hull
1990-91	Philippe Boucher, Granby
1991-92	Paul Brousseau, Hull
1992-93	Alexandre Daigle, Victoriaville
1993-94	Eric Fichaud, Chicoutimi
1994-95	Martin Biron, Beauport

Originally known as Association of Journalism of Hockey Trophy from 1980-81 through 1982-83.

EMILE "BUTCH" BOUCHARD TROPHY
(Top defenseman)

Season	Player, Team
1975-76	Jean Gagnon, Quebec
1976-77	Robert Picard, Montreal
1977-78	Mark Hardy, Montreal
1978-79	Ray Bourque, Verdun
1979-80	Gaston Therrien, Quebec
1980-81	Fred Boimistruck, Cornwall
1981-82	Paul Andre Boutilier, Sherbrooke
1982-83	J.J. Daigneault, Longueuil
1983-84	Billy Campbell, Verdun
1984-85	Yves Beaudoin, Shawinigan
1985-86	Sylvain Cote, Hull
1986-87	Jean Marc Richard, Chicoutimi
1987-88	Eric Desjardins, Granby
1988-89	Yves Racine, Victoriaville
1989-90	Claude Barthe, Victoriaville
1990-91	Patrice Brisebois, Drummondville
1991-92	Francois Groleau, Shawinigan
1992-93	Benoit Larose, Laval
1993-94	Steve Gosselin, Chicoutimi
1994-95	Stephane Julien, Sherbrooke

JACQUES PLANTE TROPHY
(Top goaltender)

Season	Player, Team
1969-70	Michael Deguise, Sorel
1970-71	Reynald Fortier, Quebec
1971-72	Richard Brodeur, Cornwall
1972-73	Pierre Perusee, Quebec
1973-74	Claude Legris, Sorel

Season	Player, Team
1974-75	Nick Sanza, Sherbrooke
1975-76	Tim Bernhardt, Cornwall
1976-77	Tim Bernhardt, Cornwall
1977-78	Tim Bernhardt, Cornwall
1978-79	Jacques Cloutier, Trois-Rivieres
1979-80	Corrado Micalef, Sherbrooke
1980-81	Michel Dufour,Sorel
1981-82	Jeff Barratt, Montreal
1982-83	Tony Haladuick, Laval
1983-84	Tony Haladuick, Laval
1984-85	Daniel Berthiaume, Chicoutimi
1985-86	Robert Desjardins, Hull
1986-87	Robert Desjardins, Longueuil
1987-88	Stephane Beauregard, St. Jean
1988-89	Stephane Fiset, Victoriaville
1989-90	Pierre Gagnon, Victoriaville
1990-91	Felix Potvin, Chicoutimi
1991-92	Jean-Francois Labbe, Trois-Rivieres
1992-93	Jocelyn Thibault, Sherbrooke
1993-94	Philippe DeRouville, Verdun
1994-95	Martin Biron, Beauport

GUY LAFLEUR TROPHY

(Playoff MVP)

Season	Player, Team
1977-78	Richard David, Trois-Rivieres
1978-79	Jean-Francois Sauve, Trois-Rivieres
1979-80	Dale Hawerchuk, Cornwall
1980-81	Alain Lemieux, Trois-Rivieres
1981-82	Michel Morissette, Sherbrooke
1982-83	Pat LaFontaine, Verdun
1983-84	Mario Lemieux, Laval
1984-85	Claude Lemieux, Verdun

Season	Player, Team
1985-86	Sylvain Cote, Hull
	Luc Robitaille, Hull
1986-87	Marc Saumier, Longueuil
1987-88	Marc Saumier, Hull
1988-89	Donald Audette, Laval
1989-90	Denis Chalifoux, Laval
1990-91	Felix Potvin, Chicoutimi
1991-92	Robert Guillet, Longueuil
1992-93	Emmanuel Fernandez, Laval
1993-94	Eric Fichaud, Chicoutimi
1994-95	Jose Theodore, Hull

ROBERT LeBEL TROPHY

(Best team defensive average)

Season	Team
1977-78	Trois-Rivieres Draveurs
1978-79	Trois-Rivieres Draveurs
1979-80	Sherbrooke Beavers
1980-81	Sorel Black Hawks
1981-82	Montreal Juniors
1982-83	Shawinigan Cataracts
1983-84	Shawinigan Cataracts
1984-85	Shawinigan Cataracts
1985-86	Hull Olympiques
1986-78	Longueuil Chevaliers
1987-88	St. Jean Castors
1988-89	Hull Olympiques
1989-90	Victoriaville Tigres
1990-91	Chicoutimi Sagueneens
1991-92	Trois-Rivieres Draveurs
1992-93	Sherbrooke Faucons
1993-94	College Francais de Verdun
1994-95	Beauport Harfangs

ALL-TIME LEAGUE CHAMPIONS

REGULAR-SEASON CHAMPION / PLAYOFF CHAMPION

Season	Team	Team (Playoff Champion)
1969-70	Quebec Remparts	Quebec Remparts
1970-71	Quebec Remparts	Quebec Remparts
1971-72	Cornwall Royals	Cornwall Royals
1972-73	Quebec Remparts	Quebec Remparts
1973-74	Sorel Black Hawks	Quebec Remparts
1974-75	Sherbrooke Beavers	Sherbrooke Beavers
1975-76	Sherbrooke Beavers	Quebec Remparts
1976-77	Quebec Remparts	Sherbrooke Beavers
1977-78	Trois-Rivieres Draveurs	Trois-Rivieres Draveurs
1978-79	Trois-Rivieres Draveurs	Trois-Rivieres Draveurs
1979-80	Sherbrooke Beavers	Cornwall Royals
1980-81	Cornwall Royals	Cornwall Royals
1981-82	Sherbrooke Beavers	Sherbrooke Beavers
1982-83	Laval Voisins	Verdun Juniors
1983-84	Laval Voisins	Laval Voisins
1984-85	Shawinigan Cataracts	Verdun Junior Canadiens
1985-86	Hull Olympiques	Hull Olympiques
1986-87	Granby Bisons	Longueuil Chevaliers
1987-88	Hull Olympiques	Hull Olympiques
1988-89	Trois-Rivieres Draveurs	Laval Titans
1989-90	Victoriaville Tigres	Laval Titans
1990-91	Chicoutimi Sagueneens	Chicoutimi Sagueneens
1991-92	Longueuil College Francais	Longueuil College Francais
1992-93	Sherbrooke Faucons	Laval Titans
1993-94	Laval Titans	Chicoutimi Sagueneens
1994-95	Laval Titans	Hull Olympiques

The QMJHL regular-season champion is awarded the John Rougeau Trophy and the playoff champion is awarded the Presidents Cup.

The John Rougeau Trophy was originally called the Governors Trophy from 1969-70 through 1982-83.

WESTERN HOCKEY LEAGUE

LEAGUE OFFICE

Note: League was known as Canadian Major Junior Hockey League in 1966-67 and Western Canadian Hockey League from 1967-68 through 1977-78.

President
Ed Chynoweth
Vice president
Richard Doerksen

Executive assistant
Norman Dueck
Statistician
Stu Judge

Address
Suite 521, 10333 Southport Road SW
Calgary, Alberta T2W 3X6
Phone
403-253-8113

1994-95 REGULAR SEASON

FINAL STANDINGS

EAST DIVISION

Team	G	W	L	T	Pts.	GF	GA
Brandon	72	45	22	5	95	315	235
Prince Albert	72	44	26	2	90	308	267
Saskatoon	72	41	23	8	90	324	254
Moose Jaw	72	39	32	1	79	315	275
Medicine Hat	72	38	32	2	78	244	229
Swift Current	72	31	34	7	69	274	284
Regina	72	26	43	3	55	269	306
Lethbridge	72	22	48	2	46	263	341
Red Deer	72	17	51	4	38	209	356

WEST DIVISION

Team	G	W	L	T	Pts.	GF	GA
Kamloops	72	52	14	6	110	375	202
Tacoma	72	43	27	2	88	294	246
Seattle	72	42	28	2	86	319	282
Tri-City	72	36	31	5	77	295	279
Spokane	72	32	36	4	68	244	261
Portland	72	23	43	6	52	240	308
Prince George	72	14	55	3	31	229	392

INDIVIDUAL LEADERS

Goals: Daymond Langkow, Tri-City (67)
Assists: Marty Murray, Brandon (88)
Points: Daymond Langkow, Tri-City (140)
Penalty minutes: Kevin Sawyer, Spokane (365)
Goaltending average: Rod Branch, Kamloops (2.60)
Shutouts: Rod Branch, Kamloops (5)

	Games	G	A	Pts.
Terry Ryan, Tri-City	70	50	60	110
Chris Wells, Seattle	69	45	63	108
Curtis Brown, Moose Jaw	70	51	53	104
Mark Deyell, Saskatoon	70	34	68	102
Chris Herperger, Seattle	59	49	52	101
Paul Vincent, Swift Current	65	59	41	100
Jan Hrdina, Seattle	69	41	59	100
Paul Buczkowski, Saskatoon	72	42	56	98
Mark Szoke, Saskatoon	66	47	48	95
Shane Doan, Kamloops	71	37	57	94
Paul Healey, Prince Albert	71	43	50	93
Scott Townsend, Lethbridge	72	36	56	92
Ladislav Kohn, Swift Current	65	32	60	92
Blair Manning, Seattle	58	32	58	90

TOP SCORERS

	Games	G	A	Pts.
Daymond Langkow, Tri-City	72	67	73	140
Darcy Tucker, Kamloops	64	64	73	137
Marty Murray, Brandon	65	40	88	128
Stacy Roest, Medicine Hat	69	37	78	115
Darren Ritchie, Brandon	69	62	52	114
Hnat Domenichelli, Kamloops	72	52	62	114

INDIVIDUAL STATISTICS

BRANDON WHEAT KINGS

SCORING

	Games	G	A	Pts.	PIM
Marty Murray	65	40	88	128	53
Darren Ritchie	69	62	52	114	12
Chris Dingman	66	40	43	83	201
Wade Redden	64	14	46	60	83
Peter Schaefer	68	27	32	59	34
Bobby Brown	72	23	28	51	128
Mark Dutiaume	62	23	21	44	80
Colin Cloutier	47	16	27	43	170
Justin Kurtz	65	8	34	42	75
Scott Laluk	60	4	19	23	48
Kevin Pozzo	50	4	17	21	81
Kelly Smart	72	11	8	19	47
Jeff Staples	57	3	16	19	176
Darren Van Oene	59	5	13	18	108
Alex Vasilevskii	23	6	11	17	39
Chris Low	37	10	6	16	15
Bryan McCabe	20	6	10	16	38
Mike LeClerc	23	5	8	13	50

	Games	G	A	Pts.	PIM
Dean Kletzel	22	2	5	7	31
Sven Butenschon	21	1	5	6	44
Oleg Tverdovsky	7	1	4	5	4
Mike Dubinsky	4	1	2	3	0
Adam Magarrell	41	0	3	3	72
Ian Walterson	40	2	0	2	27
Ryan Robson	2	1	1	2	0
Byron Penstock (goalie)	48	0	2	2	8
Paul Bailley	11	0	1	1	10
Joel Korenko	26	0	1	1	48
Darryl Stockham	1	0	0	0	0
David Darguza	2	0	0	0	0
Jeff Temple	3	0	0	0	0
Darren Smadis (goalie)	4	0	0	0	0
Brian Elder (goalie)	23	0	0	0	0

GOALTENDING

	Games	Min.	W	L	T	Goals	SO	Avg.
Darren Smadis	4	228	2	1	0	10	0	2.63
Brian Elder	23	1325	16	5	1	69	0	3.12
Byron Penstock	48	2813	27	16	4	148	4	3.16

KAMLOOPS BLAZERS

SCORING

	Games	G	A	Pts.	PIM
Darcy Tucker	64	64	73	137	94
Hnat Domenichelli	72	52	62	114	34
Shane Doan	71	37	57	94	106
Aaron Keller	71	18	62	80	34
Tyson Nash	63	34	41	75	70
Ivan Vologjaninov	66	23	49	72	35
Jarome Iginla	72	33	38	71	111
Ryan Huska	66	27	40	67	78
Brad Lukowich	63	10	35	45	125
Nolan Baumgartner	62	8	36	44	71
Jason Holland	71	9	32	41	65
Bob Maudie	67	9	29	38	34
Donnie Kinney	47	16	12	28	2
Ashley Buckberger	21	9	13	22	13
Greg Hart	60	6	9	15	9
Jason Strudwick	72	3	11	14	183
Jeff Ainsworth	53	3	6	9	31
Mike Josephson	5	2	6	8	4
Shawn McNeil	43	4	3	7	11
Jeff Jubenville	13	1	6	7	27
Keith McCambridge	21	0	6	6	90
Cam Severson	30	4	1	5	40
Jeff Henkelman	37	1	3	4	31
Bob Westerby	13	0	3	3	67
Randy Petruk (goalie)	27	0	3	3	7
Kevin McDonald	6	1	1	2	27
Jeff Antonovich	1	0	2	2	2
Jeff Oldenborger	33	1	0	1	31
Rob Skrlac	23	0	1	1	107
Rod Branch (goalie)	50	0	1	1	18
Greg Deverson	1	0	0	0	0
Mike Krooshoop	1	0	0	0	7
Cam McCormick (goalie)	1	0	0	0	0
Scott Sherwood	1	0	0	0	0
Andrei Srubko	1	0	0	0	0

GOALTENDING

	Games	Min.	W	L	T	Goals	SO	Avg.
Rod Branch	50	2864	35	11	2	124	5	2.60
Randy Petruk	27	1462	16	3	4	71	1	2.91
Cam McCormick	1	60	1	0	0	4	0	4.00

LETHBRIDGE HURRICANES

SCORING

	Games	G	A	Pts.	PIM
Scott Townsend	72	36	56	92	23
Todd MacIsaac	67	34	39	73	106
Mark Szoke	42	35	31	66	89
Randy Perry	69	7	49	56	37
Byron Ritchie	58	22	28	50	132
Mike Josephson	62	22	25	47	113
Derek Diener	68	13	29	42	104
Travis Brigley	64	14	18	32	14
Scott Grieco	72	14	18	32	141
Kory Mullin	48	6	21	27	72
Brad Mehalko	52	11	15	26	83
Kirk Dewaele	71	3	18	21	123
Chad Gans	72	11	9	20	63
Lee Sorochan	29	4	15	19	93
Derek Wood	44	6	12	18	161
Dmitri Markovsky	25	5	9	14	4
Kirby Law	24	4	10	14	38
John Bradley	53	2	8	10	64
Bryce Salvador	67	1	9	10	88
Steve Roberts	10	3	6	9	7
Mark Smith	49	3	4	7	25
Lee Hamilton	46	2	4	6	31
Jason Bird	29	2	3	5	26
Doyle McMorris	18	0	5	5	4
Mike O'Grady	21	1	2	3	124
Jamie Liedl	6	0	2	2	0
Brian Kostur	2	1	0	1	0

	Games	G	A	Pts.	PIM
Ryan Johnston	3	1	0	1	4
Jeremy Thompson	15	0	1	1	62
Andrew Kaminsky	1	0	0	0	0
Andrei Dovidnyi	4	0	0	0	2
Tim Lozinik	4	0	0	0	4
Dennis Mullen	11	0	0	0	43
David Trofimenkoff (goalie)	11	0	0	0	17
David Brumby (goalie)	19	0	0	0	9
Scott Tollestrup (goalie)	26	0	0	0	10
Darren Smadis (goalie)	30	0	0	0	2

GOALTENDING

	Games	Min.	W	L	T	Goals	SO	Avg.
David Brumby	19	1036	6	11	0	78	0	4.52
Scott Tollestrup	26	1287	4	18	1	99	0	4.62
Darren Smadis	30	1446	8	13	1	112	0	4.65
David Trofimenkoff	11	600	4	6	0	47	0	4.70

MEDICINE HAT TIGERS

SCORING

	Games	G	A	Pts.	PIM
Stacy Roest	69	37	78	115	32
Sergei Klimentiev	71	19	45	64	146
Josh Green	68	32	23	55	64
Henry Kuster	71	28	26	54	61
Mark Polak	71	18	25	43	101
Aaron Zarowny	60	20	22	42	109
Brad Wilson	71	13	19	32	110
Cal Benazic	71	9	23	32	166
Steve Cheredaryk	70	3	26	29	193
Rob Niedermayer	13	9	15	24	14
Robert Longpre	59	12	9	21	40
Don Larner	44	7	14	21	37
Ryan Petz	29	11	7	18	14
Chad Reich	26	6	9	15	30
Jeremy Schaefer	70	8	6	14	146
Trevor Wasyluk	67	6	4	10	75
Rocky Thompson	63	1	6	7	220
Blair St. Martin	65	1	6	7	112
Johnathan Aitken	53	0	5	5	71
Mike Eley	1	1	1	2	2
Bill Hooson	15	1	1	2	23
Chad Knippel	42	1	1	2	69
Paxton Schafer (goalie)	61	0	2	2	0
Jason Duda	3	1	0	1	0
Rodney Bowers	5	0	1	1	0
Clint Cabana	49	0	1	1	68
Scott Buhler (goalie)	1	0	0	0	0
Aaron Miller	1	0	0	0	0
Bryan Kondo	2	0	0	0	0
Kevin Marsh	2	0	0	0	0
Derek Shuel	2	0	0	0	9
Ashley Wesling	2	0	0	0	0
Calvin Crowe	3	0	0	0	11
Dwayne Ripley	3	0	0	0	0
Trevor Anderson (goalie)	16	0	0	0	5
Darcy Smith	24	0	0	0	16
Chris Leskiw	26	0	0	0	9

GOALTENDING

	Games	Min.	W	L	T	Goals	SO	Avg.
Trevor Anderson	16	764	6	5	0	38	0	2.98
Paxton Schafer	61	3519	32	26	2	185	0	3.15
Scott Buhler	1	60	0	1	0	5	0	5.00

MOOSE JAW WARRIORS

SCORING

	Games	G	A	Pts.	PIM
Curtis Brown	70	51	53	104	63
Ryan Smyth	50	41	45	86	66
Grady Manson	70	33	42	75	83
Chris Armstrong	66	17	54	71	61
Matt Higgins	72	36	34	70	26

	Games	G	A	Pts.	PIM
Jeff Dewar	66	21	49	70	70
Darryl LaPlante	71	22	24	46	66
Ryan Petz	41	15	31	46	32
Roman Vopat	72	23	20	43	141
Rob Trumbley	56	16	25	41	236
Paul Johnson	70	4	19	23	97
Don Halverson	50	7	11	18	30
Chris Twerdun	70	5	12	17	25
Mike Broda	58	5	11	16	35
Mike Krooshoop	49	3	13	16	146
Scott Ducharmie	22	6	7	13	12
Kevin McKay	56	1	11	12	93
Curtis Capjack	45	2	8	10	34
Milt Mastad	68	1	8	9	155
Bob Graham	22	2	6	8	6
John Wood	64	2	6	8	37
Jody Lehman (goalie)	65	0	6	6	18
Chad Reich	19	1	4	5	33
Tyler Love (goalie)	9	0	2	2	0
Devon Hanson (goalie)	13	0	2	2	10
Rob Wilson	15	0	2	2	47
Scott Spiller	25	1	0	1	28
Derek Ernest	18	0	1	1	5

GOALTENDING

	Games	Min.	W	L	T	Goals	SO	Avg.
Devon Hanson	13	563	5	4	1	34	0	3.62
Jody Lehman	65	3443	33	25	0	208	1	3.62
Tyler Love	9	336	1	3	0	27	0	4.82

PORTLAND WINTER HAWKS

SCORING

	Games	G	A	Pts.	PIM
Richard Zednik	65	35	51	86	89
Todd Robinson	67	21	57	78	40
Colin Forbes	72	24	31	55	108
Dave Scatchard	71	20	30	50	148
Adam Deadmarsh	29	28	20	48	129
Layne Roland	45	20	23	43	64
Nolan Pratt	72	6	37	43	196
Matt Davidson	72	17	20	37	51
Brad Isbister	67	16	20	36	123
Jason Wiemer	16	10	14	24	63
Brad Symes	70	8	16	24	134
Brad Swanson	65	3	18	21	91
Brian Medeiros	25	7	7	14	36
Kevin Haupt	52	4	10	14	4
Jason Horvath	33	2	10	12	52
Deny Gaudet	58	3	7	10	22
Justin Guy	51	3	5	8	49
Mike Little	64	3	4	7	15
Graeme Harder	61	2	4	6	134
Judd Casper	19	0	5	5	32
Paul Herron	59	3	1	4	105
Chris Carson	49	2	1	3	27
Rodney Bowers	12	2	0	2	2
Mark Barrie	16	1	0	1	30
Paul Ferone	2	0	1	1	5
Brent Belecki (goalie)	10	0	1	1	0
Joey Tetarenko	59	0	1	1	134
Scott Langkow (goalie)	63	0	1	1	36
Dave Cammock	1	0	0	0	4
Andrew Ferrence	2	0	0	0	4
Jake Deadmarsh	3	0	0	0	10
Brett Fizzell	7	0	0	0	16
Scott Rideout (goalie)	8	0	0	0	0
Shannon Briske	9	0	0	0	11

GOALTENDING

	Games	Min.	W	L	T	Goals	SO	Avg.
Scott Langkow	63	3638	20	36	5	240	1	3.96
Brent Belecki	10	438	3	3	0	34	0	4.66
Scott Rideout	8	317	0	4	1	31	0	5.87

PRINCE ALBERT RAIDERS

SCORING

	Games	G	A	Pts.	PIM
Paul Healey	71	43	50	93	67
Shayne Toporowski	72	36	38	74	151
Steve Kelly	68	31	41	72	153
Denis Pederson	63	30	38	68	122
Russell Hogue	72	21	32	53	34
Mike McGhan	71	19	34	53	79
Brad Church	62	26	24	50	184
Shane Willis	65	24	19	43	38
Jeff Lank	68	12	25	37	60
Shane Zulyniak	70	8	26	34	158
Shane Hnidy	72	5	29	34	169
Neil Johnston	39	12	16	28	34
Rob Hegberg	64	5	23	28	37
Jason Issel	57	9	18	27	47
Sean Robertson	50	9	12	21	19
Darren Wright	62	1	16	17	196
David Van Drunen	71	2	14	16	132
Kaleb Toth	59	9	6	15	113
Ryan Bast	42	1	10	11	149
Kris Fizzell	50	4	6	10	16
Mitch Shawara	30	1	1	2	103
Ryan Mything	1	0	1	1	0
Kevin Kellett	8	0	1	1	6
Sandy Allan (goalie)	35	0	1	1	18
Craig Hordal (goalie)	36	0	1	1	2
Justin Bekkering	1	0	0	0	0
Greg Harvey	1	0	0	0	0
Garnet Jacobsen	1	0	0	0	0
Charles Keshane	1	0	0	0	2
Mike Muzechka	1	0	0	0	0
Tim Bacik (goalie)	8	0	0	0	2

GOALTENDING

	Games	Min.	W	L	T	Goals	SO	Avg.
Sandy Allan	35	1947	19	11	2	112	1	3.45
Craig Hordal	36	1978	22	11	0	121	1	3.67
Tim Bacik	8	427	3	4	0	31	0	4.36

PRINCE GEORGE COUGARS

SCORING

	Games	G	A	Pts.	PIM
Steve Dowhy	63	44	42	86	43
Alex Vasilevskii	48	32	34	66	52
Mike LeClerc	43	20	36	56	78
Dorian Anneck	47	18	38	56	12
Ryan Smith	69	6	38	44	81
Shawn Gendron	72	17	19	36	66
Martin Hohenberger	47	10	21	31	81
Rob Butz	32	12	18	30	83
Alexander Boikov	46	5	23	28	115
Chris Petersen	39	15	10	25	41
Andrew Laming	48	8	14	22	95
Matt Van Horkick	69	7	14	21	247
Trevor Shoaf	59	5	13	18	77
James Reimer	62	4	9	13	28
Ryan Marien	68	5	6	11	16
Ronald Petrovicky	21	4	6	10	37
Clayton Catellier	71	0	10	10	287
Geoff Lynch	22	3	6	9	24
Rob Voltera	52	3	6	9	101
Ryan Brown	32	2	7	9	103
Randy Toye	10	3	3	6	19
Chris Low	23	2	4	6	7
Sheldon Souray	11	2	3	5	23
Graeme Harder	12	1	2	3	28
Ian Walterson	23	0	3	3	19
Derek Stevely	68	0	3	3	61
Brad Hammerback	5	1	0	1	6
Greg Harder	3	0	1	1	0
Jarret Smith	1	0	0	0	0
George Cooke	2	0	0	0	11
Rob Friesen	3	0	0	0	0

	Games	G	A	Pts.	PIM
Shaun Woroschuk	3	0	0	0	0
Ryan Follack	4	0	0	0	0
Chris Martin	4	0	0	0	0
Corey Laniuk	5	0	0	0	2
Brent Fritz	7	0	0	0	0
Sean Halifax	8	0	0	0	20
Ryan Ludwar (goalie)	8	0	0	0	2
Mike Walker (goalie)	16	0	0	0	2
David Trofimenkoff (goalie)	17	0	0	0	2
Chris Mason (goalie)	44	0	0	0	6

GOALTENDING

	Games	Min.	W	L	T	Goals	SO	Avg.
Chris Mason	44	2288	8	30	1	192	1	5.03
Mike Walker	16	828	0	13	0	72	0	5.22
David Trofimenkoff	17	889	4	8	2	86	0	5.80
Ryan Ludwar	8	364	2	4	0	37	0	6.10

RED DEER REBELS

SCORING

	Games	G	A	Pts.	PIM
Pete LeBoutillier	59	27	16	43	159
Jonathan Zukiwsky	71	19	24	43	38
Tony Vlastelic	60	19	17	36	35
Mike McBain	68	6	28	34	55
Peter Vandermeer	61	16	16	32	218
Terry Lindgren	72	7	23	30	139
Sean Selmser	33	11	17	28	65
Aleksei Boudaev	30	15	12	27	6
Arron Asham	62	11	16	27	126
Eddy Marchant	38	10	17	27	103
Dean Tiltgen	23	8	18	26	25
Chris Johnston	25	8	14	22	60
Chrtis Cardinal	25	7	15	22	11
Byron Briske	48	4	17	21	116
Berkley Pennock	69	6	14	20	171
Jesse Wallin	72	4	16	20	72
Greg Schmidt	58	4	12	16	89
B.J. Young	21	5	9	14	33
Dale Donaldson	70	6	7	13	80
Jay Henderson	54	3	9	12	80
Neil Johnston	28	5	5	10	49
Chris Maillet	47	1	9	10	102
Scott Lega	61	2	7	9	134
Chris Kibermanis	52	3	1	4	93
Tyler Quiring	11	1	1	2	10
Greg Johnson	14	1	1	2	34
Lewis Kinvig	16	0	2	2	6
Josh Lazzari	2	0	1	1	0
Craig Bilick	1	0	0	0	4
Mike Brown	1	0	0	0	0
Ken McKay	1	0	0	0	0
Garnet Stevenson (goalie)	2	0	0	0	0
Jason Clague (goalie)	3	0	0	0	0
Brad Leeb	3	0	0	0	4
Craig Hann (goalie)	5	0	0	0	0
Lance Ward	28	0	0	0	29
Mike Whitney (goalie)	31	0	0	0	4
Chris Wickenheiser (goalie)	47	0	0	0	25

GOALTENDING

	Games	Min.	W	L	T	Goals	SO	Avg.
Chris Wickenheiser	47	2429	13	26	3	181	1	4.47
Mike Whitney	31	1517	4	19	1	127	0	5.02
Garnet Stevenson	2	64	0	1	0	6	0	5.63
Jason Clague	3	153	0	2	0	15	0	5.88
Craig Hann	5	200	0	3	0	21	0	6.30

REGINA PATS

SCORING

	Games	G	A	Pts.	PIM
Jeff Petruic	71	46	33	79	79
Rhett Gordon	71	36	43	79	64

	Games	G	A	Pts.	PIM
Colin Foley	38	19	38	57	54
Russell Hewson	57	23	24	47	43
Jeff Friesen	25	21	23	44	22
Josh Holden	62	20	23	43	45
Perry Johnson	72	6	33	39	45
Dion Zukiwsky	68	4	28	32	83
Chris Johnston	21	13	17	30	32
Chad Wilchinski	70	7	15	22	96
Jeromie Kufflick	68	6	15	21	162
Joey Bouvier	43	7	12	19	83
Kurt Neumeier	48	7	12	19	20
Lars Pettersen	69	7	10	17	59
Wade Strand	70	4	13	17	85
Jesse Rezansoff	45	8	8	16	83
Judd Casper	46	7	9	16	67
Brad Brown	57	4	11	15	57
Shawn Collins	55	2	13	15	127
Boyd Kane	25	6	5	11	6
Jan Vasilev	23	6	2	8	0
Dmitri Markovsky	13	4	3	7	9
Jason Bird	26	3	4	7	6
Ross Parsons	66	1	5	6	107
Shannon Briske	17	2	2	4	18
Ryan Phillips	14	0	3	3	6
Mike Walker (goalie)	14	0	3	3	0
Travis Stevenson	6	0	2	2	18
Greg Harvey	17	0	2	2	36
Tim Winters (goalie)	12	0	1	1	0
Chad Mercier (goalie)	53	0	1	1	17
Rob Lenz	1	0	0	0	0
Reed Low	2	0	0	0	5
Chris Riddell	3	0	0	0	4
David Brumby (goalie)	4	0	0	0	2
Sean Donnelly	4	0	0	0	0

GOALTENDING

	Games	Min.	W	L	T	Goals	SO	Avg.
David Brumby	4	230	0	3	0	15	0	3.91
Chad Mercier	53	2860	19	26	3	188	1	3.94
Mike Walker	14	760	6	7	0	50	1	3.95
Tim Winters	12	520	1	7	0	48	0	5.54

SASKATOON BLADES

SCORING

	Games	G	A	Pts.	PIM
Mark Deyell	70	34	68	102	56
Paul Buczkowski	72	42	56	98	54
Frank Banham	70	50	39	89	63
Shane Calder	72	30	47	77	123
Trevor Hanas	70	24	41	65	77
Clarke Wilm	71	20	39	59	179
Ivan Salon	61	21	25	46	49
Chad Allan	63	14	29	43	95
Rhett Warrener	66	13	26	39	137
Ryan Tobler	61	11	19	30	81
Mark Szoke	24	12	17	29	42
Kirby Law	46	10	15	25	44
Andrew Kemper	54	3	21	24	97
Steve Roberts	29	8	12	20	6
Lee Sorochan	24	5	13	18	63
Wade Belak	72	4	14	18	290
Dmitri Markovsky	24	8	8	16	4
Nathan Rempel	61	6	5	11	94
Brent Sopel	22	1	10	11	31
Chris McAllister	65	2	8	10	134
Greg Phillips	64	3	5	8	94
Mike O'Grady	39	0	7	7	157
Doyle McMorris	41	1	2	3	8
Ian Gordon (goalie)	41	0	3	3	8
Jay Fitzpatrick	3	1	1	2	16
Trevor Ethier	6	1	1	2	10
Kevin Pozzo	11	0	2	2	20
Rob Friesen (goalie)	17	0	1	1	0
Matt Cusson	1	0	0	0	0

	Games	G	A	Pts.	PIM
Vinnie Jonasson	1	0	0	0	7
Jason Duda	2	0	0	0	0
Dennis Bassett (goalie)	4	0	0	0	0
Cory Sarich	6	0	0	0	4
Devon Hanson (goalie)	15	0	0	0	2

GOALTENDING

	Games	Min.	W	L	T	Goals	SO	Avg.
Ian Gordon	41	2476	24	9	7	129	1	3.13
Rob Friesen	17	961	9	8	0	57	0	3.56
Dennis Bassett	4	159	2	0	0	10	0	3.77
Devon Hanson	15	816	6	6	1	56	0	4.12

SEATTLE THUNDERBIRDS

SCORING

	Games	G	A	Pts.	PIM
Chris Wells	69	45	63	108	148
Chris Herperger	59	49	52	101	106
Jan Hrdina	69	41	59	100	79
Blair Manning	58	32	58	90	57
Deron Quint	65	29	60	89	82
Regan Mueller	66	29	41	70	66
Shawn Gervais	66	11	23	34	73
Chris Schmidt	61	21	11	32	31
Paul Ferone	63	6	19	25	156
Tyler Perry	49	9	13	22	19
Michal Divisek	61	0	21	21	83
Scott Burt	62	9	11	20	106
David Jesiolowski	54	8	7	15	230
Lloyd Shaw	66	3	12	15	313
Kevin Popp	70	5	8	13	257
Dave Cammock	17	6	6	12	55
Drew Palmer	67	2	10	12	215
Jake Deadmarsh	51	1	9	10	92
Jeff Connolly	9	2	6	8	19
Jason Norrie	45	3	4	7	127
Kevin Boris	39	2	4	6	15
Jason Kroffat	14	2	1	3	6
Brent Symes	10	1	2	3	0
Darrell Sandback	11	1	2	3	44
Calvin Crowe	29	1	2	3	97
Doug Bonner (goalie)	59	0	3	3	4
Paul Vincent	3	0	2	2	2
Harlan Pratt	33	1	0	1	17
Travis Stevenson	4	0	1	1	19
Scott Reid (goalie)	20	0	1	1	5
David Carson	1	0	0	0	0
Jeff Peddigrew	1	0	0	0	0
Aaron Bowal	2	0	0	0	0
Bill Russell (goalie)	2	0	0	0	0
Chad Kalmakoff	5	0	0	0	2
Darcy Smith	6	0	0	0	7
Chad Hackywicz	11	0	0	0	2

GOALTENDING

	Games	Min.	W	L	T	Goals	SO	Avg.
Doug Bonner	59	3386	33	23	1	205	1	3.63
Scott Reid	20	940	9	5	1	69	0	4.40
Bill Russell	2	26	0	0	0	6	0	13.85

SPOKANE CHIEFS

SCORING

	Games	G	A	Pts.	PIM
Jason Podollan	72	43	41	84	102
John Cirjak	69	21	37	58	58
Sean Gillam	72	16	40	56	192
Greg Leeb	72	21	34	55	48
Bryan McCabe	42	14	39	53	115
Jeremy Stasiuk	65	26	24	50	154
Joe Cardarelli	71	27	22	49	20
Darren Sinclair	71	16	20	36	81
Hugh Hamilton	60	5	28	33	102
Dmitri Leonov	43	9	17	26	62

	Games	G	A	Pts.	PIM
Trent Whitfield	48	8	17	25	26
Randy Favaro	66	8	10	18	102
Kevin Sawyer	54	7	9	16	365
Jared Hope	59	5	9	14	17
Jay Bertsch	47	5	7	12	147
Mike Haley	55	4	7	11	117
Joel Boschman	55	1	7	8	105
Derek Descoteau	21	3	4	7	22
John Shockey	38	1	6	7	70
Scott Fletcher	61	1	4	5	160
Rob Sandrock	27	0	5	5	24
Adam Magarrell	19	0	4	4	27
Ryan Berry	43	2	1	3	51
Jarrod Daniel (goalie)	64	0	2	2	10
Tomas Pisa	21	1	0	1	0
Trevor Shoaf	2	0	1	1	2
Darren Smadis (goalie)	1	0	0	0	0
Derek Schutz	2	0	0	0	2
Paul Bailley	9	0	0	0	0
Ryan Hawes	15	0	0	0	19
David Lemanowicz (goalie)	16	0	0	0	0

GOALTENDING

	Games	Min.	W	L	T	Goals	SO	Avg.
David Lemanowicz	16	761	5	5	1	41	2	3.23
Jarrod Daniel	64	3608	27	31	3	213	1	3.54
Darren Smadis	1	32	0	0	0	5	0	9.38

SWIFT CURRENT BRONCOS

SCORING

	Games	G	A	Pts.	PIM
Paul Vincent	62	59	39	98	85
Ladislav Kohn	65	32	60	92	122
Ashley Buckberger	53	23	37	60	51
Brad Larsen	62	24	33	57	73
Tyler Willis	71	21	29	50	284
Craig Millar	72	8	42	50	80
Josh St. Louis	70	25	18	43	76
Jeff Kirwan	71	16	27	43	12
John Kachur	62	15	11	26	10
Jason Becker	68	7	18	25	25
Brent Sopel	41	4	19	23	50
Vernon Beardy	62	3	18	21	29
Shane Belter	55	3	12	15	72
Bill Hooson	41	7	7	14	64
Chris Szysky	61	6	6	12	105
Keith McCambridge	48	5	7	12	120
Derek Arbez	59	4	6	10	118
Travis Stevenson	42	0	8	8	56
Jesse Rezansoff	19	4	2	6	21
Jan Vasilev	24	3	3	6	0
Aaron MacDonald (goalie)	53	0	5	5	12
Chad Beagle	53	2	2	4	80
Jeff Henkelman	19	0	4	4	8
Cam Severson	15	2	1	3	16
Dalen Hrooshkin	17	1	2	3	0
Cadrin Smart	16	0	3	3	19
Jim Gattolliat	24	0	2	2	24
Trent Dingwall	2	0	1	1	0
Mike Johnston	2	0	1	1	0
Ryan Brown	7	0	1	1	28
Chris Jensen	2	0	0	0	0
Tony Mohagen	2	0	0	0	0
Jaret Sledz	2	0	0	0	7
Adam Rettschlag	3	0	0	0	0
John Shockey	3	0	0	0	0
Craig Bilick	5	0	0	0	2
Chad Kalmakoff	5	0	0	0	6
Bill Russell (goalie)	12	0	0	0	0
Ian Gordon (goalie)	17	0	0	0	0

GOALTENDING

	Games	Min.	W	L	T	Goals	SO	Avg.
Aaron MacDonald	53	2957	24	20	6	177	4	3.59

	Games	Min.	W	L	T	Goals	SO	Avg.
Ian Gordon	17	994	6	9	1	62	1	3.74
Bill Russell	12	447	1	5	0	41	0	5.50

TACOMA ROCKETS

SCORING

	Games	G	A	Pts.	PIM
Vaclav Varada	68	50	38	88	108
John Varga	56	37	51	88	109
Marty Flichel	67	25	53	78	81
Tavis Hansen	71	32	41	73	142
Burt Henderson	72	12	49	61	88
Jason Leleurme	70	25	23	48	70
Tyler Prosofsky	71	20	27	47	161
Alexandre Alexeev	54	14	32	46	55
Brett McLean	67	11	23	34	33
Kyle McLaren	47	13	19	32	68
Rod Butler	60	10	14	24	60
Adam Smith	69	2	19	21	96
Ryan Wade	59	11	9	20	37
Dallas Thompson	71	8	12	20	259
Steve Roberts	15	6	11	17	4
Joel Kwiatkowski	70	4	13	17	66
Quinn Hancock	58	8	7	15	14
Mike Piersol	57	2	12	14	45
Dale Purinton	65	0	8	8	291
Chris Fleury	55	2	3	5	51
Jamie Butt	44	1	4	5	140
Todd MacDonald (goalie)	60	0	3	3	16
Lewis Kinvig	11	1	0	1	4
Kim Dillabaugh (goalie)	20	0	1	1	0
Luke Curtin	1	0	0	0	0
Jason Gibson	2	0	0	0	9
Scott Hannan	2	0	0	0	0

GOALTENDING

	Games	Min.	W	L	T	Goals	SO	Avg.
Todd MacDonald	60	3433	35	21	2	179	3	3.13
Kim Dillabaugh	20	943	8	6	0	64	0	4.07

TRI-CITY AMERICANS

SCORING

	Games	G	A	Pts.	PIM
Daymond Langkow	72	67	73	140	142
Terry Ryan	70	50	60	110	207
Brent Ascroft	68	26	62	88	53
Chad Cabana	68	25	34	59	252
Mark Hurley	69	25	27	52	48
Pavel Kriz	68	6	34	40	47
Boyd Olson	69	16	16	32	87
Sheldon Souray	40	2	24	26	140
Dean Tiltgen	20	9	15	24	21
Zenith Komarniski	66	5	19	24	110
Cadrin Smart	48	7	16	23	92
Geoff Lynch	36	11	8	19	24
Marc Stephan	44	8	8	16	99
Alexander Boikov	24	3	13	16	63
Ryan Marsh	60	3	13	16	177
Ronald Petrovicky	39	4	11	15	86
Jeremy Thompson	54	8	6	14	159
Rob Butz	17	4	8	12	38
B.J. Young	30	6	3	9	39
Tom Zavediuk	49	2	7	9	11
Craig Stahl	50	2	7	9	157
Ray Schultz	63	1	8	9	209
Doug Strobl	57	1	6	7	17
Mike Hurley	47	2	4	6	6
Ryan Brown	19	1	2	3	84
David Benard	1	1	0	1	0
Justin Guy	1	0	1	1	2
Byron Briske	15	0	1	1	22
David Brumby (goalie)	15	0	1	1	7
Brian Boucher (goalie)	35	0	1	1	2
Nevin Holowachuk	1	0	0	0	0
Scott Reid (goalie)	1	0	0	0	0

	Games	G	A	Pts.	PIM
John Shockey	1	0	0	0	0
Dorian Anneck	3	0	0	0	0
Dylan Gyori	3	0	0	0	0
Shane Ottenbritt	3	0	0	0	0
Jaret Sledz	3	0	0	0	0
David Trofimenkoff (goalie)	8	0	0	0	0
David Pirnak (goalie)	12	0	0	0	0
Mike Walker (goalie)	12	0	0	0	4

GOALTENDING

	Games	Min.	W	L	T	Goals	SO	Avg.
David Trofimenkoff	8	442	6	2	0	18	2	2.44
Brian Boucher	35	1969	17	11	2	108	1	3.29
David Brumby	15	851	5	6	1	60	0	4.23
David Pirnak	12	521	5	5	0	37	0	4.26
Mike Walker	12	537	2	7	2	44	0	4.92
Scott Reid	1	60	1	0	0	6	0	6.00

PLAYERS WITH TWO OR MORE TEAMS

SCORING

	Games	G	A	Pts.	PIM
Dorian Anneck, Prince George	47	18	38	56	12
Dorian Anneck, Tri-City	3	0	0	0	0
Totals	50	18	38	56	12
Paul Bailley, Brandon	11	0	1	1	10
Paul Bailley, Spokane	9	0	0	0	0
Totals	20	0	1	1	10
Craig Bilick, Red Deer	1	0	0	0	4
Craig Bilick, Swift Current	5	0	0	0	2
Totals	6	0	0	0	6
Jason Bird, Lethbridge	29	2	3	5	26
Jason Bird, Regina	26	3	4	7	6
Totals	55	5	7	12	32
Alexander Boikov, P.G.	46	5	23	28	115
Alexander Boikov, Tri-City	24	3	13	16	63
Totals	70	8	36	44	178
Rodney Bowers, Medicine Hat	5	0	1	1	0
Rodney Bowers, Portland	12	2	1	2	2
Totals	17	2	1	3	2
Byron Briske, Red Deer	48	4	17	21	116
Byron Briske, Tri-City	15	0	1	1	22
Totals	63	4	18	22	138
Shannon Briske, Portland	9	0	0	0	11
Shannon Briske, Regina	17	2	2	4	18
Totals	26	2	2	4	29
Ryan Brown, Swift Current	7	0	1	1	28
Ryan Brown, Prince George	32	2	7	9	103
Ryan Brown, Tri-City	19	1	2	3	84
Totals	58	3	10	13	215
David Brumby, Tri-City (g)	15	0	1	1	7
David Brumby, Regina (g)	4	0	0	0	2
David Brumby, Lethbridge (g)	19	0	0	0	9
Totals	38	0	1	1	18
Ashley Buckberger, S.C.	53	23	37	60	51
Ashley Buckberger, Kamloops	21	9	13	22	13
Totals	74	32	50	82	64
Rob Butz, Prince George	32	12	18	30	83
Rob Butz, Tri-City	17	4	8	12	38
Totals	49	16	26	42	121
Dave Cammock, Portland	1	0	0	0	4
Dave Cammock, Seattle	17	6	6	12	55
Totals	18	6	6	12	59
Judd Casper, Regina	46	7	9	16	67
Judd Casper, Portland	19	0	5	5	32
Totals	65	7	14	21	99
Calvin Crowe, Medicine Hat	3	0	0	0	11
Calvin Crowe, Seattle	29	1	2	3	97
Totals	32	1	2	3	108
Jake Deadmarsh, Portland	3	0	0	0	10
Jake Deadmarsh, Seattle	51	1	9	10	92
Totals	54	1	9	10	102
Jason Duda, Saskatoon	2	0	0	0	0
Jason Duda, Medicine Hat	3	1	0	1	0
Totals	5	1	0	1	0

	Games	G	A	Pts.	PIM
Paul Ferone, Portland	2	0	1	1	5
Paul Ferone, Seattle	63	6	19	25	156
Totals	65	6	20	26	161
Ian Gordon, Swift Current (g)	17	0	0	0	2
Ian Gordon, Saskatoon (g)	41	0	3	3	8
Totals	58	0	3	3	10
Justin Guy, Tri-City	1	0	1	1	2
Justin Guy, Portland	51	3	5	8	49
Totals	52	3	6	9	51
Devon Hanson, Saskatoon (g)	15	0	0	0	2
Devon Hanson, Moose Jaw (g)	13	0	2	2	10
Totals	28	0	2	2	12
Graeme Harder, Prince George	12	1	2	3	28
Graeme Harder, Portland	61	2	4	6	134
Totals	73	3	6	9	162
Greg Harvey, Prince Albert	1	0	0	0	0
Greg Harvey, Regina	17	0	2	2	36
Totals	18	0	2	2	36
Jeff Henkelman, Kamloops	37	1	3	4	31
Jeff Henkelman, Swift Current	19	0	4	4	8
Totals	56	1	7	8	39
Bill Hooson, Swift Current	41	7	7	14	64
Bill Hooson, Medicine Hat	15	1	1	2	23
Totals	56	8	8	16	87
Chris Johnston, Red Deer	25	8	14	22	60
Chris Johnston, Regina	21	13	17	30	32
Totals	46	21	31	52	92
Neil Johnston, Red Deer	28	5	5	10	49
Neil Johnston, Prince Albert	39	12	16	28	34
Totals	67	17	21	38	83
Mike Josephson, Kamloops	5	2	6	8	4
Mike Josephson, Lethbridge	62	22	25	47	113
Totals	67	24	31	55	117
Chad Kalmakoff, Swift Current	5	0	0	0	6
Chad Kalmakoff, Seattle	5	0	0	0	2
Totals	10	0	0	0	8
Lewis Kinvig, Tacoma	11	1	0	1	4
Lewis Kinvig, Red Deer	16	0	2	2	6
Totals	27	1	2	3	10
Mike Krooshoop, Kamloops	1	0	0	0	7
Mike Krooshoop, Moose Jaw	49	3	13	16	146
Totals	50	3	13	16	153
Kirby Law, Saskatoon	46	10	15	25	44
Kirby Law, Lethbridge	24	4	10	14	38
Totals	70	14	25	39	82
Mike LeClerc, Prince George	43	20	36	56	78
Mike LeClerc, Brandon	23	5	8	13	50
Totals	66	25	44	69	128
Chris Low, Brandon	37	10	6	16	15
Chris Low, Prince George	23	2	4	6	7
Totals	60	12	10	22	22
Geoff Lynch, Tri-City	36	11	8	19	24
Geoff Lynch, Prince George	22	3	6	9	24
Totals	58	14	14	28	48
Adam Magarrell, Brandon	41	0	3	3	72
Adam Magarrell, Spokane	19	0	4	4	27
Totals	60	0	7	7	99
Dmitri Markovsky, Regina	13	4	3	7	9
Dmitri Markovsky, Lethbridge	25	5	9	14	4
Dmitri Markovsky, Saskatoon	24	8	8	16	4
Totals	62	17	20	37	17
Bryan McCabe, Spokane	42	14	39	53	115
Bryan McCabe, Brandon	20	6	10	16	38
Totals	62	20	49	69	153
Keith McCambridge, S.C.	48	5	7	12	120
Keith McCambridge, Kamloops	21	0	6	6	90
Totals	69	5	13	18	210
Doyle McMorris, Saskatoon	41	1	2	3	8
Doyle McMorris, Lethbridge	18	0	5	5	4
Totals	59	1	7	8	12
Mike O'Grady, Saskatoon	39	0	7	7	157
Mike O'Grady, Lethbridge	21	1	2	3	124
Totals	60	1	9	10	281
Ronald Petrovicky, Tri-City	39	4	11	15	86
Ronald Petrovicky, P.G.	21	4	6	10	37
Totals	60	8	17	25	123
Ryan Petz, Medicine Hat	29	11	7	18	14
Ryan Petz, Moose Jaw	41	15	31	46	32
Totals	70	26	38	64	46
Kevin Pozzo, Saskatoon	11	0	2	2	20
Kevin Pozzo, Brandon	50	4	17	21	81
Totals	61	4	19	23	101
Chad Reich, Moose Jaw	19	1	4	5	33
Chad Reich, Medicine Hat	26	6	9	15	30
Totals	45	7	13	20	63
Scott Reid, Tri-City (g)	1	0	0	0	0
Scott Reid, Seattle (g)	20	0	1	1	5
Totals	21	0	1	1	5
Jesse Rezansoff, Regina	45	8	8	16	83
Jesse Rezansoff, Swift Current	19	4	2	6	21
Totals	64	12	10	22	104
Steve Roberts, Tacoma	15	6	11	17	4
Steve Roberts, Saskatoon	29	8	12	20	6
Steve Roberts, Lethbridge	10	3	6	9	7
Totals	54	17	29	46	17
Bill Russell, Seattle (g)	2	0	0	0	0
Bill Russell, Swift Current (g)	12	0	0	0	0
Totals	14	0	0	0	0
Cam Severson, Kamloops	30	4	1	5	40
Cam Severson, Swift Current	15	2	1	3	16
Totals	45	6	2	8	56
Trevor Shoaf, Spokane	2	0	1	1	2
Trevor Shoaf, Prince George	59	5	13	18	77
Totals	61	5	14	19	79
John Shockey, Tri-City	1	0	0	0	0
John Shockey, Swift Current	3	0	0	0	0
John Shockey, Spokane	38	1	6	7	70
Totals	42	1	6	7	70
Jaret Sledz, Swift Current	2	0	0	0	7
Jaret Sledz, Tri-City	3	0	0	0	0
Totals	5	0	0	0	7
Darren Smadis, Spokane (g)	1	0	0	0	0
Darren Smadis, Brandon (g)	4	0	0	0	0
Darren Smadis, Lethbridge (g)	30	0	0	0	2
Totals	35	0	0	0	2
Cadrin Smart, Tri-City	48	7	16	23	92
Cadrin Smart, Swift Current	16	0	3	3	19
Totals	64	7	19	26	111
Darcy Smith, Seattle	6	0	0	0	7
Darcy Smith, Medicine Hat	24	0	0	0	16
Totals	30	0	0	0	23
Brent Sopel, Saskatoon	22	1	10	11	31
Brent Sopel, Swift Current	41	4	19	23	50
Totals	63	5	29	34	81
Lee Sorochan, Lethbridge	29	4	15	19	93
Lee Sorochan, Saskatoon	24	5	13	18	63
Totals	53	9	28	37	156
Sheldon Souray, Tri-City	40	2	24	26	140
Sheldon Souray, Prince George	11	2	3	5	23
Totals	51	4	27	31	163
Travis Stevenson, Seattle	4	0	1	1	19
Travis Stevenson, Swift Current	42	0	8	8	56
Travis Stevenson, Regina	6	0	2	2	18
Totals	52	0	11	11	93
Mark Szoke, Lethbridge	42	35	31	66	89
Mark Szoke, Saskatoon	24	12	17	29	42
Totals	66	47	48	95	131
Jeremy Thompson, Lethbridge	15	0	1	1	62
Jeremy Thompson, Tri-City	54	8	6	14	159
Totals	69	8	7	15	221
Dean Tiltgen, Tri-City	20	9	15	24	21
Dean Tiltgen, Red Deer	23	8	18	26	25
Totals	43	17	33	50	46
David Trofimenkoff, Leth. (g)	11	0	0	0	17
David Trofimenkoff, P.G. (g)	17	0	0	0	2
David Trofimenkoff, T.C. (g)	8	0	0	0	0
Totals	36	0	0	0	19
Jan Vasilev, Swift Current	24	3	3	6	0
Jan Vasilev, Regina	23	6	2	8	0
Totals	47	9	5	14	0
Alex Vasilevskii, Prince George	48	32	34	66	52
Alex Vasilevskii, Brandon	23	6	11	17	39

	Games	G	A	Pts.	PIM
Totals	71	38	45	83	91
Paul Vincent, Seattle	3	0	2	2	2
Paul Vincent, Swift Current	62	59	39	98	85
Totals	65	59	41	100	87
Mike Walker, Regina (g)	14	0	3	3	0
Mike Walker, Tri-City (g)	12	0	0	0	4
Mike Walker, Prince George (g)	16	0	0	0	2
Totals	42	0	3	3	6
Ian Walterson, Brandon	40	2	0	2	27
Ian Walterson, Prince George	23	0	3	3	19
Totals	63	2	3	5	46
B.J. Young, Tri-City	30	6	3	9	39
B.J. Young, Red Deer	21	5	9	14	33
Totals	51	11	12	23	72

GOALTENDING

	Games	Min.	W	L	T	Goals	SO	Avg.
David Brumby, T.C..	15	851	5	6	1	60	0	4.23
David Brumby, Reg..	4	230	0	3	0	15	0	3.91
David Brumby, Leth.	19	1036	6	11	0	78	0	4.52
Totals	38	2117	11	20	1	153	0	4.34
Ian Gordon, S.C.	17	994	6	9	1	62	1	3.74
Ian Gordon, Sask.	41	2476	24	9	7	129	1	3.13

	Games	Min.	W	L	T	Goals	SO	Avg.
Totals	58	3470	30	18	8	344	2	5.95
Devon Hanson, Sask.	15	816	6	6	1	56	0	4.12
Devon Hanson, M.J..	13	563	5	4	1	34	0	3.62
Totals	28	1379	11	10	2	434	0	18.88
Scott Reid, T.C.	1	60	1	0	0	6	0	6.00
Scott Reid, Sea.	20	940	9	5	1	69	0	4.40
Totals	21	1000	10	5	1	509	0	30.54
Bill Russell, Sea.	2	26	0	0	0	6	0	13.85
Bill Russell, S.C.	12	447	1	5	0	41	0	5.50
Totals	14	473	1	5	0	556	0	70.53
Darren Smadis, Spo.	1	32	0	0	0	5	0	9.38
Darren Smadis, Bran.	4	228	2	1	0	10	0	2.63
Darren Smadis, Leth..	30	1446	8	13	1	112	0	4.65
Totals	35	1706	10	14	1	127	0	4.47
D. Trofimenkoff, Leth.	11	600	4	6	0	47	0	4.70
D. Trofimenkoff, P.G.	17	889	4	8	2	86	0	5.80
D. Trofimenkoff, T.C.	8	442	6	2	0	18	2	2.44
Totals	36	1931	14	16	2	151	2	4.69
Mike Walker, Reg....	14	760	6	7	0	50	1	3.95
Mike Walker, T.C....	12	537	2	7	2	44	0	4.92
Mike Walker, P.G....	16	828	0	13	0	72	0	5.22
Totals	42	2125	8	27	2	166	1	4.69

1995 PLAYOFFS

RESULTS

EAST DIVISION QUARTERFINALS

Series "A"

	W	L	Pts.	GF	GA
Prince Albert	4	0	8	24	15
Regina	0	4	0	15	24

(Prince Albert won series, 4-0)

Series "B"

	W	L	Pts.	GF	GA
Saskatoon	4	2	8	18	14
Swift Current	2	4	4	14	18

(Saskatoon won series, 4-2)

Series "C"

	W	L	Pts.	GF	GA
Moose Jaw	4	1	8	20	14
Medicine Hat	1	4	2	14	20

(Moose Jaw won series, 4-1)

WEST DIVISION QUARTERFINALS

Series "D"

	W	L	Pts.	GF	GA
Kamloops	3	1	6	16	8
Portland	3	1	4	13	14
Seattle	0	4	0	9	16

(Kamloops and Portland advance)

Series "E"

	W	L	Pts.	GF	GA
Spokane	3	1	6	18	15
Tri-City	2	2	4	17	18
Tacoma	1	3	2	12	14

(Spokane and Tri-City advance)

EAST DIVISION SEMIFINALS

Series "F"

	W	L	Pts.	GF	GA
Brandon	4	1	8	25	22
Moose Jaw	1	4	2	22	25

(Brandon won series, 4-1)

Series "G"

	W	L	Pts.	GF	GA
Prince Albert	4	0	8	17	10
Saskatoon	0	4	0	10	17

(Prince Albert won series, 4-0)

WEST DIVISION SEMIFINALS

Series "H"

	W	L	Pts.	GF	GA
Kamloops	4	1	8	19	11
Portland	1	4	2	11	19

(Kamloops won series, 4-1)

Series "I"

	W	L	Pts.	GF	GA
Tri-City	4	3	8	31	36
Spokane	3	4	6	36	31

(Tri-City won series, 4-3)

EAST DIVISION FINALS

Series "J"

	W	L	Pts.	GF	GA
Brandon	4	3	8	24	22
Prince Albert	3	4	6	22	24

(Brandon won series, 4-3)

WEST DIVISION FINALS

Series "K"

	W	L	Pts.	GF	GA
Kamloops	4	2	8	28	17
Tri-City	2	4	4	17	28

(Kamloops won series, 4-2)

FINALS

Series "L"

	W	L	Pts.	GF	GA
Kamloops	4	2	8	21	19
Brandon	2	4	4	19	21

(Kamloops won series, 4-2)

Goals: Darcy Tucker, Kamloops (16)
Assists: Marty Murray, Brandon (20)
Points: Darcy Tucker, Kamloops (31)
Penalty minutes: Rob Trumbley, Moose Jaw (64)
Goaltending average: Rod Branch, Kamloops (2.19)
Shutouts: Rod Branch, Kamloops (1)
Brian Elder, Brandon (1)
Ian Gordon, Saskatoon (1)

TOP SCORERS

	Games	G	A	Pts.
Darcy Tucker, Kamloops	21	16	15	31
Marty Murray, Brandon	18	9	20	29
Daymond Langkow, Tri-City	17	12	15	27
Terry Ryan, Tri-City	17	12	15	27
Denis Pederson, Prince Albert	15	11	14	25
Darren Ritchie, Brandon	18	13	9	22
Chad Cabana, Tri-City	17	10	11	21
Shayne Toporowski, Prince Albert	15	10	8	18
Hnat Domenichelli, Kamloops	19	9	9	18
Jarome Iginla, Kamloops	21	7	11	18
Brent Ascroft, Tri-City	17	6	12	18

INDIVIDUAL STATISTICS

BRANDON WHEAT KINGS

(Lost WHL finals to Kamloops, 4-2)

SCORING

	Games	G	A	Pts.	PIM
Marty Murray	18	9	20	29	16
Darren Ritchie	18	13	9	22	2
Bryan McCabe	18	4	13	17	59
Mike LeClerc	18	10	6	16	33
Wade Redden	18	5	10	15	8
Colin Cloutier	16	5	6	11	47
Alex Vasilevskii	18	3	6	9	34
Peter Schaefer	18	5	3	8	18
Bobby Brown	18	3	3	6	31
Kevin Pozzo	18	0	5	5	30
Justin Kurtz	18	2	2	4	26
Scott Laluk	11	2	1	3	2
Mark Dutiaume	17	1	2	3	33
Sven Butenschon	18	1	2	3	11
Kelly Smart	18	1	2	3	4
Darren Van Oene	18	1	1	2	34
Jeff Staples	18	0	2	2	23
Mike Dubinsky	1	1	0	1	4
Chris Dingman	3	1	0	1	9
Ryan Robson	15	1	0	1	2
Byron Penstock (goalie)	6	0	0	0	0
Darryl Stockham	7	0	0	0	0
Brian Elder (goalie)	13	0	0	0	6

GOALTENDING

	Games	Min.	W	L	T	Goals	SO	Avg.
Brian Elder	13	756	6	7	0	38	1	3.02
Byron Penstock	6	342	4	1	0	24	0	4.21

KAMLOOPS BLAZERS

(Winner of 1995 playoffs)

SCORING

	Games	G	A	Pts.	PIM
Darcy Tucker	21	16	15	31	19
Hnat Domenichelli	19	9	9	18	9
Ashley Buckberger	19	7	11	18	22
Jarome Iginla	21	7	11	18	34
Tyson Nash	21	10	7	17	30
Nolan Baumgartner	21	4	13	17	16
Shane Doan	21	6	10	16	16
Aaron Keller	15	3	13	16	6
Ryan Huska	17	7	8	15	12
Ivan Vologjaninov	13	5	5	10	2
Jason Holland	21	2	7	9	9
Brad Lukowich	18	0	7	7	21
Greg Hart	14	3	2	5	0
Jeff Antonovich	17	2	3	5	6
Donnie Kinney	18	1	4	5	4
Keith McCambridge	21	0	5	5	49
Bob Maudie	21	1	2	3	8
Jason Strudwick	21	1	1	2	39

	Games	G	A	Pts.	PIM
Bob Westerby	17	0	2	2	41
Randy Petruk (goalie)	7	0	1	1	0
Shawn McNeil	9	0	1	1	0
Jeff Ainsworth	6	0	0	0	7
Jeff Oldenborger	7	0	0	0	2
Rod Branch (goalie)	15	0	0	0	2

GOALTENDING

	Games	Min.	W	L	T	Goals	SO	Avg.
Rod Branch	15	932	10	4	0	34	1	2.19
Randy Petruk	7	423	5	2	0	19	0	2.70

MEDICINE HAT TIGERS

(Lost East Division quarterfinals to Moose Jaw, 4-1)

SCORING

	Games	G	A	Pts.	PIM
Stacy Roest	5	2	7	9	2
Josh Green	5	5	1	6	2
Sergei Klimentiev	5	4	2	6	14
Henry Kuster	5	1	3	4	6
Don Larner	5	1	2	3	10
Aaron Zarowny	5	1	1	2	6
Mark Polak	5	0	2	2	6
Trevor Wasyluk	5	0	2	2	4
Cal Benazic	5	0	1	1	19
Steve Cheredaryk	5	0	1	1	13
Johnathan Aitken	5	0	0	0	0
Bill Hooson	5	0	0	0	2
Chad Reich	5	0	0	0	6
Jeremy Schaefer	5	0	0	0	20
Paxton Schafer (goalie)	5	0	0	0	2
Darcy Smith	5	0	0	0	2
Blair St. Martin	5	0	0	0	0
Rocky Thompson	5	0	0	0	17
Brad Wilson	5	0	0	0	6

GOALTENDING

	Games	Min.	W	L	T	Goals	SO	Avg.
Paxton Schafer	5	339	1	4	0	18	0	3.19

MOOSE JAW WARRIORS

(Lost East Division semifinals to Brandon, 4-1)

SCORING

	Games	G	A	Pts.	PIM
Curtis Brown	10	8	7	15	20
Ryan Smyth	10	6	9	15	22
Chris Armstrong	10	2	12	14	22
Ryan Petz	10	6	4	10	7
Grady Manson	10	5	5	10	10
Roman Vopat	10	4	1	5	28
Mike Krooshoop	10	3	1	4	26
Darryl LaPlante	10	2	2	4	7
Jeff Dewar	10	0	4	4	23

	Games	G	A	Pts.	PIM
Rob Trumbley	10	2	1	3	64
Matt Higgins	10	1	2	3	2
Paul Johnson	10	1	2	3	24
Chris Twerdun	10	0	3	3	2
Don Halverson	5	1	1	2	5
Mike Broda	10	1	1	2	2
Kevin McKay	10	0	2	2	17
Devon Hanson (goalie)	2	0	1	1	0
John Wood	8	0	1	1	4
Derek Ernest	5	0	0	0	0
Milt Mastad	5	0	0	0	6
Curtis Capjack	7	0	0	0	0
Jody Lehman (goalie)	8	0	0	0	2

GOALTENDING

	Games	Min.	W	L	T	Goals	SO	Avg.
Jody Lehman	8	522	4	4	0	28	0	3.22
Devon Hanson	2	123	1	1	0	11	0	5.37

PORTLAND WINTER HAWKS

(Lost West Division semifinals to Kamloops, 4-1)

SCORING

	Games	G	A	Pts.	PIM
Richard Zednik	9	5	5	10	20
Todd Robinson	9	4	4	8	4
Nolan Pratt	9	1	6	7	10
Layne Roland	8	2	3	5	2
Judd Casper	9	4	0	4	4
Matt Davidson	9	1	3	4	0
Colin Forbes	9	1	3	4	10
Brian Medeiros	9	1	3	4	2
Brad Swanson	9	2	1	3	18
Dave Scatchard	8	0	3	3	21
Chris Carson	5	2	0	2	5
Graeme Harder	9	0	2	2	10
Brad Symes	9	0	2	2	27
Mike Little	9	1	0	1	5
Rodney Bowers	2	0	1	1	0
Justin Guy	7	0	1	1	13
Kevin Haupt	7	0	1	1	2
Deny Gaudet	8	0	1	1	2
Brent Belecki (goalie)	1	0	0	0	0
Scott Rideout (goalie)	1	0	0	0	0
Scott Langkow (goalie)	8	0	0	0	0
Paul Herron	9	0	0	0	0
Joey Tetarenko	9	0	0	0	8

GOALTENDING

	Games	Min.	W	L	T	Goals	SO	Avg.
Scott Rideout	1	28	1	0	0	0	0	0.00
Scott Langkow	8	510	3	5	0	30	0	3.53
Brent Belecki	1	32	0	0	0	3	0	5.63

PRINCE ALBERT RAIDERS

(Lost East Division finals to Brandon, 4-3)

SCORING

	Games	G	A	Pts.	PIM
Denis Pederson	15	11	14	25	14
Shayne Toporowski	15	10	8	18	25
Steve Kelly	15	7	9	16	35
Brad Church	15	6	9	15	32
Russell Hogue	15	5	9	14	8
Neil Johnston	15	6	6	12	17
Jeff Lank	13	2	10	12	8
Shane Hnidy	15	4	7	11	29
Paul Healey	12	3	4	7	2
Shane Willis	13	3	4	7	6
David Van Drunen	15	3	4	7	26
Mike McGhan	15	0	4	4	19
Shane Zulyniak	15	0	4	4	13
Ryan Bast	14	0	3	3	13
Kris Fizzell	4	2	0	2	0
Sandy Allan (goalie)	15	0	2	2	0

	Games	G	A	Pts.	PIM
Jason Issel	13	1	0	1	9
Sean Robertson	10	0	1	1	4
Rob Hegberg	15	0	1	1	2
Kaleb Toth	6	0	0	0	0
Mitch Shawara	7	0	0	0	20
Darren Wright	13	0	0	0	22

GOALTENDING

	Games	Min.	W	L	T	Goals	SO	Avg.
Sandy Allan	15	904	11	4	0	49	0	3.25

REGINA PATS

(Lost East Division quarterfinals to Prince Albert, 4-0)

SCORING

	Games	G	A	Pts.	PIM
Colin Foley	4	3	3	6	8
Chris Johnston	4	2	3	5	8
Josh Holden	4	3	1	4	0
Rhett Gordon	4	2	2	4	0
Perry Johnson	4	1	3	4	2
Jeff Petruic	4	2	1	3	4
Russell Hewson	4	2	0	2	6
Chad Mercier (goalie)	2	0	1	1	0
Joey Bouvier	4	0	1	1	0
Kurt Neumeier	4	0	1	1	0
Ross Parsons	4	0	1	1	0
Chad Wilchinski	4	0	1	1	4
Dion Zukiwsky	4	0	1	1	2
Shawn Collins	2	0	0	0	2
Mike Walker (goalie)	2	0	0	0	0
Tim Winters	2	0	0	0	0
Sean Donnelly	3	0	0	0	0
Lars Pettersen	3	0	0	0	2
Brad Brown	4	0	0	0	0
Boyd Kane	4	0	0	0	0
Jeromie Kufflick	4	0	0	0	10
Wade Strand	4	0	0	0	10

GOALTENDING

	Games	Min.	W	L	T	Goals	SO	Avg.
Chad Mercier	2	120	0	2	0	9	0	4.50
Mike Walker	2	120	0	2	0	13	0	6.50

SASKATOON BLADES

(Lost East Division semifinals to Prince Albert, 4-0)

SCORING

	Games	G	A	Pts.	PIM
Lee Sorochan	10	3	6	9	34
Frank Banham	8	2	6	8	12
Clarke Wilm	10	6	1	7	21
Shane Calder	10	5	2	7	8
Mark Szoke	10	4	3	7	24
Paul Buczkowski	10	2	5	7	5
Mark Deyell	10	2	5	7	14
Trevor Hanas	10	2	4	6	12
Ryan Tobler	10	1	2	3	8
Chad Allan	9	0	3	3	2
Dmitri Markovsky	10	0	3	3	2
Rhett Warrener	10	0	3	3	6
Andrew Kemper	10	0	2	2	18
Nathan Rempel	10	1	0	1	11
Cory Sarich	3	0	1	1	0
Wade Belak	9	0	0	0	36
Ian Gordon (goalie)	10	0	0	0	2
Chris McAllister	10	0	0	0	28
Greg Phillips	10	0	0	0	4
Ivan Salon	10	0	0	0	2

GOALTENDING

	Games	Min.	W	L	T	Goals	SO	Avg.
Ian Gordon	10	633	4	6	0	29	1	2.75

SEATTLE THUNDERBIRDS

(Eliminated by Kamloops and Portland in
West Division quarterfinals)

SCORING

	Games	G	A	Pts.	PIM
Chris Herperger	4	4	0	4	6
Deron Quint	3	1	2	3	6
Kevin Popp	4	1	2	3	4
Tyler Perry	4	2	0	2	2
Blair Manning	4	1	1	2	4
David Jesiolowski	4	0	2	2	0
Dave Cammock	2	0	1	1	4
Doug Bonner (goalie)	3	0	1	1	2
Chris Wells	3	0	1	1	4
Michal Divisek	4	0	1	1	10
Paul Ferone	4	0	1	1	9
Shawn Gervais	4	0	1	1	4
Jan Hrdina	4	0	1	1	8
Aaron Bowal	1	0	0	0	2
Calvin Crowe	1	0	0	0	0
Chad Hackywicz	1	0	0	0	2
Harlan Pratt	1	0	0	0	0
Scott Reid (goalie)	1	0	0	0	0
Kevin Boris	2	0	0	0	0
Jason Norrie	2	0	0	0	2
Scott Burt	3	0	0	0	7
Regan Mueller	3	0	0	0	2
Chris Schmidt	3	0	0	0	0
Lloyd Shaw	3	0	0	0	13
Jake Deadmarsh	4	0	0	0	0
Drew Palmer	4	0	0	0	8

GOALTENDING

	Games	Min.	W	L	T	Goals	SO	Avg.
Doug Bonner	3	193	0	3	0	10	0	3.11
Scott Reid	1	60	0	1	0	6	0	6.00

SPOKANE CHIEFS

(Lost West Division semifinals to Tri-City, 4-3)

SCORING

	Games	G	A	Pts.	PIM
Jeremy Stasiuk	11	8	7	15	20
Greg Leeb	11	5	10	15	10
John Cirjak	11	4	11	15	11
Trent Whitfield	11	7	6	13	5
Joe Cardarelli	11	4	9	13	0
Jason Podollan	11	5	7	12	18
Dmitri Leonov	11	6	5	11	25
Hugh Hamilton	11	3	5	8	16
John Shockey	10	1	5	6	26
Darren Sinclair	11	2	3	5	8
Jay Bertsch	9	3	0	3	34
Mike Haley	9	3	0	3	20
Randy Favaro	11	1	2	3	8
Sean Gillam	11	0	3	3	33
Kevin Sawyer	11	2	0	2	58
Joel Boschman	11	0	2	2	24
Jared Hope	4	0	1	1	0
David Lemanowicz (goalie)	1	0	0	0	0
Rob Sandrock	1	0	0	0	0
Jarrod Daniel (goalie)	11	0	0	0	0
Scott Fletcher	11	0	0	0	23
Adam Magarrell	11	0	0	0	34

GOALTENDING

	Games	Min.	W	L	T	Goals	SO	Avg.
David Lemanowicz	1	1	0	0	0	0	0	0.00
Jarrod Daniel	11	696	6	5	0	43	0	3.71

SWIFT CURRENT

(Lost East Division quarterfinals to Saskatoon, 4-2)

SCORING

	Games	G	A	Pts.	PIM
Ladislav Kohn	6	2	6	8	14
Paul Vincent	6	3	2	5	17
Josh St. Louis	6	2	2	4	2
Vernon Beardy	6	1	2	3	9
Brent Sopel	3	0	3	3	0
Cadrin Smart	6	0	3	3	8
John Kachur	6	2	0	2	2
Chris Szysky	6	2	0	2	10
Jeff Henkelman	6	1	1	2	6
Craig Millar	6	1	1	2	10
Jason Becker	6	0	2	2	4
Jeff Kirwan	6	0	2	2	0
Brad Larsen	6	0	1	1	2
Aaron MacDonald (goalie)	6	0	1	1	2
Tony Mohagen	1	0	0	0	0
Chad Beagle	4	0	0	0	2
Shane Belter	4	0	0	0	6
Derek Arbez	6	0	0	0	9
Jesse Rezansoff	6	0	0	0	2
Cam Severson	6	0	0	0	2
Tyler Willis	6	0	0	0	20

GOALTENDING

	Games	Min.	W	L	T	Goals	SO	Avg.
Aaron MacDonald	6	393	2	4	0	18	0	2.75

TACOMA ROCKETS

(Eliminated by Spokane and Tri-City in
West Division quarterfinals)

SCORING

	Games	G	A	Pts.	PIM
Vaclav Varada	4	4	3	7	11
Marty Flichel	4	2	3	5	8
Alexandre Alexeev	4	0	3	3	4
Burt Henderson	4	2	0	2	10
Luke Curtin	4	1	1	2	2
Tavis Hansen	4	1	1	2	8
Kyle McLaren	4	1	1	2	4
Mike Piersol	4	1	1	2	4
Brett McLean	4	0	1	1	0
Tyler Prosofsky	4	0	1	1	21
Adam Smith	4	0	1	1	9
Ryan Wade	4	0	1	1	0
Quinn Hancock	2	0	0	0	0
Dale Purinton	3	0	0	0	13
John Varga	3	0	0	0	7
Jamie Butt	4	0	0	0	5
Jason Leleurme	4	0	0	0	7
Joel Kwiatkowski	4	0	0	0	2
Todd MacDonald (goalie)	4	0	0	0	6
Dallas Thompson	4	0	0	0	25

GOALTENDING

	Games	Min.	W	L	T	Goals	SO	Avg.
Todd MacDonald	4	255	1	3	0	13	0	3.06

TRI-CITY AMERICANS

(Lost West Division finals to Kamloops, 4-2)

SCORING

	Games	G	A	Pts.	PIM
Daymond Langkow	17	12	15	27	52
Terry Ryan	17	12	15	27	36
Chad Cabana	17	10	11	21	47
Brent Ascroft	17	6	12	18	15
Pavel Kriz	17	5	12	17	6
Mark Hurley	17	5	5	10	29
Rob Butz	17	4	5	9	22
Boyd Olson	17	6	2	8	22
Alexander Boikov	17	1	7	8	30
Ryan Brown	16	1	6	7	49
Ryan Marsh	17	0	4	4	32
Zenith Komarniski	17	1	2	3	47

	Games	G	A	Pts.	PIM
Jeremy Thompson	15	1	1	2	47
Tom Zavediuk	17	0	2	2	4
Kevin Schurack	10	1	0	1	4
Mike Hurley	10	0	1	1	0
Blaine Russell (goalie)	1	0	0	0	0
David Trofimenkoff (goalie)	6	0	0	0	2
Doug Strobl	9	0	0	0	2
Ray Schultz	11	0	0	0	16
Brian Boucher (goalie)	13	0	0	0	2

	Games	G	A	Pts.	PIM
Byron Briske	13	0	0	0	18
Craig Stahl	17	0	0	0	31

GOALTENDING

	Games	Min.	W	L	T	Goals	SO	Avg.
Brian Boucher	13	795	6	5	0	50	0	3.77
David Trofimenkoff	6	281	2	3	0	28	0	5.98
Blaine Russell	1	20	0	1	0	3	0	9.00

1994-95 AWARD WINNERS

ALL-STAR TEAMS

EAST DIVISION

First team	Pos.	Second team
Paxton Schafer, M.H.	G	Byron Penstock, Brandon
Chad Allan, Sask.	D	Chris Armstrong, M.J.
Bryan McCabe, Brandon	D	Wade Redden, Brandon
Curtis Brown, Moose Jaw	F	Paul Healey, P.A.
Marty Murray, Brandon	F	Stacy Roest, M.H.
Darren Ritchie, Brandon	F	Ryan Smyth, Moose Jaw

WEST DIVISION

First team	Pos.	Second team
Todd MacDonald, Tacoma	G	Scott Langkow, Portland
Nolan Baumgartner, Kam.	D	Alex Alexeev, Tacoma
Deron Quint, Seattle	D	Sean Gillam, Spokane
		Aaron Keller, Kamloops
Daymond Langkow, T.C.	F	Hnat Domenichelli, Kam.
Darcy Tucker, Kamloops	F	Chris Herperger, Seattle
Chris Wells, Seattle	F	Terry Ryan, Tri-City

TROPHY WINNERS

Four Broncos Memorial Trophy: Marty Murray, Brandon
Bob Clarke Trophy: Daymond Langkow, Tri-City
Jim Piggott Memorial Trophy: Todd Robinson, Portland
Brad Hornung Trophy: Darren Ritchie, Brandon
Bill Hunter Trophy: Nolan Baumgartner, Kamloops
Del Wilson Trophy: Paxton Schafer, Medicine Hat
Dunc McCallum Memorial Trophy: Don Nachbaur, Seattle
Scott Munro Memorial Trophy: Kamloops Blazers
President's Cup: Kamloops Blazers

ALL-TIME AWARD WINNERS

FOUR BRONCOS MEMORIAL TROPHY

(Player of the year—selected by coaches)

Season	Player, Team
1966-67	Gerry Pinder, Saskatoon
1967-68	Jim Harrison, Estevan
1968-69	Bobby Clarke, Flin Flon
1969-70	Reggie Leach, Flin Flon
1970-71	Ed Dyck, Calgary
1971-72	John Davidson, Calgary
1972-73	Dennis Sobchuk, Regina
1973-74	Ron Chipperfield, Brandon
1974-75	Bryan Trottier, Lethbridge
1975-76	Bernie Federko, Saskatoon
1976-77	Barry Beck, New Westminster
1977-78	Ryan Walter, Seattle
1978-79	Perry Turnbull, Portland
1979-80	Doug Wickenheiser, Regina
1980-81	Steve Tsujiura, Medicine Hat
1981-82	Mike Vernon, Calgary
1982-83	Mike Vernon, Calgary
1983-84	Ray Ferraro, Brandon
1984-85	Cliff Ronning, New Westminster
1985-86	Emanuel Viveiros, Prince Albert (East Div.)
	Rob Brown, Kamloops (West Div.)
1986-87	Joe Sakic, Swift Current (East Division)
	Rob Brown, Kamloops (West Division)
1987-88	Joe Sakic, Swift Current
1988-89	Stu Barnes, Tri-City
1989-90	Glen Goodall, Seattle
1990-91	Ray Whitney, Spokane
1991-92	Steve Konowalchuk, Portland
1992-93	Jason Krywulak, Swift Current
1993-94	Sonny Mignacca, Medicine Hat
1994-95	Marty Murray, Brandon

The trophy was awarded to the most valuable player prior to the 1994-95 season.

BOB CLARKE TROPHY

(Top scorer)

Season	Player, Team
1966-67	Gerry Pinder, Saskatoon
1967-68	Bobby Clarke, Flin Flon
1968-69	Bobby Clarke, Flin Flon
1969-70	Reggie Leach, Flin Flon
1970-71	Chuck Arnason, Flin Flon
1971-72	Tom Lysiak, Medicine Hat
1972-73	Tom Lysiak, Medicine Hat
1973-74	Ron Chipperfield, Brandon
1974-75	Mel Bridgman, Victoria
1975-76	Bernie Federko, Saskatoon
1976-77	Bill Derlago, Brandon
1977-78	Brian Propp, Brandon
1978-79	Brian Propp, Brandon
1979-80	Doug Wickenheiser, Regina
1980-81	Brian Varga, Regina
1981-82	Jack Callander, Regina
1982-83	Dale Derkatch, Regina
1983-84	Ray Ferraro, Brandon
1984-85	Cliff Ronning, New Westminster
1985-86	Rob Brown, Kamloops
1986-87	Rob Brown, Kamloops
1987-88	Joe Sakic, Swift Current
	Theo Fleury, Moose Jaw
1988-89	Dennis Holland, Portland
1989-90	Len Barrie, Kamloops
1990-91	Ray Whitney, Spokane
1991-92	Kevin St. Jacques, Lethbridge
1992-93	Jason Krywulak, Swift Current
1993-94	Lonny Bohonos, Portland
1994-95	Daymond Langkow, Tri-City

The award was originally known as the Bob Brownridge Memorial Trophy

WHL

MAJOR JUNIOR LEAGUES

JIM PIGGOTT MEMORIAL TROPHY

(Rookie of the year)

Season	Player, Team
1966-67	Ron Garwasiuk, Regina
1967-68	Ron Fairbrother, Saskatoon
1968-69	Ron Williams, Edmonton
1969-70	Gene Carr, Flin Flon
1970-71	Stan Weir, Medicine Hat
1971-72	Dennis Sobchuk, Regina
1972-73	Rick Blight, Brandon
1973-74	Cam Connor, Flin Flon
1974-75	Don Murdoch, Medicine Hat
1975-76	Steve Tambellini, Lethbridge
1976-77	Brian Propp, Brandon
1977-78	John Orgrodnick, New Westminster
	Keith Brown, Portland
1978-79	Kelly Kisio, Calgary
1979-80	Grant Fuhr, Victoria
1980-81	Dave Michayluk, Regina
1981-82	Dale Derkatch, Regina
1982-83	Dan Hodgson, Prince Albert
1983-84	Cliff Ronning, New Westminster
1984-85	Mark Mackay, Moose Jaw
1985-86	Neil Brady, Medicine Hat (East Division)
	Ron Shudra, Kamloops, (West Division)
	Dave Waldie, Portland (West Division)
1986-87	Joe Sakic, Swift Current (East Division)
	Dennis Holland, Portland (West Division)
1987-88	Stu Barnes, New Westminster
1988-89	Wes Walz, Lethbridge
1989-90	Petr Nedved, Seattle
1990-91	Donevan Hextall, Prince Albert
1991-92	Ashley Buckberger, Swift Current
1992-93	Jeff Friesen, Regina
1993-94	Wade Redden, Brandon
1994-95	Todd Robinson, Portland

The award was originally known as the Stewart "Butch" Paul Memorial Trophy.

BRAD HORNUNG TROPHY

(Most sportsmanlike player)

Season	Player, Team
1966-67	Morris Stefaniw, Estevan
1967-68	Bernie Blanchette, Saskatoon
1968-69	Bob Liddington, Calgary
1969-70	Randy Rota, Calgary
1970-71	Lorne Henning, Estevan
1971-72	Ron Chipperfield, Brandon
1972-73	Ron Chipperfield, Brandon
1973-74	Mike Rogers, Calgary
1974-75	Danny Arndt, Saskatoon
1975-76	Blair Chapman, Saskatoon
1976-77	Steve Tambellini, Lethbridge
1977-78	Steve Tambellini, Lethbridge
1978-79	Errol Rausse, Seattle
1979-80	Steve Tsujiura, Medicine Hat
1980-81	Steve Tsujiura, Medicine Hat
1981-82	Mike Moller, Lethbridge
1982-83	Darren Boyko, Winnipeg
1983-84	Mark Lamb, Medicine Hat
1984-85	Cliff Ronning, New Westminster
1985-86	Randy Smith, Saskatoon (East Division)
	Ken Morrison, Kamloops (West Division)
1986-87	Len Nielsen, Regina (East Division)
	Dave Archibald, Portland (West Division)
1987-88	Craig Endean, Regina
1988-89	Blair Atcheynum, Moose Jaw
1989-90	Bryan Bosch, Lethbridge
1990-91	Pat Falloon, Spokane
1991-92	Steve Junker, Spokane
1992-93	Rick Girard, Swift Current
1993-94	Lonny Bohonos, Portland
1994-95	Darren Ritchie, Brandon

The award was originally known as the Frank Boucher Memorial Trophy for most gentlemanly player.

BILL HUNTER TROPHY

(Top defenseman)

Season	Player, Team
1966-67	Barry Gibbs, Estevan
1967-68	Gerry Hart, Flin Flon
1968-69	Dale Hoganson, Estevan
1969-70	Jim Hargreaves, Winnipeg
1970-71	Ron Jones, Edmonton
1971-72	Jim Watson, Calgary
1972-73	George Pesut, Saskatoon
1973-74	Pat Price, Saskatoon
1974-75	Rick LaPointe, Victoria
1975-76	Kevin McCarthy, Winnipeg
1976-77	Barry Beck, New Westminster
1977-78	Brad McCrimmon, Brandon
1978-79	Keith Brown, Portland
1979-80	David Babych, Portland
1980-81	Jim Benning, Portland
1981-82	Gary Nylund, Portland
1982-83	Gary Leeman, Regina
1983-84	Bob Rouse, Lethbridge
1984-85	Wendel Clark, Saskatoon
1985-86	Emanuel Viveiros, Prince Albert (East Division)
	Glen Wesley, Portland (West Division)
1986-87	Wayne McBean, Medicine Hat (East Division)
	Glen Wesley, Portland (West Division)
1987-88	Greg Hawgood, Kamloops
1988-89	Dan Lambert, Swift Current
1989-90	Kevin Haller, Regina
1990-91	Darryl Sydor, Kamloops
1991-92	Richard Matvichuk, Saskatoon
1992-93	Jason Smith, Regina
1993-94	Brendan Witt, Seattle
1994-95	Nolan Baumgartner, Kamloops

DEL WILSON TROPHY

(Top goaltender)

Season	Player, Team
1966-67	Ken Brown, Moose Jaw
1967-68	Chris Worthy, Flin Flon
1968-69	Ray Martyniuk, Flin Flon
1969-70	Ray Martyniuk, Flin Flon
1970-71	Ed Dyck, Calgary
1971-72	John Davidson, Calgary
1972-73	Ed Humphreys, Saskatoon
1973-74	Garth Malarchuk, Calgary
1974-75	Bill Oleschuk, Saskatoon
1975-76	Carey Walker, New Westminster
1976-77	Glen Hanlon, Brandon
1977-78	Bart Hunter, Portland
1978-79	Rick Knickle, Brandon
1979-80	Kevin Eastman, Victoria
1980-81	Grant Fuhr, Victoria
1981-82	Mike Vernon, Calgary
1982-83	Mike Vernon, Calgary
1983-84	Ken Wregget, Lethbridge
1984-85	Troy Gamble, Medicine Hat
1985-86	Mark Fitzpatrick, Medicine Hat
1986-87	Kenton Rein, Prince Albert (East Division)
	Dean Cook, Kamloops (West Division)
1987-88	Troy Gamble, Spokane
1988-89	Danny Lorenz, Seattle
1989-90	Trevor Kidd, Brandon
1990-91	Jamie McLennan, Lethbridge
1991-92	Corey Hirsch, Kamloops
1992-93	Trevor Wilson, Brandon
1993-94	Norm Maracle, Saskatoon
1994-95	Paxton Schafer, Medicine Hat

PLAYER OF THE YEAR

(Selected by fans and media)

Season	Player, Team
1974-75	Ed Staniowski, Regina

Season	Player, Team
1975-76	Bernie Federko, Saskatoon
1976-77	Kevin McCarthy, Winnipeg
1977-78	Ryan Walter, Seattle
1978-79	Brian Propp, Brandon
1979-80	Doug Wickenheiser, Regina
1980-81	Barry Pederson, Victoria
1981-82	Mike Vernon, Calgary
1982-83	Dean Evason, Kamloops
1983-84	Ray Ferraro, Brandon
1984-85	Dan Hodgson, Prince Albert
1985-86	Emanuel Viveiros, Prince Albert
1986-87	Rob Brown, Kamloops
1987-88	Joe Sakic, Swift Current
1988-89	Dennis Holland, Portland
1989-90	Wes Walz, Lethbridge
1990-91	Ray Whitney, Spokane
1991-92	Corey Hirsch, Kamloops
1992-93	Jason Krywulak, Swift Current
1993-94	Sonny Mignacca, Medicine Hat

The award merged with the Four Broncos Memorial Trophy after the 1993-94 season.

DUNC McCALLUM MEMORIAL TROPHY

(Coach of the year)

Season	Coach, Team
1968-69	Scotty Munro, Calgary

Season	Coach, Team
1969-70	Pat Ginnell, Flin Flon
1970-71	Pat Ginnell, Flin Flon
1971-72	Earl Ingarfield, Regina
1972-73	Pat Ginnell, Flin Flon
1973-74	Stan Dunn, Swift Current
1974-75	Pat Ginnell, Victoria
1975-76	Ernie McLean, New Westminster
1976-77	Dunc McCallum, Brandon
1977-78	Jack Shupe, Victoria
	Dave King, Billings
1978-79	Dunc McCallum, Brandon
1979-80	Doug Sauter, Calgary
1980-81	Ken Hodge, Portland
1981-82	Jack Sangster, Seattle
1982-83	Darryl Lubiniecki, Saskatoon
1983-84	Terry Simpson, Prince Albert
1984-85	Doug Sauter, Medicine Hat
1985-86	Terry Simpson, Prince Albert
1986-87	Ken Hitchcock, Kam. (W. Division)
	Graham James, S. Curr. (E. Div.)
1987-88	Marcel Comeau, Saskatoon
1988-89	Ron Kennedy, Medicine Hat
1989-90	Ken Hitchcock, Kamloops
1990-91	Tom Renney, Kamloops
1991-92	Bryan Maxwell, Spokane
1992-93	Marcel Comeau, Tacoma
1993-94	Lorne Molleken, Saskatoon
1994-95	Don Nachbaur, Seattle

ALL-TIME LEAGUE CHAMPIONS

Season	REGULAR-SEASON CHAMPION Team	PLAYOFF CHAMPION Team
1966-67	Edmonton Oil Kings	Moose Jaw Canucks
1967-68	Flin Flon Bombers	Estevan Bruins
1968-69	Flin Flon Bombers	Flin Flon Bombers
1969-70	Flin Flon Bombers	Flin Flon Bombers
1970-71	Edmonton Oil Kings	Edmonton Oil Kings
1971-72	Calgary Centennials	Edmonton Oil Kings
1972-73	Saskatoon Blades	Medicine Hat Tigers
1973-74	Regina Pats	Regina Pats
1974-75	Victoria Cougars	New Westminster Bruins
1975-76	New Westminster Bruins	New Westminster Bruins
1976-77	New Westminster Bruins	New Westminster Bruins
1977-78	Brandon Wheat Kings	New Westminster Bruins
1978-79	Brandon Wheat Kings	Brandon Wheat Kings
1979-80	Portland Winter Hawks	Regina Pats
1980-81	Victoria Cougars	Victoria Cougars
1981-82	Lethbridge Broncos	Portland Winter Hawks
1982-83	Saskatoon Blades	Lethbridge Broncos
1983-84	Kamloops Junior Oilers	Kamloops Junior Oilers
1984-85	Prince Albert Raiders	Prince Albert Raiders
1985-86	Medicine Hat Tigers	Kamloops Blazers
1986-87	Kamloops Blazers	Medicine Hat Tigers
1987-88	Saskatoon Blades	Medicine Hat Tigers
1988-89	Swift Current Broncos	Swift Current Broncos
1989-90	Kamloops Blazers	Kamloops Blazers
1990-91	Kamloops Blazers	Spokane Chiefs
1991-92	Kamloops Blazers	Kamloops Blazers
1992-93	Swift Current Broncos	Swift Current Broncos
1993-94	Kamloops Blazers	Kamloops Blazers
1994-95	Kamloops Blazers	Kamloops Blazers

The WHL regular-season champion is awarded the Scott Munro Memorial Trophy and the playoff champion is awarded the President's Cup.

COLLEGE HOCKEY

NCAA Division I

Central Collegiate Hockey Association

Eastern College Athletic Conference

Hockey East

Western Collegiate Hockey Association

Independents

Canadian Interuniversity Athletic Union

Canadian Colleges

NCAA DIVISION I

NCAA TOURNAMENT

EAST REGIONAL
(Worcester, Mass.)

Denver 9, New Hampshire 2
Lake Superior State 5, Clarkson 4
Maine 4, Denver 2
Boston University 6, Lake Superior State 2

WEST REGIONAL
(Madison, Wis.)

Minnesota 3, Rensselaer 0
Wisconsin 5, Michigan State 3
Minnesota 5, Colorado College 2
Michigan 4, Wisconsin 3

SEMIFINAL SERIES
(Providence, R.I.)

Maine 4, Michigan 3 (3 OT)
Boston University 7, Minnesota 2

CHAMPIONSHIP GAME
(Providence, R.I.)

Boston University 6, Maine 2

ALL-TOURNAMENT TEAM

Player	Pos.	College
Blair Allison	G	Maine
Kaj Linna	D	Boston University
Chris Imes	D	Maine
Chris O'Sullivan	F	Boston University
Shawn Bates	F	Boston University
Dan Shermerhorn	F	Maine

NCAA Most Valuable Player: Chris O'Sullivan, Boston University.

ALL-AMERICA TEAMS

EAST

First team	Pos.	Second team
Blair Allison, Maine	G	Tim Thomas, Vermont
Chris Imes, Maine	D	Kaj Linna, Boston U.
Brian Mueller, Clarkson	D	Jeff Tory, Maine
Greg Bullock, Lowell	F	Chris O'Sullivan, Boston U.
Mike Grier, Boston U.	F	Chad Quennville, Prov.
Martin St. Louis, Vermont	F	Marko Tuomainen, Clark.

WEST

First team	Pos.	Second team
Charles Thuss, Miami	G	Ryan Bach, Colorado Col.
Kelly Perrault, B. Green	D	Keith Aldridge, L. Sup. St.
Brian Rafalski, Wisconsin	D	Kent Fearns, Colorado Col.
Brian Bonin, Minnesota	F	Anson Carter, Michigan St.
Brian Holzinger, B. Green	F	Mike Knuble, Michigan
Brendan Morrison, Mich.	F	Jay McNeill, Colorado Col.

HISTORY

TOURNAMENT CHAMPIONS

Year	Champion	Coach	Score	Runner-up	Most outstanding player
1948	Michigan	Vic Heyliger	8-4	Dartmouth	Joe Riley, F, Dartmouth
1949	Boston College	John Kelley	4-3	Dartmouth	Dick Desmond, G, Dartmouth
1950	Colorado College	Cheddy Thompson	13-4	Boston University	Ralph Bevins, G, Boston University
1951	Michigan	Vic Heyliger	7-1	Brown	Ed Whiston, G, Brown
1952	Michigan	Vic Heyliger	4-1	Colorado College	Kenneth Kinsley, G, Colorado College
1953	Michigan	Vic Heyliger	7-3	Minnesota	John Matchefts, F, Michigan
1954	Rensselaer	Ned Harkness	5-4*	Minnesota	Abbie Moore, F, Rensselaer
1955	Michigan	Vic Heyliger	5-3	Colorado College	Philip Hilton, D, Colorado College
1956	Michigan	Vic Heyliger	7-5	Michigan Tech	Lorne Howes, G, Michigan
1957	Colorado College	Thomas Bedecki	13-6	Michigan	Bob McCusker, F, Colorado College
1958	Denver	Murray Armstrong	6-2	North Dakota	Murray Massier, F, Denver
1959	North Dakota	Bob May	4-3*	Michigan State	Reg Morelli, G, North Dakota
1960	Denver	Murray Armstrong	5-3	Michigan Tech	Bob Marquis, F, Boston University
					Barry Urbanski, G, Boston University
					Louis Angotti, F, Michigan Tech
1961	Denver	Murray Armstrong	12-2	St. Lawrence	Bill Masterton, F, Denver
1962	Michigan Tech	John MacInnes	7-1	Clarkson	Louis Angotti, F, Michigan Tech
1963	North Dakota	Barney Thorndycraft	6-5	Denver	Al McLean, F, North Dakota
1964	Michigan	Allen Renfrew	6-3	Denver	Bob Gray, G, Michigan
1965	Michigan Tech	John MacInnes	8-2	Boston College	Gary Milroy, F, Michigan Tech
1966	Michigan State	Amo Bessone	6-1	Clarkson	Gaye Cooley, G, Michigan State
1967	Cornell	Ned Harkness	4-1	Boston University	Walt Stanowski, D, Cornell
1968	Denver	Murray Armstrong	4-0	North Dakota	Gerry Powers, G, Denver
1969	Denver	Murray Armstrong	4-3	Cornell	Keith Magnuson, D, Denver
1970	Cornell	Ned Harkness	6-4	Clarkson	Daniel Lodboa, D, Cornell
1971	Boston University	Jack Kelley	4-2	Minnesota	Dan Brady, G, Boston University
1972	Boston University	Jack Kelley	4-0	Cornell	Tim Regan, G, Boston University
1973	Wisconsin	Bob Johnson	4-2	Vacated	Dean Talafous, F, Wisconsin
1974	Minnesota	Herb Brooks	4-2	Michigan Tech	Brad Shelstad, G, Minnesota
1975	Michigan Tech	John MacInnes	6-1	Minnesota	Jim Warden, G, Michigan Tech
1976	Minnesota	Herb Brooks	6-4	Michigan Tech	Tom Vanelli, F, Minnesota
1977	Wisconsin	Bob Johnson	6-5*	Michigan	Julian Baretta, G, Wisconsin
1978	Boston University	Jack Parker	5-3	Boston College	Jack O'Callahan, D, Boston University

Year	Champion	Coach	Score	Runner-up	Most outstanding player
1979	Minnesota	Herb Brooks	4-3	North Dakota	Steve Janaszak, G, Minnesota
1980	North Dakota	John Gasparini	5-2	Northern Michigan	Doug Smail, F, North Dakota
1981	Wisconsin	Bob Johnson	6-3	Minnesota	Marc Behrend, G, Wisconsin
1982	North Dakota	John Gasparini	5-2	Wisconsin	Phil Sykes, F, North Dakota
1983	Wisconsin	Jeff Sauer	6-2	Harvard	Marc Behrend, G, Wisconsin
1984	Bowling Green State	Jerry York	5-4*	Minnesota-Duluth	Gary Kruzich, G, Bowling Green State
1985	Rensselaer	Mike Addesa	2-1	Providence	Chris Terreri, G, Providence
1986	Michigan State	Ron Mason	6-5	Harvard	Mike Donnelly, F, Michigan State
1987	North Dakota	John Gasparini	5-3	Michigan State	Tony Hrkac, F, North Dakota
1988	Lake Superior State	Frank Anzalone	4-3*	St. Lawrence	Bruce Hoffort, G, Lake Superior State
1989	Harvard	Bill Cleary	4-3*	Minnesota	Ted Donato, F, Harvard
1990	Wisconsin	Jeff Sauer	7-3	Colgate	Chris Tancill, F, Wisconsin
1991	Northern Michigan	Rick Comley	8-7*	Boston University	Scott Beattie, F, Northern Michigan
1992	Lake Superior State	Jeff Jackson	5-3	Wisconsin	Paul Constantin, F, Lake Superior State
1993	Maine	Shawn Walsh	5-4	Lake Superior State	Jim Montgomery, F, Maine
1994	Lake Superior State	Jeff Jackson	9-1	Boston University	Sean Tallaire, F, Lake Superior State
1995	Boston University	Jack Parker	6-2	Maine	Chris O'Sullivan, F, Boston University

*Overtime.

ALL-TIME TOURNAMENT RECORDS

	Visits	W	L	GF	GA	Pct.	Finished 1st	2nd
Colgate	1	3	1	10	11	.750	0	1
†Wisconsin	16	29	14	179	131	.674	5	2
Michigan	18	26	13	221	144	.667	7	2
North Dakota	13	22	11	132	102	.667	5	3
#Lake Superior State	9	19	10	137	99	.655	3	1
Denver	12	18	10	132	79	.643	5	2
Michigan Tech	10	13	9	118	85	.591	3	4
Maine	7	14	10	99	97	.583	1	1
†Michigan State	15	22	18	168	149	.550	2	2
Minnesota	20	26	22	241	219	.542	3	6
Boston University	21	29	25	229	223	.537	4	4
Northern Michigan	6	8	7	65	65	.533	1	1
#Rensselaer Polytechnic Institute	8	8	8	52	55	.500	2	0
*Northeastern	3	3	3	30	30	.500	0	0
Merrimack	1	2	2	14	16	.500	0	0
Yale	1	1	1	7	5	.500	0	0
Cornell	9	9	10	66	71	.474	2	2
Minnesota-Duluth	4	5	6	43	41	.455	0	1
Providence	6	9	11	71	73	.450	0	1
Dartmouth	5	4	5	38	37	.444	0	2
Clarkson	13	11	16	88	116	.407	0	3
*Bowling Green State	9	8	12	66	88	.400	1	0
†Harvard	16	14	24	143	166	.368	1	2
Colorado College	10	6	11	78	89	.353	2	2
‡Lowell	2	1	2	10	16	.333	0	0
Boston College	18	13	27	141	105	.325	1	2
Alaska-Anchorage	3	2	5	22	39	.286	0	0
Brown	4	2	5	31	45	.286	0	1
New Hampshire	7	3	11	42	76	.214	0	0
St. Lawrence	12	5	21	76	123	.192	0	2
Miami of Ohio	1	0	1	1	3	.000	0	0
St. Cloud State	1	0	2	5	10	.000	0	0
Vermont	1	0	2	2	10	.000	0	0
Western Michigan	2	0	3	7	17	.000	0	0

(Denver also participated in 1973 tournament but its record was voided by the NCAA in 1977 upon discovery of violations by the University. The team had finished second in '73.)
*Bowling Green State and Northeastern played to a 2-2 tie in 1981-82.
†Harvard and Michigan State played to a 3-3 tie in 1982-83.
#Lake Superior State and RPI played to a 3-3 tie in 1984-85.
‡Wisconsin and Lowell played to a 4-4 tie in 1987-88.
Hobey Baker Memorial Trophy (Top college hockey player in U.S.): Brian Holzinger, Bowling Green State.

HOBEY BAKER AWARD WINNERS

(Top college hockey player in United States)

Year	Player, College	Year	Player, College	Year	Player, College
1981	Neal Broten, Minnesota	1986	Scott Fusco, Harvard	1991	David Emma, Boston College
1982	George McPhee, Bowling Green St.	1987	Tony Hrkac, North Dakota	1992	Scott Pellerin, Maine
1983	Mark Fusco, Harvard	1988	Robb Stauber, Minnesota	1993	Paul Kariya, Maine
1984	Tom Kurvers, Minnesota-Duluth	1989	Lane MacDonald, Harvard	1994	Chris Marinucci, Min.-Duluth
1985	Bill Watson, Minnesota-Duluth	1990	Kip Miller, Michigan State	1995	Brian Holzinger, Bowling Green St.

CENTRAL COLLEGIATE HOCKEY ASSOCIATION

FINAL STANDINGS

Team	G	W	L	T	Pts.	GF	GA
Michigan (30-8-1)...	27	22	4	1	45	151	74
Bowl. Green (25-11-2)	27	18	7	2	38	135	101
Mich. St. (25-12-3) ..	27	17	7	3	37	123	79
L. Sup. St. (23-12-6) ..	27	14	9	4	32	114	78
Mia. of Ohio (18-15-6)	27	13	8	6	32	88	87
Ferris St. (12-20-4) ..	27	9	14	4	22	82	111
W. Mich. (17-18-5)...	27	9	14	4	22	87	102
Ill.-Chi. (11-22-4)	27	8	16	3	19	99	132
Notre Dame (11-25-1)	27	7	19	1	15	77	126
Ohio State (7-29-2) ..	27	3	22	2	8	76	142

A'ka F'banks (11-21-1)   Affiliate (5-10-0 vs. CCHA teams)

Overall record in parentheses.

PLAYOFF RESULTS

FIRST ROUND

Michigan 7, Ohio State 2
Michigan 4, Ohio State 0
(Michigan won series, 2-0)

Bowling Green State 7, Notre Dame 2
Bowling Green State 5, Notre Dame 4
(Bowling Green State won series, 2-0)

Michigan State 6, Illinois-Chicago 4
Michigan State 4, Illinois-Chicago 2
(Michigan State won series, 2-0)

Lake Superior State 7, Western Michigan 2
Lake Superior State 5, Western Michigan 0
(Lake Superior State won series, 2-0)

Miami of Ohio 10, Ferris State 2
Miami of Ohio 4, Ferris State 2
(Miami of Ohio won series, 2-0)

CHAMPIONSHIP QUALIFIER

Lake Superior State 5, Miami of Ohio 2

CONFERENCE FINALS

Lake Superior State 5, Michigan 4 (OT)
Michigan State 4, Bowling Green State 3 (OT)

CHAMPIONSHIP GAME

Lake Superior State 5, Michigan State 3

ALL-STAR TEAMS

First team	Pos.	Second team
Chuck Thuss, Miami	G	Mike Buzak, Mich. State
Kelly Perrault, Bowl. Green	D	Andy Roach, Ferris State
Keith Aldridge, L.S.S.	D	Steve Halko, Michigan
Brian Holzinger, B. Green	F	Mike Knuble, Michigan
Anson Carter, Mich. State	F	Kevyn Adams, Miami
Brendan Morrison, Mich.	F	Rem Murray, Mich. State

AWARD WINNERS

Player of the year: Brian Holzinger, Bowling Green State
Rookie of the year: Marty Turco, Michigan
Coach of the year: Buddy Powers, Bowling Green State
Leading scorer: Brendan Morrison, Michigan
Playoff MVP: Wayne Strachan, Lake Superior State

INDIVIDUAL STATISTICS

ALASKA-FAIRBANKS (AFFILIATE)

SCORING

	Pos.	Class	Games	G	A	Pts.	PIM
Corey Spring	F	Sr.	33	18	15	33	56
Cody Bowtell	F	So.	33	15	15	30	2
Pat Williams	F	So.	33	16	10	26	18
Greg Milles	F	Jr.	31	9	17	26	32
Warren Carter........	F	Sr.	31	4	19	23	24
Dallas Ferguson	D	Jr.	32	3	19	22	24
Trent Schachle	F	Jr.	30	7	8	15	50
Rob Phillips	F	So.	31	6	9	15	14
Forrest Gore...........	F	Fr.	29	7	7	14	36
Mark Cotter............	D	So.	29	1	10	11	18
Kirk Patton.............	D	Sr.	27	4	6	10	44
Fred Scott	F	Jr.	30	5	4	9	18
Derek Norton	F	So.	30	4	4	8	20
Sean Fraser	F	Fr.	33	3	4	7	44
Eon MacFarlane	D	Fr.	25	1	4	5	35
Marcel Aubin	D	Sr.	33	1	4	5	30
Bob Schwark	D	Jr.	30	2	2	4	60
Kyle McDonald	D	Fr.	13	1	0	1	16
Andy Roth	G	Fr.	1	0	0	0	0
Chris Carney..........	F	Sr.	8	0	0	0	0
Dima Kulmanovsky..	F	So.	11	0	0	0	10
Chris Hodges	D	So.	12	0	0	0	6
Ryan Olier	F	So.	12	0	0	0	8
Jeff McLean	D	Fr.	16	0	0	0	4
Brian Fish	G	Sr.	18	0	0	0	8
Larry Moberg.........	G	Jr.	20	0	0	0	2

GOALTENDING

	Games	Min.	W	L	T	Goals	SO	Avg.
Andy Roth...............	1	12	0	0	0	0	0	0.00
Larry Moberg	20	998	5	9	1	66	0	3.97
Brian Fish	18	983	6	12	0	73	0	4.46

BOWLING GREEN STATE

SCORING

	Pos.	Class	Games	G	A	Pts.	PIM
Brian Holzinger......	F	Sr.	38	35	34	69	42
Mike Johnson	F	So.	37	16	33	49	35
Kelly Perrault.........	D	So.	37	16	32	48	61
Curtis Fry	F	So.	37	13	33	46	46
Jason Clark............	F	Jr.	37	17	23	40	50
Brett Punchard......	F	So.	38	13	22	35	50
Dale Crombeen	F	So.	36	9	24	33	44
Tom Glantz.............	F	Sr.	33	20	12	32	10
Mike Hall	F	Jr.	38	17	14	31	22
Chad Ackerman	F	Jr.	38	5	23	28	38
Kevin Lune.............	D	Sr.	34	12	15	27	68
David Faulkner	F	Fr.	36	7	8	15	16
Matt Eldred	D	So.	35	2	11	13	82
Brandon Carper	D	Sr.	23	2	11	13	60
Quinn Fair	D	Jr.	37	4	7	11	62
Jeff Herman	F	Jr.	25	3	6	9	24
Todd Kelman	D	So.	37	2	6	8	20
Brad Holzinger.......	F	Fr.	29	3	4	7	10
Jamie Williams	F	Jr.	26	3	1	4	20
Adam Lamarre.......	D	Fr.	21	0	3	3	14

	Pos.	Class	Games	G	A	Pts.	PIM
Kevin Armbruster ..	F	Fr.	9	0	2	2	6
Bob Petrie	G	So.	16	0	2	2	0
Will Clarke	G	Sr.	26	0	1	1	0
Noel Crawford	G	Jr.	4	0	0	0	0

GOALTENDING

	Games	Min.	W	L	T	Goals	SO	Avg.
Will Clarke	26	1454	14	6	2	75	0	3.10
Bob Petrie	16	840	11	5	0	56	0	4.00
Noel Crawford	4	19	0	0	0	3	0	9.36

FERRIS STATE
SCORING

	Pos.	Class	Games	G	A	Pts.	PIM
Tim Christian	F	Sr.	36	18	21	39	56
Jason Blake	F	Fr.	36	16	16	32	46
Val Passarelli	F	Jr.	33	9	22	31	38
Andy Roach	D	So.	36	11	19	30	26
Derek Crimin	F	Jr.	36	11	10	21	44
John Duff	F	Jr.	33	7	13	20	84
Mike Kolenda	F	Sr.	28	7	11	18	66
Gordy Hunt	F	So.	29	8	7	15	47
Keith Sergott	D	Jr.	36	3	12	15	28
Brett Colborne	D	So.	32	3	7	10	54
Gary Kitching	F	Sr.	15	3	7	10	20
Dwight Parrish	D	Jr.	36	3	6	9	76
Jim Mitchell	F	Jr.	34	4	2	6	97
Phil Sturock	F	So.	35	2	4	6	12
Dusty Anderson	D	So.	36	1	5	6	61
Colin Dodunski	D	Sr.	29	4	1	5	30
Colin Muldoon	D	So.	28	0	3	3	20
Nick Krueger	F	Fr.	30	2	0	2	10
Jeff Blashill	G	Fr.	26	0	2	2	2
Brad Burnham	F	Sr.	19	1	0	1	34
Rich Nagy	G	Sr.	12	0	1	1	0
Scot Bell	F	Jr.	16	0	1	1	4
Brett Severson	F	So.	20	0	0	0	2
Earl Rock	F	So.	10	0	0	0	18
Seth Appert	G	So.	9	0	0	0	10

GOALTENDING

	Games	Min.	W	L	T	Goals	SO	Avg.
Jeff Blashill	26	1355	10	10	3	88	0	3.90
Rich Nagy	12	437	1	6	0	32	0	4.39
Seth Appert	9	377	1	4	1	33	0	5.25

ILLINOIS-CHICAGO
SCORING

	Pos.	Class	Games	G	A	Pts.	PIM
Rob Hutson	F	Jr.	35	14	28	42	71
Mark Zdan	F	Sr.	36	13	21	34	64
Shannon Finn	D	Sr.	37	9	23	32	40
Chris MacDonald	F	Sr.	35	15	14	29	36
Derek Knorr	F	Sr.	37	9	17	26	58
Mike Peron	F	So.	35	16	9	25	54
Alan Dunbar	F	So.	34	7	15	22	87
Kevin O'Keefe	F	Fr.	33	12	9	21	8
Jeff Blum	D	Sr.	36	8	11	19	53
Matt Brenner	D	Jr.	37	7	8	15	14
Matt McElwee	F	So.	28	4	11	15	40
Trevor Mathias	F	Jr.	37	5	9	14	28
Darren Tymchyshyn	F	Jr.	32	4	10	14	8
Bob Gohde	D	Sr.	37	4	9	13	34
Rob Mottau	D	Sr.	26	8	4	12	28
Shaun Summerville..	F	So.	26	4	7	11	12
Ryan Walls	F	So.	22	2	8	10	12
Billy Allick	F	Fr.	14	3	5	8	18
Deuce Wynes	D	Fr.	36	1	7	8	10
Clay Awe	D	Fr.	26	0	5	5	46
Ryan Furness	F	Fr.	27	1	2	3	34
Sean Carter	G	So.	1	0	0	0	0
Adam Lord	G	Jr.	22	0	0	0	0
Paul Spencer	G	So.	24	0	0	0	2

GOALTENDING

	Games	Min.	W	L	T	Goals	SO	Avg.
Sean Carter	1	19	0	0	0	0	0	0.00
Paul Spencer	24	1163	6	10	2	86	0	4.44
Adam Lord	22	1027	5	12	2	82	0	4.79

LAKE SUPERIOR STATE
SCORING

	Pos.	Class	Games	G	A	Pts.	PIM
Brian Felsner	F	So.	41	24	28	52	51
Sean Tallaire	F	Jr.	41	21	28	49	38
Wayne Strachan	F	Sr.	41	22	20	42	68
Keith Aldridge	D	Jr.	40	10	31	41	89
Gerald Tallaire	F	So.	39	11	27	38	16
Mike Morin	F	Sr.	41	19	17	36	116
Rob Valicevic	F	Sr.	37	10	22	32	40
Brad Willner	D	Sr.	41	5	19	24	20
Jon Battaglia	F	Fr.	38	6	15	21	34
Jason Trzcinski	F	Jr.	38	12	6	18	43
Mike Matteucci	D	Jr.	38	3	11	14	52
Ted Laviolette	D	Fr.	40	5	8	13	50
Danny Galarneau ..	F	So.	38	6	6	12	37
Dave Lambeth	D	Fr.	38	3	9	12	28
Dan Angelelli	F	Sr.	39	5	6	11	92
Matt Alvey	F	So.	25	4	7	11	32
Joe Blaznek	F	Fr.	25	5	4	9	18
Bryan Fuss	F	Fr.	20	3	6	9	39
Terry Marchant	F	Fr.	23	2	5	7	12
Ryan Sharpe	D	Fr.	28	0	3	3	38
Gino Pulente	D	So.	8	0	2	2	8
John Grahame	G	Fr.	28	0	2	2	4
Christian Graham..	D	Fr.	13	0	1	1	14
Paul Sass	F	So.	1	0	0	0	0
Scott McCabe	F	So.	6	0	0	0	7
Sean Kulick	G	So.	15	0	0	0	0

GOALTENDING

	Games	Min.	W	L	T	Goals	SO	Avg.
John Grahame	28	1616	16	7	3	75	1	2.79
Sean Kulick	15	812	7	4	3	40	1	2.96
Paul Sass	1	62	0	1	0	6	0	5.77

MIAMI OF OHIO
SCORING

	Pos.	Class	Games	G	A	Pts.	PIM
Kevyn Adams	F	Jr.	38	20	29	49	30
Andrew Miller	F	Sr.	39	22	22	44	42
Jason Mallon	F	Sr.	39	13	18	31	46
Dan Boyle	D	Fr.	35	8	18	26	24
Marc Boxer	F	Sr.	39	6	20	26	36
Vitali Andreev	F	Fr.	35	10	12	22	10
Dan Carter	F	Sr.	30	12	6	18	61
Barry Schutte	F	So.	24	4	8	12	9
Adam Copeland	F	Fr.	39	6	4	10	28
Marc Tropper	F	Fr.	35	3	7	10	66
Joe Bodnar	F	Fr.	39	3	7	10	29
Justin Krall	D	Jr.	38	1	9	10	38
Pat Hanley	D/F	Jr.	39	4	4	8	60
Jeff Reid	D	So.	39	3	5	8	22
Jason Crane	F	Sr.	19	2	5	7	8
Tom White	F	So.	35	2	5	7	24
Todd Rohloff	D	Fr.	38	1	6	7	22
Jared Echternach..	F	Jr.	27	4	2	6	14
Tim Leahy	F	Fr.	14	3	1	4	14
Andrew Backen	D	Jr.	13	2	1	3	12
Grady Hamilton	D	So.	4	1	1	1	0
Charles Thuss	G	Sr.	34	0	1	1	6
Brooke Chateau	D	Fr.	38	0	1	1	18
Eustace King	G	Jr.	2	0	0	0	0
Derek Block	F	Sr.	3	0	0	0	0
K. Deschambeault .	G	Jr.	8	0	0	0	0

GOALTENDING

	Games	Min.	W	L	T	Goals	SO	Avg.
Charles Thuss	34	1983	16	10	6	95	2	2.87
Kevin Deschambeault	8	321	2	4	0	25	0	4.67
Eustace King	1	60	0	1	0	5	0	5.00

MICHIGAN
SCORING

	Pos.	Class	Games	G	A	Pts.	PIM
Brendan Morrison .	F	So.	39	23	53	76	42
Mike Knuble	F	Sr.	34	38	22	60	62
Kevin Hilton	F	Jr.	37	20	31	51	14
John Madden	F	So.	39	21	22	43	8
Warren Luhning	F	So.	36	17	24	41	80
Robb Gordon	F	Fr.	39	15	26	41	72
Bill Muckalt	F	Fr.	39	19	18	37	42
Mike Legg	F	So.	39	14	23	37	22
Jason Botterill	F	So.	34	14	14	28	117
Matt Herr	F	Fr.	37	11	8	19	51
Harold Schock	D	So.	37	2	16	18	42
Blake Sloan	D	So.	39	2	15	17	60
Steven Halko	D	Jr.	39	2	14	16	20
Ron Sacka	F	Sr.	30	10	5	15	31
Tim Hogan	D	Sr.	35	1	14	15	24
John Arnold	F	Jr.	24	4	8	12	8
Rick Willis	F	Sr.	35	3	6	9	78
Chris Fox	D	Fr.	13	1	5	6	12
Alan Sinclair	D	Sr.	30	0	6	6	22
Peter Bourke	D	So.	11	1	2	3	6
Chris Frescoln	D	So.	13	0	3	3	20
Mark Sakala	D	Sr.	23	0	3	3	22
Marty Turco	G	Fr.	37	0	3	3	16
Al Loges	G	Sr.	11	0	0	0	0

GOALTENDING

	Games	Min.	W	L	T	Goals	SO	Avg.
Al Loges	11	330	3	1	0	14	0	2.55
Marty Turco	37	2064	27	7	1	95	1	2.76

MICHIGAN STATE
SCORING

	Pos.	Class	Games	G	A	Pts.	PIM
Rem Murray	F	Sr.	40	20	36	56	21
Anson Carter	F	Jr.	39	34	17	51	40
Steve Guolla	F	Sr.	40	16	35	51	16
Steve Suk	F	Sr.	40	10	27	37	32
Dean Sylvester	F	Sr.	40	15	15	30	38
Chris Smith	D	Jr.	39	10	20	30	62
Tony Tuzzolino	F	So.	39	9	19	28	81
Chris Slater	D	So.	40	5	23	28	34
Richard Keyes	F	Fr.	39	16	11	27	60
Sean Berens	F	Fr.	40	16	6	22	22
Mike Watt	F	Fr.	39	12	6	18	64
Ryan Fleming	D	Jr.	36	1	15	16	8
Taylor Clarke	F	Jr.	31	7	8	15	42
Brian Crane	F	So.	36	5	6	11	40
Bart Vanstaalduinen	D	Jr.	40	1	8	9	32
Brian Clifford	F	Jr.	17	2	5	7	8
Jon Gaskins	D	Fr.	28	1	5	6	18
Tyler Harlton	D	Fr.	39	1	4	5	55
Matt Albers	F	Sr.	28	2	1	3	27
Steve Ferranti	F	So.	11	0	3	3	6
Mike Buzak	G	Sr.	31	0	3	3	2
Chris Sullivan	D	Sr.	16	0	1	1	17
Josh Wiegand	F	So.	2	0	0	0	2
Chad Alban	G	Fr.	13	0	0	0	0

GOALTENDING

	Games	Min.	W	L	T	Goals	SO	Avg.
Chad Alban	13	637	8	2	0	29	0	2.73
Mike Buzak	31	1797	17	10	3	94	0	3.14

NOTRE DAME
SCORING

	Pos.	Class	Games	G	A	Pts.	PIM
Jamie Ling	F	Jr.	36	12	30	42	49
Tim Harberts	F	So.	37	21	13	34	4
Terry Lorenz	F	So.	36	12	17	29	61
Jamie Morshead	F	Jr.	34	9	18	27	74
Garry Gruber	G	Jr.	31	4	14	18	54
Lyle Andrusiak	F	Fr.	35	10	6	16	26

	Pos.	Class	Games	G	A	Pts.	PIM
Davide Dal Grande.	D	Jr.	36	4	12	16	46
Ben Nelsen	D	So.	37	3	12	15	80
Jay Matushak	F	Jr.	36	7	7	14	2
Steve Noble	F	Fr.	37	6	8	14	25
Chris Bales	F	Jr.	23	5	9	14	34
Brett Bruininks	F	Jr.	37	10	3	13	104
Jeff Hasselman	F	Sr.	34	4	5	9	30
Jeremy Coe	D	Jr.	34	2	6	8	84
Brian McCarthy	F	So.	36	3	4	7	55
Justin Theel	D	Fr.	31	2	5	7	64
Bryan Welch	D	So.	33	2	5	7	74
John Rushin	F	Sr.	31	3	3	6	36
Carey Nemeth	F	Sr.	16	1	4	5	16
Brent Lamppa	F	Sr.	10	1	3	4	0
Matt Eisler	G	Fr.	25	0	1	1	4
Troy Cusey	F	Sr.	2	0	0	0	14
Erik Berg	G	So.	3	0	0	0	0
Kevin Young	F	Fr.	3	0	0	0	0
Ryan Thornton	F	So.	6	0	0	0	0
Sean McAlister	F	So.	7	0	0	0	6
Rob Bolton	D	Jr.	8	0	0	0	4
Wade Salzman	G	Jr.	16	0	0	0	0

GOALTENDING

	Games	Min.	W	L	T	Goals	SO	Avg.
Matt Eisler	25	1368	9	13	0	98	0	4.30
Wade Salzman	16	778	2	12	1	59	1	4.55
Erik Berg	3	75	0	0	0	7	0	5.59

OHIO STATE
SCORING

	Pos.	Class	Games	G	A	Pts.	PIM
Steve Richards	F/D	Sr.	38	13	24	37	67
Randy Holmes	F	Jr.	38	14	21	35	42
Sacha Guilbault	F	Sr.	29	13	19	32	12
Pierre Dufour	F	So.	36	14	10	24	16
Adam Smith	F	Sr.	33	6	18	24	51
Tyler McMillan	F	Fr.	38	5	15	20	48
Joe Sellers	F	Jr.	28	5	13	18	22
Sean Sutton	F	Jr.	28	8	6	14	12
Chad Power	F	So.	32	9	4	13	81
Ryan Root	D	Fr.	36	2	11	13	42
Todd Compeau	F	Fr.	14	7	2	9	6
Al DiPasquo	F	Fr.	31	3	6	9	26
Jarret Whidden	F	So.	14	4	4	8	6
Steve Brent	F	Jr.	24	2	6	8	84
Craig Paterson	D	Jr.	30	3	3	6	124
Jeff Winter	D	Jr.	30	2	4	6	72
Dan Cousineau	F	Fr.	30	1	4	5	64
Bill Rathwell	F	Jr.	34	2	2	4	36
Derek Beuselinck	D	Jr.	35	2	2	4	54
Taj Schaffnit	D	Fr.	19	1	3	4	46
Sandy Fraser	D	Sr.	31	0	3	3	27
Rick Lance	F	Fr.	2	1	0	1	0
Gary Hirst	D	Jr.	34	0	1	1	22
Mark Skogstad	F	Jr.	2	0	0	0	0
Derek Nicolson	D	So.	4	0	0	0	2
Brian Keller	D	So.	6	0	0	0	4
Kurt Brown	G	Jr.	19	0	0	0	10
Tom Askey	G	Jr.	26	0	0	0	12

GOALTENDING

	Games	Min.	W	L	T	Goals	SO	Avg.
Kurt Brown	19	900	3	10	0	67	0	4.47
Tom Askey	26	1387	4	19	2	121	0	5.23

WESTERN MICHIGAN
SCORING

	Pos.	Class	Games	G	A	Pts.	PIM
Jamal Mayers	F	Jr.	39	13	33	46	40
Chris Brooks	F	Jr.	40	7	39	46	42
Jeremy Brown	F	Jr.	39	25	17	42	28
Brian Gallentine	F	Sr.	39	23	17	40	54
Steve Duke	D	Fr.	39	9	22	31	49

	Pos.	Class	Games	G	A	Pts.	PIM
Derek Innanen	F	Jr.	35	9	14	23	80
Mike Whitton	F	Sr.	37	10	12	22	107
Kyle Millar..............	F	Jr.	39	12	7	19	36
Darren Maloney	D	Jr.	40	2	17	19	64
Shawn Zimmerman..	F	So.	39	7	9	16	39
Justin Cardwell......	F	So.	33	9	6	15	46
Jeff Rucinski..........	D	Fr.	39	3	9	12	66
Brendan Kenny	D	So.	39	1	6	7	74
Matt Cressman	F	So.	32	3	3	6	32
Carlin Nordstrom...	F	So.	33	2	4	6	22
Joel Irving	F	Fr.	30	2	3	5	20
Brent Lovett..........	D	Fr.	40	1	2	3	32
Chad Anderson	F	Fr.	9	1	1	2	6

	Pos.	Class	Games	G	A	Pts.	PIM
David Agnew..........	D	So.	14	1	1	2	8
Graham Bridel........	F	Fr.	16	1	1	2	10
Tony Code	F	So.	22	0	2	2	10
Misha Lapin	D	Jr.	15	0	1	1	22
Jim Holman	D	Jr.	4	0	0	0	6
David Mitchell........	G	Jr.	5	0	0	0	0
Brian Renfrew........	G	Sr.	40	0	0	0	4

GOALTENDING

	Games	Min.	W	L	T	Goals	SO	Avg.
Brian Renfrew	40	2356	17	18	5	139	0	3.54
David Mitchell	5	59	0	0	0	5	0	5.07

EASTERN COLLEGE
ATHLETIC CONFERENCE

FINAL STANDINGS

Team	G	W	L	T	Pts.	GF	GA
Clarkson (23-10-4) ..	22	14	5	3	31	116	70
Brown (15-12-3)	22	13	7	2	28	78	76
Harvard (14-14-2) ..	22	12	9	1	25	79	68
Colgate (20-16-1) ..	22	12	9	1	25	98	78
Vermont (19-14-2) ..	22	11	9	2	24	85	61
R.P.I. (19-14-4)	22	10	9	3	23	75	78
Princeton (17-13-4) .	22	9	10	3	21	81	83
St. Law. (15-17-1)....	22	10	12	0	20	83	110
Cornell (11-15-4)	22	8	10	4	20	72	76
Union (9-16-4)	22	6	12	4	16	70	87
Dartmouth (9-16-2) ..	22	7	13	2	16	80	111
Yale (8-17-3)	22	6	13	3	15	65	84

Overall record in parentheses.

PLAYOFF RESULTS

PRELIMINARIES

Princeton 5, Union 2
Cornell 6, St. Lawrence 2

Vermont 5, Colgate 2
Colgate 2, Vermont 0
Colgate 4, Vermont 1
(Colgate won series, 2-1)

QUARTERFINALS

Clarkson 6, Cornell 2
Clarkson 7, Cornell 2
(Clarkson won series, 2-0)
Princeton 4, Brown 3
Brown 3, Princeton 2
Princeton 3, Brown 2 (2 OT)
(Princeton won series, 2-1)
Rensselaer 2, Harvard 2
Rensselaer 3, Harvard 1
(Rensselaer won series, 1-0)

SEMIFINALS

Rensselaer 2, Colgate 1
Princeton 2, Clarkson 1

CONSOLATION GAME

Clarkson 10, Colgate 5

CHAMPIONSHIP GAME

Rensselaer 5, Princeton 1

ALL-STAR TEAMS

First team	Pos.	Second team
Tim Thomas, Vermont	G	Todd Sullivan, Yale
Brian Mueller, Clarkson	D	Adam Bartell, Rensselaer
Mike Traggio, Brown	D	Brad Dexter, Colgate
Eric Perrin, Vermont	F	Mike Harder, Colgate
Martin St. Louis, Ver.	F	Burke Murphy, St. Law.
Marko Tuomainen, Clark.	F	Patrice Robitaille, Clark.

AWARD WINNERS

Player of the year: Martin St. Louis, Vermont
Rookie of the year: Paul DiFrancesco, St. Lawrence
Coach of the year: Bob Gaudet, Brown
Leading scorer: Martin St. Louis, Vermont
Playoff MVP: Mike Tamburro, Rensselaer

INDIVIDUAL STATISTICS

BROWN

SCORING

	Pos.	Class	Games	G	A	Pts.	PIM
Ryan Mulhern	F	Jr.	30	18	16	34	108
Brian Jardine	F	Jr.	30	10	24	34	31
Eric Trach	F	Sr.	30	10	18	28	30
Charlie Humber	D	Jr.	29	7	13	20	25
Tony Martino	F	Sr.	29	13	6	19	10
Mike Flynn	F	So.	28	2	15	17	36
Scott Bradford	F	So.	26	10	5	15	58
Marty Clapton	F	So.	26	4	10	14	33
Jimmy Andersson..	D	Fr.	28	4	10	14	49
John DiRenzo	F	Fr.	28	7	5	12	12
Robert Merrill	F	So.	30	6	6	12	28
Mike Traggio..........	D	Sr.	30	5	7	12	105
Damian Prescott.....	F	Fr.	24	3	7	10	14
Mike Noble	F	So.	23	2	4	6	16
Bill McKay	D	So.	25	0	6	6	28
Scott Humber	F	Jr.	13	2	3	5	16
Patrick Thompson .	D	Sr.	30	0	4	4	46
D.J. Harding..........	D	Fr.	19	2	1	3	10
Steve Kathol	F	Jr.	14	0	2	2	17
Ron Smitko	D	Jr.	20	1	0	1	10
Jeff Reschny	F	Sr.	6	0	1	1	4
Kim Hannah	F	Sr.	9	0	1	1	6
James Mooney	D	Jr.	11	0	1	1	10
Brian Crowley	F	Fr.	1	0	0	0	0
Jeff Holowaty.........	G	Fr.	2	0	0	0	0
Brian Audette	G	So.	6	0	0	0	0
Mike Parsons.........	G	Jr.	26	0	0	0	4

GOALTENDING

	Games	Min.	W	L	T	Goals	SO	Avg.
Brian Audette	6	309	2	1	1	13	0	2.52

	Games	Min.	W	L	T	Goals	SO	Avg.
Mike Parsons...........	26	1472	13	11	2	84	1	3.42
Jeff Holowaty	2	53	0	0	0	5	0	5.61

CLARKSON

SCORING

	Pos.	Class	Games	G	A	Pts.	PIM
Marko Tuomainen .	F	Sr.	37	23	37	60	34
Patrice Robitaille ...	F	Sr.	37	30	26	56	24
Brian Mueller	D	Sr.	36	12	42	54	56
Claude Morin	F	Sr.	37	16	37	53	34
David Seitz	F	Jr.	32	16	19	35	38
Steve Palmer	F	Jr.	36	18	12	30	62
Todd White	F	So.	34	14	16	30	44
Chris Lipsett	F	Jr.	34	13	16	29	30
Chris de Ruiter	F	Jr.	34	10	14	24	78
Chris Clark	F	Fr.	32	12	11	23	92
Kevin Murphy	F	Jr.	36	8	15	23	56
Jean Francois Houle .	F	So.	34	8	11	19	42
Adam Wiesel	D	So.	36	6	13	19	28
Dana Mulvihill	F	Fr.	34	2	11	13	53
Matt Pagnutti	D	So.	31	4	7	11	36
Nicholas Windsor ..	D	Fr.	26	1	10	11	20
Scott Ricci.............	D	Fr.	35	1	10	11	20
Phil LeCavalier	D	So.	14	1	2	3	18
Buddy Wallace	F	Fr.	17	0	3	3	18
Josh Bartell............	D	Jr.	29	0	3	3	77
Dan Murphy	G	Fr.	37	0	1	1	0
Chris Bernard	G	Fr.	1	0	0	0	0
Jonathan Parrella..	G	Fr.	1	0	0	0	0
Jerry Rosenheck....	F	So.	1	0	0	0	0
Jordan Grant..........	F	Fr.	4	0	0	0	0
Kerry Blanchard	G	So.	6	0	0	0	0
Jason LaBarge	D	So.	15	0	0	0	41

GOALTENDING

	Games	Min.	W	L	T	Goals	SO	Avg.
Chris Bernard	1	4	0	0	0	0	0	0.00
Jonathan Parrella	1	12	0	0	0	0	0	0.00
Dan Murphy	37	2157	23	9	4	118	0	3.28
Kerry Blanchard	6	69	0	1	0	5	0	4.37

COLGATE

SCORING

	Pos.	Class	Games	G	A	Pts.	PIM
Mike Harder	F	So.	36	22	36	58	18
Chris DeProfio	F	Jr.	35	21	34	55	40
Earl Cronan	F	Jr.	37	21	20	41	81
Ron Fogarty	F	Sr.	37	17	22	39	32
Tim Loftsgard	F	Fr.	37	14	17	31	43
Brad Dexter	D	Jr.	31	7	23	30	36
Dave Debusschere	F	So.	37	9	18	27	32
Matt Garzone	D	Sr.	35	6	17	23	55
Bill Baaki	F	Fr.	37	7	10	17	44
Rod Pamenter	D	Jr.	35	4	12	16	74
Dru Burgess	F	Fr.	37	5	10	15	20
Rob Mara	F	33	6	8	14	30
Jack McIntosh	D	So.	35	3	11	14	58
Jason Craig	D	Sr.	27	2	9	11	14
Steve DuBarry	F	So.	29	5	3	8	12
Scott Steeves	F	So.	30	3	4	7	34
Todd Murphy	D	So.	25	2	3	5	6
Greg Lewis	F	Jr.	20	0	5	5	37
John Dance	D	So.	29	2	2	4	49
Ben Crittenden	F	Fr.	6	1	1	2	2
Clayton McCaffery	F	Sr.	17	1	1	2	20
Nigel Creightney	D	Sr.	23	0	1	1	28
Dan Brenzavich	G	Fr.	29	0	1	1	0
Matt Weder	G	Jr.	11	0	0	0	0

GOALTENDING

	Games	Min.	W	L	T	Goals	SO	Avg.
Dan Brenzavich	29	1693	15	12	1	94	3	3.33
Matt Weder	11	553	5	4	0	37	0	4.02

CORNELL

SCORING

	Pos.	Class	Games	G	A	Pts.	PIM
Jake Karam	F	Sr.	30	16	14	30	2
Mike Sancimino	F	Jr.	30	9	19	28	34
Geoff Lopatka	F	Jr.	30	13	14	27	34
Steve Wilson	F	So.	30	6	21	27	63
Ryan Smart	F	Fr.	26	13	7	20	10
Jamie Papp	F	So.	30	7	12	19	16
P.C. Drouin	F	Jr.	26	4	15	19	48
Brad Chartrand	F	Jr.	26	8	9	18	10
Mark Scollan	F	Jr.	26	6	12	18	2
Tyler McManus	F	Sr.	25	6	9	15	18
Tony Bergin	F	So.	27	5	8	13	22
Andre Doll	F	Jr.	29	1	10	11	12
Matt Cooney	F	So.	26	7	3	10	50
Bill Holowatiuk	D	Jr.	30	1	8	9	48
Chad Wilson	D	So.	30	0	9	9	30
Jason Dailey	D	Fr.	26	0	7	7	24
Christian Felli	D	Sr.	23	0	6	6	20
Dan Dufresne	D	Jr.	14	1	1	2	32
Jason Kendall	D	So.	19	1	1	2	50
Jason Weber	F	Jr.	7	0	1	1	10
Joel McArter	F	Jr.	12	0	1	1	20
Eddy Skazyk	G	Jr.	16	0	1	1	0
Andy Bandurski	G	Sr.	1	0	0	0	0
Jiri Kloboucek	F	Sr.	4	0	0	0	6
Blair Ettles	D	Sr.	5	0	0	0	4
John DeHart	F	Jr.	6	0	0	0	0
Jason Elliott	G	Fr.	16	0	0	0	2

GOALTENDING

	Games	Min.	W	L	T	Goals	SO	Avg.
Andy Bandurski	1	60	1	0	0	3	0	3.00
Eddy Skazyk	16	881	7	4	3	50	0	3.41
Jason Elliott	16	877	3	11	1	62	0	4.24

DARTMOUTH

SCORING

	Pos.	Class	Games	G	A	Pts.	PIM
Dion Del Monte	F	Sr.	26	14	22	36	22
Mike Stacchi	F	Sr.	28	15	13	28	40
Pat Turcotte	F	Sr.	27	16	9	25	22
Bill Kelleher	F	Jr.	26	6	19	25	10
David Whitworth	F	Fr.	27	8	12	20	26
Owen Hughes	F	So.	27	6	13	19	22
Trevor Dodman	D	Sr.	27	5	12	17	26
Bob Cancelli	F	Fr.	25	5	10	15	23
Dax Burkhart	D	Jr.	26	1	10	11	20
Charlie Retter	F	Fr.	22	6	2	8	28
Brent Retter	F	So.	26	4	4	8	32
Darren Wercinski	F	So.	24	3	5	8	14
Jon Sturgis	F	Sr.	27	3	5	8	10
Dan Bloom	D	Jr.	19	2	4	6	8
Yanick Roussin	D	Sr.	18	0	4	4	10
Shaun Peet	F	Fr.	14	1	2	3	28
Jeremiah Buckley	F	Fr.	21	1	2	3	2
Scott Dolesh	D	Jr.	15	0	3	3	8
Shane Ness	D	Sr.	24	0	2	2	10
Ben Butters	D	So.	23	0	1	1	34
Alex Dumas	D	So.	3	0	0	0	2
Darik Buchar	G	Fr.	4	0	0	0	0
Tom Ruzzo	F	So.	4	0	0	0	4
Brian Fleming	F	Fr.	8	0	0	0	0
Ben Heller	G	So.	12	0	0	0	0
Scott Baker	G	So.	17	0	0	0	2

GOALTENDING

	Games	Min.	W	L	T	Goals	SO	Avg.
Scott Baker	17	924	6	8	1	61	0	3.96
Ben Heller	12	592	3	7	1	59	0	5.98
Darik Buchar	4	112	0	1	0	14	0	7.51

HARVARD

SCORING

	Pos.	Class	Games	G	A	Pts.	PIM
Steve Martins	F	Sr.	28	15	23	38	93
Cory Gustafson	F	Jr.	30	10	16	26	26
Brad Konik	F	Jr.	29	11	13	24	28
Ben Coughlin	F	Sr.	30	5	19	24	34
Perry Cohagan	F	Sr.	29	9	13	22	44
Kirk Nielsen	F	Jr.	30	13	7	20	24
Ashlin Halfnight	D	So.	24	5	15	20	42
Bryan Lonsinger	D	Sr.	28	8	9	17	12
Jason Karmanos	F	Jr.	30	6	10	16	36
Tom Holmes	F	So.	30	2	13	15	45
Doug Sproule	F	Jr.	30	7	2	9	28
Jeremiah McCarthy	D	Fr.	25	3	5	8	4
Joe Craigen	F	So.	27	3	5	8	6
Henry Higdon	F	Fr.	30	3	5	8	20
Geordie Hyland	D	Fr.	20	1	6	7	22
Michel Breistroff	D	Sr.	25	1	6	7	32
Peter McLaughlin	D	Jr.	30	1	6	7	44
Stuart Swenson	F	So.	28	4	2	6	12
Tripp Tracy	G	Jr.	27	0	1	1	2
Brian Famigletti	D	Fr.	5	0	0	0	0
Steve Hermsdorf	G	Sr.	5	0	0	0	0
Keith McLean	F	Sr.	7	0	0	0	0
Marco Ferrari	D	So.	11	0	0	0	8
Geb Marret	D	Jr.	14	0	0	0	18

GOALTENDING

	Games	Min.	W	L	T	Goals	SO	Avg.
Steve Hermsdorf	5	244	1	2	0	11	0	2.71
Tripp Tracy	27	1561	13	12	2	86	0	3.31

PRINCETON

SCORING

	Pos.	Class	Games	G	A	Pts.	PIM
Jonathan Kelley	F	Jr.	33	24	16	40	55
J.P. O'Connor	F	Jr.	34	8	22	30	26

	Pos.	Class	Games	G	A	Pts.	PIM
Ian Sharp	F	Sr.	34	12	15	27	28
Mervin Kopeck	F	Sr.	35	11	16	27	32
Brent Flahr	D	Jr.	34	3	23	26	20
Casson Masters	F	Fr.	34	7	17	24	34
Ethan Early	F	Sr.	33	11	12	23	34
Mike Bois	F	Jr.	27	10	13	23	17
Matt Brush	F	Fr.	34	10	11	21	28
Tony Ranaldi	F	So.	34	5	9	14	54
Gavin Colquhoun	D	Sr.	35	2	11	13	81
Jason Smith	D	Jr.	32	3	9	12	68
Barrington Miller	D/F	Jr.	34	1	10	11	28
Dan Brown	D	Jr.	30	3	7	10	26
Robbie Sinclair	F	Fr.	23	4	4	8	8
Keith O'Brien	F	So.	33	3	5	8	39
Joey Pelle	F	So.	9	3	2	5	2
Corey Rhodes	F	Sr.	24	2	2	4	22
Jean Verdon	F	So.	23	0	4	4	10
David Scowby	D	Sr.	22	1	2	3	16
Scott Almon	D	Sr.	26	0	3	3	8
Clint Murray	G	Jr.	1	0	1	1	0
Erasmo Saltarelli	G	Fr.	8	0	1	1	0
James Konte	G	Jr.	34	0	1	1	24
Kevin Sheehan	D	So.	4	0	0	0	4

GOALTENDING

	Games	Min.	W	L	T	Goals	SO	Avg.
Erasmo Saltarelli	8	203	2	1	0	9	1	2.66
James Konte	34	1935	16	12	4	104	2	3.22

RENSSELAER POLYTECHNIC INSTITUTE
SCORING

	Pos.	Class	Games	G	A	Pts.	PIM
Bryan Richardson	F	Jr.	36	23	24	47	36
Craig Hamelin	F	Sr.	34	15	29	44	36
Tim Regan	F	Jr.	35	12	19	31	94
Wayne Clarke	F	Sr.	32	15	13	28	28
Patrick Rochon	D	Jr.	37	4	22	26	64
Jeff O'Connor	F	Jr.	32	11	14	25	54
Eric Healey	F	Fr.	37	13	11	24	33
Kelly Askew	F	Sr.	31	8	16	24	58
Adam Bartell	D	Sr.	35	3	19	22	28
Eric Perardi	F	Sr.	35	6	13	19	54
Jeff Matthews	F	Sr.	33	8	9	17	20
Jon Pirrong	D	Jr.	36	3	9	12	75
Jeff Brick	F	Sr.	33	4	5	9	48
Bryan Tapper	D	Fr.	32	4	3	7	70
Patrick Brownlee	D	Fr.	36	1	6	7	18
Chris Maye	F	Sr.	35	1	5	6	12
Doug Battaglia	F	Fr.	34	1	4	5	57
Chris Kiley	D	Jr.	30	0	5	5	8
Ken Kwasniewski	F	Sr.	15	2	1	3	0
Mike Tamburro	G	Jr.	27	0	1	1	8
Chris Aldous	D	Fr.	31	0	1	1	4
Mike Rolanti	D	So.	3	0	0	0	0
Tim Spadafore	G	Sr.	5	0	0	0	0
Bryan Masotta	G	Fr.	13	0	0	0	10

GOALTENDING

	Games	Min.	W	L	T	Goals	SO	Avg.
Tim Spadafore	5	72	1	0	0	3	0	2.51
Mike Tamburro	27	1517	13	8	4	74	1	2.93
Bryan Masotta	13	646	5	6	0	46	0	4.27

ST. LAWRENCE
SCORING

	Pos.	Class	Games	G	A	Pts.	PIM
Burke Murphy	F	Jr.	33	27	23	50	61
Paul DiFrancesco	F	Fr.	33	8	28	36	56
Thom Cullen	D	So.	32	9	19	28	67
Derek Ladouceur	F	Fr.	29	6	21	27	22
Scott Stevens	F	So.	32	12	11	23	14
Tom Perry	D	Jr.	32	4	16	20	14
Ryan Cassidy	F	So.	32	7	11	18	34
Joel Prpic	F	So.	32	7	10	17	62

	Pos.	Class	Games	G	A	Pts.	PIM
Derek McLaughlin	F	Fr.	33	10	6	16	48
Brian Kapeller	F	Sr.	33	4	9	13	72
Troy Creuer	D	So.	33	1	11	12	30
Kris Laamanen	F	So.	19	8	3	11	8
Cade Blackburn	F	Sr.	28	3	6	9	24
Dan Skene	F	Sr.	32	3	5	8	54
Jeff Kungle	D	Jr.	33	4	3	7	20
Scott Murphy	F	So.	28	2	5	7	26
Ken Ruddock	D	So.	33	0	5	5	56
Pat Dennehy	F	Jr.	13	0	4	4	0
Mark McGrath	F	Fr.	16	1	1	2	6
Chris Dashney	D	Jr.	31	0	2	2	30
Alex Gordon	F	Fr.	1	0	0	0	0
Steve Polanish	D	So.	2	0	0	0	0
Scott Smith	G	Sr.	3	0	0	0	0
Brian LaVack	D	So.	3	0	0	0	2
Jon Bracco	G	So.	18	0	0	0	0
Clint Owen	G	Fr.	21	0	0	0	2

GOALTENDING

	Games	Min.	W	L	T	Goals	SO	Avg.
Scott Smith	3	32	0	0	0	2	0	3.77
Jon Bracco	18	910	6	8	1	67	1	4.42
Clint Owen	21	1046	9	9	0	80	0	4.59

UNION
SCORING

	Pos.	Class	Games	G	A	Pts.	PIM
Cory Holbrough	F	Sr.	29	11	24	35	55
Chris Albert	F	Sr.	29	17	15	32	44
Russell Monteith	F	So.	27	12	10	22	16
Chris Ford	F	So.	28	8	14	22	28
Andrew Will	D	So.	28	7	14	21	26
Troy Stevens	F	So.	18	4	13	17	8
John Sincinski	F	So.	26	9	7	16	0
Charlie Moxham	F	Fr.	28	5	9	14	16
Jay Prentice	F	So.	28	7	6	13	4
Ryan Donovan	F	So.	25	5	8	13	41
Reid Simonton	D	Jr.	27	4	9	13	68
Dean Goulet	D	Sr.	29	1	10	11	48
Craig Reckin	F	So.	24	2	4	6	18
Seabrook Satterlund	D	So.	23	0	6	6	16
Jamie Antoine	F	So.	16	3	2	5	6
Scott Boyd	D	Jr.	19	0	5	5	14
Chad Thompson	F	So.	18	2	2	4	20
Bill Moody	D	So.	25	0	4	4	22
Boe Leslie	F	Fr.	18	1	2	3	2
Shane Holunga	D	Jr.	9	1	1	2	8
Greg Buchanan	D	So.	11	1	0	1	8
Mike Gallant	G	Sr.	7	0	1	1	0
Chris Hancock	F	Jr.	18	0	1	1	38
Luigi Villa	G	So.	9	0	0	0	2
Pat O'Flaherty	F	So.	12	0	0	0	12
Trevor Koenig	G	Fr.	20	0	0	0	2

GOALTENDING

	Games	Min.	W	L	T	Goals	SO	Avg.
Luigi Villa	9	422	3	1	0	24	0	3.41
Trevor Koenig	20	1005	7	9	2	63	0	3.76
Mike Gallant	7	330	0	4	1	25	0	4.55

VERMONT
SCORING

	Pos.	Class	Games	G	A	Pts.	PIM
Martin St. Louis	F	So.	35	23	48	71	36
Eric Perrin	F	So.	35	28	39	67	38
Dominique Ducharme	F	Sr.	35	13	23	36	28
J.C. Ruid	F	So.	24	13	14	27	60
Dale Patterson	F	Jr.	34	6	18	24	16
Matt Stelljes	F	Fr.	35	8	8	16	12
Mike Larkin	D	Sr.	33	5	11	16	70
Rob Pattison	F	Sr.	8	8	6	14	8
Jason Williams	D	Sr.	34	4	10	14	48
Bill Lincoln	F	Sr.	32	3	8	11	31

	Pos.	Class	Games	G	A	Pts.	PIM
Jason Hamilton	F	Fr.	32	2	9	11	23
Phil Eboli	F	Jr.	31	4	6	10	24
Matt Johnson	F	Jr.	32	3	6	9	22
Steve McKell	D	Jr.	34	1	8	9	28
Brian Leddy	F	Sr.	16	5	3	8	33
Eric Lavoie	F	Jr.	21	2	5	7	16
Keith Festa	F	Sr.	26	1	6	7	10
Justin Martin	F	Fr.	23	4	2	6	20
Johathan Sorg	D	So.	29	2	3	5	14
Pavel Navrat	D	So.	25	1	2	3	37
Eric Hallman	D	So.	29	0	3	3	36
Tim Thomas	G	So.	34	0	2	2	8
Jon Miyamoto	G	Sr.	4	0	0	0	0
Jason Reid	D	Fr.	5	0	0	0	4
Scott MacDonald	D	Jr.	8	0	0	0	4
Tom Quinn	D	Sr.	13	0	0	0	4

GOALTENDING

	Games	Min.	W	L	T	Goals	SO	Avg.
Tim Thomas	34	2011	18	14	2	90	3	2.69
Jon Miyamoto	4	98	1	0	0	13	1	7.97

YALE

SCORING

	Pos.	Class	Games	G	A	Pts.	PIM
Jason Cipolla	F	Sr.	28	15	19	34	38
Andy Weidenbach	F	Sr.	28	18	15	33	68
Jeff Sorem	F	Jr.	28	10	15	25	2

	Pos.	Class	Games	G	A	Pts.	PIM
Zoran Kozic	F	Sr.	28	7	15	22	18
John Emmons	F	Jr.	28	4	16	20	57
Matt Cumming	F	Fr.	27	10	7	17	28
Dan Nyberg	D	Sr.	27	4	10	14	22
Dan Brierly	D	Jr.	28	5	7	12	44
Sani Silvennoinen	D	So.	26	3	8	11	10
Richard Giroux	D	Sr.	21	1	9	10	20
Brendan Doyle	F	Jr.	27	3	6	9	18
Chris Barbanti	F	Sr.	24	3	4	7	12
Curtis Millen	D	Jr.	16	1	5	6	6
Steve Lombardi	F	Sr.	24	1	5	6	16
Michael Yoshino	F	Jr.	16	2	2	4	8
Brad Dunlap	F	Fr.	18	2	2	4	8
Geoff Kufta	F	Fr.	25	1	3	4	6
Ray Giroux	D	Fr.	27	1	3	4	8
Daryl Jones	D	Fr.	16	0	3	3	16
Todd Sullivan	G	Sr.	26	0	2	2	0
Jeff Glew	D	Fr.	3	0	1	1	0
Louie Loucks	F	So.	6	0	1	1	0
Kris Merkler	F	Fr.	13	0	1	1	10
Josh Rabjohns	F	So.	15	0	1	1	6
Andy Young	D	Fr.	1	0	0	0	0
Dan Choquette	G	So.	3	0	0	0	2
Prescott Logan	D	Jr.	3	0	0	0	0

GOALTENDING

	Games	Min.	W	L	T	Goals	SO	Avg.
Todd Sullivan	26	1552	8	15	3	92	0	3.56
Dan Choquette	3	140	0	2	0	21	0	9.00

HOCKEY EAST

FINAL STANDINGS

Team	G	W	L	T	Pts.	GF	GA
Maine (32-6-6)	24	15	3	6	88	104	63
Boston U. (31-6-3)	24	16	5	3	88	131	82
New Hamp. (22-10-4)	24	14	6	4	78	113	85
N'eastern (16-14-5)	24	11	8	5	70	98	89
Lowell (17-19-4)	24	11	12	1	58	105	116
Providence (14-17-6)	24	7	11	6	50	102	103
Merrimack (14-18-5)	24	7	12	5	48	74	91
Boston Col. (11-22-2)	24	8	14	2	45	86	119
Mass. (6-28-2)	24	3	21	0	15	64	129

Overall record in parentheses.

PLAYOFF RESULTS

QUARTERFINALS

Providence 3, New Hampshire 2 (OT)
Lowell 5, Northeastern 2
Maine 7, Massachusetts 4
Boston University 4, Merrimack 3

SEMIFINALS

Providence 7, Maine 3

Boston University 4, Lowell 2

CONSOLATION GAME

Maine 6, Lowell 0

CHAMPIONSHIP GAME

Boston University 3, Providence 2

ALL-STAR TEAMS

First team	Pos.	Second team
Blair Allison, Maine	G	Martin Legault, Merrimack
Chris Imes, Maine	D	Kaj Linna, Boston U.
Dan McGillis, Northeastern	D	Jeff Tory, Maine
Greg Bullock, Lowell	F	Eric Flinton, New Hamp.
Mike Grier, Boston U.	F	Chris O'Sullivan, Boston U.
Chad Quenneville, Prov.	F	Jordan Shields, N'eastern

AWARD WINNERS

Player of the year: Chris Imes, Maine
Rookie of the year: Mark Mowers, New Hampshire
Coach of the year: Shawn Walsh, Maine
Leading scorer: Greg Bullock, Lowell
Playoff MVP: Bob Bell, Providence

INDIVIDUAL STATISTICS

BOSTON COLLEGE

SCORING

	Pos.	Class	Games	G	A	Pts.	PIM
Ryan Haggerty	F	Sr.	35	23	22	45	20
David Hymovitz	F	Jr.	35	21	19	40	22
Don Chase	F	Jr.	35	19	12	31	74
Jamie O'Leary	F	Fr.	29	6	23	29	36
Tom Ashe	D	Jr.	34	5	18	23	68
Jerry Buckley	F	Sr.	33	8	11	19	45
Rob Laferriere	F	Sr.	31	6	10	16	40
Brian Callahan	F	So.	34	10	1	11	58
Ken Hemenway	D	Fr.	32	4	6	10	24
David Wainwright	D	So.	33	3	6	9	48
Rob Canavan	F	Sr.	35	4	4	8	30
Greg Callahan	D	Jr.	33	1	6	7	89
Jim Krayer	F	Sr.	33	3	4	7	6
Toby Harris	F	So.	31	3	4	7	30
Brad Carlson	D	So.	27	3	3	6	8
Peter Masters	D	So.	33	1	5	6	52
Joe Harney	D	So.	21	2	3	5	36
Michael McCarthy	F	Sr.	34	3	2	5	16
Timmy Lewis	F	Fr.	15	2	2	4	22
Clifton McHale	F	Jr.	27	2	2	4	21
Greg Taylor	G	So.	32	0	1	1	16
Ryan Taylor	D	So.	5	0	1	1	4
Josh Singewald	G	Sr.	3	0	0	0	0
Mike Correia	G	Fr.	7	0	0	0	2
Luke Howarth	F	Fr.	1	0	0	0	0

GOALTENDING

	Games	Min.	W	L	T	Goals	SO	Avg.
Greg Taylor	32	1803	11	19	2	128	0	4.26
Mike Correia	7	223	0	2	0	23	0	6.18
Josh Singewald	3	87	0	1	0	12	0	8.32

BOSTON UNIVERSITY

SCORING

	Pos.	Class	Games	G	A	Pts.	PIM
Chris O'Sullivan	F	So.	40	23	33	56	48
Mike Grier	F	So.	37	29	26	55	85
Jacques Joubert	F	Sr.	40	29	23	52	41
Steve Thornton	F	Sr.	39	17	24	41	14
Bob Lachance	F	Jr.	37	12	29	41	51
Mike Prendergast	F	Sr.	38	17	22	39	30
Shawn Bates	F	So.	38	18	12	30	48
Rich Brennan	D	Sr.	31	5	23	28	56
Jon Coleman	D	So.	40	5	23	28	42
Chris Drury	F	Fr.	39	12	15	27	38
Kaj Linna	D	Sr.	36	7	20	27	26
Ken Rausch	F	Sr.	37	12	12	24	6
Jay Pandolfo	F	Jr.	20	7	13	20	6
Chris Kelleher	D	Fr.	35	3	17	20	62
Mike Sylvia	F	Fr.	36	10	9	19	25
Bill Pierce	F	So.	33	5	13	18	29
Doug Wood	D	Jr.	39	6	11	17	87
Matt Wright	F	So.	35	7	9	16	27
Shane Johnson	D	So.	33	0	6	6	50
Jeff Kealty	D	Fr.	25	0	5	5	29
Derek Herlofsky	G	Sr.	24	0	3	3	2
Tom Noble	G	Fr.	18	0	2	2	0
Peter Donatelli	F	Fr.	2	0	0	0	0
Shawn Ferullo	G	So.	5	0	0	0	0
John Hynes	F	Fr.	7	0	0	0	6

GOALTENDING

	Games	Min.	W	L	T	Goals	SO	Avg.
Tom Noble	18	1003	15	2	0	46	0	2.75
Derek Herlofsky	24	1366	16	4	3	66	1	2.90
Shawn Ferullo	5	43	0	0	0	4	0	5.58

LOWELL

SCORING

	Pos.	Class	Games	G	A	Pts.	PIM
Greg Bullock	F	So.	40	25	40	65	125
Christian Sbrocca	F	Jr.	39	15	32	47	110
Jeff Daw	F	Jr.	40	27	15	42	24
Brendan Concannon	F	Jr.	40	12	23	35	19
Ed Campbell	D	So.	34	6	23	29	105
Neil Donovan	F	So.	34	15	13	28	56

	Pos.	Class	Games	G	A	Pts.	PIM
David Dartsch	F	Jr.	37	9	16	25	69
Jon Mahoney	F	Jr.	33	10	10	20	34
Mike Nicholishen	D	Fr.	40	8	10	18	40
Shannon Basaraba	F	Fr.	28	7	11	18	8
David Mayes	D	Jr.	37	1	16	17	28
Paul Botto	D	Sr.	39	2	10	12	90
Aaron Kriss	D	Sr.	40	3	8	11	56
Marc Salsman	F	So.	25	3	7	10	24
Bill Riga	F	Jr.	32	5	4	9	10
Dave Barozzino	D	Jr.	31	3	5	8	66
Chris Libett	D	Fr.	25	1	7	8	16
Mike Henderson	F	Fr.	33	4	3	7	85
Eric Brown	F	Sr.	35	3	4	7	16
Ryan Sandholm	F	So.	26	3	4	7	12
Jason Cormier	D	So.	16	2	3	5	12
Craig Lindsay	G	So.	27	0	2	2	0
Ludwig Marek	F	Jr.	5	1	0	1	4
Scott Fankhouser	G	Fr.	11	0	0	0	0
Martin Fillion	G	Fr.	10	0	0	0	2
Ryan Golden	F	So.	10	0	0	0	10

GOALTENDING

	Games	Min.	W	L	T	Goals	SO	Avg.
Martin Fillion	10	518	2	4	0	36	0	4.17
Craig Lindsay	27	1424	11	11	3	100	0	4.21
Scott Fankhouser	11	499	4	4	1	37	0	4.44

MAINE

SCORING

	Pos.	Class	Games	G	A	Pts.	PIM
Jeff Tory	D	Jr.	40	13	42	55	22
Brad Purdie	F	Jr.	44	29	19	48	28
Tim Lovell	F	So.	44	23	25	48	42
Dan Shermerhorn	F	So.	44	25	18	43	72
Jacque Rodrigue	D/F	Sr.	43	11	26	37	44
Shawn Wansborough	F	Fr.	36	14	21	35	20
Scott Parmentier	F	Fr.	42	14	19	33	22
Chris Imes	D	Sr.	43	4	29	33	18
Jamie Thompson	F	So.	43	11	15	26	22
Barry Clukey	F	So.	40	9	12	21	32
Trevor Roenick	F	So.	36	8	13	21	42
Tony Frenette	F	Jr.	44	11	10	21	60
Dave MacIsaac	D	Sr.	44	5	13	18	44
Reg Cardinal	F	Jr.	44	7	11	18	60
Wayne Conlan	F	Jr.	26	3	8	11	4
Brad Mahoney	F	So.	37	4	5	9	52
Tony Tempestilli	F	Fr.	21	4	5	9	12
Jason Dekker	D	So.	19	0	8	8	10
Jason Mansoff	D	So.	41	2	6	8	18
Jeff Libby	D/F	Fr.	22	2	4	6	6
Brian White	D	Fr.	28	1	1	2	16
Blair Marsh	G	Jr.	9	0	1	1	0
Marcel Pineau	F	So.	9	1	0	1	2
Blair Allison	G	Jr.	44	0	1	1	8
Marcus Gustafsson	F	Fr.	1	0	0	0	0
Paul Zinchenko	F	Fr.	1	0	0	0	2
Greg Hirsch	G	Jr.	5	0	0	0	0

GOALTENDING

	Games	Min.	W	L	T	Goals	SO	Avg.
Blair Marsh	9	118	0	0	0	0	0	0.00
Blair Allison	44	2572	32	6	6	115	0	2.68
Greg Hirsch	5	20	0	0	0	2	0	5.87

MASSACHUSETTS

SCORING

	Pos.	Class	Games	G	A	Pts.	PIM
Rob Bonneau	F	So.	34	14	12	26	65
Tom Perry	F	So.	35	7	18	25	30
Warren Norris	F	So.	35	13	8	21	34
Sal Manganaro	F	Jr.	27	11	9	20	52
Mike Evans	F	So.	35	7	10	17	67
Blair Wagar	F	So.	33	7	8	15	18
Chris Fawcett	F	Fr.	35	5	6	11	4

	Pos.	Class	Games	G	A	Pts.	PIM
Jon Jacques	F	Jr.	21	4	7	11	6
Gerry Cahill	F	So.	32	5	5	10	18
Dale Hooper	D	So.	20	3	7	10	30
Dean Campanale	F	Fr.	31	4	5	9	18
Keith O'Connell	D	So.	29	1	7	8	33
Dennis Wright	F	So.	30	4	3	7	60
Tiger Holland	D	So.	25	3	4	7	31
Jaynen Rissling	D	So.	35	0	7	7	42
Brian Corcoran	D	Sr.	20	3	3	6	40
Brad Norton	D	Fr.	30	0	6	6	89
Mike Gaffney	D	Fr.	33	1	4	5	38
Judd Smith	F	So.	22	1	2	3	13
Tom O'Connor	D	Fr.	34	1	1	2	44
Armand Latulippe	D	So.	10	1	0	1	4
Brian Regan	G	Fr.	22	0	1	1	0
Dave Kilduff	G	So.	14	0	1	1	0
Tony Giusto	D	So.	8	0	1	1	38
Rich Moriarty	G	So.	8	0	0	0	2
Dan Juden	F	Fr.	3	0	0	0	0
Bryan Fitzgerald	F	Fr.	1	0	0	0	0

GOALTENDING

	Games	Min.	W	L	T	Goals	SO	Avg.
Rich Moriarty	8	306	1	3	0	22	0	4.31
Brian Regan	22	1139	3	14	2	92	0	4.84
Dave Kilduff	14	728	2	11	0	64	0	5.27

MERRIMACK

SCORING

	Pos.	Class	Games	G	A	Pts.	PIM
Matt Adams	F	Sr.	37	22	22	44	58
Casey Kesselring	F	Fr.	37	14	21	35	38
Rob Beck	F	So.	37	12	19	31	64
Mark Cornforth	D	Sr.	30	8	20	28	93
Daryl Krauss	F	Jr.	34	12	8	20	44
Martin Laroche	F	Fr.	36	10	9	19	14
Tom Johnson	F	So.	36	5	14	19	35
Eric Weichselbaumer	D	So.	34	1	18	19	18
Mark Goble	F	Sr.	32	7	8	15	10
Gaetan Poirier	F	Fr.	32	8	6	14	38
Claudio Peca	F	Jr.	36	6	8	14	46
John Jakopin	D	So.	37	4	10	14	42
Chris Silvestro	D	Fr.	18	2	9	11	15
Steve McKenna	D	So.	37	1	9	10	74
Dan Hodge	D	Sr.	20	3	5	8	18
Tom Costa	D	Jr.	33	1	7	8	118
Chris Davis	F	Sr.	31	2	5	7	10
Ryan Mailhiot	F	Jr.	25	4	1	5	8
Karl Infanger	D	So.	32	0	5	5	26
Ziggy Marszalek	F	So.	20	1	2	3	12
Tom O'Grady	F	Fr.	13	1	1	2	0
Jim Sapienza	F	Fr.	10	1	1	2	6
Martin Legault	G	So.	28	0	1	1	4
Eric Thibeault	G	So.	13	0	1	1	2
Alex MacLellan	D	Jr.	5	0	0	0	0
Jim McNiff	G	So.	3	0	0	0	0
Chris Ross	D	Sr.	2	0	0	0	0
Chris Sannutti	F	Fr.	2	0	0	0	0

GOALTENDING

	Games	Min.	W	L	T	Goals	SO	Avg.
Martin Legault	28	1629	9	15	4	92	0	3.39
Eric Thibeault	13	572	5	3	1	39	0	4.09
Jim McNiff	3	30	0	0	0	3	0	6.00

NEW HAMPSHIRE

SCORING

	Pos.	Class	Games	G	A	Pts.	PIM
Eric Flinton	F	Sr.	36	22	23	45	44
Eric Royal	F	Sr.	36	18	26	44	32
Mike Sullivan	F	Jr.	36	13	26	39	14
Mark Mowers	F	Fr.	36	13	23	36	16
Nick Poole	F	Sr.	36	8	26	34	10
Eric Boguniecki	F	So.	34	12	19	31	62

	Pos.	Class	Games	G	A	Pts.	PIM
Todd Hall	D	Jr.	36	8	18	26	16
Kent Schmidke	D	Sr.	36	5	21	26	18
Eric Nikulas	F	Fr.	33	15	9	24	32
Steve Pleau	F	Jr.	29	13	9	22	24
Bryan Muir	D	Jr.	28	9	9	18	46
Ted Russell	D	Sr.	36	5	11	16	72
Tom O'Brien	F	Jr.	32	5	9	14	26
Rob Gagnon	F	Fr.	33	4	10	14	30
Dean Woodman	D	So.	30	3	8	11	32
Tim Murray	D	So.	33	0	6	6	14
Tom Nolan	F	So.	4	3	2	5	10
Brian Putnam	F	So.	26	1	3	4	12
Joey Moran	F	Fr.	20	2	1	3	6
Corey Cash	F	Jr.	11	1	1	2	4
Dylan Dellezay	F	Fr.	16	1	1	2	8
Mike Heinke	G	Sr.	17	0	1	1	2
Erik Johnson	D	Fr.	9	0	1	1	6
Eric Fitzgerald	D	So.	7	0	0	0	10
Trent Cavicchi	G	Jr.	23	0	0	0	0
Scott Robison	F	So.	7	0	0	0	2
Pat Norton	F	Jr.	3	0	0	0	0
Jeff Lenz	F	Jr.	3	0	0	0	0
Pat Bottino	D	Fr.	1	0	0	0	0
Mike McCready	F/D	So.	1	0	0	0	0
Brian Larochelle	G	Fr.	1	0	0	0	0

GOALTENDING

	Games	Min.	W	L	T	Goals	SO	Avg.
Brian Larochelle	1	8	0	0	0	0	0	0.00
Trent Cavicchi	23	1277	14	6	1	71	0	3.34
Mike Heinke	17	904	8	4	3	51	0	3.39

NORTHEASTERN
SCORING

	Pos.	Class	Games	G	A	Pts.	PIM
Jordon Shields	F	Jr.	35	21	25	46	58
Jean-Francois Aube	F	Sr.	34	21	17	38	24
Jason Melong	F	Sr.	35	15	17	32	22
Danny McGillis	D	Jr.	34	9	22	31	70
Mike Collett	F	Jr.	34	10	19	29	61
Scott Campbell	F	Fr.	35	8	16	24	32
Dan Lupo	F	Jr.	32	6	18	24	55
Francois Bouchard	D	Sr.	31	7	16	23	39
Tom Parlon	F	Sr.	33	8	9	17	40
Eric Petersen	F	So.	32	4	11	15	20
Jason Kelly	D	Sr.	30	4	10	14	50
Justin Kearns	F	Fr.	31	6	4	10	24
Hart Webb	F	So.	16	6	4	10	38
Geoff Lucas	F	Jr.	33	5	4	9	14
Tomas Persson	F	Jr.	34	5	2	7	18
Darryl MacNair	D	Sr.	35	3	4	7	66
Rick Schuhwerk	D	So.	34	2	5	7	18
Jeff Vaughan	D	So.	21	0	4	4	16

	Pos.	Class	Games	G	A	Pts.	PIM
Craig Carmody	F	Jr.	24	2	1	3	4
Brad Klyn	D	So.	13	1	2	3	8
David Penney	F	So.	1	0	0	0	2
Mike Veisor	G	Jr.	24	0	0	0	6
Todd Reynolds	G	Sr.	17	0	0	0	2
Bob Sheehan	D	Fr.	11	0	0	0	6
Marc Grande	D	Fr.	4	0	0	0	4
Justin Kummerer	D	Jr.	1	0	0	0	0
Mike Santonelli	F	So.	2	0	0	0	4
Kevin Noke	G	So.	2	0	0	0	0

GOALTENDING

	Games	Min.	W	L	T	Goals	SO	Avg.
Kevin Noke	2	16	1	0	0	0	0	0.00
Mike Veisor	24	1290	12	5	3	73	0	3.40
Todd Reynolds	17	820	4	9	2	61	0	4.46

PROVIDENCE
SCORING

	Pos.	Class	Games	G	A	Pts.	PIM
Chad Quenneville	F	Sr.	36	25	29	54	51
Brady Kramer	F	Sr.	37	23	29	52	64
George Breen	F	Sr.	36	17	18	35	51
Joe Hulbig	F	Jr.	37	14	21	35	36
Stefan Brannare	F	So.	37	18	10	28	40
Dennis Burke	F	Jr.	37	12	13	25	24
Jon Lavarre	F	Sr.	36	7	17	24	14
David Green	F	So.	37	9	13	22	28
Jay Kenney	F	Jr.	35	4	12	16	12
Justin Gould	D	Jr.	37	2	14	16	48
Scott Balboni	D	Jr.	33	4	11	15	57
Travis Dillabough	F	So.	37	3	11	14	48
Erik Sundquist	D	Jr.	23	4	7	11	30
Trevor Hanson	F	Jr.	27	5	4	9	28
Russ Guzior	F	So.	9	1	7	8	10
Mike Mader	F	Fr.	29	1	5	6	26
Nick Sinerate	F	Fr.	35	2	2	4	2
Jon Rowe	D	Jr.	25	1	3	4	14
Hal Gill	F	So.	26	1	3	4	22
David Ruhly	F	So.	24	3	0	3	8
John Tuohy	D	Fr.	16	1	1	2	18
Bob Bell	G	Jr.	20	0	2	2	2
Mike Gambino	F	Jr.	6	1	0	1	0
Dennis Sousa	D	Jr.	11	0	0	0	14
Dan Dennis	G	So.	24	0	0	0	2
Vin Martino	G	So.	1	0	0	0	0

GOALTENDING

	Games	Min.	W	L	T	Goals	SO	Avg.
Vin Martino	1	1	0	0	0	0	0	0.00
Bob Bell	20	971	7	6	3	58	1	3.58
Dan Dennis	24	1273	7	11	3	98	0	4.62

WESTERN COLLEGIATE HOCKEY ASSOCIATION

1994-95 SEASON

FINAL STANDINGS

Team	G	W	L	T	Pts.	GF	GA
Colorado C. (30-12-1)	32	22	9	1	45	155	108
Wisconsin (24-15-4)	32	17	11	4	38	128	112
Denver (25-15-2)	32	18	12	2	38	131	115
Minnesota (25-14-5)	32	16	11	5	37	121	95
St. Cloud St. (17-20-1)	32	15	16	1	31	126	113
N. Dakota (18-18-3) ..	32	14	15	3	31	120	141
M.-Duluth (16-18-4) .	32	13	15	4	30	124	127
Mich. Tech (15-20-4)	32	12	17	3	27	109	140
N. Mich. (13-24-3)	32	10	19	3	23	110	136
A'ka Anch. (11-25-0) .	32	10	22	0	20	106	142

Overall record in parentheses.

PLAYOFF RESULTS

FIRST ROUND

Colorado College 11, Alaska-Anchorage 3
Colorado College 5, Alaska-Anchorage 2
(Colorado College won series, 2-0)

Northern Michigan 4, Wisconsin 3
Wisconsin 5, Northern Michigan 4
Wisconsin 5, Northern Michigan 1
(Wisconsin won series, 2-1)

Denver 5, Michigan Tech 4 (OT)
Denver 5, Michigan Tech 2
(Denver won series, 2-0)

Minnesota 5, Minnesota-Duluth 4 (OT)
Minnesota 4, Minnesota-Duluth 3
(Minnesota won series, 2-0)

North Dakota 3, St. Cloud State 2
North Dakota 5, St. Cloud State 2
(North Dakota State won series, 2-0)

FINAL FIVE

Minnesota 3, North Dakota 2
Wisconsin 5, Denver 4
Colorado College 5, Minnesota 4 (OT)

CONSOLATION GAME

Minnesota 5, Denver 4 (OT)

CHAMPIONSHIP GAME

Wisconsin 4, Colorado College 3 (OT)

ALL-STAR TEAMS

First team	Pos.	Second team
Ryan Bach, Colorado Col.	G	Sinuhe Wallinheimo, Den.
Brian Rafalski, Wisconsin	D	Kelly Hultgren, St. Cloud St.
Nick Naumenko, N. Dakota	D	Kent Fearns, Colorado Col.
Brian Bonin, Minnesota	F	Colin Schmidt, Colo. Col.
Jay McNeill, Colorado Col.	F	Peter Geronazzo, Colo. Col.
Greg Hadden, N. Michigan	F	Brad Federenko, Min.-Dul.

AWARD WINNERS

Most Valuable Player: Brian Bonin, Minnesota
Rookie of the year: Mike Crowley, Minnesota
Coach of the year: George Gwozdecky, Denver
Leading scorer: Brian Bonin, Minnesota
Playoff MVP: Kirk Daubenspeck, Wisconsin

INDIVIDUAL STATISTICS

ALASKA-ANCHORAGE

SCORING

	Pos.	Class	Games	G	A	Pts.	PIM
Mark Stitt..............	F	Sr.	36	10	30	40	48
Paul Williams.........	F	Sr.	34	19	18	37	34
Troy Norcross........	F	Sr.	36	22	13	35	40
Jack Kowal	F	Jr.	36	7	17	24	52
Todd Bethard........	D	So.	36	10	12	22	14
Glen Thornborough..	F	Jr.	32	11	9	20	69
Jeremy Mylymok ...	D	Jr.	36	2	17	19	72
David Vallieres	F	So.	29	8	10	18	30
Stacy Prevost	F	So.	30	5	11	16	14
Mika Rautakallio ...	F	So.	27	4	9	13	6
Petri Tuomisto	D	Sr.	33	2	10	12	72
Trent Leggett	F	Sr.	32	2	7	9	22
Jason White...........	D	Jr.	34	4	4	8	38
Todd Skoglund.......	F	Sr.	10	5	2	7	19
Cotton Gore...........	F	Sr.	10	3	2	5	14
Jeff Grabinsky	F	Fr.	23	1	4	5	19
Matt Christian	F	Jr.	20	3	1	4	22
Bobby Stewart.......	F	Fr.	20	1	3	4	20
Darren Meek	D	Jr.	36	1	2	3	77
Gord McCann........	F	So.	33	2	1	3	60
Jeff Edwards.........	F	Fr.	32	0	3	3	68
Lee Schill	G	So.	26	0	1	1	0
Kirby Senden	D	So.	3	0	0	0	0
Chris Davis	G	So.	14	0	0	0	0
Conrad Sterling	F	Fr.	14	0	0	0	12
Chris Kerr..............	D	So.	16	0	0	0	10

GOALTENDING

	Games	Min.	W	L	T	Goals	SO	Avg.
Chris Davis..............	14	671	4	6	0	49	0	4.39
Lee Schill	26	1485	7	19	0	114	1	4.61

COLORADO COLLEGE

SCORING

	Pos.	Class	Games	G	A	Pts.	PIM
Peter Geronazzo	F	Sr.	43	29	28	57	111
Colin Schmidt	F	Jr.	43	26	31	57	61
Jay McNeill	F	Jr.	43	33	18	51	70
Chad Remackel......	F	Jr.	43	17	31	48	100
Ryan Reynard........	F	Sr.	43	19	28	47	119
R.J. Enga..............	F	Sr.	43	23	23	46	40
Eric Rud	D	So.	43	6	27	33	38
Kent Fearns	D	Sr.	40	7	23	30	39
Calvin Elfring	D	Fr.	43	3	23	26	34
Jason Gudmundson	F	Fr.	41	12	12	24	4
Jason Christopherson	F	Jr.	42	6	14	20	26
David Paxton	D	Sr.	42	6	12	18	50
Tim Sweezo...........	F	So.	41	8	9	17	26
Chad Hartnell........	F	So.	41	3	12	15	26
Bob Needham........	D	So.	43	1	13	14	54
John Steiner...........	D	Sr.	43	1	11	12	76
Travis Cheyne........	F	Fr.	42	5	6	11	16
Stewart Bodtker	F	Fr.	32	6	4	10	24
Geoff Herzog	D	Fr.	4	1	1	2	4
T.J. Tanberg	F	Fr.	17	1	1	2	4

	Pos.	Class	Games	G	A	Pts.	PIM
Trevor Putrah	D	Fr.	1	0	1	1	2
Steve Metzger	F	Jr.	2	0	1	1	0
Ryan Bach	G	Jr.	27	0	1	1	0
Paul Frank	G	Sr.	1	0	0	0	0
Judd Lambert	G	So.	21	0	0	0	0

GOALTENDING

	Games	Min.	W	L	T	Goals	SO	Avg.
Paul Frank	1	20	0	0	0	1	0	3.00
Judd Lambert	21	1060	12	7	0	57	1	3.23
Ryan Bach	27	1522	18	5	1	83	0	3.27

DENVER
SCORING

	Pos.	Class	Games	G	A	Pts.	PIM
Angelo Ricci	F	Sr.	42	20	27	47	73
Jason Elders	F	Sr.	42	22	19	41	18
Chris Kenady	F	Sr.	39	21	17	38	113
Warren Smith	F	So.	42	18	17	35	14
Antti Laaksonen	F	So.	40	17	18	35	42
Erik Andersson	F	Jr.	42	12	19	31	42
Craig McMillan	D	Sr.	42	4	23	27	52
Mike Naylor	F	Sr.	36	10	16	26	22
Petri Gunther	F	So.	38	8	16	24	32
Kelly Hollingshead	D	Jr.	41	7	16	23	65
Mike Dairon	F	Fr.	42	7	14	21	44
Anders Bjork	F	Fr.	39	8	12	20	22
John McLean	D	Sr.	38	4	12	16	76
Paul Koch	D	Sr.	42	5	10	15	126
Sean Ortiz	F	Sr.	38	7	7	14	30
Garrett Buzan	F	Jr.	29	6	6	12	33
Charlie Host	F	So.	39	2	6	8	28
Travis Smith	D	So.	42	1	6	7	61
Dave Klasnick	F	Jr.	27	1	3	4	8
Sinuhe Wallinheimo	G	Jr.	30	0	3	3	2
Brent Cary	F	Jr.	7	1	0	1	0
Jim Mullin	G	So.	18	0	1	1	8
Mike Corbett	D	So.	2	0	0	0	0
Mike Rotsch	F	So.	3	0	0	0	0

GOALTENDING

	Games	Min.	W	L	T	Goals	SO	Avg.
Sinuhe Wallinheimo	30	1668	16	10	1	79	1	2.84
Jim Mullin	18	875	9	5	1	65	0	4.46

MICHIGAN TECH
SCORING

	Pos.	Class	Games	G	A	Pts.	PIM
Pat Mikesch	F	Jr.	36	15	28	43	37
Brent Peterson	F	Sr.	39	20	16	36	27
Jason Wright	D	Jr.	38	2	23	25	77
Andre Savage	F	Fr.	39	7	17	24	56
Randy Stevens	F	Sr.	31	13	11	24	22
Bret Meyers	F	Fr.	32	11	9	20	42
Dave Dupont	D	Fr.	36	5	14	19	102
Kyle Peterson	F	So.	36	7	11	18	52
Jeff Mikesch	F	So.	36	9	8	17	83
Jimmy Roy	F	Fr.	38	5	11	16	62
Travis Seale	F	Sr.	25	8	7	15	12
Austyn Kryzer	F	Fr.	35	9	5	14	46
Liam Garvey	D	Sr.	31	6	7	13	52
Eric Jensen	D	So.	33	2	11	13	43
Jason Hanchuk	D	Sr.	38	4	6	10	81
Mike Figliomeni	F	Jr.	14	3	7	10	8
Tim Harris	D	Fr.	17	0	8	8	85
Jason Prokopetz	F	So.	35	3	3	6	152
Craig Perrett	F	Fr.	35	3	2	5	79
Travis VanTighem	D	So.	36	1	3	4	66
Andy Sutton	F	Fr.	19	2	1	3	42
Brian Hunter	D	So.	2	0	0	0	2
Pete Hamilton	G	Fr.	3	0	0	0	0
John Kisil	F	So.	6	0	0	0	12
Matt Kucway	G	Fr.	10	0	0	0	0
Martin Machacek	F	Jr.	10	0	0	0	6
Luciano Caravaggio	G	So.	31	0	0	0	2

GOALTENDING

	Games	Min.	W	L	T	Goals	SO	Avg.
Luciano Caravaggio	31	1777	12	15	3	119	1	4.02
Pete Hamilton	10	477	3	3	1	40	0	5.03
Matt Kucway	3	105	0	2	0	10	0	5.77

MINNESOTA
SCORING

	Pos.	Class	Games	G	A	Pts.	PIM
Brian Bonin	F	Jr.	44	32	31	63	28
Ryan Kraft	F	Fr.	44	13	33	46	44
Dan Trebil	D	Jr.	44	10	33	43	10
Justin McHugh	F	Sr.	35	24	16	40	46
Scott Bell	F	Sr.	41	18	21	39	100
Mike Crowley	D	Fr.	41	11	27	38	60
Nick Checco	F	So.	43	14	11	25	46
Dan Woog	F	Jr.	44	5	16	21	36
Andy Brink	F/D	Jr.	43	3	15	18	29
Dave Larson	F	Jr.	42	9	7	16	93
Dan Hendrickson	F	So.	40	4	12	16	69
Jed Fiebelkorn	F	Sr.	41	4	9	13	119
Brian LaFleur	D	So.	34	0	10	10	18
Casey Hankinson	F	Fr.	33	7	1	8	86
Bobby Dustin	F	Jr.	24	4	2	6	22
Charlie Wasley	D	Jr.	36	2	4	6	60
Greg Zwackman	D	Jr.	43	0	6	6	28
Joe Pankratz	F	Fr.	18	3	2	5	12
Jesse Bertogliat	F	Jr.	22	2	3	5	51
Jay Moser	D	Jr.	13	1	4	5	29
Jason Godbout	D	Fr.	32	1	4	5	28
Brandon Steege	F	Jr.	15	1	3	4	8
Jeff Callinan	G	Sr.	43	0	2	2	2
Jason Seils	F	Fr.	15	1	0	1	4
Will Anderson	F	Fr.	1	0	0	0	2
Brent Godbout	F	So.	2	0	0	0	2
Jeff Moen	G	Jr.	6	0	0	0	0

GOALTENDING

	Games	Min.	W	L	T	Goals	SO	Avg.
Jeff Callinan	43	2484	23	11	5	115	2	2.78
Jeff Moen	6	218	2	3	0	16	0	4.41

MINNESOTA-DULUTH
SCORING

	Pos.	Class	Games	G	A	Pts.	PIM
Brad Federenko	F	So.	38	30	19	49	33
Rusty Fitzgerald	F	Sr.	34	16	22	38	50
Mike Peluso	F	Fr.	38	11	23	34	38
Joe Ciccarello	F	Jr.	38	16	17	33	30
Brett Larson	D	Sr.	37	6	25	31	50
Joe Rybar	F	Fr.	35	12	17	29	36
Rod Aldoff	D	Sr.	36	11	18	29	80
Ken Dzikowski	F	Fr.	37	4	15	19	30
Chet Culic	F	So.	34	8	10	18	20
Chris Sittlow	F	Sr.	35	8	8	16	92
Jeff Romfo	F	Jr.	35	6	8	14	32
Laird Lidster	D	Fr.	37	2	11	13	50
Sergei Petrov	F	So.	30	6	6	12	46
Greg Hanson	D	Jr.	35	1	10	11	98
Marc Christian	F	Jr.	21	3	6	9	19
Joe Tamminen	F	Jr.	21	2	6	8	32
Adam Roy	F	So.	30	3	3	6	20
Brian Bolf	F	Fr.	15	1	2	3	2
Jason Garatti	D	So.	36	0	3	3	32
Taras Lendzyk	G	Jr.	37	0	3	3	6
Josh Arnold	F	Fr.	14	0	2	2	2
Chris Snell	D	Fr.	19	0	2	2	22
Jason Watt	D	Sr.	21	0	1	1	21
David Buck	D	So.	2	0	0	0	8
Paul Carey	F	Fr.	2	0	0	0	0
Niklas Axelsson	G	Sr.	3	0	0	0	0
Rick Mrozik	D	So.	3	0	0	0	2

GOALTENDING

	Games	Min.	W	L	T	Goals	SO	Avg.
Niklas Axelsson	3	99	1	0	0	6	0	3.65
Taras Lendzyk	37	2210	15	18	4	140	1	3.80

NORTH DAKOTA

SCORING

	Pos.	Class	Games	G	A	Pts.	PIM
Teeder Wynne	F	Jr.	39	22	27	49	58
Nick Naumenko	D	Jr.	39	13	26	39	78
Darcy Mitani	F	Jr.	39	15	14	29	36
Scott Kirton	F	Sr.	37	8	20	28	65
Ryan Johnson	F	Fr.	38	6	22	28	39
Brett Hryniuk	F	Sr.	34	15	11	26	58
Kevin Hoogsteen	F	So.	38	13	13	26	67
Landon Wilson	F	So.	31	7	16	23	141
Bill Trew	F	Jr.	35	10	10	20	16
Curtis Murphy	D	Fr.	33	6	10	16	28
Sean Beswick	F	Sr.	31	10	4	14	44
Mark Pivetz	D	So.	39	3	11	14	38
Corey Johnson	F	Jr.	37	7	6	13	26
Keith Murphy	F	Sr.	35	8	4	12	16
Dane Litke	D	So.	26	2	7	9	10
Tyler Rice	F	Fr.	22	1	8	9	20
Matt Henderson	F	Fr.	19	1	3	4	16
Kevin Rappana	D	Jr.	36	1	3	4	92
Tim Slukynsky	F	Fr.	21	0	4	4	4
Chad Sturrock	D	Fr.	24	0	3	3	14
Brian Zierke	F	So.	10	2	0	2	8
Mitch Vig	D	Fr.	15	0	2	2	18
Jarrod Olson	D	Sr.	22	1	0	1	16
Kevin Powell	G	Jr.	6	0	0	0	0
Jeff Lembke	G	Sr.	8	0	0	0	0
Toby Kvalevog	G	So.	32	0	0	0	6

GOALTENDING

	Games	Min.	W	L	T	Goals	SO	Avg.
Toby Kvalevog	32	1829	14	13	4	120	1	3.94
Kevin Powell	6	257	2	2	0	22	0	5.14
Jeff Lembke	8	261	2	3	0	25	0	5.75

ST. CLOUD STATE

SCORING

	Pos.	Class	Games	G	A	Pts.	PIM
Brett Lievers	F	Sr.	38	21	27	48	8
Eric Johnson	F	Sr.	38	15	29	44	22
Kelly Hultgren	D	Sr.	37	9	29	38	80
Bill Lund	F	Sr.	36	10	24	34	68
Dave Holum	F	Sr.	37	18	13	31	68
Dave Paradise	F	So.	35	14	9	23	104
Taj Melson	D	Jr.	38	4	17	21	60
Sandy Gasseau	F	Sr.	34	12	8	20	41
Chris Markstrom	F	Sr.	36	6	12	18	20
Gino Santerre	D	Sr.	35	5	11	16	98
Marc Gagnon	F	Sr.	23	7	8	15	14
Kelly Rieder	F	Jr.	32	6	8	14	14
Jeff Schmidt	F	Sr.	35	4	7	11	14
Jay Geisbauer	F	Jr.	22	5	3	8	24
P.J. Lepler	D	Jr.	38	3	3	6	68
Randy Best	D	So.	20	2	3	5	20
Jason Stewart	F	Fr.	28	1	3	4	16
Mike O'Connell	D	So.	30	1	3	4	22
Dan Reimann	D	Jr.	38	1	3	4	69
Mark Kotary	F	So.	11	1	2	3	6
Brian Leitza	G	Fr.	30	0	2	2	12
Adam Rodak	F	So.	15	1	0	1	8
Rob Klasnick	F	Fr.	13	0	1	1	0
Andy Vicari	D	Fr.	14	0	1	1	0
Jon Tykeson	F	So.	1	0	0	0	0
Jason Jiskra	G	Jr.	6	0	0	0	0
Dave Stone	G	Sr.	6	0	0	0	0

GOALTENDING

	Games	Min.	W	L	T	Goals	SO	Avg.
Jason Jiskra	6	348	3	1	1	19	0	3.27
Brian Leitza	30	1625	13	15	4	93	2	3.43
Dave Stone	6	308	1	4	0	25	0	4.86

NORTHERN MICHIGAN

SCORING

	Pos.	Class	Games	G	A	Pts.	PIM
Greg Hadden	F	Sr.	38	20	30	50	117
Bill MacGillivray	F	Sr.	40	13	34	47	32
Mike Harding	F	Sr.	40	16	22	38	68
Jason Hehr	D	Sr.	39	11	26	37	40
Dean Seymour	F	So.	39	17	19	36	54
Kory Karlander	F	Jr.	36	13	11	24	42
Brent Riplinger	F	Sr.	37	9	15	24	30
Scott Green	F	Sr.	36	7	9	16	22
Jason Welch	F	Jr.	33	6	8	14	25
Trevor Janicki	D	So.	36	4	8	12	30
Aaron Cain	F	Fr.	36	3	8	11	42
John Bossio	F	Fr.	36	6	4	10	16
Shayne Tomlinson	D	So.	27	1	8	9	46
Curtis Sheptak	F	Fr.	39	4	4	8	86
Rocky Welsing	D	Fr.	38	0	8	8	129
Justin George	F	Sr.	18	3	4	7	20
Don McCusker	F	Jr.	13	1	5	6	6
Dieter Kochan	G	So.	29	0	5	5	0
Mike Hillock	D	So.	29	3	1	4	26
Steve Hamilton	D	Jr.	14	0	4	4	23
Chad Dameworth	D	Sr.	39	0	4	4	46
Brian Barker	F	So.	24	3	0	3	4
Darcy Dallas	D	So.	2	1	0	1	0
Jason Mitchell	G	Fr.	12	0	1	1	2
Roger Lewis	F	So.	14	0	1	1	4
Mike Johnson	D	Fr.	7	0	0	0	10

GOALTENDING

	Games	Min.	W	L	T	Goals	SO	Avg.
Jason Mitchell	12	591	3	4	0	36	0	3.66
Dieter Kochan	29	1512	8	17	3	107	0	4.25

WISCONSIN

SCORING

	Pos.	Class	Games	G	A	Pts.	PIM
Max Williams	F	Jr.	43	26	26	52	60
Brian Rafalski	D	Sr.	43	11	34	45	48
Mike Strobel	F	Jr.	38	22	16	38	117
Maco Balkovec	D	Sr.	41	4	34	38	106
Jamie Spencer	F	Sr.	41	14	23	37	61
Shawn Carter	F	Jr.	43	15	13	28	98
Mickey Elick	D	Jr.	43	5	23	28	52
Erik Raygor	F	So.	43	18	9	27	58
Joe Bianchi	F	Fr.	43	11	16	27	29
Mark Strobel	D	Sr.	37	9	18	27	74
Scott Sanderson	F	Jr.	43	10	10	20	14
Dan Tompkins	F	So.	32	4	10	14	82
Brad Englehart	F	Fr.	29	6	6	12	42
Chris Tok	D	Sr.	43	5	7	12	129
Troy Howard	F	Jr.	43	4	8	12	32
E.J. Bradley	F	Fr.	40	3	4	7	22
Rick Enrico	F	Fr.	31	4	2	6	42
Darren Haley	F	So.	36	1	4	5	11
Kirk Daubenspeck	G	So.	41	0	5	5	14
Tim Krug	D	So.	27	0	1	1	22
John Sauer	G	So.	1	0	0	0	0
Steve Sabo	D	So.	3	0	0	0	0
Jake Soper	G	Fr.	3	0	0	0	2
Mark Smith	F	Fr.	7	0	0	0	12
Matt Peterson	D	Fr.	20	0	0	0	10

GOALTENDING

	Games	Min.	W	L	T	Goals	SO	Avg.
Jake Sauer	1	1	0	0	0	0	0	0.00
Kirk Daubenspeck	42	2504	23	15	4	146	0	3.50
John Soper	3	76	1	0	0	5	0	3.97

INDEPENDENTS

FINAL STANDINGS

	W	L	T	GF	GA	Pct.
Army	20	13	1	123	121	.603
Air Force	15	17	1	135	148	.470

INDIVIDUAL STATISTICS

AIR FORCE
SCORING

	Pos.	Class	Games	G	A	Pts.	PIM
Mark DeGironimo...	F	Jr.	32	20	19	39	38
John Decker	F	Sr.	33	16	23	39	76
Beau Bilek	D	Sr.	33	8	29	37	38
Andy Veneri	F	Sr.	33	20	15	35	46
Dan McAlister	F	Sr.	31	11	13	24	48
Todd Lafortune	F	So.	31	12	9	21	24
Stephen Maturo	F	So.	27	9	11	20	36
Dan Leone	D	Jr.	33	4	16	20	38
Patrick Ryan	D	Jr.	33	5	13	18	60
Justin Scott	D	So.	33	4	14	18	42
Joe Javorski	F	Sr.	30	6	7	13	46
Peter Sandness	F	So.	27	8	2	10	14
Erik Brown	F	Sr.	30	2	5	7	37
Rocky Northon	F	Sr.	30	3	3	6	52
Erik Öberg	D	Fr.	20	0	6	6	4
Chris Mitchell	F	Jr.	25	1	3	4	18
John Haberlach	F	Fr.	22	2	1	3	2
Mike Palmer	F	Fr.	20	1	2	3	4
Mike DesRoche	F	Fr.	11	2	0	2	4
Derek Sellnow	F	So.	4	0	1	1	18
David Michaud	D	Jr.	19	0	1	1	18
Pat Kielb	G	So.	27	0	1	1	0
Tate Hagland	D	Fr.	8	1	0	1	2
Mike Benson	G	Sr.	9	0	1	1	0
Jeremy Gregoire	G	Fr.	1	0	0	0	0
Phillip Vallie	F	Fr.	1	0	0	0	0
John Rimstad	D	So.	4	0	0	0	0
Brian Mulligan	F	So.	5	0	0	0	2
Tony DaCosta	D	Fr.	15	0	0	0	0

GOALTENDING

	Games	Min.	W	L	T	Goals	SO	Avg.
Jeremy Gregoire	1	60	1	0	0	1	0	1.00
Pat Kielb	27	1535	11	15	1	115	0	4.49
Mike Benson	9	394	3	2	0	32	0	4.87

ARMY
SCORING

	Pos.	Class	Games	G	A	Pts.	PIM
Ian Winer	F	Fr.	29	15	36	51	44
Frank Fede	F	So.	33	22	24	46	30
Bill Morrison	F	So.	31	22	19	41	24
Tony DiCarlo	F	So.	33	20	19	39	42
Mark Stachelski	F	Sr.	32	17	20	37	110
Joe Sharrock	F	So.	33	15	21	36	57
Troy Eigner	F	Sr.	32	8	20	28	11
Mike Mansell	D	Jr.	32	3	23	26	30
Sean Hennessy	D	Sr.	33	6	17	23	78
Leif Hansen	D	So.	34	7	11	18	32
Darren Clapprood	D	Fr.	32	5	13	18	40
Tom Deveans	F	So.	24	4	10	14	4
Eric Leetch	F	Sr.	24	5	7	12	16
Craig Fellman	F	Sr.	34	7	3	10	33
Mike Gunning	F	Jr.	33	3	7	10	22
Doug Scott	F	Fr.	18	4	5	9	4
Chris Perron	F	So.	28	2	6	8	26
Marc Dorrer	F	Jr.	11	4	3	7	8
Anthony Felice	D	Fr.	28	2	4	6	8
Mike Opdenaker	D	So.	28	1	4	5	16
James May	F	Fr.	6	1	3	4	0
Jason Dickie	D	Jr.	23	0	4	4	30
T.R. Coccaro	F	So.	1	0	0	0	0
Daryl Chamberlain	G	Fr.	10	0	0	0	2
Brian Bolio	G	Sr.	28	0	0	0	4

GOALTENDING

	Games	Min.	W	L	T	Goals	SO	Avg.
Daryl Chamberlain	10	461	5	3	0	22	2	2.86
Brian Bolio	28	1583	15	10	1	84	5	3.18

CANADIAN INTERUNIVERSITY ATHLETIC UNION

GENERAL INFORMATION

The Canadian Interuniversity Athletic Union is an alliance of three Canadian college leagues—the Atlantic Universities Athletic Association, Canada West University Athletic Association and Ontario Universities Athletic Association. After the regular season, the three leagues compete in an elimination tournament to decide the CIAU national champion. The award and trophy winners are based on regular-season play.

1995 NATIONAL CHAMPIONSHIPS

PLAYOFF STANDINGS

Team (League)	W	L	Pts.	GF	GA
Moncton (AUAA)	2	0	4	10	5
Guelph (OUAA)	1	1	1	5	6
Western Ontario (OUAA)	0	1	0	4	5
Calgary (CWUAA)	0	1	0	1	4

RESULTS

SEMIFINALS

FRIDAY, MARCH 10

Guelph 4, Calgary 1
Moncton 5, W. Ontario 4

FINAL

SUNDAY, MARCH 12

Moncton 5, Guelph 1

1994-95 AWARD WINNERS

ALL-STAR TEAMS

Pos.	Player
G	Sean Basilio, Western Ontario
	Francois Leblanc, New Brunswick
D	Jeff MacLeod, Acadia
	Mark Guy, Western Ontario
	Jamie Pegg, Calgary
	Martin Roy, Ottawa
F	Karry Biette, Manitoba
	Greg Clancy, Acadia
	Greg Hutchings, Regina
	Todd Sparks, New Brunswick
	Todd Wetzel, Guelph
	Jarret Zukiwsky, Lethbridge

TROPHY WINNERS

Player of the year: Sean Basilio, Western Ontario
Rookie of the year: Sylvain Rodrigue, Trois-Rivieres
Scholastic player of the year: Dana McKechnie, Lethbridge
Coach of the year: Tom Coolen, Acadia

TOP SCORERS

	Games	G	A	Pts.
Greg Clancy, Acadia	25	24	37	61
Yvan Bergeron, Trois-Rivieres	24	23	33	56
John Nelson, Prince Edward Island	26	18	38	56
Jarret Zukiwsky, Lethbridge	27	31	24	55
Darren Macoretta, Brock	24	25	30	55
Ryan Savoia, Brock	26	23	32	55
John Spoltore, Wilfrid Laurier	24	18	34	52
Todd Sparks, New Brunswick	26	29	23	52
Dale McTavish, St. Francis Xavier	25	25	27	52
Jean Imbeau, Moncton	26	21	30	51
Karry Biette, Manitoba	28	20	31	51
Keifer House, Dalhousie	26	25	25	50

CANADIAN COLLEGES

CANADIAN COLLEGES (vertical left margin)
COLLEGE HOCKEY (vertical left margin)
CANADIAN COLLEGES (vertical left margin)

ATLANTIC UNIVERSITIES ATHLETIC ASSOCIATION, 1994-95 SEASON

FINAL STANDINGS

KELLY DIVISION

Team	G	W	L	T	Pts.	GF	GA
Acadia University......	26	22	1	3	47	181	80
Dalhousie University..	26	18	7	1	37	158	87
St. Mary's University .	26	10	15	1	21	119	141
St. Francis Xavier U. ..	26	9	16	1	19	105	144
U. Col. of Cape Breton.	26	1	24	1	3	71	203

MAC ADAM DIVISION

Team	G	W	L	T	Pts.	GF	GA
U. of New Brunswick ..	26	18	4	4	40	161	87
Univ. de Moncton.......	26	15	7	4	34	167	112
U. of P. Edward Island	26	13	11	2	28	134	143
St. Thomas University	26	11	12	3	25	105	103
Mount Allison Univ....	26	2	22	2	6	82	183

PLAYOFF RESULTS

KELLY DIVISION SEMIFINALS

Acadia 6, St.F.X. 2
Acadia 7, St.F.X. 0

Dalhousie 8, St. Mary's 1
Dalhousie 11, St. Mary's 3

MAC ADAM DIVISION SEMIFINALS

St. Thomas 4, N. Bruns. 3 (OT)
N. Bruns. 4, St. Thomas 2
St. Thomas 9, N. Bruns. 3

Moncton 4, P.E.I. 2
Moncton 6, P.E.I. 5 (OT)

KELLY DIVISION FINALS

Dalhousie 6, Acadia 3
Acadia 7, Dalhousie 3
Acadia 4, Dalhousie 1

MAC ADAM DIVISION FINALS

Moncton 3, St. Thomas 2
Moncton 7, St. Thomas 4

LEAGUE FINALS

Moncton 5, Acadia 4
Moncton 4, Acadia 3

ALL-STAR TEAMS

Kelly Division	Pos.	MacAdam Division
Denis Sproxton, Acadia	G	Frank Leblanc, N.B.
Kevin Knopp, Acadia	D	Mike Cavanagh, N.B.
Jeff MacLeod, Acadia	D	Daryl Lavoie, P.E.I.
Greg Clancy, Acadia	F	Todd Sparks, N.B.
Dale McTavish, St.F.X.	F	Jean Imbeau, Moncton
Keifer House, Dalhousie	F	Derek Cormier, N.B.

AWARD WINNERS

Most Valuable Player: Dale McTavish, St. Francis Xavier
Rookie of the year: Christian Skoryna, Acadia
Coach of the year: Tom Coolen, Acadia
Leading scorer: Greg Clancy, Acadia

INDIVIDUAL LEADERS

Goals: Todd Sparks, New Brunswick (29)
Assists: John Nelson, P.E.I. (38)
Points: Greg Clancy, Acadia (61)
Penalty minutes: Patrick Caron, Moncton (141)
Goaltending average: Denis Sproxton, Acadia (3.34)

TOP SCORERS

	Games	G	A	Pts.
Greg Clancy, Acadia.........................	25	24	37	61
John Nelson, Prince Edward Island...	26	18	38	56
Todd Sparks, New Brunswick............	26	29	23	52
Dale McTavish, St. Francis Xavier	25	25	27	52
Jean Imbeau, Moncton	26	21	30	51
Keifer House, Dalhousie	26	25	25	50
Dominic Rheaume, Moncton	24	22	26	48
Steve Kluczkowski, St. Mary's	24	21	25	46
Stephen Maltby, Dalhousie	25	28	17	45
Tony McCabe, St. Mary's...................	26	21	24	45
Christian Skoryna, Acadia.................	23	17	28	45

CANADA WEST UNIVERSITY ATHLETIC ASSOCIATION, 1994-95 SEASON

FINAL STANDINGS

Team	G	W	L	T	Pts.	GF	GA
Calgary (30-11-2)	28	20	6	2	42	129	92
Regina (21-14-2).....	28	17	9	2	36	123	107
Manitoba (22-15-2) .	28	15	11	2	32	125	108
Leth. (16-23-1)........	28	14	13	1	29	124	107
Alberta (15-16-5).....	28	11	12	5	27	111	118
Brit. Col. (15-15-5)..	28	10	13	5	25	103	120
Brandon (12-25-2) ..	28	8	18	2	18	99	121
Sask. (10-25-1)	28	7	20	1	15	100	141

PLAYOFF RESULTS

SEMIFINALS

Calgary 3, Lethbridge 2
Calgary 5, Lethbridge 1

Manitoba 5, Regina 2
Manitoba 4, Regina 3

FINALS

Calgary 4, Manitoba 3 (OT)
Calgary 7, Manitoba 2

ALL-STAR TEAMS

First team	Pos.	Second team
Jaret Burgoyne, Cal.	G	Craig Lumbard, Regina
Jamie Pegg, Calgary	D	Brad Woods, Manitoba
Vince Boe, Calgary	D	Trevor Sherban, Alberta
Greg Hutchings, Regina	F	Greg Suchan, Calgary
Karry Biette, Manitoba	F	Tracy Katelnikoff, Calgary
Jarret Zukiwsky, Lethbridge	F	Brian Purdy, Sask.

AWARD WINNERS

Most Valuable Player: Jamie Pegg, Calgary
Rookie of the year: Karry Biette, Manitoba
Most gentlemanly player: Dana McKechnie, Lethbridge
Coach of the year: Mike Coflin, Brit. Col.
Leading scorer: Jarret Zukiwsky, Lethbridge

INDIVIDUAL LEADERS

Goals: Jarret Zukiwsky, Lethbridge (31)
Assists: David Stetch, Manitoba (33)
Points: Jarret Zukiwsky, Lethbridge (55)
Penalty minutes: Jarret Zukiwsky, Lethbridge (140)
Goaltending average: Jaret Burgoyne, Calgary (3.25)
Shutouts: Dale Baydock, Manitoba (1)

TOP SCORERS

	Games	G	A	Pts.
Jarret Zukiwsky, Lethbridge	27	31	24	55
Karry Biette, Manitoba......................	28	20	31	51
Greg Hutchings, Regina	28	27	21	48

	Games	G	A	Pts.
Cory Dosdall, Regina	25	14	30	44
Dana McKechnie, Lethbridge	28	14	29	43
David Stetch, Manitoba	28	10	33	43
Jason Krywulak, Calgary	28	19	24	43

	Games	G	A	Pts.
Todd Dutiaume, Manitoba	28	21	21	42
Greg Gatto, Lethbridge	28	16	26	42
Al Patterson, Brandon	28	19	21	40
Brian Purdy, Saskatchewan	27	11	29	40

ONTARIO UNIVERSITIES ATHLETIC ASSOCIATION. 1994-95 SEASON

FINAL STANDINGS

FAR EAST DIVISION

Team	G	W	L	T	Pts.	GF	GA
Que. at Trois-Rivieres .	24	20	1	3	43	150	59
McGill University	24	13	10	1	27	111	88
Concordia University .	24	11	9	4	26	81	89
University of Ottawa ..	24	12	10	2	26	86	71

MID EAST DIVISION

Team	G	W	L	T	Pts.	GF	GA
University of Guelph..	26	16	7	3	35	122	79
University of Toronto .	26	9	10	7	25	82	99
Queen's University	26	3	19	4	10	73	119
Royal Military College	26	0	23	3	3	56	160

MID WEST DIVISION

Team	G	W	L	T	Pts.	GF	GA
Brock University	26	17	8	1	35	123	84
York University	26	12	12	2	26	117	110
Laurentian University	26	8	17	1	17	85	128
Ryerson Poly. Inst.	26	7	19	0	14	71	149

FAR WEST DIVISION

Team	G	W	L	T	Pts.	GF	GA
U. of Western Ontario.	24	16	6	2	34	117	64
Wilfrid Laurier Univ.	24	14	8	2	30	101	73
University of Waterloo.	24	13	9	2	28	97	86
University of Windsor	24	8	11	5	21	79	93

PLAYOFF RESULTS

DIVISIONAL SEMIFINALS

McGill 3, Concordia 1
York 5, Laurentian 3
Toronto 5, Queen's 4 (OT)
Waterloo 6, Laurier 5 (2 OT)

Brock 9, York 0
York 6, Brock 3
York 5, Brock 3
W. Ontario 6, Waterloo 3
W. Ontario 3, Waterloo 1

LEAGUE SEMIFINALS

Guelph 3, Trois-Rivieres 1
Western Ontario 7, York 2

DIVISIONAL FINALS

McGill 2, Trois-Rivieres 1
Trois-Rivieres 6, McGill 3
Trois-Rivieres 6, McGill 5
Guelph 7, Toronto 3
Guelph 3, Toronto 1

LEAGUE FINALS

W. Ontario 5, Guelph 4 (2 OT)

ALL-STAR TEAMS

EAST DIVISION

First team	Pos.	Second team
J.F. Rivard, Ottawa	G	Sylvain Rodrigue, UQTR
Paul O'Hagan, Guelph	D	Dave Anderson, Guelph
Martin Roy, Ottawa	D	Alain Cote, UQTR
Todd Wetzel, Guelph	F	Jamie Coon, Toronto
Yvan Bergeron, UQTR	F	Guy Boucher, McGill
Patrick Genest, UQTR	F	Chris Clancy, Guelph

WEST DIVISION

First team	Pos.	Second team
Sean Basilio, W. Ont.	G	Joe Dimaline, York
Marc Guy, W. Ont.	D	Mark Strohack, Laurier
John Wynne, Waterloo	D	Geoff Schneider, Waterloo
Aaron Nagy, W. Ontario	F	Ben Davis, York
John Spoltore, Laurier	F	Ryan Savoia, Brock
Chris George, Laurier	F	Dave Matsos, W. Ontario

AWARD WINNERS

East Division Most Valuable Player: Todd Wetzel, Guelph
West Division Most Valuable Player: Sean Basilio, W. Ontario
East Division rookie of the year: Sylvain Rodrigue, UQTR
West Division rookie of the year: Ryan Savoia, Brock
East Division most gentlemanly player: Patrick Genest, UQTR
West Division most gentlemanly player: Aaron Nagy, W. Ontario
East Division coach of the year: Danny Dube, UQTR
West Division coaches of the year: Mike Pelino, Brock
         Graham Wise, York

Leading scorer: Yvan Bergeron, UQTR

INDIVIDUAL LEADERS

Goals: Darren Macoretta, Brock (25)
Assists: John Spoltore, Laurier (34)
Points: Yvan Bergeron, UQTR (56)
Penalty minutes: Gabe Batstone, Ryerson (86)
Goaltending average: J.F. Rivard, Ottawa (2.52)

TOP SCORERS

	Games	G	A	Pts.
Yvan Bergeron, Trois-Rivieres	24	23	33	56
Darren Macoretta, Brock	24	25	30	55
Ryan Savoia, Brock	26	23	32	55
John Spoltore, Laurier	24	18	34	52
Todd Wetzel, Guelph	26	19	29	48
Ben Davis, York	26	17	26	43
Todd Zavitz, Brock	24	11	30	41
Darren Dougan, Laurentian	26	17	23	40
Chris Clancy, Guelph	26	12	28	40
Dave Tremblay, Trois-Rivieres	24	15	24	39
Aaron Nagy, W. Ontario	24	14	25	39

INDEX OF TEAMS

NHL, MINOR LEAGUES, MAJOR JUNIOR LEAGUES

COLLEGE TEAMS

HOCKEY REGISTER

Players

NHL head coaches

EXPLANATION OF AWARDS

NHL AWARDS: Alka-Seltzer Plus Award: plus/minus leader. **Art Ross Trophy:** leading scorer. **Bill Masterton Memorial Trophy:** perseverance, sportsmanship and dedication to hockey. **Bud Light/NHL Man of the Year:** service to community; called Budweiser/NHL Man of the Year prior to 1990-91. **Budweiser/NHL Man of the Year:** service to community; renamed Bud Light/NHL Man of the Year in 1990-91. **Calder Memorial Trophy:** rookie of the year. **Conn Smythe Trophy:** most valuable player in playoffs. **Dodge Performance of the Year Award:** most outstanding achievement or single-game performance. **Dodge Performer of the Year Award:** most outstanding performer in regular season. **Dodge Ram Tough Award:** highest combined total of power-play, shorthanded, game-winning and game-tying goals. **Emery Edge Award:** plus/minus leader; awarded from 1982-83 through 1987-88. **Frank J. Selke Trophy:** best defensive forward. **Hart Memorial Trophy:** most valuable player. **Jack Adams Award:** coach of the year. **James Norris Memorial Trophy:** outstanding defenseman. **King Clancy Memorial Trophy:** humanitarian contributions. **Lady Byng Memorial Trophy:** most gentlemanly player. **Lester B. Pearson Award:** outstanding player as selected by NHL Players' Association. **Lester Patrick Trophy:** outstanding service to hockey in U.S. **Trico Goaltender Award:** best save percentage. **Vezina Trophy:** best goaltender; awarded to goalkeeper(s) having played minimum of 25 games for team with fewest goals scored against prior to 1981-82. **William M. Jennings Trophy:** goalkeeper(s) having played minimum of 25 games for team with fewest goals scored against.

MINOR LEAGUE AWARDS: Baz Bastien Trophy: top goaltender (AHL). **Bobby Orr Trophy:** best defenseman (CHL); awarded prior to 1984-85. **Bob Gassoff Award:** most improved defenseman (CHL); awarded prior to 1984-85. **Commissioner's Trophy:** coach of the year (IHL). **Dudley (Red) Garrett Memorial Trophy:** rookie of the year (AHL). **Eddie Shore Plaque:** outstanding defenseman (AHL). **Fred Hunt Memorial Award:** sportsmanship, determination and dedication (AHL). **Garry F. Longman Memorial Trophy:** outstanding rookie (IHL). **Governors Trophy:** outstanding defenseman (IHL). **Harry (Hap) Holmes Memorial Trophy:** goaltender(s) having played minimum of 25 games for team with fewest goals scored against (AHL); awarded to outstanding goaltender prior to 1983-84. **Jack Butterfield Trophy:** Calder Cup playoffs MVP (AHL). **Jake Milford Trophy:** coach of the year (CHL); awarded prior to 1984-85. **James Gatschene Memorial Trophy:** most valuable player (IHL). **James Norris Memorial Trophy:** outstanding goaltender (IHL). **John B. Sollenberger Trophy:** leading scorer (AHL); originally called Wally Kilrea Trophy, later changed to Carl Liscombe Trophy until summer of 1955. **Ken McKenzie Trophy:** outstanding U.S.-born rookie (IHL). **Ken McKenzie Trophy:** top rookie (CHL); awarded to scoring leader from 1992-93. **Leo P. Lamoureux Memorial Trophy:** leading scorer (IHL); originally called George H. Wilkinson Trophy from 1946-47 through 1959-60. **Les Cunningham Plaque:** most valuable player (AHL). **Louis A.R. Pieri Memorial Award:** top coach (AHL). **Max McNab Trophy:** playoff MVP (CHL); awarded prior to 1984-85. **N.R. (Bud) Poile Trophy:** playoff MVP (IHL); originally called Turner Cup Playoff MVP from 1984-85 through 1988-89. **Phil Esposito Trophy:** leading scorer (CHL); awarded prior to 1984-85. **Terry Sawchuk Trophy:** top goaltenders (CHL); awarded prior to 1984-85. **Tommy Ivan Trophy:** most valuable player (CHL); awarded prior to 1984-85. **Turner Cup Playoff MVP:** playoff MVP (IHL); renamed N.R. (Bud) Poile Trophy in 1989-90.

MAJOR JUNIOR LEAGUE AWARDS: Association of Journalists for Major Junior League Hockey Trophy: top pro prospect (QMJHL); renamed Michael Bossy Trophy in 1983-84. **Bill Hunter Trophy:** top defenseman (WHL); called Top Defenseman Trophy prior to 1987-88 season. **Bob Brownridge Memorial Trophy:** top scorer (WHL); later renamed Bob Clarke Trophy. **Bobby Smith Trophy:** scholastic player of the year (OHL). **Bob Clarke Trophy:** top scorer (WHL); originally called Bob Brownridge Memorial Trophy. **Brad Hornung Trophy:** most sportsmanlike player (WHL); called Frank Boucher Memorial Trophy for most gentlemanly player prior to 1987-88 season. **Dave Pinkney Trophy:** team goaltending (OHL). **Del Wilson Trophy:** top goaltender (WHL); called Top Goaltender Trophy prior to 1987-88 season. **Des Instructeurs Trophy:** rookie of the year (QMJHL); awarded to top rookie forward since 1981-82 season; renamed Michel Bergeron Trophy in 1985-86. **Dunc McCallum Memorial Trophy:** coach of the year (WHL). **Eddie Powers Memorial Trophy:** scoring champion (OHL). **Emile (Butch) Bouchard Trophy:** best defenseman (QMJHL). **Emms Family Award:** rookie of the year (OHL). **Four Broncos Memorial Trophy:** most valuable player as selected by coaches (WHL); called Most Valuable Player Trophy prior to 1987-88 season. **Frank Boucher Memorial Trophy:** most gentlemanly player (WHL); renamed Brad Hornung Trophy during 1987-88 season. **Frank J. Selke Trophy:** most gentlemanly player (QMJHL). **F.W. (Dinty) Moore Trophy:** rookie goalie with best goals-against average (OHL). **George Parsons Trophy:** sportsmanship in Memorial Cup (Can.HL). **Guy Lafleur Trophy:** most valuable player during playoffs (QMJHL). **Hap Emms Memorial Trophy:** outstanding goaltender in Memorial Cup (Can.HL). **Jacques Plante Trophy:** best goaltender (QMJHL). **Jean Beliveau Trophy:** leading point scorer (QMJHL). **Jim Mahon Memorial Trophy:** top-scoring right winger (OHL). **Jim Piggott Memorial Trophy:** rookie of the year (WHL); originally called Stewart (Butch) Paul Memorial Trophy. **Leo Lalonde Memorial Trophy:** overage player of the year (OHL). **Marcel Robert Trophy:** top scholastic/athletic performer (QMJHL). **Matt Leyden Trophy:** coach of the year (OHL); awarded to most gentlemanly player prior to 1969-70. **Max Kaminsky Trophy:** outstanding defenseman (OHL). **Michael Bossy Trophy:** top pro prospect (QMJHL); originally called Association of Journalists for Major Junior League Hockey Trophy from 1980-81 through 1982-83. **Michel Bergeron Trophy:** top rookie forward (QMJHL); awarded to rookie of the year prior to 1980-81 season. **Michel Briere Trophy:** most valuable player (QMJHL). **Most Valuable Player Trophy:** most valuable player (WHL); renamed Four Broncos Memorial Trophy during 1987-88 season. **Raymond Lagace Trophy:** top rookie defenseman or goaltender (QMJHL). **Red Tilson Trophy:** outstanding player (OHL). **Shell Cup:** awarded to offensive player of the year and defensive player of the year (QMJHL). **Stafford Smythe Memorial Trophy:** most valuable player of Memorial Cup (Can.HL). **Stewart (Butch) Paul Memorial Trophy:** rookie of the year (WHL); renamed Jim Piggott Memorial Trophy during 1987-88 season. **Top Defenseman Trophy:** top defenseman (WHL); renamed Bill Hunter Trophy during 1987-88 season. **Top Goaltender Trophy:** top goaltender (WHL); renamed Del Wilson Trophy during 1987-88 season. **William Hanley Trophy:** most gentlemanly player (OHL).

COLLEGE AWARDS: Hobey Baker Memorial Award: top college hockey player in U.S. **Senator Joseph A. Sullivan Trophy:** outstanding player in Canadian Interuniversity Athletic Union.

OTHER AWARDS: Golden Puck Award: Sweden's Player of the Year. **Golden Stick Award:** Europe's top player. **Izvestia Trophy:** leading scorer (Soviet Union).

EXPLANATION OF FOOTNOTES AND ABBREVIATIONS

* Led league.
† Tied for league lead.
‡ Overtime loss.
... Statistic unavailable, unofficial or mathematically impossible to calculate.
— Statistic inapplicable.

POSITIONS: C: center. **D:** defenseman. **G:** goaltender. **LW:** left winger. **RW:** right winger.

STATISTICS: A: assists. **Avg.:** goals-against average. **G:** goals. **GA:** goals against. **Gms.:** games. **L:** losses. **Min.:** minutes. **PIM.:** penalties in minutes. **Pts:** points. **SO:** shutouts. **T:** ties. **W:** wins.

LEAGUES: AAHL: All American Hockey League. **ACHL:** Atlantic Coast Hockey League. **AHL:** American Hockey League. **AJHL:** Alberta Junior Hockey League. **AMHL:** Alberta Minor Hockey League. **AUAA:** Atlantic Universities Athletic Association. **BCJHL:** British Columbia Junior Hockey League. **CAHL:** Central Alberta Hockey League. **CAJHL:** Central Alberta Junior Hockey League. **Can. College:** Canadian College. **Can.HL:** Canadian Hockey League. **CCHA:** Central Collegiate Hockey Association. **CHL:** Central Hockey League. **CIS:** Commonwealth of Independent States. **CJHL:** Central Junior A Hockey League. **COJHL:** Central Ontario Junior Hockey League. **CPHL:** Central Professional Hockey League. **CWUAA:** Canada West University Athletic Association. **Conn. H.S.:** Connecticut High School. **Czech.:** Czechoslovakia. **Czech Rep.:** Czechoslovakia Republic. **ECAC:** Eastern College Athletic Conference. **ECAC-II:** Eastern College Athletic Conference, Division II. **ECHL:** East Coast Hockey League. **EHL:** Eastern Hockey League. **EURO:** Euroliga. **Fin.:** Finland. **Ger.:** Germany. **GWHC:** Great Western Hockey Conference. **Hoc. East:** Hockey East. **IHL:** International Hockey League. **Ill. H.S.:** Illinois High School. **Indiana H.S.:** Indiana High School. **Int'l:** International. **KIJHL:** Kootenay International Junior Hockey League. **Mass. H.S.:** Massachusetts High School. **Md. H.S.:** Maryland High School. **Met. Bos.:** Metro Boston. **Mich. H.S.:** Michigan High School. **Minn. H.S.:** Minnesota High School. **MJHL:** Manitoba Junior Hockey League. **MTHL:** Metro Toronto Hockey League. **NAHL:** North American Hockey League. **NAJHL:** North American Junior Hockey League. **N.B. H.S.:** New Brunswick High School. **NCAA-II:** National Collegiate Athletic Association, Division II. **N.D. H.S.:** North Dakota High School. **NEJHL:** New England Junior Hockey League. **NHL:** National Hockey League. **N.H. H.S.:** New Hampshire High School. **N.J. H.S.:** New Jersey High School. **Nia. D. Jr. C:** Niagara District Junior C. **NSJHL:** Nova Scotia Junior Hockey League. **N.S.Jr.A:** Nova Scotia Junior A. **N.Y. H.S.:** New York High School. **NYMJHL:** New York Major Junior Hockey League. **NYOHL:** North York Ontario Hockey League. **ODHA:** Ottawa & District Hockey Association. **OHA:** Ontario Hockey Association. **OHA Jr. A:** Ontario Hockey Association Junior A. **OHA Mjr. Jr. A:** Ontario Hockey Association Major Junior A. **OHA Senior:** Ontario Hockey Association Senior. **OHL:** Ontario Hockey League. **O.H.S.:** Ohio High School. **OJHA:** Ontario Junior Hockey Association. **OJHL:** Ontario Junior Hockey League. **OMJHL:** Ontario Major Junior Hockey League. **OPJHL:** Ontario Provincial Junior Hockey League. **OUAA:** Ontario Universities Athletic Association. **PCJHL:** Peace Caribou Junior Hockey League. **PEIHA:** Prince Edward Island Hockey Association. **PEIJHL:** Prince Edward Island Junior Hockey League. **Penn. H.S.:** Pennsylvania High School. **QMJHL:** Quebec Major Junior Hockey League. **R.I. H.S.:** Rhode Island High School. **SAJHL:** Southern Alberta Junior Hockey League. **SJHL:** Saskatchewan Junior Hockey League. **Sask. H.S.:** Saskatchewan High School. **SOJHL:** Southern Ontario Junior Hockey League. **Swed. Jr.:** Sweden Junior. **Switz.:** Switzerland. **TBAHA:** Thunder Bay Amateur Hockey Association. **TBJHL:** Thunder Bay Junior Hockey League. **USHL:** United States Hockey League. **USHS:** United States High School. **USSR:** Union of Soviet Socialist Republics. **Vt. H.S.:** Vermont High School. **W. Germany, W. Ger.:** West Germany. **WCHA:** Western Collegiate Hockey Association. **WCHL:** Western Canada Hockey League. **WHA:** World Hockey Association. **WHL:** Western Hockey League. **Wisc. H.S.:** Wisconsin High School. **Yukon Sr.:** Yukon Senior.

Included in the Hockey Register are every player who appeared in an NHL game in 1994-95, top prospects, other players listed on NHL rosters and the NHL head coaches.

PLAYERS

AALTO, ANTTI
C, MIGHTY DUCKS

PERSONAL: Born March 4, 1975, in Lappeenranta, Finland. . . . 6-2/185. . . . Shoots left. . . . Name pronounced AN-tee AL-toh.
TRANSACTIONS/CAREER NOTES: Selected by Mighty Ducks of Anaheim in sixth round (sixth Mighty Ducks pick, 134th overall) of NHL entry draft (June 26, 1993).

Season Team	League	REGULAR SEASON					PLAYOFFS				
		Gms.	G	A	Pts.	PIM	Gms.	G	A	Pts.	PIM
91-92—SaiPa Jr.	Finland	19	10	10	20	38	—	—	—	—	—
—SaiPa	Finland	20	6	6	12	20	—	—	—	—	—
92-93—SaiPa	Finland	23	6	8	14	14	—	—	—	—	—
—TPS Jr.	Finland	14	6	8	14	18	—	—	—	—	—
—TPS Turku	Finland	1	0	0	0	0	—	—	—	—	—
93-94—TPS Turku	Finland	33	5	9	14	16	10	1	1	2	4
94-95—TPS Turku	Finland	44	11	7	18	18	5	0	1	1	2

ADAMS, GREG
LW, STARS

PERSONAL: Born August 1, 1963, in Nelson, B.C. . . . 6-3/198. . . . Shoots left. . . . Son-in-law of George Swarbrick, right winger, Oakland Seals, Pittsburgh Penguins and Philadelphia Flyers (1967-68 through 1970-71).
COLLEGE: Northern Arizona.
TRANSACTIONS/CAREER NOTES: Signed as free agent by New Jersey Devils (June 25, 1984). . . . Tore tendon in right wrist (April 1986). . . . Traded by Devils with G Kirk McLean to Vancouver Canucks for C Patrik Sundstrom, fourth-round pick in 1988 draft (LW Matt Ruchty) and the option to flip second-round picks in 1988 draft; Devils exercised option and selected LW Jeff Christian and Canucks selected D Leif Rohlin (September 10, 1987). . . . Fractured ankle (February 1989). . . . Fractured cheekbone (January 4, 1990); missed 12 games. . . . Sprained left knee (October 17, 1990); missed 12 games. . . . Sprained forearm, wrist and abdomen (February 27, 1991). . . . Suffered concussion (October 8, 1991); missed one game. . . . Suffered charley horse (January 16, 1993); missed nine games. . . . Suffered charley horse (February 15, 1993); missed 22 games. . . . Suffered stress fracture in hand requiring minor surgery (December 14, 1993); missed 14 games. . . . Bruised foot (February 22, 1994); missed one game. . . . Traded by Canucks with RW Dan Kesa and fifth-round pick in 1995 draft (traded to Los Angeles) to Dallas Stars for RW Russ Courtnall (April 7, 1995).
HONORS: Played in NHL All-Star Game (1988).
STATISTICAL PLATEAUS: Three-goal games: 1991-92 (1). . . . Four-goal games: 1987-88 (1). . . . Total hat tricks: 2.

Season Team	League	REGULAR SEASON					PLAYOFFS				
		Gms.	G	A	Pts.	PIM	Gms.	G	A	Pts.	PIM
80-81—Kelowna	BCJHL	47	40	50	90	16	—	—	—	—	—
81-82—Kelowna	BCJHL	45	31	42	73	24	—	—	—	—	—
82-83—Northern Arizona Univ.	Indep.	29	14	21	35	46	—	—	—	—	—
83-84—Northern Arizona Univ.	Indep.	47	40	50	90	16	—	—	—	—	—
84-85—Maine	AHL	41	15	20	35	12	11	3	4	7	0
—New Jersey	NHL	36	12	9	21	14	—	—	—	—	—
85-86—New Jersey	NHL	78	35	42	77	30	—	—	—	—	—
86-87—New Jersey	NHL	72	20	27	47	19	—	—	—	—	—
87-88—Vancouver	NHL	80	36	40	76	30	—	—	—	—	—
88-89—Vancouver	NHL	61	19	14	33	24	7	2	3	5	2
89-90—Vancouver	NHL	65	30	20	50	18	—	—	—	—	—
90-91—Vancouver	NHL	55	21	24	45	10	5	0	0	0	2
91-92—Vancouver	NHL	76	30	27	57	26	6	0	2	2	4
92-93—Vancouver	NHL	53	25	31	56	14	12	7	6	13	6
93-94—Vancouver	NHL	68	13	24	37	20	23	6	8	14	2
94-95—Vancouver	NHL	31	5	10	15	12	—	—	—	—	—
—Dallas	NHL	12	3	3	6	4	5	2	0	2	0
NHL totals		687	249	271	520	221	58	17	19	36	16

ADAMS, KEVYN
C, BRUINS

PERSONAL: Born October 8, 1974, in Washington, D.C. . . . 6-1/182. . . . Shoots right.
COLLEGE: Miami of Ohio.
TRANSACTIONS/CAREER NOTES: Selected by Boston Bruins in first round (first Bruins pick, 25th overall) of NHL entry draft (June 26, 1993).
HONORS: Named to CCHA All-Star second team (1994-95).

Season Team	League	REGULAR SEASON					PLAYOFFS				
		Gms.	G	A	Pts.	PIM	Gms.	G	A	Pts.	PIM
90-91—Niagara	NAJHL	55	17	20	37	24	—	—	—	—	—
91-92—Niagara	NAJHL	40	25	33	58	51	—	—	—	—	—
92-93—Miami of Ohio	CCHA	41	17	16	33	18	—	—	—	—	—
93-94—Miami of Ohio	CCHA	36	15	28	43	24	—	—	—	—	—
94-95—Miami of Ohio	CCHA	38	20	29	49	30	—	—	—	—	—

AIVAZOFF, MICAH
C/LW, OILERS

PERSONAL: Born May 4, 1969, in Powell River, B.C. . . . 6-0/185. . . . Shoots left. . . . Name pronounced MIGH-kuh AY-vuh-zahf.
TRANSACTIONS/CAREER NOTES: Selected by Los Angeles Kings in sixth round (sixth Kings pick, 109th overall) of NHL entry draft (June 11, 1988). . . . Signed as free agent by Detroit Red Wings (July 2, 1991). . . . Claimed by Pittsburgh Penguins as compensation for Red Wings claiming RW Doug

Brown in 1994-95 waiver draft (January 18, 1995).... Selected by Edmonton Oilers in 1994-95 waiver draft for cash (January 18, 1995).

			REGULAR SEASON					PLAYOFFS			
Season Team	League	Gms.	G	A	Pts.	PIM	Gms.	G	A	Pts.	PIM
85-86—Victoria	WHL	27	3	4	7	25	—	—	—	—	—
86-87—Victoria	WHL	72	18	39	57	112	5	1	0	1	2
87-88—Victoria	WHL	69	26	57	83	79	8	3	4	7	14
88-89—Victoria	WHL	70	35	65	100	136	8	5	7	12	2
89-90—New Haven	AHL	77	20	39	59	71	—	—	—	—	—
90-91—New Haven	AHL	79	11	29	40	84	—	—	—	—	—
91-92—Adirondack	AHL	61	9	20	29	50	†19	2	8	10	25
92-93—Adirondack	AHL	79	32	53	85	100	11	8	6	14	10
93-94—Detroit	NHL	59	4	4	8	38	—	—	—	—	—
94-95—Edmonton	NHL	21	0	1	1	2	—	—	—	—	—
NHL totals		80	4	5	9	40					

ALBELIN, TOMMY

D, DEVILS

PERSONAL: Born May 21, 1964, in Stockholm, Sweden.... 6-1/190.... Shoots left.... Name pronounced AL-buh-LEEN.
TRANSACTIONS/CAREER NOTES: Selected by Quebec Nordiques in eighth round (seventh Nordiques pick, 152nd overall) of NHL entry draft (June 8, 1983).... Traded by Nordiques to New Jersey Devils for fourth-round pick (LW Niclas Andersson) in 1989 draft (December 12, 1988).... Injured right knee (March 2, 1990); missed four games.... Injured groin (November 21, 1992); missed two games.... Suffered from urinary infection (1993-94 season); missed nine games.
HONORS: Named to Swedish League All-Star team (1986-87).
MISCELLANEOUS: Member of Stanley Cup championship team (1995).

			REGULAR SEASON					PLAYOFFS			
Season Team	League	Gms.	G	A	Pts.	PIM	Gms.	G	A	Pts.	PIM
82-83—Djurgarden Stockholm	Sweden	17	2	5	7	4	6	1	0	1	2
83-84—Djurgarden Stockholm	Sweden	37	9	8	17	36	4	0	1	1	2
84-85—Djurgarden Stockholm	Sweden	32	9	8	17	22	8	2	1	3	4
85-86—Djurgarden Stockholm	Sweden	35	4	8	12	26	—	—	—	—	—
86-87—Djurgarden Stockholm	Sweden	33	7	5	12	49	2	0	0	0	0
87-88—Quebec	NHL	60	3	23	26	47	—	—	—	—	—
88-89—Halifax	AHL	8	2	5	7	4	—	—	—	—	—
—Quebec	NHL	14	2	4	6	27	—	—	—	—	—
—New Jersey	NHL	46	7	24	31	40	—	—	—	—	—
89-90—New Jersey	NHL	68	6	23	29	63	—	—	—	—	—
90-91—Utica	AHL	14	4	2	6	10	—	—	—	—	—
—New Jersey	NHL	47	2	12	14	44	3	0	1	1	2
91-92—New Jersey	NHL	19	0	4	4	4	1	1	1	2	0
—Utica	AHL	11	4	6	10	4	—	—	—	—	—
92-93—New Jersey	NHL	36	1	5	6	14	5	2	0	2	0
93-94—Albany	AHL	4	0	2	2	17	—	—	—	—	—
—New Jersey	NHL	62	2	17	19	36	20	2	5	7	14
94-95—New Jersey	NHL	48	5	10	15	20	20	1	7	8	2
NHL totals		400	28	122	150	295	49	6	14	20	18

ALEXEYEV, ALEXANDER

D, JETS

PERSONAL: Born March 23, 1974, in Kiev, U.S.S.R.... 5-11/198.... Shoots left.... Name pronounced al-ihk-SAY-ehf.
TRANSACTIONS/CAREER NOTES: Selected by Winnipeg Jets in sixth round (fifth Jets pick, 132nd overall) of NHL entry draft (June 20, 1992).
HONORS: Named to WHL (West) All-Star second team (1993-94 and 1994-95).

			REGULAR SEASON					PLAYOFFS			
Season Team	League	Gms.	G	A	Pts.	PIM	Gms.	G	A	Pts.	PIM
90-91—Sokol Kiev	USSR	5	0	0	0	2	—	—	—	—	—
91-92—Sokol Kiev	CIS	25	1	5	6	22	—	—	—	—	—
92-93—Tacoma	WHL	44	3	33	36	67	7	2	7	9	4
93-94—Tacoma	WHL	64	12	48	60	106	8	0	5	5	9
94-95—Tacoma	WHL	54	14	32	46	55	4	0	3	3	4

ALFREDSSON, DANIEL

C/RW, SENATORS

PERSONAL: Born December 11, 1972, in Grums, Sweden.... 5-11/187.... Shoots right.
TRANSACTIONS/CAREER NOTES: Selected by Ottawa Senators in sixth round (fifth Senators pick, 133rd overall) of NHL entry draft (June 29, 1994).

			REGULAR SEASON					PLAYOFFS			
Season Team	League	Gms.	G	A	Pts.	PIM	Gms.	G	A	Pts.	PIM
91-92—Molndal Hockey	Swed. Dv.II	32	12	8	20	43	—	—	—	—	—
92-93—Vastra Frolunda	Sweden	20	1	5	6	8	—	—	—	—	—
93-94—Vastra Frolunda	Sweden	39	20	10	30	18	4	1	1	2	0
94-95—Vastra Frolunda	Sweden	22	7	11	18	22	—	—	—	—	—

ALLAN, CHAD

D, CANUCKS

PERSONAL: Born July 12, 1976, in Davidson, Sask.... 6-1/192.... Shoots left.
HIGH SCHOOL: Marion Graham (Regina, Sask.).
TRANSACTIONS/CAREER NOTES: Selected by Vancouver Canucks in third round (fourth Canucks pick, 65th overall) of NHL entry draft (June 29, 1994).

HONORS: Named to WHL (East) All-Star first team (1994-95).

Season Team	League	REGULAR SEASON Gms.	G	A	Pts.	PIM	PLAYOFFS Gms.	G	A	Pts.	PIM
91-92—Saskatoon	WHL	1	0	0	0	2	—	—	—	—	—
92-93—Saskatoon	WHL	69	2	10	12	67	9	0	0	0	25
93-94—Saskatoon	WHL	70	6	16	22	123	16	1	1	2	21
94-95—Saskatoon	WHL	63	14	29	43	95	9	0	3	3	2

ALLAN, SANDY
G, KINGS

PERSONAL: Born January 22, 1974, in Nassau, Bahamas. . . . 6-0/175. . . . Catches left.
HIGH SCHOOL: Chippewa Secondary School (North Bay, Ont.).
TRANSACTIONS/CAREER NOTES: Selected by Los Angeles Kings in third round (second Kings pick, 63rd overall) of NHL entry draft (June 20, 1992).
HONORS: Won F.W. (Dinty) Moore Trophy (1991-92). . . . Shared Dave Pinkney Trophy with Scott Roche (1993-94).

Season Team	League	REGULAR SEASON Gms.	Min.	W	L	T	GA	SO	Avg.	PLAYOFFS Gms.	Min.	W	L	GA	SO	Avg.
91-92—North Bay	OHL	34	1747	18	5	4	112	0	3.85	3	18	0	2	0	6.67
92-93—North Bay	OHL	39	1835	8	19	4	133	0	4.35	4	180	0	3	10	0	3.33
93-94—North Bay	OHL	45	2404	*31	†10	1	131	1	*3.27	*17	*912	†10	5	57	0	3.75
94-95—Prince Albert	WHL	35	1947	19	11	2	112	1	3.45	15	904	11	4	49	0	3.25

ALLISON, JAMIE
D, FLAMES

PERSONAL: Born May 13, 1975, in Lindsay, Ont. . . . 6-1/190. . . . Shoots left.
TRANSACTIONS/CAREER NOTES: Selected by Calgary Flames in second round (second Flames pick, 44th overall) of NHL entry draft (June 26, 1993).

Season Team	League	REGULAR SEASON Gms.	G	A	Pts.	PIM	PLAYOFFS Gms.	G	A	Pts.	PIM
90-91—Waterloo Jr. B	OHA	45	3	8	11	91	—	—	—	—	—
91-92—Windsor	OHL	59	4	8	12	52	4	1	1	2	2
92-93—Detroit	OHL	61	0	13	13	64	15	2	5	7	23
93-94—Detroit	OHL	40	2	22	24	69	17	2	9	11	35
94-95—Detroit	OHL	50	1	14	15	119	18	2	7	9	35
—Calgary	NHL	1	0	0	0	0	—	—	—	—	—
NHL totals		1	0	0	0	0					

ALLISON, JASON
C, CAPITALS

PERSONAL: Born May 29, 1975, in Toronto. . . . 6-3/205. . . . Shoots right.
TRANSACTIONS/CAREER NOTES: Selected by Washington Capitals in first round (second Capitals pick, 17th overall) of NHL entry draft (June 26, 1993).
HONORS: Won Can.HL Player of the Year Award (1993-94). . . . Won Can.HL Top Scorer Award (1993-94). . . . Won Red Tilson Trophy (1993-94). . . . Won William Hanley Trophy (1993-94). . . . Won Eddie Powers Memorial Trophy (1993-94). . . . Named to Can.HL All-Star first team (1993-94). . . . Named to OHL All-Star first team (1993-94).

Season Team	League	REGULAR SEASON Gms.	G	A	Pts.	PIM	PLAYOFFS Gms.	G	A	Pts.	PIM
91-92—London	OHL	65	11	18	29	15	7	0	0	0	0
92-93—London	OHL	66	42	76	118	50	12	7	13	20	8
93-94—London	OHL	56	55	87	*142	68	5	2	13	15	13
—Washington	NHL	2	0	1	1	0	—	—	—	—	—
—Portland	AHL	6	2	1	3	0	—	—	—	—	—
94-95—London	OHL	15	15	21	36	43	—	—	—	—	—
—Washington	NHL	12	2	1	3	6	—	—	—	—	—
—Portland	AHL	8	5	4	9	2	7	3	8	11	2
NHL totals		14	2	2	4	6					

ALVEY, MATT
C, BRUINS

PERSONAL: Born May 15, 1975, in Troy, N.Y. . . . 6-2/210. . . . Shoots right.
TRANSACTIONS/CAREER NOTES: Selected by Boston Bruins in second round (second Bruins pick, 51st overall) of NHL entry draft (June 26, 1993).

Season Team	League	REGULAR SEASON Gms.	G	A	Pts.	PIM	PLAYOFFS Gms.	G	A	Pts.	PIM
90-91—Springfield Jr. B	NEJHL	. . .	12	20	32	. . .	—	—	—	—	—
91-92—Springfield Jr. B	NEJHL	32	22	35	57	34	—	—	—	—	—
92-93—Springfield Jr. B	NEJHL	38	22	37	59	85	—	—	—	—	—
93-94—Lake Superior State	CCHA	41	6	8	14	16	—	—	—	—	—
94-95—Lake Superior State	CCHA	25	4	7	11	32	—	—	—	—	—

AMBROSIO, JEFF
LW, BLUES

PERSONAL: Born April 26, 1977, in Toronto. . . . 6-1/190. . . . Shoots left.
HIGH SCHOOL: Quinte Secondary School (Belleville, Ont.).
TRANSACTIONS/CAREER NOTES: Selected by St. Louis Blues in fifth round (fourth Blues pick, 127th overall) of NHL entry draft (July 8, 1995).

Season Team	League	REGULAR SEASON Gms.	G	A	Pts.	PIM	PLAYOFFS Gms.	G	A	Pts.	PIM
92-93—Bramalea	MTHL	2	0	1	1	0	—	—	—	—	—
93-94—Belleville	OHL	59	13	17	30	18	11	1	0	1	6
94-95—Belleville	OHL	47	10	10	20	10	16	1	7	8	8

AMBROZIAK, PETER
LW, SABRES

PERSONAL: Born September 15, 1971, in Toronto. . . . 6-0/191. . . . Shoots left. . . . Name pronounced am-BROH-zee-ak.
TRANSACTIONS/CAREER NOTES: Selected by Buffalo Sabres in fourth round (fourth Sabres pick, 72nd overall) of NHL entry draft (June 22, 1991). . . . Suffered concussion (March 30, 1995); missed one game.

			REGULAR SEASON					PLAYOFFS				
Season	Team	League	Gms.	G	A	Pts.	PIM	Gms.	G	A	Pts.	PIM
88-89—Ottawa		OHL	50	8	15	23	11	12	1	2	3	2
89-90—Ottawa		OHL	60	13	19	32	37	4	0	0	0	2
90-91—Ottawa		OHL	62	30	32	62	56	17	15	9	24	24
91-92—Rochester		AHL	2	0	1	1	0	—	—	—	—	—
—Ottawa		OHL	49	32	49	81	50	11	3	7	10	33
92-93—Rochester		AHL	50	8	10	18	37	12	4	3	7	16
93-94—Rochester		AHL	22	3	4	7	53	—	—	—	—	—
94-95—Rochester		AHL	46	14	11	25	35	4	0	0	0	6
—Buffalo		NHL	12	0	1	1	0	—	—	—	—	—
NHL totals			**12**	**0**	**1**	**1**	**0**					

AMONTE, TONY
RW, BLACKHAWKS

PERSONAL: Born August 2, 1970, in Weymouth, Mass. . . . 6-0/186. . . . Shoots left. . . . Full name: Anthony Lewis Amonte. . . . Name pronounced ah-MAHN-tee.
HIGH SCHOOL: Thayer Academy (Braintree, Mass.).
COLLEGE: Boston University.
TRANSACTIONS/CAREER NOTES: Selected by New York Rangers in fourth round (third Rangers pick, 68th overall) of NHL entry draft (June 11, 1988). . . . Separated shoulder (December 29, 1990). . . . Traded by Rangers with rights to LW Matt Oates to Chicago Blackhawks for LW Stephane Matteau and RW Brian Noonan (March 21, 1994). . . . Pulled groin (1993-94 season); missed three games. . . . Played in Europe during 1994-95 NHL lockout.
HONORS: Named to Hockey East All-Rookie team (1989-90). . . . Named to NCAA All-Tournament team (1990-91). . . . Named to Hockey East All-Star second team (1990-91). . . . Named NHL Rookie of the Year by THE SPORTING NEWS (1991-92). . . . Named to NHL All-Rookie team (1991-92).
STATISTICAL PLATEAUS: Three-goal games: 1991-92 (1).

			REGULAR SEASON					PLAYOFFS				
Season	Team	League	Gms.	G	A	Pts.	PIM	Gms.	G	A	Pts.	PIM
86-87—Thayer Academy		Mass. H.S.	25	25	32	57	. . .	—	—	—	—	—
87-88—Thayer Academy		Mass. H.S.	28	30	38	68	. . .	—	—	—	—	—
88-89—Team USA Juniors		Int'l	7	1	3	4	. . .	—	—	—	—	—
89-90—Boston University		Hockey East	41	25	33	58	52	—	—	—	—	—
90-91—Boston University		Hockey East	38	31	37	68	82	—	—	—	—	—
—New York Rangers		NHL	—	—	—	—	—	2	0	2	2	2
91-92—New York Rangers		NHL	79	35	34	69	55	13	3	6	9	2
92-93—New York Rangers		NHL	83	33	43	76	49	—	—	—	—	—
93-94—New York Rangers		NHL	72	16	22	38	31	—	—	—	—	—
—Chicago		NHL	7	1	3	4	6	6	4	2	6	4
94-95—Fassa		Italy	14	22	16	38	10	—	—	—	—	—
—Chicago		NHL	48	15	20	35	41	16	3	3	6	10
NHL totals			**289**	**100**	**122**	**222**	**182**	**37**	**10**	**13**	**23**	**18**

ANDERSON, GLENN
RW

PERSONAL: Born October 2, 1960, in Vancouver. . . . 6-1/190. . . . Shoots left. . . . Full name: Glenn Chris Anderson.
COLLEGE: Denver.
TRANSACTIONS/CAREER NOTES: Selected by Edmonton Oilers in fourth round (third Oilers pick, 69th overall) of NHL entry draft (August 9, 1979). . . . Underwent knee surgery to remove bone chips (November 1980). . . . Underwent nose surgery to correct breathing problem (spring 1982). . . . Suspended eight games by NHL for fighting (December 13, 1985). . . . Pulled side muscle (November 1988). . . . Fined $500 for deliberately breaking the cheekbone of RW Tomas Sandstrom (February 28, 1990). . . . Missed first four games of 1990-91 season due to contract dispute (October 1990). . . . Injured thigh (March 5, 1991); missed two games. . . . Traded by Oilers with G Grant Fuhr and LW Craig Berube to Toronto Maple Leafs for LW Vincent Damphousse, D Luke Richardson, G Peter Ing, C Scott Thornton and future considerations (September 19, 1991). . . . Sprained knee (December 3, 1992); missed four games. . . . Injured knee (February 3, 1993); missed one game. . . . Traded by Maple Leafs with rights to D Scott Malone and fourth-round pick in 1994 draft (D Alexander Korobolin) to New York Rangers for RW Mike Gartner (March 21, 1994). . . . Played in Europe during 1994-95 NHL lockout. . . . Signed as free agent by St. Louis Blues (February 4, 1995). . . . Suspended one playoff game and fined $1,000 by NHL for high-sticking (May 19, 1995).
HONORS: Played in NHL All-Star Game (1984-1986 and 1988).
RECORDS: Shares NHL single-game playoff record for most points in one period—4 (April 6, 1988).
STATISTICAL PLATEAUS: Three-goal games: 1980-81 (2), 1981-82 (1), 1982-83 (2), 1983-84 (2), 1984-85 (3), 1985-86 (4), 1987-88 (2), 1989-90 (1), 1991-92 (1). Total: 18. . . . Four-goal games: 1983-84 (1), 1987-88 (1), 1988-89 (1). Total: 3. . . . Total hat tricks: 21.
MISCELLANEOUS: Member of Stanley Cup championship teams (1984, 1985, 1987, 1988, 1990 and 1994).

			REGULAR SEASON					PLAYOFFS				
Season	Team	League	Gms.	G	A	Pts.	PIM	Gms.	G	A	Pts.	PIM
77-78—Bellingham Jr. A		BCJHL	58	61	64	125	96	—	—	—	—	—
—New Westminster		WCHL	1	0	1	1	2	—	—	—	—	—
78-79—Seattle		WHL	2	0	1	1	0	—	—	—	—	—
—University of Denver		WCHA	40	26	29	55	58	—	—	—	—	—
79-80—Canadian Olympic Team		Int'l	49	21	21	42	46	—	—	—	—	—
—Seattle		WHL	7	5	5	10	4	—	—	—	—	—

Season Team	League	REGULAR SEASON					PLAYOFFS				
		Gms.	G	A	Pts.	PIM	Gms.	G	A	Pts.	PIM
80-81—Edmonton	NHL	58	30	23	53	24	9	5	7	12	12
81-82—Edmonton	NHL	80	38	67	105	71	5	2	5	7	8
82-83—Edmonton	NHL	72	48	56	104	70	16	10	10	20	32
83-84—Edmonton	NHL	80	54	45	99	65	19	6	11	17	33
84-85—Edmonton	NHL	80	42	39	81	69	18	10	16	26	38
85-86—Edmonton	NHL	72	54	48	102	90	10	8	3	11	14
86-87—Edmonton	NHL	80	35	38	73	65	21	14	13	27	59
87-88—Edmonton	NHL	80	38	50	88	58	19	9	16	25	49
88-89—Edmonton	NHL	79	16	48	64	93	7	1	2	3	8
89-90—Edmonton	NHL	73	34	38	72	107	22	10	12	22	20
90-91—Edmonton	NHL	74	24	31	55	59	18	6	7	13	41
91-92—Toronto	NHL	72	24	33	57	100	—	—	—	—	—
92-93—Toronto	NHL	76	22	43	65	117	21	7	11	18	31
93-94—Toronto	NHL	73	17	18	35	50	—	—	—	—	—
—New York Rangers	NHL	12	4	2	6	12	23	3	3	6	42
94-95—Augsburg	Ger. Div. II	5	6	2	8	10	—	—	—	—	—
—Lukko	Finland	4	1	1	2	0	—	—	—	—	—
—St. Louis	NHL	36	12	14	26	37	6	1	1	2	*49
NHL totals		1097	492	593	1085	1087	214	92	117	209	436

ANDERSON, SHAWN

D/LW, FLYERS

PERSONAL: Born February 7, 1968, in Montreal. . . . 6-1/200. . . . Shoots left. **COLLEGE:** Maine.

TRANSACTIONS/CAREER NOTES: Selected by Buffalo Sabres as underage player in first round (first Sabres pick, fifth overall) of NHL entry draft (June 21, 1986). . . . Sprained knee (October 1986). . . . Separated shoulder (March 3, 1987). . . . Reseparated shoulder (March 28, 1987). . . . Injured ankle (October 1987). . . . Injured ankle (December 1987). . . . Bruised knee (February 1988). . . . Traded by Sabres to Washington Capitals for D Bill Houlder (September 30, 1990). . . . Claimed by Quebec Nordiques in 1990 NHL waiver draft for $60,000 waiver price (October 2, 1990). . . . Traded by Nordiques to Winnipeg Jets for RW Sergei Kharin (October 22, 1991). . . . Traded by Jets to Capitals for future considerations (October 23, 1991). . . . Suffered back spasms (February 20, 1993); missed six games. . . . Bruised hand (November 24, 1993); missed seven games. . . . Pulled abdominal muscle (March 29, 1994); missed three games. . . . Bruised ankle (April 12, 1994); missed one game. . . . Signed as free agent by Philadelphia Flyers (August 16, 1994).

Season Team	League	REGULAR SEASON					PLAYOFFS				
		Gms.	G	A	Pts.	PIM	Gms.	G	A	Pts.	PIM
85-86—University of Maine	Hockey East	16	5	8	13	22	—	—	—	—	—
—Canadian national team	Int'l	49	4	14	18	38	—	—	—	—	—
86-87—Rochester	AHL	15	2	5	7	11	—	—	—	—	—
—Buffalo	NHL	41	2	11	13	23	—	—	—	—	—
87-88—Buffalo	NHL	23	1	2	3	17	—	—	—	—	—
—Rochester	AHL	22	5	16	21	19	6	0	0	0	0
88-89—Rochester	AHL	31	5	14	19	24	—	—	—	—	—
—Buffalo	NHL	33	2	10	12	14	5	0	1	1	4
89-90—Rochester	AHL	39	2	16	18	41	9	1	0	1	8
—Buffalo	NHL	16	1	3	4	8	—	—	—	—	—
90-91—Quebec	NHL	31	3	10	13	21	—	—	—	—	—
—Halifax	AHL	4	0	1	1	2	—	—	—	—	—
91-92—PEV Weiswasser	Germany	38	7	15	22	83	—	—	—	—	—
92-93—Baltimore	AHL	10	1	5	6	8	—	—	—	—	—
—Washington	NHL	60	2	6	8	18	6	0	0	0	0
93-94—Washington	NHL	50	0	9	9	12	8	1	0	1	12
94-95—Hershey	AHL	31	9	21	30	18	6	2	3	5	19
—Philadelphia	NHL	1	0	0	0	0	—	—	—	—	—
NHL totals		255	11	51	62	117	19	1	1	2	16

ANDERSSON, MIKAEL

RW, LIGHTNING

PERSONAL: Born May 10, 1966, in Malmo, Sweden. . . . 5-11/185. . . . Shoots left. . . . Full name: Bo Mikael Andersson. . . . Name pronounced mih-KEHL AN-duhr-suhn.

TRANSACTIONS/CAREER NOTES: Selected by Buffalo Sabres in first round (first Sabres pick, 18th overall) of NHL entry draft (June 9, 1984). . . . Sprained ankle (March 1988). . . . Twisted ankle (March 1988). . . . Sprained neck and shoulder (December 1988). . . . Selected by Hartford Whalers in 1989 NHL waiver draft (October 2, 1989). . . . Bruised left knee (December 13, 1989). . . . Reinjured knee (February 9, 1990). . . . Pulled right hamstring (March 8, 1990). . . . Reinjured hamstring (March 17, 1990). . . . Reinjured hamstring (April 1990). . . . Underwent surgery to left knee (May 14, 1990). . . . Suffered from the flu (October 4, 1990); missed two games. . . . Pulled groin (January 1991). . . . Injured toe (October 26, 1991); missed one game. . . . Injured groin (December 17, 1991); missed three games. . . . Suffered chip fracture to foot (April 12, 1992). . . . Signed as free agent by Tampa Bay Lightning (July 8, 1992). . . . Suffered back spasms (November 21, 1992); missed four games. . . . Injured left rotator cuff (October 27, 1993); missed three games. . . . Played in Europe during 1994-95 NHL lockout. . . . Injured groin (March 4, 1995); missed four games. . . . Sprained ankle (April 8, 1995); missed six games.

STATISTICAL PLATEAUS: Three-goal games: 1992-93 (1).

Season	Team	League	REGULAR SEASON Gms.	G	A	Pts.	PIM	PLAYOFFS Gms.	G	A	Pts.	PIM
82-83—Vastra Frolunda	Sweden	1	1	0	1	...	—	—	—	—	—	
83-84—Vastra Frolunda	Sweden	12	0	2	2	6	—	—	—	—	—	
84-85—Vastra Frolunda	Sweden	32	16	11	27	18	6	3	2	5	2	
85-86—Rochester	AHL	20	10	4	14	6	—	—	—	—	—	
—Buffalo	NHL	32	1	9	10	4	—	—	—	—	—	
86-87—Rochester	AHL	42	6	20	26	14	9	1	2	3	2	
—Buffalo	NHL	16	0	3	3	0	—	—	—	—	—	
87-88—Rochester	AHL	35	12	24	36	16	—	—	—	—	—	
—Buffalo	NHL	37	3	20	23	10	1	1	0	1	0	
88-89—Buffalo	NHL	14	0	1	1	4	—	—	—	—	—	
—Rochester	AHL	56	18	33	51	12	—	—	—	—	—	
89-90—Hartford	NHL	50	13	24	37	6	5	0	3	3	2	
90-91—Hartford	NHL	41	4	7	11	8	—	—	—	—	—	
—Springfield	AHL	26	7	22	29	10	18	†10	8	18	12	
91-92—Hartford	NHL	74	18	29	47	14	7	0	2	2	6	
92-93—Tampa Bay	NHL	77	16	11	27	14	—	—	—	—	—	
93-94—Tampa Bay	NHL	76	13	12	25	23	—	—	—	—	—	
94-95—Vastra Frolunda	Sweden	7	1	0	1	31	—	—	—	—	—	
—Tampa Bay	NHL	36	4	7	11	4	—	—	—	—	—	
NHL totals		453	72	123	195	87	13	1	5	6	8	

ANDERSSON, NICLAS
LW, ISLANDERS

PERSONAL: Born May 20, 1971, in Kunglav, Sweden. . . . 5-9/175. . . . Shoots left.

TRANSACTIONS/CAREER NOTES: Selected by Quebec Nordiques in third round (fifth Nordiques pick, 68th overall) of NHL entry draft (June 17, 1989). . . . Signed as free agent by New York Islanders (July 15, 1994).

Season	Team	League	REGULAR SEASON Gms.	G	A	Pts.	PIM	PLAYOFFS Gms.	G	A	Pts.	PIM
87-88—Frolunda	Sweden	15	5	5	10	...	—	—	—	—	—	
88-89—Frolunda	Sweden	30	13	24	37	...	—	—	—	—	—	
89-90—Frolunda	Sweden	38	10	21	31	14	—	—	—	—	—	
90-91—Frolunda	Sweden	22	6	10	16	16	—	—	—	—	—	
91-92—Halifax	AHL	57	8	26	34	41	—	—	—	—	—	
92-93—Halifax	AHL	76	32	50	82	42	—	—	—	—	—	
—Quebec	NHL	3	0	1	1	2	—	—	—	—	—	
93-94—Cornwall	AHL	42	18	34	52	8	—	—	—	—	—	
94-95—Denver	IHL	66	22	39	61	28	15	8	13	21	10	
NHL totals		3	0	1	1	2						

ANDERSSON-JUNKKA, JONAS
D, PENGUINS

PERSONAL: Born May 4, 1975, in Kiruna, Sweden. . . . 6-2/165. . . . Shoots right.

TRANSACTIONS/CAREER NOTES: Selected by Pittsburgh Penguins in fourth round (fourth Penguins pick, 104th overall) of NHL entry draft (June 26, 1993).

Season	Team	League	REGULAR SEASON Gms.	G	A	Pts.	PIM	PLAYOFFS Gms.	G	A	Pts.	PIM
91-92—Kiruna	Swed. Dv.II	1	0	0	0	0	—	—	—	—	—	
92-93—Kiruna	Swed. Dv.II	30	3	7	10	32	—	—	—	—	—	
93-94—Kiruna	Swed. Dv.II	32	6	10	16	84	—	—	—	—	—	
94-95—Vastra Frolunda	Sweden	19	0	2	2	2	—	—	—	—	—	

ANDREYCHUK, DAVE
LW, MAPLE LEAFS

PERSONAL: Born September 29, 1963, in Hamilton, Ont. . . . 6-3/220. . . . Shoots right. . . . Name pronounced AN-druh-chuhk.

TRANSACTIONS/CAREER NOTES: Selected by Buffalo Sabres as underage junior in first round (third Sabres pick, 16th overall) of NHL entry draft (June 9, 1982). . . . Sprained knee (March 1983). . . . Fractured collarbone (March 1985). . . . Twisted knee (September 1985). . . . Injured right knee (September 1986). . . . Strained medial collateral ligaments in left knee (November 27, 1988). . . . Broke left thumb (February 18, 1990). . . . Suspended two off-days and fined $500 by NHL for cross-checking (November 16, 1992). . . . Traded by Sabres with G Daren Puppa and first-round pick in 1993 draft (D Kenny Jonsson) to Toronto Maple Leafs for G Grant Fuhr and fifth-round pick (D Kevin Popp) in 1995 draft (February 2, 1993). . . . Injured knee (December 27, 1993); missed one game.

HONORS: Played in NHL All-Star Game (1990 and 1994). . . . Named to THE SPORTING NEWS All-Star second team (1993-94).

STATISTICAL PLATEAUS: Three-goal games: 1987-88 (3), 1988-89 (1), 1989-90 (1), 1991-92 (1), 1992-93 (1). Total: 7. . . . Four-goal games: 1991-92 (1), 1992-93 (1). Total: 2. . . . Five-goal games: 1985-86 (1). . . . Total hat tricks: 10.

MISCELLANEOUS: Played with Team Canada in World Junior Championships (1982-83).

STATISTICAL NOTES: Led NHL with 32 power-play goals in 1992-93.

Season	Team	League	REGULAR SEASON Gms.	G	A	Pts.	PIM	PLAYOFFS Gms.	G	A	Pts.	PIM
80-81—Oshawa	OMJHL	67	22	22	44	80	10	3	2	5	20	
81-82—Oshawa	OHL	67	58	43	101	71	3	1	4	5	16	
82-83—Oshawa	OHL	14	8	24	32	6	—	—	—	—	—	
—Buffalo	NHL	43	14	23	37	16	4	1	0	1	4	

		REGULAR SEASON					PLAYOFFS			
Season Team	League	Gms.	G	A	Pts.	PIM	Gms.	G	A	Pts.	PIM
83-84—Buffalo	NHL	78	38	42	80	42	2	0	1	1	2
84-85—Buffalo	NHL	64	31	30	61	54	5	4	2	6	4
85-86—Buffalo	NHL	80	36	51	87	61	—	—	—	—	—
86-87—Buffalo	NHL	77	25	48	73	46	—	—	—	—	—
87-88—Buffalo	NHL	80	30	48	78	112	6	2	4	6	0
88-89—Buffalo	NHL	56	28	24	52	40	5	0	3	3	0
89-90—Buffalo	NHL	73	40	42	82	42	6	2	5	7	2
90-91—Buffalo	NHL	80	36	33	69	32	6	2	2	4	8
91-92—Buffalo	NHL	80	41	50	91	71	7	1	3	4	12
92-93—Buffalo	NHL	52	29	32	61	48	—	—	—	—	—
—Toronto	NHL	31	25	13	38	8	21	12	7	19	35
93-94—Toronto	NHL	83	53	46	99	98	18	5	5	10	16
94-95—Toronto	NHL	48	22	16	38	34	7	3	2	5	25
NHL totals		925	448	498	946	704	87	32	34	66	108

ANDRUSAK, GREG
D, PENGUINS

PERSONAL: Born November 14, 1969, in Cranbrook, B.C.... 6-1/185.... Shoots right. ... Full name: Greg Frederick Andrusak.... Name pronounced AN-druh-sak.
COLLEGE: Minnesota-Duluth.
TRANSACTIONS/CAREER NOTES: Selected by Pittsburgh Penguins in fifth round (fifth Penguins pick, 88th overall) of NHL entry draft (June 11, 1988).... Loaned by Penguins to Detroit Vipers (November 16, 1994).... Returned to Penguins (March 3, 1995).... Separated shoulder (March 15, 1995); missed eight games.
HONORS: Named to WCHA All-Star first team (1991-92).

		REGULAR SEASON					PLAYOFFS			
Season Team	League	Gms.	G	A	Pts.	PIM	Gms.	G	A	Pts.	PIM
86-87—Kelowna	BCJHL	45	10	24	34	95	—	—	—	—	—
87-88—Minnesota-Duluth	WCHA	37	4	5	9	42	—	—	—	—	—
88-89—Minnesota-Duluth	WCHA	35	4	8	12	74	—	—	—	—	—
—Canadian national team	Int'l	2	0	0	0	0	—	—	—	—	—
89-90—Minnesota-Duluth	WCHA	35	5	29	34	74	—	—	—	—	—
90-91—Canadian national team	Int'l	53	4	11	15	34	—	—	—	—	—
91-92—Minnesota-Duluth	WCHA	36	7	27	34	125	—	—	—	—	—
92-93—Cleveland	IHL	55	3	22	25	78	2	0	0	0	2
—Muskegon	Col.HL	2	0	3	3	7	—	—	—	—	—
93-94—Cleveland	IHL	69	13	26	39	109	—	—	—	—	—
—Pittsburgh	NHL	3	0	0	0	2	—	—	—	—	—
94-95—Cleveland	IHL	8	0	8	8	14	—	—	—	—	—
—Detroit	IHL	37	5	26	31	50	—	—	—	—	—
—Pittsburgh	NHL	7	0	4	4	6	—	—	—	—	—
NHL totals		10	0	4	4	8					

ANGER, NIKLAS
RW, CANADIENS

PERSONAL: Born July 14, 1977, in Gavle, Sweden.... 6-1/185.... Shoots left.
TRANSACTIONS/CAREER NOTES: Selected by Montreal Canadiens in fifth round (fifth Canadiens pick, 112th overall) of NHL entry draft (July 8, 1995).

		REGULAR SEASON					PLAYOFFS			
Season Team	League	Gms.	G	A	Pts.	PIM	Gms.	G	A	Pts.	PIM
93-94—Djurgarden Jr. B	Sweden	31	30	31	61	...	—	—	—	—	—
94-95—Djurgarden Jrs.	Sweden	30	14	12	26	26	—	—	—	—	—
—Djurgarden Stockholm	Sweden	1	0	0	0	0	—	—	—	—	—

ANISIMOV, ARTEM
D, FLYERS

PERSONAL: Born July 27, 1976, in Kazan, U.S.S.R.... 6-1/187.... Shoots left.
TRANSACTIONS/CAREER NOTES: Selected by Philadelphia Flyers in third round (first Flyers pick, 62nd overall) of NHL entry draft (June 29, 1994).

		REGULAR SEASON					PLAYOFFS			
Season Team	League	Gms.	G	A	Pts.	PIM	Gms.	G	A	Pts.	PIM
93-94—Itil Kazan	CIS	38	0	1	1	12	5	0	0	0	0
94-95—Itil Kazan	CIS	46	3	2	5	55	1	0	0	0	0

ANNECK, DORIAN
C, JETS

PERSONAL: Born April 24, 1976, in Winnipeg.... 6-1/183.... Shoots left.... Name pronounced AN-ihk.
TRANSACTIONS/CAREER NOTES: Selected by Winnipeg Jets in third round (second Jets pick, 56th overall) of NHL entry draft (June 29, 1994).

		REGULAR SEASON					PLAYOFFS			
Season Team	League	Gms.	G	A	Pts.	PIM	Gms.	G	A	Pts.	PIM
92-93—Victoria	WHL	63	5	6	11	19	—	—	—	—	—
93-94—Victoria	WHL	71	26	53	79	30	—	—	—	—	—
94-95—Prince George	WHL	47	18	38	56	12	—	—	—	—	—
—Tri-City	WHL	3	0	0	0	0	—	—	—	—	—

ANTOSKI, SHAWN
LW/RW, FLYERS

PERSONAL: Born May 25, 1970, in Brantford, Ont.... 6-4/235.... Shoots left.... Name pronounced an-TAH-skee.
TRANSACTIONS/CAREER NOTES: Injured knee ligament (December 1988).... Separated shoulder (March 1989).... Selected by Vancouver Canucks in first round (second

Canucks pick, 18th overall) of NHL entry draft (June 17, 1989). . . . Suffered sore back (December 1991). . . . Fractured knuckle (December 15, 1993); missed eight games. . . . Sprained thumb (January 19, 1994); missed three games. . . . Suffered sore hand (April 1, 1994); missed three games. . . . Traded by Canucks to Philadelphia Flyers for LW Josef Beranek (February 15, 1995). . . . Suffered from the flu (March 2, 1995); missed four games.

			REGULAR SEASON					PLAYOFFS				
Season	Team	League	Gms.	G	A	Pts.	PIM	Gms.	G	A	Pts.	PIM
87-88	—North Bay	OHL	52	3	4	7	163	—	—	—	—	—
88-89	—North Bay	OHL	57	6	21	27	201	9	5	3	8	24
89-90	—North Bay	OHL	59	25	31	56	201	5	1	2	3	17
90-91	—Milwaukee	IHL	62	17	7	24	330	5	1	2	3	10
	—Vancouver	NHL	2	0	0	0	0	—	—	—	—	—
91-92	—Milwaukee	IHL	52	17	16	33	346	5	2	0	2	20
	—Vancouver	NHL	4	0	0	0	29	—	—	—	—	—
92-93	—Hamilton	AHL	41	3	4	7	172	—	—	—	—	—
	—Vancouver	NHL	2	0	0	0	0	—	—	—	—	—
93-94	—Vancouver	NHL	55	1	2	3	190	16	0	1	1	36
94-95	—Vancouver	NHL	7	0	0	0	46	—	—	—	—	—
	—Philadelphia	NHL	25	0	0	0	61	13	0	1	1	10
	NHL totals		95	1	2	3	326	29	0	2	2	46

APPEL, FRANK
D, FLAMES

PERSONAL: Born May 12, 1976, in Dusseldorf, West Germany. . . . 6-4/207. . . . Shoots left.
TRANSACTIONS/CAREER NOTES: Selected by Calgary Flames in fifth round (seventh Flames pick, 123rd overall) of NHL entry draft (June 14, 1994).

			REGULAR SEASON					PLAYOFFS				
Season	Team	League	Gms.	G	A	Pts.	PIM	Gms.	G	A	Pts.	PIM
93-94	—Dusseldorf	Germany	4	0	0	0	4	—	—	—	—	—
94-95	—Eisbaren Berlin	Germany	12	0	0	0	4	—	—	—	—	—

ARCHIBALD, DAVE
C/LW, SENATORS

PERSONAL: Born April 14, 1969, in Chilliwack, B.C. . . . 6-1/211. . . . Shoots left. . . . Full name: David John Archibald.
TRANSACTIONS/CAREER NOTES: Underwent shoulder surgery (January 1984). . . . Lacerated hand (October 1986). . . . Selected as underage junior by Minnesota North Stars in first round (first North Stars pick, sixth overall) of NHL entry draft (June 13, 1987). . . . Injured shoulder (September 1987). . . . Suffered sore back (February 1989). . . . Traded by North Stars to New York Rangers for D Jayson More (November 1, 1989). . . . Traded by Rangers to Ottawa Senators for fifth-round pick (traded to Los Angeles Kings who selected G Frederick Beaubien) in 1993 draft (November 6, 1992). . . . Injured back (January 8, 1993); missed 26 games. . . . Injured groin (March 25, 1993); missed one game. . . . Injured shoulder (November 13, 1993); missed 14 games. . . . Injured groin (January 14, 1994); missed remainder of season. . . . Sprained ankle (February 17, 1995); missed 21 games. . . . Reinjured ankle (April 8, 1995); missed remainder of season.

			REGULAR SEASON					PLAYOFFS				
Season	Team	League	Gms.	G	A	Pts.	PIM	Gms.	G	A	Pts.	PIM
84-85	—Portland	WHL	47	7	11	18	10	3	0	2	2	0
85-86	—Portland	WHL	70	29	35	64	56	15	6	7	13	11
86-87	—Portland	WHL	65	50	57	107	40	20	10	18	28	11
87-88	—Minnesota	NHL	78	13	20	33	26	—	—	—	—	—
88-89	—Minnesota	NHL	72	14	19	33	14	5	0	1	1	0
89-90	—Minnesota	NHL	12	1	5	6	6	—	—	—	—	—
	—New York Rangers	NHL	19	2	3	5	6	—	—	—	—	—
	—Flint	IHL	41	14	38	52	16	4	3	2	5	0
90-91	—Canadian national team	Int'l	29	19	12	31	20	—	—	—	—	—
91-92	—Canadian national team	Int'l	58	20	43	63	62	—	—	—	—	—
	—Canadian Olympic Team	Int'l	8	7	1	8	18	—	—	—	—	—
	—Bolzon	Italy	12	12	12	24	16	—	—	—	—	—
92-93	—Binghamton	AHL	8	6	3	9	10	—	—	—	—	—
	—Ottawa	NHL	44	9	6	15	32	—	—	—	—	—
93-94	—Ottawa	NHL	33	10	8	18	14	—	—	—	—	—
94-95	—Ottawa	NHL	14	2	2	4	19	—	—	—	—	—
	NHL totals		272	51	63	114	117	5	0	1	1	0

ARMSTRONG, BILL
D, BRUINS

PERSONAL: Born May 18, 1970, in Richmond Hill, Ont. . . . 6-5/220. . . . Shoots left.
TRANSACTIONS/CAREER NOTES: Selected by Philadelphia Flyers in third round (fifth Flyers pick, 46th overall) of NHL entry draft (June 16, 1990). . . . Signed as free agent by Boston Bruins (June 23, 1993).

			REGULAR SEASON					PLAYOFFS				
Season	Team	League	Gms.	G	A	Pts.	PIM	Gms.	G	A	Pts.	PIM
86-87	—Barrie Jr. B	OHA	45	1	11	12	45	—	—	—	—	—
87-88	—Toronto	OHL	64	1	10	11	99	—	—	—	—	—
88-89	—Toronto	OHL	64	1	16	17	82	—	—	—	—	—
89-90	—Dukes of Hamilton	OHL	18	0	2	2	38	—	—	—	—	—
	—Niagara Falls	OHL	4	0	1	1	17	—	—	—	—	—
	—Oshawa	OHL	41	2	8	10	115	17	0	7	7	39
90-91	—Hershey	AHL	56	1	9	10	117	1	0	0	0	0
91-92	—Hershey	AHL	†80	2	14	16	159	3	0	0	0	2

Season Team	League	REGULAR SEASON Gms.	G	A	Pts.	PIM	PLAYOFFS Gms.	G	A	Pts.	PIM
92-93—Hershey	AHL	80	2	10	12	205	—	—	—	—	—
93-94—Providence	AHL	66	0	7	7	200	—	—	—	—	—
94-95—Providence	AHL	75	3	10	13	244	13	0	2	2	8

ARMSTRONG, BILL
LW, DEVILS

PERSONAL: Born June 25, 1966, in London, Ont. . . . 6-2/195. . . . Shoots left. . . . Full name: William Harold Armstrong.
COLLEGE: Western Michigan.
TRANSACTIONS/CAREER NOTES: Signed as free agent by Philadelphia Flyers (May 16, 1989). . . . Signed as free agent by New Jersey Devils (March 21, 1993).

Season Team	League	REGULAR SEASON Gms.	G	A	Pts.	PIM	PLAYOFFS Gms.	G	A	Pts.	PIM
86-87—Western Michigan Univ.	CCHA	43	13	20	33	86	—	—	—	—	—
87-88—Western Michigan Univ.	CCHA	41	22	17	39	88	—	—	—	—	—
88-89—Western Michigan Univ.	CCHA	40	23	19	42	97	—	—	—	—	—
89-90—Hershey	AHL	58	10	6	16	99	—	—	—	—	—
90-91—Philadelphia	NHL	1	0	1	1	0	—	—	—	—	—
—Hershey	AHL	70	36	27	63	150	6	2	8	10	19
91-92—Hershey	AHL	64	26	22	48	185	6	2	2	4	6
92-93—Cincinnati	IHL	42	14	11	25	99	—	—	—	—	—
—Utica	AHL	32	18	21	39	60	—	—	—	—	—
93-94—Albany	AHL	74	32	50	82	188	—	—	—	—	—
94-95—Albany	AHL	76	32	47	79	115	13	6	5	11	20
NHL totals		1	0	1	1	0					

ARMSTRONG, CHRIS
D, PANTHERS

PERSONAL: Born June 26, 1975, in Regina, Sask. . . . 6-0/184. . . . Shoots left.
HIGH SCHOOL: Vanier Collegiate (Moose Jaw, Sask.).
TRANSACTIONS/CAREER NOTES: Selected by Florida Panthers in third round (third Panthers pick, 57th overall) of NHL entry draft (June 26, 1993).
HONORS: Named to Can.HL All-Star second team (1993-94). . . . Named to WHL (East) All-Star first team (1993-94). . . . Named to WHL (East) All-Star second team (1994-95).

Season Team	League	REGULAR SEASON Gms.	G	A	Pts.	PIM	PLAYOFFS Gms.	G	A	Pts.	PIM
91-92—Moose Jaw	WHL	43	2	7	9	19	4	0	0	0	0
92-93—Moose Jaw	WHL	67	9	35	44	104	—	—	—	—	—
93-94—Moose Jaw	WHL	64	13	55	68	54	—	—	—	—	—
—Cincinnati	IHL	1	0	0	0	0	10	1	3	4	2
94-95—Moose Jaw	WHL	66	17	54	71	61	10	2	12	14	22
—Cincinnati	IHL	—	—	—	—	—	9	1	3	4	10

ARMSTRONG, DEREK
C, ISLANDERS

PERSONAL: Born April 23, 1973, in Ottawa. . . . 5-11/180. . . . Shoots right.
HIGH SCHOOL: Lo-Ellen Park Secondary School (Sudbury, Ont.).
TRANSACTIONS/CAREER NOTES: Selected by New York Islanders in sixth round (fifth Islanders pick, 128th overall) of NHL entry draft (June 20, 1992).

Season Team	League	REGULAR SEASON Gms.	G	A	Pts.	PIM	PLAYOFFS Gms.	G	A	Pts.	PIM
89-90—Hawkesbury	COJHL	48	8	10	18	30	—	—	—	—	—
90-91—Sudbury	OHL	2	0	2	2	0	—	—	—	—	—
—Hawkesbury	COJHL	54	27	45	72	49	—	—	—	—	—
91-92—Sudbury	OHL	66	31	54	85	22	9	2	2	4	2
92-93—Sudbury	OHL	66	44	62	106	56	14	9	10	19	26
93-94—Salt Lake City	IHL	76	23	35	58	61	—	—	—	—	—
94-95—Denver	IHL	59	13	18	31	65	6	0	2	2	0

ARNOTT, JASON
C, OILERS

PERSONAL: Born October 11, 1974, in Collingworth, Ont. . . . 6-3/195. . . . Shoots right. . . . Name pronounced AHR-niht.
HIGH SCHOOL: Henry Street (Whitby, Ont.).
TRANSACTIONS/CAREER NOTES: Selected by Edmonton Oilers in first round (first Oilers pick, seventh overall) of NHL entry draft (June 26, 1993). . . . Suffered from tonsillitis (November 3, 1993); missed one game. . . . Bruised sternum (November 27, 1993); missed one game. . . . Sprained back (December 7, 1993); missed one game. . . . Underwent appendectomy (December 28, 1993); missed three games. . . . Suffered from the flu (February 22, 1995); missed one game. . . . Suffered concussion (March 23, 1995); missed two games. . . . Strained knee (April 19, 1995); missed two games. . . . Suspended one game by NHL for game misconduct penalties (April 22, 1995).
HONORS: Named NHL Rookie of the Year by THE SPORTING NEWS (1993-94). . . . Named to NHL All-Rookie team (1993-94).
STATISTICAL PLATEAUS: Three-goal games: 1994-95 (1).

Season Team	League	REGULAR SEASON Gms.	G	A	Pts.	PIM	PLAYOFFS Gms.	G	A	Pts.	PIM
90-91—Lindsay Jr. B	OHA	42	17	44	61	10	—	—	—	—	—
91-92—Oshawa	OHL	57	9	15	24	12	—	—	—	—	—
92-93—Oshawa	OHL	56	41	57	98	74	13	9	9	18	20
93-94—Edmonton	NHL	78	33	35	68	104	—	—	—	—	—
94-95—Edmonton	NHL	42	15	22	37	128	—	—	—	—	—
NHL totals		120	48	57	105	232					

ARSENAULT, DAVID
G, RED WINGS

PERSONAL: Born March 21, 1977, in West Germany. . . . 6-1/165. . . . Catches left.
TRANSACTIONS/CAREER NOTES: Selected by Detroit Red Wings in fifth round (sixth Red Wings pick, 126th overall) of NHL entry draft (July 8, 1995).

			REGULAR SEASON								PLAYOFFS						
Season Team	League	Gms.	Min.	W	L	T	GA	SO	Avg.	Gms.	Min.	W	L	GA	SO	Avg.
94-95—St. Hyac.-Drummondv.	QMJHL	31	1332	5	15	0	115	0	5.18	2	122	0	2	8	0	3.93

ASTLEY, MARK
D, SABRES

PERSONAL: Born March 30, 1969, in Calgary. . . . 5-11/185. . . . Shoots left. . . . Name pronounced AST-lee.
COLLEGE: Lake Superior State (Mich.).
TRANSACTIONS/CAREER NOTES: Selected by Buffalo Sabres in 10th round (ninth Sabres pick, 194th overall) of NHL entry draft (June 17, 1989). . . . Hospitalized with strep pneumonia (March 14, 1990). . . . Loaned by Sabres to Canadian Olympic Team (October 15, 1993).
HONORS: Named to CCHA All-Star second team (1990-91). . . . Named to NCAA All-America West first team (1991-92). . . . Named to CCHA All-Star first team (1991-92). . . . Named to NCAA All-Tournament team (1991-92).
MISCELLANEOUS: Member of silver-medal-winning Canadian Olympic team (1994).

		REGULAR SEASON					PLAYOFFS				
Season Team	League	Gms.	G	A	Pts.	PIM	Gms.	G	A	Pts.	PIM
87-88—Calgary Canucks	AJHL	52	25	37	62	106	—	—	—	—	—
88-89—Lake Superior State	CCHA	42	3	12	15	26	—	—	—	—	—
89-90—Lake Superior State	CCHA	43	7	25	32	74	—	—	—	—	—
90-91—Lake Superior State	CCHA	45	19	27	46	50	—	—	—	—	—
91-92—Lake Superior State	CCHA	43	12	37	49	65	—	—	—	—	—
92-93—Lugano	Switzerland	30	10	12	22	57	—	—	—	—	—
—Canadian national team ..	Int'l	22	4	14	18	14	—	—	—	—	—
93-94—Buffalo.........................	NHL	1	0	0	0	0	—	—	—	—	—
—Canadian national team ..	Int'l	13	4	8	12	6	—	—	—	—	—
—Canadian Olympic Team ..	Int'l	8	0	1	1	4	—	—	—	—	—
94-95—Rochester	AHL	46	5	24	29	49	3	0	2	2	2
—Buffalo.........................	NHL	14	2	1	3	12	2	0	0	0	0
NHL totals................................		15	2	1	3	12	2	0	0	0	0

AUBIN, JEAN-SEBASTIEN
G, PENGUINS

PERSONAL: Born July 19, 1977, in Montreal. . . . 5-11/179. . . . Catches right.
TRANSACTIONS/CAREER NOTES: Selected by Pittsburgh Penguins in third round (second Penguins pick, 76th overall) of NHL entry draft (July 8, 1995).

			REGULAR SEASON								PLAYOFFS						
Season Team	League	Gms.	Min.	W	L	T	GA	SO	Avg.	Gms.	Min.	W	L	GA	SO	Avg.
94-95—Sherbrooke..................	QMJHL	27	1287	13	10	1	73	1	3.40	3	185	1	2	11	0	3.57

AUBIN, SERGE
C, PENGUINS

PERSONAL: Born February 15, 1975, in Val d'Or, Que. . . . 6-0/180. . . . Shoots left.
TRANSACTIONS/CAREER NOTES: Selected by Pittsburgh Penguins in seventh round (ninth Penguins pick, 161st overall) of NHL entry draft (June 29, 1994).

		REGULAR SEASON					PLAYOFFS				
Season Team	League	Gms.	G	A	Pts.	PIM	Gms.	G	A	Pts.	PIM
92-93—Drummondville................	QMJHL	65	16	34	50	30	8	0	1	1	16
93-94—Granby..........................	QMJHL	63	42	32	74	80	7	2	3	5	8
94-95—Granby..........................	QMJHL	60	37	73	110	55	11	8	15	23	4

AUCOIN, ADRIAN
D, CANUCKS

PERSONAL: Born July 3, 1973, in London, Ont. . . . 6-1/194. . . . Shoots right. . . . Name pronounced oh-KOYN.
COLLEGE: Boston University.
TRANSACTIONS/CAREER NOTES: Selected by Vancouver Canucks in fifth round (seventh Canucks pick, 117th overall) of NHL entry draft (June 20, 1992).
MISCELLANEOUS: Member of silver-medal-winning Canadian Olympic team (1994).

		REGULAR SEASON					PLAYOFFS				
Season Team	League	Gms.	G	A	Pts.	PIM	Gms.	G	A	Pts.	PIM
91-92—Boston University	Hockey East	33	2	10	12	62	—	—	—	—	—
92-93—Canadian national team ...	Int'l	42	8	10	18	71	—	—	—	—	—
93-94—Canadian national team ...	Int'l	59	5	12	17	80	—	—	—	—	—
—Canadian Olympic Team ..	Int'l	4	0	0	0	2	—	—	—	—	—
—Hamilton......................	AHL	13	1	2	3	19	4	0	2	2	6
94-95—Syracuse.......................	AHL	71	13	18	31	52	—	—	—	—	—
—Vancouver....................	NHL	1	1	0	1	0	4	1	0	1	0
NHL totals................................		1	1	0	1	0	4	1	0	1	0

AUDET, PHILLIPPE
LW, RED WINGS

PERSONAL: Born June 4, 1977, in Ottawa. . . . 6-2/175. . . . Shoots left.
TRANSACTIONS/CAREER NOTES: Selected by Detroit Red Wings in second round (second Red Wings pick, 52nd overall) of NHL entry draft (July 8, 1995).

Season Team	League	REGULAR SEASON					PLAYOFFS				
		Gms.	G	A	Pts.	PIM	Gms.	G	A	Pts.	PIM
94-95—Granby	QMJHL	62	19	17	36	93	7	1	3	4	4

AUDETTE, DONALD
RW, SABRES

PERSONAL: Born September 23, 1969, in Laval, Que.... 5-8/175.... Shoots right.... Name pronounced aw-DEHT.

TRANSACTIONS/CAREER NOTES: Selected by Buffalo Sabres in ninth round (eighth Sabres pick, 183rd overall) of NHL entry draft (June 17, 1989).... Broke left hand (February 11, 1990); missed seven games.... Bruised thigh (September 1990).... Bruised thigh (October 1990); missed five games.... Tore left knee ligaments (November 16, 1990).... Underwent surgery to left knee (December 10, 1990).... Sprained ankle (December 14, 1991); missed eight games.... Injured knee (March 31, 1992).... Underwent knee surgery prior to 1992-93 season; missed first 22 games of season.

HONORS: Won Guy Lafleur Trophy (1988-89).... Named to QMJHL All-Star first team (1988-89).... Won Dudley (Red) Garrett Memorial Trophy (1989-90).... Named to AHL All-Star first team (1989-90).

STATISTICAL PLATEAUS: Three-goal games: 1994-95 (1).

Season Team	League	REGULAR SEASON					PLAYOFFS				
		Gms.	G	A	Pts.	PIM	Gms.	G	A	Pts.	PIM
86-87—Laval	QMJHL	66	17	22	39	36	14	2	6	8	10
87-88—Laval	QMJHL	63	48	61	109	56	14	7	12	19	20
88-89—Laval	QMJHL	70	76	85	161	123	17	*17	12	29	43
89-90—Rochester	AHL	70	42	46	88	78	15	9	8	17	29
—Buffalo	NHL	—	—	—	—	—	2	0	0	0	0
90-91—Rochester	AHL	5	4	0	4	2	—	—	—	—	—
—Buffalo	NHL	8	4	3	7	4	—	—	—	—	—
91-92—Buffalo	NHL	63	31	17	48	75	—	—	—	—	—
92-93—Buffalo	NHL	44	12	7	19	51	8	2	2	4	6
—Rochester	AHL	6	8	4	12	10	—	—	—	—	—
93-94—Buffalo	NHL	77	29	30	59	41	7	0	1	1	6
94-95—Buffalo	NHL	46	24	13	37	27	5	1	1	2	4
NHL totals		238	100	70	170	198	22	3	4	7	16

AUGUSTA, PATRIK
RW

PERSONAL: Born November 13, 1969, in Jihlava, Czechoslovakia.... 5-10/170.... Shoots left.... Name pronounced pa-TREEK ah-GOOS-tuh.

TRANSACTIONS/CAREER NOTES: Selected by Toronto Maple Leafs in seventh round (eighth Maple Leafs pick, 149th overall) of NHL entry draft (June 20, 1992).... Signed as free agent by Los Angeles Ice Dogs (July 12, 1995).

HONORS: Named to AHL All-Star second team (1993-94).

Season Team	League	REGULAR SEASON					PLAYOFFS				
		Gms.	G	A	Pts.	PIM	Gms.	G	A	Pts.	PIM
89-90—Dukla Jihlava	Czech.	46	12	12	24	...	—	—	—	—	—
90-91—Dukla Jihlava	Czech.	49	20	22	42	18	—	—	—	—	—
91-92—Dukla Jihlava	Czech.	34	15	11	26	...	—	—	—	—	—
—Czech. Olympic Team	Int'l	8	3	2	5	...	—	—	—	—	—
92-93—St. John's	AHL	75	32	45	77	74	8	3	3	6	23
93-94—St. John's	AHL	77	*53	43	96	105	11	4	8	12	4
—Toronto	NHL	2	0	0	0	0	—	—	—	—	—
94-95—St. John's	AHL	71	37	32	69	98	4	2	0	2	7
NHL totals		2	0	0	0	0					

BABYCH, DAVE
D, CANUCKS

PERSONAL: Born May 23, 1961, in Edmonton.... 6-2/215.... Shoots left.... Full name: David Michael Babych.... Name pronounced BA-bihch.... Brother of Wayne Babych, right winger for four NHL teams (1978-79 through 1986-87).

TRANSACTIONS/CAREER NOTES: Selected by Winnipeg Jets as underage junior in first round (first Jets pick, second overall) of NHL entry draft (June 11, 1980).... Separated shoulder (March 1984).... Suffered back spasms (December 1984).... Traded by Jets to Hartford Whalers for RW Ray Neufeld (November 21, 1985).... Injured hip (January 1987); missed 12 games.... Lacerated right hand (March 16, 1989); missed six games.... Bruised neck (March 1990).... Underwent surgery to right wrist (October 29, 1990); missed 44 games.... Broke right thumb (February 8, 1991); missed remainder of season.... Selected by Minnesota North Stars in NHL expansion draft (May 30, 1991).... Traded by North Stars to Vancouver Canucks for D Craig Ludwig as part of a three-club deal in which Canucks sent D Tom Kurvers to Islanders for Ludwig (June 22, 1991).... Suffered sore back (November 3, 1991); missed one game.... Suffered hernia (September 22, 1992); missed 22 games.... Sprained knee (December 7, 1992); missed 12 games.... Suffered from the flu (March 20, 1993); missed one game.... Suffered facial lacerations (April 4, 1993); missed three games.... Suffered facial lacerations (December 15, 1993); missed two games.... Bruised foot (February 13, 1994); missed one game.... Suffered injury (February 5, 1995); missed three games.

HONORS: Won AJHL Top Defenseman Trophy (1977-78).... Won AJHL Rookie of the Year Trophy (1977-78).... Named to AJHL All-Star first team (1977-78).... Won Top Defenseman Trophy (1979-80).... Named to WHL All-Star first team (1979-80).... Played in NHL All-Star Game (1983 and 1984).

STATISTICAL PLATEAUS: Three-goal games: 1991-92 (1).

Season Team	League	REGULAR SEASON					PLAYOFFS				
		Gms.	G	A	Pts.	PIM	Gms.	G	A	Pts.	PIM
77-78—Portland	WCHL	6	1	3	4	4	—	—	—	—	—
—Fort Saskatchewan	AJHL	56	31	69	100	37	—	—	—	—	—
78-79—Portland	WHL	67	20	59	79	63	25	7	22	29	22
79-80—Portland	WHL	50	22	60	82	71	8	1	10	11	2

AB

Season	Team	League	REGULAR SEASON Gms.	G	A	Pts.	PIM	PLAYOFFS Gms.	G	A	Pts.	PIM
80-81	Winnipeg	NHL	69	6	38	44	90	—	—	—	—	—
81-82	Winnipeg	NHL	79	19	49	68	92	4	1	2	3	29
82-83	Winnipeg	NHL	79	13	61	74	56	3	0	0	0	0
83-84	Winnipeg	NHL	66	18	39	57	62	3	1	1	2	0
84-85	Winnipeg	NHL	78	13	49	62	78	8	2	7	9	6
85-86	Winnipeg	NHL	19	4	12	16	14	—	—	—	—	—
	Hartford	NHL	62	10	43	53	36	8	1	3	4	14
86-87	Hartford	NHL	66	8	33	41	44	6	1	1	2	14
87-88	Hartford	NHL	71	14	36	50	54	6	3	2	5	2
88-89	Hartford	NHL	70	6	41	47	54	4	1	5	6	2
89-90	Hartford	NHL	72	6	37	43	62	7	1	2	3	0
90-91	Hartford	NHL	8	0	6	6	4	—	—	—	—	—
91-92	Vancouver	NHL	75	5	24	29	63	13	2	6	8	10
92-93	Vancouver	NHL	43	3	16	19	44	12	2	5	7	6
93-94	Vancouver	NHL	73	4	28	32	52	24	3	5	8	12
94-95	Vancouver	NHL	40	3	11	14	18	11	2	2	4	14
NHL totals			970	132	523	655	823	109	20	41	61	109

B

BACH, RYAN
G, RED WINGS

PERSONAL: Born October 21, 1973, in Sherwood Park, Alta.... 6-1/ 180.... Catches left.
COLLEGE: Colorado College.
TRANSACTIONS/CAREER NOTES: Selected by Detroit Red Wings in 11th round (11th Red Wings pick, 262nd overall) of NHL entry draft (June 20, 1992).
HONORS: Named to NCAA All-America West second team (1994-95).... Named to WCHA All-Star first team (1994-95).

Season	Team	League	REGULAR SEASON Gms.	Min.	W	L	T	GA	SO	Avg.	PLAYOFFS Gms.	Min.	W	L	GA SO	Avg.
91-92	Notre Dame	SJHL	33	1862	...	...	...	124	0	4.00	—	—	—	—	—	—
92-93	Colorado College	WCHA	4	239	1	3	0	11	0	2.76	—	—	—	—	—	—
93-94	Colorado College	WCHA	30	1733	17	7	5	105	0	3.64	—	—	—	—	—	—
94-95	Colorado College	WCHA	27	1522	18	5	1	83	0	3.27	—	—	—	—	—	—

BAILEY, SCOTT
G, BRUINS

PERSONAL: Born May 2, 1972, in Calgary.... 5-11/ 185.... Catches left.
TRANSACTIONS/CAREER NOTES: Selected by Boston Bruins in fifth round (third Bruins pick, 112th overall) of NHL entry draft (June 20, 1992).
HONORS: Won WHL (West) Rookie of the Year Award (1990-91).... Named to WHL (West) All-Star second team (1990-91 and 1991-92).

Season	Team	League	REGULAR SEASON Gms.	Min.	W	L	T	GA	SO	Avg.	PLAYOFFS Gms.	Min.	W	L	GA SO	Avg.
88-89	Moose Jaw	WHL	2	34	...	...	...	7	0	12.35	—	—	—	—	—	—
89-90								Did not play.								
90-91	Spokane	WHL	46	2537	33	11	0	157	4	3.71	—	—	—	—	—	—
91-92	Spokane	WHL	65	3748	34	23	5	206	1	3.30	10	605	5	5	43 0	4.26
92-93	Johnstown	ECHL	36	1750	13	15	‡3	112	1	3.84	—	—	—	—	—	—
93-94	Charlotte	ECHL	36	2180	22	11	3	130	1	3.58	3	188	1	2	12 0	3.83
	Providence	AHL	7	377	2	2	2	24	0	3.82	—	—	—	—	—	—
94-95	Providence	AHL	52	2936	25	16	9	147	2	3.00	9	505	4	4	31 2	3.68

BAKER, JAMIE
C, SHARKS

PERSONAL: Born August 31, 1966, in Nepean, Ont.... 6-0/190.... Shoots left.... Full name: James Paul Baker.
HIGH SCHOOL: J.S. Woodsworth (Nepean, Ont.).
COLLEGE: St. Lawrence (N.Y.).
TRANSACTIONS/CAREER NOTES: Selected by Quebec Nordiques in NHL supplemental draft (June 10, 1988).... Broke left ankle (December 30, 1988).... Sprained ankle (January 9, 1992); missed two games.... Signed as free agent by Ottawa Senators (September 2, 1992).... Sprained ankle (December 15, 1992); missed six games.... Bruised foot (February 22, 1993); missed one game.... Signed as free agent by San Jose Sharks (August 18, 1993).... Suffered slight groin pull (October 16, 1993); missed 10 games.... Suffered from the flu (February 26, 1995); missed two games.... Injured shoulder (March 15, 1995); missed three games.

Season	Team	League	REGULAR SEASON Gms.	G	A	Pts.	PIM	PLAYOFFS Gms.	G	A	Pts.	PIM
85-86	St. Lawrence University	ECAC	31	9	16	25	52	—	—	—	—	—
86-87	St. Lawrence University	ECAC	32	8	24	32	59	—	—	—	—	—
87-88	St. Lawrence University	ECAC	38	26	28	54	44	—	—	—	—	—
88-89	St. Lawrence University	ECAC	13	11	16	27	16	—	—	—	—	—
89-90	Quebec	NHL	1	0	0	0	0	—	—	—	—	—
	Halifax	AHL	74	17	43	60	47	6	0	0	0	7
90-91	Quebec	NHL	18	2	0	2	8	—	—	—	—	—
	Halifax	AHL	50	14	22	36	85	—	—	—	—	—
91-92	Halifax	AHL	9	5	0	5	12	—	—	—	—	—
	Quebec	NHL	52	7	10	17	32	—	—	—	—	—
92-93	Ottawa	NHL	76	19	29	48	54	—	—	—	—	—
93-94	San Jose	NHL	65	12	5	17	38	14	3	2	5	30
94-95	San Jose	NHL	43	7	4	11	22	11	2	2	4	12
NHL totals			255	47	48	95	154	25	5	4	9	42

BALES, MIKE
G, SENATORS

PERSONAL: Born August 6, 1971, in Saskatoon, Sask.... 6-1/180.... Catches left.... Full name: Michael Raymond Bales.
COLLEGE: Ohio State.
TRANSACTIONS/CAREER NOTES: Selected by Boston Bruins in fifth round (fourth Bruins pick, 105th overall) of NHL entry draft (June 16, 1990).... Signed as free agent by Ottawa Senators (July 4, 1994).

			REGULAR SEASON								PLAYOFFS						
Season	Team	League	Gms.	Min.	W	L	T	GA	SO	Avg.	Gms.	Min.	W	L	GA	SO	Avg.
88-89—Estevan		SJHL	44	2412	...	...	...	197	1	4.90	—	—	—	—	—	—	—
89-90—Ohio State		CCHA	21	1117	6	13	2	95	0	5.10	—	—	—	—	—	—	—
90-91—Ohio State		CCHA	*39	*2180	11	24	3	*184	0	5.06	—	—	—	—	—	—	—
91-92—Ohio State		CCHA	36	2061	11	20	5	*180	0	5.24	—	—	—	—	—	—	—
92-93—Providence		AHL	44	2363	22	17	0	166	1	4.21	2	118	0	2	8	0	4.07
—Boston		NHL	1	25	0	0	0	1	0	2.40	—	—	—	—	—	—	—
93-94—Providence		AHL	33	1757	9	15	4	130	0	4.44	—	—	—	—	—	—	—
94-95—Prince Edward Island		AHL	45	2649	25	16	3	160	2	3.62	9	530	6	3	24	2	2.72
—Ottawa		NHL	1	3	0	0	0	0	0	0.00	—	—	—	—	—	—	—
NHL totals			2	28	0	0	0	1	0	2.14							

BALL, MATT
RW, WHALERS

PERSONAL: Born January 29, 1976, in Toronto.... 6-2/215.... Shoots right.
TRANSACTIONS/CAREER NOTES: Injured hand (1993).... Selected by Hartford Whalers in ninth round (sixth Whalers pick, 230th overall) of NHL entry draft (June 29, 1994).

			REGULAR SEASON					PLAYOFFS				
Season	Team	League	Gms.	G	A	Pts.	PIM	Gms.	G	A	Pts.	PIM
93-94—Detroit		OHL	43	3	7	10	11	17	2	0	2	0
94-95—Detroit		OHL	64	35	44	79	84	21	9	19	28	22

BANNISTER, DREW
D, LIGHTNING

PERSONAL: Born September 4, 1974, in Belleville, Ont.... 6-1/193.... Shoots right.
HIGH SCHOOL: Bawating Collegiate School (Sault Ste. Marie, Ont.).
TRANSACTIONS/CAREER NOTES: Selected by Tampa Bay Lightning in second round (second Lightning pick, 26th overall) of NHL entry draft (June 20, 1992).
HONORS: Named to Memorial Cup All-Star team (1991-92).... Named to OHL All-Star second team (1993-94).

			REGULAR SEASON					PLAYOFFS				
Season	Team	League	Gms.	G	A	Pts.	PIM	Gms.	G	A	Pts.	PIM
90-91—Sault Ste. Marie		OHL	41	2	8	10	51	4	0	0	0	0
91-92—Sault Ste. Marie		OHL	64	4	21	25	122	16	3	10	13	36
92-93—Sault Ste. Marie		OHL	59	5	28	33	114	18	2	7	9	12
93-94—Sault Ste. Marie		OHL	58	7	43	50	108	14	6	9	15	20
94-95—Atlanta		IHL	72	5	7	12	74	5	0	2	2	22

BARNABY, MATTHEW
LW, SABRES

PERSONAL: Born May 4, 1973, in Ottawa.... 6-0/170.... Shoots right.
TRANSACTIONS/CAREER NOTES: Selected by Buffalo Sabres in fourth round (fifth Sabres pick, 83rd overall) of NHL entry draft (June 20, 1992).... Suffered lower back spasms (March 28, 1995); missed one game.

			REGULAR SEASON					PLAYOFFS				
Season	Team	League	Gms.	G	A	Pts.	PIM	Gms.	G	A	Pts.	PIM
90-91—Beauport		QMJHL	52	9	5	14	262	—	—	—	—	—
91-92—Beauport		QMJHL	63	29	37	66	*476	—	—	—	—	—
92-93—Victoriaville		QMJHL	65	44	67	111	*448	6	2	4	6	44
—Buffalo		NHL	2	1	0	1	10	1	0	1	1	4
93-94—Buffalo		NHL	35	2	4	6	106	3	0	0	0	17
—Rochester		AHL	42	10	32	42	153	—	—	—	—	—
94-95—Rochester		AHL	56	21	29	50	274	—	—	—	—	—
—Buffalo		NHL	23	1	1	2	116	—	—	—	—	—
NHL totals			60	4	5	9	232	4	0	1	1	21

BARNES, STU
C, PANTHERS

PERSONAL: Born December 25, 1970, in Edmonton.... 5-11/174.... Shoots right.
TRANSACTIONS/CAREER NOTES: Selected by Winnipeg Jets in first round (first Jets pick, fourth overall) of NHL entry draft (June 17, 1989).... Traded by Jets to Florida Panthers for C Randy Gilhen (November 26, 1993).... Strained left calf (January 1, 1994); missed one game.... Suffered lacerations and bruises in and around left eye (February 15, 1995); missed seven games.
HONORS: Won Jim Piggott Memorial Trophy (1987-88).... Named to WHL All-Star second team (1987-88).... Won Four Broncos Memorial Trophy (1988-89).... Named to WHL All-Star first team (1988-89).
STATISTICAL PLATEAUS: Three-goal games: 1991-92 (1).

			REGULAR SEASON					PLAYOFFS				
Season	Team	League	Gms.	G	A	Pts.	PIM	Gms.	G	A	Pts.	PIM
86-87—St. Albert		AJHL	57	43	32	75	80	—	—	—	—	—
87-88—New Westminster		WHL	71	37	64	101	88	5	2	3	5	6
88-89—Tri-City		WHL	70	59	82	141	117	7	6	5	11	10
89-90—Tri-City		WHL	63	52	92	144	165	7	1	5	6	26
90-91—Canadian national team		Int'l	53	22	27	49	68	—	—	—	—	—
91-92—Winnipeg		NHL	46	8	9	17	26	—	—	—	—	—
—Moncton		AHL	30	13	19	32	10	11	3	9	12	6

Season	Team	League	REGULAR SEASON					PLAYOFFS				
			Gms.	G	A	Pts.	PIM	Gms.	G	A	Pts.	PIM
92-93	Moncton	AHL	42	23	31	54	58	—	—	—	—	—
	Winnipeg	NHL	38	12	10	22	10	6	1	3	4	2
93-94	Winnipeg	NHL	18	5	4	9	8	—	—	—	—	—
	Florida	NHL	59	18	20	38	30	—	—	—	—	—
94-95	Florida	NHL	41	10	19	29	8	—	—	—	—	—
NHL totals			202	53	62	115	82	6	1	3	4	2

BARON, MURRAY
D, BLUES

PERSONAL: Born June 1, 1967, in Prince George, B.C.... 6-3/215.... Shoots left.
HIGH SCHOOL: Kamloops (B.C.).
COLLEGE: North Dakota.
TRANSACTIONS/CAREER NOTES: Selected by Philadelphia Flyers as underage player in eighth round (seventh Flyers pick, 167th overall) of NHL entry draft (June 21, 1986).... Separated left shoulder (October 5, 1989).... Underwent surgery to have bone spur removed from foot (April 1990).... Traded by Flyers with C Ron Sutter to St. Louis Blues for C Rod Brind'Amour and C Dan Quinn (September 22, 1991).... Injured shoulder (December 3, 1991); missed seven games.... Broke foot (March 22, 1993); missed remainder of regular season.... Injured groin (December 1, 1993); missed three games.... Injured groin (December 11, 1993); missed three games.... Injured knee (March 7, 1994); missed one game.... Injured knee (April 18, 1995); missed last nine games of season.

Season	Team	League	REGULAR SEASON					PLAYOFFS				
			Gms.	G	A	Pts.	PIM	Gms.	G	A	Pts.	PIM
84-85	Vernon	BCJHL	37	5	9	14	93	—	—	—	—	—
85-86	Vernon	BCJHL	49	15	32	47	176	7	1	2	3	13
86-87	Univ. of North Dakota	WCHA	41	4	10	14	62	—	—	—	—	—
87-88	Univ. of North Dakota	WCHA	41	1	10	11	95	—	—	—	—	—
88-89	Univ. of North Dakota	WCHA	40	2	6	8	92	—	—	—	—	—
	Hershey	AHL	9	0	3	3	8	—	—	—	—	—
89-90	Hershey	AHL	50	0	10	10	101	—	—	—	—	—
	Philadelphia	NHL	16	2	2	4	12	—	—	—	—	—
90-91	Hershey	AHL	6	2	3	5	0	—	—	—	—	—
	Philadelphia	NHL	67	8	8	16	74	—	—	—	—	—
91-92	St. Louis	NHL	67	3	8	11	94	2	0	0	0	2
92-93	St. Louis	NHL	53	2	2	4	59	11	0	0	0	12
93-94	St. Louis	NHL	77	5	9	14	123	4	0	0	0	10
94-95	St. Louis	NHL	39	0	5	5	93	7	1	1	2	2
NHL totals			319	20	34	54	455	24	1	1	2	26

BARRASSO, TOM
G, PENGUINS

PERSONAL: Born March 31, 1965, in Boston.... 6-3/211.... Catches right.... Name pronounced buh-RAH-soh.
HIGH SCHOOL: Acton (Mass.)-Boxborough.
TRANSACTIONS/CAREER NOTES: Selected by Buffalo Sabres in first round (first Sabres pick, fifth overall) of NHL entry draft (June 8, 1983).... Suffered chip fracture of ankle (November 1987).... Pulled groin (April 9, 1988).... Traded by Sabres with third-round pick in 1990 draft (RW Joe Dziedzic) to Pittsburgh Penguins for D Doug Bodger and LW Darrin Shannon (November 12, 1988).... Pulled groin muscle (January 17, 1989).... Injured shoulder (March 1989).... Underwent surgery to right wrist (October 30, 1989); missed 21 games.... Pulled groin (February 1990). ... Granted leave of absence to be with daughter as she underwent cancer treatment in Los Angeles (February 9, 1990).... Rejoined the Penguins (March 19, 1990).... Bruised right hand (October 29, 1991); missed two games.... Bruised right ankle (December 26, 1991); missed three games.... Suffered back spasms (March 1992); missed three games.... Suffered from chicken pox (January 14, 1993); missed nine games.... Strained groin (October 7, 1993); missed four games.... Injured hip (November 18, 1993); missed 12 games.... Underwent surgery on right wrist (January 20, 1995); missed first 43 games of season.... Suffered sore wrist (May 3, 1995); missed one game.
HONORS: Won Vezina Trophy (1983-84).... Won Calder Memorial Trophy (1983-84).... Named to THE SPORTING NEWS All-Star second team (1983-84, 1984-85 and 1987-88).... Named to NHL All-Star first team (1983-84).... Named to NHL All-Rookie team (1983-84).... Shared William M. Jennings Trophy with Bob Sauve (1984-85).... Named to NHL All-Star second team (1984-85 and 1992-93).... Played in NHL All-Star Game (1985).... Named to THE SPORTING NEWS All-Star first team (1992-93).
RECORDS: Shares NHL single-season playoff records for most wins by a goaltender—16 (1992); and most consecutive wins by a goaltender—11 (1992).
MISCELLANEOUS: Member of U.S. National Junior Team (1983).... Member of Stanley Cup championship teams (1991 and 1992).

Season	Team	League	REGULAR SEASON							PLAYOFFS						
			Gms.	Min.	W	L	T	GA	SO	Avg.	Gms.	Min.	W	L	GA	SO	Avg.
81-82	Acton-Boxborough HS.	Mass. HS	23	1035	...	...	...	32	7	1.86	—	—	—	—	—	—	—
82-83	Acton-Boxborough HS.	Mass. HS	23	1035	...	...	...	17	10	0.99	—	—	—	—	—	—	—
83-84	Buffalo	NHL	42	2475	26	12	3	117	2	2.84	3	139	0	2	8	0	3.45
84-85	Rochester	AHL	5	267	3	1	1	6	1	1.35	—	—	—	—	—	—	—
	Buffalo	NHL	54	3248	25	18	10	144	*5	*2.66	5	300	2	3	22	0	4.40
85-86	Buffalo	NHL	60	*3561	29	24	5	214	2	3.61	—	—	—	—	—	—	—
86-87	Buffalo	NHL	46	2501	17	23	2	152	2	3.65	—	—	—	—	—	—	—
87-88	Buffalo	NHL	54	3133	25	18	8	173	2	3.31	4	224	1	3	16	0	4.29
88-89	Buffalo	NHL	10	545	2	7	0	45	0	4.95	—	—	—	—	—	—	—
	Pittsburgh	NHL	44	2406	18	15	7	162	0	4.04	11	631	7	4	40	0	3.80
89-90	Pittsburgh	NHL	24	1294	7	12	3	101	0	4.68	—	—	—	—	—	—	—
90-91	Pittsburgh	NHL	48	2754	27	16	3	165	1	3.59	20	1175	12	7	51	†1	*2.60

Season	Team	League	REGULAR SEASON Gms.	Min.	W	L	T	GA	SO	Avg.	PLAYOFFS Gms.	Min.	W	L	GA	SO	Avg.
91-92—Pittsburgh	NHL	57	3329	25	22	9	196	1	3.53	*21	*1233	*16	5	*58	1	2.82
92-93—Pittsburgh	NHL	63	3702	*43	14	5	186	4	3.01	12	722	7	5	35	2	2.91
93-94—Pittsburgh	NHL	44	2482	22	15	5	139	2	3.36	6	356	2	4	17	0	2.87
94-95—Pittsburgh	NHL	2	125	0	1	1	8	0	3.84	2	80	0	1	8	0	6.00
NHL totals			548	31555	266	197	61	1802	21	3.43	84	4860	47	34	255	4	3.15

BARRAULT, DOUG
RW, PANTHERS

PERSONAL: Born April 21, 1970, in Golden, B.C. . . . 6-2/205. . . . Shoots right. . . . Name pronounced buh-ROH.
TRANSACTIONS/CAREER NOTES: Selected by Minnesota North Stars in eighth round (eighth North Stars pick, 155th overall) of NHL entry draft (June 16, 1990). . . . Selected by Florida Panthers in NHL expansion draft (June 24, 1993).
HONORS: Named to WHL (West) All-Star second team (1990-91).

Season	Team	League	REGULAR SEASON Gms.	G	A	Pts.	PIM	PLAYOFFS Gms.	G	A	Pts.	PIM
88-89—Lethbridge	WHL	57	14	13	27	34	—	—	—	—	—
89-90—Lethbridge	WHL	54	14	16	30	36	19	7	3	10	0
90-91—Lethbridge	WHL	4	2	2	4	16	—	—	—	—	—
—Seattle	WHL	61	42	42	84	69	6	5	3	8	4
91-92—Kalamazoo	IHL	60	5	14	19	26	—	—	—	—	—
92-93—Kalamazoo	IHL	78	32	34	66	74	—	—	—	—	—
—Minnesota	NHL	2	0	0	0	2	—	—	—	—	—
93-94—Cincinnati	IHL	75	36	28	64	59	9	8	2	10	0
—Florida	NHL	2	0	0	0	0	—	—	—	—	—
94-95—Cincinnati	IHL	74	20	40	60	57	—	—	—	—	—
NHL totals		4	0	0	0	2					

BARRIE, LEN
C, PENGUINS

PERSONAL: Born June 4, 1969, in Kimberley, B.C. . . . 6-0/200. . . . Shoots right.
TRANSACTIONS/CAREER NOTES: Selected by Edmonton Oilers in sixth round (seventh Oilers pick, 124th overall) of NHL entry draft (June 11, 1988). . . . Broke finger (March 1989). . . . Traded by Victoria Cougars to Kamloops Blazers for RW Mark Cipriano (August 1989). . . . Signed as free agent by Philadelphia Flyers (February 8, 1990). . . . Signed as free agent by Florida Panthers (July 20, 1993). . . . Signed as free agent by Pittsburgh Penguins (August 25, 1994).
HONORS: Won CHL Plus/Minus Award (1989-90). . . . Won Bob Clarke Trophy (1989-90). . . . Named to WHL (West) All-Star first team (1989-90). . . . Named to IHL All-Star second team (1993-94).

Season	Team	League	REGULAR SEASON Gms.	G	A	Pts.	PIM	PLAYOFFS Gms.	G	A	Pts.	PIM
85-86—Calgary Spurs	AJHL	23	7	14	21	86	—	—	—	—	—
—Calgary	WHL	32	3	0	3	18	—	—	—	—	—
86-87—Calgary	WHL	34	13	13	26	81	—	—	—	—	—
—Victoria	WHL	34	7	6	13	92	5	0	1	1	15
87-88—Victoria	WHL	70	37	49	86	192	8	2	0	2	29
88-89—Victoria	WHL	67	39	48	87	157	7	5	2	7	23
89-90—Philadelphia	NHL	1	0	0	0	0	—	—	—	—	—
—Kamloops	WHL	70	*85	*100	*185	108	17	†14	23	†37	24
90-91—Hershey	AHL	63	26	32	58	60	7	4	0	4	12
91-92—Hershey	AHL	75	42	43	85	78	3	0	2	2	32
92-93—Hershey	AHL	61	31	45	76	162	—	—	—	—	—
—Philadelphia	NHL	8	2	2	4	9	—	—	—	—	—
93-94—Cincinnati	IHL	77	45	71	116	246	11	8	13	21	60
—Florida	NHL	2	0	0	0	0	—	—	—	—	—
94-95—Cleveland	IHL	28	13	30	43	137	—	—	—	—	—
—Pittsburgh	NHL	48	3	11	14	66	4	1	0	1	8
NHL totals		59	5	13	18	75	4	1	0	1	8

BARTELL, ADAM
D, DENVER

PERSONAL: Born April 27, 1973, in Buffalo, N.Y. . . . 6-1/182. . . . Shoots right.
COLLEGE: Rensselaer Polytechnic Institute (N.Y.).
TRANSACTIONS/CAREER NOTES: Selected by Quebec Nordiques in ninth round (10th Nordiques pick, 178th overall) of NHL entry draft (June 22, 1991). . . . Nordiques franchise moved to Denver for 1995-96 season.
HONORS: Named to ECAC All-Star second team (1994-95).

Season	Team	League	REGULAR SEASON Gms.	G	A	Pts.	PIM	PLAYOFFS Gms.	G	A	Pts.	PIM
91-92—R.P.I.	ECAC	31	5	13	18	18	—	—	—	—	—
92-93—R.P.I.	ECAC	32	2	17	19	46	—	—	—	—	—
93-94—R.P.I.	ECAC	27	3	10	13	24	—	—	—	—	—
94-95—R.P.I.	ECAC	35	3	19	22	28	—	—	—	—	—

BASSEN, BOB
C, STARS

PERSONAL: Born May 6, 1965, in Calgary. . . . 5-10/180. . . . Shoots left. . . . Name pronounced BA-suhn. . . . Son of Hank Bassen, goalie, Chicago Blackhawks, Detroit Red Wings and Pittsburgh Penguins (1954-55 through 1967-68).
HIGH SCHOOL: Sir Winston Churchill (Calgary).

TRANSACTIONS/CAREER NOTES: Signed as free agent by New York Islanders (October 19, 1984).... Injured knee (October 12, 1985).... Traded by Islanders with D Steve Konroyd to Chicago Blackhawks for D Gary Nylund and D Marc Bergevin (November 25, 1988).... Selected by St. Louis Blues in 1990 waiver draft for $25,000 (October 2, 1990).... Broke right foot (December 4, 1992); missed 22 games.... Broke finger (January 28, 1993); missed nine games.... Traded by Blues with C Ron Sutter and D Garth Butcher to Quebec Nordiques for D Steve Duchesne and RW Denis Chasse (January 23, 1994).... Lacerated left eye (March 30, 1994); missed one game.... Injured back (February 18, 1995); missed one game.... Signed as free agent by Dallas Stars (July 18, 1995).
HONORS: Named to WHL (East) All-Star first team (1984-85).... Named to IHL All-Star first team (1989-90).

Season	Team	League	REGULAR SEASON					PLAYOFFS				
			Gms.	G	A	Pts.	PIM	Gms.	G	A	Pts.	PIM
82-83	Medicine Hat	WHL	4	3	2	5	0	3	0	0	0	4
83-84	Medicine Hat	WHL	72	29	29	58	93	14	5	11	16	12
84-85	Medicine Hat	WHL	65	32	50	82	143	10	2	8	10	39
85-86	New York Islanders	NHL	11	2	1	3	6	3	0	1	1	0
	Springfield	AHL	54	13	21	34	111	—	—	—	—	—
86-87	New York Islanders	NHL	77	7	10	17	89	14	1	2	3	21
87-88	New York Islanders	NHL	77	6	16	22	99	6	0	1	1	23
88-89	New York Islanders	NHL	19	1	4	5	21	—	—	—	—	—
	Chicago	NHL	49	4	12	16	62	10	1	1	2	34
89-90	Indianapolis	IHL	73	22	32	54	179	12	3	8	11	33
	Chicago	NHL	6	1	1	2	8	—	—	—	—	—
90-91	St. Louis	NHL	79	16	18	34	183	13	1	3	4	24
91-92	St. Louis	NHL	79	7	25	32	167	6	0	2	2	4
92-93	St. Louis	NHL	53	9	10	19	63	11	0	0	0	10
93-94	St. Louis	NHL	46	2	7	9	44	—	—	—	—	—
	Quebec	NHL	37	11	8	19	55	—	—	—	—	—
94-95	Quebec	NHL	47	12	15	27	33	5	2	4	6	0
	NHL totals		580	78	127	205	830	68	5	14	19	116

BATES, SHAWN
C, BRUINS

PERSONAL: Born April 3, 1975, in Melrose, Mass.... 5-11/170.... Shoots right.
HIGH SCHOOL: Medford (Mass.).
COLLEGE: Boston University.
TRANSACTIONS/CAREER NOTES: Selected by Boston Bruins in fourth round (fourth Bruins pick, 103rd overall) of NHL entry draft (June 26, 1993).
HONORS: Named to Hockey East All-Rookie team (1993-94).

Season	Team	League	REGULAR SEASON					PLAYOFFS				
			Gms.	G	A	Pts.	PIM	Gms.	G	A	Pts.	PIM
90-91	Medford H.S.	Mass. H.S.	22	18	43	61	6	—	—	—	—	—
91-92	Medford H.S.	Mass. H.S.	22	38	41	79	10	—	—	—	—	—
92-93	Medford H.S.	Mass. H.S.	25	49	46	95	20	—	—	—	—	—
93-94	Boston University	Hockey East	41	10	19	29	24	—	—	—	—	—
94-95	Boston University	Hockey East	38	18	12	30	48	—	—	—	—	—

BATTAGLIA, JON
LW, MIGHTY DUCKS

PERSONAL: Born December 13, 1975, in Chicago.... 6-2/185.... Shoots left.... Name pronounced buh-TAG-lee-uh.
COLLEGE: Lake Superior State (Mich.).
TRANSACTIONS/CAREER NOTES: Selected by Mighty Ducks of Anaheim in sixth round (sixth Mighty Ducks pick, 132nd overall) of NHL entry draft (June 29, 1994).

Season	Team	League	REGULAR SEASON					PLAYOFFS				
			Gms.	G	A	Pts.	PIM	Gms.	G	A	Pts.	PIM
93-94	Caledon	Jr. A	44	15	33	48	104	—	—	—	—	—
94-95	Lake Superior State	CCHA	38	6	15	21	34	—	—	—	—	—

BATTERS, JEFF
D

PERSONAL: Born October 23, 1970, in Victoria, B.C.... 6-2/215.... Shoots right.... Full name: Jeffrey William Batters.
COLLEGE: Alaska-Anchorage.
TRANSACTIONS/CAREER NOTES: Selected by St. Louis Blues in seventh round (seventh Blues pick, 135th overall) of NHL entry draft (June 17, 1989).

Season	Team	League	REGULAR SEASON					PLAYOFFS				
			Gms.	G	A	Pts.	PIM	Gms.	G	A	Pts.	PIM
88-89	Alaska-Anchorage	Indep.	33	8	14	22	123	—	—	—	—	—
89-90	Alaska-Anchorage	Indep.	34	6	9	15	102	—	—	—	—	—
90-91	Alaska-Anchorage	Indep.	39	16	14	30	90	—	—	—	—	—
91-92	Alaska-Anchorage	Indep.	34	6	17	23	86	—	—	—	—	—
92-93	Peoria	IHL	74	5	18	23	113	4	0	0	0	10
93-94	Peoria	IHL	59	3	9	12	175	6	0	0	0	18
	St. Louis	NHL	6	0	0	0	7	—	—	—	—	—
94-95	Peoria	IHL	42	0	11	11	128	5	0	1	1	18
	St. Louis	NHL	10	0	0	0	21	—	—	—	—	—
	NHL totals		16	0	0	0	28					

BATYRSHIN, RUSLAN
D, KINGS

PERSONAL: Born February 19, 1975, in Moscow, U.S.S.R.... 6-1/180.... Shoots left.
TRANSACTIONS/CAREER NOTES: Selected by Winnipeg Jets in fourth round (fourth Jets pick, 79th overall) of NHL entry draft (June 26, 1993).... Traded

by Jets with second-round pick in 1996 draft to Los Angeles Kings for D Brent Thompson (August 8, 1994).

Season Team	League	REGULAR SEASON Gms.	G	A	Pts.	PIM	PLAYOFFS Gms.	G	A	Pts.	PIM
91-92—Dynamo Moscow	CIS Div. III	40	0	2	2	52	—	—	—	—	—
92-93—Dynamo Moscow	CIS Div. II				Statistics unavailable.						
93-94—Dynamo Moscow	CIS	19	0	0	0	10	3	0	0	0	22
94-95—Dynamo Moscow	CIS	36	2	2	4	65	12	1	1	2	6

BAUMGARTNER, KEN
D/LW, MAPLE LEAFS

PERSONAL: Born March 11, 1966, in Flin Flon, Man. . . . 6-1/205. . . . Shoots left. . . . Full name: Ken James Baumgartner.

TRANSACTIONS/CAREER NOTES: Selected by Buffalo Sabres as underage junior in 12th round (12th Sabres pick, 245th overall) of NHL entry draft (June 15, 1985). . . . Traded by Sabres with D Larry Playfair and RW Sean McKenna to Los Angeles Kings for D Brian Engblom and C Doug Smith (January 29, 1986). . . . Traded by Kings with C Hubie McDonough to New York Islanders for RW Mikko Makela (November 29, 1989). . . . Suspended one game by NHL for fighting (April 5, 1990). . . . Fractured right orbital bone (December 19, 1991); missed 14 games. . . . Traded by Islanders with C Dave McLlwain to Toronto Maple Leafs for C Claude Loiselle and RW Daniel Marois (March 10, 1992). . . . Broke bone in wrist (February 28, 1994); missed remainder of season. . . . Underwent shoulder surgery (January 31, 1995); missed remainder of season.

Season Team	League	REGULAR SEASON Gms.	G	A	Pts.	PIM	PLAYOFFS Gms.	G	A	Pts.	PIM
83-84—Prince Albert..................	WHL	57	1	6	7	203	—	—	—	—	—
84-85—Prince Albert..................	WHL	60	3	9	12	252	13	1	3	4	*89
85-86—Prince Albert..................	WHL	70	4	23	27	277	20	3	9	12	112
86-87—Chur	Switzerland				Statistics unavailable.						
—New Haven	AHL	13	0	3	3	99	6	0	0	0	60
87-88—Los Angeles	NHL	30	2	3	5	189	5	0	1	1	28
—New Haven	AHL	48	1	5	6	181	—	—	—	—	—
88-89—Los Angeles	NHL	49	1	3	4	288	5	0	0	0	8
—New Haven	AHL	10	1	3	4	26	—	—	—	—	—
89-90—Los Angeles	NHL	12	1	0	1	28	—	—	—	—	—
—New York Islanders..........	NHL	53	0	5	5	194	4	0	0	0	27
90-91—New York Islanders..........	NHL	78	1	6	7	282	—	—	—	—	—
91-92—New York Islanders..........	NHL	44	0	1	1	202	—	—	—	—	—
—Toronto......................	NHL	11	0	0	0	23	—	—	—	—	—
92-93—Toronto	NHL	63	1	0	1	155	7	1	0	1	0
93-94—Toronto	NHL	64	4	4	8	185	10	0	0	0	18
94-95—Toronto	NHL	2	0	0	0	5	—	—	—	—	—
NHL totals....................		406	10	22	32	1551	31	1	1	2	81

BAUMGARTNER, NOLAN
D, CAPITALS

PERSONAL: Born March 23, 1976, in Calgary. . . . 6-1/200. . . . Shoots right.

HIGH SCHOOL: Norkam Secondary (Kamloops, B.C.).

TRANSACTIONS/CAREER NOTES: Selected by Washington Capitals in first round (first Capitals pick, 10th overall) of NHL entry draft (June 28, 1994).

HONORS: Named to Memorial Cup All-Star team (1993-94 and 1994-95). . . . Won Can.HL Defenseman of the Year Award (1994-95). . . . Won Bill Hunter Trophy (1994-95). . . . Named to Can.HL All-Star first team (1994-95). . . . Named to WHL (West) All-Star first team (1994-95).

Season Team	League	REGULAR SEASON Gms.	G	A	Pts.	PIM	PLAYOFFS Gms.	G	A	Pts.	PIM
92-93—Kamloops	WHL	43	0	5	5	30	11	1	1	2	0
93-94—Kamloops	WHL	69	13	42	55	109	19	3	14	17	33
94-95—Kamloops	WHL	62	8	36	44	71	21	4	13	17	16

BAUTIN, SERGEI
D, RED WINGS

PERSONAL: Born March 11, 1967, in Murmansk, U.S.S.R. . . . 6-3/218. . . . Shoots left. . . . Name pronounced SAIR-gay bah-OO-tihn.

TRANSACTIONS/CAREER NOTES: Selected by Winnipeg Jets in first round (first Jets pick, 17th overall) of NHL entry draft (June 20, 1992). . . . Injured hip (December 29, 1993); missed one game. . . . Reinjured hip (January 2, 1993); missed two games. . . . Fractured foot (February 28, 1993); missed nine games. . . . Bruised foot (October 6, 1993); missed three games. . . . Traded by Jets with G Bob Essensa to Detroit Red Wings for G Tim Cheveldae and LW Dallas Drake (March 8, 1994).

Season Team	League	REGULAR SEASON Gms.	G	A	Pts.	PIM	PLAYOFFS Gms.	G	A	Pts.	PIM
90-91—Dynamo Moscow	USSR	33	2	0	2	28	—	—	—	—	—
91-92—Dynamo Moscow	CIS	37	1	3	4	88	—	—	—	—	—
—Unified Olympic Team.......	Int'l	8	0	0	0	6	—	—	—	—	—
92-93—Winnipeg	NHL	71	5	18	23	96	6	0	0	0	2
93-94—Winnipeg	NHL	59	0	7	7	78	—	—	—	—	—
—Detroit	NHL	1	0	0	0	0	—	—	—	—	—
—Adirondack	AHL	9	1	5	6	6	—	—	—	—	—
94-95—Adirondack	AHL	32	0	10	10	57	1	0	0	0	4
NHL totals....................		131	5	25	30	174	6	0	0	0	2

BEAUBIEN, FREDERICK

G, KINGS

PERSONAL: Born April 1, 1975, in Levis, Que.... 6-1/204.... Catches left.... Name pronounced boh-BYEHN.
TRANSACTIONS/CAREER NOTES: Selected by Los Angeles Kings in fifth round (fourth Kings pick, 105th overall) of NHL entry draft (June 26, 1993).

Season Team	League	Gms.	Min.	W	L	T	GA	SO	Avg.	Gms.	Min.	W	L	GA	SO	Avg.
					REGULAR SEASON							PLAYOFFS				
92-93—St. Hyacinthe	QMJHL	33	1702	8	16	3	133	0	4.69	—						
93-94—St. Hyacinthe	QMJHL	47	2663	19	19	5	168	1	3.79	7	411	3	4	33	0	4.82
94-95—St. Hyacinthe	QMJHL	51	2697	19	24	4	178	1	3.96	3	176	1	2	9	0	3.07

BEAUDOIN, NIC

LW, DENVER

PERSONAL: Born December 25, 1976, in Ottawa.... 6-3/192.... Shoots left.
TRANSACTIONS/CAREER NOTES: Selected by Denver in second round (second Denver pick, 51st overall) of NHL entry draft (July 8, 1995).

Season Team	League	Gms.	G	A	Pts.	PIM	Gms.	G	A	Pts.	PIM
			REGULAR SEASON					PLAYOFFS			
92-93—Ottawa	Tier II Jr. A	51	13	22	35	62	—				
93-94—Detroit	OHL	63	9	18	27	32	17	1	2	3	13
94-95—Detroit	OHL	11	1	3	4	16	21	5	7	12	16

B

BEAUPRE, DON

G, SENATORS

PERSONAL: Born September 19, 1961, in Kitchener, Ont.... 5-10/172.... Catches left.... Full name: Donald William Beaupre.... Name pronounced boh-PRAY.
TRANSACTIONS/CAREER NOTES: Selected by Minnesota North Stars as underage junior in second round (second North Stars pick, 37th overall) of NHL entry draft (June 11, 1980).... Bruised ribs (October 1981).... Sprained knee (February 1985).... Pulled groin muscle (December 1987).... Traded by North Stars to Washington Capitals for rights to D Claudio Scremin (November 1, 1988).... Injured ligaments in right thumb (January 31, 1990); missed nine games.... Pulled left groin (October 30, 1990); missed 12 games.... Pulled muscle (November 5, 1992); missed three games.... Pulled groin (January 2, 1993); missed two games.... Traded by Capitals to Ottawa Senators for fifth-round pick (LW Benoit Gratton) in 1995 draft (January 18, 1995).... Suffered from the flu (March 10, 1995); missed one game.
HONORS: Named to OMJHL All-Star first team (1979-80).... Played in NHL All-Star Game (1981 and 1992).

Season Team	League	Gms.	Min.	W	L	T	GA	SO	Avg.	Gms.	Min.	W	L	GA	SO	Avg.
					REGULAR SEASON							PLAYOFFS				
78-79—Sudbury	OMJHL	54	3248	...	...	...	*259	2	4.78	10	600	...	...	44	...	4.40
79-80—Sudbury	OMJHL	59	3447	28	29	2	248	0	4.32	9	552	5	4	38	0	4.13
80-81—Minnesota	NHL	44	2585	18	14	11	138	0	3.20	6	360	4	2	26	0	4.33
81-82—Nashville	CHL	5	299	2	3	0	25	0	5.02	—						
—Minnesota	NHL	29	1634	11	8	9	101	0	3.71	2	60	0	1	4	0	4.00
82-83—Birmingham	CHL	10	599	8	2	0	31	0	3.11	—						
—Minnesota	NHL	36	2011	19	10	5	120	0	3.58	4	245	2	2	20	0	4.90
83-84—Salt Lake City	CHL	7	419	2	5	0	30	0	4.30	—						
—Minnesota	NHL	33	1791	16	13	2	123	0	4.12	13	782	6	7	40	1	3.07
84-85—Minnesota	NHL	31	1770	10	17	3	109	1	3.69	4	184	1	1	12	0	3.91
85-86—Minnesota	NHL	52	3073	25	20	6	182	1	3.55	5	300	2	3	17	0	3.40
86-87—Minnesota	NHL	47	2622	17	20	6	174	1	3.98	—						
87-88—Minnesota	NHL	43	2288	10	22	3	161	0	4.22	—						
88-89—Minnesota	NHL	1	59	0	1	0	3	0	3.05	—						
—Kalamazoo	IHL	3	179	1	2	†0	9	0	3.02	—						
—Baltimore	AHL	30	1715	14	12	2	102	0	3.57	—						
—Washington	NHL	11	578	5	4	0	28	1	2.91	—						
89-90—Washington	NHL	48	2793	23	18	5	150	2	3.22	8	401	4	3	18	0	2.69
90-91—Baltimore	AHL	2	120	2	0	0	3	0	1.50	—						
—Washington	NHL	45	2572	20	18	3	113	*5	2.64	11	624	5	5	29	†1	2.79
91-92—Baltimore	AHL	3	184	1	1	1	10	0	3.26	—						
—Washington	NHL	54	3108	29	17	6	166	1	3.20	7	419	3	4	22	0	3.15
92-93—Washington	NHL	58	3282	27	23	5	181	1	3.31	2	119	1	1	9	0	4.54
93-94—Washington	NHL	53	2853	24	16	8	135	2	2.84	8	429	5	2	21	1	2.94
94-95—Ottawa	NHL	38	2161	8	25	3	121	1	3.36	—						
NHL totals		623	35180	262	246	75	2005	16	3.42	70	3923	33	31	218	3	3.33

BEAUREGARD, STEPHANE

G, JETS

PERSONAL: Born January 10, 1968, in Cowansville, Que.... 5-11/190.... Catches right.... Name pronounced steh-FAN BOH-rih-GAHRD.
TRANSACTIONS/CAREER NOTES: Selected by Winnipeg Jets in third round (third Jets pick, 52nd overall) of NHL entry draft (June 11, 1988).... Suffered hip flexor (October 29, 1991); missed four games.... Traded by Jets to Buffalo Sabres for C Christian Ruuttu and future considerations (June 15, 1992).... Traded by Sabres with future considerations to Chicago Blackhawks for G Dominik Hasek (August 7, 1992).... Traded by Blackhawks to Jets for C Christian Ruuttu and future considerations (August 10, 1992).... Traded by Jets to Philadelphia Flyers for third-round pick in 1993 draft and fifth-round pick in 1994 draft (October 1, 1992).... Traded by Flyers to Jets for third-round pick in 1993 draft and future considerations (February 8, 1993); trade nullified by NHL, citing league bylaw that prohibits trading player within month of waiver draft and reacquiring him later in season (February 9, 1993).... Traded by Flyers to Jets for fourth-round pick in 1993 draft and fifth-round pick in 1994 draft (June 11, 1993).... Suffered from the flu (October 26, 1993); missed two games.
HONORS: Won Jacques Plante Trophy (1987-88).... Won Raymond Lagace Trophy (1987-88).... Won Marcel Robert Trophy (1987-88).... Named to QMJHL All-Star first team (1987-88).

			REGULAR SEASON							PLAYOFFS						
Season Team	League	Gms.	Min.	W	L	T	GA	SO	Avg.	Gms.	Min.	W	L	GA	SO	Avg.
86-87—St. Jean	QMJHL	13	785	6	7	0	58	0	4.43	5	260	1	3	26	0	6.00
87-88—St. Jean	QMJHL	*66	*3766	38	20	3	229	2	*3.65	7	423	3	4	34	0	4.82
88-89—Moncton	AHL	15	824	4	8	2	62	0	4.51	—	—	—	—	—	—	—
—Fort Wayne	IHL	16	830	9	5	‡0	43	0	3.11	9	484	4	4	21	*1	*2.60
89-90—Fort Wayne	IHL	33	1949	20	8	‡3	115	1	3.54	—	—	—	—	—	—	—
—Winnipeg	NHL	19	1079	7	8	3	59	0	3.28	4	238	1	3	12	0	3.03
90-91—Winnipeg	NHL	16	836	3	10	1	55	0	3.95	—	—	—	—	—	—	—
—Moncton	AHL	9	504	3	4	1	20	1	2.38	1	60	1	0	1	0	1.00
—Fort Wayne	IHL	32	1761	14	13	‡2	109	0	3.71	*19	*1158	10	9	57	2	2.95
91-92—Winnipeg	NHL	26	1267	6	8	6	61	2	2.89	—	—	—	—	—	—	—
92-93—Philadelphia	NHL	16	802	3	9	0	59	0	4.41	—	—	—	—	—	—	—
—Hershey	AHL	13	794	5	5	3	48	0	3.63	—	—	—	—	—	—	—
93-94—Winnipeg	NHL	13	418	0	4	1	34	0	4.88	—	—	—	—	—	—	—
—Moncton	AHL	37	2083	18	11	6	121	1	3.49	21	*1304	†12	*9	58	*2	2.67
94-95—Springfield	AHL	24	1381	10	11	3	73	2	3.17	—	—	—	—	—	—	—
NHL totals		90	4402	19	39	11	268	2	3.65	4	238	1	3	12	0	3.03

BEDDOES, CLAYTON
C, BRUINS

PERSONAL: Born November 10, 1970, in Bentley, Alta. . . . 5-10/180. . . . Shoots left. . . . Name pronounced BEH-dohs.
HIGH SCHOOL: Bentley (Alta.).
COLLEGE: Lake Superior State (Mich.).
TRANSACTIONS/CAREER NOTES: Signed as free agent by Boston Bruins (May 24, 1994).
HONORS: Named to NCCA All-America West second team (1993-94). . . . Named to CCHA All-Star second team (1993-94).

			REGULAR SEASON				PLAYOFFS			
Season Team	League	Gms.	G	A	Pts.	PIM	Gms.	G	A	Pts.	PIM
90-91—Lake Superior State	CCHA	45	14	28	42	26	—	—	—	—	—
91-92—Lake Superior State	CCHA	42	16	28	44	26	—	—	—	—	—
92-93—Lake Superior State	CCHA	45	18	40	58	32	—	—	—	—	—
93-94—Lake Superior State	CCHA	44	23	31	54	56	—	—	—	—	—
94-95—Providence	AHL	65	16	20	36	39	13	3	1	4	18

BEERS, BOB
D, ISLANDERS

PERSONAL: Born May 20, 1967, in Pittsburgh. . . . 6-2/200. . . . Shoots right.
COLLEGE: Northern Arizona, then Maine.
TRANSACTIONS/CAREER NOTES: Selected by Boston Bruins in 11th round (10th Bruins pick, 220th overall) of NHL entry draft (June 15, 1985). . . . Broke right leg (May 9, 1990). . . . Underwent surgery to remove pin from right hip (December 10, 1990); missed four games. . . . Suffered tendinitis in right hip (January 6, 1991). . . . Traded by Bruins to Tampa Bay Lightning for D Stephane Richer (October 28, 1992). . . . Traded by Lightning to Edmonton Oilers for D Chris Joseph (November 12, 1993). . . . Signed as free agent by New York Islanders (August 29, 1994). . . . Fractured facial bones (January 16, 1995); missed 18 games. . . . Injured eye (March 5, 1995); missed one game.
HONORS: Named Hockey East Tournament Most Valuable Player (1988-89). . . . Named to NCAA All-America East second team (1988-89). . . . Named to Hockey East All-Star second team (1988-89).

			REGULAR SEASON				PLAYOFFS			
Season Team	League	Gms.	G	A	Pts.	PIM	Gms.	G	A	Pts.	PIM
85-86—Northern Arizona Univ.	Indep.	28	11	39	50	96	—	—	—	—	—
86-87—University of Maine	Hockey East	38	0	13	13	46	—	—	—	—	—
87-88—University of Maine	Hockey East	41	3	11	14	72	—	—	—	—	—
88-89—University of Maine	Hockey East	44	10	27	37	53	—	—	—	—	—
89-90—Maine	AHL	74	7	36	43	63	—	—	—	—	—
—Boston	NHL	3	0	1	1	6	14	1	1	2	18
90-91—Maine	AHL	36	2	16	18	21	—	—	—	—	—
—Boston	NHL	16	0	1	1	10	6	0	0	0	4
91-92—Boston	NHL	31	0	5	5	29	1	0	0	0	0
—Maine	AHL	33	6	23	29	24	—	—	—	—	—
92-93—Providence	AHL	6	1	2	3	10	—	—	—	—	—
—Tampa Bay	NHL	64	12	24	36	70	—	—	—	—	—
—Atlanta	IHL	1	0	0	0	0	—	—	—	—	—
93-94—Tampa Bay	NHL	16	1	5	6	12	—	—	—	—	—
—Edmonton	NHL	66	10	27	37	74	—	—	—	—	—
94-95—New York Islanders	NHL	22	2	7	9	6	—	—	—	—	—
NHL totals		218	25	70	95	207	21	1	1	2	22

BELAK, WADE
D, DENVER

PERSONAL: Born July 3, 1976, in North Battleford, Sask. . . . 6-4/213. . . . Shoots right.
HIGH SCHOOL: North Battleford (Sask.) Comprehensive.
TRANSACTIONS/CAREER NOTES: Selected by Quebec Nordiques in first round (first Nordiques pick, 12th overall) of NHL entry draft (June 28, 1994). . . . Nordiques franchise moved to Denver for 1995-96 season.

			REGULAR SEASON				PLAYOFFS			
Season Team	League	Gms.	G	A	Pts.	PIM	Gms.	G	A	Pts.	PIM
91-92—North Battleford	SJHL	57	6	20	26	186	—	—	—	—	—
92-93—North Battleford	SJHL	32	3	13	16	142	—	—	—	—	—
93-94—Saskatoon	WHL	69	4	13	17	226	16	2	2	4	43
94-95—Saskatoon	WHL	72	4	14	18	290	9	0	0	0	36
—Cornwall	AHL	—	—	—	—	—	11	1	2	3	40

BELANGER, JESSE

C, PANTHERS

PERSONAL: Born June 15, 1969, in St. Georges Beauce, Que. . . . 6-0/186. . . . Shoots right. . . . Name pronounced buh-LAHN-zhay.
TRANSACTIONS/CAREER NOTES: Signed as free agent by Montreal Canadiens (October 3, 1990). . . . Selected by Florida Panthers in NHL expansion draft (June 24, 1993). . . . Strained right Achilles tendon (October 12, 1993); missed one game. . . . Broke bone in left hand (February 13, 1994); missed 12 games. . . . Suffered from illness (March 24, 1995); missed one game.
MISCELLANEOUS: Member of Stanley Cup championship team (1993).

Season Team	League	REGULAR SEASON					PLAYOFFS				
		Gms.	G	A	Pts.	PIM	Gms.	G	A	Pts.	PIM
87-88—Granby	QMJHL	69	33	43	76	10	5	3	3	6	0
88-89—Granby	QMJHL	67	40	63	103	26	4	0	5	5	0
89-90—Granby	QMJHL	67	53	54	107	53	—	—	—	—	—
90-91—Fredericton	AHL	75	40	58	98	30	6	2	4	6	0
91-92—Fredericton	AHL	65	30	41	71	26	7	3	3	6	2
—Montreal	NHL	4	0	0	0	0	—	—	—	—	—
92-93—Fredericton	AHL	39	19	32	51	24	—	—	—	—	—
—Montreal	NHL	19	4	2	6	4	9	0	1	1	0
93-94—Florida	NHL	70	17	33	50	16	—	—	—	—	—
94-95—Florida	NHL	47	15	14	29	18	—	—	—	—	—
NHL totals		140	36	49	85	38	9	0	1	1	0

BELANGER, KEN

LW, MAPLE LEAFS

PERSONAL: Born May 14, 1974, in Sault Ste. Marie, Ont. . . . 6-4/225. . . . Shoots left. . . . Name pronounced buh-LAHN-zhay.
TRANSACTIONS/CAREER NOTES: Selected by Hartford Whalers in seventh round (seventh Whalers pick, 153rd overall) of NHL entry draft (June 20, 1992). . . . Traded by Whalers to Toronto Maple Leafs for ninth-round pick (RW Matt Ball) in 1994 draft (March 18, 1994).

Season Team	League	REGULAR SEASON					PLAYOFFS				
		Gms.	G	A	Pts.	PIM	Gms.	G	A	Pts.	PIM
91-92—Ottawa	OHL	51	4	4	8	174	11	0	0	0	24
92-93—Ottawa	OHL	34	6	12	18	139	—	—	—	—	—
—Guelph	OHL	29	10	14	24	86	5	2	1	3	14
93-94—Guelph	OHL	55	11	22	33	185	9	2	3	5	30
94-95—St. John's	AHL	47	5	5	10	246	4	0	0	0	30
—Toronto	NHL	3	0	0	0	9	—	—	—	—	—
NHL totals		3	0	0	0	9					

BELANGER, MARTIN

D, CANADIENS

PERSONAL: Born February 3, 1976, in La Salle, Que. . . . 6-0/206. . . . Shoots right. . . . Name pronounced mahr-TAN bay-lahn-ZHAY.
TRANSACTIONS/CAREER NOTES: Selected by Montreal Canadiens in third round (fifth Canadiens pick, 74th overall) of NHL entry draft (June 29, 1994).

Season Team	League	REGULAR SEASON					PLAYOFFS				
		Gms.	G	A	Pts.	PIM	Gms.	G	A	Pts.	PIM
92-93—Granby	QMJHL	49	2	19	21	24	—	—	—	—	—
93-94—Granby	QMJHL	63	8	32	40	49	7	0	1	1	28
94-95—Granby	QMJHL	43	0	11	11	32	12	0	1	1	6

BELFOUR, ED

G, BLACKHAWKS

PERSONAL: Born April 21, 1965, in Carman, Man. . . . 5-11/182. . . . Catches left.
COLLEGE: North Dakota.
TRANSACTIONS/CAREER NOTES: Signed as free agent by Chicago Blackhawks (June 18, 1987). . . . Strained hip muscle (1993-94 season); missed four games.
HONORS: Named top goaltender in MJHL (1985-86). . . . Named to NCAA All-America West second team (1986-87). . . . Named to NCAA All-Tournament team (1986-87). . . . Named to WCHA All-Star first team (1986-87). . . . Shared Garry F. Longman Memorial Trophy with John Cullen (1987-88). . . . Named to IHL All-Star first team (1987-88). . . . Named Rookie of the Year by THE SPORTING NEWS (1990-91). . . . Won Vezina Trophy (1990-91 and 1992-93). . . . Won Calder Memorial Trophy (1990-91). . . . Won William M. Jennings Trophy (1990-91, 1992-93 and 1994-95). . . . Won Trico Goaltender Award (1990-91). . . . Named to THE SPORTING NEWS All-Star first team (1990-91). . . . Named to NHL All-Star first team (1990-91 and 1992-93). . . . Named to NHL All-Rookie team (1990-91). . . . Played in NHL All-Star Game (1992 and 1993). . . . Named to THE SPORTING NEWS All-Star second team (1992-93 and 1994-95).
RECORDS: Shares NHL single-season playoff record for most consecutive wins by goaltender—11 (1992).

Season Team	League	REGULAR SEASON								PLAYOFFS						
		Gms.	Min.	W	L	T	GA	SO	Avg.	Gms.	Min.	W	L	GA	SO	Avg.
85-86—Winkler	MJHL	48	2880	...	...	...	124	1	2.58	—	—	—	—	—	—	—
86-87—Univ. of North Dakota	WCHA	34	2049	29	4	0	81	3	2.37	—	—	—	—	—	—	—
87-88—Saginaw	IHL	61	*3446	32	25	‡0	183	3	3.19	9	561	4	5	33	0	3.53
88-89—Chicago	NHL	23	1148	4	12	3	74	0	3.87	—	—	—	—	—	—	—
—Saginaw	IHL	29	1760	12	10	‡0	92	0	3.14	5	298	2	3	14	0	2.82
89-90—Can. national team	Int'l	33	1808	...	...	...	93	...	3.09	—	—	—	—	—	—	—
—Chicago	NHL	—	—	—	—	—	—	—	—	9	409	4	2	17	0	2.49
90-91—Chicago	NHL	*74	*4127	*43	19	7	170	4	*2.47	6	295	2	4	20	0	4.07
91-92—Chicago	NHL	52	2928	21	18	10	132	†5	2.70	18	949	12	4	39	1	*2.47
92-93—Chicago	NHL	*71	*4106	41	18	11	177	*7	2.59	4	249	0	4	13	0	3.13
93-94—Chicago	NHL	70	3998	37	24	6	178	†7	2.67	6	360	2	4	15	0	2.50
94-95—Chicago	NHL	42	2450	22	15	3	93	†5	2.28	16	1014	9	†7	37	1	2.19
NHL totals		332	18757	168	106	40	824	28	2.64	59	3276	29	25	141	2	2.58

BELLOWS, BRIAN

LW, LIGHTNING

PERSONAL: Born September 1, 1964, in St. Catharines, Ont. . . . 5-11/209. . . . Shoots right.

TRANSACTIONS/CAREER NOTES: Separated shoulder (November 1981); coached Kitchener Rangers for two games while recovering (became the youngest coach in OHL history at 17 years old). . . . Selected by Minnesota North Stars as underage junior in first round (first North Stars pick, second overall) of NHL entry draft (June 9, 1982). . . . Suffered tendinitis in elbow (October 1984). . . . Injured wrist (October 1986); missed 13 games. . . . Strained abdominal muscles (February 1989); missed 20 games. . . . Bruised left knee (September 1990). . . . Strained hip and groin (December 18, 1990). . . . Traded by North Stars to Montreal Canadiens for RW Russ Courtnall (August 31, 1992). . . . Injured neck (December 3, 1992); missed two games. . . . Injured rib cage (November 20, 1993); missed seven games. . . . Separated shoulder (February 18, 1995); missed two games. . . . Separated shoulder (February 25, 1995); missed five games. . . . Traded by Canadiens to Tampa Bay Lightning for C Marc Bureau (June 30, 1995).

HONORS: Named to Memorial Cup All-Star team (1980-81). . . . Won George Parsons Trophy (1981-82). . . . Named to OHL All-Star first team (1981-82). . . . Played in NHL All-Star Game (1984, 1988 and 1992). . . . Named to THE SPORTING NEWS All-Star second team (1989-90). . . . Named to NHL All-Star second team (1989-90).

STATISTICAL PLATEAUS: Three-goal games: 1987-88 (1), 1988-89 (1), 1989-90 (1), 1990-91 (1), 1991-92 (1). Total: 5. . . . Four-goal games: 1985-86 (1), 1991-92 (1), 1992-93 (1). Total: 3. . . . Total hat tricks: 8.

MISCELLANEOUS: Co-captain of Minnesota North Stars (1983-84). . . . Member of Stanley Cup championship team (1993).

Season Team	League	REGULAR SEASON					PLAYOFFS				
		Gms.	G	A	Pts.	PIM	Gms.	G	A	Pts.	PIM
80-81—Kitchener	OMJHL	66	49	67	116	23	16	14	13	27	13
81-82—Kitchener	OHL	47	45	52	97	23	15	16	13	29	11
82-83—Minnesota	NHL	78	35	30	65	27	9	5	4	9	18
83-84—Minnesota	NHL	78	41	42	83	66	16	2	12	14	6
84-85—Minnesota	NHL	78	26	36	62	72	9	2	4	6	9
85-86—Minnesota	NHL	77	31	48	79	46	5	5	0	5	16
86-87—Minnesota	NHL	65	26	27	53	34	—	—	—	—	—
87-88—Minnesota	NHL	77	40	41	81	81	—	—	—	—	—
88-89—Minnesota	NHL	60	23	27	50	55	5	2	3	5	8
89-90—Minnesota	NHL	80	55	44	99	72	7	4	3	7	10
90-91—Minnesota	NHL	80	35	40	75	43	23	10	19	29	30
91-92—Minnesota	NHL	80	30	45	75	41	7	4	4	8	14
92-93—Montreal	NHL	82	40	48	88	44	18	6	9	15	18
93-94—Montreal	NHL	77	33	38	71	36	6	1	2	3	2
94-95—Montreal	NHL	41	8	8	16	8	—	—	—	—	—
NHL totals		953	423	474	897	625	105	41	60	101	131

BELOV, OLEG

C, PENGUINS

PERSONAL: Born April 20, 1973, in Moscow, U.S.S.R. . . . 6-0/185. . . . Shoots left.

TRANSACTIONS/CAREER NOTES: Selected by Pittsburgh Penguins in fourth round (third Penguins pick, 102nd overall) of NHL entry draft (July 8, 1995).

Season Team	League	REGULAR SEASON					PLAYOFFS				
		Gms.	G	A	Pts.	PIM	Gms.	G	A	Pts.	PIM
91-92—CSKA Moscow	CIS	1	0	0	0	2	—	—	—	—	—
92-93—CSKA Moscow	CIS	42	7	4	11	18	—	—	—	—	—
93-94—CSKA Moscow	CIS	46	14	8	22	18	3	1	0	1	2
94-95—CSKA Moscow	CIS	46	21	18	39	51	—	—	—	—	—

BENNING, BRIAN

D, PANTHERS

PERSONAL: Born June 10, 1966, in Edmonton. . . . 6-0/196. . . . Shoots left. . . . Full name: Brian Anthony Benning. . . . Brother of Jim Benning, defenseman, Toronto Maple Leafs and Vancouver Canucks (1981-82 through 1989-90) and current scout, Buffalo Sabres.

HIGH SCHOOL: St. Joseph (Edmonton).

TRANSACTIONS/CAREER NOTES: Cracked bone in right wrist (December 1983); missed 38 games. . . . Selected by St. Louis Blues as underage junior in second round (first Blues pick, 26th overall) of NHL entry draft (June 9, 1984). . . . Broke right leg (December 28, 1984). . . . Traded by Blues to Los Angeles Kings for third-round pick (RW Kyle Reeves) in 1991 draft (November 10, 1989). . . . Underwent appendectomy (March 6, 1990); missed three weeks. . . . Suspended three games by NHL for cross-checking (September 28, 1990). . . . Suffered back spasms (December 1990). . . . Injured groin (October 22, 1991); missed three games. . . . Traded by Kings with D Jeff Chychrun and first-round pick in 1992 draft (traded to Philadelphia Flyers) to Pittsburgh Penguins for D Paul Coffey (February 19, 1992). . . . Traded by Penguins with RW Mark Recchi and first-round pick in 1992 draft (LW Jason Bowen) to Philadelphia Flyers for RW Rick Tocchet, D Kjell Samuelsson, G Ken Wregget and third-round pick (RW Sergei Zholtok) in 1992 draft (February 19, 1992). . . . Strained back (October 26, 1992); missed three games. . . . Traded by Flyers to Edmonton Oilers for C Josef Beranek and D Greg Hawgood (January 16, 1993). . . . Strained groin (January 23, 1993); missed five games. . . . Strained wrist (February 23, 1993); missed three games. . . . Signed as free agent by Florida Panthers (July 15, 1993). . . . Bruised left shoulder (October 12, 1993); missed five games. . . . Suspended four games by NHL for slashing (November 16, 1993).

HONORS: Named to NHL All-Rookie team (1986-87).

Season Team	League	REGULAR SEASON					PLAYOFFS				
		Gms.	G	A	Pts.	PIM	Gms.	G	A	Pts.	PIM
83-84—Portland	WHL	38	6	41	47	108	—	—	—	—	—
84-85—Kamloops	WHL	17	3	18	21	26	—	—	—	—	—
—St. Louis	NHL	4	0	2	2	0	—	—	—	—	—
85-86—Canadian national team	Int'l	60	6	13	19	43	—	—	—	—	—
—St. Louis	NHL	—	—	—	—	—	6	1	2	3	13
86-87—St. Louis	NHL	78	13	36	49	110	6	0	4	4	9
87-88—St. Louis	NHL	77	8	29	37	107	10	1	6	7	25
88-89—St. Louis	NHL	66	8	26	34	102	7	1	1	2	11

Season	Team	League	REGULAR SEASON Gms.	G	A	Pts.	PIM	PLAYOFFS Gms.	G	A	Pts.	PIM
89-90—St. Louis		NHL	7	1	1	2	2	—	—	—	—	—
—Los Angeles		NHL	48	5	18	23	104	7	0	2	2	10
90-91—Los Angeles		NHL	61	7	24	31	127	12	0	5	5	6
91-92—Los Angeles		NHL	53	2	30	32	99	—	—	—	—	—
—Philadelphia		NHL	22	2	12	14	35	—	—	—	—	—
92-93—Philadelphia		NHL	37	9	17	26	93	—	—	—	—	—
—Edmonton		NHL	18	1	7	8	59	—	—	—	—	—
93-94—Florida		NHL	73	6	24	30	107	—	—	—	—	—
94-95—Florida		NHL	24	1	7	8	18	—	—	—	—	—
NHL totals			568	63	233	296	963	48	3	20	23	74

BERANEK, JOSEF
C, CANUCKS

PERSONAL: Born October 25, 1969, in Litvinov, Czechoslovakia. . . . 6-2/189. . . . Shoots left. . . . Name pronounced JOH-sehf buh-RAH-nehk. **TRANSACTIONS/CAREER NOTES:** Selected by Edmonton Oilers in fourth round (third Oilers pick, 78th overall) of NHL entry draft (June 17, 1989). . . . Traded by Oilers with D Greg Hawgood to Philadelphia Flyers for D Brian Benning (January 16, 1993). . . . Bruised left shoulder (January 30, 1994); missed three games. . . . Played in Europe during 1994-95 NHL lockout. . . . Traded by Flyers to Vancouver Canucks for LW Shawn Antoski (February 15, 1995). **STATISTICAL PLATEAUS:** Three-goal games: 1994-95 (1).

Season	Team	League	REGULAR SEASON Gms.	G	A	Pts.	PIM	PLAYOFFS Gms.	G	A	Pts.	PIM
87-88—CHZ Litvinov		Czech.	14	7	4	11	12	—	—	—	—	—
88-89—CHZ Litvinov		Czech.	32	18	10	28	47	—	—	—	—	—
—Czechoslovakia Jr.		Czech.	5	2	7	9	2	—	—	—	—	—
89-90—Dukla Trencin		Czech.	49	16	21	37	. . .	—	—	—	—	—
90-91—CHZ Litvinov		Czech.	50	27	27	54	98	—	—	—	—	—
91-92—Edmonton		NHL	58	12	16	28	18	12	2	1	3	0
92-93—Edmonton		NHL	26	2	6	8	28	—	—	—	—	—
—Cape Breton		AHL	6	1	2	3	8	—	—	—	—	—
—Philadelphia		NHL	40	13	12	25	50	—	—	—	—	—
93-94—Philadelphia		NHL	80	28	21	49	85	—	—	—	—	—
94-95—Dadak Vsetin		Czech.	16	7	7	14	26	—	—	—	—	—
—Philadelphia		NHL	14	5	5	10	2	—	—	—	—	—
—Vancouver		NHL	37	8	13	21	28	11	1	1	2	12
NHL totals			255	68	73	141	211	23	3	2	5	12

BERARD, BRYAN
D, SENATORS

PERSONAL: Born March 5, 1977, in Woonsocket, R.I. . . . 6-1/195. . . . Shoots left. **HIGH SCHOOL:** Mount St. Charles (Woonsocket, R.I.). **COLLEGE:** University of Michigan-Dearborn. **TRANSACTIONS/CAREER NOTES:** Selected by Ottawa Senators in first round (first Senators pick, first overall) of NHL entry draft (July 8, 1995). **HONORS:** Won Can.HL Rookie of the Year Award (1994-95). . . . Won Can.HL Top Draft Prospect Award (1994-95). . . . Won Emms Family Trophy (1994-95). . . . Won Max Kaminsky Trophy (1994-95). . . . Won OHL Top Draft Prospect Award (1994-95). . . . Named to Can.HL All-Star first team (1994-95). . . . Named to Can.HL All-Rookie team (1994-95). . . . Named to OHL All-Star first team (1994-95).

Season	Team	League	REGULAR SEASON Gms.	G	A	Pts.	PIM	PLAYOFFS Gms.	G	A	Pts.	PIM
91-92—Mount St. Charles H.S.		R.I.H.S.	32	3	15	18	10	—	—	—	—	—
92-93—Mount St. Charles H.S.		R.I.H.S.	32	8	12	20	18	—	—	—	—	—
93-94—Mount St. Charles H.S.		R.I.H.S.	32	11	36	47	5	—	—	—	—	—
94-95—Detroit		OHL	58	20	55	75	97	21	4	20	24	38

BEREHOWSKY, DRAKE
D, PENGUINS

PERSONAL: Born January 3, 1972, in Toronto. . . . 6-2/211. . . . Shoots right. . . . Name pronounced BAIR-uh-HOW-skee. **TRANSACTIONS/CAREER NOTES:** Injured knees and underwent reconstructive surgery (October 13, 1989); missed remainder of season. . . . Selected by Toronto Maple Leafs in first round (first Maple Leafs pick, 10th overall) of NHL entry draft (June 16, 1990). . . . Sprained knee (April 15, 1993); missed remainder of season. . . . Underwent off-season knee surgery; missed four games. . . . Traded by Maple Leafs to Pittsburgh Penguins for D Grant Jennings (April 7, 1995). **HONORS:** Won Can.HL Defenseman of the Year Award (1991-92). . . . Won Max Kaminsky Trophy (1991-92). . . . Named to Can.HL All-Star first team (1991-92). . . . Named to OHL All-Star first team (1991-92).

Season	Team	League	REGULAR SEASON Gms.	G	A	Pts.	PIM	PLAYOFFS Gms.	G	A	Pts.	PIM
87-88—Barrie Jr. B		OHA	40	10	36	46	81	—	—	—	—	—
88-89—Kingston		OHL	63	7	39	46	85	—	—	—	—	—
89-90—Kingston		OHL	9	3	11	14	28	—	—	—	—	—
90-91—Toronto		NHL	8	0	1	1	25	—	—	—	—	—
—Kingston		OHL	13	5	13	18	28	—	—	—	—	—
—North Bay		OHL	26	7	23	30	51	10	2	7	9	21
91-92—North Bay		OHL	62	19	63	82	147	21	7	24	31	22
—Toronto		NHL	1	0	0	0	0	—	—	—	—	—
—St. John's		AHL						6	0	5	5	21

Season	Team	League	Gms.	G	A	Pts.	PIM	Gms.	G	A	Pts.	PIM
92-93—Toronto		NHL	41	4	15	19	61	—	—	—	—	—
—St. John's		AHL	28	10	17	27	38	—	—	—	—	—
93-94—Toronto		NHL	49	2	8	10	63	—	—	—	—	—
—St. John's		AHL	18	3	12	15	40	—	—	—	—	—
94-95—Toronto		NHL	25	0	2	2	15	—	—	—	—	—
—Pittsburgh		NHL	4	0	0	0	13	1	0	0	0	0
NHL totals			128	6	26	32	177	1	0	0	0	0

BEREZIN, SERGEI
RW, MAPLE LEAFS

PERSONAL: Born November 5, 1971.... 5-10/172.... Shoots right.
TRANSACTIONS/CAREER NOTES: Selected by Toronto Maple Leafs in 10th round (eighth Maple Leafs pick, 256th overall) of NHL entry draft (June 29, 1994).

Season	Team	League	Gms.	G	A	Pts.	PIM	Gms.	G	A	Pts.	PIM
93-94—Khimik Voskresensk		CIS	40	31	10	41	16	—	—	—	—	—
94-95—Koln		Germany	43	38	19	57	8	18	17	8	25	18

BERG, AKI-PETTERI
D, KINGS

PERSONAL: Born July 28, 1977, in Turku, Finland.... 6-3/196.... Shoots left.
TRANSACTIONS/CAREER NOTES: Selected by Los Angeles Kings in first round (first Kings pick, third overall) of NHL entry draft (July 8, 1995).

Season	Team	League	Gms.	G	A	Pts.	PIM	Gms.	G	A	Pts.	PIM
92-93—TPS Jr.		Finland	39	18	24	42	59	—	—	—	—	—
93-94—TPS Jr.		Finland	21	3	11	14	24	7	0	0	0	10
—TPS Turku		Finland	6	0	3	3	4	—	—	—	—	—
94-95—Kiekko-67		Finland Dv.II	20	3	9	12	34	—	—	—	—	—
—TPS Jr.		Finland	8	1	0	1	30	—	—	—	—	—
—TPS Turku		Finland	5	0	0	0	4	—	—	—	—	—

BERG, BILL
LW, MAPLE LEAFS

PERSONAL: Born October 21, 1967, in St. Catharines, Ont.... 6-1/205.... Shoots left.
TRANSACTIONS/CAREER NOTES: Broke ankle (March 1985).... Selected by New York Islanders as underage junior in third round (third Islanders pick, 59th overall) of NHL entry draft (June 21, 1986). ... Injured knee (October 1986).... Separated shoulder (May 1990).... Fractured left foot (November 9, 1991); missed 12 games.... Claimed on waivers by Toronto Maple Leafs (December 3, 1992).... Injured hip flexor (November 18, 1993); missed one game.... Sprained knee (February 6, 1995); missed 16 games.
MISCELLANEOUS: Moved from defense to left wing (1990).

Season	Team	League	Gms.	G	A	Pts.	PIM	Gms.	G	A	Pts.	PIM
84-85—Grimsby Jr. B		OHA	42	10	22	32	153	—	—	—	—	—
85-86—Toronto		OHL	64	3	35	38	143	4	0	0	0	19
86-87—Toronto		OHL	57	3	15	18	138	—	—	—	—	—
—Springfield		AHL	4	1	1	2	4	—	—	—	—	—
87-88—Springfield		AHL	76	6	26	32	148	—	—	—	—	—
—Peoria		IHL	5	0	1	1	8	7	0	3	3	31
88-89—New York Islanders		NHL	7	1	2	3	10	—	—	—	—	—
—Springfield		AHL	69	17	32	49	122	—	—	—	—	—
89-90—Springfield		AHL	74	12	42	54	74	15	5	12	17	35
90-91—New York Islanders		NHL	78	9	14	23	67	—	—	—	—	—
91-92—New York Islanders		NHL	47	5	9	14	28	—	—	—	—	—
—Capital District		AHL	3	0	2	2	16	—	—	—	—	—
92-93—New York Islanders		NHL	22	6	3	9	49	—	—	—	—	—
—Toronto		NHL	58	7	8	15	54	21	1	1	2	18
93-94—Toronto		NHL	83	8	11	19	93	18	1	2	3	10
94-95—Toronto		NHL	32	5	1	6	26	7	0	1	1	4
NHL totals			327	41	48	89	327	46	2	4	6	32

BERGERON, JEAN-CLAUDE
G, LIGHTNING

PERSONAL: Born October 14, 1968, in Hauterive, Que.... 5-9/181. ... Catches left.
TRANSACTIONS/CAREER NOTES: Selected by Montreal Canadiens in fifth round (sixth Canadiens pick, 104th overall) of NHL entry draft (June 11, 1988).... Traded by Canadiens to Tampa Bay Lightning for G Frederic Chabot (June 18, 1992).
HONORS: Won Aldege (Baz) Bastien Trophy (1989-90).... Shared Harry (Hap) Holmes Memorial Trophy with Andre Racicot (1989-90).... Named to AHL All-Star first team (1989-90).... Shared James Norris Memorial Trophy with Mike Greenlay (1993-94).

Season	Team	League	Gms.	Min.	W	L	T	GA	SO	Avg.	Gms.	Min.	W	L	GA	SO	Avg.
85-86—Shawinigan		QMJHL	33	1796	...	...	...	156	0	5.21	—	—	—	—	—	—	—
86-87—Verdun		QMJHL	52	2991	...	...	...	*306	0	6.14	—	—	—	—	—	—	—
87-88—Verdun		QMJHL	49	2715	13	31	3	*265	0	5.86	—	—	—	—	—	—	—
88-89—Verdun		QMJHL	44	2417	8	34	1	199	0	4.94	—	—	—	—	—	—	—
—Sherbrooke		AHL	5	302	4	1	0	18	0	3.58	—	—	—	—	—	—	—

Season Team	League	REGULAR SEASON								PLAYOFFS						
		Gms.	Min.	W	L	T	GA	SO	Avg.	Gms.	Min.	W	L	GA	SO	Avg.
89-90—Sherbrooke	AHL	40	2254	21	8	7	103	2	*2.74	9	497	6	2	28	0	3.38
90-91—Montreal	NHL	18	941	7	6	2	59	0	3.76	—	—	—	—	—	—	—
—Fredericton	AHL	18	1083	12	6	0	59	1	3.27	10	546	5	5	32	0	3.52
91-92—Fredericton	AHL	13	791	5	7	1	57	0	4.32	—	—	—	—	—	—	—
—Peoria	IHL	27	1632	14	9	‡3	96	1	3.53	6	352	3	3	24	0	4.09
92-93—Atlanta	IHL	31	1722	21	7	†0	92	1	3.21	6	368	3	3	19	0	3.10
—Tampa Bay	NHL	21	1163	8	10	1	71	0	3.66	—	—	—	—	—	—	—
93-94—Tampa Bay	NHL	3	134	1	1	1	7	0	3.13	—	—	—	—	—	—	—
—Atlanta	IHL	48	2755	27	11	‡7	141	0	3.07	2	153	1	1	6	0	2.35
94-95—Tampa Bay	NHL	17	883	3	9	1	49	1	3.33	—	—	—	—	—	—	—
—Atlanta	IHL	6	324	3	3	‡0	24	0	4.44	—	—	—	—	—	—	—
NHL totals		59	3121	19	26	5	186	1	3.58							

BERGEVIN, MARC

D, LIGHTNING

PERSONAL: Born August 11, 1965, in Montreal. . . . 6-1/197. . . . Shoots left. . . . Name pronounced BUHR-zhuh-van.

TRANSACTIONS/CAREER NOTES: Selected by Chicago Blackhawks as underage junior in third round (third Blackhawks pick, 59th overall) of NHL entry draft (June 8, 1983). . . . Sprained neck (March 18, 1987). . . . Traded by Blackhawks with D Gary Nylund to New York Islanders for D Steve Konroyd and C Bob Bassen (November 25, 1988). . . . Bruised ribs (November 25, 1989). . . . Broke hand (May 1990). . . . Traded by Islanders to Hartford Whalers for future considerations; Islanders received fifth-round pick (C Ryan Duthie) in 1992 draft to complete deal (October 31, 1990). . . . Signed as free agent by Tampa Bay Lightning (July 9, 1992). . . . Injured foot (March 18, 1993); missed one game. . . . Bruised back (November 19, 1993); missed one game. . . . Injured elbow (March 10, 1995); missed one game. . . . Suffered from sore neck (April 22, 1995); missed three games.

Season Team	League	REGULAR SEASON					PLAYOFFS				
		Gms.	G	A	Pts.	PIM	Gms.	G	A	Pts.	PIM
82-83—Chicoutimi	QMJHL	64	3	27	30	113	—	—	—	—	—
83-84—Chicoutimi	QMJHL	70	10	35	45	125	—	—	—	—	—
—Springfield	AHL	7	0	1	1	2	—	—	—	—	—
84-85—Chicago	NHL	60	0	6	6	54	6	0	3	3	2
—Springfield	AHL	—	—	—	—	—	4	0	0	0	0
85-86—Chicago	NHL	71	7	7	14	60	3	0	0	0	0
86-87—Chicago	NHL	66	4	10	14	66	3	1	0	1	2
87-88—Chicago	NHL	58	1	6	7	85	—	—	—	—	—
—Saginaw	IHL	10	2	7	9	20	—	—	—	—	—
88-89—Chicago	NHL	11	0	0	0	18	—	—	—	—	—
—New York Islanders	NHL	58	2	13	15	62	—	—	—	—	—
89-90—New York Islanders	NHL	18	0	4	4	30	—	—	—	—	—
—Springfield	AHL	47	7	16	23	66	17	2	11	13	16
90-91—Hartford	NHL	4	0	0	0	4	—	—	—	—	—
—Capital District	AHL	7	0	5	5	6	—	—	—	—	—
—Springfield	AHL	58	4	23	27	85	18	0	7	7	26
91-92—Hartford	NHL	75	7	17	24	64	5	0	0	0	2
92-93—Tampa Bay	NHL	78	2	12	14	66	—	—	—	—	—
93-94—Tampa Bay	NHL	83	1	15	16	87	—	—	—	—	—
94-95—Tampa Bay	NHL	44	2	4	6	51	—	—	—	—	—
NHL totals		626	26	94	120	647	17	1	3	4	6

BERGQVIST, STEFAN

D, PENGUINS

PERSONAL: Born March 10, 1975, in Leksand, Sweden. . . . 6-3/216. . . . Shoots left. . . . Brother of Jonas Bergqvist, right winger, Calgary Flames (1989-90).

TRANSACTIONS/CAREER NOTES: Selected by Pittsburgh Penguins in first round (first Penguins pick, 26th overall) of NHL entry draft (June 26, 1993).

Season Team	League	REGULAR SEASON					PLAYOFFS				
		Gms.	G	A	Pts.	PIM	Gms.	G	A	Pts.	PIM
92-93—Leksand	Sweden	15	0	0	0	6	—	—	—	—	—
93-94—Leksand	Sweden	6	0	0	0	0	—	—	—	—	—
94-95—London	OHL	64	3	17	20	93	4	0	0	0	5

BERTUZZI, TODD

LW, ISLANDERS

PERSONAL: Born February 2, 1975, in Sudbury, Ont. . . . 6-3/227. . . . Shoots left. . . . Name pronounced buhr-TOO-zee.

HIGH SCHOOL: Bishop MacDonnell (Guelph, Ont.).

TRANSACTIONS/CAREER NOTES: Selected by New York Islanders in first round (first Islanders pick, 23rd overall) of NHL entry draft (June 26, 1993).

HONORS: Named to OHL All-Star second team (1994-95).

Season Team	League	REGULAR SEASON					PLAYOFFS				
		Gms.	G	A	Pts.	PIM	Gms.	G	A	Pts.	PIM
91-92—Guelph	OHL	47	7	14	21	145	—	—	—	—	—
92-93—Guelph	OHL	59	27	32	59	164	5	2	2	4	6
93-94—Guelph	OHL	61	28	54	82	165	9	2	6	8	30
94-95—Guelph	OHL	62	54	65	119	58	14	*15	18	33	41

BERUBE, CRAIG
LW, CAPITALS

PERSONAL: Born December 17, 1965, in Calihoo, Alta. . . . 6-1/205. . . . Shoots left. . . . Name pronounced buh-ROO-bee.

TRANSACTIONS/CAREER NOTES: Signed as free agent by Philadelphia Flyers (March 19, 1986). . . . Sprained left knee (March 1988). . . . Traded by Flyers with RW Scott Mellanby and C Craig Fisher to Edmonton Oilers for RW Dave Brown, D Corey Foster and the NHL rights to RW Jari Kurri (May 30, 1991). . . . Traded by Oilers with G Grant Fuhr and RW/LW Glenn Anderson to Toronto Maple Leafs for LW Vincent Damphousse, D Luke Richardson, G Peter Ing, C Scott Thornton and future considerations (September 19, 1991). . . . Traded by Maple Leafs with D Alexander Godynyuk, RW Gary Leeman, D Michel Petit and G Jeff Reese to Calgary Flames for C Doug Gilmour, D Jamie Macoun, LW Kent Manderville, D Ric Nattress and G Rick Wamsley (January 2, 1992). . . . Traded by Flames to Washington Capitals for fifth-round pick (C Darryl LaFrance) in 1993 draft (June 26, 1993). . . . Suffered from the flu (March 31, 1995); missed three games.

Season	Team	League	Gms.	G	A	Pts.	PIM	Gms.	G	A	Pts.	PIM
82-83—	Williams Lake	PCJHL	33	9	24	33	99	—	—	—	—	—
—	Kamloops	WHL	4	0	0	0	0	—	—	—	—	—
83-84—	New Westminster	WHL	70	11	20	31	104	8	1	2	3	5
84-85—	New Westminster	WHL	70	25	44	69	191	10	3	2	5	4
85-86—	Kamloops	WHL	32	17	14	31	119	—	—	—	—	—
—	Medicine Hat	WHL	34	14	16	30	95	25	7	8	15	102
86-87—	Hershey	AHL	63	7	17	24	325	—	—	—	—	—
—	Philadelphia	NHL	7	0	0	0	57	5	0	0	0	17
87-88—	Hershey	AHL	31	5	9	14	119	—	—	—	—	—
—	Philadelphia	NHL	27	3	2	5	108	—	—	—	—	—
88-89—	Hershey	AHL	7	0	2	2	19	—	—	—	—	—
—	Philadelphia	NHL	53	1	1	2	199	16	0	0	0	56
89-90—	Philadelphia	NHL	74	4	14	18	291	—	—	—	—	—
90-91—	Philadelphia	NHL	74	8	9	17	293	—	—	—	—	—
91-92—	Toronto	NHL	40	5	7	12	109	—	—	—	—	—
—	Calgary	NHL	36	1	4	5	155	—	—	—	—	—
92-93—	Calgary	NHL	77	4	8	12	209	6	0	1	1	21
93-94—	Washington	NHL	84	7	7	14	305	8	0	0	0	21
94-95—	Washington	NHL	43	2	4	6	173	7	0	0	0	29
NHL totals			**515**	**35**	**56**	**91**	**1899**	**42**	**0**	**1**	**1**	**144**

BES, JEFF
C, WHALERS

PERSONAL: Born July 31, 1973, in Tillsonburg, Ont. . . . 6-0/190. . . . Shoots left. . . . Name pronounced BEHZ.

HIGH SCHOOL: Bishop MacDonell (Guelph, Ont.).

TRANSACTIONS/CAREER NOTES: Selected by Minnesota North Stars in third round (second North Stars pick, 58th overall) of NHL entry draft (June 20, 1992). . . . North Stars franchise moved from Minnesota to Dallas and renamed Stars for 1993-94 season. . . . Claimed on waivers by Hartford Whalers (July 31, 1995).

Season	Team	League	Gms.	G	A	Pts.	PIM	Gms.	G	A	Pts.	PIM
87-88—	Woodstock Jr. C	OHA	33	19	10	29	16	—	—	—	—	—
88-89—	St. Mary's Jr. B	OHA	37	8	22	30	37	—	—	—	—	—
89-90—	St. Mary's Jr. B	OHA	39	25	37	62	127	—	—	—	—	—
90-91—	Dukes of Hamilton	OHL	66	23	47	70	53	4	1	4	5	4
91-92—	Guelph	OHL	62	40	62	102	123	—	—	—	—	—
92-93—	Guelph	OHL	59	48	67	115	128	5	3	5	8	4
—	Kalamazoo	IHL	3	1	3	4	6	—	—	—	—	—
93-94—	Dayton	ECHL	2	2	0	2	12	—	—	—	—	—
—	Kalamazoo	IHL	30	2	12	14	30	—	—	—	—	—
94-95—	Kalamazoo	IHL	52	8	17	25	47	—	—	—	—	—

BESTER, ALLAN
G

PERSONAL: Born March 26, 1964, in Hamilton, Ont. . . . 5-7/155. . . . Catches left.

TRANSACTIONS/CAREER NOTES: Selected by Toronto Maple Leafs as underage junior in third round (third Maple Leafs pick, 48th overall) of NHL entry draft (June 8, 1983). . . . Sprained left knee ligaments (February 1988); missed 14 games. . . . Suffered phlebitis in right leg (January 1989). . . . Stretched knee ligaments (April 1989). . . . Suffered from bone spurs in right heel (October 1989). . . . Underwent surgery for calcium deposits on his heels (October 1990). . . . Traded by Maple Leafs to Detroit Red Wings for sixth-round pick (C Alexander Kuzminsky) in 1991 draft (March 5, 1991). . . . Signed as free agent by Mighty Ducks of Anaheim (September 7, 1993). . . . Signed as free agent by Orlando Solar Bears of IHL (July 10, 1995).

HONORS: Named to OHL All-Star first team (1982-83). . . . Won Jack Butterfield Trophy (1991-92).

Season	Team	League	Gms.	Min.	W	L	T	GA	SO	Avg.	Gms.	Min.	W	L	GA	SO	Avg.
81-82—	Brantford	OHL	19	970	4	11	0	68	0	4.21	—	—	—	—	—	—	—
82-83—	Brantford	OHL	56	3210	29	21	3	188	0	3.51	8	480	3	3	20	†1	*2.50
83-84—	Brantford	OHL	23	1271	12	9	1	71	1	3.35	1	60	0	1	5	0	5.00
—	Toronto	NHL	32	1848	11	16	4	134	0	4.35	—	—	—	—	—	—	—
84-85—	St. Catharines	AHL	30	1669	9	18	1	133	0	4.78	—	—	—	—	—	—	—
—	Toronto	NHL	15	767	3	9	1	54	1	4.22	—	—	—	—	—	—	—
85-86—	St. Catharines	AHL	50	2855	23	23	3	173	1	3.64	11	637	7	3	27	0	2.54
—	Toronto	NHL	1	20	0	0	0	2	0	6.00	—	—	—	—	—	—	—
86-87—	Newmarket	AHL	3	190	1	0	0	6	0	1.89	—	—	—	—	—	—	—
—	Toronto	NHL	36	1808	10	14	3	110	2	3.65	1	39	0	0	1	0	1.54
87-88—	Toronto	NHL	30	1607	8	12	5	102	2	3.81	5	253	2	3	21	0	4.98

Season	Team	League	REGULAR SEASON								PLAYOFFS						
			Gms.	Min.	W	L	T	GA	SO	Avg.	Gms.	Min.	W	L	GA	SO	Avg.
88-89—Toronto	NHL	43	2460	17	20	3	156	2	3.80	—	—	—	—	—	—	—
89-90—Newmarket	AHL	5	264	2	1	1	18	0	4.09	—	—	—	—	—	—	—
—Toronto	NHL	42	2206	20	16	0	165	0	4.49	—	—	—	—	—	—	—
90-91—Toronto	NHL	6	247	0	4	0	18	0	4.37	—	—	—	—	—	—	—
—Detroit	NHL	3	178	0	3	0	13	0	4.38	1	20	0	0	1	0	3.00
—Newmarket	AHL	19	1157	7	8	4	58	1	3.01	—	—	—	—	—	—	—
91-92—Detroit	NHL	1	31	0	0	0	2	0	3.87	—	—	—	—	—	—	—
—Adirondack	AHL	22	1268	13	8	0	78	0	3.69	†19	1174	*14	5	50	1	2.56
92-93—Adirondack	AHL	41	2268	16	15	5	133	1	3.52	10	633	7	3	26	†1	2.46
93-94—San Diego	IHL	46	2543	22	14	‡6	150	1	3.54	8	419	4	4	28	0	4.01
94-95—San Diego	IHL	58	3251	28	23	‡5	183	1	3.38	4	272	2	2	13	0	2.87
NHL totals		209	11172	69	94	16	756	7	4.06	7	312	2	3	23	0	4.42

BETS, MAXIM
LW, MIGHTY DUCKS

PERSONAL: Born January 31, 1974, in Chelyabinsk, U.S.S.R. . . . . 6-1/185. . . . Shoots left. . . . Name pronounced MAKS-eem BEHTS.
TRANSACTIONS/CAREER NOTES: Selected by St. Louis Blues in second round (first Blues pick, 37th overall) of NHL entry draft (June 26, 1993). . . . Traded by Blues with sixth-round pick in 1995 draft (traded back to St. Louis) to Mighty Ducks of Anaheim for D Alexei Kasatonov (March 21, 1994).
HONORS: Named to Can.HL All-Rookie team (1992-93).

Season	Team	League	REGULAR SEASON					PLAYOFFS				
			Gms.	G	A	Pts.	PIM	Gms.	G	A	Pts.	PIM
90-91—Traktor Juniors	CIS	60	71	37	108	. . .	—	—	—	—	—
91-92—Traktor Chelyabinsk	CIS	25	1	1	2	8	—	—	—	—	—
92-93—Spokane	WHL	54	49	57	106	130	9	5	6	11	20
93-94—Spokane	WHL	63	46	70	116	111	3	1	1	2	12
—Anaheim	NHL	3	0	0	0	0	—	—	—	—	—
—San Diego	IHL	—	—	—	—	—	9	0	2	2	0
94-95—San Diego	IHL	36	2	6	8	31	—	—	—	—	—
—Worcester	AHL	9	1	1	2	6	—	—	—	—	—
NHL totals		3	0	0	0	0	—	—	—	—	—

BETY, SEBASTIEN
D, DENVER

PERSONAL: Born May 6, 1976, in St.-Bernard Beauce, Que. . . . 6-2/201. . . . Shoots left. . . . Name pronounced BAY-tee.
TRANSACTIONS/CAREER NOTES: Selected by Quebec Nordiques in third round (fourth Nordiques pick, 61st overall) of NHL entry draft (June 29, 1994). . . . Nordiques franchise moved to Denver for 1995-96 season.

Season	Team	League	REGULAR SEASON					PLAYOFFS				
			Gms.	G	A	Pts.	PIM	Gms.	G	A	Pts.	PIM
92-93—Drummondville	QMJHL	70	1	21	22	126	10	1	2	3	24
93-94—Drummondville	QMJHL	67	3	8	11	164	10	0	0	0	17
94-95—Drummondville	QMJHL	22	1	7	8	77	—	—	—	—	—
—Chicoutimi	QMJHL	24	4	9	13	109	13	1	5	6	46

BEUKEBOOM, JEFF
D, RANGERS

PERSONAL: Born March 28, 1965, in Ajax, Ont. . . . 6-5/225. . . . Shoots right. . . . Name pronounced BOO-kuh-BOOM. . . . Nephew of Ed Kea, defenseman, Atlanta Flames and St. Louis Blues (1973-74 through 1982-83); and cousin of Joe Nieuwendyk, center, Calgary Flames.
TRANSACTIONS/CAREER NOTES: Selected by Edmonton Oilers as underage junior in first round (first Oilers pick, 19th overall) of NHL entry draft (June 8, 1983). . . . Injured knee (December 1984). . . . Lacerated knuckle (October 24, 1987). . . . Suspended 10 games by NHL for leaving the bench (October 2, 1988). . . . Sprained right knee (January 1989). . . . Suffered hairline fracture of ankle (February 22, 1991); missed two games. . . . Traded by Oilers to New York Rangers for D David Shaw (November 12, 1991), completing deal in which Oilers traded C Mark Messier with future considerations to Rangers for C Bernie Nicholls, LW Louie DeBrusk, RW Steven Rice and future considerations (October 4, 1991). . . . Strained back (March 16, 1992); missed one game. . . . Injured knee (December 21, 1992); missed one game. . . . Bruised ankle (February 1, 1993); missed one game. . . . Suspended one game by NHL for hitting from behind (May 25, 1994). . . . Suffered neck spasms (March 5, 1995); missed one game. . . . Bruised chest (March 18, 1995); missed three games.
HONORS: Named to OHL All-Star first team (1984-85).
MISCELLANEOUS: Member of Stanley Cup championship teams (1987, 1988, 1990 and 1994).

Season	Team	League	REGULAR SEASON					PLAYOFFS				
			Gms.	G	A	Pts.	PIM	Gms.	G	A	Pts.	PIM
81-82—Newmarket	OPJHL	49	5	30	35	218	—	—	—	—	—
82-83—Sault Ste. Marie	OHL	70	0	25	25	143	16	1	14	15	46
83-84—Sault Ste. Marie	OHL	61	6	30	36	178	16	1	7	8	43
84-85—Sault Ste. Marie	OHL	37	4	20	24	85	16	4	6	10	47
85-86—Nova Scotia	AHL	77	9	20	29	175	—	—	—	—	—
—Edmonton	NHL	—	—	—	—	—	1	0	0	0	4
86-87—Nova Scotia	AHL	14	1	7	8	35	—	—	—	—	—
—Edmonton	NHL	44	3	8	11	124	—	—	—	—	—
87-88—Edmonton	NHL	73	5	20	25	201	7	0	0	0	16
88-89—Cape Breton	AHL	8	0	4	4	36	—	—	—	—	—
—Edmonton	NHL	36	0	5	5	94	1	0	0	0	2

B

Season Team	League	REGULAR SEASON Gms.	G	A	Pts.	PIM	PLAYOFFS Gms.	G	A	Pts.	PIM
89-90—Edmonton	NHL	46	1	12	13	86	2	0	0	0	0
90-91—Edmonton	NHL	67	3	7	10	150	18	1	3	4	28
91-92—Edmonton	NHL	18	0	5	5	78	—	—	—	—	—
—New York Rangers	NHL	56	1	10	11	122	13	2	3	5	*47
92-93—New York Rangers	NHL	82	2	17	19	153	—	—	—	—	—
93-94—New York Rangers	NHL	68	8	8	16	170	22	0	6	6	50
94-95—New York Rangers	NHL	44	1	3	4	70	9	0	0	0	10
NHL totals		534	24	95	119	1248	73	3	12	15	157

BIALOWAS, FRANK
D

PERSONAL: Born July 11, 1969, in Winnipeg. . . . 5-11/220. . . . Shoots left. . . . Name pronounced bigh-uh-LOH-uhz.
TRANSACTIONS/CAREER NOTES: Signed as free agent by Toronto Maple Leafs (December 1992).

Season Team	League	REGULAR SEASON Gms.	G	A	Pts.	PIM	PLAYOFFS Gms.	G	A	Pts.	PIM
91-92—Roanoke	ECHL	23	4	2	6	150	3	0	0	0	4
92-93—Richmond	ECHL	60	3	18	21	261	1	0	0	0	2
—St. John's	AHL	7	1	0	1	28	1	0	0	0	0
93-94—St. John's	AHL	69	2	8	10	352	7	0	3	3	25
—Toronto	NHL	3	0	0	0	12	—	—	—	—	—
94-95—St. John's	AHL	51	2	3	5	277	4	0	0	0	12
NHL totals		3	0	0	0	12					

BICANEK, RADIM
D, SENATORS

PERSONAL: Born January 18, 1975, in Uherske Hradiste, Czechoslovakia. . . . 6-1/195. . . . Shoots left. . . . Name pronounced RA-deem BEECH-ih-nehk.
TRANSACTIONS/CAREER NOTES: Selected by Ottawa Senators in second round (second Senators pick, 27th overall) of NHL entry draft (June 26, 1993).

Season Team	League	REGULAR SEASON Gms.	G	A	Pts.	PIM	PLAYOFFS Gms.	G	A	Pts.	PIM
92-93—Jihlava	Czech.	43	2	3	5	...	—	—	—	—	—
93-94—Belleville	OHL	63	16	27	43	49	12	2	8	10	21
94-95—Belleville	OHL	49	13	26	39	61	16	6	5	11	30
—Ottawa	NHL	6	0	0	0	0	—	—	—	—	—
—Prince Edward Island	AHL	—	—	—	—	—	3	0	1	1	0
NHL totals		6	0	0	0	0					

BIENVENUE, DANIEL
LW, SABRES

PERSONAL: Born June 10, 1977, in Val d'Or, Que. . . . 6-0/195. . . . Shoots left.
TRANSACTIONS/CAREER NOTES: Selected by Buffalo Sabres in fifth round (eighth Sabres pick, 123rd overall) of NHL entry draft (July 8, 1995).

Season Team	League	REGULAR SEASON Gms.	G	A	Pts.	PIM	PLAYOFFS Gms.	G	A	Pts.	PIM
93-94—Chicoutimi	QMJHL	42	2	7	9	4	0	0	0	0	0
94-95—Val-d'Or	QMJHL	67	27	14	41	40	—	—	—	—	—

BILLINGTON, CRAIG
G, BRUINS

PERSONAL: Born September 11, 1966, in London, Ont. . . . 5-10/170. . . . Catches left.
TRANSACTIONS/CAREER NOTES: Selected by New Jersey Devils as underage junior in second round (second Devils pick, 23rd overall) of NHL entry draft (June 9, 1984). . . . Suffered from mononucleosis (July 1984). . . . Injured hamstring (February 15, 1992); missed two games. . . . Strained knee (March 11, 1992); missed six games. . . . Underwent arthroscopic knee surgery (April 13, 1992). . . . Suffered from sore throat (March 27, 1993); missed one game. . . . Traded by Devils with C/LW Troy Mallette and fourth-round pick in 1993 draft (C Cosmo Dupaul) to Ottawa Senators for G Peter Sidorkiewicz and future considerations (June 20, 1993); Senators sent LW Mike Peluso to Devils to complete deal (June 26, 1993). . . . Injured knee (January 27, 1995); missed 17 games. . . . Traded by Senators to Boston Bruins for eighth-round pick in 1996 draft (April 7, 1995).
HONORS: Won Bobby Smith Trophy (1984-85). . . . Named to OHL All-Star first team (1984-85). . . . Played in NHL All-Star Game (1993).

Season Team	League	REGULAR SEASON Gms.	Min.	W	L	T	GA	SO	Avg.	PLAYOFFS Gms.	Min.	W	L	GA	SO	Avg.
82-83—London Diamonds	OPJHL	23	1338	...	...	...	76	0	3.41	—						
83-84—Belleville	OHL	44	2335	20	19	0	162	1	4.16	1	30	0	0	3	0	6.00
84-85—Belleville	OHL	47	2544	26	19	0	180	1	4.25	14	761	7	5	47	†1	3.71
85-86—Belleville	OHL	3	180	2	1	0	11	0	3.67	†20	1133	9	6	*68	0	3.60
—New Jersey	NHL	18	701	4	9	1	77	0	6.59	—						
86-87—Maine	AHL	20	1151	9	8	2	70	0	3.65	—						
—New Jersey	NHL	22	1114	4	13	2	89	0	4.79	—						
87-88—Utica	AHL	*59	*3404	22	27	8	*208	1	3.67	—						
88-89—New Jersey	NHL	3	140	1	1	0	11	0	4.71	—						
—Utica	AHL	41	2432	17	18	6	150	2	3.70	4	219	1	3	18	0	4.93
89-90—Utica	AHL	38	2087	20	13	1	138	0	3.97	—						

Season Team	League	Gms.	Min.	W	L	T	GA	SO	Avg.	Gms.	Min.	W	L	GA	SO	Avg.
90-91—Can. national team	Int'l	34	1879	17	14	2	110	2	3.51	—	—	—	—	—	—	—
91-92—New Jersey	NHL	26	1363	13	7	1	69	2	3.04	—	—	—	—	—	—	—
92-93—New Jersey	NHL	42	2389	21	16	4	146	2	3.67	2	78	0	1	5	0	3.85
93-94—Ottawa	NHL	63	3319	11	*41	4	*254	0	4.59	—	—	—	—	—	—	—
94-95—Ottawa	NHL	9	472	0	6	2	32	0	4.07	—	—	—	—	—	—	—
—Boston	NHL	8	373	5	1	0	19	0	3.06	1	25	0	0	1	0	2.40
NHL totals		191	9871	59	94	14	697	4	4.24	3	103	0	1	6	0	3.50

BILODEAU, BRENT
D, CANADIENS

PERSONAL: Born March 27, 1973, in Dallas.... 6-4/215.... Shoots left.... Name pronounced BIHL-uh-DOH.
TRANSACTIONS/CAREER NOTES: Selected by Montreal Canadiens in first round (first Canadiens pick, 17th overall) of NHL entry draft (June 22, 1991).
HONORS: Named to WHL (East) All-Star second team (1991-92 and 1992-93).

Season Team	League	Gms.	G	A	Pts.	PIM	Gms.	G	A	Pts.	PIM
88-89—St. Albert	AJHL	55	8	17	25	167	—	—	—	—	—
89-90—Seattle	WHL	68	14	29	43	170	13	3	5	8	31
90-91—Seattle	WHL	55	7	18	25	145	6	1	0	1	12
91-92—Seattle	WHL	7	1	2	3	43	—	—	—	—	—
—Swift Current	WHL	56	10	47	57	118	8	2	3	5	11
92-93—Swift Current	WHL	59	11	57	68	77	17	5	14	19	18
93-94—Fredericton	AHL	72	2	5	7	89	—	—	—	—	—
94-95—Fredericton	AHL	50	4	8	12	146	12	3	3	6	28

BIRON, MARTIN
G, SABRES

PERSONAL: Born August 15, 1977, in Lac St. Charles, Que.... 6-1/154.... Catches left.
TRANSACTIONS/CAREER NOTES: Selected by Buffalo Sabres in first round (second Sabres pick, 16th overall) of NHL entry draft (July 8, 1995).
HONORS: Won Can.HL Goaltender of the Year Award (1994-95).... Won Raymond Lagace Trophy (1994-95).... Won Mike Bossy Trophy (1994-95).... Won Jacques Plante Trophy (1994-95).... Named to Can.HL All-Star first team (1994-95).... Named to Can.HL All-Rookie team (1994-95).

Season Team	League	Gms.	Min.	W	L	T	GA	SO	Avg.	Gms.	Min.	W	L	GA	SO	Avg.
94-95—Beauport	QMJHL	56	3193	29	16	9	132	3	2.48	16	902	8	7	37	4	2.46

BLAKE, ROB
D, KINGS

PERSONAL: Born December 10, 1969, in Simcoe, Ont.... 6-3/215.... Shoots right.... Full name: Robert Bowlby Blake.
COLLEGE: Bowling Green State.
TRANSACTIONS/CAREER NOTES: Dislocated shoulder (April 1987).... Selected by Los Angeles Kings in fourth round (fourth Kings pick, 70th overall) of NHL entry draft (June 11, 1988).... Sprained knee (April 1990).... Injured knee (February 12, 1991); missed two games.... Injured shoulder (October 8, 1991); missed 11 games.... Sprained knee ligaments (November 28, 1991); missed six games.... Suffered from the flu (January 23, 1992); missed one game.... Suffered from the flu (February 13, 1992); missed one game.... Strained shoulder (March 14, 1992); missed four games.... Broke rib (December 19, 1992); missed three games.... Suffered lower back contusion (April 3, 1993); missed final five games of regular season and one playoff game.... Strained groin (January 23, 1995); missed 11 games.... Strained groin (March 11, 1995); missed 12 games.... Strained groin (April 7, 1995); missed one game.
HONORS: Named to CCHA All-Star second team (1988-89).... Named to NCAA All-America West first team (1989-90).... Named to CCHA All-Star first team (1989-90).... Named to NHL All-Rookie team (1990-91).... Played in NHL All-Star Game (1994).

Season Team	League	Gms.	G	A	Pts.	PIM	Gms.	G	A	Pts.	PIM
86-87—Stratford Jr. B	OHA	31	11	20	31	115	—	—	—	—	—
87-88—Bowling Green State	CCHA	36	5	8	13	72	—	—	—	—	—
88-89—Bowling Green State	CCHA	46	11	21	32	140	—	—	—	—	—
89-90—Bowling Green State	CCHA	42	23	36	59	140	—	—	—	—	—
—Los Angeles	NHL	4	0	0	0	4	8	1	3	4	4
90-91—Los Angeles	NHL	75	12	34	46	125	12	1	4	5	26
91-92—Los Angeles	NHL	57	7	13	20	102	6	2	1	3	12
92-93—Los Angeles	NHL	76	16	43	59	152	23	4	6	10	46
93-94—Los Angeles	NHL	84	20	48	68	137	—	—	—	—	—
94-95—Los Angeles	NHL	24	4	7	11	38	—	—	—	—	—
NHL totals		320	59	145	204	558	49	8	14	22	88

BLOMSTEN, ARTO
D, KINGS

PERSONAL: Born March 16, 1965, in Vaasa, Finland.... 6-3/198.... Shoots left.
TRANSACTIONS/CAREER NOTES: Selected by Winnipeg Jets in 11th round (11th Jets pick, 239th overall) of NHL entry draft (June 21,1986).... Strained groin (October 29, 1993); missed two games.... Traded by Jets to Los Angeles Kings for eighth-round pick (C Frederik Loven) in 1995 draft (March 28, 1995).

Season Team	League	Gms.	G	A	Pts.	PIM	Gms.	G	A	Pts.	PIM
83-84—Djurgarden Stockholm	Sweden	3	0	0	0	4	—	—	—	—	—

Season Team	League	REGULAR SEASON					PLAYOFFS				
		Gms.	G	A	Pts.	PIM	Gms.	G	A	Pts.	PIM
84-85—Djurgarden Stockholm	Sweden	19	3	1	4	22	8	0	0	0	8
85-86—Djurgarden Stockholm	Sweden	8	0	3	3	6	—	—	—	—	—
86-87—Djurgarden Stockholm	Sweden	29	2	4	6	28	—	—	—	—	—
87-88—Djurgarden Stockholm	Sweden	39	12	6	18	36	2	1	0	1	0
88-89—Djurgarden Stockholm	Sweden	40	10	9	19	38	—	—	—	—	—
89-90—Djurgarden Stockholm	Sweden	36	5	21	26	28	8	4	1	5	6
90-91—Djurgarden Stockholm	Sweden	38	2	9	11	42	—	—	—	—	—
91-92—Djurgarden Stockholm	Sweden	39	6	8	14	34	10	2	0	2	8
92-93—Djurgarden Stockholm	Sweden	40	4	16	20	52	—	—	—	—	—
93-94—Winnipeg	NHL	18	0	2	2	6	—	—	—	—	—
—Moncton	AHL	44	6	27	33	25	20	4	10	14	8
94-95—Springfield	AHL	27	3	16	19	20	—	—	—	—	—
—Winnipeg	NHL	1	0	0	0	2	—	—	—	—	—
—Los Angeles....................	NHL	4	0	1	1	0	—	—	—	—	—
—Phoenix	IHL	2	1	2	3	0	8	3	6	9	6
NHL totals...........		23	0	3	3	8					

BLOUIN, SYLVAIN
D, RANGERS

PERSONAL: Born May 21, 1974, in Montreal.... 6-2/190.... Shoots left.
TRANSACTIONS/CAREER NOTES: Selected by New York Rangers in fourth round (fifth Rangers pick, 104th overall) of NHL entry draft (June 29, 1994).... Loaned by Rangers to Chicago Wolves (October 6, 1994).

Season Team	League	REGULAR SEASON					PLAYOFFS				
		Gms.	G	A	Pts.	PIM	Gms.	G	A	Pts.	PIM
91-92—Laval	QMJHL	28	0	0	0	23	9	0	0	0	35
92-93—Laval	QMJHL	68	0	10	10	373	13	1	0	1	*66
93-94—Laval	QMJHL	62	18	22	40	*492	21	4	13	17	*177
94-95—Binghamton	AHL	10	1	0	1	46	2	0	0	0	24
—Chicago	IHL	1	0	0	0	2	—	—	—	—	—
—Charlotte	ECHL	50	5	7	12	280	3	0	0	0	6

BLUE, JOHN
G, BRUINS

PERSONAL: Born February 9, 1966, in Huntington Beach, Calif.... 5-10/185.... Catches left.
COLLEGE: Minnesota.
TRANSACTIONS/CAREER NOTES: Selected by Winnipeg Jets in 10th round (ninth Jets pick, 197th overall) of NHL entry draft (June 21, 1986).... Traded by Jets to Minnesota North Stars for seventh-round pick (C Markus Akerbloom) in 1988 draft (March 7, 1988).... Signed as free agent by Boston Bruins (August 1, 1991).
HONORS: Named to WCHA All-Star second team (1984-85).... Named to WCHA All-Star first team (1985-86).

Season Team	League	REGULAR SEASON							PLAYOFFS						
		Gms.	Min.	W	L	T	GA	SO	Avg.	Gms.	Min.	W	L	GA	SO	Avg.
83-84—Des Moines................	USHL	15	753	...	...	...	63	...	5.02	—	—	—	—	—	—	—
84-85—Univ. of Minnesota......	WCHA	34	1964	23	10	0	111	2	3.39	—	—	—	—	—	—	—
85-86—Univ. of Minnesota......	WCHA	29	1588	20	6	0	80	3	3.02	—	—	—	—	—	—	—
86-87—Univ. of Minnesota......	WCHA	33	1889	21	9	1	99	3	3.14	—	—	—	—	—	—	—
87-88—Kalamazoo	IHL	15	847	3	8	‡4	65	0	4.60	1	40	0	1	6	0	9.00
—U.S. national team	Int'l	13	588	3	4	1	33	0	3.37	—	—	—	—	—	—	—
—U.S. Olympic Team	Int'l						Did not play.									
88-89—Kalamazoo	IHL	17	970	8	6	‡0	69	0	4.27	—	—	—	—	—	—	—
—Virginia......................	ECHL	10	570	...	...	...	38	0	4.00	—	—	—	—	—	—	—
89-90—Kalamazoo	IHL	4	232	2	1	‡1	18	0	4.66	—	—	—	—	—	—	—
—Phoenix	IHL	19	986	5	10	‡3	93	0	5.66	—	—	—	—	—	—	—
—Knoxville	ECHL	19	1000	6	10	‡1	85	...	5.10	—	—	—	—	—	—	—
90-91—Maine....................	AHL	10	545	3	4	2	22	0	2.42	1	40	0	1	7	0	10.50
—Kalamazoo	IHL	1	64	1	0	‡0	2	0	1.88	—	—	—	—	—	—	—
—Albany........................	IHL	19	1077	11	6	‡0	71	0	3.96	—	—	—	—	—	—	—
—Peoria........................	IHL	4	240	4	0	‡0	12	0	3.00	—	—	—	—	—	—	—
—Knoxville	ECHL	3	149	1	1	‡0	13	0	5.23	—	—	—	—	—	—	—
91-92—Maine....................	AHL	43	2168	11	*23	6	165	1	4.57	—	—	—	—	—	—	—
92-93—Providence	AHL	19	1159	14	4	1	67	0	3.47	—	—	—	—	—	—	—
—Boston	NHL	23	1322	9	8	4	64	1	2.90	2	96	0	1	5	0	3.13
93-94—Boston	NHL	18	944	5	8	3	47	0	2.99	—	—	—	—	—	—	—
—Providence	AHL	24	1298	7	11	4	76	1	3.51	—	—	—	—	—	—	—
94-95—Providence	AHL	10	577	6	3	0	30	0	3.12	4	220	1	3	19	0	5.18
NHL totals................		41	2266	14	16	7	111	1	2.94	2	96	0	1	5	0	3.13

BOBACK, MIKE
C

PERSONAL: Born August 13, 1970, in Mt. Clemens, Mich.... 5-11/180.... Shoots right.... Name pronounced BOH-BAK.
COLLEGE: Providence.
TRANSACTIONS/CAREER NOTES: Selected by Washington Capitals in 10th round (12th Capitals pick, 198th overall) of NHL entry draft (June 16, 1990).
HONORS: Named to Hockey East All-Star first team (1989-90 and 1991-92).

Season	Team	League	REGULAR SEASON					PLAYOFFS				
			Gms.	G	A	Pts.	PIM	Gms.	G	A	Pts.	PIM
88-89	Providence College	Hockey East	29	19	19	38	24	—	—	—	—	—
89-90	Providence College	Hockey East	31	13	29	42	28	—	—	—	—	—
90-91	Providence College	Hockey East	26	15	24	39	6	—	—	—	—	—
91-92	Providence College	Hockey East	36	24	*48	*72	34	—	—	—	—	—
92-93	Baltimore	AHL	69	11	68	79	14	5	3	3	6	6
93-94	Portland	AHL	68	16	43	59	50	17	10	17	*27	4
94-95	Portland	AHL	32	14	36	50	20	5	1	4	5	2

BODGER, DOUG
D, SABRES

PERSONAL: Born June 18, 1966, in Chemainus, B.C.... 6-2/213.... Shoots left.... Name pronounced BAH-juhr.

TRANSACTIONS/CAREER NOTES: Selected by Pittsburgh Penguins as underage junior in first round (second Penguins pick, ninth overall) of NHL entry draft (June 9, 1984).... Underwent surgery to remove bone chip on left foot (April 1985).... Sprained knee (December 1987).... Strained left knee (October 1988).... Traded by Penguins with LW Darrin Shannon to Buffalo Sabres for G Tom Barrasso and third-round pick (RW Joe Dziedzic) in 1990 draft (November 12, 1988).... Sprained left knee (October 1989); missed eight games.... Injured shoulder (December 28, 1990); missed four games.... Separated left shoulder (February 17, 1991); missed 18 games.... Reinjured left shoulder (March 30, 1991).... Injured eye (February 11, 1992); missed seven games.... Suffered sore back (December 2, 1993); missed four games.... Suffered from the flu (March 19, 1995); missed one game.... Bruised shoulder (April 28, 1995); missed last three games of season.

HONORS: Named to WHL All-Star second team (1982-83).... Named to WHL (West) All-Star first team (1983-84).

Season	Team	League	REGULAR SEASON					PLAYOFFS				
			Gms.	G	A	Pts.	PIM	Gms.	G	A	Pts.	PIM
82-83	Kamloops	WHL	72	26	66	92	98	7	0	5	5	2
83-84	Kamloops	WHL	70	21	77	98	90	17	2	15	17	12
84-85	Pittsburgh	NHL	65	5	26	31	67	—	—	—	—	—
85-86	Pittsburgh	NHL	79	4	33	37	63	—	—	—	—	—
86-87	Pittsburgh	NHL	76	11	38	49	52	—	—	—	—	—
87-88	Pittsburgh	NHL	69	14	31	45	103	—	—	—	—	—
88-89	Pittsburgh	NHL	10	1	4	5	7	—	—	—	—	—
	Buffalo	NHL	61	7	40	47	52	5	1	1	2	11
89-90	Buffalo	NHL	71	12	36	48	64	6	1	5	6	6
90-91	Buffalo	NHL	58	5	23	28	54	4	0	1	1	0
91-92	Buffalo	NHL	73	11	35	46	108	7	2	1	3	2
92-93	Buffalo	NHL	81	9	45	54	87	8	2	3	5	0
93-94	Buffalo	NHL	75	7	32	39	76	7	0	3	3	6
94-95	Buffalo	NHL	44	3	17	20	47	5	0	4	4	0
	NHL totals		762	89	360	449	780	42	6	18	24	25

BOGUNIECKI, ERIC
C, BLUES

PERSONAL: Born May 6, 1975, in New Haven, Conn.... 5-8/192.... Shoots right.
HIGH SCHOOL: Westminster (Simsbury, Conn.).
COLLEGE: New Hampshire.
TRANSACTIONS/CAREER NOTES: Selected by St. Louis Blues in eighth round (sixth Blues pick, 193rd overall) of NHL entry draft (June 29, 1993).

Season	Team	League	REGULAR SEASON					PLAYOFFS				
			Gms.	G	A	Pts.	PIM	Gms.	G	A	Pts.	PIM
92-93	Westminster School	Conn. H.S.	24	30	24	54	55	—	—	—	—	—
93-94	Univ. of New Hampshire	Hockey East	40	17	16	33	66	—	—	—	—	—
94-95	Univ. of New Hampshire	Hockey East	34	12	19	31	62	—	—	—	—	—

BOHONOS, LONNY
RW, CANUCKS

PERSONAL: Born May 20, 1973, in Winnipeg.... 5-11/190.... Shoots right.... Name pronounced boh-HOH-nohz.
TRANSACTIONS/CAREER NOTES: Signed as free agent by Vancouver Canucks (May 31, 1994).
HONORS: Won Bob Clarke Trophy (1993-94).... Won Brad Hornung Trophy (1993-94).... Named to Can.HL All-Star first team (1993-94).... Named to WHL (West) All-Star first team (1993-94).

Season	Team	League	REGULAR SEASON					PLAYOFFS				
			Gms.	G	A	Pts.	PIM	Gms.	G	A	Pts.	PIM
91-92	Moose Jaw	WHL	8	1	1	2	0	—	—	—	—	—
92-93	Seattle	WHL	46	13	13	26	27	—	—	—	—	—
	Portland	WHL	27	20	17	37	16	15	8	13	21	19
93-94	Portland	WHL	70	*62	*90	*152	80	10	8	11	19	13
94-95	Syracuse	AHL	67	30	45	75	71	—	—	—	—	—

BOILEAU, PATRICK
D, CAPITALS

PERSONAL: Born February 22, 1975, in Montreal.... 6-0/190.... Shoots right.... Name pronounced BOY-loh.
HIGH SCHOOL: CEGEP Lionel-Groulx (Que.).
TRANSACTIONS/CAREER NOTES: Selected by Washington Capitals in third round (third Capitals pick, 69th overall) of NHL entry draft (June 26, 1993).
HONORS: Named to Can.HL All-Rookie team (1992-93).... Won Marcel Robert Trophy (1993-94).... Won Can.HL Scholastic Player of the Year Award (1993-94).

B

Season	Team	League	REGULAR SEASON Gms.	G	A	Pts.	PIM	PLAYOFFS Gms.	G	A	Pts.	PIM
92-93—Laval		QMJHL	69	4	19	23	73	13	1	2	3	10
93-94—Laval		QMJHL	64	13	57	70	56	21	1	7	8	24
94-95—Laval		QMJHL	38	8	25	33	46	20	4	16	20	24

BOIVIN, CLAUDE
LW, SENATORS

PERSONAL: Born March 1, 1970, in St. Foy, Que.... 6-2/200.... Shoots left.... Name pronounced BOY-vihn.

TRANSACTIONS/CAREER NOTES: Selected by Philadelphia Flyers in first round (first Flyers pick, 14th overall) of NHL entry draft (June 11, 1988).... Traded by Drummondville Voltigeurs with D Serge Anglehart and fifth-round draft pick to Laval Titans for D Luc Doucet, D Brad MacIsaac and second- and third-round draft picks (February 15, 1990).... Separated shoulder and bruised chest (October 6, 1992); missed first five games of season.... Tore ligaments in left knee (January 2, 1993) and underwent reconstructive knee surgery (January 18, 1993); missed remainder of season.... Lacerated left elbow (October 30, 1993).... Underwent arthroscopic knee surgery (November 18, 1993); missed 18 games.... Traded by Flyers with G Kirk Daubenspeck to Ottawa Senators for C Mark Lamb (March 5, 1994).

Season	Team	League	REGULAR SEASON Gms.	G	A	Pts.	PIM	PLAYOFFS Gms.	G	A	Pts.	PIM
87-88—Drummondville		QMJHL	63	23	26	49	233	17	5	3	8	74
88-89—Drummondville		QMJHL	63	20	36	56	218	4	0	2	2	27
89-90—Laval		QMJHL	59	24	51	75	309	13	7	13	20	59
90-91—Hershey		AHL	65	13	32	45	159	7	1	5	6	28
91-92—Hershey		AHL	20	4	5	9	96	—	—	—	—	—
—Philadelphia		NHL	58	5	13	18	187	—	—	—	—	—
92-93—Philadelphia		NHL	30	5	4	9	76	—	—	—	—	—
93-94—Hershey		AHL	4	1	6	7	6	—	—	—	—	—
—Philadelphia		NHL	26	1	1	2	57	—	—	—	—	—
—Ottawa		NHL	15	1	0	1	38	—	—	—	—	—
94-95—Prince Edward Island		AHL	22	10	9	19	89	9	1	2	3	32
—Ottawa		NHL	3	0	1	1	6	—	—	—	—	—
NHL totals			132	12	19	31	364					

BOLIBRUCK, KEVIN
D, SENATORS

PERSONAL: Born February 8, 1977, in Peterborough, Ont.... 6-1/197.... Shoots left.
HIGH SCHOOL: Thomas A. Stewart S.S. (Peterborough, Ont.).
TRANSACTIONS/CAREER NOTES: Selected by Ottawa Senators in fourth round (fourth Senators pick, 89th overall) of NHL entry draft (July 8, 1995).

Season	Team	League	REGULAR SEASON Gms.	G	A	Pts.	PIM	PLAYOFFS Gms.	G	A	Pts.	PIM
93-94—Thorold		Jr. B	38	6	18	24	78	—	—	—	—	—
94-95—Peterborough		OHL	66	2	16	18	88	11	1	1	2	14

BOMBARDIR, BRAD
D, DEVILS

PERSONAL: Born May 5, 1972, in Powell River, B.C.... 6-2/187.... Shoots left.... Full name: Luke Bradley Bombardir.... Name pronounced BAHM-bahr-deer.
COLLEGE: North Dakota.
TRANSACTIONS/CAREER NOTES: Selected by New Jersey Devils in third round (fifth Devils pick, 56th overall) of NHL entry draft (June 16, 1990).

Season	Team	League	REGULAR SEASON Gms.	G	A	Pts.	PIM	PLAYOFFS Gms.	G	A	Pts.	PIM
88-89—Powell River		BCJHL	30	6	5	11	24	6	0	0	0	0
89-90—Powell River		BCJHL	60	10	35	45	93	8	2	3	5	4
90-91—Univ. of North Dakota		WCHA	33	3	6	9	18	—	—	—	—	—
91-92—Univ. of North Dakota		WCHA	35	3	14	17	54	—	—	—	—	—
92-93—Univ. of North Dakota		WCHA	38	8	15	23	34	—	—	—	—	—
93-94—Univ. of North Dakota		WCHA	38	5	17	22	38	—	—	—	—	—
94-95—Albany		AHL	77	5	22	27	22	14	0	3	3	6

BONDRA, PETER
RW, CAPITALS

PERSONAL: Born February 7, 1968, in Luck, U.S.S.R.... 6-1/200.... Shoots left.... Name pronounced BAHN-druh.
TRANSACTIONS/CAREER NOTES: Selected by Washington Capitals in eighth round (ninth Capitals pick, 156th overall) of NHL entry draft (June 16, 1990).... Dislocated left shoulder (January 17, 1991).... Suffered recurring shoulder problems (February 13, 1991); missed 13 games.... Suffered throat injury (April 4, 1993); missed one game.... Broke left hand (November 26, 1993); missed 12 games.... Played in Europe during 1994-95 NHL lockout.... Suffered from the flu (April 8, 1995); missed one game.
HONORS: Played in NHL All-Star Game (1993).
STATISTICAL PLATEAUS: Three-goal games: 1993-94 (1), 1994-95 (1). Total: 2.

Season	Team	League	REGULAR SEASON Gms.	G	A	Pts.	PIM	PLAYOFFS Gms.	G	A	Pts.	PIM
88-89—Kosice		Czech.	40	30	10	40	20	—	—	—	—	—
89-90—Kosice		Czech.	42	29	17	46	...	—	—	—	—	—
90-91—Washington		NHL	54	12	16	28	47	4	0	1	1	2
91-92—Washington		NHL	71	28	28	56	42	7	6	2	8	4
92-93—Washington		NHL	83	37	48	85	70	6	0	6	6	0

Season	Team	League		REGULAR SEASON					PLAYOFFS			
			Gms.	G	A	Pts.	PIM	Gms.	G	A	Pts.	PIM
93-94—Washington	NHL	69	24	19	43	40	9	2	4	6	4
94-95—HC Kosice	Slovakia	2	1	0	1	0	—	—	—	—	—
—Washington	NHL	47	*34	9	43	24	7	5	3	8	10
NHL totals		324	135	120	255	223	33	13	16	29	20

BONIN, BRIAN
C, PENGUINS

PERSONAL: Born November 28, 1973, in St. Paul, Minn. . . . 5-10/175. . . . Shoots left.
COLLEGE: Minnesota.
TRANSACTIONS/CAREER NOTES: Selected by Pittsburgh Penguins in ninth round (ninth Penguins pick, 211th overall) of NHL entry draft (June 20, 1992).
HONORS: Named WCHA Player of the Year (1994-95). . . . Named to NCAA All-America West first team (1994-95). . . . Named to WCHA All-Star first team (1994-95).

Season	Team	League		REGULAR SEASON					PLAYOFFS			
			Gms.	G	A	Pts.	PIM	Gms.	G	A	Pts.	PIM
92-93—University of Minnesota	WCHA	38	10	18	28	10	—	—	—	—	—
93-94—University of Minnesota	WCHA	42	24	20	44	14	—	—	—	—	—
94-95—University of Minnesota	WCHA	44	32	31	63	28	—	—	—	—	—

BONK, RADEK
C, SENATORS

PERSONAL: Born January 9, 1976, in Kronov, Czechoslovakia. . . . 6-3/215. . . . Shoots left. . . . Name pronounced RA-dihk bahnk.
TRANSACTIONS/CAREER NOTES: Selected by Ottawa Senators in first round (first Senators pick, third overall) of NHL entry draft (June 28, 1994). . . . Injured ankle (April 26, 1995); missed last five games of season.
HONORS: Won Garry F. Longman Memorial Trophy (1993-94).

Season	Team	League		REGULAR SEASON					PLAYOFFS			
			Gms.	G	A	Pts.	PIM	Gms.	G	A	Pts.	PIM
90-91—Opava	Czech.	35	47	42	89	25	—	—	—	—	—
91-92—ZPS Zlin	Czech-II	45	47	36	83	30	—	—	—	—	—
92-93—ZPS Zlin	Czech.	30	5	5	10	10	—	—	—	—	—
93-94—Las Vegas	IHL	76	42	45	87	208	5	1	2	3	10
94-95—Las Vegas	IHL	33	7	13	20	62	—	—	—	—	—
—Ottawa	NHL	42	3	8	11	28	—	—	—	—	—
—Prince Edward Island	AHL	—	—	—	—	—	1	0	0	0	0
NHL totals		42	3	8	11	28	—	—	—	—	—

BONNER, CRAIG
D, STARS

PERSONAL: Born July 25, 1972, in Edmonton. . . . 6-4/205. . . . Shoots left.
TRANSACTIONS/CAREER NOTES: Signed as free agent by Dallas Stars (July 19, 1994).

Season	Team	League		REGULAR SEASON					PLAYOFFS			
			Gms.	G	A	Pts.	PIM	Gms.	G	A	Pts.	PIM
89-90—Kamloops	WHL	64	1	17	18	77	17	1	2	3	0
90-91—Kamloops	WHL	45	5	13	18	59	1	0	0	0	0
91-92—Kamloops	WHL	67	15	28	43	122	3	0	0	0	8
92-93—Kamloops	WHL	72	8	43	51	143	13	2	5	7	14
93-94—Kalamazoo	IHL	20	0	2	2	49	1	0	0	0	0
94-95—Kalamazoo	IHL	23	0	3	3	42	—	—	—	—	—

BONNER, DOUG
G, MAPLE LEAFS

PERSONAL: Born October 15, 1976, in Tacoma, Wash. . . . 5-9/170. . . . Catches left.
TRANSACTIONS/CAREER NOTES: Selected by Toronto Maple Leafs in sixth round (third Maple Leafs pick, 139th overall) of NHL entry draft (July 8, 1995).

Season	Team	League			REGULAR SEASON						PLAYOFFS					
			Gms.	Min.	W	L	T	GA	SO	Avg.	Gms.	Min.	W	L	GA	SO	Avg.
92-93—Seattle	WHL	30	1212	7	15	0	93	1	4.60	—	—	—	—	—	—	—
93-94—Seattle	WHL	29	1481	9	15	0	111	1	4.50	—	—	—	—	—	—	—
94-95—Seattle	WHL	59	3386	33	23	1	205	1	3.63	3	193	0	3	10	0	3.11

BONSIGNORE, JASON
C, OILERS

PERSONAL: Born April 15, 1976, in Rochester, N.Y. . . . 6-4/208. . . . Shoots right. . . . Name pronounced BAHN-seen-yohr.
TRANSACTIONS/CAREER NOTES: Selected by Edmonton Oilers in first round (first Oilers pick, fourth overall) of NHL entry draft (June 28, 1994).

Season	Team	League		REGULAR SEASON					PLAYOFFS			
			Gms.	G	A	Pts.	PIM	Gms.	G	A	Pts.	PIM
92-93—Newmarket	OHL	66	22	20	42	6	—	—	—	—	—
93-94—Newmarket	OHL	17	7	17	24	22	—	—	—	—	—
—Niagara Falls	OHL	41	15	47	62	41	—	—	—	—	—
—U.S. national team	Int'l	5	0	2	2	0	—	—	—	—	—
94-95—Niagara Falls	OHL	26	12	21	33	51	—	—	—	—	—
—Edmonton	NHL	1	1	0	1	0	—	—	—	—	—
—Sudbury	OHL	23	15	14	29	45	17	13	10	23	12
NHL totals		1	1	0	1	0					

BONVIE, DENNIS
RW/D, OILERS

PERSONAL: Born July 23, 1973, in Antigonish, N.S. . . . 5-11/210. . . . Shoots right. . . . Name pronounced BAHN-vee.
TRANSACTIONS/CAREER NOTES: Signed as free agent by Edmonton Oilers (August 26, 1994).

Season Team	League	Gms.	G	A	Pts.	PIM	Gms.	G	A	Pts.	PIM
				REGULAR SEASON					PLAYOFFS		
90-91—Antigonish	N.S.Jr.A			Statistics unavailable.							
91-92—Kitchener	OHL	7	1	1	2	23	—	—	—	—	—
—North Bay	OHL	49	0	12	12	261	21	0	1	1	91
92-93—North Bay	OHL	64	3	21	24	316	5	0	0	0	34
93-94—Cape Breton	AHL	63	1	10	11	278	4	0	0	0	11
94-95—Cape Breton	AHL	74	5	15	20	422	—	—	—	—	—
—Edmonton	NHL	2	0	0	0	0	—	—	—	—	—
NHL totals		**2**	**0**	**0**	**0**	**0**					

BORDELEAU, SEBASTIEN
C, CANADIENS

PERSONAL: Born February 15, 1975, in Vancouver. . . . 5-10/176. . . . Shoots right. . . . Name pronounced BOHR-duh-loh. . . . Son of Paulin Bordeleau, coach, Fredericton Canadiens of American Hockey League.
TRANSACTIONS/CAREER NOTES: Selected by Montreal Canadiens in third round (third Canadiens pick, 73rd overall) of NHL entry draft (June 26, 1993).
HONORS: Named to QMJHL All-Star first team (1994-95).

Season Team	League	Gms.	G	A	Pts.	PIM	Gms.	G	A	Pts.	PIM
				REGULAR SEASON					PLAYOFFS		
91-92—Hull	QMJHL	62	26	32	58	91	5	0	3	3	23
92-93—Hull	QMJHL	60	18	39	57	95	10	3	8	11	20
93-94—Hull	QMJHL	60	26	57	83	147	17	6	14	20	26
94-95—Hull	QMJHL	68	52	76	128	142	18	13	19	32	25

BORSATO, LUCIANO
C, JETS

PERSONAL: Born January 7, 1966, in Richmond Hill, Ont. . . . 5-11/190. . . . Shoots right. . . . Name pronounced LOO-chee-AH-noh bohr-SAH-toh.
COLLEGE: Clarkson (N.Y.).
TRANSACTIONS/CAREER NOTES: Selected by Winnipeg Jets as underage junior in seventh round (seventh Jets pick, 135th overall) of NHL entry draft (June 9, 1984). . . . Suffered back spasms (October 28, 1992); missed three games. . . . Fractured finger (November 19, 1992); missed eight games. . . . Suffered back spasms (January 17, 1993); missed six games. . . . Suffered back spasms (February 28, 1994); missed three games.
HONORS: Named to NCAA All-America East second team (1987-88). . . . Named to ECAC All-Star second team (1987-88).

Season Team	League	Gms.	G	A	Pts.	PIM	Gms.	G	A	Pts.	PIM
				REGULAR SEASON					PLAYOFFS		
83-84—Bramalea	MTHL	37	20	36	56	59	—	—	—	—	—
84-85—Clarkson	ECAC	33	15	17	32	37	—	—	—	—	—
85-86—Clarkson	ECAC	32	17	20	37	50	—	—	—	—	—
86-87—Clarkson	ECAC	31	16	*41	57	55	—	—	—	—	—
87-88—Clarkson	ECAC	33	15	29	44	38	—	—	—	—	—
—Moncton	AHL	3	1	1	2	0	—	—	—	—	—
88-89—Tappara	Finland	44	31	36	67	69	7	0	3	3	4
—Moncton	AHL	6	2	5	7	4	—	—	—	—	—
89-90—Moncton	AHL	1	1	0	1	0	—	—	—	—	—
90-91—Moncton	AHL	41	14	24	38	40	9	3	7	10	22
—Winnipeg	NHL	1	0	1	1	2	—	—	—	—	—
91-92—Moncton	AHL	14	2	7	9	39	—	—	—	—	—
—Winnipeg	NHL	56	15	21	36	45	1	0	0	0	0
92-93—Winnipeg	NHL	67	15	20	35	38	6	1	0	1	4
93-94—Winnipeg	NHL	75	5	13	18	28	—	—	—	—	—
94-95—Winnipeg	NHL	4	0	0	0	0	—	—	—	—	—
—Springfield	AHL	22	9	11	20	14	—	—	—	—	—
NHL totals		**203**	**35**	**55**	**90**	**113**	**7**	**1**	**0**	**1**	**4**

BORSCHEVSKY, NIKOLAI
RW, FLAMES

PERSONAL: Born January 12, 1965, in Tomsk, U.S.S.R. . . . 5-9/180. . . . Shoots left. . . . Name pronounced bohr-SHEHV-skee.
TRANSACTIONS/CAREER NOTES: Selected by Toronto Maple Leafs in fourth round (third Maple Leafs pick, 77th overall) of NHL entry draft (June 20, 1992). . . . Bruised buttock (November 7, 1992); missed one game. . . . Strained neck (December 31, 1992); missed three games. . . . Strained back (March 9, 1993); missed one game. . . . Broke orbital bone (April 19, 1993); missed first five playoff games. . . . Suffered ruptured spleen (November 3, 1993); missed 22 games. . . . Separated shoulder (February 28, 1994); missed 14 games. . . . Played in Europe during 1994-95 NHL lockout. . . . Traded by Maple Leafs to Calgary Flames for sixth-round pick in 1996 draft (April 6, 1995). . . . Broke ribs (April 20, 1995); missed last five games of season and entire playoffs.
HONORS: Named CIS Player of the Year (1991-92).
MISCELLANEOUS: Member of gold-medal-winning Unified Olympic team.

Season Team	League	Gms.	G	A	Pts.	PIM	Gms.	G	A	Pts.	PIM
				REGULAR SEASON					PLAYOFFS		
83-84—Dynamo Moscow	USSR	34	4	5	9	4	—	—	—	—	—
84-85—Dynamo Moscow	USSR	34	5	9	14	6	—	—	—	—	—
85-86—Dynamo Moscow	USSR	31	6	4	10	4	—	—	—	—	—
86-87—Dynamo Moscow	USSR	28	1	4	5	8	—	—	—	—	—

Season Team	League	REGULAR SEASON					PLAYOFFS				
		Gms.	G	A	Pts.	PIM	Gms.	G	A	Pts.	PIM
87-88—Dynamo Moscow	USSR	37	11	7	18	6	—	—	—	—	—
88-89—Dynamo Moscow	USSR	43	7	8	15	18	—	—	—	—	—
89-90—Spartak Moscow	USSR	48	17	25	42	8	—	—	—	—	—
90-91—Spartak Moscow	USSR	45	19	16	35	16	—	—	—	—	—
91-92—Spartak Moscow	CIS	40	25	14	39	16	—	—	—	—	—
—Unified Olympic Team.......	Int'l	8	7	2	9	0	—	—	—	—	—
92-93—Toronto..........................	NHL	78	34	40	74	28	16	2	7	9	0
93-94—Toronto..........................	NHL	45	14	20	34	10	15	2	2	4	4
94-95—Spartak Moscow	CIS	9	5	1	6	14	—	—	—	—	—
—Toronto..........................	NHL	19	0	5	5	0	—	—	—	—	—
—Calgary..........................	NHL	8	0	5	5	0	—	—	—	—	—
NHL totals............................		150	48	70	118	38	31	4	9	13	4

BOTTERILL, JASON
LW, STARS

PERSONAL: Born May 19, 1976, in Edmonton.... 6-3/205.... Shoots left.
HIGH SCHOOL: St. Paul's Prep (Concord, N.H.).
COLLEGE: Michigan.
TRANSACTIONS/CAREER NOTES: Selected by Dallas Stars in first round (first Stars pick, 20th overall) of NHL entry draft (June 28, 1994).
HONORS: Named to CCHA All-Rookie team (1993-94).

Season Team	League	REGULAR SEASON					PLAYOFFS				
		Gms.	G	A	Pts.	PIM	Gms.	G	A	Pts.	PIM
92-93—St. Paul............................	USHL	22	22	26	48	...	—	—	—	—	—
93-94—University of Michigan	CCHA	37	21	19	40	94	—	—	—	—	—
94-95—University of Michigan	CCHA	34	14	14	28	117	—	—	—	—	—

BOUCHARD, FRANCOIS
D, LIGHTNING

PERSONAL: Born August 8, 1973, in Brossard, Que.... 6-0/185.... Shoots right.
COLLEGE: Northeastern.
TRANSACTIONS/CAREER NOTES: Selected by Tampa Bay Lightning in first round (first Lightning pick, eighth pick overall) of NHL supplemental draft (June 28, 1994).
HONORS: Named to Hockey East All-Star first team (1993-94).

Season Team	League	REGULAR SEASON					PLAYOFFS				
		Gms.	G	A	Pts.	PIM	Gms.	G	A	Pts.	PIM
91-92—Northeastern University...	Hockey East	34	4	9	13	28	—	—	—	—	—
92-93—Northeastern University...	Hockey East	26	4	6	10	20	—	—	—	—	—
93-94—Northeastern University...	Hockey East	39	15	15	30	34	—	—	—	—	—
94-95—Northeastern University...	Hockey East	31	7	16	23	39	—	—	—	—	—

BOUCHARD, JOEL
D, FLAMES

PERSONAL: Born January 23, 1974, in Montreal.... 6-0/185.... Shoots left.
TRANSACTIONS/CAREER NOTES: Selected by Calgary Flames in sixth round (sixth Flames pick, 129th overall) of NHL entry draft (June 20, 1992).
HONORS: Named to QMJHL All-Star first team (1993-94).

Season Team	League	REGULAR SEASON					PLAYOFFS				
		Gms.	G	A	Pts.	PIM	Gms.	G	A	Pts.	PIM
90-91—Longueuil	QMJHL	53	3	19	22	34	8	0	1	1	11
91-92—Verdun............................	QMJHL	70	9	37	46	55	19	1	7	8	20
92-93—Verdun............................	QMJHL	60	10	49	59	126	4	0	2	2	4
93-94—Verdun............................	QMJHL	60	15	55	70	62	4	1	0	1	6
—Saint John	AHL	1	0	0	0	0	2	0	0	0	0
94-95—Saint John	AHL	77	6	25	31	63	5	1	0	1	4
—Calgary............................	NHL	2	0	0	0	0	—	—	—	—	—
NHL totals................................		2	0	0	0	0					

BOUCHER, BRIAN
G, FLYERS

PERSONAL: Born August 1, 1977, in Woonsocket, R.I.... 6-1/180.... Catches left.
HIGH SCHOOL: Mount St. Charles Academy (Woonsocket, R.I.), then Kamiakin (Kennewick, Wash.).
TRANSACTIONS/CAREER NOTES: Selected by Philadelphia Flyers in first round (first Flyers pick, 22nd overall) of NHL entry draft (July 8, 1995).

Season Team	League	REGULAR SEASON							PLAYOFFS						
		Gms.	Min.	W	L	T	GA	SO	Avg.	Gms.	Min.	W	L	GA	SO	Avg.
93-94—Mount St. Charles H.S. .	R.I.H.S.	...	...	13	1	1	...	...	...	—	—	—	—	—	—	—
94-95—Wexford........................	Tier II Jr. A	8	425	...	...	...	23	0	3.25	—	—	—	—	—	—	—
—Tri-City	WHL	35	1969	17	11	2	108	1	3.29	13	795	6	5	50	0	3.77

BOUCHER, PHILIPPE
D, KINGS

PERSONAL: Born March 24, 1973, in St. Apollinaire, Que.... 6-2/188.... Shoots right.... Name pronounced fih-LEEP boo-SHAY.
TRANSACTIONS/CAREER NOTES: Selected by Buffalo Sabres in first round (first Sabres pick, 13th overall) of NHL entry draft (June 22, 1991).... Traded by Sabres with G Grant Fuhr and D Denis Tsygurov to Los Angeles Kings for D Alexei Zhitnik, D Charlie Huddy, G Robb Stauber and fifth-round pick (D Marian Menhart) in 1995 draft (February 14, 1995).... Sprained wrist (February 25, 1995); missed last 31

games of season.
HONORS: Won Can.HL Rookie of the Year Award (1990-91).... Won Raymond Lagace Trophy (1990-91).... Won Michael Bossy Trophy (1990-91).... Named to QMJHL All-Star second team (1990-91 and 1991-92).

Season Team	League	REGULAR SEASON					PLAYOFFS				
		Gms.	G	A	Pts.	PIM	Gms.	G	A	Pts.	PIM
90-91—Granby	QMJHL	69	21	46	67	92	—	—	—	—	—
91-92—Granby	QMJHL	49	22	37	59	47	—	—	—	—	—
—Laval	QMJHL	16	7	11	18	36	10	5	6	11	8
92-93—Laval	QMJHL	16	12	15	27	37	13	6	15	21	12
—Rochester	AHL	5	4	3	7	8	3	0	1	1	2
—Buffalo	NHL	18	0	4	4	14	—	—	—	—	—
93-94—Buffalo	NHL	38	6	8	14	29	7	1	1	2	2
—Rochester	AHL	31	10	22	32	51	—	—	—	—	—
94-95—Rochester	AHL	43	14	27	41	26	—	—	—	—	—
—Buffalo	NHL	9	1	4	5	0	—	—	—	—	—
—Los Angeles	NHL	6	1	0	1	4	—	—	—	—	—
NHL totals		71	8	16	24	47	7	1	1	2	2

BOUGHNER, BOB
D, PANTHERS

PERSONAL: Born March 8, 1971, in Windsor, Ont.... 6-1/200.... Shoots right.... Name pronounced BOOG-nuhr.
TRANSACTIONS/CAREER NOTES: Selected by Detroit Red Wings in second round (second Red Wings pick, 32nd overall) of NHL entry draft (June 17, 1989).... Signed as free agent by Florida Panthers (August 10, 1994).

Season Team	League	REGULAR SEASON					PLAYOFFS				
		Gms.	G	A	Pts.	PIM	Gms.	G	A	Pts.	PIM
87-88—St. Mary's Jr. B	OHA	36	4	18	22	177	—	—	—	—	—
88-89—Sault Ste. Marie	OHL	64	6	15	21	182	—	—	—	—	—
89-90—Sault Ste. Marie	OHL	49	7	23	30	122	—	—	—	—	—
90-91—Sault Ste. Marie	OHL	64	13	33	46	156	14	2	9	11	35
91-92—Adirondack	AHL	1	0	0	0	7	—	—	—	—	—
—Toledo	ECHL	28	3	10	13	79	5	2	0	2	15
92-93—Adirondack	AHL	69	1	16	17	190	—	—	—	—	—
93-94—Adirondack	AHL	72	8	14	22	292	10	1	1	2	18
94-95—Cincinnati	IHL	81	2	14	16	192	10	0	0	0	18

BOULIN, VLADISLAV
D, FLYERS

PERSONAL: Born May 18, 1972, in Penza, U.S.S.R.... 6-4/196.... Shoots right. ... Name pronounced BOO-leen.
TRANSACTIONS/CAREER NOTES: Selected by Philadelphia Flyers in fifth round (fourth Flyers pick, 103rd overall) of NHL entry draft (June 20, 1992).

Season Team	League	REGULAR SEASON					PLAYOFFS				
		Gms.	G	A	Pts.	PIM	Gms.	G	A	Pts.	PIM
90-91—Dizelist Penza	USSR Div. II	68	...	...		0	...	—	—	—	—	—
91-92—Dizelist Penza	CIS Div. II				Statistics unavailable.						
92-93—Dynamo Moscow	CIS	32	2	1	3	55	4	0	0	0	2
93-94—Dynamo Moscow	CIS	43	4	2	6	36	7	0	1	1	16
94-95—Hershey	AHL	52	1	7	8	30	—	—	—	—	—

BOURQUE, PHIL
LW, SENATORS

PERSONAL: Born June 8, 1962, in Chelmsford, Mass.... 6-1/196.... Shoots left.... Full name: Phillippe Richard Bourque.... Name pronounced BOHRK.
TRANSACTIONS/CAREER NOTES: Signed as free agent by Pittsburgh Penguins (October 4, 1982).... Suffered back spasms (November 1989).... Sprained wrist (December 1990). ... Suffered inflammation of left elbow (November 15, 1991); missed two games.... Strained back (December 18, 1991); missed three games.... Fractured left foot (January 10, 1992); missed nine games.... Reinjured foot (February 9, 1992); missed four games.... Signed as free agent by New York Rangers (August 31, 1992).... Suffered concussion (December 11, 1992); missed two games.... Sprained left knee (February 3, 1993); missed six games.... Bruised ankle (April 8, 1993); missed four games.... Traded by Rangers to Ottawa Senators for future considerations (March 21, 1994).... Suffered from the flu (February 8, 1995); missed one game.... Injured knee (April 24, 1995); missed remainder of season.
HONORS: Won Governors Trophy (1987-88).... Named to IHL All-Star first team (1987-88).
STATISTICAL PLATEAUS: Three-goal games: 1990-91 (1).
MISCELLANEOUS: Member of Stanley Cup championship teams (1991 and 1992).

Season Team	League	REGULAR SEASON					PLAYOFFS				
		Gms.	G	A	Pts.	PIM	Gms.	G	A	Pts.	PIM
80-81—Kingston	OMJHL	47	4	4	8	46	6	0	0	0	10
81-82—Kingston	OHL	67	11	40	51	111	4	0	0	0	0
82-83—Baltimore	AHL	65	1	15	16	93	—	—	—	—	—
83-84—Baltimore	AHL	58	5	17	22	96	—	—	—	—	—
—Pittsburgh	NHL	5	0	1	1	12	—	—	—	—	—
84-85—Baltimore	AHL	79	6	15	21	164	13	2	5	7	23
85-86—Pittsburgh	NHL	4	0	0	0	2	—	—	—	—	—
—Baltimore	AHL	74	8	18	26	226	—	—	—	—	—
86-87—Pittsburgh	NHL	22	2	3	5	32	—	—	—	—	—
—Baltimore	AHL	49	15	16	31	183	—	—	—	—	—
87-88—Muskegon	IHL	52	16	36	52	66	6	1	2	3	16

Season Team	League		REGULAR SEASON					PLAYOFFS			
		Gms.	G	A	Pts.	PIM	Gms.	G	A	Pts.	PIM
—Pittsburgh	NHL	21	4	12	16	20	—	—	—	—	—
88-89—Pittsburgh	NHL	80	17	26	43	97	11	4	1	5	66
89-90—Pittsburgh	NHL	76	22	17	39	108	—	—	—	—	—
90-91—Pittsburgh	NHL	78	20	14	34	106	24	6	7	13	16
91-92—Pittsburgh	NHL	58	10	16	26	58	†21	3	4	7	25
92-93—New York Rangers	NHL	55	6	14	20	39	—	—	—	—	—
93-94—New York Rangers	NHL	16	0	1	1	8	—	—	—	—	—
—Ottawa	NHL	11	2	3	5	0	—	—	—	—	—
94-95—Ottawa	NHL	38	4	3	7	20	—	—	—	—	—
NHL totals		464	87	110	197	502	56	13	12	25	107

BOURQUE, RAY

D, BRUINS

B

PERSONAL: Born December 28, 1960, in Montreal. . . . 5-11/210. . . . Shoots left. . . . Full name: Raymond Jean Bourque. . . . Name pronounced BOHRK.
TRANSACTIONS/CAREER NOTES: Selected by Boston Bruins in first round (first Bruins pick, eighth overall) of NHL entry draft (August 9, 1979). . . . Broke jaw (November 11, 1980). . . . Injured left shoulder (October 1981). . . . Fractured left wrist (April 21, 1982). . . . Refractured left wrist and fractured left forearm (summer 1982). . . . Broke bone over left eye (October 1982). . . . Sprained left knee ligaments (December 10, 1988). . . . Bruised hip (April 7, 1990). . . . Bruised right shoulder (October 17, 1990); missed four games. . . . Fractured finger (May 5, 1992); missed remainder of playoffs. . . . Injured back (December 19, 1992); missed two games. . . . Injured ankle (January 21, 1993); missed three games. . . . Injured knee (March 22, 1994); missed 11 games.
HONORS: Named to QMJHL All-Star first team (1977-78 and 1978-79). . . . Won Frank J. Selke Trophy (1978-79). . . . Won Emile (Butch) Bouchard Trophy (1978-79). . . . Named NHL Rookie of the Year by THE SPORTING NEWS (1979-80). . . . Won Calder Memorial Trophy (1979-80). . . . Named to NHL All-Star first team (1979-80, 1981-82, 1983-84, 1984-85, 1986-87, 1987-88 and 1989-90 through 1993-94). . . . Named to THE SPORTING NEWS All-Star second team (1980-81, 1982-83, 1985-86 and 1988-89). . . . Named to NHL All-Star second team (1980-81, 1982-83, 1985-86, 1988-89 and 1994-95). . . . Played in NHL All-Star Game (1981-1986 and 1988-1994). . . . Named to THE SPORTING NEWS All-Star first team (1981-82, 1983-84, 1984-85, 1986-87, 1987-88 and 1989-90 through 1994-95). . . . Won James Norris Memorial Trophy (1986-87, 1987-88, 1989-90, 1990-91 and 1993-94). . . . Won King Clancy Memorial Trophy (1991-92).
STATISTICAL PLATEAUS: Three-goal games: 1982-83 (1).
MISCELLANEOUS: Co-captain of Boston Bruins (1985-86 through 1987-88). . . . Captain of Bruins (1988-89 through 1994-95).

Season Team	League		REGULAR SEASON					PLAYOFFS			
		Gms.	G	A	Pts.	PIM	Gms.	G	A	Pts.	PIM
76-77—Sorel	QMJHL	69	12	36	48	61	—	—	—	—	—
77-78—Verdun	QMJHL	72	22	57	79	90	4	2	1	3	0
78-79—Verdun	QMJHL	63	22	71	93	44	11	3	16	19	18
79-80—Boston	NHL	80	17	48	65	73	10	2	9	11	27
80-81—Boston	NHL	67	27	29	56	96	3	0	1	1	2
81-82—Boston	NHL	65	17	49	66	51	9	1	5	6	16
82-83—Boston	NHL	65	22	51	73	20	17	8	15	23	10
83-84—Boston	NHL	78	31	65	96	57	3	0	2	2	0
84-85—Boston	NHL	73	20	66	86	53	5	0	3	3	4
85-86—Boston	NHL	74	19	57	76	68	3	0	0	0	0
86-87—Boston	NHL	78	23	72	95	36	4	1	2	3	0
87-88—Boston	NHL	78	17	64	81	72	23	3	18	21	26
88-89—Boston	NHL	60	18	43	61	52	10	0	4	4	6
89-90—Boston	NHL	76	19	65	84	50	17	5	12	17	16
90-91—Boston	NHL	76	21	73	94	75	19	7	18	25	12
91-92—Boston	NHL	80	21	60	81	56	12	3	6	9	12
92-93—Boston	NHL	78	19	63	82	40	4	1	0	1	2
93-94—Boston	NHL	72	20	71	91	58	13	2	8	10	0
94-95—Boston	NHL	46	12	31	43	20	5	0	3	3	0
NHL totals		1146	323	907	1230	877	157	33	106	139	133

BOWEN, CURT

LW, RED WINGS

PERSONAL: Born March 24, 1974, in Kenora, Ont. . . . 6-1/190. . . . Shoots left.
HIGH SCHOOL: Ridgemont (Ottawa).
TRANSACTIONS/CAREER NOTES: Selected by Detroit Red Wings in first round (first Red Wings pick, 22nd overall) of NHL entry draft (June 20, 1992).

Season Team	League		REGULAR SEASON					PLAYOFFS			
		Gms.	G	A	Pts.	PIM	Gms.	G	A	Pts.	PIM
90-91—Ottawa	OHL	42	12	14	26	31	—	—	—	—	—
91-92—Ottawa	OHL	65	31	45	76	94	11	3	7	10	11
92-93—Ottawa	OHL	21	9	19	28	51	—	—	—	—	—
93-94—Ottawa	OHL	52	25	37	62	98	17	8	13	21	14
94-95—Adirondack	AHL	64	6	11	17	71	4	0	2	2	4

BOWEN, JASON

D, FLYERS

PERSONAL: Born November 11, 1973, in Courtenay, B.C. . . . 6-4/208. . . . Shoots left.
TRANSACTIONS/CAREER NOTES: Selected by Philadelphia Flyers in first round (second Flyers pick, 15th overall) of NHL entry draft (June 20, 1992). . . . Suffered from hyphema in left eye (November 18, 1993); missed eight games. . . . Separated left shoulder (January 30, 1994); missed 14 games.

Season Team	League	REGULAR SEASON					PLAYOFFS				
		Gms.	G	A	Pts.	PIM	Gms.	G	A	Pts.	PIM
89-90—Tri-City	WHL	61	8	5	13	129	7	0	3	3	4
90-91—Tri-City	WHL	60	7	13	20	252	6	2	2	4	18
91-92—Tri-City	WHL	19	5	3	8	135	5	0	1	1	42
92-93—Tri-City	WHL	62	10	12	22	219	3	1	1	2	18
—Philadelphia	NHL	7	1	0	1	2	—				
93-94—Philadelphia	NHL	56	1	5	6	87	—				
94-95—Hershey	AHL	55	5	5	10	116	6	0	0	0	46
—Philadelphia	NHL	4	0	0	0	0	—				
NHL totals		67	2	5	7	89					

BOYD, KEVIN
LW, SENATORS

PERSONAL: Born May 19, 1977, in Newmarket, Ont....6-2/201....Shoots left. **HIGH SCHOOL:** Saunders Secondary (London, Ont.). **TRANSACTIONS/CAREER NOTES:** Selected by Ottawa Senators in fourth round (fifth Senators pick, 103rd overall) of NHL entry draft (July 8, 1995).

Season Team	League	REGULAR SEASON					PLAYOFFS				
		Gms.	G	A	Pts.	PIM	Gms.	G	A	Pts.	PIM
93-94—Newmarket Tier II Jr. A	OHA	30	2	7	9	51	—				
94-95—London	OHL	65	5	5	10	125	4	0	0	0	0

BOYER, ZAC
RW, STARS

PERSONAL: Born October 25, 1971, in Inuvik, Northwest Territories....6-1/199....Shoots right. **TRANSACTIONS/CAREER NOTES:** Selected by Chicago Blackhawks in fourth round (sixth Blackhawks pick, 88th overall) of NHL entry draft (June 22, 1991)....Signed as free agent by Dallas Stars (July 25, 1994).

Season Team	League	REGULAR SEASON					PLAYOFFS				
		Gms.	G	A	Pts.	PIM	Gms.	G	A	Pts.	PIM
87-88—St. Albert	AJHL	55	16	31	47	258	—				
88-89—Kamloops	WHL	42	10	17	27	22	16	9	8	17	10
89-90—Kamloops	WHL	71	24	47	71	63	17	4	4	8	8
90-91—Kamloops	WHL	64	45	60	105	58	12	6	10	16	8
91-92—Kamloops	WHL	70	40	69	109	90	17	9	*20	*29	16
92-93—Indianapolis	IHL	59	7	14	21	26	—				
93-94—Indianapolis	IHL	54	13	12	25	67	—				
94-95—Kalamazoo	IHL	22	9	7	16	22	15	3	9	12	8
—Dallas	NHL	1	0	0	0	0	2	0	0	0	0
NHL totals		1	0	0	0	0	2	0	0	0	0

BOZON, PHILIPPE
LW

PERSONAL: Born November 30, 1966, in Chamonix, France....5-10/185....Shoots left. ...Name pronounced fih-LEEP BOH-zohn. **TRANSACTIONS/CAREER NOTES:** Signed as free agent by St. Louis Blues (September 29, 1985)....On Blues inactive list while in France preparing for 1992 Olympics (1987-88 through 1990-91)....Returned to Blues (February 27, 1992)....Suffered from mononucleosis (January 30, 1993); missed 21 games....Suffered facial injury (October 16, 1993); missed one game....Injured stomach (January 13, 1994); missed one game....Suffered concussion (April 1, 1994); missed two games....Released by Blues (February 1, 1995)....Played in France (1995). **HONORS:** Named to QMJHL All-Star second team (1985-86).

Season Team	League	REGULAR SEASON					PLAYOFFS				
		Gms.	G	A	Pts.	PIM	Gms.	G	A	Pts.	PIM
84-85—St. Jean	QMJHL	67	32	50	82	82	3	1	0	1	0
85-86—St. Jean	QMJHL	65	59	52	111	72	10	10	6	16	16
—Peoria	IHL	—	—	—	—	—	5	1	0	1	0
86-87—Peoria	IHL	28	4	11	15	17	—				
—St. Jean	QMJHL	25	20	21	41	75	8	5	5	10	30
87-88—Mont-Blanc	France	18	11	15	26	34	10	15	6	21	6
—French Olympic Team	Int'l	6	3	2	5	0	—				
88-89—Mont-Blanc	France	18	11	18	29	18	11	11	17	28	38
89-90—French national team	Int'l	Statistics unavailable.									
—Grenoble	France	36	45	38	83	34	6	4	3	7	2
90-91—Grenoble	France	26	22	16	38	16	10	7	8	15	8
91-92—Chamonix	France	10	12	8	20	20	—				
—French Olympic Team	Int'l	7	3	2	5	4	—				
—St. Louis	NHL	9	1	3	4	4	6	1	0	1	27
92-93—St. Louis	NHL	54	6	6	12	55	9	1	0	1	0
—Peoria	IHL	4	3	2	5	2	—				
93-94—St. Louis	NHL	80	9	16	25	42	4	0	0	0	4
94-95—St. Louis	NHL	1	0	0	0	0	—				
—Grenoble	France	Statistics unavailable.									
NHL totals		144	16	25	41	101	19	2	0	2	31

BRADLEY, BRIAN
C, LIGHTNING

PERSONAL: Born January 21, 1965, in Kitchener, Ont....5-10/177....Shoots right.... Full name: Brian Walter Richard Bradley. **TRANSACTIONS/CAREER NOTES:** Selected by Calgary Flames as underage junior in third round (second Flames pick, 51st overall) of NHL entry draft (June 8, 1983)....Traded

by Flames with RW Peter Bakovic and future considerations to Vancouver Canucks for C Craig Coxe (March 6, 1988); Canucks received D Kevan Guy to complete deal. . . . Bruised knee (January 1989). . . . Broke thumb knuckle (February 1, 1990); missed seven games. . . . Traded by Canucks to Toronto Maple Leafs for D Tom Kurvers (January 12, 1991). . . . Sprained ankle (November 10, 1991); missed six games. . . . Suffered back spasms (December 10, 1991); missed two games. . . . Selected by Tampa Bay Lightning in NHL expansion draft (June 18, 1992). . . . Suffered injury (October 6, 1993); missed three games. . . . Injured shoulder (October 22, 1993); missed one game. . . . Suffered from the flu (January 4, 1994); missed one game. . . . Suffered charley horse (February 17, 1995); missed two games.
HONORS: Played in NHL All-Star Game (1993 and 1994).
STATISTICAL PLATEAUS: Three-goal games: 1992-93 (1).
MISCELLANEOUS: Captain of Tampa Bay Lightning (1994-95).

Season Team	League	REGULAR SEASON					PLAYOFFS				
		Gms.	G	A	Pts.	PIM	Gms.	G	A	Pts.	PIM
81-82—London	OHL	62	34	44	78	34	—	—	—	—	—
82-83—London	OHL	67	37	82	119	37	3	1	0	1	0
83-84—London	OHL	49	40	60	100	24	4	2	4	6	0
84-85—London	OHL	32	27	49	76	22	8	5	10	15	4
85-86—Calgary	NHL	5	0	1	1	0	1	0	0	0	0
—Moncton	AHL	59	23	42	65	40	10	6	9	15	4
86-87—Moncton	AHL	20	12	16	28	8	—	—	—	—	—
—Calgary	NHL	40	10	18	28	16	—	—	—	—	—
87-88—Canadian national team	Int'l	47	18	19	37	42	—	—	—	—	—
—Canadian Olympic Team	Int'l	7	0	4	4	0	—	—	—	—	—
—Vancouver	NHL	11	3	5	8	6	—	—	—	—	—
88-89—Vancouver	NHL	71	18	27	45	42	7	3	4	7	10
89-90—Vancouver	NHL	67	19	29	48	65	—	—	—	—	—
90-91—Vancouver	NHL	44	11	20	31	42	—	—	—	—	—
—Toronto	NHL	26	0	11	11	20	—	—	—	—	—
91-92—Toronto	NHL	59	10	21	31	48	—	—	—	—	—
92-93—Tampa Bay	NHL	80	42	44	86	92	—	—	—	—	—
93-94—Tampa Bay	NHL	78	24	40	64	56	—	—	—	—	—
94-95—Tampa Bay	NHL	46	13	27	40	42	—	—	—	—	—
NHL totals		527	150	243	393	429	8	3	4	7	10

BRADY, NEIL
C

PERSONAL: Born April 12, 1968, in Montreal. . . . 6-2/200. . . . Shoots left. . . . Full name: Neil Patrick Brady.
HIGH SCHOOL: Medicine Hat (Alta.).
TRANSACTIONS/CAREER NOTES: Selected by New Jersey Devils as underage junior in first round (first Devils pick, third overall) of NHL entry draft (June 21, 1986). . . . Traded by Devils to Ottawa Senators for future considerations (September 3, 1992). . . . Injured ankle (February 17, 1993); missed two games. . . . Suffered from the flu (February 23, 1993); missed two games. . . . Injured knee (March 4, 1993); missed one game. . . . Signed as free agent by Dallas Stars (December 3, 1994).
HONORS: Won WHL (East) Stewart (Butch) Paul Memorial Trophy (1985-86).

Season Team	League	REGULAR SEASON					PLAYOFFS				
		Gms.	G	A	Pts.	PIM	Gms.	G	A	Pts.	PIM
84-85—Medicine Hat	WHL	—	—	—	—	—	3	0	0	0	2
85-86—Medicine Hat	WHL	72	21	60	81	104	21	9	11	20	23
86-87—Medicine Hat	WHL	57	19	64	83	126	18	1	4	5	25
87-88—Medicine Hat	WHL	61	16	35	51	110	15	0	3	3	19
88-89—Utica	AHL	75	16	21	37	56	4	0	3	3	0
89-90—New Jersey	NHL	19	1	4	5	13	—	—	—	—	—
—Utica	AHL	38	10	13	23	21	5	0	1	1	10
90-91—New Jersey	NHL	3	0	0	0	0	—	—	—	—	—
—Utica	AHL	77	33	63	96	91	—	—	—	—	—
91-92—Utica	AHL	33	12	30	42	28	—	—	—	—	—
—New Jersey	NHL	7	1	0	1	4	—	—	—	—	—
92-93—Ottawa	NHL	55	7	17	24	57	—	—	—	—	—
—New Haven	AHL	8	6	3	9	2	—	—	—	—	—
93-94—Kalamazoo	IHL	43	10	16	26	188	5	1	1	2	10
—Dallas	NHL	5	0	1	1	21	—	—	—	—	—
94-95—Kalamazoo	IHL	70	13	45	58	140	15	5	14	19	22
NHL totals		89	9	22	31	95					

BRASHEAR, DONALD
LW, CANADIENS

PERSONAL: Born January 7, 1972, in Bedford, Ind. . . . 6-3/214. . . . Shoots left.
TRANSACTIONS/CAREER NOTES: Signed as free agent by Montreal Canadiens (July 28, 1992). . . . Bruised knee (November 23, 1993); missed one game. . . . Injured shoulder (February 27, 1995); missed one game. . . . Bruised hand (March 20, 1995); missed one game.

Season Team	League	REGULAR SEASON					PLAYOFFS				
		Gms.	G	A	Pts.	PIM	Gms.	G	A	Pts.	PIM
89-90—Longueuil	QMJHL	64	12	14	26	169	7	0	0	0	11
90-91—Longueuil	QMJHL	68	12	26	38	195	8	0	3	3	33
91-92—Verdun	QMJHL	65	18	24	42	283	18	4	2	6	98
92-93—Fredericton	AHL	76	11	3	14	261	5	0	0	0	8

B

Season	Team	League	REGULAR SEASON Gms.	G	A	Pts.	PIM	PLAYOFFS Gms.	G	A	Pts.	PIM
93-94—Fredericton		AHL	62	38	28	66	250	—	—	—	—	—
—Montreal		NHL	14	2	2	4	34	2	0	0	0	0
94-95—Montreal		NHL	20	1	1	2	63	—	—	—	—	—
—Fredericton		AHL	29	10	9	19	182	17	7	5	12	77
NHL totals			34	3	3	6	97	2	0	0	0	0

BRATHWAITE, FRED
G, OILERS

PERSONAL: Born November 24, 1972, in Ottawa. . . . 5-7/170. . . . Catches left. . . . Name pronounced BRATH-wayt.
TRANSACTIONS/CAREER NOTES: Signed as free agent by Las Vegas Thunder (August 18, 1993). . . . Signed as free agent by Edmonton Oilers (October 6, 1993).
STATISTICAL NOTES: Led OHL with 3.31 goals against average and four shutouts (1991-92).

Season	Team	League	REGULAR SEASON Gms.	Min.	W	L	T	GA	SO	Avg.	PLAYOFFS Gms.	Min.	W	L	GA	SO	Avg.
89-90—Oshawa		OHL	20	901	11	2	1	45	1	3.00	10	451	4	2	22	0	*2.93
90-91—Oshawa		OHL	39	1986	25	6	3	112	1	3.38	13	677	*9	2	43	0	3.81
91-92—Oshawa		OHL	24	1248	12	7	2	81	*0	*3.89	—	—	—	—	—	—	—
—London		OHL	23	1325	23	10	4	61	*4	*2.76	10	615	5	5	36	0	3.51
92-93—Detroit		OHL	37	2192	23	10	4	134	0	3.67	15	858	9	6	48	1	3.36
93-94—Cape Breton		AHL	2	119	1	1	0	6	0	3.03	—	—	—	—	—	—	—
—Edmonton		NHL	19	982	3	10	3	58	0	3.54	—	—	—	—	—	—	—
94-95—Edmonton		NHL	14	601	2	5	1	40	0	3.99	—	—	—	—	—	—	—
NHL totals			33	1583	5	15	4	98	0	3.71							

BREEN, GEORGE
RW, OILERS

PERSONAL: Born August 3, 1973, in Webster, Mass. . . . 6-2/200. . . . Shoots right. . . . Full name: George Bernard Breen.
HIGH SCHOOL: Shrewsbury (Mass.), then Cushing Academy (Ashburnham, Mass.).
COLLEGE: Providence.
TRANSACTIONS/CAREER NOTES: Selected by Edmonton Oilers in third round (third Oilers pick, 56th overall) of NHL entry draft (June 22, 1991).

Season	Team	League	REGULAR SEASON Gms.	G	A	Pts.	PIM	PLAYOFFS Gms.	G	A	Pts.	PIM
87-88—Shrewsbury H.S.		Mass. H.S.	20	11	9	20	. . .	—	—	—	—	—
88-89—Shrewsbury H.S.		Mass. H.S.	20	32	9	41	. . .	—	—	—	—	—
89-90—Cushing Academy		Mass. H.S.	20	9	8	17	. . .	—	—	—	—	—
90-91—Cushing Academy		Mass. H.S.	23	21	39	60	. . .	—	—	—	—	—
91-92—Providence College		Hockey East	36	8	4	12	24	—	—	—	—	—
92-93—Providence College		Hockey East	31	11	7	18	45	—	—	—	—	—
93-94—Providence College		Hockey East	32	8	14	22	22	—	—	—	—	—
94-95—Providence College		Hockey East	36	17	18	35	51	—	—	—	—	—

BRENNAN, RICH
D, DENVER

PERSONAL: Born November 26, 1972, in Schenectady, N.Y. . . . 6-2/200. . . . Shoots right.
HIGH SCHOOL: Albany (N.Y.) Academy, then Tabor Academy (Marion, Mass.).
COLLEGE: Boston University.
TRANSACTIONS/CAREER NOTES: Selected by Quebec Nordiques in third round (third Nordiques pick, 56th overall) of NHL entry draft (June 22, 1991). . . . Nordiques franchise moved to Denver for 1995-96 season.
HONORS: Named to Hockey East All-Star first team (1993-94).

Season	Team	League	REGULAR SEASON Gms.	G	A	Pts.	PIM	PLAYOFFS Gms.	G	A	Pts.	PIM
88-89—Albany Academy		N.Y. H.S.	25	17	30	47	57	—	—	—	—	—
89-90—Tabor Academy		N.Y. H.S.	33	12	14	26	68	—	—	—	—	—
90-91—Tabor Academy		N.Y. H.S.	34	13	37	50	91	—	—	—	—	—
91-92—Boston University		Hockey East	31	4	13	17	54	—	—	—	—	—
92-93—Boston University		Hockey East	40	9	11	20	68	—	—	—	—	—
93-94—Boston University		Hockey East	41	8	27	35	82	—	—	—	—	—
94-95—Boston University		Hockey East	31	5	23	28	56	—	—	—	—	—

BRIMANIS, ARIS
D, FLYERS

PERSONAL: Born March 14, 1972, in Cleveland. . . . 6-3/195. . . . Shoots right. . . . Full name: Aris Aldis Brimanis. . . . Name pronounced AIR-ihz brih-MAN-ihz.
HIGH SCHOOL: Culver (Ind.) Military Academy.
COLLEGE: Bowling Green State.
TRANSACTIONS/CAREER NOTES: Selected by Philadelphia Flyers in fourth round (third Flyers pick, 86th overall) of NHL entry draft (June 22, 1991).

Season	Team	League	REGULAR SEASON Gms.	G	A	Pts.	PIM	PLAYOFFS Gms.	G	A	Pts.	PIM
88-89—Culver Military Academy		Indiana H.S.	38	10	13	23	24	—	—	—	—	—
89-90—Culver Military Academy		Indiana H.S.	37	15	10	25	52	—	—	—	—	—
90-91—Bowling Green State		CCHA	38	3	6	9	42	—	—	—	—	—
91-92—Bowling Green State		CCHA	32	2	9	11	38	—	—	—	—	—
92-93—Brandon		WHL	71	8	50	58	110	4	2	1	3	12

Season Team	League	REGULAR SEASON					PLAYOFFS				
		Gms.	G	A	Pts.	PIM	Gms.	G	A	Pts.	PIM
93-94—Hershey	AHL	75	8	15	23	65	11	2	3	5	12
—Philadelphia	NHL	1	0	0	0	0	—	—	—	—	—
94-95—Hershey	AHL	76	8	17	25	68	6	1	1	2	14
NHL totals		1	0	0	0	0					

BRIND'AMOUR, ROD
C/LW, FLYERS

PERSONAL: Born August 9, 1970, in Ottawa. . . . 6-1/200. . . . Shoots left. . . . Full name: Rod Jean Brind'Amour. . . . Name pronounced BRIHND-uh-MOHR.
COLLEGE: Michigan State.
TRANSACTIONS/CAREER NOTES: Broke wrist (November 1985). . . . Selected by St. Louis Blues in first round (first Blues pick, ninth overall) of NHL entry draft (June 11, 1988). . . . Traded by Blues with C Dan Quinn to Philadelphia Flyers for C Ron Sutter and D Murray Baron (September 22, 1991). . . . Lacerated elbow (November 19, 1992); missed two games. . . . Bruised right hand (February 20, 1993); missed one game.
HONORS: Named CCHA Rookie of the Year (1988-89). . . . Named to CCHA All-Rookie team (1988-89). . . . Named to NHL All-Rookie team (1989-90). . . . Played in NHL All-Star Game (1992).
STATISTICAL PLATEAUS: Three-goal games: 1992-93 (1).

Season Team	League	REGULAR SEASON					PLAYOFFS				
		Gms.	G	A	Pts.	PIM	Gms.	G	A	Pts.	PIM
87-88—Notre Dame	SJHL	56	46	61	107	136	—	—	—	—	—
88-89—Michigan State	CCHA	42	27	32	59	63	—	—	—	—	—
—St. Louis	NHL	—	—	—	—	—	5	2	0	2	4
89-90—St. Louis	NHL	79	26	35	61	46	12	5	8	13	6
90-91—St. Louis	NHL	78	17	32	49	93	13	2	5	7	10
91-92—Philadelphia	NHL	80	33	44	77	100	—	—	—	—	—
92-93—Philadelphia	NHL	81	37	49	86	89	—	—	—	—	—
93-94—Philadelphia	NHL	84	35	62	97	85	—	—	—	—	—
94-95—Philadelphia	NHL	48	12	27	39	33	15	6	9	15	8
NHL totals		450	160	249	409	446	45	15	22	37	28

BRISEBOIS, PATRICE
D, CANADIENS

PERSONAL: Born January 27, 1971, in Montreal. . . . 6-2/192. . . . Shoots right. . . . Name pronounced pa-TREEZ BREES-bwah.
TRANSACTIONS/CAREER NOTES: Underwent surgery on fractured right thumb (February 1988). . . . Tore ligaments in left knee (March 1988). . . . Broke left thumb (August 1988). . . . Selected by Montreal Canadiens in second round (second Canadiens pick, 30th overall) of NHL entry draft (June 17, 1989). . . . Traded by Laval Titans with LW Allen Kerr to Drummondville Voltigeurs for second- and third-round picks in 1990 QMJHL draft (May 26, 1990). . . . Sprained right ankle (October 10, 1992); missed two games. . . . Suffered charley horse (December 16, 1992); missed two games. . . . Injured knee (October 30, 1993); missed 10 games. . . . Suffered hairline fracture of ankle (December 1, 1993); missed 14 games. . . . Sprained ankle (February 21, 1994); missed seven games. . . . Suffered acute herniated disc (April 3, 1995); missed 12 games.
HONORS: Won Michael Bossy Trophy (1988-89). . . . Named to QMJHL All-Star second team (1989-90). . . . Won Can.HL Defenseman of the Year Award (1990-91). . . . Won Emile (Butch) Bouchard Trophy (1990-91). . . . Named to QMJHL All-Star first team (1990-91). . . . Named to Memorial Cup All-Star team (1990-91).
MISCELLANEOUS: Member of Stanley Cup championship team (1993).

Season Team	League	REGULAR SEASON					PLAYOFFS				
		Gms.	G	A	Pts.	PIM	Gms.	G	A	Pts.	PIM
87-88—Laval	QMJHL	48	10	34	44	95	6	0	2	2	2
88-89—Laval	QMJHL	50	20	45	65	95	17	8	14	22	45
89-90—Laval	QMJHL	56	18	70	88	108	13	7	9	16	26
90-91—Montreal	NHL	10	0	2	2	4	—	—	—	—	—
—Drummondville	QMJHL	54	17	44	61	72	14	6	18	24	49
91-92—Fredericton	AHL	53	12	27	39	51	—	—	—	—	—
—Montreal	NHL	26	2	8	10	20	11	2	4	6	6
92-93—Montreal	NHL	70	10	21	31	79	20	0	4	4	18
93-94—Montreal	NHL	53	2	21	23	63	7	0	4	4	6
94-95—Montreal	NHL	35	4	8	12	26	—	—	—	—	—
NHL totals		194	18	60	78	192	38	2	12	14	30

BRISKE, BYRON
D, MIGHTY DUCKS

PERSONAL: Born January 23, 1976, in Jansen, Sask. . . . 6-3/194. . . . Shoots right. . . . Name pronounced BRIH-skee.
HIGH SCHOOL: Lindsay Thurber (Red Deer, Alta.).
TRANSACTIONS/CAREER NOTES: Selected by Mighty Ducks of Anaheim in fourth round (fourth Mighty Ducks pick, 80th overall) of NHL entry draft (June 29, 1994).

Season Team	League	REGULAR SEASON					PLAYOFFS				
		Gms.	G	A	Pts.	PIM	Gms.	G	A	Pts.	PIM
91-92—Victoria	WHL	1	0	0	0	0	—	—	—	—	—
92-93—Victoria	WHL	66	1	10	11	110	—	—	—	—	—
93-94—Red Deer	WHL	61	6	21	27	174	—	—	—	—	—
94-95—Red Deer	WHL	48	4	17	21	116	—	—	—	—	—
—Tri-City	WHL	15	0	1	1	22	13	0	0	0	18

B

BROCHU, MARTIN
G, CANADIENS

PERSONAL: Born March 10, 1973, in Anjou, Que. . . . 5-11/195. . . . Catches left. . . . Name pronounced MAHR-tai broh-SHOO.
TRANSACTIONS/CAREER NOTES: Signed as free agent by Montreal Canadiens (September 22, 1992).

			REGULAR SEASON							PLAYOFFS						
Season Team	League	Gms.	Min.	W	L	T	GA	SO	Avg.	Gms.	Min.	W	L	GA	SO	Avg.
91-92—Granby	QMJHL	52	2772	15	29	2	218	0	4.72	—	—	—	—	—	—	—
92-93—Hull	QMJHL	29	1453	9	15	1	137	0	5.66	2	69	0	1	7	0	6.09
93-94—Fredericton	AHL	32	1506	10	11	3	76	2	3.03	—	—	—	—	—	—	—
94-95—Fredericton	AHL	44	2475	18	18	4	145	0	3.52	—	—	—	—	—	—	—

BRODEUR, MARTIN
G, DEVILS

PERSONAL: Born May 6, 1972, in Montreal. . . . 6-1/205. . . . Catches left. . . . Name pronounced MAHR-tai broh-DOOR.
TRANSACTIONS/CAREER NOTES: Suffered pinched nerve in elbow and slight concussion (March 9, 1990). . . . Selected by New Jersey Devils in first round (first Devils pick, 20th overall) of NHL entry draft (June 16, 1990). . . . Strained knee (February 24, 1994).
HONORS: Named to QMJHL All-Star second team (1991-92). . . . Won Calder Memorial Trophy (1993-94). . . . Named to NHL All-Rookie team (1993-94).
RECORDS: Shares NHL single-season playoff record for most wins by goaltender—16 (1995).
MISCELLANEOUS: Member of Stanley Cup championship team (1995).

			REGULAR SEASON							PLAYOFFS						
Season Team	League	Gms.	Min.	W	L	T	GA	SO	Avg.	Gms.	Min.	W	L	GA	SO	Avg.
89-90—St. Hyacinthe	QMJHL	42	2333	23	13	2	156	0	4.01	12	678	5	7	46	0	4.07
90-91—St. Hyacinthe	QMJHL	52	2946	22	24	4	162	2	3.30	4	232	0	4	16	0	4.14
91-92—St. Hyacinthe	QMJHL	48	2846	27	16	4	161	2	3.39	5	317	2	3	14	0	2.65
—New Jersey	NHL	4	179	2	1	0	10	0	3.35	1	32	0	1	3	0	5.63
92-93—Utica	AHL	32	1952	14	13	5	131	0	4.03	4	258	1	3	18	0	4.19
93-94—New Jersey	NHL	47	2625	27	11	8	105	3	2.40	17	1171	8	+9	38	1	1.95
94-95—New Jersey	NHL	40	2184	19	11	6	89	3	2.45	*20	*1222	*16	4	34	*3	*1.67
NHL totals		91	4988	48	23	14	204	6	2.45	38	2425	24	14	75	4	1.86

BROS, MICHAL
C, SHARKS

PERSONAL: Born January 25, 1976, in Olomouc, Czechoslovakia. . . . 6-1/174. . . . Shoots right.
TRANSACTIONS/CAREER NOTES: Selected by San Jose Sharks in fifth round (sixth Sharks pick, 130th overall) of NHL entry draft (July 8, 1995).

			REGULAR SEASON				PLAYOFFS				
Season Team	League	Gms.	G	A	Pts.	PIM	Gms.	G	A	Pts.	PIM
94-95—HC Olomouc Jrs.	Czech Rep.				Statistics unavailable.						

BROTEN, NEAL
C, DEVILS

PERSONAL: Born November 29, 1959, in Roseau, Minn. . . . 5-9/175. . . . Shoots left. . . . Full name: Neal LaMoy Broten. . . . Name pronounced BRAH-tuhn. . . . Brother of Aaron Broten, center/left winger for six NHL teams (1980-81 through 1991-92); and brother of Paul Broten, right winger, Dallas Stars.
HIGH SCHOOL: Roseau (Minn.).
COLLEGE: Minnesota.
TRANSACTIONS/CAREER NOTES: Selected by Minnesota North Stars in second round (third North Stars pick, 42nd overall) of NHL entry draft (August 9, 1979). . . . Fractured ankle (December 26, 1981). . . . Dislocated shoulder (October 30, 1986). . . . Tore shoulder ligaments (March 1987). . . . Separated shoulder (November 1987). . . . Underwent reconstructive shoulder surgery (February 1988). . . . Suffered sterno-clavicular sprain (February 14, 1989). . . . Strained groin (December 18, 1990). . . . North Stars franchise moved from Minnesota to Dallas and renamed Stars for 1993-94 season. . . . Pulled hip muscle (October 9, 1993); missed two games. . . . Traded by Stars to New Jersey Devils for C Corey Millen (February 27, 1995).
HONORS: Won WCHA Rookie of the Year Award (1978-79). . . . Won Hobey Baker Memorial Award (1980-81). . . . Named to NCAA All-America West team (1980-81). . . . Named to WCHA All-Star first team (1980-81). . . . Named to NCAA All-Tournament team (1980-81). . . . Played in NHL All-Star Game (1983 and 1986).
STATISTICAL PLATEAUS: Three-goal games: 1983-84 (1), 1985-86 (2), 1986-87 (1), 1989-90 (1). Total: 5.
MISCELLANEOUS: Member of gold-medal-winning U.S. Olympic team (1980). . . . Member of Stanley Cup championship team (1995).

			REGULAR SEASON				PLAYOFFS				
Season Team	League	Gms.	G	A	Pts.	PIM	Gms.	G	A	Pts.	PIM
78-79—University of Minnesota	WCHA	40	21	50	71	18	—	—	—	—	—
79-80—U.S. national team	Int'l	55	25	30	55	20	—	—	—	—	—
—U.S. Olympic Team	Int'l	7	2	1	3	2	—	—	—	—	—
80-81—University of Minnesota	WCHA	36	17	54	71	56	—	—	—	—	—
—Minnesota	NHL	3	2	0	2	12	19	1	7	8	9
81-82—Minnesota	NHL	73	38	60	98	42	4	0	2	2	0
82-83—Minnesota	NHL	79	32	45	77	43	9	1	6	7	10
83-84—Minnesota	NHL	76	28	61	89	43	16	5	5	10	4
84-85—Minnesota	NHL	80	19	37	56	39	9	2	5	7	10
85-86—Minnesota	NHL	80	29	76	105	47	5	3	2	5	2
86-87—Minnesota	NHL	46	18	35	53	35	—	—	—	—	—
87-88—Minnesota	NHL	54	9	30	39	32	—	—	—	—	—
88-89—Minnesota	NHL	68	18	38	56	57	5	2	2	4	4
89-90—Minnesota	NHL	80	23	62	85	45	7	2	2	4	18
90-91—Minnesota	NHL	79	13	56	69	26	23	9	13	22	6

B

Season Team	League	REGULAR SEASON					PLAYOFFS				
		Gms.	G	A	Pts.	PIM	Gms.	G	A	Pts.	PIM
91-92—Minnesota	NHL	76	8	26	34	16	7	1	5	6	2
92-93—Minnesota	NHL	82	12	21	33	22	—	—	—	—	—
93-94—Dallas	NHL	79	17	35	52	62	9	2	1	3	6
94-95—Dallas	NHL	17	0	4	4	4	—	—	—	—	—
—New Jersey	NHL	30	8	20	28	20	20	7	12	19	6
NHL totals		1002	274	606	880	545	133	35	62	97	77

BROTEN, PAUL
RW, STARS

PERSONAL: Born October 27, 1965, in Roseau, Minn.... 5-11/190.... Shoots right.... Name pronounced BRAH-tuhn.... Brother of Aaron Broten, center/left winger for six NHL teams (1980-81 through 1991-92); and brother of Neal Broten, center, New Jersey Devils.
HIGH SCHOOL: Roseau (Minn.).
COLLEGE: Minnesota.
TRANSACTIONS/CAREER NOTES: Selected by New York Rangers in fourth round (third Rangers pick, 77th overall) of NHL entry draft (June 9, 1984).... Pulled thigh muscle (September 1990).... Selected by Dallas Stars in NHL waiver draft (October 2, 1993).
STATISTICAL PLATEAUS: Three-goal games: 1991-92 (1).

Season Team	League	REGULAR SEASON					PLAYOFFS				
		Gms.	G	A	Pts.	PIM	Gms.	G	A	Pts.	PIM
83-84—Roseau H.S.	Minn. H.S.	26	26	29	55	4	—	—	—	—	—
84-85—University of Minnesota	WCHA	44	8	8	16	26	—	—	—	—	—
85-86—University of Minnesota	WCHA	38	6	16	22	24	—	—	—	—	—
86-87—University of Minnesota	WCHA	48	17	22	39	52	—	—	—	—	—
87-88—University of Minnesota	WCHA	62	19	26	45	54	—	—	—	—	—
88-89—Denver	IHL	77	28	31	59	133	4	0	2	2	6
89-90—Flint	IHL	28	17	9	26	55	—	—	—	—	—
—New York Rangers	NHL	32	5	3	8	26	6	1	1	2	2
90-91—New York Rangers	NHL	28	4	6	10	18	5	0	0	0	2
—Binghamton	AHL	8	2	2	4	4	—	—	—	—	—
91-92—New York Rangers	NHL	74	13	15	28	102	13	1	2	3	10
92-93—New York Rangers	NHL	60	5	9	14	48	—	—	—	—	—
93-94—Dallas	NHL	64	12	12	24	30	9	1	1	2	2
94-95—Dallas	NHL	47	7	9	16	36	5	1	2	3	2
NHL totals		305	46	54	100	260	38	4	6	10	18

BROUSSEAU, PAUL
RW, DENVER

PERSONAL: Born September 18, 1973, in Montreal.... 6-1/203.... Shoots right.... Name pronounced broo-SOH.
COLLEGE: Heritage College (Fla.).
TRANSACTIONS/CAREER NOTES: Selected by Quebec Nordiques in second round (second Nordiques pick, 28th overall) of NHL entry draft (June 20, 1992).... Nordiques franchise moved to Denver for 1995-96 season.
HONORS: Won Michael Bossy Trophy (1991-92).

Season Team	League	REGULAR SEASON					PLAYOFFS				
		Gms.	G	A	Pts.	PIM	Gms.	G	A	Pts.	PIM
89-90—Chicoutimi	QMJHL	57	17	24	41	32	7	0	3	3	0
90-91—Trois-Rivieres	QMJHL	67	30	66	96	48	6	3	2	5	2
91-92—Hull	QMJHL	57	35	61	96	54	6	3	5	8	10
92-93—Hull	QMJHL	59	27	48	75	49	10	7	8	15	6
93-94—Cornwall	AHL	69	18	26	44	35	1	0	0	0	0
94-95—Cornwall	AHL	57	19	17	36	29	7	2	1	3	10

BROWN, BRAD
D, CANADIENS

PERSONAL: Born December 27, 1975, in Mississauga, Ont.... 6-3/218.... Shoots right.
HIGH SCHOOL: Chippewa (North Bay, Ont.).
TRANSACTIONS/CAREER NOTES: Selected by Montreal Canadiens in first round (first Canadiens pick, 18th overall) of NHL entry draft (June 28, 1994).

Season Team	League	REGULAR SEASON					PLAYOFFS				
		Gms.	G	A	Pts.	PIM	Gms.	G	A	Pts.	PIM
91-92—North Bay	OHL	49	2	9	11	170	18	0	6	6	43
92-93—North Bay	OHL	61	4	9	13	228	2	0	2	2	13
93-94—North Bay	OHL	66	8	24	32	196	18	3	12	15	33
94-95—North Bay	OHL	64	8	38	46	172	6	1	4	5	8

BROWN, CURTIS
C, SABRES

PERSONAL: Born February 12, 1976, in Unity, Sask.... 6-0/182.... Shoots left.
TRANSACTIONS/CAREER NOTES: Selected by Buffalo Sabres in second round (second Sabres pick, 43rd overall) of NHL entry draft (June 28, 1994).
HONORS: Named to Can.HL All-Star second team (1994-95).... Named to WHL (East) All-Star first team (1994-95).

Season Team	League	REGULAR SEASON					PLAYOFFS				
		Gms.	G	A	Pts.	PIM	Gms.	G	A	Pts.	PIM
92-93—Moose Jaw	WHL	71	13	16	29	30	—	—	—	—	—

B

Season Team	League	REGULAR SEASON					PLAYOFFS				
		Gms.	G	A	Pts.	PIM	Gms.	G	A	Pts.	PIM
93-94—Moose Jaw	WHL	72	27	38	65	82	—	—	—	—	—
94-95—Moose Jaw	WHL	70	51	53	104	63	10	8	7	15	20
—Buffalo	NHL	1	1	1	2	2	—	—	—	—	—
NHL totals		1	1	1	2	2					

BROWN, DAVE
RW, FLYERS

PERSONAL: Born October 12, 1962, in Saskatoon, Sask.... 6-5/222.... Shoots right.
TRANSACTIONS/CAREER NOTES: Selected by Philadelphia Flyers in seventh round (seventh Flyers pick, 140th overall) of NHL entry draft (June 9, 1982).... Bruised shoulder (March 1985).... Suspended five games by NHL for stick-swinging incident (March 1987).... Suspended 15 games by NHL for crosschecking (October 16, 1987).... Bruised left hand and wrist (January 1988).... Traded by Flyers to Edmonton Oilers for C Keith Acton and future considerations (February 7, 1989).... Suffered facial laceration (March 3, 1989).... Sprained hand (March 1989).... Traded by Oilers with D Corey Foster and NHL rights to RW Jari Kurri to Flyers for RW Scott Mellanby, LW Craig Berube and C Craig Fisher (May 30, 1991).... Injured shoulder (January 28, 1992); missed 10 games.
MISCELLANEOUS: Member of Stanley Cup championship team (1990).

Season Team	League	REGULAR SEASON					PLAYOFFS				
		Gms.	G	A	Pts.	PIM	Gms.	G	A	Pts.	PIM
80-81—Spokane Flyers	WHL	9	2	2	4	21	—	—	—	—	—
81-82—Saskatoon	WHL	62	11	33	44	344	5	1	0	1	4
82-83—Maine	AHL	71	8	6	14	*418	16	0	0	0	*107
—Philadelphia	NHL	2	0	0	0	5	—	—	—	—	—
83-84—Philadelphia	NHL	19	1	5	6	98	2	0	0	0	12
—Springfield	AHL	59	17	14	31	150	—	—	—	—	—
84-85—Philadelphia	NHL	57	3	6	9	165	11	0	0	0	59
85-86—Philadelphia	NHL	76	10	7	17	277	5	0	0	0	16
86-87—Philadelphia	NHL	62	7	3	10	274	26	1	2	3	59
87-88—Philadelphia	NHL	47	12	5	17	114	7	1	0	1	27
88-89—Philadelphia	NHL	50	0	3	3	100	—	—	—	—	—
—Edmonton	NHL	22	0	2	2	56	7	0	0	0	6
89-90—Edmonton	NHL	60	0	6	6	145	3	0	0	0	0
90-91—Edmonton	NHL	58	3	4	7	160	16	0	1	1	30
91-92—Philadelphia	NHL	70	4	2	6	81	—	—	—	—	—
92-93—Philadelphia	NHL	70	0	2	2	78	—	—	—	—	—
93-94—Philadelphia	NHL	71	1	4	5	137	—	—	—	—	—
94-95—Philadelphia	NHL	28	1	2	3	53	3	0	0	0	0
NHL totals		692	42	51	93	1743	80	2	3	5	209

BROWN, DOUG
RW, RED WINGS

PERSONAL: Born June 12, 1964, in Southborough, Mass.... 5-10/185.... Shoots right.... Full name: Douglas Allen Brown.... Brother of Greg Brown, defenseman, Winnipeg Jets.
HIGH SCHOOL: St. Mark's (Southborough, Mass.).
COLLEGE: Boston College.
TRANSACTIONS/CAREER NOTES: Signed as free agent by New Jersey Devils (August 6, 1986).... Broke nose (October 1988).... Injured back (November 25, 1989).... Bruised right foot (February 13, 1991).... Suspended by Devils for refusing to report to Utica (November 20, 1992).... Reinstated by Devils (November 30, 1992).... Signed as free agent by Pittsburgh Penguins (September 29, 1993).... Injured leg (March 26, 1994); missed seven games.... Selected by Detroit Red Wings in 1994-95 waiver draft (January 18, 1995); Penguins claimed C Micah Aivazoff as compensation (who was then claimed by Edmonton Oilers).
HONORS: Named to NCAA All-America East second team (1984-85 and 1985-86).... Named to Hockey East All-Star second team (1984-85 and 1985-86).

Season Team	League	REGULAR SEASON					PLAYOFFS				
		Gms.	G	A	Pts.	PIM	Gms.	G	A	Pts.	PIM
82-83—Boston College	ECAC	22	9	8	17	0	—	—	—	—	—
83-84—Boston College	ECAC	38	11	10	21	6	—	—	—	—	—
84-85—Boston College	Hockey East	45	37	31	68	10	—	—	—	—	—
85-86—Boston College	Hockey East	38	16	40	56	16	—	—	—	—	—
86-87—Maine	AHL	73	24	34	58	15	—	—	—	—	—
—New Jersey	NHL	4	0	1	1	0	—	—	—	—	—
87-88—New Jersey	NHL	70	14	11	25	20	19	5	1	6	6
—Utica	AHL	2	0	2	2	2	—	—	—	—	—
88-89—New Jersey	NHL	63	15	10	25	15	—	—	—	—	—
—Utica	AHL	4	1	4	5	0	—	—	—	—	—
89-90—New Jersey	NHL	69	14	20	34	16	6	0	1	1	2
90-91—New Jersey	NHL	58	14	16	30	4	7	2	2	4	2
91-92—New Jersey	NHL	71	11	17	28	27	—	—	—	—	—
92-93—New Jersey	NHL	15	0	5	5	2	—	—	—	—	—
—Utica	AHL	25	11	17	28	8	—	—	—	—	—
93-94—Pittsburgh	NHL	77	18	37	55	18	6	0	0	0	2
94-95—Detroit	NHL	45	9	12	21	16	18	4	8	12	2
NHL totals		472	95	129	224	118	56	11	12	23	14

BROWN, GREG

D, JETS

PERSONAL: Born March 7, 1968, in Hartford, Conn.... 6-0/185.... Shoots right.... Full name: Gregory Curtis Brown.... Brother of Doug Brown, right winger, Detroit Red Wings.
HIGH SCHOOL: St. Mark's (Southborough, Mass.).
COLLEGE: Boston College.
TRANSACTIONS/CAREER NOTES: Selected by Buffalo Sabres in second round (second Sabres pick, 26th overall) of NHL entry draft (June 21, 1986).... Signed as free agent by Pittsburgh Penguins (September 30, 1993).... Traded by Penguins to Winnipeg Jets for future considerations (April 7, 1995).
HONORS: Named to Hockey East All-Freshman team (1986-87).... Named Hockey East Player of the Year (1988-89 and 1989-90).... Named to NCAA All-America East first team (1988-89 and 1989-90).... Named to Hockey East All-Star first team (1988-89 and 1989-90).... Named to Hockey East All-Decade team (1994).

			REGULAR SEASON					PLAYOFFS				
Season Team	League	Gms.	G	A	Pts.	PIM	Gms.	G	A	Pts.	PIM
84-85—St. Marks H.S.	Mass. H.S.	24	16	24	40	12	—	—	—	—	—
85-86—St. Marks H.S.	Mass. H.S.	19	22	28	50	30	—	—	—	—	—
86-87—Boston College	Hockey East	37	10	27	37	22	—	—	—	—	—
87-88—U.S. Olympic Team	Int'l	6	0	4	4	2	—	—	—	—	—
88-89—Boston College	Hockey East	40	9	34	43	24	—	—	—	—	—
89-90—Boston College	Hockey East	42	5	35	40	42	—	—	—	—	—
90-91—Buffalo	NHL	39	1	2	3	35	—	—	—	—	—
—Rochester	AHL	31	6	17	23	16	14	1	4	5	8
91-92—Rochester	AHL	56	8	30	38	25	16	1	5	6	4
—U.S. national team	Int'l	8	0	0	0	5	—	—	—	—	—
—U.S. Olympic Team	Int'l	7	0	0	0	2	—	—	—	—	—
92-93—Rochester	AHL	61	11	38	49	46	16	3	8	11	14
—Buffalo	NHL	10	0	1	1	6	—	—	—	—	—
93-94—San Diego	IHL	42	8	25	33	26	—	—	—	—	—
—Pittsburgh	NHL	36	3	8	11	28	6	0	1	1	4
94-95—Cleveland	IHL	28	5	14	19	22	—	—	—	—	—
—Winnipeg	NHL	9	0	3	3	17	—	—	—	—	—
NHL totals		94	4	14	18	86	6	0	1	1	4

BROWN, JEFF

D, CANUCKS

PERSONAL: Born April 30, 1966, in Ottawa.... 6-1/204.... Shoots right.... Full name: Jeff Randall Brown.
HIGH SCHOOL: Sudbury (Ont.).
TRANSACTIONS/CAREER NOTES: Selected by Quebec Nordiques as underage junior in second round (second Nordiques pick, 36th overall) of NHL entry draft (June 9, 1984).... Traded by Nordiques to St. Louis Blues for G Greg Millen and C Tony Hrkac (December 13, 1989).... Broke left ankle (February 14, 1991); missed 13 games.... Broke foot (January 14, 1993); missed 11 games.... Suffered from sore foot (February 11, 1993); missed two games.... Injured hand and foot (October 30, 1993); missed three games.... Broke thumb (January 15, 1994); missed six games.... Traded by Blues with D Brett Hedican and C Nathan LaFayette to Vancouver Canucks for C Craig Janney (March 21, 1994).... Cracked bone in wrist (March 6, 1995); missed 12 games.... Sprained shoulder (April 28, 1995); missed last two games of season.
HONORS: Shared Max Kaminsky Trophy with Terry Carkner (1985-86).... Named to OHL All-Star first team (1985-86).

			REGULAR SEASON					PLAYOFFS				
Season Team	League	Gms.	G	A	Pts.	PIM	Gms.	G	A	Pts.	PIM
81-82—Hawkesbury	COJHL	49	12	47	59	72	—	—	—	—	—
82-83—Sudbury	OHL	65	9	37	46	39	—	—	—	—	—
83-84—Sudbury	OHL	68	17	60	77	39	—	—	—	—	—
84-85—Sudbury	OHL	56	16	48	64	26	—	—	—	—	—
85-86—Sudbury	OHL	45	22	28	50	24	4	0	2	2	11
—Quebec	NHL	8	3	2	5	6	1	0	0	0	0
—Fredericton	AHL	—	—	—	—	—	1	0	1	1	0
86-87—Fredericton	AHL	26	2	14	16	16	—	—	—	—	—
—Quebec	NHL	44	7	22	29	16	13	3	3	6	2
87-88—Quebec	NHL	78	16	36	52	64	—	—	—	—	—
88-89—Quebec	NHL	78	21	47	68	62	—	—	—	—	—
89-90—Quebec	NHL	29	6	10	16	18	—	—	—	—	—
—St. Louis	NHL	48	10	28	38	37	12	2	10	12	4
90-91—St. Louis	NHL	67	12	47	59	39	13	3	9	12	6
91-92—St. Louis	NHL	80	20	39	59	38	6	2	1	3	2
92-93—St. Louis	NHL	71	25	53	78	58	11	3	8	11	6
93-94—St. Louis	NHL	63	13	47	60	46	—	—	—	—	—
—Vancouver	NHL	11	1	5	6	10	24	6	9	15	37
94-95—Vancouver	NHL	33	8	23	31	16	5	1	3	4	2
NHL totals		610	142	359	501	410	85	20	43	63	59

BROWN, KEITH

D, PANTHERS

PERSONAL: Born May 6, 1960, in Corner Brook, Nfld.... 6-1/196.... Shoots right.... Full name: Keith Jeffrey Brown.
TRANSACTIONS/CAREER NOTES: Selected by Chicago Blackhawks as underage junior in first round (first Blackhawks pick, seventh overall) of NHL entry draft (August 9, 1979).... Tore ligaments in right knee (December 23, 1981).... Separated right shoulder (January 26, 1983).... Strained leg (January 1985).... Broke finger (October 1985); missed 10 games.... Tore ligaments and damaged cartilage in left knee (October 1987).... Bruised shoulder (January 1990).... Bruised ribs (February 25, 1990); missed 10 games.... Bruised elbow (April 1990).... Strained shoulder (September 1990).... Bruised ribs (November 1990).... Separated left shoulder (December 16, 1990); missed 30 games.... Strained chest muscle (March 1991).... Injured eye (October 10, 1991); missed one game....

— 353 —

Pulled groin (November 7, 1991); missed two games. . . . Reinjured groin (November 19, 1991); missed two games. . . . Reinjured groin (December 1991); missed three games. . . . Sprained right ankle (January 27, 1992); missed 14 games. . . . Underwent left shoulder surgery (September 27, 1992); missed first 47 games of 1992-93 season. . . . Pulled groin (March 25, 1993); missed two games. . . . Traded by Blackhawks to Florida Panthers for RW Darin Kimble (September 30, 1993). . . . Injured neck (October 21, 1993); missed four games. . . . Suffered from sore right knee (November 13, 1993); missed two games. . . . Suffered from sore right knee (November 18, 1993); missed two games. . . . Underwent right knee surgery (November 28, 1993); missed 15 games. . . . Strained groin (February 16, 1994); missed three games. . . . Strained groin (February 23, 1994); missed six games. . . . Underwent arthroscopic surgery on left knee to remove cartilage (February 1, 1995); missed 15 games. . . . Suffered swelling in left knee (March 11, 1995); missed three games. . . . Underwent arthroscopic surgery on left knee (March 28, 1995); missed last 17 games of season.
HONORS: Shared WCHL Rookie of the Year Award with John Ogrodnick (1977-78). . . . Named to WCHL All-Star second team (1977-78). . . . Won WHL's Top Defenseman Trophy (1978-79). . . . Named to WHL All-Star first team (1978-79).
MISCELLANEOUS: Captain of Chicago Blackhawks (1987-88).

Season Team	League	REGULAR SEASON					PLAYOFFS				
		Gms.	G	A	Pts.	PIM	Gms.	G	A	Pts.	PIM
76-77—Fort Saskatchewan	AJHL	59	14	61	75	14	—	—	—	—	—
—Portland	WCHL	2	0	0	0	0	—	—	—	—	—
77-78—Portland	WCHL	72	11	53	64	51	8	0	3	3	2
78-79—Portland	WHL	70	11	85	96	75	25	3	*30	33	21
79-80—Chicago	NHL	76	2	18	20	27	6	0	0	0	4
80-81—Chicago	NHL	80	9	34	43	80	3	0	2	2	2
81-82—Chicago	NHL	33	4	20	24	26	4	0	2	2	5
82-83—Chicago	NHL	50	4	27	31	20	7	0	0	0	11
83-84—Chicago	NHL	74	10	25	35	94	5	0	1	1	10
84-85—Chicago	NHL	56	1	22	23	55	11	2	7	9	31
85-86—Chicago	NHL	70	11	29	40	87	3	0	1	1	9
86-87—Chicago	NHL	73	4	23	27	86	4	0	1	1	6
87-88—Chicago	NHL	24	3	6	9	45	5	0	2	2	10
88-89—Chicago	NHL	74	2	16	18	84	13	1	3	4	25
89-90—Chicago	NHL	67	5	20	25	87	18	0	4	4	43
90-91—Chicago	NHL	45	1	10	11	55	6	1	0	1	8
91-92—Chicago	NHL	57	6	10	16	69	14	0	8	8	18
92-93—Chicago	NHL	33	2	6	8	39	4	0	1	1	2
93-94—Florida	NHL	51	4	8	12	60	—	—	—	—	—
94-95—Florida	NHL	13	0	0	0	2	—	—	—	—	—
NHL totals		876	68	274	342	916	103	4	32	36	184

BROWN, KEVIN
RW, KINGS

PERSONAL: Born May 11, 1974, in Birmingham, England. . . . 6-1/212. . . . Shoots right.
HIGH SCHOOL: Quinte Secondary School (Belleville, Ont.).
TRANSACTIONS/CAREER NOTES: Selected by Los Angeles Kings in fourth round (third Kings pick, 87th overall) of NHL entry draft (June 20, 1992). . . . Strained knee and hip (April 12, 1995); missed two games. . . . Sprained right shoulder (April 19, 1995); missed last seven games of season.
HONORS: Won Jim Mahon Memorial Trophy (1992-93 and 1993-94). . . . Named to OHL All-Star second team (1992-93). . . . Named to Can.HL All-Star second team (1993-94). . . . Named to OHL All-Star first team (1993-94).

Season Team	League	REGULAR SEASON					PLAYOFFS				
		Gms.	G	A	Pts.	PIM	Gms.	G	A	Pts.	PIM
89-90—Georgetown Jr. B	OHA	31	3	8	11	59	—	—	—	—	—
90-91—Waterloo Jr. B	OHA	46	25	33	58	116	—	—	—	—	—
91-92—Belleville	OHL	66	24	24	48	52	5	1	4	5	8
92-93—Belleville	OHL	6	2	5	7	4	—	—	—	—	—
—Detroit	OHL	56	48	86	134	76	15	10	18	28	18
93-94—Detroit	OHL	57	54	81	135	85	17	14	*26	*40	28
94-95—Phoenix	IHL	48	19	31	50	64	—	—	—	—	—
—Los Angeles	NHL	23	2	3	5	18	—	—	—	—	—
NHL totals		23	2	3	5	18					

BROWN, ROB
LW

PERSONAL: Born April 10, 1968, in Kingston, Ont. . . . 5-11/185. . . . Shoots left.
TRANSACTIONS/CAREER NOTES: Selected by Pittsburgh Penguins as underage junior in fourth round (fourth Penguins pick, 67th overall) of NHL entry draft (June 21, 1986). . . . Separated right shoulder (February 12, 1989); missed 12 games. . . . Traded by Penguins to Hartford Whalers for RW Scott Young (December 21, 1990). . . . Injured Adam's apple (April 5, 1991); missed one playoff game. . . . Traded by Whalers to Chicago Blackhawks for D Steve Konroyd (January 24, 1992). . . . Signed as free agent by Dallas Stars (August 6, 1993). . . . Signed as free agent by Los Angeles Kings (June 14, 1994). . . . Signed as free agent by Chicago Wolves of IHL (July 17, 1995).
HONORS: Won WHL (West) Most Valuable Player Trophy (1985-86 and 1986-87). . . . Won Bob Brownridge Memorial Trophy (1985-86). . . . Named to WHL (West) All-Star first team (1985-86 and 1986-87). . . . Won Can.HL Player of the Year Award (1986-87). . . . Won Can.HL Plus/Minus Award (1986-87). . . . Won WHL (West) Bob Brownridge Memorial Trophy (1986-87). . . . Won WHL Player of the Year Award (1986-87). . . . Played in NHL All-Star Game (1989). . . . Won James Gatschene Memorial Trophy (1993-94). . . . Won Leo P. Lamoureux Memorial Trophy (1993-94). . . . Named to IHL All-Star first team (1993-94). . . . Named to IHL All-Star second team (1994-95).
STATISTICAL PLATEAUS: Three-goal games: 1988-89 (4), 1989-90 (3). Total: 7.

Season Team	League	REGULAR SEASON					PLAYOFFS				
		Gms.	G	A	Pts.	PIM	Gms.	G	A	Pts.	PIM
83-84—Kamloops	WHL	50	16	42	58	80	15	1	2	3	17
84-85—Kamloops	WHL	60	29	50	79	95	15	8	8	16	28

Season	Team	League	Gms.	G	A	Pts.	PIM	Gms.	G	A	Pts.	PIM
			REGULAR SEASON					**PLAYOFFS**				
85-86—Kamloops	WHL	69	58	*115	*173	171	16	*18	*28	*46	14
86-87—Kamloops	WHL	63	*76	*136	*212	101	5	6	5	11	6
87-88—Pittsburgh	NHL	51	24	20	44	56	—	—	—	—	—
88-89—Pittsburgh	NHL	68	49	66	115	118	11	5	3	8	22
89-90—Pittsburgh	NHL	80	33	47	80	102	—	—	—	—	—
90-91—Pittsburgh	NHL	25	6	10	16	31	—	—	—	—	—
—Hartford	NHL	44	18	24	42	101	5	1	0	1	7
91-92—Hartford	NHL	42	16	15	31	39	—	—	—	—	—
—Chicago	NHL	25	5	11	16	34	8	2	4	6	4
92-93—Chicago	NHL	15	1	6	7	33	—	—	—	—	—
—Indianapolis	IHL	19	14	19	33	32	2	0	1	1	2
93-94—Kalamazoo	IHL	79	42	*113	*155	188	5	1	3	4	6
—Dallas	NHL	1	0	0	0	0	—	—	—	—	—
94-95—Phoenix	IHL	69	34	73	107	135	9	4	12	16	0
—Los Angeles	NHL	2	0	0	0	0	—	—	—	—	—
NHL totals		353	152	199	351	514	24	8	7	15	33

BROWN, SEAN
D, BRUINS

PERSONAL: Born November 5, 1976, in Oshawa, Ont.... 6-2/196.... Shoots left.
HIGH SCHOOL: Quinte Secondary School (Belleville, Ont.).
TRANSACTIONS/CAREER NOTES: Selected by Boston Bruins in first round (second Bruins pick, 21st overall) of NHL entry draft (July 8, 1995).

Season	Team	League	Gms.	G	A	Pts.	PIM	Gms.	G	A	Pts.	PIM
			REGULAR SEASON					**PLAYOFFS**				
92-93—Oshawa	Tier II Jr. A	15	0	1	1	9	—	—	—	—	—
93-94—Wellington	Tier II Jr. A	32	5	14	19	165	—	—	—	—	—
—Belleville	OHL	28	1	2	3	53	8	0	0	0	17
94-95—Belleville	OHL	58	2	16	18	200	16	4	2	6	67
—Phoenix	IHL	3	0	1	1	0	—	—	—	—	—

BRUCE, DAVID
LW

PERSONAL: Born October 7, 1964, in Thunder Bay, Ont.... 5-11/190.... Shoots right.
TRANSACTIONS/CAREER NOTES: Selected by Vancouver Canucks as underage junior in second round (second Canucks pick, 30th overall) of NHL entry draft (June 8, 1983).... Suffered from mononucleosis (November 1987).... Bruised foot (March 1988).... Tore cartilage near thumb on left hand and underwent surgery (March 1989).... Signed as free agent by St. Louis Blues (July 23, 1990).... Selected by San Jose Sharks in NHL expansion draft (May 30, 1991).... Tore abdominal muscle (March 19, 1992).... Strained groin (November 7, 1992); missed 17 games.... Strained groin (December 23, 1992); missed 33 games.... Strained groin (March 11, 1993); missed remainder of season.
HONORS: Named to IHL All-Star first team (1989-90 and 1990-91).... Won James Gatschene Memorial Trophy (1990-91).

Season	Team	League	Gms.	G	A	Pts.	PIM	Gms.	G	A	Pts.	PIM
			REGULAR SEASON					**PLAYOFFS**				
81-82—Thunder Bay	TBJHL	35	27	31	58	74	—	—	—	—	—
82-83—Kitchener	OHL	67	36	35	71	199	12	7	9	16	27
83-84—Kitchener	OHL	62	52	40	92	203	10	5	8	13	20
84-85—Fredericton	AHL	56	14	11	25	104	5	0	0	0	37
85-86—Fredericton	AHL	66	25	16	41	151	2	0	1	1	12
—Vancouver	NHL	12	0	1	1	14	1	0	0	0	0
86-87—Fredericton	AHL	17	7	6	13	73	—	—	—	—	—
—Vancouver	NHL	50	9	7	16	109	—	—	—	—	—
87-88—Fredericton	AHL	30	27	18	45	115	—	—	—	—	—
—Vancouver	NHL	28	7	3	10	57	—	—	—	—	—
88-89—Vancouver	NHL	53	7	7	14	65	—	—	—	—	—
89-90—Milwaukee	IHL	68	40	35	75	148	6	5	3	8	0
90-91—St. Louis	NHL	12	1	2	3	14	2	0	0	0	2
—Peoria	IHL	60	*64	52	116	78	18	*18	11	*29	40
91-92—Kansas City	IHL	7	5	5	10	6	—	—	—	—	—
—San Jose	NHL	60	22	16	38	46	—	—	—	—	—
92-93—San Jose	NHL	17	2	3	5	33	—	—	—	—	—
93-94—San Jose	NHL	2	0	0	0	0	—	—	—	—	—
—Kansas City	IHL	72	40	24	64	115	—	—	—	—	—
94-95—Kansas City	IHL	63	33	25	58	80	—	—	—	—	—
NHL totals		234	48	39	87	338	3	0	0	0	2

BRULE, STEVE
C, DEVILS

PERSONAL: Born January 15, 1975, in Montreal.... 5-11/185.... Shoots right.... Name pronounced broo-LAY.
TRANSACTIONS/CAREER NOTES: Selected by New Jersey Devils in sixth round (sixth Devils pick, 143rd overall) of NHL entry draft (June 26, 1993).
HONORS: Won Michel Bergeron Trophy (1992-93).... Named to QMJHL All-Rookie team (1992-93).... Named to QMJHL All-Star second team (1994-95).

Season	Team	League	Gms.	G	A	Pts.	PIM	Gms.	G	A	Pts.	PIM
			REGULAR SEASON					**PLAYOFFS**				
92-93—St. Jean	QMJHL	70	33	47	80	46	4	0	0	0	9

B

Season	Team	League	REGULAR SEASON					PLAYOFFS				
			Gms.	G	A	Pts.	PIM	Gms.	G	A	Pts.	PIM
93-94—St. Jean		QMJHL	66	41	64	105	46	5	2	1	3	0
94-95—St. Jean		QMJHL	69	44	64	108	42	7	3	4	7	8
—Albany		AHL	3	1	4	5	0	14	9	5	14	4

BRUNET, BENOIT
LW, CANADIENS

PERSONAL: Born August 24, 1968, in Montreal. . . . 5-11/193. . . . Shoots left. . . . Name pronounced BEHN-wah broo-nay.

TRANSACTIONS/CAREER NOTES: Selected by Montreal Canadiens as underage junior in second round (second Canadiens pick, 27th overall) of NHL entry draft (June 21, 1986). . . . Injured ankle (September 1987). . . . Tore left knee ligaments (September 24, 1990); missed 24 games. . . . Fractured ankle (December 4, 1991). . . . Sprained left knee (November 21, 1992); missed 10 games. . . . Fractured thumb (January 22, 1993); missed 14 games. . . . Bruised knee (November 17, 1993); missed four games. . . . Suffered mild concussion (February 2, 1994); missed six games. . . . Suffered sore throat (April 8, 1994); missed three games. . . . Pulled hamstring (March 18, 1995); missed two games. . . . Bruised right knee (May 3, 1995); missed one game.

HONORS: Named to QMJHL All-Star second team (1986-87). . . . Named to AHL All-Star first team (1988-89).

MISCELLANEOUS: Member of Stanley Cup championship team (1993).

Season	Team	League	REGULAR SEASON					PLAYOFFS				
			Gms.	G	A	Pts.	PIM	Gms.	G	A	Pts.	PIM
85-86—Hull		QMJHL	71	33	37	70	81	—	—	—	—	—
86-87—Hull		QMJHL	60	43	67	110	105	6	7	5	12	8
87-88—Hull		QMJHL	62	54	89	143	131	10	3	10	13	11
88-89—Montreal		NHL	2	0	1	1	0	—	—	—	—	—
—Sherbrooke		AHL	73	41	*76	117	95	6	2	0	2	4
89-90—Sherbrooke		AHL	72	32	35	67	82	12	8	7	15	20
90-91—Fredericton		AHL	24	13	18	31	16	6	5	6	11	2
—Montreal		NHL	17	1	3	4	0	—	—	—	—	—
91-92—Fredericton		AHL	6	7	9	16	27	—	—	—	—	—
—Montreal		NHL	18	4	6	10	14	—	—	—	—	—
92-93—Montreal		NHL	47	10	15	25	19	20	2	8	10	8
93-94—Montreal		NHL	71	10	20	30	20	7	1	4	5	16
94-95—Montreal		NHL	45	7	18	25	16	—	—	—	—	—
NHL totals			200	32	63	95	69	27	3	12	15	24

BRYLIN, SERGEI
C, DEVILS

PERSONAL: Born January 13, 1974, in Moscow, U.S.S.R. . . . 5-9/175. . . . Shoots left. . . . Name pronounced BRIH-lihn.

TRANSACTIONS/CAREER NOTES: Selected by New Jersey Devils in second round (second Devils pick, 42nd overall) of NHL entry draft (June 20, 1992). . . . Suffered from tonsillitis (May 3, 1995); missed last game of season.

MISCELLANEOUS: Member of Stanley Cup championship team (1995).

Season	Team	League	REGULAR SEASON					PLAYOFFS				
			Gms.	G	A	Pts.	PIM	Gms.	G	A	Pts.	PIM
91-92—CSKA Moscow		CIS	44	1	6	7	4	—	—	—	—	—
92-93—CSKA Moscow		CIS	42	5	4	9	36	—	—	—	—	—
93-94—CSKA Moscow		CIS	39	4	6	10	36	3	0	1	1	0
—Russian Penguins		IHL	13	4	5	9	18	—	—	—	—	—
94-95—Albany		AHL	63	19	35	54	78	—	—	—	—	—
—New Jersey		NHL	26	6	8	14	8	12	1	2	3	4
NHL totals			26	6	8	14	8	12	1	2	3	4

BUCHANAN, JEFF
D, BLACKHAWKS

PERSONAL: Born May 23, 1971, in Swift Current, Sask. . . . 5-10/165. . . . Shoots right.

TRANSACTIONS/CAREER NOTES: Signed as free agent by Tampa Bay Lightning (August 13, 1992). . . . Loaned by Lightning to Detroit Vipers (October 19, 1994). . . . Traded by Lightning with RW Jim Cummins and D Tom Tilley to Chicago Blackhawks for LW Paul Ysebaert and RW Rich Sutter (February 22, 1995).

Season	Team	League	REGULAR SEASON					PLAYOFFS				
			Gms.	G	A	Pts.	PIM	Gms.	G	A	Pts.	PIM
89-90—Saskatoon		WHL	66	7	12	19	96	9	0	2	2	2
90-91—Saskatoon		WHL	69	10	26	36	123	—	—	—	—	—
91-92—Saskatoon		WHL	72	17	37	54	143	—	—	—	—	—
92-93—Atlanta		IHL	68	4	18	22	282	9	0	0	0	26
93-94—Atlanta		IHL	76	5	24	29	253	14	0	1	1	20
94-95—Atlanta		IHL	4	0	1	1	9	—	—	—	—	—
—Detroit		IHL	50	4	6	10	125	—	—	—	—	—
—Indianapolis		IHL	25	3	9	12	63	—	—	—	—	—

BUCHBERGER, KELLY
RW/LW, OILERS

PERSONAL: Born December 12, 1966, in Langenburg, Sask. . . . 6-2/210. . . . Shoots left. . . . Full name: Kelly Michael Buchberger. . . . Name pronounced BUK-buhr-guhr.

HIGH SCHOOL: Langenburg (Sask.).

TRANSACTIONS/CAREER NOTES: Selected by Edmonton Oilers as underage junior in ninth round (eighth Oilers pick, 188th overall) of NHL entry draft (June 15, 1985). . . . Suspended six games by AHL for leaving bench to fight (March 30, 1988). . . .

Fractured right ankle (March 1989).... Dislocated left shoulder (March 13, 1990).... Reinjured shoulder (May 4, 1990)....
Strained shoulder (April 7, 1993); missed one game.
STATISTICAL PLATEAUS: Three-goal games: 1992-93 (1).
MISCELLANEOUS: Member of Stanley Cup championship teams (1987 and 1990).

			REGULAR SEASON					PLAYOFFS			
Season Team	League	Gms.	G	A	Pts.	PIM	Gms.	G	A	Pts.	PIM
83-84—Melville	SAJHL	60	14	11	25	139	—	—	—	—	—
84-85—Moose Jaw	WHL	51	12	17	29	114	—	—	—	—	—
85-86—Moose Jaw	WHL	72	14	22	36	206	13	11	4	15	37
86-87—Nova Scotia	AHL	70	12	20	32	257	5	0	1	1	23
—Edmonton	NHL	—	—	—	—	—	3	0	1	1	5
87-88—Edmonton	NHL	19	1	0	1	81	—	—	—	—	—
—Nova Scotia	AHL	49	21	23	44	206	2	0	0	0	11
88-89—Edmonton	NHL	66	5	9	14	234	—	—	—	—	—
89-90—Edmonton	NHL	55	2	6	8	168	19	0	5	5	13
90-91—Edmonton	NHL	64	3	1	4	160	12	2	1	3	25
91-92—Edmonton	NHL	79	20	24	44	157	16	1	4	5	32
92-93—Edmonton	NHL	83	12	18	30	133	—	—	—	—	—
93-94—Edmonton	NHL	84	3	18	21	199	—	—	—	—	—
94-95—Edmonton	NHL	48	7	17	24	82	—	—	—	—	—
NHL totals		498	53	93	146	1214	50	3	11	14	75

BUCKBERGER, ASHLEY
RW, PANTHERS

PERSONAL: Born February 19, 1975, in Esterhazy, Sask. ... 6-2/200. ... Shoots right.
HIGH SCHOOL: Swift Current (Sask.) Comprehensive.
TRANSACTIONS/CAREER NOTES: Selected by Quebec Nordiques in second round (third Nordiques pick, 49th overall) of NHL entry draft (June 26, 1993). ... Signed as free agent by Florida Panthers (July 27, 1995).
HONORS: Won Jim Piggott Memorial Trophy (1991-92).

			REGULAR SEASON					PLAYOFFS			
Season Team	League	Gms.	G	A	Pts.	PIM	Gms.	G	A	Pts.	PIM
90-91—Swift Current	WHL	10	2	3	5	0	3	0	0	0	0
91-92—Swift Current	WHL	67	23	22	45	38	8	2	1	3	2
92-93—Swift Current	WHL	72	23	44	67	41	17	6	7	13	6
93-94—Swift Current	WHL	67	42	45	87	42	7	0	1	1	6
94-95—Swift Current	WHL	53	23	37	60	51	—	—	—	—	—
—Kamloops	WHL	21	9	13	22	13	19	7	11	18	22

BUCKLEY, TOM
C, WHALERS

PERSONAL: Born May 26, 1976, in Buffalo, N.Y. ... 6-0/210. ... Shoots left.
HIGH SCHOOL: St. Joseph's Collegiate Institute (Buffalo, N.Y.).
TRANSACTIONS/CAREER NOTES: Selected by Hartford Whalers in eighth round (fourth Whalers pick, 187th overall) of NHL entry draft (June 29, 1994).

			REGULAR SEASON					PLAYOFFS			
Season Team	League	Gms.	G	A	Pts.	PIM	Gms.	G	A	Pts.	PIM
93-94—St. Joseph's	N.Y. H.S.	17	17	18	35	40	—	—	—	—	—
94-95—Detroit	OHL	64	30	36	66	49	21	10	9	19	8

BUDAYEV, ALEXEI
C, JETS

PERSONAL: Born April 24, 1975, in Elektrostal, U.S.S.R. ... 6-2/183. ... Shoots right. ... Name pronounced boo-DIGH-yehf.
TRANSACTIONS/CAREER NOTES: Selected by Winnipeg Jets in second round (third Jets pick, 43rd overall) of NHL entry draft (June 26, 1993).

			REGULAR SEASON					PLAYOFFS			
Season Team	League	Gms.	G	A	Pts.	PIM	Gms.	G	A	Pts.	PIM
92-93—Kristall Elektrostal	CIS Div. II				Statistics unavailable.						
93-94—Kristall Elektrostal	CIS Div. II	46	6	5	11	26	—	—	—	—	—
94-95—Kristall Elektrostal	CIS	25	2	1	3	12	—	—	—	—	—

BURE, PAVEL
RW/LW, CANUCKS

PERSONAL: Born March 31, 1971, in Moscow, U.S.S.R. ... 5-10/187. ... Shoots left. ... Name pronounced PA-vihl BUHR-ay. ... Brother of Valeri Bure, right winger/left winger, Montreal Canadiens.
TRANSACTIONS/CAREER NOTES: Selected by Vancouver Canucks in sixth round (fourth Canucks pick, 113th overall) of NHL entry draft (June 17, 1989). ... Strained groin (October 24, 1993); missed eight games. ... Fined $500 by NHL for flagrantly hitting another player with elbow (May 6, 1994). ... Played in Europe during 1994-95 NHL lockout. ... Suffered injury (March 17, 1995); missed two games.
HONORS: Named Soviet League Rookie of the Year (1988-89). ... Won Calder Memorial Trophy (1991-92). ... Named to THE SPORTING NEWS All-Star second team (1993-94). ... Played in NHL All-Star Game (1993 and 1994). ... Named to NHL All-Star first team (1993-94).
STATISTICAL PLATEAUS: Three-goal games: 1992-93 (1), 1993-94 (3), 1994-95 (1). Total: 5. ... Four-goal games: 1992-93 (1). ... Total hat tricks: 6.

			REGULAR SEASON					PLAYOFFS			
Season Team	League	Gms.	G	A	Pts.	PIM	Gms.	G	A	Pts.	PIM
87-88—CSKA Moscow	USSR	5	1	1	2	0	—	—	—	—	—
88-89—CSKA Moscow	USSR	32	17	9	26	8	—	—	—	—	—

Season Team	League	REGULAR SEASON					PLAYOFFS				
		Gms.	G	A	Pts.	PIM	Gms.	G	A	Pts.	PIM
89-90—CSKA Moscow	USSR	46	14	11	25	22	—	—	—	—	—
90-91—CSKA Moscow	USSR	46	35	12	47	24	—	—	—	—	—
91-92—Vancouver	NHL	65	34	26	60	30	13	6	4	10	14
92-93—Vancouver	NHL	83	60	50	110	69	12	5	7	12	8
93-94—Vancouver	NHL	76	*60	47	107	86	24	*16	15	31	40
94-95—Landshut	Germany	1	3	0	3	2	—	—	—	—	—
—Spartak Moscow	CIS	1	2	0	2	2	—	—	—	—	—
—Vancouver	NHL	44	20	23	43	47	11	7	6	13	10
NHL totals		268	174	146	320	232	60	34	32	66	72

BURE, VALERI
RW/LW, CANADIENS

PERSONAL: Born June 13, 1974, in Moscow, U.S.S.R. . . . . 5-10/168. . . . Shoots right. . . . Name pronounced BUHR-ee. . . . Brother of Pavel Bure, right winger/left winger, Vancouver Canucks.
TRANSACTIONS/CAREER NOTES: Selected by Montreal Canadiens in second round (second Canadiens pick, 33rd overall) of NHL entry draft (June 20, 1992). . . . Bruised forearm (April 3, 1995); missed two games.
HONORS: Named to WHL (West) All-Star first team (1992-93). . . . Named to WHL (West) All-Star second team (1993-94).

Season Team	League	REGULAR SEASON					PLAYOFFS				
		Gms.	G	A	Pts.	PIM	Gms.	G	A	Pts.	PIM
90-91—CSKA Moscow	USSR	3	0	0	0	0	—	—	—	—	—
91-92—Spokane	WHL	53	27	22	49	78	10	11	6	17	10
92-93—Spokane	WHL	66	68	79	147	49	9	6	11	17	14
93-94—Spokane	WHL	59	40	62	102	48	3	5	3	8	2
94-95—Fredericton	AHL	45	23	25	48	32	—	—	—	—	—
—Montreal	NHL	24	3	1	4	6	—	—	—	—	—
NHL totals		24	3	1	4	6					

BUREAU, MARC
C, CANADIENS

PERSONAL: Born May 17, 1966, in Trois-Rivieres, Que. . . . 6-1/198. . . . Shoots right. . . . Name pronounced BYOOR-oh.
TRANSACTIONS/CAREER NOTES: Traded by Chicoutimi Sagueneens with C Stephane Roy, Lee Duhemee, Sylvain Demers and D Rene L'Ecuyer to Granby Bisons for LW Greg Choules and C Stephane Richer (January 1985). . . . Signed as free agent by Calgary Flames (May 16, 1987). . . . Suffered eye contusion (March 25, 1990); missed final two weeks of season. . . . Traded by Flames to Minnesota North Stars for third-round pick (RW Sandy McCarthy) in 1991 draft (March 5, 1991). . . . Injured shoulder (January 13, 1992); missed four games. . . . Separated shoulder (February 15, 1992); missed five games. . . . Separated shoulder (March 1, 1992); missed eight games. . . . Claimed on waivers by Tampa Bay Lightning (October 16, 1992). . . . Bruised shoulder (November 17, 1992); missed six games. . . . Bruised right knee (April 3, 1993); missed remainder of season. . . . Traded by Lightning to Montreal Canadiens for LW Brian Bellows (June 30, 1995).
HONORS: Named to IHL All-Star second team (1989-90 and 1990-91).

Season Team	League	REGULAR SEASON					PLAYOFFS				
		Gms.	G	A	Pts.	PIM	Gms.	G	A	Pts.	PIM
83-84—Chicoutimi	QMJHL	56	6	16	22	14	—	—	—	—	—
84-85—Granby	QMJHL	68	50	70	120	29	—	—	—	—	—
85-86—Chicoutimi	QMJHL	63	36	62	98	69	9	3	7	10	10
86-87—Longueuil	QMJHL	66	54	58	112	68	20	17	20	37	12
87-88—Salt Lake City	IHL	69	7	20	27	86	7	0	3	3	8
88-89—Salt Lake City	IHL	76	28	36	64	119	14	7	5	12	31
89-90—Salt Lake City	IHL	67	43	48	91	173	11	4	8	12	0
—Calgary	NHL	5	0	0	0	4	—	—	—	—	—
90-91—Calgary	NHL	5	0	0	0	2	—	—	—	—	—
—Salt Lake City	IHL	54	40	48	88	101	23	3	2	5	20
—Minnesota	NHL	9	0	6	6	4	—	—	—	—	—
91-92—Minnesota	NHL	46	6	4	10	50	5	0	0	0	14
—Kalamazoo	IHL	7	2	8	10	2	—	—	—	—	—
92-93—Tampa Bay	NHL	63	10	21	31	111	—	—	—	—	—
93-94—Tampa Bay	NHL	75	8	7	15	30	—	—	—	—	—
94-95—Tampa Bay	NHL	48	2	12	14	30	—	—	—	—	—
NHL totals		251	26	50	76	231	28	3	2	5	34

BURKE, SEAN
G, WHALERS

PERSONAL: Born January 29, 1967, in Windsor, Ont. . . . 6-4/210. . . . Catches left.
TRANSACTIONS/CAREER NOTES: Selected by New Jersey Devils as underage junior in second round (second Devils pick, 24th overall) of NHL entry draft (June 15, 1985). . . . Injured groin (December 1988). . . . Underwent arthroscopic surgery to right knee (September 5, 1989). . . . Traded by Devils with D Eric Weinrich to Hartford Whalers for RW Bobby Holik, second-round pick in 1993 draft (LW Jay Pandolfo) and future considerations (August 28, 1992). . . . Sprained ankle (December 27, 1992); missed seven games. . . . Suffered back spasms (March 13, 1993); missed remainder of season. . . . Pulled hamstring (September 29, 1993); missed seven games. . . . Reinjured hamstring (October 27, 1993); missed 14 games. . . . Suffered back spasms (December 23, 1993); missed one game. . . . Strained groin (February 28, 1995); missed two games.
HONORS: Played in NHL All-Star Game (1989).
MISCELLANEOUS: Member of silver-medal-winning Canadian Olympic team (1992).

Season Team	League	Gms.	Min.	W	L	T	GA	SO	Avg.	Gms.	Min.	W	L	GA	SO	Avg.
			REGULAR SEASON								PLAYOFFS					
83-84—St. Michael's H.S.........	MTHL	25	1482	...	...	...	120	0	4.86	—	—	—	—	—	—	—
84-85—Toronto.......................	OHL	49	2987	25	21	3	211	0	4.24	5	266	1	3	25	0	5.64
85-86—Toronto.......................	OHL	47	2840	16	27	3	†233	0	4.92	4	238	0	4	24	0	6.05
—Can. national team	Int'l	5	284	...	...	...	22	0	4.65	—	—	—	—	—	—	—
86-87—Can. national team	Int'l	46	2670	...	...	...	138	0	3.10	—	—	—	—	—	—	—
87-88—Can. national team	Int'l	37	1962	19	9	2	92	1	2.81	—	—	—	—	—	—	—
—Can. Olympic Team......	Int'l	4	238	1	2	1	12	0	3.03	—	—	—	—	—	—	—
—New Jersey	NHL	13	689	10	1	0	35	1	3.05	17	1001	9	8	*57	†1	3.42
88-89—New Jersey	NHL	62	3590	22	31	9	†230	3	3.84	—	—	—	—	—	—	—
89-90—New Jersey	NHL	52	2914	22	22	6	175	0	3.60	2	125	0	2	8	0	3.84
90-91—New Jersey	NHL	35	1870	8	12	8	112	0	3.59	—	—	—	—	—	—	—
91-92—Can. national team	Int'l	31	1721	18	6	4	75	1	2.61	—	—	—	—	—	—	—
—Can. Olympic Team......	Int'l	7	429	5	2	0	17	0	2.38	—	—	—	—	—	—	—
—San Diego	IHL	7	424	4	2	‡1	17	0	2.41	3	160	0	3	13	0	4.88
92-93—Hartford.....................	NHL	50	2656	16	27	3	184	0	4.16	—	—	—	—	—	—	—
93-94—Hartford.....................	NHL	47	2750	17	24	5	137	2	2.99	—	—	—	—	—	—	—
94-95—Hartford.....................	NHL	42	2418	17	19	4	108	0	2.68	—	—	—	—	—	—	—
NHL totals............		301	16887	112	136	35	981	6	3.49	19	1126	9	10	65	1	3.46

BURR, SHAWN

LW, RED WINGS

PERSONAL: Born July 1, 1966, in Sarnia, Ont.... 6-1/195.... Shoots left.
TRANSACTIONS/CAREER NOTES: Selected by Detroit Red Wings as underage junior in first round (first Red Wings pick, seventh overall) of NHL entry draft (June 9, 1984).... Separated left shoulder (May 1988).... Suffered lower back spasms (October 20, 1992); missed three games.... Underwent surgery on wrist (December 8, 1993); missed 18 games.... Injured leg (January 25, 1994); missed seven games.
HONORS: Won Emms Family Award (1983-84).... Named to OHL All-Star second team (1985-86).
STATISTICAL PLATEAUS: Three-goal games: 1986-87 (1), 1989-90 (1). Total: 2.

Season Team	League	Gms.	G	A	Pts.	PIM	Gms.	G	A	Pts.	PIM
			REGULAR SEASON					PLAYOFFS			
83-84—Kitchener..................	OHL	68	41	44	85	50	16	5	12	17	22
84-85—Kitchener..................	OHL	38	24	42	66	50	4	3	3	6	2
—Detroit	NHL	9	0	0	0	2	—	—	—	—	—
—Adirondack	AHL	4	0	0	0	2	—	—	—	—	—
85-86—Kitchener..................	OHL	59	60	67	127	104	5	2	3	5	8
—Adirondack	AHL	3	2	2	4	2	17	5	7	12	32
—Detroit	NHL	5	1	0	1	4	—	—	—	—	—
86-87—Detroit	NHL	80	22	25	47	107	16	7	2	9	20
87-88—Detroit	NHL	78	17	23	40	97	9	3	1	4	14
88-89—Detroit	NHL	79	19	27	46	78	6	1	2	3	6
89-90—Adirondack	AHL	3	4	2	6	2	—	—	—	—	—
—Detroit	NHL	76	24	32	56	82	—	—	—	—	—
90-91—Detroit	NHL	80	20	30	50	112	7	0	4	4	15
91-92—Detroit	NHL	79	19	32	51	118	11	1	5	6	10
92-93—Detroit	NHL	80	10	25	35	74	7	2	1	3	2
93-94—Detroit	NHL	51	10	12	22	31	7	2	0	2	6
94-95—Detroit	NHL	42	6	8	14	60	16	0	2	2	6
NHL totals............		659	148	214	362	765	79	16	17	33	79

BURRIDGE, RANDY

LW, KINGS

PERSONAL: Born January 7, 1966, in Fort Erie, Ont.... 5-9/185.... Shoots left.... Name pronounced BUHR-ihdj.
TRANSACTIONS/CAREER NOTES: Selected by Boston Bruins in eighth round (seventh Bruins pick, 157th overall) of NHL entry draft (June 15, 1985).... Strained groin (March 1, 1986).... Suspended by AHL during playoffs (April 1987).... Sprained medial collateral ligament in left knee (February 6, 1990); missed 18 games.... Tore right knee ligaments (February 7, 1991).... Underwent surgery to right knee (February 13, 1991).... Traded by Bruins to Washington Capitals for RW Stephen Leach (June 21, 1991).... Partially tore left knee ligament (March 1, 1992); missed 14 games.... Underwent knee surgery (September 5, 1992); missed first 71 games of season.... Strained groin (October 6, 1993); missed three games.... Traded by Capitals to Los Angeles Kings for LW Warren Rychel (February 10, 1995).
HONORS: Played in NHL All-Star Game (1992).
STATISTICAL PLATEAUS: Three-goal games: 1988-89 (2), 1993-94 (2). Total: 4.

Season Team	League	Gms.	G	A	Pts.	PIM	Gms.	G	A	Pts.	PIM
			REGULAR SEASON					PLAYOFFS			
82-83—Fort Erie Jr. B	OHA	42	32	56	88	32	—	—	—	—	—
83-84—Peterborough	OHL	55	6	7	13	44	8	3	2	5	7
84-85—Peterborough	OHL	66	49	57	106	88	17	9	16	25	18
85-86—Peterborough	OHL	17	15	11	26	23	3	1	3	4	2
—Boston	NHL	52	17	25	42	28	3	0	4	4	12
—Moncton	AHL	—	—	—	—	—	3	0	2	2	2
86-87—Moncton	AHL	47	26	41	67	139	3	1	2	3	30
—Boston	NHL	23	1	4	5	16	2	1	0	1	2
87-88—Boston	NHL	79	27	28	55	105	23	2	10	12	16
88-89—Boston	NHL	80	31	30	61	39	10	5	2	7	8
89-90—Boston	NHL	63	17	15	32	47	21	4	11	15	14

Season	Team	League	REGULAR SEASON					PLAYOFFS				
			Gms.	G	A	Pts.	PIM	Gms.	G	A	Pts.	PIM
90-91—Boston		NHL	62	15	13	28	40	19	0	3	3	39
91-92—Washington		NHL	66	23	44	67	50	2	0	1	1	0
92-93—Baltimore		AHL	2	0	1	1	2	—	—	—	—	—
—Washington		NHL	4	0	0	0	0	4	1	0	1	0
93-94—Washington		NHL	78	25	17	42	73	11	0	2	2	12
94-95—Washington		NHL	2	0	0	0	2	—	—	—	—	—
—Los Angeles		NHL	38	4	15	19	8	—	—	—	—	—
NHL totals			547	160	191	351	408	95	13	33	46	103

BURT, ADAM
D, WHALERS

PERSONAL: Born January 15, 1969, in Detroit.... 6-0/190.... Shoots left.
TRANSACTIONS/CAREER NOTES: Broke jaw (December 1985).... Selected by Hartford Whalers as underage junior in second round (second Whalers pick, 39th overall) of NHL entry draft (June 13, 1987).... Separated left shoulder (September 13, 1988).... Bruised hip (December 1989).... Dislocated left shoulder (January 19, 1989).... Tore medial collateral ligaments in right knee (February 16, 1991); missed remainder of season.... Sprained left wrist (January 11, 1992); missed six games.... Broke bone in right foot (January 25, 1993); missed 13 games.... Sprained shoulder (February 27, 1994); missed remainder of season.
HONORS: Named to OHL All-Star second team (1987-88).
MISCELLANEOUS: Captain of Hartford Whalers (1994-95).

Season	Team	League	REGULAR SEASON					PLAYOFFS				
			Gms.	G	A	Pts.	PIM	Gms.	G	A	Pts.	PIM
85-86—North Bay		OHL	49	0	11	11	81	10	0	0	0	24
86-87—North Bay		OHL	57	4	27	31	138	24	1	6	7	68
87-88—North Bay		OHL	66	17	54	71	176	2	0	3	3	6
—Binghamton		AHL	—	—	—	—	—	2	1	1	2	0
88-89—North Bay		OHL	23	4	11	15	45	12	2	12	14	12
—Team USA Juniors		Int'l	7	1	6	7	...	—	—	—	—	—
—Binghamton		AHL	5	0	2	2	13	—	—	—	—	—
—Hartford		NHL	5	0	0	0	6	—	—	—	—	—
89-90—Hartford		NHL	63	4	8	12	105	2	0	0	0	0
90-91—Springfield		AHL	9	1	3	4	22	—	—	—	—	—
—Hartford		NHL	42	2	7	9	63	—	—	—	—	—
91-92—Hartford		NHL	66	9	15	24	93	2	0	0	0	0
92-93—Hartford		NHL	65	6	14	20	116	—	—	—	—	—
93-94—Hartford		NHL	63	1	17	18	75	—	—	—	—	—
94-95—Hartford		NHL	46	7	11	18	65	—	—	—	—	—
NHL totals			350	29	72	101	523	4	0	0	0	0

BUTCHER, GARTH
D, MAPLE LEAFS

PERSONAL: Born January 8, 1963, in Regina, Sask.... 6-0/204.... Shoots right.
HIGH SCHOOL: Thom (Regina, Sask.).
TRANSACTIONS/CAREER NOTES: Selected by Vancouver Canucks as underage junior in first round (first Canucks pick, 10th overall) of NHL entry draft (June 10, 1981).... Separated shoulder (October 1984).... Traded by Canucks with C Dan Quinn to St. Louis Blues for LW Geoff Courtnall, D Robert Dirk, C Cliff Ronning, LW Sergio Momesso and fifth-round pick (RW Brian Loney) in 1992 draft (March 5, 1991).... Fractured bone in left foot (March 7, 1992); missed final 12 games of season.... Bruised foot (December 26, 1993); missed two games.... Traded by Blues with C Bob Bassen and C Ron Sutter to Quebec Nordiques for D Steve Duchesne and RW Denis Chasse (January 23, 1994).... Bruised thigh (March 10, 1994); missed two games.... Traded by Nordiques with C Mats Sundin, LW Todd Warriner and first-round pick (traded to Washington Capitals who selected D Nolan Baumgartner) in 1994 draft to Toronto Maple Leafs for LW Wendel Clark, D Sylvain Lefebvre, RW Landon Wilson and first-round pick (D Jeffrey Kealty) in 1994 draft (June 28, 1994).... Suffered back spasms (March 12, 1995); missed three games.
HONORS: Named to WHL All-Star first team (1980-81 and 1981-82).... Played in NHL All-Star Game (1993).
MISCELLANEOUS: Captain of St. Louis Blues (1991-92).

Season	Team	League	REGULAR SEASON					PLAYOFFS				
			Gms.	G	A	Pts.	PIM	Gms.	G	A	Pts.	PIM
79-80—Regina Tier II		SJHL	51	15	31	46	236	—	—	—	—	—
—Regina		WHL	13	0	4	4	20	9	0	0	0	45
80-81—Regina		WHL	69	9	77	86	230	11	5	17	22	60
81-82—Regina		WHL	65	24	68	92	318	19	3	17	20	95
—Vancouver		NHL	5	0	0	0	9	1	0	0	0	0
82-83—Kamloops		WHL	5	4	2	6	4	6	4	8	12	16
—Vancouver		NHL	55	1	13	14	104	3	1	0	1	2
83-84—Fredericton		AHL	25	4	13	17	43	6	0	2	2	19
—Vancouver		NHL	28	2	0	2	34	—	—	—	—	—
84-85—Vancouver		NHL	75	3	9	12	152	—	—	—	—	—
—Fredericton		AHL	3	1	0	1	11	—	—	—	—	—
85-86—Vancouver		NHL	70	4	7	11	188	3	0	0	0	0
86-87—Vancouver		NHL	70	5	15	20	207	—	—	—	—	—
87-88—Vancouver		NHL	80	6	17	23	285	—	—	—	—	—
88-89—Vancouver		NHL	78	0	20	20	227	7	1	1	2	22
89-90—Vancouver		NHL	80	6	14	20	205	—	—	—	—	—
90-91—Vancouver		NHL	69	6	12	18	257	—	—	—	—	—
—St. Louis		NHL	13	0	4	4	32	13	2	1	3	54
91-92—St. Louis		NHL	68	5	15	20	189	5	1	2	3	16

Season Team	League	REGULAR SEASON					PLAYOFFS				
		Gms.	G	A	Pts.	PIM	Gms.	G	A	Pts.	PIM
92-93—St. Louis	NHL	84	5	10	15	211	11	1	1	2	20
93-94—St. Louis	NHL	43	1	6	7	76	—	—	—	—	—
—Quebec	NHL	34	3	9	12	67	—	—	—	—	—
94-95—Toronto	NHL	45	1	7	8	59	7	0	0	0	8
NHL totals		897	48	158	206	2302	50	6	5	11	122

BUTENSCHON, SVEN
D, PENGUINS

PERSONAL: Born March 22, 1976, in Itzehoe, West Germany. . . . 6-5/201. . . . Shoots left. . . . Name pronounced boot-en-SHOWN.
HIGH SCHOOL: Crocus Plains (Brandon, Man.).
TRANSACTIONS/CAREER NOTES: Selected by Pittsburgh Penguins in third round (third Penguins pick, 57th overall) of NHL entry draft (June 29, 1994).

Season Team	League	REGULAR SEASON					PLAYOFFS				
		Gms.	G	A	Pts.	PIM	Gms.	G	A	Pts.	PIM
93-94—Brandon	WHL	70	3	19	22	51	4	0	0	0	6
94-95—Brandon	WHL	21	1	5	6	44	18	1	2	3	11

BUTSAYEV, SLAVA
C, SHARKS

PERSONAL: Born June 13, 1970, in Togliatti, U.S.S.R. . . . 6-2/200. . . . Shoots left. . . . Name pronounced SLAH-vuh boot-SIGH-yehf.
TRANSACTIONS/CAREER NOTES: Selected by Philadelphia Flyers in sixth round (10th Flyers pick, 109th overall) of NHL entry draft (June 16, 1990). . . . Traded by Flyers to San Jose Sharks for D Rob Zettler (February 1, 1994). . . . Played in Europe during 1994-95 NHL lockout. . . . Injured stomach (January 20, 1995); missed eight games.
STATISTICAL PLATEAUS: Three-goal games: 1993-94 (1).

Season Team	League	REGULAR SEASON					PLAYOFFS				
		Gms.	G	A	Pts.	PIM	Gms.	G	A	Pts.	PIM
89-90—CSKA Moscow	USSR	48	13	4	17	30	—	—	—	—	—
90-91—CSKA Moscow	USSR	46	14	9	23	32	—	—	—	—	—
91-92—CSKA Moscow	USSR	36	12	13	25	26	—	—	—	—	—
—Unified Olympic Team	Int'l	8	1	1	2	4	—	—	—	—	—
92-93—CSKA Moscow	CIS	5	3	4	7	6	—	—	—	—	—
—Philadelphia	NHL	52	2	14	16	61	—	—	—	—	—
—Hershey	AHL	24	8	10	18	51	—	—	—	—	—
93-94—Philadelphia	NHL	47	12	9	21	58	—	—	—	—	—
—San Jose	NHL	12	0	2	2	10	—	—	—	—	—
94-95—Lada Togliatti	CIS	9	2	6	8	6	—	—	—	—	—
—San Jose	NHL	6	2	0	2	0	—	—	—	—	—
—Kansas City	IHL	13	4	3	7	12	3	0	0	0	2
NHL totals		117	16	25	41	129					

BUZAK, MIKE
G, BLUES

PERSONAL: Born February 10, 1973, in Edson, Alta. . . . 6-3/190. . . . Catches left.
HIGH SCHOOL: Queen Elizabeth (Edmonton).
COLLEGE: Michigan State.
TRANSACTIONS/CAREER NOTES: Selected by St. Louis Blues in seventh round (fifth Blues pick, 167th overall) of NHL entry draft (June 26, 1993).
HONORS: Named to CCHA All-Star second team (1993-94 and 1994-95).

Season Team	League	REGULAR SEASON							PLAYOFFS						
		Gms.	Min.	W	L	T	GA	SO	Avg.	Gms.	Min.	W	L	GA SO	Avg.
91-92—Michigan State	CCHA	7	311	4	0	0	22	0	4.24	—	—	—	—	— —	—
92-93—Michigan State	CCHA	38	2090	22	10	2	102	0	2.93	—	—	—	—	— —	—
93-94—Michigan State	CCHA	39	2297	21	12	5	104	2	2.72	—	—	—	—	— —	—
94-95—Michigan State	CCHA	31	1797	17	10	3	94	0	3.14	—	—	—	—	— —	—

BUZEK, PETR
D, STARS

PERSONAL: Born April 26, 1977, in Jihlava, Czechoslovakia. . . . 6-0/184. . . . Shoots left.
TRANSACTIONS/CAREER NOTES: Selected by Dallas Stars in third round (third Stars pick, 63rd overall) of NHL entry draft (July 8, 1995).

Season Team	League	REGULAR SEASON					PLAYOFFS				
		Gms.	G	A	Pts.	PIM	Gms.	G	A	Pts.	PIM
93-94—Jihlava	Czech.	29	6	16	22	...	—	—	—	—	—
—Dukla Jihlava	Czech Rep.	3	0	0	0	...	—	—	—	—	—
94-95—Dukla Jihlava	Czech Rep.	43	2	5	7	...	2	0	0	0	...

BYAKIN, ILYA
D, SHARKS

PERSONAL: Born February 2, 1963, in Sverdlovsk, U.S.S.R. . . . 5-9/185. . . . Shoots left.
TRANSACTIONS/CAREER NOTES: Selected by Edmonton Oilers in 11th round (11th Oilers pick, 267th overall) of NHL entry draft (June 26, 1993). . . . Sprained knee (November 13, 1993); missed two games. . . . Sprained left wrist (January 7, 1994); missed four games. . . . Played in Europe during 1994-95 NHL lockout. . . . Signed as free agent by San Jose Sharks (September 4, 1995).

Season Team	League	REGULAR SEASON					PLAYOFFS				
		Gms.	G	A	Pts.	PIM	Gms.	G	A	Pts.	PIM
83-84—Spartak Moscow	USSR	44	9	12	21	26	—	—	—	—	—
84-85—Spartak Moscow	USSR	46	7	11	18	56	—	—	—	—	—

Season Team	League	REGULAR SEASON Gms.	G	A	Pts.	PIM	PLAYOFFS Gms.	G	A	Pts.	PIM
85-86—Spartak Moscow	USSR	34	8	7	15	41	—	—	—	—	—
86-87—Avtomobilist Sverdlovsk ..	USSR					Did not play.					
87-88—Avtomobilist Sverdlovsk ..	USSR	30	10	10	20	37	—	—	—	—	—
88-89—Avtomobilist Sverdlovsk ..	USSR	40	11	9	20	53	—	—	—	—	—
89-90—Avtomobilist Sverdlovsk ..	USSR	27	14	7	21	20	—	—	—	—	—
90-91—CSKA Moscow	USSR	29	4	7	11	20	—	—	—	—	—
91-92—Rapperswil	Switzerland	36	27	40	67	36	—	—	—	—	—
92-93—Landshut	Germany	44	12	19	31	43	—	—	—	—	—
93-94—Cape Breton	AHL	12	2	9	11	8	—	—	—	—	—
—Edmonton	NHL	44	8	20	28	30	—	—	—	—	—
94-95—Avtomobilist Yek.	CIS	4	3	2	5	14	—	—	—	—	—
—San Jose	NHL	13	0	5	5	14	—	—	—	—	—
—Kansas City	IHL	1	0	2	2	0	16	4	10	14	43
NHL totals		57	8	25	33	44					

BYLSMA, DANIEL
LW, KINGS

PERSONAL: Born September 19, 1970, in Grand Rapids, Mich. . . . 6-2/205. . . . Shoots left. . . . Full name: Daniel Brian Bylsma. . . . Name pronounced BIGHL-smuh.
COLLEGE: Bowling Green State.
TRANSACTIONS/CAREER NOTES: Selected by Winnipeg Jets in fourth round (sixth Jets pick, 69th overall) of NHL entry draft (June 17, 1989). . . . Signed as free agent by Los Angeles Kings (July 14, 1994).

Season Team	League	REGULAR SEASON Gms.	G	A	Pts.	PIM	PLAYOFFS Gms.	G	A	Pts.	PIM
87-88—St. Mary's Jr. B	OHA	40	30	39	69	33	—	—	—	—	—
88-89—Bowling Green State	CCHA	39	4	7	11	16	—	—	—	—	—
89-90—Bowling Green State	CCHA	44	13	17	30	32	—	—	—	—	—
90-91—Bowling Green State	CCHA	40	9	12	21	48	—	—	—	—	—
91-92—Bowling Green State	CCHA	34	11	14	25	24	—	—	—	—	—
92-93—Rochester	AHL	2	0	1	1	0	—	—	—	—	—
93-94—Albany	AHL	3	0	1	1	2	—	—	—	—	—
—Moncton	AHL	50	12	16	28	25	21	3	4	7	31
—Greensboro	ECHL	25	14	16	30	52	—	—	—	—	—
94-95—Phoenix	IHL	81	19	23	42	41	—	—	—	—	—

CABANA, CHAD
LW, PANTHERS

PERSONAL: Born October 1, 1974, in Bonnyville, Alta. . . . 6-1/200. . . . Shoots left. . . . Name pronounced ka-buh-nuh.
HIGH SCHOOL: Kamiakin (Kennewick, Wash.).
TRANSACTIONS/CAREER NOTES: Selected by Florida Panthers in 11th round (11th Panthers pick, 213th overall) of NHL entry draft (June 26, 1993).

Season Team	League	REGULAR SEASON Gms.	G	A	Pts.	PIM	PLAYOFFS Gms.	G	A	Pts.	PIM
90-91—Bonnyville	Jr. B	45	35	40	75	90	—	—	—	—	—
91-92—Tri-City	WHL	57	5	8	13	145	4	0	1	1	21
92-93—Tri-City	WHL	68	19	23	42	104	4	1	0	1	10
93-94—Tri-City	WHL	67	27	33	60	201	4	2	0	2	24
94-95—Tri-City	WHL	68	25	34	59	252	17	10	11	21	47

CAIRNS, ERIC
D, RANGERS

PERSONAL: Born June 27, 1974, in Oakville, Ont. . . . 6-6/217. . . . Shoots left.
TRANSACTIONS/CAREER NOTES: Selected by New York Rangers in third round (third Rangers pick, 72nd overall) of NHL entry draft (June 20, 1992). . . . Loaned by Binghamton Rangers to Birmingham Bulls of ECHL (January 11, 1995). . . . Returned to Binghamton (February 7, 1995).

Season Team	League	REGULAR SEASON Gms.	G	A	Pts.	PIM	PLAYOFFS Gms.	G	A	Pts.	PIM
90-91—Burlington Jr. B	OHA	37	5	16	21	120	—	—	—	—	—
91-92—Detroit	OHL	64	1	11	12	237	7	0	0	0	31
92-93—Detroit	OHL	64	3	13	16	194	15	0	3	3	24
93-94—Detroit	OHL	59	7	35	42	204	17	0	4	4	46
94-95—Binghamton	AHL	27	0	3	3	134	9	1	1	2	28
—Birmingham	ECHL	11	1	3	4	49	—	—	—	—	—

CALOUN, JAN
RW, SHARKS

PERSONAL: Born December 20, 1972, in Usti-nad-Labem, Czechoslovakia. . . . 5-10/175. . . . Shoots right. . . . Name pronounced kuh-LOON.
TRANSACTIONS/CAREER NOTES: Selected by San Jose Sharks in fourth round (fourth Sharks pick, 75th overall) of NHL entry draft (June 20, 1992).

Season Team	League	REGULAR SEASON Gms.	G	A	Pts.	PIM	PLAYOFFS Gms.	G	A	Pts.	PIM
90-91—CHZ Litvinov	Czech.	50	28	19	47	12	—	—	—	—	—
91-92—Chemopetrol Litvinov	Czech.	46	39	13	52	...	—	—	—	—	—
92-93—Chemopetrol Litvinov	Czech.	47	45	22	67	...	—	—	—	—	—
93-94—Chemopetrol Litvinov	Czech Rep.	41	25	17	42	...	4	2	0	2	...
94-95—Kansas City	IHL	76	34	39	73	50	21	13	10	23	18

CAMPBELL, JIM
C, CANADIENS

PERSONAL: Born February 3, 1973, in Worcester, Mass.... 6-1/175.... Shoots right.
HIGH SCHOOL: Lawrence Academy (Groton, Mass.), then Northwood School (Lake Placid, N.Y.).
TRANSACTIONS/CAREER NOTES: Selected by Montreal Canadiens in second round (second Canadiens pick, 28th overall) of NHL entry draft (June 22, 1991).... Loaned by Canadiens to U.S. Olympic Team (September 26, 1993).

			REGULAR SEASON					PLAYOFFS			
Season Team	League	Gms.	G	A	Pts.	PIM	Gms.	G	A	Pts.	PIM
88-89—Lawrence Academy	Mass. H.S.	12	12	8	20	6	—	—	—	—	—
89-90—Lawrence Academy	Mass. H.S.	8	14	7	21	8	—	—	—	—	—
90-91—Northwood School	N.Y. H.S.	26	36	47	83	36	—	—	—	—	—
91-92—Hull	QMJHL	64	41	44	85	51	6	7	3	10	8
92-93—Hull	QMJHL	50	42	29	71	66	8	11	4	15	43
93-94—U.S. national team	Int'l	56	24	33	57	59	—	—	—	—	—
—U.S. Olympic Team	Int'l	8	0	0	0	6	—	—	—	—	—
—Fredericton	AHL	19	6	17	23	6	—	—	—	—	—
94-95—Fredericton	AHL	77	27	24	51	103	12	0	7	7	8

CAMPEAU, CHRISTIAN
RW, LIGHTNING

PERSONAL: Born June 2, 1971, in Verdun, Que.... 5-10/180.... Shoots right. ... Name pronounced KAM-poh.
TRANSACTIONS/CAREER NOTES: Signed as free agent by Tampa Bay Lightning (July 2, 1992).

			REGULAR SEASON					PLAYOFFS			
Season Team	League	Gms.	G	A	Pts.	PIM	Gms.	G	A	Pts.	PIM
89-90—Victoriaville	QMJHL	70	25	39	64	96	16	8	7	15	19
90-91—Granby	QMJHL	69	16	27	43	128	—	—	—	—	—
91-92—Rouen	France	16	3	5	8	12	—	—	—	—	—
92-93—Atlanta	IHL	66	3	5	8	40	3	0	0	0	2
93-94—Atlanta	IHL	65	8	9	17	74	14	1	0	1	2
94-95—Atlanta	IHL	76	10	13	23	96	5	1	0	1	11

C

CARBONNEAU, GUY
C, BLUES

PERSONAL: Born March 18, 1960, in Sept-Iles, Que.... 5-11/185.... Shoots right. ... Name pronounced GEE KAHR-buh-noh.
TRANSACTIONS/CAREER NOTES: Selected by Montreal Canadiens as underage junior in third round (fourth Canadiens pick, 44th overall) of NHL entry draft (August 9, 1979).... Strained right knee ligaments (October 7, 1989); missed nine games.... Broke nose (October 28, 1989).... Suffered concussion (October 8, 1990).... Fractured rib (January 13, 1992); missed six games.... Injured elbow (March 2, 1992); missed one game.... Suffered right knee tendinitis (October 1, 1992); missed five games.... Broke finger (November 14, 1992); missed three games.... Suffered knee tendinitis (February 4, 1993); missed 15 games.... Suffered from the flu (February 11, 1994); missed one game.... Traded by Canadiens to St. Louis Blues for C Jim Montgomery (August 19, 1994). ... Underwent knee surgery (March 31, 1995); missed six games.
HONORS: Named to QMJHL All-Star second team (1979-80).... Won Frank J. Selke Trophy (1987-88, 1988-89 and 1991-92).
STATISTICAL PLATEAUS: Three-goal games: 1982-83 (1), 1993-94 (1). Total: 2.
MISCELLANEOUS: Member of Stanley Cup championship teams (1986 and 1993).... Co-captain of Montreal Canadiens (1989-90).... Captain of Canadiens (1991-92 through 1993-1994).

			REGULAR SEASON					PLAYOFFS			
Season Team	League	Gms.	G	A	Pts.	PIM	Gms.	G	A	Pts.	PIM
76-77—Chicoutimi	QMJHL	59	9	20	29	8	4	1	0	1	0
77-78—Chicoutimi	QMJHL	70	28	55	83	60	—	—	—	—	—
78-79—Chicoutimi	QMJHL	72	62	79	141	47	4	2	1	3	4
79-80—Chicoutimi	QMJHL	72	72	110	182	66	12	9	15	24	28
—Nova Scotia	AHL	—	—	—	—	—	2	1	1	2	2
80-81—Montreal	NHL	2	0	1	1	0	—	—	—	—	—
—Nova Scotia	AHL	78	35	53	88	87	6	1	3	4	9
81-82—Nova Scotia	AHL	77	27	67	94	124	9	2	7	9	8
82-83—Montreal	NHL	77	18	29	47	68	3	0	0	0	2
83-84—Montreal	NHL	78	24	30	54	75	15	4	3	7	12
84-85—Montreal	NHL	79	23	34	57	43	12	4	3	7	8
85-86—Montreal	NHL	80	20	36	56	57	20	7	5	12	35
86-87—Montreal	NHL	79	18	27	45	68	17	3	8	11	20
87-88—Montreal	NHL	80	17	21	38	61	11	0	4	4	2
88-89—Montreal	NHL	79	26	30	56	44	21	4	5	9	10
89-90—Montreal	NHL	68	19	36	55	37	11	2	3	5	6
90-91—Montreal	NHL	78	20	24	44	63	13	1	5	6	10
91-92—Montreal	NHL	72	18	21	39	39	11	1	1	2	6
92-93—Montreal	NHL	61	4	13	17	20	20	3	3	6	10
93-94—Montreal	NHL	79	14	24	38	48	7	1	3	4	4
94-95—St. Louis	NHL	42	5	11	16	16	7	1	2	3	6
NHL totals		954	226	337	563	639	168	31	45	76	131

CAREY, JIM
G, CAPITALS

PERSONAL: Born May 31, 1974, in Dorchester, Mass.... 6-2/205.... Catches left.... Brother of Paul Carey, first baseman, Baltimore Orioles organization.
HIGH SCHOOL: Catholic Memorial (Boston).
COLLEGE: Wisconsin.

TRANSACTIONS/CAREER NOTES: Selected by Washington Capitals in second round (second Capitals pick, 32nd overall) of NHL entry draft (June 20, 1992).
HONORS: Won WCHA Rookie of the Year Award (1992-93).... Named to WCHA All-Star second team (1992-93).... Named to WCHA All-Rookie team (1992-93).... Named to NHL All-Rookie team (1994-95).... Won Dudley (Red) Garrett Memorial Trophy (1994-95).... Won Aldege (Baz) Bastien Trophy (1994-95).... Named to AHL All-Star first team (1994-95).

Season Team	League	Gms.	Min.	W	L	T	GA	SO	Avg.	Gms.	Min.	W	L	GA	SO	Avg.
89-90—Catholic Memorial H.S..	Mass. HS	12	...	12	0	0	...	...	...	—	—	—	—	—	—	—
90-91—Catholic Memorial H.S..	Mass. HS	14	...	13	0	0	...	6	...	—	—	—	—	—	—	—
91-92—Catholic Memorial H.S..	Mass. HS	21	1108	19	2	0	29	6	1.57	—	—	—	—	—	—	—
92-93—Univ. of Wisconsin	WCHA	26	1525	15	8	1	78	1	3.07	—	—	—	—	—	—	—
93-94—Univ. of Wisconsin	WCHA	39	*2247	*24	13	1	114	1	*3.04	—	—	—	—	—	—	—
94-95—Portland	AHL	55	3281	30	14	11	151	*6	2.76	—	—	—	—	—	—	—
—Washington	NHL	28	1604	18	6	3	57	4	2.13	7	358	2	4	25	0	4.19
NHL totals		28	1604	18	6	3	57	4	2.13	7	358	2	4	25	0	4.19

CARKNER, TERRY
D, RED WINGS

PERSONAL: Born March 7, 1966, in Smith Falls, Ont.... 6-3/210.... Shoots left.
TRANSACTIONS/CAREER NOTES: Selected by New York Rangers as underage junior in first round (first Rangers pick, 14th overall) of NHL entry draft (June 9, 1984).... Traded by Rangers with LW Jeff Jackson to Quebec Nordiques for LW John Ogrodnick and D David Shaw (September 30, 1987).... Suspended 10 games by NHL for leaving bench during fight (January 24, 1988).... Traded by Nordiques to Philadelphia Flyers for D Greg Smyth and third-round pick (G John Tanner) in 1989 draft (July 25, 1988).... Underwent surgery to left knee (September 23, 1989); missed 15 games.... Bruised ankle (March 1990).... Bruised foot (November 23, 1991); missed two games.... Bruised wrist (November 19, 1992); missed one game.... Traded by Flyers to Detroit Red Wings for D Yves Racine and fourth-round pick (LW Sebastien Vallee) in 1994 draft (October 5, 1993).... Injured left shoulder (March 19, 1994); missed 11 games.... Did not play due to contract dispute (February 24-March 15, 1995).
HONORS: Named to OHL All-Star second team (1984-85).... Shared Max Kaminsky Trophy with Jeff Brown (1985-86).... Named to OHL All-Star first team (1985-86).

Season Team	League	Gms.	G	A	Pts.	PIM	Gms.	G	A	Pts.	PIM
82-83—Brockville	COJHL	47	8	32	40	94	—	—	—	—	—
83-84—Peterborough	OHL	66	4	21	25	91	8	0	6	6	13
84-85—Peterborough	OHL	64	14	47	61	125	17	2	10	12	11
85-86—Peterborough	OHL	54	12	32	44	106	16	1	7	8	17
86-87—New Haven	AHL	12	2	6	8	56	3	1	0	1	0
—New York Rangers	NHL	52	2	13	15	120	1	0	0	0	0
87-88—Quebec	NHL	63	3	24	27	159	—	—	—	—	—
88-89—Philadelphia	NHL	78	11	32	43	149	19	1	5	6	28
89-90—Philadelphia	NHL	63	4	18	22	167	—	—	—	—	—
90-91—Philadelphia	NHL	79	7	25	32	204	—	—	—	—	—
91-92—Philadelphia	NHL	73	4	12	16	195	—	—	—	—	—
92-93—Philadelphia	NHL	83	3	16	19	150	—	—	—	—	—
93-94—Detroit	NHL	68	1	6	7	130	7	0	0	0	4
94-95—Detroit	NHL	20	1	2	3	21	—	—	—	—	—
NHL totals		579	36	148	184	1295	27	1	5	6	32

CARNBACK, PATRIK
C/LW, MIGHTY DUCKS

PERSONAL: Born February 1, 1968, in Goteborg, Sweden.... 6-0/187.... Shoots left.
TRANSACTIONS/CAREER NOTES: Selected by Montreal Canadiens in sixth round (seventh Canadiens pick, 125th overall) of NHL entry draft (June 11, 1988).... Traded by Canadiens with RW Todd Ewen to Mighty Ducks of Anaheim for third-round pick (RW Chris Murray) in 1994 draft (August 10, 1993).... Strained groin (December 20, 1993); missed five games.... Played in Europe during 1994-95 NHL lockout.
HONORS: Named Swedish League Rookie of the Year (1989-90).

Season Team	League	Gms.	G	A	Pts.	PIM	Gms.	G	A	Pts.	PIM
86-87—Vastra Frolunda	Swed. Dv.II	28	3	1	4	4	—	—	—	—	—
87-88—Vastra Frolunda	Swed. Dv.II	33	16	19	35	10	11	4	5	9	8
88-89—Vastra Frolunda	Swed. Dv.II	53	39	36	75	75	—	—	—	—	—
89-90—Vastra Frolunda	Sweden	40	26	27	53	34	—	—	—	—	—
90-91—Vastra Frolunda	Sweden	22	10	9	19	46	28	15	24	39	24
91-92—Vastra Frolunda	Sweden	33	17	24	41	32	—	—	—	—	—
—Swedish Olympic Team	Int'l	7	1	1	2	2	—	—	—	—	—
92-93—Fredericton	AHL	45	20	37	57	45	5	0	3	3	14
—Montreal	NHL	6	0	0	0	2	—	—	—	—	—
93-94—Anaheim	NHL	73	12	11	23	54	—	—	—	—	—
94-95—Vastra Frolunda	Sweden	14	2	6	8	20	—	—	—	—	—
—Anaheim	NHL	41	6	15	21	32	—	—	—	—	—
NHL totals		120	18	26	44	88	—	—	—	—	—

CARNEY, KEITH
D, BLACKHAWKS

PERSONAL: Born February 3, 1970, in Pawtucket, R.I.... 6-2/205.... Shoots left.... Full name: Keith Edward Carney.
COLLEGE: Maine.
TRANSACTIONS/CAREER NOTES: Selected by Buffalo Sabres in fourth round (third Sabres pick,

76th overall) of NHL entry draft (June 11, 1988).... Traded by Sabres to Chicago Blackhawks for D Craig Muni (October 27, 1993).
HONORS: Named to Hockey East All-Rookie team (1988-89).... Named to NCAA All-America East second team (1989-90).... Named to Hockey East All-Star second team (1989-90).... Named to NCAA All-America East first team (1990-91).... Named to Hockey East All-Star first team (1990-91).

			REGULAR SEASON					PLAYOFFS			
Season Team	League	Gms.	G	A	Pts.	PIM	Gms.	G	A	Pts.	PIM
88-89—University of Maine	Hockey East	40	4	22	26	24	—	—	—	—	—
89-90—University of Maine	Hockey East	41	3	41	44	43	—	—	—	—	—
90-91—University of Maine	Hockey East	40	7	49	56	38	—	—	—	—	—
91-92—U.S. national team	Int'l	49	2	17	19	16	—	—	—	—	—
—Rochester.........................	AHL	24	1	10	11	2	2	0	2	2	0
—Buffalo.............................	NHL	14	1	2	3	18	7	0	3	3	0
92-93—Buffalo.............................	NHL	30	2	4	6	55	8	0	3	3	6
—Rochester.........................	AHL	41	5	21	26	32	—	—	—	—	—
93-94—Louisville......................	ECHL	15	1	4	5	14	—	—	—	—	—
—Buffalo.............................	NHL	7	1	3	4	4	—	—	—	—	—
—Indianapolis	IHL	28	0	14	14	20	—	—	—	—	—
—Chicago	NHL	30	3	5	8	35	6	0	1	1	4
94-95—Chicago	NHL	18	1	0	1	11	4	0	1	1	0
NHL totals....................		99	8	14	22	123	25	0	8	8	10

CARPENTER, BOB
LW, DEVILS

PERSONAL: Born July 13, 1963, in Beverly, Mass.... 6-0/200.... Shoots left.
HIGH SCHOOL: St. John's Prep (Danvers, Mass.).
TRANSACTIONS/CAREER NOTES: Selected by Washington Capitals as underage junior in first round (first Capitals pick, third overall) of NHL entry draft (June 10, 1981)....
Traded by Capitals with second-round pick in 1989 draft (RW Jason Prosofsky) to New York Rangers for C Mike Ridley, C Kelly Miller and RW Bobby Crawford (January 1, 1987).... Traded by Rangers with D Tom Laidlaw to Los Angeles Kings for C Marcel Dionne, C Jeff Crossman and third-round pick in 1989 draft (March 10, 1987).... Tore rotator cuff (January 1988).... Broke right thumb and wrist (December 31, 1988).... Traded by Kings to Boston Bruins for C Steve Kasper and LW Jay Miller (January 23, 1989).... Tore ligaments of right wrist (April 1989).... Injured left knee (October 1990).... Suffered multiple fracture of left kneecap (December 8, 1990); missed remainder of season.... Injured left wrist and suffered stiffness in knee (April 5, 1991).... Strained calf (March 19, 1992).... Signed as free agent by Capitals (June 30, 1992).... Signed as free agent by New Jersey Devils (September 30, 1993).... Sprained ankle (February 11, 1995); missed one game.... Suffered charley horse (April 20, 1995); missed last five games of season and first three games of playoffs.
HONORS: Played in NHL All-Star Game (1985).
STATISTICAL PLATEAUS: Three-goal games: 1987-88 (1), 1989-90 (1). Total: 2.... Four-goal games: 1981-82 (1).... Total hat tricks: 3.
MISCELLANEOUS: Member of Stanley Cup championship team (1995).

			REGULAR SEASON					PLAYOFFS			
Season Team	League	Gms.	G	A	Pts.	PIM	Gms.	G	A	Pts.	PIM
79-80—St. John's Prep School......	Mass. H.S.	...	28	37	65	...	—	—	—	—	—
80-81—St. John's Prep School......	Mass. H.S.	18	14	24	38	...	—	—	—	—	—
81-82—Washington	NHL	80	32	35	67	69	—	—	—	—	—
82-83—Washington	NHL	80	32	37	69	64	4	1	0	1	2
83-84—Washington	NHL	80	28	40	68	51	8	2	1	3	25
84-85—Washington	NHL	80	53	42	95	87	5	1	4	5	8
85-86—Washington	NHL	80	27	29	56	105	9	5	4	9	12
86-87—Washington	NHL	22	5	7	12	21	—	—	—	—	—
—New York Rangers	NHL	28	2	8	10	20	—	—	—	—	—
—Los Angeles.....................	NHL	10	2	3	5	6	5	1	2	3	2
87-88—Los Angeles.....................	NHL	71	19	33	52	84	5	1	1	2	0
88-89—Los Angeles.....................	NHL	39	11	15	26	16	—	—	—	—	—
—Boston.............................	NHL	18	5	9	14	10	8	1	1	2	4
89-90—Boston.............................	NHL	80	25	31	56	97	21	4	6	10	39
90-91—Boston.............................	NHL	29	8	8	16	22	1	0	1	1	2
91-92—Boston.............................	NHL	60	25	23	48	46	8	0	1	1	6
92-93—Washington	NHL	68	11	17	28	65	6	1	4	5	6
93-94—New Jersey......................	NHL	76	10	23	33	51	20	1	7	8	20
94-95—New Jersey......................	NHL	41	5	11	16	19	17	1	4	5	6
NHL totals....................		942	300	371	671	833	117	19	36	55	132

CARSON, JIMMY
C, WHALERS

PERSONAL: Born July 20, 1968, in Southfield, Mich.... 6-1/200.... Shoots right.
TRANSACTIONS/CAREER NOTES: Selected by Los Angeles Kings as underage junior in first round (first Kings pick, second overall) of NHL entry draft (June 21, 1986).... Traded by Kings with LW Martin Gelinas and first-round picks in 1989 (traded to New Jersey), 1991 (LW Martin Rucinsky) and 1993 (D Nick Stajduhar) drafts and cash to Edmonton Oilers for C Wayne Gretzky, RW/D Marty McSorley and LW/C Mike Krushelnyski (August 9, 1988).... Bruised right knee (September 27, 1989).... Traded by Oilers with C Kevin McClelland and fifth-round pick in 1991 draft (traded to Montreal Canadiens who selected D Brad Layzell) to Detroit Red Wings for C/RW Joe Murphy, C/LW Adam Graves, LW Petr Klima and D Jeff Sharples (November 2, 1989).... Injured right knee ligaments (February 3, 1990); missed 14 games.... Suffered from tonsillitis and mononucleosis (March 1990).... Suffered sore left shoulder (November 1990).... Strained right knee (January 11, 1991); missed 15 games.... Underwent surgery to left shoulder ligaments (April 25, 1991).... Traded by Red Wings with RW Marc Potvin and C Gary Shuchuk to Kings for D Paul Coffey, RW Jim Hiller and C/LW Sylvain Couturier (January 29, 1993).... Suffered throat infection

— 365 —

(November 6, 1993); missed three games. . . . Traded by Kings to Vancouver Canucks for LW Dixon Ward and future consider-ations (January 8, 1994). . . . Signed as free agent by Hartford Whalers (July 13, 1994). . . . Injured shoulder (April 16, 1995); missed eight games.
HONORS: Won Frank J. Selke Trophy (1985-86). . . . Won Michael Bossy Trophy (1985-86). . . . Named to QMJHL All-Star sec-ond team (1985-86). . . . Named to NHL All-Rookie team (1986-87). . . . Played in NHL All-Star Game (1989).
STATISTICAL PLATEAUS: Three-goal games: 1987-88 (4), 1988-89 (1), 1989-90 (1), 1990-91 (1), 1991-92 (1), 1992-93 (1). Total: 9. . . . Four-goal games: 1987-88 (1). . . . Total hat tricks: 10.

Season Team	League	REGULAR SEASON					PLAYOFFS				
		Gms.	G	A	Pts.	PIM	Gms.	G	A	Pts.	PIM
84-85—Verdun	QMJHL	68	44	72	116	16	—	—	—	—	—
85-86—Verdun	QMJHL	69	70	83	153	46	5	2	6	8	0
86-87—Los Angeles	NHL	80	37	42	79	22	5	1	2	3	6
87-88—Los Angeles	NHL	80	55	52	107	45	5	5	3	8	4
88-89—Edmonton	NHL	80	49	51	100	36	7	2	1	3	6
89-90—Edmonton	NHL	4	1	2	3	0	—	—	—	—	—
—Detroit	NHL	44	20	16	36	8	—	—	—	—	—
90-91—Detroit	NHL	64	21	25	46	28	7	2	1	3	4
91-92—Detroit	NHL	80	34	35	69	30	11	2	3	5	0
92-93—Detroit	NHL	52	25	26	51	18	—	—	—	—	—
—Los Angeles	NHL	34	12	10	22	14	18	5	4	9	2
93-94—Los Angeles	NHL	25	4	7	11	2	—	—	—	—	—
—Vancouver	NHL	34	7	10	17	22	2	0	1	1	0
94-95—Hartford	NHL	38	9	10	19	29	—	—	—	—	—
NHL totals		615	274	286	560	254	55	17	15	32	22

CARTER, ANSON
C, DENVER

PERSONAL: Born June 6, 1974, in Toronto. . . . 6-1/175. . . . Shoots right.
COLLEGE: Michigan State.
TRANSACTIONS/CAREER NOTES: Selected by Quebec Nordiques in 10th round (10th Nor-diques pick, 220th overall) of NHL entry draft (June 20, 1992). . . . Nordiques franchise moved to Denver for 1995-96 season.
HONORS: Named to CCHA All-Star first team (1993-94 and 1994-95). . . . Named to NCAA All-America West second team (1994-95).

Season Team	League	REGULAR SEASON					PLAYOFFS				
		Gms.	G	A	Pts.	PIM	Gms.	G	A	Pts.	PIM
91-92—Wexford	OHA Jr. A	42	18	22	40	24	—	—	—	—	—
92-93—Michigan State	CCHA	36	19	11	30	20	—	—	—	—	—
93-94—Michigan State	CCHA	39	30	24	54	36	—	—	—	—	—
94-95—Michigan State	CCHA	39	34	17	51	40	—	—	—	—	—

CASEY, JON
G, BLUES

PERSONAL: Born August 29, 1962, in Grand Rapids, Minn. . . . 5-10/155. . . . Catches left.
HIGH SCHOOL: Grand Rapids (Minn.).
COLLEGE: North Dakota.
TRANSACTIONS/CAREER NOTES: Signed as free agent by Minnesota North Stars (April 1, 1984). . . . North Stars franchise moved from Minnesota to Dallas and renamed Stars for 1993-94 season. . . . Traded by Stars to Boston Bruins for G Andy Moog (June 25, 1993) to complete deal in which Bruins sent D Gord Murphy to Stars for future consider-ations (June 20, 1993). . . . Signed as free agent by St. Louis Blues (June 30, 1994).
HONORS: Named to WCHL All-Star first team (1981-82 and 1983-84). . . . Won Harry (Hap) Holmes Memorial Trophy (1984-85). . . . Won Aldege (Baz) Bastien Trophy (1984-85). . . . Named to AHL All-Star first team (1984-85). . . . Played in NHL All-Star Game (1993).

Season Team	League	REGULAR SEASON								PLAYOFFS						
		Gms.	Min.	W	L	T	GA	SO	Avg.	Gms.	Min.	W	L	GA	SO	Avg.
80-81—Univ. of North Dakota	WCHA	6	300	3	1	0	19	0	3.80	—	—	—	—	—	—	—
81-82—Univ. of North Dakota	WCHA	18	1038	15	3	0	48	1	2.77	—	—	—	—	—	—	—
82-83—Univ. of North Dakota	WCHA	17	1020	9	6	2	42	0	2.47	—	—	—	—	—	—	—
83-84—Univ. of North Dakota	WCHA	37	2180	25	10	2	115	2	3.17	—	—	—	—	—	—	—
—Minnesota	NHL	2	84	1	0	0	6	0	4.29	—	—	—	—	—	—	—
84-85—Baltimore	AHL	46	2646	30	11	4	116	†4	*2.63	13	689	8	3	38	0	3.31
85-86—Springfield	AHL	9	464	4	3	1	30	0	3.88	—	—	—	—	—	—	—
—Minnesota	NHL	26	1402	11	11	1	91	0	3.89	—	—	—	—	—	—	—
86-87—Indianapolis	CHL	31	1794	14	15	0	133	0	4.45	—	—	—	—	—	—	—
—Springfield	AHL	13	770	1	8	0	56	0	4.36	—	—	—	—	—	—	—
87-88—Kalamazoo	IHL	42	2541	24	13	‡5	154	2	3.64	7	382	3	3	26	0	4.08
—Minnesota	NHL	14	663	1	7	4	41	0	3.71	—	—	—	—	—	—	—
88-89—Minnesota	NHL	55	2961	18	17	12	151	1	3.06	4	211	1	3	16	0	4.55
89-90—Minnesota	NHL	61	3407	*31	22	4	183	3	3.22	7	415	3	4	21	1	3.04
90-91—Minnesota	NHL	55	3185	21	20	11	158	3	2.98	*23	*1205	*14	7	*61	†1	3.04
91-92—Minnesota	NHL	52	2911	19	23	5	165	2	3.40	7	437	3	4	22	0	3.02
—Kalamazoo	IHL	4	250	2	1	‡1	11	0	2.64	—	—	—	—	—	—	—
92-93—Minnesota	NHL	60	3476	26	26	5	193	3	3.33	—	—	—	—	—	—	—
93-94—Boston	NHL	57	3192	30	15	9	153	4	2.88	11	698	5	6	34	0	2.92
94-95—St. Louis	NHL	19	872	7	5	4	40	0	2.75	2	30	0	1	2	0	4.00
NHL totals		401	22153	165	146	55	1181	16	3.20	54	2996	26	25	156	2	3.12

CASSELMAN, MIKE
C, RED WINGS

PERSONAL: Born August 23, 1968, in Morrisburg, Ont. . . . 5-11/190. . . . Shoots left.
TRANSACTIONS/CAREER NOTES: Selected by Detroit Red Wings in first round (first Red Wings pick, third overall) of NHL supplemental draft (June 10, 1988).
HONORS: Named to ECHL All-Star second team (1991-92).

			REGULAR SEASON					PLAYOFFS				
Season	Team	League	Gms.	G	A	Pts.	PIM	Gms.	G	A	Pts.	PIM
87-88	Clarkson	ECAC	24	4	1	5	0	—	—	—	—	—
88-89	Clarkson	ECAC	31	3	14	17	0	—	—	—	—	—
89-90	Clarkson	ECAC	34	22	21	43	69	—	—	—	—	—
90-91	Clarkson	ECAC	40	19	35	54	44	—	—	—	—	—
91-92	Toledo	ECHL	61	39	60	99	83	5	0	1	1	6
	Adirondack	AHL	1	0	0	0	0	—	—	—	—	—
92-93	Toledo	ECHL	3	0	1	1	2	—	—	—	—	—
	Adirondack	AHL	60	12	19	31	27	8	3	3	6	0
93-94	Adirondack	AHL	77	17	38	55	34	12	2	4	6	10
94-95	Adirondack	AHL	60	17	43	60	42	4	0	0	0	2

CASSELS, ANDREW
C, WHALERS

PERSONAL: Born July 23, 1969, in Mississauga, Ont. . . . 6-0/192. . . . Shoots left. . . . Name pronounced KAZ-uhls.
TRANSACTIONS/CAREER NOTES: Broke wrist (January 1986). . . . Selected by Montreal Canadiens as underage junior in first round (first Canadiens pick, 17th overall) of NHL entry draft (June 13, 1987). . . . Sprained left knee ligaments (September 1988). . . . Separated right shoulder (November 22, 1989); missed 10 games. . . . Traded by Canadiens to Hartford Whalers for second-round pick (RW Valeri Bure) in 1992 draft (September 17, 1991). . . . Bruised kneecap (December 4, 1993); missed one game. . . . Suffered facial injury (March 13, 1994); missed four games.
HONORS: Won Emms Family Award (1986-87). . . . Won Red Tilson Trophy (1987-88). . . . Won Eddie Powers Memorial Trophy (1987-88). . . . Won William Hanley Trophy (1987-88). . . . Named to OHL All-Star first team (1987-88 and 1988-89).
MISCELLANEOUS: Captain of Hartford Whalers (1994-95).

			REGULAR SEASON					PLAYOFFS				
Season	Team	League	Gms.	G	A	Pts.	PIM	Gms.	G	A	Pts.	PIM
85-86	Bramalea Jr. B	OHA	33	18	25	43	26	—	—	—	—	—
86-87	Ottawa	OHL	66	26	66	92	28	11	5	9	14	7
87-88	Ottawa	OHL	61	48	*103	*151	39	16	8	*24	†32	13
88-89	Ottawa	OHL	56	37	97	134	66	12	5	10	15	10
89-90	Sherbrooke	AHL	55	22	45	67	25	12	2	11	13	6
	Montreal	NHL	6	2	0	2	2	—	—	—	—	—
90-91	Montreal	NHL	54	6	19	25	20	8	0	2	2	2
91-92	Hartford	NHL	67	11	30	41	18	7	2	4	6	6
92-93	Hartford	NHL	84	21	64	85	62	—	—	—	—	—
93-94	Hartford	NHL	79	16	42	58	37	—	—	—	—	—
94-95	Hartford	NHL	46	7	30	37	18	—	—	—	—	—
NHL totals			336	63	185	248	157	15	2	6	8	8

CAVALLINI, GINO
LW

PERSONAL: Born November 24, 1962, in Toronto. . . . 6-2/215. . . . Shoots left. . . . Full name: Gino John Cavallini. . . . Name pronounced KAV-uh-LEE-nee. . . . Brother of Paul Cavallini, defenseman, Dallas Stars.
COLLEGE: Bowling Green State.
TRANSACTIONS/CAREER NOTES: Signed as free agent by Calgary Flames (July 1984). . . . Traded by Flames with LW Eddy Beers and D Charles Bourgeois to St. Louis Blues for D Terry Johnson, RW Joe Mullen and D Rik Wilson (February 1, 1986). . . . Broke right hand (January 1988); missed 16 games. . . . Strained left knee (February 1989). . . . Claimed on waivers by Quebec Nordiques (February 27, 1992). . . . Sprained left knee (February 12, 1993); missed 13 games. . . . Signed as free agent by Milwaukee Admirals (September 14, 1993).
HONORS: Named to IHL All-Star second team (1994-95).
STATISTICAL PLATEAUS: Three-goal games: 1989-90 (1).

			REGULAR SEASON					PLAYOFFS				
Season	Team	League	Gms.	G	A	Pts.	PIM	Gms.	G	A	Pts.	PIM
81-82	Toronto St. Mikes	OJHL	37	27	56	83	. . .	—	—	—	—	—
82-83	Bowling Green State	CCHA	40	8	16	24	52	—	—	—	—	—
83-84	Bowling Green State	CCHA	43	25	23	48	16	—	—	—	—	—
84-85	Moncton	AHL	51	29	19	48	28	—	—	—	—	—
	Calgary	NHL	27	6	10	16	14	3	0	0	0	4
85-86	Moncton	AHL	4	3	2	5	7	—	—	—	—	—
	Calgary	NHL	27	7	7	14	26	—	—	—	—	—
	St. Louis	NHL	30	6	5	11	36	17	4	5	9	10
86-87	St. Louis	NHL	80	18	26	44	54	6	3	1	4	2
87-88	St. Louis	NHL	64	15	17	32	62	10	5	5	10	19
88-89	St. Louis	NHL	74	20	23	43	79	9	0	2	2	17
89-90	St. Louis	NHL	80	15	15	30	77	12	1	3	4	2
90-91	St. Louis	NHL	78	8	27	35	81	13	1	3	4	2
91-92	St. Louis	NHL	48	9	7	16	40	—	—	—	—	—
	Quebec	NHL	18	1	7	8	4	—	—	—	—	—
92-93	Quebec	NHL	67	9	15	24	34	4	0	0	0	0
93-94	Milwaukee	IHL	78	43	35	78	64	4	3	4	7	6
94-95	Milwaukee	IHL	80	53	35	88	54	15	7	2	9	10
NHL totals			593	114	159	273	507	74	14	19	33	56

C

CAVALLINI, PAUL
D, STARS

PERSONAL: Born October 13, 1965, in Toronto. . . . 6-1/202. . . . Shoots left. . . . Full name: Paul Edward Cavallini. . . . Name pronounced KAV-uh-LEE-nee. . . . Brother of Gino Cavallini, left winger, Calgary Flames, St. Louis Blues and Quebec Nordiques (1984-85 through 1992-93).

HIGH SCHOOL: Henry Carr (Rexdale, Ont.).
COLLEGE: Providence.
TRANSACTIONS/CAREER NOTES: Selected by Washington Capitals as underage junior in 10th round (ninth Capitals pick, 205th overall) of NHL entry draft (June 9, 1984). . . . Traded by Capitals to St. Louis Blues for second-round pick (D Wade Bartley) in 1988 draft (December 1987). . . . Broke hand (December 11, 1987). . . . Injured neck (December 11, 1988). . . . Dislocated left shoulder (February 25, 1989). . . . Lost tip of left index finger (December 22, 1990); missed 13 games. . . . Strained knee ligament (October 20, 1991); missed 13 games. . . . Traded by Blues to Capitals for C Kevin Miller (November 1, 1992). . . . Missed one game due to personal reasons (March 16, 1993). . . . Traded by Capitals to Dallas Stars for future considerations (June 20, 1993); Stars sent D Enrico Ciccone to Capitals to complete deal (June 25, 1993). . . . Fractured eye (January 16, 1994); missed five games.
HONORS: Named to Hockey East All-Freshman team (1984-85). . . . Won Alka-Seltzer Plus Award (1989-90). . . . Played in NHL All-Star Game (1990).

Season Team	League	REGULAR SEASON					PLAYOFFS				
		Gms.	G	A	Pts.	PIM	Gms.	G	A	Pts.	PIM
83-84—Henry Carr H.S.	MTHL	54	20	41	61	190	—	—	—	—	—
84-85—Providence College	Hockey East	45	5	14	19	64	—	—	—	—	—
85-86—Canadian national team	Int'l	52	1	11	12	95	—	—	—	—	—
—Binghamton	AHL	15	3	4	7	20	6	0	2	2	56
86-87—Binghamton	AHL	66	12	24	36	188	13	2	7	9	35
—Washington	NHL	6	0	2	2	8	—	—	—	—	—
87-88—Washington	NHL	24	2	3	5	66	—	—	—	—	—
—St. Louis	NHL	48	4	7	11	86	10	1	6	7	26
88-89—St. Louis	NHL	65	4	20	24	128	10	2	2	4	14
89-90—St. Louis	NHL	80	8	39	47	106	12	2	3	5	20
90-91—St. Louis	NHL	67	10	25	35	89	13	2	3	5	20
91-92—St. Louis	NHL	66	10	25	35	95	4	0	1	1	6
92-93—St. Louis	NHL	11	1	4	5	10	—	—	—	—	—
—Washington	NHL	71	5	8	13	46	6	0	2	2	18
93-94—Dallas	NHL	74	11	33	44	82	9	1	8	9	4
94-95—Dallas	NHL	44	1	11	12	28	5	0	2	2	6
NHL totals		556	56	177	233	744	69	8	27	35	114

CHABOT, FREDERIC
G, PANTHERS

PERSONAL: Born February 12, 1968, in Hebertville, Que. . . . 5-11/175. . . . Catches right. . . . Name pronounced shuh-BAHT.
TRANSACTIONS/CAREER NOTES: Selected by New Jersey Devils in 10th round (10th Devils pick, 192nd overall) of NHL entry draft (June 21, 1986). . . . Signed as free agent by Montreal Canadiens (January 16, 1990). . . . Selected by Tampa Bay Lightning in NHL expansion draft (June 18, 1992). . . . Traded by Lightning to Canadiens for G Jean-Claude Bergeron (June 18, 1992). . . . Traded by Canadiens to Philadelphia Flyers for future considerations (February 21, 1994). . . . Signed as free agent by Florida Panthers (August 15, 1994).
HONORS: Named to Memorial Cup All-Star team (1981-82). . . . Named to WHL (East) All-Star first team (1988-89). . . . Won Aldege (Baz) Bastien Trophy (1993-94).
STATISTICAL NOTES: Member of Stanley Cup championship team (1993).

Season Team	League	REGULAR SEASON							PLAYOFFS						
		Gms.	Min.	W	L	T	GA	SO	Avg.	Gms.	Min.	W	L	GA	SO	Avg.
86-87—Drummondville	QMJHL	*62	*3508	31	29	0	293	1	5.01	8	481	2	6	40	0	4.99
87-88—Drummondville	QMJHL	58	3276	27	24	4	237	1	4.34	*16	1019	10	6	56	†1	*3.30
88-89—Moose Jaw	WHL	26	1385	...	...	...	114	1	4.94	—						—
—Prince Albert	WHL	28	1572	...	...	...	88	1	3.36	4	199	1	1	16	0	4.82
89-90—Fort Wayne	IHL	23	1208	6	13	‡3	87	1	4.32	—						—
—Sherbrooke	AHL	2	119	1	1	0	8	0	4.03	—						—
90-91—Montreal	NHL	3	108	0	0	1	6	0	3.33	—						—
—Fredericton	AHL	35	1800	9	15	5	122	0	4.07	—						—
91-92—Winston-Salem	ECHL	25	1449	15	7	‡2	71	0	*2.94	—						—
—Fredericton	AHL	30	1761	17	9	4	79	2	*2.69	7	457	3	4	20	0	2.63
92-93—Fredericton	AHL	45	2544	22	17	4	141	0	3.33	4	261	1	3	16	0	3.68
—Montreal	NHL	1	40	0	0	0	1	0	1.50	—						—
93-94—Fredericton	AHL	3	143	0	1	1	12	0	5.03	—						—
—Las Vegas	IHL	2	110	1	1	‡1	5	0	2.73	—						—
—Montreal	NHL	1	60	0	1	0	5	0	5.00	—						—
—Hershey	AHL	31	1607	13	6	7	75	2	*2.80	11	665	7	4	32	0	2.89
—Philadelphia	NHL	4	70	0	1	1	5	0	4.29	—						—
94-95—Cincinnati	IHL	48	2622	25	12	‡7	128	1	2.93	5	326	3	2	16	0	2.94
NHL totals		9	278	0	2	2	17	0	3.67							

CHAMBERS, SHAWN
D, DEVILS

PERSONAL: Born October 11, 1966, in Royal Oak, Mich. . . . 6-2/200. . . . Shoots left. . . . Full name: Shawn Randall Chambers.
COLLEGE: Alaska-Fairbanks.
TRANSACTIONS/CAREER NOTES: Selected by Minnesota North Stars in NHL supplemental draft (June 13, 1987). . . . Dislocated shoulder (February 1988). . . . Separated right shoulder (September 1988). . . . Injured left knee (September 11, 1990); missed first 11 games of season. . . . Fractured left kneecap (December 5, 1990);

missed three months. . . . Underwent surgery to left knee to remove piece of loose cartilage (May 1991). . . . Traded by North Stars to Washington Capitals for C Trent Klatt and LW Steve Maltais (June 21, 1991). . . . Suffered sore knee (October 1991); missed first 47 games of season. . . . Reinjured knee (January 26, 1992); missed remainder of season. . . . Underwent arthroscopic knee surgery (February 4, 1992). . . . Selected by Tampa Bay Lightning in NHL expansion draft (June 18, 1992). . . . Underwent arthroscopic knee surgery (October 9, 1992); missed 14 games. . . . Underwent arthroscopic knee surgery (October 21, 1993); missed 14 games. . . . Injured shoulder (November 13, 1993); missed two games. . . . Suffered facial cuts (January 2, 1994). . . . Suffered strep throat (February 7, 1995); missed one game. . . . Traded by Lightning with RW Danton Cole to New Jersey Devils for C Alexander Semak and RW Ben Hankinson (March 14, 1995).

MISCELLANEOUS: Member of Stanley Cup championship team (1995).

Season Team	League	REGULAR SEASON Gms.	G	A	Pts.	PIM	PLAYOFFS Gms.	G	A	Pts.	PIM
85-86—Alaska-Fairbanks	GWHC	25	15	21	36	34	—	—	—	—	—
86-87—Alaska-Fairbanks	GWHC	17	11	19	30	...	—	—	—	—	—
—Seattle	WHL	28	8	25	33	58	—	—	—	—	—
—Fort Wayne	IHL	12	2	6	8	0	10	1	4	5	5
87-88—Minnesota	NHL	19	1	7	8	21	—	—	—	—	—
—Kalamazoo	IHL	19	1	6	7	22	—	—	—	—	—
88-89—Minnesota	NHL	72	5	19	24	80	3	0	2	2	0
89-90—Minnesota	NHL	78	8	18	26	81	7	2	1	3	10
90-91—Minnesota	NHL	29	1	3	4	24	23	0	7	7	16
—Kalamazoo	IHL	3	1	1	2	0	—	—	—	—	—
91-92—Baltimore	AHL	5	2	3	5	9	—	—	—	—	—
—Washington	NHL	2	0	0	0	2	—	—	—	—	—
92-93—Atlanta	IHL	6	0	2	2	18	—	—	—	—	—
—Tampa Bay	NHL	55	10	29	39	36	—	—	—	—	—
93-94—Tampa Bay	NHL	66	11	23	34	23	—	—	—	—	—
94-95—Tampa Bay	NHL	24	2	12	14	6	—	—	—	—	—
—New Jersey	NHL	21	2	5	7	6	20	4	5	9	2
NHL totals		366	40	116	156	279	53	6	15	21	28

CHARBONNEAU, JOE
RW, CANUCKS

PERSONAL: Born November 21, 1966, in Ferme-Neuve, Que. . . . 6-0/195. . . . Shoots right. . . . Name pronounced SHAHR-buh-noh.
TRANSACTIONS/CAREER NOTES: Separated right shoulder (November 1984). . . . Reinjured shoulder (December 1984). . . . Injured shoulder (January 1985). . . . Selected by Montreal Canadiens as underage junior in first round (first Canadiens pick, 12th overall) of NHL entry draft (June 21, 1986). . . . Traded by Canadiens to Vancouver Canucks for C Dan Woodley (January 25, 1989). . . . Suffered back spasms (December 6, 1993); missed 24 games. . . . Sprained knee (February 6, 1994); missed eight games.

Season Team	League	REGULAR SEASON Gms.	G	A	Pts.	PIM	PLAYOFFS Gms.	G	A	Pts.	PIM
83-84—Drummondville	QMJHL	65	31	59	90	110	—	—	—	—	—
84-85—Drummondville	QMJHL	46	34	40	74	91	12	5	10	15	20
85-86—Drummondville	QMJHL	57	44	45	89	158	23	16	20	36	40
86-87—Sherbrooke	AHL	72	14	27	41	94	16	5	12	17	17
87-88—Montreal	NHL	16	0	2	2	6	8	0	0	0	4
—Sherbrooke	AHL	55	30	35	65	108	—	—	—	—	—
88-89—Montreal	NHL	9	1	3	4	6	—	—	—	—	—
—Sherbrooke	AHL	33	13	15	28	95	—	—	—	—	—
—Vancouver	NHL	13	0	1	1	6	—	—	—	—	—
—Milwaukee	IHL	13	8	5	13	46	10	3	2	5	23
89-90—Milwaukee	IHL	65	23	38	61	137	5	0	1	1	8
90-91—Canadian national team	Int'l	56	22	29	51	54	—	—	—	—	—
91-92—Canadian national team	Int'l					Statistics unavailable.					
92-93—Canadian national team	Int'l	1	0	0	0	0	—	—	—	—	—
—Vancouver	NHL					Did not play.					
93-94—Vancouver	NHL	30	7	7	14	49	3	1	0	1	4
—Hamilton	AHL	7	3	2	5	8	—	—	—	—	—
94-95—Vancouver	NHL	3	1	0	1	0	—	—	—	—	—
—Las Vegas	IHL	27	8	12	20	102	9	1	1	2	71
NHL totals		71	9	13	22	67	11	1	0	1	8

CHARBONNEAU, PATRICK
G, SENATORS

PERSONAL: Born July 22, 1975, in St. Jean-sur-Richelieu, Que. . . . 5-11/205. . . . Catches left.
TRANSACTIONS/CAREER NOTES: Selected by Ottawa Senators in third round (third Senators pick, 53rd overall) of NHL entry draft (June 26, 1993).

Season Team	League	REGULAR SEASON Gms.	Min.	W	L	T	GA	SO	Avg.	PLAYOFFS Gms.	Min.	W	L	GA	SO	Avg.
91-92—Victoriaville	QMJHL	37	1943	9	23	2	163	0	5.03	—	—	—	—	—	—	—
92-93—Victoriaville	QMJHL	59	3121	35	22	0	216	0	4.15	2	92	1	0	4	0	2.61
93-94—Victoriaville	QMJHL	56	2948	11	34	2	261	0	5.31	5	212	1	4	24	0	6.79
—Prince Edward Island	AHL	3	180	2	1	0	11	0	3.67	—	—	—	—	—	—	—
94-95—Victoriaville	QMJHL	47	2339	15	27	1	201	0	5.16	4	142	0	3	20	0	8.45
—Prince Edward Island	AHL	2	120	2	0	0	4	0	2.00	3	137	0	2	12	0	5.26

CHARPENTIER, SEBASTIEN

G, CAPITALS

(July 8, 1995).

PERSONAL: Born April 18, 1977, in Drummondville, Que.... 5-9/161. ... Catches left.
TRANSACTIONS/CAREER NOTES: Selected by Washington Capitals in fourth round (fourth Capitals pick, 93rd overall) of NHL entry draft

			REGULAR SEASON								PLAYOFFS					
Season Team	League	Gms.	Min.	W	L	T	GA	SO	Avg.	Gms.	Min.	W	L	GA	SO	Avg.
94-95—Laval	QMJHL	41	2152	25	12	1	99	2	2.76	16	886	9	4	45	0	3.05

CHARRON, ERIC

D, LIGHTNING

PERSONAL: Born January 14, 1970, in Verdun, Que.... 6-3/192.... Shoots left.
TRANSACTIONS/CAREER NOTES: Selected by Montreal Canadiens in first round (first Canadiens pick, 20th overall) of NHL entry draft (June 11, 1988).... Traded by Canadiens with D Alain Cote and future considerations to Tampa Bay Lightning for D Rob Ramage (March 20, 1993); Canadiens sent D Donald Dufresne to Lightning to complete deal (June 18, 1993).

			REGULAR SEASON				PLAYOFFS			
Season Team	League	Gms.	G	A	Pts.	PIM	Gms.	G	A	Pts.	PIM
87-88—Trois-Rivieres	QMJHL	67	3	13	16	135	—	—	—	—	—
88-89—Trois-Rivieres	QMJHL	38	2	16	18	111	—	—	—	—	—
—Verdun	QMJHL	28	2	15	17	66	—	—	—	—	—
—Sherbrooke	AHL	1	0	0	0	0	—	—	—	—	—
89-90—St. Hyacinthe	QMJHL	68	13	38	51	152	11	3	4	7	67
—Sherbrooke	AHL	—	—	—	—	—	2	0	0	0	0
90-91—Fredericton	AHL	71	1	11	12	108	2	1	0	1	29
91-92—Fredericton	AHL	59	2	11	13	98	6	1	0	1	4
92-93—Fredericton	AHL	54	3	13	16	93	—	—	—	—	—
—Montreal	NHL	3	0	0	0	2	—	—	—	—	—
—Atlanta	IHL	11	0	2	2	12	3	0	1	1	6
93-94—Atlanta	IHL	66	5	18	23	144	14	1	4	5	28
—Tampa Bay	NHL	4	0	0	0	2	—	—	—	—	—
94-95—Tampa Bay	NHL	45	1	4	5	26	—	—	—	—	—
NHL totals		52	1	4	5	30					

CHARTIER, SCOTT

D, MIGHTY DUCKS

PERSONAL: Born January 19, 1972, in St. Lazare, Man.... 5-11/195.... Shoots right. ... Name pronounced SHAHR-tee-yay.
TRANSACTIONS/CAREER NOTES: Signed as free agent by Mighty Ducks of Anaheim (July 30, 1993).

			REGULAR SEASON				PLAYOFFS			
Season Team	League	Gms.	G	A	Pts.	PIM	Gms.	G	A	Pts.	PIM
91-92—Kelowna	BCJHL	55	13	33	46	...	—	—	—	—	—
92-93—Western Michigan Univ.	CCHA	38	6	22	28	84	—	—	—	—	—
93-94—San Diego	IHL	49	2	6	8	84	4	0	0	0	6
94-95—San Diego	IHL	8	0	0	0	0	—	—	—	—	—
—Greensboro	ECHL	30	6	14	20	82	18	2	3	5	41

CHASE, KELLY

RW, WHALERS

PERSONAL: Born October 25, 1967, in Porcupine Plain, Sask.... 5-11/195.... Shoots right.... Full name: Kelly Wayne Chase.
HIGH SCHOOL: Porcupine Plain (Sask.).
TRANSACTIONS/CAREER NOTES: Signed as free agent by St. Louis Blues (May 24, 1988).... Bruised right foot (January 1990).... Suffered back spasms (March 1990).... Suspended 10 games by NHL for fighting (March 18, 1991).... Injured knee (December 11, 1991); missed two games.... Sprained left wrist (January 14, 1992); missed three games.... Bruised thigh (February 2, 1992); missed five games.... Injured hand (February 23, 1992); missed four games.... Pulled groin (October 26, 1992); missed six games.... Injured wrist (January 9, 1993); missed five games.... Bruised lower leg (March 30, 1993); missed last six games of season.... Suffered from the flu (December 4, 1993); missed one game.... Injured leg (January 2, 1994); missed four games.... Injured elbow (January 28, 1994); missed three games.... Pulled groin (March 24, 1994); missed three games.... Injured hand (April 5, 1994); missed one game.... Selected by Hartford Whalers in 1994-95 waiver draft for cash (January 18, 1995).... Suffered back spasms (February 24, 1995); missed 14 games.... Suffered sore back (April 9, 1995); missed six games.

			REGULAR SEASON				PLAYOFFS			
Season Team	League	Gms.	G	A	Pts.	PIM	Gms.	G	A	Pts.	PIM
85-86—Saskatoon	WHL	57	7	18	25	172	10	3	4	7	37
86-87—Saskatoon	WHL	68	17	29	46	285	11	2	8	10	37
87-88—Saskatoon	WHL	70	21	34	55	*343	9	3	5	8	32
88-89—Peoria	IHL	38	14	7	21	278	—	—	—	—	—
89-90—Peoria	IHL	10	1	2	3	76	—	—	—	—	—
—St. Louis	NHL	43	1	3	4	244	9	1	0	1	46
90-91—Peoria	IHL	61	20	34	54	406	10	4	3	7	61
—St. Louis	NHL	2	1	0	1	15	6	0	0	0	18
91-92—St. Louis	NHL	46	1	2	3	264	1	0	0	0	7
92-93—St. Louis	NHL	49	2	5	7	204	—	—	—	—	—
93-94—St. Louis	NHL	68	2	5	7	278	4	0	1	1	6
94-95—Hartford	NHL	28	0	4	4	141	—	—	—	—	—
NHL totals		236	7	19	26	1146	20	1	1	2	77

CHASSE, DENIS
RW, BLUES

PERSONAL: Born February 7, 1970, in Montreal.... 6-2/200.... Shoots right.... Name pronounced CHA-say.

TRANSACTIONS/CAREER NOTES: Signed as free agent by Quebec Nordiques (May 14, 1991). ... Traded by Nordiques with D Steve Duchesne to St. Louis Blues for C Ron Sutter, C Bob Bassen and D Garth Butcher (January 23, 1994).... Injured neck (January 29, 1993); missed remainder of season.... Underwent neck surgery (March 9, 1994); missed remainder of season.

			REGULAR SEASON				PLAYOFFS			
Season Team	League	Gms.	G	A	Pts.	PIM	Gms.	G	A	Pts.	PIM
87-88—St. Jean	QMJHL	13	0	1	1	2	1	0	0	0	0
88-89—Verdun	QMJHL	38	12	12	24	61	—	—	—	—	—
—Drummondville	QMJHL	30	15	16	31	77	3	0	2	2	28
89-90—Drummondville	QMJHL	34	14	29	43	85	—	—	—	—	—
—Chicoutimi	QMJHL	33	19	27	46	105	7	7	4	11	50
90-91—Drummondville	QMJHL	62	47	54	101	246	13	9	11	20	56
91-92—Halifax	AHL	73	26	35	61	254	—	—	—	—	—
92-93—Halifax	AHL	75	35	41	76	242	—	—	—	—	—
93-94—Cornwall	AHL	48	27	39	66	194	—	—	—	—	—
—St. Louis	NHL	3	0	1	1	15	—	—	—	—	—
94-95—St. Louis	NHL	47	7	9	16	133	7	1	7	8	23
NHL totals		50	7	10	17	148	7	1	7	8	23

CHELIOS, CHRIS
D, BLACKHAWKS

PERSONAL: Born January 25, 1962, in Chicago.... 6-1/186.... Shoots right.... Name pronounced CHEHL-ee-ohz.

COLLEGE: Wisconsin.

TRANSACTIONS/CAREER NOTES: Selected by Montreal Canadiens as underage junior in second round (fifth Canadiens pick, 40th overall) of NHL entry draft (June 10, 1981).... Sprained right ankle (January 1985). ... Injured left knee (April 1985).... Sprained knee (December 19, 1985).... Reinjured knee (January 20, 1986).... Suffered back spasms (October 1986).... Broke finger on left hand (December 1987).... Bruised tailbone (February 7, 1988).... Strained left knee ligaments (February 1990).... Underwent surgery to repair torn abdominal muscle (April 30, 1990).... Traded by Canadiens with second-round pick in 1991 draft (C Michael Pomichter) to Chicago Blackhawks for C Denis Savard (June 29, 1990).... Lacerated left temple (February 9, 1991).... Suspended four games by NHL (October 15, 1993).... Suspended four games without pay and fined $500 by NHL for eye-scratching incident (February 5, 1994).... Played in Europe during 1994-95 NHL lockout.

HONORS: Named to NCAA All-Tournament team (1982-83).... Named to WCHA All-Star second team (1982-83).... Named to NHL All-Rookie team (1984-85).... Played in NHL All-Star game (1985 and 1990-1994).... Won James Norris Memorial Trophy (1988-89 and 1992-93).... Named to THE SPORTING NEWS All-Star first team (1988-89 and 1992-93).... Named to NHL All-Star first team (1988-89, 1992-93 and 1994-95).... Named to THE SPORTING NEWS All-Star second team (1990-91 and 1991-92).... Named to NHL All-Star second team (1990-91).

MISCELLANEOUS: Member of Stanley Cup championship team (1986).

			REGULAR SEASON				PLAYOFFS			
Season Team	League	Gms.	G	A	Pts.	PIM	Gms.	G	A	Pts.	PIM
79-80—Moose Jaw	SJHL	53	12	31	43	118	—	—	—	—	—
80-81—Moose Jaw	SJHL	54	23	64	87	175	—	—	—	—	—
81-82—University of Wisconsin ...	WCHA	43	6	43	49	50	—	—	—	—	—
82-83—University of Wisconsin ...	WCHA	45	16	32	48	62	—	—	—	—	—
83-84—U.S. national team	Int'l	60	14	35	49	58	—	—	—	—	—
—U.S. Olympic Team	Int'l	6	0	3	3	8	—	—	—	—	—
—Montreal	NHL	12	0	2	2	12	15	1	9	10	17
84-85—Montreal	NHL	74	9	55	64	87	9	2	8	10	17
85-86—Montreal	NHL	41	8	26	34	67	20	2	9	11	49
86-87—Montreal	NHL	71	11	33	44	124	17	4	9	13	38
87-88—Montreal	NHL	71	20	41	61	172	11	3	1	4	29
88-89—Montreal	NHL	80	15	58	73	185	21	4	15	19	28
89-90—Montreal	NHL	53	9	22	31	136	5	0	1	1	8
90-91—Chicago	NHL	77	12	52	64	192	6	1	7	8	46
91-92—Chicago	NHL	80	9	47	56	245	18	6	15	21	37
92-93—Chicago	NHL	84	15	58	73	282	4	0	2	2	14
93-94—Chicago	NHL	76	16	44	60	212	6	1	1	2	8
94-95—Biel-Bienne	Switzerland	3	0	3	3	4	—	—	—	—	—
—Chicago	NHL	48	5	33	38	72	16	4	7	11	12
NHL totals		767	129	471	600	1786	148	28	84	112	303

CHERBATURKIN, VLADIMIR
D, ISLANDERS

PERSONAL: Born April 23, 1975, in Tyumen, U.S.S.R.... 6-2/189. ... Shoots left.... Name pronounced CHEH-buh-TURK-in.

TRANSACTIONS/CAREER NOTES: Selected by New York Islanders in third round (third Islanders pick, 66th overall) of NHL entry draft (June 26, 1993).

			REGULAR SEASON				PLAYOFFS			
Season Team	League	Gms.	G	A	Pts.	PIM	Gms.	G	A	Pts.	PIM
92-93—Kristall Elektrostal	CIS Div. II				Statistics unavailable.						
93-94—Kristall Elektrostal	CIS Div. II	42	4	4	8	38	—	—	—	—	—
94-95—Kristall Elektrostal	CIS	52	2	6	8	90	—	—	—	—	—

CHERBAYEV, ALEXANDER
RW, SHARKS

PERSONAL: Born August 13, 1973, in Voskresensk, U.S.S.R. . . . 6-1/190. . . . Shoots left. . . . Name pronounced chuhr-BIGH-ehv.
TRANSACTIONS/CAREER NOTES: Selected by San Jose Sharks in third round (third Sharks pick, 51st overall) of NHL entry draft (June 20, 1992).

Season Team	League	REGULAR SEASON					PLAYOFFS				
		Gms.	G	A	Pts.	PIM	Gms.	G	A	Pts.	PIM
90-91—Khimik Voskresensk	USSR	16	2	2	4	0	—	—	—	—	—
91-92—Khimik Voskresensk	CIS	38	3	3	6	14	—	—	—	—	—
92-93—Khimik Voskresensk	CIS	33	18	9	27	74	2	1	0	1	0
93-94—Kansas City	IHL	43	17	15	32	100	—	—	—	—	—
94-95—Kansas City	IHL	62	17	28	45	56	6	0	1	1	10

CHEREDARYK, STEVE
D, JETS

PERSONAL: Born November 20, 1975, in Calgary. . . . 6-2/197. . . . Shoots left. . . . Name pronounced CHAIR-ih-DAIR-ihk.
HIGH SCHOOL: Medicine Hat (Alta.).
TRANSACTIONS/CAREER NOTES: Selected by Winnipeg Jets in fourth round (fourth Jets pick, 82nd overall) of NHL entry draft (June 29, 1994).

Season Team	League	REGULAR SEASON					PLAYOFFS				
		Gms.	G	A	Pts.	PIM	Gms.	G	A	Pts.	PIM
92-93—Medicine Hat	WHL	67	1	9	10	88	10	0	1	1	16
93-94—Medicine Hat	WHL	72	3	35	38	151	3	0	1	1	9
94-95—Medicine Hat	WHL	70	3	26	29	193	5	0	1	1	13
—Springfield	AHL	3	0	1	1	0	—	—	—	—	—

CHERNOMAZ, RICHARD
RW

PERSONAL: Born September 1, 1963, in Selkirk, Man. . . . 5-8/185. . . . Shoots right. . . . Name pronounced CHUHR-noh-mas.
TRANSACTIONS/CAREER NOTES: Selected by Colorado Rockies as underage junior in second round (third Rockies pick, 26th overall) of NHL entry draft (June 10, 1981). . . . Suffered recurring pain caused by separated shoulder; missed parts of 1981-82 season. . . . Injured knee ligaments (January 1983). . . . Sprained left knee and underwent arthroscopic surgery (November 27, 1984). . . . Signed as free agent by Calgary Flames (August 4, 1987). . . . Underwent surgery to remove ligament from right knee (November 1989); missed 13 games. . . . Signed as free agent by Toronto Maple Leafs (August 3, 1993).
HONORS: Named to WHL All-Star first team (1982-83). . . . Named to IHL All-Star second team (1987-88 and 1990-91). . . . Won Les Cunningham Plaque (1993-94). . . . Named to AHL All-Star first team (1993-94).

Season Team	League	REGULAR SEASON					PLAYOFFS				
		Gms.	G	A	Pts.	PIM	Gms.	G	A	Pts.	PIM
79-80—Saskatoon	SJHL	51	33	37	70	75	—	—	—	—	—
—Saskatoon	WHL	25	9	10	19	33	—	—	—	—	—
80-81—Victoria	WHL	72	49	64	113	92	15	11	15	26	38
81-82—Victoria	WHL	49	36	62	98	69	4	1	2	3	13
—Colorado	NHL	2	0	0	0	0	—	—	—	—	—
82-83—Victoria	WHL	64	71	53	124	113	12	10	5	15	18
83-84—Maine	AHL	69	17	29	46	39	2	0	1	1	0
—New Jersey	NHL	7	2	1	3	2	—	—	—	—	—
84-85—Maine	AHL	64	17	34	51	64	10	2	2	4	4
—New Jersey	NHL	3	0	2	2	2	—	—	—	—	—
85-86—Maine	AHL	78	21	28	49	82	5	0	0	0	2
86-87—Maine	AHL	58	35	27	62	65	—	—	—	—	—
—New Jersey	NHL	25	6	4	10	8	—	—	—	—	—
87-88—Calgary	NHL	2	1	0	1	0	—	—	—	—	—
—Salt Lake City	IHL	73	48	47	95	122	18	4	14	18	30
88-89—Calgary	NHL	1	0	0	0	0	—	—	—	—	—
—Salt Lake City	IHL	81	33	68	101	122	14	7	5	12	47
89-90—Salt Lake City	IHL	65	39	35	74	170	11	6	6	12	32
90-91—Salt Lake City	IHL	81	39	58	97	213	4	3	1	4	8
91-92—Salt Lake City	IHL	66	20	40	60	201	5	1	2	3	10
—Calgary	NHL	11	0	0	0	6	—	—	—	—	—
92-93—Salt Lake City	IHL	76	26	48	74	172	—	—	—	—	—
93-94—St. John's	AHL	78	45	65	110	199	11	5	11	16	18
94-95—St. John's	AHL	77	24	45	69	235	5	1	1	2	8
NHL totals		51	9	7	16	18					

CHERREY, SCOTT
LW, CAPITALS

PERSONAL: Born May 27, 1976, in Drayton, Ont. . . . 6-2/205. . . . Shoots left.
HIGH SCHOOL: Chippewa (North Bay, Ont.).
TRANSACTIONS/CAREER NOTES: Selected by Washington Capitals in second round (third Capitals pick, 41st overall) of NHL entry draft (June 28, 1994).

Season Team	League	REGULAR SEASON					PLAYOFFS				
		Gms.	G	A	Pts.	PIM	Gms.	G	A	Pts.	PIM
92-93—Listowel Jr. B	OHA	46	17	10	27	63	—	—	—	—	—
93-94—North Bay	OHL	63	15	26	41	45	18	5	3	8	10
94-95—North Bay	OHL	62	16	32	48	78	6	1	3	4	4

CHEVELDAE, TIM
G, JETS

PERSONAL: Born February 15, 1968, in Melville, Sask. . . . 5-10/195. . . . Catches left. . . . Name pronounced SHEH-vehl-day.
TRANSACTIONS/CAREER NOTES: Selected by Detroit Red Wings as underage junior in fourth round (fourth Red Wings pick, 64th overall) of NHL entry draft (June 21, 1986). . . . Sprained right knee (October 5, 1993); missed 16 games. . . . Traded by Red Wings with LW Dallas Drake to Winnipeg Jets for G Bob Essensa and D Sergei Bautin (March 8, 1994).
HONORS: Named to WHL (East) All-Star first team (1987-88). . . . Played in NHL All-Star Game (1992).

					REGULAR SEASON						PLAYOFFS				
Season	Team	League	Gms.	Min.	W	L	T	GA	SO	Avg.	Gms.	Min.	W	L	GA	SO	Avg.
84-85	Melville	SAJHL	23	1167	...	...	...	98	0	5.04	—	—	—	—	—	—	—
85-86	Saskatoon	WHL	36	2030	21	10	3	165	0	4.88	8	480	6	2	29	0	3.63
86-87	Saskatoon	WHL	33	1909	20	11	0	133	2	4.18	5	308	4	1	20	0	3.90
87-88	Saskatoon	WHL	66	3798	44	19	3	235	1	3.71	6	364	4	2	27	0	4.45
88-89	Detroit	NHL	2	122	0	2	0	9	0	4.43	—	—	—	—	—	—	—
	Adirondack	AHL	30	1694	20	8	0	98	1	3.47	2	99	1	0	9	0	5.45
89-90	Adirondack	AHL	31	1848	17	8	6	116	0	3.77	—	—	—	—	—	—	—
	Detroit	NHL	28	1600	10	9	8	101	0	3.79	—	—	—	—	—	—	—
90-91	Detroit	NHL	65	3615	30	26	5	*214	2	3.55	7	398	3	4	22	0	3.32
91-92	Detroit	NHL	*72	*4236	†38	23	9	226	2	3.20	11	597	3	7	25	†2	2.51
92-93	Detroit	NHL	67	3880	34	24	7	210	4	3.25	7	423	3	4	24	0	3.40
93-94	Detroit	NHL	30	1572	16	9	1	91	1	3.47	—	—	—	—	—	—	—
	Adirondack	AHL	2	125	1	0	1	7	0	3.36	—	—	—	—	—	—	—
	Winnipeg	NHL	14	788	5	8	1	52	1	3.96	—	—	—	—	—	—	—
94-95	Winnipeg	NHL	30	1571	8	16	3	97	0	3.70	—	—	—	—	—	—	—
NHL totals			308	17384	141	117	34	1000	10	3.45	25	1418	9	15	71	2	3.00

CHIASSON, STEVE
D, FLAMES

PERSONAL: Born April 14, 1967, in Barrie, Ont. . . . 6-1/205. . . . Shoots left. . . . Name pronounced CHAY-sahn.
TRANSACTIONS/CAREER NOTES: Selected by Detroit Red Wings as underage junior in third round (third Red Wings pick, 50th overall) of NHL entry draft (June 15, 1985). . . . Injured hand (October 1985). . . . Separated right shoulder (February 1988). . . . Injured foot (May 1988). . . . Injured groin (October 1988). . . . Bruised ribs (January 1989). . . . Injured ankle (February 1989). . . . Injured knee (November 29, 1990); missed three games. . . . Broke right ankle (January 2, 1991). . . . Reinjured right ankle (February 19, 1991); missed 26 games. . . . Reinjured right ankle (March 9, 1991). . . . Injured ankle (October 22, 1991); missed 14 games. . . . Bruised thigh (October 25, 1992); missed three games. . . . Pulled hamstring (January 21, 1993); missed one game. . . . Suffered injuries (April 2, 1994); missed two games. . . . Traded by Red Wings to Calgary Flames for G Mike Vernon (June 29, 1994). . . . Bruised left foot (February 23, 1995); missed two games.
HONORS: Won Stafford Smythe Memorial Trophy (1985-86). . . . Named to Memorial Cup All-Star team (1985-86). . . . Played in NHL All-Star Game (1993).

				REGULAR SEASON					PLAYOFFS			
Season	Team	League	Gms.	G	A	Pts.	PIM	Gms.	G	A	Pts.	PIM
83-84	Guelph	OHL	55	1	9	10	112	—	—	—	—	—
84-85	Guelph	OHL	61	8	22	30	139	—	—	—	—	—
85-86	Guelph	OHL	54	12	29	41	126	18	10	10	20	37
86-87	Detroit	NHL	45	1	4	5	73	2	0	0	0	19
87-88	Adirondack	AHL	23	6	11	17	58	—	—	—	—	—
	Detroit	NHL	29	2	9	11	57	9	2	2	4	31
88-89	Detroit	NHL	65	12	35	47	149	5	2	1	3	6
89-90	Detroit	NHL	67	14	28	42	114	—	—	—	—	—
90-91	Detroit	NHL	42	3	17	20	80	5	3	1	4	19
91-92	Detroit	NHL	62	10	24	34	136	11	1	5	6	12
92-93	Detroit	NHL	79	12	50	62	155	7	2	2	4	19
93-94	Detroit	NHL	82	13	33	46	122	7	2	3	5	2
94-95	Calgary	NHL	45	2	23	25	39	7	1	2	3	9
NHL totals			516	69	223	292	925	53	13	16	29	117

CHIBIREV, IGOR
C, WHALERS

PERSONAL: Born April 19, 1968, in Penza, U.S.S.R. . . . 6-0/170. . . . Shoots left. . . . Name pronounced EE-gohr CHEE-bihr-ehv.
TRANSACTIONS/CAREER NOTES: Selected by Hartford Whalers in 11th round (eighth Whalers pick, 266th overall) of NHL entry draft (June 26, 1993).
STATISTICAL PLATEAUS: Three-goal games: 1994-95 (1).

				REGULAR SEASON					PLAYOFFS			
Season	Team	League	Gms.	G	A	Pts.	PIM	Gms.	G	A	Pts.	PIM
87-88	CSKA Moscow	USSR	29	5	1	6	8	—	—	—	—	—
88-89	CSKA Moscow	USSR	34	7	9	16	16	—	—	—	—	—
89-90	CSKA Moscow	USSR	46	2	10	12	12	—	—	—	—	—
90-91	CSKA Moscow	USSR	40	10	9	19	4	—	—	—	—	—
91-92	CSKA Moscow	USSR	30	16	16	32	12	—	—	—	—	—
92-93	Fort Wayne	IHL	60	33	36	69	2	12	7	13	20	2
93-94	Springfield	AHL	36	28	23	51	4	—	—	—	—	—
	Hartford	NHL	37	4	11	15	2	—	—	—	—	—
94-95	Fort Wayne	IHL	56	34	28	62	10	—	—	—	—	—
	Hartford	NHL	8	3	1	4	0	—	—	—	—	—
NHL totals			45	7	12	19	2					

CHORSKE, TOM
RW, DEVILS

PERSONAL: Born September 18, 1966, in Minneapolis.... 6-1/205.... Shoots right.... Name pronounced CHOR-skee.
HIGH SCHOOL: Southwest (Minneapolis).
COLLEGE: Minnesota.
TRANSACTIONS/CAREER NOTES: Selected by Montreal Canadiens in first round (second Canadiens pick, 16th overall) of NHL entry draft (June 15, 1985).... Separated shoulder (November 18, 1988); missed 11 games.... Suffered hip pointer (October 26, 1989).... Sprained right shoulder (March 14, 1991).... Traded by Canadiens with RW Stephane Richer to New Jersey Devils for LW Kirk Muller and G Roland Melanson (September 20, 1991).... Suffered charley horse (January 14, 1993); missed two games.... Injured elbow (April 14, 1994); missed one game.... Played in Europe during 1994-95 NHL lockout.... Pulled groin (April 1, 1995); missed one game.... Bruised leg (April 20, 1995); missed two games.
HONORS: Named to WCHA All-Star first team (1988-89).
MISCELLANEOUS: Member of Stanley Cup championship team (1995).

			REGULAR SEASON					PLAYOFFS			
Season Team	League	Gms.	G	A	Pts.	PIM	Gms.	G	A	Pts.	PIM
84-85—Minn. Southwest H.S.	Minn. H.S.	23	44	26	70	...	—	—	—	—	—
85-86—University of Minnesota ...	WCHA	39	6	4	10	6	—	—	—	—	—
86-87—University of Minnesota ...	WCHA	47	20	22	42	20	—	—	—	—	—
87-88—U.S. national team	Int'l	36	9	16	25	24	—	—	—	—	—
88-89—University of Minnesota ...	WCHA	37	25	24	49	28	—	—	—	—	—
89-90—Montreal........................	NHL	14	3	1	4	2	—	—	—	—	—
—Sherbrooke..................	AHL	59	22	24	46	54	12	4	4	8	8
90-91—Montreal........................	NHL	57	9	11	20	32	—	—	—	—	—
91-92—New Jersey.....................	NHL	76	19	17	36	32	7	0	3	3	4
92-93—New Jersey.....................	NHL	50	7	12	19	25	1	0	0	0	0
—Utica..............................	AHL	6	1	4	5	2	—	—	—	—	—
93-94—New Jersey.....................	NHL	76	21	20	41	32	20	4	3	7	0
94-95—Milan.............................	Italy	7	11	5	16	6	—	—	—	—	—
—New Jersey....................	NHL	42	10	8	18	16	17	1	5	6	4
NHL totals.............................		315	69	69	138	139	45	5	11	16	8

CHOUINARD, MARC
C, JETS

PERSONAL: Born May 6, 1977, in Quebec City.... 6-5/187.... Shoots right.
TRANSACTIONS/CAREER NOTES: Selected by Winnipeg Jets in second round (second Jets pick, 32nd overall) of NHL entry draft (July 8, 1995).

			REGULAR SEASON					PLAYOFFS			
Season Team	League	Gms.	G	A	Pts.	PIM	Gms.	G	A	Pts.	PIM
93-94—Beauport	QMJHL	62	11	19	30	23	13	2	5	7	2
94-95—Beauport	QMJHL	68	24	40	64	32	18	1	6	7	4

CHRISTIAN, DAVE
RW

PERSONAL: Born May 12, 1959, in Warroad, Minn.... 5-11/195.... Shoots right.... Son of Bill Christian and nephew of Roger Christian, members of 1960 gold-medal-winning U.S. Olympic team and 1964 U.S. Olympic team; and nephew of Gordon Christian, member of 1956 U.S. Olympic team.
COLLEGE: North Dakota.
TRANSACTIONS/CAREER NOTES: Selected by Winnipeg Jets in second round (second Jets pick, 40th overall) of NHL entry draft (August 9, 1979).... Tore shoulder muscles (December 1982); missed 25 games.... Traded by Jets to Washington Capitals for first-round pick (D Bobby Dollas) in 1983 draft (June 8, 1983).... Traded by Capitals to Boston Bruins for LW Bob Joyce (December 13, 1989).... Signed as free agent by St. Louis Blues; Bruins tried to block the signing, claiming Christian was not a free agent. Blues and Bruins later arranged trade in which Boston received D Glen Featherstone and LW Dave Thomlinson for Christian, third-round (LW Vitali Prokhorov) and seventh-round (C Lance Burns) picks in 1992 draft (July 30, 1991).... Bruised ribs (January 16, 1992); missed one game.... Selected by Chicago Blackhawks in NHL waiver draft (October 4, 1992).... Signed as free agent by Minnesota Moose (September 1, 1994).
HONORS: Played in NHL All-Star Game (1991).
STATISTICAL PLATEAUS: Three-goal games: 1979-80 (1), 1987-88 (1), 1988-89 (1). Total: 3.
MISCELLANEOUS: Member of gold-medal-winning U.S. Olympic team (1980).

			REGULAR SEASON					PLAYOFFS			
Season Team	League	Gms.	G	A	Pts.	PIM	Gms.	G	A	Pts.	PIM
77-78—Univ. of North Dakota	WCHA	38	8	16	24	14	—	—	—	—	—
78-79—Univ. of North Dakota	WCHA	40	22	24	46	22	—	—	—	—	—
79-80—U.S. national team	Int'l	59	10	20	30	26	—	—	—	—	—
—U.S. Olympic Team	Int'l	7	0	8	8	6	—	—	—	—	—
—Winnipeg........................	NHL	15	8	10	18	2	—	—	—	—	—
80-81—Winnipeg........................	NHL	80	28	43	71	22	—	—	—	—	—
81-82—Winnipeg........................	NHL	80	25	51	76	28	4	0	1	1	2
82-83—Winnipeg........................	NHL	55	18	26	44	23	3	0	0	0	0
83-84—Washington	NHL	80	29	52	81	28	8	5	4	9	5
84-85—Washington	NHL	80	26	43	69	14	5	1	1	2	0
85-86—Washington	NHL	80	41	42	83	15	9	4	4	8	0
86-87—Washington	NHL	76	23	27	50	8	7	1	3	4	6
87-88—Washington	NHL	80	37	21	58	26	14	5	6	11	6
88-89—Washington	NHL	80	34	31	65	12	6	1	1	2	0
89-90—Washington	NHL	28	3	8	11	4	—	—	—	—	—
—Boston..........................	NHL	50	12	17	29	8	21	4	1	5	4
90-91—Boston..........................	NHL	78	32	21	53	41	19	8	4	12	4
91-92—St. Louis	NHL	78	20	24	44	41	4	3	0	3	0

Season	Team	League	REGULAR SEASON Gms.	G	A	Pts.	PIM	PLAYOFFS Gms.	G	A	Pts.	PIM
92-93—Chicago		NHL	60	4	14	18	12	1	0	0	0	0
93-94—Chicago		NHL	9	0	3	3	0	1	0	0	0	0
—Indianapolis		IHL	40	8	18	26	6	—	—	—	—	—
94-95—Minnesota		IHL	81	38	42	80	16	3	0	1	1	0
NHL totals			1009	340	433	773	284	102	32	25	57	27

CHRISTIAN, JEFF
LW, PENGUINS

PERSONAL: Born July 30, 1970, in Burlington, Ont.... 6-1/210.... Shoots left.
TRANSACTIONS/CAREER NOTES: Selected by New Jersey Devils in second round (second Devils pick, 23rd overall) of NHL entry draft (June 11, 1988).... Traded by London Knights to Owen Sound Platers for C Todd Hlushko and D David Noseworthy (November 27, 1989).... Suspended three games by OHL for high-sticking (March 28, 1990).... Signed as free agent by Pittsburgh Penguins (August 2, 1994).

Season	Team	League	REGULAR SEASON Gms.	G	A	Pts.	PIM	PLAYOFFS Gms.	G	A	Pts.	PIM
86-87—Dundas Jr. C		OHA	29	20	34	54	42	—	—	—	—	—
87-88—London		OHL	64	15	29	44	154	9	1	5	6	27
88-89—London		OHL	60	27	30	57	221	20	3	4	7	56
89-90—London		OHL	18	14	7	21	64	—	—	—	—	—
—Owen Sound		OHL	37	19	26	45	145	10	6	7	13	43
90-91—Utica		AHL	80	24	42	66	165	—	—	—	—	—
91-92—Utica		AHL	76	27	24	51	198	4	0	0	0	16
—New Jersey		NHL	2	0	0	0	2	—	—	—	—	—
92-93—Utica		AHL	22	4	6	10	39	—	—	—	—	—
—Cincinnati		IHL	36	5	12	17	113	—	—	—	—	—
—Hamilton		AHL	11	2	5	7	35	—	—	—	—	—
93-94—Albany		AHL	76	34	43	77	227	5	1	2	3	19
94-95—Cleveland		IHL	56	13	24	37	126	2	0	1	1	8
—Pittsburgh		NHL	1	0	0	0	0	—	—	—	—	—
NHL totals			3	0	0	0	2					

CHURCH, BRAD
LW, CAPITALS

PERSONAL: Born November 14, 1976, in Dauphin, Man.... 6-1/210.... Shoots left.
TRANSACTIONS/CAREER NOTES: Selected by Washington Capitals in first round (first Capitals pick, 17th overall) of NHL entry draft (July 8, 1995).

Season	Team	League	REGULAR SEASON Gms.	G	A	Pts.	PIM	PLAYOFFS Gms.	G	A	Pts.	PIM
92-93—Dauphin		MJHL	45	15	23	38	80	—	—	—	—	—
93-94—Prince Albert		WHL	71	33	20	53	197	—	—	—	—	—
94-95—Prince Albert		WHL	62	26	24	50	184	15	6	9	15	32

CHURLA, SHANE
RW, STARS

PERSONAL: Born June 24, 1965, in Fernie, B.C.... 6-1/200.... Shoots right. ... Name pronounced CHUR-luh.... Cousin of Mark Rypien, quarterback, St. Louis Rams.
TRANSACTIONS/CAREER NOTES: Selected by Hartford Whalers in sixth round (fourth Whalers pick, 110th overall) of NHL entry draft (June 15, 1985).... Pulled stomach muscles (October 1985).... Suspended three games by AHL (October 5, 1986).... Traded by Whalers with D Dana Murzyn to Calgary Flames for D Neil Sheehy, C Carey Wilson and the rights to LW Lane MacDonald (January 3, 1988).... Traded by Flames with C Perry Berezan to Minnesota North Stars for LW Brian MacLellan and fourth-round pick (C Robert Reichel) in 1989 draft (March 4, 1989).... Broke wrist (April 2, 1989).... Bruised right hand (November 1989).... Suspended 10 games by NHL for fighting (December 28, 1989).... Underwent surgery to wrist (April 1990).... Tore rib cartilage (November 17, 1990); missed five games.... Separated shoulder (December 11, 1990); missed seven games.... Separated right shoulder (January 17, 1991); missed 23 games.... Selected by San Jose Sharks in dispersal draft of North Stars roster (May 30, 1991).... Traded by Sharks to North Stars for C Kelly Kisio (June 3, 1991).... Suffered back spasms (January 30, 1992); missed five games. ... Injured shoulder (March 19, 1992); missed five games.... Injured shoulder (December 1, 1992); missed one game.... Injured shoulder (December 22, 1992); missed two games.... Strained neck (February 28, 1993); missed two games.... Suspended three games by NHL during 1992-93 season for game misconduct penalties.... North Stars franchise moved from Minnesota to Dallas and renamed Stars for 1993-94 season.... Pulled groin (October 23, 1993); missed two games.... Pulled leg muscle (November 24, 1993); missed nine games.... Strained bicep muscle (January 9, 1994); missed one game.... Bruised hip (April 10, 1994); missed one game.... Bruised hand (February 4, 1995); missed one game.... Suffered deep thigh bruise (February 15, 1995); missed one game.... Tore knee ligament (February 24, 1995); missed 12 games.... Suffered from the flu (April 2, 1995); missed one game.... Suspended four games without pay and fined $500 for resisting linesman (April 17, 1995).... Pulled stomach muscle (April 25, 1995); missed one game.

Season	Team	League	REGULAR SEASON Gms.	G	A	Pts.	PIM	PLAYOFFS Gms.	G	A	Pts.	PIM
83-84—Medicine Hat		WHL	48	3	7	10	115	14	1	5	6	41
84-85—Medicine Hat		WHL	70	14	20	34	*370	9	1	0	1	55
85-86—Binghamton		AHL	52	4	10	14	306	3	0	0	0	22
86-87—Binghamton		AHL	24	1	5	6	249	—	—	—	—	—
—Hartford		NHL	20	0	1	1	78	2	0	0	0	42
87-88—Binghamton		AHL	25	5	8	13	168	—	—	—	—	—
—Hartford		NHL	2	0	0	0	14	—	—	—	—	—
—Calgary		NHL	29	1	5	6	132	7	0	1	1	17

— 375 —

Season	Team	League	REGULAR SEASON					PLAYOFFS				
			Gms.	G	A	Pts.	PIM	Gms.	G	A	Pts.	PIM
88-89—Calgary	NHL		5	0	0	0	25	—	—	—	—	—
—Salt Lake City	IHL		32	3	13	16	278	—	—	—	—	—
—Minnesota	NHL		13	1	0	1	54	—	—	—	—	—
89-90—Minnesota	NHL		53	2	3	5	292	7	0	0	0	44
90-91—Minnesota	NHL		40	2	2	4	286	22	2	1	3	90
91-92—Minnesota	NHL		57	4	1	5	278	—	—	—	—	—
92-93—Minnesota	NHL		73	5	16	21	286	—	—	—	—	—
93-94—Dallas	NHL		69	6	7	13	333	9	1	3	4	35
94-95—Dallas	NHL		27	1	3	4	186	5	0	0	0	20
NHL totals			388	22	38	60	1964	52	3	5	8	248

CHYNOWETH, DEAN
D, ISLANDERS

PERSONAL: Born October 30, 1968, in Saskatoon, Sask. . . . 6-2/193. . . . Shoots right. . . . Name pronounced shih-NOWTH. . . . Son of Ed Chynoweth, president of the Western Hockey League; and brother of Jeff Chynoweth, assistant general manager, Red Deer Rebels of WHL.

TRANSACTIONS/CAREER NOTES: Broke hand (September 1985). . . . Broke hand (April 1986). . . . Broke hand (October 1986). . . . Fractured rib and punctured lung (April 1987). . . . Selected by New York Islanders as underage junior in first round (first Islanders pick, 13th overall) of NHL entry draft (June 13, 1987). . . . Injured left eye (October 27, 1988); missed two months. . . . Developed Osgood-Schlatter disease, an abnormal relationship between the muscles and the growing bones (December 1988); missed remainder of season. . . . Injured ankle (October 31, 1989). . . . Sprained ligaments in right thumb (November 1989). . . . Strained shoulder (February 24, 1994); missed one game. . . . Strained groin (March 15, 1994); missed 10 games. . . . Bruised knee (February 20, 1995); missed three games. . . . Injured groin (March 18, 1995); missed three games.

HONORS: Named to Memorial Cup All-Star team (1987-88).

Season	Team	League	REGULAR SEASON					PLAYOFFS				
			Gms.	G	A	Pts.	PIM	Gms.	G	A	Pts.	PIM
85-86—Medicine Hat	WHL		69	3	12	15	208	17	3	2	5	52
86-87—Medicine Hat	WHL		67	3	18	21	285	13	4	2	6	28
87-88—Medicine Hat	WHL		64	1	21	22	274	16	0	6	6	*87
88-89—New York Islanders	NHL		6	0	0	0	48	—	—	—	—	—
89-90—New York Islanders	NHL		20	0	2	2	39	—	—	—	—	—
—Springfield	AHL		40	0	7	7	98	17	0	4	4	36
90-91—New York Islanders	NHL		25	1	1	2	59	—	—	—	—	—
—Capital District	AHL		44	1	5	6	176	—	—	—	—	—
91-92—Capital District	AHL		43	4	6	10	164	6	1	1	2	39
—New York Islanders	NHL		11	1	0	1	23	—	—	—	—	—
92-93—Capital District	AHL		52	3	10	13	197	4	0	1	1	9
93-94—Salt Lake City	IHL		5	0	1	1	33	—	—	—	—	—
—New York Islanders	NHL		39	0	4	4	122	2	0	0	0	2
94-95—New York Islanders	NHL		32	0	2	2	77	—	—	—	—	—
NHL totals			133	2	9	11	368	2	0	0	0	2

CHYZOWSKI, DAVE
LW, ISLANDERS

PERSONAL: Born July 11, 1971, in Edmonton. . . . 6-1/190. . . . Shoots left. . . . Name pronounced chih-ZOW-skee.

TRANSACTIONS/CAREER NOTES: Selected by New York Islanders in first round (first Islanders pick, second overall) of NHL entry draft (June 17, 1989).

HONORS: Named to WHL (West) All-Star first team (1988-89).

Season	Team	League	REGULAR SEASON					PLAYOFFS				
			Gms.	G	A	Pts.	PIM	Gms.	G	A	Pts.	PIM
87-88—Kamloops	WHL		66	16	17	33	117	18	2	4	6	26
88-89—Kamloops	WHL		68	56	48	104	139	16	15	13	28	32
89-90—Kamloops	WHL		4	5	2	7	17	17	11	6	17	46
—Springfield	AHL		4	0	0	0	7	—	—	—	—	—
—New York Islanders	NHL		34	8	6	14	45	—	—	—	—	—
90-91—Capital District	AHL		7	3	6	9	22	—	—	—	—	—
—New York Islanders	NHL		56	5	9	14	61	—	—	—	—	—
91-92—New York Islanders	NHL		12	1	1	2	17	—	—	—	—	—
—Capital District	AHL		55	15	18	33	121	6	1	1	2	23
92-93—Capital District	AHL		66	15	21	36	177	3	2	0	2	0
93-94—Salt Lake City	IHL		66	27	13	40	151	—	—	—	—	—
—New York Islanders	NHL		3	1	0	1	4	2	0	0	0	0
94-95—New York Islanders	NHL		13	0	0	0	11	—	—	—	—	—
—Kalamazoo	IHL		4	0	4	4	8	16	9	5	14	27
NHL totals			118	15	16	31	138	2	0	0	0	0

CIAVAGLIA, PETER
C

PERSONAL: Born July 15, 1969, in Albany, N.Y. . . . 5-10/173. . . . Shoots left. . . . Full name: Peter Anthony Ciavaglia. . . . Name pronounced sa-VAG-lia.

COLLEGE: Harvard.

TRANSACTIONS/CAREER NOTES: Selected by Calgary Flames in seventh round (eighth Flames pick, 145th overall) of NHL entry draft (June 13, 1987). . . . Signed as free agent by Buffalo Sabres (August 1990). . . . Suffered stiff neck (February 14, 1993); missed two games.

HONORS: Named to ECAC All-Star second team (1988-89).... Named to NCAA All-America East second team (1990-91).... Named ECAC Player of the Year (1990-91).... Named to ECAC All-Star first team (1990-91).

			REGULAR SEASON					PLAYOFFS				
Season	Team	League	Gms.	G	A	Pts.	PIM	Gms.	G	A	Pts.	PIM
86-87—Nichols/Wheatfield Jr. B..	NY Jr. B	...	53	84	137	...	—	—	—	—	—
87-88—Harvard University	....	ECAC	30	10	23	33	16	—	—	—	—	—
88-89—Harvard University	....	ECAC	34	15	48	63	36	—	—	—	—	—
89-90—Harvard University	....	ECAC	28	17	18	35	22	—	—	—	—	—
90-91—Harvard University	....	ECAC	28	24	39	63	4	—	—	—	—	—
91-92—Rochester	....	AHL	77	37	61	98	16	6	2	5	7	6
—Buffalo	NHL	2	0	0	0	0	—	—	—	—	—
92-93—Rochester	....	AHL	64	35	67	102	32	17	9	16	25	12
—Buffalo	NHL	3	0	0	0	0	—	—	—	—	—
93-94—Leksand	....	Sweden	39	14	18	32	34	4	1	2	3	0
—U.S. national team	....	Int'l	18	2	9	11	6	—	—	—	—	—
—U.S. Olympic Team	....	Int'l	8	2	4	6	0	—	—	—	—	—
94-95—Detroit	....	IHL	73	22	59	81	83	5	1	1	2	6
NHL totals	....		5	0	0	0	0					

CICCARELLI, DINO
RW, RED WINGS

PERSONAL: Born February 8, 1960, in Sarnia, Ont.... 5-10/175.... Shoots right.... Name pronounced sih-sih-REHL-ee.
TRANSACTIONS/CAREER NOTES: Fractured midshaft of right femur (spring 1978).... Signed as free agent by Minnesota North Stars (September 1979).... Injured shoulder (November 1984).... Broke right wrist (December 1984).... Suspended three games by NHL for making contact with linesman (October 5, 1987).... Suspended 10 games by NHL for stick-swinging incident (January 6, 1988).... Suspended by North Stars for failure to report to training camp (September 10, 1988).... Traded by North Stars with D Bob Rouse to Washington Capitals for RW Mike Gartner and D Larry Murphy (March 7, 1989).... Suffered concussion (March 8, 1989).... Sprained left knee (April 23, 1990).... Fractured right hand (October 20, 1990); missed 21 games.... Injured groin (March 24, 1991); missed five games. . . . Injured eye (December 4, 1991); missed one game. . . . Traded by Capitals to Detroit Red Wings for RW Kevin Miller (June 20, 1992).... Suffered from the flu (January 30, 1993); missed two games.... Injured foot (January 15, 1994); missed 17 games.... Lacerated face (February 8, 1995); missed one game.... Strained right groin (April 2, 1995); missed one game.
HONORS: Won Jim Mahon Memorial Trophy (1977-78).... Named to OMJHL All-Star second team (1977-78).... Played in NHL All-Star Game (1982, 1983 and 1989).
RECORDS: Holds NHL single-season playoff records for most points by rookie—21; and most goals by rookie—14 (1981).... Shares NHL single-season playoff record for most power-play goals in one game—3 (April 29, 1993).
STATISTICAL PLATEAUS: Three-goal games: 1981-82 (3), 1982-83 (1), 1983-84 (3), 1985-86 (3), 1986-87 (1), 1988-89 (2), 1990-91 (1). Total: 14.... Four-goal games: 1980-81 (1), 1988-89 (1), 1988-89 (1), 1989-90 (1), 1993-94 (1). Total: 5. ... Total hat tricks: 19.

			REGULAR SEASON					PLAYOFFS				
Season	Team	League	Gms.	G	A	Pts.	PIM	Gms.	G	A	Pts.	PIM
76-77—London	....	OMJHL	66	39	43	82	45	—	—	—	—	—
77-78—London	....	OMJHL	68	*72	70	142	49	9	6	10	16	6
78-79—London	....	OMJHL	30	8	11	19	35	7	3	5	8	0
79-80—London	....	OMJHL	62	50	53	103	72	5	2	6	8	15
—Oklahoma City	....	CHL	6	3	2	5	0	—	—	—	—	—
80-81—Oklahoma City	....	CHL	48	32	25	57	45	—	—	—	—	—
—Minnesota	....	NHL	32	18	12	30	29	19	14	7	21	25
81-82—Minnesota	NHL	76	55	51	106	138	4	3	1	4	2
82-83—Minnesota	NHL	77	37	38	75	94	9	4	6	10	11
83-84—Minnesota	NHL	79	38	33	71	58	16	4	5	9	27
84-85—Minnesota	NHL	51	15	17	32	41	9	3	3	6	8
85-86—Minnesota	NHL	75	44	45	89	51	5	0	1	1	6
86-87—Minnesota	NHL	80	52	51	103	88	—	—	—	—	—
87-88—Minnesota	NHL	67	41	45	86	79	—	—	—	—	—
88-89—Minnesota	NHL	65	32	27	59	64	—	—	—	—	—
—Washington	....	NHL	11	12	3	15	12	6	3	3	6	12
89-90—Washington	NHL	80	41	38	79	122	8	8	3	11	6
90-91—Washington	NHL	54	21	18	39	76	11	5	4	9	22
91-92—Washington	NHL	78	38	38	76	78	7	5	4	9	14
92-93—Detroit	....	NHL	82	41	56	97	81	7	4	2	6	16
93-94—Detroit	....	NHL	66	28	29	57	73	7	5	2	7	14
94-95—Detroit	....	NHL	42	16	27	43	39	16	9	2	11	22
NHL totals	....		1015	529	528	1057	1123	124	67	43	110	185

CICCONE, ENRICO
D, LIGHTNING

PERSONAL: Born April 10, 1970, in Montreal.... 6-4/200.... Shoots left.... Name pronounced ehn-REE-koh shih-KOH-nee.
TRANSACTIONS/CAREER NOTES: Selected by Minnesota North Stars in fifth round (fifth North Stars pick, 92nd overall) of NHL entry draft (June 16, 1990).... North Stars franchise moved from Minnesota to Dallas and renamed Stars for 1993-94 season.... Traded by Stars to Washington Capitals (June 25, 1993) to complete deal in which Capitals sent D Paul Cavallini to Stars for future considerations (June 20, 1993).... Suffered pulled groin (January 25, 1994); missed seven games. . . . Traded by Capitals with third-round pick in 1994 draft (traded to Mighty Ducks of Anaheim who selected RW Craig Reichert) and conditional draft pick to Tampa Bay Lightning for D Joe Reekie (March 21, 1994).... Suffered whiplash (February 5, 1995); missed one game.... Injured neck (March 1, 1995); missed one game.... Injured shoulder (April ?6, 1995); missed two games.

C

Season Team	League	REGULAR SEASON					PLAYOFFS				
		Gms.	G	A	Pts.	PIM	Gms.	G	A	Pts.	PIM
87-88—Shawinigan	QMJHL	61	2	12	14	324	—	—	—	—	—
88-89—Shawinigan/T-Rivieres ...	QMJHL	58	7	19	26	289	—	—	—	—	—
89-90—Trois-Rivieres	QMJHL	40	4	24	28	227	3	0	0	0	15
90-91—Kalamazoo	IHL	57	4	9	13	384	4	0	1	1	32
91-92—Kalamazoo	IHL	53	4	16	20	406	10	0	1	1	58
—Minnesota	NHL	11	0	0	0	48	—	—	—	—	—
92-93—Minnesota	NHL	31	0	1	1	115	—	—	—	—	—
—Kalamazoo	IHL	13	1	3	4	50	—	—	—	—	—
—Hamilton	AHL	6	1	3	4	44	—	—	—	—	—
93-94—Washington	NHL	46	1	1	2	174	—	—	—	—	—
—Portland	AHL	6	0	0	0	27	—	—	—	—	—
—Tampa Bay	NHL	11	0	1	1	52	—	—	—	—	—
94-95—Tampa Bay	NHL	41	2	4	6	225	—	—	—	—	—
NHL totals		140	3	7	10	614					

CIERNY, JOZEF
LW, OILERS

PERSONAL: Born May 13, 1974, in Zvolen, Czechoslovakia. . . . 6-2/185. . . . Shoots left. . . . Name pronounced YOH-sehf CHEER-nee.

TRANSACTIONS/CAREER NOTES: Selected by Buffalo Sabres in second round (second Sabres pick, 35th overall) of NHL entry draft (June 20, 1992). . . . Traded by Sabres with undisclosed draft pick to Edmonton Oilers for LW Craig Simpson (September 1, 1993).

Season Team	League	REGULAR SEASON					PLAYOFFS				
		Gms.	G	A	Pts.	PIM	Gms.	G	A	Pts.	PIM
91-92—Zvolen	Czech.	26	10	3	13	8	—	—	—	—	—
92-93—Rochester	AHL	54	27	27	54	36	—	—	—	—	—
93-94—Cape Breton	AHL	73	30	27	57	88	4	1	1	2	4
—Edmonton	NHL	1	0	0	0	0	—	—	—	—	—
94-95—Cape Breton	AHL	73	28	24	52	58	—	—	—	—	—
NHL totals		1	0	0	0	0					

CIGER, ZDENO
LW, OILERS

PERSONAL: Born October 19, 1969, in Martin, Czechoslovakia. . . . 6-1/190. . . . Shoots left. . . . Name pronounced zuh-DAY-noh SEE-guhr.

TRANSACTIONS/CAREER NOTES: Selected by New Jersey Devils in third round (third Devils pick, 54th overall) of NHL entry draft (June 11, 1988). . . . Bruised left shoulder (October 6, 1990). . . . Injured elbow (January 24, 1991). . . . Fractured right wrist (September 24, 1991); missed first 59 games of season. . . . Traded by Devils with C Kevin Todd to Edmonton Oilers for C Bernie Nicholls (January 13, 1993). . . . Played in Europe during 1994-95 NHL lockout.

HONORS: Named Czechoslovakian League Rookie of the Year (1988-89).

Season Team	League	REGULAR SEASON					PLAYOFFS				
		Gms.	G	A	Pts.	PIM	Gms.	G	A	Pts.	PIM
88-89—Dukla Trencin	Czech.	32	15	21	36	18	—	—	—	—	—
89-90—Dukla Trencin	Czech.	53	18	28	46	...	—	—	—	—	—
90-91—New Jersey	NHL	45	8	17	25	8	6	0	2	2	4
—Utica	AHL	8	5	4	9	2	—	—	—	—	—
91-92—New Jersey	NHL	20	6	5	11	10	7	2	4	6	0
92-93—New Jersey	NHL	27	4	8	12	2	—	—	—	—	—
—Edmonton	NHL	37	9	15	24	6	—	—	—	—	—
93-94—Edmonton	NHL	84	22	35	57	8	—	—	—	—	—
94-95—Dukla Trencin	Slovakia	34	23	26	49	10	9	2	9	11	2
—Edmonton	NHL	5	2	2	4	0	—	—	—	—	—
NHL totals		218	51	82	133	34	13	2	6	8	4

CIRELLA, JOE
D, PANTHERS

PERSONAL: Born May 9, 1963, in Hamilton, Ont. . . . 6-3/208. . . . Shoots right. . . . Name pronounced sih-REHL-uh.

TRANSACTIONS/CAREER NOTES: Selected by Colorado Rockies as underage junior in first round (first Rockies pick, fifth overall) of NHL entry draft (June 10, 1981). . . . Injured left knee (November 26, 1985). . . . Traded by New Jersey Devils to Quebec Nordiques for C Walt Poddubny (June 17, 1989). . . . Broke right foot (January 18, 1990). . . . Strained lower back (February 28, 1990). . . . Injured knee (October 21, 1990). . . . Traded by Nordiques to New York Rangers for C Aaron Broten and fifth-round pick (LW Bill Lindsay) in 1991 draft (January 17, 1991). . . . Strained lower back (October 4, 1991); missed 10 games. . . . Selected by Florida Panthers in NHL expansion draft (June 24, 1993). . . . Fractured right cheekbone (November 23, 1993); missed three games. . . . Underwent right eye surgery (December 18, 1993); missed 12 games. . . . Broke nose (February 4, 1994); missed four games.

HONORS: Named to OHL All-Star first team (1982-83). . . . Named to Memorial Cup All-Star team (1982-83). . . . Played in NHL All-Star Game (1984).

Season Team	League	REGULAR SEASON					PLAYOFFS				
		Gms.	G	A	Pts.	PIM	Gms.	G	A	Pts.	PIM
80-81—Oshawa	OMJHL	56	5	31	36	220	11	0	2	2	41
81-82—Oshawa	OHL	3	0	1	1	10	11	7	10	17	32
—Colorado	NHL	65	7	12	19	52	—	—	—	—	—
82-83—Oshawa	OHL	56	13	55	68	110	17	4	16	20	37
—New Jersey	NHL	2	0	1	1	4	—	—	—	—	—
83-84—New Jersey	NHL	79	11	33	44	137	—	—	—	—	—

Season Team	League	REGULAR SEASON Gms.	G	A	Pts.	PIM	PLAYOFFS Gms.	G	A	Pts.	PIM
84-85—New Jersey	NHL	66	6	18	24	143	—	—	—	—	—
85-86—New Jersey	NHL	66	6	23	29	147	—	—	—	—	—
86-87—New Jersey	NHL	65	9	22	31	111	—	—	—	—	—
87-88—New Jersey	NHL	80	8	31	39	191	19	0	7	7	49
88-89—New Jersey	NHL	80	3	19	22	155	—	—	—	—	—
89-90—Quebec	NHL	56	4	14	18	67	—	—	—	—	—
90-91—Quebec	NHL	39	2	10	12	59	—	—	—	—	—
—New York Rangers	NHL	19	1	0	1	52	6	0	2	2	26
91-92—New York Rangers	NHL	67	3	12	15	121	13	0	4	4	23
92-93—New York Rangers	NHL	55	3	6	9	85	—	—	—	—	—
93-94—Florida	NHL	63	1	9	10	99	—	—	—	—	—
94-95—Florida	NHL	20	0	1	1	21	—	—	—	—	—
NHL totals		822	64	211	275	1444	38	0	13	13	98

CIRJAK, JOHN
C, DENVER

PERSONAL: Born February 10, 1977, in Vancouver. . . . 6-2/180. . . . Shoots right.
HIGH SCHOOL: Joel E. Ferris (Spokane, Wash.).
TRANSACTIONS/CAREER NOTES: Selected by Denver in sixth round (sixth Denver pick, 155th overall) of NHL entry draft (July 8, 1995).

Season Team	League	REGULAR SEASON Gms.	G	A	Pts.	PIM	PLAYOFFS Gms.	G	A	Pts.	PIM
93-94—Spokane	WHL	44	2	5	7	22	3	0	0	0	0
94-95—Spokane	WHL	69	21	37	58	58	11	4	11	15	11

CIRONE, JASON
C, PANTHERS

PERSONAL: Born February 21, 1971, in Toronto. . . . 5-9/185. . . . Shoots left. . . . Name pronounced suh-ROH-nee.
TRANSACTIONS/CAREER NOTES: Selected by Winnipeg Jets in third round (third Jets pick, 46th overall) of NHL entry draft (June 17, 1989). . . . Traded by Cornwall Royals to Windsor Spitfires for LW Rival Fullum and second-round draft pick (January 10, 1991). . . . Played in Italy (1992-93). . . . Traded by Jets to Toronto Maple Leafs for C Dave Tomlinson (August 3, 1993).

Season Team	League	REGULAR SEASON Gms.	G	A	Pts.	PIM	PLAYOFFS Gms.	G	A	Pts.	PIM
87-88—Cornwall	OHL	53	12	11	23	41	11	1	2	3	4
88-89—Cornwall	OHL	64	39	44	83	67	17	19	8	27	14
89-90—Cornwall	OHL	32	21	43	64	56	6	4	2	6	14
90-91—Cornwall	OHL	40	31	29	60	66	—	—	—	—	—
—Windsor	OHL	23	27	23	50	31	11	9	8	17	14
91-92—Moncton	AHL	64	32	27	59	124	10	1	1	2	8
—Winnipeg	NHL	3	0	0	0	2	—	—	—	—	—
92-93—Asiago	Alpenliga	25	24	14	38	36	—	—	—	—	—
—Asiago	Italy	16	6	5	11	18	2	1	5	6	18
93-94—Cincinnati	IHL	26	4	2	6	61	—	—	—	—	—
—Birmingham	ECHL	11	3	3	6	45	10	8	8	16	*67
94-95—Cincinnati	IHL	74	22	15	37	170	9	1	1	2	14
NHL totals		3	0	0	0	2					

CLARK, CHRIS
RW, FLAMES

PERSONAL: Born March 8, 1976, in South Windsor, Conn. . . . 6-0/180. . . . Shoots right.
HIGH SCHOOL: South Windsor (Conn.).
COLLEGE: Clarkson (N.Y.).
TRANSACTIONS/CAREER NOTES: Selected by Calgary Flames in third round (third Flames pick, 77th overall) of NHL entry draft (June 29, 1994).

Season Team	League	REGULAR SEASON Gms.	G	A	Pts.	PIM	PLAYOFFS Gms.	G	A	Pts.	PIM
93-94—Springfield Jr. B	NEJHL	35	31	26	57	185	—	—	—	—	—
94-95—Clarkson	ECAC	32	12	11	23	92	—	—	—	—	—

CLARK, WENDEL
LW, DENVER

PERSONAL: Born October 25, 1966, in Kelvington, Sask. . . . 5-10/194. . . . Shoots left. . . . Brother of Kerry Clark, right winger in Washington Capitals system; and cousin of Joe Kocur, right winger, New York Rangers.
TRANSACTIONS/CAREER NOTES: Selected by Toronto Maple Leafs as underage junior in first round (first Maple Leafs pick, first overall) of NHL entry draft (June 15, 1985). . . . Suffered from virus (November 1985). . . . Broke right foot (November 26, 1985); missed 14 games. . . . Suffered back spasms (November 1987); missed 23 games. . . . Suffered tendinitis in right shoulder (October 1987). . . . Reinjured back (February 1988); missed 90 regular season games (March 1, 1989). . . . Suffered recurrence of back problems (October 1989). . . . Bruised muscle above left knee (November 4, 1989); missed seven games. . . . Tore ligament of right knee (January 26, 1990); missed 29 games. . . . Separated left shoulder (December 18, 1990). . . . Pulled rib cage muscle (February 6, 1991); missed 12 games. . . . Partially tore knee ligaments (October 7, 1991); missed 12 games. . . . Strained knee ligaments (November 6, 1991); missed 24 games. . . . Injured groin (October 24, 1992); missed four games. . . . Strained rib muscle (January 17, 1993); missed 13 games. . . . Strained knee (October 13, 1993); missed two games. . . . Bruised foot (December 22, 1993); missed 17 games. . . . Traded by Maple Leafs with D Sylvain Lefebvre, RW Landon Wilson and first-round pick in 1994 draft (D Jeffrey Kealty) to Quebec Nordiques for C Mats Sundin, D Garth Butcher, LW Todd Warriner and first-round pick (traded to Washington Capitals who selected D Nolan Baumgartner) in 1994 draft (June 28, 1994). . . . Injured thigh (March 18, 1995); missed 11 games. . . . Fined $1,000 by NHL for elbowing (May 10, 1995). . . . Nordiques franchise moved to Denver for 1995-96 season.

HONORS: Won Top Defenseman Trophy (1984-85).... Named to WHL (East) All-Star first team (1984-85).... Named NHL Rookie of the Year by THE SPORTING NEWS (1985-86).... Named to NHL All-Rookie team (1985-86).... Played in NHL All-Star Game (1986).
STATISTICAL PLATEAUS: Three-goal games: 1985-86 (1), 1989-90 (1), 1991-92 (2), 1993-94 (2), 1994-95 (1). Total: 7.... Four-goal games: 1986-87 (1).... Total hat tricks: 8.
MISCELLANEOUS: Captain of Toronto Maple Leafs (1991-92 through 1993-94).

			REGULAR SEASON					PLAYOFFS			
Season Team	League	Gms.	G	A	Pts.	PIM	Gms.	G	A	Pts.	PIM
83-84—Saskatoon	WHL	72	23	45	68	225	—	—	—	—	—
84-85—Saskatoon	WHL	64	32	55	87	253	3	3	3	6	7
85-86—Toronto	NHL	66	34	11	45	227	10	5	1	6	47
86-87—Toronto	NHL	80	37	23	60	271	13	6	5	11	38
87-88—Toronto	NHL	28	12	11	23	80	—	—	—	—	—
88-89—Toronto	NHL	15	7	4	11	66	—	—	—	—	—
89-90—Toronto	NHL	38	18	8	26	116	5	1	1	2	19
90-91—Toronto	NHL	63	18	16	34	152	—	—	—	—	—
91-92—Toronto	NHL	43	19	21	40	123	—	—	—	—	—
92-93—Toronto	NHL	66	17	22	39	193	21	10	10	20	51
93-94—Toronto	NHL	64	46	30	76	115	18	9	7	16	24
94-95—Quebec	NHL	37	12	18	30	45	6	1	2	3	6
NHL totals		500	220	164	384	1388	73	32	26	58	185

CLOUTIER, COLIN
C, LIGHTNING

PERSONAL: Born January 27, 1976, in Winnipeg.... 6-3/224.... Shoots left.... Name pronounced CLOO-tee-yay.
HIGH SCHOOL: Crocus Plains (Brandon, Man.).
TRANSACTIONS/CAREER NOTES: Selected by Tampa Bay Lightning in second round (second Lightning pick, 34th overall) of NHL entry draft (June 28, 1994).

			REGULAR SEASON					PLAYOFFS			
Season Team	League	Gms.	G	A	Pts.	PIM	Gms.	G	A	Pts.	PIM
91-92—St. Boniface	MJHL	42	7	15	22	113	—	—	—	—	—
—Brandon	WHL	3	1	1	2	0	—	—	—	—	—
92-93—Brandon	WHL	60	11	15	26	138	4	0	0	0	18
93-94—Brandon	WHL	30	10	13	23	102	11	2	5	7	23
94-95—Brandon	WHL	47	16	27	43	170	16	5	6	11	47

CLOUTIER, DAN
G, RANGERS

PERSONAL: Born April 22, 1976, in Mont-Laurier, Que.... 6-1/182.... Catches left.... Name pronounced CLOO-tee-yay.... Brother of Sylvain Cloutier, center in Detroit Red Wings system.
HIGH SCHOOL: Notre-Dame-des-Grands-Lacs (Sault Ste. Marie, Ont.).
TRANSACTIONS/CAREER NOTES: Selected by New York Rangers in first round (first Rangers pick, 26th overall) of NHL entry draft (June 28, 1994).

			REGULAR SEASON							PLAYOFFS					
Season Team	League	Gms.	Min.	W	L	T	GA	SO	Avg.	Gms.	Min.	W	L	GA	SO	Avg.
91-92—St. Thomas	Jr. B	14	823	...	...	...	80	...	5.83	—	—	—	—	—	—	—
92-93—Sault Ste. Marie	OHL	12	572	4	6	0	44	0	4.62	4	231	1	2	12	0	3.12
93-94—Sault Ste. Marie	OHL	55	2934	28	14	6	174	†2	3.56	14	833	†10	4	52	0	3.75
94-95—Sault Ste. Marie	OHL	45	2517	15	25	2	184	1	4.39	—	—	—	—	—	—	—

CLOUTIER, FRANCOIS
LW, PANTHERS

PERSONAL: Born April 28, 1977, in Sherbrooke, Que.... 6-2/202.... Shoots left.
TRANSACTIONS/CAREER NOTES: Selected by Florida Panthers in fifth round (sixth Panthers pick, 114th overall) of NHL entry draft (July 8, 1995).

			REGULAR SEASON					PLAYOFFS			
Season Team	League	Gms.	G	A	Pts.	PIM	Gms.	G	A	Pts.	PIM
94-95—Hull	QMJHL	58	15	5	20	70	17	2	4	6	36

CLOUTIER, SYLVAIN
C, RED WINGS

PERSONAL: Born February 13, 1974, in Mont-Laurier, Que.... 6-0/195.... Shoots left.... Name pronounced sihl-VAY CLOO-tee-yay.... Brother of Dan Cloutier, center in New York Rangers system.
HIGH SCHOOL: Bishop MacDonnell (Guelph, Ont.).
TRANSACTIONS/CAREER NOTES: Selected by Detroit Red Wings in third round (third Red Wings pick, 70th overall) of NHL entry draft (June 20, 1992).

			REGULAR SEASON					PLAYOFFS			
Season Team	League	Gms.	G	A	Pts.	PIM	Gms.	G	A	Pts.	PIM
91-92—Guelph	OHL	62	35	31	66	74	—	—	—	—	—
92-93—Guelph	OHL	44	26	29	55	78	5	0	5	5	14
93-94—Guelph	OHL	66	45	71	116	127	9	7	9	16	32
—Adirondack	AHL	2	0	2	2	2	—	—	—	—	—
94-95—Adirondack	AHL	71	7	26	33	144	—	—	—	—	—

COFFEY, PAUL
D, RED WINGS

PERSONAL: Born June 1, 1961, in Weston, Ont. . . . 6-1/190. . . . Shoots left. . . . Full name: Paul Douglas Coffey.

TRANSACTIONS/CAREER NOTES: Selected by Edmonton Oilers in first round (first Oilers pick, sixth overall) of NHL entry draft (June 11, 1980). . . . Suffered recurring back spasms (December 1986); missed 10 games. . . . Traded by Oilers with LW Dave Hunter and RW Wayne Van Dorp to Pittsburgh Penguins for C Craig Simpson, C Dave Hannan, D Moe Mantha and D Chris Joseph (November 24, 1987). . . . Tore knee cartilage (December 1987). . . . Bruised right shoulder (November 16, 1988). . . . Broke finger (May 1990). . . . Injured back (February 27, 1991). . . . Injured hip muscle (March 9, 1991). . . . Scratched left eye cornea (April 9, 1991). . . . Broke jaw (April 1991). . . . Pulled hip muscle (February 3, 1992); missed three games. . . . Traded by Penguins to Los Angeles Kings for D Brian Benning, D Jeff Chychrun and first-round pick (LW Jason Bowen) in 1992 draft (February 19, 1992). . . . Suffered back spasms (March 3, 1992); missed three games. . . . Fractured wrist (March 17, 1992); missed five games. . . . Traded by Kings with RW Jim Hiller and C/LW Sylain Couturier to Detroit Red Wings for C Jimmy Carson, RW Marc Potvin and C Gary Shuchuk (January 29, 1993). . . . Injured groin (March 18, 1993); missed one game. . . . Injured groin and left knee (October 18, 1993); missed four games. . . . Injured back (January 28, 1995); missed two games.

HONORS: Named to OMJHL All-Star second team (1979-80). . . . Named to NHL All-Star second team (1980-81 through 1983-84 and 1989-90). . . . Named to THE SPORTING NEWS All-Star second team (1981-82 through 1983-84, 1986-87 and 1989-90). . . . Played in NHL All-Star Game (1982-1986 and 1988-1994). . . . Won James Norris Memorial Trophy (1984-85, 1985-86 and 1994-95). . . . Named to THE SPORTING NEWS All-Star first team (1984-85, 1985-86, 1988-89 and 1994-95). . . . Named to NHL All-Star first team (1984-85, 1985-86, 1988-89 and 1994-95).

RECORDS: Holds NHL career records for most goals by a defenseman—358; most assists by a defenseman—978; and most points by a defenseman—1,336. . . . Holds NHL single-season record for most goals by a defenseman—48 (1985-86). . . . Shares NHL single-game records for most points by a defenseman—8; and most assists by a defenseman—6 (March 14, 1986). . . . Holds NHL record for most consecutive games scoring points by a defenseman—28 (1985-86). . . . Holds NHL single-season playoff record for most goals by a defenseman—12; assists by a defenseman—25; and points by a defenseman—37 (1985). . . . Holds NHL single-game playoff record for most points by a defenseman—6 (May 14, 1985).

STATISTICAL PLATEAUS: Three-goal games: 1982-83 (1), 1984-85 (1), 1985-86 (1), 1987-88 (1). Total: 4. . . . Four-goal games: 1984-85 (1). . . . Total hat tricks: 5.

MISCELLANEOUS: Member of Stanley Cup championship teams (1984, 1985, 1987 and 1991).

			REGULAR SEASON					PLAYOFFS			
Season	Team	League	Gms.	G	A	Pts.	PIM	Gms.	G	A	Pts.	PIM
77-78—Kingston	OMJHL	8	2	2	4	11	—	—	—	—	—
—North York	MTHL	50	14	33	47	64	—	—	—	—	—
78-79—Sault Ste. Marie	OMJHL	68	17	72	89	99	—	—	—	—	—
79-80—Sault Ste. Marie	OMJHL	23	10	21	31	63	—	—	—	—	—
—Kitchener	OMJHL	52	19	52	71	130	—	—	—	—	—
80-81—Edmonton	NHL	74	9	23	32	130	9	4	3	7	22
81-82—Edmonton	NHL	80	29	60	89	106	5	1	1	2	6
82-83—Edmonton	NHL	80	29	67	96	87	16	7	7	14	14
83-84—Edmonton	NHL	80	40	86	126	104	19	8	14	22	21
84-85—Edmonton	NHL	80	37	84	121	97	18	12	25	37	44
85-86—Edmonton	NHL	79	48	90	138	120	10	1	9	10	30
86-87—Edmonton	NHL	59	17	50	67	49	17	3	8	11	30
87-88—Pittsburgh	NHL	46	15	52	67	93	—	—	—	—	—
88-89—Pittsburgh	NHL	75	30	83	113	195	11	2	13	15	31
89-90—Pittsburgh	NHL	80	29	74	103	95	—	—	—	—	—
90-91—Pittsburgh	NHL	76	24	69	93	128	12	2	9	11	6
91-92—Pittsburgh	NHL	54	10	54	64	62	—	—	—	—	—
—Los Angeles	NHL	10	1	4	5	25	6	4	3	7	2
92-93—Los Angeles	NHL	50	8	49	57	50	—	—	—	—	—
—Detroit	NHL	30	4	26	30	27	7	2	9	11	2
93-94—Detroit	NHL	80	14	63	77	106	7	1	6	7	8
94-95—Detroit	NHL	45	14	44	58	72	18	6	12	18	10
NHL totals		1078	358	978	1336	1546	155	53	119	172	226

COLE, DANTON
RW, DEVILS

PERSONAL: Born January 10, 1967, in Pontiac, Mich. . . . 5-11/185. . . . Shoots right. . . . Full name: Danton Edward Cole.

COLLEGE: Michigan State.

TRANSACTIONS/CAREER NOTES: Selected by Winnipeg Jets in sixth round (sixth Jets pick, 123rd overall) of NHL entry draft (June 15, 1985). . . . Strained knee (January 26, 1992); missed 11 games. . . . Traded by Jets to Tampa Bay Lightning for future considerations (June 19, 1992). . . . Tore ligament in left knee (December 15, 1992); missed 10 games. . . . Injured groin (October 23, 1993); missed one game. . . . Suffered cut to mouth (October 30, 1993); missed one game. . . . Traded by Lightning with D Shawn Chambers to New Jersey Devils for C Alexander Semak and RW Ben Hankinson (March 14, 1995).

MISCELLANEOUS: Member of Stanley Cup championship team (1995).

			REGULAR SEASON					PLAYOFFS			
Season	Team	League	Gms.	G	A	Pts.	PIM	Gms.	G	A	Pts.	PIM
84-85—Aurora	OHA	41	51	44	95	91	—	—	—	—	—
85-86—Michigan State	CCHA	43	11	10	21	22	—	—	—	—	—
86-87—Michigan State	CCHA	44	9	15	24	16	—	—	—	—	—
87-88—Michigan State	CCHA	46	20	36	56	38	—	—	—	—	—
88-89—Michigan State	CCHA	47	29	33	62	46	—	—	—	—	—
89-90—Winnipeg	NHL	2	1	1	2	0	—	—	—	—	—
—Moncton	AHL	80	31	42	73	18	—	—	—	—	—
90-91—Winnipeg	NHL	66	13	11	24	24	—	—	—	—	—
—Moncton	AHL	3	1	1	2	0	—	—	—	—	—

C

Season Team	League	REGULAR SEASON					PLAYOFFS				
		Gms.	G	A	Pts.	PIM	Gms.	G	A	Pts.	PIM
91-92—Winnipeg	NHL	52	7	5	12	32	—	—	—	—	—
92-93—Tampa Bay	NHL	67	12	15	27	23	—	—	—	—	—
—Atlanta	IHL	1	1	0	1	2	—	—	—	—	—
93-94—Tampa Bay	NHL	81	20	23	43	32	—	—	—	—	—
94-95—Tampa Bay	NHL	26	3	3	6	6	—	—	—	—	—
—New Jersey	NHL	12	1	2	3	8	1	0	0	0	0
NHL totals		306	57	60	117	125	1	0	0	0	0

COLEMAN, JONATHAN
D, RED WINGS

PERSONAL: Born March 9, 1975, in Boston.... 6-2/195.... Shoots left.
HIGH SCHOOL: Phillips Academy (Andover, Mass.).
COLLEGE: Boston University.
TRANSACTIONS/CAREER NOTES: Selected by Detroit Red Wings in second round (second Red Wings pick, 48th overall) of NHL entry draft (June 26, 1993).

Season Team	League	REGULAR SEASON					PLAYOFFS				
		Gms.	G	A	Pts.	PIM	Gms.	G	A	Pts.	PIM
89-90—Phillips Andover Acad.	Mass. H.S.	24	8	20	28	10	—	—	—	—	—
90-91—Phillips Andover Acad.	Mass. H.S.	24	11	25	36	18	—	—	—	—	—
91-92—Phillips Andover Acad.	Mass. H.S.	24	12	29	41	26	—	—	—	—	—
92-93—Phillips Andover Acad.	Mass. H.S.	23	14	33	47	72	—	—	—	—	—
93-94—Boston University	Hockey East	29	1	14	15	26	—	—	—	—	—
94-95—Boston University	Hockey East	40	5	23	28	42	—	—	—	—	—

CONACHER, PAT
LW/C, KINGS

PERSONAL: Born May 1, 1959, in Edmonton.... 5-9/190.... Shoots left.... Full name: Patrick John Conacher.... Name pronounced KAH-nih-kuhr.
TRANSACTIONS/CAREER NOTES: Selected by New York Rangers in fourth round (third Rangers pick, 76th overall) of NHL entry draft (August 9, 1979).... Fractured left ankle (September 21, 1980); missed entire 1980-81 season.... Injured shoulder (November 1982).... Signed as free agent by Edmonton Oilers (October 4, 1983).... Injured groin (December 1984).... Signed as free agent by New Jersey Devils (August 14, 1985).... Sprained back (February 1988).... Bruised left shoulder (December 1988).... Underwent major reconstructive surgery to left shoulder (April 7, 1989).... Lacerated face and lost two teeth (October 13, 1989).... Sprained left knee (April 9, 1990).... Strained left knee (September 22, 1990).... Suffered ulcer problems (February 1991).... Injured groin (October 24, 1991); missed two games.... Injured groin (December 1991).... Underwent hernia surgery (January 9, 1992); missed 34 games.... Traded by Devils to Los Angeles Kings for future considerations (September 3, 1992).... Strained lower back (November 21, 1992); missed four games.
MISCELLANEOUS: Member of Stanley Cup championship team (1984).

Season Team	League	REGULAR SEASON					PLAYOFFS				
		Gms.	G	A	Pts.	PIM	Gms.	G	A	Pts.	PIM
77-78—Billings	WCHL	72	31	44	75	105	20	15	14	29	22
78-79—Billings	WHL	39	25	37	62	50	—	—	—	—	—
—Saskatoon	WHL	33	15	32	47	37	—	—	—	—	—
79-80—New York Rangers	NHL	17	0	5	5	4	3	0	1	1	2
—New Haven	AHL	53	11	14	25	43	7	1	1	2	4
80-81—New York Rangers	NHL				Did not play—injured.						
81-82—Springfield	AHL	77	23	22	45	30	—	—	—	—	—
82-83—Tulsa	CHL	63	29	28	57	44	—	—	—	—	—
—New York Rangers	NHL	5	0	1	1	4	—	—	—	—	—
83-84—Moncton	AHL	28	7	16	23	30	—	—	—	—	—
—Edmonton	NHL	45	2	8	10	31	3	1	0	1	2
84-85—Nova Scotia	AHL	68	20	45	65	44	6	3	2	5	0
85-86—New Jersey	NHL	2	0	2	2	2	—	—	—	—	—
—Maine	AHL	69	15	30	45	83	5	1	1	2	11
86-87—Maine	AHL	56	12	14	26	47	—	—	—	—	—
87-88—Utica	AHL	47	14	33	47	32	—	—	—	—	—
—New Jersey	NHL	24	2	5	7	12	17	2	2	4	14
88-89—New Jersey	NHL	55	7	5	12	14	—	—	—	—	—
89-90—Utica	AHL	57	13	36	49	53	—	—	—	—	—
—New Jersey	NHL	19	3	3	6	4	5	1	0	1	10
90-91—Utica	AHL	4	0	1	1	6	—	—	—	—	—
—New Jersey	NHL	49	5	11	16	27	7	0	2	2	2
91-92—New Jersey	NHL	44	7	3	10	16	7	1	1	2	4
92-93—Los Angeles	NHL	81	9	8	17	20	24	6	4	10	6
93-94—Los Angeles	NHL	77	15	13	28	71	—	—	—	—	—
94-95—Los Angeles	NHL	48	7	9	16	12	—	—	—	—	—
NHL totals		466	57	73	130	217	66	11	10	21	40

CONN, ROB
RW, BLACKHAWKS

PERSONAL: Born September 3, 1968, in Calgary.... 6-2/200.... Shoots right.... Full name: Robert Phillip Conn.
COLLEGE: Alaska-Anchorage.
TRANSACTIONS/CAREER NOTES: Signed as free agent by Chicago Blackhawks (July 31, 1991).

Season Team	League	REGULAR SEASON					PLAYOFFS				
		Gms.	G	A	Pts.	PIM	Gms.	G	A	Pts.	PIM
88-89—Alaska-Anchorage..........	Indep.	33	21	17	38	46	—	—	—	—	—
89-90—Alaska-Anchorage..........	Indep.	34	27	21	48	46	—	—	—	—	—
90-91—Alaska-Anchorage..........	Indep.	43	28	32	60	53	—	—	—	—	—
91-92—Indianapolis	IHL	72	19	16	35	100	—	—	—	—	—
—Chicago	NHL	2	0	0	0	2	—	—	—	—	—
92-93—Indianapolis	IHL	75	13	14	27	81	5	0	1	1	6
93-94—Indianapolis	IHL	51	16	11	27	46	—	—	—	—	—
94-95—Indianapolis	IHL	10	4	4	8	11	—	—	—	—	—
—Albany...........................	AHL	68	35	32	67	76	14	4	6	10	16
NHL totals................................		2	0	0	0	2					

CONROY, CRAIG
C, CANADIENS

PERSONAL: Born September 4, 1971, in Potsdam, N.Y. . . . 6-2/190. . . . Shoots right.
HIGH SCHOOL: Northwood (Lake Placid, N.Y.).
COLLEGE: Clarkson (N.Y.).
TRANSACTIONS/CAREER NOTES: Selected by Montreal Canadiens in sixth round (seventh Canadiens pick, 123rd overall) of NHL entry draft (June 16, 1990).
HONORS: Named to NCAA All-America East first team (1993-94). . . . Named to NCAA All-Tournament team (1993-94). . . . Named to ECAC All-Star first team (1993-94).

Season Team	League	REGULAR SEASON					PLAYOFFS				
		Gms.	G	A	Pts.	PIM	Gms.	G	A	Pts.	PIM
90-91—Clarkson..........................	ECAC	40	8	21	29	24	—	—	—	—	—
91-92—Clarkson..........................	ECAC	31	19	17	36	36	—	—	—	—	—
92-93—Clarkson..........................	ECAC	35	10	23	33	26	—	—	—	—	—
93-94—Clarkson..........................	ECAC	34	26	40	66	66	—	—	—	—	—
94-95—Fredericton	AHL	55	26	18	44	29	11	7	3	10	6
—Montreal........................	NHL	6	1	0	1	0	—	—	—	—	—
NHL totals................................		6	1	0	1	0					

CONVERY, BRANDON
C, MAPLE LEAFS

PERSONAL: Born February 4, 1974, in Kingston, Ont. . . . 6-1/182. . . . Shoots right.
HIGH SCHOOL: Lasalle Secondary School (Sudbury, Ont.).
TRANSACTIONS/CAREER NOTES: Selected by Toronto Maple Leafs in first round (first Maple Leafs pick, eighth overall) of NHL entry draft (June 20, 1992).
HONORS: Won OHL Top Prospect Award (1991-92).

Season Team	League	REGULAR SEASON					PLAYOFFS				
		Gms.	G	A	Pts.	PIM	Gms.	G	A	Pts.	PIM
89-90—Kingston Jr. B	OHA	42	13	25	38	4	—	—	—	—	—
90-91—Sudbury...........................	OHL	56	26	22	48	18	5	1	1	2	2
91-92—Sudbury...........................	OHL	44	40	27	67	44	5	3	2	5	4
92-93—Sudbury...........................	OHL	7	7	9	16	6	—	—	—	—	—
—Niagara Falls	OHL	51	38	39	77	24	4	1	3	4	4
—St. John's	AHL	3	0	0	0	0	5	0	1	1	0
93-94—St. John's	AHL	—	—	—	—	—	1	0	0	0	0
—Belleville	OHL	23	16	19	35	22	12	4	10	14	13
94-95—St. John's	AHL	76	34	37	71	43	5	2	2	4	4

COOPER, DAVID
D, SABRES

PERSONAL: Born November 2, 1973, in Ottawa. . . . 6-2/204. . . . Shoots left.
HIGH SCHOOL: Medicine Hat (Alta.).
TRANSACTIONS/CAREER NOTES: Selected by Buffalo Sabres in first round (first Sabres pick, 11th overall) of NHL entry draft (June 20, 1992).
HONORS: Won WHL Top Prospect Award (1991-92). . . . Named to WHL (East) All-Star first team (1991-92).

Season Team	League	REGULAR SEASON					PLAYOFFS				
		Gms.	G	A	Pts.	PIM	Gms.	G	A	Pts.	PIM
89-90—Medicine Hat	WHL	61	4	11	15	65	3	0	2	2	2
90-91—Medicine Hat	WHL	64	12	31	43	66	11	1	3	4	23
91-92—Medicine Hat	WHL	72	17	47	64	176	4	1	4	5	8
92-93—Medicine Hat	WHL	63	15	50	65	88	10	2	2	4	32
—Rochester	AHL	0	0	0	0	0	2	0	0	0	2
93-94—Rochester	AHL	68	10	25	35	82	4	1	1	2	2
94-95—Rochester	AHL	21	2	4	6	48	—	—	—	—	—
—South Carolina	ECHL	39	9	19	28	90	9	3	8	11	24

COPELAND, ADAM
RW, OILERS

PERSONAL: Born June 5, 1976, in Burlington, Ont. . . . 6-2/184. . . . Shoots right.
TRANSACTIONS/CAREER NOTES: Selected by Edmonton Oilers in fourth round (sixth Oilers pick, 79th overall) of NHL entry draft (June 29, 1994).

Season Team	League	REGULAR SEASON					PLAYOFFS				
		Gms.	G	A	Pts.	PIM	Gms.	G	A	Pts.	PIM
93-94—Burlington Jr. B................	OHA	39	28	44	72	55	—	—	—	—	—
94-95—Miami of Ohio	CCHA	39	6	4	10	28	—	—	—	—	—

COPELAND, TODD
D, SABRES

PERSONAL: Born May 18, 1968, in Ridgewood, N.J. . . . . 6-2/210. . . . Shoots left. . . . Full name: John Todd Copeland.
HIGH SCHOOL: Belmont (Mass.) Hill.
COLLEGE: Michigan.
TRANSACTIONS/CAREER NOTES: Injured knee (February 1986). . . . Selected by New Jersey Devils in second round (second Devils pick, 24th overall) of NHL entry draft (June 21, 1986). . . . Signed as free agent by Winnipeg Jets (August 1993). . . . Signed as free agent by Buffalo Sabres (July 7, 1994).

			REGULAR SEASON					PLAYOFFS			
Season Team	League	Gms.	G	A	Pts.	PIM	Gms.	G	A	Pts.	PIM
84-85—Belmont Hill H.S.	Mass. H.S.	23	8	25	33	18	—	—	—	—	—
85-86—Belmont Hill H.S.	Mass. H.S.	19	4	19	23	19	—	—	—	—	—
86-87—University of Michigan	CCHA	34	2	11	13	59	—	—	—	—	—
87-88—University of Michigan	CCHA	41	3	10	13	58	—	—	—	—	—
88-89—University of Michigan	CCHA	39	5	14	19	102	—	—	—	—	—
89-90—University of Michigan	CCHA	34	6	16	22	62	—	—	—	—	—
90-91—Utica	AHL	79	6	24	30	53	—	—	—	—	—
91-92—Utica	AHL	80	4	23	27	96	4	2	2	4	2
92-93—Utica	AHL	16	3	2	5	10	—	—	—	—	—
—Cincinnati......................	IHL	37	0	3	3	47	—	—	—	—	—
—Moncton	AHL	16	1	4	5	16	5	1	3	4	2
93-94—Moncton	AHL	80	4	17	21	158	19	0	1	1	54
94-95—Rochester	AHL	77	4	12	16	152	5	1	0	1	14

CORBET, RENE
LW, DENVER

PERSONAL: Born June 25, 1973, in Victoriaville, Que. . . . . 6-0/187. . . . Shoots left. . . . Name pronounced ruh-NAY kohr-BAY.
TRANSACTIONS/CAREER NOTES: Selected by Quebec Nordiques in second round (second Nordiques pick, 24th overall) of NHL entry draft (June 22, 1991). . . . Nordiques franchise moved to Denver for 1995-96 season.
HONORS: Won Michel Bergeron Trophy (1990-91). . . . Named to QMJHL All-Rookie team (1990-91). . . . Won Jean Beliveau Trophy (1992-93). . . . Named to Can.HL All-Star first team (1992-93). . . . Named to QMJHL All-Star first team (1992-93). . . . Won Dudley (Red) Garrett Memorial Trophy (1993-94).

			REGULAR SEASON					PLAYOFFS			
Season Team	League	Gms.	G	A	Pts.	PIM	Gms.	G	A	Pts.	PIM
90-91—Drummondville.................	QMJHL	45	25	40	65	34	14	11	6	17	15
91-92—Drummondville.................	QMJHL	56	46	50	96	90	4	1	2	3	17
92-93—Drummondville.................	QMJHL	63	*79	69	*148	143	10	7	13	20	16
93-94—Cornwall	AHL	68	37	40	77	56	13	7	2	9	18
—Quebec	NHL	9	1	1	2	0	—	—	—	—	—
94-95—Cornwall	AHL	65	33	24	57	79	12	2	8	10	27
—Quebec	NHL	8	0	3	3	2	2	0	1	1	0
NHL totals		17	1	4	5	2	2	0	1	1	0

CORCORAN, BRIAN
D, MIGHTY DUCKS

PERSONAL: Born April 23, 1972, in Baldwinsville, N.Y. . . . . 6-2/247. . . . Shoots right.
HIGH SCHOOL: C.W. Baker (Baldwinsville, N.Y.).
COLLEGE: Massachusetts.
TRANSACTIONS/CAREER NOTES: Signed as free agent by Mighty Ducks of Anaheim (April 28, 1995).
MISCELLANEOUS: Also played defensive end for University of Massachusetts football team.

			REGULAR SEASON					PLAYOFFS			
Season Team	League	Gms.	G	A	Pts.	PIM	Gms.	G	A	Pts.	PIM
93-94—Univ. of Massachusetts....	Hockey East	15	1	7	8	24	—	—	—	—	—
94-95—Univ. of Massachusetts....	Hockey East	20	3	3	6	40	—	—	—	—	—

CORKUM, BOB
C/RW, MIGHTY DUCKS

PERSONAL: Born December 18, 1967, in Salisbury, Mass. . . . 6-2/212. . . . Shoots right. . . . Full name: Robert Freeman Corkum.
HIGH SCHOOL: Triton Regional (Byfield, Mass.).
COLLEGE: Maine.
TRANSACTIONS/CAREER NOTES: Selected by Buffalo Sabres in third round (third Sabres pick, 47th overall) of NHL entry draft (June 21, 1986). . . . Injured hip (March 19, 1992). . . . Selected by Mighty Ducks of Anaheim in NHL expansion draft (June 24, 1993). . . . Ruptured ankle tendon (March 27, 1994); missed remainder of season.

			REGULAR SEASON					PLAYOFFS			
Season Team	League	Gms.	G	A	Pts.	PIM	Gms.	G	A	Pts.	PIM
84-85—Triton Regional H.S.........	Mass. H.S.	18	35	36	71	. . .	—	—	—	—	—
85-86—University of Maine	Hockey East	39	7	26	33	53	—	—	—	—	—
86-87—University of Maine	Hockey East	35	18	11	29	24	—	—	—	—	—
87-88—University of Maine	Hockey East	40	14	18	32	64	—	—	—	—	—
88-89—University of Maine	Hockey East	45	17	31	48	64	—	—	—	—	—
89-90—Rochester	AHL	43	8	11	19	45	12	2	5	7	16
—Buffalo............................	NHL	8	2	0	2	4	5	1	0	1	4
90-91—Rochester	AHL	69	13	21	34	77	15	4	4	8	4
91-92—Rochester	AHL	52	16	12	28	47	8	0	6	6	8
—Buffalo............................	NHL	20	2	4	6	21	4	1	0	1	0
92-93—Buffalo............................	NHL	68	6	4	10	38	5	0	0	0	2

			REGULAR SEASON					PLAYOFFS			
Season Team	League	Gms.	G	A	Pts.	PIM	Gms.	G	A	Pts.	PIM
93-94—Anaheim	NHL	76	23	28	51	18	—	—	—	—	—
94-95—Anaheim	NHL	44	10	9	19	25	—	—	—	—	—
NHL totals		216	43	45	88	106	14	2	0	2	6

CORPSE, KELI
C, CANADIENS

PERSONAL: Born May 14, 1974, in London, Ont. . . . 5-11/174. . . . Shoots left. . . . Name pronounced KAL-ee KOHRPS.
HIGH SCHOOL: Loyalist Collegiate (Kingston, Ont.).
TRANSACTIONS/CAREER NOTES: Selected by Montreal Canadiens in second round (third Canadiens pick, 44th overall) of NHL entry draft (June 20, 1992).
HONORS: Won Can.HL Humanitarian Award (1992-93). . . . Named to OHL All-Star second team (1993-94).

			REGULAR SEASON					PLAYOFFS			
Season Team	League	Gms.	G	A	Pts.	PIM	Gms.	G	A	Pts.	PIM
89-90—London Jr. B	OHA	39	26	31	57	10	—	—	—	—	—
90-91—Kingston	OHL	58	18	33	51	34	—	—	—	—	—
91-92—Kingston	OHL	65	31	52	83	20	—	—	—	—	—
92-93—Kingston	OHL	54	32	75	107	45	16	9	20	29	10
—Canadian national team	Int'l	1	0	0	0	2	—	—	—	—	—
93-94—Kingston	OHL	63	42	84	126	55	6	1	7	8	2
94-95—Canadian national team	Int'l	32	10	7	17	16	—	—	—	—	—
—Kingston	OHL	25	12	41	53	6	6	4	9	13	10

CORSON, SHAYNE
LW, BLUES

PERSONAL: Born August 13, 1966, in Barrie, Ont. . . . 6-1/200. . . . Shoots left.
TRANSACTIONS/CAREER NOTES: Selected by Montreal Canadiens in first round (second Canadiens pick, eighth overall) of NHL entry draft (June 9, 1984). . . . Broke jaw (January 24, 1987). . . . Strained ligament in right knee (September 1987). . . . Injured groin (March 1988). . . . Injured knee (April 1988). . . . Injured knee (April 1989). . . . Bruised left shoulder (October 29, 1989). . . . Broke toe on right foot (December 1989). . . . Suffered hip pointer (November 10, 1990); missed seven games. . . . Pulled groin (February 11, 1991). . . . Traded by Canadiens with LW Vladimir Vujtek and C Brent Gilchrist to Edmonton Oilers for LW Vincent Damphousse and fourth-round pick (D Adam Wiesel) in 1993 draft (August 27, 1992). . . . Fractured fibula (February 18, 1994); missed 12 games. . . . Injured leg (March 23, 1994); missed remainder of season. . . . Signed by St. Louis Blues to an offer sheet (July 28, 1995); Oilers received Blues first-round picks in 1996 and 1997 drafts as compensation; Oilers then traded picks to Blues for rights to G Curtis Joseph and RW Michael Grier (August 4, 1995).
HONORS: Played in NHL All-Star Game (1990 and 1994).
STATISTICAL PLATEAUS: Three-goal games: 1988-89 (2), 1993-94 (1). Total: 3.
MISCELLANEOUS: Captain of Edmonton Oilers (1994-95).

			REGULAR SEASON					PLAYOFFS			
Season Team	League	Gms.	G	A	Pts.	PIM	Gms.	G	A	Pts.	PIM
82-83—Barrie	COJHL	23	13	29	42	87	—	—	—	—	—
83-84—Brantford	OHL	66	25	46	71	165	6	4	1	5	26
84-85—Hamilton	OHL	54	27	63	90	154	11	3	7	10	19
85-86—Hamilton	OHL	47	41	57	98	153	—	—	—	—	—
—Montreal	NHL	3	0	0	0	2	—	—	—	—	—
86-87—Montreal	NHL	55	12	11	23	144	17	6	5	11	30
87-88—Montreal	NHL	71	12	27	39	152	3	1	0	1	12
88-89—Montreal	NHL	80	26	24	50	193	21	4	5	9	65
89-90—Montreal	NHL	76	31	44	75	144	11	2	8	10	20
90-91—Montreal	NHL	71	23	24	47	138	13	9	6	15	36
91-92—Montreal	NHL	64	17	36	53	118	10	2	5	7	15
92-93—Edmonton	NHL	80	16	31	47	209	—	—	—	—	—
93-94—Edmonton	NHL	64	25	29	54	118	—	—	—	—	—
94-95—Edmonton	NHL	48	12	24	36	86	—	—	—	—	—
NHL totals		612	174	250	424	1304	75	24	29	53	178

CORT, JOEL
D, CAPITALS

PERSONAL: Born April 26, 1977, in Hamilton, Ont. . . . 6-3/222. . . . Shoots left.
HIGH SCHOOL: Bishop MacDonnell (Guelph, Ont.).
TRANSACTIONS/CAREER NOTES: Selected by Washington Capitals in fifth round (seventh Capitals pick, 124th overall) of NHL entry draft (July 8, 1995).

			REGULAR SEASON					PLAYOFFS			
Season Team	League	Gms.	G	A	Pts.	PIM	Gms.	G	A	Pts.	PIM
94-95—Guelph	OHL	29	1	3	4	20	—	—	—	—	—

COTE, PATRICK
LW, STARS

PERSONAL: Born January 24, 1975, in Lasalle, Que. . . . 6-2/199. . . . Shoots left.
TRANSACTIONS/CAREER NOTES: Selected by Dallas Stars in second round (second Stars pick, 37th overall) of NHL entry draft (July 8, 1995).

			REGULAR SEASON					PLAYOFFS			
Season Team	League	Gms.	G	A	Pts.	PIM	Gms.	G	A	Pts.	PIM
93-94—Beauport	QMJHL	48	2	4	6	230	12	1	0	1	61
94-95—Beauport	QMJHL	56	20	20	40	314	17	8	8	16	115

COTE, SYLVAIN
D, CAPITALS

PERSONAL: Born January 19, 1966, in Quebec City. . . . 6-0/190. . . . Shoots right. . . . Name pronounced KOH-tay. . . . Brother of Alain Cote, defenseman for five NHL teams (1985-86 through 1993-94).
TRANSACTIONS/CAREER NOTES: Selected by Hartford Whalers as underage junior in first round

(first Whalers pick, 11th overall) of NHL entry draft (June 9, 1984).... Broke toe on left foot (October 28, 1989).... Sprained left knee (December 1989).... Fractured right foot (January 22, 1990).... Traded by Whalers to Washington Capitals for second-round pick (LW Andrei Nikolishin) in 1992 draft (September 8, 1991).... Broke wrist (September 25, 1992); missed six games.... Suffered hip pointer (January 7, 1993); missed one game.... Lacerated right eye (February 26, 1995); missed one game.

HONORS: Named to QMJHL All-Star second team (1983-84).... Won Emile (Butch) Bouchard Trophy (1985-86).... Shared Guy Lafleur Trophy with Luc Robitaille (1985-86).... Named to QMJHL All-Star first team (1985-86).

Season Team	League	REGULAR SEASON					PLAYOFFS				
		Gms.	G	A	Pts.	PIM	Gms.	G	A	Pts.	PIM
82-83—Quebec	QMJHL	66	10	24	34	50	—	—	—	—	—
83-84—Quebec	QMJHL	66	15	50	65	89	5	1	1	2	0
84-85—Hartford	NHL	67	3	9	12	17	—	—	—	—	—
85-86—Hartford	NHL	2	0	0	0	0	—	—	—	—	—
—Hull	QMJHL	26	10	33	43	14	13	6	*28	34	22
86-87—Binghamton	AHL	12	2	4	6	0	—	—	—	—	—
—Hartford	NHL	67	2	8	10	20	2	0	2	2	2
87-88—Hartford	NHL	67	7	21	28	30	6	1	1	2	4
88-89—Hartford	NHL	78	8	9	17	49	3	0	1	1	4
89-90—Hartford	NHL	28	4	2	6	14	5	0	0	0	0
90-91—Hartford	NHL	73	7	12	19	17	6	0	2	2	2
91-92—Washington	NHL	78	11	29	40	31	7	1	2	3	4
92-93—Washington	NHL	77	21	29	50	34	6	1	1	2	4
93-94—Washington	NHL	84	16	35	51	66	9	1	8	9	6
94-95—Washington	NHL	47	5	14	19	53	7	1	3	4	2
NHL totals		668	84	168	252	331	51	5	20	25	28

COURTNALL, GEOFF
LW, BLUES

PERSONAL: Born August 18, 1962, in Victoria, B.C.... 6-1/195.... Shoots left.... Brother of Russ Courtnall, right winger, Vancouver Canucks.
TRANSACTIONS/CAREER NOTES: Signed as free agent by Boston Bruins (September 1983).... Traded by Bruins with G Bill Ranford to Edmonton Oilers for G Andy Moog (March 8, 1988).... Traded by Oilers to Washington Capitals for C Greg Adams (July 22, 1988).... Traded by Capitals to St. Louis Blues for C Peter Zezel and D Mike Lalor (July 13, 1990).... Traded by Blues with D Robert Dirk, C Cliff Ronning, LW Sergio Momesso and fifth-round pick in 1992 draft (RW Brian Loney) to Vancouver Canucks for C Dan Quinn and D Garth Butcher (March 5, 1991).... Lacerated foot (February 28, 1992) and suffered from chronic fatigue (March 1992); missed nine games.... Suspended two games by NHL (November 14, 1993).... Suffered injury (April 20, 1995); missed three games. ... Signed as free agent by Blues (July 14, 1995).
STATISTICAL PLATEAUS: Three-goal games: 1987-88 (1), 1987-88 (1), 1988-89 (1), 1989-90 (1). Total: 4.
MISCELLANEOUS: Member of Stanley Cup championship team (1988).

Season Team	League	REGULAR SEASON					PLAYOFFS				
		Gms.	G	A	Pts.	PIM	Gms.	G	A	Pts.	PIM
80-81—Victoria	WHL	11	3	5	8	6	15	2	1	3	7
81-82—Victoria	WHL	72	35	57	92	100	4	1	0	1	2
83-84—Victoria	WHL	71	41	73	114	186	12	6	7	13	42
—Hershey	AHL	74	14	12	26	51	—	—	—	—	—
—Boston	NHL	4	0	0	0	0	—	—	—	—	—
84-85—Hershey	AHL	9	8	4	12	4	—	—	—	—	—
—Boston	NHL	64	12	16	28	82	5	0	2	2	7
85-86—Moncton	AHL	12	8	8	16	6	—	—	—	—	—
—Boston	NHL	64	21	16	37	61	3	0	0	0	2
86-87—Boston	NHL	65	13	23	36	117	1	0	0	0	0
87-88—Boston	NHL	62	32	26	58	108	—	—	—	—	—
—Edmonton	NHL	12	4	4	8	15	19	0	3	3	23
88-89—Washington	NHL	79	42	38	80	112	6	2	5	7	12
89-90—Washington	NHL	80	35	39	74	104	15	4	9	13	32
90-91—St. Louis	NHL	66	27	30	57	56	—	—	—	—	—
—Vancouver	NHL	11	6	2	8	8	6	3	5	8	4
91-92—Vancouver	NHL	70	23	34	57	116	12	6	8	14	20
92-93—Vancouver	NHL	84	31	46	77	167	12	4	10	14	12
93-94—Vancouver	NHL	82	26	44	70	123	24	9	10	19	51
94-95—Vancouver	NHL	45	16	18	34	81	11	4	2	6	34
NHL totals		788	288	336	624	1150	114	32	54	86	197

COURTNALL, RUSS
RW, CANUCKS

PERSONAL: Born June 3, 1965, in Victoria, B.C.... 5-11/190.... Shoots right.... Brother of Geoff Courtnall, left winger, St. Louis Blues.
TRANSACTIONS/CAREER NOTES: Selected by Toronto Maple Leafs as underage junior in first round (first Maple Leafs pick, seventh overall) of NHL entry draft (June 8, 1983).... Bruised knee (November 1987).... Suffered from virus (February 1988).... Suffered back spasms (March 1988). ... Traded by Maple Leafs to Montreal Canadiens for RW John Kordic and sixth-round pick (RW Michael Doers) in 1989 draft (November 7, 1988).... Pulled muscle in right shoulder (October 8, 1991); missed 41 games.... Injured hand (January 15, 1992); missed 12 games.... Traded by Canadiens to Minnesota North Stars for LW Brian Bellows (August 31, 1992).... North Stars franchise moved from Minnesota to Dallas and renamed Stars for 1993-94 season.... Traded by Stars to Vancouver Canucks for LW Greg Adams, RW Dan Kesa and fifth-round pick (traded to Los Angeles) in 1995 draft (April 7, 1995).
HONORS: Played in NHL All-Star Game (1994).
STATISTICAL PLATEAUS: Three-goal games: 1985-86 (1), 1989-90 (1), 1992-93 (1), 1994-95 (1). Total: 4.

Season	Team	League	REGULAR SEASON Gms.	G	A	Pts.	PIM	PLAYOFFS Gms.	G	A	Pts.	PIM
82-83	Victoria	WHL	60	36	61	97	33	12	11	7	18	6
83-84	Victoria	WHL	32	29	37	66	63	—	—	—	—	—
	Canadian Olympic Team ..	Int'l	16	4	7	11	10	—	—	—	—	—
	Toronto	NHL	14	3	9	12	6	—	—	—	—	—
84-85	Toronto	NHL	69	12	10	22	44	—	—	—	—	—
85-86	Toronto	NHL	73	22	38	60	52	10	3	6	9	8
86-87	Toronto	NHL	79	29	44	73	90	13	3	4	7	11
87-88	Toronto	NHL	65	23	26	49	47	6	2	1	3	0
88-89	Toronto	NHL	9	1	1	2	4	—	—	—	—	—
	Montreal	NHL	64	22	17	39	15	21	8	5	13	18
89-90	Montreal	NHL	80	27	32	59	27	11	5	1	6	10
90-91	Montreal	NHL	79	26	50	76	29	13	8	3	11	7
91-92	Montreal	NHL	27	7	14	21	6	10	1	1	2	4
92-93	Minnesota	NHL	84	36	43	79	49	—	—	—	—	—
93-94	Dallas	NHL	84	23	57	80	59	9	1	8	9	0
94-95	Dallas	NHL	32	7	10	17	13	—	—	—	—	—
	Vancouver	NHL	13	4	14	18	4	11	4	8	12	21
	NHL totals		772	242	365	607	445	104	35	37	72	79

COURVILLE, LARRY
LW, CANUCKS

PERSONAL: Born April 2, 1975, in Timmins, Ont.... 6-1/180.... Shoots left.
HIGH SCHOOL: Huron Heights Secondary School (Newmarket, Ont.).
TRANSACTIONS/CAREER NOTES: Selected by Winnipeg Jets in fifth round (sixth Jets pick, 119th overall) of NHL entry draft (June 26, 1993).... Returned to draft pool by Jets and selected by Vancouver Canucks in third round (second Canucks pick, 61st overall) of entry draft (July 8, 1995).
HONORS: Named to OHL All-Star second team (1994-95).

Season	Team	League	REGULAR SEASON Gms.	G	A	Pts.	PIM	PLAYOFFS Gms.	G	A	Pts.	PIM
90-91	Waterloo	USHL	48	20	18	38	144	—	—	—	—	—
91-92	Cornwall	OHL	60	8	12	20	80	6	0	0	0	8
92-93	Newmarket	OHL	64	21	18	39	181	7	0	6	6	14
93-94	Newmarket	OHL	39	20	19	39	134	—	—	—	—	—
	Moncton	AHL	8	2	0	2	37	10	2	2	4	27
94-95	Sarnia	OHL	16	9	9	18	58	—	—	—	—	—
	Oshawa	OHL	28	25	30	55	72	7	4	10	14	10

COUSINEAU, MARCEL
G, MAPLE LEAFS

PERSONAL: Born April 30, 1973, in Delson, Que.... 5-10/175.... Catches left. ... Name pronounced KOO-sih-noh.
TRANSACTIONS/CAREER NOTES: Selected by Boston Bruins in third round (third Bruins pick, 62nd overall) of NHL entry draft (June 22, 1991).... Signed as free agent by Toronto Maple Leafs (November 13, 1993).
HONORS: Named to QMJHL All-Rookie team (1990-91).

Season	Team	League	REGULAR SEASON Gms.	Min.	W	L	T	GA	SO	Avg.	PLAYOFFS Gms.	Min.	W	L	GA	SO	Avg.
90-91	Beauport	QMJHL	49	2739	13	29	3	196	1	4.29	—	—	—	—	—	—	—
91-92	Beauport	QMJHL	*67	*3673	26	*32	5	*241	0	3.94	—	—	—	—	—	—	—
92-93	Drummondville	QMJHL	60	3298	20	32	2	225	0	4.09	9	498	3	6	37	1	4.46
93-94	St. John's	AHL	37	2015	13	11	9	118	0	3.51	—	—	—	—	—	—	—
94-95	St. John's	AHL	58	3342	22	27	6	171	4	3.07	3	180	0	3	9	0	3.00

COWIE, ROB
D, KINGS

PERSONAL: Born November 3, 1967, in Toronto.... 6-0/195.... Shoots left.
COLLEGE: Northeastern.
TRANSACTIONS/CAREER NOTES: Signed as free agent by Winnipeg Jets (July 4, 1991).... Signed as free agent by Hartford Whalers (August 9, 1993).... Signed as free agent by Los Angeles Kings (July 8, 1994).... Suffered from the flu (April 21, 1995); missed one game.
HONORS: Named to Hockey East All-Star second team (1988-89 and 1990-91).... Named NCAA East All-America first team (1989-90).... Named to Hockey East All-Star first team (1989-90).... Named to AHL All-Star second team (1993-94).

Season	Team	League	REGULAR SEASON Gms.	G	A	Pts.	PIM	PLAYOFFS Gms.	G	A	Pts.	PIM
87-88	Northeastern University	Hockey East	36	7	8	15	38	—	—	—	—	—
88-89	Northeastern University	Hockey East	36	7	34	41	60	—	—	—	—	—
89-90	Northeastern University	Hockey East	34	14	31	45	54	—	—	—	—	—
90-91	Northeastern University	Hockey East	33	18	23	41	56	—	—	—	—	—
91-92	Moncton	AHL	64	11	30	41	89	5	1	1	2	0
92-93	Moncton	AHL	67	12	20	32	91	5	3	5	8	2
93-94	Springfield	AHL	78	17	57	74	124	6	3	6	9	4
94-95	Phoenix	IHL	51	14	33	47	71	—	—	—	—	—
	Los Angeles	NHL	32	2	7	9	20	—	—	—	—	—
	NHL totals		32	2	7	9	20	—	—	—	—	—

CRAIG, MIKE
RW, MAPLE LEAFS

PERSONAL: Born June 6, 1971, in London, Ont. . . . 6-1/180. . . . Shoots right.
TRANSACTIONS/CAREER NOTES: Selected by Minnesota North Stars in second round (second North Stars pick, 28th overall) of NHL entry draft (June 17, 1989). . . . Broke fibula (January 28, 1990). . . . Broke right wrist (February 4, 1991); missed 17 games. . . . Sprained knee (February 25, 1993); missed 12 games. . . . North Stars franchise moved from Minnesota to Dallas and renamed Stars for 1993-94 season. . . . Signed as free agent by Toronto Maple Leafs (July 29, 1994); C Peter Zezel and RW Grant Marshall awarded to Stars as compensation (August 10, 1994). . . . Broke index finger (March 13, 1995); missed nine games.

			REGULAR SEASON					PLAYOFFS				
Season	Team	League	Gms.	G	A	Pts.	PIM	Gms.	G	A	Pts.	PIM
86-87—Woodstock Jr. C.	OHA	32	29	19	48	64	—	—	—	—	—
87-88—Oshawa	OHL	61	6	10	16	39	7	7	0	7	11
88-89—Oshawa	OHL	63	36	36	72	34	6	3	1	4	6
89-90—Oshawa	OHL	43	36	40	76	85	17	10	16	26	46
90-91—Minnesota	NHL	39	8	4	12	32	10	1	1	2	20
91-92—Minnesota	NHL	67	15	16	31	155	4	1	0	1	7
92-93—Minnesota	NHL	70	15	23	38	106	—	—	—	—	—
93-94—Dallas	NHL	72	13	24	37	139	4	0	0	0	2
94-95—Toronto	NHL	37	5	5	10	12	2	0	1	1	2
NHL totals		285	56	72	128	444	20	2	2	4	31

CRAIGWELL, DALE
C, SHARKS

PERSONAL: Born April 24, 1971, in Toronto. . . . 5-10/180. . . . Shoots left.
COLLEGE: Toronto.
TRANSACTIONS/CAREER NOTES: Selected by San Jose Sharks in 10th round (11th Sharks pick, 199th overall) of NHL entry draft (June 22, 1991). . . . Strained back (October 1992); missed two games. . . . Strained back (November 1, 1992); missed 10 games. . . . Injured groin (November 18, 1993); missed three games. . . . Broke ankle (September 4, 1994); missed entire season.
HONORS: Won William Hanley Trophy (1990-91).

			REGULAR SEASON					PLAYOFFS				
Season	Team	League	Gms.	G	A	Pts.	PIM	Gms.	G	A	Pts.	PIM
88-89—Oshawa	OHL	55	9	14	23	15	6	0	0	0	0
89-90—Oshawa	OHL	64	22	41	63	39	17	7	7	14	11
90-91—Oshawa	OHL	56	27	68	95	34	16	7	16	23	9
91-92—Kansas City	IHL	48	6	19	25	29	12	4	7	11	4
—San Jose	NHL	32	5	11	16	8	—	—	—	—	—
92-93—San Jose	NHL	8	3	1	4	4	—	—	—	—	—
—Kansas City	IHL	60	15	38	53	24	12	†7	5	12	2
93-94—Kansas City	IHL	5	3	1	4	0	—	—	—	—	—
—San Jose	NHL	58	3	6	9	16	—	—	—	—	—
94-95—San Jose	NHL				Did not play-injured.						
NHL totals		98	11	18	29	28					

CRAVEN, MURRAY
C/LW, BLACKHAWKS

PERSONAL: Born July 20, 1964, in Medicine Hat, Alta. . . . 6-2/185. . . . Shoots left.
TRANSACTIONS/CAREER NOTES: Selected by Detroit Red Wings as underage junior in first round (first Red Wings pick, 17th overall) of NHL entry draft (June 9, 1982). . . . Injured left knee cartilage (January 15, 1983). . . . Traded by Red Wings with LW/C Joe Paterson to Philadelphia Flyers for C Darryl Sittler (October 1984). . . . Broke foot (April 16, 1987). . . . Hyperextended right knee and lacerated eye (November 1988). . . . Bruised right foot (January 1989). . . . Fractured left wrist (February 24, 1989). . . . Fractured right wrist (April 5, 1989). . . . Suffered back spasms (February 1990). . . . Injured rotator cuff (March 24, 1990). . . . Traded by Flyers with fourth-round pick in 1992 draft (LW Kevin Smyth) to Hartford Whalers for RW Kevin Dineen (November 13, 1991). . . . Injured groin (January 21, 1992). . . . Traded by Whalers with fifth-round pick in 1993 draft to Vancouver Canucks for LW Robert Kron, third-round pick in 1993 draft (D Marek Malik) and future considerations (March 22, 1993). . . . Canucks sent RW Jim Sandlak to complete deal (May 17, 1993). . . . Injured hip (November 2, 1993); missed two games. . . . Strained groin (November 14, 1993); missed two games. . . . Traded by Canucks to Chicago Blackhawks for C Christian Ruuttu (March 10, 1995). . . . Suffered from sore back (1995); missed four games.
STATISTICAL PLATEAUS: Three-goal games: 1986-87 (1), 1987-88 (1), 1991-92 (1). Total: 3.

			REGULAR SEASON					PLAYOFFS				
Season	Team	League	Gms.	G	A	Pts.	PIM	Gms.	G	A	Pts.	PIM
80-81—Medicine Hat	WHL	69	5	10	15	18	5	0	0	0	2
81-82—Medicine Hat	WHL	72	35	46	81	49	—	—	—	—	—
82-83—Medicine Hat	WHL	28	17	29	46	35	—	—	—	—	—
—Detroit	NHL	31	4	7	11	6	—	—	—	—	—
83-84—Medicine Hat	WHL	48	38	56	94	53	4	5	3	8	4
—Detroit	NHL	15	0	4	4	6	—	—	—	—	—
84-85—Philadelphia	NHL	80	26	35	61	30	19	4	6	10	11
85-86—Philadelphia	NHL	78	21	33	54	34	5	0	3	3	4
86-87—Philadelphia	NHL	77	19	30	49	38	12	3	1	4	9
87-88—Philadelphia	NHL	72	30	46	76	58	7	2	5	7	4
88-89—Philadelphia	NHL	51	9	28	37	52	1	0	0	0	0
89-90—Philadelphia	NHL	76	25	50	75	42	—	—	—	—	—
90-91—Philadelphia	NHL	77	19	47	66	53	—	—	—	—	—
91-92—Philadelphia	NHL	12	3	3	6	8	—	—	—	—	—
—Hartford	NHL	61	24	30	54	38	7	3	3	6	6
92-93—Hartford	NHL	67	25	42	67	20	—	—	—	—	—
—Vancouver	NHL	10	0	10	10	12	12	4	6	10	4

Season	Team	League	REGULAR SEASON					PLAYOFFS				
			Gms.	G	A	Pts.	PIM	Gms.	G	A	Pts.	PIM
93-94—Vancouver		NHL	78	15	40	55	30	22	4	9	13	18
94-95—Chicago		NHL	16	4	3	7	2	16	5	5	10	4
NHL totals			801	224	408	632	429	101	25	38	63	60

CREIGHTON, ADAM
C, BLUES

PERSONAL: Born June 2, 1965, in Burlington, Ont. . . . 6-5/220. . . . Shoots left. . . . Son of Dave Creighton, center with four NHL teams (1948-49 through 1959-60).
TRANSACTIONS/CAREER NOTES: Selected by Buffalo Sabres in first round (third Sabres pick, 11th overall) of NHL entry draft (June 8, 1983). . . . Underwent knee surgery (January 1988). . . . Sprained knee (September 1988). . . . Traded by Sabres to Chicago Blackhawks for RW Rick Vaive (December 2, 1988). . . . Suspended five games by NHL for stick-swinging incident in preseason game (September 30, 1990). . . . Sprained right hand (February 10, 1991). . . . Traded by Blackhawks with LW Steve Thomas to New York Islanders for C Brent Sutter and RW Brad Lauer (October 25, 1991). . . . Selected by Tampa Bay Lightning in NHL waiver draft (October 4, 1992). . . . Sprained right knee ligaments (October 7, 1993); missed 14 games. . . . Reinjured right knee (November 11, 1993); missed eight games. . . . Injured groin (December 19, 1993); missed three games. . . . Traded by Lightning to St. Louis Blues for D Tom Tilley (October 6, 1994).
HONORS: Won Stafford Smythe Memorial Cup (May 1984). . . . Named to Memorial Cup All-Star team (1983-84).
STATISTICAL PLATEAUS: Three-goal games: 1988-89 (2).

Season	Team	League	REGULAR SEASON					PLAYOFFS				
			Gms.	G	A	Pts.	PIM	Gms.	G	A	Pts.	PIM
81-82—Ottawa		OHL	60	14	27	41	73	17	7	1	8	40
82-83—Ottawa		OHL	68	44	46	90	88	9	0	2	2	12
83-84—Ottawa		OHL	56	42	49	91	79	13	16	11	27	28
—Buffalo		NHL	7	2	2	4	4	—	—	—	—	—
84-85—Ottawa		OHL	10	4	14	18	23	5	6	2	8	11
—Rochester		AHL	6	5	3	8	2	5	2	1	3	20
—Buffalo		NHL	30	2	8	10	33	—	—	—	—	—
85-86—Rochester		AHL	32	17	21	38	27	—	—	—	—	—
—Buffalo		NHL	19	1	1	2	2	—	—	—	—	—
86-87—Buffalo		NHL	56	18	22	40	26	—	—	—	—	—
87-88—Buffalo		NHL	36	10	17	27	87	—	—	—	—	—
88-89—Buffalo		NHL	24	7	10	17	44	—	—	—	—	—
—Chicago		NHL	43	15	14	29	92	15	5	6	11	44
89-90—Chicago		NHL	80	34	36	70	224	20	3	6	9	59
90-91—Chicago		NHL	72	22	29	51	135	6	0	1	1	10
91-92—Chicago		NHL	11	6	6	12	16	—	—	—	—	—
—New York Islanders		NHL	66	15	9	24	102	—	—	—	—	—
92-93—Tampa Bay		NHL	83	19	20	39	110	—	—	—	—	—
93-94—Tampa Bay		NHL	53	10	10	20	37	—	—	—	—	—
94-95—St. Louis		NHL	48	14	20	34	74	7	2	0	2	16
NHL totals			628	175	204	379	986	48	10	13	23	129

CRONIN, SHAWN
D, SHARKS

PERSONAL: Born August 20, 1963, in Flushing, Mich. . . . 6-2/225. . . . Shoots left. . . . Full name: Shawn Patrick Cronin.
COLLEGE: Illinois-Chicago.
TRANSACTIONS/CAREER NOTES: Signed as free agent by Hartford Whalers (March 1986). . . . Signed as free agent by Washington Capitals (June 6, 1988). . . . Signed as free agent by Philadelphia Flyers (June 13, 1989). . . . Traded by Flyers to Winnipeg Jets for future considerations (July 1, 1989); future considerations later canceled. . . . Bruised hand (February 1990). . . . Bruised foot (October 27, 1991); missed three games. . . . Injured ribs (December 23, 1991). . . . Traded by Jets to Quebec Nordiques for D Danny Lambert (August 25, 1992). . . . Selected by Flyers in NHL waiver draft (October 4, 1992). . . . Sprained left knee (April 12, 1993); missed remainder of season. . . . Traded by Flyers to San Jose Sharks for future considerations (August 5, 1993). . . . Sprained knee (January 17, 1994); missed 12 games. . . . Suffered split finger (March 24, 1994); missed three games. . . . Injured knee (February 26, 1995); missed 10 games.

Season	Team	League	REGULAR SEASON					PLAYOFFS				
			Gms.	G	A	Pts.	PIM	Gms.	G	A	Pts.	PIM
82-83—Illinois-Chicago		CCHA	36	1	5	6	52	—	—	—	—	—
83-84—Illinois-Chicago		CCHA	32	0	4	4	41	—	—	—	—	—
84-85—Illinois-Chicago		CCHA	31	2	6	8	52	—	—	—	—	—
85-86—Illinois-Chicago		CCHA	38	3	8	11	70	—	—	—	—	—
86-87—Binghamton		AHL	12	0	1	1	60	10	0	0	0	41
—Salt Lake City		IHL	53	8	16	24	118	—	—	—	—	—
87-88—Binghamton		AHL	66	3	8	11	212	4	0	0	0	15
88-89—Washington		NHL	1	0	0	0	0	—	—	—	—	—
—Baltimore		AHL	75	3	9	12	267	—	—	—	—	—
89-90—Winnipeg		NHL	61	0	4	4	243	5	0	0	0	7
90-91—Winnipeg		NHL	67	1	5	6	189	—	—	—	—	—
91-92—Winnipeg		NHL	65	0	4	4	271	4	0	0	0	6
92-93—Philadelphia		NHL	35	2	1	3	37	—	—	—	—	—
—Hershey		AHL	7	0	1	1	12	—	—	—	—	—
93-94—San Jose		NHL	34	0	2	2	76	14	1	0	1	20
94-95—San Jose		NHL	29	0	2	2	61	9	0	0	0	5
NHL totals			292	3	18	21	877	32	1	0	1	38

C

CROSS, CORY
D, LIGHTNING

PERSONAL: Born January 3, 1971, in Prince Albert, Sask. . . . 6-5/212. . . . Shoots left. . . . Full name: Cory James Cross.
HIGH SCHOOL: Lloydminster (Alta.) Comprehensive.
COLLEGE: Alberta.
TRANSACTIONS/CAREER NOTES: Selected by Tampa Bay Lightning in NHL supplemental draft (June 19, 1992).
HONORS: Named to CWUAA All-Star second team (1992-93).

Season Team	League	REGULAR SEASON					PLAYOFFS				
		Gms.	G	A	Pts.	PIM	Gms.	G	A	Pts.	PIM
90-91—University of Alberta	CWUAA	20	2	5	7	16	—	—	—	—	—
91-92—University of Alberta	CWUAA	39	3	10	13	76	—	—	—	—	—
92-93—University of Alberta	CWUAA	43	11	28	39	105	—	—	—	—	—
—Atlanta	IHL	7	0	1	1	2	4	0	0	0	6
93-94—Atlanta	IHL	70	4	14	18	72	9	1	2	3	14
—Tampa Bay	NHL	5	0	0	0	6	—	—	—	—	—
94-95—Atlanta	IHL	41	5	10	15	67	—	—	—	—	—
—Tampa Bay	NHL	43	1	5	6	41	—	—	—	—	—
NHL totals		48	1	5	6	47					

CROWDER, TROY
RW, KINGS

PERSONAL: Born May 3, 1968, in Sudbury, Ont. . . . 6-4/220. . . . Shoots right.
TRANSACTIONS/CAREER NOTES: Selected by New Jersey Devils as underage junior in sixth round (sixth Devils pick, 108th overall) of NHL entry draft (June 21, 1986). . . . Left training camp (September 1989); returned (March 1990). . . . Injured left elbow (October 4, 1990). . . . Hyperextended elbow (November 1, 1990). . . . Lacerated right hand and damaged ligaments (December 29, 1990). . . . Signed as free agent by Detroit Red Wings (August 27, 1991); Devils received C/RW Dave Barr and RW Randy McKay as compensation. . . . Strained back (October 10, 1991); missed 73 games. . . . Reinjured back (May 6, 1992). . . . Signed as free agent by Los Angeles Kings (September 2, 1994). . . . Sprained right wrist (January 27, 1995); missed 11 games. . . . Sprained wrist (March 28, 1995); missed five games.

Season Team	League	REGULAR SEASON					PLAYOFFS				
		Gms.	G	A	Pts.	PIM	Gms.	G	A	Pts.	PIM
85-86—Hamilton	OHL	55	4	4	8	178	—	—	—	—	—
86-87—North Bay	OHL	35	6	11	17	90	23	3	9	12	99
—Belleville	OHL	21	5	5	10	52	—	—	—	—	—
87-88—North Bay	OHL	9	1	2	3	44	—	—	—	—	—
—New Jersey	NHL	—	—	—	—	—	1	0	0	0	12
—Belleville	OHL	46	12	27	39	103	6	2	3	5	24
—Utica	AHL	3	0	0	0	36	—	—	—	—	—
88-89—Utica	AHL	62	6	4	10	152	2	0	0	0	25
89-90—Nashville	ECHL	3	0	0	0	15	—	—	—	—	—
—New Jersey	NHL	10	0	0	0	23	2	0	0	0	10
90-91—New Jersey	NHL	59	6	3	9	182	—	—	—	—	—
91-92—Detroit	NHL	7	0	0	0	35	1	0	0	0	0
92-93—					Did not play.						
93-94—					Did not play.						
94-95—Los Angeles	NHL	29	1	2	3	99	—	—	—	—	—
NHL totals		105	7	5	12	339	4	0	0	0	22

CROWE, PHIL
LW, FLYERS

PERSONAL: Born April 14, 1970, in Red Deer, Alta. . . . 6-2/220. . . . Shoots left.
TRANSACTIONS/CAREER NOTES: Signed as free agent by Los Angeles Kings (November 8, 1993). . . . Signed as free agent by Philadelphia Flyers (July 19, 1994). . . . Loaned by Flyers to Hershey Bears (October 14, 1994).

Season Team	League	REGULAR SEASON					PLAYOFFS				
		Gms.	G	A	Pts.	PIM	Gms.	G	A	Pts.	PIM
91-92—Adirondack	AHL	6	0	1	1	29	—	—	—	—	—
—Columbus	ECHL	32	4	7	11	145	—	—	—	—	—
92-93—Phoenix	IHL	53	3	3	6	190	—	—	—	—	—
93-94—Fort Wayne	IHL	5	0	1	1	26	—	—	—	—	—
—Phoenix	IHL	2	0	0	0	0	—	—	—	—	—
—Los Angeles	NHL	31	0	2	2	77	—	—	—	—	—
94-95—Hershey	AHL	46	11	6	17	132	6	0	1	1	19
NHL totals		31	0	2	2	77					

CROWLEY, MIKE
D, FLYERS

PERSONAL: Born July 4, 1975, in Bloomington, Minn. . . . 5-11/165. . . . Shoots left.
HIGH SCHOOL: Thomas Jefferson (Bloomington, Minn.).
COLLEGE: Minnesota.
TRANSACTIONS/CAREER NOTES: Selected by Philadelphia Flyers in sixth round (fifth Flyers pick, 140th overall) of NHL entry draft (June 26, 1993).
HONORS: Named WCHA rookie of the year (1994-95).

Season Team	League	REGULAR SEASON					PLAYOFFS				
		Gms.	G	A	Pts.	PIM	Gms.	G	A	Pts.	PIM
90-91—Jefferson H.S.	Minn. H.S.	20	3	9	12	2	—	—	—	—	—
91-92—Jefferson H.S.	Minn. H.S.	28	5	18	23	8	—	—	—	—	—
92-93—Jefferson H.S.	Minn. H.S.	22	10	32	42	18	—	—	—	—	—

Season Team	League	REGULAR SEASON					PLAYOFFS				
		Gms.	G	A	Pts.	PIM	Gms.	G	A	Pts.	PIM
93-94—Jefferson H.S...................	Minn. H.S.	28	23	54	77	26	—	—	—	—	—
94-95—University of Minnesota ...	WCHA	41	11	27	38	60	—	—	—	—	—

CROZIER, GREG
LW, PENGUINS

PERSONAL: Born July 6, 1976, in Williamsville, N.Y. . . . 6-4/200. . . . Shoots left.
HIGH SCHOOL: Lawrence Academy (Groton, Mass.).
TRANSACTIONS/CAREER NOTES: Selected by Pittsburgh Penguins in third round (fourth Penguins pick, 73rd overall) of NHL entry draft (June 29, 1994).

Season Team	League	REGULAR SEASON					PLAYOFFS				
		Gms.	G	A	Pts.	PIM	Gms.	G	A	Pts.	PIM
90-91—Amherst.........................	Mass. H.S.	41	52	34	86	17	—	—	—	—	—
91-92—Amherst.........................	Mass. H.S.	46	61	47	108	47	—	—	—	—	—
92-93—Lawrence Academy........	Mass. H.S.	21	22	13	35	9	—	—	—	—	—
93-94—Lawrence Academy........	Mass. H.S.	19	22	26	48	10	—	—	—	—	—
94-95—Lawrence Academy........	Mass. H.S.	31	45	32	77	22	—	—	—	—	—

CULLEN, JOHN
C

PERSONAL: Born August 2, 1964, in Puslinch, Ont. . . . 5-10/180. . . . Shoots right. . . . Full name: Barry John Cullen. . . . Son of Barry Cullen, right winger, Toronto Maple Leafs and Detroit Red Wings (1955-56 through 1959-60); nephew of Brian Cullen, center, Toronto Maple Leafs and New York Rangers (1954-55 through 1960-61); and nephew of Ray Cullen, left winger, four NHL teams (1965-66 through 1970-71).
COLLEGE: Boston University.
TRANSACTIONS/CAREER NOTES: Selected by Buffalo Sabres in NHL supplemental draft (September 17, 1986). . . . Signed as free agent by Pittsburgh Penguins (July 1988). . . . Suffered from hepatitis (October 1989); missed seven games. . . . Pulled stomach muscle (November 17, 1990). . . . Traded by Penguins with D Zarley Zalapski and RW Jeff Parker to Whalers for C Ron Francis, D Ulf Samuelsson and D Grant Jennings (March 4, 1991). . . . Missed first three games of 1991-92 season due to contract dispute. . . . Traded by Whalers to Toronto Maple Leafs for second-round pick in 1993 or 1994 draft (November 24, 1992). . . . Suffered herniated disc in neck (March 2, 1993); missed 16 games. . . . Sprained ankle (January 26, 1994); missed 21 games. . . . Signed as free agent by Penguins (August 3, 1994). . . . Suffered charley horse (March 19, 1995); missed two games.
HONORS: Named ECAC Rookie of the Year (1983-84). . . . Named to Hockey East All-Star first team (1984-85 and 1985-86). . . . Named to NCAA All-America East second team (1985-86). . . . Named to Hockey East All-Star second team (1986-87). . . . Won James Gatschene Memorial Trophy (1987-88). . . . Won Leo P. Lamoureux Memorial Trophy (1987-88). . . . Shared Garry F. Longman Memorial Trophy with Ed Belfour (1987-88). . . . Named to IHL All-Star first team (1987-88). . . . Played in NHL All-Star Game (1991 and 1992). . . . Named to Hockey East All-Decade team (1994).
STATISTICAL PLATEAUS: Three-goal games: 1989-90 (1), 1990-91 (1), 1991-92 (1). Total: 3.

Season Team	League	REGULAR SEASON					PLAYOFFS				
		Gms.	G	A	Pts.	PIM	Gms.	G	A	Pts.	PIM
83-84—Boston University............	ECAC	40	23	33	56	28	—	—	—	—	—
84-85—Boston University............	Hockey East	41	27	32	59	46	—	—	—	—	—
85-86—Boston University............	Hockey East	43	25	49	74	54	—	—	—	—	—
86-87—Boston University............	Hockey East	36	23	29	52	35	—	—	—	—	—
87-88—Flint..............................	IHL	81	48	*109	*157	113	16	11	†15	26	16
88-89—Pittsburgh......................	NHL	79	12	37	49	112	11	3	6	9	28
89-90—Pittsburgh......................	NHL	72	32	60	92	138	—	—	—	—	—
90-91—Pittsburgh......................	NHL	65	31	63	94	83	—	—	—	—	—
—Hartford..........................	NHL	13	8	8	16	18	6	2	7	9	10
91-92—Hartford.........................	NHL	77	26	51	77	141	7	2	1	3	12
92-93—Hartford.........................	NHL	19	5	4	9	58	—	—	—	—	—
—Toronto...........................	NHL	47	13	28	41	53	12	2	3	5	0
93-94—Toronto..........................	NHL	53	13	17	30	67	3	0	0	0	0
94-95—Pittsburgh......................	NHL	46	13	24	37	66	9	0	2	2	8
NHL totals.................................		**471**	**153**	**292**	**445**	**736**	**48**	**9**	**19**	**28**	**58**

CULLIMORE, JASSEN
D, CANUCKS

PERSONAL: Born December 4, 1972, in Simcoe, Ont. . . . 6-5/220. . . . Shoots left. . . . Name pronounced KUHL-ih-MOHR.
TRANSACTIONS/CAREER NOTES: Selected by Vancouver Canucks in second round (second Canucks pick, 29th overall) of NHL entry draft (June 22, 1991). . . . Suffered injury (March 31, 1995); missed three games.
HONORS: Named to OHL All-Star second team (1991-92).

Season Team	League	REGULAR SEASON					PLAYOFFS				
		Gms.	G	A	Pts.	PIM	Gms.	G	A	Pts.	PIM
88-89—Peterborough	Jr. B	29	11	17	28	88	—	—	—	—	—
89-90—Peterborough	OHL	59	2	6	8	61	11	0	2	2	8
90-91—Peterborough	OHL	62	8	16	24	74	4	1	0	1	7
91-92—Peterborough	OHL	54	9	37	46	65	10	3	6	9	8
92-93—Hamilton.........................	AHL	56	5	7	12	60	—	—	—	—	—
93-94—Hamilton.........................	AHL	71	8	20	28	86	3	0	1	1	2
94-95—Syracuse	AHL	33	2	7	9	66	—	—	—	—	—
—Vancouver.....................	NHL	34	1	2	3	39	11	0	0	0	12
NHL totals.................................		**34**	**1**	**2**	**3**	**39**	**11**	**0**	**0**	**0**	**12**

CUMMINS, JIM

LW, BLACKHAWKS

PERSONAL: Born May 17, 1970, in Dearborn, Mich. . . . 6-2/205. . . . Shoots right. . . . Full name: James Stephen Cummins.
COLLEGE: Michigan State.
TRANSACTIONS/CAREER NOTES: Selected by New York Rangers in fourth round (fifth Rangers pick, 67th overall) of NHL entry draft (June 17, 1989). . . . Traded by Rangers with C Kevin Miller and D Dennis Vial to Detroit Red Wings for RW Joe Kocur and D Per Djoos (March 5, 1991). . . . Suspended 11 games by NHL for leaving penalty box to join fight (January 23, 1993). . . . Traded by Red Wings with fourth-round pick in 1993 draft (later traded to Boston which selected D Charles Paquette) to Philadelphia Flyers for rights to C Greg Johnson and future considerations (June 20, 1993). . . . Suffered slightly separated shoulder. . . . Traded by Flyers with fourth-round pick in 1995 draft to Tampa Bay Lightning for C Rob DiMaio (March 18, 1994). . . . Traded by Lightning with D Jeff Buchanan and D Tom Tilley to Chicago Blackhawks for LW Paul Ysebaert and RW Rich Sutter (February 22, 1995). . . . Sprained tricep (March 16, 1995); missed five games.

Season	Team	League	REGULAR SEASON					PLAYOFFS				
			Gms.	G	A	Pts.	PIM	Gms.	G	A	Pts.	PIM
87-88—	Detroit Compuware	NAJHL	31	11	15	26	146	—	—	—	—	—
88-89—	Michigan State	CCHA	36	3	9	12	100	—	—	—	—	—
89-90—	Michigan State	CCHA	41	8	7	15	94	—	—	—	—	—
90-91—	Michigan State	CCHA	34	9	6	15	110	—	—	—	—	—
91-92—	Adirondack	AHL	65	7	13	20	338	5	0	0	0	19
	—Detroit	NHL	1	0	0	0	7	—	—	—	—	—
92-93—	Adirondack	AHL	43	16	4	20	179	9	3	1	4	4
	—Detroit	NHL	7	1	1	2	58	—	—	—	—	—
93-94—	Philadelphia	NHL	22	1	2	3	71	—	—	—	—	—
	—Hershey	AHL	17	6	6	12	70	—	—	—	—	—
	—Atlanta	IHL	7	4	5	9	14	13	1	2	3	90
	—Tampa Bay	NHL	4	0	0	0	13	—	—	—	—	—
94-95—	Tampa Bay	NHL	10	1	0	1	41	—	—	—	—	—
	—Chicago	NHL	27	3	1	4	117	14	1	1	2	4
NHL totals			**71**	**6**	**4**	**10**	**307**	**14**	**1**	**1**	**2**	**4**

CUNNEYWORTH, RANDY

LW, SENATORS

PERSONAL: Born May 10, 1961, in Etobicoke, Ont. . . . 6-0/193. . . . Shoots left. . . . Full name: Randolph William Cunneyworth.
TRANSACTIONS/CAREER NOTES: Selected by Buffalo Sabres as underage junior in eighth round (ninth Sabres pick, 167th overall) of NHL entry draft (June 11, 1980). . . . Attended Pittsburgh Penguins training camp as unsigned free agent (summer 1985); Sabres then traded his equalization rights with RW Mike Moller to Penguins for future considerations (October 4, 1985); Penguins sent RW Pat Hughes to Sabres to complete deal (October 1985). . . . Suspended three games by NHL (January 1988). . . . Suspended five games by NHL (January 1988). . . . Fractured right foot (January 24, 1989). . . . Traded by Penguins with G Richard Tabaracci and RW Dave McLlwain to Winnipeg Jets for RW Andrew McBain, D Jim Kyte and LW Randy Gilhen (June 17, 1989). . . . Broke bone in right foot (October 1989). . . . Traded by Jets to Hartford Whalers for C Paul MacDermid (December 13, 1989). . . . Broke tibia bone in left leg (November 28, 1990); missed 38 games. . . . Strained lower back (December 1991); missed one game. . . . Strained ankle (December 21, 1991); missed two games. . . . Strained left ankle (January 16, 1992); missed three games. . . . Reinjured ankle (February 1, 1992); missed six games. . . . Bruised ribs (November 15, 1992); missed four games. . . . Suffered neck spasms (December 31, 1992); missed three games. . . . Traded by Hartford with D Gary Suter and undisclosed draft pick to Chicago Blackhawks for D Frantisek Kucera and LW Jocelyn Lemieux (March 11, 1994). . . . Signed as free agent by Ottawa Senators (June 30, 1994).
STATISTICAL PLATEAUS: Three-goal games: 1986-87 (1). . . . Four-goal games: 1986-87 (1). . . . Total hat tricks: 2.
MISCELLANEOUS: Captain of Ottawa Senators (1994-95).

Season	Team	League	REGULAR SEASON					PLAYOFFS				
			Gms.	G	A	Pts.	PIM	Gms.	G	A	Pts.	PIM
79-80—	Ottawa	OMJHL	63	16	25	41	145	11	0	1	1	13
80-81—	Ottawa	OMJHL	67	54	74	128	240	15	5	8	13	35
	—Rochester	AHL	1	0	1	1	2	—	—	—	—	—
	—Buffalo	NHL	1	0	0	0	2	—	—	—	—	—
81-82—	Rochester	AHL	57	12	15	27	86	9	4	0	4	30
	—Buffalo	NHL	20	2	4	6	47	—	—	—	—	—
82-83—	Rochester	AHL	78	23	33	56	111	16	4	4	8	35
83-84—	Rochester	AHL	54	18	17	35	85	17	5	5	10	55
84-85—	Rochester	AHL	72	30	38	68	148	5	2	1	3	16
85-86—	Pittsburgh	NHL	75	15	30	45	74	—	—	—	—	—
86-87—	Pittsburgh	NHL	79	26	27	53	142	—	—	—	—	—
87-88—	Pittsburgh	NHL	71	35	39	74	141	—	—	—	—	—
88-89—	Pittsburgh	NHL	70	25	19	44	156	11	3	5	8	26
89-90—	Winnipeg	NHL	28	5	6	11	34	—	—	—	—	—
	—Hartford	NHL	43	9	9	18	41	4	0	0	0	2
90-91—	Springfield	AHL	2	0	0	0	5	—	—	—	—	—
	—Hartford	NHL	32	9	5	14	49	1	0	0	0	0
91-92—	Hartford	NHL	39	7	10	17	71	7	3	0	3	9
92-93—	Hartford	NHL	39	5	4	9	63	—	—	—	—	—
93-94—	Hartford	NHL	63	9	8	17	87	—	—	—	—	—
	—Chicago	NHL	16	4	3	7	13	6	0	0	0	8
94-95—	Ottawa	NHL	48	5	5	10	68	—	—	—	—	—
NHL totals			**624**	**156**	**169**	**325**	**988**	**29**	**6**	**5**	**11**	**45**

— 392 —

CURRAN, BRIAN
D, CAPITALS

PERSONAL: Born November 5, 1963, in Toronto. . . . 6-4/230. . . . Shoots left.
TRANSACTIONS/CAREER NOTES: Underwent appendectomy (November 1981). . . . Selected by Boston Bruins as underage junior in second round (second Bruins pick, 22nd overall) of NHL entry draft (June 9, 1982). . . . Broke ankle (September 1982). . . . Bruised thigh (November 1984). . . . Broke leg (February 1, 1986). . . . Signed as free agent by New York Islanders (August 1986); Bruins awarded D Paul Boutilier as compensation. . . . Fractured jaw (January 12, 1988). . . . Traded by Islanders to Toronto Maple Leafs for sixth-round pick (RW Pavel Gross) in 1988 draft (March 1988). . . . Pulled pelvic muscle (November 1988). . . . Bruised spine (December 1, 1988). . . . Dislocated right wrist (February 25, 1989). . . . Bruised left wrist (November 1990). . . . Traded by Maple Leafs with LW Lou Franceschetti to Buffalo Sabres for RW Mike Foligno and eighth-round pick (C Thomas Kucharcik) in 1991 draft (December 17, 1990). . . . Injured shoulder (December 28, 1990); missed four games. . . . Signed as free agent by Edmonton Oilers (October 27, 1992). . . . Signed as free agent by Portland Pirates (July 1993).

			REGULAR SEASON					PLAYOFFS				
Season	Team	League	Gms.	G	A	Pts.	PIM	Gms.	G	A	Pts.	PIM
80-81—Portland		WHL	51	2	16	18	132	14	1	7	8	63
81-82—Portland		WHL	59	2	28	30	275	7	0	1	1	13
82-83—Portland		WHL	56	1	30	31	187	14	1	3	4	57
83-84—Hershey		AHL	23	0	2	2	94	—	—	—	—	—
—Boston		NHL	16	1	1	2	57	3	0	0	0	7
84-85—Hershey		AHL	4	0	0	0	19	—	—	—	—	—
—Boston		NHL	56	0	1	1	158	—	—	—	—	—
85-86—Boston		NHL	43	2	5	7	192	2	0	0	0	4
86-87—New York Islanders		NHL	68	0	10	10	356	8	0	0	0	51
87-88—Springfield		AHL	8	1	0	1	43	—	—	—	—	—
—New York Islanders		NHL	22	0	1	1	68	—	—	—	—	—
—Toronto		NHL	7	0	1	1	19	6	0	0	0	41
88-89—Toronto		NHL	47	1	4	5	185	—	—	—	—	—
89-90—Toronto		NHL	72	2	9	11	301	5	0	1	1	19
90-91—Toronto		NHL	4	0	0	0	7	—	—	—	—	—
—Buffalo		NHL	17	0	1	1	43	—	—	—	—	—
—Newmarket		AHL	6	0	1	1	32	—	—	—	—	—
—Rochester		AHL	10	0	0	0	36	—	—	—	—	—
91-92—Buffalo		NHL	3	0	0	0	14	—	—	—	—	—
—Rochester		AHL	36	0	3	3	122	—	—	—	—	—
92-93—Cape Breton		AHL	61	2	24	26	223	12	0	3	3	12
93-94—Portland		AHL	46	1	6	7	247	15	0	1	1	59
—Washington		NHL	26	1	0	1	61	—	—	—	—	—
94-95—Portland		AHL	59	2	10	12	328	7	0	0	0	24
NHL totals			381	7	33	40	1461	24	0	1	1	122

CZERKAWSKI, MARIUSZ
RW, BRUINS

PERSONAL: Born April 13, 1972, in Radomski, Poland. . . . 5-11/185. . . . Shoots right. . . . Name pronounced MAIR-ee-uhz chuhr-KAH-skee.
TRANSACTIONS/CAREER NOTES: Selected by Boston Bruins (fifth Bruins pick, 106th overall) of NHL entry draft (June 22, 1991). . . . Played in Europe during 1994-95 NHL lockout.

			REGULAR SEASON					PLAYOFFS				
Season	Team	League	Gms.	G	A	Pts.	PIM	Gms.	G	A	Pts.	PIM
90-91—GKS Tychy		Poland	24	25	15	40	. . .	—	—	—	—	—
91-92—Djurgarden Stockholm		Sweden	39	8	5	13	4	3	0	0	0	2
—Polish Olympic Team		Int'l	5	0	1	1	4	—	—	—	—	—
92-93—Hammarby		Swed. Dv.II	32	39	30	69	74	—	—	—	—	—
93-94—Djurgarden Stockholm		Sweden	39	13	21	34	20	—	—	—	—	—
—Boston		NHL	4	2	1	3	0	13	3	3	6	4
94-95—Kiekko-Espoo		Finland	7	9	3	12	10	—	—	—	—	—
—Boston		NHL	47	12	14	26	31	5	1	0	1	0
NHL totals			51	14	15	29	31	18	4	3	7	4

DAFOE, BYRON
G, KINGS

PERSONAL: Born February 25, 1971, in Duncan, B.C. . . . 5-11/195. . . . Catches left. . . . Full name: Byron Jaromir Dafoe.
TRANSACTIONS/CAREER NOTES: Selected by Washington Capitals in second round (second Capitals pick, 35th overall) of NHL entry draft (June 17, 1989). . . . Underwent emergency appendectomy (December 1989). . . . Traded by Capitals with LW/C Dimitri Khristich to Los Angeles Kings for first- and fourth-round picks in 1996 draft (July 8, 1995).
HONORS: Shared Harry (Hap) Holmes Memorial Trophy with Olaf Kolzig (1993-94). . . . Named to AHL All-Star first team (1993-94).

			REGULAR SEASON						PLAYOFFS					
Season	Team	League	Gms.	Min.	W	L	T	GA	SO	Avg.	Gms.	Min.	W	L	GA	SO	Avg.
87-88—Juan de Fuca		BCJHL	32	1716	. . .	. . .	. . .	129	0	4.51	—	—	—	—	—	—	—
88-89—Portland		WHL	59	3279	29	24	3	*291	1	5.32	*18	*1091	10	8	*81	*1	4.45
89-90—Portland		WHL	40	2265	14	21	3	193	0	5.11	—	—	—	—	—	—	—
90-91—Portland		WHL	8	414	1	5	1	41	0	5.94	—	—	—	—	—	—	—
—Prince Albert		WHL	32	1839	13	12	4	124	0	4.05	—	—	—	—	—	—	—
91-92—New Haven		AHL	7	364	3	2	1	22	0	3.63	—	—	—	—	—	—	—
—Baltimore		AHL	33	1847	12	16	4	119	0	3.87	—	—	—	—	—	—	—
—Hampton Roads		ECHL	10	562	6	4	‡0	26	1	2.78	—	—	—	—	—	—	—

Season Team	League	REGULAR SEASON								PLAYOFFS						
		Gms.	Min.	W	L	T	GA	SO	Avg.	Gms.	Min.	W	L	GA	SO	Avg.
92-93—Baltimore	AHL	48	2617	16	*20	7	191	1	4.38	5	241	2	3	22	0	5.48
—Washington	NHL	1	1	0	0	0	0	0	0.00	—						
93-94—Portland	AHL	47	2662	24	16	4	148	1	3.34	1	9	0	0	1	0	6.67
—Washington	NHL	5	230	2	2	0	13	0	3.39	2	118	0	2	5	0	2.54
94-95—Portland	AHL	6	330	5	0	0	16	0	2.91	7	417	3	4	29	0	4.17
—Phoenix	IHL	49	2744	25	16	‡6	169	2	3.70	—						
—Washington	NHL	4	187	1	1	1	11	0	3.53	1	20	0	0	1	0	3.00
NHL totals		10	418	3	3	1	24	0	3.44	3	138	0	2	6	0	2.61

DAHL, KEVIN

D, FLAMES

PERSONAL: Born December 30, 1968, in Regina, Sask. . . . 5-11/190. . . . Shoots right.
COLLEGE: Bowling Green State (degree in physical education).
TRANSACTIONS/CAREER NOTES: Selected by Montreal Canadiens in 11th round (12th Canadiens pick, 230th overall) of NHL entry draft (June 11, 1988). . . . Signed as free agent by Calgary Flames (August 1, 1991). . . . Suffered charley horse (November 2, 1992); missed two games. . . . Injured heel (November 28, 1992); missed one game. . . . Strained left knee (December 15, 1992); missed 18 games. . . . Fractured left foot (April 9, 1993); missed one game. . . . Separated left shoulder (November 6, 1993); missed nine games. . . . Strained left shoulder (December 7, 1993); missed 30 games. . . . Separated left shoulder (February 16, 1995); missed two games. . . . Injured rib cartilage (March 31, 1995); missed seven games.
MISCELLANEOUS: Member of silver-medal-winning Canadian Olympic team (1992).

Season Team	League	REGULAR SEASON					PLAYOFFS				
		Gms.	G	A	Pts.	PIM	Gms.	G	A	Pts.	PIM
87-88—Bowling Green State	CCHA	44	2	23	25	78	—	—	—	—	—
88-89—Bowling Green State	CCHA	46	9	26	35	51	—	—	—	—	—
89-90—Bowling Green State	CCHA	43	8	22	30	74	—	—	—	—	—
90-91—Fredericton	AHL	32	1	15	16	45	9	0	1	1	11
—Winston-Salem	ECHL	36	7	17	24	58	—	—	—	—	—
91-92—Canadian national team	Int'l	45	2	15	17	44	—	—	—	—	—
—Canadian Olympic Team	Int'l	8	2	0	2	6	—	—	—	—	—
—Salt Lake City	IHL	13	0	2	2	12	5	0	0	0	13
92-93—Calgary	NHL	61	2	9	11	56	6	0	2	2	8
93-94—Calgary	NHL	33	0	3	3	23	6	0	0	0	4
—Saint John	AHL	2	0	0	0	0	—	—	—	—	—
94-95—Calgary	NHL	34	4	8	12	38	3	0	0	0	0
NHL totals		128	6	20	26	117	15	0	2	2	12

DAHLEN, ULF

RW, SHARKS

PERSONAL: Born January 12, 1967, in Ostersund, Sweden. . . . 6-3/200. . . . Shoots right. . . . Name pronounced DAH-lihn.
TRANSACTIONS/CAREER NOTES: Selected by New York Rangers in first round (first Rangers pick, seventh overall) of NHL entry draft (June 15, 1985). . . . Bruised shin (November 1987). . . . Bruised left shoulder (November 1988). . . . Separated right shoulder (January 1989). . . . Traded by Rangers with fourth-round pick in 1990 draft (C Cal McGowan) and future considerations to Minnesota North Stars for RW Mike Gartner (March 6, 1990). . . . North Stars franchise moved from Minnesota to Dallas and renamed Stars for 1993-94 season. . . . Traded by Stars with future considerations to San Jose Sharks for D Mike Lalor and D Doug Zmolek (March 19, 1994). . . . Suffered from the flu (February 20, 1995); missed two games.
STATISTICAL PLATEAUS: Three-goal games: 1987-88 (1), 1990-91 (1), 1992-93 (1), 1993-94 (1), 1993-94 (1). Total: 5.

Season Team	League	REGULAR SEASON					PLAYOFFS				
		Gms.	G	A	Pts.	PIM	Gms.	G	A	Pts.	PIM
83-84—Ostersund	Sweden	36	15	11	26	10	—	—	—	—	—
84-85—Ostersund	Sweden	36	33	26	59	20	—	—	—	—	—
85-86—Bjorkloven	Sweden	22	4	3	7	8	—	—	—	—	—
86-87—Bjorkloven	Sweden	31	9	12	21	20	6	6	2	8	4
87-88—New York Rangers	NHL	70	29	23	52	26	—	—	—	—	—
—Colorado	IHL	2	2	2	4	0	—	—	—	—	—
88-89—New York Rangers	NHL	56	24	19	43	50	4	0	0	0	0
89-90—New York Rangers	NHL	63	18	18	36	30	—	—	—	—	—
—Minnesota	NHL	13	2	4	6	0	7	1	4	5	2
90-91—Minnesota	NHL	66	21	18	39	6	15	2	6	8	4
91-92—Minnesota	NHL	79	36	30	66	10	7	0	3	3	2
92-93—Minnesota	NHL	83	35	39	74	6	—	—	—	—	—
93-94—Dallas	NHL	65	19	38	57	10	—	—	—	—	—
—San Jose	NHL	13	6	6	12	0	14	6	2	8	0
94-95—San Jose	NHL	46	11	23	34	11	11	5	4	9	0
NHL totals		554	201	218	419	149	58	14	19	33	8

DAHLQUIST, CHRIS

D, SENATORS

PERSONAL: Born December 14, 1962, in Fridley, Minn. . . . 6-1/196. . . . Shoots left. . . . Name pronounced DAHL-KWIHST.
COLLEGE: Lake Superior State (Mich.).
TRANSACTIONS/CAREER NOTES: Signed as free agent by Pittsburgh Penguins (May 1985). . . . Traded by Penguins with Jim Johnson to Minnesota North Stars for D Peter Taglianetti and D Larry Murphy (December 11, 1990). . . . Broke left wrist (January 1991). . . . Selected by Calgary Flames in NHL waiver draft (October 4, 1992). . . . Bruised ribs (November 11, 1992); missed five games. . . . Suffered charley horse (February 26, 1993); missed two games. . . . Signed as free agent by Ottawa Senators (July 4, 1994).

Season Team	League	REGULAR SEASON					PLAYOFFS				
		Gms.	G	A	Pts.	PIM	Gms.	G	A	Pts.	PIM
81-82—Lake Superior State........	CCHA	39	4	10	14	62	—	—	—	—	—
82-83—Lake Superior State........	CCHA	35	0	12	12	63	—	—	—	—	—
83-84—Lake Superior State........	CCHA	40	4	19	23	76	—	—	—	—	—
84-85—Lake Superior State........	CCHA	44	4	15	19	18	—	—	—	—	—
85-86—Baltimore......................	AHL	65	4	21	25	64	—	—	—	—	—
—Pittsburgh	NHL	5	1	2	3	2	—	—	—	—	—
86-87—Baltimore	AHL	51	1	16	17	50	—	—	—	—	—
—Pittsburgh	NHL	19	0	1	1	20	—	—	—	—	—
87-88—Pittsburgh	NHL	44	3	6	9	69	—	—	—	—	—
88-89—Pittsburgh	NHL	43	1	5	6	42	2	0	0	0	0
—Muskegon	IHL	10	3	6	9	14	—	—	—	—	—
89-90—Muskegon	IHL	6	1	1	2	8	—	—	—	—	—
—Pittsburgh	NHL	62	4	10	14	56	—	—	—	—	—
90-91—Pittsburgh	NHL	22	1	2	3	30	—	—	—	—	—
—Minnesota	NHL	42	2	6	8	33	23	1	6	7	20
91-92—Minnesota	NHL	74	1	13	14	68	7	0	0	0	6
92-93—Calgary	NHL	74	3	7	10	66	6	3	1	4	4
93-94—Calgary	NHL	77	1	11	12	52	1	0	0	0	0
94-95—Ottawa	NHL	46	1	7	8	36	—	—	—	—	—
NHL totals...............		508	18	70	88	474	39	4	7	11	30

DAIGLE, ALEXANDRE
C, SENATORS

PERSONAL: Born February 7, 1975, in Montreal. . . . 6-0/184. . . . Shoots left. . . . Name pronounced DAYG.

TRANSACTIONS/CAREER NOTES: Selected by Ottawa Senators in first round (first Senators pick, first overall) of NHL entry draft (June 26, 1993).

HONORS: Won Can.HL Rookie of the Year Award (1991-92). . . . Named QMJHL Rookie of the Year (1991-92). . . . Won Michel Bergeron Trophy (1991-92). . . . Named to Can.HL All-Rookie team (1991-92). . . . Named to the QMJHL All-Star second team (1991-92). . . . Won Can.HL Top Draft Prospect Award (1992-93). . . . Won QMJHL Top Draft Prospect Award (1992-93). . . . Named to QMJHL All-Star first team (1992-93).
STATISTICAL PLATEAUS: Three-goal games: 1994-95 (1).

Season Team	League	REGULAR SEASON					PLAYOFFS				
		Gms.	G	A	Pts.	PIM	Gms.	G	A	Pts.	PIM
91-92—Victoriaville......................	QMJHL	66	35	75	110	63	—	—	—	—	—
92-93—Victoriaville......................	QMJHL	53	45	92	137	85	6	5	6	11	4
93-94—Ottawa............................	NHL	84	20	31	51	40	—	—	—	—	—
94-95—Victoriaville......................	QMJHL	18	14	20	34	16	—	—	—	—	—
—Ottawa	NHL	47	16	21	37	14	—	—	—	—	—
NHL totals...............		131	36	52	88	54					

DAIGLE, SYLVAIN
G, JETS

PERSONAL: Born October 20, 1976, in St. Hyacinthe, Que. . . . 5-8/185. . . . Catches right.
TRANSACTIONS/CAREER NOTES: Selected by Winnipeg Jets in sixth round (seventh Jets pick, 136th overall) of NHL entry draft (July 8, 1995).

Season Team	League	REGULAR SEASON							PLAYOFFS						
		Gms.	Min.	W	L	T	GA	SO	Avg.	Gms.	Min.	W	L	GA	SO	Avg.
93-94—Shawinigan	QMJHL	31	1645	14	11	3	113	0	4.12	—	—	—	—	—	—	—
94-95—Shawinigan	QMJHL	48	2831	27	17	3	159	3	3.37	14	824	7	6	57	0	4.15

DAIGNEAULT, J.J.
D, CANADIENS

PERSONAL: Born October 12, 1965, in Montreal. . . . 5-11/199. . . . Shoots left. . . . Name pronounced DAYN-yoh.

TRANSACTIONS/CAREER NOTES: Underwent knee surgery (March 1984). . . . Selected by Vancouver Canucks as underage junior in first round (first Canucks pick, 10th overall) of NHL entry draft (June 1984). . . . Broke finger (March 19, 1986). . . . Traded by Canucks with second-round pick in 1986 draft (C Kent Hawley) and fifth-round pick in 1987 draft to Philadelphia Flyers for RW Rich Sutter, D Dave Richter and third-round pick (D Don Gibson) in 1986 draft (June 1986). . . . Sprained ankle (April 12, 1987). . . . Traded by Flyers to Montreal Canadiens for D Scott Sandelin (November 1988). . . . Bruised shoulder (December 1990). . . . Suffered left hip pointer (March 16, 1991). . . . Injured knee (April 7, 1991). . . . Bruised left knee (November 28, 1992); missed one game. . . . Injured shoulder (December 23, 1992); missed two games. . . . Sprained right ankle (March 1, 1993); missed 11 games. . . . Suffered injury (December 22, 1993); missed one game. . . . Suspended three games and fined $500 by NHL for elbowing (January 7, 1994). . . . Sprained wrist (January 10, 1994); missed six games. . . . Suffered sore back (March 1, 1994); missed one game. . . . Injured shoulder (February 4, 1995); missed one game. . . . Suffered from cold (February 13, 1995); missed one game. . . . Bruised ankle (April 12, 1995); missed one game.
HONORS: Won Emile (Butch) Bouchard Trophy (1982-83). . . . Named to QMJHL All-Star first team (1982-83).
MISCELLANEOUS: Member of Stanley Cup championship team (1993).

Season Team	League	REGULAR SEASON					PLAYOFFS				
		Gms.	G	A	Pts.	PIM	Gms.	G	A	Pts.	PIM
81-82—Laval	QMJHL	64	4	25	29	41	18	1	3	4	2
82-83—Longueuil	QMJHL	70	26	58	84	58	15	4	11	15	35
83-84—Canadian Olympic Team ..	Int'l	62	6	15	21	40	—	—	—	—	—
—Longueuil	QMJHL	10	2	11	13	6	14	3	13	16	30
84-85—Vancouver.......................	NHL	67	4	23	27	69	—	—	—	—	—
85-86—Vancouver.......................	NHL	64	5	23	28	45	3	0	2	2	0

Season Team	League	Gms.	G	A	Pts.	PIM	Gms.	G	A	Pts.	PIM
		REGULAR SEASON					**PLAYOFFS**				
86-87—Philadelphia	NHL	77	6	16	22	56	9	1	0	1	0
87-88—Philadelphia	NHL	28	2	2	4	12	—	—	—	—	—
—Hershey	AHL	10	1	5	6	8	—	—	—	—	—
88-89—Hershey	AHL	12	0	10	10	13	—	—	—	—	—
—Sherbrooke	AHL	63	10	33	43	48	6	1	3	4	2
89-90—Sherbrooke	AHL	28	8	19	27	18	—	—	—	—	—
—Montreal	NHL	36	2	10	12	14	9	0	0	0	2
90-91—Montreal	NHL	51	3	16	19	31	5	0	1	1	0
91-92—Montreal	NHL	79	4	14	18	36	11	0	3	3	4
92-93—Montreal	NHL	66	8	10	18	57	20	1	3	4	22
93-94—Montreal	NHL	68	2	12	14	73	7	0	1	1	12
94-95—Montreal	NHL	45	3	5	8	40	—	—	—	—	—
NHL totals		581	39	131	170	433	64	2	10	12	40

DALGARNO, BRAD
RW, ISLANDERS

PERSONAL: Born August 8, 1967, in Vancouver.... 6-3/217.... Shoots right.
TRANSACTIONS/CAREER NOTES: Selected by New York Islanders as underage junior in first round (first Islanders pick, sixth overall) of NHL entry draft (June 15, 1985).... Suffered concussion (November 1988).... Fractured orbital bone of left eye (February 21, 1989).... Sat out season in retirement (1989-90).... Bruised kidney (December 9, 1990); missed four games.... Lacerated jaw (January 13, 1991); missed three games.... Sprained left shoulder (November 27, 1991); missed four games. ... Reinjured left shoulder (December 11, 1991); missed seven games.... Fractured left wrist (January 12, 1992); missed final 37 games of season.... Underwent shoulder surgery (April 1, 1992).... Bruised shoulder (February 3, 1993); missed one game.... Strained hip flexor (November 9, 1993); missed 10 games.... Suffered hernia (January 21, 1995); missed eight games.... Suffered concussion (February 23, 1995); missed one game.

Season Team	League	Gms.	G	A	Pts.	PIM	Gms.	G	A	Pts.	PIM
		REGULAR SEASON					**PLAYOFFS**				
83-84—Markham	MTHL	40	17	11	28	59	—	—	—	—	—
84-85—Hamilton	OHL	66	23	30	53	86	—	—	—	—	—
85-86—Hamilton	OHL	54	22	43	65	79	—	—	—	—	—
—New York Islanders	NHL	2	1	0	1	0	—	—	—	—	—
86-87—Hamilton	OHL	60	27	32	59	100	—	—	—	—	—
—New York Islanders	NHL	—	—	—	—	—	1	0	1	1	0
87-88—New York Islanders	NHL	38	2	8	10	58	4	0	0	0	19
—Springfield	AHL	39	13	11	24	76	—	—	—	—	—
88-89—New York Islanders	NHL	55	11	10	21	86	—	—	—	—	—
89-90—						Did not play—retired.					
90-91—New York Islanders	NHL	41	3	12	15	24	—	—	—	—	—
—Capital District	AHL	27	6	14	20	26	—	—	—	—	—
91-92—Capital District	AHL	14	7	8	15	34	—	—	—	—	—
—New York Islanders	NHL	15	2	1	3	12	—	—	—	—	—
92-93—Capital District	AHL	19	10	4	14	16	—	—	—	—	—
—New York Islanders	NHL	57	15	17	32	62	18	2	2	4	14
93-94—New York Islanders	NHL	73	11	19	30	62	4	0	1	1	4
94-95—New York Islanders	NHL	22	3	2	5	14	—	—	—	—	—
NHL totals		303	48	69	117	318	27	2	4	6	37

DAMEWORTH, CHAD
D, OILERS

PERSONAL: Born July 6, 1972, in Marquette, Mich.... 6-2/200.... Shoots left.
HIGH SCHOOL: Marquette (Mich.).
COLLEGE: Northern Michigan.
TRANSACTIONS/CAREER NOTES: Selected by Edmonton Oilers in first round (first Oilers pick, sixth overall) of NHL supplemental draft (June 28, 1994).

Season Team	League	Gms.	G	A	Pts.	PIM	Gms.	G	A	Pts.	PIM
		REGULAR SEASON					**PLAYOFFS**				
91-92—Northern Michigan Univ.	WCHA	13	0	2	2	8	—	—	—	—	—
92-93—Northern Michigan Univ.	WCHA	29	0	2	2	22	—	—	—	—	—
93-94—Northern Michigan Univ.	WCHA	36	0	4	4	26	—	—	—	—	—
94-95—Northern Michigan Univ.	WCHA	39	0	4	4	46	—	—	—	—	—
—Cape Breton	AHL	1	0	0	0	0	—	—	—	—	—

DAMPHOUSSE, VINCENT
LW, CANADIENS

PERSONAL: Born December 17, 1967, in Montreal.... 6-1/199.... Shoots left.... Name pronounced dahm-FOOZ.
TRANSACTIONS/CAREER NOTES: Selected by Toronto Maple Leafs as underage junior in first round (first Maple Leafs pick, sixth overall) of NHL entry draft (June 21, 1986).... Traded by Maple Leafs with D Luke Richardson, G Peter Ing, C Scott Thornton and future considerations to Edmonton Oilers for G Grant Fuhr, LW/RW Glenn Anderson and LW Craig Berube (September 19, 1991).... Traded by Oilers with fourth-round pick in 1993 draft (D Adam Wiesel) to Montreal Canadiens for LW Shayne Corson, LW Vladimir Vujtek and C Brent Gilchrist (August 27, 1992).... Played in Europe during 1994-95 NHL lockout.
HONORS: Named to QMJHL All-Star second team (1985-86).... Played in NHL All-Star Game (1991 and 1992).... Named All-Star Game Most Valuable Player (1991).
RECORDS: Shares NHL All-Star single-game record for most goals—4 (1991).
STATISTICAL PLATEAUS: Three-goal games: 1988-89 (1), 1989-90 (2), 1992-93 (2), 1993-94 (2). Total: 7.... Four-goal games: 1991-92 (1).... Total hat tricks: 8.
MISCELLANEOUS: Member of Stanley Cup championship team (1993).

Season Team	League	REGULAR SEASON					PLAYOFFS				
		Gms.	G	A	Pts.	PIM	Gms.	G	A	Pts.	PIM
83-84—Laval	QMJHL	66	29	36	65	25	—	—	—	—	—
84-85—Laval	QMJHL	68	35	68	103	62	—	—	—	—	—
85-86—Laval	QMJHL	69	45	110	155	70	14	9	27	36	12
86-87—Toronto	NHL	80	21	25	46	26	12	1	5	6	8
87-88—Toronto	NHL	75	12	36	48	40	6	0	1	1	10
88-89—Toronto	NHL	80	26	42	68	75	—	—	—	—	—
89-90—Toronto	NHL	80	33	61	94	56	5	0	2	2	2
90-91—Toronto	NHL	79	26	47	73	65	—	—	—	—	—
91-92—Edmonton	NHL	80	38	51	89	53	16	6	8	14	8
92-93—Montreal	NHL	84	39	58	97	98	20	11	12	23	16
93-94—Montreal	NHL	84	40	51	91	75	7	1	2	3	8
94-95—Ratingen	Germany	11	5	6	11	24	—	—	—	—	—
—Montreal	NHL	48	10	30	40	42	—	—	—	—	—
NHL totals		690	245	401	646	530	66	19	30	49	52

DANDENAULT, MATHIEU
RW, RED WINGS

PERSONAL: Born February 3, 1976, in Magog, Que. . . . 6-0/174. . . . Shoots right. . . . Name pronounced dan-dehn-OH. . . . Cousin of Eric Dandenault, defenseman in Philadelphia Flyers system.
HIGH SCHOOL: CEGEP de Sherbrooke (Que.).

TRANSACTIONS/CAREER NOTES: Selected by Detroit Red Wings in second round (second Red Wings pick, 49th overall) of NHL entry draft (June 28, 1994).

Season Team	League	REGULAR SEASON					PLAYOFFS				
		Gms.	G	A	Pts.	PIM	Gms.	G	A	Pts.	PIM
91-92—Gloucester	OPJHL	6	3	4	7	0	—	—	—	—	—
92-93—Gloucester	OPJHL	55	11	26	37	64	—	—	—	—	—
93-94—Sherbrooke	QMJHL	67	17	36	53	67	12	4	10	14	12
94-95—Sherbrooke	QMJHL	67	37	70	107	76	7	1	7	8	10

DANEYKO, KEN
D, DEVILS

PERSONAL: Born April 17, 1964, in Windsor, Ont. . . . 6-0/210. . . . Shoots left. . . . Name pronounced DAN-ih-KOH.
TRANSACTIONS/CAREER NOTES: Selected by Seattle Breakers from Spokane Flyers in WHL dispersal draft (December 1981). . . . Selected by New Jersey Devils as underage junior in first round (second Devils pick, 18th overall) of NHL entry draft (June 1982). . . . Fractured right fibula (November 2, 1983). . . . Suspended one game and fined $500 by NHL for playing in West Germany without permission (October 1985). . . . Injured wrist (February 25, 1987). . . . Broke nose (February 24, 1988). . . . Injured shoulder (March 29, 1994); missed six games. . . . Injured knee (March 8, 1995); missed 23 games.
MISCELLANEOUS: Member of Stanley Cup championship team (1995).

Season Team	League	REGULAR SEASON					PLAYOFFS				
		Gms.	G	A	Pts.	PIM	Gms.	G	A	Pts.	PIM
80-81—Spokane Flyers	WHL	62	6	13	19	140	4	0	0	0	6
81-82—Spokane Flyers	WHL	26	1	11	12	147	—	—	—	—	—
—Seattle	WHL	38	1	22	23	151	14	1	9	10	49
82-83—Seattle	WHL	69	17	43	60	150	4	1	3	4	14
83-84—Kamloops	WHL	19	6	28	34	52	17	4	9	13	28
—New Jersey	NHL	11	1	4	5	17	—	—	—	—	—
84-85—New Jersey	NHL	1	0	0	0	10	—	—	—	—	—
—Maine	AHL	80	4	9	13	206	11	1	3	4	36
85-86—Maine	AHL	21	3	2	5	75	—	—	—	—	—
—New Jersey	NHL	44	0	10	10	100	—	—	—	—	—
86-87—New Jersey	NHL	79	2	12	14	183	—	—	—	—	—
87-88—New Jersey	NHL	80	5	7	12	239	20	1	6	7	83
88-89—New Jersey	NHL	80	5	5	10	283	—	—	—	—	—
89-90—New Jersey	NHL	74	6	15	21	216	6	2	0	2	21
90-91—New Jersey	NHL	80	4	16	20	249	7	0	1	1	10
91-92—New Jersey	NHL	80	1	7	8	170	7	0	3	3	16
92-93—New Jersey	NHL	84	2	11	13	236	5	0	0	0	8
93-94—New Jersey	NHL	78	1	9	10	176	20	0	1	1	45
94-95—New Jersey	NHL	25	1	2	3	54	20	1	0	1	22
NHL totals		716	28	98	126	1933	85	4	11	15	205

DANIELS, JEFF
LW, WHALERS

PERSONAL: Born June 24, 1968, in Oshawa, Ont. . . . 6-1/200. . . . Shoots left.
TRANSACTIONS/CAREER NOTES: Selected by Pittsburgh Penguins as underage junior in sixth round (sixth Penguins pick, 109th overall) of NHL entry draft (June 21, 1986). . . . Traded by Penguins to Florida Panthers for D Greg Hawgood (March 19, 1994). . . . Loaned by Panthers to Detroit Vipers (February 14, 1995). . . . Signed as free agent by Hartford Whalers (July 18, 1995).
MISCELLANEOUS: Member of Stanley Cup championship team (1992).

Season Team	League	REGULAR SEASON					PLAYOFFS				
		Gms.	G	A	Pts.	PIM	Gms.	G	A	Pts.	PIM
84-85—Oshawa	OHL	59	7	11	18	16	—	—	—	—	—
85-86—Oshawa	OHL	62	13	19	32	23	6	0	1	1	0
86-87—Oshawa	OHL	54	14	9	23	22	15	3	2	5	5

Season	Team	League	REGULAR SEASON					PLAYOFFS				
			Gms.	G	A	Pts.	PIM	Gms.	G	A	Pts.	PIM
87-88—Oshawa	OHL	64	29	39	68	59	4	2	3	5	0
88-89—Muskegon	IHL	58	21	21	42	58	11	3	5	8	11
89-90—Muskegon	IHL	80	30	47	77	39	6	1	1	2	7
90-91—Pittsburgh	NHL	11	0	2	2	2	—	—	—	—	—
—Muskegon	IHL	62	23	29	52	18	5	1	3	4	2
91-92—Pittsburgh	NHL	2	0	0	0	0	—	—	—	—	—
—Muskegon	IHL	44	19	16	35	38	10	5	4	9	9
92-93—Pittsburgh	NHL	58	5	4	9	14	12	3	2	5	0
—Cleveland	IHL	3	2	1	3	0	—	—	—	—	—
93-94—Pittsburgh	NHL	63	3	5	8	20	—	—	—	—	—
—Florida	NHL	7	0	0	0	0	—	—	—	—	—
94-95—Florida	NHL	3	0	0	0	0	—	—	—	—	—
—Detroit	IHL	25	8	12	20	6	5	1	0	1	0
NHL totals		144	8	11	19	36	12	3	2	5	0

DANIELS, SCOTT
LW, WHALERS

PERSONAL: Born September 19, 1969, in Prince Albert, Sask.... 6-3/200.... Shoots left.
TRANSACTIONS/CAREER NOTES: Traded by Kamloops Blazers with C Mario Desjardins, Wayne MacDonald, Jason Bennings and future considerations to New Westminster Bruins for C Glenn Mulvenna and D Garth Premak (February 1987).... Selected by Hartford Whalers in seventh round (sixth Whalers pick, 136th overall) of NHL entry draft (June 17, 1989).... Injured knee (March 25, 1995); missed seven games.

Season	Team	League	REGULAR SEASON					PLAYOFFS				
			Gms.	G	A	Pts.	PIM	Gms.	G	A	Pts.	PIM
86-87—Kamloops	WHL	43	6	4	10	66	—	—	—	—	—
—New Westminster	WHL	19	4	7	11	30	—	—	—	—	—
87-88—New Westminster	WHL	37	6	11	17	157	—	—	—	—	—
—Regina	WHL	19	2	3	5	83	—	—	—	—	—
88-89—Regina	WHL	64	21	26	47	241	—	—	—	—	—
89-90—Regina	WHL	53	28	31	59	171	—	—	—	—	—
90-91—Springfield	AHL	40	2	6	8	121	—	—	—	—	—
—Louisville	ECHL	9	5	3	8	34	1	0	2	2	0
91-92—Springfield	AHL	54	7	15	22	213	10	0	0	0	32
92-93—Hartford	NHL	1	0	0	0	19	—	—	—	—	—
—Springfield	AHL	60	11	12	23	181	12	2	7	9	12
93-94—Springfield	AHL	52	9	11	20	185	6	0	1	1	53
94-95—Springfield	AHL	48	9	5	14	277	—	—	—	—	—
—Hartford	NHL	12	0	2	2	55	—	—	—	—	—
NHL totals		13	0	2	2	74					

DARBY, CRAIG
C, ISLANDERS

PERSONAL: Born September 26, 1972, in Oneida, N.Y.... 6-3/180.... Shoots right.
HIGH SCHOOL: Albany (N.Y.) Academy.
COLLEGE: Providence.
TRANSACTIONS/CAREER NOTES: Selected by Montreal Canadiens in second round (third Canadiens pick, 43rd overall) of NHL entry draft (June 22, 1991).... Traded by Canadiens with LW Kirk Muller and D Mathieu Schneider to New York Islanders for D Vladimir Malakhov and C Pierre Turgeon (April 5, 1995).
HONORS: Named Hockey East co-Rookie of the Year with Ian Moran (1991-92).... Named to Hockey East All-Rookie team (1991-92).

Season	Team	League	REGULAR SEASON					PLAYOFFS				
			Gms.	G	A	Pts.	PIM	Gms.	G	A	Pts.	PIM
89-90—Albany Academy	N.Y. H.S.	29	32	53	85	...					
90-91—Albany Academy	N.Y. H.S.	27	33	61	94	53	—	—	—	—	—
91-92—Providence College	Hockey East	35	17	24	41	47	—	—	—	—	—
92-93—Providence College	Hockey East	35	11	21	32	62	—	—	—	—	—
93-94—Fredericton	AHL	66	23	33	56	51	—	—	—	—	—
94-95—Fredericton	AHL	64	21	47	68	82	—	—	—	—	—
—Montreal	NHL	10	0	2	2	0	—	—	—	—	—
—New York Islanders	NHL	3	0	0	0	0	—	—	—	—	—
NHL totals		13	0	2	2	0					

DAVIDSON, MATT
RW, SABRES

PERSONAL: Born August 9, 1977, in Flin Flon, Man.... 6-2/190.... Shoots right.
HIGH SCHOOL: Beaverton (Ore.).
TRANSACTIONS/CAREER NOTES: Selected by Buffalo Sabres in fourth round (fifth Sabres pick, 94th overall) of NHL entry draft (July 8, 1995).

Season	Team	League	REGULAR SEASON					PLAYOFFS				
			Gms.	G	A	Pts.	PIM	Gms.	G	A	Pts.	PIM
93-94—Portland	WHL	59	4	12	16	18	10	0	0	0	4
94-95—Portland	WHL	72	17	20	37	51	9	1	3	4	0

DAVIDSSON, JOHAN
C, MIGHTY DUCKS

PERSONAL: Born January 6, 1976, in Jonkoping, Sweden.... 5-11/170.... Shoots left.

TRANSACTIONS/CAREER NOTES: Selected by Mighty Ducks of Anaheim in second round (second Mighty Ducks pick, 28th overall) of NHL entry draft (June 28, 1994).

Season	Team	League	REGULAR SEASON					PLAYOFFS				
			Gms.	G	A	Pts.	PIM	Gms.	G	A	Pts.	PIM
92-93	HV 71 Jonkoping	Sweden	8	1	0	1	0	—	—	—	—	—
93-94	HV 71 Jonkoping	Sweden	38	2	5	7	4	—	—	—	—	—
94-95	HV 71 Jonkoping	Sweden	37	4	7	11	20	13	3	2	5	0

DAVYDOV, EVGENY
LW

PERSONAL: Born May 27, 1967, in Chelyabinsk, U.S.S.R.... 6-0/200.... Shoots right. ...Name pronounced yehv-GEH-nee DAY-vuh-dahf.

TRANSACTIONS/CAREER NOTES: Selected by Winnipeg Jets in 12th round (14th Jets pick, 235th overall) of NHL entry draft (June 17, 1989).... Traded by Jets with future draft pick to Florida Panthers for future draft pick (September 30, 1993).... Suffered from the flu (November 10, 1993); missed one game.... Suffered from the flu (December 27, 1993); missed one game.... Traded by Panthers with C Scott Levins and sixth-round pick in 1994 draft (D Mike Gaffney) to Ottawa Senators for RW Bob Kudelski (January 6, 1994).... Injured wrist (April 14, 1994); missed one game.... Traded by San Diego Gulls to Chicago Wolves for LW Todd Gillingham (February 26, 1995).... Injured eye (April 26, 1995); missed two games.

STATISTICAL PLATEAUS: Three-goal games: 1992-93 (1).

MISCELLANEOUS: Member of gold-medal-winning Unified Olympic team (1992).

Season	Team	League	REGULAR SEASON					PLAYOFFS				
			Gms.	G	A	Pts.	PIM	Gms.	G	A	Pts.	PIM
84-85	Chelyabinsk	USSR	5	1	0	1	2	—	—	—	—	—
85-86	Chelyabinsk	USSR	39	11	5	16	22	—	—	—	—	—
86-87	CSKA Moscow	USSR	32	11	2	13	8	—	—	—	—	—
87-88	CSKA Moscow	USSR	44	16	7	23	18	—	—	—	—	—
88-89	CSKA Moscow	USSR	35	9	7	16	4	—	—	—	—	—
89-90	CSKA Moscow	USSR	44	17	6	23	16	—	—	—	—	—
90-91	CSKA Moscow	USSR	44	10	10	20	26	—	—	—	—	—
91-92	CSKA Moscow	CIS	27	13	12	25	14	—	—	—	—	—
	—Unified Olympic Team	Int'l	8	3	3	6	2	—	—	—	—	—
	—Winnipeg	NHL	12	4	3	7	8	7	2	2	4	2
92-93	—Winnipeg	NHL	79	28	21	49	66	4	0	0	0	0
93-94	—Florida	NHL	21	2	6	8	8	—	—	—	—	—
	—Ottawa	NHL	40	5	7	12	38	—	—	—	—	—
94-95	—San Diego	IHL	11	2	1	3	14	—	—	—	—	—
	—Chicago	IHL	18	10	12	22	26	3	1	0	1	0
	—Ottawa	NHL	3	1	2	3	0	—	—	—	—	—
NHL totals			155	40	39	79	120	11	2	2	4	2

DAWE, JASON
LW/RW, SABRES

PERSONAL: Born May 29, 1973, in North York, Ont.... 5-10/195.... Shoots left.... Name pronounced DAW.

TRANSACTIONS/CAREER NOTES: Tore ankle ligaments (September 1989).... Selected by Buffalo Sabres in second round (second Sabres pick, 35th overall) of NHL entry draft (June 22, 1991). ... Slightly sprained knee (February 11, 1995); missed three games.

HONORS: Won George Parsons Trophy (1992-93).... Named to Can.HL All-Star second team (1992-93).... Named to OHL All-Star first team (1992-93).

Season	Team	League	REGULAR SEASON					PLAYOFFS				
			Gms.	G	A	Pts.	PIM	Gms.	G	A	Pts.	PIM
89-90	Peterborough	OHL	50	15	18	33	19	12	4	7	11	4
90-91	Peterborough	OHL	66	43	27	70	43	4	3	1	4	0
91-92	Peterborough	OHL	66	53	55	108	55	4	5	0	5	0
92-93	Peterborough	OHL	59	58	68	126	80	21	18	33	51	18
	—Rochester	AHL	0	0	0	0	0	3	1	0	1	0
93-94	—Rochester	AHL	48	22	14	36	44	—	—	—	—	—
	—Buffalo	NHL	32	6	7	13	12	6	0	1	1	6
94-95	—Rochester	AHL	44	27	19	46	24	—	—	—	—	—
	—Buffalo	NHL	42	7	4	11	19	5	2	1	3	6
NHL totals			74	13	11	24	31	11	2	2	4	12

DAZE, ERIC
LW, BLACKHAWKS

PERSONAL: Born July 2, 1975, in Montreal.... 6-4/202.... Shoots left.

TRANSACTIONS/CAREER NOTES: Selected by Chicago Blackhawks in fourth round (fifth Blackhawks pick, 90th overall) of NHL entry draft (June 26, 1993).

HONORS: Named to QMJHL All-Star first team (1993-94 and 1994-95).... Won Can.HL Most Sportsmanlike Player of the Year Award (1994-95).... Won Frank J. Selke Trophy (1994-95).

Season	Team	League	REGULAR SEASON					PLAYOFFS				
			Gms.	G	A	Pts.	PIM	Gms.	G	A	Pts.	PIM
92-93	Beauport	QMJHL	68	19	36	55	24	—	—	—	—	—
93-94	Beauport	QMJHL	66	59	48	107	31	15	16	8	24	2
94-95	Beauport	QMJHL	57	54	45	99	20	16	9	12	21	23
	—Chicago	NHL	4	1	1	2	2	16	0	1	1	4
NHL totals			4	1	1	2	2	16	0	1	1	4

DEADMARSH, ADAM
RW, DENVER

PERSONAL: Born May 10, 1975, in Trail, B.C. . . . . 6-0 / 195. . . . Shoots right.
HIGH SCHOOL: Lakeridge (Fruitvale, B.C.).
TRANSACTIONS/CAREER NOTES: Selected by Quebec Nordiques in first round (second Nordiques pick, 14th overall) of NHL entry draft (June 26, 1993). . . . Nordiques franchise moved to Denver for 1995-96 season.

Season	Team	League	REGULAR SEASON					PLAYOFFS				
			Gms.	G	A	Pts.	PIM	Gms.	G	A	Pts.	PIM
91-92	Portland	WHL	68	30	30	60	81	6	3	3	6	13
92-93	Portland	WHL	58	33	36	69	126	16	7	8	15	29
93-94	Portland	WHL	65	43	56	99	212	10	9	8	17	33
94-95	Portland	WHL	29	28	20	48	129	—	—	—	—	—
	Quebec	NHL	48	9	8	17	56	6	0	1	1	0
	NHL totals		48	9	8	17	56	6	0	1	1	0

DEAN, KEVIN
D, DEVILS

PERSONAL: Born April 1, 1969, in Madison, Wis. . . . 6-2 / 195. . . . Shoots left.
HIGH SCHOOL: Culver (Ind.) Military Academy.
COLLEGE: New Hampshire.
TRANSACTIONS/CAREER NOTES: Selected by New Jersey Devils in fourth round (fourth Devils pick, 86th overall) of NHL entry draft (June 13, 1987).
HONORS: Named to AHL All-Star first team (1994-95).
MISCELLANEOUS: Member of Stanley Cup championship team (1995).

Season	Team	League	REGULAR SEASON					PLAYOFFS				
			Gms.	G	A	Pts.	PIM	Gms.	G	A	Pts.	PIM
85-86	Culver Military Academy	Indiana H.S.	35	28	44	72	48	—	—	—	—	—
86-87	Culver Military Academy	Indiana H.S.	25	19	25	44	30	—	—	—	—	—
87-88	Univ. of New Hampshire	Hockey East	27	1	6	7	34	—	—	—	—	—
88-89	Univ. of New Hampshire	Hockey East	34	1	12	13	28	—	—	—	—	—
89-90	Univ. of New Hampshire	Hockey East	39	2	6	8	42	—	—	—	—	—
90-91	Univ. of New Hampshire	Hockey East	31	10	12	22	22	—	—	—	—	—
	Utica	AHL	7	0	1	1	2	—	—	—	—	—
91-92	Utica	AHL	23	0	3	3	6	—	—	—	—	—
	Cincinnati	ECHL	30	3	22	25	43	9	1	6	7	8
92-93	Utica	AHL	57	2	16	18	76	5	1	0	1	8
	Cincinnati	IHL	13	2	1	3	15	—	—	—	—	—
93-94	Albany	AHL	70	9	33	42	92	5	0	2	2	7
94-95	Albany	AHL	68	5	37	42	66	8	0	4	4	4
	New Jersey	NHL	17	0	1	1	4	3	0	2	2	0
	NHL totals		17	0	1	1	4	3	0	2	2	0

DEAZELEY, MARK
LW, JETS

PERSONAL: Born April 8, 1972, in North York, Ont. . . . 6-4 / 240. . . . Shoots left. . . . Name pronounced DEES-lee.
TRANSACTIONS/CAREER NOTES: Signed as free agent by Winnipeg Jets (June 17, 1994).

Season	Team	League	REGULAR SEASON					PLAYOFFS				
			Gms.	G	A	Pts.	PIM	Gms.	G	A	Pts.	PIM
89-90	Oshawa Jr. B	OHA	17	4	10	14	51	—	—	—	—	—
	Oshawa	OHL	27	3	1	4	56	—	—	—	—	—
90-91	Oshawa	OHL	65	17	19	36	149	16	1	2	3	38
91-92	Oshawa	OHL	66	19	21	40	215	7	0	0	0	16
92-93	Toledo	ECHL	63	27	18	45	263	15	8	6	14	66
93-94	Toledo	ECHL	57	41	36	77	231	14	16	10	26	37
	Fort Wayne	IHL	1	0	0	0	2	—	—	—	—	—
94-95	Toledo	ECHL	14	5	1	6	136	—	—	—	—	—
	Springfield	AHL	26	2	0	2	141	—	—	—	—	—

DeBRUSK, LOUIE
LW, OILERS

PERSONAL: Born March 19, 1971, in Cambridge, Ont. . . . 6-2 / 215. . . . Shoots left. . . . Full name: Dennis Louis DeBrusk. . . . Name pronounced duh-BRUHSK.
HIGH SCHOOL: Saugeen (Port Elgin, Ont.).
TRANSACTIONS/CAREER NOTES: Selected by New York Rangers in third round (fourth Rangers pick, 49th overall) of NHL entry draft (June 17, 1989). . . . Traded by Rangers with C Bernie Nicholls, RW Steven Rice and future considerations to Edmonton Oilers for C Mark Messier and future considerations (October 4, 1991); Rangers traded D David Shaw to Oilers for D Jeff Beukeboom to complete deal (November 12, 1991). . . . Separated shoulder (January 28, 1992); missed four games. . . . Strained groin (January 1993); missed five games. . . . Strained abdominal muscle (January 1993); missed 11 games. . . . Underwent blood tests (April 17, 1995); missed one game.

Season	Team	League	REGULAR SEASON					PLAYOFFS				
			Gms.	G	A	Pts.	PIM	Gms.	G	A	Pts.	PIM
87-88	Stratford Jr. B	OHA	43	13	14	27	205	—	—	—	—	—
88-89	London	OHL	59	11	11	22	149	19	1	1	2	43
89-90	London	OHL	61	21	19	40	198	6	2	2	4	24
90-91	London	OHL	61	31	33	64	*223	7	2	2	4	14
	Binghamton	AHL	2	0	0	0	7	2	0	0	0	9
91-92	Edmonton	NHL	25	2	1	3	124	—	—	—	—	—
	Cape Breton	AHL	28	2	2	4	73	—	—	—	—	—
92-93	Edmonton	NHL	51	8	2	10	205	—	—	—	—	—

Season	Team	League	Gms.	G	A	Pts.	PIM	Gms.	G	A	Pts.	PIM
			REGULAR SEASON					PLAYOFFS				
93-94—Edmonton		NHL	48	4	6	10	185	—	—	—	—	—
—Cape Breton		AHL	5	3	1	4	58	—	—	—	—	—
94-95—Edmonton		NHL	34	2	0	2	93	—	—	—	—	—
NHL totals			158	16	9	25	607					

DeGRAY, DALE
D

PERSONAL: Born September 3, 1963, in Oshawa, Ont. . . . 6-0/206. . . . Shoots right. . . . Full name: Dale Edward DeGray.

TRANSACTIONS/CAREER NOTES: Selected by Calgary Flames as underage junior in eighth round (seventh Flames pick, 162nd overall) of NHL entry draft (June 10, 1981). . . . Traded by Flames to Toronto Maple Leafs for future considerations (September 1987). . . . Separated left shoulder (January 1988); missed 15 games. . . . Selected by Los Angeles Kings in 1988 NHL waiver draft for $12,500 (October 3, 1988). . . . Sprained knee (October 1988). . . . Suffered concussion (December 1988). . . . Traded by Kings to Buffalo Sabres for D Bob Halkidis (November 24, 1989). . . . Signed as free agent by San Diego Gulls (August 27, 1992). . . . Signed as free agent by Detroit Vipers (1994). . . . Traded by Vipers to Cleveland Lumberjacks to complete earlier trade (November 16, 1994).

HONORS: Named to AHL All-Star second team (1984-85). . . . Named to IHL All-Star second team (1992-93 and 1994-95).

Season	Team	League	Gms.	G	A	Pts.	PIM	Gms.	G	A	Pts.	PIM
			REGULAR SEASON					PLAYOFFS				
79-80—Oshawa Jr. B		ODHA	42	14	14	28	34	—	—	—	—	—
—Oshawa		OMJHL	1	0	0	0	2	—	—	—	—	—
80-81—Oshawa		OMJHL	61	11	10	21	93	8	1	1	2	19
81-82—Oshawa		OHL	66	11	22	33	162	12	3	4	7	49
82-83—Oshawa		OHL	69	20	30	50	149	17	7	7	14	36
83-84—Colorado		CHL	67	16	14	30	67	6	1	1	2	2
84-85—Moncton		AHL	77	24	37	61	63	—	—	—	—	—
85-86—Moncton		AHL	76	10	31	41	128	6	0	1	1	0
—Calgary		NHL	1	0	0	0	0	—	—	—	—	—
86-87—Moncton		AHL	45	10	22	32	57	5	2	1	3	19
—Calgary		NHL	27	6	7	13	29	—	—	—	—	—
87-88—Toronto		NHL	56	6	18	24	63	5	0	1	1	16
—Newmarket		AHL	8	2	10	12	8	—	—	—	—	—
88-89—Los Angeles		NHL	63	6	22	28	97	8	1	2	3	12
89-90—New Haven		AHL	16	2	10	12	38	—	—	—	—	—
—Rochester		AHL	50	6	25	31	118	17	5	6	11	59
—Buffalo		NHL	6	0	0	0	6	—	—	—	—	—
90-91—Rochester		AHL	64	9	25	34	121	15	3	4	7	*76
91-92—Alleghe		Italy	27	6	24	30	46	—	—	—	—	—
92-93—San Diego		IHL	79	18	64	82	181	14	3	11	14	77
93-94—San Diego		IHL	80	20	50	70	163	9	2	1	3	8
94-95—Detroit		IHL	14	1	8	9	18	—	—	—	—	—
—Cleveland		IHL	64	19	49	68	134	4	0	4	4	10
NHL totals			153	18	47	65	195	13	1	3	4	28

DELISLE, JONATHAN
RW, CANADIENS

PERSONAL: Born June 30, 1977, in Montreal. . . . 5-10/186. . . . Shoots right.
TRANSACTIONS/CAREER NOTES: Selected by Montreal Canadiens in fourth round (fourth Canadiens pick, 86th overall) of NHL entry draft (July 8, 1995).

Season	Team	League	Gms.	G	A	Pts.	PIM	Gms.	G	A	Pts.	PIM
			REGULAR SEASON					PLAYOFFS				
93-94—Verdun		QMJHL	61	16	17	33	130	4	0	1	1	14
94-95—Hull		QMJHL	60	21	38	59	218	19	11	8	19	43

DEMITRA, PAVOL
LW, SENATORS

PERSONAL: Born November 29, 1974, in Dubnica, Czechoslovakia. . . . 6-0/184. . . . Shoots left. . . . Name pronounced PA-vuhl dih-MEE-truh.
TRANSACTIONS/CAREER NOTES: Selected by Ottawa Senators in ninth round (ninth Senators pick, 227th overall) of NHL entry draft (June 26, 1993). . . . Broke ankle (October 14, 1993); missed 23 games.

Season	Team	League	Gms.	G	A	Pts.	PIM	Gms.	G	A	Pts.	PIM
			REGULAR SEASON					PLAYOFFS				
91-92—Sparta Dubnica		Czech Dv.II	28	13	10	23	12	—	—	—	—	—
92-93—Dukla Trencin		Czech.	46	11	17	28	0	—	—	—	—	—
—CAPEH Dubnica		Czech Dv.II	4	3	0	3	. . .	—	—	—	—	—
93-94—Ottawa		NHL	12	1	1	2	4	—	—	—	—	—
—Prince Edward Island		AHL	41	18	23	41	8	—	—	—	—	—
94-95—Prince Edward Island		AHL	61	26	48	74	23	5	0	7	7	0
—Ottawa		NHL	16	4	3	7	0	—	—	—	—	—
NHL totals			28	5	4	9	4					

DENIS, MARC
G, DENVER

PERSONAL: Born August 1, 1977, in Montreal. . . . 6-0/188. . . . Catches left.
TRANSACTIONS/CAREER NOTES: Selected by Denver in first round (first Denver pick, 25th overall) of NHL entry draft (July 8, 1995).

Season Team	League	REGULAR SEASON							PLAYOFFS					
		Gms.	Min.	W	L	T	GA	SO	Avg.	Gms.	Min.	W	L	GA	SO	Avg.
94-95—Chicoutimi	QMJHL	32	1688	17	9	1	98	0	3.48	6	374	4	2	19	1	3.05

DeROUVILLE, PHILLIPPE
G, PENGUINS

PERSONAL: Born August 7, 1974, in Arthabaska, Que. . . . 6-1/185. . . . Catches left.

TRANSACTIONS/CAREER NOTES: Selected by Pittsburgh Penguins in fifth round (fifth Penguins pick, 115th overall) of NHL entry draft (June 20, 1992). . . . Suffered from mild case of mononucleosis (February 16, 1995); missed seven games.

HONORS: Won Raymond Lagace Trophy (1991-92). . . . Named to QMJHL All-Star second team (1992-93 and 1993-94). . . . Won Jacques Plante Trophy (1993-94).

Season Team	League	REGULAR SEASON							PLAYOFFS					
		Gms.	Min.	W	L	T	GA	SO	Avg.	Gms.	Min.	W	L	GA	SO	Avg.
90-91—Longueuil	QMJHL	20	1030	13	6	0	50	0	2.91	—	—	—	—	—	—	—
91-92—Longueuil	QMJHL	34	1854	20	6	3	99	2	3.20	11	593	†7	2	28	†1	2.83
92-93—Verdun	QMJHL	*61	*3491	30	27	2	210	1	3.61	4	257	0	4	18	0	4.20
93-94—Verdun	QMJHL	51	2845	28	22	0	145	1	*3.06	4	210	0	4	14	0	4.00
94-95—Verdun	QMJHL	1	60	1	0	0	3	0	3.00	—	—	—	—	—	—	—
—Cleveland	IHL	41	2369	24	10	‡5	131	1	3.32	—	—	—	—	—	—	—

de RUITER, CHRIS
RW/C, MAPLE LEAFS

PERSONAL: Born February 27, 1974, in Kingston, Ont. . . . 6-2/190. . . . Shoots right.

HIGH SCHOOL: Kingston (Ont.) Collegiate and Vocational Institute.

COLLEGE: Clarkson (N.Y.).

TRANSACTIONS/CAREER NOTES: Selected by Toronto Maple Leafs in fifth round (sixth Maple Leafs pick, 106th overall) of NHL entry draft (June 20, 1992).

Season Team	League	REGULAR SEASON				PLAYOFFS			
		Gms.	G	A	Pts.	PIM	Gms.	G	A	Pts.	PIM
90-91—Kingston Jr. A	MTHL	43	8	33	41	78	—	—	—	—	—
91-92—Kingston Jr. A	MTHL	29	27	24	51	52	3	5	2	7	2
92-93—Clarkson	ECAC	32	2	5	7	40	—	—	—	—	—
93-94—Clarkson	ECAC	33	4	10	14	42	—	—	—	—	—
94-95—Clarkson	ECAC	34	10	14	24	78	—	—	—	—	—

DeSANTIS, MARK
D, MIGHTY DUCKS

PERSONAL: Born August 2, 1972, in Brampton, Ont. . . . 6-0/205. . . . Shoots right.

TRANSACTIONS/CAREER NOTES: Signed as free agent by Mighty Ducks of Anaheim (August 2, 1993).

Season Team	League	REGULAR SEASON				PLAYOFFS			
		Gms.	G	A	Pts.	PIM	Gms.	G	A	Pts.	PIM
89-90—Newmarket	OHL	59	3	17	20	79	—	—	—	—	—
90-91—Newmarket	OHL	41	7	15	22	78	—	—	—	—	—
91-92—Newmarket	OHL	66	10	45	55	105	—	—	—	—	—
92-93—Newmarket	OHL	66	19	70	89	131	7	3	11	14	14
93-94—San Diego	IHL	54	5	10	15	95	—	—	—	—	—
94-95—San Diego	IHL	8	0	0	0	23	—	—	—	—	—
—Greensboro	ECHL	57	10	34	44	196	15	0	4	4	71

DESJARDINS, ERIC
D, FLYERS

PERSONAL: Born June 14, 1969, in Rouyn, Que. . . . 6-1/200. . . . Shoots right. . . . Name pronounced deh-ZHAHR-dai.

TRANSACTIONS/CAREER NOTES: Selected by Montreal Canadiens as underage junior in second round (third Canadiens pick, 38th overall) of NHL entry draft (June 13, 1987). . . . Suffered from the flu (January 1989). . . . Pulled groin (November 2, 1989); missed seven games. . . . Sprained left ankle (January 26, 1991); missed 16 games. . . . Fractured right thumb (December 8, 1991); missed two games. . . . Traded by Canadiens with LW Gilbert Dionne and C John LeClair to Philadelphia Flyers for RW Mark Recchi and third-round pick (C Martin Hohenberger) in 1995 draft (February 9, 1995). . . . Slightly strained groin (March 28, 1995); missed one game. . . . Reinjured groin (April 1, 1995); missed three games.

HONORS: Named to QMJHL All-Star second team (1986-87). . . . Won Emile (Butch) Bouchard Trophy (1987-88). . . . Named to QMJHL All-Star first team (1987-88). . . . Played in NHL All-Star Game (1992).

RECORDS: Shares NHL single-game playoff record for most goals by defensemen—3 (June 3, 1993).

MISCELLANEOUS: Member of Stanley Cup championship team (1993).

Season Team	League	REGULAR SEASON				PLAYOFFS			
		Gms.	G	A	Pts.	PIM	Gms.	G	A	Pts.	PIM
86-87—Granby	QMJHL	66	14	24	38	75	8	3	2	5	10
87-88—Granby	QMJHL	62	18	49	67	138	5	0	3	3	10
—Sherbrooke	AHL	3	0	0	0	6	4	0	2	2	2
88-89—Montreal	NHL	36	2	12	14	26	14	1	1	2	6
89-90—Montreal	NHL	55	3	13	16	51	6	0	0	0	10
90-91—Montreal	NHL	62	7	18	25	27	13	1	4	5	8
91-92—Montreal	NHL	77	6	32	38	50	11	3	3	6	4
92-93—Montreal	NHL	82	13	32	45	98	20	4	10	14	23
93-94—Montreal	NHL	84	12	23	35	97	7	0	2	2	4
94-95—Montreal	NHL	9	0	6	6	2	—	—	—	—	—
—Philadelphia	NHL	34	5	18	23	12	15	4	4	8	10
NHL totals		439	48	154	202	363	86	13	24	37	65

DEULING, JARRETT
LW, ISLANDERS

PERSONAL: Born March 4, 1974, in Vernon, B.C. .... 5-11/194. ... Shoots left. ... Name pronounced DOO-lihng.
HIGH SCHOOL: Norkam Secondary (Kamloops, B.C.).
TRANSACTIONS/CAREER NOTES: Selected by New York Islanders in third round (second Islanders pick, 56th overall) of NHL entry draft (June 20, 1992).
HONORS: WHL Playoff Most Valuable Player Award (1991-92).

			REGULAR SEASON					PLAYOFFS			
Season Team	League	Gms.	G	A	Pts.	PIM	Gms.	G	A	Pts.	PIM
90-91—Kamloops	WHL	48	4	12	16	43	12	5	2	7	7
91-92—Kamloops	WHL	68	28	26	54	79	17	10	6	16	18
92-93—Kamloops	WHL	68	31	32	63	93	13	6	7	13	14
93-94—Kamloops	WHL	70	44	59	103	171	18	*13	8	21	43
94-95—Worcester	AHL	63	11	8	19	37	—	—	—	—	—

De VRIES, GREG
D, OILERS

PERSONAL: Born January 4, 1973, in Sundridge, Ont. .... 6-3/218. ... Shoots left.
COLLEGE: Bowling Green State.
TRANSACTIONS/CAREER NOTES: Signed as free agent by Edmonton Oilers (March 28, 1994).

			REGULAR SEASON					PLAYOFFS			
Season Team	League	Gms.	G	A	Pts.	PIM	Gms.	G	A	Pts.	PIM
91-92—Bowling Green State	CCHA	24	0	3	3	20	—	—	—	—	—
92-93—Niagara Falls	OHL	62	3	23	26	86	4	0	1	1	6
93-94—Niagara Falls	OHL	64	5	40	45	135	—	—	—	—	—
—Cape Breton	AHL	9	0	0	0	11	1	0	0	0	0
94-95—Cape Breton	AHL	77	5	19	24	68	—	—	—	—	—

DEYELL, MARK
C, MAPLE LEAFS

PERSONAL: Born March 26, 1976, in Regina, Sask. .... 5-11/165. ... Shoots right.
TRANSACTIONS/CAREER NOTES: Selected by Toronto Maple Leafs in fifth round (fourth Maple Leafs pick, 126th overall) of NHL entry draft (June 29, 1994).

			REGULAR SEASON					PLAYOFFS			
Season Team	League	Gms.	G	A	Pts.	PIM	Gms.	G	A	Pts.	PIM
93-94—Saskatoon	WHL	66	17	36	53	52	16	5	2	7	20
94-95—Saskatoon	WHL	70	34	68	102	56	10	2	5	7	14

D

DIDUCK, GERALD
D, WHALERS

PERSONAL: Born April 6, 1965, in Edmonton. .... 6-2/207. ... Shoots right. ... Name pronounced DIH-duhk.
TRANSACTIONS/CAREER NOTES: Selected by New York Islanders as underage junior in first round (second Islanders pick, 16th overall) of NHL entry draft (June 8, 1983). .... Fractured left foot (November 1987). ... Fractured right hand (November 1988). ... Injured knee (January 1989). ... Traded by Islanders to Montreal Canadiens for D Craig Ludwig (September 4, 1990). ... Traded by Canadiens to Vancouver Canucks for fourth-round pick (LW Vladimir Vujtek) in 1991 draft (January 12, 1991). ... Bruised knee (March 16, 1991). ... Strained groin (January 4, 1993); missed three games. ... Suffered stress fracture in ankle (January 1, 1994); missed 14 games. ... Bruised foot (February 17, 1994); missed six games. ... Suffered eye contusion (March 31, 1994); missed five games. ... Traded by Canucks to Chicago Blackhawks for RW Bogdan Savenko and third-round pick (LW Larry Courville) of 1995 draft (April 7, 1995). ... Signed as free agent by Hartford Whalers (August 1, 1995).

			REGULAR SEASON					PLAYOFFS			
Season Team	League	Gms.	G	A	Pts.	PIM	Gms.	G	A	Pts.	PIM
81-82—Lethbridge	WHL	71	1	15	16	81	12	0	3	3	27
82-83—Lethbridge	WHL	67	8	16	24	151	20	3	12	15	49
83-84—Lethbridge	WHL	65	10	24	34	133	5	1	4	5	27
—Indianapolis	IHL	—	—	—	—	—	10	1	6	7	19
84-85—New York Islanders	NHL	65	2	8	10	80	—	—	—	—	—
85-86—New York Islanders	NHL	10	1	2	3	2	—	—	—	—	—
—Springfield	AHL	61	6	14	20	175	—	—	—	—	—
86-87—Springfield	AHL	45	6	8	14	120	—	—	—	—	—
—New York Islanders	NHL	30	2	3	5	67	14	0	1	1	35
87-88—New York Islanders	NHL	68	7	12	19	113	6	1	0	1	42
88-89—New York Islanders	NHL	65	11	21	32	155	—	—	—	—	—
89-90—New York Islanders	NHL	76	3	17	20	163	5	0	0	0	12
90-91—Montreal	NHL	32	1	2	3	39	—	—	—	—	—
—Vancouver	NHL	31	3	7	10	66	6	1	0	1	11
91-92—Vancouver	NHL	77	6	21	27	229	5	0	0	0	10
92-93—Vancouver	NHL	80	6	14	20	171	12	4	2	6	12
93-94—Vancouver	NHL	55	1	10	11	72	24	1	7	8	22
94-95—Vancouver	NHL	22	1	3	4	15	—	—	—	—	—
—Chicago	NHL	13	1	0	1	48	16	1	3	4	22
NHL totals		624	45	120	165	1220	88	8	13	21	166

DiMAIO, ROB
C, FLYERS

PERSONAL: Born February 19, 1968, in Calgary. .... 5-10/190. ... Shoots right. ... Name pronounced duh-MIGH-oh.
TRANSACTIONS/CAREER NOTES: Traded by Kamloops Blazers with LW Dave Mackey and C Kalvin Knibbs to Medicine Hat Tigers for LW Doug Pickel and LW Sean Pass (December 1985). .... Selected by New York Islanders in sixth round (sixth Islanders pick, 118th overall) of NHL entry draft (June 13, 1987). ... Suspended two games by WHL for leaving bench during fight (January 28, 1988). ... Bruised left hand (February 1989). ...

Sprained clavicle (November 1989).... Sprained wrist (February 20, 1992); missed four games.... Reinjured wrist (February 29, 1992); missed final 17 games of season.... Underwent surgery to repair torn ligaments in wrist (March 11, 1992).... Selected by Tampa Bay Lightning in NHL expansion draft (June 18, 1992).... Bruised wrist (November 28, 1992); missed four games.... Sprained ankle (February 14, 1993); missed nine games.... Reinjured right ankle (March 20, 1993); missed three games.... Reinjured right ankle (April 1, 1993); missed remainder of season.... Broke left leg (October 16, 1993); missed 27 games.... Traded by Lightning to Philadelphia Flyers for RW Jim Cummins and fourth-round pick in 1995 draft (March 18, 1994).... Bruised foot (February 28, 1995); missed two games.... Suffered from the flu (April 16, 1995); missed one game.
HONORS: Won Stafford Smythe Memorial Trophy (1987-88).... Named to Memorial Cup All-Star team (1987-88).

Season	Team	League	REGULAR SEASON					PLAYOFFS				
			Gms.	G	A	Pts.	PIM	Gms.	G	A	Pts.	PIM
84-85	Kamloops	WHL	55	9	18	27	29	—	—	—	—	—
85-86	Kamloops	WHL	6	1	0	1	0	—	—	—	—	—
	Medicine Hat	WHL	55	20	30	50	82	—	—	—	—	—
86-87	Medicine Hat	WHL	70	27	43	70	130	20	7	11	18	46
87-88	Medicine Hat	WHL	54	47	43	90	120	14	12	19	†31	59
88-89	New York Islanders	NHL	16	1	0	1	30	—	—	—	—	—
	Springfield	AHL	40	13	18	31	67	—	—	—	—	—
89-90	New York Islanders	NHL	7	0	0	0	2	1	1	0	1	4
	Springfield	AHL	54	25	27	52	69	16	4	7	11	45
90-91	New York Islanders	NHL	1	0	0	0	0	—	—	—	—	—
	Capital District	AHL	12	3	4	7	22	—	—	—	—	—
91-92	New York Islanders	NHL	50	5	2	7	43	—	—	—	—	—
92-93	Tampa Bay	NHL	54	9	15	24	62	—	—	—	—	—
93-94	Tampa Bay	NHL	39	8	7	15	40	—	—	—	—	—
	Philadelphia	NHL	14	3	5	8	6	—	—	—	—	—
94-95	Philadelphia	NHL	36	3	1	4	53	15	2	4	6	4
	NHL totals		217	29	30	59	236	16	3	4	7	8

DINEEN, GORD
D, ISLANDERS

PERSONAL: Born September 21, 1962, in Quebec City.... 6-0/195.... Shoots right.... Son of Bill Dineen, right winger, Detroit Red Wings and Chicago Blackhawks (1953-54 through 1957-58) and former head coach, Philadelphia Flyers (1992-93); brother of Kevin Dineen, right winger, Flyers; and brother of Peter Dineen, defenseman, Los Angeles Kings and Red Wings (1986-87 and 1989-90).
HIGH SCHOOL: St. Micheal (Toronto).
TRANSACTIONS/CAREER NOTES: Selected by New York Islanders as underage junior in second round (second Islanders pick, 42nd overall) of NHL entry draft (June 10, 1981).... Bruised ribs (January 15, 1985).... Sprained left ankle (February 1988).... Traded by Islanders with future considerations to Minnesota North Stars for D Chris Pryor (March 1988).... Traded by North Stars with LW Scott Bjugstad to Pittsburgh Penguins for D Ville Siren and C Steve Gotaas (December 17, 1988).... Signed as free agent by Ottawa Senators (August 31, 1992).... Loaned to San Diego Gulls prior to 1992-93 season.... Returned to Senators (January 20, 1993).... Signed as free agent by New York Islanders (August 2, 1994).
HONORS: Won Bobby Orr Trophy (1982-83).... Won Bob Gassoff Award (1982-83).... Named to CHL All-Star first team (1982-83).... Named to IHL All-Star first team (1991-92).
MISCELLANEOUS: Captain of Ottawa Senators (1993-94).

Season	Team	League	REGULAR SEASON					PLAYOFFS				
			Gms.	G	A	Pts.	PIM	Gms.	G	A	Pts.	PIM
79-80	St. Michael's Jr. B	ODHA	42	15	35	50	103	—	—	—	—	—
80-81	Sault Ste. Marie	OMJHL	68	4	26	30	158	19	1	7	8	58
81-82	Sault Ste. Marie	OHL	68	9	45	54	185	13	1	2	3	52
82-83	Indianapolis	CHL	73	10	47	57	78	13	2	10	12	29
	New York Islanders	NHL	2	0	0	0	4	—	—	—	—	—
83-84	Indianapolis	CHL	26	4	13	17	63	—	—	—	—	—
	New York Islanders	NHL	43	1	11	12	32	9	1	1	2	28
84-85	Springfield	AHL	25	1	8	9	46	—	—	—	—	—
	New York Islanders	NHL	48	1	12	13	89	10	0	0	0	26
85-86	New York Islanders	NHL	57	1	8	9	81	3	0	0	0	2
	Springfield	AHL	11	2	3	5	20	—	—	—	—	—
86-87	New York Islanders	NHL	71	4	10	14	110	7	0	4	4	4
87-88	New York Islanders	NHL	57	4	12	16	62	—	—	—	—	—
	Minnesota	NHL	13	1	1	2	21	—	—	—	—	—
88-89	Kalamazoo	IHL	25	2	6	8	49	—	—	—	—	—
	Minnesota	NHL	2	0	1	1	2	—	—	—	—	—
	Pittsburgh	NHL	38	1	2	3	42	11	0	2	2	8
89-90	Pittsburgh	NHL	69	1	8	9	125	—	—	—	—	—
90-91	Muskegon	IHL	40	1	14	15	57	5	0	2	2	0
	Pittsburgh	NHL	9	0	0	0	6	—	—	—	—	—
91-92	Muskegon	IHL	79	8	37	45	83	14	2	4	6	33
	Pittsburgh	NHL	1	0	0	0	0	—	—	—	—	—
92-93	San Diego	IHL	41	6	23	29	36	—	—	—	—	—
	Ottawa	NHL	32	2	4	6	30	—	—	—	—	—
93-94	Ottawa	NHL	77	0	21	21	89	—	—	—	—	—
	San Diego	IHL	3	0	0	0	2	—	—	—	—	—
94-95	Denver	IHL	68	5	27	32	75	17	1	6	7	8
	New York Islanders	NHL	9	0	0	0	2	—	—	—	—	—
	NHL totals		528	16	90	106	695	40	1	7	8	68

DINEEN, KEVIN
RW, FLYERS

PERSONAL: Born October 28, 1963, in Quebec City. . . . 5-11/190. . . . Shoots right. . . . Son of Bill Dineen, right winger with Detroit Red Wings and Chicago Blackhawks (1953-54 through 1957-58) and former head coach, Philadelphia Flyers (1992-93); brother of Gord Dineen, defenseman, New York Islanders; and brother of Peter Dineen, defenseman, Los Angeles Kings and Red Wings (1986-87 and 1989-90).
HIGH SCHOOL: St. Michael (Toronto).
COLLEGE: Denver.
TRANSACTIONS/CAREER NOTES: Selected by Hartford Whalers as underage junior in third round (third Whalers pick, 56th overall) of NHL entry draft (June 9, 1982). . . . Sprained left shoulder (October 24, 1985); missed nine games. . . . Broke knuckle (January 12, 1986); missed seven games. . . . Sprained knee (February 14, 1986). . . . Suffered shoulder tendinitis (September 1988). . . . Underwent surgery to right knee cartilage (August 1, 1990). . . . Suffered hip pointer (November 28, 1990). . . . Hospitalized due to complications caused by Crohn's disease (January 1, 1991); missed eight games. . . . Injured groin (March 1991). . . . Traded by Whalers to Philadelphia Flyers for C/LW Murray Craven and fourth-round pick (LW Kevin Smyth) in 1992 draft (November 13, 1991). . . . Sprained wrist (February 4, 1992); missed one game. . . . Strained right rotator cuff (December 3, 1992); missed one game. . . . Suffered injury (October 9, 1993); missed one game. . . . Bruised right shoulder (November 13, 1993); missed two games. . . . Suffered recurrence of Crohn's disease (February 10, 1994); missed five games. . . . Separated shoulder (March 8, 1994); missed three games. . . . Strained left shoulder (January 31, 1995); missed three games. . . . Reinjured left shoulder (February 11, 1995); missed three games.
HONORS: Named to THE SPORTING NEWS All-Star second team (1986-87). . . . Played in NHL All-Star Game (1988 and 1989). . . . Named Bud Light/NHL Man of the Year (1990-91).
STATISTICAL PLATEAUS: Three-goal games: 1985-86 (1), 1986-87 (1), 1988-89 (1), 1989-90 (2), 1992-93 (3), 1993-94 (1). Total: 9. . . . Four-goal games: 1993-94 (1). . . . Total hat tricks: 10.
MISCELLANEOUS: Captain of Philadelphia Flyers (1993-94).

Season Team	League	REGULAR SEASON					PLAYOFFS				
		Gms.	G	A	Pts.	PIM	Gms.	G	A	Pts.	PIM
80-81—St. Michael's Jr. B	ODHA	40	15	28	43	167	—	—	—	—	—
81-82—University of Denver	WCHA	38	12	22	34	105	—	—	—	—	—
82-83—University of Denver	WCHA	36	16	13	29	108	—	—	—	—	—
83-84—Canadian national team	Int'l	52	5	11	16	2	—	—	—	—	—
—Canadian Olympic Team	Int'l	7	0	0	0	0	—	—	—	—	—
84-85—Binghamton	AHL	25	15	8	23	41	—	—	—	—	—
—Hartford	NHL	57	25	16	41	120	—	—	—	—	—
85-86—Hartford	NHL	57	33	35	68	124	10	6	7	13	18
86-87—Hartford	NHL	78	40	39	79	110	6	2	1	3	31
87-88—Hartford	NHL	74	25	25	50	217	6	4	4	8	8
88-89—Hartford	NHL	79	45	44	89	167	4	1	0	1	10
89-90—Hartford	NHL	67	25	41	66	164	6	3	2	5	18
90-91—Hartford	NHL	61	17	30	47	104	6	1	0	1	16
91-92—Hartford	NHL	16	4	2	6	23	—	—	—	—	—
—Philadelphia	NHL	64	26	30	56	130	—	—	—	—	—
92-93—Philadelphia	NHL	83	35	28	63	201	—	—	—	—	—
93-94—Philadelphia	NHL	71	19	23	42	113	—	—	—	—	—
94-95—Houston	IHL	17	6	4	10	42	—	—	—	—	—
—Philadelphia	NHL	40	8	5	13	39	15	6	4	10	18
NHL totals		747	302	318	620	1512	53	23	18	41	119

DINGMAN, CHRIS
LW, FLAMES

PERSONAL: Born July 6, 1976, in Edmonton. . . . 6-4/225. . . . Shoots left.
HIGH SCHOOL: Crocus Plains (Brandon, Man.).
TRANSACTIONS/CAREER NOTES: Selected by Calgary Flames in first round (first Flames pick, 19th overall) of NHL entry draft (June 28, 1994).

Season Team	League	REGULAR SEASON					PLAYOFFS				
		Gms.	G	A	Pts.	PIM	Gms.	G	A	Pts.	PIM
92-93—Brandon	WHL	50	10	17	27	64	4	0	0	0	0
93-94—Brandon	WHL	45	21	20	41	77	13	1	7	8	39
94-95—Brandon	WHL	66	40	43	83	201	3	1	0	1	9

DIONNE, GILBERT
LW, FLYERS

PERSONAL: Born September 19, 1970, in Drummondville, Que. . . . 6-0/205. . . . Shoots left. . . . Name pronounced ZHIHL-bair dee-AHN. . . . Brother of Marcel Dionne, Hall of Fame center, Detroit Red Wings, Los Angeles Kings and New York Rangers (1971-72 through 1988-89).
TRANSACTIONS/CAREER NOTES: Selected by Montreal Canadiens in fourth round (fifth Canadiens pick, 81st overall) of NHL entry draft (June 16, 1990). . . . Injured hand (December 3, 1992); missed one game. . . . Pulled groin (December 18, 1992); missed eight games. . . . Traded by Canadiens with LW John LeClair and D Eric Desjardins to Philadelphia Flyers for RW Mark Recchi and third-round pick (C Martin Hohenberger) in 1995 draft (February 9, 1995). . . . Suffered from the flu (March 9, 1995); missed two games.
HONORS: Named to NHL All-Rookie team (1991-92).
STATISTICAL PLATEAUS: Three-goal games: 1991-92 (1).
MISCELLANEOUS: Member of Stanley Cup championship team (1993).

Season Team	League	REGULAR SEASON					PLAYOFFS				
		Gms.	G	A	Pts.	PIM	Gms.	G	A	Pts.	PIM
87-88—Niagara Falls Jr. B	OHA	38	36	48	84	60	—	—	—	—	—
88-89—Kitchener	OHL	66	11	33	44	13	5	1	1	2	4
89-90—Kitchener	OHL	64	48	57	105	85	17	13	10	23	22
90-91—Fredericton	AHL	77	40	47	87	62	9	6	5	11	8
—Montreal	NHL	2	0	0	0	0	—	—	—	—	—

Season	Team	League	REGULAR SEASON					PLAYOFFS				
			Gms.	G	A	Pts.	PIM	Gms.	G	A	Pts.	PIM
91-92—Fredericton		AHL	29	19	27	46	20	—	—	—	—	—
—Montreal		NHL	39	21	13	34	10	11	3	4	7	10
92-93—Montreal		NHL	75	20	28	48	63	20	6	6	12	20
—Fredericton		AHL	3	4	3	7	0	—	—	—	—	—
93-94—Montreal		NHL	74	19	26	45	31	5	1	2	3	0
94-95—Montreal		NHL	6	0	3	3	2	—	—	—	—	—
—Philadelphia		NHL	20	0	6	6	2	3	0	0	0	4
NHL totals			216	60	76	136	108	39	10	12	22	34

DIPIETRO, PAUL
C, MAPLE LEAFS

PERSONAL: Born September 8, 1970, in Sault Ste. Marie, Ont. . . . 5-8/179. . . . Shoots right. . . . Name pronounced dee-pee-AY-troh.

TRANSACTIONS/CAREER NOTES: Selected by Montreal Canadiens in fifth round (sixth Canadiens pick, 102nd overall) of NHL entry draft (June 16, 1990). . . . Strained hip flexor (February 12, 1992). . . . Bruised thumb (November 24, 1993). . . . Suffered contusion (January 4, 1994); missed two games. . . . Separated shoulder (January 15, 1994); missed six games. . . . Traded by Canadiens to Toronto Maple Leafs for conditional fourth-round draft pick (April 6, 1995).

MISCELLANEOUS: Member of Stanley Cup championship team (1993).

Season	Team	League	REGULAR SEASON					PLAYOFFS				
			Gms.	G	A	Pts.	PIM	Gms.	G	A	Pts.	PIM
86-87—Sudbury		OHL	49	5	11	16	13	—	—	—	—	—
87-88—Sudbury		OHL	63	25	42	67	27	—	—	—	—	—
88-89—Sudbury		OHL	57	31	48	79	27	—	—	—	—	—
89-90—Sudbury		OHL	66	56	63	119	57	7	3	6	9	7
90-91—Fredericton		AHL	78	39	31	70	38	9	5	6	11	2
91-92—Fredericton		AHL	43	26	31	57	52	7	3	4	7	8
—Montreal		NHL	33	4	6	10	25	—	—	—	—	—
92-93—Fredericton		AHL	26	8	16	24	16	—	—	—	—	—
—Montreal		NHL	29	4	13	17	14	17	8	5	13	8
93-94—Montreal		NHL	70	13	20	33	37	7	2	4	6	2
94-95—Montreal		NHL	22	4	5	9	4	—	—	—	—	—
—Toronto		NHL	12	1	1	2	6	7	1	1	2	0
NHL totals			166	26	45	71	86	31	11	10	21	10

DIRK, ROBERT
D, MIGHTY DUCKS

PERSONAL: Born August 20, 1966, in Regina, Sask. . . . 6-4/210. . . . Shoots left.

TRANSACTIONS/CAREER NOTES: Selected by St. Louis Blues as underage junior in third round (fourth Blues pick, 53rd overall) of NHL entry draft (June 9, 1984). . . . Traded by Blues with LW Geoff Courtnall, C Cliff Ronning, LW Sergio Momesso and fifth-round pick in 1992 draft (RW Brian Loney) to Vancouver Canucks for C Dan Quinn and D Garth Butcher (March 5, 1991). . . . Sprained knee (February 1, 1992); missed four games. . . . Bruised ribs (March 6, 1993); missed four games. . . . Injured shoulder (September 22, 1992); missed two games. . . . Pulled groin (February 12, 1993); missed six games. . . . Traded by Canucks to Chicago Blackhawks for fourth-round pick (RW Mike Dubinsky) in 1994 draft (March 21, 1994). . . . Suffered from sore shoulder (1994); missed four games. . . . Traded by Blackhawks to Mighty Ducks of Anaheim for fourth-round pick (D Chris Van Dyk) in 1995 draft (July 12, 1994). . . . Lacerated chin (April 13, 1995); missed seven games.

HONORS: Named to WHL All-Star second team (1985-86).

Season	Team	League	REGULAR SEASON					PLAYOFFS				
			Gms.	G	A	Pts.	PIM	Gms.	G	A	Pts.	PIM
82-83—Regina		WHL	1	0	0	0	0	—	—	—	—	—
—Kelowna		BCJHL	40	8	23	31	87	—	—	—	—	—
83-84—Regina		WHL	62	2	10	12	64	23	1	12	13	24
84-85—Regina		WHL	69	10	34	44	97	8	0	0	0	4
85-86—Regina		WHL	72	19	60	79	140	10	3	5	8	8
86-87—Peoria		IHL	76	5	17	22	155	—	—	—	—	—
87-88—St. Louis		NHL	7	0	1	1	16	6	0	1	1	2
—Peoria		IHL	54	4	21	25	126	—	—	—	—	—
88-89—St. Louis		NHL	9	0	1	1	11	—	—	—	—	—
—Peoria		IHL	22	0	2	2	54	—	—	—	—	—
89-90—Peoria		IHL	24	1	2	3	79	3	0	0	0	0
—St. Louis		NHL	37	1	1	2	128	9	0	1	1	2
90-91—Peoria		IHL	3	0	0	0	2	—	—	—	—	—
—St. Louis		NHL	41	1	3	4	100	—	—	—	—	—
—Vancouver		NHL	11	1	0	1	20	6	0	0	0	13
91-92—Vancouver		NHL	72	2	7	9	126	13	0	0	0	20
92-93—Vancouver		NHL	69	4	8	12	150	9	0	0	0	6
93-94—Vancouver		NHL	65	2	3	5	105	—	—	—	—	—
—Chicago		NHL	6	0	0	0	26	2	0	0	0	15
94-95—Anaheim		NHL	38	1	3	4	56	—	—	—	—	—
NHL totals			355	12	27	39	738	45	0	2	2	58

DOAN, SHANE
RW, JETS

PERSONAL: Born October 10, 1976, in Eston, Sask. . . . 6-1/215. . . . Shoots right.
TRANSACTIONS/CAREER NOTES: Selected by Winnipeg Jets in first round (first Jets pick, seventh overall) of NHL entry draft (July 8, 1995).
HONORS: Won Stafford Smyth Memorial Trophy (1994-95). . . . Named to Memorial Cup All-Star team (1994-95).

			REGULAR SEASON				PLAYOFFS			
Season Team	League	Gms.	G	A	Pts.	PIM	Gms.	G	A	Pts.	PIM
92-93—Kamloops	WHL	51	7	12	19	55	13	0	1	1	8
93-94—Kamloops	WHL	52	24	24	48	88	—	—	—	—	—
94-95—Kamloops	WHL	71	37	57	94	106	21	6	10	16	16

DOIG, JASON
D, JETS

PERSONAL: Born January 29, 1977, in Montreal. . . . 6-3/216. . . . Shoots right.
TRANSACTIONS/CAREER NOTES: Selected by Winnipeg Jets in second round (third Jets pick, 34th overall) of NHL entry draft (July 8, 1995).

			REGULAR SEASON				PLAYOFFS			
Season Team	League	Gms.	G	A	Pts.	PIM	Gms.	G	A	Pts.	PIM
93-94—St. Jean	QMJHL	63	8	17	25	65	5	0	2	2	2
94-95—Laval	QMJHL	55	13	42	55	259	20	4	13	17	39

DOLLAS, BOBBY
D, MIGHTY DUCKS

PERSONAL: Born January 31, 1965, in Montreal. . . . 6-2/212. . . . Shoots left.
TRANSACTIONS/CAREER NOTES: Selected by Winnipeg Jets as underage junior in first round (second Jets pick, 14th overall) of NHL entry draft (June 8, 1983). . . . Traded by Jets to Quebec Nordiques for RW Stu Kulak (December 17, 1987). . . . Signed as free agent by Detroit Red Wings (October 18, 1990). . . . Suffered from the flu (December 15, 1990); missed two games. . . . Injured leg (January 9, 1991). . . . Strained abdomen (November 7, 1991); missed 15 games. . . . Selected by Mighty Ducks of Anaheim in NHL expansion draft (June 24, 1993). . . . Sprained left thumb (October 1, 1993); missed five games.
HONORS: Won Raymond Lagace Trophy (1982-83). . . . Named to QMJHL All-Star second team (1982-83). . . . Won Eddie Shore Plaque (1992-93). . . . Named to AHL All-Star first team (1992-93).

			REGULAR SEASON				PLAYOFFS			
Season Team	League	Gms.	G	A	Pts.	PIM	Gms.	G	A	Pts.	PIM
82-83—Laval	QMJHL	63	16	45	61	144	11	5	5	10	23
83-84—Laval	QMJHL	54	12	33	45	80	14	1	8	9	23
—Winnipeg	NHL	1	0	0	0	0	—	—	—	—	—
84-85—Winnipeg	NHL	9	0	0	0	0	—	—	—	—	—
—Sherbrooke	AHL	8	1	3	4	4	17	3	6	9	17
85-86—Sherbrooke	AHL	25	4	7	11	29	—	—	—	—	—
—Winnipeg	NHL	46	0	5	5	66	3	0	0	0	2
86-87—Sherbrooke	AHL	75	6	18	24	87	16	2	4	6	13
87-88—Quebec	NHL	9	0	0	0	2	—	—	—	—	—
—Moncton	AHL	26	4	10	14	20	—	—	—	—	—
—Fredericton	AHL	33	4	8	12	27	15	2	2	4	24
88-89—Halifax	AHL	57	5	19	24	65	4	1	0	1	14
—Quebec	NHL	16	0	3	3	16	—	—	—	—	—
89-90—Canadian national team	Int'l	68	8	29	37	60	—	—	—	—	—
90-91—Detroit	NHL	56	3	5	8	20	7	1	0	1	13
91-92—Detroit	NHL	27	3	1	4	20	2	0	1	1	0
—Adirondack	AHL	19	1	6	7	33	18	7	4	11	22
92-93—Adirondack	AHL	64	7	36	43	54	11	3	8	11	8
—Detroit	NHL	6	0	0	0	2	—	—	—	—	—
93-94—Anaheim	NHL	77	9	11	20	55	—	—	—	—	—
94-95—Anaheim	NHL	45	7	13	20	12	—	—	—	—	—
NHL totals		292	22	38	60	193	12	1	1	2	15

DOMENICHELLI, HNAT
C/LW, WHALERS

PERSONAL: Born February 17, 1976, in Edmonton. . . . 6-0/173. . . . Shoots left. . . . Name pronounced NAT DOHM-ih-nih-CHEH-lee.
TRANSACTIONS/CAREER NOTES: Selected by Hartford Whalers in fourth round (second Whalers pick, 83rd overall) of NHL entry draft (June 29, 1994).
HONORS: Named to WHL (West) All-Star second team (1994-95).

			REGULAR SEASON				PLAYOFFS			
Season Team	League	Gms.	G	A	Pts.	PIM	Gms.	G	A	Pts.	PIM
92-93—Kamloops	WHL	45	12	8	20	15	11	1	1	2	2
93-94—Kamloops	WHL	69	27	40	67	31	19	10	12	22	0
94-95—Kamloops	WHL	72	52	62	114	34	19	9	9	18	9

DOMI, TIE
RW, MAPLE LEAFS

PERSONAL: Born November 1, 1969, in Windsor, Ont. . . . 5-10/200. . . . Shoots . . . . Name pronounced TIGH DOH-mee.
TRANSACTIONS/CAREER NOTES: Suspended indefinitely by OHL for leaving the bench during fight (November 2, 1986). . . . Selected by Toronto Maple Leafs in second round (second Maple Leafs pick, 27th overall) of NHL entry draft (June 11, 1988). . . . Traded by Maple Leafs with G Mark Laforest to New York Rangers for RW Greg Johnston (June 28, 1990). . . . Suspended six games by AHL for pre-game fighting (November 25, 1990). . . . Sprained right knee (March 11, 1992); missed eight games. . . . Traded by Rangers with LW Kris King to Winnipeg Jets for C Ed Olczyk (December 28, 1992). . . . Fined $500 by NHI for premeditated fight (January 4, 1993). . . . Sprained knee (January 25, 1994);

missed three games. . . . Traded by Jets to Toronto Maple Leafs for C Mike Eastwood and third-round pick (RW Brad Isbister) in 1995 draft (April 7, 1995). . . . Strained groin (April 8, 1995); missed two games. . . . Suffered from the flu (April 19, 1995); missed one game.

Season Team	League	REGULAR SEASON					PLAYOFFS				
		Gms.	G	A	Pts.	PIM	Gms.	G	A	Pts.	PIM
85-86—Windsor Jr. B	OHA	32	8	17	25	346	—	—	—	—	—
86-87—Peterborough	OHL	18	1	1	2	79	—	—	—	—	—
87-88—Peterborough	OHL	60	22	21	43	*292	12	3	9	12	24
88-89—Peterborough	OHL	43	14	16	30	175	17	10	9	19	*70
89-90—Newmarket	AHL	57	14	11	25	285	—	—	—	—	—
—Toronto	NHL	2	0	0	0	42	—	—	—	—	—
90-91—New York Rangers	NHL	28	1	0	1	185	—	—	—	—	—
—Binghamton	AHL	25	11	6	17	219	7	3	2	5	16
91-92—New York Rangers	NHL	42	2	4	6	246	6	1	1	2	32
92-93—New York Rangers	NHL	12	2	0	2	95	—	—	—	—	—
—Winnipeg	NHL	49	3	10	13	249	6	1	0	1	23
93-94—Winnipeg	NHL	81	8	11	19	*347	—	—	—	—	—
94-95—Winnipeg	NHL	31	4	4	8	128	—	—	—	—	—
—Toronto	NHL	9	0	1	1	31	7	1	0	1	0
NHL totals		254	20	30	50	1323	19	3	1	4	55

DONATO, TED
C, BRUINS

PERSONAL: Born April 28, 1968, in Dedham, Mass. . . . 5-10/170. . . . Shoots left. . . . Full name: Edward Paul Donato. . . . Name pronounced duh-NAH-toh.
HIGH SCHOOL: Catholic Memorial (Boston).
COLLEGE: Harvard (degree in history).
TRANSACTIONS/CAREER NOTES: Selected by Boston Bruins in sixth round (sixth Bruins pick, 98th overall) of NHL entry draft (June 13, 1987). . . . Broke collarbone (November 18, 1989). . . . Played in Europe during 1994-95 NHL lockout.
HONORS: Named NCAA Tournament Most Valuable Player (1988-89). . . . Named to NCAA All-Tournament team (1988-89). . . . Named to ECAC All-Star first team (1990-91).

Season Team	League	REGULAR SEASON					PLAYOFFS				
		Gms.	G	A	Pts.	PIM	Gms.	G	A	Pts.	PIM
86-87—Catholic Memorial H.S.	Mass. H.S.	22	29	34	63	30	—	—	—	—	—
87-88—Harvard University	ECAC	28	12	14	26	24	—	—	—	—	—
88-89—Harvard University	ECAC	34	14	37	51	30	—	—	—	—	—
89-90—Harvard University	ECAC	16	5	6	11	34	—	—	—	—	—
90-91—Harvard University	ECAC	28	19	37	56	26	—	—	—	—	—
91-92—U.S. national team	Int'l	52	11	22	33	24	—	—	—	—	—
—U.S. Olympic Team	Int'l	8	4	3	7	8	—	—	—	—	—
—Boston	NHL	10	1	2	3	8	15	3	4	7	4
92-93—Boston	NHL	82	15	20	35	61	4	0	1	1	0
93-94—Boston	NHL	84	22	32	54	59	13	4	2	6	10
94-95—TuTo Turku	Finland	14	5	5	10	47	—	—	—	—	—
—Boston	NHL	47	10	10	20	10	5	0	0	0	4
NHL totals		223	48	64	112	138	37	7	7	14	18

DONNELLY, GORD
D/RW, STARS

PERSONAL: Born April 5, 1962, in Montreal. . . . 6-1/202. . . . Shoots right.
TRANSACTIONS/CAREER NOTES: Selected by St. Louis Blues in third round (third Blues pick, 62nd overall) of NHL entry draft (June 10, 1981). . . . Sent by Blues with D Claude Julien to Quebec Nordiques as compensation for Blues signing coach Jacques Demers (August 1983). . . . Suspended five games by NHL for kneeing (October 29, 1987). . . . Suspended five games and fined $100 by NHL for pre-game fighting (February 26, 1988). . . . Suspended 10 games by NHL for hitting with stick (March 27, 1988); missed final four games of 1987-88 season and first six games of 1988-89 season. . . . Traded by Nordiques to Winnipeg Jets for D Mario Marois (December 6, 1988). . . . Fined $500 by NHL for kicking (April 12, 1990). . . . Traded by Jets with RW Dave McIlwain, fifth-round pick in 1992 draft (LW Yuri Khmylev) and future considerations to Buffalo Sabres for LW Darrin Shannon, LW Mike Hartman and D Dean Kennedy (October 11, 1991). . . . Traded by Sabres to Dallas Stars for LW James Black and seventh-round pick (RW Steve Webb) in 1994 draft (December 15, 1993). . . . Injured elbow (January 20, 1995); missed first nine games of season.

Season Team	League	REGULAR SEASON					PLAYOFFS				
		Gms.	G	A	Pts.	PIM	Gms.	G	A	Pts.	PIM
78-79—Laval	QMJHL	71	1	14	15	79	—	—	—	—	—
79-80—Laval	QMJHL	44	5	10	15	47	—	—	—	—	—
—Chicoutimi	QMJHL	24	1	5	6	64	—	—	—	—	—
80-81—Sherbrooke	QMJHL	67	15	23	38	252	14	1	2	3	35
81-82—Sherbrooke	QMJHL	60	8	41	49	250	22	2	7	9	*106
82-83—Salt Lake City	IHL	67	3	12	15	222	6	1	1	2	8
83-84—Fredericton	AHL	30	2	3	5	146	7	1	1	2	43
—Quebec	NHL	38	0	5	5	60	—	—	—	—	—
84-85—Fredericton	AHL	42	1	5	6	134	6	0	1	1	25
—Quebec	NHL	22	0	0	0	33	—	—	—	—	—
85-86—Fredericton	AHL	37	3	5	8	103	5	0	0	0	33
—Quebec	NHL	36	2	2	4	85	1	0	0	0	0
86-87—Quebec	NHL	38	0	2	2	143	13	0	0	0	53
87-88—Quebec	NHL	63	4	3	7	301	—	—	—	—	—

Season	Team	League	REGULAR SEASON					PLAYOFFS				
			Gms.	G	A	Pts.	PIM	Gms.	G	A	Pts.	PIM
88-89	Quebec	NHL	16	4	0	4	46	—	—	—	—	—
	—Winnipeg	NHL	57	6	10	16	228	—	—	—	—	—
89-90	Winnipeg	NHL	55	3	3	6	222	6	0	1	1	8
90-91	Winnipeg	NHL	57	3	4	7	265	—	—	—	—	—
91-92	Winnipeg	NHL	4	0	0	0	11	—	—	—	—	—
	—Buffalo	NHL	67	2	3	5	305	6	0	1	1	0
92-93	Buffalo	NHL	60	3	8	11	221	—	—	—	—	—
93-94	Buffalo	NHL	7	0	0	0	31	—	—	—	—	—
	—Dallas	NHL	18	0	1	1	66	—	—	—	—	—
94-95	Dallas	NHL	16	1	0	1	52	—	—	—	—	—
	—Kalamazoo	IHL	7	2	2	4	18	—	—	—	—	—
	NHL totals		554	28	41	69	2069	26	0	2	2	61

DONNELLY, MIKE
LW, STARS

PERSONAL: Born October 10, 1963, in Livonia, Mich. . . . 5-11/185. . . . Shoots left. . . . Full name: Michael Chene Donnelly.
HIGH SCHOOL: Franklin (Livonia, Mich.).
COLLEGE: Michigan State.
TRANSACTIONS/CAREER NOTES: Signed as free agent by New York Rangers (August 1986). . . . Dislocated and fractured right index finger (November 1987). . . . Traded by Rangers with fifth-round pick in 1988 draft (RW Alexander Mogilny) to Buffalo Sabres for LW Paul Cyr and 10th-round pick (C Eric Fenton) in 1988 draft (December 1987). . . . Traded by Sabres to Los Angeles Kings for LW Mikko Makela (October 1, 1990). . . . Traded by Kings to Dallas Stars for fourth-round pick in 1996 draft (February 17, 1995). . . . Suffered concussion (March 8, 1995); missed one game.
HONORS: Named NCAA Tournament Most Valuable Player (1985-86). . . . Named to NCAA All-America West first team (1985-86). . . . Named to NCAA All-Tournament team (1985-86). . . . Named to CCHA All-Star first team (1985-86).
STATISTICAL PLATEAUS: Three-goal games: 1992-93 (1), 1993-94 (1). Total: 2.

Season	Team	League	REGULAR SEASON					PLAYOFFS				
			Gms.	G	A	Pts.	PIM	Gms.	G	A	Pts.	PIM
82-83	Michigan State	CCHA	24	7	13	20	8	—	—	—	—	—
83-84	Michigan State	CCHA	44	18	14	32	40	—	—	—	—	—
84-85	Michigan State	CCHA	44	26	21	47	48	—	—	—	—	—
85-86	Michigan State	CCHA	44	*59	38	97	65	—	—	—	—	—
86-87	New York Rangers	NHL	5	1	1	2	0	—	—	—	—	—
	—New Haven	AHL	58	27	34	61	52	7	2	0	2	9
87-88	Colorado	IHL	8	7	11	18	15	—	—	—	—	—
	—New York Rangers	NHL	17	2	2	4	8	—	—	—	—	—
	—Buffalo	NHL	40	6	8	14	44	—	—	—	—	—
88-89	Buffalo	NHL	22	4	6	10	10	—	—	—	—	—
	—Rochester	AHL	53	32	37	69	53	—	—	—	—	—
89-90	Rochester	AHL	68	43	55	98	71	16	*12	7	19	9
	—Buffalo	NHL	12	1	2	3	8	—	—	—	—	—
90-91	Los Angeles	NHL	53	7	5	12	41	12	5	4	9	6
	—New Haven	AHL	18	10	6	16	2	—	—	—	—	—
91-92	Los Angeles	NHL	80	29	16	45	20	6	1	0	1	4
92-93	Los Angeles	NHL	84	29	40	69	45	24	6	7	13	14
93-94	Los Angeles	NHL	81	21	21	42	34	—	—	—	—	—
94-95	Los Angeles	NHL	9	1	1	2	4	—	—	—	—	—
	—Dallas	NHL	35	11	14	25	29	5	0	1	1	6
	NHL totals		438	112	116	228	243	47	12	12	24	30

DONOVAN, SHEAN
RW, SHARKS

PERSONAL: Born January 22, 1975, in Timmins, Ont. . . . 6-1/172. . . . Shoots right. . . . Name pronounced SHAWN DAHN-ih-vihn.
TRANSACTIONS/CAREER NOTES: Selected by San Jose Sharks in second round (second Sharks pick, 28th overall) of NHL entry draft (June 26, 1993).

Season	Team	League	REGULAR SEASON					PLAYOFFS				
			Gms.	G	A	Pts.	PIM	Gms.	G	A	Pts.	PIM
91-92	Ottawa	OHL	58	11	8	19	14	11	1	0	1	5
92-93	Ottawa	OHL	66	29	23	52	33	—	—	—	—	—
93-94	Ottawa	OHL	62	35	49	84	63	17	10	11	21	14
94-95	Ottawa	OHL	29	22	19	41	41	—	—	—	—	—
	—San Jose	NHL	14	0	0	0	6	7	0	1	1	6
	—Kansas City	IHL	5	0	2	2	7	14	5	3	8	23
	NHL totals		14	0	0	0	6	7	0	1	1	6

DOURIS, PETER
RW, MIGHTY DUCKS

PERSONAL: Born February 19, 1966, in Toronto. . . . 6-1/195. . . . Shoots right. . . . Name pronounced DOOR-ihz.
COLLEGE: New Hampshire.
TRANSACTIONS/CAREER NOTES: Selected by Winnipeg Jets in second round (first Jets pick, 30th overall) of NHL entry draft (June 9, 1984). . . . Traded by Jets to St. Louis Blues for LW/D Kent Carlson and 12th-round pick (RW Sergei Kharin) in 1989 draft (September 29, 1988). . . . Signed as free agent by Boston Bruins (September 1989). . . . Injured ankle (December 1990). . . . Strained hip flexor (November 1991); missed three games. . . . Signed as free agent by Mighty Ducks of Anaheim (July 22, 1993). . . . Sprained left knee (September 16, 1993); missed eight games.

Season Team	League	REGULAR SEASON					PLAYOFFS				
		Gms.	G	A	Pts.	PIM	Gms.	G	A	Pts.	PIM
83-84—Univ. of New Hampshire ...	ECAC	37	19	15	34	14	—	—	—	—	—
84-85—Univ. of New Hampshire ...	Hockey East	42	27	24	51	34	—	—	—	—	—
85-86—Canadian national team ...	Int'l	33	16	7	23	18	—	—	—	—	—
—Winnipeg	NHL	11	0	0	0	0	—	—	—	—	—
86-87—Sherbrooke	AHL	62	14	28	42	24	17	7	*15	†22	16
—Winnipeg	NHL	6	0	0	0	0	—	—	—	—	—
87-88—Moncton	AHL	73	42	37	79	53	—	—	—	—	—
—Winnipeg	NHL	4	0	2	2	0	1	0	0	0	0
88-89—Peoria	IHL	81	28	41	69	32	4	1	2	3	0
89-90—Maine	AHL	38	17	20	37	14	—	—	—	—	—
—Boston	NHL	36	5	6	11	15	8	0	1	1	8
90-91—Maine	AHL	35	16	15	31	9	7	0	1	1	6
—Boston	NHL	39	5	2	7	9	2	3	0	3	2
91-92—Boston	NHL	54	10	13	23	10	7	2	3	5	0
—Maine	AHL	12	4	3	7	2	—	—	—	—	—
92-93—Providence	AHL	50	29	26	55	12	—	—	—	—	—
—Boston	NHL	19	4	4	8	4	4	1	0	1	0
93-94—Anaheim	NHL	74	12	22	34	21	—	—	—	—	—
94-95—Anaheim	NHL	46	10	11	21	12	—	—	—	—	—
NHL totals		289	46	60	106	71	22	6	4	10	10

DOWD, JIM
C, DEVILS

PERSONAL: Born December 25, 1968, in Brick, N.J. . . . 6-1/190. . . . Shoots right.
HIGH SCHOOL: Brick (N.J.) Township.
COLLEGE: Lake Superior State (Mich.).
TRANSACTIONS/CAREER NOTES: Selected by New Jersey Devils in eighth round (seventh Devils pick, 149th overall) of NHL entry draft (June 13, 1987). . . . Injured shoulder (February 2, 1995) and underwent shoulder surgery (February 15, 1995); missed 35 games.
HONORS: Named to NCAA All-America West second team (1989-90). . . . Named to CCHA All-Star second team (1989-90). . . . Named CCHA Player of the Year (1990-91). . . . Named to NCAA All-America West first team (1990-91). . . . Named to CCHA All-Star first team (1990-91).
MISCELLANEOUS: Member of Stanley Cup championship team (1995).

Season Team	League	REGULAR SEASON					PLAYOFFS				
		Gms.	G	A	Pts.	PIM	Gms.	G	A	Pts.	PIM
83-84—Brick Township H.S.	N.J. H.S.	...	19	30	49	...	—	—	—	—	—
84-85—Brick Township H.S.	N.J. H.S.	...	58	55	113	...	—	—	—	—	—
85-86—Brick Township H.S.	N.J. H.S.	...	47	51	98	...	—	—	—	—	—
86-87—Brick Township H.S.	N.J. H.S.	20	62	53	115	...	—	—	—	—	—
87-88—Lake Superior State	CCHA	45	18	27	45	16	—	—	—	—	—
88-89—Lake Superior State	CCHA	46	24	35	59	40	—	—	—	—	—
89-90—Lake Superior State	CCHA	46	25	67	92	30	—	—	—	—	—
90-91—Lake Superior State	CCHA	44	24	54	78	53	—	—	—	—	—
91-92—Utica	AHL	78	17	42	59	47	4	2	2	4	4
—New Jersey	NHL	1	0	0	0	0	—	—	—	—	—
92-93—Utica	AHL	78	27	45	72	62	5	1	7	8	10
—New Jersey	NHL	1	0	0	0	0	—	—	—	—	—
93-94—New Jersey	NHL	15	5	10	15	0	19	2	6	8	8
—Albany	AHL	58	26	37	63	76	—	—	—	—	—
94-95—New Jersey	NHL	10	1	4	5	0	11	2	1	3	8
NHL totals		27	6	14	20	0	30	4	7	11	16

DRAKE, DALLAS
C, JETS

PERSONAL: Born February 4, 1969, in Trail, B.C. . . . 6-0/180. . . . Shoots left. . . . Full name: Dallas James Drake.
COLLEGE: Northern Michigan.
TRANSACTIONS/CAREER NOTES: Selected by Detroit Red Wings in sixth round (sixth Red Wings pick, 116th overall) of NHL entry draft (June 17, 1989). . . . Bruised left leg (November 27, 1992); missed three games. . . . Suffered back spasms (December 28, 1992); missed one game. . . . Bruised kneecap (January 23, 1993); missed three games. . . . Suffered concussion (February 13, 1993); missed one game. . . . Injured right wrist (October 16, 1993); missed three games. . . . Injured tendon in right hand (December 14, 1993); missed 16 games. . . . Traded by Detroit Red Wings with G Tim Cheveldae to Winnipeg Jets for G Bob Essensa and D Sergei Bautin (March 8, 1994). . . . Suffered back spasms (March 17, 1995); missed four games.
HONORS: Won WCHA Player of the Year Award (1991-92). . . . Named to NCAA All-America West first team (1991-92). . . . Named to WCHA All-Star first team (1991-92).

Season Team	League	REGULAR SEASON					PLAYOFFS				
		Gms.	G	A	Pts.	PIM	Gms.	G	A	Pts.	PIM
84-85—Rossland	KIJHL	30	13	37	50	...	—	—	—	—	—
85-86—Rossland	KIJHL	41	53	73	126	...	—	—	—	—	—
86-87—Rossland	KIJHL	40	55	80	135	...	—	—	—	—	—
87-88—Vernon	BCJHL	47	39	85	124	50	11	9	17	26	30
88-89—Northern Michigan Univ. ..	WCHA	45	18	24	42	26	—	—	—	—	—
89-90—Northern Michigan Univ. ..	WCHA	36	13	24	37	42	—	—	—	—	—
90-91—Northern Michigan Univ. ..	WCHA	44	22	36	58	89	—	—	—	—	—
91-92—Northern Michigan Univ. ..	WCHA	40	*39	44	83	58	—	—	—	—	—

Season	Team	League	REGULAR SEASON					PLAYOFFS				
			Gms.	G	A	Pts.	PIM	Gms.	G	A	Pts.	PIM
92-93—Detroit		NHL	72	18	26	44	93	7	3	3	6	6
93-94—Detroit		NHL	47	10	22	32	37	—	—	—	—	—
—Adirondack		AHL	1	2	0	2	0	—	—	—	—	—
—Winnipeg		NHL	15	3	5	8	12	—	—	—	—	—
94-95—Winnipeg		NHL	43	8	18	26	30	—	—	—	—	—
NHL totals			177	39	71	110	172	7	3	3	6	6

DRAPER, KRIS

C, RED WINGS

PERSONAL: Born May 24, 1971, in Toronto. . . . 5-11/185. . . . Shoots left. . . . Full name: Kris Bruce Draper.

TRANSACTIONS/CAREER NOTES: Selected by Winnipeg Jets in third round (fourth Jets pick, 62nd overall) of NHL entry draft (June 17, 1989). . . . Traded by Jets to Detroit Red Wings for future considerations (June 30, 1993). . . . Sprained medial collateral ligament in right knee (February 4, 1995); missed eight games.

Season	Team	League	REGULAR SEASON					PLAYOFFS				
			Gms.	G	A	Pts.	PIM	Gms.	G	A	Pts.	PIM
88-89—Canadian national team		Int'l	60	11	15	26	16	—	—	—	—	—
89-90—Canadian national team		Int'l	61	12	22	34	44	—	—	—	—	—
90-91—Winnipeg		NHL	3	1	0	1	5	—	—	—	—	—
—Moncton		AHL	7	2	1	3	2	—	—	—	—	—
—Ottawa		OHL	39	19	42	61	35	17	8	11	19	20
91-92—Moncton		AHL	61	11	18	29	113	4	0	1	1	6
—Winnipeg		NHL	10	2	0	2	2	2	0	0	0	0
92-93—Winnipeg		NHL	7	0	0	0	2	—	—	—	—	—
—Moncton		AHL	67	12	23	35	40	5	2	2	4	18
93-94—Adirondack		AHL	46	20	23	43	49	—	—	—	—	—
—Detroit		NHL	39	5	8	13	31	7	2	2	4	4
94-95—Detroit		NHL	36	2	6	8	22	18	4	1	5	12
NHL totals			95	10	14	24	62	27	6	3	9	16

DRIVER, BRUCE

D, DEVILS

PERSONAL: Born April 29, 1962, in Toronto. . . . 6-0/185. . . . Shoots left. . . . Full name: Bruce Douglas Driver.

COLLEGE: Wisconsin.

TRANSACTIONS/CAREER NOTES: Selected by Colorado Rockies as underage junior in sixth round (sixth Rockies pick, 108th overall) of NHL entry draft (June 10, 1981). . . . Rockies franchise moved from Colorado to New Jersey and renamed Devils for 1982-83 season. . . . Underwent surgery to left knee (February 1985). . . . Reinjured knee (April 2, 1985). . . . Bruised shoulder (March 9, 1986). . . . Sprained ankle (February 1988). . . . Broke right leg in three places (December 7, 1988). . . . Broke rib (January 8, 1991); missed three games. . . . Reinjured rib (January 22, 1991); missed four games. . . . Injured shoulder (December 5, 1993); missed 14 games. . . . Dislocated shoulder (February 20, 1995); missed three games. . . . Suffered stiff neck (April 16, 1995); missed one game.

HONORS: Named to NCAA All-America West team (1981-82). . . . Named to NCAA All-Tournament team (1981-82). . . . Named to WCHA All-Star first team (1981-82). . . . Named to WCHA All-Star second team (1982-83).

MISCELLANEOUS: Captain of New Jersey Devils (1991-92). . . . Member of Stanley Cup championship team (1995).

Season	Team	League	REGULAR SEASON					PLAYOFFS				
			Gms.	G	A	Pts.	PIM	Gms.	G	A	Pts.	PIM
78-79—Royal York Royals		OPJHL	45	13	36	49	...	—	—	—	—	—
79-80—Royal York Royals		OPJHL	43	13	57	70	102	—	—	—	—	—
80-81—University of Wisconsin		WCHA	42	5	15	20	42	—	—	—	—	—
81-82—University of Wisconsin		WCHA	46	7	37	44	84	—	—	—	—	—
82-83—University of Wisconsin		WCHA	39	16	34	50	50	—	—	—	—	—
83-84—Canadian Olympic Team		Int'l	61	11	17	28	44	—	—	—	—	—
—Maine		AHL	12	2	6	8	15	16	0	10	10	8
—New Jersey		NHL	4	0	2	2	0	—	—	—	—	—
84-85—New Jersey		NHL	67	9	23	32	36	—	—	—	—	—
85-86—Maine		AHL	15	4	7	11	16	—	—	—	—	—
—New Jersey		NHL	40	3	15	18	32	—	—	—	—	—
86-87—New Jersey		NHL	74	6	28	34	36	—	—	—	—	—
87-88—New Jersey		NHL	74	15	40	55	68	20	3	7	10	14
88-89—New Jersey		NHL	27	1	15	16	24	—	—	—	—	—
89-90—New Jersey		NHL	75	7	46	53	63	6	1	5	6	6
90-91—New Jersey		NHL	73	9	36	45	62	7	1	2	3	12
91-92—New Jersey		NHL	78	7	35	42	66	7	0	4	4	2
92-93—New Jersey		NHL	83	14	40	54	66	5	1	3	4	4
93-94—New Jersey		NHL	66	8	24	32	63	20	3	5	8	12
94-95—New Jersey		NHL	41	4	12	16	18	17	1	6	7	8
NHL totals			702	83	316	399	534	82	10	32	42	58

DROLET, JIMMY

D, CANADIENS

PERSONAL: Born February 19, 1976, in Vanier, Que. . . . 6-0/168. . . . Shoots left. . . . Name pronounced droo-LAY.

TRANSACTIONS/CAREER NOTES: Selected by Montreal Canadiens in fifth round (seventh Canadiens pick, 122nd overall) of NHL entry draft (June 29, 1994).

HONORS: Won Raymond Lagace Trophy (1993-94). . . . Named to QMJHL All-Rookie team (1993-94).

D

Season	Team	League	REGULAR SEASON					PLAYOFFS				
			Gms.	G	A	Pts.	PIM	Gms.	G	A	Pts.	PIM
93-94—St. Hyacinthe		QMJHL	72	10	46	56	93	7	1	7	8	10
94-95—St. Hyacinthe		QMJHL	68	9	27	36	126	5	0	2	2	12

DROPPA, IVAN
D, BLACKHAWKS

PERSONAL: Born February 1, 1972, in Liptovsky Mikulas, Czechoslovakia. . . . 6-2/209. . . . Shoots left. . . . Name pronounced IGH-vihn DROH-puh.
TRANSACTIONS/CAREER NOTES: Selected by Chicago Blackhawks in second round (second Blackhawks pick, 37th overall) of NHL entry draft (June 16, 1990).

Season	Team	League	REGULAR SEASON					PLAYOFFS				
			Gms.	G	A	Pts.	PIM	Gms.	G	A	Pts.	PIM
89-90—Liptovsky Mikulas		Czech.				Statistics unavailable.						
90-91—VSZ Kosice		Czech.	49	1	7	8	12	—	—	—	—	—
91-92—VSZ Kosice		Czech.	43	4	9	13	. . .	—	—	—	—	—
92-93—Indianapolis		IHL	77	14	29	43	92	5	0	1	1	2
93-94—Indianapolis		IHL	55	9	10	19	71	—	—	—	—	—
—Chicago		NHL	12	0	1	1	12	—	—	—	—	—
94-95—Indianapolis		IHL	67	5	28	33	91	—	—	—	—	—
NHL totals			12	0	1	1	12					

DRUCE, JOHN
RW, KINGS

PERSONAL: Born February 23, 1966, in Peterborough, Ont. . . . 6-2/195. . . . Shoots right. . . . Name pronounced DROOZ.
TRANSACTIONS/CAREER NOTES: Broke collarbone (October 1983). . . . Tore ligaments in ankle (December 1984). . . . Selected by Washington Capitals in second round (second Capitals pick, 40th overall) of NHL entry draft (June 15, 1985). . . . Tore thumb ligaments (October 1985). . . . Fractured wrist (October 18, 1992); missed 18 games. . . . Traded by Capitals to Winnipeg Jets with conditional pick in 1993 draft for RW Pat Elynuik (October 1, 1992). . . . Signed as free agent by Los Angeles Kings (August 2, 1993). . . . Strained groin (April 7, 1995); missed two games.
STATISTICAL PLATEAUS: Three-goal games: 1991-92 (1), 1993-94 (1). Total: 2.

Season	Team	League	REGULAR SEASON					PLAYOFFS				
			Gms.	G	A	Pts.	PIM	Gms.	G	A	Pts.	PIM
83-84—Peterborough Jr. B		OHA	40	15	18	33	69	—	—	—	—	—
84-85—Peterborough		OHL	54	12	14	26	90	17	6	2	8	21
85-86—Peterborough		OHL	49	22	24	46	84	16	0	5	5	34
86-87—Binghamton		AHL	7	13	9	22	131	12	0	3	3	28
87-88—Binghamton		AHL	68	32	29	61	82	1	0	0	0	0
88-89—Washington		NHL	48	8	7	15	62	1	0	0	0	0
—Baltimore		AHL	16	2	11	13	10	—	—	—	—	—
89-90—Washington		NHL	45	8	3	11	52	15	14	3	17	23
—Baltimore		AHL	26	15	16	31	38	—	—	—	—	—
90-91—Washington		NHL	80	22	36	58	46	11	1	1	2	7
91-92—Washington		NHL	67	19	18	37	39	7	1	0	1	2
92-93—Winnipeg		NHL	50	6	14	20	37	2	0	0	0	0
93-94—Phoenix		IHL	8	5	6	11	9	—	—	—	—	—
—Los Angeles		NHL	55	14	17	31	50	—	—	—	—	—
94-95—Los Angeles		NHL	43	15	5	20	20	—	—	—	—	—
NHL totals			388	92	100	192	306	36	16	4	20	32

DRULIA, STAN
RW

PERSONAL: Born January 5, 1968, in Elmira, N.Y. . . . 5-11/190. . . . Shoots right. . . . Name pronounced DROOL-yuh.
TRANSACTIONS/CAREER NOTES: Selected by Pittsburgh Penguins as underage junior in 11th round (11th Penguins pick, 214th overall) of NHL entry draft (June 21, 1986). . . . Signed as free agent by Edmonton Oilers (May 1989). . . . Signed as free agent by Tampa Bay Lightning (September 1, 1992).
HONORS: Won Jim Mahon Memorial Trophy (1988-89). . . . Won Leo Lalonde Memorial Trophy (1988-89). . . . Named to OHL All-Star first team (1988-89). . . . Won ECHL Most Valuable Player Award (1990-91). . . . Won ECHL Top Scorer Award (1990-91). . . . Named to ECHL All-Star first team (1990-91). . . . Named to AHL All-Star second team (1991-92). . . . Named to IHL All-Star first team (1993-94 and 1994-95).

Season	Team	League	REGULAR SEASON					PLAYOFFS				
			Gms.	G	A	Pts.	PIM	Gms.	G	A	Pts.	PIM
84-85—Belleville		OHL	63	24	31	55	33	—	—	—	—	—
85-86—Belleville		OHL	66	43	37	80	73	—	—	—	—	—
86-87—Hamilton		OHL	55	27	51	78	26	—	—	—	—	—
87-88—Hamilton		OHL	65	52	69	121	44	14	8	16	24	12
88-89—Niagara Falls		OHL	47	52	93	145	59	17	11	*26	37	18
—Maine		AHL	3	1	1	2	0	—	—	—	—	—
89-90—Cape Breton		AHL	31	5	7	12	2	—	—	—	—	—
—Phoenix		IHL	16	6	3	9	2	—	—	—	—	—
90-91—Knoxville		ECHL	64	*63	77	*140	39	3	3	2	5	4
91-92—New Haven		AHL	77	49	53	102	46	5	2	4	6	4
92-93—Tampa Bay		NHL	24	2	1	3	10	—	—	—	—	—
—Atlanta		IHL	47	28	26	54	38	3	2	3	5	4
93-94—Atlanta		IHL	79	54	60	114	70	14	13	12	25	8
94-95—Atlanta		IHL	66	41	49	90	60	5	1	5	6	2
NHL totals			24	2	1	3	10					

DRURY, CHRIS
C, DENVER

PERSONAL: Born August 20, 1976, in Trumbull, Conn. . . . 5-10/180. . . . Shoots right. . . . Brother of Ted Drury, center, Hartford Whalers.
HIGH SCHOOL: Fairfield (Conn.) College Prep School.
COLLEGE: Boston University.
TRANSACTIONS/CAREER NOTES: Selected by Quebec Nordiques in third round (fifth Nordiques pick, 72nd overall) of NHL entry draft (June 29, 1994). . . . Nordiques franchise moved to Denver for 1995-96 season.

Season Team	League		REGULAR SEASON					PLAYOFFS			
		Gms.	G	A	Pts.	PIM	Gms.	G	A	Pts.	PIM
92-93—Fairfield College Prep	Conn. H.S.	24	25	32	57	15	—	—	—	—	—
93-94—Fairfield College Prep	Conn. H.S.	24	37	18	55	...	—	—	—	—	—
94-95—Boston University	Hockey East	39	12	15	27	38	—	—	—	—	—

DRURY, TED
C, WHALERS

PERSONAL: Born September 13, 1971, in Boston. . . . 6-0/185. . . . Shoots left. . . . Full name: Theodore Evans Drury. . . . Name pronounced DROO-ree. . . . Brother of Chris Drury, center in Denver's system.
HIGH SCHOOL: Fairfield (Conn.) College Prep School.
COLLEGE: Harvard.
TRANSACTIONS/CAREER NOTES: Broke ankle (January 1988). . . . Selected by Calgary Flames in second round (second Flames pick, 42nd overall) of NHL entry draft (June 17, 1989). . . . Fractured kneecap (December 22, 1993); missed 15 games. . . . Traded by Flames with D Gary Suter and LW Paul Ranheim to Hartford Whalers for C Mikael Nylander, D Zarley Zalapski and D James Patrick (March 10, 1994). . . . Strained back (March 9, 1995); missed three games.
HONORS: Named ECAC Player of the Year (1992-93). . . . Named to NCAA All-America East first team (1992-93). . . . Named to ECAC All-Star first team (1992-93).

Season Team	League		REGULAR SEASON					PLAYOFFS			
		Gms.	G	A	Pts.	PIM	Gms.	G	A	Pts.	PIM
87-88—Fairfield College Prep	Conn. H.S.	...	21	28	49	...	—	—	—	—	—
88-89—Fairfield College Prep	Conn. H.S.	...	35	31	66	...	—	—	—	—	—
89-90—Harvard University	ECAC	17	9	13	22	10	—	—	—	—	—
90-91—Harvard University	ECAC	26	18	18	36	22	—	—	—	—	—
91-92—U.S. national team	Int'l	53	11	23	34	30	—	—	—	—	—
—U.S. Olympic Team	Int'l	7	1	1	2	0	—	—	—	—	—
92-93—Harvard University	ECAC	31	22	41	*63	26	—	—	—	—	—
93-94—Calgary	NHL	34	5	7	12	26	—	—	—	—	—
—U.S. national team	Int'l	11	1	4	5	11	—	—	—	—	—
—U.S. Olympic Team	Int'l	7	1	2	3	2	—	—	—	—	—
—Hartford.........................	NHL	16	1	5	6	10	—	—	—	—	—
94-95—Hartford.........................	NHL	34	3	6	9	21	—	—	—	—	—
—Springfield...................	AHL	2	0	1	1	0	—	—	—	—	—
NHL totals................................		84	9	18	27	57					

DUBE, CHRISTIAN
C, RANGERS

PERSONAL: Born April 25, 1977, in Quebec City. . . . 5-11/170. . . . Shoots right.
TRANSACTIONS/CAREER NOTES: Selected by New York Rangers in second round (first Rangers pick, 39th overall) of NHL entry draft (July 8, 1995).
HONORS: Won Michael Bergeron Trophy (1993-94).

Season Team	League		REGULAR SEASON					PLAYOFFS			
		Gms.	G	A	Pts.	PIM	Gms.	G	A	Pts.	PIM
93-94—Sherbrooke......................	QMJHL	72	31	41	72	22	11	3	2	5	6
94-95—Sherbrooke......................	QMJHL	71	36	65	101	43	7	1	7	8	8

DUBE, YANNICK
C, CANUCKS

PERSONAL: Born June 14, 1974, in Gaspe, Que. . . . 5-9/170. . . . Shoots right. . . . Name pronounced YAH-nihk doo-BAY.
TRANSACTIONS/CAREER NOTES: Selected by Vancouver Canucks in fifth round (sixth Canucks pick, 117th overall) of NHL entry draft (June 29, 1994).
HONORS: Won Can.HL Most Sportsmanlike Player of the Year Award (1993-94). . . . Won George Parsons Trophy (1993-94). . . . Won Jean Beliveau Trophy (1993-94). . . . Won Frank J. Selke Trophy (1993-94). . . . Named to Can.HL All-Star second team (1993-94). . . . Named to QMJHL All-Star first team (1993-94).

Season Team	League		REGULAR SEASON					PLAYOFFS			
		Gms.	G	A	Pts.	PIM	Gms.	G	A	Pts.	PIM
91-92—Laval	QMJHL	65	14	19	33	8	10	0	2	2	2
92-93—Laval	QMJHL	68	45	38	83	25	13	6	7	13	6
93-94—Laval	QMJHL	64	*66	75	*141	30	21	12	18	30	8
94-95—Canadian national team ...	Int'l	24	4	6	10	16	—	—	—	—	—
—Syracuse	AHL	39	10	11	21	8	—	—	—	—	—
—Laval	QMJHL	1	0	1	1	0	16	11	3	14	12

DUBINSKY, MIKE
RW, CANUCKS

PERSONAL: Born August 26, 1976, in Edmonton. . . . 6-2/185. . . . Shoots right. . . . Name pronounced doo-BIHN-skee.
TRANSACTIONS/CAREER NOTES: Selected by Vancouver Canucks in fourth round (fifth Canucks pick, 92nd overall) of NHL entry draft (June 29, 1994).

Season Team	League		REGULAR SEASON					PLAYOFFS			
		Gms.	G	A	Pts.	PIM	Gms.	G	A	Pts.	PIM
92-93—Brandon...........................	WHL	64	10	25	35	44	3	0	0	0	0

D

Season	Team	League	Gms.	G	A	Pts.	PIM	Gms.	G	A	Pts.	PIM
93-94—Brandon		WHL	20	9	13	22	23	—	—	—	—	—
94-95—Brandon		WHL	4	1	2	3	0	1	1	0	1	4

DUBINSKY, STEVE
C, BLACKHAWKS

PERSONAL: Born July 9, 1970, in Montreal.... 6-0/190.... Shoots left.... Name pronounced doo-BIHN-skee.
COLLEGE: Clarkson (N.Y.).
TRANSACTIONS/CAREER NOTES: Selected by Chicago Blackhawks in 11th round (11th Blackhawks pick, 226th overall) of NHL entry draft (June 16, 1990).

Season	Team	League	Gms.	G	A	Pts.	PIM	Gms.	G	A	Pts.	PIM
89-90—Clarkson		ECAC	35	7	10	17	24	—	—	—	—	—
90-91—Clarkson		ECAC	38	15	23	38	26	—	—	—	—	—
91-92—Clarkson		ECAC	33	21	34	55	40	—	—	—	—	—
92-93—Clarkson		ECAC	35	18	26	44	58	—	—	—	—	—
93-94—Chicago		NHL	27	2	6	8	16	6	0	0	0	10
—Indianapolis		IHL	54	15	25	40	63	—	—	—	—	—
94-95—Indianapolis		IHL	62	16	11	27	29	—	—	—	—	—
—Chicago		NHL	16	0	0	0	8	—	—	—	—	—
NHL totals			43	2	6	8	24	6	0	0	0	10

DuBOIS, ERIC
D, LIGHTNING

PERSONAL: Born May 10, 1970, in Moncton, N.B.... 6-0/195.... Shoots right.... Name pronounced doo-BWAH.
TRANSACTIONS/CAREER NOTES: Selected by Quebec Nordiques in fourth round (sixth Nordiques pick, 76th overall) of NHL entry draft (June 17, 1989).... Signed as free agent by Tampa Bay Lightning (July 2, 1993).
HONORS: Named to QMJHL All-Star first team (1988-89).

Season	Team	League	Gms.	G	A	Pts.	PIM	Gms.	G	A	Pts.	PIM
86-87—Laval		QMJHL	61	1	17	18	29	—	—	—	—	—
87-88—Laval		QMJHL	69	8	32	40	132	14	1	7	8	12
88-89—Laval		QMJHL	68	15	44	59	126	17	1	11	12	55
89-90—Laval		QMJHL	66	9	36	45	153	13	3	8	11	29
90-91—Laval		QMJHL	57	15	45	60	122	13	3	5	8	29
91-92—New Haven		AHL	1	0	0	0	2	—	—	—	—	—
—Halifax		AHL	14	0	0	0	8	—	—	—	—	—
—Greensboro		ECHL	36	7	17	24	62	11	4	4	8	40
92-93—Greensboro		ECHL	25	5	20	25	70	—	—	—	—	—
—Atlanta		IHL	43	3	9	12	44	9	0	0	0	10
93-94—Atlanta		IHL	80	13	26	39	174	14	0	7	7	48
94-95—Atlanta		IHL	56	3	25	28	56	5	0	3	3	24

DUCHESNE, GAETAN
LW, PANTHERS

PERSONAL: Born July 11, 1962, in Quebec City.... 5-11/200.... Shoots left.... Name pronounced gay-tan doo-SHAYN.
TRANSACTIONS/CAREER NOTES: Selected by Washington Capitals in eighth round (eighth Capitals pick, 152nd overall) of NHL entry draft (June 10, 1981).... Bruised right ankle (December 30, 1981).... Broke finger (October 11, 1984).... Traded by Capitals with C Alan Haworth and first-round pick in 1987 draft (C Joe Sakic) to Quebec Nordiques for C Dale Hunter and G Clint Malarchuk (June 1987).... Sprained left knee (January 26, 1988).... Sprained left shoulder (November 1988).... Traded by Nordiques to Minnesota North Stars for C Kevin Kaminski (June 18, 1989).... Sprained right knee (November 11, 1989); missed eight games.... North Stars franchise moved from Minnesota to Dallas and renamed Stars for 1993-94 season.... Traded by Stars to San Jose Sharks for sixth-round pick in 1993 draft (June 20, 1993).... Traded by Sharks to Florida Panthers for sixth-round pick (C Timo Hakanen) in 1995 draft (April 7, 1995).

Season	Team	League	Gms.	G	A	Pts.	PIM	Gms.	G	A	Pts.	PIM
79-80—Quebec		QMJHL	46	9	28	37	22	5	0	2	2	9
80-81—Quebec		QMJHL	72	27	45	72	63	7	1	4	5	6
81-82—Washington		NHL	74	9	14	23	46	—	—	—	—	—
82-83—Hershey		AHL	1	1	0	1	0	—	—	—	—	—
—Washington		NHL	77	18	19	37	52	4	1	1	2	4
83-84—Washington		NHL	79	17	19	36	29	8	2	1	3	2
84-85—Washington		NHL	67	15	23	38	32	5	0	1	1	7
85-86—Washington		NHL	80	11	28	39	39	9	4	3	7	12
86-87—Washington		NHL	74	17	35	52	53	7	3	0	3	14
87-88—Quebec		NHL	80	24	23	47	83	—	—	—	—	—
88-89—Quebec		NHL	70	8	21	29	56	—	—	—	—	—
89-90—Minnesota		NHL	72	12	8	20	33	7	0	0	0	6
90-91—Minnesota		NHL	68	9	9	18	18	23	2	3	5	34
91-92—Minnesota		NHL	73	8	15	23	102	7	1	0	1	6
92-93—Minnesota		NHL	84	16	13	29	30	—	—	—	—	—
93-94—San Jose		NHL	84	12	18	30	28	14	1	4	5	12
94-95—San Jose		NHL	33	2	7	9	16	—	—	—	—	—
—Florida		NHL	13	1	2	3	0	—	—	—	—	—
NHL totals			1028	179	254	433	617	84	14	13	27	97

DUCHESNE, STEVE

D, SENATORS

PERSONAL: Born June 30, 1965, in Sept-Iles, Que. . . . 5-11/195. . . . Shoots left. . . . Name pronounced doo-SHAYN.

TRANSACTIONS/CAREER NOTES: Signed as free agent by Los Angeles Kings (October 1, 1984). . . . Strained left knee (January 26, 1988). . . . Separated left shoulder (November 1988). . . . Traded by Kings with C Steve Kasper and fourth-round pick in 1991 draft (D Aris Brimanis) to Philadelphia Flyers for D Jeff Chychrun and rights to RW Jari Kurri (May 30, 1991). . . . Traded by Flyers with G Ron Hextall, C Mike Ricci, C Peter Forsberg, D Kerry Huffman, first-round pick in 1993 draft (D Jocelyn Thibault), cash and future considerations to Quebec Nordiques for C Eric Lindros (June 20, 1992). . . . Flyers sent LW Chris Simon and first-round pick in 1994 draft (traded to Toronto Maple Leafs) to Nordiques to complete deal (July 21, 1992). . . . Suffered a concussion (January 2, 1993); missed one game. . . . Suffered from the flu (March 20, 1993); missed one game. . . . Refused to report to Nordiques in 1993-94 due to contract dispute. . . . Traded by Nordiques with RW Denis Chasse to St. Louis Blues for C Ron Sutter, C Bob Bassen and D Garth Butcher (January 23, 1994). . . . Injured back (March 30, 1994); missed one game. . . . Injured shoulder (March 31, 1995); missed one game. . . . Traded by Blues to Ottawa Senators for second-round pick in 1996 draft (August 4, 1995).

HONORS: Named to QMJHL All-Star first team (1984-85). . . . Named to NHL All-Rookie team (1986-87). . . . Played in NHL All-Star Game (1989, 1990 and 1993).

STATISTICAL PLATEAUS: Three-goal games: 1988-89 (1), 1991-92 (1), 1993-94 (1). Total: 3.

Season Team	League	Gms.	G	A	Pts.	PIM	Gms.	G	A	Pts.	PIM
		REGULAR SEASON					**PLAYOFFS**				
83-84—Drummondville	QMJHL	67	1	34	35	79	—	—	—	—	—
84-85—Drummondville	QMJHL	65	22	54	76	94	5	4	7	11	8
85-86—New Haven	AHL	75	14	35	49	76	5	0	2	2	9
86-87—Los Angeles	NHL	75	13	25	38	74	5	2	2	4	4
87-88—Los Angeles	NHL	71	16	39	55	109	5	1	3	4	14
88-89—Los Angeles	NHL	79	25	50	75	92	11	4	4	8	12
89-90—Los Angeles	NHL	79	20	42	62	36	10	2	9	11	6
90-91—Los Angeles	NHL	78	21	41	62	66	12	4	8	12	8
91-92—Philadelphia	NHL	78	18	38	56	86	—	—	—	—	—
92-93—Quebec	NHL	82	20	62	82	57	6	0	5	5	6
93-94—St. Louis	NHL	36	12	19	31	14	4	0	2	2	2
94-95—St. Louis	NHL	47	12	26	38	36	7	0	4	4	2
NHL totals		625	157	342	499	570	60	13	37	50	54

DUERDEN, DAVE

LW, PANTHERS

PERSONAL: Born April 11, 1977, in Oshawa, Ont. . . . 6-2/182. . . . Shoots left. **HIGH SCHOOL:** Thomas A. Stewart (Peterborough, Ont.).

TRANSACTIONS/CAREER NOTES: Selected by Florida Panthers in fourth round (fourth Panthers pick, 80th overall) of NHL entry draft (July 8, 1995).

Season Team	League	Gms.	G	A	Pts.	PIM	Gms.	G	A	Pts.	PIM
		REGULAR SEASON					**PLAYOFFS**				
93-94—Wexford	Tier II Jr. A	47	17	24	44	26	—	—	—	—	—
94-95—Peterborough	OHL	66	20	33	53	21	11	6	2	8	6

DUFFUS, PARRIS

G, JETS

PERSONAL: Born January 27, 1970, in Denver. . . . 6-2/192. . . . Catches left. . . . Name pronounced PAIR-ihz DOO-fihz. **COLLEGE:** Cornell.

TRANSACTIONS/CAREER NOTES: Selected by St. Louis Blues in ninth round (sixth Blues pick, 180th overall) of NHL entry draft (June 16, 1990). . . . Signed as free agent by Winnipeg Jets (July 21, 1995).

HONORS: Named to NCAA All-America East first team (1991-92). . . . Named to ECAC All-Star second team (1991-92).

Season Team	League	Gms.	Min.	W	L	T	GA	SO	Avg.	Gms.	Min.	W	L	GA	SO	Avg.
		REGULAR SEASON								**PLAYOFFS**						
88-89—Melfort	SJHL	39	2207	5	28	3	227	1	6.17	—	—	—	—	—	—	—
89-90—Melfort	SJHL	51	2828	17	26	3	226	2	4.79	—	—	—	—	—	—	—
90-91—Cornell University	ECAC	4	37	0	0	0	3	0	4.86	—	—	—	—	—	—	—
91-92—Cornell University	ECAC	28	1677	14	11	3	74	1	2.65	—	—	—	—	—	—	—
92-93—Hampton Roads	ECHL	4	245	3	1	†0	13	0	3.18	—	—	—	—	—	—	—
—Peoria	IHL	37	2149	16	15	†0	142	0	3.96	1	59	0	1	5	0	5.08
93-94—Peoria	IHL	36	1845	19	10	†3	141	0	4.59	2	92	0	1	6	0	3.91
94-95—Peoria	IHL	29	1581	17	7	†3	71	3	2.69	7	410	4	2	17	0	2.49

DUFRESNE, DONALD

D, BLUES

PERSONAL: Born April 10, 1967, in Quebec City. . . . 6-1/206. . . . Shoots left. . . . Name pronounced doo-FRAYN.

TRANSACTIONS/CAREER NOTES: Suffered from pneumonia (November 1984). . . . Selected by Montreal Canadiens in sixth round (eighth Canadiens pick, 117th overall) of NHL entry draft (June 15, 1985). . . . Dislocated shoulder (January 8, 1988). . . . Sprained ankle (February 1989). . . . Separated shoulder (October 5, 1989); missed 15 games. . . . Reinjured shoulder (December 9, 1989). . . . Tore ligaments in right knee (December 9, 1991); missed 15 games. . . . Sprained knee (February 20, 1993); missed three games. . . . Strained rib cage muscles (March 3, 1993); missed three games. . . . Traded by Canadiens to Tampa Bay Lightning (June 18, 1993) to complete deal in which Canadiens sent D Eric Charron, D Alain Cote and future considerations to Lightning for D Rob Ramage (March 20, 1993). . . . Suffered knee ligament sprain (January 26, 1994); missed eight games. . . . Reinjured knee (February 17, 1994); missed seven games. . . . Traded by Lightning to Los Angeles Kings for sixth-round pick (C Daniel Juden) in 1994 draft (March 19, 1994). . . . Selected by St. Louis Blues in 1994-95 waiver draft for cash (January 18, 1995).

HONORS: Named to QMJHL All-Star second team (1985-86 and 1986-87).

MISCELLANEOUS: Member of Stanley Cup championship team (

Season	Team	League	REGULAR SEASON Gms.	G	A	Pts.	PIM	PLAYOFFS Gms.	G	A	Pts.	PIM
83-84	Trois-Rivieres	QMJHL	67	7	12	19	97	—	—	—	—	—
84-85	Trois-Rivieres	QMJHL	65	5	30	35	112	7	1	3	4	12
85-86	Trois-Rivieres	QMJHL	63	8	32	40	160	1	0	0	0	0
86-87	Longueuil	QMJHL	67	5	29	34	97	20	1	8	9	38
87-88	Sherbrooke	AHL	47	1	8	9	107	6	1	1	2	34
88-89	Montreal	NHL	13	0	1	1	43	6	1	1	2	4
	—Sherbrooke	AHL	47	0	12	12	170	—	—	—	—	—
89-90	Montreal	NHL	18	0	4	4	23	10	0	1	1	18
	—Sherbrooke	AHL	38	2	11	13	104	0	0	0	0	0
90-91	Fredericton	AHL	10	1	4	5	35	1	0	0	0	0
	—Montreal	NHL	53	2	13	15	55	10	0	1	1	21
91-92	Montreal	NHL	3	0	0	0	2	—	—	—	—	—
	—Fredericton	AHL	31	8	12	20	60	7	0	0	0	10
92-93	Montreal	NHL	32	1	2	3	32	2	0	0	0	0
93-94	Tampa Bay	NHL	51	2	6	8	48	—	—	—	—	—
	—Los Angeles	NHL	9	0	0	0	10	—	—	—	—	—
94-95	St. Louis	NHL	22	0	3	3	10	3	0	0	0	4
NHL totals			201	5	29	34	223	31	1	3	4	47

DUNCANSON, CRAIG

LW, RANGERS

PERSONAL: Born March 17, 1967, in Sudbury, Ont. . . . 6-0/190. . . . Shoots left. . . . Full name: Craig Murray Duncanson.

TRANSACTIONS/CAREER NOTES: Tore knee ligaments (September 1984). . . . Selected by Los Angeles Kings as underage junior in first round (first Kings pick, ninth overall) of NHL entry draft (June 15, 1985). . . . Suffered deep leg bruise (November 23, 1986). . . . Traded by Kings to Minnesota North Stars for G Daniel Berthiaume (September 6, 1990). . . . Traded by North Stars to Winnipeg Jets for C Brian Hunt (September 6, 1990). . . . Traded by Jets with LW Brent Hughes and C Simon Wheeldon to Washington Capitals for LW Bob Joyce, D Kent Paynter and C Tyler Larter (May 21, 1991). . . . Loaned to Jets organization (February 26, 1992). . . . Signed as free agent by New York Rangers (September 4, 1992).

Season	Team	League	REGULAR SEASON Gms.	G	A	Pts.	PIM	PLAYOFFS Gms.	G	A	Pts.	PIM
82-83	St. Michael's Jr. B	ODHA	32	14	19	33	68	—	—	—	—	—
83-84	Sudbury	OHL	62	38	38	76	178	—	—	—	—	—
84-85	Sudbury	OHL	53	35	28	63	129	—	—	—	—	—
85-86	Sudbury	OHL	21	12	17	29	55	—	—	—	—	—
	—Cornwall	OHL	40	31	50	81	135	6	4	7	11	2
	—Los Angeles	NHL	2	0	1	1	0	—	—	—	—	—
	—New Haven	AHL	—	—	—	—	—	2	0	0	0	5
86-87	Cornwall	OHL	52	22	45	67	88	5	4	3	7	20
	—Los Angeles	NHL	2	0	0	0	24	—	—	—	—	—
87-88	New Haven	AHL	57	15	25	40	170	—	—	—	—	—
	—Los Angeles	NHL	9	0	0	0	12	—	—	—	—	—
88-89	New Haven	AHL	69	25	39	64	200	17	4	8	12	60
	—Los Angeles	NHL	5	0	0	0	0	—	—	—	—	—
89-90	Los Angeles	NHL	10	3	2	5	9	—	—	—	—	—
	—New Haven	AHL	51	17	30	47	152	—	—	—	—	—
90-91	Moncton	AHL	58	16	34	50	107	9	3	11	14	31
	—Winnipeg	NHL	7	2	0	2	16	—	—	—	—	—
91-92	Baltimore	AHL	46	20	26	46	98	—	—	—	—	—
	—Moncton	AHL	19	12	9	21	6	11	6	4	10	10
92-93	Binghamton	AHL	69	35	59	94	126	14	7	5	12	9
	—New York Rangers	NHL	3	0	1	1	0	—	—	—	—	—
93-94	Binghamton	AHL	70	25	44	69	83	—	—	—	—	—
94-95	Binghamton	AHL	62	21	43	64	105	11	4	4	8	16
NHL totals			38	5	4	9	61					

DUNHAM, MIKE

G, DEVILS

PERSONAL: Born June 1, 1972, in Johnson City, N.Y. . . . 6-3/185. . . . Catches left. . . . Full name: Michael Francis Dunham.

HIGH SCHOOL: Canterbury (New Milford, Conn.).

COLLEGE: Maine.

TRANSACTIONS/CAREER NOTES: Selected by New Jersey Devils in third round (fourth Devils pick, 53rd overall) of NHL entry draft (June 16, 1990).

HONORS: Named to NCAA All-America East first team (1992-93). . . . Named to Hockey East All-Star first team (1992-93). . . . Shared Harry (Hap) Holmes Memorial Trophy with Corey Schwab (1994-95). . . . Shared Jack Butterfield Trophy with Corey Schwab (1994-95).

Season	Team	League	REGULAR SEASON Gms.	Min.	W	L	T	GA	SO	Avg.	PLAYOFFS Gms.	Min.	W	L	GA	SO	Avg.
87-88	Canterbury School	Conn. HS	29	...	...	...	...	...	4	2.37	—	—	—	—	—	—	—
88-89	Canterbury School	Conn. HS	25	...	...	...	...	63	2	...	—	—	—	—	—	—	—
89-90	Canterbury School	Conn. HS	32	1558	...	...	...	55	...	2.12	—	—	—	—	—	—	—
90-91	University of Maine	Hoc. East	23	1275	14	5	2	63	2	*2.96	—	—	—	—	—	—	—
91-92	University of Maine	Hoc. East	7	382	6	0	0	14	1	2.20	—	—	—	—	—	—	—
	—U.S. national team	Int'l	3	157	0	1	1	10	0	3.82	—	—	—	—	—	—	—
	—U.S. Olympic Team	Int'l						Did not play.									

Season	Team	League	Gms.	Min.	W	L	T	GA	SO	Avg.	Gms.	Min.	W	L	GA	SO	Avg.
92-93—University of Maine	Hoc. East	25	1429	21	1	1	63	...	2.65	—	—	—	—	—	—	—	
93-94—U.S. national team	Int'l	33	1983	...	...	...	125	...	3.78	—	—	—	—	—	—	—	
—U.S. Olympic Team	Int'l	3	179	...	...	...	15	0	5.03	—	—	—	—	—	—	—	
—Albany	AHL	5	305	2	2	1	26	0	5.11	—	—	—	—	—	—	—	
94-95—Albany	AHL	35	2120	20	7	8	99	1	2.80	7	420	6	1	20	1	2.86	

DUPAUL, COSMO
C, SENATORS

PERSONAL: Born April 11, 1975, in Pointe-Claire, Que.... 6-0/185.... Shoots left.
TRANSACTIONS/CAREER NOTES: Selected by Ottawa Senators in fourth round (fourth Senators pick, 91st overall) of NHL entry draft (June 26, 1993).

			REGULAR SEASON					PLAYOFFS			
Season	Team	League	Gms.	G	A	Pts.	PIM	Gms.	G	A	Pts.	PIM
92-93—Victoriaville.....................	QMJHL	67	23	35	58	16	6	1	3	4	2
93-94—Victoriaville.....................	QMJHL	66	26	46	72	32	5	2	2	4	6
94-95—Victoriaville...................	QMJHL	71	29	44	73	60	4	3	4	7	6

DUPRE, YANICK
LW, FLYERS

PERSONAL: Born November 20, 1972, in Montreal.... 6-0/192.... Shoots left.... Name pronounced YAH-nihk doo-PRAY.
TRANSACTIONS/CAREER NOTES: Pulled ankle ligament (September 1989).... Traded by Chicoutimi Sagueneens with D Guy Lehoux and RW Eric Meloche to Drummondville Voltigeurs for RW Daniel Dore, RW Denis Chasse and D Pierre-Paul Landry (December 19, 1989).... Injured knee ligament (October 1990).... Selected by Philadelphia Flyers in third round (second Flyers pick, 50th overall) of NHL entry draft (June 22, 1991).

			REGULAR SEASON					PLAYOFFS			
Season	Team	League	Gms.	G	A	Pts.	PIM	Gms.	G	A	Pts.	PIM
89-90—Chicoutimi.....................	QMJHL	24	5	9	14	27	—	—	—	—	—
—Drummondville................	QMJHL	30	10	10	20	32	—	—	—	—	—
90-91—Drummondville................	QMJHL	58	29	38	67	87	11	8	5	13	33
91-92—Philadelphia	NHL	1	0	0	0	0	—	—	—	—	—
—Drummondville................	QMJHL	28	19	17	36	48	—	—	—	—	—
—Verdun........................	QMJHL	12	7	14	21	21	19	9	9	18	20
92-93—Hershey	AHL	63	13	24	37	22	—	—	—	—	—
93-94—Hershey	AHL	51	22	20	42	42	8	1	3	4	2
94-95—Hershey	AHL	41	15	19	34	35	—	—	—	—	—
—Philadelphia	NHL	22	0	0	0	8	—	—	—	—	—
NHL totals................................		23	0	0	0	8					

DUTHIE, RYAN
C, FLAMES

PERSONAL: Born September 2, 1974, in Strathmore, Alta.... 5-10/180.... Shoots right.... Name pronounced DUH-thee.
HIGH SCHOOL: Joel E. Ferris (Spokane, Wash.).
TRANSACTIONS/CAREER NOTES: Selected by New York Islanders in fifth round (fourth Islanders pick, 105th overall) of NHL entry draft (June 20, 1992).... Returned to the draft pool by Islanders and selected by Calgary Flames in fourth round (fourth Flames pick, 91st overall) of NHL entry draft (June 29, 1994).
HONORS: Named to WHL (West) All-Star first team (1993-94).

			REGULAR SEASON					PLAYOFFS			
Season	Team	League	Gms.	G	A	Pts.	PIM	Gms.	G	A	Pts.	PIM
91-92—Spokane	WHL	67	23	37	60	119	10	5	10	15	18
92-93—Spokane	WHL	60	26	58	84	122	9	7	2	9	8
93-94—Spokane	WHL	71	57	69	126	111	3	3	5	8	11
94-95—Saint John	AHL	72	18	21	39	70	2	0	0	0	0

DUTIAUME, MARK
LW, SABRES

PERSONAL: Born January 31, 1977, in Winnipeg.... 6-0/200.... Shoots left.
TRANSACTIONS/CAREER NOTES: Selected by Buffalo Sabres in second round (third Sabres pick, 42nd overall) of NHL entry draft (July 8, 1995).

			REGULAR SEASON					PLAYOFFS			
Season	Team	League	Gms.	G	A	Pts.	PIM	Gms.	G	A	Pts.	PIM
93-94—Tri-City	WHL	3	2	0	2	0	—	—	—	—	—
—Brandon............................	WHL	55	4	7	11	43	12	0	2	2	6
94-95—Brandon............................	WHL	62	23	21	44	80	17	1	2	3	33

DVORAK, RADEK
LW, PANTHERS

PERSONAL: Born March 9, 1977, in Ceske Budejovice, Czechoslovakia.... 6-2/185.... Shoots right.
TRANSACTIONS/CAREER NOTES: Selected by Florida Panthers in first round (first Panthers pick, 10th overall) of NHL entry draft (July 8, 1995).

			REGULAR SEASON					PLAYOFFS			
Season	Team	League	Gms.	G	A	Pts.	PIM	Gms.	G	A	Pts.	PIM
92-93—Motor Ceske-Budejovice..	Czech.	35	44	46	90	...	—	—	—	—	—
93-94—Motor Ceske-Budejovice..	Czech.	20	17	18	35	...	—	—	—	—	—
—HC Ceske Budejovice	Czech.	8	0	0	0	...	—	—	—	—	—
94-95—HC Ceske Budejovice	Czech.	10	3	5	8	...	9	5	1	6	...

D

DYKHUIS, KARL

D, FLYERS

PERSONAL: Born July 8, 1972, in Sept-Iles, Que.... 6-3/195.... Shoots left.... Name pronounced DIGH-kowz.
TRANSACTIONS/CAREER NOTES: Selected by Chicago Blackhawks in first round (first Blackhawks pick, 16th overall) of NHL entry draft (June 16, 1990).... QMJHL rights traded by Hull Olympiques to College Francais for first- and sixth-round draft picks (January 10, 1991).... Traded by Blackhawks to Philadelphia Flyers for D Bob Wilkie (February 16, 1995).
HONORS: Won Raymond Lagace Trophy (1988-89).... Won Michael Bossy Trophy (1989-90).... Named to QMJHL All-Star first team (1989-90).

Season	Team	League	REGULAR SEASON					PLAYOFFS				
			Gms.	G	A	Pts.	PIM	Gms.	G	A	Pts.	PIM
88-89	Hull	QMJHL	63	2	29	31	59	9	1	9	10	6
89-90	Hull	QMJHL	69	10	45	55	119	11	2	5	7	2
90-91	Longueuil	QMJHL	3	1	4	5	6	—	—	—	—	—
	Canadian national team	Int'l	37	2	9	11	16	—	—	—	—	—
91-92	Longueuil	QMJHL	29	5	19	24	55	17	0	12	12	14
	Chicago	NHL	6	1	3	4	4	—	—	—	—	—
92-93	Indianapolis	IHL	59	5	18	23	76	5	1	1	2	8
	Chicago	NHL	12	0	5	5	0	—	—	—	—	—
93-94	Indianapolis	IHL	73	7	25	32	132	—	—	—	—	—
94-95	Indianapolis	IHL	52	2	21	23	63	—	—	—	—	—
	Hershey	AHL	1	0	0	0	0	—	—	—	—	—
NHL totals			18	1	8	9	4					

DZIEDZIC, JOE

LW, PENGUINS

PERSONAL: Born December 18, 1971, in Minneapolis.... 6-3/220.... Shoots left.... Full name: Joseph Walter Dziedzic.
HIGH SCHOOL: Edison (Minneapolis).
COLLEGE: Minnesota.
TRANSACTIONS/CAREER NOTES: Selected by Pittsburgh Penguins in third round (second Penguins pick, 61st overall) of NHL entry draft (June 16, 1990).

Season	Team	League	REGULAR SEASON					PLAYOFFS				
			Gms.	G	A	Pts.	PIM	Gms.	G	A	Pts.	PIM
88-89	Minneapolis Edison H.S.	Minn. H.S.	25	47	27	74	34	—	—	—	—	—
89-90	Minneapolis Edison H.S.	Minn. H.S.	17	29	19	48	0	—	—	—	—	—
90-91	University of Minnesota	WCHA	20	6	4	10	26	—	—	—	—	—
91-92	University of Minnesota	WCHA	37	9	10	19	68	—	—	—	—	—
92-93	University of Minnesota	WCHA	41	11	14	25	62	—	—	—	—	—
93-94	University of Minnesota	WCHA	18	7	10	17	48	—	—	—	—	—
94-95	Cleveland	IHL	68	15	15	30	74	4	1	0	1	10

DE

EAGLES, MIKE

C, CAPITALS

PERSONAL: Born March 7, 1963, in Sussex, N.B.... 5-10/190.... Shoots left.... Full name: Michael Bryant Eagles.
TRANSACTIONS/CAREER NOTES: Selected by Quebec Nordiques as underage junior in sixth round (fifth Nordiques pick, 116th overall) of NHL entry draft (June 10, 1981).... Broke hand (October 1984).... Injured ribs (February 21, 1986).... Traded by Nordiques to Chicago Blackhawks for G Bob Mason (July 1988).... Broke left hand (February 1989).... Bruised kidney (January 15, 1990); missed eight games.... Traded by Blackhawks to Winnipeg Jets for fourth-round pick (D Igor Kravchuk) in 1991 draft (December 14, 1990).... Fractured thumb (February 17, 1992); missed 14 games.... Suffered concussion (November 30, 1993); missed one game.... Strained shoulder (March 7, 1994); missed one game.... Bruised kidneys (March 27, 1994); missed remainder of season.... Traded by Jets with D Igor Ulanov to Washington Capitals for third-round (traded to Dallas) and fifth-round picks (G Brian Elder) in 1995 draft (April 7, 1995).

Season	Team	League	REGULAR SEASON					PLAYOFFS				
			Gms.	G	A	Pts.	PIM	Gms.	G	A	Pts.	PIM
79-80	Melville	SJHL	55	46	30	76	77	—	—	—	—	—
80-81	Kitchener	OMJHL	56	11	27	38	64	18	4	2	6	36
81-82	Kitchener	OHL	62	26	40	66	148	15	3	11	14	27
82-83	Kitchener	OHL	58	26	36	62	133	12	5	7	12	27
	Quebec	NHL	2	0	0	0	2	—	—	—	—	—
83-84	Fredericton	AHL	68	13	29	42	85	4	0	0	0	5
84-85	Fredericton	AHL	36	4	20	24	80	3	0	0	0	2
85-86	Quebec	NHL	73	11	12	23	49	3	0	0	0	2
86-87	Quebec	NHL	73	13	19	32	55	4	1	0	1	10
87-88	Quebec	NHL	76	10	10	20	74	—	—	—	—	—
88-89	Chicago	NHL	47	5	11	16	44	—	—	—	—	—
89-90	Indianapolis	IHL	24	11	13	24	47	13	*10	10	20	34
	Chicago	NHL	23	1	2	3	34	—	—	—	—	—
90-91	Indianapolis	IHL	25	15	14	29	47	—	—	—	—	—
	Winnipeg	NHL	44	0	9	9	79	—	—	—	—	—
91-92	Winnipeg	NHL	65	7	10	17	118	7	0	0	0	8
92-93	Winnipeg	NHL	84	8	18	26	131	5	0	1	1	6
93-94	Winnipeg	NHL	73	4	8	12	96	—	—	—	—	—
94-95	Winnipeg	NHL	27	2	1	3	40	—	—	—	—	—
	Washington	NHL	13	1	3	4	8	7	0	2	2	4
NHL totals			600	62	103	165	730	26	1	3	4	30

EAKINS, DALLAS

D, PANTHERS

PERSONAL: Born January 20, 1967, in Dade City, Fla. . . . 6-2/195. . . . Shoots left. . . . Name pronounced AY-kihns.
TRANSACTIONS/CAREER NOTES: Selected by Washington Capitals as underage junior in 10th round (11th Capitals pick, 208th overall) of NHL entry draft (June 15, 1985). . . . Injured back (October 1988). . . . Signed as free agent by Winnipeg Jets (September 1989). . . . Signed as free agent by Florida Panthers (July 14, 1993).

			REGULAR SEASON					PLAYOFFS			
Season Team	League	Gms.	G	A	Pts.	PIM	Gms.	G	A	Pts.	PIM
84-85—Peterborough	OHL	48	0	8	8	96	7	0	0	0	18
85-86—Peterborough	OHL	60	6	16	22	134	16	0	1	1	30
86-87—Peterborough	OHL	54	3	11	14	145	12	1	4	5	37
87-88—Peterborough	OHL	64	11	27	38	129	12	3	12	15	16
88-89—Baltimore	AHL	62	0	10	10	139	—	—	—	—	—
89-90—Moncton	AHL	75	2	11	13	189	—	—	—	—	—
90-91—Moncton	AHL	75	1	12	13	132	9	0	1	1	44
91-92—Moncton	AHL	67	3	13	16	136	11	2	1	3	16
92-93—Moncton	AHL	55	4	6	10	132	—	—	—	—	—
—Winnipeg	NHL	14	0	2	2	38	—	—	—	—	—
93-94—Cincinnati	IHL	80	1	18	19	143	8	0	1	1	41
—Florida	NHL	1	0	0	0	0	—	—	—	—	—
94-95—Cincinnati	IHL	59	6	12	18	69	—	—	—	—	—
—Florida	NHL	17	0	1	1	35	—	—	—	—	—
NHL totals		32	0	3	3	73					

EASTWOOD, MIKE

C/RW, JETS

PERSONAL: Born July 1, 1967, in Cornwall, Ont. . . . 6-3/205. . . . Shoots right.
COLLEGE: Western Michigan.
TRANSACTIONS/CAREER NOTES: Selected by Toronto Maple Leafs in fifth round (fifth Maple Leafs pick, 91st overall) of NHL entry draft (June 13, 1987). . . . Traded by Maple Leafs with third-round pick in 1995 draft (RW Brad Isbister) to Winnipeg Jets for RW Tie Domi (April 7, 1995).
HONORS: Named to CCHA All-Star second team (1990-91).

			REGULAR SEASON					PLAYOFFS			
Season Team	League	Gms.	G	A	Pts.	PIM	Gms.	G	A	Pts.	PIM
86-87—Pembroke	COJHL			Statistics unavailable.							
87-88—Western Michigan Univ.	CCHA	42	5	8	13	14	—	—	—	—	—
88-89—Western Michigan Univ.	CCHA	40	10	13	23	87	—	—	—	—	—
89-90—Western Michigan Univ.	CCHA	40	25	27	52	36	—	—	—	—	—
90-91—Western Michigan Univ.	CCHA	42	29	32	61	84	—	—	—	—	—
91-92—St. John's	AHL	61	18	25	43	28	16	9	10	19	16
—Toronto	NHL	9	0	2	2	4	—	—	—	—	—
92-93—St. John's	AHL	60	24	35	59	32	—	—	—	—	—
—Toronto	NHL	12	1	6	7	21	10	1	2	3	8
93-94—Toronto	NHL	54	8	10	18	28	18	3	2	5	12
94-95—Toronto	NHL	36	5	5	10	32	—	—	—	—	—
—Winnipeg	NHL	13	3	6	9	4	—	—	—	—	—
NHL totals		124	17	29	46	89	28	4	4	8	20

EGELAND, ALLAN

C, LIGHTNING

PERSONAL: Born January 31, 1973, in Lethbridge, Alta. . . . 6-0/184. . . . Shoots left. . . . Name pronounced EHG-uh-luhnd. . . . Brother of Tracy Egeland, right winger in Philadelphia Flyers system.
TRANSACTIONS/CAREER NOTES: Selected by Tampa Bay Lightning in third round (third Lightning pick, 55th overall) of NHL entry draft (June 26, 1993).
HONORS: Named to WHL (West) All-Star first team (1992-93). . . . Named to WHL (West) All-Star second team (1993-94).

			REGULAR SEASON					PLAYOFFS			
Season Team	League	Gms.	G	A	Pts.	PIM	Gms.	G	A	Pts.	PIM
90-91—Lethbridge	WHL	67	2	16	18	57	9	0	0	0	0
91-92—Tacoma	WHL	72	35	39	74	115	4	0	1	1	18
92-93—Tacoma	WHL	71	56	57	113	119	7	9	7	16	18
93-94—Tacoma	WHL	70	47	76	123	204	8	5	3	8	26
94-95—Atlanta	IHL	60	8	16	24	112	5	0	1	1	16

EISENHUT, NEIL

C, FLAMES

PERSONAL: Born February 9, 1967, in Osoyoos, B.C. . . . 6-1/190. . . . Shoots left. . . . Name pronounced IGH-sehn-HUHT.
COLLEGE: North Dakota.
TRANSACTIONS/CAREER NOTES: Selected by Vancouver Canucks in 12th round (11th Canucks pick, 233rd overall) of NHL entry draft (June 13, 1987). . . . Signed as free agent by Calgary Flames (June 27, 1994).

			REGULAR SEASON					PLAYOFFS			
Season Team	League	Gms.	G	A	Pts.	PIM	Gms.	G	A	Pts.	PIM
86-87—Langley Eagles	BCJHL	43	41	34	75	. . .	—	—	—	—	—
87-88—North Dakota	WCHA	42	12	20	32	14	—	—	—	—	—
88-89—North Dakota	WCHA	41	22	16	38	26	—	—	—	—	—
89-90—North Dakota	WCHA	45	22	32	54	46	—	—	—	—	—
90-91—North Dakota	WCHA	20	9	15	24	10	—	—	—	—	—

Season	Team	League	REGULAR SEASON Gms.	G	A	Pts.	PIM	PLAYOFFS Gms.	G	A	Pts.	PIM
91-92	Milwaukee	IHL	76	13	23	36	26	2	1	2	3	0
92-93	Hamilton	AHL	72	22	40	62	41	—	—	—	—	—
93-94	Hamilton	AHL	60	17	36	53	30	4	1	4	5	0
	Vancouver	NHL	13	1	3	4	21	—	—	—	—	—
94-95	Saint John	AHL	75	16	39	55	30	5	1	1	2	6
	Calgary	NHL	3	0	0	0	0	—	—	—	—	—
NHL totals			16	1	3	4	21					

ELDER, BRIAN
G, JETS

PERSONAL: Born June 8, 1976, in Oak Lake, Man. . . . 6-0/175. . . . Catches left.
TRANSACTIONS/CAREER NOTES: Selected by Winnipeg Jets in fifth round (sixth Jets pick, 121st overall) of NHL entry draft (July 8, 1995).

Season	Team	League	REGULAR SEASON Gms.	Min.	W	L	T	GA	SO	Avg.	PLAYOFFS Gms.	Min.	W	L	GA	SO	Avg.
94-95	Brandon	WHL	23	1325	16	5	1	69	0	3.12	13	756	6	7	38	1	3.02

ELIAS, PATRIK
LW, DEVILS

PERSONAL: Born April 13, 1976, in Trebic, Czechoslovakia. . . . 6-0/176. . . . Shoots left.
TRANSACTIONS/CAREER NOTES: Selected by New Jersey Devils in second round (second Devils pick, 51st overall) of NHL entry draft (June 28, 1994).

Season	Team	League	REGULAR SEASON Gms.	G	A	Pts.	PIM	PLAYOFFS Gms.	G	A	Pts.	PIM
92-93	Poldi Kladno	Czech.	2	0	0	0	...	—	—	—	—	—
93-94	HC Kladno	Czech Rep.	15	1	2	3	...	11	2	2	4	...
	Czech Republic Olympic	Int'l	5	2	5	7	...	—	—	—	—	—
94-95	HC Kladno	Czech Rep.	28	4	3	7	...	7	1	2	3	...

ELIK, TODD
C, BRUINS

PERSONAL: Born April 15, 1966, in Brampton, Ont. . . . 6-2/195. . . . Shoots left. . . . Name pronounced EHL-ihk.
COLLEGE: Regina (Sask.).
TRANSACTIONS/CAREER NOTES: Signed as free agent by New York Rangers (February 26, 1988). . . . Traded by Rangers with LW Igor Liba, D Michael Boyce and future considerations to Los Angeles Kings for D Dean Kennedy and D Denis Larocque (December 12, 1988). . . . Suffered lacerations near right eye (January 1991). . . . Injured thigh (February 26, 1991); missed one game. . . . Traded by Kings to Minnesota North Stars for D Charlie Huddy, LW Randy Gilhen, RW Jim Thomson and fourth-round pick (D Alexei Zhitnik) in 1991 draft (June 22, 1991). . . . Broke foot (November 14, 1992); missed five games. . . . Suffered head injury (January 23, 1993); missed six games. . . . Traded by North Stars to Edmonton Oilers for C Brent Gilchrist (March 5, 1993). . . . Injured shoulder (April 6, 1993); missed remainder of season. . . . Claimed on waivers by San Jose Sharks (October 26, 1993). . . . Injured hip (February 6, 1995); missed four games. . . . Traded by Sharks to St. Louis Blues for LW Kevin Miller (March 23, 1995). . . . Signed as free agent by Boston Bruins (July 31, 1995).
HONORS: Named to CWUAA All-Star second team (1986-87).

Season	Team	League	REGULAR SEASON Gms.	G	A	Pts.	PIM	PLAYOFFS Gms.	G	A	Pts.	PIM
83-84	Kingston	OHL	64	5	16	21	17	—	—	—	—	—
84-85	Kingston	OHL	34	14	11	25	6	—	—	—	—	—
	North Bay	OHL	23	4	6	10	2	4	2	0	2	0
85-86	North Bay	OHL	40	12	34	46	20	10	7	6	13	0
86-87	University of Regina	CWUAA	27	26	34	60	137	—	—	—	—	—
87-88	Denver	IHL	81	44	56	100	83	12	8	12	20	9
88-89	Denver	IHL	28	20	15	35	22	—	—	—	—	—
	New Haven	AHL	43	11	25	36	31	17	10	12	22	44
89-90	Los Angeles	NHL	48	10	23	33	41	10	3	9	12	10
	New Haven	AHL	32	20	23	43	42	—	—	—	—	—
90-91	Los Angeles	NHL	74	21	37	58	58	12	2	7	9	6
91-92	Minnesota	NHL	62	14	32	46	125	5	1	1	2	2
92-93	Minnesota	NHL	46	13	18	31	48	—	—	—	—	—
	Edmonton	NHL	14	1	9	10	8	—	—	—	—	—
93-94	Edmonton	NHL	4	0	0	0	6	—	—	—	—	—
	San Jose	NHL	75	25	41	66	89	14	5	5	10	12
94-95	San Jose	NHL	22	7	10	17	18	—	—	—	—	—
	St. Louis	NHL	13	2	4	6	4	7	4	3	7	2
NHL totals			358	93	174	267	397	48	15	25	40	32

ELLETT, DAVE
D, MAPLE LEAFS

PERSONAL: Born March 30, 1964, in Cleveland. . . . 6-2/205. . . . Shoots left.
COLLEGE: Bowling Green State.
TRANSACTIONS/CAREER NOTES: Selected by Winnipeg Jets as underage junior in fourth round (third Jets pick, 75th overall) of NHL entry draft (June 9, 1982). . . . Bruised thigh (March 6, 1988); missed 10 games. . . . Sprained ankle (November 16, 1988). . . . Traded by Jets with C Paul Fenton to Toronto Maple Leafs for C Ed Olczyk and LW Mark Osborne (November 10, 1990). . . . Separated shoulder (March 2, 1993); missed 14 games. . . . Suffered rib strain (December 11, 1993); missed 10 games. . . . Separated shoulder (March 31, 1994); missed remainder of season. . . . Cracked bone in foot (February 27, 1995); missed 15 games.
HONORS: Named to NCAA All-Tournament team (1983-84). . . . Played in NHL All-Star Game (1989 and 1992). . . . Named to CCHA All-Star second team (1983-84).

Season Team	League	REGULAR SEASON					PLAYOFFS				
		Gms.	G	A	Pts.	PIM	Gms.	G	A	Pts.	PIM
81-82—Ottawa	COJHL	50	9	35	44	...	—	—	—	—	—
82-83—Bowling Green State	CCHA	40	4	13	17	34	—	—	—	—	—
83-84—Bowling Green State	CCHA	43	15	39	54	9	—	—	—	—	—
84-85—Winnipeg	NHL	80	11	27	38	85	8	1	5	6	4
85-86—Winnipeg	NHL	80	15	31	46	96	3	0	1	1	0
86-87—Winnipeg	NHL	78	13	31	44	53	10	0	8	8	2
87-88—Winnipeg	NHL	68	13	45	58	106	5	1	2	3	10
88-89—Winnipeg	NHL	75	22	34	56	62	—	—	—	—	—
89-90—Winnipeg	NHL	77	17	29	46	96	7	2	0	2	6
90-91—Winnipeg	NHL	17	4	7	11	6	—	—	—	—	—
—Toronto	NHL	60	8	30	38	69	—	—	—	—	—
91-92—Toronto	NHL	79	18	33	51	95	—	—	—	—	—
92-93—Toronto	NHL	70	6	34	40	46	21	4	8	12	8
93-94—Toronto	NHL	68	7	36	43	42	18	3	15	18	31
94-95—Toronto	NHL	33	5	10	15	26	7	0	2	2	0
NHL totals		785	139	347	486	782	79	11	41	52	61

ELOMO, MIIKKA
C/LW, CAPITALS

PERSONAL: Born April 21, 1977, in Turku, Finland. . . . 6-0/183. . . . Shoots left.
TRANSACTIONS/CAREER NOTES: Selected by Washington Capitals in first round (second Capitals pick, 23rd overall) of NHL entry draft (July 8, 1995).

Season Team	League	REGULAR SEASON					PLAYOFFS				
		Gms.	G	A	Pts.	PIM	Gms.	G	A	Pts.	PIM
93-94—TPS Jr.	Finland	30	8	5	13	24	5	1	1	2	2
94-95—Kiekko-67	Finland Dv.II	14	9	2	11	39	—	—	—	—	—
—TPS Jr.	Finland	14	3	8	11	24	—	—	—	—	—

ELYNUIK, PAT
RW, SENATORS

PERSONAL: Born October 30, 1967, in Foam Lake, Sask. . . . 6-1/192. . . . Shoots right. . . . Full name: Pat Gerald Elynuik. . . . Name pronounced EHL-ih-nuhk.
TRANSACTIONS/CAREER NOTES: Selected by Winnipeg Jets as underage junior in first round (first Jets pick, eighth overall) of NHL entry draft (June 21, 1986). . . . Separated left shoulder (March 7, 1989). . . . Strained groin (December 14, 1991); missed six games. . . . Sprained knee (February 2, 1992); missed three games. . . . Injured eye (March 17, 1992); missed five games. . . . Traded by Jets to Washington Capitals for RW John Druce and conditional pick in 1993 draft (October 1, 1992). . . . Traded by Capitals to Tampa Bay Lightning for fifth-round pick in 1995 draft (October 22, 1993). . . . Signed as free agent by Ottawa Senators (June 21, 1994). . . . Bruised ribs (April 22, 1995); missed three games.
HONORS: Named to WHL (East) All-Star first team (1985-86 and 1986-87).

Season Team	League	REGULAR SEASON					PLAYOFFS				
		Gms.	G	A	Pts.	PIM	Gms.	G	A	Pts.	PIM
84-85—Prince Albert	WHL	70	23	20	43	54	13	9	3	12	7
85-86—Prince Albert	WHL	68	53	53	106	62	20	7	9	16	17
86-87—Prince Albert	WHL	64	51	62	113	40	8	5	5	10	12
87-88—Winnipeg	NHL	13	1	3	4	12	—	—	—	—	—
—Moncton	AHL	30	11	18	29	35	—	—	—	—	—
88-89—Winnipeg	NHL	56	26	25	51	29	—	—	—	—	—
—Moncton	AHL	7	8	2	10	2	—	—	—	—	—
89-90—Winnipeg	NHL	80	32	42	74	83	7	2	4	6	2
90-91—Winnipeg	NHL	80	31	34	65	73	—	—	—	—	—
91-92—Winnipeg	NHL	60	25	25	50	65	7	2	2	4	4
92-93—Washington	NHL	80	22	35	57	66	6	2	3	5	19
93-94—Washington	NHL	4	1	1	2	0	—	—	—	—	—
—Tampa Bay	NHL	63	12	14	26	64	—	—	—	—	—
94-95—Ottawa	NHL	41	3	7	10	51	—	—	—	—	—
NHL totals		477	153	186	339	443	20	6	9	15	25

EMERSON, NELSON
C, JETS

PERSONAL: Born August 17, 1967, in Hamilton, Ont. . . . 5-11/175. . . . Shoots right. . . . Full name: Nelson Donald Emerson.
COLLEGE: Bowling Green State.
TRANSACTIONS/CAREER NOTES: Selected by St. Louis Blues in third round (second Blues pick, 44th overall) of NHL entry draft (June 15, 1985). . . . Fractured bone under his eye (December 28, 1991). . . . Injured leg (April 3, 1993); missed one game. . . . Traded by Blues with D Stephane Quintal to Winnipeg Jets for D Phil Housley (September 24, 1993). . . . Sprained neck (January 25, 1994); missed one game.
HONORS: Named CCHA Rookie of the Year (1986-87). . . . Named to NCAA All-America West second team (1987-88). . . . Named to CCHA All-Star first team (1987-88 and 1989-90). . . . Named to NCAA All-America West first team (1989-90). . . . Named to CCHA All-Star second team (1988-89). . . . Won Garry F. Longman Memorial Trophy (1990-91). . . . Named to IHL All-Star first team (1990-91).
STATISTICAL PLATEAUS: Three-goal games: 1994-95 (1).

Season Team	League	REGULAR SEASON					PLAYOFFS				
		Gms.	G	A	Pts.	PIM	Gms.	G	A	Pts.	PIM
84-85—Stratford Jr. B	OHA	40	23	38	61	70	—	—	—	—	—
85-86—Stratford Jr. B	OHA	39	54	58	112	91	—	—	—	—	—
86-87—Bowling Green State	CCHA	45	26	35	61	28	—	—	—	—	—

Season Team	League	REGULAR SEASON					PLAYOFFS				
		Gms.	G	A	Pts.	PIM	Gms.	G	A	Pts.	PIM
87-88—Bowling Green State	CCHA	45	34	49	83	54	—	—	—	—	—
88-89—Bowling Green State	CCHA	44	22	46	68	46	—	—	—	—	—
89-90—Bowling Green State	CCHA	44	30	52	82	42	—	—	—	—	—
—Peoria	IHL	3	1	1	2	0	—	—	—	—	—
90-91—St. Louis	NHL	4	0	3	3	2	—	—	—	—	—
—Peoria	IHL	73	36	79	115	91	17	9	12	21	16
91-92—St. Louis	NHL	79	23	36	59	66	6	3	3	6	21
92-93—St. Louis	NHL	82	22	51	73	62	11	1	6	7	6
93-94—Winnipeg	NHL	83	33	41	74	80	—	—	—	—	—
94-95—Winnipeg	NHL	48	14	23	37	26	—	—	—	—	—
NHL totals................................		296	92	154	246	236	17	4	9	13	27

EMMA, DAVID
C

PERSONAL: Born January 14, 1969, in Cranston, R.I. . . . 5-11/ 180. . . . Shoots left. . . . Full name: David Anaclethe Emma.
HIGH SCHOOL: Bishop Hendricken (Warwick, R.I.).
COLLEGE: Boston College.
TRANSACTIONS/CAREER NOTES: Selected by New Jersey Devils in sixth round (sixth Devils pick, 110th overall) of NHL entry draft (June 17, 1989). . . . Refused assignment and left team (March 15, 1995).
HONORS: Named to Hockey East All-Freshman team (1987-88). . . . Named to Hockey East All-Star second team (1988-89). . . . Named to Hockey East All-Star first team (1989-90 and 1990-91). . . . Won Hobey Baker Memorial Award (1990-91). . . . Named Hockey East Player of the Year (1990-91). . . . Named to NCAA All-America East first team (1989-90 and 1990-91). . . . Named to Hockey East All-Decade team (1994).
MISCELLANEOUS: Member of Stanley Cup championship team (1995).

Season Team	League	REGULAR SEASON					PLAYOFFS				
		Gms.	G	A	Pts.	PIM	Gms.	G	A	Pts.	PIM
86-87—Bishop Hendricken	R.I.H.S.				Statistics unavailable.						
87-88—Boston College	Hockey East	30	19	16	35	30	—	—	—	—	—
88-89—Boston College	Hockey East	36	20	31	51	36	—	—	—	—	—
89-90—Boston College	Hockey East	42	38	34	*72	46	—	—	—	—	—
90-91—Boston College	Hockey East	39	35	46	81	44	—	—	—	—	—
91-92—U.S. national team	Int'l	55	15	16	31	32	—	—	—	—	—
—U.S. Olympic Team	Int'l	6	0	1	1	6	—	—	—	—	—
—Utica	AHL	15	4	7	11	12	4	1	1	2	2
92-93—Utica	AHL	61	21	40	61	47	5	2	1	3	6
—New Jersey......................	NHL	2	0	0	0	0	—	—	—	—	—
93-94—New Jersey......................	NHL	15	5	5	10	2	—	—	—	—	—
—Albany..............................	AHL	56	26	29	55	53	5	1	2	3	8
94-95—New Jersey......................	NHL	6	0	1	1	0	—	—	—	—	—
—Albany..............................	AHL	1	0	0	0	0	—	—	—	—	—
NHL totals................................		23	5	6	11	2					

EMMONS, GARY
C

PERSONAL: Born December 30, 1963, in Winnipeg. . . . 5-9/170. . . . Shoots right. . . . Name pronounced EH-muhns.
COLLEGE: Northern Michigan.
TRANSACTIONS/CAREER NOTES: Selected by New York Rangers in NHL supplemental draft (September 17, 1986). . . . Signed as free agent by Edmonton Oilers (July 27, 1987). . . . Signed as free agent by Minnesota North Stars (July 11, 1989). . . . Signed as free agent by San Jose Sharks (October 18, 1993). . . . Suffered hip flexor (October 24, 1993); missed four games.
HONORS: Named CCHA co-Rookie of the Year with Bill Shibicky (1983-84). . . . Named to WCHA All-Star first team (1985-86 and 1986-87). . . . Named to NCAA All-America West second team (1986-87). . . . Named to WCHA All-Star second team (1986-87).

Season Team	League	REGULAR SEASON					PLAYOFFS				
		Gms.	G	A	Pts.	PIM	Gms.	G	A	Pts.	PIM
83-84—Northern Michigan Univ...	CCHA	40	28	21	49	42	—	—	—	—	—
84-85—Northern Michigan Univ...	WCHA	40	25	28	53	22	—	—	—	—	—
85-86—Northern Michigan Univ...	WCHA	36	45	30	75	34	—	—	—	—	—
86-87—Northern Michigan Univ...	WCHA	35	32	34	66	59	—	—	—	—	—
87-88—Milwaukee	IHL	13	3	4	7	4	—	—	—	—	—
—Nova Scotia	AHL	59	18	27	45	22	—	—	—	—	—
88-89—Canadian national team ...	Int'l	49	16	26	42	42	—	—	—	—	—
89-90—Kalamazoo	IHL	81	41	59	100	38	—	—	—	—	—
90-91—Kalamazoo	IHL	62	25	33	58	26	11	5	8	13	6
91-92—Kansas City......................	IHL	80	29	54	83	60	15	6	13	19	8
92-93—Kansas City......................	IHL	80	37	44	81	80	12	†7	6	13	8
93-94—Kansas City......................	IHL	63	20	49	69	28	—	—	—	—	—
—San Jose..........................	NHL	3	1	0	1	0	—	—	—	—	—
94-95—Kansas City......................	IHL	81	22	38	60	42	21	9	19	28	24
NHL totals................................		3	1	0	1	0					

EPANCHINTSEV, VADIM

C, LIGHTNING

PERSONAL: Born March 16, 1976, in Orsk, U.S.S.R. . . . . 5-9/170. . . . Shoots left.

TRANSACTIONS/CAREER NOTES: Selected by Tampa Bay Lightning in third round (third Lightning pick, 55th overall) of NHL entry draft (June 29, 1994).

Season Team	League	REGULAR SEASON					PLAYOFFS				
		Gms.	G	A	Pts.	PIM	Gms.	G	A	Pts.	PIM
92-93—Yuzhny Ural Ork..............	CIS	50	15	22	37	18	—	—	—	—	—
93-94—Spartak Moscow..............	CIS	46	6	5	11	16	3	0	1	1	0
94-95—Spartak Moscow..............	CIS	43	4	8	12	24	—	—	—	—	—

ERIKSSON, ANDERS

D, RED WINGS

PERSONAL: Born January 9, 1975, in Bollnas, Sweden. . . . 6-3/218. . . . Shoots left.

TRANSACTIONS/CAREER NOTES: Selected by Detroit Red Wings in first round (first Red Wings pick, 22nd overall) of NHL entry draft (June 26, 1993).

Season Team	League	REGULAR SEASON					PLAYOFFS				
		Gms.	G	A	Pts.	PIM	Gms.	G	A	Pts.	PIM
92-93—MoDo Hockey	Sweden	20	0	2	2	2	—	—	—	—	—
93-94—MoDo Hockey	Sweden	38	2	8	10	42	11	0	0	0	8
94-95—MoDo Hockey	Sweden	39	3	6	9	54	—	—	—	—	—

ERREY, BOB

LW, RED WINGS

PERSONAL: Born September 21, 1964, in Montreal. . . . 5-10/185. . . . Shoots left. . . . Name pronounced AIR-ee. . . . Cousin of Ted Lindsay, Hall of Fame left winger, Detroit Red Wings and Chicago Blackhawks (1944-45 through 1959-60 and 1964-65).

TRANSACTIONS/CAREER NOTES: Selected by Pittsburgh Penguins as underage junior in first round (first Penguins pick, 15th overall) of NHL entry draft (June 8, 1983). . . . Sprained right knee (March 18, 1987). . . . Broke right wrist (October 1987). . . . Injured shoulder (May 9, 1992). . . . Sprained ankle (September 29, 1992); missed 14 games. . . . Bruised tailbone (February 27, 1993); missed two games. . . . Traded by Penguins to Buffalo Sabres for D Mike Ramsey (March 22, 1993). . . . Sprained ankle (April 4, 1993); missed four games. . . . Injured hip (April 18, 1993); missed two games. . . . Signed as free agent by San Jose Sharks (August 17, 1993). . . . Suffered rib injury (October 10, 1993); missed three games. . . . Suffered from the flu (October 26, 1993); missed three games. . . . Suspended two games by NHL for checking from behind (December 31, 1993). . . . Suffered hyperextended knee (February 1, 1994); missed two games. . . . Sprained knee (March 22, 1994); missed five games. . . . Injured ankle (February 6, 1995); missed two games. . . . Reinjured ankle (February 17, 1995); missed two games. . . . Traded by Sharks to Detroit Red Wings for fifth-round pick (C Michal Bros) in 1995 draft (February 27, 1995).

HONORS: Named to OHL All-Star first team (1982-83).

STATISTICAL PLATEAUS: Three-goal games: 1991-92 (1).

MISCELLANEOUS: Member of Stanley Cup championship teams (1991 and 1992). . . . Captain of San Jose Sharks (1993-94).

Season Team	League	REGULAR SEASON					PLAYOFFS				
		Gms.	G	A	Pts.	PIM	Gms.	G	A	Pts.	PIM
81-82—Peterborough	OHL	68	29	31	60	39	9	3	1	4	9
82-83—Peterborough	OHL	67	53	47	100	74	4	1	3	4	7
83-84—Pittsburgh	NHL	65	9	13	22	29	—	—	—	—	—
84-85—Baltimore	AHL	59	17	24	41	14	8	3	4	7	11
—Pittsburgh	NHL	16	0	2	2	7	—	—	—	—	—
85-86—Baltimore	AHL	18	8	7	15	28	—	—	—	—	—
—Pittsburgh	NHL	37	11	6	17	8	—	—	—	—	—
86-87—Pittsburgh	NHL	72	16	18	34	46	—	—	—	—	—
87-88—Pittsburgh	NHL	17	3	6	9	18	—	—	—	—	—
88-89—Pittsburgh	NHL	76	26	32	58	124	11	1	2	3	12
89-90—Pittsburgh	NHL	78	20	19	39	109	—	—	—	—	—
90-91—Pittsburgh	NHL	79	20	22	42	115	24	5	2	7	29
91-92—Pittsburgh	NHL	78	19	16	35	119	14	3	0	3	10
92-93—Pittsburgh	NHL	54	8	6	14	76	—	—	—	—	—
—Buffalo	NHL	8	1	3	4	4	4	0	1	1	10
93-94—San Jose	NHL	64	12	18	30	126	14	3	2	5	10
94-95—San Jose	NHL	13	2	2	4	27	—	—	—	—	—
—Detroit	NHL	30	6	11	17	31	18	1	5	6	30
NHL totals............................		687	153	174	327	839	85	13	12	25	101

ESAU, LEN

D, PANTHERS

PERSONAL: Born March 16, 1968, in Meadow Lake, Sask. . . . 6-3/190. . . . Shoots right. . . . Full name: Leonard Roy Esau. . . . Name pronounced EE-saw.

COLLEGE: St. Cloud (Minn.) State.

TRANSACTIONS/CAREER NOTES: Selected by Toronto Maple Leafs in fifth round (fifth Maple Leafs pick, 86th overall) of NHL entry draft (June 11, 1988). . . . Traded by Maple Leafs to Quebec Nordiques for C Ken McRae (July 21, 1992). . . . Signed as free agent by Calgary Flames (September 6, 1993). . . . Selected by Edmonton Oilers in 1994-95 waiver draft for cash (January 18, 1995). . . . Claimed on waivers by Flames (March 7, 1995). . . . Signed as free agent by Florida Panthers (July 27, 1995).

Season Team	League	REGULAR SEASON					PLAYOFFS				
		Gms.	G	A	Pts.	PIM	Gms.	G	A	Pts.	PIM
86-87—Humboldt......................	SJHL	57	4	26	30	278	—	—	—	—	—
87-88—Humboldt......................	SJHL	57	16	37	53	229	—	—	—	—	—
88-89—St. Cloud State	WCHA	35	12	27	39	69	—	—	—	—	—
89-90—St. Cloud State	WCHA	29	8	11	19	83	—	—	—	—	—
90-91—Newmarket......................	AHL	75	4	14	18	28	—	—	—	—	—

E

Season	Team	League	REGULAR SEASON Gms.	G	A	Pts.	PIM	PLAYOFFS Gms.	G	A	Pts.	PIM
91-92—St. John's	AHL	78	9	29	38	68	13	0	2	2	14
—Toronto	NHL	2	0	0	0	0	—	—	—	—	—
92-93—Halifax	AHL	75	11	31	42	19	—	—	—	—	—
—Quebec	NHL	4	0	1	1	2	—	—	—	—	—
93-94—Saint John	AHL	75	12	36	48	129	7	2	2	4	6
—Calgary	NHL	6	0	3	3	7	—	—	—	—	—
94-95—Saint John	AHL	54	13	27	40	73	5	0	2	2	0
—Edmonton	NHL	14	0	6	6	15	—	—	—	—	—
—Calgary	NHL	1	0	0	0	0	—	—	—	—	—
NHL totals			27	0	10	10	24					

ESSENSA, BOB
G, RED WINGS

PERSONAL: Born January 14, 1965, in Toronto. . . . 6-0/180. . . . Catches left. . . . Full name: Robert Earle Essensa. . . . Name pronounced EH-sihn-zuh.
HIGH SCHOOL: Henry Carr (Rexdale, Ont.).
COLLEGE: Michigan State.
TRANSACTIONS/CAREER NOTES: Selected by Winnipeg Jets in fourth round (fifth Jets pick, 69th overall) of NHL entry draft (June 8, 1983). . . . Suffered severe lacerations to both hands and wrist (February 1985). . . . Injured groin (September 1990); missed three weeks. . . . Sprained knee (October 12, 1991); missed four games. . . . Injured left hamstring (December 8, 1991); missed four games. . . . Sprained knee (March 6, 1992); missed seven games. . . . Strained knee (March 6, 1993); missed two games. . . . Traded by Jets with D Sergei Bautin to Detroit Red Wings for G Tim Cheveldae and LW Dallas Drake (March 8, 1994). . . . Loaned by Red Wings to San Diego Gulls (January 27, 1995).
HONORS: Named to CCHA All-Star first team (1984-85). . . . Named to CCHA All-Star second team (1985-86). . . . Named to NHL All-Rookie team (1989-90).

Season	Team	League	REGULAR SEASON Gms.	Min.	W	L	T	GA	SO	Avg.	PLAYOFFS Gms.	Min.	W	L	GA	SO	Avg.
81-82—Henry Carr H.S.	MTHL	17	948	. . .	. . .	. . .	79	. . .	5.00	—	—	—	—	—	—	—
82-83—Henry Carr H.S.	MTHL	31	1840	. . .	. . .	. . .	98	2	3.20	—	—	—	—	—	—	—
83-84—Michigan State	CCHA	17	947	11	4	0	44	2	2.79	—	—	—	—	—	—	—
84-85—Michigan State	CCHA	18	1059	15	2	0	29	2	1.64	—	—	—	—	—	—	—
85-86—Michigan State	CCHA	23	1333	17	4	1	74	1	3.33	—	—	—	—	—	—	—
86-87—Michigan State	CCHA	25	1383	19	3	1	64	*2	*2.78	—	—	—	—	—	—	—
87-88—Moncton	AHL	27	1287	7	11	1	100	1	4.66	—	—	—	—	—	—	—
88-89—Winnipeg	NHL	20	1102	6	8	3	68	1	3.70	—	—	—	—	—	—	—
—Fort Wayne	IHL	22	1287	14	7	‡0	70	0	3.26	—	—	—	—	—	—	—
89-90—Moncton	AHL	6	358	3	3	0	15	0	2.51	—	—	—	—	—	—	—
—Winnipeg	NHL	36	2035	18	9	5	107	1	3.15	4	206	2	1	12	0	3.50
90-91—Moncton	AHL	2	125	1	0	1	6	0	2.88	—	—	—	—	—	—	—
—Winnipeg	NHL	55	2916	19	24	6	153	4	3.15	—	—	—	—	—	—	—
91-92—Winnipeg	NHL	47	2627	21	17	6	126	†5	2.88	1	33	0	0	3	0	5.45
92-93—Winnipeg	NHL	67	3855	33	26	6	227	2	3.53	6	367	2	4	20	0	3.27
93-94—Winnipeg	NHL	56	3136	19	30	6	201	1	3.85	—	—	—	—	—	—	—
—Detroit	NHL	13	778	4	7	2	34	1	2.62	2	109	0	2	9	0	4.95
94-95—San Diego	IHL	16	919	6	8	‡1	52	0	3.39	1	59	0	1	3	0	3.05
NHL totals		294	16449	120	121	34	916	15	3.34	13	715	4	7	44	0	3.69

EVANS, KEVIN
LW

PERSONAL: Born July 10, 1965, in Peterborough, Ont. . . . 5-11/185. . . . Shoots left. . . . Full name: Kevin Robert Evans.
TRANSACTIONS/CAREER NOTES: Signed as free agent by Minnesota North Stars (August 8, 1988). . . . Suspended three games and fined $100 by IHL for fighting (December 28, 1988). . . . Severed five tendons and an artery (February 24, 1989). . . . Suspended one game and fined $300 by IHL for fighting (November 25, 1989). . . . Underwent reconstructive knee surgery (December 1990). . . . Selected by San Jose Sharks in NHL dispersal draft (May 30, 1991). . . . Signed as free agent by North Stars (July 17, 1992). . . . North Stars franchise moved from Minnesota to Dallas and renamed Stars for 1993-94 season. . . . Signed as free agent by Peoria Rivermen (September 7, 1993). . . . Traded by Rivermen to Kansas City Blades for future considerations (February 7, 1995).

Season	Team	League	REGULAR SEASON Gms.	G	A	Pts.	PIM	PLAYOFFS Gms.	G	A	Pts.	PIM
83-84—Peterborough Jr. B	OHA	39	17	34	51	210	—	—	—	—	—
84-85—London	OHL	52	3	7	10	148	—	—	—	—	—
85-86—Victoria	WHL	66	16	39	55	*441	—	—	—	—	—
—Kalamazoo	IHL	11	3	5	8	97	6	3	0	3	56
86-87—Kalamazoo	IHL	73	19	31	50	*648	5	1	1	2	46
87-88—Kalamazoo	IHL	54	9	28	37	404	—	—	—	—	—
88-89—Kalamazoo	IHL	54	22	32	54	328	—	—	—	—	—
89-90—Kalamazoo	IHL	76	30	54	84	346	—	—	—	—	—
90-91—Minnesota	NHL	4	0	0	0	19	—	—	—	—	—
—Kalamazoo	IHL	16	10	12	22	70	—	—	—	—	—
91-92—San Jose	NHL	5	0	1	1	25	—	—	—	—	—
—Kansas City	IHL	66	10	39	49	342	14	2	13	15	70
92-93—Kalamazoo	IHL	49	7	24	31	283	—	—	—	—	—
93-94—Peoria	IHL	67	10	29	39	254	4	0	0	0	6
94-95—Peoria	IHL	29	5	9	14	121	—	—	—	—	—
—Kansas City	IHL	26	3	6	9	192	19	2	4	6	*111
NHL totals			9	0	1	1	44					

E

EVASON, DEAN

C, STARS

PERSONAL: Born August 22, 1964, in Flin Flon, Man. . . . 5-10/180. . . . Shoots right. . . . Name pronounced EH-vih-suhn.

TRANSACTIONS/CAREER NOTES: Selected by Kamloops Junior Oilers in WHL dispersal draft of players of Spokane Flyers (December 1981). . . . Selected by Washington Capitals as under-age junior in fifth round (third Capitals pick, 89th overall) of NHL entry draft (June 9, 1982). . . . Traded by Capitals with G Peter Sidorkiewicz to Hartford Whalers for LW David A. Jensen (March 1985). . . . Strained left ankle ligaments (December 14, 1988). . . . Traded by Whalers to San Jose Sharks for D Dan Keczmer (October 2, 1991). . . . Pulled stomach muscles (January 27, 1992); missed two games. . . . Traded by Sharks to Dallas Stars for sixth-round pick (LW Petri Varis) in 1993 draft (June 26, 1993). . . . Bruised ribs (February 2, 1995); missed one game.

HONORS: Won WHL Player of the Year Award (1982-83). . . . Named to WHL (West) All-Star first team (1983-84).

STATISTICAL PLATEAUS: Three-goal games: 1985-86 (1).

			REGULAR SEASON					PLAYOFFS				
Season	Team	League	Gms.	G	A	Pts.	PIM	Gms.	G	A	Pts.	PIM
80-81—Spokane Flyers		WHL	3	1	1	2	0	—	—	—	—	—
81-82—Spokane		WHL	26	8	14	22	65	—	—	—	—	—
—Kamloops		WHL	44	21	55	76	47	4	2	1	3	0
82-83—Kamloops		WHL	70	71	93	164	102	7	5	7	12	18
83-84—Kamloops		WHL	57	49	88	137	89	17	†21	20	41	33
—Washington		NHL	2	0	0	0	2	—	—	—	—	—
84-85—Binghamton		AHL	65	27	49	76	38	8	3	5	8	9
—Washington		NHL	15	3	4	7	2	—	—	—	—	—
—Hartford		NHL	2	0	0	0	0	—	—	—	—	—
85-86—Binghamton		AHL	26	9	17	26	29	—	—	—	—	—
—Hartford		NHL	55	20	28	48	65	10	1	4	5	10
86-87—Hartford		NHL	80	22	37	59	67	5	3	2	5	35
87-88—Hartford		NHL	77	10	18	28	115	6	1	1	2	2
88-89—Hartford		NHL	67	11	17	28	60	4	1	2	3	10
89-90—Hartford		NHL	78	18	25	43	138	7	2	2	4	22
90-91—Hartford		NHL	75	6	23	29	170	6	0	4	4	29
91-92—San Jose		NHL	74	11	15	26	99	—	—	—	—	—
92-93—San Jose		NHL	84	12	19	31	132	—	—	—	—	—
93-94—Dallas		NHL	80	11	33	44	66	9	0	2	2	12
94-95—Dallas		NHL	47	8	7	15	48	5	1	2	3	12
NHL totals			**736**	**132**	**226**	**358**	**964**	**52**	**9**	**19**	**28**	**132**

EWEN, DEAN

LW

PERSONAL: Born February 28, 1969, in St. Albert, Alta. . . . 6-2/225. . . . Shoots left. . . . Brother of Todd Ewen, right winger, Mighty Ducks of Anaheim.

TRANSACTIONS/CAREER NOTES: Selected by New York Islanders in third round (third Islanders pick, 55th overall) of NHL entry draft (June 13, 1987). . . . Missed entire 1992-93 season due to knee injury. . . . Signed as free agent by Mighty Ducks of Anaheim (January 21, 1994). . . . Signed as free agent by Kansas City Blades of IHL (July 19, 1995).

			REGULAR SEASON					PLAYOFFS				
Season	Team	League	Gms.	G	A	Pts.	PIM	Gms.	G	A	Pts.	PIM
88-89—Spokane		WHL	5	0	0	0	5	—	—	—	—	—
—Seattle		WHL	56	22	30	52	254	—	—	—	—	—
89-90—Springfield		AHL	34	0	7	7	. . .	—	—	—	—	—
90-91—Capital District		AHL					Did not play.					
91-92—Capital District		AHL	41	5	8	13	106	—	—	—	—	—
93-94—							Did not play—injured.					
—San Diego		IHL	19	0	3	3	45	3	1	0	1	8
94-95—San Diego		IHL	36	4	3	7	187	4	0	0	0	10

EWEN, TODD

RW, MIGHTY DUCKS

PERSONAL: Born March 22, 1966, in Saskatoon, Sask. . . . 6-2/220. . . . Shoots right. . . . Name pronounced YOO-ihn. . . . Brother of Dean Ewen, left winger, Kansas City Blades of IHL.

TRANSACTIONS/CAREER NOTES: Selected by Edmonton Oilers as underage junior in eighth round (eighth Oilers pick, 168th overall) of NHL entry draft (June 9, 1984). . . . Traded by Oilers to St. Louis Blues for D Shawn Evans (October 15, 1986). . . . Sprained ankle (October 1987). . . . Suspended one game by NHL for third game misconduct of season (January 1988). . . . Pulled groin (January 1988). . . . Tore right eye muscle (December 1988). . . . Pulled left hamstring and bruised shoulder (February 1989). . . . Suspended 10 games by NHL for coming off bench to instigate fight during playoff game (April 18, 1989); missed three playoff games and first seven games of 1989-90 season. . . . Broke right hand (October 28, 1989). . . . Traded by Blues to Montreal Canadiens for the return of a draft pick dealt to Montreal for D Mike Lalor (December 12, 1989). . . . Strained knee ligaments and underwent surgery (November 19, 1990); missed 24 games. . . . Fractured right hand at home (February 14, 1991); missed remainder of season. . . . Separated shoulder (February 12, 1992); missed two games. . . . Injured hand (January 10, 1993); missed two games. . . . Pulled muscle in back (February 20, 1993); missed three games. . . . Traded by Canadiens with C Patrik Carnback to Mighty Ducks of Anaheim for third-round pick (RW Chris Murray) in 1994 draft (August 10, 1993). . . . Broke nose (October 19, 1993); missed one game. . . . Sprained shoulder (April 2, 1994); missed five games. . . . Suffered hip pointer (January 20, 1995); missed four games. . . . Slightly pulled groin (February 24, 1995); missed three games. . . . Sprained thumb (March 31, 1995); missed five games. . . . Suffered charley horse (April 21, 1995); missed six games.

MISCELLANEOUS: Member of Stanley Cup championship team (1993).

			REGULAR SEASON					PLAYOFFS				
Season	Team	League	Gms.	G	A	Pts.	PIM	Gms.	G	A	Pts.	PIM
82-83—Vernon		BCJHL	42	20	23	43	195	—	—	—	—	—
—Kamloops		WHL	3	0	0	0	2	2	0	0	0	0

Season Team	League	REGULAR SEASON Gms.	G	A	Pts.	PIM	PLAYOFFS Gms.	G	A	Pts.	PIM
83-84—New Westminster	WHL	68	11	13	24	176	7	2	1	3	15
84-85—New Westminster	WHL	56	11	20	31	304	10	1	8	9	60
85-86—New Westminster	WHL	60	28	24	52	289	—	—	—	—	—
—Maine..............................	AHL	—	—	—	—	—	3	0	0	0	7
86-87—Peoria..........................	IHL	16	3	3	6	110	—	—	—	—	—
—St. Louis........................	NHL	23	2	0	2	84	4	0	0	0	23
87-88—St. Louis........................	NHL	64	4	2	6	227	6	0	0	0	21
88-89—St. Louis........................	NHL	34	4	5	9	171	2	0	0	0	21
89-90—Peoria..........................	IHL	2	0	0	0	12	—	—	—	—	—
—St. Louis........................	NHL	3	0	0	0	11	—	—	—	—	—
—Montreal.......................	NHL	41	4	6	10	158	10	0	0	0	4
90-91—Montreal.......................	NHL	28	3	2	5	128	—	—	—	—	—
91-92—Montreal.......................	NHL	46	1	2	3	130	3	0	0	0	18
92-93—Montreal.......................	NHL	75	5	9	14	193	1	0	0	0	0
93-94—Anaheim.......................	NHL	76	9	9	18	272	—	—	—	—	—
94-95—Anaheim.......................	NHL	24	0	0	0	90	—	—	—	—	—
NHL totals...............		**414**	**32**	**35**	**67**	**1464**	**26**	**0**	**0**	**0**	**87**

FAIR, QUINN
D, KINGS

PERSONAL: Born May 23, 1973, in Campbell River, B.C.... 6-1/210.... Shoots right.... Full name: Quinn Stanley Fair.
COLLEGE: Kent, then Bowling Green State.
TRANSACTIONS/CAREER NOTES: Selected by Los Angeles Kings in first round (first Kings pick, seventh overall) of NHL supplemental draft (June 28, 1994).

Season Team	League	REGULAR SEASON Gms.	G	A	Pts.	PIM	PLAYOFFS Gms.	G	A	Pts.	PIM
92-93—Kent..................................	CCHA	37	6	6	12	77	—	—	—	—	—
93-94—Kent..................................	CCHA	39	11	13	24	92	—	—	—	—	—
94-95—Bowling Green State	CCHA	37	4	7	11	62	—	—	—	—	—

FAIRCHILD, KELLY
C

PERSONAL: Born April 9, 1973, in Hibbing, Minn.... 5-11/180.... Shoots left.
COLLEGE: Wisconsin.
TRANSACTIONS/CAREER NOTES: Selected by Los Angeles Kings in seventh round (seventh Kings pick, 152nd overall) of NHL entry draft (June 22, 1991).... Traded by Kings with RW Dixon Ward, C Guy Leveque and RW Shayne Toporowski to Toronto Maple Leafs for LW Eric Lacroix, D Chris Snell and fourth-round pick in 1996 draft (October 3, 1994).
HONORS: Named to WCHA All-Star first team (1993-94).

Season Team	League	REGULAR SEASON Gms.	G	A	Pts.	PIM	PLAYOFFS Gms.	G	A	Pts.	PIM
91-92—University of Wisconsin ...	WCHA	37	11	10	21	45	—	—	—	—	—
92-93—University of Wisconsin ...	WCHA	42	25	29	54	54	—	—	—	—	—
93-94—University of Wisconsin ...	WCHA	42	20	44	64	81	—	—	—	—	—
94-95—St. John's	AHL	53	27	23	50	51	4	0	2	2	4

FALLOON, PAT
RW, SHARKS

PERSONAL: Born September 22, 1972, in Foxwarren, Man.... 5-11/190.... Shoots right.... Name pronounced fuh-LOON.
TRANSACTIONS/CAREER NOTES: WHL rights traded with future considerations by Regina Pats to Spokane Chiefs for RW Jamie Heward (October 1987).... Tore right knee cartilage and underwent surgery (July 24, 1990).... Selected by San Jose Sharks in first round (first Sharks pick, second overall) of NHL entry draft (June 22, 1991).... Bruised shoulder (November 19, 1992); missed one game.... Dislocated right shoulder (January 10, 1993) and underwent arthroscopic surgery (January 15, 1993); missed remainder of season.... Injured hamstring (March 2, 1995); missed one game.
HONORS: Named WHL (West) Division Rookie of the Year (1988-89).... Named to WHL All-Star second team (1988-89).... Won WHL (West) Division Most Sportsmanlike Player Award (1989-90).... Named to WHL (West) All-Star first team (1989-90 and 1990-91).... Won Can.HL Most Sportsmanlike Player of the Year Award (1990-91).... Won Brad Hornung Trophy (1990-91).... Won Stafford Smythe Memorial Trophy (1990-91).... Named to Memorial Cup All-Star team (1990-91).

Season Team	League	REGULAR SEASON Gms.	G	A	Pts.	PIM	PLAYOFFS Gms.	G	A	Pts.	PIM
87-88—Yellowbeard	Tier II	52	74	69	143	50	—	—	—	—	—
88-89—Spokane	WHL	72	22	56	78	41	5	5	8	13	4
89-90—Spokane	WHL	71	60	64	124	48	6	5	8	13	4
90-91—Spokane	WHL	61	64	74	138	33	15	10	14	24	10
91-92—San Jose.........................	NHL	79	25	34	59	16	—	—	—	—	—
92-93—San Jose.........................	NHL	41	14	14	28	12	—	—	—	—	—
93-94—San Jose.........................	NHL	83	22	31	53	18	14	1	2	3	6
94-95—San Jose.........................	NHL	46	12	7	19	25	11	3	1	4	0
NHL totals...............		**249**	**73**	**86**	**159**	**71**	**25**	**4**	**3**	**7**	**6**

FAUST, ANDRE
C, FLYERS

PERSONAL: Born October 7, 1969, in Joliette, Que.... 6-1/190.... Shoots left.
COLLEGE: Princeton.
TRANSACTIONS/CAREER NOTES: Selected by New Jersey Devils in ninth round (eighth Devils pick, 173rd overall) of NHL entry draft (June 17, 1989).... Signed as free agent by Philadel-

phia Flyers (October 14, 1992).
HONORS: Named to ECAC All-Star second team (1989-90 and 1991-92).

Season Team	League	REGULAR SEASON					PLAYOFFS				
		Gms.	G	A	Pts.	PIM	Gms.	G	A	Pts.	PIM
88-89—Princeton University........	ECAC	27	15	24	39	28	—	—	—	—	—
89-90—Princeton University........	ECAC	22	9	28	37	20	—	—	—	—	—
90-91—Princeton University........	ECAC	26	15	22	37	51	—	—	—	—	—
91-92—Princeton University........	ECAC	27	14	21	35	38	—	—	—	—	—
92-93—Hershey	AHL	62	26	25	51	71	—	—	—	—	—
—Philadelphia	NHL	10	2	2	4	4	—	—	—	—	—
93-94—Hershey	AHL	13	6	7	13	10	10	4	3	7	26
—Philadelphia	NHL	37	8	5	13	10	—	—	—	—	—
94-95—Hershey	AHL	55	12	28	40	72	6	1	5	6	12
NHL totals.................................		47	10	7	17	14					

FEARNS, KENT
D, WHALERS

PERSONAL: Born September 13, 1972, in Langley, B.C.... 6-0/180.... Shoots left.
COLLEGE: Colorado College.
TRANSACTIONS/CAREER NOTES: Selected by Hartford Whalers in NHL supplemental draft (June 25, 1993).
HONORS: Named to WCHA All-Star second team (1993-94 and 1994-95).... Named to NCAA All-America West second team (1994-95).

Season Team	League	REGULAR SEASON					PLAYOFFS				
		Gms.	G	A	Pts.	PIM	Gms.	G	A	Pts.	PIM
92-93—Colorado College..............	WCHA	33	7	15	22	78	—	—	—	—	—
93-94—Colorado College..............	WCHA	39	11	19	30	62	—	—	—	—	—
94-95—Colorado College..............	WCHA	40	7	23	30	39	—	—	—	—	—

FEATHERSTONE, GLEN
D, WHALERS

PERSONAL: Born July 8, 1968, in Toronto.... 6-4/215.... Shoots left.
TRANSACTIONS/CAREER NOTES: Selected by St. Louis Blues as underage junior in fourth round (fourth Blues pick, 73rd overall) of NHL entry draft (June 21, 1986).... Suffered sore back (March 7, 1991); missed two games.... Signed as free agent by Boston Bruins (July 25, 1991); Bruins and Blues later arranged a trade in which Bruins received Featherstone and LW Dave Thomlinson, whom they had also previously signed as free agent, for RW Dave Christian, whom the Blues had previously signed as free agent, third-round (LW Vitali Prokhorov) and either seventh-round pick in 1992 draft or sixth-round pick in 1993 draft; Blues used seventh-round pick in 1992 draft to select C Lance Burns.... Suffered hip pointer (October 5, 1991); missed three games.... Strained back (November 1991); missed remainder of season.... Underwent back surgery (November 15, 1991).... Injured groin (December 31, 1992); missed seven games.... Injured knee and thigh (March 1, 1993); missed remainder of season.... Injured shoulder (November 18, 1993); missed five games.... Suffered sore shoulder (January 24, 1994); missed four games.... Injured knee (February 12, 1994); missed four games.... Reinjured knee (March 8, 1994); missed two games.... Suffered from the flu (April 1, 1994); missed one game.... Traded by Bruins to New York Rangers for C Daniel Lacroix (August 19, 1994).... Traded by Rangers with D Michael Stewart, first-round pick in 1995 draft (G Jean-Sebastien Giguere) and fourth-round pick in 1996 draft to Hartford Whalers for RW Pat Verbeek (March 23, 1995). ... Suspended four games without pay by NHL for engaging in verbal confrontation with fans and throwing helmet into stands and injuring usher (April 4, 1995).

Season Team	League	REGULAR SEASON					PLAYOFFS				
		Gms.	G	A	Pts.	PIM	Gms.	G	A	Pts.	PIM
85-86—Windsor	OHL	49	0	6	6	135	14	1	1	2	23
86-87—Windsor	OHL	47	6	11	17	154	14	2	6	8	19
87-88—Windsor	OHL	53	7	27	34	201	12	6	9	15	47
88-89—Peoria	IHL	37	5	19	24	97	—	—	—	—	—
—St. Louis	NHL	18	0	2	2	22	6	0	0	0	0
89-90—Peoria	IHL	15	1	4	5	43	—	—	—	—	—
—St. Louis	NHL	58	0	12	12	145	12	0	2	2	47
90-91—St. Louis	NHL	68	5	15	20	204	9	0	0	0	31
91-92—Boston	NHL	7	1	0	1	20	—	—	—	—	—
92-93—Providence	AHL	8	3	4	7	60	—	—	—	—	—
—Boston	NHL	34	5	5	10	102	—	—	—	—	—
93-94—Boston	NHL	58	1	8	9	152	1	0	0	0	0
94-95—New York Rangers	NHL	6	1	0	1	18	—	—	—	—	—
—Hartford	NHL	13	1	1	2	32	—	—	—	—	—
NHL totals.................................		262	14	43	57	695	28	0	2	2	78

FEDOROV, SERGEI
C, RED WINGS

PERSONAL: Born December 13, 1969, in Minsk, U.S.S.R.... 6-1/200.... Shoots left.... Name pronounced SAIR-gay FEH-duh-rahf.
TRANSACTIONS/CAREER NOTES: Selected by Detroit Red Wings in fourth round (fourth Red Wings pick, 74th overall) of NHL entry draft (June 17, 1989).... Bruised left shoulder (October 1990).... Reinjured left shoulder (January 16, 1991).... Sprained left shoulder (November 27, 1992); missed seven games.... Suffered from the flu (January 30, 1993); missed two games.... Suffered charley horse (February 11, 1993); missed one game.... Suffered concussion (April 5, 1994); missed two games.... Suspended four games without pay and fined $500 by NHL for high-sticking incident in playoff game (May 17, 1994); suspension reduced to three games due to abbreviated 1994-95 season.... Suffered from the flu (February 7, 1995); missed one game.... Bruised right hamstring (April 9, 1995); missed one game.
HONORS: Named to NHL All-Rookie team (1990-91).... Played in NHL All-Star Game (1992 and 1994).... Named NHL Player

F

of the Year by THE SPORTING NEWS (1993-94). . . . Named to THE SPORTING NEWS All-Star first team (1993-94). . . . Won Hart Memorial Trophy (1993-94). . . . Won Frank J. Selke Trophy (1993-94). . . . Won Lester B. Pearson Award (1993-94). . . . Named to NHL All-Star first team (1993-94).
STATISTICAL PLATEAUS: Three-goal games: 1993-94 (1). . . . Four-goal games: 1994-95 (1). . . . Total hat tricks: 2.

Season Team	League	REGULAR SEASON					PLAYOFFS				
		Gms.	G	A	Pts.	PIM	Gms.	G	A	Pts.	PIM
85-86—Dynamo Minsk	USSR	15	6	1	7	10	—	—	—	—	—
86-87—CSKA Moscow	USSR	29	6	6	12	12	—	—	—	—	—
87-88—CSKA Moscow	USSR	48	7	9	16	20	—	—	—	—	—
88-89—CSKA Moscow	USSR	44	9	8	17	35	—	—	—	—	—
89-90—CSKA Moscow	USSR	48	19	10	29	20	—	—	—	—	—
90-91—Detroit	NHL	77	31	48	79	66	7	1	5	6	4
91-92—Detroit	NHL	80	32	54	86	72	11	5	5	10	8
92-93—Detroit	NHL	73	34	53	87	72	7	3	6	9	23
93-94—Detroit	NHL	82	56	64	120	34	7	1	7	8	6
94-95—Detroit	NHL	42	20	30	50	24	17	7	*17	*24	6
NHL totals		354	173	249	422	268	49	17	40	57	47

FEDOTOV, SERGEI
D, WHALERS

PERSONAL: Born January 24, 1977, in Moscow, U.S.S.R. . . . 6-1/185. . . . Shoots left.
TRANSACTIONS/CAREER NOTES: Selected by Hartford Whalers in second round (second Whalers pick, 35th overall) of NHL entry draft (July 8, 1995).

Season Team	League	REGULAR SEASON					PLAYOFFS				
		Gms.	G	A	Pts.	PIM	Gms.	G	A	Pts.	PIM
94-95—Dynamo Moscow	CIS	8	0	0	0	2	—	—	—	—	—

FEDYK, BRENT
LW, FLYERS

PERSONAL: Born March 8, 1967, in Yorkton, Sask. . . . 6-0/196. . . . Shoots right. . . . Name pronounced FEH-dihk.
TRANSACTIONS/CAREER NOTES: Selected by Detroit Red Wings as underage junior in first round (first Red Wings pick, eighth overall) of NHL entry draft (June 15, 1985). . . . Strained hip in training camp (September 1985); missed three weeks. . . . Traded by Regina Pats with RW Ken McIntyre, LW Grant Kazuik, D Gerald Bzdel and the WHL rights to LW Kevin Kowalchuk to Seattle Thunderbirds for RW Craig Endean, C Ray Savard, Grant Chorney, C Erin Ginnell and WHL rights to LW Frank Kovacs (November 1986). . . . Traded by Thunderbirds to Portland Winter Hawks for future considerations (February 1987). . . . Injured knee (December 22, 1990); missed one game. . . . Suffered deep shin bruise (January 26, 1991); missed five games. . . . Suffered concussion (March 1991). . . . Traded by Red Wings to Philadelphia Flyers for fourth-round pick (later traded to Boston which selected D Charles Paquette) in 1993 draft (October 1, 1992). . . . Strained right shoulder (December 11, 1992); missed three games. . . . Fractured thumb (January 31, 1993); missed one game. . . . Sprained left ankle (March 11, 1993); missed one game. . . . Fractured toe (April 6, 1993); missed remainder of season. . . . Strained left wrist (February 24, 1994); missed three games. . . . Suspended one game by NHL for second stick-related game misconduct (March 24, 1994). . . . Pulled right hamstring (February 16, 1995); missed three games. . . . Strained neck (March 7, 1995); missed 13 games. . . . Suffered chip fracture in first vertebrae of neck (May 26, 1995); missed remainder of playoffs.
HONORS: Named to WHL All-Star second team (1985-86).

Season Team	League	REGULAR SEASON					PLAYOFFS				
		Gms.	G	A	Pts.	PIM	Gms.	G	A	Pts.	PIM
82-83—Regina	WHL	1	0	0	0	0	—	—	—	—	—
83-84—Regina	WHL	63	15	28	43	30	23	8	7	15	6
84-85—Regina	WHL	66	35	35	70	48	8	5	4	9	0
85-86—Regina	WHL	50	43	34	77	47	5	0	1	1	0
86-87—Regina	WHL	12	9	6	15	9	—	—	—	—	—
—Seattle	WHL	13	5	11	16	9	—	—	—	—	—
—Portland	WHL	11	5	4	9	6	14	5	6	11	0
87-88—Detroit	NHL	2	0	1	1	2	—	—	—	—	—
—Adirondack	AHL	34	9	11	20	22	5	0	2	2	6
88-89—Detroit	NHL	5	2	0	2	0	—	—	—	—	—
—Adirondack	AHL	66	40	28	68	33	15	7	8	15	23
89-90—Detroit	NHL	27	1	4	5	6	—	—	—	—	—
—Adirondack	AHL	33	14	15	29	24	6	2	1	3	4
90-91—Detroit	NHL	67	16	19	35	38	6	1	0	1	2
91-92—Adirondack	AHL	1	0	2	2	0	—	—	—	—	—
—Detroit	NHL	61	5	8	13	42	1	0	0	0	2
92-93—Philadelphia	NHL	74	21	38	59	48	—	—	—	—	—
93-94—Philadelphia	NHL	72	20	18	38	74	—	—	—	—	—
94-95—Philadelphia	NHL	30	8	4	12	14	9	2	2	4	8
NHL totals		338	73	92	165	224	16	3	2	5	12

FELSNER, DENNY
LW

PERSONAL: Born April 29, 1970, in Warren, Mich. . . . 6-0/195. . . . Shoots left. . . . Full name: Denny Walter Felsner.
COLLEGE: Michigan.
TRANSACTIONS/CAREER NOTES: Selected by St. Louis Blues in third round (third Blues pick, 55th overall) of NHL entry draft (June 17, 1989). . . . Injured knee (December 29, 1989). . . . Broke ankle during off-season; missed four games. . . . Suffered sore ankle (January 25, 1994); missed seven games. . . . Suffered sore ankle (February 20, 1994); missed 11 games.
HONORS: Named to CCHA All-Rookie team (1988-89). . . . Named to NCAA All-America West second team (1990-91). . . . Named to CCHA All-Star first team (1990-91 and 1991-92). . . . Named to NCAA All-America West first team (1991-92).

F

Season Team	League	REGULAR SEASON Gms.	G	A	Pts.	PIM	PLAYOFFS Gms.	G	A	Pts.	PIM
86-87—Detroit Falcons	NAJHL	37	22	33	55	18	—	—	—	—	—
87-88—Detroit Junior Red Wings .	NAJHL	39	35	43	78	46	—	—	—	—	—
88-89—University of Michigan	CCHA	39	30	19	49	22	—	—	—	—	—
89-90—University of Michigan	CCHA	33	27	16	43	24	—	—	—	—	—
90-91—University of Michigan	CCHA	46	40	35	75	58	—	—	—	—	—
91-92—University of Michigan	CCHA	44	42	*52	*94	48	—	—	—	—	—
—St. Louis	NHL	3	0	1	1	0	1	0	0	0	0
92-93—Peoria	IHL	29	14	21	35	8	—	—	—	—	—
—St. Louis	NHL	6	0	3	3	2	9	2	3	5	2
93-94—Peoria	IHL	6	8	3	11	14	—	—	—	—	—
—St. Louis	NHL	6	1	0	1	2	—	—	—	—	—
94-95—Peoria	IHL	25	10	12	22	14	8	2	3	5	0
—St. Louis	NHL	3	0	0	0	2	—	—	—	—	—
NHL totals.............		18	1	4	5	6	10	2	3	5	2

FERGUSON, CRAIG
RW, CANADIENS

PERSONAL: Born April 8, 1970, in Castro Valley, Calif. . . . 6-0/185. . . . Shoots left.
COLLEGE: Yale.
TRANSACTIONS/CAREER NOTES: Selected by Montreal Canadiens in seventh round (seventh Canadiens pick, 146th overall) of NHL entry draft (June 22, 1991).

Season Team	League	REGULAR SEASON Gms.	G	A	Pts.	PIM	PLAYOFFS Gms.	G	A	Pts.	PIM
88-89—Yale University	ECAC	24	11	6	17	20	—	—	—	—	—
89-90—Yale University	ECAC	35	6	15	21	38	—	—	—	—	—
90-91—Yale University	ECAC	29	11	10	21	34	—	—	—	—	—
91-92—Yale University	ECAC	27	9	16	25	28	—	—	—	—	—
92-93—Wheeling	ECHL	9	6	5	11	24	—	—	—	—	—
—Fredericton	AHL	55	15	13	28	20	5	0	1	1	2
93-94—Fredericton	AHL	57	29	32	61	60	—	—	—	—	—
—Montreal	NHL	2	0	1	1	0	—	—	—	—	—
94-95—Fredericton	AHL	80	27	35	62	62	17	6	2	8	6
—Montreal	NHL	1	0	0	0	0	—	—	—	—	—
NHL totals........................		3	0	1	1	0					

FERNANDEZ, EMMANUEL
G, STARS

PERSONAL: Born August 27, 1974, in Etobicoke, Ont. . . . 6-0/185. . . . Catches left. . . . Nephew of Jacques Lemaire, center, Montreal Canadiens (1967-68 through 1978-79) and current head coach, New Jersey Devils.
TRANSACTIONS/CAREER NOTES: Selected by Quebec Nordiques in third round (fourth Nordiques pick, 52nd overall) of NHL entry draft (June 20, 1992). . . . Traded by Nordiques to Dallas Stars for D Tommy Sjodin and undisclosed draft pick (February 13, 1994).
HONORS: Won Guy Lafleur Trophy (1992-93). . . . Won Michel Briere Trophy (1993-94). . . . Named to QMJHL All-Star first team (1993-94). . . . Named to Can.HL All-Star second team (1993-94). . . . Named to QMJHL All-Star first team (1993-94). . . . Named to IHL All-Star second team (1994-95).

Season Team	League	REGULAR SEASON Gms.	Min.	W	L	T	GA	SO	Avg.	PLAYOFFS Gms.	Min.	W	L	GA	SO	Avg.
91-92—Laval	QMJHL	31	1593	14	13	2	99	1	3.73	9	468	3	5 †39	0	5.00
92-93—Laval	QMJHL	43	2348	26	14	2	141	1	3.60	13	818	12	1	42	0	3.08
93-94—Laval	QMJHL	51	2776	29	14	1	143	*5	3.09	19	1116	14	5	49 †1	*2.63
94-95—Kalamazoo	IHL	46	2470	21	10	‡9	115	2	2.79	12	655	9	1 ‡30	1	2.75
—Dallas	NHL	1	59	0	1	0	3	0	3.05	—	—	—	—	—	—	—
NHL totals............................		1	59	0	1	0	3	0	3.05							

F

FERNER, MARK
D, RED WINGS

PERSONAL: Born September 5, 1965, in Regina, Sask. . . . 6-0/193. . . . Shoots left.
TRANSACTIONS/CAREER NOTES: Selected by Buffalo Sabres in 10th round (12th Sabres pick, 194th overall) of NHL entry draft (June 8, 1983). . . . Broke foot (March 1986). . . . Traded by Sabres to Washington Capitals for C Scott McCrory (June 1, 1989). . . . Traded by Capitals to Toronto Maple Leafs for future considerations (February 27, 1992). . . . Signed as free agent by Ottawa Senators (August 6, 1992). . . . Loaned to San Diego Gulls (February 17, 1993). . . . Selected by Mighty Ducks of Anaheim in NHL expansion draft (June 24, 1993). . . . Strained groin (November 13, 1993); missed five games. . . . Suffered deep bruise (November 26, 1993); missed three games. . . . Suffered deep left thigh bruise (December 14, 1993); missed two games. . . . Traded by Mighty Ducks with LW Stu Grimson and sixth-round pick in 1996 draft to Detroit Red Wings for C/RW Mike Sillinger and D Jason York (April 4, 1995).
HONORS: Named to WHL (West) All-Star first team (1984-85). . . . Named to AHL All-Star second team (1990-91).

Season Team	League	REGULAR SEASON Gms.	G	A	Pts.	PIM	PLAYOFFS Gms.	G	A	Pts.	PIM
82-83—Kamloops	WHL	69	6	15	21	81	7	0	0	0	7
83-84—Kamloops	WHL	72	9	30	39	162	14	1	8	9	20
84-85—Kamloops	WHL	69	15	39	54	91	15	4	9	13	21
85-86—Rochester	AHL	63	3	14	17	87	—	—	—	—	—
86-87—Buffalo	NHL	13	0	3	3	9	—	—	—	—	—
—Rochester	AHL	54	0	12	12	157	—	—	—	—	—

Season Team	League	REGULAR SEASON					PLAYOFFS				
		Gms.	G	A	Pts.	PIM	Gms.	G	A	Pts.	PIM
87-88—Rochester	AHL	69	1	25	26	165	7	1	4	5	31
88-89—Buffalo	NHL	2	0	0	0	2	—	—	—	—	—
—Rochester	AHL	55	0	18	18	97	—	—	—	—	—
89-90—Washington	NHL	2	0	0	0	0	—	—	—	—	—
—Baltimore	AHL	74	7	28	35	76	11	1	2	3	21
90-91—Baltimore	AHL	61	14	40	54	38	6	1	4	5	24
—Washington	NHL	7	0	1	1	4	—	—	—	—	—
91-92—Baltimore	AHL	57	7	38	45	67	—	—	—	—	—
—St. John's	AHL	15	1	8	9	6	14	2	14	16	39
92-93—New Haven	AHL	34	5	7	12	69	—	—	—	—	—
—San Diego	IHL	26	0	15	15	34	11	1	2	3	8
93-94—Anaheim	NHL	50	3	5	8	30	—	—	—	—	—
94-95—San Diego	IHL	46	3	12	15	51	—	—	—	—	—
—Anaheim	NHL	14	0	1	1	6	—	—	—	—	—
—Adirondack	AHL	3	0	0	0	2	1	0	0	0	0
—Detroit	NHL	3	0	0	0	0	—	—	—	—	—
NHL totals		91	3	10	13	51					

FERRARO, CHRIS
RW, RANGERS

PERSONAL: Born January 24, 1973, in Port Jefferson, N.Y. . . . 5-10/175. . . . Shoots right. . . . Twin brother of Peter Ferraro, center in New York Rangers system.
COLLEGE: Maine.
TRANSACTIONS/CAREER NOTES: Selected by New York Rangers in fourth round (fourth Rangers pick, 85th overall) of NHL entry draft (June 20, 1992).
HONORS: Named to Hockey East Rookie All-Star team (1992-93).

Season Team	League	REGULAR SEASON					PLAYOFFS				
		Gms.	G	A	Pts.	PIM	Gms.	G	A	Pts.	PIM
90-91—Dubuque	USHL	45	53	44	97	. . .	—	—	—	—	—
91-92—Waterloo	USHL	38	49	50	99	106	—	—	—	—	—
92-93—University of Maine	Hockey East	39	25	26	51	46	—	—	—	—	—
93-94—U.S. national team	Int'l	48	8	34	42	58	—	—	—	—	—
—University of Maine	Hockey East	4	0	1	1	8	—	—	—	—	—
94-95—Atlanta	IHL	54	13	14	27	72	—	—	—	—	—
—Binghamton	AHL	13	6	4	10	38	10	2	3	5	16

FERRARO, PETER
C, RANGERS

PERSONAL: Born January 24, 1973, in Port Jefferson, N.Y. . . . 5-10/175. . . . Shoots right. . . . Twin brother of Chris Ferraro, right winger in New York Rangers system.
COLLEGE: Maine.
TRANSACTIONS/CAREER NOTES: Selected by New York Rangers in first round (first Rangers pick, 24th overall) of NHL entry draft (June 20, 1992).

Season Team	League	REGULAR SEASON					PLAYOFFS				
		Gms.	G	A	Pts.	PIM	Gms.	G	A	Pts.	PIM
90-91—Dubuque	USHL	29	21	31	52	83	—	—	—	—	—
91-92—Waterloo	USHL	42	48	53	101	168	—	—	—	—	—
92-93—University of Maine	Hockey East	36	18	32	50	106	—	—	—	—	—
93-94—U.S. national team	Int'l	59	28	39	67	48	—	—	—	—	—
—U.S. Olympic Team	Int'l	8	6	0	6	6	—	—	—	—	—
—University of Maine	Hockey East	4	3	6	9	16	—	—	—	—	—
94-95—Atlanta	IHL	61	15	24	39	118	—	—	—	—	—
—Binghamton	AHL	12	2	6	8	67	11	4	3	7	51

FERRARO, RAY
C, RANGERS

PERSONAL: Born August 23, 1964, in Trail, B.C. . . . 5-10/186. . . . Shoots left. . . . Name pronounced fuh-RAH-roh.
TRANSACTIONS/CAREER NOTES: Selected by Hartford Whalers as underage junior in fifth round (fifth Whalers pick, 88th overall) of NHL entry draft (June 9, 1982). . . . Traded by Whalers to New York Islanders for D Doug Crossman (November 13, 1990). . . . Fractured right fibula (December 10, 1992); missed 36 games. . . . Suffered from the flu (March 25, 1993); missed one game. . . . Injured knee (March 9, 1995); missed one game. . . . Signed as free agent by New York Rangers (July 19, 1995).
HONORS: Won WHL Most Valuable Player Trophy (1983-84). . . . Won Bob Brownridge Memorial Trophy (1983-84). . . . Won WHL Player of the Year Award (1983-84). . . . Named to WHL (East) All-Star first team (1983-84). . . . Played in NHL All-Star Game (1992).
STATISTICAL PLATEAUS: Three-goal games: 1984-85 (2), 1986-87 (1), 1988-89 (1), 1989-90 (1), 1991-92 (1). Total: 6. . . . Four-goal games: 1991-92 (1). . . . Total hat tricks: 7.

Season Team	League	REGULAR SEASON					PLAYOFFS				
		Gms.	G	A	Pts.	PIM	Gms.	G	A	Pts.	PIM
81-82—Penticton	BCJHL	48	65	70	135	50	—	—	—	—	—
82-83—Portland	WHL	50	41	49	90	39	14	14	10	24	13
83-84—Brandon	WHL	72	*108	84	*192	84	11	13	15	28	20
84-85—Binghamton	AHL	37	20	13	33	29	—	—	—	—	—
—Hartford	NHL	44	11	17	28	40	—	—	—	—	—
85-86—Hartford	NHL	76	30	47	77	57	10	3	6	9	4
86-87—Hartford	NHL	80	27	32	59	42	6	1	1	2	8

Season	Team	League	REGULAR SEASON					PLAYOFFS				
			Gms.	G	A	Pts.	PIM	Gms.	G	A	Pts.	PIM
87-88	Hartford	NHL	68	21	29	50	81	6	1	1	2	6
88-89	Hartford	NHL	80	41	35	76	86	4	2	0	2	4
89-90	Hartford	NHL	79	25	29	54	109	7	0	3	3	2
90-91	Hartford	NHL	15	2	5	7	18	—	—	—	—	—
	New York Islanders	NHL	61	19	16	35	52	—	—	—	—	—
91-92	New York Islanders	NHL	80	40	40	80	92	—	—	—	—	—
92-93	New York Islanders	NHL	46	14	13	27	40	18	13	7	20	18
	Capital District	AHL	1	0	2	2	2	—	—	—	—	—
93-94	New York Islanders	NHL	82	21	32	53	83	4	1	0	1	6
94-95	New York Islanders	NHL	47	22	21	43	30	—	—	—	—	—
NHL totals			758	273	316	589	730	55	21	18	39	48

FETISOV, SLAVA
D, RED WINGS

PERSONAL: Born May 20, 1958, in Moscow, U.S.S.R. . . . 6-1/220. . . . Shoots left. . . . Name pronounced SLAH-vuh fuh-TEE-sahf.
TRANSACTIONS/CAREER NOTES: Selected by Montreal Canadiens in 12th round (14th Canadiens pick, 201st overall) of NHL entry draft (June 15, 1978). . . . Selected by New Jersey Devils in eighth round (sixth Devils pick, 150th overall) of NHL entry draft (June 8, 1983). . . . Tore cartilage in left knee (November 22, 1989); missed six games. . . . Suffered bronchial pneumonia and hospitalized twice (November 28, 1990); missed 10 games. . . . Suffered from the flu (October 14, 1992); missed one game. . . . Sprained knee (November 30, 1993); missed four games. . . . Played in Europe during 1994-95 NHL lockout. . . . Bruised leg (February 25, 1995); missed six games. . . . Traded by Devils to Detroit Red Wings for third-round pick (RW David Gosselin) in 1995 draft (April 3, 1995).
HONORS: Named to Soviet League All-Star team (1977-78 and 1981-82 through 1987-88). . . . Won Soviet Player of the Year Award (1981-82 and 1985-86). . . . Won Golden Stick Award (1983-84, 1987-88 and 1988-89).
MISCELLANEOUS: Member of silver-medal-winning (1980) and gold-medal-winning U.S.S.R. Olympic teams (1984 and 1988).

Season	Team	League	REGULAR SEASON					PLAYOFFS				
			Gms.	G	A	Pts.	PIM	Gms.	G	A	Pts.	PIM
76-77	CSKA Moscow	USSR	28	3	4	7	14	—	—	—	—	—
77-78	CSKA Moscow	USSR	35	9	18	27	46	—	—	—	—	—
78-79	CSKA Moscow	USSR	29	10	19	29	40	—	—	—	—	—
79-80	CSKA Moscow	USSR	37	10	14	24	46	—	—	—	—	—
	Soviet Olympic Team	Int'l	7	5	4	9	10	—	—	—	—	—
80-81	CSKA Moscow	USSR	48	13	16	29	44	—	—	—	—	—
81-82	CSKA Moscow	USSR	46	15	26	41	20	—	—	—	—	—
82-83	CSKA Moscow	USSR	43	6	17	23	46	—	—	—	—	—
83-84	CSKA Moscow	USSR	44	19	30	49	38	—	—	—	—	—
	Soviet Olympic Team	Int'l	7	3	8	11	8	—	—	—	—	—
84-85	CSKA Moscow	USSR	20	13	12	25	6	—	—	—	—	—
85-86	CSKA Moscow	USSR	40	15	19	34	12	—	—	—	—	—
86-87	CSKA Moscow	USSR	39	13	20	33	18	—	—	—	—	—
87-88	CSKA Moscow	USSR	46	18	17	35	26	—	—	—	—	—
	Soviet Olympic Team	Int'l	8	4	9	13	6	—	—	—	—	—
88-89	CSKA Moscow	USSR	23	9	8	17	18	—	—	—	—	—
89-90	New Jersey	NHL	72	8	34	42	52	6	0	2	2	10
90-91	New Jersey	NHL	67	3	16	19	62	7	0	0	0	17
	Utica	AHL	1	1	1	2	0	—	—	—	—	—
91-92	New Jersey	NHL	70	3	23	26	108	6	0	3	3	8
92-93	New Jersey	NHL	76	4	23	27	158	5	0	2	2	4
93-94	New Jersey	NHL	52	1	14	15	30	14	1	0	1	8
94-95	Spartak Moscow	CIS	1	0	1	1	4	—	—	—	—	—
	New Jersey	NHL	4	0	1	1	0	—	—	—	—	—
	Detroit	NHL	14	3	11	14	2	18	0	8	8	14
NHL totals			355	22	122	144	412	56	1	15	16	61

FICHAUD, ERIC
G, ISLANDERS

PERSONAL: Born November 4, 1975, in Montreal. . . . 5-11/160. . . . Catches left. . . . Name pronounced fee-SHOH.
HIGH SCHOOL: CEGEP de Chicoutimi (Que.).
TRANSACTIONS/CAREER NOTES: Selected by Toronto Maple Leafs in first round (first Maple Leafs pick, 16th overall) of NHL entry draft (June 28, 1994). . . . Traded by Maple Leafs to New York Islanders for C Benoit Hogue, third-round pick in 1995 draft (RW Ryan Pepperall) and fifth-round pick in 1996 draft (April 6, 1995).
HONORS: Named to Memorial Cup All-Star team (1993-94). . . . Won Hap Emms Memorial Trophy (1993-94). . . . Won QMJHL Top Draft Prospect Award (1993-94). . . . Won Guy Lafleur Award (1993-94). . . . Named to QMJHL All-Star first team (1994-95).

Season	Team	League	REGULAR SEASON							PLAYOFFS						
			Gms.	Min.	W	L	T	GA	SO	Avg.	Gms.	Min.	W	L	GA	SO	Avg.
92-93	Chicoutimi	QMJHL	43	2040	18	13	1	149	0	4.38	—	—	—	—	—	—	—
93-94	Chicoutimi	QMJHL	63	3493	37	21	3	192	4	3.30	26	1560	16	10	86	†1	3.31
94-95	Chicoutimi	QMJHL	46	2637	21	19	4	151	4	3.44	7	430	2	5	20	0	2.79

FILIMONOV, DIMITRI
D, SENATORS

PERSONAL: Born October 14, 1971, in Perm, U.S.S.R. . . . 6-4/220. . . . Shoots right. . . . Name pronounced fih-lih-MAH-nahf.
TRANSACTIONS/CAREER NOTES: Selected by Winnipeg Jets in third round (second Jets pick, 49th overall) of NHL entry draft (June 22, 1991). . . . Traded by Jets to Ottawa Senators for fourth-round pick in 1993 draft (D Ruslan Batyrshin) and future considerations (March 15, 1993).

Season Team	League	REGULAR SEASON					PLAYOFFS				
		Gms.	G	A	Pts.	PIM	Gms.	G	A	Pts.	PIM
90-91—Dynamo Moscow	USSR	45	4	6	10	12	—	—	—	—	—
91-92—Dynamo Moscow	CIS	38	3	2	5	12	—	—	—	—	—
92-93—Dynamo Moscow	CIS	42	2	3	5	30	10	1	2	3	2
93-94—Ottawa	NHL	30	1	4	5	18	—	—	—	—	—
—Prince Edward Island	AHL	48	10	16	26	14	—	—	—	—	—
94-95—Prince Edward Island	AHL	32	6	19	25	14	9	0	1	1	2
NHL totals		30	1	4	5	18					

FINLEY, JEFF
D, JETS

PERSONAL: Born April 14, 1967, in Edmonton.... 6-2/205.... Shoots left.
TRANSACTIONS/CAREER NOTES: Selected by New York Islanders as underage junior in third round (fourth Islanders pick, 55th overall) of NHL entry draft (June 15, 1985).... Suffered swollen left knee (September 1988).... Traded by Islanders to Ottawa Senators for D Chris Luongo (June 30, 1993).... Signed as free agent by Philadelphia Flyers (August 2, 1993).... Traded by Flyers to Winnipeg Jets for LW Russ Romaniuk (June 27, 1995).

Season Team	League	REGULAR SEASON					PLAYOFFS				
		Gms.	G	A	Pts.	PIM	Gms.	G	A	Pts.	PIM
83-84—Portland	WHL	5	0	0	0	0	5	0	1	1	4
—Summerland	BCJHL	49	0	21	21	14	—	—	—	—	—
84-85—Portland	WHL	69	6	44	50	57	6	1	2	3	2
85-86—Portland	WHL	70	11	59	70	83	15	1	7	8	16
86-87—Portland	WHL	72	13	53	66	113	20	1	†21	22	27
87-88—Springfield	AHL	52	5	18	23	50	—	—	—	—	—
—New York Islanders	NHL	10	0	5	5	15	1	0	0	0	2
88-89—New York Islanders	NHL	4	0	0	0	6	—	—	—	—	—
—Springfield	AHL	65	3	16	19	55	—	—	—	—	—
89-90—New York Islanders	NHL	11	0	1	1	0	5	0	2	2	2
—Springfield	AHL	57	1	15	16	41	13	1	4	5	23
90-91—Capital District	AHL	67	10	34	44	34	—	—	—	—	—
—New York Islanders	NHL	11	0	0	0	4	—	—	—	—	—
91-92—Capital District	AHL	20	1	9	10	6	—	—	—	—	—
—New York Islanders	NHL	51	1	10	11	26	—	—	—	—	—
92-93—Capital District	AHL	61	6	29	35	34	4	0	1	1	0
93-94—Philadelphia	NHL	55	1	8	9	24	—	—	—	—	—
94-95—Hershey	AHL	36	2	9	11	33	6	0	1	1	8
NHL totals		142	2	24	26	75	6	0	2	2	4

FINN, STEVEN
D, DENVER

PERSONAL: Born August 20, 1966, in Laval, Que.... 6-0/191.... Shoots left.
TRANSACTIONS/CAREER NOTES: Selected by Quebec Nordiques as underage junior in third round (third Nordiques pick, 57th overall) of NHL entry draft (June 9, 1984).... Separated left shoulder (January 31, 1990).... Lacerated right index finger (October 25, 1990); missed five games. ... Sprained wrist (November 25, 1991); missed six games.... Sprained right wrist (February 15, 1992); missed seven games. ... Injured eye (January 22, 1993); missed one game.... Bruised left arm (March 8, 1993); missed one game.... Suffered from stomach virus (December 17, 1993); missed one game.... Bruised knee (March 22, 1995); missed three games.... Nordiques franchise moved to Denver for 1995-96 season.
HONORS: Named to QMJHL All-Star first team (1983-84).... Named to QMJHL All-Star second team (1984-85).
MISCELLANEOUS: Captain of Quebec Nordiques (1990-91).

Season Team	League	REGULAR SEASON					PLAYOFFS				
		Gms.	G	A	Pts.	PIM	Gms.	G	A	Pts.	PIM
82-83—Laval	QMJHL	69	7	30	37	108	6	0	2	2	6
83-84—Laval	QMJHL	68	7	39	46	159	14	1	6	7	27
84-85—Laval	QMJHL	61	20	33	53	169	—	—	—	—	—
—Fredericton	AHL	4	0	0	0	14	6	1	1	2	4
85-86—Laval	QMJHL	29	4	15	19	111	14	6	16	22	57
—Quebec	NHL	17	0	1	1	28	—	—	—	—	—
86-87—Fredericton	AHL	38	7	19	26	73	—	—	—	—	—
—Quebec	NHL	36	2	5	7	40	13	0	2	2	29
87-88—Quebec	NHL	75	3	7	10	198	—	—	—	—	—
88-89—Quebec	NHL	77	2	6	8	235	—	—	—	—	—
89-90—Quebec	NHL	64	3	9	12	208	—	—	—	—	—
90-91—Quebec	NHL	71	6	13	19	228	—	—	—	—	—
91-92—Quebec	NHL	65	4	7	11	194	—	—	—	—	—
92-93—Quebec	NHL	80	5	9	14	160	6	0	1	1	8
93-94—Quebec	NHL	80	4	13	17	159	—	—	—	—	—
94-95—Quebec	NHL	40	0	3	3	64	4	0	1	1	2
NHL totals		605	29	73	102	1514	23	0	4	4	39

FINNSTROM, JOHAN
D, FLAMES

PERSONAL: Born March 27, 1976, in Broby, Sweden.... 6-3/205.... Shoots left.
TRANSACTIONS/CAREER NOTES: Selected by Calgary Flames in fourth round (fifth Flames pick, 97th overall) of NHL entry draft (June 29, 1994).

Season Team	League	REGULAR SEASON					PLAYOFFS				
		Gms.	G	A	Pts.	PIM	Gms.	G	A	Pts.	PIM
93-94—Rogle	Sweden	7	1	1	2	2	—	—	—	—	—
94-95—Rogle	Sweden	19	0	0	0	10	—	—	—	—	—

FISET, STEPHANE
G, DENVER

PERSONAL: Born June 17, 1970, in Montreal. . . . 6-1/195. . . . Catches left. . . . Name pronounced fih-SEHT.

TRANSACTIONS/CAREER NOTES: Selected by Quebec Nordiques in second round (third Nordiques pick, 24th overall) of NHL entry draft (June 13, 1987). . . . Underwent shoulder surgery (May 1989). . . . Twisted knee (December 9, 1990). . . . Sprained left knee (January 14, 1992); missed 12 games. . . . Suffered slipped disc (November 4, 1993); missed 18 games. . . . Injured groin (February 28, 1995); missed two games. . . . Nordiques franchise moved to Denver for 1995-96 season.

HONORS: Won Can.HL Goaltender of the Year Award (1988-89). . . . Won Jacques Plante Trophy (1988-89). . . . Named to QMJHL All-Star first team (1988-89).

Season Team	League	REGULAR SEASON								PLAYOFFS							
		Gms.	Min.	W	L	T	GA	SO	Avg.	Gms.	Min.	W	L	GA	SO	Avg.
87-88—Victoriaville	QMJHL	40	2221	14	17	4	146	1	3.94	2	163	0	2	10	0	3.68
88-89—Victoriaville	QMJHL	43	2401	25	14	0	138	1	*3.45	12	711	9	2	33	0	*2.78
89-90—Victoriaville	QMJHL	24	1383	14	6	3	63	1	2.73	*14	*790	7	6	*49	0	3.72
—Quebec	NHL	6	342	0	5	1	34	0	5.96	—	—	—	—	—	—	—
90-91—Quebec	NHL	3	186	0	2	1	12	0	3.87	—	—	—	—	—	—	—
—Halifax	AHL	36	1902	10	15	8	131	0	4.13	—	—	—	—	—	—	—
91-92—Halifax	AHL	29	1675	8	14	6	110	+3	3.94	—	—	—	—	—	—	—
—Quebec	NHL	23	1133	7	10	2	71	1	3.76	—	—	—	—	—	—	—
92-93—Quebec	NHL	37	1939	18	9	4	110	0	3.40	1	21	0	0	1	0	2.86
—Halifax	AHL	3	180	2	1	0	11	0	3.67	—	—	—	—	—	—	—
93-94—Cornwall	AHL	1	60	0	1	0	4	0	4.00	—	—	—	—	—	—	—
—Quebec	NHL	50	2798	20	25	4	158	2	3.39	—	—	—	—	—	—	—
94-95—Quebec	NHL	32	1879	17	10	3	87	2	2.78	4	209	1	2	16	0	4.59
NHL totals		151	8277	62	61	15	472	5	3.42	5	230	1	2	17	0	4.43

FISHER, CRAIG
C, BLACKHAWKS

PERSONAL: Born June 30, 1970, in Oshawa, Ont. . . . 6-3/180. . . . Shoots left. . . . Full name: Craig Francis Fisher.

COLLEGE: Miami of Ohio.

TRANSACTIONS/CAREER NOTES: Suffered concussion (October 1987). . . . Selected by Philadelphia Flyers in third round (third Flyers pick, 56th overall) of NHL entry draft (June 11, 1988). . . . Traded by Flyers with RW Scott Mellanby and LW Craig Berube to Edmonton Oilers for RW Dave Brown, D Corey Foster and the NHL rights to RW Jari Kurri (May 30, 1991). . . . Traded by Oilers to Winnipeg Jets for future considerations (December 9, 1993). . . . Signed as free agent by Chicago Blackhawks (June 23, 1994).

HONORS: Named to CCHA All-Rookie team (1988-89). . . . Named to CCHA All-Star first team (1989-90).

Season Team	League	REGULAR SEASON					PLAYOFFS				
		Gms.	G	A	Pts.	PIM	Gms.	G	A	Pts.	PIM
86-87—Oshawa Jr. B	OHA	34	22	26	48	18	—	—	—	—	—
87-88—Oshawa Jr. B	OHA	36	42	34	76	48	—	—	—	—	—
88-89—Miami of Ohio	CCHA	37	22	20	42	37	—	—	—	—	—
89-90—Miami of Ohio	CCHA	39	37	29	66	38	—	—	—	—	—
—Philadelphia	NHL	2	0	0	0	0	—	—	—	—	—
90-91—Hershey	AHL	77	43	36	79	46	7	5	3	8	2
—Philadelphia	NHL	2	0	0	0	0	—	—	—	—	—
91-92—Cape Breton	AHL	60	20	25	45	28	1	0	0	0	0
92-93—Cape Breton	AHL	75	32	29	61	74	1	0	0	0	2
93-94—Cape Breton	AHL	16	5	5	10	11	—	—	—	—	—
—Moncton	AHL	46	26	35	61	36	21	11	11	22	28
—Winnipeg	NHL	4	0	0	0	2	—	—	—	—	—
94-95—Indianapolis	IHL	77	53	40	93	65	—	—	—	—	—
NHL totals		8	0	0	0	2	—	—	—	—	—

F

FITZGERALD, RUSTY
C, PENGUINS

PERSONAL: Born October 4, 1972, in Minneapolis. . . . 6-1/195. . . . Shoots left.

HIGH SCHOOL: William M. Kelley (Silver Bay, Minn.), then Silver Bay (Minn.), then East (Duluth, Minn.).

COLLEGE: Minnesota-Duluth.

TRANSACTIONS/CAREER NOTES: Selected by Pittsburgh Penguins in second round (second Penguins pick, 38th overall) of NHL entry draft (June 22, 1991).

Season Team	League	REGULAR SEASON					PLAYOFFS				
		Gms.	G	A	Pts.	PIM	Gms.	G	A	Pts.	PIM
87-88—William M. Kelley H.S.	Minn. H.S.	20	19	26	45	18	—	—	—	—	—
88-89—William M. Kelley H.S.	Minn. H.S.	22	24	25	49	26	—	—	—	—	—
89-90—William M. Kelley H.S.	Minn. H.S.	21	25	26	51	24	—	—	—	—	—
—Northland Jr. B	Minn.	20	11	5	16	12	—	—	—	—	—
—Silver Bay H.S.	Minn. H.S.	21	25	26	51	24	—	—	—	—	—
90-91—Duluth East High School	Minn. H.S.	15	14	11	25	...	—	—	—	—	—
91-92—Minnesota-Duluth	WCHA	37	9	11	20	40	—	—	—	—	—
92-93—Minnesota-Duluth	WCHA	39	24	23	47	58	—	—	—	—	—

Season	Team	League	REGULAR SEASON					PLAYOFFS				
			Gms.	G	A	Pts.	PIM	Gms.	G	A	Pts.	PIM
93-94—Minnesota-Duluth	WCHA	37	11	25	36	59	—	—	—	—	—
94-95—Minnesota-Duluth	WCHA	34	16	22	38	50	—	—	—	—	—
—Pittsburgh	NHL	4	1	0	1	0	5	0	0	0	4
—Cleveland	IHL	2	0	1	1	0	3	3	0	3	6
NHL totals................		4	1	0	1	0	5	0	0	0	4

FITZGERALD, TOM
RW/C, PANTHERS

PERSONAL: Born August 28, 1968, in Melrose, Mass. . . . 6-1/191. . . . Shoots right. . . . Full name: Thomas James Fitzgerald.
HIGH SCHOOL: Austin Prep (Reading, Mass.).
COLLEGE: Providence.
TRANSACTIONS/CAREER NOTES: Selected by New York Islanders in first round (first Islanders pick, 17th overall) of NHL entry draft (June 21, 1986). . . . Bruised left knee (November 7, 1990). . . . Strained abdominal muscle (October 22, 1991); missed 16 games. . . . Tore rib cage muscle (October 24, 1992); missed four games. . . . Selected by Florida Panthers in NHL expansion draft (June 24, 1993). . . . Sore hip (March 18, 1994); missed one game.
RECORDS: Shares NHL single-game playoff record for most shorthanded goals—2 (May 8, 1993).

Season	Team	League	REGULAR SEASON					PLAYOFFS				
			Gms.	G	A	Pts.	PIM	Gms.	G	A	Pts.	PIM
84-85—Austin Prep.	Mass. H.S.	18	20	21	41	...	—	—	—	—	—
85-86—Austin Prep.	Mass. H.S.	24	35	38	73	...	—	—	—	—	—
86-87—Providence College	Hockey East	27	8	14	22	22	—	—	—	—	—
87-88—Providence College	Hockey East	36	19	15	34	50	—	—	—	—	—
88-89—Springfield	AHL	61	24	18	42	43	—	—	—	—	—
—New York Islanders..........	NHL	23	3	5	8	10	—	—	—	—	—
89-90—Springfield	AHL	53	30	23	53	32	14	2	9	11	13
—New York Islanders..........	NHL	19	2	5	7	4	4	1	0	1	4
90-91—New York Islanders.........	NHL	41	5	5	10	24	—	—	—	—	—
—Capital District..............	AHL	27	7	7	14	50	—	—	—	—	—
91-92—New York Islanders.........	NHL	45	6	11	17	28	—	—	—	—	—
—Capital District..............	AHL	4	1	1	2	4	—	—	—	—	—
92-93—New York Islanders.........	NHL	77	9	18	27	34	18	2	5	7	18
93-94—Florida	NHL	83	18	14	32	54	—	—	—	—	—
94-95—Florida	NHL	48	3	13	16	31	—	—	—	—	—
NHL totals................		336	46	71	117	185	22	3	5	8	22

FITZPATRICK, MARK
G, PANTHERS

PERSONAL: Born November 13, 1968, in Toronto. . . . 6-2/198. . . . Catches left.
TRANSACTIONS/CAREER NOTES: Injured knee (February 1987). . . . Selected by Los Angeles Kings as underage junior in second round (second Kings pick, 27th overall) of NHL entry draft (June 13, 1987). . . . Traded by Kings with D Wayne McBean and future considerations to New York Islanders for G Kelly Hrudey (February 22, 1989); Kings sent D Doug Crossman to Islanders to complete deal (May 23, 1989). . . . Developed Eosinophilic Myalgia Syndrome (EMS) after a reaction to L-Trytophan, an ingredient in a vitamin supplement (September 1990); returned to play (March 1991). . . . Suffered recurrence of EMS and underwent biopsy on right thigh (October 22, 1991); missed 10 games. . . . Strained abdominal muscle (December 15, 1992); missed five games. . . . Traded by Islanders with first-round pick in 1993 draft (C Adam Deadmarsh) to Quebec Nordiques for G Ron Hextall and first-round pick (C/RW Todd Bertuzzi) in 1993 draft (June 20, 1993). . . . Selected by Florida Panthers in NHL expansion draft (June 24, 1993). . . . Suspended two games without pay and fined $500 by NHL for high-sticking incident (February 16, 1994). . . . Sprained lower back (April 22, 1995); missed one game. . . . Suffered recurring back spasms (April 26, 1995); missed last four games of season.
HONORS: Won Top Goaltender Trophy (1985-86). . . . Named to WHL All-Star second team (1985-86 and 1987-88). . . . Named to Memorial Cup All-Star team (1986-87 and 1987-88). . . . Won Bill Masterton Memorial Trophy (1991-92).

Season	Team	League	REGULAR SEASON							PLAYOFFS						
			Gms.	Min.	W	L	T	GA	SO	Avg.	Gms.	Min.	W	L	GA	SO	Avg.
83-84—Revelstoke...................	BCJHL	21	1019	...	...	...	90	0	5.30	—	—	—	—	—	—	—
84-85—Medicine Hat	WHL	3	180	...	...	...	9	0	3.00	—	—	—	—	—	—	—
85-86—Medicine Hat	WHL	41	2074	26	6	1	99	1	*2.86	*19	986	12	5	*58	0	3.53
86-87—Medicine Hat	WHL	50	2844	31	11	4	159	*4	3.35	*20	*1224	12	8	71	+1	3.48
87-88—Medicine Hat	WHL	63	3600	36	15	6	194	+2	*3.23	16	959	12	4	52	+1	*3.25
88-89—New Haven	AHL	18	980	10	5	1	54	1	3.31	—	—	—	—	—	—	—
—Los Angeles...................	NHL	17	957	6	7	3	64	0	4.01	—	—	—	—	—	—	—
—New York Islanders.........	NHL	11	627	3	5	2	41	0	3.92	—	—	—	—	—	—	—
89-90—New York Islanders.........	NHL	47	2653	19	19	5	150	3	3.39	4	152	0	2	13	0	5.13
90-91—Capital District.............	AHL	12	734	3	7	2	47	0	3.84	—	—	—	—	—	—	—
—New York Islanders.........	NHL	2	120	1	1	0	6	0	3.00	—	—	—	—	—	—	—
91-92—Capital District.............	AHL	14	782	6	5	1	39	0	2.99	—	—	—	—	—	—	—
—New York Islanders.........	NHL	30	1743	11	13	5	93	0	3.20	—	—	—	—	—	—	—
92-93—New York Islanders.........	NHL	39	2253	17	15	5	130	0	3.46	3	77	0	1	4	0	3.12
—Capital District.............	AHL	5	284	1	3	1	18	0	3.80	—	—	—	—	—	—	—
93-94—Florida	NHL	28	1603	12	8	6	73	1	2.73	—	—	—	—	—	—	—
94-95—Florida	NHL	15	819	6	7	2	36	2	2.64	—	—	—	—	—	—	—
NHL totals................		189	10775	75	75	28	593	6	3.30	7	229	0	3	17	0	4.45

F

FITZPATRICK, RORY
D, CANADIENS

PERSONAL: Born January 11, 1975, in Rochester, N.Y. . . . 6-1/190. . . . Shoots right.
TRANSACTIONS/CAREER NOTES: Selected by Montreal Canadiens in second round (second Canadiens pick, 47th overall) of NHL entry draft (June 26, 1993).
HONORS: Named to OHL All-Rookie team (1992-93).

			REGULAR SEASON					PLAYOFFS				
Season	Team	League	Gms.	G	A	Pts.	PIM	Gms.	G	A	Pts.	PIM
90-91	Rochester Jr. B	OHA	40	0	5	5	—	—	—	—	—	—
91-92	Rochester Jr. B	OHA	28	8	28	36	141	—	—	—	—	—
92-93	Sudbury	OHL	58	4	20	24	68	14	0	0	0	17
93-94	Sudbury	OHL	65	12	34	46	112	10	2	5	7	10
94-95	Sudbury	OHL	56	12	36	48	72	18	3	15	18	21
	Fredericton	AHL						10	1	2	3	5

FLAHERTY, WADE
G, SHARKS

PERSONAL: Born January 11, 1968, in Terrace, B.C. . . . 6-0/190. . . . Catches right.
TRANSACTIONS/CAREER NOTES: Selected by Buffalo Sabres in ninth round (181st Sabres pick, 181st overall) of NHL entry draft (June 11, 1988). . . . Signed as free agent by San Jose Sharks (September 3, 1991). . . . Injured ribs (February 28, 1995); missed three games.
HONORS: Named to WHL All-Star second team (1987-88). . . . Won ECHL Playoff Most Valuable Player Award (1989-90). . . . Shared James Norris Memorial Trophy with Arturs Irbe (1991-92). . . . Named to IHL All-Star second team (1992-93 and 1993-94).

			REGULAR SEASON								PLAYOFFS						
Season	Team	League	Gms.	Min.	W	L	T	GA	SO	Avg.	Gms.	Min.	W	L	GA	SO	Avg.
84-85	Kelowna Wings	WHL	1	55	0	0	0	5	0	5.45	—	—	—	—	—	—	—
85-86	Seattle	WHL	9	271	1	3	0	36	0	7.97	—	—	—	—	—	—	—
	Spokane	WHL	5	161	0	3	0	21	0	7.83	—	—	—	—	—	—	—
86-87	Nanaimo	BCJHL	15	830				53	0	3.83	—	—	—	—	—	—	—
	Victoria	WHL	3	127	0	2	0	16	0	7.56	—	—	—	—	—	—	—
87-88	Victoria	WHL	36	2052	20	15	0	135	0	3.95	5	300	2	3	18	0	3.60
88-89	Victoria	WHL	42	2408	21	19	0	180	0	4.49	8	480	3	5	35	0	4.38
89-90	Kalamazoo	IHL	1	13	0	0	‡0	0	0	0.00	—	—	—	—	—	—	—
	Greensboro	ECHL	27	1308	12	10	‡0	96	. . .	4.40	‡9	567	*8	1	21	0	*2.22
90-91	Kansas City	IHL	‡56	2990	16	31	‡4	*224	0	4.49	—	—	—	—	—	—	—
91-92	Kansas City	IHL	43	2603	26	14	‡3	140	1	3.23	1	1	0	0	0	0	0.00
	San Jose	NHL	3	178	0	3	0	13	0	4.38	—	—	—	—	—	—	—
92-93	Kansas City	IHL	61	*3642	*34	19	‡0	*195	2	3.21	12	*733	6	*5	‡34	*1	2.78
	San Jose	NHL	1	60	0	1	0	5	0	5.00	—	—	—	—	—	—	—
93-94	Kansas City	IHL	60	*3564	32	19	‡9	202	0	3.40	—	—	—	—	—	—	—
94-95	San Jose	NHL	18	852	5	6	1	44	1	3.10	7	377	2	3	31	0	4.93
NHL totals			22	1090	5	10	1	62	1	3.41	7	377	2	3	31	0	4.93

FLATLEY, PATRICK
RW, ISLANDERS

PERSONAL: Born October 3, 1963, in Toronto. . . . 6-2/201. . . . Shoots right. . . . Full name: Patrick William Flatley.
HIGH SCHOOL: Henry Carr (Rexdale, Ont.).
COLLEGE: Wisconsin.
TRANSACTIONS/CAREER NOTES: Selected by New York Islanders as underage junior in first round (first Islanders pick, 21st overall) of NHL entry draft (June 9, 1982). . . . Broke bone in left hand (April 1985). . . . Strained left knee ligaments (February 4, 1987). . . . Separated right shoulder (November 1987). . . . Injured right knee (January 1988). . . . Underwent reconstructive knee surgery (February 1988). . . . Injured right knee (December 1988). . . . Suffered sore right ankle (February 1989). . . . Re-injured right knee (March 1989). . . . Bruised right ankle (October 1989). . . . Pulled groin muscle (February 13, 1990). . . . Re-injured groin (March 2, 1990); missed six games. . . . Sprained right knee (October 13, 1990). . . . Bruised left knee (November 30, 1990). . . . Fractured finger on left hand (February 16, 1991). . . . Fractured right thumb (December 19, 1991); missed 42 games. . . . Broke ribs (January 5, 1993); missed four games. . . . Broke jaw (October 22, 1993); missed eight games. . . . Suffered sore foot (January 8, 1994); missed one game. . . . Pulled abdominal muscle (March 27, 1994); missed 10 games. . . . Suffered hip flexor (March 26, 1995); missed two games.
HONORS: Named to NCAA All-America West team (1982-83). . . . Named to NCAA All-Tournament team (1982-83). . . . Named to WCHA All-Star first team (1982-83).
STATISTICAL PLATEAUS: Three-goal games: 1990-91 (1). . . . Four-goal games: 1985-86 (1). . . . Total hat tricks: 2.
MISCELLANEOUS: Captain of New York Islanders (1991-92 through 1994-95).

			REGULAR SEASON					PLAYOFFS				
Season	Team	League	Gms.	G	A	Pts.	PIM	Gms.	G	A	Pts.	PIM
80-81	Henry Carr H.S.	MTHL	42	30	61	91	122	—	—	—	—	—
81-82	University of Wisconsin	WCHA	33	17	20	37	65	—	—	—	—	—
82-83	University of Wisconsin	WCHA	43	25	44	69	76	—	—	—	—	—
83-84	Canadian Olympic Team	Int'l	57	33	17	50	136	—	—	—	—	—
	New York Islanders	NHL	16	2	7	9	6	21	9	6	15	14
84-85	New York Islanders	NHL	78	20	31	51	106	4	1	0	1	6
85-86	New York Islanders	NHL	73	18	34	52	66	3	0	0	0	21
86-87	New York Islanders	NHL	63	16	35	51	81	11	3	2	5	6
87-88	New York Islanders	NHL	40	9	15	24	28	—	—	—	—	—
88-89	New York Islanders	NHL	41	10	15	25	31	—	—	—	—	—
	Springfield	AHL	2	1	1	2	2	—	—	—	—	—
89-90	New York Islanders	NHL	62	17	32	49	101	5	3	0	3	2
90-91	New York Islanders	NHL	56	20	25	45	74	—	—	—	—	—

Season Team	League	REGULAR SEASON Gms.	G	A	Pts.	PIM	PLAYOFFS Gms.	G	A	Pts.	PIM
91-92—New York Islanders..........	NHL	38	8	28	36	31	—	—	—	—	—
92-93—New York Islanders..........	NHL	80	13	47	60	63	15	2	7	9	12
93-94—New York Islanders..........	NHL	64	12	30	42	40	—	—	—	—	—
94-95—New York Islanders..........	NHL	45	7	20	27	12	—	—	—	—	—
NHL totals.......................................		656	152	319	471	639	59	18	15	33	61

FLEMING, GERRY
D, CANADIENS

PERSONAL: Born October 16, 1967, in Montreal.... 6-5/240.... Shoots left.
COLLEGE: University of Prince Edward Island.
TRANSACTIONS/CAREER NOTES: Signed as free agent by Montreal Canadiens (February 17, 1992).

Season Team	League	REGULAR SEASON Gms.	G	A	Pts.	PIM	PLAYOFFS Gms.	G	A	Pts.	PIM
89-90—Fredericton	AHL	24	12	18	30	83	—	3	6	9	—
90-91—Prince Edward Island U....	AUAA			Statistics unavailable.							
91-92—Fredericton	AHL	37	4	6	10	133	1	0	0	0	7
92-93—Fredericton	AHL	64	9	17	26	262	5	1	2	3	14
93-94—Fredericton	AHL	46	6	16	22	188	—	—	—	—	—
—Montreal............................	NHL	5	0	0	0	25	—	—	—	—	—
94-95—Montreal	NHL	6	0	0	0	17	—	—	—	—	—
—Fredericton	AHL	16	3	3	6	60	10	2	0	2	67
NHL totals.......................................		11	0	0	0	42					

FLEURY, THEO
C/RW, FLAMES

PERSONAL: Born June 29, 1968, in Oxbow, Sask.... 5-6/160.... Shoots right.... Name pronounced FLUH-ree.
TRANSACTIONS/CAREER NOTES: Selected by Calgary Flames in eighth round (ninth Flames pick, 166th overall) of NHL entry draft (June 13, 1987).... Played in Europe during 1994-95 NHL lockout.
HONORS: Named to WHL (East) All-Star first team (1986-87).... Shared Bob Clarke Trophy with Joe Sakic (1987-88).... Named to WHL All-Star second team (1987-88).... Shared Alka-Seltzer Plus Award with Marty McSorley (1990-91).... Played in NHL All-Star Game (1991 and 1992).... Named to NHL All-Star second team (1994-95).
RECORDS: Holds NHL single-game record for highest plus-minus rating—9 (February 10, 1993).
STATISTICAL PLATEAUS: Three-goal games: 1990-91 (5), 1992-93 (1), 1993-94 (1). Total: 7.
MISCELLANEOUS: Member of Stanley Cup championship team (1989).

Season Team	League	REGULAR SEASON Gms.	G	A	Pts.	PIM	PLAYOFFS Gms.	G	A	Pts.	PIM
84-85—Moose Jaw	WHL	71	29	46	75	82	—	—	—	—	—
85-86—Moose Jaw	WHL	72	43	65	108	124	—	—	—	—	—
86-87—Moose Jaw	WHL	66	61	68	129	110	9	7	9	16	34
87-88—Moose Jaw	WHL	65	68	92	†160	235	—	—	—	—	—
—Salt Lake City..................	IHL	2	3	4	7	7	8	11	5	16	16
88-89—Salt Lake City..................	IHL	40	37	37	74	81	—	—	—	—	—
—Calgary............................	NHL	36	14	20	34	46	22	5	6	11	24
89-90—Calgary	NHL	80	31	35	66	157	6	2	3	5	10
90-91—Calgary	NHL	79	51	53	104	136	7	2	5	7	14
91-92—Calgary	NHL	80	33	40	73	133	—	—	—	—	—
92-93—Calgary	NHL	83	34	66	100	88	6	5	7	12	27
93-94—Calgary	NHL	83	40	45	85	186	7	6	4	10	5
94-95—Tappara	Finland	10	8	9	17	22	—	—	—	—	—
—Calgary............................	NHL	47	29	29	58	112	7	7	7	14	2
NHL totals.......................................		488	232	288	520	858	55	27	32	59	82

FLICHEL, MARTY
RW, STARS

PERSONAL: Born March 6, 1976, in Hodgeville, Sask.... 5-11/175.... Shoots left.
TRANSACTIONS/CAREER NOTES: Selected by Dallas Stars in ninth round (sixth Stars pick, 228th overall) of NHL entry draft (June 29, 1994).

Season Team	League	REGULAR SEASON Gms.	G	A	Pts.	PIM	PLAYOFFS Gms.	G	A	Pts.	PIM
92-93—Tacoma	WHL	61	21	20	41	19	7	0	0	0	8
93-94—Tacoma	WHL	72	27	48	75	69	8	1	4	5	13
94-95—Tacoma	WHL	67	25	53	78	81	4	2	3	5	8

FLINTON, ERIC
LW, SENATORS

PERSONAL: Born February 2, 1972, in Will Lake, B.C.... 6-2/200.... Shoots left.
COLLEGE: New Hampshire.
TRANSACTIONS/CAREER NOTES: Selected by Ottawa Senators in NHL supplemental draft (June 25, 1993).
HONORS: Named to Hockey East All-Star second team (1994-95).

Season Team	League	REGULAR SEASON Gms.	G	A	Pts.	PIM	PLAYOFFS Gms.	G	A	Pts.	PIM
92-93—Univ. of New Hampshire ...	Hockey East	37	18	18	36	14	—	—	—	—	—
93-94—Univ. of New Hampshire ...	Hockey East	40	16	25	41	36	—	—	—	—	—
94-95—Univ. of New Hampshire ...	Hockey East	36	22	23	45	44	—	—	—	—	—

FOGARTY, BRYAN
D, CANADIENS

PERSONAL: Born June 11, 1969, in Montreal. . . . 6-2/206. . . . Shoots left.
TRANSACTIONS/CAREER NOTES: Selected by Quebec Nordiques as underage junior in first round (first Nordiques pick, ninth overall) of NHL entry draft (June 13, 1987). . . . Traded by Kingston Raiders to Niagara Falls Thunder for D Garth Joy, LW Jason Simon, Kevin Lune and fourth-round pick in 1989 draft (August 1988). . . . Underwent appendectomy (September 1989). . . . Underwent substance-abuse treatment (February 1991); missed one month. . . . Left Nordiques to report to halfway house (March 28, 1991). . . . Suffered from the flu (November 30, 1991); missed five games. . . . Traded by Nordiques to Pittsburgh Penguins for rights to RW Scott Young (March 10, 1992). . . . Suspended by Penguins for leaving Cleveland Lumberjacks without approval (January 28, 1993). . . . Reinstated by Penguins (March 16, 1993). . . . Suffered from amygdalitis, a throat condition (April 6, 1993); missed four games. . . . Signed as free agent by Tampa Bay Lightning (September 1, 1993). . . . Traded by Las Vegas Thunder to Kansas City Blades for future considerations (February 12, 1994). . . . Signed as free agent by Montreal Canadiens (February 26, 1994). . . . Suffered from the flu (March 25, 1995); missed one game. . . . Suffered from the flu (April 14, 1995); missed three games.
HONORS: Named to OHL All-Star first team (1986-87 and 1988-89). . . . Won Can.HL Player of the Year Award (1988-89). . . . Won Can.HL Defenseman of the Year Award (1988-89). . . . Won Can.HL Plus/Minus Award (1988-89). . . . Won Red Tilson Trophy (1988-89). . . . Won Eddie Powers Memorial Trophy (1988-89). . . . Won Max Kaminsky Trophy (1988-89).
STATISTICAL PLATEAUS: Three-goal games: 1990-91 (1).

			REGULAR SEASON					PLAYOFFS				
Season	Team	League	Gms.	G	A	Pts.	PIM	Gms.	G	A	Pts.	PIM
84-85—Aurora		OHA	66	18	39	57	180	—	—	—	—	—
85-86—Kingston		OHL	47	2	19	21	14	10	1	3	4	4
86-87—Kingston		OHL	56	20	50	70	46	12	2	3	5	5
87-88—Kingston		OHL	48	11	36	47	50	—	—	—	—	—
88-89—Niagara Falls		OHL	60	47	*108	*155	88	17	10	22	32	36
89-90—Quebec		NHL	45	4	10	14	31	—	—	—	—	—
—Halifax		AHL	22	5	14	19	6	6	4	2	6	0
90-91—Halifax		AHL	5	0	2	2	0	—	—	—	—	—
—Quebec		NHL	45	9	22	31	24	—	—	—	—	—
91-92—Quebec		NHL	20	3	12	15	16	—	—	—	—	—
—Halifax		AHL	2	0	0	0	2	—	—	—	—	—
—New Haven		AHL	4	0	1	1	6	—	—	—	—	—
—Muskegon		IHL	8	2	4	6	30	—	—	—	—	—
92-93—Pittsburgh		NHL	12	0	4	4	4	—	—	—	—	—
—Cleveland		IHL	15	2	5	7	8	3	0	1	1	17
93-94—Atlanta		IHL	8	1	5	6	4	—	—	—	—	—
—Las Vegas		IHL	33	3	16	19	38	—	—	—	—	—
—Kansas City		IHL	3	2	1	3	2	—	—	—	—	—
—Montreal		NHL	13	1	2	3	10	—	—	—	—	—
94-95—Montreal		NHL	21	5	2	7	34	—	—	—	—	—
NHL totals			**156**	**22**	**52**	**74**	**119**					

FOOTE, ADAM
D, DENVER

PERSONAL: Born July 10, 1971, in Toronto. . . . 6-1/202. . . . Shoots right. . . . Full name: Adam David Vernon Foote. . . . Name pronounced FUT.
TRANSACTIONS/CAREER NOTES: Selected by Quebec Nordiques in second round (second Nordiques pick, 22nd overall) of NHL entry draft (June 17, 1989). . . . Fractured right thumb (February 1992); missed remainder of season. . . . Injured knee (October 21, 1992); missed one game. . . . Suffered from the flu (January 28, 1993); missed two games. . . . Injured groin (January 18, 1994); missed eight games. . . . Suffered herniated disc (February 11, 1994); underwent surgery and missed remainder of season. . . . Injured back (February 9, 1995); missed two games. . . . Injured groin (February 28, 1995); missed two games. . . . Injured groin (March 26, 1995); missed four games. . . . Reinjured groin (April 6, 1995); missed five games. . . . Nordiques franchise moved to Denver for 1995-96 season.
HONORS: Named to OHL All-Star first team (1990-91).

			REGULAR SEASON					PLAYOFFS				
Season	Team	League	Gms.	G	A	Pts.	PIM	Gms.	G	A	Pts.	PIM
88-89—Sault Ste. Marie		OHL	66	7	32	39	120	—	—	—	—	—
89-90—Sault Ste. Marie		OHL	61	12	43	55	199	—	—	—	—	—
90-91—Sault Ste. Marie		OHL	59	18	51	69	93	14	5	12	17	28
91-92—Quebec		NHL	46	2	5	7	44	—	—	—	—	—
—Halifax		AHL	6	0	1	1	2	—	—	—	—	—
92-93—Quebec		NHL	81	4	12	16	168	6	0	1	1	2
93-94—Quebec		NHL	45	2	6	8	67	—	—	—	—	—
94-95—Quebec		NHL	35	0	7	7	52	6	0	1	1	14
NHL totals			**207**	**8**	**30**	**38**	**331**	**12**	**0**	**2**	**2**	**16**

FORBES, COLIN
C, FLYERS

PERSONAL: Born February 16, 1976, in New Westminister, B.C. . . . 6-3/190. . . . Shoots left.
TRANSACTIONS/CAREER NOTES: Selected by Philadelphia Flyers in seventh round (fifth Flyers pick, 166th overall) of NHL entry draft (June 29, 1994).

			REGULAR SEASON					PLAYOFFS				
Season	Team	League	Gms.	G	A	Pts.	PIM	Gms.	G	A	Pts.	PIM
93-94—Sherwood Park		AJHL	47	18	22	40	76	—	—	—	—	—
94-95—Portland		WHL	72	24	31	55	108	9	1	3	4	10

FORSBERG, PETER
C, DENVER

PERSONAL: Born July 20, 1973, in Ornskoldsvik, Sweden. . . . 5-11/190. . . . Shoots left.
TRANSACTIONS/CAREER NOTES: Selected by Philadelphia Flyers in first round (first Flyers pick, sixth overall) of NHL entry draft (June 22, 1991). . . . Traded by Flyers with G Ron Hextall, C Mike Ricci, D Steve Duchesne, D Kerry Huffman, first-round pick in 1993

F

draft (G Jocelyn Thibault), cash and future considerations to Quebec Nordiques for C Eric Lindros (June 20, 1992); Flyers sent LW Chris Simon and first-round pick in 1994 draft (traded to Toronto Maple Leafs) to Nordiques to complete deal (July 21, 1992).... Played in Europe during 1994-95 NHL lockout.... Suffered from the flu (March 1, 1995); missed one game.... Nordiques franchise moved to Denver for 1995-96 season.

HONORS: Named to Swedish League All-Star team (1991-92).... Named Swedish League Player of the Year (1993-94).... Named NHL Rookie of the Year by THE SPORTING NEWS (1994-95).... Won Calder Memorial Trophy (1994-95).... Named to NHL All-Rookie team (1994-95).

MISCELLANEOUS: Member of gold-medal-winning Swedish Olympic team (1994).

			REGULAR SEASON					PLAYOFFS				
Season	Team	League	Gms.	G	A	Pts.	PIM	Gms.	G	A	Pts.	PIM
89-90—MoDo		Sweden Jr.	30	15	12	27	42	—	—	—	—	—
90-91—MoDo Hockey		Sweden	23	7	10	17	22	—	—	—	—	—
91-92—MoDo Hockey		Sweden	39	9	19	28	78	—	—	—	—	—
92-93—MoDo Hockey		Sweden	39	23	24	47	92	3	4	1	5	0
93-94—MoDo Hockey		Sweden	39	18	26	44	82	11	9	7	16	14
—Swedish Olympic Team		Int'l	8	2	6	8	6	—	—	—	—	—
94-95—MoDo Hockey		Sweden	11	5	9	14	20	—	—	—	—	—
—Quebec		NHL	47	15	35	50	16	6	2	4	6	4
NHL totals			47	15	35	50	16	6	2	4	6	4

FOSTER, COREY
D, SENATORS

PERSONAL: Born October 27, 1969, in Ottawa.... 6-3/204.... Shoots left.
TRANSACTIONS/CAREER NOTES: Selected by New Jersey Devils in first round (first Devils pick, 12th overall) of NHL entry draft (June 11, 1988).... Traded by Devils to Edmonton Oilers for first-round pick (C Jason Miller) in 1989 draft (June 17, 1989).... Traded by Oilers with RW Dave Brown and rights to RW Jari Kurri to Philadelphia Flyers for RW Scott Mellanby, LW Craig Berube and C Craig Fisher (May 30, 1991).... Fractured collarbone during preseason (September 1991); missed 14 games.... Signed as free agent by Ottawa Senators (June 20, 1994).

			REGULAR SEASON					PLAYOFFS				
Season	Team	League	Gms.	G	A	Pts.	PIM	Gms.	G	A	Pts.	PIM
86-87—Peterborough		OHL	30	3	4	7	4	1	0	0	0	0
87-88—Peterborough		OHL	66	13	31	44	58	11	5	9	14	13
88-89—Peterborough		OHL	55	14	42	56	42	17	1	17	18	12
—New Jersey		NHL	2	0	0	0	0	—	—	—	—	—
89-90—Cape Breton		AHL	54	7	17	24	32	1	0	0	0	0
90-91—Cape Breton		AHL	67	14	11	25	51	4	2	4	6	4
91-92—Philadelphia		NHL	25	3	4	7	20	—	—	—	—	—
—Hershey		AHL	19	5	9	14	26	6	1	1	2	5
92-93—Hershey		AHL	80	9	25	34	102	—	—	—	—	—
93-94—Hershey		AHL	66	21	37	58	96	9	2	5	7	10
94-95—Prince Edward Island		AHL	78	13	34	47	61	11	2	5	7	12
NHL totals			27	3	4	7	20					

FOUNTAIN, MIKE
G, CANUCKS

PERSONAL: Born January 26, 1972, in Gravenhurst, Ont.... 6-1/176.... Catches left.
COLLEGE: Trent (Ont.).
TRANSACTIONS/CAREER NOTES: Selected by Vancouver Canucks in second round (third Canucks pick, 45th overall) of NHL entry draft (June 20, 1992).
HONORS: Named to OHL All-Star first team (1991-92).... Named to Can.HL All-Star second team (1991-92).... Named to AHL All-Star second team (1993-94).

			REGULAR SEASON							PLAYOFFS						
Season	Team	League	Gms.	Min.	W	L	T	GA	SO	Avg.	Gms.	Min.	W	L	GA	SO	Avg.
88-89—Huntsville Jr. C		OHA	22	1306	...	...	...	82	0	3.77	—	—	—	—	—	—	—
89-90—Chatham Jr. B		OHA	21	1249	...	...	...	76	0	3.65	—	—	—	—	—	—	—
90-91—Sault Ste. Marie		OHL	7	380	5	2	0	19	0	3.00	—	—	—	—	—	—	—
—Oshawa		OHL	30	1483	17	5	1	84	0	3.40	8	292	1	4	26	0	5.34
91-92—Oshawa		OHL	40	2260	18	13	6	149	1	3.96	7	428	3	4	26	0	3.64
92-93—Can. national team		Int'l	13	...	7	5	1	37	1	2.98	—	—	—	—	—	—	—
—Hamilton		AHL	12	618	2	8	0	46	0	4.47	—	—	—	—	—	—	—
93-94—Hamilton		AHL	*70	*4005	*34	28	6	241	*4	3.61	3	146	0	2	12	0	4.93
94-95—Syracuse		AHL	61	*3618	25	*29	7	225	2	3.73	—	—	—	—	—	—	—

FRANCIS, RON
C, PENGUINS

PERSONAL: Born March 1, 1963, in Sault Ste. Marie, Ont.... 6-2/200.... Shoots left.... Cousin of Mike Liut, goaltender, St. Louis Blues, Hartford Whalers and Washington Capitals (1979-80 through 1991-92) and Cincinnati Stingers of WHA (1977-78 and 1978-79).
TRANSACTIONS/CAREER NOTES: Selected by Hartford Whalers as underage junior in first round (first Whalers pick, fourth overall) of NHL entry draft (June 10, 1981).... Injured eye (January 27, 1982); missed three weeks.... Strained ligaments in right knee (November 30, 1983).... Broke left ankle (January 18, 1986); missed 27 games. ... Broke left index finger (January 28, 1989); missed 11 games.... Broke nose (November 24, 1990).... Traded by Whalers with D Ulf Samuelsson and D Grant Jennings to Pittsburgh Penguins for C John Cullen, D Zarley Zalapski and RW Jeff Parker (March 4, 1991).... Suffered from the flu (February 19, 1995); missed one game.... Suffered back spasms (February 21, 1995); missed three games.
HONORS: Played in NHL All-Star Game (1983, 1985 and 1990).... Won Lady Byng Memorial Trophy (1994-95).... Won Frank J. Selke Trophy (1994-95).... Won NHL Alka-Seltzer Plus award (1994-95).
STATISTICAL PLATEAUS: Three-goal games: 1982-83 (1), 1984-85 (1), 1985-86 (2), 1987-88 (1), 1988-89 (1), 1989-90 (1),

1990-91 (1). Total: 8.... Four-goal games: 1983-84 (1).... Total hat tricks: 9.
MISCELLANEOUS: Member of Stanley Cup championship teams (1991 and 1992).... Captain of Hartford Whalers (1984-85 through 1990- 1991).... Captain of Pittsburgh Penguins (1994-95).

Season Team	League	REGULAR SEASON					PLAYOFFS				
		Gms.	G	A	Pts.	PIM	Gms.	G	A	Pts.	PIM
80-81—Sault Ste. Marie	OMJHL	64	26	43	69	33	19	7	8	15	34
81-82—Sault Ste. Marie	OHL	25	18	30	48	46	—	—	—	—	—
—Hartford	NHL	59	25	43	68	51	—	—	—	—	—
82-83—Hartford	NHL	79	31	59	90	60	—	—	—	—	—
83-84—Hartford	NHL	72	23	60	83	45	—	—	—	—	—
84-85—Hartford	NHL	80	24	57	81	66	—	—	—	—	—
85-86—Hartford	NHL	53	24	53	77	24	10	1	2	3	4
86-87—Hartford	NHL	75	30	63	93	45	6	2	2	4	6
87-88—Hartford	NHL	80	25	50	75	87	6	2	5	7	2
88-89—Hartford	NHL	69	29	48	77	36	4	0	2	2	0
89-90—Hartford	NHL	80	32	69	101	73	7	3	3	6	8
90-91—Hartford	NHL	67	21	55	76	51	—	—	—	—	—
—Pittsburgh	NHL	14	2	9	11	21	24	7	10	17	24
91-92—Pittsburgh	NHL	70	21	33	54	30	21	8	*19	27	6
92-93—Pittsburgh	NHL	84	24	76	100	68	12	6	11	17	19
93-94—Pittsburgh	NHL	82	27	66	93	62	6	0	2	2	6
94-95—Pittsburgh	NHL	44	11	*48	59	18	12	6	13	19	4
NHL totals		1008	349	789	1138	737	108	35	69	104	79

FRASER, IAIN
C, OILERS

PERSONAL: Born August 10, 1969, in Scarborough, Ont.... 5- 10/ 175.... Shoots left.
TRANSACTIONS/CAREER NOTES: Selected by New York Islanders in 12th round (14th Islanders pick, 233rd overall) of NHL entry draft (June 17, 1989).... Signed as free agent by Quebec Nordiques (August 3, 1993).... Injured mouth (October 15, 1993); missed one game.... Suffered from the flu (November 22, 1993); missed one game.... Bruised left foot (December 28, 1993); missed three games.... Bruised right knee (January 26, 1994); missed one game.... Injured back (February 21, 1994); missed six games.... Traded by Nordiques to Dallas Stars for undisclosed pick in 1996 draft (January 31, 1995).... Claimed on waivers by Edmonton Oilers (March 3, 1995).... Loaned by Oilers to Denver Grizzlies of IHL (April 10, 1995).
HONORS: Won Leo LaLonde Memorial Trophy (1989-90).... Won Stafford Smythe Memorial Trophy (1989-90).... Named to Memorial Cup All-Star team (1989-90).... Named to AHL All-Star second team (1992-93).

Season Team	League	REGULAR SEASON					PLAYOFFS				
		Gms.	G	A	Pts.	PIM	Gms.	G	A	Pts.	PIM
86-87—Oshawa Jr. B	OHA	31	18	22	40	119	—	—	—	—	—
87-88—Oshawa	OHL	16	4	4	8	22	6	2	3	5	2
88-89—Oshawa	OHL	62	33	57	90	87	6	2	8	10	12
89-90—Oshawa	OHL	56	40	65	105	75	17	10	*22	32	8
90-91—Richmond	ECHL	3	1	1	2	0	—	—	—	—	—
—Capital District	AHL	32	5	13	18	16	—	—	—	—	—
91-92—Capital District	AHL	45	9	11	20	24	—	—	—	—	—
92-93—Capital District	AHL	74	41	69	110	16	4	0	1	1	0
—New York Islanders	NHL	7	2	2	4	2	—	—	—	—	—
93-94—Quebec	NHL	60	17	20	37	23	—	—	—	—	—
—Canadian national team	Int'l	4	0	1	1	4	—	—	—	—	—
94-95—Dallas	NHL	4	0	0	0	0	—	—	—	—	—
—Edmonton	NHL	9	3	0	3	0	—	—	—	—	—
—Denver	IHL	1	0	0	0	0	—	—	—	—	—
NHL totals		80	22	22	44	25					

FREDERICK, JOE
RW, RED WINGS

PERSONAL: Born August 6, 1969, in St. Hubert, Que.... 6- 1/ 190.... Shoots right.
COLLEGE: Northern Michigan.
TRANSACTIONS/CAREER NOTES: Selected by Detroit Red Wings in 12th round (13th Red Wings pick, 242nd overall) of NHL entry draft (June 17, 1989).
HONORS: Named to WCHA All-Star second team (1992-93).

Season Team	League	REGULAR SEASON					PLAYOFFS				
		Gms.	G	A	Pts.	PIM	Gms.	G	A	Pts.	PIM
90-91—Northern Michigan Univ.	WCHA	40	9	11	20	77	—	—	—	—	—
91-92—Northern Michigan Univ.	WCHA	36	23	8	31	100	—	—	—	—	—
92-93—Northern Michigan Univ.	WCHA	29	28	20	48	100	—	—	—	—	—
—Adirondack	AHL	5	0	1	1	2	8	0	0	0	6
93-94—Adirondack	AHL	68	28	30	58	130	12	11	4	15	22
94-95—Adirondack	AHL	71	27	28	55	124	4	0	0	0	10

FREER, MARK
C

PERSONAL: Born July 14, 1968, in Peterborough, Ont.... 5- 10/ 180.... Shoots left.... Name pronounced FREER.
HIGH SCHOOL: Crestwood (Peterborough, Ont.).
TRANSACTIONS/CAREER NOTES: Signed as free agent by Philadelphia Flyers (September 1986).... Selected by Ottawa Senators in NHL expansion draft (June 18, 1992).... Suffered charley horse (October 24, 1992); missed 14 games.... Signed as free agent by Calgary Flames (August 10, 1993).

Season	Team	League	REGULAR SEASON Gms.	G	A	Pts.	PIM	PLAYOFFS Gms.	G	A	Pts.	PIM
85-86—Peterborough		OHL	65	16	28	44	24	14	3	4	7	13
86-87—Peterborough		OHL	65	39	43	82	44	12	2	6	8	5
—Philadelphia		NHL	1	0	1	1	0	—	—	—	—	—
87-88—Philadelphia		NHL	1	0	0	0	0	—	—	—	—	—
—Peterborough		OHL	63	38	71	109	63	12	5	12	17	4
88-89—Philadelphia		NHL	5	0	1	1	0	—	—	—	—	—
—Hershey		AHL	75	30	49	79	77	12	4	6	10	2
89-90—Hershey		AHL	65	28	36	64	31	—	—	—	—	—
90-91—Hershey		AHL	77	18	44	62	45	7	1	3	4	17
91-92—Hershey		AHL	31	13	11	24	38	6	0	3	3	2
—Philadelphia		NHL	50	6	7	13	18	—	—	—	—	—
92-93—Ottawa		NHL	63	10	14	24	39	—	—	—	—	—
93-94—Saint John		AHL	77	33	53	86	45	7	2	4	6	16
—Calgary		NHL	2	0	0	0	4	—	—	—	—	—
94-95—Houston		IHL	80	38	42	80	54	4	0	1	1	4
NHL totals			122	16	23	39	61					

FRIESEN, JEFF
C/LW, SHARKS

PERSONAL: Born August 5, 1976, in Meadow Lake, Sask.... 6-1/190.... Shoots left.... Name pronounced FREE-sehn.
HIGH SCHOOL: Robert Usher (Regina, Sask.).
TRANSACTIONS/CAREER NOTES: Selected by San Jose Sharks in first round (first Sharks pick, 11th overall) of NHL entry draft (June 28, 1994).
HONORS: Won Can.HL Rookie of the Year Award (1992-93).... Won Jim Piggott Memorial Trophy (1992-93).... Named to NHL All-Rookie team (1994-95).

Season	Team	League	REGULAR SEASON Gms.	G	A	Pts.	PIM	PLAYOFFS Gms.	G	A	Pts.	PIM
91-92—Regina		WHL	4	3	1	4	2	—	—	—	—	—
92-93—Regina		WHL	70	45	38	83	23	13	7	10	17	8
93-94—Regina		WHL	66	51	67	118	48	4	3	2	5	2
94-95—Regina		WHL	25	21	23	44	22	—	—	—	—	—
—San Jose		NHL	48	15	10	25	14	11	1	5	6	4
NHL totals			48	15	10	25	14	11	1	5	6	4

FUHR, GRANT
G, BLUES

PERSONAL: Born September 28, 1962, in Spruce Grove, Alta.... 5-9/190.... Catches right.... Name pronounced FYOOR.
TRANSACTIONS/CAREER NOTES: Selected by Edmonton Oilers in first round (first Oilers pick, eighth overall) of NHL entry draft (June 10, 1981).... Suffered partial separation of right shoulder (December 1981).... Strained left knee ligaments and underwent surgery (December 13, 1983).... Separated shoulder (February 1985).... Bruised left shoulder (November 3, 1985); missed 10 games.... Bruised left shoulder (November 1987).... Injured right knee (November 1987).... Suffered cervical neck strain (January 18, 1989).... Underwent appendectomy (September 14, 1989); missed first six games of season.... Underwent reconstructive surgery to left shoulder (December 27, 1989).... Tore adhesions in left shoulder (March 13, 1990).... Suspended six months by NHL for admitting to using drugs earlier in career (September 27, 1990).... Traded by Oilers with RW/LW Glenn Anderson and LW Craig Berube to Toronto Maple Leafs for LW Vincent Damphousse, D Luke Richardson, G Peter Ing, C Scott Thornton and future considerations (September 19, 1991).... Sprained thumb (October 17, 1991); missed two games.... Pulled groin (November 12, 1991); missed three games.... Sprained knee (February 11, 1992); missed four games.... Sprained knee (October 20, 1992); missed 10 games.... Strained shoulder (December 5, 1992); missed three games.... Bruised shoulder muscle (January 17, 1993); missed four games.... Traded by Maple Leafs with fifth-round pick in 1995 draft (D Kevin Popp) to Buffalo Sabres for LW Dave Andreychuk, G Daren Puppa and first-round pick (D Kenny Jonsson) in 1993 draft (February 2, 1993).... Injured knee (November 24, 1993); missed 24 games.... Traded by Sabres with D Philippe Boucher and D Denis Tsygurov to Los Angeles Kings for D Alexei Zhitnik, D Charlie Huddy, G Robb Stauber and fifth-round pick (D Marian Menhart) in 1995 draft (February 14, 1995).... Signed as free agent by St. Louis Blues (July 11, 1995).
HONORS: Won Stewart (Butch) Paul Memorial Trophy (1979-80).... Named to WHL All-Star first team (1979-80 and 1980-81).... Won WHL Top Goaltender Trophy (1980-81).... Named to THE SPORTING NEWS All-Star second team (1981-82 and 1985-86).... Named to NHL All-Star second team (1981-82).... Played in NHL All-Star Game (1982, 1984-1986, 1988 and 1989).... Named All-Star Game Most Valuable Player (1986).... Won Vezina Trophy (1987-88).... Named to THE SPORTING NEWS All-Star first team (1987-88).... Named to NHL All-Star first team (1987-88).... Shared William M. Jennings Trophy with Dominik Hasek (1993-94).
RECORDS: Holds NHL single-season records for most points by a goaltender—14 (1983-84); and most games by a goaltender—75 (1987-88).... Shares NHL single-season playoff record for most wins by a goaltender—16 (1987-88).
MISCELLANEOUS: Member of Stanley Cup championship teams (1984, 1985, 1987, 1988 and 1990).

Season	Team	League	REGULAR SEASON Gms.	Min.	W	L	T	GA	SO	Avg.	PLAYOFFS Gms.	Min.	W	L	GA	SO	Avg.
79-80—Victoria		WHL	43	2488	30	12	0	130	2	3.14	8	465	5	3	22	0	2.84
80-81—Victoria		WHL	59	*3448	48	9	1	160	+4	*2.78	15	899	12	3	45	1	3.00
81-82—Edmonton		NHL	48	2847	28	5	14	157	0	3.31	5	309	2	3	26	0	5.05
82-83—Moncton		AHL	10	604	4	5	1	40	0	3.97	—	—	—	—	—	—	—
—Edmonton		NHL	32	1803	13	12	5	129	0	4.29	1	11	0	0	0	0	0.00
83-84—Edmonton		NHL	45	2625	30	10	4	171	1	3.91	16	883	11	4	44	1	2.99
84-85—Edmonton		NHL	46	2559	26	8	7	165	1	3.87	+18	*1064	*15	3	55	0	3.10
85-86—Edmonton		NHL	40	2184	29	8	0	143	0	3.93	9	541	5	4	28	0	3.11
86-87—Edmonton		NHL	44	2388	22	13	3	137	0	3.44	19	1148	14	5	47	0	2.46

Season Team	League	REGULAR SEASON								PLAYOFFS						
		Gms.	Min.	W	L	T	GA	SO	Avg.	Gms.	Min.	W	L	GA	SO	Avg.
87-88—Edmonton	NHL	*75	*4304	40	24	9	*246	†4	3.43	*19	*1136	*16	2	55	0	2.90
88-89—Edmonton	NHL	59	3341	23	26	6	213	1	3.83	7	417	3	4	24	1	3.45
89-90—Cape Breton	AHL	2	120	2	0	0	6	0	3.00	—	—	—	—	—	—	—
—Edmonton	NHL	21	1081	9	7	3	70	1	3.89	—	—	—	—	—	—	—
90-91—Cape Breton	AHL	4	240	2	2	0	17	0	4.25	—	—	—	—	—	—	—
—Edmonton	NHL	13	778	6	4	3	39	1	3.01	17	1019	8	7	51	0	3.00
91-92—Toronto	NHL	65	3774	25	*33	5	*230	2	3.66	—	—	—	—	—	—	—
92-93—Toronto	NHL	29	1665	13	9	4	87	1	3.14	—	—	—	—	—	—	—
—Buffalo	NHL	29	1694	11	15	2	98	0	3.47	8	474	3	4	27	1	3.42
93-94—Buffalo	NHL	32	1726	13	12	3	106	2	3.68	—	—	—	—	—	—	—
—Rochester	AHL	5	310	3	0	2	10	0	1.94	—	—	—	—	—	—	—
94-95—Buffalo	NHL	3	180	1	2	0	12	0	4.00	—	—	—	—	—	—	—
—Los Angeles	NHL	14	698	1	7	3	47	0	4.04	—	—	—	—	—	—	—
NHL totals		595	33647	290	195	71	2050	14	3.66	119	7002	77	36	357	3	3.06

GAGE, JOAQUIN
G, OILERS

PERSONAL: Born October 19, 1973, in Vancouver.... 6-0/200.... Catches left.... Name pronounced wah-KEEN GAYJ.
COLLEGE: Portland (Ore.) Community College.
TRANSACTIONS/CAREER NOTES: Selected by Edmonton Oilers in fifth round (sixth Oilers pick, 109th overall) of NHL entry draft (June 20, 1992).

Season Team	League	REGULAR SEASON								PLAYOFFS						
		Gms.	Min.	W	L	T	GA	SO	Avg.	Gms.	Min.	W	L	GA	SO	Avg.
90-91—Bellingham Jr. A	BCJHL	16	751	...	...	...	64	0	5.11	—	—	—	—	—	—	—
—Portland	WHL	3	180	0	3	0	17	0	5.67	—	—	—	—	—	—	—
91-92—Portland	WHL	63	3635	27	30	4	269	2	4.44	6	366	2	4	28	0	4.59
92-93—Portland	WHL	38	2302	21	16	1	153	2	3.99	8	427	5	2	30	0	4.22
93-94—Prince Albert	WHL	53	3041	24	25	3	212	1	4.18	—	—	—	—	—	—	—
94-95—Cape Breton	AHL	54	3010	17	28	5	207	0	4.13	—	—	—	—	—	—	—
—Edmonton	NHL	2	99	0	2	0	7	0	4.24	—	—	—	—	—	—	—
NHL totals		2	99	0	2	0	7	0	4.24							

GAGE, JODY
RW, SABRES

PERSONAL: Born November 29, 1959, in Toronto.... 6-0/190.... Shoots right.... Full name: Joseph William Gage.
TRANSACTIONS/CAREER NOTES: Selected by Detroit Red Wings in third round (second Red Wings pick, 46th overall) of NHL entry draft (August 9, 1979).... Signed as free agent by Buffalo Sabres (August 1985).... Strained ankle and knee ligaments in preseason game (September 27, 1988); missed two months.
HONORS: Named to AHL All-Star first team (1985-86, 1987-88 and 1990-91).... Won Les Cunningham Plaque (1987-88).

Season Team	League	REGULAR SEASON				PLAYOFFS			
		Gms.	G	A	Pts.	PIM	Gms.	G	A	Pts.	PIM
76-77—St. Catharines	OMJHL	47	13	20	33	2	—	—	—	—	—
77-78—Hamilton Fincups	OMJHL	32	15	18	33	19	—	—	—	—	—
—Kitchener	OMJHL	36	17	27	44	21	9	4	3	7	4
78-79—Kitchener	OMJHL	59	46	43	89	40	10	1	2	3	6
79-80—Adirondack	AHL	63	25	21	46	15	5	2	1	3	0
—Kalamazoo	IHL	14	17	12	29	0	—	—	—	—	—
80-81—Detroit	NHL	16	2	2	4	22	—	—	—	—	—
—Adirondack	AHL	59	17	31	48	44	17	9	6	15	12
81-82—Detroit	NHL	31	9	10	19	2	—	—	—	—	—
—Adirondack	AHL	47	21	20	41	21	—	—	—	—	—
82-83—Adirondack	AHL	65	23	30	53	33	6	1	5	6	8
83-84—Detroit	NHL	3	0	0	0	0	—	—	—	—	—
—Adirondack	AHL	73	40	32	72	32	6	3	4	7	2
84-85—Adirondack	AHL	78	27	33	60	55	—	—	—	—	—
85-86—Buffalo	NHL	7	3	2	5	0	—	—	—	—	—
—Rochester	AHL	73	42	57	99	56	—	—	—	—	—
86-87—Rochester	AHL	70	26	39	65	60	17	*14	5	19	24
87-88—Rochester	AHL	76	*60	44	104	46	5	2	5	7	10
—Buffalo	NHL	2	0	0	0	0	—	—	—	—	—
88-89—Rochester	AHL	65	31	38	69	50	—	—	—	—	—
89-90—Rochester	AHL	75	45	38	83	42	17	4	6	10	12
90-91—Rochester	AHL	73	42	43	85	34	15	6	10	16	14
91-92—Rochester	AHL	67	40	40	80	54	16	5	9	14	10
—Buffalo	NHL	9	0	1	1	2	—	—	—	—	—
92-93—Rochester	AHL	71	40	40	80	76	9	5	8	13	2
93-94—Rochester	AHL	44	18	21	39	57	—	—	—	—	—
94-95—Rochester	AHL	23	4	5	9	20	2	0	0	0	0
NHL totals		68	14	15	29	26					

FG

GAGNER, DAVE
LW/C, STARS

PERSONAL: Born December 11, 1964, in Chatham, Ont.... 5-10/180.... Shoots left.... Name pronounced GAHN-yay.
TRANSACTIONS/CAREER NOTES: Selected by New York Rangers as underage junior in first round (first Rangers pick, 12th overall) of NHL entry draft (June 8, 1983).... Fractured ankle

(February 5, 1986).... Underwent emergency appendectomy (December 1986).... Traded by Rangers with RW Jay Caufield to Minnesota North Stars for D Jari Gronstrand and D Paul Boutilier (October 8, 1987).... Broke kneecap (March 31, 1989). ... Underwent surgery to left knee cartilage (November 11, 1990).... Underwent arthroscopic knee surgery (December 18, 1991); missed one game.... Hyperextended knee (March 17, 1992); missed one game.... North Stars franchise moved from Minnesota to Dallas and renamed Stars for 1993-94 season.... Separated shoulder (November 1, 1993); missed seven games. ... Played in Europe during 1994-95 NHL lockout.

HONORS: Won Bobby Smith Trophy (1982-83).... Named to OHL All-Star second team (1982-83).... Played in NHL All-Star Game (1991).

RECORDS: Shares NHL single-game playoff record for most points in one period—4 (April 8, 1991, first period).

STATISTICAL PLATEAUS: Three-goal games: 1988-89 (2), 1990-91 (1). Total: 3.... Four-goal games: 1993-94 (1).... Total hat tricks: 4.

Season Team	League	REGULAR SEASON					PLAYOFFS				
		Gms.	G	A	Pts.	PIM	Gms.	G	A	Pts.	PIM
81-82—Brantford	OHL	68	30	46	76	31	11	3	6	9	6
82-83—Brantford	OHL	70	55	66	121	57	8	5	5	10	4
83-84—Canadian Olympic Team	Int'l	50	19	18	37	26	—	—	—	—	—
—Brantford	OHL	12	7	13	20	4	6	0	4	4	6
84-85—New Haven	AHL	38	13	20	33	23	—	—	—	—	—
—New York Rangers	NHL	38	6	6	12	16	—	—	—	—	—
85-86—New York Rangers	NHL	32	4	6	10	19	—	—	—	—	—
—New Haven	AHL	16	10	11	21	11	4	1	2	3	2
86-87—New York Rangers	NHL	10	1	4	5	12	—	—	—	—	—
—New Haven	AHL	56	22	41	63	50	7	1	5	6	18
87-88—Kalamazoo	IHL	14	16	10	26	26	—	—	—	—	—
—Minnesota	NHL	51	8	11	19	55	—	—	—	—	—
88-89—Minnesota	NHL	75	35	43	78	104	—	—	—	—	—
—Kalamazoo	IHL	1	0	1	1	4	—	—	—	—	—
89-90—Minnesota	NHL	79	40	38	78	54	7	2	3	5	16
90-91—Minnesota	NHL	73	40	42	82	114	23	12	15	27	28
91-92—Minnesota	NHL	78	31	40	71	107	7	2	4	6	8
92-93—Minnesota	NHL	84	33	43	76	143	—	—	—	—	—
93-94—Dallas	NHL	76	32	29	61	83	9	5	1	6	2
94-95—Courmaosta	Italy	1	0	4	4	0	—	—	—	—	—
—Dallas	NHL	48	14	28	42	42	5	1	1	2	4
NHL totals		**644**	**244**	**290**	**534**	**749**	**51**	**22**	**24**	**46**	**58**

GAGNON, JOEL
G, MIGHTY DUCKS

PERSONAL: Born March 14, 1975, in Hearst, Ont.... 6-0/194.... Catches left.... Name pronounced GAN-yahn.

TRANSACTIONS/CAREER NOTES: Selected by Mighty Ducks of Anaheim in fourth round (fourth Mighty Ducks pick, 82nd overall) of NHL entry draft (June 26, 1993).

Season Team	League	REGULAR SEASON								PLAYOFFS							
		Gms.	Min.	W	L	T	GA	SO	Avg.	Gms.	Min.	W	L	GA	SO	Avg.
92-93—Oshawa	OHL	48	2248	19	19	1	159	0	4.24	7	285	3	0	21	0	4.42
93-94—Oshawa	OHL	23	1089	4	11	3	100	0	5.51	—	—	—	—	—	—	—
94-95—Oshawa	OHL	15	789	6	7	2	50	1	3.80	—	—	—	—	—	—	—
—North Bay	OHL	21	1021	8	9	1	59	0	3.47	2	35	0	0	2	0	3.43

GALANOV, MAXIM
D, RANGERS

PERSONAL: Born March 13, 1974, in Krasnoyarsk, U.S.S.R.... 6-1/167.... Shoots left. ... Name pronounced guh-LAH-nahf.

TRANSACTIONS/CAREER NOTES: Selected by New York Rangers in third round (third Rangers pick, 61st overall) of NHL entry draft (June 26, 1993).

Season Team	League	REGULAR SEASON					PLAYOFFS				
		Gms.	G	A	Pts.	PIM	Gms.	G	A	Pts.	PIM
92-93—Lada Togliatti	CIS	41	4	2	6	12	10	1	1	2	12
93-94—Lada Togliatti	CIS	7	1	0	1	4	12	1	0	1	8
94-95—Lada Togliatti	CIS	45	5	6	11	54	9	0	1	1	12

G

GALLANT, GERARD
LW, LIGHTNING

PERSONAL: Born September 2, 1963, in Summerside, P.E.I.... 5-10/190.... Shoots left.... Name pronounced guh-LANT.

TRANSACTIONS/CAREER NOTES: Selected by Detroit Red Wings in sixth round (fourth Red Wings pick, 107th overall) of NHL entry draft (June 10, 1981).... Broke jaw (December 11, 1985); missed 25 games.... Fined $500 by NHL for stick-swinging incident (April 8, 1989).... Suspended five games by NHL for slashing (October 7, 1989).... Suspended three games by NHL for hitting linesman (January 13, 1990).... Suffered sore back (November 1990); missed eight games.... Suffered back spasms (December 1990); missed 18 games.... Underwent surgery to remove bone spur in back (March 14, 1991); missed remainder of season.... Injured hand (February 1992); missed five games.... Strained back (March 20, 1992); missed five games.... Injured hip (December 15, 1992); missed three games.... Suffered from the flu (January 17, 1993); missed one game.... Signed as free agent by Tampa Bay Lightning (July 21, 1993).... Sprained back (November 17, 1993); missed four games. ... Sprained back (April 1, 1994); missed six games.

HONORS: Named to NHL All-Star second team (1988-89).

STATISTICAL PLATEAUS: Three-goal games: 1987-88 (3), 1988-89 (1). Total: 4.

Season Team	League	REGULAR SEASON					PLAYOFFS				
		Gms.	G	A	Pts.	PIM	Gms.	G	A	Pts.	PIM
79-80—Summerside	PEIHA	45	60	55	115	90	—	—	—	—	—
80-81—Sherbrooke	QMJHL	68	41	60	101	220	14	6	13	19	46
81-82—Sherbrooke	QMJHL	58	34	58	92	260	22	14	24	38	84
82-83—St. Jean	QMJHL	33	28	25	53	139	—	—	—	—	—
—Verdun	QMJHL	29	26	49	75	105	15	†14	19	33	*84
83-84—Adirondack	AHL	77	31	33	64	195	7	1	3	4	34
84-85—Adirondack	AHL	46	18	29	47	131	—	—	—	—	—
—Detroit	NHL	32	6	12	18	66	3	0	0	0	11
85-86—Detroit	NHL	52	20	19	39	106	—	—	—	—	—
86-87—Detroit	NHL	80	38	34	72	216	16	8	6	14	43
87-88—Detroit	NHL	73	34	39	73	242	16	6	9	15	55
88-89—Detroit	NHL	76	39	54	93	230	6	1	2	3	40
89-90—Detroit	NHL	69	36	44	80	254	—	—	—	—	—
90-91—Detroit	NHL	45	10	16	26	111	—	—	—	—	—
91-92—Detroit	NHL	69	14	22	36	187	11	2	2	4	25
92-93—Detroit	NHL	67	10	20	30	188	6	1	2	3	4
93-94—Tampa Bay	NHL	51	4	9	13	74	—	—	—	—	—
94-95—Atlanta	IHL	16	3	3	6	31	—	—	—	—	—
—Tampa Bay	NHL	1	0	0	0	0	—	—	—	—	—
NHL totals		615	211	269	480	1674	58	18	21	39	178

GALLEY, GARRY

D, SABRES

PERSONAL: Born April 16, 1963, in Ottawa.... 6-0/204.... Shoots left.
COLLEGE: Bowling Green State.

TRANSACTIONS/CAREER NOTES: Selected by Los Angeles Kings in fifth round (fourth Kings pick, 100th overall) of NHL entry draft (June 8, 1983).... Injured knee (December 8, 1985).... Traded by Kings to Washington Capitals for G Al Jensen (February 14, 1987).... Signed as free agent by Boston Bruins; third-round pick in 1989 draft awarded to Capitals as compensation (July 8, 1988).... Sprained left shoulder (September 30, 1989); missed first nine games of season.... Suffered lacerations to cheek, both lips and part of neck (October 6, 1990).... Dislocated right shoulder (December 22, 1990).... Bruised left kneecap (March 23, 1991); missed two games.... Pulled hamstring (April 17, 1991); missed three playoff games.... Traded by Bruins with C Wes Walz and future considerations to Philadelphia Flyers for D Gord Murphy, RW Brian Dobbin and third-round pick (LW Sergei Zholtok) in 1992 draft (January 2, 1992).... Bruised ribs (January 9, 1992); missed one game.... Fractured foot (March 3, 1992); missed two games.... Bruised jaw (February 24, 1993); missed one game.... Strained shoulder (March 6, 1994); missed three games. ... Sprained wrist (February 13, 1995); missed three games.... Traded by Flyers to Buffalo Sabres for D Petr Svoboda (April 7, 1995).

HONORS: Named to CCHA All-Star first team (1982-83 and 1983-84).... Named to NCAA All-Tournament team (1983-84). ... Played in NHL All-Star Game (1991 and 1994).

Season Team	League	REGULAR SEASON					PLAYOFFS				
		Gms.	G	A	Pts.	PIM	Gms.	G	A	Pts.	PIM
81-82—Bowling Green State	CCHA	42	3	36	39	48	—	—	—	—	—
82-83—Bowling Green State	CCHA	40	17	29	46	40	—	—	—	—	—
83-84—Bowling Green State	CCHA	44	15	52	67	61	—	—	—	—	—
84-85—Los Angeles	NHL	78	8	30	38	82	3	1	0	1	2
85-86—Los Angeles	NHL	49	9	13	22	46	—	—	—	—	—
—New Haven	AHL	4	2	6	8	6	—	—	—	—	—
86-87—Los Angeles	NHL	30	5	11	16	57	—	—	—	—	—
—Washington	NHL	18	1	10	11	10	2	0	0	0	0
87-88—Washington	NHL	58	7	23	30	44	13	2	4	6	13
88-89—Boston	NHL	78	8	21	29	80	9	0	1	1	33
89-90—Boston	NHL	71	8	27	35	75	21	3	3	6	34
90-91—Boston	NHL	70	6	21	27	84	16	1	5	6	17
91-92—Boston	NHL	38	2	12	14	83	—	—	—	—	—
—Philadelphia	NHL	39	3	15	18	34	—	—	—	—	—
92-93—Philadelphia	NHL	83	13	49	62	115	—	—	—	—	—
93-94—Philadelphia	NHL	81	10	60	70	91	—	—	—	—	—
94-95—Philadelphia	NHL	33	2	20	22	20	—	—	—	—	—
—Buffalo	NHL	14	1	9	10	10	5	0	3	3	4
NHL totals		740	83	321	404	831	69	7	16	23	103

GARDINER, BRUCE

C, SENATORS

PERSONAL: Born February 11, 1971, in Barrie, Ont.... 6-1/185.... Shoots right.
COLLEGE: Colgate.

TRANSACTIONS/CAREER NOTES: Selected by St. Louis Blues in sixth round (sixth Blues pick, 131st overall) of NHL entry draft (June 22, 1991).... Signed as free agent by Ottawa Senators (June 14, 1994).

HONORS: Named to ECAC All-Star second team (1993-94).

Season Team	League	REGULAR SEASON					PLAYOFFS				
		Gms.	G	A	Pts.	PIM	Gms.	G	A	Pts.	PIM
90-91—Colgate University	ECAC	27	4	9	13	72	—	—	—	—	—
91-92—Colgate University	ECAC	23	7	8	15	77	—	—	—	—	—
92-93—Colgate University	ECAC	33	17	12	29	64	—	—	—	—	—
93-94—Colgate University	ECAC	33	23	23	46	68	—	—	—	—	—
—Peoria	IHL	3	0	0	0	0	—	—	—	—	—
94-95—Prince Edward Island	AHL	72	17	20	37	132	7	4	1	5	4

G

GARPENLOV, JOHAN

LW, PANTHERS

PERSONAL: Born March 21, 1968, in Stockholm, Sweden. . . . 5-11/184. . . . Shoots left. . . . Name pronounced YOH-hahn GAHR-pehn-LAHV.

TRANSACTIONS/CAREER NOTES: Selected by Detroit Red Wings in fifth round (fifth Red Wings pick, 85th overall) of NHL entry draft (June 9, 1984). . . . Traded by Red Wings to San Jose Sharks for D Bob McGill and eighth-round pick (G C.J. Denomme) in 1992 draft (March 10, 1992). . . . Strained back (October 20, 1992); missed three games. . . . Suffered from the flu (March 25, 1993); missed one game. . . . Injured thigh (October 10, 1993); missed one game. . . . Sprained groin (January 30, 1995); missed six games. . . . Traded by Sharks to Florida Panthers for conditional fifth-round pick in 1998 draft (March 3, 1995).

STATISTICAL PLATEAUS: Three-goal games: 1990-91 (1), 1992-93 (1). Total: 2. . . . Four-goal games: 1990-91 (1). . . . Total hat tricks: 3.

Season Team	League	REGULAR SEASON					PLAYOFFS				
		Gms.	G	A	Pts.	PIM	Gms.	G	A	Pts.	PIM
86-87—Djurgarden Stockholm	Sweden	29	5	8	13	20	—	—	—	—	—
87-88—Djurgarden Stockholm	Sweden	30	7	10	17	12	—	—	—	—	—
88-89—Djurgarden Stockholm	Sweden	36	12	19	31	20	—	—	—	—	—
89-90—Djurgarden Stockholm	Sweden	39	20	13	33	36	8	2	4	6	4
90-91—Detroit	NHL	71	18	22	40	18	6	0	1	1	4
91-92—Detroit	NHL	16	1	1	2	4	—	—	—	—	—
—Adirondack	AHL	9	3	3	6	6	—	—	—	—	—
—San Jose..........................	NHL	12	5	6	11	4	—	—	—	—	—
92-93—San Jose	NHL	79	22	44	66	56	—	—	—	—	—
93-94—San Jose	NHL	80	18	35	53	28	14	4	6	10	6
94-95—San Jose	NHL	13	1	1	2	2	—	—	—	—	—
—Florida	NHL	27	3	9	12	0	—	—	—	—	—
NHL totals................................		**298**	**68**	**118**	**186**	**112**	**20**	**4**	**7**	**11**	**10**

GARTNER, MIKE

RW, MAPLE LEAFS

PERSONAL: Born October 29, 1959, in Ottawa. . . . 6-0/187. . . . Shoots right. . . . Full name: Michael Alfred Gartner.

TRANSACTIONS/CAREER NOTES: Signed as underage junior by Cincinnati Stingers (August 1978). . . . Selected by Washington Capitals in first round (first Capitals pick, fourth overall) of NHL entry draft (August 9, 1979). . . . Injured eye (February 1983). . . . Underwent arthroscopic surgery to repair torn cartilage in left knee (March 1986). . . . Sprained right knee (November 1988). . . . Traded by Capitals with D Larry Murphy to Minnesota North Stars for RW Dino Ciccarelli and D Bob Rouse (March 7, 1989). . . . Underwent surgery to repair cartilage in left knee (April 14, 1989). . . . Traded by North Stars to New York Rangers for C Ulf Dahlen, fourth-round pick in 1990 draft (C Cal McGowan) and future considerations (March 6, 1990). . . . Underwent arthroscopic surgery to repair elbow (January 27, 1994); missed one game. . . . Traded by Rangers to Toronto Maple Leafs for RW Glenn Anderson, rights to D Scott Malone and fourth-round pick (D Alexander Korobolin) in 1994 draft (March 21, 1994). . . . Suffered partially collapsed lung (February 3, 1995); missed seven games. . . . Suffered hairline fracture in foot (March 17, 1995); missed three games.

HONORS: Won Emms Family Award (1976-77). . . . Named to OMJHL All-Star first team (1977-78). . . . Played in NHL All-Star Game (1980, 1985, 1986, 1988, 1990 and 1993). . . . Named All-Star Game Most Valuable Player (1993).

RECORDS: Holds NHL career record for most consecutive 30-goal seasons—15 (1979-80 through 1993-94). . . . Shares NHL career record for most 30-or-more goal seasons—15. . . . Holds NHL All-Star Game records for fastest two goals from start of game—3:37 (1993); and fastest two goals from start of period—3:37 (1993). . . . Shares NHL All-Star Game record for most goals—4 (1991).

STATISTICAL PLATEAUS: Three-goal games: 1979-80 (2), 1980-81 (1), 1981-82 (1), 1982-83 (1), 1983-84 (1), 1984-85 (1), 1985-86 (3), 1987-88 (1), 1989-90 (2), 1991-92 (1). Total: 14. . . . Four-goal games: 1980-81 (1), 1986-87 (1). Total: 2. . . . Total hat tricks: 16.

Season Team	League	REGULAR SEASON					PLAYOFFS				
		Gms.	G	A	Pts.	PIM	Gms.	G	A	Pts.	PIM
75-76—St. Catharines	OHA Mj. Jr. A	3	1	3	4	0	—	—	—	—	—
76-77—Niagara Falls	OMJHL	62	33	42	75	125	—	—	—	—	—
77-78—Niagara Falls	OMJHL	64	41	49	90	56	—	—	—	—	—
78-79—Cincinnati	WHA	78	27	25	52	123	3	0	2	2	2
79-80—Washington	NHL	77	36	32	68	66	—	—	—	—	—
80-81—Washington	NHL	80	48	46	94	100	—	—	—	—	—
81-82—Washington	NHL	80	35	45	80	121	—	—	—	—	—
82-83—Washington	NHL	73	38	38	76	54	4	0	0	0	4
83-84—Washington	NHL	80	40	45	85	90	8	3	7	10	16
84-85—Washington	NHL	80	50	52	102	71	5	4	3	7	9
85-86—Washington	NHL	74	35	40	75	63	9	2	10	12	4
86-87—Washington	NHL	78	41	32	73	61	7	4	3	7	14
87-88—Washington	NHL	80	48	33	81	73	14	3	4	7	14
88-89—Washington	NHL	56	26	29	55	71	—	—	—	—	—
—Minnesota	NHL	13	7	7	14	6	5	0	0	0	0
89-90—Minnesota	NHL	67	34	36	70	32	—	—	—	—	—
—New York Rangers	NHL	12	11	5	16	6	10	5	3	8	12
90-91—New York Rangers	NHL	79	49	20	69	53	6	1	1	2	0
91-92—New York Rangers	NHL	76	40	41	81	55	13	8	8	16	4
92-93—New York Rangers	NHL	84	45	23	68	59	—	—	—	—	—
93-94—New York Rangers	NHL	71	28	24	52	58	—	—	—	—	—
—Toronto	NHL	10	6	6	12	4	18	5	6	11	14
94-95—Toronto	NHL	38	12	8	20	6	5	2	2	4	2
WHA totals................................		**78**	**27**	**25**	**52**	**123**	**3**	**0**	**2**	**2**	**2**
NHL totals................................		**1208**	**629**	**562**	**1191**	**1049**	**104**	**37**	**47**	**84**	**93**

G

GAUDREAU, ROB
RW, SENATORS

PERSONAL: Born January 20, 1970, in Cranston, R.I. . . . . 5-11/185. . . . Shoots right. . . . Full name: Robert Rene Gaudreau. . . . Name pronounced guh-DROH. . . . Son of Bob Gaudreau, member of 1968 U.S. Olympic hockey team.
HIGH SCHOOL: Bishop Hendricken (Warwick, R.I.).

COLLEGE: Providence.
TRANSACTIONS/CAREER NOTES: Separated shoulder (February 1987). . . . Selected by Pittsburgh Penguins in ninth round (eighth Penguins pick, 127th overall) of NHL entry draft (June 11, 1988). . . . Traded by Penguins to Minnesota North Stars for C Richard Zemlak (November 1, 1988). . . . Selected by San Jose Sharks in NHL dispersal draft (May 30, 1991). . . . Bruised hand (March 21, 1993); missed one game. . . . Selected by Ottawa Senators in 1994-95 waiver draft for cash (January 18, 1995). . . . Tore knee ligaments (April 10, 1995); missed remainder of season.
HONORS: Named Hockey East co-Rookie of the Year with Scott Pellerin (1988-89). . . . Named to Hockey East All-Rookie team (1988-89). . . . Named to Hockey East All-Star second team (1990-91). . . . Named to NCAA All-America East second team (1991-92). . . . Named to Hockey East All-Star first team (1991-92). . . . Named to Hockey East All-Decade team (1994).
STATISTICAL PLATEAUS: Three-goal games: 1992-93 (2), 1993-94 (1). Total: 3.

Season Team	League	REGULAR SEASON					PLAYOFFS				
		Gms.	G	A	Pts.	PIM	Gms.	G	A	Pts.	PIM
86-87—Bishop Hendricken	R.I.H.S.	33	41	39	80	...	—	—	—	—	—
87-88—Bishop Hendricken	R.I.H.S.	...	52	60	112	...	—	—	—	—	—
88-89—Providence College	Hockey East	42	28	29	57	32	—	—	—	—	—
89-90—Providence College	Hockey East	32	20	18	38	12	—	—	—	—	—
90-91—Providence College	Hockey East	36	34	27	61	20	—	—	—	—	—
91-92—Providence College	Hockey East	36	21	34	55	22	—	—	—	—	—
92-93—Kansas City....................	IHL	19	8	6	14	6	—	—	—	—	—
—San Jose........................	NHL	59	23	20	43	18	—	—	—	—	—
93-94—San Jose........................	NHL	84	15	20	35	28	14	2	0	2	0
94-95—Ottawa..........................	NHL	36	5	9	14	8	—	—	—	—	—
NHL totals.................		179	43	49	92	54	14	2	0	2	0

GAUTHIER, DANIEL
C, BLACKHAWKS

PERSONAL: Born May 17, 1970, in Charlemagne, Que. . . . 6-2/192. . . . Shoots left. . . . Name pronounced GOH-chay.
TRANSACTIONS/CAREER NOTES: Selected by Pittsburgh Penguins in third round (third Penguins pick, 62nd overall) of NHL entry draft (June 11, 1988). . . . Left Victoria-ville (January 2, 1990); returned (January 16, 1990). . . . Signed as free agent by Florida Panthers (July 27, 1993). . . . Signed as free agent by Chicago Blackhawks (June 23, 1994).
HONORS: Won ECHL Rookie of the Year Award (1990-91). . . . Named to ECHL All-Star first team (1990-91).

Season Team	League	REGULAR SEASON					PLAYOFFS				
		Gms.	G	A	Pts.	PIM	Gms.	G	A	Pts.	PIM
86-87—Longueuil	QMJHL	64	23	22	45	23	18	4	5	9	15
87-88—Victoriaville....................	QMJHL	66	43	47	90	53	5	2	1	3	0
88-89—Victoriaville....................	QMJHL	64	41	75	116	84	16	12	17	29	30
89-90—Victoriaville....................	QMJHL	62	45	69	114	32	16	8	*19	27	16
90-91—Albany	IHL	1	1	0	1	0	—	—	—	—	—
—Knoxville	ECHL	61	41	*93	134	40	2	0	4	4	4
91-92—Muskegon	IHL	68	19	18	37	28	9	3	6	9	8
92-93—Cleveland	IHL	80	40	66	106	88	4	2	2	4	14
93-94—Cincinnati....................	IHL	74	30	34	64	101	10	2	3	5	14
94-95—Indianapolis....................	IHL	66	22	50	72	53	—	—	—	—	—
—Chicago	NHL	5	0	0	0	0	—	—	—	—	—
NHL totals.................		5	0	0	0	0	—	—	—	—	—

GAUTHIER, DENIS
D, FLAMES

PERSONAL: Born October 1, 1976, in Montreal. . . . 6-1/195. . . . Shoots left. . . . Name pronounced GOH-chay.
TRANSACTIONS/CAREER NOTES: Selected by Calgary Flames in first round (first Flames pick, 20th overall) of NHL entry draft (July 8, 1995).

Season Team	League	REGULAR SEASON					PLAYOFFS				
		Gms.	G	A	Pts.	PIM	Gms.	G	A	Pts.	PIM
92-93—Drummondville................	QMJHL	61	1	7	8	136	10	0	5	5	40
93-94—Drummondville................	QMJHL	60	0	7	7	176	9	2	0	2	41
94-95—Drummondville................	QMJHL	64	9	31	40	190	4	0	5	5	12

GAUTHIER, SEAN
G, JETS

PERSONAL: Born March 28, 1971, in Sudbury, Ont. . . . 5-11/202. . . . Catches left. . . . Name pronounced GOH-chay.
TRANSACTIONS/CAREER NOTES: Selected by Winnipeg Jets in ninth round (seventh Jets pick, 181st overall) of NHL entry draft (June 22, 1991).
HONORS: Shared Dave Pinkney Trophy with Jeff Wilson (1992-93).

Season Team	League	REGULAR SEASON							PLAYOFFS					
		Gms.	Min.	W	L	T	GA	SO	Avg.	Gms.	Min.	W	L	GA	SO	Avg.
90-91—Kingston......................	OHL	*59	3200	16	36	3	282	0	5.29	—	—	—	—	—	—	—
91-92—Fort Wayne	IHL	18	978	10	4	‡2	59	1	3.62	2	48	0	0	7	0	8.75
—Moncton	AHL	25	1415	8	10	5	88	1	3.73	2	26	0	0	2	0	4.62
92-93—Moncton	AHL	38	2196	10	16	9	145	0	3.96	2	75	0	1	6	0	4.80
93-94—Moncton	AHL	13	617	3	5	1	41	0	3.99	—	—	—	—	—	—	—
—Fort Wayne	IHL	22	1139	9	9	‡3	66	0	3.48	—	—	—	—	—	—	—
94-95—Fort Wayne	IHL	5	218	0	2	‡1	15	0	4.13	—	—	—	—	—	—	—
—Can. national team	Int'l	24	1326	16	6	0	53	0	2.40	—	—	—	—	—	—	—

G

GAVEY, AARON
C, LIGHTNING

PERSONAL: Born February 22, 1974, in Sudbury, Ont. . . . 6-1/169. . . . Shoots left. . . . Name pronounced gay-vee.

TRANSACTIONS/CAREER NOTES: Selected by Tampa Bay Lightning in fourth round (fourth Lightning pick, 74th overall) of NHL entry draft (June 20, 1992).

Season Team	League	REGULAR SEASON					PLAYOFFS				
		Gms.	G	A	Pts.	PIM	Gms.	G	A	Pts.	PIM
90-91—Peterborough Jr. B	OHA	42	26	30	56	68	—	—	—	—	—
91-92—Sault Ste. Marie	OHL	48	7	11	18	27	19	5	1	6	10
92-93—Sault Ste. Marie	OHL	62	45	39	84	114	18	5	9	14	36
93-94—Sault Ste. Marie	OHL	60	42	60	102	116	14	11	10	21	22
94-95—Atlanta	IHL	66	18	17	35	85	5	0	1	1	9

GELINAS, MARTIN
LW, CANUCKS

PERSONAL: Born June 5, 1970, in Shawinigan, Que. . . . 5-11/195. . . . Shoots left. . . . Name pronounced MAHR-tai ZHEHL-ih-nuh.

HIGH SCHOOL: Polyvalente Val-Maurice (Shawinigan, Que.).

TRANSACTIONS/CAREER NOTES: Broke left clavicle (November 1983). . . . Suffered hairline fracture of clavicle (July 1986). . . . Selected by Los Angeles Kings in first round (first Kings pick, seventh overall) of NHL entry draft (June 11, 1988). . . . Traded by Kings with C Jimmy Carson, first-round picks in 1989 (traded to New Jersey Devils), 1991 (LW Martin Rucinsky) and 1993 (D Nick Stajduhar) drafts and cash to Edmonton Oilers for C Wayne Gretzky, RW/D Marty McSorley and LW/C Mike Krushelnyski (August 9, 1988). . . . Suspended five games (March 9, 1990). . . . Underwent shoulder surgery (June 1990). . . . Traded by Oilers with sixth-round pick in 1993 draft (C Nicholas Checco) to Quebec Nordiques for LW Scott Pearson (June 20, 1993). . . . Injured thigh (October 20, 1993); missed one game. . . . Separated left shoulder (November 25, 1993); missed 10 games. . . . Claimed on waivers by Vancouver Canucks (January 15, 1994). . . . Suffered charley horse (March 27, 1994); missed six games. . . . Injured knee (April 30, 1995); missed last game of season and eight playoff games.

HONORS: Won Can.HL Rookie of the Year Award (1987-88). . . . Won Michel Bergeron Trophy (1987-88). . . . Named to QMJHL All-Star first team (1987-88).

STATISTICAL PLATEAUS: Three-goal games: 1989-90 (1).

MISCELLANEOUS: Member of Stanley Cup championship team (1990).

Season Team	League	REGULAR SEASON					PLAYOFFS				
		Gms.	G	A	Pts.	PIM	Gms.	G	A	Pts.	PIM
87-88—Hull	QMJHL	65	63	68	131	74	17	15	18	33	32
88-89—Edmonton	NHL	6	1	2	3	0	—	—	—	—	—
—Hull	QMJHL	41	38	39	77	31	9	5	4	9	14
89-90—Edmonton	NHL	46	17	8	25	30	20	2	3	5	6
90-91—Edmonton	NHL	73	20	20	40	34	18	3	6	9	25
91-92—Edmonton	NHL	68	11	18	29	62	15	1	3	4	10
92-93—Edmonton	NHL	65	11	12	23	30	—	—	—	—	—
93-94—Quebec	NHL	31	6	6	12	8	—	—	—	—	—
—Vancouver	NHL	33	8	8	16	26	24	5	4	9	14
94-95—Vancouver	NHL	46	13	10	23	36	3	0	1	1	0
NHL totals		368	87	84	171	226	80	11	17	28	55

GENDRON, MARTIN
RW, CAPITALS

PERSONAL: Born February 15, 1974, in Valleyfield, Que. . . . 5-9/190. . . . Shoots right. . . . Name pronounced MAHR-tai ZHEHN-drah.

TRANSACTIONS/CAREER NOTES: Selected by Washington Capitals in third round (fourth Capitals pick, 71st overall) of NHL entry draft (June 20, 1992).

HONORS: Named to QMJHL All-Rookie team (1990-91). . . . Won Can.HL Most Sportsmanlike Player of the Year Award (1991-92). . . . Won Shell Cup (1991-92). . . . Won Frank J. Selke Trophy (1991-92 and 1992-93). . . . Named to QMJHL All-Star first team (1991-92). . . . Named to Can.HL All-Star first team (1992-93). . . . Named to QMJHL All-Star second team (1992-93).

Season Team	League	REGULAR SEASON					PLAYOFFS				
		Gms.	G	A	Pts.	PIM	Gms.	G	A	Pts.	PIM
90-91—St. Hyacinthe	QMJHL	55	34	23	57	33	4	1	2	3	0
91-92—St. Hyacinthe	QMJHL	69	*71	66	137	45	6	7	4	11	14
92-93—St. Hyacinthe	QMJHL	63	73	61	134	44	—	—	—	—	—
—Baltimore	AHL	10	1	2	3	2	3	0	0	0	0
93-94—Canadian national team	Int'l	19	4	5	9	2	—	—	—	—	—
—Hull	QMJHL	37	39	36	75	18	20	*21	17	38	8
94-95—Portland	AHL	72	36	32	68	54	4	5	1	6	2
—Washington	NHL	8	2	1	3	2	—	—	—	—	—
NHL totals		8	2	1	3	2					

GERNANDER, KEN
LW, RANGERS

PERSONAL: Born June 30, 1969, in Grand Rapids, Minn. . . . 5-10/175. . . . Shoots left. . . . Full name: Kenneth Robert Gernander. . . . Name pronounced juhr-NAN-duhr.

HIGH SCHOOL: Greenway (Coleraine, Minn.).

COLLEGE: Minnesota.

TRANSACTIONS/CAREER NOTES: Selected by Winnipeg Jets in fifth round (fourth Jets pick, 96th overall) of NHL entry draft (June 13, 1987). . . . Signed as free agent by New York Rangers (September 9, 1994).

Season Team	League	REGULAR SEASON					PLAYOFFS				
		Gms.	G	A	Pts.	PIM	Gms.	G	A	Pts.	PIM
85-86—Greenway H.S.	Minn. H.S.	23	14	23	37	. . .	—	—	—	—	—
86-87—Greenway H.S.	Minn. H.S.	26	35	34	69	. . .	—	—	—	—	—
87-88—University of Minnesota	WCHA	44	14	14	28	14	—	—	—	—	—

Season	Team	League	Gms.	G	A	Pts.	PIM	Gms.	G	A	Pts.	PIM
88-89—University of Minnesota ...		WCHA	44	9	11	20	2	—	—	—	—	—
89-90—University of Minnesota ...		WCHA	44	32	17	49	24	—	—	—	—	—
90-91—University of Minnesota ...		WCHA	44	23	20	43	24	—	—	—	—	—
91-92—Moncton		AHL	43	8	18	26	9	8	1	1	2	2
—Fort Wayne		IHL	13	7	6	13	2	—	—	—	—	—
92-93—Moncton		AHL	71	18	29	47	20	5	1	4	5	0
93-94—Moncton		AHL	71	22	25	47	12	19	6	1	7	0
94-95—Binghamton		AHL	80	28	25	53	24	11	2	2	4	6

GIGUERE, JEAN
G, WHALERS

PERSONAL: Born May 16, 1977, in Montreal.... 6-0/ 178.... Catches left.... Full name: Jean Sebastien Giguere.
TRANSACTIONS/CAREER NOTES: Selected by Hartford Whalers in first round (first Whalers pick, 13th overall) of NHL entry draft (July 8, 1995).

			REGULAR SEASON							PLAYOFFS				
Season	Team	League	Gms.	Min.	W	L	T	GA	SO	Avg.	Gms.	Min.	W	L	GA	SO	Avg.
93-94—Verdun		QMJHL	25	1234	13	5	2	66	0	3.21	—	—	—	—	—	—	—
94-95—Halifax		QMJHL	47	2755	14	27	5	181	2	3.94	7	417	3	4	17	1	2.45

GILBERT, GREG
LW, BLUES

PERSONAL: Born January 22, 1967, in Mississauga, Ont.... 6-1/ 191.... Shoots left.... Full name: Gregory Scott Gilbert.
TRANSACTIONS/CAREER NOTES: Sprained ankle (December 1979).... Selected by New York Islanders as underage junior in fourth round (fifth Islanders pick, 80th overall) of NHL entry draft (June 11, 1980).... Stretched ligaments in left ankle (September 1984).... Injured ligaments in knee and underwent arthroscopic surgery then major reconstructive surgery (February 27, 1985).... Broke jaw (October 11, 1986); missed 10 games.... Bruised thigh (December 7, 1986).... Bruised hip (February 1987).... Separated right shoulder (March 1987). ... Bruised right knee (February 20, 1988).... Injured left foot (April 1988).... Suffered back spasms and injured left shoulder (February 1989).... Traded by Islanders to Chicago Blackhawks for fifth-round pick (RW Steve Young) in 1989 draft (March 7, 1989).... Broke foot (March 1989).... Strained abdominal muscle during practice (March 8, 1990).... Bruised left shoulder (September 28, 1990); missed first eight games of season.... Hyperextended left knee (April 1991).... Pulled lateral muscle (November 13, 1991); missed two games.... Fractured ankle (February 16, 1992).... Slightly strained left knee (April 4, 1992).... Suspended three off-days and fined $500 by NHL for fighting (February 26, 1993).... Suffered from the flu (March 5, 1993); missed two games.... Signed as free agent by New York Rangers (July 29, 1993).... Suffered injury (January 14, 1994); missed two games.... Sprained right knee (January 25, 1994); missed six games.... Selected by St. Louis Blues in 1994-95 waiver draft for cash (January 18, 1995).... Injured leg (March 12, 1995); missed one game.... Reinjured leg (April 23, 1995); missed one game.
STATISTICAL PLATEAUS: Three-goal games: 1983-84 (1), 1987-88 (1). Total: 2.
MISCELLANEOUS: Member of Stanley Cup championship teams (1982, 1983 and 1990).

			REGULAR SEASON					PLAYOFFS				
Season	Team	League	Gms.	G	A	Pts.	PIM	Gms.	G	A	Pts.	PIM
79-80—Toronto		OMJHL	68	10	11	21	35	—	—	—	—	—
80-81—Toronto		OMJHL	64	30	37	67	73	5	2	6	8	16
81-82—Toronto		OHL	65	41	67	108	119	10	4	12	16	23
—New York Islanders		NHL	1	1	0	1	0	4	1	1	2	2
82-83—Indianapolis		CHL	24	11	16	27	23	—	—	—	—	—
—New York Islanders		NHL	45	8	11	19	30	10	1	0	1	14
83-84—New York Islanders		NHL	79	31	35	66	59	21	5	7	12	39
84-85—New York Islanders		NHL	58	13	25	38	36	—	—	—	—	—
85-86—Springfield		AHL	2	0	0	0	2	—	—	—	—	—
—New York Islanders		NHL	60	9	19	28	82	2	0	0	0	9
86-87—New York Islanders		NHL	51	6	7	13	26	10	2	2	4	6
87-88—New York Islanders		NHL	76	17	28	45	46	4	0	0	0	6
88-89—New York Islanders		NHL	55	8	13	21	45	—	—	—	—	—
—Chicago		NHL	4	0	0	0	0	15	1	5	6	20
89-90—Chicago		NHL	70	12	25	37	54	19	5	8	13	34
90-91—Chicago		NHL	72	10	15	25	58	5	0	1	1	2
91-92—Chicago		NHL	50	7	5	12	35	10	1	3	4	16
92-93—Chicago		NHL	77	13	19	32	57	3	0	0	0	0
93-94—New York Rangers		NHL	76	4	11	15	29	23	1	3	4	8
94-95—St. Louis		NHL	46	11	14	25	11	7	0	3	3	6
NHL totals			820	150	227	377	568	133	17	33	50	162

GILCHRIST, BRENT
LW, STARS

PERSONAL: Born April 3, 1967, in Moose Jaw, Sask.... 5-11/ 185.... Shoots left.
TRANSACTIONS/CAREER NOTES: Strained medial collateral ligament (January 1985). ... Selected by Montreal Canadiens as underage junior in sixth round (sixth Canadiens pick, 79th overall) of NHL entry draft (June 15, 1985).... Injured knee (January 1987).... Broke right index finger (November 17, 1990); missed 19 games.... Separated left shoulder (February 6, 1991); missed two games.... Reinjured left shoulder (February 13, 1991); missed five games.... Traded by Canadiens with LW Shayne Corson and LW Vladimir Vujtek to Edmonton Oilers for LW Vincent Damphousse and fourth-round pick (D Adam Wiesel) in 1993 draft (August 27, 1992).... Suffered concussion (October 1992); missed two games.... Fractured nose (December 21, 1992); missed two games.... Traded by Oilers to Minnesota North Stars for C Todd Elik (March 5, 1993).... Separated shoulder (March 18, 1993); missed remainder of season.... North Stars franchise moved from Minnesota to Dallas and renamed Stars for 1993-94 season.... Strained shoulder (October 27, 1993); missed four games.... Pulled groin (November 21,

G

1993); missed four games.... Underwent oral surgery (February 2, 1995); missed no games.... Strained groin (February 20, 1995); missed two games.... Strained groin and sprained wrist (February 26, 1995); missed 13 games.... Suffered from sore wrist (April 11, 1995); missed one game.
STATISTICAL PLATEAUS: Three-goal games: 1991-92 (1).

Season Team	League	REGULAR SEASON					PLAYOFFS				
		Gms.	G	A	Pts.	PIM	Gms.	G	A	Pts.	PIM
83-84—Kelowna Wings	WHL	69	16	11	27	16	—	—	—	—	—
84-85—Kelowna Wings	WHL	51	35	38	73	58	6	5	2	7	8
85-86—Spokane	WHL	52	45	45	90	57	9	6	7	13	19
86-87—Spokane	WHL	46	45	55	100	71	5	2	7	9	6
—Sherbrooke	AHL	—	—	—	—	—	10	2	7	9	2
87-88—Sherbrooke	AHL	77	26	48	74	83	6	1	3	4	6
88-89—Montreal	NHL	49	8	16	24	16	9	1	1	2	10
—Sherbrooke	AHL	7	6	5	11	7	—	—	—	—	—
89-90—Montreal	NHL	57	9	15	24	28	8	2	0	2	2
90-91—Montreal	NHL	51	6	9	15	10	13	5	3	8	6
91-92—Montreal	NHL	79	23	27	50	57	11	2	4	6	6
92-93—Edmonton	NHL	60	10	10	20	47	—	—	—	—	—
—Minnesota	NHL	8	0	1	1	2	—	—	—	—	—
93-94—Dallas	NHL	76	17	14	31	31	9	3	1	4	2
94-95—Dallas	NHL	32	9	4	13	16	5	0	1	1	2
NHL totals		412	82	96	178	207	55	13	10	23	28

GILHEN, RANDY

C, JETS

PERSONAL: Born June 13, 1963, in Zweibrucken, West Germany.... 6-0/190.... Shoots left. ... Name pronounced GIHL-ihn.
TRANSACTIONS/CAREER NOTES: Selected by Hartford Whalers as underage junior in sixth round (sixth Whalers pick, 109th overall) of NHL entry draft (June 9, 1982).... Signed as free agent by Winnipeg Jets (August 1985).... Separated shoulder (November 16, 1988).... Traded by Jets with RW Andrew McBain and D Jim Kyte to Pittsburgh Penguins for C/LW Randy Cunneyworth, G Richard Tabaracci and RW Dave McIlwain (June 17, 1989).... Sprained knee (November 2, 1989).... Selected by Minnesota North Stars in NHL expansion draft (May 30, 1991).... Traded by North Stars with D Charlie Huddy, RW Jim Thomson and fourth-round pick in 1991 draft (D Alexei Zhitnik) to Los Angeles Kings for C Todd Elik (June 22, 1991).... Traded by Kings to New York Rangers for C Corey Millen (December 23, 1991).... Sprained right knee (January 30, 1993); missed seven games.... Traded by Rangers to Tampa Bay Lightning for LW Mike Hartman (March 22, 1993).... Selected by Florida Panthers in NHL expansion draft (June 24, 1993). ... Traded by Panthers to Jets for C Stu Barnes (November 26, 1993).... Underwent elbow surgery (January 16, 1994); missed four games.... Dislocated shoulder (March 7, 1994); missed 15 games.
MISCELLANEOUS: Member of Stanley Cup championship team (1991).

Season Team	League	REGULAR SEASON					PLAYOFFS				
		Gms.	G	A	Pts.	PIM	Gms.	G	A	Pts.	PIM
79-80—Saskatoon	SJHL	55	18	34	52	112	—	—	—	—	—
—Saskatoon	WHL	9	2	2	4	20	—	—	—	—	—
80-81—Saskatoon	WHL	68	10	5	15	154	—	—	—	—	—
81-82—Winnipeg	WHL	61	41	37	78	87	—	—	—	—	—
82-83—Winnipeg	WHL	71	57	44	101	84	3	2	2	4	0
—Hartford	NHL	2	0	1	1	0	—	—	—	—	—
—Binghamton	AHL	—	—	—	—	—	5	2	0	2	2
83-84—Binghamton	AHL	73	8	12	20	72	—	—	—	—	—
84-85—Salt Lake City	IHL	57	20	20	40	28	—	—	—	—	—
—Binghamton	AHL	18	3	3	6	9	8	4	1	5	16
85-86—Fort Wayne	IHL	82	44	40	84	48	15	10	8	18	6
86-87—Winnipeg	NHL	2	0	0	0	0	—	—	—	—	—
—Sherbrooke	AHL	75	36	29	65	44	17	7	13	20	10
87-88—Winnipeg	NHL	13	3	2	5	15	4	1	0	1	10
—Moncton	AHL	68	40	47	87	51	—	—	—	—	—
88-89—Winnipeg	NHL	64	5	3	8	38	—	—	—	—	—
89-90—Pittsburgh	NHL	61	5	11	16	54	—	—	—	—	—
90-91—Pittsburgh	NHL	72	15	10	25	51	16	1	0	1	14
91-92—Los Angeles	NHL	33	3	6	9	14	—	—	—	—	—
—New York Rangers	NHL	40	7	7	14	14	13	1	2	3	2
92-93—New York Rangers	NHL	33	3	2	5	8	—	—	—	—	—
—Tampa Bay	NHL	11	0	2	2	6	—	—	—	—	—
93-94—Florida	NHL	20	4	4	8	16	—	—	—	—	—
—Winnipeg	NHL	40	3	3	6	34	—	—	—	—	—
94-95—Winnipeg	NHL	44	5	6	11	52	—	—	—	—	—
NHL totals		435	53	57	110	302	33	3	2	5	26

GILL, TODD

D, MAPLE LEAFS

PERSONAL: Born November 9, 1965, in Brockville, Ont.... 6-0/180.... Shoots left.
TRANSACTIONS/CAREER NOTES: Selected by Toronto Maple Leafs as underage junior in second round (second Maple Leafs pick, 25th overall) of NHL entry draft (June 9, 1984).... Broke bone in right foot (October 1987).... Bruised shoulder (March 1989).... Fractured finger (October 15, 1991); missed three games.... Strained back (February 8, 1992); missed three games.... Injured back prior to 1992-93 season; missed first two games of season.... Bruised foot (November 14, 1992); missed 11 games.... Strained groin (November 1, 1993); missed 26 games.... Suffered back spasms (February 24, 1994); missed 13 games.... Injured shoulder (March 17, 1995); missed one game.

Season	Team	League	Gms.	G	A	Pts.	PIM	Gms.	G	A	Pts.	PIM
82-83—Windsor		OHL	70	12	24	36	108	3	0	0	0	11
83-84—Windsor		OHL	68	9	48	57	184	3	1	1	2	10
84-85—Toronto		NHL	10	1	0	1	13	—	—	—	—	—
—Windsor		OHL	53	17	40	57	148	4	0	1	1	14
85-86—St. Catharines		AHL	58	8	25	33	90	10	1	6	7	17
—Toronto		NHL	15	1	2	3	28	1	0	0	0	0
86-87—Newmarket		AHL	11	1	8	9	33	—	—	—	—	—
—Toronto		NHL	61	4	27	31	92	13	2	2	4	42
87-88—Newmarket		AHL	2	0	1	1	2	—	—	—	—	—
—Toronto		NHL	65	8	17	25	131	6	1	3	4	20
88-89—Toronto		NHL	59	11	14	25	72	—	—	—	—	—
89-90—Toronto		NHL	48	1	14	15	92	5	0	3	3	16
90-91—Toronto		NHL	72	2	22	24	113	—	—	—	—	—
91-92—Toronto		NHL	74	2	15	17	91	—	—	—	—	—
92-93—Toronto		NHL	69	11	32	43	66	21	1	10	11	26
93-94—Toronto		NHL	45	4	24	28	44	18	1	5	6	37
94-95—Toronto		NHL	47	7	25	32	64	7	0	3	3	6
NHL totals			565	52	192	244	806	71	5	26	31	147

GILLAM, SEAN
D, RED WINGS

PERSONAL: Born May 7, 1976, in Lethbridge, Alta. . . . 6-2/187. . . . Shoots right.
HIGH SCHOOL: Spokane (Wash.).
TRANSACTIONS/CAREER NOTES: Selected by Detroit Red Wings in third round (third Red Wings pick, 75th overall) of NHL entry draft (June 29, 1994).
HONORS: Named to WHL (West) All-Star second team (1994-95).

Season	Team	League	Gms.	G	A	Pts.	PIM	Gms.	G	A	Pts.	PIM
92-93—Spokane		WHL	70	6	27	33	121	10	0	2	2	10
93-94—Spokane		WHL	70	7	17	24	106	3	0	0	0	6
94-95—Spokane		WHL	72	16	40	56	192	11	0	3	3	33

GILMOUR, DOUG
C, MAPLE LEAFS

PERSONAL: Born June 25, 1963, in Kingston, Ont. . . . 5-11/172. . . . Shoots left.
TRANSACTIONS/CAREER NOTES: Selected by St. Louis Blues as underage junior in seventh round (fourth Blues pick, 134th overall) of NHL entry draft (June 9, 1982). . . . Sprained ankle (October 7, 1985); missed four games. . . . Suffered concussion (January 1988). . . . Bruised shoulder (March 1988). . . . Traded by Blues with RW Mark Hunter, LW Steve Bozek and D/RW Michael Dark to Calgary Flames for C Mike Bullard, C Craig Coxe and D Tim Corkery (September 5, 1988). . . . Suffered abscessed jaw (March 1989); missed six games. . . . Broke bone in right foot (August 12, 1989). . . . Traded by Flames with D Ric Nattress, D Jamie Macoun, LW Kent Manderville and G Rick Wamsley to Toronto Maple Leafs for LW Craig Berube, D Alexander Godynyuk, LW Gary Leeman, D Michel Petit and G Jeff Reese (January 2, 1992). . . . Suspended eight off-days and fined $500 by NHL for slashing (November 27, 1992). . . . Suspended one preseason game and fined $500 by NHL for headbutting (September 26, 1993). . . . Played in Europe during 1994-95 NHL lockout. . . . Pinched nerve in neck (February 8, 1995); missed one game. . . . Broke nose (April 7, 1995); missed three games.
HONORS: Won Red Tilson Trophy (1982-83). . . . Won Eddie Powers Memorial Trophy (1982-83). . . . Named to OHL All-Star first team (1982-83). . . . Won Frank J. Selke Trophy (1992-93). . . . Named to THE SPORTING NEWS All-Star second team (1992-93). . . . Played in NHL All-Star Game (1993 and 1994).
STATISTICAL PLATEAUS: Three-goal games: 1985-86 (1), 1987-88 (1), 1993-94 (1). Total: 3.
MISCELLANEOUS: Member of Stanley Cup championship team (1989). . . . Captain of Toronto Maple Leafs (1994-95).

Season	Team	League	Gms.	G	A	Pts.	PIM	Gms.	G	A	Pts.	PIM
80-81—Cornwall		QMJHL	51	12	23	35	35	—	—	—	—	—
81-82—Cornwall		OHL	67	46	73	119	42	5	6	9	15	2
82-83—Cornwall		OHL	68	*70	*107	*177	62	8	8	10	18	16
83-84—St. Louis		NHL	80	25	28	53	57	11	2	9	11	10
84-85—St. Louis		NHL	78	21	36	57	49	3	1	1	2	2
85-86—St. Louis		NHL	74	25	28	53	41	19	9	12	†21	25
86-87—St. Louis		NHL	80	42	63	105	58	6	2	2	4	16
87-88—St. Louis		NHL	72	36	50	86	59	10	3	14	17	18
88-89—Calgary		NHL	72	26	59	85	44	22	11	11	22	20
89-90—Calgary		NHL	78	24	67	91	54	6	3	1	4	8
90-91—Calgary		NHL	78	20	61	81	144	7	1	1	2	0
91-92—Calgary		NHL	38	11	27	38	46	—	—	—	—	—
—Toronto		NHL	40	15	34	49	32	—	—	—	—	—
92-93—Toronto		NHL	83	32	95	127	100	21	10	25	35	30
93-94—Toronto		NHL	83	27	84	111	105	18	6	22	28	42
94-95—Rapperswil		Switz. Div. II	9	2	13	15	16	—	—	—	—	—
—Toronto		NHL	44	10	23	33	26	7	0	6	6	6
NHL totals			900	314	655	969	815	130	48	104	152	177

GIRARD, RICK
C, CANUCKS

PERSONAL: Born May 1, 1974, in Edmonton. . . . 5-11/180. . . . Shoots left.
TRANSACTIONS/CAREER NOTES: Selected by Vancouver Canucks in second round (second Canucks pick, 46th overall) of NHL entry draft (June 26, 1993).
HONORS: Won Brad Hornung Trophy (1992-93). . . . Won Can.HL Most Sportsmanlike Player of

G

the Year Award (1992-93).... Named to WHL (East) All-Star first team (1992-93).... Named to WHL (East) All-Star first team (1993-94).

Season	Team	League	REGULAR SEASON Gms.	G	A	Pts.	PIM	PLAYOFFS Gms.	G	A	Pts.	PIM
91-92—Swift Current		WHL	45	14	17	31	6	8	2	0	2	2
92-93—Swift Current		WHL	72	71	70	141	25	17	9	17	26	10
93-94—Swift Current		WHL	58	40	49	89	43	7	1	8	9	6
—Hamilton		AHL	1	1	1	2	0	—	—	—	—	—
94-95—Syracuse		AHL	26	10	13	23	22	—	—	—	—	—

GLYNN, BRIAN
D, WHALERS

PERSONAL: Born November 23, 1967, in Iserlohn, West Germany.... 6-4/224.... Shoots left. ... Full name: Brian Thomas Glynn. **TRANSACTIONS/CAREER NOTES:** Selected by Calgary Flames in second round (second Flames pick, 37th overall) of NHL entry draft (June 21, 1986).... Traded by Flames to Minnesota North Stars for D Frantisek Musil (October 26, 1990).... Traded by North Stars to Edmonton Oilers for D David Shaw (January 21, 1992).... Injured knee (March 15, 1992); missed seven games.... Injured knee (November 4, 1992); missed two games. ... Traded by Oilers to Ottawa Senators for eighth-round pick (D Rob Guinn) in 1994 draft (September 14, 1993).... Claimed on waivers by Vancouver Canucks (February 5, 1994).... Selected by Hartford Whalers in 1994-95 waiver draft for cash (January 18, 1995).
HONORS: Won Governors Trophy (1989-90).... Named to IHL All-Star first team (1989-90).

Season	Team	League	REGULAR SEASON Gms.	G	A	Pts.	PIM	PLAYOFFS Gms.	G	A	Pts.	PIM
84-85—Saskatoon		SJHL	12	1	0	1	2	3	0	0	0	0
85-86—Saskatoon		WHL	66	7	25	32	131	13	0	3	3	30
86-87—Saskatoon		WHL	44	2	26	28	163	11	1	3	4	19
87-88—Calgary		NHL	67	5	14	19	87	1	0	0	0	0
88-89—Salt Lake City		IHL	31	3	10	13	105	14	3	7	10	31
—Calgary		NHL	9	0	1	1	19	—	—	—	—	—
89-90—Calgary		NHL	1	0	0	0	0	—	—	—	—	—
—Salt Lake City		IHL	80	17	44	61	164	—	—	—	—	—
90-91—Salt Lake City		IHL	8	1	3	4	18	—	—	—	—	—
—Minnesota		NHL	66	8	11	19	83	23	2	6	8	18
91-92—Minnesota		NHL	37	2	12	14	24	—	—	—	—	—
—Edmonton		NHL	25	2	6	8	6	16	4	1	5	12
92-93—Edmonton		NHL	64	4	12	16	60	—	—	—	—	—
93-94—Ottawa		NHL	48	2	13	15	41	—	—	—	—	—
—Vancouver		NHL	16	0	0	0	12	17	0	3	3	10
94-95—Hartford		NHL	43	1	6	7	32	—	—	—	—	—
NHL totals			376	24	75	99	364	57	6	10	16	40

GODYNYUK, ALEXANDER
D, WHALERS

PERSONAL: Born January 27, 1970, in Kiev, U.S.S.R. .... 6-0/207. ... Shoots left.... Name pronounced goh-DIHN-yuhk. **TRANSACTIONS/CAREER NOTES:** Selected by Toronto Maple Leafs in sixth round (fifth Maple Leafs pick, 115th overall) of NHL entry draft (June 16, 1990).... Traded by Maple Leafs with LW Craig Berube, RW Gary Leeman, D Michel Petit and G Jeff Reese to Calgary Flames for C Doug Gilmour, D Jamie Macoun, LW Kent Manderville, D Ric Nattress and G Rick Wamsley (January 2, 1992).... Injured shoulder (February 23, 1993); missed one game.... Selected by Florida Panthers in NHL expansion draft (June 24, 1993).... Strained stomach muscle (November 14, 1993); missed two games.... Traded by Panthers to Hartford Whalers for D Jim McKenzie (December 16, 1993).... Bruised knee (December 28, 1993); missed one game.... Injured knee (March 25, 1994); missed remainder of season.... Injured groin (March 7, 1995); missed four games.

Season	Team	League	REGULAR SEASON Gms.	G	A	Pts.	PIM	PLAYOFFS Gms.	G	A	Pts.	PIM
86-87—Sokol Kiev		USSR	9	0	1	1	2	—	—	—	—	—
87-88—Sokol Kiev		USSR	2	0	0	0	2	—	—	—	—	—
88-89—Sokol Kiev		USSR	30	3	3	6	12	—	—	—	—	—
89-90—Sokol Kiev		USSR	37	3	2	5	31	—	—	—	—	—
90-91—Sokol Kiev		USSR	19	3	1	4	20	—	—	—	—	—
—Toronto		NHL	18	0	3	3	16	—	—	—	—	—
—Newmarket		AHL	11	0	1	1	29	—	—	—	—	—
91-92—Toronto		NHL	31	3	6	9	59	—	—	—	—	—
—Calgary		NHL	6	0	1	1	4	—	—	—	—	—
—Salt Lake City		IHL	17	2	1	3	24	—	—	—	—	—
92-93—Calgary		NHL	27	3	4	7	19	—	—	—	—	—
93-94—Florida		NHL	26	0	10	10	35	—	—	—	—	—
—Hartford		NHL	43	3	9	12	40	—	—	—	—	—
94-95—Hartford		NHL	14	0	0	0	8	—	—	—	—	—
NHL totals			165	9	33	42	181	—	—	—	—	—

GOLOKHVASTOV, KONSTANTIN
RW, LIGHTNING

PERSONAL: Born February 6, 1977, in Dneprodzerzhinsk, U.S.S.R. ... 6-1/185. ... Shoots right. **TRANSACTIONS/CAREER NOTES:** Selected by Tampa Bay Lightning in fifth round (fourth Lightning pick, 108th overall) of NHL entry draft (July 8, 1995).

G

Season	Team	League	REGULAR SEASON Gms.	G	A	Pts.	PIM	PLAYOFFS Gms.	G	A	Pts.	PIM
94-95—Dynamo Moscow		CIS	6	0	0	0	2	—	—	—	—	—

GOLUBOVSKY, YAN
D, RED WINGS

PERSONAL: Born March 9, 1976, in Novosibirsk, U.S.S.R. . . . 6-3/185. . . . Shoots right. . . . Name pronounced YAHN gohl-uh-BAHF-skee.
TRANSACTIONS/CAREER NOTES: Selected by Detroit Red Wings in first round (first Red Wings pick, 23rd overall) of NHL entry draft (June 28, 1994).

Season	Team	League	REGULAR SEASON Gms.	G	A	Pts.	PIM	PLAYOFFS Gms.	G	A	Pts.	PIM
93-94—Dynamo-2 Moscow		CIS Div. III	10	0	1	1	. . .	—	—	—	—	—
—Russian Penguins		IHL	8	0	0	0	23	—	—	—	—	—
94-95—Adirondack		AHL	57	4	2	6	39	—	—	—	—	—

GONCHAR, SERGEI
D, CAPITALS

PERSONAL: Born April 13, 1974, in Chelyabinsk, U.S.S.R. . . . 6-2/212. . . . Shoots left. . . . Name pronounced GAHN-chahr.
TRANSACTIONS/CAREER NOTES: Selected by Washington Capitals in first round (first Capitals pick, 14th overall) of NHL entry draft (June 20, 1992).

Season	Team	League	REGULAR SEASON Gms.	G	A	Pts.	PIM	PLAYOFFS Gms.	G	A	Pts.	PIM
90-91—Mechel Chelyabinsk		USSR	2	0	0	0	0	—	—	—	—	—
91-92—Traktor Chelyabinsk		CIS	31	1	0	1	6	—	—	—	—	—
92-93—Dynamo Moscow		CIS	31	1	3	4	70	10	0	0	0	12
93-94—Dynamo Moscow		CIS	44	4	5	9	36	10	0	3	3	14
—Portland		AHL	—	—	—	—	—	2	0	0	0	0
94-95—Portland		AHL	61	10	32	42	67	—	—	—	—	—
—Washington		NHL	31	2	5	7	22	7	2	2	4	2
NHL totals			31	2	5	7	22	7	2	2	4	2

GONEAU, DANIEL
LW, BRUINS

PERSONAL: Born January 16, 1976, in Lachine, Que. . . . 6-1/196. . . . Shoots left. . . . Name pronounced guh-NOH.
TRANSACTIONS/CAREER NOTES: Selected by Boston Bruins in second round (second Bruins pick, 47th overall) of NHL entry draft (June 28, 1994).

Season	Team	League	REGULAR SEASON Gms.	G	A	Pts.	PIM	PLAYOFFS Gms.	G	A	Pts.	PIM
92-93—Laval		QMJHL	62	16	25	41	44	13	0	4	4	4
93-94—Laval		QMJHL	68	29	57	86	81	19	8	21	29	45
94-95—Laval		QMJHL	56	16	31	47	78	20	5	10	15	33

GORDIOUK, VIKTOR
RW, SABRES

PERSONAL: Born April 11, 1970, in Moscow, U.S.S.R. . . . 5-10/176. . . . Shoots right. . . . Name pronounced GOHR-dee-yuhk.
TRANSACTIONS/CAREER NOTES: Selected by Buffalo Sabres in seventh round (sixth Sabres pick, 142nd overall) of NHL entry draft (June 16, 1990).

Season	Team	League	REGULAR SEASON Gms.	G	A	Pts.	PIM	PLAYOFFS Gms.	G	A	Pts.	PIM
86-87—Soviet Wings		USSR	2	0	0	0	0	—	—	—	—	—
87-88—Soviet Wings		USSR	26	2	2	4	6	—	—	—	—	—
88-89—Soviet Wings		USSR	41	5	1	6	10	—	—	—	—	—
89-90—Soviet Wings		USSR	48	11	4	15	24	—	—	—	—	—
90-91—Soviet Wings		USSR	46	12	10	22	22	—	—	—	—	—
91-92—Soviet Wings		CIS	42	16	7	23	24	—	—	—	—	—
92-93—Buffalo		NHL	16	3	6	9	0	—	—	—	—	—
—Rochester		AHL	35	11	14	25	8	17	9	9	18	4
93-94—Rochester		AHL	74	28	39	67	26	4	3	0	3	2
94-95—Rochester		AHL	63	31	30	61	36	3	0	2	2	0
—Buffalo		NHL	10	0	2	2	0	—	—	—	—	—
NHL totals			26	3	8	11	0	—	—	—	—	—

G

GORDON, ROBB
C, CANUCKS

PERSONAL: Born January 13, 1976, in Surrey, B.C. . . . 5-11/170. . . . Shoots right.
HIGH SCHOOL: Max Cameron (Powell River, B.C.).
COLLEGE: Michigan.
TRANSACTIONS/CAREER NOTES: Selected by Vancouver Canucks in second round (second Canucks pick, 39th overall) of NHL entry draft (June 28, 1994).

Season	Team	League	REGULAR SEASON Gms.	G	A	Pts.	PIM	PLAYOFFS Gms.	G	A	Pts.	PIM
92-93—Powell River		BCJHL	60	55	38	93	76	18	8	10	18	24
93-94—Powell River		BCJHL	60	69	89	158	141	10	11	14	25	29
94-95—University of Michigan		CCHA	39	15	26	41	72	—	—	—	—	—

GOSSELIN, DAVID
RW, DEVILS

PERSONAL: Born June 22, 1977, in Levis, Que.... 6-0/175.... Shoots right.
TRANSACTIONS/CAREER NOTES: Selected by New Jersey Devils in third round (fourth Devils pick, 78th overall) of NHL entry draft (July 8, 1995).

Season Team	League	REGULAR SEASON					PLAYOFFS				
		Gms.	G	A	Pts.	PIM	Gms.	G	A	Pts.	PIM
94-95—Sherbrooke	QMJHL	58	8	8	16	36	7	0	0	0	2

GOVEDARIS, CHRIS
LW, RED WINGS

PERSONAL: Born February 2, 1970, in Toronto.... 6-0/200.... Shoots left.... Name pronounced goh-vih-DAIR-ihz.
TRANSACTIONS/CAREER NOTES: Suspended two games by OHL (October 1986).... Selected by Hartford Whalers in first round (first Whalers pick, 11th overall) of NHL entry draft (June 11, 1988).... Suspended 15 games by OHL for shattering stick across another player's hip (January 22, 1989).... Bruised right leg (January 23, 1991); missed five games.... Suspended by Whalers for failure to report to AHL game (October 31, 1991); reinstated (January 3, 1992).... Signed as free agent by Toronto Maple Leafs (September 7, 1993). ... Traded by Maple Leafs to Detroit Red Wings for D Gord Kruppke (February 17, 1995).

Season Team	League	REGULAR SEASON					PLAYOFFS				
		Gms.	G	A	Pts.	PIM	Gms.	G	A	Pts.	PIM
85-86—Toronto Young Nationals	MTHL	38	35	50	85	...	—	—	—	—	—
86-87—Toronto	OHL	64	36	28	64	148	—	—	—	—	—
87-88—Toronto	OHL	62	42	38	80	118	4	2	1	3	10
88-89—Toronto	OHL	49	41	38	79	117	6	2	3	5	0
89-90—Hartford	NHL	12	0	1	1	6	2	0	0	0	2
—Binghamton	AHL	14	3	3	6	4	—	—	—	—	—
—Dukes of Hamilton	OHL	23	11	21	32	53	—	—	—	—	—
90-91—Hartford	NHL	14	1	3	4	4	—	—	—	—	—
—Springfield	AHL	56	26	36	62	133	9	2	5	7	36
91-92—Springfield	AHL	43	14	25	39	55	11	3	2	5	25
92-93—Springfield	AHL	65	31	24	55	58	15	7	4	11	18
—Hartford	NHL	7	1	0	1	0	—	—	—	—	—
93-94—St. John's	AHL	62	35	35	70	76	11	6	5	11	22
—Toronto	NHL	12	2	2	4	14	2	0	0	0	0
94-95—Milwaukee	IHL	54	34	25	59	71	—	—	—	—	—
—Adirondack	AHL	24	19	11	30	34	4	2	1	3	10
NHL totals		45	4	6	10	24	4	0	0	0	2

GRAHAM, DIRK
LW/RW

PERSONAL: Born July 29, 1959, in Regina, Sask.... 5-11/198.... Shoots right.... Full name: Dirk Milton Graham.
TRANSACTIONS/CAREER NOTES: Selected by Vancouver Canucks in fifth round (fifth Canucks pick, 89th overall) of NHL entry draft (August 9, 1979).... Signed as free agent by Minnesota North Stars (August 17, 1983).... Sprained wrist (November 1987); missed seven games.... Traded by North Stars to Chicago Blackhawks for LW Curt Fraser (January 4, 1988).... Fined $500 by NHL for fighting (December 28, 1989).... Fractured left kneecap (March 17, 1990); missed six weeks.... Underwent surgery to left knee (May 1990).... Separated shoulder (February 18, 1994); missed 17 games.... Sprained knee (February 19, 1995); missed eight games.... Announced retirement and named assistant coach of Blackhawks (summer 1995).
HONORS: Named to WHL All-Star second team (1978-79).... Named to IHL All-Star second team (1980-81).... Named to IHL All-Star first team (1982-83).... Named to CHL All-Star first team (1983-84).... Won Frank J. Selke Trophy (1990-91).
STATISTICAL PLATEAUS: Three-goal games: 1989-90 (1).
MISCELLANEOUS: Captain of Chicago Blackhawks (1988-1989 through 1994-95).

Season Team	League	REGULAR SEASON					PLAYOFFS				
		Gms.	G	A	Pts.	PIM	Gms.	G	A	Pts.	PIM
75-76—Regina Blues	SJHL	54	36	32	68	82	—	—	—	—	—
—Regina	WCHL	2	0	0	0	0	6	1	1	2	5
76-77—Regina	WCHL	65	37	28	65	66	—	—	—	—	—
77-78—Regina	WCHL	72	49	61	110	87	13	15	19	34	37
78-79—Regina	WHL	71	48	60	108	252	—	—	—	—	—
79-80—Dallas	CHL	62	17	15	32	96	—	—	—	—	—
80-81—Fort Wayne	IHL	6	1	2	3	12	—	—	—	—	—
—Toledo	IHL	61	40	45	85	88	—	—	—	—	—
81-82—Toledo	IHL	72	49	56	105	68	13	10	11	21	8
82-83—Toledo	IHL	78	70	55	125	86	11	13	7	†20	30
83-84—Minnesota	NHL	6	1	1	2	0	1	0	0	0	2
—Salt Lake City	CHL	57	37	57	94	72	5	3	8	11	2
84-85—Springfield	AHL	37	20	28	48	41	—	—	—	—	—
—Minnesota	NHL	36	12	11	23	23	9	0	4	4	7
85-86—Minnesota	NHL	80	22	33	55	87	5	3	1	4	2
86-87—Minnesota	NHL	76	25	29	54	142	—	—	—	—	—
87-88—Minnesota	NHL	28	7	5	12	39	—	—	—	—	—
—Chicago	NHL	42	17	19	36	32	4	1	2	3	4
88-89—Chicago	NHL	80	33	45	78	89	16	2	4	6	38
89-90—Chicago	NHL	73	22	32	54	102	5	1	5	6	2
90-91—Chicago	NHL	80	24	21	45	88	6	1	2	3	17
91-92—Chicago	NHL	80	17	30	47	89	18	7	5	12	8
92-93—Chicago	NHL	84	20	17	37	139	4	0	0	0	0
93-94—Chicago	NHL	67	15	18	33	45	6	0	1	1	4
94-95—Chicago	NHL	40	4	9	13	42	16	2	3	5	8
NHL totals		772	219	270	489	917	90	17	27	44	92

G

GRANATO, TONY

RW, KINGS

PERSONAL: Born July 25, 1964, in Downers Grove, Ill. . . . 5-10/185. . . . Shoots right. . . . Full name: Anthony Lewis Granato.
HIGH SCHOOL: Northwood School (Lake Placid, N.Y.).
COLLEGE: Wisconsin.
TRANSACTIONS/CAREER NOTES: Selected by New York Rangers in sixth round (fifth Rangers pick, 120th overall) of NHL entry draft (June 9, 1982). . . . Bruised foot (February 1989). . . . Traded by Rangers with RW Tomas Sandstrom to Los Angeles Kings for C Bernie Nicholls (January 20, 1990). . . . Pulled groin (January 25, 1990); missed 12 games. . . . Injured knee (March 20, 1990). . . . Tore rib cartilage (December 18, 1990); missed 10 games. . . . Strained back (October 6, 1992); missed three games. . . . Strained back (December 4, 1993); missed one game. . . . Strained lower back (December 13, 1993); missed nine games. . . . Suspended 15 games without pay and fined $500 by NHL for slashing incident (February 16, 1994). . . . Strained back (April 3, 1994); missed remainder of season. . . . Strained hip flexor (March 13, 1995); missed one game. . . . Broke bone in foot (April 6, 1995); missed 13 games.
HONORS: Named to NCAA All-America West second team (1984-85 and 1986-87). . . . Named to WCHA All-Star second team (1986-87). . . . Named to NHL All-Rookie team (1988-89).
STATISTICAL PLATEAUS: Three-goal games: 1988-89 (2), 1991-92 (1), 1994-95 (1). Total: 4. . . . Four-goal games: 1988-89 (1). . . . Total hat tricks: 5.

Season Team	League	REGULAR SEASON					PLAYOFFS				
		Gms.	G	A	Pts.	PIM	Gms.	G	A	Pts.	PIM
81-82—Northwood School	N.Y. H.S.					Statistics unavailable.					
82-83—Northwood School	N.Y. H.S.					Statistics unavailable.					
83-84—University of Wisconsin	WCHA	35	14	17	31	48	—	—	—	—	—
84-85—University of Wisconsin	WCHA	42	33	34	67	94	—	—	—	—	—
85-86—University of Wisconsin	WCHA	32	25	24	49	36	—	—	—	—	—
86-87—University of Wisconsin	WCHA	42	28	45	73	64	—	—	—	—	—
87-88—U.S. national team	Int'l	49	40	31	71	55	—	—	—	—	—
—U.S. Olympic Team	Int'l	6	1	7	8	4	—	—	—	—	—
—Denver	IHL	22	13	14	27	36	8	9	4	13	16
88-89—New York Rangers	NHL	78	36	27	63	140	4	1	1	2	21
89-90—New York Rangers	NHL	37	7	18	25	77	—	—	—	—	—
—Los Angeles	NHL	19	5	6	11	45	10	5	4	9	12
90-91—Los Angeles	NHL	68	30	34	64	154	12	1	4	5	28
91-92—Los Angeles	NHL	80	39	29	68	187	6	1	5	6	10
92-93—Los Angeles	NHL	81	37	45	82	171	24	6	11	17	50
93-94—Los Angeles	NHL	50	7	14	21	150	—	—	—	—	—
94-95—Los Angeles	NHL	33	13	11	24	68	—	—	—	—	—
NHL totals		446	174	184	358	992	56	14	25	39	121

GRATTON, BENOIT

LW, CAPITALS

PERSONAL: Born December 28, 1976, in Montreal. . . . 5-10/163. . . . Shoots left.
TRANSACTIONS/CAREER NOTES: Selected by Washington Capitals in fifth round (sixth Capitals pick, 105th overall) of NHL entry draft (July 8, 1995).

Season Team	League	REGULAR SEASON					PLAYOFFS				
		Gms.	G	A	Pts.	PIM	Gms.	G	A	Pts.	PIM
93-94—Laval	QMJHL	51	9	14	23	70	20	2	1	3	19
94-95—Laval	QMJHL	71	30	58	88	199	20	8	21	29	42

GRATTON, CHRIS

C, LIGHTNING

PERSONAL: Born July 5, 1975, in Brantford, Ont. . . . 6-3/202. . . . Shoots left.
HIGH SCHOOL: Loyalist Collegiate (Brantford, Ont.).
TRANSACTIONS/CAREER NOTES: Selected by Tampa Bay Lightning in first round (first Lightning pick, third overall) of NHL entry draft (June 26, 1993). . . . Bruised shoulder (April 2, 1995); missed two games.
HONORS: Won Emms Family Award (1991-92). . . . Named to OHL Rookie All-Star team (1991-92). . . . Won OHL Top Draft Prospect Award (1992-93).

Season Team	League	REGULAR SEASON					PLAYOFFS				
		Gms.	G	A	Pts.	PIM	Gms.	G	A	Pts.	PIM
90-91—Brantford Jr. B	OHA	31	30	30	60	28	—	—	—	—	—
91-92—Kingston	OHL	62	27	39	66	35	—	—	—	—	—
92-93—Kingston	OHL	58	55	54	109	125	16	11	18	29	42
93-94—Tampa Bay	NHL	84	13	29	42	123	—	—	—	—	—
94-95—Tampa Bay	NHL	46	7	20	27	89	—	—	—	—	—
NHL totals		130	20	49	69	212					

GRAVES, ADAM

LW, RANGERS

PERSONAL: Born April 12, 1968, in Toronto. . . . 6-0/207. . . . Shoots left.
TRANSACTIONS/CAREER NOTES: Bruised shoulder (February 1986). . . . Selected by Detroit Red Wings as underage junior in second round (second Red Wings pick, 22nd overall) of NHL entry draft (June 21, 1986). . . . Traded by Red Wings with C/RW Joe Murphy, LW Petr Klima and D Jeff Sharples to Edmonton Oilers for C Jimmy Carson, C Kevin McClelland and fifth-round pick (traded to Montreal Canadiens who selected D Brad Layzell) in 1991 draft (November 2, 1989). . . . Signed as free agent by New York Rangers (September 2, 1991); Oilers received C/LW Troy Mallette as compensation (September 9, 1991). . . . Suffered from infected elbow (February 11, 1995); missed one game.
HONORS: Won King Clancy Memorial Trophy (1993-94). . . . Named to THE SPORTING NEWS All-Star first team (1993-94). . . . Named to NHL All-Star second team (1993-94). . . . Played in NHL All-Star Game (1994).
STATISTICAL PLATEAUS: Three-goal games: 1989-90 (1), 1991-92 (1), 1992-93 (1), 1993-94 (1), 1994-95 (1). Total: 5.
MISCELLANEOUS: Member of Stanley Cup championship teams (1990 and 1994).

G

Season Team	League	REGULAR SEASON Gms.	G	A	Pts.	PIM	PLAYOFFS Gms.	G	A	Pts.	PIM
84-85—King City Jr. B.	OHA	25	23	33	56	29	—	—	—	—	—
85-86—Windsor	OHL	62	27	37	64	35	16	5	11	16	10
86-87—Windsor	OHL	66	45	55	100	70	14	9	8	17	32
—Adirondack	AHL	—	—	—	—	—	5	0	1	1	0
87-88—Detroit	NHL	9	0	1	1	8	—	—	—	—	—
—Windsor	OHL	37	28	†32	60	107	12	14	18	†32	16
88-89—Detroit	NHL	56	7	5	12	60	5	0	0	0	4
—Adirondack	AHL	14	10	11	21	28	14	11	7	18	17
89-90—Detroit	NHL	13	0	1	1	13	—	—	—	—	—
—Edmonton	NHL	63	9	12	21	123	22	5	6	11	17
90-91—Edmonton	NHL	76	7	18	25	127	18	2	4	6	22
91-92—New York Rangers	NHL	80	26	33	59	139	10	5	3	8	22
92-93—New York Rangers	NHL	84	36	29	65	148	—	—	—	—	—
93-94—New York Rangers	NHL	84	52	27	79	127	23	10	7	17	24
94-95—New York Rangers	NHL	47	17	14	31	51	10	4	4	8	8
NHL totals		512	154	140	294	796	88	26	24	50	97

GREEN, TRAVIS
C, ISLANDERS

PERSONAL: Born December 20, 1970, in Creston, B.C. . . . 6-2/195. . . . Shoots right.
TRANSACTIONS/CAREER NOTES: Selected by New York Islanders in second round (second Islanders pick, 23rd overall) of NHL entry draft (June 17, 1989). . . . Traded by Spokane Chiefs to Medicine Hat Tigers for RW Mark Woolf, D/LW Chris Lafreniere and C Frank Esposito (January 26, 1990).
STATISTICAL PLATEAUS: Three-goal games: 1993-94 (1).

Season Team	League	REGULAR SEASON Gms.	G	A	Pts.	PIM	PLAYOFFS Gms.	G	A	Pts.	PIM
85-86—Castlegar	KIJHL	35	30	40	70	41	—	—	—	—	—
86-87—Spokane	WHL	64	8	17	25	27	3	0	0	0	0
87-88—Spokane	WHL	72	33	53	86	42	15	10	10	20	13
88-89—Spokane	WHL	72	51	51	102	79	—	—	—	—	—
89-90—Spokane	WHL	50	45	44	89	80	—	—	—	—	—
—Medicine Hat	WHL	25	15	24	39	19	3	0	0	0	2
90-91—Capital District	AHL	73	21	34	55	26	—	—	—	—	—
91-92—Capital District	AHL	71	23	27	50	10	7	0	4	4	21
92-93—Capital District	AHL	20	12	11	23	39	—	—	—	—	—
—New York Islanders	NHL	61	7	18	25	43	12	3	1	4	6
93-94—New York Islanders	NHL	83	18	22	40	44	4	0	0	0	2
94-95—New York Islanders	NHL	42	5	7	12	25	—	—	—	—	—
NHL totals		186	30	47	77	112	16	3	1	4	8

GREENLAY, MIKE
G, FLYERS

PERSONAL: Born September 15, 1968, in Calgary. . . . 6-3/210. . . . Catches left. . . . Full name: Michael Ronald Greenlay.
COLLEGE: Lake Superior State (Mich.).
TRANSACTIONS/CAREER NOTES: Selected by Edmonton Oilers in ninth round (ninth Oilers pick, 189th overall) of NHL entry draft (June 21, 1986). . . . Loaned by Oilers to Knoxville Cherokees (December 2, 1991); returned (January 6, 1992). . . . Loaned by Oilers to Cherokees (January 1992); returned (February 13, 1992). . . . Signed as free agent by Tampa Bay Lightning (July 29, 1992). . . . Traded by Lightning to Philadelphia Flyers to G Scott LaGrand (February 2, 1995).
HONORS: Named to Memorial Cup All-Star team (1988-89). . . . Shared James Norris Memorial Trophy with Jean-Claude Bergeron (1993-94).

Season Team	League	REGULAR SEASON Gms.	Min.	W	L	T	GA	SO	Avg.	PLAYOFFS Gms.	Min.	W	L	GA	SO	Avg.
86-87—Lake Superior State	CCHA	17	744	7	5	0	44	0	3.55	—	—	—	—	—	—	—
87-88—Lake Superior State	CCHA	19	1023	10	3	3	57	0	3.34	—	—	—	—	—	—	—
88-89—Lake Superior State	CCHA	2	85	1	1	0	6	0	4.24	—	—	—	—	—	—	—
—Saskatoon	WHL	20	1128	10	8	1	86	0	4.57	6	174	2	0	16	0	5.52
89-90—Cape Breton	AHL	46	2595	19	18	5	146	2	3.38	5	306	1	3	26	0	5.10
—Edmonton	NHL	2	20	0	0	0	4	0	12.00	—	—	—	—	—	—	—
90-91—Knoxville	ECHL	29	1725	17	9	‡2	108	2	3.76	—	—	—	—	—	—	—
—Cape Breton	AHL	11	493	5	2	0	33	0	4.02	—	—	—	—	—	—	—
91-92—Cape Breton	AHL	3	144	1	1	1	12	0	5.00	—	—	—	—	—	—	—
—Knoxville	ECHL	27	1415	8	12	‡2	113	1	4.79	—	—	—	—	—	—	—
92-93—Louisville	ECHL	27	1437	12	11	‡2	96	1	4.01	—	—	—	—	—	—	—
—Atlanta	IHL	12	637	5	3	‡2	40	0	3.77	—	—	—	—	—	—	—
93-94—Atlanta	IHL	34	1741	16	10	‡4	104	0	3.58	13	749	*11	1	29	†1	*2.32
94-95—Atlanta	IHL	20	1059	9	7	‡0	72	0	4.08	—	—	—	—	—	—	—
—Hershey	AHL	16	704	5	5	2	46	0	3.92	5	270	2	3	12	0	2.67
NHL totals		2	20	0	0	0	4	0	12.00							

GREIG, MARK
RW, FLAMES

PERSONAL: Born January 25, 1970, in High River, Alta. . . . 5-11/190. . . . Shoots right. . . . Name pronounced GRAYG.
TRANSACTIONS/CAREER NOTES: Selected by Hartford Whalers in first round (first Whalers pick, 15th overall) of NHL entry draft (June 16, 1990). . . . Injured right knee (April 11, 1993); missed

G

final three games of regular season. . . . Traded by Whalers with sixth-round pick in 1995 draft (G Doug Bonner) to Toronto Maple Leafs for D Ted Crowley (January 25, 1994). . . . Strained hip flexor (February 21, 1994); missed one game. . . . Signed as free agent by Calgary Flames (August 9, 1994).

HONORS: Named to WHL (East) All-Star first team (1989-90).

			REGULAR SEASON					PLAYOFFS			
Season Team	League	Gms.	G	A	Pts.	PIM	Gms.	G	A	Pts.	PIM
86-87—Calgary	WHL	5	0	0	0	0	—	—	—	—	—
87-88—Lethbridge	WHL	65	9	18	27	38	—	—	—	—	—
88-89—Lethbridge	WHL	71	36	72	108	113	8	5	5	10	16
89-90—Lethbridge	WHL	65	55	80	135	149	18	11	21	32	35
90-91—Hartford	NHL	4	0	0	0	0	—	—	—	—	—
—Springfield	AHL	73	32	55	87	73	17	2	6	8	22
91-92—Hartford	NHL	17	0	5	5	6	—	—	—	—	—
—Springfield	AHL	50	20	27	47	38	9	1	1	2	20
92-93—Hartford	NHL	22	1	7	8	27	—	—	—	—	—
—Springfield	AHL	55	20	38	58	86	—	—	—	—	—
93-94—Hartford	NHL	31	4	5	9	31	—	—	—	—	—
—Springfield	AHL	4	0	4	4	21	—	—	—	—	—
—Toronto	NHL	13	2	2	4	10	—	—	—	—	—
—St. John's	AHL	9	4	6	10	0	11	4	2	6	26
94-95—Saint John	AHL	67	31	50	81	82	2	0	1	1	0
—Calgary	NHL	8	1	1	2	2	—	—	—	—	—
NHL totals		95	8	20	28	76					

GRETZKY, BRENT
C, LIGHTNING

PERSONAL: Born February 20, 1972, in Brantford, Ont. . . . 5-10/160. . . . Shoots left. . . . Brother of Wayne Gretzky, center, Los Angeles Kings.
HIGH SCHOOL: Quinte Secondary School (Belleville, Ont.).
TRANSACTIONS/CAREER NOTES: Selected by Tampa Bay Lightning in third round (third Lightning pick, 49th overall) of NHL entry draft (June 20, 1992).

			REGULAR SEASON					PLAYOFFS			
Season Team	League	Gms.	G	A	Pts.	PIM	Gms.	G	A	Pts.	PIM
87-88—Brantford Jr. B	OHA	14	4	11	15	2	—	—	—	—	—
88-89—Brantford Jr. B	OHA	40	29	47	76	57	—	—	—	—	—
89-90—Belleville	OHL	40	29	47	76	57	11	0	0	0	2
90-91—Belleville	OHL	66	26	56	82	25	6	3	3	6	2
91-92—Belleville	OHL	62	43	78	121	37	—	—	—	—	—
92-93—Atlanta	IHL	77	20	34	54	84	9	3	2	5	8
93-94—Atlanta	IHL	54	17	23	40	30	14	1	1	2	2
—Tampa Bay	NHL	10	1	2	3	2	—	—	—	—	—
94-95—Atlanta	IHL	67	19	32	51	42	5	4	1	5	4
—Tampa Bay	NHL	3	0	1	1	0	—	—	—	—	—
NHL totals		13	1	3	4	2					

GRETZKY, WAYNE
C, KINGS

PERSONAL: Born January 26, 1961, in Brantford, Ont. . . . 6-0/170. . . . Shoots left. . . . Full name: Wayne Douglas Gretzky. . . . Brother of Brent Gretzky, center in Tampa Bay Lightning system.
TRANSACTIONS/CAREER NOTES: Signed as underage junior by Indianapolis Racers to multi-year contract (May 1978). . . . Traded by Racers with LW Peter Driscoll and G Ed Mio to Edmonton Oilers for cash and future considerations (November 1978). . . . Bruised right shoulder (January 28, 1984). . . . Underwent surgery on left ankle to remove benign growth (June 1984). . . . Twisted right knee (December 30, 1987). . . . Suffered corneal abrasion to left eye (February 19, 1988); missed three games. . . . Traded by Oilers with RW/D Marty McSorley and LW/C Mike Krushelnyski to Los Angeles Kings for C Jimmy Carson, LW Martin Gelinas, first-round picks in 1989 (traded to New Jersey), 1991 (LW Martin Rucinsky) and 1993 (D Nick Stajduhar) drafts and cash (August 9, 1988). . . . Injured groin (March 17, 1990). . . . Strained lower back (March 22, 1990); missed five regular-season games and two playoff games. . . . Missed five games due to personal reasons (October 1991). . . . Sprained knee (February 25, 1992); missed one game. . . . Suffered herniated thoracic disc prior to 1992-93 season; missed first 39 games of season. . . . Sprained left knee (April 9, 1994).
HONORS: Won William Hanley Trophy (1977-78). . . . Won Emms Family Award (1977-78). . . . Named to OMJHL All-Star second team (1977-78). . . . Named WHA Rookie of the Year by THE SPORTING NEWS (1978-79). . . . Won WHA Rookie of the Year Award (1978-79). . . . Named to WHA All-Star second team (1978-79). . . . Won Hart Memorial Trophy (1979-80 through 1986-87 and 1988-89). . . . Won Lady Byng Memorial Trophy (1979-80, 1990-91, 1991-92 and 1993-94). . . . Named to THE SPORTING NEWS All-Star second team (1979-80, 1987-88, 1988-89, 1991-92 and 1993-94). . . . Named to NHL All-Star second team (1979-80, 1987-88 through 1989-90 and 1993-94). . . . Named NHL Player of Year by THE SPORTING NEWS (1980-81 through 1986-87, 1989-90, 1990-91 and 1993-94). . . . Won Art Ross Memorial Trophy (1980-81 through 1986-87 and 1990-91). . . . Named to THE SPORTING NEWS All-Star first team (1980-81 through 1986-87 and 1990-91). . . . Named to NHL All-Star first team (1980-81 through 1986-87 and 1990-91). . . . Played in NHL All-Star Game (1980-1986 and 1988-1994). . . . Named Man of the Year by THE SPORTING NEWS (1981). . . . Won Lester B. Pearson Award (1981-82 through 1984-85 and 1986-87). . . . Won Emery Edge Award (1983-84, 1984-85 and 1986-87). . . . Named All-Star Game Most Valuable Player (1983 and 1989). . . . Named Canadian Athlete of the Year (1985). . . . Won Conn Smythe Trophy (1984-85 and 1987-88). . . . Won Dodge Performer of the Year Award (1984-85 through 1986-87). . . . Won Dodge Performance of the Year Award (1988-89). . . . Won Lester Patrick Trophy (1993-94).
RECORDS: Holds NHL career records for points—2,506; assists—1,692; overtime assists—11; points by a center—2,506; goals by a center—814; assists by a center—1,692; most points including playoffs—2,852; most goals including playoffs—924; most assists including playoffs—1,928; most games with three or more goals—49; most 40-or-more goal seasons—12; most consecutive 40-or-more goal seasons—12 (1979-80 through 1990-91); most 60-or-more goal seasons—5; most consecutive

G

60-or-more goal seasons—4 (1981-82 through 1984-85); most 100-or-more point seasons—14; most consecutive 100-or-more point seasons—13 (1979-80 through 1991-92); highest assist-per-game average—1.442; and highest points-per-game average—2.136. . . . Shares NHL career records for most 50-or-more goal seasons—9; and most 60-or-more goal seasons—5. . . . Holds NHL single-season records for most goals—92 (1981-82); assists—163 (1985-86); points—215 (1985-86); games with three or more goals—10 (1981-82 and 1983-84); highest goals-per-game average—1.18 (1983-84); highest assists-per-game average—2.04 (1985-86); highest points-per-game average—2.77 (1983-84); most points including playoffs—255 (1984-85); most goals including playoffs—100 (1983-84); most assists including playoffs—174 (1985-86); most points by a center—215 (1985-86); most goals by a center—92 (1981-82); most assists by a center—163 (1985-86); and most goals, 50 games from start of season—61 (1981-82 and 1983-84). . . . Shares NHL single-game records for most assists—7 (February 15, 1980; December 11, 1985; and February 14, 1986); most assists for road game—7 (December 11, 1985); and most goals in one period—4 (February 18, 1981). . . . Holds NHL records for most consecutive games scoring points—51 (October 5, 1983 through January 28, 1984); longest point-scoring streak from start of season—51 (1983-84); most consecutive games with an assist—23 (1990-91); and most assists in game by rookie—7 (February 15, 1980). . . . Holds NHL career playoff records for most points—346; most goals—110; most assists—236; and most games with three-or-more goals—8. . . . Shares NHL career playoff record for most game-winning goals—21. . . . Holds NHL single-season playoff records for most assists—31 (1988); and most points—47 (1985). . . . Shares NHL single-season playoff record for most shorthanded goals—3 (1983). . . . Holds NHL final-series playoff records for most assists—10 (1988); and most points—13 (1988). . . . Shares NHL single-series playoff record for most assists—14 (1985). . . . Shares NHL single-game playoff records for most assists—6 (April 9, 1987); most shorthanded goals—2 (April 6, 1983); most assists in one period—3 (done five times); and most points in one period—4 (April 12, 1987). . . . Holds NHL career All-Star Game record for most goals—12. . . . Holds NHL All-Star Game records for most goals in one period—4 (1983); and most points in one period—4 (1983). . . . Shares NHL All-Star Game record for most goals—4 (February 8, 1983).

STATISTICAL PLATEAUS: Three-goal games: 1979-80 (2), 1980-81 (2), 1981-82 (6), 1982-83 (2), 1983-84 (6), 1984-85 (5), 1985-86 (3), 1986-87 (3), 1987-88 (1), 1988-89 (2), 1989-90 (1), 1990-91 (2), 1991-92 (1). Total: 36. . . . Four-goal games: 1980-81 (1), 1981-82 (3), 1983-84 (4), 1986-87 (1). Total: 9. . . . Five-goal games: 1980-81 (1), 1981-82 (1), 1984-85 (1), 1987-88 (1). Total: 4. . . . Total hat tricks: 49.

MISCELLANEOUS: Member of Stanley Cup championship teams (1984, 1985, 1987 and 1988). . . . Captain of Edmonton Oilers (1983-84 through 1987-88). . . . Captain of Los Angeles Kings (1989-90 through 1994-95).

Season Team	League	REGULAR SEASON					PLAYOFFS				
		Gms.	G	A	Pts.	PIM	Gms.	G	A	Pts.	PIM
76-77—Peterborough	OMJHL	3	0	3	3	0	—	—	—	—	—
77-78—Sault Ste. Marie	OMJHL	64	70	112	182	14	13	6	20	26	0
78-79—Indianapolis	WHA	8	3	3	6	0	—	—	—	—	—
—Edmonton	WHA	72	43	61	104	19	13	†10	10	*20	2
79-80—Edmonton	NHL	79	51	*86	†137	21	3	2	1	3	0
80-81—Edmonton	NHL	80	55	*109	*164	28	9	7	14	21	4
81-82—Edmonton	NHL	80	*92	*120	*212	26	5	5	7	12	8
82-83—Edmonton	NHL	80	*71	*125	*196	59	16	12	*26	*38	4
83-84—Edmonton	NHL	74	*87	*118	*205	39	19	13	*22	*35	12
84-85—Edmonton	NHL	80	*73	*135	*208	52	18	17	*30	*47	4
85-86—Edmonton	NHL	80	52	*163	*215	46	10	8	11	19	2
86-87—Edmonton	NHL	79	*62	*121	*183	28	21	5	*29	*34	6
87-88—Edmonton	NHL	64	40	*109	149	24	19	12	*31	*43	16
88-89—Los Angeles	NHL	78	54	†114	168	26	11	5	17	22	0
89-90—Los Angeles	NHL	73	40	*102	*142	42	7	3	7	10	0
90-91—Los Angeles	NHL	78	41	*122	*163	16	12	4	11	15	2
91-92—Los Angeles	NHL	74	31	*90	*121	34	6	2	5	7	2
92-93—Los Angeles	NHL	45	16	49	65	6	24	15	25	40	4
93-94—Los Angeles	NHL	81	38	*92	*130	20	—	—	—	—	—
94-95—Los Angeles	NHL	48	11	37	48	6	—	—	—	—	—
WHA totals		80	46	64	110	19	13	10	10	20	2
NHL totals		1173	814	1692	2506	473	180	110	236	346	64

GRIER, MIKE
RW, OILERS

PERSONAL: Born January 5, 1975, in Detroit. . . . 6-0/242. . . . Shoots right.
HIGH SCHOOL: St. Sebastian's (Needham, Mass.).
COLLEGE: Boston University.
TRANSACTIONS/CAREER NOTES: Selected by St. Louis Blues in ninth round (seventh Blues pick, 219th overall) of NHL entry draft (June 26, 1993). . . . Rights traded by Blues with rights to G Curtis Joseph for first-round picks in 1996 and 1997 drafts (August 4, 1995); picks had been awarded earlier to Oilers as compensation for Blues signing free agent LW Shayne Corson (July 28, 1995).
HONORS: Named to NCAA All-America East first team (1994-95). . . . Named to Hockey East All-Star first team (1994-95).

Season Team	League	REGULAR SEASON					PLAYOFFS				
		Gms.	G	A	Pts.	PIM	Gms.	G	A	Pts.	PIM
92-93—St. Sebastian's	Mass. H.S.	22	16	27	43	32	—	—	—	—	—
93-94—Boston University	Hockey East	39	9	9	18	56	—	—	—	—	—
94-95—Boston University	Hockey East	37	29	26	55	85	—	—	—	—	—

GRIEVE, BRENT
LW, BLACKHAWKS

PERSONAL: Born May 9, 1969, in Oshawa, Ont. . . . 6-1/205. . . . Shoots left. . . . Name pronounced GREEV.
TRANSACTIONS/CAREER NOTES: Selected by New York Islanders in fourth round (fourth Islanders pick, 65th overall) of NHL entry draft (June 17, 1989). . . . Traded by Islanders to Edmonton Oilers for D Marc Laforge (December 15, 1993). . . . Signed as free agent by Chicago Blackhawks (July 6, 1994). . . . Tore knee ligaments (February 28, 1995); missed 18 games.
STATISTICAL PLATEAUS: Three-goal games: 1993-94 (1).

Season Team	League	REGULAR SEASON					PLAYOFFS				
		Gms.	G	A	Pts.	PIM	Gms.	G	A	Pts.	PIM
86-87—Oshawa	OHL	60	9	19	28	102	24	3	8	11	22
87-88—Oshawa	OHL	56	19	20	39	122	7	0	1	1	8
88-89—Oshawa	OHL	49	34	33	67	105	6	4	3	7	4
89-90—Oshawa	OHL	62	46	47	93	125	17	10	10	20	26
90-91—Kansas City	IHL	5	2	2	4	2	—	—	—	—	—
—Capital District	AHL	61	14	13	27	80	—	—	—	—	—
91-92—Capital District	AHL	74	34	32	66	84	7	3	1	4	16
92-93—Capital District	AHL	79	34	28	62	122	4	1	1	2	10
93-94—Salt Lake City	IHL	22	9	5	14	30	—	—	—	—	—
—New York Islanders	NHL	3	0	0	0	7	—	—	—	—	—
—Cape Breton	AHL	20	10	11	21	14	4	2	4	6	16
—Edmonton	NHL	24	13	5	18	14	—	—	—	—	—
94-95—Chicago	NHL	24	1	5	6	23	—	—	—	—	—
NHL totals		51	14	10	24	44					

GRILLO, DEAN
RW, SHARKS

PERSONAL: Born December 8, 1972, in Bemidji, Minn. . . . 6-2/210. . . . Shoots right. . . . Son of Chuck Grillo, vice president/director of player personnel, San Jose Sharks. **HIGH SCHOOL:** Warroad (Minn.). **COLLEGE:** North Dakota.
TRANSACTIONS/CAREER NOTES: Selected by San Jose Sharks in eighth round (ninth Sharks pick, 155th overall) of NHL entry draft (June 22, 1991).

Season Team	League	REGULAR SEASON					PLAYOFFS				
		Gms.	G	A	Pts.	PIM	Gms.	G	A	Pts.	PIM
90-91—Warroad H.S.	Minn. H.S.	24	20	15	35	. . .	—	—	—	—	—
91-92—Waterloo	USHL	48	27	38	65	42	4	4	2	6	4
92-93—North Dakota	WCHA	29	7	4	11	14	—	—	—	—	—
93-94—North Dakota	WCHA	38	11	14	25	14	—	—	—	—	—
94-95—Kansas City	IHL	72	15	21	36	24	18	3	5	8	18

GRIMSON, STU
LW, RED WINGS

PERSONAL: Born May 20, 1965, in Kamloops, B.C. . . . 6-5/227. . . . Shoots left. **COLLEGE:** Manitoba.
TRANSACTIONS/CAREER NOTES: Fractured forearm (February 1983). . . . Selected by Detroit Red Wings in 10th round (11th Red Wings pick, 186th overall) of NHL entry draft (June 8, 1983). . . . Returned to draft pool and selected by Calgary Flames in seventh round (eighth Flames pick, 143rd overall) of NHL entry draft (June 15, 1985). . . . Broke cheekbone (January 9, 1990). . . . Claimed on waivers by Chicago Blackhawks (October 1, 1990). . . . Injured eye (February 3, 1993). . . . Selected by Mighty Ducks of Anaheim in NHL expansion draft (June 24, 1993). . . . Lacerated hand (January 16, 1994); missed one game. . . . Lacerated hand (March 9, 1994); missed one game. . . . Lacerated hand (March 26, 1994); missed five games. . . . Traded by Mighty Ducks with D Mark Ferner and sixth-round pick in 1996 draft to Red Wings for C/RW Mike Sillinger and D Jason York (April 4, 1995).

Season Team	League	REGULAR SEASON					PLAYOFFS				
		Gms.	G	A	Pts.	PIM	Gms.	G	A	Pts.	PIM
82-83—Regina	WHL	48	0	1	1	144	5	0	0	0	14
83-84—Regina	WHL	63	8	8	16	131	21	0	1	1	29
84-85—Regina	WHL	71	24	32	56	248	8	1	2	3	14
85-86—University of Manitoba	CWUAA	12	7	4	11	113	3	1	1	2	20
86-87—University of Manitoba	CWUAA	29	8	8	16	67	14	4	2	6	28
87-88—Salt Lake City	IHL	38	9	5	14	268	—	—	—	—	—
88-89—Calgary	NHL	1	0	0	0	5	—	—	—	—	—
—Salt Lake City	IHL	72	9	18	27	*397	15	2	3	5	*86
89-90—Salt Lake City	IHL	62	8	8	16	319	4	0	0	0	8
—Calgary	NHL	3	0	0	0	17	—	—	—	—	—
90-91—Chicago	NHL	35	0	1	1	183	5	0	0	0	46
91-92—Chicago	NHL	54	2	2	4	234	14	0	1	1	10
—Indianapolis	IHL	5	1	1	2	17	—	—	—	—	—
92-93—Chicago	NHL	78	1	1	2	193	2	0	0	0	4
93-94—Anaheim	NHL	77	1	5	6	199	—	—	—	—	—
94-95—Anaheim	NHL	31	0	1	1	110	—	—	—	—	—
—Detroit	NHL	11	0	0	0	37	11	1	0	1	26
NHL totals		290	4	10	14	978	32	1	1	2	86

G

GROLEAU, FRANCOIS
D, DENVER

PERSONAL: Born January 23, 1973, in Longueuil, Que. . . . 6-0/195. . . . Shoots left. . . . Name pronounced FRAN-swah GROH-loh.
TRANSACTIONS/CAREER NOTES: Selected by Calgary Flames in second round (second Flames pick, 41st overall) of NHL entry draft (June 22, 1991). . . . Traded by Flames to Quebec Nordiques for D Ed Ward (March 24, 1995). . . . Nordiques franchise moved to Denver for 1995-96 season.
HONORS: Won Raymond Lagace Trophy (1989-90). . . . Named to QMJHL All-Star second team (1989-90). . . . Won Emile (Butch) Bouchard Trophy (1991-92). . . . Named to QMJHL All-Star first team (1991-92).

Season Team	League	Gms.	G	A	Pts.	PIM	Gms.	G	A	Pts.	PIM
89-90—Shawinigan	QMJHL	60	11	54	65	80	6	0	1	1	12
90-91—Shawinigan	QMJHL	70	9	60	69	70	6	0	3	3	2
91-92—Shawinigan	QMJHL	65	8	70	78	74	10	5	15	20	8
92-93—St. Jean	QMJHL	48	7	38	45	66	4	0	1	1	14
93-94—Saint John	AHL	73	8	14	22	49	7	0	1	1	2
94-95—Saint John	AHL	65	6	34	40	28	—	—	—	—	—
—Cornwall	AHL	8	1	2	3	7	14	2	7	9	16

GRONMAN, TUOMAS
D, DENVER

PERSONAL: Born March 22, 1974, in Vitasaari, Finland. . . . 6-2/193. . . . Shoots left.
TRANSACTIONS/CAREER NOTES: Selected by Quebec Nordiques in second round (third Nordiques pick, 29th overall) of NHL entry draft (June 20, 1992). . . . Nordiques franchise moved to Denver for 1995-96 season.

Season Team	League	Gms.	G	A	Pts.	PIM	Gms.	G	A	Pts.	PIM
90-91—Rauman Lukko	Finland	40	15	20	35	60	—	—	—	—	—
91-92—Tacoma	WHL	61	5	18	23	102	4	0	1	1	2
—Finnish national Jr. team .	Int'l	7	1	0	1	10	—	—	—	—	—
92-93—Rauman Lukko	Finland	45	2	11	13	46	—	—	—	—	—
93-94—Lukko	Finland	44	4	12	16	40	9	0	1	1	14
94-95—TPS Turku	Finland	47	4	20	24	66	13	2	2	4	43

GRONVALL, JANNE
D, MAPLE LEAFS

PERSONAL: Born July 17, 1973, in Rauma, Finland. . . . 6-3/195. . . . Shoots left. . . . Name pronounced GRAHN-vehl.
TRANSACTIONS/CAREER NOTES: Selected by Toronto Maple Leafs in fifth round (fifth Maple Leafs pick, 101st overall) of NHL entry draft (June 20, 1992).
HONORS: Named Finnish Rookie of the Year (1990-91).

Season Team	League	Gms.	G	A	Pts.	PIM	Gms.	G	A	Pts.	PIM
89-90—Lukko	Finland	5	0	0	0	0	—	—	—	—	—
90-91—Lukko	Finland	40	2	8	10	30	—	—	—	—	—
91-92—Lukko	Finland	42	2	6	8	40	2	0	0	0	0
92-93—Tappara	Finland	46	1	7	8	54	—	—	—	—	—
93-94—Tappara	Finland	47	2	9	11	54	10	0	4	4	31
—St. John's	AHL	—	—	—	—	—	9	0	0	0	2
94-95—St. John's	AHL	76	8	29	37	75	5	0	0	0	0

GROSEK, MICHAL
LW, JETS

PERSONAL: Born June 1, 1975, in Gottwaldov, Czechoslovakia. . . . 6-2/200. . . . Shoots right. . . . Name pronounced GROH-sehk.
TRANSACTIONS/CAREER NOTES: Selected by Winnipeg Jets in sixth round (seventh Jets pick, 145th overall) of NHL entry draft (June 26, 1993). . . . Sprained knee ligaments (February 15, 1995); missed four games. . . . Fractured foot (April 5, 1995); missed last 14 games of season.

Season Team	League	Gms.	G	A	Pts.	PIM	Gms.	G	A	Pts.	PIM
92-93—ZPS Zlin	Czech.	17	1	3	4	0	—	—	—	—	—
93-94—Moncton	AHL	20	1	2	3	47	2	0	0	0	0
—Tacoma	WHL	30	25	20	45	106	7	2	2	4	30
—Winnipeg	NHL	3	1	0	1	0	—	—	—	—	—
94-95—Springfield	AHL	45	10	22	32	98	—	—	—	—	—
—Winnipeg	NHL	24	2	2	4	21	—	—	—	—	—
NHL totals		27	3	2	5	21					

GRUDEN, JOHN
D, BRUINS

PERSONAL: Born April 6, 1970, in Hastings, Minn. . . . 6-0/180. . . . Shoots left. . . . Name pronounced GROO-dihn.
COLLEGE: Ferris State (Mich.).
TRANSACTIONS/CAREER NOTES: Selected by Boston Bruins in seventh round (seventh Bruins pick, 168th overall) of NHL entry draft (June 16, 1990). . . . Suffered back spasms (March 15, 1995); missed two games.
HONORS: Named to NCCA All-America first team (1993-94). . . . Named to CCHA All-Star first team (1993-94).

Season Team	League	Gms.	G	A	Pts.	PIM	Gms.	G	A	Pts.	PIM
90-91—Ferris State	CCHA	37	4	11	15	27	—	—	—	—	—
91-92—Ferris State	CCHA	37	9	14	23	24	—	—	—	—	—
92-93—Ferris State	CCHA	41	16	14	30	58	—	—	—	—	—
93-94—Ferris State	CCHA	38	11	25	36	52	—	—	—	—	—
—Boston	NHL	7	0	1	1	2	—	—	—	—	—
94-95—Boston	NHL	38	0	6	6	22	—	—	—	—	—
—Providence	AHL	1	0	1	1	0	—	—	—	—	—
NHL totals		45	0	7	7	24					

GUERARD, DANIEL
RW, SENATORS

PERSONAL: Born April 9, 1974, in La Salle, Que. . . . 6-4/215. . . . Shoots right. . . . Name pronounced gay-RAHR.
TRANSACTIONS/CAREER NOTES: Selected by Ottawa Senators in fifth round (fifth Senators pick, 98th overall) of NHL entry draft (June 20, 1992).

			REGULAR SEASON					PLAYOFFS				
Season	Team	League	Gms.	G	A	Pts.	PIM	Gms.	G	A	Pts.	PIM
91-92—Victoriaville	QMJHL	31	5	16	21	66	—	—	—	—	—
92-93—Verdun	QMJHL	58	31	26	57	131	4	1	1	2	17
—New Haven	AHL	2	2	1	3	0	—	—	—	—	—
93-94—Verdun	QMJHL	53	31	34	65	169	4	3	1	4	4
—Prince Edward Island	AHL	3	0	0	0	17	—	—	—	—	—
94-95—Prince Edward Island	AHL	68	20	22	42	95	8	0	1	1	16
—Ottawa	NHL	2	0	0	0	0	—	—	—	—	—
NHL totals		2	0	0	0	0					

GUERIN, BILL
RW/C, DEVILS

PERSONAL: Born November 9, 1970, in Wilbraham, Mass. . . . 6-2/200. . . . Shoots right. . . . Full name: William Robert Guerin. . . . Name pronounced GAIR-ihn.
COLLEGE: Boston College.
TRANSACTIONS/CAREER NOTES: Selected by New Jersey Devils in first round (first Devils pick, fifth overall) of NHL entry draft (June 17, 1989). . . . Suffered from the flu (February 1992); missed three games. . . . Suffered from sore leg (March 19, 1994); missed two games.
MISCELLANEOUS: Member of Stanley Cup championship team (1995).

			REGULAR SEASON					PLAYOFFS				
Season	Team	League	Gms.	G	A	Pts.	PIM	Gms.	G	A	Pts.	PIM
85-86—Springfield Jr. B	NEJHL	48	26	19	45	71	—	—	—	—	—
86-87—Springfield Jr. B	NEJHL	32	34	20	54	40	—	—	—	—	—
87-88—Springfield Jr. B	NEJHL	38	31	44	75	146	—	—	—	—	—
88-89—Springfield Jr. B	NEJHL	31	32	37	69	90	—	—	—	—	—
89-90—Boston College	Hockey East	39	14	11	25	64	—	—	—	—	—
90-91—Boston College	Hockey East	38	26	19	45	102	—	—	—	—	—
91-92—U.S. national team	Int'l	46	12	15	27	67	—	—	—	—	—
—Utica	AHL	22	13	10	23	6	4	1	3	4	14
—New Jersey	NHL	5	0	1	1	9	6	3	0	3	4
92-93—New Jersey	NHL	65	14	20	34	63	5	1	1	2	4
—Utica	AHL	18	10	7	17	47	—	—	—	—	—
93-94—New Jersey	NHL	81	25	19	44	101	17	2	1	3	35
94-95—New Jersey	NHL	48	12	13	25	72	20	3	8	11	30
NHL totals		199	51	53	104	245	48	9	10	19	73

GUILLET, ROBERT
RW, CANADIENS

PERSONAL: Born February 22, 1972, in Montreal. . . . 5-11/189. . . . Shoots right. . . . Name pronounced gee-YEHT.
TRANSACTIONS/CAREER NOTES: Selected by Montreal Canadiens in third round (fourth Canadiens pick, 60th overall) of NHL entry draft (June 16, 1990).
HONORS: Named to QMJHL All-Star first team (1990-91). . . . Won Guy Lafleur Trophy (1991-92). . . . Named to QMJHL All-Star second team (1991-92).

			REGULAR SEASON					PLAYOFFS				
Season	Team	League	Gms.	G	A	Pts.	PIM	Gms.	G	A	Pts.	PIM
89-90—Longueuil	QMJHL	69	32	40	72	132	7	2	1	3	16
90-91—Longueuil	QMJHL	69	55	32	87	96	8	4	7	11	27
91-92—Longueuil	QMJHL	67	56	62	118	104	19	†14	11	*25	26
92-93—Fredericton	AHL	42	16	15	31	38	1	0	0	0	0
—Wheeling	ECHL	15	16	14	30	8	—	—	—	—	—
93-94—Fredericton	AHL	78	38	40	78	48	—	—	—	—	—
94-95—Fredericton	AHL	48	14	15	29	23	17	*10	6	16	28

GUOLLA, STEVE
LW, SENATORS

PERSONAL: Born March 15, 1973, in Scarborough, Ont. . . . 6-0/180. . . . Shoots left.
HIGH SCHOOL: Stephen Leacock (Agincourt, Ont.).
COLLEGE: Michigan State.
TRANSACTIONS/CAREER NOTES: Selected by Ottawa Senators (first Senators pick, third overall) in NHL supplemental draft (June 28, 1994).
HONORS: Named to NCCA All-America West second team (1993-94). . . . Named to CCHA All-Star second team (1993-94).

			REGULAR SEASON					PLAYOFFS				
Season	Team	League	Gms.	G	A	Pts.	PIM	Gms.	G	A	Pts.	PIM
91-92—Michigan State	CCHA	33	4	9	13	8	—	—	—	—	—
92-93—Michigan State	CCHA	39	19	35	54	6	—	—	—	—	—
93-94—Michigan State	CCHA	41	23	46	69	16	—	—	—	—	—
94-95—Michigan State	CCHA	40	16	35	51	16	—	—	—	—	—

GUREN, MIROSLAV
D, CANADIENS

PERSONAL: Born September 24, 1976, in Gottwaldov, Czechoslovakia. . . . 6-2/205. . . . Shoots left.
TRANSACTIONS/CAREER NOTES: Selected by Montreal Canadiens in third round (second Canadiens pick, 60th overall) of NHL entry draft (July 8, 1995).

G

Season	Team	League	REGULAR SEASON					PLAYOFFS				
			Gms.	G	A	Pts.	PIM	Gms.	G	A	Pts.	PIM
93-94—ZPS Zlin		Czech. Rep.	22	1	5	6	...	3	0	0	0	...
94-95—ZPS Zlin		Czech. Rep.	32	3	7	10	...	12	1	0	1	...

GUSAROV, ALEXEI
D, DENVER

PERSONAL: Born July 8, 1964, in Leningrad, U.S.S.R. ... 6-3/185. ... Shoots left. ... Name pronounced goo-SAH-rahf.

TRANSACTIONS/CAREER NOTES: Selected by Quebec Nordiques in 11th round (11th Nordiques pick, 213th overall) in the NHL entry draft (June 11, 1988). ... Suffered hairline fracture of left ankle (December 15, 1990); missed seven games. ... Hyperextended right knee (February 28, 1991). ... Fractured finger (October 13, 1991); missed four games. ... Suffered from the flu (February 9, 1993); missed two games. ... Suffered concussion (March 31, 1993); missed two games. ... Bruised left thumb (November 13, 1993); missed one game. ... Suffered from the flu (January 11, 1994); missed two games. ... Suffered from sinusitis (March 30, 1994); missed two games. ... Injured foot (January 21, 1995); missed nine games. ... Reinjured foot (February 11, 1995); missed six games. ... Injured knee (March 26, 1995); missed last 17 games of season and entire playoffs. ... Nordiques franchise moved to Denver for 1995-96 season.

MISCELLANEOUS: Member of gold-medal-winning U.S.S.R. Olympic team (1988).

Season	Team	League	REGULAR SEASON					PLAYOFFS				
			Gms.	G	A	Pts.	PIM	Gms.	G	A	Pts.	PIM
81-82—SKA Leningrad		USSR	20	1	2	3	16	—	—	—	—	—
82-83—SKA Leningrad		USSR	42	2	1	3	32	—	—	—	—	—
83-84—SKA Leningrad		USSR	43	2	3	5	32	—	—	—	—	—
84-85—CSKA Moscow		USSR	36	3	2	5	26	—	—	—	—	—
85-86—CSKA Moscow		USSR	40	3	5	8	30	—	—	—	—	—
86-87—CSKA Moscow		USSR	38	4	7	11	24	—	—	—	—	—
87-88—CSKA Moscow		USSR	39	3	2	5	28	—	—	—	—	—
88-89—CSKA Moscow		USSR	42	5	4	9	37	—	—	—	—	—
89-90—CSKA Moscow		USSR	42	4	7	11	42	—	—	—	—	—
90-91—CSKA Moscow		USSR	15	0	0	0	12	—	—	—	—	—
—Quebec		NHL	36	3	9	12	12	—	—	—	—	—
—Halifax		AHL	2	0	3	3	2	—	—	—	—	—
91-92—Quebec		NHL	68	5	18	23	22	—	—	—	—	—
—Halifax		AHL	3	0	0	0	0	—	—	—	—	—
92-93—Quebec		NHL	79	8	22	30	57	5	0	1	1	0
93-94—Quebec		NHL	76	5	20	25	38	—	—	—	—	—
94-95—Quebec		NHL	14	1	2	3	6	—	—	—	—	—
NHL totals			**273**	**22**	**71**	**93**	**135**	**5**	**0**	**1**	**1**	**0**

GUSEV, SERGEI
D, STARS

PERSONAL: Born July 31, 1975, in Nizhny Tagil, U.S.S.R. ... 5-11/176. ... Shoots left.
TRANSACTIONS/CAREER NOTES: Selected by Dallas Stars in third round (fourth Stars pick, 69th overall) of NHL entry draft (July 8, 1995).

Season	Team	League	REGULAR SEASON					PLAYOFFS				
			Gms.	G	A	Pts.	PIM	Gms.	G	A	Pts.	PIM
94-95—CSK VVS Samara		CIS	50	3	5	8	58	—	—	—	—	—

GUSMANOV, RAVIL
RW/LW, JETS

PERSONAL: Born July 22, 1972, in Naberezhnye Chelny, U.S.S.R. ... 6-2/185. ... Shoots left. ... Name pronounced RA-vihl goos-MAH-nahf.
TRANSACTIONS/CAREER NOTES: Selected by Winnipeg Jets in fourth round (fifth Jets pick, 93rd overall) of NHL entry draft (June 26, 1993).

Season	Team	League	REGULAR SEASON					PLAYOFFS				
			Gms.	G	A	Pts.	PIM	Gms.	G	A	Pts.	PIM
90-91—Traktor Chelyabinsk		USSR	15	0	0	0	10	—	—	—	—	—
91-92—Traktor Chelyabinsk		CIS	38	4	4	8	20	—	—	—	—	—
92-93—Traktor Chelyabinsk		CIS	39	15	8	23	30	8	4	0	4	2
93-94—Traktor Chelyabinsk		CIS	43	18	9	27	51	6	4	3	7	10
—Russian Olympic team		Int'l	8	3	1	4	0	—	—	—	—	—
94-95—Springfield		AHL	72	18	15	33	14	—	—	—	—	—

HACKETT, JEFF
G, BLACKHAWKS

PERSONAL: Born June 1, 1968, in London, Ont. ... 6-1/185. ... Catches left.
TRANSACTIONS/CAREER NOTES: Selected by New York Islanders as underage junior in second round (second Islanders pick, 34th overall) of NHL entry draft (June 13, 1987). ... Strained groin (May 13, 1990). ... Selected by San Jose Sharks in NHL expansion draft (May 30, 1991). ... Injured groin and hamstring (December 3, 1991); missed nine games. ... Injured knee (March 23, 1992). ... Injured groin (October 30, 1992); missed 12 games. ... Suffered from the flu (February 20, 1993); missed five games. ... Traded by Sharks to Chicago Blackhawks for third-round pick (C Alexei Yegorov) in 1994 draft (July 13, 1993).

HONORS: Won F.W. (Dinty) Moore Trophy (1986-87). ... Shared Dave Pinkney Trophy with Sean Evoy (1986-87). ... Won Jack Butterfield Trophy (1989-90).

Season	Team	League	REGULAR SEASON							PLAYOFFS					
			Gms.	Min.	W	L	T	GA	SO	Avg.	Gms.	Min.	W	L	GA	SO	Avg.
85-86—London Jr. B		OHA	19	1150	...	...	...	66	0	3.44	—	—	—	—	—	—	—
86-87—Oshawa		OHL	31	1672	18	9	2	85	2	3.05	15	895	8	7	40	0	2.68
87-88—Oshawa		OHL	53	3165	30	21	2	205	0	3.89	7	438	3	4	31	0	4.25

Season	Team	League	Gms.	Min.	W	L	T	GA	SO	Avg.	Gms.	Min.	W	L	GA	SO	Avg.
			REGULAR SEASON								PLAYOFFS						
88-89	New York Islanders......	NHL	13	662	4	7	0	39	0	3.53	—	—	—	—	—	—	—
	—Springfield..................	AHL	29	1677	12	14	2	116	0	4.15	—	—	—	—	—	—	—
89-90	Springfield..................	AHL	54	3045	24	25	3	187	1	3.68	†17	934	10	5	*60	0	3.85
90-91	New York Islanders......	NHL	30	1508	5	18	1	91	0	3.62	—	—	—	—	—	—	—
91-92	San Jose......................	NHL	42	2314	11	27	1	148	0	3.84	—	—	—	—	—	—	—
92-93	San Jose......................	NHL	36	2000	2	30	1	176	0	5.28	—	—	—	—	—	—	—
93-94	Chicago......................	NHL	22	1084	2	12	3	62	0	3.43	—	—	—	—	—	—	—
94-95	Chicago......................	NHL	7	328	1	3	2	13	0	2.38	2	26	0	0	1	0	2.31
NHL totals...............			150	7896	25	97	8	529	0	4.02	2	26	0	0	1	0	2.31

HAGGERTY, RYAN
C, OILERS

PERSONAL: Born May 2, 1973, in Rye, N.Y.... 6-1/186.... Shoots left.... Brother of Sean Haggerty, left winger in Toronto Maple Leafs system.
HIGH SCHOOL: Westminster School (Simsbury, Conn.).
COLLEGE: Boston College.
TRANSACTIONS/CAREER NOTES: Selected by Edmonton Oilers in fifth round (sixth Oilers pick, 93rd overall) of NHL entry draft (June 22, 1991).

Season	Team	League	Gms.	G	A	Pts.	PIM	Gms.	G	A	Pts.	PIM
			REGULAR SEASON					PLAYOFFS				
90-91	Westminster Prep............	Conn. H.S.	25	34	38	72	...	—	—	—	—	—
91-92	Boston College	Hockey East	34	12	5	17	16	—	—	—	—	—
92-93	Boston College	Hockey East	32	6	5	11	12	—	—	—	—	—
93-94	Boston College	Hockey East	36	17	23	40	16	—	—	—	—	—
94-95	Boston College	Hockey East	35	23	22	45	20	—	—	—	—	—

HAGGERTY, SEAN
LW, MAPLE LEAFS

PERSONAL: Born February 11, 1976, in Greenwich, Conn.... 6-1/186.... Shoots left.... Brother of Ryan Haggerty, center in Edmonton Oilers system.
HIGH SCHOOL: Westminster School (Simsbury, Conn.).
TRANSACTIONS/CAREER NOTES: Selected by Toronto Maple Leafs in second round (second Maple Leafs pick, 48th overall) of NHL entry draft (June 28, 1994).
HONORS: Named to OHL All-Rookie team (1993-94).... Named to Memorial Cup All-Star team (1994-95).

Season	Team	League	Gms.	G	A	Pts.	PIM	Gms.	G	A	Pts.	PIM
			REGULAR SEASON					PLAYOFFS				
90-91	Westminster Prep............	Conn. H.S.	25	20	22	42	...	—	—	—	—	—
91-92	Westminster Prep............	Conn. H.S.	25	24	36	60	...	—	—	—	—	—
92-93	Boston	NEJHL	72	70	111	181	80	—	—	—	—	—
93-94	Detroit	OHL	60	31	32	63	21	17	9	10	19	11
94-95	Detroit	OHL	61	40	49	89	37	21	13	24	37	18

HAKANEN, TIMO
C, SHARKS

PERSONAL: Born March 26, 1977, in Pori, Finland.... 6-2/189.... Shoots left.
TRANSACTIONS/CAREER NOTES: Selected by San Jose Sharks in sixth round (sixth Sharks pick, 140th overall) of NHL entry draft (July 8, 1995).

Season	Team	League	Gms.	G	A	Pts.	PIM	Gms.	G	A	Pts.	PIM
			REGULAR SEASON					PLAYOFFS				
94-95	Assat Pori Jrs.	Finland	36	23	21	44	6	5	0	0	0	0

HALKIDIS, BOB
D, LIGHTNING

PERSONAL: Born March 5, 1966, in Toronto.... 5-11/205.... Shoots left.... Name pronounced hal-KEE-duhz.
TRANSACTIONS/CAREER NOTES: Broke ankle (September 1982).... Reinjured ankle (November 1982); missed two weeks.... Selected by Buffalo Sabres as underage junior in fourth round (fourth Sabres pick, 81st overall) of NHL entry draft (June 9, 1984).... Dislocated right shoulder (December 4, 1985); missed 15 games.... Suspended six games by AHL for fighting (October 23, 1987).... Injured ankle (December 1987).... Injured shoulder (December 1988).... Traded by Sabres to Los Angeles Kings for D Dale DeGray (November 24, 1989).... Underwent surgery to left shoulder (May 1990).... Underwent surgery to left shoulder (October 16, 1990).... Signed as free agent by Toronto Maple Leafs (July 24, 1991).... Pulled groin (November 21, 1991); missed three games.... Signed as free agent by Detroit Red Wings (September 2, 1993).... Torn left medial collateral ligament (December 21, 1993); missed 18 games.... Claimed on waivers by Tampa Bay Lightning (February 9, 1995).
HONORS: Won Max Kaminsky Trophy (1984-85).... Named to OHL All-Star first team (1984-85).

Season	Team	League	Gms.	G	A	Pts.	PIM	Gms.	G	A	Pts.	PIM
			REGULAR SEASON					PLAYOFFS				
82-83	London	OHL	37	3	12	15	52	—	—	—	—	—
83-84	London	OHL	51	9	22	31	123	8	0	2	2	27
84-85	London	OHL	62	14	50	64	154	8	3	6	9	22
	—Buffalo..........................	NHL	—	—	—	—	—	4	0	0	0	19
85-86	Buffalo..........................	NHL	37	1	9	10	115	—	—	—	—	—
86-87	Buffalo..........................	NHL	6	1	1	2	19	—	—	—	—	—
	—Rochester......................	AHL	59	1	8	9	144	8	0	0	0	43
87-88	Rochester......................	AHL	15	2	5	7	50	—	—	—	—	—
	—Buffalo..........................	NHL	30	0	3	3	115	4	0	0	0	22
88-89	Buffalo..........................	NHL	16	0	1	1	66	—	—	—	—	—
	—Rochester......................	AHL	16	0	6	6	64					

H

Season	Team	League	Gms.	G	A	Pts.	PIM	Gms.	G	A	Pts.	PIM
89-90	—Rochester	AHL	18	1	13	14	70	—	—	—	—	—
	—Los Angeles	NHL	20	0	4	4	56	—	—	—	—	—
	—New Haven	AHL	30	3	17	20	67	—	—	—	—	—
90-91	—Phoenix	IHL	4	1	5	6	6	—	—	—	—	—
	—New Haven	AHL	7	1	3	4	10	—	—	—	—	—
	—Los Angeles	NHL	34	1	3	4	133	3	0	0	0	0
91-92	—Toronto	NHL	46	3	3	6	145	—	—	—	—	—
92-93	—St. John's	AHL	29	2	13	15	61	—	—	—	—	—
	—Milwaukee	IHL	26	0	9	9	79	5	0	1	1	27
93-94	—Adirondack	AHL	15	0	6	6	46	—	—	—	—	—
	—Detroit	NHL	28	1	4	5	93	1	0	0	0	2
94-95	—Detroit	NHL	4	0	1	1	6	—	—	—	—	—
	—Tampa Bay	NHL	27	1	3	4	40	—	—	—	—	—
NHL totals			248	8	32	40	788	12	0	0	0	43

HALKO, STEVEN
D, WHALERS

PERSONAL: Born March 8, 1974, in Etobicoke, Ont. . . . 6-1/183. . . . Shoots right.
COLLEGE: Michigan.
TRANSACTIONS/CAREER NOTES: Selected by Hartford Whalers in 10th round (10th Whalers pick, 225th overall) of NHL entry draft (June 20, 1992).
HONORS: Named to CCHA All-Star second team (1994-95).

Season	Team	League	Gms.	G	A	Pts.	PIM	Gms.	G	A	Pts.	PIM
91-92	—Thornhill	OHA Jr. A	44	15	46	61	43	—	—	—	—	—
92-93	—University of Michigan	CCHA	39	1	12	13	12	—	—	—	—	—
93-94	—University of Michigan	CCHA	41	2	13	15	32	—	—	—	—	—
94-95	—University of Michigan	CCHA	39	2	14	16	20	—	—	—	—	—

HALLER, KEVIN
D, FLYERS

PERSONAL: Born December 5, 1970, in Trochu, Alta. . . . 6-2/183. . . . Name pronounced HAH-luhr.
TRANSACTIONS/CAREER NOTES: Broke leg (October 1986). . . . Broke leg (May 1987). . . . Selected by Buffalo Sabres in first round (first Sabres pick, 14th overall) of NHL entry draft (June 17, 1989). . . . Separated shoulder (May 7, 1991); missed seven games. . . . Traded by Sabres to Montreal Canadiens for D Petr Svoboda (March 10, 1992). . . . Suspended four games and fined $500 by NHL for slashing (November 2, 1993). . . . Traded by Canadiens to Philadelphia Flyers for D Yves Racine (June 29, 1994). . . . Pulled right groin (January 26, 1995); missed four games. . . . Strained groin (March 15, 1995); missed six games. . . . Suffered from the flu (March 2, 1995); missed two games.
HONORS: Won Bill Hunter Trophy (1989-90). . . . Named to WHL (East) All-Star first team (1989-90).
MISCELLANEOUS: Member of Stanley Cup championship team (1993).

Season	Team	League	Gms.	G	A	Pts.	PIM	Gms.	G	A	Pts.	PIM
87-88	—Olds	AJHL	54	13	31	44	58	—	—	—	—	—
88-89	—Regina	WHL	72	10	31	41	99	—	—	—	—	—
89-90	—Regina	WHL	58	16	37	53	93	11	2	9	11	16
	—Buffalo	NHL	2	0	0	0	0	—	—	—	—	—
90-91	—Rochester	AHL	52	2	8	10	53	10	2	1	3	6
	—Buffalo	NHL	21	1	8	9	20	6	1	4	5	10
91-92	—Buffalo	NHL	58	6	15	21	75	—	—	—	—	—
	—Rochester	AHL	4	0	0	0	18	—	—	—	—	—
	—Montreal	NHL	8	2	2	4	17	9	0	0	0	6
92-93	—Montreal	NHL	73	11	14	25	117	17	1	6	7	16
93-94	—Montreal	NHL	68	4	9	13	118	7	1	1	2	19
94-95	—Philadelphia	NHL	36	2	8	10	48	15	4	4	8	10
NHL totals			266	26	56	82	395	54	7	15	22	61

HAMEL, DENIS
LW, BLUES

PERSONAL: Born May 10, 1977, in Lachute, Que. . . . 6-2/175. . . . Shoots left.
TRANSACTIONS/CAREER NOTES: Selected by St. Louis Blues in sixth round (fifth Blues pick, 153rd overall) of NHL entry draft (July 8, 1995).

Season	Team	League	Gms.	G	A	Pts.	PIM	Gms.	G	A	Pts.	PIM
94-95	—Chicoutimi	QMJHL	66	15	12	27	155	13	2	0	2	29

HAMILTON, HUGH
D, WHALERS

PERSONAL: Born February 11, 1977, in Saskatoon, Sask. . . . 6-1/175. . . . Shoots left.
HIGH SCHOOL: Joel E. Ferris (Spokane, Wash.).
TRANSACTIONS/CAREER NOTES: Selected by Hartford Whalers in fifth round (fifth Whalers pick, 113th overall) of NHL entry draft (July 8, 1995).

Season	Team	League	Gms.	G	A	Pts.	PIM	Gms.	G	A	Pts.	PIM
93-94	—Spokane	WHL	64	5	9	14	70	3	0	0	0	0
94-95	—Spokane	WHL	60	5	28	33	102	11	3	5	8	16

HAMMOND, KEN

D

PERSONAL: Born August 23, 1963, in London, Ont. . . . 6-1/190. . . . Shoots left. . . . Full name: Kenneth Paul Hammond.
HIGH SCHOOL: Saunders (London, Ont.).
COLLEGE: Rensselaer Polytechnic Institute (N.Y.).
TRANSACTIONS/CAREER NOTES: Selected by Los Angeles Kings in eighth round (eighth Kings pick, 147th overall) of NHL entry draft (June 8, 1983). . . . Sprained knee (March 13, 1988). . . . Selected by Edmonton Oilers in NHL waiver draft for $30,000 (October 3, 1988). . . . Claimed on waivers by New York Rangers (November 1, 1988). . . . Traded by Rangers to Toronto Maple Leafs for LW Chris McRae (February 19, 1989). . . . Suffered back spasms (March 1989). . . . Sold by Maple Leafs to Boston Bruins (August 20, 1990). . . . Signed as free agent by San Jose Sharks (August 9, 1991). . . . Pulled groin (January 23, 1992); missed five games. . . . Fractured hand (February 21, 1992); missed seven games. . . . Traded by Sharks to Vancouver Canucks for eighth-round pick in 1992 draft (traded to Detroit Red Wings who selected G C.J. Denomme) (March 9, 1992). . . . Underwent surgery to hand (March 1992). . . . Selected by Ottawa Senators in NHL expansion draft (June 18, 1992). . . . Signed as free agent by Kansas City Blades (July 8, 1994).
HONORS: Named to NCAA All-America East first team (1984-85). . . . Named to NCAA All-Tournament team (1984-85). . . . Named to ECAC All-Star first team (1984-85).

Season	Team	League	REGULAR SEASON					PLAYOFFS				
			Gms.	G	A	Pts.	PIM	Gms.	G	A	Pts.	PIM
81-82	R.P.I.	ECAC	29	2	3	5	54	—	—	—	—	—
82-83	R.P.I.	ECAC	28	4	13	17	54	—	—	—	—	—
83-84	R.P.I.	ECAC	34	5	11	16	72	—	—	—	—	—
84-85	R.P.I.	ECAC	38	11	28	39	90	—	—	—	—	—
	Los Angeles	NHL	3	1	0	1	0	3	0	0	0	4
85-86	New Haven	AHL	67	4	12	16	96	4	0	0	0	7
	Los Angeles	NHL	3	0	1	1	2	—	—	—	—	—
86-87	New Haven	AHL	66	1	15	16	76	6	0	1	1	21
	Los Angeles	NHL	10	0	2	2	11	—	—	—	—	—
87-88	New Haven	AHL	26	3	8	11	27	—	—	—	—	—
	Los Angeles	NHL	46	7	9	16	69	2	0	0	0	4
88-89	Edmonton	NHL	5	0	1	1	8	—	—	—	—	—
	New York Rangers	NHL	3	0	0	0	0	—	—	—	—	—
	Toronto	NHL	14	0	2	2	12	—	—	—	—	—
	Denver	IHL	38	5	18	23	24	—	—	—	—	—
89-90	Newmarket	AHL	75	9	45	54	106	—	—	—	—	—
90-91	Boston	NHL	1	1	0	1	2	8	0	0	0	10
	Maine	AHL	80	10	41	51	159	2	0	1	1	16
91-92	San Jose	NHL	46	5	10	15	82	—	—	—	—	—
	Vancouver	NHL	—	—	—	—	—	2	0	0	0	6
92-93	Ottawa	NHL	62	4	4	8	104	—	—	—	—	—
	New Haven	AHL	4	0	1	1	4	—	—	—	—	—
93-94	Providence	AHL	65	12	45	57	100	—	—	—	—	—
94-95	Kansas City	IHL	76	3	24	27	151	21	1	4	5	45
NHL totals			193	18	29	47	290	15	0	0	0	24

HAMR, RADEK

D, SENATORS

PERSONAL: Born June 15, 1974, in Prague, Czechoslovakia. . . . 5-11/175. . . . Shoots left. . . . Name pronounced RA-dehk HAM-uhr.
TRANSACTIONS/CAREER NOTES: Selected by Ottawa Senators in fourth round (fourth Senators pick, 73rd overall) of NHL entry draft (June 20, 1992).

Season	Team	League	REGULAR SEASON					PLAYOFFS				
			Gms.	G	A	Pts.	PIM	Gms.	G	A	Pts.	PIM
91-92	Sparta Prague	Czech.	3	0	0	0	0	—	—	—	—	—
92-93	New Haven	AHL	59	4	21	25	18	—	—	—	—	—
	Ottawa	NHL	4	0	0	0	0	—	—	—	—	—
93-94	Prince Edward Island	AHL	69	10	26	36	44	—	—	—	—	—
	Ottawa	NHL	7	0	0	0	0	—	—	—	—	—
94-95	Fort Wayne	IHL	58	3	13	16	14	1	0	0	0	0
	Prince Edward Island	AHL	7	0	1	1	2	8	0	1	1	16
NHL totals			11	0	0	0	0					

HAMRLIK, MARTIN

D, BLUES

PERSONAL: Born May 6, 1973, in Zlin, Czechoslovakia. . . . 5-11/176. . . . Shoots right. . . . Name pronounced HAM-uhr-lihk. . . . Brother of Roman Hamrlik, defenseman, Tampa Bay Lightning.
TRANSACTIONS/CAREER NOTES: Selected by Hartford Whalers in second round (second Whalers pick, 31st overall) of NHL entry draft (June 22, 1991). . . . Suffered from Lyme disease (October 1991); missed remainder of season. . . . Traded by Whalers to St. Louis Blues for cash (November 13, 1993).

Season	Team	League	REGULAR SEASON					PLAYOFFS				
			Gms.	G	A	Pts.	PIM	Gms.	G	A	Pts.	PIM
89-90	TJ Zlin	Czech.	11	2	0	2	. . .	—	—	—	—	—
90-91	TJ Zlin	Czech.	50	8	14	22	44	—	—	—	—	—
91-92	ZPS Zlin	Czech.	4	0	2	2	. . .	—	—	—	—	—
92-93	Ottawa	OHL	26	4	11	15	41	—	—	—	—	—
	Springfield	AHL	8	1	3	4	16	—	—	—	—	—
93-94	Peoria	IHL	47	1	11	12	61	6	0	1	1	2
	Springfield	AHL	1	0	0	0	0	—	—	—	—	—
94-95	Peoria	IHL	77	5	13	18	120	3	0	0	0	2

H

HAMRLIK, ROMAN
D, LIGHTNING

PERSONAL: Born April 12, 1974, in Gottwaldov, Czechoslovakia. . . . 6-2/189. . . . Shoots left. . . . Name pronounced ROH-muhn HAM-uhr-lihk. . . . Brother of Martin Hamrlik, defenseman in St. Louis Blues system.
TRANSACTIONS/CAREER NOTES: Selected by Tampa Bay Lightning in first round (first Lightning pick, first overall) of NHL entry draft (June 20, 1992). . . . Bruised shoulder (November 3, 1993); missed six games. . . . Bruised shoulder (March 1, 1994); missed seven games. . . . Played in Europe during 1994-95 NHL lockout.

Season Team	League	REGULAR SEASON					PLAYOFFS				
		Gms.	G	A	Pts.	PIM	Gms.	G	A	Pts.	PIM
90-91—TJ Zlin	Czech.	14	2	2	4	18	—	—	—	—	—
91-92—ZPS Zlin	Czech.	34	5	5	10	34	—	—	—	—	—
92-93—Tampa Bay	NHL	67	6	15	21	71	—	—	—	—	—
—Atlanta	IHL	2	1	1	2	2	—	—	—	—	—
93-94—Tampa Bay	NHL	64	3	18	21	135	—	—	—	—	—
94-95—ZPS Zlin	Czech Rep.	2	1	0	1	10	—	—	—	—	—
—Tampa Bay	NHL	48	12	11	23	86	—	—	—	—	—
NHL totals		179	21	44	65	292					

HANDZUS, MICHAL
C, BLUES

PERSONAL: Born March 11, 1977, in Banska Bystrica, Czechoslovakia. . . . 6-3/191. . . . Shoots left.
TRANSACTIONS/CAREER NOTES: Selected by St. Louis Blues in fourth round (third Blues pick, 101st overall) of NHL entry draft (July 8, 1995).

Season Team	League	REGULAR SEASON					PLAYOFFS				
		Gms.	G	A	Pts.	PIM	Gms.	G	A	Pts.	PIM
93-94—IS Banska Bystrica Jr.	Slovakia	40	23	36	59	. . .	—	—	—	—	—
94-95—IS Banska Bystrica	Slovak Div. II	22	15	14	29	10	—	—	—	—	—

HANKINSON, BEN
RW, LIGHTNING

PERSONAL: Born January 5, 1969, in Edina, Minn. . . . 6-2/215. . . . Shoots right. . . . Full name: Benjamin John Hankinson. . . . Brother of Casey Hankinson, left winger in Chicago Blackhawks system.
HIGH SCHOOL: Edina (Minn.).
COLLEGE: Minnesota.
TRANSACTIONS/CAREER NOTES: Selected by New Jersey Devils in sixth round (fifth Devils pick, 107th overall) of NHL entry draft (June 13, 1987). . . . Traded by Devils with C Alexander Semak to Tampa Bay Lightning for D Shawn Chambers and RW Danton Cole (March 14, 1995).
HONORS: Named to WCHA All-Star first team (1989-90).

Season Team	League	REGULAR SEASON					PLAYOFFS				
		Gms.	G	A	Pts.	PIM	Gms.	G	A	Pts.	PIM
85-86—Edina High School	Minn. H.S.	. . .	9	21	30	. . .	—	—	—	—	—
86-87—Edina High School	Minn. H.S.	26	14	20	34	. . .	—	—	—	—	—
87-88—University of Minnesota	WCHA	24	4	7	11	36	—	—	—	—	—
88-89—University of Minnesota	WCHA	43	7	11	18	115	—	—	—	—	—
89-90—University of Minnesota	WCHA	46	25	41	66	34	—	—	—	—	—
90-91—University of Minnesota	WCHA	43	19	21	40	133	—	—	—	—	—
91-92—Utica	AHL	77	17	16	33	186	4	3	1	4	2
92-93—Utica	AHL	75	35	27	62	145	5	2	2	4	6
—New Jersey	NHL	4	2	1	3	9	—	—	—	—	—
93-94—New Jersey	NHL	13	1	0	1	23	2	1	0	1	4
—Albany	AHL	29	9	14	23	80	5	3	1	4	6
94-95—New Jersey	NHL	8	0	0	0	7	—	—	—	—	—
—Albany	AHL	1	1	0	1	6	—	—	—	—	—
—Tampa Bay	NHL	18	0	2	2	6	—	—	—	—	—
NHL totals		43	3	3	6	45	2	1	0	1	4

HANNAN, DAVE
C, SABRES

PERSONAL: Born November 26, 1961, in Sudbury, Ont. . . . 5-10/180. . . . Shoots left.
TRANSACTIONS/CAREER NOTES: Bruised shoulder; missed part of 1980-81 season. . . . Selected by Pittsburgh Penguins in 10th round (ninth Penguins pick, 196th overall) of NHL entry draft (June 10, 1981). . . . Injured knee and underwent surgery (January 9, 1987). . . . Traded by Penguins with C Craig Simpson, D Chris Joseph and D Moe Mantha to Edmonton Oilers for D Paul Coffey, LW Dave Hunter and RW Wayne Van Dorp (November 24, 1987). . . . Selected by Penguins in NHL waiver draft (October 3, 1988); LW Dave Hunter was taken by Oilers as compensation. . . . Suffered hip pointer (October 1988). . . . Sprained knee (March 1989). . . . Selected by Toronto Maple Leafs in NHL waiver draft for $7,500 (October 2, 1989). . . . Injured left knee ligaments (November 22, 1989). . . . Underwent surgery to left knee (December 18, 1989); missed 23 games. . . . Traded by Maple Leafs to Buffalo Sabres for fifth-round pick (RW Chris de Ruiter) in 1992 draft (March 10, 1992). . . . Injured shoulder (April 12, 1992). . . . Broke toe (January 19, 1993); missed three games. . . . Strained back (March 13, 1995); missed four games. . . . Suffered sore groin (April 9, 1995); missed one game.
STATISTICAL PLATEAUS: Three-goal games: 1987-88 (1).
MISCELLANEOUS: Member of Stanley Cup championship team (1988). . . . Member of silver-medal-winning Canadian Olympic team (1992).

Season Team	League	REGULAR SEASON					PLAYOFFS				
		Gms.	G	A	Pts.	PIM	Gms.	G	A	Pts.	PIM
77-78—Windsor	OMJHL	68	14	16	30	43	—	—	—	—	—
78-79—Sault Ste. Marie	OMJHL	26	7	8	15	13	—	—	—	—	—
79-80—Sault Ste. Marie	OMJHL	28	11	10	21	31	—	—	—	—	—
—Brantford	OMJHL	25	5	10	15	26	—	—	—	—	—

Season	Team	League	Gms.	G	A	Pts.	PIM	Gms.	G	A	Pts.	PIM
80-81	Brantford	OMJHL	56	46	35	81	155	6	2	4	6	20
81-82	Erie	AHL	76	33	37	70	129	—	—	—	—	—
	—Pittsburgh	NHL	1	0	0	0	0	—	—	—	—	—
82-83	Baltimore	AHL	5	2	2	4	13	—	—	—	—	—
	—Pittsburgh	NHL	74	11	22	33	127	—	—	—	—	—
83-84	Baltimore	AHL	47	18	24	42	98	10	2	6	8	27
	—Pittsburgh	NHL	24	2	3	5	33	—	—	—	—	—
84-85	Baltimore	AHL	49	20	25	45	91	—	—	—	—	—
	—Pittsburgh	NHL	30	6	7	13	43	—	—	—	—	—
85-86	Pittsburgh	NHL	75	17	18	35	91	—	—	—	—	—
86-87	Pittsburgh	NHL	58	10	15	25	56	—	—	—	—	—
87-88	Pittsburgh	NHL	21	4	3	7	23	—	—	—	—	—
	—Edmonton	NHL	51	9	11	20	43	12	1	1	2	8
88-89	Pittsburgh	NHL	72	10	20	30	157	8	0	1	1	4
89-90	Toronto	NHL	39	6	9	15	55	3	1	0	1	4
90-91	Toronto	NHL	74	11	23	34	82	—	—	—	—	—
91-92	Toronto	NHL	35	2	2	4	16	—	—	—	—	—
	—Canadian national team	Int'l	3	0	0	0	2	—	—	—	—	—
	—Canadian Olympic Team	Int'l	8	3	5	8	8	—	—	—	—	—
	—Buffalo	NHL	12	2	4	6	48	7	2	0	2	2
92-93	Buffalo	NHL	55	5	15	20	43	8	1	1	2	18
93-94	Buffalo	NHL	83	6	15	21	53	7	1	0	1	6
94-95	Buffalo	NHL	42	4	12	16	32	5	0	2	2	2
NHL totals			746	105	179	284	902	50	6	5	11	44

HANSEN, TAVIS
C/RW, JETS

PERSONAL: Born June 17, 1975, in Prince Albert, Sask. . . . 6-1/180. . . . Shoots right.
TRANSACTIONS/CAREER NOTES: Selected by Winnipeg Jets in third round (third Jets pick, 58th overall) of NHL entry draft (June 29, 1994).

Season	Team	League	Gms.	G	A	Pts.	PIM	Gms.	G	A	Pts.	PIM
93-94	Tacoma	WHL	71	23	31	54	122	8	1	3	4	17
94-95	Tacoma	WHL	71	32	41	73	142	4	1	1	2	8

HARDING, MIKE
RW, WHALERS

PERSONAL: Born February 24, 1971, in Edsow, Alta. . . . 6-4/221. . . . Shoots right.
COLLEGE: Northern Michigan.
TRANSACTIONS/CAREER NOTES: Selected by Hartford Whalers in sixth round (sixth Whalers pick, 119th overall) of NHL entry draft (June 22, 1991).
HONORS: Named to WCHA All-Star second team (1993-94).

Season	Team	League	Gms.	G	A	Pts.	PIM	Gms.	G	A	Pts.	PIM
91-92	Northern Michigan Univ.	WCHA	28	6	8	14	46	—	—	—	—	—
92-93	Northern Michigan Univ.	WCHA	39	17	18	35	66	—	—	—	—	—
93-94	Northern Michigan Univ.	WCHA	38	24	25	49	66	—	—	—	—	—
94-95	Northern Michigan Univ.	WCHA	40	16	22	38	68	—	—	—	—	—

HARKINS, BRETT
LW/C, PANTHERS

PERSONAL: Born July 2, 1970, in North Ridgefield, O. . . . 6-1/170. . . . Shoots left. . . . Full name: Brett Alan Harkins. . . . Brother of Todd Harkins, right winger in Florida Panthers system.
COLLEGE: Bowling Green State.
TRANSACTIONS/CAREER NOTES: Selected by New York Islanders in seventh round (ninth Islanders pick, 133rd overall) of NHL entry draft (June 17, 1989). . . . Signed as free agent by Adirondack Red Wings (1993). . . . Signed as free agent by Boston Bruins (July 6, 1994). . . . Signed as free agent by Florida Panthers (July 19, 1995).
HONORS: Named to CCHA All-Rookie team (1989-90).

Season	Team	League	Gms.	G	A	Pts.	PIM	Gms.	G	A	Pts.	PIM
87-88	Brockville	COJHL	55	21	55	76	36	—	—	—	—	—
88-89	Detroit Compuware	NAJHL	38	23	46	69	94	—	—	—	—	—
89-90	Bowling Green State	CCHA	41	11	43	54	45	—	—	—	—	—
90-91	Bowling Green State	CCHA	40	22	38	60	30	—	—	—	—	—
91-92	Bowling Green State	CCHA	34	8	39	47	32	—	—	—	—	—
92-93	Bowling Green State	CCHA	35	19	28	47	28	—	—	—	—	—
93-94	Adirondack	AHL	80	22	47	69	23	10	1	5	6	4
94-95	Providence	AHL	80	23	†69	92	32	13	8	14	22	4
	—Boston	NHL	1	0	1	1	0	—	—	—	—	—
NHL totals			1	0	1	1	0					

HARKINS, TODD
RW, PANTHERS

PERSONAL: Born October 8, 1968, in Cleveland. . . . 6-3/210. . . . Shoots right. . . . Full name: Todd Michael Harkins. . . . Brother of Brett Harkins, left winger/center in Florida Panthers system.
COLLEGE: Miami of Ohio.
TRANSACTIONS/CAREER NOTES: Selected by Calgary Flames in second round (second Flames pick, 42nd overall) of NHL entry

H

draft (June 11, 1988). . . . Traded by Flames to Hartford Whalers for LW Scott Morrow (January 24, 1994). . . . Fined $500 by Whalers for involvement in bar brawl (April 1, 1994). . . . Suffered from the flu (April 2, 1994); missed two games. . . . Signed as free agent by Chicago Wolves (September 9, 1994). . . . Traded by Wolves with D Ted Crowley to Houston Aeros for F Clayton Young, D Steve Gosselin and RW Brian Pellerin (February 16, 1995). . . . Signed as free agent by Florida Panthers (June 12, 1995).

				REGULAR SEASON					PLAYOFFS			
Season Team	League	Gms.	G	A	Pts.	PIM		Gms.	G	A	Pts.	PIM
86-87—Aurora Jr. B.	OHA	40	19	29	48	102		—	—	—	—	—
87-88—Miami of Ohio	CCHA	34	9	7	16	133		—	—	—	—	—
88-89—Miami of Ohio	CCHA	36	8	7	15	77		—	—	—	—	—
89-90—Miami of Ohio	CCHA	40	27	17	44	78		—	—	—	—	—
90-91—Salt Lake City	IHL	79	15	27	42	113		3	0	0	0	2
91-92—Salt Lake City	IHL	72	32	30	62	67		5	1	1	2	6
—Calgary	NHL	5	0	0	0	7		—	—	—	—	—
92-93—Salt Lake City	IHL	53	13	21	34	90		—	—	—	—	—
—Calgary	NHL	15	2	3	5	22		—	—	—	—	—
93-94—Saint John	AHL	38	13	9	22	64		—	—	—	—	—
—Springfield	AHL	1	0	3	3	0		—	—	—	—	—
—Hartford	NHL	28	1	0	1	49		—	—	—	—	—
94-95—Chicago	IHL	52	18	25	43	136		—	—	—	—	—
—Houston	IHL	25	9	10	19	77		4	1	1	2	28
NHL totals		48	3	3	6	78						

HARLOCK, DAVID
D, MAPLE LEAFS

PERSONAL: Born March 16, 1971, in Toronto. . . . 6-2/205. . . . Shoots left. . . . Full name: David Alan Harlock.
COLLEGE: Michigan.
TRANSACTIONS/CAREER NOTES: Injured knee (October 1988). . . . Selected by New Jersey Devils in second round (second Devils pick, 24th overall) of NHL entry draft (June 16, 1990). . . . Signed as free agent by Toronto Maple Leafs (August 20, 1993). . . . Loaned by Maple Leafs to Canadian Olympic Team (October 3, 1993).
MISCELLANEOUS: Member of silver-medal-winning Canadian Olympic team (1994).

				REGULAR SEASON					PLAYOFFS			
Season Team	League	Gms.	G	A	Pts.	PIM		Gms.	G	A	Pts.	PIM
86-87—Toronto Red Wings	MTHL	86	17	55	72	60		—	—	—	—	—
87-88—Toronto Red Wings	MTHL	70	16	56	72	100		—	—	—	—	—
88-89—St. Michael's Jr. B	ODHA	25	4	15	19	34		—	—	—	—	—
89-90—University of Michigan	CCHA	42	2	13	15	44		—	—	—	—	—
90-91—University of Michigan	CCHA	39	2	8	10	70		—	—	—	—	—
91-92—University of Michigan	CCHA	44	1	6	7	80		—	—	—	—	—
92-93—University of Michigan	CCHA	38	3	9	12	58		—	—	—	—	—
93-94—Canadian national team	Int'l	41	0	3	3	28		—	—	—	—	—
—Canadian Olympic Team	Int'l	8	0	0	0	8		—	—	—	—	—
—Toronto	NHL	6	0	0	0	0		—	—	—	—	—
—St. John's	AHL	10	0	3	3	2		9	0	0	0	6
94-95—St. John's	AHL	58	0	6	6	44		5	0	0	0	0
—Toronto	NHL	1	0	0	0	0		—	—	—	—	—
NHL totals		7	0	0	0	0						

HARLTON, TYLER
D, BLUES

PERSONAL: Born January 11, 1976, in Regina, Sask. . . . 6-3/201. . . . Shoots left.
COLLEGE: Michigan State.
TRANSACTIONS/CAREER NOTES: Selected by St. Louis Blues in fourth round (second Blues pick, 94th overall) of NHL entry draft (June 29, 1994).

				REGULAR SEASON					PLAYOFFS			
Season Team	League	Gms.	G	A	Pts.	PIM		Gms.	G	A	Pts.	PIM
93-94—Vernon	BCJHL	60	3	18	21	102		—	—	—	—	—
94-95—Michigan State	CCHA	39	1	4	5	55		—	—	—	—	—

HARTMAN, MIKE
LW, RANGERS

PERSONAL: Born February 7, 1967, in West Bloomfield, Mich. . . . 6-0/192. . . . Shoots left. . . . Full name: Michael Jay Hartman.
TRANSACTIONS/CAREER NOTES: Selected by Buffalo Sabres in seventh round (eighth Sabres pick, 131st overall) of NHL entry draft (June 21, 1986). . . . Suffered sore back (January 1989). . . . Sprained right ankle (December 1, 1989); missed five games. . . . Reinjured right ankle (December 29, 1989); missed five games. . . . Injured ankle (March 10, 1990). . . . Injured elbow (November 3, 1990); missed seven games. . . . Traded by Sabres with LW Darrin Shannon and D Dean Kennedy to Winnipeg Jets for RW Dave McLlwain, D Gordon Donnelly, fifth-round pick in 1992 draft (LW Yuri Khmylev) and future considerations (October 11, 1991). . . . Suffered from the flu (December 1991); missed one game. . . . Selected by Tampa Bay Lightning in NHL expansion draft (June 18, 1992). . . . Cut forearm (October 20, 1992); missed four games. . . . Bruised ribs (December 5, 1992); missed three games. . . . Traded by Lightning to New York Rangers for C Randy Gilhen (March 22, 1993). . . . Suffered injury (November 10, 1993); missed two games. . . . Loaned by Rangers to Detroit Vipers of IHL (March 8, 1995).
MISCELLANEOUS: Member of Stanley Cup championship team (1994).

				REGULAR SEASON					PLAYOFFS			
Season Team	League	Gms.	G	A	Pts.	PIM		Gms.	G	A	Pts.	PIM
84-85—Belleville	OHL	49	13	12	25	119		—	—	—	—	—

Season	Team	League	REGULAR SEASON Gms.	G	A	Pts.	PIM	PLAYOFFS Gms.	G	A	Pts.	PIM
85-86	—Belleville	OHL	4	2	1	3	5	—	—	—	—	—
	—North Bay	OHL	53	19	16	35	205	10	2	4	6	34
86-87	—North Bay	OHL	32	15	24	39	144	19	7	8	15	88
	—Buffalo	NHL	17	3	3	6	69	—	—	—	—	—
87-88	—Rochester	AHL	57	13	14	27	283	4	1	0	1	22
	—Buffalo	NHL	18	3	1	4	90	6	0	0	0	35
88-89	—Buffalo	NHL	70	8	9	17	316	5	0	0	0	34
89-90	—Buffalo	NHL	60	11	10	21	211	6	0	0	0	18
90-91	—Buffalo	NHL	60	9	3	12	204	2	0	0	0	17
91-92	—Winnipeg	NHL	75	4	4	8	264	2	0	0	0	2
92-93	—Tampa Bay	NHL	58	4	4	8	154	—	—	—	—	—
	—New York Rangers	NHL	3	0	0	0	6	—	—	—	—	—
93-94	—New York Rangers	NHL	35	1	1	2	70	—	—	—	—	—
94-95	—New York Rangers	NHL	1	0	0	0	4	—	—	—	—	—
	—Detroit	IHL	6	1	0	1	52	1	0	0	0	0
NHL totals			397	43	35	78	1388	21	0	0	0	106

HARVEY, TODD
RW/C, STARS

PERSONAL: Born February 17, 1975, in Hamilton, Ont.... 6-0/195.... Shoots right.
TRANSACTIONS/CAREER NOTES: Selected by Dallas Stars in first round (first Stars pick, ninth overall) of NHL entry draft (June 26, 1993).... Strained back (March 13, 1995); missed one game.
HONORS: Named to Can.HL All-Rookie team (1991-92).... Named to OHL Rookie All-Star team (1991-92).
STATISTICAL PLATEAUS: Three-goal games: 1994-95 (1).

Season	Team	League	REGULAR SEASON Gms.	G	A	Pts.	PIM	PLAYOFFS Gms.	G	A	Pts.	PIM
89-90	—Cambridge Jr. B	OHA	41	35	27	62	213	—	—	—	—	—
90-91	—Cambridge Jr. B	OHA	35	32	39	71	174	—	—	—	—	—
91-92	—Detroit	OHL	58	21	43	64	141	7	3	5	8	32
92-93	—Detroit	OHL	55	50	50	100	83	15	9	12	21	39
93-94	—Detroit	OHL	49	34	51	85	75	17	10	12	22	26
94-95	—Detroit	OHL	11	8	14	22	12	—	—	—	—	—
	—Dallas	NHL	40	11	9	20	67	5	0	0	0	8
NHL totals			40	11	9	20	67	5	0	0	0	8

HASEK, DOMINIK
G, SABRES

PERSONAL: Born January 29, 1965, in Pardubice, Czechoslovakia.... 5-11/168.... Catches left.... Name pronounced HA-shihk.
TRANSACTIONS/CAREER NOTES: Selected by Chicago Blackhawks in 10th round (11th Blackhawks pick, 199th overall) of NHL entry draft (June 8, 1983).... Traded by Blackhawks to Buffalo Sabres for G Stephane Beauregard and future considerations (August 7, 1992).... Injured groin (November 25, 1992); missed three games.... Pulled stomach muscle (January 6, 1993); missed six games.... Played in Europe during 1994-95 NHL lockout.... Strained rotator cuff (March 16, 1995); missed three games.
HONORS: Named Czechoslovakian League Player of the Year (1986-87, 1988-89 and 1989-90).... Named to Czechoslovakian League All-Star team (1988-89 and 1989-90).... Named to IHL All-Star first team (1990-91).... Named to NHL All-Rookie team (1991-92).... Won Vezina Trophy (1993-94 and 1994-95).... Shared William M. Jennings Trophy with Grant Fuhr (1993-94).... Named to THE SPORTING NEWS All-Star second team (1993-94).... Named to NHL All-Star first team (1993-94 and 1994-95).... Named to THE SPORTING NEWS All-Star first team (1994-95).

Season	Team	League	REGULAR SEASON Gms.	Min.	W	L	T	GA	SO	Avg.	PLAYOFFS Gms.	Min.	W	L	GA	SO	Avg.
81-82	—Pardubice	Czech.	12	661	...	...	...	34	0	3.09	—	—	—	—	—	—	—
82-83	—Pardubice	Czech.	42	2358	...	...	...	105	0	2.67	—	—	—	—	—	—	—
83-84	—Pardubice	Czech.	40	2304	...	...	...	108	0	2.81	—	—	—	—	—	—	—
84-85	—Pardubice	Czech.	42	2419	...	...	...	131	0	3.25	—	—	—	—	—	—	—
85-86	—Pardubice	Czech.	45	2689	...	...	...	138	0	3.08	—	—	—	—	—	—	—
86-87	—Pardubice	Czech.	23	2515	...	...	...	103	0	2.46	—	—	—	—	—	—	—
87-88	—Pardubice	Czech.	31	2265	...	...	...	98	0	2.60	—	—	—	—	—	—	—
	—Czech. Olympic Team	Int'l	8	217				18	...	4.98	—						
88-89	—Pardubice	Czech.	42	2507	...	...	...	114	0	2.73	—	—	—	—	—	—	—
89-90	—Dukla Jihlava	Czech.	40	2251	...	...	...	80	0	2.13	—	—	—	—	—	—	—
90-91	—Chicago	NHL	5	195	3	0	1	8	0	2.46	3	69	0	0	3	0	2.61
	—Indianapolis	IHL	33	1903	20	11	‡4	80	*5	*2.52	1	60	1	0	3	0	3.00
91-92	—Indianapolis	IHL	20	1162	7	10	‡3	69	1	3.56	—	—	—	—	—	—	—
	—Chicago	NHL	20	1014	10	4	1	44	1	2.60	3	158	0	2	8	0	3.04
92-93	—Buffalo	NHL	28	1429	11	10	4	75	0	3.15	1	45	1	0	1	0	1.33
93-94	—Buffalo	NHL	58	3358	30	20	6	109	†7	*1.95	7	484	3	4	13	2	*1.61
94-95	—HC Pardubice	Czech Rp	2	125	...	...	...	6	...	2.88	—	—	—	—	—	—	—
	—Buffalo	NHL	41	2416	19	14	7	85	†5	*2.11	5	309	1	4	18	0	3.50
NHL totals			152	8412	73	48	19	321	13	2.29	19	1065	5	10	43	2	2.42

HATCHER, DERIAN
D, STARS

PERSONAL: Born June 4, 1972, in Sterling Heights, Mich.... 6-5/225.... Shoots left. ... Brother of Kevin Hatcher, defenseman, Dallas Stars.
TRANSACTIONS/CAREER NOTES: Underwent knee surgery (January 1989).... Selected by Minnesota North Stars in first round (first North Stars pick, eighth overall) of NHL

entry draft (June 16, 1990). . . . Suspended 10 games by NHL (December 1991). . . . Fractured ankle in off-ice incident (January 19, 1992); missed 21 games. . . . Sprained knee (January 6, 1993); missed 14 games. . . . Suspended one game by NHL for game misconduct penalties (March 9, 1993). . . . North Stars franchise moved from Minnesota to Dallas and renamed Stars for 1993-94 season. . . . Sprained ankle (February 2, 1995); missed one game. . . . Suffered staph infection on little finger (February 14, 1995); missed four games. . . . Injured medial collateral ligament in right knee (May 1, 1995); missed entire playoffs.

Season Team	League	REGULAR SEASON					PLAYOFFS				
		Gms.	G	A	Pts.	PIM	Gms.	G	A	Pts.	PIM
88-89—Detroit G.P.D.	MNHL	51	19	35	54	100	—	—	—	—	—
89-90—North Bay	OHL	64	14	38	52	81	5	2	3	5	8
90-91—North Bay	OHL	64	13	50	63	163	10	2	10	12	28
91-92—Minnesota	NHL	43	8	4	12	88	5	0	2	2	8
92-93—Minnesota	NHL	67	4	15	19	178	—	—	—	—	—
—Kalamazoo	IHL	2	1	2	3	21	—	—	—	—	—
93-94—Dallas	NHL	83	12	19	31	211	9	0	2	2	14
94-95—Dallas	NHL	43	5	11	16	105	—	—	—	—	—
NHL totals		236	29	49	78	582	14	0	4	4	22

HATCHER, KEVIN
D, STARS

PERSONAL: Born September 9, 1966, in Detroit. . . . 6-4/225. . . . Shoots right. . . . Full name: Kevin John Hatcher. . . . Brother of Derian Hatcher, defenseman, Dallas Stars.
TRANSACTIONS/CAREER NOTES: Selected by Washington Capitals as underage junior in first round (first Capitals pick, 17th overall) of NHL entry draft (June 9, 1984). . . . Tore cartilage in left knee (October 1987). . . . Pulled groin (January 1989). . . . Fractured two metatarsal bones in left foot (February 5, 1989); missed 15 games. . . . Sprained left knee (April 27, 1990). . . . Did not attend Capitals training camp due to contract dispute (September 1990). . . . Injured right knee (November 10, 1990). . . . Suspended one game by NHL for game misconduct penalties (February 2, 1993). . . . Fractured right hand (December 23, 1993); missed 10 games. . . . Suffered from the flu (March 29, 1994); missed one game. . . . Pulled thigh (April 9, 1994); missed one game. . . . Traded by Capitals to Dallas Stars for D Mark Tinordi and rights to D Rick Mrozik (January 18, 1995).
HONORS: Named to OHL All-Star second team (1984-85). . . . Played in NHL All-Star Game (1990 through 1992).
STATISTICAL PLATEAUS: Three-goal games: 1992-93 (1).

Season Team	League	REGULAR SEASON					PLAYOFFS				
		Gms.	G	A	Pts.	PIM	Gms.	G	A	Pts.	PIM
83-84—North Bay	OHL	67	10	39	49	61	4	2	2	4	11
84-85—North Bay	OHL	58	26	37	63	75	8	5	8	13	9
—Washington	NHL	2	1	0	1	0	1	0	0	0	0
85-86—Washington	NHL	79	9	10	19	119	9	1	1	2	19
86-87—Washington	NHL	78	8	16	24	144	7	1	0	1	20
87-88—Washington	NHL	71	14	27	41	137	14	5	7	12	55
88-89—Washington	NHL	62	13	27	40	101	6	1	4	5	20
89-90—Washington	NHL	80	13	41	54	102	11	0	8	8	32
90-91—Washington	NHL	79	24	50	74	69	11	3	3	6	8
91-92—Washington	NHL	79	17	37	54	105	7	2	4	6	19
92-93—Washington	NHL	83	34	45	79	114	6	0	1	1	14
93-94—Washington	NHL	72	16	24	40	108	11	3	4	7	37
94-95—Dallas	NHL	47	10	19	29	66	5	2	1	3	2
NHL totals		732	159	296	455	1065	88	18	33	51	226

HAWERCHUK, DALE
C, BLUES

PERSONAL: Born April 4, 1963, in Toronto. . . . 5-11/190. . . . Shoots left. . . . Name pronounced HOW-uhr-CHUHK.
TRANSACTIONS/CAREER NOTES: Selected by Winnipeg Jets as underage junior in first round (first Jets pick, first overall) of NHL entry draft (June 10, 1981). . . . Broke rib (April 13, 1985). . . . Fractured cheekbone (February 1, 1989). . . . Traded by Jets with first-round pick in 1990 draft (LW Brad May) to Buffalo Sabres for D Phil Housley, LW Scott Arniel, RW Jeff Parker and first-round pick (C Keith Tkachuk) in 1990 draft (June 16, 1990). . . . Injured hip (March 8, 1992); missed one game. . . . Sprained right knee (February 12, 1993); missed three games. . . . Pulled groin (February 25, 1995); missed six games. . . . Suffered partial groin tear (March 14, 1995); missed nine games. . . . Strained hip (April 14, 1995); missed last 10 games of season and first three playoff games. . . . Signed as free agent by St. Louis Blues (July 8, 1995).
HONORS: Won Instructeurs Trophy (1979-80). . . . Won Guy Lafleur Trophy (1979-80). . . . Named to Memorial Cup All-Star team (1979-80 and 1980-81). . . . Won Can.HL Player of the Year Award (1980-81). . . . Won Michel Briere Trophy (1980-81). . . . Won Jean Beliveau Trophy (1980-81). . . . Won Association of Journalists for Major Junior League Hockey Trophy (1980-81). . . . Won CCM Trophy (1980-81). . . . Named to QMJHL All-Star first team (1980-81). . . . Named NHL Rookie of the Year by THE SPORTING NEWS (1981-82). . . . Won Calder Memorial Trophy (1981-82). . . . Played in NHL All-Star Game (1982, 1985, 1986 and 1988). . . . Named to THE SPORTING NEWS All-Star second team (1984-85). . . . Named to NHL All-Star second team (1984-85).
RECORDS: Holds NHL single-game record for most assists in one period—5 (March 6, 1984).
STATISTICAL PLATEAUS: Three-goal games: 1981-82 (2), 1982-83 (3), 1983-84 (1), 1984-85 (3), 1988-89 (2), 1990-91 (1), 1991-92 (1). Total: 13.
MISCELLANEOUS: Captain of Winnipeg Jets (1984-85 through 1989-90).
STATISTICAL NOTES: Youngest player in NHL history to have 100-point season (18 years, 351 days).

Season Team	League	REGULAR SEASON					PLAYOFFS				
		Gms.	G	A	Pts.	PIM	Gms.	G	A	Pts.	PIM
79-80—Cornwall	QMJHL	72	37	66	103	21	18	20	25	45	0
80-81—Cornwall	QMJHL	72	*81	*102	*183	69	19	15	20	35	0
81-82—Winnipeg	NHL	80	45	58	103	47	4	1	7	8	5
82-83—Winnipeg	NHL	79	40	51	91	31	3	1	4	5	8

Season Team	League	REGULAR SEASON					PLAYOFFS				
		Gms.	G	A	Pts.	PIM	Gms.	G	A	Pts.	PIM
83-84—Winnipeg	NHL	80	37	65	102	73	3	1	1	2	0
84-85—Winnipeg	NHL	80	53	77	130	74	3	2	1	3	4
85-86—Winnipeg	NHL	80	46	59	105	44	3	0	3	3	0
86-87—Winnipeg	NHL	80	47	53	100	54	10	5	8	13	4
87-88—Winnipeg	NHL	80	44	77	121	59	5	3	4	7	16
88-89—Winnipeg	NHL	75	41	55	96	28	—	—	—	—	—
89-90—Winnipeg	NHL	79	26	55	81	60	7	3	5	8	2
90-91—Buffalo	NHL	80	31	58	89	32	6	2	4	6	10
91-92—Buffalo	NHL	77	23	75	98	27	7	2	5	7	0
92-93—Buffalo	NHL	81	16	80	96	52	8	5	9	14	2
93-94—Buffalo	NHL	81	35	51	86	91	7	0	7	7	4
94-95—Buffalo	NHL	23	5	11	16	2	2	0	0	0	0
NHL totals		1055	489	825	1314	674	68	25	58	83	55

HAWGOOD, GREG
D, PENGUINS

PERSONAL: Born August 10, 1968, in St. Albert, Alta. . . . 5-10/190. . . . Shoots left. . . . Full name: Gregory William Hawgood.
TRANSACTIONS/CAREER NOTES: Selected by Boston Bruins as underage junior in 10th round (ninth Bruins pick, 202nd overall) of NHL entry draft (June 21, 1986). . . . Announced that he would play in Italy for 1990-91 season (July 1990). . . . Traded by Bruins to Edmonton Oilers for C Vladimir Ruzicka (October 22, 1990). . . . Traded by Oilers with C Josef Beranek to Philadelphia Flyers for D Brian Benning (January 16, 1993). . . . Traded by Flyers to Florida Panthers for future considerations (November 28, 1993). . . . Bruised left thumb (January 13, 1994); missed seven games. . . . Traded by Panthers to Pittsburgh Penguins for LW Jeff Daniels (March 19, 1994). . . . Dislocated left shoulder (February 14, 1995); missed eight games.
HONORS: Named to WHL (West) All-Star first team (1985-86 through 1987-88). . . . Won Can.HL Defenseman of the Year Award (1987-88). . . . Won Bill Hunter Trophy (1987-88). . . . Won Eddie Shore Plaque (1991-92). . . . Named to AHL All-Star first team (1991-92).

Season Team	League	REGULAR SEASON					PLAYOFFS				
		Gms.	G	A	Pts.	PIM	Gms.	G	A	Pts.	PIM
83-84—Kamloops	WHL	49	10	23	33	39	—	—	—	—	—
84-85—Kamloops	WHL	66	25	40	65	72	—	—	—	—	—
85-86—Kamloops	WHL	71	34	85	119	86	16	9	22	31	16
86-87—Kamloops	WHL	61	30	93	123	139	—	—	—	—	—
87-88—Boston	NHL	1	0	0	0	0	3	1	0	1	0
—Kamloops	WHL	63	48	85	133	142	16	10	16	26	33
88-89—Boston	NHL	56	16	24	40	84	10	0	2	2	2
—Maine	AHL	21	2	9	11	41	—	—	—	—	—
89-90—Boston	NHL	77	11	27	38	76	15	1	3	4	12
90-91—Asiago	Italy	2	. . .	. . .	0	. . .	—	—	—	—	—
—Maine	AHL	5	0	1	1	13	—	—	—	—	—
—Cape Breton	AHL	55	10	32	42	73	4	0	3	3	23
—Edmonton	NHL	6	0	1	1	6	—	—	—	—	—
91-92—Cape Breton	AHL	56	20	55	75	26	3	2	2	4	0
—Edmonton	NHL	20	2	11	13	22	13	0	3	3	23
92-93—Edmonton	NHL	29	5	13	18	35	—	—	—	—	—
—Philadelphia	NHL	40	6	22	28	39	—	—	—	—	—
93-94—Philadelphia	NHL	19	3	12	15	19	—	—	—	—	—
—Florida	NHL	33	2	14	16	9	—	—	—	—	—
—Pittsburgh	NHL	12	1	2	3	8	1	0	0	0	0
94-95—Cleveland	IHL	—	—	—	—	—	3	1	0	1	4
NHL totals		293	46	126	172	298	42	2	8	10	37

HAY, DWAYNE
LW, CAPITALS

PERSONAL: Born February 11, 1977, in London, Ont. . . . 6-1/183. . . . Shoots left.
HIGH SCHOOL: Bishop MacDonnell (Guelph, Ont.).
TRANSACTIONS/CAREER NOTES: Selected by Washington Capitals in second round (third Capitals pick, 43rd overall) of NHL entry draft (July 8, 1995).

Season Team	League	REGULAR SEASON					PLAYOFFS				
		Gms.	G	A	Pts.	PIM	Gms.	G	A	Pts.	PIM
93-94—Listowel Jr. B	OHA	48	10	24	34	56	—	—	—	—	—
94-95—Guelph	OHL	65	26	28	54	37	14	5	7	12	6

HEALEY, PAUL
RW, FLYERS

PERSONAL: Born March 20, 1975, in Edmonton. . . . 6-2/185. . . . Shoots right.
TRANSACTIONS/CAREER NOTES: Selected by Philadelphia Flyers in eighth round (seventh Flyers pick, 192nd overall) of NHL entry draft (June 26, 1993).
HONORS: Named to WHL (East) All-Star second team (1994-95).

Season Team	League	REGULAR SEASON					PLAYOFFS				
		Gms.	G	A	Pts.	PIM	Gms.	G	A	Pts.	PIM
92-93—Prince Albert	WHL	72	12	20	32	66	—	—	—	—	—
93-94—Prince Albert	WHL	63	23	26	49	70	—	—	—	—	—
94-95—Prince Albert	WHL	71	43	50	93	67	12	3	4	7	2

H

HEALY, GLENN

G, RANGERS

PERSONAL: Born August 23, 1962, in Pickering, Ont.... 5-10/183.... Catches left.
COLLEGE: Western Michigan.
TRANSACTIONS/CAREER NOTES: Signed as free agent by Los Angeles Kings (June 13, 1985)....
Signed as free agent by New York Islanders (August 16, 1989); Kings received fourth-round pick in 1990 draft (traded to Minnesota) as compensation.... Strained left ankle ligaments (October 13, 1990); missed eight games.... Fractured right index finger (November 10, 1991); missed five games.... Fractured right thumb (January 3, 1992); missed 10 games.... Severed tip of finger in practice and underwent reconstructive surgery (March 2, 1992); missed 13 games.... Suffered from tendinitis in right wrist (January 9, 1993); missed four games.... Selected by Mighty Ducks of Anaheim in NHL expansion draft (June 24, 1993).... Selected by Tampa Bay Lightning in Phase II of NHL expansion draft (June 25, 1993).... Traded by Lightning to New York Rangers for third-round pick in 1993 draft; Lightning reacquired their original pick which they had traded away earlier (June 25, 1993).
HONORS: Named to NCAA All-America West second team (1984-85).... Named to CCHA All-Star second team (1984-85).
MISCELLANEOUS: Member of Stanley Cup championship team (1994).

Season Team	League	REGULAR SEASON							PLAYOFFS						
		Gms.	Min.	W	L	T	GA	SO	Avg.	Gms.	Min.	W	L	GA	SO	Avg.
81-82—Western Michigan U.....	CCHA	27	1569	7	19	1	116	0	4.44	—	—	—	—	—	—	—
82-83—Western Michigan U.....	CCHA	30	1733	8	19	2	116	0	4.02	—	—	—	—	—	—	—
83-84—Western Michigan U.....	CCHA	38	2242	19	16	3	146	0	3.91	—	—	—	—	—	—	—
84-85—Western Michigan U.....	CCHA	37	2172	21	14	2	118	...	3.26	—	—	—	—	—	—	—
85-86—Toledo	IHL	7	402	...	...	...	28	0	4.18	—	—	—	—	—	—	—
—New Haven	AHL	43	2410	21	15	4	160	0	3.98	2	119	0	2	11	0	5.55
—Los Angeles	NHL	1	51	0	0	0	6	0	7.06	—	—	—	—	—	—	—
86-87—New Haven	AHL	47	2828	21	15	0	173	1	3.67	7	427	3	4	19	0	2.67
87-88—Los Angeles	NHL	34	1869	12	18	1	135	1	4.33	4	240	1	3	20	0	5.00
88-89—Los Angeles	NHL	48	2699	25	19	2	192	0	4.27	3	97	0	1	6	0	3.71
89-90—New York Islanders	NHL	39	2197	12	19	6	128	2	3.50	4	166	1	2	9	0	3.25
90-91—New York Islanders	NHL	53	2999	18	24	9	166	0	3.32	—	—	—	—	—	—	—
91-92—New York Islanders	NHL	37	1960	14	16	4	124	1	3.80	—	—	—	—	—	—	—
92-93—New York Islanders	NHL	47	2655	22	20	2	146	1	3.30	18	1109	9	8	59	0	3.19
93-94—New York Rangers	NHL	29	1368	10	12	2	69	2	3.03	2	68	0	1	0	0	0.88
94-95—New York Rangers	NHL	17	888	8	6	1	35	1	2.36	5	230	2	1	13	0	3.39
NHL totals............		305	16686	121	134	27	1001	8	3.60	36	1910	13	15	108	0	3.39

HEBERT, GUY

G, MIGHTY DUCKS

PERSONAL: Born January 7, 1967, in Troy, N.Y.... 5-11/185.... Catches left.... Full name: Guy Andrew Hebert.... Name pronounced GEE ay-BAIR.
HIGH SCHOOL: LaSalle Institute (Troy, N.Y.).
COLLEGE: Hamilton (N.Y.).
TRANSACTIONS/CAREER NOTES: Selected by St. Louis Blues in eighth round (eighth Blues choice, 159th overall) of NHL entry draft (June 13, 1987).... Selected by Mighty Ducks of Anaheim in NHL expansion draft (June 24, 1993).... Suffered concussion (April 30, 1995); missed one game.
HONORS: Shared James Norris Memorial Trophy with Pat Jablonski (1990-91).... Named to IHL All-Star second team (1990-91).

Season Team	League	REGULAR SEASON							PLAYOFFS						
		Gms.	Min.	W	L	T	GA	SO	Avg.	Gms.	Min.	W	L	GA	SO	Avg.
85-86—Hamilton College..........	Div. II	18	1011	4	12	2	69	2	4.09	—	—	—	—	—	—	—
86-87—Hamilton College..........	Div. II	18	1070	12	5	0	40	0	2.24	—	—	—	—	—	—	—
87-88—Hamilton College..........	Div. II	8	450	5	3	0	19	0	2.53	—	—	—	—	—	—	—
88-89—Hamilton College..........	Div. II	25	1453	18	7	0	62	0	2.56	—	—	—	—	—	—	—
89-90—Peoria	IHL	30	1706	7	13	‡7	124	1	4.36	2	76	0	1	5	0	3.95
90-91—Peoria	IHL	36	2093	24	10	‡1	100	2	*2.87	8	458	3	4	32	0	4.19
91-92—Peoria	IHL	29	1731	20	9	‡0	98	0	3.40	4	239	3	1	9	0	*2.26
—St. Louis	NHL	13	738	5	5	1	36	0	2.93	—	—	—	—	—	—	—
92-93—St. Louis	NHL	24	1210	8	8	2	74	1	3.67	1	2	0	0	0	0	0.00
93-94—Anaheim	NHL	52	2991	20	27	3	141	2	2.83	—	—	—	—	—	—	—
94-95—Anaheim	NHL	39	2092	12	20	4	109	2	3.13	—	—	—	—	—	—	—
NHL totals...........		128	7031	45	60	10	360	5	3.07	1	2	0	0	0		0

HECHT, JOCHEN

C, BLUES

PERSONAL: Born June 21, 1977, in Mannheim, Germany.... 6-1/180.... Shoots left.
TRANSACTIONS/CAREER NOTES: Selected by St. Louis Blues in second round (first Blues pick, 49th overall) of NHL entry draft (July 8, 1995).

Season Team	League	REGULAR SEASON					PLAYOFFS				
		Gms.	G	A	Pts.	PIM	Gms.	G	A	Pts.	PIM
94-95—Mannheim	Germany	43	11	12	23	68	10	5	4	9	12

HEDICAN, BRET

D, CANUCKS

PERSONAL: Born August 10, 1970, in St. Paul, Minn.... 6-2/195.... Shoots left.... Full name: Bret Michael Hedican.... Name pronounced HEHD-ih-kuhn.
HIGH SCHOOL: North St. Paul (Minn.).
COLLEGE: St. Cloud (Minn.) State.
TRANSACTIONS/CAREER NOTES: Selected by St. Louis Blues in 10th round (10th Blues pick, 198th overall) of NHL entry draft (June 11, 1988).... Sprained knee ligaments (September 27, 1992); missed first 15 games of season.... Injured shoulder (October 23, 1993); missed three games.... Injured groin (January 18, 1994); missed six games.... Traded by Blues with D Jeff Brown and C Nathan LaFayette to Vancouver Canucks for C Craig Janney (March 21, 1994).... Strained groin (March 27, 1994); missed three games.
HONORS: Named to WCHA All-Star first team (1990-91).

Season	Team	League	REGULAR SEASON Gms.	G	A	Pts.	PIM	PLAYOFFS Gms.	G	A	Pts.	PIM
88-89	St. Cloud State	WCHA	28	5	3	8	28	—	—	—	—	—
89-90	St. Cloud State	WCHA	36	4	17	21	37	—	—	—	—	—
90-91	St. Cloud State	WCHA	41	18	30	48	52	—	—	—	—	—
91-92	U.S. national team	Int'l	54	1	8	9	59	—	—	—	—	—
	U.S. Olympic Team	Int'l	8	0	0	0	4	—	—	—	—	—
	St. Louis	NHL	4	1	0	1	0	5	0	0	0	0
92-93	Peoria	IHL	19	0	8	8	10	—	—	—	—	—
	St. Louis	NHL	42	0	8	8	30	10	0	0	0	14
93-94	St. Louis	NHL	61	0	11	11	64	—	—	—	—	—
	Vancouver......................	NHL	8	0	1	1	0	24	1	6	7	16
94-95	Vancouver......................	NHL	45	2	11	13	34	11	0	2	2	6
	NHL totals................		160	3	31	34	128	50	1	8	9	36

HEINZE, STEVE
RW, BRUINS

PERSONAL: Born January 30, 1970, in Lawrence, Mass. . . . 5-11/180. . . . Shoots right. . . . Full name: Stephen Herbert Heinze. . . . Name pronounced HIGHNS.
HIGH SCHOOL: Lawrence Academy (Groton, Mass.).
COLLEGE: Boston College.
TRANSACTIONS/CAREER NOTES: Selected by Boston Bruins in second round (second Bruins pick, 60th overall) of NHL entry draft (June 11, 1988). . . . Injured shoulder (May 1, 1992). . . . Injured shoulder (March 20, 1993); missed 11 games. . . . Injured knee (February 18, 1994); missed five games. . . . Reinjured knee (March 26, 1994); missed two games.
HONORS: Named to Hockey East All-Rookie team (1988-89). . . . Named to NCAA All-America East first team (1989-90). . . . Named to Hockey East All-Star first team (1989-90).
STATISTICAL PLATEAUS: Three-goal games: 1992-93 (1).

Season	Team	League	REGULAR SEASON Gms.	G	A	Pts.	PIM	PLAYOFFS Gms.	G	A	Pts.	PIM
86-87	Lawrence Academy	Mass. H.S.	23	26	24	50	...	—	—	—	—	—
87-88	Lawrence Academy	Mass. H.S.	23	30	25	55	...	—	—	—	—	—
88-89	Boston College	Hockey East	36	26	23	49	26	—	—	—	—	—
89-90	Boston College	Hockey East	40	27	36	63	41	—	—	—	—	—
90-91	Boston College	Hockey East	35	21	26	47	35	—	—	—	—	—
91-92	U.S. national team	Int'l	49	18	15	33	38	—	—	—	—	—
	U.S. Olympic Team	Int'l	8	1	3	4	8	—	—	—	—	—
	Boston	NHL	14	3	4	7	6	7	0	3	3	17
92-93	Boston	NHL	73	18	13	31	24	4	1	1	2	2
93-94	Boston	NHL	77	10	11	21	32	13	2	3	5	7
94-95	Boston	NHL	36	7	9	16	23	5	0	0	0	0
	NHL totals................		200	38	37	75	85	29	3	7	10	26

HEJDUK, MILAN
RW, DENVER

PERSONAL: Born February 14, 1976, in Usti-nad-Labem, Czechoslovakia. . . . 5-11/163. . . . Shoots right.
TRANSACTIONS/CAREER NOTES: Selected by Quebec Nordiques in fourth round (sixth Nordiques pick, 72nd overall) of NHL entry draft (June 29, 1994). . . . Nordiques franchise moved to Denver for 1995-96 season.
HONORS: Named Czech Republic League Rookie of the Year (1993-94).

Season	Team	League	REGULAR SEASON Gms.	G	A	Pts.	PIM	PLAYOFFS Gms.	G	A	Pts.	PIM
93-94	HC Pardubice	Czech Rep.	22	6	3	9	...	10	5	1	6	...
94-95	HC Pardubice	Czech Rep.	43	11	13	24	...	—	—	—	—	—

HENDRICKSON, DARBY
C, MAPLE LEAFS

PERSONAL: Born August 28, 1972, in Richfield, Minn. . . . 6-0/185. . . . Shoots left.
HIGH SCHOOL: Richfield (Minn.).
COLLEGE: Minnesota.
TRANSACTIONS/CAREER NOTES: Selected by Toronto Maple Leafs in fourth round (third Maple Leafs pick, 73rd overall) of NHL entry draft (June 16, 1990).
HONORS: Won WCHA Rookie of the Year Award (1991-92). . . . Named to WCHA All-Rookie team (1991-92).

Season	Team	League	REGULAR SEASON Gms.	G	A	Pts.	PIM	PLAYOFFS Gms.	G	A	Pts.	PIM
87-88	Richfield H.S....................	Minn. H.S.	22	12	9	21	10	—	—	—	—	—
88-89	Richfield H.S....................	Minn. H.S.	22	22	20	42	12	—	—	—	—	—
89-90	Richfield H.S....................	Minn. H.S.	24	23	27	50	49	—	—	—	—	—
90-91	Richfield H.S....................	Minn. H.S.	27	32	29	61	...	—	—	—	—	—
91-92	University of Minnesota ...	WCHA	41	25	28	53	61	—	—	—	—	—
92-93	University of Minnesota ...	WCHA	31	12	15	27	35	—	—	—	—	—
93-94	U.S. national team	Int'l	59	12	16	28	30	—	—	—	—	—
	U.S. Olympic Team	Int'l	8	0	0	0	6	—	—	—	—	—
	St. John's	AHL	6	4	1	5	4	3	1	1	2	0
	Toronto..........................	NHL	—	—	—	—	—	2	0	0	0	0
94-95	St. John's	AHL	59	16	20	36	48	—	—	—	—	—
	Toronto..........................	NHL	8	0	1	1	4	—	—	—	—	—
	NHL totals................		8	0	1	1	4	2	0	0	0	0

H

HERPERGER, CHRIS
LW, FLYERS

PERSONAL: Born February 24, 1974, in Esterhazy, Sask.... 6-0/195.... Shoots left.
TRANSACTIONS/CAREER NOTES: Signed by Philadelphia Flyers in 10th round (10th Flyers pick, 223rd overall) of NHL entry draft (June 20, 1992).
HONORS: Named to WHL (West) All-Star second team (1994-95).

			REGULAR SEASON				PLAYOFFS				
Season Team	League	Gms.	G	A	Pts.	PIM	Gms.	G	A	Pts.	PIM
90-91—Swift Current	WHL	10	0	1	1	5	—	—	—	—	—
91-92—Swift Current	WHL	72	14	19	33	44	8	0	1	1	9
92-93—Seattle	WHL	66	29	18	47	61	5	1	1	2	6
93-94—Seattle	WHL	71	44	51	95	110	9	12	10	22	12
94-95—Seattle	WHL	59	49	52	101	106	4	4	0	4	6
—Hershey	AHL	4	0	0	0	0	—	—	—	—	—

HERR, MATT
C, CAPITALS

PERSONAL: Born May 26, 1976, in New Windsor, N.Y.... 6-1/180.... Shoots left.
HIGH SCHOOL: Hotchkiss (Lakeville, Conn.).
COLLEGE: Michigan.
TRANSACTIONS/CAREER NOTES: Selected by Washington Capitals in fourth round (fourth Capitals pick, 93rd overall) of NHL entry draft (June 29, 1994).

			REGULAR SEASON				PLAYOFFS				
Season Team	League	Gms.	G	A	Pts.	PIM	Gms.	G	A	Pts.	PIM
90-91—Hotchkiss	Conn. H.S.	26	9	5	14	...	—	—	—	—	—
91-92—Hotchkiss	Conn. H.S.	25	17	16	33	...	—	—	—	—	—
92-93—Hotchkiss	Conn. H.S.	24	48	30	78	...	—	—	—	—	—
93-94—Hotchkiss	Conn. H.S.	20	28	19	47	...	—	—	—	—	—
94-95—University of Michigan	CCHA	37	11	8	19	51	—	—	—	—	—

HERTER, JASON
D, STARS

PERSONAL: Born October 2, 1970, in Hafford, Sask.... 6-1/190.... Shoots right.
COLLEGE: North Dakota.
TRANSACTIONS/CAREER NOTES: Strained shoulder (September 1988).... Selected by Vancouver Canucks in first round (first Canucks pick, eighth overall) of NHL entry draft (June 17, 1989).... Signed as free agent by Dallas Stars (August 5, 1993).
HONORS: Named to WCHA All-Star second team (1989-90 and 1990-91).

			REGULAR SEASON				PLAYOFFS				
Season Team	League	Gms.	G	A	Pts.	PIM	Gms.	G	A	Pts.	PIM
87-88—Notre Dame	SJHL	54	5	33	38	152	—	—	—	—	—
88-89—Univ. of North Dakota	WCHA	41	8	24	32	62	—	—	—	—	—
89-90—Univ. of North Dakota	WCHA	38	11	39	50	40	—	—	—	—	—
90-91—Univ. of North Dakota	WCHA	39	11	26	37	52	—	—	—	—	—
91-92—Milwaukee	IHL	56	7	18	25	34	1	0	0	0	2
92-93—Hamilton	AHL	70	7	16	23	68	—	—	—	—	—
93-94—Kalamazoo	IHL	68	14	28	42	92	5	3	0	3	14
94-95—Kalamazoo	IHL	60	12	20	32	70	16	2	8	10	10

HEWSON, RUSS
LW, JETS

PERSONAL: Born January 12, 1975, in Lloydminster, B.C.... 6-0/191.... Shoots left.
HIGH SCHOOL: Swift Current (Sask.) Comprehensive.
TRANSACTIONS/CAREER NOTES: Selected by Winnipeg Jets in 11th round (13th Jets pick, 285th overall) of NHL entry draft (June 26, 1993).

			REGULAR SEASON				PLAYOFFS				
Season Team	League	Gms.	G	A	Pts.	PIM	Gms.	G	A	Pts.	PIM
92-93—Swift Current	WHL	70	6	20	26	39	17	2	4	6	4
93-94—Swift Current	WHL	48	15	25	40	31	—	—	—	—	—
—Regina	WHL	22	8	12	20	24	4	1	2	3	2
94-95—Regina	WHL	57	23	24	47	43	4	2	0	2	6

HEXTALL, RON
G, FLYERS

PERSONAL: Born May 3, 1964, in Winnipeg.... 6-3/192.... Catches left.
TRANSACTIONS/CAREER NOTES: Selected by Philadelphia Flyers as underage junior in sixth round (sixth Flyers pick, 119th overall) of NHL entry draft (June 9, 1982).... Suspended eight games by NHL for slashing (May 1987).... Pulled hamstring (March 7, 1989).... Suspended first 12 games of 1989-90 season by NHL for attacking opposing player in final playoff game (May 11, 1989).... Did not attend training camp due to a contract dispute (September 1989).... Pulled groin (November 4, 1989).... Pulled hamstring (November 15, 1989).... Tore right groin muscle (December 13, 1989); missed 29 games.... Injured left groin (March 8, 1990).... Pulled groin (October 11, 1990); missed five games.... Sprained medial collateral ligament in left knee (October 27, 1990); missed five weeks.... Tore groin muscle (March 12, 1991); missed nine games.... Suffered from the flu (November 14, 1991); missed one game.... Developed shoulder tendinitis (November 27, 1991); missed nine games.... Traded by Flyers with C Mike Ricci, C Peter Forsberg, D Steve Duchesne, D Kerry Huffman, first-round pick in 1993 draft (G Jocelyn Thibault), cash and future considerations to Quebec Nordiques for C Eric Lindros (June 20, 1992); Flyers sent LW Chris Simon and first-round pick in 1994 draft (traded to Toronto Maple Leafs) to Nordiques to complete deal (July 21, 1992).... Strained muscle in left thigh (February 20, 1993); missed 14 games.... Traded by Nordiques with first-round pick in 1993 draft to New York Islanders for G Mark Fitzpatrick and first-round pick (C Adam Deadmarsh) in 1993 draft (June 20, 1993).... Traded by Islanders with sixth-round pick in 1995 draft (D Dimitri Tertyshny) to Flyers for G Tommy Soderstrom (September 22, 1994).... Injured groin (February 3, 1995); missed three games.
HONORS: Won Dudley (Red) Garrett Memorial Trophy (1985-86).... Named to AHL All-Star first team (1985-86).... Named NHL Rookie of the Year by THE SPORTING NEWS (1986-87).... Won Vezina Trophy (1986-87).... Won Conn Smythe Trophy

(1986-87). . . . Named to THE SPORTING NEWS All-Star second team (1986-87). . . . Named to NHL All-Star first team (1986-87). . . . Named to NHL All-Rookie team (1986-87). . . . Played in NHL All-Star Game (1988).
STATISTICAL NOTES: Scored a goal into a Washington empty net, becoming the first goalie to score a goal in Stanley Cup play (April 11, 1989).

Season	Team	League	Gms.	Min.	W	L	T	GA	SO	Avg.	Gms.	Min.	W	L	GA	SO	Avg.
80-81—Melville		SJHL	42	2127	...	...	...	254	0	7.17	—	—	—	—	—	—	—
81-82—Brandon		WHL	30	1398	12	11	0	133	0	5.71	3	103	0	2	16	0	9.32
82-83—Brandon		WHL	44	2589	13	30	0	249	0	5.77	—	—	—	—	—	—	—
83-84—Brandon		WHL	46	2670	29	13	2	190	0	4.27	10	592	5	5	37	0	3.75
84-85—Kalamazoo		IHL	19	1103	6	11	‡1	80	0	4.35	—	—	—	—	—	—	—
—Hershey		AHL	11	555	4	6	0	34	0	3.68	—	—	—	—	—	—	—
85-86—Hershey		AHL	*53	*3061	30	19	2	174	*5	3.41	13	780	5	7	42	*1	3.23
86-87—Philadelphia		NHL	*66	*3799	37	21	6	190	1	3.00	*26	*1540	15	11	*71	†2	2.77
87-88—Philadelphia		NHL	62	3561	30	22	7	208	0	3.50	7	379	2	4	30	0	4.75
88-89—Philadelphia		NHL	64	3756	30	28	6	202	0	3.23	15	886	8	7	49	0	3.32
89-90—Philadelphia		NHL	8	419	4	2	1	29	0	4.15	—	—	—	—	—	—	—
—Hershey		AHL	1	49	1	0	0	3	0	3.67	—	—	—	—	—	—	—
90-91—Philadelphia		NHL	36	2035	13	16	5	106	0	3.13	—	—	—	—	—	—	—
91-92—Philadelphia		NHL	45	2668	16	21	6	151	3	3.40	—	—	—	—	—	—	—
92-93—Quebec		NHL	54	2988	29	16	5	172	0	3.45	6	372	2	4	18	0	2.90
93-94—New York Islanders		NHL	65	3581	27	26	6	184	5	3.08	3	158	0	3	16	0	6.08
94-95—Philadelphia		NHL	31	1824	17	9	4	88	1	2.89	15	897	10	5	*42	0	2.81
NHL totals			431	24631	203	161	46	1330	10	3.24	72	4232	37	34	226	2	3.20

HILL, SEAN
D, SENATORS

PERSONAL: Born February 14, 1970, in Duluth, Minn. . . . 6-0/196. . . . Shoots right. . . . Full name: Sean Ronald Hill.
COLLEGE: Wisconsin.
TRANSACTIONS/CAREER NOTES: Selected by Montreal Canadiens in eighth round (ninth Canadiens pick, 167th overall) of NHL entry draft (June 11, 1988). . . . Injured knee (December 29, 1990). . . . Suspended two games by WCHA for elbowing (January 18, 1991). . . . Suffered abdominal strain (October 13, 1992); missed 14 games. . . . Selected by Mighty Ducks of Anaheim in NHL expansion draft (June 24, 1993). . . . Sprained shoulder (January 6, 1994); missed nine games. . . . Traded by Mighty Ducks with ninth-round pick in 1994 draft (G Frederic Cassivi) to Ottawa Senators for third-round pick (traded to Tampa Bay Lightning who selected C Vadim Yepanchintsev) in 1994 draft (June 29, 1994).
HONORS: Named to WCHA All-Star second team (1989-90 and 1990-91). . . . Named to NCAA All-America West second team (1990-91).
MISCELLANEOUS: Member of Stanley Cup championship team (1993).

Season	Team	League	Gms.	G	A	Pts.	PIM	Gms.	G	A	Pts.	PIM
88-89—University of Wisconsin		WCHA	45	2	23	25	69	—	—	—	—	—
89-90—University of Wisconsin		WCHA	42	14	39	53	78	—	—	—	—	—
90-91—University of Wisconsin		WCHA	37	19	32	51	122	—	—	—	—	—
—Fredericton		AHL	—	—	—	—	—	3	0	2	2	2
—Montreal		NHL	—	—	—	—	—	1	0	0	0	0
91-92—Fredericton		AHL	42	7	20	27	65	7	1	3	4	6
—U.S. national team		Int'l	12	4	3	7	16	—	—	—	—	—
—U.S. Olympic Team		Int'l	8	2	0	2	6	—	—	—	—	—
—Montreal		NHL	—	—	—	—	—	4	1	0	1	2
92-93—Montreal		NHL	31	2	6	8	54	3	0	0	0	4
—Fredericton		AHL	6	1	3	4	10	—	—	—	—	—
93-94—Anaheim		NHL	68	7	20	27	78	—	—	—	—	—
94-95—Ottawa		NHL	45	1	14	15	30	—	—	—	—	—
NHL totals			144	10	40	50	162	8	1	0	1	6

HILLER, JIM
RW, RANGERS

PERSONAL: Born May 15, 1969, in Port Alberni, B.C. . . . 6-0/190. . . . Shoots right.
COLLEGE: Northern Michigan.
TRANSACTIONS/CAREER NOTES: Selected by Los Angeles Kings in 10th round (10th Kings pick, 207th overall) of NHL entry draft (June 10, 1989). . . . Strained back (November 21, 1992); missed four games. . . . Traded by Kings with D Paul Coffey and C/LW Sylvain Couturier to Detroit Red Wings for C Jimmy Carson, RW Marc Potvin and C Gary Shuchuk (January 29, 1993). . . . Separated shoulder (March 18, 1993); missed four games. . . . Claimed on waivers by New York Rangers (October 12, 1993). . . . Loaned by Binghamton Rangers to Atlanta Knights of IHL (March 10, 1995).
HONORS: Named to NCAA All-America West second team (1991-92). . . . Named WCHA All-Star second team (1991-92).

Season	Team	League	Gms.	G	A	Pts.	PIM	Gms.	G	A	Pts.	PIM
89-90—Northern Michigan Univ.		WCHA	39	23	33	56	52	—	—	—	—	—
90-91—Northern Michigan Univ.		WCHA	43	22	41	63	59	—	—	—	—	—
91-92—Northern Michigan Univ.		WCHA	39	28	52	80	115	—	—	—	—	—
92-93—Los Angeles		NHL	40	6	6	12	90	—	—	—	—	—
—Phoenix		IHL	3	0	2	2	2	—	—	—	—	—
—Detroit		NHL	21	2	6	8	19	2	0	0	0	4
93-94—Binghamton		AHL	67	27	34	61	61	—	—	—	—	—
—New York Rangers		NHL	2	0	0	0	7	—	—	—	—	—

H

Season Team	League	Gms.	G	A	Pts.	PIM	Gms.	G	A	Pts.	PIM
94-95—Binghamton	AHL	49	15	13	28	44	—	—	—	—	—
—Atlanta	IHL	17	5	10	15	28	5	0	3	3	8
NHL totals		63	8	12	20	116	2	0	0	0	4

HILTON, KEVIN
C, RED WINGS

PERSONAL: Born January 12, 1975, in Trenton, Mich.... 5-11/170.... Shoots left.
COLLEGE: Michigan.
TRANSACTIONS/CAREER NOTES: Selected by Detroit Red Wings in third round (third Red Wings pick, 74th overall) of NHL entry draft (June 26, 1993).

		—REGULAR SEASON—					—PLAYOFFS—				
Season Team	League	Gms.	G	A	Pts.	PIM	Gms.	G	A	Pts.	PIM
91-92—Detroit Compuware	NAJHL	39	35	42	77	42	—	—	—	—	—
92-93—University of Michigan	CCHA	38	16	15	31	8	—	—	—	—	—
93-94—University of Michigan	CCHA	39	11	12	23	16	—	—	—	—	—
94-95—University of Michigan	CCHA	37	20	31	51	14	—	—	—	—	—

HIRSCH, COREY
G, CANUCKS

PERSONAL: Born July 1, 1972, in Medicine Hat, Alta.... 5-10/160.... Catches left.
TRANSACTIONS/CAREER NOTES: Selected by New York Rangers in eighth round (seventh Rangers pick, 169th overall) of NHL entry draft (June 22, 1991).... Loaned by Rangers to Canadian Olympic Team (October 1, 1993).... Returned to Rangers (March 8, 1994).... Traded by Rangers to Vancouver Canucks for C Nathan LaFayette (April 7, 1995).
HONORS: Named to WHL (West) All-Star second team (1989-90).... Won Can.HL Goaltender of the Year Award (1991-92). ... Won Hap Emms Memorial Trophy (1991-92).... Won Del Wilson Trophy (1991-92).... Won WHL Player of the Year Award (1991-92).... Named to Can.HL All-Star first team (1991-92).... Named to Memorial Cup All-Star first team (1991-92). ... Named to WHL (West) All-Star first team (1991-92).... Won Aldege (Baz) Bastien Trophy (1992-93).... Won Dudley (Red) Garrett Memorial Trophy (1992-93).... Shared Harry (Hap) Holmes Memorial Trophy with Boris Rousson (1992-93). ... Named to AHL All-Star first team (1992-93).
MISCELLANEOUS: Member of silver-medal-winning Canadian Olympic team (1994).

		—REGULAR SEASON—							—PLAYOFFS—						
Season Team	League	Gms.	Min.	W	L	T	GA	SO	Avg.	Gms.	Min.	W	L	GA	SO	Avg.
88-89—Kamloops	WHL	32	1516	11	12	2	106	2	4.20	5	245	3	2	19	0	4.65
89-90—Kamloops	WHL	63	3608	48	13	0	230	3	3.82	17	1043	14	3	60	0	3.45
90-91—Kamloops	WHL	38	1970	26	7	1	100	3	3.05	11	623	5	6	42	0	4.04
91-92—Kamloops	WHL	48	2732	35	10	2	124	*5	*2.72	*16	*954	*11	5	35	*2	*2.20
92-93—Binghamton	AHL	46	2692	*35	4	5	125	1	*2.79	14	831	7	7	46	0	3.32
—New York Rangers	NHL	4	224	1	2	1	14	0	3.75	—	—	—	—	—	—	—
93-94—Can. national team	Int'l	37	2158	19	15	2	107	0	2.97	—	—	—	—	—	—	—
—Can. Olympic Team	Int'l	8	495	5	2	1	17	0	2.06	—	—	—	—	—	—	—
—Binghamton	AHL	10	611	5	4	1	38	0	3.73	—	—	—	—	—	—	—
94-95—Binghamton	AHL	57	3371	31	20	5	175	0	3.11	—	—	—	—	—	—	—
NHL totals		4	224	1	2	1	14	0	3.75							

HLAVAC, JAN
LW, ISLANDERS

PERSONAL: Born September 20, 1976, in Prague, Czechoslovakia.... 6-0/185.... Shoots left.
TRANSACTIONS/CAREER NOTES: Selected by New York Islanders in second round (second Islanders pick, 28th overall) of NHL entry draft (July 8, 1995).

		—REGULAR SEASON—					—PLAYOFFS—				
Season Team	League	Gms.	G	A	Pts.	PIM	Gms.	G	A	Pts.	PIM
93-94—Sparta Prague Jrs.	Czech Rep.	27	12	15	27	...	—	—	—	—	—
—Sparta Prague	Czech Rep.	9	1	1	2	...	—	—	—	—	—
94-95—Sparta Prague	Czech Rep.	38	7	6	13	...	5	0	2	2	...

HLUSHKO, TODD
LW, FLAMES

PERSONAL: Born February 7, 1970, in Toronto.... 5-11/185.... Shoots left.... Name pronounced huh-LOOSH-koh.
TRANSACTIONS/CAREER NOTES: Selected by Washington Capitals in 14th round (14th Capitals pick, 240th overall) in NHL entry draft (June 16, 1990).... Signed as free agent by Philadelphia Flyers (March 6, 1994).... Signed as free agent by Calgary Flames (June 27, 1994).... Separated shoulder (February 11, 1995); missed 25 games.

		—REGULAR SEASON—					—PLAYOFFS—				
Season Team	League	Gms.	G	A	Pts.	PIM	Gms.	G	A	Pts.	PIM
88-89—Guelph	OHL	66	28	18	46	71	7	5	3	8	18
89-90—Owen Sound	OHL	25	9	17	26	31	—	—	—	—	—
—London	OHL	40	27	17	44	39	6	2	4	6	10
90-91—Baltimore	AHL	66	9	14	23	55	—	—	—	—	—
91-92—Baltimore	AHL	74	16	35	51	113	—	—	—	—	—
92-93—Canadian national team	Int'l	58	22	26	48	10	—	—	—	—	—
93-94—Canadian national team	Int'l	55	22	6	28	61	—	—	—	—	—
—Canadian Olympic Team	Int'l	8	5	0	5	6	—	—	—	—	—
—Philadelphia	NHL	2	1	0	1	0	—	—	—	—	—
—Hershey	AHL	9	6	0	6	4	6	2	1	3	4

H

Season	Team	League	REGULAR SEASON Gms.	G	A	Pts.	PIM	PLAYOFFS Gms.	G	A	Pts.	PIM
94-95—Saint John		AHL	46	22	10	32	36	4	2	2	4	22
—Calgary		NHL	2	0	1	1	2	1	0	0	0	2
NHL totals			4	1	1	2	2	1	0	0	0	2

HNILICKA, MILAN
G, ISLANDERS

PERSONAL: Born June 24, 1973, in Kladno, Czechoslovakia. . . . 6-0/180. . . . Catches left. . . . Name pronounced MEE-lahn nun-LEECH-kuh.

TRANSACTIONS/CAREER NOTES: Selected by New York Islanders in fourth round (fourth Islanders pick, 70th overall) of NHL entry draft (June 22, 1991).

Season	Team	League	REGULAR SEASON Gms.	Min.	W	L	T	GA	SO	Avg.	PLAYOFFS Gms.	Min.	W	L	GA	SO	Avg.
89-90—Poldi Kladno		Czech.	24	1113	...	...	...	70	...	3.77	—	—	—	—	—	—	—
90-91—Poldi Kladno		Czech.	35	2122	...	...	...	98	...	2.77	—	—	—	—	—	—	—
91-92—Poldi Kladno		Czech.	30	1788	...	...	...	107	...	3.59	—	—	—	—	—	—	—
92-93—Swift Current		WHL	65	3679	*46	12	2	206	2	3.36	17	1017	12	5	54	*2	3.19
93-94—Salt Lake City		IHL	9	381	5	1	‡0	25	0	3.94	—	—	—	—	—	—	—
—Richmond		ECHL	43	2299	18	16	‡5	155	0	4.05	—	—	—	—	—	—	—
94-95—Denver		IHL	15	798	9	4	‡1	47	1	3.53	—	—	—	—	—	—	—

HOCKING, JUSTIN
D, KINGS

PERSONAL: Born January 9, 1974, in Stettler, Alta. . . . 6-4/206. . . . Shoots right. . . . Name pronounced HAH-kihng.

COLLEGE: Spokane (Wash.) Falls Community College.

TRANSACTIONS/CAREER NOTES: Selected by Los Angeles Kings in second round (first Kings pick, 39th overall) of NHL entry draft (June 20, 1992). . . . Loaned by Phoenix Roadrunners to Syracuse Crunch (December 8, 1994).

HONORS: Named to WHL (East) All-Star second team (1993-94).

Season	Team	League	REGULAR SEASON Gms.	G	A	Pts.	PIM	PLAYOFFS Gms.	G	A	Pts.	PIM
90-91—Fort Saskatchewan		AJHL	38	4	6	10	84	—	—	—	—	—
91-92—Spokane		WHL	71	4	6	10	309	10	0	3	3	28
92-93—Spokane		WHL	16	0	1	1	75	—	—	—	—	—
—Medicine Hat		WHL	54	1	9	10	119	10	0	1	1	75
93-94—Medicine Hat		WHL	68	7	26	33	236	3	0	0	0	6
—Phoenix		IHL	3	0	0	0	15	—	—	—	—	—
—Los Angeles		NHL	1	0	0	0	0	—	—	—	—	—
94-95—Phoenix		IHL	20	1	1	2	50	1	0	0	0	0
—Syracuse		AHL	7	0	0	0	24	—	—	—	—	—
—Portland		AHL	9	0	1	1	34	—	—	—	—	—
—Knoxville		ECHL	20	0	6	6	70	4	0	0	0	26
NHL totals			1	0	0	0	0					

HODSON, KEVIN
G, RED WINGS

PERSONAL: Born March 27, 1972, in Winnipeg. . . . 6-0/182. . . . Catches left.

TRANSACTIONS/CAREER NOTES: Signed as free agent by Chicago Blackhawks (August 27, 1992). . . . Signed as free agent by Detroit Red Wings (May 3, 1993).

HONORS: Won Hap Emms Memorial Trophy (1992-93).

Season	Team	League	REGULAR SEASON Gms.	Min.	W	L	T	GA	SO	Avg.	PLAYOFFS Gms.	Min.	W	L	GA	SO	Avg.
90-91—S.S. Marie		OHL	30	1638	18	11	0	88	2	*3.22	10	600	*9	1	28	0	2.80
91-92—S.S. Marie		OHL	50	2722	28	12	4	151	0	3.33	18	1116	12	6	59	1	3.17
92-93—S.S. Marie		OHL	26	1470	18	5	2	76	1	*3.10	8	448	8	0	17	0	2.28
—Indianapolis		IHL	14	777	5	9	0	53	0	4.09	—	—	—	—	—	—	—
93-94—Adirondack		AHL	37	2083	20	10	5	102	2	2.94	3	89	0	2	10	0	6.74
94-95—Adirondack		AHL	51	2731	19	22	8	161	1	3.54	4	238	0	4	14	0	3.53

HOGUE, BENOIT
LW, MAPLE LEAFS

PERSONAL: Born October 28, 1966, in Repentigny, Que. . . . 5-10/194. . . . Shoots left. . . . Name pronounced behn-wah HOHG.

TRANSACTIONS/CAREER NOTES: Selected by Buffalo Sabres as underage junior in second round (second Sabres pick, 35th overall) of NHL entry draft (June 15, 1985). . . . Suspended six games by AHL for fighting (October 1987). . . . Suffered sore back (March 1988). . . . Broke left cheekbone (October 11, 1989); missed 20 games. . . . Sprained left ankle (March 14, 1990). . . . Traded by Sabres with C Pierre Turgeon, D Uwe Krupp and C Dave McLlwain to New York Islanders for C Pat LaFontaine, LW Randy Wood, D Randy Hillier and future considerations; Sabres later received fourth-round pick (D Dean Melanson) in 1992 draft (October 25, 1991). . . . Suffered stiff neck (December 7, 1992); missed five games. . . . Suffered sore hand and foot (January 14, 1993); missed three games. . . . Sprained knee ligament (March 14, 1993); missed six games. . . . Traded by Islanders with third-round pick in 1995 draft (RW Ryan Pepperall) and fifth-round pick in 1996 draft to Toronto Maple Leafs for G Eric Fichaud (April 6, 1995). . . . Injured shoulder (February 4, 1993); missed one game.

STATISTICAL PLATEAUS: Three-goal games: 1992-93 (1).

Season	Team	League	REGULAR SEASON Gms.	G	A	Pts.	PIM	PLAYOFFS Gms.	G	A	Pts.	PIM
83-84—St. Jean		QMJHL	59	14	11	25	42	—	—	—	—	—
84-85—St. Jean		QMJHL	63	46	44	90	92	—	—	—	—	—

H

Season Team	League	REGULAR SEASON					PLAYOFFS				
		Gms.	G	A	Pts.	PIM	Gms.	G	A	Pts.	PIM
85-86—St. Jean	QMJHL	65	54	54	108	115	9	6	4	10	26
86-87—Rochester	AHL	52	14	20	34	52	12	5	4	9	8
87-88—Buffalo	NHL	3	1	1	2	0	—	—	—	—	—
—Rochester	AHL	62	24	31	55	141	7	6	1	7	46
88-89—Buffalo	NHL	69	14	30	44	120	5	0	0	0	17
89-90—Buffalo	NHL	45	11	7	18	79	3	0	0	0	10
90-91—Buffalo	NHL	76	19	28	47	76	5	3	1	4	10
91-92—Buffalo	NHL	3	0	1	1	0	—	—	—	—	—
—New York Islanders	NHL	72	30	45	75	67	—	—	—	—	—
92-93—New York Islanders	NHL	70	33	42	75	108	18	6	6	12	31
93-94—New York Islanders	NHL	83	36	33	69	73	4	0	1	1	4
94-95—New York Islanders	NHL	33	6	4	10	34	—	—	—	—	—
—Toronto	NHL	12	3	3	6	0	7	0	0	0	6
NHL totals		466	153	194	347	557	42	9	8	17	78

HOHENBERGER, MARTIN
LW, CANADIENS

PERSONAL: Born January 29, 1977, in Villach, Austria. . . . 6-1/185. . . . Shoots left.
TRANSACTIONS/CAREER NOTES: Selected by Montreal Canadiens in third round (third Canadiens pick, 74th overall) of NHL entry draft (July 8, 1995).

Season Team	League	REGULAR SEASON					PLAYOFFS				
		Gms.	G	A	Pts.	PIM	Gms.	G	A	Pts.	PIM
93-94—Victoria	WHL	61	3	13	16	28	—	—	—	—	—
94-95—Prince George	WHL	47	10	21	31	81	—	—	—	—	—

HOLAN, MILOS
D, MIGHTY DUCKS

PERSONAL: Born April 22, 1971, in Bilovec, Czechoslovakia. . . . 5-11/191. . . . Shoots left. . . . Name pronounced MEE-lohz HOH-lihn.
TRANSACTIONS/CAREER NOTES: Selected by Philadelphia Flyers in third round (third Flyers pick, 77th overall) of NHL entry draft (June 26, 1993). . . . Traded by Flyers to Mighty Ducks of Anaheim for C Anatoli Semenov (March 8, 1995).

Season Team	League	REGULAR SEASON					PLAYOFFS				
		Gms.	G	A	Pts.	PIM	Gms.	G	A	Pts.	PIM
88-89—TJ Vitkovice	Czech.	7	0	0	0	0	—	—	—	—	—
89-90—TJ Vitkovice	Czech.	50	8	8	16	. . .	—	—	—	—	—
90-91—Dukla Trencin	Czech.	53	6	13	19	. . .	—	—	—	—	—
91-92—Dukla Trencin	Czech.	51	13	22	35	32	—	—	—	—	—
92-93—TJ Vitkovice	Czech.	53	35	33	68	. . .	—	—	—	—	—
93-94—Philadelphia	NHL	8	1	1	2	4	—	—	—	—	—
—Hershey	AHL	27	7	22	29	16	—	—	—	—	—
94-95—Hershey	AHL	55	22	27	49	75	—	—	—	—	—
—Anaheim	NHL	25	2	8	10	14	—	—	—	—	—
NHL totals		33	3	9	12	18					

HOLIK, BOBBY
RW, DEVILS

PERSONAL: Born January 1, 1971, in Jihlava, Czechoslovakia. . . . 6-3/200. . . . Shoots right. . . . Name pronounced hoh-LEEK.
TRANSACTIONS/CAREER NOTES: Selected by Hartford Whalers in first round (first Whalers pick, 10th overall) of NHL entry draft (June 17, 1989). . . . Broke right thumb (February 1990). . . . Traded by Whalers with second-round pick in 1993 draft (LW Jay Pandolfo) and future considerations to New Jersey Devils for G Sean Burke and D Eric Weinrich (August 28, 1992). . . . Fractured right thumb (January 22, 1993); missed 22 games. . . . Bruised left shoulder (December 8, 1993); missed 11 games.
STATISTICAL PLATEAUS: Three-goal games: 1992-93 (2).
MISCELLANEOUS: Member of Stanley Cup championship team (1995).

Season Team	League	REGULAR SEASON					PLAYOFFS				
		Gms.	G	A	Pts.	PIM	Gms.	G	A	Pts.	PIM
87-88—Dukla Jihlava	Czech.	31	5	9	14	. . .	—	—	—	—	—
88-89—Dukla Jihlava	Czech.	24	7	10	17	. . .	—	—	—	—	—
89-90—Czech. national team	Int'l	10	1	5	6	0	—	—	—	—	—
—Dukla Jihlava	Czech.	42	15	26	41	. . .	—	—	—	—	—
90-91—Hartford	NHL	78	21	22	43	113	6	0	0	0	7
91-92—Hartford	NHL	76	21	24	45	44	7	0	1	1	6
92-93—Utica	AHL	1	0	0	0	2	—	—	—	—	—
—New Jersey	NHL	61	20	19	39	76	5	1	1	2	6
93-94—New Jersey	NHL	70	13	20	33	72	20	0	3	3	6
94-95—New Jersey	NHL	48	10	10	20	18	20	4	4	8	22
NHL totals		333	85	95	180	323	58	5	9	14	47

HOLLAND, JASON
D, ISLANDERS

PERSONAL: Born April 30, 1976, in Morinville, Alta. . . . 6-3/190. . . . Shoots right.
HIGH SCHOOL: Norkam (Kamloops, B.C.).
TRANSACTIONS/CAREER NOTES: Selected by New York Islanders in second round (second Islanders pick, 38th overall) of NHL entry draft (June 28, 1994).

Season Team	League	REGULAR SEASON Gms.	G	A	Pts.	PIM	PLAYOFFS Gms.	G	A	Pts.	PIM
92-93—Kamloops	WHL	4	0	0	0	2	—	—	—	—	—
93-94—Kamloops	WHL	59	14	15	29	80	18	2	3	5	4
94-95—Kamloops	WHL	71	9	32	41	65	21	2	7	9	9

HOLLINGER, TERRY
D

PERSONAL: Born February 24, 1971, in Regina, Sask. . . . 6-1/200. . . . Shoots left.
TRANSACTIONS/CAREER NOTES: Selected by St. Louis Blues in sixth round (sixth Blues pick, 153rd overall) of NHL entry draft (June 22, 1991).

Season Team	League	REGULAR SEASON Gms.	G	A	Pts.	PIM	PLAYOFFS Gms.	G	A	Pts.	PIM
87-88—Regina	WHL	7	1	1	2	4	—	—	—	—	—
88-89—Regina	WHL	65	2	27	29	49	—	—	—	—	—
89-90—Regina	WHL	70	14	43	57	40	11	1	3	4	10
90-91—Regina	WHL	8	1	6	7	6	—	—	—	—	—
—Lethbridge	WHL	62	9	32	41	113	16	3	14	17	22
91-92—Lethbridge	WHL	65	23	62	85	155	5	1	2	3	13
—Peoria	IHL	1	0	2	2	0	5	0	1	1	0
92-93—Peoria	IHL	72	2	28	30	67	4	1	1	2	0
93-94—Peoria	IHL	78	12	31	43	96	6	0	3	3	31
—St. Louis	NHL	2	0	0	0	0	—	—	—	—	—
94-95—Peoria	IHL	69	7	25	32	137	4	2	4	6	8
—St. Louis	NHL	5	0	0	0	2	—	—	—	—	—
NHL totals		7	0	0	0	2					

HOLT, TODD
RW, SHARKS

PERSONAL: Born January 20, 1973, in Estevan, Sask. . . . 5-7/155. . . . Shoots right.
TRANSACTIONS/CAREER NOTES: Selected by San Jose Sharks in eighth round (10th Sharks pick, 184th overall) of NHL entry draft (June 26, 1993).

Season Team	League	REGULAR SEASON Gms.	G	A	Pts.	PIM	PLAYOFFS Gms.	G	A	Pts.	PIM
89-90—Swift Current	WHL	63	26	22	48	29	4	1	0	1	2
90-91—Swift Current	WHL	69	47	27	74	72	3	1	0	1	0
91-92—Swift Current	WHL	66	47	54	101	155	8	4	5	9	10
92-93—Swift Current	WHL	67	56	57	113	90	16	10	12	22	18
93-94—Swift Current	WHL	56	40	47	87	59	7	11	7	18	8
94-95—Kansas City	IHL	28	4	4	8	12	—	—	—	—	—
—Roanoke	ECHL	2	0	2	2	0	—	—	—	—	—

HOLZINGER, BRIAN
C, SABRES

PERSONAL: Born October 10, 1972, in Parma, O. . . . 5-11/180. . . . Shoots right.
HIGH SCHOOL: Parma (O.).
COLLEGE: Bowling Green State.
TRANSACTIONS/CAREER NOTES: Selected by Buffalo Sabres in sixth round (seventh Sabres pick, 124th overall) of NHL entry draft (June 22, 1991).
HONORS: Named to CCHA All-Star second team (1993-94). . . . Won Hobey Baker Memorial Award (1994-95). . . . Named CCHA Player of the Year (1994-95). . . . Named to NCAA All-America West first team (1994-95). . . . Named to CCHA All-Star first team (1994-95).

Season Team	League	REGULAR SEASON Gms.	G	A	Pts.	PIM	PLAYOFFS Gms.	G	A	Pts.	PIM
91-92—Bowling Green State	CCHA	30	14	8	22	36	—	—	—	—	—
92-93—Bowling Green State	CCHA	41	31	26	57	44	—	—	—	—	—
93-94—Bowling Green State	CCHA	38	22	15	37	24	—	—	—	—	—
94-95—Bowling Green State	CCHA	38	35	34	69	42	—	—	—	—	—
—Buffalo	NHL	4	0	3	3	0	4	2	1	3	2
NHL totals		4	0	3	3	0	4	2	1	3	2

HORACEK, TONY
LW, BLACKHAWKS

PERSONAL: Born February 3, 1967, in Vancouver. . . . 6-4/215. . . . Shoots left. . . . Name pronounced HOHR-uh-CHEHK.
TRANSACTIONS/CAREER NOTES: Selected by Philadelphia Flyers as underage junior in seventh round (eighth Flyers pick, 147th overall) of NHL entry draft (June 15, 1985). . . . Suspended one game by WHL for swinging stick at fans (November 1, 1987). . . . Suspended eight games by WHL for fighting (November 27, 1987). . . . Suffered broken knuckle (December 1989). . . . Injured left eye (March 19, 1991); missed six games. . . . Traded by Flyers to Chicago Blackhawks for D Ryan McGill (February 7, 1992). . . . Suffered hip pointer (February 25, 1992); missed nine games.
STATISTICAL PLATEAUS: Three-goal games: 1989-90 (1).

Season Team	League	REGULAR SEASON Gms.	G	A	Pts.	PIM	PLAYOFFS Gms.	G	A	Pts.	PIM
84-85—Kelowna Wings	WHL	67	9	18	27	114	6	0	1	1	11
85-86—Spokane	WHL	64	19	28	47	129	9	4	5	9	29
86-87—Spokane	WHL	64	23	37	60	177	5	1	3	4	18
—Hershey	AHL	1	0	0	0	0	1	0	0	0	0
87-88—Hershey	AHL	1	0	0	0	0	—	—	—	—	—
—Spokane	WHL	24	17	23	40	63	—	—	—	—	—
—Kamloops	WHL	26	14	17	31	51	18	6	4	10	73

H

Season Team	League	REGULAR SEASON					PLAYOFFS				
		Gms.	G	A	Pts.	PIM	Gms.	G	A	Pts.	PIM
88-89—Hershey	AHL	10	0	0	0	38	—	—	—	—	—
—Indianapolis	IHL	43	11	13	24	138	—	—	—	—	—
89-90—Philadelphia	NHL	48	5	5	10	117	—	—	—	—	—
—Hershey	AHL	12	0	5	5	25	—	—	—	—	—
90-91—Hershey	AHL	19	5	3	8	35	4	2	0	2	14
—Philadelphia	NHL	34	3	6	9	49	—	—	—	—	—
91-92—Philadelphia	NHL	34	1	3	4	51	—	—	—	—	—
—Chicago	NHL	12	1	4	5	21	2	1	0	1	2
92-93—Indianapolis	IHL	6	1	1	2	28	5	3	2	5	18
93-94—Indianapolis	IHL	29	6	7	13	63	—	—	—	—	—
—Chicago	NHL	7	0	0	0	53	—	—	—	—	—
94-95—Indianapolis	IHL	51	7	19	26	201	—	—	—	—	—
—Chicago	NHL	19	0	1	1	25	—	—	—	—	—
NHL totals		154	10	19	29	316	2	1	0	1	2

HOUDA, DOUG
D, SABRES

PERSONAL: Born June 3, 1966, in Blairmore, Alta. . . . 6-2/190. . . . Shoots right. . . . Name pronounced HOO-duh.

TRANSACTIONS/CAREER NOTES: Selected by Detroit Red Wings as underage junior in second round (second Red Wings pick, 28th overall) of NHL entry draft (June 9, 1984). . . . Fractured left cheekbone (September 23, 1988). . . . Injured knee and underwent surgery (November 21, 1989). . . . Traded by Red Wings to Hartford Whalers for D Doug Crossman (February 20, 1991). . . . Separated shoulder (February 28, 1994); missed three games. . . . Strained shoulder (March 15, 1994); missed two games. . . . Traded by Whalers to Los Angeles Kings for RW Marc Potvin (November 3, 1993). . . . Traded by Kings to Buffalo Sabres for D Sean O'Donnell (July 26, 1994). . . . Severed tendon in hand (February 11, 1995); missed 12 games.

HONORS: Named to WHL All-Star second team (1984-85). . . . Named to AHL All-Star first team (1987-88).

Season Team	League	REGULAR SEASON					PLAYOFFS				
		Gms.	G	A	Pts.	PIM	Gms.	G	A	Pts.	PIM
81-82—Calgary	WHL	3	0	0	0	0	—	—	—	—	—
82-83—Calgary	WHL	71	5	23	28	99	16	1	3	4	44
83-84—Calgary	WHL	69	6	30	36	195	4	0	0	0	7
84-85—Calgary	WHL	65	20	54	74	182	8	3	4	7	29
—Kalamazoo	IHL	—	—	—	—	—	7	0	2	2	10
85-86—Calgary	WHL	16	4	10	14	60	—	—	—	—	—
—Medicine Hat	WHL	35	9	23	32	80	25	4	19	23	64
—Detroit	NHL	6	0	0	0	4	—	—	—	—	—
86-87—Adirondack	AHL	77	6	23	29	142	11	1	8	9	50
87-88—Detroit	NHL	11	1	1	2	10	—	—	—	—	—
—Adirondack	AHL	71	10	32	42	169	11	0	3	3	44
88-89—Adirondack	AHL	7	0	3	3	8	—	—	—	—	—
—Detroit	NHL	57	2	11	13	67	6	0	1	1	0
89-90—Detroit	NHL	73	2	9	11	127	—	—	—	—	—
90-91—Adirondack	AHL	38	9	17	26	67	—	—	—	—	—
—Detroit	NHL	22	0	4	4	43	—	—	—	—	—
—Hartford	NHL	19	1	2	3	41	6	0	0	0	8
91-92—Hartford	NHL	56	3	6	9	125	6	0	2	2	13
92-93—Hartford	NHL	60	2	6	8	167	—	—	—	—	—
93-94—Hartford	NHL	7	0	0	0	23	—	—	—	—	—
—Los Angeles	NHL	54	2	6	8	165	—	—	—	—	—
94-95—Buffalo	NHL	28	1	2	3	68	—	—	—	—	—
NHL totals		393	14	47	61	840	18	0	3	3	21

HOUGH, MIKE
LW, PANTHERS

PERSONAL: Born February 6, 1963, in Montreal. . . . 6-1/197. . . . Shoots left. . . . Name pronounced HUHF.

TRANSACTIONS/CAREER NOTES: Selected by Quebec Nordiques as underage junior in ninth round (seventh Nordiques pick, 181st overall) of NHL entry draft (June 9, 1982). . . . Sprained left shoulder and developed tendinitis (November 5, 1989); missed 14 games. . . . Broke right thumb (January 23, 1990); missed 12 games. . . . Injured back (November 8, 1990); missed nine games. . . . Separated left shoulder (January 15, 1991); missed three games. . . . Suffered concussion (February 10, 1991). . . . Injured knee (December 28, 1991); missed three games. . . . Fractured left thumb (February 15, 1992); missed 14 games. . . . Suffered concussion in preseason (October 1992); missed first two games of season. . . . Sprained right shoulder (April 6, 1993); missed four games. . . . Traded by Nordiques to Washington Capitals for RW Paul MacDermid and RW Reggie Savage (June 20, 1993). . . . Selected by Florida Panthers in NHL expansion draft (June 24, 1993). . . . Hyperextended left knee (October 30, 1993); missed five games.

MISCELLANEOUS: Captain of Quebec Nordiques (1991-92).

Season Team	League	REGULAR SEASON					PLAYOFFS				
		Gms.	G	A	Pts.	PIM	Gms.	G	A	Pts.	PIM
80-81—Dixie	OPJHL	24	15	20	35	84	—	—	—	—	—
81-82—Kitchener	OHL	58	14	34	48	172	14	1	5	6	16
82-83—Kitchener	OHL	61	17	27	44	156	12	5	4	9	30
83-84—Fredericton	AHL	69	11	16	27	142	1	0	0	0	7
84-85—Fredericton	AHL	76	21	27	48	49	6	1	1	2	2
85-86—Fredericton	AHL	74	21	33	54	68	6	0	3	3	8
86-87—Quebec	NHL	56	6	8	14	79	9	0	3	3	26
—Fredericton	AHL	10	1	3	4	20	—	—	—	—	—

H

Season Team	League	REGULAR SEASON					PLAYOFFS				
		Gms.	G	A	Pts.	PIM	Gms.	G	A	Pts.	PIM
87-88—Fredericton	AHL	46	16	25	41	133	15	4	8	12	55
—Quebec	NHL	17	3	2	5	2	—	—	—	—	—
88-89—Halifax	AHL	22	11	10	21	87	—	—	—	—	—
—Quebec	NHL	46	9	10	19	39	—	—	—	—	—
89-90—Quebec	NHL	43	13	13	26	84	—	—	—	—	—
90-91—Quebec	NHL	63	13	20	33	111	—	—	—	—	—
91-92—Quebec	NHL	61	16	22	38	77	—	—	—	—	—
92-93—Quebec	NHL	77	8	22	30	69	6	0	1	1	2
93-94—Florida	NHL	78	6	23	29	62	—	—	—	—	—
94-95—Florida	NHL	48	6	7	13	38	—	—	—	—	—
NHL totals		489	80	127	207	561	15	0	4	4	28

HOULDER, BILL

D, LIGHTNING

PERSONAL: Born March 11, 1967, in Thunder Bay, Ont. . . . 6-3/218. . . . Shoots left.
TRANSACTIONS/CAREER NOTES: Selected by Washington Capitals as underage junior in fourth round (fourth Capitals pick, 82nd overall) of NHL entry draft (June 15, 1985). . . . Pulled groin (January 1989). . . . Traded by Capitals to Buffalo Sabres for D Shawn Anderson (September 30, 1990). . . . Selected by Mighty Ducks of Anaheim in NHL expansion draft (June 24, 1993). . . . Traded by Mighty Ducks to St. Louis Blues for D Jason Marshall (August 29, 1994). . . . Signed as free agent by Tampa Bay Lightning (August 1, 1995).
HONORS: Named to AHL All-Star first team (1990-91). . . . Won Governors Trophy (1992-93). . . . Named to IHL All-Star first team (1992-93).

Season Team	League	REGULAR SEASON					PLAYOFFS				
		Gms.	G	A	Pts.	PIM	Gms.	G	A	Pts.	PIM
83-84—Thunder Bay Beavers	TBAHA	23	4	18	22	37	—	—	—	—	—
84-85—North Bay	OHL	66	4	20	24	37	8	0	0	0	2
85-86—North Bay	OHL	59	5	30	35	97	10	1	6	7	12
86-87—North Bay	OHL	62	17	51	68	68	22	4	19	23	20
87-88—Washington	NHL	30	1	2	3	10	—	—	—	—	—
—Fort Wayne	IHL	43	10	14	24	32	—	—	—	—	—
88-89—Baltimore	AHL	65	10	36	46	50	—	—	—	—	—
—Washington	NHL	8	0	3	3	4	—	—	—	—	—
89-90—Baltimore	AHL	26	3	7	10	12	7	0	2	2	2
—Washington	NHL	41	1	11	12	28	—	—	—	—	—
90-91—Rochester	AHL	69	13	53	66	28	15	5	13	18	4
—Buffalo	NHL	7	0	2	2	4	—	—	—	—	—
91-92—Rochester	AHL	42	8	26	34	16	16	5	6	11	4
—Buffalo	NHL	10	1	0	1	8	—	—	—	—	—
92-93—San Diego	IHL	64	24	48	72	39	—	—	—	—	—
—Buffalo	NHL	15	3	5	8	6	8	0	2	2	4
93-94—Anaheim	NHL	80	14	25	39	40	—	—	—	—	—
94-95—St. Louis	NHL	41	5	13	18	20	4	1	1	2	0
NHL totals		232	25	61	86	120	12	1	3	4	4

HOULE, JEAN-FRANCOIS

LW, CANADIENS

PERSONAL: Born January 14, 1975, in La Salle, Que. . . . 5-8/145. . . . Shoots left. . . . Son of Rejean Houle, left winger/right winger, Montreal Canadiens (1969-70 through 1972-73 and 1976-77 through 1982-83) and Quebec Nordiques of WHA (1973-74 through 1975-76).
HIGH SCHOOL: Northwood (Lake Placid, N.Y.).
COLLEGE: Clarkson (N.Y.).
TRANSACTIONS/CAREER NOTES: Selected by Montreal Canadiens in fourth round (fifth Canadiens pick, 99th overall) of NHL entry draft (June 26, 1993).

Season Team	League	REGULAR SEASON					PLAYOFFS				
		Gms.	G	A	Pts.	PIM	Gms.	G	A	Pts.	PIM
92-93—Northwood School	N.Y. H.S.	28	37	45	82	. . .	—	—	—	—	—
93-94—Clarkson	ECAC	34	6	19	25	18	—	—	—	—	—
94-95—Clarkson	ECAC	34	8	11	19	42	—	—	—	—	—

HOUSLEY, PHIL

D, FLAMES

PERSONAL: Born March 9, 1964, in St. Paul, Minn. . . . 5-10/185. . . . Shoots left.
HIGH SCHOOL: South St. Paul (Minn.).
TRANSACTIONS/CAREER NOTES: Selected by Buffalo Sabres as underage player in first round (first Sabres pick, sixth overall) of NHL entry draft (June 9, 1982). . . . Bruised shoulder (January 1984). . . . Suspended three games by NHL (October 1984). . . . Injured back (November 1987). . . . Bruised back (January 12, 1989). . . . Suffered hip pointer and bruised back (March 18, 1989). . . . Pulled shoulder ligaments while playing at World Cup Tournament (April 1989). . . . Traded by Sabres with LW Scott Arniel, RW Jeff Parker and first-round pick (C Keith Tkachuk) in 1990 draft to Winnipeg Jets for C Dale Hawerchuk and first-round pick (LW Brad May) in 1990 draft (June 16, 1990). . . . Strained abdomen (February 26, 1992); missed five games. . . . Strained groin (October 31, 1992); missed two games. . . . Sprained wrist (January 19, 1993); missed two games. . . . Traded by Jets to St. Louis Blues for RW Nelson Emerson and D Stephane Quintal (September 24, 1993). . . . Suffered back spasms (October 26, 1993); missed five games. . . . Suffered sore back (November 18, 1993). . . . Underwent back surgery (January 4, 1994); missed 53 games. . . . Traded by Blues with second-round pick in 1996 and 1997 drafts to Calgary Flames for free-agent rights to D Al MacInnis and fourth-round pick in 1997 draft (July 4, 1994). . . . Played in Europe during 1994-95 NHL lockout. . . . Crushed right pinky (February 9, 1995); missed five games.

H

HONORS: Named to NHL All-Rookie team (1982-83).... Played in NHL All-Star Game (1984 and 1989-1993).... Named to THE SPORTING NEWS All-Star second team (1991-92).... Named to NHL All-Star second team (1991-92).
STATISTICAL PLATEAUS: Three-goal games: 1982-83 (1), 1987-88 (1). Total: 2.
MISCELLANEOUS: Member of Team U.S.A. at World Junior Championships (1982).... Member of Team U.S.A. at World Cup Tournament (1982).

Season Team	League	REGULAR SEASON					PLAYOFFS				
		Gms.	G	A	Pts.	PIM	Gms.	G	A	Pts.	PIM
80-81—St. Paul	USHL	6	7	7	14	6	—	—	—	—	—
81-82—South St. Paul H.S.	Minn. H.S.	22	31	34	65	18	—	—	—	—	—
82-83—Buffalo	NHL	77	19	47	66	39	10	3	4	7	2
83-84—Buffalo	NHL	75	31	46	77	33	3	0	0	0	6
84-85—Buffalo	NHL	73	16	53	69	28	5	3	2	5	2
85-86—Buffalo	NHL	79	15	47	62	54	—	—	—	—	—
86-87—Buffalo	NHL	78	21	46	67	57	—	—	—	—	—
87-88—Buffalo	NHL	74	29	37	66	96	6	2	4	6	6
88-89—Buffalo	NHL	72	26	44	70	47	5	1	3	4	2
89-90—Buffalo	NHL	80	21	60	81	32	6	1	4	5	4
90-91—Winnipeg	NHL	78	23	53	76	24	—	—	—	—	—
91-92—Winnipeg	NHL	74	23	63	86	92	7	1	4	5	0
92-93—Winnipeg	NHL	80	18	79	97	52	6	0	7	7	2
93-94—St. Louis	NHL	26	7	15	22	12	4	2	1	3	4
94-95—Grasshoppers	Switz. Div. II	10	6	8	14	34	—	—	—	—	—
—Calgary	NHL	43	8	35	43	18	7	0	9	9	0
NHL totals		909	257	625	882	584	59	13	38	51	28

HOWE, MARK
D, RED WINGS

PERSONAL: Born May 28, 1955, in Detroit.... 5-11/185.... Shoots left.... Full name: Mark Steven Howe.... Son of Gordie Howe, Hall of Fame right winger, Detroit Red Wings and Hartford Whalers (1946-47 through 1970-71 and 1979-80) and Houston Aeros and New England Whalers of WHA (1973-74 through 1978-79); and brother of Marty Howe, defenseman, Hartford Whalers and Boston Bruins (1979-80 through 1984-85) and Houston Aeros and New England Whalers of WHA (1973-74 through 1978-79).

TRANSACTIONS/CAREER NOTES: Signed by Houston Aeros (June 1972).... Traded by London Knights to Toronto Marlboros for D Larry Goodenough and C Dennis Maruk (August 1972).... Underwent corrective knee surgery; missed most of 1971-72 season.... Selected by Boston Bruins from Marlboros in second round (second Bruins pick, 25th overall) of amateur draft (May 28, 1974).... Separated shoulder; missed part of 1976-77 season.... Signed as free agent by New England Whalers (June 1977).... Injured ribs; missed part of 1977-78 season.... Selected by Boston Bruins in NHL reclaim draft, but remained Hartford Whalers property as a priority selection for the expansion draft (June 9, 1979).... Suffered five-inch puncture wound to upper thigh (December 27, 1980).... Traded by Whalers to Philadelphia Flyers for C Ken Linseman, C Greg Adams and first-round pick (LW David A. Jensen) in 1983 draft and exchange of third-round picks in 1983 draft (August 19, 1982).... Injured shoulder (February 1984).... Bruised collarbone (January 1985).... Suffered back spasms (January 1987).... Broke rib and vertebrae (September 1987).... Strained back (March 1988).... Bruised right foot (October 1988).... Pulled groin muscle (December 1988).... Sprained cruciate ligament in left knee (February 1989); missed eight games.... Reinjured left knee (February 27, 1989).... Injured groin (December 22, 1989).... Injured back (November 3, 1990); missed four games.... Reinjured back (November 25, 1990).... Underwent surgery for herniated disk (January 18, 1991); missed 54 games.... Aggravated back injury (October 4, 1991); missed seven games.... Fractured thumb (November 23, 1991); missed 24 games.... Signed as free agent by Detroit Red Wings (July 8, 1992).... Injured back (November 28, 1992); missed three games.... Injured rib (December 28, 1992); missed three games.... Injured back (January 17, 1993); missed two games.... Sprained neck (March 18, 1993); missed eight games.... Sprained left knee (October 5, 1993); missed four games.... Suffered back spasms (December 5, 1993); missed two games.... Strained back (January 6, 1994); missed 22 games.... Bruised left knee (January 22, 1995); missed two games.... Suffered lower back spasms (February 7, 1995); missed two games.... Reinjured back (March 9, 1995); missed five games.... Separated left shoulder (April 2, 1995); missed 13 games.

HONORS: Won Most Valuable Player and Outstanding Forward Awards (1970-71).... Named to SOJHL All-Star first team (1970-71).... Won WHA Rookie of the Year Award (1973-74).... Named to WHA All-Star second team (1973-74 and 1976-77).... Named to WHA All-Star first team (1978-79).... Named to THE SPORTING NEWS All-Star second team (1979-80).... Played in NHL All-Star Game (1981, 1983, 1986 and 1988).... Named to THE SPORTING NEWS All-Star first team (1982-83, 1985-86 and 1986-87).... Named to NHL All-Star first team (1982-83, 1985-86 and 1986-87).... Won Emery Edge Award (1985-86).

STATISTICAL PLATEAUS: Three-goal games: 1980-81 (1).

Season Team	League	REGULAR SEASON					PLAYOFFS				
		Gms.	G	A	Pts.	PIM	Gms.	G	A	Pts.	PIM
70-71—Detroit Junior Red Wings	SOJHL	44	37	*70	*107	...	—	—	—	—	—
71-72—Detroit Junior Red Wings	SOJHL	9	5	9	14	...	—	—	—	—	—
—U.S. Olympic Team	Int'l				Statistics unavailable.						
72-73—Toronto	OHA Mj. Jr. A	60	38	66	104	27	—	—	—	—	—
73-74—Houston	WHA	76	38	41	79	20	14	9	10	19	4
74-75—Houston	WHA	74	36	40	76	30	13	†10	12	*22	0
75-76—Houston	WHA	72	39	37	76	38	†17	6	10	16	18
76-77—Houston	WHA	57	23	52	75	46	10	4	10	14	2
77-78—New England	WHA	70	30	61	91	32	14	8	7	15	18
78-79—New England	WHA	77	42	65	107	32	6	4	2	6	6
79-80—Hartford	NHL	74	24	56	80	20	3	1	2	3	2
80-81—Hartford	NHL	63	19	46	65	54	—	—	—	—	—
81-82—Hartford	NHL	76	8	45	53	18	—	—	—	—	—
82-83—Philadelphia	NHL	76	20	47	67	18	3	0	2	2	4

Season	Team	League	REGULAR SEASON					PLAYOFFS				
			Gms.	G	A	Pts.	PIM	Gms.	G	A	Pts.	PIM
83-84—Philadelphia		NHL	71	19	34	53	44	3	0	0	0	2
84-85—Philadelphia		NHL	73	18	39	57	31	19	3	8	11	6
85-86—Philadelphia		NHL	77	24	58	82	36	5	0	4	4	0
86-87—Philadelphia		NHL	69	15	43	58	37	26	2	10	12	4
87-88—Philadelphia		NHL	75	19	43	62	62	7	3	6	9	4
88-89—Philadelphia		NHL	52	9	29	38	45	19	0	15	15	10
89-90—Philadelphia		NHL	40	7	21	28	24	—	—	—	—	—
90-91—Philadelphia		NHL	19	0	10	10	8	—	—	—	—	—
91-92—Philadelphia		NHL	42	7	18	25	18	—	—	—	—	—
92-93—Detroit		NHL	60	3	31	34	22	7	1	3	4	2
93-94—Detroit		NHL	44	4	20	24	8	6	0	1	1	0
94-95—Detroit		NHL	18	1	5	6	10	3	0	0	0	0
WHA totals			426	208	296	504	198	74	41	51	92	48
NHL totals			929	197	545	742	455	101	10	51	61	34

HRDINA, JAN
RW, PENGUINS

PERSONAL: Born February 5, 1976, in Hradec Kralove, Czechoslovakia. . . . 5-11/180. . . . Shoots right.
TRANSACTIONS/CAREER NOTES: Selected by Pittsburgh Penguins in fifth round (fourth Penguins pick, 128th overall) of NHL entry draft (July 8, 1995).

Season	Team	League	REGULAR SEASON					PLAYOFFS				
			Gms.	G	A	Pts.	PIM	Gms.	G	A	Pts.	PIM
93-94—Stadion Hradec Kralove		Czech Rep.	21	1	5	6	. . .	—	—	—	—	—
94-95—Seattle		WHL	69	41	59	100	79	4	0	1	1	8

HRKAC, TONY
C

PERSONAL: Born July 7, 1966, in Thunder Bay, Ont. . . . 5-11/185. . . . Shoots left. . . . Name pronounced HUHR-kihz.
COLLEGE: North Dakota.
TRANSACTIONS/CAREER NOTES: Selected by St. Louis Blues as underage junior in second round (second Blues pick, 32nd overall) of NHL entry draft (June 9, 1984). . . . Suspended six games by coach for disciplinary reasons (January 1985). . . . Bruised left leg (January 1987). . . . Sprained shoulder (January 12, 1988). . . . Lacerated ankle (March 1988). . . . Bruised left shoulder (November 28, 1989). . . . Traded by Blues with G Greg Millen to Quebec Nordiques for D Jeff Brown (December 13, 1989). . . . Traded by Nordiques to San Jose Sharks for RW Greg Paslawski (May 30, 1991). . . . Injured wrist during preseason (September 1991); missed first 27 games of season. . . . Traded by Sharks to Chicago Blackhawks for conditional pick in 1993 draft (February 7, 1992). . . . Signed as free agent by Blues (July 30, 1993).
HONORS: Won Hobey Baker Memorial Award (1986-87). . . . Won WCHA Most Valuable Player Award (1986-87). . . . Named NCAA Tournament Most Valuable Player (1986-87). . . . Named to NCAA All-America West first team (1986-87). . . . Named to WCHA All-Star first team (1986-87). . . . Named to NCAA All-Tournament team (1986-87). . . . Won James Gatschene Memorial Trophy (1992-93). . . . Won Leo P. Lamoureux Memorial Trophy (1992-93). . . . Named to IHL All-Star first team (1992-93).

Season	Team	League	REGULAR SEASON					PLAYOFFS				
			Gms.	G	A	Pts.	PIM	Gms.	G	A	Pts.	PIM
83-84—Orillia		OHA	42	*52	54	*106	20	—	—	—	—	—
84-85—Univ. of North Dakota		WCHA	36	18	36	54	16	—	—	—	—	—
85-86—Canadian national team		Int'l	62	19	30	49	36	—	—	—	—	—
86-87—Univ. of North Dakota		WCHA	48	46	*70	*116	48	—	—	—	—	—
—St. Louis		NHL	—	—	—	—	—	3	0	0	0	0
87-88—St. Louis		NHL	67	11	37	48	22	10	6	1	7	4
88-89—St. Louis		NHL	70	17	28	45	8	4	1	1	2	0
89-90—St. Louis		NHL	28	5	12	17	8	—	—	—	—	—
—Quebec		NHL	22	4	8	12	2	—	—	—	—	—
—Halifax		AHL	20	12	21	33	4	6	5	9	14	4
90-91—Halifax		AHL	3	4	1	5	2	—	—	—	—	—
—Quebec		NHL	70	16	32	48	16	—	—	—	—	—
91-92—San Jose		NHL	22	2	10	12	4	—	—	—	—	—
—Chicago		NHL	18	1	2	3	6	3	0	0	0	2
92-93—Indianapolis		IHL	80	45	*87	*132	70	5	0	2	2	2
93-94—St. Louis		NHL	36	6	5	11	8	4	0	0	0	0
—Peoria		IHL	45	30	51	81	25	1	1	2	3	0
94-95—Milwaukee		IHL	71	24	67	91	26	15	4	9	13	16
NHL totals			333	62	134	196	74	24	7	2	9	6

HRUDEY, KELLY
G, KINGS

PERSONAL: Born January 13, 1961, in Edmonton. . . . 5-10/189. . . . Catches left. . . . Full name: Kelly Stephen Hrudey. . . . Name pronounced ROO-dee.
TRANSACTIONS/CAREER NOTES: Selected by New York Islanders as underage junior in second round (second Islanders pick, 38th overall) of NHL entry draft (June 11, 1980). . . . Traded by Islanders to Los Angeles Kings for D Wayne McBean, G Mark Fitzpatrick and future considerations (February 27, 1989); Kings sent D Doug Crossman to Islanders to complete deal (May 23, 1989). . . . Suffered from the flu (April 1989). . . . Suffered from mononucleosis (February 1990); missed 14 games. . . . Bruised ribs (April 20, 1990). . . . Suffered from the flu (March 11, 1993); missed one game. . . . Suffered from the flu (March 26, 1993); missed one game. . . . Bruised right kneecap (January 22, 1995); missed four games.
HONORS: Named to WHL All-Star second team (1980-81). . . . Shared Terry Sawchuk Trophy with Robert Holland (1981-82

H

and 1982-83).... Won Max McNab Trophy (1981-82).... Named to CHL All-Star first team (1981-82 and 1982-83)....
Won Tommy Ivan Trophy (1982-83).

				REGULAR SEASON							PLAYOFFS					
Season	Team	League	Gms.	Min.	W	L	T	GA	SO	Avg.	Gms.	Min.	W	L	GA	SO	Avg.
78-79	Medicine Hat	WHL	57	3093	12	34	7	*318	0	6.17	—	—			—	—	—
79-80	Medicine Hat	WHL	57	3049	25	23	4	212	1	4.17	13	638	6	6	48	0	4.51
80-81	Medicine Hat	WHL	55	3023	32	19	1	200	†4	3.97	4	244	...	...	17	0	4.18
	Indianapolis	CHL	—	—	—	—	—	—	—	—	2	135	...	...	8	0	3.56
81-82	Indianapolis	CHL	51	3033	27	19	4	149	1	*2.95	13	842	11	2	34	*1	*2.42
82-83	Indianapolis	CHL	47	2744	26	17	1	139	2	3.04	10	†637	*7	3	28	0	*2.64
83-84	Indianapolis	CHL	6	370	3	2	1	21	0	3.41	—	—			—	—	—
	New York Islanders	NHL	12	535	7	2	0	28	0	3.14	—	—			—	—	—
84-85	New York Islanders	NHL	41	2335	19	17	3	141	2	3.62	5	281	1	3	8	0	1.71
85-86	New York Islanders	NHL	45	2563	19	15	8	137	1	3.21	2	120	0	2	6	0	3.00
86-87	New York Islanders	NHL	46	2634	21	15	7	145	0	3.30	14	842	7	7	38	0	2.71
87-88	New York Islanders	NHL	47	2751	22	17	5	153	3	3.34	6	381	2	4	23	0	3.62
88-89	New York Islanders	NHL	50	2800	18	24	3	183	0	3.92	—	—			—	—	—
	Los Angeles	NHL	16	974	10	4	2	47	1	2.90	10	566	4	6	35	0	3.71
89-90	Los Angeles	NHL	52	2860	22	21	6	194	2	4.07	9	539	4	4	39	0	4.34
90-91	Los Angeles	NHL	47	2730	26	13	6	132	3	2.90	12	798	6	6	37	0	2.78
91-92	Los Angeles	NHL	60	3509	26	17	*13	197	1	3.37	6	355	2	4	22	0	3.72
92-93	Los Angeles	NHL	50	2718	18	21	6	175	2	3.86	20	1261	10	10	74	0	3.52
93-94	Los Angeles	NHL	64	3713	22	31	7	228	1	3.68	—	—			—	—	—
94-95	Los Angeles	NHL	35	1894	14	13	5	99	0	3.14	—	—			—	—	—
NHL totals			565	32016	244	210	71	1859	16	3.48	84	5143	36	46	282	0	3.29

HRUSKA, DAVID
RW, SENATORS

PERSONAL: Born January 8, 1977, in Sokolov, Czechoslovakia.... 6-0/189.... Shoots right.
TRANSACTIONS/CAREER NOTES: Selected by Ottawa Senators in sixth round (sixth Senators pick, 131st overall) of NHL entry draft (July 8, 1995).

				REGULAR SEASON					PLAYOFFS			
Season	Team	League	Gms.	G	A	Pts.	PIM	Gms.	G	A	Pts.	PIM
94-95	Banik Sokolov	Czech Dv.II				Statistics unavailable.						

HUARD, BILL
LW, DENVER

PERSONAL: Born June 24, 1967, in Alland, Ont.... 6-1/215.... Shoots left.... Name pronounced HYOO-ahrd.
TRANSACTIONS/CAREER NOTES: Signed as free agent by New Jersey Devils (October 1, 1989)....
Signed as free agent by Boston Bruins (December 4, 1992).... Signed as free agent by Ottawa Senators (July 20, 1993).... Injured hip (December 9, 1993); missed three games.... Strained back (February 23, 1994); missed nine games.... Strained groin (March 29, 1995); missed five games.... Traded by Senators to Quebec Nordiques for rights to D Mika Stromberg and fourth-round pick (LW Kevin Boyd) in 1995 draft (April 7, 1995).... Nordiques franchise moved to Denver for 1995-96 season.

				REGULAR SEASON					PLAYOFFS			
Season	Team	League	Gms.	G	A	Pts.	PIM	Gms.	G	A	Pts.	PIM
86-87	Peterborough	OHL	61	14	11	25	61	12	5	2	7	19
87-88	Peterborough	OHL	66	28	33	61	132	12	7	8	15	33
88-89	Carolina	ECHL	40	27	21	48	177	10	7	2	9	70
89-90	Utica	AHL	27	1	7	8	67	5	0	1	1	33
	Nashville	ECHL	34	24	27	51	212	—	—	—	—	—
90-91	Utica	AHL	72	11	16	27	359	—	—	—	—	—
91-92	Utica	AHL	62	9	11	20	233	4	1	1	2	4
92-93	Providence	AHL	72	18	19	37	302	6	3	0	3	9
	Boston	NHL	2	0	0	0	0	—	—	—	—	—
93-94	Ottawa	NHL	63	2	2	4	162	—	—	—	—	—
94-95	Ottawa	NHL	26	1	1	2	64	—	—	—	—	—
	Quebec	NHL	7	2	2	4	13	1	0	0	0	0
NHL totals			98	5	5	10	239	1	0	0	0	0

HUDDY, CHARLIE
D, SABRES

PERSONAL: Born June 2, 1959, in Oshawa, Ont.... 6-0/210.... Shoots left.... Full name: Charles William Huddy.... Name pronounced HUH-dee.
TRANSACTIONS/CAREER NOTES: Signed as free agent by Edmonton Oilers (September 14, 1979).... Injured shoulder (November 10, 1980).... Suffered back spasms (February 1986); missed three games.... Broke finger (April 1986).... Suffered hematoma of left thigh and underwent surgery (May 7, 1988); missed six playoff games.... Strained hamstring (January 2, 1989).... Sprained right ankle (December 22, 1990); missed 17 games.... Broke left toe (February 16, 1991); missed nine games.... Twisted back (March 1991).... Selected by Minnesota North Stars in NHL expansion draft (May 30, 1991).... Traded by North Stars with LW Randy Gilhen, RW Jim Thomson and fourth-round pick in 1991 draft (D Alexei Zhitnik) to Los Angeles Kings for C Todd Elik (June 22, 1991).... Injured groin (October 10, 1991); missed seven games.... Strained groin (November 7, 1991); missed five games.... Suffered chest contusion (February 1, 1992); missed seven games.... Suffered chest contusion (March 3, 1992); missed five games. ... Suffered from the flu (January 14, 1993); missed one game.... Strained groin (October 27, 1993); missed five games.... Traded by Kings with D Alexei Zhitnik, G Robb Stauber and fifth-round pick in 1995 draft (D Marian Menhart) to Buffalo Sabres for G Grant Fuhr, D Philippe Boucher and D Denis Tsygurov (February 14, 1995).
HONORS: Won Emery Edge Award (1982-83).
MISCELLANEOUS: Member of Stanley Cup championship teams (1984, 1985, 1987, 1988 and 1990).

Season	Team	League	REGULAR SEASON					PLAYOFFS				
			Gms.	G	A	Pts.	PIM	Gms.	G	A	Pts.	PIM
77-78	Oshawa	OMJHL	59	17	18	35	81	6	2	1	3	10
78-79	Oshawa	OMJHL	64	20	38	58	108	5	3	4	7	12
79-80	Houston	CHL	79	14	34	48	46	6	1	0	1	2
80-81	Edmonton	NHL	12	2	5	7	6	—	—	—	—	—
	Wichita	CHL	47	8	36	44	71	17	3	11	14	10
81-82	Wichita	CHL	32	7	19	26	51	—	—	—	—	—
	Edmonton	NHL	41	4	11	15	46	5	1	2	3	14
82-83	Edmonton	NHL	76	20	37	57	58	15	1	6	7	10
83-84	Edmonton	NHL	75	8	34	42	43	12	1	9	10	8
84-85	Edmonton	NHL	80	7	44	51	46	18	3	17	20	17
85-86	Edmonton	NHL	76	6	35	41	55	7	0	2	2	0
86-87	Edmonton	NHL	58	4	15	19	35	21	1	7	8	21
87-88	Edmonton	NHL	77	13	28	41	71	13	4	5	9	10
88-89	Edmonton	NHL	76	11	33	44	52	7	2	0	2	4
89-90	Edmonton	NHL	70	1	23	24	56	22	0	6	6	11
90-91	Edmonton	NHL	53	5	22	27	32	18	3	7	10	10
91-92	Los Angeles	NHL	56	4	19	23	43	6	1	1	2	10
92-93	Los Angeles	NHL	82	2	25	27	64	23	1	4	5	12
93-94	Los Angeles	NHL	79	5	13	18	71	—	—	—	—	—
94-95	Los Angeles	NHL	9	0	1	1	6	—	—	—	—	—
	Buffalo	NHL	32	2	4	6	36	3	0	0	0	0
NHL totals			952	94	349	443	720	170	18	66	84	127

HUDSON, MIKE
C, PENGUINS

PERSONAL: Born February 6, 1967, in Guelph, Ont. . . . 6-1/205. . . . Shoots left. **TRANSACTIONS/CAREER NOTES:** Traded by Hamilton Steelhawks with D Keith Vanrooyen to Sudbury Wolves for C Brad Belland (October 1985). . . . Selected by Chicago Blackhawks as underage junior in seventh round (sixth Blackhawks pick, 140th overall) of NHL entry draft (June 21, 1986). . . . Lacerated right hand (December 21, 1989); missed 12 games. . . . Suffered elbow tendinitis (September 1990). . . . Underwent elbow surgery (May 1991). . . . Suffered viral infection (December 20, 1992); missed 21 games. . . . Traded by Blackhawks to Edmonton Oilers for D Craig Muni (March 22, 1993). . . . Suffered nerve disorder in left shoulder (March 1993); missed two games. . . . Fractured left hand (October 9, 1993); missed 16 games. . . . Selected by New York Rangers in 1993 waiver draft (October 3, 1993). . . . Suspended one game for high-sticking incident (March 13, 1994). . . . Suspended 10 games and fined $500 by NHL for hitting another player with a two-handed swing (March 16, 1994). . . . Selected by Pittsburgh Penguins in 1994-95 waiver draft for cash (January 18, 1995). . . . Strained upper back (April 11, 1995); missed three games. . . . Suffered stiff neck (April 22, 1995); missed three games. . . . Suffered stiff neck (May 2, 1995); missed last two games of season.
MISCELLANEOUS: Member of Stanley Cup championship team (1994).

Season	Team	League	REGULAR SEASON					PLAYOFFS				
			Gms.	G	A	Pts.	PIM	Gms.	G	A	Pts.	PIM
84-85	Hamilton	OHL	50	10	12	22	13	—	—	—	—	—
85-86	Hamilton	OHL	7	3	2	5	4	—	—	—	—	—
	Sudbury	OHL	59	35	42	77	20	4	2	5	7	7
86-87	Sudbury	OHL	63	40	57	97	18	—	—	—	—	—
87-88	Saginaw	IHL	75	18	30	48	44	10	2	3	5	20
88-89	Chicago	NHL	41	7	16	23	20	10	1	2	3	18
	Saginaw	IHL	30	15	17	32	10	—	—	—	—	—
89-90	Chicago	NHL	49	9	12	21	56	4	0	0	0	2
90-91	Chicago	NHL	55	7	9	16	62	6	0	2	2	8
	Indianapolis	IHL	3	1	2	3	0	—	—	—	—	—
91-92	Chicago	NHL	76	14	15	29	92	16	3	5	8	26
92-93	Chicago	NHL	36	1	6	7	44	—	—	—	—	—
	Edmonton	NHL	5	0	1	1	2	—	—	—	—	—
93-94	New York Rangers	NHL	48	4	7	11	47	—	—	—	—	—
94-95	Pittsburgh	NHL	40	2	9	11	34	11	0	0	0	6
NHL totals			350	44	75	119	357	47	4	9	13	60

HUFFMAN, KERRY
D, SENATORS

PERSONAL: Born January 3, 1968, in Peterborough, Ont. . . . 6-2/214. . . . Shoots left. . . . Brother-in-law of Mike Posavad, defenseman, St. Louis Blues (1985-86 and 1986-87). **TRANSACTIONS/CAREER NOTES:** Selected by Philadelphia Flyers as underage junior in first round (first Flyers pick, 20th overall) of NHL entry draft (June 21, 1986). . . . Sprained ankle (November 1987). . . . Suffered calcium deposits in thigh (January 1988); missed 22 games. . . . Bruised right knee (March 15, 1990). . . . Suspended by Flyers after leaving team in dispute over ice time (November 16, 1990). . . . Returned to Flyers (December 10, 1990). . . . Suffered from tonsillitis (October 1991); missed one game. . . . Traded by Flyers with G Ron Hextall, C Mike Ricci, C Peter Forsberg, D Steve Duchesne, first-round pick in 1993 draft (G Jocelyn Thibault), cash and future considerations to Quebec Nordiques for C Eric Lindros (June 20, 1992); Flyers sent LW Chris Simon and first-round pick in 1994 draft (traded to Toronto Maple Leafs) to Nordiques to complete deal (July 21, 1992). . . . Broke ribs (October 17, 1992); missed three games. . . . Injured shoulder (November 28, 1992); missed 14 games. . . . Fractured finger (March 8, 1993); missed 10 games. . . . Claimed on waivers by Ottawa Senators (January 15, 1994). . . . Suffered back spasms (March 23, 1994); missed two games. . . . Injured groin (February 1, 1995); missed two games. . . . Injured shoulder (April 24, 1995); missed remainder of season.
HONORS: Won Max Kaminsky Trophy (1986-87). . . . Named to OHL All-Star first team (1986-87).

H

Season	Team	League	REGULAR SEASON					PLAYOFFS				
			Gms.	G	A	Pts.	PIM	Gms.	G	A	Pts.	PIM
84-85—Peterborough Jr. B..........		OHA	24	2	5	7	53	—	—	—	—	—
85-86—Guelph		OHL	56	3	24	27	35	20	1	10	11	10
86-87—Guelph		OHL	44	4	31	35	20	5	0	2	2	8
—Hershey		AHL	3	0	1	1	0	4	0	0	0	0
—Philadelphia		NHL	9	0	0	0	2	—	—	—	—	—
87-88—Philadelphia		NHL	52	6	17	23	34	2	0	0	0	0
88-89—Hershey		AHL	29	2	13	15	16	—	—	—	—	—
—Philadelphia		NHL	29	0	11	11	31	—	—	—	—	—
89-90—Philadelphia		NHL	43	1	12	13	34	—	—	—	—	—
90-91—Hershey		AHL	45	5	29	34	20	7	1	2	3	0
—Philadelphia		NHL	10	1	2	3	10	—	—	—	—	—
91-92—Philadelphia		NHL	60	14	18	32	41	—	—	—	—	—
92-93—Quebec		NHL	52	4	18	22	54	3	0	0	0	0
93-94—Quebec		NHL	28	0	6	6	28	—	—	—	—	—
—Ottawa		NHL	34	4	8	12	12	—	—	—	—	—
94-95—Ottawa		NHL	37	2	4	6	46	—	—	—	—	—
NHL totals.............			354	32	96	128	292	5	0	0	0	0

HUGHES, BRENT
LW, BRUINS

PERSONAL: Born April 5, 1966, in New Westminster, B.C.... 5-11/180.... Shoots left.... Full name: Brent Allen Hughes.

TRANSACTIONS/CAREER NOTES: Traded by New Westminster Bruins to Victoria Cougars for future considerations (October 1986).... Signed as free agent by Winnipeg Jets (July 1987).... Traded by Jets with LW Craig Duncanson and C Simon Wheeldon to Washington Capitals for LW Bob Joyce, D Kent Paynter and C Tyler Larter (May 21, 1991).... Traded by Capitals with future considerations to Boston Bruins for RW John Byce and D Dennis Smith (February 24, 1992).... Separated shoulder (November 28, 1992); missed 11 games.

HONORS: Named to WHL (West) All-Star first team (1986-87).

Season	Team	League	REGULAR SEASON					PLAYOFFS				
			Gms.	G	A	Pts.	PIM	Gms.	G	A	Pts.	PIM
83-84—New Westminster		WHL	67	21	18	39	133	9	2	2	4	27
84-85—New Westminster		WHL	64	25	32	57	135	11	2	1	3	37
85-86—New Westminster		WHL	71	28	52	80	180	—	—	—	—	—
86-87—New Westminster		WHL	8	5	4	9	22	—	—	—	—	—
—Victoria............................		WHL	61	38	61	99	146	5	4	1	5	8
87-88—Moncton		AHL	77	13	19	32	206	—	—	—	—	—
88-89—Winnipeg		NHL	28	3	2	5	82	—	—	—	—	—
—Moncton		AHL	54	34	34	68	286	10	9	4	13	40
89-90—Moncton		AHL	65	31	29	60	277	—	—	—	—	—
—Winnipeg		NHL	11	1	2	3	33	—	—	—	—	—
90-91—Moncton		AHL	63	21	22	43	144	3	0	0	0	7
91-92—Baltimore.......................		AHL	55	25	29	54	190	—	—	—	—	—
—Maine		AHL	12	6	4	10	34	—	—	—	—	—
—Boston		NHL	8	1	1	2	38	10	2	0	2	20
92-93—Boston		NHL	62	5	4	9	191	1	0	0	0	2
93-94—Providence		AHL	6	2	5	7	4	—	—	—	—	—
—Boston		NHL	77	13	11	24	143	13	2	1	3	27
94-95—Boston		NHL	44	6	6	12	139	5	0	0	0	4
NHL totals.............			230	29	26	55	626	29	4	1	5	53

HULBIG, JOE
LW, OILERS

PERSONAL: Born September 29, 1973, in Wrentham, Mass.... 6-3/215.... Shoots left.

HIGH SCHOOL: St. Sebastian's Country Day (Needham, Mass.).

COLLEGE: Providence.

TRANSACTIONS/CAREER NOTES: Selected by Edmonton Oilers in first round (first Oilers pick, 13th overall) of NHL entry draft (June 20, 1992).

Season	Team	League	REGULAR SEASON					PLAYOFFS				
			Gms.	G	A	Pts.	PIM	Gms.	G	A	Pts.	PIM
89-90—St. Sebastian's................		Mass. H.S.	30	13	12	25	...	—	—	—	—	—
90-91—St. Sebastian's..............		Mass. H.S.	...	23	19	42	...	—	—	—	—	—
91-92—St. Sebastian's................		Mass. H.S.	17	19	24	43	30	—	—	—	—	—
92-93—Providence College		Hockey East	26	3	13	16	22	—	—	—	—	—
93-94—Providence College		Hockey East	28	6	4	10	36	—	—	—	—	—
94-95—Providence College		Hockey East	37	14	21	35	36	—	—	—	—	—

HULL, BRETT
RW, BLUES

PERSONAL: Born August 9, 1964, in Belleville, Ont. ... 5-10/200. ... Shoots right. ... Son of Bobby Hull, Hall of Fame left winger, Chicago Blackhawks, Winnipeg Jets and Hartford Whalers (1957-58 through 1971-72 and 1979-80) and Winnipeg Jets of WHA (1972-73 through 1978-79); and nephew of Dennis Hull, left winger, Blackhawks and Detroit Red Wings (1964-65 through 1977-78).

COLLEGE: Minnesota-Duluth.

TRANSACTIONS/CAREER NOTES: Selected by Calgary Flames in sixth round (sixth Flames pick, 117th overall) of NHL entry draft (June 9, 1984).... Traded by Flames with LW Steve Bozek to St. Louis Blues for D Rob Ramage and G Rick Wamsley (March 7, 1988).... Sprained left ankle (January 15, 1991); missed two regular-season games and All-Star Game.... Suffered back spasms (March 12, 1992); missed seven games.... Suffered sore wrist (March 20, 1993); missed four games.... Suffered

abdominal injury (October 7, 1993); missed three games.
HONORS: Won WCHA Freshman of the Year Award (1984-85).... Named to WCHA All-Star first team (1985-86).... Won Dudley (Red) Garrett Memorial Trophy (1986-87).... Named to AHL All-Star first team (1986-87).... Won Lady Byng Memorial Trophy (1989-90).... Won Dodge Ram Tough Award (1989-90 and 1990-91).... Named to THE SPORTING NEWS All-Star first team (1989-90 through 1991-92).... Named to NHL All-Star first team (1989-90 through 1991-92).... Played in NHL All-Star Game (1989, 1990 and 1992-1994).... Named NHL Player of the Year by THE SPORTING NEWS (1990-91). ... Won Hart Memorial Trophy (1990-91).... Won Lester B. Pearson Award (1990-91).... Won Pro Set NHL Player of the Year Award (1990-91).... Named All-Star Game Most Valuable Player (1992).
RECORDS: Holds NHL single-season record for most goals by a right winger—86 (1990-91).
STATISTICAL PLATEAUS: Three-goal games: 1987-88 (1), 1989-90 (5), 1990-91 (4), 1991-92 (8), 1993-94 (3), 1994-95 (1). Total: 22.... Four-goal games: 1994-95 (1).... Total hat tricks: 23.
MISCELLANEOUS: Shares distinction with Bobby Hull of being the first father-son duo to win the same NHL trophy (both the Lady Byng Memorial and Hart Memorial trophies).... Captain of St. Louis Blues (1992-93 through 1994-95).
STATISTICAL NOTES: Became the first son of an NHL 50-goal scorer to score 50 goals in one season (1989-90).

Season Team	League	REGULAR SEASON					PLAYOFFS				
		Gms.	G	A	Pts.	PIM	Gms.	G	A	Pts.	PIM
82-83—Penticton	BCJHL	50	48	56	104	27	—	—	—	—	—
83-84—Penticton	BCJHL	56	*105	83	*188	20	—	—	—	—	—
84-85—Minnesota-Duluth	WCHA	48	32	28	60	24	—	—	—	—	—
85-86—Minnesota-Duluth	WCHA	42	*52	32	84	46	—	—	—	—	—
—Calgary	NHL	—	—	—	—	—	2	0	0	0	0
86-87—Moncton	AHL	67	50	42	92	16	3	2	2	4	2
—Calgary	NHL	5	1	0	1	0	4	2	1	3	0
87-88—Calgary	NHL	52	26	24	50	12	—	—	—	—	—
—St. Louis	NHL	13	6	8	14	4	10	7	2	9	4
88-89—St. Louis	NHL	78	41	43	84	33	10	5	5	10	6
89-90—St. Louis	NHL	80	*72	41	113	24	12	13	8	21	17
90-91—St. Louis	NHL	78	*86	45	131	22	13	11	8	19	4
91-92—St. Louis	NHL	73	*70	39	109	48	6	4	4	8	4
92-93—St. Louis	NHL	80	54	47	101	41	11	8	5	13	2
93-94—St. Louis	NHL	81	57	40	97	38	4	2	1	3	0
94-95—St. Louis	NHL	48	29	21	50	10	7	6	2	8	0
NHL totals		588	442	308	750	232	79	58	36	94	37

HULL, JODY
RW, PANTHERS

PERSONAL: Born February 2, 1969, in Petrolia, Ont.... 6-2/195.... Shoots right.
HIGH SCHOOL: Thomas A. Stewart (Peterborough, Ont.).
TRANSACTIONS/CAREER NOTES: Strained ankle ligaments (September 1986).... Pulled groin (February 1987).... Selected by Hartford Whalers as underage junior in first round (first Whalers pick, 18th overall) of NHL entry draft (June 13, 1987).... Pulled hamstring (March 1989).... Traded by Whalers to New York Rangers for C Carey Wilson and third-round pick (C Mikael Nylander) in 1991 draft (July 9, 1990).... Sprained muscle in right hand (October 6, 1990).... Bruised left big toe (November 19, 1990); missed six games... Injured knee (March 13, 1991).... Traded by Rangers to Ottawa Senators for future considerations (July 28, 1992).... Injured groin (December 7, 1992); missed three games.... Suffered concussion (January 10, 1993); missed one game.... Sprained ankle (January 19, 1993); missed eight games.... Sprained left ankle (April 1, 1993); missed two games.... Signed as free agent by Florida Panthers (August 10, 1993).... Bruised right shoulder (February 1, 1994); missed one game.... Separated right shoulder (March 4, 1994); missed three games.... Separated right shoulder (March 18, 1994); missed six games.... Suffered viral illness (February 1, 1995); missed two games.
HONORS: Named to OHL All-Star second team (1987-88).
STATISTICAL PLATEAUS: Three-goal games: 1988-89 (1).

Season Team	League	REGULAR SEASON					PLAYOFFS				
		Gms.	G	A	Pts.	PIM	Gms.	G	A	Pts.	PIM
84-85—Cambridge Jr. B	OHA	38	13	17	30	39	—	—	—	—	—
85-86—Peterborough	OHL	61	20	22	42	29	16	1	5	6	4
86-87—Peterborough	OHL	49	18	34	52	22	12	4	9	13	14
87-88—Peterborough	OHL	60	50	44	94	33	12	10	8	18	8
88-89—Hartford	NHL	60	16	18	34	10	1	0	0	0	2
89-90—Binghamton	AHL	21	7	10	17	6	—	—	—	—	—
—Hartford	NHL	38	7	10	17	21	5	0	1	1	2
90-91—New York Rangers	NHL	47	5	8	13	10	—	—	—	—	—
91-92—New York Rangers	NHL	3	0	0	0	2	—	—	—	—	—
—Binghamton	AHL	69	34	31	65	28	11	5	2	7	4
92-93—Ottawa	NHL	69	13	21	34	14	—	—	—	—	—
93-94—Florida	NHL	69	13	13	26	8	—	—	—	—	—
94-95—Florida	NHL	46	11	8	19	8	—	—	—	—	—
NHL totals		332	65	78	143	73	6	0	1	1	4

HULSE, CALE
D, DEVILS

PERSONAL: Born November 10, 1973, in Edmonton.... 6-3/210.... Shoots right.... Name pronounced HUHLS.
COLLEGE: Portland.
TRANSACTIONS/CAREER NOTES: Selected by New Jersey Devils in third round (third Devils pick, 66th overall) of NHL entry draft (June 20, 1992).

Season Team	League	REGULAR SEASON					PLAYOFFS				
		Gms.	G	A	Pts.	PIM	Gms.	G	A	Pts.	PIM
90-91—Calgary Royals	AJHL	49	3	23	26	220	—	—	—	—	—

H

Season Team	League	REGULAR SEASON					PLAYOFFS				
		Gms.	G	A	Pts.	PIM	Gms.	G	A	Pts.	PIM
91-92—Portland	WHL	70	4	18	22	250	6	0	2	2	27
92-93—Portland	WHL	72	10	26	36	284	16	4	4	8	*65
93-94—Albany	AHL	79	7	14	21	186	5	0	3	3	11
94-95—Albany	AHL	77	5	13	18	215	12	1	1	2	17

HULST, KENT
C, CAPITALS

PERSONAL: Born April 8, 1968, in St. Thomas, Ont.... 6-0/200.... Shoots left. **TRANSACTIONS/CAREER NOTES:** Selected by Toronto Maple Leafs as underage junior in fourth round (fourth Maple Leafs pick, 69th overall) of NHL entry draft (June 21, 1986).... Separated shoulder (September 1988).... Signed as free agent by Quebec Nordiques (September 20, 1991).... Signed as free agent by Portland Pirates (1993).... Fined $100 by AHL (November 30, 1994).

Season Team	League	REGULAR SEASON					PLAYOFFS				
		Gms.	G	A	Pts.	PIM	Gms.	G	A	Pts.	PIM
84-85—St. Thomas Jr. B	OHA	47	21	25	46	29	—	—	—	—	—
85-86—Belleville	OHL	43	6	17	23	20	—	—	—	—	—
—Windsor	OHL	17	6	10	16	9	—	—	—	—	—
86-87—Windsor	OHL	37	18	20	38	49	—	—	—	—	—
—Belleville	OHL	27	13	10	23	17	6	1	1	2	0
87-88—Belleville	OHL	66	42	43	85	48	6	3	1	4	7
88-89—Belleville	OHL	45	21	41	62	43	—	—	—	—	—
—Flint	IHL	7	0	1	1	4	—	—	—	—	—
—Newmarket	AHL	—	—	—	—	—	2	1	1	2	2
89-90—Newmarket	AHL	80	26	34	60	29	—	—	—	—	—
90-91—Newmarket	AHL	79	28	37	65	57	—	—	—	—	—
91-92—New Haven	AHL	†80	21	39	60	59	5	2	2	4	0
93-94—Portland	AHL	72	34	33	67	68	17	4	6	10	14
94-95—Portland	AHL	29	10	17	27	80	7	3	1	4	2

HUNTER, DALE
C, CAPITALS

PERSONAL: Born July 31, 1960, in Petrolia, Ont.... 5-10/200.... Shoots left.... Full name: Dale Robert Hunter.... Brother of Mark Hunter, right winger for four NHL teams (1981-82 through 1992-93); and brother of Dave Hunter, left winger, Edmonton Oilers of WHA (1978-79); and Edmonton Oilers, Pittsburgh Penguins and Winnipeg Jets (1979-80 through 1988-89).
TRANSACTIONS/CAREER NOTES: Selected by Quebec Nordiques as underage junior in second round (second Nordiques pick, 41st overall) of NHL entry draft (August 9, 1979).... Suspended three games by NHL (March 1984).... Suffered hand infection (April 21, 1985).... Broke lower fibula of left leg (November 25, 1986).... Traded by Nordiques with G Clint Malarchuk to Washington Capitals for C Alan Haworth, LW Gaetan Duchesne and first-round pick (C Joe Sakic) in 1987 draft (June 13, 1987).... Broke thumb (September 1988).... Suspended four games by NHL for elbowing D Gord Murphy (February 10, 1991).... Suspended for first 21 games of 1993-94 season by NHL for blindside check on player (May 4, 1993).... Injured medial collateral knee ligament (November 26, 1993); missed 10 games.... Bruised left knee (February 13, 1995); missed three games.
RECORDS: Holds NHL career playoff record for most penalty minutes—637.
STATISTICAL PLATEAUS: Three-goal games: 1981-82 (2), 1983-84 (1), 1991-92 (1). Total: 4.
MISCELLANEOUS: Captain of Washington Capitals (1994-95).

Season Team	League	REGULAR SEASON					PLAYOFFS				
		Gms.	G	A	Pts.	PIM	Gms.	G	A	Pts.	PIM
77-78—Kitchener	OMJHL	68	22	42	64	115	—	—	—	—	—
78-79—Sudbury	OMJHL	59	42	68	110	188	10	4	12	16	47
79-80—Sudbury	OMJHL	61	34	51	85	189	9	6	9	15	45
80-81—Quebec	NHL	80	19	44	63	226	5	4	2	6	34
81-82—Quebec	NHL	80	22	50	72	272	16	3	7	10	52
82-83—Quebec	NHL	80	17	46	63	206	4	2	1	3	24
83-84—Quebec	NHL	77	24	55	79	232	9	2	3	5	41
84-85—Quebec	NHL	80	20	52	72	209	17	4	6	10	*97
85-86—Quebec	NHL	80	28	42	70	265	3	0	0	0	15
86-87—Quebec	NHL	46	10	29	39	135	13	1	7	8	56
87-88—Washington	NHL	79	22	37	59	240	14	7	5	12	98
88-89—Washington	NHL	80	20	37	57	219	6	0	4	4	29
89-90—Washington	NHL	80	23	39	62	233	15	4	8	12	61
90-91—Washington	NHL	76	16	30	46	234	11	1	9	10	41
91-92—Washington	NHL	80	28	50	78	205	7	1	4	5	16
92-93—Washington	NHL	84	20	59	79	198	6	7	1	8	35
93-94—Washington	NHL	52	9	29	38	131	7	0	3	3	14
94-95—Washington	NHL	45	8	15	23	101	7	4	4	8	24
NHL totals		1099	286	614	900	3106	140	40	64	104	637

HUNTER, TIM
LW/RW, CANUCKS

PERSONAL: Born September 10, 1960, in Calgary.... 6-2/202.... Shoots right.... Full name: Timothy Robert Hunter.
TRANSACTIONS/CAREER NOTES: Selected by Atlanta Flames in third round (fourth Flames pick, 54th overall) of NHL entry draft (August 9, 1979).... Flames franchise moved to Calgary (May 21, 1980).... Bruised hand (October 1987).... Injured right eye (October 17, 1988).... Suspended 10 games and fined $500 by NHL for leaving bench to fight (November 1, 1989).... Tore shoulder muscles (October 6, 1990); missed four games.... Reinjured shoulder (October 18, 1990); missed 21 games.... Reinjured shoulder (December 2, 1990); missed 20 games....

Suffered back spasms (October 1991); missed one game. . . . Fractured left ankle (December 8, 1991); missed 39 games. . . . Selected by Tampa Bay Lightning in NHL expansion draft (June 18, 1992). . . . Traded by Lightning to Quebec Nordiques for future considerations (June 22, 1992); Nordiques sent RW Martin Simard to Lightning to complete deal (September 14, 1992). . . . Bruised knee (December 29, 1992); missed one game. . . . Suffered back spasms (January 28, 1993); missed three games. . . . Claimed on waivers by Vancouver Canucks (February 12, 1993). . . . Sprained knee (November 2, 1993); missed 14 games. . . . Suffered back spasms (March 3, 1994); missed seven games. . . . Suspended three games by NHL for wrestling with linesman (March 26, 1994). . . . Injured shoulder (April 9, 1995); missed last 12 games of season.
MISCELLANEOUS: Co-captain of Calgary Flames (1988-89). . . . Member of Stanley Cup championship team (1989).

			REGULAR SEASON					PLAYOFFS			
Season Team	League	Gms.	G	A	Pts.	PIM	Gms.	G	A	Pts.	PIM
77-78—Kamloops	BCJHL	51	9	28	37	266	—	—	—	—	—
—Seattle	WCHL	3	1	2	3	4	—	—	—	—	—
78-79—Seattle	WHL	70	8	41	49	300	—	—	—	—	—
79-80—Seattle	WHL	72	14	53	67	311	12	1	2	3	41
80-81—Birmingham	CHL	58	3	5	8	*236	—	—	—	—	—
—Nova Scotia	AHL	17	0	0	0	62	6	0	1	1	45
81-82—Oklahoma City	CHL	55	4	12	16	222	—	—	—	—	—
—Calgary	NHL	2	0	0	0	9	—	—	—	—	—
82-83—Calgary	NHL	16	1	0	1	54	9	1	0	1	*70
—Colorado	CHL	46	5	12	17	225	—	—	—	—	—
83-84—Calgary	NHL	43	4	4	8	130	7	0	0	0	21
84-85—Calgary	NHL	71	11	11	22	259	4	0	0	0	24
85-86—Calgary	NHL	66	8	7	15	291	19	0	3	3	108
86-87—Calgary	NHL	73	6	15	21	361	6	0	0	0	51
87-88—Calgary	NHL	68	8	5	13	337	9	4	0	4	32
88-89—Calgary	NHL	75	3	9	12	*375	19	0	4	4	32
89-90—Calgary	NHL	67	2	3	5	279	6	0	0	0	4
90-91—Calgary	NHL	34	5	2	7	143	7	0	0	0	10
91-92—Calgary	NHL	30	1	3	4	167	—	—	—	—	—
92-93—Quebec	NHL	48	5	3	8	94	—	—	—	—	—
—Vancouver	NHL	26	0	4	4	99	11	0	0	0	26
93-94—Vancouver	NHL	56	3	4	7	171	24	0	0	0	26
94-95—Vancouver	NHL	34	3	2	5	120	11	0	0	0	22
NHL totals		709	60	72	132	2889	132	5	7	12	426

HURLBUT, MIKE
D, DENVER

PERSONAL: Born July 10, 1966, in Massena, N.Y. . . . 6-2/200. . . . Shoots left. . . . Full name: Michael Ray Hurlbut.
HIGH SCHOOL: Northwood (Lake Placid, N.Y.).
COLLEGE: St. Lawrence (N.Y.).
TRANSACTIONS/CAREER NOTES: Selected by New York Rangers in NHL supplemental draft (June 10, 1988). . . . Sprained left knee (January 25, 1993); missed 13 games. . . . Traded by Rangers to Quebec Nordiques for D Alexander Karpovtsev (September 9, 1993). . . . Nordiques franchise moved to Denver for 1995-96 season.
HONORS: Named to NCAA All-America East first team (1988-89). . . . Named to ECAC All-Star first team (1988-89). . . . Named to AHL All-Star second team (1994-95).

			REGULAR SEASON					PLAYOFFS			
Season Team	League	Gms.	G	A	Pts.	PIM	Gms.	G	A	Pts.	PIM
84-85—Northwood School	N.Y. H.S.	34	20	27	47	30	—	—	—	—	—
85-86—St. Lawrence University	ECAC	25	2	10	12	40	—	—	—	—	—
86-87—St. Lawrence University	ECAC	35	8	15	23	44	—	—	—	—	—
87-88—St. Lawrence University	ECAC	38	6	12	18	18	—	—	—	—	—
88-89—St. Lawrence University	ECAC	36	8	25	33	30	—	—	—	—	—
—Flint	IHL	8	0	2	2	13	4	1	2	3	2
89-90—Flint	IHL	74	3	34	37	38	3	0	1	1	2
90-91—Binghamton	AHL	33	2	11	13	27	3	0	1	1	0
—San Diego	IHL	2	1	0	1	0	—	—	—	—	—
91-92—Binghamton	AHL	79	16	39	55	64	11	2	7	9	8
92-93—Binghamton	AHL	46	11	25	36	46	14	2	5	7	12
—New York Rangers	NHL	23	1	8	9	16	—	—	—	—	—
93-94—Cornwall	AHL	77	13	33	46	100	13	3	7	10	12
—Quebec	NHL	1	0	0	0	0	—	—	—	—	—
94-95—Cornwall	AHL	74	11	49	60	69	3	1	0	1	15
NHL totals		24	1	8	9	16					

HUSCROFT, JAMIE
D, BRUINS

PERSONAL: Born January 9, 1967, in Creston, B.C. . . . 6-2/200. . . . Shoots right. . . . Name pronounced HUHZ-krawft.
TRANSACTIONS/CAREER NOTES: Selected by New Jersey Devils as underage junior in ninth round (ninth Devils pick, 171st overall) of NHL entry draft (June 15, 1985). . . . Fractured arm (October 1986); missed eight weeks. . . . Traded by Seattle Thunderbirds to Medicine Hat Tigers for C Mike Schwengler (February 1987). . . . Fractured right wrist (October 1988). . . . Injured groin (December 1988). . . . Broke foot (January 1989); missed 19 games. . . . Signed as free agent by Boston Bruins (July 16, 1992).

			REGULAR SEASON					PLAYOFFS			
Season Team	League	Gms.	G	A	Pts.	PIM	Gms.	G	A	Pts.	PIM
83-84—Portland	WHL	63	0	12	12	77	5	0	0	0	15
84-85—Seattle	WHL	69	3	13	16	273					

H

Season Team	League	REGULAR SEASON					PLAYOFFS				
		Gms.	G	A	Pts.	PIM	Gms.	G	A	Pts.	PIM
85-86—Seattle	WHL	66	6	20	26	394	5	0	1	1	18
86-87—Seattle	WHL	21	1	18	19	99	20	0	3	3	0
—Medicine Hat	WHL	35	4	21	25	170	20	0	3	3	*125
87-88—Flint	IHL	3	1	0	1	2	16	0	1	1	110
—Utica	AHL	71	5	7	12	316	—	—	—	—	—
88-89—Utica	AHL	41	2	10	12	215	5	0	0	0	40
—New Jersey	NHL	15	0	2	2	51	—				
89-90—New Jersey	NHL	42	2	3	5	149	5	0	0	0	16
—Utica	AHL	22	3	6	9	122	—				
90-91—New Jersey	NHL	8	0	1	1	27	3	0	0	0	6
—Utica	AHL	59	3	15	18	339	—				
91-92—Utica	AHL	50	4	7	11	224	—				
92-93—Providence	AHL	69	2	15	17	257	2	0	1	1	6
93-94—Providence	AHL	32	1	10	11	157	—				
—Boston	NHL	36	0	1	1	144	—				
94-95—Boston	NHL	34	0	6	6	103	5	0	0	0	11
NHL totals		135	2	13	15	474	17	0	0	0	42

HUSKA, RYAN
LW, BLACKHAWKS

PERSONAL: Born July 2, 1975, in Cranbrook, B.C. . . . 6-2/194. . . . Shoots left. . . . Name pronounced HOO-skuh.
HIGH SCHOOL: Norkam Secondary (Kamloops, B.C.).
TRANSACTIONS/CAREER NOTES: Selected by Chicago Blackhawks in third round (fourth Blackhawks pick, 76th overall) of NHL entry draft (June 26, 1993).

Season Team	League	REGULAR SEASON					PLAYOFFS				
		Gms.	G	A	Pts.	PIM	Gms.	G	A	Pts.	PIM
91-92—Kamloops	WHL	44	4	5	9	23	6	0	1	1	0
92-93—Kamloops	WHL	68	17	15	32	50	13	2	6	8	4
93-94—Kamloops	WHL	69	23	31	54	66	19	9	5	14	23
94-95—Kamloops	WHL	66	27	40	67	78	17	7	8	15	12

IAFRATE, AL
D, BRUINS

PERSONAL: Born March 21, 1966, in Dearborn, Mich. . . . 6-3/220. . . . Shoots left. . . . Full name: Al Anthony Iafrate. . . . Name pronounced IGH-ih-FRAY-tee.
TRANSACTIONS/CAREER NOTES: Selected by Toronto Maple Leafs as underage junior in first round (first Maple Leafs pick, fourth overall) of NHL entry draft (June 9, 1984). . . . Bruised knee (February 1985). . . . Broke nose (October 2, 1985); missed five games. . . . Strained neck (January 29, 1986); missed six games. . . . Suffered stiff back (January 1988). . . . Broke back (October 22, 1988). . . . Lacerated hand (December 9, 1988). . . . Tore right knee ligament (March 24, 1990). . . . Underwent knee surgery (April 9, 1990). . . . Traded by Maple Leafs to Washington Capitals for D Bob Rouse and C Peter Zezel (January 16, 1991). . . . Took a leave of absence due to mental exhaustion (March 30, 1991). . . . Injured eye (February 19, 1992); missed one game. . . . Pulled hamstring (April 10, 1993); missed three games. . . . Sprained right knee (December 21, 1993); missed four games. . . . Suffered sore right knee (January 2, 1994); missed one game. . . . Traded by Capitals to Boston Bruins for LW Joe Juneau (March 21, 1994). . . . Underwent off-season knee surgery; missed entire 1994-95 season.
HONORS: Played in NHL All-Star Game (1988, 1990, 1993 and 1994). . . . Named to THE SPORTING NEWS All-Star second team (1992-93). . . . Named to NHL All-Star second team (1992-93).
RECORDS: Shares NHL single-game playoff record for most goals by defenseman—3 (April 26, 1993).

Season Team	League	REGULAR SEASON					PLAYOFFS				
		Gms.	G	A	Pts.	PIM	Gms.	G	A	Pts.	PIM
83-84—U.S. national team	Int'l	55	4	17	21	26	—				
—U.S. Olympic Team	Int'l	6	0	0	0	2	—				
—Belleville	OHL	10	2	4	6	2	3	0	1	1	2
84-85—Toronto	NHL	68	5	16	21	51	—				
85-86—Toronto	NHL	65	8	25	33	40	10	0	3	3	4
86-87—Toronto	NHL	80	9	21	30	55	13	1	3	4	11
87-88—Toronto	NHL	77	22	30	52	80	6	3	4	7	6
88-89—Toronto	NHL	65	13	20	33	72	—				
89-90—Toronto	NHL	75	21	42	63	135	—				
90-91—Toronto	NHL	42	3	15	18	113	—				
—Washington	NHL	30	6	8	14	124	10	1	3	4	22
91-92—Washington	NHL	78	17	34	51	180	7	4	2	6	14
92-93—Washington	NHL	81	25	41	66	169	6	6	0	6	4
93-94—Washington	NHL	67	10	35	45	143	—				
—Boston	NHL	12	5	8	13	20	13	3	1	4	6
94-95—Boston	NHL			Did not play—injured.							
NHL totals		740	144	295	439	1182	65	18	16	34	67

IGINLA, JAROME
C/RW, STARS

PERSONAL: Born July 1, 1977, in Edmonton. . . . 6-2/195. . . . Shoots right.
TRANSACTIONS/CAREER NOTES: Selected by Dallas Stars in first round (first Stars pick, 11th overall) of NHL entry draft (July 8, 1995).
HONORS: Won George Parsons Trophy (1994-95).

Season Team	League	REGULAR SEASON					PLAYOFFS				
		Gms.	G	A	Pts.	PIM	Gms.	G	A	Pts.	PIM
93-94—Kamloops	WHL	48	6	23	29	33	19	3	6	9	10
94-95—Kamloops	WHL	72	33	38	71	111	21	7	11	18	34

IMES, CHRIS

D

PERSONAL: Born August 27, 1972, in Birchdale, Mich. . . . 5-11/195. . . . Shoots right. . . . Name pronounced IGHMS.
COLLEGE: Maine.
TRANSACTIONS/CAREER NOTES: Selected by Florida Panthers in NHL supplemental draft (June 25, 1993). . . . Signed as free agent by Minnesota Moose (April 7, 1995).
HONORS: Named to NCAA All-America East first team (1992-93). . . . Named to NCAA All-Tournament team (1992-93). . . . Named to Hockey East All-Star first team (1992-93 and 1994-95). . . . Named Hockey East Player of the Year (1994-95).

Season Team	League	REGULAR SEASON					PLAYOFFS				
		Gms.	G	A	Pts.	PIM	Gms.	G	A	Pts.	PIM
90-91—University of Maine	Hockey East	37	6	8	14	16	—	—	—	—	—
91-92—University of Maine	Hockey East	31	4	19	23	22	—	—	—	—	—
92-93—University of Maine	Hockey East	45	12	23	35	24	—	—	—	—	—
93-94—U.S. national team	Int'l	58	6	10	16	12	—	—	—	—	—
—U.S. Olympic Team	Int'l	8	0	0	0	2	—	—	—	—	—
94-95—University of Maine	Hockey East	43	4	29	33	18	—	—	—	—	—
—Minnesota	IHL	2	0	0	0	4	3	0	0	0	0

INTRANUOVO, RALPH

C, OILERS

PERSONAL: Born December 11, 1973, in Scarborough, Ont. . . . 5-8/185. . . . Shoots left. . . . Name pronounced ihn-trah-NOH-voh.
TRANSACTIONS/CAREER NOTES: Selected by Edmonton Oilers in fourth round (fifth Oilers pick, 96th overall) of NHL entry draft (June 20, 1992).
HONORS: Won Stafford Smythe Memorial Trophy (1992-93). . . . Named to AHL All-Star second team (1994-95).

Season Team	League	REGULAR SEASON					PLAYOFFS				
		Gms.	G	A	Pts.	PIM	Gms.	G	A	Pts.	PIM
90-91—Sault Ste. Marie	OHL	63	25	42	67	22	14	7	13	20	17
91-92—Sault Ste. Marie	OHL	65	50	63	113	44	18	10	14	24	12
92-93—Sault Ste. Marie	OHL	54	31	47	78	61	18	10	16	26	30
93-94—Cape Breton	AHL	66	21	31	52	39	4	1	2	3	2
94-95—Cape Breton	AHL	70	46	47	93	62	—	—	—	—	—
—Edmonton	NHL	1	0	1	1	0	—	—	—	—	—
NHL totals		**1**	**0**	**1**	**1**	**0**					

IRBE, ARTURS

G, SHARKS

PERSONAL: Born February 2, 1967, in Riga, U.S.S.R. . . . 5-8/190. . . . Catches left. . . . Name pronounced AHR-tuhrs UHR-bay.
TRANSACTIONS/CAREER NOTES: Selected by Minnesota North Stars in 10th round (11th North Stars pick, 196th overall) of NHL entry draft (June 17, 1989). . . . Selected by San Jose Sharks in NHL dispersal draft (May 30, 1991). . . . Sprained knee (November 27, 1992); missed 19 games. . . . Injured foot (February 15, 1995); missed one game.
HONORS: Named Soviet League Rookie of the Year (1987-88). . . . Shared James Norris Memorial Trophy with Wade Flaherty (1991-92). . . . Named to IHL All-Star first team (1991-92). . . . Played in NHL All-Star Game (1994).
RECORDS: Holds NHL single-season record for most minutes played by goaltender—4,412 (1993-94).

Season Team	League	REGULAR SEASON								PLAYOFFS						
		Gms.	Min.	W	L	T	GA	SO	Avg.	Gms.	Min.	W	L	GA	SO	Avg.
86-87—Dynamo Riga	USSR	2	27	...	...	...	1	0	2.22	—	—	—	—	—	—	—
87-88—Dynamo Riga	USSR	34	1870	...	...	...	84	0	2.70	—	—	—	—	—	—	—
88-89—Dynamo Riga	USSR	41	2460	...	...	...	117	0	2.85	—	—	—	—	—	—	—
89-90—Dynamo Riga	USSR	48	2880	...	...	...	116	0	2.42	—	—	—	—	—	—	—
90-91—Dynamo Riga	USSR	46	2713	...	...	...	133	0	2.94	—	—	—	—	—	—	—
91-92—Kansas City	IHL	32	1955	24	7	†1	80	0	*2.46	15	914	12	3	44	0	2.89
—San Jose	NHL	13	645	2	6	3	48	0	4.47	—	—	—	—	—	—	—
92-93—Kansas City	IHL	6	364	3	3	†0	20	0	3.30	—	—	—	—	—	—	—
—San Jose	NHL	36	2074	7	26	0	142	1	4.11	—	—	—	—	—	—	—
93-94—San Jose	NHL	*74	*4412	30	28	*16	209	3	2.84	14	806	7	7	50	0	3.72
94-95—San Jose	NHL	38	2043	14	19	3	111	4	3.26	6	316	2	4	27	0	5.13
NHL totals		**161**	**9174**	**53**	**79**	**22**	**510**	**8**	**3.34**	**20**	**1122**	**9**	**11**	**77**	**0**	**4.12**

ISBISTER, BRAD

RW, JETS

PERSONAL: Born March 7, 1977, in Edmonton. . . . 6-2/198. . . . Shoots right.
HIGH SCHOOL: Milwaukie (Ore.).
TRANSACTIONS/CAREER NOTES: Selected by Winnipeg Jets in third round (fourth Jets pick, 67th overall) of NHL entry draft (July 8, 1995).

Season Team	League	REGULAR SEASON					PLAYOFFS				
		Gms.	G	A	Pts.	PIM	Gms.	G	A	Pts.	PIM
93-94—Portland	WHL	64	7	10	17	45	10	0	2	2	0
94-95—Portland	WHL	67	16	20	36	123	—	—	—	—	—

ISRAEL, AARON

G, FLYERS

PERSONAL: Born June 4, 1973, in Boston. . . . 6-2/176. . . . Catches left.
COLLEGE: Harvard.
TRANSACTIONS/CAREER NOTES: Selected by Philadelphia Flyers in seventh round (sixth Flyers pick, 166th overall) of NHL entry draft (June 26, 1993).
HONORS: Named to NCAA All-Tournament team (1993-94).

Season Team	League	REGULAR SEASON								PLAYOFFS						
		Gms.	Min.	W	L	T	GA	SO	Avg.	Gms.	Min.	W	L	GA	SO	Avg.
92-93—Harvard University	ECAC	14	843	9	4	1	43	0	3.06	—	—	—	—	—	—	—
93-94—Harvard University	ECAC	18	1045	12	2	2	40	0	2.30	—	—	—	—	—	—	—
94-95—Johnstown	ECHL	30	1775	17	10	‡2	119	1	4.02	3	157	2	1	14	0	5.35
—Hershey	AHL	7	245	2	1	0	16	0	3.92	1	21	0	0	1	0	2.86

JABLONSKI, PAT
G, MAPLE LEAFS

PERSONAL: Born June 20, 1967, in Toledo, O. . . . 6-0/180. . . . Catches right.
TRANSACTIONS/CAREER NOTES: Selected by St. Louis Blues in seventh round (sixth Blues pick, 138th overall) of NHL entry draft (June 15, 1985). . . . Pulled groin (December 7, 1991); missed 26 games. . . . Traded by Blues with D Rob Robinson, RW Darin Kimble and RW Steve Tuttle to Tampa Bay Lightning for future considerations (June 19, 1992). . . . Traded by Lightning to Toronto Maple Leafs for future considerations (February 21, 1994). . . . Loaned by Maple Leafs to Chicago Wolves (February 17, 1995). . . . Returned to Maple Leafs (March 6, 1995). . . . Loaned by Maple Leafs to Houston Aeros (March 29, 1995). . . . Returned to Maple Leafs (April 7, 1995).
HONORS: Shared James Norris Memorial Trophy with Guy Hebert (1990-91).

Season Team	League	REGULAR SEASON								PLAYOFFS						
		Gms.	Min.	W	L	T	GA	SO	Avg.	Gms.	Min.	W	L	GA	SO	Avg.
84-85—Detroit Compuware	NAJHL	29	1483	. . .	. . .	. . .	95	0	3.84	—	—	—	—	—	—	—
85-86—Windsor	OHL	29	1600	6	16	4	119	1	4.46	6	263	0	3	20	0	4.56
86-87—Windsor	OHL	41	2328	22	14	2	128	†3	3.30	12	710	8	4	38	0	3.21
87-88—Windsor	OHL	18	994	14	3	0	48	2	*2.90	9	537	8	0	28	0	3.13
—Peoria	IHL	5	285	2	2	‡1	17	0	3.58	—	—	—	—	—	—	—
88-89—Peoria	IHL	35	2051	11	20	‡3	163	1	4.77	3	130	0	2	13	0	6.00
89-90—St. Louis	NHL	4	208	0	3	0	17	0	4.90	—	—	—	—	—	—	—
—Peoria	IHL	36	2043	14	17	‡4	165	0	4.85	4	223	1	3	19	0	5.11
90-91—St. Louis	NHL	8	492	2	3	3	25	0	3.05	3	90	0	0	5	0	3.33
—Peoria	IHL	29	1738	23	3	‡2	87	0	3.00	10	532	7	2	23	0	*2.59
91-92—St. Louis	NHL	10	468	3	6	0	38	0	4.87	—	—	—	—	—	—	—
—Peoria	IHL	8	493	6	1	‡1	29	1	3.53	—	—	—	—	—	—	—
92-93—Tampa Bay	NHL	43	2268	8	24	4	150	1	3.97	—	—	—	—	—	—	—
93-94—Tampa Bay	NHL	15	834	5	6	3	54	0	3.88	—	—	—	—	—	—	—
—St. John's	AHL	16	963	12	3	1	49	1	3.05	—	—	—	—	—	—	—
94-95—Chicago	IHL	4	217	0	4	‡0	17	0	4.70	—	—	—	—	—	—	—
—Houston	IHL	3	179	1	1	‡1	9	0	3.02	—	—	—	—	—	—	—
NHL totals		80	4270	18	42	10	284	1	3.99	3	90	0	0	5	0	3.33

JACKSON, DANE
RW, CANUCKS

PERSONAL: Born May 17, 1970, in Winnipeg. . . . 6-1/200. . . . Shoots right.
COLLEGE: North Dakota.
TRANSACTIONS/CAREER NOTES: Selected by Vancouver Canucks in third round (third Canucks pick, 44th overall) of NHL entry draft (June 11, 1988). . . . Bruised shoulder (January 9, 1994); missed two games.

Season Team	League	REGULAR SEASON				PLAYOFFS			
		Gms.	G	A	Pts.	PIM	Gms.	G	A	Pts.	PIM
87-88—Vernon	BCJHL	50	28	32	60	99	13	7	10	17	49
88-89—Univ. of North Dakota	WCHA	30	4	5	9	33	—	—	—	—	—
89-90—Univ. of North Dakota	WCHA	44	15	11	26	56	—	—	—	—	—
90-91—Univ. of North Dakota	WCHA	37	17	9	26	79	—	—	—	—	—
91-92—Univ. of North Dakota	WCHA	39	23	19	42	81	—	—	—	—	—
92-93—Hamilton	AHL	68	23	20	43	59	—	—	—	—	—
93-94—Hamilton	AHL	60	25	35	60	75	4	2	2	4	16
—Vancouver	NHL	12	5	1	6	9	—	—	—	—	—
94-95—Syracuse	AHL	78	30	28	58	162	—	—	—	—	—
—Vancouver	NHL	3	1	0	1	4	6	0	0	0	10
NHL totals		15	6	1	7	13	6	0	0	0	10

JAGR, JAROMIR
RW, PENGUINS

PERSONAL: Born February 15, 1972, in Kladno, Czechoslovakia. . . . 6-2/208. . . . Shoots left. . . . Name pronounced YAH-guhr.
TRANSACTIONS/CAREER NOTES: Selected by Pittsburgh Penguins in first round (first Penguins pick, fifth overall) of NHL entry draft (June 16, 1990). . . . Separated shoulder (February 23, 1993); missed three games. . . . Strained groin (January 21, 1994); missed four games. . . . Played in Europe during 1994-95 NHL lockout.
HONORS: Named to Czechoslovakian League All-Star team (1989-90). . . . Named to NHL All-Rookie team (1990-91). . . . Played in NHL All-Star Game (1992 and 1993). . . . Won Art Ross Trophy (1994-95). . . . Named to THE SPORTING NEWS All-Star first team (1994-95). . . . Named to NHL All-Star first team (1994-95).
STATISTICAL PLATEAUS: Three-goal games: 1990-91 (1), 1994-95 (1). Total: 2.
MISCELLANEOUS: Member of Stanley Cup championship teams (1991 and 1992).

Season Team	League	REGULAR SEASON				PLAYOFFS			
		Gms.	G	A	Pts.	PIM	Gms.	G	A	Pts.	PIM
88-89—Poldi Kladno	Czech.	39	8	10	18	. . .	—	—	—	—	—
89-90—Poldi Kladno	Czech.	51	30	30	60	. . .	—	—	—	—	—
90-91—Pittsburgh	NHL	80	27	30	57	42	24	3	10	13	6
91-92—Pittsburgh	NHL	70	32	37	69	34	†21	11	13	24	6
92-93—Pittsburgh	NHL	81	34	60	94	61	12	5	4	9	23

Season	Team	League	REGULAR SEASON					PLAYOFFS				
			Gms.	G	A	Pts.	PIM	Gms.	G	A	Pts.	PIM
93-94—Pittsburgh		NHL	80	32	67	99	61	6	2	4	6	16
94-95—HC Kladno		Czech.	11	8	14	22	10	—	—	—	—	—
—HC Bolzano		EURO	5	8	8	16	4	—	—	—	—	—
—HC Bolzano		Italy	1	0	0	0	0	—	—	—	—	—
—Schalker Haie		Ger. Div. II	1	1	10	11	0	—	—	—	—	—
—Pittsburgh		NHL	48	32	38	†70	37	12	10	5	15	6
NHL totals			359	157	232	389	235	75	31	36	67	57

JAKOPIN, JOHN
LW, RED WINGS

PERSONAL: Born July 2, 1975, in Cranbrook, B.C. . . . 6-2/194. . . . Shoots left.
HIGH SCHOOL: St. Michael's (Victoria, B.C.).
COLLEGE: Merrimack (Mass.).
TRANSACTIONS/CAREER NOTES: Selected by Detroit Red Wings in fourth round (fourth Red Wings pick, 97th overall) of NHL entry draft (June 26, 1993).
HONORS: Named to Hockey East All-Rookie team (1993-94).

Season	Team	League	REGULAR SEASON					PLAYOFFS				
			Gms.	G	A	Pts.	PIM	Gms.	G	A	Pts.	PIM
92-93—St. Michael's H.S.		Jr. A	45	9	21	30	42	—	—	—	—	—
93-94—Merrimack College		Hockey East	36	2	8	10	64	—	—	—	—	—
94-95—Merrimack College		Hockey East	37	4	10	14	42	—	—	—	—	—

JAKS, PAULI
G, KINGS

PERSONAL: Born January 25, 1972, in Schaffhausen, Switzerland. . . . 6-0/194. . . . Catches left. . . . Name pronounced YAHKS.
TRANSACTIONS/CAREER NOTES: Selected by Los Angeles Kings in fifth round (fourth Kings pick, 108th overall) of NHL entry draft (June 22, 1991).

Season	Team	League	REGULAR SEASON							PLAYOFFS						
			Gms.	Min.	W	L	T	GA	SO	Avg.	Gms.	Min.	W	L	GA SO	Avg.
90-91—Ambri Piotta		Switz.	22	1247	...	...	...	100	0	4.81	—	—	—	—	— —	—
91-92—Ambri Piotta		Switz.	33	1890	25	7	1	97	2	3.08	—	—	—	—	— —	—
92-93—Ambri Piotta		Switz.	29	...	20	8	1	92	...	3.17	—	—	—	—	— —	—
93-94—Phoenix		IHL	33	1712	16	13	‡1	101	0	3.54	—	—	—	—	— —	—
94-95—Phoenix		IHL	15	636	2	4	‡4	44	0	4.15	—	—	—	—	— —	—
—Los Angeles		NHL	1	40	0	0	0	2	0	3.00	—	—	—	—	— —	—
NHL totals			1	40	0	0	0	2	0	3.00						

JANNEY, CRAIG
C, SHARKS

PERSONAL: Born September 26, 1967, in Hartford, Conn. . . . 6-1/190. . . . Shoots left. . . . Full name: Craig Harlan Janney.
HIGH SCHOOL: Deerfield (Mass.) Academy.
COLLEGE: Boston College.
TRANSACTIONS/CAREER NOTES: Broke collarbone (December 1985). . . . Selected by Boston Bruins in first round (first Bruins pick, 13th overall) of NHL entry draft (June 21, 1986). . . . Suffered from mononucleosis (December 1986). . . . Pulled right groin (December 1988); missed seven games. . . . Tore right groin muscle (October 26, 1989); missed 21 games. . . . Strained left shoulder (April 5, 1990). . . . Sprained left shoulder (December 13, 1990). . . . Sprained right ankle (March 30, 1991). . . . Traded by Bruins with D Stephane Quintal to St. Louis Blues for C Adam Oates (February 7, 1992). . . . Suffered leg laceration (December 1, 1993); missed one game. . . . Strained knee (February 20, 1994); missed 11 games. . . . Awarded to Vancouver Canucks with second-round pick in 1994 draft (C Dave Scatchard) as compensation for Blues signing free agent C Petr Nedved (March 14, 1994). . . . Traded by Canucks to Blues for D Jeff Brown, D Bret Hedican and C Nathan LaFayette (March 21, 1994). . . . Left Blues for personal reasons (February 17-March 6, 1995). . . . Traded by Blues to San Jose Sharks for D Jeff Norton, fourth-round pick in 1997 draft and future considerations (March 6, 1995).
HONORS: Named to NCAA All-America East first team (1986-87). . . . Named to Hockey East All-Star first team (1986-87). . . . Named to Hockey East All-Decade team (1994).
STATISTICAL PLATEAUS: Three-goal games: 1987-88 (1), 1991-92 (1), 1992-93 (1). Total: 3.

Season	Team	League	REGULAR SEASON					PLAYOFFS				
			Gms.	G	A	Pts.	PIM	Gms.	G	A	Pts.	PIM
84-85—Deerfield Academy		Mass. H.S.	17	33	35	68	6	—	—	—	—	—
85-86—Boston College		Hockey East	34	13	14	27	8	—	—	—	—	—
86-87—Boston College		Hockey East	37	28	*55	*83	6	—	—	—	—	—
87-88—U.S. national team		Int'l	52	26	44	70	6	—	—	—	—	—
—U.S. Olympic Team		Int'l	5	3	1	4	2	—	—	—	—	—
—Boston		NHL	15	7	9	16	0	23	6	10	16	11
88-89—Boston		NHL	62	16	46	62	12	10	4	9	13	21
89-90—Boston		NHL	55	24	38	62	4	18	3	19	22	2
90-91—Boston		NHL	77	26	66	92	8	18	4	18	22	11
91-92—Boston		NHL	53	12	39	51	20	—	—	—	—	—
—St. Louis		NHL	25	6	30	36	2	6	0	6	6	0
92-93—St. Louis		NHL	84	24	82	106	12	11	2	9	11	0
93-94—St. Louis		NHL	69	16	68	84	24	4	1	3	4	0
94-95—St. Louis		NHL	8	2	5	7	0	—	—	—	—	—
—San Jose		NHL	27	5	15	20	10	11	3	4	7	4
NHL totals			475	138	398	536	92	101	23	78	101	49

JANSSENS, MARK

C, WHALERS

PERSONAL: Born May 19, 1968, in Surrey, B.C.... 6-3/216.... Shoots left.
TRANSACTIONS/CAREER NOTES: Selected by New York Rangers as underage junior in fourth round (fourth Rangers pick, 72nd overall) of NHL entry draft (June 21, 1986).... Fractured skull and suffered cerebral concussion (December 10, 1988).... Traded by Rangers to Minnesota North Stars for C Mario Thyer and third-round pick (D Maxim Galanov) in 1993 draft (March 10, 1992).... Traded by North Stars to Hartford Whalers for C James Black (September 3, 1992).... Separated shoulder (December 26, 1992); missed five games.... Fined $500 by Whalers for involvement in bar brawl (April 1, 1994).... Suffered slight concussion (February 4, 1995); missed two games.

			REGULAR SEASON					PLAYOFFS				
Season	Team	League	Gms.	G	A	Pts.	PIM	Gms.	G	A	Pts.	PIM
84-85—Regina		WHL	70	8	22	30	51	5	1	1	2	0
85-86—Regina		WHL	71	25	38	63	146	9	0	2	2	17
86-87—Regina		WHL	68	24	38	62	209	3	0	1	1	14
87-88—Regina		WHL	71	39	51	90	202	4	3	4	7	6
—New York Rangers		NHL	1	0	0	0	0	—	—	—	—	—
—Colorado		IHL	6	2	2	4	24	12	3	2	5	20
88-89—New York Rangers		NHL	5	0	0	0	0	—	—	—	—	—
—Denver		IHL	38	19	19	38	104	4	3	0	3	18
89-90—New York Rangers		NHL	80	5	8	13	161	9	2	1	3	10
90-91—New York Rangers		NHL	67	9	7	16	172	6	3	0	3	6
91-92—New York Rangers		NHL	4	0	0	0	5	—	—	—	—	—
—Binghamton		AHL	55	10	23	33	109	—	—	—	—	—
—Minnesota		NHL	3	0	0	0	0	—	—	—	—	—
—Kalamazoo		IHL	2	0	0	0	2	11	1	2	3	22
92-93—Hartford		NHL	76	12	17	29	237	—	—	—	—	—
93-94—Hartford		NHL	84	2	10	12	137	—	—	—	—	—
94-95—Hartford		NHL	46	2	5	7	93	—	—	—	—	—
NHL totals			366	30	47	77	805	15	5	1	6	16

JEAN, YANICK

D, CAPITALS

PERSONAL: Born November 26, 1975, in Alma, Que.... 6-1/198.... Shoots left.... Name pronounced YAH-neek ZHAHN.
HIGH SCHOOL: CEGEP de Chicoutimi (Que.).
TRANSACTIONS/CAREER NOTES: Selected by Washington Capitals in fifth round (fifth Capitals pick, 119th overall) of NHL entry draft (June 29, 1994).

			REGULAR SEASON					PLAYOFFS				
Season	Team	League	Gms.	G	A	Pts.	PIM	Gms.	G	A	Pts.	PIM
92-93—Chicoutimi		QMJHL	50	2	2	4	40	3	0	0	0	0
93-94—Chicoutimi		QMJHL	65	11	30	41	177	27	8	12	20	82
94-95—Chicoutimi		QMJHL	71	7	46	53	155	13	2	7	9	25

JENNINGS, GRANT

D

PERSONAL: Born May 5, 1965, in Hudson Bay, Sask.... 6-3/200.... Shoots left.
TRANSACTIONS/CAREER NOTES: Injured shoulder (1984-85)... Signed as free agent by Washington Capitals (June 25, 1985).... Injured knee (October 1986).... Traded by Capitals with RW Ed Kastelic to Hartford Whalers for D Neil Sheehy and RW Mike Millar (July 6, 1988).... Broke left hand (October 6, 1988).... Bruised right foot (October 1988).... Sprained left shoulder (December 1988).... Underwent surgery to left shoulder (April 14, 1989).... Sprained left knee (February 7, 1990).... Twisted knee (March 14, 1990).... Strained left ankle (September 1990).... Bruised shoulder (December 1, 1990); missed six games.... Injured shoulder (February 13, 1991).... Traded by Whalers with C Ron Francis and D Ulf Samuelsson to Pittsburgh Penguins for C John Cullen, D Zarley Zalapski and RW Jeff Parker (March 4, 1991).... Separated left shoulder (March 1991).... Bruised hand (February 15, 1992); missed seven games.... Bruised right hand (March 15, 1992); missed one game.... Bruised left foot (March 11, 1993); missed one game.... Injured groin (December 11, 1993); missed two games.... Sprained knee (December 28, 1993); missed 14 games.... Bruised shoulder (January 31, 1994); missed one game.... Injured hand (March 8, 1994); missed one game.... Injured groin (January 25, 1995); missed three games.... Reinjured groin (February 7, 1995); missed three games.... Reinjured groin (February 25, 1995); missed three games.... Traded by Penguins to Toronto Maple Leafs for D Drake Berehowsky (April 7, 1995).... Injured groin (April 21, 1995); missed one game.... Released by Maple Leafs (June 28, 1995).
MISCELLANEOUS: Member of Stanley Cup championship teams (1991 and 1992).

			REGULAR SEASON					PLAYOFFS				
Season	Team	League	Gms.	G	A	Pts.	PIM	Gms.	G	A	Pts.	PIM
83-84—Saskatoon		WHL	64	5	13	18	102	—	—	—	—	—
84-85—Saskatoon		WHL	47	10	24	34	134	2	1	0	1	2
85-86—Binghamton		AHL	51	0	4	4	109	—	—	—	—	—
86-87—Fort Wayne		IHL	3	0	0	0	0	—	—	—	—	—
—Binghamton		AHL	47	1	5	6	125	13	0	2	2	17
87-88—Binghamton		AHL	56	2	12	14	195	3	1	0	1	15
—Washington		NHL	—	—	—	—	—	1	0	0	0	0
88-89—Hartford		NHL	55	3	10	13	159	4	1	0	1	17
—Binghamton		AHL	2	0	0	0	2	—	—	—	—	—
89-90—Hartford		NHL	64	3	6	9	171	7	0	0	0	13
90-91—Hartford		NHL	44	1	4	5	82	—	—	—	—	—
—Pittsburgh		NHL	13	1	3	4	26	13	1	1	2	16
91-92—Pittsburgh		NHL	53	4	5	9	104	10	0	0	0	12
92-93—Pittsburgh		NHL	58	0	5	5	65	12	0	0	0	8
93-94—Pittsburgh		NHL	61	2	4	6	126	3	0	0	0	2

Season	Team	League	Gms.	G	A	Pts.	PIM	Gms.	G	A	Pts.	PIM
94-95—Pittsburgh	NHL	25	0	4	4	36	—	—	—	—	—	
—Toronto	NHL	10	0	2	2	7	4	0	0	0	0	
NHL totals			383	14	43	57	776	54	2	1	3	68

JENSEN, CHRIS
RW

PERSONAL: Born October 28, 1963, in Fort St. John, B.C. . . . 5-11/180. . . . Shoots right.
COLLEGE: North Dakota.
TRANSACTIONS/CAREER NOTES: Selected by New York Rangers as underage player in fourth round (fourth Rangers pick, 78th overall) of NHL entry draft (June 9, 1982). . . . Injured knee (October 1985). . . . Strained shoulder (October 1986). . . . Underwent shoulder surgery (April 1987). . . . Traded by Rangers to Philadelphia Flyers for D Michael Boyce (September 28, 1988). . . . Underwent surgery to knee (February 1989); missed five weeks. . . . Injured hand (October 1989). . . . Signed as free agent by Portland Pirates (July 1993). . . . Signed as free agent by Minnesota Moose (June 20, 1995).

Season	Team	League	Gms.	G	A	Pts.	PIM	Gms.	G	A	Pts.	PIM
80-81—Kelowna	BCJHL	53	51	45	96	120	—	—	—	—	—	
81-82—Kelowna	BCJHL	48	46	46	92	212	—	—	—	—	—	
82-83—Univ. of North Dakota	WCHA	13	3	3	6	28	—	—	—	—	—	
83-84—Univ. of North Dakota	WCHA	44	24	25	49	100	—	—	—	—	—	
84-85—Univ. of North Dakota	WCHA	40	25	27	52	80	—	—	—	—	—	
85-86—Univ. of North Dakota	WCHA	34	25	40	65	53	—	—	—	—	—	
—New York Rangers	NHL	9	1	3	4	0	—	—	—	—	—	
86-87—New York Rangers	NHL	37	6	7	13	21	—	—	—	—	—	
—New Haven	AHL	14	4	9	13	41	—	—	—	—	—	
87-88—New York Rangers	NHL	7	0	1	1	2	—	—	—	—	—	
—Colorado	IHL	43	10	23	33	68	10	3	7	10	8	
88-89—Hershey	AHL	45	27	31	58	66	10	4	5	9	29	
89-90—Philadelphia	NHL	1	0	0	0	2	—	—	—	—	—	
—Hershey	AHL	43	16	26	42	101	—	—	—	—	—	
90-91—Philadelphia	NHL	18	2	1	3	2	—	—	—	—	—	
—Hershey	AHL	50	26	20	46	83	6	2	2	4	10	
91-92—Hershey	AHL	71	38	33	71	134	6	0	1	1	2	
—Philadelphia	NHL	2	0	0	0	0	—	—	—	—	—	
92-93—Hershey	AHL	74	33	47	80	95	—	—	—	—	—	
93-94—Portland	AHL	56	33	28	61	52	16	6	10	16	22	
94-95—Portland	AHL	67	35	42	77	89	7	4	3	7	0	
NHL totals			74	9	12	21	27						

JINMAN, LEE
C, STARS

PERSONAL: Born January 10, 1976, in Scarborough, Ont. . . . 5-10/160. . . . Shoots right.
HIGH SCHOOL: Chippewa (North Bay, Ont.).
TRANSACTIONS/CAREER NOTES: Selected by Dallas Stars in second round (second Stars pick, 46th overall) of NHL entry draft (June 28, 1994).
HONORS: Named to Can.HL All-Rookie team (1993-94). . . . Named to OHL All-Rookie team (1993-94).

Season	Team	League	Gms.	G	A	Pts.	PIM	Gms.	G	A	Pts.	PIM
92-93—Wexford	Tier II Jr. A	42	37	53	90	14	—	—	—	—	—	
93-94—North Bay	OHL	66	31	66	97	33	18	*18	19	37	8	
94-95—North Bay	OHL	63	39	65	104	41	6	5	5	10	4	

JOBIN, FREDERIC
D, CAPITALS

PERSONAL: Born January 28, 1977, in Montreal. . . . 6-0/210. . . . Shoots left.
TRANSACTIONS/CAREER NOTES: Selected by Washington Capitals in sixth round (eighth Capitals pick, 147th overall) of NHL entry draft (July 8, 1995).

Season	Team	League	Gms.	G	A	Pts.	PIM	Gms.	G	A	Pts.	PIM
93-94—Laval	QMJHL	67	4	11	15	150	21	2	1	3	40	
94-95—Laval	QMJHL	70	0	13	13	285	20	1	1	2	106	

JOHANSSON, CALLE
D, CAPITALS

PERSONAL: Born February 14, 1967, in Goteborg, Sweden. . . . 5-11/200. . . . Shoots left. . . . Name pronounced KAL-ee yoh-HAHN-sehn.
TRANSACTIONS/CAREER NOTES: Selected by Buffalo Sabres in first round (first Sabres pick, 14th overall) of NHL entry draft (June 15, 1985). . . . Dislocated thumb (October 9, 1988). . . . Traded by Sabres with second-round pick in 1989 draft (G Byron Dafoe) to Washington Capitals for D Grant Ledyard and G Clint Malarchuk (March 6, 1989). . . . Injured back (October 7, 1989); missed 10 games. . . . Bruised ribs (January 9, 1993); missed seven games. . . . Played in Europe during 1994-95 NHL lockout. . . . Suffered from the flu (March 25, 1995); missed two games.
HONORS: Named to NHL All-Rookie team (1987-88).

Season	Team	League	Gms.	G	A	Pts.	PIM	Gms.	G	A	Pts.	PIM
83-84—Vastra Frolunda	Sweden	34	5	10	15	20	—	—	—	—	—	
84-85—Vastra Frolunda	Sweden	36	14	15	29	20	6	1	2	3	4	
85-86—Bjorkloven	Sweden	17	1	1	2	14	—	—	—	—	—	

Season Team	League	REGULAR SEASON Gms.	G	A	Pts.	PIM	PLAYOFFS Gms.	G	A	Pts.	PIM
86-87—Bjorkloven	Sweden	30	2	13	15	18	6	1	3	4	6
87-88—Buffalo	NHL	71	4	38	42	37	6	0	1	1	0
88-89—Buffalo	NHL	47	2	11	13	33	—	—	—	—	—
—Washington	NHL	12	1	7	8	4	6	1	2	3	0
89-90—Washington	NHL	70	8	31	39	25	15	1	6	7	4
90-91—Washington	NHL	80	11	41	52	23	10	2	7	9	8
91-92—Washington	NHL	80	14	42	56	49	7	0	5	5	4
92-93—Washington	NHL	77	7	38	45	56	6	0	5	5	4
93-94—Washington	NHL	84	9	33	42	59	6	1	3	4	4
94-95—Kloten	Switzerland	5	1	2	3	8	—	—	—	—	—
—Washington	NHL	46	5	26	31	35	7	3	1	4	0
NHL totals		567	61	267	328	321	63	8	30	38	24

JOHANSSON, MATHIAS
C, FLAMES

PERSONAL: Born February 22, 1974, in Oskarshamn, Sweden. . . . 6-2/187. . . . Shoots left.

TRANSACTIONS/CAREER NOTES: Selected by Calgary Flames in third round (third Flames pick, 54th overall) of NHL entry draft (June 20, 1992).

Season Team	League	REGULAR SEASON Gms.	G	A	Pts.	PIM	PLAYOFFS Gms.	G	A	Pts.	PIM
90-91—Farjestad Karlstad	Sweden	3	0	0	0	0	—	—	—	—	—
91-92—Farjestad Karlstad	Sweden	16	0	0	0	2	1	0	0	0	0
92-93—Farjestad Karlstad	Sweden	11	2	1	3	4	3	0	0	0	0
93-94—Farjestad Karlstad	Sweden	16	2	1	3	4	—	—	—	—	—
94-95—Farjestad Karlstad	Sweden	40	7	8	15	30	4	4	3	7	2

JOHANSSON, ROGER
D, BLACKHAWKS

PERSONAL: Born April 17, 1967, in Ljungby, Sweden. . . . 6-3/190. . . . Shoots left. . . . Name pronounced joh-HAN-suhn.

TRANSACTIONS/CAREER NOTES: Selected by Calgary Flames in fourth round (fifth Flames pick, 80th overall) of NHL entry draft (June 15, 1985). . . . Suffered intestinal infection (November 24, 1990); missed 11 games. . . . Suffered infected elbow (December 12, 1992); missed two games. . . . Selected by Chicago Blackhawks in 1994-95 waiver draft for cash (January 18, 1995). . . . Played in Europe during 1994-95 NHL lockout.

MISCELLANEOUS: Member of gold-medal-winning Swedish Olympic team (1994).

Season Team	League	REGULAR SEASON Gms.	G	A	Pts.	PIM	PLAYOFFS Gms.	G	A	Pts.	PIM
83-84—Troja Sr.	Sweden	8	2	1	3	8	—	—	—	—	—
84-85—Troja Sr.	Sweden	30	1	10	11	28	—	—	—	—	—
85-86—Troja Sr.	Sweden	32	5	16	21	42	—	—	—	—	—
86-87—Farjestad Karlstad	Sweden	31	6	11	17	22	7	1	1	2	8
87-88—Farjestad Karlstad	Sweden	24	3	11	14	20	—	—	—	—	—
88-89—Farjestad Karlstad	Sweden	40	5	15	20	36	—	—	—	—	—
89-90—Calgary	NHL	35	0	5	5	48	—	—	—	—	—
90-91—Calgary	NHL	38	4	13	17	47	—	—	—	—	—
91-92—Leksand	Sweden	22	3	9	12	42	—	—	—	—	—
92-93—Calgary	NHL	77	4	16	20	62	5	0	1	1	2
93-94—Leksand	Sweden	38	6	15	21	56	4	0	1	1	0
—Swedish Olympic Team	Int'l	8	2	0	2	8	—	—	—	—	—
94-95—Leksand	Sweden	7	0	0	0	14	—	—	—	—	—
—Chicago	NHL	11	1	0	1	6	—	—	—	—	—
NHL totals		161	9	34	43	163	5	0	1	1	2

JOHNSON, BRENT
G, DENVER

PERSONAL: Born March 12, 1977, in Farmington, Mich. . . . 6-1/175. . . . Catches left.

TRANSACTIONS/CAREER NOTES: Selected by Denver in fifth round (fifth Denver pick, 129th overall) of NHL entry draft (July 8, 1995).

Season Team	League	REGULAR SEASON Gms.	Min.	W	L	T	GA	SO	Avg.	PLAYOFFS Gms.	Min.	W	L	GA	SO	Avg.
94-95—Owen Sound	OHL	18	904	3	9	1	75	0	4.98	—	—	—	—	—	—	—

JOHNSON, CRAIG
LW, BLUES

PERSONAL: Born March 18, 1972, in St. Paul, Minn. . . . 6-2/185. . . . Shoots left.

HIGH SCHOOL: Hill-Murray (St. Paul, Minn.).

COLLEGE: Minnesota.

TRANSACTIONS/CAREER NOTES: Suffered stress fracture of vertebrae (February 1987). . . . Selected by St. Louis Blues in second round (first Blues pick, 33rd overall) of NHL entry draft (June 16, 1990). . . . Separated shoulder (December 1990).

HONORS: Named to WCHA All-Rookie Team (1990-91).

Season Team	League	REGULAR SEASON Gms.	G	A	Pts.	PIM	PLAYOFFS Gms.	G	A	Pts.	PIM
87-88—Hill Murray H.S.	Minn. H.S.	28	14	20	34	4	—	—	—	—	—
88-89—Hill Murray H.S.	Minn. H.S.	24	22	30	52	10	—	—	—	—	—
89-90—Hill Murray H.S.	Minn. H.S.	23	15	36	51	. . .	—	—	—	—	—

Season Team	League	REGULAR SEASON					PLAYOFFS				
		Gms.	G	A	Pts.	PIM	Gms.	G	A	Pts.	PIM
90-91—University of Minnesota ...	WCHA	33	13	18	31	34	—	—	—	—	—
91-92—University of Minnesota ...	WCHA	44	19	39	58	70	—	—	—	—	—
92-93—University of Minnesota ...	WCHA	42	22	24	46	70	—	—	—	—	—
93-94—U.S. national team	Int'l	54	25	26	51	64	—	—	—	—	—
—U.S. Olympic Team	Int'l	8	0	4	4	4	—	—	—	—	—
94-95—Peoria	IHL	16	2	6	8	25	9	0	4	4	10
—St. Louis	NHL	15	3	3	6	6	1	0	0	0	2
NHL totals................		15	3	3	6	6	1	0	0	0	2

JOHNSON, GREG
C/RW, RED WINGS

PERSONAL: Born March 16, 1971, in Thunder Bay, Ont. . . . 5-10/174. . . . Shoots left. . . . Brother of Ryan Johnson, center in Florida Panthers system.
COLLEGE: North Dakota.
TRANSACTIONS/CAREER NOTES: Selected by Philadelphia Flyers in second round (first Flyers pick, 33rd overall) of NHL entry draft (June 17, 1989). . . . Separated right shoulder (November 24, 1990). . . . Rights traded by Flyers with future considerations to Detroit Red Wings for RW Jim Cummins and fourth-round pick (traded to Boston Bruins who selected D Charles Paquette) in 1993 draft (June 20, 1993). . . . Loaned to Canadian Olympic Team (January 19, 1994). . . . Returned to Red Wings (March 1, 1994). . . . Sprained left ankle (April 14, 1995); missed last nine games of season.
HONORS: Named to USHL All-Star first team (1988-89). . . . Named Canadian Junior A Player of the Year (1989). . . . Named to Centennial Cup All-Star first team (1989). . . . Named to NCAA All-America West first team (1990-91 and 1992-93). . . . Named to WCHA All-Star first team (1990-91 through 1992-93). . . . Named to NCAA West All-America second team (1991-92).
MISCELLANEOUS: Member of silver-medal-winning Canadian Olympic team (1994).

Season Team	League	REGULAR SEASON					PLAYOFFS				
		Gms.	G	A	Pts.	PIM	Gms.	G	A	Pts.	PIM
88-89—Thunder Bay Jrs.	USHL	47	32	64	96	4	12	5	13	18	0
89-90—Univ. of North Dakota.......	WCHA	44	17	38	55	11	—	—	—	—	—
90-91—Univ. of North Dakota.......	WCHA	38	18	*61	79	6	—	—	—	—	—
91-92—Univ. of North Dakota.......	WCHA	39	20	54	74	8	—	—	—	—	—
92-93—Canadian national team ...	Int'l	23	6	14	20	2	—	—	—	—	—
—Univ. of North Dakota.......	WCHA	34	19	45	64	18	—	—	—	—	—
93-94—Detroit	NHL	52	6	11	17	22	7	2	2	4	2
—Canadian national team ...	Int'l	6	2	6	8	4	—	—	—	—	—
—Canadian Olympic Team ..	Int'l	8	0	3	3	0	—	—	—	—	—
—Adirondack	AHL	3	2	4	6	0	4	0	4	4	2
94-95—Detroit	NHL	22	3	5	8	14	1	0	0	0	0
NHL totals................		74	9	16	25	36	8	2	2	4	2

JOHNSON, JIM
D, CAPITALS

PERSONAL: Born August 9, 1962, in New Hope, Minn. . . . 6-1/190. . . . Shoots left. . . . Full name: James Erik Johnson.
HIGH SCHOOL: Cooper (New Hope, Minn.).
COLLEGE: Minnesota-Duluth.
TRANSACTIONS/CAREER NOTES: Signed as free agent by Pittsburgh Penguins (June 9, 1985). . . . Tore cartilage in right knee (January 1988). . . . Suffered back pain (October 1990). . . . Injured neck (November 12, 1990); missed three games. . . . Traded by Penguins with D Chris Dahlquist to Minnesota North Stars for D Peter Taglianetti and D Larry Murphy (December 11, 1990). . . . Sprained back (February 12, 1991); missed two games. . . . Bruised hip (April 1991). . . . Injured groin (December 7, 1991); missed five games. . . . Strained hamstring (March 10, 1992); missed two games. . . . Lacerated face (November 14, 1992); missed two games. . . . Broke finger (January 3, 1993); missed one game. . . . Sprained knee (April 14, 1993); missed final two games of season. . . . North Stars franchise moved from Minnesota to Dallas and renamed Stars for 1993-94 season. . . . Sprained knee (October 23, 1993); missed three games. . . . Injured neck (January 18, 1994); missed 14 games. . . . Traded by Stars to Washington Capitals for LW Alan May and seventh-round pick (RW Jeff Dewar) in 1995 draft (March 21, 1994). . . . Tore medial collateral knee ligament (April 5, 1994); missed remainder of season. . . . Bruised arm (February 13, 1995); missed one game.

Season Team	League	REGULAR SEASON					PLAYOFFS				
		Gms.	G	A	Pts.	PIM	Gms.	G	A	Pts.	PIM
81-82—Minnesota-Duluth	WCHA	40	0	10	10	62	—	—	—	—	—
82-83—Minnesota-Duluth	WCHA	44	3	18	21	118	—	—	—	—	—
83-84—Minnesota-Duluth	WCHA	43	3	13	16	116	—	—	—	—	—
84-85—Minnesota-Duluth	WCHA	47	7	29	36	49	—	—	—	—	—
85-86—Pittsburgh	NHL	80	3	26	29	115	—	—	—	—	—
86-87—Pittsburgh	NHL	80	5	25	30	116	—	—	—	—	—
87-88—Pittsburgh	NHL	55	1	12	13	87	—	—	—	—	—
88-89—Pittsburgh	NHL	76	2	14	16	163	11	0	5	5	44
89-90—Pittsburgh	NHL	75	3	13	16	154	—	—	—	—	—
90-91—Pittsburgh	NHL	24	0	5	5	23	—	—	—	—	—
—Minnesota	NHL	44	1	9	10	100	14	0	1	1	52
91-92—Minnesota	NHL	71	4	10	14	102	7	1	3	4	18
92-93—Minnesota	NHL	79	3	20	23	105	—	—	—	—	—
93-94—Dallas	NHL	53	0	7	7	51	—	—	—	—	—
—Washington	NHL	8	0	0	0	12	—	—	—	—	—
94-95—Washington	NHL	47	0	13	13	43	7	0	2	2	8
NHL totals................		692	22	154	176	1071	39	1	11	12	122

JOHNSON, MATT
LW, KINGS

PERSONAL: Born November 23, 1975, in Pelham, Ont.... 6-5/223.... Shoots left.
TRANSACTIONS/CAREER NOTES: Selected by Los Angeles Kings in second round (second Kings pick, 33rd overall) of NHL entry draft (June 28, 1994).... Suffered from the flu (February 25, 1995); missed one game.... Bruised right hand (April 3, 1995); missed four games.

			REGULAR SEASON					PLAYOFFS				
Season Team	League	Gms.	G	A	Pts.	PIM		Gms.	G	A	Pts.	PIM
91-92—Welland	Jr. B	38	6	19	25	214		—	—	—	—	—
92-93—Peterborough	OHL	66	8	17	25	211		16	1	1	2	54
93-94—Peterborough	OHL	50	13	24	37	233		—	—	—	—	—
94-95—Peterborough	OHL	14	1	2	3	43		—	—	—	—	—
—Los Angeles	NHL	14	1	0	1	102		—	—	—	—	—
NHL totals		14	1	0	1	102						

JOHNSON, RYAN
C, PANTHERS

PERSONAL: Born June 14, 1976, in Thunder Bay, Ont.... 6-2/180.... Shoots left.... Brother of Greg Johnson, center/right winger, Detroit Red Wings.
COLLEGE: North Dakota.
TRANSACTIONS/CAREER NOTES: Selected by Florida Panthers in second round (fourth Panthers pick, 36th overall) of NHL entry draft (June 28, 1994).

			REGULAR SEASON					PLAYOFFS				
Season Team	League	Gms.	G	A	Pts.	PIM		Gms.	G	A	Pts.	PIM
93-94—Thunder Bay Jrs.	USHL	48	14	36	50	28		—	—	—	—	—
94-95—Univ. of North Dakota	WCHA	38	6	22	28	39		—	—	—	—	—

JOMPHE, JEAN-FRANCOIS
C, MIGHTY DUCKS

PERSONAL: Born December 28, 1972, in Harve St. Pierre, Que.... 6-1/193.... Shoots left.... Name pronounced ZHOHMF.
TRANSACTIONS/CAREER NOTES: Signed as free agent by Mighty Ducks of Anaheim (September 7, 1993).... Loaned by Mighty Ducks to Canadian national team (September 28, 1994).

			REGULAR SEASON					PLAYOFFS				
Season Team	League	Gms.	G	A	Pts.	PIM		Gms.	G	A	Pts.	PIM
90-91—Shawinigan	QMJHL	42	17	22	39	14		6	2	1	3	2
91-92—Shawinigan	QMJHL	44	28	33	61	69		10	6	10	16	10
92-93—Sherbrooke	QMJHL	60	43	43	86	86		15	10	13	23	18
93-94—San Diego	IHL	29	2	3	5	12		—	—	—	—	—
—Greensboro	ECHL	25	9	9	18	41		1	1	0	1	0
94-95—Canadian national team	Int'l	52	33	25	58	85		—	—	—	—	—

JONES, KEITH
RW, CAPITALS

PERSONAL: Born November 8, 1968, in Brantford, Ont.... 6-0/200.... Shoots left.
COLLEGE: Western Michigan.
TRANSACTIONS/CAREER NOTES: Selected by Washington Capitals in seventh round (seventh Capitals pick, 141st overall) of NHL entry draft (June 11, 1988).... Suffered from the flu (January 21, 1993); missed two games.... Sprained wrist (January 25, 1994); missed six games.... Injured foot (March 16, 1995); missed one game.... Separated ribs and bruised foot (March 29, 1995); missed six games.
HONORS: Named to CCHA All-Star first team (1991-92).

			REGULAR SEASON					PLAYOFFS				
Season Team	League	Gms.	G	A	Pts.	PIM		Gms.	G	A	Pts.	PIM
87-88—Niagara Falls	OHA	40	50	80	130	...		—	—	—	—	—
88-89—Western Michigan Univ.	CCHA	37	9	12	21	51		—	—	—	—	—
89-90—Western Michigan Univ.	CCHA	40	19	18	37	82		—	—	—	—	—
90-91—Western Michigan Univ.	CCHA	41	30	19	49	106		—	—	—	—	—
91-92—Western Michigan Univ.	CCHA	35	25	31	56	77		—	—	—	—	—
—Baltimore	AHL	6	2	4	6	0		—	—	—	—	—
92-93—Baltimore	AHL	8	7	3	10	4		—	—	—	—	—
—Washington	NHL	71	12	14	26	124		6	0	0	0	10
93-94—Washington	NHL	68	16	19	35	149		11	0	1	1	36
—Portland	AHL	6	5	7	12	4		—	—	—	—	—
94-95—Washington	NHL	40	14	6	20	65		7	4	4	8	22
NHL totals		179	42	39	81	338		24	4	5	9	68

JONSSON, KENNY
D, MAPLE LEAFS

PERSONAL: Born October 5, 1974, in Angelholm, Sweden.... 6-3/195.... Shoots left.... Name pronounced YAHN-suhn.
TRANSACTIONS/CAREER NOTES: Selected by Toronto Maple Leafs in first round (first Maple Leafs pick, 12th overall) of NHL entry draft (June 26, 1993).... Played in Europe during 1994-95 NHL lockout.... Suffered from the flu (February 13, 1995); missed two games.... Strained hip flexor (February 27, 1995); missed one game.... Suffered hip pointer (April 7, 1995); missed one game.... Suffered from the flu (April 19, 1995); missed one game.
HONORS: Named Swedish League Rookie of the Year (1992-93).... Named to NHL All-Rookie team (1994-95).

			REGULAR SEASON					PLAYOFFS				
Season Team	League	Gms.	G	A	Pts.	PIM		Gms.	G	A	Pts.	PIM
91-92—Rogle	Sweden	30	4	11	15	24		—	—	—	—	—
92-93—Rogle	Sweden	39	3	10	13	42		—	—	—	—	—

Season	Team	League	REGULAR SEASON Gms.	G	A	Pts.	PIM	PLAYOFFS Gms.	G	A	Pts.	PIM
94-95	—Rogle	Sweden	8	3	1	4	20	—	—	—	—	—
	—St. John's	AHL	10	2	5	7	2	—	—	—	—	—
	—Toronto	NHL	39	2	7	9	16	4	0	0	0	0
NHL totals			39	2	7	9	16	4	0	0	0	0

JOSEPH, CHRIS

D, PENGUINS

PERSONAL: Born September 10, 1969, in Burnaby, B.C.... 6-2/210.... Shoots right.... Full name: Robin Christopher Joseph.
HIGH SCHOOL: Alpha (Burnaby, B.C.).
TRANSACTIONS/CAREER NOTES: Selected by Pittsburgh Penguins in first round (first Penguins pick, fifth overall) of NHL entry draft (June 13, 1987).... Traded by Penguins with C Craig Simpson, C Dave Hannan and D Moe Mantha to Edmonton Oilers for D Paul Coffey, LW Dave Hunter and RW Wayne Van Dorp (November 24, 1987)....
Strained knee ligaments (January 1989).... Traded by Oilers to Tampa Bay Lightning for D Bob Beers (November 12, 1993). ... Selected by Pittsburgh Penguins in 1994-95 waiver draft for cash (January 18, 1995).... Damaged right knee ligaments (March 2, 1995); missed 14 games.

Season	Team	League	REGULAR SEASON Gms.	G	A	Pts.	PIM	PLAYOFFS Gms.	G	A	Pts.	PIM
85-86	—Seattle	WHL	72	4	8	12	50	5	0	3	3	12
86-87	—Seattle	WHL	67	13	45	58	155	—	—	—	—	—
87-88	—Pittsburgh	NHL	17	0	4	4	12	—	—	—	—	—
	—Edmonton	NHL	7	0	4	4	6	—	—	—	—	—
	—Nova Scotia	AHL	8	0	2	2	8	4	0	0	0	9
	—Seattle	WHL	23	5	14	19	49	—	—	—	—	—
88-89	—Cape Breton	AHL	5	1	1	2	18	—	—	—	—	—
	—Edmonton	NHL	44	4	5	9	54	—	—	—	—	—
89-90	—Edmonton	NHL	4	0	2	2	2	—	—	—	—	—
	—Cape Breton	AHL	61	10	20	30	69	6	2	1	3	4
90-91	—Edmonton	NHL	49	5	17	22	59	—	—	—	—	—
91-92	—Edmonton	NHL	7	0	0	0	8	5	1	3	4	2
	—Cape Breton	AHL	63	14	29	43	72	5	0	2	2	8
92-93	—Edmonton	NHL	33	2	10	12	48	—	—	—	—	—
93-94	—Edmonton	NHL	10	1	1	2	28	—	—	—	—	—
	—Tampa Bay	NHL	66	10	19	29	108	—	—	—	—	—
94-95	—Pittsburgh	NHL	33	5	10	15	46	10	1	1	2	12
NHL totals			270	27	72	99	371	15	2	4	6	14

JOSEPH, CURTIS

G, OILERS

PERSONAL: Born April 29, 1967, in Keswick, Ont.... 5-10/182.... Catches left.... Full name: Curtis Shayne Joseph.
HIGH SCHOOL: Huron Heights (Newmarket, Ont.).
COLLEGE: Wisconsin.
TRANSACTIONS/CAREER NOTES: Signed as free agent by St. Louis Blues (June 16, 1989).... Dislocated left shoulder (April 11, 1990).... Underwent surgery to left shoulder (May 10, 1990).... Sprained right knee (February 26, 1991); missed remainder of season.... Injured ankle (March 12, 1992); missed seven games.... Suffered sore knee (January 2, 1993); missed three games.... Suffered from the flu (February 9, 1993); missed one game.... Slightly strained groin (January 26, 1995); missed three games.... Pulled hamstring (April 16, 1995); missed four games.... Rights traded by Blues with rights to RW Mike Grier for first-round picks in 1996 and 1997 drafts (August 4, 1995); picks had been awarded earlier to Oilers as compensation for Blues signing free agent LW Shayne Corson (July 28, 1995).
HONORS: Named OHA Most Valuable Player (1986-87).... Won WCHA Most Valuable Player Award (1988-89).... Won WCHA Rookie of the Year Award (1988-89).... Named to NCAA All-America West second team (1988-89).... Named to WCHA All-Star first team (1988-89).... Played in NHL All-Star Game (1994).

Season	Team	League	REGULAR SEASON Gms.	Min.	W	L	T	GA	SO	Avg.	PLAYOFFS Gms.	Min.	W	L	GA	SO	Avg.
86-87	—Richmond Hill	OHA						Statistics unavailable.									
87-88	—Notre Dame	SCMHL	36	2174	25	4	7	94	1	2.59	—	—	—	—	—	—	—
88-89	—Univ. of Wisconsin	WCHA	38	2267	21	11	5	94	1	2.49	—	—	—	—	—	—	—
89-90	—Peoria	IHL	23	1241	10	8	‡2	80	0	3.87	—	—	—	—	—	—	—
	—St. Louis	NHL	15	852	9	5	1	48	0	3.38	6	327	4	1	18	0	3.30
90-91	—St. Louis	NHL	30	1710	16	10	2	89	0	3.12	—	—	—	—	—	—	—
91-92	—St. Louis	NHL	60	3494	27	20	10	175	2	3.01	6	379	2	4	23	0	3.64
92-93	—St. Louis	NHL	68	3890	29	28	9	196	1	3.02	11	715	7	4	27	2	2.27
93-94	—St. Louis	NHL	71	4127	36	23	11	213	1	3.10	4	246	0	4	15	0	3.66
94-95	—St. Louis	NHL	36	1914	20	10	1	89	1	2.79	7	392	3	3	24	0	3.67
NHL totals			280	15987	137	96	34	810	5	3.04	34	2059	16	16	107	2	3.12

JOUBERT, JACQUES

C

PERSONAL: Born March 23, 1971, in South Bend, Ind.... 6-1/191.... Shoots left. ... Name pronounced zhoh-BAIR.
COLLEGE: Boston University.
TRANSACTIONS/CAREER NOTES: Selected by Dallas Stars in NHL supplemental draft (June 25, 1993).
HONORS: Named to Hockey East All-Star first team (1993-94).

Season	Team	League	REGULAR SEASON Gms.	G	A	Pts.	PIM	PLAYOFFS Gms.	G	A	Pts.	PIM
92-93	—Boston University	Hockey East	40	17	18	35	54	—	—	—	—	—

Season Team	League	REGULAR SEASON Gms.	G	A	Pts.	PIM	PLAYOFFS Gms.	G	A	Pts.	PIM
93-94—Boston University	Hockey East	41	20	24	44	82	—	—	—	—	—
94-95—Boston University	Hockey East	40	29	23	52	41	—	—	—	—	—

JOVANOVSKI, ED
D, PANTHERS

PERSONAL: Born June 26, 1976, in Windsor, Ont. . . . 6-2/210. . . . Shoots left. . . . Name pronounced JOH-vuh-NAHF-skee.
HIGH SCHOOL: Riverside Secondary (Windsor, Ont.).
TRANSACTIONS/CAREER NOTES: Selected by Florida Panthers in first round (first Panthers pick, first overall) of NHL entry draft (June 28, 1994).
HONORS: Named to Can.HL All-Rookie team (1993-94). . . . Named to OHL All-Star second team (1993-94). . . . Named to OHL All-Rookie team (1993-94). . . . Named to Can.HL All-Star second team (1994-95). . . . Named to OHL All-Star first team (1994-95).

Season Team	League	REGULAR SEASON Gms.	G	A	Pts.	PIM	PLAYOFFS Gms.	G	A	Pts.	PIM
92-93—Windsor	OHL Jr. B	48	7	46	53	88	—	—	—	—	—
93-94—Windsor	OHL	62	15	35	50	221	4	0	0	0	15
94-95—Windsor	OHL	50	23	42	65	198	9	2	7	9	39

JUHLIN, PATRIK
LW, FLYERS

PERSONAL: Born April 24, 1970, in Huddinge, Sweden. . . . 6-0/187. . . . Shoots left. . . . Name pronounced YOO-lihn.
TRANSACTIONS/CAREER NOTES: Selected by Philadelphia Flyers in second round (second Flyers pick, 34th overall) of NHL entry draft (June 17, 1989). . . . Played in Europe during 1994-95 NHL lockout. . . . Sprained left knee (April 26, 1995); missed last three games of season.
MISCELLANEOUS: Member of gold-medal-winning Swedish Olympic team (1994).

Season Team	League	REGULAR SEASON Gms.	G	A	Pts.	PIM	PLAYOFFS Gms.	G	A	Pts.	PIM
87-88—Vasteras	Sweden	28	25	10	35	. . .	—	—	—	—	—
88-89—Vasteras	Sweden	30	29	13	42	. . .	—	—	—	—	—
89-90—Vasteras	Sweden	35	10	13	23	18	2	0	0	0	0
90-91—Vasteras	Sweden	40	13	9	22	24	—	—	—	—	—
91-92—Vasteras	Sweden	39	15	12	27	40	—	—	—	—	—
92-93—Vasteras	Sweden	34	14	12	26	22	3	0	1	1	0
93-94—Vasteras	Sweden	40	15	16	31	20	4	1	1	2	0
—Swedish Olympic Team	Int'l	8	7	1	8	16	—	—	—	—	—
94-95—Vasteras	Sweden	11	5	9	14	8	—	—	—	—	—
—Philadelphia	NHL	42	4	3	7	6	13	1	0	1	2
NHL totals...............		42	4	3	7	6	13	1	0	1	2

JUNEAU, JOE
C, CAPITALS

PERSONAL: Born January 5, 1968, in Pont-Rouge, Que. . . . 6-0/195. . . . Shoots left. . . . Name pronounced zhoh-AY ZHOO-noh.
COLLEGE: Rensselaer Polytechnic Institute (N.Y.).
TRANSACTIONS/CAREER NOTES: Selected by Boston Bruins in fourth round (third Bruins pick, 81st overall) of NHL entry draft (June 11, 1988). . . . Suffered ligament problem in back (November 1990). . . . Broke jaw (November 7, 1993); missed seven games. . . . Reinjured jaw (February 18, 1994); missed two games. . . . Traded by Bruins to Washington Capitals for D Al Iafrate (March 21, 1994). . . . Sustained hip flexor (January 29, 1995); missed one game. . . . Strained back (February 15, 1995); missed one game. . . . Bruised arm (April 11, 1995); missed one game. . . . Injured leg (April 30, 1995); missed one game.
HONORS: Named to NCAA All-America East first team (1989-90). . . . Named to ECAC All-Star first team (1989-90). . . . Named to NCAA All-America East second team (1990-91). . . . Named to ECAC All-Star second team (1990-91). . . . Named to NHL All-Rookie team (1992-93).
RECORDS: Holds NHL single-season record for most assists by a left winger—70 (1992-93). . . . Holds NHL single-season record for most assists by a rookie—70 (1992-93).
STATISTICAL PLATEAUS: Three-goal games: 1992-93 (1).
MISCELLANEOUS: Member of silver-medal-winning Canadian Olympic team (1992).

Season Team	League	REGULAR SEASON Gms.	G	A	Pts.	PIM	PLAYOFFS Gms.	G	A	Pts.	PIM
87-88—R.P.I.	ECAC	31	16	29	45	18	—	—	—	—	—
88-89—R.P.I.	ECAC	30	12	23	35	40	—	—	—	—	—
89-90—R.P.I.	ECAC	34	18	*52	*70	31	—	—	—	—	—
90-91—R.P.I.	ECAC	29	23	40	63	70	—	—	—	—	—
91-92—Canadian national team ...	Int'l	60	20	49	69	35	—	—	—	—	—
—Canadian Olympic Team ..	Int'l	8	6	9	15	4	—	—	—	—	—
—Boston	NHL	14	5	14	19	4	15	4	8	12	21
92-93—Boston	NHL	84	32	70	102	33	4	2	4	6	6
93-94—Boston	NHL	63	14	58	72	35	—	—	—	—	—
—Washington	NHL	11	5	8	13	6	11	4	5	9	6
94-95—Washington	NHL	44	5	38	43	8	7	2	6	8	2
NHL totals...............		216	61	188	249	86	37	12	23	35	35

JUNKER, STEVE
RW, ISLANDERS

PERSONAL: Born June 26, 1972, in Castlegar, B.C. . . . 6-0/191. . . . Shoots left.
TRANSACTIONS/CAREER NOTES: Selected by New York Islanders in fifth round (fifth Islanders pick, 92nd overall) of NHL entry draft (June 22, 1991).

Season	Team	League	REGULAR SEASON					PLAYOFFS				
			Gms.	G	A	Pts.	PIM	Gms.	G	A	Pts.	PIM
90-91	Spokane	WHL	71	39	38	77	86	15	5	13	18	6
91-92	Spokane	WHL	58	28	32	60	110	10	6	7	13	18
92-93	Capital District	AHL	79	16	31	47	20	4	0	0	0	0
	New York Islanders	NHL	—	—	—	—	—	3	0	1	1	0
93-94	Salt Lake City	IHL	71	9	14	23	36	—	—	—	—	—
	New York Islanders	NHL	5	0	0	0	0	—	—	—	—	—
94-95	Denver	IHL	72	13	16	29	37	11	3	4	7	4
NHL totals			5	0	0	0	0	3	0	1	1	0

JUNKIN, DALE
LW, WHALERS

PERSONAL: Born May 23, 1973, in Oshawa, Ont. . . . 5-11/196. . . . Shoots left.
TRANSACTIONS/CAREER NOTES: Signed as free agent by Hartford Whalers (September 23, 1994).

Season	Team	League	REGULAR SEASON					PLAYOFFS				
			Gms.	G	A	Pts.	PIM	Gms.	G	A	Pts.	PIM
90-91	Kingston	OHL	63	6	7	13	28	—	—	—	—	—
91-92	Niagara Falls	OHL	62	20	19	39	22	17	4	4	8	12
92-93	Niagara Falls	OHL	65	29	49	78	50	4	1	3	4	0
93-94	Niagara Falls	OHL	41	28	18	46	39	—	—	—	—	—
	Detroit	OHL	23	13	17	30	6	17	13	13	26	6

KACIR, MARIAN
RW, LIGHTNING

PERSONAL: Born September 29, 1974, in Hodonin, Czechoslovakia. . . . 6-1/183. . . . Shoots left. . . . Name pronounced kuh-SIHR.
TRANSACTIONS/CAREER NOTES: Selected by Tampa Bay Lightning in fourth round (fourth Lightning pick, 81st overall) of NHL entry draft (June 26, 1993). . . . Loaned to Chicago Wolves (October 14, 1994).

Season	Team	League	REGULAR SEASON					PLAYOFFS				
			Gms.	G	A	Pts.	PIM	Gms.	G	A	Pts.	PIM
91-92	Czechoslovakia Jr.	Czech.	6	6	4	10	2	8	3	5	8	4
92-93	Owen Sound	OHL	56	20	36	56	8	8	3	5	8	4
93-94	Owen Sound	OHL	66	23	64	87	26	9	5	4	9	2
94-95	Chicago	IHL	29	4	6	10	6	—	—	—	—	—
	Charlotte	ECHL	5	2	3	5	2	—	—	—	—	—
	Nashville	ECHL	9	1	7	8	2	4	1	2	3	6

KALLIO, TOMI
LW, DENVER

PERSONAL: Born January 27, 1977, in Turku, Finland. . . . 6-1/176. . . . Shoots left.
TRANSACTIONS/CAREER NOTES: Selected by Denver in fourth round (fourth Denver pick, 81st overall) of NHL entry draft (July 8, 1995).

Season	Team	League	REGULAR SEASON					PLAYOFFS				
			Gms.	G	A	Pts.	PIM	Gms.	G	A	Pts.	PIM
93-94	TPS Jr.	Finland	33	9	7	16	16	6	0	1	1	2
94-95	Kiekko-67	Finland Dv.II	25	8	5	13	16	7	3	1	4	6
	TPS Jr.	Finland	14	5	12	17	24	—	—	—	—	—

KAMENSKY, VALERI
LW, DENVER

PERSONAL: Born April 18, 1966, in Voskresensk, U.S.S.R. . . . 6-2/198. . . . Shoots right. . . . Name pronounced kuh-MEHN-skee.
TRANSACTIONS/CAREER NOTES: Selected by Quebec Nordiques in seventh round (eighth Nordiques pick, 129th overall) of NHL entry draft (June 11, 1988). . . . Fractured leg (October 1991); missed 57 games. . . . Broke left thumb (October 17, 1992); missed three games. . . . Broke right ankle (October 27, 1992); missed 47 games. . . . Bruised left foot (October 21, 1993); missed two games. . . . Bruised right foot (December 21, 1993); missed one game. . . . Played in Europe during 1994-95 NHL lockout. . . . Suffered kidney infection (February 26, 1995); missed eight games. . . . Nordiques franchise moved to Denver for 1995-96 season.
HONORS: Won Soviet Player of the Year Award (1990-91).
MISCELLANEOUS: Member of gold-medal-winning U.S.S.R. Olympic team (1988).

Season	Team	League	REGULAR SEASON					PLAYOFFS				
			Gms.	G	A	Pts.	PIM	Gms.	G	A	Pts.	PIM
82-83	Khimik	USSR	5	0	0	0	0	—	—	—	—	—
83-84	Khimik	USSR	20	2	2	4	6	—	—	—	—	—
84-85	Khimik	USSR	45	9	3	12	24	—	—	—	—	—
85-86	CSKA Moscow	USSR	40	15	9	24	8	—	—	—	—	—
86-87	CSKA Moscow	USSR	37	13	8	21	16	—	—	—	—	—
87-88	CSKA Moscow	USSR	51	26	20	46	40	—	—	—	—	—
	Soviet Olympic Team	Int'l	8	4	2	6	4	—	—	—	—	—
88-89	CSKA Moscow	USSR	40	18	10	28	30	—	—	—	—	—
89-90	CSKA Moscow	USSR	45	19	18	37	38	—	—	—	—	—
90-91	CSKA Moscow	USSR	46	20	26	46	66	—	—	—	—	—
91-92	Quebec	NHL	23	7	14	21	14	—	—	—	—	—
92-93	Quebec	NHL	32	15	22	37	14	6	0	1	1	6
93-94	Quebec	NHL	76	28	37	65	42	—	—	—	—	—
94-95	Ambri Piotta	Switzerland	12	13	6	19	2	—	—	—	—	—
	Quebec	NHL	40	10	20	30	22	2	1	0	1	0
NHL totals			171	60	93	153	92	8	1	1	2	6

KAMINSKI, KEVIN
C, CAPITALS

PERSONAL: Born March 13, 1969, in Churchbridge, Sask. . . . 5-10/190. . . . Shoots left.
TRANSACTIONS/CAREER NOTES: Selected by Minnesota North Stars as underage junior in third round (third North Stars pick, 48th overall) of NHL entry draft (June 13, 1987). . . . Suspended 12 games by WHL for cross-checking (November 4, 1987). . . . Traded by North Stars to Quebec Nordiques for LW Gaetan Duchesne (June 18, 1989). . . . Separated shoulder in training camp (September 1989). . . . Suspended two games by AHL for head-butting (January 26, 1990). . . . Traded by Nordiques to Washington Capitals for D Mark Matier (June 15, 1993). . . . Suspended three games by AHL for postgame altercation (November 30, 1994).

			REGULAR SEASON					PLAYOFFS			
Season	Team	League	Gms.	G	A	Pts.	PIM	Gms.	G	A	Pts.	PIM
84-85—Saskatoon	WHL	5	0	1	1	17	—	—	—	—	—
85-86—Saskatoon	WHL	4	1	1	2	35	—	—	—	—	—
86-87—Saskatoon	WHL	67	26	44	70	235	11	5	6	11	45
87-88—Saskatoon	WHL	55	38	61	99	247	10	5	7	12	37
88-89—Saskatoon	WHL	52	25	43	68	199	8	4	9	13	25
—Minnesota	NHL	1	0	0	0	0	—	—	—	—	—
89-90—Quebec	NHL	1	0	0	0	0	—	—	—	—	—
—Halifax	AHL	19	3	4	7	128	2	0	0	0	5
90-91—Halifax	AHL	7	1	0	1	44	—	—	—	—	—
—Fort Wayne	IHL	56	9	15	24	*455	19	4	2	6	*169
91-92—Halifax	AHL	63	18	27	45	329	—	—	—	—	—
—Quebec	NHL	5	0	0	0	45	—	—	—	—	—
92-93—Halifax	AHL	79	27	37	64	*345	—	—	—	—	—
93-94—Portland	AHL	39	10	22	32	263	16	4	5	9	*91
—Washington	NHL	13	0	5	5	87	—	—	—	—	—
94-95—Portland	AHL	34	15	20	35	292	—	—	—	—	—
—Washington	NHL	27	1	1	2	102	5	0	0	0	36
NHL totals		47	1	6	7	234	5	0	0	0	36

KAMINSKY, YAN
RW, ISLANDERS

PERSONAL: Born July 28, 1971, in Penza, U.S.S.R. . . . 6-1/176. . . . Shoots left. . . . Name pronounced YAHN kuh-MIHN-skee.
TRANSACTIONS/CAREER NOTES: Selected by Winnipeg Jets in fifth round (fourth Jets pick, 99th overall) of NHL entry draft (June 22, 1991). . . . Separated shoulder (January 6, 1994); missed six games. . . . Traded by Jets to New York Islanders for D Wayne McBean (February 1, 1994).

			REGULAR SEASON					PLAYOFFS			
Season	Team	League	Gms.	G	A	Pts.	PIM	Gms.	G	A	Pts.	PIM
89-90—Dynamo Moscow	USSR	6	1	0	1	4	—	—	—	—	—
90-91—Dynamo Moscow	USSR	25	10	5	15	2	—	—	—	—	—
91-92—Dynamo Moscow	CIS	42	9	7	16	22	—	—	—	—	—
92-93—Dynamo Moscow	CIS	39	15	14	29	12	10	2	5	7	8
93-94—Moncton	AHL	33	9	13	22	6	—	—	—	—	—
—Winnipeg	NHL	1	0	0	0	0	—	—	—	—	—
—New York Islanders	NHL	23	2	1	3	4	2	0	0	0	4
94-95—Denver	IHL	38	17	16	33	14	15	6	6	12	0
—New York Islanders	NHL	2	1	1	2	0	—	—	—	—	—
NHL totals		26	3	2	5	4	2	0	0	0	4

KAPANEN, SAMI
LW, WHALERS

PERSONAL: Born June 14, 1973, in Vantaa, Finland. . . . 5-10/169. . . . Shoots left.
TRANSACTIONS/CAREER NOTES: Selected by Hartford Whalers in fourth round (fourth Whalers pick, 87th overall) of NHL entry draft (July 8, 1995).

			REGULAR SEASON					PLAYOFFS			
Season	Team	League	Gms.	G	A	Pts.	PIM	Gms.	G	A	Pts.	PIM
90-91—KalPa Kuopio	Finland	14	1	1	2	2	8	2	1	3	2
91-92—KalPa Kuopio	Finland	42	15	10	25	8	—	—	—	—	—
92-93—KalPa Kuopio	Finland	37	4	17	21	12	—	—	—	—	—
93-94—KalPa Kuopio	Finland	48	23	32	55	16	—	—	—	—	—
94-95—HIFK Helsinki	Finland	49	14	28	42	42	3	0	0	0	0

KARABIN, LADISLAV
LW, PENGUINS

PERSONAL: Born February 16, 1970, in Bratislava, Czechoslovakia. . . . 6-1/189. . . . Shoots left.
TRANSACTIONS/CAREER NOTES: Selected by Pittsburgh Penguins in ninth round (ninth Penguins pick, 173rd overall) of NHL entry draft (June 16, 1990).

			REGULAR SEASON					PLAYOFFS			
Season	Team	League	Gms.	G	A	Pts.	PIM	Gms.	G	A	Pts.	PIM
91-92—Bratislava	Czech.	24	4	8	12	. . .	—	—	—	—	—
92-93—Bratislava	Czech.	39	21	23	44	. . .	—	—	—	—	—
93-94—Cleveland	IHL	58	13	26	39	48	—	—	—	—	—
—Pittsburgh	NHL	9	0	0	0	2	—	—	—	—	—
94-95—Cleveland	IHL	47	15	25	40	26	4	0	0	0	2
NHL totals		9	0	0	0	2					

KARAMNOV, VITALI
LW

PERSONAL: Born July 6, 1968, in Moscow, U.S.S.R. . . . 6-2/198. . . . Shoots left. . . . Name pronounced vee-TAL-ee kuh-RAHM-nahf.
TRANSACTIONS/CAREER NOTES: Selected by St. Louis Blues in third round (second Blues pick, 62nd overall) of NHL entry draft (June 20, 1992). . . . Pulled groin (October 15, 1992); missed 14 games. . . . Injured ankle (January 28, 1994); missed four games. . . . Reinjured ankle (February 5, 1994); missed five games. . . . Suffered from the flu (March 13, 1994); missed one game.

			REGULAR SEASON					PLAYOFFS			
Season	Team	League	Gms.	G	A	Pts.	PIM	Gms.	G	A	Pts.	PIM
86-87	Dynamo Moscow	USSR	4	0	0	0	0	—	—	—	—	—
87-88	Dynamo Moscow	USSR	2	0	1	1	0	—	—	—	—	—
88-89	Dynamo Kharkov	USSR	23	4	1	5	19	—	—	—	—	—
89-90	Torpedo Yaroslavl	USSR	47	6	7	13	32	—	—	—	—	—
90-91	Torpedo Yaroslavl	USSR	45	14	7	21	30	—	—	—	—	—
91-92	Dynamo Moscow	CIS	40	13	19	32	25	—	—	—	—	—
92-93	St. Louis	NHL	7	0	1	1	0	—	—	—	—	—
	Peoria	IHL	23	8	12	20	47	—	—	—	—	—
93-94	St. Louis	NHL	59	9	12	21	51	—	—	—	—	—
	Peoria	IHL	3	0	1	1	2	1	0	1	1	0
94-95	St. Louis	NHL	26	3	7	10	14	2	0	0	0	2
	Peoria	IHL	15	6	9	15	7	—	—	—	—	—
NHL totals			92	12	20	32	65	2	0	0	0	2

KARIYA, PAUL
LW, MIGHTY DUCKS

PERSONAL: Born October 16, 1974, in Vancouver. . . . 5-11/175. . . . Shoots left. . . . Name pronounced kuh-REE-uh.
COLLEGE: Maine.
TRANSACTIONS/CAREER NOTES: Selected by Mighty Ducks of Anaheim in first round (first Mighty Ducks pick, fourth overall) of NHL entry draft (June 26, 1993). . . . Suffered lower back spasms (February 12, 1995); missed one game.
HONORS: Won Hobey Baker Memorial Award (1992-93). . . . Named Hockey East Player of the Year (1992-93). . . . Named Hockey East Rookie of the Year (1992-93). . . . Named to NCAA All-America East first team (1992-93). . . . Named to NCAA All-Tournament team (1992-93). . . . Named to Hockey East All-Star first team (1992-93). . . . Named to Hockey East All-Rookie team (1992-93). . . . Named to Hockey East All-Decade team (1994). . . . Named to NHL All-Rookie team (1994-95).
MISCELLANEOUS: Member of silver-medal-winning Canadian Olympic team (1994).

			REGULAR SEASON					PLAYOFFS			
Season	Team	League	Gms.	G	A	Pts.	PIM	Gms.	G	A	Pts.	PIM
90-91	Penticton	BCJHL	54	45	67	112	8	—	—	—	—	—
91-92	Penticton	BCJHL	40	46	86	132	16	—	—	—	—	—
92-93	University of Maine	Hockey East	39	25	*75	*100	12	—	—	—	—	—
93-94	Canadian national team	Int'l	23	7	34	41	2	—	—	—	—	—
	Canadian Olympic Team	Int'l	8	3	4	7	2	—	—	—	—	—
	University of Maine	Hockey East	12	8	16	24	4	—	—	—	—	—
94-95	Anaheim	NHL	47	18	21	39	4	—	—	—	—	—
NHL totals			47	18	21	39	4					

KARPA, DAVID
D, MIGHTY DUCKS

PERSONAL: Born May 7, 1971, in Regina, Sask. . . . 6-1/202. . . . Shoots right. . . . Full name: David James Karpa.
COLLEGE: Ferris State (Mich.).
TRANSACTIONS/CAREER NOTES: Selected by Quebec Nordiques in fourth round (fourth Nordiques pick, 68th overall) of NHL entry draft (June 22, 1991). . . . Broke right wrist (January 26, 1994); missed 18 games. . . . Traded by Nordiques to Los Angeles Kings for fourth-round pick in 1995 or 1996 draft (February 28, 1995); trade invalidated by NHL because Karpa failed his physical examination (March 3, 1995). . . . Traded by Nordiques to Mighty Ducks of Anaheim for fourth-round pick in 1997 draft (March 8, 1995). . . . Underwent right wrist surgery (May 9, 1995).

			REGULAR SEASON					PLAYOFFS			
Season	Team	League	Gms.	G	A	Pts.	PIM	Gms.	G	A	Pts.	PIM
88-89	Notre Dame	SCMHL	. . .	16	37	53	. . .	—	—	—	—	—
89-90	Notre Dame	SCMHL	43	9	19	28	271	—	—	—	—	—
90-91	Ferris State	CCHA	41	6	19	25	109	—	—	—	—	—
91-92	Ferris State	CCHA	34	7	12	19	124	—	—	—	—	—
	Halifax	AHL	2	0	0	0	4	—	—	—	—	—
	Quebec	NHL	4	0	0	0	14	—	—	—	—	—
92-93	Halifax	AHL	71	4	27	31	167	—	—	—	—	—
	Quebec	NHL	12	0	1	1	13	3	0	0	0	0
93-94	Quebec	NHL	60	5	12	17	148	—	—	—	—	—
	Cornwall	AHL	1	0	0	0	0	12	2	2	4	27
94-95	Cornwall	AHL	6	0	2	2	19	—	—	—	—	—
	Quebec	NHL	2	0	0	0	0	—	—	—	—	—
	Anaheim	NHL	28	1	5	6	91	—	—	—	—	—
NHL totals			106	6	18	24	266	3	0	0	0	0

KARPOV, VALERI
RW/LW, MIGHTY DUCKS

PERSONAL: Born August 5, 1971, in Chelyabinsk, U.S.S.R. . . . 5-10/176. . . . Shoots left. . . . Name pronounced vuh-LAIR-ee KAHR-pahf.
TRANSACTIONS/CAREER NOTES: Selected by Mighty Ducks of Anaheim in third round (third Mighty Ducks pick, 56th overall) of NHL entry draft (June 26, 1993). . . . Played in Europe during 1994-95 NHL lockout.

K

HONORS: Named to CIS All-Star team (1992-93 and 1993-94).

Season Team	League	REGULAR SEASON					PLAYOFFS				
		Gms.	G	A	Pts.	PIM	Gms.	G	A	Pts.	PIM
88-89—Traktor Chelyabinsk........	USSR	5	0	0	0	0	—	—	—	—	—
89-90—Traktor Chelyabinsk........	USSR	24	1	2	3	6	—	—	—	—	—
90-91—Traktor Chelyabinsk........	USSR	25	8	4	12	15	—	—	—	—	—
91-92—Traktor Chelyabinsk........	CIS	44	16	10	26	34	—	—	—	—	—
92-93—CSKA Moscow.................	CIS	9	2	6	8	0	—	—	—	—	—
—Traktor Chelyabinsk........	CIS	38	12	21	33	6	8	0	1	1	10
93-94—Traktor Chelyabinsk........	CIS	32	11	19	30	18	6	2	5	7	2
—Russian Olympic team......	Int'l	8	3	1	4	2	—	—	—	—	—
94-95—Traktor Chelyabinsk........	CIS	10	6	8	14	8	—	—	—	—	—
—Anaheim.........................	NHL	30	4	7	11	6	—	—	—	—	—
—San Diego.......................	IHL	5	3	3	6	0	—	—	—	—	—
NHL totals................................		30	4	7	11	6					

KARPOVTSEV, ALEXANDER
D, RANGERS

PERSONAL: Born April 7, 1970, in Moscow, U.S.S.R. . . . 6-1/210. . . . Shoots left. . . . Name pronounced KAHR-puht-sehf.

TRANSACTIONS/CAREER NOTES: Selected by Quebec Nordiques in seventh round (seventh Nordiques pick, 158th overall) of NHL entry draft (June 16, 1990). . . . Traded by Nordiques to New York Rangers for D Mike Hurlbut (September 9, 1993). . . . Bruised buttocks (October 9, 1993); missed one game. . . . Bruised hip (November 3, 1993); missed six games. . . . Reinjured hip (November 23, 1993); missed one game. . . . Suffered facial injury (February 28, 1994); missed two games. . . . Suffered injury (March 14, 1994); missed two games. . . . Played in Europe during 1994-95 NHL lockout. . . . Suffered sore ankle (April 14, 1995); missed one game.

MISCELLANEOUS: Member of Stanley Cup championship team (1994).

Season Team	League	REGULAR SEASON					PLAYOFFS				
		Gms.	G	A	Pts.	PIM	Gms.	G	A	Pts.	PIM
89-90—Dynamo Moscow	USSR	35	1	1	2	27	—	—	—	—	—
90-91—Dynamo Moscow	USSR	40	0	5	5	15	—	—	—	—	—
91-92—Dynamo Moscow	CIS	28	3	2	5	22	—	—	—	—	—
92-93—Dynamo Moscow	CIS	40	3	11	14	100	—	—	—	—	—
93-94—New York Rangers	NHL	67	3	15	18	58	17	0	4	4	12
94-95—Dynamo Moscow	CIS	13	0	2	2	10	—	—	—	—	—
—New York Rangers	NHL	47	4	8	12	30	8	1	0	1	0
NHL totals................................		114	7	23	30	88	25	1	4	5	12

KASATONOV, ALEXEI
D, BRUINS

PERSONAL: Born October 14, 1959, in Leningrad, U.S.S.R. . . . 6-1/215. . . . Shoots left. . . . Name pronounced ah-LEHK-suh-nahf.

TRANSACTIONS/CAREER NOTES: Selected by New Jersey Devils in 12th round (ninth Devils pick, 225th overall) of NHL entry draft (June 8, 1983). . . . Broke toe on right foot (February 1990). . . . Suffered from hemorrhoids (December 1991); missed three games. . . . Injured left hand (October 6, 1992); missed three games. . . . Suffered from the flu (December 27, 1992); missed two games. . . . Selected by Mighty Ducks of Anaheim in NHL expansion draft (June 24, 1993). . . . Suffered from the flu (October 30, 1993); missed one game. . . . Bruised right foot (January 26, 1994); missed three games. . . . Suffered hairline fracture of right foot (February 20, 1994); missed 11 games with Mighty Ducks and first four games with St. Louis Blues. . . . Traded by Mighty Ducks to Blues for LW Maxim Bets and sixth-round pick (traded back to St. Louis) in 1995 draft (March 21, 1994). . . . Signed as free agent by Boston Bruins (June 22, 1994). . . . Played in Europe during 1994-95 NHL lockout. . . . Injured ankle (April 1995); missed four games.

HONORS: Named to Soviet League All-Star first team (1979-80 through 1987-88). . . . Played in NHL All-Star Game (1994).

MISCELLANEOUS: Member of silver-medal-winning U.S.S.R. Olympic team (1980) and gold-medal-winning U.S.S.R. Olympic team (1984 and 1988).

Season Team	League	REGULAR SEASON					PLAYOFFS				
		Gms.	G	A	Pts.	PIM	Gms.	G	A	Pts.	PIM
76-77—SKA Leningrad.................	USSR	7	0	0	0	0	—	—	—	—	—
77-78—SKA Leningrad.................	USSR	35	4	7	11	15	—	—	—	—	—
78-79—CSKA Moscow.................	USSR	40	5	14	19	30	—	—	—	—	—
79-80—CSKA Moscow.................	USSR	37	5	8	13	26	—	—	—	—	—
—Soviet Olympic Team........	Int'l	7	2	5	7	8	—	—	—	—	—
80-81—CSKA Moscow.................	USSR	47	10	12	22	38	—	—	—	—	—
81-82—CSKA Moscow.................	USSR	46	12	27	39	45	—	—	—	—	—
82-83—CSKA Moscow.................	USSR	44	12	19	31	37	—	—	—	—	—
83-84—CSKA Moscow.................	USSR	39	12	24	36	20	—	—	—	—	—
—Soviet Olympic Team........	Int'l	7	3	2	5	0	—	—	—	—	—
84-85—CSKA Moscow.................	USSR	40	18	18	36	26	—	—	—	—	—
85-86—CSKA Moscow.................	USSR	40	6	17	23	27	—	—	—	—	—
86-87—CSKA Moscow.................	USSR	40	13	17	30	16	—	—	—	—	—
87-88—CSKA Moscow.................	USSR	43	8	12	20	8	—	—	—	—	—
—Soviet Olympic Team........	Int'l	7	2	6	8	0	—	—	—	—	—
88-89—CSKA Moscow.................	USSR	41	8	14	22	8	—	—	—	—	—
89-90—New Jersey.....................	NHL	39	6	15	21	16	6	0	3	3	14
—Utica.................................	AHL	3	0	2	2	7	—	—	—	—	—
90-91—New Jersey.....................	NHL	78	10	31	41	76	7	1	3	4	8
91-92—New Jersey.....................	NHL	76	12	28	40	70	7	1	1	2	12

					REGULAR SEASON					PLAYOFFS			
Season	Team	League	Gms.	G	A	Pts.	PIM	Gms.	G	A	Pts.	PIM
92-93—New Jersey		NHL	64	3	14	17	57	4	0	0	0	0
93-94—Anaheim		NHL	55	4	18	22	43	—	—	—	—	—
—St. Louis		NHL	8	0	2	2	19	4	2	0	2	2
94-95—CSKA Moscow		CIS	9	2	3	5	6	—	—	—	—	—
—Boston		NHL	44	2	14	16	33	5	0	0	0	2
NHL totals			364	37	122	159	314	33	4	7	11	38

KASPARAITIS, DARIUS
D, ISLANDERS

PERSONAL: Born October 16, 1972, in Elektrenai, U.S.S.R. . . . 5-11/190. . . . Shoots left. . . . Name pronounced KAZ-puhr-IGH-tihz.
TRANSACTIONS/CAREER NOTES: Selected by New York Islanders in first round (first Islanders pick, fifth overall) of NHL entry draft (June 20, 1992). . . . Suffered back spasms (February 12, 1993); missed two games. . . . Strained back (April 15, 1993); missed one game. . . . Strained lower back (November 10, 1993); missed two games. . . . Jammed wrist (March 5, 1994); missed four games. . . . Tore anterior cruciate ligament (February 20, 1995); missed remainder of season.
MISCELLANEOUS: Member of gold-medal-winning Unified Olympic team (1992).

					REGULAR SEASON					PLAYOFFS			
Season	Team	League	Gms.	G	A	Pts.	PIM	Gms.	G	A	Pts.	PIM
88-89—Dynamo Moscow		USSR	3	0	0	0	0	—	—	—	—	—
89-90—Dynamo Moscow		USSR	1	0	0	0	0	—	—	—	—	—
90-91—Dynamo Moscow		USSR	17	0	1	1	10	—	—	—	—	—
91-92—Dynamo Moscow		CIS	31	2	10	12	14	—	—	—	—	—
—Unified Olympic Team		Int'l	8	0	2	2	2	—	—	—	—	—
92-93—Dynamo Moscow		CIS	7	1	3	4	8	—	—	—	—	—
—New York Islanders		NHL	79	4	17	21	166	18	0	5	5	31
93-94—New York Islanders		NHL	76	1	10	11	142	4	0	0	0	8
94-95—New York Islanders		NHL	13	0	1	1	22	—	—	—	—	—
NHL totals			168	5	28	33	330	22	0	5	5	39

KEALTY, JEFF
D, DENVER

PERSONAL: Born April 9, 1976, in Framingham, Mass. . . . 6-4/175. . . . Shoots left.
HIGH SCHOOL: Catholic Memorial (Boston).
COLLEGE: Boston University.
TRANSACTIONS/CAREER NOTES: Selected by Quebec Nordiques in first round (second Nordiques pick, 22nd overall) of NHL entry draft (June 28, 1994). . . . Nordiques franchise moved to Denver for 1995-96 season.

					REGULAR SEASON					PLAYOFFS			
Season	Team	League	Gms.	G	A	Pts.	PIM	Gms.	G	A	Pts.	PIM
90-91—Catholic Memorial H.S.		Mass. H.S.	5	0	2	2	0	—	—	—	—	—
91-92—Catholic Memorial H.S.		Mass. H.S.	25	2	13	15	8	—	—	—	—	—
92-93—Catholic Memorial H.S.		Mass. H.S.	24	3	22	25	10	—	—	—	—	—
93-94—Catholic Memorial H.S.		Mass. H.S.	25	10	22	32	. . .	—	—	—	—	—
94-95—Boston University		Hockey East	25	0	5	5	29	—	—	—	—	—

KEANE, MIKE
RW, CANADIENS

PERSONAL: Born May 29, 1967, in Winnipeg. . . . 5-10/180. . . . Shoots right.
TRANSACTIONS/CAREER NOTES: Signed as free agent by Montreal Canadiens (March 1987). . . . Separated right shoulder (December 21, 1988). . . . Lacerated left kneecap (October 31, 1990); missed seven games. . . . Injured neck (March 1991). . . . Sprained ankle (January 16, 1992); missed four games. . . . Resprained ankle (February 1, 1992); missed 10 games. . . . Bruised ankle (March 11, 1992); missed one game. . . . Suspended four off-days and fined $500 by NHL for swinging stick in preseason game (October 13, 1992). . . . Suffered wrist tendinitis (January 26, 1993); missed three games. . . . Suffered back spasms (February 12, 1993); missed two games. . . . Fractured toe (February 27, 1993); missed two games. . . . Suffered back spasms (October 16, 1993); missed one game. . . . Suffered back spasms (January 12, 1994); missed three games.
MISCELLANEOUS: Member of Stanley Cup championship team (1993). . . . Captain of Montreal Canadiens (1994-95).

					REGULAR SEASON					PLAYOFFS			
Season	Team	League	Gms.	G	A	Pts.	PIM	Gms.	G	A	Pts.	PIM
83-84—Winnipeg		WHL	1	0	0	0	0	—	—	—	—	—
84-85—Moose Jaw		WHL	65	17	26	43	141	—	—	—	—	—
85-86—Moose Jaw		WHL	67	34	49	83	162	13	6	8	14	9
86-87—Moose Jaw		WHL	53	25	45	70	107	9	3	9	12	11
—Sherbrooke		AHL	—	—	—	—	—	9	2	2	4	16
87-88—Sherbrooke		AHL	78	25	43	68	70	6	1	1	2	18
88-89—Montreal		NHL	69	16	19	35	69	21	4	3	7	17
89-90—Montreal		NHL	74	9	15	24	78	11	0	1	1	8
90-91—Montreal		NHL	73	13	23	36	50	12	3	2	5	6
91-92—Montreal		NHL	67	11	30	41	64	8	1	1	2	16
92-93—Montreal		NHL	77	15	45	60	95	19	2	13	15	6
93-94—Montreal		NHL	80	16	30	46	119	6	3	1	4	4
94-95—Montreal		NHL	48	10	10	20	15	—	—	—	—	—
NHL totals			488	90	172	262	490	77	13	21	34	57

KECZMER, DAN
D, FLAMES

PERSONAL: Born May 25, 1968, in Mt. Clemens, Mich. . . . 6-1/190. . . . Shoots left. . . . Full name: Daniel Leonard Keczmer. . . . Name pronounced KEHS-muhr.
COLLEGE: Lake Superior State (Mich.).
TRANSACTIONS/CAREER NOTES: Selected by Minnesota North Stars in 10th round (11th North Stars pick, 201st overall) of NHL entry draft (June 21, 1986). . . . Injured shoulder (February 2, 1990). . . . Claimed by San Jose Sharks as part of ownership change with North Stars (October 1990). . . . Traded by Sharks to Hartford Whalers for C Dean Evason (October 2, 1991). . . . Released by U.S. National team prior to Olympics (January 1992). . . . Suffered right leg contusion (February 8, 1993); missed three games. . . . Traded by Whalers to Calgary Flames for G Jeff Reese and future considerations (November 19, 1993). . . . Separated right shoulder (February 16, 1995); missed 10 games.
HONORS: Named to CCHA All-Star second team (1989-90).

			REGULAR SEASON					PLAYOFFS				
Season	Team	League	Gms.	G	A	Pts.	PIM	Gms.	G	A	Pts.	PIM
86-87—Lake Superior State		CCHA	38	3	5	8	28	—	—	—	—	—
87-88—Lake Superior State		CCHA	41	2	15	17	34	—	—	—	—	—
88-89—Lake Superior State		CCHA	46	3	26	29	70	—	—	—	—	—
89-90—Lake Superior State		CCHA	43	13	23	36	48	—	—	—	—	—
90-91—Minnesota		NHL	9	0	1	1	6	—	—	—	—	—
—Kalamazoo		IHL	60	4	20	24	60	9	1	2	3	10
91-92—U.S. national team		Int'l	51	3	11	14	56	—	—	—	—	—
—Springfield		AHL	18	3	4	7	10	4	0	0	0	6
—Hartford		NHL	1	0	0	0	0	—	—	—	—	—
92-93—Springfield		AHL	37	1	13	14	38	12	0	4	4	14
—Hartford		NHL	23	4	4	8	28	—	—	—	—	—
93-94—Hartford		NHL	12	0	1	1	12	—	—	—	—	—
—Springfield		AHL	7	0	1	1	4	—	—	—	—	—
—Calgary		NHL	57	1	20	21	48	3	0	0	0	4
94-95—Calgary		NHL	28	2	3	5	10	7	0	1	1	2
NHL totals			130	7	29	36	104	10	0	1	1	6

KELLY, STEVE
C, OILERS

PERSONAL: Born October 26, 1976, in Vancouver. . . . 6-1/188. . . . Shoots left.
TRANSACTIONS/CAREER NOTES: Selected by Edmonton Oilers in first round (first Oilers pick, sixth overall) of NHL entry draft (July 8, 1995).

			REGULAR SEASON					PLAYOFFS				
Season	Team	League	Gms.	G	A	Pts.	PIM	Gms.	G	A	Pts.	PIM
92-93—Prince Albert		WHL	65	11	9	20	75	—	—	—	—	—
93-94—Prince Albert		WHL	65	19	42	61	106	—	—	—	—	—
94-95—Prince Albert		WHL	68	31	41	72	153	15	7	9	16	35

KENADY, CHRIS
RW, BLUES

PERSONAL: Born April 10, 1973, in Mound, Minn. . . . 6-2/195. . . . Shoots right.
HIGH SCHOOL: Mound (Minn.) Westonka.
COLLEGE: Denver.
TRANSACTIONS/CAREER NOTES: Selected by St. Louis Blues in eighth round (eighth Blues pick, 175th overall) of NHL entry draft (June 22, 1991).

			REGULAR SEASON					PLAYOFFS				
Season	Team	League	Gms.	G	A	Pts.	PIM	Gms.	G	A	Pts.	PIM
91-92—University of Denver		WCHA	36	8	5	13	56	—	—	—	—	—
92-93—University of Denver		WCHA	38	8	16	24	95	—	—	—	—	—
93-94—University of Denver		WCHA	37	14	11	25	125	—	—	—	—	—
94-95—University of Denver		WCHA	39	21	17	38	113	—	—	—	—	—

KENNEDY, DEAN
D, OILERS

PERSONAL: Born January 18, 1963, in Redvers, Sask. . . . 6-2/212. . . . Shoots right. . . . Full name: Edward Dean Kennedy.
TRANSACTIONS/CAREER NOTES: Selected by Los Angeles Kings as underage junior in second round (second Kings pick, 39th overall) of NHL entry draft (June 10, 1981). . . . Suspended four games by NHL for off-ice altercation (February 18, 1983). . . . Injured knee; missed part of 1981-82 season. . . . Suffered hip pointer (March 1987). . . . Broke finger (November 1987). . . . Injured groin (March 1988). . . . Suffered concussion (November 10, 1988). . . . Traded by Kings with D Denis Larocque to New York Rangers for LW Igor Liba, C Todd Elik, D Michael Boyce and future considerations (December 12, 1988). . . . Traded by Rangers to Los Angeles Kings for fifth-round pick in 1990 draft (February 3, 1989). . . . Traded by Kings to Buffalo Sabres for fourth-round pick in 1990 draft (October 4, 1989). . . . Suffered hip pointer (January 31, 1991); missed nine games. . . . Broke jaw (April 5, 1991). . . . Traded by Sabres with LW Darrin Shannon and D Mike Hartman to Winnipeg Jets for RW Dave McLlwain, D Gordon Donnelly, fifth-round pick in 1992 draft (LW Yuri Khmylev) and future considerations (October 11, 1991). . . . Injured knee (November 20, 1991). . . . Suffered back spasms (December 21, 1992); missed two games. . . . Selected by Edmonton Oilers in 1994-95 waiver draft for cash (January 18, 1995).
MISCELLANEOUS: Captain of Winnipeg Jets (1992-93 and 1993-94).

			REGULAR SEASON					PLAYOFFS				
Season	Team	League	Gms.	G	A	Pts.	PIM	Gms.	G	A	Pts.	PIM
79-80—Weyburn		SJHL	57	12	20	32	64	—	—	—	—	—
—Brandon		WHL	1	0	0	0	0	—	—	—	—	—
80-81—Brandon		WHL	71	3	29	32	157	5	0	2	2	7
81-82—Brandon		WHL	49	5	38	43	103	—	—	—	—	—
82-83—Brandon		WHL	14	2	15	17	22	—	—	—	—	—
—Los Angeles		NHL	55	0	12	12	97	—	—	—	—	—
—Saskatoon		WHL	—	—	—	—	—	4	0	3	3	0

Season	Team	League	REGULAR SEASON					PLAYOFFS				
			Gms.	G	A	Pts.	PIM	Gms.	G	A	Pts.	PIM
83-84—New Haven	AHL	26	1	7	8	23	—	—	—	—	—
—Los Angeles	NHL	37	1	5	6	50	—	—	—	—	—
84-85—New Haven	AHL	76	3	14	17	104	—	—	—	—	—
85-86—Los Angeles	NHL	78	2	10	12	132	—	—	—	—	—
86-87—Los Angeles	NHL	66	6	14	20	91	5	0	2	2	10
87-88—Los Angeles	NHL	58	1	11	12	158	4	0	1	1	10
88-89—New York Rangers	NHL	16	0	1	1	40	—	—	—	—	—
—Los Angeles	NHL	51	3	10	13	63	11	0	2	2	8
89-90—Buffalo	NHL	80	2	12	14	53	6	1	1	2	12
90-91—Buffalo	NHL	64	4	8	12	119	2	0	1	1	17
91-92—Winnipeg	NHL	18	2	4	6	21	2	0	0	0	0
92-93—Winnipeg	NHL	78	1	7	8	105	6	0	0	0	2
93-94—Winnipeg	NHL	76	2	8	10	164	—	—	—	—	—
94-95—Edmonton	NHL	40	2	8	10	25	—	—	—	—	—
NHL totals		717	26	110	136	1118	36	1	7	8	59

KENNEDY, MIKE
LW, STARS

PERSONAL: Born April 3, 1972, in Vancouver.... 6-1/170.... Shoots right.
COLLEGE: British Columbia.
TRANSACTIONS/CAREER NOTES: Selected by Minnesota North Stars in fifth round (third North Stars pick, 97th overall) of NHL entry draft (June 22, 1991).... North Stars franchise moved from Minnesota to Dallas and renamed Stars for 1993-94 season.

Season	Team	League	REGULAR SEASON					PLAYOFFS				
			Gms.	G	A	Pts.	PIM	Gms.	G	A	Pts.	PIM
89-90—British Columbia	CWUAA	9	5	7	12	0	—	—	—	—	—
90-91—British Columbia	CWUAA	28	17	17	34	18	—	—	—	—	—
91-92—Seattle	WHL	71	42	47	89	134	15	11	6	17	20
92-93—Kalamazoo	IHL	77	21	30	51	39	—	—	—	—	—
93-94—Kalamazoo	IHL	63	20	18	38	42	—	—	—	—	—
94-95—Kalamazoo	IHL	42	20	28	48	29	—	—	—	—	—
—Dallas	NHL	44	6	12	18	33	5	0	0	0	9
NHL totals		44	6	12	18	33	5	0	0	0	9

KENNEDY, SHELDON
RW, FLAMES

PERSONAL: Born June 15, 1969, in Brandon, Man.... 5-11/180.... Shoots right.
TRANSACTIONS/CAREER NOTES: Broke ankle (January 18, 1987); missed six weeks.... Selected by Detroit Red Wings in fourth round (fifth Red Wings pick, 80th overall) of NHL entry draft (June 11, 1988).... Separated shoulder (December 5, 1989).... Injured thumb (March 2, 1990).... Took leave of absence to attend alcohol treatment program (March 21, 1990).... Injured left arm in automobile accident (summer 1990); missed 48 games.... Suffered from tonsillitis (February 8, 1991); missed two games.... Suffered from food poisoning (February 19, 1991).... Sent to alcohol treatment center for evaluation (March 27, 1991).... Bruised ribs (November 27, 1993); missed two games.... Injured sternum (March 22, 1994); missed five games.... Traded by Red Wings to Winnipeg Jets for third-round pick (C Darryl Laplante) in 1995 draft (May 25, 1994).... Selected by Calgary Flames in 1994-95 waiver draft for cash (January 18, 1995).... Sprained left shoulder (January 26, 1995); missed one game.... Suffered charley horse (January 28, 1995); missed 10 games.... Suffered from the flu (February 28, 1995); missed one game.... Sprained left shoulder (April 8, 1995); missed six games.... Fined $1,000 by NHL for high-sticking (May 10, 1995).
HONORS: Named to Memorial Cup All-Star team (1988-89).

Season	Team	League	REGULAR SEASON					PLAYOFFS				
			Gms.	G	A	Pts.	PIM	Gms.	G	A	Pts.	PIM
86-87—Swift Current	WHL	49	23	41	64	64	4	0	3	3	4
87-88—Swift Current	WHL	59	53	64	117	45	10	8	9	17	12
88-89—Swift Current	WHL	51	58	48	106	92	—	—	—	—	—
89-90—Detroit	NHL	20	2	7	9	10	—	—	—	—	—
—Adirondack	AHL	26	11	15	26	35	—	—	—	—	—
90-91—Adirondack	AHL	11	1	3	4	8	—	—	—	—	—
—Detroit	NHL	7	1	0	1	12	—	—	—	—	—
91-92—Adirondack	AHL	46	25	24	49	56	16	5	9	14	12
—Detroit	NHL	27	3	8	11	24	—	—	—	—	—
92-93—Detroit	NHL	68	19	11	30	46	7	1	1	2	2
93-94—Detroit	NHL	61	6	7	13	30	7	1	2	3	0
94-95—Calgary	NHL	30	7	8	15	45	7	3	1	4	16
NHL totals		213	38	41	79	167	21	5	4	9	18

KENNY, SHANE
D, FLYERS

PERSONAL: Born March 1, 1977, in Oromocto, N.B.... 6-2/242.... Shoots left.
HIGH SCHOOL: St. Mary's (Edmundston, N.B.).
TRANSACTIONS/CAREER NOTES: Selected by Philadelphia Flyers in second round (second Flyers pick, 48th overall) of NHL entry draft (July 8, 1995).

Season	Team	League	REGULAR SEASON					PLAYOFFS				
			Gms.	G	A	Pts.	PIM	Gms.	G	A	Pts.	PIM
93-94—Owen Sound	OHL	54	4	9	13	138	2	0	0	0	6
94-95—Owen Sound	OHL	65	13	19	32	134	9	0	2	2	8

K

KERCH, ALEXANDER
LW, OILERS

during 1994-95 NHL lockout.

PERSONAL: Born March 16, 1967, in Arkhangelsk, U.S.S.R. . . . . 5-10/190. . . . Shoots right. . . . Name pronounced KUHRSH.
TRANSACTIONS/CAREER NOTES: Selected by Edmonton Oilers in third round (fifth Oilers pick, 60th overall) of NHL entry draft (June 26, 1993). . . . Played in Europe

Season Team	League	REGULAR SEASON					PLAYOFFS				
		Gms.	G	A	Pts.	PIM	Gms.	G	A	Pts.	PIM
84-85—Dynamo Riga	USSR	8	0	0	0	6	—	—	—	—	—
85-86—Dynamo Riga	USSR	23	5	2	7	16	—	—	—	—	—
86-87—Dynamo Riga	USSR	26	5	4	9	10	—	—	—	—	—
87-88—Dynamo Riga	USSR	50	14	4	18	28	—	—	—	—	—
88-89—Dynamo Riga	USSR	39	6	7	13	41	—	—	—	—	—
89-90—Dynamo Riga	USSR	46	9	11	20	22	—	—	—	—	—
90-91—Dynamo Riga	USSR	46	16	17	33	46	—	—	—	—	—
91-92—HC Riga	CIS	42	23	14	37	28	—	—	—	—	—
92-93—Riga Stars	CIS	42	23	14	37	28	2	1	2	3	12
93-94—Cape Breton	AHL	57	24	38	62	16	4	1	1	2	2
—Edmonton	NHL	5	0	0	0	2	—	—	—	—	—
94-95—Pardaugava Riga	CIS	11	4	0	4	4	—	—	—	—	—
—Providence	AHL	1	0	0	0	15	4	0	2	2	0
NHL totals		5	0	0	0	2					

KESA, DAN
RW, STARS

PERSONAL: Born November 23, 1971, in Vancouver. . . . 6-0/198. . . . Shoots right. . . . Name pronounced KEH-suh.
TRANSACTIONS/CAREER NOTES: Selected by Vancouver Canucks in fifth round (fifth Canucks pick, 95th overall) of NHL entry draft (June 22, 1991). . . . Loaned by Syracuse Crunch to Canadian national team (April 6, 1995). . . . Traded by Canucks with LW Greg Adams and fifth-round pick (traded to Los Angeles Kings) in 1995 draft to Dallas Stars for RW Russ Courtnall (April 7, 1995).

Season Team	League	REGULAR SEASON					PLAYOFFS				
		Gms.	G	A	Pts.	PIM	Gms.	G	A	Pts.	PIM
88-89—Richmond	BCJHL	44	21	21	42	71	—	—	—	—	—
89-90—Richmond	BCJHL	54	39	38	77	103	—	—	—	—	—
90-91—Prince Albert	WHL	69	30	23	53	116	3	1	1	2	0
91-92—Prince Albert	WHL	62	46	51	97	201	10	9	10	19	27
92-93—Hamilton	AHL	62	16	24	40	76	—	—	—	—	—
93-94—Hamilton	AHL	53	37	33	70	33	4	1	4	5	4
—Vancouver	NHL	19	2	4	6	18	—	—	—	—	—
94-95—Syracuse	AHL	70	34	44	78	81	—	—	—	—	—
NHL totals		19	2	4	6	18					

KETTERER, MARKUS
G, SABRES

PERSONAL: Born August 23, 1967, in Helsinki, Finland. . . . 5-11/165. . . . Catches left. . . . Name pronounced KEHT-uh-ruhr.
TRANSACTIONS/CAREER NOTES: Selected by Buffalo Sabres in fifth round (sixth Sabres pick, 107th overall) of NHL entry draft (June 20, 1992).

Season Team	League	REGULAR SEASON							PLAYOFFS						
		Gms.	Min.	W	L	T	GA	SO	Avg.	Gms.	Min.	W	L	GA	SO	Avg.
87-88—Jokerit	Finland	21	...	...	...	...	61	0	...	—	—	—	—	—	—	—
88-89—TPS Turku	Finland	34	2021	...	...	...	95	2	2.82	3	139	...	...	6	0	2.59
89-90—TPS Turku	Finland	29	1709	...	...	...	68	1	2.39	7	422	...	...	15	1	2.13
90-91—TPS Turku	Finland	36	2022	...	...	...	85	2	2.52	8	440	...	...	13	2	1.77
91-92—Finnish Olympic Team	Int'l	3	180	...	...	...	8	0	2.67	—	—	—	—	—	—	—
—Jokerit	Finland	37	2128	...	...	...	97	0	2.73	10	634	7	3	20	3	1.89
92-93—Jokerit	Finland	37	2064	...	...	...	96	...	2.79	2	130	0	0	11	0	5.08
93-94—Rochester	AHL	32	1775	9	15	5	110	1	3.72	4	199	0	3	13	0	3.92
94-95—Rochester	AHL	47	2563	19	20	3	154	1	3.61	—	—	—	—	—	—	—

KHABIBULIN, NIKOLAI
G, JETS

PERSONAL: Born January 13, 1973, in Sverdlovsk, U.S.S.R. . . . 6-1/176. . . . Catches left. . . . Name pronounced kah-bih-BOO-lihn.
TRANSACTIONS/CAREER NOTES: Selected by Winnipeg Jets in ninth round (eighth Jets pick, 204th overall) of NHL entry draft (June 20, 1992).

Season Team	League	REGULAR SEASON							PLAYOFFS						
		Gms.	Min.	W	L	T	GA	SO	Avg.	Gms.	Min.	W	L	GA	SO	Avg.
88-89—Avtomobilist Sverdlovsk	USSR	1	3	0	0	0	0	0	0.00	—	—	—	—	—	—	—
89-90—Avtomo. Sverdlovsk Jr.	USSR					Statistics unavailable.										
90-91—Sputnik Nizhny Tagil	USSR Dv.III					Statistics unavailable.										
91-92—CSKA Moscow	CIS	2	34	...	...	...	2	...	3.53	—	—	—	—	—	—	—
92-93—CSKA Moscow	CIS	13	491	...	...	...	27	...	3.30	—	—	—	—	—	—	—
93-94—CSKA Moscow	CIS	46	2625	...	...	...	116	5	2.65	3	193	1	2	11	0	3.42
—Russian Penguins	IHL	12	639	2	9	‡2	47	0	4.41	—	—	—	—	—	—	—
94-95—Springfield	AHL	23	1240	9	9	3	80	0	3.87	—	—	—	—	—	—	—
—Winnipeg	NHL	26	1339	8	9	4	76	0	3.41	—	—	—	—	—	—	—
NHL totals		26	1339	8	9	4	76	0	3.41							

KHARLAMOV, ALEXANDER
LW, CAPITALS

PERSONAL: Born September 23, 1975, in Moscow, U.S.S.R. . . . 5-10/180. . . . Shoots left. . . . Name pronounced HAR-la-moff. . . . Son of Valery Kharlamov, left winger, CSKA Moscow and Soviet national team (1968-81).

TRANSACTIONS/CAREER NOTES: Selected by Washington Capitals in first round (second Capitals pick, 15th overall) of NHL entry draft (June 28, 1994).

			REGULAR SEASON					PLAYOFFS				
Season	Team	League	Gms.	G	A	Pts.	PIM	Gms.	G	A	Pts.	PIM
92-93—CSKA Moscow		CIS	42	8	4	12	12	—	—	—	—	—
93-94—CSKA Moscow		CIS	46	7	7	14	26	3	1	0	1	2
—Russian Penguins		IHL	12	2	2	4	4	—	—	—	—	—
94-95—CSKA Moscow		CIS	45	8	4	12	12	—	—	—	—	—

KHMYLEV, YURI
LW, SABRES

PERSONAL: Born August 9, 1964, in Moscow, U.S.S.R. . . . 6-1/189. . . . Shoots right. . . . Name pronounced HIHM-ih-lehf.

TRANSACTIONS/CAREER NOTES: Selected by Buffalo Sabres in fifth round (seventh Sabres pick, 108th overall) of NHL entry draft (June 20, 1992). . . . Strained right shoulder (November 2, 1992); missed two games. . . . Strained neck (September 19, 1993); missed six games. . . . Suffered left fibula hairline fracture (March 27, 1994); missed six games.

STATISTICAL PLATEAUS: Three-goal games: 1992-93 (1).

MISCELLANEOUS: Member of gold-medal-winning Unified Olympic team (1992).

			REGULAR SEASON					PLAYOFFS				
Season	Team	League	Gms.	G	A	Pts.	PIM	Gms.	G	A	Pts.	PIM
81-82—Soviet Wings		USSR	8	2	2	4	2	—	—	—	—	—
82-83—Soviet Wings		USSR	51	9	7	16	14	—	—	—	—	—
83-84—Soviet Wings		USSR	43	7	8	15	10	—	—	—	—	—
84-85—Soviet Wings		USSR	30	11	4	15	24	—	—	—	—	—
85-86—Soviet Wings		USSR	40	24	9	33	22	—	—	—	—	—
86-87—Soviet Wings		USSR	40	15	15	30	48	—	—	—	—	—
87-88—Soviet Wings		USSR	48	21	8	29	46	—	—	—	—	—
88-89—Soviet Wings		USSR	44	16	18	34	38	—	—	—	—	—
89-90—Soviet Wings		USSR	44	14	13	27	30	—	—	—	—	—
90-91—Soviet Wings		USSR	45	25	14	39	26	—	—	—	—	—
91-92—Soviet Wings		CIS	42	19	17	36	20	—	—	—	—	—
—Unified Olympic Team		Int'l	8	4	6	10	. . .	—	—	—	—	—
92-93—Buffalo		NHL	68	20	19	39	28	8	4	3	7	4
93-94—Buffalo		NHL	72	27	31	58	49	7	3	1	4	8
94-95—Buffalo		NHL	48	8	17	25	14	5	0	1	1	8
NHL totals			188	55	67	122	91	20	7	5	12	20

KHRISTICH, DIMITRI
LW, KINGS

PERSONAL: Born July 23, 1969, in Kiev, U.S.S.R. . . . 6-2/200. . . . Shoots right. . . . Name pronounced KRIH-stihch.

TRANSACTIONS/CAREER NOTES: Selected by Washington Capitals in sixth round (sixth Capitals pick, 120th overall) of NHL entry draft (June 11, 1988). . . . Injured hip (February 16, 1990); missed six games. . . . Broke foot (October 3, 1992); missed 20 games. . . . Traded by Capitals with G Byron Dafoe to Los Angeles Kings for first- and fourth-round picks in 1996 draft (July 8, 1995).

STATISTICAL PLATEAUS: Three-goal games: 1992-93 (2).

			REGULAR SEASON					PLAYOFFS				
Season	Team	League	Gms.	G	A	Pts.	PIM	Gms.	G	A	Pts.	PIM
88-89—Sokol Kiev		USSR	42	17	8	25	15	—	—	—	—	—
89-90—Sokol Kiev		USSR	47	14	22	36	32	—	—	—	—	—
90-91—Sokol Kiev		USSR	28	10	12	22	20	—	—	—	—	—
—Baltimore		AHL	3	0	0	0	0	—	—	—	—	—
—Washington		NHL	40	13	14	27	21	11	1	3	4	6
91-92—Washington		NHL	80	36	37	73	35	7	3	2	5	15
92-93—Washington		NHL	64	31	35	66	28	6	2	5	7	2
93-94—Washington		NHL	83	29	29	58	73	11	2	3	5	10
94-95—Washington		NHL	48	12	14	26	41	7	1	4	5	0
NHL totals			315	121	129	250	198	42	9	17	26	33

KIBERMANIS, CHRIS
D, JETS

PERSONAL: Born March 24, 1976, in Calgary. . . . 6-5/184. . . . Shoots right. . . . Name pronounced KIGH-buhr-MAN-ihz.

HIGH SCHOOL: Lindsay Thurber (Red Deer, Alta.).

TRANSACTIONS/CAREER NOTES: Selected by Winnipeg Jets in sixth round (seventh Jets pick, 146th overall) of NHL entry draft (June 29, 1994).

			REGULAR SEASON					PLAYOFFS				
Season	Team	League	Gms.	G	A	Pts.	PIM	Gms.	G	A	Pts.	PIM
93-94—Red Deer		WHL	49	1	5	6	57	4	0	0	0	7
94-95—Red Deer		WHL	52	3	1	4	93	—	—	—	—	—

KIDD, TREVOR
G, FLAMES

PERSONAL: Born March 29, 1972, in St. Boniface, Man. . . . 6-2/190. . . . Catches left.

TRANSACTIONS/CAREER NOTES: Broke finger (December 1987). . . . Selected by Calgary Flames in first round (first Flames pick, 11th overall) of NHL entry draft (June 16, 1990). . . . Traded by Brandon Wheat Kings with D Bart Cote to Spokane Chiefs for RW Bobby House, C Marty Murray

and G Don Blishen (January 21, 1991).... Sprained left ankle (October 18, 1993); missed one game.
HONORS: Won Del Wilson Trophy (1989-90).... Named to WHL (West) All-Star first team (1989-90).
MISCELLANEOUS: Member of silver-medal-winning Canadian Olympic team (1992).

Season Team	League	REGULAR SEASON								PLAYOFFS						
		Gms.	Min.	W	L	T	GA	SO	Avg.	Gms.	Min.	W	L	GA	SO	Avg.
88-89—Brandon	WHL	32	1509	...	...	...	102	0	4.06	—	—	—	—	—	—	—
89-90—Brandon	WHL	*63	*3676	24	32	2	254	2	4.15	—	—	—	—	—	—	—
90-91—Brandon	WHL	30	1730	10	19	1	117	0	4.06	—	—	—	—	—	—	—
—Spokane	WHL	14	749	8	3	0	44	0	3.52	15	926	*14	1	32	*2	*2.07
91-92—Can. national team	Int'l	28	1349	18	4	4	79	2	3.51	—						
—Can. Olympic Team	Int'l	1	60	1	0	0	0	1	0.00	—						
—Calgary	NHL	2	120	1	1	0	8	0	4.00	—						
92-93—Salt Lake City	IHL	30	1696	10	16	‡0	111	1	3.93	—						
93-94—Calgary	NHL	31	1614	13	7	6	85	0	3.16	—						
94-95—Calgary	NHL	43	2463	22	14	6	107	3	2.61	7	434	3	4	26	1	3.59
NHL totals		76	4197	36	22	12	200	3	2.86	7	434	3	4	26	1	3.59

KILGER, CHAD
C, MIGHTY DUCKS

PERSONAL: Born November 27, 1976, in Cornwall, Ont.... 6-3/204.... Shoots left.... Son of Bob Kilger, former NHL referee (1970-71 through 1979-80) and current deputy speaker in House of Commons in Canadian Parliament.
TRANSACTIONS/CAREER NOTES: Selected by Mighty Ducks of Anaheim in first round (first Mighty Ducks pick, fourth overall) of NHL entry draft (July 8, 1995).

Season Team	League	REGULAR SEASON					PLAYOFFS			
		Gms.	G	A	Pts.	PIM	Gms.	G	A	Pts.	PIM
92-93—Cornwall	CJHL	55	30	36	66	26	—				
93-94—Kingston	OHL	66	17	35	52	23	6	7	2	9	8
94-95—Kingston	OHL	65	42	53	95	95	6	5	2	7	10

KIMBLE, DARIN
RW, BLACKHAWKS

PERSONAL: Born November 22, 1968, in Lucky Lake, Sask.... 6-2/205.... Shoots right.
TRANSACTIONS/CAREER NOTES: Traded by Brandon Wheat Kings with Kerry Angus to Prince Albert Raiders for C Graham Garden, C Ryan Stewart and Kim Rasmussen (September 1986).... Selected by Quebec Nordiques in fourth round (fifth Nordiques pick, 66th overall) of NHL entry draft (June 11, 1988).... Suspended eight games by NHL for slashing (March 23, 1989); missed final four games of 1988-89 season and first four games of 1989-90.... Sprained right wrist (September 1989).... Bruised ribs (November 5, 1989).... Pulled abdominal muscle (December 1990).... Bruised right hand (January 24, 1991).... Traded by Nordiques to St. Louis Blues for RW Herb Raglan, D Tony Twist and LW Andy Rymsha (February 4, 1991).... Broke nose (February 1992). ... Traded by Blues with D Rob Robinson, G Pat Jablonski and RW Steve Tuttle to Tampa Bay Lightning for future considerations (June 19, 1992).... Traded by Lightning with future considerations to Boston Bruins for C Ken Hodge and D Matt Hervey (September 4, 1992).... Signed as free agent by Florida Panthers (July 14, 1993).... Traded by Panthers to Chicago Blackhawks for LW Evgeny Davydov (September 30, 1993).

Season Team	League	REGULAR SEASON					PLAYOFFS			
		Gms.	G	A	Pts.	PIM	Gms.	G	A	Pts.	PIM
84-85—Swift Current Jr. A	SAJHL	59	28	32	60	264	—				
—Calgary	WHL	—	—	—	—	—	1	0	0	0	0
85-86—Calgary	WHL	37	14	8	22	93	—				
—New Westminster	WHL	11	1	1	2	22	—				
—Brandon	WHL	15	1	6	7	39	—				
86-87—Prince Albert	WHL	68	17	13	30	190	—				
87-88—Prince Albert	WHL	67	35	36	71	307	10	3	2	5	4
88-89—Halifax	AHL	39	8	6	14	188	—				
—Quebec	NHL	26	3	1	4	149	—				
89-90—Quebec	NHL	44	5	5	10	185	—				
—Halifax	AHL	18	6	6	12	37	6	1	1	2	61
90-91—Halifax	AHL	7	1	4	5	20	—				
—Quebec	NHL	35	2	5	7	114	—				
—St. Louis	NHL	26	1	1	2	128	13	0	0	0	38
91-92—St. Louis	NHL	46	1	3	4	166	5	0	0	0	7
92-93—Providence	AHL	12	1	4	5	34	—				
—Boston	NHL	55	7	3	10	177	4	0	0	0	2
93-94—Chicago	NHL	65	4	2	6	133	1	0	0	0	5
94-95—Chicago	NHL	14	0	0	0	30	—				
NHL totals		311	23	20	43	1082	23	0	0	0	52

KING, DEREK
LW, ISLANDERS

PERSONAL: Born February 11, 1967, in Hamilton, Ont.... 6-1/206.... Shoots left.
TRANSACTIONS/CAREER NOTES: Selected by New York Islanders as underage junior in first round (second Islanders pick, 13th overall) of NHL entry draft (June 15, 1985).... Sprained right knee (September 1985).... Fractured left wrist (December 12, 1987).... Separated shoulder (November 23, 1988).... Suffered concussion (November 2, 1990).... Separated right shoulder (February 14, 1991).... Bruised hip (November 27, 1992); missed two games.... Suffered hip pointer (December 26, 1992); missed four games.... Broke finger on left hand (April 3, 1993); missed one game.... Suffered hip pointer (January 8, 1994); missed knee (March 9, 1995); missed one game.... Injured elbow (April 28, 1995); missed two games.
HONORS: Won Emms Family Award (1984-85).... Named to OHL All-Star first team (1986-87).
STATISTICAL PLATEAUS: Three-goal games: 1989-90 (1), 1991-92 (2), 1993-94 (1). Total: 4.... Four-goal games: 1990-91 (1).... Total hat tricks: 5.

Season Team	League	REGULAR SEASON					PLAYOFFS				
		Gms.	G	A	Pts.	PIM	Gms.	G	A	Pts.	PIM
83-84—Hamilton Jr. A.	OHA	37	10	14	24	142	—	—	—	—	—
84-85—Sault Ste. Marie	OHL	63	35	38	73	106	16	3	13	16	11
85-86—Sault Ste. Marie	OHL	25	12	17	29	33	—	—	—	—	—
—Oshawa	OHL	19	8	13	21	15	6	3	2	5	13
86-87—Oshawa	OHL	57	53	53	106	74	17	14	10	24	40
—New York Islanders	NHL	2	0	0	0	0	—	—	—	—	—
87-88—New York Islanders	NHL	55	12	24	36	30	5	0	2	2	2
—Springfield	AHL	10	7	6	13	6	—	—	—	—	—
88-89—Springfield	AHL	4	4	0	4	0	—	—	—	—	—
—New York Islanders	NHL	60	14	29	43	14	—	—	—	—	—
89-90—Springfield	AHL	21	11	12	23	33	—	—	—	—	—
—New York Islanders	NHL	46	13	27	40	20	4	0	0	0	4
90-91—New York Islanders	NHL	66	19	26	45	44	—	—	—	—	—
91-92—New York Islanders	NHL	80	40	38	78	46	—	—	—	—	—
92-93—New York Islanders	NHL	77	38	38	76	47	18	3	11	14	14
93-94—New York Islanders	NHL	78	30	40	70	59	4	0	1	1	0
94-95—New York Islanders	NHL	43	10	16	26	41	—	—	—	—	—
NHL totals		507	176	238	414	301	31	3	14	17	20

KING, KRIS

LW, JETS

PERSONAL: Born February 18, 1966, in Bracebridge, Ont. . . . 5-11/208. . . . Shoots left.
TRANSACTIONS/CAREER NOTES: Selected by Washington Capitals as underage junior in fourth round (fourth Capitals pick, 80th overall) of NHL entry draft (June 9, 1984). . . . Signed as free agent by Detroit Red Wings (June 1987). . . . Traded by Red Wings to New York Rangers for LW Chris McRae and fifth-round pick (D Tony Burns) in 1990 draft (September 7, 1989). . . . Sprained knee (January 7, 1991); missed six games. . . . Traded by Rangers with RW Tie Domi to Winnipeg Jets for C Ed Olczyk (December 28, 1992).

Season Team	League	REGULAR SEASON					PLAYOFFS				
		Gms.	G	A	Pts.	PIM	Gms.	G	A	Pts.	PIM
82-83—Gravenhurst	SOJHL	32	72	53	125	115	—	—	—	—	—
83-84—Peterborough	OHL	62	13	18	31	168	8	3	3	6	14
84-85—Peterborough	OHL	61	18	35	53	222	16	2	8	10	28
85-86—Peterborough	OHL	58	19	40	59	254	8	4	0	4	21
86-87—Peterborough	OHL	46	23	33	56	160	12	5	8	13	41
—Binghamton	AHL	7	0	0	0	18	—	—	—	—	—
87-88—Adirondack	AHL	78	21	32	53	337	10	4	4	8	53
—Detroit	NHL	3	1	0	1	2	—	—	—	—	—
88-89—Detroit	NHL	55	2	3	5	168	2	0	0	0	2
89-90—New York Rangers	NHL	68	6	7	13	286	10	0	1	1	38
90-91—New York Rangers	NHL	72	11	14	25	154	6	2	0	2	36
91-92—New York Rangers	NHL	79	10	9	19	224	13	4	1	5	14
92-93—New York Rangers	NHL	30	0	3	3	67	—	—	—	—	—
—Winnipeg	NHL	48	8	8	16	136	6	1	1	2	4
93-94—Winnipeg	NHL	83	4	8	12	205	—	—	—	—	—
94-95—Winnipeg	NHL	48	4	2	6	85	—	—	—	—	—
NHL totals		486	46	54	100	1327	37	7	3	10	94

KING, STEVEN

LW, MIGHTY DUCKS

PERSONAL: Born July 22, 1969, in East Greenwich, R.I. . . . 6-0/195. . . . Shoots right.
COLLEGE: Brown.
TRANSACTIONS/CAREER NOTES: Selected by New York Rangers in NHL supplemental draft (June 21, 1991). . . . Selected by Mighty Ducks of Anaheim in NHL expansion draft (June 24, 1993). . . . Sprained shoulder (January 1, 1994); missed six games. . . . Underwent reconstructive shoulder surgery (February 3, 1994); missed remainder of season. . . . Underwent shoulder surgery (January 5, 1995); missed entire 1994-95 season.

Season Team	League	REGULAR SEASON					PLAYOFFS				
		Gms.	G	A	Pts.	PIM	Gms.	G	A	Pts.	PIM
87-88—Brown University	ECAC	24	10	5	15	30	—	—	—	—	—
88-89—Brown University	ECAC	26	8	5	13	73	—	—	—	—	—
89-90—Brown University	ECAC	27	19	8	27	53	—	—	—	—	—
90-91—Brown University	ECAC	27	19	15	34	76	—	—	—	—	—
91-92—Binghamton	AHL	66	27	15	42	56	10	2	0	2	14
92-93—Binghamton	AHL	53	35	33	68	100	14	7	9	16	26
—New York Rangers	NHL	24	7	5	12	16	—	—	—	—	—
93-94—Anaheim	NHL	36	8	3	11	44	—	—	—	—	—
94-95—Anaheim	NHL				Did not play—injured.						
NHL totals		60	15	8	23	60					

KIPRUSOFF, MARKO

D, CANADIENS

PERSONAL: Born June 6, 1972, in Turku, Finland. . . . 6-0/194. . . . Shoots right.
TRANSACTIONS/CAREER NOTES: Selected by Montreal Canadiens in fourth round (fourth Canadiens pick, 70th overall) of NHL entry draft (June 29, 1994).
HONORS: Named to Finnish League All-Star team (1993-94).

Season Team	League	REGULAR SEASON					PLAYOFFS				
		Gms.	G	A	Pts.	PIM	Gms.	G	A	Pts.	PIM
90-91—TPS Turku	Finland	3	0	0	0	0	—	—	—	—	—

			REGULAR SEASON					PLAYOFFS				
Season Team	League	Gms.	G	A	Pts.	PIM	Gms.	G	A	Pts.	PIM
91-92—TPS Turku	Finland	23	0	2	2	0	—	—	—	—	—
—HPK Hameenlinna	Finland	3	0	0	0	0	—	—	—	—	—
92-93—TPS Turku	Finland	43	3	7	10	14	12	2	3	5	6
93-94—TPS Turku	Finland	48	5	19	24	8	11	0	6	6	4
94-95—TPS Turku	Finland	50	10	21	31	16	13	0	9	9	2

KIPRUSOFF, MIIKKA
G, SHARKS

PERSONAL: Born October 26, 1976, in Turku, Finland. . . . 6-0/176. . . . Catches left.
TRANSACTIONS/CAREER NOTES: Selected by San Jose Sharks in fifth round (fifth Sharks pick, 115 overall) of NHL entry draft (July 8, 1995).

			REGULAR SEASON							PLAYOFFS						
Season Team	League	Gms.	Min.	W	L	T	GA	SO	Avg.	Gms.	Min.	W	L	GA	SO	Avg.
93-94—TPS Jr.	Finland	35	. . .	. . .	. . . . . .	. . .	. . . . . .	2.88	6	. . . .						4.23
94-95—TPS Jr.	Finland	31	1880	. . .	. . . . . .	. . .	93	. . .	2.97	—	—	—	—	—	—	—
—TPS Turku	Finland	4	240	. . .	. . . . . .	. . .	12	. . .	3.00	2	120	. . .	. . .	7	. . .	3.50

KISIO, KELLY
C, FLAMES

PERSONAL: Born September 18, 1959, in Peace River, Alta. . . . 5-10/185. . . . Shoots right. . . . Name pronounced KIHZ-ee-oh.
HIGH SCHOOL: Lindsay Thurber (Red Deer, Alta.).
TRANSACTIONS/CAREER NOTES: Traded by Toledo Goaldiggers to Kalamazoo Wings for LW/C Jean Chouinard (February 1981). . . . Signed as free agent by Detroit Red Wings (February 1983). . . . Suspended five games by NHL for stick-swinging incident (February 1985). . . . Traded by Red Wings with RW Lane Lambert, D Jim Leavins and fifth-round pick in 1988 draft to New York Rangers for G Glen Hanlon, third-round picks in 1987 (C Dennis Holland) and 1988 (C Guy Dupuis) drafts and future considerations (July 29, 1986). . . . Dislocated left shoulder (October 1986). . . . Underwent shoulder surgery (April 1987). . . . Bruised and twisted left knee (February 1988). . . . Fractured left hand (October 1988); missed five games. . . . Suffered back spasms (November 1988). . . . Bruised left thigh and suffered back spasms (November 9, 1989); missed 11 games. . . . Tore ligaments and suffered chip fracture of right ankle (October 6, 1990); missed 18 games. . . . Bruised thigh (December 7, 1990). . . . Injured groin (January 17, 1991). . . . Selected by Minnesota North Stars in NHL expansion draft (May 30, 1991). . . . Traded by North Stars to San Jose Sharks for RW Shane Churla (June 3, 1991). . . . Injured ankle (October 17, 1991); missed 18 games. . . . Strained abdominal muscle (February 4, 1992); missed two games. . . . Injured shoulder (March 19, 1992). . . . Suffered sore body (January 1993); missed one game. . . . Strained groin (February 22, 1993); missed four games. . . . Signed as free agent by Calgary Flames (August 18, 1993). . . . Fractured right kneecap (October 1, 1993); missed 18 games. . . . Fractured rib (January 2, 1994); missed 12 games. . . . Fractured cheekbone (March 11, 1994); missed three games. . . . Cracked ribs (January 22, 1995); missed 27 games. . . . Strained left shoulder (April 17, 1995); missed seven games.
HONORS: Named to AJHL All-Star first team (1977-78). . . . Played in NHL All-Star Game (1993).
MISCELLANEOUS: Captain of New York Rangers (1987-88 through 1990-91).

			REGULAR SEASON					PLAYOFFS				
Season Team	League	Gms.	G	A	Pts.	PIM	Gms.	G	A	Pts.	PIM
76-77—Red Deer	AJHL	60	53	48	101	101	—	—	—	—	—
77-78—Red Deer	AJHL	58	74	68	142	66	—	—	—	—	—
78-79—Calgary	WHL	70	60	61	121	73	—	—	—	—	—
79-80—Calgary	WHL	71	65	73	138	64	—	—	—	—	—
80-81—Adirondack	AHL	41	10	14	24	43	—	—	—	—	—
—Kalamazoo	IHL	31	27	16	43	48	8	7	7	14	13
81-82—Dallas	CHL	78	*62	39	101	59	16	*12	†17	*29	38
82-83—Davos HC	Switzerland	. . .	49	38	87	. . .	—	—	—	—	—
—Detroit	NHL	15	4	3	7	0	—	—	—	—	—
83-84—Detroit	NHL	70	23	37	60	34	4	1	0	1	4
84-85—Detroit	NHL	75	20	41	61	56	3	0	2	2	2
85-86—Detroit	NHL	76	21	48	69	85	—	—	—	—	—
86-87—New York Rangers	NHL	70	24	40	64	73	4	0	1	1	2
87-88—New York Rangers	NHL	77	23	55	78	88	—	—	—	—	—
88-89—New York Rangers	NHL	70	26	36	62	91	4	0	0	0	9
89-90—New York Rangers	NHL	68	22	44	66	105	10	2	8	10	8
90-91—New York Rangers	NHL	51	15	20	35	58	—	—	—	—	—
91-92—San Jose	NHL	48	11	26	37	54	—	—	—	—	—
92-93—San Jose	NHL	78	26	52	78	90	—	—	—	—	—
93-94—Calgary	NHL	51	7	23	30	28	7	0	2	2	8
94-95—Calgary	NHL	12	7	4	11	6	7	3	2	5	19
NHL totals		761	229	429	658	768	39	6	15	21	52

KLATT, TRENT
RW, STARS

PERSONAL: Born January 30, 1971, in Robbinsdale, Minn. . . . 6-1/205. . . . Shoots right. . . . Full name: Trent Thomas Klatt.
HIGH SCHOOL: Osseo (Minn.).
COLLEGE: Minnesota.
TRANSACTIONS/CAREER NOTES: Selected by Washington Capitals in fourth round (fifth Capitals pick, 82nd overall) of NHL entry draft (June 17, 1989). . . . Rights traded by Capitals with LW Steve Maltais to Minnesota North Stars for D Sean Chambers (June 21, 1991). . . . Injured finger (January 7, 1993); missed three games. . . . North Stars franchise moved from Minnesota to Dallas and renamed Stars for 1993-94 season. . . . Strained back (November 9, 1993); missed one game. . . . Sprained knee (November 11, 1993); missed two games. . . . Sprained knee (February 6, 1994); missed three games.

Season	Team	League	REGULAR SEASON					PLAYOFFS				
			Gms.	G	A	Pts.	PIM	Gms.	G	A	Pts.	PIM
87-88—Osseo H.S.		Minn. H.S.	22	19	17	36	...	—	—	—	—	—
88-89—Osseo H.S.		Minn. H.S.	22	24	39	63	...	—	—	—	—	—
89-90—University of Minnesota		WCHA	38	22	14	36	16	—	—	—	—	—
90-91—University of Minnesota		WCHA	39	16	28	44	58	—	—	—	—	—
91-92—University of Minnesota		WCHA	44	30	36	66	78	—	—	—	—	—
—Minnesota		NHL	1	0	0	0	0	6	0	0	0	2
92-93—Kalamazoo		IHL	31	8	11	19	18	—	—	—	—	—
—Minnesota		NHL	47	4	19	23	38	—	—	—	—	—
93-94—Dallas		NHL	61	14	24	38	30	9	2	1	3	4
—Kalamazoo		IHL	6	3	2	5	4	—	—	—	—	—
94-95—Dallas		NHL	47	12	10	22	26	5	1	0	1	0
NHL totals			156	30	53	83	94	20	3	1	4	6

KLEE, KEN

D, CAPITALS

PERSONAL: Born April 24, 1971, in Indianapolis. ... 6-1/205. ... Shoots right. ... Full name: Kenneth William Klee.
HIGH SCHOOL: Rockhurst (Kansas City, Mo.).
COLLEGE: St. Michael's College (Vt.), then Bowling Green State.
TRANSACTIONS/CAREER NOTES: Selected by Washington Capitals in ninth round (11th Capitals pick, 177th overall) of NHL entry draft (June 16, 1990). ... Injured foot (January 27, 1995); missed six games.

Season	Team	League	REGULAR SEASON					PLAYOFFS				
			Gms.	G	A	Pts.	PIM	Gms.	G	A	Pts.	PIM
89-90—Bowling Green State		CCHA	39	0	5	5	52	—	—	—	—	—
90-91—Bowling Green State		CCHA	37	7	28	35	50	—	—	—	—	—
91-92—Bowling Green State		CCHA	10	0	1	1	14	—	—	—	—	—
92-93—Baltimore		AHL	77	4	14	18	68	7	0	1	1	15
93-94—Portland		AHL	65	2	9	11	87	17	1	2	3	14
94-95—Portland		AHL	49	5	7	12	89	—	—	—	—	—
—Washington		NHL	23	3	1	4	41	7	0	0	0	4
NHL totals			23	3	1	4	41	7	0	0	0	4

KLEMM, JON

D, DENVER

PERSONAL: Born January 6, 1970, in Cranbrook, B.C. ... 6-3/200. ... Shoots right. ... Full name: Jonathan Darryl Klemm.
TRANSACTIONS/CAREER NOTES: Signed as free agent by Quebec Nordiques (May 1991). ... Injured abdomen (March 28, 1995); missed five games. ... Reinjured abdomen (April 8, 1995); missed last 10 games of season and entire playoffs. ... Nordiques franchise moved to Denver for 1995-96 season.
HONORS: Named to WHL (West) All-Star second team (1990-91).

Season	Team	League	REGULAR SEASON					PLAYOFFS				
			Gms.	G	A	Pts.	PIM	Gms.	G	A	Pts.	PIM
87-88—Seattle		WHL	68	6	7	13	24	—	—	—	—	—
88-89—Seattle		WHL	2	1	1	2	0	—	—	—	—	—
—Spokane		WHL	66	6	34	40	42	—	—	—	—	—
89-90—Spokane		WHL	66	3	28	31	100	6	1	1	2	5
90-91—Spokane		WHL	72	7	58	65	65	15	3	6	9	8
91-92—Halifax		AHL	70	6	13	19	40	—	—	—	—	—
—Quebec		NHL	4	0	1	1	0	—	—	—	—	—
92-93—Halifax		AHL	80	3	20	23	32	—	—	—	—	—
93-94—Cornwall		AHL	66	4	26	30	78	13	1	2	3	6
—Quebec		NHL	7	0	0	0	4	—	—	—	—	—
94-95—Cornwall		AHL	65	6	13	19	84	—	—	—	—	—
—Quebec		NHL	4	1	0	1	2	—	—	—	—	—
NHL totals			15	1	1	2	6	—	—	—	—	—

KLEVAKIN, DMITRI

RW, LIGHTNING

PERSONAL: Born February 20, 1976, in Angarsk, U.S.S.R. ... 5-11/165. ... Shoots left.
TRANSACTIONS/CAREER NOTES: Selected by Tampa Bay Lightning in fourth round (fourth Lightning pick, 86th overall) of NHL entry draft (June 29, 1994).

Season	Team	League	REGULAR SEASON					PLAYOFFS				
			Gms.	G	A	Pts.	PIM	Gms.	G	A	Pts.	PIM
92-93—Spartak Moscow		CIS	8	1	1	2	0	—	—	—	—	—
93-94—Spartak Moscow		CIS	42	6	3	9	6	4	1	0	1	0
94-95—Spartak Moscow		CIS	52	12	10	22	4	—	—	—	—	—

KLIMA, PETR

LW/RW, LIGHTNING

PERSONAL: Born December 23, 1964, in Chaomutov, Czechoslovakia. ... 6-0/190. ... Shoots right. ... Name pronounced KLEE-muh.
TRANSACTIONS/CAREER NOTES: Selected by Detroit Red Wings in fifth round (fifth Red Wings pick, 88th overall) of NHL entry draft (June 8, 1983). ... Broke right thumb (May 1988). ... Sprained right ankle (November 12, 1988). ... Pulled groin (December 1988). ... Injured back (February 1989). ... Traded by Red Wings with C/RW Joe Murphy, C/LW Adam Graves and D Jeff Sharples to Edmonton Oilers for C Jimmy Carson, C Kevin McClelland and fifth-round pick (traded to Montreal Canadiens who selected D Brad Layzell) in 1991 draft (November 2, 1989).

... Suspended four games by NHL for butt-ending player (October 25, 1990).... Pulled groin (March 15, 1991).... Scratched cornea in right eye (November 18, 1991); missed one game.... Strained groin (February 2, 1992); missed six games.... Strained left knee ligaments (October 14, 1992); missed six games.... Strained groin (January 7, 1993); missed eight games. ... Traded by Oilers to Tampa Bay Lightning for future considerations (June 16, 1993).... Slightly separated shoulder (February 27, 1994); missed eight games.... Played in Europe during 1994-95 NHL lockout.
STATISTICAL PLATEAUS: Three-goal games: 1985-86 (2), 1986-87 (1), 1990-91 (3). Total: 6.
MISCELLANEOUS: Member of Stanley Cup championship team (1990).

			REGULAR SEASON					PLAYOFFS				
Season	Team	League	Gms.	G	A	Pts.	PIM	Gms.	G	A	Pts.	PIM
82-83—Czech. national team		Int'l	44	19	17	36	74	—	—	—	—	—
83-84—Dukla Jihlava		Czech.	41	20	16	36	46	—	—	—	—	—
—Czech. national team		Int'l	7	6	5	11	...	—	—	—	—	—
84-85—Dukla Jihlava		Czech.	35	23	22	45	...	—	—	—	—	—
85-86—Detroit		NHL	74	32	24	56	16	—	—	—	—	—
86-87—Detroit		NHL	77	30	23	53	42	13	1	2	3	4
87-88—Detroit		NHL	78	37	25	62	46	12	10	8	18	10
88-89—Adirondack		AHL	5	5	1	6	4	—	—	—	—	—
—Detroit		NHL	51	25	16	41	44	6	2	4	6	19
89-90—Detroit		NHL	13	5	5	10	6	—	—	—	—	—
—Edmonton		NHL	63	25	28	53	66	21	5	0	5	8
90-91—Edmonton		NHL	70	40	28	68	113	18	7	6	13	16
91-92—Edmonton		NHL	57	21	13	34	52	15	1	4	5	8
92-93—Edmonton		NHL	68	32	16	48	100	—	—	—	—	—
93-94—Tampa Bay		NHL	75	28	27	55	76	—	—	—	—	—
94-95—Wolfsburg		Ger. Div. II	12	27	11	38	28	—	—	—	—	—
—ZPS Zlin		Czech. Rep.	1	1	0	1	...	—	—	—	—	—
—Tampa Bay		NHL	47	13	13	26	26	—	—	—	—	—
NHL totals			**673**	**288**	**218**	**506**	**587**	**85**	**26**	**24**	**50**	**65**

KLIMENTIEV, SERGEI
D, SABRES

PERSONAL: Born April 5, 1975, in Kiev, U.S.S.R.... 5-11/200.... Shoots left.
TRANSACTIONS/CAREER NOTES: Selected by Buffalo Sabres in fifth round (fourth Sabres pick, 121st overall) of NHL entry draft (June 29, 1994).

			REGULAR SEASON					PLAYOFFS				
Season	Team	League	Gms.	G	A	Pts.	PIM	Gms.	G	A	Pts.	PIM
91-92—SVSM Kiev		CIS Div. III	42	4	15	19	...	—	—	—	—	—
92-93—Sokol-Eskulap Kiev		CIS	3	0	0	0	4	1	0	0	0	0
93-94—Medicine Hat		WHL	72	16	26	42	165	3	0	0	0	4
94-95—Medicine Hat		WHL	71	19	45	64	146	5	4	2	6	14
—Rochester		AHL	7	0	0	0	8	1	0	0	0	0

KLIMOVICH, SERGEI
C, BLACKHAWKS

PERSONAL: Born May 8, 1974, in Novosibirsk, U.S.S.R.... 6-2/189.... Shoots right.
TRANSACTIONS/CAREER NOTES: Selected by Chicago Blackhawks in second round (third Blackhawks pick, 41st overall) of NHL entry draft (June 20, 1992).

			REGULAR SEASON					PLAYOFFS				
Season	Team	League	Gms.	G	A	Pts.	PIM	Gms.	G	A	Pts.	PIM
91-92—Dynamo Moscow		CIS	3	0	0	0	0	—	—	—	—	—
92-93—Dynamo Moscow		CIS	30	4	1	5	14	10	1	0	1	2
93-94—Dynamo Moscow		CIS	39	7	4	11	14	12	2	3	5	6
94-95—Dynamo Moscow		CIS	4	1	0	1	2	—	—	—	—	—
—Indianapolis		IHL	71	14	30	44	20	—	—	—	—	—

KNICKLE, RICK
G

PERSONAL: Born February 26, 1960, in Chatham, N.B.... 5-10/175.... Catches left.
TRANSACTIONS/CAREER NOTES: Selected by Buffalo Sabres as underage junior in sixth round (seventh Buffalo pick, 116th overall) of NHL entry draft (August 9, 1979).... Sprained thumb (February 1981).... Signed as free agent by Montreal Canadiens (February 8, 1985). ... Signed as free agent by Springfield Indians (1991).... Signed as free agent by Los Angeles Kings (February 15, 1993).... Suspended indefinitely by Phoenix Roadrunners for failing to report on temporary assignment to Fort Wayne Komets (January 25, 1994).
HONORS: Won Top Goaltender Trophy (1978-79).... Named to WHL All-Star first team (1978-79).... Named to AHL All-Star first team (1980-81).... Named to IHL All-Star second team (1983-84 and 1991-92).... Won James Norris Memorial Trophy (1988-89).... Named to IHL All-Star first team (1988-89 and 1992-93).... Shared James Norris Memorial Trophy with Clint Malarchuk (1992-93).

			REGULAR SEASON							PLAYOFFS					
Season	Team	League	Gms.	Min.	W	L	T	GA	SO	Avg.	Gms.	Min.	W	L	GA	SO	Avg.
77-78—Brandon		WCHL	49	2806	34	5	7	182	0	3.89	8	450	...	...	36	0	4.80
78-79—Brandon		WHL	38	2240	26	3	8	118	1	*3.16	16	886	12	3	41	*1	*2.78
79-80—Brandon		WHL	33	1604	11	14	1	125	0	4.68	—	—	—	—	—	—	—
—Muskegon		IHL	16	829	...	...	...	51	0	3.69	3	156	...	...	17	0	6.54
80-81—Erie		AHL	43	2347	...	...	...	125	1	*3.20	*8	*446	...	...	14	0	*1.88
81-82—Rochester		AHL	31	1753	10	12	5	108	1	3.70	3	125	0	2	7	0	3.36
82-83—Flint		IHL	27	1638	...	...	...	92	+2	3.37	3	193	...	...	10	0	3.11
—Rochester		AHL	4	143	...	...	...	11	0	4.62	—	—	—	—	—	—	—

Season Team	League	REGULAR SEASON Gms.	Min.	W	L	T	GA	SO	Avg.	PLAYOFFS Gms.	Min.	W	L	GA	SO	Avg.
83-84—Flint	IHL	60	3518	32	21	‡5	203	3	3.46	8	480	8	0	24	0	*3.00
84-85—Sherbrooke	AHL	14	780	7	6	0	53	0	4.08	—						
—Flint	IHL	36	2018	18	11	‡3	115	2	3.42	7	401	3	4	27	0	4.04
85-86—Saginaw	IHL	39	2235	16	15	‡0	135	2	3.62	3	193	2	1	12	0	3.73
86-87—Saginaw	IHL	26	1413	9	13	‡0	113	0	4.80	5	329	1	4	21	0	3.83
87-88—Flint	IHL	1	60	0	1	‡0	4	0	4.00	—						
—Peoria	IHL	13	705	2	8	‡1	58	0	4.94	6	294	3	3	20	0	4.08
88-89—Fort Wayne	IHL	47	2719	22	16	‡0	141	1	3.11	4	173	1	2	15	0	5.20
89-90—Flint	IHL	55	2998	25	24	‡1	210	1	4.20	2	101	0	2	13	0	7.72
90-91—Springfield	AHL	9	509	6	0	2	28	0	3.30	—						
91-92—San Diego	IHL	46	2686	*28	13	‡4	155	0	3.46	2	78	0	1	3	0	2.31
92-93—San Diego	IHL	41	2437	33	4	‡0	88	*4	*2.17	—						
—Los Angeles	NHL	10	532	6	4	0	35	0	3.95	—						
93-94—Los Angeles	NHL	4	174	1	2	0	9	0	3.10	—						
—Phoenix	IHL	25	1292	8	9	‡3	89	1	4.13	—						
94-95—Detroit	IHL	49	2726	24	15	‡5	134	†3	2.95	—						
NHL totals		14	706	7	6	0	44	0	3.74							

KNIPSCHEER, FRED
C, BRUINS

PERSONAL: Born September 3, 1969, in Fort Wayne, Ind. . . . 5-11/ 185. . . . Shoots left. . . . Name pronounced kuh-NIHP-sheer.
COLLEGE: St. Cloud (Minn.) State.
TRANSACTIONS/CAREER NOTES: Signed as free agent by Boston Bruins (April 30, 1993) . . . . Injured shoulder (April 2, 1995); missed four games.

Season Team	League	REGULAR SEASON Gms.	G	A	Pts.	PIM	PLAYOFFS Gms.	G	A	Pts.	PIM
90-91—St. Cloud State	WCHA	40	9	10	19	57	—				—
91-92—St. Cloud State	WCHA	33	15	17	32	48	—				—
92-93—St. Cloud State	WCHA	36	34	26	60	68	—				—
93-94—Boston	NHL	11	3	2	5	14	12	2	1	3	6
—Providence	AHL	62	26	13	39	50	—				—
94-95—Providence	AHL	71	29	34	63	81	—				—
—Boston	NHL	16	3	1	4	2	4	0	0	0	0
NHL totals		27	6	3	9	16	16	2	1	3	6

KNUBLE, MICHAEL
RW, RED WINGS

PERSONAL: Born July 4, 1972, in Toronto. . . . 6-3/200. . . . Shoots right.
HIGH SCHOOL: East Kentwood (Mich.).
COLLEGE: Michigan.
TRANSACTIONS/CAREER NOTES: Selected by Detroit Red Wings in fourth round (fourth Red Wings pick, 76th overall) of NHL entry draft (June 22, 1991).
HONORS: Named to CCHA All-Star first team (1993-94). . . . Named to NCAA All-America West second team (1994-95). . . . Named to CCHA All-Star second team (1994-95).

Season Team	League	REGULAR SEASON Gms.	G	A	Pts.	PIM	PLAYOFFS Gms.	G	A	Pts.	PIM
88-89—East Kentwood H.S.	Mich. H.S.	28	52	37	89	60	—				—
89-90—East Kentwood H.S.	Mich. H.S.	29	63	40	103	40	—				—
90-91—Kalamazoo	NAJHL	36	18	24	42	30	—				—
91-92—University of Michigan	CCHA	43	7	8	15	48	—				—
92-93—University of Michigan	CCHA	39	26	16	42	57	—				—
93-94—University of Michigan	CCHA	41	32	26	58	71	—				—
94-95—University of Michigan	CCHA	34	38	22	60	62	—				—

KOCHAN, DIETER
G, CANUCKS

PERSONAL: Born November 5, 1974, in Saskatoon, Sask. . . . 6-1/ 165. . . . Catches left.
HIGH SCHOOL: North (Sioux City, Ia.).
COLLEGE: Northern Michigan.
TRANSACTIONS/CAREER NOTES: Selected by Vancouver Canucks in fourth round (third Canucks pick, 98th overall) of NHL entry draft (June 26, 1993).

Season Team	League	REGULAR SEASON Gms.	Min.	W	L	T	GA	SO	Avg.	PLAYOFFS Gms.	Min.	W	L	GA	SO	Avg.
91-92—Sioux City	USHL	23	1131	7	10	0	100	. . .	5.31	—						
92-93—Kelowna	BCJHL	44	2582	34	8	9	137	1	*3.18	—						
93-94—N. Michigan U.	WCHA	16	984	9	7	0	57	0	3.48	—						
94-95—N. Michigan U.	WCHA	29	1512	8	17	3	107	0	4.25	—						

KOCUR, JOEY
RW, RANGERS

PERSONAL: Born December 21, 1964, in Calgary. . . . 6-0/201. . . . Shoots right. . . . Name pronounced KOH-suhr. . . . Cousin of Wendell Clark, left winger, Denver; and cousin of Kory Kocur, right winger in Detroit Red Wings system.
TRANSACTIONS/CAREER NOTES: Stretched knee ligaments (December 1981). . . . Selected by Detroit Red Wings as underage junior in fifth round (sixth Red Wings pick, 88th overall) of NHL entry draft (June 8, 1983). . . . Lacerated right hand (January 1985). . . . Sprained thumb (December 11, 1985). . . . Strained ligaments (March 26, 1986). . . . Suffered sore right elbow (October 1987). . . . Strained sternum and collarbone (November 1987). . . . Injured shoulder (December 1987). . . . Separated shoulder (May 1988). . . . Injured knee (November 1988). . . . Injured back (February 1989). . . . Bruised right foot (February 16, 1990). . . . Strained right knee ligaments (March 1990). . . . Injured right hand and arm (De-

cember 1, 1990); missed three weeks.... Traded by Red Wings with D Per Djoos to New York Rangers for C Kevin Miller, D Dennis Vial and RW Jim Cummins (March 5, 1991).... Suspended four games by NHL for high-sticking (March 10, 1991).... Suspended additional four games by NHL for high-sticking during appeal of March 10 incident (March 14, 1991); missed final seven games of 1990-91 season and first game of 1991-92 season.... Underwent surgery to middle knuckle of right hand (May 10, 1991).... Injured hip flexor (October 1991); missed first five games of season.... Separated shoulder (January 28, 1992); missed 13 games.... Slightly sprained right knee (March 5, 1992); missed six games.... Sprained leg (November 21, 1992); missed one game.... Injured back (February 10, 1993); missed two games.... Injured back (February 20, 1993); missed two games.... Pulled groin (April 9, 1993); missed three games.... Bruised hand (January 28, 1994); missed three games.... Reinjured hand (February 9, 1994); missed four games.... Suffered back spasms (April 4, 1994); missed two games.

MISCELLANEOUS: Member of Stanley Cup championship team (1994).

			REGULAR SEASON					PLAYOFFS				
Season	Team	League	Gms.	G	A	Pts.	PIM	Gms.	G	A	Pts.	PIM
80-81—Yorkton		SJHL	48	6	9	15	307	—	—	—	—	—
81-82—Yorkton		SJHL	47	20	21	41	199	—	—	—	—	—
82-83—Saskatoon		WHL	62	23	17	40	289	6	2	3	5	25
83-84—Saskatoon		WHL	69	40	41	81	258	—	—	—	—	—
84-85—Detroit		NHL	17	1	0	1	64	3	1	0	1	5
—Adirondack		AHL	47	12	7	19	171	—	—	—	—	—
85-86—Adirondack		AHL	9	6	2	8	34	—	—	—	—	—
—Detroit		NHL	59	9	6	15	*377	—	—	—	—	—
86-87—Detroit		NHL	77	9	9	18	276	16	2	3	5	71
87-88—Detroit		NHL	64	7	7	14	263	10	0	1	1	13
88-89—Detroit		NHL	60	9	9	18	213	3	0	1	1	6
89-90—Detroit		NHL	71	16	20	36	268	—	—	—	—	—
90-91—Detroit		NHL	52	5	4	9	253	—	—	—	—	—
—New York Rangers		NHL	5	0	0	0	36	6	0	2	2	21
91-92—New York Rangers		NHL	51	7	4	11	121	12	1	1	2	38
92-93—New York Rangers		NHL	65	3	6	9	131	—	—	—	—	—
93-94—New York Rangers		NHL	71	2	1	3	129	20	1	1	2	17
94-95—New York Rangers		NHL	48	1	2	3	71	10	0	0	0	8
NHL totals			640	69	68	137	2202	80	5	9	14	179

KOHN, LADISLAV
RW, FLAMES

PERSONAL: Born March 4, 1975, in Uherske Hradiste, Czechoslovakia.... 5-10/175.... Shoots left.
TRANSACTIONS/CAREER NOTES: Selected by Calgary Flames in seventh round (ninth Flames pick, 175th overall) in NHL entry draft (June 29, 1994).

			REGULAR SEASON					PLAYOFFS				
Season	Team	League	Gms.	G	A	Pts.	PIM	Gms.	G	A	Pts.	PIM
93-94—Brandon		WHL	2	0	0	0	0	—	—	—	—	—
—Swift Current		WHL	69	33	35	68	68	7	5	4	9	8
94-95—Swift Current		WHL	65	32	60	92	122	6	2	6	8	14
—Saint John		AHL	1	0	0	0	0	—	—	—	—	—

KOIVU, SAKU
C, CANADIENS

PERSONAL: Born November 23, 1974, in Turku, Finland.... 5-9/163.... Shoots left.
TRANSACTIONS/CAREER NOTES: Selected by Montreal Canadiens in first round (first Canadiens pick, 21st overall) of NHL entry draft (June 26, 1993).
MISCELLANEOUS: Member of bronze-medal-winning Finnish Olympic team (1994).

			REGULAR SEASON					PLAYOFFS				
Season	Team	League	Gms.	G	A	Pts.	PIM	Gms.	G	A	Pts.	PIM
91-92—TPS Jr.		Finland	42	30	37	67	63	—	—	—	—	—
92-93—TPS Turku		Finland	46	3	7	10	28	—	—	—	—	—
93-94—TPS Turku		Finland	47	23	30	53	42	11	4	8	12	16
—Finnish Olympic Team		Int'l	8	4	3	7	12	—	—	—	—	—
94-95—TPS Turku		Finland	45	27	47	74	73	13	7	10	17	16

KOLESAR, MARK
LW, MAPLE LEAFS

PERSONAL: Born January 23, 1973, in Brampton, Ont.... 6-1/188.... Shoots right.... Name pronounced KOHL-SAHR.
TRANSACTIONS/CAREER NOTES: Signed as free agent by Toronto Maple Leafs (May 24, 1994).

			REGULAR SEASON					PLAYOFFS				
Season	Team	League	Gms.	G	A	Pts.	PIM	Gms.	G	A	Pts.	PIM
91-92—Brandon		WHL	56	6	7	13	36	—	—	—	—	—
92-93—Brandon		WHL	68	27	33	60	110	4	0	0	0	4
93-94—Brandon		WHL	59	29	37	66	131	14	8	3	11	48
94-95—St. John's		AHL	65	12	18	30	62	5	1	0	1	2

KOLKUNOV, ALEXEI
C, PENGUINS

PERSONAL: Born February 3, 1977, in Belgorod, U.S.S.R.... 6-0/185.... Shoots right.
TRANSACTIONS/CAREER NOTES: Selected by Pittsburgh Penguins in sixth round (fifth Penguins pick, 154th overall) of NHL entry draft (July 8, 1995).

			REGULAR SEASON					PLAYOFFS				
Season	Team	League	Gms.	G	A	Pts.	PIM	Gms.	G	A	Pts.	PIM
94-95—Soviet Wings		CIS	7	0	0	0	0	4	1	0	1	0

KOLZIG, OLAF

G, CAPITALS

PERSONAL: Born April 6, 1970, in Johannesburg, South Africa.... 6-3/225.... Catches left.... Name pronounced OH-lahf KOHL-zihg.
TRANSACTIONS/CAREER NOTES: Underwent surgery to right knee (November 1988).... Selected by Washington Capitals in first round (first Capitals pick, 19th overall) of NHL entry draft (June 17, 1989).... Loaned by Capitals to Rochester Americans (October 2, 1992).... Dislocated kneecap (October 13, 1993); missed 14 games.
HONORS: Shared Harry (Hap) Holmes Memorial Trophy with Byron Dafoe (1993-94).... Won Jack Butterfield Trophy (1993-94).

			REGULAR SEASON							PLAYOFFS						
Season	Team	League	Gms.	Min.	W	L	T	GA	SO	Avg.	Gms.	Min.	W	L	GA	SO	Avg.
87-88—New Westminster		WHL	15	650	6	5	0	48	1	4.43	3	149	0	0	11	0	4.43
88-89—Tri-City		WHL	30	1671	16	10	2	97	1	*3.48	—	—	—	—	—	—	—
89-90—Washington		NHL	2	120	0	2	0	12	0	6.00	—	—	—	—	—	—	—
—Tri-City		WHL	48	2504	27	27	3	187	1	4.48	6	318	4	0	27	0	5.09
90-91—Baltimore		AHL	26	1367	10	12	1	72	0	3.16	—	—	—	—	—	—	—
—Hampton Roads		ECHL	21	1248	11	9	‡1	71	2	3.41	3	180	1	2	14	0	4.67
91-92—Baltimore		AHL	28	1503	5	17	2	105	1	4.19	—	—	—	—	—	—	—
—Hampton Roads		ECHL	14	847	11	3	‡0	41	0	2.90	—	—	—	—	—	—	—
92-93—Rochester		AHL	49	2737	25	16	4	168	0	3.68	17	*1040	9	*8	61	0	3.52
—Washington		NHL	1	20	0	0	0	2	0	6.00	—	—	—	—	—	—	—
93-94—Portland		AHL	29	1726	16	8	5	88	3	3.06	17	1035	†12	5	44	0	*2.55
—Washington		NHL	7	224	0	3	0	20	0	5.36	—	—	—	—	—	—	—
94-95—Washington		NHL	14	724	2	8	2	30	0	2.49	2	44	1	0	1	0	1.36
—Portland		AHL	2	125	1	0	1	3	0	1.44	—	—	—	—	—	—	—
NHL totals			**24**	**1088**	**2**	**13**	**2**	**64**	**0**	**3.53**	**2**	**44**	**1**	**0**	**1**	**0**	**1.36**

KOMAROV, PAVEL

D, RANGERS

PERSONAL: Born February 28, 1974, in Gorky, U.S.S.R.... 6-2/183.... Shoots left.
TRANSACTIONS/CAREER NOTES: Selected by New York Rangers in 11th round (12th Rangers pick, 261st overall) of NHL entry draft (June 29, 1993).

			REGULAR SEASON					PLAYOFFS				
Season	Team	League	Gms.	G	A	Pts.	PIM	Gms.	G	A	Pts.	PIM
91-92—Torpedo Nizhny Novgorod		CIS	10	0	1	1	0	—	—	—	—	—
92-93—Torpedo Nizhny Novgorod		CIS	28	0	0	0	25	—	—	—	—	—
93-94—Torpedo Nizhny Novgorod		CIS	18	1	0	1	20	1	0	0	0	2
—Binghamton		AHL	1	1	0	1	2	—	—	—	—	—
94-95—Torpedo Nizhny Novgorod		CIS	26	0	1	1	38	3	0	0	0	0

KONOWALCHUK, STEVE

C, CAPITALS

PERSONAL: Born November 11, 1972, in Salt Lake City.... 6-1/195.... Shoots left.... Full name: Steven Reed Konowalchuk.... Name pronounced kahn-uh-WAHL-chuhk.
TRANSACTIONS/CAREER NOTES: Selected by Washington Capitals in third round (fifth Capitals pick, 58th overall) of NHL entry draft (June 22, 1991).
HONORS: Won Four Broncos Memorial Trophy (1991-92).... Named to Can.HL All-Star second team (1991-92).... Named to WHL (West) All-Star first team (1991-92).

			REGULAR SEASON					PLAYOFFS				
Season	Team	League	Gms.	G	A	Pts.	PIM	Gms.	G	A	Pts.	PIM
90-91—Portland		WHL	72	43	49	92	78	—	—	—	—	—
91-92—Portland		WHL	64	51	53	104	95	6	3	6	9	12
—Baltimore		AHL	3	1	1	2	0	—	—	—	—	—
—Washington		NHL	1	0	0	0	0	—	—	—	—	—
92-93—Baltimore		AHL	37	18	28	46	74	—	—	—	—	—
—Washington		NHL	36	4	7	11	16	2	0	1	1	0
93-94—Portland		AHL	8	11	4	15	4	—	—	—	—	—
—Washington		NHL	62	12	14	26	33	11	0	1	1	10
94-95—Washington		NHL	46	11	14	25	44	7	2	5	7	12
NHL totals			**145**	**27**	**35**	**62**	**93**	**20**	**2**	**7**	**9**	**22**

KONROYD, STEVE

D

PERSONAL: Born February 10, 1961, in Scarborough, Ont.... 6-1/195.... Shoots left.... Full name: Stephen Mark Konroyd.
TRANSACTIONS/CAREER NOTES: Selected by Calgary Flames as underage junior in second round (fourth Flames pick, 39th overall) of NHL entry draft (June 11, 1980).... Dislocated elbow (December 1984).... Pulled chest muscle (February 1986).... Traded by Flames with LW Richard Kromm to New York Islanders for LW/C John Tonelli (March 1986).... Bruised collarbone (December 1986).... Suspended four games by NHL for stick-swinging incident (January 1988).... Traded by Islanders with C Bob Bassen to Chicago Blackhawks for D Gary Nylund and D Marc Bergevin (November 25, 1988).... Bruised thigh (January 1990).... Suffered back spasms (February 10, 1991).... Broke knuckle on little finger of right hand (March 10, 1991); missed 18 days.... Traded by Blackhawks to Hartford Whalers for RW Rob Brown (January 24, 1992).... Traded by Whalers to Detroit Red Wings for sixth-round pick (traded back to Red Wings who selected RW Tim Spitzig) in 1993 draft (March 22, 1993).... Traded by Red Wings to Ottawa

Senators for G Daniel Berthiaume (March 21, 1994). . . . Suffered back spasms (March 31, 1994); missed three games. . . . Signed as free agent by Chicago Wolves (March 7, 1995). . . . Signed as free agent by Flames (April 7, 1995).
HONORS: Won Bobby Smith Trophy (1979-80). . . . Named to OMJHL All-Star second team (1980-81).

Season	Team	League	REGULAR SEASON					PLAYOFFS				
			Gms.	G	A	Pts.	PIM	Gms.	G	A	Pts.	PIM
78-79	—Oshawa	OMJHL	65	4	19	23	63	—	—	—	—	—
79-80	—Oshawa	OMJHL	62	11	23	34	133	7	0	2	2	14
80-81	—Calgary	NHL	4	0	0	0	4	—	—	—	—	—
	—Oshawa	OMJHL	59	19	49	68	232	11	3	11	14	35
81-82	—Oklahoma City	CHL	14	2	3	5	15	—	—	—	—	—
	—Calgary	NHL	63	3	14	17	78	3	0	0	0	12
82-83	—Calgary	NHL	79	4	13	17	73	9	2	1	3	18
83-84	—Calgary	NHL	80	1	13	14	94	8	1	2	3	8
84-85	—Calgary	NHL	64	3	23	26	73	4	1	4	5	2
85-86	—Calgary	NHL	59	7	20	27	64	—	—	—	—	—
	—New York Islanders	NHL	14	0	5	5	16	3	0	0	0	6
86-87	—New York Islanders	NHL	72	5	16	21	70	14	1	4	5	10
87-88	—New York Islanders	NHL	62	2	15	17	99	6	1	0	1	4
88-89	—New York Islanders	NHL	21	1	5	6	2	—	—	—	—	—
	—Chicago	NHL	57	5	7	12	40	16	2	0	2	10
89-90	—Chicago	NHL	75	3	14	17	34	20	1	3	4	19
90-91	—Chicago	NHL	70	0	12	12	40	6	1	0	1	8
91-92	—Chicago	NHL	49	2	14	16	65	—	—	—	—	—
	—Hartford	NHL	33	2	10	12	32	7	0	1	1	2
92-93	—Hartford	NHL	59	3	11	14	63	—	—	—	—	—
	—Detroit	NHL	6	0	1	1	4	1	0	0	0	0
93-94	—Detroit	NHL	19	0	0	0	10	—	—	—	—	—
	—Ottawa	NHL	8	0	2	2	2	—	—	—	—	—
94-95	—Chicago	IHL	16	2	2	4	4	3	0	1	1	2
	—Calgary	NHL	1	0	0	0	0	—	—	—	—	—
NHL totals			895	41	195	236	863	97	10	15	25	99

KONSTANTINOV, VLADIMIR
D, RED WINGS

PERSONAL: Born March 19, 1967, in Murmansk, U.S.S.R. . . . 6-0/190. . . . Shoots right. . . . Name pronounced KAHN-stan-TEE-nahf.

TRANSACTIONS/CAREER NOTES: Selected by Detroit Red Wings in 11th round (12th Red Wings pick, 221st overall) of NHL entry draft (June 17, 1989). . . . Injured groin (December 3, 1992); missed two games. . . . Sprained knee (October 27, 1993); missed four games. . . . Played in Europe during 1994-95 NHL lockout.

HONORS: Named to NHL All-Rookie team (1991-92).

Season	Team	League	REGULAR SEASON					PLAYOFFS				
			Gms.	G	A	Pts.	PIM	Gms.	G	A	Pts.	PIM
84-85	—CSKA Moscow	USSR	40	1	4	5	10	—	—	—	—	—
85-86	—CSKA Moscow	USSR	26	4	3	7	12	—	—	—	—	—
86-87	—CSKA Moscow	USSR	35	2	2	4	19	—	—	—	—	—
87-88	—CSKA Moscow	USSR	50	3	6	9	32	—	—	—	—	—
88-89	—CSKA Moscow	USSR	37	7	8	15	20	—	—	—	—	—
89-90	—CSKA Moscow	USSR	47	14	13	27	44	—	—	—	—	—
90-91	—CSKA Moscow	USSR	45	5	12	17	42	—	—	—	—	—
91-92	—Detroit	NHL	79	8	26	34	172	11	0	1	1	16
92-93	—Detroit	NHL	82	5	17	22	137	7	0	1	1	8
93-94	—Detroit	NHL	80	12	21	33	138	7	0	2	2	4
94-95	—Wedemark	Ger. Div. II	15	13	17	30	51	—	—	—	—	—
	—Detroit	NHL	47	3	11	14	101	18	1	1	2	22
NHL totals			288	28	75	103	548	43	1	5	6	50

KORDIC, DAN
D, FLYERS

PERSONAL: Born April 18, 1971, in Edmonton. . . . 6-5/220. . . . Shoots left. . . . Name pronounced KOHR-dihk. . . . Brother of John Kordic, right winger for four NHL teams (1985-86 through 1991-92).

TRANSACTIONS/CAREER NOTES: Selected by Philadelphia Flyers in fifth round (eighth Flyers pick, 88th overall) of NHL entry draft (June 16, 1990). . . . Suffered from the flu (January 1992); missed five games.

Season	Team	League	REGULAR SEASON					PLAYOFFS				
			Gms.	G	A	Pts.	PIM	Gms.	G	A	Pts.	PIM
87-88	—Medicine Hat	WHL	63	1	5	6	75	—	—	—	—	—
88-89	—Medicine Hat	WHL	70	1	13	14	190	—	—	—	—	—
89-90	—Medicine Hat	WHL	59	4	12	16	182	3	0	0	0	9
90-91	—Medicine Hat	WHL	67	8	15	23	150	12	2	6	8	42
91-92	—Philadelphia	NHL	46	1	3	4	126	—	—	—	—	—
92-93	—Hershey	AHL	14	0	2	2	17	—	—	—	—	—
93-94	—Hershey	AHL	64	0	4	4	164	11	0	3	3	26
	—Philadelphia	NHL	4	0	0	0	5	—	—	—	—	—
94-95	—Hershey	AHL	37	0	2	2	121	6	0	1	1	21
NHL totals			50	1	3	4	131					

KOROBOLIN, ALEXANDER
D, RANGERS

PERSONAL: Born March 12, 1976, in Chelyabinsk, U.S.S.R. . . . 6-2/189. . . . Shoots left.
TRANSACTIONS/CAREER NOTES: Selected by New York Rangers in fourth round (fourth Rangers pick, 100th overall) of NHL entry draft (June 29, 1994).

			REGULAR SEASON					PLAYOFFS				
Season	Team	League	Gms.	G	A	Pts.	PIM	Gms.	G	A	Pts.	PIM
93-94—Mechel Chelyabinsk		CIS Div. II	32	0	0	0	30	—	—	—	—	—
94-95—Mechel Chelyabinsk		CIS Div. II			Statistics unavailable.							

KOROLEV, IGOR
RW/C, JETS

PERSONAL: Born September 6, 1970, in Moscow, U.S.S.R. . . . 6-1/187. . . . Shoots left. . . . Name pronounced EE-gohr KOHR-ih-lehv.
TRANSACTIONS/CAREER NOTES: Selected by St. Louis Blues in second round (first Blues pick, 38th overall) of NHL entry draft (June 20, 1992). . . . Suffered from the flu (March 3, 1994); missed one game. . . . Injured hip (March 12, 1994); missed three games. . . . Selected by Winnipeg Jets in 1994-95 waiver draft for cash (January 18, 1995). . . . Played in Europe during 1994-95 NHL lockout.

			REGULAR SEASON					PLAYOFFS				
Season	Team	League	Gms.	G	A	Pts.	PIM	Gms.	G	A	Pts.	PIM
88-89—Dynamo Moscow		USSR	1	0	0	0	2	—	—	—	—	—
89-90—Dynamo Moscow		USSR	17	3	2	5	2	—	—	—	—	—
90-91—Dynamo Moscow		USSR	38	12	4	16	12	—	—	—	—	—
91-92—Dynamo Moscow		CIS	39	15	12	27	16	—	—	—	—	—
92-93—Dynamo Moscow		CIS	5	1	2	3	4	—	—	—	—	—
—St. Louis		NHL	74	4	23	27	20	3	0	0	0	0
93-94—St. Louis		NHL	73	6	10	16	40	2	0	0	0	0
94-95—Dynamo Moscow		CIS	13	4	6	10	18	—	—	—	—	—
—Winnipeg		NHL	45	8	22	30	10	—	—	—	—	—
NHL totals			192	18	55	73	70	5	0	0	0	0

KOROLYUK, ALEXANDER
RW, SHARKS

PERSONAL: Born January 15, 1976, in Moscow, U.S.S.R. . . . 5-9/165. . . . Shoots left.
TRANSACTIONS/CAREER NOTES: Selected by San Jose Sharks in sixth round (sixth Sharks pick, 141st overall) of NHL entry draft (June 29, 1994).

			REGULAR SEASON					PLAYOFFS				
Season	Team	League	Gms.	G	A	Pts.	PIM	Gms.	G	A	Pts.	PIM
93-94—Soviet Wings		CIS	22	4	4	8	20	3	1	0	1	4
94-95—Soviet Wings		CIS	52	16	13	29	62	4	1	2	3	4

KOVALENKO, ANDREI
RW, DENVER

PERSONAL: Born July 7, 1970, in Gorky, U.S.S.R. . . . 5-10/200. . . . Shoots left. . . . Name pronounced koh-vuh-LEHN-koh.
TRANSACTIONS/CAREER NOTES: Selected by Quebec Nordiques in eighth round (sixth Nordiques pick, 148th overall) of NHL entry draft (June 16, 1990). . . . Suffered from tonsillitis (December 22, 1992); missed two games. . . . Suffered from the flu (March 15, 1993); missed one game. . . . Suffered concussion (November 4, 1993); missed five games. . . . Bruised ribs (January 11, 1994); missed two games. . . . Injured shoulder (January 25, 1994); missed 14 games. . . . Suffered from tonsillitis (April 3, 1994); missed two games. . . . Played in Europe during 1994-95 NHL lockout. . . . Pulled groin (March 9, 1995); missed one game. . . . Injured neck (April 5, 1995); missed one game. . . . Injured thumb (April 20, 1995); missed one game. . . . Nordiques franchise moved to Denver for 1995-96 season.
STATISTICAL PLATEAUS: Three-goal games: 1992-93 (1).
MISCELLANEOUS: Member of gold-medal-winning Unified Olympic team (1992).

			REGULAR SEASON					PLAYOFFS				
Season	Team	League	Gms.	G	A	Pts.	PIM	Gms.	G	A	Pts.	PIM
88-89—CSKA Moscow		USSR	10	1	0	1	0	—	—	—	—	—
89-90—CSKA Moscow		USSR	48	8	5	13	18	—	—	—	—	—
90-91—CSKA Moscow		USSR	45	13	8	21	26	—	—	—	—	—
91-92—CSKA Moscow		CIS	44	19	13	32	32	—	—	—	—	—
—Unified Olympic Team		Int'l	8	1	1	2	2	—	—	—	—	—
92-93—CSKA Moscow		CIS	3	3	1	4	4	—	—	—	—	—
—Quebec		NHL	81	27	41	68	57	4	1	0	1	2
93-94—Quebec		NHL	58	16	17	33	46	—	—	—	—	—
94-95—Lada Togliatti		CIS	11	9	2	11	14	—	—	—	—	—
—Quebec		NHL	45	14	10	24	31	6	0	1	1	2
NHL totals			184	57	68	125	134	10	1	1	2	4

KOVALEV, ALEXEI
RW, RANGERS

PERSONAL: Born February 24, 1973, in Moscow, U.S.S.R. . . . 6-0/200. . . . Shoots left. . . . Name pronounced KOH-vuh-lehf.
TRANSACTIONS/CAREER NOTES: Selected by New York Rangers in first round (first Rangers pick, 15th overall) of NHL entry draft (June 22, 1991). . . . Suffered back spasms (January 16, 1993); missed one game. . . . Suspended one game by NHL (November 10, 1993). . . . Suspended five games by NHL for tripping (November 30, 1993). . . . Suspended two games by NHL (February 12, 1994). . . . Played in Europe during 1994-95 NHL lockout.
STATISTICAL PLATEAUS: Three-goal games: 1992-93 (1).

MISCELLANEOUS: Member of gold-medal-winning Unified Olympic team (1992).... Member of Stanley Cup championship team (1994).

			REGULAR SEASON					PLAYOFFS			
Season	Team	League	Gms.	G	A	Pts.	PIM	Gms.	G	A	Pts.	PIM
89-90—Dynamo Moscow		USSR	1	0	0	0	0	—	—	—	—	—
90-91—Dynamo Moscow		USSR	18	1	2	3	4	—	—	—	—	—
91-92—Dynamo Moscow		CIS	33	16	9	25	20	—	—	—	—	—
—Unified Olympic Team		Int'l	8	1	2	3	14	—	—	—	—	—
92-93—New York Rangers		NHL	65	20	18	38	79	—	—	—	—	—
—Binghamton		AHL	13	13	11	24	35	9	3	5	8	14
93-94—New York Rangers		NHL	76	23	33	56	154	23	9	12	21	18
94-95—Lada Togliatti		CIS	12	8	8	16	49	—	—	—	—	—
—New York Rangers		NHL	48	13	15	28	30	10	4	7	11	10
NHL totals			189	56	66	122	263	33	13	19	32	28

KOZLOV, SLAVA
LW, RED WINGS

PERSONAL: Born May 3, 1972, in Voskresensk, U.S.S.R.... 5-10/180.... Shoots left.... Name pronounced KAHS-lahf.

TRANSACTIONS/CAREER NOTES: Selected by Detroit Red Wings in third round (second Red Wings pick, 45th overall) of NHL entry draft (June 16, 1990).... Played in Europe during 1994-95 NHL lockout.... Bruised left foot (April 16, 1995); missed one game.

HONORS: Named Soviet League Rookie of the Year (1989-90).

STATISTICAL PLATEAUS: Three-goal games: 1993-94 (1).

			REGULAR SEASON					PLAYOFFS			
Season	Team	League	Gms.	G	A	Pts.	PIM	Gms.	G	A	Pts.	PIM
89-90—Khimik		USSR	45	14	12	26	38	—	—	—	—	—
90-91—Khimik		USSR	45	11	13	24	46	—	—	—	—	—
91-92—CSKA Moscow		CIS	11	6	5	11	12	—	—	—	—	—
—Detroit		NHL	7	0	2	2	2	—	—	—	—	—
92-93—Detroit		NHL	17	4	1	5	14	4	0	2	2	2
—Adirondack		AHL	45	23	36	59	54	4	1	1	2	4
93-94—Detroit		NHL	77	34	39	73	50	7	2	5	7	12
—Adirondack		AHL	3	0	1	1	15	—	—	—	—	—
94-95—CSKA Moscow		CIS	10	3	4	7	14	—	—	—	—	—
—Detroit		NHL	46	13	20	33	45	18	9	7	16	10
NHL totals			147	51	62	113	111	29	11	14	25	24

KOZLOV, VIKTOR
LW, SHARKS

PERSONAL: Born February 14, 1975, in Togliatti, U.S.S.R.... 6-5/209.... Shoots right.

TRANSACTIONS/CAREER NOTES: Selected by San Jose Sharks in first round (first Sharks pick, sixth overall) of NHL entry draft (June 26, 1993).... Suffered displaced ankle fracture (November 27, 1994); missed 13 games.... Played in Europe during 1994-95 NHL lockout.

			REGULAR SEASON					PLAYOFFS			
Season	Team	League	Gms.	G	A	Pts.	PIM	Gms.	G	A	Pts.	PIM
90-91—Lada Togliatti		USSR Div. II	2	2	0	2	0	—	—	—	—	—
91-92—Lada Togliatti		CIS	3	0	0	0	0	—	—	—	—	—
92-93—Dynamo Moscow		CIS	30	6	5	11	4	10	3	0	3	0
93-94—Dynamo Moscow		CIS	42	16	9	25	14	7	3	2	5	0
94-95—Dynamo Moscow		CIS	3	1	1	2	2	—	—	—	—	—
—San Jose		NHL	16	2	0	2	2	—	—	—	—	—
—Kansas City		IHL	—	—	—	—	—	13	4	5	9	12
NHL totals			16	2	0	2	2					

KRAVCHUK, IGOR
D, OILERS

PERSONAL: Born September 13, 1966, in Ufa, U.S.S.R.... 6-1/200.... Shoots left.... Name pronounced EE-gohr KRAV-chuk.

TRANSACTIONS/CAREER NOTES: Selected by Chicago Blackhawks in fourth round (fifth Blackhawks pick, 71st overall) of NHL entry draft (June 22, 1991).... Sprained knee (October 25, 1992); missed four games.... Sprained left ankle (December 29, 1992); missed 18 games.... Traded by Blackhawks with C Dean McAmmond to Edmonton Oilers for RW Joe Murphy (February 25, 1993).... Sprained left knee (April 6, 1993); missed remainder of season.... Strained groin (November 15, 1993); missed three games.... Injured left knee (January 30, 1995) and underwent surgery (February 6, 1995); missed 12 games.

MISCELLANEOUS: Member of gold-medal-winning U.S.S.R. Olympic team (1988) and gold-medal-winning Unified Olympic team (1992).

			REGULAR SEASON					PLAYOFFS			
Season	Team	League	Gms.	G	A	Pts.	PIM	Gms.	G	A	Pts.	PIM
87-88—CSKA Moscow		USSR	47	1	8	9	12	—	—	—	—	—
88-89—CSKA Moscow		USSR	27	3	4	7	2	—	—	—	—	—
89-90—CSKA Moscow		USSR	48	1	3	4	16	—	—	—	—	—
90-91—CSKA Moscow		USSR	41	6	5	11	16	—	—	—	—	—
91-92—CSKA Moscow		CIS	30	3	7	10	2	—	—	—	—	—
—Unified Olympic Team		Int'l	8	3	2	5	...	—	—	—	—	—
—Chicago		NHL	18	1	8	9	4	18	2	6	8	8

Season Team	League	REGULAR SEASON					PLAYOFFS				
		Gms.	G	A	Pts.	PIM	Gms.	G	A	Pts.	PIM
92-93—Chicago	NHL	38	6	9	15	30	—	—	—	—	—
—Edmonton	NHL	17	4	8	12	2	—	—	—	—	—
93-94—Edmonton	NHL	81	12	38	50	16	—	—	—	—	—
94-95—Edmonton	NHL	36	7	11	18	29	—	—	—	—	—
NHL totals		190	30	74	104	81	18	2	6	8	8

KRIVCHENKOV, ALEXEI
D, PENGUINS

PERSONAL: Born June 11, 1974, in Novosibirsk, U.S.S.R. . . . 6-0/185. . . . Shoots left.
TRANSACTIONS/CAREER NOTES: Selected by Pittsburgh Penguins in third round (fifth Penguins pick, 76th overall) of NHL entry draft (June 29, 1994).

Season Team	League	REGULAR SEASON					PLAYOFFS				
		Gms.	G	A	Pts.	PIM	Gms.	G	A	Pts.	PIM
93-94—Sibir Novosibirsk	CIS Div. II	37	1	3	4	48	—	—	—	—	—
—CSKA Moscow	CIS	4	0	0	0	2	3	0	0	0	0
94-95—CSKA Moscow	CIS	46	1	4	5	43	2	0	0	0	0

KRIVOKRASOV, SERGEI
RW, BLACKHAWKS

PERSONAL: Born April 15, 1974, in Angarsk, U.S.S.R. . . . 5-11/175. . . . Shoots left. . . . Name pronounced SAIR-gay kree-vuh-KRA-sahff.
TRANSACTIONS/CAREER NOTES: Selected by Chicago Blackhawks in first round (first Blackhawks pick, 12th overall) of NHL entry draft (June 20, 1992).

Season Team	League	REGULAR SEASON					PLAYOFFS				
		Gms.	G	A	Pts.	PIM	Gms.	G	A	Pts.	PIM
90-91—CSKA Moscow	USSR	41	4	0	4	8	—	—	—	—	—
91-92—CSKA Moscow	CIS	42	10	8	18	35	—	—	—	—	—
92-93—Chicago	NHL	4	0	0	0	2	—	—	—	—	—
—Indianapolis	IHL	78	36	33	69	157	5	3	1	4	2
93-94—Indianapolis	IHL	53	19	26	45	145	—	—	—	—	—
—Chicago	NHL	9	1	0	1	4	—	—	—	—	—
94-95—Indianapolis	IHL	29	12	15	27	41	—	—	—	—	—
—Chicago	NHL	41	12	7	19	33	10	0	0	0	8
NHL totals		54	13	7	20	39	10	0	0	0	8

KRIZ, PAVEL
D, BLACKHAWKS

PERSONAL: Born January 2, 1977, in Numburk, Czech Republic. . . . 6-0/205. . . . Shoots right.
TRANSACTIONS/CAREER NOTES: Selected by Chicago Blackhawks in fourth round (fifth Blackhawks pick, 97th overall) of NHL entry draft (July 8, 1995).

Season Team	League	REGULAR SEASON					PLAYOFFS				
		Gms.	G	A	Pts.	PIM	Gms.	G	A	Pts.	PIM
92-93—Kladno	Czech. Jrs.	30	10	14	24	50	—	—	—	—	—
93-94—Kladno	Czech. Jrs.	45	20	25	45	52	—	—	—	—	—
94-95—Tri-City	WHL	68	6	34	40	47	17	5	12	17	6

KRON, ROBERT
LW, WHALERS

PERSONAL: Born February 27, 1967, in Brno, Czechoslovakia. . . . 5-10/180. . . . Shoots right. . . . Name pronounced KRAHN.
TRANSACTIONS/CAREER NOTES: Selected by Vancouver Canucks in fourth round (fifth Canucks pick, 88th overall) of NHL entry draft (June 15, 1985). . . . Played entire season with a broken bone in left wrist (1990-91). . . . Underwent surgery to repair torn knee ligaments and wrist fracture (March 22, 1991). . . . Fractured ankle (January 28, 1992); missed 22 games. . . . Traded by Canucks with third-round pick in 1993 draft (D Marek Malik) and future considerations to Hartford Whalers for C/LW Murray Craven and fifth-round pick (D Scott Walker) in 1993 draft (March 22, 1993); Canucks sent RW Jim Sandlak to Whalers to complete deal (May 17, 1993). . . . Sprained shoulder (February 26, 1994); missed seven games. . . . Broke thumb (March 29, 1995); missed 11 games.

Season Team	League	REGULAR SEASON					PLAYOFFS				
		Gms.	G	A	Pts.	PIM	Gms.	G	A	Pts.	PIM
86-87—Zetor Brno	Czech.	28	14	11	25	. . .	—	—	—	—	—
87-88—Zetor Brno	Czech.	32	12	6	18	. . .	—	—	—	—	—
88-89—Zetor Brno	Czech.	43	28	19	47	. . .	—	—	—	—	—
89-90—Dukla Trencin	Czech.	39	22	22	44	. . .	—	—	—	—	—
90-91—Vancouver	NHL	76	12	20	32	21	—	—	—	—	—
91-92—Vancouver	NHL	36	2	2	4	2	11	1	2	3	2
92-93—Vancouver	NHL	32	10	11	21	14	—	—	—	—	—
—Hartford	NHL	13	4	2	6	4	—	—	—	—	—
93-94—Hartford	NHL	77	24	26	50	8	—	—	—	—	—
94-95—Hartford	NHL	37	10	8	18	10	—	—	—	—	—
NHL totals		271	62	69	131	59	11	1	2	3	2

KROUPA, VLASTIMIL
D, SHARKS

PERSONAL: Born April 27, 1975, in Most, Czechoslovakia. . . . 6-2/176. . . . Shoots left. . . . Name pronounced VLAS-tuh-meel KROO-pah.
TRANSACTIONS/CAREER NOTES: Selected by San Jose Sharks in second round (third Sharks pick, 45th overall) of NHL entry draft (June 26, 1993).

K

Season	Team	League	REGULAR SEASON Gms.	G	A	Pts.	PIM	PLAYOFFS Gms.	G	A	Pts.	PIM
91-92	Litvinov	Czech. Jrs.	37	9	16	25	...	—	—	—	—	—
92-93	Chemopetrol Litvinov	Czech.	9	0	1	1	...	—	—	—	—	—
93-94	San Jose	NHL	27	1	3	4	20	14	1	2	3	21
	Kansas City	IHL	39	3	12	15	12	—	—	—	—	—
94-95	Kansas City	IHL	51	4	8	12	49	12	2	4	6	22
	San Jose	NHL	14	0	2	2	16	6	0	0	0	4
NHL totals			41	1	5	6	36	20	1	2	3	25

KRUPP, UWE
D, DENVER

PERSONAL: Born June 24, 1965, in Cologne, West Germany.... 6-6/235.... Shoots right.... Name pronounced YOO-ee KROOP.
TRANSACTIONS/CAREER NOTES: Selected by Buffalo Sabres in 11th round (13th Sabres pick, 214th overall) of NHL entry draft (June 8, 1983).... Bruised hip (November 1987).... Injured head (April 1988).... Broke rib (January 6, 1989).... Banned from international competition for 18 months by IIHF after failing random substance test (April 20, 1990).... Suffered from cyst on foot (January 2, 1991).... Traded by Sabres with C Pierre Turgeon, RW Benoit Hogue and C Dave McLlwain to New York Islanders for C Pat LaFontaine, LW Randy Wood, D Randy Hillier and future considerations; Sabres received fourth-round pick in 1992 draft (D Dean Melanson) to complete deal (October 25, 1991).... Sprained left knee (December 28, 1991); missed five games.... Bruised thigh (February 7, 1992).... Suffered from the flu (March 2, 1993); missed one game.... Suffered sore shoulder (April 10, 1993); missed three games.... Broke toe (October 10, 1993); missed three games.... Fractured sinus bone (October 26, 1993); missed 17 games.... Suffered severely sprained hamstring (December 19, 1993); missed nine games.... Suffered from the flu, bruised jaw and sprained wrist (February 27, 1994); missed four games.... Sprained wrist (March 5, 1994); missed nine games.... Traded by Islanders with first-round pick in 1994 draft (D Wade Belak) to Quebec Nordiques for C Ron Sutter and first-round pick (RW Brett Lindros) in 1994 draft (June 28, 1994).... Played in Europe during 1994-95 NHL lockout.... Injured hip (February 23, 1995); missed two games.... Suffered hip flexor (April 18, 1995); missed two games.... Nordiques franchise moved to Denver for 1995-96 season.
HONORS: Played in NHL All-Star Game (1991).
STATISTICAL PLATEAUS: Three-goal games: 1994-95 (1).

Season	Team	League	REGULAR SEASON Gms.	G	A	Pts.	PIM	PLAYOFFS Gms.	G	A	Pts.	PIM
83-84	KEC	W. Germany	40	0	4	4	22	—	—	—	—	—
84-85	KEC	W. Germany	39	11	8	19	36	—	—	—	—	—
85-86	KEC	W. Germany	45	10	21	31	83	—	—	—	—	—
86-87	Rochester	AHL	42	3	19	22	50	17	1	11	12	16
	Buffalo	NHL	26	1	4	5	23	—	—	—	—	—
87-88	Buffalo	NHL	75	2	9	11	151	6	0	0	0	15
88-89	Buffalo	NHL	70	5	13	18	55	5	0	1	1	4
89-90	Buffalo	NHL	74	3	20	23	85	6	0	0	0	4
90-91	Buffalo	NHL	74	12	32	44	66	6	1	1	2	6
91-92	Buffalo	NHL	8	2	0	2	6	—	—	—	—	—
	New York Islanders	NHL	59	6	29	35	43	—	—	—	—	—
92-93	New York Islanders	NHL	80	9	29	38	67	18	1	5	6	12
93-94	New York Islanders	NHL	41	7	14	21	30	4	0	1	1	4
94-95	Landshut	Germany	5	1	2	3	6	—	—	—	—	—
	Quebec	NHL	44	6	17	23	20	5	0	2	2	2
NHL totals			551	53	167	220	546	50	2	10	12	47

KRUPPKE, GORD
D, RED WINGS

PERSONAL: Born April 2, 1969, in Edmonton.... 6-1/200.... Shoots right.... Name pronounced KRUHP-kee.
TRANSACTIONS/CAREER NOTES: Underwent surgery to have spleen removed (December 1986).... Selected by Detroit Red Wings as underage junior in second round (second Red Wings pick, 32nd overall) of NHL entry draft (June 13, 1987).... Injured left knee ligaments (October 1987).... Bruised elbow (December 2, 1992); missed one game.... Traded by Red Wings to Toronto Maple Leafs for LW Chris Govedaris (February 17, 1995).... Traded by Maple Leafs to Red Wings for other considerations (April 7, 1995).
HONORS: Named to WHL All-Star second team (1988-89).

Season	Team	League	REGULAR SEASON Gms.	G	A	Pts.	PIM	PLAYOFFS Gms.	G	A	Pts.	PIM
85-86	Prince Albert	WHL	62	1	8	9	81	20	4	4	8	22
86-87	Prince Albert	WHL	49	2	10	12	129	8	0	0	0	9
87-88	Prince Albert	WHL	54	8	8	16	113	10	0	0	0	46
88-89	Prince Albert	WHL	62	6	26	32	254	3	0	0	0	11
89-90	Adirondack	AHL	59	2	12	14	103	—	—	—	—	—
90-91	Adirondack	AHL	45	1	8	9	153	—	—	—	—	—
	Detroit	NHL	4	0	0	0	0	—	—	—	—	—
91-92	Adirondack	AHL	65	3	9	12	208	16	0	1	1	52
92-93	Adirondack	AHL	41	2	12	14	197	9	1	2	3	20
	Detroit	NHL	10	0	0	0	20	—	—	—	—	—
93-94	Adirondack	AHL	54	2	9	11	210	12	1	3	4	32
	Detroit	NHL	9	0	0	0	12	—	—	—	—	—
94-95	Adirondack	AHL	48	2	9	11	157	—	—	—	—	—
	St. John's	AHL	3	0	1	1	6	—	—	—	—	—
NHL totals			23	0	0	0	32					

KRUSE, PAUL

LW, FLAMES

PERSONAL: Born March 15, 1970, in Merritt, B.C. . . . 6-0/205. . . . Shoots left. . . . Name pronounced KROOS.
TRANSACTIONS/CAREER NOTES: Selected by Calgary Flames in fourth round (sixth Flames pick, 83rd overall) of NHL entry draft (June 16, 1990). . . . Injured eye (March 8, 1992); missed four games. . . . Suffered hip pointer (March 21, 1993); missed one game. . . . Broke toe on right foot (September 27, 1993); missed 12 games. . . . Bruised left foot (March 2, 1995); missed one game. . . . Bruised left knee (April 29, 1995); missed one game.

			REGULAR SEASON					PLAYOFFS				
Season	Team	League	Gms.	G	A	Pts.	PIM	Gms.	G	A	Pts.	PIM
86-87—Merritt		BCJHL	35	8	15	23	120	—	—	—	—	—
87-88—Merritt		BCJHL	44	12	32	44	227	4	1	4	5	18
—Moose Jaw		WHL	1	0	0	0	0	—	—	—	—	—
88-89—Kamloops		WHL	68	8	15	23	209	—	—	—	—	—
89-90—Kamloops		WHL	67	22	23	45	291	17	3	5	8	†79
90-91—Salt Lake City		IHL	83	24	20	44	313	4	1	1	2	4
—Calgary		NHL	1	0	0	0	7	—	—	—	—	—
91-92—Salt Lake City		IHL	57	14	15	29	267	5	1	2	3	19
—Calgary		NHL	16	3	1	4	65	—	—	—	—	—
92-93—Salt Lake City		IHL	35	1	4	5	206	—	—	—	—	—
—Calgary		NHL	27	2	3	5	41	—	—	—	—	—
93-94—Calgary		NHL	68	3	8	11	185	7	0	0	0	14
94-95—Calgary		NHL	45	11	5	16	141	7	4	2	6	10
NHL totals			157	19	17	36	439	14	4	2	6	24

KRUSHELNYSKI, MIKE

C/LW, RED WINGS

PERSONAL: Born April 27, 1960, in Montreal. . . . 6-2/200. . . . Shoots left. . . . Name pronounced KROO-shihl-NIH-skee.
TRANSACTIONS/CAREER NOTES: Started 1978-79 season at St. Louis University then returned to junior hockey. . . . Selected by Boston Bruins as underage junior in sixth round (seventh Bruins pick, 120th overall) of NHL entry draft (August 9, 1979). . . . Separated right shoulder (January 1984). . . . Traded by Bruins to Edmonton Oilers for C Ken Linseman (June 1984). . . . Sprained right knee (December 10, 1985); missed 17 games. . . . Twisted knee (February 14, 1986); missed nine games. . . . Suspended by Oilers for not reporting to training camp (September 1987). . . . Traded by Oilers with C Wayne Gretzky and RW/D Marty McSorley to Los Angeles Kings for C Jimmy Carson, LW Martin Gelinas, first-round picks in 1989 (traded to New Jersey), 1991 (LW Martin Rucinsky) and 1993 (D Nick Stajduhar) drafts and cash (August 9, 1988). . . . Fractured left wrist (October 5, 1989); missed 17 games. . . . Traded by Kings to Toronto Maple Leafs for C John McIntyre (November 9, 1990). . . . Suffered back disc irritation (January 4, 1994); missed 17 games. . . . Signed as free agent by Detroit Red Wings (August 1, 1994). . . . Injured left knee (January 30, 1995); missed two games. . . . Injured lower left leg (February 7, 1995); missed eight games. . . . Sprained left knee (March 8, 1995); missed 13 games.
HONORS: Played in NHL All-Star Game (1985).
STATISTICAL PLATEAUS: Three-goal games: 1984-85 (1).
MISCELLANEOUS: Member of Stanley Cup championship teams (1985, 1987 and 1988).

			REGULAR SEASON					PLAYOFFS				
Season	Team	League	Gms.	G	A	Pts.	PIM	Gms.	G	A	Pts.	PIM
78-79—Montreal		QMJHL	46	15	29	44	42	11	3	4	7	8
79-80—Montreal		QMJHL	72	39	61	100	78	6	2	3	5	2
80-81—Springfield		AHL	80	25	38	63	47	7	1	1	2	29
81-82—Erie		AHL	62	31	52	83	44	—	—	—	—	—
—Boston		NHL	17	3	3	6	2	1	0	0	0	2
82-83—Boston		NHL	79	23	42	65	43	17	8	6	14	12
83-84—Boston		NHL	66	25	20	45	55	2	0	0	0	0
84-85—Edmonton		NHL	80	43	45	88	60	18	5	8	13	22
85-86—Edmonton		NHL	54	16	24	40	22	10	4	5	9	16
86-87—Edmonton		NHL	80	16	35	51	67	21	3	4	7	18
87-88—Edmonton		NHL	76	20	27	47	64	19	4	6	10	12
88-89—Los Angeles		NHL	78	26	36	62	110	11	1	4	5	4
89-90—Los Angeles		NHL	63	16	25	41	50	10	1	3	4	12
90-91—Los Angeles		NHL	15	1	5	6	10	—	—	—	—	—
—Toronto		NHL	59	17	22	39	48	—	—	—	—	—
91-92—Toronto		NHL	72	9	15	24	72	—	—	—	—	—
92-93—Toronto		NHL	84	19	20	39	62	16	3	7	10	8
93-94—Toronto		NHL	54	5	6	11	28	6	0	0	0	0
94-95—Detroit		NHL	20	2	3	5	6	8	0	0	0	0
NHL totals			897	241	328	569	699	139	29	43	72	106

KRYGIER, TODD

LW, MIGHTY DUCKS

PERSONAL: Born October 12, 1965, in Northville, Mich. . . . 6-0/185. . . . Shoots left. . . . Full name: Todd Andrew Krygier. . . . Name pronounced KREE-guhr.
COLLEGE: Connecticut.
TRANSACTIONS/CAREER NOTES: Selected by Hartford Whalers in NHL supplemental draft (June 10, 1988). . . . Bruised heel (March 13, 1990). . . . Traded by Whalers to Washington Capitals for fourth-round pick (traded to Calgary Flames who selected D Jason Smith) in 1993 draft (October 3, 1991). . . . Separated right shoulder (December 28, 1993); missed seven games. . . . Traded by Capitals to Mighty Ducks of Anaheim for fourth-round pick in 1996 draft (February 2, 1995). . . . Slightly strained groin (March 11, 1995); missed three games. . . . Strained groin (March 30, 1995); missed three games.
STATISTICAL PLATEAUS: Three-goal games: 1993-94 (1).

K

Season	Team	League	Gms.	G	A	Pts.	PIM	Gms.	G	A	Pts.	PIM
84-85—University of Connecticut.		ECAC-II	14	14	11	25	12	—	—	—	—	—
85-86—University of Connecticut.		ECAC-II	32	29	27	56	46	—	—	—	—	—
86-87—University of Connecticut.		ECAC-II	28	24	24	48	44	—	—	—	—	—
87-88—University of Connecticut.		ECAC-II	27	32	39	71	38	—	—	—	—	—
—New Haven		AHL	13	1	5	6	34	—	—	—	—	—
88-89—Binghamton		AHL	76	26	42	68	77	—	—	—	—	—
89-90—Binghamton		AHL	12	1	9	10	16	—	—	—	—	—
—Hartford		NHL	58	18	12	30	52	7	2	1	3	4
90-91—Hartford		NHL	72	13	17	30	95	6	0	2	2	0
91-92—Washington		NHL	67	13	17	30	107	5	2	1	3	4
92-93—Washington		NHL	77	11	12	23	60	6	1	1	2	4
93-94—Washington		NHL	66	12	18	30	60	5	2	0	2	10
94-95—Anaheim		NHL	35	11	11	22	10	—	—	—	—	—
NHL totals			375	78	87	165	384	29	7	5	12	22

KUCERA, FRANTISEK
D, WHALERS

PERSONAL: Born February 3, 1968, in Prague, Czechoslovakia. . . . 6-2/205. . . . Shoots right. . . . Name pronounced koo-CHAIR-uh.
TRANSACTIONS/CAREER NOTES: Selected by Chicago Blackhawks in fourth round (third Blackhawks pick, 77th overall) of NHL entry draft (June 21, 1986). . . . Pulled groin (March 20, 1993); missed 11 games. . . . Pulled groin (1993-94 season); missed five games. . . . Traded by Blackhawks with LW Jocelyn Lemieux to Hartford Whalers for LW Randy Cunneyworth and D Gary Suter (March 11, 1994). . . . Played in Europe during 1994-95 NHL lockout.

Season	Team	League	Gms.	G	A	Pts.	PIM	Gms.	G	A	Pts.	PIM
85-86—Sparta Prague		Czech.	15	0	0	0	. . .	—	—	—	—	—
86-87—Sparta Prague		Czech.	33	7	2	9	14	—	—	—	—	—
87-88—Sparta Prague		Czech.	34	4	2	6	30	—	—	—	—	—
88-89—Dukla Jihlava		Czech.	45	10	9	19	28	—	—	—	—	—
89-90—Dukla Jihlava		Czech.	43	9	10	19	. . .	—	—	—	—	—
90-91—Chicago		NHL	40	2	12	14	32	—	—	—	—	—
—Indianapolis		IHL	35	8	19	27	23	7	0	1	1	15
91-92—Chicago		NHL	61	3	10	13	36	6	0	0	0	0
—Indianapolis		IHL	7	1	2	3	4	—	—	—	—	—
92-93—Chicago		NHL	71	5	14	19	59	—	—	—	—	—
93-94—Chicago		NHL	60	4	13	17	34	—	—	—	—	—
—Hartford		NHL	16	1	3	4	14	—	—	—	—	—
94-95—Sparta Prague		Czech.	16	1	2	3	14	—	—	—	—	—
—Hartford		NHL	48	3	17	20	30	—	—	—	—	—
NHL totals			296	18	69	87	205	6	0	0	0	0

KUCHARCIK, TOMAS
C/RW, MAPLE LEAFS

PERSONAL: Born May 10, 1970, in Vlasim, Czechoslovakia. . . . 6-2/200. . . . Shoots left. . . . Name pronounced koo-HARH-chihk.
TRANSACTIONS/CAREER NOTES: Selected by Toronto Maple Leafs in eighth round (11th Maple Leafs pick, 167th overall) of NHL entry draft (June 22, 1991).

Season	Team	League	Gms.	G	A	Pts.	PIM	Gms.	G	A	Pts.	PIM
90-91—Dukla Jihlava		Czech.	23	7	6	13	6	—	—	—	—	—
91-92—Dukla Jihlava		Czech.	37	13	17	30	. . .	—	—	—	—	—
92-93—Dukla Jihlava		Czech.	39	17	20	37	. . .	—	—	—	—	—
93-94—St. John's		AHL	8	2	3	5	4	10	3	4	7	2
—Skoda Plzen		Czech Rep.	32	10	10	20	. . .	5	2	6	8	. . .
94-95—Skoda Plzen		Czech Rep.	40	14	4	18	. . .	3	0	0	0	. . .

KUDASHOV, ALEXEI
C, PANTHERS

PERSONAL: Born July 21, 1971, in Elektrostal, U.S.S.R. . . . 6-0/190. . . . Shoots right. . . . Name pronounced KOO-duh-shahf.
TRANSACTIONS/CAREER NOTES: Selected by Toronto Maple Leafs in fifth round (third Maple Leafs pick, 102nd overall) of NHL entry draft (June 22, 1991). . . . Loaned by Maple Leafs to Russian Olympic Team (February 1, 1994). . . . Returned to Maple Leafs (March 1, 1994). . . . Signed as free agent by Florida Panthers (July 27, 1995).

Season	Team	League	Gms.	G	A	Pts.	PIM	Gms.	G	A	Pts.	PIM
90-91—Soviet Wings		USSR	45	9	5	14	10	—	—	—	—	—
91-92—Soviet Wings		CIS	36	8	16	24	12	—	—	—	—	—
92-93—Soviet Wings		CIS	41	8	20	28	24	7	1	3	4	4
93-94—Toronto		NHL	25	1	0	1	4	—	—	—	—	—
—St. John's		AHL	27	7	15	22	21	—	—	—	—	—
—Russian Olympic team		Int'l	8	1	2	3	4	—	—	—	—	—
94-95—St. John's		AHL	75	25	54	79	17	5	1	4	5	2
NHL totals			25	1	0	1	4					

KUDELSKI, BOB
RW, PANTHERS

PERSONAL: Born March 3, 1964, in Springfield, Mass.... 6-1/206.... Shoots right.... Name pronounced kuh-DEHL-skee.
HIGH SCHOOL: Cathedral (Springfield, Mass.).
COLLEGE: Yale.
TRANSACTIONS/CAREER NOTES: Selected by Los Angeles Kings in NHL supplemental draft (September 17, 1986).... Broke knuckle on left hand (November 22, 1989); missed 15 games.... Strained medial collateral knee ligament (April 24, 1991).... Traded by Kings with C Shawn McCosh to Ottawa Senators for RW Jim Thomson and C Marc Fortier (December 20, 1992).... Traded by Senators to Florida Panthers for C Scott Levins, LW Evgeny Davydov and sixth-round pick (D Mike Gaffney) in 1994 draft (January 6, 1994).
HONORS: Named to ECAC All-Star first team (1986-87).... Played in NHL All-Star Game (1994).
STATISTICAL PLATEAUS: Three-goal games: 1990-91 (1), 1991-92 (1), 1992-93 (1), 1993-94 (1). Total: 4.

			REGULAR SEASON					PLAYOFFS				
Season	Team	League	Gms.	G	A	Pts.	PIM	Gms.	G	A	Pts.	PIM
83-84	Yale University	ECAC	21	14	12	26	12	—	—	—	—	—
84-85	Yale University	ECAC	32	21	23	44	38	—	—	—	—	—
85-86	Yale University	ECAC	31	18	23	41	48	—	—	—	—	—
86-87	Yale University	ECAC	30	25	22	47	34	—	—	—	—	—
87-88	New Haven	AHL	50	15	19	34	41	—	—	—	—	—
	Los Angeles	NHL	26	0	1	1	8	—	—	—	—	—
88-89	New Haven	AHL	60	32	19	51	43	17	8	5	13	12
	Los Angeles	NHL	14	1	3	4	17	—	—	—	—	—
89-90	Los Angeles	NHL	62	23	13	36	49	8	1	2	3	2
90-91	Los Angeles	NHL	72	23	13	36	46	8	3	2	5	2
91-92	Los Angeles	NHL	80	22	21	43	42	6	0	0	0	0
92-93	Los Angeles	NHL	15	3	3	6	8	—	—	—	—	—
	Ottawa	NHL	48	21	14	35	22	—	—	—	—	—
93-94	Ottawa	NHL	42	26	15	41	14	—	—	—	—	—
	Florida	NHL	44	14	15	29	10	—	—	—	—	—
94-95	Florida	NHL	26	6	3	9	2	—	—	—	—	—
NHL totals			429	139	101	240	218	22	4	4	8	4

KUDRNA, JAROSLAV
LW, SHARKS

PERSONAL: Born December 5, 1975, in Hradec Kralove, Czechoslovakia.... 5-11/176.... Shoots left.
TRANSACTIONS/CAREER NOTES: Selected by San Jose Sharks in sixth round (eighth Sharks pick, 142nd overall) of NHL entry draft (July 8, 1995).

			REGULAR SEASON					PLAYOFFS				
Season	Team	League	Gms.	G	A	Pts.	PIM	Gms.	G	A	Pts.	PIM
92-93	Stadion H. Kralove Jrs.	Czech.	40	30	30	60	45	—	—	—	—	—
93-94	Stadion H. Kralove Jrs.	Czech Rep.	43	40	29	69	60	—	—	—	—	—
	Stadion H. Kralove	Czech Rep.	5	0	0	0	...	2	0	1	1	...
94-95	Penticton	BCJHL	58	60	55	115	148	—	—	—	—	—

KUKI, ARTO
C, CANADIENS

PERSONAL: Born February 22, 1976, in Espoo, Finland.... 6-3/205.... Shoots left.
TRANSACTIONS/CAREER NOTES: Selected by Montreal Canadiens in fourth round (sixth Canadiens pick, 96th overall) of NHL entry draft (June 29, 1994).

			REGULAR SEASON					PLAYOFFS				
Season	Team	League	Gms.	G	A	Pts.	PIM	Gms.	G	A	Pts.	PIM
93-94	Kiekko-Espoo	Finland	26	1	10	11	28	—	—	—	—	—
94-95	Kiekko-Espoo Jrs.	Finland	33	7	10	17	36	—	—	—	—	—
	Kiekko-Espoo	Finland	4	0	1	1	0	—	—	—	—	—

KUNTAR, LES
G, FLYERS

PERSONAL: Born July 28, 1969, in Buffalo, N.Y.... 6-2/195.... Catches left.... Full name: Leslie Steven Kuntar.
HIGH SCHOOL: Nichols School (Buffalo, N.Y.).
COLLEGE: St. Lawrence (N.Y.).
TRANSACTIONS/CAREER NOTES: Selected by Montreal Canadiens in sixth round (sixth Canadiens pick, 122nd overall) of NHL entry draft (June 13, 1987).... Traded by Worcester Ice Cats to Hershey Bears for future considerations (January 16, 1995). ... Signed as free agent by Philadelphia Flyers (March 5, 1995).
HONORS: Named to NCAA All-America East first team (1990-91).... Named to ECAC All-Star first team (1990-91).

			REGULAR SEASON							PLAYOFFS						
Season	Team	League	Gms.	Min.	W	L	T	GA	SO	Avg.	Gms.	Min.	W	L	GA	SO	Avg.
86-87	Nichols School	N.Y. H.S.	22	1585	...	...	...	56	3	2.12	—	—	—	—	—	—	—
87-88	St. Lawrence Univ.	ECAC	10	488	6	1	0	27	0	3.32	—	—	—	—	—	—	—
88-89	St. Lawrence Univ.	ECAC	14	786	11	2	0	31	0	2.37	—	—	—	—	—	—	—
89-90	St. Lawrence Univ.	ECAC	19	1076	7	11	1	76	1	4.24	—	—	—	—	—	—	—
90-91	St. Lawrence Univ.	ECAC	*33	*1794	*19	11	1	97	2	*3.24	—	—	—	—	—	—	—
91-92	Fredericton	AHL	11	638	7	3	0	26	0	2.45	—	—	—	—	—	—	—
	U.S. national team	Int'l	2	100	...	...	...	4	0	2.40	—	—	—	—	—	—	—
92-93	Fredericton	AHL	42	2315	16	14	7	130	0	3.37	1	64	0	1	6	0	5.63
93-94	Fredericton	AHL	34	1804	10	17	3	109	1	3.63	—	—	—	—	—	—	—
	Montreal	NHL	6	302	2	2	0	16	0	3.18	—	—	—	—	—	—	—
94-95	Worcester	AHL	24	1241	6	10	5	77	2	3.72	—	—	—	—	—	—	—
	Hershey	AHL	32	1802	15	13	2	89	0	2.96	2	70	0	1	5	0	4.29
NHL totals			6	302	2	2	0	16	0	3.18							

K

KURRI, JARI
RW, KINGS

PERSONAL: Born May 18, 1960, in Helsinki, Finland. . . . 6-1/195. . . . Shoots right. . . . Name pronounced YAH-ree KUHR-ee.

TRANSACTIONS/CAREER NOTES: Selected by Edmonton Oilers in fourth round (third Oilers pick, 69th overall) of NHL entry draft (June 11, 1980). . . . Pulled groin (November 24, 1981). . . . Pulled groin muscle (January 1984); missed 16 games. . . . Sprained medial collateral ligament in left knee (February 12, 1989). . . . Signed two-year contract with Milan Devils of Italian Hockey League (July 30, 1990). . . . Injured knee (January 1991). . . . Rights traded by Oilers with RW Dave Brown and D Corey Foster to Philadelphia Flyers for RW Scott Mellanby, LW Craig Berube and C Craig Fisher (May 30, 1991). . . . Rights traded by Flyers to Los Angeles Kings for D Steve Duchesne, C Steve Kasper and fourth-round pick (D Aris Brimanis) in 1991 draft (May 30, 1991). . . . Sprained shoulder (November 12, 1991); missed three games. . . . Suffered from the flu (January 1992); missed two games. . . . Suffered knee contusion (November 6, 1993); missed two games. . . . Played in Europe during 1994-95 NHL lockout. . . . Strained hip flexor (March 11, 1995); missed two games. . . . Strained groin (March 20, 1995); missed two games. . . . Strained groin (March 26, 1995); missed five games. . . . Strained groin (April 7, 1995); missed one game.

HONORS: Named to NHL All-Star second team (1983-84, 1985-86 and 1988-89). . . . Played in NHL All-Star Game (1983, 1985, 1986, 1988-1990 and 1993). . . . Won Lady Byng Memorial Trophy (1984-85). . . . Named to THE SPORTING NEWS All-Star first team (1984-85). . . . Named to NHL All-Star first team (1984-85 and 1986-87). . . . Named to THE SPORTING NEWS All-Star second team (1985-86 and 1988-89).

RECORDS: Shares NHL career record for most overtime goals—7. . . . Holds NHL single-season playoff record for most three-or-more-goal games—4 (1985). . . . Shares NHL single-season playoff records for most goals—19 (1985); and most game-winning goals—5 (1987). . . . Holds NHL single-series playoff records for most goals—12 (1985); and most three-or-more-goal games—3 (1985). . . . Shares NHL single-game playoff records for most shorthanded goals—2 (April 24, 1983); most shorthanded goals in one period—2 (April 24, 1983); and most power-play goals—3 (April 9, 1987).

STATISTICAL PLATEAUS: Three-goal games: 1980-81 (3), 1982-83 (2), 1983-84 (3), 1984-85 (5), 1985-86 (2), 1986-87 (1), 1988-89 (2), 1991-92 (1), 1992-93 (1). Total: 20. . . . Four-goal games: 1985-86 (1). . . . Five-goal games: 1983-84 (1). . . . Total hat tricks: 22.

MISCELLANEOUS: Member of Stanley Cup championship teams (1984, 1985, 1987, 1988 and 1990).

			REGULAR SEASON					PLAYOFFS			
Season	Team	League	Gms.	G	A	Pts.	PIM	Gms.	G	A	Pts.	PIM
77-78—Jokerit	Finland	29	2	9	11	12	—	—	—	—	—
78-79—Jokerit	Finland	33	16	14	30	12	—	—	—	—	—
79-80—Jokerit	Finland	33	23	16	39	22	6	7	2	9	13
—Finnish Olympic Team	Int'l	7	2	1	3	6	—	—	—	—	—
80-81—Edmonton	NHL	75	32	43	75	40	9	5	7	12	4
81-82—Edmonton	NHL	71	32	54	86	32	5	2	5	7	10
82-83—Edmonton	NHL	80	45	59	104	22	16	8	15	23	8
83-84—Edmonton	NHL	64	52	61	113	14	19	*14	14	28	13
84-85—Edmonton	NHL	73	71	64	135	30	18	*19	12	31	6
85-86—Edmonton	NHL	78	*68	63	131	22	10	2	10	12	4
86-87—Edmonton	NHL	79	54	54	108	41	21	*15	10	25	20
87-88—Edmonton	NHL	80	43	53	96	30	19	*14	17	31	12
88-89—Edmonton	NHL	76	44	58	102	69	7	3	5	8	6
89-90—Edmonton	NHL	78	33	60	93	48	22	10	15	25	18
90-91—Milan	Italy	40	60	40	97	8	10	10	12	22	2
91-92—Los Angeles	NHL	73	23	37	60	24	4	1	2	3	4
92-93—Los Angeles	NHL	82	27	60	87	38	24	9	8	17	12
93-94—Los Angeles	NHL	81	31	46	77	48	—	—	—	—	—
94-95—Jokerit Helsinki	Finland	20	10	9	19	10	—	—	—	—	—
—Los Angeles	NHL	38	10	19	29	24	—	—	—	—	—
NHL totals		1028	565	731	1296	482	174	102	120	222	117

KURTZ, JUSTIN
D, JETS

PERSONAL: Born January 14, 1977, in Winnipeg. . . . 5-11/188. . . . Shoots left.

TRANSACTIONS/CAREER NOTES: Selected by Winnipeg Jets in fourth round (fifth Jets pick, 84th overall) of NHL entry draft (July 8, 1995).

			REGULAR SEASON					PLAYOFFS			
Season	Team	League	Gms.	G	A	Pts.	PIM	Gms.	G	A	Pts.	PIM
93-94—Brandon	WHL	63	3	13	16	37	14	1	3	4	24
94-95—Brandon	WHL	65	8	34	42	75	18	2	2	4	26

KURVERS, TOM
D, MIGHTY DUCKS

PERSONAL: Born September 14, 1962, in Minneapolis. . . . 6-0/195. . . . Shoots left. . . . Full name: Thomas James Kurvers.

COLLEGE: Minnesota-Duluth.

TRANSACTIONS/CAREER NOTES: Selected by Montreal Canadiens as underage player in seventh round (10th Canadiens pick, 145th overall) of NHL entry draft (June 10, 1981). . . . Suffered facial injuries (October 23, 1984); missed five games. . . . Traded by Canadiens to Buffalo Sabres for second-round pick (LW Martin St. Amour) in 1988 draft (November 18, 1986). . . . Traded by Sabres to New Jersey Devils for third-round pick (LW Andrew MacVicar) in 1988 draft (June 13, 1987). . . . Fractured left index finger (November 1987). . . . Pulled groin (February 1988). . . . Injured right thumb (May 1988). . . . Pulled groin (November 17, 1988). . . . Traded by Devils to Toronto Maple Leafs for first-round pick (D Scott Niedermayer) in 1991 draft (October 16, 1989). . . . Injured knee (March 8, 1990). . . . Underwent arthroscopic knee surgery (November 15, 1990). . . . Traded by Maple Leafs to Canucks for C Brian Bradley (January 12, 1991). . . . Traded by Canucks to New York Islanders as part of three-way deal in which Minnesota North Stars sent D Dave Babych to Canucks and Islanders sent D Craig Ludwig to North Stars (June 22, 1991). . . . Fractured thumb (November 30, 1993); missed seven games. . . . Traded by Islanders to Mighty Ducks of Anaheim for LW Troy Loney (June 29, 1994). . . . Sprained wrist (February, 17, 1995); missed three games. . . . Sprained wrist (March 11, 1995); missed three games.

HONORS: Won Hobey Baker Memorial Award (1983-84).... Named to NCAA All-America West team (1983-84).... Named to WCHA All-Star first team (1983-84).
MISCELLANEOUS: Member of Stanley Cup championship team (1986).

			REGULAR SEASON					PLAYOFFS			
Season Team	League	Gms.	G	A	Pts.	PIM	Gms.	G	A	Pts.	PIM
80-81—Minnesota-Duluth	WCHA	39	6	24	30	48	—	—	—	—	—
81-82—Minnesota-Duluth	WCHA	37	11	31	42	18	—	—	—	—	—
82-83—Minnesota-Duluth	WCHA	45	8	36	44	42	—	—	—	—	—
83-84—Minnesota-Duluth	WCHA	43	18	58	76	46	—	—	—	—	—
84-85—Montreal	NHL	75	10	35	45	30	12	0	6	6	6
85-86—Montreal	NHL	62	7	23	30	36	—	—	—	—	—
86-87—Montreal	NHL	1	0	0	0	0	—	—	—	—	—
—Buffalo	NHL	55	6	17	23	24	—	—	—	—	—
87-88—New Jersey	NHL	56	5	29	34	46	19	6	9	15	38
88-89—New Jersey	NHL	74	16	50	66	38	—	—	—	—	—
89-90—New Jersey	NHL	1	0	0	0	0	—	—	—	—	—
—Toronto	NHL	70	15	37	52	29	5	0	3	3	4
90-91—Toronto	NHL	19	0	3	3	8	—	—	—	—	—
—Vancouver	NHL	32	4	23	27	20	6	2	2	4	12
91-92—New York Islanders	NHL	74	9	47	56	30	—	—	—	—	—
92-93—New York Islanders	NHL	52	8	30	38	38	12	0	2	2	6
—Capital District	AHL	7	3	4	7	8	—	—	—	—	—
93-94—New York Islanders	NHL	66	9	31	40	47	3	0	0	0	2
94-95—Anaheim	NHL	22	4	3	7	6	—	—	—	—	—
NHL totals.................		**659**	**93**	**328**	**421**	**352**	**57**	**8**	**22**	**30**	**68**

KUZNETSOV, MAXIM
D, RED WINGS

PERSONAL: Born March 24, 1977, in Pavlodar, U.S.S.R. .... 6-5/198. .... Shoots left.
TRANSACTIONS/CAREER NOTES: Selected by Detroit Red Wings in first round (first Red Wings pick, 26th overall) of NHL entry draft (July 8, 1995).

			REGULAR SEASON					PLAYOFFS			
Season Team	League	Gms.	G	A	Pts.	PIM	Gms.	G	A	Pts.	PIM
94-95—Dynamo Moscow	CIS	11	0	0	0	8	—	—	—	—	—

KYPREOS, NICK
LW, RANGERS

PERSONAL: Born June 4, 1966, in Toronto. .... 6-0/195. .... Shoots left. .... Full name: Nicholas George Kypreos. .... Name pronounced KIHP-ree-ohz.
TRANSACTIONS/CAREER NOTES: Signed as free agent by Philadelphia Flyers (September 30, 1984).... Underwent surgery to right knee (summer 1988); missed first 52 games of 1988-89 season.... Selected by Washington Capitals in NHL waiver draft for $20,000 (October 2, 1989).... Underwent surgery to right knee (February 8, 1990).... Traded by Capitals to Hartford Whalers for RW Mark Hunter and future considerations (June 15, 1992); Whalers sent LW Yvon Corriveau to Capitals to complete deal (August 20, 1992).... Suspended two games by NHL for game misconduct penalties (February 3, 1993).... Injured abdominal muscle (April 3, 1993); missed remainder of season.... Traded by Whalers with RW Steve Larmer, D Barry Richter and sixth-round pick in 1994 draft (C Yuri Litvinov) to New York Rangers for D James Patrick and C Darren Turcotte (November 2, 1993).... Suspended five games and fined $500 by NHL for deliberately injuring player with late hit (November 2, 1993).... Underwent root canal surgery (April 1, 1994); missed one game.
HONORS: Named to OHL All-Star first team (1985-86).... Named to OHL All-Star second team (1986-87).
MISCELLANEOUS: Member of Stanley Cup championship team (1994).

			REGULAR SEASON					PLAYOFFS			
Season Team	League	Gms.	G	A	Pts.	PIM	Gms.	G	A	Pts.	PIM
83-84—North Bay	OHL	51	12	11	23	36	4	3	2	5	9
84-85—North Bay	OHL	64	41	36	77	71	8	2	2	4	15
85-86—North Bay	OHL	64	62	35	97	112	—	—	—	—	—
86-87—North Bay	OHL	46	49	41	90	54	24	11	5	16	78
—Hershey	AHL	10	0	1	1	4	—	—	—	—	—
87-88—Hershey	AHL	71	24	20	44	101	12	0	2	2	17
88-89—Hershey	AHL	28	12	15	27	19	12	4	5	9	11
89-90—Washington	NHL	31	5	4	9	82	7	1	0	1	15
—Baltimore	AHL	14	6	5	11	6	7	4	1	5	17
90-91—Washington	NHL	79	9	9	18	196	9	0	1	1	38
91-92—Washington	NHL	65	4	6	10	206	—	—	—	—	—
92-93—Hartford	NHL	75	17	10	27	325	—	—	—	—	—
93-94—Hartford	NHL	10	0	0	0	37	—	—	—	—	—
—New York Rangers	NHL	46	3	5	8	102	3	0	0	0	2
94-95—New York Rangers	NHL	40	1	3	4	93	10	0	2	2	6
NHL totals.................		**346**	**39**	**37**	**76**	**1041**	**29**	**1**	**3**	**4**	**61**

KYTE, JIM
D, SHARKS

PERSONAL: Born March 21, 1964, in Ottawa. .... 6-5/220. .... Shoots left.
TRANSACTIONS/CAREER NOTES: Broke left wrist (March 1980).... Selected by Winnipeg Jets as underage junior in first round (first Jets pick, 12th overall) of NHL entry draft (June 9, 1982).... Suffered stress fracture in lower back (February 1988).... Sprained shoulder (March 1989).... Traded by Jets with RW Andrew McBain and RW Randy Gilhen to Pittsburgh Penguins for C/LW Randy Cunneyworth, G Richard Tabaracci and RW Dave McIlwain (June 17, 1989).... Traded by Penguins to Calgary Flames for C Jiri Hrdina (December 13, 1990).... Fractured bone in left hand during preseason (September 1991).... Fractured right ankle (January 27, 1991); missed remain-

der of season.... Signed as free agent by Ottawa Senators (September 10, 1992).... Signed as free agent by San Jose Sharks (March 30, 1995).

			REGULAR SEASON					PLAYOFFS				
Season Team	League	Gms.	G	A	Pts.	PIM	Gms.	G	A	Pts.	PIM
80-81—Hawkesbury	COJHL	42	2	24	26	133	—	—	—	—	—
81-82—Cornwall	OHL	52	4	13	17	148	5	0	0	0	10
82-83—Cornwall	OHL	65	6	30	36	195	8	0	2	2	24
—Winnipeg	NHL	2	0	0	0	0	—	—	—	—	—
83-84—Winnipeg	NHL	58	1	2	3	55	3	0	0	0	11
84-85—Winnipeg	NHL	71	0	3	3	111	8	0	0	0	14
85-86—Winnipeg	NHL	71	1	3	4	126	3	0	0	0	12
86-87—Winnipeg	NHL	72	5	5	10	162	10	0	4	4	36
87-88—Winnipeg	NHL	51	1	3	4	128	—	—	—	—	—
88-89—Winnipeg	NHL	74	3	9	12	190	—	—	—	—	—
89-90—Pittsburgh	NHL	56	3	1	4	125	—	—	—	—	—
90-91—Muskegon	IHL	25	2	5	7	157	—	—	—	—	—
—Pittsburgh	NHL	1	0	0	0	2	—	—	—	—	—
—Calgary	NHL	42	0	9	9	153	7	0	0	0	7
91-92—Calgary	NHL	21	0	1	1	107	—	—	—	—	—
—Salt Lake City	IHL	6	0	1	1	9	—	—	—	—	—
92-93—New Haven	AHL	63	6	18	24	163	—	—	—	—	—
—Ottawa	NHL	4	0	1	1	4	—	—	—	—	—
93-94—Las Vegas	IHL	75	2	16	18	246	4	0	1	1	51
94-95—Las Vegas	IHL	76	3	17	20	195	—	—	—	—	—
—San Jose	NHL	18	2	5	7	33	11	0	2	2	14
NHL totals		541	16	42	58	1196	42	0	6	6	94

LABBE, JEAN-FRANCOIS
G, SENATORS

PERSONAL: Born June 15, 1972, in Sherbrooke, Quebec.... 5-9/170.... Catches left.... Name pronounced luh-BAY.
TRANSACTIONS/CAREER NOTES: Signed as free agent by Ottawa Senators (1993).
HONORS: Won Jacques Plante Trophy (1991-92).... Named to QMJHL All-Star first team (1991-92).... Named Col.HL Rookie of the Year (1993-94).... Named Col.HL Playoff Most Valuable Player (1993-94).... Named to Col.HL All-Star first team (1993-94).

				REGULAR SEASON								PLAYOFFS				
Season Team	League	Gms.	Min.	W	L	T	GA	SO	Avg.	Gms.	Min.	W	L	GA	SO	Avg.
89-90—Trois-Rivieres	QMJHL	28	1499	13	10	0	106	1	4.24	3	132	1	1	8	0	3.64
90-91—Trois-Rivieres	QMJHL	54	2870	35	14	0	158	5	3.30	5	230	1	4	19	0	4.96
91-92—Trois-Rivieres	QMJHL	48	2749	31	13	3	142	3	*3.10	15	791	10	3	33	†1	*2.50
92-93—Hull	QMJHL	46	2701	25	16	2	155	2	3.44	10	518	6	3	24	†1	*2.78
93-94—Prince Edward Island	AHL	7	390	4	3	0	22	0	3.38	—	—	—	—	—	—	—
—Thunder Bay	Col.HL	52	*2900	*35	11	4	150	*2	*3.10	8	493	7	1	18	*2	*2.19
94-95—Prince Edward Island	AHL	32	1817	13	14	3	94	2	3.10	—	—	—	—	—	—	—

LABRAATEN, JAN
LW, FLAMES

PERSONAL: Born February 17, 1977, in Karlstad, Sweden.... 6-2/198.... Shoots right. ... Cousin of Dan Labraaten, left winger, Detroit Red Wings and Calgary Flames (1978-79 through 1981-82) and Winnipeg Jets of WHA (1976-77 and 1977-78).
TRANSACTIONS/CAREER NOTES: Selected by Calgary Flames in fourth round (fourth Flames pick, 98th overall) of NHL entry draft (July 8, 1995).

			REGULAR SEASON					PLAYOFFS				
Season Team	League	Gms.	G	A	Pts.	PIM	Gms.	G	A	Pts.	PIM
94-95—Farjestad Jrs.	Sweden	25	10	6	16	20	—	—	—	—	—
—Farjestad Karlstad	Sweden	2	0	1	1	2	1	0	0	0	0

LABRECQUE, PATRICK
G, CANADIENS

PERSONAL: Born March 6, 1971, in Laval, Que.... 6-0/187.... Catches left. ... Name pronounced luh-BREHK.
TRANSACTIONS/CAREER NOTES: Selected by Quebec Nordiques in fifth round (fifth Nordiques pick, 90th overall) of NHL entry draft (June 22, 1991).... Signed as free agent by Montreal Canadiens (June 21, 1994).

				REGULAR SEASON								PLAYOFFS				
Season Team	League	Gms.	Min.	W	L	T	GA	SO	Avg.	Gms.	Min.	W	L	GA	SO	Avg.
89-90—St. Jean	QMJHL	48	2630	...	...	...	196	0	4.47	—	—	—	—	—	—	—
90-91—St. Jean	QMJHL	59	3375	17	34	6	216	1	3.84	—	—	—	—	—	—	—
91-92—Halifax	AHL	29	1570	5	12	8	114	0	4.36	—	—	—	—	—	—	—
92-93—Halifax	AHL	20	914	3	12	2	76	0	4.99	—	—	—	—	—	—	—
—Greensboro	ECHL	11	650	6	3	†2	31	0	2.86	1	59	0	1	5	0	5.08
93-94—Cornwall	AHL	4	198	1	2	0	8	1	2.42	—	—	—	—	—	—	—
—Greensboro	ECHL	29	1609	17	8	2	89	0	3.32	1	22	0	0	4	0	10.91
94-95—Wheeling	ECHL	5	281	2	3	†0	22	0	4.70	—	—	—	—	—	—	—
—Fredericton	AHL	35	1913	15	17	1	104	1	3.26	16	*968	*10	*6	40	1	2.48

LACHANCE, BOB
RW, BLUES

PERSONAL: Born February 1, 1974, in North Hampton, Mass. ... 5-11/175.... Shoots right.... Brother of Scott Lachance, defenseman, New York Islanders.
COLLEGE: Boston University.
TRANSACTIONS/CAREER NOTES: Selected by St. Louis Blues in sixth round (fifth Blues pick,

KL

134th overall) of NHL entry draft (June 20, 1992).

			REGULAR SEASON					PLAYOFFS				
Season Team	League	Gms.	G	A	Pts.	PIM	Gms.	G	A	Pts.	PIM
91-92—Springfield Jr. B	NEJHL	46	40	98	138	87	—	—	—	—	—
92-93—Boston University	Hockey East	33	4	10	14	24	—	—	—	—	—
93-94—Boston University	Hockey East	32	13	19	32	42	—	—	—	—	—
94-95—Boston University	Hockey East	37	12	29	41	51	—	—	—	—	—

LACHANCE, SCOTT
D, ISLANDERS

PERSONAL: Born October 22, 1972, in Charlottesville, Va. . . . 6-2/ 198. . . . Shoots left. . . . Full name: Scott Joseph Lachance. . . . Brother of Bob Lachance, right winger in St. Louis Blues system.
COLLEGE: Boston University.
TRANSACTIONS/CAREER NOTES: Selected by New York Islanders in first round (first Islanders pick, fourth overall) of NHL entry draft (June 22, 1991). . . . Sprained wrist (April 13, 1993); missed remainder of season. . . . Underwent wrist surgery (April 30, 1993). . . . Suffered mild separation of right shoulder (October 8, 1993); missed four games. . . . Broke ankle (February 25, 1995); missed 22 games.
HONORS: Named to Hockey East All-Rookie team (1990-91).

			REGULAR SEASON					PLAYOFFS				
Season Team	League	Gms.	G	A	Pts.	PIM	Gms.	G	A	Pts.	PIM
88-89—Springfield Jr. B	NEJHL	36	8	28	36	20	—	—	—	—	—
89-90—Springfield Jr. B	NEJHL	34	25	41	66	62	—	—	—	—	—
90-91—Boston University	Hockey East	31	5	19	24	48	—	—	—	—	—
91-92—U.S. national team	Int'l	36	1	10	11	34	—	—	—	—	—
—U.S. Olympic Team	Int'l	8	0	1	1	6	—	—	—	—	—
—New York Islanders.........	NHL	17	1	4	5	9	—	—	—	—	—
92-93—New York Islanders.........	NHL	75	7	17	24	67	—	—	—	—	—
93-94—New York Islanders.........	NHL	74	3	11	14	70	3	0	0	0	0
94-95—New York Islanders.........	NHL	26	6	7	13	26	—	—	—	—	—
NHL totals...........................		192	17	39	56	172	3	0	0	0	0

LACHER, BLAINE
G, BRUINS

PERSONAL: Born September 5, 1970, in Medicine Hat, Alta. . . . 6-1/205. . . . Catches left. . . . Name pronounced LAH-kuhr.
COLLEGE: Lake Superior State.
TRANSACTIONS/CAREER NOTES: Signed as free agent by Boston Bruins (May 19, 1994). . . . Injured hamstring (February 10, 1995); missed four games.

			REGULAR SEASON							PLAYOFFS						
Season Team	League	Gms.	Min.	W	L	T	GA	SO	Avg.	Gms.	Min.	W	L	GA	SO	Avg.
91-92—Lake Superior State	CCHA	10	413	5	3	0	23	0	3.34	—	—	—	—	—	—	—
92-93—Lake Superior State	CCHA	34	1915	24	5	3	86	...	2.69	—	—	—	—	—	—	—
93-94—Lake Superior State	CCHA	30	1785	20	5	4	59	6	1.98	—	—	—	—	—	—	—
94-95—Boston	NHL	35	1965	19	11	2	79	4	2.41	5	283	1	4	12	0	2.54
—Providence	AHL	1	59	0	1	0	3	0	3.05	—	—	—	—	—	—	—
NHL totals............................		35	1965	19	11	2	79	4	2.41	5	283	1	4	12	0	2.54

LACROIX, DANIEL
C, RANGERS

PERSONAL: Born March 11, 1969, in Montreal. . . . 6-3/205. . . . Shoots left. . . . Name pronounced luh-KWAH.
TRANSACTIONS/CAREER NOTES: Selected as underage junior by New York Rangers in second round (second Rangers pick, 31st overall) of NHL entry draft (June 13, 1987). . . . Traded by Rangers to Boston Bruins for D Glen Featherstone (August 19, 1994). . . . Claimed on waivers by Rangers (March 23, 1995).
HONORS: Won Marcel Robert Trophy (1988-89).

			REGULAR SEASON					PLAYOFFS				
Season Team	League	Gms.	G	A	Pts.	PIM	Gms.	G	A	Pts.	PIM
86-87—Granby............................	QMJHL	54	9	16	25	311	8	1	2	3	22
87-88—Granby............................	QMJHL	58	24	50	74	468	5	0	4	4	12
88-89—Granby............................	QMJHL	70	45	49	94	320	4	1	1	2	57
—Denver	IHL	2	0	1	1	0	2	0	1	1	0
89-90—Flint	IHL	61	12	16	28	128	4	2	0	2	24
90-91—Binghamton	AHL	54	7	12	19	237	5	1	0	1	24
91-92—Binghamton	AHL	52	12	20	32	149	11	2	4	6	28
92-93—Binghamton	AHL	73	21	22	43	255	—	—	—	—	—
93-94—New York Rangers	NHL	4	0	0	0	0	—	—	—	—	—
—Binghamton	AHL	59	20	23	43	278	—	—	—	—	—
94-95—Providence	AHL	40	15	11	26	266	—	—	—	—	—
—Boston	NHL	23	1	0	1	38	—	—	—	—	—
—New York Rangers	NHL	1	0	0	0	0	—	—	—	—	—
NHL totals............................		28	1	0	1	38					

LACROIX, ERIC
LW, KINGS

PERSONAL: Born July 15, 1971, in Montreal. . . . 6-1/200. . . . Shoots left. . . . Name pronounced luh-KWAH.
HIGH SCHOOL: Governor Dummer (Byfield, Mass.).
COLLEGE: St. Lawrence (N.Y.).

TRANSACTIONS/CAREER NOTES: Selected by Toronto Maple Leafs in seventh round (sixth Maple Leafs pick, 136th overall) of NHL entry draft (June 16, 1990).... Separated shoulder (November 27, 1993); missed eight games.... Traded by Maple Leafs with D Chris Snell and fourth-round pick in 1996 draft to Los Angeles Kings for RW Dixon Ward, C Guy Leveque, RW Shayne Toporowski and C Kelly Fairchild (October 3, 1994).... Sprained knee (February 4, 1995); missed one game.... Sprained knee (February 23, 1995); missed two games.

Season	Team	League	REGULAR SEASON					PLAYOFFS				
			Gms.	G	A	Pts.	PIM	Gms.	G	A	Pts.	PIM
89-90—	Governor Dummer...........	Mass. H.S.	...	23	18	41	...	—	—	—	—	—
90-91—	St. Lawrence University...	ECAC	35	13	11	24	35	—	—	—	—	—
91-92—	St. Lawrence University...	ECAC	34	11	20	31	40	—	—	—	—	—
92-93—	St. John's	AHL	76	15	19	34	59	9	5	3	8	4
93-94—	St. John's	AHL	59	17	22	39	69	11	5	3	8	6
	—Toronto...........................	NHL	3	0	0	0	2	2	0	0	0	0
94-95—	St. John's	AHL	1	0	0	0	2	—	—	—	—	—
	—Phoenix...........................	IHL	25	7	1	8	31	—	—	—	—	—
	—Los Angeles....................	NHL	45	9	7	16	54	—	—	—	—	—
NHL totals................			48	9	7	16	56	2	0	0	0	0

LADOUCEUR, RANDY
D, MIGHTY DUCKS

PERSONAL: Born June 30, 1960, in Brockville, Ont.... 6-2/220.... Shoots left.... Name pronounced LAD-uh-SOOR.

TRANSACTIONS/CAREER NOTES: Signed as free agent by Detroit Red Wings (November 1, 1979).... Suffered back spasms (March 1986).... Traded by Red Wings to Hartford Whalers for C Dave Barr (January 12, 1987).... Sprained right knee (March 1990).... Sprained knee (January 10, 1991); missed 10 games.... Bruised knee (October 28, 1992); missed one game.... Suffered right elbow infection (December 8, 1992); missed three games.... Suffered right foot contusion (March 3, 1993); missed two games.... Selected by Mighty Ducks of Anaheim in NHL expansion draft (June 24, 1993).... Bruised right thigh (January 10, 1994); missed three games.... Suffered from sore ankle (March 9, 1995); missed four games.

MISCELLANEOUS: Captain of Hartford Whalers (1991-92).... Captain of Mighty Ducks of Anaheim (1994-95).

Season	Team	League	REGULAR SEASON					PLAYOFFS				
			Gms.	G	A	Pts.	PIM	Gms.	G	A	Pts.	PIM
78-79—	Brantford..........................	OMJHL	64	3	17	20	141	—	—	—	—	—
79-80—	Brantford..........................	OMJHL	37	6	15	21	125	8	0	5	5	18
80-81—	Kalamazoo........................	IHL	80	7	30	37	52	8	1	3	4	10
81-82—	Adirondack	AHL	78	4	28	32	78	5	1	1	2	6
82-83—	Adirondack	AHL	48	11	21	32	54	—	—	—	—	—
	—Detroit............................	NHL	27	0	4	4	16	—	—	—	—	—
83-84—	Adirondack	AHL	11	3	5	8	12	—	—	—	—	—
	—Detroit............................	NHL	71	3	17	20	58	4	1	0	1	6
84-85—	Detroit..............................	NHL	80	3	27	30	108	3	1	0	1	0
85-86—	Detroit..............................	NHL	78	5	13	18	196	—	—	—	—	—
86-87—	Detroit..............................	NHL	34	3	6	9	70	—	—	—	—	—
	—Hartford..........................	NHL	36	2	3	5	51	6	0	2	2	12
87-88—	Hartford............................	NHL	67	1	7	8	91	6	1	1	2	4
88-89—	Hartford............................	NHL	75	2	5	7	95	1	0	0	0	10
89-90—	Hartford............................	NHL	71	3	12	15	126	7	1	0	1	10
90-91—	Hartford............................	NHL	67	1	3	4	118	6	1	4	5	6
91-92—	Hartford............................	NHL	74	1	9	10	127	7	0	1	1	11
92-93—	Hartford............................	NHL	62	2	4	6	109	—	—	—	—	—
93-94—	Anaheim...........................	NHL	81	1	9	10	74	—	—	—	—	—
94-95—	Anaheim...........................	NHL	44	2	4	6	36	—	—	—	—	—
NHL totals................			867	29	123	152	1275	40	5	8	13	59

LaFAYETTE, NATHAN
C, RANGERS

PERSONAL: Born February 17, 1973, in New Westminster, B.C.... 6-1/195.... Shoots right.... Name pronounced LAH-fay-eht.

TRANSACTIONS/CAREER NOTES: Traded by Kingston Frontenacs with Joel Sandie to Cornwall Royals for D Rod Pasma and Shawn Caplice (January 6, 1991).... Selected by St. Louis Blues in third round (third Blues pick, 65th overall) of NHL entry draft (June 22, 1991).... Traded by Blues with D Jeff Brown and D Bret Hedican to Vancouver Canucks for C Craig Janney (March 21, 1994).... Traded by Canucks to New York Rangers for G Corey Hirsch (April 7, 1995).

HONORS: Won Bobby Smith Trophy (1990-91 and 1991-92).... Won Can.HL Scholastic Player of the Year Award (1991-92).

Season	Team	League	REGULAR SEASON					PLAYOFFS				
			Gms.	G	A	Pts.	PIM	Gms.	G	A	Pts.	PIM
89-90—	Kingston...........................	OHL	53	6	8	14	14	7	0	1	1	0
90-91—	Kingston...........................	OHL	35	13	13	26	10	—	—	—	—	—
	—Cornwall........................	OHL	28	16	22	38	25	—	—	—	—	—
91-92—	Cornwall...........................	OHL	66	28	45	73	26	6	2	5	7	16
92-93—	Newmarket........................	OHL	58	49	38	87	26	7	4	6	10	19
93-94—	Peoria...............................	IHL	27	13	11	24	20	—	—	—	—	—
	—St. Louis.........................	NHL	38	2	3	5	14	—	—	—	—	—
	—Vancouver......................	NHL	11	1	1	2	4	20	2	7	9	4
94-95—	Syracuse	AHL	27	9	9	18	10	—	—	—	—	—
	—Vancouver......................	NHL	27	4	4	8	2	—	—	—	—	—
	—New York Rangers	NHL	12	0	0	0	0	—	—	—	—	—
NHL totals................			88	7	8	15	20	20	2	7	9	4

LAFLAMME, CHRISTIAN
D, BLACKHAWKS

PERSONAL: Born November 24, 1976, in St. Charles, Que.... 6-1/195.... Shoots right.
TRANSACTIONS/CAREER NOTES: Selected by Chicago Blackhawks in second round (second Blackhawks pick, 45th overall) of NHL entry draft (July 8, 1995).
HONORS: Named to QMJHL All-Rookie team (1992-93).... Named to QMJHL All-Star second team (1994-95).

			REGULAR SEASON					PLAYOFFS			
Season Team	League	Gms.	G	A	Pts.	PIM	Gms.	G	A	Pts.	PIM
92-93—Verdun	QMJHL	69	2	17	19	70	3	0	2	2	6
93-94—Verdun	QMJHL	72	4	34	38	85	4	0	3	3	4
94-95—Beauport	QMJHL	67	6	41	47	82	8	1	4	5	6

LaFONTAINE, PAT
C, SABRES

PERSONAL: Born February 22, 1965, in St. Louis.... 5-10/180.... Shoots right.... Name pronounced luh-FAHN-tayn.
TRANSACTIONS/CAREER NOTES: Selected by New York Islanders as underage junior in first round (first Islanders pick, third overall) of NHL entry draft (June 8, 1983).... Damaged ligaments in left knee (August 16, 1984).... Suffered from mononucleosis (January 1985).... Separated right shoulder (January 25, 1986).... Bruised knee (March 1988).... Broke nose (October 7, 1988); played entire season with injury.... Sprained ligaments in right wrist (November 5, 1988).... Strained left hamstring (October 13, 1990); missed three games.... Traded by Islanders with LW Randy Wood, D Randy Hillier and future considerations to Buffalo Sabres for C Pierre Turgeon, RW Benoit Hogue, D Uwe Krupp and C Dave McIlwain; Sabres later received fourth-round pick (D Dean Melanson) in 1992 draft (October 25, 1991).... Fractured jaw (November 16, 1991); missed 13 games.... Injured knee (November 13, 1993); missed remainder of season and first 24 games of 1994-95 season.
HONORS: Won Can.HL Player of the Year Award (1982-83).... Won Michel Briere Trophy (1982-83).... Won Jean Beliveau Trophy (1982-83).... Won Frank J. Selke Trophy (1982-83).... Won Des Instructeurs Trophy (1982-83).... Won Guy Lafleur Trophy (1982-83).... Named to QMJHL All-Star first team (1982-83).... Played in NHL All-Star Game (1988-1991 and 1993).... Won Dodge Performer of the Year Award (1989-90).... Named to THE SPORTING NEWS All-Star second team (1989-90).... Named to NHL All-Star second team (1992-93).... Won Bill Masterton Memorial Trophy (1994-95).
RECORDS: Holds NHL playoff record for fastest two goals from the start of a period—35 seconds (May 19, 1984).
STATISTICAL PLATEAUS: Three-goal games: 1983-84 (1), 1987-88 (1), 1988-89 (2), 1989-90 (2), 1990-91 (1), 1991-92 (4), 1992-93 (1). Total: 12.
MISCELLANEOUS: Captain of Buffalo Sabres (1992-93 through 1994-95).

			REGULAR SEASON					PLAYOFFS			
Season Team	League	Gms.	G	A	Pts.	PIM	Gms.	G	A	Pts.	PIM
82-83—Verdun	QMJHL	70	*104	*130	*234	10	15	11	*24	*35	4
83-84—U.S. national team	Int'l	58	56	55	111	22	—	—	—	—	—
—U.S. Olympic Team	Int'l	6	5	3	8	0	—	—	—	—	—
—New York Islanders	NHL	15	13	6	19	6	16	3	6	9	8
84-85—New York Islanders	NHL	67	19	35	54	32	9	1	2	3	4
85-86—New York Islanders	NHL	65	30	23	53	43	3	1	0	1	0
86-87—New York Islanders	NHL	80	38	32	70	70	14	5	7	12	10
87-88—New York Islanders	NHL	75	47	45	92	52	6	4	5	9	8
88-89—New York Islanders	NHL	79	45	43	88	26	—	—	—	—	—
89-90—New York Islanders	NHL	74	54	51	105	38	2	0	1	1	0
90-91—New York Islanders	NHL	75	41	44	85	42	—	—	—	—	—
91-92—Buffalo	NHL	57	46	47	93	98	7	8	3	11	4
92-93—Buffalo	NHL	84	53	95	148	63	7	2	10	12	0
93-94—Buffalo	NHL	16	5	13	18	2	—	—	—	—	—
94-95—Buffalo	NHL	22	12	15	27	4	5	2	2	4	2
NHL totals		709	403	449	852	476	69	26	36	62	36

LAFOREST, MARK
G

PERSONAL: Born July 10, 1962, in Welland, Ont.... 5-11/190.... Catches left.... Full name: Mark Andrew Laforest.
TRANSACTIONS/CAREER NOTES: Signed as free agent by Detroit Red Wings (September 1983).... Traded by Red Wings to Philadelphia Flyers for second-round pick (D Bob Wilkie) in 1987 draft (June 1987).... Sprained knee (March 16, 1989).... Traded by Flyers to Toronto Maple Leafs for sixth- and seventh-round picks in 1991 draft (September 8, 1989).... Twisted left ankle (January 11, 1990); missed five weeks.... Traded by Maple Leafs with RW Tie Domi to New York Rangers for RW Greg Johnston (June 18, 1990).... Selected by Ottawa Senators in NHL expansion draft (June 18, 1992).
HONORS: Won Aldege (Baz) Bastien Trophy (1986-87 and 1990-91).... Named to AHL All-Star second team (1990-91).

			REGULAR SEASON						PLAYOFFS					
Season Team	League	Gms.	Min.	W	L	T	GA	SO	Avg.	Gms.	Min.	W	L	GA SO	Avg.
81-82—Niagara Falls	OHL	24	1365	10	13	1	105	1	4.62	5	300	1	2	19 0	3.80
82-83—North Bay	OHL	54	3140	34	17	1	195	0	3.73	8	474	4	4	31 0	3.92
83-84—Adirondack	AHL	7	351	3	3	1	29	0	4.96	—	—	—	—	— —	—
—Kalamazoo	IHL	13	718	4	5	‡2	48	1	4.01	—	—	—	—	— —	—
84-85—Mohawk Valley Stars	ACHL	8	420	...	...	...	60	0	8.57	—	—	—	—	— —	—
—Adirondack	AHL	11	430	2	3	1	35	0	4.88	—	—	—	—	— —	—
85-86—Adirondack	AHL	19	1142	13	5	1	57	0	2.99	*17	*1075	12	5	*58 0	3.24
—Detroit	NHL	28	1383	4	21	0	114	1	4.95	—	—	—	—	— —	—
86-87—Adirondack	AHL	37	2229	23	8	0	105	3	2.83	—	—	—	—	— —	—
—Detroit	NHL	5	219	2	1	0	12	0	3.29	—	—	—	—	— —	—
87-88—Hershey	AHL	5	309	2	1	2	13	0	2.52	—	—	—	—	— —	—
—Philadelphia	NHL	21	972	5	9	2	60	1	3.70	2	48	1	0	1 0	1.25

Season	Team	League	Gms.	Min.	W	L	T	GA	SO	Avg.	Gms.	Min.	W	L	GA	SO	Avg.
88-89—Philadelphia	NHL	17	933	5	7	2	64	0	4.12	—	—	—	—	—	—	—
—Hershey	AHL	3	185	2	0	0	9	0	2.92	12	744	7	5	27	1	*2.18
89-90—Toronto	NHL	27	1343	9	14	0	87	0	3.89	—	—	—	—	—	—	—
—Newmarket	AHL	10	604	6	4	0	33	1	3.28	—	—	—	—	—	—	—
90-91—Binghamton	AHL	45	2452	25	14	2	129	0	3.16	9	442	3	4	28	*1	3.80
91-92—Binghamton	AHL	43	2559	25	15	3	146	1	3.42	11	662	7	4	34	0	3.08
92-93—New Haven	AHL	30	1688	10	18	1	121	1	4.30	—	—	—	—	—	—	—
—Brantford	Col.HL	10	565	5	3	‡1	35	†1	3.72	—	—	—	—	—	—	—
93-94—Prince Edward Island	AHL	43	2359	9	25	5	161	0	4.09	—	—	—	—	—	—	—
—Ottawa	NHL	5	182	0	2	0	17	0	5.60	—	—	—	—	—	—	—
94-95—Milwaukee	IHL	42	2326	19	13	‡7	123	2	3.17	15	938	8	7	40	*2	2.56
NHL totals		103	5032	25	54	4	354	2	4.22	2	48	1	0	1	0	1.25

LAFORGE, MARC

RW/D, OILERS

PERSONAL: Born January 3, 1968, in Sudbury, Ont. . . . 6-2/210. . . . Shoots left.
TRANSACTIONS/CAREER NOTES: Selected by Hartford Whalers as underage junior in second round (second Whalers pick, 32nd overall) of NHL entry draft (June 21, 1986). . . . Suspended nine games by OHL (October 1986). . . . Suspended two years by OHL for attacking several members of opposing team in game-ending fight (November 6, 1987). . . . Suspended three games by AHL for head-butting (November 26, 1988). . . . Suspended six games for leaving bench to start fight (December 8, 1988). . . . Suspended by Whalers for refusing to report to Indianapolis (December 28, 1988). . . . Whalers lifted suspension when he reported to Indianapolis (January 19, 1989). . . . Suffered sore back (November 1989). . . . Suspended five games by AHL for head-butting (February 5, 1990). . . . Traded by Whalers to Edmonton Oilers for rights to D Cam Brauer (March 6, 1990). . . . Suspended 10 games by AHL for cross-checking and kneeing (December 3, 1990). . . . Suspended 10 games by AHL for cross-checking (January 13, 1991). . . . Suspended six games by AHL for leaving the bench to start fight (February 1991). . . . Suspended 10 games by NHL (September 26, 1991). . . . Suffered groin strain (October 29, 1993); missed three games. . . . Traded by Oilers to New York Islanders for LW Brent Grieve (December 15, 1993). . . . Suspended six games by AHL for fighting (October 11, 1994). . . . Signed as free agent by Oilers (August 26, 1994). . . . Loaned by Cape Breton Oilers to Syracuse Crunch (January 3, 1995).

Season	Team	League	Gms.	G	A	Pts.	PIM	Gms.	G	A	Pts.	PIM
84-85—Kingston	OHL	57	1	5	6	214	—	—	—	—	—
85-86—Kingston	OHL	60	1	13	14	248	10	0	1	1	30
86-87—Kingston	OHL	53	2	10	12	224	12	1	0	1	79
—Binghamton	AHL	—	—	—	—	—	4	0	0	0	7
87-88—Sudbury	OHL	14	0	2	2	68	—	—	—	—	—
88-89—Indianapolis	IHL	14	0	2	2	138	—	—	—	—	—
—Binghamton	AHL	38	2	2	4	179	—	—	—	—	—
89-90—Hartford	NHL	9	0	0	0	43	—	—	—	—	—
—Binghamton	AHL	25	2	6	8	111	—	—	—	—	—
—Cape Breton	AHL	3	0	1	1	24	3	0	0	0	27
90-91—Cape Breton	AHL	49	1	7	8	217	—	—	—	—	—
91-92—Cape Breton	AHL	59	0	14	14	341	4	0	0	0	24
92-93—Cape Breton	AHL	77	1	12	13	208	15	1	2	3	*78
93-94—Cape Breton	AHL	14	0	0	0	91	—	—	—	—	—
—Salt Lake City	IHL	43	0	2	2	242	—	—	—	—	—
—Edmonton	NHL	5	0	0	0	21	—	—	—	—	—
94-95—Cape Breton	AHL	18	0	1	1	80	—	—	—	—	—
—Syracuse	AHL	39	1	5	6	202	—	—	—	—	—
NHL totals		14	0	0	0	64					

LaFRANCE, DARRYL

C, FLAMES

PERSONAL: Born March 20, 1974, in Sudbury, Ont. . . . 5-11/175. . . . Shoots right.
HIGH SCHOOL: Henry Street (Whitby, Ont.).
TRANSACTIONS/CAREER NOTES: Selected by Calgary Flames in fifth round (sixth Flames pick, 121st overall) of NHL entry draft (June 26, 1993).

Season	Team	League	Gms.	G	A	Pts.	PIM	Gms.	G	A	Pts.	PIM
91-92—Oshawa	OHL	48	12	20	32	24	7	0	1	1	2
92-93—Oshawa	OHL	66	35	51	86	24	13	8	8	16	0
93-94—Oshawa	OHL	61	45	61	106	17	5	1	9	10	0
94-95—Oshawa	OHL	57	55	67	122	10	7	6	7	13	2

LaGRAND, SCOTT

G, LIGHTNING

PERSONAL: Born February 11, 1970, in Potsdam, N.Y. . . . 6-0/170. . . . Catches left.
HIGH SCHOOL: Hotchkiss School (Lakeville, Conn.).
COLLEGE: Boston College.
TRANSACTIONS/CAREER NOTES: Selected by Philadelphia Flyers in fourth round (fifth Flyers pick, 77th overall) of NHL entry draft (June 11, 1988). . . . Traded by Flyers to Tampa Bay Lightning for G Mike Greenlay (February 2, 1995).
HONORS: Named Hockey East Tournament Most Valuable Player (1989-90). . . . Named to Hockey East All-Star first team (1990-91). . . . Named to NCAA All-America East second team (1991-92).

Season	Team	League	Gms.	Min.	W	L	T	GA	SO	Avg.	Gms.	Min.	W	L	GA	SO	Avg.
86-87—Hotchkiss	Conn. HS	17	1020	...	...	...	36	0	2.12	—	—	—	—	—	—	—	
87-88—Hotchkiss	Conn. HS									Statistics unavailable.							
88-89—Hotchkiss	Conn. HS									Statistics unavailable.							
89-90—Boston College	Hoc. East	24	1268	17	4	0	57	0	2.70	—	—	—	—	—	—	—
90-91—Boston College	Hoc. East	23	1153	12	8	0	63	2	3.28	—	—	—	—	—	—	—
91-92—Boston College	Hoc. East	30	1750	11	16	2	108	1	3.70	—	—	—	—	—	—	—
92-93—Hershey	AHL	32	1854	8	17	4	145	0	4.69	—	—	—	—	—	—	—
93-94—Hershey	AHL	40	2032	16	13	3	117	2	3.45	—	—	—	—	—	—	—
94-95—Hershey	AHL	21	1104	7	9	3	71	1	3.86	—	—	—	—	—	—	—
—Atlanta	IHL	21	994	7	7	‡3	67	0	4.04	3	102	0	2	10	0	5.88

LALIME, PATRICK
G, PENGUINS

PERSONAL: Born July 7, 1974, in St. Bonaventure, Que.... 6-2/170.... Catches left.... Name pronounced luh-LEEM.

TRANSACTIONS/CAREER NOTES: Selected by Pittsburgh Penguins in sixth round (sixth Penguins pick, 156th overall) of NHL entry draft (June 26, 1993).

Season	Team	League	Gms.	Min.	W	L	T	GA	SO	Avg.	Gms.	Min.	W	L	GA	SO	Avg.
92-93—Shawinigan	QMJHL	44	2467	10	24	4	192	0	4.67	—	—	—	—	—	—	—
93-94—Shawinigan	QMJHL	48	2733	22	20	2	192	1	4.22	5	223	1	3	25	0	6.73
94-95—Hampton Roads	ECHL	26	1471	15	7	3	82	2	3.34	—	—	—	—	—	—	—
—Cleveland	IHL	23	1230	7	10	‡4	91	0	4.44	—	—	—	—	—	—	—

LALOR, MIKE
D, STARS

PERSONAL: Born March 8, 1963, in Fort Erie, Ont.... 6-0/200.... Shoots left.... Full name: John Michael Lalor.... Name pronounced LAH-luhr.

TRANSACTIONS/CAREER NOTES: Signed as free agent by Montreal Canadiens (September 1983). ... Suffered from bursitis in right ankle (September 1987).... Suffered stress fracture of left ankle (November 1, 1988).... Traded by Canadiens to St. Louis Blues for option to flip first-round picks in 1990 draft and second- or third-round picks in 1991 draft; Canadiens exercised option (January 16, 1989).... Traded by Blues with C Peter Zezel to Washington Capitals for LW Geoff Courtnall (July 13, 1990).... Traded by Capitals to Winnipeg Jets for RW Paul MacDermid (March 2, 1992).... Broke finger (November 12, 1992); missed 13 games.... Strained neck (January 8, 1993); missed one game.... Suffered rib contusion (March 23, 1993); missed two games.... Strained knee ligaments (October 26, 1993); missed 22 games.... Traded by San Jose Sharks with D Doug Zmolek to Dallas Stars for LW Ulf Dahlen and future considerations (March 19, 1994).

MISCELLANEOUS: Member of Stanley Cup championship team (1986).

Season	Team	League	Gms.	G	A	Pts.	PIM	Gms.	G	A	Pts.	PIM
81-82—Brantford	OHL	64	3	13	16	114	11	0	6	6	11
82-83—Brantford	OHL	65	10	30	40	113	6	1	3	4	20
83-84—Nova Scotia	AHL	67	5	11	16	80	12	0	2	2	13
84-85—Sherbrooke	AHL	79	9	23	32	114	17	3	5	8	36
85-86—Montreal	NHL	62	3	5	8	56	17	1	2	3	29
86-87—Montreal	NHL	57	0	10	10	47	13	2	1	3	29
87-88—Montreal	NHL	66	1	10	11	113	11	0	0	0	11
88-89—Montreal	NHL	12	1	4	5	15	—	—	—	—	—
—St. Louis	NHL	36	1	14	15	54	10	1	1	2	14
89-90—St. Louis	NHL	78	0	16	16	81	12	0	2	2	31
90-91—Washington	NHL	68	1	5	6	61	10	1	2	3	22
91-92—Washington	NHL	64	5	7	12	64	—	—	—	—	—
—Winnipeg	NHL	15	2	3	5	14	7	0	0	0	19
92-93—Winnipeg	NHL	64	1	8	9	76	4	0	2	2	4
93-94—San Jose	NHL	23	0	2	2	8	—	—	—	—	—
—Dallas	NHL	12	0	1	1	6	5	0	0	0	6
94-95—Dallas	NHL	12	0	0	0	9	3	0	0	0	2
—Kalamazoo	IHL	5	0	1	1	11	—	—	—	—	—
NHL totals		569	15	85	100	604	92	5	10	15	167

LAMB, MARK
C, CANADIENS

PERSONAL: Born August 3, 1964, in Swift Current, Sask.... 5-9/180.... Shoots left.

HIGH SCHOOL: Swift Current (Sask.).

TRANSACTIONS/CAREER NOTES: Selected by Calgary Flames as underage junior in fourth round (fifth Flames pick, 72nd overall) of NHL entry draft (June 9, 1982).... Refused to dress for a game after Nanaimo Islanders released coach Les Calder; asked to be traded (December 1982).... Traded by Islanders to Medicine Hat Tigers for Glen Kulka and G Daryl Reaugh (December 1982).... Signed as free agent by Detroit Red Wings (July 1, 1986).... Selected by Edmonton Oilers in NHL waiver draft (October 5, 1987).... Pinched nerve in neck (October 21, 1990). ... Selected by Ottawa Senators in NHL expansion draft (June 18, 1992).... Suffered sore foot (October 24, 1992); missed two games.... Injured neck (December 17, 1992); missed 10 games.... Traded by Senators to Philadelphia Flyers for LW Claude Boivin and G Kirk Daubenspeck (March 5, 1994).... Traded by Flyers to Montreal Canadiens for cash (February 10, 1995).

HONORS: Won Frank Boucher Memorial Trophy (1983-84).... Named to WHL (East) All-Star first team (1983-84).

MISCELLANEOUS: Member of Stanley Cup championship team (1990).... Captain of Ottawa Senators (1993-94).

Season	Team	League	Gms.	G	A	Pts.	PIM	Gms.	G	A	Pts.	PIM
80-81—Billings	WHL	24	1	8	9	12	—	—	—	—	—
81-82—Billings	WHL	72	45	56	101	46	5	4	6	10	4

Season	Team	League	Gms.	G	A	Pts.	PIM	Gms.	G	A	Pts.	PIM
82-83—Nanaimo	WHL	30	14	37	51	16	—	—	—	—	—
—Medicine Hat	WHL	46	22	43	65	33	5	3	2	5	4
—Colorado	CHL	—	—	—	—	—	6	0	2	2	0
83-84—Medicine Hat	WHL	72	59	77	136	30	14	12	11	23	6
84-85—Medicine Hat	WHL	—	—	—	—	—	6	3	2	5	2
—Moncton	AHL	80	23	49	72	53	—	—	—	—	—
85-86—Calgary	NHL	1	0	0	0	0	—	—	—	—	—
—Moncton	AHL	79	26	50	76	51	10	2	6	8	17
86-87—Detroit	NHL	22	2	1	3	8	11	0	0	0	11
—Adirondack	AHL	49	14	36	50	45	—	—	—	—	—
87-88—Nova Scotia	AHL	69	27	61	88	45	5	0	5	5	6
—Edmonton	NHL	2	0	0	0	0	—	—	—	—	—
88-89—Cape Breton	AHL	54	33	49	82	29	—	—	—	—	—
—Edmonton	NHL	20	2	8	10	14	6	0	2	2	8
89-90—Edmonton	NHL	58	12	16	28	42	22	6	11	17	2
90-91—Edmonton	NHL	37	4	8	12	25	15	0	5	5	20
91-92—Edmonton	NHL	59	6	22	28	46	16	1	1	2	10
92-93—Ottawa	NHL	71	7	19	26	64	—	—	—	—	—
93-94—Ottawa	NHL	66	11	18	29	56	—	—	—	—	—
—Philadelphia	NHL	19	1	6	7	16	—	—	—	—	—
94-95—Philadelphia	NHL	8	0	2	2	2	—	—	—	—	—
—Montreal	NHL	39	1	0	1	18	—	—	—	—	—
NHL totals		402	46	100	146	291	70	7	19	26	51

LAMBERT, DENNY
LW, MIGHTY DUCKS

PERSONAL: Born January 7, 1970, in Wawa, Ont. . . . 5-11/200. . . . Shoots left. . . . Name pronounced lam-BAIR.
TRANSACTIONS/CAREER NOTES: Signed as free agent by Mighty Ducks of Anaheim (August 16, 1993).

Season	Team	League	Gms.	G	A	Pts.	PIM	Gms.	G	A	Pts.	PIM
88-89—Sault Ste. Marie	OHL	61	14	15	29	203	—	—	—	—	—
89-90—Sault Ste. Marie	OHL	61	23	29	52	*276	—	—	—	—	—
90-91—Sault Ste. Marie	OHL	59	28	39	67	169	14	7	9	16	48
91-92—San Diego	IHL	71	17	14	31	229	3	0	0	0	10
92-93—St. Thomas	Col.HL	5	2	6	8	9	—	—	—	—	—
—San Diego	IHL	56	18	12	30	277	14	1	1	2	44
93-94—San Diego	IHL	79	13	14	27	314	6	1	0	1	45
94-95—San Diego	IHL	75	25	35	60	222	—	—	—	—	—
—Anaheim	NHL	13	1	3	4	4	—	—	—	—	—
NHL totals		13	1	3	4	4	—	—	—	—	—

LAMOTHE, MARC
G, CANADIENS

PERSONAL: Born February 27, 1974, in New Liskeard, Ont. . . . 6-2/186. . . . Catches left. . . . Name pronounced luh-MAHT.
TRANSACTIONS/CAREER NOTES: Selected by Montreal Canadiens in fourth round (sixth Canadiens pick, 92nd overall) of NHL entry draft (June 20, 1992).

Season	Team	League	Gms.	Min.	W	L	T	GA	SO	Avg.	Gms.	Min.	W	L	GA	SO	Avg.
90-91—Ottawa	OHA Mj Jr.A	25	1220	. . .	. . .	. . .	82	1	4.03	—	—	—	—	—	—	—
91-92—Kingston	OHL	42	2378	10	25	2	189	1	4.77	—	—	—	—	—	—	—
92-93—Kingston	OHL	45	2489	23	12	6	162	†1	3.91	15	733	8	5	46	†1	3.77
93-94—Kingston	OHL	48	2828	23	20	5	177	†2	3.76	6	224	2	2	12	0	3.21
94-95—Fredericton	AHL	9	428	2	5	0	32	0	4.49	—	—	—	—	—	—	—
—Wheeling	ECHL	13	737	9	2	‡1	38	0	3.09	—	—	—	—	—	—	—

LANG, CHAD
G, STARS

PERSONAL: Born February 11, 1975, in Newmarket, Ont. . . . 5-10/188. . . . Catches left. . . . Cousin of Gerard Gallant, left winger, Tampa Bay Lightning.
TRANSACTIONS/CAREER NOTES: Selected by Dallas Stars in fourth round (third Stars pick, 87th overall) of NHL entry draft (June 26, 1993).
HONORS: Shared Dave Pinkney Trophy with Ryan Douglas (1992-93). . . . Named to OHL All-Star second team (1992-93).

Season	Team	League	Gms.	Min.	W	L	T	GA	SO	Avg.	Gms.	Min.	W	L	GA	SO	Avg.
90-91—Newmarket	Jr. B	34	1733	. . .	. . .	. . .	149	1	5.16	—	—	—	—	—	—	—
91-92—Peterborough	OHL	16	886	7	5	1	63	0	4.27	2	65	0	0	9	0	8.31
92-93—Peterborough	OHL	43	2554	*32	6	4	140	†1	3.29	*21	*1224	*12	*8	*74	†1	3.63
93-94—Peterborough	OHL	48	2732	11	27	7	225	0	4.94	7	391	3	4	24	0	3.68
94-95—Peterborough	OHL	43	2214	14	19	1	163	0	4.42	6	376	2	4	25	0	3.99

LANG, ROBERT
C, KINGS

PERSONAL: Born December 19, 1970, in Teplice, Czechoslovakia. . . . 6-2/180. . . . Shoots right. . . . Name pronounced LUHNG.
TRANSACTIONS/CAREER NOTES: Selected by Los Angeles Kings in seventh round (sixth Kings pick, 133rd overall) of NHL entry draft (June 16, 1990). . . . Dislocated shoulder (April 3,

1994); missed remainder of season. . . . Played in Europe during 1994-95 NHL lockout. . . . Strained left shoulder (March 26, 1995); missed one game.

			REGULAR SEASON					PLAYOFFS				
Season	Team	League	Gms.	G	A	Pts.	PIM	Gms.	G	A	Pts.	PIM
88-89—Litvinov		Czech.	7	3	2	5	0	—	—	—	—	—
89-90—Litvinov		Czech.	39	11	10	21	20	—	—	—	—	—
90-91—Litvinov		Czech.	56	26	26	52	38	—	—	—	—	—
91-92—Litvinov		Czech.	43	12	31	43	34	—	—	—	—	—
—Czech. national team		Int'l	8	5	8	13	8	—	—	—	—	—
—Czech. Olympic Team		Int'l	8	5	8	13	8	—	—	—	—	—
92-93—Los Angeles		NHL	11	0	5	5	2	—	—	—	—	—
—Phoenix		IHL	38	9	21	30	20	—	—	—	—	—
93-94—Phoenix		IHL	44	11	24	35	34	—	—	—	—	—
—Los Angeles		NHL	32	9	10	19	10	—	—	—	—	—
94-95—Chemopetrol Litvinov		Czech Rep.	16	4	19	23	28	—	—	—	—	—
—Los Angeles		NHL	36	4	8	12	4	—	—	—	—	—
NHL totals			79	13	23	36	16					

LANGDON, DARREN
LW, RANGERS

PERSONAL: Born January 8, 1971, in Deer Lake, Nfld. . . . 6-1/200. . . . Shoots left.
TRANSACTIONS/CAREER NOTES: Signed as free agent by New York Rangers (August 16, 1993).

			REGULAR SEASON					PLAYOFFS				
Season	Team	League	Gms.	G	A	Pts.	PIM	Gms.	G	A	Pts.	PIM
91-92—Summerside		MJHL	44	34	49	83	441	—	—	—	—	—
92-93—Binghamton		AHL	18	3	4	7	115	8	0	1	1	14
—Dayton		ECHL	54	23	22	45	429	3	0	1	1	40
93-94—Binghamton		AHL	54	2	7	9	327	11	1	3	4	*84
94-95—Binghamton		AHL	55	6	14	20	296	11	1	3	4	84
—New York Rangers		NHL	18	1	1	2	62	—	—	—	—	—
NHL totals			18	1	1	2	62					

LANGENBRUNNER, JAMIE
C, STARS

PERSONAL: Born April 21, 1975, in Edmonton. . . . 5-11/185. . . . Shoots right. . . . Name pronounced LANG-ihn-BROO-nuhr.
HIGH SCHOOL: Cloquet (Minn.).
TRANSACTIONS/CAREER NOTES: Selected by Dallas Stars in second round (second Stars pick, 35th overall) of NHL entry draft (June 26, 1993).

			REGULAR SEASON					PLAYOFFS				
Season	Team	League	Gms.	G	A	Pts.	PIM	Gms.	G	A	Pts.	PIM
90-91—Cloquet H.S.		Minn. H.S.	20	6	16	22	8	—	—	—	—	—
91-92—Cloquet H.S.		Minn. H.S.	23	16	23	39	24	—	—	—	—	—
92-93—Cloquet H.S.		Minn. H.S.	27	27	62	89	18	—	—	—	—	—
93-94—Peterborough		OHL	62	33	58	91	53	7	4	6	10	2
94-95—Peterborough		OHL	62	42	57	99	84	11	8	14	22	12
—Dallas		NHL	2	0	0	0	2	—	—	—	—	—
—Kalamazoo		IHL	—	—	—	—	—	11	1	3	4	2
NHL totals			2	0	0	0	2					

LANGKOW, DAYMOND
C, LIGHTNING

PERSONAL: Born September 27, 1976, in Edmonton. . . . 5-11/175. . . . Shoots left.
TRANSACTIONS/CAREER NOTES: Selected by Tampa Bay Lightning in first round (first Lightning pick, fifth overall) of NHL entry draft (July 8, 1995).
HONORS: Won Bob Clarke Trophy (1994-95). . . . Named to Can.HL All-Star first team (1994-95). . . . Named to WHL (West) All-Star first team (1994-95).

			REGULAR SEASON					PLAYOFFS				
Season	Team	League	Gms.	G	A	Pts.	PIM	Gms.	G	A	Pts.	PIM
91-92—Tri-City		WHL	1	0	0	0	0	4	2	2	4	15
92-93—Tri-City		WHL	65	22	42	64	96	4	1	0	1	4
93-94—Tri-City		WHL	61	40	43	83	174	4	2	2	4	15
94-95—Tri-City		WHL	72	67	73	140	142	17	12	15	27	52

LANGKOW, SCOTT
G, JETS

PERSONAL: Born April 21, 1975, in Edmonton. . . . 5-11/190. . . . Catches left. . . . Name pronounced LANG-koh.
HIGH SCHOOL: Aloha (Beaverton, Ore.).
TRANSACTIONS/CAREER NOTES: Selected by Winnipeg Jets in second round (second Jets pick, 31st overall) of NHL entry draft (June 26, 1993).
HONORS: Named to WHL (West) All-Star second team (1993-94 and 1994-95).

			REGULAR SEASON						PLAYOFFS					
Season	Team	League	Gms.	Min.	W	L	T	GA	SO	Avg.	Gms.	Min.	W	L	GA	SO	Avg.
91-92—Portland		WHL	1	33	0	0	0	2	0	3.64	—	—	—	—	—	—	—
92-93—Portland		WHL	34	2064	24	8	2	119	2	3.46	9	535	6	3	31	0	3.48
93-94—Portland		WHL	39	2302	27	9	1	121	2	3.15	10	600	6	4	34	0	3.40
94-95—Portland		WHL	63	3638	20	36	5	240	1	3.96	8	510	3	5	30	0	3.53

LAPERRIERE, DAN
D, SENATORS

PERSONAL: Born March 28, 1969, in Laval, Que. . . . 6-1/180. . . . Shoots left. . . . Full name: Daniel Jacques Laperriere. . . . Name pronounced luh-PAIR-ee-YAIR. . . . Son of Jacques Laperriere, Hall of Fame defenseman, Montreal Canadiens (1962-63 through 1973-74) and current assistant coach, Canadiens.
COLLEGE: St. Lawrence (N.Y.).
TRANSACTIONS/CAREER NOTES: Selected by St. Louis Blues in fifth round (fourth Blues pick, 93rd overall) of NHL entry draft (June 17, 1989). . . . Suffered from the flu (October 9, 1992); missed two games. . . . Traded by Blues to Ottawa Senators for ninth-round pick (D Libor Zabransky) in 1995 draft (April 7, 1995).
HONORS: Named to ECAC All-Star second team (1990-91). . . . Named ECAC Player of the Year (1991-92). . . . Named ECAC Playoff Most Valuable Player (1991-92). . . . Named to NCAA All-America East first team (1991-92). . . . Named to ECAC All-Star first team (1991-92).

			REGULAR SEASON					PLAYOFFS				
Season	Team	League	Gms.	G	A	Pts.	PIM	Gms.	G	A	Pts.	PIM
88-89	St. Lawrence University...	ECAC	34	1	11	12	14	—	—	—	—	—
89-90	St. Lawrence University...	ECAC	29	6	19	25	16	—	—	—	—	—
90-91	St. Lawrence University...	ECAC	34	7	32	39	18	—	—	—	—	—
91-92	St. Lawrence University...	ECAC	32	8	*45	53	36	—	—	—	—	—
92-93	St. Louis	NHL	5	0	1	1	0	—	—	—	—	—
	Peoria	IHL	54	4	20	24	28	—	—	—	—	—
93-94	Peoria	IHL	56	10	37	47	16	6	0	2	2	2
	St. Louis	NHL	20	1	3	4	8	—	—	—	—	—
94-95	Peoria	IHL	65	19	33	52	42	—	—	—	—	—
	St. Louis	NHL	4	0	0	0	15	—	—	—	—	—
	Ottawa	NHL	13	1	1	2	0	—	—	—	—	—
NHL totals			42	2	5	7	23					

LAPERRIERE, IAN
C, BLUES

PERSONAL: Born January 19, 1974, in Montreal. . . . 6-1/195. . . . Shoots right. . . . Name pronounced EE-ihn luh-PAIR-ee-YAIR.
TRANSACTIONS/CAREER NOTES: Selected by St. Louis Blues in seventh round (sixth Blues pick, 158th overall) of NHL entry draft (June 20, 1992). . . . Suffered concussion (March 26, 1995); missed three games.
HONORS: Named to QMJHL All-Star second team (1992-93).

			REGULAR SEASON					PLAYOFFS				
Season	Team	League	Gms.	G	A	Pts.	PIM	Gms.	G	A	Pts.	PIM
90-91	Drummondville	QMJHL	65	19	29	48	117	—	—	—	—	—
91-92	Drummondville	QMJHL	70	28	49	77	160	—	—	—	—	—
92-93	Drummondville	QMJHL	60	44	+96	140	188	10	6	13	19	20
93-94	Drummondville	QMJHL	62	41	72	113	150	9	4	6	10	35
	St. Louis	NHL	1	0	0	0	0	—	—	—	—	—
	Peoria	IHL	—	—	—	—	—	5	1	3	4	2
94-95	Peoria	IHL	51	16	32	48	111	—	—	—	—	—
	St. Louis	NHL	37	13	14	27	85	7	0	4	4	21
NHL totals			38	13	14	27	85	7	0	4	4	21

LAPLANTE, DARRYL
C, RED WINGS

PERSONAL: Born March 28, 1977, in Calgary. . . . 6-1/177. . . . Shoots right.
COLLEGE: Vanier (Edson, Alta.).
TRANSACTIONS/CAREER NOTES: Selected by Detroit Red Wings in third round (third Red Wings pick, 58th overall) of NHL entry draft (July 8, 1995).

			REGULAR SEASON					PLAYOFFS				
Season	Team	League	Gms.	G	A	Pts.	PIM	Gms.	G	A	Pts.	PIM
94-95	Moose Jaw	WHL	71	22	24	46	66	10	2	2	4	7

LAPOINTE, CLAUDE
C, DENVER

PERSONAL: Born October 11, 1968, in Ville Emard, Que. . . . 5-9/181. . . . Shoots left. . . . Name pronounced KLOHD luh-pwah.
TRANSACTIONS/CAREER NOTES: Traded by Trois-Rivieres Draveurs with G Alain Dubeau and third-round pick in QMJHL draft (D Patrice Brisebois) to Laval Titans for D Raymond Saumier, LW Mike Gober, D Eric Gobeil and second-round pick (D Eric Charron) in QMJHL draft (May 1987). . . . Selected by Quebec Nordiques in 12th round (12th Nordiques pick, 234th overall) of NHL entry draft (June 11, 1988). . . . Tore groin muscle (February 9, 1991). . . . Injured groin (October 23, 1991); missed one game. . . . Injured back in training camp (September 1992); missed five games. . . . Bruised hip (April 6, 1993); missed two games. . . . Sprained left knee (October 18, 1993); missed 13 games. . . . Sprained back (February 1, 1994); missed nine games. . . . Injured back (March 19, 1994); missed three games. . . . Suffered lower back pain (January 21, 1995); missed 16 games. . . . Suffered from the flu (April 16, 1995); missed one game. . . . Injured hip (April 30, 1995); missed one game. . . . Nordiques franchise moved to Denver for 1995-96 season.

			REGULAR SEASON					PLAYOFFS				
Season	Team	League	Gms.	G	A	Pts.	PIM	Gms.	G	A	Pts.	PIM
85-86	Trois-Rivieres	QMJHL	72	19	38	57	74	—	—	—	—	—
86-87	Trois-Rivieres	QMJHL	70	47	57	104	123	—	—	—	—	—
87-88	Laval	QMJHL	69	37	83	120	143	13	2	17	19	53
88-89	Laval	QMJHL	63	32	72	104	158	17	5	14	19	66
89-90	Halifax	AHL	63	18	19	37	51	6	1	1	2	34
90-91	Quebec	NHL	13	2	2	4	4	—	—	—	—	—
	Halifax	AHL	43	17	17	34	46	—	—	—	—	—

Season Team	League	REGULAR SEASON					PLAYOFFS				
		Gms.	G	A	Pts.	PIM	Gms.	G	A	Pts.	PIM
91-92—Quebec	NHL	78	13	20	33	86	—	—	—	—	—
92-93—Quebec	NHL	74	10	26	36	98	6	2	4	6	8
93-94—Quebec	NHL	59	11	17	28	70	—	—	—	—	—
94-95—Quebec	NHL	29	4	8	12	41	5	0	0	0	8
NHL totals		253	40	73	113	299	11	2	4	6	16

LAPOINTE, MARTIN
RW, RED WINGS

PERSONAL: Born September 12, 1973, in Lachine, Que. . . . 5-11/200. . . . Shoots right. . . . Name pronounced MAHR-tai luh-POYNT.
TRANSACTIONS/CAREER NOTES: Selected by Detroit Red Wings in first round (first Red Wings pick, 10th overall) of NHL entry draft (June 22, 1991). . . . Fractured wrist (October 9, 1991); missed 22 games.
HONORS: Won Michel Bergeron Trophy (1989-90). . . . Named to QMJHL All-Star first team (1989-90 and 1992-93). . . . Named to QMJHL All-Star second team (1990-91).

Season Team	League	REGULAR SEASON					PLAYOFFS				
		Gms.	G	A	Pts.	PIM	Gms.	G	A	Pts.	PIM
89-90—Laval	QMJHL	65	42	54	96	77	14	8	17	25	54
90-91—Laval	QMJHL	64	44	54	98	66	13	7	14	21	26
91-92—Detroit	NHL	4	0	1	1	5	3	0	1	1	4
—Laval	QMJHL	31	25	30	55	84	10	4	10	14	32
—Adirondack	AHL	—	—	—	—	—	8	2	2	4	4
92-93—Adirondack	AHL	8	1	2	3	9	—	—	—	—	—
—Detroit	NHL	3	0	0	0	0	—	—	—	—	—
—Laval	QMJHL	35	38	51	89	41	13	*13	*17	*30	22
93-94—Adirondack	AHL	28	25	21	46	47	4	1	1	2	8
—Detroit	NHL	50	8	8	16	55	4	0	0	0	6
94-95—Adirondack	AHL	39	29	16	45	80	—	—	—	—	—
—Detroit	NHL	39	4	6	10	73	2	0	1	1	8
NHL totals		96	12	15	27	133	9	0	2	2	18

LARAQUE, GEORGES
RW, OILERS

PERSONAL: Born December 7, 1976, in Montreal. . . . 6-3/225. . . . Shoots right.
TRANSACTIONS/CAREER NOTES: Selected by Edmonton Oilers in second round (second Oilers pick, 31st overall) of NHL entry draft (July 8, 1995).

Season Team	League	REGULAR SEASON					PLAYOFFS				
		Gms.	G	A	Pts.	PIM	Gms.	G	A	Pts.	PIM
93-94—St. Jean	QMJHL	70	11	11	22	142	4	0	0	0	7
94-95—St. Jean	QMJHL	62	19	22	41	259	7	1	1	2	42

LARIONOV, IGOR
C, SHARKS

PERSONAL: Born December 3, 1960, in Voskresensk, U.S.S.R. . . . 5-9/170. . . . Shoots left. . . . Name pronounced EE-gohr lair-ee-AH-nahf.
TRANSACTIONS/CAREER NOTES: Selected by Vancouver Canucks in 11th round (11th Canucks pick, 214th overall) of NHL entry draft (June 15, 1985). . . . Injured groin (October 25, 1990); missed four games. . . . Sprained ankle (January 8, 1991). . . . Reinjured ankle (January 30, 1991); missed seven games. . . . Signed to play with Lugano of Switzerland (July 14, 1992). . . . Selected by San Jose Sharks in NHL waiver draft (October 4, 1992). . . . Injured shoulder (September 30, 1993); missed four games. . . . Reinjured shoulder (October 16, 1993); missed four games. . . . Suffered from the flu (November 7, 1993); missed two games. . . . Sprained knee (December 12, 1993); missed 10 games. . . . Suffered from respiratory infection (February 11, 1994); missed one game. . . . Suffered from the flu (February 26, 1994); missed two games. . . . Injured groin (February 15, 1995); missed three games. . . . Injured foot (February 26, 1995); missed 12 games.
HONORS: Named to Soviet League All-Star team (1982-83 and 1985-86 through 1987-88). . . . Won Soviet Player of the Year Award (1987-88).
STATISTICAL PLATEAUS: Three-goal games: 1991-92 (2), 1993-94 (2). Total: 4.
MISCELLANEOUS: Member of gold-medal-winning U.S.S.R. Olympic teams (1984 and 1988).

Season Team	League	REGULAR SEASON					PLAYOFFS				
		Gms.	G	A	Pts.	PIM	Gms.	G	A	Pts.	PIM
77-78—Khimik Voskresensk	USSR	6	3	0	3	4	—	—	—	—	—
78-79—Khimik Voskresensk	USSR	25	3	4	7	12	—	—	—	—	—
79-80—Khimik Voskresensk	USSR	42	11	7	18	24	—	—	—	—	—
80-81—Khimik Voskresensk	USSR	56	22	23	45	36	—	—	—	—	—
81-82—CSKA Moscow	USSR	46	31	22	53	6	—	—	—	—	—
82-83—CSKA Moscow	USSR	44	20	19	39	20	—	—	—	—	—
83-84—CSKA Moscow	USSR	43	15	26	41	30	—	—	—	—	—
—Soviet Olympic Team	Int'l	7	1	4	5	6	—	—	—	—	—
84-85—CSKA Moscow	USSR	40	18	28	46	20	—	—	—	—	—
85-86—CSKA Moscow	USSR	40	21	31	52	33	—	—	—	—	—
86-87—CSKA Moscow	USSR	39	20	26	46	34	—	—	—	—	—
87-88—CSKA Moscow	USSR	51	25	32	57	54	—	—	—	—	—
—Soviet Olympic Team	Int'l	8	4	9	13	4	—	—	—	—	—
88-89—CSKA Moscow	USSR	31	15	12	27	22	—	—	—	—	—
89-90—Vancouver	NHL	74	17	27	44	20	—	—	—	—	—
90-91—Vancouver	NHL	64	13	21	34	14	6	1	0	1	6
91-92—Vancouver	NHL	72	21	44	65	54	13	3	7	10	4

Season Team	League	REGULAR SEASON Gms.	G	A	Pts.	PIM	PLAYOFFS Gms.	G	A	Pts.	PIM
92-93—Lugano	Switzerland	24	10	19	29	44	—	—	—	—	—
93-94—San Jose	NHL	60	18	38	56	40	14	5	13	18	10
94-95—San Jose	NHL	33	4	20	24	14	11	1	8	9	2
NHL totals		303	73	150	223	142	44	10	28	38	22

LARMER, STEVE
RW, RANGERS

PERSONAL: Born June 16, 1961, in Peterborough, Ont. . . . 5-11/185. . . . Shoots left. . . . Full name: Steve Donald Larmer. . . . Brother of Jeff Larmer, left winger, Colorado Rockies, New Jersey Devils and Chicago Blackhawks (1981-82 through 1985-86).

TRANSACTIONS/CAREER NOTES: Selected by Chicago Blackhawks as underage junior in sixth round (11th Blackhawks pick, 120th overall) of NHL entry draft (June 11, 1980). . . . Traded by Blackhawks with D Bryan Marchment to Hartford for LW Patrick Poulin and D Eric Weinrich (November 2, 1993). . . . Traded by Whalers with LW Nick Kypreos, D Barry Richter and sixth-round pick in 1994 draft (C Yuri Litvinov) to New York Rangers for D James Patrick and C Darren Turcotte (November 2, 1993). . . . Broke right hand (January 5, 1994); missed three games. . . . Suffered sore back (March 23, 1995); missed one game.

HONORS: Named to OMJHL All-Star second team (1980-81). . . . Named to AHL All-Star second team (1981-82). . . . Named NHL Rookie of the Year by THE SPORTING NEWS (1982-83). . . . Won Calder Memorial Trophy (1982-83). . . . Named to NHL All-Rookie team (1982-83). . . . Played in NHL All-Star Game (1990 and 1991).

STATISTICAL PLATEAUS: Three-goal games: 1982-83 (2), 1985-86 (1), 1987-88 (1), 1990-91 (1), 1991-92 (2), 1992-93 (2). Total: 9.

MISCELLANEOUS: Member of Stanley Cup championship team (1994).

Season Team	League	REGULAR SEASON Gms.	G	A	Pts.	PIM	PLAYOFFS Gms.	G	A	Pts.	PIM
77-78—Peterborough	OMJHL	62	24	17	41	51	18	5	7	12	27
78-79—Niagara Falls	OMJHL	66	37	47	84	108	—	—	—	—	—
79-80—Niagara Falls	OMJHL	67	45	69	114	71	10	5	9	14	15
80-81—Niagara Falls	OMJHL	61	55	78	133	73	12	13	8	21	24
—Chicago	NHL	4	0	1	1	0	—	—	—	—	—
81-82—New Brunswick	AHL	74	38	44	82	46	15	6	6	12	0
—Chicago	NHL	3	0	0	0	0	—	—	—	—	—
82-83—Chicago	NHL	80	43	47	90	28	11	5	7	12	8
83-84—Chicago	NHL	80	35	40	75	34	5	2	2	4	7
84-85—Chicago	NHL	80	46	40	86	16	15	9	13	22	14
85-86—Chicago	NHL	80	31	45	76	47	3	0	3	3	4
86-87—Chicago	NHL	80	28	56	84	22	4	0	0	0	2
87-88—Chicago	NHL	80	41	48	89	42	5	1	6	7	0
88-89—Chicago	NHL	80	43	44	87	54	16	8	9	17	22
89-90—Chicago	NHL	80	31	59	90	40	20	7	15	22	2
90-91—Chicago	NHL	80	44	57	101	79	6	5	1	6	4
91-92—Chicago	NHL	80	29	45	74	65	18	8	7	15	6
92-93—Chicago	NHL	84	35	35	70	48	4	0	3	3	0
93-94—New York Rangers	NHL	68	21	39	60	41	23	9	7	16	14
94-95—New York Rangers	NHL	47	14	15	29	16	10	2	2	4	6
NHL totals		1006	441	571	1012	532	140	56	75	131	89

LAROSE, GUY
C/LW, BRUINS

PERSONAL: Born July 31, 1967, in Hull, Que. . . . 5-10/175. . . . Shoots left. . . . Name pronounced GEE luh-ROHS. . . . Son of Claude Larose, right winger, Montreal Canadiens, Minnesota North Stars and St. Louis Blues (1962-63 through 1977-78).

TRANSACTIONS/CAREER NOTES: Fractured third left metacarpal (February 22, 1985). . . . Selected by Buffalo Sabres as underage junior in 11th round (11th Sabres pick, 224th overall) of NHL entry draft (June 15, 1985). . . . Signed as free agent by Winnipeg Jets (July 21, 1987). . . . Traded by Jets to New York Rangers for D Rudy Poeschek (January 22, 1991). . . . Traded by Rangers to Toronto Maple Leafs for C/LW Mike Stevens (December 26, 1991). . . . Injured stomach before season (1992); missed first two games of season. . . . Claimed on waivers by Calgary Flames (January 1, 1994). . . . Bruised ribs (January 2, 1994); missed eight games. . . . Signed as free agent by Boston Bruins (July 6, 1994).

Season Team	League	REGULAR SEASON Gms.	G	A	Pts.	PIM	PLAYOFFS Gms.	G	A	Pts.	PIM
83-84—Ottawa	COJHL	54	37	66	103	66	—	—	—	—	—
84-85—Guelph	OHL	58	30	30	60	63	—	—	—	—	—
85-86—Guelph	OHL	37	12	36	48	55	—	—	—	—	—
—Ottawa	OHL	28	19	25	44	63	—	—	—	—	—
86-87—Ottawa	OHL	66	28	49	77	77	11	2	8	10	27
87-88—Moncton	AHL	77	22	31	53	127	—	—	—	—	—
88-89—Winnipeg	NHL	3	0	1	1	6	—	—	—	—	—
—Moncton	AHL	72	32	27	59	176	10	4	4	8	37
89-90—Moncton	AHL	79	44	26	70	232	—	—	—	—	—
90-91—Moncton	AHL	35	14	10	24	60	—	—	—	—	—
—Binghamton	AHL	34	21	15	36	48	10	8	5	13	37
—Winnipeg	NHL	7	0	0	0	8	—	—	—	—	—
91-92—Binghamton	AHL	30	10	11	21	36	—	—	—	—	—
—St. John's	AHL	15	7	7	14	26	—	—	—	—	—
—Toronto	NHL	34	9	5	14	27	—	—	—	—	—
92-93—Toronto	NHL	9	0	0	0	8	—	—	—	—	—
—St. John's	AHL	5	0	1	1	8	9	5	2	7	6

Season Team	League	REGULAR SEASON					PLAYOFFS				
		Gms.	G	A	Pts.	PIM	Gms.	G	A	Pts.	PIM
93-94—St. John's	AHL	23	13	16	29	41	—	—	—	—	—
—Toronto	NHL	10	1	2	3	10	—	—	—	—	—
—Calgary	NHL	7	0	1	1	4	—	—	—	—	—
—Saint John	AHL	15	11	11	22	20	7	3	2	5	22
94-95—Providence	AHL	68	25	33	58	93	12	4	6	10	22
—Boston	NHL	—	—	—	—	—	4	0	0	0	0
NHL totals		70	10	9	19	63	4	0	0	0	0

LAROUCHE, STEVE
C, SENATORS

PERSONAL: Born April 14, 1971, in Rouyn, Que.... 6-0/184.... Shoots right. **TRANSACTIONS/CAREER NOTES:** Selected by Montreal Canadiens in second round (third Canadiens pick, 41st overall) of NHL entry draft (June 17, 1989).... Injured shoulder (October 8, 1989).... QMJHL rights traded by Trois-Rivieres Draveurs with C Sabastien Parent and sixth-round pick in 1990 QMJHL draft to Chicoutimi Sagueneens for Paul Brosseau and Jasmin Ouellet (May 26, 1990).... Tore left knee ligaments (October 5, 1990); missed two months.... Sent home by Chicoutimi coach Joe Canale for indifferent play (January 1991).... Signed as free agent by Ottawa Senators (September 3, 1994).
HONORS: Named to QMJHL All-Star second team (1989-90).... Won Les Cunningham Plaque (1994-95).... Won Fred Hunt Memorial Award (1994-95).... Named to AHL All-Star first team (1994-95).
STATISTICAL PLATEAUS: Three-goal games: 1994-95 (1).

Season Team	League	REGULAR SEASON					PLAYOFFS				
		Gms.	G	A	Pts.	PIM	Gms.	G	A	Pts.	PIM
87-88—Trois-Rivieres	QMJHL	66	11	29	40	25	—	—	—	—	—
88-89—Trois-Rivieres	QMJHL	70	51	102	153	53	4	4	2	6	6
89-90—Trois-Rivieres	QMJHL	60	55	90	145	40	7	3	5	8	8
90-91—Chicoutimi	QMJHL	45	35	41	76	64	17	†13	*20	*33	20
91-92—Fredericton	AHL	74	21	35	56	41	7	1	0	1	0
92-93—Fredericton	AHL	77	27	65	92	52	5	2	5	7	6
93-94—Atlanta	IHL	80	43	53	96	73	14	*16	10	*26	16
94-95—Prince Edward Island	AHL	70	*53	48	101	54	2	1	0	1	0
—Ottawa	NHL	18	8	7	15	6	—	—	—	—	—
NHL totals		18	8	7	15	6					

LARSEN, BRAD
LW, SENATORS

PERSONAL: Born June 28, 1977, in Nakusp, B.C.... 6-0/196.... Shoots left. **TRANSACTIONS/CAREER NOTES:** Selected by Ottawa Senators in third round (third Senators pick, 53rd overall) of NHL entry draft (July 8, 1995).

Season Team	League	REGULAR SEASON					PLAYOFFS				
		Gms.	G	A	Pts.	PIM	Gms.	G	A	Pts.	PIM
92-93—Nelson	Tier II Jr. A	42	31	37	68	164	—	—	—	—	—
93-94—Swift Current	WHL	64	15	18	33	37	7	1	2	3	4
94-95—Swift Current	WHL	62	24	33	57	73	6	0	1	1	2

LARSON, BRETT
D, RED WINGS

PERSONAL: Born August 20, 1972, in Duluth, Minn.... 6-0/175.... Shoots right. **COLLEGE:** Minnesota-Duluth. **TRANSACTIONS/CAREER NOTES:** Selected by Detroit Red Wings in 11th round (10th Red Wings pick, 213th overall) of NHL entry draft (June 16, 1990).

Season Team	League	REGULAR SEASON					PLAYOFFS				
		Gms.	G	A	Pts.	PIM	Gms.	G	A	Pts.	PIM
91-92—Minnesota-Duluth	WCHA	26	2	1	3	20	—	—	—	—	—
92-93—Minnesota-Duluth	WCHA	32	2	3	5	8	—	—	—	—	—
93-94—Minnesota-Duluth	WCHA	38	14	14	28	40	—	—	—	—	—
94-95—Minnesota-Duluth	WCHA	37	6	25	31	50	—	—	—	—	—

LAUER, BRAD
LW, PENGUINS

PERSONAL: Born October 27, 1966, in Humboldt, Sask.... 6-0/195.... Shoots left. **TRANSACTIONS/CAREER NOTES:** Selected by New York Islanders as underage junior in second round (third Islanders pick, 34th overall) of NHL entry draft (June 15, 1985).... Fractured left kneecap (October 1988).... Reinjured left knee (March 1989).... Strained abdomen (February 1990).... Bruised right quadricep (April 1990).... Traded by Islanders with C Brent Sutter to Chicago Blackhawks for C Adam Creighton and LW Steve Thomas (October 25, 1991).... Signed as free agent by Las Vegas Thunder (July 19, 1993). ... Signed as free agent by Ottawa Senators (January 1, 1994).... Injured hip flexor (March 13, 1994); missed three games. ... Suspended by Las Vegas Thunder for failing to report from Senators (March 26, 1994).... Signed as free agent by Pittsburgh Penguins (September 6, 1994).
HONORS: Named to IHL All-Star first team (1992-93).

Season Team	League	REGULAR SEASON					PLAYOFFS				
		Gms.	G	A	Pts.	PIM	Gms.	G	A	Pts.	PIM
83-84—Regina	WHL	60	5	7	12	51	16	0	1	1	24
84-85—Regina	WHL	72	33	46	79	57	8	6	6	12	9
85-86—Regina	WHL	57	36	38	74	69	10	4	5	9	2
86-87—New York Islanders	NHL	61	7	14	21	65	6	2	0	2	4
87-88—New York Islanders	NHL	69	17	18	35	67	5	3	1	4	4
88-89—Springfield	AHL	8	1	5	6	0	—	—	—	—	—
—New York Islanders	NHL	14	3	2	5	2	—	—	—	—	—

Season Team	League	REGULAR SEASON Gms.	G	A	Pts.	PIM	PLAYOFFS Gms.	G	A	Pts.	PIM
89-90—New York Islanders..........	NHL	63	6	18	24	19	4	0	2	2	10
—Springfield.......................	AHL	7	4	2	6	0	—	—	—	—	—
90-91—New York Islanders..........	NHL	44	4	8	12	45	—	—	—	—	—
—Capital District................	AHL	11	5	11	16	14	—	—	—	—	—
91-92—New York Islanders..........	NHL	8	1	0	1	2	—	—	—	—	—
—Indianapolis	IHL	57	24	30	54	46	—	—	—	—	—
—Chicago	NHL	6	0	0	0	4	7	1	1	2	2
92-93—Indianapolis	IHL	62	*50	41	91	80	5	3	1	4	6
—Chicago	NHL	7	0	1	1	2	—	—	—	—	—
93-94—Ottawa...........................	NHL	30	2	5	7	6	—	—	—	—	—
—Las Vegas........................	IHL	32	21	21	42	30	4	1	0	1	2
94-95—Cleveland.......................	IHL	51	32	27	59	48	4	4	2	6	6
NHL totals............................		**302**	**40**	**66**	**106**	**212**	**22**	**6**	**4**	**10**	**20**

LAUKKANEN, JANNE
D, DENVER

PERSONAL: Born March 19, 1970, in Lahti, Finland. . . . 6-0/180. . . . Shoots left. . . . Name pronounced YAH-nee LOW-kuh-nehn.

TRANSACTIONS/CAREER NOTES: Selected by Quebec Nordiques in eighth round (eighth Nordiques pick, 156th overall) of NHL entry draft (June 22, 1991). . . . Injured groin (April 14, 1995); missed four games. . . . Reinjured groin (April 30, 1995); missed last game of season. . . . Nordiques franchise moved to Denver for 1995-96 season.

MISCELLANEOUS: Member of bronze-medal-winning Finnish Olympic team (1994).

Season Team	League	REGULAR SEASON Gms.	G	A	Pts.	PIM	PLAYOFFS Gms.	G	A	Pts.	PIM
89-90—Ilves Tampere	Finland	39	5	6	11	10	—	—	—	—	—
90-91—Reipas.............................	Finland	44	8	14	22	56	—	—	—	—	—
91-92—Helsinki HPK	Finland	43	5	14	19	62	—	—	—	—	—
—Finnish Olympic Team......	Int'l	8	0	1	1	6	—	—	—	—	—
92-93—HPK Hameenlinna...........	Finland	47	8	21	29	76	12	1	4	5	10
93-94—HPK Hameenlinna...........	Finland	48	5	24	29	46	—	—	—	—	—
—Finnish Olympic Team......	Int'l	8	0	2	2	12	—	—	—	—	—
94-95—Cornwall.........................	AHL	55	8	26	34	41	—	—	—	—	—
—Quebec............................	NHL	11	0	3	3	4	6	1	0	1	2
NHL totals............................		**11**	**0**	**3**	**3**	**4**	**6**	**1**	**0**	**1**	**2**

LAUS, PAUL
D, PANTHERS

PERSONAL: Born September 26, 1970, in Beamsville, Ont. . . . 6-1/216. . . . Shoots right. . . . Name pronounced LAWS.

TRANSACTIONS/CAREER NOTES: Suffered inflamed knuckles (September 1988). . . . Suspended three playoff games by OHL for spearing (April 28, 1989). . . . Selected by Pittsburgh Penguins in second round (second Penguins pick, 37th overall) of NHL entry draft (June 17, 1989). . . . Selected by Florida Panthers in NHL expansion draft (June 24, 1993). . . . Strained groin (February 19, 1995); missed six games. . . . Separated left shoulder (April 16, 1995); missed two games.

Season Team	League	REGULAR SEASON Gms.	G	A	Pts.	PIM	PLAYOFFS Gms.	G	A	Pts.	PIM
86-87—St. Catharines Jr. B..........	OHA	40	1	8	9	56	—	—	—	—	—
87-88—Hamilton.........................	OHL	56	1	9	10	171	14	0	0	0	28
88-89—Niagara Falls	OHL	49	1	10	11	225	15	0	5	5	56
89-90—Niagara Falls	OHL	60	13	35	48	231	16	6	16	22	71
90-91—Muskegon.......................	IHL	35	3	4	7	103	4	0	0	0	13
—Albany.............................	IHL	7	0	0	0	7	—	—	—	—	—
—Knoxville..........................	ECHL	20	6	12	18	83	—	—	—	—	—
91-92—Muskegon.......................	IHL	75	0	21	21	248	14	2	5	7	70
92-93—Cleveland.......................	IHL	76	8	18	26	427	4	1	0	1	27
93-94—Florida............................	NHL	39	2	0	2	109	—	—	—	—	—
94-95—Florida............................	NHL	37	0	7	7	138	—	—	—	—	—
NHL totals............................		**76**	**2**	**7**	**9**	**247**					

LAVIGNE, ERIC
D, KINGS

PERSONAL: Born November 14, 1972, in Victoriaville, Que. . . . 6-3/194. . . . Shoots left. . . . Name pronounced luh-VEEN.

TRANSACTIONS/CAREER NOTES: Selected by Washington Capitals in second round (third Capitals pick, 25th overall) of NHL entry draft (June 22, 1991). . . . Signed as free agent by Los Angeles Kings (October 13, 1993).

Season Team	League	REGULAR SEASON Gms.	G	A	Pts.	PIM	PLAYOFFS Gms.	G	A	Pts.	PIM
89-90—Hull	QMJHL	69	7	11	18	203	11	0	0	0	32
90-91—Hull	QMJHL	66	11	11	22	153	4	0	1	1	16
91-92—Hull	QMJHL	46	4	17	21	101	6	0	0	0	32
92-93—Hull	QMJHL	59	7	20	27	221	10	2	4	6	47
93-94—Phoenix	IHL	62	3	11	14	168	—	—	—	—	—
94-95—Phoenix	IHL	69	4	10	14	233	—	—	—	—	—
—Los Angeles......................	NHL	1	0	0	0	0	—	—	—	—	—
—Detroit.............................	IHL	1	0	0	0	2	5	0	0	0	26
NHL totals............................		**1**	**0**	**0**	**0**	**0**					

LAWRENCE, MARK
RW, STARS

PERSONAL: Born January 27, 1972, in Burlington, Ont.... 6-4/215.... Shoots right.
TRANSACTIONS/CAREER NOTES: Selected by Dallas Stars in sixth round (fourth Stars pick, 118th overall) of NHL entry draft (June 22, 1991).

Season	Team	League	Gms.	G	A	Pts.	PIM	Gms.	G	A	Pts.	PIM
				REGULAR SEASON					**PLAYOFFS**			
87-88	Burlington Jr. B	OHA	40	11	12	23	90	—	—	—	—	—
88-89	Niagara Falls	OHL	63	9	27	36	142	—	—	—	—	—
89-90	Niagara Falls	OHL	54	15	18	33	123	16	2	5	7	42
90-91	Detroit	OHL	66	27	38	65	53	—	—	—	—	—
91-92	Detroit	OHL	28	19	26	45	54	—	—	—	—	—
	North Bay	OHL	24	13	14	27	21	21	*23	12	35	36
92-93	Dayton	ECHL	20	8	14	22	46	—	—	—	—	—
	Kalamazoo	IHL	57	22	13	35	47	—	—	—	—	—
93-94	Kalamazoo	IHL	64	17	20	37	90	—	—	—	—	—
94-95	Kalamazoo	IHL	77	21	29	50	92	16	3	7	10	28
	Dallas	NHL	2	0	0	0	0	—	—	—	—	—
NHL totals			**2**	**0**	**0**	**0**	**0**					

LEACH, STEVE
RW, BRUINS

PERSONAL: Born January 16, 1966, in Cambridge, Mass.... 5-11/200.... Shoots right.
HIGH SCHOOL: Matignon (Cambridge, Mass.).
COLLEGE: New Hampshire.
TRANSACTIONS/CAREER NOTES: Selected by Washington Capitals in second round (second Capitals pick, 34th overall) of NHL entry draft (June 9, 1984).... Strained left knee (February 1989).... Injured thumb (March 1990).... Suffered concussion (October 10, 1990).... Separated right shoulder (February 2, 1991); missed four games.... Traded by Capitals to Boston Bruins for LW Randy Burridge (June 21, 1991).... Injured thigh (October 1992); missed one game.... Injured ribs (January 1993); missed four games.... Injured knee (January 8, 1994); missed 25 games.... Reinjured knee (March 7, 1994); missed 15 games.... Broke foot (April 8, 1995).
HONORS: Named to Hockey East All-Freshman team (1984-85).

Season	Team	League	Gms.	G	A	Pts.	PIM	Gms.	G	A	Pts.	PIM
				REGULAR SEASON					**PLAYOFFS**			
83-84	Matignon H.S.	Mass. H.S.	21	27	22	49	49	—	—	—	—	—
84-85	Univ. of New Hampshire	Hockey East	41	12	25	37	53	—	—	—	—	—
85-86	Univ. of New Hampshire	Hockey East	25	22	6	28	30	—	—	—	—	—
	Washington	NHL	11	1	1	2	2	6	0	1	1	0
86-87	Binghamton	AHL	54	18	21	39	39	13	3	1	4	6
	Washington	NHL	15	1	0	1	6	—	—	—	—	—
87-88	U.S. national team	Int'l	53	26	20	46	...	—	—	—	—	—
	U.S. Olympic Team	Int'l	6	1	2	3	0	—	—	—	—	—
	Washington	NHL	8	1	1	2	17	9	2	1	3	0
88-89	Washington	NHL	74	11	19	30	94	6	1	0	1	12
89-90	Washington	NHL	70	18	14	32	104	14	2	2	4	6
90-91	Washington	NHL	68	11	19	30	99	9	1	2	3	8
91-92	Boston	NHL	78	31	29	60	147	15	4	0	4	10
92-93	Boston	NHL	79	26	25	51	126	4	1	1	2	2
93-94	Boston	NHL	42	5	10	15	74	5	0	1	1	2
94-95	Boston	NHL	35	5	6	11	68	—	—	—	—	—
NHL totals			**480**	**110**	**124**	**234**	**737**	**68**	**11**	**8**	**19**	**40**

LEBEAU, STEPHAN
C

PERSONAL: Born February 28, 1968, in Sherbrooke, Que.... 5-10/173.... Shoots right.... Name pronounced STEH-fihn luh-BOH.... Brother of Patrick Lebeau, left winger, Montreal Canadiens, Calgary Flames and Florida Panthers (1990-91 through 1993-94).
TRANSACTIONS/CAREER NOTES: Signed as free agent by Montreal Canadiens (September 27, 1986).... Injured thigh (January 25, 1992); missed one game.... Injured ankle (February 26, 1993); missed four games.... Reinjured ankle (March 17, 1993); missed nine games.... Bruised foot (November 17, 1993); missed five games.... Injured ankle (December 1, 1993); missed five games.... Reinjured ankle (January 14, 1994); missed 14 games.... Traded by Canadiens to Mighty Ducks of Anaheim for G Ron Tugnutt (February 20, 1994).... Suffered sore right ankle (February 7, 1995); missed two games.... Signed to play with Lugano of Swiss League (May 18, 1995).
HONORS: Named to QMJHL All-Star second team (1986-87 and 1987-88).... Won Frank J. Selke Trophy (1987-88).... Won Les Cunningham Plaque (1988-89).... Won John B. Sollenberger Trophy (1988-89).... Won Dudley (Red) Garrett Memorial Trophy (1988-89).... Named to AHL All-Star first team (1988-89).
STATISTICAL PLATEAUS: Three-goal games: 1991-92 (1).
MISCELLANEOUS: Member of Stanley Cup championship team (1993).

Season	Team	League	Gms.	G	A	Pts.	PIM	Gms.	G	A	Pts.	PIM
				REGULAR SEASON					**PLAYOFFS**			
84-85	Shawinigan	QMJHL	66	41	38	79	18	9	4	5	9	4
85-86	Shawinigan	QMJHL	72	69	77	146	22	5	4	2	6	4
86-87	Shawinigan	QMJHL	65	*77	90	167	60	14	9	20	29	20
87-88	Shawinigan	QMJHL	67	*94	94	188	66	11	†17	9	26	10
	Sherbrooke	AHL	—	—	—	—	—	1	0	1	1	0
88-89	Sherbrooke	AHL	78	*70	64	*134	47	6	1	4	5	8
	Montreal	NHL	1	0	1	1	2	—	—	—	—	—
89-90	Montreal	NHL	57	15	20	35	11	2	3	0	3	0
90-91	Montreal	NHL	73	22	31	53	24	7	2	1	3	2

Season Team	League	REGULAR SEASON					PLAYOFFS				
		Gms.	G	A	Pts.	PIM	Gms.	G	A	Pts.	PIM
91-92—Montreal	NHL	77	27	31	58	14	8	1	3	4	4
92-93—Montreal	NHL	71	31	49	80	20	13	3	3	6	6
93-94—Montreal	NHL	34	9	7	16	8	—	—	—	—	—
—Anaheim	NHL	22	6	4	10	14	—	—	—	—	—
94-95—Anaheim	NHL	38	8	16	24	12	—	—	—	—	—
NHL totals		373	118	159	277	105	30	9	7	16	12

LeBLANC, JOHN
LW

PERSONAL: Born January 21, 1964, in Campbellton, N.B. . . . 6-1/190. . . . Shoots left. . . . Full name: John Glenn LeBlanc.
TRANSACTIONS/CAREER NOTES: Suffered ankle contusion (February 1992); missed three games. . . . Signed as free agent by Vancouver Canucks (April 12, 1986). . . . Traded by Canucks with fifth-round pick in 1989 draft (LW Peter White) to Edmonton Oilers for C Doug Smith and LW Greg C. Adams (March 7, 1989). . . . Traded by Oilers with 10th-round pick in 1992 draft (C Teemu Numminen) to Winnipeg Jets for fifth-round pick (C Ryan Haggerty) in 1991 draft (June 12, 1991). . . . Signed as free agent by Orlando Solar Bears of IHL (July 10, 1995).
HONORS: Won Senator Joseph A. Sullivan Trophy (1985-86).

Season Team	League	REGULAR SEASON					PLAYOFFS				
		Gms.	G	A	Pts.	PIM	Gms.	G	A	Pts.	PIM
83-84—Hull	QMJHL	69	39	35	74	32	—	—	—	—	—
84-85—New Brunswick	AUAA	24	25	34	59	32	—	—	—	—	—
85-86—New Brunswick	AUAA	24	38	28	66	35	—	—	—	—	—
86-87—Vancouver	NHL	2	1	0	1	0	—	—	—	—	—
—Fredericton	AHL	75	40	30	70	27	—	—	—	—	—
87-88—Vancouver	NHL	41	12	10	22	18	—	—	—	—	—
—Fredericton	AHL	35	26	25	51	54	15	6	7	13	34
88-89—Milwaukee	IHL	61	39	31	70	42	—	—	—	—	—
—Edmonton	NHL	2	1	0	1	0	1	0	0	0	0
—Cape Breton	AHL	3	4	0	4	0	—	—	—	—	—
89-90—Cape Breton	AHL	77	*54	34	88	50	6	4	0	4	4
90-91—Cape Breton	AHL				Did not play.						
91-92—Moncton	AHL	56	31	22	53	24	10	3	2	5	8
—Winnipeg	NHL	16	6	1	7	6	—	—	—	—	—
92-93—Winnipeg	NHL	3	0	0	0	2	—	—	—	—	—
—Moncton	AHL	77	48	40	88	29	5	2	1	3	6
93-94—Moncton	AHL	41	25	26	51	38	20	3	6	9	6
—Winnipeg	NHL	17	6	2	8	2	—	—	—	—	—
94-95—Springfield	AHL	65	39	34	73	32	—	—	—	—	—
—Winnipeg	NHL	2	0	0	0	0	—	—	—	—	—
NHL totals		83	26	13	39	28	1	0	0	0	0

LeBOUTILLIER, PETER
RW, MIGHTY DUCKS

PERSONAL: Born January 11, 1975, in Minnedosa, Man. . . . 6-1/198. . . . Shoots right. . . . Name pronounced luh-BOO-tih-LAY.
HIGH SCHOOL: Lindsay Thurber (Red Deer, Alta.).
TRANSACTIONS/CAREER NOTES: Selected by New York Islanders in sixth round (sixth Islanders pick, 144th overall) of NHL entry draft (June 26, 1993). . . . Returned to draft pool by Islanders and selected by Mighty Ducks of Anaheim in sixth round (fifth Mighty Ducks pick, 133rd overall) of entry draft (July 8, 1995).

Season Team	League	REGULAR SEASON					PLAYOFFS				
		Gms.	G	A	Pts.	PIM	Gms.	G	A	Pts.	PIM
91-92—Neepawa	Jr. A	35	11	14	25	99	—	—	—	—	—
92-93—Red Deer	WHL	67	8	26	34	284	2	0	1	1	5
93-94—Red Deer	WHL	66	19	20	39	300	2	0	1	1	4
94-95—Red Deer	WHL	59	27	16	43	159	—	—	—	—	—

LeCLAIR, JOHN
C, FLYERS

PERSONAL: Born July 5, 1969, in St. Albans, Vt. . . . 6-2/220. . . . Shoots left. . . . Full name: John Clark LeClair.
HIGH SCHOOL: Bellows Free Academy (St. Albans, Vt.).
COLLEGE: Vermont.
TRANSACTIONS/CAREER NOTES: Selected by Montreal Canadiens in second round (second Canadiens pick, 33rd overall) of NHL entry draft (June 13, 1987). . . . Injured thigh; missed 16 games during 1988-89 season. . . . Injured knee and underwent surgery (January 20, 1990); missed remainder of season. . . . Injured shoulder (January 15, 1992); missed four games. . . . Suffered charley horse (January 20, 1993); missed four games. . . . Sprained knee (October 2, 1993); missed eight games. . . . Bruised sternum (March 28, 1994); missed two games. . . . Traded by Canadiens with LW Gilbert Dionne and D Eric Desjardins to Philadelphia Flyers for RW Mark Recchi and third-round pick (C Martin Hohenberger) in 1995 draft (February 9, 1995). . . . Strained right hip (April 18, 1995); missed one game.
HONORS: Named to ECAC All-Star second team (1990-91). . . . Named to THE SPORTING NEWS All-Star first team (1994-95). . . . Named to NHL All-Star first team (1994-95).
STATISTICAL PLATEAUS: Three-goal games: 1994-95 (2).
MISCELLANEOUS: Member of Stanley Cup championship team (1993).

Season Team	League	REGULAR SEASON					PLAYOFFS				
		Gms.	G	A	Pts.	PIM	Gms.	G	A	Pts.	PIM
85-86—Bellows Free Academy	Vt. H.S.	22	41	28	69	14	—	—	—	—	—
86-87—Bellows Free Academy	Vt. H.S.	23	44	40	84	25	—	—	—	—	—

Season	Team	League	REGULAR SEASON					PLAYOFFS				
			Gms.	G	A	Pts.	PIM	Gms.	G	A	Pts.	PIM
87-88—University of Vermont		ECAC	31	12	22	34	62	—	—	—	—	—
88-89—University of Vermont		ECAC	19	9	12	21	40	—	—	—	—	—
89-90—University of Vermont		ECAC	10	10	6	16	38	—	—	—	—	—
90-91—University of Vermont		ECAC	33	25	20	45	58	—	—	—	—	—
—Montreal..........................		NHL	10	2	5	7	2	3	0	0	0	0
91-92—Montreal.......................		NHL	59	8	11	19	14	8	1	1	2	4
—Fredericton		AHL	8	7	7	14	10	2	0	0	0	4
92-93—Montreal.......................		NHL	72	19	25	44	33	20	4	6	10	14
93-94—Montreal.......................		NHL	74	19	24	43	32	7	2	1	3	8
94-95—Montreal.......................		NHL	9	1	4	5	10	—	—	—	—	—
—Philadelphia		NHL	37	25	24	49	20	15	5	7	12	4
NHL totals...................................			261	74	93	167	111	53	12	15	27	30

LECLERC, MIKE
LW, MIGHTY DUCKS

PERSONAL: Born November 10, 1976, in Winnipeg.... 6-1/205.... Shoots left.
TRANSACTIONS/CAREER NOTES: Selected by Mighty Ducks of Anaheim in third round (third Mighty Ducks pick, 55th overall) of NHL entry draft (July 8, 1995).

Season	Team	League	REGULAR SEASON					PLAYOFFS				
			Gms.	G	A	Pts.	PIM	Gms.	G	A	Pts.	PIM
91-92—St. Boniface......................		Tier II Jr. A	43	16	12	28	25	—	—	—	—	—
—Victoria............................		WHL	2	0	0	0	0	—	—	—	—	—
92-93—Victoria.........................		WHL	70	4	11	15	118	—	—	—	—	—
93-94—Victoria.........................		WHL	68	29	11	40	112	—	—	—	—	—
94-95—Prince George..................		WHL	43	20	36	56	78	—	—	—	—	—
—Brandon...........................		WHL	23	5	8	13	50	18	10	6	16	33

LECOMPTE, ERIC
LW, BLACKHAWKS

PERSONAL: Born April 4, 1975, in Montreal.... 6-4/190.... Shoots left.
TRANSACTIONS/CAREER NOTES: Selected by Chicago Blackhawks in first round (first Blackhawks pick, 24th overall) of NHL entry draft (June 26, 1993).

Season	Team	League	REGULAR SEASON					PLAYOFFS				
			Gms.	G	A	Pts.	PIM	Gms.	G	A	Pts.	PIM
91-92—Hull		QMJHL	60	16	17	33	138	6	1	0	1	4
92-93—Hull		QMJHL	66	33	38	71	149	10	4	4	8	52
93-94—Hull		QMJHL	62	39	49	88	171	20	10	10	20	68
94-95—Hull		QMJHL	12	11	9	20	58	—	—	—	—	—
—St. Jean		QMJHL	18	9	10	19	54	—	—	—	—	—
—Sherbrooke.....................		QMJHL	34	22	29	51	111	4	2	2	4	4
—Indianapolis		IHL	3	2	0	2	2	—	—	—	—	—

LEDYARD, GRANT
D, STARS

PERSONAL: Born November 19, 1961, in Winnipeg.... 6-2/195.... Shoots left.
TRANSACTIONS/CAREER NOTES: Signed as free agent by New York Rangers (July 7, 1982).... Injured hip (October 1984).... Traded by Rangers to Los Angeles Kings for LW Brian MacLellan and fourth-round pick in 1987 draft (C Michael Sullivan); Rangers also sent second-round pick in 1986 draft (D Neil Wilkinson) and fourth-round pick in 1987 draft (RW John Weisbrod) to Minnesota North Stars and the North Stars sent G Roland Melanson to the Kings as part of the same deal (December 1986).... Sprained ankle (October 1987).... Traded by Kings to Washington Capitals for RW Craig Laughlin (February 9, 1988).... Traded by Capitals with G Clint Malarchuk and sixth-round pick in 1991 draft to Buffalo Sabres for D Calle Johansson and second-round pick (G Byron Dafoe) in 1989 draft (March 6, 1989).... Injured knee (February 12, 1991).... Injured shoulder (March 2, 1991).... Bruised ankle (March 14, 1992); missed four games.... Broke finger (October 28, 1992); missed 25 games.... Injured eye (March 7, 1993); missed three games.... Signed as free agent by Dallas Stars (August 13, 1993).... Sprained ankle (February 13, 1994); missed two games.... Fractured ankle (April 16, 1995); missed last eight games of season and first game of playoffs.... Suffered from the flu (May 14, 1995); missed one game.
HONORS: Named MJHL Most Valuable Player (1981-82).... Named to MJHL All-Star first team (1981-82).... Won Bob Gassoff Award (1983-84).... Won Max McNab Trophy (1983-84).

Season	Team	League	REGULAR SEASON					PLAYOFFS				
			Gms.	G	A	Pts.	PIM	Gms.	G	A	Pts.	PIM
79-80—Fort Garry		MJHL	49	13	24	37	90	—	—	—	—	—
80-81—Saskatoon		WHL	71	9	28	37	148	—	—	—	—	—
81-82—Fort Garry		MJHL	63	25	45	70	150	—	—	—	—	—
82-83—Tulsa		CHL	80	13	29	42	115	—	—	—	—	—
83-84—Tulsa		CHL	58	9	17	26	71	9	5	4	9	10
84-85—New Haven		AHL	36	6	20	26	18	—	—	—	—	—
—New York Rangers		NHL	42	8	12	20	53	3	0	2	2	4
85-86—New York Rangers		NHL	27	2	9	11	20	—	—	—	—	—
—Los Angeles		NHL	52	7	18	25	78	—	—	—	—	—
86-87—Los Angeles		NHL	67	14	23	37	93	5	0	0	0	10
87-88—New Haven		AHL	3	2	1	3	4	—	—	—	—	—
—Los Angeles		NHL	23	1	7	8	52	—	—	—	—	—
—Washington		NHL	21	4	3	7	14	14	1	0	1	30
88-89—Washington		NHL	61	3	11	14	43	—	—	—	—	—
—Buffalo		NHL	13	1	5	6	8	5	1	2	3	2
89-90—Buffalo		NHL	67	2	13	15	37	—	—	—	—	—
90-91—Buffalo		NHL	60	8	23	31	46	6	3	3	6	10

L

Season Team	League	REGULAR SEASON					PLAYOFFS				
		Gms.	G	A	Pts.	PIM	Gms.	G	A	Pts.	PIM
91-92—Buffalo	NHL	50	5	16	21	45	—	—	—	—	—
92-93—Buffalo	NHL	50	2	14	16	45	8	0	0	0	8
—Rochester	AHL	5	0	2	2	8	—	—	—	—	—
93-94—Dallas	NHL	84	9	37	46	42	9	1	2	3	6
94-95—Dallas	NHL	38	5	13	18	20	3	0	0	0	2
NHL totals		655	71	204	275	596	53	6	9	15	72

LEEMAN, GARY
RW

PERSONAL: Born February 19, 1964, in Toronto. . . . 5-11/186. . . . Shoots right.
TRANSACTIONS/CAREER NOTES: Selected by Toronto Maple Leafs as underage junior in second round (second Maple Leafs pick, 24th overall) of NHL entry draft (June 9, 1982). . . . Broke finger (January 1984). . . . Broke wrist (March 1984). . . . Separated shoulder (March 1985). . . . Cracked kneecap (April 14, 1987). . . . Cracked bone in right hand (April 1988). . . . Fractured bone behind left ear (October 22, 1988). . . . Injured back (January 1988). . . . Separated right shoulder (November 10, 1990); missed 21 games. . . . Suffered back spasms (November 18, 1991); missed one game. . . . Traded by Maple Leafs with D Alexander Godynyuk, LW Craig Berube, D Michel Petit and G Jeff Reese to Calgary Flames for C Doug Gilmour, D Jamie Macoun, LW Kent Manderville, D Ric Nattress and G Rick Wamsley (January 2, 1992). . . . Bruised thigh (February 1992). . . . Sprained ankle (February 21, 1992); missed eight games. . . . Traded by Flames to Montreal Canadiens for C Brian Skrudland (January 28, 1993). . . . Bruised lower back (February 3, 1993); missed four games. . . . Injured ankle (April 2, 1993); missed five games. . . . Injured shoulder (January 12, 1994); missed two games. . . . Fractured forearm (April 11, 1994); missed remainder of season.
HONORS: Won Top Defenseman Trophy (1982-83). . . . Named to WHL All-Star first team (1982-83). . . . Played in NHL All-Star Game (1989).
STATISTICAL PLATEAUS: Three-goal games: 1986-87 (1), 1988-89 (1), 1989-90 (2), 1992-93 (2). Total: 6.
MISCELLANEOUS: Member of Stanley Cup championship team (1993).

Season Team	League	REGULAR SEASON					PLAYOFFS				
		Gms.	G	A	Pts.	PIM	Gms.	G	A	Pts.	PIM
81-82—Regina	WHL	72	19	41	60	112	3	2	2	4	0
82-83—Regina	WHL	63	24	62	86	88	5	1	5	6	4
—Toronto	NHL	—	—	—	—	—	2	0	0	0	0
83-84—Toronto	NHL	52	4	8	12	31	—	—	—	—	—
84-85—St. Catharines	AHL	7	2	2	4	11	—	—	—	—	—
—Toronto	NHL	53	5	26	31	72	—	—	—	—	—
85-86—St. Catharines	AHL	25	15	13	28	6	—	—	—	—	—
—Toronto	NHL	53	9	23	32	20	10	2	10	12	2
86-87—Toronto	NHL	80	21	31	52	66	5	0	1	1	14
87-88—Toronto	NHL	80	30	31	61	62	2	2	0	2	2
88-89—Toronto	NHL	61	32	43	75	66	—	—	—	—	—
89-90—Toronto	NHL	80	51	44	95	63	5	3	3	6	16
90-91—Toronto	NHL	52	17	12	29	39	—	—	—	—	—
91-92—Toronto	NHL	34	7	13	20	44	—	—	—	—	—
—Calgary	NHL	29	2	7	9	27	—	—	—	—	—
92-93—Calgary	NHL	30	9	5	14	10	—	—	—	—	—
—Montreal	NHL	20	6	12	18	14	11	1	2	3	2
93-94—Montreal	NHL	31	4	11	15	17	1	0	0	0	0
—Fredericton	AHL	23	18	8	26	16	—	—	—	—	—
94-95—Vancouver	NHL	10	2	0	2	0	—	—	—	—	—
NHL totals		665	199	266	465	531	36	8	16	24	36

LEETCH, BRIAN
D, RANGERS

PERSONAL: Born March 3, 1968, in Corpus Christi, Tex. . . . 5-11/195. . . . Shoots left. . . . Full name: Brian Joseph Leetch.
HIGH SCHOOL: Avon (Conn.) Old Farms School for Boys.
COLLEGE: Boston College.
TRANSACTIONS/CAREER NOTES: Selected by New York Rangers in first round (first Rangers pick, ninth overall) of NHL entry draft (June 21, 1986). . . . Sprained ligaments in left knee at U.S. Olympic Festival (July 1987). . . . Fractured bone in left foot (December 1988). . . . Suffered hip pointer (March 15, 1989). . . . Fractured left ankle (March 14, 1990). . . . Injured ankle (November 21, 1992); missed one game. . . . Suffered stretched nerve in neck (December 17, 1992); missed 34 games. . . . Broke ankle (March 19, 1993) and underwent ankle surgery (March 31, 1993); missed remainder of season.
HONORS: Named Hockey East Player of the Year (1986-87). . . . Named Hockey East Rookie of the Year (1986-87). . . . Named Hockey East Tournament Most Valuable Player (1986-87). . . . Named to NCAA All-America East first team (1986-87). . . . Named to Hockey East All-Star first team (1986-87). . . . Named to Hockey East All-Freshman team (1986-87). . . . Named NHL Rookie of the Year by THE SPORTING NEWS (1988-89). . . . Won Calder Memorial Trophy (1988-89). . . . Named to NHL All-Rookie team (1988-89). . . . Named to THE SPORTING NEWS All-Star second team (1990-91 and 1993-94). . . . Named to NHL All-Star second team (1990-91 and 1993-94). . . . Played in NHL All-Star Game (1990-1992 and 1994). . . . Won James Norris Memorial Trophy (1991-92). . . . Named to THE SPORTING NEWS All-Star first team (1991-92). . . . Named to NHL All-Star first team (1991-92). . . . Won Conn Smythe Trophy (1993-94). . . . Named to Hockey East All-Decade team (1994).
RECORDS: Holds NHL single-season record for most goals by a rookie defenseman—23 (1988-89).
MISCELLANEOUS: Member of Stanley Cup championship team (1994).

Season Team	League	REGULAR SEASON					PLAYOFFS				
		Gms.	G	A	Pts.	PIM	Gms.	G	A	Pts.	PIM
84-85—Avon Old Farms H.S.	Conn. H.S.	26	30	46	76	15	—	—	—	—	—
85-86—Avon Old Farms H.S.	Conn. H.S.	28	40	44	84	18	—	—	—	—	—
86-87—Boston College	Hockey East	37	9	38	47	10	—	—	—	—	—

			REGULAR SEASON					PLAYOFFS			
Season	Team	League	Gms.	G	A	Pts.	PIM	Gms.	G	A	Pts.	PIM
87-88—	U.S. national team	Int'l	60	13	61	74	38	—	—	—	—	—
	—U.S. Olympic Team	Int'l	6	1	5	6	4	—	—	—	—	—
	—New York Rangers	NHL	17	2	12	14	0	—	—	—	—	—
88-89—	New York Rangers	NHL	68	23	48	71	50	4	3	2	5	2
89-90—	New York Rangers	NHL	72	11	45	56	26	—	—	—	—	—
90-91—	New York Rangers	NHL	80	16	72	88	42	6	1	3	4	0
91-92—	New York Rangers	NHL	80	22	80	102	26	13	4	11	15	4
92-93—	New York Rangers	NHL	36	6	30	36	26	—	—	—	—	—
93-94—	New York Rangers	NHL	84	23	56	79	67	23	11	*23	*34	6
94-95—	New York Rangers	NHL	48	9	32	41	18	10	6	8	14	8
	NHL totals..		485	112	375	487	255	56	25	47	72	20

LEFEBVRE, SYLVAIN

D, DENVER

PERSONAL: Born October 14, 1967, in Richmond, Que. . . . 6-2/205. . . . Shoots left. . . . Name pronounced luh-FAYV.

TRANSACTIONS/CAREER NOTES: Signed as free agent by Montreal Canadiens (September 24, 1986). . . . Traded by Canadiens to Toronto Maple Leafs for third-round pick (D Martin Belanger) in 1994 draft (August 20, 1992). . . . Traded by Maple Leafs with LW Wendel Clark, RW Landon Wilson and first-round pick in 1994 draft (D Jeffrey Kealty) to Quebec Nordiques for C Mats Sundin, D Garth Butcher, LW Todd Warriner and first-round pick (traded to Washington Capitals who selected D Nolan Baumgartner) in 1994 draft (June 28, 1994). . . . Nordiques franchise moved to Denver for 1995-96 season.

HONORS: Named to AHL All-Star second team (1988-89).

			REGULAR SEASON					PLAYOFFS			
Season	Team	League	Gms.	G	A	Pts.	PIM	Gms.	G	A	Pts.	PIM
84-85—	Laval	QMJHL	66	7	5	12	31	—	—	—	—	—
85-86—	Laval	QMJHL	71	8	17	25	48	14	1	0	1	25
86-87—	Laval	QMJHL	70	10	36	46	44	15	1	6	7	12
87-88—	Sherbrooke......................	AHL	79	3	24	27	73	6	2	3	5	4
88-89—	Sherbrooke......................	AHL	77	15	32	47	119	6	1	3	4	4
89-90—	Montreal........................	NHL	68	3	10	13	61	6	0	0	0	2
90-91—	Montreal........................	NHL	63	5	18	23	30	11	1	0	1	6
91-92—	Montreal........................	NHL	69	3	14	17	91	2	0	0	0	2
92-93—	Toronto..........................	NHL	81	2	12	14	90	21	3	3	6	20
93-94—	Toronto..........................	NHL	84	2	9	11	79	18	0	3	3	16
94-95—	Quebec	NHL	48	2	11	13	17	6	0	2	2	2
	NHL totals..		413	17	74	91	368	64	4	8	12	48

LEGACE, MANNY

G, WHALERS

PERSONAL: Born February 4, 1973, in Toronto. . . . 5-9/162. . . . Catches left. . . . Name pronounced LEHG-uh-see.

HIGH SCHOOL: Stamford Collegiate (Niagara Falls, Ont.).

TRANSACTIONS/CAREER NOTES: Selected by Hartford Whalers in eighth round (fifth Whalers pick, 188th overall) of NHL entry draft (June 26, 1993).

HONORS: Named to Can.HL All-Star second team (1992-93). . . . Named to OHL All-Star first team (1992-93).

MISCELLANEOUS: Member of silver-medal-winning Canadian Olympic team (1994).

			REGULAR SEASON							PLAYOFFS						
Season	Team	League	Gms.	Min.	W	L	T	GA	SO	Avg.	Gms.	Min.	W	L	GA	SO	Avg.
89-90—	Vaughan-Thornhill	OHA Jr. B	29	1660	...	...	...	119	1	4.30	—	—			—	—	—
90-91—	Niagara Falls	OHL	30	1515	...	...	...	107	0	4.24	4	119	...	...	10	0	5.04
91-92—	Niagara Falls	OHL	43	2384	...	...	...	143	0	3.60	14	791	...	...	56	0	4.25
92-93—	Niagara Falls	OHL	†48	*2630	22	19	3	*170	0	3.88	4	240	0	4	18	0	4.50
93-94—	Can. national team	Int'l	16	859	8	6	0	36	2	2.51	—	—	—	—	—	—	—
94-95—	Springfield...................	AHL	39	2169	12	17	6	128	2	3.54	—	—	—	—	—	—	—

LEGG, MIKE

RW, DEVILS

PERSONAL: Born May 25, 1975, in London, Ont. . . . 5-11/164. . . . Shoots right.

HIGH SCHOOL: Westminster (London, Ont.).

COLLEGE: Michigan.

TRANSACTIONS/CAREER NOTES: Selected by New Jersey Devils in 11th round (11th Devils pick, 273rd overall) of NHL entry draft (June 26, 1993).

			REGULAR SEASON					PLAYOFFS			
Season	Team	League	Gms.	G	A	Pts.	PIM	Gms.	G	A	Pts.	PIM
90-91—	Westminster H.S.	Ont. H.S.	31	25	35	60	10	—	—	—	—	—
91-92—	London Jr. B	OHA	45	26	34	60	16	—	—	—	—	—
92-93—	London Jr. B	OHA	52	49	55	104	32	—	—	—	—	—
93-94—	University of Michigan	CCHA	37	10	13	23	20	—	—	—	—	—
94-95—	University of Michigan	CCHA	39	14	23	37	22	—	—	—	—	—

LEHOUX, GUY

D, MAPLE LEAFS

PERSONAL: Born October 19, 1971, in Disraeli, Que. . . . 5-11/210. . . . Shoots left. . . . Name pronounced leh-HOO.

TRANSACTIONS/CAREER NOTES: Selected by Toronto Maple Leafs in ninth round (ninth Maple Leafs pick, 179th overall) of NHL entry draft (June 22, 1991).

Season	Team	League	REGULAR SEASON					PLAYOFFS				
			Gms.	G	A	Pts.	PIM	Gms.	G	A	Pts.	PIM
89-90—Drummondville		QMJHL	66	4	17	21	178	—	—	—	—	—
90-91—Drummondville		QMJHL	63	8	26	34	107	14	1	7	8	24
91-92—St. John's		AHL	67	1	7	8	134	—	—	—	—	—
92-93—St. John's		AHL	42	3	2	5	89	—	—	—	—	—
—Brantford		Col.HL	13	0	5	5	28	4	0	1	1	15
93-94—St. John's		AHL	71	2	8	10	217	9	1	1	2	8
94-95—St. John's		AHL	77	4	9	13	255	5	0	0	0	2

LEHTINEN, JERE
RW, STARS

PERSONAL: Born June 24, 1973, in Espoo, Finland.... 6-0/185.... Shoots right.... Name pronounced YAIR-ee LEH-tih-nehn.
TRANSACTIONS/CAREER NOTES: Selected by Minnesota North Stars in fourth round (third North Stars pick, 88th overall) of NHL entry draft (June 20, 1992).... North Stars franchise moved from Minnesota to Dallas and renamed Stars for 1993-94 season.
MISCELLANEOUS: Member of bronze-medal-winning Finnish Olympic team (1994).

Season	Team	League	REGULAR SEASON					PLAYOFFS				
			Gms.	G	A	Pts.	PIM	Gms.	G	A	Pts.	PIM
90-91—Kiekko-Espoo		Finland	32	15	9	24	12	—	—	—	—	—
91-92—Kiekko-Espoo		Finland	43	32	17	49	6	—	—	—	—	—
92-93—Kiekko-Espoo		Finland	45	13	14	27	6	—	—	—	—	—
93-94—TPS Turku		Finland	42	19	20	39	6	11	11	2	13	2
—Finnish Olympic Team		Int'l	8	3	0	3	11	—	—	—	—	—
94-95—TPS Turku		Finland	39	19	23	42	33	13	8	6	14	4

LEITZA, BRIAN
G, PENGUINS

PERSONAL: Born August 31, 1975, in Lake Villa, Ill.... 6-2/185.... Catches left.
HIGH SCHOOL: Antioch (Ill.) Community.
COLLEGE: St. Cloud (Minn.) State.
TRANSACTIONS/CAREER NOTES: Selected by Pittsburgh Penguins in 11th round (14th Penguins pick, 284th overall) of NHL entry draft (June 29, 1994).
HONORS: Named to WCHA All-Rookie team (1994-95).

Season	Team	League	REGULAR SEASON							PLAYOFFS					
			Gms.	Min.	W	L	T	GA	SO	Avg.	Gms.	Min.	W	L	GA	SO	Avg.
93-94—Sioux City		USHL	32	1793	...	...	...	98	0	3.28	—	—	—	—	—	—	—
94-95—St. Cloud State		WCHA	30	1625	13	15	0	93	2	3.43	—	—	—	—	—	—	—

LEMIEUX, CLAUDE
RW, DEVILS

PERSONAL: Born July 16, 1965, in Buckingham, Que.... 6-1/215.... Shoots right.... Name pronounced luh-MYOO.... Brother of Jocelyn Lemieux, right winger, Hartford Whalers.
TRANSACTIONS/CAREER NOTES: Selected by Montreal Canadiens as underage junior in second round (second Canadiens pick, 26th overall) of NHL entry draft (June 8, 1983).... Tore ankle ligaments (October 1987).... Fractured orbital bone above right eye (January 14, 1988).... Pulled groin (March 1989).... Underwent surgery to repair torn stomach muscle (November 1, 1989); missed 41 games.... Traded by Canadiens to New Jersey Devils for LW Sylvain Turgeon (September 4, 1990).... Suffered contusion of right eye retina (February 25, 1991).... Suffered sore back (November 27, 1991); missed four games.... Injured ankle (March 11, 1992); missed two games.... Suffered back spasms (October 24, 1992); missed three games.... Injured right elbow (March 21, 1993); missed one game.... Suspended three games and fined $500 by NHL for altercation with opponent's bench (March 28, 1995).
HONORS: Named to QMJHL All-Star second team (1983-84).... Won Guy Lafleur Trophy (1984-85).... Named to QMJHL All-Star first team (1984-85).... Won Conn Smythe Trophy (1994-95).
STATISTICAL PLATEAUS: Three-goal games: 1988-89 (1), 1990-91 (2), 1992-93 (1). Total: 4.
MISCELLANEOUS: Member of Stanley Cup championship teams (1986 and 1995).

Season	Team	League	REGULAR SEASON					PLAYOFFS				
			Gms.	G	A	Pts.	PIM	Gms.	G	A	Pts.	PIM
82-83—Trois-Rivieres		QMJHL	62	28	38	66	187	4	1	0	1	30
83-84—Verdun		QMJHL	51	41	45	86	225	9	8	12	20	63
—Montreal		NHL	8	1	1	2	12	—	—	—	—	—
—Nova Scotia		AHL	—	—	—	—	—	2	1	0	1	0
84-85—Verdun		QMJHL	52	58	66	124	152	14	*23	17	*40	38
—Montreal		NHL	1	0	1	1	7	—	—	—	—	—
85-86—Sherbrooke		AHL	58	21	32	53	145	—	—	—	—	—
—Montreal		NHL	10	1	2	3	22	20	10	6	16	68
86-87—Montreal		NHL	76	27	26	53	156	17	4	9	13	41
87-88—Montreal		NHL	78	31	30	61	137	11	3	2	5	20
88-89—Montreal		NHL	69	29	22	51	136	18	4	3	7	58
89-90—Montreal		NHL	39	8	10	18	106	11	1	3	4	38
90-91—New Jersey		NHL	78	30	17	47	105	7	4	0	4	34
91-92—New Jersey		NHL	74	41	27	68	109	7	4	3	7	26
92-93—New Jersey		NHL	77	30	51	81	155	5	2	0	2	19
93-94—New Jersey		NHL	79	18	26	44	86	20	7	11	18	44
94-95—New Jersey		NHL	45	6	13	19	86	20	*13	3	16	20
NHL totals			634	222	226	448	1117	136	52	40	92	368

LEMIEUX, JOCELYN
RW, WHALERS

PERSONAL: Born November 18, 1967, in Mont-Laurier, Que. ... 5-10/200. ... Shoots left. ... Name pronounced luh-MYOO. ... Brother of Claude Lemieux, right winger, New Jersey Devils.

TRANSACTIONS/CAREER NOTES: Selected by St. Louis Blues as underage junior in first round (first Blues pick, 10th overall) of NHL entry draft (June 21, 1986). ... Severed tendon in left little finger (December 1986). ... Broke left leg and tore ligaments (January 1988). ... Traded by Blues with G Darrell May and second-round pick in 1989 draft (D Patrice Brisebois) to Montreal Canadiens for LW Sergio Momesso and G Vincent Riendeau (August 9, 1988). ... Traded by Canadiens to Chicago Blackhawks for third-round pick (D Charles Poulin) in 1990 draft (January 5, 1990). ... Suffered concussion and cracked orbital bone above right eye (February 26, 1991); missed a month. ... Traded by Blackhawks with D Frantisek Kucera to Hartford Whalers for LW Randy Cunneyworth and D Gary Suter (March 11, 1994). ... Injured shoulder (March 14, 1995); missed seven games.

HONORS: Named to QMJHL All-Star first team (1985-86).

STATISTICAL PLATEAUS: Three-goal games: 1989-90 (1), 1993-94 (1). Total: 2.

Season Team	League	REGULAR SEASON					PLAYOFFS				
		Gms.	G	A	Pts.	PIM	Gms.	G	A	Pts.	PIM
84-85—Laval	QMJHL	68	13	19	32	92	—	—	—	—	—
85-86—Laval	QMJHL	71	57	68	125	131	14	9	15	24	37
86-87—St. Louis	NHL	53	10	8	18	94	5	0	1	1	6
87-88—Peoria	IHL	8	0	5	5	35	—	—	—	—	—
—St. Louis	NHL	23	1	0	1	42	5	0	0	0	0
88-89—Montreal	NHL	1	0	1	1	0	—	—	—	—	—
—Sherbrooke	AHL	73	25	28	53	134	4	3	1	4	6
89-90—Montreal	NHL	34	4	2	6	61	—	—	—	—	—
—Chicago	NHL	39	10	11	21	47	18	1	8	9	28
90-91—Chicago	NHL	67	6	7	13	119	4	0	0	0	0
91-92—Chicago	NHL	78	6	10	16	80	18	3	1	4	33
92-93—Chicago	NHL	81	10	21	31	111	4	1	0	1	2
93-94—Chicago	NHL	66	12	8	20	63	—	—	—	—	—
—Hartford	NHL	16	6	1	7	19	—	—	—	—	—
94-95—Hartford	NHL	41	6	5	11	32	—	—	—	—	—
NHL totals		499	71	74	145	668	54	5	10	15	69

LEMIEUX, MARIO
C, PENGUINS

PERSONAL: Born October 5, 1965, in Montreal. ... 6-4/220. ... Shoots right. ... Name pronounced luh-MYOO. ... Brother of Alain Lemieux, center, St. Louis Blues, Quebec Nordiques and Pittsburgh Penguins (1981-82 through 1986-87).

TRANSACTIONS/CAREER NOTES: Selected by Pittsburgh Penguins as underage junior in first round (first Penguins pick, first overall) of NHL entry draft (June 9, 1984). ... Sprained left knee (September 1984). ... Reinjured knee (December 2, 1984). ... Sprained right knee (December 20, 1986). ... Bruised right shoulder (November 1987). ... Sprained right wrist (November 3, 1988). ... Suffered herniated disk (February 14, 1990); missed 21 games. ... Underwent surgery to remove part of herniated disk (July 11, 1990); missed first 50 games of season. ... Suffered back spasms (October 1991); missed three games. ... Suffered back spasms (January 4, 1992); missed three games. ... Injured back (January 29, 1992); missed six games. ... Suffered from the flu (February 1992); missed one game. ... Fractured bone in hand (May 5, 1992). ... Injured heel (December 1992); missed one game. ... Injured back (January 5, 1993); missed three games. ... Diagnosed with Hodgkin's Disease (January 12, 1993) and underwent radiation treatment (February 1-March 2); missed 20 games. ... Injured back prior to 1993-94 season; missed first 10 games of season. ... Injured back (October 28, 1993); missed one game. ... Injured back (November 2, 1993); missed one game. ... Suffered from the flu (November 9, 1993); missed one game. ... Injured back (November 11, 1993); missed 38 games. ... Injured back (February 13, 1994); missed two games. ... Injured back (February 19, 1994); missed two games. ... Injured back (March 12, 1994); missed four games. ... Fined $500 by NHL for charging at a referee (April 6, 1994). ... On medical leave of absence (entire 1994-95 season).

HONORS: Named to QMJHL All-Star second team (1982-83). ... Won Can.HL Player of the Year Award (1983-84). ... Won Michel Briere Trophy (1983-84). ... Won Jean Beliveau Trophy (1983-84). ... Won Michael Bossy Trophy (1983-84). ... Won Guy Lafleur Trophy (1983-84). ... Named to QMJHL All-Star first team (1983-84). ... Named NHL Rookie of the Year by THE SPORTING NEWS (1984-85). ... Won Calder Memorial Trophy (1984-85). ... Named to NHL All-Rookie team (1984-85). ... Won Lester B. Pearson Award (1985-86, 1987-88 and 1992-93). ... Named to THE SPORTING NEWS All-Star second team (1985-86). ... Named to NHL All-Star second team (1985-86, 1986-87 and 1991-92). ... Played in NHL All-Star Game (1985, 1986, 1988-1990 and 1992). ... Named All-Star Game Most Valuable Player (1985, 1988 and 1990). ... Named NHL Player of the Year by THE SPORTING NEWS (1987-88, 1988-89 and 1992-93). ... Won Hart Memorial Trophy (1987-88 and 1992-93). ... Won Art Ross Memorial Trophy (1987-88, 1988-89, 1991-92 and 1992-93). ... Won Dodge Performance of the Year Award (1987-88). ... Won Dodge Performer of the Year Award (1987-88 and 1988-89). ... Named to THE SPORTING NEWS All-Star first team (1987-88, 1988-89 and 1992-93). ... Named to NHL All-Star first team (1987-88, 1988-89 and 1992-93). ... Won Dodge Ram Tough Award (1988-89). ... Won Conn Smythe Trophy (1990-91 and 1991-92). ... Won Pro Set NHL Player of the Year Award (1991-92). ... Won Bill Masterton Memorial Trophy (1992-93).

RECORDS: Holds NHL career records for highest goals-per-game average—.825; and most overtime points—14. ... Shares NHL career record for most overtime goals—7. ... Holds NHL single-season record for most shorthanded goals—13 (1988-89). ... Shares NHL single-game playoff records for most goals—5 (April 25, 1989); most single-season playoff game-winning goals—5 (1992); most points—8 (April 25, 1989); most goals in one period—4 (April 25, 1989); and most points in one period—4 (April 25, 1989 and April 23, 1992). ... Holds NHL All-Star single-game record for most points—6 (1988). ... Shares NHL All-Star single-game record for most goals—4 (1990).

STATISTICAL PLATEAUS: Three-goal games: 1986-87 (5), 1987-88 (3), 1988-89 (7), 1989-90 (3), 1990-91 (1), 1991-92 (1), 1992-93 (1). Total: 21. ... Four-goal games: 1985-86 (1), 1986-87 (1), 1987-88 (2), 1988-89 (1), 1989-90 (1), 1992-93 (2). Total: 8. ... Five-goal games: 1988-89 (1), 1992-93 (1). Total: 2. ... Total hat tricks: 31.

MISCELLANEOUS: Member of Stanley Cup championship teams (1991 and 1992). ... Captain of Pittsburgh Penguins (1987-88 through 1993-94).

Season Team	League	REGULAR SEASON					PLAYOFFS				
		Gms.	G	A	Pts.	PIM	Gms.	G	A	Pts.	PIM
81-82—Laval	QMJHL	64	30	66	96	22	18	5	9	14	31
82-83—Laval	QMJHL	66	84	100	184	76	12	†14	18	32	18

Season Team	League	REGULAR SEASON					PLAYOFFS				
		Gms.	G	A	Pts.	PIM	Gms.	G	A	Pts.	PIM
83-84—Laval	QMJHL	70	*133	*149	*282	92	14	*29	*23	*52	29
84-85—Pittsburgh	NHL	73	43	57	100	54	—	—	—	—	—
85-86—Pittsburgh	NHL	79	48	93	141	43	—	—	—	—	—
86-87—Pittsburgh	NHL	63	54	53	107	57	—	—	—	—	—
87-88—Pittsburgh	NHL	77	*70	98	*168	92	—	—	—	—	—
88-89—Pittsburgh	NHL	76	*85	†114	*199	100	11	12	7	19	16
89-90—Pittsburgh	NHL	59	45	78	123	78	—	—	—	—	—
90-91—Pittsburgh	NHL	26	19	26	45	30	23	16	*28	*44	16
91-92—Pittsburgh	NHL	64	44	87	*131	94	15	*16	18	*34	2
92-93—Pittsburgh	NHL	60	69	91	*160	38	11	8	10	18	10
93-94—Pittsburgh	NHL	22	17	20	37	32	6	4	3	7	2
94-95—Pittsburgh	NHL					Did not play.					
NHL totals		599	494	717	1211	618	66	56	66	122	46

LEROUX, FRANCOIS

D, PENGUINS

PERSONAL: Born April 18, 1970, in St. Adele, Que. . . . 6-6/234. . . . Shoots left. . . . Name pronounced FRAN-swah luh-ROO.

TRANSACTIONS/CAREER NOTES: Selected by Edmonton Oilers in first round (first Oilers pick, 19th overall) of NHL entry draft (June 11, 1988). . . . Separated shoulder (March 20, 1989). . . . Traded by St. Jean Lynx with LW Patrick Lebeau and LW Jean Blouin to Victoriaville Tigres for RW Trevor Duhaime, second- and third-round draft picks and future considerations (February 15, 1990). . . . Tore left knee ligaments (March 18, 1990). . . . Underwent surgery to left knee (March 22, 1990). . . . Claimed on waivers by Ottawa Senators (October 6, 1993). . . . Fractured left thumb (December 6, 1993); missed 16 games. . . . Selected by Pittsburgh Penguins in 1994-95 waiver draft for cash (January 18, 1995). . . . Suffered from the flu (February 16, 1995); missed one game. . . . Twisted knee (March 9, 1995); missed two games. . . . Suffered back spasms (April 23, 1995); missed one game.

Season Team	League	REGULAR SEASON					PLAYOFFS				
		Gms.	G	A	Pts.	PIM	Gms.	G	A	Pts.	PIM
87-88—St. Jean	QMJHL	58	3	8	11	143	7	2	0	2	21
88-89—Edmonton	NHL	2	0	0	0	0	—	—	—	—	—
—St. Jean	QMJHL	57	8	34	42	185	—	—	—	—	—
89-90—Edmonton	NHL	3	0	1	1	0	—	—	—	—	—
—St. Jean/Victoriaville	QMJHL	54	4	33	37	160	—	—	—	—	—
90-91—Cape Breton	AHL	71	2	7	9	124	4	0	1	1	19
—Edmonton	NHL	1	0	2	2	0	—	—	—	—	—
91-92—Cape Breton	AHL	61	7	22	29	114	5	0	0	0	8
—Edmonton	NHL	4	0	0	0	7	—	—	—	—	—
92-93—Cape Breton	AHL	55	10	24	34	139	16	0	5	5	29
—Edmonton	NHL	1	0	0	0	4	—	—	—	—	—
93-94—Ottawa	NHL	23	0	1	1	70	—	—	—	—	—
—Prince Edward Island	AHL	25	4	6	10	52	—	—	—	—	—
94-95—Prince Edward Island	AHL	45	4	14	18	137	—	—	—	—	—
—Pittsburgh	NHL	40	0	2	2	114	12	0	2	2	14
NHL totals		74	0	6	6	195	12	0	2	2	14

LEROUX, JEAN-YVES

LW, BLACKHAWKS

PERSONAL: Born June 24, 1976, in Montreal. . . . 6-2/193. . . . Shoots left. . . . Name pronounced zhan-eev lair-OO.

TRANSACTIONS/CAREER NOTES: Selected by Chicago Blackhawks in second round (second Blackhawks pick, 40th overall) of NHL entry draft (June 28, 1994).

Season Team	League	REGULAR SEASON					PLAYOFFS				
		Gms.	G	A	Pts.	PIM	Gms.	G	A	Pts.	PIM
92-93—Beauport	QMJHL	62	20	25	45	33	—	—	—	—	—
93-94—Beauport	QMJHL	45	14	25	39	43	15	7	6	13	33
94-95—Beauport	QMJHL	59	19	33	52	125	17	4	6	10	39

LESCHYSHYN, CURTIS

D, DENVER

PERSONAL: Born September 21, 1969, in Thompson, Man. . . . 6-1/205. . . . Shoots left. . . . Full name: Curtis Michael Leschyshyn. . . . Name pronounced luh-SIH-shuhn.

TRANSACTIONS/CAREER NOTES: Selected by Quebec Nordiques in first round (first Nordiques pick, third overall) of NHL entry draft (June 11, 1988). . . . Separated shoulder (January 10, 1989). . . . Sprained left knee (November 1989). . . . Damaged knee ligaments (February 18, 1991) and underwent surgery (February 20, 1991); missed final 19 games of 1990-91 season and first 30 games of 1991-92 season. . . . Strained back (October 13, 1992); missed two games. . . . Strained right collar bone (December 30, 1994); missed two games. . . . Pulled thigh muscle (March 19, 1994); missed two games. . . . Injured groin (March 31, 1994); missed remainder of season. . . . Lacerated groin (April 22, 1995); missed last four games of season. . . . Nordiques franchise moved to Denver for 1995-96 season.

HONORS: Named to WHL (East) All-Star first team (1987-88).

Season Team	League	REGULAR SEASON					PLAYOFFS				
		Gms.	G	A	Pts.	PIM	Gms.	G	A	Pts.	PIM
85-86—Saskatoon	WHL	1	0	0	0	0	—	—	—	—	—
86-87—Saskatoon	WHL	70	14	26	40	107	11	1	5	6	14
87-88—Saskatoon	WHL	56	14	41	55	86	10	2	5	7	16
88-89—Quebec	NHL	71	4	9	13	71	—	—	—	—	—
89-90—Quebec	NHL	68	2	6	8	44	—	—	—	—	—

Season	Team	League	REGULAR SEASON					PLAYOFFS				
			Gms.	G	A	Pts.	PIM	Gms.	G	A	Pts.	PIM
90-91—Quebec	NHL	55	3	7	10	49	—	—	—	—	—
91-92—Quebec	NHL	42	5	12	17	42	—	—	—	—	—
—Halifax	AHL	6	0	2	2	4	—	—	—	—	—
92-93—Quebec	NHL	82	9	23	32	61	6	1	1	2	6
93-94—Quebec	NHL	72	5	17	22	65	—	—	—	—	—
94-95—Quebec	NHL	44	2	13	15	20	3	0	1	1	4
NHL totals			434	30	87	117	352	9	1	2	3	10

LESLIE, LEE
LW, SHARKS

PERSONAL: Born August 15, 1972, in Prince George, B.C. . . . 6-4/190. . . . Shoots left. **HIGH SCHOOL:** Carlton Comprensive (Prince Albert, Sask.). **TRANSACTIONS/CAREER NOTES:** Selected by St. Louis Blues in fourth round (fourth Blues pick, 86th overall) of NHL entry draft (June 20, 1992). . . . Signed as free agent by San Jose Sharks (June 21, 1993).

Season	Team	League	REGULAR SEASON					PLAYOFFS				
			Gms.	G	A	Pts.	PIM	Gms.	G	A	Pts.	PIM
88-89—Prince George	BCJHL	50	19	23	42	62	—	—	—	—	—
89-90—Prince Albert	WHL	62	14	16	30	13	14	2	3	5	4
90-91—Prince Albert	WHL	72	29	42	71	68	3	0	0	0	5
91-92—Prince Albert	WHL	72	52	48	100	70	10	6	6	12	12
92-93—Peoria	IHL	72	22	24	46	46	4	0	3	3	2
93-94—Kansas City	IHL	43	8	7	15	21	—	—	—	—	—
94-95—Kansas City	IHL	10	2	5	7	4	—	—	—	—	—
—Canadian national team	Int'l	17	6	0	6	16	—	—	—	—	—

LEVEQUE, GUY
C, MAPLE LEAFS

PERSONAL: Born December 28, 1972, in Kingston, Ont. . . . 5-11/166. . . . Shoots right. . . . Full name: Guy Scott Leveque. . . . Name pronounced GIGH luh-VEHK. . . . Cousin of Mike Murray, center, Philadelphia Flyers (1987-88). **TRANSACTIONS/CAREER NOTES:** Selected by Los Angeles Kings in second round (first Kings pick, 42nd overall) of NHL entry draft (June 22, 1991). . . . Traded by Kings with RW Dixon Ward, RW Shayne Toporowski and C Kelly Fairchild to Toronto Maple Leafs for LW Eric Lacroix, D Chris Snell and fourth-round pick in 1996 draft (October 3, 1994). . . . Loaned by Maple Leafs to Canadian national team (November 16, 1994).

Season	Team	League	REGULAR SEASON					PLAYOFFS				
			Gms.	G	A	Pts.	PIM	Gms.	G	A	Pts.	PIM
89-90—Cornwall	OHL	62	10	15	25	30	3	0	0	0	4
90-91—Cornwall	OHL	66	41	56	97	34	—	—	—	—	—
91-92—Cornwall	OHL	37	23	36	59	40	6	3	5	8	2
92-93—Phoenix	IHL	56	27	30	57	71	—	—	—	—	—
—Los Angeles	NHL	12	2	1	3	19	—	—	—	—	—
93-94—Phoenix	IHL	39	10	16	26	47	—	—	—	—	—
—Los Angeles	NHL	5	0	1	1	2	—	—	—	—	—
94-95—Canadian national team	Int'l	31	17	17	34	14	—	—	—	—	—
—Phoenix	IHL	2	0	0	0	15	—	—	—	—	—
—St. John's	AHL	37	8	14	22	31	3	0	0	0	0
NHL totals			17	2	2	4	21					

LEVINS, SCOTT
C/RW, SENATORS

PERSONAL: Born January 30, 1970, in Portland, Ore. . . . 6-4/216. . . . Shoots right. . . . Name pronounced LEH-vihns. **TRANSACTIONS/CAREER NOTES:** Selected by Winnipeg Jets in fourth round (fourth Jets pick, 75th overall) of NHL entry draft (June 16, 1990). . . . Bruised shoulder (November 17, 1992); missed four games. . . . Selected by Florida Panthers in NHL expansion draft (June 24, 1993). . . . Fractured hip bone (October 17, 1993); missed eight games. . . . Traded by Panthers with LW Evgeny Davydov and sixth-round pick (D Mike Gaffney) in 1994 draft to Ottawa Senators for RW Bob Kudelski (January 6, 1994). . . . Injured eye (January 10, 1994); missed one game. . . . Injured left knee (February 12, 1994); missed one game. . . . Injured back (March 15, 1994); missed four games. . . . Suffered ear infection (April 12, 1995); missed two games. **HONORS:** Named to WHL All-Star second team (1989-90).

Season	Team	League	REGULAR SEASON					PLAYOFFS				
			Gms.	G	A	Pts.	PIM	Gms.	G	A	Pts.	PIM
88-89—Penticton	BCJHL	50	27	58	85	154	—	—	—	—	—
89-90—Tri-City	WHL	71	25	37	62	132	6	2	3	5	18
90-91—Moncton	AHL	74	12	26	38	133	4	0	0	0	4
91-92—Moncton	AHL	69	15	18	33	271	11	3	4	7	30
92-93—Moncton	AHL	54	22	26	48	158	5	1	3	4	14
—Winnipeg	NHL	9	0	1	1	18	—	—	—	—	—
93-94—Florida	NHL	29	5	6	11	69	—	—	—	—	—
—Ottawa	NHL	33	3	5	8	93	—	—	—	—	—
94-95—Ottawa	NHL	24	5	6	11	51	—	—	—	—	—
—Prince Edward Island	AHL	6	0	4	4	14	—	—	—	—	—
NHL totals			95	13	18	31	231					

LIDSTER, DOUG

D, RANGERS

PERSONAL: Born October 18, 1960, in Kamloops, B.C. . . . 6-1/201. . . . Shoots right. . . . Full name: John Douglas Andrew Lidster.
COLLEGE: Colorado College.
TRANSACTIONS/CAREER NOTES: Selected by Vancouver Canucks in seventh round (sixth Canucks pick, 133rd overall) of NHL entry draft (June 11, 1980). . . . Strained left knee (January 1988). . . . Hyperextended elbow (October 1988). . . . Broke hand (November 13, 1988). . . . Fractured cheekbone (March 1989). . . . Separated shoulder (March 1, 1992); missed 13 games. . . . Sprained knee (December 13, 1992); missed nine games. . . . Suffered from the flu (February 24, 1993); missed one game. . . . Traded by Canucks to New York Rangers (June 25, 1993) to complete deal in which Rangers sent G John Vanbiesbrouck to Canucks for future considerations (June 20, 1993). . . . Traded by Rangers with LW Esa Tikkanen to St. Louis Blues for C Petr Nedved (July 24, 1994); trade arranged as compensation for Blues signing Coach Mike Keenan. . . . Broke nose (April 27, 1995); missed two games. . . . Traded by Blues to Rangers for D Jay Wells (July 31, 1995).
HONORS: Named to WCHA All-Star first team (1981-82 and 1982-83). . . . Named to NCAA All-America West team (1982-83).
MISCELLANEOUS: Captain of Vancouver Canucks (1990-91). . . . Member of Stanley Cup championship team (1994).

Season Team	League	REGULAR SEASON					PLAYOFFS				
		Gms.	G	A	Pts.	PIM	Gms.	G	A	Pts.	PIM
77-78—Seattle	WHL	2	0	0	0	0	—	—	—	—	—
78-79—Kamloops	BCJHL	59	36	47	83	50	—	—	—	—	—
79-80—Colorado College	WCHA	39	18	25	43	52	—	—	—	—	—
80-81—Colorado College	WCHA	36	10	30	40	54	—	—	—	—	—
81-82—Colorado College	WCHA	36	13	22	35	32	—	—	—	—	—
82-83—Colorado College	WCHA	34	15	41	56	30	—	—	—	—	—
83-84—Canadian Olympic Team	Int'l	59	6	20	26	28	—	—	—	—	—
—Vancouver	NHL	8	0	0	0	4	2	0	1	1	0
84-85—Vancouver	NHL	78	6	24	30	55	—	—	—	—	—
85-86—Vancouver	NHL	78	12	16	28	56	3	0	1	1	2
86-87—Vancouver	NHL	80	12	51	63	40	—	—	—	—	—
87-88—Vancouver	NHL	64	4	32	36	105	—	—	—	—	—
88-89—Vancouver	NHL	63	5	17	22	78	7	1	1	2	9
89-90—Vancouver	NHL	80	8	28	36	36	—	—	—	—	—
90-91—Vancouver	NHL	78	6	32	38	77	6	0	2	2	6
91-92—Vancouver	NHL	66	6	23	29	39	11	1	2	3	11
92-93—Vancouver	NHL	71	6	19	25	36	12	0	3	3	8
93-94—New York Rangers	NHL	34	0	2	2	33	9	2	0	2	10
94-95—St. Louis	NHL	37	2	7	9	12	4	0	0	0	2
NHL totals		737	67	251	318	571	54	4	10	14	48

LIDSTROM, NICKLAS

D, RED WINGS

PERSONAL: Born April 28, 1970, in Vasteras, Sweden. . . . 6-2/185. . . . Shoots left. . . . Name pronounced NIHK-luhs LIHD-struhm.
TRANSACTIONS/CAREER NOTES: Selected by Detroit Red Wings in third round (third Red Wings pick, 53rd overall) of NHL entry draft (June 17, 1989). . . . Played in Europe during 1994-95 NHL lockout. . . . Suffered back spasms (April 9, 1995); missed five games.
HONORS: Named to Swedish League All-Star team (1990-91). . . . Named to NHL All-Rookie team (1991-92).

Season Team	League	REGULAR SEASON					PLAYOFFS				
		Gms.	G	A	Pts.	PIM	Gms.	G	A	Pts.	PIM
88-89—Vasteras	Sweden	19	0	2	2	4	—	—	—	—	—
89-90—Vasteras	Sweden	39	8	8	16	14	—	—	—	—	—
90-91—Vasteras	Sweden	20	2	12	14	14	—	—	—	—	—
91-92—Detroit	NHL	80	11	49	60	22	11	1	2	3	0
92-93—Detroit	NHL	84	7	34	41	28	7	1	0	1	0
93-94—Detroit	NHL	84	10	46	56	26	7	3	2	5	0
94-95—Vasteras	Sweden	13	2	10	12	4	—	—	—	—	—
—Detroit	NHL	43	10	16	26	6	18	4	12	16	8
NHL totals		291	38	145	183	82	43	9	16	25	8

LILLEY, JOHN

RW, MIGHTY DUCKS

PERSONAL: Born August 3, 1972, in Wakefield, Mass. . . . 5-0/170. . . . Shoots right.
COLLEGE: Boston University.
TRANSACTIONS/CAREER NOTES: Selected by Winnipeg Jets in eighth round (eighth Jets pick, 140th overall) of NHL entry draft (June 16, 1990). . . . Signed as free agent by Mighty Ducks of Anaheim (March 9, 1994).

Season Team	League	REGULAR SEASON					PLAYOFFS				
		Gms.	G	A	Pts.	PIM	Gms.	G	A	Pts.	PIM
91-92—Boston University	Hockey East	23	9	9	18	43	—	—	—	—	—
92-93—Boston University	Hockey East	4	0	1	1	13	—	—	—	—	—
—Seattle	WHL	45	22	28	50	55	5	1	3	4	9
93-94—U.S. national team	Int'l	58	27	23	50	117	—	—	—	—	—
—U.S. Olympic Team	Int'l	8	3	1	4	16	—	—	—	—	—
—San Diego	IHL	2	2	1	3	0	—	—	—	—	—
—Anaheim	NHL	13	1	6	7	8	—	—	—	—	—
94-95—San Diego	IHL	45	9	15	24	71	2	0	0	0	2
—Anaheim	NHL	9	2	2	4	5	—	—	—	—	—
NHL totals		22	3	8	11	13					

LIND, JUHA
C, STARS

PERSONAL: Born January 2, 1974, in Helsinki, Finland. . . . 5-11/160. . . . Shoots left.
TRANSACTIONS/CAREER NOTES: Selected by Minnesota North Stars in eighth round (sixth North Stars pick, 178th overall) of NHL entry draft (June 26, 1992). . . . North Stars franchise moved from Minnesota to Dallas and renamed Stars for 1993-94 season.

			REGULAR SEASON					PLAYOFFS			
Season Team	League	Gms.	G	A	Pts.	PIM	Gms.	G	A	Pts.	PIM
91-92—Jokerit Helsinki Jrs.	Finland	28	16	24	40	10	—	—	—	—	—
92-93—Vantaa HT	Finland Dv.II	25	8	12	20	8	—	—	—	—	—
—Jokerit Helsinki	Finland	6	0	0	0	2	1	0	0	0	0
93-94—Jokerit Helsinki	Finland	47	17	11	28	37	11	2	5	7	4
94-95—Jokerit Helsinki	Finland	50	10	8	18	12	11	1	2	3	6

LINDEN, JAMIE
RW, PANTHERS

PERSONAL: Born July 19, 1972, in Medicine Hat, Alta. . . . 6-3/185. . . . Shoots right. . . . Brother of Trevor Linden, right winger, Vancouver Canucks.
TRANSACTIONS/CAREER NOTES: Signed as free agent by Florida Panthers (October 4, 1993).

			REGULAR SEASON					PLAYOFFS			
Season Team	League	Gms.	G	A	Pts.	PIM	Gms.	G	A	Pts.	PIM
90-91—Prince Albert	WHL	64	9	12	21	114	3	0	0	0	0
91-92—Prince Albert	WHL	4	2	1	3	8	—	—	—	—	—
—Spokane	WHL	60	7	10	17	302	10	0	0	0	69
92-93—Medicine Hat	WHL	65	12	10	22	205	—	—	—	—	—
93-94—Cincinnati	IHL	47	1	5	6	55	2	0	0	0	2
—Birmingham	ECHL	16	3	7	10	38	—	—	—	—	—
94-95—Cincinnati	IHL	51	3	6	9	173	—	—	—	—	—
—Florida	NHL	4	0	0	0	17	—	—	—	—	—
NHL totals		4	0	0	0	17					

LINDEN, TREVOR
RW, CANUCKS

PERSONAL: Born April 11, 1970, in Medicine Hat, Alta. . . . 6-4/210. . . . Shoots right. . . . Brother of Jamie Linden, right winger in Florida Panthers system.
TRANSACTIONS/CAREER NOTES: Selected by Vancouver Canucks in first round (first Canucks pick, second overall) of NHL entry draft (June 11, 1988). . . . Hyperextended elbow (October 1989). . . . Separated shoulder (March 17, 1990).
HONORS: Named to WHL All-Star second team (1987-88). . . . Named to Memorial Cup All-Star team (1987-88). . . . Named to NHL All-Rookie team (1988-89). . . . Played in NHL All-Star Game (1991 and 1992).
STATISTICAL PLATEAUS: Three-goal games: 1988-89 (2), 1990-91 (1). Total: 3.
MISCELLANEOUS: Captain of Vancouver Canucks (1990-91 through 1994-95).

			REGULAR SEASON					PLAYOFFS			
Season Team	League	Gms.	G	A	Pts.	PIM	Gms.	G	A	Pts.	PIM
85-86—Medicine Hat	WHL	5	2	0	2	0	—	—	—	—	—
86-87—Medicine Hat	WHL	72	14	22	36	59	20	5	4	9	17
87-88—Medicine Hat	WHL	67	46	64	110	76	16	†13	12	25	19
88-89—Vancouver	NHL	80	30	29	59	41	7	3	4	7	8
89-90—Vancouver	NHL	73	21	30	51	43	—	—	—	—	—
90-91—Vancouver	NHL	80	33	37	70	65	6	0	7	7	2
91-92—Vancouver	NHL	80	31	44	75	101	13	4	8	12	6
92-93—Vancouver	NHL	84	33	39	72	64	12	5	8	13	16
93-94—Vancouver	NHL	84	32	29	61	73	24	12	13	25	18
94-95—Vancouver	NHL	48	18	22	40	40	11	2	6	8	12
NHL totals		529	198	230	428	427	73	26	46	72	62

LINDGREN, MATS
C, OILERS

PERSONAL: Born October 1, 1974, in Skelleftea, Sweden. . . . 6-1/190. . . . Shoots left.
HIGH SCHOOL: Lindsay Thurber (Red Deer, Alta.).
TRANSACTIONS/CAREER NOTES: Selected by Winnipeg Jets in first round (first Jets pick, 15th overall) of NHL entry draft (June 26, 1993). . . . Traded by Jets with D Boris Mironov and first-round (C Jason Bonsignore) and fourth-round (RW Adam Copeland) picks in 1994 draft to Edmonton Oilers for D Dave Manson and sixth-round pick in 1994 draft (March 15, 1994). . . . Strained lower back (March 17, 1995); missed 23 games.
HONORS: Named Swedish League Rookie of the Year (1993-94).

			REGULAR SEASON					PLAYOFFS			
Season Team	League	Gms.	G	A	Pts.	PIM	Gms.	G	A	Pts.	PIM
90-91—Skelleftea	Swed. Dv.II	1	0	0	0	0	—	—	—	—	—
91-92—Skelleftea	Swed. Dv.II	29	14	8	22	14	—	—	—	—	—
92-93—Skelleftea	Swed. Dv.II	32	20	14	34	18	—	—	—	—	—
93-94—Farjestad Karlstad	Sweden	22	11	6	17	26	—	—	—	—	—
94-95—Farjestad Karlstad	Sweden	37	17	15	32	20	3	0	0	0	4

LINDROS, BRETT
RW, ISLANDERS

PERSONAL: Born December 2, 1975, in Toronto. . . . 6-4/215. . . . Shoots right. . . . Name pronounced LIHND-rahz. . . . Brother of Eric Lindros, center, Philadelphia Flyers.
TRANSACTIONS/CAREER NOTES: Injured left knee (January 6, 1994). . . . Selected by New York Islanders in first round (first Islanders pick, ninth overall) of NHL entry draft (June 28, 1994). . . . Injured wrist (January 31, 1995); missed one game. . . . Suffered concussion (February 9, 1995); missed eight games. . . . Sprained knee (March 14, 1995); missed two games. . . . Suffered from back spasms (April 8, 1995); missed three games.

L

Season Team	League	REGULAR SEASON					PLAYOFFS				
		Gms.	G	A	Pts.	PIM	Gms.	G	A	Pts.	PIM
91-92—St. Michaels Tier II	Jr. A	34	21	21	42	210	—	—	—	—	—
92-93—Kingston	OHL	31	11	11	22	162	—	—	—	—	—
—Canadian national team ...	Int'l	11	1	6	7	33	—	—	—	—	—
93-94—Kingston	OHL	15	4	6	10	94	3	0	0	0	18
—Canadian national team ...	Int'l	44	7	7	14	118	—	—	—	—	—
94-95—Kingston	OHL	26	24	23	47	63	—	—	—	—	—
—New York Islanders..........	NHL	33	1	3	4	100	—	—	—	—	—
NHL totals.................		33	1	3	4	100	—	—	—	—	—

LINDROS, ERIC

C, FLYERS

PERSONAL: Born February 28, 1973, in London, Ont. . . . 6-4/229. . . . Shoots right. . . . Name pronounced LIHND-rahz. . . . Brother of Brett Lindros, right winger, New York Islanders.
TRANSACTIONS/CAREER NOTES: Selected by Sault Ste. Marie Greyhounds in OHL priority draft; refused to report (August 30, 1989); played for Detroit Compuware. . . . Rights traded by Greyhounds to Oshawa Generals for RW Mike DeCoff, RW Jason Denomme, G Mike Lenarduzzi, second-round picks in 1991 and 1992 drafts and cash (December 17, 1989). . . . Suspended two games by OHL for fighting (February 7, 1990). . . . Selected by Quebec Nordiques in first round (first Nordiques pick, first overall) of NHL entry draft (June 22, 1991); refused to report. . . . Traded by Nordiques to Philadelphia Flyers for G Ron Hextall, C Mike Ricci, C Peter Forsberg, D Steve Duchesne, D Kerry Huffman, first-round pick in 1993 draft (G Jocelyn Thibault), cash and future considerations (June 20, 1992); Flyers sent LW Chris Simon and first-round pick in 1994 draft (traded to Toronto Maple Leafs) to Nordiques to complete deal (July 21, 1992). . . . Sprained medial collateral ligament (November 22, 1992); missed nine games. . . . Injured knee (December 29, 1992); missed two games. . . . Reinjured knee (January 10, 1993); missed 12 games. . . . Tore ligament in right knee (November 12, 1993); missed 14 games. . . . Suffered back spasms (March 6, 1994); missed one game. . . . Sprained shoulder (April 4, 1994); missed remainder of season. . . . Suffered from the flu (January 29, 1995); missed one game. . . . Bruised eye (April 30, 1995); missed last game of season and first three playoff games.
HONORS: Named to Memorial Cup All-Star Team (1989-90). . . . Won Can.HL Player of the Year Award (1990-91). . . . Won Can.HL Plus/Minus Award (1990-91). . . . Won Can.HL Top Draft Prospect Award (1990-91). . . . Won Red Tilson Trophy (1990-91). . . . Won Eddie Powers Memorial Trophy (1990-91). . . . Named to OHL All-Star first team (1990-91). . . . Named to NHL All-Rookie team (1992-93). . . . Played in NHL All-Star Game (1994). . . . Named NHL Player of the Year by THE SPORTING NEWS (1994-95). . . . Won Hart Memorial Trophy (1994-95). . . . Named to THE SPORTING NEWS All-Star first team (1994-95). . . . Named to NHL All-Star first team (1994-95).
STATISTICAL PLATEAUS: Three-goal games: 1992-93 (3), 1993-94 (1), 1994-95 (3). Total: 7.
MISCELLANEOUS: Member of silver-medal-winning Canadian Olympic team (1992). . . . Captain of Philadelphia Flyers (1994-95).

Season Team	League	REGULAR SEASON					PLAYOFFS				
		Gms.	G	A	Pts.	PIM	Gms.	G	A	Pts.	PIM
88-89—St. Michaels	MTHL	37	24	43	67	193	—	—	—	—	—
89-90—Detroit Compuware..........	NAJHL	14	23	29	52	123	—	—	—	—	—
—Oshawa	OHL	25	17	19	36	61	17	*18	18	36	*76
90-91—Oshawa	OHL	57	*71	78	*149	189	16	*18	20	*38	*93
91-92—Oshawa	OHL	13	9	22	31	54	—	—	—	—	—
—Canadian national team ...	Int'l	24	19	16	35	34	—	—	—	—	—
—Canadian Olympic Team ..	Int'l	8	5	6	11	6	—	—	—	—	—
92-93—Philadelphia	NHL	61	41	34	75	147	—	—	—	—	—
93-94—Philadelphia	NHL	65	44	53	97	103	—	—	—	—	—
94-95—Philadelphia	NHL	46	29	41	†70	60	12	4	11	15	18
NHL totals.................		172	114	128	242	310	12	4	11	15	18

LINDSAY, BILL

LW, PANTHERS

PERSONAL: Born May 17, 1971, in Big Fork, Mont. . . . 5-11/190. . . . Shoots left. . . . Full name: William Hamilton Lindsay.
TRANSACTIONS/CAREER NOTES: Selected by Quebec Nordiques in fifth round (sixth Nordiques pick, 103rd overall) of NHL entry draft (June 22, 1991). . . . Separated right shoulder (December 26, 1992); missed four games. . . . Selected by Florida Panthers in NHL expansion draft (June 24, 1993).
HONORS: Named to WHL (West) All-Star second team (1991-92).

Season Team	League	REGULAR SEASON					PLAYOFFS				
		Gms.	G	A	Pts.	PIM	Gms.	G	A	Pts.	PIM
89-90—Tri-City	WHL	72	40	45	85	84	—	—	—	—	—
90-91—Tri-City	WHL	63	46	47	93	151	—	—	—	—	—
91-92—Tri-City	WHL	42	34	59	93	111	3	2	3	5	16
—Quebec	NHL	23	2	4	6	14	—	—	—	—	—
92-93—Quebec	NHL	44	4	9	13	16	—	—	—	—	—
—Halifax............................	AHL	20	11	13	24	18	—	—	—	—	—
93-94—Florida	NHL	84	6	6	12	97	—	—	—	—	—
94-95—Florida	NHL	48	10	9	19	46	—	—	—	—	—
NHL totals.................		199	22	28	50	173	—	—	—	—	—

LING, DAVID

RW, DENVER

PERSONAL: Born January 9, 1975, in Halifax, N.S. . . . 5-9/185. . . . Shoots right.
TRANSACTIONS/CAREER NOTES: Selected by Quebec Nordiques in seventh round (ninth Nordiques pick, 179th overall) of NHL entry draft (June 29, 1993). . . . Nordiques franchise moved to Denver for 1995-96 season.
HONORS: Won Can.HL Player of the Year Award (1994-95). . . . Won Jim Mahon Memorial Trophy (1994-95). . . . Won Red Tilson Trophy (1994-95). . . . Named to Can.HL All-Star first team (1994-95). . . . Named to OHL All-Star first team (1994-95).

Season	Team	League	Gms.	G	A	Pts.	PIM	Gms.	G	A	Pts.	PIM
92-93—Kingston	OHL	64	17	46	63	275	16	3	12	15	72
93-94—Kingston	OHL	61	37	40	77	254	6	4	2	6	16
94-95—Kingston	OHL	62	*61	74	135	136	6	7	8	15	12

LiPUMA, CHRIS
D, LIGHTNING

PERSONAL: Born March 23, 1971, in Chicago. . . . 6-0/ 183. . . . Shoots left. . . . Name pronounced luh-POO-muh.

TRANSACTIONS/CAREER NOTES: Signed as free agent by Tampa Bay Lightning (August 24, 1992). . . . Sprained left knee (February 7, 1995); missed nine games.

			REGULAR SEASON					PLAYOFFS				
Season	Team	League	Gms.	G	A	Pts.	PIM	Gms.	G	A	Pts.	PIM
88-89—Kitchener	OHL	59	7	13	20	101	—	—	—	—	—
89-90—Kitchener	OHL	63	11	26	37	125	17	1	4	5	6
90-91—Kitchener	OHL	61	6	30	36	145	4	0	1	1	4
91-92—Kitchener	OHL	61	13	59	72	115	14	4	9	13	34
92-93—Atlanta	IHL	66	4	14	18	379	9	1	1	2	35
—Tampa Bay	NHL	15	0	5	5	34	—	—	—	—	—
93-94—Tampa Bay	NHL	27	0	4	4	77	—	—	—	—	—
—Atlanta	IHL	42	2	10	12	254	11	1	1	2	28
94-95—Atlanta	IHL	41	5	12	17	191	—	—	—	—	—
—Tampa Bay	NHL	1	0	0	0	0	—	—	—	—	—
—Nashville	ECHL	1	0	0	0	0	—	—	—	—	—
NHL totals		43	0	9	9	111					

LITTLE, NEIL
G, FLYERS

PERSONAL: Born December 18, 1971, in Medicine Hat, Alta. . . . 6-1/ 180. . . . Catches left.
COLLEGE: Rensselaer Polytechnic Institute (N.Y.).
TRANSACTIONS/CAREER NOTES: Selected by Philadelphia Flyers in 11th round (10th Flyers pick, 226th overall) of NHL entry draft (June 22, 1991).
HONORS: Named SJHL Rookie of the Year (1989-90). . . . Named to SJHL All-Star first team (1989-90). . . . Named NCAA All-America East second team (1992-93). . . . Named to ECAC All-Star first team (1992-93).

			REGULAR SEASON							PLAYOFFS						
Season	Team	League	Gms.	Min.	W	L	T	GA	SO	Avg.	Gms.	Min.	W	L	GA	SO	Avg.
89-90—Estevan	SJHL	46	2707	21	19	4	150	1	3.32	—	—	—	—	—	—	—
90-91—R.P.I.	ECAC	18	1032	9	8	0	71	0	4.13	—	—	—	—	—	—	—
91-92—R.P.I.	ECAC	28	1532	11	11	3	96	0	3.76	—	—	—	—	—	—	—
92-93—R.P.I.	ECAC	31	1801	19	9	3	88	0	2.93	—	—	—	—	—	—	—
93-94—R.P.I.	ECAC	27	1570	16	7	4	88	0	3.36	—	—	—	—	—	—	—
—Hershey	AHL	1	18	0	0	0	1	0	3.33	—	—	—	—	—	—	—
94-95—Hershey	AHL	19	919	5	7	3	60	0	3.92	—	—	—	—	—	—	—
—Johnstown	ECHL	16	897	7	6	‡1	55	0	3.68	3	145	0	2	11	0	4.55

LOACH, LONNIE
LW

PERSONAL: Born April 14, 1968, in New Liskeard, Ont. . . . 5-10/ 181. . . . Shoots left.
TRANSACTIONS/CAREER NOTES: Selected by Chicago Blackhawks as underage junior in fifth round (fourth Blackhawks pick, 98th overall) of NHL entry draft (June 21, 1986). . . . Signed as free agent by Fort Wayne Komets (August 1990). . . . Signed as free agent by Detroit Red Wings (April 20, 1991). . . . Selected by Ottawa Senators in NHL expansion draft (June 18, 1992). . . . Claimed on waivers by Los Angeles Kings (October 21, 1992). . . . Fractured thumb (December 13, 1992); missed 11 games. . . . Selected by Mighty Ducks of Anaheim in NHL expansion draft (June 24, 1993). . . . Traded by San Diego Gulls to Detroit Vipers for C Ron Wilson (November 8, 1994).
HONORS: Won Emms Family Award (1985-86). . . . Won Leo P. Lamoureux Memorial Trophy (1990-91). . . . Named to IHL All-Star second team (1990-91).

			REGULAR SEASON					PLAYOFFS				
Season	Team	League	Gms.	G	A	Pts.	PIM	Gms.	G	A	Pts.	PIM
84-85—St. Mary's Jr. B	OHA	44	26	36	62	113	—	—	—	—	—
85-86—Guelph	OHL	65	41	42	83	63	20	7	8	15	16
86-87—Guelph	OHL	56	31	24	55	42	5	2	1	3	2
87-88—Guelph	OHL	66	43	49	92	75	—	—	—	—	—
88-89—Saginaw	IHL	32	7	6	13	27	—	—	—	—	—
—Flint	IHL	41	22	26	48	30	—	—	—	—	—
89-90—Indianapolis	IHL	3	0	1	1	0	—	—	—	—	—
—Fort Wayne	IHL	54	15	33	48	40	5	4	2	6	15
90-91—Fort Wayne	IHL	81	55	76	*131	45	19	5	11	16	13
91-92—Adirondack	AHL	67	37	49	86	69	†19	*13	4	17	10
92-93—Ottawa	NHL	3	0	0	0	0	—	—	—	—	—
—Los Angeles	NHL	50	10	13	23	27	1	0	0	0	0
—Phoenix	IHL	4	2	3	5	10	—	—	—	—	—
93-94—San Diego	IHL	74	42	49	91	65	9	4	10	14	6
—Anaheim	NHL	3	0	0	0	2	—	—	—	—	—
94-95—San Diego	IHL	13	3	10	13	21	—	—	—	—	—
—Detroit	IHL	64	32	43	75	45	3	2	1	3	2
NHL totals		56	10	13	23	29	1	0	0	0	0

L

LOMAKIN, ANDREI

LW, PANTHERS

PERSONAL: Born April 3, 1964, in Voskresensk, U.S.S.R. . . . 5-10/178. . . . Shoots left. . . . Name pronounced AHN-dray loh-MAH-kihn.

TRANSACTIONS/CAREER NOTES: Selected by Philadelphia Flyers in seventh round (sixth Flyers pick, 107th overall) of NHL entry draft (June 22, 1991). . . . Fractured thumb (January 23, 1992); missed 15 games. . . . Bruised ribs prior to 1992-93 season; missed first game of season. . . . Bruised right foot (November 27, 1992); missed one game. . . . Separated shoulder (February 14, 1993); missed 10 games. . . . Selected by Florida Panthers in NHL expansion draft (June 24, 1993). . . . Bruised tendon in right knee (October 14, 1993); missed one game. . . . Bruised left shoulder (October 28, 1993); missed six games.

MISCELLANEOUS: Member of gold-medal-winning U.S.S.R. Olympic team (1988).

			REGULAR SEASON					PLAYOFFS				
Season	Team	League	Gms.	G	A	Pts.	PIM	Gms.	G	A	Pts.	PIM
81-82—Khimik Voskresensk		USSR	8	1	1	2	2	—	—	—	—	—
82-83—Khimik Voskresensk		USSR	56	15	8	23	32	—	—	—	—	—
83-84—Khimik Voskresensk		USSR	44	10	8	18	26	—	—	—	—	—
84-85—Khimik Voskresensk		USSR	52	13	10	23	24	—	—	—	—	—
86-87—Dynamo Moscow		USSR	40	15	14	29	30	—	—	—	—	—
87-88—Dynamo Moscow		USSR	45	10	15	25	24	—	—	—	—	—
88-89—Dynamo Moscow		USSR	44	9	16	25	22	—	—	—	—	—
89-90—Dynamo Moscow		USSR	48	11	15	26	36	—	—	—	—	—
90-91—Dynamo Moscow		USSR	45	16	17	33	22	—	—	—	—	—
91-92—Philadelphia		NHL	57	14	16	30	26	—	—	—	—	—
92-93—Philadelphia		NHL	51	8	12	20	34	—	—	—	—	—
93-94—Florida		NHL	76	19	28	47	26	—	—	—	—	—
94-95—Florida		NHL	31	1	6	7	6	—	—	—	—	—
NHL totals			215	42	62	104	92					

LONEY, BRIAN

RW, CANUCKS

PERSONAL: Born August 9, 1972, in Winnipeg. . . . 6-2/195. . . . Shoots right.

COLLEGE: Ohio State.

TRANSACTIONS/CAREER NOTES: Selected by Vancouver Canucks in fifth round (sixth Canucks pick, 110th overall) of NHL entry draft (June 20, 1992).

HONORS: Named CCHA Rookie of the Year (1991-92).

			REGULAR SEASON					PLAYOFFS				
Season	Team	League	Gms.	G	A	Pts.	PIM	Gms.	G	A	Pts.	PIM
91-92—Ohio State		CCHA	37	21	34	55	109	—	—	—	—	—
92-93—Red Deer		WHL	66	39	36	75	147	4	1	1	2	19
—Canadian national team		Int'l	1	0	1	1	0	—	—	—	—	—
—Hamilton		AHL	3	0	2	2	0	—	—	—	—	—
93-94—Hamilton		AHL	67	18	16	34	76	4	0	0	0	8
94-95—Syracuse		AHL	67	23	17	40	98	—	—	—	—	—

LONEY, TROY

LW, RANGERS

PERSONAL: Born September 21, 1963, in Bow Island, Alta. . . . 6-3/210. . . . Shoots left. . . . Name pronounced LOH-nee.

TRANSACTIONS/CAREER NOTES: Selected by Pittsburgh Penguins as underage junior in third round (third Penguins pick, 52nd overall) of NHL entry draft (June 9, 1982). . . . Suspended by AHL (December 1986). . . . Sprained right shoulder (January 17, 1987). . . . Underwent knee surgery (October 1987). . . . Suspended 10 games by NHL for leaving bench to fight (November 13, 1988). . . . Broke right hand (November 24, 1989); missed 12 games. . . . Underwent surgery to right knee (June 1990); missed first two months of season. . . . Bruised neck (November 8, 1992); missed two games. . . . Selected by Mighty Ducks of Anaheim in NHL expansion draft (June 24, 1993). . . . Bruised right knee (October 28, 1993); missed four games. . . . Underwent arthroscopic knee surgery (November 17, 1993); missed 17 games. . . . Traded by Mighty Ducks to New York Islanders for D Tom Kurvers (June 29, 1994). . . . Claimed on waivers by New York Rangers (April 7, 1995).

MISCELLANEOUS: Member of Stanley Cup championship teams (1991 and 1992). . . . Captain of Mighty Ducks of Anaheim (1993-94).

			REGULAR SEASON					PLAYOFFS				
Season	Team	League	Gms.	G	A	Pts.	PIM	Gms.	G	A	Pts.	PIM
80-81—Lethbridge		WHL	71	18	13	31	100	9	2	3	5	14
81-82—Lethbridge		WHL	71	26	31	57	152	12	3	3	6	10
82-83—Lethbridge		WHL	72	33	34	67	156	20	10	7	17	43
83-84—Baltimore		AHL	63	18	13	31	147	10	0	2	2	19
—Pittsburgh		NHL	13	0	0	0	9	—	—	—	—	—
84-85—Baltimore		AHL	15	4	2	6	25	—	—	—	—	—
—Pittsburgh		NHL	46	10	8	18	59	—	—	—	—	—
85-86—Baltimore		AHL	33	12	11	23	84	—	—	—	—	—
—Pittsburgh		NHL	47	3	9	12	95	—	—	—	—	—
86-87—Baltimore		AHL	40	13	14	27	134	—	—	—	—	—
—Pittsburgh		NHL	23	8	7	15	22	—	—	—	—	—
87-88—Pittsburgh		NHL	65	5	13	18	151	—	—	—	—	—
88-89—Pittsburgh		NHL	69	10	6	16	165	11	1	3	4	24
89-90—Pittsburgh		NHL	67	11	16	27	168	—	—	—	—	—
90-91—Muskegon		IHL	2	0	0	0	5	—	—	—	—	—
—Pittsburgh		NHL	44	7	9	16	85	24	2	2	4	41
91-92—Pittsburgh		NHL	76	10	16	26	127	†21	4	5	9	32
92-93—Pittsburgh		NHL	82	5	16	21	99	10	1	4	5	0
93-94—Anaheim		NHL	62	13	6	19	88	—	—	—	—	—

Season Team	League	REGULAR SEASON					PLAYOFFS				
		Gms.	G	A	Pts.	PIM	Gms.	G	A	Pts.	PIM
94-95—New York Islanders..........	NHL	26	5	4	9	23	—	—	—	—	—
—New York Rangers	NHL	4	0	0	0	0	1	0	0	0	0
NHL totals.................................		624	87	110	197	1091	67	8	14	22	97

LORENZ, DANNY
G, PANTHERS

PERSONAL: Born December 12, 1969, in Murrayville, B.C.... 5-10/187.... Catches left.... Name pronounced luh-REHNS.

TRANSACTIONS/CAREER NOTES: Selected by New York Islanders in third round (fourth Islanders pick, 58th overall) of NHL entry draft (June 11, 1988).... Loaned by Islanders to Springfield Indians (February 2, 1994).... Signed as free agent by Florida Panthers (June 14, 1994).

HONORS: Won Del Wilson Trophy (1988-89).... Named to WHL (West) All-Star first team (1988-89 and 1989-90).

Season Team	League	REGULAR SEASON								PLAYOFFS						
		Gms.	Min.	W	L	T	GA	SO	Avg.	Gms.	Min.	W	L	GA	SO	Avg.
86-87—Seattle	WHL	38	2103	12	21	2	199	0	5.68	—	—	—	—	—	—	—
87-88—Seattle	WHL	62	3302	20	37	2	*314	0	5.71	—	—	—	—	—	—	—
88-89—Seattle	WHL	*68	*4003	31	33	4	240	*3	3.60	—	—	—	—	—	—	—
—Springfield....................	AHL	4	210	2	1	0	12	0	3.43	—	—	—	—	—	—	—
89-90—Seattle	WHL	56	3226	37	15	2	221	0	4.11	13	751	6	7	40	0	*3.20
90-91—New York Islanders......	NHL	2	80	0	1	0	5	0	3.75	—	—	—	—	—	—	—
—Capital District.............	AHL	17	940	5	9	2	70	0	4.47	—	—	—	—	—	—	—
—Richmond	ECHL	20	1020	6	9	‡2	75	0	4.41	—	—	—	—	—	—	—
91-92—Capital District.............	AHL	53	3050	22	22	7	*181	2	3.56	7	442	3	4	25	0	3.39
—New York Islanders......	NHL	2	120	0	2	0	10	0	5.00	—	—	—	—	—	—	—
92-93—Capital District.............	AHL	44	2412	16	17	5	146	1	3.63	4	219	0	3	12	0	3.29
—New York Islanders......	NHL	4	157	1	2	0	10	0	3.82	—	—	—	—	—	—	—
93-94—Salt Lake City..............	IHL	20	982	4	12	‡0	91	0	5.56	—	—	—	—	—	—	—
—Springfield....................	AHL	14	802	5	7	1	59	0	4.41	2	35	0	0	0	0	0.00
94-95—Cincinnati....................	IHL	41	2223	24	10	‡3	126	0	3.40	5	308	2	3	16	0	3.12
NHL totals.................................		8	357	1	5	0	25	0	4.20							

LOWE, KEVIN
D, RANGERS

PERSONAL: Born April 15, 1959, in Lachute, Que.... 6-2/195.... Shoots left.... Full name: Kevin Hugh Lowe.... Name pronounced LOH.... Husband of Karen Percy, Canadian Olympic bronze-medal-winning downhill skier (1988); and brother of Ken Lowe, athletic trainer for Edmonton Oilers.

TRANSACTIONS/CAREER NOTES: Selected by Edmonton Oilers in first round (first Oilers pick, 21st overall) of NHL entry draft (August 9, 1979).... Broke index finger (March 7, 1986); missed six games.... Broke left wrist (March 9, 1988).... Pulled rib muscle (September 1988).... Suffered concussion (October 14, 1988).... Suffered back spasms (April 8, 1990).... Bruised back (December 28, 1991); missed one game.... Strained rotator cuff (January 28, 1992); missed three games.... Restrained rotator cuff (February 5, 1992); missed 21 games.... Strained groin (April 12, 1992); missed playoffs.... Did not report to Oilers in 1992-93 season because of contract dispute; missed 30 games.... Traded by Oilers to New York Rangers for RW Roman Oksiuta and third-round pick in 1993 draft (December 11, 1992).... Suffered stiff neck (December 19, 1992); missed one game.... Suffered from the flu (December 23, 1992); missed one game.... Injured back (February 15, 1993); missed one game.... Injured back (February 24, 1993); missed one game.... Suspended three preseason games and fined $500 by NHL for high-sticking incident (September 28, 1993).... Bruised right foot (October 9, 1993); missed two games.... Bruised thigh (October 15, 1993); missed one game.... Suffered from the flu (December 31, 1993); missed one game.... Injured back (February 28, 1994); missed one game.... Reinjured back (March 10, 1994); missed one game.... Reinjured back (March 14, 1994); missed two games.... Sprained wrist (April 2, 1994); missed five games.... Suffered from the flu (March 18, 1995); missed one game.... Pinched nerve in neck (April 23, 1995); missed two games.

HONORS: Named to QMJHL All-Star second team (1977-78 and 1978-79).... Played in NHL All-Star Game (1984-1986, 1988-1990 and 1993).... Won King Clancy Memorial Trophy (1989-90).... Named Budweiser/NHL Man of the Year (1989-90).

MISCELLANEOUS: Member of Stanley Cup championship teams (1984, 1985, 1987, 1988, 1990 and 1994).... Captain of Edmonton Oilers (1991-92).

Season Team	League	REGULAR SEASON					PLAYOFFS				
		Gms.	G	A	Pts.	PIM	Gms.	G	A	Pts.	PIM
76-77—Quebec	QMJHL	69	3	19	22	39	—	—	—	—	—
77-78—Quebec	QMJHL	64	13	52	65	86	4	1	2	3	6
78-79—Quebec	QMJHL	68	26	60	86	120	6	1	7	8	36
79-80—Edmonton	NHL	64	2	19	21	70	3	0	1	1	0
80-81—Edmonton	NHL	79	10	24	34	94	9	0	2	2	11
81-82—Edmonton	NHL	80	9	31	40	63	5	0	3	3	0
82-83—Edmonton	NHL	80	6	34	40	43	16	1	8	9	10
83-84—Edmonton	NHL	80	4	42	46	59	19	3	7	10	16
84-85—Edmonton	NHL	80	4	22	26	104	16	0	5	5	8
85-86—Edmonton	NHL	74	2	16	18	90	10	1	3	4	15
86-87—Edmonton	NHL	77	8	29	37	94	21	2	4	6	22
87-88—Edmonton	NHL	70	9	15	24	89	19	0	2	2	26
88-89—Edmonton	NHL	76	7	18	25	98	7	1	2	3	4
89-90—Edmonton	NHL	78	7	26	33	140	20	0	2	2	10
90-91—Edmonton	NHL	73	3	13	16	113	14	1	1	2	14
91-92—Edmonton	NHL	55	2	8	10	107	11	0	3	3	16
92-93—New York Rangers..........	NHL	49	3	12	15	58	—	—	—	—	—
93-94—New York Rangers..........	NHL	71	5	14	19	70	22	1	0	1	20
94-95—New York Rangers..........	NHL	44	1	7	8	58	10	0	1	1	12
NHL totals.................................		1130	82	330	412	1350	202	10	44	54	184

LOWRY, DAVE
LW, PANTHERS

PERSONAL: Born January 14, 1965, in Sudbury, Ont. . . . 6-1/200. . . . Shoots left. . . . Name pronounced LOW-ree.
HIGH SCHOOL: Sir Wilfrid Laurier (London, Ont.).
TRANSACTIONS/CAREER NOTES: Underwent arthroscopic knee surgery (December 1982). . . . Selected as underage junior by Vancouver Canucks in sixth round (fourth Canucks pick, 110th overall) of NHL entry draft (June 8, 1983). . . . Traded by Canucks to St. Louis Blues for C Ernie Vargas (September 29, 1988). . . . Injured groin (March 1990). . . . Sprained shoulder (October 1991); missed two games. . . . Injured knee (October 26, 1992); missed 26 games. . . . Selected by Florida Panthers in NHL expansion draft (June 24, 1993). . . . Fractured cheekbone (November 26, 1993); missed three games. . . . Injured knee (December 12, 1993); missed one game. . . . Suffered abrasion to right cornea (April 28, 1995); missed three games.
HONORS: Named to OHL All-Star first team (1984-85).

Season Team	League		REGULAR SEASON					PLAYOFFS			
		Gms.	G	A	Pts.	PIM	Gms.	G	A	Pts.	PIM
82-83—London	OHL	42	11	16	27	48	3	0	0	0	14
83-84—London	OHL	66	29	47	76	125	8	6	6	12	41
84-85—London	OHL	61	60	60	120	94	8	6	5	11	10
85-86—Vancouver	NHL	73	10	8	18	143	3	0	0	0	0
86-87—Vancouver	NHL	70	8	10	18	176	—	—	—	—	—
87-88—Fredericton	AHL	46	18	27	45	59	14	7	3	10	72
—Vancouver	NHL	22	1	3	4	38	—	—	—	—	—
88-89—Peoria	IHL	58	31	35	66	45	—	—	—	—	—
—St. Louis	NHL	21	3	3	6	11	10	0	5	5	4
89-90—St. Louis	NHL	78	19	6	25	75	12	2	1	3	39
90-91—St. Louis	NHL	79	19	21	40	168	13	1	4	5	35
91-92—St. Louis	NHL	75	7	13	20	77	6	0	1	1	20
92-93—St. Louis	NHL	58	5	8	13	101	11	2	0	2	14
93-94—Florida	NHL	80	15	22	37	64	—	—	—	—	—
94-95—Florida	NHL	45	10	10	20	25	—	—	—	—	—
NHL totals		**601**	**97**	**104**	**201**	**878**	**55**	**5**	**11**	**16**	**112**

LUDWIG, CRAIG
D, STARS

PERSONAL: Born March 15, 1961, in Rhinelander, Wis. . . . 6-3/217. . . . Shoots left. . . . Full name: Craig Lee Ludwig. . . . Name pronounced LUHD-wihg.
COLLEGE: North Dakota.
TRANSACTIONS/CAREER NOTES: Selected by Montreal Canadiens in third round (fifth Canadiens pick, 61st overall) of NHL entry draft (June 11, 1980). . . . Fractured knuckle in left hand (October 1984). . . . Broke hand (December 2, 1985); missed nine games. . . . Broke right facial bone (January 1988); missed five games. . . . Suspended five games by NHL for elbowing (November 19, 1988). . . . Separated right shoulder (March 21, 1990). . . . Traded by Canadiens to New York Islanders for D Gerald Diduck (September 4, 1990). . . . Traded by Islanders to Minnesota North Stars as part of a three-way deal in which North Stars sent D Dave Babych to Vancouver Canucks and Canucks sent D Tom Kurvers to Islanders (June 22, 1991). . . . Injured foot (December 8, 1991); missed six games. . . . Injured foot (January 30, 1993); missed two games. . . . Pinched nerve in neck (March 18, 1993); missed two games. . . . North Stars franchise moved from Minnesota to Dallas and renamed Stars for 1993-94 season. . . . Suffered sore back (April 2, 1995); missed one game.
HONORS: Named to WCHA All-Star second team (1981-82).
MISCELLANEOUS: Member of Stanley Cup championship team (1986).

Season Team	League		REGULAR SEASON					PLAYOFFS			
		Gms.	G	A	Pts.	PIM	Gms.	G	A	Pts.	PIM
79-80—Univ. of North Dakota	WCHA	33	1	8	9	32	—	—	—	—	—
80-81—Univ. of North Dakota	WCHA	34	4	8	12	48	—	—	—	—	—
81-82—Univ. of North Dakota	WCHA	47	5	26	31	70	—	—	—	—	—
82-83—Montreal	NHL	80	0	25	25	59	3	0	0	0	2
83-84—Montreal	NHL	80	7	18	25	52	15	0	3	3	23
84-85—Montreal	NHL	72	5	14	19	90	12	0	2	2	6
85-86—Montreal	NHL	69	2	4	6	63	20	0	1	1	48
86-87—Montreal	NHL	75	4	12	16	105	17	2	3	5	30
87-88—Montreal	NHL	74	4	10	14	69	11	1	1	2	6
88-89—Montreal	NHL	74	3	13	16	73	21	0	2	2	24
89-90—Montreal	NHL	73	1	15	16	108	11	0	1	1	16
90-91—New York Islanders	NHL	75	1	8	9	77	—	—	—	—	—
91-92—Minnesota	NHL	73	2	9	11	54	7	0	1	1	19
92-93—Minnesota	NHL	78	1	10	11	153	—	—	—	—	—
93-94—Dallas	NHL	84	1	13	14	123	9	0	3	3	8
94-95—Dallas	NHL	47	2	7	9	61	4	0	1	1	2
NHL totals		**954**	**33**	**158**	**191**	**1087**	**130**	**3**	**18**	**21**	**184**

LUHNING, WARREN
RW, ISLANDERS

PERSONAL: Born July 3, 1975, in Edmonton. . . . 6-2/185. . . . Shoots right.
COLLEGE: Michigan.
TRANSACTIONS/CAREER NOTES: Selected by New York Islanders in fourth round (fourth Islanders pick, 92nd overall) of NHL entry draft (June 26, 1993).

Season Team	League		REGULAR SEASON					PLAYOFFS			
		Gms.	G	A	Pts.	PIM	Gms.	G	A	Pts.	PIM
92-93—Calgary Royals	AJHL	46	18	25	43	287	—	—	—	—	—
93-94—University of Michigan	CCHA	38	13	6	19	83	—	—	—	—	—
94-95—University of Michigan	CCHA	36	17	24	41	80	—	—	—	—	—

LUKOWICH, BRAD
D, ISLANDERS

PERSONAL: Born August 12, 1976, in Surrey, B.C. . . . . 6-0/170. . . . Shoots left.
HIGH SCHOOL: Norkam Secondary (Kamloops, B.C.).
TRANSACTIONS/CAREER NOTES: Selected by New York Islanders in fourth round (fourth Islanders pick, 90th overall) of NHL entry draft (June 29, 1994).

Season Team	League	REGULAR SEASON					PLAYOFFS				
		Gms.	G	A	Pts.	PIM	Gms.	G	A	Pts.	PIM
92-93—Cranbook	Tier II Jr. A	54	21	41	62	162	—	—	—	—	—
—Kamloops	WHL	1	0	0	0	0	—	—	—	—	—
93-94—Kamloops	WHL	42	5	11	16	166	16	0	1	1	35
94-95—Kamloops	WHL	63	10	35	45	125	18	0	7	7	21

LUMME, JYRKI
D, CANUCKS

PERSONAL: Born July 16, 1966, in Tampere, Finland. . . . 6-1/207. . . . Shoots left. . . . Name pronounced LOO-mee.
TRANSACTIONS/CAREER NOTES: Selected by Montreal Canadiens in third round (third Canadiens pick, 57th overall) of NHL entry draft (June 21, 1986). . . . Strained left knee ligaments (December 1988). . . . Stretched knee ligaments (February 21, 1989). . . . Bruised right foot (November 1989). . . . Traded by Canadiens to Vancouver Canucks for second-round pick (C Craig Darby) in 1991 draft (March 6, 1990). . . . Lacerated eye (November 19, 1991); missed three games. . . . Sprained knee (January 19, 1993); missed nine games. . . . Played in Europe during 1994-95 NHL lockout. . . . Injured knee (February 15, 1995); missed six games. . . . Bruised ribs (March 1, 1995); missed five games.
MISCELLANEOUS: Member of silver-medal-winning Finnish Olympic team (1988).

Season Team	League	REGULAR SEASON					PLAYOFFS				
		Gms.	G	A	Pts.	PIM	Gms.	G	A	Pts.	PIM
84-85—Koo Vee	Finland	30	6	4	10	44	—	—	—	—	—
85-86—Ilves Tampere	Finland	31	1	5	6	4	—	—	—	—	—
86-87—Ilves Tampere	Finland	43	12	12	24	52	4	0	1	1	0
87-88—Ilves Tampere	Finland	43	8	22	30	75	—	—	—	—	—
—Finnish Olympic Team	Int'l	6	0	1	1	2	—	—	—	—	—
88-89—Montreal	NHL	21	1	3	4	10	—	—	—	—	—
—Sherbrooke	AHL	26	4	11	15	10	6	1	3	4	4
89-90—Montreal	NHL	54	1	19	20	41	—	—	—	—	—
—Vancouver	NHL	11	3	7	10	8	—	—	—	—	—
90-91—Vancouver	NHL	80	5	27	32	59	6	2	3	5	0
91-92—Vancouver	NHL	75	12	32	44	65	13	2	3	5	4
92-93—Vancouver	NHL	74	8	36	44	55	12	0	5	5	6
93-94—Vancouver	NHL	83	13	42	55	50	24	2	11	13	16
94-95—Ilves Tampere	Finland	12	4	4	8	24	—	—	—	—	—
—Vancouver	NHL	36	5	12	17	26	11	2	6	8	8
NHL totals		434	48	178	226	314	66	8	28	36	34

LUONGO, CHRISTOPHER
D, ISLANDERS

PERSONAL: Born March 17, 1967, in Detroit. . . . 6-0/199. . . . Shoots right. . . . Full name: Christopher John Luongo. . . . Name pronounced loo-WAHN-goh.
HIGH SCHOOL: Notre Dame (Harper Woods, Mich.).
COLLEGE: Michigan State.
TRANSACTIONS/CAREER NOTES: Selected by Detroit Red Wings in fifth round (fifth Red Wings pick, 92nd overall) of NHL entry draft (June 15, 1985). . . . Signed as free agent by Ottawa Senators (September 9, 1992). . . . Traded by Senators to New York Islanders for D Jeff Finley (June 30, 1993).
HONORS: Named to NCAA All-Tournament team (1986-87). . . . Named to CCHA All-Star second team (1988-89).

Season Team	League	REGULAR SEASON					PLAYOFFS				
		Gms.	G	A	Pts.	PIM	Gms.	G	A	Pts.	PIM
84-85—St. Clair Shores	NAJHL	41	2	25	27	. . .	—	—	—	—	—
85-86—Michigan State	CCHA	38	1	5	6	29	—	—	—	—	—
86-87—Michigan State	CCHA	27	4	16	20	38	—	—	—	—	—
87-88—Michigan State	CCHA	45	3	15	18	49	—	—	—	—	—
88-89—Michigan State	CCHA	47	4	21	25	42	—	—	—	—	—
89-90—Adirondack	AHL	53	9	14	23	37	3	0	0	0	0
—Phoenix	IHL	23	5	9	14	41	—	—	—	—	—
90-91—Detroit	NHL	4	0	1	1	4	—	—	—	—	—
—Adirondack	AHL	76	14	25	39	71	2	0	0	0	7
91-92—Adirondack	AHL	80	6	20	26	60	19	3	5	8	10
92-93—Ottawa	NHL	76	3	9	12	68	—	—	—	—	—
—New Haven	AHL	7	0	2	2	2	—	—	—	—	—
93-94—Salt Lake City	IHL	51	9	31	40	54	—	—	—	—	—
—New York Islanders	NHL	17	1	3	4	13	—	—	—	—	—
94-95—Denver	IHL	41	1	14	15	26	—	—	—	—	—
—New York Islanders	NHL	47	1	3	4	36	—	—	—	—	—
NHL totals		144	5	16	21	121					

MacDERMID, PAUL
RW, DENVER

PERSONAL: Born April 14, 1963, in Chesley, Ont. . . . 6-1/205. . . . Shoots right.
TRANSACTIONS/CAREER NOTES: Selected by Hartford Whalers as underage junior in third round (second Whalers pick, 61st overall) of NHL entry draft (June 10, 1981). . . . Injured knee (December 1982). . . . Injured neck and shoulder (December 6, 1988). . . . Sprained right knee ligament (February 4, 1989). . . . Traded by Whalers to Winnipeg Jets for C/LW Randy Cun-

neyworth (December 13, 1989). . . . Suffered back spasms (November 3, 1990); missed six games. . . . Strained knee (December 1990). . . . Traded by Jets to Washington Capitals for D Mike Lalor (March 2, 1992). . . . Traded by Capitals with RW Reggie Savage to Quebec Nordiques for LW Mike Hough (June 20, 1993). . . . Sprained right ankle (October 14, 1993); missed nine games. . . . Suffered lumbar sprain (November 22, 1993); missed 21 games. . . . Suffered lumbar sprain (April 5, 1994); missed four games. . . . Suffered back spasms (January 21, 1995); missed 19 games. . . . Suffered sore back (March 1, 1995); missed one game. . . . Suffered back spasms (April 27, 1995); missed last three games of season and three playoff games. . . . Nordiques franchise moved to Denver for 1995-96 season.

Season Team	League	REGULAR SEASON					PLAYOFFS				
		Gms.	G	A	Pts.	PIM	Gms.	G	A	Pts.	PIM
79-80—Port Elgin Jr. C	OHA	30	23	20	43	87	—	—	—	—	—
80-81—Windsor	OMJHL	68	15	17	32	106	—	—	—	—	—
81-82—Windsor	OHL	65	26	45	71	179	9	6	4	10	17
—Hartford	NHL	3	1	0	1	2	—	—	—	—	—
82-83—Windsor	OHL	42	35	45	80	90	—	—	—	—	—
—Hartford	NHL	7	0	0	0	2	—	—	—	—	—
83-84—Hartford	NHL	3	0	1	1	0	—	—	—	—	—
—Binghamton	AHL	70	31	30	61	130	—	—	—	—	—
84-85—Binghamton	AHL	48	9	31	40	87	—	—	—	—	—
—Hartford	NHL	31	4	7	11	29	—	—	—	—	—
85-86—Hartford	NHL	74	13	10	23	160	10	2	1	3	20
86-87—Hartford	NHL	72	7	11	18	202	6	2	1	3	34
87-88—Hartford	NHL	80	20	15	35	139	6	0	5	5	14
88-89—Hartford	NHL	74	17	27	44	141	4	1	1	2	16
89-90—Hartford	NHL	29	6	12	18	69	—	—	—	—	—
—Winnipeg	NHL	44	7	10	17	100	7	0	2	2	8
90-91—Winnipeg	NHL	69	15	21	36	128	—	—	—	—	—
91-92—Winnipeg	NHL	59	10	11	21	151	—	—	—	—	—
—Washington	NHL	15	2	5	7	43	7	0	1	1	22
92-93—Washington	NHL	72	9	8	17	80	—	—	—	—	—
93-94—Quebec	NHL	44	2	3	5	35	—	—	—	—	—
94-95—Quebec	NHL	14	3	1	4	22	3	0	0	0	2
NHL totals		690	116	142	258	1303	43	5	11	16	116

MacDONALD, AARON
G, PANTHERS

PERSONAL: Born August 29, 1977, in Grande Prairie, Alta. . . . 6-1/186. . . . Catches left.
TRANSACTIONS/CAREER NOTES: Selected by Florida Panthers in second round (second Panthers pick, 36th overall) of NHL entry draft (July 8, 1995).

Season Team	League	REGULAR SEASON							PLAYOFFS						
		Gms.	Min.	W	L	T	GA	SO	Avg.	Gms.	Min.	W	L	GA SO	Avg.
93-94—Swift Current	WHL	18	710	6	6	0	48	0	4.06	1	1	0	0	0 0	0.00
94-95—Swift Current	WHL	53	2957	24	20	6	177	4	3.59	6	393	2	4	18 0	2.75

MacDONALD, DOUG
LW, SABRES

PERSONAL: Born February 8, 1969, in Port Moody, B.C. . . . 6-0/192. . . . Shoots left. . . . Full name: Douglas Bruce MacDonald.
COLLEGE: Wisconsin.
TRANSACTIONS/CAREER NOTES: Selected by Buffalo Sabres in fourth round (third Sabres pick, 77th overall) of NHL entry draft (June 17, 1989). . . . Injured knee (December 29, 1990).

Season Team	League	REGULAR SEASON					PLAYOFFS				
		Gms.	G	A	Pts.	PIM	Gms.	G	A	Pts.	PIM
85-86—Langley Eagles	BCJHL	42	19	37	56	16	—	—	—	—	—
86-87—Delta	BCJHL	51	28	49	77	61	—	—	—	—	—
87-88—Delta	BCJHL	51	50	54	104	70	9	5	9	14	16
88-89—University of Wisconsin	WCHA	44	23	25	48	50	—	—	—	—	—
89-90—University of Wisconsin	WCHA	44	16	35	51	52	—	—	—	—	—
90-91—University of Wisconsin	WCHA	31	20	26	46	50	—	—	—	—	—
91-92—University of Wisconsin	WCHA	33	16	28	44	76	—	—	—	—	—
92-93—Rochester	AHL	64	25	33	58	58	7	0	2	2	4
—Buffalo	NHL	5	1	0	1	2	—	—	—	—	—
93-94—Rochester	AHL	63	25	19	44	46	4	1	1	2	8
—Buffalo	NHL	4	0	0	0	0	—	—	—	—	—
94-95—Rochester	AHL	58	21	25	46	73	5	0	1	1	0
—Buffalo	NHL	2	0	0	0	0	—	—	—	—	—
NHL totals		11	1	0	1	2					

MacDONALD, KEVIN
D

PERSONAL: Born February 24, 1966, in Prescott, Ont. . . . 6-0/200. . . . Shoots left.
TRANSACTIONS/CAREER NOTES: Signed as free agent by Los Angeles Kings (July 1990). . . . Signed as free agent by Ottawa Senators (December 3, 1993).

Season Team	League	REGULAR SEASON					PLAYOFFS				
		Gms.	G	A	Pts.	PIM	Gms.	G	A	Pts.	PIM
88-89—Muskegon	IHL	64	2	13	15	190	11	2	3	5	22
89-90—New Haven	AHL	27	0	1	1	111	—	—	—	—	—
—Phoenix	IHL	30	1	5	6	201	—	—	—	—	—
90-91—Phoenix	IHL	74	1	9	10	327	11	0	1	1	22

M

			REGULAR SEASON					PLAYOFFS				
Season	Team	League	Gms.	G	A	Pts.	PIM	Gms.	G	A	Pts.	PIM
91-92—Phoenix		IHL	76	7	14	21	304	—	—	—	—	—
92-93—Phoenix		IHL	6	0	1	1	23	—	—	—	—	—
—Fort Wayne		IHL	65	4	9	13	283	11	0	0	0	21
93-94—Fort Wayne		IHL	29	0	3	3	140	15	0	4	4	76
—Prince Edward Island		AHL	40	2	4	6	245	—	—	—	—	—
—Ottawa		NHL	1	0	0	0	2	—	—	—	—	—
94-95—Chicago		IHL	75	1	12	13	*390	3	0	0	0	17
NHL totals			1	0	0	0	2					

MacDONALD, TODD
G, PANTHERS

PERSONAL: Born July 5, 1975, in Charlottetown, P.E.I. . . . . 6-0/155. . . . Catches left.
TRANSACTIONS/CAREER NOTES: Selected by Florida Panthers in fifth round (seventh Panthers pick, 109th overall) of NHL entry draft (June 26, 1993).
HONORS: Named to WHL (West) All-Star first team (1994-95).

			REGULAR SEASON						PLAYOFFS					
Season	Team	League	Gms.	Min.	W	L	T	GA	SO	Avg.	Gms.	Min.	W	L	GA	SO	Avg.
91-92—Kingston		OHA Mj Jr.A	28	1680	...	...	...	84	0	3.00	—	—	—	—	—	—	—
92-93—Tacoma		WHL	19	823	6	6	0	59	0	4.30	—	—	—	—	—	—	—
93-94—Tacoma		WHL	29	1606	13	10	2	109	1	4.07	—	—	—	—	—	—	—
94-95—Tacoma		WHL	60	3433	35	21	2	179	3	3.13	4	255	1	3	13	0	3.06

MacDONALD, TOM
C, LIGHTNING

PERSONAL: Born April 14, 1974, in Toronto. . . . 5-11/190. . . . Shoots left.
TRANSACTIONS/CAREER NOTES: Selected by Tampa Bay Lightning in 11th round (11th Lightning pick, 241st overall) of NHL entry draft (June 20, 1992).

			REGULAR SEASON					PLAYOFFS				
Season	Team	League	Gms.	G	A	Pts.	PIM	Gms.	G	A	Pts.	PIM
90-91—S.S. Marie		OHL	41	3	6	9	71	6	0	1	1	19
91-92—S.S. Marie		OHL	52	11	15	26	139	19	3	7	10	31
92-93—S.S. Marie		OHL	50	13	24	37	134	18	5	9	14	62
93-94—S.S. Marie		OHL	55	34	36	70	175	14	3	7	10	38
94-95—Nashville		ECHL	55	9	12	21	137	13	2	7	9	55

MacINNIS, AL
D, BLUES

PERSONAL: Born July 11, 1963, in Inverness, N.S. . . . 6-2/196. . . . Shoots right. . . . Name pronounced mah-KIH-niz.
TRANSACTIONS/CAREER NOTES: Selected by Calgary Flames as underage junior in first round (first Flames pick, 15th overall) of NHL entry draft (June 10, 1981). . . . Twisted knee (February 1985). . . . Lacerated hand (March 23, 1986). . . . Stretched ligaments of knee (April 8, 1990). . . . Separated shoulder (November 22, 1991); missed eight games. . . . Dislocated left hip (November 12, 1992); missed 34 games. . . . Strained shoulder (December 22, 1993); missed one game. . . . Strained shoulder (January 2, 1994); missed four games. . . . Bruised knee (February 24, 1994); missed four games. . . . Traded by Flames with fourth-round pick in 1997 draft to St. Louis Blues for D Phil Housley and second-round pick in 1996 and 1997 drafts (July 4, 1994). . . . Injured shoulder (January 31, 1995); missed eight games. . . . Suffered from the flu (April 9, 1995); missed three games. . . . Injured shoulder (April 25, 1995); missed last five games of season.
HONORS: Named to OHL All-Star first team (1981-82 and 1982-83). . . . Named to Memorial Cup All-Star team (1981-82). . . . Won Max Kaminsky Trophy (1982-83). . . . Played in NHL All-Star Game (1985, 1988, 1990 through 1992 and 1994). . . . Named to NHL All-Star second team (1986-87, 1988-89 and 1993-94). . . . Won Conn Smythe Trophy (1988-89). . . . Named to THE SPORTING NEWS All-Star first team (1989-90 and 1990-91). . . . Named to THE SPORTING NEWS All-Star second team (1993-94). . . . Named to NHL All-Star first team (1989-90 and 1990-91).
STATISTICAL PLATEAUS: Three-goal games: 1991-92 (1).
MISCELLANEOUS: Member of Stanley Cup championship team (1989).

			REGULAR SEASON					PLAYOFFS				
Season	Team	League	Gms.	G	A	Pts.	PIM	Gms.	G	A	Pts.	PIM
79-80—Regina Blues		SJHL	59	20	28	48	110	—	—	—	—	—
80-81—Kitchener		OMJHL	47	11	28	39	59	18	4	12	16	20
81-82—Kitchener		OHL	59	25	50	75	145	15	5	10	15	44
—Calgary		NHL	2	0	0	0	0	—	—	—	—	—
82-83—Kitchener		OHL	51	38	46	84	67	8	3	8	11	9
—Calgary		NHL	14	1	3	4	9	—	—	—	—	—
83-84—Colorado		CHL	19	5	14	19	22	—	—	—	—	—
—Calgary		NHL	51	11	34	45	42	11	2	12	14	13
84-85—Calgary		NHL	67	14	52	66	75	4	1	2	3	8
85-86—Calgary		NHL	77	11	57	68	76	21	4	*15	19	30
86-87—Calgary		NHL	79	20	56	76	97	4	1	0	1	0
87-88—Chicago		NHL	80	25	58	83	114	7	3	6	9	18
88-89—Calgary		NHL	79	16	58	74	126	22	7	*24	*31	46
89-90—Calgary		NHL	79	28	62	90	82	6	2	3	5	8
90-91—Calgary		NHL	78	28	75	103	90	7	2	3	5	8
91-92—Calgary		NHL	72	20	57	77	83	—	—	—	—	—
92-93—Calgary		NHL	50	11	43	54	61	6	1	6	7	10
93-94—Calgary		NHL	75	28	54	82	95	7	2	6	8	12
94-95—St. Louis		NHL	32	8	20	28	43	7	1	5	6	10
NHL totals			835	221	629	850	993	102	26	82	108	163

M

MacINTYRE, ANDY
LW, BLACKHAWKS

PERSONAL: Born April 16, 1974, in Thunder Bay, Ont. . . . 6-2/195. . . . Shoots left.
HIGH SCHOOL: Marion Graham (Saskatoon, Sask.).
TRANSACTIONS/CAREER NOTES: Selected by Chicago Blackhawks in fourth round (fourth Blackhawks pick, 89th overall) of NHL entry draft (June 20, 1992).
HONORS: Named to WHL (East) All-Star second team (1993-94).

Season Team	League	REGULAR SEASON					PLAYOFFS				
		Gms.	G	A	Pts.	PIM	Gms.	G	A	Pts.	PIM
89-90—Elk Valley	BCJHL	40	24	22	46	14	—	—	—	—	—
90-91—Seattle	WHL	71	16	13	29	52	6	0	0	0	2
91-92—Seattle	WHL	12	6	2	8	18	—	—	—	—	—
—Saskatoon	WHL	55	22	13	35	66	22	10	2	12	17
92-93—Saskatoon	WHL	72	35	29	64	82	9	3	2	5	2
93-94—Saskatoon	WHL	72	54	35	89	58	16	6	6	12	16
94-95—Indianapolis	IHL	51	9	8	17	17	—	—	—	—	—
—Columbus	ECHL	22	7	8	15	5	—	—	—	—	—

MACIVER, NORM
D, PENGUINS

PERSONAL: Born September 8, 1964, in Thunder Bay, Ont. . . . 5-11/185. . . . Shoots left. . . . Full name: Norman Steven Maciver.
HIGH SCHOOL: Sir Winston Churchill (Thunder Bay, Ont.).
COLLEGE: Minnesota-Duluth.
TRANSACTIONS/CAREER NOTES: Signed as free agent by New York Rangers (September 8, 1986). . . . Dislocated right shoulder (March 1988). . . . Suffered hip pointer (November 1988). . . . Traded by Rangers with LW Don Maloney and C Brian Lawton to Hartford Whalers for C Carey Wilson and fifth-round pick (C Lubos Rob) in 1990 draft (December 26, 1988). . . . Traded by Whalers to Edmonton Oilers for D Jim Ennis (October 9, 1989). . . . Selected by Ottawa Senators in NHL waiver draft (October 4, 1992). . . . Suffered sore back (December 9, 1992); missed one game. . . . Injured back (January 19, 1993); missed one game. . . . Injured wrist (January 28, 1993); missed two games. . . . Suffered chest contusion (October 26, 1993); missed 10 games. . . . Injured left knee (January 13, 1994); missed three games. . . . Injured ankle (March 2, 1994); missed 15 games. . . . Broke leg (April 10, 1994); missed three games. . . . Pulled groin (1995); missed one game. . . . Bruised ribs (1995); missed three games. . . . Suffered slight concussion (March 29, 1995); missed one game. . . . Traded by Senators with C Troy Murray to Pittsburgh Penguins for C Martin Straka (April 7, 1995).
HONORS: Named to WCHA All-Star second team (1983-84). . . . Named to NCAA All-America West first team (1984-85 and 1985-86). . . . Named to WCHA All-Star first team (1984-85 and 1985-86). . . . Won Eddie Shore Plaque (1990-91). . . . Named to AHL All-Star first team (1990-91).

Season Team	League	REGULAR SEASON					PLAYOFFS				
		Gms.	G	A	Pts.	PIM	Gms.	G	A	Pts.	PIM
82-83—Minnesota-Duluth	WCHA	45	1	26	27	40	6	0	2	2	2
83-84—Minnesota-Duluth	WCHA	31	13	28	41	28	8	1	10	11	8
84-85—Minnesota-Duluth	WCHA	47	14	47	61	63	10	3	3	6	6
85-86—Minnesota-Duluth	WCHA	42	11	51	62	36	4	2	3	5	2
86-87—New Haven	AHL	71	6	30	36	73	7	0	0	0	9
—New York Rangers	NHL	3	0	1	1	0	—	—	—	—	—
87-88—Colorado	IHL	27	6	20	26	22	—	—	—	—	—
—New York Rangers	NHL	37	9	15	24	14	—	—	—	—	—
88-89—New York Rangers	NHL	26	0	10	10	14	—	—	—	—	—
—Hartford	NHL	37	1	22	23	24	1	0	0	0	2
89-90—Binghamton	AHL	2	0	0	0	0	—	—	—	—	—
—Cape Breton	AHL	68	13	37	50	55	6	0	7	7	10
—Edmonton	NHL	1	0	0	0	0	—	—	—	—	—
90-91—Cape Breton	AHL	56	13	46	59	60	—	—	—	—	—
—Edmonton	NHL	21	2	5	7	14	18	0	4	4	8
91-92—Edmonton	NHL	57	6	34	40	38	13	1	2	3	10
92-93—Ottawa	NHL	80	17	46	63	84	—	—	—	—	—
93-94—Ottawa	NHL	53	3	20	23	26	—	—	—	—	—
94-95—Ottawa	NHL	28	4	7	11	10	—	—	—	—	—
—Pittsburgh	NHL	13	0	9	9	6	12	1	4	5	8
NHL totals		356	42	169	211	230	44	2	10	12	28

MacLEAN, DONALD
C, KINGS

PERSONAL: Born January 14, 1977, in Sydney, N.S. . . . 6-2/174. . . . Shoots left.
TRANSACTIONS/CAREER NOTES: Selected by Los Angeles Kings in second round (second Kings pick, 33rd overall) of NHL entry draft (July 8, 1995).

Season Team	League	REGULAR SEASON					PLAYOFFS				
		Gms.	G	A	Pts.	PIM	Gms.	G	A	Pts.	PIM
94-95—Beauport	QMJHL	64	15	27	42	37	17	4	4	8	6

MacLEAN, JOHN
RW, DEVILS

PERSONAL: Born November 20, 1964, in Oshawa, Ont. . . . 6-0/200. . . . Shoots right. . . . Name pronounced muh-KLAYN.
TRANSACTIONS/CAREER NOTES: Selected by New Jersey Devils as underage junior in first round (first Devils pick, sixth overall) of NHL entry draft (June 8, 1983). . . . Bruised shoulder (November 1984). . . . Injured right knee (January 25, 1985). . . . Reinjured knee and underwent arthroscopic surgery (January 31, 1985). . . . Bruised ankle (November 2, 1986). . . . Sprained right elbow (December 1988). . . . Bruised ribs (March 1, 1989). . . . Suffered concussion and stomach contusions (October 1990). . . . Suffered concussion (December 11, 1990). . . . Tore ligament in right knee (September 30, 1991); missed entire 1991-92 season. . . . Underwent surgery to right knee (November 23, 1991). . . . Injured forearm (November 3, 1993); missed two games. . . . Lacerated eye (February 24, 1994); missed one game. . . . Bruised foot (April 9, 1995); missed one game.

HONORS: Named to Memorial Cup All-Star team (1982-83).... Played in NHL All-Star Game (1989 and 1991).
STATISTICAL PLATEAUS: Three-goal games: 1987-88 (1), 1988-89 (3), 1990-91 (2). Total: 6.
MISCELLANEOUS: Member of Stanley Cup championship team (1995).

			REGULAR SEASON					PLAYOFFS			
Season Team	League	Gms.	G	A	Pts.	PIM	Gms.	G	A	Pts.	PIM
81-82—Oshawa	OHL	67	17	22	39	197	12	3	6	9	63
82-83—Oshawa	OHL	66	47	51	98	138	17	*18	20	†38	35
83-84—New Jersey	NHL	23	1	0	1	10	—	—	—	—	—
—Oshawa	OHL	30	23	36	59	58	7	2	5	7	18
84-85—New Jersey	NHL	61	13	20	33	44	—	—	—	—	—
85-86—New Jersey	NHL	74	21	36	57	112	—	—	—	—	—
86-87—New Jersey	NHL	80	31	36	67	120	—	—	—	—	—
87-88—New Jersey	NHL	76	23	16	39	147	20	7	11	18	60
88-89—New Jersey	NHL	74	42	45	87	122	—	—	—	—	—
89-90—New Jersey	NHL	80	41	38	79	80	6	4	1	5	12
90-91—New Jersey	NHL	78	45	33	78	150	7	5	3	8	20
91-92—New Jersey	NHL			Did not play—injured.							
92-93—New Jersey	NHL	80	24	24	48	102	5	0	1	1	10
93-94—New Jersey	NHL	80	37	33	70	95	20	6	10	16	22
94-95—New Jersey	NHL	46	17	12	29	32	20	5	13	18	14
NHL totals		752	295	293	588	1014	78	27	39	66	138

MacNEIL, IAN
C, WHALERS

PERSONAL: Born April 27, 1977, in Halifax, N.S.... 6-2/175.... Shoots left.
TRANSACTIONS/CAREER NOTES: Selected by Hartford Whalers in fourth round (third Whalers pick, 85th overall) of NHL entry draft (July 8, 1995).

			REGULAR SEASON					PLAYOFFS			
Season Team	League	Gms.	G	A	Pts.	PIM	Gms.	G	A	Pts.	PIM
94-95—Oshawa	OHL	60	7	21	28	57	7	0	2	2	0

MACOUN, JAMIE
D, MAPLE LEAFS

PERSONAL: Born August 17, 1961, in Newmarket, Ont.... 6-2/200.... Shoots left.... Name pronounced muh-KOW-uhn.
COLLEGE: Ohio State.
TRANSACTIONS/CAREER NOTES: Signed as free agent by Calgary Flames (January 30, 1983).... Fractured cheekbone (December 26, 1984).... Suffered nerve damage to left arm in automobile accident (May 1987).... Suffered concussion (January 23, 1989).... Traded by Flames with C Doug Gilmour, LW Kent Manderville, D Ric Nattress and G Rick Wamsley to Toronto Maple Leafs for LW Craig Berube, D Alexander Godynyuk, LW Gary Leeman, D Michel Petit and G Jeff Reese (January 2, 1992).... Pulled groin (February 27, 1993); missed four games.... Suspended for one game for two stick-related game misconducts (March 9, 1994).... Suffered from the flu (March 10, 1994); missed one game. ...Strained hip muscle (April 2, 1995); missed two games.
HONORS: Named to NHL All-Rookie team (1983-84).
MISCELLANEOUS: Member of Stanley Cup championship team (1989).

			REGULAR SEASON					PLAYOFFS			
Season Team	League	Gms.	G	A	Pts.	PIM	Gms.	G	A	Pts.	PIM
80-81—Ohio State	CCHA	38	9	20	29	83	—	—	—	—	—
81-82—Ohio State	CCHA	25	2	18	20	89	—	—	—	—	—
82-83—Ohio State	CCHA	19	6	21	27	54	—	—	—	—	—
—Calgary	NHL	22	1	4	5	25	9	0	2	2	8
83-84—Calgary	NHL	72	9	23	32	97	11	1	0	1	0
84-85—Calgary	NHL	70	9	30	39	67	4	1	0	1	4
85-86—Calgary	NHL	77	11	21	32	81	22	1	6	7	23
86-87—Calgary	NHL	79	7	33	40	111	3	0	1	1	8
87-88—Calgary	NHL			Did not play—injured.							
88-89—Calgary	NHL	72	8	19	27	76	22	3	6	9	30
89-90—Calgary	NHL	78	8	27	35	70	6	0	3	3	10
90-91—Calgary	NHL	79	7	15	22	84	7	0	1	1	4
91-92—Calgary	NHL	37	2	12	14	53	—	—	—	—	—
—Toronto	NHL	39	3	13	16	18	—	—	—	—	—
92-93—Toronto	NHL	77	4	15	19	55	21	0	6	6	36
93-94—Toronto	NHL	82	3	27	30	115	18	1	1	2	12
94-95—Toronto	NHL	46	2	8	10	75	7	1	2	3	8
NHL totals		830	74	247	321	927	130	8	28	36	143

MacTAVISH, CRAIG
C, FLYERS

PERSONAL: Born August 15, 1958, in London, Ont.... 6-1/195.... Shoots left.
HIGH SCHOOL: Westminster (London, Ont.).
COLLEGE: Lowell (Mass.).
TRANSACTIONS/CAREER NOTES: Selected by Boston Bruins in ninth round (ninth Bruins pick, 153rd overall) of NHL amateur draft (June 15, 1978).... Involved in automobile accident in which another driver was killed (January 25, 1984); pleaded guilty to vehicular homicide, driving while under the influence of alcohol and reckless driving and sentenced to a year in prison (May 1984); missed 1984-85 season.... Signed as free agent by Edmonton Oilers (February 1, 1985).... Strained lower back (January 1993); missed one game.... Suffered concussion (March 10, 1993); missed one game.... Strained wrist (October 18, 1993); missed one game.... Reinjured wrist (December 7, 1993); missed one game. ... Suffered whiplash (December 15, 1993); missed four games.... Bruised foot (December 30, 1993); missed one game.... Traded by Oilers to New York Rangers for C Todd Marchant (March 21, 1994).... Signed as free agent by Philadelphia Flyers (July 6, 1994).... Injured foot (January 24, 1995); missed one game.... Bruised foot (April 14, 1995); missed two games.

M

HONORS: Named ECAC Division II Rookie of the Year (1977-78).... Named to ECAC Division II All-Star second team (1977-78).... Named ECAC Division II Player of the Year (1978-79).... Named to NCAA All-America East (College Division) first team (1978-79).... Named to ECAC Division II All-Star first team (1978-79).
STATISTICAL PLATEAUS: Three-goal games: 1985-86 (1), 1990-91 (1). Total: 2.
MISCELLANEOUS: Does not wear a helmet.... Member of Stanley Cup championship teams (1987, 1988, 1990 and 1994).... Captain of Edmonton Oilers (1992-93 and 1993-94).

| Season Team | League | REGULAR SEASON | | | | | PLAYOFFS | | | | |
		Gms.	G	A	Pts.	PIM	Gms.	G	A	Pts.	PIM
77-78—University of Lowell	ECAC-II	24	26	19	45	...	—	—	—	—	—
78-79—University of Lowell	ECAC-II	31	36	52	*88	...	—	—	—	—	—
79-80—Binghamton	AHL	34	17	15	32	20	—	—	—	—	—
—Boston	NHL	46	11	17	28	8	10	2	3	5	7
80-81—Boston	NHL	24	3	5	8	13	—	—	—	—	—
—Springfield	AHL	53	19	24	43	89	7	5	4	9	8
81-82—Erie	AHL	72	23	32	55	37	—	—	—	—	—
—Boston	NHL	2	0	1	1	0	—	—	—	—	—
82-83—Boston	NHL	75	10	20	30	18	17	3	1	4	18
83-84—Boston	NHL	70	20	23	43	35	1	0	0	0	0
84-85—Boston	NHL					Did not play.					
85-86—Edmonton	NHL	74	23	24	47	70	10	4	4	8	11
86-87—Edmonton	NHL	79	20	19	39	55	21	1	9	10	16
87-88—Edmonton	NHL	80	15	17	32	47	19	0	1	1	31
88-89—Edmonton	NHL	80	21	31	52	55	7	0	1	1	8
89-90—Edmonton	NHL	80	21	22	43	89	22	2	6	8	29
90-91—Edmonton	NHL	80	17	15	32	76	18	3	3	6	20
91-92—Edmonton	NHL	80	12	18	30	98	16	3	0	3	28
92-93—Edmonton	NHL	82	10	20	30	110	—	—	—	—	—
93-94—Edmonton	NHL	66	16	10	26	80	—	—	—	—	—
—New York Rangers	NHL	12	4	2	6	11	23	1	4	5	22
94-95—Philadelphia	NHL	45	3	9	12	23	15	1	4	5	20
NHL totals		975	206	253	459	788	179	20	36	56	210

MADELEY, DARRIN
G, SENATORS

PERSONAL: Born February 25, 1968, in Holland Landing, Ont.... 5-11/168.... Catches left.... Name pronounced MAY-duh-lee.
HIGH SCHOOL: Aurora (Ont.).
COLLEGE: Lake Superior State (Mich.).
TRANSACTIONS/CAREER NOTES: Signed as free agent by Ottawa Senators (June 20, 1992).... Bruised back (November 15, 1993); missed two games.... Loaned by Senators to Detroit Vipers (March 12, 1995).
HONORS: Named to CCHA All-Star second team (1989-90).... Named to NCAA All-America West first team (1990-91).... Named to CCHA All-Star first team (1990-91 and 1991-92).... Named NCAA Tournament Most Valuable Player (1991-92).... Named CCHA Playoff Most Valuable Player (1991-92).... Named to NCAA All-Tournament team (1991-92).... Named to AHL All-Star second team (1992-93).

| Season Team | League | REGULAR SEASON | | | | | | | PLAYOFFS | | | | | |
		Gms.	Min.	W	L	T	GA	SO	Avg.	Gms.	Min.	W	L	GA	SO	Avg.
89-90—Lake Superior State	CCHA	30	1683	21	7	1	68	...	2.42	—	—	—	—	—	—	—
90-91—Lake Superior State	CCHA	36	2137	29	3	3	93	...	2.61	—	—	—	—	—	—	—
91-92—Lake Superior State	CCHA	36	2024	25	6	4	69	...	2.05	—	—	—	—	—	—	—
92-93—New Haven	AHL	41	2295	10	16	9	127	0	3.32	—	—	—	—	—	—	—
—Ottawa	NHL	2	90	0	2	0	10	0	6.67	—	—	—	—	—	—	—
93-94—Ottawa	NHL	32	1583	3	18	5	115	0	4.36	—	—	—	—	—	—	—
—Prince Edward Island	AHL	6	270	0	4	0	26	0	5.78	—	—	—	—	—	—	—
94-95—Ottawa	NHL	5	255	1	3	0	15	0	3.53	—	—	—	—	—	—	—
—Prince Edward Island	AHL	3	185	1	1	1	8	0	2.59	—	—	—	—	—	—	—
—Detroit	IHL	9	498	7	2	‡0	20	1	2.41	—	—	—	—	—	—	—
NHL totals		39	1928	4	23	5	140	0	4.36							

MAGARRELL, ADAM
D, FLYERS

PERSONAL: Born February 1, 1976, in Dormain, Man.... 6-3/178.... Shoots left.
HIGH SCHOOL: Crocus Plains (Brandon, Man.).
TRANSACTIONS/CAREER NOTES: Selected by Philadelphia Flyers in fourth round (second Flyers pick, 88th overall) of NHL entry draft (June 29, 1994).

| Season Team | League | REGULAR SEASON | | | | | PLAYOFFS | | | | |
		Gms.	G	A	Pts.	PIM	Gms.	G	A	Pts.	PIM
92-93—Brandon	WHL	8	0	0	0	0	—	—	—	—	—
93-94—Brandon	WHL	40	2	1	3	69	13	0	2	2	32
94-95—Brandon	WHL	41	0	3	3	72	—	—	—	—	—
—Spokane	WHL	19	0	4	4	27	11	0	0	0	34

MAGLIARDITI, MARC
G, BLACKHAWKS

PERSONAL: Born July 9, 1976, in Niagara Falls, N.Y.... 5-11/170.... Catches left.
TRANSACTIONS/CAREER NOTES: Selected by Chicago Blackhawks in sixth round (sixth Blackhawk pick, 146th overall) of NHL entry draft (July 8, 1995).

| Season Team | League | REGULAR SEASON | | | | | | | PLAYOFFS | | | | | |
		Gms.	Min.	W	L	T	GA	SO	Avg.	Gms.	Min.	W	L	GA	SO	Avg.
94-95—Des Moines	USHL	29	1727	...	...	...	82	0	2.85	—	—	—	—	—	—	—

MAGUIRE, DEREK
D, CANADIENS

PERSONAL: Born December 9, 1971, in Delbarton, N.J. . . . 6-0/185. . . . Shoots right.
COLLEGE: Harvard.
TRANSACTIONS/CAREER NOTES: Selected by Montreal Canadiens in ninth round (10th Canadiens pick, 186th overall) of NHL entry draft (June 16, 1990).
HONORS: Named to NCAA All-America East second team (1993-94). . . . Named to NCAA All-Tournament team (1993-94). . . . Named to ECAC All-Star second team (1993-94).

			REGULAR SEASON					PLAYOFFS			
Season Team	League	Gms.	G	A	Pts.	PIM	Gms.	G	A	Pts.	PIM
90-91—Harvard University	ECAC	25	3	14	17	12	—	—	—	—	—
91-92—Harvard University	ECAC	25	1	16	17	16	—	—	—	—	—
92-93—Harvard University	ECAC	16	3	9	12	10	—	—	—	—	—
93-94—Harvard University	ECAC	31	6	32	38	14	—	—	—	—	—
94-95—Fredericton	AHL	52	6	14	20	19	17	0	4	4	17

MAILLET, CHRIS
D, LIGHTNING

PERSONAL: Born January 28, 1976, in Moncton, Alta. . . . 6-5/188. . . . Shoots left. . . . Name pronounced MIGH-yeht.
TRANSACTIONS/CAREER NOTES: Selected by Tampa Bay Lightning in seventh round (seventh Lightning pick, 164th overall) of NHL entry draft (June 29, 1994).

			REGULAR SEASON					PLAYOFFS			
Season Team	League	Gms.	G	A	Pts.	PIM	Gms.	G	A	Pts.	PIM
93-94—Red Deer	WHL	52	0	0	0	102	1	0	0	0	5
94-95—Red Deer	WHL	47	1	9	10	102	—	—	—	—	—

MAKAROV, SERGEI
RW, SHARKS

PERSONAL: Born June 19, 1958, in Chelyabinsk, U.S.S.R. . . . 5-11/195. . . . Shoots left. . . . Name pronounced SAIR-gay muh-kah-rahf.
TRANSACTIONS/CAREER NOTES: Selected by Calgary Flames in 12th round (14th Flames pick, 231st overall) of NHL entry draft (June 8, 1983). . . . Traded by Flames to Hartford Whalers for future considerations (June 20, 1993). . . . Traded by Whalers with first-round (RW Victor Kozlov), second-round (D Vlastimil Kroupa) and third-round (LW Ville Peltonen) picks in 1993 draft to San Jose Sharks for first-round pick (D Chris Pronger) in 1993 draft (June 26, 1993). . . . Bruised big toe (March 22, 1994); missed one game. . . . Suspended one game by NHL for spearing (March 8, 1995).
HONORS: Won Golden Stick Award (1979-80 and 1985-86). . . . Won Soviet Player of the Year Award (1979-80, 1984-85 and 1988-89). . . . Won Izvestia Trophy (1979-80 through 1981-82 and 1983-84 through 1988-89). . . . Named to Soviet League All-Star team (1978-79 and 1980-81 through 1987-88). . . . Won Calder Memorial Trophy (1989-90). . . . Named to NHL All-Rookie team (1989-90).
STATISTICAL PLATEAUS: Three-goal games: 1990-91 (2), 1992-93 (1), 1993-94 (1). Total: 4.
MISCELLANEOUS: Member of silver-medal-winning U.S.S.R. Olympic team (1980) and gold-medal-winning U.S.S.R. Olympic team (1984 and 1988).

			REGULAR SEASON					PLAYOFFS			
Season Team	League	Gms.	G	A	Pts.	PIM	Gms.	G	A	Pts.	PIM
76-77—Traktor Chelyabinsk	USSR	11	1	0	1	4	—	—	—	—	—
77-78—Traktor Chelyabinsk	USSR	36	18	13	31	10	—	—	—	—	—
78-79—CSKA Moscow	USSR	44	18	21	39	12	—	—	—	—	—
79-80—CSKA Moscow	USSR	44	29	39	*68	16	—	—	—	—	—
—Soviet Olympic Team	Int'l	7	5	6	11	2	—	—	—	—	—
80-81—CSKA Moscow	USSR	49	42	37	*79	22	—	—	—	—	—
81-82—CSKA Moscow	USSR	46	32	43	*75	18	—	—	—	—	—
82-83—CSKA Moscow	USSR	30	25	17	42	6	—	—	—	—	—
83-84—CSKA Moscow	USSR	44	36	37	*73	28	—	—	—	—	—
—Soviet Olympic Team	Int'l	7	3	3	6	6	—	—	—	—	—
84-85—CSKA Moscow	USSR	40	26	39	*65	28	—	—	—	—	—
85-86—CSKA Moscow	USSR	40	30	32	*62	28	—	—	—	—	—
86-87—CSKA Moscow	USSR	40	21	32	*53	26	—	—	—	—	—
87-88—CSKA Moscow	USSR	51	23	45	*68	50	—	—	—	—	—
—Soviet Olympic Team	Int'l	8	3	8	11	10	—	—	—	—	—
88-89—CSKA Moscow	USSR	44	21	33	*54	42	—	—	—	—	—
89-90—Calgary	NHL	80	24	62	86	55	6	0	6	6	0
90-91—Calgary	NHL	78	30	49	79	44	3	1	0	1	0
91-92—Calgary	NHL	68	22	48	70	60	—	—	—	—	—
92-93—Calgary	NHL	71	18	39	57	40	—	—	—	—	—
93-94—San Jose	NHL	80	30	38	68	78	14	8	2	10	4
94-95—San Jose	NHL	43	10	14	24	40	11	3	3	6	4
NHL totals		**420**	**134**	**250**	**384**	**317**	**34**	**12**	**11**	**23**	**8**

MAKELA, MIKKO
LW, BRUINS

PERSONAL: Born February 28, 1965, in Tampere, Finland. . . . 6-2/200. . . . Shoots left. . . . Name pronounced MEE-koh MAK-uh-luh.
TRANSACTIONS/CAREER NOTES: Selected by New York Islanders in fourth round (fifth Islanders pick, 65th overall) of 1983 entry draft (June 8, 1983). . . . Injured back (November 1, 1985); missed 15 games. . . . Suffered elbow infection (February 1988). . . . Traded by Islanders to Los Angeles Kings for D Ken Baumgartner and C Hubie McDonough (November 29, 1989). . . . Bruised shoulder (December 13, 1989). . . . Traded by Kings to Buffalo Sabres for LW Mike Donnelly (October 1, 1990). . . . Signed as free agent by Boston Bruins (May 25, 1994). . . . Played in Europe during 1994-95 NHL lockout.
HONORS: Won Most Gentlemanly Player Trophy (1984-85). . . . Named to Finnish League All-Star first team (1984-85).
STATISTICAL PLATEAUS: Three-goal games: 1987-88 (1).

Season Team	League	REGULAR SEASON					PLAYOFFS				
		Gms.	G	A	Pts.	PIM	Gms.	G	A	Pts.	PIM
83-84—Ilves Tampere	Finland	35	17	11	28	26	2	0	1	1	0
84-85—Ilves Tampere	Finland	36	*34	25	59	24	9	4	7	11	10
85-86—Springfield......................	AHL	2	1	1	2	0	—	—	—	—	—
—New York Islanders..........	NHL	58	16	20	36	28	—	—	—	—	—
86-87—New York Islanders.........	NHL	80	24	33	57	24	11	2	4	6	8
87-88—New York Islanders.........	NHL	73	36	40	76	22	6	1	4	5	6
88-89—New York Islanders.........	NHL	76	17	28	45	22	—	—	—	—	—
89-90—New York Islanders.........	NHL	20	2	3	5	2	—	—	—	—	—
—Los Angeles..................	NHL	45	7	14	21	16	1	0	0	0	0
90-91—Buffalo..........................	NHL	60	15	7	22	25	—	—	—	—	—
91-92—TPS Turku	Finland	44	25	45	70	38	3	2	3	5	0
—Finnish Olympic Team......	Int'l	5	3	3	6	. . .					
92-93—TPS Turku	Finland	38	17	24	41	22	11	4	8	12	0
93-94—Malmo..........................	Sweden	37	15	21	36	20	11	4	7	11	2
—Finnish Olympic Team......	Int'l	8	2	3	5	4	—	—	—	—	—
94-95—Ilves Tampere	Finland	18	3	11	14	4	—	—	—	—	—
—Boston	NHL	11	1	2	3	0	—	—	—	—	—
—Providence	AHL	—	—	—	—	—	7	2	4	6	2
NHL totals...............		423	118	147	265	139	18	3	8	11	14

MAKINEN, MARKO
RW, SHARKS

PERSONAL: Born March 31, 1977, in Turku, Finland.... 6-4/198.... Shoots right.
TRANSACTIONS/CAREER NOTES: Selected by San Jose Sharks in third round (third Sharks pick, 64th overall) of NHL entry draft (July 8, 1995).

Season Team	League	REGULAR SEASON					PLAYOFFS				
		Gms.	G	A	Pts.	PIM	Gms.	G	A	Pts.	PIM
93-94—TPS Turku Jrs.	Finland	24	6	5	11	28	—	—	—	—	—
94-95—TPS Turku Jrs.	Finland	26	7	1	8	34	7	3	4	7	14
—Kiekko-67	Finland Dv.II	5	0	0	0	0	—	—	—	—	—

MALAKHOV, VLADIMIR
D, CANADIENS

PERSONAL: Born August 30, 1968, in Sverdlovsk, U.S.S.R.... 6-3/220.... Shoots.... Name pronounced MAL-ih-kahf.
TRANSACTIONS/CAREER NOTES: Selected by New York Islanders in 10th round (12th Islanders pick, 191st overall) of NHL entry draft (June 17, 1989)....
Suffered sore groin prior to 1992-93 season; missed first two games of season.... Injured right shoulder (January 16, 1993); missed eight games.... Sprained shoulder (March 14, 1993); missed five games.... Suffered concussion (December 7, 1993); missed one game.... Strained lower back (December 28, 1993); missed six games.... Suffered hip flexor (February 9, 1995); missed five games.... Suffered charley horse (March 14, 1995); missed two games.... Traded by Islanders with C Pierre Turgeon to Montreal Canadiens for LW Kirk Muller, D Mathieu Schneider and C Craig Darby (April 5, 1995).... Suffered hip flexor (April 24, 1995); missed one game.
HONORS: Named to NHL All-Rookie team (1992-93).
MISCELLANEOUS: Member of gold-medal-winning Unified Olympic team (1992).

Season Team	League	REGULAR SEASON					PLAYOFFS				
		Gms.	G	A	Pts.	PIM	Gms.	G	A	Pts.	PIM
86-87—Spartak Moscow	USSR	22	0	1	1	12	—	—	—	—	—
87-88—Spartak Moscow	USSR	28	2	2	4	26	—	—	—	—	—
88-89—CSKA Moscow	USSR	34	6	2	8	16	—	—	—	—	—
89-90—CSKA Moscow	USSR	48	2	10	12	34	—	—	—	—	—
90-91—CSKA Moscow	USSR	46	5	13	18	22	—	—	—	—	—
91-92—Unified Olympic Team.......	Int'l	8	3	0	3	4	—	—	—	—	—
—CSKA Moscow	CIS	40	1	9	10	12	—	—	—	—	—
92-93—Capital District................	AHL	3	2	1	3	11	—	—	—	—	—
—New York Islanders.........	NHL	64	14	38	52	59	17	3	6	9	12
93-94—New York Islanders.........	NHL	76	10	47	57	80	4	0	0	0	6
94-95—New York Islanders.........	NHL	26	3	13	16	32	—	—	—	—	—
—Montreal	NHL	14	1	4	5	14	—	—	—	—	—
NHL totals...............		180	28	102	130	185	21	3	6	9	18

MALARCHUK, CLINT
G

PERSONAL: Born May 1, 1961, in Grande Prairie, Alta.... 6-0/185.... Catches left.... Name pronounced muh-LAHR-chuhk.
TRANSACTIONS/CAREER NOTES: Selected by Quebec Nordiques in fourth round (third Nordiques pick, 74th overall) of NHL entry draft (June 11, 1981)....
Traded by Nordiques with C Dale Hunter to Washington Capitals for C Alan Haworth, LW Gaetan Duchesne and first-round pick (C Joe Sakic) in 1987 draft (June 1987).... Traded by Capitals with D Grant Ledyard to Buffalo Sabres for D Calle Johansson and second-round pick (G Byron Dafoe) in 1989 draft (March 6, 1989).... Suffered severed jugular vein (March 22, 1989). ... Strained neck and shoulder (January 23, 1991); missed 14 games.... Suffered from strep throat (November 2, 1991); missed three games.... Suffered from medicine reaction (January 27, 1992); missed six games.... Loaned to San Diego Gulls (October 12, 1992).... Named goaltenders coach of Las Vegas Thunder (July 24, 1995).
HONORS: Shared Harry (Hap) Holmes Memorial Trophy with Brian Ford (1982-83).... Shared James Norris Memorial Trophy with Rick Knickle (1992-93).

Season	Team	League	Gms.	Min.	W	L	T	GA	SO	Avg.	Gms.	Min.	W	L	GA	SO	Avg.
78-79—Portland	WHL	2	120	...	...	...	4	0	2.00	—	—	—	—	—	—	—
79-80—Portland	WHL	37	1948	21	10	0	147	0	4.53	1	40	0	0	3	0	4.50
80-81—Portland	WHL	38	2235	28	8	0	142	3	3.81	4	307	0	0	21	0	4.10
81-82—Quebec	NHL	2	120	0	1	1	14	0	7.00	—	—	—	—	—	—	—
—Fredericton	AHL	51	2962	15	34	2	*253	0	5.12	—	—	—	—	—	—	—
82-83—Quebec	NHL	15	900	8	5	2	71	0	4.73	—	—	—	—	—	—	—
—Fredericton	AHL	25	1506	0	0	0	78	1	*3.11	—	—	—	—	—	—	—
83-84—Fredericton	AHL	11	663	5	5	1	40	0	3.62	—	—	—	—	—	—	—
—Quebec	NHL	23	1215	10	9	2	80	0	3.95	—	—	—	—	—	—	—
84-85—Fredericton	AHL	*56	*3347	26	25	4	*198	2	3.55	6	379	2	4	20	0	3.17
85-86—Quebec	NHL	46	2657	26	12	4	142	4	3.21	3	143	0	2	11	0	4.62
86-87—Quebec	NHL	54	3092	18	26	9	175	1	3.40	3	140	0	2	8	0	3.43
87-88—Washington	NHL	54	2926	24	20	4	154	†4	3.16	4	193	0	2	15	0	4.66
88-89—Washington	NHL	42	2428	16	18	7	141	1	3.48	1	59	0	1	5	0	5.08
—Buffalo	NHL	7	326	3	1	1	13	1	2.39	—	—	—	—	—	—	—
89-90—Buffalo	NHL	29	1596	14	11	2	89	0	3.35	—	—	—	—	—	—	—
90-91—Buffalo	NHL	37	2131	12	14	10	119	1	3.35	4	246	2	2	17	0	4.15
91-92—Buffalo	NHL	29	1639	10	13	3	102	0	3.73	—	—	—	—	—	—	—
—Rochester	AHL	2	120	2	0	0	3	1	1.50	—	—	—	—	—	—	—
92-93—San Diego	IHL	27	1516	17	3	†0	72	3	2.85	†12	668	6	3	†34	0	3.05
93-94—Las Vegas	IHL	55	3076	*34	10	†7	172	1	3.36	5	257	1	2	16	0	3.74
94-95—Las Vegas	IHL	38	2039	15	13	†3	127	0	3.74	2	32	0	2	0	0	3.75
NHL totals		338	19030	141	130	45	1100	12	3.47	15	781	2	9	56	0	4.30

MALGUNAS, STEWART
D, FLYERS

PERSONAL: Born April 21, 1970, in Prince George, B.C. . . . 6-0/200. . . . Shoots left. . . . Name pronounced MAL-goo-nihz.

TRANSACTIONS/CAREER NOTES: Selected by Detroit Red Wings in fourth round (third Red Wings pick, 66th overall) of NHL entry draft (June 16, 1990). . . . Injured knee (September 26, 1992); missed first 10 games of season. . . . Traded by Red Wings to Philadelphia Flyers for fifth-round pick (G Frederic Deschenes) in 1994 draft (September 8, 1993). . . . Sprained medial collateral ligament in left knee (February 5, 1994); missed 12 games.

HONORS: Named to WHL (West) All-Star first team (1989-90).

Season	Team	League	Gms.	G	A	Pts.	PIM	Gms.	G	A	Pts.	PIM
87-88—Prince George	BCJHL	54	12	34	46	99	—	—	—	—	—
—New Westminster	WHL	6	0	0	0	0	—	—	—	—	—
88-89—Seattle	WHL	72	11	41	52	51	—	—	—	—	—
89-90—Seattle	WHL	63	15	48	63	116	13	2	9	11	32
90-91—Adirondack	AHL	78	5	19	24	70	2	0	0	0	4
91-92—Adirondack	AHL	69	4	28	32	82	18	2	6	8	28
92-93—Adirondack	AHL	45	3	12	15	39	11	3	3	6	8
93-94—Philadelphia	NHL	67	1	3	4	86	—	—	—	—	—
94-95—Hershey	AHL	32	3	5	8	28	6	2	1	3	31
—Philadelphia	NHL	4	0	0	0	4	—	—	—	—	—
NHL totals		71	1	3	4	90					

MALIK, MAREK
D, WHALERS

PERSONAL: Born June 24, 1975, in Ostrava, Czechoslovakia. . . . 6-5/190. . . . Shoots left. . . . Name pronounced muh-REHK muh-LEEK.

TRANSACTIONS/CAREER NOTES: Selected by Hartford Whalers in third round (second Whalers pick, 72nd overall) of NHL entry draft (June 26, 1993).

Season	Team	League	Gms.	G	A	Pts.	PIM	Gms.	G	A	Pts.	PIM
91-92—TJ Vitkovice Jrs	Czech. Jrs.				Statistics unavailable.						
92-93—TJ Vitkovice	Czech.	20	5	10	15	16	—	—	—	—	—
93-94—HC Vitkovice	Czech Rep.	38	3	3	6	...	3	0	1	1	0
94-95—Springfield	AHL	58	11	30	41	91	—	—	—	—	—
—Hartford	NHL	1	0	1	1	0	—	—	—	—	—
NHL totals		1	0	1	1	0					

MALLETTE, TROY
LW, SENATORS

PERSONAL: Born February 25, 1970, in Sudbury, Ont. . . . 6-2/214. . . . Shoots left. . . . Full name: Troy Matthew Mallette. . . . Name pronounced muh-LEHT.

TRANSACTIONS/CAREER NOTES: Selected by New York Rangers in second round (first Rangers pick, 22nd overall) of NHL entry draft (June 11, 1988). . . . Fined $500 by NHL for head-butting (March 19, 1990). . . . Sprained left knee ligaments (September 1990). . . . Fined $500 by NHL for attempting to injure another player (October 28, 1990). . . . Reinjured knee (October 29, 1990). . . . Injured shoulder (January 13, 1991). . . . Awarded to Edmonton Oilers as compensation for Rangers signing free agent C/LW Adam Graves (September 9, 1991). . . . Strained knee ligament (November 1991); missed two games. . . . Traded by Oilers to New Jersey Devils for LW David Maley (January 12, 1992). . . . Sprained right ankle (January 24, 1992); missed four games. . . . Suffered pinched nerve in neck (January 2, 1993); missed one game. . . . Traded by Devils with G Craig Billington and fourth-round pick in 1993 draft (C Cosmo Dupaul) to Ottawa Senators for G Peter Sidorkiewicz and future considerations (June 20, 1993); Senators sent LW Mike Peluso to Devils to complete deal (June 26, 1993). . . . Bruised ribs (February 24, 1995); missed five games.

M

Season Team	League	REGULAR SEASON					PLAYOFFS				
		Gms.	G	A	Pts.	PIM	Gms.	G	A	Pts.	PIM
86-87—Sault Ste. Marie	OHL	65	20	25	45	157	4	0	2	2	2
87-88—Sault Ste. Marie	OHL	62	18	30	48	186	6	1	3	4	12
88-89—Sault Ste. Marie	OHL	64	39	37	76	172	—	—	—	—	—
89-90—New York Rangers	NHL	79	13	16	29	305	10	2	2	4	81
90-91—New York Rangers	NHL	71	12	10	22	252	5	0	0	0	18
91-92—Edmonton	NHL	15	1	3	4	36	—	—	—	—	—
—New Jersey	NHL	17	3	4	7	43	—	—	—	—	—
92-93—New Jersey	NHL	34	4	3	7	56	—	—	—	—	—
—Utica	AHL	5	3	3	6	17	—	—	—	—	—
93-94—Ottawa	NHL	82	7	16	23	166	—	—	—	—	—
94-95—Ottawa	NHL	23	3	5	8	35	—	—	—	—	—
—Prince Edward Island	AHL	5	1	5	6	9	—	—	—	—	—
NHL totals...........................		321	43	57	100	893	15	2	2	4	99

MALONE, SCOTT
D, RANGERS

PERSONAL: Born January 16, 1971, in Boston.... 6-0/180.... Shoots left.
COLLEGE: New Hampshire.
TRANSACTIONS/CAREER NOTES: Selected by Toronto Maple Leafs in 11th round (10th Maple Leafs pick, 220th overall) of NHL entry draft (June 16, 1990).... Rights traded by Maple Leafs with D Glenn Anderson and fourth-round pick in 1994 draft (D Alexander Korobolin) to New York Rangers for RW Mike Gartner (March 21, 1994).
HONORS: Named to Hockey East All-Star second team (1993-94).

Season Team	League	REGULAR SEASON					PLAYOFFS				
		Gms.	G	A	Pts.	PIM	Gms.	G	A	Pts.	PIM
91-92—Univ. of New Hampshire ...	Hockey East	27	0	4	4	52	—	—	—	—	—
92-93—Univ. of New Hampshire ...	Hockey East	36	5	6	11	96	—	—	—	—	—
93-94—Univ. of New Hampshire ...	Hockey East	40	14	6	20	162	—	—	—	—	—
94-95—Birmingham	ECHL	8	1	4	5	36	—	—	—	—	—
—Binghamton	AHL	48	3	14	17	85	11	0	2	2	12

MALTAIS, STEVE
LW

PERSONAL: Born January 25, 1969, in Arvida, Ont.... 6-2/210.... Shoots left.... Name pronounced MAHL-tay.
TRANSACTIONS/CAREER NOTES: Selected by Washington Capitals as underage junior in third round (second Capitals pick, 57th overall) of NHL entry draft (June 13, 1987).... Traded by Capitals with C Trent Klatt to Minnesota North Stars for D Shawn Chambers (June 21, 1991).... Traded by North Stars to Quebec Nordiques for C Kip Miller (March 8, 1992).... Selected by Tampa Bay Lightning in NHL expansion draft (June 18, 1992).... Traded by Lightning to Detroit Red Wings for D Dennis Vial (June 8, 1993).... Signed as free agent by Chicago Wolves (September 8, 1994).
HONORS: Named to OHL All-Star second team (1988-89).... Named to IHL All-Star first team (1994-95).

Season Team	League	REGULAR SEASON					PLAYOFFS				
		Gms.	G	A	Pts.	PIM	Gms.	G	A	Pts.	PIM
85-86—Wexford Jr. B	MTHL	33	35	19	54	38	—	—	—	—	—
86-87—Cornwall	OHL	65	32	12	44	29	5	0	0	0	2
87-88—Cornwall	OHL	59	39	46	85	30	11	9	6	15	33
88-89—Cornwall	OHL	58	53	70	123	67	18	14	16	30	16
—Fort Wayne	IHL	—	—	—	—	—	4	2	1	3	0
89-90—Washington	NHL	8	0	0	0	2	1	0	0	0	0
—Baltimore	AHL	67	29	37	66	54	12	6	10	16	6
90-91—Baltimore	AHL	73	36	43	79	97	6	1	4	5	10
—Washington	NHL	7	0	0	0	2	—	—	—	—	—
91-92—Kalamazoo	IHL	48	25	31	56	51	—	—	—	—	—
—Minnesota	NHL	12	2	1	3	2	—	—	—	—	—
—Halifax	AHL	10	3	3	6	0	—	—	—	—	—
92-93—Atlanta	IHL	16	14	10	24	22	—	—	—	—	—
—Tampa Bay	NHL	63	7	13	20	35	—	—	—	—	—
93-94—Adirondack	AHL	73	35	49	84	79	12	5	11	16	14
—Detroit	NHL	4	0	1	1	0	—	—	—	—	—
94-95—Chicago	IHL	79	*57	40	97	145	3	1	1	2	0
NHL totals...........................		94	9	15	24	41	1	0	0	0	0

MALTBY, KIRK
RW, OILERS

PERSONAL: Born December 22, 1972, in Guelph, Ont.... 6-0/180.... Shoots right.
COLLEGE: Georgian (Ont.).
TRANSACTIONS/CAREER NOTES: Selected by Edmonton Oilers in third round (fourth Oilers pick, 65th overall) of NHL entry draft (June 20, 1992).... Suffered chip fracture of ankle bone (February 2, 1994); missed 13 games.... Lacerated right eye (March 1, 1995); missed last game of season.

Season Team	League	REGULAR SEASON					PLAYOFFS				
		Gms.	G	A	Pts.	PIM	Gms.	G	A	Pts.	PIM
88-89—Cambridge Jr. B	OHA	48	28	18	46	138	—	—	—	—	—
89-90—Owen Sound	OHL	61	12	15	27	90	12	1	6	7	15
90-91—Owen Sound	OHL	66	34	32	66	100	—	—	—	—	—
91-92—Owen Sound	OHL	64	50	41	91	99	5	3	3	6	18
92-93—Cape Breton	AHL	73	22	23	45	130	16	3	3	6	45

Season Team	League	REGULAR SEASON					PLAYOFFS				
		Gms.	G	A	Pts.	PIM	Gms.	G	A	Pts.	PIM
93-94—Edmonton	NHL	68	11	8	19	74	—	—	—	—	—
94-95—Edmonton	NHL	47	8	3	11	49	—	—	—	—	—
NHL totals		115	19	11	30	123					

MANDERVILLE, KENT
LW, MAPLE LEAFS

PERSONAL: Born April 12, 1971, in Edmonton. . . . 6-3/207. . . . Shoots left. . . . Full name: Kent Stephen Manderville.
COLLEGE: Cornell.
TRANSACTIONS/CAREER NOTES: Selected by Calgary Flames in second round (first Flames pick, 24th overall) of NHL entry draft (June 17, 1989). . . . Traded by Flames with C Doug Gilmour, D Jamie Macoun, D Ric Nattress and G Rick Wamsley to Toronto Maple Leafs for LW Craig Berube, D Alexander Godynyuk, RW Gary Leeman, D Michel Petit and G Jeff Reese (January 2, 1992). . . . Bruised hand (October 5, 1993); missed one game. . . . Suffered from the flu (December 17, 1993); missed two games. . . . Sprained ankle (January 30, 1995); missed one game.
HONORS: Named ECAC Rookie of the Year (1989-90). . . . Named to ECAC All-Rookie team (1989-90).
MISCELLANEOUS: Member of silver-medal-winning Canadian Olympic team (1992).

Season Team	League	REGULAR SEASON					PLAYOFFS				
		Gms.	G	A	Pts.	PIM	Gms.	G	A	Pts.	PIM
88-89—Notre Dame	SJHL	58	39	36	75	165	—	—	—	—	—
89-90—Cornell University	ECAC	26	11	15	26	28	—	—	—	—	—
90-91—Cornell University	ECAC	28	17	14	31	60	—	—	—	—	—
—Canadian national team	Int'l	3	1	2	3	0	—	—	—	—	—
91-92—Canadian national team	Int'l	63	16	23	39	75	—	—	—	—	—
—Canadian Olympic Team	Int'l	8	1	2	3	0	—	—	—	—	—
—Toronto	NHL	15	0	4	4	0	—	—	—	—	—
—St. John's	AHL	—	—	—	—	—	12	5	9	14	14
92-93—Toronto	NHL	18	1	1	2	17	18	1	0	1	8
—St. John's	AHL	56	19	28	47	86	2	0	2	2	0
93-94—Toronto	NHL	67	7	9	16	63	12	1	0	1	4
94-95—Toronto	NHL	36	0	1	1	22	7	0	0	0	6
NHL totals		136	8	15	23	102	37	2	0	2	18

MANELUK, MIKE
LW, MIGHTY DUCKS

PERSONAL: Born October 1, 1973, in Winnipeg. . . . 5-11/188. . . . Shoots right. . . . Name pronounced MAN-ih-luhk.
TRANSACTIONS/CAREER NOTES: Signed as free agent by Mighty Ducks of Anaheim (January 28, 1994).

Season Team	League	REGULAR SEASON					PLAYOFFS				
		Gms.	G	A	Pts.	PIM	Gms.	G	A	Pts.	PIM
90-91—St. Boniface	MJHL	45	29	41	70	199	—	—	—	—	—
91-92—Brandon	WHL	68	23	30	53	102	—	—	—	—	—
92-93—Brandon	WHL	72	36	51	87	75	4	2	1	3	2
93-94—Brandon	WHL	63	50	47	97	112	13	11	3	14	23
—San Diego	IHL	—	—	—	—	—	1	0	0	0	0
94-95—San Diego	IHL	10	0	1	1	4	—	—	—	—	—
—Canadian national team	Int'l	44	36	24	60	34	—	—	—	—	—

MANLOW, ERIC
C, BLACKHAWKS

PERSONAL: Born April 7, 1975, in Belleville, Ont. . . . 6-0/190. . . . Shoots left.
TRANSACTIONS/CAREER NOTES: Selected by Chicago Blackhawks in second round (second Blackhawks pick, 50th overall) of NHL entry draft (June 26, 1993).

Season Team	League	REGULAR SEASON					PLAYOFFS				
		Gms.	G	A	Pts.	PIM	Gms.	G	A	Pts.	PIM
91-92—Kitchener	OHL	59	12	20	32	17	14	2	5	7	8
92-93—Kitchener	OHL	53	26	21	47	31	4	0	1	1	2
93-94—Kitchener	OHL	49	28	32	60	25	3	0	1	1	4
94-95—Kitchener	OHL	44	25	29	54	26	—	—	—	—	—
—Detroit	OHL	16	4	16	20	11	21	11	10	21	18

MANN, CAMERON
RW, BRUINS

PERSONAL: Born April 20, 1977, in Thompson, Man. . . . 5-11/185. . . . Shoots right.
HIGH SCHOOL: Thomas A. Stewart (Peterborough, Ont.).
TRANSACTIONS/CAREER NOTES: Selected by Boston Bruins in fourth round (fifth Bruins pick, 99th overall) of NHL entry draft (July 8, 1995).

Season Team	League	REGULAR SEASON					PLAYOFFS				
		Gms.	G	A	Pts.	PIM	Gms.	G	A	Pts.	PIM
93-94—Peterborough	Tier II Jr.A	16	3	14	17	23	—	—	—	—	—
—Peterborough	OHL	49	8	17	25	18	7	1	1	2	2
94-95—Peterborough	OHL	64	18	25	43	40	11	3	8	11	4

MANSON, DAVE
D, JETS

PERSONAL: Born January 27, 1967, in Prince Albert, Sask. . . . 6-2/202. . . . Shoots left.
HIGH SCHOOL: Carleton (Prince Albert, Sask.).
TRANSACTIONS/CAREER NOTES: Selected by Chicago Blackhawks as underage junior in first round (first Blackhawks pick, 11th overall) of NHL entry draft (June 15, 1985). . . . Sus-

M

pended three games by NHL for pushing linesman (October 8, 1989).... Bruised right thigh (December 8, 1989).... Suspended 13 games by NHL for abusing linesman and returning to ice to fight (December 23, 1989).... Suspended three games by NHL for biting (February 27, 1990).... Suspended four games by NHL for attempting to injure another player (October 20, 1990).... Traded by Blackhawks with third-round pick in 1992 draft (RW Kirk Maltby) to Edmonton Oilers for D Steve Smith (October 2, 1991).... Suspended five off-days and fined $500 by NHL for spearing (October 19, 1992).... Strained ligaments in left knee (December 7, 1992); missed one game.... Separated shoulder (October 22, 1993); missed 13 games.... Traded by Oilers with sixth-round pick in 1994 draft to Winnipeg Jets for C Mats Lindgren, D Boris Mironov and first-round (C Jason Bonsignore) and fourth-round (RW Adam Copeland) picks in 1994 draft (March 15, 1994).... Bruised kidneys (January 21, 1995); missed one game.... Bruised hand (April 19, 1995); missed two games.

HONORS: Named to WHL All-Star second team (1985-86).... Played in NHL All-Star Game (1989 and 1993).

			REGULAR SEASON					PLAYOFFS				
Season	Team	League	Gms.	G	A	Pts.	PIM	Gms.	G	A	Pts.	PIM
83-84—Prince Albert		WHL	70	2	7	9	233	5	0	0	0	4
84-85—Prince Albert		WHL	72	8	30	38	247	13	1	0	1	34
85-86—Prince Albert		WHL	70	14	34	48	177	20	1	8	9	63
86-87—Chicago		NHL	63	1	8	9	146	3	0	0	0	10
87-88—Saginaw		IHL	6	0	3	3	37	—	—	—	—	—
—Chicago		NHL	54	1	6	7	185	5	0	0	0	27
88-89—Chicago		NHL	79	18	36	54	352	16	0	8	8	*84
89-90—Chicago		NHL	59	5	23	28	301	20	2	4	6	46
90-91—Chicago		NHL	75	14	15	29	191	6	0	1	1	36
91-92—Edmonton		NHL	79	15	32	47	220	16	3	9	12	44
92-93—Edmonton		NHL	83	15	30	45	210	—	—	—	—	—
93-94—Edmonton		NHL	57	3	13	16	140	—	—	—	—	—
—Winnipeg		NHL	13	1	4	5	51	—	—	—	—	—
94-95—Winnipeg		NHL	44	3	15	18	139	—	—	—	—	—
NHL totals			606	76	182	258	1935	66	5	22	27	247

MARACLE, NORM
G, RED WINGS

PERSONAL: Born October 2, 1974, in Belleville, Ont.... 5-9/175.... Catches left.... Name pronounced MAIR-ih-kuhl.

HIGH SCHOOL: Marion Graham (Regina, Sask.).

TRANSACTIONS/CAREER NOTES: Selected by Detroit Red Wings in fifth round (sixth Red Wings pick, 126th overall) of NHL entry draft (June 26, 1993).

HONORS: Named to Can.HL All-Rookie team (1991-92).... Named to WHL (East) All-Star second team (1992-93).... Won Can.HL Goaltender-of-the-Year Award (1993-94).... Won Del Wilson Trophy (1993-94).... Named to Can.HL All-Star first team (1993-94).... Named to WHL (East) All-Star first team (1993-94).

			REGULAR SEASON							PLAYOFFS						
Season	Team	League	Gms.	Min.	W	L	T	GA	SO	Avg.	Gms.	Min.	W	L	GA	SO	Avg.
91-92—Saskatoon		WHL	29	1529	13	6	3	87	1	3.41	15	860	9	5	37	0	2.58
92-93—Saskatoon		WHL	53	2939	27	18	3	160	1	3.27	9	569	4	5	33	0	3.48
93-94—Saskatoon		WHL	56	3219	*41	13	1	148	2	2.76	16	939	†11	5	48	†1	3.07
94-95—Adirondack		AHL	39	1997	12	15	2	119	0	3.58	—	—	—	—	—	—	—

MARCHANT, TODD
C/LW, OILERS

PERSONAL: Born August 12, 1973, in Buffalo, N.Y.... 6-0/190.... Shoots left.... Name pronounced MAHR-shahnt.... Brother of Terry Marchant, left winger in Edmonton Oilers system.

COLLEGE: Clarkson (N.Y.).

TRANSACTIONS/CAREER NOTES: Selected by New York Rangers in seventh round (eighth Rangers pick, 164th overall) of NHL entry draft (June 26, 1993).... Traded by Rangers to Edmonton Oilers for C Craig MacTavish (March 21, 1994).

			REGULAR SEASON					PLAYOFFS				
Season	Team	League	Gms.	G	A	Pts.	PIM	Gms.	G	A	Pts.	PIM
91-92—Clarkson		ECAC	33	20	12	32	32	—	—	—	—	—
92-93—Clarkson		ECAC	33	18	28	46	38	—	—	—	—	—
93-94—U.S. national team		Int'l	59	28	39	67	48	—	—	—	—	—
—U.S. Olympic Team		Int'l	8	1	1	2	6	—	—	—	—	—
—Binghamton		AHL	8	2	7	9	6	—	—	—	—	—
—New York Rangers		NHL	1	0	0	0	0	—	—	—	—	—
—Edmonton		NHL	3	0	1	1	2	—	—	—	—	—
—Cape Breton		AHL	3	1	4	5	2	5	1	1	2	0
94-95—Cape Breton		AHL	38	22	25	47	25	—	—	—	—	—
—Edmonton		NHL	45	13	14	27	32	—	—	—	—	—
NHL totals			49	13	15	28	34					

MARCHMENT, BRYAN
D, OILERS

PERSONAL: Born May 1, 1969, in Scarborough, Ont.... 6-1/198.... Shoots left.

TRANSACTIONS/CAREER NOTES: Suspended three games by OHL (October 1, 1986).... Selected by Winnipeg Jets as underage junior in first round (first Jets pick, 16th overall) of NHL entry draft (June 13, 1987).... Suspended six games by AHL for fighting (December 10, 1989).... Sprained shoulder (March 1990).... Suffered back spasms (March 13, 1991).... Traded by Jets with D Chris Norton to Chicago Blackhawks for C Troy Murray and LW Warren Rychel (July 22, 1991).... Fractured cheekbone (December 12, 1991); missed 12 games.... Suspended one preseason game and fined $500 by NHL for headbutting (September 30, 1993).... Traded with RW Steve Larmer by Blackhawks to Hartford Whalers for LW Patrick Poulin and D Eric Weinrich (November 2, 1993).... Suspended two games and fined $500 by NHL for illegal check (December 21, 1993).... Sprained ankle (January 14, 1994); missed three games.... Sprained ankle (February 19, 1994);

missed remainder of season.... Awarded to Edmonton Oilers as compensation for Whalers signing free agent RW Steven Rice (August 30, 1994).... Strained lower back (April 15, 1995); missed two games.... Suspended one game by NHL for game misconduct penalties (March 22, 1995).... Suspended two games by NHL for game misconduct penalties (March 27, 1995). ... Suspended three games and fined $500 by NHL for fighting player from bench (April 29, 1995).
HONORS: Named to OHL All-Star second team (1988-89).

			REGULAR SEASON					PLAYOFFS				
Season	Team	League	Gms.	G	A	Pts.	PIM	Gms.	G	A	Pts.	PIM
84-85—Toronto Nationals...........		MTHL	...	14	35	49	229	—	—	—	—	—
85-86—Belleville.........................		OHL	57	5	15	20	225	21	0	7	7	*83
86-87—Belleville.........................		OHL	52	6	38	44	238	6	0	4	4	17
87-88—Belleville.........................		OHL	56	7	51	58	200	6	1	3	4	19
88-89—Belleville.........................		OHL	43	14	36	50	198	5	0	1	1	12
—Winnipeg.........................		NHL	2	0	0	0	2	—	—	—	—	—
89-90—Winnipeg.........................		NHL	7	0	2	2	28	—	—	—	—	—
—Moncton.........................		AHL	56	4	19	23	217	—	—	—	—	—
90-91—Winnipeg.........................		NHL	28	2	2	4	91	—	—	—	—	—
—Moncton.........................		AHL	33	2	11	13	101	—	—	—	—	—
91-92—Chicago.........................		NHL	58	5	10	15	168	16	1	0	1	36
92-93—Chicago.........................		NHL	78	5	15	20	313	4	0	0	0	12
93-94—Chicago.........................		NHL	13	1	4	5	42	—	—	—	—	—
—Hartford.........................		NHL	42	3	7	10	124	—	—	—	—	—
94-95—Edmonton.........................		NHL	40	1	5	6	184	—	—	—	—	—
NHL totals................................			268	17	45	62	952	20	1	0	1	48

MARHA, JOSEF
C, DENVER

PERSONAL: Born June 2, 1976, in Havl. Brod, Czechoslovakia.... 6-0/176.... Shoots left.... Name pronounced mar-HA.
TRANSACTIONS/CAREER NOTES: Selected by Quebec Nordiques in second round (third Nordiques pick, 35th overall) of NHL entry draft (June 28, 1994).... Nordiques franchise moved to Denver for 1995-96 season.

			REGULAR SEASON					PLAYOFFS				
Season	Team	League	Gms.	G	A	Pts.	PIM	Gms.	G	A	Pts.	PIM
91-92—Jihlava.............................		Czech.	25	12	13	25	0	—	—	—	—	—
92-93—Dukla Jihlava		Czech.	7	2	2	4	4	—	—	—	—	—
93-94—Dukla Jihlava		Czech Rep.	41	7	2	9	...	3	0	1	1	...
94-95—Dukla Jihlava		Czech Rep.	35	3	7	10	...	—	—	—	—	—

MARINUCCI, CHRIS
LW, ISLANDERS

PERSONAL: Born December 29, 1971, in Grand Rapids, Minn.... 6-0/175.... Shoots left.... Full name: Christopher Jon Marinucci.
HIGH SCHOOL: Grand Rapids (Minn.).
COLLEGE: Minnesota-Duluth.
TRANSACTIONS/CAREER NOTES: Selected by New York Islanders in fifth round (fourth Islanders pick, 90th overall) of NHL entry draft (June 16, 1990).
HONORS: Named to WCHA All-Star second team (1992-93).... Won Hobey Baker Memorial Award (1993-94).... Named WCHA Player of the Year (1993-94).... Named to WCHA All-Star first team (1993-94).... Won Ken McKenzie Trophy (1994-95).

			REGULAR SEASON					PLAYOFFS				
Season	Team	League	Gms.	G	A	Pts.	PIM	Gms.	G	A	Pts.	PIM
88-89—Grand Rapids H.S.............		Minn. H.S.	25	24	18	42	...	—	—	—	—	—
89-90—Grand Rapids H.S.............		Minn. H.S.	28	24	39	63	0	—	—	—	—	—
90-91—Minnesota-Duluth		WCHA	36	6	10	16	20	—	—	—	—	—
91-92—Minnesota-Duluth		WCHA	37	6	13	19	41	—	—	—	—	—
92-93—Minnesota-Duluth		WCHA	40	35	42	77	52	—	—	—	—	—
93-94—Minnesota-Duluth		WCHA	38	*30	31	61	65	—	—	—	—	—
94-95—Denver..........................		IHL	74	29	40	69	42	14	3	4	7	12
—New York Islanders..........		NHL	12	1	4	5	2	—	—	—	—	—
NHL totals................................			12	1	4	5	2					

MARK, GORD
D, OILERS

PERSONAL: Born September 10, 1964, in Edmonton.... 6-4/220.... Shoots right.
TRANSACTIONS/CAREER NOTES: Selected by New Jersey Devils in sixth round (fourth Devils pick, 108th overall) of NHL entry draft (June 8, 1983).... Retired from 1988-89 through 1991-92 season.... Played for Stony Plain Eagles of Alberta Senior A League during retirement.... Broke kneecap (September 1992).... Signed as free agent by Edmonton Oilers (November 10, 1992).

			REGULAR SEASON					PLAYOFFS				
Season	Team	League	Gms.	G	A	Pts.	PIM	Gms.	G	A	Pts.	PIM
82-83—Kamloops		WHL	71	12	20	32	135	7	1	1	2	8
83-84—Kamloops		WHL	67	12	30	42	202	17	2	6	8	27
84-85—Kamloops		WHL	32	11	23	34	68	7	1	2	3	10
85-86—Maine.............................		AHL	77	9	13	22	134	5	0	1	1	9
86-87—New Jersey.....................		NHL	36	3	5	8	82	—	—	—	—	—
—Maine.............................		AHL	29	4	10	14	66	—	—	—	—	—
87-88—New Jersey.....................		NHL	19	0	2	2	27	—	—	—	—	—
—Utica.............................		AHL	50	5	21	26	96	—	—	—	—	—
88-89—..						Did not play—retired.						

M

Season	Team	League	Gms.	G	A	Pts.	PIM	Gms.	G	A	Pts.	PIM
89-90—						Did not play—retired.						
90-91—						Did not play—retired.						
91-92—						Did not play—retired.						
92-93—Cape Breton		AHL	60	3	21	24	78	16	1	7	8	20
93-94—Cape Breton		AHL	49	11	20	31	116	5	0	2	2	6
—Edmonton		NHL	12	0	1	1	43	—	—	—	—	—
94-95—Edmonton		NHL	18	0	2	2	35	—	—	—	—	—
NHL totals			85	3	10	13	187	19				

MARLEAU, DOMINIC
D, STARS

PERSONAL: Born February 11, 1977, in La Salle, Que. . . . 6-2/195. . . . Shoots right.
TRANSACTIONS/CAREER NOTES: Selected by Dallas Stars in sixth round (sixth Stars pick, 141st overall) of NHL entry draft (July 8, 1995).

Season	Team	League	Gms.	G	A	Pts.	PIM	Gms.	G	A	Pts.	PIM
93-94—Victoriaville		QMJHL	67	2	10	12	45	5	0	1	1	4
94-95—Victoriaville		QMJHL	63	3	13	16	78	3	0	0	0	11

MAROIS, DANIEL
RW, BRUINS

PERSONAL: Born October 3, 1968, in Montreal. . . . 6-0/190. . . . Shoots right. . . . Name pronounced MAIR-WAH.
TRANSACTIONS/CAREER NOTES: Selected by Toronto Maple Leafs as underage junior in second round (second Maple Leafs pick, 28th overall) of NHL entry draft (June 13, 1987). . . . Suffered from the flu (January 1989). . . . Damaged ligaments in right knee and underwent surgery (April 2, 1989). . . . Bruised left shoulder (November 12, 1989); missed 11 games. . . . Injured wrist (October 25, 1991); missed two games. . . . Traded by Maple Leafs with C Claude Loiselle to New York Islanders for LW Ken Baumgartner and C Dave McIlwain (March 10, 1992). . . . Strained lower back (December 23, 1992); missed three games. . . . Strained lower back (March 7, 1993); missed five games. . . . Traded by Islanders to Boston Bruins for eighth-round pick (C Peter Hogarth) in 1994 draft (March 18, 1993). . . . Underwent back surgery (April 1, 1993). . . . Injured shoulder (October 22, 1993); missed 54 games. . . . Underwent back surgery (December 1994); missed entire season.
STATISTICAL PLATEAUS: Three-goal games: 1988-89 (2), 1989-90 (1). Total: 3.

Season	Team	League	Gms.	G	A	Pts.	PIM	Gms.	G	A	Pts.	PIM
85-86—Verdun		QMJHL	58	42	35	77	110	5	4	2	6	6
86-87—Chicoutimi		QMJHL	40	22	26	48	143	16	7	14	21	25
87-88—Verdun		QMJHL	67	52	36	88	153	—				—
—Newmarket		AHL	8	4	4	8	4	—				—
—Toronto		NHL	—			—	—	3	1	0	1	0
88-89—Toronto		NHL	76	31	23	54	76	—				—
89-90—Toronto		NHL	68	39	37	76	82	5	2	2	4	12
90-91—Toronto		NHL	78	21	9	30	112	—				—
91-92—Toronto		NHL	63	15	11	26	76	—				—
—New York Islanders		NHL	12	2	5	7	18	—				—
92-93—New York Islanders		NHL	28	2	5	7	35	—				—
—Capital District		AHL	4	2	0	2	0	—				—
93-94—Boston		NHL	22	7	3	10	18	11	0	1	1	16
—Providence		AHL	6	1	2	3	6	—				—
94-95—Boston		NHL				Did not play—injured.						
NHL totals			347	117	93	210	417	19	3	3	6	28

MARSHALL, GRANT
RW, STARS

PERSONAL: Born June 9, 1973, in Toronto. . . . 6-1/185. . . . Shoots right.
HIGH SCHOOL: Hillcrest (Thunder Bay, Ont.).
TRANSACTIONS/CAREER NOTES: Selected by Toronto Maple Leafs in first round (second Maple Leafs pick, 23rd overall) of NHL entry draft (June 20, 1992). . . . Awarded to Dallas Stars with C Peter Zezel as compensation for Maple Leafs signing free-agent RW Mike Craig (August 10, 1994).

Season	Team	League	Gms.	G	A	Pts.	PIM	Gms.	G	A	Pts.	PIM
90-91—Ottawa		OHL	26	6	11	17	25	1	0	0	0	0
91-92—Ottawa		OHL	61	32	51	83	132	11	6	11	17	11
92-93—Newmarket		OHL	31	12	25	37	85	7	4	7	11	20
—Ottawa		OHL	30	14	28	42	83	—				—
—St. John's		AHL	2	0	0	0	0	2	0	0	0	2
93-94—St. John's		AHL	67	11	29	40	155	11	1	5	6	17
94-95—Kalamazoo		IHL	61	17	29	46	96	16	9	3	12	27
—Dallas		NHL	2	0	1	1	0	—				—
NHL totals			2	0	1	1	0					

MARSHALL, JASON
D, MIGHTY DUCKS

PERSONAL: Born February 22, 1971, in Cranbrook, B.C. . . . 6-2/195. . . . Shoots right.
TRANSACTIONS/CAREER NOTES: WHL rights traded by Regina Pats with RW Devin Derksen to Tri-City Americans for RW Mark Cipriano (August 1988). . . . Selected by St. Louis Blues in first round (first Blues pick, ninth overall) of NHL entry draft (June 17, 1989). . . . Traded by Blues to Mighty Ducks of Anaheim for D Bill Houlder (August 29, 1994).

Season Team	League	Gms.	G	A	Pts.	PIM	Gms.	G	A	Pts.	PIM
87-88—Columbia Valley	KIJHL	40	4	28	32	150	—	—	—	—	—
88-89—Vernon	BCJHL	48	10	30	40	197	31	6	6	12	141
—Canadian national team	Int'l	2	0	1	1	0	—	—	—	—	—
89-90—Canadian national team	Int'l	72	1	11	12	57	—	—	—	—	—
90-91—Tri-City	WHL	59	10	34	44	236	7	1	2	3	20
—Peoria	IHL	—	—	—	—	—	18	0	1	1	48
91-92—Peoria	IHL	78	4	18	22	178	10	0	1	1	16
—St. Louis	NHL	2	1	0	1	4	—	—	—	—	—
92-93—Peoria	IHL	77	4	16	20	229	4	0	0	0	20
93-94—Peoria	IHL	20	1	1	2	72	3	2	0	2	2
—Canadian national team	Int'l	41	3	10	13	60	—	—	—	—	—
94-95—San Diego	IHL	80	7	18	25	218	5	0	1	1	8
—Anaheim	NHL	1	0	0	0	0	—	—	—	—	—
NHL totals		3	1	0	1	4					

MARTIN, CRAIG
RW, JETS

PERSONAL: Born January 21, 1971, in Amherst, N.S.... 6-2/215.... Shoots right. **TRANSACTIONS/CAREER NOTES:** Suspended by QMJHL for opening game of 1990-91 season for fighting in a playoff game (April 14, 1990).... Selected by Winnipeg Jets in fifth round (sixth Jets pick, 98th overall) of NHL entry draft (June 16, 1990).... Suspended by QMJHL for striking referee with stick (December 9, 1990).... Signed as free agent by Detroit Red Wings (July 28, 1993).... Selected by Jets in 1994-95 NHL waiver draft for cash (January 18, 1995).

Season Team	League	Gms.	G	A	Pts.	PIM	Gms.	G	A	Pts.	PIM
87-88—Hull	QMJHL	66	5	5	10	137	—	—	—	—	—
88-89—Hull	QMJHL	70	14	29	43	260	—	—	—	—	—
89-90—Hull	QMJHL	66	14	31	45	299	11	2	1	3	65
90-91—Hull	QMJHL	18	5	6	11	166	—	—	—	—	—
—St. Hyacinthe	QMJHL	36	8	9	17	87	—	—	—	—	—
91-92—Fort Wayne	IHL	24	0	0	0	115	—	—	—	—	—
—Moncton	AHL	11	1	1	2	70	—	—	—	—	—
92-93—Moncton	AHL	64	5	13	18	198	5	0	1	1	22
93-94—Adirondack	AHL	76	15	24	39	297	12	2	2	4	63
94-95—Winnipeg	NHL	20	0	1	1	19	—	—	—	—	—
—Springfield	AHL	6	0	1	1	21	—	—	—	—	—
NHL totals		20	0	1	1	19					

MARTIN, MATT
D, MAPLE LEAFS

PERSONAL: Born April 30, 1971, in Hamden, Conn.... 6-3/205.... Shoots left. **HIGH SCHOOL:** Avon (Conn.) Old Farms School for Boys. **COLLEGE:** Maine. **TRANSACTIONS/CAREER NOTES:** Selected by Toronto Maple Leafs in fourth round (fourth Maple Leaf pick, 66th overall) of 1989 NHL entry draft (June 17, 1989).... Loaned to U.S. Olympic Team (October 5, 1993).... Returned to Maple Leafs (October 19, 1993).... Loaned to U.S. Olympic Team (October 28, 1993).... Returned to Maple Leafs (November 3, 1993).... Loaned to U.S. Olympic Team (November 15, 1993).... Returned to Maple Leafs (March 1, 1994).... Suffered hip pointer (April 8, 1995); missed three games.

Season Team	League	Gms.	G	A	Pts.	PIM	Gms.	G	A	Pts.	PIM
88-89—Avon Old Farms H.S.	Conn. H.S.	...	9	23	32	...	—	—	—	—	—
89-90—				Statistics Unavailable							
90-91—University of Maine	Hockey East	35	3	12	15	48	—	—	—	—	—
91-92—University of Maine	Hockey East	30	4	14	18	46	—	—	—	—	—
92-93—University of Maine	Hockey East	44	6	26	32	88	—	—	—	—	—
—St. John's	AHL	2	0	0	0	2	9	1	5	6	4
93-94—U.S. national team	Int'l	39	7	8	15	127	—	—	—	—	—
—Toronto	NHL	12	0	1	1	6	—	—	—	—	—
—U.S. Olympic Team	Int'l	8	0	2	2	8	—	—	—	—	—
—St. John's	AHL	12	1	5	6	9	11	1	5	6	33
94-95—St. John's	AHL	49	2	16	18	54	—	—	—	—	—
—Toronto	NHL	15	0	0	0	13	—	—	—	—	—
NHL totals		27	0	1	1	19					

MARTIN, MIKE
D, RANGERS

PERSONAL: Born October 27, 1976, in Stratford, Ont.... 6-2/204.... Shoots right. **TRANSACTIONS/CAREER NOTES:** Selected by New York Rangers in third round (second Rangers pick, 65th overall) of NHL entry draft (July 8, 1995).

Season Team	League	Gms.	G	A	Pts.	PIM	Gms.	G	A	Pts.	PIM
91-92—Stratford	OPJHL	16	2	3	5	14	—	—	—	—	—
92-93—Windsor	OHL	61	2	7	9	80	4	1	2	3	4
93-94—Windsor	OHL	64	2	29	31	94	4	1	2	3	4
94-95—Windsor	OHL	53	9	28	37	79	10	1	3	4	21

M

MARTINI, DARCY

D, OILERS

PERSONAL: Born January 30, 1969, in Castlegar, B.C.... 6-4/220.... Shoots left.
COLLEGE: Michigan Tech.
TRANSACTIONS/CAREER NOTES: Selected by Edmonton Oilers in eighth round (eighth Oilers pick, 162nd overall) of NHL entry draft (June 17, 1989).... Suspended six games by AHL for fighting (October 11, 1994).

			REGULAR SEASON					PLAYOFFS				
Season Team	League	Gms.	G	A	Pts.	PIM	Gms.	G	A	Pts.	PIM
84-85—Castlegar	KIJHL	38	4	17	21	58	—	—	—	—	—
85-86—Castlegar	KIJHL	38	8	28	36	180	—	—	—	—	—
86-87—Castlegar	KIJHL	40	12	53	65	260	—	—	—	—	—
87-88—Vernon	BCJHL	48	9	26	35	193	12	2	9	11	28
88-89—Michigan Tech	WCHA	37	1	2	3	107	—	—	—	—	—
89-90—Michigan Tech	WCHA	36	3	16	19	150	—	—	—	—	—
90-91—Michigan Tech	WCHA	34	10	13	23	*184	—	—	—	—	—
91-92—Michigan Tech	WCHA	17	5	13	18	58	—	—	—	—	—
92-93—Cape Breton	AHL	47	1	6	7	36	2	0	1	1	0
—Wheeling	ECHL	6	0	2	2	2	—	—	—	—	—
93-94—Cape Breton	AHL	65	18	38	56	131	5	1	3	4	26
—Edmonton	NHL	2	0	0	0	0	—	—	—	—	—
94-95—Cape Breton	AHL	31	2	13	15	75	—	—	—	—	—
—Portland	AHL	22	3	6	9	28	—	—	—	—	—
—Minnesota	IHL	10	3	1	4	10	1	0	0	0	2
NHL totals		2	0	0	0	0					

MARTINS, STEVE

C, WHALERS

PERSONAL: Born April 13, 1972, in Gatineau, Que.... 5-9/175.... Shoots left.
HIGH SCHOOL: Choate Rosemary Hall (Wallingford, Conn.).
COLLEGE: Harvard.
TRANSACTIONS/CAREER NOTES: Selected by Hartford Whalers in first round (first Whalers pick, fifth overall) of NHL supplemental draft (June 24, 1994).
HONORS: Named to NCAA All-America East first team (1993-94).... Named to NCAA All-Tournament team (1993-94).... Named to ECAC All-Star first team (1993-94).

			REGULAR SEASON					PLAYOFFS				
Season Team	League	Gms.	G	A	Pts.	PIM	Gms.	G	A	Pts.	PIM
91-92—Harvard University	ECAC	20	13	14	27	26	—	—	—	—	—
92-93—Harvard University	ECAC	18	6	8	14	40	—	—	—	—	—
93-94—Harvard University	ECAC	32	25	35	60	93	—	—	—	—	—
94-95—Harvard University	ECAC	28	15	23	38	93	—	—	—	—	—

MASON, CHRIS

G, DEVILS

PERSONAL: Born April 20, 1976, in Red Deer, Alta.... 5-11/180.... Catches left.
TRANSACTIONS/CAREER NOTES: Selected by New Jersey Devils in fifth round (seventh Devils pick, 122nd overall) of NHL entry draft (July 8, 1995).

			REGULAR SEASON							PLAYOFFS					
Season Team	League	Gms.	Min.	W	L	T	GA	SO	Avg.	Gms.	Min.	W	L	GA	SO	Avg.
94-95—Prince George	WHL	44	2288	8	30	1	192	1	5.03	—	—	—	—	—	—	—

MASOTTA, BRYAN

G, SENATORS

PERSONAL: Born May 30, 1975, in New Haven, Conn.... 6-2/195.... Catches left.
HIGH SCHOOL: Taft Prep (Watertown, Conn.), then Hotchkiss School (Lakeville, Conn.).
COLLEGE: Rensselaer Polytechnic Institute (N.Y.).
TRANSACTIONS/CAREER NOTES: Selected by Ottawa Senators in fourth round (third Senators pick, 81st overall) of NHL entry draft (June 29, 1994).

			REGULAR SEASON							PLAYOFFS					
Season Team	League	Gms.	Min.	W	L	T	GA	SO	Avg.	Gms.	Min.	W	L	GA	SO	Avg.
91-92—Taft	Conn. HS	14	...	...	...	...	...	1	3.10	—	—	—	—	—	—	—
92-93—Hotchkiss	Conn. HS	29	...	...	...	...	...	8	2.00	—	—	—	—	—	—	—
93-94—Hotchkiss	Conn. HS	18	856	...	...	...	38	8	2.66	—	—	—	—	—	—	—
94-95—R.P.I.	ECAC	13	646	5	6	0	46	0	4.27	—	—	—	—	—	—	—

MASTAD, MILT

D, BRUINS

PERSONAL: Born March 5, 1975, in Regina, Sask.... 6-3/205.... Shoots left.... Name pronounced MIHZ-tahd.
HIGH SCHOOL: Meadowdale (Lynnwood, Wash.).
TRANSACTIONS/CAREER NOTES: Selected by Boston Bruins in sixth round (sixth Bruins pick, 155th overall) of NHL entry draft (June 26, 1993).

			REGULAR SEASON					PLAYOFFS				
Season Team	League	Gms.	G	A	Pts.	PIM	Gms.	G	A	Pts.	PIM
91-92—Surrey Jr. A	BCJHL	55	1	13	14	122	—	—	—	—	—
92-93—Seattle	WHL	60	1	1	2	123	5	0	1	1	14
93-94—Seattle	WHL	29	1	3	4	59	—	—	—	—	—
—Moose Jaw	WHL	41	2	8	10	74	—	—	—	—	—
94-95—Moose Jaw	WHL	68	1	8	9	155	5	0	0	0	6

MATHIESON, JIM
D, CAPITALS

PERSONAL: Born January 24, 1970, in Kindersley, Sask. . . . 6-1/210. . . . Shoots left. . . . Full name: James Johnson Mathieson.
TRANSACTIONS/CAREER NOTES: Selected by Washington Capitals in third round (third Capitals pick, 59th overall) of NHL entry draft (June 17, 1989).

			REGULAR SEASON					PLAYOFFS				
Season Team	League	Gms.	G	A	Pts.	PIM	Gms.	G	A	Pts.	PIM
86-87—Regina	WHL	40	0	9	9	40	3	0	1	1	2
87-88—Regina	WHL	72	3	12	15	115	4	0	2	2	4
88-89—Regina	WHL	62	5	22	27	151	—	—	—	—	—
89-90—Regina	WHL	67	1	26	27	158	11	0	7	7	16
—Baltimore	AHL	—	—	—	—	—	3	0	0	0	4
—Washington	NHL	2	0	0	0	4	—	—	—	—	—
90-91—Baltimore	AHL	65	3	5	8	168	4	1	0	1	6
91-92—Baltimore	AHL	74	2	9	11	206	—	—	—	—	—
92-93—Baltimore	AHL	46	3	5	8	88	3	0	1	1	23
93-94—Portland	AHL	43	0	7	7	89	12	0	1	1	36
94-95—Portland	AHL	35	5	5	10	119	7	1	0	1	4
NHL totals		2	0	0	0	4					

MATTE, CHRISTIAN
RW, DENVER

PERSONAL: Born January 20, 1975, in Hull, Que. . . . 5-11/166. . . . Shoots right. . . . Name pronounced muh-TAY.
TRANSACTIONS/CAREER NOTES: Selected by Quebec Nordiques in sixth round (eighth Nordiques pick, 153rd overall) of NHL entry draft (June 26, 1993). . . . Nordiques franchise moved to Denver for 1995-96 season.
HONORS: Named to QMJHL All-Star second team (1993-94).

			REGULAR SEASON					PLAYOFFS				
Season Team	League	Gms.	G	A	Pts.	PIM	Gms.	G	A	Pts.	PIM
92-93—Granby	QMJHL	68	17	36	53	56	—	—	—	—	—
93-94—Granby	QMJHL	59	50	47	97	103	7	5	5	10	12
—Cornwall	AHL	1	0	0	0	0	—	—	—	—	—
94-95—Granby	QMJHL	66	50	66	116	86	13	11	7	18	12
—Cornwall	AHL	—	—	—	—	—	3	0	1	1	2

MATTEAU, STEPHANE
LW, RANGERS

PERSONAL: Born September 2, 1969, in Rouyn, Que. . . . 6-3/210. . . . Shoots left. . . . Name pronounced ma-TOH.
TRANSACTIONS/CAREER NOTES: Selected by Calgary Flames as underage junior in second round (second Flames pick, 25th overall) of NHL entry draft (June 13, 1987). . . . Bruised thigh (October 10, 1991); missed 43 games. . . . Traded by Flames to Chicago Blackhawks for D Trent Yawney (December 16, 1991). . . . Fractured left foot (January 27, 1992); missed 12 games. . . . Suffered tonsillitis (September 1992); missed first three games of 1992-93 season. . . . Pulled groin (December 17, 1993); missed three games. . . . Traded by Blackhawks with RW Brian Noonan to New York Rangers for RW Tony Amonte and rights to LW Matt Oates (March 21, 1994). . . . Suffered from the flu (February 1, 1995); missed one game. . . . Suffered back spasms (April 24, 1995); missed two games.
MISCELLANEOUS: Member of Stanley Cup championship team (1994).

			REGULAR SEASON					PLAYOFFS				
Season Team	League	Gms.	G	A	Pts.	PIM	Gms.	G	A	Pts.	PIM
85-86—Hull	QMJHL	60	6	8	14	19	4	0	0	0	0
86-87—Hull	QMJHL	69	27	48	75	113	8	3	7	10	8
87-88—Hull	QMJHL	57	17	40	57	179	18	5	14	19	84
88-89—Hull	QMJHL	59	44	45	89	202	9	8	6	14	30
—Salt Lake City	IHL	—	—	—	—	—	9	0	4	4	13
89-90—Salt Lake City	IHL	81	23	35	58	130	10	6	3	9	38
90-91—Calgary	NHL	78	15	19	34	93	5	0	1	1	0
91-92—Calgary	NHL	4	1	0	1	19	—	—	—	—	—
—Chicago	NHL	20	5	8	13	45	18	4	6	10	24
92-93—Chicago	NHL	79	15	18	33	98	3	0	1	1	2
93-94—Chicago	NHL	65	15	16	31	55	—	—	—	—	—
—New York Rangers	NHL	12	4	3	7	2	23	6	3	9	20
94-95—New York Rangers	NHL	41	3	5	8	25	9	0	1	1	10
NHL totals		299	58	69	127	337	58	10	12	22	56

MATTSSON, JESPER
C, FLAMES

PERSONAL: Born May 13, 1975, in Malmo, Sweden. . . . 6-0/173. . . . Shoots right.
TRANSACTIONS/CAREER NOTES: Selected by Calgary Flames in first round (first Flames pick, 18th overall) of NHL entry draft (June 26, 1993).

			REGULAR SEASON					PLAYOFFS				
Season Team	League	Gms.	G	A	Pts.	PIM	Gms.	G	A	Pts.	PIM
91-92—Malmo	Sweden	24	0	1	1	2	—	—	—	—	—
92-93—Malmo	Sweden	40	9	8	17	14	5	0	0	0	0
93-94—Malmo	Sweden	40	3	6	9	14	9	1	2	3	2
94-95—Malmo	Sweden	37	9	6	15	18	9	2	0	2	18

M

MATVICHUK, RICHARD

D, STARS

PERSONAL: Born February 5, 1973, in Edmonton. . . . 6-2/190. . . . Shoots left. . . . Name pronounced MAT-vih-chuhk.
TRANSACTIONS/CAREER NOTES: Selected by Minnesota North Stars in first round (first North Stars pick, eighth overall) of 1991 NHL entry draft (June 22, 1991). . . . Strained lower back (November 9, 1992); missed two games. . . . Sprained ankle (December 27, 1992); missed 10 games. . . . North Stars franchise moved from Minnesota to Dallas and renamed Stars for 1993-94 season. . . . Bruised shoulder (April 5, 1994); missed one game. . . . Tore knee ligaments and underwent knee surgery (September 20, 1994); missed first 16 games of season.
HONORS: Won Bill Hunter Trophy (1991-92). . . . Named to Can.HL All-Star second team (1991-92). . . . Named to WHL (East) All-Star first team (1991-92).

			REGULAR SEASON					PLAYOFFS				
Season	Team	League	Gms.	G	A	Pts.	PIM	Gms.	G	A	Pts.	PIM
88-89—Fort Saskatchewan		AJHL	58	7	36	43	147	—	—	—	—	—
89-90—Saskatoon		WHL	56	8	24	32	126	10	2	8	10	16
90-91—Saskatoon		WHL	68	13	36	49	117	—	—	—	—	—
91-92—Saskatoon		WHL	58	14	40	54	126	22	1	9	10	61
92-93—Minnesota		NHL	53	2	3	5	26	—	—	—	—	—
—Kalamazoo		IHL	3	0	1	1	6	—	—	—	—	—
93-94—Kalamazoo		IHL	43	8	17	25	84	—	—	—	—	—
—Dallas		NHL	25	0	3	3	22	7	1	1	2	12
94-95—Dallas		NHL	14	0	2	2	14	5	0	2	2	4
—Kalamazoo		IHL	17	0	6	6	16	—	—	—	—	—
NHL totals			92	2	8	10	62	12	1	3	4	16

MAY, ALAN

RW, FLAMES

PERSONAL: Born January 14, 1965, in Swan Hills, Alta. . . . 6-1/200. . . . Shoots right. . . . Full name: Alan Randy May.
TRANSACTIONS/CAREER NOTES: Signed as free agent by Boston Bruins (September 1987). . . . Traded by Bruins to Edmonton Oilers for LW Moe Lemay (March 8, 1988). . . . Traded by Oilers with D Jim Wiemer to Los Angeles Kings for C Brian Wilks and D John English (March 7, 1989). . . . Traded by Kings to Washington Capitals for fifth-round pick (G Tom Newman) in 1989 draft (June 17, 1989). . . . Fractured knuckle on left hand (October 20, 1990). . . . Strained shoulder (December 8, 1990). . . . Underwent surgery to nose (March 1992); missed two games. . . . Traded by Capitals with seventh-round pick in 1995 draft (RW Jeff Dewar) to Dallas Stars for D Jim Johnson (March 21, 1994). . . . Broke left hand (November 10, 1993); missed 12 games. . . . Traded by Stars to Calgary Flames for eighth-round pick (RW Sergei Luchinkin) in 1995 draft (April 7, 1995).
HONORS: Named to ECHL All-Star second team (1986-87).

			REGULAR SEASON					PLAYOFFS				
Season	Team	League	Gms.	G	A	Pts.	PIM	Gms.	G	A	Pts.	PIM
84-85—Estevan		SAJHL	64	51	47	98	409	—	—	—	—	—
85-86—Medicine Hat		WHL	6	1	0	1	25	—	—	—	—	—
86-87—New Westminster		WHL	32	8	9	17	81	—	—	—	—	—
—Springfield		AHL	4	0	2	2	11	—	—	—	—	—
—Carolina		ECHL	42	23	14	37	310	5	2	2	4	57
87-88—Maine		AHL	61	14	11	25	357	—	—	—	—	—
—Boston		NHL	3	0	0	0	15	—	—	—	—	—
—Nova Scotia		AHL	12	4	1	5	54	4	0	0	0	51
88-89—Edmonton		NHL	3	1	0	1	7	—	—	—	—	—
—Cape Breton		AHL	50	12	13	25	214	—	—	—	—	—
—New Haven		AHL	12	2	8	10	99	16	6	3	9	*105
89-90—Washington		NHL	77	7	10	17	339	15	0	0	0	37
90-91—Washington		NHL	67	4	6	10	264	11	1	1	2	37
91-92—Washington		NHL	75	6	9	15	221	7	0	0	0	0
92-93—Washington		NHL	83	6	10	16	268	6	0	1	1	6
93-94—Washington		NHL	43	4	7	11	97	—	—	—	—	—
—Dallas		NHL	8	1	0	1	18	1	0	0	0	0
94-95—Dallas		NHL	27	1	1	2	106	—	—	—	—	—
—Calgary		NHL	7	1	2	3	13	—	—	—	—	—
NHL totals			393	31	45	76	1348	40	1	2	3	80

MAY, BRAD

LW, SABRES

PERSONAL: Born November 29, 1971, in Toronto. . . . 6-1/210. . . . Shoots left.
TRANSACTIONS/CAREER NOTES: Selected by Buffalo Sabres in first round (first Sabres pick, 14th overall) of NHL entry draft (June 16, 1990). . . . Injured knee (August 1990). . . . Injured left knee ligaments (November 1990). . . . Broke bone in hand (March 11, 1995); missed 15 games.
HONORS: Named to OHL All-Star second team (1989-90 and 1990-91).

			REGULAR SEASON					PLAYOFFS				
Season	Team	League	Gms.	G	A	Pts.	PIM	Gms.	G	A	Pts.	PIM
87-88—Markham Jr. B		OHA	6	1	1	2	21	—	—	—	—	—
88-89—Niagara Falls		OHL	65	8	14	22	304	17	0	1	1	55
89-90—Niagara Falls		OHL	61	33	58	91	223	16	9	13	22	64
90-91—Niagara Falls		OHL	34	37	32	69	93	14	11	14	25	53
91-92—Buffalo		NHL	69	11	6	17	309	7	1	4	5	2
92-93—Buffalo		NHL	82	13	13	26	242	8	1	1	2	14
93-94—Buffalo		NHL	84	18	27	45	171	7	0	2	2	9
94-95—Buffalo		NHL	33	3	3	6	87	4	0	0	0	2
NHL totals			268	45	49	94	809	26	2	7	9	27

MAYERS, JAMAL
C, BLUES

PERSONAL: Born October 24, 1974, in Toronto. . . . 6-0/190. . . . Shoots right. . . . Name pronounced MAY-ohrs.
HIGH SCHOOL: Erindale Secondary (Mississauga, Ont.).
COLLEGE: Western Michigan.
TRANSACTIONS/CAREER NOTES: Selected by St. Louis Blues in fourth round (third Blues pick, 89th overall) of NHL entry draft (June 26, 1993).

				REGULAR SEASON					PLAYOFFS			
Season	Team	League	Gms.	G	A	Pts.	PIM	Gms.	G	A	Pts.	PIM
90-91—Thornhill		Jr. A	44	12	24	36	78	—	—	—	—	—
91-92—Thornhill		Jr. A	56	38	69	107	36	—	—	—	—	—
92-93—Western Michigan Univ.		CCHA	38	8	17	25	26	—	—	—	—	—
93-94—Western Michigan Univ.		CCHA	40	17	32	49	40	—	—	—	—	—
94-95—Western Michigan Univ.		CCHA	39	13	33	46	40	—	—	—	—	—

McALLISTER, CHRIS
D, CANUCKS

PERSONAL: Born June 16, 1975, in Saskatoon, Sask. . . . 6-0/236. . . . Shoots left.
TRANSACTIONS/CAREER NOTES: Selected by Vancouver Canucks in second round (first Canucks pick, 40th overall) of NHL entry draft (July 8, 1995).

				REGULAR SEASON					PLAYOFFS			
Season	Team	League	Gms.	G	A	Pts.	PIM	Gms.	G	A	Pts.	PIM
93-94—Humboldt		Tier II Jr.A	50	3	5	8	150	—	—	—	—	—
—Saskatoon		WHL	2	0	0	0	5	—	—	—	—	—
94-95—Saskatoon		WHL	65	2	8	10	134	10	0	0	0	28

McALPINE, CHRIS
D, DEVILS

PERSONAL: Born December 1, 1971, in Roseville, Minn. . . . 6-0/190. . . . Shoots right.
HIGH SCHOOL: Roseville (Minn.).
COLLEGE: Minnesota.
TRANSACTIONS/CAREER NOTES: Selected by New Jersey Devils in seventh round (seventh Devils pick, 137th overall) of NHL entry draft (June 16, 1990). . . . Injured thumb (March 26, 1995); missed four games.
HONORS: Named to NCCA All-America West second team (1993-94). . . . Named to WCHA All-Star first team (1993-94).
MISCELLANEOUS: Member of Stanley Cup championship team (1995).

				REGULAR SEASON					PLAYOFFS			
Season	Team	League	Gms.	G	A	Pts.	PIM	Gms.	G	A	Pts.	PIM
89-90—Roseville		Minn. H.S.	25	15	13	28	. . .	—	—	—	—	—
90-91—Univ. of Minnesota		WCHA	38	7	9	16	112	—	—	—	—	—
91-92—Univ. of Minnesota		WCHA	39	3	9	12	126	—	—	—	—	—
92-93—Univ. of Minnesota		WCHA	41	14	9	23	82	—	—	—	—	—
93-94—Univ. of Minnesota		WCHA	36	12	18	30	121	—	—	—	—	—
94-95—Albany		AHL	48	4	18	22	49	—	—	—	—	—
—New Jersey		NHL	24	0	3	3	17	—	—	—	—	—
NHL totals			24	0	3	3	17					

McAMMOND, DEAN
C, OILERS

PERSONAL: Born June 15, 1973, in Grand Cache, Alta. . . . 5-11/185. . . . Shoots left.
TRANSACTIONS/CAREER NOTES: Selected by Chicago Blackhawks in first round (first Blackhawks pick, 22nd overall) of NHL entry draft (June 22, 1991). . . . Traded by Blackhawks with D Igor Kravchuk to Edmonton Oilers for RW Joe Murphy (February 25, 1993). . . . Severed left Achilles tendon (February 1, 1995); missed last 41 games of season.
HONORS: Won Can.HL Plus/Minus Award (1991-92).

				REGULAR SEASON					PLAYOFFS			
Season	Team	League	Gms.	G	A	Pts.	PIM	Gms.	G	A	Pts.	PIM
89-90—Prince Albert		WHL	53	11	11	22	49	14	2	3	5	18
90-91—Prince Albert		WHL	71	33	35	68	108	2	0	1	1	6
91-92—Prince Albert		WHL	63	37	54	91	189	10	12	11	23	26
—Chicago		NHL	5	0	2	2	0	3	0	0	0	2
92-93—Prince Albert		WHL	30	19	29	48	44	—	—	—	—	—
—Swift Current		WHL	18	10	13	23	29	17	*16	19	35	20
93-94—Edmonton		NHL	45	6	21	27	16	—	—	—	—	—
—Cape Breton		AHL	28	9	12	21	38	—	—	—	—	—
94-95—Edmonton		NHL	6	0	0	0	0	—	—	—	—	—
NHL totals			56	6	23	29	16	3	0	0	0	2

McARTHUR, MARK
G, ISLANDERS

PERSONAL: Born November 16, 1975, in East York, Ont. . . . 5-11/179. . . . Catches left.
HIGH SCHOOL: Bishop MacDonnell (Guelph, Ont.).
TRANSACTIONS/CAREER NOTES: Selected by New York Islanders in fifth round (fifth Islanders pick, 112th overall) of NHL entry draft (June 29, 1994).
HONORS: Shared Dave Pinkney Trophy with Andy Adams (1994-95). . . . Named to OHL All-Star second team (1994-95).

				REGULAR SEASON						PLAYOFFS					
Season	Team	League	Gms.	Min.	W	L	T	GA	SO	Avg.	Gms.	Min.	W	L	GA	SO	Avg.
91-92—Peterborough		Jr. B	25	1198	. . .	. . .	. . .	98	0	4.91	—	—	—	—	—	—	—
92-93—Guelph		OHL	35	1853	14	14	3	180	0	5.83	—	—	—	—	—	—	—
93-94—Guelph		OHL	51	2936	25	18	5	201	0	4.11	9	561	4	5	38	0	4.06
94-95—Guelph		OHL	48	2776	34	8	4	130	1	*2.81	13	797	9	4	44	0	3.31

M

McBAIN, JASON
D, WHALERS

PERSONAL: Born April 12, 1974, in Ilion, N.Y. . . . 6-2/178. . . . Shoots right. . . . Brother of Mike McBain, defenseman in Tampa Bay Lightning system.
TRANSACTIONS/CAREER NOTES: Selected by Hartford Whalers in fourth round (fifth Whalers pick, 81st overall) of NHL entry draft (June 20, 1992).

			REGULAR SEASON					PLAYOFFS			
Season Team	League	Gms.	G	A	Pts.	PIM	Gms.	G	A	Pts.	PIM
90-91—Lethbridge	WHL	52	2	7	9	39	1	0	0	0	0
91-92—Lethbridge	WHL	13	0	1	1	12	—	—	—	—	—
—Portland	WHL	54	9	23	32	95	6	1	0	1	13
92-93—Portland	WHL	71	9	35	44	76	16	2	12	14	14
93-94—Portland	WHL	63	15	51	66	86	10	2	7	9	14
94-95—Springfield	AHL	77	16	28	44	92	—	—	—	—	—

McBAIN, MIKE
D, LIGHTNING

PERSONAL: Born January 12, 1977, in Kimberley, B.C. . . . 6-0/191. . . . Shoots left. . . . Brother of Jason McBain, defenseman in Hartford Whalers system.
TRANSACTIONS/CAREER NOTES: Selected by Tampa Bay Lightning in second round (second Lightning pick, 30th overall) of NHL entry draft (July 8, 1995).

			REGULAR SEASON					PLAYOFFS			
Season Team	League	Gms.	G	A	Pts.	PIM	Gms.	G	A	Pts.	PIM
92-93—Kingston	Tier II Jr.A	38	31	29	60	18	—	—	—	—	—
93-94—Red Deer	WHL	58	4	13	17	41	4	0	0	0	0
94-95—Red Deer	WHL	68	6	28	34	55	—	—	—	—	—

McBEAN, WAYNE
D, PENGUINS

PERSONAL: Born February 21, 1969, in Calgary. . . . 6-2/185. . . . Shoots left.
TRANSACTIONS/CAREER NOTES: Selected by Los Angeles Kings as underage junior in first round (first Kings pick, fourth overall) of NHL entry draft (June 13, 1987). . . . Traded by Kings with G Mark Fitzpatrick and future considerations to New York Islanders for G Kelly Hrudey (February 22, 1989); Kings sent D Doug Crossman to Islanders to complete deal. . . . Injured left knee (December 23, 1991); missed final 47 games of season. . . . Underwent arthroscopic surgery to left knee (December 31, 1991). . . . Sprained left wrist (October 12, 1993); missed five games. . . . Suffered from sore left knee (November 21, 1993); missed three games. . . . Traded by Islanders to Winnipeg Jets for RW Yan Kaminsky (February 1, 1994). . . . Selected by Pittsburgh Penguins in 1994-95 waiver draft for cash (January 18, 1995). . . . Underwent offseason wrist surgery; missed entire 1994-95 season.
HONORS: Won Top Defenseman Trophy East (1986-87). . . . Named to WHL (East) All-Star first team (1986-87). . . . Named to Memorial Cup All-Star team (1986-87).

			REGULAR SEASON					PLAYOFFS			
Season Team	League	Gms.	G	A	Pts.	PIM	Gms.	G	A	Pts.	PIM
85-86—Medicine Hat	WHL	67	1	14	15	73	25	1	5	6	36
86-87—Medicine Hat	WHL	71	12	41	53	163	20	2	8	10	40
87-88—Los Angeles	NHL	27	0	1	1	26	—	—	—	—	—
—Medicine Hat	WHL	30	15	30	45	48	16	6	17	23	50
88-89—New Haven	AHL	7	1	1	2	2	—	—	—	—	—
—Los Angeles	NHL	33	0	5	5	23	—	—	—	—	—
—New York Islanders	NHL	19	0	1	1	12	—	—	—	—	—
89-90—Springfield	AHL	68	6	33	39	48	17	4	11	15	31
—New York Islanders	NHL	5	0	1	1	2	2	1	1	2	0
90-91—Capital District	AHL	22	9	9	18	19	—	—	—	—	—
—New York Islanders	NHL	52	5	14	19	47	—	—	—	—	—
91-92—New York Islanders	NHL	25	2	4	6	18	—	—	—	—	—
92-93—Capital District	AHL	20	1	9	10	35	3	0	1	1	9
93-94—New York Islanders	NHL	19	1	4	5	16	—	—	—	—	—
—Salt Lake City	IHL	5	0	6	6	2	—	—	—	—	—
—Winnipeg	NHL	31	2	9	11	24	—	—	—	—	—
94-95—Pittsburgh	NHL			Did not play-injured.							
NHL totals		211	10	39	49	168	2	1	1	2	0

McCABE, BRYAN
D, ISLANDERS

PERSONAL: Born June 8, 1975, in St. Catharines, Ont. . . . 6-1/200. . . . Shoots left.
HIGH SCHOOL: Joel E. Ferris (Spokane, Wash.).
TRANSACTIONS/CAREER NOTES: Selected by New York Islanders in second round (second Islanders pick, 40th overall) of NHL entry draft (June 26, 1993).
HONORS: Named to WHL (West) All-Star second team (1992-93). . . . Named to WHL (West) All-Star first team (1993-94). . . . Named to WHL (East) All-Star first team (1994-95). . . . Named to Memorial Cup All-Star team (1994-95).

			REGULAR SEASON					PLAYOFFS			
Season Team	League	Gms.	G	A	Pts.	PIM	Gms.	G	A	Pts.	PIM
91-92—Medicine Hat	WHL	68	6	24	30	157	4	0	0	0	6
92-93—Medicine Hat	WHL	14	0	13	13	83	—	—	—	—	—
—Spokane	WHL	46	3	44	47	134	10	1	5	6	28
93-94—Spokane	WHL	64	22	62	84	218	3	0	4	4	4
94-95—Spokane	WHL	42	14	39	53	115	—	—	—	—	—
—Brandon	WHL	20	6	10	16	38	18	4	13	17	59

McCAMBRIDGE, KEITH
D, FLAMES

PERSONAL: Born February 1, 1974, in Thompson, Man. . . . 6-2/205. . . . Shoots left.
TRANSACTIONS/CAREER NOTES: Selected by Calgary Flames in eighth round (10th Flames pick, 201st overall) of NHL entry draft (June 29, 1994).

Season Team	League	Gms.	G	A	Pts.	PIM	Gms.	G	A	Pts.	PIM
91-92—Swift Current	WHL	72	1	4	5	84	8	0	0	0	2
92-93—Swift Current	WHL	70	0	6	6	87	17	0	1	1	27
93-94—Swift Current	WHL	71	0	10	10	179	7	0	0	0	4
94-95—Swift Current	WHL	48	5	7	12	120	—	—	—	—	—
—Kamloops	WHL	21	0	6	6	90	21	0	5	5	49

McCARTHY, SANDY
RW, FLAMES

PERSONAL: Born June 15, 1972, in Toronto.... 6-3/225.... Shoots right. **TRANSACTIONS/CAREER NOTES:** Suspended one game by QMJHL for attempting to injure another player (October 2, 1989).... Suspended one playoff game by QMJHL for pre-game fight (March 19, 1990).... Selected by Calgary Flames in third round (third Flames pick, 52nd overall) of NHL entry draft (June 22, 1991).... Strained right shoulder (December 18, 1993); missed two games.... Strained shoulder (December 27, 1993); missed one game.... Strained right knee (January 20, 1995); missed five games.... Suffered hernia (February 3, 1995); missed six games.

Season Team	League	Gms.	G	A	Pts.	PIM	Gms.	G	A	Pts.	PIM
89-90—Laval	QMJHL	65	10	11	21	269	—	—	—	—	—
90-91—Laval	QMJHL	68	21	19	40	297	—	—	—	—	—
91-92—Laval	QMJHL	62	39	51	90	326	8	4	5	9	81
92-93—Salt Lake City	IHL	77	18	20	38	220	—	—	—	—	—
93-94—Calgary	NHL	79	5	5	10	173	7	0	0	0	34
94-95—Calgary	NHL	37	5	3	8	101	6	0	1	1	17
NHL totals		116	10	8	18	274	13	0	1	1	51

McCARTY, DARREN
RW, RED WINGS

PERSONAL: Born April 1, 1972, in Burnaby, B.C.... 6-1/210.... Shoots right. **HIGH SCHOOL:** Quinte Secondary School (Belleville, Ont.). **TRANSACTIONS/CAREER NOTES:** Selected by Detroit Red Wings in second round (second Red Wings pick, 46th overall) of NHL entry draft (June 20, 1992).... Injured groin (January 29, 1994); missed five games.... Injured shoulder (March 23, 1994); missed five games.... Separated right shoulder (February 7, 1995); missed eight games.... Injured right hand (March 30, 1995); missed two games.... Injured left knee (April 9, 1995); missed five games.
HONORS: Won Jim Mahon Memorial Trophy (1991-92).... Named to Can.HL All-Star first team (1991-92).... Named to OHL All-Star first team (1991-92).

Season Team	League	Gms.	G	A	Pts.	PIM	Gms.	G	A	Pts.	PIM
88-89—Peterborough Jr. B	OHA	34	18	17	35	135	—	—	—	—	—
89-90—Belleville	OHL	63	12	15	27	142	11	1	1	2	21
90-91—Belleville	OHL	60	30	37	67	151	6	2	2	4	13
91-92—Belleville	OHL	65	*55	72	127	177	5	1	4	5	13
92-93—Adirondack	AHL	73	17	19	36	278	11	0	1	1	33
93-94—Detroit	NHL	67	9	17	26	181	7	2	2	4	8
94-95—Detroit	NHL	31	5	8	13	88	18	3	2	5	14
NHL totals		98	14	25	39	269	25	5	4	9	22

McCAULEY, ALYN
C, DEVILS

PERSONAL: Born May 29, 1977, in Brockville, Ont.... 5-10/185.... Shoots left. **HIGH SCHOOL:** Canterbury (Ottawa, Ont.). **TRANSACTIONS/CAREER NOTES:** Selected by New Jersey Devils in fourth round (fifth Devils pick, 79th overall) of NHL entry draft (July 8, 1995).

Season Team	League	Gms.	G	A	Pts.	PIM	Gms.	G	A	Pts.	PIM
92-93—Kingston Jr. A	MTHL	38	31	29	60	18	—	—	—	—	—
93-94—Ottawa	OHL	38	13	23	36	10	13	5	14	19	4
94-95—Ottawa	OHL	65	16	38	54	20	—	—	—	—	—

McCAULEY, BILL
C, BRUINS

PERSONAL: Born April 20, 1975, in Detroit.... 6-0/173.... Shoots left. **TRANSACTIONS/CAREER NOTES:** Selected by Florida Panthers in fourth round (sixth Panthers pick, 83rd overall) of NHL entry draft (June 26, 1993).... Returned to draft pool by Panthers and selected by Boston Bruins in third round (third Bruins pick, 73rd overall) of entry draft (July 8, 1995).

Season Team	League	Gms.	G	A	Pts.	PIM	Gms.	G	A	Pts.	PIM
91-92—Detroit Junior Red Wings	NAJHL	38	25	35	60	64	—	—	—	—	—
92-93—Detroit	OHL	65	13	37	50	24	15	1	4	5	6
93-94—Detroit	OHL	59	18	39	57	51	16	4	7	11	25
94-95—Detroit	OHL	66	41	61	102	43	21	12	*27	*39	12

McCOSH, SHAWN
C, RANGERS

PERSONAL: Born June 5, 1969, in Oshawa, Ont.... 6-0/188.... Shoots right. **TRANSACTIONS/CAREER NOTES:** Selected by Detroit Red Wings in fifth round (fifth Red Wings pick, 95th overall) of NHL entry draft (June 17, 1989).... Traded by Red Wings to Los Angeles Kings for eighth-round pick (D Justin Krall) in 1992 draft (August 15, 1990).... Traded by Kings with RW Bob Kudelski to Ottawa Senators for RW Jim Thomson and C Marc Fortier (December 20, 1992).... Signed as free agent by New York Rangers (August 17, 1993).

M

Season Team	League	REGULAR SEASON					PLAYOFFS				
		Gms.	G	A	Pts.	PIM	Gms.	G	A	Pts.	PIM
86-87—Hamilton	OHL	50	11	17	28	49	6	1	0	1	2
87-88—Hamilton	OHL	64	17	36	53	96	14	6	8	14	14
88-89—Niagara Falls	OHL	56	41	62	103	75	14	4	13	17	23
89-90—Niagara Falls	OHL	9	6	10	16	24	—	—	—	—	—
—Dukes of Hamilton	OHL	39	24	28	52	65	—	—	—	—	—
90-91—New Haven	AHL	66	16	21	37	104	—	—	—	—	—
91-92—Los Angeles	NHL	4	0	0	0	4	—	—	—	—	—
—Phoenix	IHL	71	21	32	53	118	—	—	—	—	—
—New Haven	AHL	—	—	—	—	—	5	0	1	1	0
92-93—Phoenix	IHL	22	9	8	17	36	—	—	—	—	—
—New Haven	AHL	46	22	32	54	54	—	—	—	—	—
93-94—Binghamton	AHL	75	31	44	75	68	—	—	—	—	—
94-95—Binghamton	AHL	67	23	60	83	73	8	3	9	12	6
—New York Rangers	NHL	5	1	0	1	2	—	—	—	—	—
NHL totals		9	1	0	1	6					

McCOSH, SHAYNE

D, WHALERS

PERSONAL: Born January 27, 1974, in Oshawa, Ont. . . . 6-0/ 193. . . . Shoots left.
TRANSACTIONS/CAREER NOTES: Signed as free agent by Hartford Whalers (October 5, 1992).

Season Team	League	REGULAR SEASON					PLAYOFFS				
		Gms.	G	A	Pts.	PIM	Gms.	G	A	Pts.	PIM
90-91—Kitchener	OHL	62	3	22	25	26	6	0	1	1	4
91-92—Kitchener	OHL	62	7	36	43	46	14	1	2	3	28
92-93—Kitchener	OHL	32	7	25	32	43	—	—	—	—	—
—Windsor	OHL	36	5	35	40	38	—	—	—	—	—
93-94—Windsor	OHL	34	3	21	24	46	—	—	—	—	—
—Detroit	OHL	25	3	18	21	33	17	3	8	11	24
94-95—Springfield	AHL	18	2	3	5	4	—	—	—	—	—
—Detroit	OHL	26	4	21	25	32	20	7	16	23	12

M

McCRIMMON, BRAD

D, WHALERS

PERSONAL: Born March 29, 1959, in Dodsland, Sask. . . . 5-11/ 197. . . . Shoots left. . . . Full name: Byron Brad McCrimmon.
TRANSACTIONS/CAREER NOTES: Selected by Boston Bruins in first round (second Bruins pick, 15th overall) of NHL entry draft (August 9, 1979). . . . Traded by Bruins to Philadelphia Flyers for G Pete Peeters (June 1982). . . . Broke bone in right hand (February 2, 1985); missed 13 games. . . . Separated left shoulder and underwent surgery (May 9, 1985). . . . Missed start of 1986-87 season due to contract dispute. . . . Traded by Flyers to Calgary Flames for third-round pick in 1988 draft (G Dominic Roussel) and first-round pick in 1989 draft (August 1987). . . . Suffered from skin rash (February 1989). . . . Fractured ankle (March 1989). . . . Traded by Flames to Detroit Red Wings for second-round pick (traded to New Jersey Devils who selected D David Harlock) for in 1990 draft (June 16, 1990). . . . Fractured right ankle (January 12, 1991); missed 16 games. . . . Suffered from the flu (October 24, 1992); missed one game. . . . Traded by Red Wings to Hartford Whalers for sixth-round pick in 1993 draft (June 1, 1993).
HONORS: Named to WCHL All-Star second team (1976-77). . . . Won Top Defenseman Trophy (1977-78). . . . Named to WCHL All-Star first team (1977-78). . . . Named to WHL All-Star first team (1978-79). . . . Named to Memorial Cup All-Star team (1978-79). . . . Won Emery Edge Award (1987-88). . . . Named to THE SPORTING NEWS All-Star second team (1987-88). . . . Named to NHL All-Star second team (1987-88). . . . Played in NHL All-Star Game (1988).
MISCELLANEOUS: Member of Stanley Cup championship team (1989). . . . Captain of Calgary Flames (1989-90).

Season Team	League	REGULAR SEASON					PLAYOFFS				
		Gms.	G	A	Pts.	PIM	Gms.	G	A	Pts.	PIM
76-77—Brandon	WCHL	72	18	66	84	96	—	—	—	—	—
77-78—Brandon	WCHL	65	19	78	97	245	8	2	11	13	20
78-79—Brandon	WHL	66	24	74	98	139	22	9	19	28	34
79-80—Boston	NHL	72	5	11	16	94	10	1	1	2	28
80-81—Boston	NHL	78	11	18	29	148	3	0	1	1	2
81-82—Boston	NHL	78	1	8	9	83	2	0	0	0	2
82-83—Philadelphia	NHL	79	4	21	25	61	3	0	0	0	4
83-84—Philadelphia	NHL	71	0	24	24	76	1	0	0	0	4
84-85—Philadelphia	NHL	66	8	35	43	81	11	2	1	3	15
85-86—Philadelphia	NHL	80	13	42	55	85	5	2	0	2	2
86-87—Philadelphia	NHL	71	10	29	39	52	26	3	5	8	30
87-88—Calgary	NHL	80	7	43	50	98	9	2	3	5	22
88-89—Calgary	NHL	72	5	17	22	96	22	0	3	3	30
89-90—Calgary	NHL	79	4	15	19	78	6	0	2	2	8
90-91—Detroit	NHL	64	0	13	13	81	7	1	1	2	21
91-92—Detroit	NHL	79	7	22	29	118	11	0	1	1	8
92-93—Detroit	NHL	60	1	14	15	71	—	—	—	—	—
93-94—Hartford	NHL	65	1	5	6	72	—	—	—	—	—
94-95—Hartford	NHL	33	0	1	1	42	—	—	—	—	—
NHL totals		1127	77	318	395	1336	116	11	18	29	176

McDONOUGH, HUBIE
C

PERSONAL: Born August 7, 1963, in Manchester, N.H. . . . 5-9/180. . . . Shoots left.
HIGH SCHOOL: Memorial (Manchester, N.H.).
COLLEGE: St. Anselm (N.H.).
TRANSACTIONS/CAREER NOTES: Signed as free agent by Los Angeles Kings (October 1987). . . . Traded by Kings with D Ken Baumgartner to New York Islanders for RW Mikko Makela (November 29, 1989). . . . Injured knee (September 1990). . . . Fractured left thumb (October 22, 1991). . . . Traded by Islanders to San Jose Sharks for cash (August 31, 1992). . . . Loaned to San Diego Gulls (September 29, 1992). . . . Returned to Sharks (January 6, 1993). . . . Loaned to Gulls (March 20, 1993). . . . Signed as free agent by Gulls (August 11, 1993). . . . Signed as free agent by Los Angeles Ice Dogs (June 6, 1995).
HONORS: Named to IHL All-Star second team (1992-93 and 1994-95).

Season Team	League	REGULAR SEASON					PLAYOFFS				
		Gms.	G	A	Pts.	PIM	Gms.	G	A	Pts.	PIM
82-83—St. Anselm College	ECAC-II	27	24	21	45	12	—	—	—	—	—
83-84—St. Anselm College	ECAC-II	26	37	15	52	20	—	—	—	—	—
84-85—St. Anselm College	ECAC-II	26	41	30	71	48	—	—	—	—	—
85-86—St. Anselm College	ECAC-II	25	22	20	42	16	—	—	—	—	—
86-87—Flint	IHL	82	27	52	79	59	6	3	2	5	0
87-88—New Haven	AHL	78	30	29	59	43	—	—	—	—	—
88-89—New Haven	AHL	74	37	55	92	41	17	10	*21	*31	6
—Los Angeles	NHL	4	0	1	1	0	—	—	—	—	—
89-90—Los Angeles	NHL	22	3	4	7	10	—	—	—	—	—
—New York Islanders	NHL	54	18	11	29	26	5	1	0	1	4
90-91—Capital District	AHL	17	9	9	18	4	—	—	—	—	—
—New York Islanders	NHL	52	6	6	12	10	—	—	—	—	—
91-92—Capital District	AHL	21	11	18	29	14	—	—	—	—	—
—New York Islanders	NHL	33	7	2	9	15	—	—	—	—	—
92-93—San Diego	IHL	48	26	49	75	26	14	4	7	11	6
—San Jose	NHL	30	6	2	8	6	—	—	—	—	—
93-94—San Diego	IHL	69	31	48	79	61	8	0	7	7	6
94-95—San Diego	IHL	80	43	55	98	10	5	0	1	1	4
NHL totals		195	40	26	66	67	5	1	0	1	4

McEACHERN, SHAWN
C, BRUINS

PERSONAL: Born February 28, 1969, in Waltham, Mass. . . . 6-0/195. . . . Shoots left. . . . Name pronounced muh-GEH-kruhn.
HIGH SCHOOL: Matignon (Cambridge, Mass.).
COLLEGE: Boston University.
TRANSACTIONS/CAREER NOTES: Selected by Pittsburgh Penguins in sixth round (sixth Penguins pick, 110th overall) of NHL entry draft (June 13, 1987). . . . Traded by Penguins to Los Angeles Kings for D Marty McSorley (August 27, 1993). . . . Traded by Kings to Penguins for D Marty McSorley and D Jim Paek (February 15, 1994). . . . Played in Europe during 1994-95 NHL lockout. . . . Suspended for first three games of 1994-95 season by NHL and fined $500 for slashing (September 21, 1994); suspension reduced to two games due to abbreviated 1994-95 season. . . . Traded by Penguins with LW Kevin Stevens to Boston Bruins for C Bryan Smolinski and RW Glen Murray (August 2, 1995).
HONORS: Named to Hockey East All-Star second team (1989-90). . . . Named Hockey East Tournament Most Valuable Player (1990-91). . . . Named to NCAA All-America East first team (1990-91). . . . Named to Hockey East All-Star first team (1990-91).
MISCELLANEOUS: Member of Stanley Cup championship team (1992).

Season Team	League	REGULAR SEASON					PLAYOFFS				
		Gms.	G	A	Pts.	PIM	Gms.	G	A	Pts.	PIM
85-86—Matignon H.S.	Mass. H.S.	20	32	20	52	...	—	—	—	—	—
86-87—Matignon H.S.	Mass. H.S.	16	29	28	57	...	—	—	—	—	—
87-88—Matignon H.S.	Mass. H.S.	...	52	40	92	...	—	—	—	—	—
88-89—Boston University	Hockey East	36	20	28	48	32	—	—	—	—	—
89-90—Boston University	Hockey East	43	25	31	56	78	—	—	—	—	—
90-91—Boston University	Hockey East	41	34	48	82	43	—	—	—	—	—
91-92—U.S. national team	Int'l	57	26	23	49	38	—	—	—	—	—
—U.S. Olympic Team	Int'l	8	1	0	1	10	—	—	—	—	—
—Pittsburgh	NHL	15	0	4	4	0	19	2	7	9	4
92-93—Pittsburgh	NHL	84	28	33	61	46	12	3	2	5	10
93-94—Los Angeles	NHL	49	8	13	21	24	—	—	—	—	—
—Pittsburgh	NHL	27	12	9	21	10	6	1	0	1	2
94-95—Kiekko-Espoo	Finland	8	1	3	4	6	—	—	—	—	—
—Pittsburgh	NHL	44	13	13	26	22	11	0	2	2	8
NHL totals		219	61	72	133	102	48	6	11	17	24

McGARRY, PAT
G, SHARKS

PERSONAL: Born November 3, 1970, in Ottawa. . . . 6-2/200.
COLLEGE: Dalhousie (Halifax, N.S.).
TRANSACTIONS/CAREER NOTES: Selected by Toronto Maple Leafs in NHL supplemental draft (June 21, 1991). . . . Signed as free agent by San Jose Sharks (April 8, 1995).

Season Team	League	REGULAR SEASON								PLAYOFFS						
		Gms.	Min.	W	L	T	GA	SO	Avg.	Gms.	Min.	W	L	GA	SO	Avg.
92-93—Springfield	AHL	3	117	0	1	0	12	0	6.15	—	—	—	—	—	—	—
—Louisville	ECHL	18	926	7	6	1	78	0	5.05	—	—	—	—	—	—	—
93-94—Fort Worth	CHL	47	2690	19	22	2	194	0	4.33	—	—	—	—	—	—	—
94-95—Fort Worth	CHL	46	2444	21	16	‡6	166	1	4.08	—	—	—	—	—	—	—
—Kansas City	IHL	7	371	2	2	‡1	20	0	3.23	—	—	—	—	—	—	—

McGILL, RYAN
D, OILERS

PERSONAL: Born February 28, 1969, in Prince Albert, Sask.... 6-2/205.... Shoots right. **TRANSACTIONS/CAREER NOTES:** Sprained ankle (January 1986).... Underwent knee surgery (July 1986).... Selected by Chicago Blackhawks as underage junior in second round (second Blackhawks pick, 29th overall) of NHL entry draft (June 13, 1987).... Traded by Swift Current Broncos to Medicine Hat Tigers for G Kelly Hitching (September 1987).... Traded by Blackhawks with C Mike McNeil to Quebec Nordiques for LW Dan Vincelette and C Paul Gillis (March 5, 1991).... Traded by Nordiques to Blackhawks for C Mike Dagenais (September 26, 1991).... Traded by Blackhawks to Philadelphia Flyers for LW Tony Horacek (February 7, 1992). ... Bruised left wrist (October 15, 1993); missed one game.... Sprained left wrist (December 7, 1993); missed eight games. ... Traded by Flyers to Edmonton Oilers for LW Brad Zavisha and sixth-round pick (D Jamie Sokolsky) in 1995 draft (March 13, 1995).... Suffered detached retina in right eye (April 5, 1995); missed last 13 games of season.
HONORS: Named to IHL All-Star second team (1990-91).

			REGULAR SEASON					PLAYOFFS				
Season	Team	League	Gms.	G	A	Pts.	PIM	Gms.	G	A	Pts.	PIM
85-86—Lethbridge		WHL	64	5	10	15	171	10	0	1	1	9
86-87—Swift Current		WHL	71	12	36	48	226	4	1	0	1	9
87-88—Medicine Hat		WHL	67	5	30	35	224	15	7	3	10	47
88-89—Medicine Hat		WHL	57	26	45	71	172	3	0	2	2	15
—Saginaw		IHL	8	2	0	2	12	6	0	0	0	42
89-90—Indianapolis		IHL	77	11	17	28	215	14	2	2	4	29
90-91—Indianapolis		IHL	63	11	40	51	200	—	—	—	—	—
—Halifax		AHL	7	0	4	4	6	—	—	—	—	—
91-92—Indianapolis		IHL	40	7	19	26	170	—	—	—	—	—
—Chicago		NHL	9	0	2	2	20	—	—	—	—	—
—Hershey		AHL	17	3	5	8	67	6	1	1	2	4
92-93—Hershey		AHL	4	0	2	2	26	—	—	—	—	—
—Philadelphia		NHL	72	3	10	13	238	—	—	—	—	—
93-94—Philadelphia		NHL	50	1	3	4	112	—	—	—	—	—
94-95—Philadelphia		NHL	12	0	0	0	13	—	—	—	—	—
—Edmonton		NHL	8	0	0	0	8	—	—	—	—	—
NHL totals			151	4	15	19	391					

McGILLIS, DANIEL
D, RED WINGS

PERSONAL: Born July 1, 1972, in Hawkesbury, Ont.... 6-2/220.... Shoots left. **COLLEGE:** Northeastern. **TRANSACTIONS/CAREER NOTES:** Selected by Detroit Red Wings in 10th round (10th Red Wings pick, 238th overall) of NHL entry draft (June 20, 1992).
HONORS: Named to Hockey East All-Star first team (1994-95).

			REGULAR SEASON					PLAYOFFS				
Season	Team	League	Gms.	G	A	Pts.	PIM	Gms.	G	A	Pts.	PIM
91-92—Hawkesbury		Tier II Jr.A	36	5	19	24	106	—	—	—	—	—
92-93—Northeastern University		Hockey East	35	5	12	17	42	—	—	—	—	—
93-94—Northeastern University		Hockey East	38	4	25	29	82	—	—	—	—	—
94-95—Northeastern University		Hockey East	34	9	22	31	70	—	—	—	—	—

McHUGH, MIKE
LW, FLYERS

PERSONAL: Born August 16, 1965, in Bowdoin, Mass.... 5-10/190.... Shoots left. **COLLEGE:** Maine. **TRANSACTIONS/CAREER NOTES:** Selected by Minnesota North Stars in NHL supplemental draft (June 10, 1988).... Selected by San Jose Sharks in NHL dispersal draft (May 30, 1991).... Traded by Sharks to Hartford Whalers for LW Paul Fenton (October 18, 1991).... Signed as free agent by Hershey Bears (1993).
HONORS: Named Hockey East Player of the Year (1987-88).... Named to NCAA All-America East second team (1987-88).... Named to Hockey East All-Rookie team (1987-88).

			REGULAR SEASON					PLAYOFFS				
Season	Team	League	Gms.	G	A	Pts.	PIM	Gms.	G	A	Pts.	PIM
84-85—University of Maine		Hockey East	25	9	8	17	9	—	—	—	—	—
85-86—University of Maine		Hockey East	38	9	10	19	24	—	—	—	—	—
86-87—University of Maine		Hockey East	42	21	29	50	40	—	—	—	—	—
87-88—University of Maine		Hockey East	44	29	37	66	90	—	—	—	—	—
88-89—Kalamazoo		IHL	70	17	29	46	89	6	3	1	4	17
—Minnesota		NHL	3	0	0	0	2	—	—	—	—	—
89-90—Kalamazoo		IHL	73	14	17	31	96	10	0	6	6	16
—Minnesota		NHL	3	0	0	0	0	—	—	—	—	—
90-91—Kalamazoo		IHL	69	27	38	65	82	11	3	8	11	6
—Minnesota		NHL	6	0	0	0	0	—	—	—	—	—
91-92—San Jose		NHL	8	1	0	1	14	—	—	—	—	—
—Springfield		AHL	70	23	31	54	51	11	4	7	11	25
92-93—Springfield		AHL	67	19	27	46	111	11	5	2	7	12
93-94—Hershey		AHL	80	27	43	70	58	11	9	3	12	14
94-95—Hershey		AHL	68	24	26	50	102	6	3	2	5	6
NHL totals			20	1	0	1	16					

McINNIS, MARTY
C/LW, ISLANDERS

PERSONAL: Born June 2, 1970, in Weymouth, Mass.... 6-0/183.... Shoots right.... Full name: Martin Edward McInnis.... Name pronounced muh-KIH-nihz. **HIGH SCHOOL:** Milton (Mass.) Academy. **COLLEGE:** Boston College.

TRANSACTIONS/CAREER NOTES: Selected by New York Islanders in eighth round (10th Islanders pick, 163rd overall) of NHL entry draft (June 11, 1988).... Injured eye (March 9, 1993); missed two games.... Fractured patella (March 27, 1993); missed remainder of regular season and 14 playoff games.... Sprained wrist (April 18, 1995); missed one game.

Season Team	League	REGULAR SEASON					PLAYOFFS				
		Gms.	G	A	Pts.	PIM	Gms.	G	A	Pts.	PIM
86-87—Milton Academy	Mass. H.S.	...	21	19	40	...	—	—	—	—	—
87-88—Milton Academy	Mass. H.S.	...	26	25	51	...	—	—	—	—	—
88-89—Boston College	Hockey East	39	13	19	32	8	—	—	—	—	—
89-90—Boston College	Hockey East	41	24	29	53	43	—	—	—	—	—
90-91—Boston College	Hockey East	38	21	36	57	40	—	—	—	—	—
91-92—U.S. national team	Int'l	54	15	19	34	20	—	—	—	—	—
—U.S. Olympic Team	Int'l	8	5	2	7	4	—	—	—	—	—
—New York Islanders	NHL	15	3	5	8	0	—	—	—	—	—
92-93—New York Islanders	NHL	56	10	20	30	24	3	0	1	1	0
—Capital District	AHL	10	4	12	16	2	—	—	—	—	—
93-94—New York Islanders	NHL	81	25	31	56	24	4	0	0	0	0
94-95—New York Islanders	NHL	41	9	7	16	8	—	—	—	—	—
NHL totals		193	47	63	110	56	7	0	1	1	0

McINTYRE, IAN
LW, DENVER

PERSONAL: Born February 12, 1974, in Montreal.... 6-0/184.... Shoots left.
TRANSACTIONS/CAREER NOTES: Selected by Quebec Nordiques in fourth round (fifth Nordiques pick, 76th overall) of NHL entry draft (June 20, 1992).... Nordiques franchise moved to Denver for 1995-96 season.
HONORS: Named to Can.HL All-Rookie team (1991-92).... Named to QMJHL All-Rookie team (1991-92).

Season Team	League	REGULAR SEASON					PLAYOFFS				
		Gms.	G	A	Pts.	PIM	Gms.	G	A	Pts.	PIM
91-92—Beauport	QMJHL	63	29	32	61	250	—	—	—	—	—
92-93—Beauport	QMJHL	44	14	18	32	115	—	—	—	—	—
93-94—Beauport	QMJHL	71	23	53	76	129	12	3	11	14	27
94-95—Beauport	QMJHL	56	10	33	43	149	18	1	4	5	49

McINTYRE, JOHN
C/LW, CANUCKS

PERSONAL: Born April 29, 1969, in Ravenswood, Ont.... 6-1/180.... Shoots left.
TRANSACTIONS/CAREER NOTES: Broke ankle (November 1985).... Severed nerve in right leg (February 1987).... Selected by Toronto Maple Leafs as underage junior in third round (third Maple Leafs pick, 49th overall) of NHL entry draft (June 13, 1987)....
Traded by Maple Leafs to Los Angeles Kings for LW/C Mike Krushelnyski (November 9, 1990).... Sprained left thumb (October 22, 1991); missed two games.... Broke nose (March 9, 1992); missed five games.... Traded by Kings to New York Rangers for D Mike Hardy and fifth-round pick (G Frederick Beaubien) in 1993 draft (March 22, 1993).... Selected by Vancouver Canucks in 1993 waiver draft (October 3, 1993).... Suffered concussion (October 21, 1993); missed four games.... Fractured foot (November 5, 1993); missed 16 games.
HONORS: Won Bobby Smith Trophy (1986-87).

Season Team	League	REGULAR SEASON					PLAYOFFS				
		Gms.	G	A	Pts.	PIM	Gms.	G	A	Pts.	PIM
84-85—Strathroy Jr. B	OHA	48	21	23	44	49	—	—	—	—	—
85-86—Guelph	OHL	30	4	6	10	25	20	1	5	6	31
86-87—Guelph	OHL	47	8	22	30	95	—	—	—	—	—
87-88—Guelph	OHL	39	24	18	42	109	—	—	—	—	—
88-89—Guelph	OHL	52	30	26	56	129	7	5	4	9	25
—Newmarket	AHL	3	0	2	2	7	5	1	1	2	20
89-90—Newmarket	AHL	6	2	2	4	12	—	—	—	—	—
—Toronto	NHL	59	5	12	17	117	2	0	0	0	2
90-91—Toronto	NHL	13	0	3	3	25	—	—	—	—	—
—Los Angeles	NHL	56	8	5	13	115	12	0	1	1	24
91-92—Los Angeles	NHL	73	5	19	24	100	6	0	4	4	12
92-93—Los Angeles	NHL	49	2	5	7	80	—	—	—	—	—
—New York Rangers	NHL	11	1	0	1	4	—	—	—	—	—
93-94—Vancouver	NHL	62	3	6	9	38	24	0	1	1	16
94-95—Vancouver	NHL	28	0	4	4	37	—	—	—	—	—
NHL totals		351	24	54	78	516	44	0	6	6	54

McKAY, KEVIN
D, BLACKHAWKS

PERSONAL: Born January 4, 1977, in North Battleford, Sask.... 6-2/198.... Shoots left.
HIGH SCHOOL: Vanier Collegiate (Moose Jaw, Sask.).
TRANSACTIONS/CAREER NOTES: Selected by Chicago Blackhawks in third round (third Blackhawks pick, 71st overall) of NHL entry draft (July 8, 1995).

Season Team	League	REGULAR SEASON					PLAYOFFS				
		Gms.	G	A	Pts.	PIM	Gms.	G	A	Pts.	PIM
93-94—Moose Jaw	WHL	6	0	0	0	2	—	—	—	—	—
94-95—Moose Jaw	WHL	56	1	11	12	93	10	0	2	2	17

McKAY, RANDY
RW, DEVILS

PERSONAL: Born January 25, 1967, in Montreal.... 6-1/205.... Shoots right.... Full name: Hugh Randall McKay.
COLLEGE: Michigan Tech.
TRANSACTIONS/CAREER NOTES: Selected by Detroit Red Wings in sixth round (sixth Red

Wings pick, 113th overall) of NHL entry draft (June 15, 1985).... Injured knee (February 1989).... Lacerated forearm (February 23, 1991).... Sent by Red Wings with C Dave Barr to New Jersey Devils as compensation for Red Wings signing free agent RW Troy Crowder (September 9,1991).... Sprained knee (January 16, 1993); missed nine games.... Bruised shoulder (November 3, 1993); missed three games.... Bruised shoulder (January 24, 1994); missed three games.... Injured groin (February 24, 1995); missed nine games.... Reinjured groin (March 18, 1995); missed six games.... Suffered charley horse (May 26, 1995); missed one playoff game.

MISCELLANEOUS: Member of Stanley Cup championship team (1995).

			REGULAR SEASON					PLAYOFFS			
Season Team	League	Gms.	G	A	Pts.	PIM	Gms.	G	A	Pts.	PIM
84-85—Michigan Tech	WCHA	25	4	5	9	32	—	—	—	—	—
85-86—Michigan Tech	WCHA	40	12	22	34	46	—	—	—	—	—
86-87—Michigan Tech	WCHA	39	5	11	16	46	—	—	—	—	—
87-88—Michigan Tech	WCHA	41	17	24	41	70	—	—	—	—	—
—Adirondack	AHL	10	0	3	3	12	6	0	4	4	0
88-89—Adirondack	AHL	58	29	34	63	170	14	4	7	11	60
—Detroit	NHL	3	0	0	0	0	2	0	0	0	2
89-90—Detroit	NHL	33	3	6	9	51	—	—	—	—	—
—Adirondack	AHL	36	16	23	39	99	6	3	0	3	35
90-91—Detroit	NHL	47	1	7	8	183	5	0	1	1	41
91-92—New Jersey	NHL	80	17	16	33	246	7	1	3	4	10
92-93—New Jersey	NHL	73	11	11	22	206	5	0	0	0	16
93-94—New Jersey	NHL	78	12	15	27	244	20	1	2	3	24
94-95—New Jersey	NHL	33	5	7	12	44	19	8	4	12	11
NHL totals		347	49	62	111	974	58	10	10	20	104

McKEE, JAY
D, SABRES

PERSONAL: Born September 8, 1977, in Kingston, Ont.... 6-2/ 175.... Shoots left.
HIGH SCHOOL: Stamford (Niagara Falls, Ont.).
TRANSACTIONS/CAREER NOTES: Selected by Buffalo Sabres in first round (first Sabres pick, 14th overall) of NHL entry draft (July 8, 1995).

			REGULAR SEASON					PLAYOFFS			
Season Team	League	Gms.	G	A	Pts.	PIM	Gms.	G	A	Pts.	PIM
92-93—Ernestown	Jr. C	36	0	17	17	37	—	—	—	—	—
93-94—Sudbury	OHL	51	0	1	1	51	3	0	0	0	0
94-95—Sudbury	OHL	39	6	6	12	91	—	—	—	—	—
—Niagara Falls	OHL	26	3	13	16	60	6	2	3	5	10

M

McKENZIE, JIM
LW, ISLANDERS

PERSONAL: Born November 3, 1969, in Gull Lake, Sask.... 6-3/205.... Shoots left.
TRANSACTIONS/CAREER NOTES: Selected by Hartford Whalers in fourth round (third Whalers pick, 73rd overall) of NHL entry draft (June 17, 1989).... Injured elbow (January 31, 1992); missed two games.... Suffered hip flexor (November 11, 1992); missed three games. ... Suffered hip flexor (December 5, 1992); missed four games.... Suffered back spasms (January 24, 1993); missed three games.... Suspended two games by NHL for game misconduct penalties (April 3, 1993).... Suspended three games by NHL for game misconduct penalties (April 10, 1993).... Traded by Whalers to Florida Panthers for D Alexander Godynyuk (December 16, 1993).... Traded by Panthers to Dallas Stars for fourth-round pick (LW Jamie Wright) in 1994 draft (December 16, 1993).... Traded by Stars to Pittsburgh Penguins for RW Mike Needham (March 21, 1994).... Broke toe (November 24, 1993); missed four games.... Bruised hand (March 11, 1995); missed one game.... Sprained wrist (April 5, 1995); missed seven games.... Signed as free agent by New York Islanders (July 31, 1995).

			REGULAR SEASON					PLAYOFFS			
Season Team	League	Gms.	G	A	Pts.	PIM	Gms.	G	A	Pts.	PIM
85-86—Moose Jaw	WHL	3	0	2	2	0	—	—	—	—	—
86-87—Moose Jaw	WHL	65	5	3	8	125	9	0	0	0	7
87-88—Moose Jaw	WHL	62	1	17	18	134	—	—	—	—	—
88-89—Victoria	WHL	67	15	27	42	176	8	1	4	5	30
89-90—Binghamton	AHL	56	4	12	16	149	—	—	—	—	—
—Hartford	NHL	5	0	0	0	4	—	—	—	—	—
90-91—Springfield	AHL	24	3	4	7	102	—	—	—	—	—
—Hartford	NHL	41	4	3	7	108	6	0	0	0	8
91-92—Hartford	NHL	67	5	1	6	87	—	—	—	—	—
92-93—Hartford	NHL	64	3	6	9	202	—	—	—	—	—
93-94—Hartford	NHL	26	1	2	3	67	—	—	—	—	—
—Dallas	NHL	34	2	3	5	63	—	—	—	—	—
—Pittsburgh	NHL	11	0	0	0	16	3	0	0	0	0
94-95—Pittsburgh	NHL	39	2	1	3	63	5	0	0	0	4
NHL totals		287	17	16	33	610	14	0	0	0	12

McKIM, ANDREW
C, RED WINGS

PERSONAL: Born July 6, 1970, in St. Johns, N.B. ... 5-7/170. ... Shoots right. ... Full name: Andrew Harry McKim.
TRANSACTIONS/CAREER NOTES: Traded by Verdun Jr. Canadiens with C Trevor Boland to Hull Olympiques for third-round pick (G Martin Brodeur) in 1989 QMJHL draft (May 26, 1989).... Signed as free agent by Calgary Flames (October 5, 1990).... Signed as free agent by Boston Bruins (July 16, 1992).... Broke jaw (January 2, 1993); missed 17 games.... Signed as free agent by Detroit Red Wings (August 2, 1994).
HONORS: Won Can.HL Most Sportsmanlike Player of the Year Award (1989-90).... Won Frank J. Selke Trophy (1989-90).... Won Michel Briere Trophy (1989-90).... Named to QMJHL All-Star first team (1989-90).

Season Team	League	REGULAR SEASON					PLAYOFFS				
		Gms.	G	A	Pts.	PIM	Gms.	G	A	Pts.	PIM
86-87—Verdun	QMJHL	70	28	59	87	12	—	—	—	—	—
87-88—Verdun	QMJHL	62	27	32	59	27	—	—	—	—	—
88-89—Verdun	QMJHL	68	50	56	106	36	—	—	—	—	—
89-90—Hull	QMJHL	70	66	64	130	44	11	8	10	18	8
90-91—Salt Lake City	IHL	74	30	30	60	48	4	0	2	2	6
91-92—St. John's	AHL	79	43	50	93	79	16	11	12	23	4
92-93—Providence	AHL	61	23	46	69	64	6	2	2	4	0
—Boston	NHL	7	1	3	4	0	—	—	—	—	—
93-94—Providence	AHL	46	13	24	37	49	—	—	—	—	—
—Boston	NHL	29	0	1	1	4	—	—	—	—	—
94-95—Adirondack	AHL	77	39	55	94	22	4	3	3	6	0
—Detroit	NHL	2	0	0	0	2	—	—	—	—	—
NHL totals		38	1	4	5	6					

McLAREN, KYLE
D, BRUINS

PERSONAL: Born June 18, 1977, in Coaldale, Alta. . . . 6-4/210. . . . Shoots left.
TRANSACTIONS/CAREER NOTES: Selected by Boston Bruins in first round (first Bruins pick, ninth overall) of NHL entry draft (July 8, 1995).

Season Team	League	REGULAR SEASON					PLAYOFFS				
		Gms.	G	A	Pts.	PIM	Gms.	G	A	Pts.	PIM
93-94—Tacoma	WHL	62	1	9	10	53	6	1	4	5	6
94-95—Tacoma	WHL	47	13	19	32	68	4	1	1	2	4

McLAREN, STEVE
D, BLACKHAWKS

PERSONAL: Born February 3, 1975, in Owen Sound, Ont. . . . 6-0/194. . . . Shoots left.
HIGH SCHOOL: Widdlifield (North Bay, Ont.).
TRANSACTIONS/CAREER NOTES: Selected by Chicago Blackhawks in fourth round (third Blackhawks pick, 85th overall) of NHL entry draft (June 29, 1994).

Season Team	League	REGULAR SEASON					PLAYOFFS				
		Gms.	G	A	Pts.	PIM	Gms.	G	A	Pts.	PIM
93-94—North Bay	OHL	55	2	15	17	130	18	0	3	3	50
94-95—North Bay	OHL	27	3	10	13	119	6	2	1	3	23

McLAUGHLIN, MIKE
LW, RANGERS

PERSONAL: Born March 29, 1970, in Springfield, Mass. . . . 6-1/175. . . . Shoots left.
. . . Full name: Michael Sean McLaughlin.
HIGH SCHOOL: Choate Rosemary Hall (Wallingford, Conn.).
COLLEGE: Vermont.
TRANSACTIONS/CAREER NOTES: Selected by Buffalo Sabres in sixth round (seventh Sabres pick, 118th overall) of NHL entry draft (June 11, 1988). . . . Signed as free agent by New York Rangers (August 17, 1993).

Season Team	League	REGULAR SEASON					PLAYOFFS				
		Gms.	G	A	Pts.	PIM	Gms.	G	A	Pts.	PIM
86-87—Choate Rosemary Hall	Conn. H.S.	. . .	19	18	37	. . .	—	—	—	—	—
87-88—Choate Rosemary Hall	Conn. H.S.	. . .	17	18	35	. . .	—	—	—	—	—
88-89—University of Vermont	ECAC	32	5	6	11	12	—	—	—	—	—
89-90—University of Vermont	ECAC	29	11	12	23	37	—	—	—	—	—
90-91—University of Vermont	ECAC	32	12	14	26	26	—	—	—	—	—
91-92—University of Vermont	ECAC	30	9	9	18	34	—	—	—	—	—
92-93—Rochester	AHL	71	19	35	54	27	16	4	2	6	8
93-94—Binghamton	AHL	56	11	13	24	33	—	—	—	—	—
94-95—Binghamton	AHL	60	10	16	26	27	8	0	3	3	0

McLEAN, JEFF
C

PERSONAL: Born October 6, 1969, in Port Moody, B.C. . . . 5-10/185. . . . Shoots left.
COLLEGE: North Dakota.
TRANSACTIONS/CAREER NOTES: Selected by San Jose Sharks in NHL supplemental draft (June 22, 1991).

Season Team	League	REGULAR SEASON					PLAYOFFS				
		Gms.	G	A	Pts.	PIM	Gms.	G	A	Pts.	PIM
87-88—North Dakota	WCHA	37	0	3	3	14	—	—	—	—	—
88-89—New Westminster	BCJHL	60	70	91	161	128	—	—	—	—	—
89-90—North Dakota	WCHA	45	10	16	26	42	—	—	—	—	—
90-91—North Dakota	WCHA	42	19	26	45	22	—	—	—	—	—
91-92—North Dakota	WCHA	39	27	43	70	40	—	—	—	—	—
92-93—Kansas City	IHL	60	21	23	44	45	10	3	1	4	2
93-94—Kansas City	IHL	69	27	30	57	44	—	—	—	—	—
—San Jose	NHL	6	1	0	1	0	—	—	—	—	—
94-95—Kalamazoo	IHL	41	16	18	34	22	4	1	4	5	0
NHL totals		6	1	0	1	0					

McLEAN, KIRK
G, CANUCKS

PERSONAL: Born June 26, 1966, in Willowdale, Ont. . . . 6-0/180. . . . Catches left.
TRANSACTIONS/CAREER NOTES: Selected by New Jersey Devils as underage junior in sixth round (sixth Devils pick, 107th overall) of NHL entry draft (June 9, 1984). . . . Traded by Devils with C Greg Adams and second-round pick in 1988 draft to Vancouver Canucks for C Patrik Sund-

M

strom, second-round and fourth-round (LW Matt Ruchty) picks in 1988 draft (September 15, 1987).... Suffered tendinitis in left wrist (February 25, 1991).
HONORS: Played in NHL All-Star Game (1990 and 1992).... Named to THE SPORTING NEWS All-Star second team (1991-92). ... Named to NHL All-Star second team (1991-92).
RECORDS: Holds NHL single-season playoff record for most minutes played by a goaltender—1,544 (1994).

Season	Team	League	Gms.	Min.	W	L	T	GA	SO	Avg.	Gms.	Min.	W	L	GA	SO	Avg.
			REGULAR SEASON								PLAYOFFS						
83-84—Oshawa		OHL	17	940	5	9	0	67	0	4.28	—	—	—	—	—	—	—
84-85—Oshawa		OHL	47	2581	23	17	2	143	1	*3.32	5	271	1	3	21	0	4.65
85-86—Oshawa		OHL	51	2830	24	21	2	169	1	3.58	4	201	1	2	18	0	5.37
—New Jersey		NHL	2	111	1	1	0	11	0	5.95	—	—	—	—	—	—	—
86-87—New Jersey		NHL	4	160	1	1	0	10	0	3.75	—	—	—	—	—	—	—
—Maine		AHL	45	2606	15	23	4	140	1	3.22	—	—	—	—	—	—	—
87-88—Vancouver		NHL	41	2380	11	27	3	147	1	3.71	—	—	—	—	—	—	—
88-89—Vancouver		NHL	42	2477	20	17	3	127	4	3.08	5	302	2	3	18	0	3.58
89-90—Vancouver		NHL	*63	*3739	21	30	10	*216	0	3.47	—	—	—	—	—	—	—
90-91—Vancouver		NHL	41	1969	10	22	3	131	0	3.99	2	123	1	1	7	0	3.41
91-92—Vancouver		NHL	65	3852	†38	17	9	176	†5	2.74	13	785	6	7	33	†2	2.52
92-93—Vancouver		NHL	54	3261	28	21	5	184	3	3.39	12	754	6	6	42	0	3.34
93-94—Vancouver		NHL	52	3128	23	26	3	156	3	2.99	24	*1544	15	*9	59	*4	2.29
94-95—Vancouver		NHL	40	2374	18	12	10	109	1	2.75	11	660	4	†7	36	0	3.27
NHL totals			404	23451	171	174	46	1267	17	3.24	67	4168	34	33	195	6	2.81

McLENNAN, JAMIE
G, ISLANDERS

PERSONAL: Born June 30, 1971, in Edmonton.... 6-0/189.... Catches left.
TRANSACTIONS/CAREER NOTES: Selected by New York Islanders in third round (third Islanders pick, 48th overall) of NHL entry draft (June 22, 1991).
HONORS: Won Del Wilson Trophy (1990-91).... Named to WHL (East) All-Star first team (1990-91).

Season	Team	League	Gms.	Min.	W	L	T	GA	SO	Avg.	Gms.	Min.	W	L	GA	SO	Avg.
			REGULAR SEASON								PLAYOFFS						
88-89—Spokane		WHL	11	578	...	...	...	63	0	6.54	—	—	—	—	—	—	—
—Lethbridge		WHL	7	368	...	...	...	22	0	3.59	—	—	—	—	—	—	—
89-90—Lethbridge		WHL	34	1690	20	4	2	110	1	3.91	13	677	6	5	44	0	3.90
90-91—Lethbridge		WHL	56	3230	32	18	4	205	0	3.81	*16	*970	8	8	*56	0	3.46
91-92—Capital District		AHL	18	952	4	10	2	60	1	3.78	—	—	—	—	—	—	—
—Richmond		ECHL	32	1837	16	12	‡2	114	0	3.72	—	—	—	—	—	—	—
92-93—Capital District		AHL	38	2171	17	14	6	117	1	3.23	1	20	0	1	5	0	15.00
93-94—Salt Lake City		IHL	24	1320	8	12	‡2	80	0	3.64	—	—	—	—	—	—	—
—New York Islanders		NHL	22	1287	8	7	6	61	0	2.84	2	82	0	1	6	0	4.39
94-95—New York Islanders		NHL	21	1185	6	11	2	67	0	3.39	—	—	—	—	—	—	—
—Denver		IHL	4	240	3	0	‡1	12	0	3.00	11	641	8	2	23	1	*2.15
NHL totals			43	2472	14	18	8	128	0	3.11	2	82	0	1	6	0	4.39

McLLWAIN, DAVID
C/RW, SENATORS

PERSONAL: Born January 9, 1967, in Seaforth, Ont.... 6-0/185.... Shoots right.... Name pronounced MAK-ihl-wayn.
TRANSACTIONS/CAREER NOTES: Traded by Kitchener Rangers with D John Keller and RW Todd Stromback to North Bay Centennials for RW Ron Sanko, RW Peter Lisy, Richard Hawkins and D Brett MacDonald (November 1985).... Selected by Pittsburgh Penguins as underage junior in ninth round (ninth Penguins pick, 172nd overall) of NHL entry draft (June 21, 1986).... Traded by Penguins with C/LW Randy Cunneyworth and G Richard Tabaracci to Winnipeg Jets for RW Andrew McBain, D Jim Kyte and LW Randy Gilhen (June 17, 1989).... Injured wrist (October 28, 1990).... Tore medial collateral ligament of right knee (December 3, 1990); missed 16 games.... Traded by Jets with D Gord Donnelly, fifth-round pick in 1992 draft (LW Yuri Khmylev) and future considerations to Buffalo Sabres for LW Darrin Shannon, LW Mike Hartman and D Dean Kennedy (October 11, 1991).... Traded by Sabres with C Pierre Turgeon, RW Benoit Hogue and D Uwe Krupp to New York Islanders for C Pat LaFontaine, LW Randy Wood, D Randy Hillier and future considerations (October 25, 1991); Sabres received fourth-round pick in 1992 draft (D Dean Melanson) to complete deal.... Traded by Islanders with LW Ken Baumgartner to Toronto Maple Leafs for C Claude Loiselle and RW Daniel Marois (March 10, 1992).... Selected by Ottawa Senators in 1993 waiver draft (October 3, 1993).... Separated left shoulder (December 30, 1993); missed 17 games.... Suffered charley horse (April 7, 1994); missed one game.... Bruised ribs (February 6, 1995); missed two games.... Injured knee (April 10, 1995); missed one game.
HONORS: Named to OHL All-Star second team (1986-87).

Season	Team	League	Gms.	G	A	Pts.	PIM	Gms.	G	A	Pts.	PIM
			REGULAR SEASON					PLAYOFFS				
84-85—Kitchener		OHL	61	13	21	34	29	—	—	—	—	—
85-86—Kitchener		OHL	13	7	7	14	12	—	—	—	—	—
—North Bay		OHL	51	30	28	58	25	10	4	4	8	2
86-87—North Bay		OHL	60	46	73	119	35	24	7	18	25	40
87-88—Muskegon		IHL	9	4	6	10	23	6	2	3	5	8
—Pittsburgh		NHL	66	11	8	19	40	—	—	—	—	—
88-89—Muskegon		IHL	46	37	35	72	51	7	8	2	10	6
—Pittsburgh		NHL	24	1	2	3	4	3	0	1	1	0
89-90—Winnipeg		NHL	80	25	26	51	60	7	0	1	1	2
90-91—Winnipeg		NHL	60	14	11	25	46	—	—	—	—	—

Season	Team	League	REGULAR SEASON Gms.	G	A	Pts.	PIM	PLAYOFFS Gms.	G	A	Pts.	PIM
91-92—	Winnipeg	NHL	3	1	1	2	2	—	—	—	—	—
	Buffalo	NHL	5	0	0	0	2	—	—	—	—	—
	New York Islanders	NHL	54	8	15	23	28	—	—	—	—	—
	Toronto	NHL	11	1	2	3	4	—	—	—	—	—
92-93—	Toronto	NHL	66	14	4	18	30	4	0	0	0	0
93-94—	Ottawa	NHL	66	17	26	43	48	—	—	—	—	—
94-95—	Ottawa	NHL	43	5	6	11	22	—	—	—	—	—
NHL totals			**478**	**97**	**101**	**198**	**286**	**14**	**0**	**2**	**2**	**2**

McPHEE, MIKE
LW

PERSONAL: Born February 14, 1960, in Sydney, N.S. . . . 6-1/205. . . . Shoots left. . . . Full name: Michael Joseph McPhee.
COLLEGE: Rensselaer Polytechnic Institute (N.Y.).
TRANSACTIONS/CAREER NOTES: Selected by Montreal Canadiens in sixth round (eighth Canadiens pick, 124th overall) of NHL entry draft (June 11, 1980). . . . Broke hand (September 1982). . . . Injured ankle (January 10, 1986); missed 10 games. . . . Broke little toe on left foot (February 1989). . . . Pulled muscle in rib cage (April 8, 1989). . . . Tore abdominal muscle (October 7, 1989); missed 13 games. . . . Injured groin, knee and thumb (November 13, 1990); missed 16 games. . . . Bruised thigh (February 26, 1992); missed one game. . . . Traded by Canadiens to Minnesota North Stars for fifth-round pick (D Jeff Lank) in 1993 draft (August 17, 1992). . . . North Stars franchise moved from Minnesota to Dallas and renamed Stars for 1993-94 season. . . . Strained back (December 9, 1993); missed three games. . . . Bruised knee (February 13, 1994); missed one game. . . . Strained knee ligaments (September 1994); missed entire season.
HONORS: Played in NHL All-Star Game (1989).
STATISTICAL PLATEAUS: Three-goal games: 1984-85 (1), 1985-86 (1), 1990-91 (1). Total: 3.
MISCELLANEOUS: Member of Stanley Cup championship team (1986).

Season	Team	League	REGULAR SEASON Gms.	G	A	Pts.	PIM	PLAYOFFS Gms.	G	A	Pts.	PIM
78-79—	R.P.I.	ECAC	26	14	19	33	16	—	—	—	—	—
79-80—	R.P.I.	ECAC	27	15	21	36	22	—	—	—	—	—
80-81—	R.P.I.	ECAC	29	28	18	46	22	—	—	—	—	—
81-82—	R.P.I.	ECAC	6	0	3	3	4	—	—	—	—	—
82-83—	Nova Scotia	AHL	42	10	15	25	29	7	1	1	2	14
83-84—	Nova Scotia	AHL	67	22	33	55	101	—	—	—	—	—
	Montreal	NHL	14	5	2	7	41	15	1	0	1	31
84-85—	Montreal	NHL	70	17	22	39	120	12	4	1	5	32
85-86—	Montreal	NHL	70	19	21	40	69	20	3	4	7	45
86-87—	Montreal	NHL	79	18	21	39	58	17	7	2	9	13
87-88—	Montreal	NHL	77	23	20	43	53	11	4	3	7	8
88-89—	Montreal	NHL	73	19	22	41	74	20	4	7	11	30
89-90—	Montreal	NHL	56	23	18	41	47	9	1	1	2	16
90-91—	Montreal	NHL	64	22	21	43	56	13	1	7	8	12
91-92—	Montreal	NHL	78	16	15	31	63	8	1	1	2	4
92-93—	Minnesota	NHL	84	18	22	40	44	—	—	—	—	—
93-94—	Dallas	NHL	79	20	15	35	36	9	2	1	3	2
94-95—	Dallas	NHL					Did not play.					
NHL totals			**744**	**200**	**199**	**399**	**661**	**134**	**28**	**27**	**55**	**193**

McRAE, BASIL
LW, BLUES

PERSONAL: Born January 5, 1961, in Beaverton, Ont. . . . 6-2/210. . . . Shoots left. . . . Full name: Basil Paul McRae. . . . Name pronounced BA-zihl muh-KRAY. . . . Brother of Chris McRae, left winger, Toronto Maple Leafs and Detroit Red Wings (1987-88 through 1989-90).
TRANSACTIONS/CAREER NOTES: Selected by Quebec Nordiques as underage junior in fifth round (third Nordiques pick, 87th overall) of NHL entry draft (June 11, 1980). . . . Traded by Nordiques to Toronto Maple Leafs for D Richard Turmel (August 12, 1983). . . . Signed as free agent by Detroit Red Wings (August 1985). . . . Traded by Red Wings with LW John Ogrodnick and RW Doug Shedden to Nordiques for LW Brent Ashton, RW Mark Kumpel and D Gilbert Delorme (January 17, 1987). . . . Signed as free agent by Minnesota North Stars (July 1987). . . . Strained right knee ligaments (October 10, 1989); missed nine games. . . . Suspended five games and fined $500 by NHL for fighting (December 28, 1989). . . . Strained abdominal muscle (October 1990). . . . Underwent abdominal surgery (November 29, 1990); missed 35 games. . . . Severed tendon (February 29, 1992); missed final 17 games of regular season. . . . Selected by Tampa Bay Lightning in NHL expansion draft (June 18, 1992). . . . Fractured bone in lower leg (October 11, 1992); missed 35 games. . . . Traded by Lightning with D Doug Crossman and fourth-round pick in 1996 draft to St. Louis Blues for LW Jason Ruff (January 28, 1993). . . . Suffered allergic reaction (November 16, 1993); missed two games. . . . Pulled abdominal muscle (January 3, 1994); missed seven games. . . . Underwent abdominal surgery (February 10, 1994); missed 18 games. . . . Injured abdomen (March 22, 1994); missed three games. . . . Injured rib (April 1, 1994); missed remainder of season. . . . Injured back (February 13, 1995); missed nine games.

Season	Team	League	REGULAR SEASON Gms.	G	A	Pts.	PIM	PLAYOFFS Gms.	G	A	Pts.	PIM
77-78—	Seneca Jr. B	OHA	36	21	38	59	80	—	—	—	—	—
78-79—	London	OMJHL	66	13	28	41	79	—	—	—	—	—
79-80—	London	OMJHL	67	23	35	58	116	5	0	0	0	18
80-81—	London	OMJHL	65	29	23	52	266	—	—	—	—	—
81-82—	Fredericton	AHL	47	11	15	26	175	—	—	—	—	—
	Quebec	NHL	20	4	3	7	69	9	1	0	1	34
82-83—	Fredericton	AHL	53	22	19	41	146	12	1	5	6	75
	Quebec	NHL	22	1	1	2	59	—	—	—	—	—

M

Season Team	League		REGULAR SEASON					PLAYOFFS			
		Gms.	G	A	Pts.	PIM	Gms.	G	A	Pts.	PIM
83-84—Toronto	NHL	3	0	0	0	19	—	—	—	—	—
—St. Catharines	AHL	78	14	25	39	187	6	0	0	0	40
84-85—St. Catharines	AHL	72	30	25	55	186	—	—	—	—	—
—Toronto	NHL	1	0	0	0	0	—	—	—	—	—
85-86—Detroit	NHL	4	0	0	0	5	—	—	—	—	—
—Adirondack	AHL	69	22	30	52	259	17	5	4	9	101
86-87—Detroit	NHL	36	2	2	4	193	—	—	—	—	—
—Quebec	NHL	33	9	5	14	149	13	3	1	4	*99
87-88—Minnesota	NHL	80	5	11	16	382	—	—	—	—	—
88-89—Minnesota	NHL	78	12	19	31	365	5	0	0	0	58
89-90—Minnesota	NHL	66	9	17	26	*351	7	1	0	1	24
90-91—Minnesota	NHL	40	1	3	4	224	22	1	1	2	*94
91-92—Minnesota	NHL	59	5	8	13	245	—	—	—	—	—
92-93—Tampa Bay	NHL	14	2	3	5	71	—	—	—	—	—
—St. Louis	NHL	33	1	3	4	98	11	0	1	1	24
93-94—St. Louis	NHL	40	1	2	3	103	2	0	0	0	12
94-95—St. Louis	NHL	21	0	5	5	72	7	2	1	3	4
—Peoria	IHL	2	0	0	0	12	—	—	—	—	—
NHL totals		550	52	82	134	2405	76	8	4	12	349

McRAE, KEN
RW, OILERS

PERSONAL: Born April 23, 1968, in Finch, Ont. . . . 6-1/195. . . . Shoots right. . . . Full name: Kenneth Duncan McRae.
TRANSACTIONS/CAREER NOTES: Selected by Quebec Nordiques as underage junior in first round (first Nordiques pick, 18th overall) of NHL entry draft (June 21, 1986). . . . Traded by Sudbury Wolves with C Andy Paquette and D Ken Alexander to Hamilton Steelhawks for C Dan Hie, C Joe Simon, RW Steve Locke, C Shawn Heaphy and D Jordan Fois (December 1986). . . . Lacerated right elbow (December 26, 1989); missed seven games. . . . Bruised shoulder (March 10, 1990). . . . Traded by Nordiques to Toronto Maple Leafs for D Leonard Esau (July 21, 1992). . . . Signed as free agent by Edmonton Oilers (September 2, 1994).

Season Team	League		REGULAR SEASON					PLAYOFFS			
		Gms.	G	A	Pts.	PIM	Gms.	G	A	Pts.	PIM
84-85—Hawkesbury	COJHL	51	38	50	88	77	—	—	—	—	—
85-86—Sudbury	OHL	66	25	40	65	127	4	2	1	3	12
86-87—Sudbury	OHL	21	12	15	27	40	—	—	—	—	—
—Hamilton	OHL	20	7	12	19	25	7	1	1	2	12
87-88—Fredericton	AHL	—	—	—	—	—	3	0	0	0	8
—Quebec	NHL	1	0	0	0	0	—	—	—	—	—
—Hamilton	OHL	62	30	55	85	158	14	13	9	22	35
88-89—Halifax	AHL	41	20	21	41	87	—	—	—	—	—
—Quebec	NHL	37	6	11	17	68	—	—	—	—	—
89-90—Quebec	NHL	66	7	8	15	191	—	—	—	—	—
90-91—Quebec	NHL	12	0	0	0	36	—	—	—	—	—
—Halifax	AHL	60	10	36	46	193	—	—	—	—	—
91-92—Halifax	AHL	52	30	41	71	184	—	—	—	—	—
—Quebec	NHL	10	0	1	1	31	—	—	—	—	—
92-93—St. John's	AHL	64	30	44	74	135	9	6	6	12	27
—Toronto	NHL	2	0	0	0	2	—	—	—	—	—
93-94—St. John's	AHL	65	23	41	64	200	—	—	—	—	—
—Toronto	NHL	9	1	1	2	36	6	0	0	0	4
94-95—Detroit	IHL	24	4	9	13	38	—	—	—	—	—
—Phoenix	IHL	2	2	0	2	0	9	3	8	11	21
NHL totals		137	14	21	35	364	6	0	0	0	4

McREYNOLDS, BRIAN
C, KINGS

PERSONAL: Born January 5, 1965, in Penetanguishene, Ont. . . . 6-1/192. . . . Shoots left.
COLLEGE: Michigan State.
TRANSACTIONS/CAREER NOTES: Selected by New York Rangers as underage junior in sixth round (sixth Rangers pick, 112th overall) of NHL entry draft (June 15, 1985). . . . Signed as free agent by Winnipeg Jets (July 1989). . . . Traded by Jets to Rangers for C Simon Wheeldon (July 10, 1990). . . . Signed as free agent by Los Angeles Kings (July 29, 1993). . . . Loaned by Kings from Phoenix Roadrunners to Atlanta Knights (March 18, 1995).

Season Team	League		REGULAR SEASON					PLAYOFFS			
		Gms.	G	A	Pts.	PIM	Gms.	G	A	Pts.	PIM
84-85—Orillia	OHA	48	40	54	94	...	—	—	—	—	—
85-86—Michigan State	CCHA	45	14	24	38	78	—	—	—	—	—
86-87—Michigan State	CCHA	45	16	24	40	68	—	—	—	—	—
87-88—Michigan State	CCHA	43	10	24	34	50	—	—	—	—	—
88-89—Canadian national team	Int'l	58	5	25	30	59	—	—	—	—	—
89-90—Winnipeg	NHL	9	0	2	2	4	—	—	—	—	—
—Moncton	AHL	72	18	41	59	87	—	—	—	—	—
90-91—Binghamton	AHL	77	30	42	72	74	10	0	4	4	6
—New York Rangers	NHL	1	0	0	0	0	—	—	—	—	—
91-92—Binghamton	AHL	48	19	28	47	22	7	2	2	4	12
92-93—Binghamton	AHL	79	30	70	100	88	14	3	10	13	18

Season	Team	League	Gms.	G	A	Pts.	PIM	Gms.	G	A	Pts.	PIM
93-94—Phoenix		IHL	51	14	33	47	65	—	—	—	—	—
—Los Angeles		NHL	20	1	3	4	4	—	—	—	—	—
94-95—Phoenix		IHL	55	5	27	32	60	—	—	—	—	—
—Atlanta		IHL	11	5	7	12	14	5	4	5	9	4
NHL totals			30	1	5	6	8					

McSORLEY, MARTY
D/RW, KINGS

PERSONAL: Born May 18, 1963, in Hamilton, Ont. . . . 6-1/225. . . . Shoots right. . . . Full name: Martin James McSorley.

TRANSACTIONS/CAREER NOTES: Signed as free agent by Pittsburgh Penguins (April 1983). . . . Traded by Penguins with C Tim Hrynewich to Edmonton Oilers for G Gilles Meloche (August 1985). . . . Suspended by NHL for AHL incident (March 1987). . . . Sprained knee (November 1987). . . . Suspended three playoff games by NHL for spearing (April 23, 1988). . . . Traded by Oilers with C Wayne Gretzky and LW/C Mike Krushelnyski to Los Angeles Kings for C Jimmy Carson, LW Martin Gelinas, first-round picks in 1989 (traded to New Jersey), 1991 (LW Martin Rucinsky) and 1993 (D Nick Stajduhar) drafts and cash (August 9, 1988). . . . Injured shoulder (December 31, 1988). . . . Sprained knee (February 1989). . . . Suspended four games by NHL for game-misconduct penalties (1989-90). . . . Twisted right knee (October 14, 1990); missed four games. . . . Twisted ankle (February 9, 1991). . . . Suspended three games by NHL for striking another player with a gloved hand (March 2, 1991). . . . Suffered from throat virus (November 23, 1991); missed six games. . . . Sprained shoulder (February 19, 1992); missed three games. . . . Suspended six off-days and fined $500 by NHL for cross-checking (October 31, 1992). . . . Suspended one game by NHL for game misconduct penalties (November 27, 1992). . . . Traded by Kings to Pittsburgh Penguins for C Shawn McEachern (August 27, 1993). . . . Sprained ankle (November 16, 1993); missed eight games. . . . Traded by Penguins with D Jim Paek to Los Angeles Kings for RW Thomas Sandstrom and C Shawn McEachern (February 15, 1993). . . . Suspended four games without pay and fined $500 for eye-gouging incident (February 23, 1994). . . . Sprained abdomen (April 7, 1994); missed remainder of season. . . . Strained groin (February 12, 1995); missed seven games.

HONORS: Shared Alka-Seltzer Plus Award with Theoren Fleury (1990-91).

MISCELLANEOUS: Member of Stanley Cup championship teams (1987 and 1988).

Season	Team	League	Gms.	G	A	Pts.	PIM	Gms.	G	A	Pts.	PIM
81-82—Belleville		OHL	58	6	13	19	234	—	—	—	—	—
82-83—Belleville		OHL	70	10	41	51	183	4	0	0	0	7
—Baltimore		AHL	2	0	0	0	22	—	—	—	—	—
83-84—Pittsburgh		NHL	72	2	7	9	224	—	—	—	—	—
84-85—Baltimore		AHL	58	6	24	30	154	14	0	7	7	47
—Pittsburgh		NHL	15	0	0	0	15	—	—	—	—	—
85-86—Edmonton		NHL	59	11	12	23	265	8	0	2	2	50
—Nova Scotia		AHL	9	2	4	6	34	—	—	—	—	—
86-87—Edmonton		NHL	41	2	4	6	159	21	4	3	7	65
—Nova Scotia		AHL	7	2	2	4	48	—	—	—	—	—
87-88—Edmonton		NHL	60	9	17	26	223	16	0	3	3	67
88-89—Los Angeles		NHL	66	10	17	27	350	11	0	2	2	33
89-90—Los Angeles		NHL	75	15	21	36	322	10	1	3	4	18
90-91—Los Angeles		NHL	61	7	32	39	221	12	0	1	0	58
91-92—Los Angeles		NHL	71	7	22	29	268	6	1	0	1	21
92-93—Los Angeles		NHL	81	15	26	41	*399	24	4	6	10	60
93-94—Pittsburgh		NHL	47	3	18	21	139	—	—	—	—	—
—Los Angeles		NHL	18	4	6	10	55	—	—	—	—	—
94-95—Los Angeles		NHL	41	3	18	21	83	—	—	—	—	—
NHL totals			707	88	200	288	2723	108	10	19	29	372

McSWEEN, DON
D, MIGHTY DUCKS

PERSONAL: Born June 9, 1964, in Detroit. . . . 5-11/197. . . . Shoots left. . . . Full name: Donald Kennedy McSween.

COLLEGE: Michigan State.

TRANSACTIONS/CAREER NOTES: Selected by Buffalo Sabres in eighth round (10th Sabres pick, 154th overall) of NHL entry draft (June 8, 1983). . . . Signed as free agent by Detroit Red Wings (August 29, 1992). . . . Loaned to San Diego Gulls (October 6, 1992). . . . Signed as free agent by Mighty Ducks of Anaheim (January 12, 1994). . . . Suffered from chicken pox (March 7, 1994); missed seven games. . . . Lacerated right forearm (January 21, 1995); missed remainder of season.

HONORS: Named to NCAA All-America West second team (1985-86 and 1986-87). . . . Named to CCHA All-Star first team (1985-86 and 1986-87). . . . Named to NCAA All-Tournament team (1986-87). . . . Named to AHL All-Star first team (1989-90).

Season	Team	League	Gms.	G	A	Pts.	PIM	Gms.	G	A	Pts.	PIM
83-84—Michigan State		CCHA	46	10	26	36	30	—	—	—	—	—
84-85—Michigan State		CCHA	44	2	23	25	52	—	—	—	—	—
85-86—Michigan State		CCHA	45	9	29	38	18	—	—	—	—	—
86-87—Michigan State		CCHA	45	7	23	30	34	—	—	—	—	—
87-88—Rochester		AHL	63	9	29	38	108	6	0	1	1	15
—Buffalo		NHL	5	0	1	1	6	—	—	—	—	—
88-89—Rochester		AHL	66	7	22	29	45	—	—	—	—	—
89-90—Buffalo		NHL	4	0	0	0	6	—	—	—	—	—
—Rochester		AHL	70	16	43	59	43	17	3	10	13	12
90-91—Rochester		AHL	74	7	44	51	57	15	2	5	7	8

Season Team	League	REGULAR SEASON					PLAYOFFS				
		Gms.	G	A	Pts.	PIM	Gms.	G	A	Pts.	PIM
91-92—Rochester	AHL	75	6	32	38	60	16	5	6	11	18
92-93—San Diego	IHL	80	15	40	55	85	14	1	2	3	10
93-94—San Diego	IHL	38	5	13	18	36	—	—	—	—	—
—Anaheim	NHL	32	3	9	12	39	—	—	—	—	—
94-95—Anaheim	NHL	2	0	0	0	0	—	—	—	—	—
NHL totals		43	3	10	13	51					

MELANSON, DEAN
D, SABRES

PERSONAL: Born November 19, 1973, in Antigonish, N.S. ... 5-11/211. ... Shoots right. ... Name pronounced muh-LAHN-suhn.
TRANSACTIONS/CAREER NOTES: Selected by Buffalo Sabres in fourth round (fourth Sabres pick, 80th overall) of NHL entry draft (June 20, 1992).

Season Team	League	REGULAR SEASON					PLAYOFFS				
		Gms.	G	A	Pts.	PIM	Gms.	G	A	Pts.	PIM
90-91—St. Hyacinthe	QMJHL	69	10	17	27	110	4	0	1	1	2
91-92—St. Hyacinthe	QMJHL	42	8	19	27	158	6	1	2	3	25
92-93—St. Hyacinthe	QMJHL	57	13	29	42	253	—	—	—	—	—
—Rochester	AHL	8	0	1	1	6	14	1	6	7	18
93-94—Rochester	AHL	80	1	21	22	138	4	0	1	1	2
94-95—Rochester	AHL	43	4	7	11	84	—	—	—	—	—
—Buffalo	NHL	5	0	0	0	4	—	—	—	—	—
NHL totals		5	0	0	0	4					

MELLANBY, SCOTT
RW, PANTHERS

PERSONAL: Born June 11, 1966, in Montreal. ... 6-1/199. ... Shoots right. ... Full name: Scott Edgar Mellanby.
HIGH SCHOOL: Henry Carr (Rexdale, Ont.).
COLLEGE: Wisconsin.
TRANSACTIONS/CAREER NOTES: Selected by Philadelphia Flyers as underage junior in second round (first Flyers pick, 27th overall) of NHL entry draft (June 9, 1984). ... Lacerated right index finger (October 1987). ... Severed nerve and damaged tendon in left forearm (August 1989); missed first 20 games of season. ... Suffered viral infection (November 1989). ... Traded by Flyers with LW Craig Berube and C Craig Fisher to Edmonton Oilers for RW Dave Brown, D Corey Foster and rights to RW Jari Kurri (May 30, 1991). ... Injured shoulder (February 14, 1993); missed 15 games. ... Selected by Florida Panthers in NHL expansion draft (June 24, 1993). ... Fractured nose and lacerated face (February 1, 1994); missed four games.

Season Team	League	REGULAR SEASON					PLAYOFFS				
		Gms.	G	A	Pts.	PIM	Gms.	G	A	Pts.	PIM
83-84—Henry Carr H.S.	MTHL	39	37	37	74	97	—	—	—	—	—
84-85—University of Wisconsin	WCHA	40	14	24	38	60	—	—	—	—	—
85-86—University of Wisconsin	WCHA	32	21	23	44	89	—	—	—	—	—
—Philadelphia	NHL	2	0	0	0	0	—	—	—	—	—
86-87—Philadelphia	NHL	71	11	21	32	94	24	5	5	10	46
87-88—Philadelphia	NHL	75	25	26	51	185	7	0	1	1	16
88-89—Philadelphia	NHL	76	21	29	50	183	19	4	5	9	28
89-90—Philadelphia	NHL	57	6	17	23	77	—	—	—	—	—
90-91—Philadelphia	NHL	74	20	21	41	155	—	—	—	—	—
91-92—Edmonton	NHL	80	23	27	50	197	16	2	1	3	29
92-93—Edmonton	NHL	69	15	17	32	147	—	—	—	—	—
93-94—Florida	NHL	80	30	30	60	149	—	—	—	—	—
94-95—Florida	NHL	48	13	12	25	90	—	—	—	—	—
NHL totals		632	164	200	364	1277	66	11	12	23	119

MELYAKOV, IGOR
RW, KINGS

PERSONAL: Born December 25, 1976, in Lipetsk, U.S.S.R. ... 5-10/175. ... Shoots left.
TRANSACTIONS/CAREER NOTES: Selected by Los Angeles Kings in sixth round (sixth Kings pick, 137th overall) of NHL entry draft (July 8, 1995).

Season Team	League	REGULAR SEASON					PLAYOFFS				
		Gms.	G	A	Pts.	PIM	Gms.	G	A	Pts.	PIM
93-94—Torpedo Yaroslavl	CIS	39	3	4	7	10	4	0	0	0	0
94-95—Torpedo Yaroslavl	CIS	50	6	8	14	34	4	0	1	1	0

MENHART, MARIAN
D, SABRES

PERSONAL: Born February 2, 1977, in Most, Czechoslovakia. ... 6-3/220. ... Shoots left.
TRANSACTIONS/CAREER NOTES: Selected by Buffalo Sabres in fifth round (fifth Sabres pick, 111 overall) of NHL entry draft (July 8, 1995).

Season Team	League	REGULAR SEASON					PLAYOFFS				
		Gms.	G	A	Pts.	PIM	Gms.	G	A	Pts.	PIM
94-95—Litvinov	Czech. Jrs.	36	15	19	34	...	—	—	—	—	—

MESSIER, JOBY
D, RANGERS

PERSONAL: Born March 2, 1970, in Regina, Sask. ... 6-0/193. ... Shoots right. ... Full name: Marcus Cyril Messier. ... Name pronounced MEHZ-yay. ... Brother of Mitch Messier, center/right winger in Dallas Stars system; cousin of Mark Messier, center, New York Rangers; and cousin of Paul Messier, center, Colorado Rockies (1978-79).

COLLEGE: Michigan State.
TRANSACTIONS/CAREER NOTES: Broke right arm (December 1984).... Broke right arm (September 1987).... Selected by New York Rangers in sixth round (seventh Rangers pick, 118th overall) of NHL entry draft (June 17, 1989).
HONORS: Named to NCAA All-America West first team (1991-92).... Named to CCHA All-Star first team (1991-92).
MISCELLANEOUS: Member of Stanley Cup championship team (1994).

Season Team	League	REGULAR SEASON					PLAYOFFS				
		Gms.	G	A	Pts.	PIM	Gms.	G	A	Pts.	PIM
87-88—Notre Dame	SJHL	53	9	22	31	208	—	—	—	—	—
88-89—Michigan State	CCHA	46	2	10	12	70	—	—	—	—	—
89-90—Michigan State	CCHA	42	1	11	12	58	—	—	—	—	—
90-91—Michigan State	CCHA	39	5	11	16	71	—	—	—	—	—
91-92—Michigan State	CCHA	44	13	16	29	85	—	—	—	—	—
92-93—Binghamton	AHL	60	5	16	21	63	14	1	1	2	6
—New York Rangers	NHL	11	0	0	0	6	—	—	—	—	—
93-94—New York Rangers	NHL	4	0	2	2	0	—	—	—	—	—
—Binghamton	AHL	42	6	14	20	58	—	—	—	—	—
94-95—Binghamton	AHL	25	2	9	11	36	1	0	0	0	0
—New York Rangers	NHL	10	0	2	2	18	—	—	—	—	—
NHL totals		**25**	**0**	**4**	**4**	**24**					

MESSIER, MARK

C, RANGERS

PERSONAL: Born January 18, 1961, in Edmonton.... 6-1/210.... Shoots left.... Full name: Mark Douglas Messier.... Name pronounced MEHZ-yay.... Brother of Paul Messier, center, Colorado Rockies (1978-79); cousin of Mitch Messier, center/right winger in Dallas Stars system; cousin of Joby Messier, defenseman in New York Rangers system; and brother-in-law of John Blum, defenseman for four NHL teams (1982-83 through 1989-90).
TRANSACTIONS/CAREER NOTES: Given five-game trial by Indianapolis Racers (November 1978).... Signed as free agent by Cincinnati Stingers (January 1979).... Selected by Edmonton Oilers in third round (second Oilers pick, 48th overall) of NHL entry draft (August 9, 1979).... Injured ankle (November 7, 1981).... Chipped bone in wrist (March 1983).... Suspended six games by NHL for hitting another player with stick (January 18, 1984).... Sprained knee ligaments (November 1984).... Suspended 10 games by NHL for injuring another player (December 26, 1984).... Bruised left foot (December 3, 1985); missed 17 games.... Suspended and fined by Oilers after refusing to report to training camp (October 1987); missed three weeks of camp.... Suspended six games by NHL for injuring another player with his stick (October 23, 1988).... Twisted left knee (January 28, 1989).... Strained right knee (February 3, 1989).... Bruised left knee (February 12, 1989).... Sprained left knee ligaments (October 16, 1990); missed 10 games.... Reinjured left knee (December 12, 1990); missed three games.... Reinjured knee (December 22, 1990); missed nine games.... Broke left thumb (February 11, 1991); missed eight games.... Missed one game due to contract dispute (October 1991).... Traded by Oilers with future considerations to New York Rangers for C Bernie Nicholls, LW Louie DeBrusk, RW Steven Rice and future considerations (October 4, 1991); Oilers traded D Jeff Beukeboom to Rangers for D David Shaw to complete deal (November 12, 1991).... Sprained ligament in wrist (January 19, 1993); missed six games.... Strained rib cage muscle (February 27, 1993); missed two games.... Strained rib cage muscle (March 11, 1993); missed one game.... Suspended three off-days and fined $500 by NHL for stick-swinging incident (March 18, 1993).... Sprained wrist (December 22, 1993); missed six games.... Bruised thigh (March 16, 1994); missed two games.... Suffered back spasms (April 30, 1995); missed two games.
HONORS: Named to THE SPORTING NEWS All-Star first team (1981-82, 1982-83, 1989-90 and 1991-92).... Named to NHL All-Star first team (1981-82, 1982-83, 1989-90 and 1991-92).... Played in NHL All-Star Game (1982-1984, 1986, 1988-1992 and 1994).... Won Conn Smythe Trophy (1983-84).... Named to NHL All-Star second team (1983-84).... Named to THE SPORTING NEWS All-Star second team (1986-87).... Named NHL Player of the Year by THE SPORTING NEWS (1989-90 and 1991-92).... Won Hart Memorial Trophy (1989-90 and 1991-92).... Won Lester B. Pearson Award (1989-90 and 1991-92).
RECORDS: Holds NHL career playoff record for most shorthanded goals—11.... Shares NHL single-game playoff record for most shorthanded goals—2 (April 21, 1992).
STATISTICAL PLATEAUS: Three-goal games: 1980-81 (1), 1981-82 (2), 1982-83 (1), 1983-84 (2), 1985-86 (1), 1987-88 (1), 1989-90 (2), 1991-92 (2). Total: 12.... Four-goal games: 1982-83 (1), 1988-89 (1), 1989-90 (1), 1991-92 (1). Total: 4.... Total hat tricks: 16.
MISCELLANEOUS: Member of Stanley Cup championship teams (1984, 1985, 1987, 1988, 1990 and 1994).... Captain of Edmonton Oilers (1988-89 through 1990-91).... Captain of New York Rangers (1991-92 through 1994-95).

Season Team	League	REGULAR SEASON					PLAYOFFS				
		Gms.	G	A	Pts.	PIM	Gms.	G	A	Pts.	PIM
76-77—Spruce Grove	AJHL	57	27	39	66	91	—	—	—	—	—
77-78—St. Albert	AJHL			Statistics unavailable.							
—Portland	WHL	—	—	—	—	—	7	4	1	5	2
78-79—Indianapolis	WHA	5	0	0	0	0	—	—	—	—	—
—Cincinnati	WHA	47	1	10	11	58	—	—	—	—	—
79-80—Houston	CHL	4	0	3	3	4	—	—	—	—	—
—Edmonton	NHL	75	12	21	33	120	3	1	2	3	2
80-81—Edmonton	NHL	72	23	40	63	102	9	2	5	7	13
81-82—Edmonton	NHL	78	50	38	88	119	5	1	2	3	8
82-83—Edmonton	NHL	77	48	58	106	72	15	15	6	21	14
83-84—Edmonton	NHL	73	37	64	101	165	19	8	18	26	19
84-85—Edmonton	NHL	55	23	31	54	57	18	12	13	25	12
85-86—Edmonton	NHL	63	35	49	84	68	10	4	6	10	18
86-87—Edmonton	NHL	77	37	70	107	73	21	12	16	28	16
87-88—Edmonton	NHL	77	37	74	111	103	19	11	23	34	29
88-89—Edmonton	NHL	72	33	61	94	130	7	1	11	12	8
89-90—Edmonton	NHL	79	45	84	129	79	22	9	*22	†31	20
90-91—Edmonton	NHL	53	12	52	64	34	18	4	11	15	16

M

Season Team	League	REGULAR SEASON Gms.	G	A	Pts.	PIM	PLAYOFFS Gms.	G	A	Pts.	PIM
91-92—New York Rangers	NHL	79	35	72	107	76	11	7	7	14	6
92-93—New York Rangers	NHL	75	25	66	91	72	—	—	—	—	—
93-94—New York Rangers	NHL	76	26	58	84	76	23	12	18	30	33
94-95—New York Rangers	NHL	46	14	39	53	40	10	3	10	13	8
WHA totals		52	1	10	11	58					
NHL totals		1127	492	877	1369	1386	210	102	170	272	222

METLYUK, DENIS
C, FLYERS

PERSONAL: Born January 30, 1972, in Togliatti, U.S.S.R. . . . 5-10/183. . . . Shoots left. . . . Name pronounced MEHT-lee-ook.
TRANSACTIONS/CAREER NOTES: Selected by Philadelphia Flyers in second round (third Flyers pick, 31st overall) of NHL entry draft (June 20, 1992). . . . Played in Europe during 1994-95 NHL lockout.

Season Team	League	REGULAR SEASON Gms.	G	A	Pts.	PIM	PLAYOFFS Gms.	G	A	Pts.	PIM
90-91—Lada Togliatti	USSR	25	5	6	11	8	—	—	—	—	—
91-92—Lada Togliatti	CIS	26	0	1	1	6	—	—	—	—	—
92-93—Lada Togliatti	CIS	39	7	12	19	20	10	0	1	1	2
93-94—Hershey	AHL	73	8	13	21	46	11	4	2	6	4
94-95—Lada Togliatti	CIS	25	8	6	14	10	12	4	5	9	10
—Hershey	AHL	7	1	0	1	8	—	—	—	—	—

MICHAYLUK, DAVE
LW, PENGUINS

PERSONAL: Born May 18, 1962, in Wakaw, Sask. . . . 5-10/185. . . . Shoots left.
TRANSACTIONS/CAREER NOTES: Selected by Philadelphia Flyers as underage junior in fourth round (fifth Flyers pick, 65th overall) of NHL entry draft (June 10, 1981). . . . Lacerated right arm (May 1989). . . . Signed as free agent by Pittsburgh Penguins (May 24, 1989).
HONORS: Won Stewart (Butch) Paul Memorial Trophy (1980-81). . . . Named to WHL All-Star second team (1980-81 and 1981-82). . . . Named to IHL All-Star second team (1984-85, 1991-92 and 1992-93). . . . Named to IHL All-Star first team (1986-87 through 1989-90). . . . Won James Gatschene Memorial Trophy (1988-89). . . . Won Leo P. Lamoureux Memorial Trophy (1988-89). . . . Named Turner Cup Playoff Most Valuable Player (1988-89).
MISCELLANEOUS: Member of Stanley Cup championship team (1992).

Season Team	League	REGULAR SEASON Gms.	G	A	Pts.	PIM	PLAYOFFS Gms.	G	A	Pts.	PIM
79-80—Prince Albert	AJHL	60	46	67	113	49	—	—	—	—	—
80-81—Regina	WHL	72	62	71	133	39	11	5	12	17	8
81-82—Regina	WHL	72	62	111	173	128	12	16	24	*40	23
—Philadelphia	NHL	1	0	0	0	0	—	—	—	—	—
82-83—Philadelphia	NHL	13	2	6	8	8	—	—	—	—	—
—Maine	AHL	69	32	40	72	16	8	0	2	2	0
83-84—Springfield	AHL	79	18	44	62	37	4	0	0	0	2
84-85—Hershey	AHL	3	0	2	2	2	—	—	—	—	—
—Kalamazoo	IHL	82	*66	33	99	49	11	7	7	14	0
85-86—Nova Scotia	AHL	3	0	1	1	0	—	—	—	—	—
—Muskegon	IHL	77	52	52	104	73	14	6	9	15	12
86-87—Muskegon	IHL	82	47	53	100	69	15	2	14	16	8
87-88—Muskegon	IHL	81	*56	81	137	46	6	2	0	2	18
88-89—Muskegon	IHL	80	50	72	*122	84	13	†9	12	†21	24
89-90—Muskegon	IHL	79	*51	51	102	80	15	8	†14	*22	10
90-91—Muskegon	IHL	83	40	62	102	116	5	2	2	4	4
91-92—Muskegon	IHL	82	39	63	102	154	13	9	8	17	4
—Pittsburgh	NHL	—	—	—	—	—	7	1	1	2	0
92-93—Cleveland	IHL	82	47	65	112	104	4	1	2	3	4
93-94—Cleveland	IHL	81	48	51	99	92	—	—	—	—	—
94-95—Cleveland	IHL	60	19	17	36	22	1	0	0	0	0
NHL totals		14	2	6	8	8	7	1	1	2	0

MIETTINEN, TOMMI
C/LW, MIGHTY DUCKS

PERSONAL: Born December 3, 1975, in Kuopio, Finland. . . . 5-10/165. . . . Shoots left.
TRANSACTIONS/CAREER NOTES: Selected by the Mighty Ducks of Anaheim in the 10th round (10th Mighty Ducks pick, 236th overall) of NHL entry draft (June 29, 1994).

Season Team	League	REGULAR SEASON Gms.	G	A	Pts.	PIM	PLAYOFFS Gms.	G	A	Pts.	PIM
92-93—KalPa Juniors	Finland Jrs.	26	16	27	43	14	—	—	—	—	—
—KalPa Kuopio	Finland	14	0	0	0	0	—	—	—	—	—
93-94—KalPa Kuopio	Finland	47	5	7	12	14	—	—	—	—	—
94-95—KalPa Kuopio	Finland	48	13	16	29	26	3	1	1	2	2

MIGNACCA, SONNY
G, CANUCKS

PERSONAL: Born January 4, 1974, in Winnipeg. . . . 5-8/175. . . . Catches left. . . . Name pronounced migh-NAH-kuh.
TRANSACTIONS/CAREER NOTES: Selected by Vancouver in ninth round (10th Canucks pick, 213th overall) of NHL entry draft (June 20, 1992).

HONORS: Named to WHL (East) All-Star second team (1991-92 and 1993-94).... Won Four Broncos Memorial Trophy (1993-94).... Named WHL Player of the Year (1993-94).

			REGULAR SEASON							PLAYOFFS						
Season	Team	League	Gms.	Min.	W	L	T	GA	SO	Avg.	Gms.	Min.	W	L	GA	SO	Avg.
90-91—Medicine Hat		WHL	33	1743	17	9	2	121	0	4.17	1	13	0	0	2	0	9.23
91-92—Medicine Hat		WHL	56	3207	35	19	0	189	2	3.54	4	240	0	4	17	0	4.25
92-93—Medicine Hat		WHL	50	2724	18	25	2	210	1	4.63	10	605	5	5	36	0	3.57
93-94—Medicine Hat		WHL	60	3361	26	23	5	183	2	3.27	3	180	0	3	17	0	5.67
94-95—Syracuse		AHL	19	1097	4	11	2	85	0	4.65	—	—	—	—	—	—	—

MIKULCHIK, OLEG
D, MIGHTY DUCKS

PERSONAL: Born June 27, 1964, in Minsk, U.S.S.R.... 6-2/200.... Shoots right.... Name pronounced OH-lehg mih-KOOL-chihk.
TRANSACTIONS/CAREER NOTES: Signed as free agent by Winnipeg Jets (July 1992).... Sprained elbow (December 22, 1993); missed five games.... Fractured toe (March 14, 1995); missed three games.... Signed as free agent by Mighty Ducks of Anaheim (July 28, 1995).

			REGULAR SEASON					PLAYOFFS				
Season	Team	League	Gms.	G	A	Pts.	PIM	Gms.	G	A	Pts.	PIM
83-84—Dynamo Moscow		USSR	17	0	0	0	6	—	—	—	—	—
84-85—Dynamo Moscow		USSR	30	1	3	4	26	—	—	—	—	—
85-86—Dynamo Moscow		USSR	40	0	1	1	36	—	—	—	—	—
86-87—Dynamo Moscow		USSR	39	5	3	8	34	—	—	—	—	—
87-88—Dynamo Moscow		USSR	48	7	8	15	63	—	—	—	—	—
88-89—Dynamo Moscow		USSR	43	4	7	11	52	—	—	—	—	—
89-90—Dynamo Moscow		USSR	32	1	3	4	31	—	—	—	—	—
90-91—Dynamo Moscow		USSR	36	2	6	8	40	—	—	—	—	—
91-92—Khimik		CIS	15	3	2	5	20	—	—	—	—	—
—New Haven		AHL	30	3	3	6	63	5	0	0	0	4
92-93—Moncton		AHL	75	6	20	26	159	4	1	3	4	6
93-94—Moncton		AHL	67	9	38	47	121	21	2	10	12	18
—Winnipeg		NHL	4	0	1	1	17	—	—	—	—	—
94-95—Springfield		AHL	50	5	16	21	59	—	—	—	—	—
—Winnipeg		NHL	25	0	2	2	12	—	—	—	—	—
NHL totals			29	0	3	3	29					

MILLEN, COREY
C, STARS

PERSONAL: Born April 29, 1964, in Cloquet, Minn.... 5-7/170.... Shoots right.
HIGH SCHOOL: Cloquet (Minn.).
COLLEGE: Minnesota.
TRANSACTIONS/CAREER NOTES: Selected by New York Rangers as underage player in third round (third Rangers pick, 57th overall) of NHL entry draft (June 9, 1982).... Injured knee and underwent surgery (November 1982).... Injured shoulder (October 1984).... Tested positive for a non-anabolic steroid in a random test at World Cup Tournament and was banned from play (April 1989).... Sprained left knee ligaments and underwent surgery (September 18, 1989); missed four months.... Underwent surgery to left knee (August 1990); missed four months.... Traded by Rangers to Los Angeles Kings for C Randy Gilhen (December 23, 1991).... Suffered shoulder contusion (February 29, 1992); missed one game.... Strained back (October 13, 1992); missed four games.... Strained groin (December 22, 1992); missed 38 games.... Traded by Kings to New Jersey Devils for fifth-round pick (G Jason Saal) in 1993 draft (June 26, 1993).... Traded by Devils to Dallas Stars for C Neal Broten (February 27, 1995).... Bruised foot (April 17, 1995); missed one game.
HONORS: Named to WCHA All-Star second team (1984-85 through 1986-87).... Named to NCAA All-America West second team (1985-86).... Named to NCAA All-Tournament team (1986-87).

			REGULAR SEASON					PLAYOFFS				
Season	Team	League	Gms.	G	A	Pts.	PIM	Gms.	G	A	Pts.	PIM
81-82—Cloquet H.S.		Minn. H.S.	18	46	35	81	...	—	—	—	—	—
82-83—University of Minnesota		WCHA	21	14	15	29	18	—	—	—	—	—
83-84—U.S. national team		Int'l	45	15	11	26	10	—	—	—	—	—
—U.S. Olympic Team		Int'l	6	0	0	0	2	—	—	—	—	—
84-85—University of Minnesota		WCHA	38	28	36	64	60	—	—	—	—	—
85-86—University of Minnesota		WCHA	48	41	42	83	64	—	—	—	—	—
86-87—University of Minnesota		WCHA	42	36	29	65	62	—	—	—	—	—
87-88—U.S. national team		Int'l	47	41	43	84	26	—	—	—	—	—
—U.S. Olympic Team		Int'l	6	6	5	11	4	—	—	—	—	—
88-89—Ambri Piotta		Switzerland	36	32	22	54	18	6	4	3	7	0
89-90—New York Rangers		NHL	4	0	0	0	2	—	—	—	—	—
—Flint		IHL	11	4	5	9	2	—	—	—	—	—
90-91—Binghamton		AHL	40	19	37	56	68	6	0	7	7	8
—New York Rangers		NHL	4	3	1	4	0	6	1	2	3	0
91-92—New York Rangers		NHL	11	1	4	5	10	—	—	—	—	—
—Binghamton		AHL	15	8	7	15	44	—	—	—	—	—
—Los Angeles		NHL	46	20	21	41	44	6	0	1	1	6
92-93—Los Angeles		NHL	42	23	16	39	42	23	2	4	6	12
93-94—New Jersey		NHL	78	20	30	50	52	7	1	0	1	2
94-95—New Jersey		NHL	17	2	3	5	8	—	—	—	—	—
—Dallas		NHL	28	3	15	18	28	5	1	0	1	2
NHL totals			230	72	90	162	186	47	5	7	12	22

MILLER, AARON
D, DENVER

PERSONAL: Born August 11, 1971, in Buffalo, N.Y. . . . 6-3/197. . . . Shoots right. . . . Full name: Aaron Michael Miller.
COLLEGE: Vermont.
TRANSACTIONS/CAREER NOTES: Selected by New York Rangers in fifth round (sixth Rangers pick, 88th overall) of NHL entry draft (June 17, 1989). . . . Traded by Rangers with fifth-round pick in 1991 draft (LW Bill Lindsay) to Quebec Nordiques for D Joe Cirella (January 17, 1991). . . . Nordiques franchise moved to Denver for 1995-96 season.
HONORS: Named to ECAC All-Rookie team (1989-90). . . . Named to NCAA All-America East second team (1992-93). . . . Named to ECAC All-Star first team (1992-93).

			REGULAR SEASON					PLAYOFFS				
Season	Team	League	Gms.	G	A	Pts.	PIM	Gms.	G	A	Pts.	PIM
87-88	Niagara	NAJHL	30	4	9	13	2	—	—	—	—	—
88-89	Niagara	NAJHL	59	24	38	62	60	—	—	—	—	—
89-90	University of Vermont	ECAC	31	1	15	16	24	—	—	—	—	—
90-91	University of Vermont	ECAC	30	3	7	10	22	—	—	—	—	—
91-92	University of Vermont	ECAC	31	3	16	19	36	—	—	—	—	—
92-93	University of Vermont	ECAC	30	4	13	17	16	—	—	—	—	—
93-94	Cornwall	AHL	64	4	10	14	49	13	0	2	2	10
	Quebec	NHL	1	0	0	0	0	—	—	—	—	—
94-95	Cornwall	AHL	76	4	18	22	69	—	—	—	—	—
	Quebec	NHL	9	0	3	3	6	—	—	—	—	—
NHL totals			10	0	3	3	6					

MILLER, JASON
C, RED WINGS

PERSONAL: Born March 1, 1971, in Edmonton. . . . 6-1/195. . . . Shoots left.
TRANSACTIONS/CAREER NOTES: Separated shoulder (May 1986). . . . Selected by New Jersey Devils in first round (second Devils pick, 18th overall) of NHL entry draft (June 17, 1989). . . . Suffered sore back (January 23, 1993); missed two games. . . . Signed as free agent by Detroit Red Wings (July 28, 1994).
HONORS: Named to WHL (East) All-Star second team (1990-91).

			REGULAR SEASON					PLAYOFFS				
Season	Team	League	Gms.	G	A	Pts.	PIM	Gms.	G	A	Pts.	PIM
87-88	Medicine Hat	WHL	71	11	18	29	28	15	0	1	1	2
88-89	Medicine Hat	WHL	72	51	55	106	44	3	1	2	3	2
89-90	Medicine Hat	WHL	66	43	56	99	40	3	3	2	5	0
90-91	New Jersey	NHL	1	0	0	0	0	—	—	—	—	—
	Medicine Hat	WHL	66	60	76	136	31	12	9	10	19	8
91-92	Utica	AHL	71	23	32	55	31	4	1	3	4	0
	New Jersey	NHL	3	0	0	0	0	—	—	—	—	—
92-93	Utica	AHL	72	28	42	70	43	5	4	4	8	2
	New Jersey	NHL	2	0	0	0	0	—	—	—	—	—
93-94	Albany	AHL	77	22	53	75	65	5	1	1	2	4
94-95	Adirondack	AHL	77	32	33	65	39	4	1	0	1	0
NHL totals			6	0	0	0	0					

MILLER, KELLY
LW, CAPITALS

PERSONAL: Born March 3, 1963, in Lansing, Mich. . . . 5-11/195. . . . Shoots left. . . . Full name: Kelly David Miller. . . . Brother of Kevin Miller, left winger, San Jose Sharks; and brother of Kip Miller, center in New York Islanders system.
HIGH SCHOOL: Eastern (Lansing, Mich.).
COLLEGE: Michigan State.
TRANSACTIONS/CAREER NOTES: Selected by New York Rangers in ninth round (ninth Rangers pick, 183rd overall) of NHL entry draft (June 9, 1982). . . . Injured ankle (September 1985). . . . Sprained knee (January 27, 1986); missed five games. . . . Traded by Rangers with C Mike Ridley and RW Bobby Crawford to Washington Capitals for C Bobby Carpenter and second-round pick (RW Jason Prosofsky) in 1989 draft (January 1, 1987). . . . Pulled groin (November 1988). . . . Sprained knee (September 22, 1990).
HONORS: Named to NCAA All-America West first team (1984-85). . . . Named to CCHA All-Star first team (1984-85).

			REGULAR SEASON					PLAYOFFS				
Season	Team	League	Gms.	G	A	Pts.	PIM	Gms.	G	A	Pts.	PIM
81-82	Michigan State	CCHA	40	11	19	30	21	—	—	—	—	—
82-83	Michigan State	CCHA	36	16	19	35	12	—	—	—	—	—
83-84	Michigan State	CCHA	46	28	21	49	12	—	—	—	—	—
84-85	Michigan State	CCHA	43	27	23	50	21	—	—	—	—	—
	New York Rangers	NHL	5	0	2	2	2	3	0	0	0	2
85-86	New York Rangers	NHL	74	13	20	33	52	16	3	4	7	4
86-87	New York Rangers	NHL	38	6	14	20	22	—	—	—	—	—
	Washington	NHL	39	10	12	22	26	7	2	2	4	0
87-88	Washington	NHL	80	9	23	32	35	14	4	4	8	10
88-89	Washington	NHL	78	19	21	40	45	6	1	0	1	2
89-90	Washington	NHL	80	18	22	40	49	15	3	5	8	23
90-91	Washington	NHL	80	24	26	50	29	11	4	2	6	6
91-92	Washington	NHL	78	14	38	52	49	7	1	2	3	4
92-93	Washington	NHL	84	18	27	45	32	6	0	3	3	2
93-94	Washington	NHL	84	14	25	39	32	11	2	7	9	0
94-95	Washington	NHL	48	10	13	23	6	7	0	3	3	4
NHL totals			768	155	243	398	379	103	20	32	52	57

M

MILLER, KEVIN
LW, SHARKS

PERSONAL: Born August 9, 1965, in Lansing, Mich. . . . 5-11/190. . . . Shoots right. . . . Full name: Kevin Bradley Miller. . . . Brother of Kelly Miller, left winger, Washington Capitals; and brother of Kip Miller, center in New York Islanders system.
HIGH SCHOOL: Eastern (Lansing, Mich.).
COLLEGE: Michigan State.
TRANSACTIONS/CAREER NOTES: Selected by New York Rangers in 10th round (10th Rangers pick, 202nd overall) of NHL entry draft (June 9, 1984). . . . Pulled groin (September 1990). . . . Sprained shoulder (December 1990). . . . Traded by Rangers with D Dennis Vial and RW Jim Cummings to Detroit Red Wings for RW Joe Kocur and D Per Djoos (March 5, 1991). . . . Traded by Red Wings to Washington Capitals for RW Dino Ciccarelli (June 20, 1992). . . . Traded by Capitals to St. Louis Blues for D Paul Cavallini (November 1, 1992). . . . Suffered sore knee (November 3, 1993); missed two games. . . . Injured knee (November 24, 1993); missed two games. . . . Injured hip (March 30, 1994); missed one game. . . . Suffered sore groin (April 8, 1994); missed three games. . . . Traded by Blues to San Jose Sharks for C Todd Elik (March 23, 1995).
STATISTICAL PLATEAUS: Three-goal games: 1991-92 (1), 1993-94 (1). Total: 3.

			REGULAR SEASON					PLAYOFFS				
Season	Team	League	Gms.	G	A	Pts.	PIM	Gms.	G	A	Pts.	PIM
84-85—Michigan State		CCHA	44	11	29	40	84	—	—	—	—	—
85-86—Michigan State		CCHA	45	19	52	71	112	—	—	—	—	—
86-87—Michigan State		CCHA	42	25	56	81	63	—	—	—	—	—
87-88—Michigan State		CCHA	9	6	3	9	18	—	—	—	—	—
—U.S. Olympic Team		Int'l	50	32	34	66	. . .	—	—	—	—	—
88-89—New York Rangers		NHL	24	3	5	8	2	—	—	—	—	—
—Denver		IHL	55	29	47	76	19	4	2	1	3	2
89-90—New York Rangers		NHL	16	0	5	5	2	1	0	0	0	0
—Flint		IHL	48	19	23	42	41	—	—	—	—	—
90-91—New York Rangers		NHL	63	17	27	44	63	—	—	—	—	—
—Detroit		NHL	11	5	2	7	4	7	3	2	5	20
91-92—Detroit		NHL	80	20	26	46	53	9	0	2	2	4
92-93—Washington		NHL	10	0	3	3	35	—	—	—	—	—
—St. Louis		NHL	72	24	22	46	65	10	0	3	3	11
93-94—St. Louis		NHL	75	23	25	48	83	3	1	0	1	4
94-95—St. Louis		NHL	15	2	5	7	0	—	—	—	—	—
—San Jose		NHL	21	6	7	13	13	6	0	0	0	2
NHL totals			387	100	127	227	320	36	4	7	11	41

MILLER, KIP
C, ISLANDERS

PERSONAL: Born June 11, 1969, in Lansing, Mich. . . . 5-10/185. . . . Shoots left. . . . Full name: Kip Charles Miller. . . . Brother of Kelly Miller, left winger, Washington Capitals; and brother of Kevin Miller, left winger, San Jose Sharks.
HIGH SCHOOL: Eastern (Lansing, Mich.).
COLLEGE: Michigan State.
TRANSACTIONS/CAREER NOTES: Selected by Quebec Nordiques in fourth round (fourth Nordiques pick, 72nd overall) of NHL entry draft (June 13, 1987). . . . Injured hand and forearm in off-ice accident (November 1987). . . . Traded by Nordiques to Minnesota North Stars for LW Steve Maltais (March 8, 1992). . . . North Stars franchise moved from Minnesota to Dallas and renamed Stars for 1993-94 season. . . . Signed as free agent by San Jose Sharks (August 10, 1993). . . . Signed as free agent by New York Islanders (August 2, 1994).
HONORS: Named to NCAA All-America West first team (1988-89 and 1989-90). . . . Named to CCHA All-Star first team (1988-89 and 1989-90). . . . Won Hobey Baker Memorial Award (1989-90). . . . Named CCHA Player of the Year (1989-90). . . . Won N.R. (Bud) Poile Trophy (1994-95).

			REGULAR SEASON					PLAYOFFS				
Season	Team	League	Gms.	G	A	Pts.	PIM	Gms.	G	A	Pts.	PIM
86-87—Michigan State		CCHA	41	20	19	39	92	—	—	—	—	—
87-88—Michigan State		CCHA	39	16	25	41	51	—	—	—	—	—
88-89—Michigan State		CCHA	47	32	45	77	94	—	—	—	—	—
89-90—Michigan State		CCHA	45	*48	53	*101	60	—	—	—	—	—
90-91—Quebec		NHL	13	4	3	7	7	—	—	—	—	—
—Halifax		AHL	66	36	33	69	40	—	—	—	—	—
91-92—Quebec		NHL	36	5	10	15	12	—	—	—	—	—
—Halifax		AHL	24	9	17	26	8	—	—	—	—	—
—Minnesota		NHL	3	1	2	3	2	—	—	—	—	—
—Kalamazoo		IHL	6	1	8	9	4	12	3	9	12	12
92-93—Kalamazoo		IHL	61	17	39	56	59	—	—	—	—	—
93-94—San Jose		NHL	11	2	2	4	6	—	—	—	—	—
—Kansas City		IHL	71	38	54	92	51	—	—	—	—	—
94-95—Denver		IHL	71	46	60	106	54	17	*15	14	29	8
—New York Islanders		NHL	8	0	1	1	0	—	—	—	—	—
NHL totals			71	12	18	30	27	—	—	—	—	—

MILLS, CRAIG
RW, JETS

PERSONAL: Born August 27, 1976, in Toronto. . . . 5-11/174. . . . Shoots right.
TRANSACTIONS/CAREER NOTES: Selected by Winnipeg Jets in fifth round (fifth Jets pick, 108th overall) of NHL entry draft (June 29, 1994).

			REGULAR SEASON					PLAYOFFS				
Season	Team	League	Gms.	G	A	Pts.	PIM	Gms.	G	A	Pts.	PIM
92-93—St. Michaels Tier II		Jr. A	44	8	12	20	51	—	—	—	—	—
93-94—Belleville		OHL	63	15	18	33	88	12	2	1	3	11
94-95—Belleville		OHL	62	39	41	80	104	13	7	9	16	8

M

MINARD, MIKE
G, OILERS

PERSONAL: Born January 11, 1976, in Owen Sound, Ont. . . . 6-3/205. . . . Catches left.
TRANSACTIONS/CAREER NOTES: Selected by Edmonton Oilers in fourth round (fourth Oilers pick, 83rd overall) of NHL entry draft (July 8, 1995).

			REGULAR SEASON							PLAYOFFS						
Season	Team	League	Gms.	Min.	W	L	T	GA	SO	Avg.	Gms.	Min.	W	L	GA	SO	Avg.
94-95—Chilliwack		BCJHL	40	2330	. . .	. . .	. . .	136	0	3.50	—	—	—	—	—	—	—

MIRONOV, BORIS
D, OILERS

PERSONAL: Born March 21, 1972, in Moscow, U.S.S.R. . . . 6-3/220. . . . Shoots right. . . . Name pronounced MIHR-in-nahf. . . . Brother of Dmitri Mironov, defenseman, Pittsburgh Penguins.
TRANSACTIONS/CAREER NOTES: Selected by Winnipeg Jets in second round (second Jets pick, 27th overall) of NHL entry draft (June 20, 1992). . . . Bruised back (February 2, 1994); missed three games. . . . Traded by Jets with C Mats Lindgren and first-round (C Jason Bonsignore) and fourth-round (RW Adam Copeland) picks in 1994 draft to Edmonton Oilers for D Dave Manson and sixth-round pick in 1994 draft (March 15, 1994). . . . Bruised ankle (April 3, 1995); missed one game. . . . Strained lower back (April 13, 1995); missed 10 games.
HONORS: Named to NHL All-Rookie team (1993-94).

			REGULAR SEASON					PLAYOFFS				
Season	Team	League	Gms.	G	A	Pts.	PIM	Gms.	G	A	Pts.	PIM
88-89—CSKA Moscow		USSR	1	0	0	0	0	—	—	—	—	—
89-90—CSKA Moscow		USSR	7	0	0	0	0	—	—	—	—	—
90-91—CSKA Moscow		USSR	36	1	5	6	16	—	—	—	—	—
91-92—CSKA Moscow		CIS	36	2	1	3	22	—	—	—	—	—
92-93—CSKA Moscow		CIS	19	0	5	5	20	—	—	—	—	—
93-94—Winnipeg		NHL	65	7	22	29	96	—	—	—	—	—
—Edmonton		NHL	14	0	2	2	14	—	—	—	—	—
94-95—Cape Breton		AHL	4	2	5	7	23	—	—	—	—	—
—Edmonton		NHL	29	1	7	8	40	—	—	—	—	—
NHL totals			108	8	31	39	150					

MIRONOV, DMITRI
D, PENGUINS

PERSONAL: Born December 25, 1965, in Moscow, U.S.S.R. . . . 6-2/214. . . . Shoots right. . . . Name pronounced MIH-rih-nahf. . . . Brother of Boris Mironov, defenseman, Edmonton Oilers.
TRANSACTIONS/CAREER NOTES: Selected by Toronto Maple Leafs in eighth round (seventh Maple Leafs pick, 160th overall) of NHL entry draft (June 22, 1991). . . . Broke nose (March 23, 1992). . . . Suffered infected tooth (March 18, 1993); missed 10 games. . . . Suffered quad contusion (December 28, 1993); missed one game. . . . Lacerated lip (March 7, 1994); missed two games. . . . Suffered rib and muscle strain (April 2, 1994); missed remainder of season. . . . Bruised thigh (February 18, 1995); missed one game. . . . Separated shoulder (March 27, 1995); missed 14 games. . . . Traded by Maple Leafs with second-round pick in 1996 draft to Pittsburgh Penguins for D Larry Murphy (July 8, 1995).
MISCELLANEOUS: Member of gold-medal-winning Unified Olympic team (1992).

			REGULAR SEASON					PLAYOFFS				
Season	Team	League	Gms.	G	A	Pts.	PIM	Gms.	G	A	Pts.	PIM
90-91—Soviet Wings		USSR	45	16	12	28	22	—	—	—	—	—
91-92—Soviet Wings		USSR	35	15	16	31	62	—	—	—	—	—
—Unified Olympic Team		Int'l	8	3	1	4	4	—	—	—	—	—
—Toronto		NHL	7	1	0	1	0	—	—	—	—	—
92-93—Toronto		NHL	59	7	24	31	40	14	1	2	3	2
93-94—Toronto		NHL	76	9	27	36	78	18	6	9	15	6
94-95—Toronto		NHL	33	5	12	17	28	6	2	1	3	2
NHL totals			175	22	63	85	146	38	9	12	21	10

MITCHELL, JEFF
C/RW, STARS

PERSONAL: Born May 16, 1975, in Wayne, Mich. . . . 6-1/175. . . . Shoots right.
TRANSACTIONS/CAREER NOTES: Selected by Los Angeles Kings in third round (second Kings pick, 68th overall) of NHL entry draft (June 26, 1993). . . . Traded by Kings to Dallas Stars for fifth-round pick (C Jason Morgan) in 1995 draft (June 6, 1995).

			REGULAR SEASON					PLAYOFFS				
Season	Team	League	Gms.	G	A	Pts.	PIM	Gms.	G	A	Pts.	PIM
92-93—Detroit		OHL	62	10	15	25	100	15	3	3	6	16
93-94—Detroit		OHL	59	25	18	43	99	17	3	5	8	22
94-95—Detroit		OHL	61	30	30	60	121	21	9	12	21	48

MODANO, MIKE
RW/C, STARS

PERSONAL: Born June 7, 1970, in Livonia, Mich. . . . 6-3/190. . . . Shoots left. . . . Name pronounced muh-DAH-noh.
TRANSACTIONS/CAREER NOTES: Selected by Minnesota North Stars in first round (first North Stars pick, first overall) of NHL entry draft (June 11, 1988). . . . Fractured scaphoid bone in left wrist (January 24, 1989). . . . Broke nose (March 4, 1990). . . . Pulled groin (November 30, 1992); missed two games. . . . North Stars franchise moved from Minnesota to Dallas and renamed Stars for 1993-94 season. . . . Strained medial collateral knee ligament (January 6, 1994); missed six games. . . . Suffered concussion (February 26, 1994); missed two games. . . . Bruised ankle (March 12, 1995); missed four games. . . . Ruptured tendons in ankle (April 4, 1995) and underwent surgery (April 11, 1995); missed last 14 games of season and entire playoffs.
HONORS: Named to WHL (East) All-Star first team (1988-89). . . . Named to NHL All-Rookie team (1989-90). . . . Played in NHL All-Star Game (1993).
STATISTICAL PLATEAUS: Three-goal games: 1989-90 (1), 1993-94 (1). Total: 2.

Season Team	League	REGULAR SEASON Gms.	G	A	Pts.	PIM	PLAYOFFS Gms.	G	A	Pts.	PIM
86-87—Prince Albert	WHL	70	32	30	62	96	8	1	4	5	4
87-88—Prince Albert	WHL	65	47	80	127	80	9	7	11	18	18
88-89—Prince Albert	WHL	41	39	66	105	74	—	—	—	—	—
—Minnesota	NHL	—	—	—	—	—	2	0	0	0	0
89-90—Minnesota	NHL	80	29	46	75	63	7	1	1	2	12
90-91—Minnesota	NHL	79	28	36	64	65	23	8	12	20	16
91-92—Minnesota	NHL	76	33	44	77	46	7	3	2	5	4
92-93—Minnesota	NHL	82	33	60	93	83	—	—	—	—	—
93-94—Dallas	NHL	76	50	43	93	54	9	7	3	10	16
94-95—Dallas	NHL	30	12	17	29	8	—	—	—	—	—
NHL totals		423	185	246	431	319	48	19	18	37	48

MODIN, FREDRIK
LW, MAPLE LEAFS

PERSONAL: Born October 8, 1974, in Jonkoping, Sweden.... 6-3/202.... Shoots left.
TRANSACTIONS/CAREER NOTES: Selected by Toronto Maple Leafs in third round (third Maple Leafs pick, 64th overall) of NHL entry draft (June 29, 1994).

Season Team	League	REGULAR SEASON Gms.	G	A	Pts.	PIM	PLAYOFFS Gms.	G	A	Pts.	PIM
91-92—Sundsvall Timra	Swed. Dv.II	11	1	0	1	0	—	—	—	—	—
92-93—Sundsvall Timra	Swed. Dv.II	30	5	7	12	12	—	—	—	—	—
93-94—Sundsvall Timra	Swed. Dv.II	30	16	15	31	36	—	—	—	—	—
94-95—Brynas Gavle	Sweden	38	9	10	19	33	14	4	4	8	6

MODRY, JAROSLAV
D, SENATORS

PERSONAL: Born February 27, 1971, in Ceske-Budejovice, Czechoslovakia.... 6-2/195.... Shoots left.... Name pronounced moh-DREE.
TRANSACTIONS/CAREER NOTES: Selected by New Jersey Devils in ninth round (10th Devils pick, 179th overall) of NHL entry draft (June 16, 1990).... Played in Europe during 1994-95 NHL lockout.... Injured ankle (January 31, 1995); missed two games.... Reinjured ankle (February 18, 1995); missed three games.... Traded by Devils to Ottawa Senators for fourth-round pick (C Alyn McCauley) in 1995 draft (July 8, 1995).

Season Team	League	REGULAR SEASON Gms.	G	A	Pts.	PIM	PLAYOFFS Gms.	G	A	Pts.	PIM
88-89—Budejovice	Czech.	28	0	1	1	...	—	—	—	—	—
89-90—Budejovice	Czech.	41	2	2	4	...	—	—	—	—	—
90-91—Dukla Trencin	Czech.	33	1	9	10	6	—	—	—	—	—
91-92—Dukla Trencin	Czech.	18	0	4	4	...	—	—	—	—	—
—Budejovice	Czech II	14	4	10	14	...	—	—	—	—	—
92-93—Utica	AHL	80	7	35	42	62	5	0	2	2	2
93-94—New Jersey	NHL	41	2	15	17	18	—	—	—	—	—
—Albany	AHL	19	1	5	6	25	—	—	—	—	—
94-95—HC Ceske Budejovice	Czech. Rep.	19	1	3	4	30	—	—	—	—	—
—New Jersey	NHL	11	0	0	0	0	—	—	—	—	—
—Albany	AHL	18	5	6	11	14	14	3	3	6	4
NHL totals		52	2	15	17	18					

MOGER, SANDY
RW, BRUINS

PERSONAL: Born March 21, 1969, in 100 Mile House, B.C.... 6-2/190.... Shoots right.... Full name: Alexander Sandy Moger.... Name pronounced MOH-guhr.
COLLEGE: Lake Superior State (Mich.).
TRANSACTIONS/CAREER NOTES: Broke wrist (September 1988).... Selected by Vancouver Canucks in ninth round (seventh Canucks pick, 176th overall) of NHL entry draft (June 17, 1989).... Signed as free agent by Boston Bruins (July 6, 1994).... Broke arm (April 28, 1995); missed remainder of season and entire playoffs.
HONORS: Named to CCHA All-Star second team (1991-92).

Season Team	League	REGULAR SEASON Gms.	G	A	Pts.	PIM	PLAYOFFS Gms.	G	A	Pts.	PIM
86-87—Vernon	BCJHL	13	5	4	9	10	—	—	—	—	—
87-88—Yorkton	SJHL	60	39	41	80	144	—	—	—	—	—
88-89—Lake Superior State	CCHA	31	4	6	10	28	—	—	—	—	—
89-90—Lake Superior State	CCHA	46	17	15	32	76	—	—	—	—	—
90-91—Lake Superior State	CCHA	45	27	21	48	*172	—	—	—	—	—
91-92—Lake Superior State	CCHA	42	26	25	51	111	—	—	—	—	—
92-93—Hamilton	AHL	78	23	26	49	57	—	—	—	—	—
93-94—Hamilton	AHL	29	9	8	17	41	—	—	—	—	—
94-95—Providence	AHL	63	32	29	61	105	—	—	—	—	—
—Boston	NHL	18	2	6	8	6	—	—	—	—	—
NHL totals		18	2	6	8	6					

MOGILNY, ALEXANDER
RW, CANUCKS

PERSONAL: Born February 18, 1969, in Khabarovsk, U.S.S.R.... 5-11/187.... Shoots left.... Name pronounced moh-GIHL-nee.
TRANSACTIONS/CAREER NOTES: Selected by Buffalo Sabres in fifth round (fourth Sabres pick, 89th overall) of NHL entry draft (June 11, 1988).... Suffered from the flu (November 26, 1989).... Missed games due to fear of flying (January 22, 1990); spent remainder of season traveling on ground.... Separated shoulder (February 8, 1991); missed six games.... Suffered from the flu (November

M

1991); missed two games. . . . Suffered from the flu (December 18, 1991); missed one game. . . . Bruised shoulder (October 10, 1992); missed six games. . . . Broke fibula and tore ankle ligaments (May 6, 1993); missed remainder of 1992-93 playoffs and first nine games of 1993-94 season. . . . Suffered sore ankle (February 2, 1994); missed four games. . . . Suffered inflamed tendon in ankle (February 15, 1994); missed four games. . . . Played in Europe during 1994-95 NHL lockout. . . . Pinched nerve in neck (April 9, 1995); missed three games. . . . Traded by Sabres with fifth-round pick in 1995 draft (LW Todd Norman) to Vancouver Canucks for RW Mike Peca, D Mike Wilson and first-round pick (D Jay McKee) in 1995 draft (July 8, 1995).

HONORS: Played in NHL All-Star Game (1992 through 1994). . . . Named to THE SPORTING NEWS All-Star second team (1992-93). . . . Named to NHL All-Star second team (1992-93).

RECORDS: Shares NHL record for fastest goal from start of a game—5 seconds (December 21, 1991).

STATISTICAL PLATEAUS: Three-goal games: 1990-91 (1), 1991-92 (1), 1992-93 (5), 1993-94 (1). Total: 8. . . . Four-goal games: 1992-93 (2). . . . Total hat tricks: 10.

MISCELLANEOUS: Member of gold-medal-winning U.S.S.R. Olympic team (1988). . . . Captain of Buffalo Sabres (1993-94 and 1994-95).

			REGULAR SEASON					PLAYOFFS			
Season	Team	League	Gms.	G	A	Pts.	PIM	Gms.	G	A	Pts.	PIM
86-87—CSKA Moscow	USSR	28	15	1	16	4	—	—	—	—	—
87-88—CSKA Moscow	USSR	39	12	8	20	20	—	—	—	—	—
88-89—CSKA Moscow	USSR	31	11	11	22	24	—	—	—	—	—
89-90—Buffalo	NHL	65	15	28	43	16	4	0	1	1	2
90-91—Buffalo	NHL	62	30	34	64	16	6	0	6	6	2
91-92—Buffalo	NHL	67	39	45	84	73	2	0	2	2	0
92-93—Buffalo	NHL	77	†76	51	127	40	7	7	3	10	6
93-94—Buffalo	NHL	66	32	47	79	22	7	4	2	6	6
94-95—Spartak Moscow	CIS	1	0	1	1	0	—	—	—	—	—
—Buffalo	NHL	44	19	28	47	36	5	3	2	5	2
NHL totals		381	211	233	444	203	31	14	16	30	18

MOLLER, RANDY
D, PANTHERS

PERSONAL: Born August 23, 1963, in Red Deer, Alta. . . . 6-2/210. . . . Shoots right. . . . Name pronounced MOH-luhr. . . . Brother of Mike Moller, right winger, Buffalo Sabres and Edmonton Oilers (1980-81 through 1986-87).

TRANSACTIONS/CAREER NOTES: Tore knee ligaments and underwent surgery (December 1980). . . . Selected by Quebec Nordiques in first round (first Nordiques pick, 11th overall) of NHL entry draft (June 10, 1981). . . . Broke hand (October 28, 1986). . . . Suffered lingering neck problem (November 1987). . . . Injured knee (January 1988). . . . Suffered back spasms (March 1988). . . . Separated shoulder (October 29, 1988). . . . Broke toe (September 1989). . . . Traded by Nordiques to New York Rangers for D Michel Petit (October 5, 1989). . . . Dislocated right shoulder (December 13, 1989). . . . Suffered back spasms (March 21, 1990); missed six games. . . . Dislocated left shoulder (November 7, 1990); missed 15 games. . . . Separated shoulder (January 22, 1992); missed four games. . . . Traded by Rangers to Buffalo Sabres for D Jay Wells (March 9, 1992). . . . Suffered knee ligament damage (November 11, 1992); missed 25 games. . . . Strained back muscle (January 17, 1993); missed 21 games. . . . Signed as free agent by Florida Panthers (July 12, 1994). . . . Sprained knee (March 4, 1995); missed 17 games.

HONORS: Named to WHL All-Star second team (1981-82).

			REGULAR SEASON					PLAYOFFS			
Season	Team	League	Gms.	G	A	Pts.	PIM	Gms.	G	A	Pts.	PIM
79-80—Red Deer	AJHL	56	3	34	37	253	—	—	—	—	—
80-81—Lethbridge	WHL	46	4	21	25	176	9	0	4	4	24
81-82—Lethbridge	WHL	60	20	55	75	249	12	4	6	10	65
—Quebec	NHL	—	—	—	—	—	1	0	0	0	0
82-83—Quebec	NHL	75	2	12	14	145	4	1	0	1	4
83-84—Quebec	NHL	74	4	14	18	147	9	1	0	1	45
84-85—Quebec	NHL	79	7	22	29	120	18	2	2	4	40
85-86—Quebec	NHL	69	5	18	23	141	3	0	0	0	26
86-87—Quebec	NHL	71	5	9	14	144	13	1	4	5	23
87-88—Quebec	NHL	66	3	22	25	169	—	—	—	—	—
88-89—Quebec	NHL	74	7	22	29	136	—	—	—	—	—
89-90—New York Rangers	NHL	60	1	12	13	139	10	1	6	7	32
90-91—New York Rangers	NHL	61	4	19	23	161	6	0	2	2	11
91-92—New York Rangers	NHL	43	2	7	9	78	—	—	—	—	—
—Binghamton	AHL	3	0	1	1	0	—	—	—	—	—
—Buffalo	NHL	13	1	2	3	59	7	0	0	0	8
92-93—Buffalo	NHL	35	2	7	9	83	—	—	—	—	—
—Rochester	AHL	3	1	0	1	10	—	—	—	—	—
93-94—Buffalo	NHL	78	2	11	13	154	7	0	2	2	8
94-95—Florida	NHL	17	0	3	3	16	—	—	—	—	—
NHL totals		815	45	180	225	1692	78	6	16	22	197

MOMESSO, SERGIO
LW, MAPLE LEAFS

PERSONAL: Born September 4, 1965, in Montreal. . . . 6-3/215. . . . Shoots left. . . . Name pronounced moh-MEH-soh.

TRANSACTIONS/CAREER NOTES: Selected by Montreal Canadiens as underage junior in second round (third Canadiens pick, 27th overall) of NHL entry draft (June 8, 1983). . . . Tore cruciate ligament in left knee and underwent surgery (December 5, 1985); missed remainder of season. . . . Tore ligaments, injured cartilage and fractured left knee (December 5, 1986). . . . Lacerated leg (February 1988). . . . Traded by Canadiens with G Vincent Riendeau to St. Louis Blues for LW Jocelyn Lemieux, G Darrell May and second-round pick (D Patrice Brisebois) in 1989 draft (August 9, 1988). . . . Fractured right ankle (November 12, 1988). . . . Traded by Blues with LW Geoff Courtnall, D Robert Dirk, C Cliff Ronning and fifth-round pick in 1992 draft (RW Brian Loney) to Vancouver Canucks for C Dan

Quinn and D Garth Butcher (March 5, 1991).... Separated shoulder (December 3, 1991); missed 22 games.... Sprained knee (November 30, 1993); missed 11 games.... Suspended two games and fined $500 by NHL for stick-swinging incident (March 28, 1994).... Played in Europe during 1994-95 NHL lockout.... Traded by Canucks to Toronto Maple Leafs for C Mike Ridley (July 8, 1995).
HONORS: Named to QMJHL All-Star first team (1984-85).
STATISTICAL PLATEAUS: Three-goal games: 1987-88 (1).
MISCELLANEOUS: Member of Stanley Cup championship team (1987).

			REGULAR SEASON					PLAYOFFS				
Season	Team	League	Gms.	G	A	Pts.	PIM	Gms.	G	A	Pts.	PIM
82-83—Shawinigan		QMJHL	70	27	42	69	93	10	5	4	9	55
83-84—Nova Scotia		AHL	—	—	—	—	—	8	0	2	2	4
—Shawinigan		QMJHL	68	42	88	130	235	6	4	4	8	13
—Montreal		NHL	1	0	0	0	0	—	—	—	—	—
84-85—Shawinigan		QMJHL	64	56	90	146	216	8	7	8	15	17
85-86—Montreal		NHL	24	8	7	15	46	—	—	—	—	—
86-87—Montreal		NHL	59	14	17	31	96	11	1	3	4	31
—Sherbrooke		AHL	6	1	6	7	10	—	—	—	—	—
87-88—Montreal		NHL	53	7	14	21	101	6	0	2	2	16
88-89—St. Louis		NHL	53	9	17	26	139	10	2	5	7	24
89-90—St. Louis		NHL	79	24	32	56	199	12	3	2	5	63
90-91—St. Louis		NHL	59	10	18	28	131	—	—	—	—	—
—Vancouver		NHL	11	6	2	8	43	6	0	3	3	25
91-92—Vancouver		NHL	58	20	23	43	198	13	0	5	5	30
92-93—Vancouver		NHL	84	18	20	38	200	12	3	0	3	30
93-94—Vancouver		NHL	68	14	13	27	149	24	3	4	7	56
94-95—Milan		Italy	2	1	4	5	2	—	—	—	—	—
—Vancouver		NHL	48	10	15	25	65	11	3	1	4	16
NHL totals			597	140	178	318	1367	105	15	25	40	291

MONGEAU, MICHEL
C

PERSONAL: Born February 9, 1965, in Nun's Island, Que.... 5-9/180.... Shoots left. ... Name pronounced mahn-ZHOW.
TRANSACTIONS/CAREER NOTES: Signed as free agent by St. Louis Blues (August 21, 1989).... Selected by Tampa Bay Lightning in NHL expansion draft (June 18, 1992).... Loaned to Milwaukee Admirals at beginning of 1992-93 season.... Traded by Lightning with RW Martin Simard and RW Steve Tuttle to Quebec Nordiques for RW Herb Raglan (February 12, 1993).
HONORS: Named to QMJHL All-Star second team (1985-86).... Won Garry F. Longman Memorial Trophy (1986-87).... Won James Gatschene Memorial Trophy (1989-90).... Won Leo P. Lamoureux Memorial Trophy (1989-90).... Named to IHL All-Star first team (1989-90).... Won N.R. (Bud) Poile Trophy (1990-91).... Named to IHL All-Star second team (1990-91).

			REGULAR SEASON					PLAYOFFS				
Season	Team	League	Gms.	G	A	Pts.	PIM	Gms.	G	A	Pts.	PIM
83-84—Laval		QMJHL	60	45	49	94	30	—	—	—	—	—
84-85—Laval		QMJHL	67	60	84	144	56	—	—	—	—	—
85-86—Laval		QMJHL	72	71	109	180	45	—	—	—	—	—
86-87—Saginaw		IHL	76	42	53	95	34	10	3	6	9	10
87-88—Played in France		France	30	31	21	52	...	—	—	—	—	—
88-89—Flint		IHL	82	41	*76	117	57	—	—	—	—	—
89-90—St. Louis		NHL	7	1	5	6	2	2	0	1	1	0
—Peoria		IHL	73	39	*78	*117	53	5	3	4	7	6
90-91—St. Louis		NHL	7	1	1	2	0	—	—	—	—	—
—Peoria		IHL	73	41	65	106	114	19	10	*16	26	32
91-92—Peoria		IHL	32	21	34	55	77	10	5	14	19	8
—St. Louis		NHL	36	3	12	15	6	—	—	—	—	—
92-93—Milwaukee		IHL	45	24	41	65	69	4	1	4	5	4
—Tampa Bay		NHL	4	1	1	2	2	—	—	—	—	—
—Halifax		AHL	22	13	18	31	10	—	—	—	—	—
93-94—Cornwall		AHL	7	3	11	14	4	—	—	—	—	—
—Peoria		IHL	52	29	36	65	50	—	—	—	—	—
94-95—Peoria		IHL	74	30	52	82	72	—	—	—	—	—
NHL totals			54	6	19	25	10	2	0	1	1	0

MONTGOMERY, JIM
C, FLYERS

PERSONAL: Born June 30, 1969, in Montreal.... 5-9/180.... Shoots right.
COLLEGE: Maine.
TRANSACTIONS/CAREER NOTES: Signed as free agent by St. Louis Blues (June 2, 1993).... Suspended four games and fined $500 by NHL for high-sticking incident (October 4, 1993).... Traded by Blues to Montreal Canadiens for C Guy Carbonneau (August 19, 1994).... Claimed on waivers by Philadelphia Flyers (February 10, 1995).
HONORS: Named to NCAA All-America East second team (1990-91 and 1992-93).... Named to Hockey East All-Star second team (1990-91 and 1991-92).... Named NCAA Tournament Most Valuable Player (1992-93).... Named Hockey East Tournament Most Valuable Player (1992-93).... Named to NCAA All-Tournament team (1992-93).... Named to Hockey East All-Star first team (1992-93).... Named to Hockey East All-Decade team (1994).

			REGULAR SEASON					PLAYOFFS				
Season	Team	League	Gms.	G	A	Pts.	PIM	Gms.	G	A	Pts.	PIM
89-90—University of Maine		Hockey East	45	26	34	60	35	—	—	—	—	—
90-91—University of Maine		Hockey East	43	24	57	81	44	—	—	—	—	—

M

Season	Team	League	Gms.	G	A	Pts.	PIM	Gms.	G	A	Pts.	PIM
			REGULAR SEASON					PLAYOFFS				
91-92	University of Maine	Hockey East	37	21	44	65	46	—	—	—	—	—
92-93	University of Maine	Hockey East	45	32	63	95	40	—	—	—	—	—
93-94	St. Louis	NHL	67	6	14	20	44	—	—	—	—	—
	Peoria	IHL	12	7	8	15	10	—	—	—	—	—
94-95	Montreal	NHL	5	0	0	0	2	—	—	—	—	—
	Philadelphia	NHL	8	1	1	2	6	7	1	0	1	2
	Hershey	AHL	16	8	6	14	14	6	3	2	5	25
NHL totals			80	7	15	22	52	7	1	0	1	2

MONTREUIL, ERIC
C, PANTHERS

PERSONAL: Born May 18, 1975, in Verdun, Que. . . . 6-1/170. . . . Shoots left. . . . Name pronounced MAHN-tray.
TRANSACTIONS/CAREER NOTES: Selected by Florida Panthers in 11th round (13th Panthers pick, 265th overall) of NHL entry draft (June 26, 1993).

Season	Team	League	Gms.	G	A	Pts.	PIM	Gms.	G	A	Pts.	PIM
			REGULAR SEASON					PLAYOFFS				
92-93	Chicoutimi	QMJHL	70	19	13	32	98	4	0	1	1	2
93-94	Beauport	QMJHL	67	31	40	71	122	15	4	8	12	39
94-95	Beauport	QMJHL	70	21	39	60	186	18	5	10	15	72

MOOG, ANDY
G, STARS

PERSONAL: Born February 18, 1960, in Penticton, B.C. . . . 5-8/170. . . . Catches left. . . . Full name: Donald Andrew Moog. . . . Name pronounced MOHG.
TRANSACTIONS/CAREER NOTES: Selected by Edmonton Oilers in seventh round (sixth Oilers pick, 132nd overall) of NHL entry draft (June 11, 1980). . . . Suffered viral infection (December 1983). . . . Injured ligaments in both knees (March 1, 1985). . . . Traded by Oilers to Boston Bruins for LW Geoff Courtnall and G Bill Ranford (March 1988). . . . Hyperextended right knee (January 31, 1991); missed three weeks. . . . Injured back (January 1993); missed three games. . . . Injured hamstring (February 1993); missed four games. . . . Traded by Bruins to Dallas Stars for G Jon Casey (June 25, 1993) to complete deal in which Bruins sent D Gord Murphy to Stars for future considerations (June 20, 1993). . . . Strained groin (November 24, 1993); missed five games. . . . Strained hip muscle (March 30, 1995); missed two games. . . . Strained hamstring (April 11, 1995); missed one game. . . . Reinjured hamstring (April 19, 1995); missed five games.
HONORS: Named to WHL All-Star team (1979-80). . . . Named to CHL All-Star second team (1981-82). . . . Named to THE SPORTING NEWS All-Star second team (1982-83). . . . Played in NHL All-Star Game (1985, 1986 and 1991). . . . Shared William M. Jennings Trophy with Rejean Lemelin (1989-90).
MISCELLANEOUS: Member of Stanley Cup championship teams (1984, 1985 and 1987).

Season	Team	League	Gms.	Min.	W	L	T	GA	SO	Avg.	Gms.	Min.	W	L	GA	SO	Avg.
			REGULAR SEASON								PLAYOFFS						
76-77	Kamloops	BCJHL	44	2735	...	...	...	173	0	*3.80	—	—	—	—	—	—	—
	Kamloops	WCHL	1	35	...	...	...	6	0	10.29	—	—	—	—	—	—	—
77-78	Penticton	BCJHL	39	2243	...	...	...	191	0	5.11	—	—	—	—	—	—	—
78-79	Billings	WHL	26	1306	13	5	4	90	*3	4.13	5	229	1	3	21	0	5.50
79-80	Billings	WHL	46	2435	23	14	1	149	1	3.67	3	190	2	1	10	0	3.16
80-81	Wichita	CHL	29	1602	14	13	1	89	0	3.33	5	300	3	2	16	0	3.20
	Edmonton	NHL	7	313	3	3	0	20	0	3.83	9	526	5	4	32	0	3.65
81-82	Edmonton	NHL	8	399	3	5	0	32	0	4.81	—	—	—	—	—	—	—
	Wichita	CHL	40	2391	23	13	3	119	1	2.99	7	434	3	4	23	0	3.18
82-83	Edmonton	NHL	50	2833	33	8	7	167	1	3.54	16	949	11	5	48	0	3.03
83-84	Edmonton	NHL	38	2212	27	8	1	139	1	3.77	7	263	4	0	12	0	2.74
84-85	Edmonton	NHL	39	2019	22	9	3	111	1	3.30	2	20	0	0	0	0	0.00
85-86	Edmonton	NHL	47	2664	27	9	7	164	1	3.69	1	60	1	0	1	0	1.00
86-87	Edmonton	NHL	46	2461	28	11	3	144	0	3.51	2	120	2	0	8	0	4.00
87-88	Can. national team	Int'l	27	1438	10	7	5	86	0	3.59	—	—	—	—	—	—	—
	Can. Olympic Team	Int'l	4	240	4	0	0	9	1	2.25	—	—	—	—	—	—	—
	Boston	NHL	6	360	4	2	0	17	1	2.83	7	354	1	4	25	0	4.24
88-89	Boston	NHL	41	2482	18	14	8	133	1	3.22	6	359	4	2	14	0	2.34
89-90	Boston	NHL	46	2536	24	10	7	122	3	2.89	20	1195	13	7	44	*2	*2.21
90-91	Boston	NHL	51	2844	25	13	9	136	4	2.87	19	1133	10	9	60	0	3.18
91-92	Boston	NHL	62	3640	28	22	9	196	1	3.23	15	866	8	7	46	1	3.19
92-93	Boston	NHL	55	3194	37	14	3	168	3	3.16	3	161	0	3	14	0	5.22
93-94	Dallas	NHL	55	3121	24	20	7	170	2	3.27	4	246	1	3	12	0	2.93
94-95	Dallas	NHL	31	1770	10	12	7	72	2	2.44	5	277	1	4	16	0	3.47
NHL totals			582	32848	313	160	71	1791	21	3.27	116	6529	61	48	332	3	3.05

MORAN, IAN
D, PENGUINS

PERSONAL: Born August 24, 1972, in Cleveland. . . . 5-11/175. . . . Shoots right.
HIGH SCHOOL: Belmont Hill (Mass.).
COLLEGE: Boston College.
TRANSACTIONS/CAREER NOTES: Underwent knee surgery (June 1988). . . . Separated shoulder (March 1989). . . . Selected by Pittsburgh Penguins in sixth round (fifth Penguins pick, 107th overall) of NHL entry draft (June 16, 1990).
HONORS: Named Hockey East co-Rookie of the Year with Craig Darby (1991-92). . . . Named to Hockey East All-Rookie team (1991-92).

M

Season Team	League	REGULAR SEASON					PLAYOFFS				
		Gms.	G	A	Pts.	PIM	Gms.	G	A	Pts.	PIM
87-88—Belmont Hill H.S.	Mass. H.S.	25	3	13	16	15	—	—	—	—	—
88-89—Belmont Hill H.S.	Mass. H.S.	23	7	25	32	8	—	—	—	—	—
89-90—Belmont Hill H.S.	Mass. H.S.	...	10	36	46	0	—	—	—	—	—
90-91—Belmont Hill H.S.	Mass. H.S.	23	7	44	51	12	—	—	—	—	—
91-92—Boston College	Hockey East	30	2	16	18	44	—	—	—	—	—
92-93—Boston College	Hockey East	31	8	12	20	32	—	—	—	—	—
93-94—U.S. national team	Int'l	50	8	15	23	69	—	—	—	—	—
—Cleveland	IHL	33	5	13	18	39	—	—	—	—	—
94-95—Cleveland	IHL	64	7	31	38	94	4	0	1	1	2
—Pittsburgh	NHL	—	—	—	—	—	8	0	0	0	0
NHL totals		0					8	0	0	0	0

MORE, JAY
D, SHARKS

PERSONAL: Born January 12, 1969, in Souris, Man.... 6-2/210.... Shoots right.
TRANSACTIONS/CAREER NOTES: Selected by New York Rangers as underage junior in first round (first Rangers pick, 10th overall) of NHL entry draft (June 13, 1987).... Traded by Rangers to Minnesota North Stars for C Dave Archibald (November 1, 1989).... Traded by North Stars to Montreal Canadiens for G Brian Hayward (November 7, 1990).... Selected by San Jose Sharks in NHL expansion draft (May 30, 1991).... Injured foot during preseason (September 1991); missed 16 games.... Injured knee (March 1992).... Pulled groin (December 9, 1992); missed four games.... Reaggravated groin injury (December 23, 1992); missed four games.... Suspended one game by NHL for accumulating three game misconduct penalties (January 27, 1993).... Strained hip (March 7, 1993); missed one game.... Suspended for last game of season and first game of 1993-94 season for accumulating four game misconduct penalties (April 11, 1993).... Fractured wrist (October 23, 1993); missed 25 games.... Bruised hand (February 18, 1995); missed two games.... Injured leg (April 7, 1995); missed one game.
HONORS: Named to WHL (West) All-Star first team (1987-88).

Season Team	League	REGULAR SEASON					PLAYOFFS				
		Gms.	G	A	Pts.	PIM	Gms.	G	A	Pts.	PIM
84-85—Lethbridge	WHL	71	3	9	12	101	4	1	0	1	7
85-86—Lethbridge	WHL	61	7	18	25	155	9	0	2	2	36
86-87—New Westminster	WHL	64	8	29	37	217	—	—	—	—	—
87-88—New Westminster	WHL	70	13	47	60	270	5	0	2	2	26
88-89—Denver	IHL	62	7	15	22	138	3	0	1	1	26
—New York Rangers	NHL	1	0	0	0	0	—	—	—	—	—
89-90—Flint	IHL	9	1	5	6	41	—	—	—	—	—
—Kalamazoo	IHL	64	9	25	34	216	10	0	3	3	13
—Minnesota	NHL	5	0	0	0	16	—	—	—	—	—
90-91—Kalamazoo	IHL	10	0	5	5	46	—	—	—	—	—
—Fredericton	AHL	57	7	17	24	152	9	1	1	2	34
91-92—San Jose	NHL	46	4	13	17	85	—	—	—	—	—
—Kansas City	IHL	2	0	2	2	4	—	—	—	—	—
92-93—San Jose	NHL	73	5	6	11	179	—	—	—	—	—
93-94—San Jose	NHL	49	1	6	7	63	13	0	2	2	32
—Kansas City	IHL	2	1	0	1	25	—	—	—	—	—
94-95—San Jose	NHL	45	0	6	6	71	11	0	4	4	6
NHL totals		219	10	31	41	414	24	0	6	6	38

MOREAU, ETHAN
LW, BLACKHAWKS

PERSONAL: Born September 22, 1975, in Orillia, Ont.... 6-2/205.... Shoots left.... Name pronounced MOHR-oh.
TRANSACTIONS/CAREER NOTES: Selected by Chicago Blackhawks in first round (first Blackhawks pick, 14th overall) of NHL entry draft (June 28, 1994).
HONORS: Won Bobby Smith Trophy (1993-94).

Season Team	League	REGULAR SEASON					PLAYOFFS				
		Gms.	G	A	Pts.	PIM	Gms.	G	A	Pts.	PIM
90-91—Orillia	OHA	42	17	22	39	26	—	—	—	—	—
91-92—Niagara Falls	OHL	62	20	35	55	39	17	4	6	10	4
92-93—Niagara Falls	OHL	65	32	41	73	69	4	0	3	3	4
93-94—Niagara Falls	OHL	59	44	54	98	100	—	—	—	—	—
94-95—Niagara Falls	OHL	39	25	41	66	69	—	—	—	—	—
—Sudbury	OHL	23	13	17	30	22	18	6	12	18	26

MORGAN, JASON
C, KINGS

PERSONAL: Born October 9, 1976, in Kitchener, Ont.... 6-1/199.... Shoots left.
HIGH SCHOOL: Loyalist C & VI (Kingston, Ont.).
TRANSACTIONS/CAREER NOTES: Selected by Los Angeles Kings in fifth round (fifth Kings pick, 118th overall) of NHL entry draft (July 8, 1995).

Season Team	League	REGULAR SEASON					PLAYOFFS				
		Gms.	G	A	Pts.	PIM	Gms.	G	A	Pts.	PIM
93-94—Kitchener	OHL	65	6	15	21	16	5	1	0	1	0
94-95—Kitchener	OHL	35	3	15	18	25	—	—	—	—	—
—Kingston	OHL	20	0	3	3	14	6	0	2	2	0

M

MORIN, STEPHANE

C

PERSONAL: Born March 27, 1969, in Montreal. . . . 6-0/175. . . . Shoots left. . . . Name pronounced moh-RAI.

TRANSACTIONS/CAREER NOTES: Traded by Shawinigan Cataractes with second-round pick in QMJHL draft to Chicoutimi Sagueneens for D Daniel Bock (December 1987). . . . Selected by Quebec Nordiques in third round (third Nordiques pick, 43rd overall) of NHL entry draft (June 17, 1989). . . . Stretched right knee ligaments (January 8, 1991); missed six games. . . . Broke finger on right hand (February 20, 1991); missed eight games. . . . Sprained knee (October 12, 1991); missed nine games. . . . Signed as free agent by Vancouver Canucks (October 5, 1992).

HONORS: Won Michel Briere Trophy (1988-89). . . . Won Jean Beliveau Trophy (1988-89). . . . Named to QMJHL All-Star first team (1988-89). . . . Named to AHL All-Star second team (1993-94). . . . Won Leo P. Lamoureux Memorial Trophy (1994-95). . . . Named to IHL All-Star first team (1994-95).

Season Team	League	REGULAR SEASON					PLAYOFFS				
		Gms.	G	A	Pts.	PIM	Gms.	G	A	Pts.	PIM
86-87—Shawinigan	QMJHL	65	9	14	23	28	14	1	3	4	27
87-88—Shawinigan-Chicoutimi	QMJHL	68	38	45	83	18	6	3	8	11	2
88-89—Chicoutimi	QMJHL	70	77	*109	*186	71	—	—	—	—	—
89-90—Quebec	NHL	6	0	2	2	2	—	—	—	—	—
—Halifax	AHL	65	28	32	60	60	6	3	4	7	6
90-91—Halifax	AHL	17	8	14	22	18	—	—	—	—	—
—Quebec	NHL	48	13	27	40	30	—	—	—	—	—
91-92—Quebec	NHL	30	2	8	10	14	—	—	—	—	—
—Halifax	AHL	30	17	13	30	29	—	—	—	—	—
92-93—Hamilton	AHL	70	31	54	85	49	—	—	—	—	—
—Vancouver	NHL	1	0	1	1	0	—	—	—	—	—
93-94—Hamilton	AHL	69	38	71	109	48	4	3	2	5	4
—Vancouver	NHL	5	1	1	2	6	—	—	—	—	—
94-95—Minnesota	IHL	81	33	*81	*114	53	2	0	1	1	0
NHL totals		90	16	39	55	52					

MORO, MARC

D, SENATORS

PERSONAL: Born July 17, 1977, in Toronto. . . . 6-0/209. . . . Shoots left.

HIGH SCHOOL: Loyalist C & VI (Kingston, Ont.).

TRANSACTIONS/CAREER NOTES: Selected by Ottawa Senators in second round (second Senators pick, 27th overall) of NHL entry draft (July 8, 1995).

Season Team	League	REGULAR SEASON					PLAYOFFS				
		Gms.	G	A	Pts.	PIM	Gms.	G	A	Pts.	PIM
92-93—Mississauga	Jr. A	2	0	0	0	0	—	—	—	—	—
93-94—Kingston	Tier II Jr. A	12	0	2	2	20	—	—	—	—	—
—Kingston	OHL	43	0	3	3	81	—	—	—	—	—
94-95—Kingston	OHL	64	4	12	16	255	6	0	0	0	23

MOROZOV, ALEXEI

RW, PENGUINS

PERSONAL: Born February 16, 1977, in Moscow, U.S.S.R. . . . 6-1/174. . . . Shoots left. . . . Brother of Valentin Morozov, center in Pittsburgh Penguins system.

TRANSACTIONS/CAREER NOTES: Selected by Pittsburgh Penguins in first round (first Penguins pick, 24th overall) of NHL entry draft (July 8, 1995).

Season Team	League	REGULAR SEASON					PLAYOFFS				
		Gms.	G	A	Pts.	PIM	Gms.	G	A	Pts.	PIM
93-94—Soviet Wings	CIS	7	0	0	0	0	3	0	0	0	2
94-95—Soviet Wings	CIS	48	15	12	27	53	4	0	3	3	0

MORRISON, BRENDAN

C, DEVILS

PERSONAL: Born August 12, 1975, in North Vancouver. . . . 5-11/170. . . . Shoots left.

HIGH SCHOOL: Pitt Meadow (B.C.) Secondary.

COLLEGE: Michigan.

TRANSACTIONS/CAREER NOTES: Selected by New Jersey Devils in second round (third Devils pick, 39th overall) of NHL entry draft (June 26, 1993).

HONORS: Won CCHA Rookie of Year Award (1993-94). . . . Named to CCHA All-Rookie team (1993-94). . . . Named to NCAA All-America West first team (1994-95). . . . Named to CCHA All-Star first team (1994-95).

Season Team	League	REGULAR SEASON					PLAYOFFS				
		Gms.	G	A	Pts.	PIM	Gms.	G	A	Pts.	PIM
92-93—Penticton	BCJHL	56	35	59	94	45	—	—	—	—	—
93-94—University of Michigan	CCHA	38	20	28	48	24	—	—	—	—	—
94-95—University of Michigan	CCHA	39	23	53	76	42	—	—	—	—	—

MORROW, SCOTT

LW, FLAMES

PERSONAL: Born June 18, 1969, in Chicago. . . . 6-1/190. . . . Shoots left. . . . Brother of Steve Morrow, defenseman in Philadelphia Flyers system.

HIGH SCHOOL: Northwood School (Lake Placid, N.Y.).

COLLEGE: New Hampshire.

TRANSACTIONS/CAREER NOTES: Selected by Hartford Whalers in fifth round (fourth Whalers pick, 95th overall) of NHL entry draft (June 11, 1988). . . . Broke ankle (November 18, 1988). . . . Traded by Whalers to Calgary Flames for C Todd Harkins (January 24, 1994).

HONORS: Named to Hockey East All-Star second team (1991-92).

		REGULAR SEASON					PLAYOFFS				
Season Team	League	Gms.	G	A	Pts.	PIM	Gms.	G	A	Pts.	PIM
87-88—Northwood School	N.Y. H.S.	24	10	13	23	...	—	—	—	—	—
88-89—Univ. of New Hampshire	Hockey East	19	6	7	13	14	—	—	—	—	—
89-90—Univ. of New Hampshire	Hockey East	29	10	11	21	35	—	—	—	—	—
90-91—Univ. of New Hampshire	Hockey East	31	11	11	22	52	—	—	—	—	—
91-92—Univ. of New Hampshire	Hockey East	35	30	23	53	65	—	—	—	—	—
—Springfield	AHL	2	0	1	1	0	5	0	0	0	9
92-93—Springfield	AHL	70	22	29	51	80	15	6	9	15	21
93-94—Springfield	AHL	30	12	15	27	28	—	—	—	—	—
—Saint John	AHL	8	2	2	4	0	7	2	1	3	10
94-95—Saint John	AHL	64	18	21	39	105	5	2	0	2	4
—Calgary	NHL	4	0	0	0	0	—	—	—	—	—
NHL totals		4	0	0	0	0					

MOSS, TYLER

G, LIGHTNING

PERSONAL: Born June 29, 1975, in Ottawa. . . . 6-0/168. . . . Catches right.
TRANSACTIONS/CAREER NOTES: Selected by Tampa Bay Lightning in second round (second Lightning pick, 29th overall) of NHL entry draft (June 26, 1993).
HONORS: Named to OHL All-Rookie team (1992-93). . . . Named to OHL All-Star first team (1994-95).

		REGULAR SEASON								PLAYOFFS						
Season Team	League	Gms.	Min.	W	L	T	GA	SO	Avg.	Gms.	Min.	W	L	GA	SO	Avg.
91-92—Nepean	COJHL	26	1335	...	...	...	109	0	4.90	—	—	—	—	—	—	—
92-93—Kingston	OHL	31	1537	13	7	5	97	0	3.79	6	228	1	2	19	0	5.00
93-94—Kingston	OHL	13	795	6	4	3	42	1	3.17	3	136	0	2	8	0	3.53
94-95—Kingston	OHL	57	3249	33	17	5	164	1	3.03	6	333	2	4	27	0	4.86

MROZIK, RICK

D, CAPITALS

PERSONAL: Born January 2, 1975, in Duluth, Minn. . . . 6-2/185. . . . Shoots left. . . . Name pronounced MROH-zihk.
HIGH SCHOOL: Cloquet (Minn.).
COLLEGE: Minnesota-Duluth.
TRANSACTIONS/CAREER NOTES: Selected by Dallas Stars in sixth round (fourth Stars pick, 136th overall) of NHL entry draft (June 26, 1993). . . . Rights traded by Stars with D Mark Tinordi to Washington Capitals for D Kevin Hatcher (January 18, 1995).

		REGULAR SEASON					PLAYOFFS				
Season Team	League	Gms.	G	A	Pts.	PIM	Gms.	G	A	Pts.	PIM
92-93—Cloquet H.S.	Minn. H.S.	28	9	38	47	12	—	—	—	—	—
93-94—Minnesota-Duluth	WCHA	38	2	9	11	38	—	—	—	—	—
94-95—Minnesota-Duluth	WCHA	3	0	0	0	2	—	—	—	—	—

MUELLER, BRIAN

D, WHALERS

PERSONAL: Born June 2, 1972, in Liverpool, N.Y. . . . 5-11/225. . . . Shoots left.
HIGH SCHOOL: South Kent (Conn.) Prep.
COLLEGE: Clarkson.
TRANSACTIONS/CAREER NOTES: Selected by Hartford Whalers in seventh round (seventh Whalers pick, 141st overall) of NHL entry draft (June 22, 1991).
HONORS: Named to ECAC All-Rookie team (1991-92). . . . Named to NCAA All-America East first team (1993-94 and 1994-95). . . . Named to ECAC All-Star first team (1993-94 and 1994-95).

		REGULAR SEASON					PLAYOFFS				
Season Team	League	Gms.	G	A	Pts.	PIM	Gms.	G	A	Pts.	PIM
90-91—Kent	Conn. H.S.	32	21	30	51	...	—	—	—	—	—
91-92—Clarkson	ECAC	29	4	13	17	32	—	—	—	—	—
92-93—Clarkson	ECAC	32	6	23	29	12	—	—	—	—	—
93-94—Clarkson	ECAC	34	17	39	56	58	—	—	—	—	—
94-95—Clarkson	ECAC	36	12	42	54	56	—	—	—	—	—

MULLEN, JOE

RW, PENGUINS

PERSONAL: Born February 26, 1957, in New York. . . . 5-9/180. . . . Shoots right. . . . Full name: Joseph Patrick Mullen. . . . Brother of Brian Mullen, right winger for four NHL teams (1982-83 through 1992-93) and current NHL director of off-ice programs.
COLLEGE: Boston College.
TRANSACTIONS/CAREER NOTES: Signed as free agent by St. Louis Blues (August 16, 1979). . . . Injured leg (October 18, 1982). . . . Tore ligaments in left knee and underwent surgery (January 29, 1983); missed remainder of season. . . . Traded by Blues with D Terry Johnson and D Rik Wilson to Calgary Flames for LW Eddy Beers, LW Gino Cavallini and D Charles Bourgeois (February 1, 1986). . . . Bruised knee (April 1988). . . . Suffered from the flu (April 1989). . . . Traded by Flames to Pittsburgh Penguins for second-round pick (D Nicolas Perreault) in 1990 draft (June 16, 1990). . . . Injured neck (January 22, 1991). . . . Underwent neck surgery for herniated disk (February 6, 1991); missed remainder of season. . . . Damaged ligament in knee (May 5, 1992); missed remainder of playoffs and first 11 games of 1992-93 season. . . . Strained muscle in upper back (March 28, 1995); missed three games.
HONORS: Named NYMJHL Most Valuable Player (1974-75). . . . Named to NCAA All-America East (University Division) first team (1977-78 and 1978-79). . . . Named to ECAC All-Star first team (1977-78 and 1978-79). . . . Won Ken McKenzie Trophy (1979-80). . . . Named to CHL All-Star second team (1979-80). . . . Won Tommy Ivan Trophy (1980-81). . . . Won Phil Esposito Trophy (1980-81). . . . Named to CHL All-Star first team (1980-81). . . . Won Lady Byng Memorial Trophy (1986-87 and 1988-89). . . . Named to THE SPORTING NEWS All-Star first team (1988-89). . . . Named to NHL All-Star first team (1988-89). . . . Played in NHL All-Star Game (1989, 1990 and 1994). . . . Named to THE SPORTING NEWS All-Star second

team (1991-92).
STATISTICAL PLATEAUS: Three-goal games: 1983-84 (1), 1984-85 (1), 1988-89 (2), 1989-90 (1), 1991-92 (1), 1992-93 (1). Total: 7.... Four-goal games: 1988-89 (2), 1991-92 (2). Total: 4.... Total hat tricks: 11.
MISCELLANEOUS: Member of Stanley Cup championship teams (1989, 1991 and 1992).

Season Team	League	REGULAR SEASON					PLAYOFFS				
		Gms.	G	A	Pts.	PIM	Gms.	G	A	Pts.	PIM
71-72—New York 14th Precinct....	NYMJHL	30	13	11	24	2	—	—	—	—	—
72-73—New York Westsiders	NYMJHL	40	14	28	42	8	—	—	—	—	—
73-74—New York Westsiders	NYMJHL	†42	71	49	120	41	7	9	9	18	0
74-75—New York Westsiders	NYMJHL	40	*110	72	*182	20	13	*24	13	*37	2
75-76—Boston College	ECAC	24	16	18	34	4	—	—	—	—	—
76-77—Boston College	ECAC	28	28	26	54	8	—	—	—	—	—
77-78—Boston College	ECAC	34	34	34	68	12	—	—	—	—	—
78-79—Boston College	ECAC	25	32	24	56	8	—	—	—	—	—
79-80—Salt Lake City..................	IHL	75	40	32	72	21	13	†9	11	20	0
—St. Louis	NHL	—	—	—	—	—	1	0	0	0	0
80-81—Salt Lake City..................	IHL	80	59	58	*117	8	17	11	9	20	0
81-82—Salt Lake City..................	IHL	27	21	27	48	12	—	—	—	—	—
—St. Louis	NHL	45	25	34	59	4	10	7	11	18	4
82-83—St. Louis	NHL	49	17	30	47	6	—	—	—	—	—
83-84—St. Louis	NHL	80	41	44	85	19	6	2	0	2	0
84-85—St. Louis	NHL	79	40	52	92	6	3	0	0	0	0
85-86—St. Louis	NHL	48	28	24	52	10	—	—	—	—	—
—Calgary	NHL	29	16	22	38	11	21	*12	7	19	4
86-87—Calgary	NHL	79	47	40	87	14	6	2	1	3	0
87-88—Calgary	NHL	80	40	44	84	30	7	2	4	6	10
88-89—Calgary	NHL	79	51	59	110	16	21	*16	8	24	4
89-90—Calgary	NHL	78	36	33	69	24	6	3	0	3	0
90-91—Pittsburgh	NHL	47	17	22	39	6	22	8	9	17	4
91-92—Pittsburgh	NHL	77	42	45	87	30	9	3	1	4	4
92-93—Pittsburgh	NHL	72	33	37	70	14	12	4	2	6	6
93-94—Pittsburgh	NHL	84	38	32	70	41	6	1	0	1	2
94-95—Pittsburgh	NHL	45	16	21	37	6	12	0	3	3	4
NHL totals.............................		971	487	539	1026	237	142	60	46	106	42

MULLER, KIRK
LW, ISLANDERS

M

PERSONAL: Born February 8, 1966, in Kingston, Ont.... 6-0/205.... Shoots left.... Name pronounced MUH-luhr.
TRANSACTIONS/CAREER NOTES: Selected by New Jersey Devils as underage junior in first round (first Devils pick, second overall) of NHL entry draft (June 9, 1984).... Strained knee (January 13, 1986).... Fractured ribs (April 1986).... Traded by Devils with G Roland Melanson to Montreal Canadiens for RW Stephane Richer and RW Tom Chorske (September 1991).... Injured eye (January 21, 1992); missed one game.... Bruised ribs (November 7, 1992); missed one game.... Sprained wrist (March 6, 1993); missed two games.... Injured shoulder (October 11, 1993); missed eight games.... Traded by Canadiens with D Mathieu Schneider and C Craig Darby to New York Islanders for C Pierre Turgeon and D Vladimir Malakhov (April 5, 1995).
HONORS: Won William Hanley Trophy (1982-83).... Played in NHL All-Star Game (1985, 1986, 1988, 1990, 1992 and 1993).
STATISTICAL PLATEAUS: Three-goal games: 1986-87 (1), 1987-88 (3), 1991-92 (2). Total: 6.
MISCELLANEOUS: Captain of New Jersey Devils (1987-88 through 1990-91).... Member of Stanley Cup championship team (1993).... Captain of Montreal Canadiens (1994-95).

Season Team	League	REGULAR SEASON					PLAYOFFS				
		Gms.	G	A	Pts.	PIM	Gms.	G	A	Pts.	PIM
80-81—Kingston	OMJHL	2	0	0	0	0	—	—	—	—	—
81-82—Kingston	OHL	67	12	39	51	27	4	5	1	6	4
82-83—Guelph	OHL	66	52	60	112	41	—	—	—	—	—
83-84—Canadian Olympic Team ..	Int'l	15	2	2	4	6	—	—	—	—	—
—Guelph	OHL	49	31	63	94	27	—	—	—	—	—
84-85—New Jersey	NHL	80	17	37	54	69	—	—	—	—	—
85-86—New Jersey	NHL	77	25	41	66	45	—	—	—	—	—
86-87—New Jersey	NHL	79	26	50	76	75	—	—	—	—	—
87-88—New Jersey	NHL	80	37	57	94	114	20	4	8	12	37
88-89—New Jersey	NHL	80	31	43	74	119	—	—	—	—	—
89-90—New Jersey	NHL	80	30	56	86	74	6	1	3	4	11
90-91—New Jersey	NHL	80	19	51	70	76	7	0	2	2	10
91-92—Montreal	NHL	78	36	41	77	86	11	4	3	7	31
92-93—Montreal	NHL	80	37	57	94	77	20	10	7	17	18
93-94—Montreal	NHL	76	23	34	57	96	7	6	2	8	4
94-95—Montreal	NHL	33	8	11	19	33	—	—	—	—	—
—New York Islanders..........	NHL	12	3	5	8	14	—	—	—	—	—
NHL totals.............................		835	292	483	775	878	71	25	25	50	111

MULLER, MIKE
D, JETS

PERSONAL: Born September 18, 1971, in Minneapolis.... 6-2/205.... Shoots left.... Full name: Mike Todd Muller.
HIGH SCHOOL: Wayzata (Plymouth, Minn.).
COLLEGE: Minnesota.
TRANSACTIONS/CAREER NOTES: Selected by Winnipeg Jets in second round (second Jets pick, 35th overall) of NHL entry draft (June 16, 1990).

Season	Team	League	Gms.	G	A	Pts.	PIM	Gms.	G	A	Pts.	PIM
88-89—Wayzata H.S.	Minn. H.S.		24	10	11	21	56	—	—	—	—	—
89-90—Wayzata H.S.	Minn. H.S.		23	11	15	26	45	—	—	—	—	—
90-91—University of Minnesota	WCHA		33	4	4	8	44	—	—	—	—	—
91-92—University of Minnesota	WCHA		44	4	12	16	60	—	—	—	—	—
92-93—Dynamo Moscow	CIS		11	1	0	1	8	—	—	—	—	—
93-94—Moncton	AHL		61	2	14	16	88	—	—	—	—	—
94-95—Springfield	AHL		64	2	5	7	61	—	—	—	—	—

MUNI, CRAIG
D, SABRES

PERSONAL: Born July 19, 1962, in Toronto.... 6-3/208.... Shoots left.... Full name: Craig Douglas Muni.... Name pronounced MYOO-nee.
TRANSACTIONS/CAREER NOTES: Selected by Toronto Maple Leafs as underage junior in second round (first Maple Leafs pick, 25th overall) of NHL entry draft (June 11, 1980).... Tore left knee ligaments (September 1981).... Broke ankle (January 1983).... Signed as free agent by Edmonton Oilers (August 18, 1986). ... Traded by Oilers to Buffalo Sabres for cash (October 2, 1986).... Traded by Sabres to Pittsburgh Penguins for future considerations (October 3, 1986).... Traded by Penguins to Oilers to complete earlier trade for G Gilles Meloche (October 6, 1986).... Bruised kidney (May 1987).... Bruised ankle (January 1988).... Bruised ankle (December 17, 1988).... Strained right shoulder (January 1989).... Broke little finger of right hand (January 27, 1990); missed eight games.... Suffered pinched nerve (January 15, 1992); missed 17 games.... Injured knee (March 19, 1992); missed eight games.... Suspended two games by NHL during playoffs for kneeing (May 22, 1992); missed final 1992 playoff game and first game of 1992-93 regular season.... Suffered from the flu (December 1992); missed one game.... Injured eye (February 18, 1993); missed two games.... Traded by Oilers to Chicago Blackhawks for C Mike Hudson (March 22, 1993).... Traded by Blackhawks to Buffalo Sabres for D Keith Carney (October 27, 1993).... Pulled left hamstring (February 15, 1995); missed six games.
MISCELLANEOUS: Member of Stanley Cup championship teams (1987, 1988 and 1990).

Season	Team	League	Gms.	G	A	Pts.	PIM	Gms.	G	A	Pts.	PIM
79-80—Kingston	OMJHL		66	6	28	34	114	—	—	—	—	—
80-81—Kingston	OMJHL		38	2	14	16	65	—	—	—	—	—
—Windsor	OMJHL		25	5	11	16	41	11	1	4	5	14
—New Brunswick	AHL		—	—	—	—	—	2	0	1	1	10
81-82—Toronto	NHL		3	0	0	0	2	—	—	—	—	—
—Windsor	OHL		49	5	32	37	92	9	2	3	5	16
—Cincinnati	CHL		—	—	—	—	—	3	0	2	2	2
82-83—Toronto	NHL		2	0	1	1	0	—	—	—	—	—
—St. Catharines	AHL		64	6	32	38	52	—	—	—	—	—
83-84—St. Catharines	AHL		64	4	16	20	79	7	0	1	1	0
84-85—St. Catharines	AHL		68	7	17	24	54	—	—	—	—	—
—Toronto	NHL		8	0	0	0	0	—	—	—	—	—
85-86—Toronto	NHL		6	0	1	1	4	—	—	—	—	—
—St. Catharines	AHL		73	3	34	37	91	13	0	5	5	16
86-87—Edmonton	NHL		79	7	22	29	85	14	0	2	2	17
87-88—Edmonton	NHL		72	4	15	19	77	19	0	4	4	31
88-89—Edmonton	NHL		69	5	13	18	71	7	0	3	3	8
89-90—Edmonton	NHL		71	5	12	17	81	22	0	3	3	16
90-91—Edmonton	NHL		76	1	9	10	77	18	0	3	3	20
91-92—Edmonton	NHL		54	2	5	7	34	3	0	0	0	2
92-93—Edmonton	NHL		72	0	11	11	67	—	—	—	—	—
—Chicago	NHL		9	0	0	0	8	4	0	0	0	2
93-94—Chicago	NHL		9	0	4	4	4	—	—	—	—	—
—Buffalo	NHL		73	2	8	10	62	7	0	0	0	4
94-95—Buffalo	NHL		40	0	6	6	36	5	0	1	1	2
NHL totals			643	26	107	133	608	99	0	16	16	102

MURPHY, BURKE
LW, FLAMES

PERSONAL: Born June 5, 1973, in Gloucester, Ont.... 6-0/180.... Shoots left.
COLLEGE: St. Lawrence (N.Y.).
TRANSACTIONS/CAREER NOTES: Selected by Calgary Flames in 11th round (11th Flames pick, 278th overall) in NHL entry draft (June 29, 1993).
HONORS: Named to ECAC All-Star second team (1994-95).

Season	Team	League	Gms.	G	A	Pts.	PIM	Gms.	G	A	Pts.	PIM
92-93—St. Lawrence University	ECAC		32	19	10	29	32	—	—	—	—	—
93-94—St. Lawrence University	ECAC		30	20	17	37	42	—	—	—	—	—
94-95—St. Lawrence University	ECAC		33	27	23	50	51	—	—	—	—	—

MURPHY, GORD
D, PANTHERS

PERSONAL: Born February 23, 1967, in Willowdale, Ont.... 6-2/191.... Shoots right.
TRANSACTIONS/CAREER NOTES: Injured clavicle (January 1985).... Selected by Philadelphia Flyers as underage junior in ninth round (10th Flyers pick, 189th overall) of NHL entry draft (June 15, 1985).... Injured left foot and suffered hip pointer (March 24, 1990).... Traded by Flyers with RW Brian Dobbin and third-round pick in 1992 draft (LW Sergei Zholtok) to Boston Bruins for D Garry Galley, C Wes Walz and future considerations (January 2, 1992).... Injured ankle (January 1993); missed 16 games.... Traded by Bruins to Dallas Stars for future considerations (June 20, 1993); Bruins sent G Andy Moog to Stars for G Jon Casey to complete deal (June 25, 1993).... Selected by Florida Panthers in NHL expansion draft (June 24, 1993).... Suffered illness (March 26, 1995); missed one game.... Sprained left ankle (April 5, 1995); missed one game.
HONORS: Named to Memorial Cup All-Star team (1986-87).

Season Team	League	REGULAR SEASON					PLAYOFFS				
		Gms.	G	A	Pts.	PIM	Gms.	G	A	Pts.	PIM
83-84—Don Mills Flyers	MTHL	65	24	42	66	130	—	—	—	—	—
84-85—Oshawa	OHL	59	3	12	15	25	—	—	—	—	—
85-86—Oshawa	OHL	64	7	15	22	56	6	1	1	2	6
86-87—Oshawa	OHL	56	7	30	37	95	24	6	16	22	22
87-88—Hershey	AHL	62	8	20	28	44	12	0	8	8	12
88-89—Philadelphia	NHL	75	4	31	35	68	19	2	7	9	13
89-90—Philadelphia	NHL	75	14	27	41	95	—	—	—	—	—
90-91—Philadelphia	NHL	80	11	31	42	58	—	—	—	—	—
91-92—Philadelphia	NHL	31	2	8	10	33	—	—	—	—	—
—Boston	NHL	42	3	6	9	51	15	1	0	1	12
92-93—Boston	NHL	49	5	12	17	62	—	—	—	—	—
—Providence	AHL	2	1	3	4	2	—	—	—	—	—
93-94—Florida	NHL	84	14	29	43	71	—	—	—	—	—
94-95—Florida	NHL	46	6	16	22	24	—	—	—	—	—
NHL totals		482	59	160	219	462	34	3	7	10	25

MURPHY, JOE

RW, BLACKHAWKS

PERSONAL: Born October 16, 1967, in London, Ont. . . . 6-1/190. . . . Shoots left. . . . Full name: Joseph Patrick Murphy.
COLLEGE: Michigan State.
TRANSACTIONS/CAREER NOTES: Selected by Detroit Red Wings in first round (first Red Wings pick, first overall) of NHL entry draft (June 21, 1986). . . . Sprained right ankle (January 1988). . . . Traded by Red Wings with C/LW Adam Graves, LW Petr Klima and D Jeff Sharples to Edmonton Oilers for C Jimmy Carson, C Kevin McClelland and fifth-round pick (traded to Montreal Canadiens who selected D Brad Layzell) in 1991 draft (November 2, 1989). . . . Bruised both thighs (March 1990). . . . Did not report to Oilers in 1992-93 season because of contract dispute; missed 63 games. . . . Traded by Oilers to Chicago Blackhawks for D Igor Kravchuk and C Dean McAmmond (February 25, 1993). . . . Pulled groin (February 3, 1995); missed three games. . . . Reinjured groin (March 6, 1995); missed four games. . . . Sprained knee (March 21, 1995); missed one game.
HONORS: Named BCJHL Rookie of the Year (1984-85). . . . Named CCHA Rookie of the Year (1985-86).
MISCELLANEOUS: Member of Stanley Cup championship team (1990).

Season Team	League	REGULAR SEASON					PLAYOFFS				
		Gms.	G	A	Pts.	PIM	Gms.	G	A	Pts.	PIM
84-85—Penticton	BCJHL	51	68	84	*152	92	—	—	—	—	—
85-86—Michigan State	CCHA	35	24	37	61	50	—	—	—	—	—
—Canadian national team	Int'l	8	3	3	6	2	—	—	—	—	—
86-87—Adirondack	AHL	71	21	38	59	61	10	2	1	3	33
—Detroit	NHL	5	0	1	1	2	—	—	—	—	—
87-88—Adirondack	AHL	6	5	6	11	4	—	—	—	—	—
—Detroit	NHL	50	10	9	19	37	8	0	1	1	6
88-89—Detroit	NHL	26	1	7	8	28	—	—	—	—	—
—Adirondack	AHL	47	31	35	66	66	16	6	11	17	17
89-90—Detroit	NHL	9	3	1	4	4	—	—	—	—	—
—Edmonton	NHL	62	7	18	25	56	22	6	8	14	16
90-91—Edmonton	NHL	80	27	35	62	35	15	2	5	7	14
91-92—Edmonton	NHL	80	35	47	82	52	16	8	16	24	12
92-93—Chicago	NHL	19	7	10	17	18	4	0	0	0	8
93-94—Chicago	NHL	81	31	39	70	111	6	1	3	4	25
94-95—Chicago	NHL	40	23	18	41	89	16	9	3	12	29
NHL totals		452	144	185	329	432	87	26	36	62	110

MURPHY, LARRY

D, MAPLE LEAFS

PERSONAL: Born March 8, 1961, in Scarborough, Ont. . . . 6-2/210. . . . Shoots right. . . . Full name: Lawrence Thomas Murphy.
TRANSACTIONS/CAREER NOTES: Selected by Los Angeles Kings as underage junior in first round (first Kings pick, fourth overall) of NHL entry draft (June 11, 1980). . . . Traded by Kings to Washington Capitals for D Brian Engblom and RW Ken Houston (October 18, 1983). . . . Injured foot (October 29, 1985). . . . Broke ankle (May 1988). . . . Traded by Capitals with RW Mike Gartner to Minnesota North Stars for RW Dino Ciccarelli and D Bob Rouse (March 7, 1989). . . . Traded by North Stars with D Peter Taglianetti to Pittsburgh Penguins for D Jim Johnson and D Chris Dahlquist (December 11, 1990). . . . Fractured right foot (February 22, 1991); played until March 5 then missed five games. . . . Suffered back spasms (March 28, 1993); missed one game. . . . Traded by Penguins to Toronto Maple Leafs for D Dmitri Mironov and second-round pick in 1996 draft (July 8, 1995).
HONORS: Won Max Kaminsky Trophy (1979-80). . . . Named to OMJHL All-Star first team (1979-80). . . . Named to Memorial Cup All-Star team (1979-80). . . . Named to THE SPORTING NEWS All-Star second team (1986-87 and 1992-93). . . . Named to NHL All-Star second team (1986-87, 1992-93 and 1994-95). . . . Played in NHL All-Star Game (1994).
RECORDS: Holds NHL rookie-season records for most points by a defenseman—76; and most assists by a defenseman—60 (1980-81).
MISCELLANEOUS: Member of Stanley Cup championship teams (1991 and 1992).

Season Team	League	REGULAR SEASON					PLAYOFFS				
		Gms.	G	A	Pts.	PIM	Gms.	G	A	Pts.	PIM
78-79—Peterborough	OMJHL	66	6	21	27	82	19	1	9	10	42
79-80—Peterborough	OMJHL	68	21	68	89	88	14	4	13	17	20
80-81—Los Angeles	NHL	80	16	60	76	79	4	3	0	3	2
81-82—Los Angeles	NHL	79	22	44	66	95	10	2	8	10	12
82-83—Los Angeles	NHL	77	14	48	62	81	—	—	—	—	—

Season	Team	League	REGULAR SEASON					PLAYOFFS				
			Gms.	G	A	Pts.	PIM	Gms.	G	A	Pts.	PIM
83-84—Los Angeles		NHL	6	0	3	3	0	—	—	—	—	—
—Washington		NHL	72	13	33	46	50	8	0	3	3	6
84-85—Washington		NHL	79	13	42	55	51	5	2	3	5	0
85-86—Washington		NHL	78	21	44	65	50	9	1	5	6	6
86-87—Washington		NHL	80	23	58	81	39	7	2	2	4	6
87-88—Washington		NHL	79	8	53	61	72	13	4	4	8	33
88-89—Washington		NHL	65	7	29	36	70	—	—	—	—	—
—Minnesota		NHL	13	4	6	10	12	5	0	2	2	8
89-90—Minnesota		NHL	77	10	58	68	44	7	1	2	3	31
90-91—Minnesota		NHL	31	4	11	15	38	—	—	—	—	—
—Pittsburgh		NHL	44	5	23	28	30	23	5	18	23	44
91-92—Pittsburgh		NHL	77	21	56	77	48	†21	6	10	16	19
92-93—Pittsburgh		NHL	83	22	63	85	73	12	2	11	13	10
93-94—Pittsburgh		NHL	84	17	56	73	44	6	0	5	5	0
94-95—Pittsburgh		NHL	48	13	25	38	18	12	2	13	15	0
NHL totals			1152	233	712	945	894	142	30	86	116	177

MURRAY, CHRIS
RW, CANADIENS

PERSONAL: Born October 25, 1974, in Port Hardy, B.C. . . . 6-2/214. . . . Shoots right.
TRANSACTIONS/CAREER NOTES: Selected by Montreal Canadiens in third round (third Canadiens pick, 54th overall) of NHL entry draft (June 29, 1994).

Season	Team	League	REGULAR SEASON					PLAYOFFS				
			Gms.	G	A	Pts.	PIM	Gms.	G	A	Pts.	PIM
90-91—Bellingham Jr. A		BCJHL	54	5	8	13	150	—	—	—	—	—
91-92—Kamloops		WHL	33	1	1	2	168	5	0	0	0	10
92-93—Kamloops		WHL	62	6	10	16	217	13	0	4	4	34
93-94—Kamloops		WHL	59	14	16	30	260	15	4	2	6	107
94-95—Fredericton		AHL	55	6	12	18	234	12	1	1	2	50
—Montreal		NHL	3	0	0	0	4	—	—	—	—	—
NHL totals			3	0	0	0	4					

MURRAY, GLEN
RW, PENGUINS

PERSONAL: Born November 1, 1972, in Halifax, N.S. . . . 6-2/200. . . . Shoots right.
TRANSACTIONS/CAREER NOTES: Selected by Boston Bruins in first round (first Bruins pick, 18th overall) of NHL entry draft (June 22, 1991). . . . Injured elbow (December 15, 1993); missed two games. . . . Traded by Bruins with C Bryan Smolinski to Pittsburgh Penguins for LW Kevin Stevens and C Shawn McEachern (August 2, 1995).

Season	Team	League	REGULAR SEASON					PLAYOFFS				
			Gms.	G	A	Pts.	PIM	Gms.	G	A	Pts.	PIM
89-90—Sudbury		OHL	62	8	28	36	17	7	0	0	0	4
90-91—Sudbury		OHL	66	27	38	65	82	5	8	4	12	10
91-92—Sudbury		OHL	54	37	47	84	93	11	7	4	11	18
—Boston		NHL	5	3	1	4	0	15	4	2	6	10
92-93—Providence		AHL	48	30	26	56	42	6	1	4	5	4
—Boston		NHL	27	3	4	7	8	—	—	—	—	—
93-94—Boston		NHL	81	18	13	31	48	13	4	5	9	14
94-95—Boston		NHL	35	5	2	7	46	2	0	0	0	2
NHL totals			148	29	20	49	102	30	8	7	15	26

MURRAY, MARTY
C, FLAMES

PERSONAL: Born February 16, 1975, in Deloraine, Man. . . . 5-9/170. . . . Shoots left.
TRANSACTIONS/CAREER NOTES: Selected by Calgary Flames in fourth round (fifth Flames pick, 96th overall) of NHL entry draft (June 26, 1993).
HONORS: Named to Can.HL All-Star second team (1993-94). . . . Named to WHL (East) All-Star first team (1993-94 and 1994-95). . . . Won Four Broncos Memorial Trophy (1994-95).

Season	Team	League	REGULAR SEASON					PLAYOFFS				
			Gms.	G	A	Pts.	PIM	Gms.	G	A	Pts.	PIM
91-92—Brandon		WHL	68	20	36	56	12	—	—	—	—	—
92-93—Brandon		WHL	67	29	65	94	50	4	1	3	4	0
93-94—Brandon		WHL	64	43	71	114	33	14	6	14	20	14
94-95—Brandon		WHL	65	40	88	128	53	18	9	20	29	16

MURRAY, REM
LW/C, KINGS

PERSONAL: Born October 9, 1972, in Stratford, Ont. . . . 6-1/183. . . . Shoots left.
COLLEGE: Michigan State.
TRANSACTIONS/CAREER NOTES: Selected by Los Angeles Kings in sixth round (fifth Kings pick, 135th overall) of NHL entry draft (June 20, 1992).
HONORS: Named to CCHA All-Star second team (1994-95).

Season	Team	League	REGULAR SEASON					PLAYOFFS				
			Gms.	G	A	Pts.	PIM	Gms.	G	A	Pts.	PIM
90-91—Stratford Jr. B		OHA	48	39	59	98	22	—	—	—	—	—
91-92—Michigan State		CCHA	44	12	36	48	16	—	—	—	—	—
92-93—Michigan State		CCHA	40	22	35	57	24	—	—	—	—	—
93-94—Michigan State		CCHA	41	16	38	54	18	—	—	—	—	—
94-95—Michigan State		CCHA	40	20	36	56	21	—	—	—	—	—

M

MURRAY, ROB
C, JETS

PERSONAL: Born April 4, 1967, in Toronto.... 6-1/180.... Shoots right.
TRANSACTIONS/CAREER NOTES: Selected by Washington Capitals as underage junior in third round (third Capitals pick, 61st overall) of NHL entry draft (June 15, 1985).... Suspended two games by OHL (November 2, 1986).... Injured right hip (December 21, 1989); missed 10 games.... Selected by Minnesota North Stars in NHL expansion draft (May 30, 1991).... Traded by North Stars with future considerations to Winnipeg Jets for seventh-round pick in 1991 draft (G Geoff Finch) and future considerations (May 30, 1991).... Strained groin (November 2, 1992); missed three games.... Suffered back spasms (December 15, 1992); missed six games.

			REGULAR SEASON						PLAYOFFS			
Season	Team	League	Gms.	G	A	Pts.	PIM	Gms.	G	A	Pts.	PIM
83-84—Mississauga		OHA	35	18	36	54	32	—	—	—	—	—
84-85—Peterborough		OHL	63	12	9	21	155	17	2	7	9	45
85-86—Peterborough		OHL	52	14	18	32	125	16	1	2	3	50
86-87—Peterborough		OHL	62	17	37	54	204	3	1	4	5	8
87-88—Fort Wayne		IHL	80	12	21	33	139	6	0	2	2	16
88-89—Baltimore		AHL	80	11	23	34	235	—	—	—	—	—
89-90—Baltimore		AHL	23	5	4	9	63	—	—	—	—	—
—Washington		NHL	41	2	7	9	58	9	0	0	0	18
90-91—Baltimore		AHL	48	6	20	26	177	4	0	0	0	12
—Washington		NHL	17	0	3	3	19	—	—	—	—	—
91-92—Moncton		AHL	60	16	15	31	247	8	0	1	1	56
—Winnipeg		NHL	9	0	1	1	18	—	—	—	—	—
92-93—Moncton		AHL	56	16	21	37	147	3	0	0	0	6
—Winnipeg		NHL	10	1	0	1	6	—	—	—	—	—
93-94—Moncton		AHL	69	25	32	57	280	21	2	3	5	60
—Winnipeg		NHL	6	0	0	0	2	—	—	—	—	—
94-95—Springfield		AHL	78	16	38	54	373	—	—	—	—	—
—Winnipeg		NHL	10	0	2	2	2	—	—	—	—	—
NHL totals			93	3	13	16	105	9	0	0	0	18

MURRAY, TROY
C, PENGUINS

PERSONAL: Born July 31, 1962, in Winnipeg.... 6-1/195.... Shoots right.... Full name: Troy Norman Murray.
COLLEGE: North Dakota.
TRANSACTIONS/CAREER NOTES: Selected by Chicago Blackhawks in third round (sixth Blackhawks pick, 57th overall) of NHL entry draft (June 11, 1980).... Injured knee ligaments (November 1983).... Lacerated face (December 1988).... Injured right elbow and underwent surgery (December 26, 1989); missed 11 games.... Developed bursitis on right elbow and hospitalized (February 8, 1990).... Traded by Blackhawks with LW Warren Rychel to Winnipeg Jets for D Bryan Marchment and D Chris Norton (July 22, 1991).... Separated shoulder (October 23, 1991); missed four games. ... Lacerated knee (December 14, 1991); missed three games.... Separated shoulder (October 7, 1992); missed five games. ... Suffered hip pointer (November 10, 1992); missed two games.... Fractured foot (December 19, 1992); missed 22 games. ... Traded by Jets to Chicago Blackhawks for D Steve Bancroft and undisclosed pick in 1993 draft (February 21, 1993).... Traded by Blackhawks to Ottawa Senators for future considerations (March 11, 1994).... Bruised ribs (February 8, 1995); missed one game.... Traded by Senators with D Norm Maciver to Pittsburgh Penguins for C Martin Straka (April 7, 1995).
HONORS: Won WCHA Freshman of the Year Award (1980-81).... Named to WCHA All-Star second team (1980-81 and 1981-82).... Won Frank J. Selke Trophy (1985-86).
STATISTICAL PLATEAUS: Three-goal games: 1985-86 (3), 1989-90 (1). Total: 4.
MISCELLANEOUS: Co-captain of Chicago Blackhawks (1987-88).... Captain of Winnipeg Jets (1991-92 and 1992-93).

			REGULAR SEASON						PLAYOFFS			
Season	Team	League	Gms.	G	A	Pts.	PIM	Gms.	G	A	Pts.	PIM
79-80—St. Albert		AJHL	60	53	47	100	101	—	—	—	—	—
80-81—Univ. of North Dakota		WCHA	38	33	45	78	28	—	—	—	—	—
81-82—Univ. of North Dakota		WCHA	42	22	29	51	62	—	—	—	—	—
—Chicago		NHL	1	0	0	0	0	7	1	0	1	5
82-83—Chicago		NHL	54	8	8	16	27	2	0	0	0	0
83-84—Chicago		NHL	61	15	15	30	45	5	1	0	1	7
84-85—Chicago		NHL	80	26	40	66	82	15	5	14	19	24
85-86—Chicago		NHL	80	45	54	99	94	2	0	0	0	2
86-87—Chicago		NHL	77	28	43	71	59	4	0	0	0	5
87-88—Chicago		NHL	79	22	36	58	96	5	1	0	1	8
88-89—Chicago		NHL	79	21	30	51	113	16	3	6	9	25
89-90—Chicago		NHL	68	17	38	55	86	20	4	4	8	2
90-91—Chicago		NHL	75	14	23	37	74	6	0	1	1	12
91-92—Winnipeg		NHL	74	17	30	47	69	7	0	0	0	2
92-93—Winnipeg		NHL	29	3	4	7	34	—	—	—	—	—
—Chicago		NHL	22	1	3	4	25	4	0	0	0	2
93-94—Chicago		NHL	12	0	1	1	6	—	—	—	—	—
—Indianapolis		IHL	8	3	3	6	12	—	—	—	—	—
—Ottawa		NHL	15	2	3	5	4	—	—	—	—	—
94-95—Ottawa		NHL	33	4	10	14	16	—	—	—	—	—
—Pittsburgh		NHL	13	0	2	2	23	12	2	1	3	12
NHL totals			852	223	340	563	853	105	17	26	43	106

MURZYN, DANA
D, CANUCKS

PERSONAL: Born December 9, 1966, in Regina, Sask.... 6-2/210.... Shoots left.... Name pronounced MUHR-zihn.
TRANSACTIONS/CAREER NOTES: Selected by Hartford Whalers as underage junior in first round (first Whalers pick, fifth overall) of NHL entry draft (June 15, 1985).... Traded by

M

Whalers with RW Shane Churla to Calgary Flames for C Carey Wilson, D Neil Sheehy and LW Lane MacDonald (January 3, 1988).... Strained knee (March 13, 1989).... Pulled groin (February 4, 1990).... Bruised hip (October 25, 1990); missed 11 games.... Separated shoulder (December 1, 1990); missed 34 games.... Traded by Flames to Vancouver Canucks for RW Ron Stern, D Kevan Guy and option to switch fourth-round picks in 1992 draft; Flames did not exercise option (March 5, 1991).... Suffered from the flu (February 26, 1993); missed two games.... Underwent minor knee surgery (January 21, 1995); missed five games.... Sprained knee (April 30, 1995); missed last game of season.
HONORS: Named to WHL (East) All-Star first team (1984-85).... Named to NHL All-Rookie team (1985-86).
STATISTICAL PLATEAUS: Three-goal games: 1989-90 (1).
MISCELLANEOUS: Member of Stanley Cup championship team (1989).

Season Team	League	REGULAR SEASON					PLAYOFFS				
		Gms.	G	A	Pts.	PIM	Gms.	G	A	Pts.	PIM
83-84—Calgary	WHL	65	11	20	31	135	2	0	0	0	0
84-85—Calgary	WHL	72	32	60	92	233	8	1	11	12	16
85-86—Hartford	NHL	78	3	23	26	125	4	0	0	0	10
86-87—Hartford	NHL	74	9	19	28	95	6	2	1	3	29
87-88—Hartford	NHL	33	1	6	7	45	—	—	—	—	—
—Calgary	NHL	41	6	5	11	94	5	2	0	2	13
88-89—Calgary	NHL	63	3	19	22	142	21	0	3	3	20
89-90—Calgary	NHL	78	7	13	20	140	6	2	2	4	2
90-91—Calgary	NHL	19	0	2	2	30	—	—	—	—	—
—Vancouver	NHL	10	1	0	1	8	6	0	1	1	8
91-92—Vancouver	NHL	70	3	11	14	147	1	0	0	0	15
92-93—Vancouver	NHL	79	5	11	16	196	12	3	2	5	18
93-94—Vancouver	NHL	80	6	14	20	109	7	0	0	0	4
94-95—Vancouver	NHL	40	0	8	8	129	8	0	1	1	22
NHL totals		665	44	131	175	1260	76	9	10	19	141

MUSIL, FRANK
D, FLAMES

PERSONAL: Born December 17, 1964, in Pardubice, Czechoslovakia.... 6-3/215.... Shoots left.... Name pronounced moo-SIHL.
TRANSACTIONS/CAREER NOTES: Selected by Minnesota North Stars in second round (third North Stars pick, 38th overall) of NHL entry draft (June 8, 1983).... Separated shoulder (December 9, 1986).... Fractured foot (December 17, 1988).... Suffered concussion (February 9, 1989).... Strained lower back muscles (February 18, 1989).... Suffered back spasms (November 2, 1989); missed 10 games.... Separated right shoulder (April 1990).... Traded by North Stars to Calgary Flames for D Brian Glynn (October 26, 1990).... Suffered back spasms (November 8, 1993); missed one game.... Strained neck (December 28, 1993); missed four games.... Hyperextended elbow (March 22, 1994); missed four games.... Played in Europe during 1994-95 NHL lockout.... Bruised right knee (January 24, 1995); missed one game.... Sprained right knee (February 9, 1995); missed three games.... Suffered back spasms (February 28, 1995); missed one game.... Sprained right knee (April 7, 1995); missed seven games.

Season Team	League	REGULAR SEASON					PLAYOFFS				
		Gms.	G	A	Pts.	PIM	Gms.	G	A	Pts.	PIM
85-86—Dukla Jihlava	Czech.	35	3	7	10	85	—	—	—	—	—
86-87—Minnesota	NHL	72	2	9	11	148	—	—	—	—	—
87-88—Minnesota	NHL	80	9	8	17	213	—	—	—	—	—
88-89—Minnesota	NHL	55	1	19	20	54	5	1	1	2	4
89-90—Minnesota	NHL	56	2	8	10	109	4	0	0	0	14
90-91—Minnesota	NHL	8	0	2	2	23	—	—	—	—	—
—Calgary	NHL	67	7	14	21	160	7	0	0	0	10
91-92—Calgary	NHL	78	4	8	12	103	—	—	—	—	—
92-93—Calgary	NHL	80	6	10	16	131	6	1	1	2	7
93-94—Calgary	NHL	75	1	8	9	50	7	0	1	1	4
94-95—Sparta Prague	Czech. Rep.	19	1	4	5	30	—	—	—	—	—
—Sachsen	Germany	1	0	0	0	2	—	—	—	—	—
—Calgary	NHL	35	0	5	5	61	5	0	1	1	0
NHL totals		606	32	91	123	1052	34	2	4	6	39

MUZZATTI, JASON
G, FLAMES

PERSONAL: Born February 3, 1970, in Toronto.... 6-1/190.... Catches left.... Full name: Jason Mark Muzzatti.... Name pronounced moo-ZAH-tee.
COLLEGE: Michigan State.
TRANSACTIONS/CAREER NOTES: Selected by Calgary Flames in first round (first Flames pick, 21st overall) of NHL entry draft (June 11, 1988).... Loaned to Indianapolis Ice (January 11, 1993).... Suffered from the flu (November 4, 1993); missed four games.
HONORS: Named to CCHA All-Star second team (1987-88).... Named to NCAA All-America West second team (1989-90).... Named to CCHA All-Star first team (1989-90).... Named to CCHA All-Tournament team (1989-90).

Season Team	League	REGULAR SEASON							PLAYOFFS					
		Gms.	Min.	W	L	T	GA	SO	Avg.	Gms.	Min.	W	L	GA	SO	Avg.
86-87—St. Mikes Jr. B	MTHL	20	1054	...	...	...	69	1	3.93	—	—	—	—	—	—	—
87-88—Michigan State	CCHA	33	1916	19	9	3	109	1	3.41	—	—	—	—	—	—	—
88-89—Michigan State	CCHA	42	2515	32	9	1	127	3	3.03	—	—	—	—	—	—	—
89-90—Michigan State	CCHA	33	1976	24	6	0	99	0	3.01	—	—	—	—	—	—	—
90-91—Michigan State	CCHA	22	1204	8	10	2	75	0	3.74	—	—	—	—	—	—	—
91-92—Salt Lake City	IHL	52	3033	24	22	‡5	167	2	3.30	4	247	1	3	18	0	4.37
92-93—Salt Lake City	IHL	13	747	5	6	‡0	52	0	4.18	—	—	—	—	—	—	—
—Can. national team	Int'l	16	880	6	9	0	53	0	3.61	—	—	—	—	—	—	—
—Indianapolis	IHL	12	707	5	6	‡0	48	0	4.07	—	—	—	—	—	—	—

M

Season Team	League	Gms.	Min.	W	L	T	GA	SO	Avg.	Gms.	Min.	W	L	GA	SO	Avg.
93-94—Calgary	NHL	1	60	0	1	0	8	0	8.00	—	—	—	—	—	—	—
—Saint John	AHL	51	2939	26	21	3	183	2	3.74	7	415	3	4	19	0	2.75
94-95—Saint John	AHL	31	1741	10	14	4	101	2	3.48	—	—	—	—	—	—	—
—Calgary	NHL	1	10	0	0	0	0	0	0.00	—	—	—	—	—	—	—
NHL totals		2	70	0	1	0	8	0	6.86							

MYHRES, BRANTT
LW, LIGHTNING

PERSONAL: Born March 18, 1974, in Edmonton. . . . 6-3/195. . . . Shoots right. . . . Name pronounced MIGHRS.
HIGH SCHOOL: Sir Winston Churchill (Calgary).
TRANSACTIONS/CAREER NOTES: Selected by Tampa Bay Lightning in fifth round (fifth Lightning pick, 97th overall) of NHL entry draft (June 20, 1992). . . . Injured shoulder (April 11, 1995); missed one game.

			REGULAR SEASON					PLAYOFFS			
Season Team	League	Gms.	G	A	Pts.	PIM	Gms.	G	A	Pts.	PIM
90-91—Portland	WHL	59	2	7	9	125	—	—	—	—	—
91-92—Portland	WHL	4	0	2	2	22	—	—	—	—	—
—Lethbridge	WHL	53	4	11	15	359	5	0	0	0	36
92-93—Lethbridge	WHL	64	13	35	48	277	3	0	0	0	11
93-94—Atlanta	IHL	2	0	0	0	17	—	—	—	—	—
—Lethbridge	WHL	34	10	21	31	103	—	—	—	—	—
—Spokane	WHL	27	10	22	32	139	3	1	4	5	7
94-95—Atlanta	IHL	40	5	5	10	213	—	—	—	—	—
—Tampa Bay	NHL	15	2	0	2	81	—	—	—	—	—
NHL totals		15	2	0	2	81					

MYRVOLD, ANDERS
D, DENVER

PERSONAL: Born August 12, 1975, in Lorenskog, Norway. . . . 6-1/178. . . . Shoots left.
TRANSACTIONS/CAREER NOTES: Selected by Quebec Nordiques in fifth round (sixth Nordiques pick, 127th overall) of NHL entry draft (June 26, 1993). . . . Nordiques franchise moved to Denver for 1995-96 season.
HONORS: Named to Can.HL All-Rookie team (1994-95).

			REGULAR SEASON					PLAYOFFS			
Season Team	League	Gms.	G	A	Pts.	PIM	Gms.	G	A	Pts.	PIM
92-93—Farjestad Karlstad	Sweden	2	0	0	0	0	—	—	—	—	—
93-94—Grums	Swed. Dv.II	24	1	0	1	59	—	—	—	—	—
94-95—Laval	QMJHL	64	14	50	64	173	20	4	10	14	68
—Cornwall	AHL	—	—	—	—	—	3	0	1	1	2

NABOKOV, DIMITRI
C/LW, BLACKHAWKS

PERSONAL: Born January 4, 1977, in Novosibirsk, U.S.S.R. . . . 6-2/209. . . . Shoots right.
TRANSACTIONS/CAREER NOTES: Selected by Chicago Blackhawks in first round (first Blackhawks pick, 19th overall) of NHL entry draft (July 8, 1995).

			REGULAR SEASON					PLAYOFFS			
Season Team	League	Gms.	G	A	Pts.	PIM	Gms.	G	A	Pts.	PIM
93-94—Soviet Wings	CIS	17	0	2	2	6	3	0	0	0	0
94-95—Soviet Wings	CIS	49	15	12	27	32	4	5	0	5	6

NAMESTNIKOV, JOHN
D, CANUCKS

PERSONAL: Born October 9, 1971, in Novgorod, U.S.S.R. . . . 5-11/190. . . . Shoots right. . . . Name pronounced nuh-MEHZ-nih-kahf.
TRANSACTIONS/CAREER NOTES: Selected by Vancouver Canucks in sixth round (fifth Canucks pick, 117th overall) of NHL entry draft (June 22, 1991). . . . Sprained ankle (May 7, 1995); missed 10 playoff games.

			REGULAR SEASON					PLAYOFFS			
Season Team	League	Gms.	G	A	Pts.	PIM	Gms.	G	A	Pts.	PIM
88-89—Torpedo Gorky	USSR	2	0	0	0	2	—	—	—	—	—
89-90—Torpedo Gorky	USSR	23	0	0	0	25	—	—	—	—	—
90-91—Torpedo Nizhny Novgorod	USSR	45	1	2	3	49	—	—	—	—	—
91-92—CSKA Moscow	CIS	42	1	1	2	47	—	—	—	—	—
92-93—CSKA Moscow	CIS	42	5	5	10	68	—	—	—	—	—
93-94—Hamilton	AHL	59	7	27	34	97	4	0	2	2	19
—Vancouver	NHL	17	0	5	5	10	—	—	—	—	—
94-95—Syracuse	AHL	59	11	22	33	59	—	—	—	—	—
—Vancouver	NHL	16	0	3	3	4	1	0	0	0	2
NHL totals		33	0	8	8	14	1	0	0	0	2

NASH, TYSON
LW, CANUCKS

PERSONAL: Born March 11, 1975, in Edmonton. . . . 6-0/180. . . . Shoots left.
TRANSACTIONS/CAREER NOTES: Selected by Vancouver Canucks in 10th round (eighth Canucks pick, 247th overall) of NHL entry draft (June 29, 1994).

MN

Season Team	League	REGULAR SEASON Gms.	G	A	Pts.	PIM	PLAYOFFS Gms.	G	A	Pts.	PIM
90-91—Kamloops	WHL	3	0	0	0	0	—	—	—	—	—
91-92—Kamloops	WHL	33	1	6	7	32	4	0	0	0	0
92-93—Kamloops	WHL	61	10	16	26	78	13	3	2	5	32
93-94—Kamloops	WHL	65	20	36	56	137	16	3	3	6	12
94-95—Kamloops	WHL	63	34	41	75	70	21	10	7	17	30

NASLUND, MARKUS
LW, PENGUINS

PERSONAL: Born July 30, 1973, in Harnosand, Sweden. . . . 5-11/185. . . . Shoots left. . . . Name pronounced NAZ-luhnd.
TRANSACTIONS/CAREER NOTES: Selected by Pittsburgh Penguins in first round (first Penguins pick, 16th overall) of NHL entry draft (June 22, 1991).

Season Team	League	REGULAR SEASON Gms.	G	A	Pts.	PIM	PLAYOFFS Gms.	G	A	Pts.	PIM
89-90—MoDo	Sweden Jr.	33	43	35	78	20	—	—	—	—	—
90-91—MoDo Hockey	Sweden	32	10	9	19	14	—	—	—	—	—
91-92—MoDo Hockey	Sweden	39	22	18	40	54	—	—	—	—	—
92-93—MoDo Hockey	Sweden	39	22	17	39	67	3	3	2	5	0
93-94—Pittsburgh	NHL	71	4	7	11	27	—	—	—	—	—
—Cleveland	IHL	5	1	6	7	4	—	—	—	—	—
94-95—Pittsburgh	NHL	14	2	2	4	2	—	—	—	—	—
—Cleveland	IHL	7	3	4	7	6	4	1	3	4	8
NHL totals		85	6	9	15	29					

NASLUND, MATS
LW, BRUINS

PERSONAL: Born October 31, 1959, in Timra, Sweden. . . . 5-7/160. . . . Shoots left.
TRANSACTIONS/CAREER NOTES: Selected by Montreal Canadiens in second round (second Canadiens pick, 37th overall) of NHL entry draft (August 9, 1979). . . . Injured mouth (September 25, 1988). . . . Sprained ankle (January 31, 1989); missed All-Star Game. . . . Bruised shoulder (October 7, 1989). . . . Injured groin (March 21, 1990). . . . Signed to play for Lugano, Italy (May 4, 1990). . . . Played in Sweden (1991-92 through 1993-94). . . . Signed as free agent by Boston Bruins (February 21, 1995).
HONORS: Named to NHL All-Rookie team (1982-83). . . . Named to NHL All-Star second team (1985-86). . . . Played in NHL All-Star Game (1984, 1986 and 1988). . . . Won Lady Byng Memorial Trophy (1987-88).
MISCELLANEOUS: Member of gold-medal-winning Swedish Olympic team (1994).

Season Team	League	REGULAR SEASON Gms.	G	A	Pts.	PIM	PLAYOFFS Gms.	G	A	Pts.	PIM
77-78—Timra	Sweden	35	13	6	19	14	—	—	—	—	—
78-79—Swedish national team	Int'l	13	8	3	11	12	—	—	—	—	—
—Brynas Gavle	Sweden	36	12	12	24	19	—	—	—	—	—
79-80—Swedish national team	Int'l	21	3	11	14	10	—	—	—	—	—
—Swedish Olympic Team	Int'l	7	3	7	10	6	—	—	—	—	—
—Brynas Gavle	Sweden	36	18	19	37	34	7	2	2	4	4
80-81—Swedish national team	Int'l	25	4	6	10	20	—	—	—	—	—
—Brynas Gavle	Sweden	36	17	25	42	34	—	—	—	—	—
81-82—Swedish national team	Int'l	24	6	9	15	40	—	—	—	—	—
—Brynas Gavle	Sweden	36	24	18	42	16	—	—	—	—	—
82-83—Montreal	NHL	74	26	45	71	10	3	1	0	1	0
83-84—Montreal	NHL	77	29	35	64	4	15	6	8	14	4
84-85—Montreal	NHL	80	42	37	79	14	12	7	4	11	6
85-86—Montreal	NHL	80	43	67	110	16	20	8	11	19	4
86-87—Montreal	NHL	79	25	55	80	16	17	7	15	22	11
87-88—Montreal	NHL	78	24	59	83	14	6	0	7	7	2
88-89—Montreal	NHL	77	33	51	84	14	21	4	11	15	6
89-90—Montreal	NHL	72	21	20	41	19	3	1	1	2	0
90-91—Lugano	Switzerland	31	27	29	56	. . .	11	4	8	12	0
91-92—Malmo	Sweden	39	15	24	39	10	10	3	2	5	0
—Swedish Olympic Team	Int'l	8	1	5	6	27	—	—	—	—	—
92-93—Malmo	Sweden	33	10	22	32	10	—	—	—	—	—
93-94—Malmo	Sweden	40	14	20	34	8	—	—	—	—	—
—Swedish Olympic Team	Int'l	8	0	7	7	0	—	—	—	—	—
94-95—Boston	NHL	34	8	14	22	4	5	1	0	1	0
NHL totals		651	251	383	634	111	102	35	57	92	33

NASREDDINE, ALAIN
D, PANTHERS

PERSONAL: Born July 10, 1975, in Montreal. . . . 6-1/201. . . . Shoots left. . . . Name pronounced AL-ay NAS-ruh-deen.
TRANSACTIONS/CAREER NOTES: Selected by Florida Panthers in sixth round (eighth Panthers pick, 135th overall) of NHL entry draft (June 26, 1993).
HONORS: Named to QMJHL All-Star second team (1994-95).

Season Team	League	REGULAR SEASON Gms.	G	A	Pts.	PIM	PLAYOFFS Gms.	G	A	Pts.	PIM
91-92—Drummondville	QMJHL	61	1	9	10	78	4	0	0	0	17
92-93—Drummondville	QMJHL	64	0	14	14	137	10	0	1	1	36
93-94—Chicoutimi	QMJHL	60	3	24	27	218	26	2	10	12	118
94-95—Chicoutimi	QMJHL	67	8	31	39	342	13	3	5	8	40

N

NAUMENKO, NICK
D, BLUES

PERSONAL: Born July 7, 1974, in Chicago.... 5-11/185.... Shoots right.
COLLEGE: North Dakota.
TRANSACTIONS/CAREER NOTES: Selected by St. Louis Blues in eighth round (ninth Blues pick, 182nd overall) of NHL entry draft (June 20, 1992).
HONORS: Named to WCHA All-Star first team (1994-95).

			REGULAR SEASON					PLAYOFFS			
Season Team	League	Gms.	G	A	Pts.	PIM	Gms.	G	A	Pts.	PIM
91-92—Dubuque	USHL	24	6	19	25	4	—	—	—	—	—
92-93—North Dakota	WCHA	38	10	24	34	26	—	—	—	—	—
93-94—North Dakota	WCHA	32	4	22	26	22	—	—	—	—	—
94-95—North Dakota	WCHA	39	13	26	39	78	—	—	—	—	—

NAZAROV, ANDREI
LW, SHARKS

PERSONAL: Born March 21, 1972, in Chelyabinsk, U.S.S.R.... 6-6/230.... Shoots right.... Name pronounced nuh-ZAH-rahf.
TRANSACTIONS/CAREER NOTES: Selected by San Jose Sharks in first round (second Sharks pick, 10th overall) of NHL entry draft (June 20, 1992).... Suspended four games and fined $500 by NHL for head-butting (March 8, 1995).

			REGULAR SEASON					PLAYOFFS			
Season Team	League	Gms.	G	A	Pts.	PIM	Gms.	G	A	Pts.	PIM
90-91—Mechel Chelyabinsk	USSR	2	0	0	0	0	—	—	—	—	—
91-92—Dynamo Moscow	CIS	2	1	0	1	2	—	—	—	—	—
92-93—Dynamo Moscow	CIS	42	8	2	10	79	10	1	1	2	8
93-94—Kansas City	IHL	71	15	18	33	64	—	—	—	—	—
—San Jose	NHL	1	0	0	0	0	—	—	—	—	—
94-95—Kansas City	IHL	43	15	10	25	55	—	—	—	—	—
—San Jose	NHL	26	3	5	8	94	6	0	0	0	9
NHL totals		27	3	5	8	94	6	0	0	0	9

NDUR, RUMUN
D, SABRES

PERSONAL: Born July 7, 1975, in Zaria, Nigeria.... 6-2/200.... Shoots left.... Name pronounced roo-MOHN EHN-duhr.
HIGH SCHOOL: Bishop MacDonnell (Guelph, Ont.).
TRANSACTIONS/CAREER NOTES: Selected by Buffalo Sabres in third round (third Sabres pick, 69th overall) of NHL entry draft (June 29, 1994).

			REGULAR SEASON					PLAYOFFS			
Season Team	League	Gms.	G	A	Pts.	PIM	Gms.	G	A	Pts.	PIM
91-92—Clearwater	Jr. C	4	0	4	4	4	—	—	—	—	—
—Sarnia	Jr. B	30	2	5	7	46	—	—	—	—	—
92-93—Guelph	Jr. B	24	7	8	15	202	—	—	—	—	—
—Guelph	OHL	22	1	3	4	30	4	0	1	1	4
93-94—Guelph	OHL	61	6	33	39	176	9	4	1	5	24
94-95—Guelph	OHL	63	10	21	31	187	14	0	4	4	28

NEATON, PATRICK
D, PENGUINS

PERSONAL: Born May 21, 1971, in Redford, Mich.... 6-0/180.... Shoots left.
COLLEGE: Michigan.
TRANSACTIONS/CAREER NOTES: Selected by Pittsburgh Penguins in seventh round (ninth Penguins pick, 145th overall) of NHL entry draft (June 16, 1990).... Loaned by Penguins to San Diego Gulls of IHL (October 21, 1994).
HONORS: Named to CCHA All-Star second team (1990-91).... Named to CCHA All-Star first team (1992-93).

			REGULAR SEASON					PLAYOFFS			
Season Team	League	Gms.	G	A	Pts.	PIM	Gms.	G	A	Pts.	PIM
89-90—University of Michigan	CCHA	42	3	23	26	36	—	—	—	—	—
90-91—University of Michigan	CCHA	44	15	28	43	78	—	—	—	—	—
91-92—University of Michigan	CCHA	43	10	20	30	62	—	—	—	—	—
92-93—University of Michigan	CCHA	38	10	18	28	37	—	—	—	—	—
93-94—Cleveland	IHL	71	8	24	32	78	—	—	—	—	—
—Pittsburgh	NHL	9	1	1	2	12	—	—	—	—	—
94-95—Cleveland	IHL	2	0	0	0	4	—	—	—	—	—
—San Diego	IHL	71	8	27	35	86	5	0	1	1	0
NHL totals		9	1	1	2	12					

NECKAR, STANISLAV
D, SENATORS

PERSONAL: Born December 22, 1975, in Ceske Budejovice, Czechoslovakia.... 6-0/196.... Shoots left.... Name pronounced NEHK-uhr.
TRANSACTIONS/CAREER NOTES: Selected by Ottawa Senators in second round (second Senators pick, 29th overall) of NHL entry draft (June 28, 1994).

			REGULAR SEASON					PLAYOFFS			
Season Team	League	Gms.	G	A	Pts.	PIM	Gms.	G	A	Pts.	PIM
91-92—Budejovice	Czech. Div II	18	1	3	4	...	—	—	—	—	—
92-93—Motor Ceske-Budejovice	Czech.	42	2	9	11	12	—	—	—	—	—
93-94—HC Ceske Budejovice	Czech Rep.	12	3	2	5	2	3	0	0	0	0
94-95—Detroit	IHL	15	2	2	4	15	—	—	—	—	—
—Ottawa	NHL	48	1	3	4	37	—	—	—	—	—
NHL totals		48	1	3	4	37					

NEDVED, PETR
C, RANGERS

PERSONAL: Born December 9, 1971, in Liberec, Czechoslovakia. . . . 6-3/195. . . . Shoots left. . . . Name pronounced NEHD-VEHD. . . . Brother of Zdenek Nedved, right winger in Toronto Maple Leafs system.
TRANSACTIONS/CAREER NOTES: Defected from Czechoslovakia to Canada when Czechoslovakian midget team was playing in Calgary (January 1989). . . . WHL rights traded by Moose Jaw Warriors with D Brian Ilkuf to Seattle Thunderbirds for D Corey Beaulieu (February 3, 1989). . . . Selected by Vancouver Canucks in first round (first Canucks pick, second overall) of NHL entry draft (June 16, 1990). . . . Signed as free agent by St. Louis Blues (March 4, 1994); C Craig Janney and second-round pick in 1994 draft (C Dave Scatchard) awarded to Canucks as compensation (March 14, 1994). . . . Traded by Blues to New York Rangers for LW Esa Tikkanen and D Doug Lidster (July 24, 1994); trade arranged as compensation for Blues signing Coach Mike Keenan. . . . Strained abdomen (February 27, 1995); missed two games.
HONORS: Won Can.HL Rookie of the Year Award (1989-90). . . . Won Jim Piggott Memorial Trophy (1989-90).
MISCELLANEOUS: Member of silver-medal-winning Canadian Olympic team (1994).

			REGULAR SEASON					PLAYOFFS			
Season	Team	League	Gms.	G	A	Pts.	PIM	Gms.	G	A	Pts.	PIM
88-89—Litvinov		Czech. Jrs.	20	32	19	51	12	—	—	—	—	—
89-90—Seattle		WHL	71	65	80	145	80	11	4	9	13	2
90-91—Vancouver		NHL	61	10	6	16	20	6	0	1	1	0
91-92—Vancouver		NHL	77	15	22	37	36	10	1	4	5	16
92-93—Vancouver		NHL	84	38	33	71	96	12	2	3	5	2
93-94—Canadian national team		Int'l	17	19	12	31	16	—	—	—	—	—
—Canadian Olympic Team		Int'l	8	5	1	6	6	—	—	—	—	—
—St. Louis		NHL	19	6	14	20	8	4	0	1	1	4
94-95—New York Rangers		NHL	46	11	12	23	26	10	3	2	5	6
NHL totals			287	80	87	167	186	42	6	11	17	28

NEDVED, ZDENEK
RW, MAPLE LEAFS

PERSONAL: Born March 3, 1975, in Lany, Czechoslovakia. . . . 6-0/180. . . . Shoots left. . . . Name pronounced NEHD-VEHD. . . . Brother of Petr Nedved, center, New York Rangers.
TRANSACTIONS/CAREER NOTES: Selected by Toronto Maple Leafs in fifth round (third Maple Leafs pick, 123rd overall) of NHL entry draft (June 26, 1993).

			REGULAR SEASON					PLAYOFFS			
Season	Team	League	Gms.	G	A	Pts.	PIM	Gms.	G	A	Pts.	PIM
91-92—PZ Kladno		Czech.	19	15	12	27	22	—	—	—	—	—
92-93—Sudbury		OHL	18	3	9	12	6	—	—	—	—	—
93-94—Sudbury		OHL	60	50	50	100	42	10	7	8	15	10
94-95—Sudbury		OHL	59	47	51	98	36	18	12	16	28	16
—Toronto		NHL	1	0	0	0	2	—	—	—	—	—
NHL totals			1	0	0	0	2	—	—	—	—	—

NEELY, CAM
RW, BRUINS

PERSONAL: Born June 6, 1965, in Comox, B.C. . . . 6-1/210. . . . Shoots right. . . . Full name: Cameron Michael Neely.
TRANSACTIONS/CAREER NOTES: Selected by Vancouver Canucks as underage junior in first round (first Canucks pick, ninth overall) of NHL entry draft (June 8, 1983). . . . Dislocated kneecap (October 1984). . . . Traded by Canucks with first-round pick in 1987 draft (D Glen Wesley) to Boston Bruins for C Barry Pederson (June 6, 1986). . . . Slipped right kneecap (March 1988). . . . Fractured right thumb and inflamed right knee (December 1988). . . . Suffered recurrence of right knee inflammation (March 1989). . . . Hyperextended knee (October 1989). . . . Pulled groin (March 1990). . . . Suspended five games by NHL for high-sticking (November 23, 1990). . . . Injured thigh (May 11, 1991); missed first 38 games of 1991-92 season. . . . Suffered knee inflammation (January 1992). . . . Underwent knee surgery (February 3, 1992); missed remainder of season. . . . Underwent arthroscopic knee surgery (September 17, 1992); missed first 60 games of season. . . . Injured knee (March 1993); missed eight games. . . . Injured knee (April 1993); missed three games. . . . Reinjured knee (October 9, 1993); missed three games. . . . Injured groin (February 10, 1994); missed one game. . . . Injured knee (March 22, 1994); missed 12 games.
HONORS: Named to THE SPORTING NEWS All-Star first team (1987-88 and 1993-94). . . . Named to NHL All-Star second team (1987-88, 1989-90, 1990-91 and 1993-94). . . . Played in NHL All-Star Game (1988-1991). . . . Named to THE SPORTING NEWS All-Star second team (1989-90 and 1990-91). . . . Won Bill Masterton Memorial Trophy (1993-94).
RECORDS: Shares NHL single-season playoff record for most power-play goals—9 (1991).
STATISTICAL PLATEAUS: Three-goal games: 1986-87 (1), 1987-88 (3), 1988-89 (1), 1989-90 (1), 1990-91 (2), 1993-94 (3), 1994-95 (2). Total: 13.

			REGULAR SEASON					PLAYOFFS			
Season	Team	League	Gms.	G	A	Pts.	PIM	Gms.	G	A	Pts.	PIM
82-83—Portland		WHL	72	56	64	120	130	14	9	11	20	17
83-84—Portland		WHL	19	8	18	26	29	—	—	—	—	—
—Vancouver		NHL	56	16	15	31	57	4	2	0	2	2
84-85—Vancouver		NHL	72	21	18	39	137	—	—	—	—	—
85-86—Vancouver		NHL	73	14	20	34	126	3	0	0	0	6
86-87—Boston		NHL	75	36	36	72	143	4	5	1	6	8
87-88—Boston		NHL	69	42	27	69	175	23	9	8	17	51
88-89—Boston		NHL	74	37	38	75	190	10	7	2	9	8
89-90—Boston		NHL	76	55	37	92	117	21	12	16	28	51
90-91—Boston		NHL	69	51	40	91	98	19	16	4	20	36
91-92—Boston		NHL	9	9	3	12	16	—	—	—	—	—
92-93—Boston		NHL	13	11	7	18	25	4	4	1	5	4
93-94—Boston		NHL	49	50	24	74	54	—	—	—	—	—
94-95—Boston		NHL	42	27	14	41	72	5	2	0	2	2
NHL totals			677	369	279	648	1210	93	57	32	89	168

N

NEILSON, COREY
D, OILERS

PERSONAL: Born August 22, 1976, in Oromocto, N.B. . . . 6-5/207. . . . Shoots right.
TRANSACTIONS/CAREER NOTES: Selected by Edmonton Oilers in third round (fourth Oilers pick, 53rd overall) of NHL entry draft (June 29, 1994).
HONORS: Named to OHL All-Rookie team (1993-94).

			REGULAR SEASON					PLAYOFFS			
Season Team	League	Gms.	G	A	Pts.	PIM	Gms.	G	A	Pts.	PIM
93-94—North Bay	OHL	62	3	35	38	46	18	1	5	6	10
94-95—North Bay	OHL	64	6	27	33	86	6	3	3	6	9

NELSON, JEFF
C, CAPITALS

PERSONAL: Born December 18, 1972, in Prince Albert, Sask. . . . 6-0/190. . . . Shoots left. . . . Full name: Jeffrey Arthur Nelson. . . . Brother of Todd Nelson, defenseman in Pittsburgh Penguins system.
TRANSACTIONS/CAREER NOTES: Selected by Washington Capitals in second round (fourth Capitals pick, 36th overall) of NHL entry draft (June 22, 1991).
HONORS: Won Can.HL Scholastic Player of the Year Award (1988-89 and 1989-90). . . . Named WHL Scholastic Player of the Year (1988-89 and 1989-90). . . . Named WHL (East) Player of the Year (1990-91). . . . Named to WHL All-Star second team (1990-91). . . . Named to WHL (East) All-Star second team (1991-92).

			REGULAR SEASON					PLAYOFFS			
Season Team	League	Gms.	G	A	Pts.	PIM	Gms.	G	A	Pts.	PIM
88-89—Prince Albert	WHL	71	30	57	87	74	4	0	3	3	4
89-90—Prince Albert	WHL	72	28	69	97	79	14	2	11	13	10
90-91—Prince Albert	WHL	72	46	74	120	58	3	1	1	2	4
91-92—Prince Albert	WHL	64	48	65	113	84	9	7	14	21	18
92-93—Baltimore	AHL	72	14	38	52	12	7	1	3	4	2
93-94—Portland	AHL	80	34	73	107	92	17	10	5	15	20
94-95—Portland	AHL	64	33	50	83	57	7	1	4	5	8
—Washington	NHL	10	1	0	1	2	—	—	—	—	—
NHL totals		10	1	0	1	2					

NEMCHINOV, SERGEI
C, RANGERS

PERSONAL: Born January 14, 1964, in Moscow, U.S.S.R. . . . 6-0/210. . . . Shoots left. . . . Name pronounced SAIR-gay nehm-CHEE-nahf.
TRANSACTIONS/CAREER NOTES: Selected by New York Rangers in 12th round (14th Rangers pick, 244th overall) of NHL entry draft (June 16, 1990). . . . Sprained knee (November 4, 1991); missed seven games. . . . Strained buttock (April 4, 1993); missed three games. . . . Suspended eight games and fined $500 by NHL for hitting another player (March 16, 1994). . . . Bruised Achilles tendon (January 30, 1995); missed one game.
STATISTICAL PLATEAUS: Three-goal games: 1992-93 (1).
MISCELLANEOUS: Member of Stanley Cup championship team (1994).

			REGULAR SEASON					PLAYOFFS			
Season Team	League	Gms.	G	A	Pts.	PIM	Gms.	G	A	Pts.	PIM
81-82—Soviet Wings	USSR	15	1	0	1	0	—	—	—	—	—
82-83—CSKA Moscow	USSR	11	0	0	0	2	—	—	—	—	—
83-84—CSKA Moscow	USSR	20	6	5	11	4	—	—	—	—	—
84-85—CSKA Moscow	USSR	31	2	4	6	4	—	—	—	—	—
85-86—Soviet Wings	USSR	39	7	12	19	28	—	—	—	—	—
86-87—Soviet Wings	USSR	40	13	9	22	24	—	—	—	—	—
87-88—Soviet Wings	USSR	48	17	11	28	26	—	—	—	—	—
88-89—Soviet Wings	USSR	43	15	14	29	28	—	—	—	—	—
89-90—Soviet Wings	USSR	48	17	16	33	34	—	—	—	—	—
90-91—Soviet Wings	USSR	46	21	24	45	30	—	—	—	—	—
91-92—New York Rangers	NHL	73	30	28	58	15	13	1	4	5	8
92-93—New York Rangers	NHL	81	23	31	54	34	—	—	—	—	—
93-94—New York Rangers	NHL	76	22	27	49	36	23	2	5	7	6
94-95—New York Rangers	NHL	47	7	6	13	16	10	4	5	9	2
NHL totals		277	82	92	174	101	46	7	14	21	16

NEMIROVSKY, DAVID
RW, PANTHERS

PERSONAL: Born August 1, 1976, in Toronto. . . . 6-1/176. . . . Shoots right. . . . Name pronounced nehm-uhr-AHF-skee.
TRANSACTIONS/CAREER NOTES: Selected by Florida Panthers in fourth round (fifth Panthers pick, 84th overall) of NHL entry draft (June 29, 1994).

			REGULAR SEASON					PLAYOFFS			
Season Team	League	Gms.	G	A	Pts.	PIM	Gms.	G	A	Pts.	PIM
91-92—Pickering-Weston	Jr. A	38	27	23	50	70	—	—	—	—	—
92-93—Weston-North York	MTHL	40	19	23	42	27	—	—	—	—	—
93-94—Ottawa	OHL	64	21	31	52	18	17	10	10	20	2
94-95—Ottawa	OHL	59	27	29	56	25	—	—	—	—	—

NICHOLLS, BERNIE
C, BLACKHAWKS

PERSONAL: Born June 24, 1961, in Haliburton, Ont. . . . 6-0/185. . . . Shoots right. . . . Full name: Bernard Irvine Nicholls.
TRANSACTIONS/CAREER NOTES: Selected by Los Angeles Kings as underage junior in fourth round (fourth Kings pick, 73rd overall) of NHL entry draft (June 11, 1980). . . . Partially tore medial collateral ligament in right knee (November 18, 1982). . . . Broke jaw (February 1984); missed two games.

... Fractured left index finger in three places (October 8, 1987).... Traded by Kings to New York Rangers for RW Tomas Sandstrom and LW Tony Granato (January 20, 1990).... Separated left shoulder (January 22, 1991); missed five games.... Suspended three games by NHL for stick-swinging incident (February 14, 1991).... Traded by Rangers with LW Louie De-Brusk, RW Steven Rice and future considerations to Edmonton Oilers for C Mark Messier and future considerations (October 4, 1991); Rangers traded D David Shaw to Oilers for D Jeff Beukeboom to complete the deal (November 12, 1991).... Did not report to Oilers to be with his wife for the birth of their child (October 4, 1991); missed 27 games.... Reported to Oilers (December 6, 1991).... Strained abdominal muscle (February 16, 1992); missed two games.... Suspended seven off-days and fined $500 by NHL for swinging stick in preseason game (October 13, 1992).... Traded by Oilers to New Jersey Devils for C Kevin Todd and LW Zdeno Ciger (January 13, 1993).... Fractured left foot (February 27, 1993); missed 13 games.... Sprained left knee (December 4, 1993); missed nine games.... Injured hand (April 10, 1994); missed one game.... Suspended one game by NHL for cross-check to neck (May 21, 1994).... Signed as free agent by Chicago Blackhawks (July 14, 1994).
HONORS: Played in NHL All-Star Game (1984, 1989 and 1990).
STATISTICAL PLATEAUS: Three-goal games: 1981-82 (3), 1983-84 (1), 1984-85 (1), 1985-86 (1), 1986-87 (1), 1987-88 (1), 1988-89 (4), 1993-94 (1), 1994-95 (1). Total: 14.... Four-goal games: 1983-84 (1), 1984-85 (1), 1994-95 (2). Total: 4. ... Total hat tricks: 18.

Season Team	League	REGULAR SEASON					PLAYOFFS				
		Gms.	G	A	Pts.	PIM	Gms.	G	A	Pts.	PIM
78-79—Kingston	OMJHL	2	0	1	1	0	—	—	—	—	—
79-80—Kingston	OMJHL	68	36	43	79	85	3	1	0	1	10
80-81—Kingston	OMJHL	65	63	89	152	109	14	8	10	18	17
81-82—New Haven	AHL	55	41	30	71	31	—	—	—	—	—
—Los Angeles	NHL	22	14	18	32	27	10	4	0	4	23
82-83—Los Angeles	NHL	71	28	22	50	124	—	—	—	—	—
83-84—Los Angeles	NHL	78	41	54	95	83	—	—	—	—	—
84-85—Los Angeles	NHL	80	46	54	100	76	3	1	1	2	9
85-86—Los Angeles	NHL	80	36	61	97	78	—	—	—	—	—
86-87—Los Angeles	NHL	80	33	48	81	101	5	2	5	7	6
87-88—Los Angeles	NHL	65	32	46	78	114	5	2	6	8	11
88-89—Los Angeles	NHL	79	70	80	150	96	11	7	9	16	12
89-90—Los Angeles	NHL	47	27	48	75	66	—	—	—	—	—
—New York Rangers	NHL	32	12	25	37	20	10	7	5	12	16
90-91—New York Rangers	NHL	71	25	48	73	96	5	4	3	7	8
91-92—New York Rangers	NHL	1	0	0	0	0	—	—	—	—	—
—Edmonton	NHL	49	20	29	49	60	16	8	11	19	25
92-93—Edmonton	NHL	46	8	32	40	40	—	—	—	—	—
—New Jersey	NHL	23	5	15	20	40	5	0	0	0	6
93-94—New Jersey	NHL	61	19	27	46	86	16	4	9	13	28
94-95—Chicago	NHL	48	22	29	51	32	16	1	11	12	8
NHL totals		933	438	636	1074	1139	102	40	60	100	152

NIECKAR, BARRY

LW, ISLANDERS

PERSONAL: Born December 16, 1967, in Rama, Sask. ... 6-3/200. ... Shoots left. ... Name pronounced NIGH-kahr.
TRANSACTIONS/CAREER NOTES: Signed as free agent by Hartford Whalers (September 1992).... Signed as free agent by Calgary Flames (February 10, 1995).... Signed as free agent by New York Islanders (July 25, 1995).

Season Team	League	REGULAR SEASON					PLAYOFFS				
		Gms.	G	A	Pts.	PIM	Gms.	G	A	Pts.	PIM
91-92—Phoenix	IHL	5	0	0	0	9	—	—	—	—	—
—Raleigh	ECHL	46	10	18	28	229	4	4	0	4	22
92-93—Springfield	AHL	21	2	4	6	65	6	1	0	1	14
—Hartford	NHL	2	0	0	0	2	—	—	—	—	—
93-94—Springfield	AHL	30	0	2	2	67	—	—	—	—	—
94-95—Saint John	AHL	65	8	7	15	*491	4	0	0	0	22
—Calgary	NHL	3	0	0	0	12	—	—	—	—	—
NHL totals		5	0	0	0	14					

NIEDERMAYER, ROB

C, PANTHERS

PERSONAL: Born December 28, 1974, in Cassiar, B.C. ... 6-2/201. ... Shoots left. ... Name pronounced nee-duhr-MIGH-uhr. ... Brother of Scott Niedermayer, defenseman, New Jersey Devils.
COLLEGE: Medicine Hat.
TRANSACTIONS/CAREER NOTES: Selected by Florida Panthers in first round (first Panthers pick, fifth overall) of NHL entry draft (June 26, 1993).... Separated right shoulder (November 18, 1993); missed 17 games.
HONORS: Won WHL Top Draft Prospect Award (1992-93).... Named to WHL (East) All-Star first team (1992-93).

Season Team	League	REGULAR SEASON					PLAYOFFS				
		Gms.	G	A	Pts.	PIM	Gms.	G	A	Pts.	PIM
90-91—Medicine Hat	WHL	71	24	26	50	8	12	3	7	10	2
91-92—Medicine Hat	WHL	71	32	46	78	77	4	2	3	5	2
92-93—Medicine Hat	WHL	52	43	34	77	67	—	—	—	—	—
93-94—Florida	NHL	65	9	17	26	51	—	—	—	—	—
94-95—Medicine Hat	WHL	13	9	15	24	14	—	—	—	—	—
—Florida	NHL	48	4	6	10	36	—	—	—	—	—
NHL totals		113	13	23	36	87					

N

NIEDERMAYER, SCOTT
D, DEVILS

PERSONAL: Born August 31, 1973, in Edmonton. . . . 6-0/200. . . . Shoots left. . . . Name pronounced NEE-duhr-MIGH-uhr. . . . Brother of Rob Niedermayer, center, Florida Panthers.
TRANSACTIONS/CAREER NOTES: Stretched left knee ligaments (March 12, 1991); missed nine games. . . . Selected by New Jersey Devils in first round (first Devils pick, third overall) of NHL entry draft (June 22, 1991). . . . Suffered sore back (December 9, 1992); missed four games.
HONORS: Won Can.HL Scholastic Player of the Year Award (1990-91). . . . Named WHL Scholastic Player of the Year (1990-91). . . . Named to WHL (West) All-Star first team (1990-91 and 1991-92). . . . Won Stafford Smythe Memorial Trophy (1991-92). . . . Named to Can.HL All-Star first team (1991-92). . . . Named to Memorial Cup All-Star team (1991-92). . . . Named to NHL All-Rookie team (1992-93).
MISCELLANEOUS: Member of Stanley Cup championship team (1995).

			REGULAR SEASON					PLAYOFFS				
Season	Team	League	Gms.	G	A	Pts.	PIM	Gms.	G	A	Pts.	PIM
89-90—Kamloops		WHL	64	14	55	69	64	17	2	14	16	35
90-91—Kamloops		WHL	57	26	56	82	52	—	—	—	—	—
91-92—New Jersey		NHL	4	0	1	1	2	—	—	—	—	—
—Kamloops		WHL	35	7	32	39	61	17	9	14	23	28
92-93—New Jersey		NHL	80	11	29	40	47	5	0	3	3	2
93-94—New Jersey		NHL	81	10	36	46	42	20	2	2	4	8
94-95—New Jersey		NHL	48	4	15	19	18	20	4	7	11	10
NHL totals			213	25	81	106	109	45	6	12	18	20

NIELSEN, JEFF
RW, RANGERS

PERSONAL: Born September 20, 1971, in Grand Rapids, Minn. . . . 6-0/170. . . . Shoots right. . . . Full name: Jeffrey Michael Nielsen.
HIGH SCHOOL: Grand Rapids (Minn.).
COLLEGE: Minnesota.
TRANSACTIONS/CAREER NOTES: Selected by New York Rangers in fourth round (fourth Rangers pick, 69th overall) of NHL entry draft (June 16, 1990).
HONORS: Named to WCHA All-Star second team (1993-94).

			REGULAR SEASON					PLAYOFFS				
Season	Team	League	Gms.	G	A	Pts.	PIM	Gms.	G	A	Pts.	PIM
87-88—Grand Rapids H.S.		Minn. H.S.	21	9	11	20	14	—	—	—	—	—
88-89—Grand Rapids H.S.		Minn. H.S.	25	13	17	30	26	—	—	—	—	—
89-90—Grand Rapids H.S.		Minn. H.S.	28	32	25	57	...	—	—	—	—	—
90-91—University of Minnesota		WCHA	45	11	14	25	50	—	—	—	—	—
91-92—University of Minnesota		WCHA	44	15	15	30	74	—	—	—	—	—
92-93—University of Minnesota		WCHA	42	21	20	41	80	—	—	—	—	—
93-94—University of Minnesota		WCHA	41	29	16	45	94	—	—	—	—	—
94-95—Binghamton		AHL	76	24	13	37	139	7	0	0	0	22

NIEUWENDYK, JOE
C, FLAMES

PERSONAL: Born September 10, 1966, in Oshawa, Ont. . . . 6-1/195. . . . Shoots left. . . . Name pronounced NOO-ihn-DIGHK. . . . Cousin of Jeff Beukeboom, defenseman, New York Rangers.
COLLEGE: Cornell.
TRANSACTIONS/CAREER NOTES: Selected by Calgary Flames in second round (second Flames pick, 27th overall) of NHL entry draft (June 15, 1985). . . . Suffered concussion (November 1987). . . . Bruised ribs (May 25, 1989). . . . Tore anterior cruciate ligament of left knee (April 17, 1990). . . . Underwent arthroscopic knee surgery (September 28, 1991); missed 12 games. . . . Suffered from the flu (November 19, 1992); missed one game. . . . Strained right knee (March 26, 1993); missed four games. . . . Suffered from charley horse (November 13, 1993); missed three games. . . . Strained right knee ligaments (February 24, 1994); missed 17 games. . . . Strained back (April 29, 1995); missed two games.
HONORS: Won Ivy League Rookie of the Year Trophy (1984-85). . . . Named to NCAA All-America East first team (1985-86 and 1986-87). . . . Named to ECAC All-Star first team (1985-86 and 1986-87). . . . Named ECAC Player of the Year (1986-87). . . . Named NHL Rookie of the Year by THE SPORTING NEWS (1987-88). . . . Won Calder Memorial Trophy (1987-88). . . . Won Dodge Ram Tough Award (1987-88). . . . Named to NHL All-Rookie team (1987-88). . . . Played in NHL All-Star Game (1988-1990 and 1994). . . . Won King Clancy Trophy (1994-95).
RECORDS: Shares NHL single-game record for most goals in one period—4 (January 11, 1989).
STATISTICAL PLATEAUS: Three-goal games: 1987-88 (2), 1988-89 (1), 1989-90 (1), 1992-93 (1), 1993-94 (1), 1994-95 (1). Total: 7. . . . Four-goal games: 1987-88 (2). . . . Five-goal games: 1988-89 (1). . . . Total hat tricks: 10.
MISCELLANEOUS: Member of Stanley Cup championship team (1989). . . . Captain of Calgary Flames (1991-92 through 1994-95).
STATISTICAL NOTES: Third player in NHL history to score 50 goals in each of his first two seasons.

			REGULAR SEASON					PLAYOFFS				
Season	Team	League	Gms.	G	A	Pts.	PIM	Gms.	G	A	Pts.	PIM
83-84—Pickering Jr. B		MTHL	38	30	28	58	35	—	—	—	—	—
84-85—Cornell University		ECAC	23	18	21	39	20	—	—	—	—	—
85-86—Cornell University		ECAC	21	21	21	42	45	—	—	—	—	—
86-87—Cornell University		ECAC	23	26	26	52	26	—	—	—	—	—
—Calgary		NHL	9	5	1	6	0	6	2	2	4	0
87-88—Calgary		NHL	75	51	41	92	23	8	3	4	7	2
88-89—Calgary		NHL	77	51	31	82	40	22	10	4	14	10
89-90—Calgary		NHL	79	45	50	95	40	6	4	6	10	4
90-91—Calgary		NHL	79	45	40	85	36	7	4	1	5	10
91-92—Calgary		NHL	69	22	34	56	55	—	—	—	—	—
92-93—Calgary		NHL	79	38	37	75	52	6	3	6	9	10

N

Season Team	League	REGULAR SEASON Gms.	G	A	Pts.	PIM	PLAYOFFS Gms.	G	A	Pts.	PIM
93-94—Calgary	NHL	64	36	39	75	51	6	2	2	4	0
94-95—Calgary	NHL	46	21	29	50	33	5	4	3	7	0
NHL totals		577	314	302	616	330	66	32	28	60	36

NIINIMAA, JANNE
D, FLYERS

PERSONAL: Born May 22, 1975, in Raahe, Finland. . . . 6-1/196. . . . Shoots left.
TRANSACTIONS/CAREER NOTES: Selected by Philadelphia Flyers in second round (first Flyers pick, 36th overall) of NHL entry draft (June 26, 1993).

Season Team	League	REGULAR SEASON Gms.	G	A	Pts.	PIM	PLAYOFFS Gms.	G	A	Pts.	PIM
91-92—Karpat Oulu	Finland Dv.II	41	2	11	13	49	—	—	—	—	—
92-93—Karpat Oulu	Finland Dv.II	29	2	3	5	14	—	—	—	—	—
—Karpat Jr.	Finland	10	3	9	12	16	—	—	—	—	—
93-94—Jokerit Helsinki	Finland	45	3	8	11	24	12	1	1	2	4
94-95—Jokerit Helsinki	Finland	42	7	10	17	36	10	1	4	5	35

NIKOLISHIN, ANDREI
C, WHALERS

PERSONAL: Born March 25, 1973, in Vorkuta, U.S.S.R. . . . 5-11/180. . . . Shoots left. . . . Name pronounced nih-koh-LEE-shihn.
TRANSACTIONS/CAREER NOTES: Selected by Hartford Whalers in second round (second Whalers pick, 47th overall) of NHL entry draft (June 20, 1992). . . . Played in Europe during 1994-95 NHL lockout.
HONORS: Named to CIS All-Star team (1993-94). . . . Named CIS Player of the Year (1993-94).

Season Team	League	REGULAR SEASON Gms.	G	A	Pts.	PIM	PLAYOFFS Gms.	G	A	Pts.	PIM
90-91—Dynamo Moscow	USSR	2	0	0	0	0	—	—	—	—	—
91-92—Dynamo Moscow	CIS	18	1	0	1	4	—	—	—	—	—
92-93—Dynamo Moscow	CIS	42	5	7	12	30	10	2	1	3	8
93-94—Dynamo Moscow	CIS	41	8	12	20	30	9	1	3	4	4
—Russian Olympic team	Int'l	8	2	5	7	6	—	—	—	—	—
94-95—Dynamo Moscow	CIS	12	7	2	9	6	—	—	—	—	—
—Hartford	NHL	39	8	10	18	10	—	—	—	—	—
NHL totals		39	8	10	18	10					

NIKOLOV, ANGEL
D, SHARKS

PERSONAL: Born November 18, 1975, in Most, Czechoslovakia. . . . 6-1/176. . . . Shoots left.
TRANSACTIONS/CAREER NOTES: Selected by San Jose Sharks in second round (second Sharks pick, 37th overall) of NHL entry draft (June 28, 1994).

Season Team	League	REGULAR SEASON Gms.	G	A	Pts.	PIM	PLAYOFFS Gms.	G	A	Pts.	PIM
93-94—Chemopetrol Litvinov	Czech Rep.	10	2	2	4	. . .	3	0	0	0	. . .
94-95—Chemopetrol Litvinov	Czech Rep.	41	1	4	5	. . .	4	0	0	0	. . .

NIKULIN, IGOR
RW, MIGHTY DUCKS

PERSONAL: Born August 26, 1972, in Cherepovets, U.S.S.R. . . . 6-1/180. . . . Shoots left.
TRANSACTIONS/CAREER NOTES: Selected by Mighty Ducks of Anaheim in fifth round (fourth Mighty Ducks pick, 107th overall) of NHL entry draft (July 8, 1995).

Season Team	League	REGULAR SEASON Gms.	G	A	Pts.	PIM	PLAYOFFS Gms.	G	A	Pts.	PIM
92-93—Metallurg Cherepovets	CIS	42	11	11	22	22	—	—	—	—	—
93-94—Metallurg Cherepovets	CIS	44	14	15	29	52	2	1	0	1	1
94-95—Severstal Cherepovets	CIS	52	14	12	26	28	—	—	—	—	—

NILSSON, FREDRICK
C, SHARKS

PERSONAL: Born April 16, 1971, in Vasteras, Sweden. . . . 6-1/200. . . . Shoots left. . . . Name pronounced NEEL-son.
TRANSACTIONS/CAREER NOTES: Selected by San Jose Sharks in sixth round (seventh Sharks pick, 111th overall) of NHL entry draft (June 22, 1991).

Season Team	League	REGULAR SEASON Gms.	G	A	Pts.	PIM	PLAYOFFS Gms.	G	A	Pts.	PIM
89-90—Vasteras	Sweden	23	1	1	2	4	1	0	0	0	0
90-91—Vasteras	Sweden	35	13	7	20	20	—	—	—	—	—
91-92—Vasteras	Sweden	40	5	14	19	40	—	—	—	—	—
92-93—Vasteras	Sweden	40	14	15	29	69	1	1	1	2	0
93-94—Kansas City	IHL	13	2	7	9	2	—	—	—	—	—
94-95—Kansas City	IHL	13	3	0	3	2	12	3	2	5	4

NILSSON, KENT
C

PERSONAL: Born August 31, 1956, in Nynashaman, Sweden. . . . 6-1/185. . . . Shoots left.
TRANSACTIONS/CAREER NOTES: Selected by Atlanta Flames in fourth round (fifth Flames pick, 64th overall) of NHL amateur draft (May 24, 1976). . . . Signed as free agent by Winnipeg Jets of WHA (June 1977). . . . Selected by Flames in NHL reclaim draft (June 9, 1979). . . . Flames franchise moved from Atlanta to Calgary for 1980-81 season. . . . Dislocated shoulder (November 1, 1981). .

.. Fractured left ankle (March 1984).... Traded by Calgary Flames with third-round pick (D Brad Turner) in 1986 draft to Minnesota North Stars for second-round pick (C Joe Nieuwendyk) in 1985 draft and second-round pick (LW Stephane Matteau) in 1987 draft (June 15, 1985).... Injured back and developed viral infection (November 9, 1985); missed nine games. Separated shoulder (January 7, 1986); missed three games.... Pulled groin (March 21, 1986). Bruised ribs (December 15, 1986).... Traded by North Stars to Edmonton Oilers for 1988 draft considerations (March 1987).... Turned down contract offer by Oilers to play in Italy (June 1987).... Announced retirement (March 14, 1995).

HONORS: Named WHA Rookie of the Year by THE SPORTING NEWS (1977-78).... Named WHA Rookie of the Year (1977-78). ... Named WHA's Most Gentlemanly Player (1978-79).

STATISTICAL PLATEAUS: Three-goal games: 1979-80 (1), 1980-81 (3), 1981-82 (1), 1982-83 (5), 1984-85 (3). Total: 13.... Four-goal games: 1981-82 (1).... Total hat tricks: 14.

MISCELLANEOUS: Member of Stanley Cup championship team (1987).

Season Team	League		REGULAR SEASON					PLAYOFFS			
		Gms.	G	A	Pts.	PIM	Gms.	G	A	Pts.	PIM
75-76—Djurgarden Stockholm	Sweden	36	28	26	54	12	—	—	—	—	—
—Swedish national team	Int'l	6	0	0	0	0	—	—	—	—	—
76-77—AIK	Sweden	36	30	18	48	18	—	—	—	—	—
77-78—Winnipeg	WHA	80	42	65	107	8	9	2	8	10	10
78-79—Winnipeg	WHA	78	39	68	107	8	10	3	11	14	4
79-80—Atlanta	NHL	80	40	53	93	10	4	0	0	0	2
80-81—Calgary	NHL	80	49	82	131	26	14	3	9	12	2
81-82—Calgary	NHL	41	26	29	55	8	3	0	3	3	2
82-83—Calgary	NHL	80	46	58	104	10	9	1	11	12	2
83-84—Calgary	NHL	67	31	49	80	22	—	—	—	—	—
84-85—Calgary	NHL	77	37	62	99	14	3	0	1	1	0
85-86—Minnesota	NHL	61	16	44	60	10	5	1	4	5	0
86-87—Minnesota	NHL	44	13	33	46	12	—	—	—	—	—
—Edmonton	NHL	17	5	12	17	4	21	6	13	19	6
94-95—Edmonton	NHL	6	1	0	1	0	—	—	—	—	—
WHA totals		158	81	133	214	16	19	5	19	24	14
NHL totals		553	264	422	686	116	59	11	41	52	14

NOLAN, OWEN
RW, DENVER

PERSONAL: Born February 12, 1972, in Belfast, Northern Ireland.... 6-1/201.... Shoots right. **TRANSACTIONS/CAREER NOTES:** Separated shoulder (February 22, 1990); missed eight games. ... Selected by Quebec Nordiques in first round (first Nordiques pick, first overall) of NHL entry draft (June 16, 1990).... Suffered concussion, sore knee and sore back (October 1990). ... Suspended four off-days by NHL for cross-checking (December 7, 1992).... Bruised hand (March 2, 1993); missed three games.... Suffered shoulder contusion (March 15, 1993); eight games.... Injured right shoulder (October 19, 1993); missed 11 games.... Dislocated left shoulder (November 12, 1993); missed remainder of season.... Bruised shoulder (April 16, 1995); missed two games.... Nordiques franchise moved to Denver for 1995-96 season.

HONORS: Won Emms Family Award (1988-89).... Won Jim Mahon Memorial Trophy (1989-90).... Named to OHL All-Star first team (1989-90).... Played in NHL All-Star Game (1992).

STATISTICAL PLATEAUS: Three-goal games: 1991-92 (2), 1992-93 (2), 1994-95 (3). Total: 7.

Season Team	League		REGULAR SEASON					PLAYOFFS			
		Gms.	G	A	Pts.	PIM	Gms.	G	A	Pts.	PIM
88-89—Cornwall	OHL	62	34	25	59	213	18	5	11	16	41
89-90—Cornwall	OHL	58	51	59	110	240	6	7	5	12	26
90-91—Quebec	NHL	59	3	10	13	109	—	—	—	—	—
—Halifax	AHL	6	4	4	8	11	—	—	—	—	—
91-92—Quebec	NHL	75	42	31	73	183	—	—	—	—	—
92-93—Quebec	NHL	73	36	41	77	185	5	1	0	1	2
93-94—Quebec	NHL	6	2	2	4	8	—	—	—	—	—
94-95—Quebec	NHL	46	30	19	49	46	6	2	3	5	6
NHL totals		259	113	103	216	531	11	3	3	6	8

NOONAN, BRIAN
RW, BLUES

PERSONAL: Born May 29, 1965, in Boston.... 6-1/200.... Shoots right. **HIGH SCHOOL:** Archbishop Williams (Braintree, Mass.). **TRANSACTIONS/CAREER NOTES:** Selected by Chicago Blackhawks in ninth round (10th Blackhawks pick, 179th overall) of NHL entry draft (June 8, 1983).... Separated shoulder (April 3, 1988).... Refused to report to Indianapolis (October 18, 1990); suspended without pay by Blackhawks.... Suffered death in family (February 28, 1991); missed six games.... Damaged left knee ligaments (January 30, 1992); missed 12 games.... Bruised shoulder (October 31, 1992); missed four games.... Suspended one game by NHL for accumulating three game misconduct penalties (January 21, 1993).... Suffered from the flu (February 25, 1993); missed three games.... Traded by Blackhawks with LW Stephane Matteau to New York Rangers for RW Tony Amonte and rights to LW Matt Oates (March 21, 1994).... Sprained right knee (April 2, 1995); missed three games.... Strained groin (May 6, 1995); missed five playoff games.... Signed as free agent by St. Louis Blues (July 11, 1995).

HONORS: Won Ken McKenzie Trophy (1985-86).... Named to IHL All-Star second team (1989-90).... Named to IHL All-Star first team (1990-91).

STATISTICAL PLATEAUS: Three-goal games: 1991-92 (2), 1994-95 (1). Total: 3.... Four-goal games: 1991-92 (1).... Total hat tricks: 4.

MISCELLANEOUS: Member of Stanley Cup championship team (1994).

Season Team	League		REGULAR SEASON					PLAYOFFS			
		Gms.	G	A	Pts.	PIM	Gms.	G	A	Pts.	PIM
82-83—Archbishop Williams H.S..	Mass. H.S.	21	26	17	43	...	—	—	—	—	—
83-84—Archbishop Williams H.S..	Mass. H.S.	17	14	23	37	...	—	—	—	—	—
84-85—New Westminster	WHL	72	50	66	116	76	11	8	7	15	4
85-86—Saginaw	IHL	76	39	39	78	69	11	6	3	9	6

Season	Team	League	Gms.	G	A	Pts.	PIM	Gms.	G	A	Pts.	PIM
	—Nova Scotia	AHL	2	0	0	0	0	—	—	—	—	—
86-87	—Nova Scotia	AHL	70	25	26	51	30	5	3	1	4	4
87-88	—Chicago	NHL	77	10	20	30	44	3	0	0	0	4
88-89	—Chicago	NHL	45	4	12	16	28	1	0	0	0	0
	—Saginaw	IHL	19	18	13	31	36	1	0	0	0	0
89-90	—Chicago	NHL	8	0	2	2	6	—	—	—	—	—
	—Indianapolis	IHL	56	40	36	76	85	14	6	9	15	20
90-91	—Indianapolis	IHL	59	38	53	91	67	7	6	4	10	18
	—Chicago	NHL	7	0	4	4	2	—	—	—	—	—
91-92	—Chicago	NHL	65	19	12	31	81	18	6	9	15	30
92-93	—Chicago	NHL	63	16	14	30	82	4	3	0	3	4
93-94	—Chicago	NHL	64	14	21	35	57	—	—	—	—	—
	—New York Rangers	NHL	12	4	2	6	12	22	4	7	11	17
94-95	—New York Rangers	NHL	45	14	13	27	26	5	0	0	0	8
	NHL totals		386	81	100	181	338	53	13	16	29	63

NORMAN, TODD
LW, CANUCKS

PERSONAL: Born January 29, 1977, in Palmerston, Ont. . . . 5-10/186. . . . Shoots left.
HIGH SCHOOL: Bishop MacDonnell (Guelph, Ont.).
TRANSACTIONS/CAREER NOTES: Selected by Vancouver Canucks in fifth round (fifth Canucks pick, 120th overall) of NHL entry draft (July 8, 1995).

Season	Team	League	Gms.	G	A	Pts.	PIM	Gms.	G	A	Pts.	PIM
92-93	—Stratford	Jr. B	45	5	23	28	18	—	—	—	—	—
93-94	—Guelph	OHL	57	11	12	23	14	9	0	0	0	6
94-95	—Guelph	OHL	64	30	43	73	40	13	3	2	5	4

NORRIS, CLAYTON
RW, FLYERS

PERSONAL: Born March 8, 1972, in Edmonton. . . . 6-2/205. . . . Shoots right.
TRANSACTIONS/CAREER NOTES: Selected by Philadelphia Flyers in sixth round (fifth Flyers pick, 116th overall) of NHL entry draft (June 22, 1991).
HONORS: Named to WHL (East) All-Star second team (1991-92).

Season	Team	League	Gms.	G	A	Pts.	PIM	Gms.	G	A	Pts.	PIM
88-89	—Medicine Hat	WHL	66	4	9	13	122	3	0	0	0	2
89-90	—Medicine Hat	WHL	72	13	18	31	176	3	0	0	0	15
90-91	—Medicine Hat	WHL	71	26	27	53	165	12	5	4	9	41
91-92	—Medicine Hat	WHL	69	26	39	65	300	2	0	0	0	9
92-93	—Medicine Hat	WHL	41	21	16	37	128	10	3	2	5	14
	—Hershey	AHL	4	0	0	0	5	—	—	—	—	—
	—Roanoke	ECHL	4	0	0	0	0	—	—	—	—	—
93-94	—Hershey	AHL	62	8	10	18	217	10	1	0	1	18
94-95	—Hershey	AHL	76	12	21	33	287	4	0	0	0	8

NORRIS, DWAYNE
RW, DENVER

PERSONAL: Born January 8, 1970, in St. John's, Nfld. . . . 5-10/175. . . . Shoots right. . . . Full name: Dwayne Carl Norris.
COLLEGE: Michigan State.
TRANSACTIONS/CAREER NOTES: Selected by Quebec Nordiques in seventh round (fifth Nordiques pick, 127th overall) of NHL entry draft (June 16, 1990). . . . Nordiques franchise moved to Denver for 1995-96 season.
HONORS: Named CCHA Player of the Year (1991-92). . . . Named to NCAA All-America West first team (1991-92). . . . Named to CCHA All-Star first team (1991-92). . . . Named AHL All-Star first team (1994-95).
MISCELLANEOUS: Member of silver-medal-winning Canadian Olympic team (1994).

Season	Team	League	Gms.	G	A	Pts.	PIM	Gms.	G	A	Pts.	PIM
88-89	—Michigan State	CCHA	40	16	21	37	32	—	—	—	—	—
89-90	—Michigan State	CCHA	33	18	25	43	30	—	—	—	—	—
90-91	—Michigan State	CCHA	40	26	25	51	60	—	—	—	—	—
91-92	—Michigan State	CCHA	44	*44	39	83	62	—	—	—	—	—
92-93	—Halifax	AHL	50	25	28	53	62	—	—	—	—	—
93-94	—Canadian national team	Int'l	48	18	14	32	22	—	—	—	—	—
	—Canadian Olympic Team	Int'l	8	2	2	4	4	—	—	—	—	—
	—Quebec	NHL	4	1	1	2	4	—	—	—	—	—
	—Cornwall	AHL	9	2	9	11	0	13	7	4	11	17
94-95	—Cornwall	AHL	60	30	43	73	61	12	7	8	15	4
	—Quebec	NHL	13	1	2	3	2	—	—	—	—	—
	NHL totals		17	2	3	5	6					

NORSTROM, MATTIAS
D, RANGERS

PERSONAL: Born January 2, 1972, in Stockholm, Sweden. . . . 6-1/205. . . . Shoots left. . . . Name pronounced mat-EE-uhz NOHR-struhm.
TRANSACTIONS/CAREER NOTES: Selected by New York Rangers in second round (second Rangers pick, 48th overall) of NHL entry draft (June 20, 1992). . . . Suffered from the flu (April 28, 1995); missed two games.
MISCELLANEOUS: Member of Stanley Cup championship team (1994).

Season	Team	League	REGULAR SEASON Gms.	G	A	Pts.	PIM	PLAYOFFS Gms.	G	A	Pts.	PIM
91-92—AIK Solna		Sweden	39	4	4	8	28	—	—	—	—	—
92-93—AIK Solna		Sweden	22	0	1	1	16	—	—	—	—	—
93-94—New York Rangers		NHL	9	0	2	2	6	—	—	—	—	—
—Binghamton		AHL	55	1	9	10	70	—	—	—	—	—
94-95—Binghamton		AHL	63	9	10	19	91	—	—	—	—	—
—New York Rangers		NHL	9	0	3	3	2	3	0	0	0	0
NHL totals			18	0	5	5	8	3	0	0	0	0

NORTON, JEFF
D, BLUES

PERSONAL: Born November 25, 1965, in Cambridge, Mass. . . . 6-2/200. . . . Shoots left. . . . Full name: Jeffrey Zaccari Norton.
HIGH SCHOOL: Cushing Academy (Ashburnham, Mass.).
COLLEGE: Michigan.
TRANSACTIONS/CAREER NOTES: Selected by New York Islanders in third round (third Islanders pick, 62nd overall) of NHL entry draft (June 9, 1984). . . . Bruised ribs (November 16, 1988). . . . Injured groin (February 1990). . . . Strained groin and abdominal muscles (March 2, 1990); missed games. . . . Suffered concussion (April 9, 1990). . . . Suspended eight games by NHL for intentionally injuring another player in preseason game (September 30, 1990). . . . Dislocated right shoulder (November 3, 1990). . . . Reinjured shoulder (December 27, 1990); missed five games. . . . Reinjured shoulder and underwent surgery (February 23, 1991); missed remainder of season. . . . Suffered concussion (October 26, 1991); missed one game. . . . Tore ligaments in left wrist (January 3, 1992); missed final 42 games of season. . . . Underwent surgery to left wrist (January 8, 1992). . . . Suffered hip flexor (October 23, 1992); missed five games. . . . Suffered sore shoulder (December 31, 1992); missed one game. . . . Pulled groin (February 25, 1993); missed two games. . . . Traded by Islanders to San Jose Sharks for third-round pick (D Jason Strudwick) in 1994 draft (June 20, 1993). . . . Sprained ankle (December 11, 1993); missed nine games. . . . Reinjured ankle (January 4, 1994); missed five games. . . . Sprained ankle (February 19, 1994); missed five games. . . . Suffered from the flu (January 28, 1995); missed one game. . . . Traded by Sharks with fourth-round pick in 1997 draft and future considerations to St. Louis Blues for C Craig Janney (March 6, 1995). . . . Injured hand (March 7, 1995); missed one game.
HONORS: Named to CCHA All-Star second team (1986-87).

Season	Team	League	REGULAR SEASON Gms.	G	A	Pts.	PIM	PLAYOFFS Gms.	G	A	Pts.	PIM
83-84—Cushing Academy		Mass. H.S.	21	22	33	55	. . .	—	—	—	—	—
84-85—University of Michigan		CCHA	37	8	16	24	103	—	—	—	—	—
85-86—University of Michigan		CCHA	37	15	30	45	99	—	—	—	—	—
86-87—University of Michigan		CCHA	39	12	37	49	92	—	—	—	—	—
87-88—U.S. national team		Int'l	57	7	25	32	. . .	—	—	—	—	—
—U.S. Olympic Team		Int'l	6	0	4	4	4	—	—	—	—	—
—New York Islanders		NHL	15	1	6	7	14	3	0	2	2	13
88-89—New York Islanders		NHL	69	1	30	31	74	—	—	—	—	—
89-90—New York Islanders		NHL	60	4	49	53	65	4	1	3	4	17
90-91—New York Islanders		NHL	44	3	25	28	16	—	—	—	—	—
91-92—New York Islanders		NHL	28	1	18	19	18	—	—	—	—	—
92-93—New York Islanders		NHL	66	12	38	50	45	10	1	1	2	4
93-94—San Jose		NHL	64	7	33	40	36	14	1	5	6	20
94-95—San Jose		NHL	20	1	9	10	39	—	—	—	—	—
—St. Louis		NHL	28	2	18	20	33	7	1	1	2	11
NHL totals			394	32	226	258	340	38	4	12	16	65

NUMMINEN, TEPPO
D, JETS

PERSONAL: Born July 3, 1968, in Tampere, Finland. . . . 6-1/190. . . . Shoots right. . . . Full name: Teppo Kalevi Numminen. . . . Name pronounced TEH-poh NOO-mih-nehn.
TRANSACTIONS/CAREER NOTES: Selected by Winnipeg Jets in second round (second Jets pick, 29th overall) of NHL entry draft (June 21, 1986). . . . Separated shoulder (March 5, 1989). . . . Broke thumb (April 14, 1990). . . . Fractured foot (January 28, 1993); missed 17 games. . . . Dislocated thumb (February 9, 1994); missed remainder of season. . . . Played in Europe during 1994-95 NHL lockout. . . . Suffered from stomach flu (January 23, 1995); missed one game. . . . Suffered surface stress fracture in right knee (February 22, 1995); missed five games.
MISCELLANEOUS: Member of silver-medal-winning Finnish Olympic team (1988).

Season	Team	League	REGULAR SEASON Gms.	G	A	Pts.	PIM	PLAYOFFS Gms.	G	A	Pts.	PIM
84-85—Tappara		Finland	30	14	17	31	10	—	—	—	—	—
85-86—Tappara		Finland	39	2	4	6	6	8	0	0	0	0
86-87—Tappara		Finland	44	9	9	18	16	9	4	1	5	4
87-88—Tappara		Finland	44	10	10	20	29	10	6	6	12	6
—Finnish Olympic Team		Int'l	6	1	4	5	0	—	—	—	—	—
88-89—Winnipeg		NHL	69	1	14	15	36	—	—	—	—	—
89-90—Winnipeg		NHL	79	11	32	43	20	7	1	2	3	10
90-91—Winnipeg		NHL	80	8	25	33	28	—	—	—	—	—
91-92—Winnipeg		NHL	80	5	34	39	32	7	0	0	0	0
92-93—Winnipeg		NHL	66	7	30	37	33	6	1	1	2	2
93-94—Winnipeg		NHL	57	5	18	23	28	—	—	—	—	—
94-95—TuTo Turku		Finland	12	3	8	11	4	—	—	—	—	—
—Winnipeg		NHL	42	5	16	21	16	—	—	—	—	—
NHL totals			473	42	169	211	193	20	2	3	5	12

NYLANDER, MICHAEL
C, FLAMES

PERSONAL: Born October 3, 1972, in Stockholm, Sweden. . . . 5-11/190. . . . Shoots left. . . . Name pronounced NEE-lan-duhr.
TRANSACTIONS/CAREER NOTES: Selected by Hartford Whalers in third round (fourth Whalers pick, 59th overall) of NHL entry draft (June 22, 1991). . . . Broke jaw (January 23, 1993); missed 15 games. . . . Traded by Whalers with D Zarley Zalapski and D James Patrick to Calgary Flames for D Gary Suter, LW Paul Ranheim and C Ted Drury (March 10, 1994). . . . Played in Europe during 1994-95 NHL lockout. . . . Broke left wrist and forearm (January 24, 1995); missed 42 games.
HONORS: Named Swedish League Rookie of the Year (1991-92).
STATISTICAL PLATEAUS: Three-goal games: 1992-93 (1).

Season	Team	League	REGULAR SEASON					PLAYOFFS				
			Gms.	G	A	Pts.	PIM	Gms.	G	A	Pts.	PIM
89-90	Huddinge	Sweden	31	7	15	22	4	—	—	—	—	—
90-91	Huddinge	Sweden	33	14	20	34	10	—	—	—	—	—
91-92	AIK Solna	Sweden	40	11	17	28	30	—	—	—	—	—
	Swedish national Jr. team...	Sweden	7	8	9	17	...	—	—	—	—	—
	Swedish national team	Int'l	6	0	1	1	0	—	—	—	—	—
92-93	Hartford	NHL	59	11	22	33	36	—	—	—	—	—
93-94	Hartford	NHL	58	11	33	44	24	—	—	—	—	—
	Springfield	AHL	4	0	9	9	0	—	—	—	—	—
	Calgary	NHL	15	2	9	11	6	3	0	0	0	0
94-95	JyP HT	Finland	16	11	19	30	63	—	—	—	—	—
	Calgary	NHL	6	0	1	1	2	6	0	6	6	2
NHL totals			138	24	65	89	68	9	0	6	6	2

OATES, ADAM
C, BRUINS

PERSONAL: Born August 27, 1962, in Weston, Ont. . . . 5-11/190. . . . Shoots right. . . . Name pronounced OHTZ.
COLLEGE: Rensselaer Polytechnic Institute (N.Y.).
TRANSACTIONS/CAREER NOTES: Signed as free agent by Detroit Red Wings (June 28, 1985). . . . Pulled abdominal muscle (October 1987). . . . Suffered from chicken pox (November 1988). . . . Bruised thigh (December 1988). . . . Traded by Red Wings with RW Paul MacLean to St. Louis Blues for RW Tony McKegney and C Bernie Federko (June 15, 1989). . . . Tore rib and abdominal muscles (November 5, 1990); missed 18 games. . . . Traded by Blues to Boston Bruins for C Craig Janney and D Stephane Quintal (February 7, 1992). . . . Injured groin (January 6, 1994); missed seven games.
HONORS: Named to ECAC All-Star second team (1983-84). . . . Named to NCAA All-America East first team (1984-85). . . . Named to NCAA All-Tournament team (1984-85). . . . Named to ECAC All-Star first team (1984-85). . . . Named to THE SPORTING NEWS All-Star second team (1990-91). . . . Named to NHL All-Star second team (1990-91). . . . Played in NHL All-Star Game (1991-1994).
RECORDS: Holds NHL All-Star Game record for most assists in one period—4 (first period, 1993).
STATISTICAL PLATEAUS: Three-goal games: 1992-93 (3), 1993-94 (2). Total: 5.

Season	Team	League	REGULAR SEASON					PLAYOFFS				
			Gms.	G	A	Pts.	PIM	Gms.	G	A	Pts.	PIM
82-83	R.P.I.	ECAC	22	9	33	42	8	—	—	—	—	—
83-84	R.P.I.	ECAC	38	26	57	83	15	—	—	—	—	—
84-85	R.P.I.	ECAC	38	31	60	91	29	—	—	—	—	—
85-86	Adirondack	AHL	34	18	28	46	4	17	7	14	21	4
	Detroit	NHL	38	9	11	20	10	—	—	—	—	—
86-87	Detroit	NHL	76	15	32	47	21	16	4	7	11	6
87-88	Detroit	NHL	63	14	40	54	20	16	8	12	20	6
88-89	Detroit	NHL	69	16	62	78	14	6	0	8	8	2
89-90	St. Louis	NHL	80	23	79	102	30	12	2	12	14	4
90-91	St. Louis	NHL	61	25	90	115	29	13	7	13	20	10
91-92	St. Louis	NHL	54	10	59	69	12	—	—	—	—	—
	Boston	NHL	26	10	20	30	10	15	5	14	19	4
92-93	Boston	NHL	84	45	*97	142	32	4	0	9	9	4
93-94	Boston	NHL	77	32	80	112	45	13	3	9	12	8
94-95	Boston	NHL	48	12	41	53	8	5	1	0	1	2
NHL totals			676	211	611	822	231	100	30	84	114	46

O'CONNOR, MYLES
D, MIGHTY DUCKS

PERSONAL: Born April 2, 1967, in Calgary. . . . 5-11/190. . . . Shoots left. . . . Full name: Myles Alexander O'Connor.
HIGH SCHOOL: Notre Dame (Sask.).
COLLEGE: Michigan.
TRANSACTIONS/CAREER NOTES: Selected by New Jersey Devils in third round (fourth Devils pick, 45th overall) of NHL entry draft (June 15, 1985). . . . Fractured ankle (February 18, 1991). . . . Signed as free agent by Mighty Ducks of Anaheim (July 22, 1993). . . . Strained groin (October 29, 1993). . . . Suffered from chicken pox (March 8, 1994); missed seven games.
HONORS: Named to NCAA All-America West first team (1988-89). . . . Named to CCHA All-Star first team (1988-89).

Season	Team	League	REGULAR SEASON					PLAYOFFS				
			Gms.	G	A	Pts.	PIM	Gms.	G	A	Pts.	PIM
84-85	Notre Dame H.S.	Sask. H.S.	40	20	35	55	40	—	—	—	—	—
85-86	University of Michigan	CCHA	37	6	19	25	73	—	—	—	—	—
	Canadian national team...	Int'l	8	0	0	0	0	—	—	—	—	—
86-87	University of Michigan	CCHA	39	15	30	45	111	—	—	—	—	—
87-88	University of Michigan	CCHA	40	9	25	34	78	—	—	—	—	—
88-89	University of Michigan	CCHA	40	3	31	34	91	—	—	—	—	—
	Utica	AHL	1	0	0	0	0	—	—	—	—	—

NO

Season	Team	League	REGULAR SEASON					PLAYOFFS				
			Gms.	G	A	Pts.	PIM	Gms.	G	A	Pts.	PIM
89-90—Utica		AHL	76	14	33	47	124	5	1	2	3	26
90-91—New Jersey		NHL	22	3	1	4	41	—	—	—	—	—
—Utica		AHL	33	6	17	23	62	—	—	—	—	—
91-92—Utica		AHL	66	9	39	48	184	—	—	—	—	—
—New Jersey		NHL	9	0	2	2	13	—	—	—	—	—
92-93—Utica		AHL	9	1	5	6	10	—	—	—	—	—
—New Jersey		NHL	7	0	0	0	9	—	—	—	—	—
93-94—Anaheim		NHL	5	0	1	1	6	—	—	—	—	—
—San Diego		IHL	39	1	13	14	117	9	1	4	5	83
94-95—San Diego		IHL	16	1	4	5	50	5	0	1	1	0
NHL totals			43	3	4	7	69					

ODELEIN, LYLE

D, CANADIENS

PERSONAL: Born July 21, 1968, in Quill Lake, Sask. . . . 5-10/206. . . . Shoots right. . . . Name pronounced OH-duh-LIGHN.
TRANSACTIONS/CAREER NOTES: Selected by Montreal Canadiens as underage junior in seventh round (eighth Canadiens pick, 141st overall) of NHL entry draft (June 21, 1986). . . . Bruised right ankle (January 22, 1991); missed five games. . . . Twisted right ankle (February 9, 1991). . . . Suspended one game by NHL for game misconduct penalties (March 1, 1993). . . . Bruised shoulder (January 24, 1994); missed three games.
STATISTICAL PLATEAUS: Three-goal games: 1993-94 (1).
MISCELLANEOUS: Member of Stanley Cup championship team (1993).

Season	Team	League	REGULAR SEASON					PLAYOFFS				
			Gms.	G	A	Pts.	PIM	Gms.	G	A	Pts.	PIM
85-86—Moose Jaw		WHL	67	9	37	46	117	13	1	6	7	34
86-87—Moose Jaw		WHL	59	9	50	59	70	9	2	5	7	26
87-88—Moose Jaw		WHL	63	15	43	58	166	—	—	—	—	—
88-89—Sherbrooke		AHL	33	3	4	7	120	3	0	2	2	5
—Peoria		IHL	36	2	8	10	116	—	—	—	—	—
89-90—Sherbrooke		AHL	68	7	24	31	265	12	6	5	11	79
—Montreal		NHL	8	0	2	2	33	—	—	—	—	—
90-91—Montreal		NHL	52	0	2	2	259	12	0	0	0	54
91-92—Montreal		NHL	71	1	7	8	212	7	0	0	0	11
92-93—Montreal		NHL	83	2	14	16	205	20	1	5	6	30
93-94—Montreal		NHL	79	11	29	40	276	7	0	0	0	17
94-95—Montreal		NHL	48	3	7	10	152	—	—	—	—	—
NHL totals			341	17	61	78	1137	46	1	5	6	112

ODGERS, JEFF

RW, SHARKS

PERSONAL: Born May 31, 1969, in Spy Hill, Sask. . . . 6-0/195. . . . Shoots right. . . . Name pronounced AHD-juhrs.
TRANSACTIONS/CAREER NOTES: Signed as free agent by San Jose Sharks (September 3, 1991). . . . Injured hand (December 21, 1991); missed four games. . . . Broke hand (November 5, 1992); missed 15 games. . . . Suspended one game by NHL for accumulating three game misconduct penalties (January 29, 1993). . . . Suspended two games by NHL for accumulating four game misconduct penalties (February 19, 1993).
MISCELLANEOUS: Captain of San Jose Sharks (1994-95).

Season	Team	League	REGULAR SEASON					PLAYOFFS				
			Gms.	G	A	Pts.	PIM	Gms.	G	A	Pts.	PIM
86-87—Brandon		WHL	70	7	14	21	150	—	—	—	—	—
87-88—Brandon		WHL	70	17	18	35	202	4	1	1	2	14
88-89—Brandon		WHL	71	31	29	60	277	—	—	—	—	—
89-90—Brandon		WHL	64	37	28	65	209	—	—	—	—	—
90-91—Kansas City		IHL	77	12	19	31	*318	—	—	—	—	—
91-92—Kansas City		IHL	12	2	2	4	56	9	3	0	3	13
—San Jose		NHL	61	7	4	11	217	—	—	—	—	—
92-93—San Jose		NHL	66	12	15	27	253	—	—	—	—	—
93-94—San Jose		NHL	81	13	8	21	222	11	0	0	0	11
94-95—San Jose		NHL	48	4	3	7	117	11	1	1	2	23
NHL totals			256	36	30	66	809	22	1	1	2	34

ODJICK, GINO

LW, CANUCKS

PERSONAL: Born September 7, 1970, in Maniwaki, Que. . . . 6-3/210. . . . Shoots left. . . . Name pronounced OH-jihk.
TRANSACTIONS/CAREER NOTES: Suspended five games by QMJHL for attempting to attack another player (May 1, 1989). . . . Suspended one game by QMJHL for fighting (March 19, 1990). . . . Suspended one game by QMJHL for fighting (April 14, 1990). . . . Selected by Vancouver Canucks in fifth round (fifth Canucks pick, 86th overall) of NHL entry draft (June 16, 1990). . . . Broke cheekbone (February 27, 1991). . . . Suspended six games by NHL for stick foul (November 26, 1991). . . . Underwent arthroscopic knee surgery (February 11, 1993); missed five games. . . . Suspended one game by NHL for accumulating three game misconduct penalties (January 27, 1993). . . . Suspended one game by NHL for accumulating four game misconduct penalties (March 26, 1993). . . . Suspended two games by NHL for stick incident (April 8, 1993). . . . Separated shoulder (November 27, 1993); missed two games. . . . Suspended by NHL for 10 games (September 1994); NHL reduced suspension to six games due to abbreviated 1994-95 season (January 19, 1995). . . . Strained groin (March 10, 1995); missed six games. . . . Strained abdomen (April 7, 1995); missed last 13 games of season.

Season	Team	League	Gms.	G	A	Pts.	PIM	Gms.	G	A	Pts.	PIM
88-89—Laval		QMJHL	50	9	15	24	278	16	0	9	9	*129
89-90—Laval		QMJHL	51	12	26	38	280	13	6	5	11	*110
90-91—Milwaukee		IHL	17	7	3	10	102	—	—	—	—	—
—Vancouver		NHL	45	7	1	8	296	6	0	0	0	18
91-92—Vancouver		NHL	65	4	6	10	348	4	0	0	0	6
92-93—Vancouver		NHL	75	4	13	17	370	1	0	0	0	0
93-94—Vancouver		NHL	76	16	13	29	271	10	0	0	0	18
94-95—Vancouver		NHL	23	4	5	9	109	5	0	0	0	47
NHL totals			284	35	38	73	1394	26	0	0	0	89

O'DONNELL, SEAN
D, KINGS

PERSONAL: Born September 13, 1971, in Ottawa.... 6-3/225.... Shoots left.
TRANSACTIONS/CAREER NOTES: Selected by Buffalo Sabres in sixth round (sixth Sabres pick, 123rd overall) of NHL entry draft (June 22, 1991).... Traded by Sabres to Los Angeles Kings for D Doug Houda (July 26, 1994).... Bruised sternum (February 4, 1995); missed two games.

Season	Team	League	Gms.	G	A	Pts.	PIM	Gms.	G	A	Pts.	PIM
90-91—Sudbury		OHL	66	8	23	31	114	5	1	4	5	10
91-92—Rochester		AHL	73	4	9	13	193	16	1	2	3	21
92-93—Rochester		AHL	74	3	18	21	203	17	1	6	7	38
93-94—Rochester		AHL	64	2	10	12	242	4	0	1	1	21
94-95—Phoenix		IHL	61	2	18	20	132	9	0	1	1	21
—Los Angeles		NHL	15	0	2	2	49	—	—	—	—	—
NHL totals			15	0	2	2	49					

O'GRADY, MIKE
D, PANTHERS

PERSONAL: Born March 22, 1977, in Neilburg, Sask.... 6-3/200.... Shoots left.
TRANSACTIONS/CAREER NOTES: Selected by Florida Panthers in third round (third Panthers pick, 62nd overall) of NHL entry draft (July 8, 1995).

Season	Team	League	Gms.	G	A	Pts.	PIM	Gms.	G	A	Pts.	PIM
93-94—Saskatoon		WHL	13	0	1	1	29	—	—	—	—	—
94-95—Saskatoon		WHL	39	0	7	7	157	—	—	—	—	—
—Lethbridge		WHL	21	1	2	3	124	—	—	—	—	—

OHLUND, MATTIAS
D, CANUCKS

PERSONAL: Born September 9, 1976, in Pitea, Sweden.... 6-3/209.... Shoots left.
TRANSACTIONS/CAREER NOTES: Selected by Vancouver Canucks in first round (first Canucks pick, 13th overall) of NHL entry draft (June 28, 1994).

Season	Team	League	Gms.	G	A	Pts.	PIM	Gms.	G	A	Pts.	PIM
92-93—Pitea		Swed. Dv.II	22	0	6	6	16	—	—	—	—	—
93-94—Pitea		Swed. Dv.II	28	7	10	17	62	—	—	—	—	—
94-95—Lulea		Sweden	34	6	10	16	34	9	4	0	4	16

OKSIUTA, ROMAN
RW, CANUCKS

PERSONAL: Born August 21, 1970, in Murmansk, U.S.S.R.... 6-3/229.... Shoots left. ... Name pronounced ohk-see-OO-tuh.
TRANSACTIONS/CAREER NOTES: Selected by New York Rangers in 10th round (11th Rangers pick, 202nd overall) of NHL entry draft (June 17, 1989).... Traded by Rangers with third-round draft pick in 1993 draft (RW Alexander Kerch) to Edmonton Oilers for D Kevin Lowe (December 11, 1992). ... Traded by Oilers to Vancouver Canucks for D Jiri Slegr (April 7, 1995).

Season	Team	League	Gms.	G	A	Pts.	PIM	Gms.	G	A	Pts.	PIM
87-88—Khimik Voskresensk		USSR	11	1	0	1	4	—	—	—	—	—
88-89—Khimik Voskresensk		USSR	34	13	3	16	14	—	—	—	—	—
89-90—Khimik Voskresensk		USSR	37	13	6	19	16	—	—	—	—	—
90-91—Khimik Voskresensk		USSR	41	12	8	20	24	—	—	—	—	—
91-92—Khimik Voskresensk		CIS	42	24	20	*44	28	—	—	—	—	—
92-93—Cape Breton		AHL	43	26	25	51	22	16	9	19	28	12
93-94—Edmonton		NHL	10	1	2	3	4	—	—	—	—	—
—Cape Breton		AHL	47	31	22	53	90	4	2	2	4	22
94-95—Cape Breton		AHL	25	9	7	16	20	—	—	—	—	—
—Edmonton		NHL	26	11	2	13	8	—	—	—	—	—
—Vancouver		NHL	12	5	2	7	2	10	2	3	5	0
NHL totals			48	17	6	23	14	10	2	3	5	0

OKTYABREV, ARTUR
D, CANUCKS

PERSONAL: Born November 26, 1973, in Irkutsk, U.S.S.R.... 5-11/183.... Shoots left.
TRANSACTIONS/CAREER NOTES: Selected by Winnipeg Jets in sixth round (sixth Jets pick, 155th overall) of NHL entry draft (June 20, 1992).... Traded by Jets to Vancouver Canucks for sixth-round pick (G Steve Vezina) in 1994 NHL entry draft (June 29, 1994).

O

Season Team	League	REGULAR SEASON					PLAYOFFS				
		Gms.	G	A	Pts.	PIM	Gms.	G	A	Pts.	PIM
91-92—CSKA Moscow	CIS	38	1	2	3	19	—	—	—	—	—
92-93—CSKA Moscow	CIS	41	0	5	5	44	—	—	—	—	—
93-94—CSKA Moscow	CIS	45	1	1	2	46	3	0	0	0	4
—Russian Penguins	IHL	10	0	2	2	12	—	—	—	—	—
94-95—CSKA Moscow	CIS	46	1	3	4	36	—	—	—	—	—
—Syracuse	AHL	7	1	1	2	2	—	—	—	—	—

OLAUSSON, FREDRIK
D, OILERS

PERSONAL: Born October 5, 1966, in Vaxsjo, Sweden. . . . 6-2/195. . . . Shoots right. . . . Name pronounced OHL-uh-suhn.

TRANSACTIONS/CAREER NOTES: Selected by Winnipeg Jets in fourth round (fourth Jets pick, 81st overall) of NHL entry draft (June 15, 1985). . . . Dislocated shoulder (August 1987). . . . Underwent shoulder surgery (November 1987). . . . Signed five-year contract with Farjestad, Sweden (June 19, 1989); Farjestad agreed to allow Olausson to remain in Winnipeg. . . . Sprained knee (January 22, 1993); missed 11 games. . . . Lacerated ankle (November 8, 1993); missed two games. . . . Suffered from the flu (January 18, 1993); missed one game. . . . Sprained knee (January 23, 1993); missed 11 games. . . . Suffered from the flu (March 4, 1993); missed one game. . . . Traded by Jets with seventh-round pick in 1994 draft (LW Curtis Sheptak) to Edmonton Oilers for third-round pick (C Tavis Hansen) in 1994 draft (December 5, 1993). . . . Strained knee (January 11, 1994). . . . Played in Europe during 1994-95 NHL lockout. . . . Suffered from the flu (February 17, 1995); missed one game. . . . Suffered colitis (March 3, 1995); missed 10 games.

HONORS: Named to Swedish League All-Star team (1985-86).

Season Team	League	REGULAR SEASON					PLAYOFFS				
		Gms.	G	A	Pts.	PIM	Gms.	G	A	Pts.	PIM
83-84—Nybro	Sweden	28	8	14	22	32	—	—	—	—	—
84-85—Farjestad Karlstad	Sweden	34	6	12	18	24	3	1	0	1	0
85-86—Farjestad Karlstad	Sweden	33	5	12	17	14	8	3	2	5	6
86-87—Winnipeg	NHL	72	7	29	36	24	10	2	3	5	4
87-88—Winnipeg	NHL	38	5	10	15	18	5	1	1	2	0
88-89—Winnipeg	NHL	75	15	47	62	32	—	—	—	—	—
89-90—Winnipeg	NHL	77	9	46	55	32	7	0	2	2	2
90-91—Winnipeg	NHL	71	12	29	41	24	—	—	—	—	—
91-92—Winnipeg	NHL	77	20	42	62	34	7	1	5	6	4
92-93—Winnipeg	NHL	68	16	41	57	22	6	0	2	2	2
93-94—Winnipeg	NHL	18	2	5	7	10	—	—	—	—	—
—Edmonton	NHL	55	9	19	28	20	—	—	—	—	—
94-95—Ehrwald	Austria	10	4	3	7	8	—	—	—	—	—
—Edmonton	NHL	33	0	10	10	20	—	—	—	—	—
NHL totals		584	95	278	373	236	35	4	13	17	12

OLCZYK, EDDIE
C, JETS

PERSONAL: Born August 16, 1966, in Chicago. . . . 6-1/205. . . . Shoots left. . . . Name pronounced OHL-chehk.

TRANSACTIONS/CAREER NOTES: Selected by Chicago Blackhawks in first round (first Blackhawks pick, third overall) of NHL entry draft (June 9, 1984). . . . Hyperextended knee (September 3, 1984). . . . Broke bone in left foot (December 16, 1984). . . . Traded by Blackhawks with LW Al Secord to Toronto Maple Leafs for RW Rick Vaive, LW Steve Thomas and D Bob McGill (September 1987). . . . Pinched nerve in left knee (January 3, 1990). . . . Traded by Maple Leafs with LW Mark Osborne to Winnipeg Jets for D Dave Ellett and LW Paul Fenton (November 10, 1990). . . . Dislocated elbow and sprained ankle (January 8, 1992); missed 15 games. . . . Sprained knee (November 24, 1992); missed nine games. . . . Traded by Jets to New York Rangers for LW Kris King and RW Tie Domi (December 28, 1992). . . . Fractured right thumb (January 31, 1994); missed 24 games. . . . Suffered from kidney stones (January 24, 1995); missed six games. . . . Suffered back spasms (March 3, 1995); missed three games. . . . Traded by Rangers to Jets for fifth-round pick (D Alexei Vasiliev) in 1995 draft (April 7, 1995).

STATISTICAL PLATEAUS: Three-goal games: 1988-89 (1), 1989-90 (1), 1992-93 (1). Total: 3.

MISCELLANEOUS: Member of Stanley Cup championship team (1994).

Season Team	League	REGULAR SEASON					PLAYOFFS				
		Gms.	G	A	Pts.	PIM	Gms.	G	A	Pts.	PIM
83-84—U.S. national team	Int'l	56	19	40	59	36	—	—	—	—	—
—U.S. Olympic Team	Int'l	6	2	6	8	0	—	—	—	—	—
84-85—Chicago	NHL	70	20	30	50	67	15	6	5	11	11
85-86—Chicago	NHL	79	29	50	79	47	3	0	0	0	0
86-87—Chicago	NHL	79	16	35	51	119	4	1	1	2	4
87-88—Toronto	NHL	80	42	33	75	55	6	5	4	9	2
88-89—Toronto	NHL	80	38	52	90	75	—	—	—	—	—
89-90—Toronto	NHL	79	32	56	88	78	5	1	2	3	14
90-91—Toronto	NHL	18	4	10	14	13	—	—	—	—	—
—Winnipeg	NHL	61	26	31	57	69	—	—	—	—	—
91-92—Winnipeg	NHL	64	32	33	65	67	6	2	1	3	4
92-93—Winnipeg	NHL	25	8	12	20	26	—	—	—	—	—
—New York Rangers	NHL	46	13	16	29	26	—	—	—	—	—
93-94—New York Rangers	NHL	37	3	5	8	28	1	0	0	0	0
94-95—New York Rangers	NHL	20	2	1	3	4	—	—	—	—	—
—Winnipeg	NHL	13	2	8	10	8	—	—	—	—	—
NHL totals		751	267	372	639	682	40	15	13	28	35

OLIMPIYEV, SERGEI
LW, RANGERS

PERSONAL: Born January 12, 1975, in Minsk, U.S.S.R. . . . 5-10/172. . . . Shoots left. . . . Name pronounced SAIR-gay oh-LIHM-pee-YEHF.
TRANSACTIONS/CAREER NOTES: Selected by New York Rangers in fourth round (fourth Rangers pick, 86th overall) of NHL entry draft (June 26, 1993).

Season Team	League	REGULAR SEASON					PLAYOFFS				
		Gms.	G	A	Pts.	PIM	Gms.	G	A	Pts.	PIM
91-92—Traktor Lipetsk	CIS Div. III	20	0	0	0	2	—	—	—	—	—
92-93—Dynamo Minsk	CIS	6	1	0	1	2	—	—	—	—	—
93-94—Ottawa	OHL	20	3	5	8	4	—	—	—	—	—
—Kitchener	OHL	21	6	5	11	24	5	0	0	0	0
94-95—Kitchener	OHL	25	4	9	13	27	—	—	—	—	—

OLIVER, DAVID
RW, OILERS

PERSONAL: Born April 17, 1971, in Sechelt, B.C. . . . 5-11/185. . . . Shoots right.
COLLEGE: Michigan.
TRANSACTIONS/CAREER NOTES: Selected by Edmonton Oilers in seventh round (seventh Oilers pick, 144th overall) of NHL entry draft (June 22, 1991).
HONORS: Named to CCHA All-Star second team (1992-93). . . . Named CCHA Player of the Year (1993-94). . . . Named to NCAA All-America West first team (1993-94).
STATISTICAL PLATEAUS: Three-goal games: 1994-95 (1).

Season Team	League	REGULAR SEASON					PLAYOFFS				
		Gms.	G	A	Pts.	PIM	Gms.	G	A	Pts.	PIM
90-91—University of Michigan	CCHA	27	13	11	24	34	—	—	—	—	—
91-92—University of Michigan	CCHA	44	31	27	58	32	—	—	—	—	—
92-93—University of Michigan	CCHA	40	35	20	55	18	—	—	—	—	—
93-94—University of Michigan	CCHA	41	28	40	68	16	—	—	—	—	—
94-95—Cape Breton	AHL	32	11	18	29	8	—	—	—	—	—
—Edmonton	NHL	44	16	14	30	20	—	—	—	—	—
NHL totals		44	16	14	30	20					

OLIWA, KRZYSZTOF
LW, DEVILS

PERSONAL: Born April 12, 1973, in Tychy, Poland. . . . 6-5/220. . . . Shoots left. . . . Name pronounced KHRIH-stahf oh-LEE-vuh.
TRANSACTIONS/CAREER NOTES: Selected by New Jersey Devils in third round (fourth Devils pick, 65th overall) of NHL entry draft (June 26, 1993). . . . Loaned by Devils to Detroit Vipers of IHL (January 31, 1995). . . . Returned by Vipers to Albany (February 9, 1995). . . . Loaned by Devils to Saint John of AHL (February 17, 1995).

Season Team	League	REGULAR SEASON					PLAYOFFS				
		Gms.	G	A	Pts.	PIM	Gms.	G	A	Pts.	PIM
90-91—GKS Katowice	Poland Jrs.	5	4	4	8	10	—	—	—	—	—
91-92—GKS Tychy	Poland	10	3	7	10	6	—	—	—	—	—
92-93—Welland Jr. B	OHA	30	13	21	34	127	—	—	—	—	—
93-94—Albany	AHL	33	2	4	6	151	—	—	—	—	—
—Raleigh	ECHL	15	0	2	2	65	9	0	0	0	35
94-95—Albany	AHL	20	1	1	2	77	—	—	—	—	—
—Detroit	IHL	4	0	1	1	24	—	—	—	—	—
—Saint John	AHL	14	1	4	5	79	—	—	—	—	—
—Raleigh	ECHL	5	0	2	2	32	—	—	—	—	—

OLSON, BOYD
C, CANADIENS

PERSONAL: Born April 4, 1976, in Edmonton. . . . 6-1/170. . . . Shoots left.
TRANSACTIONS/CAREER NOTES: Selected by Montreal Canadiens in sixth round (sixth Canadiens pick, 138th overall) of NHL entry draft (July 8, 1995).

Season Team	League	REGULAR SEASON					PLAYOFFS				
		Gms.	G	A	Pts.	PIM	Gms.	G	A	Pts.	PIM
93-94—Tri-City	WHL	2	0	1	1	0	—	—	—	—	—
94-95—Tri-City	WHL	69	16	16	32	87	17	6	2	8	22

O'NEILL, JEFF
C, WHALERS

PERSONAL: Born February 23, 1976, in Richmond Hill, Ont. . . . 6-0/176. . . . Shoots right.
HIGH SCHOOL: Bishop MacDonnell (Guelph, Ont.).
TRANSACTIONS/CAREER NOTES: Selected by Hartford Whalers in first round (first Whalers pick, fifth overall) of NHL entry draft (June 28, 1994).
HONORS: Won Emms Family Award (1992-93). . . . Named to Can.HL All-Rookie team (1992-93). . . . Named to OHL All-Rookie team (1992-93). . . . Won Can.HL Top Draft Prospect Award (1993-94). . . . Named to Can.HL All-Star second team (1994-95). . . . Named to OHL All-Star first team (1994-95).

Season Team	League	REGULAR SEASON					PLAYOFFS				
		Gms.	G	A	Pts.	PIM	Gms.	G	A	Pts.	PIM
91-92—Thornhill	Tier II Jr. A	43	27	53	80	48	—	—	—	—	—
92-93—Guelph	OHL	65	32	47	79	88	5	2	2	4	6
93-94—Guelph	OHL	66	45	81	126	95	9	2	11	13	31
94-95—Guelph	OHL	57	43	81	124	56	14	8	18	26	34

O'NEILL, MIKE
G, MIGHTY DUCKS

PERSONAL: Born November 3, 1967, in Montreal. . . . 5-7/160. . . . Catches left. . . . Full name: Michael Anthony O'Neill Jr.
COLLEGE: Yale.
TRANSACTIONS/CAREER NOTES: Selected by Winnipeg Jets in NHL supplemental draft (June 10,

1988). . . . Dislocated shoulder (April 8, 1991); missed remainder of playoffs. . . . Dislocated shoulder (February 1, 1993); missed two games. . . . Underwent shoulder surgery (February 12, 1993); missed remainder of season. . . . Injured knee (March 16, 1994); missed one game. . . . Signed as free agent by Mighty Ducks of Anaheim (July 28, 1995).

HONORS: Named to ECAC All-Star first team (1986-87 and 1988-89). . . . Named to NCAA All-America East first team (1988-89).

Season Team	League	REGULAR SEASON							PLAYOFFS					
		Gms.	Min.	W	L	T	GA	SO	Avg.	Gms.	Min.	W	L	GA	SO	Avg.
85-86—Yale University	ECAC	6	389	3	1	0	17	0	2.62	—	—	—	—	—	—	—
86-87—Yale University	ECAC	16	964	9	6	1	55	2	3.42	—	—	—	—	—	—	—
87-88—Yale University	ECAC	24	1385	6	17	0	101	0	4.38	—	—	—	—	—	—	—
88-89—Yale University	ECAC	25	1490	10	14	1	93	0	3.74	—	—	—	—	—	—	—
89-90—Tappara	Finland	41	2369	23	13	5	127	2	3.22	—	—	—	—	—	—	—
90-91—Fort Wayne	IHL	8	490	5	2	‡1	31	0	3.80	—	—	—	—	—	—	—
—Moncton	AHL	30	1613	13	7	6	84	0	3.12	8	435	3	4	29	0	4.00
91-92—Fort Wayne	IHL	33	1858	22	6	‡3	97	†4	3.13	—	—	—	—	—	—	—
—Moncton	AHL	32	1902	14	16	2	108	1	3.41	11	670	4	†7	43	1	3.85
—Winnipeg	NHL	1	13	0	0	0	1	0	4.62	—	—	—	—	—	—	—
92-93—Moncton	AHL	30	1649	13	10	4	88	1	3.20	—	—	—	—	—	—	—
—Winnipeg	NHL	2	73	0	0	1	6	0	4.93	—	—	—	—	—	—	—
93-94—Moncton	AHL	12	717	8	4	0	33	1	2.76	—	—	—	—	—	—	—
—Fort Wayne	IHL	11	642	4	4	‡3	38	0	3.55	—	—	—	—	—	—	—
—Winnipeg	NHL	17	738	0	9	1	51	0	4.15	—	—	—	—	—	—	—
94-95—Fort Wayne	IHL	28	1603	11	12	‡4	109	0	4.08	—	—	—	—	—	—	—
—Phoenix	IHL	21	1257	13	4	‡4	64	1	3.05	9	536	4	5	33	0	3.69
NHL totals		20	824	0	9	2	58	0	4.22							

ORSAGH, VLADIMIR
LW, ISLANDERS

PERSONAL: Born May 24, 1977, in Banska Bystrica, Czechoslovakia. . . . 5-10/172. . . . Shoots left.

TRANSACTIONS/CAREER NOTES: Selected by New York Islanders in fifth round (fourth Islanders pick, 106th overall) of NHL entry draft (July 8, 1995).

Season Team	League	REGULAR SEASON					PLAYOFFS				
		Gms.	G	A	Pts.	PIM	Gms.	G	A	Pts.	PIM
93-94—IS Banska Bystrica Jrs.	Slovakia	. . .	38	27	65	. . .	—	—	—	—	—
94-95—IS Banska Bystrica	Slovak Div. II	38	18	12	30	. . .	—	—	—	—	—
—Martimex ZTS Martin	Slovakia	1	0	0	0	0	—	—	—	—	—

OSADCHY, ALEXANDER
D, SHARKS

PERSONAL: Born July 19, 1975, in Kharkov, U.S.S.R. . . . 5-11/190. . . . Shoots right.

TRANSACTIONS/CAREER NOTES: Selected by San Jose Sharks in fourth round (fifth Sharks pick, 80th overall) of NHL entry draft (June 26, 1993).

Season Team	League	REGULAR SEASON					PLAYOFFS				
		Gms.	G	A	Pts.	PIM	Gms.	G	A	Pts.	PIM
92-93—CSKA Moscow	CIS	37	0	1	1	60	—	—	—	—	—
93-94—CSKA Moscow	CIS	46	5	2	7	33	3	0	0	0	0
—Russian Penguins	IHL	11	0	5	5	24	—	—	—	—	—
94-95—CSKA Moscow	CIS	52	8	4	12	100	2	0	0	0	0

OSBORNE, MARK
LW, RANGERS

PERSONAL: Born August 13, 1961, in Toronto. . . . 6-2/200. . . . Shoots left. . . . Full name: Mark Anatole Osborne.

TRANSACTIONS/CAREER NOTES: Selected by Detroit Red Wings as underage junior in third round (second Red Wings pick, 46th overall) of NHL entry draft (June 11, 1980). . . . Traded by Red Wings with D Willie Huber and RW Mike Blaisdell to New York Rangers for RW Ron Duguay, G Eddie Mio and RW Ed Johnstone (June 13, 1983). . . . Injured hip (October 1984). . . . Sprained ankle (February 12, 1986); missed 12 games. . . . Suffered laceration behind left knee (February 1987). . . . Traded by Rangers to Toronto Maple Leafs for third-round pick (C Rob Zamuner) in 1989 draft (March 5, 1987). . . . Separated left shoulder (April 1988). . . . Traded by Maple Leafs with C/RW Ed Olczyk to Winnipeg Jets for D Dave Ellett and C Paul Fenton (November 10, 1990). . . . Fractured left thumb and injured ligaments (December 3, 1990); missed 21 games. . . . Separated shoulder (October 29, 1991); missed three games. . . . Fractured ankle (January 1992); missed 14 games. . . . Traded by Jets to Maple Leafs for RW Lucien Deblois (March 10, 1992). . . . Sprained knee (March 28, 1993); missed seven games. . . . Strained rib muscle (November 24, 1993); missed eight games. . . . Signed as free agent by Rangers (September 6, 1994). . . . Suffered from the flu (February 4, 1995); missed one game. . . . Suffered from the flu (March 18, 1995); missed one game.

STATISTICAL PLATEAUS: Three-goal games: 1981-82 (1).

Season Team	League	REGULAR SEASON					PLAYOFFS				
		Gms.	G	A	Pts.	PIM	Gms.	G	A	Pts.	PIM
78-79—Niagara Falls	OMJHL	62	17	25	42	53	—	—	—	—	—
79-80—Niagara Falls	OMJHL	52	10	33	43	104	10	2	1	3	23
80-81—Niagara Falls	OMJHL	54	39	41	80	140	12	11	10	21	20
—Adirondack	AHL	—	—	—	—	—	13	2	3	5	2
81-82—Detroit	NHL	80	26	41	67	61	—	—	—	—	—
82-83—Detroit	NHL	80	19	24	43	83	—	—	—	—	—
83-84—New York Rangers	NHL	73	23	28	51	88	5	0	1	1	7
84-85—New York Rangers	NHL	23	4	4	8	33	3	0	0	0	4
85-86—New York Rangers	NHL	62	16	24	40	80	15	2	3	5	26

Season Team	League	Gms.	G	A	Pts.	PIM	Gms.	G	A	Pts.	PIM
		REGULAR SEASON					PLAYOFFS				
86-87—New York Rangers	NHL	58	17	15	32	101	—	—	—	—	—
—Toronto	NHL	16	5	10	15	12	9	1	3	4	6
87-88—Toronto	NHL	79	23	37	60	102	6	1	3	4	16
88-89—Toronto	NHL	75	16	30	46	112	—	—	—	—	—
89-90—Toronto	NHL	78	23	50	73	91	5	2	3	5	12
90-91—Toronto	NHL	18	3	3	6	4	—	—	—	—	—
—Winnipeg	NHL	37	8	8	16	59	—	—	—	—	—
91-92—Winnipeg	NHL	43	4	12	16	65	—	—	—	—	—
—Toronto	NHL	11	3	1	4	8	—	—	—	—	—
92-93—Toronto	NHL	76	12	14	26	89	19	1	1	2	16
93-94—Toronto	NHL	73	9	15	24	145	18	4	2	6	52
94-95—New York Rangers	NHL	37	1	3	4	19	7	1	0	1	2
NHL totals		919	212	319	531	1152	87	12	16	28	141

OSGOOD, CHRIS
G, RED WINGS

PERSONAL: Born November 26, 1972, in Peace River, Alta. . . . 5-10/160. . . . Catches left.
TRANSACTIONS/CAREER NOTES: Selected by Detroit Red Wings in third round (third Red Wings pick, 54th overall) of NHL entry draft (June 22, 1991).
HONORS: Named to WHL (East) All-Star second team (1990-91).

Season Team	League	Gms.	Min.	W	L	T	GA	SO	Avg.	Gms.	Min.	W	L	GA	SO	Avg.
		REGULAR SEASON								PLAYOFFS						
89-90—Medicine Hat	WHL	57	3094	24	28	2	228	0	4.42	3	173	3	4	17	0	5.90
90-91—Medicine Hat	WHL	46	2630	23	18	3	173	2	3.95	12	714	7	5	42	0	3.53
91-92—Medicine Hat	WHL	15	819	10	3	0	44	0	3.22	—	—	—	—	—	—	—
—Brandon	WHL	16	890	3	10	1	60	1	4.04	—	—	—	—	—	—	—
—Seattle	WHL	21	1217	12	7	1	65	1	3.20	15	904	9	6	51	0	3.38
92-93—Adirondack	AHL	45	2438	19	19	2	159	0	3.91	1	59	0	1	2	0	2.03
93-94—Adirondack	AHL	4	240	3	1	0	13	0	3.25	—	—	—	—	—	—	—
—Detroit	NHL	41	2206	23	8	5	105	2	2.86	6	307	3	2	12	1	2.35
94-95—Adirondack	AHL	2	120	1	1	0	6	0	3.00	—	—	—	—	—	—	—
—Detroit	NHL	19	1087	14	5	0	41	1	2.26	2	68	0	0	2	0	1.76
NHL totals		60	1110	22	10	105	146	3	7.89	8	375	3	2	14	1	2.24

O'SULLIVAN, CHRIS
D, FLAMES

PERSONAL: Born May 15, 1974, in Dorchester, Mass. . . . 6-2/180. . . . Shoots left.
HIGH SCHOOL: Catholic Memorial (Boston).
COLLEGE: Boston University.
TRANSACTIONS/CAREER NOTES: Selected by Calgary Flames in second round (second Flames pick, 30th overall) of NHL entry draft (June 20, 1992).
HONORS: Named to NCAA All-America second team (1994-95).

Season Team	League	Gms.	G	A	Pts.	PIM	Gms.	G	A	Pts.	PIM
		REGULAR SEASON					PLAYOFFS				
91-92—Catholic Memorial H.S.	Mass. H.S.	26	26	23	49	65	—	—	—	—	—
92-93—Boston University	Hockey East	5	0	2	2	4	—	—	—	—	—
93-94—Boston University	Hockey East	32	5	18	23	25	—	—	—	—	—
94-95—Boston University	Hockey East	40	23	33	56	48	—	—	—	—	—

OTTO, JOEL
C, FLYERS

PERSONAL: Born October 29, 1961, in Elk River, Minn. . . . 6-4/220. . . . Shoots right. . . . Full name: Joel Stuart Otto.
COLLEGE: Bemidji (Minn.) State.
TRANSACTIONS/CAREER NOTES: Signed as free agent by Calgary Flames (September 11, 1984). . . . Tore cartilage in right knee (March 10, 1987). . . . Strained right knee ligaments (October 8, 1987). . . . Bruised ribs (November 1989). . . . Hospitalized after being crosschecked from behind (January 13, 1990). . . . Injured ankle (March 10, 1992); missed two games. . . . Suffered rib injury (January 5, 1993); missed eight games. . . . Bruised foot (February 2, 1993); missed one game. . . . Signed as free agent by Philadelphia Flyers (July 20, 1995).
STATISTICAL PLATEAUS: Three-goal games: 1986-87 (1), 1993-94 (1). Total: 2.
MISCELLANEOUS: Member of Stanley Cup championship team (1989).

Season Team	League	Gms.	G	A	Pts.	PIM	Gms.	G	A	Pts.	PIM
		REGULAR SEASON					PLAYOFFS				
80-81—Bemidji State	NCAA-II	23	5	11	16	10	—	—	—	—	—
81-82—Bemidji State	NCAA-II	31	19	33	52	24	—	—	—	—	—
82-83—Bemidji State	NCAA-II	37	33	28	61	68	—	—	—	—	—
83-84—Bemidji State	NCAA-II	31	32	43	75	32	—	—	—	—	—
84-85—Moncton	AHL	56	27	36	63	89	—	—	—	—	—
—Calgary	NHL	17	4	8	12	30	3	2	1	3	10
85-86—Calgary	NHL	79	25	34	59	188	22	5	10	15	80
86-87—Calgary	NHL	68	19	31	50	185	2	0	2	2	6
87-88—Calgary	NHL	62	13	39	52	194	9	3	2	5	26
88-89—Calgary	NHL	72	23	30	53	213	22	6	13	19	46
89-90—Calgary	NHL	75	13	20	33	116	6	2	2	4	2
90-91—Calgary	NHL	76	19	20	39	183	7	1	2	3	8
91-92—Calgary	NHL	78	13	21	34	161	—	—	—	—	—
92-93—Calgary	NHL	75	19	33	52	150	6	4	2	6	4

Season Team	League	REGULAR SEASON					PLAYOFFS				
		Gms.	G	A	Pts.	PIM	Gms.	G	A	Pts.	PIM
93-94—Calgary	NHL	81	11	12	23	92	3	0	1	1	4
94-95—Calgary	NHL	47	8	13	21	130	7	0	3	3	2
NHL totals		730	167	261	428	1642	87	23	38	61	188

OZOLINSH, SANDIS
D, SHARKS

PERSONAL: Born August 3, 1972, in Riga, U.S.S.R. . . . 6-3/205. . . . Shoots left. . . . Name pronounced SAN-dihz OH-zoh-LIHNCH.
TRANSACTIONS/CAREER NOTES: Selected by San Jose Sharks in second round (third Sharks pick, 30th overall) of NHL entry draft (June 22, 1991). . . . Strained back (November 7, 1992); missed one game. . . . Tore knee ligaments (December 30, 1992) and underwent surgery to repair anterior cruciate ligament; missed remainder of season. . . . Injured knee (December 11, 1993); missed one game.
HONORS: Played in NHL All-Star Game (1994).

Season Team	League	REGULAR SEASON					PLAYOFFS				
		Gms.	G	A	Pts.	PIM	Gms.	G	A	Pts.	PIM
90-91—Dynamo Riga	USSR	44	0	3	3	49	—	—	—	—	—
91-92—HC Riga	CIS	30	5	0	5	42	—	—	—	—	—
—Kansas City	IHL	34	6	9	15	20	15	2	5	7	22
92-93—San Jose	NHL	37	7	16	23	40	—	—	—	—	—
93-94—San Jose	NHL	81	26	38	64	24	14	0	10	10	8
94-95—San Jose	NHL	48	9	16	25	30	11	3	2	5	6
NHL totals		166	42	70	112	94	25	3	12	15	14

PADEN, KEVIN
C/LW, OILERS

PERSONAL: Born February 12, 1975, in Woodhaven, Mich. . . . 6-3/175. . . . Shoots left. . . . Name pronounced PAY-dehn.
TRANSACTIONS/CAREER NOTES: Selected by Edmonton Oilers in third round (fourth Oilers pick, 59th overall) of NHL entry draft (June 26, 1993).

Season Team	League	REGULAR SEASON					PLAYOFFS				
		Gms.	G	A	Pts.	PIM	Gms.	G	A	Pts.	PIM
92-93—Detroit	OHL	54	14	9	23	41	15	1	1	2	2
93-94—Detroit	OHL	38	10	19	29	54	—	—	—	—	—
—Windsor	OHL	24	0	11	11	30	4	0	1	1	4
94-95—Windsor	OHL	57	15	24	39	50	—	—	—	—	—

PAEK, JIM
D, SENATORS

PERSONAL: Born April 7, 1967, in Seoul, South Korea. . . . 6-1/200. . . . Shoots left. . . . Name pronounced PAK.
TRANSACTIONS/CAREER NOTES: Selected by Pittsburgh Penguins as underage junior in ninth round (ninth Penguins pick, 170th overall) of NHL entry draft (June 15, 1985). . . . Suspended two games by OHL for being involved in bench-clearing incident (November 2, 1986). . . . Dislocated finger on left hand (January 10, 1992); missed 14 games. . . . Suspended three off-days and fined $500 by NHL for fighting (February 26, 1993). . . . Injured eye (September 26, 1993); missed 13 games. . . . Traded by Penguins to Los Angeles Kings for RW Tomas Sandstrom and C Shawn McEachern (February 15, 1994). . . . Traded by Kings to Ottawa Senators for future considerations (June 25, 1994).
MISCELLANEOUS: Member of Stanley Cup championship teams (1991 and 1992).

Season Team	League	REGULAR SEASON					PLAYOFFS				
		Gms.	G	A	Pts.	PIM	Gms.	G	A	Pts.	PIM
84-85—Oshawa	OHL	54	2	13	15	57	5	1	0	1	9
85-86—Oshawa	OHL	64	5	21	26	122	6	0	1	1	9
86-87—Oshawa	OHL	57	5	17	22	75	26	1	14	15	43
87-88—Muskegon	IHL	82	7	52	59	141	6	0	0	0	29
88-89—Muskegon	IHL	80	3	54	57	96	14	1	10	11	24
89-90—Muskegon	IHL	81	9	41	50	115	15	1	10	11	41
90-91—Canadian national team	Int'l	48	2	12	14	24	—	—	—	—	—
—Pittsburgh	NHL	3	0	0	0	9	8	1	0	1	2
91-92—Pittsburgh	NHL	49	1	7	8	36	19	0	4	4	6
92-93—Pittsburgh	NHL	77	3	15	18	64	—	—	—	—	—
93-94—Pittsburgh	NHL	41	0	4	4	8	—	—	—	—	—
—Los Angeles	NHL	18	1	1	2	10	—	—	—	—	—
94-95—Ottawa	NHL	29	0	2	2	28	—	—	—	—	—
NHL totals		217	5	29	34	155	27	1	4	5	8

PALFFY, ZIGMUND
RW, ISLANDERS

PERSONAL: Born May 5, 1972, in Skalica, Czechoslovakia. . . . 5-10/169. . . . Shoots left. . . . Name pronounced PAHL-fee.
TRANSACTIONS/CAREER NOTES: Selected by New York Islanders in second round (second Islanders pick, 26th overall) of NHL entry draft (June 22, 1991). . . . Loaned to Slovak Olympic Team (January 31, 1994).
HONORS: Named Czechoslovakian League Rookie of the Year (1990-91). . . . Named to Czechoslovakian League All-Star team (1991-92).

Season Team	League	REGULAR SEASON					PLAYOFFS				
		Gms.	G	A	Pts.	PIM	Gms.	G	A	Pts.	PIM
90-91—Nitra	Czech.	50	34	16	50	18	—	—	—	—	—
91-92—Dukla Trencin	Czech.	32	23	25	*48	. . .	—	—	—	—	—

OP

Season	Team	League	REGULAR SEASON					PLAYOFFS				
			Gms.	G	A	Pts.	PIM	Gms.	G	A	Pts.	PIM
92-93—Dukla Trencin	Czech.	43	38	41	79	...	—	—	—	—	—
93-94—Salt Lake City..................	IHL	57	25	32	57	83	—	—	—	—	—
—Slovakian Olympic team...	Int'l	8	3	7	10	8	—	—	—	—	—
—New York Islanders..........	NHL	5	0	0	0	0	—	—	—	—	—
94-95—Denver	IHL	33	20	23	43	40	—	—	—	—	—
—New York Islanders..........	NHL	33	10	7	17	6	—	—	—	—	—
NHL totals................		38	10	7	17	6	—	—	—	—	—

PANDOLFO, JAY
LW, DEVILS

PERSONAL: Born December 27, 1974, in Winchester, Mass. . . . 6-1/195. . . . Shoots left.
HIGH SCHOOL: Burlington (Mass.).
COLLEGE: Boston University.
TRANSACTIONS/CAREER NOTES: Selected by New Jersey Devils in second round (second Devils pick, 32nd overall) of NHL entry draft (June 26, 1993).

Season	Team	League	REGULAR SEASON					PLAYOFFS				
			Gms.	G	A	Pts.	PIM	Gms.	G	A	Pts.	PIM
90-91—Burlington H.S.................	Mass. H.S.	20	19	27	46	10	—	—	—	—	—
91-92—Burlington H.S.................	Mass. H.S.	20	35	34	69	14	—	—	—	—	—
92-93—Boston University	Hockey East	39	17	23	40	16	—	—	—	—	—
93-94—Boston University	Hockey East	37	17	25	42	27	—	—	—	—	—
94-95—Boston University	Hockey East	20	7	13	20	6	—	—	—	—	—

PANKEWICZ, GREG
RW, CAPITALS

PERSONAL: Born October 6, 1970, in Valley, Alta. . . . 6-0/189. . . . Shoots right. . . . Name pronounced PAN-kuh-WIHTS.
TRANSACTIONS/CAREER NOTES: Signed as free agent by Ottawa Senators (May 27, 1993). . . . Signed as free agent by Washington Capitals (July 2, 1995).

Season	Team	League	REGULAR SEASON					PLAYOFFS				
			Gms.	G	A	Pts.	PIM	Gms.	G	A	Pts.	PIM
89-90—Regina	WHL	63	14	24	38	136	10	1	3	4	19
90-91—Regina	WHL	72	39	41	80	134	8	4	7	11	12
91-92—Knoxville	ECHL	59	41	39	80	214	—	—	—	—	—
92-93—New Haven	AHL	62	23	20	43	163	—	—	—	—	—
93-94—Prince Edward Island	AHL	69	33	29	62	241	—	—	—	—	—
—Ottawa	NHL	3	0	0	0	2	—	—	—	—	—
94-95—Prince Edward Island	AHL	75	37	30	67	161	6	1	1	2	24
NHL totals................		3	0	0	0	2					

PANTELEEV, GRIGORI
LW/RW, BRUINS

PERSONAL: Born November 13, 1972, in Riga, U.S.S.R. . . . 5-9/194. . . . Shoots left. . . . Name pronounced grih-GOHR-ee PAN-tuh-LAY-ehf.
TRANSACTIONS/CAREER NOTES: Selected by Boston Bruins in sixth round (fifth Bruins pick, 136th overall) of NHL entry draft (June 20, 1992).

Season	Team	League	REGULAR SEASON					PLAYOFFS				
			Gms.	G	A	Pts.	PIM	Gms.	G	A	Pts.	PIM
90-91—Dynamo Riga....................	USSR	23	4	1	5	4	—	—	—	—	—
91-92—HC Riga...........................	CIS	26	4	8	12	4	—	—	—	—	—
92-93—Providence	AHL	39	17	30	47	22	3	0	0	0	10
—Boston	NHL	39	8	6	14	12	—	—	—	—	—
93-94—Providence	AHL	55	24	26	50	20	—	—	—	—	—
—Boston	NHL	10	0	0	0	0	—	—	—	—	—
94-95—Providence	AHL	70	20	23	43	36	13	8	11	19	6
—Boston	NHL	1	0	0	0	0	—	—	—	—	—
NHL totals................		50	8	6	14	12					

PAQUETTE, CHARLES
D, BRUINS

PERSONAL: Born June 17, 1975, in Lachute, Que. . . . 6-1/193. . . . Shoots left. . . . Name pronounced pa-KEHT.
TRANSACTIONS/CAREER NOTES: Selected by Boston Bruins in fourth round (third Bruins pick, 88th overall) of NHL entry draft (June 26, 1993).
HONORS: Named to QMJHL All-Star first team (1994-95).

Season	Team	League	REGULAR SEASON					PLAYOFFS				
			Gms.	G	A	Pts.	PIM	Gms.	G	A	Pts.	PIM
91-92—Trois-Rivieres................	QMJHL	60	1	7	8	101	6	0	0	0	2
92-93—Sherbrooke......................	QMJHL	54	2	5	7	104	15	0	0	0	33
93-94—Sherbrooke......................	QMJHL	63	5	14	19	165	8	0	2	2	15
94-95—Sherbrooke......................	QMJHL	53	15	26	41	186	5	1	1	2	18

PAQUIN, PATRICE
LW, FLYERS

PERSONAL: Born June 26, 1974, in St. Jerome, Que. . . . 6-2/192. . . . Shoots left.
TRANSACTIONS/CAREER NOTES: Selected by Philadelphia Flyers in 11th round (11th Flyers pick, 247th overall) of NHL entry draft (June 20, 1992).

P

Season	Team	League	Gms.	G	A	Pts.	PIM	Gms.	G	A	Pts.	PIM
91-92—Beauport	QMJHL	60	10	15	25	169	—	—	—	—	—
92-93—Beauport	QMJHL	59	17	23	40	271	—	—	—	—	—
93-94—Beauport	QMJHL	45	22	24	46	188	15	1	7	8	39
94-95—Beauport	QMJHL	1	1	1	2	2	—	—	—	—	—
—St. Jean	QMJHL	53	22	32	54	147	5	2	2	4	6

PARK, RICHARD
C, PENGUINS

PERSONAL: Born May 27, 1976, in Seoul, South Korea. . . . 6-0/187. . . . Shoots right.
TRANSACTIONS/CAREER NOTES: Selected by Pittsburgh Penguins in second round (second Penguins pick, 50th overall) of NHL entry draft (June 28, 1994).

			REGULAR SEASON					PLAYOFFS				
Season	Team	League	Gms.	G	A	Pts.	PIM	Gms.	G	A	Pts.	PIM
91-92—Williams Lake	PCJHL	76	49	58	107	91	—	—	—	—	—
92-93—Belleville	OHL	66	23	38	61	38	5	0	0	0	14
93-94—Belleville	OHL	59	27	49	76	70	12	3	5	8	18
94-95—Belleville	OHL	45	28	51	79	35	16	9	18	27	12
—Pittsburgh	NHL	1	0	1	1	2	3	0	0	0	2
NHL totals		1	0	1	1	2	3	0	0	0	2

PASSMORE, STEVE
G, OILERS

PERSONAL: Born January 29, 1973, in Thunder Bay, Ont. . . . 5-9/165. . . . Catches left.
TRANSACTIONS/CAREER NOTES: Selected by Quebec Nordiques in ninth round (10th Nordiques pick, 196th overall) of NHL entry draft (June 20, 1992). . . . Traded by Nordiques to Edmonton Oilers for D Brad Werenka (March 21, 1994).
HONORS: Named to WHL (West) All-Star first team (1992-93 and 1993-94).

			REGULAR SEASON							PLAYOFFS						
Season	Team	League	Gms.	Min.	W	L	T	GA	SO	Avg.	Gms.	Min.	W	L	GA	SO	Avg.
88-89—Tri-City	WHL	1	60	. . .	. . .	. . .	6	0	6.00	—	—	—	—	—	—	—
89-90—Tri-City	WHL	4	215	. . .	. . .	. . .	17	0	4.74	—	—	—	—	—	—	—
90-91—Victoria	WHL	35	1838	3	25	1	190	0	6.20	—	—	—	—	—	—	—
91-92—Victoria	WHL	*71	*4228	15	50	7	347	0	4.92	—	—	—	—	—	—	—
92-93—Victoria	WHL	43	2402	14	24	2	150	1	3.75	—	—	—	—	—	—	—
—Kamloops	WHL	25	1479	19	6	0	69	1	2.80	7	401	4	2	22	1	3.29
93-94—Kamloops	WHL	36	1927	22	9	2	88	1	*2.74	18	1099†11	7	60	0	3.28
94-95—Cape Breton	AHL	25	1455	8	13	3	93	0	3.84	—	—	—	—	—	—	—

PATRICK, JAMES
D, FLAMES

PERSONAL: Born June 14, 1963, in Winnipeg. . . . 6-2/200. . . . Shoots right. . . . Brother of Steve Patrick, right winger, Buffalo Sabres, New York Rangers and Quebec Nordiques (1980-81 through 1985-86).
COLLEGE: North Dakota.
TRANSACTIONS/CAREER NOTES: Selected by New York Rangers as underage junior in first round (first Rangers pick, ninth overall) of NHL entry draft (June 10, 1981). . . . Injured groin (October 1984). . . . Pinched nerve (December 15, 1985). . . . Strained left knee ligaments (March 1988). . . . Bruised shoulder and chest (December 1988). . . . Pulled groin (March 13, 1989). . . . Sprained shoulder (November 4, 1992); missed three games. . . . Bruised right shoulder (November 27, 1992); missed three games. . . . Sprained left knee (January 27, 1993); missed four games. . . . Suffered herniated disc (February 24, 1993); missed two games. . . . Suffered herniated disc (March 28, 1993); missed remainder of season. . . . Traded by Rangers with C Darren Turcotte to Hartford Whalers for RW Steve Larmer, LW Nick Kypreos and sixth-round pick (C Yuri Litvinov) in 1994 draft (November 2, 1993). . . . Suffered herniated disc (December 7, 1993); missed five games. . . . Traded by Whalers with C Mikael Nylander and D Zarley Zalapski to Calgary Flames for D Gary Suter, LW Paul Ranheim and C Ted Drury (March 10, 1994). . . . Strained left hip (March 10, 1995); missed five games.
HONORS: Named SJHL Player of the Year (1980-81). . . . Named to SJHL All-Star first team (1980-81). . . . Won WCHA Rookie of the Year Award (1981-82). . . . Named to WCHA All-Star second team (1981-82). . . . Named to NCAA All-Tournament team (1981-82). . . . Named to NCAA All-America West team (1982-83). . . . Named to WCHA All-Star first team (1982-83).

			REGULAR SEASON					PLAYOFFS				
Season	Team	League	Gms.	G	A	Pts.	PIM	Gms.	G	A	Pts.	PIM
80-81—Prince Albert	SJHL	59	21	61	82	162	4	1	6	7	0
81-82—Univ. of North Dakota	WCHA	42	5	24	29	26	—	—	—	—	—
82-83—Univ. of North Dakota	WCHA	36	12	36	48	29	—	—	—	—	—
83-84—Canadian Olympic Team	Int'l	63	7	24	31	52	—	—	—	—	—
—New York Rangers	NHL	12	1	7	8	2	5	0	3	3	2
84-85—New York Rangers	NHL	75	8	28	36	71	3	0	0	0	4
85-86—New York Rangers	NHL	75	14	29	43	88	16	1	5	6	34
86-87—New York Rangers	NHL	78	10	45	55	62	6	1	2	3	2
87-88—New York Rangers	NHL	70	17	45	62	52	—	—	—	—	—
88-89—New York Rangers	NHL	68	11	36	47	41	4	0	1	1	2
89-90—New York Rangers	NHL	73	14	43	57	50	10	3	8	11	0
90-91—New York Rangers	NHL	74	10	49	59	58	6	0	0	0	6
91-92—New York Rangers	NHL	80	14	57	71	54	13	0	7	7	12
92-93—New York Rangers	NHL	60	5	21	26	61	—	—	—	—	—
93-94—New York Rangers	NHL	6	0	3	3	2	—	—	—	—	—
—Hartford	NHL	47	8	20	28	32	—	—	—	—	—
—Calgary	NHL	15	2	2	4	6	7	0	1	1	6
94-95—Calgary	NHL	43	0	10	10	14	5	0	1	1	0
NHL totals		776	114	395	509	593	75	5	28	33	68

P

PATTERSON, ED
RW, PENGUINS

PERSONAL: Born November 14, 1972, in Delta, B.C. . . . 6-2/210. . . . Shoots right.
TRANSACTIONS/CAREER NOTES: Selected by Pittsburgh Penguins in seventh round (seventh Penguins pick, 148th overall) of NHL entry draft (June 22, 1991).

Season	Team	League	Gms.	G	A	Pts.	PIM	Gms.	G	A	Pts.	PIM
				REGULAR SEASON					PLAYOFFS			
90-91	Swift Current	WHL	7	2	7	9	0	—	—	—	—	—
	Kamloops	WHL	55	14	33	47	134	5	0	0	0	7
91-92	Kamloops	WHL	38	19	25	44	120	1	0	0	0	0
92-93	Cleveland	IHL	63	4	16	20	131	3	1	1	2	2
93-94	Cleveland	IHL	55	21	32	53	73	—	—	—	—	—
	Pittsburgh	NHL	27	3	1	4	10	—	—	—	—	—
94-95	Cleveland	IHL	58	13	17	30	93	4	1	2	3	6
NHL totals			27	3	1	4	10					

PEAKE, PAT
RW, CAPITALS

PERSONAL: Born May 28, 1973, in Detroit. . . . 6-1/195. . . . Shoots right. . . . Full name: Patrick Michael Peake. . . . Name pronounced PEEK.
TRANSACTIONS/CAREER NOTES: Injured wrist (August 31, 1990). . . . Selected by Washington Capitals in first round (first Capitals pick, 14th overall) of NHL entry draft (June 22, 1991). . . . Suffered sore ankle (October 30, 1993); missed two games. . . . Suffered sore shoulder (December 23, 1993); missed six games. . . . Suffered from the flu (February 2, 1994); missed two games. . . . Bruised ribs (February 21, 1994); missed 14 games. . . . Suffered from the flu (February 15, 1995); missed one game. . . . Suffered from mononeucleosis (March 2, 1995); missed nine games.
HONORS: Won Can.HL Player of the Year Award (1992-93). . . . Won Red Tilson Trophy (1992-93). . . . Won William Hanley Trophy (1992-93). . . . Named to Can.HL All-Star first team (1992-93). . . . Named to OHL All-Star first team (1992-93).

Season	Team	League	Gms.	G	A	Pts.	PIM	Gms.	G	A	Pts.	PIM
				REGULAR SEASON					PLAYOFFS			
89-90	Detroit Compuware	NAJHL	40	36	37	73	57	—	—	—	—	—
90-91	Detroit	OHL	63	39	51	90	54	—	—	—	—	—
91-92	Detroit	OHL	53	41	52	93	44	7	8	9	17	10
	Baltimore	AHL	3	1	0	1	4	—	—	—	—	—
92-93	Detroit	OHL	46	58	78	136	64	2	1	3	4	2
93-94	Portland	AHL	4	0	5	5	2	—	—	—	—	—
	Washington	NHL	49	11	18	29	39	8	0	1	1	8
94-95	Washington	NHL	18	0	4	4	12	—	—	—	—	—
	Portland	AHL	5	1	3	4	2	4	0	3	3	6
NHL totals			67	11	22	33	51	8	0	1	1	8

PEARSON, ROB
RW, CAPITALS

PERSONAL: Born August 3, 1971, in Oshawa, Ont. . . . 6-3/200. . . . Shoots right.
TRANSACTIONS/CAREER NOTES: Broke wrist (November 13, 1988). . . . Selected by Toronto Maple Leafs in first round (second Maple Leafs pick, 12th overall) of NHL entry draft (June 17, 1989). . . . Dislocated right knee (August 15, 1989). . . . Suspended five games by OHL for checking from behind (February 7, 1990). . . . Broke collarbone (August 1990). . . . Traded by Belleville Bulls to Oshawa Generals for C Jarrod Skalde (November 18, 1990). . . . Partially tore knee ligament (October 23, 1993); missed 13 games. . . . Traded by Maple Leafs with first-round pick in 1994 draft (D Nolan Baumgartner) to Washington Capitals for C Mike Ridley and first-round pick (G Eric Fichaud) in 1994 draft (June 28, 1994).
HONORS: Won Jim Mahon Memorial Trophy (1990-91). . . . Named to OHL All-Star first team (1990-91).

Season	Team	League	Gms.	G	A	Pts.	PIM	Gms.	G	A	Pts.	PIM
				REGULAR SEASON					PLAYOFFS			
88-89	Belleville	OHL	26	8	12	20	51	—	—	—	—	—
89-90	Belleville	OHL	58	48	40	88	174	11	5	5	10	26
90-91	Belleville	OHL	10	6	3	9	27	—	—	—	—	—
	Oshawa	OHL	41	57	52	109	76	16	16	17	33	39
	Newmarket	AHL	3	0	0	0	29	—	—	—	—	—
91-92	Toronto	NHL	47	14	10	24	58	—	—	—	—	—
	St. John's	AHL	27	15	14	29	107	13	5	4	9	40
92-93	Toronto	NHL	78	23	14	37	211	14	2	2	4	31
93-94	Toronto	NHL	67	12	18	30	189	14	1	0	1	32
94-95	Washington	NHL	32	0	6	6	96	3	1	0	1	17
NHL totals			224	49	48	97	554	31	4	2	6	80

PEARSON, SCOTT
LW, SABRES

PERSONAL: Born December 19, 1969, in Cornwall, Ont. . . . 6-1/205. . . . Shoots left.
TRANSACTIONS/CAREER NOTES: Underwent surgery to left wrist (May 1988). . . . Selected by Toronto Maple Leafs in first round (first Maple Leafs pick, sixth overall) of NHL entry draft (June 11, 1988). . . . Traded by Maple Leafs with second-round picks in 1991 draft (D Eric Lavigne) and 1992 draft (D Tuomas Gronman) to Quebec Nordiques for C/LW Aaron Broten, D Michel Petit and RW Lucien Deblois (November 17, 1990). . . . Sprained left knee (September 27, 1992); missed first 22 games of season. . . . Traded by Nordiques to Edmonton Oilers for LW Martin Gelinas and sixth-round pick (C Nicholas Checco) in 1993 draft (June 20, 1993). . . . Sprained medial collateral knee ligament (February 8, 1994); missed 11 games. . . . Traded by Oilers to Buffalo Sabres for D Ken Sutton (April 7, 1995).

Season	Team	League	Gms.	G	A	Pts.	PIM	Gms.	G	A	Pts.	PIM
				REGULAR SEASON					PLAYOFFS			
85-86	Kingston	OHL	63	16	23	39	56	—	—	—	—	—
86-87	Kingston	OHL	62	30	24	54	101	9	3	3	6	42

P

Season	Team	League	REGULAR SEASON Gms.	G	A	Pts.	PIM	PLAYOFFS Gms.	G	A	Pts.	PIM
87-88	Kingston	OHL	46	26	32	58	118	—	—	—	—	—
88-89	Kingston	OHL	13	9	8	17	34	—	—	—	—	—
	Niagara Falls	OHL	32	26	34	60	90	17	14	10	24	53
	Toronto	NHL	9	0	1	1	2	—	—	—	—	—
89-90	Newmarket	AHL	18	12	11	23	64	—	—	—	—	—
	Toronto	NHL	41	5	10	15	90	2	2	0	2	10
90-91	Toronto	NHL	12	0	0	0	20	—	—	—	—	—
	Quebec	NHL	35	11	4	15	86	—	—	—	—	—
	Halifax	AHL	24	12	15	27	44	—	—	—	—	—
91-92	Quebec	NHL	10	1	2	3	14	—	—	—	—	—
	Halifax	AHL	5	2	1	3	4	—	—	—	—	—
92-93	Halifax	AHL	5	3	1	4	25	—	—	—	—	—
	Quebec	NHL	41	13	1	14	95	3	0	0	0	0
93-94	Edmonton	NHL	72	19	18	37	165	—	—	—	—	—
94-95	Edmonton	NHL	28	1	4	5	54	—	—	—	—	—
	Buffalo	NHL	14	2	1	3	20	5	0	0	0	4
NHL totals			262	52	41	93	546	10	2	0	2	14

PECA, MIKE
RW/C, SABRES

PERSONAL: Born March 26, 1974, in Toronto. . . . 5-11/175. . . . Shoots right. . . . Name pronounced PEH-kuh.
HIGH SCHOOL: LaSalle Secondary (Kinston, Ont.).
TRANSACTIONS/CAREER NOTES: Selected by Vancouver Canucks in second round (second Canucks pick, 40th overall) of NHL entry draft (June 20, 1992). . . . Cracked cheek bone (February 9, 1995); missed 12 games. . . . Injured wrist (April 26, 1995); missed one game. . . . Traded by Canucks with D Mike Wilson and first-round pick in 1995 draft (D Jay McKee) to Buffalo Sabres for RW Alexander Mogilny and fifth-round pick (LW Todd Norman) in 1995 draft (July 8, 1995).

Season	Team	League	REGULAR SEASON Gms.	G	A	Pts.	PIM	PLAYOFFS Gms.	G	A	Pts.	PIM
90-91	Sudbury	OHL	62	14	27	41	24	5	1	0	1	7
91-92	Sudbury	OHL	39	16	34	50	61	—	—	—	—	—
	Ottawa	OHL	27	8	17	25	32	11	6	10	16	6
92-93	Ottawa	OHL	55	38	64	102	80	—	—	—	—	—
	Hamilton	AHL	9	6	3	9	11	—	—	—	—	—
93-94	Ottawa	OHL	55	50	63	113	101	17	7	22	29	30
	Vancouver	NHL	4	0	0	0	2	—	—	—	—	—
94-95	Syracuse	AHL	35	10	24	34	75	—	—	—	—	—
	Vancouver	NHL	33	6	6	12	30	5	0	1	1	8
NHL totals			37	6	6	12	32	5	0	1	1	8

PEDERSON, DENIS
C, DEVILS

PERSONAL: Born September 10, 1975, in Prince Albert, Sask. . . . 6-2/190. . . . Shoots right.
HIGH SCHOOL: Carlton Comprehensive (Prince Albert, Sask.).
TRANSACTIONS/CAREER NOTES: Selected by New Jersey Devils in first round (first Devils pick, 13th overall) of NHL entry draft (June 26, 1993).
HONORS: Named to WHL All-Rookie team (1992-93). . . . Named to WHL (East) All-Star second team (1993-94).

Season	Team	League	REGULAR SEASON Gms.	G	A	Pts.	PIM	PLAYOFFS Gms.	G	A	Pts.	PIM
91-92	Prince Albert	WHL	10	0	0	0	6	7	0	1	1	13
92-93	Prince Albert	WHL	72	33	40	73	134	—	—	—	—	—
93-94	Prince Albert	WHL	71	53	45	98	157	—	—	—	—	—
94-95	Prince Albert	WHL	63	30	38	68	122	15	11	14	25	14
	Albany	AHL	—	—	—	—	—	3	0	0	0	2

PEDERSON, TOM
D, SHARKS

PERSONAL: Born January 14, 1970, in Bloomington, Minn. . . . 5-9/180. . . . Shoots right. . . . Full name: Thomas Stuart Pederson.
HIGH SCHOOL: Thomas Jefferson (Bloomington, Minn.).
COLLEGE: Minnesota.
TRANSACTIONS/CAREER NOTES: Selected by Minnesota North Stars in 11th round (12th North Stars pick, 217th overall) of NHL entry draft (June 17, 1989). . . . Selected by San Jose Sharks in NHL dispersal draft (May 30, 1991). . . . Strained back (January 8, 1993); missed one game. . . . Injured shoulder (January 30, 1993); missed four games. . . . Strained groin (February 22, 1993); missed five games.

Season	Team	League	REGULAR SEASON Gms.	G	A	Pts.	PIM	PLAYOFFS Gms.	G	A	Pts.	PIM
87-88	Jefferson H.S.	Minn. H.S.	22	16	27	43	. . .	—	—	—	—	—
88-89	University of Minnesota	WCHA	42	5	24	29	46	—	—	—	—	—
89-90	University of Minnesota	WCHA	43	8	30	38	58	—	—	—	—	—
90-91	University of Minnesota	WCHA	36	12	20	32	46	—	—	—	—	—
91-92	U.S. national team	Int'l	44	3	11	14	41	—	—	—	—	—
	Kansas City	IHL	20	6	9	15	16	13	1	6	7	14
92-93	Kansas City	IHL	26	6	15	21	10	12	1	6	7	2
	San Jose	NHL	44	7	13	20	31	—	—	—	—	—

P

Season Team	League	REGULAR SEASON					PLAYOFFS				
		Gms.	G	A	Pts.	PIM	Gms.	G	A	Pts.	PIM
93-94—Kansas City	IHL	7	3	1	4	0	—	—	—	—	—
—San Jose	NHL	74	6	19	25	31	14	1	6	7	2
94-95—San Jose	NHL	47	5	11	16	31	10	0	5	5	8
NHL totals		165	18	43	61	93	24	1	11	12	10

PELLERIN, SCOTT
LW, DEVILS

PERSONAL: Born January 9, 1970, in Shediac, N.B. . . . 5-11/180. . . . Shoots left. . . . Full name: Jaque-Frederick Scott Pellerin. . . . Name pronounced PEHL-ih-rihn.
COLLEGE: Maine.
TRANSACTIONS/CAREER NOTES: Selected by New Jersey Devils in third round (fourth Devils pick, 47th overall) of NHL entry draft (June 17, 1989).
HONORS: Named Hockey East co-Rookie of the Year with Rob Gaudreau (1988-89). . . . Named to Hockey East All-Rookie team (1988-89). . . . Won Hobey Baker Memorial Award (1991-92). . . . Named Hockey East Player of the Year (1991-92). . . . Named Hockey East Tournament Most Valuable Player (1991-92). . . . Named to NCAA All-America East first team (1991-92). . . . Named to Hockey East All-Star first team (1991-92). . . . Named to Hockey East All-Decade team (1994).

Season Team	League	REGULAR SEASON					PLAYOFFS				
		Gms.	G	A	Pts.	PIM	Gms.	G	A	Pts.	PIM
87-88—Notre Dame	SJHL	57	37	49	86	139	—	—	—	—	—
88-89—University of Maine	Hockey East	45	29	33	62	92	—	—	—	—	—
89-90—University of Maine	Hockey East	42	22	34	56	68	—	—	—	—	—
90-91—University of Maine	Hockey East	43	23	25	48	60	—	—	—	—	—
91-92—University of Maine	Hockey East	37	†32	25	57	54	—	—	—	—	—
—Utica	AHL	—	—	—	—	—	3	1	0	1	0
92-93—Utica	AHL	27	15	18	33	33	2	0	1	1	0
—New Jersey	NHL	45	10	11	21	41	—	—	—	—	—
93-94—Albany	IHL	73	28	46	74	84	5	2	1	3	11
—New Jersey	NHL	1	0	0	0	2	—	—	—	—	—
94-95—Albany	AHL	74	23	33	56	95	14	6	4	10	8
NHL totals		46	10	11	21	43					

PELTONEN, VILLE
LW/RW, SHARKS

PERSONAL: Born May 24, 1973, in Vantaa, Finland. . . . 5-10/172. . . . Shoots left.
TRANSACTIONS/CAREER NOTES: Selected by San Jose Sharks in third round (fourth Sharks pick, 58th overall) of NHL entry draft (June 26, 1993).
MISCELLANEOUS: Member of bronze-medal-winning Finnish Olympic team (1994).

Season Team	League	REGULAR SEASON					PLAYOFFS				
		Gms.	G	A	Pts.	PIM	Gms.	G	A	Pts.	PIM
91-92—HIFK Helsinki	Finland	6	0	0	0	0	—	—	—	—	—
92-93—HIFK Helsinki	Finland	46	13	24	37	16	4	0	2	2	2
93-94—HIFK Helsinki	Finland	43	16	22	38	14	3	0	0	0	2
—Finnish Olympic Team	Int'l	8	4	3	7	0	—	—	—	—	—
94-95—HIFK Helsinki	Finland	45	20	16	36	16	3	0	0	0	0

PELUSO, MIKE
C, FLAMES

PERSONAL: Born September 2, 1974, in Denver, Colo. . . . 6-0/200. . . . Shoots right.
COLLEGE: Minnesota-Duluth.
TRANSACTIONS/CAREER NOTES: Selected by Calgary Flames in 10th round (11th Flames pick, 253rd overall) of NHL entry draft (June 29, 1994).
HONORS: Named to WCHA All-Rookie team (1994-95).

Season Team	League	REGULAR SEASON					PLAYOFFS				
		Gms.	G	A	Pts.	PIM	Gms.	G	A	Pts.	PIM
93-94—Omaha	USHL	48	36	29	65	77	—	—	—	—	—
94-95—Minnesota-Duluth	WCHA	38	11	23	34	38	—	—	—	—	—

PELUSO, MIKE
LW, DEVILS

PERSONAL: Born November 8, 1965, in Hibbing, Minn. . . . 6-4/200. . . . Shoots left. . . . Full name: Michael David Peluso. . . . Name pronounced puh-LOO-soh.
HIGH SCHOOL: Greenway (Coleraine, Minn.).
COLLEGE: Alaska-Anchorage.
TRANSACTIONS/CAREER NOTES: Selected by New Jersey Devils in 10th round (10th Devils pick, 190th overall) of NHL entry draft (June 15, 1985). . . . Signed as free agent by Chicago Blackhawks (September 7, 1989). . . . Bruised jaw and cheek (November 8, 1990); missed five games. . . . Suspended 10 games by NHL for fighting (March 17, 1991). . . . Selected by Ottawa Senators in NHL expansion draft (June 18, 1992). . . . Suspended one game by NHL for accumulating three game misconduct penalties (February 1, 1993). . . . Pinched nerve in neck (March 27, 1993); missed two games. . . . Traded by Senators to Devils (June 26, 1993) to complete deal in which Devils sent G Craig Billington, C/LW Troy Mallette and fourth-round pick in 1993 draft (C Cosmo Dupaul) to Senators for G Peter Sidorkiewicz and future considerations (June 20, 1993). . . . Suffered concussion (December 18, 1993); missed two games. . . . Suspended one game by NHL for non-stick related game misconduct (January 7, 1994). . . . Suspended two games by NHL for non-stick related game misconduct (February 4, 1994). . . . Suspended three games by NHL for non-stick related game misconduct (March 7, 1994). . . . Suffered sore neck (March 8, 1995); missed one game. . . . Suffered from the flu (April 5, 1995); missed one game. . . . Fined $1,000 by NHL for throwing an elbow (May 12, 1995).
MISCELLANEOUS: Member of Stanley Cup championship team (1995).

P

Season Team	League	Gms.	G	A	Pts.	PIM	Gms.	G	A	Pts.	PIM
83-84—Greenway H.S.	Minn. H.S.	12	5	15	20	30	—	—	—	—	—
84-85—Stratford	OPJHL	52	11	45	56	114	—	—	—	—	—
85-86—Alaska-Anchorage..........	Indep.	32	2	11	13	59	—	—	—	—	—
86-87—Alaska-Anchorage..........	Indep.	30	5	21	26	68	—	—	—	—	—
87-88—Alaska-Anchorage..........	Indep.	35	4	33	37	76	—	—	—	—	—
88-89—Alaska-Anchorage..........	Indep.	33	10	27	37	75	—	—	—	—	—
89-90—Indianapolis	IHL	75	7	10	17	279	14	0	1	1	58
—Chicago	NHL	2	0	0	0	15	—	—	—	—	—
90-91—Indianapolis	IHL	6	2	1	3	21	5	0	2	2	40
—Chicago	NHL	53	6	1	7	320	3	0	0	0	2
91-92—Chicago	NHL	63	6	3	9	*408	17	1	2	3	8
—Indianapolis	IHL	4	0	1	1	15	—	—	—	—	—
92-93—Ottawa...........................	NHL	81	15	10	25	318	—	—	—	—	—
93-94—New Jersey....................	NHL	69	4	16	20	238	17	1	0	1	*64
94-95—New Jersey....................	NHL	46	2	9	11	167	20	1	2	3	8
NHL totals............		314	33	39	72	1466	57	3	4	7	82

PENNEY, CHAD
LW, SENATORS

PERSONAL: Born September 18, 1973, in Labrador City, Nfld. . . . 6-0/195. . . . Shoots left. . . . Full name: Chadwick Paul Penney.
HIGH SCHOOL: Chippewa Secondary (North Bay, Ont.).
TRANSACTIONS/CAREER NOTES: Selected by Ottawa Senators in second round (second Senators pick, 25th overall) of NHL entry draft (June 20 1992).

Season Team	League	Gms.	G	A	Pts.	PIM	Gms.	G	A	Pts.	PIM
90-91—North Bay	OHL	66	33	34	67	56	10	2	6	8	12
91-92—North Bay	OHL	57	25	27	52	93	21	13	17	30	9
—Can. national Jr. team	Int'l	7	0	0	0	2	—	—	—	—	—
92-93—North Bay	OHL	18	8	7	15	19	—	—	—	—	—
—Sault Ste. Marie	OHL	48	29	44	73	67	18	7	10	17	18
93-94—Prince Edward Island	AHL	73	20	30	50	66	—	—	—	—	—
—Ottawa	NHL	3	0	0	0	2	—	—	—	—	—
94-95—Prince Edward Island	AHL	66	16	16	32	19	11	2	2	4	2
NHL totals............		3	0	0	0	2					

PEPLINSKI, JIM
C, FLAMES

PERSONAL: Born October 24, 1960, in Renfrew, Ont. . . . 6-3/210. . . . Shoots right. . . . Full name: Jim Desmond Peplinski.
TRANSACTIONS/CAREER NOTES: Selected by Atlanta Flames as underage junior in fourth round (fifth Flames pick, 75th overall) of NHL entry draft (August 9, 1979). . . . Flames franchise moved from Atlanta to Calgary for 1980-81 season. . . . Fractured sinus (September 1987). . . . Announced retirement (October 31, 1989). . . . Signed as free agent by Flames (April 7, 1995).
STATISTICAL PLATEAUS: Four-goal games: 1981-82 (1).
MISCELLANEOUS: Co-captain of Calgary Flames (1984-85 through 1988-89). . . . Member of Stanley Cup championship team (1989).

Season Team	League	Gms.	G	A	Pts.	PIM	Gms.	G	A	Pts.	PIM
77-78—Toronto............................	OMJHL	66	13	28	41	44	—	—	—	—	—
78-79—Toronto............................	OMJHL	66	23	32	55	88	3	0	1	1	0
79-80—Toronto............................	OMJHL	67	35	66	101	89	4	1	2	3	15
80-81—Calgary............................	NHL	80	13	25	38	108	16	2	3	5	41
81-82—Calgary............................	NHL	74	30	37	67	115	3	1	0	1	13
82-83—Calgary............................	NHL	80	15	26	41	134	8	1	1	2	45
83-84—Calgary............................	NHL	74	11	22	33	114	11	3	4	7	21
84-85—Calgary............................	NHL	80	16	29	45	111	4	1	3	4	11
85-86—Calgary............................	NHL	77	24	35	59	214	22	5	9	14	107
86-87—Calgary............................	NHL	80	18	32	50	181	6	1	0	1	24
87-88—Calgary............................	NHL	75	20	31	51	234	9	0	5	5	45
—Canadian Olympic Team ..	Int'l	7	0	1	1	6	—	—	—	—	—
88-89—Calgary............................	NHL	79	13	25	38	241	20	1	6	7	75
89-90—Calgary............................	NHL	6	1	0	1	4	0	0	0	0	0
90-91—					Did not play.						
91-92—					Did not play.						
92-93—					Did not play.						
93-94—					Did not play.						
94-95—Calgary............................	NHL	6	0	1	1	11	—	—	—	—	—
NHL totals............		711	161	263	424	1467	99	15	31	46	382

P

PEPPERALL, RYAN
RW, MAPLE LEAFS

PERSONAL: Born January 26, 1977, in Niagara Falls, Ont. . . . 6-1/175. . . . Shoots right.
HIGH SCHOOL: Eastwood Secondaire (Kitchener, Ont.).
TRANSACTIONS/CAREER NOTES: Selected by Toronto Maple Leafs in third round (second Maple Leaf pick, 54th overall) of NHL entry draft (July 8, 1995).

Season Team	League	REGULAR SEASON Gms.	G	A	Pts.	PIM	PLAYOFFS Gms.	G	A	Pts.	PIM
93-94—Chippewa	Jr. C	8	4	8	12	39	—	—	—	—	—
—Niagara Falls	Jr. B	37	14	20	34	156	—	—	—	—	—
94-95—Kitchener	OHL	62	17	16	33	86	5	2	2	4	8

PERREAULT, YANIC
C, KINGS

PERSONAL: Born April 4, 1971, in Sherbrooke, Que.... 5-11/182.... Shoots left.... Name pronounced YAH-nihk puh-ROH.
TRANSACTIONS/CAREER NOTES: Selected by Toronto Maple Leafs in third round (first Maple Leafs pick, 47th overall) of NHL entry draft (June 22, 1991).... Signed as free agent by Los Angeles Kings (July 14, 1994).
HONORS: Won Can.HL Rookie of the Year Award (1988-89).... Won Michel Bergeron Trophy (1988-89).... Won Marcel Robert Trophy (1989-90).... Won Michel Briere Trophy (1990-91).... Won Jean Beliveau Trophy (1990-91).... Won Frank J. Selke Trophy (1990-91).... Won Shell Cup (1990-91).... Named to QMJHL All-Star first team (1990-91).

Season Team	League	REGULAR SEASON Gms.	G	A	Pts.	PIM	PLAYOFFS Gms.	G	A	Pts.	PIM
88-89—Trois-Rivieres	QMJHL	70	53	55	108	48	—	—	—	—	—
89-90—Trois-Rivieres	QMJHL	63	51	63	114	75	7	6	5	11	19
90-91—Trois-Rivieres	QMJHL	67	*87	98	*185	103	6	4	7	11	6
91-92—St. John's	AHL	62	38	38	76	19	16	7	8	15	4
92-93—St. John's	AHL	79	49	46	95	56	9	4	5	9	2
93-94—St. John's	AHL	62	45	60	105	38	11	*12	6	18	14
—Toronto	NHL	13	3	3	6	0	—	—	—	—	—
94-95—Phoenix	IHL	68	51	48	99	52	—	—	—	—	—
—Los Angeles	NHL	26	2	5	7	20	—	—	—	—	—
NHL totals		39	5	8	13	20					

PERROTT, NATHAN
RW, DEVILS

PERSONAL: Born December 8, 1976, in Owen Sound, Ont.... 6-0/213.... Shoots right.
HIGH SCHOOL: Henry Street (Whitby, Ont.).
TRANSACTIONS/CAREER NOTES: Selected by New Jersey Devils in second round (second Devils pick, 44th overall) of NHL entry draft (July 8, 1995).

Season Team	League	REGULAR SEASON Gms.	G	A	Pts.	PIM	PLAYOFFS Gms.	G	A	Pts.	PIM
93-94—St. Mary's	OHA Jr. B	41	11	26	37	249	—	—	—	—	—
94-95—Oshawa	OHL	63	18	28	46	233	2	1	1	2	9

PERRY, TYLER
C, RED WINGS

PERSONAL: Born August 31, 1977, in Grandview, B.C.... 6-1/170.... Shoots right.
TRANSACTIONS/CAREER NOTES: Selected by Detroit Red Wings in sixth round (seventh Red Wings pick, 156th overall) of NHL entry draft (July 8, 1995).

Season Team	League	REGULAR SEASON Gms.	G	A	Pts.	PIM	PLAYOFFS Gms.	G	A	Pts.	PIM
93-94—Richmond	BCJHL	40	28	35	63	8	—	—	—	—	—
94-95—Seattle	WHL	49	9	13	22	19	4	2	0	2	2

PERSHIN, EDUARD
RW, LIGHTNING

PERSONAL: Born September 1, 1977, in Nizhnekamsk, U.S.S.R.... 6-0/190.... Shoots left.
TRANSACTIONS/CAREER NOTES: Selected by Tampa Bay Lightning in sixth round (fifth Lightning pick, 134th overall) of NHL entry draft (July 8, 1995).

Season Team	League	REGULAR SEASON Gms.	G	A	Pts.	PIM	PLAYOFFS Gms.	G	A	Pts.	PIM
94-95—Dynamo Moscow	CIS	4	1	1	2	2	3	0	0	0	2

PERSSON, JOAKIM
G, BRUINS

PERSONAL: Born May 4, 1970, in Stockholm, Sweden.... 5-11/180.... Catches left.
TRANSACTIONS/CAREER NOTES: Selected by Boston Bruins in 10th round (10th Bruins pick, 259th overall) of NHL entry draft (June 26, 1993).

Season Team	League	REGULAR SEASON Gms.	Min.	W	L	T	GA	SO	Avg.	PLAYOFFS Gms.	Min.	W	L	GA	SO	Avg.
91-92—Hemmarby Stockholm	Sweden						Statistics unavailable.									
92-93—Hemmarby Stockholm	Sweden						Statistics unavailable.									
93-94—Hemmarby Stockholm	Sweden	23	...	...	...	...	59	...	2.57	—	—	—	—	—	—	—
—Providence	AHL	1	25	0	0	0	0	0	0.00	—	—	—	—	—	—	—
94-95—AIK	Sweden	38	...	...	...	...	103	...	3.43	—	—	—	—	—	—	—

PERSSON, RICKARD
D, DEVILS

PERSONAL: Born August 24, 1969, in Ostersund, Sweden.... 6-1/205.... Shoots left.
TRANSACTIONS/CAREER NOTES: Selected by New Jersey Devils in second round (second Devils pick, 23rd overall) of NHL entry draft (June 13, 1987).

Season Team	League	REGULAR SEASON Gms.	G	A	Pts.	PIM	PLAYOFFS Gms.	G	A	Pts.	PIM
85-86—Ostersund	Swed. Dv.II	24	2	2	4	16	—	—	—	—	—
86-87—Ostersund	Swed. Dv.II	31	10	11	21	28	—	—	—	—	—

P

Season	Team	League	REGULAR SEASON Gms.	G	A	Pts.	PIM	PLAYOFFS Gms.	G	A	Pts.	PIM
87-88—Leksand	Sweden	31	2	0	2	8	2	0	1	1	2
88-89—Leksand	Sweden	33	2	4	6	28	9	0	1	1	6
89-90—Leksand	Sweden	43	9	10	19	62	3	0	0	0	6
90-91—Leksand	Sweden	37	6	9	15	42	—	—	—	—	—
91-92—Leksand	Sweden	21	0	7	7	28	—	—	—	—	—
92-93—Leksand	Sweden	36	7	15	22	63	2	0	2	2	0
93-94—Malmo	Sweden	40	11	9	20	38	11	2	0	2	12
94-95—Malmo	Sweden	31	3	13	16	38	9	0	2	2	8
—Albany	AHL	—	—	—	—	—	9	3	5	8	7

PETERSON, BRENT
LW, LIGHTNING

PERSONAL: Born July 20, 1972, in Calgary.... 6-3/ 195.... Shoots left.
COLLEGE: Michigan Tech.
TRANSACTIONS/CAREER NOTES: Selected by Tampa Bay Lightning in NHL supplemental draft (June 25, 1993).

Season	Team	League	REGULAR SEASON Gms.	G	A	Pts.	PIM	PLAYOFFS Gms.	G	A	Pts.	PIM
91-92—Michigan Tech	WCHA	39	11	9	20	18	—	—	—	—	—
92-93—Michigan Tech	WCHA	37	24	18	42	32	—	—	—	—	—
93-94—Michigan Tech	WCHA	43	25	21	46	30	—	—	—	—	—
94-95—Michigan Tech	WCHA	39	20	16	36	27	—	—	—	—	—

PETERSON, KYLE
C, STARS

PERSONAL: Born April 17, 1974, in Calgary.... 6-3/ 195.... Shoots left.
TRANSACTIONS/CAREER NOTES: Selected by Minnesota North Stars in seventh round (eighth North Stars pick, 154th overall) of NHL entry draft (June 20, 1992).... North Stars franchise moved from Minnesota to Dallas and renamed Stars for 1993-94 season.

Season	Team	League	REGULAR SEASON Gms.	G	A	Pts.	PIM	PLAYOFFS Gms.	G	A	Pts.	PIM
92-93—Thunder Bay Flyers	USHL	28	8	23	31	22	—	—	—	—	—
93-94—Michigan Tech	WCHA	45	5	9	14	82	—	—	—	—	—
94-95—Michigan Tech	WCHA	36	7	11	18	52	—	—	—	—	—

PETIT, MICHEL
D, KINGS

PERSONAL: Born February 12, 1964, in St. Malo, Que.... 6-1/ 185.... Shoots right.... Name pronounced puh-TEE.
TRANSACTIONS/CAREER NOTES: Selected by Vancouver Canucks as underage junior in first round (first Canucks pick, 11th overall) of NHL entry draft (June 9, 1982).... Separated shoulder (March 1984).... Injured knee (February 1987).... Traded by Canucks to New York Rangers for D Willie Huber and D Larry Melnyk (November 1987).... Pulled groin (December 1988).... Fractured right collarbone (December 27, 1988); missed 1 games.... Traded by Rangers to Quebec Nordiques for D Randy Moller (October 5, 1989).... Traded by Nordiques with C/LW Aaron Broten and RW Lucien DeBlois to Toronto Maple Leafs for LW Scott Pearson and second-round picks in 1991 draft (D Eric Lavigne) and 1992 draft (D Tuomas Gronman) (November 17, 1990).... Sprained knee (February 4, 1991); missed five games.... Sprained thumb (November 9, 1991); missed six games.... Traded by Maple Leafs with D Alexander Godynyuk, RW Gary Leeman, LW Craig Berube and G Jeff Reese to Calgary Flames for C Doug Gilmour, D Jamie Macoun, LW Kent Manderville, D Ric Nattress and G Rick Wamsley (January 2, 1992).... Suffered back spasms (March 3, 1992); missed four games.... Pulled groin prior to 1992-93 season; missed first four games of season.... Dislocated right shoulder (October 22, 1992); missed 29 games.... Suffered hip pointer (October 21, 1993); missed one game.... Suffered concussion (January 15, 1994); missed two games.... Pulled groin (February 2, 1994); missed four games.... Signed as free agent by Los Angeles Kings (June 16, 1994).... Strained groin (February 2, 1995); missed three games.... Strained groin (February 15, 1995); missed four games.... Sprained knee (April 17, 1995); missed one game.
HONORS: Won Raymond Lagace Trophy (1981-82).... Won Association of Journalists of Hockey Trophy (1981-82).... Named to QMJHL All-Star first team (1981-82 and 1982-83).

Season	Team	League	REGULAR SEASON Gms.	G	A	Pts.	PIM	PLAYOFFS Gms.	G	A	Pts.	PIM
81-82—Sherbrooke	QMJHL	63	10	39	49	106	22	5	20	25	24
82-83—St. Jean	QMJHL	62	19	67	86	196	3	0	0	0	35
—Vancouver	NHL	2	0	0	0	0	—	—	—	—	—
83-84—Canadian Olympic Team	Int'l	19	3	10	13	58	—	—	—	—	—
—Vancouver	NHL	44	6	9	15	53	1	0	0	0	0
84-85—Vancouver	NHL	69	5	26	31	127	—	—	—	—	—
85-86—Fredericton	AHL	25	0	13	13	79	—	—	—	—	—
—Vancouver	NHL	32	1	6	7	27	—	—	—	—	—
86-87—Vancouver	NHL	69	12	13	25	131	—	—	—	—	—
87-88—Vancouver	NHL	10	0	3	3	35	—	—	—	—	—
—New York Rangers	NHL	64	9	24	33	223	—	—	—	—	—
88-89—New York Rangers	NHL	69	8	25	33	154	4	0	2	2	27
89-90—Quebec	NHL	63	12	24	36	215	—	—	—	—	—
90-91—Quebec	NHL	19	4	7	11	47	—	—	—	—	—
—Toronto	NHL	54	9	19	28	132	—	—	—	—	—
91-92—Toronto	NHL	34	1	13	14	85	—	—	—	—	—
—Calgary	NHL	36	3	10	13	79	—	—	—	—	—
92-93—Calgary	NHL	35	3	9	12	54	—	—	—	—	—
93-94—Calgary	NHL	63	2	21	23	110	—	—	—	—	—
94-95—Los Angeles	NHL	40	5	12	17	84	—	—	—	—	—
NHL totals			**703**	**80**	**221**	**301**	**1556**	**5**	**0**	**2**	**2**	**27**

P

PETRENKO, SERGEI

LW, SABRES

PERSONAL: Born September 10, 1968, in Kharkov, U.S.S.R. . . . 5-11/167. . . . Shoots left. . . . Name pronounced SAIR-gay puh-TREHN-koh.

TRANSACTIONS/CAREER NOTES: Selected by Buffalo Sabres in seventh round (fifth Sabres pick, 168th overall) of NHL entry draft (June 26, 1993).

MISCELLANEOUS: Member of gold-medal-winning Unified Olympic team (1992).

			REGULAR SEASON					PLAYOFFS				
Season	Team	League	Gms.	G	A	Pts.	PIM	Gms.	G	A	Pts.	PIM
87-88—Dynamo Moscow		USSR	31	2	5	7	4	—	—	—	—	—
88-89—Dynamo Moscow		USSR	23	4	6	10	6	—	—	—	—	—
89-90—Dynamo Moscow		USSR	33	5	4	9	8	—	—	—	—	—
90-91—Dynamo Moscow		USSR	43	14	13	27	10	—	—	—	—	—
91-92—Dynamo Moscow		CIS	31	9	10	19	10	—	—	—	—	—
—Unified Olympic Team		Int'l	8	3	2	5	0	—	—	—	—	—
92-93—Dynamo Moscow		CIS	41	12	11	23	...	—	—	—	—	—
93-94—Buffalo		NHL	14	0	4	4	0	—	—	—	—	—
—Rochester		AHL	38	16	15	31	8	—	—	—	—	—
94-95—Rochester		AHL	43	12	16	28	16	—	—	—	—	—
NHL totals			**14**	**0**	**4**	**4**	**0**					

PETROCHININ, YEVGENY

D, STARS

PERSONAL: Born February 7, 1976, in Murmansk, U.S.S.R. . . . 5-9/165. . . . Shoots left.

TRANSACTIONS/CAREER NOTES: Selected by Dallas Stars in sixth round (fifth Stars pick, 150th overall) of NHL entry draft (June 29, 1994).

			REGULAR SEASON					PLAYOFFS				
Season	Team	League	Gms.	G	A	Pts.	PIM	Gms.	G	A	Pts.	PIM
93-94—Spartak Moscow		CIS	2	0	0	0	0	—	—	—	—	—
94-95—Spartak Moscow		CIS	45	0	2	2	14	—	—	—	—	—

PETROV, OLEG

RW, CANADIENS

PERSONAL: Born April 18, 1971, in Moscow, U.S.S.R. . . . 5-9/166. . . . Shoots left. . . . Name pronounced PAY-trahf.

TRANSACTIONS/CAREER NOTES: Selected by Montreal Canadiens in sixth round (ninth Canadiens pick, 127th overall) of NHL entry draft (June 22, 1991). . . . Suffered injury (January 5, 1994); missed one game. . . . Sprained ankle (April 6, 1994); missed three games.

HONORS: Named to NHL All-Rookie team (1993-94).

STATISTICAL PLATEAUS: Three-goal games: 1993-94 (1).

			REGULAR SEASON					PLAYOFFS				
Season	Team	League	Gms.	G	A	Pts.	PIM	Gms.	G	A	Pts.	PIM
90-91—CSKA Moscow		USSR	43	7	4	11	8	—	—	—	—	—
91-92—CSKA Moscow		CIS	34	8	13	21	6	—	—	—	—	—
92-93—Montreal		NHL	9	2	1	3	10	1	0	0	0	0
—Fredericton		AHL	55	26	29	55	36	5	4	1	5	0
93-94—Fredericton		AHL	23	8	20	28	18	—	—	—	—	—
—Montreal		NHL	55	12	15	27	2	2	0	0	0	0
94-95—Montreal		NHL	12	2	3	5	4	—	—	—	—	—
—Fredericton		AHL	17	7	11	18	12	17	5	6	11	10
NHL totals			**76**	**16**	**19**	**35**	**16**	**3**	**0**	**0**	**0**	**0**

PETROVICKY, ROBERT

C, WHALERS

PERSONAL: Born October 26, 1973, in Kosice, Czechoslovakia. . . . 5-11/172. . . . Shoots left. . . . Name pronounced PEHT-roh-VEETS-kee.

TRANSACTIONS/CAREER NOTES: Selected by Hartford Whalers in first round (first Whalers pick, ninth overall) of NHL entry draft (June 20, 1992). . . . Sprained left ankle (February 28, 1993); missed five games. . . . Loaned to Slovakian Olympic Team (February 11, 1994). . . . Returned to Whalers (February 28, 1994).

HONORS: Named to Czechoslovakian League All-Star team (1991-92).

			REGULAR SEASON					PLAYOFFS				
Season	Team	League	Gms.	G	A	Pts.	PIM	Gms.	G	A	Pts.	PIM
90-91—Dukla Trencin		Czech.	33	9	14	23	12	—	—	—	—	—
91-92—Dukla Trencin		Czech.	46	25	36	61	...	—	—	—	—	—
92-93—Hartford		NHL	42	3	6	9	45	—	—	—	—	—
—Springfield		AHL	16	5	3	8	39	15	5	6	11	14
93-94—Hartford		NHL	33	6	5	11	39	—	—	—	—	—
—Springfield		AHL	30	16	8	24	39	4	0	2	2	4
—Slovakian Olympic team		Int'l	8	1	6	7	18	—	—	—	—	—
94-95—Springfield		AHL	74	30	52	82	121	—	—	—	—	—
—Hartford		NHL	2	0	0	0	0	—	—	—	—	—
NHL totals			**77**	**9**	**11**	**20**	**84**					

PHILPOTT, ETHAN

RW, SABRES

PERSONAL: Born February 11, 1975, in Rochester, Minn. . . . 6-4/230. . . . Shoots right.

HIGH SCHOOL: Phillips Academy (Andover, Mass.).

COLLEGE: Harvard.

TRANSACTIONS/CAREER NOTES: Selected by Buffalo Sabres in third round (second Sabres pick, 64th overall) of NHL entry draft (June 26, 1993).

P

Season Team	League	REGULAR SEASON					PLAYOFFS				
		Gms.	G	A	Pts.	PIM	Gms.	G	A	Pts.	PIM
90-91—Phillips Andover Acad......	Mass. H.S.	20	13	7	20	0	—	—	—	—	—
91-92—Phillips Andover Acad......	Mass. H.S.	22	7	20	27	16	—	—	—	—	—
92-93—Phillips Andover Acad......	Mass. H.S.	18	17	19	36	22	—	—	—	—	—
93-94—Harvard University	ECAC	8	1	0	1	8	—	—	—	—	—
94-95—Des Moines....................	USHL	48	19	42	61	57	—	—	—	—	—

PICARD, MICHEL
LW, SENATORS

PERSONAL: Born November 7, 1969, in Beauport, Que.... 5-11/190.... Shoots left.
TRANSACTIONS/CAREER NOTES: Selected by Hartford Whalers in ninth round (eighth Whalers pick, 178th overall) of NHL entry draft (June 17, 1989).... Separated shoulder (November 14, 1991); missed seven games.... Traded by Whalers to San Jose Sharks for future considerations (October 9, 1992); Sharks sent LW Yvon Corriveau to Whalers to complete deal (January 21, 1993).... Signed as free agent by Portland Pirates (1993).... Signed as free agent by Ottawa Senators (June 23, 1994).
HONORS: Named to QMJHL All-Star second team (1988-89).... Named to AHL All-Star first team (1990-91 and 1994-95).... Named to AHL All-Star second team (1993-94).

Season Team	League	REGULAR SEASON					PLAYOFFS				
		Gms.	G	A	Pts.	PIM	Gms.	G	A	Pts.	PIM
86-87—Trois-Rivieres.................	QMJHL	66	33	35	68	53	—	—	—	—	—
87-88—Trois-Rivieres.................	QMJHL	69	40	55	95	71	—	—	—	—	—
88-89—Trois-Rivieres.................	QMJHL	66	59	81	140	107	4	1	3	4	2
89-90—Binghamton	AHL	67	16	24	40	98	—	—	—	—	—
90-91—Hartford........................	NHL	5	1	0	1	2	—	—	—	—	—
—Springfield................	AHL	77	*56	40	96	61	18	8	13	21	18
91-92—Hartford........................	NHL	25	3	5	8	6	—	—	—	—	—
—Springfield................	AHL	40	21	17	38	44	11	2	0	2	34
92-93—Kansas City...................	IHL	33	7	10	17	51	12	3	2	5	20
—San Jose..................	NHL	25	4	0	4	24	—	—	—	—	—
93-94—Portland.......................	AHL	61	41	44	85	99	17	11	10	21	22
94-95—Prince Edward Island	AHL	57	32	57	89	58	8	4	4	8	6
—Ottawa.....................	NHL	24	5	8	13	14	—	—	—	—	—
NHL totals..............................		79	13	13	26	46					

PIERCE, BILL
C, DENVER

PERSONAL: Born October 6, 1974, in Woburn, Mass.... 6-1/190.... Shoots left.
HIGH SCHOOL: Lawrence Academy (Groton, Mass.).
COLLEGE: Boston University.
TRANSACTIONS/CAREER NOTES: Selected by Quebec Nordiques in third round (fourth Nordiques pick, 75th overall) of NHL entry draft (June 26, 1993).... Nordiques franchise moved to Denver for 1995-96 season.

Season Team	League	REGULAR SEASON					PLAYOFFS				
		Gms.	G	A	Pts.	PIM	Gms.	G	A	Pts.	PIM
90-91—Lawrence Academy	Mass. H.S.	20	10	25	35	...	—	—	—	—	—
91-92—Lawrence Academy	Mass. H.S.	20	20	26	46	26	—	—	—	—	—
92-93—Lawrence Academy	Mass. H.S.	20	12	26	38	22	—	—	—	—	—
93-94—Boston University	Hockey East	31	4	4	8	28	—	—	—	—	—
94-95—Boston University	Hockey East	33	5	13	18	29	—	—	—	—	—

PIETRANGELO, FRANK
G, ISLANDERS

PERSONAL: Born December 17, 1964, in Niagara Falls, Ont.... 5-10/185.... Catches left.... Name pronounced PEE-tuhr-AN-juh-loh.
COLLEGE: Minnesota.
TRANSACTIONS/CAREER NOTES: Selected by Pittsburgh Penguins in fourth round (fourth Penguins pick, 63rd overall) of NHL entry draft (June 8, 1983).... Pulled groin (February 1989).... Pulled groin (February 3, 1991); missed eight games.... Injured back (November 9, 1991); missed four games.... Traded by Penguins to Hartford Whalers for conditional draft pick (March 10, 1992); arbitrator later ruled that Penguins would receive third-round (D Sven Butenschon) and seventh-round (C Serge Aubin) picks in 1994 draft (September 14, 1992).... Injured groin (October 17, 1992); missed one game.... Fractured kneecap (December 5, 1992); missed six games.... Suffered from the flu (February 15, 1993); missed one game.... Bruised ribs (March 3, 1993); missed nine games.... Reinjured bruised ribs (April 1, 1993); missed remainder of season.... Suffered hip flexor (November 17, 1993); missed one game ... Injured back (November 24, 1993); missed five games.... Signed as free agent by New York Islanders (August 2, 1994).... Loaned by Islanders to Minnesota Moose of IHL (September 30, 1994).
MISCELLANEOUS: Member of Stanley Cup championship team (1991).

Season Team	League	REGULAR SEASON							PLAYOFFS						
		Gms.	Min.	W	L	T	GA	SO	Avg.	Gms.	Min.	W	L	GA	SO	Avg.
82-83—Univ. of Minnesota.......	WCHA	25	1348	15	6	1	80	1	3.56	—	—	—	—	—	—	—
83-84—Univ. of Minnesota.......	WCHA	20	1141	13	7	0	66	0	3.47	—	—	—	—	—	—	—
84-85—Univ. of Minnesota.......	WCHA	17	912	8	3	3	52	0	3.42	—	—	—	—	—	—	—
85-86—Univ. of Minnesota.......	WCHA	23	1284	15	7	0	76	0	3.55	—	—	—	—	—	—	—
86-87—Muskegon....................	IHL	35	2090	23	11	0	119	2	3.42	15	923	10	4	46	0	*2.99
87-88—Pittsburgh...................	NHL	21	1207	9	11	0	80	1	3.98	—	—	—	—	—	—	—
—Muskegon...............	IHL	15	868	11	3	†1	43	2	2.97	—	—	—	—	—	—	—
88-89—Pittsburgh...................	NHL	15	669	5	3	0	45	0	4.04	—	—	—	—	—	—	—
—Muskegon...............	IHL	13	760	10	1	‡0	38	1	3.00	9	566	8	1	29	0	3.07
89-90—Muskegon....................	IHL	12	691	9	2	‡1	38	0	3.30	—	—	—	—	—	—	—
—Pittsburgh..............	NHL	21	1066	8	6	2	77	0	4.33	—	—	—	—	—	—	—
90-91—Pittsburgh...................	NHL	25	1311	10	11	1	86	0	3.94	5	288	4	1	15	†1	3.13

Season	Team	League	REGULAR SEASON								PLAYOFFS						
			Gms.	Min.	W	L	T	GA	SO	Avg.	Gms.	Min.	W	L	GA	SO	Avg.
91-92—Pittsburgh	NHL	5	225	2	1	0	20	0	5.33	—	—	—	—	—	—	—
—Hartford	NHL	5	306	3	1	1	12	0	2.35	7	425	3	4	19	0	2.68
92-93—Hartford	NHL	30	1373	4	15	1	111	0	4.85	—	—	—	—	—	—	—
93-94—Hartford	NHL	19	984	5	11	1	59	0	3.60	—	—	—	—	—	—	—
—Springfield	AHL	23	1315	9	10	2	73	0	3.33	—	—	—	—	—	—	—
94-95—Minnesota	IHL	15	757	3	8	‡1	52	0	4.12	—	—	—	—	—	—	—
NHL totals			141	7141	46	59	6	490	1	4.12	12	713	7	5	34	1	2.86

PILON, RICH
D, ISLANDERS

PERSONAL: Born April 30, 1968, in Saskatoon, Sask. . . . 6-0/205. . . . Shoots left. . . . Name pronounced PEE-lahn.

TRANSACTIONS/CAREER NOTES: Selected by New York Islanders as underage junior in seventh round (ninth Islanders pick, 143rd overall) of NHL entry draft (June 21, 1986). . . . Injured right leg (December 1988). . . . Injured right eye (November 4, 1989); missed remainder of season. . . . Injured medial collateral ligament in left knee (February 23, 1991). . . . Suffered sore left shoulder (January 9, 1992); missed three games. . . . Lacerated finger (January 30, 1992); missed four games. . . . Bruised hand (October 31, 1992); missed two games. . . . Bruised hand (November 22, 1992); missed four games. . . . Sprained left knee (December 10, 1992); missed eight games. . . . Injured lower back (January 10, 1993); missed 11 games. . . . Injured left shoulder (November 13, 1993); missed seven games. . . . Reinjured left shoulder (December 3, 1993); missed 32 games. . . . Reinjured left shoulder (March 17, 1994); missed 14 games. . . . Suffered sore groin (February 22, 1995); missed four games. . . . Sprained ankle (March 5, 1995); missed 17 games. . . . Broke wrist (April 18, 1995); missed last seven games of season.

HONORS: Named to WHL All-Star second team (1987-88).

Season	Team	League	REGULAR SEASON					PLAYOFFS				
			Gms.	G	A	Pts.	PIM	Gms.	G	A	Pts.	PIM
85-86—Prince Albert	WHL	6	0	0	0	0	—	—	—	—	—
86-87—Prince Albert	WHL	68	4	21	25	192	7	1	6	7	17
87-88—Prince Albert	WHL	65	13	34	47	177	9	0	6	6	38
88-89—New York Islanders	NHL	62	0	14	14	242	—	—	—	—	—
89-90—New York Islanders	NHL	14	0	2	2	31	—	—	—	—	—
90-91—New York Islanders	NHL	60	1	4	5	126	—	—	—	—	—
91-92—New York Islanders	NHL	65	1	6	7	183	—	—	—	—	—
92-93—New York Islanders	NHL	44	1	3	4	164	15	0	0	0	50
—Capital District	AHL	6	0	1	1	8	—	—	—	—	—
93-94—New York Islanders	NHL	28	1	4	5	75	—	—	—	—	—
—Salt Lake City	IHL	2	0	0	0	8	—	—	—	—	—
94-95—New York Islanders	NHL	20	1	1	2	40	—	—	—	—	—
—Chicago	IHL	2	0	0	0	0	—	—	—	—	—
NHL totals			293	5	34	39	861	15	0	0	0	50

PITLICK, LANCE
D, SENATORS

PERSONAL: Born November 5, 1967, in Fridley, Minn. . . . 6-0/190. . . . Shoots right.

HIGH SCHOOL: Cooper (New Hope, Minn.).

COLLEGE: Minnesota.

TRANSACTIONS/CAREER NOTES: Selected by Minnesota North Stars in ninth round (10th North Stars pick, 180th overall) of NHL entry draft (June 21, 1986). . . . Severely pulled lower abdominal muscles (December 1, 1989). . . . Underwent surgery to have tendons sewn onto his abdominal muscle for reinforcement (January 18, 1990). . . . Signed as free agent by Philadelphia Flyers (September 5, 1990). . . . Signed as free agent by Ottawa Senators (June 22, 1994). . . . Bruised ribs (March 27, 1995); missed two games.

Season	Team	League	REGULAR SEASON					PLAYOFFS				
			Gms.	G	A	Pts.	PIM	Gms.	G	A	Pts.	PIM
84-85—Cooper H.S.	Minn. H.S.	23	8	4	12	. . .	—	—	—	—	—
85-86—Cooper H.S.	Minn. H.S.	21	17	8	25	. . .	—	—	—	—	—
86-87—University of Minnesota	WCHA	45	0	9	9	88	10	0	2	2	4
87-88—University of Minnesota	WCHA	38	3	9	12	76	8	1	1	2	14
88-89—University of Minnesota	WCHA	47	4	9	13	95	8	2	1	3	95
89-90—University of Minnesota	WCHA	14	3	2	5	26	—	—	—	—	—
90-91—Hershey	AHL	64	6	15	21	75	3	0	0	0	9
91-92—U.S. national team	Int'l	19	0	1	1	38	—	—	—	—	—
—Hershey	AHL	4	0	0	0	6	3	0	0	0	4
92-93—Hershey	AHL	53	5	10	15	77	—	—	—	—	—
93-94—Hershey	AHL	58	4	13	17	93	11	1	0	1	11
94-95—Prince Edward Island	AHL	61	8	19	27	55	11	1	4	5	10
—Ottawa	NHL	15	0	1	1	6	—	—	—	—	—
NHL totals			15	0	1	1	6	—	—	—	—	—

PITTIS, DOMENIC
C, PENGUINS

PERSONAL: Born October 1, 1974, in Calgary. . . . 5-11/180. . . . Shoots left. . . . Name pronounced PIH-tihz.

HIGH SCHOOL: Catholic Central (Lethbridge, Alta.).

TRANSACTIONS/CAREER NOTES: Selected by Pittsburgh Penguins in second round (second Penguins pick, 52nd overall) of NHL entry draft (June 26, 1993).

HONORS: Named to WHL (East) All-Star second team (1993-94).

P

Season Team	League	REGULAR SEASON					PLAYOFFS				
		Gms.	G	A	Pts.	PIM	Gms.	G	A	Pts.	PIM
91-92—Lethbridge	WHL	65	6	17	23	48	5	0	2	2	4
92-93—Lethbridge	WHL	66	46	73	119	69	4	3	3	6	8
93-94—Lethbridge	WHL	72	58	69	127	93	8	4	11	15	16
94-95—Cleveland	IHL	62	18	32	50	66	3	0	2	2	2

PIVONKA, MICHAL
C, CAPITALS

PERSONAL: Born January 28, 1966, in Kladno, Czechoslovakia. . . . 6-2/195. . . . Shoots left. . . . Name pronounced puh-VAHN-kuh.
TRANSACTIONS/CAREER NOTES: Selected by Washington Capitals in third round (third Capitals pick, 59th overall) of NHL entry draft (June 9, 1984). . . . Strained ankle ligaments (March 1987). . . . Sprained right wrist (October 1987). . . . Sprained left ankle (March 1988). . . . Sprained left knee (March 9, 1990). . . . Pulled groin (October 10, 1992); missed three games. . . . Pulled groin (October 21, 1992); missed 12 games. . . . Suffered concussion (March 25, 1994); missed one game. . . . Played in Europe during 1994-95 NHL lockout. . . . Injured leg (April 30, 1995); missed one game.
STATISTICAL PLATEAUS: Three-goal games: 1991-92 (1).

Season Team	League	REGULAR SEASON					PLAYOFFS				
		Gms.	G	A	Pts.	PIM	Gms.	G	A	Pts.	PIM
85-86—Dukla Jihlava	Czech.	42	5	13	18	...	—	—	—	—	—
86-87—Washington	NHL	73	18	25	43	41	7	1	1	2	2
87-88—Washington	NHL	71	11	23	34	28	14	4	9	13	4
88-89—Baltimore	AHL	31	12	24	36	19	—	—	—	—	—
—Washington	NHL	52	8	19	27	30	6	3	1	4	10
89-90—Washington	NHL	77	25	39	64	54	11	0	2	2	6
90-91—Washington	NHL	79	20	50	70	34	11	2	3	5	8
91-92—Washington	NHL	80	23	57	80	47	7	1	5	6	13
92-93—Washington	NHL	69	21	53	74	66	6	0	2	2	0
93-94—Washington	NHL	82	14	36	50	38	7	4	4	8	4
94-95—Klagenfurt	Austria	7	2	4	6	4	—	—	—	—	—
—Washington	NHL	46	10	23	33	50	7	1	4	5	21
NHL totals		629	150	325	475	388	76	16	31	47	68

PLANTE, DAN
RW, ISLANDERS

PERSONAL: Born October 5, 1971, in St. Louis. . . . 6-0/207. . . . Shoots right. . . . Full name: Daniel Leon Plante. . . . Name pronounced PLANT.
HIGH SCHOOL: Edina (Minn.).
COLLEGE: Wisconsin.
TRANSACTIONS/CAREER NOTES: Selected by New York Islanders in third round (third Islanders pick, 48th overall) of NHL entry draft (June 16, 1990). . . . Injured knee (September 1994).

Season Team	League	REGULAR SEASON					PLAYOFFS				
		Gms.	G	A	Pts.	PIM	Gms.	G	A	Pts.	PIM
88-89—Edina High School	Minn. H.S.	27	10	26	36	12	—	—	—	—	—
89-90—Edina High School	Minn. H.S.	24	8	18	26	...	—	—	—	—	—
90-91—University of Wisconsin	WCHA	33	1	2	3	54	—	—	—	—	—
91-92—University of Wisconsin	WCHA	40	15	16	31	113	—	—	—	—	—
92-93—University of Wisconsin	WCHA	42	26	31	57	142	—	—	—	—	—
93-94—Salt Lake City	IHL	66	7	17	24	148	—	—	—	—	—
—New York Islanders	NHL	12	0	1	1	4	1	1	0	1	2
94-95—Denver	IHL	2	0	0	0	4	—	—	—	—	—
NHL totals		12	0	1	1	4	1	1	0	1	2

PLANTE, DEREK
C, SABRES

PERSONAL: Born January 17, 1971, in Cloquet, Minn. . . . 5-11/180. . . . Shoots left. . . . Full name: Derek John Plante. . . . Name pronounced PLANT.
HIGH SCHOOL: Cloquet (Minn.).
COLLEGE: Minnesota-Duluth.
TRANSACTIONS/CAREER NOTES: Broke arm (March 1988). . . . Selected by Buffalo Sabres in eighth round (seventh Sabres pick, 161st overall) of NHL entry draft (June 17, 1989). . . . Injured collarbone (December 15, 1989). . . . Reinjured collarbone (January 20, 1990). . . . Bruised left shoulder (March 8, 1994); missed two games.
HONORS: Named WCHA Player of the Year (1992-93). . . . Named to NCAA All-America West first team (1992-93). . . . Named to WCHA All-Star first team (1992-93).
STATISTICAL PLATEAUS: Three-goal games: 1993-94 (1).

Season Team	League	REGULAR SEASON					PLAYOFFS				
		Gms.	G	A	Pts.	PIM	Gms.	G	A	Pts.	PIM
87-88—Cloquet H.S.	Minn. H.S.	23	16	25	41	...	—	—	—	—	—
88-89—Cloquet H.S.	Minn. H.S.	24	30	33	63	...	—	—	—	—	—
89-90—Minnesota-Duluth	WCHA	28	10	11	21	12	—	—	—	—	—
90-91—Minnesota-Duluth	WCHA	36	23	20	43	6	—	—	—	—	—
91-92—Minnesota-Duluth	WCHA	37	27	36	63	28	—	—	—	—	—
92-93—Minnesota-Duluth	WCHA	37	*36	*56	*92	30	—	—	—	—	—
93-94—U.S. national team	Int'l	2	...	1	1	...	—	—	—	—	—
—Buffalo	NHL	77	21	35	56	24	7	1	0	1	0
94-95—Buffalo	NHL	47	3	19	22	12	—	—	—	—	—
NHL totals		124	24	54	78	36	7	1	0	1	0

P

PLAVSIC, ADRIEN
D, LIGHTNING

PERSONAL: Born January 13, 1970, in Montreal. . . . 6-1/200. . . . Shoots left. . . . Name pronounced PLAV-sihk.
COLLEGE: New Hampshire.
TRANSACTIONS/CAREER NOTES: Selected by St. Louis Blues in second round (second Blues pick, 30th overall) of NHL entry draft (June 11, 1988). . . . Suffered concussion (September 25, 1989). . . . Traded by Blues with first-round pick in 1990 draft (LW/RW Shawn Antoski) and second-round pick in 1991 draft to Vancouver Canucks for RW Rich Sutter, D Harold Snepsts and second-round pick (LW Craig Johnson) in 1990 draft (March 6, 1990). . . . Sprained knee (November 9, 1990); missed 15 games. . . . Suffered from the flu (February 22, 1993); missed one game. . . . Suffered concussion (December 4, 1993); missed four games. . . . Traded by Canucks to Tampa Bay Lightning for fifth-round pick in 1997 draft (March 22, 1995).
MISCELLANEOUS: Member of silver-medal-winning Canadian Olympic team (1992).

			REGULAR SEASON					PLAYOFFS				
Season	Team	League	Gms.	G	A	Pts.	PIM	Gms.	G	A	Pts.	PIM
87-88	—Univ. of New Hampshire ...	Hockey East	30	5	6	11	45	—	—	—	—	—
88-89	—Canadian national team ...	Int'l	62	5	10	15	25	—	—	—	—	—
89-90	—Peoria	IHL	51	7	14	21	87	—	—	—	—	—
	—St. Louis	NHL	4	0	1	1	2	—	—	—	—	—
	—Vancouver	NHL	11	3	2	5	8	—	—	—	—	—
	—Milwaukee	IHL	3	1	2	3	14	6	1	3	4	6
90-91	—Vancouver	NHL	48	2	10	12	62	—	—	—	—	—
91-92	—Canadian national team	Int'l	38	6	9	15	29	—	—	—	—	—
	—Canadian Olympic Team ..	Int'l	8	0	2	2	0	—	—	—	—	—
	—Vancouver	NHL	16	1	9	10	14	13	1	7	8	4
92-93	—Vancouver	NHL	57	6	21	27	53	—	—	—	—	—
93-94	—Vancouver	NHL	47	1	9	10	6	—	—	—	—	—
	—Hamilton	AHL	2	0	0	0	0	—	—	—	—	—
94-95	—Vancouver	NHL	3	0	1	1	4	—	—	—	—	—
	—Tampa Bay	NHL	15	2	1	3	4	—	—	—	—	—
	NHL totals		201	15	54	69	153	13	1	7	8	4

POAPST, STEVE
D, CAPITALS

PERSONAL: Born January 3, 1969, in Cornwall, Ont. . . . 6-0/180. . . . Shoots left. . . . Name pronounced PAHPS.
COLLEGE: Colgate.
TRANSACTIONS/CAREER NOTES: Signed as free agent by Portland Pirates (July 1993). . . . Signed as free agent by Washington Capitals (January 1995).

			REGULAR SEASON					PLAYOFFS				
Season	Team	League	Gms.	G	A	Pts.	PIM	Gms.	G	A	Pts.	PIM
89-90	—Colgate University	ECAC	38	4	15	19	54	—	—	—	—	—
90-91	—Colgate University	ECAC	32	6	15	21	43	—	—	—	—	—
91-92	—Hampton Roads	ECHL	55	8	20	28	29	14	1	4	5	12
92-93	—Hampton Roads	ECHL	63	10	35	45	57	4	0	1	1	4
	—Baltimore	AHL	7	0	1	1	4	7	0	3	3	6
93-94	—Portland	AHL	78	14	21	35	47	12	0	3	3	8
94-95	—Portland	AHL	71	8	22	30	60	7	0	1	1	16

PODEIN, SHJON
LW, FLYERS

PERSONAL: Born March 5, 1968, in Rochester, Minn. . . . 6-2/200. . . . Shoots left. . . . Name pronounced SHAWN poh-DEEN.
COLLEGE: Minnesota-Duluth.
TRANSACTIONS/CAREER NOTES: Selected by Edmonton Oilers in eighth round (ninth Oilers pick, 166th overall) of NHL entry draft (June 11, 1988). . . . Injured knee (March 9, 1994); missed five games. . . . Signed as free agent by Philadelphia Flyers (July 27, 1994).

			REGULAR SEASON					PLAYOFFS				
Season	Team	League	Gms.	G	A	Pts.	PIM	Gms.	G	A	Pts.	PIM
87-88	—Minnesota-Duluth	WCHA	30	4	4	8	48	—	—	—	—	—
88-89	—Minnesota-Duluth	WCHA	36	7	5	12	46	—	—	—	—	—
89-90	—Minnesota-Duluth	WCHA	35	21	18	39	36	—	—	—	—	—
90-91	—Cape Breton	AHL	63	14	15	29	65	4	0	0	0	5
91-92	—Cape Breton	AHL	80	30	24	54	46	5	3	1	4	2
92-93	—Cape Breton	AHL	38	18	21	39	32	9	2	2	4	29
	—Edmonton	NHL	40	13	6	19	25	—	—	—	—	—
93-94	—Edmonton	NHL	28	3	5	8	8	—	—	—	—	—
	—Cape Breton	AHL	5	4	4	8	4	—	—	—	—	—
94-95	—Philadelphia	NHL	44	3	7	10	33	15	1	3	4	10
	NHL totals		112	19	18	37	66	15	1	3	4	10

PODOLLAN, JASON
RW/C, PANTHERS

PERSONAL: Born February 18, 1976, in Vernon, B.C. . . . 6-1/181. . . . Shoots right.
HIGH SCHOOL: University (Spokane, Wash.).
TRANSACTIONS/CAREER NOTES: Selected by Florida Panthers in second round (third Panthers pick, 31st overall) of NHL entry draft (June 28, 1994).

			REGULAR SEASON					PLAYOFFS				
Season	Team	League	Gms.	G	A	Pts.	PIM	Gms.	G	A	Pts.	PIM
91-92	—Penticton	Jr. A	59	20	26	46	66	—	—	—	—	—
	—Spokane	WHL	2	0	0	0	2	10	3	1	4	16

P

Season Team	League	REGULAR SEASON					PLAYOFFS				
		Gms.	G	A	Pts.	PIM	Gms.	G	A	Pts.	PIM
92-93—Spokane	WHL	72	36	33	69	108	10	4	4	8	14
93-94—Spokane	WHL	69	29	37	66	108	3	3	0	3	2
94-95—Spokane	WHL	72	43	41	84	102	11	5	7	12	18
—Cincinnati	IHL	—	—	—	—	—	3	0	0	0	2

POESCHEK, RUDY
D, LIGHTNING

PERSONAL: Born September 29, 1966, in Terrace, B.C. . . . 6-2/210. . . . Shoots right. . . . Full name: Rudolph Leopold Poeschek. . . . Name pronounced POH-shehk. **TRANSACTIONS/CAREER NOTES:** Injured knee (December 1984). . . . Selected by New York Rangers as underage junior in 12th round (12th Rangers pick, 238th overall) of NHL entry draft (June 15, 1985). . . . Injured shoulder (November 1986). . . . Bruised right hand (February 1989). . . . Suspended six games by AHL for a pre-game fight (November 25, 1990). . . . Traded by Rangers to Winnipeg Jets for C Guy Larose (January 22, 1991). . . . Signed as free agent by Tampa Bay Lightning (August 13, 1993). . . . Sprained ankle (February 7, 1995); missed two games. . . . Reinjured ankle (February 14, 1995); missed nine games. . . . Broke thumb (April 16, 1995); missed last eight games of season.

Season Team	League	REGULAR SEASON					PLAYOFFS				
		Gms.	G	A	Pts.	PIM	Gms.	G	A	Pts.	PIM
83-84—Kamloops	WHL	47	3	9	12	93	8	0	2	2	7
84-85—Kamloops	WHL	34	6	7	13	100	15	0	3	3	56
85-86—Kamloops	WHL	32	3	13	16	92	16	3	7	10	40
86-87—Kamloops	WHL	54	13	18	31	153	15	2	4	6	37
87-88—New York Rangers	NHL	1	0	0	0	2	—	—	—	—	—
—Colorado	IHL	82	7	31	38	210	12	2	2	4	31
88-89—Denver	IHL	2	0	0	0	6	—	—	—	—	—
—New York Rangers	NHL	52	0	2	2	199	—	—	—	—	—
89-90—Flint	IHL	38	8	13	21	109	4	0	0	0	16
—New York Rangers	NHL	15	0	0	0	55	—	—	—	—	—
90-91—Binghamton	AHL	38	1	3	4	162	—	—	—	—	—
—Moncton	AHL	23	2	4	6	67	9	1	1	2	41
—Winnipeg	NHL	1	0	0	0	5	—	—	—	—	—
91-92—Moncton	AHL	63	4	18	22	170	11	0	2	2	46
—Winnipeg	NHL	4	0	0	0	17	—	—	—	—	—
92-93—St. John's	AHL	78	7	24	31	189	9	0	4	4	13
93-94—Tampa Bay	NHL	71	3	6	9	118	—	—	—	—	—
94-95—Tampa Bay	NHL	25	1	1	2	92	—	—	—	—	—
NHL totals		169	4	9	13	488					

POIRIER, JOEL
LW, CAPITALS

PERSONAL: Born January 15, 1975, in Richmond Hill, Ont. . . . 6-0/190. . . . Shoots left. . . . Name pronounced POH-ree-yay. **HIGH SCHOOL:** Lasalle Secondary School (Sudbury, Ont.). **TRANSACTIONS/CAREER NOTES:** Selected by Washington Capitals in eighth round (seventh Capitals pick, 199th overall) of NHL entry draft (June 26, 1993).

Season Team	League	REGULAR SEASON					PLAYOFFS				
		Gms.	G	A	Pts.	PIM	Gms.	G	A	Pts.	PIM
91-92—Waterloo Jr. B	OHA	41	4	18	22	104	—	—	—	—	—
92-93—Sudbury	OHL	64	18	15	33	94	14	0	3	3	8
93-94—Sudbury	OHL	28	17	5	22	44	—	—	—	—	—
—Windsor	OHL	13	6	8	14	20	—	—	—	—	—
94-95—Windsor	OHL	64	24	39	63	50	10	4	5	9	10

POLASEK, LIBOR
C, CANUCKS

PERSONAL: Born April 22, 1974, in Vitkovice, Czechoslovakia. . . . 6-3/198. . . . Shoots right. . . . Name pronounced LEE-bohr poh-LA-sihk. **TRANSACTIONS/CAREER NOTES:** Selected by Vancouver Canucks in first round (first Canucks pick, 21st overall) of NHL entry draft (June 20, 1992).

Season Team	League	REGULAR SEASON					PLAYOFFS				
		Gms.	G	A	Pts.	PIM	Gms.	G	A	Pts.	PIM
91-92—TJ Vitkovice	Czech.	17	2	2	4	2	—	—	—	—	—
92-93—Hamilton	AHL	60	7	12	19	34	—	—	—	—	—
93-94—Hamilton	AHL	76	11	12	23	40	3	0	0	0	0
94-95—Syracuse	AHL	45	2	8	10	16	—	—	—	—	—
—South Carolina	ECHL	7	0	0	0	6	—	—	—	—	—

POMICHTER, MIKE
C, BLACKHAWKS

PERSONAL: Born September 10, 1973, in New Haven, Conn. . . . 6-1/200. . . . Shoots left. . . . Name pronounced PAHM-ih-chuhr. **HIGH SCHOOL:** North Haven (Conn.). **COLLEGE:** Boston University. **TRANSACTIONS/CAREER NOTES:** Selected by Chicago Blackhawks in second round (second Blackhawks pick, 39th overall) of NHL entry draft (June 22, 1991).

Season Team	League	REGULAR SEASON					PLAYOFFS				
		Gms.	G	A	Pts.	PIM	Gms.	G	A	Pts.	PIM
88-89—North Haven H.S.	Conn. H.S.	22	52	22	74	. . .	—	—	—	—	—

Season Team	League	REGULAR SEASON					PLAYOFFS				
		Gms.	G	A	Pts.	PIM	Gms.	G	A	Pts.	PIM
89-90—Springfield Jr. B	NEJHL	39	37	31	68	8	—	—	—	—	—
90-91—Springfield Jr. B	NEJHL	38	61	64	125	22	—	—	—	—	—
91-92—Boston University	Hockey East	35	11	27	38	14	—	—	—	—	—
92-93—Boston University	Hockey East	30	16	14	30	23	—	—	—	—	—
93-94—Boston University	Hockey East	40	28	26	54	37	—	—	—	—	—
94-95—Indianapolis	IHL	76	13	9	22	47	—	—	—	—	—

POPOVIC, PETER
D, CANADIENS

PERSONAL: Born February 10, 1968, in Koping, Sweden. . . . 6-5/241. . . . Shoots right. . . . Name pronounced PAH-poh-VIHK.

TRANSACTIONS/CAREER NOTES: Selected by Montreal Canadiens in fifth round (fifth Canadiens pick, 93rd overall) of NHL entry draft (June 11, 1988). . . . Injured knee (November 20, 1993); missed six games. . . . Bruised shoulder (December 22, 1993); missed seven games. . . . Played in Europe during 1994-95 NHL lockout. . . . Lacerated face (March 11, 1995); missed six games.

Season Team	League	REGULAR SEASON					PLAYOFFS				
		Gms.	G	A	Pts.	PIM	Gms.	G	A	Pts.	PIM
86-87—Vasteras	Sweden	24	1	2	3	10	—	—	—	—	—
87-88—Vasteras	Sweden	28	3	17	20	16	—	—	—	—	—
88-89—Vasteras	Sweden	22	1	4	5	32	—	—	—	—	—
89-90—Vasteras	Sweden	30	2	10	12	24	2	0	1	1	2
90-91—Vasteras	Sweden	40	3	2	5	62	4	0	0	0	4
91-92—Vasteras	Sweden	34	7	10	17	30	—	—	—	—	—
92-93—Vasteras	Sweden	39	6	12	18	46	3	0	1	1	2
93-94—Montreal	NHL	47	2	12	14	26	6	0	1	1	0
94-95—Vasteras	Sweden	11	0	3	3	10	—	—	—	—	—
—Montreal	NHL	33	0	5	5	8	—	—	—	—	—
NHL totals		80	2	17	19	34	6	0	1	1	0

POPP, KEVIN
D, SABRES

PERSONAL: Born February 26, 1976, in Surrey, B.C. . . . 6-1/198. . . . Shoots right.

TRANSACTIONS/CAREER NOTES: Selected by Buffalo Sabres in fifth round (seventh Sabres pick, 119th overall) of NHL entry draft (July 8, 1995).

Season Team	League	REGULAR SEASON					PLAYOFFS				
		Gms.	G	A	Pts.	PIM	Gms.	G	A	Pts.	PIM
92-93—New Westminster	Tier II Jr. A	40	9	9	18	325	—	—	—	—	—
93-94—Spokane	WHL	43	0	4	4	126	2	0	0	0	0
94-95—Seattle	WHL	70	5	8	13	257	4	1	2	3	4

POTOMSKI, BARRY
LW, KINGS

PERSONAL: Born November 24, 1972, in Windsor, Ont. . . . 6-2/215. . . . Shoots left.

TRANSACTIONS/CAREER NOTES: Signed as free agent by Los Angeles Kings (July 7, 1994).

Season Team	League	REGULAR SEASON					PLAYOFFS				
		Gms.	G	A	Pts.	PIM	Gms.	G	A	Pts.	PIM
90-91—London	OHL	65	14	17	31	202	7	0	2	2	10
91-92—London	OHL	61	19	32	51	224	10	5	1	6	22
92-93—Toledo	ECHL	43	5	18	23	184	14	5	2	7	73
—Erie	ECHL	5	1	1	2	31	—	—	—	—	—
93-94—Toledo	ECHL	13	9	4	13	81	—	—	—	—	—
—Adirondack	AHL	50	9	5	14	224	11	1	1	2	44
94-95—Phoenix	IHL	42	5	6	11	171	—	—	—	—	—

POTVIN, FELIX
G, MAPLE LEAFS

PERSONAL: Born June 23, 1971, in Anjou, Que. . . . 6-0/190. . . . Catches left. . . . Name pronounced PAHT-vihn.

TRANSACTIONS/CAREER NOTES: Selected by Toronto Maple Leafs in second round (second Maple Leafs pick, 31st overall) of NHL entry draft (June 16, 1990).

HONORS: Named to QMJHL All-Star second team (1989-90). . . . Won Can.HL Goaltender of the Year Award (1990-91). . . . Won Hap Emms Memorial Trophy (1990-91). . . . Won Jacques Plante Trophy (1990-91). . . . Won Shell Cup (1990-91). . . . Won Guy Lafleur Trophy (1990-91). . . . Named to Memorial Cup All-Star team (1990-91). . . . Named to QMJHL All-Star first team (1990-91). . . . Won Aldege (Baz) Bastien Trophy (1991-92). . . . Won Dudley (Red) Garrett Memorial Trophy (1991-92). . . . Named to AHL All-Star first team (1991-92). . . . Named to NHL All-Rookie team (1992-93). . . . Played in NHL All-Star Game (1994).

Season Team	League	REGULAR SEASON							PLAYOFFS						
		Gms.	Min.	W	L	T	GA	SO	Avg.	Gms.	Min.	W	L	GA	SO	Avg.
88-89—Chicoutimi	QMJHL	*65	*3489	25	31	1	*271	†2	4.66	—	—	—	—	—	—	—
89-90—Chicoutimi	QMJHL	*62	*3478	31	26	2	231	†2	3.99	—	—	—	—	—	—	—
90-91—Chicoutimi	QMJHL	54	3216	33	15	4	145	*6	†2.71	*16	*992	*11	5	46	0	*2.78
91-92—St. John's	AHL	35	2070	18	10	6	101	2	2.93	11	642	7	4	41	0	3.83
—Toronto	NHL	4	210	0	2	1	8	0	2.29	—	—	—	—	—	—	—
92-93—Toronto	NHL	48	2781	25	15	7	116	2	*2.50	21	1308	11	10	62	1	2.84
—St. John's	AHL	5	309	3	0	2	18	0	3.50	—	—	—	—	—	—	—
93-94—Toronto	NHL	66	3883	34	22	9	187	3	2.89	18	1124	9	†9	46	3	2.46
94-95—Toronto	NHL	36	2144	15	13	7	104	0	2.91	7	424	3	4	20	1	2.83
NHL totals		154	9018	74	52	24	415	5	2.76	46	2856	23	23	128	5	2.69

P

POTVIN, MARC
RW, BRUINS

PERSONAL: Born January 29, 1967, in Ottawa. . . . 6-1/215. . . . Shoots right. . . . Full name: Marc Richard Potvin. . . . Name pronounced PAHT-vihn. . . . Cousin of Denis Potvin, defenseman, New York Islanders (1973-74 through 1987-88).
COLLEGE: Bowling Green State.

TRANSACTIONS/CAREER NOTES: Selected by Detroit Red Wings in ninth round (ninth Red Wings pick, 169th overall) of NHL entry draft (June 21, 1986). . . . Traded by Red Wings with C Jimmy Carson and C Gary Shuchuk to Los Angeles Kings for D Paul Coffey, RW Jim Hiller and C/LW Sylvain Couturier (January 29, 1993). . . . Broke nose (February 18, 1993); missed one game. . . . Traded by Kings to Hartford Whalers for D Doug Houda (November 3, 1993). . . . Suffered from post-concussion syndrome (March 9, 1994); missed six games. . . . Fined $500 by Whalers for involvement in bar brawl (April 1, 1994). . . . Signed as free agent by Boston Bruins (June 28, 1994).

			REGULAR SEASON					PLAYOFFS				
Season Team	League	Gms.	G	A	Pts.	PIM		Gms.	G	A	Pts.	PIM
85-86—Stratford	OPJHL	63	5	6	11	117		—	—	—	—	—
86-87—Bowling Green State	CCHA	43	5	15	20	74		—	—	—	—	—
87-88—Bowling Green State	CCHA	45	15	21	36	80		—	—	—	—	—
88-89—Bowling Green State	CCHA	46	23	12	35	63		—	—	—	—	—
89-90—Bowling Green State	CCHA	40	19	17	36	72		—	—	—	—	—
—Adirondack	AHL	5	2	1	3	9		4	0	1	1	23
90-91—Adirondack	AHL	63	9	13	22	†365		—	—	—	—	—
—Detroit	NHL	9	0	0	0	55		6	0	0	0	32
91-92—Adirondack	AHL	51	13	16	29	314		†19	5	4	9	57
—Detroit	NHL	5	1	0	1	52		1	0	0	0	0
92-93—Adirondack	AHL	37	8	12	20	109		—	—	—	—	—
—Los Angeles	NHL	20	0	1	1	61		1	0	0	0	0
93-94—Los Angeles	NHL	3	0	0	0	26		—	—	—	—	—
—Hartford	NHL	51	2	3	5	246		—	—	—	—	—
94-95—Boston	NHL	6	0	1	1	4		—	—	—	—	—
—Providence	AHL	21	4	14	18	84		12	2	4	6	25
NHL totals		94	3	5	8	444		8	0	0	0	32

POULIN, DAVE
C

PERSONAL: Born December 17, 1958, in Mississauga, Ont. . . . 5-11/190. . . . Shoots left. . . . Full name: David James Poulin. . . . Name pronounced POO-lihn.
COLLEGE: Notre Dame.

TRANSACTIONS/CAREER NOTES: Signed as free agent by Philadelphia Flyers (February 1983). . . . Pulled hamstring and groin muscle (November 1986). . . . Fractured rib (April 16, 1987). . . . Pulled groin (February 1988). . . . Separated shoulder (November 1988). . . . Sent home due to irregular heartbeat (December 15, 1988). . . . Bruised right hand (January 1989). . . . Fractured right ring finger (April 8, 1989). . . . Suffered multiple fracture of left thumb (May 1989). . . . Bruised abdomen (October 1989). . . . Broke left thumb (October 28, 1989). . . . Traded by Flyers to Boston Bruins for C Ken Linseman (January 16, 1990). . . . Stretched nerve in neck and left arm (April 21, 1990). . . . Pulled groin (October 15, 1990); missed 17 games. . . . Broke jaw (December 28, 1990); missed 14 games. . . . Broke right shoulder blade (February 2, 1991); missed 15 games. . . . Strained groin and abdomen during preseason (September 1991); missed first 61 games of season. . . . Underwent surgery to groin and abdomen (December 6, 1991). . . . Signed as free agent by Washington Capitals (August 3, 1993). . . . Underwent root canal (October 27, 1993); missed one game. . . . Suffered from asthma (January 25, 1994); missed five games. . . . Suffered from asthma (February 10, 1994); missed 12 games. . . . Pulled groin (March 2, 1995); missed eight games. . . . Pulled groin (March 25, 1995); missed 11 games. . . . Announced retirement and named head coach of University of Notre Dame (April 25, 1995).
HONORS: Named to CCHA All-Star second team (1981-82). . . . Won Frank J. Selke Trophy (1986-87). . . . Played in NHL All-Star Game (1986 and 1988). . . . Won King Clancy Memorial Trophy (1992-93).
STATISTICAL PLATEAUS: Three-goal games: 1983-84 (2), 1984-85 (1), 1985-86 (1), 1986-87 (1). Total: 5.
MISCELLANEOUS: Captain of Philadelphia Flyers (1989-90).

			REGULAR SEASON					PLAYOFFS				
Season Team	League	Gms.	G	A	Pts.	PIM		Gms.	G	A	Pts.	PIM
78-79—University of Notre Dame	WCHA	37	28	31	59	32		—	—	—	—	—
79-80—University of Notre Dame	WCHA	24	19	24	43	46		—	—	—	—	—
80-81—University of Notre Dame	WCHA	35	13	22	35	53		—	—	—	—	—
81-82—University of Notre Dame	WCHA	39	29	30	59	44		—	—	—	—	—
82-83—Rogle	Sweden	33	35	18	53	...		—	—	—	—	—
—Maine	AHL	16	7	9	16	2		—	—	—	—	—
—Philadelphia	NHL	2	2	0	2	2		3	1	3	4	9
83-84—Philadelphia	NHL	73	31	45	76	47		3	0	0	0	2
84-85—Philadelphia	NHL	73	30	44	74	59		11	3	5	8	6
85-86—Philadelphia	NHL	79	27	42	69	49		5	2	0	2	2
86-87—Philadelphia	NHL	75	25	45	70	53		15	3	3	6	14
87-88—Philadelphia	NHL	68	19	32	51	32		7	2	6	8	4
88-89—Philadelphia	NHL	69	18	17	35	49		19	6	5	11	16
89-90—Philadelphia	NHL	28	9	8	17	12		—	—	—	—	—
—Boston	NHL	32	6	19	25	12		18	8	5	13	8
90-91—Boston	NHL	31	8	12	20	25		16	0	9	9	20
91-92—Boston	NHL	18	4	4	8	18		15	3	3	6	22
92-93—Boston	NHL	84	16	33	49	62		4	1	1	2	10
93-94—Washington	NHL	63	6	19	25	52		11	2	2	4	19
94-95—Washington	NHL	29	4	5	9	10		2	0	0	0	0
NHL totals		724	205	325	530	482		129	31	42	73	132

P

POULIN, PATRICK
LW, BLACKHAWKS

PERSONAL: Born April 23, 1973, in Vanier, Que. . . . 6-1/208. . . . Shoots left. . . . Name pronounced POO-lai.
TRANSACTIONS/CAREER NOTES: Broke wrist (January 15, 1991). . . . Selected by Hartford Whalers in first round (first Whalers pick, ninth overall) of NHL entry draft (June 22, 1991). . . . Traded by Whalers with D Eric Weinrich to Chicago Blackhawks for RW Steve Larmer and D Bryan Marchment (November 2, 1993).
HONORS: Won Jean Beliveau Trophy (1991-92). . . . Named to Can.HL All-Star first team (1991-92). . . . Named to QMJHL All-Star first team (1991-92).

			REGULAR SEASON					PLAYOFFS				
Season Team	League	Gms.	G	A	Pts.	PIM	Gms.	G	A	Pts.	PIM
89-90—St. Hyacinthe	QMJHL	60	25	26	51	55	12	1	9	10	5
90-91—St. Hyacinthe	QMJHL	56	32	38	70	82	4	0	2	2	23
91-92—St. Hyacinthe	QMJHL	56	52	86	*138	58	5	2	2	4	4
—Springfield	AHL	—	—	—	—	—	1	0	0	0	0
—Hartford	NHL	1	0	0	0	2	7	2	1	3	0
92-93—Hartford	NHL	81	20	31	51	37	—	—	—	—	—
93-94—Hartford	NHL	9	2	1	3	11	—	—	—	—	—
—Chicago	NHL	58	12	13	25	40	4	0	0	0	0
94-95—Chicago	NHL	45	15	15	30	53	16	4	1	5	8
NHL totals		194	49	60	109	143	27	6	2	8	8

PRATT, NOLAN
D, WHALERS

PERSONAL: Born August 14, 1975, in Fort McMurray, Alta. . . . 6-2/190. . . . Shoots left.
HIGH SCHOOL: Sunset (Beaverton, Ore.).
TRANSACTIONS/CAREER NOTES: Selected by Hartford Whalers in fifth round (fourth Whalers pick, 115th overall) of NHL entry draft (June 26, 1993).

			REGULAR SEASON					PLAYOFFS				
Season Team	League	Gms.	G	A	Pts.	PIM	Gms.	G	A	Pts.	PIM
91-92—Portland	WHL	22	2	9	11	13	6	1	3	4	12
92-93—Portland	WHL	70	4	19	23	97	16	2	7	9	31
93-94—Portland	WHL	72	4	32	36	105	10	1	2	3	14
94-95—Portland	WHL	72	6	37	43	196	9	1	6	7	10

PRESLEY, WAYNE
RW, RANGERS

PERSONAL: Born March 23, 1965, in Dearborn, Mich. . . . 5-11/180. . . . Shoots right.
TRANSACTIONS/CAREER NOTES: Selected by Chicago Blackhawks as an underage junior in second round (second Blackhawks pick, 39th overall) of NHL entry draft (June 8, 1983). . . . Traded by Kitchener Rangers to Sault Ste. Marie Greyhounds for RW Shawn Tyers (January 1985). . . . Underwent surgery to repair ligaments and cartilage in right knee (November 1987); missed 36 games. . . . Dislocated shoulder (May 6, 1989). . . . Traded by Blackhawks to San Jose Sharks for third-round pick in 1993 draft (September 20, 1991). . . . Injured knee (November 17, 1991). . . . Injured hand (December 3, 1991); missed eight games. . . . Traded by Sharks to Buffalo Sabres for C Dave Snuggerud (March 9, 1992). . . . Bruised foot (October 8, 1992); missed one game. . . . Injured knee (October 1993); missed four games. . . . Pulled groin (April 18, 1995); missed one game. . . . Signed as free agent by New York Rangers (August 2, 1995).
HONORS: Won Jim Mahon Memorial Trophy (1983-84). . . . Named to OHL All-Star first team (1983-84).
RECORDS: Shares NHL single-season and single-series playoff records for most shorthanded goals—3 (1989).
STATISTICAL PLATEAUS: Three-goal games: 1987-88 (1).

			REGULAR SEASON					PLAYOFFS				
Season Team	League	Gms.	G	A	Pts.	PIM	Gms.	G	A	Pts.	PIM
82-83—Kitchener	OHL	70	39	48	87	99	12	1	4	5	9
83-84—Kitchener	OHL	70	63	76	139	156	16	12	16	28	38
84-85—Kitchener	OHL	31	25	21	46	77	—	—	—	—	—
—Sault Ste. Marie	OHL	11	5	9	14	14	16	13	9	22	13
—Chicago	NHL	3	0	1	1	0	—	—	—	—	—
85-86—Nova Scotia	AHL	29	6	9	15	22	—	—	—	—	—
—Chicago	NHL	38	7	8	15	38	3	0	0	0	0
86-87—Chicago	NHL	80	32	29	61	114	4	1	0	1	9
87-88—Chicago	NHL	42	12	10	22	52	5	0	0	0	4
88-89—Chicago	NHL	72	21	19	40	100	14	7	5	12	18
89-90—Chicago	NHL	49	6	7	13	69	19	9	6	15	29
90-91—Chicago	NHL	71	15	19	34	122	6	0	1	1	38
91-92—San Jose	NHL	47	8	14	22	76	—	—	—	—	—
—Buffalo	NHL	12	2	2	4	57	7	3	3	6	14
92-93—Buffalo	NHL	79	15	17	32	96	8	1	0	1	6
93-94—Buffalo	NHL	65	17	8	25	103	7	2	1	3	14
94-95—Buffalo	NHL	46	14	5	19	41	5	3	1	4	8
NHL totals		604	149	139	288	868	78	26	17	43	140

PRIMEAU, KEITH
C, RED WINGS

PERSONAL: Born November 24, 1971, in Toronto. . . . 6-4/220. . . . Shoots left. . . . Name pronounced PREE-moh. . . . Brother of Wayne Primeau, center in Buffalo Sabres system.
TRANSACTIONS/CAREER NOTES: Selected by Detroit Red Wings in first round (first Red Wings pick, third overall) of NHL entry draft (June 16, 1990). . . . Suffered from the flu (January 13, 1993); missed two games. . . . Sprained right shoulder (February 9, 1993); missed one game. . . . Sprained right knee (March 2, 1993); missed two games. . . . Sprained right knee (April 1, 1993); missed four games. . . . Injured right thumb (February 10, 1995); missed one game. . . . Suffered from the flu (February 25, 1995); missed one game. . . . Reinjured thumb (March 2, 1995); missed one game.
HONORS: Won Eddie Powers Memorial Trophy (1989-90). . . . Named to OHL All-Star second team (1989-90).

P

Season Team	League	REGULAR SEASON Gms.	G	A	Pts.	PIM	PLAYOFFS Gms.	G	A	Pts.	PIM
87-88—Hamilton	OHL	47	6	6	12	69	11	0	2	2	2
88-89—Niagara Falls	OHL	48	20	35	55	56	17	9	6	15	12
89-90—Niagara Falls	OHL	65	*57	70	*127	97	16	*16	17	*33	49
90-91—Detroit	NHL	58	3	12	15	106	5	1	1	2	25
—Adirondack	AHL	6	3	5	8	8	—	—	—	—	—
91-92—Detroit	NHL	35	6	10	16	83	11	0	0	0	14
—Adirondack	AHL	42	21	24	45	89	9	1	7	8	27
92-93—Detroit	NHL	73	15	17	32	152	7	0	2	2	26
93-94—Detroit	NHL	78	31	42	73	173	7	0	2	2	6
94-95—Detroit	NHL	45	15	27	42	99	17	4	5	9	45
NHL totals		289	70	108	178	613	47	5	10	15	116

PRIMEAU, WAYNE
C, SABRES

PERSONAL: Born June 4, 1976, in Scarborough, Ont. . . . 6-3/193. . . . Shoots left. . . . Name pronounced PREE-moh. . . . Brother of Keith Primeau, center, Detroit Red Wings. **HIGH SCHOOL:** St. Mary's (Owen Sound, Ont.).
TRANSACTIONS/CAREER NOTES: Selected by Buffalo Sabres in first round (first Sabres pick, 17th overall) of NHL entry draft (June 28, 1994).

Season Team	League	REGULAR SEASON Gms.	G	A	Pts.	PIM	PLAYOFFS Gms.	G	A	Pts.	PIM
92-93—Owen Sound	OHL	66	10	27	37	110	8	1	4	5	0
93-94—Owen Sound	OHL	65	25	50	75	75	9	1	6	7	8
94-95—Owen Sound	OHL	66	34	62	96	84	10	4	9	13	15
—Buffalo	NHL	1	1	0	1	0	—	—	—	—	—
NHL totals		1	1	0	1	0					

PROBERT, BOB
LW, BLACKHAWKS

PERSONAL: Born June 5, 1965, in Windsor, Ont. . . . 6-3/215. . . . Shoots left. . . . Name pronounced PROH-burt.
TRANSACTIONS/CAREER NOTES: Selected by Detroit Red Wings as underage junior in third round (third Red Wings pick, 46th overall) of NHL entry draft (June 8, 1983). . . . Entered in-patient alcohol abuse treatment center (July 22, 1986). . . . Suspended six games by NHL during the 1987-88 season for game misconduct penalties. . . . Suspended without pay by Red Wings for skipping practice and missing team buses, flights and curfews (September 23, 1988). . . . Reactivated by Red Wings (November 23, 1988). . . . Suspended three games by NHL for hitting another player (December 10, 1988). . . . Removed from team after showing up late for a game (January 26, 1989). . . . Reactivated by Red Wings (February 15, 1989). . . . Charged with smuggling cocaine into the United States (March 2, 1989). . . . Expelled from the NHL (March 4, 1989). . . . Reinstated by NHL (March 14, 1990). . . . Unable to play any games in Canada while appealing deportation order by U.S. Immigration Department during 1990-91 and 1991-92 seasons. . . . Fractured left wrist (December 1, 1990); missed 12 games. . . . Suspended one game by NHL for game misconduct penalties (February 9, 1993). . . . Bruised tailbone (November 20, 1993); missed eight games. . . . Suspended four games by NHL for stick-swinging incident (October 16, 1993). . . . Suspended two games and fined $500 by NHL for head-butting (April 7, 1994). . . . Signed as free agent by Chicago Blackhawks (July 23, 1994). . . . Placed on inactive status by NHL for violating substance abuse policies (September 2, 1994). . . . Reinstated by NHL and declared eligible for 1995-96 season (April 28, 1995).
HONORS: Played in NHL All-Star Game (1988).
STATISTICAL PLATEAUS: Three-goal games: 1987-88 (1).

Season Team	League	REGULAR SEASON Gms.	G	A	Pts.	PIM	PLAYOFFS Gms.	G	A	Pts.	PIM
82-83—Brantford	OHL	51	12	16	28	133	8	2	2	4	23
83-84—Brantford	OHL	65	35	38	73	189	6	0	3	3	16
84-85—Hamilton	OHL	4	0	1	1	21	—	—	—	—	—
—Sault Ste. Marie	OHL	44	20	52	72	172	15	6	11	17	*60
85-86—Adirondack	AHL	32	12	15	27	152	10	2	3	5	68
—Detroit	NHL	44	8	13	21	186	—	—	—	—	—
86-87—Detroit	NHL	63	13	11	24	221	16	3	4	7	63
—Adirondack	AHL	7	1	4	5	15	—	—	—	—	—
87-88—Detroit	NHL	74	29	33	62	*398	16	8	13	21	51
88-89—Detroit	NHL	25	4	2	6	106	—	—	—	—	—
89-90—Detroit	NHL	4	3	0	3	21	—	—	—	—	—
90-91—Detroit	NHL	55	16	23	39	315	6	1	2	3	50
91-92—Detroit	NHL	63	20	24	44	276	11	1	6	7	28
92-93—Detroit	NHL	80	14	29	43	292	7	0	3	3	10
93-94—Detroit	NHL	66	7	10	17	275	7	1	1	2	8
94-95—Chicago	NHL	Did not play.									
NHL totals		474	114	145	259	2090	63	14	29	43	210

PROCHAZKA, MARTIN
RW, MAPLE LEAFS

PERSONAL: Born March 3, 1972, in Slany, Czechoslovakia. . . . 5-11/180. . . . Shoots right. . . . Name pronounced pro-HAHS-kah.
TRANSACTIONS/CAREER NOTES: Selected by Toronto Maple Leafs in seventh round (eighth Maple Leafs pick, 135th overall) of NHL entry draft (June 22, 1991).

Season Team	League	REGULAR SEASON Gms.	G	A	Pts.	PIM	PLAYOFFS Gms.	G	A	Pts.	PIM
89-90—Kladno	Czech.	49	18	12	30	...	—	—	—	—	—
90-91—Kladno	Czech.	50	19	10	29	21	—	—	—	—	—

P

Season Team	League	REGULAR SEASON					PLAYOFFS				
		Gms.	G	A	Pts.	PIM	Gms.	G	A	Pts.	PIM
91-92—Dukla Jihlava	Czech.	44	18	11	29	2	—	—	—	—	—
92-93—Kladno	Czech.	46	26	12	38	38	—	—	—	—	—
93-94—HC Kladno	Czech. Rep.	43	24	16	40	...	2	2	0	2	...
94-95—HC Kladno	Czech. Rep.	41	25	33	58	...	11	8	4	12	...

PROKHOROV, VITALI
LW

PERSONAL: Born December 25, 1966, in Moscow, U.S.S.R. . . . 5-9/185. . . . Shoots left. . . . Name pronounced vee-TAL-ee PROH-kuh-RAHF.
TRANSACTIONS/CAREER NOTES: Selected by St. Louis Blues in third round (third Blues pick, 64th overall) of NHL entry draft (June 20, 1992). . . . Injured shoulder (November 10, 1992); missed two games. . . . Injured shoulder (December 17, 1992); missed 14 games. . . . Reinjured shoulder (February 10, 1993); missed remainder of season. . . . Broke toe (October 9, 1993); missed six games. . . . Played in Europe during 1994-95 NHL lockout.
STATISTICAL PLATEAUS: Three-goal games: 1992-93 (1).
MISCELLANEOUS: Member of gold-medal-winning Unified Olympic team (1992).

Season Team	League	REGULAR SEASON					PLAYOFFS				
		Gms.	G	A	Pts.	PIM	Gms.	G	A	Pts.	PIM
83-84—Spartak Moscow	USSR	5	0	0	0	0	—	—	—	—	—
84-85—Spartak Moscow	USSR	31	1	1	2	10	—	—	—	—	—
85-86—Spartak Moscow	USSR	29	3	9	12	4	—	—	—	—	—
86-87—Spartak Moscow	USSR	27	1	6	7	2	—	—	—	—	—
87-88—Spartak Moscow	USSR	19	5	0	5	4	—	—	—	—	—
88-89—Spartak Moscow	USSR	37	11	5	16	10	—	—	—	—	—
89-90—Spartak Moscow	USSR	43	13	8	21	35	—	—	—	—	—
90-91—Spartak Moscow	USSR	43	21	10	31	29	—	—	—	—	—
91-92—Spartak Moscow	CIS	38	13	19	32	68	—	—	—	—	—
—Unified Olympic Team	Int'l	8	2	4	6	6	—	—	—	—	—
92-93—St. Louis	NHL	26	4	1	5	15	—	—	—	—	—
93-94—St. Louis	NHL	55	15	10	25	24	4	0	0	0	0
—Peoria	IHL	19	13	10	23	16	—	—	—	—	—
94-95—Spartak Moscow	CIS	8	1	4	5	8	—	—	—	—	—
—St. Louis	NHL	2	0	0	0	0	—	—	—	—	—
—Peoria	IHL	20	6	3	9	6	9	4	7	11	6
NHL totals		83	19	11	30	35	4	0	0	0	0

PROKOPEC, MIKE
RW, BLACKHAWKS

PERSONAL: Born May 17, 1974, in Toronto. . . . 6-2/190. . . . Shoots right. . . . Name pronounced PROH-kuh-pehk.
TRANSACTIONS/CAREER NOTES: Selected by Chicago Blackhawks in seventh round (seventh Blackhawks pick, 161st overall) of NHL entry draft (June 20, 1992).

Season Team	League	REGULAR SEASON					PLAYOFFS				
		Gms.	G	A	Pts.	PIM	Gms.	G	A	Pts.	PIM
91-92—Cornwall	OHL	59	12	15	27	75	6	0	0	0	0
92-93—Newmarket	OHL	40	6	14	20	70	—	—	—	—	—
—Guelph	OHL	28	10	14	24	27	5	1	0	1	14
93-94—Guelph	OHL	66	52	58	110	93	9	12	4	16	17
94-95—Indianapolis	IHL	70	21	12	33	80	—	—	—	—	—

PRONGER, CHRIS
D, BLUES

PERSONAL: Born October 10, 1974, in Dryden, Ont. . . . 6-5/190. . . . Shoots left. . . . Brother of Sean Pronger, center in Vancouver Canucks system.
COLLEGE: Trent (Ont.).
TRANSACTIONS/CAREER NOTES: Selected by Hartford Whalers in first round (first Whalers pick, second overall) of NHL entry draft (June 26, 1993). . . . Bruised left wrist (March 29, 1994); missed three games. . . . Fined $500 by Whalers for involvement in bar brawl (April 1, 1994). . . . Injured left shoulder (January 21, 1995); missed five games. . . . Traded by Whalers to St. Louis Blues for LW Brendan Shanahan (July 27, 1995).
HONORS: Named to Can.HL All-Rookie team (1991-92). . . . Named to OHL Rookie All-Star team (1991-92). . . . Won Can.HL Plus/Minus Award (1992-93). . . . Won Can.HL Top Defenseman Award (1992-93). . . . Won Max Kaminsky Award (1992-93). . . . Named to Can.HL All-Star first team (1992-93). . . . Named to OHL All-Star first team (1992-93). . . . Named to NHL All-Rookie team (1993-94).

Season Team	League	REGULAR SEASON					PLAYOFFS				
		Gms.	G	A	Pts.	PIM	Gms.	G	A	Pts.	PIM
90-91—Stratford	OPJHL	48	15	37	52	132	—	—	—	—	—
91-92—Peterborough	OHL	63	17	45	62	90	10	1	8	9	28
92-93—Peterborough	OHL	61	15	62	77	108	21	15	25	40	51
93-94—Hartford	NHL	81	5	25	30	113	—	—	—	—	—
94-95—Hartford	NHL	43	5	9	14	54	—	—	—	—	—
NHL totals		124	10	34	44	167					

P

PRONGER, SEAN
C, CANUCKS

PERSONAL: Born November 30, 1972, in Thunder Bay, Ont. . . . 6-3/195. . . . Shoots left. . . . Full name: Sean James Pronger. . . . Brother of Chris Pronger, defenseman, St. Louis Blues.
COLLEGE: Bowling Green State.

Season	Team	League	REGULAR SEASON Gms.	G	A	Pts.	PIM	PLAYOFFS Gms.	G	A	Pts.	PIM
89-90	Thunder Bay Flyers	USHL	48	18	34	52	61	—	—	—	—	—
90-91	Bowling Green State	CCHA	40	3	7	10	30	—	—	—	—	—
91-92	Bowling Green State	CCHA	34	9	7	16	28	—	—	—	—	—
92-93	Bowling Green State	CCHA	39	23	23	46	35	—	—	—	—	—
93-94	Bowling Green State	CCHA	38	17	17	34	38	—	—	—	—	—
94-95	Knoxville	ECHL	34	18	23	41	55	—	—	—	—	—
	Greensboro	ECHL	2	0	2	2	0	—	—	—	—	—
	San Diego	IHL	8	0	0	0	2	—	—	—	—	—

PROSPAL, VACLAV
C, FLYERS

PERSONAL: Born February 17, 1975, in Ceske-Budejovice, Czechoslovakia.... 6-2/ 167.... Shoots left.... Name pronounced VA-slav PRAHS-puhl.
TRANSACTIONS/CAREER NOTES: Selected by Philadelphia Flyers in third round (second Flyers pick, 71st overall) of NHL entry draft (June 26, 1993).

Season	Team	League	REGULAR SEASON Gms.	G	A	Pts.	PIM	PLAYOFFS Gms.	G	A	Pts.	PIM
91-92	Motor Ceske-Budejovice	Czech. Jrs.	36	16	16	32	12	—	—	—	—	—
92-93	Motor Ceske-Budejovice	Czech. Jrs.	36	26	31	57	24	—	—	—	—	—
93-94	Hershey	AHL	55	14	21	35	38	2	0	0	0	2
94-95	Hershey	AHL	69	13	32	45	36	2	1	0	1	4

PUPPA, DAREN
G, LIGHTNING

PERSONAL: Born March 23, 1965, in Kirkland Lake, Ont.... 6-3/205.... Catches right.... Full name: Daren James Puppa.... Name pronounced POO-puh.
COLLEGE: Rensselaer Polytechnic Institute (N.Y.).
TRANSACTIONS/CAREER NOTES: Selected by Buffalo Sabres in fourth round (sixth Sabres pick, 74th overall) of NHL entry draft (June 8, 1983).... Injured knee (February 1986).... Fractured left index finger (October 1987).... Sprained right wrist (January 14, 1989).... Broke right arm (January 27, 1989).... Injured back (November 21, 1990); missed nine games.... Pulled groin and stomach muscles (February 19, 1991).... Fractured arm (November 12, 1991); missed 16 games.... Suffered sore knee (January 21, 1993); missed seven games.... Traded by Sabres with LW Dave Andreychuk and first-round pick in 1993 draft (D Kenny Jonsson) to Toronto Maple Leafs for G Grant Fuhr and fifth-round pick (D Kevin Popp) in 1995 draft (February 2, 1993).... Selected by Florida Panthers in NHL expansion draft (June 24, 1993).... Selected by Tampa Bay Lightning in Phase II of NHL expansion draft (June 25, 1993).... Suffered from tonsillitis (December 11, 1993); missed two games.... Sprained lower back (February 5, 1994); missed two games.... Injured hand (April 2, 1995); missed two games.
HONORS: Named to AHL All-Star first team (1986-87).... Named to THE SPORTING NEWS All-Star second team (1989-90). ... Named to NHL All-Star second team (1989-90).... Played in NHL All-Star Game (1990).

Season	Team	League	REGULAR SEASON Gms.	Min.	W	L	T	GA	SO	Avg.	PLAYOFFS Gms.	Min.	W	L	GA	SO	Avg.
83-84	R.P.I.	ECAC	32	1816	24	6	0	89	...	2.94	—	—	—	—	—	—	—
84-85	R.P.I.	ECAC	32	1830	31	1	0	78	0	2.56	—	—	—	—	—	—	—
85-86	Buffalo	NHL	7	401	3	4	0	21	1	3.14	—	—	—	—	—	—	—
	Rochester	AHL	20	1092	8	11	0	79	0	4.34	—	—	—	—	—	—	—
86-87	Buffalo	NHL	3	185	0	2	1	13	0	4.22	—	—	—	—	—	—	—
	Rochester	AHL	57	3129	33	14	0	146	1	*2.80	*16	*944	10	6	*48	*1	3.05
87-88	Rochester	AHL	26	1415	14	8	2	65	2	2.76	2	108	0	1	5	0	2.78
	Buffalo	NHL	17	874	8	6	1	61	0	4.19	3	142	1	1	11	0	4.65
88-89	Buffalo	NHL	37	1908	17	10	6	107	1	3.36	—	—	—	—	—	—	—
89-90	Buffalo	NHL	56	3241	31	16	6	156	1	2.89	6	370	2	4	15	0	2.43
90-91	Buffalo	NHL	38	2092	15	11	6	118	2	3.38	2	81	0	1	10	0	7.41
91-92	Buffalo	NHL	33	1757	11	14	4	114	0	3.89	—	—	—	—	—	—	—
	Rochester	AHL	2	119	0	2	0	9	0	4.54	—	—	—	—	—	—	—
92-93	Buffalo	NHL	24	1306	11	5	4	78	0	3.58	—	—	—	—	—	—	—
	Toronto	NHL	8	479	6	2	0	18	2	2.25	1	20	0	0	1	0	3.00
93-94	Tampa Bay	NHL	63	3653	22	33	6	165	4	2.71	—	—	—	—	—	—	—
94-95	Tampa Bay	NHL	36	2013	14	19	2	90	1	2.68	—	—	—	—	—	—	—
NHL totals			322	17909	138	122	36	941	12	3.15	12	613	3	6	37	0	3.62

PURINGTON, DALE
D, RANGERS

PERSONAL: Born October 11, 1976, in Fort Wayne, Ind.... 6-1/201.... Shoots left.
TRANSACTIONS/CAREER NOTES: Selected by New York Rangers in fifth round (fourth Ranger pick, 117th overall) of NHL entry draft (July 8, 1995).

Season	Team	League	REGULAR SEASON Gms.	G	A	Pts.	PIM	PLAYOFFS Gms.	G	A	Pts.	PIM
93-94	Vernon	Tier II Jr. A	42	1	6	7	194	—	—	—	—	—
94-95	Tacoma	WHL	65	0	8	8	291	3	0	0	0	13

PUSHOR, JAMIE
D, RED WINGS

PERSONAL: Born February 11, 1973, in Lethbridge, Alta.... 6-3/192.... Shoots right.... Name pronounced PUSH-uhr.
TRANSACTIONS/CAREER NOTES: Selected by Detroit Red Wings in second round (second Red Wings pick, 32nd overall) of NHL entry draft (June 22, 1991).

Season	Team	League	Gms.	G	A	Pts.	PIM	Gms.	G	A	Pts.	PIM
89-90—Lethbridge		WHL	10	0	2	2	2	—	—	—	—	—
90-91—Lethbridge		WHL	71	1	13	14	193	—	—	—	—	—
91-92—Lethbridge		WHL	49	2	15	17	232	5	0	0	0	33
92-93—Lethbridge		WHL	72	6	22	28	200	4	0	1	1	9
93-94—Adirondack		AHL	73	1	17	18	124	12	0	0	0	22
94-95—Adirondack		AHL	58	2	11	13	129	4	0	1	1	0

PYSZ, PATRIK
C, BLACKHAWKS

PERSONAL: Born January 15, 1975, in Zakopane, Poland.... 5-11/187.... Shoots left.
TRANSACTIONS/CAREER NOTES: Selected by Chicago Blackhawks in fourth round (sixth Blackhawks pick, 102nd overall) of NHL entry draft (June 26, 1993).

Season	Team	League	Gms.	G	A	Pts.	PIM	Gms.	G	A	Pts.	PIM
91-92—Podhale Nowy Targ		Poland				Statistics unavailable.						
92-93—Augsburg		Ger. Div. II	36	7	5	12	12	8	2	1	3	0
93-94—Augsburg		Ger. Div. II	41	4	17	21	26	9	5	5	10	8
94-95—Augsburg		Germany	41	5	13	18	61	5	0	2	2	6

QUINN, DAN
C, SENATORS

PERSONAL: Born June 1, 1965, in Ottawa.... 5-11/182.... Shoots left.
TRANSACTIONS/CAREER NOTES: Selected by Calgary Flames as underage junior in first round (first Flames pick, 13th overall) of NHL entry draft (June 8, 1983).... Traded by Flames to Pittsburgh Penguins for C Mike Bullard (November 1986).... Broke left wrist (October 1987).... Traded by Penguins with RW Andrew McBain and C Dave Capuano to Vancouver Canucks for RW Tony Tanti, C Barry Pederson and D Rod Buskas (January 8, 1990).... Bruised shoulder (January 1991).... Traded by Canucks with D Garth Butcher to St. Louis Blues for LW Geoff Courtnall, D Robert Dirk, C Cliff Ronning, LW Sergio Momesso and fifth-round pick (RW Brian Loney) in 1992 draft (March 5, 1991).... Traded by Blues with C Rod Brind'Amour to Philadelphia Flyers for C Ron Sutter and D Murray Baron (September 22, 1991).... Signed as free agent by Minnesota North Stars (October 5, 1992).... Signed as free agent by Ottawa Senators (March 15, 1993).... Signed as free agent by Los Angeles Kings (September 2, 1994).... Played in Europe during 1994-95 NHL lockout.... Strained groin (February 18, 1995); missed one game.... Signed as free agent by Senators (July 20, 1995).
STATISTICAL PLATEAUS: Three-goal games: 1987-88 (3), 1989-90 (1). Total: 4.
MISCELLANEOUS: Captain of Vancouver Canucks (1990-91).

Season	Team	League	Gms.	G	A	Pts.	PIM	Gms.	G	A	Pts.	PIM
81-82—Belleville		OHL	67	19	32	51	41	—	—	—	—	—
82-83—Belleville		OHL	70	59	88	147	27	4	2	6	8	2
83-84—Belleville		OHL	24	23	36	59	12	—	—	—	—	—
—Calgary		NHL	54	19	33	52	20	8	3	5	8	4
84-85—Calgary		NHL	74	20	38	58	22	3	0	0	0	0
85-86—Calgary		NHL	78	30	42	72	44	18	8	7	15	10
86-87—Calgary		NHL	16	3	6	9	14	—	—	—	—	—
—Pittsburgh		NHL	64	28	43	71	40	—	—	—	—	—
87-88—Pittsburgh		NHL	70	40	39	79	50	—	—	—	—	—
88-89—Pittsburgh		NHL	79	34	60	94	102	11	6	3	9	10
89-90—Pittsburgh		NHL	41	9	20	29	22	—	—	—	—	—
—Vancouver		NHL	37	16	18	34	27	—	—	—	—	—
90-91—Vancouver		NHL	64	18	31	49	46	—	—	—	—	—
—St. Louis		NHL	14	4	7	11	20	13	4	7	11	32
91-92—Philadelphia		NHL	67	11	26	37	26	—	—	—	—	—
92-93—Minnesota		NHL	11	0	4	4	6	—	—	—	—	—
93-94—Ottawa		NHL	13	7	0	7	6	—	—	—	—	—
—Bern		Switzerland	25	12	22	34	50	—	—	—	—	—
94-95—Zug		Switzerland	7	7	6	13	26	—	—	—	—	—
—Los Angeles		NHL	44	14	17	31	32	—	—	—	—	—
NHL totals			726	253	384	637	477	53	21	22	43	56

QUINNEY, KEN
RW

PERSONAL: Born May 23, 1965, in New Westminster, B.C.... 5-10/186.... Shoots right.
TRANSACTIONS/CAREER NOTES: Selected by Quebec Nordiques as underage junior in 10th round (ninth Nordiques pick, 203rd overall) of NHL entry draft (June 9, 1984).... Broke wrist (February 1986).... Strained right thumb ligament (December 31, 1990); missed 12 games.... Signed as free agent by Detroit Red Wings (August 1991).... Signed as free agent by Las Vegas Thunder (August 5, 1993).
HONORS: Named to WHL (East) All-Star first team (1984-85).... Named to IHL All-Star first team (1993-94).

Season	Team	League	Gms.	G	A	Pts.	PIM	Gms.	G	A	Pts.	PIM
81-82—Calgary		WHL	63	11	17	28	55	2	0	0	0	15
82-83—Calgary		WHL	71	26	25	51	71	16	6	1	7	46
83-84—Calgary		WHL	71	64	54	118	38	4	5	2	7	0
84-85—Calgary		WHL	56	47	67	114	65	7	6	4	10	15
85-86—Fredericton		AHL	61	11	26	37	34	6	2	2	4	9
86-87—Quebec		NHL	25	2	7	9	16	—	—	—	—	—
—Fredericton		AHL	48	14	27	41	20	—	—	—	—	—

Season	Team	League	Gms.	G	A	Pts.	PIM	Gms.	G	A	Pts.	PIM
			REGULAR SEASON					**PLAYOFFS**				
87-88—Fredericton	AHL	58	37	39	76	39	13	3	5	8	35
—Quebec	NHL	15	2	2	4	5	—	—	—	—	—
88-89—Halifax	AHL	72	41	49	90	65	4	3	0	3	0
89-90—Halifax	AHL	44	9	16	25	63	2	0	0	0	2
90-91—Quebec	NHL	19	3	4	7	2	—	—	—	—	—
—Halifax	AHL	44	20	20	40	76	—	—	—	—	—
91-92—Adirondack	AHL	63	31	29	60	33	19	7	12	19	9
92-93—Adirondack	AHL	63	32	34	66	15	10	2	9	11	9
93-94—Las Vegas	IHL	79	*55	53	108	52	5	3	3	6	2
94-95—Las Vegas	IHL	78	40	42	82	40	10	3	2	5	9
NHL totals		59	7	13	20	23					

QUINT, DERON

D, JETS

PERSONAL: Born March 12, 1976, in Dover, N.H. . . . . 6-1/182. . . . Shoots left.
HIGH SCHOOL: Meadowdale (Lynnwood, Wash.).
TRANSACTIONS/CAREER NOTES: Selected by Winnipeg Jets in second round (first Jets pick, 30th overall) of NHL entry draft (June 28, 1994).
HONORS: Won WHL Top Draft Choice Award (1993-94). . . . Named to Can.HL All-Rookie team (1993-94). . . . Named to WHL (West) All-Star first team (1994-95).

Season	Team	League	Gms.	G	A	Pts.	PIM	Gms.	G	A	Pts.	PIM
			REGULAR SEASON					**PLAYOFFS**				
90-91—Cardigan Prep School	N.H. H.S.	31	67	54	121	. . .	—	—	—	—	—
91-92—Cardigan Prep School	N.H. H.S.	32	111	68	179	. . .	—	—	—	—	—
92-93—Tabor Academy	N.Y. H.S.	28	15	26	41	30	1	0	2	2	0
93-94—Seattle	WHL	63	15	29	44	47	9	4	12	16	8
94-95—Seattle	WHL	65	29	60	89	82	3	1	2	3	6

QUINTAL, STEPHANE

D, CANADIENS

PERSONAL: Born October 22, 1968, in Boucherville, Que. . . . 6-3/215. . . . Shoots right. . . . Name pronounced steh-FAN KIHN-tahl.
HIGH SCHOOL: Polyvalente de Mortagne (Boucherville, Que.).
TRANSACTIONS/CAREER NOTES: Broke wrist (December 1985). . . . Selected by Boston Bruins as underage junior in first round (second Bruins pick, 14th overall) of NHL entry draft (June 13, 1987). . . . Broke bone near eye (October 1988). . . . Injured knee (January 1989). . . . Sprained right knee (October 17, 1989); missed eight games. . . . Fractured left ankle (April 9, 1991); missed remainder of playoffs. . . . Traded by Bruins with C Craig Janney to St. Louis Blues for C Adam Oates (February 7, 1992). . . . Traded by Blues with RW Nelson Emerson to Winnipeg Jets for D Phil Housley (September 24, 1993). . . . Sprained wrist (January 16, 1994); missed two games. . . . Sprained neck (April 6, 1994); missed one game. . . . Sprained ankle (February 6, 1995); missed five games. . . . Traded by Jets to Montreal Canadiens for second-round pick (D Jason Doig) in 1995 draft (July 8, 1995).
HONORS: Named to QMJHL All-Star first team (1986-87).

Season	Team	League	Gms.	G	A	Pts.	PIM	Gms.	G	A	Pts.	PIM
			REGULAR SEASON					**PLAYOFFS**				
85-86—Granby	QMJHL	67	2	17	19	144	—	—	—	—	—
86-87—Granby	QMJHL	67	13	41	54	178	8	0	9	9	10
87-88—Hull	QMJHL	38	13	23	36	138	19	7	12	19	30
88-89—Maine	AHL	16	4	10	14	28	—	—	—	—	—
—Boston	NHL	26	0	1	1	29	—	—	—	—	—
89-90—Boston	NHL	38	2	2	4	22	—	—	—	—	—
—Maine	AHL	37	4	16	20	27	—	—	—	—	—
90-91—Maine	AHL	23	1	5	6	30	—	—	—	—	—
—Boston	NHL	45	2	6	8	89	3	0	1	1	7
91-92—Boston	NHL	49	4	10	14	77	—	—	—	—	—
—St. Louis	NHL	26	0	6	6	32	4	1	2	3	6
92-93—St. Louis	NHL	75	1	10	11	100	9	0	0	0	8
93-94—Winnipeg	NHL	81	8	18	26	119	—	—	—	—	—
94-95—Winnipeg	NHL	43	6	17	23	78	—	—	—	—	—
NHL totals		383	23	70	93	546	16	1	3	4	21

QUINTIN, J.F.

LW, SHARKS

PERSONAL: Born May 28, 1969, in St. Jean, Que. . . . 6-0/185. . . . Shoots left. . . . Name pronounced kihn-TAN.
TRANSACTIONS/CAREER NOTES: Fractured knee (October 1985). . . . Selected by Minnesota North Stars in fourth round (fourth North Stars pick, 75th overall) of NHL entry draft (June 17, 1989). . . . Selected by San Jose Sharks in NHL dispersal draft (May 30, 1991).
HONORS: Named to QMJHL All-Star second team (1988-89).

Season	Team	League	Gms.	G	A	Pts.	PIM	Gms.	G	A	Pts.	PIM
			REGULAR SEASON					**PLAYOFFS**				
86-87—Shawinigan	QMJHL	43	1	9	10	17	—	—	—	—	—
87-88—Shawinigan	QMJHL	70	28	70	98	143	11	5	8	13	26
88-89—Shawinigan	QMJHL	69	52	100	152	105	10	9	15	24	16
89-90—Kalamazoo	IHL	68	20	18	38	38	10	8	4	12	14
90-91—Kalamazoo	IHL	78	31	43	74	64	9	1	5	6	11
91-92—Kansas City	IHL	21	4	6	10	29	13	2	10	12	29
—San Jose	NHL	8	3	0	3	0	—	—	—	—	—

Season Team	League	REGULAR SEASON					PLAYOFFS				
		Gms.	G	A	Pts.	PIM	Gms.	G	A	Pts.	PIM
92-93—San Jose	NHL	14	2	5	7	4	—	—	—	—	—
—Kansas City	IHL	64	20	29	49	169	11	2	1	3	16
93-94—Kansas City	IHL	41	14	19	33	117	—	—	—	—	—
94-95—Kansas City	IHL	63	23	35	58	130	19	2	9	11	57
NHL totals		22	5	5	10	4					

RABY, MATHIEU
D, LIGHTNING

PERSONAL: Born January 19, 1975, in Hull, Que. . . . 6-2/204. . . . Shoots right. . . . Name pronounced RAY-bee.
TRANSACTIONS/CAREER NOTES: Selected by Tampa Bay Lightning in seventh round (seventh Lightning pick, 159th overall) of NHL entry draft (June 26, 1993).

Season Team	League	REGULAR SEASON					PLAYOFFS				
		Gms.	G	A	Pts.	PIM	Gms.	G	A	Pts.	PIM
92-93—Victoriaville	QMJHL	53	2	2	4	103	2	0	0	0	0
93-94—Victoriaville	QMJHL	67	3	7	10	264	5	0	0	0	22
94-95—Victoriaville	QMJHL	38	5	11	16	238	—	—	—	—	—
—Sherbrooke	QMJHL	25	2	2	4	106	7	0	1	1	24

RACICOT, ANDRE
G, KINGS

PERSONAL: Born June 9, 1969, in Rouyn-Noranda, Que. . . . 5-11/176. . . . Catches left. . . . Name pronounced RAH-sih-KOH.
TRANSACTIONS/CAREER NOTES: Selected by Montreal Canadiens in fourth round (fifth Canadiens pick, 83rd overall) of NHL draft (June 17, 1989). . . . Injured knee (October 20, 1993); missed 11 games. . . . Signed as free agent by Los Angeles Kings (September 22, 1994).
HONORS: Shared Harry (Hap) Holmes Memorial Trophy with Jean-Claude Bergeron (1989-90). . . . Named to QMJHL All-Star second team (1988-89).
MISCELLANEOUS: Member of Stanley Cup championship team (1993).

Season Team	League	REGULAR SEASON							PLAYOFFS					
		Gms.	Min.	W	L	T	GA	SO	Avg.	Gms.	Min.	W	L	GA SO Avg.
86-87—Longueuil	QMJHL	3	180	1	2	0	19	0	6.33	—	—	—	—	—
87-88—Hull/Granby	QMJHL	30	1547	15	11	1	105	1	4.07	5	298	1	4	23 0 4.63
88-89—Granby	QMJHL	54	2944	22	24	3	198	0	4.04	4	218	0	4	18 0 4.95
89-90—Sherbrooke	AHL	33	1948	19	11	2	97	1	2.99	5	227	0	4	18 0 4.76
—Montreal	NHL	1	13	0	0	0	3	0	13.85	—	—	—	—	—
90-91—Fredericton	AHL	22	1252	13	8	1	60	1	2.88	—	—	—	—	—
—Montreal	NHL	21	975	7	9	2	52	1	3.20	2	12	0	1	2 0 10.00
91-92—Fredericton	AHL	28	1666	14	8	5	86	0	3.10	—	—	—	—	—
—Montreal	NHL	9	436	0	3	3	23	0	3.17	1	1	0	0	0 0 0.00
92-93—Montreal	NHL	26	1433	17	5	1	81	1	3.39	1	18	0	0	2 0 6.67
93-94—Montreal	NHL	11	500	2	6	2	37	0	4.44	—	—	—	—	—
—Fredericton	AHL	6	293	1	4	0	16	0	3.28	—	—	—	—	—
94-95—Portland	AHL	19	1080	10	7	0	53	1	2.94	—	—	—	—	—
—Phoenix	IHL	3	132	1	0	‡0	8	0	3.64	2	21	0	0	0 0 0.00
NHL totals		68	3357	26	23	8	196	2	3.50	4	31	0	1	4 0 7.74

RACINE, BRUCE
G

PERSONAL: Born August 9, 1966, in Cornwall, Ont. . . . 6-0/178. . . . Catches left. . . . Full name: Bruce Michael Racine.
HIGH SCHOOL: St. Pius X (Ottawa).
COLLEGE: Northeastern.
TRANSACTIONS/CAREER NOTES: Selected by Pittsburgh Penguins in third round (third Penguins pick, 58th overall) of NHL entry draft (June 15, 1985). . . . Signed as free agent by Toronto Maple Leafs (August 3, 1993).
HONORS: Named to Hockey East All-Star second team (1984-85). . . . Named to Hockey East All-Freshman team (1984-85). . . . Named to NCAA All-America East first team (1986-87 and 1987-88). . . . Named to Hockey East All-Star first team (1986-87). . . . Named Hockey East Tournament Most Valuable Player (1987-88). . . . Named to Hockey East All-Decade team (1994).

Season Team	League	REGULAR SEASON							PLAYOFFS					
		Gms.	Min.	W	L	T	GA	SO	Avg.	Gms.	Min.	W	L	GA SO Avg.
84-85—Northeastern Univ.	Hoc. East	26	1615	11	14	1	103	1	3.83	—	—	—	—	—
85-86—Northeastern Univ.	Hoc. East	37	2212	17	14	1	171	0	4.64	—	—	—	—	—
86-87—Northeastern Univ.	Hoc. East	33	1966	12	18	3	133	0	4.06	—	—	—	—	—
87-88—Northeastern Univ.	Hoc. East	30	1809	15	11	4	108	1	3.58	—	—	—	—	—
88-89—Muskegon	IHL	51	*3039	37	11	‡0	184	*3	3.63	5	300	4	1	15 0 3.00
89-90—Muskegon	IHL	49	2911	29	15	‡4	182	1	3.75	—	—	—	—	—
90-91—Albany	IHL	29	1567	7	18	‡1	104	0	3.98	—	—	—	—	—
—Muskegon	IHL	9	516	4	4	‡1	40	0	4.65	—	—	—	—	—
91-92—Muskegon	IHL	27	1559	‡3	10	‡3	91	1	3.50	1	60	0	1	6 0 6.00
92-93—Cleveland	IHL	35	1949	13	16	‡0	140	1	4.31	2	37	0	0	2 0 3.24
93-94—St. John's	AHL	37	1875	20	9	2	116	0	3.71	—	—	—	—	—
94-95—St. John's	AHL	27	1492	11	10	4	85	1	3.42	2	119	1	1	3 0 1.51

RACINE, YVES
D, CANADIENS

PERSONAL: Born February 7, 1969, in Matane, Que. . . . 6-0/200. . . . Shoots left. . . . Name pronounced EEV ruh-SEEN.
TRANSACTIONS/CAREER NOTES: Selected by Detroit Red Wings as underage junior in first round (first Red Wings pick, 11th overall) of NHL entry draft (June 13, 1987). . . . Injured shoulder

(March 22, 1991); missed four games. . . . Sprained left shoulder (November 11, 1992); missed four games. . . . Traded by Red Wings with fourth-round pick in 1994 draft (LW Sebastien Vallee) to Philadelphia Flyers for D Terry Carkner (October 5, 1993). . . . Tore medial lateral ligament in knee (October 16, 1993); missed 15 games. . . . Traded by Flyers to Montreal Canadiens for D Kevin Haller (June 29, 1994). . . . Suffered from the flu (March 8, 1995); missed one game.

HONORS: Named to QMJHL All-Star first team (1987-88 and 1988-89). . . . Won Emile (Butch) Bouchard Trophy (1988-89).

Season Team	League	REGULAR SEASON					PLAYOFFS				
		Gms.	G	A	Pts.	PIM	Gms.	G	A	Pts.	PIM
86-87—Longueuil	QMJHL	70	7	43	50	50	20	3	11	14	14
87-88—Victoriaville	QMJHL	69	10	84	94	150	5	0	0	0	13
—Adirondack	AHL	—	—	—	—	—	9	4	2	6	2
88-89—Victoriaville	QMJHL	63	23	85	108	95	18	3	*30	*33	41
—Adirondack	AHL	—	—	—	—	—	2	1	1	2	0
89-90—Detroit	NHL	28	4	9	13	23	—	—	—	—	—
—Adirondack	AHL	46	8	27	35	31	—	—	—	—	—
90-91—Adirondack	AHL	16	3	9	12	10	—	—	—	—	—
—Detroit	NHL	62	7	40	47	33	7	2	0	2	0
91-92—Detroit	NHL	61	2	22	24	94	11	2	1	3	10
92-93—Detroit	NHL	80	9	31	40	80	7	1	3	4	27
93-94—Philadelphia	NHL	67	9	43	52	48	—	—	—	—	—
94-95—Montreal	NHL	47	4	7	11	42	—	—	—	—	—
NHL totals		345	35	152	187	320	25	5	4	9	37

RAGNARSSON, MARCUS
D, SHARKS

PERSONAL: Born August 13, 1971, in Ostervala, Sweden. . . . 6-1/200. . . . Shoots left.

TRANSACTIONS/CAREER NOTES: Selected by San Jose Sharks in fifth round (fifth Sharks pick, 99th overall) of NHL entry draft (June 20, 1992).

Season Team	League	REGULAR SEASON					PLAYOFFS				
		Gms.	G	A	Pts.	PIM	Gms.	G	A	Pts.	PIM
89-90—Djurgarden Stockholm	Sweden	13	0	2	2	0	1	0	0	0	0
90-91—Djurgarden Stockholm	Sweden	35	4	1	5	12	7	0	0	0	6
91-92—Djurgarden Stockholm	Sweden	40	8	5	13	14	—	—	—	—	—
92-93—Djurgarden Stockholm	Sweden	35	3	3	6	53	6	0	2	2	0
93-94—Djurgarden Stockholm	Sweden	19	0	4	4	24	—	—	—	—	—
94-95—Djurgarden Stockholm	Sweden	38	7	9	16	20	3	0	0	0	4

RAM, JAMIE
G, RANGERS

PERSONAL: Born January 18, 1971, in Scarborough, Ont. . . . 5-11/175. . . . Catches left.
COLLEGE: Michigan Tech.
TRANSACTIONS/CAREER NOTES: Selected by New York Rangers in 10th round (ninth Rangers pick, 213th overall) of NHL entry draft (June 22, 1991).
HONORS: Named to NCAA All-America West first team (1992-93 and 1993-94). . . . Named to WCHA All-Star first team (1992-93 and 1993-94).

Season Team	League	REGULAR SEASON							PLAYOFFS					
		Gms.	Min.	W	L	T	GA	SO	Avg.	Gms.	Min.	W	L	GA	SO	Avg.
90-91—Michigan Tech	WCHA	14	826	5	9	0	57	0	4.14	—	—	—	—	—	—	—
91-92—Michigan Tech	WCHA	23	1144	9	9	1	83	0	4.35	—	—	—	—	—	—	—
92-93—Michigan Tech	WCHA	*36	*2078	16	14	5	115	0	3.32	—	—	—	—	—	—	—
93-94—Michigan Tech	WCHA	39	2192	12	20	5	117	*1	3.20	—	—	—	—	—	—	—
94-95—Binghamton	AHL	26	1472	12	10	2	81	1	3.30	11	664	6	5	29	1	2.62

RAMSEY, MIKE
D, RED WINGS

PERSONAL: Born December 3, 1960, in Minneapolis. . . . 6-3/195. . . . Shoots left. . . . Full name: Michael Allen Ramsey.
COLLEGE: Minnesota.
TRANSACTIONS/CAREER NOTES: Selected by Buffalo Sabres in first round (first Sabres pick, 11th overall) of NHL entry draft (August 9, 1979). . . . Dislocated thumb (December 4, 1983). . . . Injured groin (October 1987). . . . Fractured bone in right hand (November 2, 1988). . . . Pulled groin (January 12, 1989). . . . Pulled rib cage muscle (November 26, 1990); missed seven games. . . . Injured groin (November 22, 1991); missed five games. . . . Injured groin (January 31, 1992); missed three games. . . . Injured groin (March 8, 1992); missed three games. . . . Injured leg (April 12, 1992). . . . Underwent shoulder surgery (August 8, 1992); missed first nine games of season. . . . Strained groin (November 7, 1992); missed four games. . . . Bruised hand (November 18, 1992); missed six games. . . . Sprained knee (January 29, 1993); missed four games. . . . Traded by Sabres to Pittsburgh Penguins for LW Bob Errey (March 22, 1993). . . . Broke toe (November 11, 1993); missed nine games. . . . Signed as free agent by Detroit Red Wings (August 3, 1994). . . . Injured groin (January 24, 1995); missed one game. . . . Strained left hip flexor (March 6, 1995); missed five games.
HONORS: Played in NHL All-Star Game (1982, 1983, 1985 and 1986).
MISCELLANEOUS: Member of gold-medal-winning U.S. Olympic team (1980). . . . Captain of Buffalo Sabres (1990-91 through 1992-93).

Season Team	League	REGULAR SEASON					PLAYOFFS				
		Gms.	G	A	Pts.	PIM	Gms.	G	A	Pts.	PIM
78-79—University of Minnesota	WCHA	26	6	11	17	30	—	—	—	—	—
79-80—U.S. national team	Int'l	56	11	22	33	55	—	—	—	—	—
—U.S. Olympic Team	Int'l	7	0	2	2	8	—	—	—	—	—
—Buffalo	NHL	13	1	6	7	6	13	1	2	3	12
80-81—Buffalo	NHL	72	3	14	17	56	8	0	3	3	20
81-82—Buffalo	NHL	80	7	23	30	56	4	1	1	2	14

R

Season	Team	League	Gms.	G	A	Pts.	PIM	Gms.	G	A	Pts.	PIM
			REGULAR SEASON					**PLAYOFFS**				
82-83	Buffalo	NHL	77	8	30	38	55	10	4	4	8	15
83-84	Buffalo	NHL	72	9	22	31	82	3	0	1	1	6
84-85	Buffalo	NHL	79	8	22	30	102	5	0	1	1	23
85-86	Buffalo	NHL	76	7	21	28	117	—	—	—	—	—
86-87	Buffalo	NHL	80	8	31	39	109	—	—	—	—	—
87-88	Buffalo	NHL	63	5	16	21	77	6	0	3	3	29
88-89	Buffalo	NHL	56	2	14	16	84	5	1	0	1	11
89-90	Buffalo	NHL	73	4	21	25	47	6	0	1	1	8
90-91	Buffalo	NHL	71	6	14	20	46	5	1	0	1	12
91-92	Buffalo	NHL	66	3	14	17	67	7	0	2	2	8
92-93	Buffalo	NHL	33	2	8	10	20	—	—	—	—	—
	Pittsburgh	NHL	12	1	2	3	8	12	0	6	6	4
93-94	Pittsburgh	NHL	65	2	2	4	22	1	0	0	0	0
94-95	Detroit	NHL	33	1	2	3	23	15	0	1	1	4
NHL totals			1021	77	262	339	977	100	8	25	33	166

RANFORD, BILL
G, OILERS

PERSONAL: Born December 14, 1966, in Brandon, Man. . . . 5-11/185. . . . Catches left. **HIGH SCHOOL:** New Westminster (B.C.). **TRANSACTIONS/CAREER NOTES:** Selected by Boston Bruins as underage junior in third round (second Bruins pick, 52nd overall) of NHL entry draft (June 15, 1985). . . . Traded by Bruins with LW Geoff Courtnall and second-round pick in 1988 draft (C Petro Koivunen) to Edmonton Oilers for G Andy Moog (March 1988). . . . Sprained ankle (February 14, 1990); missed six games. . . . Strained groin (January 4, 1992); missed two games. . . . Strained hamstring (January 29, 1992); missed five games. . . . Strained right quadriceps (November 12, 1992); missed two games. . . . Strained left hamstring (April 7, 1993); missed two games. . . . Bruised hand (March 23, 1993); missed one game. . . . Strained hamstring (April 5, 1994); missed three games. . . . Suffered back spasms (April 29, 1995); missed three games.
HONORS: Named to WHL All-Star second team (1985-86). . . . Won Conn Smythe Trophy (1989-90). . . . Played in NHL All-Star Game (1991).
RECORDS: Shares NHL single-season playoff record for most wins by a goaltender—16 (1990).
MISCELLANEOUS: Member of Stanley Cup championship teams (1988 and 1990).

Season	Team	League	Gms.	Min.	W	L	T	GA	SO	Avg.	Gms.	Min.	W	L	GA	SO	Avg.
			REGULAR SEASON								**PLAYOFFS**						
83-84	New Westminster	WHL	27	1450	10	14	0	130	0	5.38	1	27	0	0	2	0	4.44
84-85	New Westminster	WHL	38	2034	19	17	0	142	0	4.19	7	309	2	3	26	0	5.05
85-86	New Westminster	WHL	53	2791	17	29	1	225	1	4.84	—	—	—	—	—	—	—
	Boston	NHL	4	240	3	1	0	10	0	2.50	2	120	0	2	7	0	3.50
86-87	Moncton	AHL	3	180	3	0	0	6	0	2.00	—	—	—	—	—	—	—
	Boston	NHL	41	2234	16	20	2	124	3	3.33	2	123	0	2	8	0	3.90
87-88	Maine	AHL	51	2856	27	16	6	165	1	3.47	—	—	—	—	—	—	—
	Edmonton	NHL	6	325	3	0	2	16	0	2.95	—	—	—	—	—	—	—
88-89	Edmonton	NHL	29	1509	15	8	2	88	1	3.50	—	—	—	—	—	—	—
89-90	Edmonton	NHL	56	3107	24	16	9	165	1	3.19	*22	*1401	*16	6	*59	1	2.53
90-91	Edmonton	NHL	60	3415	27	27	3	182	0	3.20	3	135	1	2	8	0	3.56
91-92	Edmonton	NHL	67	3822	27	26	10	228	1	3.58	16	909	8	*8	51	†2	3.37
92-93	Edmonton	NHL	67	3753	17	38	6	240	1	3.84	—	—	—	—	—	—	—
93-94	Edmonton	NHL	71	4070	22	34	11	236	1	3.48	—	—	—	—	—	—	—
94-95	Edmonton	NHL	40	2203	15	20	3	133	2	3.62	—	—	—	—	—	—	—
NHL totals			441	24678	169	190	48	1422	10	3.46	45	2688	25	20	133	3	2.97

RANHEIM, PAUL
RW, WHALERS

PERSONAL: Born January 25, 1966, in St. Louis. . . . 6-0/195. . . . Shoots right. . . . Full name: Paul Stephen Ranheim. . . . Name pronounced RAN-HIGHM. **HIGH SCHOOL:** Edina (Minn.). **COLLEGE:** Wisconsin.
TRANSACTIONS/CAREER NOTES: Selected by Calgary Flames in second round (third Flames pick, 38th overall) of NHL entry draft (June 8, 1983). . . . Broke right ankle (December 11, 1990); missed 41 games. . . . Traded by Flames with D Gary Suter and C Ted Drury to Hartford Whalers for C Michael Nylander, D Zarley Zalapski and D James Patrick (March 10, 1994).
HONORS: Named to WCHA All-Star second team (1986-87). . . . Named to NCAA All-America West first team (1987-88). . . . Named to WCHA All-Star first team (1987-88). . . . Won Garry F. Longman Memorial Trophy (1988-89). . . . Won Ken McKenzie Trophy (1988-89). . . . Named to IHL All-Star second team (1988-89).
STATISTICAL PLATEAUS: Three-goal games: 1991-92 (1).

Season	Team	League	Gms.	G	A	Pts.	PIM	Gms.	G	A	Pts.	PIM
			REGULAR SEASON					**PLAYOFFS**				
82-83	Edina High School	Minn. H.S.	26	12	25	37	4	—	—	—	—	—
83-84	Edina High School	Minn. H.S.	26	16	24	40	6	—	—	—	—	—
84-85	University of Wisconsin	WCHA	42	11	11	22	40	—	—	—	—	—
85-86	University of Wisconsin	WCHA	33	17	17	34	34	—	—	—	—	—
86-87	University of Wisconsin	WCHA	42	24	35	59	54	—	—	—	—	—
87-88	University of Wisconsin	WCHA	44	36	26	62	63	—	—	—	—	—
88-89	Calgary	NHL	5	0	0	0	0	—	—	—	—	—
	Salt Lake City	IHL	75	*68	29	97	16	14	5	5	10	8
89-90	Calgary	NHL	80	26	28	54	23	6	1	3	4	2
90-91	Calgary	NHL	39	14	16	30	4	7	2	2	4	0

Season Team	League	REGULAR SEASON					PLAYOFFS				
		Gms.	G	A	Pts.	PIM	Gms.	G	A	Pts.	PIM
91-92—Calgary	NHL	80	23	20	43	32	—	—	—	—	—
92-93—Calgary	NHL	83	21	22	43	26	6	0	1	1	0
93-94—Calgary	NHL	67	10	14	24	20	—	—	—	—	—
—Hartford	NHL	15	0	3	3	2	—	—	—	—	—
94-95—Hartford	NHL	47	6	14	20	10	—	—	—	—	—
NHL totals		416	100	117	217	117	19	3	6	9	2

R

RATHJE, MIKE
D, SHARKS

PERSONAL: Born May 11, 1974, in Manville, Alta.... 6-6/220.... Shoots left.... Name pronounced RATH-jee.
HIGH SCHOOL: Medicine Hat (Alta.).
TRANSACTIONS/CAREER NOTES: Selected by San Jose Sharks in first round (first Sharks pick, third overall) of NHL entry draft (June 20, 1992).... Strained abdomen (February 19, 1994); missed three games.... Sprained knee (February 26, 1994); missed four games.... Sprained knee (February 2, 1995); missed three games.... Injured foot (February 15, 1995); missed one game.... Suffered hip flexor (April 25, 1995); missed two games.
HONORS: Named to Can.HL All-Star second team (1992-93).... Named to WHL (East) All-Star second team (1991-92 and 1992-93).

Season Team	League	REGULAR SEASON					PLAYOFFS				
		Gms.	G	A	Pts.	PIM	Gms.	G	A	Pts.	PIM
90-91—Medicine Hat	WHL	64	1	16	17	28	12	0	4	4	2
91-92—Medicine Hat	WHL	67	11	23	34	109	4	0	1	1	2
92-93—Medicine Hat	WHL	57	12	37	49	103	10	3	3	6	12
—Kansas City	IHL	—	—	—	—	—	5	0	0	0	12
93-94—San Jose	NHL	47	1	9	10	59	1	0	0	0	0
—Kansas City	IHL	6	0	2	2	0	—	—	—	—	—
94-95—Kansas City	IHL	6	0	1	1	7	—	—	—	—	—
—San Jose	NHL	42	2	7	9	29	11	5	2	7	4
NHL totals		89	3	16	19	88	12	5	2	7	4

RAY, ROB
LW, SABRES

PERSONAL: Born June 8, 1968, in Stirling, Ont.... 6-0/203.... Shoots left.
TRANSACTIONS/CAREER NOTES: Broke jaw (January 1987).... Selected by Buffalo Sabres in fifth round (fifth Sabres pick, 97th overall) of NHL entry draft (June 11, 1988).... Tore ligament in right knee (April 11, 1993); missed remainder of season.... Suffered from the flu (March 11, 1995); missed one game.

Season Team	League	REGULAR SEASON					PLAYOFFS				
		Gms.	G	A	Pts.	PIM	Gms.	G	A	Pts.	PIM
84-85—Whitby Lawmen	OPJHL	35	5	10	15	318	—	—	—	—	—
85-86—Cornwall	OHL	53	6	13	19	253	6	0	0	0	26
86-87—Cornwall	OHL	46	17	20	37	158	5	1	1	2	16
87-88—Cornwall	OHL	61	11	41	52	179	11	2	3	5	33
88-89—Rochester	AHL	74	11	18	29	*446	—	—	—	—	—
89-90—Buffalo	NHL	27	2	1	3	99	—	—	—	—	—
—Rochester	AHL	43	2	13	15	335	17	1	3	4	*115
90-91—Rochester	AHL	8	1	1	2	15	—	—	—	—	—
—Buffalo	NHL	66	8	8	16	*350	6	1	1	2	56
91-92—Buffalo	NHL	63	5	3	8	354	7	0	0	0	2
92-93—Buffalo	NHL	68	3	2	5	211	—	—	—	—	—
93-94—Buffalo	NHL	82	3	4	7	274	7	1	0	1	43
94-95—Buffalo	NHL	47	0	3	3	173	5	0	0	0	14
NHL totals		353	21	21	42	1461	25	2	1	3	115

RECCHI, MARK
RW, CANADIENS

PERSONAL: Born February 1, 1968, in Kamloops, B.C.... 5-10/185.... Shoots left.... Name pronounced REH-kee.
TRANSACTIONS/CAREER NOTES: Broke ankle (January 1987).... Selected by Pittsburgh Penguins in fourth round (fourth Penguins pick, 67th overall) of NHL entry draft (June 11, 1988).... Injured left shoulder (December 23, 1990).... Sprained right knee (March 30, 1991).... Traded by Penguins with D Brian Benning and first-round pick in 1992 draft (LW Jason Bowen) to Philadelphia Flyers for RW Rick Tocchet, D Kjell Samuelsson, G Ken Wregget and third-round pick in 1992 draft (February 19, 1992).... Traded by Flyers with third-round pick in 1995 draft (C Martin Hohenberger) to Montreal Canadiens for D Eric Desjardins, LW Gilbert Dionne and LW John LeClair (February 9, 1995).
HONORS: Named to WHL (West) All-Star team (1987-88).... Named to IHL All-Star second team (1988-89).... Named to NHL All-Star second team (1991-92).... Played in NHL All-Star Game (1991, 1993 and 1994).
STATISTICAL PLATEAUS: Three-goal games: 1991-92 (1).
MISCELLANEOUS: Member of Stanley Cup championship team (1991).

Season Team	League	REGULAR SEASON					PLAYOFFS				
		Gms.	G	A	Pts.	PIM	Gms.	G	A	Pts.	PIM
84-85—Langley Eagles	BCJHL	51	26	39	65	39	—	—	—	—	—
85-86—New Westminster	WHL	72	21	40	61	55	—	—	—	—	—
86-87—Kamloops	WHL	40	26	50	76	63	13	3	16	19	17
87-88—Kamloops	WHL	62	61	*93	154	75	17	10	*21	†31	18
88-89—Pittsburgh	NHL	15	1	1	2	0	—	—	—	—	—
—Muskegon	IHL	63	50	49	99	86	14	7	*14	†21	28

— 650 —

Season	Team	League	REGULAR SEASON Gms.	G	A	Pts.	PIM	PLAYOFFS Gms.	G	A	Pts.	PIM
89-90—Muskegon		IHL	4	7	4	11	2	—	—	—	—	—
—Pittsburgh		NHL	74	30	37	67	44	—	—	—	—	—
90-91—Pittsburgh		NHL	78	40	73	113	48	24	10	24	34	33
91-92—Pittsburgh		NHL	58	33	37	70	78	—	—	—	—	—
—Philadelphia		NHL	22	10	17	27	18	—	—	—	—	—
92-93—Philadelphia		NHL	84	53	70	123	95	—	—	—	—	—
93-94—Philadelphia		NHL	84	40	67	107	46	—	—	—	—	—
94-95—Philadelphia		NHL	10	2	3	5	12	—	—	—	—	—
—Montreal		NHL	39	14	29	43	16	—	—	—	—	—
NHL totals			464	223	334	557	357	24	10	24	34	33

REDDEN, WADE

D, ISLANDERS

PERSONAL: Born June 12, 1977, in Lloydminster, Sask. . . . 6-1/193. . . . Shoots left. **HIGH SCHOOL:** Crocus Plaines (Brandon, Man.). **TRANSACTIONS/CAREER NOTES:** Selected by New York Islanders in first round (first Islanders pick, second overall) of NHL entry draft (July 8, 1995).
HONORS: Won Jim Piggott Memorial Trophy (1993-94). . . . Won WHL Top Draft Prospect Award (1994-95). . . . Named to Can.HL All-Star second team (1994-95). . . . Named to WHL (East) All-Star second team (1994-95).

Season	Team	League	REGULAR SEASON Gms.	G	A	Pts.	PIM	PLAYOFFS Gms.	G	A	Pts.	PIM
92-93—Lloydminster		SJHL	34	4	11	15	64	—	—	—	—	—
93-94—Brandon		WHL	64	4	35	39	98	14	2	4	6	10
94-95—Brandon		WHL	64	14	46	60	83	18	5	10	15	8

REDDICK, POKEY

G

PERSONAL: Born October 6, 1964, in Halifax, N.S. . . . 5-8/170. . . . Catches left. **TRANSACTIONS/CAREER NOTES:** Traded by New Westminster Bruins to Brandon Wheat Kings for D Jayson Meyer and D Lee Trim (October 1984). . . . Signed as free agent by Winnipeg Jets (September 27, 1985). . . . Traded by Jets to Edmonton Oilers for future considerations (September 28, 1989). . . . Signed as free agent by Florida Panthers (July 13, 1993). . . . Signed as free agent by Las Vegas Thunder (June 14, 1994).
HONORS: Named to WHL All-Star second team (1983-84). . . . Shared James Norris Memorial Trophy with Rick St. Croix (1985-86). . . . Won N.R. (Bud) Poile Trophy (1992-93).
MISCELLANEOUS: Member of Stanley Cup championship team (1990).

Season	Team	League	REGULAR SEASON Gms.	Min.	W	L	T	GA	SO	Avg.	PLAYOFFS Gms.	Min.	W	L	GA	SO	Avg.
81-82—Billings		WHL	1	60	...	...	...	7	0	7.00	—	—	—	—	—	—	—
82-83—Nanaimo		WHL	*66	*3549	19	38	1	*383	0	6.48	—	—	—	—	—	—	—
83-84—New Westminster		WHL	50	2930	24	22	2	215	0	4.40	9	542	4	5	53	0	5.87
84-85—Brandon		WHL	47	2585	14	30	1	243	0	5.64	—	—	—	—	—	—	—
—Fort Wayne		IHL	10	491	...	...	...	32	2	3.91	4	246	...	...	17	0	4.15
85-86—Fort Wayne		IHL	32	1811	15	11	†0	92	†3	3.05	—	—	—	—	—	—	—
86-87—Winnipeg		NHL	48	2762	21	21	4	149	0	3.24	3	166	0	2	10	0	3.61
87-88—Winnipeg		NHL	28	1487	9	13	3	102	0	4.12	—	—	—	—	—	—	—
—Moncton		AHL	9	545	2	6	1	26	0	2.86	—	—	—	—	—	—	—
88-89—Winnipeg		NHL	41	2109	11	17	7	144	0	4.10	—	—	—	—	—	—	—
89-90—Edmonton		NHL	11	604	5	4	2	31	0	3.08	1	2	0	0	0	0	0.00
—Cape Breton		AHL	15	821	9	4	1	54	0	3.95	—	—	—	—	—	—	—
—Phoenix		IHL	3	185	2	1	†0	7	0	2.27	—	—	—	—	—	—	—
90-91—Edmonton		NHL	2	120	0	2	0	9	0	4.50	—	—	—	—	—	—	—
—Cape Breton		AHL	31	1673	19	10	0	97	2	3.48	2	124	0	2	10	0	4.84
91-92—Cape Breton		AHL	16	765	5	3	3	45	0	3.53	—	—	—	—	—	—	—
—Fort Wayne		IHL	14	787	6	5	†2	40	1	3.05	7	369	3	4	18	0	2.93
92-93—Fort Wayne		IHL	54	3043	33	16	†0	156	3	3.08	12	723	*12	0	18	0	*1.49
93-94—Florida		NHL	2	80	0	1	0	8	0	6.00	—	—	—	—	—	—	—
—Cincinnati		IHL	54	2894	31	12	†6	147	*2	3.05	10	498	6	2	21	†1	2.53
94-95—Las Vegas		IHL	40	2075	23	13	†1	104	†3	3.01	10	592	4	6	31	0	3.14
NHL totals			132	7162	46	58	16	443	0	3.71	4	168	0	2	10	0	3.57

REDMOND, KEITH

LW, KINGS

PERSONAL: Born October 25, 1972, in Richmond Hill, Ont. . . . 6-3/208. . . . Shoots left. . . . Full name: Keith Christopher Redmond.
COLLEGE: Bowling Green State.
TRANSACTIONS/CAREER NOTES: Selected by Los Angeles Kings in fourth round (second Kings pick, 79th overall) of NHL entry draft (June 22, 1991).

Season	Team	League	REGULAR SEASON Gms.	G	A	Pts.	PIM	PLAYOFFS Gms.	G	A	Pts.	PIM
88-89—Nepean		COJHL	59	3	12	15	110	—	—	—	—	—
89-90—Nepean		COJHL	40	14	10	24	169	—	—	—	—	—
90-91—Bowling Green State		CCHA	35	1	3	4	72	—	—	—	—	—
91-92—Bowling Green State		CCHA	8	0	0	0	14	—	—	—	—	—
—Belleville		OHL	16	1	7	8	52	—	—	—	—	—
—Detroit		OHL	25	6	12	18	61	7	1	3	4	49

R

Season Team	League	REGULAR SEASON					PLAYOFFS				
		Gms.	G	A	Pts.	PIM	Gms.	G	A	Pts.	PIM
92-93—Muskegon	Col.HL	4	1	0	1	46	—	—	—	—	—
—Phoenix	IHL	53	6	10	16	285	—	—	—	—	—
93-94—Los Angeles	NHL	12	1	0	1	20	—	—	—	—	—
—Phoenix	IHL	43	8	10	18	196	—	—	—	—	—
94-95—Phoenix	IHL	20	0	3	3	81	6	2	1	3	29
NHL totals		12	1	0	1	20					

REEKIE, JOE
D, CAPITALS

PERSONAL: Born February 22, 1965, in Victoria, B.C. . . . 6-3/220. . . . Shoots left. . . . Full name: Joseph James Reekie.

TRANSACTIONS/CAREER NOTES: Selected by Hartford Whalers as underage junior in seventh round (eighth Whalers pick, 124th overall) of NHL entry draft (June 8, 1983). . . . Released by Whalers (June 1984). . . . Selected by Buffalo Sabres in sixth round (sixth Sabres pick, 119th overall) of NHL entry draft (June 15, 1985). . . . Injured ankle (March 14, 1987). . . . Injured shoulder (October 1987). . . . Broke kneecap (November 15, 1987). . . . Underwent surgery to left knee (September 1988). . . . Traded by Sabres to New York Islanders for sixth-round pick (G Bill Pye) in 1989 draft (June 17, 1989). . . . Sprained right knee (November 1989). . . . Broke two bones in left hand and suffered facial cuts in automobile accident and underwent surgery (December 7, 1989). . . . Broke left middle finger (March 21, 1990). . . . Injured eye (January 12, 1991); missed six games. . . . Fractured knuckle on left hand (January 3, 1992); missed 22 games. . . . Selected by Tampa Bay Lightning in NHL expansion draft (June 18, 1992). . . . Broke left leg (January 16, 1993); missed remainder of season. . . . Traded by Lightning to Washington Capitals for D Enrico Ciccone, third-round pick in 1994 draft (RW Craig Reichert) and conditional draft pick (March 21, 1994).

Season Team	League	REGULAR SEASON					PLAYOFFS				
		Gms.	G	A	Pts.	PIM	Gms.	G	A	Pts.	PIM
81-82—Nepean	COJHL	16	2	5	7	4	—	—	—	—	—
82-83—North Bay	OHL	59	2	9	11	49	8	0	1	1	11
83-84—North Bay	OHL	9	1	0	1	18	—	—	—	—	—
—Cornwall	OHL	53	6	27	33	166	3	0	0	0	4
84-85—Cornwall	OHL	65	19	63	82	134	9	4	13	17	18
85-86—Rochester	AHL	77	3	25	28	178	—	—	—	—	—
—Buffalo	NHL	3	0	0	0	14	—	—	—	—	—
86-87—Buffalo	NHL	56	1	8	9	82	—	—	—	—	—
—Rochester	AHL	22	0	6	6	52	—	—	—	—	—
87-88—Buffalo	NHL	30	1	4	5	68	2	0	0	0	4
88-89—Rochester	AHL	21	2	3	5	56	—	—	—	—	—
—Buffalo	NHL	15	1	3	4	26	—	—	—	—	—
89-90—New York Islanders	NHL	31	1	8	9	43	—	—	—	—	—
—Springfield	AHL	15	1	4	5	24	—	—	—	—	—
90-91—Capital District	AHL	2	1	0	1	0	—	—	—	—	—
—New York Islanders	NHL	66	3	16	19	96	—	—	—	—	—
91-92—New York Islanders	NHL	54	4	12	16	85	—	—	—	—	—
—Capital District	AHL	3	2	2	4	2	—	—	—	—	—
92-93—Tampa Bay	NHL	42	2	11	13	69	—	—	—	—	—
93-94—Tampa Bay	NHL	73	1	11	12	127	—	—	—	—	—
—Washington	NHL	12	0	5	5	29	11	2	1	3	29
94-95—Washington	NHL	48	1	6	7	97	7	0	0	0	2
NHL totals		430	15	84	99	736	20	2	1	3	35

REESE, JEFF
G, WHALERS

PERSONAL: Born March 24, 1966, in Brantford, Ont. . . . 5-9/175. . . . Catches left.

TRANSACTIONS/CAREER NOTES: Selected by Toronto Maple Leafs as underage junior in fourth round (third Maple Leafs pick, 67th overall) of NHL entry draft (June 9, 1984). . . . Broke left kneecap (October 23, 1989); missed two months. . . . Bruised left kneecap (April 12, 1990). . . . Broke transverse processes (March 23, 1991); missed remainder of season. . . . Traded by Maple Leafs with D Alexander Godynyuk, RW Gary Leeman, D Michel Petit and LW Craig Berube to Calgary Flames for C Doug Gilmour, D Jamie Macoun, LW Kent Manderville, D Ric Nattress and G Rick Wamsley (January 2, 1992). . . . Lacerated hand prior to 1992-93 season; missed first three games of season. . . . Strained shoulder (October 31, 1993); missed three games. . . . Traded by Flames with future considerations to Hartford Whalers for D Dan Keczmer (November 19, 1993). . . . Suffered hip flexor (December 23, 1993); missed six games.

RECORDS: Holds NHL single-game record for most assists by a goaltender—3 (February 10, 1993).

Season Team	League	REGULAR SEASON								PLAYOFFS						
		Gms.	Min.	W	L	T	GA	SO	Avg.	Gms.	Min.	W	L	GA	SO	Avg.
82-83—Hamilton A's	OJHL	40	2380	...	...	...	176	0	4.44	—	—	—	—	—	—	—
83-84—London	OHL	43	2308	18	19	0	173	0	4.50	6	327	3	3	27	0	4.95
84-85—London	OHL	50	2878	31	15	1	186	1	3.88	8	440	5	2	20	+1	*2.73
85-86—London	OHL	*57	*3281	25	26	3	215	0	3.93	5	299	0	4	25	0	5.02
86-87—Newmarket	AHL	50	2822	11	29	0	193	1	4.10	—	—	—	—	—	—	—
87-88—Newmarket	AHL	28	1587	10	14	3	103	0	3.89	—	—	—	—	—	—	—
—Toronto	NHL	5	249	1	2	1	17	0	4.10	—	—	—	—	—	—	—
88-89—Toronto	NHL	10	486	2	6	1	40	0	4.94	—	—	—	—	—	—	—
—Newmarket	AHL	37	2072	17	14	3	132	0	3.82	—	—	—	—	—	—	—
89-90—Newmarket	AHL	7	431	3	2	2	29	0	4.04	—	—	—	—	—	—	—
—Toronto	NHL	21	1101	9	6	3	81	0	4.41	2	108	1	1	6	0	3.33
90-91—Toronto	NHL	30	1430	6	13	3	92	1	3.86	—	—	—	—	—	—	—
—Newmarket	AHL	3	180	2	1	0	7	0	2.33	—	—	—	—	—	—	—

Season Team	League	Gms.	Min.	W	L	T	GA	SO	Avg.	Gms.	Min.	W	L	GA	SO	Avg.
91-92—Toronto	NHL	8	413	1	5	1	20	1	2.91	—	—	—	—	—	—	—
—Calgary	NHL	12	587	3	2	2	37	0	3.78	—	—	—	—	—	—	—
92-93—Calgary	NHL	26	1311	14	4	1	70	1	3.20	4	209	1	3	17	0	4.88
93-94—Calgary	NHL	1	13	0	0	0	1	0	4.62	—	—	—	—	—	—	—
—Hartford	NHL	19	1086	5	9	3	56	1	3.09	—	—	—	—	—	—	—
94-95—Hartford	NHL	11	477	2	5	1	26	0	3.27	—	—	—	—	—	—	—
NHL totals		143	7153	43	52	16	440	4	3.69	6	317	2	4	23	0	4.35

REHNBERG, HENRIK
D, DEVILS

PERSONAL: Born July 20, 1977, in Grava, Sweden. . . . 6-2/194. . . . Shoots left.
TRANSACTIONS/CAREER NOTES: Selected by New Jersey Devils in fourth round (sixth Devils pick, 96th overall) of NHL entry draft (July 8, 1995).

Season Team	League	Gms.	G	A	Pts.	PIM	Gms.	G	A	Pts.	PIM
94-95—Farjestad Jrs	Sweden	24	1	2	3	. . .	—	—	—	—	—

REICHEL, MARTIN
RW/C, OILERS

PERSONAL: Born November 7, 1973, in Most, Czechoslovakia. . . . 6-1/183. . . . Shoots left. . . . Name pronounced RIGH-kuhl. . . . Brother of Robert Reichel, center, Calgary Flames.
TRANSACTIONS/CAREER NOTES: Selected by Edmonton Oilers in second round (second Oilers pick, 37th overall) of NHL entry draft (June 20, 1992).

Season Team	League	Gms.	G	A	Pts.	PIM	Gms.	G	A	Pts.	PIM
90-91—Freiburg	Germany	23	7	8	15	19	—	—	—	—	—
91-92—Freiburg	Germany	27	15	16	31	8	4	1	1	2	4
92-93—Freiburg	Germany	37	13	9	22	27	9	4	4	8	11
93-94—Rosenheim	Germany	20	5	15	20	6	—	—	—	—	—
94-95—Rosenheim	Germany	43	11	26	37	36	7	3	3	6	37

REICHEL, ROBERT
C, FLAMES

PERSONAL: Born June 25, 1971, in Litvinov, Czechoslovakia. . . . 5-10/185. . . . Shoots right. . . . Name pronounced RIGH-kuhl. . . . Brother of Martin Reichel, right winger/center in Edmonton Oilers system.
TRANSACTIONS/CAREER NOTES: Selected by Calgary Flames in fourth round (fifth Flames pick, 70th overall) of NHL entry draft (June 17, 1989). . . . Strained right knee (March 16, 1993); missed three games. . . . Played in Europe during 1994-95 NHL lockout.
HONORS: Named to Czechoslovakian League All-Star team (1989-90).
STATISTICAL PLATEAUS: Three-goal games: 1992-93 (2), 1993-94 (2). Total: 4.

Season Team	League	Gms.	G	A	Pts.	PIM	Gms.	G	A	Pts.	PIM
88-89—Litvinov	Czech.	. . .	20	31	51	. . .	—	—	—	—	—
89-90—Litvinov	Czech.	52	49	34	*83	. . .	—	—	—	—	—
90-91—Calgary	NHL	66	19	22	41	22	6	1	1	2	0
91-92—Calgary	NHL	77	20	34	54	32	—	—	—	—	—
92-93—Calgary	NHL	80	40	48	88	54	6	2	4	6	2
93-94—Calgary	NHL	84	40	53	93	58	7	0	5	5	0
94-95—Frankfurt	Germany	21	19	24	43	41	—	—	—	—	—
—Calgary	NHL	48	18	17	35	28	7	2	4	6	4
NHL totals		355	137	174	311	194	26	5	14	19	6

REICHERT, CRAIG
RW, MIGHTY DUCKS

PERSONAL: Born May 11, 1974, in Winnipeg. . . . 6-1/196. . . . Shoots right. . . . Name pronounced RIGH-kurht.
HIGH SCHOOL: Dr. E.P. Scarlett (Calgary).
TRANSACTIONS/CAREER NOTES: Selected by Mighty Ducks of Anaheim in third round (third Mighty Ducks pick, 67th overall) of NHL entry draft (June 29, 1994).

Season Team	League	Gms.	G	A	Pts.	PIM	Gms.	G	A	Pts.	PIM
91-92—Spokane	WHL	68	14	30	44	86	4	1	0	1	4
92-93—Red Deer	WHL	66	32	33	65	62	4	3	1	4	2
93-94—Red Deer	WHL	72	52	67	119	153	4	2	2	4	8
94-95—San Diego	IHL	49	4	12	16	28	—	—	—	—	—

REID, DAVID
LW, BRUINS

PERSONAL: Born May 15, 1964, in Toronto. . . . 6-1/205. . . . Shoots left.
TRANSACTIONS/CAREER NOTES: Selected by Boston Bruins as underage junior in third round (fourth Bruins pick, 60th overall) of NHL entry draft (June 9, 1982). . . . Underwent knee surgery (December 1986). . . . Separated shoulder (November 1987); missed 10 games. . . . Signed as free agent by Toronto Maple Leafs (August 1988). . . . Suffered from pneumonia (March 1992); missed 10 games. . . . Injured knee (March 25, 1993); missed remainder of season. . . . Signed as free agent by Bruins (November 22, 1991). . . . Injured hip (April 1995); missed two games.

Season Team	League	Gms.	G	A	Pts.	PIM	Gms.	G	A	Pts.	PIM
81-82—Peterborough	OHL	68	10	32	42	41	9	2	3	5	11
82-83—Peterborough	OHL	70	23	34	57	33	4	3	1	4	0

Season	Team	League	Gms.	G	A	Pts.	PIM	Gms.	G	A	Pts.	PIM
83-84—Peterborough		OHL	60	33	64	97	12	—	—	—	—	—
—Boston		NHL	8	1	0	1	2	—	—	—	—	—
84-85—Hershey		AHL	43	10	14	24	6	—	—	—	—	—
—Boston		NHL	35	14	13	27	27	5	1	0	1	0
85-86—Moncton		AHL	26	14	18	32	4	—	—	—	—	—
—Boston		NHL	37	10	10	20	10	—	—	—	—	—
86-87—Boston		NHL	12	3	3	6	0	2	0	0	0	0
—Moncton		AHL	40	12	22	34	23	5	0	1	1	0
87-88—Maine		AHL	63	21	37	58	40	10	6	7	13	0
—Boston		NHL	3	0	0	0	0	—	—	—	—	—
88-89—Toronto		NHL	77	9	21	30	22	—	—	—	—	—
89-90—Toronto		NHL	70	9	19	28	9	3	0	0	0	0
90-91—Toronto		NHL	69	15	13	28	18	—	—	—	—	—
91-92—Maine		AHL	12	1	5	6	4	—	—	—	—	—
—Boston		NHL	43	7	7	14	27	15	2	5	7	4
92-93—Boston		NHL	65	20	16	36	10	—	—	—	—	—
93-94—Boston		NHL	83	6	17	23	25	13	2	1	3	2
94-95—Boston		NHL	38	5	5	10	10	5	0	0	0	0
NHL totals			540	99	124	223	160	43	5	6	11	6

REID, JARRET
C, WHALERS

PERSONAL: Born March 10, 1973, in Sault Ste. Marie, Ont. . . . 5-10/180. . . . Shoots right.
HIGH SCHOOL: St. Mary's College (Sault Ste. Marie, Ont.).
TRANSACTIONS/CAREER NOTES: Selected by Hartford Whalers in sixth round (sixth Whalers pick, 143rd overall) of NHL entry draft (June 20, 1992).

Season	Team	League	Gms.	G	A	Pts.	PIM	Gms.	G	A	Pts.	PIM
90-91—Sault Ste. Marie		OHL	63	37	29	66	18	14	5	12	17	14
91-92—Sault Ste. Marie		OHL	61	53	40	93	67	19	5	13	18	17
92-93—Sault Ste. Marie		OHL	64	36	60	96	28	18	19	16	35	20
93-94—Springfield		AHL	6	2	0	2	2	—	—	—	—	—
—Raleigh		ECHL	10	3	6	9	8	—	—	—	—	—
—Belleville		OHL	25	15	23	38	16	12	5	7	12	6
94-95—Springfield		AHL	8	1	2	3	0	—	—	—	—	—

REID, SHAWN
D, RANGERS

PERSONAL: Born September 21, 1970, in Toronto. . . . 6-0/195. . . . Shoots left.
COLLEGE: Colorado College.
TRANSACTIONS/CAREER NOTES: Signed as free agent by New York Rangers (July 6, 1994).
HONORS: Named to NCAA All-America West first team (1993-94). . . . Named to WCHA All-Star first team (1993-94).

Season	Team	League	Gms.	G	A	Pts.	PIM	Gms.	G	A	Pts.	PIM
90-91—Colorado College		WCHA	38	10	8	18	36	—	—	—	—	—
91-92—Colorado College		WCHA	41	12	22	34	64	—	—	—	—	—
92-93—Colorado College		WCHA	32	3	11	14	54	—	—	—	—	—
93-94—Colorado College		WCHA	39	7	20	27	25	—	—	—	—	—
94-95—Fort Wayne		IHL	42	4	8	12	28	—	—	—	—	—
—Binghamton		AHL	18	3	4	7	8	9	0	3	3	6

RENBERG, MIKAEL
LW, FLYERS

PERSONAL: Born May 5, 1972, in Pitea, Sweden. . . . 6-2/218. . . . Shoots left.
TRANSACTIONS/CAREER NOTES: Selected by Philadelphia Flyers in second round (third Flyers pick, 40th overall) of NHL entry draft (June 16, 1990). . . . Played in Europe during 1994-95 NHL lockout. . . . Suffered sore shoulder (March 25, 1995); missed one game.
HONORS: Named to NHL All-Rookie team (1993-94).
STATISTICAL PLATEAUS: Three-goal games: 1993-94 (1).

Season	Team	League	Gms.	G	A	Pts.	PIM	Gms.	G	A	Pts.	PIM
88-89—Pitea		Sweden	12	6	3	9	...	—	—	—	—	—
89-90—Pitea		Sweden	29	15	19	34	...	—	—	—	—	—
90-91—Lulea		Sweden	29	11	6	17	12	5	1	1	2	4
91-92—Lulea		Sweden	38	8	15	23	20	2	0	0	0	0
92-93—Lulea		Sweden	39	19	13	32	61	11	4	4	8	0
93-94—Philadelphia		NHL	83	38	44	82	36	—	—	—	—	—
94-95—Lulea		Sweden	10	9	4	13	16	—	—	—	—	—
—Philadelphia		NHL	47	26	31	57	20	15	6	7	13	6
NHL totals			130	64	75	139	56	15	6	7	13	6

RHODES, DAMIAN
G, MAPLE LEAFS

PERSONAL: Born May 28, 1969, in St. Paul, Minn. . . . 6-0/190. . . . Catches left.
HIGH SCHOOL: Richfield (Minn.).
COLLEGE: Michigan Tech.
TRANSACTIONS/CAREER NOTES: Selected by Toronto Maple Leafs in sixth round (sixth Maple Leafs pick, 112th overall) of NHL entry draft (June 13, 1987).

Season	Team	League	REGULAR SEASON							PLAYOFFS					
			Gms.	Min.	W	L	T	GA	SO	Avg.	Gms.	Min.	W	L	GA	SO	Avg.
85-86	Richfield H.S.	Minn. HS	16	720	...	...	...	56	0	4.67	—	—	—	—	—	—	—
86-87	Richfield H.S.	Minn. HS	19	673	...	...	...	51	1	4.55	—	—	—	—	—	—	—
87-88	Michigan Tech	WCHA	29	1623	16	10	1	114	0	4.21	—	—	—	—	—	—	—
88-89	Michigan Tech	WCHA	37	2216	15	22	0	163	0	4.41	—	—	—	—	—	—	—
89-90	Michigan Tech	WCHA	25	1358	6	17	0	119	0	5.26	—	—	—	—	—	—	—
90-91	Toronto	NHL	1	60	1	0	0	1	0	1.00	—	—	—	—	—	—	—
	Newmarket	AHL	38	2154	8	24	3	144	1	4.01	—	—	—	—	—	—	—
91-92	St. John's	AHL	43	2454	20	16	5	148	0	3.62	6	331	4	1	16	0	2.90
92-93	St. John's	AHL	52	*3074	27	16	8	184	1	3.59	9	538	4	5	37	0	4.13
93-94	Toronto	NHL	22	1213	9	7	3	53	0	2.62	1	0	0	0	0	0	0.00
94-95	Toronto	NHL	13	760	6	6	1	34	0	2.68	—	—	—	—	—	—	—
NHL totals			36	2033	16	13	4	88	0	2.60	1	0	0	0	0	0	0

RICCI, MIKE
C, DENVER

PERSONAL: Born October 27, 1971, in Scarborough, Ont. . . . 6-0/190. . . . Shoots left. . . . Name pronounced REE-CHEE.

TRANSACTIONS/CAREER NOTES: Separated right shoulder (December 1989). . . . Selected by Philadelphia Flyers in first round (first Flyers pick, fourth overall) of NHL entry draft (June 16, 1990). . . . Broke right index finger and thumb (October 4, 1990); missed nine games. . . . Traded by Flyers with G Ron Hextall, C Peter Forsberg, D Steve Duchesne, D Kerry Huffman, first-round pick in 1993 draft (G Jocelyn Thibault), cash and future considerations to Quebec Nordiques for C Eric Lindros (June 20, 1992); Flyers sent LW Chris Simon and first-round pick in 1994 draft (traded to Toronto Maple Leafs) to Nordiques to complete deal (July 21, 1992). . . . Sprained left wrist (November 3, 1992); missed four games. . . . Suffered from the flu (January 5, 1993); missed two games. . . . Nordiques franchise moved to Denver for 1995-96 season.

HONORS: Named to OHL All-Star second team (1988-89). . . . Won Can.HL Player of the Year Award (1989-90). . . . Won Red Tilson Trophy (1989-90). . . . Won William Hanley Trophy (1989-90). . . . Named to OHL All-Star first team (1989-90).

STATISTICAL PLATEAUS: Five-goal games: 1993-94 (1).

Season	Team	League	REGULAR SEASON					PLAYOFFS				
			Gms.	G	A	Pts.	PIM	Gms.	G	A	Pts.	PIM
87-88	Peterborough	OHL	41	24	37	61	20	8	5	5	10	4
88-89	Peterborough	OHL	60	54	52	106	43	17	19	16	35	18
89-90	Peterborough	OHL	60	52	64	116	39	12	5	7	12	26
90-91	Philadelphia	NHL	68	21	20	41	64	—	—	—	—	—
91-92	Philadelphia	NHL	78	20	36	56	93	—	—	—	—	—
92-93	Quebec	NHL	77	27	51	78	123	6	0	6	6	8
93-94	Quebec	NHL	83	30	21	51	113	—	—	—	—	—
94-95	Quebec	NHL	48	15	21	36	40	6	1	3	4	8
NHL totals			354	113	149	262	433	12	1	9	10	16

RICE, STEVE
RW, WHALERS

PERSONAL: Born May 26, 1971, in Waterloo, Ont. . . . 6-0/215. . . . Shoots right.

TRANSACTIONS/CAREER NOTES: Underwent knee surgery (October 1986). . . . Selected by New York Rangers in first round (first Rangers pick, 20th overall) of NHL entry draft (June 17, 1989). . . . Suffered back spasms (September 14, 1989). . . . Injured left shoulder (October 1990). . . . Traded by Rangers with C Bernie Nicholls, LW Louie DeBrusk and future considerations to Edmonton Oilers for C Mark Messier and future considerations (October 4, 1991); Rangers later traded D David Shaw to Oilers for D Jeff Beukeboom to complete deal (November 12, 1991). . . . Bruised right hip (March 1993); missed two games. . . . Fractured hand (February 12, 1994); missed 16 games. . . . Signed as free agent by Hartford Whalers (August 18, 1994); D Bryan Marchment awarded to Oilers as compensation (August 30, 1994). . . . Injured shoulder (April 4, 1995); missed three games. . . . Suffered concussion (April 26, 1995); missed three games.

HONORS: Named to Memorial Cup All-Star team (1989-90). . . . Named to OHL All-Star second team (1990-91). . . . Named to AHL All-Star second team (1992-93).

STATISTICAL PLATEAUS: Three-goal games: 1994-95 (1).

Season	Team	League	REGULAR SEASON					PLAYOFFS				
			Gms.	G	A	Pts.	PIM	Gms.	G	A	Pts.	PIM
87-88	Kitchener	OHL	59	11	14	25	43	4	0	1	1	0
88-89	Kitchener	OHL	64	36	31	67	42	5	2	1	3	8
89-90	Kitchener	OHL	58	39	37	76	102	16	4	8	12	24
90-91	New York Rangers	NHL	11	1	1	2	4	2	2	1	3	6
	Binghamton	AHL	8	4	1	5	12	5	2	0	2	2
	Kitchener	OHL	29	30	30	60	43	6	5	6	11	2
91-92	Edmonton	NHL	3	0	0	0	2	—	—	—	—	—
	Cape Breton	AHL	45	32	20	52	38	5	4	4	8	10
92-93	Cape Breton	AHL	51	34	28	62	63	14	4	6	10	22
	Edmonton	NHL	28	2	5	7	28	—	—	—	—	—
93-94	Edmonton	NHL	63	17	15	32	36	—	—	—	—	—
94-95	Hartford	NHL	40	11	10	21	61	—	—	—	—	—
NHL totals			145	31	31	62	131	2	2	1	3	6

RICHARD, JEAN-MARC
D

PERSONAL: Born October 8, 1966, in St. Raymond, Que. . . . 5-11/178. . . . Shoots left. . . . Name pronounced ZHAWN-MAHRK rih-SHAHRD.

TRANSACTIONS/CAREER NOTES: Signed as free agent by Quebec Nordiques (April 1987). . . . Loaned to Fort Wayne Komets (March 1991). . . . Signed

as free agent by Komets (September 1991).... Signed as free agent by Las Vegas Thunder (July 8, 1993).
HONORS: Won Emile (Butch) Bouchard Trophy (1986-87).... Named to QMJHL All-Star first team (1985-86 and 1986-87).
.... Won Governors Trophy (1991-92).... Named to IHL All-Star first team (1991-92 and 1993-94).

			REGULAR SEASON					PLAYOFFS			
Season Team	League	Gms.	G	A	Pts.	PIM	Gms.	G	A	Pts.	PIM
83-84—Chicoutimi	QMJHL	61	1	20	21	41	—	—	—	—	—
84-85—Chicoutimi	QMJHL	68	10	61	71	57	—	—	—	—	—
85-86—Chicoutimi	QMJHL	72	19	88	107	111	9	3	5	8	14
86-87—Chicoutimi	QMJHL	67	21	81	102	105	16	6	25	31	28
87-88—Fredericton	AHL	68	14	42	56	52	7	2	1	3	4
—Quebec	NHL	4	2	1	3	2	—	—	—	—	—
88-89—Halifax	AHL	57	8	25	33	38	4	1	0	1	4
89-90—Quebec	NHL	1	0	0	0	0	—	—	—	—	—
—Halifax	AHL	40	1	24	25	38	—	—	—	—	—
90-91—Halifax	AHL	80	7	41	48	76	—	—	—	—	—
—Fort Wayne	IHL	1	0	0	0	0	19	3	9	12	8
91-92—Fort Wayne	IHL	82	18	68	86	109	7	0	5	5	20
92-93—San Diego	IHL	6	1	0	1	4	—	—	—	—	—
—Fort Wayne	IHL	52	10	33	43	48	12	6	11	17	6
93-94—Las Vegas	IHL	59	15	33	48	44	5	0	3	3	0
94-95—Las Vegas	IHL	81	16	41	57	76	10	0	3	3	4
NHL totals		5	2	1	3	2					

RICHARDS, TODD
D

PERSONAL: Born October 20, 1966, in Robbinsdale, Minn.... 6-0/190.... Shoots right.
HIGH SCHOOL: Armstrong (Plymouth, Minn.).
COLLEGE: Minnesota.
TRANSACTIONS/CAREER NOTES: Selected by Montreal Canadiens in second round (third Canadiens pick, 33rd overall) of NHL entry draft (June 15, 1985).... Traded by Canadiens to Hartford Whalers for future considerations (October 1990).... Bruised knee (October 14, 1991); missed two games.... Signed as free agent by Las Vegas Thunder (July 14, 1993).... Signed as free agent by Orlando Solar Bears of IHL (July 10, 1995).
HONORS: Named to WCHA All-Star second team (1987-88 and 1988-89).... Named to NCAA All-America West second team (1988-89).... Named to NCAA All-Tournament team (1988-89).... Named to IHL All-Star second team (1993-94).... Won Governors Trophy (1994-95).... Named to IHL All-Star first team (1994-95).

			REGULAR SEASON					PLAYOFFS			
Season Team	League	Gms.	G	A	Pts.	PIM	Gms.	G	A	Pts.	PIM
84-85—Armstrong H.S.	Minn. H.S.	24	10	23	33	24	—	—	—	—	—
85-86—University of Minnesota	WCHA	38	6	23	29	38	—	—	—	—	—
86-87—University of Minnesota	WCHA	49	8	43	51	70	—	—	—	—	—
87-88—University of Minnesota	WCHA	34	10	30	40	26	—	—	—	—	—
88-89—University of Minnesota	WCHA	46	6	32	38	60	—	—	—	—	—
89-90—Sherbrooke	AHL	71	6	18	24	73	5	1	2	3	6
90-91—Fredericton	AHL	3	0	1	1	2	—	—	—	—	—
—Springfield	AHL	71	10	41	51	62	14	2	8	10	2
—Hartford	NHL	2	0	4	4	2	6	0	0	0	2
91-92—Hartford	NHL	6	0	0	0	2	5	0	3	3	4
—Springfield	AHL	43	6	23	29	33	8	0	3	3	2
92-93—Springfield	AHL	78	13	42	55	53	9	1	5	6	2
93-94—Las Vegas	IHL	80	11	35	46	122	5	1	4	5	18
94-95—Las Vegas	IHL	80	12	49	61	130	9	1	2	3	6
NHL totals		8	0	4	4	4	11	0	3	3	6

RICHARDS, TRAVIS
D, STARS

PERSONAL: Born March 22, 1970, in Crystal, Minn.... 6-1/185.... Shoots right.
COLLEGE: Minnesota.
TRANSACTIONS/CAREER NOTES: Selected by Minnesota North Stars in ninth round (ninth North Stars pick, 169th overall) of NHL entry draft (June 11, 1988)....
North Stars franchise moved from Minnesota to Dallas and renamed Stars for 1993-94 season.

			REGULAR SEASON					PLAYOFFS			
Season Team	League	Gms.	G	A	Pts.	PIM	Gms.	G	A	Pts.	PIM
89-90—University of Minnesota	WCHA	45	4	24	28	38	—	—	—	—	—
90-91—University of Minnesota	WCHA	45	9	25	34	28	—	—	—	—	—
91-92—University of Minnesota	WCHA	44	10	23	33	65	—	—	—	—	—
92-93—University of Minnesota	WCHA	42	12	26	38	54	—	—	—	—	—
93-94—U.S. national team	Int'l	51	1	11	12	12	—	—	—	—	—
—U.S. Olympic Team	Int'l	8	0	0	0	2	—	—	—	—	—
—Kalamazoo	IHL	19	2	10	12	20	4	1	1	2	0
94-95—Kalamazoo	IHL	63	4	16	20	53	15	1	5	6	12
—Dallas	NHL	2	0	0	0	0	—	—	—	—	—
NHL totals		2	0	0	0	0					

RICHARDSON, LUKE
D, OILERS

PERSONAL: Born March 26, 1969, in Ottawa.... 6-4/210.... Shoots left.... Full name: Luke Glen Richardson.
TRANSACTIONS/CAREER NOTES: Selected by Toronto Maple Leafs as underage junior in first round (first Maple Leafs pick, seventh overall) of NHL entry draft (June 13,

1987). . . . Traded by Maple Leafs with LW Vincent Damphousse, G Peter Ing, C Scott Thornton and future considerations to Edmonton Oilers for G Grant Fuhr, LW Glenn Anderson and LW Craig Berube (September 19, 1991). . . . Strained clavicular joint (February 11, 1992); missed three games. . . . Suffered from the flu (March 1993); missed one game. . . . Fractured cheekbone (January 7, 1994); missed 15 games. . . . Suffered from the flu (February 28, 1995); missed two games.

			REGULAR SEASON					PLAYOFFS				
Season Team	League	Gms.	G	A	Pts.	PIM	Gms.	G	A	Pts.	PIM
84-85—Ottawa Jr. B	ODHA	35	5	26	31	72	—	—	—	—	—
85-86—Peterborough	OHL	63	6	18	24	57	16	2	1	3	50
86-87—Peterborough	OHL	59	13	32	45	70	12	0	5	5	24
87-88—Toronto	NHL	78	4	6	10	90	2	0	0	0	0
88-89—Toronto	NHL	55	2	7	9	106	—	—	—	—	—
89-90—Toronto	NHL	67	4	14	18	122	5	0	0	0	22
90-91—Toronto	NHL	78	1	9	10	238	—	—	—	—	—
91-92—Edmonton	NHL	75	2	19	21	118	16	0	5	5	45
92-93—Edmonton	NHL	82	3	10	13	142	—	—	—	—	—
93-94—Edmonton	NHL	69	2	6	8	131	—	—	—	—	—
94-95—Edmonton	NHL	46	3	10	13	40	—	—	—	—	—
NHL totals		550	21	81	102	987	23	0	5	5	67

RICHER, STEPHANE
D, PANTHERS

PERSONAL: Born April 28, 1966, in Hull, Que. . . . 5-11/190. . . . Shoots right. . . . Full name: Stephane J.G. Richer. . . . Name pronounced steh-FAN REE-shay.
TRANSACTIONS/CAREER NOTES: Signed as free agent by Montreal Canadiens (January 9, 1988). . . . Signed as free agent by Los Angeles Kings (July 11, 1990). . . . Signed as free agent by Canadiens (September 1, 1991). . . . Signed as free agent by Tampa Bay Lightning (July 29, 1992). . . . Traded by Lightning to Boston Bruins for D Bob Beers (October 28, 1992). . . . Selected by Florida Panthers in NHL expansion draft (June 24, 1993). . . . Underwent right shoulder surgery (November 22, 1993); missed three games.
HONORS: Named to AHL All-Star second team (1991-92). . . . Named to IHL All-Star second team (1993-94 and 1994-95).

			REGULAR SEASON					PLAYOFFS				
Season Team	League	Gms.	G	A	Pts.	PIM	Gms.	G	A	Pts.	PIM
83-84—Hull	QMJHL	70	8	38	46	42	—	—	—	—	—
84-85—Hull	QMJHL	67	21	56	77	98	—	—	—	—	—
85-86—Hull	QMJHL	71	14	52	66	166	—	—	—	—	—
86-87—Hull	QMJHL	33	6	22	28	74	8	3	4	7	17
87-88—Baltimore	AHL	22	0	3	3	6	—	—	—	—	—
—Sherbrooke	AHL	41	4	7	11	46	5	1	0	1	10
88-89—Sherbrooke	AHL	70	7	26	33	158	6	1	2	3	18
89-90—Sherbrooke	AHL	60	10	12	22	85	12	4	9	13	16
90-91—Phoenix	IHL	67	11	38	49	48	11	4	6	10	6
—New Haven	AHL	3	0	1	1	0	—	—	—	—	—
91-92—Fredericton	AHL	80	17	47	64	74	7	0	5	5	18
92-93—Tampa Bay	NHL	3	0	0	0	0	—	—	—	—	—
—Providence	AHL	53	8	29	37	60	—	—	—	—	—
—Boston	NHL	21	1	4	5	18	3	0	0	0	0
93-94—Cincinnati	IHL	66	9	55	64	80	11	2	9	11	26
—Florida	NHL	2	0	1	1	0	—	—	—	—	—
94-95—Cincinnati	IHL	80	16	53	69	67	—	—	—	—	—
—Florida	NHL	1	0	0	0	2	—	—	—	—	—
NHL totals		27	1	5	6	20	3	0	0	0	0

RICHER, STEPHANE
RW, DEVILS

PERSONAL: Born June 7, 1966, in Buckingham, Que. . . . 6-2/215. . . . Shoots right. . . . Full name: Stephane Joseph Jean Richer. . . . Name pronounced REE-shay.
TRANSACTIONS/CAREER NOTES: Selected by Montreal Canadiens as underage junior in second round (third Canadiens pick, 29th overall) of NHL entry draft (June 9, 1984). . . . Traded by Granby Bisons with LW Greg Choules to Chicoutimi Sagueneens for C Stephane Roy, RW Marc Bureau, Lee Duhemee, Sylvain Demers and D Rene L'Ecuyer (January 1985). . . . Sprained ankle (November 18, 1985); missed 13 games. . . . Bruised right hand (March 12, 1988). . . . Broke right thumb (April 1988). . . . Sprained right thumb (September 1988). . . . Suspended 10 games by NHL for slashing (November 16, 1988). . . . Suffered from the flu (March 15, 1989). . . . Bruised right shoulder (September 1989). . . . Bruised left foot (February 1990). . . . Injured left ankle (April 21, 1990). . . . Injured knee (December 12, 1990). . . . Traded by Canadiens with RW Tom Chorske to New Jersey Devils for LW Kirk Muller and G Roland Melanson (September 20, 1991). . . . Injured groin (October 22, 1991); missed two games. . . . Injured left knee (March 24, 1992); missed three games. . . . Injured back (December 6, 1992); missed two games. . . . Pulled groin (March 14, 1995); missed two games. . . . Reinjured groin (March 22, 1995); missed one game.
HONORS: Named QMJHL Rookie of the Year (1983-84). . . . Named to QMJHL All-Star second team (1984-85). . . . Played in NHL All-Star Game (1990).
STATISTICAL PLATEAUS: Three-goal games: 1987-88 (1), 1989-90 (2), 1990-91 (1), 1991-92 (1), 1992-93 (1). Total: 6. . . . Four-goal games: 1985-86 (1), 1987-88 (1). Total: 2. . . . Total hat tricks: 8.
MISCELLANEOUS: Member of Stanley Cup championship team (1986 and 1993).

			REGULAR SEASON					PLAYOFFS				
Season Team	League	Gms.	G	A	Pts.	PIM	Gms.	G	A	Pts.	PIM
83-84—Granby	QMJHL	67	39	37	76	58	3	1	1	2	4
84-85—Granby/Chicoutimi	QMJHL	57	61	59	120	71	12	13	13	26	25
—Montreal	NHL	1	0	0	0	0	—	—	—	—	—
—Sherbrooke	AHL	—	—	—	—	—	9	6	3	9	10

Season Team	League	REGULAR SEASON					PLAYOFFS				
		Gms.	G	A	Pts.	PIM	Gms.	G	A	Pts.	PIM
85-86—Montreal	NHL	65	21	16	37	50	16	4	1	5	23
86-87—Sherbrooke	AHL	12	10	4	14	11	—				
—Montreal	NHL	57	20	19	39	80	5	3	2	5	0
87-88—Montreal	NHL	72	50	28	78	72	8	7	5	12	6
88-89—Montreal	NHL	68	25	35	60	61	21	6	5	11	14
89-90—Montreal	NHL	75	51	40	91	46	9	7	3	10	2
90-91—Montreal	NHL	75	31	30	61	53	13	9	5	14	6
91-92—New Jersey	NHL	74	29	35	64	25	7	1	2	3	0
92-93—New Jersey	NHL	78	38	35	73	44	5	2	2	4	2
93-94—New Jersey	NHL	80	36	36	72	16	20	7	5	12	6
94-95—New Jersey	NHL	45	23	16	39	10	19	6	15	21	2
NHL totals		690	324	290	614	457	123	52	45	97	61

RICHTER, BARRY
D, RANGERS

PERSONAL: Born September 11, 1970, in Madison, Wis. . . . 6-2/203. . . . Shoots left. . . . Full name: Barron Patrick Richter. . . . Son of Pat Richter, tight end, Washington Redskins (1963-1970).
HIGH SCHOOL: Culver (Ind.) Military Academy.
COLLEGE: Wisconsin.
TRANSACTIONS/CAREER NOTES: Selected by Hartford Whalers in second round (second Whalers pick, 32nd overall) of NHL entry draft (June 11, 1988). . . . Traded by Whalers with RW Steve Larmer, LW Nick Kypreos and sixth-round pick in 1994 draft (C Yuri Litvinov) to New York Rangers for D James Patrick and C Darren Turcotte (November 2, 1993).
HONORS: Named to NCAA All-Tournament team (1991-92). . . . Named to NCAA All-America West first team (1992-93). . . . Named to WCHA All-Star first team (1992-93).

Season Team	League	REGULAR SEASON					PLAYOFFS				
		Gms.	G	A	Pts.	PIM	Gms.	G	A	Pts.	PIM
86-87—Culver Military Academy..	Indiana H.S.	35	19	26	45	. . .	—	—	—	—	—
87-88—Culver Military Academy..	Indiana H.S.	35	24	29	53	18	—	—	—	—	—
88-89—Culver Military Academy..	Indiana H.S.	19	21	29	50	16	—	—	—	—	—
89-90—University of Wisconsin ...	WCHA	42	13	23	36	26	—	—	—	—	—
90-91—University of Wisconsin ...	WCHA	43	15	20	35	42	—	—	—	—	—
91-92—University of Wisconsin ...	WCHA	39	10	25	35	62	—	—	—	—	—
92-93—University of Wisconsin ...	WCHA	42	14	32	46	74	—	—	—	—	—
93-94—U.S. national team	Int'l	56	7	16	23	50	—	—	—	—	—
—U.S. Olympic Team	Int'l	8	0	3	3	4	—	—	—	—	—
—Binghamton	AHL	21	0	9	9	12	—	—	—	—	—
94-95—Binghamton	AHL	73	15	41	56	54	11	4	5	9	12

RICHTER, MIKE
G, RANGERS

PERSONAL: Born September 22, 1966, in Philadelphia. . . . 5-11/182. . . . Catches left. . . . Full name: Michael Thomas Richter. . . . Name pronounced RIHK-tuhr.
HIGH SCHOOL: Northwood School (Lake Placid, N.Y.).
COLLEGE: Wisconsin.
TRANSACTIONS/CAREER NOTES: Selected by New York Rangers in second round (second Rangers pick, 28th overall) of NHL entry draft (June 15, 1985). . . . Bruised thigh (January 30, 1992); missed 12 games.
HONORS: Won WCHA Rookie of the Year Award (1985-86). . . . Named to WCHA All-Star second team (1985-86 and 1986-87). . . . Played in NHL All-Star Game (1992 and 1994). . . . Named All-Star Game Most Valuable Player (1994).
MISCELLANEOUS: Member of Stanley Cup championship team (1994).

Season Team	League	REGULAR SEASON							PLAYOFFS						
		Gms.	Min.	W	L	T	GA	SO	Avg.	Gms.	Min.	W	L	GA SO	Avg.
84-85—Northwood School	N.Y. H.S.	24	1374				52	2	2.27	—	—			—	—
85-86—Univ. of Wisconsin	WCHA	24	1394	14	9	0	92	1	3.96	—	—			—	—
86-87—Univ. of Wisconsin	WCHA	36	2136	19	16	1	126	0	3.54	—	—			—	—
87-88—U.S. national team	Int'l	29	1559	17	7	2	86	0	3.31	—	—			—	—
—U.S. Olympic Team	Int'l	4	230	2	2	0	15	0	3.91	—	—			—	—
—Colorado....................	IHL	22	1298	16	5	‡0	68	1	3.14	10	536	5	3	35 0	3.92
88-89—Denver........................	IHL	*57	3031	23	26	‡0	*217	1	4.30	4	210	0	4	21 0	6.00
—New York Rangers	NHL	—	—	—	—	—	—	—	—	1	58	0	1	4 0	4.14
89-90—New York Rangers	NHL	23	1320	12	5	5	66	0	3.00	6	330	3	2	19 0	3.45
—Flint	IHL	13	782	7	4	‡2	49	0	3.76	—	—			—	—
90-91—New York Rangers	NHL	45	2596	21	13	7	135	0	3.12	6	313	2	4	14 †1	2.68
91-92—New York Rangers	NHL	41	2298	23	12	2	119	3	3.11	7	412	4	2	24 1	3.50
92-93—New York Rangers	NHL	38	2105	13	19	3	134	1	3.82	—	—			—	—
—Binghamton	AHL	5	305	4	0	1	6	0	1.18	—	—			—	—
93-94—New York Rangers	NHL	68	3710	*42	12	6	159	5	2.57	23	1417	*16	7	49 †4	2.07
94-95—New York Rangers	NHL	35	1993	14	17	2	97	2	2.92	7	384	2	5	23 0	3.59
NHL totals........		250	14022	125	78	25	710	11	3.04	50	2914	27	21	133 6	2.74

RIDLEY, MIKE
C, CANUCKS

PERSONAL: Born July 8, 1963, in Winnipeg. . . . 6-0/195. . . . Shoots left.
COLLEGE: Manitoba.
TRANSACTIONS/CAREER NOTES: Signed as free agent by New York Rangers (September 1985). . . . Traded by Rangers with LW Kelly Miller and RW Bobby Crawford to Washington Capitals for C Bobby Carpenter and second-round pick (RW Jason Prosofsky) in 1989 draft (January 1987). . . . Suffered collapsed left lung (March 9, 1990); missed six games. . . . Bruised ribs (April 5, 1990). . . . Suffered from stomach flu (February 21, 1994);

missed one game. . . . Traded by Capitals with first-round pick in 1994 draft (G Eric Fichaud) to Toronto Maple Leafs for RW Rob Pearson and first-round pick (D Nolan Baumgartner) in 1994 draft (June 28, 1994). . . . Traded by Maple Leafs to Vancouver Canucks for LW Sergio Momesso (July 8, 1995).
HONORS: Won Senator Joseph A. Sullivan Trophy (1983-84). . . . Named to CIAU All-Canadian team (1983-84 and 1984-85). . . . Named to NHL All-Rookie team (1985-86). . . . Played in NHL All-Star Game (1989).
STATISTICAL PLATEAUS: Three-goal games: 1986-87 (1), 1988-89 (1), 1990-91 (1). Total: 3. . . . Four-goal games: 1988-89 (1). . . . Total hat tricks: 4.

			REGULAR SEASON					PLAYOFFS				
Season	Team	League	Gms.	G	A	Pts.	PIM	Gms.	G	A	Pts.	PIM
83-84—University of Manitoba		CWUAA	46	39	41	80	...	—	—	—	—	—
84-85—University of Manitoba		CWUAA	30	29	38	67	48	—	—	—	—	—
85-86—New York Rangers		NHL	80	22	43	65	69	16	6	8	14	26
86-87—New York Rangers		NHL	38	16	20	36	20	—	—	—	—	—
—Washington		NHL	40	15	19	34	20	7	2	1	3	6
87-88—Washington		NHL	70	28	31	59	22	14	6	5	11	10
88-89—Washington		NHL	80	41	48	89	49	6	0	5	5	2
89-90—Washington		NHL	74	30	43	73	27	14	3	4	7	8
90-91—Washington		NHL	79	23	48	71	26	11	3	4	7	8
91-92—Washington		NHL	80	29	40	69	38	7	0	11	11	0
92-93—Washington		NHL	84	26	56	82	44	6	1	5	6	0
93-94—Washington		NHL	81	26	44	70	24	11	4	6	10	6
94-95—Toronto		NHL	48	10	27	37	14	7	3	1	4	2
NHL totals			754	266	419	685	353	99	28	50	78	68

RIENDEAU, VINCE
G, BRUINS

PERSONAL: Born April 20, 1966, in St. Hyacinthe, Que. . . . 5-10/185. . . . Catches left. . . . Name pronounced ree-AYN-doh.
COLLEGE: Sherbrooke (Que.).
TRANSACTIONS/CAREER NOTES: Signed as free agent by Montreal Canadiens (October 9, 1985). . . . Suffered skin rash (November 1987). . . . Broke leg (April 10, 1988). . . . Traded by Canadiens with LW Sergio Momesso to St. Louis Blues for LW Jocelyn Lemieux, G Darrell May and second-round pick (D Patrice Brisebois) in 1989 draft (August 9, 1988). . . . Suffered compound fracture of little finger of left hand (October 4, 1989); missed 10 games. . . . Pulled groin (February 17, 1991); missed seven games. . . . Traded by Blues to Detroit Red Wings for D Rick Zombo (October 18, 1991). . . . Sprained knee (October 25, 1991); missed 59 games. . . . Strained hip (January 2, 1993); missed six games. . . . Traded by Red Wings to Boston Bruins for fifth-round pick (D Chad Wilchynski) in 1995 draft (January 17, 1994).
HONORS: Named to QMJHL All-Star second team (1985-86). . . . Won Harry (Hap) Holmes Memorial Trophy (1986-87). . . . Shared Harry (Hap) Holmes Memorial Trophy with Jocelyn Perreault (1987-88). . . . Named to AHL All-Star second team (1987-88).

			REGULAR SEASON							PLAYOFFS					
Season	Team	League	Gms.	Min.	W	L	T	GA	SO	Avg.	Gms.	Min.	W	L	GA	SO	Avg.
83-84—Verdun		QMJHL	41	2133	...	...	...	147	†2	4.14	—	—	—	—	—	—	—
84-85—Univ. of Sherbrooke		Can. Coll.						Statistics unavailable.									
85-86—Drummondville		QMJHL	57	3336	33	20	3	215	0	3.87	*23	*1271	10	13	*106	1	5.00
86-87—Sherbrooke		AHL	41	2363	25	14	0	114	2	2.89	13	742	8	5	47	0	3.80
87-88—Sherbrooke		AHL	44	2521	27	13	3	112	*4	*2.67	2	127	0	2	7	0	3.31
—Montreal		NHL	1	36	0	0	0	5	0	8.33	—	—	—	—	—	—	—
88-89—St. Louis		NHL	32	1842	11	15	5	108	0	3.52	—	—	—	—	—	—	—
89-90—St. Louis		NHL	43	2551	17	19	5	149	1	3.50	8	397	3	4	24	0	3.63
90-91—St. Louis		NHL	44	2671	29	9	6	134	3	3.01	13	687	6	7	35	†1	3.06
91-92—St. Louis		NHL	3	157	1	2	0	11	0	4.20	—	—	—	—	—	—	—
—Detroit		NHL	2	87	2	0	0	2	0	1.38	2	73	1	0	4	0	3.29
—Adirondack		AHL	3	179	2	1	0	8	0	2.68	—	—	—	—	—	—	—
92-93—Detroit		NHL	22	1193	13	4	2	64	0	3.22	—	—	—	—	—	—	—
93-94—Boston		NHL	18	976	7	6	1	50	1	3.07	2	120	1	1	8	0	4.00
—Adirondack		AHL	10	583	6	3	0	30	0	3.09	—	—	—	—	—	—	—
—Detroit		NHL	8	345	2	4	0	23	0	4.00	—	—	—	—	—	—	—
94-95—Boston		NHL	11	565	3	6	1	27	0	2.87	—	—	—	—	—	—	—
—Providence		AHL	—	—	—	—	—	—	—	—	1	60	1	0	3	0	3.00
NHL totals			184	10423	85	65	20	573	5	3.30	25	1277	11	12	71	1	3.34

RIIHIJARVI, TEEMU
RW, SHARKS

PERSONAL: Born March 1, 1977, in Espoo, Finland. . . . 6-6/202. . . . Shoots left.
TRANSACTIONS/CAREER NOTES: Selected by San Jose Sharks in first round (first Sharks pick, 12th overall) of NHL entry draft (July 8, 1995).

			REGULAR SEASON					PLAYOFFS				
Season	Team	League	Gms.	G	A	Pts.	PIM	Gms.	G	A	Pts.	PIM
93-94—Kiekko-Espoo Jrs.		Finland	29	8	5	13	22	—	—	—	—	—
—Kiekko-Espoo		Finland	13	1	1	2	6	—	—	—	—	—
94-95—Kiekko-Espoo Jrs.		Finland	30	10	4	14	50	—	—	—	—	—
—Kiekko-Espoo		Finland	13	1	0	1	4	—	—	—	—	—

RIVERS, JAMIE
D, BLUES

PERSONAL: Born March 16, 1975, in Ottawa. . . . 6-0/180. . . . Shoots left. . . . Brother of Shawn Rivers, defenseman in Tampa Bay Lightning system.
HIGH SCHOOL: Lasalle Secondary (Sudbury, Ont.).
TRANSACTIONS/CAREER NOTES: Selected by St. Louis Blues in third round (second Blues pick, 63rd overall) of NHL entry draft (June 26, 1993).

			REGULAR SEASON					PLAYOFFS			
Season Team	League	Gms.	G	A	Pts.	PIM	Gms.	G	A	Pts.	PIM
90-91—Ottawa	OHA Jr. A	55	4	30	34	74	—	—	—	—	—
91-92—Sudbury	OHL	55	3	13	16	20	8	0	0	0	0
92-93—Sudbury	OHL	62	12	43	55	20	14	7	19	26	4
93-94—Sudbury	OHL	65	32	*89	121	58	10	1	9	10	14
94-95—Sudbury	OHL	46	9	56	65	30	18	7	26	33	22

RIVET, CRAIG
D, CANADIENS

PERSONAL: Born September 13, 1974, in North Bay, Ont.... 6-2/172.... Shoots right.... Name pronounced REE-vay.

TRANSACTIONS/CAREER NOTES: Selected by Montreal Canadiens in third round (fourth Canadiens pick, 68th overall) of NHL entry draft (June 20, 1992).

			REGULAR SEASON					PLAYOFFS			
Season Team	League	Gms.	G	A	Pts.	PIM	Gms.	G	A	Pts.	PIM
90-91—Barrie Jr. B	OHA	42	9	17	26	55	—	—	—	—	—
91-92—Kingston	OHL	66	5	21	26	97	—	—	—	—	—
92-93—Kingston	OHL	64	19	55	74	117	16	5	7	12	39
93-94—Fredericton	AHL	4	0	2	2	2	—	—	—	—	—
—Kingston	OHL	61	12	52	64	100	6	0	3	3	6
94-95—Fredericton	AHL	78	5	27	32	126	12	0	4	4	17
—Montreal	NHL	5	0	1	1	5	—	—	—	—	—
NHL totals		5	0	1	1	5					

ROBERGE, MARIO
LW, CANADIENS

PERSONAL: Born January 31, 1964, in Quebec City.... 5-10/200.... Shoots left.... Name pronounced roh-BAIRZH.... Brother of Serge Roberge, right winger in Denver's system.

TRANSACTIONS/CAREER NOTES: Signed as free agent by Sherbrooke Canadiens (January 1988).... Signed as free agent by Montreal Canadiens (October 5, 1988).... Injured thigh (December 22, 1991).... Suspended one off-day and fined $500 by NHL for fighting with taped hand (March 3, 1993).... Suffered hairline fracture of ankle (March 23, 1994); missed remainder of season.... Named player/assistant coach of Fredericton Canadiens (January 16, 1995).... Bruised ankle (April 1, 1995); missed three games.

MISCELLANEOUS: Member of Stanley Cup championship team (1993).

			REGULAR SEASON					PLAYOFFS			
Season Team	League	Gms.	G	A	Pts.	PIM	Gms.	G	A	Pts.	PIM
81-82—Quebec	QMJHL	8	0	3	3	2	—	—	—	—	—
82-83—Quebec	QMJHL	69	3	27	30	153	—	—	—	—	—
83-84—Quebec	QMJHL	60	12	28	40	253	—	—	—	—	—
84-85—						Did not play.					
85-86—						Did not play.					
86-87—						Did not play.					
87-88—Port Aux Basques	Nova Scotia	35	25	64	89	152	—	—	—	—	—
88-89—Sherbrooke	AHL	58	4	9	13	249	6	0	2	2	8
89-90—Sherbrooke	AHL	73	13	27	40	247	12	5	2	7	53
90-91—Fredericton	AHL	68	12	27	39	†365	2	0	2	2	5
—Montreal	NHL	5	0	0	0	21	12	0	0	0	24
91-92—Montreal	NHL	20	2	1	3	62	—	—	—	—	—
—Fredericton	AHL	6	1	2	3	20	7	0	2	2	20
92-93—Montreal	NHL	50	4	4	8	142	3	0	0	0	0
93-94—Montreal	NHL	28	1	2	3	55	—	—	—	—	—
94-95—Fredericton	AHL	28	8	12	20	91	6	1	1	2	6
—Montreal	NHL	9	0	0	0	34	—	—	—	—	—
NHL totals		112	7	7	14	314	15	0	0	0	24

ROBERGE, SERGE
RW, DENVER

PERSONAL: Born March 31, 1965, in Quebec City.... 6-1/195.... Shoots right.... Brother of Mario Roberge, left winger, Montreal Canadiens.

TRANSACTIONS/CAREER NOTES: Signed as free agent by Montreal Canadiens (January 25, 1988).... Signed as free agent by Quebec Nordiques (December 28, 1990).... Nordiques franchise moved to Denver for 1995-96 season.

			REGULAR SEASON					PLAYOFFS			
Season Team	League	Gms.	G	A	Pts.	PIM	Gms.	G	A	Pts.	PIM
82-83—Quebec	QMJHL	9	0	0	0	30	—	—	—	—	—
—Hull	QMJHL	22	0	4	4	115	—	—	—	—	—
83-84—Drummondville	QMJHL	58	1	7	8	287	10	0	2	2	*105
84-85—Drummondville	QMJHL	45	8	19	27	299	—	—	—	—	—
85-86—						Did not play.					
86-87—Virginia	ACHL	49	9	16	25	*353	12	4	2	6	*104
87-88—Sherbrooke	AHL	30	0	1	1	130	5	0	0	0	21
88-89—Sherbrooke	AHL	65	5	7	12	352	6	0	1	1	10
89-90—Sherbrooke	AHL	66	8	5	13	*343	12	2	0	2	44
90-91—Halifax	AHL	52	0	5	5	152	—	—	—	—	—
—Quebec	NHL	9	0	0	0	24	—	—	—	—	—

Season Team	League	REGULAR SEASON					PLAYOFFS				
		Gms.	G	A	Pts.	PIM	Gms.	G	A	Pts.	PIM
91-92—Halifax	AHL	66	2	8	10	319	—	—	—	—	—
92-93—Halifax	AHL	16	2	2	4	34	—	—	—	—	—
—Utica	AHL	28	0	3	3	85	1	0	0	0	0
93-94—Cape Breton	AHL	51	3	5	8	130	1	0	0	0	0
94-95—Cornwall	AHL	73	0	3	3	342	11	0	0	0	29
NHL totals		9	0	0	0	24					

ROBERTS, DAVE
C/LW, BLUES

PERSONAL: Born May 28, 1970, in Alameda, Calif.... 6-0/185.... Shoots left.... Full name: David Lance Roberts.... Son of Doug Roberts, defenseman for four NHL teams (1965-66 through 1974-75) and New England Whalers of WHA (1975-76 and 1976-77); and nephew of Gord Roberts, defenseman for New England Whalers of WHA (1975-76 through 1978-79) and six NHL teams (1979-80 through 1993-94).
HIGH SCHOOL: Avon (Conn.) Old Farms School for Boys.
COLLEGE: Michigan.
TRANSACTIONS/CAREER NOTES: Selected by St. Louis Blues in sixth round (fifth Blues pick, 114th overall) of NHL entry draft (June 17, 1989).... Injured elbow (March 7, 1995); missed one game.... Suffered illness (April 9, 1995); missed one game.
HONORS: Named CCHA Rookie of the Year (1989-90).... Named to CCHA All-Rookie team (1989-90).... Named to NCAA All-America West second team (1990-91).... Named to CCHA All-Star second team (1990-91 and 1992-93).

Season Team	League	REGULAR SEASON					PLAYOFFS				
		Gms.	G	A	Pts.	PIM	Gms.	G	A	Pts.	PIM
87-88—Avon Old Farms H.S.	Conn. H.S.	...	18	39	57	...	—	—	—	—	—
88-89—Avon Old Farms H.S.	Conn. H.S.	...	28	48	76	...	—	—	—	—	—
89-90—University of Michigan	CCHA	42	21	32	53	46	—	—	—	—	—
90-91—University of Michigan	CCHA	43	40	35	75	58	—	—	—	—	—
91-92—University of Michigan	CCHA	44	16	42	58	68	—	—	—	—	—
92-93—University of Michigan	CCHA	40	27	38	65	40	—	—	—	—	—
93-94—U.S. national team	Int'l	49	17	28	45	68	—	—	—	—	—
—U.S. Olympic Team	Int'l	8	1	5	6	4	—	—	—	—	—
—Peoria	IHL	10	4	6	10	4	—	—	—	—	—
—St. Louis	NHL	1	0	0	0	2	3	0	0	0	12
94-95—Peoria	IHL	65	30	38	68	65	—	—	—	—	—
—St. Louis	NHL	19	6	5	11	10	6	0	0	0	4
NHL totals		20	6	5	11	12	9	0	0	0	16

ROBERTS, GARY
LW, FLAMES

PERSONAL: Born May 23, 1966, in North York, Ont.... 6-1/190.... Shoots left.
TRANSACTIONS/CAREER NOTES: Selected by Calgary Flames as underage junior in first round (first Flames pick, 12th overall) of NHL entry draft (June 9, 1984).... Injured back (January 1989).... Suffered whiplash (November 9, 1991); missed one game.... Suffered from the flu (January 19, 1993); missed one game.... Suffered left quadricep hematoma (February 16, 1993); missed 25 games.... Suspended one game by NHL for high-sticking (November 19, 1993).... Suspended four games and fined $500 by NHL for two slashing incidents and fined $500 for high-sticking (January 7, 1994).... Fractured thumb (March 20, 1994); missed one game.... Fractured thumb (April 3, 1994); missed last five games of season.... Suffered neck and spinal injury (February 4, 1995); underwent surgery and missed last 40 games of season.
HONORS: Named to OHL All-Star second team (1984-85 and 1985-86).... Played in NHL All-Star Game (1992 and 1993).
STATISTICAL PLATEAUS: Three-goal games: 1989-90 (1), 1991-92 (2), 1992-93 (2), 1993-94 (1). Total: 6.... Four-goal games: 1993-94 (1).... Total hat tricks: 7.
MISCELLANEOUS: Member of Stanley Cup championship team (1989).

Season Team	League	REGULAR SEASON					PLAYOFFS				
		Gms.	G	A	Pts.	PIM	Gms.	G	A	Pts.	PIM
82-83—Ottawa	OHL	53	12	8	20	83	5	1	0	1	19
83-84—Ottawa	OHL	48	27	30	57	144	13	10	7	17	*62
84-85—Ottawa	OHL	59	44	62	106	186	5	2	8	10	10
—Moncton	AHL	7	4	2	6	7	—	—	—	—	—
85-86—Ottawa	OHL	24	26	25	51	83	—	—	—	—	—
—Guelph	OHL	23	18	15	33	65	20	18	13	31	43
86-87—Moncton	AHL	38	20	18	38	72	—	—	—	—	—
—Calgary	NHL	32	5	10	15	85	2	0	0	0	4
87-88—Calgary	NHL	74	13	15	28	282	9	2	3	5	29
88-89—Calgary	NHL	71	22	16	38	250	22	5	7	12	57
89-90—Calgary	NHL	78	39	33	72	222	6	2	5	7	41
90-91—Calgary	NHL	80	22	31	53	252	7	1	3	4	18
91-92—Calgary	NHL	76	53	37	90	207	—	—	—	—	—
92-93—Calgary	NHL	58	38	41	79	172	5	1	6	7	43
93-94—Calgary	NHL	73	41	43	84	145	7	2	6	8	24
94-95—Calgary	NHL	8	2	2	4	43	—	—	—	—	—
NHL totals		550	235	228	463	1658	58	13	30	43	216

ROBERTSSON, BERT
D, CANUCKS

PERSONAL: Born June 30, 1974, in Sodertalje, Sweden.... 6-2/198.... Shoots left.... Name pronounced ROH-behrt-suhn.
TRANSACTIONS/CAREER NOTES: Selected by Vancouver Canucks in 10th round (eighth Canucks pick, 254th overall) of NHL entry draft (June 29, 1993).

R

Season	Team	League	Gms.	G	A	Pts.	PIM	Gms.	G	A	Pts.	PIM
			REGULAR SEASON					PLAYOFFS				
92-93—Sodertalje		Swed. Dv.II	23	1	2	3	24	—	—	—	—	—
93-94—Sodertalje		Swed. Dv.II	28	0	1	1	12	—	—	—	—	—
94-95—Sodertalje		Swed. Dv.II	23	1	2	3	24	—	—	—	—	—

ROBINS, TREVOR
G, SHARKS

PERSONAL: Born May 31, 1972, in Brandon, Man. . . . 5-11/190. . . . Catches left.
TRANSACTIONS/CAREER NOTES: Traded by Saskatoon Blades to Brandon Wheat Kings (summer 1992). . . . Signed as free agent by San Jose Sharks (December 5, 1992).
HONORS: Named to WHL (East) All-Star first team (1991-92 and 1992-93). . . . Won Del Wilson Trophy (1992-93).

Season	Team	League	Gms.	Min.	W	L	T	GA	SO	Avg.	Gms.	Min.	W	L	GA	SO	Avg.
			REGULAR SEASON								PLAYOFFS						
89-90—Saskatoon		WHL	51	2616	21	21	1	203	1	4.66	10	587	5	4	53	0	5.42
90-91—Saskatoon		WHL	49	2560	16	24	2	200	2	4.69	—	—	—	—	—	—	—
91-92—Saskatoon		WHL	50	2794	24	23	2	163	0	3.50	9	473	5	3	32	0	4.06
92-93—Brandon		WHL	59	3470	36	17	4	183	2	3.16	4	258	1	3	11	0	2.56
93-94—Fort Worth		CHL	9	452	2	6	0	42	0	5.58	—	—	—	—	—	—	—
—Kansas City		IHL	4	199	1	2	0	21	0	6.33	—	—	—	—	—	—	—
94-95—Kansas City		IHL	39	2230	15	20	‡1	144	1	3.87	—	—	—	—	—	—	—
—Milwaukee		IHL	1	60	1	0	‡0	1	0	1.00	1	20	0	0	3	0	9.00

ROBITAILLE, LUC
LW, PENGUINS

PERSONAL: Born February 17, 1966, in Montreal. . . . 6-1/195. . . . Shoots left. . . . Name pronounced ROH-bih-TIGH.
TRANSACTIONS/CAREER NOTES: Selected by Los Angeles Kings as underage junior in ninth round (ninth Kings pick, 171st overall) of NHL entry draft (June 9, 1984). . . . Suspended four games by NHL games for cross-checking from behind (November 10, 1990). . . . Underwent surgery to repair slight fracture of right ankle (June 15, 1994). . . . Traded by Kings to Pittsburgh Penguins for RW Rick Tocchet and second-round pick (RW Pavel Rosa) in 1995 draft (July 29, 1994). . . . Suspended by NHL for two games for high-sticking (February 7, 1995).
HONORS: Named to QMJHL All-Star second team (1984-85). . . . Won Can.HL Player of the Year Award (1985-86). . . . Shared Guy Lafleur Trophy with Sylvain Cote (1985-86). . . . Named to QMJHL All-Star first team (1985-86). . . . Named to Memorial Cup All-Star team (1985-86). . . . Won Calder Memorial Trophy (1986-87). . . . Named to THE SPORTING NEWS All-Star second team (1986-87 and 1991-92). . . . Named to NHL All-Star second team (1986-87 and 1991-92). . . . Named to NHL All-Rookie team (1986-87). . . . Named to THE SPORTING NEWS All-Star first team (1987-88 through 1990-91 and 1992-93). . . . Played in NHL All-Star Game (1988-1993). . . . Named to NHL All-Star first team (1987-88 through 1990-91 and 1992-93).
RECORDS: Holds NHL single-season records for most points by a left-winger—125 (1992-93); and most goals by a left-winger—63 (1992-93).
STATISTICAL PLATEAUS: Three-goal games: 1986-87 (1), 1987-88 (3), 1988-89 (1), 1989-90 (2), 1992-93 (2). Total: 9. . . . Four-goal games: 1991-92 (1), 1993-94 (1), 1994-95 (1). Total: 3. . . . Total hat tricks: 12.

Season	Team	League	Gms.	G	A	Pts.	PIM	Gms.	G	A	Pts.	PIM
			REGULAR SEASON					PLAYOFFS				
83-84—Hull		QMJHL	70	32	53	85	48	—	—	—	—	—
84-85—Hull		QMJHL	64	55	94	149	115	5	4	2	6	27
85-86—Hull		QMJHL	63	68	*123	†191	93	15	17	27	*44	28
86-87—Los Angeles		NHL	79	45	39	84	28	5	1	4	5	2
87-88—Los Angeles		NHL	80	53	58	111	82	5	2	5	7	18
88-89—Los Angeles		NHL	78	46	52	98	65	11	2	6	8	10
89-90—Los Angeles		NHL	80	52	49	101	38	10	5	5	10	10
90-91—Los Angeles		NHL	76	45	46	91	68	12	12	4	16	22
91-92—Los Angeles		NHL	80	44	63	107	95	6	3	4	7	12
92-93—Los Angeles		NHL	84	63	62	125	100	24	9	13	22	28
93-94—Los Angeles		NHL	83	44	42	86	86	—	—	—	—	—
94-95—Pittsburgh		NHL	46	23	19	42	37	12	7	4	11	26
NHL totals			686	415	430	845	599	85	41	45	86	128

ROCHE, DAVE
LW, PENGUINS

PERSONAL: Born June 13, 1975, in Lindsay, Ont. . . . 6-4/224. . . . Shoots left. . . . Name pronounced roh-SHAY. . . . Brother of Scott Roche, goaltender in St. Louis Blues system.
TRANSACTIONS/CAREER NOTES: Selected by Pittsburgh Penguins in third round (third Penguins pick, 62nd overall) of NHL entry draft (June 26, 1993).

Season	Team	League	Gms.	G	A	Pts.	PIM	Gms.	G	A	Pts.	PIM
			REGULAR SEASON					PLAYOFFS				
90-91—Peterborough Jr. B		OHA	40	22	17	39	85	—	—	—	—	—
91-92—Peterborough		OHL	62	10	17	27	105	10	0	0	0	34
92-93—Peterborough		OHL	56	·40	60	100	105	21	14	15	29	42
93-94—Peterborough		OHL	34	15	22	37	127	—	—	—	—	—
—Windsor		OHL	29	14	20	34	73	4	1	1	2	15
94-95—Windsor		OHL	66	55	59	114	180	10	9	6	15	16

ROCHE, SCOTT
G, BLUES

PERSONAL: Born March 19, 1977, in Peterborough, Ont. . . . 6-4/220. . . . Catches left. . . . Brother of Dave Roche, left winger in Pittsburgh Penguins system.
HIGH SCHOOL: Chippewa (North Bay, Ont.).
TRANSACTIONS/CAREER NOTES: Selected by St. Louis Blues in third round (second Blues pick,

75th overall) of NHL entry draft (July 8, 1995).
HONORS: Shared Dave Pinkney Trophy with Sandy Allan (1993-94). . . . Won F.W. (Dinty) Moore Trophy (1993-94). . . . Named to OHL All-Star first team (1994-95).

			REGULAR SEASON							PLAYOFFS					
Season	Team	League	Gms.	Min.	W	L	T	GA	SO	Avg.	Gms.	Min.	W	L	GA	SO	Avg.
93-94—North Bay		OHL	32	1587	15	5	4	93	0	3.52	5	191	2	1	9	0	2.83
94-95—North Bay		OHL	47	2599	24	17	2	167	2	3.86	6	348	2	4	30	0	5.17

ROED, PETER
C, SHARKS

PERSONAL: Born November 15, 1976, in St. Paul, Minn. . . . 5-10/210. . . . Shoots left.
HIGH SCHOOL: White Bear Lake (Minn.).
TRANSACTIONS/CAREER NOTES: Selected by San Jose Sharks in second round (second Sharks pick, 38th overall) of NHL entry draft (July 8, 1995).

			REGULAR SEASON					PLAYOFFS			
Season	Team	League	Gms.	G	A	Pts.	PIM	Gms.	G	A	Pts.	PIM
94-95—White Bear Lake H.S.		Minn. H.S.	28	20	39	59	22	—	—	—	—	—

ROENICK, JEREMY
C, BLACKHAWKS

PERSONAL: Born January 17, 1970, in Boston. . . . 6-0/170. . . . Shoots right. . . . Name pronounced ROH-nihk. . . . Brother of Trevor Roenick, right winger in Hartford Whalers system.
HIGH SCHOOL: Thayer Academy (Braintree, Mass.).
TRANSACTIONS/CAREER NOTES: Selected by Chicago Blackhawks in first round (first Blackhawks pick, eighth overall) of NHL entry draft (June 11, 1988). . . . Sprained knee ligaments (January 9, 1989); missed one month. . . . Played in Europe during 1994-95 NHL lockout. . . . Sprained anterior cruciate ligament (April 2, 1995); missed remainder of season and first eight games of playoffs.
HONORS: Named to QMJHL All-Star second team (1988-89). . . . Named NHL Rookie of the Year by THE SPORTING NEWS (1989-90). . . . Played in NHL All-Star Game (1991-1994).
STATISTICAL PLATEAUS: Three-goal games: 1989-90 (1), 1990-91 (2), 1992-93 (1). Total: 4. . . . Four-goal games: 1991-92 (1), 1993-94 (1). Total: 2. . . . Total hat tricks: 6.

			REGULAR SEASON					PLAYOFFS			
Season	Team	League	Gms.	G	A	Pts.	PIM	Gms.	G	A	Pts.	PIM
86-87—Thayer Academy		Mass. H.S.	24	31	34	65	. . .	—	—	—	—	—
87-88—Thayer Academy		Mass. H.S.	24	34	50	84	. . .	—	—	—	—	—
88-89—U.S. national team		Int'l	11	8	8	16	0	—	—	—	—	—
—Chicago		NHL	20	9	9	18	4	10	1	3	4	7
—Hull		QMJHL	28	34	36	70	14	—	—	—	—	—
89-90—Chicago		NHL	78	26	40	66	54	20	11	7	18	8
90-91—Chicago		NHL	79	41	53	94	80	6	3	5	8	4
91-92—Chicago		NHL	80	53	50	103	98	18	12	10	22	12
92-93—Chicago		NHL	84	50	57	107	86	4	1	2	3	2
93-94—Chicago		NHL	84	46	61	107	125	6	1	6	7	2
94-95—Koln		Germany	3	3	1	4	2	—	—	—	—	—
—Chicago		NHL	33	10	24	34	14	8	1	2	3	16
NHL totals			458	235	294	529	461	72	30	35	65	51

ROENICK, TREVOR
RW, WHALERS

PERSONAL: Born October 7, 1974, in Derby, Conn. . . . 6-1/200. . . . Shoots right. . . . Brother of Jeremy Roenick, center, Chicago Blackhawks.
HIGH SCHOOL: Thayer Academy (Braintree, Mass.).
COLLEGE: Maine.
TRANSACTIONS/CAREER NOTES: Selected by Hartford Whalers in fourth round (third Whalers pick, 84th overall) of NHL entry draft (June 26, 1993).

			REGULAR SEASON					PLAYOFFS			
Season	Team	League	Gms.	G	A	Pts.	PIM	Gms.	G	A	Pts.	PIM
90-91—Thayer Academy		Mass. H.S.	17	10	7	17	0	—	—	—	—	—
91-92—Thayer Academy		Mass. H.S.	26	16	16	32	8	—	—	—	—	—
92-93—Boston		NEJHL	58	61	48	109	94	—	—	—	—	—
93-94—University of Maine		Hockey East	32	4	3	7	18	—	—	—	—	—
94-95—University of Maine		Hockey East	36	8	13	21	42	—	—	—	—	—

ROGLES, CHRIS
G, BLACKHAWKS

PERSONAL: Born January 22, 1969, in St. Louis. . . . 5-11/175. . . . Catches left.
HIGH SCHOOL: DeSmet (St. Louis).
COLLEGE: Clarkson (N.Y.).
TRANSACTIONS/CAREER NOTES: Signed as free agent by Chicago Blackhawks (June 21, 1993).
HONORS: Won Ken McKenzie Trophy (1993-94).

			REGULAR SEASON							PLAYOFFS					
Season	Team	League	Gms.	Min.	W	L	T	GA	SO	Avg.	Gms.	Min.	W	L	GA	SO	Avg.
89-90—Clarkson		ECAC	7	142	1	0	0	7	0	2.96	—	—	—	—	—	—	—
90-91—Clarkson		ECAC	28	1359	16	6	0	76	3	3.36	—	—	—	—	—	—	—
91-92—Clarkson		ECAC	19	998	11	3	0	51	0	3.07	—	—	—	—	—	—	—
92-93—Clarkson		ECAC	27	1482	16	4	4	60	3	2.43	—	—	—	—	—	—	—
93-94—Indianapolis		IHL	44	2421	14	20	†6	147	†2	3.64	—	—	—	—	—	—	—
94-95—Indianapolis		IHL	43	2269	14	22	‡2	140	0	3.70	—	—	—	—	—	—	—

ROHLIN, LEIF
D, CANUCKS

PERSONAL: Born February 26, 1968, in Vasteras, Sweden. . . . 6-1/198. . . . Shoots left. . . . Name pronounced roh-LEEN.
TRANSACTIONS/CAREER NOTES: Selected by Vancouver Canucks in second round (second Canucks pick, 33rd overall) of NHL entry draft (June 11, 1988).

		REGULAR SEASON					PLAYOFFS				
Season Team	League	Gms.	G	A	Pts.	PIM	Gms.	G	A	Pts.	PIM
86-87—Vasteras	Swed. Dv.II	27	2	5	7	12	12	0	2	2	8
87-88—Vasteras	Swed. Dv.II	30	2	15	17	46	7	0	4	4	8
88-89—Vasteras	Sweden	22	3	7	10	18	—				
89-90—Vasteras	Sweden	32	3	6	9	40	2	0	0	0	2
90-91—Vasteras	Sweden	40	4	10	14	46	4	0	1	1	8
91-92—Vasteras	Sweden	39	4	6	10	52	—				
92-93—Vasteras	Sweden	37	5	7	12	24	2	0	0	0	0
93-94—Vasteras	Sweden	40	6	14	20	26	4	0	1	1	6
94-95—Vasteras	Sweden	39	15	15	30	46	4	2	0	2	2

ROHLOFF, JON
D, BRUINS

PERSONAL: Born October 3, 1969, in Mankato, Minn. . . . 6-0/200. . . . Shoots right. . . . Full name: Jon Richard Rohloff. . . . Name pronounced ROH-lahf.
HIGH SCHOOL: Grand Rapids (Minn.).
COLLEGE: Minnesota-Duluth.
TRANSACTIONS/CAREER NOTES: Selected by Boston Bruins in ninth round (seventh Bruins pick, 186th overall) of NHL entry draft (June 11, 1988).
HONORS: Named to WCHA All-Star second team (1992-93).

		REGULAR SEASON					PLAYOFFS				
Season Team	League	Gms.	G	A	Pts.	PIM	Gms.	G	A	Pts.	PIM
86-87—Grand Rapids H.S.	Minn. H.S.	21	12	23	35	16	—				
87-88—Grand Rapids H.S.	Minn. H.S.	23	10	13	23	. . .	—				
88-89—Minnesota-Duluth	WCHA	39	1	2	3	44	—				
89-90—Minnesota-Duluth	WCHA	5	0	1	1	6	—				
90-91—Minnesota-Duluth	WCHA	32	6	11	17	38	—				
91-92—Minnesota-Duluth	WCHA	27	9	9	18	48	—				
92-93—Minnesota-Duluth	WCHA	36	15	19	34	87	—				
93-94—Providence	AHL	55	12	23	35	59	—				
94-95—Boston	NHL	34	3	8	11	39	5	0	0	0	6
—Providence	AHL	4	2	1	3	6	—				
NHL totals		34	3	8	11	39	5	0	0	0	6

ROLOSON, DWAYNE
G, FLAMES

PERSONAL: Born October 12, 1969, in Simcoe, Ont. . . . 6-1/185. . . . Catches left.
COLLEGE: Massachusetts-Lowell.
TRANSACTIONS/CAREER NOTES: Signed as free agent by Calgary Flames (July 4, 1994).
HONORS: Named Hockey East Tournament Most Valuable Player (1993-94).

		REGULAR SEASON							PLAYOFFS					
Season Team	League	Gms.	Min.	W	L	T	GA	SO	Avg.	Gms.	Min.	W	L	GA	SO	Avg.
90-91—Massachusetts-Lowell	Hoc. East	15	823	5	9	0	63	0	4.59	—						
91-92—Massachusetts-Lowell	Hoc. East	12	660	3	8	0	52	0	4.73	—						
92-93—Massachusetts-Lowell	Hoc. East	39	2342	20	17	2	150	0	3.84	—						
93-94—Massachusetts-Lowell	Hoc. East	40	2305	23	10	7	106	0	2.76	—						
94-95—Saint John	AHL	46	2734	16	21	8	156	1	3.42	5	299	1	4	13	0	2.61

ROLSTON, BRIAN
C, DEVILS

PERSONAL: Born February 21, 1973, in Flint, Mich. . . . 6-2/185. . . . Shoots left.
COLLEGE: Lake Superior State (Mich.).
TRANSACTIONS/CAREER NOTES: Selected by New Jersey Devils in first round (second Devils pick, 11th overall) of NHL entry draft (June 22, 1991). . . . Loaned by Devils to U.S. Olympic Team (November 2, 1993).
HONORS: Named to NCAA All-Tournament team (1991-92 and 1992-93). . . . Named to NCAA All-America West second team (1992-93). . . . Named to CCHA All-Star first team (1992-93).
MISCELLANEOUS: Member of Stanley Cup championship team (1995).

		REGULAR SEASON					PLAYOFFS				
Season Team	League	Gms.	G	A	Pts.	PIM	Gms.	G	A	Pts.	PIM
89-90—Detroit Compuware	NAJHL	40	36	37	73	57	—				
90-91—Detroit Compuware	NAJHL	36	49	46	95	14	—				
91-92—Lake Superior State	CCHA	41	18	28	46	16	—				
92-93—Lake Superior State	CCHA	39	33	31	64	20	—				
93-94—U.S. national team	Int'l	41	20	28	48	36	—				
—U.S. Olympic Team	Int'l	8	7	0	7	8	—				
—Albany	AHL	17	5	5	10	8	5	1	2	3	0
94-95—Albany	AHL	18	9	11	20	10	—				
—New Jersey	NHL	40	7	11	18	17	6	2	1	3	4
NHL totals		40	7	11	18	17	6	2	1	3	4

ROMANIUK, RUSS

LW, FLYERS

PERSONAL: Born June 9, 1970, in Winnipeg. . . . 6-0/195. . . . Shoots left. . . . Full name: Russell James Romaniuk. . . . Name pronounced ROH-muh-NUHK.
COLLEGE: North Dakota.
TRANSACTIONS/CAREER NOTES: Suffered chip fracture of left knee (December 1987). . . . Sprained right shoulder (February 1988). . . . Selected by Winnipeg Jets in second round (second Jets pick, 31st overall) of NHL entry draft (June 11, 1988). . . . Fractured knuckle (October 27, 1991); missed six games. . . . Sprained wrist (December 10, 1991); missed one game. . . . Sprained knee (November 17, 1992); missed one game. . . . Sprained ankle (December 17, 1992); missed 10 games. . . . Traded by Jets to Philadelphia Flyers for D Jeff Finley (June 27, 1995).
HONORS: Named to WCHA All-Tournament team (1989-90). . . . Named to WCHA All-Star first team (1990-91).

Season Team	League	REGULAR SEASON					PLAYOFFS				
		Gms.	G	A	Pts.	PIM	Gms.	G	A	Pts.	PIM
87-88—St. Boniface	MJHL				Statistics unavailable.						
88-89—Univ. of North Dakota	WCHA	39	17	14	31	32	—	—	—	—	—
89-90—Canadian national team	Int'l	3	1	0	1	0	—	—	—	—	—
—Univ. of North Dakota	WCHA	45	36	15	51	54	—	—	—	—	—
90-91—Univ. of North Dakota	WCHA	39	40	28	68	30	—	—	—	—	—
91-92—Winnipeg	NHL	27	3	5	8	18	—	—	—	—	—
—Moncton	AHL	45	16	15	31	25	10	5	4	9	19
92-93—Winnipeg	NHL	28	3	1	4	22	1	0	0	0	0
—Fort Wayne	IHL	4	2	0	2	7	—	—	—	—	—
—Moncton	AHL	28	18	8	26	40	5	0	4	4	2
93-94—Canadian national team	Int'l	34	8	9	17	17	—	—	—	—	—
—Moncton	AHL	18	16	8	24	24	17	2	6	8	30
—Winnipeg	NHL	24	4	8	12	6	—	—	—	—	—
94-95—Winnipeg	NHL	6	0	0	0	0	—	—	—	—	—
—Springfield	AHL	17	5	7	12	29	—	—	—	—	—
NHL totals		85	10	14	24	46	1	0	0	0	0

RONAN, ED

RW, CANADIENS

PERSONAL: Born March 21, 1968, in Quincy, Mass. . . . 6-0/197. . . . Shoots right.
COLLEGE: Boston University.
TRANSACTIONS/CAREER NOTES: Selected by Montreal Canadiens in 11th round (13th Canadiens pick, 227th overall) of NHL entry draft (June 13, 1987). . . . Suffered concussion (October 6, 1993); missed four games. . . . Suffered from the flu (March 6, 1994); missed one game.
MISCELLANEOUS: Member of Stanley Cup championship team (1993).

Season Team	League	REGULAR SEASON					PLAYOFFS				
		Gms.	G	A	Pts.	PIM	Gms.	G	A	Pts.	PIM
87-88—Boston University	Hockey East	31	2	5	7	20	—	—	—	—	—
88-89—Boston University	Hockey East	36	4	11	15	34	—	—	—	—	—
89-90—Boston University	Hockey East	44	17	23	40	50	—	—	—	—	—
90-91—Boston University	Hockey East	41	16	19	35	38	—	—	—	—	—
91-92—Fredericton	AHL	78	25	34	59	82	7	5	1	6	6
—Montreal	NHL	3	0	0	0	0	—	—	—	—	—
92-93—Montreal	NHL	53	5	7	12	20	14	2	3	5	10
—Fredericton	AHL	16	10	5	15	15	5	2	4	6	6
93-94—Montreal	NHL	61	6	8	14	42	7	1	0	1	0
94-95—Montreal	NHL	30	1	4	5	12	—	—	—	—	—
NHL totals		147	12	19	31	74	21	3	3	6	10

RONNING, CLIFF

C, CANUCKS

PERSONAL: Born October 1, 1965, in Vancouver. . . . 5-8/180. . . . Shoots left.
HIGH SCHOOL: Burnaby North (B.C.).
TRANSACTIONS/CAREER NOTES: Selected by St. Louis Blues as underage junior in seventh round (ninth Blues pick, 134th overall) of NHL entry draft (June 9, 1984). . . . Injured groin (November 1988). . . . Agreed to play in Italy for 1989-90 season (August 1989). . . . Fractured right index finger (November 12, 1990); missed 12 games. . . . Traded by Blues with LW Geoff Courtnall, D Robert Dirk, LW Sergio Momesso and fifth-round pick in 1992 draft (RW Brian Loney) to Vancouver Canucks for C Dan Quinn and D Garth Butcher (March 5, 1991). . . . Sprained hand (January 4, 1993); missed five games. . . . Separated shoulder (January 8, 1994); missed eight games. . . . Strained groin (February 9, 1995); missed four games.
HONORS: Won Stewart (Butch) Paul Memorial Trophy (1983-84). . . . Named to WHL All-Star second team (1983-84). . . . Won WHL Most Valuable Player Trophy (1984-85). . . . Won Bob Brownridge Memorial Trophy (1984-85). . . . Won Frank Boucher Memorial Trophy (1984-85). . . . Named to WHL (West) All-Star first team (1984-85).
STATISTICAL PLATEAUS: Three-goal games: 1986-87 (1), 1992-93 (1). Total: 2.

Season Team	League	REGULAR SEASON					PLAYOFFS				
		Gms.	G	A	Pts.	PIM	Gms.	G	A	Pts.	PIM
82-83—New Westminster	BCJHL	52	82	68	150	42	—	—	—	—	—
83-84—New Westminster	WHL	71	69	67	136	10	9	8	13	21	10
84-85—New Westminster	WHL	70	*89	108	*197	20	11	10	14	24	4
85-86—Canadian national team	Int'l	71	55	63	118	53	—	—	—	—	—
—St. Louis	NHL	—	—	—	—	—	5	1	1	2	2
86-87—Canadian national team	Int'l	26	16	16	32	12	—	—	—	—	—
—St. Louis	NHL	42	11	14	25	6	4	0	1	1	0
87-88—St. Louis	NHL	26	5	8	13	12	—	—	—	—	—
88-89—St. Louis	NHL	64	24	31	55	18	7	1	3	4	0
—Peoria	IHL	12	11	20	31	8	—	—	—	—	—
89-90—Asiago	Italy	42	76	60	136	30	6	7	12	19	4

Season Team	League	REGULAR SEASON					PLAYOFFS				
		Gms.	G	A	Pts.	PIM	Gms.	G	A	Pts.	PIM
90-91—St. Louis	NHL	48	14	18	32	10	—	—	—	—	—
—Vancouver	NHL	11	6	6	12	0	6	6	3	9	12
91-92—Vancouver	NHL	80	24	47	71	42	13	8	5	13	6
92-93—Vancouver	NHL	79	29	56	85	30	12	2	9	11	6
93-94—Vancouver	NHL	76	25	43	68	42	24	5	10	15	16
94-95—Vancouver	NHL	41	6	19	25	27	11	3	5	8	2
NHL totals		467	144	242	386	187	82	26	37	63	44

ROSA, PAVEL
RW, KINGS

PERSONAL: Born June 7, 1977, in Most, Czechoslovakia. . . . 5-11/178. . . . Shoots right.
TRANSACTIONS/CAREER NOTES: Selected by Los Angeles Kings in second round (third Kings pick, 50th overall) of NHL entry draft (July 8, 1995).

Season Team	League	REGULAR SEASON					PLAYOFFS				
		Gms.	G	A	Pts.	PIM	Gms.	G	A	Pts.	PIM
94-95—Chemopetrol Litvinov Jrs.	Czech. Rep.	40	56	42	98	...	—	—	—	—	—
—Chemopetrol Litvinov	Czech. Rep.	—	—	—	—	—	1	0	0	0	...

ROUSE, BOB
D, RED WINGS

PERSONAL: Born June 18, 1964, in Surrey, B.C. . . . 6-2/210. . . . Shoots right. . . . Name pronounced ROWS.
TRANSACTIONS/CAREER NOTES: Selected by Minnesota North Stars as underage junior in fourth round (third North Stars pick, 80th overall) of NHL entry draft (June 9, 1982). . . . Suffered hip contusions (January 1988). . . . Traded by North Stars with RW Dino Ciccarelli to Washington Capitals for RW Mike Gartner and D Larry Murphy (March 7, 1989). . . . Sprained right knee (December 12, 1989); missed eight games. . . . Traded by Capitals with C Peter Zezel to Toronto Maple Leafs for D Al Iafrate (January 16, 1991). . . . Broke collarbone (February 16, 1991). . . . Suspended four games by NHL for stick-swinging incident (October 14, 1993). . . . Strained knee (December 29, 1993); missed three games. . . . Tore knee cartilage (January 29, 1994); missed 14 games. . . . Signed as free agent by Detroit Red Wings (August 5, 1994).
HONORS: Won Top Defenseman Trophy (1983-84). . . . Named to WHL (East) All-Star first team (1983-84).
MISCELLANEOUS: Captain of Minnesota North Stars (1988-89).

Season Team	League	REGULAR SEASON					PLAYOFFS				
		Gms.	G	A	Pts.	PIM	Gms.	G	A	Pts.	PIM
80-81—Billings	WHL	70	0	13	13	116	5	0	0	0	2
81-82—Billings	WHL	71	7	22	29	209	5	0	2	2	10
82-83—Nanaimo	WHL	29	7	20	27	86	—	—	—	—	—
—Lethbridge	WHL	42	8	30	38	82	20	2	13	15	55
83-84—Lethbridge	WHL	71	18	42	60	101	5	0	1	1	28
—Minnesota	NHL	1	0	0	0	0	—	—	—	—	—
84-85—Springfield	AHL	8	0	3	3	6	—	—	—	—	—
—Minnesota	NHL	63	2	9	11	113	—	—	—	—	—
85-86—Minnesota	NHL	75	1	14	15	151	3	0	0	0	2
86-87—Minnesota	NHL	72	2	10	12	179	—	—	—	—	—
87-88—Minnesota	NHL	74	0	12	12	168	—	—	—	—	—
88-89—Minnesota	NHL	66	4	13	17	124	—	—	—	—	—
—Washington	NHL	13	0	2	2	36	6	2	0	2	4
89-90—Washington	NHL	70	4	16	20	123	15	2	3	5	47
90-91—Washington	NHL	47	5	15	20	65	—	—	—	—	—
—Toronto	NHL	13	2	4	6	10	—	—	—	—	—
91-92—Toronto	NHL	79	3	19	22	97	—	—	—	—	—
92-93—Toronto	NHL	82	3	11	14	130	21	3	8	11	29
93-94—Toronto	NHL	63	5	11	16	101	18	0	3	3	29
94-95—Detroit	NHL	48	1	7	8	36	18	0	3	3	8
NHL totals		766	32	143	175	1333	81	7	17	24	119

ROUSSEL, DOMINIC
G, FLYERS

PERSONAL: Born February 22, 1970, in Hull, Que. . . . 6-1/190. . . . Catches left. . . . Name pronounced roo-SEHL.
TRANSACTIONS/CAREER NOTES: Selected by Philadelphia Flyers as underage junior in third round (fourth Flyers pick, 63rd overall) of NHL entry draft (June 11, 1988). . . . Pulled groin (November 29, 1992); missed three games. . . . Reinjured groin (December 11, 1992); missed 11 games. . . . Suffered from the flu (March 24, 1994); missed three games. . . . Suffered inner ear infection (March 2, 1995); missed five games.

Season Team	League	REGULAR SEASON							PLAYOFFS					
		Gms.	Min.	W	L	T	GA	SO	Avg.	Gms.	Min.	W	L	GA	SO	Avg.
87-88—Trois-Rivieres	QMJHL	51	2905	18	25	4	251	0	5.18	—	—	—	—	—	—	—
88-89—Shawinigan	QMJHL	46	2555	24	15	2	171	0	4.02	10	638	6	4	36	0	3.39
89-90—Shawinigan	QMJHL	37	1985	20	14	1	133	0	4.02	2	120	1	1	12	0	6.00
90-91—Hershey	AHL	45	2507	20	14	7	151	1	3.61	7	366	3	4	21	0	3.44
91-92—Hershey	AHL	35	2040	15	11	6	121	1	3.56	—	—	—	—	—	—	—
—Philadelphia	NHL	17	922	7	8	2	40	1	2.60	—	—	—	—	—	—	—
92-93—Philadelphia	NHL	34	1769	13	11	5	111	1	3.76	—	—	—	—	—	—	—
—Hershey	AHL	6	372	0	3	3	23	0	3.71	—	—	—	—	—	—	—
93-94—Philadelphia	NHL	60	3285	29	20	5	183	1	3.34							

Season	Team	League	REGULAR SEASON								PLAYOFFS						
			Gms.	Min.	W	L	T	GA	SO	Avg.	Gms.	Min.	W	L	GA	SO	Avg.
94-95—Philadelphia		NHL	19	1075	11	7	0	42	1	2.34	1	23	0	0	0	0	0.00
—Hershey		AHL	1	59	0	1	0	5	0	5.08	—	—	—	—	—	—	—
NHL totals			130	7051	60	46	12	376	4	3.20	1	23	0	0	0	0	0.00

ROY, ANDRE
LW, BRUINS

PERSONAL: Born February 8, 1975, in Port Chester, N.Y.... 6-3/178.... Shoots left.... Name pronounced ROY.

TRANSACTIONS/CAREER NOTES: Selected by Boston Bruins in sixth round (fifth Bruins pick, 151st overall) of NHL entry draft (June 29, 1994).

Season	Team	League	REGULAR SEASON					PLAYOFFS				
			Gms.	G	A	Pts.	PIM	Gms.	G	A	Pts.	PIM
93-94—Beauport		QMJHL	33	6	7	13	125	—	—	—	—	—
—Chicoutimi		QMJHL	32	4	14	18	152	25	3	6	9	94
94-95—Chicoutimi		QMJHL	20	15	8	23	90	—	—	—	—	—
—Drummondville		QMJHL	34	18	13	31	233	4	2	0	2	34

R

ROY, JEAN-YVES
RW, RANGERS

PERSONAL: Born February 17, 1969, in Rosemere, Que.... 5-10/185.... Shoots left.... Name pronounced ZHAHN-eev WAH.

COLLEGE: Maine.

TRANSACTIONS/CAREER NOTES: Signed as free agent by New York Rangers (July 20, 1992).

HONORS: Named to NCAA All-America East second team (1989-90).... Named to Hockey East All-Rookie team (1989-90).... Named to NCAA All-America East first team (1990-91 and 1991-92).... Named to NCAA All-Tournament team (1990-91). ... Named to Hockey East All-Star first team (1990-91).... Named to Hockey East All-Star second team (1991-92).

MISCELLANEOUS: Member of silver-medal-winning Canadian Olympic team (1994).

Season	Team	League	REGULAR SEASON					PLAYOFFS				
			Gms.	G	A	Pts.	PIM	Gms.	G	A	Pts.	PIM
89-90—University of Maine		Hockey East	46	39	26	65	52	—	—	—	—	—
90-91—University of Maine		Hockey East	43	37	45	82	26	—	—	—	—	—
91-92—University of Maine		Hockey East	35	32	24	56	62	—	—	—	—	—
92-93—Canadian national team		Int'l	23	9	6	15	35	—	—	—	—	—
—Binghamton		AHL	49	13	15	28	21	14	5	2	7	4
93-94—Binghamton		AHL	65	41	24	65	33	—	—	—	—	—
—Canadian national team		Int'l	6	3	2	5	2	—	—	—	—	—
—Canadian Olympic Team		Int'l	8	1	0	1	19	—	—	—	—	—
94-95—Binghamton		AHL	67	41	36	77	28	11	4	6	10	12
—New York Rangers		NHL	3	1	0	1	2	—	—	—	—	—
NHL totals			3	1	0	1	2					

ROY, PATRICK
G, CANADIENS

PERSONAL: Born October 5, 1965, in Quebec City.... 6-0/192.... Catches left.... Name pronounced WAH.

TRANSACTIONS/CAREER NOTES: Selected by Montreal Canadiens as underage junior in third round (fourth Canadiens pick, 51st overall) of NHL entry draft (June 9, 1984).... Suspended eight games by NHL for slashing (October 19, 1987).... Sprained medial collateral ligaments in left knee (December 12, 1990); missed nine games.... Tore left ankle ligaments (January 27, 1991); missed 14 games.... Reinjured left ankle (March 16, 1991).... Strained hip flexor (March 6, 1993); missed two games.... Suffered stiff neck (December 11, 1993); missed two games.... Strained neck (December 22, 1993); missed four games.

HONORS: Won Conn Smythe Trophy (1985-86 and 1992-93).... Named to NHL All-Rookie team (1985-86).... Shared William M. Jennings Trophy with Brian Hayward (1986-87 through 1988-89).... Named to NHL All-Star second team (1987-88 and 1990-91).... Named to THE SPORTING NEWS All-Star first team (1988-89, 1989-90 and 1991-92).... Won Trico Goaltender Award (1988-89 and 1989-90).... Named to NHL All-Star first team (1988-89, 1989-90 and 1991-92).... Won Vezina Trophy (1988-89, 1989-90 and 1991-92).... Played in NHL All-Star Game (1988 and 1990-1994).... Named to THE SPORTING NEWS All-Star second team (1990-91).... Won William M. Jennings Trophy (1991-92).

RECORDS: Shares NHL single-season playoff records for most wins by goaltender—16 (1993); and most consecutive wins by goaltender—11 (1993).

MISCELLANEOUS: Member of Stanley Cup championship teams (1986 and 1993).

Season	Team	League	REGULAR SEASON							PLAYOFFS						
			Gms.	Min.	W	L	T	GA	SO	Avg.	Gms.	Min.	W	L	GA	SO	Avg.
82-83—Granby		QMJHL	54	2808	...	...	...	293	0	6.26	—	—	—	—	—	—	—
83-84—Granby		QMJHL	61	3585	29	29	1	265	0	4.44	4	244	0	4	22	0	5.41
84-85—Granby		QMJHL	44	2463	16	25	1	228	0	5.55	—	—	—	—	—	—	—
—Montreal		NHL	1	20	1	0	0	0	0	0.00	—	—	—	—	—	—	—
—Sherbrooke		AHL	1	60	1	0	0	4	0	4.00	*13	*769	10	3	37	0	*2.89
85-86—Montreal		NHL	47	2651	23	18	3	148	1	3.35	20	1218	*15	5	39	†1	1.92
86-87—Montreal		NHL	46	2686	22	16	6	131	1	2.93	6	330	4	2	22	0	4.00
87-88—Montreal		NHL	45	2586	23	12	9	125	3	2.90	8	430	3	4	24	0	3.35
88-89—Montreal		NHL	48	2744	33	5	6	113	4	*2.47	19	1206	13	6	42	2	*2.09
89-90—Montreal		NHL	54	3173	31	16	5	134	3	2.53	11	641	5	6	26	1	2.43
90-91—Montreal		NHL	48	2835	25	15	6	128	1	2.71	13	785	7	5	40	0	3.06
91-92—Montreal		NHL	67	3935	36	22	8	155	†5	*2.36	11	686	4	7	30	1	2.62
92-93—Montreal		NHL	62	3595	31	25	5	192	2	3.20	20	1293	16	4	46	0	2.13

Season Team	League	Gms.	Min.	W	L	T	GA	SO	Avg.	Gms.	Min.	W	L	GA	SO	Avg.
			REGULAR SEASON								**PLAYOFFS**					
93-94—Montreal	NHL	68	3867	35	17	11	161	†7	2.50	6	375	3	3	16	0	2.56
94-95—Montreal	NHL	43	2566	17	20	6	127	1	2.97	—	—	—	—	—	—	—
NHL totals		529	30658	277	166	65	1414	28	2.77	114	6964	70	42	285	5	2.46

ROY, STEPHANE
C, BLUES

PERSONAL: Born January 26, 1976, in Ste.-Martine, Que. . . . 5-10/173. . . . Shoots left. . . . Name pronounced WAH.

TRANSACTIONS/CAREER NOTES: Selected by St. Louis Blues in third round (first Blues pick, 68th overall) of NHL entry draft (June 29, 1994).

Season Team	League	Gms.	G	A	Pts.	PIM	Gms.	G	A	Pts.	PIM
			REGULAR SEASON					**PLAYOFFS**			
93-94—Val-d'Or	QMJHL	72	25	28	53	116	—	—	—	—	—
94-95—St. Jean	QMJHL	68	19	52	71	113	—	—	—	—	—

RUCCHIN, STEVE
C, MIGHTY DUCKS

PERSONAL: Born July 4, 1971, in London, Ont. . . . 6-3/210. . . . Shoots left. . . . Name pronounced ROO-shihn.

COLLEGE: Western Ontario.

TRANSACTIONS/CAREER NOTES: Selected by Mighty Ducks of Anaheim in first round (first Mighty Ducks pick, second overall) of NHL supplemental draft (June 28, 1994). . . . Suffered from the flu (March 7, 1995); missed two games.

HONORS: Named OUAA Player of the Year (1993-94). . . . Named to CIAU All-Star first team (1993-94).

Season Team	League	Gms.	G	A	Pts.	PIM	Gms.	G	A	Pts.	PIM
			REGULAR SEASON					**PLAYOFFS**			
90-91—Univ. of Western Ontario	OUAA	34	13	16	29	14	—	—	—	—	—
91-92—Univ. of Western Ontario	OUAA	37	28	34	62	36	—	—	—	—	—
92-93—Univ. of Western Ontario	OUAA	34	22	26	48	16	—	—	—	—	—
93-94—Univ. of Western Ontario	OUAA	35	30	23	53	30	—	—	—	—	—
94-95—San Diego	IHL	41	11	15	26	14	—	—	—	—	—
—Anaheim	NHL	43	6	11	17	23	—	—	—	—	—
NHL totals		43	6	11	17	23					

RUCHTY, MATT
D, DEVILS

PERSONAL: Born November 27, 1969, in Kitchener, Ont. . . . 6-1/210. . . . Shoots left. . . . Full name: Matthew Kerry Ruchty. . . . Name pronounced RUHK-tee.

COLLEGE: Bowling Green State.

TRANSACTIONS/CAREER NOTES: Selected by New Jersey Devils in fourth round (fourth Devils pick, 65th overall) of NHL entry draft (June 11, 1988).

Season Team	League	Gms.	G	A	Pts.	PIM	Gms.	G	A	Pts.	PIM
			REGULAR SEASON					**PLAYOFFS**			
87-88—Bowling Green State	CCHA	41	6	15	21	78	—	—	—	—	—
88-89—Bowling Green State	CCHA	43	11	21	32	110	—	—	—	—	—
89-90—Bowling Green State	CCHA	42	28	21	49	135	—	—	—	—	—
90-91—Bowling Green State	CCHA	38	13	18	31	147	—	—	—	—	—
91-92—Utica	AHL	73	9	14	23	250	4	0	0	0	25
92-93—Utica	AHL	74	4	14	18	253	4	0	2	2	15
93-94—Albany	AHL	68	11	11	22	303	5	0	1	1	18
94-95—Albany	AHL	78	26	23	49	348	12	5	10	15	43

RUCINSKY, MARTIN
LW, DENVER

PERSONAL: Born March 11, 1971, in Most, Czechoslovakia. . . . 6-0/190. . . . Shoots left. . . . Name pronounced roo-SHIHN-skee.

TRANSACTIONS/CAREER NOTES: Selected by Edmonton Oilers in first round (second Oilers pick, 20th overall) of NHL entry draft (June 22, 1991). . . . Traded by Oilers to Quebec Nordiques for G Ron Tugnutt and LW Brad Zavisha (March 10, 1992). . . . Suffered from the flu (February 28, 1993); missed one game. . . . Bruised left buttock (December 3, 1994); missed one game. . . . Sprained right wrist (January 11, 1994); missed one game. . . . Broke left cheek (January 30, 1994); missed four games. . . . Suffered hairline fracture of right wrist (March 7, 1994); missed one game. . . . Suffered hairline fracture of right wrist (March 21, 1994); missed six games. . . . Suffered hairline fracture of right wrist (April 5, 1994); missed one game. . . . Played in Europe during 1994-95 NHL lockout. . . . Separated shoulder (February 25, 1995); missed 17 games. . . . Reinjured shoulder (April 6, 1995); missed last 11 games of season and entire playoffs. . . . Nordiques franchise moved to Denver for 1995-96 season.

Season Team	League	Gms.	G	A	Pts.	PIM	Gms.	G	A	Pts.	PIM
			REGULAR SEASON					**PLAYOFFS**			
88-89—CHZ Litvinov	Czech.	3	1	0	1	2	—	—	—	—	—
89-90—CHZ Litvinov	Czech.	47	12	6	18	. . .	—	—	—	—	—
90-91—CHZ Litvinov	Czech.	49	23	18	41	79	—	—	—	—	—
—Czechoslovakia Jr.	Czech.	7	9	5	14	2	—	—	—	—	—
91-92—Cape Breton	AHL	35	11	12	23	34	—	—	—	—	—
—Edmonton	NHL	2	0	0	0	0	—	—	—	—	—
—Halifax	AHL	7	1	1	2	6	—	—	—	—	—
—Quebec	NHL	4	1	1	2	2	—	—	—	—	—
92-93—Quebec	NHL	77	18	30	48	51	6	1	1	2	4
93-94—Quebec	NHL	60	9	23	32	58	—	—	—	—	—

Season Team	League	REGULAR SEASON					PLAYOFFS				
		Gms.	G	A	Pts.	PIM	Gms.	G	A	Pts.	PIM
94-95—Chemopetrol Litvinov	Czech. Rep.	13	12	10	22	34	—	—	—	—	—
—Quebec	NHL	20	3	6	9	14	—	—	—	—	—
NHL totals..................		163	31	60	91	125	6	1	1	2	4

RUFF, JASON

LW, LIGHTNING

PERSONAL: Born January 27, 1970, in Kelowna, B.C. . . . 6-2/192. . . . Shoots left.
TRANSACTIONS/CAREER NOTES: Underwent heel surgery (May 1988). . . . Selected by St. Louis Blues in fifth round (third Blues pick, 96th overall) of NHL entry draft (June 16, 1990). . . . Traded by Blues to Tampa Bay Lightning for LW Basil McRae, D Doug Crossman and fourth-round pick in 1996 draft (January 28, 1993).
HONORS: Named to WHL (East) All-Star first team (1990-91).

Season Team	League	REGULAR SEASON					PLAYOFFS				
		Gms.	G	A	Pts.	PIM	Gms.	G	A	Pts.	PIM
86-87—Kelowna	BCJHL	45	25	20	45	70	—	—	—	—	—
87-88—Lethbridge......................	WHL	69	25	22	47	109	—	—	—	—	—
88-89—Lethbridge......................	WHL	69	42	38	80	127	—	—	—	—	—
89-90—Lethbridge......................	WHL	72	55	64	119	114	19	9	10	19	18
90-91—Lethbridge......................	WHL	66	61	75	136	154	16	12	17	29	18
—Peoria	IHL	—	—	—	—	—	5	0	0	0	2
91-92—Peoria	IHL	67	27	45	72	148	10	7	7	14	19
92-93—Peoria	IHL	40	22	21	43	81	—	—	—	—	—
—St. Louis	NHL	7	2	1	3	8	—	—	—	—	—
—Tampa Bay......................	NHL	1	0	0	0	0	—	—	—	—	—
—Atlanta	IHL	26	11	14	25	90	7	2	1	3	26
93-94—Atlanta	IHL	71	24	25	49	122	14	6	*17	23	41
—Tampa Bay......................	NHL	6	1	2	3	2	—	—	—	—	—
94-95—Atlanta	IHL	64	42	34	76	161	3	3	1	4	10
NHL totals..................		14	3	3	6	10					

RUMBLE, DARREN

D, SENATORS

PERSONAL: Born January 23, 1969, in Barrie, Ont. . . . 6-1/200. . . . Shoots left. . . . Full name: Darren William Rumble.
HIGH SCHOOL: Eastview (Barrie, Ont.).
TRANSACTIONS/CAREER NOTES: Selected by Philadelphia Flyers as underage junior in first round (first Flyers pick, 20th overall) of NHL entry draft (June 13, 1987). . . . Stretched knee ligaments (November 27, 1988). . . . Selected by Ottawa Senators in NHL expansion draft (June 18, 1992). . . . Bruised thigh (November 29, 1993); missed four games. . . . Injured thumb (March 5, 1994); missed one game.
HONORS: Named to AHL All-Star second team (1994-95).

Season Team	League	REGULAR SEASON					PLAYOFFS				
		Gms.	G	A	Pts.	PIM	Gms.	G	A	Pts.	PIM
85-86—Barrie Jr. B	OHA	46	14	32	46	91	—	—	—	—	—
86-87—Kitchener........................	OHL	64	11	32	43	44	4	0	1	1	9
87-88—Kitchener........................	OHL	55	15	50	65	64	—	—	—	—	—
88-89—Kitchener........................	OHL	46	11	28	39	25	5	1	0	1	2
89-90—Hershey..........................	AHL	57	2	13	15	31	—	—	—	—	—
90-91—Philadelphia	NHL	3	1	0	1	0	—	—	—	—	—
—Hershey............................	AHL	73	6	35	41	48	3	0	5	5	2
91-92—Hershey..........................	AHL	79	12	54	66	118	6	0	3	3	2
92-93—Ottawa............................	NHL	69	3	13	16	61	—	—	—	—	—
—New Haven	AHL	2	1	0	1	0	—	—	—	—	—
93-94—Ottawa............................	NHL	70	6	9	15	116	—	—	—	—	—
—Prince Edward Island	AHL	3	2	0	2	0	—	—	—	—	—
94-95—Prince Edward Island	AHL	70	7	46	53	77	11	0	6	6	4
NHL totals..................		142	10	22	32	177					

RUSSELL, CAM

D, BLACKHAWKS

PERSONAL: Born January 12, 1969, in Halifax, N.S. . . . 6-4/206. . . . Shoots left.
TRANSACTIONS/CAREER NOTES: Selected by Chicago Blackhawks as underage junior in third round (third Blackhawks pick, 50th overall) of NHL entry draft (June 13, 1987). . . . Suffered from the flu (December 26, 1992); missed one game. . . . Suspended one game by NHL for accumulating three game misconduct penalties (February 11, 1993). . . . Underwent surgery for a herniated disc in neck (March 18, 1994); missed remainder of season. . . . Broke bone in hand (April 2, 1995); missed remainder of season.

Season Team	League	REGULAR SEASON					PLAYOFFS				
		Gms.	G	A	Pts.	PIM	Gms.	G	A	Pts.	PIM
85-86—Hull	QMJHL	56	3	4	7	24	15	0	2	2	4
86-87—Hull	QMJHL	66	3	16	19	119	8	0	1	1	16
87-88—Hull	QMJHL	53	9	18	27	141	19	2	5	7	39
88-89—Hull	QMJHL	66	8	32	40	109	9	2	6	8	6
89-90—Indianapolis	IHL	46	3	15	18	114	9	0	1	1	24
—Chicago	NHL	19	0	1	1	27	1	0	0	0	0
90-91—Indianapolis	IHL	53	5	9	14	125	6	0	2	2	30
—Chicago	NHL	3	0	0	0	5	1	0	0	0	0
91-92—Indianapolis	IHL	41	4	9	13	78	—	—	—	—	—
—Chicago	NHL	19	0	0	0	34	12	0	2	2	2

R

Season Team	League	REGULAR SEASON					PLAYOFFS				
		Gms.	G	A	Pts.	PIM	Gms.	G	A	Pts.	PIM
92-93—Chicago	NHL	67	2	4	6	151	4	0	0	0	0
93-94—Chicago	NHL	67	1	7	8	200	—	—	—	—	—
94-95—Chicago	NHL	33	1	3	4	88	16	0	3	3	8
NHL totals		208	4	15	19	505	34	0	5	5	10

RUUTTU, CHRISTIAN
C, CANUCKS

PERSONAL: Born February 20, 1964, in Lappeenranta, Finland. . . . 5-11/190. . . . Shoots left. . . . Name pronounced ROO-TOO.
TRANSACTIONS/CAREER NOTES: Selected by Buffalo Sabres in seventh round (ninth Sabres pick, 134th overall) of NHL entry draft (June 8, 1983). . . . Injured knee (February 1988). . . . Sprained knee (September 1988). . . . Tore pectoral muscle (October 22, 1988). . . . Separated left shoulder (April 5, 1989). . . . Injured leg (January 21, 1992); missed four games. . . . Suffered from the flu (March 16, 1992); missed three games. . . . Traded by Sabres with future considerations to Winnipeg Jets for G Stephane Beauregard (June 15, 1992). . . . Traded by Jets with future considerations to Chicago Blackhawks for G Stephane Beauregard (August 10, 1992). . . . Broke right ankle (1993-94 season); missed 28 games. . . . Played in Europe during 1994-95 NHL lockout. . . . Traded by Blackhawks to Vancouver Canucks for C Murray Craven (March 10, 1995). . . . Suffered injury (April 22, 1995); missed one game.
HONORS: Named to Finnish League All-Star team (1985-86). . . . Played in NHL All-Star Game (1988).

Season Team	League	REGULAR SEASON					PLAYOFFS				
		Gms.	G	A	Pts.	PIM	Gms.	G	A	Pts.	PIM
82-83—Assat Pori	Finland	36	15	18	33	34	—	—	—	—	—
83-84—Assat Pori	Finland	37	18	42	60	72	9	2	5	7	12
84-85—Assat Pori	Finland	32	14	32	46	34	8	1	6	7	8
85-86—Helsinki IFK	Finland	36	14	42	56	41	10	3	6	9	8
86-87—Buffalo	NHL	76	22	43	65	62	—	—	—	—	—
87-88—Buffalo	NHL	73	26	45	71	85	6	2	5	7	4
88-89—Buffalo	NHL	67	14	46	60	98	2	0	0	0	0
89-90—Buffalo	NHL	75	19	41	60	66	6	0	0	0	4
90-91—Buffalo	NHL	77	16	34	50	96	6	1	3	4	29
91-92—Buffalo	NHL	70	4	21	25	76	3	0	0	0	6
92-93—Chicago	NHL	84	17	37	54	134	4	0	0	0	2
93-94—Chicago	NHL	54	9	20	29	68	6	0	0	0	2
94-95—HIFK Helsinki	Finland	20	4	8	12	24	—	—	—	—	—
—Chicago	NHL	20	2	5	7	6	—	—	—	—	—
—Vancouver	NHL	25	5	6	11	23	9	1	1	2	0
NHL totals		621	134	298	432	714	42	4	9	13	47

RYABCHIKOV, YEVGENI
G, BRUINS

PERSONAL: Born January 16, 1974, in Yaroslavl, U.S.S.R. . . . 5-11/167. . . . Catches left. . . . Name pronounced EHV-gih-nee ree-AB-chih-kahf.
TRANSACTIONS/CAREER NOTES: Selected by Boston Bruins in first round (first Bruins pick, 21st overall) of NHL entry draft (June 28, 1994). . . . Played in Europe during 1994-95 NHL lockout.
HONORS: Named CIS Rookie of the Year (1993-94).

Season Team	League	REGULAR SEASON							PLAYOFFS					
		Gms.	Min.	W	L	T	GA	SO	Avg.	Gms.	Min.	W	L	GA	SO	Avg.
93-94—Molot Perm	CIS	28	1572	...	...	...	96	...	3.66	—	—	—	—	—	—	—
94-95—Metallurg Cherepovets	CIS	1	60	...	...	...	1	...	1.00	—	—	—	—	—	—	—
—Providence	AHL	14	721	6	3	1	42	0	3.50	—	—	—	—	—	—	—

RYABYKIN, DMITRI
D, FLAMES

PERSONAL: Born March 24, 1976, in Moscow, U.S.S.R. . . . 6-1/183. . . . Shoots right.
TRANSACTIONS/CAREER NOTES: Selected by Calgary Flames in second round (second Flames pick, 45th overall) of NHL entry draft (June 28, 1994).

Season Team	League	REGULAR SEASON					PLAYOFFS				
		Gms.	G	A	Pts.	PIM	Gms.	G	A	Pts.	PIM
93-94—Dynamo-2 Moscow	CIS Div. III				Statistics unavailable.						
94-95—Dynamo Moscow	CIS	48	0	0	0	12	11	0	2	2	0

RYAN, TERRY
LW, CANADIENS

PERSONAL: Born January 14, 1977, in St. John's, Nfld. . . . 6-1/207. . . . Shoots left.
TRANSACTIONS/CAREER NOTES: Selected by Montreal Canadiens in first round (first Canadiens pick, eighth overall) of NHL entry draft (July 8, 1995).
HONORS: Named to WHL (West) All-Star second team (1994-95).

Season Team	League	REGULAR SEASON					PLAYOFFS				
		Gms.	G	A	Pts.	PIM	Gms.	G	A	Pts.	PIM
91-92—Quesnel	PCJHL	65	35	40	75	260	—	—	—	—	—
92-93—Quesnel	PCJHL	46	45	40	85	222	—	—	—	—	—
—Tri-City	WHL	1	0	0	0	0	1	0	1	1	5
93-94—Tri-City	WHL	61	16	17	33	176	4	0	1	1	25
94-95—Tri-City	WHL	70	50	60	110	207	17	12	15	27	36

RYCHEL, WARREN
LW, MAPLE LEAFS

PERSONAL: Born May 12, 1967, in Tecumseh, Ont. . . . 6-0/202. . . . Shoots left. . . . Full name: Warren Stanley Rychel. . . . Name pronounced RIGH-kuhl.
TRANSACTIONS/CAREER NOTES: Signed as free agent by Chicago Blackhawks (September 19, 1986). . . . Hyperextended left knee (February 1989). . . . Traded by Blackhawks with C Troy Murray to Winnipeg Jets for D Bryan Marchment and D Chris Norton (July 22, 1991). . . . Traded by Jets to Minnesota North Stars for RW Tony Joseph and future considerations (December 30, 1991). . . . Signed as free agent by San Diego Gulls (August 11, 1992). . . . Signed as free agent by Los Angeles Kings (October 3, 1992). . . . Bruised ankle (December 1, 1992); missed 14 games. . . . Traded by Kings to Washington Capitals for LW Randy Burridge (February 10, 1995). . . . Traded by Capitals to Toronto Maple Leafs for fourth-round pick (G Sebastien Charpentier) in 1995 draft (February 10, 1995). . . . Suspended two games and fined $500 by NHL for spearing (March 2, 1995). . . . Strained groin (April 17, 1995); missed three games.

			REGULAR SEASON					PLAYOFFS			
Season Team	League	Gms.	G	A	Pts.	PIM	Gms.	G	A	Pts.	PIM
83-84—Essex Jr. C	OHA	24	11	16	27	86	—	—	—	—	—
84-85—Sudbury	OHL	35	5	8	13	74	—	—	—	—	—
—Guelph	OHL	29	1	3	4	48	—	—	—	—	—
85-86—Guelph	OHL	38	14	5	19	119	—	—	—	—	—
—Ottawa	OHL	29	11	18	29	54	—	—	—	—	—
86-87—Ottawa	OHL	28	11	7	18	57	—	—	—	—	—
—Kitchener	OHL	21	5	5	10	39	4	0	0	0	9
87-88—Saginaw	IHL	51	2	7	9	113	1	0	0	0	0
—Peoria	IHL	7	2	1	3	7	—	—	—	—	—
88-89—Saginaw	IHL	50	15	14	29	226	6	0	0	0	51
—Chicago	NHL	2	0	0	0	17	—	—	—	—	—
89-90—Indianapolis	IHL	77	23	16	39	374	14	1	3	4	64
90-91—Indianapolis	IHL	68	33	30	63	338	5	2	1	3	30
—Chicago	NHL	—	—	—	—	—	3	1	3	4	2
91-92—Moncton	AHL	36	14	15	29	211	—	—	—	—	—
—Kalamazoo	IHL	45	15	20	35	165	8	0	3	3	51
92-93—Los Angeles	NHL	70	6	7	13	314	23	6	7	13	39
93-94—Los Angeles	NHL	80	10	9	19	322	—	—	—	—	—
94-95—Los Angeles	NHL	7	0	0	0	19	—	—	—	—	—
—Toronto	NHL	26	1	6	7	101	3	0	0	0	0
NHL totals		**185**	**17**	**22**	**39**	**773**	**29**	**7**	**10**	**17**	**41**

RYDMARK, DANIEL
C, KINGS

PERSONAL: Born February 23, 1970, in Vasteras, Sweden. . . . 5-10/180. . . . Shoots left.
TRANSACTIONS/CAREER NOTES: Selected by Los Angeles Kings in sixth round (fifth Kings pick, 123rd overall) of NHL entry draft (June 17, 1989).

			REGULAR SEASON					PLAYOFFS			
Season Team	League	Gms.	G	A	Pts.	PIM	Gms.	G	A	Pts.	PIM
86-87—Farjestad Karlstad	Sweden	4	0	1	1	0	—	—	—	—	—
87-88—Farjestad Karlstad	Sweden	28	2	1	3	10	5	0	0	0	2
88-89—Farjestad Karlstad	Sweden	35	9	9	18	24	—	—	—	—	—
89-90—Farjestad Karlstad	Sweden	35	9	12	21	20	5	0	0	0	4
90-91—Malmo	Sweden	39	14	13	27	34	1	0	0	0	0
91-92—Malmo	Sweden	30	17	15	32	56	7	0	3	3	6
—Swedish Olympic Team	Int'l	6	1	1	2	2	—	—	—	—	—
92-93—Malmo	Sweden	39	18	13	31	70	6	5	4	9	8
93-94—Malmo	Sweden	38	14	18	32	48	11	3	7	10	18
—Swedish Olympic Team	Int'l	8	0	0	0	8	—	—	—	—	—
94-95—Malmo	Sweden	23	8	7	15	24	9	1	2	3	31

SAAL, JASON
G, MAPLE LEAFS

PERSONAL: Born February 1, 1975, in Detroit. . . . 5-9/165. . . . Catches left. . . . Name pronounced SAHL.
TRANSACTIONS/CAREER NOTES: Selected by Los Angeles Kings in fifth round (fifth Kings pick, 117th overall) of NHL entry draft (June 26, 1993). . . . Signed as free agent by Toronto Maple Leafs (August 3, 1995).
HONORS: Won Hap Emms Memorial Trophy (1994-95). . . . Named to Memorial Cup All-Star team (1994-95).

				REGULAR SEASON						PLAYOFFS					
Season Team	League	Gms.	Min.	W	L	T	GA	SO	Avg.	Gms.	Min.	W	L	GA	SO	Avg.
92-93—Detroit	OHL	23	1289	11	8	1	85	0	3.96	3	42	0	0	2	0	2.86
93-94—Detroit	OHL	45	2551	28	11	3	143	0	3.36	7	346	5	0	23	0	3.99
94-95—Detroit	OHL	51	2887	32	13	3	153	1	3.18	18	1083	13	4	52	*3	*2.88

SABOURIN, KEN
D

PERSONAL: Born April 28, 1966, in Scarborough, Ont. . . . 6-3/210. . . . Shoots left. . . . Name pronounced SAB-uhr-ihn.
TRANSACTIONS/CAREER NOTES: Selected by Calgary Flames as underage junior in second round (second Flames pick, 33rd overall) of NHL entry draft (June 9, 1984). . . . Traded by Sault Ste. Marie Greyhounds to Cornwall Royals for Kent Trolley and fifth-round pick in 1986 OHL priority draft (March 1986). . . . Traded by Flames to Washington Capitals for C Paul Fenton (January 24, 1991). . . . Traded by Capitals to Flames for future considerations (December 15, 1992).

Season Team	League	REGULAR SEASON					PLAYOFFS				
		Gms.	G	A	Pts.	PIM	Gms.	G	A	Pts.	PIM
82-83—Sault Ste. Marie	OHL	58	0	8	8	90	10	0	0	0	14
83-84—Sault Ste. Marie	OHL	63	7	13	20	157	9	0	1	1	25
84-85—Sault Ste. Marie	OHL	63	5	19	24	139	16	1	4	5	10
85-86—Sault Ste. Marie	OHL	25	1	5	6	77	—	—	—	—	—
—Cornwall	OHL	37	3	12	15	94	6	1	2	3	6
—Moncton	AHL	3	0	0	0	0	6	0	1	1	2
86-87—Moncton	AHL	75	1	10	11	166	6	0	1	1	27
87-88—Salt Lake City	IHL	71	2	8	10	186	16	1	6	7	57
88-89—Calgary	NHL	6	0	1	1	26	1	0	0	0	0
—Salt Lake City	IHL	74	2	18	20	197	11	0	1	1	26
89-90—Calgary	NHL	5	0	0	0	10	—	—	—	—	—
—Salt Lake City	IHL	76	5	19	24	336	11	0	2	2	40
90-91—Salt Lake City	IHL	28	2	15	17	77	—	—	—	—	—
—Calgary	NHL	16	1	3	4	36	—	—	—	—	—
—Washington	NHL	28	1	4	5	81	11	0	0	0	34
91-92—Baltimore	AHL	30	3	8	11	106	—	—	—	—	—
—Washington	NHL	19	0	0	0	48	—	—	—	—	—
92-93—Baltimore	AHL	30	5	14	19	68	—	—	—	—	—
—Salt Lake City	IHL	52	2	11	13	140	—	—	—	—	—
93-94—Milwaukee	IHL	81	6	13	19	279	4	0	0	0	10
94-95—Milwaukee	IHL	75	3	16	19	297	15	1	1	2	69
NHL totals		74	2	8	10	201	12	0	0	0	34

SACCO, DAVID
LW/RW, MIGHTY DUCKS

PERSONAL: Born July 31, 1970, in Medford, Mass. . . . 6-0/180. . . . Shoots right. . . . Full name: David Anthony Sacco. . . . Name pronounced SAK-oh. . . . Brother of Joe Sacco, left winger, Mighty Ducks of Anaheim.
HIGH SCHOOL: Medford (Mass.).
COLLEGE: Boston University.
TRANSACTIONS/CAREER NOTES: Selected by Toronto Maple Leafs in 10th round (ninth Maple Leafs pick, 195th overall) of NHL entry draft (June 11, 1988). . . . Loaned to U.S. Olympic Team (February 27, 1994). . . . Returned to Maple Leafs (March 1, 1994). . . . Traded by Maple Leafs to Mighty Ducks of Anaheim for RW Terry Yake (September 28, 1994).
HONORS: Named to NCAA All-America East first team (1991-92 and 1992-93). . . . Named to Hockey East All-Star first team (1991-92 and 1992-93).

Season Team	League	REGULAR SEASON					PLAYOFFS				
		Gms.	G	A	Pts.	PIM	Gms.	G	A	Pts.	PIM
88-89—Boston University	Hockey East	35	14	29	43	40	—	—	—	—	—
89-90—Boston University	Hockey East	3	0	4	4	2	—	—	—	—	—
90-91—Boston University	Hockey East	40	21	40	61	24	—	—	—	—	—
91-92—Boston University	Hockey East	35	14	33	47	30	—	—	—	—	—
92-93—Boston University	Hockey East	40	25	37	62	86	—	—	—	—	—
93-94—U.S. national team	Int'l	32	8	20	28	88	—	—	—	—	—
—U.S. Olympic Team	Int'l	8	3	5	8	12	—	—	—	—	—
—Toronto	NHL	4	1	1	2	4	—	—	—	—	—
—St. John's	AHL	5	3	1	4	2	—	—	—	—	—
94-95—San Diego	IHL	45	11	25	36	57	4	3	1	4	0
—Anaheim	NHL	8	0	2	2	0	—	—	—	—	—
NHL totals		12	1	3	4	4					

SACCO, JOE
RW, MIGHTY DUCKS

PERSONAL: Born February 4, 1969, in Medford, Mass. . . . 6-1/195. . . . Shoots left. . . . Full name: Joseph William Sacco. . . . Name pronounced SAK-oh. . . . Brother of David Sacco, center in Mighty Ducks of Anaheim system.
HIGH SCHOOL: Medford (Mass.).
COLLEGE: Boston University.
TRANSACTIONS/CAREER NOTES: Selected by Toronto Maple Leafs in fourth round (fourth Maple Leafs pick, 71st overall) of NHL entry draft (June 13, 1987). . . . Selected by Mighty Ducks of Anaheim in NHL expansion draft (June 24, 1993). . . . Bruised left thumb (February 5, 1995); missed seven games.

Season Team	League	REGULAR SEASON					PLAYOFFS				
		Gms.	G	A	Pts.	PIM	Gms.	G	A	Pts.	PIM
85-86—Medford H.S.	Mass. H.S.	20	30	30	60	...	—	—	—	—	—
86-87—Medford H.S.	Mass. H.S.	21	22	32	54	...	—	—	—	—	—
87-88—Boston University	Hockey East	34	14	22	36	38	—	—	—	—	—
88-89—Boston University	Hockey East	33	21	19	40	66	—	—	—	—	—
89-90—Boston University	Hockey East	44	28	24	52	70	—	—	—	—	—
90-91—Newmarket	AHL	49	18	17	35	24	—	—	—	—	—
—Toronto	NHL	20	0	5	5	2	—	—	—	—	—
91-92—U.S. national team	Int'l	50	11	26	37	51	—	—	—	—	—
—U.S. Olympic Team	Int'l	8	0	2	2	0	—	—	—	—	—
—Toronto	NHL	17	7	4	11	4	—	—	—	—	—
—St. John's	AHL	—	—	—	—	—	1	1	1	2	0
92-93—Toronto	NHL	23	4	4	8	8	—	—	—	—	—
—St. John's	AHL	37	14	16	30	45	7	6	4	10	2

Season	Team	League	REGULAR SEASON Gms.	G	A	Pts.	PIM	PLAYOFFS Gms.	G	A	Pts.	PIM
93-94—Anaheim		NHL	84	19	18	37	61	—	—	—	—	—
94-95—Anaheim		NHL	41	10	8	18	23	—	—	—	—	—
NHL totals			185	40	39	79	98	—	—	—	—	—

ST. PIERRE, DAVID
C, FLAMES

PERSONAL: Born March 22, 1972, in Montreal. . . . 6-0/180. . . . Shoots right.
TRANSACTIONS/CAREER NOTES: Selected by Calgary Flames in eighth round (ninth Flames pick, 173rd overall) in NHL entry draft (June 22, 1991).

Season	Team	League	REGULAR SEASON Gms.	G	A	Pts.	PIM	PLAYOFFS Gms.	G	A	Pts.	PIM
89-90—Longueuil		QMJHL	63	33	24	57	24	7	2	2	4	8
90-91—Longueuil		QMJHL	66	34	45	79	51	8	4	4	8	8
91-92—Verdun		QMJHL	69	40	55	95	98	15	3	6	9	15
92-93—Salt Lake City		IHL	35	7	8	15	18	—	—	—	—	—
93-94—Saint John		AHL	77	19	30	49	42	5	0	2	2	0
94-95—Canadian national team		Int'l	40	15	13	28	10	—	—	—	—	—
—Saint John		AHL	17	4	2	6	0	3	2	0	2	0

SAKIC, JOE
C, DENVER

PERSONAL: Born July 7, 1969, in Burnaby, B.C. . . . 5-11/185. . . . Shoots left. . . . Full name: Joseph Steve Sakic. . . . Name pronounced SAK-ihk.
TRANSACTIONS/CAREER NOTES: Selected by Quebec Nordiques as underage junior in first round (second Nordiques pick, 15th overall) of NHL entry draft (June 13, 1987). . . . Sprained right ankle (November 28, 1988). . . . Developed bursitis in left ankle (January 21, 1992); missed three games. . . . Suffered recurrence of bursitis in left ankle (January 30, 1992); missed eight games. . . . Injured eye (January 2, 1993); missed six games. . . . Nordiques franchise moved to Denver for 1995-96 season.
HONORS: Won WHL (East) Most Valuable Player Trophy (1986-87). . . . Won WHL (East) Stewart (Butch) Paul Memorial Trophy (1986-87). . . . Named to WHL All-Star second team (1986-87). . . . Won Can.HL Player of the Year Award (1987-88). . . . Won Four Broncos Memorial Trophy (1987-88). . . . Shared Bob Clarke Trophy with Theoren Fleury (1987-88). . . . Won WHL Player of the Year Award (1987-88). . . . Named to WHL (East) All-Star first team (1987-88). . . . Played in NHL All-Star Game (1990-1994).
STATISTICAL PLATEAUS: Three-goal games: 1988-89 (2), 1989-90 (1), 1990-91 (1). Total: 4. . . . Four-goal games: 1991-92 (1). . . . Total hat tricks: 5.
MISCELLANEOUS: Captain of Quebec Nordiques (1990-91 through 1994-95).

Season	Team	League	REGULAR SEASON Gms.	G	A	Pts.	PIM	PLAYOFFS Gms.	G	A	Pts.	PIM
86-87—Swift Current		WHL	72	60	73	133	31	4	0	1	1	0
87-88—Swift Current		WHL	64	†78	82	†160	64	10	11	13	24	12
88-89—Quebec		NHL	70	23	39	62	24	—	—	—	—	—
89-90—Quebec		NHL	80	39	63	102	27	—	—	—	—	—
90-91—Quebec		NHL	80	48	61	109	24	—	—	—	—	—
91-92—Quebec		NHL	69	29	65	94	20	—	—	—	—	—
92-93—Quebec		NHL	78	48	57	105	40	6	3	3	6	2
93-94—Quebec		NHL	84	28	64	92	18	—	—	—	—	—
94-95—Quebec		NHL	47	19	43	62	30	6	4	1	5	0
NHL totals			508	234	392	626	183	12	7	4	11	2

SALO, TOMMY
G, ISLANDERS

PERSONAL: Born February 1, 1971, in Surahammar, Sweden. . . . 5-11/161. . . . Catches left. . . . Name pronounced SAL-oh.
TRANSACTIONS/CAREER NOTES: Selected by New York Islanders in fifth round (fifth Islanders pick, 118th overall) of NHL entry draft (June 26, 1993).
HONORS: Won James Gatchene Memorial Trophy (1994-95). . . . Won James Norris Memorial Trophy (1994-95). . . . Won Garry F. Longman Memorial Trophy (1994-95). . . . Named to IHL All-Star first team (1994-95).
MISCELLANEOUS: Member of gold-medal-winning Swedish Olympic team (1994).

Season	Team	League	REGULAR SEASON Gms.	Min.	W	L	T	GA	SO	Avg.	PLAYOFFS Gms.	Min.	W	L	GA	SO	Avg.
90-91—Vasteras		Sweden	2	100	. . .	. . .	. . .	11	0	6.60	—	—	—	—	—	—	—
91-92—Vasteras		Sweden						Did not play.									
92-93—Vasteras		Sweden	24	1431	. . .	. . .	. . .	59	2	2.47	—	—	—	—	—	—	—
93-94—Vasteras		Sweden	32	1896	. . .	. . .	. . .	106	. . .	3.35	—	—	—	—	—	—	—
—Swedish Olympic Team		Int'l	6	370	. . .	. . .	. . .	13	1	2.11	—	—	—	—	—	—	—
94-95—Denver		IHL	65	*3810	*45	14	‡4	165	†3	*2.60	8	390	7	0	20	0	3.08
—New York Islanders		NHL	6	358	1	5	0	18	0	3.02	—	—	—	—	—	—	—
NHL totals			6	358	1	5	0	18	0	3.02							

SALVADOR, BRYCE
D, LIGHTNING

PERSONAL: Born February 11, 1994, in Brandon, Man. . . . 6-1/194. . . . Shoots left.
TRANSACTIONS/CAREER NOTES: Selected by Tampa Bay Lightning in sixth round (sixth Lightning pick, 138th overall) of NHL entry draft (June 29, 1994).

Season	Team	League	REGULAR SEASON Gms.	G	A	Pts.	PIM	PLAYOFFS Gms.	G	A	Pts.	PIM
92-93—Lethbridge		WHL	64	1	4	5	29	4	0	0	0	0
93-94—Lethbridge		WHL	61	4	14	18	36	9	0	1	1	2
94-95—Lethbridge		WHL	67	1	9	10	88	—	—	—	—	—

S

SAMUELSSON, KJELL

D, FLYERS

PERSONAL: Born October 18, 1958, in Tyngsryd, Sweden. . . . 6-6/233. . . . Shoots right. . . . Name pronounced SHEHL SAM-yuhl-suhn.
TRANSACTIONS/CAREER NOTES: Selected by New York Rangers in sixth round (fifth Rangers pick, 119th overall) of NHL entry draft (June 9, 1984). . . . Traded by Rangers with second-round pick in 1989 draft (LW Patrik Juhlin) to Philadelphia Flyers for G Bob Froese (December 18, 1986). . . . Pulled groin (February 1988). . . . Suffered herniated disc (October 1988). . . . Bruised hand (March 1989). . . . Bruised right shoulder (November 22, 1989); missed 13 games. . . . Underwent shoulder surgery (March 1990). . . . Traded by Flyers with RW Rick Tocchet, G Ken Wregget and third-round pick in 1992 draft to Pittsburgh Penguins for RW Mark Recchi, D Brian Benning and first-round pick (LW Jason Bowen) in 1992 draft (February 19, 1992). . . . Bruised knee (November 27, 1992); missed one game. . . . Broke bone in foot (December 1, 1992); missed nine games. . . . Fractured cheekbone (December 27, 1992); missed nine games. . . . Suffered from the flu (March 18, 1993); missed one game. . . . Injured groin (October 19, 1993); missed nine games. . . . Injured groin (December 28, 1993); missed 13 games. . . . Suffered from the flu (February 27, 1995); missed four games. . . . Injured groin (April 8, 1995); missed one game. . . . Suffered from the flu (April 28, 1995); missed two games. . . . Signed as free agent by Flyers (July 7, 1995).
HONORS: Played in NHL All-Star Game (1988).
MISCELLANEOUS: Member of Stanley Cup championship team (1992).

Season Team	League	REGULAR SEASON Gms.	G	A	Pts.	PIM	PLAYOFFS Gms.	G	A	Pts.	PIM
82-83—Tyngsryd	Sweden	32	11	6	17	57	—	—	—	—	—
83-84—Leksand	Sweden	36	6	7	13	59	—	—	—	—	—
84-85—Leksand	Sweden	35	9	5	14	34	—	—	—	—	—
85-86—New York Rangers	NHL	9	0	0	0	10	9	0	1	1	8
—New Haven	AHL	56	6	21	27	87	3	0	0	0	10
86-87—New York Rangers	NHL	30	2	6	8	50	—	—	—	—	—
—Philadelphia	NHL	46	1	6	7	86	26	0	4	4	25
87-88—Philadelphia	NHL	74	6	24	30	184	7	2	5	7	23
88-89—Philadelphia	NHL	69	3	14	17	140	19	1	3	4	24
89-90—Philadelphia	NHL	66	5	17	22	91	—	—	—	—	—
90-91—Philadelphia	NHL	78	9	19	28	82	—	—	—	—	—
91-92—Philadelphia	NHL	54	4	9	13	76	—	—	—	—	—
—Pittsburgh	NHL	20	1	2	3	34	15	0	3	3	12
92-93—Pittsburgh	NHL	63	3	6	9	106	12	0	3	3	2
93-94—Pittsburgh	NHL	59	5	8	13	118	6	0	0	0	26
94-95—Pittsburgh	NHL	41	1	6	7	54	11	0	1	1	32
NHL totals		**609**	**40**	**117**	**157**	**1031**	**105**	**3**	**20**	**23**	**152**

SAMUELSSON, ULF

D, PENGUINS

PERSONAL: Born March 26, 1964, in Fagersta, Sweden. . . . 6-1/195. . . . Shoots left. . . . Name pronounced UHLF SAM-yuhl-suhn.
TRANSACTIONS/CAREER NOTES: Selected by Hartford Whalers in fourth round (fourth Whalers pick, 67th overall) of NHL entry draft (June 9, 1982). . . . Suffered from the flu (December 1988); missed nine games. . . . Tore ligaments in right knee and underwent surgery (August 1989); missed part of 1989-90 season. . . . Traded by Whalers with C Ron Francis and D Grant Jennings to Pittsburgh Penguins for C John Cullen, D Zarley Zalapski and RW Jeff Parker (March 4, 1991). . . . Injured hip flexor (October 29, 1991); missed six games. . . . Underwent surgery to right elbow (December 1991); missed four games. . . . Bruised left hand (February 8, 1992); missed one game. . . . Suffered from the flu (February 1992); missed one game. . . . Strained shoulder (November 10, 1992); missed two games. . . . Broke cheekbone (November 27, 1992); missed two games. . . . Bruised knee (January 1993); missed one game. . . . Suspended one game by NHL (February 1993). . . . Suspended three off-days by NHL for stick-swinging incident (March 18, 1993). . . . Suffered back spasms (April 4, 1993); missed one game. . . . Injured knee (November 2, 1993); missed one game. . . . Bruised foot (December 14, 1993); missed two games. . . . Played in Europe during 1994-95 NHL lockout. . . . Strained right elbow (March 21, 1995) and underwent elbow surgery (March 23, 1995); missed three games. . . . Bruised knee (April 28, 1995); missed one game.
MISCELLANEOUS: Member of Stanley Cup championship teams (1991 and 1992).

Season Team	League	REGULAR SEASON Gms.	G	A	Pts.	PIM	PLAYOFFS Gms.	G	A	Pts.	PIM
83-84—Leksand	Sweden	36	5	10	15	53	—	—	—	—	—
84-85—Binghamton	AHL	36	5	11	16	92	—	—	—	—	—
—Hartford	NHL	41	2	6	8	83	—	—	—	—	—
85-86—Hartford	NHL	80	5	19	24	174	10	1	2	3	38
86-87—Hartford	NHL	78	2	31	33	162	5	0	1	1	41
87-88—Hartford	NHL	76	8	33	41	159	5	0	0	0	8
88-89—Hartford	NHL	71	9	26	35	181	4	0	2	2	4
89-90—Hartford	NHL	55	2	11	13	177	7	1	0	1	2
90-91—Hartford	NHL	62	3	18	21	174	—	—	—	—	—
—Pittsburgh	NHL	14	1	4	5	37	20	3	2	5	34
91-92—Pittsburgh	NHL	62	1	14	15	206	21	0	2	2	39
92-93—Pittsburgh	NHL	77	3	26	29	249	12	1	5	6	24
93-94—Pittsburgh	NHL	80	5	24	29	199	6	0	1	1	18
94-95—Leksand	Sweden	2	0	0	0	8	—	—	—	—	—
—Pittsburgh	NHL	44	1	15	16	113	7	0	2	2	8
NHL totals		**740**	**42**	**227**	**269**	**1914**	**97**	**6**	**17**	**23**	**216**

SANDERSON, GEOFF

LW, WHALERS

PERSONAL: Born February 1, 1972, in Hay River, Northwest Territories. . . . 6-0/185. . . . Shoots left.
TRANSACTIONS/CAREER NOTES: Selected by Hartford Whalers in second round (second Whalers pick, 36th overall) of NHL entry draft (June 16, 1990). . . . Bruised

shoulder (October 14, 1991); missed one game. . . . Injured groin (November 13, 1991); missed three games. . . . Bruised knee (December 7, 1991); missed five games. . . . Suffered from the flu (February 1, 1994). . . . Fined $500 by Whalers for involvement in bar brawl (April 1, 1994). . . . Played in Europe during 1994-95 NHL lockout.
HONORS: Played in NHL All-Star Game (1994).
STATISTICAL PLATEAUS: Three-goal games: 1992-93 (2), 1994-95 (1). Total: 3.

			REGULAR SEASON					PLAYOFFS			
Season	Team	League	Gms.	G	A	Pts.	PIM	Gms.	G	A	Pts.	PIM
88-89—Swift Current		WHL	58	17	11	28	16	12	3	5	8	6
89-90—Swift Current		WHL	70	32	62	94	56	4	1	4	5	8
90-91—Swift Current		WHL	70	62	50	112	57	3	1	2	3	4
—Hartford		NHL	2	1	0	1	0	3	0	0	0	0
—Springfield		AHL	—	—	—	—	—	1	0	0	0	2
91-92—Hartford		NHL	64	13	18	31	18	7	1	0	1	2
92-93—Hartford		NHL	82	46	43	89	28	—	—	—	—	—
93-94—Hartford		NHL	82	41	26	67	42	—	—	—	—	—
94-95—HPK Hameenlinna		Finland	12	6	4	10	24	—	—	—	—	—
—Hartford		NHL	46	18	14	32	24	—	—	—	—	—
NHL totals			276	119	101	220	112	10	1	0	1	2

SANDLAK, JIM
RW, WHALERS

PERSONAL: Born December 12, 1966, in Kitchener, Ont. . . . 6-4/219. . . . Shoots right.
TRANSACTIONS/CAREER NOTES: Selected by Vancouver Canucks as underage junior in first round (first Canucks pick, fourth overall) of NHL entry draft (June 15, 1985). . . . Ruptured ligaments in right thumb (January 1986). . . . Bruised shoulder (October 1988). . . . Suffered sore back (November 5, 1991). . . . Sprained hand (December 1, 1991); missed seven games. . . . Strained groin (December 31, 1991). . . . Sprained knee (March 1992); missed seven games. . . . Strained back and suffered bulging disc (November 18, 1992); missed 17 games. . . . Sprained hand (April 1, 1993); missed remainder of season. . . . Traded by Canucks to Hartford Whalers (May 17, 1993); to complete deal in which Canucks sent LW Robert Kron, third-round pick in 1993 draft (D Marek Malik) and future considerations to Whalers for LW Murray Craven and fifth-round pick in 1993 draft (March 22, 1993). . . . Injured right wrist (October 19, 1993); missed two games. . . . Broke bone in right foot (October 27, 1993); missed 17 games. . . . Bruised knee (January 12, 1994); missed eight games. . . . Injured ankle (February 6, 1994); missed remainder of season. . . . Broke heel (March 16, 1995); missed 21 games.
HONORS: Named to NHL All-Rookie team (1986-87).
STATISTICAL PLATEAUS: Three-goal games: 1988-89 (1).

			REGULAR SEASON					PLAYOFFS			
Season	Team	League	Gms.	G	A	Pts.	PIM	Gms.	G	A	Pts.	PIM
82-83—Kitchener		OHL	38	26	25	51	100	—	—	—	—	—
83-84—London		OHL	68	23	18	41	143	8	1	11	12	13
84-85—London		OHL	58	40	24	64	128	8	3	2	5	14
85-86—London		OHL	16	7	13	20	36	5	2	3	5	24
—Vancouver		NHL	23	1	3	4	10	3	0	1	1	0
86-87—Vancouver		NHL	78	15	21	36	66	—	—	—	—	—
87-88—Vancouver		NHL	49	16	15	31	81	—	—	—	—	—
—Fredericton		AHL	24	10	15	25	47	—	—	—	—	—
88-89—Vancouver		NHL	72	20	20	40	99	6	1	1	2	2
89-90—Vancouver		NHL	70	15	8	23	104	—	—	—	—	—
90-91—Vancouver		NHL	59	7	6	13	125	—	—	—	—	—
91-92—Vancouver		NHL	66	16	24	40	176	13	4	6	10	22
92-93—Vancouver		NHL	59	10	18	28	122	6	2	2	4	4
93-94—Hartford		NHL	27	6	2	8	32	—	—	—	—	—
94-95—Hartford		NHL	13	0	0	0	0	—	—	—	—	—
NHL totals			516	106	117	223	815	28	7	10	17	28

SANDSTROM, TOMAS
RW, PENGUINS

PERSONAL: Born September 4, 1964, in Jakobstad, Finland. . . . 6-2/200. . . . Shoots left.
TRANSACTIONS/CAREER NOTES: Selected by New York Rangers in second round (second Rangers pick, 36th overall) of NHL entry draft (June 9, 1982). . . . Suffered concussion (February 24, 1986). . . . Fractured right ankle (February 11, 1987). . . . Fractured right index finger (November 1987). . . . Traded by Rangers with LW Tony Granato to Los Angeles Kings for C Bernie Nicholls (January 20, 1990). . . . Fractured vertebrae (November 29, 1990); missed 10 games. . . . Partially dislocated shoulder (December 28, 1991); missed 26 games. . . . Fractured left forearm (November 21, 1992); missed 24 games. . . . Fractured jaw (February 28, 1993); missed 21 games. . . . Pulled hamstring (October 26, 1993); missed four games. . . . Traded by Kings to Pittsburgh Penguins for D Marty McSorley and D Jim Peak (February 15, 1994). . . . Played in Europe during 1994-95 NHL lockout. . . . Sprained foot (January 22, 1995); missed one game.
HONORS: Named to NHL All-Rookie team (1984-85). . . . Played in NHL All-Star Game (1988 and 1991).
RECORDS: Shares NHL career record for most overtime goals—7.
STATISTICAL PLATEAUS: Three-goal games: 1986-87 (3), 1990-91 (3), 1992-93 (1). Total: 7. . . . Four-goal games: 1986-87 (1). . . . Total hat tricks: 8.

			REGULAR SEASON					PLAYOFFS			
Season	Team	League	Gms.	G	A	Pts.	PIM	Gms.	G	A	Pts.	PIM
81-82—Fagersta		Sweden 2	32	28	11	39	74	—	—	—	—	—
82-83—Brynas Gavle		Sweden	36	22	14	36	36	—	—	—	—	—
83-84—Brynas Gavle		Sweden	34	20	10	30	...	—	—	—	—	—
—Swedish Olympic Team		Int'l	7	2	1	3	6	—	—	—	—	—

S

Season Team	League	REGULAR SEASON					PLAYOFFS				
		Gms.	G	A	Pts.	PIM	Gms.	G	A	Pts.	PIM
84-85—New York Rangers	NHL	74	29	29	58	51	3	0	2	2	0
85-86—New York Rangers	NHL	73	25	29	54	109	16	4	6	10	20
86-87—New York Rangers	NHL	64	40	34	74	60	6	1	2	3	20
87-88—New York Rangers	NHL	69	28	40	68	95	—	—	—	—	—
88-89—New York Rangers	NHL	79	32	56	88	148	4	3	2	5	12
89-90—New York Rangers	NHL	48	19	19	38	100	—	—	—	—	—
—Los Angeles......................	NHL	28	13	20	33	28	10	5	4	9	19
90-91—Los Angeles...................	NHL	68	45	44	89	106	10	4	4	8	14
91-92—Los Angeles...................	NHL	49	17	22	39	70	6	0	3	3	8
92-93—Los Angeles...................	NHL	39	25	27	52	57	24	8	17	25	12
93-94—Los Angeles...................	NHL	51	17	24	41	59	—	—	—	—	—
—Pittsburgh......................	NHL	27	6	11	17	24	6	0	0	0	4
94-95—Malmo......................	Sweden	12	10	5	15	14	—	—	—	—	—
—Pittsburgh......................	NHL	47	21	23	44	42	12	3	3	6	16
NHL totals.................		716	317	378	695	949	97	28	43	71	125

SAPOZHNIKOV, ANDREI
D, BRUINS

PERSONAL: Born June 15, 1971, in Chelyabinsk, U.S.S.R. . . . . 6-1/185. . . . Shoots left. . . . Name pronounced suh-PAHZH-nih-kahf.
TRANSACTIONS/CAREER NOTES: Selected by Boston Bruins in fifth round (fifth Bruins pick, 129th overall) of NHL entry draft (June 26, 1993).
HONORS: Named to CIS All-Star team (1993-94).

Season Team	League	REGULAR SEASON					PLAYOFFS				
		Gms.	G	A	Pts.	PIM	Gms.	G	A	Pts.	PIM
90-91—Traktor Chelyabinsk........	USSR	28	0	0	0	14	—	—	—	—	—
91-92—Traktor Chelyabinsk........	CIS	43	3	4	7	22	—	—	—	—	—
92-93—Traktor Chelyabinsk........	CIS	40	2	7	9	30	8	0	1	1	6
93-94—Traktor Chelyabinsk........	CIS	40	4	8	12	34	6	0	0	0	0
94-95—Providence	AHL	19	1	5	6	23	—	—	—	—	—

SARAULT, YVES
LW, CANADIENS

PERSONAL: Born December 23, 1972, in Valleyfield, Que. . . . 6-1/170. . . . Shoots left. . . . Name pronounced EEV SA-roh.
TRANSACTIONS/CAREER NOTES: Traded by Victoriaville Tigers with D Jason Downey to St. Jean Lynx for D Sylvain Bourgeois (May 26, 1990). . . . Selected by Montreal Canadiens in third round (fourth Canadiens pick, 61st overall) of NHL entry draft (June 22, 1991).
HONORS: Named to QMJHL All-Star second team (1991-92).

Season Team	League	REGULAR SEASON					PLAYOFFS				
		Gms.	G	A	Pts.	PIM	Gms.	G	A	Pts.	PIM
89-90—Victoriaville......................	QMJHL	70	12	28	40	140	16	0	3	3	26
90-91—St. Jean	QMJHL	56	22	24	46	113	—	—	—	—	—
91-92—St. Jean	QMJHL	50	28	38	66	96	—	—	—	—	—
—Trois-Rivieres......................	QMJHL	18	16	14	30	10	15	10	10	20	18
92-93—Fredericton	AHL	59	14	17	31	41	3	0	1	1	2
—Wheeling	ECHL	2	1	3	4	0	—	—	—	—	—
93-94—Fredericton	AHL	60	13	14	27	72	—	—	—	—	—
94-95—Fredericton	AHL	69	24	21	45	96	13	2	1	3	33
—Montreal......................	NHL	8	0	1	1	0	—	—	—	—	—
NHL totals.................		8	0	1	1	0					

SARJEANT, GEOFF
G, BLUES

PERSONAL: Born November 30, 1969, in Orillia, Ont. . . . 5-9/180. . . . Catches left. . . . Full name: Geoff Ian Sarjeant. . . . Name pronounced JAWF SAHR-jehnt.
HIGH SCHOOL: Newmarket (Ont.).
COLLEGE: Michigan Tech.
TRANSACTIONS/CAREER NOTES: Selected by St. Louis Blues in NHL supplemental draft (June 15, 1990).
HONORS: Named to IHL All-Star first team (1993-94).

Season Team	League	REGULAR SEASON							PLAYOFFS						
		Gms.	Min.	W	L	T	GA	SO	Avg.	Gms.	Min.	W	L	GA SO	Avg.
88-89—Michigan Tech	WCHA	6	329	0	3	2	22	0	4.01	—	—	—	—	— —	—
89-90—Michigan Tech	WCHA	19	1043	4	13	0	94	0	5.41	—	—	—	—	— —	—
90-91—Michigan Tech	WCHA	28	1540	6	16	3	97	1	3.78	—	—	—	—	— —	—
91-92—Michigan Tech	WCHA	23	1246	7	13	0	90	1	4.33	—	—	—	—	— —	—
92-93—Peoria	IHL	41	2356	22	14	‡3	130	0	3.31	3	179	0	3	13 0	4.36
93-94—Peoria	IHL	41	2275	25	9	‡2	93	†2	*2.45	4	211	2	2	13 0	3.70
94-95—Peoria	IHL	55	3147	32	12	‡8	158	0	3.01	4	207	0	3	20 0	5.80
—St. Louis	NHL	4	120	1	0	0	6	0	3.00	—	—	—	—	— —	—
NHL totals.................		4	120	1	0	0	6	0	3.00						

SATAN, MIROSLAV
C, OILERS

PERSONAL: Born October 22, 1974, in Topolcany, Czechoslovakia. . . . 6-1/176. . . . Shoots left. . . . Name pronounced shuh-TEEN.
TRANSACTIONS/CAREER NOTES: Selected by Edmonton Oilers in fifth round (sixth Oilers pick, 111th overall) of NHL entry draft (June 26, 1993). . . . Signed as free agent by Detroit Vipers (July 27, 1994). . . . Loaned by Vipers to San Diego Gulls (December 22, 1994).

Season	Team	League	REGULAR SEASON Gms.	G	A	Pts.	PIM	PLAYOFFS Gms.	G	A	Pts.	PIM
91-92—VTJ Topolcany		Czech Dv.II	9	2	1	3	6	—	—	—	—	—
—VTJ Topolcany Jrs		Czech. Jrs.	31	30	22	52	...	—	—	—	—	—
92-93—Dukla Trencin		Czech.	38	11	6	17	...	—	—	—	—	—
93-94—Dukla Trencin		Slovakia	30	32	16	48	16	—	—	—	—	—
—Slovakian Olympic team...		Int'l	8	9	0	9	0	—	—	—	—	—
94-95—Detroit		IHL	8	1	3	4	4	—	—	—	—	—
—San Diego		IHL	6	0	2	2	6	—	—	—	—	—
—Cape Breton		AHL	25	24	16	40	15	—	—	—	—	—

SAVAGE, BRIAN
C, CANADIENS

PERSONAL: Born February 24, 1971, in Sudbury, Ont.... 6-1/196.... Shoots left.
HIGH SCHOOL: Lo-Ellen Park Secondary (Sudbury, Ont.).
COLLEGE: Miami of Ohio.
TRANSACTIONS/CAREER NOTES: Selected by Montreal Canadiens in eighth round (11th Canadiens pick, 171st overall) of NHL entry draft (June 22, 1991).... Bruised knee (February 4, 1995); missed 10 games.... Bruised knee (April 5, 1995); missed one game.
HONORS: Named to NCAA All-America West second team (1992-93).... Named CCHA Player of the Year (1992-93).... Named to CCHA All-Star first team (1992-93).
MISCELLANEOUS: Member of silver-medal-winning Canadian Olympic team (1994).

Season	Team	League	REGULAR SEASON Gms.	G	A	Pts.	PIM	PLAYOFFS Gms.	G	A	Pts.	PIM
90-91—Miami of Ohio		CCHA	28	5	6	11	26	—	—	—	—	—
91-92—Miami of Ohio		CCHA	40	24	16	40	43	—	—	—	—	—
92-93—Miami of Ohio		CCHA	38	37	21	58	44	—	—	—	—	—
—Canadian national team...		Int'l	9	3	0	3	12	—	—	—	—	—
93-94—Canadian national team...		Int'l	51	20	26	46	38	—	—	—	—	—
—Canadian Olympic Team ..		Int'l	8	2	2	4	6	—	—	—	—	—
—Fredericton		AHL	17	12	15	27	4	—	—	—	—	—
—Montreal		NHL	3	1	0	1	0	3	0	2	2	0
94-95—Montreal		NHL	37	12	7	19	27	—	—	—	—	—
NHL totals			40	13	7	20	27	3	0	2	2	0

SAVAGE, REGGIE
RW, DENVER

PERSONAL: Born May 1, 1970, in Montreal.... 5-10/192.... Shoots left.... Full name: Reginald David Savage.
TRANSACTIONS/CAREER NOTES: Selected by Washington Capitals in first round (first Capitals pick, 15th overall) of NHL entry draft (June 11, 1988).... Suspended six games by QMJHL for stick-swinging incident (February 19, 1989).... Traded by Capitals with RW Paul MacDermid to Quebec Nordiques for LW Mike Hough (June 20, 1993).... Suffered charley horse (October 20, 1993); missed one game.... Broke left wrist (February 14, 1994); missed remainder of season.... Nordiques franchise moved to Denver for 1995-96 season.

Season	Team	League	REGULAR SEASON Gms.	G	A	Pts.	PIM	PLAYOFFS Gms.	G	A	Pts.	PIM
87-88—Victoriaville		QMJHL	68	68	54	122	77	5	2	3	5	8
88-89—Victoriaville		QMJHL	54	58	55	113	178	16	15	13	28	52
89-90—Victoriaville		QMJHL	63	51	43	94	79	16	13	10	23	40
90-91—Baltimore		AHL	62	32	29	61	10	6	1	1	2	6
—Washington		NHL	1	0	0	0	0	—	—	—	—	—
91-92—Baltimore		AHL	77	42	28	70	51	—	—	—	—	—
92-93—Baltimore		AHL	40	37	18	55	28	—	—	—	—	—
—Washington		NHL	16	2	3	5	12	—	—	—	—	—
93-94—Quebec		NHL	17	3	4	7	16	—	—	—	—	—
—Cornwall		AHL	33	21	13	34	56	—	—	—	—	—
94-95—Cornwall		AHL	34	13	7	20	56	14	5	6	11	40
NHL totals			34	5	7	12	28					

SAVARD, DENIS
C, BLACKHAWKS

PERSONAL: Born February 4, 1961, in Pointe Gatineau, Que.... 5-10/175.... Shoots right. ... Full name: Denis Joseph Savard.... Name pronounced suh-VAHRD.
TRANSACTIONS/CAREER NOTES: Selected by Chicago Blackhawks as underage junior in first round (first Blackhawks pick, third overall) of NHL entry draft (June 11, 1980).... Strained knee (October 15, 1980).... Broke nose (January 7, 1984).... Injured ankle (October 13, 1984).... Bruised ribs (March 22, 1987).... Broke right ankle (January 21, 1989); missed 19 games.... Sprained left ankle (January 17, 1990).... Broke left index finger (January 26, 1990); missed 17 games.... Traded by Blackhawks to Montreal Canadiens for D Chris Chelios and second-round pick (C Michael Pomichter) in 1991 draft (June 29, 1990).... Suffered sinus infection (January 17, 1991); missed five games.... Injured right thumb (March 16, 1991).... Injured eye (October 30, 1991); missed two games. ... Suffered from the flu (November 22, 1992); missed two games.... Sprained knee (January 2, 1993); missed four games. ... Suspended one game by NHL for game misconduct penalties (January 23, 1993).... Separated shoulder (February 17, 1993); missed 10 games.... Signed as free agent by Tampa Bay Lightning (July 29, 1993).... Suspended four games and fined $500 by NHL for slashing (November 22, 1993).... Separated shoulder (March 7, 1995); missed three games.... Traded by Lightning to Blackhawks for sixth-round pick in 1996 draft (April 6, 1995).
HONORS: Won Michel Briere Trophy (1979-80).... Named to QMJHL All-Star first team (1979-80).... Named to THE SPORTING NEWS All-Star second team (1982-83).... Named to NHL All-Star second team (1982-83).... Played in NHL All-Star Game (1982-1984, 1986, 1988 and 1991).
RECORDS: Shares NHL record for fastest goal from start of period—4 seconds (January 12, 1986).

STATISTICAL PLATEAUS: Three-goal games: 1983-84 (1), 1984-85 (3), 1985-86 (1), 1986-87 (3), 1987-88 (2), 1989-90 (1), 1991-92 (1). Total: 12.
MISCELLANEOUS: Co-captain of Chicago Blackhawks (1987-88).... Member of Stanley Cup championship team (1993).

Season Team	League	REGULAR SEASON					PLAYOFFS				
		Gms.	G	A	Pts.	PIM	Gms.	G	A	Pts.	PIM
77-78—Montreal	QMJHL	72	37	79	116	22	—	—	—	—	—
78-79—Montreal	QMJHL	70	46	*112	158	88	11	5	6	11	46
79-80—Montreal	QMJHL	72	63	118	181	93	10	7	16	23	8
80-81—Chicago	NHL	76	28	47	75	47	3	0	0	0	0
81-82—Chicago	NHL	80	32	87	119	82	15	11	7	18	52
82-83—Chicago	NHL	78	35	86	121	99	13	8	9	17	22
83-84—Chicago	NHL	75	37	57	94	71	5	1	3	4	9
84-85—Chicago	NHL	79	38	67	105	56	15	9	20	29	20
85-86—Chicago	NHL	80	47	69	116	111	3	4	1	5	6
86-87—Chicago	NHL	70	40	50	90	108	4	1	0	1	12
87-88—Chicago	NHL	80	44	87	131	95	5	4	3	7	17
88-89—Chicago	NHL	58	23	59	82	110	16	8	11	19	10
89-90—Chicago	NHL	60	27	53	80	56	20	7	15	22	41
90-91—Montreal	NHL	70	28	31	59	52	13	2	11	13	35
91-92—Montreal	NHL	77	28	42	70	73	11	3	9	12	8
92-93—Montreal	NHL	63	16	34	50	90	14	0	5	5	4
93-94—Tampa Bay	NHL	74	18	28	46	106	—	—	—	—	—
94-95—Tampa Bay	NHL	31	6	11	17	10	—	—	—	—	—
—Chicago	NHL	12	4	4	8	8	16	7	11	18	10
NHL totals		1063	451	812	1263	1174	153	65	105	170	246

SAVARD, MARC
C, RANGERS

PERSONAL: Born July 17, 1977, in Ottawa.... 5-10/174.... Shoots left.
HIGH SCHOOL: Henry Street (Whitby, Ont.).
TRANSACTIONS/CAREER NOTES: Selected by New York Rangers in fourth round (third Rangers pick, 91st overall) of NHL entry draft (July 8, 1995).
HONORS: Won Can.HL Top Scorer Award (1994-95).... Won Eddie Powers Memorial Trophy (1994-95).... Named to OHL All-Star second team (1994-95).

Season Team	League	REGULAR SEASON					PLAYOFFS				
		Gms.	G	A	Pts.	PIM	Gms.	G	A	Pts.	PIM
92-93—Metcalfe	Jr. B	31	46	53	99	26	—	—	—	—	—
93-94—Oshawa	OHL	61	18	39	57	24	5	4	3	7	8
94-95—Oshawa	OHL	66	43	96	*139	78	7	5	6	11	8

SAVENKO, BOGDAN
RW, CANUCKS

PERSONAL: Born November 20, 1974, in Kiev, U.S.S.R.... 6-1/192.... Shoots right.... Name pronounced BAHG-dahn sah-VEHN-koh.
HIGH SCHOOL: Niagara Falls (Ont.).
TRANSACTIONS/CAREER NOTES: Selected by Chicago Blackhawks in third round (third Blackhawks pick, 54th overall) of NHL entry draft (June 26, 1993).... Traded by Blackhawks with third-round pick in 1995 draft (LW Larry Courville) to Vancouver Canucks for D Gerald Diduck (April 7, 1995).

Season Team	League	REGULAR SEASON					PLAYOFFS				
		Gms.	G	A	Pts.	PIM	Gms.	G	A	Pts.	PIM
90-91—SVSM Kiev	USSR Div. II	40	30	18	48	24	—	—	—	—	—
91-92—Sokol Kiev	CIS	25	3	1	4	4	—	—	—	—	—
92-93—Niagara Falls	OHL	51	29	19	48	15	2	1	0	1	2
93-94—Niagara Falls	OHL	62	42	49	91	22	—	—	—	—	—
94-95—Indianapolis	IHL	62	18	17	35	49	—	—	—	—	—

SAVOIE, CLAUDE
RW, SENATORS

PERSONAL: Born March 12, 1973, in Montreal.... 5-11/200.... Shoots right.... Name pronounced sav-WAH.
TRANSACTIONS/CAREER NOTES: Selected by Ottawa Senators in ninth round (ninth Senators pick, 194th overall) of NHL entry draft (June 20, 1992).

Season Team	League	REGULAR SEASON					PLAYOFFS				
		Gms.	G	A	Pts.	PIM	Gms.	G	A	Pts.	PIM
89-90—Victoriaville	QMJHL	61	6	6	12	24	16	0	0	0	2
90-91—Victoriaville	QMJHL	61	20	22	42	101	—	—	—	—	—
91-92—Victoriaville	QMJHL	69	39	40	79	140	—	—	—	—	—
92-93—Victoriaville	QMJHL	67	70	61	131	113	6	4	5	9	6
—New Haven	AHL	2	1	1	2	2	—	—	—	—	—
93-94—Prince Edward Island	AHL	77	13	15	28	118	—	—	—	—	—
94-95—Prince Edward Island	AHL	59	9	14	23	67	4	2	0	2	7

SAWYER, KEVIN
LW, BLUES

PERSONAL: Born February 18, 1974, in Christina Lake, B.C.... 6-2/205.... Shoots left.
TRANSACTIONS/CAREER NOTES: Signed as free agent by St. Louis Blues (February 16, 1995).

Season Team	League	REGULAR SEASON					PLAYOFFS				
		Gms.	G	A	Pts.	PIM	Gms.	G	A	Pts.	PIM
92-93—Spokane	WHL	62	4	3	7	274	—	—	—	—	—

Season	Team	League	Gms.	G	A	Pts.	PIM	Gms.	G	A	Pts.	PIM
93-94—Spokane		WHL	60	10	15	25	350	3	0	1	1	6
94-95—Spokane		WHL	54	7	9	16	365	11	2	0	2	58
—Peoria		IHL	—	—	—	—	—	2	0	0	0	12

SCATCHARD, DAVE
C, CANUCKS

PERSONAL: Born February 20, 1976, in Hinton, Alta. . . . 6-2/185. . . . Shoots right.
TRANSACTIONS/CAREER NOTES: Selected by Vancouver Canucks in second round (third Canucks pick, 42nd overall) of NHL entry draft (June 28, 1994).

Season	Team	League	Gms.	G	A	Pts.	PIM	Gms.	G	A	Pts.	PIM
92-93—Kimberley		Tier II Jr. A	51	20	23	43	61	—	—	—	—	—
93-94—Portland		WHL	47	9	11	20	46	10	2	1	3	4
94-95—Portland		WHL	71	20	30	50	148	8	0	3	3	21

SCHAEFER, PETER
LW, CANUCKS

PERSONAL: Born July 12, 1977, in Yellow Grass, Sask. . . . 5-11/178. . . . Shoots left.
HIGH SCHOOL: Crocus Plains (Brandon, Man.).
TRANSACTIONS/CAREER NOTES: Selected by Vancouver Canucks in third round (third Canucks pick, 66th overall) of NHL entry draft (July 8, 1995).

Season	Team	League	Gms.	G	A	Pts.	PIM	Gms.	G	A	Pts.	PIM
93-94—Brandon		WHL	2	1	0	1	0	—	—	—	—	—
94-95—Brandon		WHL	68	27	32	59	34	18	5	3	8	18

SCHAFER, PAXTON
G, BRUINS

PERSONAL: Born February 26, 1976, in Medicine Hat, Alta. . . . 5-9/152. . . . Catches left.
COLLEGE: Medicine Hat (Alta.).
TRANSACTIONS/CAREER NOTES: Selected by Boston Bruins in second round (third Bruins pick, 47th overall) of NHL entry draft (July 8, 1995).
HONORS: Named to Can.HL All-Star first team (1994-95). . . . Won Del Wilson Trophy (1994-95). . . . Named to WHL (East) All-Star first team (1994-95).

Season	Team	League	Gms.	Min.	W	L	T	GA	SO	Avg.	Gms.	Min.	W	L	GA	SO	Avg.
93-94—Medicine Hat		WHL	19	909	6	9	1	67	0	4.42	—	—	—	—	—	—	—
94-95—Medicine Hat		WHL	61	3519	32	26	2	185	0	3.15	5	339	1	4	18	0	3.19

SCHMIDT, COLIN
C, OILERS

PERSONAL: Born February 3, 1974, in Regina, Sask. . . . 5-11/185. . . . Shoots left.
COLLEGE: Colorado College.
TRANSACTIONS/CAREER NOTES: Selected by Edmonton Oilers in eighth round (ninth Oilers pick, 190th overall) of NHL entry draft (June 20, 1992).
HONORS: Named to WCHA All-Star second team (1994-95).

Season	Team	League	Gms.	G	A	Pts.	PIM	Gms.	G	A	Pts.	PIM
92-93—Colorado College		WCHA	27	8	13	21	26	—	—	—	—	—
93-94—Colorado College		WCHA	38	14	22	36	49	—	—	—	—	—
94-95—Colorado College		WCHA	43	26	31	57	61	—	—	—	—	—

SCHNEIDER, MATHIEU
D, ISLANDERS

PERSONAL: Born June 12, 1969, in New York. . . . 5-11/189. . . . Shoots left.
HIGH SCHOOL: Mount St. Charles Academy (Woonsocket, R.I.).
TRANSACTIONS/CAREER NOTES: Selected by Montreal Canadiens in third round (fourth Canadiens pick, 44th overall) of NHL entry draft (June 13, 1987). . . . Bruised left shoulder (February 1990). . . . Sprained left ankle (January 26, 1991); missed nine games. . . . Sprained ankle (January 27, 1993); missed 24 games. . . . Separated shoulder (April 18, 1993); missed seven playoff games. . . . Injured ankle (December 6, 1993); missed two games. . . . Underwent arthroscopic elbow surgery (March 29, 1994); missed five games. . . . Suffered from cold (February 27, 1995); missed one game. . . . Traded by Canadiens with LW Kirk Muller and C Craig Darby to New York Islanders for D Vladimir Malakhov and C Pierre Turgeon (April 5, 1995).
HONORS: Named to OHL All-Star first team (1987-88 and 1988-89).
MISCELLANEOUS: Member of Stanley Cup championship team (1993).

Season	Team	League	Gms.	G	A	Pts.	PIM	Gms.	G	A	Pts.	PIM
85-86—Mount St. Charles H.S.		R.I.H.S.	19	3	27	30	. . .	—	—	—	—	—
86-87—Cornwall		OHL	63	7	29	36	75	5	0	0	0	22
87-88—Montreal		NHL	4	0	0	0	2	—	—	—	—	—
—Cornwall		OHL	48	21	40	61	85	11	2	6	8	14
—Sherbrooke		AHL	—	—	—	—	—	3	0	3	3	12
88-89—Cornwall		OHL	59	16	57	73	96	18	7	20	27	30
89-90—Sherbrooke		AHL	28	6	13	19	20	—	—	—	—	—
—Montreal		NHL	44	7	14	21	25	9	1	3	4	31
90-91—Montreal		NHL	69	10	20	30	63	13	2	7	9	18
91-92—Montreal		NHL	78	8	24	32	72	10	1	4	5	6
92-93—Montreal		NHL	60	13	31	44	91	11	1	2	3	16
93-94—Montreal		NHL	75	20	32	52	62	1	0	0	0	0
94-95—Montreal		NHL	30	5	15	20	49	—	—	—	—	—
—New York Islanders		NHL	13	3	6	9	30	—	—	—	—	—
NHL totals			373	66	142	208	394	44	5	16	21	71

— 679 —

SCHWAB, COREY
G, DEVILS

PERSONAL: Born November 4, 1970, in Battleford, Sask. . . . 6-0/180. . . . Catches left. . . . Name pronounced SHWAHB.

TRANSACTIONS/CAREER NOTES: Selected by New Jersey Devils in 10th round (12th Devils pick, 200th overall) of NHL entry draft (June 16, 1990).

HONORS: Shared Harry (Hap) Holmes Memorial Trophy with Mike Dunham (1994-95). . . . Shared Jack Butterfield Trophy with Mike Dunham (1994-95). . . . Named to AHL All-Star second team (1994-95).

Season Team	League	REGULAR SEASON								PLAYOFFS						
		Gms.	Min.	W	L	T	GA	SO	Avg.	Gms.	Min.	W	L	GA	SO	Avg.
88-89—Seattle	WHL	10	386	2	2	0	31	0	4.82	—	—	—	—	—	—	—
89-90—Seattle	WHL	27	1150	15	2	1	69	0	3.60	3	49	0	0	2	0	2.45
90-91—Seattle	WHL	58	3289	32	18	3	224	1	4.09	6	382	1	5	25	0	3.93
91-92—Utica	AHL	24	1322	9	12	1	95	1	4.31	—	—	—	—	—	—	—
—Cincinnati	AHL	8	450	6	0	1	31	0	4.13	9	540	6	3	29	0	3.22
92-93—Utica	AHL	40	2387	18	16	5	169	2	4.25	1	59	0	1	6	0	6.10
—Cincinnati	IHL	3	185	1	2	0	17	0	5.51	—	—	—	—	—	—	—
93-94—Albany	AHL	51	3059	27	21	3	184	0	3.61	5	298	1	4	20	0	4.03
94-95—Albany	AHL	45	2711	25	10	9	117	3	*2.59	7	425	6	1	19	0	2.68

SELANNE, TEEMU
RW, JETS

PERSONAL: Born July 3, 1970, in Helsinki, Finland. . . . 6-0/200. . . . Shoots right. . . . Name pronounced TAY-moo suh-LAH-nay.

TRANSACTIONS/CAREER NOTES: Selected by Winnipeg Jets in first round (first Jets pick, 10th overall) of NHL entry draft (June 11, 1988). . . . Broke left leg (October 19, 1989). . . . Severed Achilles tendon (January 26, 1994); missed 33 games. . . . Played in Europe during 1994-95 NHL lockout. . . . Suffered from patella tendonitis (February 28, 1995); missed one game. . . . Suspended two games and fined $500 by NHL (March 28, 1995).

HONORS: Named to Finnish League All-Star team (1990-91 and 1991-92). . . . Named NHL Rookie of the Year by THE SPORTING NEWS (1992-93). . . . Won Calder Memorial Trophy (1992-93). . . . Named to THE SPORTING NEWS All-Star first team (1992-93). . . . Named to NHL All-Star first team (1992-93). . . . Named to NHL All-Rookie team (1992-93). . . . Played in NHL All-Star Game (1993 and 1994).

RECORDS: Holds NHL rookie-season records for most points—132; and goals—76 (1992).

STATISTICAL PLATEAUS: Three-goal games: 1992-93 (4), 1993-94 (2). Total: 6. . . . Four-goal games: 1992-93 (1). . . . Total hat tricks: 7.

Season Team	League	REGULAR SEASON					PLAYOFFS				
		Gms.	G	A	Pts.	PIM	Gms.	G	A	Pts.	PIM
87-88—Jokerit Helsinki	Finland	33	42	23	65	18	5	4	3	7	2
88-89—Jokerit Helsinki	Finland	34	35	33	68	12	5	7	3	10	4
89-90—Jokerit Helsinki	Finland	11	4	8	12	0	—	—	—	—	—
90-91—Jokerit Helsinki	Finland	42	*33	25	58	12	—	—	—	—	—
91-92—Finnish Olympic Team	Int'l	8	7	4	11	...	—	—	—	—	—
—Jokerit Helsinki	Finland	44	39	23	62	20	—	—	—	—	—
92-93—Winnipeg	NHL	84	†76	56	132	45	6	4	2	6	2
93-94—Winnipeg	NHL	51	25	29	54	22	—	—	—	—	—
94-95—Jokerit Helsinki	Finland	20	7	12	19	6	—	—	—	—	—
—Winnipeg	NHL	45	22	26	48	2	—	—	—	—	—
NHL totals		180	123	111	234	69	6	4	2	6	2

SELIVANOV, ALEXANDER
RW, LIGHTNING

PERSONAL: Born March 23, 1971, in Moscow, U.S.S.R. . . . 6-0/180. . . . Shoots left. . . . Name pronounced sehl-ih-VAN-ahf.

TRANSACTIONS/CAREER NOTES: Selected by Philadelphia Flyers in sixth round (sixth Flyers pick, 140th overall) of NHL entry draft (June 29, 1994). . . . Rights traded by Flyers to Tampa Bay Lightning for fourth-round pick in 1995 draft (September 6, 1994). . . . Loaned by Lightning to Chicago Wolves (December 14, 1994).

Season Team	League	REGULAR SEASON					PLAYOFFS				
		Gms.	G	A	Pts.	PIM	Gms.	G	A	Pts.	PIM
88-89—Spartak Moscow	USSR	1	0	0	0	0	—	—	—	—	—
89-90—Spartak Moscow	USSR	4	0	0	0	0	—	—	—	—	—
90-91—Spartak Moscow	USSR	21	3	1	4	6	—	—	—	—	—
91-92—Spartak Moscow	CIS	31	6	7	13	16	—	—	—	—	—
92-93—Spartak Moscow	CIS	42	12	19	31	16	3	2	0	2	2
93-94—Spartak Moscow	CIS	45	30	11	41	50	6	5	1	6	2
94-95—Atlanta	IHL	4	0	3	3	2	—	—	—	—	—
—Chicago	IHL	14	4	1	5	8	—	—	—	—	—
—Tampa Bay	NHL	43	10	6	16	14	—	—	—	—	—
NHL totals		43	10	6	16	14	—	—	—	—	—

SEMAK, ALEXANDER
C, LIGHTNING

PERSONAL: Born February 11, 1966, in Ufa, U.S.S.R. . . . 5-10/185. . . . Shoots left. . . . Name pronounced SEE-mahk.

TRANSACTIONS/CAREER NOTES: Selected by New Jersey Devils in 10th round (12th Devils pick, 207th overall) of NHL entry draft (June 11, 1988). . . . Injured shoulder (February 8, 1992); missed seven games. . . . Suffered injury (November 30, 1993); missed two games. . . . Strained knee (December 11, 1993); missed 17 games. . . . Played in Europe during 1994-95 NHL lockout. . . . Traded by Devils with RW Ben Hankinson to Tampa Bay Lightning for D Shawn Chambers and RW Danton Cole (March 14, 1995).

STATISTICAL PLATEAUS: Three-goal games: 1993-94 (1).

Season	Team	League	Gms.	G	A	Pts.	PIM	Gms.	G	A	Pts.	PIM
82-83—Salavat Yulayev Ufa	USSR		13	2	1	3	4	—	—	—	—	—
83-84—Salavat Yulayev Ufa	USSR					Statistics unavailable.						
84-85—Salavat Yulayev Ufa	USSR		47	19	17	36	64	—	—	—	—	—
85-86—Salavat Yulayev Ufa	USSR		22	9	7	16	22	—	—	—	—	—
86-87—Dynamo Moscow	USSR		40	20	8	28	32	—	—	—	—	—
87-88—Dynamo Moscow	USSR		47	21	14	35	40	—	—	—	—	—
88-89—Dynamo Moscow	USSR		44	18	10	28	22	—	—	—	—	—
89-90—Dynamo Moscow	USSR		43	23	11	34	33	—	—	—	—	—
90-91—Dynamo Moscow	USSR		46	17	21	38	48	—	—	—	—	—
91-92—Dynamo Moscow	CIS		18	6	11	17	18	—	—	—	—	—
—Utica	AHL		7	3	2	5	0	—	—	—	—	—
—New Jersey	NHL		25	5	6	11	0	1	0	0	0	0
92-93—New Jersey	NHL		82	37	42	79	70	5	1	1	2	0
93-94—New Jersey	NHL		54	12	17	29	22	2	0	0	0	0
94-95—Salavat Yulayev Ufa	CIS		9	9	6	15	4	—	—	—	—	—
—New Jersey	NHL		19	2	6	8	13	—	—	—	—	—
—Tampa Bay	NHL		22	5	5	10	12	—	—	—	—	—
NHL totals			202	61	76	137	117	8	1	1	2	0

SEMENOV, ANATOLI
C/LW, FLYERS

PERSONAL: Born March 5, 1962, in Moscow, U.S.S.R. . . . 6-2/190. . . . Shoots left. . . . Name pronounced AN-uh-TOH-lee SEH-muh-nahfhf.

TRANSACTIONS/CAREER NOTES: Selected by Edmonton Oilers in sixth round (fifth Oilers pick, 120th overall) of NHL entry draft (June 17, 1989). . . . Bruised ribs (March 1, 1991); missed five games. . . . Suffered hairline fracture in left foot (October 1991); missed four games. . . . Suffered concussion (November 1991); missed two games. . . . Injured shoulder (January 4, 1992); missed six games. . . . Sprained ankle (February 28, 1992); missed one game. . . . Selected by Tampa Bay Lightning in NHL expansion draft (June 18, 1992). . . . Traded by Lightning to Vancouver Canucks for C Dave Capuano and fourth-round pick (traded to New Jersey Devils) in 1994 draft (November 3, 1992). . . . Strained knee (January 9, 1993); missed six games. . . . Selected by Mighty Ducks of Anaheim in NHL expansion draft (June 24, 1993). . . . Dislocated elbow (December 7, 1993); missed 21 games. . . . Aggravated elbow injury (January 28, 1994); missed two games. . . . Traded by Mighty Ducks to Philadelphia Flyers for D Milos Holan (March 8, 1995).
HONORS: Named to Soviet League All-Star team (1984-85).
MISCELLANEOUS: Member of gold-medal-winning U.S.S.R. Olympic team (1988).

Season	Team	League	Gms.	G	A	Pts.	PIM	Gms.	G	A	Pts.	PIM
79-80—Dynamo Moscow	USSR		8	3	0	3	2	—	—	—	—	—
80-81—Dynamo Moscow	USSR		47	18	14	32	18	—	—	—	—	—
81-82—Dynamo Moscow	USSR		44	12	14	26	28	—	—	—	—	—
82-83—Dynamo Moscow	USSR		44	22	18	40	26	—	—	—	—	—
83-84—Dynamo Moscow	USSR		19	10	5	15	14	—	—	—	—	—
84-85—Dynamo Moscow	USSR		30	17	12	29	32	—	—	—	—	—
85-86—Dynamo Moscow	USSR		32	18	17	35	19	—	—	—	—	—
86-87—Dynamo Moscow	USSR		40	15	29	44	32	—	—	—	—	—
87-88—Dynamo Moscow	USSR		32	17	8	25	22	—	—	—	—	—
88-89—Dynamo Moscow	USSR		31	9	12	21	24	—	—	—	—	—
89-90—Dynamo Moscow	USSR		48	13	20	33	16	—	—	—	—	—
—Edmonton	NHL		—	—	—	—	—	2	0	0	0	0
90-91—Edmonton	NHL		57	15	16	31	26	12	5	5	10	6
91-92—Edmonton	NHL		59	20	22	42	16	8	1	1	2	6
92-93—Tampa Bay	NHL		13	2	3	5	4	—	—	—	—	—
—Vancouver	NHL		62	10	34	44	28	12	1	3	4	0
93-94—Anaheim	NHL		49	11	19	30	12	—	—	—	—	—
94-95—Anaheim	NHL		15	3	4	7	4	—	—	—	—	—
—Philadelphia	NHL		26	1	2	3	6	15	2	4	6	0
NHL totals			281	62	100	162	96	49	9	13	22	12

SEROWIK, JEFF
D, BRUINS

PERSONAL: Born October 1, 1967, in Manchester, N.H. . . . 6-0/190. . . . Shoots right. . . . Full name: Jeff Michael Serowik. . . . Name pronounced sair-OH-wihk.
HIGH SCHOOL: West (Manchester, N.H.), then Lawrence Academy (Groton, Mass.).
COLLEGE: Providence.
TRANSACTIONS/CAREER NOTES: Broke left ankle (April 1982). . . . Broke right ankle (March 1983). . . . Selected by Toronto Maple Leafs in fifth round (fifth Maple Leafs pick, 85th overall) of NHL entry draft (June 15, 1985). . . . Signed as free agent by Florida Panthers (July 20, 1993). . . . Signed as free agent by Boston Bruins (June 29, 1994).
HONORS: Named to Hockey East All-Star second team (1989-90). . . . Named to AHL All-Star second team (1992-93). . . . Won Eddie Shore Plaque (1994-95). . . . Named to AHL All-Star first team (1994-95).

Season	Team	League	Gms.	G	A	Pts.	PIM	Gms.	G	A	Pts.	PIM
83-84—Manchester West H.S.	N.H. H.S.		21	12	12	24	. . .	—	—	—	—	—
84-85—Lawrence Academy	Mass. H.S.		24	8	25	33	. . .	—	—	—	—	—
85-86—Lawrence Academy	Mass. H.S.					Statistics unavailable.						
86-87—Providence College	Hockey East		33	3	8	11	22	—	—	—	—	—
87-88—Providence College	Hockey East		33	3	9	12	44	—	—	—	—	—

Season Team	League	REGULAR SEASON					PLAYOFFS				
		Gms.	G	A	Pts.	PIM	Gms.	G	A	Pts.	PIM
88-89—Providence College	Hockey East	35	3	14	17	48	—	—	—	—	—
89-90—Providence College	Hockey East	35	6	19	25	34	—	—	—	—	—
90-91—Toronto	NHL	1	0	0	0	0	—	—	—	—	—
—Newmarket	AHL	60	8	15	23	45	—	—	—	—	—
91-92—St. John's	AHL	78	11	34	45	60	16	4	9	13	22
92-93—St. John's	AHL	77	19	35	54	92	9	1	5	6	8
93-94—Cincinnati	IHL	79	6	21	27	98	7	0	1	1	8
94-95—Providence	AHL	78	28	34	62	102	13	4	6	10	10
—Boston	NHL	1	0	0	0	0	—	—	—	—	—
NHL totals		2	0	0	0	0					

SEVERYN, BRENT
D, ISLANDERS

PERSONAL: Born February 22, 1966, in Vegreville, Alta. . . . 6-2/210. . . . Shoots left. . . . Full name: Brent Leonard Severyn.
COLLEGE: Alberta.
TRANSACTIONS/CAREER NOTES: Selected by Winnipeg Jets in fifth round (fifth Jets pick, 99th overall) of NHL entry draft (June 9, 1984). . . . Injured knee (October 1985). . . . Signed as free agent by Quebec Nordiques (July 15, 1988). . . . Traded by Nordiques to New Jersey Devils for D Dave Marcinyshyn (June 3, 1991). . . . Traded by Devils to Jets for sixth-round pick (C Ryan Smart) in 1994 draft (September 30, 1993). . . . Traded by Jets to Florida Panthers for D Milan Tichy (October 3, 1993). . . . Suffered left eye abrasion (November 23, 1993); missed one game. . . . Traded by Panthers to New York Islanders for fourth-round pick (LW Dave Duerden) in 1995 draft (March 3, 1995). . . . Injured knee (March 16, 1995); missed four games.
HONORS: Named to CWUAA All-Star team (1987-88). . . . Named to AHL All-Star first team (1992-93).

Season Team	League	REGULAR SEASON					PLAYOFFS				
		Gms.	G	A	Pts.	PIM	Gms.	G	A	Pts.	PIM
82-83—Vegreville	CAJHL	21	20	22	42	10	—	—	—	—	—
83-84—Seattle	WHL	72	14	22	36	49	5	2	1	3	2
84-85—Seattle	WHL	38	8	32	40	54	—	—	—	—	—
—Brandon	WHL	26	7	16	23	57	—	—	—	—	—
85-86—Seattle	WHL	33	11	20	31	164	5	0	4	4	4
—Saskatoon	WHL	9	1	4	5	38	—	—	—	—	—
86-87—University of Alberta	CWUAA	43	7	19	26	171	—	—	—	—	—
87-88—University of Alberta	CWUAA	46	21	29	50	178	—	—	—	—	—
88-89—Halifax	AHL	47	2	12	14	141	—	—	—	—	—
89-90—Quebec	NHL	35	0	2	2	42	—	—	—	—	—
—Halifax	AHL	43	6	9	15	105	6	1	2	3	49
90-91—Halifax	AHL	50	7	26	33	202	—	—	—	—	—
91-92—Utica	AHL	80	11	33	44	211	4	0	1	1	4
92-93—Utica	AHL	77	20	32	52	240	5	0	0	0	35
93-94—Florida	NHL	67	4	7	11	156	—	—	—	—	—
94-95—Florida	NHL	9	1	1	2	37	—	—	—	—	—
—New York Islanders	NHL	19	1	3	4	34	—	—	—	—	—
NHL totals		130	6	13	19	269					

SEVIGNY, PIERRE
LW, CANADIENS

PERSONAL: Born September 8, 1971, in Trois-Rivieres, Que. . . . 6-0/189. . . . Shoots left. . . . Name pronounced SEH-vehn-yee.
TRANSACTIONS/CAREER NOTES: Selected by Montreal Canadiens in third round (fourth Canadiens pick, 51st overall) of NHL entry draft (June 17, 1989). . . . Severed knee ligament in off-ice accident (March 25, 1991). . . . Tore knee ligaments (December 6, 1993); missed 23 games.
HONORS: Named to QMJHL All-Star second team (1989-90 and 1990-91).

Season Team	League	REGULAR SEASON					PLAYOFFS				
		Gms.	G	A	Pts.	PIM	Gms.	G	A	Pts.	PIM
88-89—Verdun	QMJHL	67	27	43	70	88	—	—	—	—	—
89-90—St. Hyacinthe	QMJHL	67	47	72	119	205	12	8	8	16	42
90-91—St. Hyacinthe	QMJHL	60	36	46	82	203	—	—	—	—	—
91-92—Fredericton	AHL	74	22	37	59	145	7	1	1	2	26
92-93—Fredericton	AHL	80	36	40	76	113	5	1	1	2	2
93-94—Montreal	NHL	43	4	5	9	42	3	0	1	1	0
94-95—Montreal	NHL	19	0	0	0	15	—	—	—	—	—
NHL totals		62	4	5	9	57	3	0	1	1	0

SHALDYBIN, YEVEGNY
D, BRUINS

PERSONAL: Born July 29, 1975, in Novosibirsk, U.S.S.R. . . . 6-1/198. . . . Shoots left.
TRANSACTIONS/CAREER NOTES: Selected by Boston Bruins in sixth round (fifth Bruin pick, 151st overall) of NHL entry draft (July 8, 1995).

Season Team	League	REGULAR SEASON					PLAYOFFS				
		Gms.	G	A	Pts.	PIM	Gms.	G	A	Pts.	PIM
93-94—Torpedo Yaroslavl	CIS	14	0	0	0	0	—	—	—	—	—
94-95—Torpedo Yaroslavl	CIS	42	2	5	7	10	4	0	1	1	0

S

SHANAHAN, BRENDAN

LW, WHALERS

PERSONAL: Born January 23, 1969, in Mimico, Ont. . . . 6-3/215. . . . Shoots right. . . . Full name: Brendan Frederick Shanahan.
HIGH SCHOOL: Michael Power/St. Joseph's (Islington, Ont.).
TRANSACTIONS/CAREER NOTES: Bruised tendons in shoulder (January 1987). . . . Selected by New Jersey Devils as underage junior in first round (first Devils pick, second overall) of NHL entry draft (June 13, 1987). . . . Broke nose (December 1987). . . . Suffered back spasms (March 1989). . . . Suspended five games by NHL for stick-fighting (January 13, 1990). . . . Suffered lower abdominal strain (February 1990). . . . Suffered lacerations to lower right side of face and underwent surgery (January 8, 1991); missed five games. . . . Signed as free agent by St. Louis Blues (July 25, 1991); D Scott Stevens awarded to Devils as compensation (September 3, 1991). . . . Pulled groin (October 24, 1992); missed 12 games. . . . Suspended six off-days and fined $500 by NHL for hitting another player in face with his stick (January 7, 1993). . . . Suspended one game by NHL for high-sticking incident (February 23, 1993). . . . Suffered viral infection (November 18, 1993); missed one game. . . . Injured hamstring (March 22, 1994); missed two games. . . . Played in Europe during 1994-95 NHL lockout. . . . Suffered viral infection (January 20, 1995); missed three games. . . . Broke ankle (May 15, 1995); missed last two games of playoffs. . . . Traded by Blues to Hartford Whalers for D Chris Pronger (July 27, 1995).
HONORS: Played in NHL All-Star Game (1994). . . . Named to NHL All-Star first team (1993-94).
STATISTICAL PLATEAUS: Three-goal games: 1992-93 (1), 1993-94 (4). Total: 5.

Season Team	League	REGULAR SEASON					PLAYOFFS				
		Gms.	G	A	Pts.	PIM	Gms.	G	A	Pts.	PIM
84-85—Mississauga	MTHL	36	20	21	41	26	—	—	—	—	—
85-86—London	OHL	59	28	34	62	70	5	5	5	10	5
86-87—London	OHL	56	39	53	92	128	—	—	—	—	—
87-88—New Jersey	NHL	65	7	19	26	131	12	2	1	3	44
88-89—New Jersey	NHL	68	22	28	50	115	—	—	—	—	—
89-90—New Jersey	NHL	73	30	42	72	137	6	3	3	6	20
90-91—New Jersey	NHL	75	29	37	66	141	7	3	5	8	12
91-92—St. Louis	NHL	80	33	36	69	171	6	2	3	5	14
92-93—St. Louis	NHL	71	51	43	94	174	11	4	3	7	18
93-94—St. Louis	NHL	81	52	50	102	211	4	2	5	7	4
94-95—Dusseldorf	Germany	3	5	3	8	4	—	—	—	—	—
—St. Louis	NHL	45	20	21	41	136	5	4	5	9	14
NHL totals		558	244	276	520	1216	51	20	25	45	126

SHANK, DANIEL

RW

PERSONAL: Born May 12, 1967, in Montreal. . . . 5-11/200. . . . Shoots right.
TRANSACTIONS/CAREER NOTES: Signed as free agent by Detroit Red Wings (July 13, 1988). . . . Traded by Red Wings to Hartford Whalers for C/LW Chris Tancill (December 18, 1991). . . . Traded by Detroit Vipers to Las Vegas Thunder for LW Alex Hicks and cash (August 3, 1995).
HONORS: Named to IHL All-Star first team (1992-93).

Season Team	League	REGULAR SEASON					PLAYOFFS				
		Gms.	G	A	Pts.	PIM	Gms.	G	A	Pts.	PIM
85-86—Shawinigan	QMJHL	51	34	38	72	184	—	—	—	—	—
86-87—Hull	QMJHL	46	26	43	69	325	—	—	—	—	—
87-88—Hull	QMJHL	52	31	42	73	343	19	10	19	29	*106
88-89—Adirondack	AHL	42	5	20	25	113	17	11	8	19	102
89-90—Detroit	NHL	57	11	13	24	143	—	—	—	—	—
—Adirondack	AHL	14	8	8	16	36	—	—	—	—	—
90-91—Detroit	NHL	7	0	1	1	14	—	—	—	—	—
—Adirondack	AHL	60	26	49	75	278	—	—	—	—	—
91-92—Adirondack	AHL	27	13	21	34	112	—	—	—	—	—
—Hartford	NHL	13	2	0	2	18	5	0	0	0	22
—Springfield	AHL	31	9	19	28	83	8	8	0	8	48
92-93—San Diego	IHL	77	39	53	92	*495	14	5	10	15	*131
93-94—San Diego	IHL	63	27	36	63	273	—	—	—	—	—
—Phoenix	IHL	7	4	6	10	26	—	—	—	—	—
94-95—Minnesota	IHL	19	4	11	15	30	—	—	—	—	—
—Detroit	IHL	54	44	27	71	142	5	2	2	4	6
NHL totals		77	13	14	27	175	5	0	0	0	22

SHANNON, DARRIN

LW, JETS

PERSONAL: Born December 8, 1969, in Barrie, Ont. . . . 6-2/210. . . . Shoots left. . . . Brother of Darryl Shannon, defenseman, Winnipeg Jets.
TRANSACTIONS/CAREER NOTES: Separated right shoulder (November 1986). . . . Dislocated left elbow (November 1987). . . . Separated left shoulder (January 1988). . . . Selected by Pittsburgh Penguins in first round (first Penguins pick, fourth overall) of NHL entry draft (June 11, 1988). . . . Traded by Penguins with D Doug Bodger to Buffalo Sabres for G Tom Barrasso and third-round pick (LW Joe Dziedzic) in 1990 draft (November 12, 1988). . . . Strained knee ligaments (May 1990). . . . Injured jaw (January 8, 1991); missed five games. . . . Traded by Sabres with LW Mike Hartman and D Dean Kennedy to Winnipeg Jets for RW Dave McLlwain, D Gordon Donnelly, fifth-round pick in 1992 draft (LW Yuri Khmylev) and future considerations (October 11, 1991). . . . Injured knee (November 20, 1991). . . . Injured eye (November 25, 1991); missed one game. . . . Sprained leg (December 31, 1991); missed seven games. . . . Strained calf (October 1, 1993); missed five games. . . . Fractured rib (February 4, 1995); missed seven games. . . . Strained abdomen (March 11, 1995); missed one game. . . . Strained left groin (March 20, 1995); missed last 21 games of season.
HONORS: Named to OHL All-Scholastic team (1986-87). . . . Won Bobby Smith Trophy (1987-88). . . . Named to Memorial Cup All-Star team (1987-88).

Season Team	League	REGULAR SEASON					PLAYOFFS				
		Gms.	G	A	Pts.	PIM	Gms.	G	A	Pts.	PIM
85-86—Barrie Jr. B	OHA	40	13	22	35	21	—	—	—	—	—
86-87—Windsor	OHL	60	16	67	83	116	14	4	6	10	8
87-88—Windsor	OHL	43	33	41	74	49	12	6	12	18	9

Season Team	League	REGULAR SEASON					PLAYOFFS				
		Gms.	G	A	Pts.	PIM	Gms.	G	A	Pts.	PIM
88-89—Windsor	OHL	54	33	48	81	47	4	1	6	7	2
—Buffalo	NHL	3	0	0	0	0	2	0	0	0	0
89-90—Buffalo	NHL	17	2	7	9	4	6	0	1	1	4
—Rochester	AHL	50	20	23	43	25	9	4	1	5	2
90-91—Rochester	AHL	49	26	34	60	56	10	3	5	8	22
—Buffalo	NHL	34	8	6	14	12	6	1	2	3	4
91-92—Buffalo	NHL	1	0	1	1	0	—	—	—	—	—
—Winnipeg	NHL	68	13	26	39	41	7	0	1	1	10
92-93—Winnipeg	NHL	84	20	40	60	91	6	2	4	6	6
93-94—Winnipeg	NHL	77	21	37	58	87	—	—	—	—	—
94-95—Winnipeg	NHL	19	5	3	8	14	—	—	—	—	—
NHL totals		303	69	120	189	249	27	3	8	11	24

SHANNON, DARRYL
D, JETS

PERSONAL: Born June 21, 1968, in Barrie, Ont. . . . 6-2/200. . . . Shoots left. . . . Brother of Darrin Shannon, left winger, Winnipeg Jets.
TRANSACTIONS/CAREER NOTES: Selected by Toronto Maple Leafs in second round (second Maple Leafs pick, 36th overall) of NHL entry draft (June 21, 1986). . . . Broke right leg and right thumb, bruised chest and suffered slipped disk in automobile accident (June 20, 1990). . . . Signed as free agent with Winnipeg Jets (July 8, 1993).
HONORS: Named to OHL All-Star second team (1986-87). . . . Won Max Kaminsky Trophy (1987-88). . . . Named to OHL All-Star first team (1987-88). . . . Named to Memorial Cup All-Star team (1987-88).

Season Team	League	REGULAR SEASON					PLAYOFFS				
		Gms.	G	A	Pts.	PIM	Gms.	G	A	Pts.	PIM
84-85—Barrie Jr. B	OHA	39	5	23	28	50	—	—	—	—	—
85-86—Windsor	OHL	57	6	21	27	52	16	5	6	11	22
86-87—Windsor	OHL	64	23	27	50	83	14	4	8	12	18
87-88—Windsor	OHL	60	16	70	86	116	12	3	8	11	17
88-89—Toronto	NHL	14	1	3	4	6	—	—	—	—	—
—Newmarket	AHL	61	5	24	29	37	5	0	3	3	10
89-90—Newmarket	AHL	47	4	15	19	58	—	—	—	—	—
—Toronto	NHL	10	0	1	1	12	—	—	—	—	—
90-91—Toronto	NHL	10	0	1	1	0	—	—	—	—	—
—Newmarket	AHL	47	2	14	16	51	—	—	—	—	—
91-92—Toronto	NHL	48	2	8	10	23	—	—	—	—	—
92-93—Toronto	NHL	16	0	0	0	11	—	—	—	—	—
—St. John's	AHL	7	1	1	2	4	—	—	—	—	—
93-94—Moncton	AHL	37	1	10	11	62	20	1	7	8	32
—Winnipeg	NHL	20	0	4	4	18	—	—	—	—	—
94-95—Winnipeg	NHL	40	5	9	14	48	—	—	—	—	—
NHL totals		158	8	26	34	118					

SHANTZ, JEFF
C, BLACKHAWKS

PERSONAL: Born October 10, 1973, in Edmonton. . . . 6-0/185. . . . Shoots right.
HIGH SCHOOL: Robert Usher (Regina, Sask.).
TRANSACTIONS/CAREER NOTES: Selected by Chicago Blackhawks in second round (second Blackhawks pick, 36th overall) of NHL entry draft (June 20, 1992). . . . Bruised right shoulder (1993-94 season); missed six games.
HONORS: Named to WHL (East) All-Star first team (1992-93).

Season Team	League	REGULAR SEASON					PLAYOFFS				
		Gms.	G	A	Pts.	PIM	Gms.	G	A	Pts.	PIM
89-90—Regina	WHL	1	0	0	0	0	—	—	—	—	—
90-91—Regina	WHL	69	16	21	37	22	8	2	2	4	2
91-92—Regina	WHL	72	39	50	89	75	—	—	—	—	—
92-93—Regina	WHL	64	29	54	83	75	13	2	12	14	14
93-94—Chicago	NHL	52	3	13	16	30	6	0	0	0	6
—Indianapolis	IHL	19	5	9	14	20	—	—	—	—	—
94-95—Indianapolis	IHL	32	9	15	24	20	—	—	—	—	—
—Chicago	NHL	45	6	12	18	33	16	3	1	4	2
NHL totals		97	9	25	34	63	22	3	1	4	8

SHARIFIJANOV, VADIM
RW, DEVILS

PERSONAL: Born December 23, 1975, in Ufa, U.S.S.R. . . . 6-0/183. . . . Shoots left. . . . Name pronounced SHARE-in-off.
TRANSACTIONS/CAREER NOTES: Selected by New Jersey Devils in first round (first Devils pick, 25th overall) of NHL entry draft (June 28, 1994).

Season Team	League	REGULAR SEASON					PLAYOFFS				
		Gms.	G	A	Pts.	PIM	Gms.	G	A	Pts.	PIM
92-93—Salavat Yulayev Ufa	CIS	37	6	4	10	16	2	1	0	1	0
93-94—Salavat Yulayev Ufa	CIS	46	10	6	16	36	5	3	0	3	4
94-95—CSKA Moscow	CIS	34	7	3	10	26	2	0	0	0	0
—Albany	AHL	1	1	1	2	0	9	3	3	6	10

SHARPLES, JEFF
D

PERSONAL: Born July 28, 1967, in Terrace, B.C. . . . . 6-1/195. . . . Shoots left.
TRANSACTIONS/CAREER NOTES: Selected by Detroit Red Wings as underage junior in second round (second Red Wings pick, 29th overall) of NHL entry draft (June 15, 1985). . . . Injured ankle (February 1989). . . . Separated shoulder (October 20, 1989). . . . Traded by Detroit Red Wings with C/RW Joe Murphy, C/LW Adam Graves and LW Petr Klima to Edmonton Oilers for C Jimmy Carson, C Kevin McClelland and fifth-round pick (traded to Montreal Canadiens who selected D Brad Layzell) in 1991 draft (November 2, 1989). . . . Traded by Oilers to New Jersey Devils for D Reijo Ruotsalainen (March 6, 1990). . . . Signed as free agent by Kansas City Blades (November 30, 1992). . . . Signed as free agent by Las Vegas Thunder (August 31, 1993).
HONORS: Named to WHL All-Star second team (1984-85).

Season Team	League	REGULAR SEASON					PLAYOFFS				
		Gms.	G	A	Pts.	PIM	Gms.	G	A	Pts.	PIM
83-84—Kelowna Wings	WHL	72	9	24	33	51	—	—	—	—	—
84-85—Kelowna Wings	WHL	72	12	41	53	90	6	0	1	1	6
85-86—Portland	WHL	19	2	6	8	44	15	2	6	8	6
—Spokane	WHL	3	0	0	0	4	—	—	—	—	—
86-87—Portland	WHL	44	25	35	60	92	20	7	15	22	23
—Detroit	NHL	3	0	1	1	2	2	0	0	0	2
87-88—Detroit	NHL	56	10	25	35	42	4	0	3	3	4
—Adirondack	AHL	4	2	1	3	4	—	—	—	—	—
88-89—Adirondack	AHL	10	0	4	4	8	—	—	—	—	—
—Detroit	NHL	46	4	9	13	26	1	0	0	0	0
89-90—Adirondack	AHL	9	2	5	7	6	—	—	—	—	—
—Cape Breton	AHL	38	4	13	17	28	—	—	—	—	—
—Utica	AHL	13	2	5	7	19	5	1	2	3	15
90-91—Utica	AHL	64	16	29	45	42	—	—	—	—	—
91-92—Capital District	AHL	31	3	12	15	18	7	6	5	11	4
92-93—Kansas City	IHL	39	5	21	26	43	8	0	0	0	6
93-94—Las Vegas	IHL	68	18	32	50	68	5	2	1	3	6
94-95—Las Vegas	IHL	72	20	33	53	63	10	4	4	8	18
NHL totals		105	14	35	49	70	7	0	3	3	6

SHAW, BRAD
D, SENATORS

PERSONAL: Born April 28, 1964, in Cambridge, Ont. . . . 6-0/190. . . . Shoots right. . . . Full name: Bradley William Shaw.
HIGH SCHOOL: Canterbury (Ottawa), then Eastwood (Kitchener, Ont.).
TRANSACTIONS/CAREER NOTES: Selected by Detroit Red Wings as underage junior in fifth round (fifth Red Wings pick, 86th overall) of NHL entry draft (June 9, 1982). . . . Traded by Red Wings to Hartford Whalers for eighth-round pick (LW Lars Karlsson) in 1984 draft (May 29, 1984). . . . Fractured finger on left hand (February 1988). . . . Broke nose (October 21, 1989). . . . Suffered back spasms (November 12, 1989). . . . Bruised right foot (February 28, 1990). . . . Injured groin (October 28, 1991); missed two games. . . . Injured knee (January 31, 1992); missed four games. . . . Bruised knee (February 29, 1992); missed four games. . . . Injured groin (March 14, 1992); missed three games. . . . Traded by Whalers to New Jersey Devils for future considerations (June 15, 1992). . . . Selected by Ottawa Senators in NHL expansion draft (June 18, 1992). . . . Suffered slight concussion (October 8, 1992); missed two games. . . . Suffered back spasms (December 22, 1993); missed five games. . . . Suffered back spasms (March 4, 1994); missed nine games. . . . Pulled abdominal muscle (September 1994); missed first 10 games of season. . . . Loaned by Senators to Atlanta Knights of IHL (February 10, 1995).
HONORS: Won Max Kaminsky Trophy (1983-84). . . . Named to OHL All-Star first team (1983-84). . . . Won Eddie Shore Plaque (1986-87). . . . Named to AHL All-Star first team (1986-87 and 1987-88). . . . Named to NHL All-Rookie team (1989-90).
MISCELLANEOUS: Captain of Ottawa Senators (1993-94).

Season Team	League	REGULAR SEASON					PLAYOFFS				
		Gms.	G	A	Pts.	PIM	Gms.	G	A	Pts.	PIM
81-82—Ottawa	OHL	68	13	59	72	24	15	1	13	14	4
82-83—Ottawa	OHL	63	12	66	78	24	9	2	9	11	4
83-84—Ottawa	OHL	68	11	71	82	75	13	2	*27	29	9
84-85—Salt Lake City	IHL	44	3	29	32	25	—	—	—	—	—
—Binghamton	AHL	24	1	10	11	4	8	1	8	9	6
85-86—Hartford	NHL	8	0	2	2	4	—	—	—	—	—
—Binghamton	AHL	64	10	44	54	33	5	0	2	2	6
86-87—Hartford	NHL	2	0	0	0	0	—	—	—	—	—
—Binghamton	AHL	77	9	30	39	43	12	1	8	9	2
87-88—Binghamton	AHL	73	12	50	62	50	4	0	5	5	4
—Hartford	NHL	1	0	0	0	0	—	—	—	—	—
88-89—Verice	Italy	35	10	30	40	44	11	4	8	12	13
—Hartford	NHL	3	1	0	1	0	3	1	0	1	0
—Canadian national team	Int'l	4	1	0	1	2	—	—	—	—	—
89-90—Hartford	NHL	64	3	32	35	30	7	2	5	7	0
90-91—Hartford	NHL	72	4	28	32	29	6	1	2	3	2
91-92—Hartford	NHL	62	3	22	25	44	3	0	1	1	4
92-93—Ottawa	NHL	81	7	34	41	34	—	—	—	—	—
93-94—Ottawa	NHL	66	4	19	23	59	—	—	—	—	—
94-95—Ottawa	NHL	2	0	0	0	0	—	—	—	—	—
—Atlanta	IHL	26	1	18	19	17	5	3	4	7	9
NHL totals		361	22	137	159	200	19	4	8	12	6

S

SHAW, DAVID
D, BRUINS

PERSONAL: Born May 25, 1964, in St. Thomas, Ont.... 6-2/204.... Shoots right.
TRANSACTIONS/CAREER NOTES: Selected by Quebec Nordiques as underage junior in first round (first Nordiques pick, 13th overall) of NHL entry draft (June 9, 1982).... Sprained wrist (December 18, 1985).... Traded by Nordiques with LW John Ogrodnick to New York Rangers for LW Jeff Jackson and D Terry Carkner (September 30, 1987).... Separated shoulder (October 1987).... Suspended 12 games by NHL for slashing (October 27, 1988).... Bruised shoulder (March 15, 1989).... Dislocated right shoulder (November 2, 1989).... Reinjured right shoulder (November 22, 1989); missed 10 games.... Underwent surgery to right shoulder (February 7, 1990).... Bruised finger (September 1990).... Bruised left big toe (October 31, 1990).... Sprained knee (October 20, 1991).... Traded by Rangers to Edmonton Oilers for D Jeff Beukeboom (November 12, 1991) to complete deal in which Rangers traded C Bernie Nicholls, LW Louie DeBrusk, RW Steven Rice and future considerations to Oilers for C Mark Messier and future considerations (October 4, 1991).... Traded by Oilers to Minnesota North Stars for D Brian Glynn (January 21, 1992).... Traded by North Stars to Boston Bruins for future considerations (September 2, 1992).... Injured thigh (October 1992); missed one game.... Injured foot (December 1992); missed one game.... Injured ribs (March 1993); missed five games.... Suffered pinched nerve (December 26, 1993); missed three games.... Suffered charley horse (January 6, 1994); missed seven games.... Injured knee (January 28, 1994); missed 17 games.... Injured shoulder (April 1995); missed three games.
HONORS: Named to OHL All-Star first team (1983-84).... Named to Memorial Cup All-Star team (1983-84).

Season Team	League	REGULAR SEASON					PLAYOFFS				
		Gms.	G	A	Pts.	PIM	Gms.	G	A	Pts.	PIM
80-81—Stratford Jr. B	OHA	41	12	19	31	30	—	—	—	—	—
81-82—Kitchener	OHL	68	6	25	31	99	15	2	2	4	51
82-83—Kitchener	OHL	57	18	56	74	78	12	2	10	12	18
—Quebec	NHL	2	0	0	0	0	—	—	—	—	—
83-84—Kitchener	OHL	58	14	34	48	73	16	4	9	13	12
—Quebec	NHL	3	0	0	0	0	—	—	—	—	—
84-85—Guelph	OHL	2	0	0	0	0	—	—	—	—	—
—Fredericton	AHL	48	7	6	13	73	2	0	0	0	7
—Quebec	NHL	14	0	0	0	11	—	—	—	—	—
85-86—Quebec	NHL	73	7	19	26	78	—	—	—	—	—
86-87—Quebec	NHL	75	0	19	19	69	—	—	—	—	—
87-88—New York Rangers	NHL	68	7	25	32	100	—	—	—	—	—
88-89—New York Rangers	NHL	63	6	11	17	88	4	0	2	2	30
89-90—New York Rangers	NHL	22	2	10	12	22	—	—	—	—	—
90-91—New York Rangers	NHL	77	2	10	12	89	6	0	0	0	11
91-92—New York Rangers	NHL	10	0	1	1	15	—	—	—	—	—
—Edmonton	NHL	12	1	1	2	8	—	—	—	—	—
—Minnesota	NHL	37	0	7	7	49	7	2	2	4	10
92-93—Boston	NHL	77	10	14	24	108	4	0	1	1	6
93-94—Boston	NHL	55	1	9	10	85	13	1	2	3	16
94-95—Boston	NHL	44	3	4	7	36	5	0	1	1	4
NHL totals		632	39	130	169	758	39	3	8	11	77

SHAW, LLOYD
D, CANUCKS

PERSONAL: Born September 26, 1976, in Regina, Sask.... 6-3/215.... Shoots right.
HIGH SCHOOL: Lake Washington Senior (Kirkland, Wash.).
TRANSACTIONS/CAREER NOTES: Selected by Vancouver Canucks in fourth round (fourth Canucks pick, 92nd overall) of NHL entry draft (July 8, 1995).

Season Team	League	REGULAR SEASON					PLAYOFFS				
		Gms.	G	A	Pts.	PIM	Gms.	G	A	Pts.	PIM
93-94—Seattle	WHL	47	0	4	4	107	8	0	0	0	23
94-95—Seattle	WHL	66	3	12	15	313	3	0	0	0	13

SHEPPARD, RAY
RW, RED WINGS

PERSONAL: Born May 27, 1966, in Pembroke, Ont.... 6-1/195.... Shoots right.
TRANSACTIONS/CAREER NOTES: Selected by Buffalo Sabres as underage junior in third round (third Sabres pick, 60th overall) of NHL entry draft (June 9, 1984).... Injured left knee (September 1986); missed Sabres training camp.... Bruised back during training camp (September 1988).... Suffered facial lacerations (November 25, 1988).... Suffered facial lacerations (November 27, 1988).... Suffered from the flu (December 1988).... Sprained ankle (January 30, 1989).... Injured left knee (March 16, 1990).... Traded by Sabres to New York Rangers for future considerations and cash (July 10, 1990).... Sprained medial collateral ligaments of right knee (February 18, 1991); missed 13 games.... Dislocated left shoulder (March 24, 1991).... Signed as free agent by Detroit Red Wings (August 5, 1991).... Strained lower abdomen (March 20, 1992); missed five games.... Injured knee (October 8, 1992); missed five games.... Reinjured knee (October 28, 1992); missed two games.... Suffered back spasms (February 13, 1993); missed three games.... Strained back (March 2, 1993); missed two games.... Injured back (February 22, 1995); missed two games.
HONORS: Won Red Tilson Trophy (1985-86).... Won Eddie Powers Memorial Trophy (1985-86).... Won Jim Mahon Memorial Trophy (1985-86).... Named to OHL All-Star first team (1985-86).... Named to NHL All-Rookie team (1987-88).
STATISTICAL PLATEAUS: Three-goal games: 1987-88 (2), 1991-92 (1), 1993-94 (2), 1994-95 (1). Total: 6.

Season Team	League	REGULAR SEASON					PLAYOFFS				
		Gms.	G	A	Pts.	PIM	Gms.	G	A	Pts.	PIM
82-83—Brockville	COJHL	48	27	36	63	81	—	—	—	—	—
83-84—Cornwall	OHL	68	44	36	80	69	—	—	—	—	—
84-85—Cornwall	OHL	49	25	33	58	51	9	2	12	14	4
85-86—Cornwall	OHL	63	*81	61	*142	25	6	7	4	11	0
86-87—Rochester	AHL	55	18	13	31	11	15	12	3	15	2
87-88—Buffalo	NHL	74	38	27	65	14	6	1	1	2	2
88-89—Buffalo	NHL	67	22	21	43	15	1	0	1	1	0
89-90—Buffalo	NHL	18	4	2	6	0	—	—	—	—	—
—Rochester	AHL	5	3	5	8	2	17	8	7	15	9

Season Team	League	REGULAR SEASON					PLAYOFFS				
		Gms.	G	A	Pts.	PIM	Gms.	G	A	Pts.	PIM
90-91—New York Rangers	NHL	59	24	23	47	21	—	—	—	—	—
91-92—Detroit	NHL	74	36	26	62	27	11	6	2	8	4
92-93—Detroit	NHL	70	32	34	66	29	7	2	3	5	0
93-94—Detroit	NHL	82	52	41	93	26	7	2	1	3	4
94-95—Detroit	NHL	43	30	10	40	17	17	4	3	7	5
NHL totals		487	238	184	422	149	49	15	11	26	15

SHEVALIER, JEFF
LW/C, KINGS

PERSONAL: Born March 14, 1974, in Mississauga, Ont. . . . 5-11/180. . . . Shoots left. . . . Name pronounced shuh-VAHL-yay.
HIGH SCHOOL: Chippewa Secondary (North Bay, Ont.).
TRANSACTIONS/CAREER NOTES: Selected by Los Angeles Kings in fifth round (fourth Kings pick, 111th overall) of NHL entry draft (June 20, 1992).
HONORS: Named to OHL All-Star first team (1993-94).

Season Team	League	REGULAR SEASON					PLAYOFFS				
		Gms.	G	A	Pts.	PIM	Gms.	G	A	Pts.	PIM
90-91—Oakville Jr.B	OHA	5	1	4	5	0	—	—	—	—	—
—Georgetown Jr. B	OHA	12	11	11	22	8	—	—	—	—	—
—Acton Jr. C	OHA	28	29	31	60	62	—	—	—	—	—
91-92—North Bay	OHL	64	28	29	57	26	21	5	11	16	25
92-93—North Bay	OHL	62	59	54	113	46	2	1	2	3	4
93-94—North Bay	OHL	64	52	49	101	52	17	8	14	22	18
94-95—Phoenix	IHL	68	31	39	70	44	9	5	4	9	0
—Los Angeles	NHL	1	1	0	1	0	—	—	—	—	—
NHL totals		1	1	0	1	0					

SHIELDS, STEVE
G, SABRES

PERSONAL: Born July 19, 1972, in Toronto. . . . 6-3/210. . . . Catches left.
COLLEGE: Michigan.
TRANSACTIONS/CAREER NOTES: Selected by Buffalo Sabres in fifth round (fifth Sabres pick, 101st overall) of NHL entry draft (June 22, 1991).
HONORS: Named to NCCA All-America West second team (1992-93 and 1993-94). . . . Named to CCHA All-Star first team (1992-93 and 1993-94).

Season Team	League	REGULAR SEASON							PLAYOFFS					
		Gms.	Min.	W	L	T	GA	SO	Avg.	Gms.	Min.	W	L	GA	SO	Avg.
90-91—University of Michigan	CCHA	37	1963	26	6	3	106	0	3.24	—	—	—	—	—	—	—
91-92—University of Michigan	CCHA	*37	*2091	*27	7	2	98	1	2.81	—	—	—	—	—	—	—
92-93—University of Michigan	CCHA	*39	2027	*30	6	2	75	...	*2.22	—	—	—	—	—	—	—
93-94—University of Michigan	CCHA	36	1961	*28	6	1	87	2	2.66	—	—	—	—	—	—	—
94-95—South Carolina	ECHL	21	1158	11	5	‡2	52	2	2.69	3	144	0	2	11	0	4.58
—Rochester	AHL	13	673	3	8	0	53	0	4.73	1	20	0	0	3	0	9.00

SHTALENKOV, MIKHAIL
G, MIGHTY DUCKS

PERSONAL: Born October 20, 1965, in Moscow, U.S.S.R. . . . 6-2/180. . . . Catches left. . . . Name pronounced mihk-HIGHL shtuh-LEHN-kahf.
TRANSACTIONS/CAREER NOTES: Selected by Mighty Ducks of Anaheim in fifth round (fifth Mighty Ducks pick, 108th overall) of NHL entry draft (June 26, 1993).
HONORS: Named Soviet League Rookie of the Year (1986-87). . . . Won Garry F. Longman Memorial Trophy (1992-93).

Season Team	League	REGULAR SEASON							PLAYOFFS					
		Gms.	Min.	W	L	T	GA	SO	Avg.	Gms.	Min.	W	L	GA	SO	Avg.
86-87—Dynamo Moscow	USSR	17	893	...	...	...	36	1	2.42	—	—	—	—	—	—	—
87-88—Dynamo Moscow	USSR	25	1302	...	...	...	72	1	3.32	—	—	—	—	—	—	—
88-89—Dynamo Moscow	USSR	4	80	...	...	...	3	0	2.25	—	—	—	—	—	—	—
89-90—Dynamo Moscow	USSR	6	20	...	...	...	1	0	3.00	—	—	—	—	—	—	—
90-91—Dynamo Moscow	USSR	31	1568	...	...	...	56	2	2.14	—	—	—	—	—	—	—
91-92—Dynamo Moscow	CIS	27	1268	...	...	...	45	1	2.13	—	—	—	—	—	—	—
—Unified Olympic Team	Int'l	8	440	...	...	...	12	3	1.64	—	—	—	—	—	—	—
92-93—Milwaukee	IHL	47	2669	26	14	‡5	135	2	3.03	3	209	1	1	11	0	3.16
93-94—San Diego	IHL	28	1616	15	11	‡2	93	0	3.45	—	—	—	—	—	—	—
—Anaheim	NHL	10	543	3	4	1	24	0	2.65	—	—	—	—	—	—	—
94-95—Anaheim	NHL	18	810	4	7	1	49	0	3.63	—	—	—	—	—	—	—
NHL totals		28	1353	7	11	2	73	0	3.24							

SHUCHUK, GARY
RW/C, KINGS

PERSONAL: Born February 17, 1967, in Edmonton. . . . 5-10/185. . . . Shoots right. . . . Full name: Gary Robert Shuchuk. . . . Name pronounced SHOO-chuhk.
COLLEGE: Wisconsin.
TRANSACTIONS/CAREER NOTES: Selected by Detroit Red Wings in NHL supplemental draft (June 10, 1988). . . . Traded by Red Wings with C Jimmy Carson and RW Marc Potvin to Los Angeles Kings for D Paul Coffey, RW Jim Hiller and C/LW Sylvain Couturier (January 29, 1993). . . . Hyperextended right elbow (February 20, 1993); missed four games. . . . Sprained knee (January 29, 1994); missed 10 games.
HONORS: Won WCHA Most Valuable Player Award (1989-90). . . . Named to NCAA All-America West first team (1989-90). . . . Named to WCHA All-Star first team (1989-90).

Season	Team	League		REGULAR SEASON					PLAYOFFS				
			Gms.	G	A	Pts.	PIM	Gms.	G	A	Pts.	PIM
86-87—University of Wisconsin ...		WCHA	42	19	11	30	72	—	—	—	—	—
87-88—University of Wisconsin ...		WCHA	44	7	22	29	70	—	—	—	—	—
88-89—University of Wisconsin ...		WCHA	46	18	19	37	102	—	—	—	—	—
89-90—University of Wisconsin ...		WCHA	45	*41	39	*80	70	—	—	—	—	—
90-91—Detroit		NHL	6	1	2	3	6	3	0	0	0	0
—Adirondack		AHL	59	23	24	47	32	—	—	—	—	—
91-92—Adirondack		AHL	79	32	48	80	48	†19	4	9	13	18
92-93—Adirondack		AHL	47	24	53	77	66	—	—	—	—	—
—Los Angeles		NHL	25	2	4	6	16	17	2	2	4	12
93-94—Los Angeles		NHL	56	3	4	7	30	—	—	—	—	—
94-95—Los Angeles		NHL	22	3	6	9	6	—	—	—	—	—
—Phoenix		IHL	13	8	7	15	12	—	—	—	—	—
NHL totals			109	9	16	25	58	20	2	2	4	12

SIDORKIEWICZ, PETER

G, DEVILS

PERSONAL: Born June 29, 1963, in Dabrown Bialostocka, Poland.... 5-9/180.... Catches left.... Full name: Peter Paul Sidorkiewicz.... Name pronounced sih-DOHR-kuh-VIHCH.
HIGH SCHOOL: O'Neill (Oshawa, Ont.).

TRANSACTIONS/CAREER NOTES: Selected by Washington Capitals as underage junior in fifth round (fifth Capitals pick, 91st overall) of NHL entry draft (June 10, 1981).... Sprained right ankle (March 3, 1991).... Traded by Capitals with C Dean Evason to Hartford Whalers for LW David Jensen (March 1985).... Selected by Ottawa Senators in NHL expansion draft (June 18, 1992).... Traded by Senators with future considerations to New Jersey Devils for G Craig Billington and C/LW Troy Mallette and fourth-round pick (C Cosmo Dupaul) in 1993 draft (June 20, 1993); Senators sent LW Mike Peluso to Devils to complete deal (June 26, 1993).... Loaned to Fort Wayne Komets of IHL (February 2, 1995).
HONORS: Shared Dave Pinkney Trophy with Jeff Hogg (1982-83).... Named to Memorial Cup All-Star team (1982-83).... Named to AHL All-Star second team (1986-87).... Named to NHL All-Rookie team (1988-89).... Played in NHL All-Star Game (1993).

Season	Team	League		REGULAR SEASON							PLAYOFFS						
			Gms.	Min.	W	L	T	GA	SO	Avg.	Gms.	Min.	W	L	GA	SO	Avg.
80-81—Oshawa		OMJHL	7	308	3	3	0	24	0	4.68	5	266	2	2	20	0	4.51
81-82—Oshawa		OHL	29	1553	14	11	1	123	*2	4.75	1	13	0	0	1	0	4.62
82-83—Oshawa		OHL	60	3536	36	20	3	213	0	3.61	*17	*1020	15	1	*60	0	3.53
83-84—Oshawa		OHL	52	2966	28	21	1	205	1	4.15	7	420	3	4	27	†1	3.86
84-85—Fort Wayne		IHL	10	590	4	4	‡2	43	0	4.37	—	—	—	—	—	—	—
—Binghamton		AHL	45	2691	31	9	5	137	3	3.05	8	481	4	4	31	0	3.87
85-86—Binghamton		AHL	49	2819	21	22	3	150	2	*3.19	4	235	1	3	12	0	3.06
86-87—Binghamton		AHL	57	3304	23	16	0	161	4	2.92	13	794	6	7	36	0	*2.72
87-88—Hartford		NHL	1	60	0	1	0	6	0	6.00	—	—	—	—	—	—	—
—Binghamton		AHL	42	2346	19	17	3	144	0	3.68	3	147	0	2	8	0	3.27
88-89—Hartford		NHL	44	2635	22	18	4	133	4	3.03	2	124	0	2	8	0	3.87
89-90—Hartford		NHL	46	2703	19	19	7	161	1	3.57	7	429	3	4	23	0	3.22
90-91—Hartford		NHL	52	2953	21	22	7	164	1	3.33	6	359	2	4	24	0	4.01
91-92—Hartford		NHL	35	1995	9	19	6	111	2	3.34	—	—	—	—	—	—	—
92-93—Ottawa		NHL	64	3388	8	*46	3	*250	0	4.43	—	—	—	—	—	—	—
93-94—New Jersey		NHL	3	130	0	3	0	6	0	2.77	—	—	—	—	—	—	—
—Albany		AHL	15	908	6	7	2	60	0	3.96	—	—	—	—	—	—	—
—Fort Wayne		IHL	11	591	6	3	‡0	27	†2	2.74	18	*1054	10	*6	59	†1	3.36
94-95—Fort Wayne		IHL	16	942	8	6	‡1	58	1	3.69	3	144	1	2	12	0	5.00
NHL totals			245	13864	79	128	27	831	8	3.60	15	912	5	10	55	0	3.62

SILLINGER, MIKE

LW/C, MIGHTY DUCKS

PERSONAL: Born June 29, 1971, in Regina, Sask.... 5-10/190.... Shoots right.... Name pronounced SIHL-ihn-juhr.
TRANSACTIONS/CAREER NOTES: Selected by Detroit Red Wings in first round (first Red Wings pick, 11th overall) of NHL entry draft (June 17, 1989).... Fractured rib in training camp (September 1990).... Suffered from the flu (March 5, 1993); missed three games.... Strained rotator cuff (October 9, 1993); missed four games.... Played in Europe during 1994-95 NHL lockout.... Injured eye (January 17, 1995); missed four games.... Traded by Red Wings with D Jason York to Mighty Ducks of Anaheim for LW Stu Grimson, D Mark Ferner and sixth-round pick in 1996 draft (April 4, 1995).
HONORS: Named to WHL All-Star second team (1989-90).... Named to WHL (East) All-Star first team (1990-91).

Season	Team	League		REGULAR SEASON					PLAYOFFS				
			Gms.	G	A	Pts.	PIM	Gms.	G	A	Pts.	PIM
87-88—Regina		WHL	67	18	25	43	17	4	2	2	4	0
88-89—Regina		WHL	72	53	78	131	52	—	—	—	—	—
89-90—Regina		WHL	70	57	72	129	41	11	12	10	22	2
—Adirondack		AHL	—	—	—	—	—	1	0	0	0	0
90-91—Regina		WHL	57	50	66	116	42	8	6	9	15	4
—Detroit		NHL	3	0	1	1	0	3	0	1	1	0
91-92—Adirondack		AHL	64	25	41	66	26	15	9	*19	*28	12
—Detroit		NHL	—	—	—	—	—	8	2	2	4	2
92-93—Detroit		NHL	51	4	17	21	16	—	—	—	—	—
—Adirondack		AHL	15	10	20	30	31	11	5	13	18	10
93-94—Detroit		NHL	62	8	21	29	10	—	—	—	—	—

S

Season	Team	League	REGULAR SEASON					PLAYOFFS				
			Gms.	G	A	Pts.	PIM	Gms.	G	A	Pts.	PIM
94-95	Wien	Austria	13	13	14	27	10	—	—	—	—	—
	Detroit	NHL	13	2	6	8	2	—	—	—	—	—
	Anaheim	NHL	15	2	5	7	6	—	—	—	—	—
NHL totals			144	16	50	66	34	11	2	3	5	2

SIMON, CHRIS
LW, DENVER

PERSONAL: Born January 30, 1972, in Wawa, Ont. . . . 6-3/219. . . . Shoots left. . . . Name pronounced SIGH-muhn.

TRANSACTIONS/CAREER NOTES: Suspended six games by OHL for shooting the puck in frustration and striking another player (January 20, 1990). . . . Selected by Philadelphia Flyers in second round (second Flyers pick, 25th overall) of NHL entry draft (June 16, 1990). . . . Underwent surgery to repair left rotator cuff and torn muscle (September 1990). . . . Traded by Flyers with first-round pick in 1994 draft (traded to Toronto Maple Leafs) to Quebec Nordiques (July 21, 1992); completed deal in which Flyers sent G Ron Hextall, C Mike Ricci, C Peter Forsberg, D Steve Duchesne, first-round pick in 1993 draft (G Jocelyn Thibault) and cash to Nordiques for C Eric Lindros (June 20, 1992). . . . Suffered from the flu (March 13, 1993); missed one game. . . . Injured back (December 1, 1993); missed 31 games. . . . Injured back (February 16, 1994); missed one game. . . . Injured back (March 6, 1994); missed one game. . . . Injured back (March 18, 1994); missed remainder of season. . . . Injured back (January 31, 1995); missed six games. . . . Injured shoulder (March 22, 1995); missed 13 games. . . . Nordiques franchise moved to Denver for 1995-96 season.

Season	Team	League	REGULAR SEASON					PLAYOFFS				
			Gms.	G	A	Pts.	PIM	Gms.	G	A	Pts.	PIM
87-88	Sault Ste. Marie	OHA	55	42	36	78	172	—	—	—	—	—
88-89	Ottawa	OHL	36	4	2	6	31	—	—	—	—	—
89-90	Ottawa	OHL	57	36	38	74	146	3	2	1	3	4
90-91	Ottawa	OHL	20	16	6	22	69	17	5	9	14	59
91-92	Ottawa	OHL	2	1	1	2	24	—	—	—	—	—
	Sault Ste. Marie	OHL	31	19	25	44	143	11	5	8	13	49
92-93	Halifax	AHL	36	12	6	18	131	—	—	—	—	—
	Quebec	NHL	16	1	1	2	67	5	0	0	0	26
93-94	Quebec	NHL	37	4	4	8	132	—	—	—	—	—
94-95	Quebec	NHL	29	3	9	12	106	6	1	1	2	19
NHL totals			82	8	14	22	305	11	1	1	2	45

SIMON, JASON
LW, JETS

PERSONAL: Born March 21, 1969, in Sarnia, Ont. . . . 6-1/190. . . . Shoots left.

TRANSACTIONS/CAREER NOTES: Selected by New Jersey Devils in ninth round (ninth Devils pick, 215th overall) of NHL entry draft (June 26, 1993). . . . Signed as free agent by New York Islanders (January 6, 1994). . . . Signed as free agent by Winnipeg Jets (July 21, 1995).

Season	Team	League	REGULAR SEASON					PLAYOFFS				
			Gms.	G	A	Pts.	PIM	Gms.	G	A	Pts.	PIM
86-87	London	OHL	33	1	2	3	33	—	—	—	—	—
	Sudbury	OHL	26	2	3	5	50	—	—	—	—	—
87-88	Sudbury	OHL	26	5	7	12	35	—	—	—	—	—
	Hamilton	OHL	29	5	13	18	124	11	0	2	2	15
88-89	Windsor	OHL	62	23	39	62	193	4	1	4	5	13
89-90	Utica	AHL	16	3	4	7	28	2	0	0	0	12
	Nashville	ECHL	13	4	3	7	81	5	1	3	4	17
90-91	Johnstown	ECHL	22	11	9	20	55	—	—	—	—	—
	Utica	AHL	50	2	12	14	189	—	—	—	—	—
91-92	Utica	AHL	1	0	0	0	12	—	—	—	—	—
	San Diego	IHL	13	1	4	5	45	3	0	1	1	9
92-93	Flint	Col.HL	44	17	32	49	202	—	—	—	—	—
	Detroit	Col.HL	11	7	13	20	38	6	1	2	3	40
93-94	Detroit	Col.HL	13	9	16	25	87	—	—	—	—	—
	Salt Lake City	IHL	50	7	7	14	*323	—	—	—	—	—
	New York Islanders	NHL	4	0	0	0	34	—	—	—	—	—
94-95	Denver	IHL	61	3	6	9	300	1	0	0	0	12
NHL totals			4	0	0	0	34					

SIMON, TODD
C

PERSONAL: Born April 21, 1972, in Toronto. . . . 5-10/188. . . . Shoots right.

TRANSACTIONS/CAREER NOTES: Selected by Buffalo Sabres in ninth round (10th Sabres pick, 203rd overall) of NHL entry draft (June 20, 1992). . . . Signed as free agent by Las Vegas Thunder (August 5, 1995).

HONORS: Won Eddie Powers Memorial Trophy (1991-92). . . . Won Red Tilson Trophy (1991-92).

Season	Team	League	REGULAR SEASON					PLAYOFFS				
			Gms.	G	A	Pts.	PIM	Gms.	G	A	Pts.	PIM
89-90	Niagara Falls	OHL	9	0	1	1	2	11	3	1	4	2
90-91	Niagara Falls	OHL	65	51	74	125	35	14	7	8	15	12
91-92	Niagara Falls	OHL	66	53	93	*146	70	17	17	24	†41	36
92-93	Rochester	AHL	68	27	66	93	54	12	3	14	17	15
93-94	Rochester	AHL	55	33	52	85	79	—	—	—	—	—
	Buffalo	NHL	15	0	1	1	0	5	1	0	1	0
94-95	Rochester	AHL	69	25	65	90	78	5	0	2	2	21
NHL totals			15	0	1	1	0	5	1	0	1	0

S

SIMPSON, CRAIG

LW, SABRES

PERSONAL: Born February 15, 1967, in London, Ont. . . . 6-2/195. . . . Shoots right. . . . Full name: Craig Andrew Simpson.
COLLEGE: Michigan State.
TRANSACTIONS/CAREER NOTES: Selected by Pittsburgh Penguins in first round (first Penguins pick, second overall) of NHL entry draft (June 15, 1985). . . . Pulled muscle in right hip (March 1987). . . . Sprained right wrist (March 14, 1987). . . . Traded by Penguins with C Dave Hannan, D Chris Joseph and D Moe Mantha to Edmonton Oilers for D Paul Coffey, LW Dave Hunter and RW Wayne Van Dorp (November 24, 1987). . . . Broke right ankle (December 4, 1988). . . . Suspended three games by NHL for injuring an opposing player (January 23, 1991); missed one game. . . . Bruised chest (November 1991); missed one game. . . . Bruised shoulder (April 18, 1992). . . . Strained lower back (January 5, 1993); missed four games. . . . Strained lower back (February 23, 1993); missed three games. . . . Suffered protruded disk (March 1993); missed remainder of season. . . . Signed as free agent by San Jose Sharks (July 17, 1993); deal invalidated by NHL (July 26, 1993). . . . Traded by Oilers to Buffalo Sabres for LW Jozef Cierny and undisclosed draft pick (September 1, 1993). . . . Suffered sore back (December 1, 1993); missed 42 games. . . . Pulled hamstring (February 25, 1995); missed five games. . . . Suffered lower back pain (March 21, 1995); missed 13 games. . . . Suffered lower back pain (May 3, 1995); missed entire playoffs.
HONORS: Named to NCAA All-America West first team (1984-85). . . . Named to CCHA All-Star first team (1984-85).
STATISTICAL PLATEAUS: Three-goal games: 1986-87 (1), 1987-88 (1), 1988-89 (1). Total: 3.
MISCELLANEOUS: Member of Stanley Cup championship teams (1988 and 1990).

Season Team	League	REGULAR SEASON					PLAYOFFS				
		Gms.	G	A	Pts.	PIM	Gms.	G	A	Pts.	PIM
82-83—London Jr. B	OHA	. . .	48	63	*111	. . .	—	—	—	—	—
83-84—Michigan State	CCHA	30	8	28	36	22	—	—	—	—	—
84-85—Michigan State	CCHA	42	31	53	84	33	—	—	—	—	—
85-86—Pittsburgh	NHL	76	11	17	28	49	—	—	—	—	—
86-87—Pittsburgh	NHL	72	26	25	51	57	—	—	—	—	—
87-88—Pittsburgh	NHL	21	13	13	26	34	—	—	—	—	—
—Edmonton	NHL	59	43	21	64	43	19	13	6	19	26
88-89—Edmonton	NHL	66	35	41	76	80	7	2	0	2	10
89-90—Edmonton	NHL	80	29	32	61	180	22	*16	15	†31	8
90-91—Edmonton	NHL	75	30	27	57	66	18	5	11	16	12
91-92—Edmonton	NHL	79	24	37	61	80	1	0	0	0	0
92-93—Edmonton	NHL	60	24	22	46	36	—	—	—	—	—
93-94—Buffalo	NHL	22	8	8	16	8	—	—	—	—	—
94-95—Buffalo	NHL	24	4	7	11	26	—	—	—	—	—
NHL totals		634	247	250	497	659	67	36	32	68	56

SIMPSON, REID

LW, DEVILS

PERSONAL: Born May 21, 1969, in Flin Flon, Man. . . . 6-1/210. . . . Shoots left.
TRANSACTIONS/CAREER NOTES: Selected by Philadelphia Flyers in fourth round (third Flyers pick, 72nd overall) of NHL entry draft (June 17, 1989). . . . Signed as free agent by Minnesota North Stars (December 13, 1992). . . . North Stars franchise moved from Minnesota to Dallas and renamed Stars for 1993-94 season. . . . Traded by Stars with D Roy Mitchell to New Jersey Devils for future considerations (March 21, 1994).

Season Team	League	REGULAR SEASON					PLAYOFFS				
		Gms.	G	A	Pts.	PIM	Gms.	G	A	Pts.	PIM
85-86—Flin Flon	MJHL	40	20	21	41	200	—	—	—	—	—
—New Westminster	WHL	2	0	0	0	0	—	—	—	—	—
86-87—Prince Albert	WHL	47	3	8	11	105	—	—	—	—	—
87-88—Prince Albert	WHL	72	13	14	27	164	10	1	0	1	43
88-89—Prince Albert	WHL	59	26	29	55	264	4	2	1	3	30
89-90—Prince Albert	WHL	29	15	17	32	121	14	4	7	11	34
—Hershey	AHL	28	2	2	4	175	—	—	—	—	—
90-91—Hershey	AHL	54	9	15	24	183	1	0	0	0	0
91-92—Hershey	AHL	60	11	7	18	145	—	—	—	—	—
—Philadelphia	NHL	1	0	0	0	0	—	—	—	—	—
92-93—Kalamazoo	IHL	45	5	5	10	193	—	—	—	—	—
—Minnesota	NHL	1	0	0	0	5	—	—	—	—	—
93-94—Albany	AHL	37	9	5	14	135	5	1	1	2	18
—Kalamazoo	IHL	5	0	0	0	16	—	—	—	—	—
94-95—Albany	AHL	70	18	25	43	268	14	1	8	9	13
—New Jersey	NHL	9	0	0	0	27	—	—	—	—	—
NHL totals		11	0	0	0	32					

SITTLER, RYAN

LW/C, FLYERS

PERSONAL: Born January 28, 1974, in London, Ont. . . . 6-2/185. . . . Shoots left. . . . Son of Darryl Sittler, Hall of Fame center, Toronto Maple Leafs, Philadelphia Flyers and Detroit Red Wings (1970-71 through 1984-85).
HIGH SCHOOL: Nichols School (Buffalo, N.Y.).
COLLEGE: Michigan.
TRANSACTIONS/CAREER NOTES: Selected by Philadelphia Flyers in first round (first Flyers pick, seventh overall) of NHL entry draft (June 20, 1992).

Season Team	League	REGULAR SEASON					PLAYOFFS				
		Gms.	G	A	Pts.	PIM	Gms.	G	A	Pts.	PIM
90-91—Nichols School	N.Y. H.S.	7	8	9	17	8	—	—	—	—	—
—Buffalo	AHAUS	20	25	34	59	26	—	—	—	—	—
91-92—Nichols School	N.Y. H.S.	21	19	29	48	38	—	—	—	—	—
—Buffalo	AHAUS	30	39	54	93	. . .	—	—	—	—	—

Season	Team	League	REGULAR SEASON Gms.	G	A	Pts.	PIM	PLAYOFFS Gms.	G	A	Pts.	PIM
92-93—University of Michigan		CCHA	35	9	24	33	43	—	—	—	—	—
93-94—University of Michigan		CCHA	26	9	9	18	14	—	—	—	—	—
94-95—Hershey		AHL	42	2	7	9	48	—	—	—	—	—
—Johnstown		ECHL	1	1	1	2	0	—	—	—	—	—

SKALDE, JARROD
C, MIGHTY DUCKS

PERSONAL: Born February 26, 1971, in Niagara Falls, Ont. . . . 6-0/ 170. . . . Shoots left. . . . Name pronounced SKAHL -dee. **TRANSACTIONS/CAREER NOTES:** Selected by New Jersey Devils in second round (third Devils pick, 26th overall) of NHL entry draft (June 17, 1989). . . . Traded by Oshawa Generals to Belleville Bulls for RW Rob Pearson (November 18, 1990). . . . Selected by Mighty Ducks of Anaheim in NHL expansion draft (June 24, 1993). . . . Signed as free agent by Las Vegas Thunder (August 18, 1994). . . . Signed as free agent by Mighty Ducks (May 31, 1995).
HONORS: Named to OHL All-Star second team (1990-91).

Season	Team	League	REGULAR SEASON Gms.	G	A	Pts.	PIM	PLAYOFFS Gms.	G	A	Pts.	PIM
86-87—Fort Erie Jr. B		OHA	41	27	34	61	36	—	—	—	—	—
87-88—Oshawa		OHL	60	12	16	28	24	7	2	1	3	2
88-89—Oshawa		OHL	65	38	38	76	36	6	1	5	6	2
89-90—Oshawa		OHL	62	40	52	92	66	17	10	7	17	6
90-91—New Jersey		NHL	1	0	1	1	0	—	—	—	—	—
—Utica		AHL	3	3	2	5	0	—	—	—	—	—
—Oshawa		OHL	15	8	14	22	14	—	—	—	—	—
—Belleville		OHL	40	30	52	82	21	6	9	6	15	10
91-92—Utica		AHL	62	20	20	40	56	4	3	1	4	8
—New Jersey		NHL	15	2	4	6	4	—	—	—	—	—
92-93—Cincinnati		IHL	4	1	2	3	4	—	—	—	—	—
—Utica		AHL	59	21	39	60	76	5	0	2	2	19
—New Jersey		NHL	11	0	2	2	4	—	—	—	—	—
93-94—San Diego		IHL	57	25	38	63	79	9	3	12	15	10
—Anaheim		NHL	20	5	4	9	10	—	—	—	—	—
94-95—Las Vegas		IHL	74	34	41	75	103	9	2	4	6	8
NHL totals.............................			47	7	11	18	18					

SKOREPA, ZDENEK
RW, DEVILS

PERSONAL: Born August 10, 1976, in Duchcov, Czechoslavakia. . . . 6-0/ 187. . . . Shoots left. **TRANSACTIONS/CAREER NOTES:** Selected by New Jersey Devils in fourth round (fourth Devils pick, 103rd overall) of NHL entry draft (June 29, 1994).

Season	Team	League	REGULAR SEASON Gms.	G	A	Pts.	PIM	PLAYOFFS Gms.	G	A	Pts.	PIM
93-94—Chemopetrol Litvinov		Czech Rep.	20	4	7	11	...	4	0	0	0	...
94-95—Chemopetrol Litvinov		Czech Rep.	28	3	3	6	...	3	0	0	0	...

SKRUDLAND, BRIAN
C, PANTHERS

PERSONAL: Born July 31, 1963, in Peace River, Alta. . . . 6-0/ 196. . . . Shoots left. . . . Name pronounced SKROOD-luhnd. . . . Cousin of Barry Pederson, center for four NHL teams (1980-81 through 1991-92). **TRANSACTIONS/CAREER NOTES:** Signed as free agent by Montreal Canadiens (August 1983). . . . Injured groin (February 1988). . . . Strained left knee ligaments (December 27, 1988). . . . Bruised right foot (January 1989). . . . Sprained right ankle (October 7, 1989); missed 21 games. . . . Pulled hip muscle (November 4, 1990); missed six games. . . . Broke foot (January 17, 1991); missed 14 games including All-Star Game. . . . Broke left thumb (October 5, 1991); missed five games. . . . Sprained knee (October 26, 1991); missed 25 games. . . . Broke nose (January 25, 1992); missed eight games. . . . Tore right knee ligaments (October 6, 1992); missed 27 games. . . . Injured shoulder (January 14, 1993); missed one game. . . . Traded by Canadiens to Calgary Flames for RW Gary Leeman (January 28, 1993). . . . Sprained ankle (February 16, 1993); missed four games. . . . Broke thumb (March 2, 1993); missed 12 games. . . . Lacerated right ear (April 11, 1993); missed one game. . . . Selected by Florida Panthers in NHL expansion draft (June 24, 1993). . . . Sprained right ankle (April 4, 1994); missed five games. . . . Strained left hip flexor (March 22, 1995); missed one game.
HONORS: Won Jack Butterfield Trophy (1984-85).
MISCELLANEOUS: Member of Stanley Cup championship team (1986). . . . Captain of Florida Panthers (1994-95).

Season	Team	League	REGULAR SEASON Gms.	G	A	Pts.	PIM	PLAYOFFS Gms.	G	A	Pts.	PIM
80-81—Saskatoon		WHL	66	15	27	42	97	—	—	—	—	—
81-82—Saskatoon		WHL	71	27	29	56	135	5	0	1	1	2
82-83—Saskatoon		WHL	71	35	59	94	42	6	1	3	4	19
83-84—Nova Scotia		AHL	56	13	12	25	55	12	2	8	10	14
84-85—Sherbrooke		AHL	70	22	28	50	109	17	9	8	17	23
85-86—Montreal		NHL	65	9	13	22	57	20	2	4	6	76
86-87—Montreal		NHL	79	11	17	28	107	14	1	5	6	29
87-88—Montreal		NHL	79	12	24	36	112	11	1	5	6	24
88-89—Montreal		NHL	71	12	29	41	84	21	3	7	10	40
89-90—Montreal		NHL	59	11	31	42	56	11	3	5	8	30
90-91—Montreal		NHL	57	15	19	34	85	13	3	10	13	42
91-92—Montreal		NHL	42	3	3	6	36	11	1	1	2	20

Season Team	League	REGULAR SEASON					PLAYOFFS				
		Gms.	G	A	Pts.	PIM	Gms.	G	A	Pts.	PIM
92-93—Montreal	NHL	23	5	3	8	55	—	—	—	—	—
—Calgary	NHL	16	2	4	6	10	6	0	3	3	12
93-94—Florida	NHL	79	15	25	40	136	—	—	—	—	—
94-95—Florida	NHL	47	5	9	14	88	—	—	—	—	—
NHL totals		617	100	177	277	826	107	14	40	54	273

SLAMIAR, PETER
LW/RW, RANGERS

PERSONAL: Born February 26, 1977, in Zvolen, Czecholovakia. . . . 5-11/174. . . . Shoots right.

TRANSACTIONS/CAREER NOTES: Selected by New York Rangers in sixth round (sixth Rangers pick, 143rd overall) of NHL entry draft (July 8, 1995).

Season Team	League	REGULAR SEASON					PLAYOFFS				
		Gms.	G	A	Pts.	PIM	Gms.	G	A	Pts.	PIM
94-95—ZTK Zvolen Jrs.	Slovakia	30	19	18	37	. . .	—	—	—	—	—
—ZTK Zvolen	Slovakia-II	11	4	1	5	. . .	—	—	—	—	—

SLANEY, JOHN
D, DENVER

PERSONAL: Born February 7, 1972, in St. John's, Nfld. . . . 6-0/195. . . . Shoots left.

TRANSACTIONS/CAREER NOTES: Selected by Washington Capitals in first round (first Capitals pick, ninth overall) of NHL entry draft (June 16, 1990). . . . Sprained right ankle (March 9, 1994); missed six games. . . . Traded by Capitals to Denver for third-round pick in 1996 draft (July 12, 1995).

HONORS: Won Max Kaminsky Trophy (1989-90). . . . Named to OHL All-Star first team (1989-90). . . . Named to OHL All-Star second team (1990-91).

Season Team	League	REGULAR SEASON					PLAYOFFS				
		Gms.	G	A	Pts.	PIM	Gms.	G	A	Pts.	PIM
88-89—Cornwall	OHL	66	16	43	59	23	18	8	16	24	10
89-90—Cornwall	OHL	64	38	59	97	60	6	0	8	8	11
90-91—Cornwall	OHL	34	21	25	46	28	—	—	—	—	—
91-92—Cornwall	OHL	34	19	41	60	43	6	3	8	11	0
—Baltimore	AHL	6	2	4	6	0	—	—	—	—	—
92-93—Baltimore	AHL	79	20	46	66	60	7	0	7	7	8
93-94—Portland	AHL	29	14	13	27	17	—	—	—	—	—
—Washington	NHL	47	7	9	16	27	11	1	1	2	2
94-95—Washington	NHL	16	0	3	3	6	—	—	—	—	—
—Portland	AHL	8	3	10	13	4	7	1	3	4	4
NHL totals		63	7	12	19	33	11	1	1	2	2

SLEGR, JIRI
D, OILERS

PERSONAL: Born May 30, 1971, in Litvinov, Czechoslovakia. . . . 6-1/205. . . . Shoots left. . . . Name pronounced YOO-ree SLAY-guhr. . . . Son of Jiri Bubla, defenseman, Vancouver Canucks (1981-82 through 1985-86).

TRANSACTIONS/CAREER NOTES: Selected by Vancouver Canucks in second round (third Canucks pick, 23rd overall) of NHL entry draft (June 16, 1990). . . . Played in Europe during 1994-95 NHL lockout. . . . Traded by Canucks to Edmonton Oilers for RW Roman Oksiuta (April 7, 1995).

HONORS: Named to Czechoslovakian League All-Star team (1990-91).

Season Team	League	REGULAR SEASON					PLAYOFFS				
		Gms.	G	A	Pts.	PIM	Gms.	G	A	Pts.	PIM
88-89—Litvinov	Czech.	8	0	0	0	. . .	—	—	—	—	—
89-90—Litvinov	Czech.	51	4	15	19	. . .	—	—	—	—	—
90-91—Litvinov	Czech.	39	10	33	43	26	—	—	—	—	—
91-92—Litvinov	Czech.	38	7	22	29	30	—	—	—	—	—
—Czech. Olympic Team	Int'l	8	1	1	2	. . .	—	—	—	—	—
92-93—Vancouver	NHL	41	4	22	26	109	5	0	3	3	4
—Hamilton	AHL	21	4	14	18	42	—	—	—	—	—
93-94—Vancouver	NHL	78	5	33	38	86	—	—	—	—	—
94-95—Chemopetrol Litvinov	Czech Rep.	11	3	10	13	43	—	—	—	—	—
—Vancouver	NHL	19	1	5	6	32	—	—	—	—	—
—Edmonton	NHL	12	1	5	6	14	—	—	—	—	—
NHL totals		150	11	65	76	241	5	0	3	3	4

SMEHLIK, RICHARD
D, SABRES

PERSONAL: Born January 23, 1970, in Ostrava, Czechoslovakia. . . . 6-3/208. . . . Shoots left. . . . Name pronounced SHMEHL-ihk.

TRANSACTIONS/CAREER NOTES: Selected by Buffalo Sabres in fifth round (third Sabres pick, 97th overall) of NHL entry draft (June 16, 1990). . . . Injured hip (October 30, 1992); missed two games. . . . Played in Europe during 1994-95 NHL lockout. . . . Bruised shoulder (January 27, 1995); missed six games.

Season Team	League	REGULAR SEASON					PLAYOFFS				
		Gms.	G	A	Pts.	PIM	Gms.	G	A	Pts.	PIM
88-89—Vitkovice	Czech.	38	2	5	7	12	—	—	—	—	—
89-90—Vitkovice	Czech.	43	4	3	7	. . .	—	—	—	—	—
90-91—Dukla Jihlava	Czech.	51	4	2	6	22	—	—	—	—	—

Season	Team	League	REGULAR SEASON Gms.	G	A	Pts.	PIM	PLAYOFFS Gms.	G	A	Pts.	PIM
91-92—Vitkovice	Czech.	47	9	10	19	...	—	—	—	—	—	
—Czech. Olympic Team	Int'l	8	0	1	1	2	—	—	—	—	—	
92-93—Buffalo	NHL	80	4	27	31	59	8	0	4	4	2	
93-94—Buffalo	NHL	84	14	27	41	69	7	0	2	2	10	
94-95—HC Vitkovice	Czech Rep.	13	5	2	7	12	—	—	—	—	—	
—Buffalo	NHL	39	4	7	11	46	5	0	0	0	2	
NHL totals		203	22	61	83	174	20	0	6	6	14	

SMIRNOV, PAVEL
RW, FLAMES

PERSONAL: Born May 12, 1977, in Perm, U.S.S.R. . . . 6-3/191. . . . Shoots left.
TRANSACTIONS/CAREER NOTES: Selected by Calgary Flames in second round (second Flames pick, 46th overall) of NHL entry draft (July 8, 1995).

Season	Team	League	REGULAR SEASON Gms.	G	A	Pts.	PIM	PLAYOFFS Gms.	G	A	Pts.	PIM
93-94—Molot Perm	CIS	8	0	0	0	0	—	—	—	—	—	
94-95—Molot Perm	CIS	48	2	2	4	34	—	—	—	—	—	

SMIRNOV, YURI
LW, LIGHTNING

PERSONAL: Born January 10, 1976, in Moscow, Russia. . . . 5-11/172. . . . Shoots left.
TRANSACTIONS/CAREER NOTES: Selected by Tampa Bay Lightning in ninth round (ninth Lightning pick, 216th overall) of NHL entry draft (June 29, 1994).

Season	Team	League	REGULAR SEASON Gms.	G	A	Pts.	PIM	PLAYOFFS Gms.	G	A	Pts.	PIM
93-94—Spartak Moscow	CIS	27	2	3	5	4	—	—	—	—	—	
94-95—Spartak Moscow	CIS	22	1	0	1	0	—	—	—	—	—	

SMITH, ADAM
D, RANGERS

PERSONAL: Born April 24, 1976, in Digby, N.S. . . . 6-0/200. . . . Shoots left.
HIGH SCHOOL: Clover Park (Tacoma, Wash.).
TRANSACTIONS/CAREER NOTES: Selected by New York Rangers in third round (third Rangers pick, 78th overall) of NHL entry draft (June 29, 1994).

Season	Team	League	REGULAR SEASON Gms.	G	A	Pts.	PIM	PLAYOFFS Gms.	G	A	Pts.	PIM
91-92—Kelowna	BCJHL	58	4	4	8	60	—	—	—	—	—	
92-93—Tacoma	WHL	67	0	12	12	43	7	0	1	1	4	
93-94—Tacoma	WHL	66	4	19	23	119	8	0	0	0	10	
94-95—Tacoma	WHL	69	2	19	21	96	4	0	1	1	9	

SMITH, D.J.
D, ISLANDERS

PERSONAL: Born May 13, 1977, in Windsor, Ont. . . . 6-1/210. . . . Shoots left.
HIGH SCHOOL: Holy Names (Winsor, Ont.).
TRANSACTIONS/CAREER NOTES: Selected by New York Islanders in second round (third Islanders pick, 41st overall) of NHL entry draft (July 8, 1995).

Season	Team	League	REGULAR SEASON Gms.	G	A	Pts.	PIM	PLAYOFFS Gms.	G	A	Pts.	PIM
92-93—Belle River	Jr. C	50	11	29	40	101	—	—	—	—	—	
93-94—Windsor	Jr. B	51	8	34	42	267	—	—	—	—	—	
94-95—Windsor	OHL	61	4	13	17	201	10	1	3	4	41	

SMITH, GEOFF
D, PANTHERS

PERSONAL: Born March 7, 1969, in Edmonton. . . . 6-3/194. . . . Shoots left. . . . Full name: Geoff Arthur Smith.
HIGH SCHOOL: Harry Ainlay (Edmonton).
COLLEGE: North Dakota.
TRANSACTIONS/CAREER NOTES: Selected by Edmonton Oilers in third round (third Oilers pick, 63rd overall) of NHL entry draft (June 13, 1987). . . . Fractured ankle (October 1988); missed first 10 games of season. . . . Left University of North Dakota and signed to play with Kamloops Blazers (January 1989). . . . Broke jaw (March 1989). . . . Pulled back muscle (February 8, 1991); missed eight games. . . . Bruised shoulder (April 26, 1992). . . . Traded by Oilers to Florida Panthers for third-round (D Corey Neilson) and sixth-round picks in 1994 draft (December 6, 1993). . . . Lacerated left leg (December 10, 1993); missed two games.
HONORS: Named to WHL All-Star first team (1988-89). . . . Named to NHL All-Rookie team (1989-90).
MISCELLANEOUS: Member of Stanley Cup championship team (1990).

Season	Team	League	REGULAR SEASON Gms.	G	A	Pts.	PIM	PLAYOFFS Gms.	G	A	Pts.	PIM
86-87—St. Albert	AJHL	57	7	28	35	101	—	—	—	—	—	
87-88—Univ. of North Dakota	WCHA	9	0	1	1	8	—	—	—	—	—	
88-89—Kamloops	WHL	32	4	31	35	29	6	1	3	4	12	
89-90—Edmonton	NHL	74	4	11	15	52	3	0	0	0	0	
90-91—Edmonton	NHL	59	1	12	13	55	4	0	0	0	0	
91-92—Edmonton	NHL	74	2	16	18	43	5	0	1	1	6	
92-93—Edmonton	NHL	78	4	14	18	30	—	—	—	—	—	
93-94—Edmonton	NHL	21	0	3	3	12	—	—	—	—	—	
—Florida	NHL	56	1	5	6	38	—	—	—	—	—	
94-95—Florida	NHL	47	2	4	6	22	—	—	—	—	—	
NHL totals		409	14	65	79	252	12	0	1	1	6	

S

SMITH, JASON

D, DEVILS

PERSONAL: Born November 2, 1973, in Calgary.... 6-3/195.... Shoots right.
TRANSACTIONS/CAREER NOTES: Selected by New Jersey Devils in first round (first Devils pick, 18th overall) of NHL entry draft (June 20, 1992).... Injured right knee (November 5, 1994); missed 37 games.

HONORS: Named to Can.HL All-Rookie team (1991-92).... Won Bill Hunter Trophy (1992-93).... Named to Can.HL All-Star first team (1992-93).... Named to WHL (East) All-Star first team (1992-93).

			REGULAR SEASON					PLAYOFFS			
Season Team	League	Gms.	G	A	Pts.	PIM	Gms.	G	A	Pts.	PIM
90-91—Calgary Canucks	AJHL	45	3	15	18	69	—	—	—	—	—
—Regina	WHL	2	0	0	0	7	—	—	—	—	—
91-92—Regina	WHL	62	9	29	38	168	—	—	—	—	—
92-93—Regina	WHL	64	14	52	66	175	13	4	8	12	39
93-94—New Jersey	NHL	41	0	5	5	43	6	0	0	0	7
—Albany	AHL	20	6	3	9	31	—	—	—	—	—
94-95—Albany	AHL	7	0	2	2	15	11	2	2	4	19
—New Jersey	NHL	2	0	0	0	0	—	—	—	—	—
NHL totals		43	0	5	5	43	6	0	0	0	7

SMITH, STEVE

D, BLACKHAWKS

PERSONAL: Born April 30, 1963, in Glasgow, Scotland.... 6-4/215.... Shoots left.... Full name: James Stephen Smith.
TRANSACTIONS/CAREER NOTES: Selected by Edmonton Oilers as underage junior in sixth round (fifth Oilers pick, 111th overall) of NHL entry draft (June 10, 1981).... Strained right shoulder (November 1, 1985).... Pulled stomach muscle (February 1986).... Separated left shoulder (September 20, 1988).... Aggravated shoulder injury (October 1988).... Dislocated left shoulder and tore cartilage (January 2, 1989).... Underwent surgery to left shoulder (January 23, 1989); missed 45 games.... Traded by Oilers to Chicago Blackhawks for D Dave Manson and third-round pick in either 1992 or 1993 draft; Oilers used third-round pick in 1992 draft to select RW Kirk Maltby (September 26, 1991).... Pulled rib-cage muscle (December 31, 1991); missed three games.... Strained back muscle (December 27, 1992); missed four games.... Suspended four games and fined $500 by NHL for slashing (November 22, 1993).... Broke left leg (February 24, 1994); missed remainder of season.
HONORS: Played in NHL All-Star Game (1991).
MISCELLANEOUS: Member of Stanley Cup championship teams (1987, 1988 and 1990).

			REGULAR SEASON					PLAYOFFS			
Season Team	League	Gms.	G	A	Pts.	PIM	Gms.	G	A	Pts.	PIM
80-81—London	OMJHL	62	4	12	16	141	—	—	—	—	—
81-82—London	OHL	58	10	36	46	207	4	1	2	3	13
82-83—London	OHL	50	6	35	41	133	3	1	0	1	10
—Moncton	AHL	2	0	0	0	0	—	—	—	—	—
83-84—Moncton	AHL	64	1	8	9	176	—	—	—	—	—
84-85—Nova Scotia	AHL	68	2	28	30	161	5	0	3	3	40
—Edmonton	NHL	2	0	0	0	2	—	—	—	—	—
85-86—Nova Scotia	AHL	4	0	2	2	11	—	—	—	—	—
—Edmonton	NHL	55	4	20	24	166	6	0	1	1	14
86-87—Edmonton	NHL	62	7	15	22	165	15	1	3	4	45
87-88—Edmonton	NHL	79	12	43	55	286	19	1	11	12	55
88-89—Edmonton	NHL	35	3	19	22	97	7	2	2	4	20
89-90—Edmonton	NHL	75	7	34	41	171	22	5	10	15	37
90-91—Edmonton	NHL	77	13	41	54	193	18	1	2	3	45
91-92—Chicago	NHL	76	9	21	30	304	18	1	11	12	16
92-93—Chicago	NHL	78	10	47	57	214	4	0	0	0	10
93-94—Chicago	NHL	57	5	22	27	174	—	—	—	—	—
94-95—Chicago	NHL	48	1	12	13	128	16	0	1	1	26
NHL totals		644	71	274	345	1900	125	11	41	52	268

SMOLINSKI, BRYAN

C, PENGUINS

PERSONAL: Born December 27, 1971, in Toledo, O.... 6-0/185.... Shoots right.... Full name: Bryan Anthony Smolinski.
COLLEGE: Michigan State.
TRANSACTIONS/CAREER NOTES: Selected by Boston Bruins in first round (first Bruins pick, 21st overall) of NHL entry draft (June 16, 1990).... Injured knee (April 14, 1994); missed one game.... Suffered charley horse (April 1995); missed four games.... Traded by Bruins with RW Glen Murray to Pittsburgh Penguins for LW Kevin Stevens and C Shawn McEachern (August 2, 1995).
HONORS: Named to CCHA All-Rookie team (1989-90).... Named to NCAA All-America West first team (1992-93).... Named to CCHA All-Star first team (1992-93).
STATISTICAL PLATEAUS: Three-goal games: 1994-95 (1).

			REGULAR SEASON					PLAYOFFS			
Season Team	League	Gms.	G	A	Pts.	PIM	Gms.	G	A	Pts.	PIM
87-88—Detroit Little Caesars	MNHL	80	43	77	120	...	—	—	—	—	—
88-89—Stratford Jr. B	OHA	46	32	62	94	132	—	—	—	—	—
89-90—Michigan State	CCHA	39	10	17	27	45	—	—	—	—	—
90-91—Michigan State	CCHA	35	9	12	21	24	—	—	—	—	—
91-92—Michigan State	CCHA	44	30	35	65	59	—	—	—	—	—
92-93—Michigan State	CCHA	40	31	37	*68	93	—	—	—	—	—
—Boston	NHL	9	1	3	4	0	4	1	0	1	2
93-94—Boston	NHL	83	31	20	51	82	13	5	4	9	4
94-95—Boston	NHL	44	18	13	31	31	5	0	1	1	4
NHL totals		136	50	36	86	113	22	6	5	11	10

SMYTH, GREG

D, BLACKHAWKS

PERSONAL: Born April 23, 1966, in Oakville, Ont. . . . 6-3/212. . . . Shoots right. . . . Name pronounced SMIHTH.

TRANSACTIONS/CAREER NOTES: Selected by Philadelphia Flyers as underage junior in second round (first Flyers pick, 22nd overall) of NHL entry draft (June 9, 1984). . . . Suspended 10 games by OHL for fighting with fans (December 1984). . . . Suspended by London Knights (October 1985). . . . Suspended eight games by OHL (November 7, 1985). . . . Traded by Flyers with third-round pick in 1989 draft (G John Tanner) to Quebec Nordiques for D Terry Carkner (July 25, 1988). . . . Broke two bones in right hand during training camp (September 1988). . . . Suspended eight games by AHL for fighting (December 17, 1988). . . . Injured back (February 15, 1990). . . . Recalled from Halifax by Quebec and refused to report (February 10, 1991). . . . Traded by Nordiques to Calgary Flames for RW Martin Simard (March 10, 1992). . . . Strained stomach (October 6, 1992); missed first four games of season. . . . Injured ribs (December 4, 1992); missed four games. . . . Signed as free agent by Florida Panthers (July 14, 1993). . . . Underwent surgery to right elbow (October 6, 1993); missed five games. . . . Traded by Panthers to Toronto Maple Leafs for future considerations (December 7, 1993). . . . Claimed on waivers by Chicago Blackhawks (January 9, 1994). . . . Pulled rib cage muscle (January 27, 1994); missed four games.

HONORS: Named to OHL All-Star second team (1985-86).

			REGULAR SEASON					PLAYOFFS				
Season	Team	League	Gms.	G	A	Pts.	PIM	Gms.	G	A	Pts.	PIM
83-84	—London	OHL	64	4	21	25	*252	6	1	0	1	24
84-85	—London	OHL	47	7	16	23	188	8	2	2	4	27
85-86	—London	OHL	46	12	42	54	197	4	1	2	3	28
	—Hershey	AHL	2	0	1	1	5	8	0	0	0	60
86-87	—Hershey	AHL	35	0	2	2	158	2	0	0	0	19
	—Philadelphia	NHL	1	0	0	0	0	1	0	0	0	2
87-88	—Hershey	AHL	21	0	10	10	102	—	—	—	—	—
	—Philadelphia	NHL	48	1	6	7	192	5	0	0	0	38
88-89	—Halifax	AHL	43	3	9	12	310	4	0	1	1	35
	—Quebec	NHL	10	0	1	1	70	—	—	—	—	—
89-90	—Quebec	NHL	13	0	0	0	57	—	—	—	—	—
	—Halifax	AHL	49	5	14	19	235	6	1	0	1	52
90-91	—Quebec	NHL	1	0	0	0	0	—	—	—	—	—
	—Halifax	AHL	56	6	23	29	340	—	—	—	—	—
91-92	—Quebec	NHL	29	0	2	2	138	—	—	—	—	—
	—Halifax	AHL	9	1	3	4	35	—	—	—	—	—
	—Calgary	NHL	7	1	1	2	15	—	—	—	—	—
92-93	—Calgary	NHL	35	1	2	3	95	—	—	—	—	—
	—Salt Lake City	IHL	5	0	1	1	31	—	—	—	—	—
93-94	—Florida	NHL	12	1	0	1	37	—	—	—	—	—
	—Toronto	NHL	11	0	1	1	38	—	—	—	—	—
	—Chicago	NHL	38	0	0	0	108	6	0	0	0	0
94-95	—Chicago	NHL	22	0	3	3	33	—	—	—	—	—
	—Indianapolis	IHL	2	0	0	0	0	—	—	—	—	—
	NHL totals		227	4	16	20	783	12	0	0	0	40

SMYTH, KEVIN

LW, WHALERS

PERSONAL: Born November 22, 1973, in Banff, Alta. . . . 6-2/217. . . . Shoots left. . . . Name pronounced SMIHTH. . . . Brother of Ryan Smyth, left winger in Edmonton Oilers system.

TRANSACTIONS/CAREER NOTES: Selected by Hartford Whalers in fourth round (fourth Whalers pick, 79th overall) of NHL entry draft (June 20, 1992). . . . Bruised spleen (February 11, 1994); missed six games. . . . Injured shoulder (March 22, 1994); missed four games.

			REGULAR SEASON					PLAYOFFS				
Season	Team	League	Gms.	G	A	Pts.	PIM	Gms.	G	A	Pts.	PIM
90-91	—Moose Jaw	WHL	66	30	45	75	96	6	1	1	2	0
91-92	—Moose Jaw	WHL	71	30	55	85	114	4	1	3	4	6
92-93	—Moose Jaw	WHL	64	44	38	82	111	—	—	—	—	—
93-94	—Springfield	AHL	42	22	27	49	72	6	4	5	9	0
	—Hartford	NHL	21	3	2	5	10	—	—	—	—	—
94-95	—Springfield	AHL	57	17	22	39	72	—	—	—	—	—
	—Hartford	NHL	16	1	5	6	13	—	—	—	—	—
	NHL totals		37	4	7	11	23					

SMYTH, RYAN

LW, OILERS

PERSONAL: Born February 21, 1976, in Banff, Alta. . . . 6-1/185. . . . Shoots left. . . . Name pronounced SMIHTH. . . . Brother of Kevin Smyth, left winger in Hartford Whalers system.

HIGH SCHOOL: Vanier Comm. Catholic (Edson, Alta.).

TRANSACTIONS/CAREER NOTES: Selected by Edmonton Oilers in first round (second Oilers pick, sixth overall) of NHL entry draft (June 28, 1994).

HONORS: Named to Can.HL All-Star first team (1994-95). . . . Named to WHL (East) All-Star second team (1994-95).

			REGULAR SEASON					PLAYOFFS				
Season	Team	League	Gms.	G	A	Pts.	PIM	Gms.	G	A	Pts.	PIM
91-92	—Moose Jaw	WHL	2	0	0	0	0	—	—	—	—	—
92-93	—Moose Jaw	WHL	64	19	14	33	59	—	—	—	—	—
93-94	—Moose Jaw	WHL	72	50	55	105	88	—	—	—	—	—
94-95	—Moose Jaw	WHL	50	41	45	86	66	10	6	9	15	22
	—Edmonton	NHL	3	0	0	0	0	—	—	—	—	—
	NHL totals		3	0	0	0	0					

S

SNELL, CHRIS
D, KINGS

PERSONAL: Born May 12, 1971, in Regina, Sask. . . . 5-10/200. . . . Shoots left.
TRANSACTIONS/CAREER NOTES: Signed as free agent by Toronto Maple Leafs (August 3, 1993).
. . . Traded by Maple Leafs with LW Eric Lacroix and fourth-round pick in 1996 draft to Los Angeles Kings for RW Dixon Ward, C Guy Leveque, RW Shayne Toporowski and C Kelly Fairchild (October 3, 1994). . . . Suffered from the flu (April 23, 1995); missed one game.
HONORS: Named to OHL All-Star first team (1989-90). . . . Won Eddie Shore Plaque (1993-94). . . . Named to AHL All-Star first team (1993-94). . . . Named to IHL All-Star first team (1994-95).

			REGULAR SEASON					PLAYOFFS				
Season	Team	League	Gms.	G	A	Pts.	PIM	Gms.	G	A	Pts.	PIM
89-90—Ottawa	OHL	63	18	62	80	36	3	2	4	6	4
90-91—Ottawa	OHL	54	23	59	82	58	17	3	14	17	8
91-92—Rochester	AHL	65	5	27	32	66	10	2	1	3	6
92-93—Rochester	AHL	76	14	57	71	83	17	5	8	13	39
93-94—St. John's	AHL	75	22	74	96	92	11	1	15	16	10
—Toronto	NHL	2	0	0	0	2	—	—	—	—	—
94-95—Phoenix	IHL	57	15	49	64	122	—	—	—	—	—
—Los Angeles	NHL	32	2	7	9	22	—	—	—	—	—
NHL totals		**34**	**2**	**7**	**9**	**24**					

SNOPEK, JAN
D, OILERS

PERSONAL: Born June 22, 1976, in Prague, Czechoslovakia. . . . 6-3/212. . . . Shoots right.
HIGH SCHOOL: Henry Street (Whitby, Ont.).
TRANSACTIONS/CAREER NOTES: Selected by Edmonton Oilers in fifth round (fifth Oilers pick, 109th overall) of NHL entry draft (July 8, 1995).

			REGULAR SEASON					PLAYOFFS				
Season	Team	League	Gms.	G	A	Pts.	PIM	Gms.	G	A	Pts.	PIM
92-93—Sparta Prague	Czech.	40	3	8	11	80	—	—	—	—	—
93-94—Oshawa	OHL	52	0	5	5	51	—	—	—	—	—
94-95—Oshawa	OHL	64	14	30	44	97	7	0	1	1	4

SNOW, GARTH
G, FLYERS

PERSONAL: Born July 28, 1969, in Wrentham, Mass. . . . 6-3/200. . . . Catches left.
HIGH SCHOOL: Mount St. Charles Academy (Woonsocket, R.I.).
COLLEGE: Maine.
TRANSACTIONS/CAREER NOTES: Selected by Quebec Nordiques in sixth round (sixth Nordiques pick, 114th overall) of NHL entry draft (June 13, 1987). . . . Traded by Nordiques to Philadelphia Flyers for third- and sixth-round picks in 1996 draft (July 12, 1995).
HONORS: Named to NCAA All-Tournament team (1992-93). . . . Named to Hockey East All-Star second team (1992-93).

			REGULAR SEASON							PLAYOFFS						
Season	Team	League	Gms.	Min.	W	L	T	GA	SO	Avg.	Gms.	Min.	W	L	GA	SO	Avg.
88-89—University of Maine	Hoc. East	5	241	2	2	0	14	1	3.49	—	—	—	—	—	—	—
89-90—University of Maine	Hoc. East						Did not play.			—	—	—	—	—	—	—
90-91—University of Maine	Hoc. East	25	1290	18	4	0	64	0	2.98	—	—	—	—	—	—	—
91-92—University of Maine	Hoc. East	31	1792	25	4	2	73	2	2.44	—	—	—	—	—	—	—
92-93—University of Maine	Hoc. East	23	1210	21	0	1	42	1	2.08	—	—	—	—	—	—	—
93-94—U.S. national team	Int'l	23	1324	...	...	...	71	...	3.22	—	—	—	—	—	—	—
—Quebec	NHL	5	279	3	2	0	16	0	3.44	—	—	—	—	—	—	—
—U.S. Olympic Team	Int'l	5	299	...	...	...	17	0	3.41	—	—	—	—	—	—	—
—Cornwall	AHL	16	927	6	5	3	51	0	3.30	13	790	8	5	42	0	3.19
94-95—Cornwall	AHL	62	3558	*32	20	7	162	3	2.73	8	402	4	3	14	+2	*2.09
—Quebec	NHL	2	119	1	1	0	11	0	5.55	1	9	0	0	1	0	6.67
NHL totals		**7**	**398**	**4**	**3**	**0**	**27**	**0**	**4.07**	**1**	**9**	**0**	**0**	**1**	**0**	**6.67**

SODERSTROM, TOMMY
G, ISLANDERS

PERSONAL: Born July 17, 1969, in Stockholm, Sweden. . . . 5-9/156. . . . Catches left. . . . Name pronounced SAH-duhr-struhm.
TRANSACTIONS/CAREER NOTES: Selected by Philadelphia Flyers in 11th round (14th Flyers pick, 214th overall) of NHL entry draft (June 16, 1990). . . . Underwent procedure to correct Wolff-Parkinson-White syndrome (November 3, 1993); missed six games. . . . Traded by Flyers to New York Islanders for G Ron Hextall and sixth-round pick (D Dmitri Tertyshny) in 1995 draft (September 22, 1994).
HONORS: Named Swedish League Rookie of the Year (1990-91). . . . Named to Swedish League All-Star team (1991-92).

			REGULAR SEASON							PLAYOFFS						
Season	Team	League	Gms.	Min.	W	L	T	GA	SO	Avg.	Gms.	Min.	W	L	GA	SO	Avg.
89-90—Djurgarden Stockholm	Sweden	4	240	...	...	...	14	0	3.50	—	—	—	—	—	—	—
90-91—Djurgarden Stockholm	Sweden	39	2340	22	12	6	104	3	2.67	7	423	...	...	10	2	1.42
91-92—Djurgarden Stockholm	Sweden	31	2357	15	8	11	112	1	2.85	10	635	...	...	28	0	2.65
—Swedish Olympic Team	Int'l	5	296	...	...	...	13	0	2.64	—	—	—	—	—	—	—
92-93—Hershey	AHL	7	373	4	1	0	15	0	2.41	—	—	—	—	—	—	—
—Philadelphia	NHL	44	2512	20	17	6	143	5	3.42	—	—	—	—	—	—	—
93-94—Philadelphia	NHL	34	1736	6	18	4	116	2	4.01	—	—	—	—	—	—	—
—Hershey	AHL	9	462	3	4	1	37	0	4.81	—	—	—	—	—	—	—
94-95—New York Islanders	NHL	26	1350	8	12	3	70	1	3.11	—	—	—	—	—	—	—
NHL totals		**104**	**5598**	**34**	**47**	**13**	**329**	**8**	**3.53**							

S

SOKOLSKY, JAMIE
D, FLYERS

PERSONAL: Born March 11, 1977, in Toronto.... 6-2/202.... Shoots right.
HIGH SCHOOL: Huron Heights Secondary School (Newmarket, Ont.).
TRANSACTIONS/CAREER NOTES: Selected by Philadelphia Flyers in sixth round (fifth Flyers pick, 135th overall) of NHL entry draft (July 8, 1995).

			REGULAR SEASON					PLAYOFFS				
Season	Team	League	Gms.	G	A	Pts.	PIM	Gms.	G	A	Pts.	PIM
92-93—Caledon		Jr. A	3	1	0	1	4	—	—	—	—	—
93-94—Newmarket		OHL	41	0	3	3	11	—	—	—	—	—
94-95—Belleville		OHL	63	4	18	22	28	16	3	6	9	14

SOMIK, RADOVAN
LW, FLYERS

PERSONAL: Born May 5, 1977, in Martin, Czechoslovakia.... 6-2/194.... Shoots right.
TRANSACTIONS/CAREER NOTES: Selected by Philadelphia Flyers in fourth round (third Flyers pick, 100th overall) of NHL entry draft (July 8, 1995).

			REGULAR SEASON					PLAYOFFS				
Season	Team	League	Gms.	G	A	Pts.	PIM	Gms.	G	A	Pts.	PIM
93-94—Martimex ZTS Martin		Slovakia	1	0	0	0	0	—	—	—	—	—
94-95—Martimex ZTS Martin		Slovakia	28	4	0	4	31	3	1	0	1	2

SOPEL, BRENT
D, CANUCKS

PERSONAL: Born January 7, 1977, in Calgary.... 6-1/185.... Shoots right.
TRANSACTIONS/CAREER NOTES: Selected by Vancouver Canucks in sixth round (sixth Canucks pick, 144th overall) of NHL entry draft (July 8, 1995).

			REGULAR SEASON					PLAYOFFS				
Season	Team	League	Gms.	G	A	Pts.	PIM	Gms.	G	A	Pts.	PIM
93-94—Saskatoon		WHL	11	2	2	4	2	—	—	—	—	—
94-95—Saskatoon		WHL	22	1	10	11	31	—	—	—	—	—
—Swift Current		WHL	41	4	19	23	50	3	0	3	3	0

SOROCHAN, LEE
D, RANGERS

PERSONAL: Born September 9, 1975, in Edmonton.... 5-11/208... Shoots left.... Name pronounced suh-RAH-kuhn.
HIGH SCHOOL: Gibbons (Alta.).
TRANSACTIONS/CAREER NOTES: Selected by New York Rangers in second round (second Rangers pick, 34th overall) of NHL entry draft (June 26, 1993).

			REGULAR SEASON					PLAYOFFS				
Season	Team	League	Gms.	G	A	Pts.	PIM	Gms.	G	A	Pts.	PIM
91-92—Lethbridge		WHL	67	2	9	11	105	5	0	2	2	6
92-93—Lethbridge		WHL	69	8	32	40	208	4	0	1	1	12
93-94—Lethbridge		WHL	46	5	27	32	123	9	4	3	7	16
94-95—Lethbridge		WHL	29	4	15	19	93	—	—	—	—	—
—Saskatoon		WHL	24	5	13	18	63	10	3	6	9	34
—Binghamton		AHL	—	—	—	—	—	8	0	0	0	11

SOUCY, CHRISTIAN
G, BLACKHAWKS

PERSONAL: Born September 14, 1970, in Gatineau, Que.... 5-11/160.... Catches left.... Name pronounced SOO-see.
COLLEGE: Vermont.
TRANSACTIONS/CAREER NOTES: Signed as free agent by Chicago Blackhawks (June 21, 1993).
HONORS: Named to NCAA All-America East second team (1991-92).... Named to ECAC All-Star second team (1992-93).

			REGULAR SEASON							PLAYOFFS					
Season	Team	League	Gms.	Min.	W	L	T	GA	SO	Avg.	Gms.	Min.	W	L	GA	SO	Avg.
89-90—Pembroke		CJHL	47	2721	16	24	4	212	1	4.67	—	—	—	—	—	—	—
90-91—Pembroke		CJHL	54	3109	27	24	1	198	2	3.82	—	—	—	—	—	—	—
91-92—University of Vermont		ECAC	30	1783	15	11	3	84	1	2.83	—	—	—	—	—	—	—
92-93—University of Vermont		ECAC	29	1708	11	15	3	90	2	3.16	—	—	—	—	—	—	—
93-94—Indianapolis		IHL	46	2302	14	*25	‡1	159	1	4.14	—	—	—	—	—	—	—
—Chicago		NHL	1	3	0	0	0	0	0	0.00	—	—	—	—	—	—	—
94-95—Indianapolis		IHL	42	2217	15	17	‡5	148	0	4.01	—	—	—	—	—	—	—
NHL totals			1	3	0	0	0	0	0	0.00							

SOULLIERE, STEPHANE
LW, KINGS

PERSONAL: Born May 30, 1975, in Greenfield Park, Que.... 5-11/181.... Shoots left.... Name pronounced soo-lee-YAIR.
TRANSACTIONS/CAREER NOTES: Signed as free agent by Los Angeles Kings (July 14, 1994).

			REGULAR SEASON					PLAYOFFS				
Season	Team	League	Gms.	G	A	Pts.	PIM	Gms.	G	A	Pts.	PIM
92-93—Oshawa		OHL	65	11	7	18	77	13	1	0	1	19
93-94—Oshawa		OHL	63	25	24	49	120	5	0	1	1	12
94-95—Oshawa		OHL	18	9	21	30	27	—	—	—	—	—
—Sarnia		OHL	22	10	9	19	38	—	—	—	—	—
—Guelph		OHL	22	10	8	18	48	14	3	2	5	21

S

SOURAY, SHELDON
D, DEVILS

PERSONAL: Born July 13, 1976, in Elk Point, Alta. . . . 6-3/210. . . . Shoots left.
TRANSACTIONS/CAREER NOTES: Selected by New Jersey Devils in third round (third Devils pick, 71st overall) of NHL entry draft (June 29, 1994).

			REGULAR SEASON					PLAYOFFS				
Season	Team	League	Gms.	G	A	Pts.	PIM	Gms.	G	A	Pts.	PIM
92-93—Fort Saskatchewan		AJHL	35	0	12	12	125	—	—	—	—	—
—Tri-City		WHL	2	0	0	0	0	—	—	—	—	—
93-94—Tri-City		WHL	42	3	6	9	122	—	—	—	—	—
94-95—Tri-City		WHL	40	2	24	26	140	—	—	—	—	—
—Prince George..................		WHL	11	2	3	5	23	—	—	—	—	—
—Albany..............................		AHL	7	0	2	2	8	—	—	—	—	—

SPANHEL, MARTIN
LW, FLYERS

PERSONAL: Born July 1, 1977, in Gottwaldov, Czechoslovakia. . . . 6-2/187. . . . Shoots left.
TRANSACTIONS/CAREER NOTES: Selected by Philadelphia Flyers in sixth round (fifth Flyers pick, 152nd overall) of NHL entry draft (July 8, 1995).

			REGULAR SEASON					PLAYOFFS				
Season	Team	League	Gms.	G	A	Pts.	PIM	Gms.	G	A	Pts.	PIM
94-95—ZPS Zlin Jrs.....................		Czech. Jrs.	33	25	16	41	...	—	—	—	—	—
—ZPS Zlin...........................		Czech Rep.	1	0	0	0	...	—	—	—	—	—

STAIOS, STEVE
D, BLUES

PERSONAL: Born July 28, 1973, in Hamilton, Ont. . . . 6-0/183. . . . Shoots right. . . . Name pronounced STAY-ohz.
TRANSACTIONS/CAREER NOTES: Selected by St. Louis Blues in second round (first Blues pick, 27th overall) of NHL entry draft (June 22, 1991).

			REGULAR SEASON					PLAYOFFS				
Season	Team	League	Gms.	G	A	Pts.	PIM	Gms.	G	A	Pts.	PIM
89-90—Hamilton Jr. B		OHA	40	9	27	36	66	—	—	—	—	—
90-91—Niagara Falls		OHL	66	17	29	46	115	12	2	3	5	10
91-92—Niagara Falls		OHL	65	11	42	53	122	17	7	8	15	27
92-93—Niagara Falls		OHL	12	4	14	18	30	—	—	—	—	—
—Sudbury..........................		OHL	53	13	44	57	67	11	5	6	11	22
93-94—Peoria		IHL	38	3	9	12	42	—	—	—	—	—
94-95—Peoria		IHL	60	3	13	16	64	6	0	0	0	10

STAJDUHAR, NICK
D, OILERS

PERSONAL: Born December 6, 1974, in Kitchener, Ont. . . . 6-2/1195. . . . Shoots left. . . . Name pronounced STAJ-doo-hahr.
TRANSACTIONS/CAREER NOTES: Selected by Edmonton Oilers in first round (second Oilers pick, 16th overall) of NHL entry draft (June 26, 1993).
HONORS: Named to OHL All-Star first team (1993-94).

			REGULAR SEASON					PLAYOFFS				
Season	Team	League	Gms.	G	A	Pts.	PIM	Gms.	G	A	Pts.	PIM
90-91—London		OHL	66	3	12	15	39	7	0	0	0	2
91-92—London		OHL	66	6	15	21	62	10	1	4	5	10
92-93—London		OHL	49	15	46	61	58	12	4	11	15	10
93-94—London		OHL	52	34	52	86	58	5	0	2	2	8
94-95—Cape Breton		AHL	54	12	26	38	55	—	—	—	—	—

STANTON, PAUL
D, ISLANDERS

PERSONAL: Born June 22, 1967, in Boston. . . . 6-1/200. . . . Shoots right. . . . Full name: Paul Fredrick Stanton.
HIGH SCHOOL: Catholic Memorial (Boston).
COLLEGE: Wisconsin.
TRANSACTIONS/CAREER NOTES: Selected by Pittsburgh Penguins in eighth round (eighth Penguins pick, 149th overall) of NHL entry draft (June 15, 1985). . . . Injured knee ligament (October 31, 1991); missed 16 games. . . . Traded by Penguins to Boston Bruins for third-round pick (LW Greg Crozier) in 1994 draft (October 8, 1993). . . . Suffered from the flu (April 7, 1994); missed one game. . . . Traded by Bruins to New York Islanders for future considerations (February 11, 1995).
HONORS: Named to NCAA All-America West first team (1987-88). . . . Named to WCHA All-Star first team (1988-89).
MISCELLANEOUS: Member of Stanley Cup championship teams (1991 and 1992).

			REGULAR SEASON					PLAYOFFS				
Season	Team	League	Gms.	G	A	Pts.	PIM	Gms.	G	A	Pts.	PIM
83-84—Catholic Memorial H.S.		Mass. H.S.	...	15	20	35	...	—	—	—	—	—
84-85—Catholic Memorial H.S.		Mass. H.S.	20	16	21	37	17	—	—	—	—	—
85-86—University of Wisconsin		WCHA	36	4	6	10	16	—	—	—	—	—
86-87—University of Wisconsin ...		WCHA	41	5	17	22	70	—	—	—	—	—
87-88—University of Wisconsin ...		WCHA	45	9	38	47	98	—	—	—	—	—
88-89—University of Wisconsin ...		WCHA	45	7	29	36	126	—	—	—	—	—
89-90—Muskegon.......................		IHL	77	5	27	32	61	15	2	4	6	21
90-91—Pittsburgh		NHL	75	5	18	23	40	22	1	2	3	24
91-92—Pittsburgh		NHL	54	2	8	10	62	†21	1	7	8	42
92-93—Pittsburgh		NHL	77	4	12	16	97	1	0	1	1	0
93-94—Boston		NHL	71	3	7	10	54	—	—	—	—	—

Season	Team	League	REGULAR SEASON Gms.	G	A	Pts.	PIM	PLAYOFFS Gms.	G	A	Pts.	PIM
94-95—Providence		AHL	8	4	4	8	4	—	—	—	—	—
—Denver		IHL	11	2	6	8	15	—	—	—	—	—
—New York Islanders		NHL	18	0	4	4	9	—	—	—	—	—
NHL totals			295	14	49	63	262	44	2	10	12	66

STAPLETON, MIKE
C/RW, OILERS

PERSONAL: Born May 5, 1966, in Sarnia, Ont. . . . 5-10/185. . . . Shoots right. . . . Son of Pat Stapleton, defenseman, Boston Bruins and Chicago Blackhawks (1961-62 through 1972-73); and Chicago Cougars, Indianapolis Racers and Cincinnati Stingers of WHA (1973-74 through 1977-78).

TRANSACTIONS/CAREER NOTES: Selected by Chicago Blackhawks in seventh round (seventh Blackhawks pick, 132nd overall) of NHL entry draft (June 9, 1984). . . . Signed as free agent by Pittsburgh Penguins (September 4, 1992). . . . Claimed on waivers by Edmonton Oilers (February 19, 1994).

Season	Team	League	REGULAR SEASON Gms.	G	A	Pts.	PIM	PLAYOFFS Gms.	G	A	Pts.	PIM
82-83—Strathroy Jr. B		OHA	40	39	38	77	99	—	—	—	—	—
83-84—Cornwall		OHL	70	24	45	69	94	3	1	2	3	4
84-85—Cornwall		OHL	56	41	44	85	68	9	2	4	6	23
85-86—Cornwall		OHL	56	39	65	104	74	6	2	3	5	2
86-87—Canadian national team		Int'l	21	2	4	6	4	—	—	—	—	—
—Chicago		NHL	39	3	6	9	6	4	0	0	0	2
87-88—Saginaw		IHL	31	11	19	30	52	10	5	6	11	10
—Chicago		NHL	53	2	9	11	59	—	—	—	—	—
88-89—Chicago		NHL	7	0	1	1	7	—	—	—	—	—
—Saginaw		IHL	69	21	47	68	162	6	1	3	4	4
89-90—Arvika		Sweden	30	15	18	33	...	—	—	—	—	—
—Indianapolis		IHL	16	5	10	15	6	13	9	10	19	38
90-91—Chicago		NHL	7	0	1	1	2	—	—	—	—	—
—Indianapolis		IHL	75	29	52	81	76	7	1	4	5	0
91-92—Indianapolis		IHL	59	18	40	58	65	—	—	—	—	—
—Chicago		NHL	19	4	4	8	8	—	—	—	—	—
92-93—Pittsburgh		NHL	78	4	9	13	10	4	0	0	0	0
93-94—Pittsburgh		NHL	58	7	4	11	18	—	—	—	—	—
—Edmonton		NHL	23	5	9	14	28	—	—	—	—	—
94-95—Edmonton		NHL	46	6	11	17	21	—	—	—	—	—
NHL totals			330	31	54	85	159	8	0	0	0	2

STAROSTENKO, DIMITRI
RW, RANGERS

PERSONAL: Born March 18, 1973, in Minsk, U.S.S.R. . . . 6-0/185. . . . Shoots left. . . . Name pronounced STAIR-ih-STEHN-koh.

TRANSACTIONS/CAREER NOTES: Selected by New York Rangers in fifth round (fifth Rangers pick, 120th overall) of NHL entry draft (June 20, 1992).

Season	Team	League	REGULAR SEASON Gms.	G	A	Pts.	PIM	PLAYOFFS Gms.	G	A	Pts.	PIM
89-90—Dynamo Minsk		USSR	7	0	0	0	2	—	—	—	—	—
90-91—CSKA Moscow		USSR	20	2	1	3	4	—	—	—	—	—
91-92—CSKA Moscow		CIS	32	3	1	4	12	—	—	—	—	—
92-93—CSKA Moscow		CIS	42	15	12	27	22	—	—	—	—	—
93-94—Binghamton		AHL	41	12	9	21	10	—	—	—	—	—
94-95—Binghamton		AHL	69	19	22	41	40	5	1	1	2	0

STASTNY, PETER
C, BLUES

PERSONAL: Born September 18, 1956, in Bratislava, Czechoslovakia. . . . 6-1/200. . . . Shoots left. . . . Name pronounced STAST-nee. . . . Brother of Anton Stastny, left winger, Quebec Nordiques (1980-81 through 1988-89); and brother of Marian Stastny, right winger, Quebec Nordiques and Toronto Maple Leafs (1981-82 through 1985-86).

TRANSACTIONS/CAREER NOTES: Signed as free agent by Quebec Nordiques (August 26, 1980). . . . Injured knee (December 18, 1982). . . . Suspended five games by NHL (October 1984). . . . Injured lower back (November 1987). . . . Sprained left shoulder (December 1988). . . . Suffered sore left knee (December 1989). . . . Traded by Nordiques to New Jersey Devils for D Craig Wolanin and future considerations (March 6, 1990); Devils sent D Randy Velischek to Nordiques to complete deal (August 1990). . . . Suffered from digestive virus (February 29, 1992); missed eight games. . . . Suffered from minor knee sprain and the flu (March 21, 1992); missed five games. . . . Missed first five games of regular season due to contract dispute (October 1992). . . . Suffered from the flu (January 22, 1993); missed two games. . . . Bruised shoulder (March 7, 1993); missed one game. . . . Signed as free agent by St. Louis Blues (March 9, 1994). . . . Injured knee (February 7, 1995); missed 14 games.

HONORS: Named to Czechoslovakian League All-Star second team (1977-78). . . . Named to Czechoslovakian League All-Star first team (1978-79). . . . Named Czechoslovakian League Player of the Year (1979-80). . . . Named NHL Rookie of the Year by THE SPORTING NEWS (1980-81). . . . Won Calder Memorial Trophy (1980-81). . . . Played in NHL All-Star Game (1981, 1982-1984, 1986 and 1988).

RECORDS: Shares NHL single-season record for most assists by a rookie—70 (1980-81). . . . Shares NHL single-game records for most points by a rookie—8 (February 22, 1981); and most points for road game—8 (February 22, 1981).

STATISTICAL PLATEAUS: Three-goal games: 1980-81 (1), 1981-82 (2), 1982-83 (4), 1985-86 (2), 1987-88 (3), 1988-89 (1), 1989-90 (1), 1991-92 (1). Total: 15. . . . Four-goal games: 1980-81 (1), 1988-89 (1). Total: 2. . . . Total hat tricks: 17.

MISCELLANEOUS: Captain of Quebec Nordiques (1985-86 through 1989-90).

STATISTICAL NOTES: One of three players to score 100 points in each of their first six NHL seasons (Wayne Gretzky and Mario Lemieux).

Season Team	League	REGULAR SEASON Gms.	G	A	Pts.	PIM	PLAYOFFS Gms.	G	A	Pts.	PIM
77-78—Slovan Bratislava	Czech.	44	29	24	53	...	—	—	—	—	—
—Czech. national team	Int'l	16	5	2	7	...	—	—	—	—	—
78-79—Slovan Bratislava	Czech.	44	32	23	55	...	—	—	—	—	—
—Czech. national team	Int'l	18	12	9	21	...	—	—	—	—	—
79-80—Slovan Bratislava	Czech.	40	28	30	58	...	—	—	—	—	—
—Czech. Olympic Team	Int'l	6	7	7	14	6	—	—	—	—	—
80-81—Quebec	NHL	77	39	70	109	37	5	2	8	10	7
81-82—Quebec	NHL	80	46	93	139	91	12	7	11	18	10
82-83—Quebec	NHL	75	47	77	124	78	4	3	2	5	10
83-84—Quebec	NHL	80	46	73	119	73	9	2	7	9	31
84-85—Quebec	NHL	75	32	68	100	95	18	4	19	23	24
85-86—Quebec	NHL	76	41	81	122	60	3	0	1	1	2
86-87—Quebec	NHL	64	24	53	77	43	13	6	9	15	12
87-88—Quebec	NHL	76	46	65	111	69	—	—	—	—	—
88-89—Quebec	NHL	72	35	50	85	117	—	—	—	—	—
89-90—Quebec	NHL	62	24	38	62	24	—	—	—	—	—
—New Jersey	NHL	12	5	6	11	16	6	3	2	5	4
90-91—New Jersey	NHL	77	18	42	60	53	7	3	4	7	2
91-92—New Jersey	NHL	66	24	38	62	42	7	3	7	10	19
92-93—New Jersey	NHL	62	17	23	40	22	5	0	2	2	2
93-94—Slovan Bratislava	Slovakia	4	0	4	4	0	—	—	—	—	—
—Slovakian Olympic team...	Int'l	8	5	4	9	9	—	—	—	—	—
—St. Louis	NHL	17	5	11	16	4	4	0	0	0	2
94-95—St. Louis	NHL	6	1	1	2	0	—	—	—	—	—
NHL totals..		977	450	789	1239	824	93	33	72	105	125

STAUBER, ROBB
G, SABRES

PERSONAL: Born November 25, 1967, in Duluth, Minn. ... 5-11/180. ... Catches left. ... Name pronounced STAW-buhr.
HIGH SCHOOL: Denfeld (Duluth, Minn.).
COLLEGE: Minnesota.
TRANSACTIONS/CAREER NOTES: Selected by Los Angeles Kings in sixth round (fifth Kings pick, 107th overall) of NHL entry draft (June 21, 1986). ... Twisted left knee and ankle (December 3, 1988); missed 14 games. ... Injured groin and back (October 1989). ... Underwent knee surgery (March 1991). ... Strained shoulder (November 6, 1993); missed four games. ... Broke tip of right ring-finger (January 22, 1995); missed nine games. ... Traded by Kings with D Alexei Zhitnik, D Charlie Huddy and fifth-round pick in 1995 draft (D Marian Menhart) to Buffalo Sabres for G Grant Fuhr, D Philippe Boucher and D Denis Tsygurov (February 14, 1995). ... Sprained knee (April 24, 1995); missed two games.
HONORS: Won Hobey Baker Memorial Award (1987-88). ... Won WCHA Most Valuable Player Award (1987-88). ... Won WCHA Goaltender of the Year Award (1987-88 and 1988-89). ... Named to NCAA All-America West first team (1987-88). ... Named to WCHA All-Star first team (1987-88). ... Named to WCHA All-Star second team (1988-89).

Season Team	League	REGULAR SEASON Gms.	Min.	W	L	T	GA	SO	Avg.	PLAYOFFS Gms.	Min.	W	L	GA	SO	Avg.
84-85—Duluth Denfeld H.S.	Minn. HS	22	990	...	...	...	37	0	2.24	—	—	—	—	—	—	—
85-86—Duluth Denfeld H.S.	Minn. HS	27	1215	...	...	...	66	0	3.26	—	—	—	—	—	—	—
86-87—Univ. of Minnesota.......	WCHA	20	1072	13	5	0	63	0	3.53	—	—	—	—	—	—	—
87-88—Univ. of Minnesota.......	WCHA	44	2621	34	10	0	119	5	2.72	—	—	—	—	—	—	—
88-89—Univ. of Minnesota.......	WCHA	34	2024	26	8	0	82	0	2.43	—	—	—	—	—	—	—
89-90—New Haven	AHL	14	851	6	6	2	43	0	3.03	5	302	2	3	24	0	4.77
—Los Angeles...................	NHL	2	83	0	1	0	11	0	7.95	—	—	—	—	—	—	—
90-91—Phoenix	IHL	4	160	1	2	‡0	11	0	4.13	—	—	—	—	—	—	—
—New Haven	AHL	33	1882	13	16	4	115	1	3.67	—	—	—	—	—	—	—
91-92—Phoenix	IHL	22	1242	8	12	‡1	80	0	3.86	—	—	—	—	—	—	—
92-93—Los Angeles................	NHL	31	1735	15	8	4	111	0	3.84	4	240	3	1	16	0	4.00
93-94—Los Angeles................	NHL	22	1144	4	11	5	65	1	3.41	—	—	—	—	—	—	—
—Phoenix	IHL	3	121	1	1	‡0	13	0	6.45	—	—	—	—	—	—	—
94-95—Los Angeles................	NHL	1	16	0	0	0	2	0	7.50	—	—	—	—	—	—	—
—Buffalo	NHL	6	317	2	3	0	20	0	3.79	—	—	—	—	—	—	—
NHL totals..		62	3295	21	23	9	209	1	3.81	4	240	3	1	16	0	4.00

STEEN, THOMAS
C, JETS

PERSONAL: Born June 8, 1960, in Tocksmark, Sweden. ... 5-11/185. ... Shoots left. ... Cousin of Dan Labraaten, right winger, Detroit Red Wings and Calgary Flames (1978-79 through 1981-82).
TRANSACTIONS/CAREER NOTES: Selected by Winnipeg Jets in fifth round (fifth Jets pick, 103rd overall) of NHL entry draft (June 11, 1979). ... Lacerated elbow during Canada Cup (September 1981). ... Injured knee in training camp (October 1981). ... Suffered protruding disk (December 1989); missed 22 games. ... Fractured right ankle (November 28, 1990); missed 20 games. ... Suffered lower back spasms during preseason (September 1991); missed first 24 games of season. ... Suffered ankle contusion (December 1991); missed 10 games. ... Suffered recurrence of back spasms (January 1992); missed six games. ... Suffered hip pointer (October 31, 1992); missed one game. ... Suffered from the flu (February 12, 1993); missed three games. ... Strained groin (November 26, 1993); missed four games. ... Strained groin (December 12, 1993); missed four games. ... Suffered back spasms (February 17, 1995); missed two games. ... Sprained left knee ligaments (April 5, 1995); missed six games. ... Suffered back spasms (April 25, 1995); missed four games.

HONORS: Named Swedish League Player of the Year (1980-81).
STATISTICAL PLATEAUS: Three-goal games: 1982-83 (1), 1986-87 (1), 1988-89 (1), 1992-93 (1). Total: 4.
MISCELLANEOUS: Captain of Winnipeg Jets (1990-91).

Season Team	League	REGULAR SEASON					PLAYOFFS				
		Gms.	G	A	Pts.	PIM	Gms.	G	A	Pts.	PIM
76-77—Leksand	Sweden	2	1	1	2	2	—	—	—	—	—
77-78—Leksand	Sweden	35	5	6	11	30	—	—	—	—	—
78-79—Leksand	Sweden	25	13	4	17	35	2	0	0	0	0
—Swedish national team	Int'l	2	0	0	0	0	—	—	—	—	—
79-80—Leksand	Sweden	18	7	7	14	14	2	0	0	0	6
80-81—Farjestad Karlstad	Sweden	32	16	23	39	30	7	4	2	6	8
—Swedish national team	Int'l	19	2	5	7	12	—	—	—	—	—
81-82—Winnipeg	NHL	73	15	29	44	42	4	0	4	4	2
82-83—Winnipeg	NHL	75	26	33	59	60	3	0	2	2	0
83-84—Winnipeg	NHL	78	20	45	65	69	3	0	1	1	9
84-85—Winnipeg	NHL	79	30	54	84	80	8	2	3	5	17
85-86—Winnipeg	NHL	78	17	47	64	76	3	1	1	2	4
86-87—Winnipeg	NHL	75	17	33	50	59	10	3	4	7	8
87-88—Winnipeg	NHL	76	16	38	54	53	5	1	5	6	2
88-89—Winnipeg	NHL	80	27	61	88	80	—	—	—	—	—
89-90—Winnipeg	NHL	53	18	48	66	35	7	2	5	7	16
90-91—Winnipeg	NHL	58	19	48	67	49	—	—	—	—	—
91-92—Winnipeg	NHL	38	13	25	38	29	7	2	4	6	2
92-93—Winnipeg	NHL	80	22	50	72	75	6	1	3	4	2
93-94—Winnipeg	NHL	76	19	32	51	32	—	—	—	—	—
94-95—Winnipeg	NHL	31	5	10	15	14	—	—	—	—	—
NHL totals		950	264	553	817	753	56	12	32	44	62

STEINER, ONDREJ
C, SABRES

PERSONAL: Born February 12, 1974, in Plzen, Czechoslovakia.... 6-1/176.... Shoots left.... Name pronounced AHN-drehzh STIGH-nuhr.
TRANSACTIONS/CAREER NOTES: Selected by Buffalo Sabres in third round (third Sabres pick, 59th overall) of NHL entry draft (June 20, 1992).

Season Team	League	REGULAR SEASON					PLAYOFFS				
		Gms.	G	A	Pts.	PIM	Gms.	G	A	Pts.	PIM
91-92—Skoda Plzen	Czech.	4	0	1	1	...	—	—	—	—	—
92-93—Skoda Plzen	Czech.	29	1	7	8	...	—	—	—	—	—
93-94—Skoda Plzen	Czech Rep.	31	3	6	9	...	—	—	—	—	—
94-95—Skoda Plzen	Czech Rep.	20	2	4	6	...	3	1	1	2	...

STERN, RONNIE
RW, FLAMES

PERSONAL: Born January 11, 1967, in Ste. Agatha Des Mont, Que.... 6-0/195.... Shoots right.
TRANSACTIONS/CAREER NOTES: Selected by Vancouver Canucks as underage junior in fourth round (third Canucks pick, 70th overall) of NHL entry draft (June 21, 1986).... Bruised shoulder (April 1989).... Suffered laceration near eye and dislocated shoulder (March 19, 1990).... Fractured wrist (October 30, 1990); missed 10 weeks.... Traded by Canucks with D Kevan Guy and option to switch fourth-round picks in 1992 draft to Calgary Flames for D Dana Murzyn; Flames did not exercise option (March 5, 1991).... Suffered back spasms (October 11, 1992); missed 11 games.... Broke bone in right foot (October 11, 1993); missed three games.... Bruised shoulder (December 7, 1993); missed one game.... Bruised shoulder (December 28, 1993); missed six games.... Sprained left ankle (February 6, 1995); missed four games.... Strained thigh (April 25, 1995); missed three games.... Suspended two games by NHL for accumulating four game misconduct penalties (1995).
STATISTICAL PLATEAUS: Three-goal games: 1991-92 (1), 1992-93 (1), 1994-95 (1). Total: 3.

Season Team	League	REGULAR SEASON					PLAYOFFS				
		Gms.	G	A	Pts.	PIM	Gms.	G	A	Pts.	PIM
84-85—Longueuil	QMJHL	67	6	14	20	176	—	—	—	—	—
85-86—Longueuil	QMJHL	70	39	33	72	317	—	—	—	—	—
86-87—Longueuil	QMJHL	56	32	39	71	266	19	11	9	20	55
87-88—Fredericton	AHL	2	1	0	1	4	—	—	—	—	—
—Flint	IHL	55	14	19	33	294	16	8	8	16	94
—Vancouver	NHL	15	0	0	0	52	—	—	—	—	—
88-89—Milwaukee	IHL	45	19	23	42	280	5	1	0	1	11
—Vancouver	NHL	17	1	0	1	49	3	0	1	1	17
89-90—Milwaukee	IHL	26	8	9	17	165	—	—	—	—	—
—Vancouver	NHL	34	2	3	5	208	—	—	—	—	—
90-91—Milwaukee	IHL	7	2	2	4	81	—	—	—	—	—
—Vancouver	NHL	31	2	3	5	171	—	—	—	—	—
—Calgary	NHL	13	1	3	4	69	7	1	3	4	14
91-92—Calgary	NHL	72	13	9	22	338	—	—	—	—	—
92-93—Calgary	NHL	70	10	15	25	207	6	0	0	0	43
93-94—Calgary	NHL	71	9	20	29	243	7	2	0	2	12
94-95—Calgary	NHL	39	9	4	13	163	7	3	1	4	8
NHL totals		362	47	57	104	1500	30	6	5	11	94

STEVENS, JOHN
D, WHALERS

PERSONAL: Born May 4, 1966, in Completon, N.B. . . . 6-1/195. . . . Shoots left.
TRANSACTIONS/CAREER NOTES: Selected by Philadelphia Flyers as underage junior in third round (fifth Flyers pick, 47th overall) of NHL entry draft (June 9, 1984). . . . Underwent knee surgery (September 1984). . . . Signed as free agent by Hartford Whalers (July 16, 1990).

			REGULAR SEASON					PLAYOFFS				
Season	Team	League	Gms.	G	A	Pts.	PIM	Gms.	G	A	Pts.	PIM
82-83—Newmarket	OHA	48	2	9	11	111	—	—	—	—	—
83-84—Oshawa	OHL	70	1	10	11	71	7	0	1	1	6
84-85—Oshawa	OHL	45	2	10	12	61	5	0	2	2	4
—Hershey	AHL	3	0	0	0	2	—	—	—	—	—
85-86—Oshawa	OHL	65	1	7	8	146	6	0	2	2	14
—Kalamazoo	IHL	6	0	1	1	8	6	0	3	3	9
86-87—Hershey	AHL	63	1	15	16	131	3	0	0	0	7
—Philadelphia	NHL	6	0	2	2	14	—	—	—	—	—
87-88—Philadelphia	NHL	3	0	0	0	0	—	—	—	—	—
—Hershey	AHL	59	1	15	16	108	—	—	—	—	—
88-89—Hershey	AHL	78	3	13	16	129	12	1	1	2	29
89-90—Hershey	AHL	79	3	10	13	193	—	—	—	—	—
90-91—Hartford	NHL	14	0	1	1	11	—	—	—	—	—
—Springfield	AHL	65	0	12	12	139	18	0	6	6	35
91-92—Springfield	AHL	45	1	12	13	73	11	1	3	4	27
—Hartford	NHL	21	0	4	4	19	—	—	—	—	—
92-93—Springfield	AHL	74	1	19	20	111	15	0	1	1	18
93-94—Springfield	AHL	71	3	9	12	85	3	0	0	0	0
—Hartford	NHL	9	0	3	3	4	—	—	—	—	—
94-95—Springfield	AHL	79	5	15	20	122	—	—	—	—	—
NHL totals			53	0	10	10	48					

STEVENS, KEVIN
LW, BRUINS

PERSONAL: Born April 15, 1965, in Brockton, Mass. . . . 6-3/217. . . . Shoots left. . . . Full name: Kevin Michael Stevens.
HIGH SCHOOL: Silver Lake (Mass.).
COLLEGE: Boston College.
TRANSACTIONS/CAREER NOTES: Selected by Los Angeles Kings in sixth round (sixth Kings pick, 108th overall) of NHL entry draft (June 8, 1983). . . . Traded by Kings to Pittsburgh Penguins for LW Anders Hakansson (September 9, 1983). . . . Damaged cartilage in left knee (November 5, 1992) and underwent arthroscopic surgery (November 6, 1992); missed nine games. . . . Suspended one game by NHL (March 1993). . . . Suffered from bronchitis (April 3, 1993); missed two games. . . . Fractured left ankle (February 4, 1995); missed 21 games. . . . Traded by Penguins with C Shawn McEachern to Boston Bruins for C Bryan Smolinski and RW Glen Murray (August 2, 1995).
HONORS: Named to NCAA All-America East second team (1986-87). . . . Named to Hockey East All-Star first team (1986-87). . . . Named to THE SPORTING NEWS All-Star second team (1990-91 and 1992-93). . . . Named to NHL All-Star second team (1990-91 and 1992-93). . . . Named to THE SPORTING NEWS All-Star first team (1991-92). . . . Named to NHL All-Star first team (1991-92). . . . Played in NHL All-Star Game (1991-1993).
STATISTICAL PLATEAUS: Three-goal games: 1989-90 (1), 1990-91 (1), 1991-92 (3), 1992-93 (2), 1993-94 (1). Total: 8. . . . Four-goal games: 1991-92 (1), 1992-93 (1). Total: 2. . . . Total hat tricks: 10.
MISCELLANEOUS: Member of Stanley Cup championship teams (1991 and 1992).

			REGULAR SEASON					PLAYOFFS				
Season	Team	League	Gms.	G	A	Pts.	PIM	Gms.	G	A	Pts.	PIM
82-83—Silver Lake H.S.	Minn. H.S.	18	24	27	51	...	—	—	—	—	—
83-84—Boston College	ECAC	37	6	14	20	36	—	—	—	—	—
84-85—Boston College	Hockey East	40	13	23	36	36	—	—	—	—	—
85-86—Boston College	Hockey East	42	17	27	44	56	—	—	—	—	—
86-87—Boston College	Hockey East	39	*35	35	70	54	—	—	—	—	—
87-88—U.S. national team	Int'l	44	22	23	45	52	—	—	—	—	—
—U.S. Olympic Team	Int'l	5	1	3	4	2	—	—	—	—	—
—Pittsburgh	NHL	16	5	2	7	8	—	—	—	—	—
88-89—Pittsburgh	NHL	24	12	3	15	19	11	3	7	10	16
—Muskegon	IHL	45	24	41	65	113	—	—	—	—	—
89-90—Pittsburgh	NHL	76	29	41	70	171	—	—	—	—	—
90-91—Pittsburgh	NHL	80	40	46	86	133	24	*17	16	33	53
91-92—Pittsburgh	NHL	80	54	69	123	254	†21	13	15	28	28
92-93—Pittsburgh	NHL	72	55	56	111	177	12	5	11	16	22
93-94—Pittsburgh	NHL	83	41	47	88	155	6	1	1	2	10
94-95—Pittsburgh	NHL	27	15	12	27	51	12	4	7	11	21
NHL totals			458	251	276	527	968	86	43	57	100	150

STEVENS, RANDY
RW, JETS

PERSONAL: Born August 9, 1973, in Sault Ste. Marie, Mich. . . . 6-0/190. . . . Shoots right.
COLLEGE: Michigan Tech.
TRANSACTIONS/CAREER NOTES: Selected by Winnipeg Jets in first round (first Jets pick, fourth overall) of NHL supplemental draft (June 28, 1994).

			REGULAR SEASON					PLAYOFFS				
Season	Team	League	Gms.	G	A	Pts.	PIM	Gms.	G	A	Pts.	PIM
91-92—Michigan Tech	WCHA	28	1	3	4	16	—	—	—	—	—
92-93—Michigan Tech	WCHA	37	12	12	24	28	—	—	—	—	—
93-94—Michigan Tech	WCHA	42	21	12	33	42	—	—	—	—	—
94-95—Michigan Tech	WCHA	31	13	11	24	22	—	—	—	—	—

STEVENS, ROD
C, CANUCKS

PERSONAL: Born April 5, 1974, in Fort St. John, B.C. . . . 5-10/175. . . . Shoots left.
TRANSACTIONS/CAREER NOTES: Signed as free agent by Vancouver Canucks (October 4, 1993).
HONORS: Named to Memorial Cup All-Star team (1993-94).

			REGULAR SEASON					PLAYOFFS			
Season	Team	League	Gms.	G	A	Pts.	PIM	Gms.	G	A	Pts.	PIM
91-92—Kamloops		WHL	57	8	13	21	20	15	2	2	4	0
92-93—Kamloops		WHL	68	26	28	54	42	13	9	2	11	4
93-94—Kamloops		WHL	62	51	58	109	31	19	9	12	21	10
94-95—Syracuse		AHL	78	21	21	42	63	—	—	—	—	—

STEVENS, SCOTT
D, DEVILS

PERSONAL: Born April 1, 1964, in Kitchener, Ont. . . . 6-2/210. . . . Shoots left. . . . Brother of Mike Stevens, center/left winger in New York Rangers system.
TRANSACTIONS/CAREER NOTES: Selected by Washington Capitals as underage junior in first round (first Capitals pick, fifth overall) of NHL entry draft (June 9, 1982). . . . Bruised right knee (November 6, 1985); missed seven games. . . . Broke right index finger (December 14, 1986). . . . Bruised shoulder (April 1988). . . . Suffered from poison oak (November 1988). . . . Lacerated face during World Cup (April 21, 1989). . . . Broke left foot (December 29, 1989); missed 17 games. . . . Suspended three games by NHL for scratching (February 27, 1990). . . . Bruised left shoulder (March 27, 1990). . . . Dislocated left shoulder (May 3, 1990). . . . Signed as free agent by St. Louis Blues (July 9, 1990); Blues owed Capitals two first-round draft picks among the top seven over next two years and $100,000 cash; upon failing to get a pick in the top seven in 1991, Blues forfeited their first-round pick in 1991 (LW Trevor Halverson), 1992 (D Sergei Gonchar), 1993 (D Brendan Witt), 1994 (traded to Toronto Maple Leafs) and 1995 (LW Miika Elomo) drafts to Capitals (July 9, 1990). . . . Awarded to New Jersey Devils as compensation for Blues signing free agent RW/LW Brendan Shanahan (September 3, 1991). . . . Strained right knee (February 20, 1992); missed 12 games. . . . Suffered concussion (December 27, 1992); missed three games. . . . Strained knee (November 19, 1993); missed one game.
HONORS: Named to NHL All-Rookie team (1982-83). . . . Played in NHL All-Star Game (1985, 1989 and 1991-1994). . . . Named to THE SPORTING NEWS All-Star second team (1987-88). . . . Named to NHL All-Star first team (1987-88 and 1993-94). . . . Named to NHL All-Star second team (1991-92). . . . Named to THE SPORTING NEWS All-Star first team (1993-94).
MISCELLANEOUS: Captain of St. Louis Blues (1990-91). . . . Captain of New Jersey Devils (1992-93 and 1994-95). . . . Member of Stanley Cup championship team (1995).

			REGULAR SEASON					PLAYOFFS			
Season	Team	League	Gms.	G	A	Pts.	PIM	Gms.	G	A	Pts.	PIM
80-81—Kitchener Jr. B		OHA	39	7	33	40	82	—	—	—	—	—
—Kitchener		OHL	1	0	0	0	0	—	—	—	—	—
81-82—Kitchener		OHL	68	6	36	42	158	15	1	10	11	71
82-83—Washington		NHL	77	9	16	25	195	4	1	0	1	26
83-84—Washington		NHL	78	13	32	45	201	8	1	8	9	21
84-85—Washington		NHL	80	21	44	65	221	5	0	1	1	20
85-86—Washington		NHL	73	15	38	53	165	9	3	8	11	12
86-87—Washington		NHL	77	10	51	61	283	7	0	5	5	19
87-88—Washington		NHL	80	12	60	72	184	13	1	11	12	46
88-89—Washington		NHL	80	7	61	68	225	6	1	4	5	11
89-90—Washington		NHL	56	11	29	40	154	15	2	7	9	25
90-91—St. Louis		NHL	78	5	44	49	150	13	0	3	3	36
91-92—New Jersey		NHL	68	17	42	59	124	7	2	1	3	29
92-93—New Jersey		NHL	81	12	45	57	120	5	2	2	4	10
93-94—New Jersey		NHL	83	18	60	78	112	20	2	9	11	42
94-95—New Jersey		NHL	48	2	20	22	56	20	1	7	8	24
NHL totals			959	152	542	694	2190	132	16	66	82	321

STEVENSON, TURNER
RW, CANADIENS

PERSONAL: Born May 18, 1972, in Port Alberni, B.C. . . . 6-3/224. . . . Shoots right.
TRANSACTIONS/CAREER NOTES: Underwent surgery to remove growth in chest (August 1987). . . . Injured shoulder (December 1987). . . . Selected by Montreal Canadiens in first round (first Canadiens pick, 12th overall) of NHL entry draft (June 16, 1990).
HONORS: Named to Can.HL All-Star second team (1991-92). . . . Named to Memorial Cup All-Star team (1991-92). . . . Named to WHL (West) All-Star first team (1991-92).

			REGULAR SEASON					PLAYOFFS			
Season	Team	League	Gms.	G	A	Pts.	PIM	Gms.	G	A	Pts.	PIM
88-89—Seattle		WHL	69	15	12	27	84	—	—	—	—	—
89-90—Seattle		WHL	62	29	32	61	276	13	3	2	5	35
90-91—Seattle		WHL	57	36	27	63	222	6	1	5	6	15
—Fredericton		AHL	—	—	—	—	—	4	0	0	0	5
91-92—Seattle		WHL	58	20	32	52	264	15	9	3	12	55
92-93—Fredericton		AHL	79	25	34	59	102	5	2	3	5	11
—Montreal		NHL	1	0	0	0	0	—	—	—	—	—
93-94—Fredericton		AHL	66	19	28	47	155	—	—	—	—	—
—Montreal		NHL	2	0	0	0	2	3	0	2	2	0
94-95—Fredericton		AHL	37	12	12	24	109	—	—	—	—	—
—Montreal		NHL	41	6	1	7	86	—	—	—	—	—
NHL totals			44	6	1	7	88	3	0	2	2	0

S

STEWART, CAM
C, BRUINS

PERSONAL: Born September 18, 1971, in Kitchener, Ont. . . . 5-10/188. . . . Shoots left.
COLLEGE: Michigan.
TRANSACTIONS/CAREER NOTES: Strained knee ligaments (June 1989). . . . Selected by Boston Bruins in third round (second Bruins pick, 63rd overall) of NHL entry draft (June 16, 1990). . . . Fractured finger (November 13, 1993); missed seven games.

			REGULAR SEASON					PLAYOFFS			
Season Team	League	Gms.	G	A	Pts.	PIM	Gms.	G	A	Pts.	PIM
88-89—Elmira Jr. B	OHA	43	38	50	88	138	—	—	—	—	—
89-90—Elmira Jr. B	OHA	46	44	95	139	172	—	—	—	—	—
90-91—University of Michigan	CCHA	44	8	24	32	122	—	—	—	—	—
91-92—University of Michigan	CCHA	44	13	15	28	106	—	—	—	—	—
92-93—University of Michigan	CCHA	39	20	39	59	69	—	—	—	—	—
93-94—Boston	NHL	57	3	6	9	66	8	0	3	3	7
—Providence	AHL	14	3	2	5	5	—	—	—	—	—
94-95—Boston	NHL	5	0	0	0	2	—	—	—	—	—
—Providence	AHL	31	13	11	24	38	9	2	5	7	0
NHL totals		62	3	6	9	68	8	0	3	3	7

STEWART, MICHAEL
D, WHALERS

PERSONAL: Born March 30, 1972, in Calgary. . . . 6-2/210. . . . Shoots left. . . . Full name: Michael Donald Stewart.
COLLEGE: Michigan State.
TRANSACTIONS/CAREER NOTES: Selected by New York Rangers in first round (first Rangers pick, 13th overall) of NHL entry draft (June 16, 1990). . . . Traded by Rangers with D Glen Featherstone, first-round pick in 1995 draft (G Jean-Sebastien Giguere) and fourth-round pick in 1996 draft to Hartford Whalers for RW Pat Verbeek (March 23, 1995).
HONORS: Named to CCHA All-Rookie team (1989-90).

			REGULAR SEASON					PLAYOFFS			
Season Team	League	Gms.	G	A	Pts.	PIM	Gms.	G	A	Pts.	PIM
89-90—Michigan State	CCHA	45	2	6	8	45	—	—	—	—	—
90-91—Michigan State	CCHA	37	3	12	15	58	—	—	—	—	—
91-92—Michigan State	CCHA	8	1	3	4	6	—	—	—	—	—
92-93—Binghamton	AHL	68	2	10	12	71	1	0	0	0	0
93-94—Binghamton	AHL	79	8	42	50	75	—	—	—	—	—
94-95—Binghamton	AHL	68	6	21	27	83	—	—	—	—	—
—Springfield	AHL	7	0	3	3	21	—	—	—	—	—

STILLMAN, CORY
C, FLAMES

PERSONAL: Born December 20, 1973, in Peterborough, Ont. . . . 6-0/185. . . . Shoots left.
HIGH SCHOOL: Herman E. Fawcett (Brantford, Ont.).
TRANSACTIONS/CAREER NOTES: Selected by Calgary Flames in first round (first Flames pick, sixth overall) of NHL entry draft (June 20, 1992). . . . Suspended four games by AHL for incident involving on-ice official (March 29, 1995).
HONORS: Won Emms Family Award (1990-91).

			REGULAR SEASON					PLAYOFFS			
Season Team	League	Gms.	G	A	Pts.	PIM	Gms.	G	A	Pts.	PIM
89-90—Peterborough Jr. B	OHA	41	30	54	84	76	—	—	—	—	—
90-91—Windsor	OHL	64	31	70	101	31	11	3	6	9	8
91-92—Windsor	OHL	53	29	61	90	59	7	2	4	6	8
92-93—Peterborough	OHL	61	25	55	80	55	18	3	8	11	18
—Canadian national team	Int'l	1	0	0	0	0	—	—	—	—	—
93-94—Saint John	AHL	79	35	48	83	52	7	2	4	6	16
94-95—Saint John	AHL	63	28	53	81	70	5	0	2	2	2
—Calgary	NHL	10	0	2	2	2	—	—	—	—	—
NHL totals		10	0	2	2	2	—	—	—	—	—

STOJANOV, ALEX
LW, CANUCKS

PERSONAL: Born April 25, 1973, in Windsor, Ont. . . . 6-4/230. . . . Shoots left. . . . Name pronounced STOY-uh-nahf.
TRANSACTIONS/CAREER NOTES: Dislocated shoulder (July 1989). . . . Selected by Vancouver Canucks in first round (first Canucks pick, seventh overall) of NHL entry draft (June 22, 1991).

			REGULAR SEASON					PLAYOFFS			
Season Team	League	Gms.	G	A	Pts.	PIM	Gms.	G	A	Pts.	PIM
89-90—Dukes of Hamilton	OHL	37	4	4	8	91	—	—	—	—	—
90-91—Dukes of Hamilton	OHL	62	25	20	45	179	4	1	1	2	14
91-92—Guelph	OHL	33	12	15	27	91	—	—	—	—	—
92-93—Guelph	OHL	35	27	28	55	11	—	—	—	—	—
—Newmarket	OHL	14	9	7	16	21	7	1	3	4	26
—Hamilton	AHL	4	4	0	4	0	—	—	—	—	—
93-94—Hamilton	AHL	4	0	1	1	5	—	—	—	—	—
94-95—Syracuse	AHL	73	18	12	30	270	—	—	—	—	—
—Vancouver	NHL	4	0	0	0	13	5	0	0	0	2
NHL totals		4	0	0	0	13	5	0	0	0	2

STORM, JIM
LW, WHALERS

PERSONAL: Born February 5, 1971, in Detroit. . . . 6-2/200. . . . Shoots left. . . . Full name: James David Storm.
COLLEGE: Michigan Tech.
TRANSACTIONS/CAREER NOTES: Selected by Hartford Whalers in fourth round (fifth Whalers pick, 75th overall) of NHL entry draft (June 22, 1991). . . . Joined U.S. national team (October 6-November 6, 1993).

			REGULAR SEASON					PLAYOFFS				
Season	Team	League	Gms.	G	A	Pts.	PIM	Gms.	G	A	Pts.	PIM
88-89—Detroit Compuware		NAJHL	60	30	45	75	50	—	—	—	—	—
89-90—Detroit Compuware		NAJHL	55	38	73	111	58	—	—	—	—	—
90-91—Michigan Tech		WCHA	36	16	17	33	46	—	—	—	—	—
91-92—Michigan Tech		WCHA	39	25	33	58	12	—	—	—	—	—
92-93—Michigan Tech		WCHA	33	22	32	54	30	—	—	—	—	—
93-94—Hartford		NHL	68	6	10	16	27	—	—	—	—	—
—U.S. national team		Int'l	28	8	12	20	14	—	—	—	—	—
94-95—Springfield		AHL	33	11	11	22	29	—	—	—	—	—
—Hartford		NHL	6	0	3	3	0	—	—	—	—	—
NHL totals			74	6	13	19	27					

STORR, JAMIE
G, KINGS

PERSONAL: Born December 28, 1975, in Brampton, Ont. . . . 6-2/192. . . . Catches left.
HIGH SCHOOL: West Hill (Owen Sound, Ont.).
TRANSACTIONS/CAREER NOTES: Selected by Los Angeles Kings in first round (first Kings pick, seventh overall) of NHL entry draft (June 28, 1994).
HONORS: Named to OHL All-Star first team (1993-94).

			REGULAR SEASON							PLAYOFFS						
Season	Team	League	Gms.	Min.	W	L	T	GA	SO	Avg.	Gms.	Min.	W	L	GA	SO	Avg.
90-91—Brampton		Jr. B	24	1145	...	...	...	91	0	4.77	—	—	—	—	—	—	—
91-92—Owen Sound		OHL	34	1733	11	16	1	128	0	4.43	5	299	1	4	28	0	5.62
92-93—Owen Sound		OHL	41	2362	20	17	3	180	0	4.57	8	454	4	4	35	0	4.63
93-94—Owen Sound		OHL	35	2004	21	11	1	120	1	3.59	9	547	4	5	44	0	4.83
94-95—Owen Sound		OHL	17	977	5	9	2	64	0	3.93	—	—	—	—	—	—	—
—Los Angeles		NHL	5	263	1	3	1	17	0	3.88	—	—	—	—	—	—	—
—Windsor		OHL	4	241	3	1	0	8	1	1.99	10	520	6	3	34	1	3.92
NHL totals			5	263	1	3	1	17	0	3.88							

STRAKA, MARTIN
C, SENATORS

PERSONAL: Born September 3, 1972, in Plzen, Czechoslovakia. . . . 5-10/180. . . . Shoots left. . . . Name pronounced STRAH-kuh.
TRANSACTIONS/CAREER NOTES: Selected by Pittsburgh Penguins in first round (first Penguins pick, 19th overall) of NHL entry draft (June 20, 1992). . . . Played in Europe during 1994-95 NHL lockout. . . . Suffered from the flu (February 14, 1995); missed four games. . . . Traded by Penguins to Ottawa Senators for D Norm Maciver and C Troy Murray (April 7, 1995). . . . Strained knee (April 19, 1995); missed remainder of season.
HONORS: Named to Czechoslovakian League All-Star team (1991-92).
STATISTICAL PLATEAUS: Three-goal games: 1993-94 (1).

			REGULAR SEASON					PLAYOFFS				
Season	Team	League	Gms.	G	A	Pts.	PIM	Gms.	G	A	Pts.	PIM
89-90—Skoda Plzen		Czech.	1	0	3	3	...	—	—	—	—	—
90-91—Skoda Plzen		Czech.	47	7	24	31	6	—	—	—	—	—
91-92—Skoda Plzen		Czech.	50	27	28	55	20	—	—	—	—	—
92-93—Pittsburgh		NHL	42	3	13	16	29	11	2	1	3	2
—Cleveland		IHL	4	4	3	7	0	—	—	—	—	—
93-94—Pittsburgh		NHL	84	30	34	64	24	6	1	0	1	2
94-95—Interconex Plzen		Czech.	19	10	11	21	18	—	—	—	—	—
—Pittsburgh		NHL	31	4	12	16	16	—	—	—	—	—
—Ottawa		NHL	6	1	1	2	0	—	—	—	—	—
NHL totals			163	38	60	98	69	17	3	1	4	4

STRAND, WADE
D, STARS

PERSONAL: Born May 4, 1976, in Regina, Sask. . . . 6-3/185. . . . Shoots right.
TRANSACTIONS/CAREER NOTES: Selected by Dallas Stars in fifth round (fifth Stars pick, 115th overall) of NHL entry draft (July 8, 1995).

			REGULAR SEASON					PLAYOFFS				
Season	Team	League	Gms.	G	A	Pts.	PIM	Gms.	G	A	Pts.	PIM
94-95—Regina		WHL	70	4	13	17	85	4	0	0	0	10

STROMBERG, MIKA
D, SENATORS

PERSONAL: Born February 28, 1970, in Helsinki, Finland. . . . 5-11/178. . . . Shoots left.
TRANSACTIONS/CAREER NOTES: Selected by Quebec Nordiques in 10th round (10th Nordiques pick, 211st overall) of NHL entry draft (June 16, 1990). . . . Rights traded by Nordiques with fourth-round pick in 1995 draft (LW Kevin Boyd) to Ottawa Senators for LW Bill Huard (April 7, 1995).

			REGULAR SEASON					PLAYOFFS				
Season	Team	League	Gms.	G	A	Pts.	PIM	Gms.	G	A	Pts.	PIM
88-89—Jokerit Helsinki		Finland	39	6	12	18	...	—	—	—	—	—
89-90—Jokerit Helsinki		Finland	42	2	15	17	...	—	—	—	—	—

Season Team	League	REGULAR SEASON					PLAYOFFS				
		Gms.	G	A	Pts.	PIM	Gms.	G	A	Pts.	PIM
90-91—Jokerit Helsinki	Finland	44	4	16	20	38	—	—	—	—	—
91-92—Jokerit Helsinki	Finland	36	7	14	21	32	—	—	—	—	—
92-93—Jokerit Helsinki	Finland	16	2	5	7	6	3	1	2	3	4
93-94—Jokerit Helsinki	Finland	48	17	8	25	53	12	1	3	4	8
—Swedish Olympic Team	Int'l	7	2	2	4	10	—	—	—	—	—
94-95—Jokerit Helsinki	Finland	50	15	25	40	52	11	5	5	10	10

STRUDWICK, JASON
D, ISLANDERS

PERSONAL: Born July 17, 1975, in Edmonton.... 6-3/210.... Shoots left.
COLLEGE: University College of the Cariboo (Kamloops, B.C.).
TRANSACTIONS/CAREER NOTES: Selected by New York Islanders in third round (third Islanders pick, 63rd overall) of NHL entry draft (June 29, 1994).

Season Team	League	REGULAR SEASON					PLAYOFFS				
		Gms.	G	A	Pts.	PIM	Gms.	G	A	Pts.	PIM
93-94—Kamloops	WHL	61	6	8	14	118	19	0	4	4	24
94-95—Kamloops	WHL	72	3	11	14	183	21	1	1	2	39

STUMPEL, JOZEF
LW, BRUINS

PERSONAL: Born June 20, 1972, in Nitra, Czechoslovakia.... 6-1/190.... Shoots right.
... Name pronounced JOH-sehf STUHM-puhl.
TRANSACTIONS/CAREER NOTES: Selected by Boston Bruins in second round (second Bruins pick, 40th overall) of NHL entry draft (June 22, 1991).... Injured shoulder (December 1992); missed nine games.... Injured knee (March 17, 1994); missed nine games.... Played in Europe during 1994-95 NHL lockout.... Injured knee (April 1995).

Season Team	League	REGULAR SEASON					PLAYOFFS				
		Gms.	G	A	Pts.	PIM	Gms.	G	A	Pts.	PIM
89-90—Nitra	Czech.	38	12	11	23	0	—	—	—	—	—
90-91—Nitra	Czech.	49	23	22	45	14	—	—	—	—	—
91-92—Boston	NHL	4	1	0	1	0	—	—	—	—	—
—Koln	Germany	33	19	18	37	35	—	—	—	—	—
92-93—Providence	AHL	56	31	61	92	26	6	4	4	8	0
—Boston	NHL	13	1	3	4	4	—	—	—	—	—
93-94—Boston	NHL	59	8	15	23	14	13	1	7	8	4
—Providence	AHL	17	5	12	17	4	—	—	—	—	—
94-95—Koln	Germany	25	16	23	39	18	—	—	—	—	—
—Boston	NHL	44	5	13	18	8	5	0	0	0	0
NHL totals		120	15	31	46	26	18	1	7	8	4

SULLIVAN, BRIAN
LW, MIGHTY DUCKS

PERSONAL: Born April 23, 1969, in South Windsor, Conn.... 6-4/195.... Shoots right. ... Full name: Brian Scott Sullivan.
HIGH SCHOOL: South Windsor (Conn.).
COLLEGE: Northeastern.
TRANSACTIONS/CAREER NOTES: Selected by New Jersey Devils in fourth round (third Devils pick, 65th overall) of NHL entry draft (June 13, 1987).... Bruised shoulder (November 1989).... Signed as free agent by Mighty Ducks of Anaheim (September 2, 1994).

Season Team	League	REGULAR SEASON					PLAYOFFS				
		Gms.	G	A	Pts.	PIM	Gms.	G	A	Pts.	PIM
85-86—South Windsor H.S.	Conn. H.S.	...	39	50	89	...	—	—	—	—	—
86-87—Springfield Jr. B	NEJHL	...	30	35	65	...	—	—	—	—	—
87-88—Northeastern University	Hockey East	37	20	12	32	18	—	—	—	—	—
88-89—Northeastern University	Hockey East	34	13	14	27	65	—	—	—	—	—
89-90—Northeastern University	Hockey East	34	24	21	45	72	—	—	—	—	—
90-91—Northeastern University	Hockey East	32	17	23	40	75	—	—	—	—	—
91-92—Utica	AHL	70	23	24	47	58	4	0	4	4	6
92-93—Utica	AHL	75	30	27	57	88	5	0	0	0	12
—New Jersey	NHL	2	0	1	1	0	—	—	—	—	—
93-94—Albany	AHL	77	31	30	61	140	5	1	1	2	18
94-95—San Diego	IHL	74	24	23	47	97	5	0	1	1	7
NHL totals		2	0	1	1	0					

SULLIVAN, MIKE
LW, FLAMES

PERSONAL: Born February 28, 1968, in Marshfield, Mass.... 6-2/190.... Shoots left.... Full name: Michael Barry Sullivan.
HIGH SCHOOL: Boston College.
COLLEGE: Boston University.
TRANSACTIONS/CAREER NOTES: Selected by New York Rangers in fourth round (fourth Rangers pick, 69th overall) of NHL entry draft (June 13, 1987).... Traded by Rangers with D Mark Tinordi, D Paul Jerrard, RW Brett Barnett and third-round pick in 1989 draft (C Murray Garbutt) to Minnesota North Stars for LW Igor Liba, C Brian Lawton and rights to LW Eric Bennett (October 11, 1988).... Signed as free agent by San Jose Sharks (August 9, 1991).... Sprained left knee (April 6, 1993); missed remainder of season.... Claimed on waivers by Calgary Flames (January 6, 1994).... Pulled groin (January 29, 1994); missed 13 games.... Bruised knee (April 6, 1994); missed one game.... Bruised left foot (March 17, 1995); missed two games.... Sprained right ankle (April 13, 1995); missed last eight games of season.

Season Team	League	REGULAR SEASON Gms.	G	A	Pts.	PIM	PLAYOFFS Gms.	G	A	Pts.	PIM
85-86—Boston College H.S.	Mass. H.S.	22	26	33	59	...	—	—	—	—	—
86-87—Boston University	Hockey East	37	13	18	31	18	—	—	—	—	—
87-88—Boston University	Hockey East	30	18	22	40	30	—	—	—	—	—
88-89—Boston University	Hockey East	36	19	17	36	30	—	—	—	—	—
—Virginia	ECHL	2	0	0	0	0	—	—	—	—	—
90-91—San Diego	IHL	74	12	23	35	27	—	—	—	—	—
91-92—Kansas City	IHL	10	2	8	10	8	—	—	—	—	—
—San Jose	NHL	64	8	11	19	15	—	—	—	—	—
92-93—San Jose	NHL	81	6	8	14	30	—	—	—	—	—
93-94—San Jose	NHL	26	2	2	4	4	—	—	—	—	—
—Kansas City	IHL	6	3	3	6	0	—	—	—	—	—
—Saint John	AHL	5	2	0	2	4	—	—	—	—	—
—Calgary	NHL	19	2	3	5	6	7	1	1	2	8
94-95—Calgary	NHL	38	4	7	11	14	7	3	5	8	2
NHL totals		228	22	31	53	69	14	4	6	10	10

SULLIVAN, STEVE
C, DEVILS

PERSONAL: Born July 6, 1974, in Timmins, Ont. . . . 5-9/155. . . . Shoots right.
TRANSACTIONS/CAREER NOTES: Selected by New Jersey Devils in ninth round (10th Devils pick, 233rd overall) of NHL entry draft (June 29, 1994).

Season Team	League	REGULAR SEASON Gms.	G	A	Pts.	PIM	PLAYOFFS Gms.	G	A	Pts.	PIM
92-93—Timmins	USHL	47	66	55	121	141	—	—	—	—	—
93-94—Sault Ste. Marie	OHL	63	51	62	113	82	14	9	16	25	22
94-95—Albany	AHL	75	31	50	81	124	14	4	7	11	10

SUNDBLAD, NIKLAS
RW, FLAMES

PERSONAL: Born January 3, 1973, in Stockholm, Sweden. . . . 6-1/200. . . . Shoots right.
TRANSACTIONS/CAREER NOTES: Selected by Calgary Flames in first round (first Flames pick, 19th overall) of NHL entry draft (June 22, 1991).

Season Team	League	REGULAR SEASON Gms.	G	A	Pts.	PIM	PLAYOFFS Gms.	G	A	Pts.	PIM
90-91—AIK	Sweden	39	1	3	4	14	—	—	—	—	—
91-92—AIK	Sweden	33	9	2	11	24	3	3	1	4	0
92-93—AIK	Sweden	22	5	4	9	56	—	—	—	—	—
93-94—Saint John	AHL	76	13	19	32	75	4	1	1	2	2
94-95—Saint John	AHL	72	9	5	14	151	2	0	0	0	6

SUNDERLAND, MATHIEU
RW, SABRES

PERSONAL: Born November 30, 1976, in Quebec City. . . . 6-4/192. . . . Shoots right.
TRANSACTIONS/CAREER NOTES: Selected by Buffalo Sabres in third round (fourth Sabres pick, 68th overall) of NHL entry draft (July 8, 1995).

Season Team	League	REGULAR SEASON Gms.	G	A	Pts.	PIM	PLAYOFFS Gms.	G	A	Pts.	PIM
93-94—Drummondville	QMJHL	60	19	13	32	118	5	0	0	0	19
94-95—Drummondville	QMJHL	66	21	24	45	185	3	2	4	6	12

SUNDIN, MATS
RW, MAPLE LEAFS

PERSONAL: Born February 13, 1971, in Sollentuna, Sweden. . . . 6-4/215. . . . Shoots right. . . . Full name: Mats Johan Sundin. . . . Name pronounced suhn-DEEN.
TRANSACTIONS/CAREER NOTES: Selected by Quebec Nordiques in first round (first Nordiques pick, first overall) of NHL entry draft (June 17, 1989). . . . Separated right shoulder (January 2, 1993); missed three games. . . . Suspended one game by NHL for second stick-related infraction (March 2, 1993). . . . Traded by Nordiques with D Garth Butcher, LW Todd Warriner and first-round pick in 1994 draft (traded to Washington Capitals who selected D Nolan Baumgartner) to Toronto Maple Leafs for LW Wendel Clark, D Sylvain Lefebvre, RW Landon Wilson and first-round pick (D Jeffrey Kealty) in 1994 draft (June 28, 1994). . . . Played in Europe during 1994-95 NHL lockout. . . . Sprained shoulder (March 25, 1995); missed one game.
HONORS: Named to Swedish League All-Star team (1990-91 and 1991-92).
STATISTICAL PLATEAUS: Three-goal games: 1990-91 (2), 1992-93 (1). Total: 3. . . . Five-goal games: 1991-92 (1). . . . Total hat tricks: 4.

Season Team	League	REGULAR SEASON Gms.	G	A	Pts.	PIM	PLAYOFFS Gms.	G	A	Pts.	PIM
88-89—Nacka	Sweden	25	10	8	18	18	—	—	—	—	—
89-90—Djurgarden Stockholm	Sweden	34	10	8	18	16	8	7	0	7	4
90-91—Quebec	NHL	80	23	36	59	58	—	—	—	—	—
91-92—Quebec	NHL	80	33	43	76	103	—	—	—	—	—
92-93—Quebec	NHL	80	47	67	114	96	6	3	1	4	6
93-94—Quebec	NHL	84	32	53	85	60	—	—	—	—	—
94-95—Djurgarden Stockholm	Sweden	12	7	2	9	14	—	—	—	—	—
—Toronto	NHL	47	23	24	47	14	7	5	4	9	4
NHL totals		371	158	223	381	331	13	8	5	13	10

SUNDSTROM, NIKLAS

LW, RANGERS

PERSONAL: Born June 6, 1975, in Ornskoldsvik, Sweden. . . . 5-11/183. . . . Shoots left.

TRANSACTIONS/CAREER NOTES: Selected by New York Rangers in first round (first Rangers pick, eighth overall) of NHL entry draft (June 26, 1993).

			REGULAR SEASON					PLAYOFFS				
Season Team	League	Gms.	G	A	Pts.	PIM	Gms.	G	A	Pts.	PIM
91-92—MoDo Hockey	Sweden	9	1	3	4	0	—	—	—	—	—
92-93—MoDo Hockey	Sweden	40	7	11	18	18	—	—	—	—	—
93-94—MoDo Hockey	Sweden	37	7	12	19	28	11	4	3	7	2
94-95—MoDo Hockey	Sweden	33	8	13	21	30	—	—	—	—	—

SUNDSTROM, OLIE

G, PENGUINS

PERSONAL: Born April 24, 1968, in Leksand, Sweden. . . . 5-11/178. . . . Catches left.

TRANSACTIONS/CAREER NOTES: Signed as free agent by Pittsburgh Penguins (December 16, 1993).

				REGULAR SEASON							PLAYOFFS					
Season Team	League	Gms.	Min.	W	L	T	GA	SO	Avg.	Gms.	Min.	W	L	GA	SO	Avg.
92-93—Nashville	ECHL	21	1087	8	7	‡0	99	0	5.46	—	—	—	—	—	—	—
—Columbus	ECHL	8	416	4	3	‡0	28	0	4.04	—	—	—	—	—	—	—
93-94—Cleveland	IHL	46	2521	20	19	‡4	172	0	4.09	—	—	—	—	—	—	—
94-95—Cleveland	IHL	23	1235	3	17	‡1	104	0	5.05	—	—	—	—	—	—	—

SUTER, GARY

D, BLACKHAWKS

PERSONAL: Born June 24, 1964, in Madison, Wis. . . . 6-0/190. . . . Shoots left. . . . Full name: Gary Lee Suter. . . . Name pronounced SOO-tuhr.

COLLEGE: Wisconsin.

TRANSACTIONS/CAREER NOTES: Selected by Calgary Flames in ninth round (ninth Flames pick, 180th overall) of NHL entry draft (June 9, 1984). . . . Stretched knee ligament (December 1986). . . . Suspended first four games of regular season and next six international games in which NHL participates for high-sticking during Canada Cup (September 4, 1987). . . . Injured left knee (February 1988). . . . Pulled hamstring (February 1989). . . . Ruptured appendix (February 22, 1989); missed 16 games. . . . Broke jaw (April 11, 1989). . . . Bruised knee (December 12, 1991); missed 10 games. . . . Injured ribs (March 16, 1993); missed one game. . . . Suffered from the flu (March 30, 1993); missed one game. . . . Tore left knee ligaments (November 4, 1993); missed 33 games. . . . Strained left leg muscle (January 24, 1994); missed 10 games. . . . Traded by Flames with LW Paul Ranheim and C Ted Drury to Hartford Whalers for C Michael Nylander, D Zarley Zalapski and D James Patrick (March 10, 1994). . . . Traded by Hartford with LW Randy Cunneyworth and third-round pick in 1995 draft (traded to Vancouver Canucks) to Chicago Blackhawks for D Frantisek Kucera and LW Jocelyn Lemieux (March 11, 1994). . . . Cracked bone in hand (May 25, 1995); missed four playoff games.

HONORS: Named USHL Top Defenseman (1982-83). . . . Named to USHL All-Star first team (1982-83). . . . Won Calder Memorial Trophy (1985-86). . . . Named to NHL All-Rookie team (1985-86). . . . Played in NHL All-Star Game (1986, 1988, 1989 and 1991). . . . Named to THE SPORTING NEWS All-Star first team (1987-88). . . . Named to NHL All-Star second team (1987-88). . . . Named to THE SPORTING NEWS All-Star second team (1988-89).

RECORDS: Shares NHL single-game record for most assists by a defenseman—6 (April 4, 1986).

MISCELLANEOUS: Member of Stanley Cup championship team (1989).

			REGULAR SEASON					PLAYOFFS				
Season Team	League	Gms.	G	A	Pts.	PIM	Gms.	G	A	Pts.	PIM
81-82—Dubuque	USHL	18	3	4	7	32	—	—	—	—	—
82-83—Dubuque	USHL	41	9	10	19	112	—	—	—	—	—
83-84—University of Wisconsin	WCHA	35	4	18	22	68	—	—	—	—	—
84-85—University of Wisconsin	WCHA	39	12	39	51	110	—	—	—	—	—
85-86—Calgary	NHL	80	18	50	68	141	10	2	8	10	8
86-87—Calgary	NHL	68	9	40	49	70	6	0	3	3	10
87-88—Calgary	NHL	75	21	70	91	124	9	1	9	10	6
88-89—Calgary	NHL	63	13	49	62	78	5	0	3	3	10
89-90—Calgary	NHL	76	16	60	76	97	6	0	1	1	14
90-91—Calgary	NHL	79	12	58	70	102	7	1	6	7	12
91-92—Calgary	NHL	70	12	43	55	128	—	—	—	—	—
92-93—Calgary	NHL	81	23	58	81	112	6	2	3	5	8
93-94—Calgary	NHL	25	4	9	13	20	—	—	—	—	—
—Chicago	NHL	16	2	3	5	18	6	3	2	5	6
94-95—Chicago	NHL	48	10	27	37	42	12	2	5	7	10
NHL totals		**681**	**140**	**467**	**607**	**932**	**67**	**11**	**40**	**51**	**84**

SUTTER, BRENT

C, BLACKHAWKS

PERSONAL: Born June 10, 1962, in Viking, Alta. . . . 5-11/180. . . . Shoots right. . . . Full name: Brent Colin Sutter. . . . Name pronounced SUH-tuhr. . . . Brother of Brian Sutter, left winger, St. Louis Blues (1976-77 through 1987-88) and head coach, Blues and Boston Bruins (1988-89 through 1994-95); brother of Darryl Sutter, left winger, Chicago Blackhawks (1979-80 through 1986-87) and head coach, Blackhawks (1992-93 through 1994-95); brother of Duane Sutter, right winger, New York Islanders and Blackhawks (1979-80 through 1989-90); brother of Rich Sutter, right winger with seven NHL teams (1982-83 through 1994-95); and brother of Ron Sutter, center, New York Islanders.

TRANSACTIONS/CAREER NOTES: Selected by New York Islanders as underage junior in first round (first Islanders pick, 17th overall) of NHL entry draft (June 11, 1980). . . . Damaged tendon and developed infection in right hand (January 1984); missed 11 games. . . . Separated shoulder (March 1985). . . . Bruised left shoulder (October 19, 1985); missed 12 games. . . . Bruised shoulder (December 21, 1985); missed seven games. . . . Strained abductor muscle in right leg (March 1987). . . . Suffered non-displaced fracture of right thumb (December 1987). . . . Lacerated right leg (January 19, 1990). . . . Hospitalized with an infection in right leg after stitches were removed (January 28, 1990); missed seven games. . . . Traded by Islanders with RW

Brad Lauer to Chicago Blackhawks for C Adam Creighton and LW Steve Thomas (October 25, 1991).... Injured abdomen (March 11, 1992).... Broke foot (September 25, 1992); missed 14 games.... Bruised index finger (January 19, 1993); missed three games.... Injured eye (March 9, 1993); missed two games.... Strained back (February 1994); missed five games.
HONORS: Played in NHL All-Star Game (1985).
STATISTICAL PLATEAUS: Three-goal games: 1981-82 (1), 1983-84 (1), 1984-85 (2), 1986-87 (1), 1989-90 (1). Total: 6.
MISCELLANEOUS: Member of Stanley Cup championship teams (1982 and 1983).... Captain of New York Islanders (1987-88 through 1991-92).

Season Team	League	Gms.	G	A	Pts.	PIM	Gms.	G	A	Pts.	PIM
			REGULAR SEASON					PLAYOFFS			
77-78—Red Deer	AJHL	60	12	18	30	33	—	—	—	—	—
78-79—Red Deer	AJHL	60	42	42	84	79	—	—	—	—	—
79-80—Red Deer	AJHL	59	70	101	171	131	—	—	—	—	—
—Lethbridge	WHL	5	1	0	1	2	—	—	—	—	—
80-81—New York Islanders	NHL	3	2	2	4	0	—	—	—	—	—
—Lethbridge	WHL	68	54	54	108	116	9	6	4	10	51
81-82—Lethbridge	WHL	34	46	34	80	162	—	—	—	—	—
—New York Islanders	NHL	43	21	22	43	114	19	2	6	8	36
82-83—New York Islanders	NHL	80	21	19	40	128	20	10	11	21	26
83-84—New York Islanders	NHL	69	34	15	49	69	20	4	10	14	18
84-85—New York Islanders	NHL	72	42	60	102	51	10	3	3	6	14
85-86—New York Islanders	NHL	61	24	31	55	74	3	0	1	1	2
86-87—New York Islanders	NHL	69	27	36	63	73	5	1	0	1	4
87-88—New York Islanders	NHL	70	29	31	60	55	6	2	1	3	18
88-89—New York Islanders	NHL	77	29	34	63	77	—	—	—	—	—
89-90—New York Islanders	NHL	67	33	35	68	65	5	2	3	5	2
90-91—New York Islanders	NHL	75	21	32	53	49	—	—	—	—	—
91-92—New York Islanders	NHL	8	4	6	10	6	—	—	—	—	—
—Chicago	NHL	61	18	32	50	30	18	3	5	8	22
92-93—Chicago	NHL	65	20	34	54	67	4	1	1	2	4
93-94—Chicago	NHL	73	9	29	38	43	6	0	0	0	2
94-95—Chicago	NHL	47	7	8	15	51	16	1	2	3	4
NHL totals		940	341	426	767	952	132	29	43	72	152

SUTTER, RICH
RW

PERSONAL: Born December 2, 1963, in Viking, Alta.... 5-11/188.... Shoots right.... Name pronounced SUH-tuhr.... Brother of Brian Sutter, left winger, St. Louis Blues (1976-77 through 1987-88) and head coach, Blues and Boston Bruins (1988-89 through 1994-95); brother of Brent Sutter, center, Chicago Blackhawks; brother of Darryl Sutter, left winger, Blackhawks (1979-80 through 1986-87) and head coach, Blackhawks (1992-93 through 1994-95); brother of Duane Sutter, right winger, New York Islanders and Blackhawks (1979-80 through 1989-90); and twin brother of Ron Sutter, center, New York Islanders.
HIGH SCHOOL: Winston Churchill (Lethbridge, Alta.).
TRANSACTIONS/CAREER NOTES: Selected as underage junior by Pittsburgh Penguins in first round (first Penguins pick, 10th overall) of NHL entry draft (June 9, 1982).... Traded by Penguins with second-round (D Greg Smyth) and third-round (LW David McLay) picks in 1984 draft to Philadelphia Flyers for C Ron Flockhart, C/LW Mark Taylor, LW Andy Brickley, first-round (RW/C Roger Belanger) and third-round picks in 1984 draft (October 1983).... Traded by Flyers with D Dave Richter and third-round pick in 1986 draft to Vancouver Canucks for D J.J. Daigneault, second-round pick in 1986 draft (C Kent Hawley) and fifth-round pick in 1987 draft (June 1986).... Lost four teeth (October 23, 1988).... Injured lower back (January 17, 1989).... Broke nose (March 24, 1989).... Suspended five games by NHL for slashing (January 27, 1990).... Traded by Canucks with D Harold Snepsts and second-round pick in 1990 draft (previously acquired from St. Louis Blues) to Blues for D Adrien Plavsic, first-round pick in 1990 draft (traded to Montreal Canadiens) and second-round pick in 1991 draft (March 6, 1990).... Suffered concussion (November 1, 1991); missed two games.... Selected by Chicago Blackhawks in 1993 waiver draft (October 3, 1993).... Traded by Blackhawks with LW Paul Ysebaert to Tampa Bay Lightning for RW Jim Cummins, D Jeff Buchanan and D Tom Tilley (February 22, 1995).... Traded by Lightning to Toronto Maple Leafs for future considerations (March 13, 1995).... Released by Maple Leafs (June 28, 1995).
STATISTICAL PLATEAUS: Three-goal games: 1989-90 (1).

Season Team	League	Gms.	G	A	Pts.	PIM	Gms.	G	A	Pts.	PIM
			REGULAR SEASON					PLAYOFFS			
79-80—Red Deer	AJHL	60	13	19	32	157	—	—	—	—	—
80-81—Lethbridge	WHL	72	23	18	41	255	9	3	1	4	35
81-82—Lethbridge	WHL	57	38	31	69	263	12	3	3	6	55
82-83—Lethbridge	WHL	64	37	30	67	200	17	14	9	23	43
—Pittsburgh	NHL	4	0	0	0	0	—	—	—	—	—
83-84—Baltimore	AHL	2	0	1	1	0	—	—	—	—	—
—Pittsburgh	NHL	5	0	0	0	0	—	—	—	—	—
—Philadelphia	NHL	70	16	12	28	93	3	0	0	0	15
84-85—Hershey	AHL	13	3	7	10	14	—	—	—	—	—
—Philadelphia	NHL	56	6	10	16	89	11	3	0	3	10
85-86—Philadelphia	NHL	78	14	25	39	199	5	2	0	2	19
86-87—Vancouver	NHL	74	20	22	42	113	—	—	—	—	—
87-88—Vancouver	NHL	80	15	15	30	165	—	—	—	—	—
88-89—Vancouver	NHL	75	17	15	32	122	7	2	1	3	12
89-90—Vancouver	NHL	62	9	9	18	133	—	—	—	—	—
—St. Louis	NHL	12	2	0	2	22	12	2	1	3	39
90-91—St. Louis	NHL	77	16	11	27	122	13	4	2	6	16

Season Team	League	REGULAR SEASON					PLAYOFFS				
		Gms.	G	A	Pts.	PIM	Gms.	G	A	Pts.	PIM
91-92—St. Louis	NHL	77	9	16	25	107	6	0	0	0	8
92-93—St. Louis	NHL	84	13	14	27	100	11	0	1	1	10
93-94—Chicago	NHL	83	12	14	26	108	6	0	0	0	2
94-95—Chicago	NHL	15	0	0	0	28	—	—	—	—	—
—Tampa Bay	NHL	4	0	0	0	0	—	—	—	—	—
—Atlanta	IHL	4	0	5	5	0	—	—	—	—	—
—Toronto	NHL	18	0	3	3	10	4	0	0	0	2
NHL totals		874	149	166	315	1411	78	13	5	18	133

SUTTER, RON
C, ISLANDERS

PERSONAL: Born December 2, 1963, in Viking, Alta. . . . 6-0/180. . . . Shoots right. . . . Name pronounced SUH-tuhr. . . . Brother of Brian Sutter, left winger, St. Louis Blues (1976-77 through 1987-88) and head coach, Blues and Boston Bruins (1988-89 through 1994-95); brother of Brent Sutter, center, Chicago Blackhawks; brother of Darryl Sutter, left winger, Blackhawks (1979-80 through 1986-87) and head coach, Blackhawks (1992-93 through 1994-95); brother of Duane Sutter, right winger, New York Islanders and Blackhawks (1979-80 through 1989-90); and twin brother of Rich Sutter, right winger with seven NHL teams (1982-83 through 1994-95).
HIGH SCHOOL: Winston Churchill (Lethbridge, Ont.).
TRANSACTIONS/CAREER NOTES: Selected by Philadelphia Flyers as underage junior in first round (first Flyers pick, fourth overall) of NHL entry draft (June 9, 1982). . . . Broke ankle (November 27, 1981). . . . Bruised ribs (March 1985). . . . Suffered stress fracture in lower back (January 1987). . . . Tore rib cartilage (March 1988). . . . Fractured jaw (October 29, 1988). . . . Pulled groin (March 1989). . . . Traded by Flyers with D Murray Baron to St. Louis Blues for C Rod Brind'Amour and C Dan Quinn (September 22, 1991). . . . Strained ligament in right knee (February 1, 1992); missed 10 games. . . . Suffered abdominal pull (September 1992); missed first 18 games of season. . . . Separated shoulder (March 30, 1993); missed remainder of season. . . . Underwent abdominal surgery during off-season; missed nine games. . . . Traded by Blues with C Bob Bassen and D Garth Butcher to Quebec Nordiques for D Steve Duchesne and RW Denis Chasse (January 23, 1994). . . . Suffered sore neck (November 16, 1993); missed two games. . . . Traded by Nordiques with first-round pick in 1994 draft (RW Brett Lindros) to New York Islanders for D Uwe Krupp and first-round pick (D Wade Belak) in 1994 draft (June 28, 1994). . . . Sprained right ankle (February 7, 1995); missed 18 games.
MISCELLANEOUS: Captain of Philadelphia Flyers (1989-90 and 1990-91).

Season Team	League	REGULAR SEASON					PLAYOFFS				
		Gms.	G	A	Pts.	PIM	Gms.	G	A	Pts.	PIM
79-80—Red Deer	AJHL	60	12	33	45	44	—	—	—	—	—
80-81—Lethbridge	WHL	72	13	32	45	152	9	2	5	7	29
81-82—Lethbridge	WHL	59	38	54	92	207	12	6	5	11	28
82-83—Lethbridge	WHL	58	35	48	83	98	20	*22	†19	*41	45
—Philadelphia	NHL	10	1	1	2	9	—	—	—	—	—
83-84—Philadelphia	NHL	79	19	32	51	101	3	0	0	0	22
84-85—Philadelphia	NHL	73	16	29	45	94	19	4	8	12	28
85-86—Philadelphia	NHL	75	18	42	60	159	5	0	2	2	10
86-87—Philadelphia	NHL	39	10	17	27	69	16	1	7	8	12
87-88—Philadelphia	NHL	69	8	25	33	146	7	0	1	1	26
88-89—Philadelphia	NHL	55	26	22	48	80	19	1	9	10	51
89-90—Philadelphia	NHL	75	22	26	48	104	—	—	—	—	—
90-91—Philadelphia	NHL	80	17	28	45	92	—	—	—	—	—
91-92—St. Louis	NHL	68	19	27	46	91	6	1	3	4	8
92-93—St. Louis	NHL	59	12	15	27	99	—	—	—	—	—
93-94—St. Louis	NHL	36	6	12	18	46	—	—	—	—	—
—Quebec	NHL	37	9	13	22	44	—	—	—	—	—
94-95—New York Islanders	NHL	27	1	4	5	21	—	—	—	—	—
NHL totals		782	184	293	477	1155	75	7	30	37	157

SUTTON, KEN
D, OILERS

PERSONAL: Born May 11, 1969, in Edmonton. . . . 6-0/198. . . . Shoots left.
TRANSACTIONS/CAREER NOTES: Selected by Buffalo Sabres in fifth round (fourth Sabres pick, 98th overall) of NHL entry draft (June 17, 1989). . . . Separated shoulder (March 3, 1992); missed six games. . . . Broke ankle (September 15, 1992); missed first 19 games of season. . . . Broke finger (February 15, 1995); missed 10 games. . . . Traded by Sabres to Edmonton Oilers for LW Scott Pearson (April 7, 1995).
HONORS: Named to Memorial Cup All-Star team (1988-89).

Season Team	League	REGULAR SEASON					PLAYOFFS				
		Gms.	G	A	Pts.	PIM	Gms.	G	A	Pts.	PIM
87-88—Calgary Canucks	AJHL	53	13	43	56	228	—	—	—	—	—
88-89—Saskatoon	WHL	71	22	31	53	104	8	2	5	7	12
89-90—Rochester	AHL	57	5	14	19	83	11	1	6	7	15
90-91—Buffalo	NHL	15	3	6	9	13	6	0	1	1	2
—Rochester	AHL	62	7	24	31	65	3	1	1	2	14
91-92—Buffalo	NHL	64	2	18	20	71	7	0	2	2	4
92-93—Buffalo	NHL	63	8	14	22	30	8	3	1	4	8
93-94—Buffalo	NHL	78	4	20	24	71	4	0	0	0	2
94-95—Buffalo	NHL	12	1	2	3	30	—	—	—	—	—
—Edmonton	NHL	12	3	1	4	12	—	—	—	—	—
NHL totals		244	21	61	82	227	25	3	4	7	16

S

SVARTVADET, PER

LW/C, STARS

PERSONAL: Born May 17, 1975, in Ornskoldsvik, Sweden. . . . 6-1/180. . . . Shoots left. . . . Name pronounced SVAHRT-vuh-DEHT.

TRANSACTIONS/CAREER NOTES: Selected by Dallas Stars in sixth round (fifth Stars pick, 139th overall) of NHL entry draft (June 26, 1993).

			REGULAR SEASON					PLAYOFFS			
Season	Team	League	Gms.	G	A	Pts.	PIM	Gms.	G	A	Pts.	PIM
91-92—MoDo		Sweden Jr.	30	17	19	36	36	—	—	—	—	—
92-93—MoDo Hockey		Sweden	2	0	0	0	0	—	—	—	—	—
—MoDo		Sweden Jr.	22	19	27	46	38	—	—	—	—	—
93-94—MoDo Hockey		Sweden	36	2	1	3	4	11	0	0	0	6
94-95—MoDo Hockey		Sweden	40	6	9	15	31	—	—	—	—	—

SVEHLA, ROBERT

D, PANTHERS

PERSONAL: Born January 2, 1969, in Martin, Czechoslovakia. . . . 6-1/190. . . . Shoots left. . . . Name pronounced SVEE-luh.

TRANSACTIONS/CAREER NOTES: Selected by Calgary Flames in fourth round (fourth Flames pick, 78th overall) of NHL entry draft (June 20, 1992). . . . Traded by Flames with D Magnus Svensson to Florida Panthers for third-round pick in 1996 draft and future considerations (September 29, 1994). . . . Sprained left rotator cuff (April 22, 1995); missed two games. . . . Reinjured left rotator cuff (April 28, 1995); missed one game.

HONORS: Named Czechoslovakian League Player of the Year (1991-92). . . . Named to Czechoslovakian League All-Star team (1991-92).

MISCELLANEOUS: Member of bronze-medal-winning Czechoslovakian Olympic team (1992).

			REGULAR SEASON					PLAYOFFS			
Season	Team	League	Gms.	G	A	Pts.	PIM	Gms.	G	A	Pts.	PIM
89-90—Dukla Trencin		Czech.	29	4	3	7	...	—	—	—	—	—
90-91—Dukla Trencin		Czech.	58	16	9	25	...	—	—	—	—	—
91-92—Dukla Trencin		Czech.	51	23	28	51	0	—	—	—	—	—
—Czech. Olympic Team		Int'l	8	2	1	3	...	—	—	—	—	—
92-93—Malmo		Sweden	40	19	10	29	86	6	0	1	1	0
93-94—Malmo		Sweden	37	14	25	39	*127	10	5	1	6	23
—Slovakian Olympic team		Int'l	8	2	4	6	26	—	—	—	—	—
94-95—Malmo		Sweden	32	11	13	24	83	9	2	3	5	6
—Florida		NHL	5	1	1	2	0	—	—	—	—	—
NHL totals			5	1	1	2	0					

SVENSSON, MAGNUS

D, PANTHERS

PERSONAL: Born March 1, 1963, in Tranas, Sweden. . . . 5-11/180. . . . Shoots left.

TRANSACTIONS/CAREER NOTES: Selected by Calgary Flames in 12th round (13th Flames pick, 250th overall) of NHL entry draft (June 14, 1987). . . . Traded by Flames with D Robert Svehla to Florida Panthers for third-round pick in 1996 draft and future considerations (September 29, 1994).

			REGULAR SEASON					PLAYOFFS			
Season	Team	League	Gms.	G	A	Pts.	PIM	Gms.	G	A	Pts.	PIM
83-84—Leksand		Sweden	35	3	8	11	20	—	—	—	—	—
84-85—Leksand		Sweden	35	8	7	15	22	—	—	—	—	—
85-86—Leksand		Sweden	36	6	9	15	62	—	—	—	—	—
86-87—Leksand		Sweden	33	8	16	24	42	—	—	—	—	—
87-88—Leksand		Sweden	40	12	11	23	20	3	0	0	0	8
88-89—Leksand		Sweden	39	15	22	37	40	9	3	5	8	8
89-90—Leksand		Sweden	26	11	12	23	60	1	0	0	0	0
90-91—Lugano		Switzerland	33	16	20	36	...	11	3	2	5	0
91-92—Leksand		Sweden	22	4	10	14	32	—	—	—	—	—
92-93—Leksand		Sweden	37	10	17	27	36	2	0	2	2	0
93-94—Leksand		Sweden	39	13	16	29	22	4	3	1	4	0
94-95—Davos HC		Switzerland	35	8	25	33	46	5	2	2	4	8
—Florida		NHL	19	2	5	7	10	—	—	—	—	—
NHL totals			19	2	5	7	10					

SVOBODA, PETR

D, FLYERS

PERSONAL: Born February 14, 1966, in Most, Czechoslovakia. . . . 6-1/175. . . . Shoots left. . . . Name pronounced svuh-BOH-duh.

TRANSACTIONS/CAREER NOTES: Selected by Montreal Canadiens in first round (first Canadiens pick, fifth overall) of NHL entry draft (June 9, 1984). . . . Suffered back spasms (January 1988). . . . Suffered hip pointer (March 1988). . . . Sprained right wrist (November 21, 1988); missed five games. . . . Injured back (March 1989). . . . Separated shoulder (November 1989). . . . Pulled groin (November 22, 1989). . . . Aggravated groin injury (December 11, 1989); missed 15 games. . . . Bruised left foot (March 11, 1990). . . . Suffered stomach disorder (November 28, 1990); missed five games. . . . Broke left foot (January 15, 1991); missed 15 games. . . . Injured mouth (December 4, 1991). . . . Sprained ankle (February 17, 1992); missed seven games. . . . Traded by Canadiens to Buffalo Sabres for D Kevin Haller (March 10, 1992). . . . Bruised knee (October 28, 1992); missed four games. . . . Tore ligament in right knee (January 17, 1993); missed remainder of season. . . . Injured knee (October 12, 1993); missed three games. . . . Suffered knee inflammation (October 16, 1993); missed seven games. . . . Sprained left knee (March 17, 1994); missed 12 games. . . . Played in Europe during 1994-95 NHL lockout. . . . Fractured jaw (March 16, 1995); missed one game. . . . Separated shoulder (March 2, 1995); missed two games. . . . Traded by Sabres to Philadelphia Flyers for D Garry Galley (April 7, 1995). . . . Strained neck (April 26, 1995); missed one game.

MISCELLANEOUS: Member of Stanley Cup championship team (1986).

S

Season	Team	League	REGULAR SEASON					PLAYOFFS				
			Gms.	G	A	Pts.	PIM	Gms.	G	A	Pts.	PIM
83-84—Czechoslovakia Jr.	Czech.	40	15	21	36	14	—	—	—	—	—
84-85—Montreal............................	NHL	73	4	27	31	65	7	1	1	2	12
85-86—Montreal............................	NHL	73	1	18	19	93	8	0	0	0	21
86-87—Montreal............................	NHL	70	5	17	22	63	14	0	5	5	10
87-88—Montreal............................	NHL	69	7	22	29	149	10	0	5	5	12
88-89—Montreal............................	NHL	71	8	37	45	147	21	1	11	12	16
89-90—Montreal............................	NHL	60	5	31	36	98	10	0	5	5	2
90-91—Montreal............................	NHL	60	4	22	26	52	2	0	1	1	2
91-92—Montreal............................	NHL	58	5	16	21	94	—	—	—	—	—
—Buffalo	NHL	13	1	6	7	52	7	1	4	5	6
92-93—Buffalo	NHL	40	2	24	26	59	—	—	—	—	—
93-94—Buffalo	NHL	60	2	14	16	89	3	0	0	0	4
94-95—Chemopetrol Litvinov	Czech Rep.	8	2	0	2	40	—	—	—	—	—
—Buffalo	NHL	26	0	5	5	60	—	—	—	—	—
—Philadelphia	NHL	11	0	3	3	10	14	0	4	4	8
NHL totals................		**684**	**44**	**242**	**286**	**1031**	**96**	**3**	**36**	**39**	**93**

SWEENEY, BOB
C, SABRES

PERSONAL: Born January 25, 1964, in Boxborough, Mass. . . . 6-3/200. . . . Shoots right. . . . Full name: Robert Emmett Sweeney. . . . Brother of Tim Sweeney, center, Calgary Flames, Boston Bruins and Mighty Ducks of Anaheim (1990-91 through 1994-95).
HIGH SCHOOL: Acton (Mass.)-Boxborough.
COLLEGE: Boston College.
TRANSACTIONS/CAREER NOTES: Selected by Boston Bruins in sixth round (sixth Bruins pick, 123rd overall) of NHL entry draft (June 9, 1982). . . . Pulled rib muscle (November 1989); missed six games. . . . Injured left shoulder (April 23, 1991). . . . Sprained knee (February 4, 1992); missed 11 games. . . . Claimed on waivers by Buffalo Sabres and Calgary Flames; NHL awarded rights to Sabres (October 9, 1992). . . . Injured rib (November 7, 1993); missed five games. . . . Injured right knee (March 9, 1994); missed 14 games. . . . Suspended three games by NHL for fighting (October 11, 1993). . . . Bruised shoulder (January 25, 1995); missed two games.
HONORS: Named to NCAA All-America East second team (1984-85). . . . Named to Hockey East All-Star second team (1984-85).
RECORDS: Shares NHL career record for most overtime goals—7.
STATISTICAL PLATEAUS: Three-goal games: 1989-90 (1).

Season	Team	League	REGULAR SEASON					PLAYOFFS				
			Gms.	G	A	Pts.	PIM	Gms.	G	A	Pts.	PIM
82-83—Boston College	ECAC	30	17	11	28	10	—	—	—	—	—
83-84—Boston College	ECAC	23	14	7	21	10	—	—	—	—	—
84-85—Boston College	Hockey East	44	32	32	64	43	—	—	—	—	—
85-86—Boston College	Hockey East	41	15	24	39	52	—	—	—	—	—
86-87—Boston	NHL	14	2	4	6	21	3	0	0	0	0
—Moncton	AHL	58	29	26	55	81	4	0	2	2	13
87-88—Boston	NHL	80	22	23	45	73	23	6	8	14	66
88-89—Boston	NHL	75	14	14	28	99	10	2	4	6	19
89-90—Boston	NHL	70	22	24	46	93	20	0	2	2	30
90-91—Boston	NHL	80	15	33	48	115	17	4	2	6	45
91-92—Boston	NHL	63	6	14	20	103	14	1	0	1	25
—Maine	AHL	1	1	0	1	0	—	—	—	—	—
92-93—Buffalo	NHL	80	21	26	47	118	8	2	2	4	8
93-94—Buffalo	NHL	60	11	14	25	94	1	0	0	0	0
94-95—Buffalo	NHL	45	5	4	9	18	5	0	0	0	4
NHL totals................		**567**	**118**	**156**	**274**	**734**	**101**	**15**	**18**	**33**	**197**

SWEENEY, DON
D, BRUINS

PERSONAL: Born August 17, 1966, in St. Stephen, N.B. . . . 5-11/170. . . . Shoots left. . . . Full name: Donald Clark Sweeney.
HIGH SCHOOL: St. Paul (N.B.).
COLLEGE: Harvard.
TRANSACTIONS/CAREER NOTES: Selected by Boston Bruins in eighth round (eighth Bruins pick, 166th overall) of NHL entry draft (June 9, 1984). . . . Bruised left heel (February 22, 1990). . . . Injured knee (October 12, 1991); missed four games. . . . Sprained knee (October 5, 1993); missed six games. . . . Injured ribs (December 15, 1993); missed three games.
HONORS: Named to NCAA All-America East second team (1987-88). . . . Named to ECAC All-Star first team (1987-88).

Season	Team	League	REGULAR SEASON					PLAYOFFS				
			Gms.	G	A	Pts.	PIM	Gms.	G	A	Pts.	PIM
83-84—St. Paul N.B. H.S.	N.B. H.S.	22	33	26	59	...	—	—	—	—	—
84-85—Harvard University	ECAC	29	3	7	10	30	—	—	—	—	—
85-86—Harvard University	ECAC	31	4	5	9	29	—	—	—	—	—
86-87—Harvard University	ECAC	34	7	14	21	22	—	—	—	—	—
87-88—Harvard University	ECAC	30	6	23	29	37	—	—	—	—	—
—Maine	AHL	—	—	—	—	—	6	1	3	4	0
88-89—Maine..............................	AHL	42	8	17	25	24	—	—	—	—	—
—Boston	NHL	36	3	5	8	20	—	—	—	—	—
89-90—Boston	NHL	58	3	5	8	58	21	1	5	6	18
—Maine	AHL	11	0	8	8	8	—	—	—	—	—
90-91—Boston	NHL	77	8	13	21	67	19	3	0	3	25

Season Team	League	REGULAR SEASON					PLAYOFFS				
		Gms.	G	A	Pts.	PIM	Gms.	G	A	Pts.	PIM
91-92—Boston	NHL	75	3	11	14	74	15	0	0	0	10
92-93—Boston	NHL	84	7	27	34	68	4	0	0	0	4
93-94—Boston	NHL	75	6	15	21	50	12	2	1	3	4
94-95—Boston	NHL	47	3	19	22	24	5	0	0	0	4
NHL totals		452	33	95	128	361	76	6	6	12	65

SWEENEY, TIM
C

PERSONAL: Born April 12, 1967, in Boston.... 5-11/185.... Shoots left.... Full name: Timothy Paul Sweeney.... Brother of Bob Sweeney, center, Buffalo Sabres.
HIGH SCHOOL: Weymouth (Mass.).
COLLEGE: Boston College.
TRANSACTIONS/CAREER NOTES: Selected by Calgary Flames in sixth round (seventh Flames pick, 122nd overall) of NHL entry draft (June 15, 1985).... Fractured index finger (January 26, 1988).... Bruised ankle (May 1990).... Signed as free agent by Boston Bruins (September 1992).... Selected by Mighty Ducks of Anaheim in NHL expansion draft (June 24, 1993).... Suffered injury (November 26, 1993); missed four games.... Released by Mighty Ducks (April 9, 1995).... Signed as free agent by Providence Bruins (April 9, 1995).
HONORS: Named to NCAA All-America East second team (1988-89).... Named to Hockey East All-Star first team (1988-89). ... Won Ken McKenzie Trophy (1989-90).... Named to IHL All-Star second team (1989-90).... Named to AHL All-Star second team (1992-93).

Season Team	League	REGULAR SEASON					PLAYOFFS				
		Gms.	G	A	Pts.	PIM	Gms.	G	A	Pts.	PIM
83-84—Weymouth North H.S.	Mass. H.S.	23	33	26	59	...	—	—	—	—	—
84-85—Weymouth North H.S.	Mass. H.S.	22	32	56	88	...	—	—	—	—	—
85-86—Boston College	Hockey East	32	8	4	12	8	—	—	—	—	—
86-87—Boston College	Hockey East	38	31	16	47	28	—	—	—	—	—
87-88—Boston College	Hockey East	18	9	11	20	18	—	—	—	—	—
88-89—Boston College	Hockey East	39	29	44	73	26	—	—	—	—	—
89-90—Salt Lake City	IHL	81	46	51	97	32	11	5	4	9	4
90-91—Calgary	NHL	42	7	9	16	8	—	—	—	—	—
—Salt Lake City	IHL	31	19	16	35	8	4	3	3	6	0
91-92—Calgary	NHL	11	1	2	3	4	—	—	—	—	—
—U.S. national team	Int'l	21	9	11	20	10	—	—	—	—	—
—U.S. Olympic Team	Int'l	8	3	4	7	6	—	—	—	—	—
92-93—Providence	AHL	60	41	55	96	32	3	2	2	4	0
—Boston	NHL	14	1	7	8	6	3	0	0	0	0
93-94—Anaheim	NHL	78	16	27	43	49	—	—	—	—	—
94-95—Anaheim	NHL	13	1	1	2	2	—	—	—	—	—
—Providence	AHL	2	2	2	4	0	13	8	*17	*25	6
NHL totals		158	26	46	72	69	3	0	0	0	0

SWINSON, WES
D, WHALERS

PERSONAL: Born May 26, 1975, in Peterborough, Ont.... 6-2/183.... Shoots left.
TRANSACTIONS/CAREER NOTES: Selected by Hartford Whalers in 10th round (seventh Whalers pick, 240th overall) of NHL entry draft (June 29, 1994).
HONORS: Named to OHL All-Star second team (1994-95).

Season Team	League	REGULAR SEASON					PLAYOFFS				
		Gms.	G	A	Pts.	PIM	Gms.	G	A	Pts.	PIM
92-93—Kitchener	OHL	61	0	16	16	103	6	0	2	2	14
93-94—Kitchener	OHL	64	26	46	72	111	5	2	6	8	18
94-95—Kitchener	OHL	42	12	38	50	71	—	—	—	—	—
—Kingston	OHL	20	7	20	27	16	6	2	7	9	6

SYDOR, DARRYL
D, KINGS

PERSONAL: Born May 13, 1972, in Edmonton.... 6-0/205.... Shoots left.... Full name: Darryl Marion Sydor.... Name pronounced sih-DOHR.
TRANSACTIONS/CAREER NOTES: Selected by Los Angeles Kings in first round (first Kings pick, seventh overall) of NHL entry draft (June 16, 1990).... Bruised hip (November 27, 1992); missed two games.... Sprained right shoulder (March 15, 1993); missed two games.
HONORS: Named to WHL (West) All-Star first team (1989-90 through 1991-92).... Won Bill Hunter Trophy (1990-91).... Named to Can.HL All-Star second team (1991-92)

Season Team	League	REGULAR SEASON					PLAYOFFS				
		Gms.	G	A	Pts.	PIM	Gms.	G	A	Pts.	PIM
88-89—Kamloops	WHL	65	12	14	26	86	15	1	4	5	19
89-90—Kamloops	WHL	67	29	66	95	129	17	2	9	11	28
90-91—Kamloops	WHL	66	27	78	105	88	12	3	*22	25	10
91-92—Kamloops	WHL	29	9	39	48	43	17	3	15	18	18
—Los Angeles	NHL	18	1	5	6	22	—	—	—	—	—
92-93—Los Angeles	NHL	80	6	23	29	63	24	3	8	11	16
93-94—Los Angeles	NHL	84	8	27	35	94	—	—	—	—	—
94-95—Los Angeles	NHL	48	4	19	23	36	—	—	—	—	—
NHL totals		230	19	74	93	215	24	3	8	11	16

SYKORA, MICHAL
D, SHARKS

PERSONAL: Born July 5, 1973, in Pardubice, Czechoslovakia. . . . 6-5/225. . . . Shoots left. . . . Name pronounced sih-KOHR-uh.
TRANSACTIONS/CAREER NOTES: Selected by San Jose Sharks in sixth round (sixth Sharks pick, 123rd overall) of NHL entry draft (June 20, 1992). . . . Strained knee (November 11, 1993); missed four games. . . . Injured shoulder (February 24, 1995); missed remainder of season.
HONORS: Named to Can.HL All-Star second team (1992-93). . . . Named to WHL (West) All-Star first team (1992-93).

Season Team	League	Gms.	G	A	Pts.	PIM	Gms.	G	A	Pts.	PIM
		REGULAR SEASON					**PLAYOFFS**				
90-91—Pardubice	Czech.	2	0	0	0	. . .	—	—	—	—	—
91-92—Tacoma	WHL	61	13	23	36	66	4	0	2	2	2
92-93—Tacoma	WHL	70	23	50	73	73	7	4	8	12	2
93-94—San Jose	NHL	22	1	4	5	14	—	—	—	—	—
—Kansas City	IHL	47	5	11	16	30	—	—	—	—	—
94-95—Kansas City	IHL	36	1	10	11	30	—	—	—	—	—
—San Jose	NHL	16	0	4	4	10	—	—	—	—	—
NHL totals		38	1	8	9	24					

SYKORA, PETR
C, DEVILS

PERSONAL: Born November 19, 1976, in Plzen, Czechoslovakia. . . . 5-11/180. . . . Shoots left.
TRANSACTIONS/CAREER NOTES: Signed as free agent by Cleveland Lumberjacks (January 31, 1994). . . . Rights traded by Lumberjacks to Detroit Vipers for cash and future considerations (July 27, 1994). . . . Injured shoulder (1995); missed remainder of season. . . . Selected by New Jersey Devils in first round (first Devils pick, 18th overall) of NHL entry draft (July 8, 1995).

Season Team	League	Gms.	G	A	Pts.	PIM	Gms.	G	A	Pts.	PIM
		REGULAR SEASON					**PLAYOFFS**				
91-92—Skoda Plzen	Czech.	30	50	50	100	. . .	—	—	—	—	—
92-93—Skoda Plzen	Czech.	19	12	5	17	. . .	—	—	—	—	—
93-94—Skoda Plzen	Czech Rep.	37	10	16	26	. . .	4	0	1	1	. . .
—Cleveland	AHL	13	4	5	9	8	—	—	—	—	—
94-95—Detroit	IHL	29	12	17	29	16	—	—	—	—	—

SYMES, BRAD
D, OILERS

PERSONAL: Born April 26, 1976, in Edmonton. . . . 6-2/210. . . . Shoots left.
TRANSACTIONS/CAREER NOTES: Selected by Edmonton Oilers in third round (fifth Oilers pick, 60th overall) of NHL entry draft (June 29, 1994).

Season Team	League	Gms.	G	A	Pts.	PIM	Gms.	G	A	Pts.	PIM
		REGULAR SEASON					**PLAYOFFS**				
91-92—Sherwood Park	AJHL	17	3	7	10	92	—	—	—	—	—
92-93—Portland	WHL	68	4	2	6	107	16	0	1	1	7
93-94—Portland	WHL	71	7	15	22	170	7	0	0	0	21
94-95—Portland	WHL	70	8	16	24	134	9	0	2	2	27

TABARACCI, RICK
G, FLAMES

PERSONAL: Born January 2, 1969, in Toronto. . . . 5-11/180. . . . Catches right. . . . Full name: Richard Stephen Tabaracci. . . . Name pronounced tab-uh-RA-chee.
TRANSACTIONS/CAREER NOTES: Selected by Pittsburgh Penguins as underage junior in second round (second Penguins pick, 26th overall) of NHL entry draft (June 13, 1987). . . . Traded by Penguins with C/LW Randy Cunneyworth and RW Dave McLlwain to Winnipeg Jets for RW Andrew McBain, D Jim Kyte and LW Randy Gilhen (June 17, 1989). . . . Pulled right hamstring (December 11, 1990); missed seven games. . . . Strained back (October 10, 1992); missed one game. . . . Suffered back spasms (December 1, 1992); missed one game. . . . Suffered back spasms (January 19, 1993); missed seven games. . . . Traded by Jets to Washington Capitals for G Jim Hrivnak and future considerations (March 22, 1993). . . . Tore knee ligaments (September 16, 1993); missed seven games. . . . Slightly sprained knee (February 20, 1994); missed 21 games. . . . Strained hamstring (February 13, 1995). . . . Loaned by Capitals to Chicago Wolves (March 27, 1995). . . . Traded by Capitals to Calgary Flames for fifth-round pick (D Joel Cort) in 1995 draft (April 7, 1995).
HONORS: Named to OHL All-Star first team (1987-88). . . . Named to OHL All-Star second team (1988-89).

Season Team	League	Gms.	Min.	W	L	T	GA	SO	Avg.	Gms.	Min.	W	L	GA	SO	Avg.
		REGULAR SEASON								**PLAYOFFS**						
85-86—Markham Jr. B	OHA	40	2176	. . .	. . .	. . .	188	1	5.18	—	—	—	—	—	—	—
86-87—Cornwall	OHL	*59	*3347	23	32	3	*290	1	5.20	5	303	1	4	26	0	5.15
87-88—Cornwall	OHL	58	3448	33	18	6	200	†3	3.48	11	642	5	6	37	0	3.46
—Muskegon	IHL	—	—	—	—	—	—	—	—	1	13	0	0	1	0	4.62
88-89—Cornwall	OHL	50	2974	24	20	5	*210	1	4.24	18	1080	10	8	65	†1	3.61
—Pittsburgh	NHL	1	33	0	0	0	4	0	7.27	—	—	—	—	—	—	—
89-90—Moncton	AHL	27	1580	10	15	2	107	2	4.06	—	—	—	—	—	—	—
—Fort Wayne	IHL	22	1064	8	9	†1	73	0	4.12	3	159	1	2	19	0	7.17
90-91—Moncton	AHL	11	645	4	5	2	41	0	3.81	—	—	—	—	—	—	—
—Winnipeg	NHL	24	1093	4	9	4	71	1	3.90	—	—	—	—	—	—	—
91-92—Moncton	AHL	23	1313	10	11	1	80	0	3.66	—	—	—	—	—	—	—
—Winnipeg	NHL	18	966	6	7	3	52	0	3.23	7	387	3	4	26	0	4.03
92-93—Winnipeg	NHL	19	959	5	10	0	70	0	4.38	—	—	—	—	—	—	—
—Moncton	AHL	5	290	2	1	2	18	0	3.72	—	—	—	—	—	—	—
—Washington	NHL	6	343	3	2	0	10	2	1.75	4	304	1	3	14	0	2.76
93-94—Portland	AHL	3	177	3	0	0	8	0	2.71	—	—	—	—	—	—	—
—Washington	NHL	32	1770	13	14	2	91	2	3.08	2	111	0	2	6	0	3.24

Season	Team	League	REGULAR SEASON							PLAYOFFS						
			Gms.	Min.	W	L	T	GA	SO	Avg.	Gms.	Min.	W	L	GA	SO	Avg.
94-95	—Washington	NHL	8	394	1	3	2	16	0	2.44	—	—	—	—	—	—	—
	—Chicago	IHL	2	120	1	1	‡0	9	0	4.50	—	—	—	—	—	—	—
	—Calgary	NHL	5	202	2	0	1	5	0	1.49	1	19	0	0	0	0	0.00
	NHL totals		113	5760	34	45	12	319	5	3.32	14	821	4	9	46	0	3.36

TAGLIANETTI, PETER
D

PERSONAL: Born August 15, 1963, in Framingham, Mass. ... 6-2/195. ... Shoots left. ... Full name: Peter Anthony Taglianetti. ... Name pronounced TAG-lee-uh-NEH-tee.
COLLEGE: Providence.
TRANSACTIONS/CAREER NOTES: Selected by Winnipeg Jets in third round (fourth Jets pick, 43rd overall) of NHL entry draft (June 8, 1983). ... Dislocated shoulder during training camp (October 1985). ... Dislocated shoulder (February 20, 1986). ... Underwent surgery to correct recurring shoulder dislocations (March 1986). ... Damaged right knee cartilage during training camp and underwent surgery (September 1988). ... Injured knee and underwent surgery (October 6, 1989). ... Suspended five games by NHL for attempting to injure opposing player (February 20, 1990). ... Bruised ribs (April 1990). ... Traded by Jets to Minnesota North Stars for future considerations (September 23, 1990). ... Traded by North Stars with D Larry Murphy to Pittsburgh Penguins for D Jim Johnson and D Chris Dahlquist (December 11, 1990). ... Suffered collapsed lung (February 11, 1991); missed nine games. ... Injured back (December 21, 1991); missed two games. ... Injured back (March 7, 1992); missed final 15 games of season. ... Underwent back surgery (April 5, 1992); missed entire playoffs. ... Selected by Tampa Bay Lightning in NHL expansion draft (June 18, 1992). ... Suffered concussion (March 20, 1993); missed one game. ... Traded by Lightning to Penguins for third-round pick in 1993 draft (March 22, 1993). ... Injured neck (November 6, 1993); missed seven games. ... Injured back (January 2, 1994); missed three games. ... Broke finger (March 6, 1994); missed two games. ... Bruised right knee (March 7, 1995); missed four games.
HONORS: Named to ECAC All-Star second team (1983-84). ... Named to NCAA All-America East second team (1984-85). ... Named to Hockey East All-Star first team (1984-85).
MISCELLANEOUS: Member of Stanley Cup championship teams (1991 and 1992).

Season	Team	League	REGULAR SEASON					PLAYOFFS				
			Gms.	G	A	Pts.	PIM	Gms.	G	A	Pts.	PIM
81-82	—Providence College	ECAC	2	0	0	0	2	—	—	—	—	—
82-83	—Providence College	ECAC	43	4	17	21	68	—	—	—	—	—
83-84	—Providence College	ECAC	30	4	25	29	68	—	—	—	—	—
84-85	—Providence College	Hockey East	43	8	21	29	114	—	—	—	—	—
	—Winnipeg	NHL	1	0	0	0	0	1	0	0	0	0
85-86	—Sherbrooke	AHL	24	1	8	9	75	—	—	—	—	—
	—Winnipeg	NHL	18	0	0	0	48	3	0	0	0	2
86-87	—Winnipeg	NHL	3	0	0	0	12	—	—	—	—	—
	—Sherbrooke	AHL	54	5	14	19	104	10	2	5	7	25
87-88	—Winnipeg	NHL	70	6	17	23	182	5	1	1	2	12
88-89	—Winnipeg	NHL	66	1	14	15	226	—	—	—	—	—
89-90	—Moncton	AHL	3	0	2	2	2	—	—	—	—	—
	—Winnipeg	NHL	49	3	6	9	136	5	0	0	0	6
90-91	—Minnesota	NHL	16	0	1	1	14	—	—	—	—	—
	—Pittsburgh	NHL	39	3	8	11	93	19	0	3	3	49
91-92	—Pittsburgh	NHL	44	1	3	4	57	—	—	—	—	—
92-93	—Tampa Bay	NHL	61	1	8	9	150	—	—	—	—	—
	—Pittsburgh	NHL	11	1	4	5	34	11	1	2	3	16
93-94	—Pittsburgh	NHL	60	2	12	14	142	5	0	2	2	16
94-95	—Pittsburgh	NHL	13	0	1	1	12	4	0	0	0	2
	—Cleveland	IHL	3	0	1	1	7	4	0	0	0	19
	NHL totals		451	18	74	92	1106	53	2	8	10	103

TAMER, CHRIS
D, PENGUINS

PERSONAL: Born November 17, 1970, in Dearborn, Mich. ... 6-2/185. ... Shoots left. ... Full name: Chris Thomas Tamer.
COLLEGE: Michigan.
TRANSACTIONS/CAREER NOTES: Selected by Pittsburgh Penguins in fourth round (third Penguins pick, 68th overall) of NHL entry draft (June 16, 1990). ... Injured shoulder (March 27, 1994); missed four games. ... Fractured ankle (May 6, 1995); missed eight playoff games.

Season	Team	League	REGULAR SEASON					PLAYOFFS				
			Gms.	G	A	Pts.	PIM	Gms.	G	A	Pts.	PIM
87-88	—Redford	NAJHL	40	10	20	30	217	—	—	—	—	—
88-89	—Redford	NAJHL	31	6	13	19	79	—	—	—	—	—
89-90	—University of Michigan	CCHA	42	2	7	9	147	—	—	—	—	—
90-91	—University of Michigan	CCHA	45	8	19	27	130	—	—	—	—	—
91-92	—University of Michigan	CCHA	43	4	15	19	*125	—	—	—	—	—
92-93	—University of Michigan	CCHA	39	5	18	23	113	—	—	—	—	—
93-94	—Cleveland	IHL	53	1	2	3	160	—	—	—	—	—
	—Pittsburgh	NHL	12	0	0	0	9	5	0	0	0	2
94-95	—Cleveland	IHL	48	4	10	14	204	—	—	—	—	—
	—Pittsburgh	NHL	36	2	0	2	82	4	0	0	0	18
	NHL totals		48	2	0	2	91	9	0	0	0	20

TANCILL, CHRIS
LW, SHARKS

PERSONAL: Born February 7, 1968, in Livonia, Mich. . . . 5-10/185. . . . Shoots left. . . . Full name: Christopher William Tancill.
COLLEGE: Wisconsin.
TRANSACTIONS/CAREER NOTES: Selected by Hartford Whalers in NHL supplemental draft (June 16, 1989). . . . Traded by Whalers to Detroit Red Wings for RW Daniel Shank (December 18, 1991). . . . Signed as free agent by Dallas Stars (August 27, 1993). . . . Signed as free agent by San Jose Sharks (August 31, 1994).
HONORS: Named NCAA Tournament Most Valuable Player (1989-90). . . . Named to NCAA All-Tournament team (1989-90). . . . Named to AHL All-Star first team (1991-92 and 1992-93).

			REGULAR SEASON					PLAYOFFS				
Season	Team	League	Gms.	G	A	Pts.	PIM	Gms.	G	A	Pts.	PIM
86-87—	University of Wisconsin ...	WCHA	40	9	23	32	26	—	—	—	—	—
87-88—	University of Wisconsin ...	WCHA	44	13	14	27	48	—	—	—	—	—
88-89—	University of Wisconsin ...	WCHA	44	20	23	43	50	—	—	—	—	—
89-90—	University of Wisconsin ...	WCHA	45	39	32	71	44	—	—	—	—	—
90-91—	Hartford	NHL	9	1	1	2	4	—	—	—	—	—
	—Springfield	AHL	72	37	35	72	46	17	8	4	12	32
91-92—	Springfield	AHL	17	12	7	19	20	—	—	—	—	—
	—Hartford	NHL	10	0	0	0	2	—	—	—	—	—
	—Adirondack	AHL	50	36	34	70	42	19	7	9	16	31
	—Detroit	NHL	1	0	0	0	0	—	—	—	—	—
92-93—	Adirondack	AHL	68	*59	43	102	62	10	7	7	14	10
	—Detroit	NHL	4	1	0	1	2	—	—	—	—	—
93-94—	Dallas	NHL	12	1	3	4	8	—	—	—	—	—
	—Kalamazoo	IHL	60	41	54	95	55	5	0	2	2	8
94-95—	San Jose	NHL	26	3	11	14	10	11	1	1	2	8
	—Kansas City	IHL	64	31	28	59	40	—	—	—	—	—
NHL totals			62	6	15	21	26	11	1	1	2	8

TARDIF, PATRICE
RW/C, BLUES

PERSONAL: Born October 30, 1970, in Thetford Mines, Que. . . . 6-2/202. . . . Shoots left. . . . Name pronounced TAHR-dih f.
COLLEGE: Champlain Regional (Que.), then Maine.
TRANSACTIONS/CAREER NOTES: Selected by St. Louis Blues in third round (second Blues pick, 54th overall) of NHL entry draft (June 16, 1990).
HONORS: Named to Hockey East All-Rookie team (1990-91).

			REGULAR SEASON					PLAYOFFS				
Season	Team	League	Gms.	G	A	Pts.	PIM	Gms.	G	A	Pts.	PIM
89-90—	Champlain Junior College	Can. Coll.	27	58	36	94	36	—	—	—	—	—
90-91—	University of Maine	Hockey East	36	13	12	25	18	—	—	—	—	—
91-92—	University of Maine	Hockey East	31	18	20	38	14	—	—	—	—	—
92-93—	University of Maine	Hockey East	45	23	25	48	22	—	—	—	—	—
93-94—	University of Maine	Hockey East	34	18	15	33	42	—	—	—	—	—
	—Peoria	IHL	11	4	4	8	21	4	2	0	2	4
94-95—	Peoria	IHL	53	27	18	45	83	—	—	—	—	—
	—St. Louis	NHL	27	3	10	13	29	—	—	—	—	—
NHL totals			27	3	10	13	29					

TARVAINEN, JUSSI
C, OILERS

PERSONAL: Born May 31, 1976, in Lahti, Finland. . . . 6-2/187. . . . Shoots right.
TRANSACTIONS/CAREER NOTES: Selected by Edmonton Oilers in fourth round (seventh Oilers pick, 95th overall) of NHL entry draft (June 29, 1994).

			REGULAR SEASON					PLAYOFFS				
Season	Team	League	Gms.	G	A	Pts.	PIM	Gms.	G	A	Pts.	PIM
92-93—	KalPa Juniors	Finland Jrs.	17	3	6	9	35	—	—	—	—	—
93-94—	KalPa	Finland	42	3	4	7	20	—	—	—	—	—
94-95—	KalPa	Finland	45	10	7	17	34	3	0	0	0	2

TAYLOR, CHRIS
C, ISLANDERS

PERSONAL: Born March 6, 1972, in Stratford, Ont. . . . 6-1/198. . . . Shoots left. . . . Brother of Tim Taylor, left winger, Detroit Red Wings.
TRANSACTIONS/CAREER NOTES: Tore knee ligaments (March 1989). . . . Selected by New York Islanders in second round (second Islanders pick, 27th overall) of NHL entry draft (June 16, 1990).

			REGULAR SEASON					PLAYOFFS				
Season	Team	League	Gms.	G	A	Pts.	PIM	Gms.	G	A	Pts.	PIM
88-89—	London	OHL	62	7	16	23	52	15	0	2	2	15
89-90—	London	OHL	66	45	60	105	60	6	3	2	5	6
90-91—	London	OHL	65	50	78	128	50	7	4	8	12	6
91-92—	London	OHL	66	48	74	122	57	10	8	16	24	9
92-93—	Roanoke	ECHL	5	2	1	3	0	—	—	—	—	—
	—Capital District.................	AHL	77	19	43	62	32	4	0	1	1	2
93-94—	Raleigh	ECHL	2	0	0	0	0	—	—	—	—	—
	—Salt Lake City...................	IHL	79	21	20	41	38	—	—	—	—	—
94-95—	Denver	IHL	78	38	48	86	47	14	7	6	13	10
	—Roanoke	ECHL	1	0	0	0	2	—	—	—	—	—
	—New York Islanders..........	NHL	10	0	3	3	2	—	—	—	—	—
NHL totals			10	0	3	3	2					

TAYLOR, TIM
LW, RED WINGS

PERSONAL: Born February 6, 1969, in Stratford, Ont. . . . 6-1/185. . . . Shoots left. . . . Full name: Tim Robertson Taylor. . . . Brother of Chris Taylor, center in New York Islanders system.
TRANSACTIONS/CAREER NOTES: Suffered from mononucleosis (October 1986). . . . Selected by Washington Capitals in second round (second Capitals pick, 36th overall) of NHL entry draft (June 11, 1988). . . . Traded by Capitals to Vancouver Canucks for C Eric Murano (January 29, 1993). . . . Signed as free agent by Detroit Red Wings (July 28, 1993).
HONORS: Won John B. Sollenberger Trophy (1993-94). . . . Named to AHL All-Star first team (1993-94).

Season	Team	League	REGULAR SEASON Gms.	G	A	Pts.	PIM	PLAYOFFS Gms.	G	A	Pts.	PIM
86-87	London	OHL	34	7	9	16	11	—	—	—	—	—
87-88	London	OHL	64	46	50	96	66	12	9	9	18	26
88-89	London	OHL	61	34	80	114	93	21	*21	25	*46	58
89-90	Baltimore	AHL	74	22	21	43	63	9	2	2	4	13
90-91	Baltimore	AHL	79	25	42	67	75	5	0	1	1	4
91-92	Baltimore	AHL	65	9	18	27	131	—	—	—	—	—
92-93	Baltimore	AHL	41	15	16	31	49	—	—	—	—	—
	—Hamilton	AHL	36	15	22	37	37	—	—	—	—	—
93-94	Adirondack	AHL	79	36	*81	117	86	12	2	10	12	12
	—Detroit	NHL	1	1	0	1	0	—	—	—	—	—
94-95	Detroit	NHL	22	0	4	4	16	6	0	1	1	12
	NHL totals		23	1	4	5	16	6	0	1	1	12

TERRERI, CHRIS
G, DEVILS

PERSONAL: Born November 15, 1964, in Warwick, R.I. . . . 5-8/160. . . . Catches left. . . . Full name: Christopher Arnold Terreri. . . . Name pronounced tuh-RAIR-ee.
COLLEGE: Providence.
TRANSACTIONS/CAREER NOTES: Selected by New Jersey Devils in fifth round (third Devils pick, 87th overall) of NHL entry draft (June 8, 1983). . . . Strained knee (October 1986). . . . Strained lower back (March 21, 1992); missed five games.
HONORS: Named NCAA Tournament Most Valuable Player (1984-85). . . . Named Hockey East Player of the Year (1984-85). . . . Named Hockey East Tournament Most Valuable Player (1984-85). . . . Named to NCAA All-Tournament team (1984-85). . . . Named to NCAA All-America East first team (1984-85). . . . Named to Hockey East All-Star first team (1984-85). . . . Named to NCAA All-America East second team (1985-86). . . . Named to Hockey East All-Decade team (1994).
MISCELLANEOUS: Member of Stanley Cup championship team (1995).

Season	Team	League	REGULAR SEASON Gms.	Min.	W	L	T	GA	SO	Avg.	PLAYOFFS Gms.	Min.	W	L	GA	SO	Avg.
82-83	Providence College	ECAC	11	529	7	1	0	17	2	1.93	—	—	—	—	—	—	—
83-84	Providence College	ECAC	10	391	4	2	0	20	0	3.07	—	—	—	—	—	—	—
84-85	Providence College	Hoc. East	41	2515	15	13	5	131	1	3.13	—	—	—	—	—	—	—
85-86	Providence College	Hoc. East	27	1540	6	16	0	96	0	3.74	—	—	—	—	—	—	—
86-87	Maine	AHL	14	765	4	9	1	57	0	4.47	—	—	—	—	—	—	—
	—New Jersey	NHL	7	286	0	3	1	21	0	4.41	—	—	—	—	—	—	—
87-88	U.S. national team	Int'l	26	1430	17	7	2	81	0	3.40	—	—	—	—	—	—	—
	—U.S. Olympic Team	Int'l	3	128	1	1	0	14	0	6.56	—	—	—	—	—	—	—
	—Utica	AHL	7	399	5	1	0	18	0	2.71	—	—	—	—	—	—	—
88-89	New Jersey	NHL	8	402	0	4	2	18	0	2.69	—	—	—	—	—	—	—
	—Utica	AHL	39	2314	20	15	3	132	0	3.42	2	80	0	1	6	0	4.50
89-90	New Jersey	NHL	35	1931	15	12	3	110	0	3.42	4	238	2	2	13	0	3.28
90-91	New Jersey	NHL	53	2970	24	21	7	144	1	2.91	7	428	3	4	21	0	2.94
91-92	New Jersey	NHL	54	3186	22	22	10	169	1	3.18	7	386	3	3	23	0	3.58
92-93	New Jersey	NHL	48	2672	19	21	3	151	2	3.39	4	219	1	3	17	0	4.66
93-94	New Jersey	NHL	44	2340	20	11	4	106	2	2.72	4	200	3	0	9	0	2.70
94-95	New Jersey	NHL	15	734	3	7	2	31	0	2.53	1	8	0	0	0	0	0.00
	NHL totals		264	14521	103	101	32	750	6	3.10	27	1479	12	12	83	0	3.37

TERTYSHNY, DMITRI
D, FLYERS

PERSONAL: Born July 25, 1976, in Chelyabinsk, U.S.S.R. . . . 5-10/174. . . . Shoots left. . . . Name pronounced tair-TIHSH-nee.
TRANSACTIONS/CAREER NOTES: Selected by Philadelphia Flyers in sixth round (fourth Flyers pick, 132nd overall) of NHL entry draft (July 8, 1995).

Season	Team	League	REGULAR SEASON Gms.	G	A	Pts.	PIM	PLAYOFFS Gms.	G	A	Pts.	PIM
94-95	Traktor Chelyabinsk	CIS	38	0	3	3	14	—	—	—	—	—

TERTYSHNY, SERGEI
D, CAPITALS

PERSONAL: Born June 3, 1970, in Chelyabinsk, U.S.S.R. . . . 6-0/187. . . . Shoots left. . . . Name pronounced tair-TIHSH-nee.
TRANSACTIONS/CAREER NOTES: Selected by Washington Capitals in 11th round (11th Capitals pick, 275th overall) of NHL entry draft (June 29, 1994).

Season	Team	League	REGULAR SEASON Gms.	G	A	Pts.	PIM	PLAYOFFS Gms.	G	A	Pts.	PIM
87-88	Chelyabinsk	USSR	19	0	0	0	4	—	—	—	—	—
88-89	SKA Sverdlovsk	USSR Div. II				Statistics unavailable.						
89-90	SKA Leningrad	USSR	4	0	0	0	0	—	—	—	—	—
90-91	SKA Leningrad	USSR	28	2	2	4	12	—	—	—	—	—
91-92	Traktor Chelyabinsk	CIS	44	4	2	6	20	—	—	—	—	—

T

Season	Team	League	Gms.	G	A	Pts.	PIM	Gms.	G	A	Pts.	PIM
92-93—Traktor Chelyabinsk	CIS	41	8	3	11	10	8	2	0	2	4
93-94—Traktor Chelyabinsk	CIS	37	8	8	16	22	6	0	1	1	0
94-95—Portland	AHL	55	0	17	17	12	—	—	—	—	—

THEODORE, JOSE
G, CANADIENS

PERSONAL: Born September 13, 1976, in Laval, Que.... 5-10/176.... Catches right.... Name pronounced ZHOH-zee tee-oh-DAHR.
TRANSACTIONS/CAREER NOTES: Selected by Montreal Canadiens in second round (second Canadiens pick, 44th overall) of NHL entry draft (June 28, 1994).
HONORS: Named to QMJHL All-Star second team (1994-95).

				REGULAR SEASON							PLAYOFFS					
Season	Team	League	Gms.	Min.	W	L	T	GA	SO	Avg.	Gms.	Min.	W	L	GA	SO	Avg.
92-93—St. Jean	QMJHL	34	1776	12	16	2	112	0	3.78	3	175	0	2	11	0	3.77
93-94—St. Jean	QMJHL	57	3225	20	29	6	194	0	3.61	5	296	1	4	18	1	3.65
94-95—Hull	QMJHL	58	3348	32	22	2	193	5	3.46	21	1263	15	6	59	1	2.80
—Fredericton	AHL	—	—	—	—	—	—	—	—	1	60	0	1	3	0	3.00

THERIAULT, JOEL
D, CAPITALS

PERSONAL: Born October 30, 1976, in Montreal.... 6-3/201.... Shoots right.
TRANSACTIONS/CAREER NOTES: Selected by Washington Capitals in fourth round (fifth Capitals pick, 95th overall) of NHL entry draft (July 8, 1995).

Season	Team	League	Gms.	G	A	Pts.	PIM	Gms.	G	A	Pts.	PIM
93-94—St. Jean	QMJHL	57	3	0	3	63	5	0	1	1	0
94-95—St. Jean	QMJHL	18	2	7	9	94	—	—	—	—	—
—Beauport	QMJHL	51	2	5	7	293	18	3	6	9	162

THERIEN, CHRIS
D, FLYERS

PERSONAL: Born December 14, 1971, in Ottawa.... 6-4/230.... Shoots left.... Name pronounced THAIR-ee-ihn.
HIGH SCHOOL: Northwood School (Lake Placid, N.Y.).
COLLEGE: Providence.
TRANSACTIONS/CAREER NOTES: Selected by Philadelphia Flyers in third round (seventh Flyers pick, 47th overall) of NHL entry draft (June 16, 1990).
HONORS: Named to Hockey East All-Rookie Team (1990-91).... Named to Hockey East All-Star second team (1992-93).... Named to NHL All-Rookie team (1994-95).

Season	Team	League	Gms.	G	A	Pts.	PIM	Gms.	G	A	Pts.	PIM
89-90—Northwood School	N.Y. H.S.	31	35	37	72	54	—	—	—	—	—
90-91—Providence College	Hockey East	36	4	18	22	36	—	—	—	—	—
91-92—Providence College	Hockey East	36	16	25	41	38	—	—	—	—	—
92-93—Providence College	Hockey East	33	8	11	19	52	—	—	—	—	—
—Canadian national team	Int'l	8	1	4	5	8	—	—	—	—	—
93-94—Canadian national team	Int'l	59	7	15	22	46	—	—	—	—	—
—Canadian Olympic Team	Int'l	4	0	0	0	4	—	—	—	—	—
—Hershey	AHL	6	0	0	0	2	—	—	—	—	—
94-95—Hershey	AHL	34	3	13	16	27	—	—	—	—	—
—Philadelphia	NHL	48	3	10	13	38	15	0	0	0	10
NHL totals		48	3	10	13	38	15	0	0	0	10

THIBAULT, JOCELYN
G, DENVER

PERSONAL: Born January 12, 1975, in Montreal.... 5-11/170.... Catches left.... Name pronounced TEE-boh.
TRANSACTIONS/CAREER NOTES: Selected by Quebec Nordiques in first round (first Nordiques pick, 10th overall) of NHL entry draft (June 26, 1993).... Sprained shoulder (March 28, 1995); missed 10 games.... Nordiques franchise moved to Denver for 1995-96 season.
HONORS: Named to QMJHL All-Rookie team (1991-92).... Won Can.HL Goaltender-of-the-Year Award (1992-93).... Won Jacques Plante Trophy (1992-93).... Won Michel Briere Trophy (1992-93).... Won Marcel Robert Trophy (1992-93).... Named to Can.HL All-Star first team (1992-93).... Named to QMJHL All-Star first team (1992-93).

				REGULAR SEASON							PLAYOFFS					
Season	Team	League	Gms.	Min.	W	L	T	GA	SO	Avg.	Gms.	Min.	W	L	GA	SO	Avg.
91-92—Trois-Rivieres	QMJHL	30	1497	14	7	1	77	0	3.09	3	300	...	...	20	0	4.00
92-93—Sherbrooke	QMJHL	56	3190	34	14	5	159	*3	*2.99	15	883	9	6	57	0	3.87
93-94—Cornwall	AHL	4	240	4	0	0	9	1	2.25	—	—	—	—	—	—	—
—Quebec	NHL	29	1504	8	13	3	83	0	3.31	—	—	—	—	—	—	—
94-95—Sherbrooke	QMJHL	13	776	6	6	1	38	1	2.94	—	—	—	—	—	—	—
—Quebec	NHL	18	898	12	2	2	35	1	2.34	3	148	1	2	8	0	3.24
NHL totals		47	2402	20	15	5	118	1	2.95	3	148	1	2	8	0	3.24

THIESSEN, TRAVIS
D, BLACKHAWKS

PERSONAL: Born November 7, 1972, in North Battleford, Sask.... 6-3/202.... Shoots left.... Name pronounced THEE-sehn.
TRANSACTIONS/CAREER NOTES: Selected by Pittsburgh Penguins in third round (third Penguins pick, 67th overall) of NHL entry draft (June 20, 1992).... Signed as free agent by Chicago Blackhawks (June 23, 1994).... Loaned by Blackhawks to Saint John (March 15, 1995).

Season Team	League	REGULAR SEASON					PLAYOFFS				
		Gms.	G	A	Pts.	PIM	Gms.	G	A	Pts.	PIM
90-91—Moose Jaw	WHL	69	4	14	18	80	8	0	0	0	10
91-92—Moose Jaw	WHL	72	9	50	59	112	4	0	2	2	8
92-93—Cleveland	IHL	64	3	7	10	69	4	0	0	0	16
93-94—Cleveland	IHL	74	2	13	15	75	—	—	—	—	—
94-95—Indianapolis	IHL	41	2	3	5	36	—	—	—	—	—
—Flint	Col.HL	5	0	1	1	2	—	—	—	—	—
—Saint John	AHL	9	1	2	3	12	5	0	1	1	0

THOMAS, SCOTT
RW, SABRES

PERSONAL: Born January 18, 1970, in Buffalo, N.Y. . . . 6-2/195. . . . Shoots right. . . . Full name: John Scott Thomas.
HIGH SCHOOL: Nichols (Buffalo, N.Y.).
COLLEGE: Clarkson (N.Y.).
TRANSACTIONS/CAREER NOTES: Selected by Buffalo Sabres in third round (second Sabres pick, 56th overall) of NHL entry draft (June 17, 1989). . . . Broke left thumb (December 1990).
HONORS: Named to ECAC All-Rookie team (1989-90).

Season Team	League	REGULAR SEASON					PLAYOFFS				
		Gms.	G	A	Pts.	PIM	Gms.	G	A	Pts.	PIM
87-88—Nichols School	N.Y. H.S.	16	23	39	62	82	—	—	—	—	—
88-89—Nichols School	N.Y. H.S.	. . .	38	52	90	. . .	—	—	—	—	—
89-90—Clarkson	ECAC	34	19	13	32	95	—	—	—	—	—
90-91—Clarkson	ECAC	40	28	14	42	90	—	—	—	—	—
91-92—Clarkson	ECAC	30	†25	21	46	62	—	—	—	—	—
—Rochester	AHL	—	—	—	—	—	9	0	1	1	17
92-93—Rochester	AHL	66	32	27	59	38	17	8	5	13	6
—Buffalo	NHL	7	1	1	2	15	—	—	—	—	—
93-94—Buffalo	NHL	32	2	2	4	8	—	—	—	—	—
—Rochester	AHL	11	4	5	9	0	—	—	—	—	—
94-95—Rochester	AHL	55	21	25	46	115	5	4	0	4	4
NHL totals		39	3	3	6	23					

THOMAS, STEVE
LW/RW, ISLANDERS

PERSONAL: Born July 15, 1963, in Stockport, England. . . . 5-11/184. . . . Shoots left.
TRANSACTIONS/CAREER NOTES: Signed as free agent by Toronto Maple Leafs (June 1984). . . . Broke wrist during training camp (September 1984). . . . Traded by Maple Leafs with RW Rick Vaive and D Bob McGill to Chicago Blackhawks for LW Al Secord and RW Ed Olczyk (September 3, 1987). . . . Pulled stomach muscle (October 1987). . . . Separated left shoulder (February 20, 1988); underwent surgery (May 1988). . . . Pulled back muscle (October 18, 1988). . . . Separated right shoulder (December 21, 1988). . . . Underwent surgery to repair chronic shoulder separation problem (January 25, 1989). . . . Strained knee ligaments during training camp (September 1990); missed first 11 games of season. . . . Traded by Blackhawks with C Adam Creighton to New York Islanders for C Brent Sutter and RW Brad Lauer (October 25, 1991). . . . Bruised ribs (March 10, 1992); missed one game. . . . Bruised ribs (November 21, 1992); missed three games. . . . Suffered neck muscle spasms (January 4, 1994); missed five games. . . . Injured back and thumb (January 24, 1995); missed one game.
HONORS: Won Dudley (Red) Garrett Memorial Trophy (1984-85). . . . Named to AHL All-Star first team (1984-85).
STATISTICAL PLATEAUS: Three-goal games: 1987-88 (1), 1989-90 (1), 1990-91 (1), 1993-94 (1). Total: 4. . . . Four-goal games: 1989-90 (1), 1991-92 (1). Total: 2. . . . Total hat tricks: 6.

Season Team	League	REGULAR SEASON					PLAYOFFS				
		Gms.	G	A	Pts.	PIM	Gms.	G	A	Pts.	PIM
81-82—Markham Tier II Jr. A	OHA	48	68	57	125	113	—	—	—	—	—
82-83—Toronto	OHL	61	18	20	38	42	—	—	—	—	—
83-84—Toronto	OHL	70	51	54	105	77	—	—	—	—	—
84-85—Toronto	NHL	18	1	1	2	2	—	—	—	—	—
—St. Catharines	AHL	64	42	48	90	56	—	—	—	—	—
85-86—St. Catharines	AHL	19	18	14	32	35	—	—	—	—	—
—Toronto	NHL	65	20	37	57	36	10	6	8	14	9
86-87—Toronto	NHL	78	35	27	62	114	13	2	3	5	13
87-88—Chicago	NHL	30	13	13	26	40	3	1	2	3	6
88-89—Chicago	NHL	45	21	19	40	69	12	3	5	8	10
89-90—Chicago	NHL	76	40	30	70	91	20	7	6	13	33
90-91—Chicago	NHL	69	19	35	54	129	6	1	2	3	15
91-92—Chicago	NHL	11	2	6	8	26	—	—	—	—	—
—New York Islanders	NHL	71	28	42	70	71	—	—	—	—	—
92-93—New York Islanders	NHL	79	37	50	87	111	18	9	8	17	37
93-94—New York Islanders	NHL	78	42	33	75	139	4	1	0	1	8
—Rochester	AHL	11	4	5	9	0	—	—	—	—	—
94-95—New York Islanders	NHL	47	11	15	26	60	—	—	—	—	—
NHL totals		667	269	308	577	888	86	30	34	64	131

THOMAS, TIM
G, DENVER

PERSONAL: Born April 15, 1974, in Flint, Mich. . . . 5-11/180. . . . Catches left.
COLLEGE: Vermont.
TRANSACTIONS/CAREER NOTES: Selected by Quebec Nordiques in ninth round (11th Nordiques pick, 217th overall) of NHL entry draft (June 29, 1994). . . . Nordiques franchise moved to Denver for 1995-96 season.
HONORS: Named to NCAA All-America East second team (1994-95). . . . Named to ECAC All-Star first team (1994-95).

Season	Team	League	Gms.	Min.	W	L	T	GA	SO	Avg.	Gms.	Min.	W	L	GA	SO	Avg.
					REGULAR SEASON								**PLAYOFFS**				
92-93—Lakeland		Tier II	27	1580	...	...	...	87	...	3.30	—	—	—	—	—	—	—
93-94—University of Vermont ..		ECAC	33	1863	15	11	6	95	1	3.06	—	—	—	—	—	—	—
94-95—University of Vermont ..		ECAC	34	2011	18	14	2	90	3	2.69	—	—	—	—	—	—	—

THOMLINSON, DAVE
LW, KINGS.

PERSONAL: Born October 22, 1966, in Edmonton.... 6-1/215.... Shoots left.... Name pronounced TAHM-lihn-suhn.

TRANSACTIONS/CAREER NOTES: Separated shoulder (November 1983).... Separated shoulder (November 1984).... Selected by Toronto Maple Leafs as underage junior in third round (third Maple Leafs pick, 43rd overall) of NHL entry draft (June 15, 1985).... Signed as free agent by St. Louis Blues (July 1987).... Bruised foot (February 1990).... Signed as free agent by Boston Bruins; Bruins and Blues later arranged trade in which Bruins received Thomlinson and D Glen Featherstone, whom they had also previously signed as free agent, for RW Dave Christian, whom the Blues had previously signed as free agent, third-round pick in 1992 draft (LW Vitali Prokhorov) and seventh-round pick (C Lance Burns) in 1992 draft (July 1991).... Suffered sore back (December 1991). ... Signed as free agent by New York Rangers (September 4, 1992).... Signed as free agent by Los Angeles Kings (July 22, 1993).... Fractured hand (February 14, 1994); missed remainder of the season.

Season	Team	League	Gms.	G	A	Pts.	PIM	Gms.	G	A	Pts.	PIM
				REGULAR SEASON					**PLAYOFFS**			
83-84—Brandon............................		WHL	41	17	12	29	62	—	—	—	—	—
84-85—Brandon............................		WHL	26	13	14	27	70	—	—	—	—	—
85-86—Brandon............................		WHL	53	25	20	45	116	—	—	—	—	—
86-87—Brandon............................		WHL	2	0	1	1	9	—	—	—	—	—
—Moose Jaw		WHL	69	44	36	80	126	9	7	3	10	19
87-88—Peoria		IHL	74	27	30	57	56	7	4	3	7	11
88-89—Peoria		IHL	64	27	29	56	154	3	0	1	1	8
89-90—St. Louis		NHL	19	1	2	3	12	—	—	—	—	—
—Peoria		IHL	59	27	40	67	87	5	1	1	2	15
90-91—Peoria		IHL	80	53	54	107	107	11	6	7	13	28
—St. Louis		NHL	3	0	0	0	0	9	3	1	4	4
91-92—Boston		NHL	12	0	1	1	17	—	—	—	—	—
—Maine		AHL	25	9	11	20	36	—	—	—	—	—
92-93—Binghamton		AHL	54	25	35	60	61	12	2	5	7	8
93-94—Los Angeles....................		NHL	7	0	0	0	21	—	—	—	—	—
—Phoenix		IHL	39	10	15	25	70	—	—	—	—	—
94-95—Phoenix		IHL	77	30	40	70	87	9	5	3	8	8
—Los Angeles....................		NHL	1	0	0	0	0	—	—	—	—	—
NHL totals........................			42	1	3	4	50	9	3	1	4	4

THOMPSON, BRENT
D, JETS

PERSONAL: Born January 9, 1971, in Calgary.... 6-2/200.... Shoots left.... Full name: Brenton Keith Thompson.

TRANSACTIONS/CAREER NOTES: Stretched knee ligaments and separated shoulder (September 1987).... Selected by Los Angeles Kings in second round (first Kings pick, 39th overall) of NHL entry draft (June 17, 1989).... Suffered hip flexor prior to 1992-93 season; missed first six games of season.... Strained abdomen (January 23, 1992); missed 17 games.... Traded by Kings to Winnipeg Jets for D Ruslan Batyrshin and second-round pick in 1996 draft (August 8, 1994).

HONORS: Named to WHL (East) All-Star second team (1990-91).

Season	Team	League	Gms.	G	A	Pts.	PIM	Gms.	G	A	Pts.	PIM
				REGULAR SEASON					**PLAYOFFS**			
88-89—Medicine Hat		WHL	72	3	10	13	160	3	0	0	0	2
89-90—Medicine Hat		WHL	68	10	35	45	167	3	0	1	1	14
90-91—Medicine Hat		WHL	51	5	40	45	87	12	1	7	8	16
—Phoenix		IHL	—	—	—	—	—	4	0	1	1	6
91-92—Phoenix		IHL	42	4	13	17	139	—	—	—	—	—
—Los Angeles.....................		NHL	27	0	5	5	89	4	0	0	0	4
92-93—Phoenix		IHL	22	0	5	5	112	—	—	—	—	—
—Los Angeles.....................		NHL	30	0	4	4	76	—	—	—	—	—
93-94—Phoenix		IHL	26	1	11	12	118	—	—	—	—	—
—Los Angeles.....................		NHL	24	1	0	1	81	—	—	—	—	—
94-95—Winnipeg		NHL	29	0	0	0	78	—	—	—	—	—
NHL totals........................			110	1	9	10	324	4	0	0	0	4

THOMPSON, ROCKY
D, FLAMES

PERSONAL: Born August 8, 1977, in Calgary.... 6-2/189.... Shoots right.

HIGH SCHOOL: Medicine Hat (Alta.).

TRANSACTIONS/CAREER NOTES: Selected by Calgary Flames in third round (third Flames pick, 72nd overall) of NHL entry draft (July 8, 1995).

Season	Team	League	Gms.	G	A	Pts.	PIM	Gms.	G	A	Pts.	PIM
				REGULAR SEASON					**PLAYOFFS**			
93-94—Medicine Hat		WHL	68	1	4	5	166	3	0	0	0	2
94-95—Medicine Hat		WHL	63	1	6	7	220	5	0	0	0	17

THOMSON, JIM
RW, MIGHTY DUCKS

PERSONAL: Born December 30, 1965, in Edmonton. . . . 6-1/220. . . . Shoots right.
TRANSACTIONS/CAREER NOTES: Selected by Washington Capitals as underage junior in ninth round (eighth Capitals pick, 185th overall) of NHL entry draft (June 9, 1984). . . . Traded by Capitals to Hartford Whalers for D Scot Kleinendorst (March 6, 1989). . . . Traded by Whalers to New Jersey Devils for RW Chris Cichocki (October 31, 1989). . . . Signed as free agent by Los Angeles Kings (July 11, 1990). . . . Fractured foot (January 19, 1991). . . . Selected by Minnesota North Stars in NHL expansion draft (May 30, 1991). . . . Traded by North Stars with D Charlie Huddy, LW Randy Gilhen and fourth-round pick in 1991 draft (D Alexei Zhitnik) to Kings for C Todd Elik (June 22, 1991). . . . Hyperextended elbow (November 11, 1991); missed four games. . . . Selected by Ottawa Senators in NHL expansion draft (June 18, 1992). . . . Traded by Senators with C Marc Fortier to Kings for RW Bob Kudelski and C Shawn McCosh (December 20, 1992). . . . Selected by Mighty Ducks of Anaheim in NHL expansion draft (June 24, 1993). . . . Injured shoulder (October 10, 1993); missed remainder of season. . . . Underwent reconstructive shoulder surgery (December 26, 1993). . . . Underwent shoulder surgery (December 27, 1994); missed entire season.

			REGULAR SEASON					PLAYOFFS			
Season	Team	League	Gms.	G	A	Pts.	PIM	Gms.	G	A	Pts.	PIM
82-83—Markham Waxers	OPJHL	35	6	7	13	81	—	—	—	—	—
83-84—Toronto	OHL	60	10	18	28	68	9	1	0	1	26
84-85—Toronto	OHL	63	23	28	51	122	5	3	1	4	25
—Binghamton	AHL	4	0	0	0	2	—	—	—	—	—
85-86—Binghamton	AHL	59	15	9	24	195	—	—	—	—	—
86-87—Binghamton	AHL	57	13	10	23	*360	10	0	1	1	40
—Washington	NHL	10	0	0	0	35	—	—	—	—	—
87-88—Binghamton	AHL	25	8	9	17	64	4	1	2	3	7
88-89—Baltimore	AHL	41	25	16	41	129	—	—	—	—	—
—Washington	NHL	14	2	0	2	53	—	—	—	—	—
—Hartford	NHL	5	0	0	0	14	—	—	—	—	—
89-90—Binghamton	AHL	8	1	2	3	30	—	—	—	—	—
—Utica	AHL	60	20	23	43	124	4	1	0	1	19
—New Jersey	NHL	3	0	0	0	31	—	—	—	—	—
90-91—New Haven	AHL	27	5	8	13	121	—	—	—	—	—
—Los Angeles	NHL	8	1	0	1	19	—	—	—	—	—
91-92—Los Angeles	NHL	45	1	2	3	162	—	—	—	—	—
—Phoenix	IHL	2	1	0	1	0	—	—	—	—	—
92-93—Ottawa	NHL	15	0	1	1	41	—	—	—	—	—
—Los Angeles	NHL	9	0	0	0	56	1	0	0	0	0
—Phoenix	IHL	14	4	5	9	44	—	—	—	—	—
93-94—Anaheim	NHL	6	0	0	0	5	—	—	—	—	—
94-95—Anaheim	NHL					Did not play—injured.					
NHL totals		115	4	3	7	416	1	0	0	0	0

THORNTON, SCOTT
C, OILERS

PERSONAL: Born January 9, 1971, in London, Ont. . . . 6-2/200. . . . Shoots left.
TRANSACTIONS/CAREER NOTES: Selected by Toronto Maple Leafs in first round (first Maple Leafs pick, third overall) of NHL entry draft (June 17, 1989). . . . Suspended 12 games by OHL for refusing to leave ice following penalty (February 7, 1990). . . . Separated shoulder (January 24, 1991); missed eight games. . . . Traded by Maple Leafs with LW Vincent Damphousse, D Luke Richardson, G Peter Ing and future considerations to Edmonton Oilers for G Grant Fuhr, RW/LW Glenn Anderson and LW Craig Berube (September 19, 1991). . . . Suffered concussion (November 23, 1991); missed one game. . . . Sprained ankle (October 6, 1993); missed 13 games. . . . Suffered back spasms (November 21, 1993); missed one game. . . . Bruised wrist (April 14, 1994); missed one game.

			REGULAR SEASON					PLAYOFFS			
Season	Team	League	Gms.	G	A	Pts.	PIM	Gms.	G	A	Pts.	PIM
86-87—London Diamonds	OPJHL	31	10	7	17	10	—	—	—	—	—
87-88—Belleville	OHL	62	11	19	30	54	6	0	1	1	2
88-89—Belleville	OHL	59	28	34	62	103	5	1	1	2	6
89-90—Belleville	OHL	47	21	28	49	91	11	2	10	12	15
90-91—Belleville	OHL	3	2	1	3	2	6	0	7	7	14
—Newmarket	AHL	5	1	0	1	4	—	—	—	—	—
—Toronto	NHL	33	1	3	4	30	—	—	—	—	—
91-92—Edmonton	NHL	15	0	1	1	43	1	0	0	0	0
—Cape Breton	AHL	49	9	14	23	40	5	1	0	1	8
92-93—Cape Breton	AHL	58	23	27	50	102	16	1	2	3	35
—Edmonton	NHL	9	0	1	1	0	—	—	—	—	—
93-94—Edmonton	NHL	61	4	7	11	104	—	—	—	—	—
—Cape Breton	AHL	2	1	1	2	31	—	—	—	—	—
94-95—Edmonton	NHL	47	10	12	22	89	—	—	—	—	—
NHL totals		165	15	24	39	266	1	0	0	0	0

TICHY, MILAN
D, ISLANDERS

PERSONAL: Born September 22, 1969, in Plzen, Czechoslovakia. . . . 6-3/198. . . . Shoots left. . . . Name pronounced TEE-SHEE.
TRANSACTIONS/CAREER NOTES: Selected by Chicago Blackhawks in eighth round (sixth Blackhawks pick, 153rd overall) of NHL entry draft (June 17, 1989). . . . Selected by Florida Panthers in NHL expansion draft (June 24, 1993). . . . Traded by Panthers to Winnipeg Jets for D Brent Severyn (October 3, 1993). . . . Signed as free agent by New York Islanders (August 2, 1994).

Season Team	League	REGULAR SEASON					PLAYOFFS				
		Gms.	G	A	Pts.	PIM	Gms.	G	A	Pts.	PIM
87-88—Skoda Plzen	Czech.	30	1	3	4	20	—	—	—	—	—
88-89—Skoda Plzen	Czech.	36	1	12	13	44	—	—	—	—	—
89-90—Dukla Trencin	Czech.	51	14	8	22	87	—	—	—	—	—
90-91—Dukla Trencin	Czech.	39	9	11	20	72	—	—	—	—	—
91-92—Indianapolis	IHL	49	6	23	29	28	—	—	—	—	—
92-93—Indianapolis	IHL	49	7	32	39	62	4	0	5	5	14
—Chicago	NHL	13	0	1	1	30	—	—	—	—	—
93-94—Moncton	AHL	48	1	20	21	103	20	3	3	6	12
94-95—Denver	IHL	71	18	36	54	90	17	4	9	13	12
—New York Islanders	NHL	2	0	0	0	2	—	—	—	—	—
NHL totals		15	0	1	1	32					

TIKKANEN, ESA
LW, BLUES

PERSONAL: Born January 25, 1968, in Helsinki, Finland. . . . 6-1/200. . . . Shoots left. . . . Full name: Esa Kalervo Tikkanen. . . . Name pronounced EH-suh TEE-kuh-nihn.
TRANSACTIONS/CAREER NOTES: Selected by Edmonton Oilers in fourth round (fourth Oilers pick, 82nd overall) of NHL entry draft (August 8, 1983). . . . Broke foot (December 10, 1985). . . . Lacerated elbow, developed bursitis and underwent surgery (December 9, 1986). . . . Fractured left wrist (January 1989). . . . Injured right knee (October 28, 1989). . . . Underwent left knee surgery (August 1990); missed first 10 days of training camp. . . . Sprained wrist (December 1, 1991); missed one game. . . . Sprained wrist (December 20, 1991); missed two games. . . . Fractured shoulder (January 4, 1992); missed 37 games. . . . Suffered from the flu (December 1992); missed one game. . . . Suffered elbow infection (February 1993); missed two games. . . . Traded by Oilers to New York Rangers for C Doug Weight (March 17, 1993). . . . Bruised knee (January 14, 1994); missed one game. . . . Traded by Rangers with D Doug Lidster to St. Louis Blues for C Petr Nedved (July 24, 1994); trade arranged as compensation for Blues signing Coach Mike Keenan. . . . Played in Europe during 1994-95 NHL lockout. . . . Injured shoulder (April 3, 1995); missed one game. . . . Suffered illness (April 28, 1995); missed two games. . . . Injured leg (May 1, 1995); missed two games.
STATISTICAL PLATEAUS: Three-goal games: 1986-87 (2), 1987-88 (1), 1988-89 (1), 1990-91 (1). Total: 5.
MISCELLANEOUS: Member of Stanley Cup championship team (1985, 1987, 1988, 1990 and 1994).

Season Team	League	REGULAR SEASON					PLAYOFFS				
		Gms.	G	A	Pts.	PIM	Gms.	G	A	Pts.	PIM
81-82—Regina	WHL	2	0	0	0	0	—	—	—	—	—
82-83—Helsinki Junior IFK	Finland	30	34	31	65	104	4	4	3	7	10
—Helsinki IFK	Finland	—	—	—	—	—	1	0	0	0	2
83-84—Helsinki IFK	Finland	36	19	11	30	30	2	0	0	0	0
—Helsinki Junior IFK	Finland	6	5	9	14	13	4	4	3	7	8
84-85—Helsinki IFK	Finland	36	21	33	54	42	—	—	—	—	—
—Edmonton	NHL	—	—	—	—	—	3	0	0	0	2
85-86—Nova Scotia	AHL	15	4	8	12	17	—	—	—	—	—
—Edmonton	NHL	35	7	6	13	28	8	3	2	5	7
86-87—Edmonton	NHL	76	34	44	78	120	21	7	2	9	22
87-88—Edmonton	NHL	80	23	51	74	153	19	10	17	27	72
88-89—Edmonton	NHL	67	31	47	78	92	7	1	3	4	12
89-90—Edmonton	NHL	79	30	33	63	161	22	13	11	24	26
90-91—Edmonton	NHL	79	27	42	69	85	18	12	8	20	24
91-92—Edmonton	NHL	40	12	16	28	44	16	5	3	8	8
92-93—Edmonton	NHL	66	14	19	33	76	—	—	—	—	—
—New York Rangers	NHL	15	2	5	7	18	—	—	—	—	—
93-94—New York Rangers	NHL	83	22	32	54	114	23	4	4	8	34
94-95—HIFK Helsinki	Finland	19	2	11	13	16	—	—	—	—	—
—St. Louis	NHL	43	12	23	35	22	7	2	2	4	20
NHL totals		663	214	318	532	913	144	57	52	109	227

TILLEY, TOM
D, BLACKHAWKS

PERSONAL: Born March 28, 1965, in Trenton, Ont. . . . 6-0/190. . . . Shoots right. . . . Full name: Thomas Robert Tilley.
COLLEGE: Michigan State.
TRANSACTIONS/CAREER NOTES: Selected by St. Louis Blues as underage junior in 10th round (13th Blues pick, 196th overall) of NHL entry draft (June 9, 1984). . . . Collapsed on bench during game due to the flu (January 28, 1989). . . . Bruised left shoulder (March 1989). . . . Strained lower back (October 14, 1989); missed eight games. . . . Played in Italy (1991-92 and 1992-93). . . . Signed as free agent by Blues (July 30, 1993). . . . Injured foot (November 3, 1993); missed one game. . . . Injured groin (December 1, 1993); missed six games. . . . Suffered from the flu (December 12, 1993); missed two games. . . . Bruised knee (December 29, 1993); missed three games. . . . Injured groin (February 3, 1994); missed four games. . . . Suffered facial injury (March 23, 1994); missed two games. . . . Traded by Blues to Tampa Bay Lightning for C Adam Creighton (October 6, 1994). . . . Traded by Lightning with D Jeff Buchanan and RW Jim Cummins to Chicago Blackhawks for LW Paul Ysebaert and RW Rich Sutter (February 22, 1995).
HONORS: Named to CCHA All-Star first team (1987-88). . . . Named to IHL All-Star second team (1990-91).

Season Team	League	REGULAR SEASON					PLAYOFFS				
		Gms.	G	A	Pts.	PIM	Gms.	G	A	Pts.	PIM
83-84—Orillia	OHA	38	16	35	51	113	—	—	—	—	—
84-85—Michigan State	CCHA	37	1	5	6	58	—	—	—	—	—
85-86—Michigan State	CCHA	42	9	25	34	48	—	—	—	—	—
86-87—Michigan State	CCHA	42	7	14	21	46	—	—	—	—	—
87-88—Michigan State	CCHA	46	8	18	26	44	—	—	—	—	—
88-89—St. Louis	NHL	70	1	22	23	47	10	1	2	3	17

Season Team	League	REGULAR SEASON					PLAYOFFS				
		Gms.	G	A	Pts.	PIM	Gms.	G	A	Pts.	PIM
89-90—St. Louis	NHL	34	0	5	5	6	—	—	—	—	—
—Salt Lake City	IHL	22	1	8	9	13	—	—	—	—	—
90-91—Peoria	IHL	48	7	38	45	53	13	2	9	11	25
—St. Louis	NHL	22	2	4	6	4	—	—	—	—	—
91-92—Milan	Italy	18	7	13	20	12	12	5	12	17	10
92-93—Milan	Alpenliga	32	5	17	22	21	—	—	—	—	—
—Milan	Italy	14	8	3	11	2	8	1	5	6	4
93-94—St. Louis	NHL	48	1	7	8	32	4	0	1	1	2
94-95—Atlanta	IHL	10	2	6	8	14	—	—	—	—	—
—Indianapolis	IHL	25	2	13	15	19	—	—	—	—	—
NHL totals		174	4	38	42	89	14	1	3	4	19

TIMANDER, MATTIAS

D, BRUINS

PERSONAL: Born April 16, 1974, in Solleftea, Sweden. . . . 6-1/194. . . . Shoots left.

TRANSACTIONS/CAREER NOTES: Selected by Boston Bruins in seventh round (seventh Bruins pick, 208th overall) of NHL entry draft (June 21, 1992).

Season Team	League	REGULAR SEASON					PLAYOFFS				
		Gms.	G	A	Pts.	PIM	Gms.	G	A	Pts.	PIM
92-93—MoDo Hockey	Sweden	1	0	0	0	0	—	—	—	—	—
93-94—MoDo Hockey	Sweden	23	2	2	4	6	11	2	0	2	10
94-95—MoDo Hockey	Sweden	39	8	9	17	24	—	—	—	—	—

TINORDI, MARK

D, CAPITALS

PERSONAL: Born May 9, 1966, in Red Deer, Alta. . . . 6-4/213. . . . Shoots left. . . . Name pronounced tuh-NOHR-dee.

TRANSACTIONS/CAREER NOTES: Signed as free agent by New York Rangers (January 4, 1987). . . . Suffered abdominal pains (January 1988). . . . Underwent left knee surgery (October 6, 1988). . . . Traded by Rangers with D Paul Jerrard, C Mike Sullivan, RW Brett Barnett and third-round pick in 1989 draft (C Murray Garbutt) to Minnesota North Stars for LW Igor Liba, C Brian Lawton and rights to LW Eric Bennett (October 11, 1988). . . . Underwent knee surgery (April 1989). . . . Suspended four games by NHL for cross-checking in a preseason game (September 27, 1989). . . . Bruised shoulder (December 1989). . . . Fined $500 by NHL for fighting (December 28, 1989). . . . Suffered concussion (January 17, 1990); missed six games. . . . Suspended 10 games by NHL for leaving penalty box to fight during a preseason game (September 26, 1990). . . . Suffered from foot palsy (October 15, 1991); missed 17 games. . . . Sprained knee (January 19, 1993); missed four games. . . . Broke collarbone (March 16, 1993); missed remainder of season. . . . North Stars franchise moved from Minnesota to Dallas and renamed Stars for 1993-94 season. . . . Suffered from the flu (December 27, 1993); missed one game. . . . Fractured femur (February 23, 1994); missed 22 games. . . . Traded by Stars with rights to D Rick Mrozik to Washington Capitals for D Kevin Hatcher (January 18, 1995). . . . Bruised ribs (February 24, 1995); missed two games. . . . Sprained knee (April 24, 1995); missed last four games of season.

HONORS: Named to WHL (East) All-Star first team (1986-87). . . . Played in NHL All-Star Game (1992).

MISCELLANEOUS: Captain of Minnesota North Stars (1991-92 and 1992-93). . . . Captain of Dallas Stars (1993-94).

Season Team	League	REGULAR SEASON					PLAYOFFS				
		Gms.	G	A	Pts.	PIM	Gms.	G	A	Pts.	PIM
82-83—Lethbridge	WHL	64	0	4	4	50	20	1	1	2	6
83-84—Lethbridge	WHL	72	5	14	19	53	5	0	1	1	7
84-85—Lethbridge	WHL	58	10	15	25	134	4	0	2	2	12
85-86—Lethbridge	WHL	58	8	30	38	139	8	1	3	4	15
86-87—Calgary	WHL	61	29	37	66	148	—	—	—	—	—
—New Haven	AHL	2	0	0	0	2	2	0	0	0	0
87-88—New York Rangers	NHL	24	1	2	3	50	—	—	—	—	—
—Colorado	IHL	41	8	19	27	150	11	1	5	6	31
88-89—Minnesota	NHL	47	2	3	5	107	5	0	0	0	0
—Kalamazoo	IHL	10	0	0	0	35	—	—	—	—	—
89-90—Minnesota	NHL	66	3	7	10	240	7	0	1	1	16
90-91—Minnesota	NHL	69	5	27	32	189	23	5	6	11	78
91-92—Minnesota	NHL	63	4	24	28	179	7	1	2	3	11
92-93—Minnesota	NHL	69	15	27	42	157	—	—	—	—	—
93-94—Dallas	NHL	61	6	18	24	143	—	—	—	—	—
94-95—Washington	NHL	42	3	9	12	71	1	0	0	0	2
NHL totals		441	39	117	156	1136	43	6	9	15	107

TITOV, GERMAN

C, FLAMES

PERSONAL: Born October 16, 1965, in Borovsk, U.S.S.R. . . . 6-0/190. . . . Shoots left. . . . Name pronounced GUHR-mihn TEE-tahf.

TRANSACTIONS/CAREER NOTES: Selected by Calgary Flames in 10th round (252nd overall) of NHL entry draft (June 26, 1993). . . . Fractured nose (December 31, 1993); missed four games. . . . Bruised hand (February 18, 1994); missed two games. . . . Bruised hand (April 2, 1994); missed one game. . . . Played in Europe during 1994-95 NHL lockout. . . . Pulled groin (March 28, 1995); missed eight games.

STATISTICAL PLATEAUS: Three-goal games: 1994-95 (1).

Season Team	League	REGULAR SEASON					PLAYOFFS				
		Gms.	G	A	Pts.	PIM	Gms.	G	A	Pts.	PIM
82-83—Khimik	USSR	16	0	2	2	4	—	—	—	—	—
83-84—Khimik	USSR				Did not play.						
84-85—Khimik	USSR				Did not play.						

Season	Team	League		REGULAR SEASON					PLAYOFFS			
			Gms.	G	A	Pts.	PIM	Gms.	G	A	Pts.	PIM
85-86	Khimik	USSR				Did not play.						
86-87	Khimik	USSR	23	1	0	1	10	—	—	—	—	—
87-88	Khimik	USSR	39	6	5	11	10	—	—	—	—	—
88-89	Khimik	USSR	44	10	3	13	24	—	—	—	—	—
89-90	Khimik	USSR	44	6	14	20	19	—	—	—	—	—
90-91	Khimik	USSR	45	13	11	24	28	—	—	—	—	—
91-92	Khimik	CIS	42	18	13	31	35	—	—	—	—	—
92-93	TPS Turku	Finland	47	25	19	44	49	—	—	—	—	—
93-94	Calgary	NHL	76	27	18	45	28	7	2	1	3	4
94-95	TPS Turku	Finland	14	6	6	12	20	—	—	—	—	—
	Calgary	NHL	40	12	12	24	16	7	5	3	8	10
	NHL totals		116	39	30	69	44	14	7	4	11	14

TJALLDEN, MIKAEL
D, PANTHERS

PERSONAL: Born February 16, 1975, in Ornskoldsvik, Sweden. . . . 6-2/194. . . . Shoots left. . . . Name pronounced shal-DEEN.
TRANSACTIONS/CAREER NOTES: Selected by Florida Panthers in third round (fourth Panthers pick, 67th overall) of NHL entry draft (June 26, 1993).

Season	Team	League		REGULAR SEASON					PLAYOFFS			
			Gms.	G	A	Pts.	PIM	Gms.	G	A	Pts.	PIM
91-92	MoDo	Sweden Jr.				Did not play.						
92-93	MoDo	Sweden Jr.				Statistics unavailable.						
93-94	Sundsvall Timra	Swed. Dv.II	24	4	5	9	32	—	—	—	—	—
94-95	Sundsvall Timra	Swed. Dv.II	21	0	9	9	20	—	—	—	—	—

TJARNQVIST, DANIEL
D, PANTHERS

PERSONAL: Born October 14, 1976, in Umea, Sweden. . . . 6-2/176. . . . Shoots left.
TRANSACTIONS/CAREER NOTES: Selected by Florida Panthers in fourth round (fifth Panthers pick, 88th overall) of NHL entry draft (July 8, 1995).

Season	Team	League		REGULAR SEASON					PLAYOFFS			
			Gms.	G	A	Pts.	PIM	Gms.	G	A	Pts.	PIM
94-95	Rogle Angelholm	Sweden	33	2	4	6	2	—	—	—	—	—

TKACHUK, KEITH
LW, JETS

PERSONAL: Born March 28, 1972, in Melrose, Mass. . . . 6-2/210. . . . Shoots left. . . . Full name: Keith Matthew Tkachuk. . . . Name pronounced kuh-CHUHK.
HIGH SCHOOL: Malden (Mass.) Catholic.
COLLEGE: Boston University.
TRANSACTIONS/CAREER NOTES: Selected by Winnipeg Jets in first round (first Jets pick, 19th overall) of NHL entry draft (June 16, 1990). . . . Lacerated forearm (November 12, 1993); missed one game.
HONORS: Named to Hockey East All-Rookie team (1990-91). . . . Named to NHL All-Star second team (1994-95).
STATISTICAL PLATEAUS: Three-goal games: 1993-94 (1).
MISCELLANEOUS: Captain of Winnipeg Jets (1993-94 and 1994-95).

Season	Team	League		REGULAR SEASON					PLAYOFFS			
			Gms.	G	A	Pts.	PIM	Gms.	G	A	Pts.	PIM
88-89	Malden Catholic H.S.	Mass. H.S.	21	30	16	46	. . .	—	—	—	—	—
89-90	Malden Catholic H.S.	Mass. H.S.	6	12	14	26	. . .	—	—	—	—	—
90-91	Boston University	Hockey East	36	17	23	40	70	—	—	—	—	—
91-92	U.S. national team	Int'l	45	10	10	20	141	—	—	—	—	—
	U.S. Olympic Team	Int'l	8	1	1	2	12	—	—	—	—	—
	Winnipeg	NHL	17	3	5	8	28	7	3	0	3	30
92-93	Winnipeg	NHL	83	28	23	51	201	6	4	0	4	14
93-94	Winnipeg	NHL	84	41	40	81	255	—	—	—	—	—
94-95	Winnipeg	NHL	48	22	29	51	152	—	—	—	—	—
	NHL totals		232	94	97	191	636	13	7	0	7	44

TOCCHET, RICK
RW, KINGS

PERSONAL: Born April 9, 1964, in Scarborough, Ont. . . . 6-0/205. . . . Shoots right. . . . Name pronounced TAH-kiht.
TRANSACTIONS/CAREER NOTES: Selected by Philadelphia Flyers as underage junior in sixth round (fifth Flyers pick, 121st overall) of NHL entry draft (June 8, 1983). . . . Bruised right knee (November 23, 1985); missed seven games. . . . Separated left shoulder (February 1988). . . . Suspended 10 games by NHL for injuring an opposing player during a fight (October 27, 1988). . . . Hyperextended right knee (April 21, 1989). . . . Suffered viral infection (November 1989). . . . Tore tendon in left groin area (January 26, 1991); missed five games. . . . Reinjured groin (March 1991); missed five games. . . . Sprained knee (November 29, 1991); missed five games. . . . Bruised heel (January 18, 1991); missed 10 games. . . . Traded by Flyers with G Ken Wregget, D Kjell Samuelsson and third-round pick in 1992 draft to Pittsburgh Penguins for RW Mark Recchi, D Brian Benning and first-round pick (LW Jason Bowen) in 1992 draft (February 19, 1992). . . . Fractured jaw (March 15, 1992); missed three games. . . . Bruised left foot (October 10, 1992); missed two games. . . . Bruised foot (February 8, 1993); missed one game. . . . Bruised ribs (November 13, 1993); missed two games. . . . Suffered back spasms (December 2, 1993); missed two games. . . . Suffered back spasms (December 31, 1993); missed 12 games. . . . Injured back (February 21, 1994); missed one game. . . . Injured back (February 28, 1994); missed 10 games. . . . Underwent back surgery (June 8, 1994). . . . Traded by Penguins with second-round pick in 1995 draft (RW Pavel Rosa) to Los Angeles Kings for LW Luc Robitaille (July 29, 1994). . . . Strained lower back (April 1, 1995); missed five games. . . . Suffered back spasms (April 17, 1995); missed six games. . . . Suffered back spasms (May 3, 1995); missed one game.

HONORS: Played in NHL All-Star Game (1989-1991 and 1993).
RECORDS: Shares NHL All-Star Game record for fastest goal from start of period—19 seconds (1993, second period).
STATISTICAL PLATEAUS: Three-goal games: 1987-88 (2), 1988-89 (2), 1989-90 (1), 1990-91 (1), 1991-92 (1), 1992-93 (2), 1994-95 (1). Total: 10.... Four-goal games: 1987-88 (1), 1989-90 (1). Total: 2.... Total hat tricks: 12.
MISCELLANEOUS: Captain of Philadelphia Flyers (1991-92).... Member of Stanley Cup championship team (1992).

			REGULAR SEASON					PLAYOFFS			
Season	Team	League	Gms.	G	A	Pts.	PIM	Gms.	G	A	Pts.	PIM
81-82—Sault Ste. Marie		OHL	59	7	15	22	184	11	1	1	2	28
82-83—Sault Ste. Marie		OHL	66	32	34	66	146	16	4	13	17	*67
83-84—Sault Ste. Marie		OHL	64	44	64	108	209	16	*22	14	†36	41
84-85—Philadelphia		NHL	75	14	25	39	181	19	3	4	7	72
85-86—Philadelphia		NHL	69	14	21	35	284	5	1	2	3	26
86-87—Philadelphia		NHL	69	21	26	47	288	26	11	10	21	72
87-88—Philadelphia		NHL	65	31	33	64	301	5	1	4	5	55
88-89—Philadelphia		NHL	66	45	36	81	183	16	6	6	12	69
89-90—Philadelphia		NHL	75	37	59	96	196	—	—	—	—	—
90-91—Philadelphia		NHL	70	40	31	71	150	—	—	—	—	—
91-92—Philadelphia		NHL	42	13	16	29	102	—	—	—	—	—
—Pittsburgh		NHL	19	14	16	30	49	14	6	13	19	24
92-93—Pittsburgh		NHL	80	48	61	109	252	12	7	6	13	24
93-94—Pittsburgh		NHL	51	14	26	40	134	6	2	3	5	20
94-95—Los Angeles		NHL	36	18	17	35	70	—	—	—	—	—
NHL totals			717	309	367	676	2190	103	37	48	85	362

TOCHER, RYAN
D, DENVER

PERSONAL: Born June 14, 1975, in Hamilton, Ont.... 6-1/194.... Shoots right.
HIGH SCHOOL: St. Paul (Nepean, Ont.).
TRANSACTIONS/CAREER NOTES: Selected by Quebec Nordiques in fourth round (fifth Nordiques pick, 101st overall) of NHL entry draft (June 26, 1993).... Nordiques franchise moved to Denver for 1995-96 season.

			REGULAR SEASON					PLAYOFFS			
Season	Team	League	Gms.	G	A	Pts.	PIM	Gms.	G	A	Pts.	PIM
90-91—Hamilton Jr. B		OHA	38	2	11	13	90	—	—	—	—	—
91-92—Niagara Falls		OHL	58	4	8	12	53	16	0	0	0	2
92-93—Niagara Falls		OHL	59	6	17	23	58	4	0	0	0	4
93-94—Niagara Falls		OHL	13	5	6	11	30	—	—	—	—	—
—Newmarket		OHL	48	7	19	26	71	—	—	—	—	—
94-95—Sarnia		OHL	12	1	5	6	17	—	—	—	—	—
—Oshawa		OHL	36	6	14	20	60	7	1	7	8	2

TODD, KEVIN
C, KINGS

PERSONAL: Born May 4, 1968, in Winnipeg.... 5-10/180.... Shoots left.... Full name: Kevin Lee Todd.
HIGH SCHOOL: Tec Voc (Winnipeg).
TRANSACTIONS/CAREER NOTES: Stretched knee ligaments (December 1985).... Selected by New Jersey Devils as underage junior in seventh round (seventh Devils pick, 129th overall) of NHL entry draft (June 21, 1986).... Injured thigh (October 31, 1992); missed one game.... Reinjured thigh (November 13, 1992); missed three games.... Bruised shoulder (December 15, 1992); missed five games.... Traded by Devils with LW Zdeno Ciger to Edmonton Oilers for C Bernie Nicholls (January 13, 1993).... Separated left shoulder (March 14, 1993); missed remainder of season.... Traded by Oilers to Chicago Blackhawks for D Adam Bennett (October 7, 1993).... Injured knee (November 18, 1993); missed 12 games.... Traded by Blackhawks to Los Angeles Kings for fourth-round pick (D Steve McLaren) in 1994 draft (March 21, 1994).... Tore cartilage in knee (March 9, 1995); missed 15 games.
HONORS: Won Les Cunningham Plaque (1990-91).... Won John B. Sollenberger Trophy (1990-91).... Named to AHL All-Star first team (1990-91).... Named to NHL All-Rookie team (1991-92).

			REGULAR SEASON					PLAYOFFS			
Season	Team	League	Gms.	G	A	Pts.	PIM	Gms.	G	A	Pts.	PIM
85-86—Prince Albert		WHL	55	14	25	39	19	20	7	6	13	29
86-87—Prince Albert		WHL	71	39	46	85	92	8	2	5	7	17
87-88—Prince Albert		WHL	72	49	72	121	83	10	8	11	19	27
88-89—New Jersey		NHL	1	0	0	0	0	—	—	—	—	—
—Utica		AHL	78	26	45	71	62	4	2	0	2	6
89-90—Utica		AHL	71	18	36	54	72	5	2	4	6	2
90-91—Utica		AHL	75	37	*81	*118	75	—	—	—	—	—
—New Jersey		NHL	1	0	0	0	0	1	0	0	0	6
91-92—New Jersey		NHL	80	21	42	63	69	7	3	2	5	8
92-93—New Jersey		NHL	30	5	5	10	16	—	—	—	—	—
—Utica		AHL	2	2	1	3	0	—	—	—	—	—
—Edmonton		NHL	25	4	9	13	10	—	—	—	—	—
93-94—Chicago		NHL	35	5	6	11	16	—	—	—	—	—
—Los Angeles		NHL	12	3	8	11	8	—	—	—	—	—
94-95—Los Angeles		NHL	33	3	8	11	12	—	—	—	—	—
NHL totals			217	41	78	119	131	8	3	2	5	14

TOMLINSON, DAVE
C, PANTHERS

PERSONAL: Born May 8, 1968, in North Vancouver.... 5-11/180.... Shoots left.
COLLEGE: Boston University.
TRANSACTIONS/CAREER NOTES: Selected by Toronto Maple Leafs in NHL supplemental draft (June 16, 1989).... Traded by Maple Leafs to Florida Panthers for future considerations (August 3, 1993).... Traded by Panthers to Winnipeg Jets for C Jason Cirone (August 3, 1993).... Signed as free agent by Panthers (June 23, 1994).

Season Team	League	REGULAR SEASON					PLAYOFFS				
		Gms.	G	A	Pts.	PIM	Gms.	G	A	Pts.	PIM
87-88—Boston University	Hockey East	34	16	20	36	28	—	—	—	—	—
88-89—Boston University	Hockey East	34	16	30	46	40	—	—	—	—	—
89-90—Boston University	Hockey East	43	15	22	37	53	—	—	—	—	—
90-91—Boston University	Hockey East	41	30	30	60	55	—	—	—	—	—
91-92—St. John's	AHL	75	23	34	57	75	12	4	5	9	6
—Toronto	NHL	3	0	0	0	2	—	—	—	—	—
92-93—St. John's	AHL	70	36	48	84	115	9	1	4	5	8
—Toronto	NHL	3	0	0	0	2	—	—	—	—	—
93-94—Moncton	AHL	39	23	23	46	38	20	6	6	12	24
—Winnipeg	NHL	31	1	3	4	24	—	—	—	—	—
94-95—Cincinnati	IHL	78	38	72	110	79	10	7	3	10	8
—Florida	NHL	5	0	0	0	0	—	—	—	—	—
NHL totals		42	1	3	4	28					

TOMPKINS, DAN
LW, FLAMES

PERSONAL: Born January 31, 1975, in Minnesota.... 6-2/205.... Shoots left.
HIGH SCHOOL: Hopkins (Minnetonka, Minn.).
COLLEGE: Wisconsin.
TRANSACTIONS/CAREER NOTES: Selected by Calgary Flames in third round (third Flames pick, 70th overall) of NHL entry draft (June 26, 1993).

Season Team	League	REGULAR SEASON					PLAYOFFS				
		Gms.	G	A	Pts.	PIM	Gms.	G	A	Pts.	PIM
90-91—Hopkins H.S.	Minn. H.S.	25	17	12	29	26	—	—	—	—	—
91-92—Hopkins H.S.	Minn. H.S.	17	10	12	22	20	—	—	—	—	—
92-93—Omaha	Jr. A	43	16	34	50	48	—	—	—	—	—
93-94—University of Wisconsin	WCHA	18	1	0	1	31	—	—	—	—	—
94-95—University of Wisconsin	WCHA	32	4	10	14	82	—	—	—	—	—

TOMS, JEFF
LW, LIGHTNING

PERSONAL: Born June 4, 1974, in Swift Current, Sask.... 6-3/180.... Shoots left.
TRANSACTIONS/CAREER NOTES: Selected by New Jersey Devils in ninth round (10th Devils pick, 210th overall) of NHL entry draft (June 26, 1993).... Traded by Devils to Tampa Bay Lightning for fourth-round pick (traded to Calgary Flames who selected C Ryan Duthie) in 1994 draft (May 31, 1994).

Season Team	League	REGULAR SEASON					PLAYOFFS				
		Gms.	G	A	Pts.	PIM	Gms.	G	A	Pts.	PIM
91-92—Sault Ste. Marie	OHL	36	9	5	14	0	16	0	1	1	2
92-93—Sault Ste. Marie	OHL	59	16	23	39	20	16	4	4	8	7
93-94—Sault Ste. Marie	OHL	64	52	45	97	19	14	11	4	15	2
94-95—Atlanta	IHL	40	7	8	15	10	4	0	0	0	4

TOPOROWSKI, KERRY
RW

PERSONAL: Born April 9, 1971, in Prince Albert, Sask.... 6-2/212.... Shoots right.... Name pronounced toh-poh-ROW-skee.
TRANSACTIONS/CAREER NOTES: Selected by San Jose Sharks in fourth round (fourth Sharks pick, 67th overall) of NHL entry draft (June 22, 1991).... Traded by Sharks with second-round pick in 1992 draft to Chicago Blackhawks for D Doug Wilson (September 6, 1991).

Season Team	League	REGULAR SEASON					PLAYOFFS				
		Gms.	G	A	Pts.	PIM	Gms.	G	A	Pts.	PIM
89-90—Spokane	WHL	65	1	13	14	*384	6	0	0	0	37
90-91—Spokane	WHL	65	11	16	27	*505	15	2	2	4	*108
91-92—Indianapolis	IHL	18	1	2	3	206	—	—	—	—	—
92-93—Indianapolis	IHL	17	0	0	0	57	—	—	—	—	—
93-94—Indianapolis	IHL	32	1	4	5	126	—	—	—	—	—
—Las Vegas	IHL	13	1	0	1	129	2	0	0	0	31
94-95—Las Vegas	IHL	37	1	4	5	300	5	0	1	1	69

TOPOROWSKI, SHAYNE
RW, MAPLE LEAFS

PERSONAL: Born August 6, 1975, in Prince Albert, Sask.... 6-2/205.... Shoots right.... Name pronounced TAHP-uhr-OW-skee.
HIGH SCHOOL: Carlton Comprehensive (Paddockwood, Sask.).
TRANSACTIONS/CAREER NOTES: Selected by Los Angeles Kings in second round (first Kings pick, 42nd overall) of NHL entry draft (June 26, 1993).... Traded by Kings with RW Dixon Ward, C Guy Leveque and C Kelly Fairchild to Toronto Maple Leafs for LW Eric Lacroix, D Chris Snell and fourth-round pick in 1996 draft (October 3, 1994).

Season Team	League	REGULAR SEASON					PLAYOFFS				
		Gms.	G	A	Pts.	PIM	Gms.	G	A	Pts.	PIM
91-92—Prince Albert	WHL	6	2	0	2	2	7	2	1	3	6
92-93—Prince Albert	WHL	72	25	32	57	235	—	—	—	—	—

Season	Team	League	Gms.	G	A	Pts.	PIM	Gms.	G	A	Pts.	PIM
93-94—Prince Albert	WHL	68	37	45	82	183	—	—	—	—	—
94-95—Prince Albert	WHL	72	36	38	74	151	15	10	8	18	25

TORCHIA, MIKE
G, CAPITALS

PERSONAL: Born February 23, 1972, in Toronto. . . . 5-11/215. . . . Catches left. . . . Name pronounced TOHR-chuh.
TRANSACTIONS/CAREER NOTES: Broke ankle (July 1989). . . . Selected by Minnesota North Stars in fourth round (second North Stars pick, 74th overall) of NHL entry draft (June 22, 1991). . . . North Stars franchise moved from Minnesota to Dallas and renamed Stars for 1993-94 season. . . . Traded by Stars to Washington Capitals for future considerations (July 14, 1995).
HONORS: Won Hap Emms Memorial Trophy (1989-90). . . . Named to Memorial Cup All-Star team (1989-90). . . . Named to OHL All-Star first team (1990-91).

				REGULAR SEASON							PLAYOFFS					
Season	Team	League	Gms.	Min.	W	L	T	GA	SO	Avg.	Gms.	Min.	W	L	GA	SO	Avg.
88-89—Kitchener	OHL	30	1672	14	9	4	112	0	4.02	2	126	0	2	8	0	3.81
89-90—Kitchener	OHL	40	2280	25	11	2	136	1	3.58	*17	*1023	*11	6	60	0	3.52
90-91—Kitchener	OHL	57	*3317	25	24	7	219	0	3.96	6	382	2	4	30	0	4.71
91-92—Kitchener	OHL	55	3042	25	24	3	203	1	4.00	14	900	7	7	47	0	3.13
92-93—Can. national team	Int'l	5	300	5	0	0	11	1	2.20	—	—	—	—	—	—	—
—Kalamazoo	IHL	48	2729	19	17	‡9	173	0	3.80	—	—	—	—	—	—	—
93-94—Kalamazoo	IHL	43	2168	23	12	‡2	133	0	3.68	4	221	1	2	14	†1	3.80
94-95—Kalamazoo	IHL	41	2140	19	14	‡5	106	†3	2.97	6	257	0	4	17	0	3.97
—Dallas	NHL	6	327	3	2	1	18	0	3.30	—	—	—	—	—	—	—
NHL totals		6	327	3	2	1	18	0	3.30							

TORMANNEN, ANTTI
RW, SENATORS

PERSONAL: Born September 19, 1970, in Espoo, Finland. . . . 6-1/198. . . . Shoots left. . . . Name pronounced AN-tee TOHR-muh-nehn.
TRANSACTIONS/CAREER NOTES: Selected by Ottawa Senators in 11th round (10th Senators pick, 274th overall) of NHL entry draft (June 29, 1994).

				REGULAR SEASON					PLAYOFFS			
Season	Team	League	Gms.	G	A	Pts.	PIM	Gms.	G	A	Pts.	PIM
91-92—Jokerit	Finland	40	18	11	29	18	—	—	—	—	—
92-93—Jokerit	Finland	21	2	0	2	8	—	—	—	—	—
93-94—Jokerit	Finland	46	20	18	38	46	—	—	—	—	—
94-95—Jokerit	Finland	50	19	13	32	32	11	7	4	11	20

TOSKALA, VESA
G, SHARKS

PERSONAL: Born May 20, 1977, in Tampere, Finland. . . . 5-9/172. . . . Catches left.
TRANSACTIONS/CAREER NOTES: Selected by San Jose Sharks in fourth round (fourth Sharks pick, 90th overall) of NHL entry draft (July 8, 1995).

				REGULAR SEASON						PLAYOFFS					
Season	Team	League	Gms.	Min.	W	L	T	GA	SO	Avg.	Gms.	Min.	W	L	GA	SO	Avg.
93-94—Ilves Jrs.	Finland	2	...	...	...	...	...	...	...	—	—	—	—	—	—	—
94-95—Ilves Jrs.	Finland	17	956	...	...	...	36	...	2.26	—	—	—	—	—	—	—

TRAVERSE, PATRICK
D, SENATORS

PERSONAL: Born March 14, 1974, in Montreal. . . . 6-3/200. . . . Shoots left.
TRANSACTIONS/CAREER NOTES: Selected by Ottawa Senators in third round (third Senators pick, 50th overall) of NHL entry draft (June 20, 1992).

				REGULAR SEASON					PLAYOFFS			
Season	Team	League	Gms.	G	A	Pts.	PIM	Gms.	G	A	Pts.	PIM
91-92—Shawinigan	QMJHL	59	3	11	14	12	10	0	0	0	4
92-93—St. Jean	QMJHL	68	6	30	36	24	4	0	1	1	2
—New Haven	AHL	2	0	0	0	2	—	—	—	—	—
93-94—Prince Edward Island	AHL	3	0	1	1	2	—	—	—	—	—
—St. Jean	QMJHL	66	15	37	52	30	5	0	4	4	4
94-95—Prince Edward Island	AHL	70	5	13	18	19	7	0	2	2	0

TREFILOV, ANDREI
G, SABRES

PERSONAL: Born August 31, 1969, in Moscow, U.S.S.R. . . . 6-0/180. . . . Catches left. . . . Name pronounced AHN-dray TREH-fee-lahf.
TRANSACTIONS/CAREER NOTES: Selected by Calgary Flames in 12th round (14th Flames pick, 261st overall) of NHL entry draft (June 22, 1991). . . . Twisted right knee ligament (February 2, 1994); missed 23 games. . . . Signed as free agent by Buffalo Sabres (July 13, 1995).
MISCELLANEOUS: Member of gold-medal-winning Unified Olympic team (1992).

				REGULAR SEASON						PLAYOFFS					
Season	Team	League	Gms.	Min.	W	L	T	GA	SO	Avg.	Gms.	Min.	W	L	GA	SO	Avg.
90-91—Dynamo Moscow	USSR	20	1070	...	...	...	36	0	2.02	—	—	—	—	—	—	—
91-92—Dynamo Moscow	CIS	28	1326	...	...	...	35	0	1.58	—	—	—	—	—	—	—
—Unified Olympic Team	Int'l	4	38	...	...	...	2	2	3.16	—	—	—	—	—	—	—
92-93—Salt Lake City	IHL	44	2536	23	17	‡0	135	0	3.19	—	—	—	—	—	—	—
—Calgary	NHL	1	65	0	0	1	5	0	4.62	—	—	—	—	—	—	—

Season	Team	League	Gms.	Min.	W	L	T	GA	SO	Avg.	Gms.	Min.	W	L	GA	SO	Avg.
93-94—Saint John		AHL	28	1629	10	10	7	93	0	3.43	—	—	—	—	—	—	—
—Calgary		NHL	11	623	3	4	2	26	2	2.50	—	—	—	—	—	—	—
94-95—Saint John		AHL	7	383	1	5	1	20	0	3.13	—	—	—	—	—	—	—
—Calgary		NHL	6	236	0	3	0	16	0	4.07	—	—	—	—	—	—	—
NHL totals			18	924	3	7	3	47	2	3.05							

TREMBLAY, YANNICK
D, MAPLE LEAFS

PERSONAL: Born November 15, 1975, in Pointe-aux-Trembles, Que. . . . 6-2/ 185. . . . Shoots right.
COLLEGE: St. Thomas (N.B.).
TRANSACTIONS/CAREER NOTES: Selected by Toronto Maple Leafs in sixth round (fourth Maple Leafs pick, 145th overall) of NHL entry draft (July 8, 1995).

Season	Team	League	Gms.	G	A	Pts.	PIM	Gms.	G	A	Pts.	PIM
93-94—St. Thomas University		AUAA	25	2	3	5	10	—	—	—	—	—
94-95—Beauport		QMJHL	70	10	32	42	22	17	6	8	14	6

TRIPP, JOHN
RW, DENVER

PERSONAL: Born May 4, 1977, in Kingston, Ont. . . . 6-2/208. . . . Shoots right.
HIGH SCHOOL: Henry Street (Whitby, Ont.).
TRANSACTIONS/CAREER NOTES: Selected by Denver in third round (third Denver pick, 77th overall) of NHL entry draft (July 8, 1995).

Season	Team	League	Gms.	G	A	Pts.	PIM	Gms.	G	A	Pts.	PIM
93-94—St. Mary's Jr. B		OHA	42	15	29	44	116	—	—	—	—	—
94-95—Oshawa		OHL	58	6	11	17	53	7	0	1	1	4

TRNKA, PAVEL
D, MIGHTY DUCKS

PERSONAL: Born July 27, 1976, in Plzen, Czechoslovakia. . . . 6-3/ 187. . . . Shoots left.
TRANSACTIONS/CAREER NOTES: Selected by Mighty Ducks of Anaheim in fifth round (fifth Mighty Ducks pick, 106th overall) of NHL entry draft (June 29, 1994).

Season	Team	League	Gms.	G	A	Pts.	PIM	Gms.	G	A	Pts.	PIM
92-93—Skoda Plzen		Czech. Jrs.				Statistics unavailable.						
93-94—Skoda Plzen		Czech Rep.	12	0	1	1	. . .	—	—	—	—	—
94-95—HC Kladno		Czech Rep.	28	0	5	5	. . .	—	—	—	—	—
—Skoda Plzen		Czech Rep.	6	0	0	0	. . .	6	0	0	0	. . .

TROMBLEY, RHETT
RW, PANTHERS

PERSONAL: Born December 9, 1974, in Humboldt, Sask. . . . 6-3/230. . . . Shoots right.
TRANSACTIONS/CAREER NOTES: Signed as free agent by Florida Panthers (June 12, 1995).

Season	Team	League	Gms.	G	A	Pts.	PIM	Gms.	G	A	Pts.	PIM
91-92—Tacoma		WHL	7	0	0	0	32	—	—	—	—	—
—Saskatoon		WHL	50	3	4	7	181	—	—	—	—	—
92-93—Saskatoon		WHL	27	0	0	0	47	—	—	—	—	—
—Victoria		WHL	12	0	0	0	66	—	—	—	—	—
93-94—Victoria		WHL	21	0	3	3	67	—	—	—	—	—
94-95—Toledo		ECHL	13	0	2	2	80	—	—	—	—	—
—Las Vegas		IHL	30	4	0	4	141	3	0	0	0	10

TSULYGIN, NIKOLAI
D, MIGHTY DUCKS

PERSONAL: Born May 29, 1975, in Ufa, U.S.S.R. . . . 6-3/ 196. . . . Shoots right. . . . Name pronounced tsoo-LEE-guhn.
TRANSACTIONS/CAREER NOTES: Selected by Mighty Ducks of Anaheim in second round (second Mighty Ducks pick, 30th overall) of NHL entry draft (June 26, 1993).

Season	Team	League	Gms.	G	A	Pts.	PIM	Gms.	G	A	Pts.	PIM
92-93—Salavat Yulayev Ufa		CIS	42	5	4	9	21	2	0	0	0	0
93-94—Salavat Yulayev Ufa		CIS	43	0	14	14	24	5	0	1	1	0
94-95—CSKA Moscow		CIS	16	0	0	0	12	—	—	—	—	—
—Salavat Yulayev Ufa		CIS	13	2	2	4	10	7	0	0	0	4

TSYGUROV, DENIS
D, KINGS

PERSONAL: Born February 26, 1971, in Chelyabinsk, U.S.S.R. . . . 6-3/ 198. . . . Shoots left. . . . Name pronounced tsuh-GOOR-ahf.
TRANSACTIONS/CAREER NOTES: Selected by Buffalo Sabres in second round (first Sabres pick, 38th overall) of NHL entry draft (June 26, 1993). . . . Suffered deep thigh bruise (September 25, 1993); missed 11 games. . . . Played in Europe during 1994-95 NHL lockout. . . . Traded by Sabres with G Grant Fuhr and D Philippe Boucher to Los Angeles Kings for D Alexei Zhitnik, D Charlie Huddy, G Robb Stauber and fifth-round pick (D Marian Menhart) in 1995 draft (February 14, 1995). . . . Suffered facial contusion (March 8, 1995); missed two games. . . . Strained groin (March 27, 1995); missed four games.
HONORS: Named to CIS All-Star team (1992-93).

Season Team	League	REGULAR SEASON Gms.	G	A	Pts.	PIM	PLAYOFFS Gms.	G	A	Pts.	PIM
88-89—Traktor Chelyabinsk	USSR	8	0	0	0	2	—	—	—	—	—
89-90—Traktor Chelyabinsk	USSR	27	0	1	1	18	—	—	—	—	—
90-91—Traktor Chelyabinsk	USSR	26	0	1	1	16	—	—	—	—	—
91-92—Lada Togliatti	CIS	29	3	2	5	6	—	—	—	—	—
92-93—Lada Togliatti	CIS	37	7	13	20	29	10	1	1	2	6
93-94—Buffalo	NHL	8	0	0	0	8	—	—	—	—	—
—Rochester	AHL	24	1	10	11	10	1	0	1	1	0
94-95—Lada Togliatti	CIS	10	3	7	10	6	—	—	—	—	—
—Buffalo	NHL	4	0	0	0	4	—	—	—	—	—
—Los Angeles	NHL	21	0	0	0	11	—	—	—	—	—
NHL totals		33	0	0	0	23					

TSYPLAKOV, VLADIMIR
LW, KINGS

PERSONAL: Born April 18, 1969, in Inta, U.S.S.R. . . . . 6-2/194. . . . Shoots left.

TRANSACTIONS/CAREER NOTES: Selected by Los Angeles Kings in third round (fourth Kings pick, 59th overall) of NHL entry draft (July 8, 1995).

Season Team	League	REGULAR SEASON Gms.	G	A	Pts.	PIM	PLAYOFFS Gms.	G	A	Pts.	PIM
88-89—Dynamo Minsk	USSR	19	6	1	7	4	—	—	—	—	—
89-90—Dynamo Minsk	USSR	47	11	6	17	20	—	—	—	—	—
90-91—Dynamo Minsk	USSR	28	6	5	11	14	—	—	—	—	—
91-92—Dynamo Minsk	CIS	29	10	9	19	16	—	—	—	—	—
92-93—Detroit	Col.HL	44	33	43	76	20	6	5	4	9	6
—Indianapolis	IHL	11	6	8	14	16	5	1	1	2	2
93-94—Fort Wayne	IHL	63	31	32	63	51	14	6	8	14	16
94-95—Fort Wayne	IHL	79	38	40	78	39	—	—	—	—	—

TUCKER, DARCY
C, CANADIENS

PERSONAL: Born March 15, 1975, in Castor, Alta. . . . 5-10/163. . . . Shoots left.
TRANSACTIONS/CAREER NOTES: Selected by Montreal Canadiens in sixth round (eighth Canadiens pick, 151st overall) of NHL entry draft (June 26, 1993).
HONORS: Won Stafford Smythe Memorial Trophy (1993-94). . . . Named to Can.HL All-Star first team (1993-94). . . . Named to WHL (West) All-Star first team (1993-94). . . . Named to Memorial Cup All-Star team (1993-94). . . . Named to WHL (West) All-Star first team (1994-95). . . . Named to Memorial Cup All-Star team (1994-95).

Season Team	League	REGULAR SEASON Gms.	G	A	Pts.	PIM	PLAYOFFS Gms.	G	A	Pts.	PIM
91-92—Kamloops	WHL	26	3	10	13	42	9	0	1	1	16
92-93—Kamloops	WHL	67	31	58	89	155	13	7	6	13	34
93-94—Kamloops	WHL	66	52	88	140	143	19	9	*18	*27	43
94-95—Kamloops	WHL	64	64	73	137	94	21	16	15	31	19

TUCKER, JOHN
RW, LIGHTNING

PERSONAL: Born September 29, 1964, in Windsor, Ont. . . . 6-0/200. . . . Shoots right.
TRANSACTIONS/CAREER NOTES: Selected by Buffalo Sabres as underage junior in second round (fourth Sabres pick, 31st overall) of NHL entry draft (June 8, 1983). . . . Broke bone in foot (November 7, 1984). . . . Injured disk in back (January 28, 1987); underwent surgery following season. . . . Tore knee ligaments (November 7, 1987). . . . Injured shoulder (December 1987). . . . Injured shoulder (February 25, 1988). . . . Injured back (January 1989); missed 16 games. . . . Traded by Sabres to Washington Capitals for conditional pick in 1990 draft (January 4, 1990). . . . Contract sold by Capitals to Sabres (July 3, 1990). . . . Traded by Sabres to New York Islanders for future considerations (January 21, 1991). . . . Signed as free agent by Tampa Bay Lightning (July 21, 1992). . . . Injured knee (March 16, 1993); missed six games. . . . Sprained right knee (November 26, 1993); missed 18 games. . . . Injured shoulder (April 26, 1995); missed two games.
HONORS: Won Red Tilson Trophy (1983-84). . . . Named to OHL All-Star first team (1983-84).
STATISTICAL PLATEAUS: Three-goal games: 1983-84 (1).
MISCELLANEOUS: Captain of Tampa Bay Lightning (1994-95).

Season Team	League	REGULAR SEASON Gms.	G	A	Pts.	PIM	PLAYOFFS Gms.	G	A	Pts.	PIM
81-82—Kitchener	OHL	67	16	32	48	32	15	2	3	5	2
82-83—Kitchener	OHL	70	60	80	140	33	11	5	9	14	10
83-84—Kitchener	OHL	39	40	60	100	25	12	12	18	30	8
—Buffalo	NHL	21	12	4	16	4	3	1	0	1	0
84-85—Buffalo	NHL	64	22	27	49	21	5	1	5	6	0
85-86—Buffalo	NHL	75	31	34	65	39	—	—	—	—	—
86-87—Buffalo	NHL	54	17	34	51	21	—	—	—	—	—
87-88—Buffalo	NHL	45	19	19	38	20	6	7	3	10	18
88-89—Buffalo	NHL	60	13	31	44	31	3	0	3	3	0
89-90—Buffalo	NHL	8	1	2	3	2	—	—	—	—	—
—Washington	NHL	38	9	19	28	10	12	1	7	8	4
90-91—Buffalo	NHL	18	1	3	4	4	—	—	—	—	—
—New York Islanders	NHL	20	3	4	7	4	—	—	—	—	—
91-92—Asiago	Italy	36	38	53	91	...	12	9	10	19	22
92-93—Tampa Bay	NHL	78	17	39	56	69	—	—	—	—	—

Season Team	League	REGULAR SEASON					PLAYOFFS				
		Gms.	G	A	Pts.	PIM	Gms.	G	A	Pts.	PIM
93-94—Tampa Bay	NHL	66	17	23	40	28	—	—	—	—	—
94-95—Tampa Bay	NHL	46	12	13	25	14	—	—	—	—	—
NHL totals		593	174	252	426	267	29	10	18	28	22

TUGNUTT, RON
G, CANADIENS

PERSONAL: Born October 22, 1967, in Scarborough, Ont. . . . 5-11/155. . . . Catches left. . . . Full name: Ronald Frederick Bradley Tugnutt.
TRANSACTIONS/CAREER NOTES: Selected by Quebec Nordiques as underage junior in fourth round (fourth Nordiques pick, 81st overall) of NHL entry draft (June 21, 1986). . . . Sprained ankle (March 1989). . . . Sprained knee (January 13, 1990). . . . Injured hamstring (January 29, 1991); missed 11 games. . . . Traded by Nordiques with LW Brad Zavisha to Edmonton Oilers for LW Martin Rucinsky (March 10, 1992). . . . Selected by Mighty Ducks of Anaheim in NHL expansion draft (June 24, 1993). . . . Traded by Mighty Ducks to Montreal Canadiens for C Stephan Lebeau (February 20, 1994). . . . Strained knee (Jan 28, 1995); missed five games.
HONORS: Won F.W. (Dinty) Moore Trophy (1984-85). . . . Shared Dave Pinkney Trophy with Kay Whitmore (1985-86). . . . Named to OHL All-Star first team (1986-87).

Season Team	League	REGULAR SEASON							PLAYOFFS						
		Gms.	Min.	W	L	T	GA	SO	Avg.	Gms.	Min.	W	L	GA	SO	Avg.
84-85—Peterborough	OHL	18	938	7	4	2	59	0	3.77	—	—	—	—	—	—	—
85-86—Peterborough	OHL	26	1543	18	7	0	74	1	2.88	3	133	2	0	6	0	2.71
86-87—Peterborough	OHL	31	1891	21	7	2	88	2	*2.79	6	374	3	3	21	1	3.37
87-88—Quebec	NHL	6	284	2	3	0	16	0	3.38	—	—	—	—	—	—	—
—Fredericton	AHL	34	1962	20	9	4	118	1	3.61	4	204	1	2	11	0	3.24
88-89—Quebec	NHL	26	1367	10	10	3	82	0	3.60	—	—	—	—	—	—	—
—Halifax	AHL	24	1368	14	7	2	79	1	3.46	—	—	—	—	—	—	—
89-90—Quebec	NHL	35	1978	5	24	3	152	0	4.61	—	—	—	—	—	—	—
—Halifax	AHL	6	366	1	5	0	23	0	3.77	—	—	—	—	—	—	—
90-91—Halifax	AHL	2	100	0	1	0	8	0	4.80	—	—	—	—	—	—	—
—Quebec	NHL	56	3144	12	†29	10	212	0	4.05	—	—	—	—	—	—	—
91-92—Quebec	NHL	30	1583	6	17	3	106	1	4.02	—	—	—	—	—	—	—
—Halifax	AHL	8	447	3	3	1	30	0	4.03	—	—	—	—	—	—	—
—Edmonton	NHL	3	124	1	1	0	10	0	4.84	2	60	0	0	3	0	3.00
92-93—Edmonton	NHL	26	1338	9	12	2	93	0	4.17	—	—	—	—	—	—	—
93-94—Anaheim	NHL	28	1520	10	15	1	76	1	3.00	—	—	—	—	—	—	—
—Montreal	NHL	8	378	2	3	1	24	0	3.81	1	59	0	1	5	0	5.08
94-95—Montreal	NHL	7	346	1	3	1	18	0	3.12	—	—	—	—	—	—	—
NHL totals		225	12062	58	117	24	789	2	3.92	3	119	0	1	8	0	4.03

TULLY, BRENT
D, CANUCKS

PERSONAL: Born March 26, 1974, in Peterborough, Ont. . . . 6-3/185. . . . Shoots right.
HIGH SCHOOL: Thomas A. Stewart (Peterborough, Ont.).
TRANSACTIONS/CAREER NOTES: Selected by Vancouver Canucks in fourth round (fifth Canucks pick, 93rd overall) of NHL entry draft (June 20, 1992).
HONORS: Named to OHL All-Star second team (1992-93).

Season Team	League	REGULAR SEASON					PLAYOFFS				
		Gms.	G	A	Pts.	PIM	Gms.	G	A	Pts.	PIM
90-91—Peterborough Jr. B	OHA	9	3	0	3	23	—	—	—	—	—
—Peterborough	OHL	45	3	5	8	35	2	0	0	0	0
91-92—Peterborough	OHL	65	9	23	32	65	10	0	0	0	2
92-93—Peterborough	OHL	59	15	45	60	81	21	8	24	32	32
93-94—Canadian national team	Int'l	1	0	1	1	0	—	—	—	—	—
—Peterborough	OHL	37	17	26	43	81	7	5	3	8	12
—Hamilton	AHL	1	0	0	0	0	1	1	0	1	0
94-95—Syracuse	AHL	63	6	3	9	106	—	—	—	—	—

TUOMAINEN, MARKO
RW, OILERS

PERSONAL: Born April 25, 1972, in Kuopio, Finland. . . . 6-2/190. . . . Shoots right.
COLLEGE: Clarkson (N.Y.).
TRANSACTIONS/CAREER NOTES: Selected by Edmonton Oilers in ninth round (10th Oilers pick, 205th overall) of NHL entry draft (June 20, 1992).
HONORS: Named to ECAC All-Star first team (1992-93 and 1994-95). . . . Named to NCAA All-America East second team (1994-95).

Season Team	League	REGULAR SEASON					PLAYOFFS				
		Gms.	G	A	Pts.	PIM	Gms.	G	A	Pts.	PIM
89-90—KalPa	Finland	5	0	0	0	0	—	—	—	—	—
90-91—KalPa	Finland	30	2	1	3	2	8	0	0	0	6
91-92—Clarkson	ECAC	28	11	12	23	32	—	—	—	—	—
92-93—Clarkson	ECAC	35	25	30	55	26	—	—	—	—	—
93-94—Clarkson	ECAC	34	23	29	52	60	—	—	—	—	—
94-95—Clarkson	ECAC	37	23	37	60	34	—	—	—	—	—
—Edmonton	NHL	4	0	0	0	0	—	—	—	—	—
NHL totals		4	0	0	0	0					

TURCO, MARTY
G, STARS

PERSONAL: Born August 13, 1975, in Sault Ste. Marie, Ont. . . . 5- 11/ 175. . . . Catches left.
HIGH SCHOOL: St. Mary's College (Sault Ste. Marie, Ont.).
COLLEGE: Michigan.
TRANSACTIONS/CAREER NOTES: Selected by Dallas Stars in fifth round (fourth Stars pick, 124th overall) of NHL entry draft (June 29, 1994).
HONORS: Named CCHA Rookie of the year (1994-95).

Season Team	League	Gms.	Min.	W	L	T	GA	SO	Avg.	Gms.	Min.	W	L	GA	SO	Avg.
93-94—Cambridge Jr. B	OHA	34	1937	...	...	...	114	0	3.53	—	—	—	—	—	—	—
94-95—University of Michigan .	CCHA	37	2064	27	7	1	95	1	2.76	—	—	—	—	—	—	—

TURCOTTE, DARREN
C, WHALERS

PERSONAL: Born March 2, 1968, in Boston. . . . 6-0/ 178. . . . Shoots left. . . . Name pronounced TUHR-kaht.
TRANSACTIONS/CAREER NOTES: Selected by New York Rangers as underage junior in sixth round (sixth Rangers pick, 114th overall) of NHL entry draft (June 21, 1986). . . . Separated shoulder (October 1987); missed 34 games. . . . Suffered concussion (March 1989). . . . Sprained left ankle (October 1989). . . . Injured knee (April 11, 1990). . . . Broke left foot (April 27, 1990). . . . Suffered contusion above left ankle (November 13, 1991); missed two games. . . . Bruised right foot (March 4, 1992); missed one game. . . . Reinjured right foot (March 9, 1992); missed two games. . . . Sprained ankle (January 2, 1993); missed one game. . . . Suffered hairline fracture in foot (February 10, 1993); missed 11 games. . . . Traded by Rangers with D James Patrick to Hartford Whalers for RW Steve Larmer, LW Nick Kypreos and sixth-round pick (C Yuri Litvinov) in 1994 draft (November 2, 1993). . . . Underwent medial collateral ligament surgery (December 9, 1993); missed 50 games.
HONORS: Played in NHL All-Star Game (1991).
STATISTICAL PLATEAUS: Three-goal games: 1988-89 (1), 1989-90 (1), 1990-91 (1), 1991-92 (1). Total: 4.

Season Team	League		REGULAR SEASON					PLAYOFFS			
		Gms.	G	A	Pts.	PIM	Gms.	G	A	Pts.	PIM
84-85—North Bay	OHL	62	33	32	65	28	8	0	2	2	0
85-86—North Bay	OHL	62	35	37	72	35	10	3	4	7	8
86-87—North Bay	OHL	55	30	48	78	20	18	12	8	20	6
87-88—Colorado	IHL	8	4	3	7	9	6	2	6	8	8
—North Bay	OHL	32	30	33	63	16	4	3	0	3	4
88-89—Denver	IHL	40	21	28	49	32	—	—	—	—	—
—New York Rangers	NHL	20	7	3	10	4	1	0	0	0	0
89-90—New York Rangers	NHL	76	32	34	66	32	10	1	6	7	4
90-91—New York Rangers	NHL	74	26	41	67	37	6	1	2	3	0
91-92—New York Rangers	NHL	71	30	23	53	57	8	4	0	4	6
92-93—New York Rangers	NHL	71	25	28	53	40	—	—	—	—	—
93-94—New York Rangers	NHL	13	2	4	6	13	—	—	—	—	—
—Hartford	NHL	19	2	11	13	4	—	—	—	—	—
94-95—Hartford	NHL	47	17	18	35	22	—	—	—	—	—
NHL totals............		**391**	**141**	**162**	**303**	**209**	**25**	**6**	**8**	**14**	**10**

TURGEON, PIERRE
C, CANADIENS

PERSONAL: Born August 29, 1969, in Rouyn, Que. . . . 6-1/ 195. . . . Shoots left. . . . Name pronounced TUHR-zhaw. . . . Brother of Sylvain Turgeon, left winger, Ottawa Senators.
TRANSACTIONS/CAREER NOTES: Underwent knee surgery (June 1985). . . . Selected by Buffalo Sabres as underage junior in first round (first Sabres pick, first overall) of NHL entry draft (June 13, 1987). . . . Traded by Sabres with RW Benoit Hogue, D Uwe Krupp and C Dave McLlwain to New York Islanders for C Pat LaFontaine, LW Randy Wood, D Randy Hillier and future considerations; Sabres received fourth-round pick in 1992 draft (D Dean Melanson) to complete deal (October 25, 1991). . . . Injured right knee (January 3, 1992); missed three games. . . . Separated shoulder (April 28, 1993); missed six playoff games. . . . Suffered from tendinitis in right wrist (October 5, 1993); missed one game. . . . Suffered from the flu (December 29, 1993); missed one game. . . . Fractured cheekbone (January 26, 1994); missed 12 games. . . . Traded by Islanders with D Vladimir Malakhov to Montreal Canadiens for LW Kirk Muller, D Mathieu Schneider and C Craig Darby (April 5, 1995).
HONORS: Won Michel Bergeron Trophy (1985-86). . . . Won Michael Bossy Trophy (1986-87). . . . Played in NHL All-Star Game (1990, 1993 and 1994). . . . Won Lady Byng Memorial Trophy (1992-93).
STATISTICAL PLATEAUS: Three-goal games: 1989-90 (1), 1990-91 (1), 1991-92 (2), 1992-93 (4), 1993-94 (2), 1994-95 (1). Total: 11.

Season Team	League		REGULAR SEASON					PLAYOFFS		
		Gms.	G	A	Pts.	PIM	Gms.	G	A	Pts.	PIM
85-86—Granby..........................	QMJHL	69	47	67	114	31	—	—	—	—	—
86-87—Granby..........................	QMJHL	58	69	85	154	8	7	9	6	15	15
87-88—Buffalo..........................	NHL	76	14	28	42	34	6	4	3	7	4
88-89—Buffalo..........................	NHL	80	34	54	88	26	5	3	5	8	2
89-90—Buffalo..........................	NHL	80	40	66	106	29	6	2	4	6	2
90-91—Buffalo..........................	NHL	78	32	47	79	26	6	3	1	4	6
91-92—Buffalo..........................	NHL	8	2	6	8	4	—	—	—	—	—
—New York Islanders..........	NHL	69	38	49	87	16	—	—	—	—	—
92-93—New York Islanders..........	NHL	83	58	74	132	26	11	6	7	13	0
93-94—New York Islanders..........	NHL	69	38	56	94	18	4	0	1	1	0
94-95—New York Islanders..........	NHL	34	13	14	27	10	—	—	—	—	—
—Montreal........................	NHL	15	11	9	20	4	—	—	—	—	—
NHL totals........................		**592**	**280**	**403**	**683**	**193**	**38**	**18**	**21**	**39**	**14**

TURGEON, SYLVAIN

LW, SENATORS

PERSONAL: Born January 17, 1965, in Noranda, Que. . . . 6-0/195. . . . Shoots left. . . . Full name: Sylvain Dorila Turgeon. . . . Name pronounced TUHR-zhaw. . . . Brother of Pierre Turgeon, center, Montreal Canadiens.

TRANSACTIONS/CAREER NOTES: Selected by Hartford Whalers as underage junior in first round (first Whalers pick, second overall) of NHL entry draft (June 8, 1983). . . . Pulled abdominal muscles (October 1984). . . . Underwent surgery to repair torn abdominal muscle (November 14, 1986); missed 39 games. . . . Broke left arm during Team Canada practice (August 11, 1987). . . . Sprained right knee during training camp (September 1988). . . . Separated left shoulder (December 21, 1988); missed 36 games. . . . Burned both eyes from ultra-violet light produced by welder's torch while working on car (February 28, 1989). . . . Traded by Whalers to New Jersey Devils for RW/LW Pat Verbeek (June 17, 1989). . . . Aggravated groin injury (March 20, 1990). . . . Underwent hernia surgery (August 23, 1990); missed first 33 games of season. . . . Traded by Devils to Montreal Canadiens for RW Claude Lemieux (September 4, 1990). . . . Broke right kneecap (February 6, 1991); missed remainder of regular season. . . . Selected by Ottawa Senators in NHL expansion draft (June 18, 1992). . . . Suspended one game by NHL for receiving two major stick fouls in one game (October 23, 1992). . . . Injured groin (February 8, 1993); missed 11 games. . . . Fractured left forearm (October 25, 1993); missed 37 games.

HONORS: Won Des Instructeurs Trophy (1981-82). . . . Won Association of Journalists of Hockey Trophy (1982-83). . . . Named to QMJHL All-Star first team (1982-83). . . . Named to NHL All-Rookie team (1983-84). . . . Played in NHL All-Star Game (1986).

STATISTICAL PLATEAUS: Three-goal games: 1984-85 (1), 1985-86 (1), 1986-87 (1), 1989-90 (1), 1993-94 (1). Total: 5.

Season Team	League	REGULAR SEASON					PLAYOFFS				
		Gms.	G	A	Pts.	PIM	Gms.	G	A	Pts.	PIM
81-82—Hull	QMJHL	57	33	40	73	78	14	11	11	22	16
82-83—Hull	QMJHL	67	54	109	163	103	7	8	7	15	10
83-84—Hartford	NHL	76	40	32	72	55	—	—	—	—	—
84-85—Hartford	NHL	64	31	31	62	67	—	—	—	—	—
85-86—Hartford	NHL	76	45	34	79	88	9	2	3	5	4
86-87—Hartford	NHL	41	23	13	36	45	6	1	2	3	4
87-88—Hartford	NHL	71	23	26	49	71	6	0	0	0	4
88-89—Hartford	NHL	42	16	14	30	40	4	0	2	2	4
89-90—New Jersey	NHL	72	30	17	47	81	1	0	0	0	0
90-91—Montreal	NHL	19	5	7	12	20	5	0	0	0	2
91-92—Montreal	NHL	56	9	11	20	39	5	1	0	1	4
92-93—Ottawa	NHL	72	25	18	43	104	—	—	—	—	—
93-94—Ottawa	NHL	47	11	15	26	52	—	—	—	—	—
94-95—Ottawa	NHL	33	11	8	19	29	—	—	—	—	—
NHL totals		669	269	226	495	691	36	4	7	11	22

TVERDOVSKY, OLEG

D, MIGHTY DUCKS

PERSONAL: Born May 18, 1976, in Donetsk, U.S.S.R. . . . 6-0/183. . . . Shoots left. . . . Name pronounced tuh-VAIR-dahf-skee.

TRANSACTIONS/CAREER NOTES: Selected by Mighty Ducks of Anaheim in first round (first Mighty Ducks pick, second overall) of NHL entry draft (June 28, 1994). . . . Suffered from pink eye (March 15, 1995); missed two games.

Season Team	League	REGULAR SEASON					PLAYOFFS				
		Gms.	G	A	Pts.	PIM	Gms.	G	A	Pts.	PIM
92-93—Soviet Wings	CIS	21	0	1	1	6	6	0	0	0	0
93-94—Soviet Wings	CIS	46	4	10	14	22	3	1	0	1	2
94-95—Brandon	WHL	7	1	4	5	4	—	—	—	—	—
—Anaheim	NHL	36	3	9	12	14	—	—	—	—	—
NHL totals		36	3	9	12	14	—	—	—	—	—

TWIST, TONY

LW, BLUES

PERSONAL: Born May 9, 1968, in Sherwood Park, Alta. . . . 6-1/220. . . . Shoots left. . . . Full name: Anthony Rory Twist.

TRANSACTIONS/CAREER NOTES: Suspended three games and fined $250 by WHL for leaving the penalty box to fight (January 28, 1988). . . . Selected by St. Louis Blues in ninth round (ninth Blues pick, 177th overall) of NHL entry draft (June 11, 1988). . . . Suspended 13 games by IHL for checking goaltender after play stopped (December 15, 1990). . . . Traded by Blues with RW Herb Raglan and LW Andy Rymsha to Quebec Nordiques for RW Darin Kimble (February 4, 1991). . . . Injured shoulder (December 18, 1993); missed six games. . . . Hyperextended right elbow (March 30, 1994); missed five games. . . . Signed as free agent by Blues (August 3, 1994). . . . Injured shoulder (March 26, 1995); missed last 20 games of season.

Season Team	League	REGULAR SEASON					PLAYOFFS				
		Gms.	G	A	Pts.	PIM	Gms.	G	A	Pts.	PIM
86-87—Saskatoon	WHL	64	0	8	8	181	—	—	—	—	—
87-88—Saskatoon	WHL	55	1	8	9	226	10	1	1	2	6
88-89—Peoria	IHL	67	3	8	11	312	—	—	—	—	—
89-90—St. Louis	NHL	28	0	0	0	124	—	—	—	—	—
—Peoria	IHL	36	1	5	6	200	5	0	1	1	8
90-91—Peoria	IHL	38	2	10	12	244	—	—	—	—	—
—Quebec	NHL	24	0	0	0	104	—	—	—	—	—
91-92—Quebec	NHL	44	0	1	1	164	—	—	—	—	—
92-93—Quebec	NHL	34	0	2	2	64	—	—	—	—	—
93-94—Quebec	NHL	49	0	4	4	101	—	—	—	—	—
94-95—St. Louis	NHL	28	3	0	3	89	1	0	0	0	6
NHL totals		207	3	7	10	646	1	0	0	0	6

ULANOV, IGOR
D, CAPITALS

PERSONAL: Born October 1, 1969, in Kraskokamsk, U.S.S.R. . . . 6-2/202. . . . Shoots right. . . . Name pronounced EE-gohr oo-LAH-nahf.
TRANSACTIONS/CAREER NOTES: Selected by Winnipeg Jets in 10th round (eighth Jets pick, 203rd overall) of NHL entry draft (June 22, 1991). . . . Suffered back spasms (March 7, 1992); missed five games. . . . Fractured foot (March 15, 1995); missed 19 games. . . . Traded by Jets with C Mike Eagles to Washington Capitals for third-round (traded to Dallas Stars) and fifth-round (G Brian Elder) picks in 1995 draft (April 7, 1995).

Season Team	League	Gms.	G	A	Pts.	PIM	Gms.	G	A	Pts.	PIM
				REGULAR SEASON					PLAYOFFS		
90-91—Khimik	USSR	41	2	2	4	52	—	—	—	—	—
91-92—Khimik	CIS	27	1	4	5	24	—	—	—	—	—
—Winnipeg	NHL	27	2	9	11	67	7	0	0	0	39
—Moncton	AHL	3	0	1	1	16	—	—	—	—	—
92-93—Moncton	AHL	9	1	3	4	26	—	—	—	—	—
—Fort Wayne	IHL	3	0	1	1	29	—	—	—	—	—
—Winnipeg	NHL	56	2	14	16	124	4	0	0	0	4
93-94—Winnipeg	NHL	74	0	17	17	165	—	—	—	—	—
94-95—Winnipeg	NHL	19	1	3	4	27	—	—	—	—	—
—Washington	NHL	3	0	1	1	2	2	0	0	0	4
NHL totals		179	5	44	49	385	13	0	0	0	47

USTORF, STEFAN
C, CAPITALS

PERSONAL: Born January 3, 1974, in Kaufbeuren, West Germany. . . . 6-0/185. . . . Shoots left. . . . Name pronounced OOS-tohrf.
TRANSACTIONS/CAREER NOTES: Selected by Washington Capitals in third round (third Capitals pick, 53rd overall) of NHL entry draft (June 20, 1992).

Season Team	League	Gms.	G	A	Pts.	PIM	Gms.	G	A	Pts.	PIM
				REGULAR SEASON					PLAYOFFS		
91-92—Kaufbeuren	Germany	41	2	22	24	46	—	—	—	—	—
92-93—Kaufbeuren	Germany	37	14	18	32	32	3	1	0	1	10
93-94—Kaufbeuren	Germany	38	10	20	30	21	3	0	0	0	4
—German Olympic team	Int'l	8	1	2	3	2	—	—	—	—	—
94-95—Portland	AHL	63	21	38	59	51	7	1	6	7	7

USTYUGOV, ANATOLY
LW, RED WINGS

PERSONAL: Born June 26, 1977, in Yaroslavl, U.S.S.R. . . . 5-10/165. . . . Shoots left.
TRANSACTIONS/CAREER NOTES: Selected by Detroit Red Wings in fourth round (fourth Red Wings pick, 104th overall) of NHL entry draft (July 8, 1995).

Season Team	League	Gms.	G	A	Pts.	PIM	Gms.	G	A	Pts.	PIM
				REGULAR SEASON					PLAYOFFS		
94-95—Torpedo Yaroslavl	CIS	5	0	0	0	0	—	—	—	—	—

VALK, GARRY
LW/RW, MIGHTY DUCKS

PERSONAL: Born November 27, 1967, in Edmonton. . . . 6-1/205. . . . Shoots left. . . . Name pronounced VAHLK.
COLLEGE: North Dakota.
TRANSACTIONS/CAREER NOTES: Selected by Vancouver Canucks in sixth round (fifth Canucks pick, 108th overall) of NHL entry draft (June 13, 1987). . . . Sprained thumb (November 24, 1991); missed one game. . . . Sprained shoulder (January 21, 1992); missed eight games. . . . Sprained knee (February 26, 1993); missed 12 games. . . . Selected by Mighty Ducks of Anaheim in NHL waiver draft (October 3, 1993). . . . Suffered concussion (December 5, 1993); missed one game. . . . Suffered post-concussion syndrome (December 5, 1993); missed four games. . . . Sprained left knee (January 16, 1995); missed 10 games.

Season Team	League	Gms.	G	A	Pts.	PIM	Gms.	G	A	Pts.	PIM
				REGULAR SEASON					PLAYOFFS		
85-86—Sherwood Park	AJHL	40	20	26	46	116	—	—	—	—	—
86-87—Sherwood Park	AJHL	59	42	44	86	204	—	—	—	—	—
87-88—Univ. of North Dakota	WCHA	38	23	12	35	64	—	—	—	—	—
88-89—Univ. of North Dakota	WCHA	40	14	17	31	71	—	—	—	—	—
89-90—Univ. of North Dakota	WCHA	43	22	17	39	92	—	—	—	—	—
90-91—Vancouver	NHL	59	10	11	21	67	5	0	0	0	20
—Milwaukee	IHL	10	12	4	16	13	3	0	0	0	2
91-92—Vancouver	NHL	65	8	17	25	56	4	0	0	0	5
92-93—Vancouver	NHL	48	6	7	13	77	7	0	1	1	12
—Hamilton	AHL	7	3	6	9	6	—	—	—	—	—
93-94—Anaheim	NHL	78	18	27	45	100	—	—	—	—	—
94-95—Anaheim	NHL	36	3	6	9	34	—	—	—	—	—
NHL totals		286	45	68	113	334	16	0	1	1	37

VALLEE, SEBASTIEN
LW, FLYERS

PERSONAL: Born January 2, 1976, in Thetford Mines, Que. . . . 6-4/180. . . . Shoots left. . . . Name pronounced val-AY.
TRANSACTIONS/CAREER NOTES: Selected by Philadelphia Flyers in fourth round (third Flyers pick, 101st overall) of NHL entry draft (June 29, 1994).

Season Team	League	Gms.	G	A	Pts.	PIM	Gms.	G	A	Pts.	PIM
				REGULAR SEASON					PLAYOFFS		
91-92—Surrey Jr. A	BCJHL	27	0	1	1	20	—	—	—	—	—

UV

Season Team	League	Gms.	G	A	Pts.	PIM	Gms.	G	A	Pts.	PIM
		REGULAR SEASON					PLAYOFFS				
92-93—Surrey Jr. A	BCJHL	60	5	37	42	210	—	—	—	—	—
93-94—Victoriaville	QMJHL	72	17	22	39	22	1	0	0	0	0
94-95—Victoriaville	QMJHL	72	23	32	55	52	4	1	0	1	0

VAN ALLEN, SHAUN
C, MIGHTY DUCKS

PERSONAL: Born August 29, 1967, in Shaunavon, Sask. . . . 6-1/200. . . . Shoots left. . . . Full name: Shaun Kelly Van Allen. **HIGH SCHOOL:** Walter Murray (Saskatoon, Sask.). **TRANSACTIONS/CAREER NOTES:** Selected by Edmonton Oilers in fifth round (fifth Oilers pick, 105th overall) of NHL entry draft (June 13, 1987). . . . Suffered concussion (January 9, 1993); missed 11 games. . . . Signed as free agent by Mighty Ducks of Anaheim (July 22, 1993). . . . Suffered back spasms (February 7, 1995); missed two games. . . . Suffered from the flu (May 1, 1995); missed one game. **HONORS:** Named to AHL All-Star second team (1990-91). . . . Won John B. Sollenberger Trophy (1991-92). . . . Named to AHL All-Star first team (1991-92).

Season Team	League	Gms.	G	A	Pts.	PIM	Gms.	G	A	Pts.	PIM
		REGULAR SEASON					PLAYOFFS				
84-85—Swift Current	SAJHL	61	12	20	32	136	—	—	—	—	—
85-86—Saskatoon	WHL	55	12	11	23	43	13	4	8	12	28
86-87—Saskatoon	WHL	72	38	59	97	116	11	4	6	10	24
87-88—Nova Scotia	AHL	19	4	10	14	17	4	1	1	2	4
—Milwaukee	IHL	40	14	28	42	34	—	—	—	—	—
88-89—Cape Breton	AHL	76	32	42	74	81	—	—	—	—	—
89-90—Cape Breton	AHL	61	25	44	69	83	4	0	2	2	8
90-91—Edmonton	NHL	2	0	0	0	0	—	—	—	—	—
—Cape Breton	AHL	76	25	75	100	182	4	0	1	1	8
91-92—Cape Breton	AHL	77	29	*84	*113	80	5	3	7	10	14
92-93—Cape Breton	AHL	43	14	62	76	68	15	8	9	17	18
—Edmonton	NHL	21	1	4	5	6	—	—	—	—	—
93-94—Anaheim	NHL	80	8	25	33	64	—	—	—	—	—
94-95—Anaheim	NHL	45	8	21	29	32	—	—	—	—	—
NHL totals		148	17	50	67	102					

VAN DYK, CHRIS
D, BLACKHAWKS

PERSONAL: Born February 18, 1977, in Welland, Ont. . . . 6-2/185. . . . Shoots right. **HIGH SCHOOL:** Herman Secondary School (Brantford, Ont.). **TRANSACTIONS/CAREER NOTES:** Selected by Chicago Blackhawks in fourth round (fourth Blackhawks pick, 82nd overall) of NHL entry draft (July 8, 1995).

Season Team	League	Gms.	G	A	Pts.	PIM	Gms.	G	A	Pts.	PIM
		REGULAR SEASON					PLAYOFFS				
93-94—Welland	Jr. B	39	4	21	25	34	—	—	—	—	—
94-95—Windsor	OHL	51	4	23	27	55	10	0	2	2	4

VAN IMPE, DARREN
D, MIGHTY DUCKS

PERSONAL: Born May 18, 1973, in Saskatoon, Sask. . . . 6-0/195. . . . Shoots left. . . . Name pronounced VAN-IHMP. **TRANSACTIONS/CAREER NOTES:** Selected by New York Islanders in seventh round (seventh Islanders pick, 170th overall) of NHL entry draft (June 26, 1993). . . . Traded by Islanders to Mighty Ducks of Anaheim for ninth-round pick (LW Mike Broda) in 1995 draft (September 2, 1994). **HONORS:** Named to WHL (East) All-Star first team (1992-93 and 1993-94).

Season Team	League	Gms.	G	A	Pts.	PIM	Gms.	G	A	Pts.	PIM
		REGULAR SEASON					PLAYOFFS				
92-93—Red Deer	WHL	54	23	47	70	118	4	2	5	7	16
93-94—Red Deer	WHL	58	20	64	84	125	4	2	4	6	6
94-95—San Diego	IHL	76	6	17	23	74	5	0	0	0	0
—Anaheim	NHL	1	0	1	1	4	—	—	—	—	—
NHL totals		1	0	1	1	4					

VANBIESBROUCK, JOHN
G, PANTHERS

PERSONAL: Born September 4, 1963, in Detroit. . . . 5-8/176. . . . Catches left. . . . Name pronounced van-BEES-bruk. **TRANSACTIONS/CAREER NOTES:** Selected by New York Rangers in fourth round (fifth Rangers pick, 72nd overall) of NHL entry draft (June 10, 1981). . . . Fractured jaw (October 1987). . . . Severely lacerated wrist (June 1988). . . . Underwent knee surgery (May 11, 1990). . . . Suffered lower back spasms (February 25, 1992); missed 11 games. . . . Pulled groin (November 2, 1992); missed four games. . . . Traded by Rangers to Vancouver Canucks for future considerations (June 20, 1993); Canucks sent D Doug Lidster to Rangers to complete deal (June 25, 1993). . . . Selected by Florida Panthers in NHL expansion draft (June 24, 1993). . . . Lacerated hand (February 1, 1994); missed seven games. **HONORS:** Won F.W. (Dinty) Moore Trophy (1980-81). . . . Shared Dave Pinkney Trophy with Marc D'Amour (1981-82). . . . Named to OHL All-Star second team (1982-83). . . . Shared Tommy Ivan Trophy with D Bruce Affleck (1983-84). . . . Shared Terry Sawchuk Trophy with Ron Scott (1983-84). . . . Named to CHL All-Star first team (1983-84). . . . Won Vezina Trophy (1985-86). . . . Named to THE SPORTING NEWS All-Star first team (1985-86 and 1993-94). . . . Named to NHL All-Star first team (1985-86). . . . Played in NHL All-Star Game (1994). . . . Named to NHL All-Star second team (1993-94).

V

Season Team	League	REGULAR SEASON								PLAYOFFS						
		Gms.	Min.	W	L	T	GA	SO	Avg.	Gms.	Min.	W	L	GA	SO	Avg.
80-81—Sault Ste. Marie	OMJHL	56	2941	31	16	1	203	0	4.14	11	457	3	3	24	1	3.15
81-82—Sault Ste. Marie	OHL	31	1686	12	12	2	102	0	3.63	7	276	1	4	20	0	4.35
—New York Rangers	NHL	1	60	1	0	0	1	0	1.00	—	—	—	—	—	—	—
82-83—Sault Ste. Marie	OHL	*62	3471	39	21	1	209	0	3.61	16	944	7	6	56	†1	3.56
83-84—New York Rangers	NHL	3	180	2	1	0	10	0	3.33	1	1	0	0	0	0	0.00
—Tulsa	CHL	37	2153	20	13	2	124	*3	3.46	4	240	4	0	10	0	*2.50
84-85—New York Rangers	NHL	42	2358	12	24	3	166	1	4.22	1	20	0	0	0	0	0.00
85-86—New York Rangers	NHL	61	3326	31	21	5	184	3	3.32	16	899	8	8	49	†1	3.27
86-87—New York Rangers	NHL	50	2656	18	20	5	161	0	3.64	4	195	1	3	11	1	3.38
87-88—New York Rangers	NHL	56	3319	27	22	7	187	2	3.38	—	—	—	—	—	—	—
88-89—New York Rangers	NHL	56	3207	28	21	4	197	0	3.69	2	107	0	1	6	0	3.36
89-90—New York Rangers	NHL	47	2734	19	19	7	154	1	3.38	6	298	2	3	15	0	3.02
90-91—New York Rangers	NHL	40	2257	15	18	6	126	3	3.35	1	52	0	0	1	0	1.15
91-92—New York Rangers	NHL	45	2526	27	13	3	120	2	2.85	7	368	2	5	23	0	3.75
92-93—New York Rangers	NHL	48	2757	20	18	7	152	4	3.31	—	—	—	—	—	—	—
93-94—Florida	NHL	57	3440	21	25	11	145	1	2.53	—	—	—	—	—	—	—
94-95—Florida	NHL	37	2087	14	15	4	86	4	2.47	—	—	—	—	—	—	—
NHL totals...........		543	30907	235	217	62	1689	21	3.28	38	1940	13	20	105	2	3.25

VARADA, VACLAV
LW, SHARKS

PERSONAL: Born April 26, 1976, in Valasske Mezirici, Czechoslovakia.... 6-0/198....
Shoots left.
TRANSACTIONS/CAREER NOTES: Selected by San Jose Sharks in fourth round (fourth Sharks pick, 89th overall) of NHL entry draft (June 29, 1994).

Season Team	League	REGULAR SEASON					PLAYOFFS				
		Gms.	G	A	Pts.	PIM	Gms.	G	A	Pts.	PIM
92-93—TJ Vitkovice	Czech.	1	0	0	0	...	—	—	—	—	—
93-94—HC Vitkovice....................	Czech Rep.	24	6	7	13	...	5	1	1	2	...
94-95—Tacoma	WHL	68	50	38	88	108	4	4	3	7	11

VARGA, JOHN
LW

PERSONAL: Born January 31, 1974, in Chicago.... 5-10/170.... Shoots left.
HIGH SCHOOL: Clover Park (Tacoma, Wash.).
TRANSACTIONS/CAREER NOTES: Selected by Washington Capitals in fifth round (fifth Capitals pick, 119th overall) of NHL entry draft (June 20, 1992).
HONORS: Named to WHL (West) All-Star second team (1993-94).

Season Team	League	REGULAR SEASON					PLAYOFFS				
		Gms.	G	A	Pts.	PIM	Gms.	G	A	Pts.	PIM
91-92—Tacoma	WHL	72	25	34	59	93	4	1	2	3	0
92-93—Tacoma	WHL	61	32	32	64	63	7	1	1	2	8
93-94—Tacoma	WHL	65	60	62	122	122	8	2	8	10	14
94-95—Tacoma	WHL	56	37	51	88	109	3	0	0	0	7
—Portland	AHL	2	0	1	1	0	—	—	—	—	—
—Milwaukee....................	IHL	1	0	0	0	0	—	—	—	—	—

VARIS, PETRI
LW, SHARKS

PERSONAL: Born May 13, 1969, in Varkaus, Finland.... 6-1/200.... Shoots left.... Name pronounced PEHT-ree VAHR-ihz.
TRANSACTIONS/CAREER NOTES: Selected by San Jose Sharks in sixth round (seventh Sharks pick, 132nd overall) of NHL entry draft (June 26, 1993).
HONORS: Named Finnish League Rookie of the Year (1991-92).
MISCELLANEOUS: Member of bronze-medal-winning Finnish Olympic team (1994).

Season Team	League	REGULAR SEASON					PLAYOFFS				
		Gms.	G	A	Pts.	PIM	Gms.	G	A	Pts.	PIM
90-91—KooKoo Kouvola..............	Finland Dv.II	44	20	31	51	42	—	—	—	—	—
91-92—Assat Pori	Finland	36	13	23	36	24	—	—	—	—	—
92-93—Assat Pori	Finland	46	14	35	49	42	8	2	2	4	12
93-94—Jokerit Helsinki	Finland	31	14	15	29	16	11	3	4	7	6
—Finnish Olympic Team......	Int'l	5	1	1	2	2	—	—	—	—	—
94-95—Jokerit Helsinki	Finland	47	21	20	41	53	11	7	2	9	10

VARVIO, JARKKO
LW, STARS

PERSONAL: Born April 28, 1972, in Tampere, Finland.... 5-9/172.... Shoots right.... Name pronounced VAHR-vee-oh.
TRANSACTIONS/CAREER NOTES: Selected by Minnesota North Stars in second round (first North Stars pick, 34th overall) of NHL entry draft (June 20, 1992).... North Stars franchise moved from Minnesota to Dallas and renamed Stars for 1993-94 season.... Played in Europe during 1994-95 NHL lockout.

Season Team	League	REGULAR SEASON					PLAYOFFS				
		Gms.	G	A	Pts.	PIM	Gms.	G	A	Pts.	PIM
89-90—Ilves Tampere	Finland	1	0	0	0	0	—	—	—	—	—
90-91—Ilves Tampere	Finland	37	10	7	17	6	—	—	—	—	—
91-92—HPK Hameenlinna	Finland	41	25	9	34	6	—	—	—	—	—
92-93—HPK Hameenlinna	Finland	40	29	19	48	16	12	3	2	5	8

Season Team	League	REGULAR SEASON Gms.	G	A	Pts.	PIM	PLAYOFFS Gms.	G	A	Pts.	PIM
93-94—Dallas	NHL	8	2	3	5	4	—	—	—	—	—
—Kalamazoo	IHL	58	29	16	45	18	1	0	0	0	0
94-95—HPK Hameenlinna	Finland	19	7	8	15	4	—	—	—	—	—
—Dallas	NHL	5	1	1	2	0	—	—	—	—	—
—Kalamazoo	IHL	7	0	0	0	2	—	—	—	—	—
NHL totals		13	3	4	7	4					

VASILEVSKII, ALEX
RW, BLUES

PERSONAL: Born January 8, 1975, in Kiev, U.S.S.R. . . . 5-11/190. . . . Shoots left. . . . Name pronounced vaz-ih-LAHF-skee.
TRANSACTIONS/CAREER NOTES: Selected by St. Louis Blues in 11th round (ninth Blues pick, 271st overall) of NHL entry draft (June 26, 1993).

Season Team	League	REGULAR SEASON Gms.	G	A	Pts.	PIM	PLAYOFFS Gms.	G	A	Pts.	PIM
92-93—Victoria	WHL	71	27	25	52	52	—	—	—	—	—
93-94—Victoria	WHL	69	34	51	85	78	—	—	—	—	—
94-95—Prince George	WHL	48	32	34	66	52	—	—	—	—	—
—Brandon	WHL	23	6	11	17	39	18	3	6	9	34

VASILIEV, ANDREI
LW

PERSONAL: Born March 30, 1972, in Voskresensk, U.S.S.R. . . . 5-9/180. . . . Shoots right.
TRANSACTIONS/CAREER NOTES: Selected by New York Islanders in 11th round (11th Islanders pick, 248th overall) of NHL entry draft (June 26, 1993). . . . Selected by Orlando Solar Bears in IHL expansion draft (July 13, 1995).

Season Team	League	REGULAR SEASON Gms.	G	A	Pts.	PIM	PLAYOFFS Gms.	G	A	Pts.	PIM
91-92—CSKA Moscow	CIS	28	7	2	9	2	—	—	—	—	—
92-93—Khimik	CIS	34	4	8	12	20	—	—	—	—	—
93-94—CSKA Moscow	CIS	46	17	6	23	8	3	1	0	1	0
94-95—Denver	IHL	74	28	37	65	48	13	9	4	13	22
—New York Islanders	NHL	2	0	0	0	2	—	—	—	—	—
NHL totals		2	0	0	0	2					

VASILJEV, ALEXEI
D, RANGERS

PERSONAL: Born September 1, 1977, in Yaroslavl, U.S.S.R. . . . 6-0/185. . . . Shoots left.
TRANSACTIONS/CAREER NOTES: Selected by New York Rangers in fifth round (fourth Rangers pick, 110th overall) of NHL entry draft (July 8, 1995).

Season Team	League	REGULAR SEASON Gms.	G	A	Pts.	PIM	PLAYOFFS Gms.	G	A	Pts.	PIM
94-95—Torpedo-2 Yaroslavl	CIS Div. II			Statistics unavailable.							

VASKE, DENNIS
D, ISLANDERS

PERSONAL: Born October 11, 1967, in Rockford, Ill. . . . 6-2/210. . . . Shoots left. . . . Full name: Dennis James Vaske. . . . Name pronounced VAS-kee.
HIGH SCHOOL: Armstrong (Plymouth, Minn.).
COLLEGE: Minnesota-Duluth.
TRANSACTIONS/CAREER NOTES: Selected by New York Islanders in second round (second Islanders pick, 38th overall) of NHL entry draft (June 21, 1986). . . . Lacerated forehead (April 8, 1993); missed three games. . . . Broke foot (December 19, 1993); missed 13 games. . . . Broke ankle (April 18, 1995); missed last seven games of season.

Season Team	League	REGULAR SEASON Gms.	G	A	Pts.	PIM	PLAYOFFS Gms.	G	A	Pts.	PIM
84-85—Armstrong H.S.	Minn. H.S.	22	5	18	23	. . .	—	—	—	—	—
85-86—Armstrong H.S.	Minn. H.S.	20	9	13	22	. . .	—	—	—	—	—
86-87—Minnesota-Duluth	WCHA	33	0	2	2	40	—	—	—	—	—
87-88—Minnesota-Duluth	WCHA	39	1	6	7	90	—	—	—	—	—
88-89—Minnesota-Duluth	WCHA	37	9	19	28	86	—	—	—	—	—
89-90—Minnesota-Duluth	WCHA	37	5	24	29	72	—	—	—	—	—
90-91—New York Islanders	NHL	5	0	0	0	2	—	—	—	—	—
—Capital District	AHL	67	10	10	20	65	—	—	—	—	—
91-92—Capital District	AHL	31	1	11	12	59	—	—	—	—	—
—New York Islanders	NHL	39	0	1	1	39	—	—	—	—	—
92-93—Capital District	AHL	42	4	15	19	70	—	—	—	—	—
—New York Islanders	NHL	27	1	5	6	32	18	0	6	6	14
93-94—New York Islanders	NHL	65	2	11	13	76	4	0	1	1	2
94-95—New York Islanders	NHL	41	1	11	12	53	—	—	—	—	—
NHL totals		177	4	28	32	202	22	0	7	7	16

VEISOR, MIKE
G, BLUES

PERSONAL: Born December 7, 1972, in Dallas. . . . 6-2/195. . . . Catches right.
COLLEGE: Northeastern.
TRANSACTIONS/CAREER NOTES: Selected by St. Louis Blues in 12th round (12th Blues pick, 263rd overall) of NHL entry draft (June 22, 1991).

Season Team	League	REGULAR SEASON							PLAYOFFS						
		Gms.	Min.	W	L	T	GA	SO	Avg.	Gms.	Min.	W	L	GA	SO	Avg.
91-92—Springfield Jr. B	NEJHL	46	2226	...	...	...	153	...	4.12	—	—	—	—	—	—	—
92-93—Northeastern Univ.	Hoc. East	30	1699	8	19	1	151	0	5.33	—	—	—	—	—	—	—
93-94—Northeastern Univ.	Hoc. East	15	775	7	3	2	55	0	4.26	—	—	—	—	—	—	—
94-95—Northeastern Univ.	Hoc. East	24	1290	12	5	3	73	0	3.40	—	—	—	—	—	—	—

VERBEEK, PAT
RW, RANGERS

PERSONAL: Born May 24, 1964, in Sarnia, Ont.... 5-9/190.... Shoots right.
TRANSACTIONS/CAREER NOTES: Selected by New Jersey Devils as underage junior in third round (third Devils pick, 43rd overall) of NHL entry draft (June 9, 1982).... Suffered severed left thumb between knuckles in a corn-planting machine on his farm and underwent surgery to have thumb reconnected (May 15, 1985).... Pulled side muscle (March 1987).... Bruised chest (October 28, 1988).... Traded by Devils to Hartford Whalers for LW Sylvain Turgeon (June 17, 1989).... Missed first three games of 1991-92 season due to contract dispute.... Fined $500 by Whalers for involvement in bar brawl (April 1, 1994).... Traded by Whalers to New York Rangers for D Glen Featherstone, D Michael Stewart, first-round pick in 1995 draft (G Jean-Sebastien Giguere) and fourth-round pick in 1996 draft (March 23, 1995).
HONORS: Won Emms Family Award (1981-82).... Played in NHL All-Star Game (1991).
STATISTICAL PLATEAUS: Three-goal games: 1985-86 (1), 1986-87 (1), 1987-88 (1), 1988-89 (1), 1992-93 (2), 1993-94 (2). Total: 8.... Four-goal games: 1987-88 (1).... Total hat tricks: 9.
STATISTICAL NOTES: Only NHL player ever to lead his team in goals scored and penalty minutes (1989-90 and 1990-91).... Captain of Hartford Whalers (1992-93 through 1993-94).

Season Team	League	REGULAR SEASON					PLAYOFFS				
		Gms.	G	A	Pts.	PIM	Gms.	G	A	Pts.	PIM
80-81—Petrolia Jr. B.	OPJHL	42	44	44	88	155	—	—	—	—	—
81-82—Sudbury...........................	OHL	66	37	51	88	180	—	—	—	—	—
82-83—Sudbury...........................	OHL	61	40	67	107	184	—	—	—	—	—
—New Jersey..................	NHL	6	3	2	5	8	—	—	—	—	—
83-84—New Jersey..................	NHL	79	20	27	47	158	—	—	—	—	—
84-85—New Jersey..................	NHL	78	15	18	33	162	—	—	—	—	—
85-86—New Jersey..................	NHL	76	25	28	53	79	—	—	—	—	—
86-87—New Jersey..................	NHL	74	35	24	59	120	—	—	—	—	—
87-88—New Jersey..................	NHL	73	46	31	77	227	20	4	8	12	51
88-89—New Jersey..................	NHL	77	26	21	47	189	—	—	—	—	—
89-90—Hartford........................	NHL	80	44	45	89	228	7	2	2	4	26
90-91—Hartford........................	NHL	80	43	39	82	246	6	3	2	5	40
91-92—Hartford........................	NHL	76	22	35	57	243	7	0	2	2	12
92-93—Hartford........................	NHL	84	39	43	82	197	—	—	—	—	—
93-94—Hartford........................	NHL	84	37	38	75	177	—	—	—	—	—
94-95—Hartford........................	NHL	29	7	11	18	53	—	—	—	—	—
—New York Rangers	NHL	19	10	5	15	18	10	4	6	10	20
NHL totals............		915	372	367	739	2105	50	13	20	33	149

VERCIK, RUDOLF
LW, RANGERS

PERSONAL: Born March 19, 1976, in Bratislava, Czechoslovakia.... 6-1/189.... Shoots left.
TRANSACTIONS/CAREER NOTES: Selected by New York Rangers in second round (second Rangers pick, 52nd overall) of NHL entry draft (June 28, 1994).

Season Team	League	REGULAR SEASON					PLAYOFFS				
		Gms.	G	A	Pts.	PIM	Gms.	G	A	Pts.	PIM
93-94—Slovan Bratislava	Slovakia	17	1	4	5	14	—	—	—	—	—
94-95—Slovan Bratislava	Slovakia	33	14	9	23	22	—	—	—	—	—

VERNON, MIKE
G, RED WINGS

PERSONAL: Born February 24, 1963, in Calgary.... 5-9/165.... Catches left.
TRANSACTIONS/CAREER NOTES: Selected by Calgary Flames in third round (second Flames pick, 56th overall) of NHL entry draft (June 10, 1981).... Injured hip (March 2, 1988).... Suffered back spasms (February 1989).... Suffered back spasms (March 1990); missed 10 games. ... Suffered lacerated forehead (October 25, 1992); missed five games.... Suffered from the flu (November 15, 1993); missed two games.... Twisted knee (December 30, 1993); missed 14 games.... Traded by Flames to Detroit Red Wings for D Steve Chiasson (June 29, 1994).
HONORS: Won WHL Most Valuable Player Trophy (1981-82 and 1982-83).... Won WHL Top Goaltender Trophy (1981-82 and 1982-83).... Won WHL Player of the Year Award (1981-82).... Named to WHL All-Star first team (1981-82 and 1982-83). ... Named to CHL All-Star second team (1983-84).... Named to THE SPORTING NEWS All-Star second team (1988-89).... Named to NHL All-Star second team (1988-89).... Played in NHL All-Star Game (1988-1991 and 1993).
RECORDS: Shares NHL single-season playoff record for most wins by a goaltender—16 (1989).
MISCELLANEOUS: Member of Stanley Cup championship team (1989).

Season Team	League	REGULAR SEASON							PLAYOFFS						
		Gms.	Min.	W	L	T	GA	SO	Avg.	Gms.	Min.	W	L	GA	SO	Avg.
80-81—Calgary........................	WHL	59	3154	33	17	1	198	1	3.77	22	1271	...	...	82	1	3.87
81-82—Calgary........................	WHL	42	2329	22	14	2	143	*3	*3.68	9	527	...	...	30	0	*3.42
—Oklahoma City	CHL	—	—	—	—	—	—	—	—	1	70	0	1	4	0	3.43
82-83—Calgary........................	WHL	50	2856	19	18	2	155	*3	*3.26	16	925	9	7	60	0	3.89
—Calgary........................	NHL	2	100	0	2	0	11	0	6.60	—	—	—	—	—	—	—
83-84—Calgary........................	NHL	1	11	0	1	0	4	0	21.82	—	—	—	—	—	—	—
—Colorado....................	CHL	`46	*2648	30	13	2	148	1	*3.35	6	347	2	4	21	0	3.63

Season Team	League	REGULAR SEASON								PLAYOFFS					
		Gms.	Min.	W	L	T	GA	SO	Avg.	Gms.	Min.	W	L	GA	SO	Avg.
84-85—Moncton	AHL	41	2050	10	20	4	134	0	3.92	—	—	—	—	—	—	—
85-86—Salt Lake City	IHL	10	601	. . .	. . .	. . .	34	1	3.39	—	—	—	—	—	—	—
—Moncton	AHL	6	374	3	1	2	21	0	3.37	—	—	—	—	—	—	—
—Calgary	NHL	18	921	9	3	3	52	1	3.39	*21	*1229	12	*9	*60	0	2.93
86-87—Calgary	NHL	54	2957	30	21	1	178	1	3.61	5	263	2	3	16	0	3.65
87-88—Calgary	NHL	64	3565	39	16	7	210	1	3.53	9	515	4	4	34	0	3.96
88-89—Calgary	NHL	52	2938	*37	6	5	130	0	2.65	*22	*1381	*16	5	*52	*3	2.26
89-90—Calgary	NHL	47	2795	23	14	9	146	0	3.13	6	342	2	3	19	0	3.33
90-91—Calgary	NHL	54	3121	31	19	3	172	1	3.31	7	427	3	4	21	0	2.95
91-92—Calgary	NHL	63	3640	24	30	9	217	0	3.58	—	—	—	—	—	—	—
92-93—Calgary	NHL	64	3732	29	26	4	203	2	3.26	4	150	1	1	15	0	6.00
93-94—Calgary	NHL	48	2798	26	17	5	131	3	2.81	7	466	3	4	23	0	2.96
94-95—Detroit	NHL	30	1807	19	6	4	76	1	2.52	18	1063	12	6	41	1	2.31
NHL totals		497	28385	267	161	55	1530	10	3.23	99	5836	55	39	281	4	2.89

VIAL, DENNIS
D, SENATORS

PERSONAL: Born April 10, 1969, in Sault Ste. Marie, Ont. . . . 6-1/222. . . . Shoots left. . . . Name pronounced vee-AL.

TRANSACTIONS/CAREER NOTES: Suspended three games by OHL for spearing (October 1986). . . . Selected by New York Rangers in sixth round (fifth Rangers pick, 110th overall) of NHL entry draft (June 11, 1988). . . . Suspended indefinitely by OHL for leaving the bench to fight (March 23, 1989). . . . Traded by Rangers with C Kevin Miller and RW Jim Cummins to Detroit Red Wings for RW Joe Kocur and D Per Djoos (March 5, 1991). . . . Injured right knee and ankle (December 7, 1991); missed two games. . . . Traded by Red Wings with D Doug Crossman to Quebec Nordiques for cash (June 15, 1992). . . . Traded by Nordiques to Red Wings for cash (September 9, 1992). . . . Separated right shoulder (January 19, 1993); missed 15 games. . . . Traded by Red Wings to Tampa Bay Lightning for LW Steve Maltais (June 8, 1993). . . . Selected by Mighty Ducks of Anaheim in NHL expansion draft (June 24, 1993). . . . Selected by Ottawa Senators in Phase II of NHL expansion draft (June 25, 1993). . . . Injured left foot (November 10, 1993); missed 12 games. . . . Fractured left hand (December 21, 1993); missed 13 games. . . . Suspended one game and fined $500 by NHL for shooting a puck into opposing team's bench (March 23, 1994). . . . Suffered ankle contusion (March 27, 1995); missed one game.

Season Team	League	REGULAR SEASON					PLAYOFFS				
		Gms.	G	A	Pts.	PIM	Gms.	G	A	Pts.	PIM
85-86—Hamilton	OHL	31	1	1	2	66	—	—	—	—	—
86-87—Hamilton	OHL	53	1	8	9	194	8	0	0	0	8
87-88—Hamilton	OHL	52	3	17	20	229	13	2	2	4	49
88-89—Niagara Falls	OHL	50	10	27	37	227	15	1	7	8	44
89-90—Flint	IHL	79	6	29	35	351	4	0	0	0	10
90-91—Binghamton	AHL	40	2	7	9	250	—	—	—	—	—
—New York Rangers	NHL	21	0	0	0	61	—	—	—	—	—
—Detroit	NHL	9	0	0	0	16	—	—	—	—	—
91-92—Detroit	NHL	27	1	0	1	72	—	—	—	—	—
—Adirondack	AHL	20	2	4	6	107	17	1	3	4	43
92-93—Detroit	NHL	9	0	1	1	20	—	—	—	—	—
—Adirondack	AHL	30	2	11	13	177	11	1	1	2	14
93-94—Ottawa	NHL	55	2	5	7	214	—	—	—	—	—
94-95—Ottawa	NHL	27	0	4	4	65	—	—	—	—	—
NHL totals		148	3	10	13	448					

VIITAKOSKI, VESA
LW, FLAMES

PERSONAL: Born February 13, 1971, in Lappeenranta, Finland. . . . 6-3/210. . . . Shoots left. . . . Name pronounced VEH-suh vee-tuh-KAH-skee.

TRANSACTIONS/CAREER NOTES: Selected by Calgary Flames in second round (third Flames pick, 32nd overall) of NHL entry draft (June 16, 1990). . . . Sprained knee (April 13, 1994); missed one game. . . . Lacerated lip (March 22, 1995); missed one game.

Season Team	League	REGULAR SEASON					PLAYOFFS				
		Gms.	G	A	Pts.	PIM	Gms.	G	A	Pts.	PIM
89-90—SaiPa	Finland	44	24	10	34	. . .	—	—	—	—	—
90-91—Tappara	Finland	41	17	23	40	14	—	—	—	—	—
91-92—Tappara	Finland	44	19	19	38	39	—	—	—	—	—
92-93—Tappara	Finland	48	27	27	54	28	—	—	—	—	—
93-94—Calgary	NHL	8	1	2	3	0	—	—	—	—	—
—Saint John	AHL	67	28	39	67	24	5	1	2	3	2
94-95—Saint John	AHL	56	17	26	43	8	4	0	1	1	2
—Calgary	NHL	10	1	2	3	6	—	—	—	—	—
NHL totals		18	2	4	6	6					

VINCENT, PAUL
C, MAPLE LEAFS

PERSONAL: Born January 4, 1975, in Utica, N.Y. . . . 6-4/200. . . . Shoots left.
HIGH SCHOOL: Cushing Academy (Ashburnham, Mass.).
TRANSACTIONS/CAREER NOTES: Selected by Toronto Maple Leafs in sixth round (fourth Maple Leafs pick, 149th overall) of NHL entry draft (June 26, 1993).

Season Team	League	REGULAR SEASON					PLAYOFFS				
		Gms.	G	A	Pts.	PIM	Gms.	G	A	Pts.	PIM
90-91—Cushing Academy	Mass. H.S.	30	4	2	6	8	—	—	—	—	—
91-92—Cushing Academy	Mass. H.S.	30	22	41	63	16	—	—	—	—	—

Season Team	League	Gms.	G	A	Pts.	PIM	Gms.	G	A	Pts.	PIM
92-93—Cushing Academy...........	Mass. H.S.	25	30	32	62	62	—	—	—	—	—
93-94—Seattle	WHL	66	27	26	53	57	8	1	3	4	8
94-95—Seattle	WHL	3	0	2	2	2	—	—	—	—	—
—Swift Current..................	WHL	62	59	39	98	85	6	3	2	5	17
—St. John's	AHL	2	0	2	2	0	—	—	—	—	—

VISHEAU, MARK
D, JETS

PERSONAL: Born June 27, 1973, in Burlington, Ont. . . . 6-4/200. . . . Shoots right. . . . Full name: Mark Andrew Visheau. . . . Name pronounced VEE-SHOO.
HIGH SCHOOL: Saunders Secondary School (London, Ont.).
TRANSACTIONS/CAREER NOTES: Selected by Winnipeg Jets in fourth round (fourth Jets pick, 84th overall) of NHL entry draft (June 20, 1992).

Season Team	League	Gms.	G	A	Pts.	PIM	Gms.	G	A	Pts.	PIM
89-90—Burlington Jr. B................	OHA	42	11	22	33	53	—	—	—	—	—
90-91—London	OHL	59	4	11	15	40	7	0	1	1	6
91-92—London	OHL	66	5	31	36	104	10	0	4	4	27
92-93—London	OHL	62	8	52	60	88	12	0	5	5	26
93-94—Moncton	AHL	48	4	5	9	58	—	—	—	—	—
—Winnipeg	NHL	1	0	0	0	0	—	—	—	—	—
94-95—Springfield.......................	AHL	35	0	4	4	94	—	—	—	—	—
NHL totals................................		**1**	**0**	**0**	**0**	**0**					

VOLKOV, MIKHAIL
RW, SABRES

PERSONAL: Born March 9, 1972, in Voronezh, U.S.S.R. . . . 5-10/174. . . . Shoots left. . . . Name pronounced mee-KIGHL VOHL-kahf.
TRANSACTIONS/CAREER NOTES: Selected by the Buffalo Sabres in 11th round (12th Sabres pick, 233rd overall) of NHL entry draft (June 22, 1991).

Season Team	League	Gms.	G	A	Pts.	PIM	Gms.	G	A	Pts.	PIM
89-90—Soviet Wings	USSR	24	0	2	2	4	—	—	—	—	—
90-91—Soviet Wings	USSR	40	8	4	12	8	—	—	—	—	—
91-92—Soviet Wings	CIS	37	3	6	9	16	—	—	—	—	—
92-93—Soviet Wings	CIS	33	9	6	15	11	5	0	1	1	2
93-94—Rochester	AHL	62	12	26	38	28	4	0	2	2	2
94-95—Rochester	AHL	56	17	27	44	52	4	1	0	1	2

VON STEFENELLI, PHIL
D, BRUINS

PERSONAL: Born April 10, 1969, in Vancouver. . . . 6-1/183. . . . Shoots left. . . . Name pronounced VAHN-STEH-fuh-NEHL-ee.
COLLEGE: Boston University.
TRANSACTIONS/CAREER NOTES: Selected by Vancouver Canucks in sixth round (fifth Canucks pick, 122nd overall) of NHL entry draft (June 11, 1988). . . . Signed as free agent by Boston Bruins (July 6, 1993).

Season Team	League	Gms.	G	A	Pts.	PIM	Gms.	G	A	Pts.	PIM
85-86—Richmond	BCJHL	41	6	11	17	28	12	1	1	2	14
86-87—Richmond	BCJHL	52	5	32	37	51	—	—	—	—	—
87-88—Boston University	Hockey East	34	3	13	16	38	—	—	—	—	—
88-89—Boston University	Hockey East	33	2	6	8	34	—	—	—	—	—
89-90—Boston University	Hockey East	44	8	20	28	40	—	—	—	—	—
90-91—Boston University	Hockey East	41	7	23	30	32	—	—	—	—	—
91-92—Milwaukee	IHL	80	2	34	36	40	5	1	2	3	2
92-93—Hamilton	AHL	78	11	20	31	75	—	—	—	—	—
93-94—Hamilton	AHL	80	10	31	41	89	4	1	0	1	2
94-95—Providence	AHL	75	6	13	19	93	13	2	4	6	6

VOPAT, JAN
D, KINGS

PERSONAL: Born March 22, 1973, in Most, Czechoslovakia. . . . 6-0/198. . . . Shoots left. . . . Name pronounced YAHN VOH-paht.
TRANSACTIONS/CAREER NOTES: Selected by Hartford Whalers in third round (third Whalers pick, 57th overall) of NHL entry draft (June 20, 1992). . . . Traded by Whalers to Los Angeles Kings for fourth-round pick (C Ian MacNeil) in 1995 draft (May 31, 1995).

Season Team	League	Gms.	G	A	Pts.	PIM	Gms.	G	A	Pts.	PIM
90-91—CHZ Litvinov	Czech.	25	1	4	5	4	—	—	—	—	—
91-92—Chemopetrol Litvinov	Czech.	46	4	2	6	6	—	—	—	—	—
92-93—Chemopetrol Litvinov	Czech.	45	12	10	22	...	—	—	—	—	—
93-94—Chemopetrol Litvinov	Czech Rep.	41	9	19	28	...	4	1	1	2	...
—Czech Republic Olympic ...	Int'l	8	0	1	1	8	—	—	—	—	—
94-95—Chemopetrol Litvinov	Czech Rep.	42	7	18	25	...	4	0	2	2	...

VOPAT, ROMAN
C, BLUES

PERSONAL: Born April 21, 1976, in Litvinov, Czechoslovakia.... 6-3/216.... Shoots left.... Name pronounced VOH-paht.
TRANSACTIONS/CAREER NOTES: Selected by St. Louis Blues in seventh round (fourth Blues pick, 172nd overall) of NHL entry draft (June 29, 1994).

			REGULAR SEASON					PLAYOFFS			
Season	Team	League	Gms.	G	A	Pts.	PIM	Gms.	G	A	Pts.	PIM
93-94—Chemopetrol Litvinov		Czech Rep.	7	0	0	0	...	—	—	—	—	—
94-95—Moose Jaw		WHL	72	23	20	43	141	10	4	1	5	28
—Peoria		IHL	—	—	—	—	—	6	0	2	2	2

VUJTEK, VLADIMIR
C, OILERS

PERSONAL: Born February 17, 1972, in Ostrava, Severomoravsky, Czechoslovakia. ... 6-1/190.... Shoots left.... Name pronounced VWEE-tehk.
TRANSACTIONS/CAREER NOTES: Selected by Montreal Canadiens in fourth round (fifth Canadiens pick, 73rd overall) of NHL entry draft (June 22, 1991).... Traded by Canadiens with LW Shayne Corson and C Brent Gilchrist to Edmonton Oilers for LW Vincent Damphousse and fourth-round pick (D Adam Wiesel) in 1993 draft (August 27, 1992).... Suffered charley horse (October 6, 1992); missed eight games.... Suspended by Oilers after failing to report to assigned team (January 4, 1993).... Strained lower back (March 17, 1993); missed five games.... Injured shoulder (January 11, 1994); missed seven games.... Injured shoulder and underwent surgery (February 14, 1994); missed remainder of season.... Played in Europe during 1994-95 NHL lockout.
HONORS: Named to WHL (West) All-Star first team (1991-92).

			REGULAR SEASON					PLAYOFFS			
Season	Team	League	Gms.	G	A	Pts.	PIM	Gms.	G	A	Pts.	PIM
89-90—Vitkovice		Czech.	29	3	4	7	...	—	—	—	—	—
90-91—Tri-City		WHL	37	26	18	44	25	—	—	—	—	—
—Vitkovice		Czech.	26	7	4	11	...	—	—	—	—	—
91-92—Tri-City		WHL	53	41	61	102	114	—	—	—	—	—
—Montreal		NHL	2	0	0	0	0	—	—	—	—	—
92-93—Edmonton		NHL	30	1	10	11	8	—	—	—	—	—
—Cape Breton		AHL	20	10	9	19	14	1	0	0	0	0
93-94—Edmonton		NHL	40	4	15	19	14	—	—	—	—	—
94-95—HC Vitkovice		Czech Rep.	18	5	7	12	51	—	—	—	—	—
—Cape Breton		AHL	30	10	11	21	30	—	—	—	—	—
—Las Vegas		IHL	1	0	0	0	0	—	—	—	—	—
NHL totals			72	5	25	30	22					

VUKOTA, MICK
RW, ISLANDERS

PERSONAL: Born September 14, 1966, in Saskatoon, Sask.... 6-2/215.... Shoots right.... Name pronounced vuh-KOH-tuh.
TRANSACTIONS/CAREER NOTES: Signed as free agent by New York Islanders (September 1987). ... Suspended six games by AHL for returning from locker room to fight (November 20, 1987).... Suffered sore back (February 1990).... Separated left shoulder (March 18, 1990).... Suspended 10 games by NHL for fighting (April 5, 1990); missed final four games of 1989-90 season and first six games of 1990-91 season.... Injured shoulder prior to 1992-93 season; missed first two games of season.... Bruised left hand (October 26, 1993); missed two games.... Suspended 10 games and fined $10,000 by NHL for leaving bench to fight (January 7, 1994).... Suspended two games without pay and fined $500 by NHL for improper conduct in playoff game (May 17, 1994).
STATISTICAL PLATEAUS: Three-goal games: 1989-90 (1).

			REGULAR SEASON					PLAYOFFS			
Season	Team	League	Gms.	G	A	Pts.	PIM	Gms.	G	A	Pts.	PIM
83-84—Winnipeg		WHL	3	1	1	2	10	—	—	—	—	—
84-85—Kelowna Wings		WHL	66	10	6	16	247	—	—	—	—	—
85-86—Spokane		WHL	64	19	14	33	369	9	6	4	10	68
86-87—Spokane		WHL	61	25	28	53	*337	4	0	0	0	40
87-88—New York Islanders		NHL	17	1	0	1	82	2	0	0	0	23
—Springfield		AHL	52	7	9	16	372	—	—	—	—	—
88-89—Springfield		AHL	3	1	0	1	33	—	—	—	—	—
—New York Islanders		NHL	48	2	2	4	237	—	—	—	—	—
89-90—New York Islanders		NHL	76	4	8	12	290	1	0	0	0	17
90-91—Capital District		AHL	2	0	0	0	9	—	—	—	—	—
—New York Islanders		NHL	60	2	4	6	238	—	—	—	—	—
91-92—New York Islanders		NHL	74	0	6	6	293	—	—	—	—	—
92-93—New York Islanders		NHL	74	2	5	7	216	15	0	0	0	16
93-94—New York Islanders		NHL	72	3	1	4	237	4	0	0	0	17
94-95—New York Islanders		NHL	40	0	2	2	109	—	—	—	—	—
NHL totals			461	14	28	42	1702	22	0	0	0	73

VYBORNY, DAVID
C, OILERS

PERSONAL: Born January 22, 1975, in Jihlava, Czechoslovakia.... 5-10/174.... Shoots left.... Name pronounced vigh-BOHR-nee.
TRANSACTIONS/CAREER NOTES: Selected by Edmonton Oilers in second round (third Oilers pick, 33rd overall) of NHL entry draft (June 26, 1993).
HONORS: Named Czechoslovakian League Rookie of the Year (1991-92).

			REGULAR SEASON					PLAYOFFS			
Season	Team	League	Gms.	G	A	Pts.	PIM	Gms.	G	A	Pts.	PIM
90-91—Sparta Prague		Czech.	3	0	0	0	0	—	—	—	—	—
91-92—Sparta Prague		Czech.	32	6	9	15	2	—	—	—	—	—

Season Team	League	REGULAR SEASON Gms.	G	A	Pts.	PIM	PLAYOFFS Gms.	G	A	Pts.	PIM
92-93—Sparta Prague	Czech.	52	20	24	44	...	—	—	—	—	—
93-94—Sparta Prague	Czech Rep.	44	15	20	35	...	6	4	7	11	...
94-95—Cape Breton	AHL	76	23	38	61	30	—	—	—	—	—

VYSHEDKEVICH, SERGEI
D, DEVILS

PERSONAL: Born January 3, 1975, in Moscow, U.S.S.R. ... 6-0/185. ... Shoots left.
TRANSACTIONS/CAREER NOTES: Selected by New Jersey Devils in third round (third Devils pick, 70th overall) of NHL entry draft (July 8, 1995).

Season Team	League	REGULAR SEASON Gms.	G	A	Pts.	PIM	PLAYOFFS Gms.	G	A	Pts.	PIM
93-94—Dynamo Moscow	CIS	—	—	—	—	—	4	0	2	2	2
94-95—Dynamo Moscow	CIS	49	6	7	13	67	14	2	0	2	12

WAITE, JIMMY
G, BLACKHAWKS

PERSONAL: Born April 15, 1969, in Sherbrooke, Que. ... 6-1/180. ... Catches left. ... Name pronounced WAYT.
TRANSACTIONS/CAREER NOTES: Selected by Chicago Blackhawks as underage junior in first round (first Blackhawks pick, eighth overall) of NHL entry draft (June 13, 1987). ... Broke collarbone (December 6, 1988). ... Sprained ankle (October 12, 1991); missed one game. ... Loaned to Hershey Bears for part of 1991-92 season. ... Traded by Blackhawks to San Jose Sharks for future considerations (June 18, 1993); Sharks sent D Neil Wilkinson to Blackhawks to complete deal (July 9, 1993). ... Sprained knee (January 11, 1994); missed two games. ... Underwent arthroscopic knee surgery (March 7, 1994); missed eight games. ... Traded by Sharks to Blackhawks for fourth-round pick in 1997 draft (February 6, 1995).
HONORS: Won Raymond Lagace Trophy (1986-87). ... Named to QMJHL All-Star second team (1986-87). ... Won James Norris Memorial Trophy (1989-90). ... Named to IHL All-Star first team (1989-90).

Season Team	League	REGULAR SEASON Gms.	Min.	W	L	T	GA	SO	Avg.	PLAYOFFS Gms.	Min.	W	L	GA	SO	Avg.
86-87—Chicoutimi	QMJHL	50	2569	23	17	3	209	†2	4.88	11	576	4	6	54	*1	5.63
87-88—Chicoutimi	QMJHL	36	2000	17	16	1	150	0	4.50	4	222	1	2	17	0	4.59
88-89—Chicago	NHL	11	494	0	7	1	43	0	5.22	—	—	—	—	—	—	—
—Saginaw	IHL	5	304	3	1	‡0	10	0	1.97	—	—	—	—	—	—	—
89-90—Indianapolis	IHL	54	*3207	34	14	‡5	135	*5	*2.53	†10	*602	9	1	19	†1	*1.89
—Chicago	NHL	4	183	2	0	0	14	0	4.59	—	—	—	—	—	—	—
90-91—Indianapolis	IHL	49	2888	26	18	‡4	167	3	3.47	6	369	2	4	20	0	3.25
—Chicago	NHL	1	60	1	0	0	2	0	2.00	—	—	—	—	—	—	—
91-92—Chicago	NHL	17	877	4	7	4	54	0	3.69	—	—	—	—	—	—	—
—Indianapolis	IHL	13	702	4	7	‡1	53	0	4.53	—	—	—	—	—	—	—
—Hershey	AHL	11	631	6	4	1	44	0	4.18	6	360	2	4	19	0	3.17
92-93—Chicago	NHL	20	996	6	7	1	49	2	2.95	—	—	—	—	—	—	—
93-94—San Jose	NHL	15	697	3	7	0	50	0	4.30	2	40	0	0	3	0	4.50
94-95—Chicago	NHL	2	119	1	1	0	5	0	2.52	—	—	—	—	—	—	—
—Indianapolis	IHL	4	239	2	1	‡1	13	0	3.26	—	—	—	—	—	—	—
NHL totals		70	3426	17	29	6	217	2	3.80	2	40	0	0	3	0	4.50

WAKALUK, DARCY
G, STARS

PERSONAL: Born March 14, 1966, in Pincher Creek, Alta. ... 5-11/180. ... Catches left. ... Name pronounced WAHK-uh-LUHK.
TRANSACTIONS/CAREER NOTES: Selected by Buffalo Sabres as underage junior in seventh round (seventh Sabres pick, 144th overall) of NHL entry draft (June 9, 1984). ... Traded by Sabres to Minnesota North Stars for eighth-round pick in 1991 draft (D Jiri Kuntos) and future considerations (May 26, 1991). ... Hyperextended knee (February 17, 1993); missed two games. ... North Stars franchise moved from Minnesota to Dallas and renamed Stars for 1993-94 season. ... Broke hand (March 16, 1995); missed nine games. ... Strained back (April 14, 1995); missed three games.
HONORS: Shared Harry (Hap) Holmes Memorial Trophy with David Littman (1990-91).
MISCELLANEOUS: First goalie in AHL history to score goal (December 5, 1987, vs. Utica).

Season Team	League	REGULAR SEASON Gms.	Min.	W	L	T	GA	SO	Avg.	PLAYOFFS Gms.	Min.	W	L	GA	SO	Avg.
83-84—Kelowna Wings	WHL	31	1555	...	...	...	163	0	6.29	—	—	—	—	—	—	—
84-85—Kelowna Wings	WHL	54	3094	19	30	4	244	0	4.73	5	282	1	4	22	0	4.68
85-86—Spokane	WHL	47	2562	21	22	1	224	1	5.25	7	419	3	4	37	0	5.30
86-87—Rochester	AHL	11	545	2	2	0	26	0	2.86	5	141	2	0	11	0	4.68
87-88—Rochester	AHL	55	2763	27	16	3	159	0	3.45	6	328	3	3	22	0	4.02
88-89—Buffalo	NHL	6	214	1	3	0	15	0	4.21	—	—	—	—	—	—	—
—Rochester	AHL	33	1566	11	14	0	97	1	3.72	—	—	—	—	—	—	—
89-90—Rochester	AHL	56	3095	31	16	4	173	2	3.35	†17	*1001	10	6	50	*3.00	
90-91—Buffalo	NHL	16	630	4	5	3	35	0	3.33	2	37	0	1	2	0	3.24
—Rochester	AHL	26	1363	10	10	3	68	*4	*2.99	9	544	6	3	30	0	3.31
91-92—Minnesota	NHL	36	1905	13	19	1	104	1	3.28	—	—	—	—	—	—	—
—Kalamazoo	IHL	1	60	1	0	‡0	7	0	7.00	—	—	—	—	—	—	—
92-93—Minnesota	NHL	29	1596	10	12	5	97	1	3.65	—	—	—	—	—	—	—
93-94—Dallas	NHL	36	2000	18	9	6	88	3	2.64	5	307	4	1	15	0	2.93
94-95—Dallas	NHL	15	754	4	8	0	40	2	3.18	1	20	0	1	1	0	3.00
NHL totals		138	7099	50	56	15	379	7	3.20	8	364	4	2	18	0	2.97

VW

WALBY, STEFFON
RW, MAPLE LEAFS

PERSONAL: Born November 22, 1972, in Madison, Wis. . . . 6-1/198. . . . Shoots right.
TRANSACTIONS/CAREER NOTES: Signed as free agent by Toronto Maple Leafs (August 20, 1993).

Season	Team	League	REGULAR SEASON					PLAYOFFS				
			Gms.	G	A	Pts.	PIM	Gms.	G	A	Pts.	PIM
92-93	Kelowna	BCJHL	59	53	68	121	76	—	—	—	—	—
93-94	St. John's	AHL	63	15	22	37	79	2	0	0	0	2
94-95	St. John's	AHL	70	23	23	46	30	5	1	1	2	4

WALKER, SCOTT
RW, CANUCKS

PERSONAL: Born July 19, 1973, in Montreal. . . . 5-9/185. . . . Shoots right.
TRANSACTIONS/CAREER NOTES: Selected by Vancouver Canucks in fifth round (fourth Canucks pick, 124th overall) of NHL entry draft (June 26, 1993).
HONORS: Named to OHL All-Star second team (1992-93).

Season	Team	League	REGULAR SEASON					PLAYOFFS				
			Gms.	G	A	Pts.	PIM	Gms.	G	A	Pts.	PIM
89-90	Kitchener-Cambridge Jr.B	OHA	33	7	27	34	91	—	—	—	—	—
90-91	Cambridge Jr. B	OHA	45	10	27	37	241	—	—	—	—	—
91-92	Owen Sound	OHL	53	7	31	38	128	5	0	7	7	8
92-93	Owen Sound	OHL	57	23	68	91	110	8	1	5	6	16
	Canadian national team	Int'l	2	3	0	3	0	—	—	—	—	—
93-94	Hamilton	AHL	77	10	29	39	272	4	0	1	1	25
94-95	Syracuse	AHL	74	14	38	52	334	—	—	—	—	—
	Vancouver	NHL	11	0	1	1	33	—	—	—	—	—
NHL totals			11	0	1	1	33					

WALZ, WES
C, FLAMES

PERSONAL: Born May 15, 1970, in Calgary. . . . 5-10/185. . . . Shoots right. . . . Name pronounced WAHLS.
TRANSACTIONS/CAREER NOTES: Selected by Boston Bruins in third round (third Bruins pick, 57th overall) of NHL entry draft (June 17, 1989). . . . Traded by Bruins with D Garry Galley and future considerations to Philadelphia Flyers for D Gord Murphy, RW Brian Dobbin and third-round pick (LW Sergei Zholtok) in 1992 draft (January 2, 1992). . . . Signed as free agent by Calgary Flames (August 31, 1993). . . . Strained hip (February 26, 1995); missed one game.
HONORS: Won Jim Piggott Memorial Trophy (1988-89). . . . Won WHL Player of the Year Award (1989-90). . . . Named to WHL (East) All-Star first team (1989-90).

Season	Team	League	REGULAR SEASON					PLAYOFFS				
			Gms.	G	A	Pts.	PIM	Gms.	G	A	Pts.	PIM
87-88	Prince Albert	WHL	1	1	1	2	0	—	—	—	—	—
88-89	Lethbridge	WHL	63	29	75	104	32	8	1	5	6	6
89-90	Boston	NHL	2	1	1	2	0	—	—	—	—	—
	Lethbridge	WHL	56	54	86	140	69	19	13	*24	†37	33
90-91	Maine	AHL	20	8	12	20	19	2	0	0	0	21
	Boston	NHL	56	8	8	16	32	2	0	0	0	0
91-92	Boston	NHL	15	0	3	3	12	—	—	—	—	—
	Maine	AHL	21	13	11	24	38	—	—	—	—	—
	Hershey	AHL	41	13	28	41	37	6	1	2	3	0
	Philadelphia	NHL	2	1	0	1	0	—	—	—	—	—
92-93	Hershey	AHL	78	35	45	80	106	—	—	—	—	—
93-94	Calgary	NHL	53	11	27	38	16	6	3	0	3	2
	Saint John	AHL	15	6	6	12	14	—	—	—	—	—
94-95	Calgary	NHL	39	6	12	18	11	1	0	0	0	0
NHL totals			167	27	51	78	71	9	3	0	3	2

WARD, AARON
D, RED WINGS

PERSONAL: Born January 17, 1973, in Windsor, Ont. . . . 6-2/200. . . . Shoots right. . . . Full name: Aaron Christian Ward.
COLLEGE: Michigan.
TRANSACTIONS/CAREER NOTES: Selected by Winnipeg Jets in first round (first Jets pick, fifth overall) of NHL entry draft (June 22, 1991). . . . Traded by Jets with fourth-round pick in 1993 draft (D John Jakopin) and future considerations to Detroit Red Wings for RW Paul Ysebaert (June 11, 1993); Jets sent RW Alan Kerr to Red Wings to complete deal (June 18, 1993).
HONORS: Named to CCHA All-Rookie Team (1990-91). . . . Named to CCHA All-Tournament Team (1990-91).

Season	Team	League	REGULAR SEASON					PLAYOFFS				
			Gms.	G	A	Pts.	PIM	Gms.	G	A	Pts.	PIM
88-89	Nepean	COJHL	56	2	17	19	44	—	—	—	—	—
89-90	Nepean	COJHL	52	6	33	39	85	—	—	—	—	—
90-91	University of Michigan	CCHA	46	8	11	19	126	—	—	—	—	—
91-92	University of Michigan	CCHA	42	7	12	19	64	—	—	—	—	—
92-93	University of Michigan	CCHA	30	5	8	13	73	—	—	—	—	—
	Canadian national team	Int'l	4	0	0	0	8	—	—	—	—	—
93-94	Detroit	NHL	5	1	0	1	4	—	—	—	—	—
	Adirondack	AHL	58	4	12	16	87	9	2	6	8	6
94-95	Adirondack	AHL	76	11	24	35	87	4	0	1	1	0
	Detroit	NHL	1	0	1	1	2	—	—	—	—	—
NHL totals			6	1	1	2	6					

WARD, DIXON
RW

PERSONAL: Born September 23, 1968, in Edmonton. . . . 6-0/195. . . . Shoots right.
COLLEGE: North Dakota.
TRANSACTIONS/CAREER NOTES: Selected by Vancouver Canucks in seventh round (sixth Canucks pick, 128th overall) of NHL entry draft (June 11, 1988). . . . Separated left shoulder (December 1990). . . . Sprained ankle (March 14, 1993); missed four games. . . . Suspended three games and fined $500 by NHL for checking from behind (October 15, 1993). . . . Traded by Canucks with future considerations to Los Angeles Kings for C Jimmy Carson (January 8, 1994). . . . Traded by Kings with C Guy Leveque, RW Shayne Toporowski and C Kelly Fairchild to Toronto Maple Leafs for LW Eric Lacroix, D Chris Snell and fourth-round pick in 1996 draft (October 3, 1994). . . . Loaned by Maple Leafs to Chicago Wolves of IHL (March 16, 1995). . . . Released by Maple Leafs (June 28, 1995).
HONORS: Named to WCHA All-Star second team (1990-91 and 1991-92).

Season Team	League	Gms.	G	A	Pts.	PIM	Gms.	G	A	Pts.	PIM
		REGULAR SEASON					PLAYOFFS				
86-87—Red Deer	AJHL	59	46	40	86	153	—	—	—	—	—
87-88—Red Deer	AJHL	51	60	71	131	167	—	—	—	—	—
88-89—Univ. of North Dakota	WCHA	37	8	9	17	26	—	—	—	—	—
89-90—Univ. of North Dakota	WCHA	45	35	34	69	44	—	—	—	—	—
90-91—Univ. of North Dakota	WCHA	43	34	35	69	84	—	—	—	—	—
91-92—Univ. of North Dakota	WCHA	38	33	31	64	90	—	—	—	—	—
92-93—Vancouver	NHL	70	22	30	52	82	9	2	3	5	0
93-94—Vancouver	NHL	33	6	1	7	37	—	—	—	—	—
—Los Angeles	NHL	34	6	2	8	45	—	—	—	—	—
94-95—Toronto	NHL	22	0	3	3	31	—	—	—	—	—
—St. John's	AHL	6	3	3	6	19	—	—	—	—	—
—Detroit	IHL	7	3	6	9	7	5	3	0	3	7
NHL totals		159	34	36	70	195	9	2	3	5	0

WARD, ED
RW, FLAMES

PERSONAL: Born November 10, 1969, in Edmonton. . . . 6-3/205. . . . Shoots right. . . . Full name: Edward John Ward.
COLLEGE: Northern Michigan.
TRANSACTIONS/CAREER NOTES: Tore knee cartilage (August 1987). . . . Selected by Quebec Nordiques in sixth round (seventh Nordiques pick, 108th overall) of NHL entry draft (June 11, 1988). . . . Traded by Nordiques to Calgary Flames for D Francois Groleau (March 24, 1995).

Season Team	League	Gms.	G	A	Pts.	PIM	Gms.	G	A	Pts.	PIM
		REGULAR SEASON					PLAYOFFS				
86-87—Sherwood Park	AJHL	60	18	28	46	272	—	—	—	—	—
87-88—Northern Michigan Univ.	WCHA	25	0	2	2	40	—	—	—	—	—
88-89—Northern Michigan Univ.	WCHA	42	5	15	20	36	—	—	—	—	—
89-90—Northern Michigan Univ.	WCHA	39	5	11	16	77	—	—	—	—	—
90-91—Northern Michigan Univ.	WCHA	46	13	18	31	109	—	—	—	—	—
91-92—Halifax	AHL	51	7	11	18	65	—	—	—	—	—
—Greensboro	ECHL	12	4	8	12	21	—	—	—	—	—
92-93—Halifax	AHL	70	13	19	32	56	—	—	—	—	—
93-94—Cornwall	AHL	60	12	30	42	65	12	1	3	4	14
—Quebec	NHL	7	1	0	1	5	—	—	—	—	—
94-95—Cornwall	AHL	56	10	14	24	118	—	—	—	—	—
—Saint John	AHL	11	4	5	9	20	5	1	0	1	10
—Calgary	NHL	2	1	1	2	2	—	—	—	—	—
NHL totals		9	2	1	3	7					

WARE, JEFF
D, MAPLE LEAFS

PERSONAL: Born May 19, 1977, in Toronto. . . . 6-4/214. . . . Shoots left.
HIGH SCHOOL: Henry Street (Whitby, Ont.).
TRANSACTIONS/CAREER NOTES: Selected by Toronto Maple Leafs in first round (first Maple Leafs pick, 15th overall) of NHL entry draft (July 8, 1995).

Season Team	League	Gms.	G	A	Pts.	PIM	Gms.	G	A	Pts.	PIM
		REGULAR SEASON					PLAYOFFS				
93-94—Wexford	Tier II Jr. A	45	1	9	10	75	—	—	—	—	—
94-95—Oshawa	OHL	55	2	11	13	86	7	1	1	2	6

WARRENER, RHETT
D, PANTHERS

PERSONAL: Born January 27, 1976, in Shaunavon, Sask. . . . 6-1/209. . . . Shoots right. . . . Name pronounced REHT WAHR-uh-nuhr.
TRANSACTIONS/CAREER NOTES: Selected by Florida Panthers in second round (second Panthers pick, 27th overall) of NHL entry draft (June 28, 1994).

Season Team	League	Gms.	G	A	Pts.	PIM	Gms.	G	A	Pts.	PIM
		REGULAR SEASON					PLAYOFFS				
91-92—Saskatoon	WHL	2	0	0	0	0	—	—	—	—	—
92-93—Saskatoon	WHL	68	2	17	19	100	9	0	0	0	14
93-94—Saskatoon	WHL	61	7	19	26	131	16	0	5	5	33
94-95—Saskatoon	WHL	66	13	26	39	137	10	0	3	3	6

WARRINER, TODD
LW/C, MAPLE LEAFS

PERSONAL: Born January 3, 1974, in Chatham, Ont. . . . 6-1/188. . . . Shoots left. . . . Name pronounced WOHR-ih-nuhr.
HIGH SCHOOL: Herman E. Fawcett (Brantford, Ont.).
TRANSACTIONS/CAREER NOTES: Selected by Quebec Nordiques in first round (first Nor-

W

diques pick, fourth overall) of NHL entry draft (June 20, 1992).... Traded by Nordiques with C Mats Sundin, D Garth Butcher and first-round pick in 1994 draft (traded to Washington Capitals who selected D Nolan Baumgartner) to Toronto Maple Leafs for LW Wendel Clark, D Sylvain Lefebvre, RW Landon Wilson and first-round pick (D Jeffrey Kealty) in 1994 draft (June 28, 1994).

HONORS: Won Can.HL Top Draft Prospect Award (1991-92).... Won OHL Top Draft Prospect Award (1991-92).... Named to Can.HL All-Star second team (1991-92).... Named to OHL All-Star first team (1991-92).

MISCELLANEOUS: Member of silver-medal-winning Canadian Olympic team (1994).

			REGULAR SEASON				PLAYOFFS				
Season	Team	League	Gms.	G	A	Pts.	PIM	Gms.	G	A	Pts.	PIM
88-89—Blenheim Jr. C		OHA	10	1	4	5	0	—	—	—	—	—
89-90—Chatham Jr. B		OHA	40	24	21	45	12	—	—	—	—	—
90-91—Windsor		OHL	57	36	28	64	26	11	5	6	11	12
91-92—Windsor		OHL	50	41	42	83	66	7	5	4	9	6
92-93—Windsor		OHL	23	13	21	34	29	—	—	—	—	—
—Kitchener		OHL	32	19	24	43	35	7	5	14	19	14
93-94—Canadian national team		Int'l	50	11	20	31	33	—	—	—	—	—
—Canadian Olympic Team		Int'l	4	1	1	2	0	—	—	—	—	—
—Kitchener		OHL	—	—	—	—	—	1	0	1	1	0
—Cornwall		AHL	—	—	—	—	—	10	1	4	5	4
94-95—St. John's		AHL	46	8	10	18	22	4	1	0	1	2
—Toronto		NHL	5	0	0	0	0	—	—	—	—	—
NHL totals			**5**	**0**	**0**	**0**	**0**					

WASHBURN, STEVE
C, PANTHERS

PERSONAL: Born April 10, 1975, in Ottawa.... 6-1/185.... Shoots left.
TRANSACTIONS/CAREER NOTES: Selected by Florida Panthers in third round (fifth Panthers pick, 78th overall) of NHL entry draft (June 26, 1993).

			REGULAR SEASON				PLAYOFFS				
Season	Team	League	Gms.	G	A	Pts.	PIM	Gms.	G	A	Pts.	PIM
90-91—Gloucester		OPJHL	56	21	30	51	47	—	—	—	—	—
91-92—Ottawa		OHL	59	5	17	22	10	11	2	3	5	4
92-93—Ottawa		OHL	66	20	38	58	54	—	—	—	—	—
93-94—Ottawa		OHL	65	30	50	80	88	17	7	16	23	10
94-95—Ottawa		OHL	63	43	63	106	72	—	—	—	—	—
—Cincinnati		IHL	6	3	1	4	0	9	1	3	4	4

WATT, MIKE
LW/C, OILERS

PERSONAL: Born March 31, 1976, in Seaforth, Ont.... 6-2/210.... Shoots left.
COLLEGE: Michigan State.
TRANSACTIONS/CAREER NOTES: Selected by Edmonton Oilers in second round (third Oilers pick, 32nd overall) of NHL entry draft (June 28, 1994).

			REGULAR SEASON				PLAYOFFS				
Season	Team	League	Gms.	G	A	Pts.	PIM	Gms.	G	A	Pts.	PIM
91-92—Stratford Jr. B		OHA	46	5	26	31	...	—	—	—	—	—
92-93—Stratford Jr. B		OHA	45	20	35	55	100	—	—	—	—	—
93-94—Stratford Jr. B		OHA	48	34	34	68	165	—	—	—	—	—
94-95—Michigan State		CCHA	39	12	6	18	64	—	—	—	—	—

WATTERS, TIMOTHY
D

PERSONAL: Born July 25, 1959, in Kamloops, B.C.... 5-11/185.... Shoots left. ...Full name: Timothy John Watters.
COLLEGE: Michigan Tech.
TRANSACTIONS/CAREER NOTES: Selected by Winnipeg Jets in sixth round (sixth Jets pick, 124th overall) of NHL draft (August 9, 1979).... Pulled hamstring (October 1983).... Broke wrist (December 1984).... Suffered back spasms (February 1986).... Strained knee (December 1987).... Signed as free agent by Los Angeles Kings (July 1988).... Bruised calf (March 1989).... Bruised ankle (December 23, 1989); missed nine games.... Bruised ankle (April 1990).... Bruised ribs (October 14, 1990); missed six games.... Twisted right knee (January 12, 1991).... Injured ankle (October 28, 1991); missed 14 games.... Injured ankle (December 1991).... Strained groin (February 17, 1995); missed 25 games.... Named assistant coach of Boston Bruins (June 20, 1995).

HONORS: Named to NCAA All-America West team (1980-81).... Named to NCAA All-Tournament team (1980-81).... Named to WCHA All-Star first team (1980-81).

			REGULAR SEASON				PLAYOFFS				
Season	Team	League	Gms.	G	A	Pts.	PIM	Gms.	G	A	Pts.	PIM
76-77—Kamloops		BCJHL	60	10	38	48	...	—	—	—	—	—
77-78—Michigan Tech		WCHA	37	1	15	16	47	—	—	—	—	—
78-79—Michigan Tech		WCHA	31	6	21	27	48	—	—	—	—	—
79-80—Canadian national team		Int'l	56	8	21	29	43	—	—	—	—	—
—Canadian Olympic Team		Int'l	6	1	1	2	0	—	—	—	—	—
80-81—Michigan Tech		WCHA	43	12	38	50	36	—	—	—	—	—
81-82—Tulsa		CHL	5	1	2	3	0	—	—	—	—	—
—Winnipeg		NHL	69	2	22	24	97	4	0	1	1	8
82-83—Winnipeg		NHL	77	5	18	23	98	3	0	0	0	2
83-84—Winnipeg		NHL	74	3	20	23	169	3	1	0	1	2
84-85—Winnipeg		NHL	63	2	20	22	74	8	0	1	1	16
85-86—Winnipeg		NHL	56	6	8	14	97	—	—	—	—	—
86-87—Winnipeg		NHL	63	3	13	16	119	10	0	0	0	21

W

— 744 —

Season	Team	League	REGULAR SEASON Gms.	G	A	Pts.	PIM	PLAYOFFS Gms.	G	A	Pts.	PIM
87-88	—Winnipeg	NHL	36	0	0	0	106	4	0	0	0	4
	—Canadian national team	Int'l	2	0	2	2	0	—	—	—	—	—
	—Canadian Olympic Team	Int'l	8	0	1	1	2	—	—	—	—	—
88-89	—Los Angeles	NHL	76	3	18	21	168	11	0	1	1	6
89-90	—Los Angeles	NHL	62	1	10	11	92	4	0	0	0	6
90-91	—Los Angeles	NHL	45	0	4	4	92	7	0	0	0	12
91-92	—Los Angeles	NHL	37	0	7	7	92	6	0	0	0	8
	—Phoenix	IHL	5	0	3	3	6	—	—	—	—	—
92-93	—Phoenix	IHL	31	3	3	6	43	—	—	—	—	—
	—Los Angeles	NHL	22	0	2	2	18	22	0	2	2	30
93-94	—Los Angeles	NHL	60	1	9	10	67	—	—	—	—	—
94-95	—Phoenix	IHL	36	1	8	9	58	7	0	1	1	10
	—Los Angeles	NHL	1	0	0	0	0	—	—	—	—	—
NHL totals			741	26	151	177	1289	82	1	5	6	115

WEEKES, KEVIN

G, PANTHERS

PERSONAL: Born April 4, 1975, in Toronto. . . . 6-0/158. . . . Catches left. . . . Name pronounced WEEKS.
HIGH SCHOOL: West Hill (Ont.) Secondary.
TRANSACTIONS/CAREER NOTES: Selected by Florida Panthers in second round (second Panthers pick, 41st overall) of NHL entry draft (June 26, 1993).

Season	Team	League	REGULAR SEASON Gms.	Min.	W	L	T	GA	SO	Avg.	PLAYOFFS Gms.	Min.	W	L	GA	SO	Avg.
91-92	—St. Michaels Tier II	Jr. A	2	127	...	...	...	11	0	5.20	—	—	—	—	—	—	—
92-93	—Owen Sound	OHL	29	1645	9	12	5	143	0	5.22	1	26	0	0	5	0	11.54
93-94	—Owen Sound	OHL	34	1974	13	19	1	158	0	4.80	—	—	—	—	—	—	—
94-95	—Ottawa	OHL	41	2266	13	23	4	154	1	4.08	—	—	—	—	—	—	—

WEIGHT, DOUG

C, OILERS

PERSONAL: Born January 21, 1971, in Warren, Mich. . . . 5-11/191. . . . Shoots left. . . . Name pronounced WAYT.
COLLEGE: Lake Superior State (Mich.).
TRANSACTIONS/CAREER NOTES: Selected by New York Rangers in second round (second Rangers pick, 34th overall) of NHL entry draft (June 16, 1990). . . . Sprained elbow (October 14, 1991); missed three games. . . . Damaged ligaments (January 11, 1991). . . . Suspended four off-days and fined $500 by NHL for cross-checking (November 5, 1992). . . . Traded by Rangers to Edmonton Oilers for LW Esa Tikkanen (March 17, 1993). . . . Played in Europe during 1994-95 NHL lockout.
HONORS: Named to CCHA All-Rookie team (1989-90). . . . Named to NCAA All-America West second team (1990-91). . . . Named to CCHA All-Star first team (1990-91).

Season	Team	League	REGULAR SEASON Gms.	G	A	Pts.	PIM	PLAYOFFS Gms.	G	A	Pts.	PIM
88-89	—Bloomfield	NAJHL	34	26	53	79	105	—	—	—	—	—
89-90	—Lake Superior State	CCHA	46	21	48	69	44	—	—	—	—	—
90-91	—Lake Superior State	CCHA	42	29	46	75	86	—	—	—	—	—
	—New York Rangers	NHL	—	—	—	—	—	1	0	0	0	0
91-92	—New York Rangers	NHL	53	8	22	30	23	7	2	2	4	0
	—Binghamton	AHL	9	3	14	17	2	4	1	4	5	6
92-93	—New York Rangers	NHL	65	15	25	40	55	—	—	—	—	—
	—Edmonton	NHL	13	2	6	8	10	—	—	—	—	—
93-94	—Edmonton	NHL	84	24	50	74	47	—	—	—	—	—
94-95	—Rosenheim	Germany	8	2	3	5	18	—	—	—	—	—
	—Edmonton	NHL	48	7	33	40	69	—	—	—	—	—
NHL totals			263	56	136	192	204	8	2	2	4	0

WEINRICH, ERIC

D, BLACKHAWKS

PERSONAL: Born December 19, 1966, in Roanoke, Va. . . . 6-0/210. . . . Shoots left. . . . Full name: Eric John Weinrich. . . . Name pronounced WIGHN-rihch. . . . Brother of Jason Weinrich, defenseman in New York Rangers system.
HIGH SCHOOL: North Yarmouth (Maine) Academy.
COLLEGE: Maine.
TRANSACTIONS/CAREER NOTES: Dislocated shoulder (December 1984). . . . Selected by New Jersey Devils in second round (third Devils pick, 32nd overall) of NHL entry draft (June 15, 1985). . . . Traded by Devils with G Sean Burke to Hartford Whalers for RW Bobby Holik, second-round pick in 1993 draft (LW Jay Pandolfo) and future considerations (August 28, 1992). . . . Suffered concussion (November 25, 1992); missed two games. . . . Sprained knee (September 22, 1993); missed five games. . . . Signed as free agent by Hartford Whalers (September 25, 1993). . . . Injured right knee (October 5, 1993); missed five games. . . . Traded with LW Patrick Poulin by Whalers to the Chicago Blackhawks for RW Steve Larmer and D Bryan Marchment (November 2, 1993). . . . Broke jaw (February 24, 1994); missed 17 games.
HONORS: Named to NCAA All-America East second team (1986-87). . . . Named to Hockey East All-Star first team (1986-87). . . . Won Eddie Shore Plaque (1989-90). . . . Named to AHL All-Star first team (1989-90). . . . Named to NHL All-Rookie team (1990-91).

Season	Team	League	REGULAR SEASON Gms.	G	A	Pts.	PIM	PLAYOFFS Gms.	G	A	Pts.	PIM
83-84	—North Yarmouth Acad.	Maine H.S.	17	23	33	56	...	—	—	—	—	—
84-85	—North Yarmouth Acad.	Maine H.S.	20	6	21	27	...	—	—	—	—	—

Season	Team	League	REGULAR SEASON					PLAYOFFS				
			Gms.	G	A	Pts.	PIM	Gms.	G	A	Pts.	PIM
85-86	University of Maine	Hockey East	34	0	15	15	26	—	—	—	—	—
86-87	University of Maine	Hockey East	41	12	32	44	59	—	—	—	—	—
87-88	University of Maine	Hockey East	8	4	7	11	22	—	—	—	—	—
	U.S. national team	Int'l	39	3	9	12	24	—	—	—	—	—
	U.S. Olympic Team	Int'l	3	0	0	0	24	—	—	—	—	—
88-89	Utica	AHL	80	17	27	44	70	5	0	1	1	8
	New Jersey	NHL	2	0	0	0	0	—	—	—	—	—
89-90	Utica	AHL	57	12	48	60	38	—	—	—	—	—
	New Jersey	NHL	19	2	7	9	11	6	1	3	4	17
90-91	New Jersey	NHL	76	4	34	38	48	7	1	2	3	6
91-92	New Jersey	NHL	76	7	25	32	55	7	0	2	2	4
92-93	Hartford	NHL	79	7	29	36	76	—	—	—	—	—
93-94	Hartford	NHL	8	1	1	2	2	—	—	—	—	—
	Chicago	NHL	54	3	23	26	31	6	0	2	2	6
94-95	Chicago	NHL	48	3	10	13	33	16	1	5	6	4
NHL totals			362	27	129	156	256	42	3	14	17	37

WELLS, CHRIS
C, PENGUINS

PERSONAL: Born November 12, 1975, in Calgary.... 6-6/215.... Shoots left.
HIGH SCHOOL: Meadowdale (Lynnwood, Wash.).
TRANSACTIONS/CAREER NOTES: Selected by Pittsburgh Penguins in first round (first Penguins pick, 24th overall) of NHL entry draft (June 28, 1994).
HONORS: Named to WHL (West) All-Star first team (1994-95).

Season	Team	League	REGULAR SEASON					PLAYOFFS				
			Gms.	G	A	Pts.	PIM	Gms.	G	A	Pts.	PIM
90-91	Calgary Royals	AJHL	35	13	14	27	33	—	—	—	—	—
91-92	Seattle	WHL	64	13	8	21	70	11	0	0	0	15
92-93	Seattle	WHL	63	18	37	55	111	5	2	3	5	4
93-94	Seattle	WHL	69	30	44	74	150	9	6	5	11	23
94-95	Seattle	WHL	69	45	63	108	148	3	0	1	1	4
	Cleveland	IHL	3	0	1	1	2	—	—	—	—	—

WELLS, JAY
D, BLUES

PERSONAL: Born May 18, 1959, in Paris, Ont.... 6-1/210.... Shoots left.... Full name: Gordon Jay Wells.
TRANSACTIONS/CAREER NOTES: Selected by Los Angeles Kings in first round (first Kings pick, 16th overall) of NHL entry draft (August 9, 1979).... Broke right hand in team practice (October 16, 1981).... Tore medial collateral ligament in right knee (December 14, 1982).... Sprained ankle (December 1983).... Struck in eye during team practice (February 1987).... Strained lower back (November 1987).... Traded by Kings to Philadelphia Flyers for D Doug Crossman (September 29, 1988).... Bruised right shoulder (October 1988).... Broke knuckle on right hand (January 1989).... Broke toe (November 1989).... Traded by Flyers with fourth-round pick in 1991 draft to Buffalo Sabres for RW Kevin Maguire and second-round pick (RW Mikael Renberg) in 1990 draft (March 5, 1990).... Fractured right ankle (March 6, 1990).... Tore medial collateral ligament of right knee (October 13, 1990); missed 18 games.... Traded by Sabres to New York Rangers for D Randy Moller (March 9, 1992).... Sprained right knee (January 27, 1993); missed 27 games.... Sprained wrist (March 25, 1994); missed one game.... Suffered from the flu (April 2, 1994); missed one game.... Traded by Rangers to St. Louis Blues for D Doug Lidster (July 31, 1995).
HONORS: Named to OMJHL All-Star first team (1978-79).
MISCELLANEOUS: Member of Stanley Cup championship team (1994).

Season	Team	League	REGULAR SEASON					PLAYOFFS				
			Gms.	G	A	Pts.	PIM	Gms.	G	A	Pts.	PIM
76-77	Kingston	OMJHL	59	4	7	11	90	—	—	—	—	—
77-78	Kingston	OMJHL	68	9	13	22	195	5	1	2	3	6
78-79	Kingston	OMJHL	48	6	21	27	100	11	2	7	9	29
79-80	Los Angeles	NHL	43	0	0	0	113	4	0	0	0	11
	Binghamton	AHL	28	0	6	6	48	—	—	—	—	—
80-81	Los Angeles	NHL	72	5	13	18	155	4	0	0	0	27
81-82	Los Angeles	NHL	60	1	8	9	145	10	1	3	4	41
82-83	Los Angeles	NHL	69	3	12	15	167	—	—	—	—	—
83-84	Los Angeles	NHL	69	3	18	21	141	—	—	—	—	—
84-85	Los Angeles	NHL	77	2	9	11	185	3	0	1	1	0
85-86	Los Angeles	NHL	79	11	31	42	226	—	—	—	—	—
86-87	Los Angeles	NHL	77	7	29	36	155	5	1	2	3	10
87-88	Los Angeles	NHL	58	2	23	25	159	5	1	2	3	21
88-89	Philadelphia	NHL	67	2	19	21	184	18	0	2	2	51
89-90	Philadelphia	NHL	59	3	16	19	129	—	—	—	—	—
	Buffalo	NHL	1	0	1	1	0	6	0	0	0	12
90-91	Buffalo	NHL	43	1	2	3	86	1	0	1	1	0
91-92	Buffalo	NHL	41	2	9	11	157	—	—	—	—	—
	New York Rangers	NHL	11	0	0	0	24	13	0	2	2	10
92-93	New York Rangers	NHL	53	1	9	10	107	—	—	—	—	—
93-94	New York Rangers	NHL	79	2	7	9	110	23	0	0	0	20
94-95	New York Rangers	NHL	43	2	7	9	36	10	0	0	0	8
NHL totals			1001	47	213	260	2279	102	3	13	16	211

WERENKA, BRAD

D, DENVER

PERSONAL: Born February 12, 1969, in Two Hills, Alta.... 6-2/205.... Shoots left.... Full name: John Bradley Werenka.... Name pronounced wuh-REHN-kuh.
HIGH SCHOOL: Fort Saskatchewan (Alta.).
COLLEGE: Northern Michigan.
TRANSACTIONS/CAREER NOTES: Selected by Edmonton Oilers as underage junior in second round (second Oilers pick, 42nd overall) of NHL entry draft (June 13, 1987).... Tore stomach muscles (October 1988).... Sprained right knee (November 3, 1989).... Loaned by Oilers to Canadian Olympic Team (February 10, 1994).... Traded by Oilers to Quebec Nordiques for G Steve Passmore (March 21, 1994).... Nordiques franchise moved to Denver for 1995-96 season.
HONORS: Named to NCAA All-America West first team (1990-91).... Named to NCAA All-Tournament team (1990-91).... Named to WCHA All-Star first team (1990-91).
MISCELLANEOUS: Member of silver-medal-winning Canadian Olympic team (1994).

Season	Team	League	REGULAR SEASON Gms.	G	A	Pts.	PIM	PLAYOFFS Gms.	G	A	Pts.	PIM
85-86	Fort Saskatchewan	AJHL	29	12	23	35	24	—	—	—	—	—
86-87	Northern Michigan Univ...	WCHA	30	4	4	8	35	—	—	—	—	—
87-88	Northern Michigan Univ...	WCHA	34	7	23	30	26	—	—	—	—	—
88-89	Northern Michigan Univ...	WCHA	28	7	13	20	16	—	—	—	—	—
89-90	Northern Michigan Univ...	WCHA	8	2	5	7	8	—	—	—	—	—
90-91	Northern Michigan Univ...	WCHA	47	20	43	63	36	—	—	—	—	—
91-92	Cape Breton	AHL	66	6	21	27	95	5	0	3	3	6
92-93	Canadian national team	Int'l	18	3	7	10	10	—	—	—	—	—
	—Edmonton	NHL	27	5	3	8	24	—	—	—	—	—
	—Cape Breton	AHL	4	1	1	2	4	16	4	17	21	12
93-94	Cape Breton	AHL	25	6	17	23	19	—	—	—	—	—
	—Edmonton	NHL	15	0	4	4	14	—	—	—	—	—
	—Canadian Olympic Team	Int'l	8	2	2	4	8	—	—	—	—	—
	—Quebec	NHL	11	0	7	7	8	—	—	—	—	—
94-95	Milwaukee	IHL	80	8	45	53	161	15	3	10	13	36
	NHL totals		53	5	14	19	46					

WERENKA, DARCY

D, RANGERS

PERSONAL: Born May 13, 1973, in Edmonton.... 6-1/210.... Shoots right.... Name pronounced wuh-REHN-kuh.
TRANSACTIONS/CAREER NOTES: Selected by New York Rangers in second round (second Rangers pick, 37th overall) of NHL entry draft (June 22, 1991).
HONORS: Named to WHL (East) All-Star second team (1990-91).

Season	Team	League	REGULAR SEASON Gms.	G	A	Pts.	PIM	PLAYOFFS Gms.	G	A	Pts.	PIM
89-90	Lethbridge	WHL	63	1	18	19	16	19	0	2	2	4
90-91	Lethbridge	WHL	72	13	37	50	39	16	1	7	8	4
91-92	Lethbridge	WHL	69	17	58	75	56	5	2	1	3	0
92-93	Lethbridge	WHL	19	4	17	21	12	—	—	—	—	—
	—Brandon	WHL	36	4	25	29	19	3	0	0	0	2
	—Binghamton	AHL	3	0	1	1	2	3	0	0	0	0
93-94	Binghamton	AHL	53	5	22	27	10	—	—	—	—	—
94-95	Binghamton	AHL	73	17	29	46	12	11	4	3	7	2

WESENBERG, BRIAN

RW, MIGHTY DUCKS

PERSONAL: Born May 9, 1977, in Peterborough, Ont.... 6-3/173.... Shoots right.
HIGH SCHOOL: Bishop MacDonnell (Guelph, Ont.).
TRANSACTIONS/CAREER NOTES: Selected by Mighty Ducks of Anaheim in second round (second Mighty Ducks pick, 29th overall) of NHL entry draft (July 8, 1995).

Season	Team	League	REGULAR SEASON Gms.	G	A	Pts.	PIM	PLAYOFFS Gms.	G	A	Pts.	PIM
93-94	Cobourg	Tier II Jr. A	40	14	18	32	81	—	—	—	—	—
94-95	Guelph	OHL	66	17	27	44	81	14	2	3	5	18

WESLEY, GLEN

D, WHALERS

PERSONAL: Born October 2, 1968, in Red Deer, Alta.... 6-1/195.... Shoots left.
TRANSACTIONS/CAREER NOTES: Selected by Boston Bruins as underage junior in first round (first Bruins pick, third overall) of NHL entry draft (June 13, 1987).... Sprained left knee (October 1988).... Broke foot (November 24, 1992); missed 14 games.... Injured groin (February 1993); missed one game.... Injured groin (March 1993); missed three games.... Injured groin (April 1993); missed two games.... Injured kidney (March 3, 1994); missed three games.... Traded by Bruins to Hartford Whalers for first-round picks in 1995 (D Kyle McLaren), 1996 and 1997 drafts (August 26, 1994).
HONORS: Won WHL West Top Defenseman Trophy (1985-86 and 1986-87).... Named to WHL (West) All-Star first team (1985-86 and 1986-87).... Named to NHL All-Rookie team (1987-88).... Played in NHL All-Star Game (1989).
STATISTICAL PLATEAUS: Three-goal games: 1993-94 (1).
MISCELLANEOUS: Captain of Hartford Whalers (1994-95).

Season	Team	League	REGULAR SEASON Gms.	G	A	Pts.	PIM	PLAYOFFS Gms.	G	A	Pts.	PIM
83-84	Red Deer	AJHL	57	9	20	29	40	—	—	—	—	—
	—Portland	WHL	3	1	2	3	0	—	—	—	—	—
84-85	Portland	WHL	67	16	52	68	76	6	1	6	7	8
85-86	Portland	WHL	69	16	75	91	96	15	3	11	14	29
86-87	Portland	WHL	63	16	46	62	72	20	8	18	26	27

W

Season Team	League	REGULAR SEASON					PLAYOFFS				
		Gms.	G	A	Pts.	PIM	Gms.	G	A	Pts.	PIM
87-88—Boston	NHL	79	7	30	37	69	23	6	8	14	22
88-89—Boston	NHL	77	19	35	54	61	10	0	2	2	4
89-90—Boston	NHL	78	9	27	36	48	21	2	6	8	36
90-91—Boston	NHL	80	11	32	43	78	19	2	9	11	19
91-92—Boston	NHL	78	9	37	46	54	15	2	4	6	16
92-93—Boston	NHL	64	8	25	33	47	4	0	0	0	0
93-94—Boston	NHL	81	14	44	58	64	13	3	3	6	12
94-95—Hartford	NHL	48	2	14	16	50	—	—	—	—	—
NHL totals		585	79	244	323	471	105	15	32	47	109

WHITE, BRIAN
D, LIGHTNING

PERSONAL: Born February 7, 1976, in Winchester, Mass. . . . 6-1/180. . . . Shoots right. **HIGH SCHOOL:** Arlington (Mass.) Catholic. **COLLEGE:** Maine. **TRANSACTIONS/CAREER NOTES:** Selected by Tampa Bay Lightning in 11th round (11th Lightning pick, 268th overall) of NHL entry draft (June 29, 1994).

Season Team	League	REGULAR SEASON					PLAYOFFS				
		Gms.	G	A	Pts.	PIM	Gms.	G	A	Pts.	PIM
92-93—Arlington Catholic	Mass. H.S.	. . .	7	25	32	. . .	—	—	—	—	—
93-94—Arlington Catholic	Mass. H.S.	26	10	29	39	. . .	—	—	—	—	—
94-95—University of Maine	Hockey East	28	1	1	2	16	—	—	—	—	—

WHITE, KAM
D, MAPLE LEAFS

PERSONAL: Born February 13, 1976, in Chicago. . . . 6-3/195. . . . Shoots left. **COLLEGE:** Lambton (Ont.). **TRANSACTIONS/CAREER NOTES:** Selected by Toronto Maple Leafs in sixth round (fifth Maple Leafs pick, 152nd overall) of NHL entry draft (June 29, 1994).

Season Team	League	REGULAR SEASON					PLAYOFFS				
		Gms.	G	A	Pts.	PIM	Gms.	G	A	Pts.	PIM
92-93—Newmarket	OHL	8	0	0	0	8	—	—	—	—	—
—St. Michaels Tier II	Jr. A	32	2	7	9	63	—	—	—	—	—
93-94—Newmarket	OHL	44	0	5	5	125	—	—	—	—	—
94-95—Sarnia	OHL	31	0	4	4	77	—	—	—	—	—
—North Bay	OHL	20	1	1	2	84	6	0	1	1	10

WHITE, PETER
C, OILERS

PERSONAL: Born March 15, 1969, in Montreal. . . . 5-11/200. . . . Shoots left. . . . Full name: Peter Toby White. **COLLEGE:** Michigan State. **TRANSACTIONS/CAREER NOTES:** Selected by Edmonton Oilers in fifth round (fourth Oilers pick, 92nd overall) of NHL entry draft (June 17, 1989). **HONORS:** Named to CCHA All-Rookie team (1988-89). . . . Named CCHA Playoff Most Valuable Player (1989-90). . . . Named to CCHA All-Tournament team (1989-90). . . . Won John B. Sellenberger Trophy (1994-95). . . . Named to AHL All-Star second team (1994-95).

Season Team	League	REGULAR SEASON					PLAYOFFS				
		Gms.	G	A	Pts.	PIM	Gms.	G	A	Pts.	PIM
87-88—Pembroke	COJHL	56	90	136	226	32	—	—	—	—	—
88-89—Michigan State	CCHA	46	20	33	53	17	—	—	—	—	—
89-90—Michigan State	CCHA	45	22	40	62	6	—	—	—	—	—
90-91—Michigan State	CCHA	37	7	31	38	28	—	—	—	—	—
91-92—Michigan State	CCHA	44	26	51	77	32	—	—	—	—	—
92-93—Cape Breton	AHL	64	12	28	40	10	16	3	3	6	12
93-94—Cape Breton	AHL	45	21	49	70	12	5	2	3	5	2
—Edmonton	NHL	26	3	5	8	2	—	—	—	—	—
94-95—Cape Breton	AHL	65	36	†69	*105	30	—	—	—	—	—
—Edmonton	NHL	9	2	4	6	0	—	—	—	—	—
NHL totals		35	5	9	14	2	—	—	—	—	—

WHITMORE, KAY
G, CANUCKS

PERSONAL: Born April 10, 1967, in Sudbury, Ont. . . . 5-11/180. . . . Catches left. **TRANSACTIONS/CAREER NOTES:** Selected by Hartford Whalers as underage junior in second round (second Whalers pick, 26th overall) of NHL entry draft (June 15, 1985). . . . Traded by Whalers to Vancouver Canucks for G Corrie D'Alessio and conditional pick in 1993 draft (October 1, 1992). **HONORS:** Shared Dave Pinkney Trophy with Ron Tugnutt (1985-86). . . . Named to OHL All-Star first team (1985-86). . . . Won Jack Butterfield Trophy (1990-91).

Season Team	League	REGULAR SEASON							PLAYOFFS						
		Gms.	Min.	W	L	T	GA	SO	Avg.	Gms.	Min.	W	L	GA	SO	Avg.
83-84—Peterborough	OHL	29	1471	17	8	0	110	0	4.49	—	—	—	—	—	—	—
84-85—Peterborough	OHL	*53	*3077	35	16	2	172	†2	3.35	*17	*1020	10	4	58	0	3.41
85-86—Peterborough	OHL	41	2467	27	12	2	114	†3	*2.77	14	837	8	5	40	0	2.87
86-87—Peterborough	OHL	36	2159	14	17	5	118	1	3.28	7	366	3	3	17	1	2.79
87-88—Binghamton	AHL	38	2137	17	15	4	121	3	3.40	2	118	0	2	10	0	5.08
88-89—Binghamton	AHL	*56	*3200	21	29	4	*241	1	4.52	—	—	—	—	—	—	—
—Hartford	NHL	3	180	2	1	0	10	0	3.33	2	135	0	2	10	0	4.44

W

Season Team	League	REGULAR SEASON								PLAYOFFS						
		Gms.	Min.	W	L	T	GA	SO	Avg.	Gms.	Min.	W	L	GA	SO	Avg.
89-90—Binghamton	AHL	24	1386	3	19	2	109	0	4.72	—	—	—	—	—	—	—
—Hartford	NHL	9	442	4	2	1	26	0	3.53	—	—	—	—	—	—	—
90-91—Hartford	NHL	18	850	3	9	3	52	0	3.67	—	—	—	—	—	—	—
—Springfield	AHL	33	1916	22	9	1	98	1	3.07	*15	*926	11	4	*37	0	*2.40
91-92—Hartford	NHL	45	2567	14	21	6	155	3	3.62	1	19	0	0	1	0	3.16
92-93—Vancouver	NHL	31	1817	18	8	4	94	1	3.10	—	—	—	—	—	—	—
93-94—Vancouver	NHL	32	1921	18	14	0	113	0	3.53	—	—	—	—	—	—	—
94-95—Vancouver	NHL	11	558	0	6	2	37	0	3.98	1	20	0	0	2	0	6.00
NHL totals		149	8335	59	61	16	487	4	3.51	4	174	0	2	13	0	4.48

WHITNEY, RAY
C, SHARKS

PERSONAL: Born May 8, 1972, in Edmonton. . . . 5-10/170. . . . Shoots right.
TRANSACTIONS/CAREER NOTES: Selected by San Jose Sharks in second round (second Sharks pick, 23rd overall) of NHL entry draft (June 22, 1991). . . . Sprained knee (October 30, 1993); missed 18 games. . . . Suffered from the flu (December 15, 1993); missed one game. . . . Injured ankle (February 20, 1995) and suffered eye infection (February 28, 1995); missed seven games. . . . Suffered eye infection (March 21, 1995); missed one game. . . . Suffered from the flu (April 9, 1995); missed one game.
HONORS: Won Four Broncos Memorial Trophy (1990-91). . . . Won Bob Clarke Trophy (1990-91). . . . Won WHL West Player of the Year Award (1990-91). . . . Won George Parsons Trophy (1990-91). . . . Named to Memorial Cup All-Star team (1990-91). . . . Named to WHL (West) All-Star first team (1990-91).

Season Team	League	REGULAR SEASON					PLAYOFFS				
		Gms.	G	A	Pts.	PIM	Gms.	G	A	Pts.	PIM
88-89—Spokane	WHL	71	17	33	50	16	—	—	—	—	—
89-90—Spokane	WHL	71	57	56	113	50	6	3	4	7	6
90-91—Spokane	WHL	72	67	118	*185	36	15	13	18	*31	12
91-92—San Diego	IHL	63	36	54	90	12	4	0	0	0	0
—San Jose	NHL	2	0	3	3	0	—	—	—	—	—
—Koln	Germany	10	3	6	9	4	—	—	—	—	—
92-93—Kansas City	IHL	46	20	33	53	14	12	5	7	12	2
—San Jose	NHL	26	4	6	10	4	—	—	—	—	—
93-94—San Jose	NHL	61	14	26	40	14	14	0	4	4	8
94-95—San Jose	NHL	39	13	12	25	14	11	4	4	8	2
NHL totals		128	31	47	78	32	25	4	8	12	10

WIDMER, JASON
D, ISLANDERS

PERSONAL: Born August 1, 1973, in Calgary. . . . 6-0/205. . . . Shoots left. . . . Name pronounced WIHD-muhr.
TRANSACTIONS/CAREER NOTES: Selected by New York Islanders in the eighth round (eighth Islanders pick, 176th overall) of the NHL entry draft (June 20, 1992).

Season Team	League	REGULAR SEASON					PLAYOFFS				
		Gms.	G	A	Pts.	PIM	Gms.	G	A	Pts.	PIM
89-90—Moose Jaw	WHL	58	1	8	9	33	—	—	—	—	—
90-91—Lethbridge	WHL	58	2	12	14	55	16	0	1	1	12
91-92—Lethbridge	WHL	40	2	19	21	181	5	0	4	4	9
92-93—Lethbridge	WHL	55	3	15	18	140	4	0	3	3	2
—Capital District	AHL	4	0	0	0	2	—	—	—	—	—
93-94—Lethbridge	WHL	64	11	31	42	191	9	3	5	8	34
94-95—Canadian national team	Int'l	6	1	4	5	4	—	—	—	—	—
—Worcester	AHL	73	8	26	34	136	—	—	—	—	—
—New York Islanders	NHL	1	0	0	0	0	—	—	—	—	—
NHL totals		1	0	0	0	0					

WIEMER, JASON
LW, LIGHTNING

PERSONAL: Born April 14, 1976, in Kimberley, B.C. . . . 6-1/215. . . . Shoots left. . . . Name pronounced WEE-muhr.
TRANSACTIONS/CAREER NOTES: Selected by Tampa Bay Lightning in first round (first Lightning pick, eighth overall) of NHL entry draft (June 28, 1994). . . . Suffered from the flu (March 2, 1995); missed one game.

Season Team	League	REGULAR SEASON					PLAYOFFS				
		Gms.	G	A	Pts.	PIM	Gms.	G	A	Pts.	PIM
91-92—Portland	WHL	2	0	1	1	0	—	—	—	—	—
—Kimberley	Tier II Jr. A	45	34	33	67	211	—	—	—	—	—
92-93—Portland	WHL	68	18	34	52	159	16	7	3	10	27
93-94—Portland	WHL	72	45	51	96	236	10	4	4	8	32
94-95—Portland	WHL	16	10	14	24	63	—	—	—	—	—
—Tampa Bay	NHL	36	1	4	5	44	—	—	—	—	—
NHL totals		36	1	4	5	44					

WIESEL, ADAM
D, CANADIENS

PERSONAL: Born January 25, 1975, in Holyoke, Mass. . . . 6-3/201. . . . Shoots right. . . . Name pronounced WEE-zul.
HIGH SCHOOL: South Hadley (Mass.).
COLLEGE: Clarkson (N.Y.).
TRANSACTIONS/CAREER NOTES: Selected by Montreal Canadiens in fourth round (fourth Canadiens pick, 85th overall) of NHL entry draft (June 26, 1993).

W

Season	Team	League	Gms.	G	A	Pts.	PIM	Gms.	G	A	Pts.	PIM
			REGULAR SEASON					PLAYOFFS				
90-91—Springfield Jr. B		NEJHL	43	8	17	25	28	—	—	—	—	—
91-92—Springfield Jr. B		NEJHL	47	6	13	19	25	—	—	—	—	—
92-93—Springfield Jr. B		NEJHL	41	11	20	31	34	—	—	—	—	—
93-94—Clarkson		ECAC	33	3	7	10	28	—	—	—	—	—
94-95—Clarkson		ECAC	36	6	13	19	28	—	—	—	—	—

WILCHYNSKI, CHAD
D, RED WINGS

PERSONAL: Born April 4, 1977, in Regina, Sask. . . . 6-3/179. . . . Shoots left.
TRANSACTIONS/CAREER NOTES: Selected by Detroit Red Wings in fifth round (fifth Red Wing pick, 125 overall) of NHL entry draft (July 8, 1995).

Season	Team	League	Gms.	G	A	Pts.	PIM	Gms.	G	A	Pts.	PIM
			REGULAR SEASON					PLAYOFFS				
93-94—Regina		WHL	2	0	0	0	2	—	—	—	—	—
94-95—Regina		WHL	70	7	15	22	96	4	0	1	1	4

WILFORD, MARTY
D, BLACKHAWKS

PERSONAL: Born April 17, 1977, in Cobourg, Ont. . . . 6-0/207. . . . Shoots left.
HIGH SCHOOL: Henry Street (Whitby, Ont.).
TRANSACTIONS/CAREER NOTES: Selected by Chicago Blackhawks in sixth round (seventh Blackhawks pick, 149th overall) of NHL entry draft (July 8, 1995).

Season	Team	League	Gms.	G	A	Pts.	PIM	Gms.	G	A	Pts.	PIM
			REGULAR SEASON					PLAYOFFS				
93-94—Peterborough		OHA Jr. A	40	3	19	22	107	—	—	—	—	—
94-95—Oshawa		OHL	63	1	6	7	95	7	1	1	2	4

WILKIE, BOB
D, BLACKHAWKS

PERSONAL: Born February 11, 1969, in Calgary. . . . 6-2/220. . . . Shoots right.
TRANSACTIONS/CAREER NOTES: Selected by Detroit Red Wings as underage junior in second round (third Red Wings pick, 41st overall) of NHL entry draft (June 13, 1987). . . . Fractured kneecap (January 1990). . . . Traded by Red Wings to Philadelphia Flyers for future considerations (February 2, 1993). . . . Traded by Flyers to Chicago Blackhawks for D Karl Dykhuis (February 16, 1995).
HONORS: Named to AHL All-Star second team (1993-94).

Season	Team	League	Gms.	G	A	Pts.	PIM	Gms.	G	A	Pts.	PIM
			REGULAR SEASON					PLAYOFFS				
85-86—Calgary		WHL	63	8	19	27	56	—	—	—	—	—
86-87—Swift Current		WHL	65	12	38	50	50	4	1	3	4	2
87-88—Swift Current		WHL	67	12	68	80	124	10	4	12	16	8
88-89—Swift Current		WHL	62	18	67	85	89	12	1	11	12	47
89-90—Adirondack		AHL	58	5	33	38	64	6	1	4	5	2
90-91—Detroit		NHL	8	1	2	3	2	—	—	—	—	—
—Adirondack		AHL	43	6	18	24	71	2	1	0	1	2
91-92—Adirondack		AHL	7	1	4	5	6	16	2	5	7	12
92-93—Adirondack		AHL	14	0	5	5	20	—	—	—	—	—
—Fort Wayne		IHL	32	7	14	21	82	12	4	6	10	10
—Hershey		AHL	28	7	25	32	18	—	—	—	—	—
93-94—Hershey		AHL	69	8	53	61	100	9	1	4	5	8
—Philadelphia		NHL	10	1	3	4	8	—	—	—	—	—
94-95—Hershey		AHL	50	9	30	39	46	—	—	—	—	—
—Indianapolis		IHL	29	5	22	27	30	—	—	—	—	—
NHL totals			18	2	5	7	10					

WILKIE, DAVID
D, CANADIENS

PERSONAL: Born May 30, 1974, in Ellensburg, Wash. . . . 6-2/202. . . . Shoots right.
COLLEGE: Cariboo (B.C.).
TRANSACTIONS/CAREER NOTES: Selected by Montreal Canadiens in first round (first Canadiens pick, 20th overall) of NHL entry draft (June 20, 1992). . . . Injured right thigh (April 14, 1995); missed last nine games of season.

Season	Team	League	Gms.	G	A	Pts.	PIM	Gms.	G	A	Pts.	PIM
			REGULAR SEASON					PLAYOFFS				
89-90—Northwest Americans Jr. B		WCHL	41	21	27	48	59	—	—	—	—	—
90-91—Seattle		WHL	25	1	1	2	22	—	—	—	—	—
91-92—Kamloops		WHL	71	12	28	40	153	16	6	5	11	19
92-93—Kamloops		WHL	53	11	26	37	109	6	4	2	6	2
93-94—Kamloops		WHL	27	11	18	29	18	—	—	—	—	—
—Regina		WHL	29	27	21	48	16	4	1	4	5	4
94-95—Fredericton		AHL	70	10	43	53	34	1	0	0	0	0
—Montreal		NHL	1	0	0	0	0	—	—	—	—	—
NHL totals			1	0	0	0	0					

WILKINSON, DEREK
G, LIGHTNING

PERSONAL: Born July 29, 1974, in Windsor, Ont. . . . 6-0/160. . . . Catches left.
TRANSACTIONS/CAREER NOTES: Selected by Tampa Bay Lightning in eighth round (eighth Lightning pick, 170th overall) of NHL entry draft (June 20, 1992).

			REGULAR SEASON								PLAYOFFS						
Season	Team	League	Gms.	Min.	W	L	T	GA	SO	Avg.	Gms.	Min.	W	L	GA	SO	Avg.
91-92	—Detroit	OHL	38	1943	16	17	1	138	1	4.26	7	313	3	2	28	0	5.37
92-93	—Detroit	OHL	4	245	1	2	1	18	0	4.41	—	—	—	—	—	—	—
	—Belleville	OHL	59	3370	21	24	11	237	0	4.22	7	434	3	4	29	0	4.01
93-94	—Belleville	OHL	56	2860	24	16	4	179	2	3.76	12	700	6	†6	39	*1	3.34
94-95	—Atlanta	IHL	46	2415	22	17	‡2	121	1	3.01	4	197	2	1	8	0	2.44

WILKINSON, NEIL

D, JETS

PERSONAL: Born August 15, 1967, in Selkirk, Man. . . . 6-3/190. . . . Shoots right. . . . Full name: Neil John Wilkinson.

COLLEGE: Michigan State.

TRANSACTIONS/CAREER NOTES: Suffered concussion and broke nose (January 1986). . . . Selected by Minnesota North Stars in second round (second North Stars pick, 30th overall) of NHL entry draft (June 21, 1986). . . . Twisted knee ligaments during training camp (September 1988). . . . Bruised left instep (November 9, 1989). . . . Strained back (January 1990). . . . Tore left thumb ligaments (March 6, 1991); missed five games. . . . Selected by San Jose Sharks in NHL dispersal draft (May 30, 1991). . . . Injured groin (December 16, 1991); missed four games. . . . Injured eye (January 8, 1992); missed three games. . . . Strained back (February 4, 1992); missed 13 games. . . . Suffered facial contusions (October 28, 1992); missed two games. . . . Strained back (November 10, 1992); missed 14 games. . . . Injured hand (December 18, 1992); missed one game. . . . Strained back (February 10, 1993); missed six games. . . . Traded by Sharks to Chicago Blackhawks (July 9, 1993); completed deal in which Blackhawks sent G Jimmy Waite to Sharks for future considerations (June 18, 1993). . . . Traded by Blackhawks to Winnipeg Jets for third-round pick in 1995 draft (June 3, 1994). . . . Bruised back (April 7, 1995); missed six games.

			REGULAR SEASON					PLAYOFFS				
Season	Team	League	Gms.	G	A	Pts.	PIM	Gms.	G	A	Pts.	PIM
85-86	—Selkirk	MJHL	42	14	35	49	91	—	—	—	—	—
86-87	—Michigan State	CCHA	19	3	4	7	18	—	—	—	—	—
87-88	—Medicine Hat	WHL	55	11	21	32	157	5	1	0	1	2
88-89	—Kalamazoo	IHL	39	5	15	20	96	—	—	—	—	—
89-90	—Kalamazoo	IHL	20	6	7	13	62	—	—	—	—	—
	—Minnesota	NHL	36	0	5	5	100	7	0	2	2	11
90-91	—Kalamazoo	IHL	10	0	3	3	38	—	—	—	—	—
	—Minnesota	NHL	50	2	9	11	117	22	3	3	6	12
91-92	—San Jose	NHL	60	4	15	19	107	—	—	—	—	—
92-93	—San Jose	NHL	59	1	7	8	96	—	—	—	—	—
93-94	—Chicago	NHL	72	3	9	12	116	4	0	0	0	0
94-95	—Winnipeg	NHL	40	1	4	5	75	—	—	—	—	—
	NHL totals		317	11	49	60	611	33	3	5	8	23

WILLIAMS, DAVID

D, MIGHTY DUCKS

PERSONAL: Born August 25, 1967, in Plainfield, N.J. . . . 6-2/195. . . . Shoots right. . . . Full name: David Andrew Williams.

HIGH SCHOOL: Choate Rosemary Hall (Wallingford, Conn.).

COLLEGE: Dartmouth.

TRANSACTIONS/CAREER NOTES: Selected by New Jersey Devils as underage junior in 12th round (12th Devils pick, 234th overall) of NHL entry draft (June 15, 1985). . . . Signed as free agent by San Jose Sharks (August 9, 1991). . . . Selected by Mighty Ducks of Anaheim in NHL expansion draft (June 24, 1993). . . . Suffered from virus (December 1, 1993); missed three games.

HONORS: Named to NCAA All-America East second team (1988-89). . . . Named to ECAC All-Star first team (1988-89).

			REGULAR SEASON					PLAYOFFS				
Season	Team	League	Gms.	G	A	Pts.	PIM	Gms.	G	A	Pts.	PIM
86-87	—Dartmouth College	ECAC	23	2	19	21	20	—	—	—	—	—
87-88	—Dartmouth College	ECAC	25	8	14	22	30	—	—	—	—	—
88-89	—Dartmouth College	ECAC	25	4	11	15	28	—	—	—	—	—
89-90	—Dartmouth College	ECAC	26	3	12	15	32	—	—	—	—	—
90-91	—Knoxville	ECHL	38	12	15	27	40	3	0	0	0	4
	—Muskegon	IHL	14	1	2	3	4	—	—	—	—	—
91-92	—Kansas City	IHL	18	2	3	5	22	—	—	—	—	—
	—San Jose	NHL	56	3	25	28	40	—	—	—	—	—
92-93	—Kansas City	IHL	31	1	11	12	28	—	—	—	—	—
	—San Jose	NHL	40	1	11	12	49	—	—	—	—	—
93-94	—San Diego	IHL	16	1	6	7	17	—	—	—	—	—
	—Anaheim	NHL	56	5	15	20	42	—	—	—	—	—
94-95	—Anaheim	NHL	21	2	2	4	26	—	—	—	—	—
	—San Diego	IHL	2	0	1	1	0	5	1	0	1	0
	NHL totals		173	11	53	64	157					

W

WILLIS, SHANE

RW, LIGHTNING

PERSONAL: Born June 13, 1977, in Edmonton. . . . 6-0/170. . . . Shoots right.

TRANSACTIONS/CAREER NOTES: Selected by Tampa Bay Lightning in third round (third Lightning pick, 56th overall) of NHL entry draft (July 8, 1995).

HONORS: Named to Can.HL All-Rookie team (1994-95).

			REGULAR SEASON					PLAYOFFS				
Season	Team	League	Gms.	G	A	Pts.	PIM	Gms.	G	A	Pts.	PIM
94-95	—Prince Albert	WHL	65	24	19	43	38	13	3	4	7	6

WILM, CLARKE
C, FLAMES

PERSONAL: Born October 24, 1976, in Central Butte, Sask. . . . 5- 11/204. . . . Shoots left.
TRANSACTIONS/CAREER NOTES: Selected by Calgary Flames in sixth round (fifth Flames pick, 150th overall) of NHL entry draft (July 8, 1995).

			REGULAR SEASON					PLAYOFFS			
Season Team	League	Gms.	G	A	Pts.	PIM	Gms.	G	A	Pts.	PIM
91-92—Saskatoon	WHL	—	—	—	—	—	1	0	0	0	0
92-93—Saskatoon	WHL	69	14	19	33	71	9	4	2	6	13
93-94—Saskatoon	WHL	70	18	32	50	181	16	0	9	9	19
94-95—Saskatoon	WHL	71	20	39	59	179	10	6	1	7	21

WILSON, LANDON
RW, DENVER

PERSONAL: Born March 15, 1975, in St. Louis. . . . 6-2/202. . . . Shoots right. . . . Son of Rick Wilson, defenseman, Montreal Canadiens, St. Louis Blues and Detroit Red Wings (1973-74 through 1976-77).
COLLEGE: North Dakota.
TRANSACTIONS/CAREER NOTES: Selected by Toronto Maple Leafs in first round (second Maple Leafs pick, 19th overall) of NHL entry draft (June 26, 1993). . . . Traded by Maple Leafs with LW Wendel Clark, D Sylvain Lefebvre and first-round pick in 1994 draft (D Jeffrey Kealty) to Quebec Nordiques for C Mats Sundin, D Garth Butcher, LW Todd Warriner and first-round pick (traded to Washington Capitals who selected D Nolan Baumgartner) in 1994 draft (June 28, 1994). . . . Nordiques franchise moved to Denver for 1995-96 season.
HONORS: Named WCHA Rookie of the Year (1993-94). . . . Named to WCHA All-Rookie team (1993-94).

			REGULAR SEASON					PLAYOFFS			
Season Team	League	Gms.	G	A	Pts.	PIM	Gms.	G	A	Pts.	PIM
92-93—Dubuque	USHL	43	29	36	65	284	—	—	—	—	—
93-94—Univ. of North Dakota	WCHA	35	18	15	33	147	—	—	—	—	—
94-95—Univ. of North Dakota	WCHA	31	7	16	23	141	—	—	—	—	—
—Cornwall	AHL	8	4	4	8	25	13	3	4	7	68

WILSON, MIKE
D, SABRES

PERSONAL: Born February 26, 1975, in Brampton, Ont. . . . 6-5/180. . . . Shoots left.
TRANSACTIONS/CAREER NOTES: Selected by Vancouver Canucks in first round (first Canucks pick, 20th overall) of NHL entry draft (June 26, 1993). . . . Traded by Canucks with RW Mike Peca and first-round pick in 1995 draft (D Jay McKee) to Buffalo Sabres for RW Alexander Mogilny and fifth-round pick (LW Todd Norman) in 1995 draft (July 8, 1995).
HONORS: Named to Can.HL All-Rookie team (1992-93). . . . Named to OHL All-Rookie team (1992-93).

			REGULAR SEASON					PLAYOFFS			
Season Team	League	Gms.	G	A	Pts.	PIM	Gms.	G	A	Pts.	PIM
91-92—Georgetown Jr. B	OHA	41	9	13	22	65	—	—	—	—	—
92-93—Sudbury	OHL	53	6	7	13	58	14	1	1	2	21
93-94—Sudbury	OHL	60	4	22	26	62	9	1	3	4	8
94-95—Sudbury	OHL	64	13	34	47	46	18	1	8	9	10

WINNES, CHRIS
RW, FLYERS

PERSONAL: Born February 12, 1968, in Ridgefield, Conn. . . . 6-0/170. . . . Shoots right. . . . Name pronounced WIH-nihz.
HIGH SCHOOL: Ridgefield (Conn.), then Northwood (Lake Placid, N.Y.).
COLLEGE: New Hampshire.
TRANSACTIONS/CAREER NOTES: Selected by Boston Bruins in eighth round (ninth Bruins pick, 161st overall) of NHL entry draft (June 13, 1987). . . . Broke nose (February 23, 1992). . . . Signed as free agent by Philadelphia Flyers (August 4, 1993).
HONORS: Named to Hockey East All-Freshman team (1987-88).

W

			REGULAR SEASON					PLAYOFFS			
Season Team	League	Gms.	G	A	Pts.	PIM	Gms.	G	A	Pts.	PIM
85-86—Ridgefield H.S.	Conn. H.S.	24	40	30	70	. . .	—	—	—	—	—
86-87—Northwood School	N.Y. H.S.	27	25	25	50	. . .	—	—	—	—	—
87-88—Univ. of New Hampshire	Hockey East	30	17	19	36	28	—	—	—	—	—
88-89—Univ. of New Hampshire	Hockey East	30	11	20	31	22	—	—	—	—	—
89-90—Univ. of New Hampshire	Hockey East	24	10	13	23	12	—	—	—	—	—
90-91—Univ. of New Hampshire	Hockey East	33	15	16	31	24	—	—	—	—	—
—Maine	AHL	7	3	1	4	0	1	0	2	2	0
—Boston	NHL	—	—	—	—	—	1	0	0	0	0
91-92—Maine	AHL	45	12	35	47	30	—	—	—	—	—
—Boston	NHL	24	1	3	4	6	—	—	—	—	—
92-93—Providence	AHL	64	23	36	59	34	4	0	2	2	5
—Boston	NHL	5	0	1	1	0	—	—	—	—	—
93-94—Hershey	AHL	70	29	21	50	20	7	1	3	4	0
—Philadelphia	NHL	4	0	2	2	0	—	—	—	—	—
94-95—Hershey	AHL	78	26	40	66	39	6	2	2	4	17
NHL totals		33	1	6	7	6	1	0	0	0	0

WITT, BRENDAN
D, CAPITALS

PERSONAL: Born February 20, 1975, in Humboldt, Sask. . . . 6-1/205. . . . Shoots left.
HIGH SCHOOL: Meadowdale (Lynnwood, Wash.).
TRANSACTIONS/CAREER NOTES: Selected by Washington Capitals in first round (first Capitals pick, 11th overall) of NHL entry draft (June 26, 1993).
HONORS: Named to WHL (West) All-Star first team (1992-93 and 1993-94). . . . Won Bill Hunter Trophy (1993-94). . . . Named to Can.HL All-Star first team (1993-94).

Season	Team	League	REGULAR SEASON					PLAYOFFS				
			Gms.	G	A	Pts.	PIM	Gms.	G	A	Pts.	PIM
90-91—Seattle		WHL	—	—	—	—	—	1	0	0	0	0
91-92—Seattle		WHL	67	3	9	12	212	15	1	1	2	84
92-93—Seattle		WHL	70	2	26	28	239	5	1	2	3	30
93-94—Seattle		WHL	56	8	31	39	235	9	3	8	11	23
94-95—								Did not play.				

WOLANIN, CRAIG
D, DENVER

PERSONAL: Born July 27, 1967, in Grosse Point, Mich. . . . 6-3/205. . . . Shoots left. . . . Name pronounced woh-LAN-ihn.
TRANSACTIONS/CAREER NOTES: Selected by New Jersey Devils as underage junior in first round (first Devils pick, third overall) of NHL entry draft (June 15, 1985). . . . Bruised left shoulder (October 31, 1985). . . . Broke ring finger on left hand (February 1, 1986). . . . Underwent surgery to finger (February 19, 1986). . . . Suffered sore left hip (December 1987). . . . Sprained right knee (November 15, 1988). . . . Underwent surgery to right knee (December 1988). . . . Injured finger (November 22, 1989). . . . Traded by Devils with future considerations to Quebec Nordiques for C Peter Stastny (March 6, 1990); Devils sent D Randy Velischek to Nordiques to complete deal (August 13, 1990). . . . Injured knee (April 1, 1990). . . . Injured groin (October 17, 1991); missed three games. . . . Injured knee (January 8, 1992); missed four games. . . . Pulled muscle in right thigh (October 13, 1992); missed 24 games. . . . Bruised ribs (December 20, 1992); missed six games. . . . Injured groin (January 16, 1993); missed 28 games. . . . Pulled groin (April 1, 1993); missed one game. . . . Strained left groin (October 18, 1993); missed 11 games. . . . Bruised right knee (November 27, 1993); missed one game. . . . Strained left hip flexors (January 4, 1994); missed six games. . . . Injured groin (January 21, 1995); missed four games. . . . Bruised knee (February 25, 1995); missed four games. . . . Nordiques franchise moved to Denver for 1995-96 season.

Season	Team	League	REGULAR SEASON					PLAYOFFS				
			Gms.	G	A	Pts.	PIM	Gms.	G	A	Pts.	PIM
84-85—Kitchener		OHL	60	5	16	21	95	4	1	1	2	2
85-86—New Jersey		NHL	44	2	16	18	74	—	—	—	—	—
86-87—New Jersey		NHL	68	4	6	10	109	—	—	—	—	—
87-88—New Jersey		NHL	78	6	25	31	170	18	2	5	7	51
88-89—New Jersey		NHL	56	3	8	11	69	—	—	—	—	—
89-90—Utica		AHL	6	2	4	6	2	—	—	—	—	—
—New Jersey		NHL	37	1	7	8	47	—	—	—	—	—
—Quebec		NHL	13	0	3	3	10	—	—	—	—	—
90-91—Quebec		NHL	80	5	13	18	89	—	—	—	—	—
91-92—Quebec		NHL	69	2	11	13	80	—	—	—	—	—
92-93—Quebec		NHL	24	1	4	5	49	4	0	0	0	4
93-94—Quebec		NHL	63	6	10	16	80	—	—	—	—	—
94-95—Quebec		NHL	40	3	6	9	40	6	1	1	2	4
NHL totals			572	33	109	142	817	28	3	6	9	59

WOOD, DODY
C/LW, SHARKS

PERSONAL: Born May 8, 1972, in Chetywynd, B.C. . . . 5-11/180. . . . Shoots left.
TRANSACTIONS/CAREER NOTES: Selected by San Jose Sharks in third round (fourth Sharks pick, 45th overall) of NHL entry draft (June 22, 1991).

Season	Team	League	REGULAR SEASON					PLAYOFFS				
			Gms.	G	A	Pts.	PIM	Gms.	G	A	Pts.	PIM
89-90—Fort St. John		PCJHL	44	51	73	124	270	—	—	—	—	—
—Seattle		WHL	—	—	—	—	—	5	0	0	0	2
90-91—Seattle		WHL	69	28	37	65	272	6	0	1	1	2
91-92—Seattle		WHL	37	13	19	32	232	—	—	—	—	—
—Swift Current		WHL	3	0	2	2	14	7	2	1	3	37
92-93—Kansas City		IHL	36	3	2	5	216	6	0	1	1	15
—San Jose		NHL	13	1	1	2	71	—	—	—	—	—
93-94—Kansas City		IHL	48	5	15	20	320	—	—	—	—	—
94-95—Kansas City		IHL	44	5	13	18	255	21	7	10	17	87
—San Jose		NHL	9	1	1	2	29	—	—	—	—	—
NHL totals			22	2	2	4	100					

WOOD, RANDY
LW, MAPLE LEAFS

PERSONAL: Born October 12, 1963, in Princeton, N.J. . . . 6-0/195. . . . Shoots left.
COLLEGE: Yale.
TRANSACTIONS/CAREER NOTES: Signed as free agent by New York Islanders (August 1986). . . . Suspended four games by NHL for stick-swinging incident (October 17, 1989). . . . Strained right shoulder (March 17, 1990). . . . Traded by Islanders with C Pat LaFontaine, D Randy Hillier and future considerations to Buffalo Sabres for C Pierre Turgeon, RW Benoit Hogue, D Uwe Krupp and C Dave McLlwain; Sabres later received fourth-round pick (D Dean Melanson) in 1992 draft (October 25, 1991). . . . Selected by Toronto Maple Leafs in 1994-95 waiver draft for cash (January 18, 1995).
HONORS: Named to ECAC All-Star second team (1984-85). . . . Named to ECAC All-Star first team (1985-86).
STATISTICAL PLATEAUS: Three-goal games: 1989-90 (1).

Season	Team	League	REGULAR SEASON					PLAYOFFS				
			Gms.	G	A	Pts.	PIM	Gms.	G	A	Pts.	PIM
82-83—Yale University		ECAC	26	5	14	19	10	—	—	—	—	—
83-84—Yale University		ECAC	18	7	7	14	10	—	—	—	—	—
84-85—Yale University		ECAC	32	25	28	53	23	—	—	—	—	—
85-86—Yale University		ECAC	31	25	30	55	26	—	—	—	—	—

W

Season Team	League	REGULAR SEASON					PLAYOFFS				
		Gms.	G	A	Pts.	PIM	Gms.	G	A	Pts.	PIM
86-87—Springfield	AHL	75	23	24	47	57	—	—	—	—	—
—New York Islanders	NHL	6	1	0	1	4	13	1	3	4	14
87-88—New York Islanders	NHL	75	22	16	38	80	5	1	0	1	6
—Springfield	AHL	1	0	1	1	0	—	—	—	—	—
88-89—Springfield	AHL	1	1	1	2	0	—	—	—	—	—
—New York Islanders	NHL	77	15	13	28	44	—	—	—	—	—
89-90—New York Islanders	NHL	74	24	24	48	39	5	1	1	2	4
90-91—New York Islanders	NHL	76	24	18	42	45	—	—	—	—	—
91-92—New York Islanders	NHL	8	2	2	4	21	—	—	—	—	—
—Buffalo	NHL	70	20	16	36	65	7	2	1	3	6
92-93—Buffalo	NHL	82	18	25	43	77	8	1	4	5	4
93-94—Buffalo	NHL	84	22	16	38	71	6	0	0	0	0
94-95—Toronto	NHL	48	13	11	24	34	7	2	0	2	6
NHL totals		600	161	141	302	480	51	8	9	17	40

WOODS, MARTIN
D, JETS

PERSONAL: Born May 14, 1975, in Hull, Que. . . . 5-11/205. . . . Shoots right.
TRANSACTIONS/CAREER NOTES: Selected by Winnipeg Jets in seventh round (eighth Jets pick, 171st overall) of NHL entry draft (June 26, 1993).

Season Team	League	REGULAR SEASON					PLAYOFFS				
		Gms.	G	A	Pts.	PIM	Gms.	G	A	Pts.	PIM
91-92—Victoriaville	QMJHL	60	3	12	15	193	—	—	—	—	—
92-93—Victoriaville	QMJHL	65	13	27	40	433	4	2	1	3	41
93-94—Victoriaville	QMJHL	18	2	7	9	41	—	—	—	—	—
—Granby	QMJHL	40	6	13	19	181	3	1	2	3	17
94-95—Granby	QMJHL	19	6	16	22	116	—	—	—	—	—
—Drummondville	QMJHL	22	8	15	23	82	4	2	2	4	11

WOOLLEY, JASON
D, PANTHERS

PERSONAL: Born July 27, 1969, in Toronto. . . . 6-0/188. . . . Shoots left. . . . Full name: Jason Douglas Woolley.
COLLEGE: Michigan State.
TRANSACTIONS/CAREER NOTES: Selected by Washington Capitals in third round (fourth Capitals pick, 61st overall) of NHL entry draft (June 17, 1989). . . . Broke wrist (October 12, 1992); missed 24 games. . . . Tore abdominal muscle (January 2, 1994). . . . Signed as free agent by Detroit Vipers (October 7, 1994). . . . Contract sold by Vipers to Florida Panthers (February 14, 1995).
HONORS: Named to CCHA All-Rookie team (1988-89). . . . Named to NCAA All-America West first team (1990-91). . . . Named to CCHA All-Star first team (1990-91).
MISCELLANEOUS: Member of silver-medal-winning Canadian Olympic team (1992). •

Season Team	League	REGULAR SEASON					PLAYOFFS				
		Gms.	G	A	Pts.	PIM	Gms.	G	A	Pts.	PIM
87-88—St. Michael's Jr. B	ODHA	31	19	37	56	22	—	—	—	—	—
88-89—Michigan State	CCHA	47	12	25	37	26	—	—	—	—	—
89-90—Michigan State	CCHA	45	10	38	48	26	—	—	—	—	—
90-91—Michigan State	CCHA	40	15	44	59	24	—	—	—	—	—
91-92—Canadian national team	Int'l	60	14	30	44	36	—	—	—	—	—
—Canadian Olympic Team	Int'l	8	0	5	5	4	—	—	—	—	—
—Baltimore	AHL	15	1	10	11	6	—	—	—	—	—
—Washington	NHL	1	0	0	0	0	—	—	—	—	—
92-93—Baltimore	AHL	29	14	27	41	22	1	0	2	2	0
—Washington	NHL	26	0	2	2	10	—	—	—	—	—
93-94—Portland	AHL	41	12	29	41	14	9	2	2	4	4
—Washington	NHL	10	1	2	3	4	4	1	0	1	4
94-95—Detroit	IHL	48	8	28	36	38	—	—	—	—	—
—Florida	NHL	34	4	9	13	18	—	—	—	—	—
NHL totals		71	5	13	18	32	4	1	0	1	4

WORTMAN, KEVIN
D, SHARKS

PERSONAL: Born February 22, 1969, in Sagus, Mass. . . . 6-0/200. . . . Shoots right.
COLLEGE: American International (Mass.).
TRANSACTIONS/CAREER NOTES: Selected by Calgary Flames in eighth round (eighth Flames pick, 168th overall) of NHL entry draft (June 20, 1992). . . . Signed as free agent by San Jose Sharks (August 31, 1994).
HONORS: Named to IHL All-Star second team (1992-93).

Season Team	League	REGULAR SEASON					PLAYOFFS				
		Gms.	G	A	Pts.	PIM	Gms.	G	A	Pts.	PIM
90-91—American Int'l	NCAA	28	21	25	46	6	—	—	—	—	—
91-92—Salt Lake City	IHL	82	12	34	46	34	5	1	0	1	0
92-93—Salt Lake City	IHL	82	13	50	63	24	—	—	—	—	—
93-94—Saint John	AHL	72	17	32	49	32	7	1	5	6	16
—Calgary	NHL	5	0	0	0	2	—	—	—	—	—
94-95—Kansas City	IHL	80	6	28	34	22	21	1	1	2	4
NHL totals		5	0	0	0	2					

W

WOTTON, MARK

D, CANUCKS

PERSONAL: Born November 16, 1973, in Foxwarren, Man. . . . 6-0/190. . . . Shoots left.
TRANSACTIONS/CAREER NOTES: Selected by Vancouver Canucks in 10th round (11th Canucks pick, 237th overall) of NHL entry draft (June 20, 1992). . . . Suffered blood clot in eye (May 17, 1995); missed six playoff games.
HONORS: Named to WHL (East) All-Star second team (1993-94).

			REGULAR SEASON					PLAYOFFS				
Season	Team	League	Gms.	G	A	Pts.	PIM	Gms.	G	A	Pts.	PIM
90-91—Saskatoon		WHL	45	4	11	15	37	—	—	—	—	—
91-92—Saskatoon		WHL	64	11	25	36	92	—	—	—	—	—
92-93—Saskatoon		WHL	71	15	51	66	90	9	6	5	11	18
93-94—Saskatoon		WHL	65	12	34	46	108	16	3	12	15	32
94-95—Syracuse		AHL	75	12	29	41	50	—	—	—	—	—
—Vancouver		NHL	1	0	0	0	0	5	0	0	0	4
NHL totals			**1**	**0**	**0**	**0**	**0**	**5**	**0**	**0**	**0**	**4**

WREGGET, KEN

G, PENGUINS

PERSONAL: Born March 25, 1964, in Brandon, Man. . . . 6-1/195. . . . Catches left.
TRANSACTIONS/CAREER NOTES: Selected by Toronto Maple Leafs as underage junior in third round (fourth Maple Leafs pick, 45th overall) of NHL entry draft (June 9, 1982). . . . Injured knee (December 26, 1985). . . . Traded by Maple Leafs to Philadelphia Flyers for two first-round picks (RW Rob Pearson and D Steve Bancroft) in 1989 draft (March 6, 1989). . . . Tore hamstring (November 1, 1989); missed seven games. . . . Pulled hamstring (March 24, 1990). . . . Strained right hip flexor (November 4, 1990); missed 15 games. . . . Traded by Flyers with RW Rick Tocchet, D Kjell Samuelsson and conditional pick in 1992 draft to Pittsburgh Penguins for RW Mark Recchi, D Brian Benning and first-round pick (LW Jason Bowen) in 1992 draft (February 19, 1992). . . . Bruised right knee (February 27, 1993); missed one game. . . . Injured foot (April 4, 1994); missed five games. . . . Strained ankle (March 24, 1995); missed two games. . . . Strained ankle (April 5, 1995); missed four games.
HONORS: Won WHL Top Goaltender Trophy (1983-84). . . . Named to WHL (East) All-Star first team (1983-84).
MISCELLANEOUS: Member of Stanley Cup championship team (1992).

			REGULAR SEASON								PLAYOFFS					
Season	Team	League	Gms.	Min.	W	L	T	GA	SO	Avg.	Gms.	Min.	W	L	GA	SO	Avg.
81-82—Lethbridge	WHL	36	1713	19	12	0	118	1	4.13	3	84	. . . .	. . . .	3	0	2.14
82-83—Lethbridge	WHL	48	2696	26	17	1	157	1	3.49	*20	*1154	14	5	58	*1	*3.02
83-84—Lethbridge	WHL	53	*3053	32	20	0	161	0	*3.16	4	210	1	3	18	0	5.14
—Toronto	NHL	3	165	1	1	1	14	0	5.09	—						
84-85—Toronto	NHL	23	1278	2	15	3	103	0	4.84	—						
—St. Catharines	AHL	12	688	2	8	1	48	0	4.19	—						
85-86—St. Catharines	AHL	18	1058	8	9	0	78	1	4.42	—						
—Toronto	NHL	30	1566	9	13	4	113	0	4.33	10	607	6	4	32	†1	3.16
86-87—Toronto	NHL	56	3026	22	28	3	200	0	3.97	13	761	7	6	29	1	*2.29
87-88—Toronto	NHL	56	3000	12	35	4	222	2	4.44	2	108	0	1	11	0	6.11
88-89—Toronto	NHL	32	1888	9	20	2	139	0	4.42	—						
—Philadelphia	NHL	3	130	1	1	0	13	0	6.00	5	268	2	2	10	0	2.24
89-90—Philadelphia	NHL	51	2961	22	24	3	169	0	3.42	—						
90-91—Philadelphia	NHL	30	1484	10	14	3	88	0	3.56	—						
91-92—Philadelphia	NHL	23	1259	9	8	3	75	0	3.57	—						
—Pittsburgh	NHL	9	448	5	3	0	31	0	4.15	1	40	0	0	4	0	6.00
92-93—Pittsburgh	NHL	25	1368	13	7	2	78	0	3.42	—						
93-94—Pittsburgh	NHL	42	2456	21	12	7	138	1	3.37	—						
94-95—Pittsburgh	NHL	38	2208	*25	9	2	118	0	3.21	11	661	5	6	33	1	3.00
NHL totals		**421**	**23237**	**161**	**190**	**37**	**1501**	**3**	**3.88**	**42**	**2445**	**20**	**19**	**119**	**3**	**2.92**

WREN, BOB

LW, WHALERS

PERSONAL: Born September 16, 1974, in Preston, Ont. . . . 5-10/175. . . . Shoots left.
TRANSACTIONS/CAREER NOTES: Selected by Los Angeles Kings in fourth round (third Kings pick, 94th overall) of NHL entry draft (June 26, 1993). . . . Signed as free agent by Hartford Whalers (September 6, 1994).
HONORS: Named to OHL All-Star second team (1992-93 and 1993-94).

			REGULAR SEASON					PLAYOFFS				
Season	Team	League	Gms.	G	A	Pts.	PIM	Gms.	G	A	Pts.	PIM
89-90—Guelph		Jr. B	48	24	36	60	12	—	—	—	—	—
90-91—Kingston		Jr. B	32	27	28	55	85	—	—	—	—	—
91-92—Detroit		OHL	62	13	36	49	58	7	3	4	7	19
92-93—Detroit		OHL	63	57	88	145	91	15	4	11	15	20
93-94—Detroit		OHL	57	45	64	109	81	17	12	18	30	20
94-95—Springfield		AHL	61	16	15	31	118	—	—	—	—	—
—Richmond		ECHL	2	0	1	1	0	—	—	—	—	—

WRIGHT, DARREN

D, BRUINS

PERSONAL: Born January 19, 1976, in Duncan, B.C. . . . 6-1/182. . . . Shoots left.
TRANSACTIONS/CAREER NOTES: Selected by Boston Bruins in fifth round (fourth Bruins pick, 125th overall) of NHL entry draft (June 29, 1994).

			REGULAR SEASON					PLAYOFFS				
Season	Team	League	Gms.	G	A	Pts.	PIM	Gms.	G	A	Pts.	PIM
91-92—Prince Albert		WHL	2	0	0	0	2	—	—	—	—	—
92-93—Prince Albert		WHL	53	0	4	4	131	—	—	—	—	—

W

Season Team	League	Gms.	G	A	Pts.	PIM	Gms.	G	A	Pts.	PIM
		REGULAR SEASON					**PLAYOFFS**				
93-94—Prince Albert	WHL	56	0	5	5	151	—	—	—	—	—
94-95—Prince Albert	WHL	62	1	16	17	196	13	0	0	0	22

WRIGHT, JAMIE
LW, STARS

PERSONAL: Born May 13, 1976, in Kitchener, Ont. . . . 6-0/172. . . . Shoots left.
HIGH SCHOOL: Bishop MacDonnell (Guelph, Ont.).
TRANSACTIONS/CAREER NOTES: Selected by Dallas Stars in fourth round (third Stars pick, 98th overall) of NHL entry draft (June 29, 1994).
HONORS: Won Bobby Smith Trophy (1994-95).

Season Team	League	Gms.	G	A	Pts.	PIM	Gms.	G	A	Pts.	PIM
		REGULAR SEASON					**PLAYOFFS**				
91-92—Elmira Jr. B	OHA	44	17	11	28	46	—	—	—	—	—
92-93—Elmira Jr. B	OHA	47	22	32	54	52	—	—	—	—	—
93-94—Guelph	OHL	65	17	15	32	34	8	2	1	3	10
94-95—Guelph	OHL	65	43	39	82	36	14	6	8	14	6

WRIGHT, SHAYNE
D, SABRES

PERSONAL: Born June 30, 1975, in Welland, Ont. . . . 6-0/189. . . . Shoots left.
TRANSACTIONS/CAREER NOTES: Selected by Buffalo Sabres in 11th round (12th Sabres pick, 277th overall) of NHL entry draft (June 29, 1994).

Season Team	League	Gms.	G	A	Pts.	PIM	Gms.	G	A	Pts.	PIM
		REGULAR SEASON					**PLAYOFFS**				
92-93—Owen Sound	OHL	62	9	21	30	101	8	2	0	2	5
93-94—Owen Sound	OHL	64	11	24	35	95	9	1	10	11	4
94-95—Owen Sound	OHL	63	12	50	62	114	10	1	9	10	34
—Rochester	AHL	2	0	0	0	0	4	0	1	1	0

WRIGHT, TYLER
C, OILERS

PERSONAL: Born April 6, 1973, in Canora, Sask. . . . 5-11/185. . . . Shoots right.
TRANSACTIONS/CAREER NOTES: Selected by Edmonton Oilers in first round (first Oilers pick, 12th overall) of NHL entry draft (June 22, 1991).

Season Team	League	Gms.	G	A	Pts.	PIM	Gms.	G	A	Pts.	PIM
		REGULAR SEASON					**PLAYOFFS**				
89-90—Swift Current	WHL	67	14	18	32	119	4	0	0	0	12
90-91—Swift Current	WHL	66	41	51	92	157	3	0	0	0	6
91-92—Swift Current	WHL	63	36	46	82	295	8	2	5	7	16
92-93—Swift Current	WHL	37	24	41	65	76	17	9	17	26	49
—Edmonton	NHL	7	1	1	2	19	—	—	—	—	—
93-94—Cape Breton	AHL	65	14	27	41	160	5	2	0	2	11
—Edmonton	NHL	5	0	0	0	4	—	—	—	—	—
94-95—Cape Breton	AHL	70	16	15	31	184	—	—	—	—	—
—Edmonton	NHL	6	1	0	1	14	—	—	—	—	—
NHL totals		18	2	1	3	37					

YACHMENEV, VITALI
RW, KINGS

PERSONAL: Born January 8, 1975, in Chelyabinsk, U.S.S.R. . . . 5-9/180. . . . Shoots left. . . . Name pronounced YAHK-mehn-ehf.
TRANSACTIONS/CAREER NOTES: Selected by Los Angeles Kings in third round (third Kings pick, 59th overall) of NHL entry draft (June 29, 1994).
HONORS: Named Can.HL Rookie of the Year (1993-94). . . . Won Emms Family Award (1993-94). . . . Named to Can.HL All-Rookie team (1993-94). . . . Named to OHL All-Rookie team (1993-94). . . . Won William Hanley Trophy (1994-95).

Season Team	League	Gms.	G	A	Pts.	PIM	Gms.	G	A	Pts.	PIM
		REGULAR SEASON					**PLAYOFFS**				
90-91—Traktor Chelyabinsk	USSR	80	88	60	148	72	—	—	—	—	—
91-92—Traktor Chelyabinsk	CIS	80	82	70	152	20	—	—	—	—	—
92-93—Mechel Chelyabinsk	CIS Div. II	51	23	20	43	12	—	—	—	—	—
93-94—North Bay	OHL	66	*61	52	113	18	18	13	19	32	12
94-95—North Bay	OHL	59	53	52	105	8	6	1	8	9	2
—Phoenix	IHL	—	—	—	—	—	4	1	0	1	0

YAKE, TERRY
RW

PERSONAL: Born October 22, 1968, in New Westminster, B.C. . . . 5-11/175. . . . Shoots right.
TRANSACTIONS/CAREER NOTES: Selected by Hartford Whalers in fourth round (third Whalers pick, 81st overall) of NHL entry draft (June 13, 1987). . . . Selected by Mighty Ducks of Anaheim in NHL expansion draft (June 24, 1993). . . . Traded by Mighty Ducks to Toronto Maple Leafs for RW David Sacco (September 28, 1994). . . . Loaned by Maple Leafs to Denver Grizzlies (April 5, 1995). . . . Released by Maple Leafs (June 28, 1995).
STATISTICAL PLATEAUS: Three-goal games: 1993-94 (1).

Season Team	League	Gms.	G	A	Pts.	PIM	Gms.	G	A	Pts.	PIM
		REGULAR SEASON					**PLAYOFFS**				
84-85—Brandon	WHL	11	1	1	2	0	—	—	—	—	—
85-86—Brandon	WHL	72	26	26	52	49	—	—	—	—	—
86-87—Brandon	WHL	71	44	58	102	64	—	—	—	—	—

WY

Season	Team	League	REGULAR SEASON					PLAYOFFS				
			Gms.	G	A	Pts.	PIM	Gms.	G	A	Pts.	PIM
87-88—Brandon	WHL	72	55	85	140	59	3	4	2	6	7
88-89—Hartford	NHL	2	0	0	0	0	—	—	—	—	—
—Binghamton	AHL	75	39	56	95	57	—	—	—	—	—
89-90—Hartford	NHL	2	0	1	1	0	—	—	—	—	—
—Binghamton	AHL	77	13	42	55	37	—	—	—	—	—
90-91—Hartford	NHL	19	1	4	5	10	6	1	1	2	16
—Springfield	AHL	60	35	42	77	56	15	9	9	18	10
91-92—Hartford	NHL	15	1	1	1	2	—	—	—	—	—
—Springfield	AHL	53	21	34	55	63	8	3	4	7	2
92-93—Springfield	AHL	16	8	14	22	27	—	—	—	—	—
—Hartford	NHL	66	22	31	53	46	—	—	—	—	—
93-94—Anaheim	NHL	82	21	31	52	44	—	—	—	—	—
94-95—Toronto	NHL	19	3	2	5	2	—	—	—	—	—
—Denver	IHL	2	0	3	3	2	17	4	11	15	16
NHL totals		205	48	70	118	106	6	1	1	2	16

YASHIN, ALEXEI
C, SENATORS

PERSONAL: Born November 5, 1973, in Sverdlovsk, U.S.S.R. ... 6-3/216. ... Shoots left. ... Name pronounced YA-shihn.
TRANSACTIONS/CAREER NOTES: Selected by Ottawa Senators in first round (first Senators pick, second overall) of NHL entry draft (June 20, 1992). ... Suffered strep throat (December 4, 1993); missed one game. ... Signed by Las Vegas Thunder (October 24, 1994).
HONORS: Named to CIS All-Star team (1992-93). ... Played in NHL All-Star Game (1994).
STATISTICAL PLATEAUS: Three-goal games: 1993-94 (1), 1994-95 (1). Total: 2.

Season	Team	League	REGULAR SEASON					PLAYOFFS				
			Gms.	G	A	Pts.	PIM	Gms.	G	A	Pts.	PIM
90-91—Avtomobilist Sverdlovsk	USSR	26	2	1	3	10	—	—	—	—	—
91-92—Dynamo Moscow	CIS	35	7	5	12	19	—	—	—	—	—
92-93—Dynamo Moscow	CIS	27	10	12	22	18	10	7	3	10	18
93-94—Ottawa	NHL	83	30	49	79	22	—	—	—	—	—
94-95—Las Vegas	IHL	24	15	20	35	32	—	—	—	—	—
—Ottawa	NHL	47	21	23	44	20	—	—	—	—	—
NHL totals		130	51	72	123	42					

YAWNEY, TRENT
D, FLAMES

PERSONAL: Born September 29, 1965, in Hudson Bay, Sask. ... 6-3/195. ... Shoots left.
TRANSACTIONS/CAREER NOTES: Selected by Chicago Blackhawks as underage junior in third round (second Blackhawks pick, 45th overall) of NHL entry draft (June 9, 1984). ... Bruised left shoulder (March 1989). ... Strained right knee (April 24, 1989). ... Bruised kidney (November 11, 1989). ... Bruised thigh (January 1990). ... Strained knee (October 1990). ... Traded by Blackhawks to Calgary Flames for LW Stephane Matteau (December 16, 1991). ... Fractured right clavicle (September 26, 1992); missed first 20 games of season. ... Tore muscle in shoulder (September 9, 1993); missed 25 games. ... Strained left thumb ligaments (January 28, 1995); missed five games. ... Reinjured left thumb (February 11, 1995); missed two games. ... Strained right thumb ligaments (March 22, 1995); missed one game.

Season	Team	League	REGULAR SEASON					PLAYOFFS				
			Gms.	G	A	Pts.	PIM	Gms.	G	A	Pts.	PIM
81-82—Saskatoon	WHL	6	1	0	1	0	—	—	—	—	—
82-83—Saskatoon	WHL	59	6	31	37	44	6	0	2	2	0
83-84—Saskatoon	WHL	72	13	46	59	81	—	—	—	—	—
84-85—Saskatoon	WHL	72	16	51	67	158	3	1	6	7	7
85-86—Canadian national team	Int'l	73	6	15	21	60	—	—	—	—	—
86-87—Canadian national team	Int'l	51	4	15	19	37	—	—	—	—	—
87-88—Canadian national team	Int'l	60	4	12	16	81	—	—	—	—	—
—Canadian Olympic Team	Int'l	8	1	1	2	6	—	—	—	—	—
—Chicago	NHL	15	2	8	10	15	5	0	4	4	8
88-89—Chicago	NHL	69	5	19	24	116	15	3	6	9	20
89-90—Chicago	NHL	70	5	15	20	82	20	3	5	8	27
90-91—Chicago	NHL	61	3	13	16	77	1	0	0	0	0
91-92—Indianapolis	IHL	9	2	3	5	12	—	—	—	—	—
—Calgary	NHL	47	4	9	13	45	—	—	—	—	—
92-93—Calgary	NHL	63	1	16	17	67	6	3	2	5	6
93-94—Calgary	NHL	58	6	15	21	60	7	0	0	0	16
94-95—Calgary	NHL	37	0	2	2	108	2	0	0	0	2
NHL totals		420	26	97	123	570	56	9	17	26	79

YEGOROV, ALEXEI
C, SHARKS

PERSONAL: Born May 21, 1975, in Leningrad, U.S.S.R. ... 5-9/174. ... Shoots left.
TRANSACTIONS/CAREER NOTES: Selected by San Jose Sharks in third round (third Sharks pick, 66th overall) of NHL entry draft (June 29, 1994).

Season	Team	League	REGULAR SEASON					PLAYOFFS				
			Gms.	G	A	Pts.	PIM	Gms.	G	A	Pts.	PIM
92-93—SKA St. Petersburg	CIS	17	1	2	3	10	6	3	1	4	6
93-94—SKA St. Petersburg	CIS	23	5	3	8	18	6	0	0	0	4
94-95—SKA St. Petersburg	CIS	10	2	1	3	10	—	—	—	—	—
—Fort Worth	CHL	18	4	10	14	15	—	—	—	—	—

Y

YELLE, STEPHANE
C, DENVER

PERSONAL: Born May 9, 1974, in Ottawa. . . . 6-1/162. . . . Shoots left. . . . Name pronounced YEHL-ee.
TRANSACTIONS/CAREER NOTES: Selected by New Jersey Devils in eighth round (ninth Devils pick, 186th overall) of NHL entry draft (June 20, 1992). . . . Traded by Devils with 11th-round pick in 1994 draft (D Stephen Low) to Quebec Nordiques for 11th-round pick (C Mike Hansen) in 1994 draft (June 1, 1994). . . . Nordiques franchise moved to Denver for 1995-96 season.

Season	Team	League	REGULAR SEASON Gms.	G	A	Pts.	PIM	PLAYOFFS Gms.	G	A	Pts.	PIM
91-92—	Oshawa	OHL	55	12	14	26	20	7	2	0	2	1
92-93—	Oshawa	OHL	66	24	50	74	20	10	2	4	6	4
93-94—	Oshawa	OHL	66	35	69	104	22	5	1	7	8	2
94-95—	Cornwall	AHL	40	18	15	33	22	13	7	7	14	8

YLONEN, JUHA
C, JETS

PERSONAL: Born February 13, 1972, in Helsinki, Finland. . . . 6-0/180. . . . Shoots left. . . . Name pronounced YOO-hah YOO-lih-nehn.
TRANSACTIONS/CAREER NOTES: Selected by Winnipeg Jets in fifth round (fifth Jets pick, 91st overall) of NHL entry draft (June 22, 1991).

Season	Team	League	REGULAR SEASON Gms.	G	A	Pts.	PIM	PLAYOFFS Gms.	G	A	Pts.	PIM
90-91—	Kiekko-Espoo	Finland Dv.II	40	12	21	33	4	—	—	—	—	—
91-92—	HPK Hameenlinna	Finland	43	7	11	18	8	—	—	—	—	—
92-93—	HPK Hameenlinna	Finland	48	8	18	26	22	12	3	5	8	2
93-94—	Jokerit Helsinki	Finland	37	5	11	16	2	12	1	3	4	8
94-95—	Jokerit Helsinki	Finland	50	13	15	28	10	11	3	2	5	0

YORK, JASON
D, MIGHTY DUCKS

PERSONAL: Born May 20, 1970, in Nepean, Ont. . . . 6-0/205. . . . Shoots right.
TRANSACTIONS/CAREER NOTES: Selected by Detroit Red Wings in seventh round (sixth Red Wings pick, 129th overall) of NHL entry draft (June 16, 1990). . . . Traded by Red Wings with C/RW Mike Sillinger to Mighty Ducks of Anaheim for LW Stu Grimson, D Mark Ferner and sixth-round pick in 1996 draft (April 4, 1995).
HONORS: Named to AHL All-Star first team (1993-94).

Season	Team	League	REGULAR SEASON Gms.	G	A	Pts.	PIM	PLAYOFFS Gms.	G	A	Pts.	PIM
89-90—	Windsor	OHL	39	9	30	39	38	—	—	—	—	—
	—Kitchener	OHL	25	11	25	36	17	17	3	19	22	10
90-91—	Windsor	OHL	66	13	80	93	40	11	3	10	13	12
91-92—	Adirondack	AHL	49	4	20	24	32	5	0	1	1	0
92-93—	Adirondack	AHL	77	15	40	55	86	11	0	3	3	18
	—Detroit	NHL	2	0	0	0	0	—	—	—	—	—
93-94—	Adirondack	AHL	74	10	56	66	98	12	3	11	14	22
	—Detroit	NHL	7	1	2	3	2	—	—	—	—	—
94-95—	Adirondack	AHL	5	1	3	4	4	—	—	—	—	—
	—Detroit	NHL	10	1	2	3	2	—	—	—	—	—
	—Anaheim	NHL	15	0	8	8	12	—	—	—	—	—
NHL totals			**34**	**2**	**12**	**14**	**16**					

YOUNG, ADAM
D, DEVILS

PERSONAL: Born January 15, 1975, in Toronto. . . . 6-4/222. . . . Shoots left.
TRANSACTIONS/CAREER NOTES: Selected by New Jersey Devils in sixth round (eighth Devils pick, 148th overall) of NHL entry draft (July 8, 1995).

Season	Team	League	REGULAR SEASON Gms.	G	A	Pts.	PIM	PLAYOFFS Gms.	G	A	Pts.	PIM
92-93—	Windsor	OHL	62	3	3	6	65	—	—	—	—	—
93-94—	Windsor	OHL	45	8	9	17	105	4	0	0	0	7
94-95—	Windsor	OHL	63	4	10	14	260	10	2	1	3	36

YOUNG, JASON
LW, SABRES

PERSONAL: Born December 16, 1972, in Sudbury, Ont. . . . 5-10/190. . . . Shoots left.
TRANSACTIONS/CAREER NOTES: Suspended remainder of season by OHL for checking opposing player from behind and breaking his neck (December 4, 1990); reinstated because of career record of 86 penalty minutes in 99 games and because he had no penalties in 71 of the 99 games (March 4, 1991). . . . Selected by Buffalo Sabres in third round (third Sabres pick, 57th overall) of NHL entry draft (June 22, 1991).

Season	Team	League	REGULAR SEASON Gms.	G	A	Pts.	PIM	PLAYOFFS Gms.	G	A	Pts.	PIM
89-90—	Sudbury	OHL	62	26	47	73	64	—	—	—	—	—
90-91—	Sudbury	OHL	37	21	38	59	22	5	0	4	4	10
91-92—	Sudbury	OHL	55	26	56	82	49	11	3	2	5	14
92-93—	Rochester	AHL	59	20	20	40	60	14	3	4	7	31
93-94—	Rochester	AHL	68	17	26	43	84	4	2	2	4	8
94-95—	Rochester	AHL	51	18	17	35	80	4	1	0	1	16

Y

YOUNG, SCOTT

RW, DENVER

PERSONAL: Born October 1, 1967, in Clinton, Mass. . . . 6-0/190. . . . Shoots right. . . . Full name: Scott Allen Young.
HIGH SCHOOL: St. Mark's (Southborough, Mass.).
COLLEGE: Boston University.
TRANSACTIONS/CAREER NOTES: Selected by Hartford Whalers in first round (first Whalers pick, 11th overall) of NHL entry draft (June 21, 1986). . . . Suffered lacerations above right eye (October 8, 1988). . . . Lacerated face (February 18, 1990). . . . Traded by Whalers to Pittsburgh Penguins for RW Rob Brown (December 21, 1990). . . . Traded by Penguins to Quebec Nordiques for D Bryan Fogarty (March 10, 1992). . . . Injured rib (February 14, 1993); missed one game. . . . Bruised ribs (February 23, 1993); missed one game. . . . Sprained right ankle (October 5, 1993); missed eight games. . . . Played in Europe during 1994-95 NHL lockout. . . . Nordiques franchise moved to Denver for 1995-96 season.
HONORS: Named Hockey East Rookie of the Year (1985-86).
STATISTICAL PLATEAUS: Three-goal games: 1992-93 (1), 1993-94 (1), 1994-95 (1). Total: 3.
MISCELLANEOUS: Member of Stanley Cup championship team (1991).

			REGULAR SEASON					PLAYOFFS				
Season Team	League	Gms.	G	A	Pts.	PIM	Gms.	G	A	Pts.	PIM
84-85—St. Marks H.S.	Mass. H.S.	23	28	41	69	...	—	—	—	—	—
85-86—Boston University	Hockey East	38	16	13	29	31	—	—	—	—	—
86-87—Boston University	Hockey East	33	15	21	36	24	—	—	—	—	—
87-88—U.S. Olympic Team	Int'l	59	13	53	66	...	—	—	—	—	—
—Hartford	NHL	7	0	0	0	2	4	1	0	1	0
88-89—Hartford	NHL	76	19	40	59	27	4	2	0	2	4
89-90—Hartford	NHL	80	24	40	64	47	7	2	0	2	2
90-91—Hartford	NHL	34	6	9	15	8	—	—	—	—	—
—Pittsburgh	NHL	43	11	16	27	33	17	1	6	7	2
91-92—U.S. national team	Int'l	10	2	4	6	21	—	—	—	—	—
—U.S. Olympic Team	Int'l	8	2	1	3	2	—	—	—	—	—
—Bolzano	Italy	18	22	17	39	6	—	—	—	—	—
92-93—Quebec	NHL	82	30	30	60	20	6	4	1	5	0
93-94—Quebec	NHL	76	26	25	51	14	—	—	—	—	—
94-95—Frankfurt	Germany	1	1	0	1	0	—	—	—	—	—
—Landshut	Germany	4	6	1	7	6	—	—	—	—	—
—Quebec	NHL	48	18	21	39	14	6	3	3	6	2
NHL totals		446	134	181	315	165	44	13	10	23	10

YOUNG, WENDELL

G

PERSONAL: Born August 1, 1963, in Halifax, N.S. . . . 5-9/181. . . . Catches left.
TRANSACTIONS/CAREER NOTES: Selected by Vancouver Canucks as underage junior in fourth round (third Canucks pick, 73rd overall) of NHL entry draft (June 10, 1981). . . . Traded by Canucks with third-round pick in 1990 draft (C Kimbi Daniels) to Philadelphia Flyers for D Daryl Stanley and G Darren Jensen (August 28, 1987). . . . Traded by Flyers with seventh-round pick in 1990 draft (C Mike Valila) to Pittsburgh Penguins for third-round pick (D Chris Therien) in 1990 draft (September 1, 1988). . . . Strained ankle (October 1988). . . . Dislocated right shoulder (February 26, 1991); missed remainder of season. . . . Fractured right hand (February 5, 1992); missed six games. . . . Selected by Tampa Bay Lightning in NHL expansion draft (June 18, 1992). . . . Dislocated shoulder (November 1, 1992); missed five games. . . . Injured shoulder (March 20, 1993); missed remainder of season. . . . Injured right shoulder (September 12, 1993); missed 53 games. . . . Loaned by Lightning to Chicago Wolves (September 29, 1994). . . . Traded by Lightning to Pittsburgh Penguins for future considerations (February 16, 1995). . . . Signed as free agent by Wolves (July 10, 1995).
HONORS: Won Aldege (Baz) Bastien Trophy (1987-88). . . . Won Jack Butterfield Trophy (1987-88). . . . Named to AHL All-Star first team (1987-88).
MISCELLANEOUS: Member of Stanley Cup championship teams (1991 and 1992).

		REGULAR SEASON							PLAYOFFS						
Season Team	League	Gms.	Min.	W	L	T	GA	SO	Avg.	Gms.	Min.	W	L	GA	SO	Avg.
79-80—Cole Harbour	NSJHL	—	1446	—	—	—	94	0	3.90	—	—	—	—	—	—	—
80-81—Kitchener	OMJHL	42	2215	19	15	0	164	1	4.44	14	800	9	1	42	1	3.15
81-82—Kitchener	OHL	*60	*3470	38	17	2	195	1	3.37	15	900	12	1	35	*1	*2.33
82-83—Kitchener	OHL	61	*3611	41	19	0	231	1	3.84	12	720	6	5	43	0	3.58
83-84—Salt Lake City	IHL	20	1094	11	6	‡0	80	0	4.39	4	122	0	2	11	0	5.41
—Fredericton	AHL	11	569	7	3	0	39	1	4.11	—	—	—	—	—	—	—
—Milwaukee	IHL	6	339	...	...	...	17	0	3.01	—	—	—	—	—	—	—
84-85—Fredericton	AHL	22	1242	7	11	3	83	0	4.01	—	—	—	—	—	—	—
85-86—Fredericton	AHL	24	1457	12	8	4	78	0	3.21	—	—	—	—	—	—	—
—Vancouver	NHL	22	1023	4	9	3	61	0	3.58	1	60	0	1	5	0	5.00
86-87—Fredericton	AHL	30	1676	11	16	0	118	0	4.22	—	—	—	—	—	—	—
—Vancouver	NHL	8	420	1	6	1	35	0	5.00	—	—	—	—	—	—	—
87-88—Philadelphia	NHL	6	320	3	2	0	20	0	3.75	—	—	—	—	—	—	—
—Hershey	AHL	51	2922	33	15	1	135	1	2.77	†12	*767	12	0	28	*1	*2.19
88-89—Pittsburgh	NHL	22	1150	12	9	0	92	0	4.80	1	39	0	0	1	0	1.54
—Muskegon	IHL	2	125	...	...	...	7	0	3.36	—	—	—	—	—	—	—
89-90—Pittsburgh	NHL	43	2318	16	20	3	161	1	4.17	—	—	—	—	—	—	—
90-91—Pittsburgh	NHL	18	773	4	6	2	52	0	4.04	—	—	—	—	—	—	—
91-92—Pittsburgh	NHL	18	838	7	6	0	53	0	3.79	—	—	—	—	—	—	—
92-93—Tampa Bay	NHL	31	1591	7	19	2	97	0	3.66	—	—	—	—	—	—	—
—Atlanta	IHL	3	183	3	0	‡0	8	0	2.62	—	—	—	—	—	—	—
93-94—Tampa Bay	NHL	9	480	2	3	1	20	1	2.50	—	—	—	—	—	—	—
—Atlanta	IHL	2	120	2	0	‡0	6	0	3.00	—	—	—	—	—	—	—

Season	Team	League	Gms.	G	A	Pts.	PIM			Gms.	G	A	Pts.	PIM
94-95—Chicago		IHL	37	1882	14	11	‡7	112	0	3.57	—	—	—	—	—
—Pittsburgh		NHL	10	497	3	6	0	27	0	3.26	—	—	—	—	—
NHL totals			187	9410	59	86	12	618	2	3.94	2	99	0	1	6	0	3.64

YSEBAERT, PAUL
LW, LIGHTNING

PERSONAL: Born May 15, 1966, in Sarnia, Ont.... 6-1/190.... Shoots left.... Full name: Paul Robert Ysebaert.... Name pronounced IGHS-bahrt.
COLLEGE: Bowling Green State.
TRANSACTIONS/CAREER NOTES: Selected by New Jersey Devils in fourth round (fourth Devils pick, 74th overall) of NHL entry draft (June 9, 1984).... Pulled stomach and groin muscles (December 1988).... Suffered contusion to left thigh (March 1989).... Traded by New Jersey Devils to Detroit Red Wings for D Lee Norwood and future considerations; Devils later received fourth-round pick in 1992 draft (D Scott McCabe) to complete deal (November 27, 1990). ... Injured knee (December 1991); missed one game.... Suffered from the flu (December 22, 1992); missed one game.... Suffered from the flu (March 5, 1993); missed one game.... Suffered from the flu (March 10, 1993); missed one game.... Traded by Red Wings to Winnipeg Jets for D Aaron Ward, fourth-round pick in 1993 draft (D John Jakopin) and future considerations (June 11, 1993); Jets sent RW Alan Kerr to Red Wings to complete deal (June 18, 1993).... Traded by Jets to Chicago Blackhawks for third-round pick in 1995 draft (March 21, 1994).... Traded by Blackhawks with RW Rich Sutter to Tampa Bay Lightning for RW Jim Cummins, D Jeff Buchanan and D Tom Tilley (February 22, 1995).... Injured groin (March 24, 1995); missed two games.
HONORS: Named CCHA Rookie of the Year (1984-85).... Named to CCHA All-Star second team (1985-86 and 1986-87).... Won Les Cunningham Plaque (1989-90).... Won John B. Sollenberger Trophy (1989-90).... Named to AHL All-Star first team (1989-90).... Won Alka-Seltzer Plus Award (1991-92).
STATISTICAL PLATEAUS: Three-goal games: 1991-92 (1).

Season	Team	League	Gms.	G	A	Pts.	PIM	Gms.	G	A	Pts.	PIM
83-84—Petrolia Jr. B	OHA	33	35	42	77	20	—	—	—	—	—
84-85—Bowling Green State	CCHA	42	23	32	55	54	—	—	—	—	—
85-86—Bowling Green State	CCHA	42	23	45	68	50	—	—	—	—	—
86-87—Bowling Green State	CCHA	45	27	58	85	44	—	—	—	—	—
—Canadian national team	Int'l	5	1	0	1	4	—	—	—	—	—
87-88—Utica	AHL	78	30	49	79	60	—	—	—	—	—
88-89—Utica	AHL	56	36	44	80	22	5	0	1	1	4
—New Jersey	NHL	5	0	4	4	0	—	—	—	—	—
89-90—New Jersey	NHL	5	1	2	3	0	—	—	—	—	—
—Utica	AHL	74	53	52	*105	61	5	2	4	6	0
90-91—New Jersey	NHL	11	4	3	7	6	—	—	—	—	—
—Detroit	NHL	51	15	18	33	16	2	0	2	2	0
91-92—Detroit	NHL	79	35	40	75	55	10	1	0	1	10
92-93—Detroit	NHL	80	34	28	62	42	7	3	1	4	2
93-94—Winnipeg	NHL	60	9	18	27	18	—	—	—	—	—
—Chicago	NHL	11	5	3	8	8	6	0	0	0	8
94-95—Chicago	NHL	15	4	5	9	6	—	—	—	—	—
—Tampa Bay	NHL	29	8	11	19	12	—	—	—	—	—
NHL totals		346	115	132	247	163	25	4	3	7	20

YULE, STEVE
D, WHALERS

PERSONAL: Born May 27, 1972, in Gleichen, Alta.... 6-0/210.... Shoots right.
TRANSACTIONS/CAREER NOTES: Selected by Hartford Whalers in eighth round (eighth Whalers pick, 163rd overall) of NHL entry draft (June 22, 1991).

Season	Team	League	Gms.	G	A	Pts.	PIM	Gms.	G	A	Pts.	PIM
88-89—Kamloops	WHL	65	1	12	13	90	15	0	0	0	17
89-90—Kamloops	WHL	44	4	11	15	99	17	1	4	5	10
90-91—Kamloops	WHL	66	7	16	23	141	6	0	1	1	8
91-92—Kamloops	WHL	61	7	10	17	257	17	2	1	3	37
92-93—Springfield	AHL	38	0	4	4	52	—	—	—	—	—
93-94—Springfield	AHL	61	4	13	17	133	5	0	4	4	8
94-95—Springfield	AHL	61	1	10	11	143	—	—	—	—	—

YUSHKEVICH, DIMITRI
D, FLYERS

PERSONAL: Born November 19, 1971, in Yaroslavl, U.S.S.R.... 5-11/208.... Shoots left.... Name pronounced yoosh-KAY-vihch.
TRANSACTIONS/CAREER NOTES: Selected by Philadelphia Flyers in sixth round (sixth Flyers pick, 122nd overall) of NHL entry draft (June 22, 1991).... Sprained wrist (January 28, 1993); missed two games.... Strained groin (February 18, 1994); missed four games.... Played in Europe during 1994-95 NHL lockout.... Suffered from sore back (February 23, 1995); missed three games.... Sprained left knee (April 16, 1995); missed five games.

Season	Team	League	Gms.	G	A	Pts.	PIM	Gms.	G	A	Pts.	PIM
88-89—Torpedo Yaroslavl	USSR	23	2	1	3	8	—	—	—	—	—
89-90—Torpedo Yaroslavl	USSR	41	2	3	5	39	—	—	—	—	—
90-91—Torpedo Yaroslavl	USSR	43	10	4	14	22	—	—	—	—	—
91-92—Dynamo Moscow	CIS	41	6	7	13	14	—	—	—	—	—
—Unified Olympic Team	Int'l	8	1	2	3	4	—	—	—	—	—

Season	Team	League	Gms.	G	A	Pts.	PIM	Gms.	G	A	Pts.	PIM
92-93—Philadelphia	NHL	82	5	27	32	71	—	—	—	—	—	
93-94—Philadelphia	NHL	75	5	25	30	86	—	—	—	—	—	
94-95—Torpedo Yaroslavl	CIS	10	3	4	7	8	—	—	—	—	—	
—Philadelphia	NHL	40	5	9	14	47	15	1	5	6	12	
NHL totals		197	15	61	76	204	15	1	5	6	12	

YZERMAN, STEVE
C, RED WINGS

PERSONAL: Born May 9, 1965, in Cranbrook, B.C. ... 5-11/185. ... Shoots right. ... Name pronounced IGH-zuhr-muhn.

TRANSACTIONS/CAREER NOTES: Selected by Detroit Red Wings as underage junior in first round (first Red Wings pick, fourth overall) of NHL entry draft (June 8, 1983). ... Fractured collarbone (January 31, 1986). ... Injured ligaments of right knee and underwent surgery (March 1, 1988). ... Injured right knee in playoff game (April 8, 1991). ... Suffered herniated disc (October 21, 1993); missed 26 games. ... Sprained knee (May 27, 1995); missed three playoff games.

HONORS: Named NHL Rookie of the Year by THE SPORTING NEWS (1983-84). ... Named to NHL All-Rookie team (1983-84). ... Played in NHL All-Star Game (1984, 1988-1993). ... Won Lester B. Pearson Award (1988-89).

STATISTICAL PLATEAUS: Three-goal games: 1983-84 (1), 1984-85 (1), 1987-88 (2), 1988-89 (2), 1989-90 (2), 1990-91 (3), 1991-92 (3), 1992-93 (3). Total: 17. ... Four-goal games: 1989-90 (1). ... Total hat tricks: 18.

MISCELLANEOUS: Captain of Detroit Red Wings (1986-87 through 1994-95).

STATISTICAL NOTES: Became youngest person (18) to play in NHL All-Star Game (January 31, 1984).

Season	Team	League	Gms.	G	A	Pts.	PIM	Gms.	G	A	Pts.	PIM
81-82—Peterborough	OHL	58	21	43	64	65	6	0	1	1	16	
82-83—Peterborough	OHL	56	42	49	91	33	4	1	4	5	0	
83-84—Detroit	NHL	80	39	48	87	33	4	3	3	6	0	
84-85—Detroit	NHL	80	30	59	89	58	3	2	1	3	2	
85-86—Detroit	NHL	51	14	28	42	16	—	—	—	—	—	
86-87—Detroit	NHL	80	31	59	90	43	16	5	13	18	8	
87-88—Detroit	NHL	64	50	52	102	44	3	1	3	4	6	
88-89—Detroit	NHL	80	65	90	155	61	6	5	5	10	2	
89-90—Detroit	NHL	79	62	65	127	79	—	—	—	—	—	
90-91—Detroit	NHL	80	51	57	108	34	7	3	3	6	4	
91-92—Detroit	NHL	79	45	58	103	64	11	3	5	8	12	
92-93—Detroit	NHL	84	58	79	137	44	7	4	3	7	4	
93-94—Detroit	NHL	58	24	58	82	36	3	1	3	4	0	
94-95—Detroit	NHL	47	12	26	38	40	15	4	8	12	0	
NHL totals		862	481	679	1160	552	75	31	47	78	38	

ZALAPSKI, ZARLEY
D, FLAMES

PERSONAL: Born April 22, 1968, in Edmonton. ... 6-1/215. ... Shoots left.

TRANSACTIONS/CAREER NOTES: Selected by Pittsburgh Penguins in first round (first Penguins pick, fourth overall) of NHL entry draft (June 21, 1986). ... Suffered from Spondylosis, deterioration of the structure of the spine (October 1987). ... Tore ligaments in right knee (December 29, 1988). ... Broke right collarbone (October 25, 1989). ... Sprained right knee (February 24, 1990); missed 13 games. ... Traded by Penguins with C John Cullen and RW Jeff Parker to Hartford Whalers for C Ron Francis, D Ulf Samuelsson and D Grant Jennings (March 4, 1991). ... Suffered from the flu (March 3, 1993); missed one game. ... Sprained knee (October 14, 1993); missed 10 games. ... Traded by Hartford Whalers with C Michael Nylander and D James Patrick to Calgary Flames for D Gary Suter, LW Paul Ranheim and C Ted Drury (March 10, 1994). ... Bruised thigh (February 16, 1994); missed one game.

HONORS: Named to NHL All-Rookie team (1988-89). ... Played in NHL All-Star Game (1993).

Season	Team	League	Gms.	G	A	Pts.	PIM	Gms.	G	A	Pts.	PIM
84-85—Fort Saskatchewan	AJHL	23	17	30	47	14	—	—	—	—	—	
85-86—Fort Saskatchewan	AJHL	27	20	33	53	46	—	—	—	—	—	
—Canadian national team	Int'l	32	2	4	6	10	—	—	—	—	—	
86-87—Canadian national team	Int'l	74	11	29	40	28	—	—	—	—	—	
87-88—Canadian national team	Int'l	47	3	13	16	32	—	—	—	—	—	
—Canadian Olympic Team	Int'l	8	1	3	4	2	—	—	—	—	—	
—Pittsburgh	NHL	15	3	8	11	7	—	—	—	—	—	
88-89—Pittsburgh	NHL	58	12	33	45	57	11	1	8	9	13	
89-90—Pittsburgh	NHL	51	6	25	31	37	—	—	—	—	—	
90-91—Pittsburgh	NHL	66	12	36	48	59	—	—	—	—	—	
—Hartford	NHL	11	3	3	6	6	6	1	3	4	8	
91-92—Hartford	NHL	79	20	37	57	120	7	2	3	5	6	
92-93—Hartford	NHL	83	14	51	65	94	—	—	—	—	—	
93-94—Hartford	NHL	56	7	30	37	56	—	—	—	—	—	
—Calgary	NHL	13	3	7	10	18	7	0	3	3	2	
94-95—Calgary	NHL	48	4	24	28	46	7	0	4	4	4	
NHL totals		480	84	254	338	500	38	4	21	25	33	

ZAMUNER, ROB
LW/C, LIGHTNING

PERSONAL: Born September 17, 1969, in Oakville, Ont. ... 6-2/202. ... Shoots left. ... Name pronounced ZAM-nuhr.

TRANSACTIONS/CAREER NOTES: Selected by New York Rangers in third round (third Rangers pick, 45th overall) of NHL entry draft (June 17, 1989). ... Signed as free agent by Tampa

YZ

Bay Lightning (July 14, 1992); Rangers awarded third-round pick in 1993 draft as compensation (July 23, 1992).... Hyper-extended elbow (March 19, 1995); missed five games.

			REGULAR SEASON					PLAYOFFS				
Season Team	League	Gms.	G	A	Pts.	PIM	Gms.	G	A	Pts.	PIM
86-87—Guelph	OHL	62	6	15	21	8	—	—	—	—	—
87-88—Guelph	OHL	58	20	41	61	18	—	—	—	—	—
88-89—Guelph	OHL	66	46	65	111	38	7	5	5	10	9
89-90—Flint	IHL	77	44	35	79	32	4	1	0	1	6
90-91—Binghamton	AHL	80	25	58	83	50	9	7	6	13	35
91-92—Binghamton	AHL	61	19	53	72	42	11	8	9	17	8
—New York Rangers	NHL	9	1	2	3	2	—	—	—	—	—
92-93—Tampa Bay	NHL	84	15	28	43	74	—	—	—	—	—
93-94—Tampa Bay	NHL	59	6	6	12	42	—	—	—	—	—
94-95—Tampa Bay	NHL	43	9	6	15	24	—	—	—	—	—
NHL totals		195	31	42	73	142					

ZAVISHA, BRAD
LW/C, FLYERS

PERSONAL: Born January 4, 1972, in Hines Creek, Alta.... 6-2/205.... Shoots left.... Name pronounced zuh-VEE-shuh.
TRANSACTIONS/CAREER NOTES: Selected by Quebec Nordiques in third round (third Nordiques pick, 43rd overall) of NHL entry draft (June 16, 1990).... Traded by Nordiques with G Ron Tugnutt to Edmonton Oilers for LW Martin Rucinsky (March 10, 1992).... Injured knee (September 1992); missed entire 1992-93 season.... Traded by Oilers with sixth-round pick in 1995 draft (D Jamie Sokolsky) to Philadelphia Flyers for D Ryan McGill (March 13, 1995).
HONORS: Named to WHL (East) All-Star first team (1991-92).

			REGULAR SEASON					PLAYOFFS				
Season Team	League	Gms.	G	A	Pts.	PIM	Gms.	G	A	Pts.	PIM
88-89—Seattle	WHL	52	8	13	21	43	—	—	—	—	—
89-90—Seattle	WHL	69	22	38	60	124	13	1	6	7	16
90-91—Seattle	WHL	24	15	12	27	40	—	—	—	—	—
—Portland	WHL	48	25	22	47	41	—	—	—	—	—
91-92—Portland	WHL	11	7	4	11	18	—	—	—	—	—
—Lethbridge	WHL	59	44	40	84	160	5	3	1	4	18
93-94—Cape Breton	AHL	58	19	15	34	114	2	0	0	0	2
—Edmonton	NHL	2	0	0	0	0	—	—	—	—	—
94-95—Cape Breton	AHL	62	13	20	33	55	—	—	—	—	—
—Hershey	AHL	9	3	0	3	12	—	—	—	—	—
NHL totals		2	0	0	0	0					

ZEDNIK, RICHARD
LW, CAPITALS

PERSONAL: Born January 6, 1976, in Bystrica, Czechoslovakia.... 5-11/172.... Shoots left.... Name pronounced ZEHD-nihk.
TRANSACTIONS/CAREER NOTES: Selected by Washington Capitals in 10th round (10th Capitals pick, 249th overall) of NHL entry draft (June 29, 1994).

			REGULAR SEASON					PLAYOFFS				
Season Team	League	Gms.	G	A	Pts.	PIM	Gms.	G	A	Pts.	PIM
93-94—Banska Bystrica	Slovakia	25	3	6	9	...	—	—	—	—	—
94-95—Portland	WHL	65	35	51	86	89	9	5	5	10	20

ZELEPUKIN, VALERI
RW, DEVILS

PERSONAL: Born September 17, 1968, in Voskresensk, U.S.S.R.... 5-11/180.... Shoots left.... Name pronounced zehl-ih-POO-kihn.
TRANSACTIONS/CAREER NOTES: Selected by New Jersey Devils in 11th round (13th Devils pick, 221st overall) of NHL entry draft (June 22, 1990).... Bruised shoulder (January 22, 1993); missed five games.... Bruised left shoulder (December 22, 1993); missed one game.... Injured chest (April 14, 1994); missed one game.... Injured eye (January 24, 1995); missed first 42 games of season.... Bruised finger (April 26, 1995); missed one game.
MISCELLANEOUS: Member of Stanley Cup championship team (1995).

			REGULAR SEASON					PLAYOFFS				
Season Team	League	Gms.	G	A	Pts.	PIM	Gms.	G	A	Pts.	PIM
84-85—Khimik	USSR	5	0	0	0	2	—	—	—	—	—
85-86—Khimik	USSR	33	2	2	4	10	—	—	—	—	—
86-87—Khimik	USSR	19	1	0	1	4	—	—	—	—	—
87-88—SKA Leningrad	USSR	18	18	6	24	...	—	—	—	—	—
—CSKA Moscow	USSR	19	3	1	4	8	—	—	—	—	—
88-89—CSKA Moscow	USSR	17	2	3	5	2	—	—	—	—	—
89-90—Khimik	USSR	46	17	14	31	26	—	—	—	—	—
90-91—Khimik	USSR	46	12	19	31	22	—	—	—	—	—
91-92—Utica	AHL	22	20	9	29	8	—	—	—	—	—
—New Jersey	NHL	44	13	18	31	28	4	1	1	2	2
92-93—New Jersey	NHL	78	23	41	64	70	5	0	2	2	0
93-94—New Jersey	NHL	82	26	31	57	70	20	5	2	7	14
94-95—New Jersey	NHL	4	1	2	3	6	18	1	2	3	12
NHL totals		208	63	92	155	174	47	7	7	14	28

ZENT, JASON

PERSONAL: Born April 15, 1971, in Buffalo, N.Y. . . . 5-11/180. . . . Shoots left. . . . Full name: Jason William Zent.
HIGH SCHOOL: Nichols School (Buffalo, N.Y.).
COLLEGE: Wisconsin.
TRANSACTIONS/CAREER NOTES: Selected by New York Islanders in third round (third Islanders pick, 44th overall) of NHL entry draft (June 17, 1989). . . . Sprained ankle playing racquetball (January 1991). . . . Traded by Islanders to Ottawa Senators for fifth-round pick in 1996 draft (October 15, 1994).
HONORS: Named to WCHA All-Rookie team (1990-91). . . . Named to NCAA All-Tournament team (1991-92).

			REGULAR SEASON					PLAYOFFS			
Season Team	League	Gms.	G	A	Pts.	PIM	Gms.	G	A	Pts.	PIM
87-88—Nichols School	N.Y. H.S.	21	20	16	36	28	—	—	—	—	—
88-89—Nichols School	N.Y. H.S.	29	49	32	81	26	—	—	—	—	—
89-90—Nichols School	N.Y. H.S.			Statistics unavailable.							
90-91—University of Wisconsin ...	WCHA	39	19	18	37	51	—	—	—	—	—
91-92—University of Wisconsin ...	WCHA	43	27	17	44	134	—	—	—	—	—
92-93—University of Wisconsin ...	WCHA	40	26	12	38	88	—	—	—	—	—
93-94—University of Wisconsin ...	WCHA	42	20	21	41	120	—	—	—	—	—
94-95—Prince Edward Island	AHL	55	15	11	26	46	9	6	1	7	6

ZETTLER, ROB

PERSONAL: Born March 8, 1968, in Sept-Iles, Que. . . . 6-3/200. . . . Shoots left.
TRANSACTIONS/CAREER NOTES: Selected by Minnesota North Stars as underage junior in fifth round (fifth North Stars pick, 55th overall) of NHL entry draft (June 21, 1986). . . . Tore hip flexor (January 21, 1991); missed 11 games. . . . Selected by San Jose Sharks in NHL dispersal draft (May 30, 1991). . . . Strained back (October 20, 1992); missed three games. . . . Injured groin (April 8, 1993); missed one game. . . . Traded by Sharks to Philadelphia Flyers for C Viacheslav Butsayev (February 1, 1994). . . . Traded by Flyers to Toronto Maple Leafs for fifth-round pick in 1996 draft (July 8, 1995).

			REGULAR SEASON					PLAYOFFS			
Season Team	League	Gms.	G	A	Pts.	PIM	Gms.	G	A	Pts.	PIM
84-85—Sault Ste. Marie	OHL	60	2	14	16	37	—	—	—	—	—
85-86—Sault Ste. Marie	OHL	57	5	23	28	92	—	—	—	—	—
86-87—Sault Ste. Marie	OHL	64	13	22	35	89	4	0	0	0	0
87-88—Sault Ste. Marie	OHL	64	7	41	48	77	6	2	2	4	9
—Kalamazoo	IHL	2	0	1	1	0	7	0	2	2	2
88-89—Minnesota	NHL	2	0	0	0	0	—	—	—	—	—
—Kalamazoo	IHL	80	5	21	26	79	6	0	1	1	26
89-90—Minnesota	NHL	31	0	8	8	45	—	—	—	—	—
—Kalamazoo	IHL	41	6	10	16	64	7	0	0	0	6
90-91—Kalamazoo	IHL	1	0	0	0	2	—	—	—	—	—
—Minnesota	NHL	47	1	4	5	119	—	—	—	—	—
91-92—San Jose	NHL	74	1	8	9	99	—	—	—	—	—
92-93—San Jose	NHL	80	0	7	7	150	—	—	—	—	—
93-94—San Jose	NHL	42	0	3	3	65	—	—	—	—	—
—Philadelphia	NHL	33	0	4	4	69	—	—	—	—	—
94-95—Philadelphia	NHL	32	0	1	1	34	1	0	0	0	2
NHL totals.............................		341	2	35	37	581	1	0	0	0	2

ZEZEL, PETER

PERSONAL: Born April 22, 1965, in Toronto. . . . 5-11/209. . . . Shoots left. . . . Name pronounced ZEH-zuhl.
TRANSACTIONS/CAREER NOTES: Selected by Philadelphia Flyers as underage junior in second round (first Flyers pick, 41st overall) of NHL entry draft (June 8, 1983). . . . Broke hand (November 1984). . . . Tore medial cartilage in left knee (March 1987). . . . Sprained right ankle (November 1987). . . . Separated left shoulder (March 1988). . . . Traded by Flyers to St. Louis Blues for C Mike Bullard (November 29, 1988). . . . Pulled groin (December 1988). . . . Bruised sternum (January 1989). . . . Sprained right knee (March 5, 1989). . . . Bruised right hip (March 11, 1990). . . . Traded by Blues with D Mike Lalor to Washington Capitals for LW Geoff Courtnall (July 13, 1990). . . . Sprained left ankle (October 23, 1990); missed 23 games. . . . Reinjured ankle (December 28, 1990); missed two games. . . . Traded by Capitals with D Bob Rouse to Toronto Maple Leafs for D Al Iafrate (January 16, 1991). . . . Sprained knee (November 14, 1991); missed five games. . . . Strained knee (March 5, 1992). . . . Bruised knee (November 5, 1992); missed five games. . . . Sprained wrist (January 6, 1993); missed three games. . . . Sprained neck (March 25, 1993); missed five games. . . . Injured back (October 16, 1993); missed 41 games. . . . Suffered back spasms (January 30, 1994); missed one game. . . . Awarded to Dallas Stars with RW Grant Marshall as compensation for Maple Leafs signing free-agent RW Mike Craig (August 10, 1994). . . . Strained knee (January 20, 1995); missed first 16 games of season.
STATISTICAL PLATEAUS: Three-goal games: 1986-87 (1).
MISCELLANEOUS: Played three games as a striker for Toronto Blizzard in the North American Soccer League (1982).

			REGULAR SEASON					PLAYOFFS			
Season Team	League	Gms.	G	A	Pts.	PIM	Gms.	G	A	Pts.	PIM
81-82—Don Mills Flyers	MTHL	40	43	51	94	36	—	—	—	—	—
82-83—Toronto............................	OHL	66	35	39	74	28	4	2	4	6	0
83-84—Toronto............................	OHL	68	47	86	133	31	9	7	5	12	4
84-85—Philadelphia	NHL	65	15	46	61	26	19	1	8	9	28
85-86—Philadelphia	NHL	79	17	37	54	76	5	3	1	4	4
86-87—Philadelphia	NHL	71	33	39	72	71	25	3	10	13	10
87-88—Philadelphia	NHL	69	22	35	57	42	7	3	2	5	7
88-89—Philadelphia	NHL	26	4	13	17	15	—	—	—	—	—
—St. Louis	NHL	52	17	36	53	27	10	6	6	12	4

Z

Season Team	League	REGULAR SEASON					PLAYOFFS				
		Gms.	G	A	Pts.	PIM	Gms.	G	A	Pts.	PIM
89-90—St. Louis	NHL	73	25	47	72	30	12	1	7	8	4
90-91—Washington	NHL	20	7	5	12	10	—	—	—	—	—
—Toronto	NHL	32	14	14	28	4	—	—	—	—	—
91-92—Toronto	NHL	64	16	33	49	26	—	—	—	—	—
92-93—Toronto	NHL	70	12	23	35	24	20	2	1	3	6
93-94—Toronto	NHL	41	8	8	16	19	18	2	4	6	8
94-95—Dallas	NHL	30	6	5	11	19	3	1	0	1	0
—Kalamazoo	IHL	2	0	0	0	0	—	—	—	—	—
NHL totals		692	196	341	537	389	119	22	39	61	71

ZHAMNOV, ALEXEI
C, JETS

PERSONAL: Born October 1, 1970, in Moscow, U.S.S.R. . . . 6-1/195. . . . Shoots left. . . . Name pronounced ZHAM-nahf.

TRANSACTIONS/CAREER NOTES: Selected by Winnipeg Jets in fourth round (fifth Jets pick, 77th overall) of NHL entry draft (June 16, 1990). . . . Suffered hip flexor (November 2, 1992); missed two games. . . . Suffered back spasms (January 27, 1993); missed one game. . . . Suffered back spasms (February 3, 1993); missed one game. . . . Suffered back spasms (February 12, 1993); missed 12 games. . . . Suffered left quad contusion (October 26, 1993); missed three games. . . . Sprained back (December 27, 1993); missed eight games. . . . Suffered back spasms (March 19, 1994); missed remainder of season.

HONORS: Named to NHL All-Star second team (1994-95).

STATISTICAL PLATEAUS: Three-goal games: 1993-94 (2), 1994-95 (1). Total: 3. . . . Five-goal games: 1994-95 (1). . . . . Total hat tricks: 4.

MISCELLANEOUS: Member of gold-medal-winning Unified Olympic team (1992).

Season Team	League	REGULAR SEASON					PLAYOFFS				
		Gms.	G	A	Pts.	PIM	Gms.	G	A	Pts.	PIM
88-89—Dynamo Moscow	USSR	4	0	0	0	0	—	—	—	—	—
89-90—Dynamo Moscow	USSR	43	11	6	17	23	—	—	—	—	—
90-91—Dynamo Moscow	USSR	46	16	12	28	24	—	—	—	—	—
91-92—Dynamo Moscow	CIS	39	15	21	36	28	—	—	—	—	—
—Unified Olympic Team	Int'l	8	0	3	3	8	—	—	—	—	—
92-93—Winnipeg	NHL	68	25	47	72	58	6	0	2	2	2
93-94—Winnipeg	NHL	61	26	45	71	62	—	—	—	—	—
94-95—Winnipeg	NHL	48	30	35	65	20	—	—	—	—	—
NHL totals		177	81	127	208	140	6	0	2	2	2

ZHITNIK, ALEXEI
D, SABRES

PERSONAL: Born October 10, 1972, in Kiev, U.S.S.R. . . . 5-11/190. . . . Shoots left. . . . Name pronounced ZHIHT-nihk.

TRANSACTIONS/CAREER NOTES: Selected by Los Angeles Kings in fourth round (third Kings pick, 81st overall) of NHL entry draft (June 22, 1991). . . . Suffered from the flu (January 12, 1993); missed five games. . . . Suspended one game by NHL for cross-checking (November 30, 1993). . . . Traded by Kings with D Charlie Huddy, G Robb Stauber and fifth-round pick in 1995 draft (D Marian Menhart) to Buffalo Sabres for G Grant Fuhr, D Philippe Boucher and D Denis Tsygurov (February 14, 1995). . . . Broke thumb (February 19, 1995); missed three games. . . . Reinjured thumb (March 8, 1995); missed one game. . . . Ruptured calf muscle (March 19, 1995); missed 11 games.

MISCELLANEOUS: Member of gold-medal-winning Unified Olympic team (1992).

Season Team	League	REGULAR SEASON					PLAYOFFS				
		Gms.	G	A	Pts.	PIM	Gms.	G	A	Pts.	PIM
90-91—Sokol Kiev	USSR	40	1	4	5	46	—	—	—	—	—
91-92—CSKA Moscow	CIS	36	2	7	9	48	—	—	—	—	—
—Unified Olympic Team	Int'l	8	1	0	1	0	—	—	—	—	—
92-93—Los Angeles	NHL	78	12	36	48	80	24	3	9	12	26
93-94—Los Angeles	NHL	81	12	40	52	101	—	—	—	—	—
94-95—Los Angeles	NHL	11	2	5	7	27	—	—	—	—	—
—Buffalo	NHL	21	2	5	7	34	5	0	1	1	14
NHL totals		191	28	86	114	242	29	3	10	13	40

ZHOLTOK, SERGEI
LW, BRUINS

PERSONAL: Born December 2, 1972, in Riga, U.S.S.R. . . . 6-0/185. . . . Shoots left. . . . Name pronounced SAIR-gay ZHOHL-tahk.

TRANSACTIONS/CAREER NOTES: Selected by Boston Bruins in third round (second Bruins pick, 56th overall) of NHL entry draft (June 20, 1992).

Season Team	League	REGULAR SEASON					PLAYOFFS				
		Gms.	G	A	Pts.	PIM	Gms.	G	A	Pts.	PIM
90-91—Dynamo Riga	USSR	39	4	0	4	16	—	—	—	—	—
91-92—HC Riga	CIS	27	6	3	9	6	—	—	—	—	—
92-93—Providence	AHL	64	31	35	66	57	6	3	5	8	4
—Boston	NHL	1	0	1	1	0	—	—	—	—	—
93-94—Providence	AHL	54	29	33	62	16	—	—	—	—	—
—Boston	NHL	24	2	1	3	2	—	—	—	—	—
94-95—Providence	AHL	78	23	35	58	42	13	8	5	13	6
NHL totals		25	2	2	4	2					

Z

ZIB, LUKAS
D, OILERS

PERSONAL: Born February 24, 1977, in Budejovice, Czechoslovakia.... 6-1/198.... Shoots right.
TRANSACTIONS/CAREER NOTES: Selected by Edmonton Oilers in third round (third Oilers pick, 57th overall) of NHL entry draft (July 8, 1995).

			REGULAR SEASON					PLAYOFFS			
Season	Team	League	Gms.	G	A	Pts.	PIM	Gms.	G	A	Pts.	PIM
94-95—HC Ceske Budejovice		Czech Rep.	13	2	0	2	...	9	1	0	1	...

ZMOLEK, DOUG
D, STARS

PERSONAL: Born November 3, 1970, in Rochester, Minn.... 6-2/220.... Shoots left.... Full name: Doug Allan Zmolek.... Name pronounced zuh-MOH-lihk.
HIGH SCHOOL: John Marshall (Rochester, Minn.).
COLLEGE: Minnesota.
TRANSACTIONS/CAREER NOTES: Selected by Minnesota North Stars in first round (first North Stars pick, seventh overall) of NHL entry draft (June 17, 1989).... Selected by San Jose Sharks in NHL dispersal draft (May 30, 1991).... Traded by Sharks with D Mike Lalor to Dallas Stars for RW Ulf Dahlen and future considerations (March 19, 1994).... Sprained thumb (March 12, 1994); missed one game.... Separated shoulder (March 31, 1994); missed five games.... Lacerated hand (March 6, 1995); missed no games.... Bruised kneecap (April 7, 1995); missed six games.
HONORS: Named to NCAA All-America West second team (1991-92).... Named to WCHA All-Star second team (1991-92).

			REGULAR SEASON					PLAYOFFS			
Season	Team	League	Gms.	G	A	Pts.	PIM	Gms.	G	A	Pts.	PIM
87-88—Rochester John Marshall HS		Minn. H.S.	27	4	32	36	...	—	—	—	—	—
88-89—Rochester John Marshall HS		Minn. H.S.	29	17	41	58	...	—	—	—	—	—
89-90—University of Minnesota ...		WCHA	40	1	10	11	52	—	—	—	—	—
90-91—University of Minnesota ...		WCHA	42	3	15	18	94	—	—	—	—	—
91-92—University of Minnesota ...		WCHA	44	6	21	27	88	—	—	—	—	—
92-93—San Jose......................		NHL	84	5	10	15	229	—	—	—	—	—
93-94—San Jose......................		NHL	68	0	4	4	122	—	—	—	—	—
—Dallas		NHL	7	1	0	1	11	7	0	1	1	4
94-95—Dallas		NHL	42	0	5	5	67	5	0	0	0	10
NHL totals..................			**201**	**6**	**19**	**25**	**429**	**12**	**0**	**1**	**1**	**14**

ZOMBO, RICK
D, BLUES

PERSONAL: Born May 8, 1963, in Des Plaines, Ill.... 6-1/202.... Shoots right.
COLLEGE: North Dakota.
TRANSACTIONS/CAREER NOTES: Selected by Detroit Red Wings in eighth round (sixth Red Wings pick, 149th overall) of NHL entry draft (June 10, 1981).... Injured knee (December 1984).... Injured shoulder (December 1987).... Strained knee (December 1988).... Suspended three games by NHL for high-sticking (December 27, 1989).... Traded by Red Wings to St. Louis Blues for G Vincent Riendeau (October 18, 1991).... Fractured bone in left foot (March 14, 1992); missed seven games.... Suffered from injury (October 13, 1992); missed one game.... Suspended 10 games by NHL for slashing and shoving linesman (January 13, 1994).... Sprained ankle (January 24, 1995); missed two games.... Reinjured ankle (January 31, 1995); missed three games.... Reinjured ankle (February 9, 1995); missed eight games.... Reinjured ankle (March 5, 1995); missed 12 games.
HONORS: Named USHL Best Defenseman (1980-81).... Named to USHL All-Star first team (1980-81).

			REGULAR SEASON					PLAYOFFS			
Season	Team	League	Gms.	G	A	Pts.	PIM	Gms.	G	A	Pts.	PIM
80-81—Austin.............................		USHL	43	10	26	36	73	—	—	—	—	—
81-82—North Dakota		WCHA	45	1	15	16	31	—	—	—	—	—
82-83—North Dakota		WCHA	33	5	11	16	41	—	—	—	—	—
83-84—North Dakota		WCHA	34	7	24	31	40	—	—	—	—	—
84-85—Adirondack		AHL	56	3	32	35	70	—	—	—	—	—
—Detroit		NHL	1	0	0	0	0	—	—	—	—	—
85-86—Adirondack		AHL	69	7	34	41	94	17	0	4	4	40
—Detroit		NHL	14	0	1	1	16	—	—	—	—	—
86-87—Adirondack		AHL	25	0	6	6	22	—	—	—	—	—
—Detroit		NHL	44	1	4	5	59	7	0	1	1	9
87-88—Detroit		NHL	62	3	14	17	96	16	0	6	6	55
88-89—Detroit		NHL	75	1	20	21	106	6	0	1	1	16
89-90—Detroit		NHL	77	5	20	25	95	—	—	—	—	—
90-91—Detroit		NHL	77	4	19	23	55	7	1	0	1	10
91-92—Detroit		NHL	3	0	0	0	15	—	—	—	—	—
—St. Louis		NHL	64	3	15	18	46	6	0	2	2	12
92-93—St. Louis		NHL	71	0	15	15	78	11	0	1	1	12
93-94—St. Louis		NHL	74	2	8	10	85	4	0	0	0	11
94-95—St. Louis		NHL	23	1	4	5	24	3	0	0	0	2
NHL totals..................			**585**	**20**	**120**	**140**	**675**	**60**	**1**	**11**	**12**	**127**

ZUBOV, SERGEI
D, RANGERS

PERSONAL: Born July 22, 1970, in Moscow, U.S.S.R.... 6-1/200.... Shoots right.... Name pronounced SAIR-gay ZOO-bahf.
TRANSACTIONS/CAREER NOTES: Selected by New York Rangers in fifth round (sixth Rangers pick, 85th overall) of NHL entry draft (June 16, 1990).... Suffered concussion (February 26, 1993); missed one game.... Suffered from the flu (February 4, 1995); missed one game.... Underwent wrist surgery (February 27, 1995); missed nine games.
MISCELLANEOUS: Member of Stanley Cup championship team (1994).... Member of gold-medal-winning Unified Olympic team (1992).

Z

Season	Team	League	REGULAR SEASON					PLAYOFFS				
			Gms.	G	A	Pts.	PIM	Gms.	G	A	Pts.	PIM
88-89—CSKA Moscow	USSR	29	1	4	5	10	—	—	—	—	—
89-90—CSKA Moscow	USSR	48	6	2	8	16	—	—	—	—	—
90-91—CSKA Moscow	USSR	41	6	5	11	12	—	—	—	—	—
91-92—CSKA Moscow	CIS	36	4	7	11	6	—	—	—	—	—
—Unified Olympic Team	Int'l	8	0	1	1	0	—	—	—	—	—
92-93—CSKA Moscow	CIS	1	0	1	1	0	—	—	—	—	—
—Binghamton	AHL	30	7	29	36	14	11	5	5	10	2
—New York Rangers	NHL	49	8	23	31	4	—	—	—	—	—
93-94—New York Rangers	NHL	78	12	77	89	39	22	5	14	19	0
—Binghamton	AHL	2	1	2	3	0	—	—	—	—	—
94-95—New York Rangers	NHL	38	10	26	36	18	10	3	8	11	2
NHL totals		165	30	126	156	61	32	8	22	30	2

Z

NHL HEAD COACHES

BOWMAN, SCOTTY
RED WINGS

PERSONAL: Born September 18, 1933, in Montreal. . . . Full name: William Scott Bowman.
HONORS: Inducted into Hall of Fame (1991).

HEAD COACHING RECORD

BACKGROUND: Minor league hockey supervisor, Montreal Canadiens organization (1954-55 through 1956-57). . . . Coach, Team Canada (1976 and 1981). . . . Director of hockey operations/general manager, Buffalo Sabres (1979-80 through 1986-87). . . . Director of player development, Pittsburgh Penguins (1990-91). . . .Director of player personnel, Detroit Red Wings (1994-95 through present).
HONORS: Won Jack Adams Award (1976-77). . . . Named NHL Executive of the Year by THE SPORTING NEWS (1979-80).
RECORDS: Holds NHL career regular-season records for wins—913; and winning percentage—.656. . . . Holds NHL career playoff records for wins—152; and games—244.

			REGULAR SEASON					PLAYOFFS		
Season	Team	League	W	L	T	Pct.	Finish	W	L	Pct.
67-68—St. Louis	NHL		23	21	14	.517	3rd/Western Division	8	10	.444
68-69—St. Louis	NHL		37	25	14	.579	1st/Western Division	8	4	.667
69-70—St. Louis	NHL		37	27	12	.566	1st/Western Division	8	8	.500
70-71—St. Louis	NHL		13	10	5	.554	2nd/West Division	2	4	.333
71-72—Montreal	NHL		46	16	16	.692	3rd/East Division	2	4	.333
72-73—Montreal	NHL		52	10	16	.769	1st/East Division	12	5	.706
73-74—Montreal	NHL		45	24	9	.635	2nd/East Division	2	4	.333
74-75—Montreal	NHL		47	14	19	.706	1st/Adams Division	6	5	.545
75-76—Montreal	NHL		58	11	11	.794	1st/Adams Division	12	1	.923
76-77—Montreal	NHL		60	8	12	.825	1st/Adams Division	12	2	.857
77-78—Montreal	NHL		59	10	11	.806	1st/Adams Division	12	3	.800
78-79—Montreal	NHL		52	17	11	.719	1st/Adams Division	12	4	.750
79-80—Buffalo	NHL		47	17	16	.688	1st/Adams Division	9	5	.643
81-82—Buffalo	NHL		18	10	7	.614	3rd/Adams Division	1	3	.250
82-83—Buffalo	NHL		38	29	13	.556	3rd/Adams Division	6	4	.600
83-84—Buffalo	NHL		48	25	7	.644	2nd/Adams Division	0	3	.000
84-85—Buffalo	NHL		38	28	14	.563	3rd/Adams Division	2	3	.400
85-86—Buffalo	NHL		18	18	1	.500	5th/Adams Division	—	—	—
86-87—Buffalo	NHL		3	7	2	.333	5th/Adams Division	—	—	—
91-92—Pittsburgh	NHL		39	32	9	.544	3rd/Adams Division	16	5	.762
92-93—Pittsburgh	NHL		56	21	7	.726	1st/Patrick Division	7	5	.583
93-94—Detroit	NHL		46	30	8	.595	1st/Central Division	3	4	.429
94-95—Detroit	NHL		33	11	4	.729	1st/Central Division	12	6	.666
NHL totals (23 years)			**913**	**421**	**238**	**.656**	**NHL totals (21 years)**	**152**	**92**	**.623**

NOTES:
1968— Defeated Philadelphia in Western Division finals; defeated Minnesota in Stanley Cup semifinals; lost to Montreal in Stanley Cup finals.
1969— Defeated Philadelphia in Stanley Cup quarterfinals; defeated Los Angeles in Stanley Cup semifinals; lost to Montreal in Stanley Cup finals.
1970— Defeated Minnesota in Stanley Cup quarterfinals; defeated Pittsburgh in Stanley Cup quarterfinals; lost to Boston in Stanley Cup finals.
1971— Lost to Minnesota in Stanley Cup quarterfinals.
1972— Lost to New York Rangers in Stanley Cup quarterfinals.
1973— Defeated Buffalo in Stanley Cup quarterfinals; defeated Philadelphia in Stanley Cup semifinals; defeated Chicago in Stanley Cup finals.
1974— Lost to New York Rangers in Stanley Cup quarterfinals.
1975— Defeated Vancouver in Stanley Cup quarterfinals; lost to Buffalo in Stanley Cup semifinals.
1976— Defeated Chicago in Stanley Cup quarterfinals; defeated New York Islanders in Stanley Cup semifinals; defeated Philadelphia in Stanley Cup finals.
1977— Defeated St. Louis in Stanley Cup quarterfinals; defeated New York Islanders in Stanley Cup semifinals; defeated Boston in Stanley Cup finals.
1978— Defeated Detroit in Stanley Cup quarterfinals; defeated Toronto in Stanley Cup semifinals; defeated Boston in Stanley Cup finals.
1979— Defeated Toronto in Stanley Cup quarterfinals; defeated Boston in Stanley Cup semifinals; defeated New York Rangers in Stanley Cup finals.
1980— Defeated Vancouver in Stanley Cup preliminary round; defeated Chicago in Stanley Cup quarterfinals; lost to New York Islanders in Stanley Cup semifinals.
1982— Lost to Boston in Stanley Cup preliminary rounds.
1983— Defeated Montreal in Adams Division semifinals; lost to Boston in Adams Division finals.
1984— Lost to Quebec in Adams Division semifinals.
1985— Lost to Quebec in Adams Division semifinals.
1992— Defeated Washington in Patrick Division semifinals; defeated New York Rangers in Patrick Division finals; defeated Boston in Wales Conference finals; defeated Chicago in Stanley Cup finals.
1993— Defeated New Jersey in Patrick Division semifinals; lost to New York Islanders in Patrick Division finals.
1994— Lost to San Jose in Western Conference quarterfinals.
1995— Defeated Dallas in Western Conference quarterfinals; defeated San Jose in Western Conference semifinals; defeated Chicago in Western Conference finals; lost to New Jersey in Stanley Cup finals.

BOWNESS, RICK
SENATORS

PERSONAL: Born January 25, 1955, in Moncton, N.B. . . . . 6-1/185. . . . Shot right. . . . Full name: Richard Gary Bowness. . . . Name pronounced BOH-nihz.
HIGH SCHOOL: Halifax (N.S.).
COLLEGE: St. Mary's (N.S.).
TRANSACTIONS/CAREER NOTES: Selected by Atlanta Flames from Montreal Juniors in second round (second Flames pick, 26th overall) of NHL amateur draft (June 3, 1975). . . . Sold by Atlanta Flames to Detroit Red Wings (September 1977). . . . Sold by Red Wings to St. Louis Blues (September 1978). . . . Traded by Blues to Winnipeg Jets for D Craig Norwich (June 19, 1980).
MISCELLANEOUS: Played right wing.

Season	Team	League	REGULAR SEASON Gms.	G	A	Pts.	PIM	PLAYOFFS Gms.	G	A	Pts.	PIM
72-73	Quebec	QMJHL	30	2	7	9	2	—	—	—	—	—
73-74	Montreal	QMJHL	67	25	46	71	95	—	—	—	—	—
74-75	Montreal	QMJHL	71	24	76	100	130	—	—	—	—	—
75-76	Tulsa	CHL	64	25	38	63	160	9	4	3	7	12
	Nova Scotia	AHL	2	0	1	1	0	—	—	—	—	—
	Atlanta	NHL	5	0	0	0	0	—	—	—	—	—
76-77	Tulsa	CHL	39	15	15	30	72	8	0	1	1	20
	Atlanta	NHL	28	0	4	4	29	—	—	—	—	—
77-78	Detroit	NHL	61	8	11	19	76	4	0	0	0	2
78-79	St. Louis	NHL	24	1	3	4	30	—	—	—	—	—
	Salt Lake City	CHL	48	25	28	53	92	10	5	4	9	27
79-80	Salt Lake City	CHL	71	25	46	71	135	13	5	9	14	39
	St. Louis	NHL	10	1	2	3	11	—	—	—	—	—
80-81	Tulsa	CHL	35	12	20	32	82	—	—	—	—	—
	Winnipeg	NHL	45	8	17	25	45	1	0	0	0	0
81-82	Tulsa	CHL	79	34	53	87	201	3	0	2	2	2
82-83	Sherbrooke	AHL	65	17	31	48	117	—	—	—	—	—
NHL totals			173	18	37	55	191	5	0	0	0	2

HEAD COACHING RECORD

BACKGROUND: Player/assistant coach, Sherbrooke, Winnipeg Jets organization (1982-83). . . . Assistant coach, Jets (1983-84 through 1986-87). . . . General manager/coach, Moncton, Jets organization (1987-88).

Season	Team	League	REGULAR SEASON W	L	T	Pct.	Finish	PLAYOFFS W	L	Pct.
87-88	Moncton	AHL	27	45	8	.388	6th/North Division	—	—	—
88-89	Moncton	AHL	37	34	9	.519	3rd/North Division	—	—	—
	Winnipeg	NHL	8	17	3	.339	5th/Smythe Division	—	—	—
89-90	Maine	AHL	31	38	11	.456	5th/North Division	—	—	—
90-91	Maine	AHL	34	34	12	.500	5th/North Division	—	—	—
91-92	Boston	NHL	36	32	12	.525	2nd/Adams Division	8	7	.533
92-93	Ottawa	NHL	10	70	4	.143	6th/Adams Division	—	—	—
93-94	Ottawa	NHL	14	61	9	.220	7th/Northeast Division	—	—	—
94-95	Ottawa	NHL	9	34	5	.240	7th/Northeast Division	—	—	—
NHL totals (5 years)			77	214	33	.289	**NHL totals (1 year)**	8	7	.533

NOTES:
1992— Defeated Buffalo in Adams Division semifinals; defeated New York Rangers in Adams Division finals; lost to Pittsburgh in Wales Conference finals.

BURNS, PAT
MAPLE LEAFS

PERSONAL: Born April 4, 1952, in St.-Henri, Que.
MISCELLANEOUS: Served 17 years with the Gastineau (Quebec) and Ottawa Police Departments before assuming a professional hockey coaching career.

HEAD COACHING RECORD

BACKGROUND: Assistant coach, Canadian national team (1986). . . . Assistant coach, Canadian national junior team (1987).
HONORS: Named NHL Coach of the Year by THE SPORTING NEWS (1988-89 and 1992-93). . . . Won Jack Adams Award (1988-89 and 1992-93).

Season	Team	League	REGULAR SEASON W	L	T	Pct.	Finish	PLAYOFFS W	L	Pct.
83-84	Hull	QMJHL	25	45	0	.357	6th/LeBel Division	—	—	—
84-85	Hull	QMJHL	33	34	1	.493	2nd/LeBel Division	1	4	.200
85-86	Hull	QMJHL	54	18	0	.750	1st/LeBel Division	15	0	1.000
86-87	Hull	QMJHL	26	39	5	.407	4th/LeBel Division	4	4	.500
87-88	Sherbrooke	AHL	42	34	4	.550	3rd/North Division	2	4	.333
88-89	Montreal	NHL	53	18	9	.719	1st/Adams Division	14	7	.667
89-90	Montreal	NHL	41	28	11	.581	3rd/Adams Division	5	6	.455
90-91	Montreal	NHL	39	30	11	.556	2nd/Adams Division	7	6	.538
91-92	Montreal	NHL	41	28	11	.581	1st/Adams Division	4	7	.364
92-93	Toronto	NHL	44	29	11	.589	3rd/Norris Division •	11	10	.524
93-94	Toronto	NHL	43	29	12	.583	2nd/Central Division	9	9	.500
94-95	Toronto	NHL	21	19	8	.521	4th/Central Division	3	4	.429
NHL totals (7 years)			282	181	73	.594	**NHL totals (7 years)**	52	50	.510

NOTES:
1985— Lost to Verdun in President Cup quarterfinals.

1986— Defeated Shawinigan in President Cup quarterfinals; defeated St. Jean in President Cup semifinals; defeated Drummondville in President Cup finals.
1987— Eliminated in President Cup quarterfinal round-robin series.
1988— Lost to Fredericton in Calder Cup quarterfinals.
1989— Defeated Hartford in Adams Division semifinals; defeated Boston in Adams Division finals; defeated Philadelphia in Wales Conference finals; lost to Calgary in Stanley Cup finals.
1990— Defeated Buffalo in Adams Division semifinals; lost to Boston in Adams Division finals.
1991— Defeated Buffalo in Adams Division semifinals; lost to Boston in Adams Division finals.
1992— Defeated Hartford in Adams Division semifinals; lost to Boston in Adams Division finals.
1993— Defeated Detroit in Norris Division semifinals; defeated St. Louis in Norris Division finals; lost to Los Angeles in Campbell Conference finals.
1994— Defeated Chicago in Western Conference quarterfinals; defeated San Jose in Western Conference semifinals; lost to Vancouver in Western Conference finals.
1995— Lost to Chicago in Western Conference quarterfinals.

CAMPBELL, COLIN
RANGERS

PERSONAL: Born January 28, 1953, in London, Ont. . . . 5-9/190. . . . Shot left. . . . Full name: Colin John Campbell.
TRANSACTIONS/CAREER NOTES: Selected by Pittsburgh Penguins in second round (third Penguins pick, 27th overall) of NHL amateur draft (May 15, 1973). . . . Selected by Vancouver Blazers in WHA amateur draft (May 1973). . . . Missed part of 1975-76 season due to elbow surgery. . . . Rights transferred by Penguins to Colorado Rockies for 1976-77 season as part compensation for earlier deal in which Penguins received G Denis Herron from Rockies for Simon Nolet and G Michel Plasse (September 1, 1976). . . . Loaned by Rockies to Oklahoma City Blazers (January 1977). . . . Returned by Rockies to Penguins for future considerations (May 1977). . . . Claimed by Edmonton Oilers from Penguins in NHL expansion draft (June 13, 1979). . . . Claimed by Vancouver Canucks from Oilers in waiver draft (October 10, 1980). . . . Broke wrist (December 10, 1980). . . . Signed as free agent by Detroit Red Wings (July 26, 1982). . . . Injured ribs (November 1982). . . . Injured ribs (November 10, 1983). . . . Underwent arthroscopic surgery to knee (March 1985). . . . Announced retirement and named assistant coach of Red Wings (July 1985).
MISCELLANEOUS: Played defense.

Season Team	League	REGULAR SEASON					PLAYOFFS				
		Gms.	G	A	Pts.	PIM	Gms.	G	A	Pts.	PIM
70-71—Peterborough	OHA Jr. A	59	5	18	23	160	—	—	—	—	—
71-72—Peterborough	OHA Jr. A	50	2	23	25	158	—	—	—	—	—
72-73—Peterborough	OHA Jr. A	60	7	40	47	189	—	—	—	—	—
73-74—Vancouver	WHA	78	3	20	23	191	—	—	—	—	—
74-75—Hershey	AHL	16	1	3	4	55	—	—	—	—	—
—Pittsburgh	NHL	59	4	15	19	172	9	1	3	4	21
75-76—Pittsburgh	NHL	64	7	10	17	105	3	0	0	0	0
76-77—Oklahoma City	CHL	7	1	2	3	9	—	—	—	—	—
—Colorado	NHL	54	3	8	11	67	—	—	—	—	—
77-78—Pittsburgh	NHL	55	1	9	10	103	—	—	—	—	—
78-79—Pittsburgh	NHL	65	2	18	20	137	7	1	4	5	30
79-80—Edmonton	NHL	72	2	11	13	196	3	0	0	0	11
80-81—Vancouver	NHL	42	1	8	9	75	3	0	1	1	9
81-82—Vancouver	NHL	47	0	8	8	131	16	2	2	4	89
82-83—Detroit	NHL	53	1	7	8	74	—	—	—	—	—
83-84—Detroit	NHL	68	3	4	7	108	4	0	0	0	21
84-85—Detroit	NHL	57	1	5	6	124	—	—	—	—	—
WHA totals		78	3	20	23	191					
NHL totals		636	25	103	128	1292	45	4	10	14	181

HEAD COACHING RECORD
BACKGROUND: Assistant coach, Detroit Red Wings (1985-86 through 1989-90). . . . Assistant coach, New York Rangers (August 1990 through January 4, 1993 and 1993-94 season).

Season Team	League	REGULAR SEASON					PLAYOFFS		
		W	L	T	Pct.	Finish	W	L	Pct.
92-93—Binghamton Rangers	AHL	29	8	5	.750	1st/Southern Division	7	7	.500
94-95—New York Rangers	NHL	22	23	3	.490	4th/Atlantic Division	4	6	.400
NHL totals (1 year)		22	23	3	.490	**NHL totals (1 year)**	4	6	.400

NOTES:
1995— Defeated Quebec in Eastern Conference quarterfinals; lost to Philadelphia in Eastern Conference semifinals.

CONSTANTINE, KEVIN
SHARKS

PERSONAL: Born December 27, 1958, in International Falls, Minn. . . . 5-10/165. . . . Full name: Kevin Lars Constantine.
HIGH SCHOOL: International Falls (Minn.).
COLLEGE: Rensselaer Polytechnic Institute (N.Y.), then Nevada-Reno.
TRANSACTIONS/CAREER NOTES: Selected by Montreal Canadiens in ninth round (11th Canadiens pick, 154th overall) in NHL entry draft (June 15, 1978). . . . Invited to Canadiens tryout camp (1980).
MISCELLANEOUS: Played goalie.

Season Team	League	REGULAR SEASON								PLAYOFFS					
		Gms.	Min.	W	L	T	GA	SO	Avg.	Gms.	Min.	W	L	GA	SO	Avg.
77-78—R.P.I.	ECAC	6	229	2	2	0	13	0	3.41	—	—	—	—	—	—	—
78-79—R.P.I.	ECAC	5	233	3	2	0	15	0	3.86	—	—	—	—	—	—	—
79-80—R.P.I.	ECAC	24	1342	11	9	0	89	1	3.98	—	—	—	—	—	—	—

HEAD COACHING RECORD

BACKGROUND: Junior varsity coach, Northwood Prep School, Lake Placid, N.Y. (1986-87).... Assistant coach, Kalamazoo, Minnesota North Stars organization (1988-89 through 1990-91).
HONORS: Won Commissioner's Trophy (1991-92).

Season	Team	League	W	L	T	Pct.	Finish	W	L	Pct.
							REGULAR SEASON		PLAYOFFS	
85-86	North Iowa	USHL	17	31	0	.396	6th/USHL	2	3	.400
87-88	Rochester	USHL	39	7	2	.844	T1st/USHL	7	4	.636
91-92	Kansas City	IHL	56	22	4	.707	1st/West Division	12	3	.800
92-93	Kansas City	IHL	46	26	10	.622	2nd/Midwest Division	6	6	.500
93-94	San Jose	NHL	33	35	16	.488	3rd/Pacific Division	7	7	.500
94-95	San Jose	NHL	19	25	4	.438	3rd/Pacific Division	4	7	.364
	NHL totals (2 years)		52	60	20	.470	NHL totals (2 years)	11	14	.440

NOTES:
1986— Lost to Sioux City in USHL quarterfinals.
1988— Defeated Sioux City in USHL quarterfinals; defeated St. Paul in USHL semifinals; lost to Thunder Bay in USHL finals. Finished first in USA Jr. A National Championships.
1992— Defeated Salt Lake in Turner Cup quarterfinals; defeated Peoria in Turner Cup semifinals; defeated Muskegon in Turner Cup finals.
1993— Defeated Milwaukee in Turner Cup quarterfinals; lost to San Diego in Turner Cup semifinals.
1994— Defeated Detroit in Western Conference quarterfinals; lost to Toronto in Western Conference semifinals.
1995— Defeated Calgary in Western Conference quarterfinals; lost to Detroit in Western Conference semifinals.

CRAWFORD, MARC
DENVER

PERSONAL: Born February 13, 1961, in Belleville, Ont.... 5-11/185.... Shot left.... Full name: Marc Joseph John Crawford.... Brother of Bob Crawford right winger for four NHL teams (1979-80 through 1986-87).
TRANSACTIONS/CAREER NOTES: Selected by Vancouver Canucks in fourth round (third Canucks pick, 70th overall) of NHL entry draft (June 11, 1980).... Suspended three games by NHL for leaving the bench to fight (February 3, 1987).
MISCELLANEOUS: Played left wing.

Season	Team	League	Gms.	G	A	Pts.	PIM	Gms.	G	A	Pts.	PIM
				REGULAR SEASON					PLAYOFFS			
79-80	Cornwall	OHL	54	27	36	63	127	18	8	20	28	48
80-81	Cornwall	OHL	63	42	57	99	242	19	20	15	35	27
81-82	Dallas	CHL	34	13	21	34	71	—	—	—	—	—
	Vancouver	NHL	40	4	8	12	29	14	1	0	1	11
82-83	Vancouver	NHL	41	4	5	9	28	3	0	1	1	25
	Fredericton	AHL	30	15	9	24	59	9	1	3	4	10
83-84	Vancouver	NHL	19	0	1	1	9	—	—	—	—	—
	Fredericton	AHL	56	9	22	31	96	7	4	2	6	23
84-85	Vancouver	NHL	1	0	0	0	4	—	—	—	—	—
85-86	Vancouver	NHL	54	11	14	25	92	3	0	1	1	8
	Fredericton	AHL	26	10	14	24	55	—	—	—	—	—
86-87	Vancouver	NHL	21	0	3	3	67	—	—	—	—	—
	Fredericton	AHL	25	8	11	19	21	—	—	—	—	—
87-88	Fredericton	AHL	43	5	13	18	90	2	0	0	0	14
88-89	Milwaukee	IHL	53	23	30	53	166	11	2	5	7	26
	NHL totals		122	19	31	50	229	20	1	2	3	44

HEAD COACHING RECORD

BACKGROUND: Player/assistant coach, Fredericton Express (1987-88).... Nordiques franchise moved to Denver for 1995-96 season.
HONORS: Won Louis A.R. Pieri Memorial Award (1992-93).... Named NHL Coach of the Year by THE SPORTING NEWS (1994-95).... Won Jack Adams Award (1994-95).

Season	Team	League	W	L	T	Pct.	Finish	W	L	Pct.
							REGULAR SEASON		PLAYOFFS	
89-90	Cornwall	OHL	24	38	4	.394	6th/Leyden Division	2	4	.333
90-91	Cornwall	OHL	23	42	1	.356	7th/Leyden Division	—	—	—
91-92	St. John's	AHL	39	29	12	.562	2nd/Atlantic Division	11	5	.688
92-93	St. John's	AHL	41	26	13	.594	1st/Atlantic Division	4	5	.444
93-94	St. John's	AHL	45	23	12	.638	1st/Atlantic Division	6	5	.545
94-95	Quebec	NHL	30	13	5	.677	1st/Northeast Division	2	4	.333
	NHL totals (1 year)		30	13	5	.677	NHL totals (1 year)	2	4	.333

NOTES:
1990— Lost to Oshawa in Leyden Division quarterfinals.
1992— Defeated Cape Breton in first round of Calder Cup playoffs; defeated Moncton in second round of Calder Cup playoffs; lost to Adirondack in Calder Cup finals.
1993— Defeated Moncton in first round of Calder Cup playoffs; lost to Cape Breton in second round of Calder Cup playoffs.
1994— Defeated Cape Breton in first round of Calder Cup playoffs; lost to Moncton in second round of Calder Cup playoffs.
1995— Lost to New York Rangers in first round of Eastern Conference quarterfinals.

CRISP, TERRY
LIGHTNING

PERSONAL: Born May 28, 1943, in Parry Sound, Ont.... 5-10/180.... Shot left.... Full name: Terrance Arthur Crisp.
TRANSACTIONS/CAREER NOTES: Underwent appendectomy and hernia operation; missed part of 1963-64 season.... Selected by St. Louis Blues from Boston Bruins in NHL expansion draft

(June 6, 1967). . . . Selected by New York Islanders from Blues in expansion draft (June 6, 1972). . . . Traded by Islanders to Philadelphia Flyers for D Jean Potvin and future considerations (March 5, 1973); Islanders received D Glen Irwin to complete deal (May 18, 1973).
MISCELLANEOUS: Played center. . . . Member of Stanley Cup championship teams (1974 and 1975).

			REGULAR SEASON					PLAYOFFS			
Season Team	League	Gms.	G	A	Pts.	PIM	Gms.	G	A	Pts.	PIM
60-61—St. Mary's	OHA					Did not play.					
61-62—Niagara Falls	OHA	50	16	22	38	0	—	—	—	—	—
62-63—Niagara Falls	OHA	50	39	35	74	0	—	—	—	—	—
63-64—Minneapolis	CPHL	42	15	20	35	22	—	—	—	—	—
64-65—Minneapolis	CPHL	70	28	34	62	22	5	0	2	2	0
65-66—Boston	NHL	3	0	0	0	0	—	—	—	—	—
—Oklahoma City	CPHL	61	11	22	33	35	9	1	5	6	0
66-67—Oklahoma City	CPHL	69	31	42	73	37	11	3	7	10	0
67-68—St. Louis	NHL	73	9	20	29	10	18	1	5	6	6
68-69—Kansas City	CHL	4	1	1	2	4	—	—	—	—	—
—St. Louis	NHL	57	6	9	15	14	12	3	4	7	20
69-70—St. Louis	NHL	26	5	6	11	2	16	2	3	5	2
—Buffalo	AHL	51	15	34	49	14	—	—	—	—	—
70-71—St. Louis	NHL	54	5	11	16	13	6	1	0	1	2
71-72—St. Louis	NHL	75	13	18	31	12	11	1	3	4	2
72-73—New York Islanders	NHL	54	4	16	20	6	—	—	—	—	—
—Philadelphia	NHL	12	1	5	6	2	11	3	2	5	2
73-74—Philadelphia	NHL	71	10	21	31	28	17	2	2	4	4
74-75—Philadelphia	NHL	71	8	19	27	20	9	2	4	6	0
75-76—Philadelphia	NHL	38	6	9	15	28	10	0	5	5	2
76-77—Philadelphia	NHL	2	0	0	0	0	—	—	—	—	—
NHL totals		536	67	134	201	135	110	15	28	43	40

HEAD COACHING RECORD

BACKGROUND: Assistant coach, Philadelphia Flyers (1977-78 and 1978-79). . . . Assistant coach, Canadian national team (1990 through 1992).
HONORS: Won Matt Leyden Trophy (1982-83 and 1984-85). . . . Named NHL Coach of the Year by THE SPORTING NEWS (1987-88).

		REGULAR SEASON					PLAYOFFS		
Season Team	League	W	L	T	Pct.	Finish	W	L	Pct.
79-80—Sault Ste. Marie	OHL	22	45	1	.331	6th/Leyden Division	—	—	—
80-81—Sault Ste. Marie	OHL	47	19	2	.706	1st/Leyden Division	8	7	.526
81-82—Sault Ste. Marie	OHL	40	25	3	.610	2nd/Emms Division	4	6	.423
82-83—Sault Ste. Marie	OHL	48	21	1	.693	1st/Emms Division	7	6	.531
83-84—Sault Ste. Marie	OHL	38	28	4	.571	3rd/Emms Division	8	4	.625
84-85—Sault Ste. Marie	OHL	54	11	1	.826	1st/Emms Division	12	2	.813
85-86—Moncton	AHL	34	34	12	.500	3rd/North Division	5	5	.500
86-87—Moncton	AHL	43	31	6	.575	3rd/North Division	2	4	.333
87-88—Calgary	NHL	48	23	9	.656	1st/Smythe Division	4	5	.444
88-89—Calgary	NHL	54	17	9	.731	1st/Smythe Division	16	6	.727
89-90—Calgary	NHL	42	23	15	.619	1st/Smythe Division	2	4	.333
92-93—Tampa Bay	NHL	23	54	7	.315	6th/Norris Division	—	—	—
93-94—Tampa Bay	NHL	30	43	11	.423	7th/Atlantic Division	—	—	—
94-95—Tampa Bay	NHL	17	28	3	.385	6th/Atlantic Division	—	—	—
NHL totals (6 years)		214	188	54	.529	**NHL totals (3 years)**	22	15	.595

NOTES:
1981— Sault Ste. Marie had four playoff ties.
1982— Defeated Brantford in Emms Division semifinals; lost to Kitchener in Emms Division finals. Sault Ste. Marie had three playoff ties.
1983— Defeated Brantford in Emms Division semifinals; defeated Kitchener in Emms Division finals; lost to Oshawa in Robertson Cup finals. Sault Ste. Marie had three playoff ties.
1984— Defeated Windsor in Emms Division quarterfinals; defeated Brantford in Emms Division semifinals; lost to Kitchener in Emms Division finals. Sault Ste. Marie had four playoff ties.
1985— Defeated Kitchener in Emms Division quarterfinals; defeated Hamilton in Emms Division finals; defeated Peterborough in Robertson Cup finals. Sault Ste. Marie had two playoff ties.
1986— Defeated Maine in Calder Cup quarterfinals; lost to Adirondack in Calder Cup semifinals.
1987— Lost to Adirondack in Calder Cup quarterfinals.
1988— Defeated Los Angeles in Smythe Division semifinals; lost to Edmonton in Smythe Division finals.
1989— Defeated Vancouver in Smythe Division semifinals; defeated Los Angeles in Smythe Division finals; defeated Chicago in Campbell Conference finals; defeated Montreal in Stanley Cup finals.
1990— Lost to Los Angeles in Smythe Division semifinals.

DEMERS, JACQUES
CANADIENS

PERSONAL: Born August 25, 1944, in Montreal.

HEAD COACHING RECORD

BACKGROUND: Director of player personnel, Chicago Cougars of WHA (1972-73).
HONORS: Won Louis A.R. Pieri Memorial Award (1982-83). . . . Named NHL Coach of the Year by THE SPORTING NEWS (1985-86 and 1986-87). . . . Won Jack Adams Award (1986-87 and 1987-88).

Season Team	League	REGULAR SEASON					PLAYOFFS		
		W	L	T	Pct.	Finish	W	L	Pct.
79-80—Quebec	NHL	25	44	11	.381	5th/Adams Division	—	—	—
81-82—Fredericton	AHL	20	55	5	.281	5th/Northern Division	—	—	—
82-83—Fredericton	AHL	45	27	8	.544	1st/Northern Division	6	6	.500
83-84—St. Louis	NHL	32	41	7	.444	2nd/Norris Division	6	5	.545
84-85—St. Louis	NHL	37	31	12	.538	1st/Norris Division	0	3	.000
85-86—St. Louis	NHL	37	34	9	.519	3rd/Norris Division	10	9	.526
86-87—Detroit	NHL	34	36	10	.488	2nd/Norris Division	9	7	.563
87-88—Detroit	NHL	41	28	11	.581	1st/Norris Division	9	7	.563
88-89—Detroit	NHL	34	34	12	.500	1st/Norris Division	2	4	.333
89-90—Detroit	NHL	28	38	14	.438	5th/Norris Division	—	—	—
92-93—Montreal	NHL	48	30	6	.607	3rd/Adams Division	16	4	.800
93-94—Montreal	NHL	41	29	14	.571	3rd/Northeast Division	3	4	.429
94-95—Montreal	NHL	18	23	7	.448	6th/Northeast Division	—	—	—
NHL totals (11 years)		375	368	113	.504	NHL totals (8 years)	55	43	.561

NOTES:
1983— Defeated Adirondack in Calder Cup quarterfinals; lost to Maine in Calder Cup semifinals.
1984— Defeated Detroit in Norris Division semifinals; lost to Minnesota in Norris Division finals.
1985— Lost to Minnesota in Norris Division semifinals.
1986— Defeated Minnesota in Norris Division semifinals; defeated Toronto in Norris Division finals; lost to Calgary in Campbell Conference finals.
1987— Defeated Chicago in Norris Division semifinals; defeated Toronto in Norris Division finals; lost to Edmonton in Campbell Conference finals.
1988— Defeated Toronto in Norris Division semifinals; defeated St. Louis in Norris Division finals; lost to Edmonton in Campbell Conference finals.
1989— Lost to Chicago in Norris Division semifinals.
1993— Defeated Quebec in Adams Division semifinals; defeated Buffalo in Adams Division finals; defeated New York Islanders in Wales Conference finals; defeated Los Angeles in Stanley Cup finals.
1994— Lost to Boston in Eastern Conference quarterfinals.

GAINEY, BOB
STARS

PERSONAL: Born December 13, 1953, in Peterborough, Ont. . . . 6-2/195. . . . Shot left. . . . Full name: Robert Michael Gainey.
HIGH SCHOOL: Peterborough (Ont.) Secondaire.
TRANSACTIONS/CAREER NOTES: Selected by Montreal Canadiens in first round (first Canadiens pick, eighth overall) of NHL amateur draft (May 15, 1973). . . . Separated shoulder; missed part of 1977-78 season. . . . Tore ligaments in left knee (October 5, 1986). . . . Pulled groin (March 14, 1987). . . . Bruised ankle (April 1988). . . . Bruised left foot (October 15, 1988). . . . Broke bone in right foot (January 9, 1989); missed two months. . . . Injured left knee (March 17, 1989). . . . Reinjured left knee (April 5, 1989). . . . Released by Canadiens when he announced he would play the 1989-90 season with Epinal Ecureuils (Squirrels), a second-division team in France.
HONORS: Won Frank J. Selke Award (1977-78 through 1980-81). . . . Played in NHL All-Star Game (1977, 1978, 1980 and 1981). . . . Won Conn Smythe Trophy (1978-79). . . . Inducted into Hall of Fame (1992).
STATISTICAL PLATEAUS: Three-goal games: 1987-88 (1).
MISCELLANEOUS: Played left wing. . . . Member of Stanley Cup championship teams (1976-79 and 1986). . . . Captain of Montreal Canadiens (1981-82 through 1988-89).

Season Team	League	REGULAR SEASON					PLAYOFFS			
		Gms.	G	A	Pts.	PIM	Gms.	G	A	Pts.	PIM
70-71—Peterborough	OHA Jr. A	4	0	0	0	0	—	—	—	—	—
71-72—Peterborough	OHA Mj. Jr. A	4	2	1	3	33	—	—	—	—	—
72-73—Peterborough	OHA Mj. Jr. A	52	22	21	43	99	—	—	—	—	—
73-74—Nova Scotia	AHL	6	2	5	7	4	—	—	—	—	—
—Montreal	NHL	66	3	7	10	34	6	0	0	0	6
74-75—Montreal	NHL	80	17	20	37	49	11	2	4	6	4
75-76—Montreal	NHL	78	15	13	28	57	13	1	3	4	20
76-77—Montreal	NHL	80	14	19	33	41	14	4	1	5	25
77-78—Montreal	NHL	66	15	16	31	57	15	2	7	9	14
78-79—Montreal	NHL	79	20	18	38	44	16	6	10	16	10
79-80—Montreal	NHL	64	14	19	33	32	10	1	1	2	4
80-81—Montreal	NHL	78	23	24	47	36	3	0	0	0	2
81-82—Montreal	NHL	79	21	24	45	24	5	0	1	1	8
82-83—Montreal	NHL	80	12	18	30	43	3	0	0	0	4
83-84—Montreal	NHL	77	17	22	39	41	15	1	5	6	9
84-85—Montreal	NHL	79	19	13	32	40	12	1	3	4	13
85-86—Montreal	NHL	80	20	23	43	20	20	5	5	10	12
86-87—Montreal	NHL	47	8	8	16	19	17	1	3	4	6
87-88—Montreal	NHL	78	11	11	22	14	6	0	1	1	6
88-89—Montreal	NHL	49	10	7	17	34	16	1	4	5	8
89-90—Epinal	France				Statistics unavailable.						
NHL totals		1160	239	262	501	585	182	25	48	73	151

HEAD COACHING RECORD

BACKGROUND: Player/coach for Epinal, a second-division team in France (1989-90). . . . General manager, Minnesota North Stars (1992-93 through present). . . . North Stars franchise moved from Minnesota to Dallas and renamed Stars for 1993-94 season.

Season Team	League	W	L	T	Pct.	Finish	W	L	Pct.
						REGULAR SEASON		PLAYOFFS	
89-90—Epinal	France					Record unavailable.			
90-91—Minnesota	NHL	27	39	14	.425	4th/Norris Division	14	9	.609
91-92—Minnesota	NHL	32	42	6	.438	4th/Norris Division	3	4	.429
92-93—Minnesota	NHL	36	38	10	.488	5th/Norris Division	—	—	—
93-94—Dallas	NHL	42	29	13	.577	3rd/Central Division	5	4	.556
94-95—Dallas	NHL	17	23	8	.438	5th/Central Division	1	4	.200
NHL totals (5 years)		154	171	51	.477	NHL totals (4 years)	23	21	.523

NOTES:
1991— Defeated Chicago in Norris Division semifinals; defeated St. Louis in Norris Division finals; defeated Edmonton in Campbell Conference finals; lost to Pittsburgh in Stanley Cup finals.
1992— Lost to Detroit in Norris Division semifinals.
1994— Defeated St. Louis in Western Conference quarterfinals; lost to Vancouver in Western Conference semifinals.
1995— Lost to Detroit in Western Conference quarterfinals.

HARTSBURG, CRAIG
BLACKHAWKS

PERSONAL: Born June 29, 1959, in Stratford, Ont. . . . 6-1/190. . . . Shot left.
TRANSACTIONS/CAREER NOTES: Selected by Minnesota North Stars in first round (first North Stars pick, sixth overall) of NHL entry draft (August 9, 1979). . . . Torn ligaments in left knee (September 1977). . . . Separated shoulder (September 1980). . . . Underwent surgery to remove bone spur on knee (October 10, 1983). . . . Injured ligaments in left knee (January 10, 1984). . . . Suffered hip pointer (October 1984). . . . Suffered fractured femur (December 1984). . . . Injured groin (January 16, 1986); missed four games. . . . Suffered herniated disc (February 1987). . . . Strained knee ligaments (March 1987). . . . Suffered concussion (November 7, 1987). . . . Injured left hip and separated shoulder (March 1988). . . . Underwent shoulder surgery (March 1988). . . . Suffered staph infection on right ankle and required hospitalization (October 11, 1988). . . . Re-injured right ankle (January 2, 1989).
HONORS: Won Max Kaminsky Memorial Trophy (1976-77). . . . Named to OHA All-Star second team (1976-77). . . . Played in NHL All-Star Game (1980, 1982 and 1983).
STATISTICAL PLATEAUS: Three-goal games: 1986-87 (1).
MISCELLANEOUS: Played defense. . . . Captain of Minnesota North Stars (1982-83 through 1987-88).

Season Team	League	Gms.	G	A	Pts.	PIM	Gms.	G	A	Pts.	PIM
				REGULAR SEASON					PLAYOFFS		
75-76—Sault Ste. Marie	OHA	64	9	19	28	65	—	—	—	—	—
76-77—Sault Ste. Marie	OHA	61	29	64	93	142	9	0	11	11	27
77-78—Sault Ste. Marie	OHA	36	15	42	57	101	13	4	8	12	24
78-79—Birmingham	WHA	77	9	40	49	73	—	—	—	—	—
79-80—Minnesota	NHL	79	14	30	44	81	15	3	1	4	17
80-81—Minnesota	NHL	74	13	30	43	124	19	3	12	15	16
81-82—Minnesota	NHL	76	17	60	77	117	4	1	2	3	14
82-83—Minnesota	NHL	78	12	50	62	109	9	3	8	11	7
83-84—Minnesota	NHL	26	7	7	14	37	—	—	—	—	—
84-85—Minnesota	NHL	32	7	11	18	54	9	5	3	8	14
85-86—Minnesota	NHL	75	10	47	57	127	5	0	1	1	2
86-87—Minnesota	NHL	73	11	50	61	93	—	—	—	—	—
87-88—Minnesota	NHL	27	3	16	19	29	—	—	—	—	—
88-89—Minnesota	NHL	30	4	14	18	47	—	—	—	—	—
WHA totals		77	9	40	49	73					
NHL totals		570	98	315	413	818	61	15	27	42	70

HEAD COACHING RECORD
BACKGROUND: Assistant coach, Minnesota North Stars (1989-90). . . . Assistant coach, Philadelphia Flyers (1990-91 through 1993-94).

Season Team	League	W	L	T	Pct.	Finish	W	L	Pct.
						REGULAR SEASON		PLAYOFFS	
94-95—Guelph	OHL	47	14	5	.712	1st/Central Division	10	4	.714

NOTES:
1995— Defeated Owen Sound in second round of OHL playoffs; defeated Belleville in third round of OHL playoffs; lost to Detroit in J. Ross Robertson Cup finals.

HOLMGREN, PAUL
WHALERS

PERSONAL: Born December 2, 1955, in St. Paul, Minn. . . . 6-3/210. . . . Shot right. . . . Full name: Paul Howard Holmgren.
COLLEGE: Minnesota.
TRANSACTIONS/CAREER NOTES: Selected by Edmonton Oilers in fifth round (fifth Oilers pick, 67th overall) of WHA amateur draft (May 1974). . . . WHA rights traded by Oilers to Minnesota Fighting Saints for future considerations (May 1974). . . . Selected by Philadelphia Flyers in sixth round (fifth Flyers pick, 108th overall) of NHL amateur draft (June 3, 1975). . . . Signed by Flyers following demise of Minnesota Fighting Saints (March 1976). . . . Scratched cornea and underwent eye surgery (1976). . . . Separated right shoulder; missed parts of 1976-77 and 1977-78 seasons. . . . Separated shoulder during Team U.S.A. training camp (August 1981). . . . Suspended five games for assaulting referee (December 12, 1981). . . . Injured knee (January 1982). . . . Sprained left knee (October 1983). . . . Bruised left shoulder (January 1984). . . . Traded by Flyers to Minnesota North Stars for RW Paul Guay and third-round pick (G Darryl Gilmour) in 1985 draft (February 1984). . . . Injured shoulder (March 1984). . . . Underwent shoulder surgery (April 1984). . . . Separated shoulder (October 1984). . . . Underwent surgery to left shoulder (December 1984). . . . Announced retirement and named assistant coach of Flyers (July 1985).
HONORS: Played in NHL All-Star Game (1981).
MISCELLANEOUS: Played right wing.

Season	Team	League	Gms.	G	A	Pts.	PIM	Gms.	G	A	Pts.	PIM
			REGULAR SEASON					**PLAYOFFS**				
73-74—St. Paul Jr. B	OHA		55	22	59	81	183	—	—	—	—	—
74-75—University of Minnesota ...	WCHA		37	10	21	31	108	—	—	—	—	—
75-76—Johnstown	NAHL		6	3	12	15	12	—	—	—	—	—
—Minnesota	WHA		51	14	16	30	121	—	—	—	—	—
—Richmond	AHL		6	4	4	8	23	—	—	—	—	—
—Philadelphia	NHL		1	0	0	0	2	—	—	—	—	—
76-77—Philadelphia	NHL		59	14	12	26	201	10	1	1	2	25
77-78—Philadelphia	NHL		62	16	18	34	190	12	1	4	5	26
78-79—Philadelphia	NHL		57	19	10	29	168	8	1	5	6	22
79-80—Philadelphia	NHL		74	30	35	65	267	18	10	10	20	47
80-81—Philadelphia	NHL		77	22	37	59	306	12	5	9	14	49
81-82—Philadelphia	NHL		41	9	22	31	183	4	1	2	3	6
82-83—Philadelphia	NHL		77	19	24	43	178	3	0	0	0	6
83-84—Philadelphia	NHL		52	9	13	22	105	—	—	—	—	—
—Minnesota	NHL		11	2	5	7	46	12	0	1	1	6
84-85—Philadelphia	NHL		16	4	3	7	38	3	0	0	0	8
WHA totals............			51	14	16	30	121					
NHL totals............			527	144	179	323	1684	82	19	32	51	195

HEAD COACHING RECORD

BACKGROUND: Assistant coach Philadelphia Flyers (1985-86 through 1987-88). .... General manager, Hartford Whalers (1993-94).

Season	Team	League	W	L	T	Pct.	Finish	W	L	Pct.
			REGULAR SEASON					**PLAYOFFS**		
88-89—Philadelphia	NHL		36	36	8	.500	4th/Patrick Division	10	9	.526
89-90—Philadelphia	NHL		30	39	11	.444	6th/Patrick Division	—	—	—
90-91—Philadelphia	NHL		33	37	10	.475	5th/Patrick Division	—	—	—
91-92—Philadelphia	NHL		8	14	2	.380		—	—	—
92-93—Hartford..........................	NHL		26	52	6	.345	5th/Adams Division	—	—	—
93-94—Hartford..........................	NHL		4	11	2	.294		—	—	—
94-95—Hartford..........................	NHL		19	24	5	.448	4th/Northeast Division	—	—	—
NHL totals (7 years)............			156	213	44	.431	**NHL totals (1 year)**............	10	9	.526

NOTES:
1989— Defeated Washington in Patrick Division semifinals; defeated Pittsburgh in Patrick Division finals; lost to Montreal in Wales Conference finals.
1993— Replaced as head coach by Pierre McGuire (November 16), with club in seventh place.
1994— Re-named as head coach (June 28).

JOHNSTON, EDDIE
PENGUINS

PERSONAL: Born November 24, 1935, in Montreal. .... 6-0/190. .... Shot left. .... Full name: Edward Joseph Johnston.
TRANSACTIONS/CAREER NOTES: Drafted by Boston Bruins from Montreal Canadiens (June 1962). .... Traded by Boston to Toronto Maple Leafs to complete deal in which Boston received G Jacques Plante and Toronto's third-round pick in 1973 amateur draft (C Doug Gibson) for Boston's first-round pick (D Ian Turnbull) in 1973 amateur draft (May 22, 1973). .... Traded by Maple Leafs to St. Louis Blues for RW Gary Sabourin (May 27, 1974). .... Sold by Blues to Chicago Blackhawks (January 27, 1978).
HONORS: Won EPHL Leading Goalie Award (1960-61).
STATISTICAL NOTES: Played in every minute of every game in 1963-64, the last player to do so in NHL.
MISCELLANEOUS: Played goalie. .... Member of Stanley Cup Championship teams (1970 and 1972).

Season	Team	League	Gms.	Min.	W	L	T	GA	SO	Avg.	Gms.	Min.	W	L	GA	SO	Avg.
			REGULAR SEASON								**PLAYOFFS**						
54-55—Trois Rivieres Flambeaux	QJHL		46	...	...	...	...	169	1	3.67	—	—	—	—	—	—	—
55-56—Chatham.......................	OHA		7	420	...	...	...	31	0	4.43	—	—	—	—	—	—	—
—Amherst......................	ACSHL		1	60	...	...	...	2	0	2.00	—	—	—	—	—	—	—
56-57—Winnipeg	WHL		50	...	...	...	...	193	2	3.86	—	—	—	—	—	—	—
57-58—Shawinigan Falls	QHL		63	...	...	...	...	230	*5	3.65	14	0	...	...	49	1	3.50
58-59—Edmonton....................	WHL		49	...	...	...	...	163	1	3.32	3	180	...	...	12	0	4.00
59-60—Johnstown	EHL		63	...	...	...	...	169	4	2.69	—	—	—	—	—	—	—
60-61—Hull-Ottawa	EPHL		70	...	...	...	...	187	*11	*2.67	14	0	...	...	28	0	*2.00
61-62—Spokane	WHL		70	...	...	...	...	237	3	3.30	16	0	...	...	58	*1	3.63
62-63—Boston	NHL		50	2907	11	27	11	196	1	4.05	—	—	—	—	—	—	—
63-64—Boston	NHL		70	*4200	18	*40	12	211	6	3.01	—	—	—	—	—	—	—
64-65—Boston	NHL		47	2820	12	31	4	163	3	3.47	—	—	—	—	—	—	—
65-66—Los Angeles	WHL		5	...	...	...	...	10	1	2.31	—	—	—	—	—	—	—
—Boston	NHL		33	1743	10	19	2	108	1	3.72	—	—	—	—	—	—	—
66-67—Boston	NHL		34	1880	9	21	2	116	0	3.70	—	—	—	—	—	—	—
67-68—Boston	NHL		28	1524	11	8	5	73	0	2.87	—	—	—	—	—	—	—
68-69—Boston	NHL		24	1440	14	6	4	74	2	3.08	1	65	0	1	4	0	3.69
69-70—Boston	NHL		37	2176	16	9	11	108	3	2.98	1	60	0	1	4	0	4.00
70-71—Boston	NHL		38	2280	30	6	2	96	4	2.53	1	60	0	1	7	0	7.00
71-72—Boston	NHL		38	2260	27	8	3	102	2	2.71	7	420	*6	1	13	1	*1.86
72-73—Boston	NHL		45	2510	24	17	1	137	5	3.27	3	160	1	2	9	0	3.38
73-74—Toronto.......................	NHL		26	1516	12	9	4	78	1	3.09	1	60	0	1	6	0	6.00
74-75—St. Louis	NHL		30	1800	12	13	5	93	2	3.10	1	60	0	1	5	0	5.00

Season	Team	League	Gms.	Min.	W	L	T	GA	SO	Avg.	Gms.	Min.	W	L	GA	SO	Avg.
								REGULAR SEASON						**PLAYOFFS**			
75-76	St. Louis	NHL	38	2152	11	17	9	130	1	3.62	—	—	—	—	—	—	—
76-77	St. Louis	NHL	38	2111	13	16	5	108	1	3.07	3	138	0	2	9	0	3.91
77-78	St. Louis	NHL	12	650	5	6	1	45	0	4.15	—	—	—	—	—	—	—
	Chicago	NHL	4	240	1	3	0	17	0	4.25	—	—	—	—	—	—	—
NHL totals			592	34209	236	256	81	1855	32	3.25	18	1023	7	10	57	1	3.34

HEAD COACHING RECORD

BACKGROUND: General manager, Pittsburgh Penguins (1983-84 through 1987-88).... Assistant general manager, Penguins (1988-89).... Vice president/general manager, Hartford Whalers (1989-90 through 1991-92).

Season	Team	League	W	L	T	Pct.	Finish	W	L	Pct.
							REGULAR SEASON	**PLAYOFFS**		
78-79	New Brunswick	AHL	41	29	10	.575	2nd/Northern Division	2	3	.400
79-80	Chicago	NHL	34	27	19	.544	1st/Smythe Division	3	4	.429
80-81	Pittsburgh	NHL	30	37	13	.456	3rd/Norris Division	2	3	.400
81-82	Pittsburgh	NHL	31	36	13	.469	4th/Patrick Division	2	3	.400
82-83	Pittsburgh	NHL	18	53	9	.281	6th/Patrick Division	—	—	—
93-94	Pittsburgh	NHL	44	27	13	.601	1st/Northeast Division	2	4	.333
94-95	Pittsburgh	NHL	29	16	3	.635	2nd/Northeast Division	5	7	.417
NHL totals (6 years)			186	196	70	.489	**NHL totals (5 years)**	14	21	.400

NOTES:
1979— Lost to Nova Scotia in Calder Cup quarterfinals.
1980— Defeated St. Louis in Stanley Cup preliminary round; lost to Buffalo in Stanley Cup quarterfinals.
1981— Lost to St. Louis in Stanley Cup preliminary round.
1982— Lost to New York Islanders in Stanley Cup preliminary round.
1994— Lost to Washington in Eastern Conference quarterfinals.
1995— Defeated Washington in Eastern Conference quarterfinals; lost to New Jersey in Eastern Conference semifinals.

KASPER, STEVE
BRUINS

PERSONAL: Born September 28, 1961, in Montreal.... 5-8/175.... Shot left.... Full name: Stephen Neil Kasper.

TRANSACTIONS/CAREER NOTES: Selected by Boston Bruins in fourth round (third Bruins pick, 81st overall) of NHL entry draft (June 11, 1980).... Suffered hip pointer (October 17, 1981).... Underwent surgery to remove torn shoulder cartilage (November 9, 1982).... Underwent surgery to left shoulder for torn capsule (December 7, 1982).... Suffered concussion (April 1983).... Separated left shoulder (November 1983).... Underwent surgery to shoulder (January 7, 1984).... Reinjured shoulder (February 1984).... Traded by Bruins with LW Jay Miller to Los Angeles Kings for C Bobby Carpenter (January 23, 1989).... Ruptured sinus cavity and fractured eye socket (January 2, 1991); missed 10 games.... Traded by Kings with D Steve Duchesne and fourth-round pick in 1991 draft (D Aris Brimanis) to Philadelphia Flyers for D Jeff Chychrun and rights to RW Jari Kurri (May 30, 1991).... Tore knee ligaments (November 20, 1991); missed remainder of season.... Traded by Flyers to Tampa Bay Lightning for LW Dan Vincelette (December 8, 1992).... Bruised shoulder (January 30, 1993); missed two games.
HONORS: Won Frank J. Selke Trophy (1981-82).
STATISTICAL PLATEAUS: Three-goal games: 1984-85 (1), 1985-86 (1), 1987-88 (1). Total: 3.
MISCELLANEOUS: Played center.

Season	Team	League	Gms.	G	A	Pts.	PIM	Gms.	G	A	Pts.	PIM
					REGULAR SEASON					**PLAYOFFS**		
77-78	Verdun	QMJHL	63	26	45	71	16	—	—	—	—	—
78-79	Verdun	QMJHL	67	37	67	104	53	11	7	6	13	22
79-80	Sorel	QMJHL	70	57	65	122	117	—	—	—	—	—
80-81	Sorel	QMJHL	2	5	2	7	0	—	—	—	—	—
	Boston	NHL	76	21	35	56	94	3	0	1	1	0
81-82	Boston	NHL	73	20	31	51	72	11	3	6	9	22
82-83	Boston	NHL	24	2	6	8	24	12	2	1	3	10
83-84	Boston	NHL	27	3	11	14	19	3	0	0	0	7
84-85	Boston	NHL	77	16	24	40	33	5	1	0	1	9
85-86	Boston	NHL	80	17	23	40	73	3	1	0	1	4
86-87	Boston	NHL	79	20	30	50	51	3	0	2	2	0
87-88	Boston	NHL	79	26	44	70	35	23	7	6	13	10
88-89	Boston	NHL	49	10	16	26	49	—	—	—	—	—
	Los Angeles	NHL	29	9	15	24	14	11	1	5	6	10
89-90	Los Angeles	NHL	77	17	28	45	27	10	1	1	2	2
90-91	Los Angeles	NHL	67	9	19	28	33	10	4	6	10	8
91-92	Philadelphia	NHL	16	3	2	5	10	—	—	—	—	—
92-93	Philadelphia	NHL	21	1	3	4	2	—	—	—	—	—
	Tampa Bay	NHL	47	3	4	7	18	—	—	—	—	—
NHL totals			821	177	291	468	554	94	20	28	48	82

HEAD COACHING RECORD

BACKGROUND: Assistant coach, Boston Bruins (1993-94).

Season	Team	League	W	L	T	Pct.	Finish	W	L	Pct.
							REGULAR SEASON	**PLAYOFFS**		
94-95	Providence	AHL	39	30	11	.556	3rd/Northern Division	6	7	.462

NOTES:
1995— Defeated Portland in AHL Division semifinals; lost to Albany in Division finals.

KEENAN, MIKE
BLUES

PERSONAL: Born October 21, 1949, in Whitby, Ont. . . . 5-10/180. . . . Shot right. . . . Full name: Michael Edward Keenan.
HIGH SCHOOL: Denis O'Connor (Ajax, Ont.).
COLLEGE: St. Lawrence (N.Y.).

Season Team	League	REGULAR SEASON					PLAYOFFS				
		Gms.	G	A	Pts.	PIM	Gms.	G	A	Pts.	PIM
69-70—St. Lawrence University...	ECAC	10	0	4	4	32	—	—	—	—	—
70-71—St. Lawrence University...	ECAC	22	4	12	16	35	—	—	—	—	—
71-72—St. Lawrence University...	ECAC	25	13	16	29	52	—	—	—	—	—

HEAD COACHING RECORD

BACKGROUND: Coach, Canadian national junior team (1980). . . . Coach, NHL All-Star team (1985-86, 1987-88, 1992-93). . . . Coach, Team Canada (1987). . . . General manager, Chicago Blackhawks (1989-90 through 1991-92). . . . General manager/coach, Team Canada (1991). . . . Coach, Canadian national team (1993).
HONORS: Named NHL Coach of the Year by THE SPORTING NEWS (1984-85). . . . Won Jack Adams Award (1984-85).

Season Team	League	REGULAR SEASON					PLAYOFFS		
		W	L	T	Pct.	Finish	W	L	Pct.
79-80—Peterborough	OHL	47	20	1	.699	1st/Leyden Division	15	3	.833
80-81—Rochester	AHL	30	42	8	.425	5th/Southern Division	—	—	—
81-82—Rochester	AHL	40	31	9	.556	2nd/Southern Division	4	5	.444
82-83—Rochester	AHL	46	25	9	.631	1st/Southern Division	12	4	.750
83-84—University of Toronto	OUAA	41	5	3	.867	1st/OUAA	9	0	1.000
84-85—Philadelphia	NHL	53	20	7	.706	1st/Patrick Division	12	7	.632
85-86—Philadelphia	NHL	53	23	4	.688	1st/Patrick Division	2	3	.400
86-87—Philadelphia	NHL	46	26	8	.625	1st/Patrick Division	15	11	.577
87-88—Philadelphia	NHL	38	33	9	.513	3rd/Patrick Division	3	4	.429
88-89—Chicago	NHL	27	41	12	.413	4th/Norris Division	9	7	.563
89-90—Chicago	NHL	41	33	6	.550	1st/Norris Division	10	10	.500
90-91—Chicago	NHL	49	23	8	.663	1st/Norris Division	2	4	.333
91-92—Chicago	NHL	36	29	15	.544	2nd/Norris Division	12	6	.667
93-94—New York Rangers	NHL	52	24	8	.667	1st/Atlantic Division	16	7	.696
94-95—St. Louis	NHL	28	15	5	.635	2nd/Central Division	3	4	.429
NHL totals (10 years)		**423**	**267**	**82**	**.601**	**NHL totals (10 years)**	**84**	**63**	**.571**

NOTES:
1982— Defeated New Haven in Calder Cup quarterfinals; lost to Binghamton in Calder Cup semifinals.
1983— Defeated Binghamton in Calder Cup quarterfinals; defeated New Haven in Calder Cup semifinals; defeated Maine in Calder Cup finals.
1984— Defeated Guelph in OUAA semifinals; defeated Western Ontario in OUAA finals; defeated New Brunswick in East Regional Qualifying Round; defeated Trois-Rivieres in CIAU Championship Tournament semifinals; defeated Concordia in CIAU Championship Tournament finals.
1985— Defeated New York Rangers in Patrick Division semifinals; defeated New York Islanders in Patrick Division finals; defeated Quebec in Wales Conference finals; lost to Edmonton in Stanley Cup finals.
1986— Lost to New York Rangers in Patrick Division semifinals.
1987— Defeated New York Rangers in Patrick Division semifinals; defeated New York Islanders in Patrick Division finals; defeated Montreal in Wales Conference finals; lost to Edmonton in Stanley Cup finals.
1988— Lost to Washington in Patrick Division semifinals.
1989— Defeated Detroit in Norris Division semifinals; defeated St. Louis in Norris Division finals; lost to Calgary in Campbell Conference finals.
1990— Defeated Minnesota in Norris Division semifinals; defeated St. Louis in Norris Division finals; lost to Edmonton in Campbell Conference finals.
1991— Lost to Minnesota in Norris Division semifinals.
1992— Defeated St. Louis in Norris Division semifinals; defeated Detroit in Norris Division finals; defeated Edmonton in Campbell Conference finals; lost to Pittsburgh in Stanley Cup finals.
1993— Finished fourth in World Championships.
1994— Defeated New York Islanders in Eastern Conference quarterfinals; defeated Washington in Eastern Conference semifinals; defeated New Jersey in Eastern Conference finals; defeated Vancouver in Stanley Cup finals.
1995— Lost to Vancouver in Western Conference quarterfinals.

LEMAIRE, JACQUES
DEVILS

PERSONAL: Born September 7, 1945, in Ville LaSalle, Que. . . . 5-10/180. . . . Shot left. . . . Full name: Jacques Gerard Lemaire. . . . Name pronounced luh-MAYR.
HONORS: Inducted into Hall of Fame (1984).
MISCELLANEOUS: Played center and left wing. . . . Member of Stanley Cup Championship teams (1968, 1969, 1971, 1973 and 1976-1979).

Season Team	League	REGULAR SEASON					PLAYOFFS				
		Gms.	G	A	Pts.	PIM	Gms.	G	A	Pts.	PIM
62-63—Lachine	QJHL	42	41	63	104	...	—	—	—	—	—
63-64—Montreal Jr. Canadiens	OHA Jr. A	42	25	30	55	...	—	—	—	—	—
64-65—Montreal Jr. Canadiens	OHA Jr. A	56	25	47	72	...	—	—	—	—	—
—Quebec	AHL	1	0	0	0	0	—	—	—	—	—
65-66—Montreal Jr. Canadiens	OHA Jr. A	48	41	52	93	69	—	—	—	—	—
66-67—Houston	CPHL	69	19	30	49	19	6	0	1	1	0
67-68—Montreal	NHL	69	22	20	42	16	13	7	6	13	6
68-69—Montreal	NHL	75	29	34	63	29	14	4	2	6	6
69-70—Montreal	NHL	69	32	28	60	16	—	—	—	—	—
70-71—Montreal	NHL	78	28	28	56	18	20	9	10	19	17

Season	Team	League		REGULAR SEASON					PLAYOFFS			
			Gms.	G	A	Pts.	PIM	Gms.	G	A	Pts.	PIM
71-72	Montreal	NHL	77	32	49	81	26	6	2	1	3	2
72-73	Montreal	NHL	77	44	51	95	16	17	7	13	20	2
73-74	Montreal	NHL	66	29	38	67	10	6	0	4	4	2
74-75	Montreal	NHL	80	36	56	92	20	11	5	7	12	4
75-76	Montreal	NHL	61	20	32	52	20	13	3	3	6	2
76-77	Montreal	NHL	75	34	41	75	22	14	7	12	19	6
77-78	Montreal	NHL	75	36	61	97	14	15	6	8	14	10
78-79	Montreal	NHL	50	24	31	55	10	16	11	12	23	6
NHL totals			852	366	469	835	217	145	61	78	139	63

HEAD COACHING RECORD

BACKGROUND: Assistant coach, University of Plattsburgh (1981-82).... Assistant coach, Montreal Canadiens (October 1982 - February 1983).... Assistant to managing director/director of hockey personnel, Canadiens (1985-86 through 1987-88).... Assistant to managing director of Verdun, Canadiens organization (1988-89).... Assistant to managing director, Canadiens (1989-90 and 1990-91).... Assistant to managing director of Fredericton, Canadiens organization (1991-92 and 1992-93).... Served as interim coach of Montreal Canadiens while Jacques Demers was hospitalized with chest pains (March 10 and 11, 1993; team was 1-1 during that time).

HONORS: Named NHL Coach of the Year by THE SPORTING NEWS (1993-94).... Won Jack Adams Award (1993-94).

Season	Team	League			REGULAR SEASON					PLAYOFFS	
			W	L	T	Pct.	Finish		W	L	Pct.
79-80	Sierre	Swiss					Record unavailable.				
80-81	Sierre	Swiss					Record unavailable.				
82-83	Longueuil	QMJHL	37	29	4	.557	3rd/LeBel Division		8	7	.533
83-84	Montreal	NHL	7	10	0	.412	4th/Adams Division		9	6	.600
84-85	Montreal	NHL	41	27	12	.588	1st/Adams Division		6	6	.500
93-94	New Jersey	NHL	47	25	12	.631	2nd/Atlantic Division		11	9	.550
94-95	New Jersey	NHL	22	18	8	.542	2nd/Atlantic Division		16	4	.800
NHL totals (4 years)			117	80	32	.580	**NHL totals (4 years)**		42	25	.627

NOTES—
1983— Defeated Chicoutimi in President Cup quarterfinals; defeated Laval in President Cup semifinals; lost to Verdun in President Cup finals.
1984— Defeated Boston in Adams Division semifinals; defeated Quebec in Adams Division finals; lost to New York Islanders in Wales Conference finals.
1985— Defeated Boston in Adams Division semifinals; lost to Quebec in Adams Division finals.
1994— Defeated Buffalo in Eastern Conference quarterfinals; defeated Boston in Eastern Conference semifinals; lost to New York Rangers in Eastern Conference finals.
1995— Defeated Boston in Eastern Conference quarterfinals; defeated Pittsburgh in Eastern Conference semifinals; defeated Philadelphia in Eastern Conference finals; defeated Detroit in Stanley Cup finals.

LEY, RICK

CANUCKS

PERSONAL: Born November 2, 1948, in Orillia, Ont.... 6-0/175.... Shot left.... Full name: Rick Norman Ley.

TRANSACTIONS/CAREER NOTES: Selected by Toronto Maple Leafs (third Maple Leafs pick, 16th overall) in NHL amateur draft (April 25, 1966).... Missed part of 1969-70 season with cartilage and ligament damage to knee.... Reclaimed by Maple Leafs from Hartford Whalers prior to expansion draft (June 9, 1979).... Claimed by Whalers from Maple Leafs in expansion draft (June 13, 1979).

HONORS: Named Outstanding defenseman of WHA (1978-79).

MISCELLANEOUS: Captain of Hartford Whalers (1979-80 and 1980-81).

Season	Team	League		REGULAR SEASON					PLAYOFFS			
			Gms.	G	A	Pts.	PIM	Gms.	G	A	Pts.	PIM
64-65	Niagara Falls Jr. B	OHA	50	0	11	11	...	—	—	—	—	—
65-66	Niagara Falls Jr. B	OHA	46	3	13	16	180	—	—	—	—	—
66-67	Niagara Falls Jr. B	OHA	48	10	27	37	128	—	—	—	—	—
67-68	Niagara Falls Jr. B	OHA	53	16	48	64	81	—	—	—	—	—
68-69	Tulsa	CHL	19	0	5	5	23	—	—	—	—	—
—	Toronto	NHL	38	1	11	12	39	3	0	0	0	9
69-70	Toronto	NHL	48	2	13	15	102	—	—	—	—	—
70-71	Toronto	NHL	76	4	16	20	151	6	0	2	2	4
71-72	Toronto	NHL	67	1	14	15	124	5	0	0	0	7
72-73	New England	WHA	76	3	27	30	108	15	3	7	10	24
73-74	New England	WHA	72	6	35	41	148	7	1	5	6	18
74-75	New England	WHA	62	6	36	42	50	6	1	1	2	32
75-76	New England	WHA	67	8	30	38	78	17	1	4	5	49
76-77	New England	WHA	55	2	21	23	102	5	0	4	4	4
77-78	New England	WHA	73	3	41	44	95	14	1	8	9	4
78-79	New England	WHA	73	7	20	27	135	9	0	4	4	11
79-80	Hartford	NHL	65	4	16	20	92	—	—	—	—	—
80-81	Hartford	NHL	16	0	2	2	20	—	—	—	—	—
WHA totals			543	39	226	265	808	73	7	33	40	142
NHL totals			310	12	72	84	528	14	0	2	2	20

HEAD COACHING RECORD

BACKGROUND: Assistant coach, Vancouver Canucks organization (1991-92 through 1993-94).

Season	Team	League	W	L	T	Pct.	Finish	W	L	Pct.
						REGULAR SEASON			**PLAYOFFS**	
82-83—Binghamton		AHL	22	17	5	.534		1	4	.200
83-84—Mohawk Valley		ACHL	29	39	7	.433		1	4	.200
84-85—Muskegon		IHL	50	29	3	.628	1st/East Division	11	6	.647
85-86—Muskegon		IHL	50	32	0	.610	1st/East Division	12	2	.857
86-87—Muskegon		IHL	47	30	5	.604	1st/East Division	10	5	.667
87-88—Muskegon		IHL	58	14	10	.768	1st/East Division	2	4	.333
88-89—Muskegon		IHL	54	23	5	.689	1st/East Division	5	6	.455
89-90—Hartford		NHL	38	33	9	.531	4th/Adams Division	3	4	.429
90-91—Hartford		NHL	31	38	11	.456	4th/Adams Division	2	4	.333
94-95—Vancouver		NHL	18	18	12	.500	2nd/Pacific Division	3	7	.300
NHL totals (3 years)			87	89	32	.495	**NHL totals (3 years)**	8	15	.348

NOTES:
1985— Defeated Toledo in East Division quarterfinals; defeated Kalamazoo in East Division semifinals; lost to Peoria in Turner Cup finals.
1986— Defeated Indianapolis in East Division quarterfinals; defeated Saginaw in East Division semifinals; defeated Fort Wayne in Turner Cup finals.
1987— Defeated Kalamazoo in East Division quarterfinals; defeated Saginaw in East Division semifinals; lost to Salt Lake in Turner Cup finals.
1988— Lost to Flint in East Division quarterfinals.
1989— Defeated Peoria in East Division quarterfinals; defeated Fort Wayne in East Division semifinals; defeated Salt Lake in Turner Cup finals,
1990— Lost to Boston in Adams Division quarterfinals.
1991— Lost to Boston in Adams Division quarterfinals.
1995— Defeated St. Louis in Western Division quarterfinals; lost to Chicago in Western Division semifinals.

LOW, RON
OILERS

PERSONAL: Born June 21, 1950, in Birtle, Man.... 6-1/205.... Full name: Ron Albert Low.
TRANSACTIONS/CAREER NOTES: Selected by Toronto Maple Leafs in eighth round (eighth Maple Leafs pick, 103rd overall) of NHL amateur draft (June 11, 1970).... Claimed by Washington Capitals from Maple Leafs in expansion draft (June 12, 1974).... Signed as free agent by Detroit Red Wings (August 17, 1977).... Claimed by Quebec Nordiques from Red Wings in expansion draft (June 13, 1979).... Traded to Edmonton Oilers by Nordiques for C Ron Chipperfield (March 11, 1980).... Traded to New Jersey Devils By Oilers with D Jim McTaggart for G Lindsay Middlebrook and C Paul Miller (February 19, 1983).
HONORS: Named to CHL All-Star second team (1973-74).... Won Tommy Ivan Trophy (1978-79).... Named to CHL All-Star first team (1978-79).
MISCELLANEOUS: Played goalie.

Season	Team	League	Gms.	Min.	W	L	T	GA	SO	Avg.	Gms.	Min.	W	L	GA	SO	Avg.
								REGULAR SEASON							**PLAYOFFS**		
70-71—Jacksonville		EHL	49	2940	...	...	...	293	1	5.98	—	—	—	—	—	—	—
—Tulsa		CHL	4	192	...	...	...	11	0	3.44	—	—	—	—	—	—	—
71-72—Richmond		AHL	1	60	...	...	...	2	0	2.00	—	—	—	—	—	—	—
—Tulsa		CHL	43	2428	...	...	...	135	1	3.34	8	474	...	...	15	1	1.90
72-73—Toronto		NHL	42	2343	12	24	4	152	1	3.89	—	—	—	—	—	—	—
73-74—Tulsa		CHL	56	3213	...	...	...	169	1	3.16	—	—	—	—	—	—	—
74-75—Washington		NHL	48	2588	8	36	2	235	1	5.45	—	—	—	—	—	—	—
75-76—Washington		NHL	43	2289	6	31	2	208	0	5.45	—	—	—	—	—	—	—
76-77—Washington		NHL	54	2918	16	27	5	188	0	3.87	—	—	—	—	—	—	—
77-78—Detroit		NHL	32	1816	9	12	9	102	1	3.37	4	240	1	3	17	0	4.25
78-79—Kansas City		CHL	63	3795	...	...	...	244	0	3.86	4	237	...	...	15	...	3.80
79-80—Syracuse		AHL	15	905	5	9	1	70	0	4.64	—	—	—	—	—	—	—
—Quebec		NHL	15	828	5	7	2	51	0	3.70	—	—	—	—	—	—	—
—Edmonton		NHL	11	650	8	2	1	37	0	3.42	3	212	0	3	12	...	3.40
80-81—Edmonton		NHL	24	1260	5	13	3	93	0	4.43	—	—	—	—	—	—	—
—Wichita		CHL	2	120	0	2	0	10	...	5.00	—	—	—	—	—	—	—
81-82—Edmonton		NHL	29	1554	17	7	1	100	0	3.86	—	—	—	—	—	—	—
82-83—Edmonton		NHL	3	104	0	1	0	10	0	5.77	—	—	—	—	—	—	—
—New Jersey		NHL	11	608	2	7	1	41	0	4.05	—	—	—	—	—	—	—
83-84—New Jersey		NHL	44	2218	8	25	4	161	0	4.36	—	—	—	—	—	—	—
84-85—New Jersey		NHL	26	1326	6	11	4	85	1	3.85	—	—	—	—	—	—	—
NHL totals			382	20502	102	203	38	1463	4	4.28	7	452	1	6	29	0	3.85

HEAD COACHING RECORD
BACKGROUND: Player/assistant coach, Nova Scotia Oilers (1985-86).... Assistant coach, Nova Scotia Oilers (1986-87).... Assistant coach, Edmonton Oilers (August 3,1989 through 1994-95).

Season	Team	League	W	L	T	Pct.	Finish	W	L	Pct.
						REGULAR SEASON			**PLAYOFFS**	
87-88—Nova Scotia		AHL	35	36	9	.506	4th/Northern Division	—	—	—
88-89—Cape Breton		AHL	27	47	6	.375	7th/Northern Division	—	—	—
94-95—Edmonton		NHL	5	7	1	.423	5th/Pacific Division	—	—	—
NHL totals (1 year)			5	7	1	.423		—	—	—

MacLEAN, DOUG
PANTHERS

PERSONAL: Born April 12, 1954, in Summerside, P.E.I.
COLLEGE: Prince Edward Island, then Western Ontario (master's degree in educational psychology).

HEAD COACHING RECORD

BACKGROUND: Assistant coach, London Knights of OHL (1984-85).... Assistant coach, St. Louis Blues (1986-87 and 1987-88).... Assistant coach, Washington Capitals (1988-89 and 1989-90).... Assistant coach, Detroit Red Wings (1990-91 and 1991-92).... Assistant general manager, Red Wings (1992-93 and 1993-94).... General manager, Adirondack, Red Wings organization (1992-93 and 1993-94).... Director of player development/scout, Florida Panthers (1994-95).

Season Team	League	W	L	T	Pct.	Finish	W	L	Pct.
				REGULAR SEASON				PLAYOFFS	
85-86—Univ. of New Brunswick . AUAA		33	46	5	.423	4th/Pacific Division	—	—	—
89-90—Baltimore...................... AHL		17	13	5	.557	3rd/Southern Division	6	6	.500

MILBURY, MIKE
ISLANDERS

PERSONAL: Born June 17, 1952, in Brighton, Mass.... 6-1/195.... Shot left.... Full name: Michael James Milbury.... Cousin of Dave Silk, center, New York Rangers, Boston Bruins and Detroit Red Wings (1979-80 through 1984-85).
COLLEGE: Colgate.

TRANSACTIONS/CAREER NOTES: Signed as free agent by Boston Bruins (September 1974).... Suspended six games by NHL for fight in stands (December 26, 1979).... Strained ligaments in right knee (March 11, 1982).... Broke kneecap (March 29, 1983).... Underwent surgery to repair ligament damage in right knee (October 26, 1986).
MISCELLANEOUS: Played defense.

Season Team	League	Gms.	G	A	Pts.	PIM	Gms.	G	A	Pts.	PIM
			REGULAR SEASON					PLAYOFFS			
72-73—Colgate University	ECAC	27	4	25	29	81	—	—	—	—	—
73-74—Colgate University	ECAC	23	2	19	21	68	—	—	—	—	—
—Boston	AHL	5	0	0	0	7	—	—	—	—	—
74-75—Rochester	AHL	71	2	15	17	246	8	0	3	3	24
75-76—Rochester	AHL	73	3	15	18	199	3	0	1	1	13
—Boston	NHL	3	0	0	0	9	11	0	0	0	29
76-77—Boston	NHL	77	6	18	24	166	13	2	2	4	47
77-78—Boston	NHL	80	8	30	38	151	15	1	8	9	27
78-79—Boston	NHL	74	1	34	35	149	11	1	7	8	7
79-80—Boston	NHL	72	10	13	23	59	10	0	2	2	50
80-81—Boston	NHL	77	0	18	18	222	2	0	1	1	10
81-82—Boston	NHL	51	2	10	12	71	11	0	4	4	6
82-83—Boston	NHL	78	9	15	24	216	—	—	—	—	—
83-84—Boston	NHL	74	2	17	19	159	3	0	0	0	12
84-85—Boston	NHL	78	3	13	16	152	5	0	0	0	10
85-86—Boston	NHL	22	2	5	7	102	1	0	0	0	17
86-87—Boston	NHL	68	6	16	22	96	4	0	0	0	4
NHL totals..................		**754**	**49**	**189**	**238**	**1552**	**86**	**4**	**24**	**28**	**219**

HEAD COACHING RECORD

BACKGROUND: Assistant coach, Boston Bruins (May 6, 1985 through February 1986).... Co-coach, Bruins (November 8, 1986).... Player/assistant coach (November 1986 through 1987).... Assistant general manager, Bruins (May 16, 1989 through 1993-94).... Head coach, Boston College (March 30-June 2, 1994).... Hockey analyst, ESPN television (1994-95).
HONORS: Named AHL Coach of the Year (1987-88).... Named NHL Coach of the Year by THE SPORTING NEWS (1989-90).

Season Team	League	W	L	T	Pct.	Finish	W	L	Pct.
				REGULAR SEASON				PLAYOFFS	
87-88—Maine........................ AHL		44	29	7	.594	1st/North Division	5	5	.500
88-89—Maine........................ AHL		32	40	8	.450	5th/North Division	—	—	—
89-90—Boston .... NHL		46	25	9	.631	1st/Adams Division	13	8	.619
90-91—Boston .... NHL		44	24	12	.625	1st/Adams Division	10	9	.526
NHL totals (2 years)..............................		**90**	**49**	**21**	**.628**	**NHL totals (2 years)**	**23**	**17**	**.575**

NOTES:
1990— Defeated Hartford in Adams Division semifinals; defeated Montreal in Adams Division finals; defeated Washington in Wales Conference finals; lost to Edmonton in Stanley Cup finals.
1991— Defeated Hartford in Adams Division semifinals; defeated Montreal in Adams Division finals; lost to Pittsburgh in Wales Conference finals.

MURRAY, TERRY
FLYERS

PERSONAL: Born July 20, 1950, in Shawville, Que. ... 6-2/190. ... Shot right. ... Full name: Terry Rodney Murray.... Brother of Bryan Murray, general manager, Florida Panthers.
HIGH SCHOOL: Shawville (Que.).

TRANSACTIONS/CAREER NOTES: Selected by Oakland Seals in seventh round (seventh Seals pick, 88th overall) of NHL amateur draft (June 11, 1970).... Loaned to Boston Braves (February 1972).... Broke leg (1973-74).... Traded by Philadelphia Flyers with RW Dave Kelly, RW Steve Coates and LW Bob Ritchie to Detroit Red Wings for D Mike Korney and D Rick LaPointe (February 1977).... Contract sold by Red Wings to Flyers (November 1977).... Selected by Washington Capitals in NHL waiver draft (October 1981).
HONORS: Won Eddie Shore Plaque (1977-78 and 1978-79).... Named to AHL All-Star first team (1975-76, 1977-78 and 1978-79).
MISCELLANEOUS: Played defense.

Season	Team	League	REGULAR SEASON Gms.	G	A	Pts.	PIM	PLAYOFFS Gms.	G	A	Pts.	PIM
67-68—Ottawa	OHA Jr. A		52	0	4	4	59	—	—	—	—	—
68-69—Ottawa	OHA Jr. A		50	1	16	17	39	—	—	—	—	—
69-70—Ottawa	OHA Jr. A		50	4	24	28	43	—	—	—	—	—
70-71—Providence	AHL		57	1	22	23	47	10	0	1	1	5
71-72—Baltimore	AHL		30	0	5	5	13	—	—	—	—	—
—Boston	AHL		9	0	0	0	0	—	—	—	—	—
—Oklahoma City	CPHL		17	1	1	2	19	6	0	0	0	2
72-73—Salt Lake City	WHL		39	3	8	11	30	9	0	6	6	14
—California	NHL		23	0	3	3	4	—	—	—	—	—
73-74—California	NHL		58	0	12	12	48	—	—	—	—	—
74-75—Salt Lake City	CHL		62	5	30	35	122	11	2	2	4	30
—California	NHL		9	0	2	2	8	—	—	—	—	—
75-76—Richmond	AHL		67	8	48	56	95	6	1	4	5	2
—Philadelphia	NHL		3	0	0	0	2	6	0	1	1	0
76-77—Philadelphia	NHL		36	0	13	13	14	—	—	—	—	—
—Detroit	NHL		23	0	7	7	10	—	—	—	—	—
77-78—Philadelphia	AHL		7	2	1	3	13	—	—	—	—	—
—Maine	AHL		68	9	40	49	53	12	1	7	8	28
78-79—Philadelphia	NHL		5	0	0	0	0	—	—	—	—	—
—Maine	AHL		55	14	23	37	14	10	1	5	6	6
79-80—Maine	AHL		68	3	19	22	26	12	2	2	4	10
80-81—Maine	AHL		2	0	1	1	0	—	—	—	—	—
—Philadelphia	NHL		71	1	17	18	53	12	2	1	3	10
81-82—Washington	NHL		74	3	22	25	60	—	—	—	—	—
NHL totals			302	4	76	80	199	18	2	2	4	10

HEAD COACHING RECORD

BACKGROUND: Assistant coach, Washington Capitals (1982-83 through 1987-1988).

Season	Team	League	REGULAR SEASON W	L	T	Pct.	Finish	PLAYOFFS W	L	Pct.
88-89—Baltimore	AHL		30	46	4	.400	6th/South Division	—	—	—
89-90—Baltimore	AHL		26	17	1	.646		—	—	—
—Washington	NHL		18	14	2	.559	3rd/Patrick Division	8	7	.533
90-91—Washington	NHL		37	36	7	.506	3rd/Patrick Division	5	6	.455
91-92—Washington	NHL		45	27	8	.613	2nd/Patrick Division	3	4	.429
92-93—Washington	NHL		43	34	7	.554	2nd/Patrick Division	2	4	.333
93-94—Washington	NHL		20	23	4	.468		—	—	—
—Cincinnati	IHL		17	7	4	.679	2nd/Central Division	6	5	.545
94-95—Philadelphia	NHL		28	16	4	.625	1st/Atlantic Division	10	5	.667
NHL totals (6 years)			191	150	32	.555	**NHL totals (5 years)**	28	26	.519

NOTES:

1990— Defeated New Jersey in Patrick Division semifinals; defeated New York Rangers in Patrick Division finals; lost to Boston in Wales Conference finals.

1991— Defeated New York Rangers in Patrick Division semifinals; lost to Pittsburgh in Patrick Division finals.

1992— Lost to Pittsburgh in Patrick Division semifinals.

1993— Lost to New York Islanders in Patrick Division semifinals.

1994— Replaced as head coach by Jim Schoenfeld (January 27), with club in fifth place. Loaned to Florida Panthers (February 18) to coach Cincinnati Cyclones of IHL. Defeated Kalamazoo in Turner Cup quarterfinals; lost to Fort Wayne in Turner Cup semifinals.

1995— Defeated Buffalo in Atlantic Division quarterfinals; Defeated New York Rangers in Atlantic Division semifinals; lost to New Jersey Devils in Atlantic Division finals.

NOLAN, TED
SABRES

PERSONAL: Born April 7, 1958, in Sault Ste. Marie.... 6-0/185.... Shot left.... Full name: Theodore John Nolan.

TRANSACTIONS/CAREER NOTES: Selected by Detroit Red Wings in fifth round (seventh Red Wings pick, 78th overall) of NHL amateur draft (June 15, 1978).... Injured knee (October 1983).... Signed as free agent by Buffalo Sabres (March 7, 1985).... Traded by Sabres to Pittsburgh Penguins for future considerations (September 1985).... Injured back (January 25, 1986).... Signed as free agent by Sabres (August 1986).

MISCELLANEOUS: Played center.

Season	Team	League	REGULAR SEASON Gms.	G	A	Pts.	PIM	PLAYOFFS Gms.	G	A	Pts.	PIM
76-77—Sault Ste. Marie	OHA		60	8	16	24	109	9	1	2	3	19
77-78—Sault Ste. Marie	OHA		66	14	30	44	106	13	1	3	4	20
78-79—Kansas City	CHL		73	12	38	50	66	4	1	2	3	0
79-80—Adirondack	AHL		75	16	24	40	106	5	0	1	1	0
80-81—Adirondack	AHL		76	22	28	50	86	18	6	10	16	11
81-82—Adirondack	AHL		39	12	18	30	81	—	—	—	—	—
—Detroit	NHL		41	4	13	17	45	—	—	—	—	—
82-83—Adirondack	AHL		78	24	40	64	103	6	2	5	7	14
83-84—Detroit	NHL		19	1	2	3	26	—	—	—	—	—
—Adirondack	AHL		31	10	16	26	76	7	2	3	5	18
84-85—Rochester	AHL		65	28	34	62	152	5	4	0	4	18

Season Team	League	REGULAR SEASON Gms.	G	A	Pts.	PIM	PLAYOFFS Gms.	G	A	Pts.	PIM
85-86—Pittsburgh	NHL	18	1	1	2	34	—	—	—	—	—
—Baltimore	AHL	10	4	4	8	19	—	—	—	—	—
NHL totals		78	6	16	22	105	—	—	—	—	—

HEAD COACHING RECORD

BACKGROUND: Assistant coach, Hartford Whalers (June 29, 1994 through July 17, 1995).

Season Team	League	REGULAR SEASON W	L	T	Pct.	Finish	PLAYOFFS W	L	Pct.
88-89—Sault Ste. Marie	OHL	21	43	2	.318	8th/Emms Division	—	—	—
89-90—Sault Ste. Marie	OHL	18	42	6	.273	7th/Emms Division	—	—	—
90-91—Sault Ste. Marie	OHL	42	21	3	.636	1st/Emms Division	12	2	.857
91-92—Sault Ste. Marie	OHL	41	19	6	.621	1st/Emms Division	12	7	.632
92-93—Sault Ste. Marie	OHL	38	23	5	.576	1st/Emms Division	9	5	.643
93-94—Sault Ste. Marie	OHL	35	24	7	.530	2nd/Emms Division	10	4	.714

NOTES:
1991— Defeated Hamilton in OHL quarterfinals; defeated Niagara Falls in OHL semifinals; defeated Oshawa in J. Ross Robertson Cup finals.
1992— Defeated Kitchener in OHL semifinals; defeated Niagara Falls in OHL finals; defeated North Bay in J. Ross Robertson Cup finals.
1993— Defeated Owen Sound in OHL semifinals; defeated Detroit in OHL finals; lost to Peterborough in J. Ross Robertson Cup finals.
1994— Defeated Windsor in OHL quarterfinals; defeated Guelph in OHL semifinals; lost to Detroit in J. Ross Robertson Cup finals.

PAGE, PIERRE
FLAMES

PERSONAL: Born April 30, 1948, in St. Hermas, Que.
COLLEGE: Rigaud College, then St. Francis-Xavier (N.S.), then Dalhousie (N.S.).

Season Team	League	REGULAR SEASON Gms.	G	A	Pts.	PIM	PLAYOFFS Gms.	G	A	Pts.	PIM
69-70—St. Francis-Xavier		22	16	33	49	...	—	—	—	—	—
70-71—St. Francis-Xavier		25	23	54	77	...	—	—	—	—	—

HEAD COACHING RECORD

BACKGROUND: Consultant, Nova Scotia, Montreal Canadiens organization (1973-74 through 1979-80).... Assistant coach, Canadian Olympic team (1980).... Assistant coach, Calgary Flames (1980-81 through 1981-82 and 1985-86 through 1987-88).... General manager/coach, Colorado Flames (1982-83 and 1983-84).... General manager/coach, Moncton, Flames organization (1984-85).... General manager, Quebec Nordiques (1990-91 through 1993-94).

Season Team	League	REGULAR SEASON W	L	T	Pct.	Finish	PLAYOFFS W	L	Pct.
71-72—Dalhousie University	AUAA	10	8	0	.556	3rd/AUAA	—	—	—
72-73—Dalhousie University	AUAA	7	14	0	.333	8th/AUAA	—	—	—
73-74—Dalhousie University	AUAA	6	11	4	.381	4th/Kelly Division	—	—	—
74-75—Dalhousie University	AUAA	12	6	0	.667	3rd/AUAA	—	—	—
75-76—Dalhousie University	AUAA	6	9	1	.406	6th/AUAA	—	—	—
76-77—Dalhousie University	AUAA	6	13	1	.325	6th/AUAA	—	—	—
77-78—Dalhousie University	AUAA	9	9	2	.500	5th/AUAA	—	—	—
78-79—Dalhousie University	AUAA	13	7	0	.650	2nd/AUAA	6	2	.750
79-80—Dalhousie University	AUAA	20	1	1	.932	1st/Kelly Division	2	3	.400
82-83—Colorado	CHL	41	36	3	.531	2nd/CHL	2	4	.333
83-84—Colorado	CHL	48	25	3	.619	1st/CHL	2	4	.333
84-85—Moncton	AHL	32	40	8	.450	6th/North Division	—	—	—
88-89—Minnesota	NHL	27	37	16	.438	4th/Norris Division	1	4	.200
89-90—Minnesota	NHL	36	40	4	.475	4th/Norris Division	3	4	.429
91-92—Quebec	NHL	17	34	11	.363	5th/Adams Division	—	—	—
92-93—Quebec	NHL	47	27	10	.619	2nd/Adams Division	2	4	.333
93-94—Quebec	NHL	34	42	8	.452	5th/Northeast Division	—	—	—
NHL totals (5 years)		161	180	49	.476	**NHL totals (3 years)**	6	12	.333

NOTES:
1979— Defeated Moncton in AUAA semifinals; defeated Saint Mary's in AUAA semifinals; defeated Guelph in CIAU Championship round; defeated Chicoutimi in CIAU Championship round; lost to Alberta in CIAU Championship finals.
1980— Defeated St. Francis-Xavier in AUAA semifinals; lost to Moncton in AUAA finals.
1983— Lost to Birmingham in Adams Cup semifinals.
1984— Lost to Indianapolis in Adams Cup semifinals.
1989— Lost to Chicago in Norris Division semifinals.
1990— Lost to St. Louis in Norris Division semifinals.
1993— Lost to Montreal in Adams Division semifinals.

ROBINSON, LARRY
KINGS

PERSONAL: Born June 2, 1951, in Winchester, Ont.... 6-4/225.... Shot left.... Full name: Larry Clark Robinson.... Brother of Moe Robinson, defenseman, Montreal Canadiens (1979-80).
TRANSACTIONS/CAREER NOTES: Selected by Montreal Canadiens in second round (fourth Canadiens pick, 20th overall) of NHL amateur draft (June 10, 1971).... Injured knee; missed part of 1978-79 season.

... Separated right shoulder (March 6, 1980).... Injured groin (October 1980).... Separated left shoulder (November 14, 1980).... Broke nose (January 8, 1981).... Injured left shoulder (October 1982).... Suffered skin infection behind right knee (October 1983).... Hyperextended left elbow (March 1985).... Strained ligaments in right ankle (March 9, 1987).... Broke right leg (August 1987).... Sprained right wrist (December 1987).... Hyperextended knee (May 23, 1989).... Signed as free agent by Los Angeles Kings (July 26, 1989).... Suffered food poisoning (March 1990); missed games.... Injured eye (November 26, 1991); missed two games.

HONORS: Named to COJHL All-Star first team (1969-70).... Played in NHL All-Star Game (1974, 1976-1978, 1980, 1982, 1986, 1988, 1989 and 1992).... Won James Norris Memorial Trophy (1976-77 and 1979-80).... Named to THE SPORTING NEWS All-Star first team (1976-77 through 1979-80).... Named to NHL All-Star first team (1976-77, 1978-79 and 1979-80).... Won Conn Smythe Trophy (1977-78).... Named to NHL All-Star second team (1977-78, 1980-81 and 1985-86).... Named to THE SPORTING NEWS All-Star second team (1980-81, 1981-82 and 1985-86).

RECORDS: Holds NHL career playoff records for most games—227; and most consecutive years in playoffs—20 (1972-73 through 1991-92).... Shares NHL career playoff record for most years in playoffs—20 (1972-73 through 1991-92).

STATISTICAL PLATEAUS: Three-goal games: 1985-86 (1).

MISCELLANEOUS: Played defense.... Member of Stanley Cup championship teams (1973, 1976-1979 and 1986).

Season Team	League	REGULAR SEASON					PLAYOFFS				
		Gms.	G	A	Pts.	PIM	Gms.	G	A	Pts.	PIM
68-69—Brockville	COJHL					Statistics unavailable.					
69-70—Brockville	COJHL	40	22	29	51	74	—	—	—	—	—
70-71—Kitchener	OHA Jr. A	61	12	39	51	65	—	—	—	—	—
71-72—Nova Scotia	AHL	74	10	14	24	54	15	2	10	12	31
72-73—Nova Scotia	AHL	38	6	33	39	33	—	—	—	—	—
—Montreal	NHL	36	2	4	6	20	11	1	4	5	9
73-74—Montreal	NHL	78	6	20	26	66	6	0	1	1	26
74-75—Montreal	NHL	80	14	47	61	76	11	0	4	4	27
75-76—Montreal	NHL	80	10	30	40	59	13	3	3	6	10
76-77—Montreal	NHL	77	19	66	85	45	14	2	10	12	12
77-78—Montreal	NHL	80	13	52	65	39	15	4	*17	†21	6
78-79—Montreal	NHL	67	16	45	61	33	16	6	9	15	8
79-80—Montreal	NHL	72	14	61	75	39	10	0	4	4	2
80-81—Montreal	NHL	65	12	38	50	37	3	0	1	1	2
81-82—Montreal	NHL	71	12	47	59	41	5	0	1	1	8
82-83—Montreal	NHL	71	14	49	63	33	3	0	0	0	2
83-84—Montreal	NHL	74	9	34	43	39	15	0	5	5	22
84-85—Montreal	NHL	76	14	33	47	44	12	3	8	11	8
85-86—Montreal	NHL	78	19	63	82	39	20	0	13	13	22
86-87—Montreal	NHL	70	13	37	50	44	17	3	17	20	6
87-88—Montreal	NHL	53	6	34	40	30	11	1	4	5	4
88-89—Montreal	NHL	74	4	26	30	22	21	2	8	10	12
89-90—Los Angeles	NHL	64	7	32	39	34	10	2	3	5	10
90-91—Los Angeles	NHL	62	1	22	23	16	12	1	4	5	15
91-92—Los Angeles	NHL	56	3	10	13	37	2	0	0	0	0
NHL totals		1384	208	750	958	793	227	28	116	144	211

HEAD COACHING RECORD

BACKGROUND: Assistant coach, New Jersey Devils (1993-94 and 1994-95).

SCHOENFELD, JIM
CAPITALS

PERSONAL: Born September 4, 1952, in Galt, Ont.... 6-2/208.... Shot left.... Full name: James Grant Schoenfeld.... Name pronounced SHAHN-fehld.

TRANSACTIONS/CAREER NOTES: Traded by London Knights with D Ken Southwick and RW Rick Kehoe to Hamilton Red Wings for D Gary Geldhart, RW Gordon Brooks, LW Dave Gilmour and Mike Craig (December 1969).... Traded by Red Wings to Niagara Falls Flyers for C Russ Friesen and D Mike Healey (January 1971).... Selected by New York Raiders in WHA player selection draft (February 1972).... Selected by Buffalo Sabres in first round (first Sabres pick, fifth overall) of NHL amateur draft (June 8, 1972).... Damaged nerve in leg (1972); underwent corrective surgery following season.... Ruptured spinal disc (1973); missed most of season.... Underwent back surgery (1973).... Broke left foot (1974).... Suffered from mononucleosis (1975).... Suffered from viral pneumonia (1976).... Broke right foot (1978).... Separated shoulder (1978).... Strained knee (1978).... Injured hand and suffered from the flu (December 1980); missed nine games.... Broke left little finger (September 1981).... Broke metatarsal bone in right foot (October 18, 1981).... Traded by Sabres with RW Danny Gare, G Bob Sauve and C Derek Smith to Red Wings for C Dale McCourt, RW Mike Foligno, C Brent Peterson and future considerations (December 1981).... Separated ribs (October 1982).... Released by Red Wings (June 1983).... Signed as free agent by Boston Bruins (August 1983).... Fractured and separated left shoulder (November 11, 1983); underwent surgery... Injured shoulder (February 27, 1984).... Announced retirement (September 1984).... Recalled to active player status by Sabres (December 19, 1984).... Stress fracture in right foot (January, 1985); missed 13 games.... Announced retirement (June 1985).

HONORS: Named to the NHL All-Star second team (1979-80).... Played in NHL All-Star Game (1976-77 and 1979-80).

MISCELLANEOUS: Played defense.... Captain of Buffalo Sabres (1974-75 through 1976-77).

Season Team	League	REGULAR SEASON					PLAYOFFS				
		Gms.	G	A	Pts.	PIM	Gms.	G	A	Pts.	PIM
69-70—London	OHA Mj. Jr. A	16	1	4	5	81	—	—	—	—	—
—Hamilton Jr. A.	OHA	32	2	12	14	54	—	—	—	—	—
70-71—Hamilton Jr. A.	OHA	25	3	19	22	120	—	—	—	—	—
—Niagara Falls	OHA	30	3	9	12	85	—	—	—	—	—
71-72—Niagara Falls	OHA	40	6	46	52	*225	—	—	—	—	—
72-73—Buffalo	NHL	66	4	15	19	178	6	2	1	3	4
73-74—Cincinnati	AHL	2	0	2	2	4	—	—	—	—	—
—Buffalo	NHL	28	1	8	9	56	—	—	—	—	—

Season	Team	League		Gms.	G	A	Pts.	PIM		Gms.	G	A	Pts.	PIM
				REGULAR SEASON						**PLAYOFFS**				
74-75	Buffalo	NHL		68	1	19	20	184		17	1	4	5	38
75-76	Buffalo	NHL		56	2	22	24	114		8	0	3	3	33
76-77	Buffalo	NHL		65	7	25	32	97		6	0	0	0	12
77-78	Buffalo	NHL		60	2	20	22	89		8	0	1	1	28
78-79	Buffalo	NHL		46	8	17	25	67		3	0	1	1	0
79-80	Buffalo	NHL		77	9	27	36	72		14	0	3	3	18
80-81	Buffalo	NHL		71	8	25	33	110		8	0	0	0	14
81-82	Buffalo	NHL		13	3	2	5	30		—	—	—	—	—
	Detroit	NHL		39	5	9	14	69		—	—	—	—	—
82-83	Detroit	NHL		57	1	10	11	18		—	—	—	—	—
83-84	Boston	NHL		39	0	2	2	20		—	—	—	—	—
84-85	Buffalo	NHL		34	0	3	3	28		5	0	0	0	4
NHL totals				719	51	204	255	1132		75	3	13	16	151

HEAD COACHING RECORD

Season	Team	League	W	L	T	Pct.	Finish		W	L	Pct.
							REGULAR SEASON		**PLAYOFFS**		
84-85	Rochester	AHL	17	6	2	.720	3rd/South Division		—	—	—
85-86	Buffalo	NHL	19	19	5	.500	5th/Adams Division		—	—	—
87-88	New Jersey	NHL	17	12	1	.583	6th/Patrick Division		11	9	.550
88-89	New Jersey	NHL	27	41	12	.413	5th/Patrick Division		—	—	—
89-90	New Jersey	NHL	6	6	2	.500			—	—	—
93-94	Washington	NHL	19	12	6	.595	3rd/Atlantic Division		5	6	.455
94-95	Washington	NHL	22	18	8	.541	3rd/Atlantic Division		3	4	.429
NHL totals (6 years)			110	108	34	.503	**NHL totals (3 years)**		19	19	.500

NOTES:
1988— Defeated New York Islanders in Patrick Division semifinals; defeated Washington in Patrick Division final; lost to Boston in Campbell Conference finals.
1994— Defeated Pittsburgh Penguins in Eastern Conference quarterfinals; lost to New York Rangers in Eastern Conference semifinals.
1995— Lost to Pittsburgh in Eastern Conference quarterfinals.

SIMPSON, TERRY
JETS

PERSONAL: Born August 30, 1943, in Brantford, Ont.

HEAD COACHING RECORD

BACKGROUND: Coach, Prince Albert Raiders, Saskatchewan Junior Hockey League (1972-73 through 1981-82).... Assistant coach, Canadian national junior team (1984 and 1985).... Coach, Canadian national junior team (1986).... Assistant coach, Winnipeg Jets (1990-91 through 1992-93).
HONORS: Won Dunc McCallum Memorial Trophy (1983-84 and 1985-86).

Season	Team	League	W	L	T	Pct.	Finish		W	L	Pct.
							REGULAR SEASON		**PLAYOFFS**		
82-83	Prince Albert	WHL	16	55	1	.229	8th/East Division		—	—	—
83-84	Prince Albert	WHL	41	29	2	.583	5th/East Division		1	4	.200
84-85	Prince Albert	WHL	58	11	3	.826	1st/East Division		12	1	.923
85-86	Prince Albert	WHL	52	17	3	.743	2nd/East Division		6	4	.600
86-87	N.Y. Islanders	NHL	35	33	12	.513	3rd/Patrick Division		7	7	.500
87-88	N.Y. Islanders	NHL	39	31	10	.550	1st/Patrick Division		2	4	.333
88-89	N.Y. Islanders	NHL	7	18	2	.296			—	—	—
93-94	Philadelphia	NHL	35	39	10	.476	6th/Atlantic Division		—	—	—
94-95	Winnipeg	NHL	7	7	1	.500	6th/Central Division		—	—	—
NHL totals (5 years)			123	128	35	.491	**NHL totals (2 years)**		9	11	.450

NOTES:
1984— Lost to Medicine Hat in East Division quarterfinals.
1985— Defeated Calgary in East Division semifinals; defeated Medicine Hat in East Division finals; defeated Kamloops in WHL finals.
1986— Defeated Saskatoon in East Division semifinals; lost to Medicine Hat in East Division finals.
1987— Defeated Washington in Patrick Division semifinals; lost to Philadelphia in Patrick Division finals.
1988— Lost to New Jersey in Patrick Division semifinals.

WILSON, RON
MIGHTY DUCKS

PERSONAL: Born May 28, 1955, in Windsor, Ont.... 5-11/175.... Shot right.... Full name: Ronald Lawrence Wilson. ... Son of Larry Wilson, center, Detroit Red Wings and Chicago Blackhawks (1949-50 through 1955-56) and coach, Red Wings (1976-77); and nephew of Johnny Wilson, left winger with four NHL teams (1949-50 through 1961-62) and coach with four NHL teams and two WHA teams (1969-70 through 1979-80).
COLLEGE: Providence (bachelor of arts degree in economics).
TRANSACTIONS/CAREER NOTES: Selected by Toronto Maple Leafs in seventh round (seventh Maple Leafs pick, 132nd overall) in NHL entry draft (June 3, 1975).... Loaned by Davos club to Minnesota North Stars for remainder of NHL season and playoffs (March 1985).... Loaned by Davos club to North Stars for remainder of NHL season and playoffs (March 1986).... Traded by Davos to North Stars for Craig Levie (May 1986).... Separated shoulder (March 9, 1987).
HONORS: Named to NCAA All-America East first team (1974-75 and 1975-76).
MISCELLANEOUS: Played defense.

Season	Team	League	REGULAR SEASON					PLAYOFFS				
			Gms.	G	A	Pts.	PIM	Gms.	G	A	Pts.	PIM
73-74	Providence College	ECAC	26	16	22	38	...	—	—	—	—	—
74-75	Providence College	ECAC	27	26	61	87	12	—	—	—	—	—
	U.S. national team	Int'l	27	5	32	37	42	—	—	—	—	—
75-76	Providence College	ECAC	28	19	47	66	44	—	—	—	—	—
76-77	Providence College	ECAC	30	17	42	59	62	—	—	—	—	—
	Dallas	CHL	4	1	0	1	2	—	—	—	—	—
77-78	Dallas	CHL	67	31	38	69	18	—	—	—	—	—
	Toronto	NHL	13	2	1	3	0	—	—	—	—	—
78-79	New Brunswick	AHL	31	11	20	31	13	—	—	—	—	—
	Toronto	NHL	46	5	12	17	4	3	0	1	1	0
79-80	New Brunswick	AHL	43	20	43	63	10	—	—	—	—	—
	Toronto	NHL	5	0	2	2	2	3	1	2	3	2
80-81	Davos HC	Switzerland					Statistics unavailable.					
81-82	Davos HC	Switzerland					Statistics unavailable.					
82-83	Davos HC	Switzerland					Statistics unavailable.					
83-84	Davos HC	Switzerland					Statistics unavailable.					
84-85	Davos HC	Switzerland					Statistics unavailable.					
	Minnesota	NHL	13	4	8	12	2	9	1	6	7	2
85-86	Davos HC	Switzerland					Statistics unavailable.					
	Minnesota	NHL	11	1	3	4	8	5	2	4	6	4
86-87	Minnesota	NHL	65	12	29	41	36	—	—	—	—	—
87-88	Minnesota	NHL	24	2	12	14	16	—	—	—	—	—
	NHL totals		131	21	55	76	64					

HEAD COACHING RECORD

BACKGROUND: Assistant coach, Milwaukee, Vancouver Canucks organization (1989-90).... Served as interim coach of Milwaukee while Ron Lapointe was hospitalized for cancer treatments (February and March 1990; team went 9-10).... Assistant coach, Canucks (1990-91 through 1992-93).

Season	Team	League	REGULAR SEASON					PLAYOFFS		
			W	L	T	Pct.	Finish	W	L	Pct.
93-94	Anaheim	NHL	33	46	5	.423	4th/Pacific Division	—	—	—
94-95	Anaheim	NHL	16	27	5	.385	6th/Pacific Division	—	—	—
	NHL totals (2 years)		49	73	10	.409				